Submarine Periscopes

There is over half a century of experience in the design and manufacture of Barr & Stroud periscopes. In service with the Royal Navy and many other navies. In all classes of submarine, from midget to nuclear. Optical system achieves maximum light transmission and image quality. Periscope design tailored to individual specification.

- Diameters 180mm, 240mm and 254mm.
- Dual Magnification.
- Anti vibration.
- Sextant – natural or artificial horizon.
- Photography – standard or motorised 35mm.
- Low light television.
- Image intensifier.
- Thermal Imager.
- Electronic support measures.
- Laser rangefinder.

Masts for medium and large submarines supplied for radar navigation, wide band radar warning, direction finding and vhf communication. Also snort induction and exhaust masts.

For further details contact Barr & Stroud Limited
Melrose House, 4 - 6 Savile Row, London W1X 1AF, England
Telephone: 01-437 9652 Telex: 261877
A member of the Pilkington Group.

Barr & Stroud

No more ships will pass in the night.

Rank nightsights perform outstandingly well across water. They're simple and self contained. They're passive, using image intensifiers. No complicated systems. They're effective on pitch dark nights, light nights, moon and starlit nights, in nights partly made visible by artificial lighting. Even in battle flash they automatically compensate.

There are Rank nightsights for all types of direct fire weapons. From small arms to the biggest ship's guns. There's even a Rank nightsight that combines day and night vision, injects ballistic information and incorporates laser range finding for ships' guns controlled from turrets. All Rank nightsights detect infra-red and can be used with infra-red search lights.

There are four Rank nightsights for surveillance alone, in varying ranges according to the situation.

Rank nightsights are superbly practicable. They're sealed against water. They're rugged and easy to operate and simple to maintain. Many parts are interchangeable. You have a single source for spares and service.

Ship to ship. Ship to shore. In man overboard emergencies. For flying and observing from helicopters.

Quite simply, Rank nightsights are the world's best nightsights. On land or at sea.

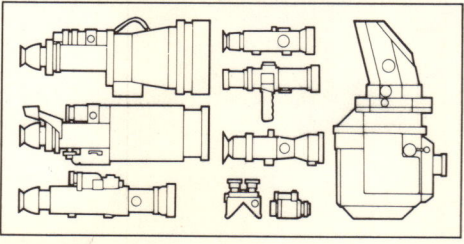

RANK PRECISION INDUSTRIES
RANK PULLIN CONTROLS

Langston Road, Debden, Loughton, Essex, England.
Tel.: 01-508 5522. Telex: 23855. Cables: Survey, Loughton.

JANE'S FIGHTING SHIPS
1979-80

Alphabetical list of advertisers

A

ABMTM Ltd
20 Park Street, London W1Y 4NA, England ...... [65]

Accumulatorenfabriken Wilhelm Hagen AG
Thomastr 27/28, PO Box 5, 4770 Soest
Federal Republic of Germany .... [86]

AEG Telefunken
Nachrichten-und Verkehrstechnik, Lyoner Strasse 26,
6000 Frankfurt 71, Federal Republic of Germany [128]

Aerimpianti SpA
Via Bergamo 21, 20100 Milan, Italy .... [63]

Aermarelli (Ercole Marelli Group)
Viale V. Lancetti 43-20158 Milan, Italy .... [91]

Aérospatiale
Division Engins Tactiques, 2 rue Béranger,
Châtillon 92320, France .... [95]

Agusta (Construzioni Aeronautiche Giovanni Agusta)
Cascina Costa, 20151 Gallarate, Italy .... [103]

AIFO (A Subsidiary Company of FIAT)
Via Carducci 29, 20123 Milan, Italy .... [115]

Ailsa Shipbuilding Co Ltd
Harbour Road, Troon, Ayrshire, Scotland .... [86]

Alsthom-Atlantique
2 quai de Seine, 93 St Denis, France .... [142]

Ameeco (Hydrospace) Ltd
Bilton Road, Manor Road, Erith, Kent,
England .... [100] & [126]

Ansaldo Societa Generale Elettromeccanica SpA
Via Nicola Lorenzi 8,
16152 Genoa-Cornigliano, Italy .... [113]

ARESA (Astilleros Reunidos SA)
Arenys de Mar, Barcelona, Spain .... [78]

Ateliers Chantiers du Havre
(Sté Nouvelle des Ateliers)
30 rue J.J. Rousseau, 76600 Le Havre, France ... [126]

Avco Lycoming
550 South Main Street, Stratford,
Connecticut 06479, USA .... [49]

B

Barr & Stroud Ltd
Melrose House, 4-6 Saville Row,
London W1X 1AF, England ... *facing inside front cover*

Bergens Mekaniske Verksteder A/S
PO Box 858, N 5001 Bergen, Norway .... [37]

Blohm & Voss AG
PO Box 100720, D-2000 Hamburg 1,
Federal Republic of Germany .... [101]

Bofors AB
Ordnance Division, Box 500,
S-690 20 Bofors, Sweden .... [146]

Borletti Fratelli SpA
Defence Products Division, Via Washington 70,
20146 Milan, Italy .... [61]

Breda Meccanica Bresciana SpA
Via Lunga 2, 25100 Brescia, Italy .... [148]

British Aerospace Aircraft Group
Richmond Road, Kingston upon Thames,
Surrey KT2 5QS, England .... [56] & [57]

British Aerospace Dynamics Group
Six Hills Way, Stevenage,
Hertfordshire SG1 2DA, England .... [17]

British Hovercraft Corporation
East Cowes, Isle of Wight, England .... [150]

Brooke Marine Ltd
Heath Road, Lowestoft, Suffolk NR33 9LZ,
England .... [40] & [41]

C

Cantiere Navale Breda SpA
Via Delle Industrie 18,
Venice Marghera, Italy .... [52] & [53]

Cantiere Navaltecnica SpA
22 Via S Raineri, 98100 Messina, Italy .... [107]

Cantieri Baglietto SpA
17019 Varozze, Italy .... [104] & [105]

Cantieri Navali di Pisa
Via Aurelia KM 334, Darsena,
56100 Pisa, Italy .... [59]

Castoldi SpA
Viale Mazzini 161, 20081 Abbiategrosse,
Milan, Italy .... [42]

CIS (Consorzio Italiano Sistemi Deg Roma)
Via GB Morgagni 30/E, 00161 Rome, Italy .... [111]

CIT Alcatel/Sintra
Department DSM, 1 av Aristide-Briand,
94117 Arcueil, France .... [102]

CNIM
50 avenue des Champs-Elysées,
75008 Paris, France .... [78]

CNR (Cantieri Navali Riuniti SpA)
Via Cipro 11, 16129 Genoa, Italy .... [38] & [39]

Cobham, Alan Engineering Ltd
Blandford, Dorset, England .... [74]

Crestitalia SpA
Via Gallarate 36, 20151 Milan, Italy .... [79]

Creusot Loire
Division de la méchanique spécialisée,
15 rue Pasquier, 75383 Paris, France .... [129]

CRM SrL
Via Manzoni 12, 20100 Milan, Italy.............. [5]

CSEE
2-8 rue Caroline, 75850 Paris,
Cedex 17, France .... [74]

Cutler-Hammer Italiana SpA
Piazza de Angeli 1, 20146 Milan, Italy .... [70]

D

Decca Navigator Co Ltd, The
Decca Radar Ltd, 9 Albert Embankment,
London SE1 7SW, England .... [31]

De Vries Shipyards
PO Box 258, Aalsmeer, The Netherlands .... [70]

DMS Inc
DMS Building, 100 Northfield Street,
Greenwich, Connecticut 06830, USA .... [122]

The UK's largest exporter of SONAR

Graseby

Graseby Ltd., Kingston-By-Pass, Surbiton, Surrey, KT6 7LR, England
Telephone: 01-397 5311, Telex: 262795

Original painting by Donal McGrory

ALPHABETICAL LIST OF ADVERTISERS

DMS Inc
31 Station Road, Henley-on-Thames, Oxfordshire,
England .... [122]

Dravo SteelShip Corporation
Route 4, Box 167, Pine Bluff, Arkansas 71602,
USA .... [126]

DTCN
2 rue Royale, Bôite Postale No 1,
75200 Paris Naval, France .... [124] & [140]

E

Edo Corporation
13-10 111th Street, College Point,
New York 11356, USA .... [109]

Elettronica San Giorgio SpA (ELSAG)
Via Hermada 6, 16154, Genoa/Sestri, Italy . [72] & [73]

Elmer Montedel SpA
PO Box 189, Viale dell'Industria 4,
00040 Pomezia, Rome, Italy .... [47]

Empresa Nacional Bazan SA
65 Castellana, Madrid 1, Spain .... [98]

Ente Fiera di Genova
Fiera Internazionale di Genova-Consornautica,
16129 Genoa, Italy .... [152]

F

Fairey Marine Ltd
Hamble, Southampton, Hampshire SO3 5NB,
England .... [9]

Ferranti Computer Systems Ltd
Bracknell Division, Bracknell,
Berkshire RG12 1RA, England .... [93]

Fiat Aviazione SpA
Via Nizza 312, 10127 Turin, Italy .... [99]

Fincantieri
(Societa Finanziaria Cantieri Navali)
Via Sardegna 40, 00187 Rome, Italy .... [119]

G

Garrett Corporation, The
Marine Gas Turbines,
AiResearch Manufacturing Co of Arizona,
PO Box 5217, Phoenix, Arizona 85010, USA ..... [97]

Gould Ocean Systems
18901 Euclid Avenue, Cleveland,
Ohio 44117, USA .... [64]

Grandi Motori Trieste
PO Box 497, 34100 Trieste, Italy .... [11]

Graseby Instruments Ltd
Kingston-by-Pass, Surbiton, Surrey KT6 7LR,
England .... [3]

H

Halter Marine Services Inc
PO Box 29266, New Orleans,
Louisiana 70189, USA .... [21]

Hatch & Kirk Export Co Inc
5111 Leary Avenue NW, Seattle,
Washington 98107, USA .... [67]

Hollandse Signaalapparaten BV
PO Box 42, Hengelo, The Netherlands ..... [88] & [89]

Howaldtswerke-Deutsche Werft AG
PO Box 146309, D-2300 Kiel 14,
Federal Republic of Germany .... [90]

Hycor Inc
North Woburn Industrial Park, Woburn,
Massachusetts 01801, USA .... [29]

I

Ingenieurkontor Lübeck
PO Box 1690, Niels-Bohr-Ring 5, D-2400
Lübeck 1, Federal Republic of Germany .... [90]

INMA SpA
(Industrie Navali Meccaniche Affini)
Viale S Bartolomeo 362, 19100 La Spezia,
Italy .... [84]

Isotta Fraschini Motori Breda SpA
Via Milan 7, 21047 Saronno, Varese, Italy ...... [108]

Israel Aircraft Industries
Ben Gurion International Airport, Israel .... [33]

Israel Shipyards
Haifa, Israel .... [114]

Italcantieri SpA
Corso Cavour 1, 54132 Trieste, Italy .... [69]

Italcraft (Cantieri Navali Italcraft)
Via Paolo Frisi 9, 00197 Rome, Italy .... [55]

Italsider SpA
Pizza Dante 7, 16121 Genoa, Italy .... [66]

Italtel SpA
(Societa Italiana Telecomunicazioni)
12 Pizzale Zavattari, 20149 Milan, Italy .... [96]

K

Kollmorgen Corporation
Electro-Optical Division, Northampton,
Massachusetts 01060, USA .... [98]

Korody-Colyer Corporation
112 North Avalon Boulevard, Wilmington,
California 90744, USA .... [46]

L

Lockheed Electronics
Plainfield, New Jersey 07061, USA .... [43]

Lürssen Werft
PO Box 70 00 30, Friedrick-Klippert Strasse,
D-2820 Bremen 70, Federal Republic of
Germany .... [80] & [81]

M

MacTaggart Scott & Co Ltd
PO Box 1, Hunter Avenue, Loanhead,
Midlothian EH20 9SP, Scotland .... [106]

Marconi Space & Defence Systems Ltd
The Grove, Warren Lane, Stanmore,
Middlesex HA7 4LY, England .... [132]

Melara Club
c/o Elettronica San Giorgio (ELSAG), Via Hermada 6,
16153 Genoa/Sestri, Italy .... [116] & [117]

Misar SpA
Via Gavardo 6, 25016 Ghedi (Brescia), Italy ..... [75]

MTU (Motoren-und Turbinen-Union GmbH)
Olgastrasse 75, D-7990 Friedrichshafen 1,
Federal Republic of Germany .... [71]

N

Nevesbu
(BV Nederlandse Verenigde Scheepsbouw Bureaus)
PO Box 289-2501 CG, The Hague,
The Netherlands .... [62]

O

Oerlikon-Bührle Ltd
PO Box 888, CH-8050 Zurich, Switzerland .... [92]

Officine Galileo
Montedison Group, Via Carlo Bini 44,
50134 Florence, Italy .... [34]

An engine for all seasons

Connecting rod and link rod on engine shaft

Engine shaft

Cam shaft

gearing distribution

Lower crankcase section with engine shaft

All boat engines may be seaworthy, but they are certainly not all engines for all seasons.
Those who have tried CRM marine engines know all too well what a difference this can mean, because they can be sure of the reliability of the technical solutions inherent in every model designed by CRM.
Just ask the navy and the customs officers, for example: ask them what the V-type 12 cylinder engines installed on their minesweepers and coastal defence vessels are like, and you are sure to be told that CRM engines are the ideal engines for all seasons.
But the last in the line, the 12 D/SS-YE, is not just an engine for all seasons, like the others; it merits above all your choice, because it reflects in its powerful, compact 1,800 Kgs all the outstanding features of the entire CRM range of great marine engines: engines for all seas.

CRM

making seafaring history

CRM. Via Manzoni, 12 - MILANO - phone 02/708326 ● 784118 - telex 334382 CREMME

ALPHABETICAL LIST OF ADVERTISERS

Officine Panerai SrL
2 Piazza G Ferraris, 50131 Florence, Italy .... [100]

OTO Melara SpA
Via Valdilocchi 15, 19100 La Spezia, Italy .... [136]

P

Paxman Diesels Ltd
PO Box 8, Paxman Works, Colchester,
Essex CO1 2HW, England .... [13]

Philips Elektronikindustrier AB
Defense Elektronics, S-17520 Järfälla 1,
Sweden .... [77]

Philips USFA BV
Meerenakkerweg 1, Eindhoven 5600 MD,
The Netherlands .... [54]

Picchiotti Commercial Ltd
PO Box 4, Sarisbury Green,
Southampton, Hampshire S03 6YU, England .... [94]

Picchiotti SpA
Cantiere Navale Viareggio, 55049, Italy .... [94]

Plessey Marine
Uppark Drive, Ilford, Essex IG1 4AQ,
England .... *inside front cover*

R

Rank Pullin Controls/Rank Precision Industries
Langston Road, Debden, Loughton, Essex,
England...................... *front endpaper iv*

Raytheon Inc
141 Spring Street, Lexington,
Massachusetts 02173, USA .... [120] & [121]

Redifon Telecommunications Ltd
Naval Communications Systems,
Broomhill Road, London SW18 4JQ, England ... [27]

Rinaldo Piaggio SpA
Viale Brigata Bisagno 14, 16129 Genoa, Italy .... [87]

Riva Calzoni SpA
Via Emilia Ponente, 72 Bollogna, Italy .... [48]

RSV (Rhine-Schelde-Verolme) BV
kon Mij "de Schelde", Glacisstraat 165,
PO Box 16, Vlissingen, The Netherlands .... [85]

S

SACM
157 Avenue Charles de Gaulle, F 92521
Neuilly sur Seine, Cedex, France .... [83]

Safare-Crouzet
BP 171, 06005 Nice, Cedex, France .... [34]

Sea Power Magazine
Navy League of the United States,
818 18th Street NW,
Washington DC 20006, USA .... [118]

Selenia
(Industrie Elettroniche Associate SpA)
Special Equipment & Systems Division,
Via dei Castelli Romani 2,
00040 Pomezia, Rome, Italy .... [51]

SEPA SpA
Lungo Stura Lazio 45, 10156 Turin, Italy .... [127]

SFCN
(Société Française de Constructions Navales)
66 quai Alfred Sisley,
92390 Valleneuve-la-Garenne, France .... [110]

Sippican Corporation, The
Oceanographic Systems Division, 7 Barnabas Road,
Massachusetts 02738, USA .... [7]

Sistel-Sistemi Elettronica SpA
The Montedison Group, Via Tiburtina 1210,
00131 Rome, Italy .... [123]

SMA SpA
Via del Ferrone 5, Casella Postale 200,
50100 Florence, Italy .... [125]

Snia Viscosa SpA
Defence & Space Division, Via Sicilia 162,
00187 Rome, Italy .... [36]

Sofrexan
30 rue d'Astorg, 75008 Paris, France .... [122]

Sperry Gyroscope
Downshire Way, Bracknell,
Berkshire RG12 1QL, England .... [134]

T

Termomeccanica Italiana SpA
Via del Molo 1, 19100 La Spezia, Italy .... [112]

Thomson CSF/ASM
BP 53, 06802 Cagnes-Sur-Mer, France .... [58]

Thomson CSF/AVS
178 BP, Gabriel Peri, 92240 Malakoff, France .... [44]

Thomson CSF/DRS/TVT
1 rue des Mathurins, BP 10,
92222 Bagneux, France .... [68]

Thomson CSF/DSE
1 rue des Mathurins, BP 10,
92222 Bagneux, France .... [60]

Trieste Club
c/o Selenia, Via Tiburtina km 12.400,
00131 Rome, Italy .... [76]

U

USEA SpA
Corso Via G. Matteotti 63,
19030 Pugliola di Lerici, La Spezia, Italy .... [100]

V

Valtec Italiana SrL
Via Valtellina 65, Milan, Italy .... [23]

Varo Inc
555 N. Fifth Street, PO Box 401267,
Garland, Texas 75040, USA .... [35]

Vickers Shipbuilding Group Ltd
Barrow-in-Furness, Cumbria, England .... [25]

Vitro Selenia
Via Tiburtina 1020, 00156 Rome, Italy .... [82]

Vosper Singapore Ltd
200 Tanjong Rhu Road, Singapore 15 .... [15]

Vosper Thornycroft (UK) Limited
Vosper House, Southampton Road, Paulsgrove,
Portsmouth, Hampshire PO6 4QA, England ..... [45]

Y

Yarrow (Shipbuilders) Ltd
Scotstoun, Glasgow G14 0XN, Scotland .... [144]

Z

Zahnradfabrik Friedrichshafen AG
PO Box 2520, D-7990 Friedrichshafen 1,
Federal Republic of Germany .... [19]

Supporting the fleet with environmental measurements.

SSXBT / Sippican
Ocean Systems

The Submarine Expendable Bathythermograph (SSXBT) has entered its third year of production and is at sea aboard the USS Groton (SSN 694) and many other submarines. SSXBT equipped vessels now have the ability to measure the temperature profile to a depth of 2500 feet while remaining submerged and underway. Sippican continues to support the fleet in the collection and data processing of environmental measurements with submarine and surface ship instrumentation and systems.

Manufacturer: Sippican Ocean Systems, Marion, Massachusetts 02738   Telex 929437

Distributors:
Plessey Marine
The Plessey Co., Ltd.
Ilford, Essex, England

Tsurumi Seiki Co., Ltd.
Yokohama, Japan

Telecommunications
Radioelectriques et Telephoniques
Paris, France

Classified list of advertisers

The companies advertising in this publication have informed us that they are involved in the fields of manufacture indicated below:

Acoustic sweeps
Sperry Gyroscope
Trieste Club

Acoustic transducers
Graseby Instruments
Trieste Club

Action information systems
Decca Navigator

Active information systems
Ferranti
Plessey Radar
SMA
Vickers

Active information trainers
DTCN
Ferranti
SEPA

Air compressors
CIT Alcatel
Fincantieri
Garrett Corporation

Aircraft, anti-submarine patrol
British Aerospace Aircraft Group
Rinaldo Piaggio

Aircraft arresting gear
Aérospatiale
MacTaggart Scott

Aircraft carriers
Cantieri Navali Riuniti
DTCN
Fincantieri
Vickers

Aircraft countermeasure dispenser systems
Hycor

Aircraft instruments
DTCN
Edo Corporation
Ferranti
Sperry Gyroscope
Thomson CSF

Aircraft, maritime reconnaissance
British Aerospace Aircraft Group
DTCN
Rinaldo Piaggio

Air cushion vehicles
British Hovercraft Corporation
DTCN
Halter Marine
Vosper Thornycroft

Airframe manufacturers
Aérospatiale
Agusta
British Aerospace Aircraft Group
British Hovercraft Corporation
Rinaldo Piaggio

Alignment equipment
British Aerospace Dynamics Group

Alternators
DTCN

Ammunition
Bofors
DTCN
Empresa Nacional Bazan
Oerlikon-Bührle
Snia Viscosa

Ammunition fuses
Borletti
DTCN
Empresa Nacional Bazan
Oerlikon-Bührle
Thomson CSF

Ammunition hoists
Blohm & Voss
DTCN
MacTaggart Scott
OTO Melara
Vickers

Antennae
British Aerospace Dynamics Group
Decca Navigator
Hollandse Signaalapparaten
Philips Elektronikindustrier
Plessey Radar
Selenia
Thomson CSF
Trieste Club

Anti-ship missile defence systems
CSEE
Hycor
MSDS
Raytheon

Anti-submarine launchers
DTCN
Plessey Marine
Trieste Club
Vickers

Anti-submarine rocket launchers
Bofors
DTCN
Trieste Club
Vickers

Anti-submarine rockets
Bofors
CIT Alcatel
DTCN
Empresa Nacional Bazan
Trieste Club

Anti-submarine weapon systems, long range
British Aerospace Dynamics Group
ELSAG
SEPA
Trieste Club

Assault craft
Blohm & Voss
British Hovercraft Corporation
Brooke Marine
Cantieri Baglietto
Crestitalia
De Vries Shipyards
Dravo Steelship
Empresa Nacional Bazan
Fairey Marine
Fincantieri
Halter Marine
SFCN
Vosper Singapore
Vosper Thornycroft
Yarrow (Shipbuilders)

Assault ships
Blohm & Voss
Brooke Marine
Cantieri Navali Riuniti
De Vries Shipyards
Dravo Steelship
DTCN
Empresa Nacional Bazan
Fincantieri
Howaldtswerke-Deutsche Werft
SFCN
Vickers
Vosper Singapore
Vosper Thornycroft
Yarrow (Shipbuilders)

ASW weapon control systems
DTCN
Ferranti
Graseby Instruments
Hollandse Signaalapparaten
Philips Elektronikindustrier
Plessey Radar
Selenia
Thomson CSF

Audio ancillary test sets
Safare-Crouzet

Automatic control systems
CIT Alcatel
DTCN
Ferranti
MTU
Officine Galileo
Selenia
SEPA
Sperry Gyroscope
Thomson CSF

Automatic steering
Decca Navigator
Sperry Gyroscope

Auxiliary machinery
Blohm & Voss
DTCN
Empresa Nacional Bazan
Fincantieri
MTU

Batteries
ACC Wilhelm Hagen

Binoculars
Barr & Stroud
British Aerospace Dynamics Group
DTCN
Kollmorgen
Montedison Group
Officine Galileo

Binnacles, compass
Decca Navigator

Boilers
Blohm & Voss
Bremer Vulkan
Cantieri Navali Riuniti
DTCN
Empresa Nacional Bazan
Howaldtswerke-Deutsche Werft
Paxman Diesels
Rhine-Schelde-Verolme
Yarrow (Shipbuilders)

Books, naval
Vosper Thornycroft

Bulk carriers
Ailsa Shipbuilding
Blohm & Voss
Bremer Vulkan
Cantieri Navali Riuniti
Dubigeon-Normandie
Empresa Nacional Bazan
Fincantieri
Howaldtswerke-Deutsche Werft
Italcantieri
Lürssen Werft
Rhine-Schelde-Verolme
Sippican Corporation
Vickers

B-OSS in sternframe
Italsider

Cable glands
Graseby Instruments

Cable looms (with or without caissons)
DTCN

CLASSIFIED LIST OF ADVERTISERS

Capstans and windlasses
Cantieri Navali Riuniti
MacTaggart Scott
Riva Calzoni

Car ferries
Ailsa Shipbuilding
Blohm & Voss
Bremer Vulkan
British Hovercraft Corporation
Brooke Marine
Cantieri Navali Riuniti
Chantiers de la Perriere
CNIM
DTCN
Dubigeon-Normandie
Empresa Nacional Bazan
Fincantieri
Halter Marine
Italcantieri
Lürssen Werft
Rhine-Schelde-Verolme
Vickers

Cargo handling equipment
Blohm & Voss
Fincantieri
MacTaggart Scott

Cargo ships
Ailsa Shipbuilding
Blohm & Voss
Bremer Vulkan
Brooke Marine
Cantieri Navali Riuniti
Chantiers de la Perriere
De Vries Shipyards
Dubigeon-Normandie
Empresa Nacional Bazan
Fincantieri
Halter Marine
Howaldtswerke-Deutsche Werft
Italcantieri
Lürssen Werft
Rhine-Schelde-Verolme
Vickers

Castings, aluminium-bronze
Barr & Stroud
DTCN
Empresa Nacional Bazan
Vickers

Castings, high duty iron
Bremer Vulkan
DTCN
Empresa Nacional Bazan

Castings, non-ferrous
DTCN
Vickers

Castings, shell moulded
Bremer Vulkan
DTCN
Ferranti

Castings, sg iron
Bremer Vulkan
DTCN
Ferranti

Castings, steel
Bremer Vulkan
DTCN
Empresa Nacional Bazan
Italsider

Cathodic protection equipment
Marconi
Thomson CSF
Vickers

Centralised and automatic control
CIT Alcatel
Selenia
Thomson CSF
Vosper Thornycroft

Chaff
Hycor
Snia Viscosa

Chaff dispensers
Hycor

Charts, nautical and aeronautical
Decca Navigator

Clear view screens
Decca Navigator

Coastal and inshore minesweepers
British Hovercraft Corporation
Brooke Marine
Cantieri Baglietto
DTCN
Empresa Nacional Bazan
Fincantieri
Halter Marine
Italcantieri
Nevesbu
Rhine-Schelde-Verolme
Vickers
Vosper Thornycroft
Yarrow (Shipbuilders)

Coast guard/patrol ships
Aresa
Bergens Mekaniske

Command/control/communications systems
AEG-Telefunken
DTCN
Ferranti
Graseby Instruments
Hollandse Signaalapparaten
Kollmorgen
MSDS
Oerlikon-Bührle
Officine Panerai
Philips Elektronikindustrier
Plessey Radar
Raytheon
Redifon
Selenia
Sippican Corporation
Thomson CSF
Trieste Club
Vosper Thornycroft

Command/control real-time displays
Ferranti
Hollandse Signaalapparaten
Philips Elektronikindustrier
Plessey Radar
Raytheon
Selenia
Thomson CSF

Communications systems
MSDS
Raytheon
Redifon
Trieste Club

Compressed air starters for gas turbines and diesel engines
DTCN
Garrett Corporation
Hatch & Kirk

Compressors
CIT Alcatel
DTCN
Fincantieri

Computer-assisted communications systems
Redifon

Computer guidance
Garrett Corporation
Raytheon
SEPA

Computer services
British Aerospace Dynamics Group
Decca Navigator
Ferranti
Plessey Radar
SEPA
Thomson CSF
Vickers
Yarrow (Shipbuilders)

Computers
CIT Alcatel
Decca Navigator
Ferranti
Hollandse Signaalapparaten
Montedison Group
OTO Melara
Philips Elektronikindustrier
Selenia
SEPA
Sperry Gyroscope
Thomson CSF

Condenser tubes
Fincantieri
Rhine-Schelde-Verolme

Condensers
Blohm & Voss
Cantieri Navali Riuniti
Fincantieri
Empresa Nacional Bazan
Howaldtswerke-Deutsche Werft
Rhine-Schelde-Verolme
Thomson CSF

Container ships
Blohm & Voss
Cantieri Navali Riuniti
DTCN
Dubigeon-Normandie
Empresa Nacional Bazan
Fincantieri
Halter Marine
Howaldtswerke-Deutsche Werft
Italcantieri
Rhine-Schelde-Verolme
Vickers

Control desks, electric
Lürssen Werft
SEPA
Thomson CSF
Vosper Thornycroft
Whipp & Bourne

Control gear
Paxman Diesels
Philips Elektronikindustrier
Vosper Thornycroft

Control gear—automated
Garrett Corporation

Corvettes
Blohm & Voss
Bremer Vulkan
Brooke Marine
Cantieri Navali Riuniti
Crestitalia
De Vries Shipyards
DTCN
Dubigeon-Normandie
Empresa Nacional Bazan
Fincantieri
Halter Marine
Howaldtswerke-Deutsche Werft
INMA
Italcantieri
Lürssen Werft
Nevesbu
Rhine-Schelde-Verolme
Sofrexan
Vickers
Vosper Singapore
Vosper Thornycroft
Yarrow (Shipbuilders)

Cranes, ships
DTCN
Dubigeon-Normandie
Howaldtswerke-Deutsche Werft
Rhine-Schelde-Verolme

Crankshafts for low-speed diesel engines
Hatch & Kirk
Italsider
Rhine-Schelde-Verolme

Crankshafts in continuous-grain-flow for medium speed engines
Hatch & Kirk
Italsider

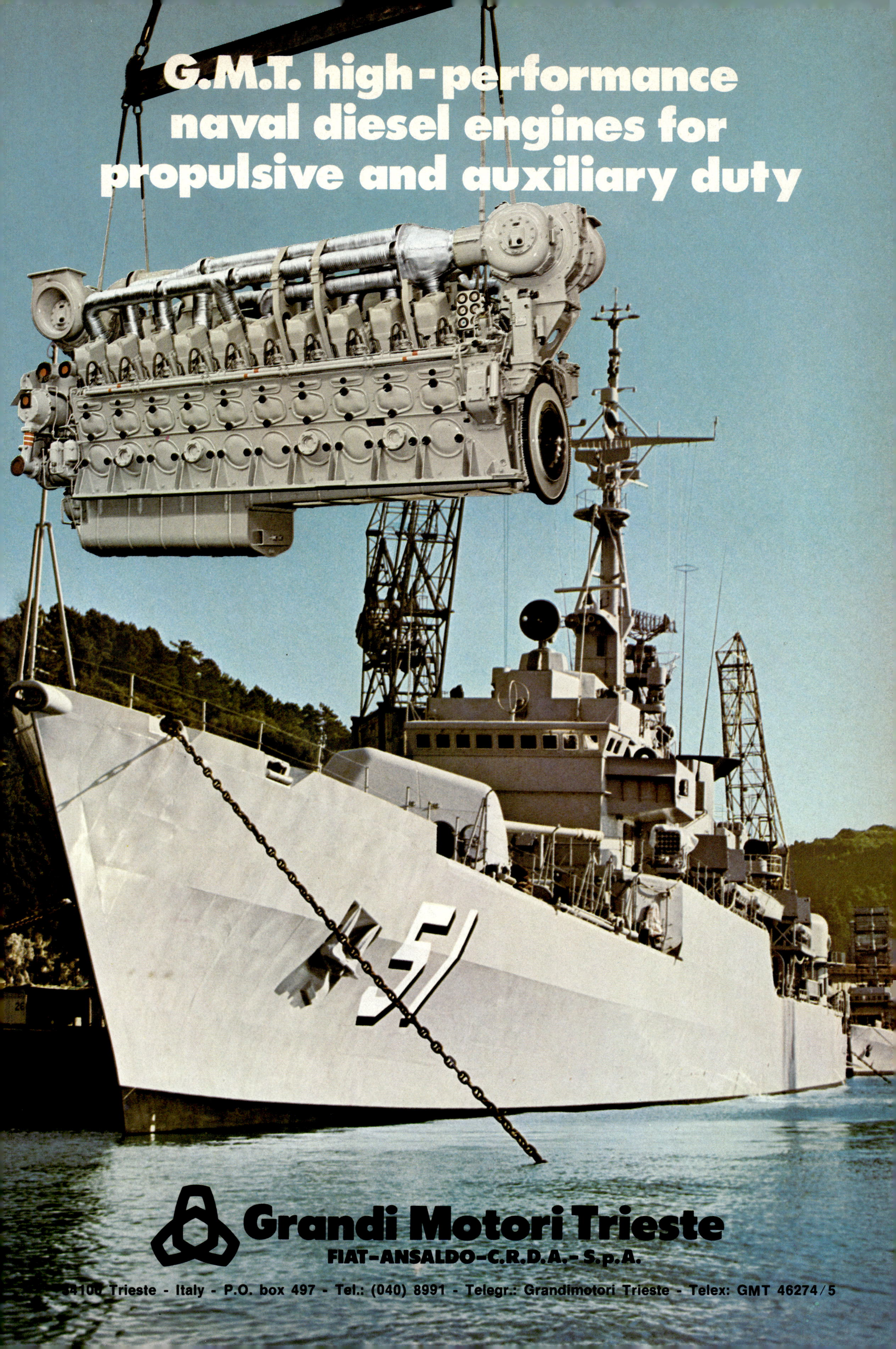
G.M.T. high-performance naval diesel engines for propulsive and auxiliary duty
Grandi Motori Trieste
FIAT-ANSALDO-C.R.D.A.-S.p.A.
34100 Trieste - Italy - P.O. box 497 - Tel.: (040) 8991 - Telegr.: Grandimotori Trieste - Telex: GMT 46274/5

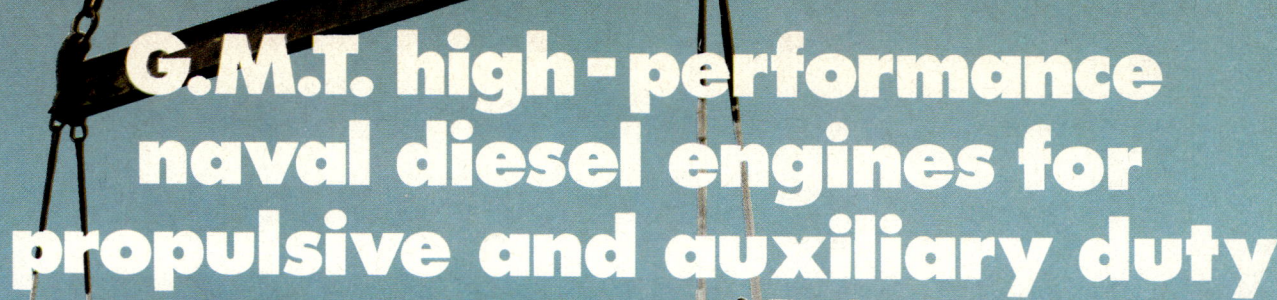

CLASSIFIED LIST OF ADVERTISERS

Cruisers
ARESA
Brooke Marine
Cantieri Navali Riuniti
Crestitalia
Dubigeon-Normandie
Empresa Nacional Bazan
Fincantieri
Italcantieri
Nevesbu
Rhine-Schelde-Verolme
Vickers
Vosper Thornycroft

Cylinder covers, forged and cast
Hatch & Kirk
Italsider
Rhine-Schelde-Verolme

Data recording systems
AEG-Telefunken
British Aerospace Dynamics Group
Decca Navigator
Garrett Corporation
Plessey Radar
SEPA
Sperry Gyroscope
Thomson CSF

Deck machinery
Cantieri Navali Riunti
DTCN
Fincantieri
Graseby Instruments
MacTaggart Scott
Rhine-Schelde-Verolme

Design-systems study and management services
Decca Navigator
Empresa Nacional Bazan
Howaldtswerke-Deutsche Werft
Ingenieurkontor Lübeck

Destroyers
Blohm & Voss
Cantieri Navali Riuniti
DTCN
Dubigeon-Normandie
Empresa Nacional Bazan
Fincantieri
Italcantieri
Nevesbu
Rhine-Schelde-Verolme
Sofrexan
Vickers
Vosper Thornycroft
Yarrow (Shipbuilders)

Diesel engine spare parts
Blohm & Voss
Bremer Vulkan
CRM
DTCN
Empresa Nacional Bazan
Grandi Motori Trieste
Fincantieri
Hatch & Kirk
Korody-Colyer
MTU
Paxman Diesels
Rhine-Schelde-Verolme
Vickers

Diesel engines, auxiliary
AIFO
Alsthom-Atlantique
Blohm & Voss
Bremer Vulkan
CRM
DTCN
Empresa Nacional Bazan
Fincantieri
Grandi Motori Trieste
Isotta Fraschini
Korody-Colyer
MTU
Paxman Diesels
Rhine-Schelde-Verolme
SACM
Trieste Club
Vickers

Diesel engines, main propulsion
AIFO
Alsthom Atlantique
Blohm & Voss
Bremer Vulkan
CRM
DTCN
Empresa Nacional Bazan
Fincantieri
Grandi Motori Trieste
Isotta Fraschini
Korody-Colyer
MTU
Paxman Diesels
Rhine-Schelde-Verolme
SACM
Trieste Club
Vickers

Diesel, fuel injection equipment
Cobham, Alan
DTCN
Hatch & Kirk
Korody-Colyer
Rhine-Schelde-Verolme

Diesel fuel filters
Cobham, Alan

Display systems
CSEE
Graseby Instruments
Hollandse Signaalapparaten
Philips Elektronikindustrier
Plessey Radar
Raytheon
Selenia
SEPA
Thomson CSF
Trieste Club

Diving equipment
DTCN
Graseby Instruments
Ingenieurkontor Lübeck
MSDS
Officine Panerai
Safare-Crouzet
Sillinger

Diving vessels
Chantiers de la Perriere
Fairey Marine

Dock gates
DTCN
Dubigeon-Normandie
Fincantieri
Howaldstwerke-Deutsche Werft
Vickers

Doppler aircraft navigation systems
Decca Navigator

Dredgers
Ailsa Shipbuilding
Brooke Marine
DTCN
Dubigeon-Normandie
Empresa Nacional Bazan
Fincantieri
SFCN

Dry cargo vessels
Ailsa Shipbuilding
Blohm & Voss
Bremer Vulkan
Brooke Marine
Cantieri Navali Riuniti
Dubigeon-Normandie
Empresa Nacional Bazan
Fincantieri
Halter Marine
Howaldtswerke-Deutsche Werft
Italcantieri
Lürssen Werft
Rhine-Schelde-Verolme
Vickers

Dry dock proprietors
Ailsa Shipbuilding
Blohm & Voss
Cantieri Navali Riuniti
CIT Alcatel
Empresa Nacional Bazan
Fincantieri
Rhine-Schelde-Verolme
Yarrow (Shipbuilders)

Dynamic positioning
British Hovercraft Corporation
DTCN
SEPA
Thomson CSF
Vosper Thornycroft

Early warning systems
Kollmorgen
MSDS
Raytheon

Echo sounders
DTCN
Edo Corporation
Graseby Instruments
Marconi
Thomson CSF
Trieste Club

Electric cables
British Hovercraft Corporation

Electric countermeasures
Bofors
Decca Navigator
DTCN
Kollmorgen
Sperry Gyroscope
Thomson CSF

Electrical auxiliaries
DTCN
Garrett Corporation
Paxman Diesels

Electrical equipment
DTCN
Garrett Corporation
Officine Panerai
SEPA
Vosper Thornycroft

Electrical fittings
DTCN

Electrical installations and repairs
AEG-Telefunken
Bremer Vulkan
DTCN
Fincantieri
Vickers
Vitroselenia
Vosper Singapore
Vosper Thornycroft

Electrical switchgear
DTCN
Garrett Corporation
Lürssen Werft
Thomson CSF
Vosper Singapore
Vosper Thornycroft
Whipp & Bourne

Electro-hydraulic auxiliaries
Cantieri Navali Riuniti
DTCN
Fincantieri
MacTaggart Scott
Trieste Club
Vosper Thornycroft

Electronic countermeasures
CSEE
DTCN
Elmer Montedel
Hollandse Signaalapparaten
Kollmorgen
MSDS
Philips Elektronikindustrier
Plessey Radar
Raytheon
Selenia
Thomson CSF

Paxman power... for Navies planning to grow!

The Paxman Valenta is a high-performance, low-weight diesel engine which offers substantial long-term advantages to developing maritime forces. The compact Valenta is available in 6, 8, 12, 16 and 18-cylinder forms, power range 1000 to 4500 bhp, and complies with the stringent specifications laid down by the Royal Navy for fighting ships. It is designed to meet shock requirements for combat, and to be simply maintained in service.

The wide power range achieved from the Valenta in its different configurations means a high degree of parts standardization for different power requirements and applications. In logistic terms this means smaller spares holdings, simplified base facilities and reduced training requirements. In this important respect, the Paxman Valenta offers Navies and Coastguards of the world a unique possibility to meet all their requirements for diesel propulsion and power generation, present and future, afloat and ashore, with logic and economy.

The Paxman Valenta has an extensive naval service record, both in propulsion and auxiliary duties.

You are invited to send for full technical specifications and information on how the Valenta range can meet the needs of your fleet.

Paxman Diesels Limited, PO Box 8, Paxman Works, Colchester, Essex CO1 2HW, England.
Telephone: (0206) 5151 Telex: 98151

Paxman Diesels Limited

A management company of GEC Diesels Limited
Holding Company – The General Electric Company Limited

CLASSIFIED LIST OF ADVERTISERS

Electronic engine room telegraph
Garrett Corporation
Officine Panerai
SEPA
Vosper Thornycroft

Electronic equipment
AEG-Telefunken
British Hovercraft Corporation
CIT Alcatel
CSEE
Decca Navigator
DTCN
Ferranti
Garrett Corporation
Howaldtswerke-Deutsche Werft
MSDS
Montedel
MTU
Officine Panerai
OTO Melara
Plessey Marine
Plessey Radar
Philips Elektronikindustrier
Raytheon
Selenia
SEPA
Sippican Corporation
SMA
Sperry Gyroscope
Thomson CSF
USEA
Vickers
Vosper Thornycroft

Electronic equipment refits
Edo Corporation
DTCN
Ferranti
Philips Elektronikindustrier
Plessey Marine
Plessey Radar
Sperry Gyroscope
Thomson CSF
Vitroselenia
Vosper Thornycroft

Electronic power systems
Varo

Engine monitors and data loggers
British Hovercraft Corporation
Garrett Corporation
SEPA
Vosper Thornycroft

Engine parts, diesel
Bremer Vulkan
CRM
DTCN
Empresa Nacional Bazan
Fincantieri
Grandi Motori Trieste
Hatch & Kirk
Korody-Colyer
Paxman Diesels
Vickers

Engine speed controls
DTCN
Vosper Thornycroft

Engine start and shut-down controls
DTCN
Garrett Corporation
Hatch & Kirk
SEPA
Vosper Thornycroft

Engines, aircraft
Avco Lycoming
Fiat
MTU
Rinaldo Piaggio

Engines, diesel
Alsthom-Atlantique
Blohm & Voss
Bremer Vulkan
DTCN
Empresa Nacional Bazan
Fincantieri
Isotta Fraschini
Korody-Colyer
MTU
Paxman Diesels
Rhine-Schelde-Verolme
SACM

Engines, gas turbine
Avco Lycoming
CIT Alcatel
DTCN
Fiat
Garrett Corporation
MTU
Rhine-Schelde-Verolme
Rinaldo Piaggio
SACM

Engines, steam turbine
Blohm & Voss
Cantieri Navali Riuniti
Empresa Nacional Bazan
Fincantieri
Rhine-Schelde-Verolme

Epicyclic gears
British Hovercraft Corporation
Vickers

Equipment for helicopter night deck landing
DTCN
Officine Panerai

Escort vessels
Ailsa Shipbuilding
Blohm & Voss
Bremer Vulkan
Brooke Marine
Cantieri Navali Riuniti
De Vries Shipyards
DTCN
Empresa Nacional Bazan
Fairey Marine
Fincantieri
Halter Marine
Italcantieri
Lürssen Werft
Nevesbu
Rhine-Schelde-Verolme
SFCN
Sofrexan
Vickers
Yarrow (Shipbuilders)

Fast patrol craft
Ailsa Shipbuilding
ARESA
British Hovercraft Corporation
Brooke Marine
Cantieri Baglietto
Cantieri Navali Riuniti
Chantiers de la Perriere
Crestitalia
De Vries Shipyards
Dravo Steelship
DTCN
Empresa Nacional Bazan
Fairey Marine
Fincantieri
Halter Marine
INMA
Italcraft
Lürssen Werft
Nevesbu
Rhine-Schelde-Verolme
SFCN
Sillinger
Sofrexan
Vosper Singapore
Vosper Thornycroft
Yarrow (Shipbuilders)

Fast warship design service
Brooke Marine
Cantieri Navali Riuniti
DTCN
Empresa Nacional Bazan
Italcantieri
Lürssen Werft
Rhine-Schelde-Verolme
Vickers
Vosper Singapore
Vosper Thornycroft
Yarrow (Shipbuilders)

Feed water heaters
Blohm & Voss
Cantieri Navali Riuniti
Fincantieri

Ferries
Bremer Vulkan
British Hovercraft Corporation
Brooke Marine
Cantieri Navali Riuniti
DTCN
Dubigeon-Normandie
Empresa Nacional Bazan
Fincantieri
Halter Marine
Howaldtswerke-Deutsche Werft
Italcantieri
Rhine-Schelde-Verolme
SFCN
Vickers

Fibre optics
Barr & Stroud
DTCN
Plessey Radar

Fibreglass vessels and other products
ARESA
Crestitalia
DTCN
Empresa Nacional Bazan
Halter Marine
Lürssen Werft
Vickers
Vosper Singapore
Vosper Thornycroft

Filters
DTCN

Filters, electronic
Barr & Stroud

Fire and salvage vessels
Brooke Marine
Chantiers de la Perriere
Crestitalia
De Vries Shipyards
Fincantieri
Halter Marine
Rhine-Schelde-Verolme
SFCN

Fire control
Raytheon

Fire control and gunnery equipment
Bofors
CSEE
ELSAG
Ferranti
Hollandse Signaalapparaten
Kollmorgen
MSDS
Montedison Group
Oerlikon-Bührle
OTO Melara
Philips Elektronikindustrier
Plessey Marine
Plessey Radar
Sperry Gyroscope
Thomson CSF
Vickers

Fittings, ships
DTCN
Fincantieri
Rhine-Schelde-Verolme
Vosper Singapore

We design — fast patrol craft.....

We are ideally based in Singapore....

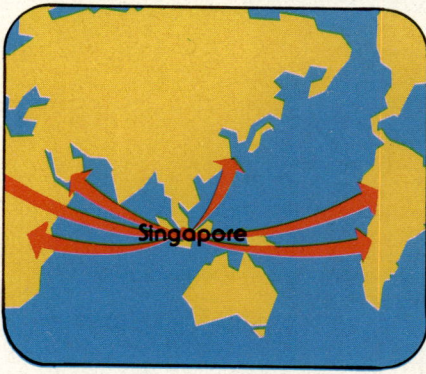

We build to the highest standards at the most competitive cost.....

We are the only shipbuilder in S.E. Asia that can design as well as build fast patrol craft and other high speed vessels for navies, police, customs and other special government departments. Since our inception in 1923 we have gained wide experience in this field.

We are based in Singapore, where there is a highly trained, low cost labour force, which makes Singapore an ideal location for the Vosper shipyard. This benefit, together with the high qualifications of Vosper's technical personnel means that we can design and build to the highest standards at the most competitive cost.

And we can deliver on time.

We are......

VOSPER SINGAPORE

VOSPER PRIVATE LIMITED 200 Tanjong Rhu Road, Singapore 15.
Tel: 4467144 Telex: RS21219 Cable: VOSPER SINGAPORE

uspneedham vs/15/7

CLASSIFIED LIST OF ADVERTISERS

Flares
Hycor
Misar

Forgings, steel
Italsider

Frigates
Blohm & Voss
Bremer Vulkan
Brooke Marine
Cantieri Navali Riuniti
DTCN
Dubigeon-Normandie
Empresa Nacional Bazan
Fincantieri
Italcantieri
Nevesbu
Rhine-Schelde-Verolme
Sofrexen
Vickers
Vosper Thornycroft
Yarrow (Shipbuilders)

Fuel filtration equipment
Cobham, Alan
DTCN
Fincantieri
Vickers

Fuel injectors, oil
DTCN

Gas turbine boats
Avco Lycoming
Blohm & Voss
Cantieri Baglietto
DTCN
Halter Marine
Vickers
Vosper Thornycroft

Gas turbines
Avco Lycoming
CIT Alcatel
DTCN
Fiat
Garrett Corporation
MTU
Rhine-Schelde-Verolme
SACM

Gear casings
Bremer Vulkan
Cantieri Navali Riuniti
Fiat
Fincantieri
Rhine-Schelde-Verolme
Vickers

Gears
Cantieri Navali Riuniti
Empresa Nacional Bazan
Howaldstwerke-Deutsche Werft
Isotta Fraschini
Rhine-Schelde-Verolme

Gears and gearing
Bremer Vulkan
Cantieri Navali Riuniti
Fiat
Fincantieri
Howaldstwerke-Deutsche Werft
Rhine-Schelde-Verolme
Vickers
Vosper Thornycroft

Gears, hypoid
Empresa Nacional Bazan
Rhine-Schelde-Verolme

Gears, reverse-reduction
CRM
Empresa Nacional Bazan
Isotta Fraschini
Korody-Colyer
MTU
Rhine-Schelde-Verolme
Vickers
Vosper Thornycroft
Zahnradfabrik

Gears, spiral bevel
Rhine-Schelde-Verolme

Gears, spur
Fiat
Rhine-Schelde-Verolme

Gears, vee drive
CRM
Vosper Thornycroft
Isotta Fraschini
Zahnradfabrik

Generators, electric
AIFO
DTCN
Empresa Nacional Bazan
Ferranti
Garrett Corporation
Paxman Diesels

Ground influence mines
Misar

Governors
DTCN
Fincantieri
Hatch & Kirk

Governors, engine speed
DTCN
Hatch & Kirk
Korody-Colyer

Guided missile servicing equipment
Aérospatiale
British Aerospace Dynamics Group
Fincantieri
OTO Melara
Rhine-Schelde-Verolme
Selenia
Thomson
CSF
Vitroselenia

Guided missile ships
Blohm & Voss
Brooke Marine
Cantieri Navali Riuniti
Dravo Steelship
DTCN
Empresa Nacional Bazan
Fincantieri
Halter Marine
Howaldstwerke-Deutsche Werft
Italcantieri
Lürssen Werft
Montedison Group
Nevesbu
Rhine-Schelde-Verolme
Selenia
SFCN
Vickers
Vosper Thornycroft
Yarrow (Shipbuilders)

Guided missiles
Aérospatiale
Bofors
British Aerospace Dynamics Group
DTCN
ELSAG
Montedison Group
OTO Melara
Raytheon
Sistel-Sistemi
SMA
Sperry Gyroscope

Gun boats
Ailsa Shipbuilding
ARESA
Brooke Marine
Cantieri Baglietto
Cantieri Navali Riuniti
Crestitalia
De Vries Shipyards
DTCN
Empresa Nacional Bazan
Fairey Marine
Fincantieri
Halter Marine
INMA
Nevesbu
OTO Melara
SFCN
Vosper Singapore
Vosper Thornycroft
Yarrow (Shipbuilders)

Guns and mountings
Bofors
Breda Meccanica
DTCN
Empresa Nacional Bazan
Oerlikon-Bührle
OTO Melara
Vickers

Gun mounts
Bofors
Breda Meccanica
DTCN
Empresa Nacional Bazan
Oerlikon-Bührle
OTO Melara
Vickers

Gun-sighting apparatus and height finders
DTCN
Kollmorgen
Montedison Group
Oerlikon-Burhle
Officine Galileo
Philips Elektronikindustrier
Thomson CSF
Vickers

Gyroscopic compasses
Decca Navigator
DTCN
Sperry Gyroscope
Thomson CSF

Gyroscopic compasses, aircraft
Sperry Gyroscope

Gyroscopic compasses, land vehicles
Sperry Gyroscope

Gyroscopic compasses, ships
Sperry Gyroscope
Trieste Club

Handsets
Thomson CSF

Headphones
DTCN
Marconi
Thomson CSF

Headsets
Thomson CSF

Heat exchangers
Blohm & Voss
Bremer Vulkan
Cantieri Navali Riuniti
Empresa Nacional Bazan
Hatch & Kirk
Howaldstwerke-Deutsche Werft
Korody-Colyer

Heated windows
Kollmorgen

Heavy duty mooring motorboats
Chantiers de la Perriere
DTCN
Fairey Marine

Helicopter, anti-submarine patrol
Agusta

Helicopter, maritime reconnaissance
Agusta

Helm indicators
Decca Navigator

High level liquid alarm systems
Officine Panerai

Hovercraft
Aérospatiale
British Hovercraft Corporation
DTCN
Halter Marine
Vosper Thornycroft

Two unique Royal Navy answers to missile attack on warships

...at close range

Seawolf is the only ship-borne point defence missile system with proven anti-missile as well as anti-aircraft capability – and missiles, not aircraft, are the real threat to today's warships. No comparable system has demonstrated the ability to intercept and destroy small, supersonic, anti-ship missiles. Successful sea trials on the British frigate HMS Penelope have cleared the way for Seawolf's service with entry into the Royal Navy in the late 1970s. The standard version is fully automatic and all-weather. Lighter-weight "blindfire", "darkfire" and "visual-only" variants are suitable for ships from 400–2,000 tons.

...at long range

Sea Skua is the only helicopter launched lightweight weapon which has been developed to counter the threat from missile-carrying fast patrol craft, launching their attacks from over the horizon. The combination of the wide radius of action of modern helicopters and Sea Skua's own considerable range ensures that the threat can be neutralised before the attacking craft can approach within effective missile-launching distance. Already at an advanced stage of development, Sea Skua will be widely used on frigate-borne Lynx helicopters of the Royal Navy from the late 1970s onwards.

Seawolf
Ship-borne anti-missile and anti-aircraft system

Sea Skua
Lightweight helicopter borne anti-ship system

BRITISH AEROSPACE DYNAMICS GROUP
Stevenage Herts England

A World Leader in Missile Defence Systems, Space Satellites and related technologies

CLASSIFIED LIST OF ADVERTISERS

Hydraulic equipment
DTCN
Fincantieri
Garrett Corporation
MacTaggart Scott
Officine Galileo
OTO Melara
Riva Calzoni
Vickers
Vosper Thornycroft

Hydraulic machinery
DTCN
Fincantieri
Garrett Corporation
MacTaggart Scott
Riva Calzoni
Trieste Club
Vickers
Vosper Thornycroft

Hydraulic plant
Aerimpianti
Cantieri Navali Riuniti
DTCN
Fincantieri
Garrett Corporation
MacTaggart Scott
Riva Calzoni
Vosper Thornycroft

Hydrofoils
Aérospatiale
Blohm & Voss
Cantiere Navaltecnica
Cantieri Navali Riuniti
DTCN
Fincantieri
Vosper Thornycroft

Hydrographic survey equipment
DTCN
Edo Corporation
MSDS

Hydrophones
Graseby Instruments

IFF Mk 10 systems
DTCN
Plessey Radar
Thomson CSF

IFF radar
DTCN
Hollandse Signaalapparaten
Philips Elektronikindustrier
Plessey Radar
Thomson CSF
Trieste Club

Indicators, electric
DTCN
Thomson CSF
Vosper Thornycroft

Inertial gyro calibration equipment
Graseby Instruments

Inertial navigation systems
British Aerospace Dynamics Group
DTCN
Ferranti
Sperry Gyroscope

Infra-red countermeasure systems
CSEE
Hycor

Infra-red materials
Barr & Stroud
DTCN
Philips Usfa

Infra-red systems
Barr & Stroud
British Aerospace Dynamics Group
DTCN
Hollandse Signaalapparaten
Kollmorgen
Montedison Group
Officine Galileo
Philips Usfa
Selenia
Thomson CSF
Vickers

Injectors, fuel
Hatch & Kirk
Korody-Colyer

Instrument calibration services
British Aerospace Dynamics Group
Vickers
Vitroselenia

Instrument components, mechanical
British Aerospace Dynamics Group
Thomson CSF

Instruments, electronic
Bofors
Decca Navigator
Ferranti
Garrett Corporation
Howaldtswerke-Deutsche Werft
Safare-Crouzet
SEPA
Sperry Gyroscope
Thomson CSF

Instruments, nautical
DTCN
Sippican Corporation
Sperry Gyroscope
Trieste Club

Instrument panels
Ferranti
Decca Navigator
Lürssen Werft
Thomson CSF

Instruments, precision
British Aerospace Dynamics Group
DTCN
Ferranti
Sperry Gyroscope

Instruments, test equipment
DTCN
Ferranti
Hatch & Kirk
SEPA
Sperry Gyroscope
Thomson CSF
Vickers
Vitroselenia

Intercommunications systems
Redifon

Interior design and furnishing for ships
Blohm & Voss
DTCN
Vickers
Vosper Thornycroft

Inverters and battery chargers
Ferranti

Landing craft
Ailsa Shipbuilding
Brooke Marine
Cantieri Baglietto
Cantieri Navali Riuniti
Chantiers de la Perriere
CNIM
DTCN
Empresa Nacional Bazan
Halter Marine
Howaldtswerke-Deutsche Werft
INMA
Lürssen Werft
Nevesbu
Rhine-Schelde-Verolme
SFCN
Sillinger
Vosper Singapore
Vosper Thornycroft
Yarrow (Shipbuilders)

Landing craft: logistic
Brooke Marine

Laser rangefinders
Barr & Stroud
Bofors
DTCN
Ferranti
Hollandse Signaalapparaten
Kollmorgen
Selenia
Thomson CSF

Laser systems
Barr & Stroud
CSEE
DTCN
Ferranti
Kollmorgen
Montedison Group
Officine Galileo
Raytheon
Selenia
Thomson CSF
Vickers

Launches: patrol
ARESA

Lifeboats
Crestitalia
DTCN
Fairey Marine
SFCN
Sillinger
Vosper Thornycroft

Lifts, hydraulic
MacTaggart Scott

Lights and lighting
Officine Panerai

Liquid petroleum gas carriers
CNIM
DTCN
Dubigeon-Normandie
Fincantieri
Howaldtswerke-Deutsche Werft
Italcantieri
SFCN
Vickers

Loudspeaker equipment
Safare-Crouzet
Thomson CSF

Machined parts, ferrous
Blohm & Voss
Bremer Vulkan
DTCN
Vickers

Machined parts, non-ferrous
Blohm & Voss
Bremer Vulkan
DTCN
Vickers

Maintenance and repair ships
Bremer Vulkan
Brooke Marine
Cantiere Navaltecnica
Cantieri Navali Riuniti
DTCN
Dubigeon-Normandie
Empresa Nacional Bazan
Fincantieri
Howaldtswerke-Deutsche Werft
Vickers
Vosper Singapore
Vosper Thornycroft

Marine architects
ABMTM
ARESA
DTCN
Empresa Nacional Bazan
Fincantieri
Ingenieurkontor Lübeck
Lürssen Werft
Nevesbu
Rhine-Schelde-Verolme
Vickers
Vosper Singapore
Vosper Thornycroft

Marine consultants
ABMTM
ARESA
Empresa Nacional Bazan
Ingenieurkontor Lübeck

Marine engine monitoring and data recording systems
Decca Navigator
DTCN
Garrett Corporation
Hatch & Kirk
SEPA

ZF gearboxes...
big on performance – small in size.

ZF – Europe's No. 1 gearbox specialist – is also taking the lead in the marine industry. More and more top designers are showing a preference for ZF drive units.

Marine quality and performance standards are among the most exacting. As with every other piece of equipment used on board, the utmost operational reliability is demanded of the reversing gearbox – coupled with quiet running and long life. The gearbox must not only match the performance of the high speed diesel engines, but not take up too much valuable space in the process.

ZF gearboxes meet the requirement precisely. They are compact, surprisingly light – give outstanding performance in ratings up to 5000 hp. Which is why they are being so widely chosen... on land, on sea and in the air.

If you have a driving problem you only have to say. ZF's gearbox specialists almost certainly have the answer.

ZF – the sign of progress

ZAHNRADFABRIK FRIEDRICHSHAFEN AG
D-7990 Friedrichshafen 1
P. O. Box 2520 W.-Germany

CLASSIFIED LIST OF ADVERTISERS

Marine management
ABMTM

Marine radar
Decca Navigator
DTCN
Ferranti
Hollandse Signaalapparaten
Graseby Instruments
Oerlikon-Bührle
Philips Elektronikindustrier
Plessey Radar
Raytheon
Selenia
SMA
Thomson CSF
Trieste Club

Materials handling equipment
DTCN
MacTaggart Scott

Market intelligence reports
DMS

Memory storage systems for military vehicles
Sperry Gyroscope

Merchant ships
Ailsa Shipbuilding
Blohm & Voss
Bremer Vulkan
Cantieri Navali Riuniti
Chantiers de la Perriere
Dubigeon-Normandie
Empresa Nacional Bazan
Fincantieri
Halter Marine
Howaldstwerke-Deutsche Werft
Italcantieri
Lürssen Werft
Rhine-Schelde-Verolme
SFCN
Vickers

Message processing systems
Sperry Gyroscope

Microphone equipment
DTCN
Thomson CSF
Trieste Club

Microwave systems
Kollmorgen

Mine countermeasure vessels
Yarrow (Shipbuilders)

Mine countermeasures
CIT Alcatel
Decca Navigator
DTCN
Edo Corporation
MSDS
Paxman Diesel
Philips Elektronikindustrier
Plessey Marine
SMA
Sperry Gyroscope

Mine hunting equipment
Decca Navigator
MSDS
Sperry Gyroscope

Minelayers
Blohm & Voss
British Hovercraft Corporation
Cantieri Navali Riuniti
DTCN
Dubigeon-Normandie
Empresa Nacional Bazan
Fincantieri
Halter Marine
Nevesbu
Rhine-Schelde-Verolme
Vickers
Vosper Thornycroft
Yarrow (Shipbuilders)

Minesweeping equipment
Sperry Gyroscope

Minesweepers
Blohm & Voss
British Hovercraft Corporation
Cantieri Baglietto
Cantieri Navali Riuniti
DTCN
Dubigeon-Normandie
Edo Corporation
Empresa Nacional Bazan
Fincantieri
Halter Marine
Italcantieri
Nevesbu
Rhine-Schelde-Verolme
Thomson CSF
Vickers
Vosper Thornycroft
Yarrow (Shipbuilders)

Missile control systems
Aérospatiale
British Aerospace Dynamics Group
CIT Alcatel
DTCN
ELSAG
Ferranti
Oerlikon-Bührle
Montedison Group
MSDS
Officine Galileo
OTO Melara
Philips Elektronikindustrier
Plessey Radar
Raytheon
Selenia
Sistel-Sistemi
Sperry Gyroscope
Thomson CSF
Vickers

Missile installations
Aérospatiale
British Aerospace Dynamics Group
DTCN
Montedison Group
OTO Melara
Raytheon
Selenia
Sistel-Sistemi
Thomson CSF
Vickers
Vitroselenia
Vosper Singapore

Missile launching systems
Aérospatiale
British Aerospace Dynamics Group
CIT Alcatel
DTCN
Ferranti
Montedison Group
OTO Melara
Raytheon
Selenia
Sistel-Sistemi
Vickers
Vitroselenia

Missile ships
Blohm & Voss
Brooke Marine
Cantiere Navaltecnica
Cantieri Baglietto
Cantieri Navali Riuniti
Dravo Steelship
DTCN
Empresa Nacional Bazan
Fincantieri
Italcantieri
Lürssen Werft
Montedison Group
Nevesbu
Rhine-Schelde-Verolme
Sofrexen
Vickers
Vosper Singapore
Yarrow (Shipbuilders)

Model makers and designers
British Hovercraft Corporation
Fincantieri
Ingenieurkontor Lübeck
Nevesbu
Vickers
Vosper Thornycroft

Model test towing tank service
British Hovercraft Corporation
Vickers

Motor control gear
Bremer Vulkan
British Hovercraft Corporation
Thomson CSF
Vosper Singapore

Motor starters
Thomson CSF
Vosper Singapore

Motor torpedo boats
Brooke Marine
Cantieri Baglietto
Cantieri Navali Riuniti
DTCN
Dubigeon-Normandie
Empresa Nacional Bazan
Halter Marine
INMA
Lürssen Werft
Nevesbu
Rhine-Schelde-Verolme
SFCN
Thomson CSF
Trieste Club
Vosper Thornycroft

Motors, electric
Thomson CSF

Naval guns
Bofors
Breda Meccanica
DTCN
Empresa Nacional Bazan
Garrett Corporation
Oerlikon-Bührle
OTO Melara
Vickers

Naval radar
DTCN
ELSAG
Ferranti
Hollandse Signaalapparaten
Oerlikon-Bührle
Philips Elektronikindustrier
Plessey Radar
Raytheon
Selenia
SMA
Sperry Gyroscope
Thomson CSF
Trieste Club

Navigation aids
AEG-Telefunken
CSEE
Decca Navigator
DTCN
Elmer Montedel
Sperry Gyroscope
Thomson CSF
USEA
Vitroselenia

Night vision systems
Barr & Stroud
DTCN
ELSAG
Kollmorgen
Montedison Group
MSDS
Officine Galileo
Philips Usfa
Thomson CSF

CLASSIFIED LIST OF ADVERTISERS

Non-magnetic minesweepers
Cantieri Baglietto
DTCN
Dubigeon-Normandie
Empresa Nacional Bazan
Fincantieri
Korody-Colyer
Rhine-Schelde-Verolme
Sperry Gyroscope
Vickers
Vosper Thornycroft

Oceanographic electronic systems
DTCN
Howaldtswerke-Deutsche Werft
MSDS
Safare-Crouzet
SEPA
Sippican Corporation
Thomson CSF

Oceanographic survey ships
Brooke Marine
Cantieri Navali Riuniti
Chantiers de la Perriere
DTCN
Empresa Nacional Bazan
Fairey Marine
Fincantieri
Halter Marine
Lürssen Werft
Nevesbu
Rhine-Schelde-Verolme
SFCN
Vickers
Yarrow (Shipbuilders)

Offshore countermeasures
DTCN
Dubigeon-Normandie

Oil drilling rigs
CIT Alcatel
Fincantieri
Howaldtswerke-Deutsche Werft
Vickers

Oil fuel heaters
Blohm & Voss
Fincantieri
Vosper Thornycroft

Oil fuel systems and burners
Vosper Thornycroft

Oil rig supply vessels and work boats
Brooke Marine
Chantiers de la Perriere
Crestitalia
Dubigeon-Normandie
Fairey Marine
Fincantieri
Halter Marine
Vosper Singapore

Optical equipment
Barr & Stroud
British Aerospace Dynamics Group
DTCN
ELSAG
Kollmorgen
Officine Galileo
Officine Panerai
Vickers

Optical filters
Barr & Stroud
DTCN
Officine Galileo

Optronics
CSEE
ELSAG
Hollandse Signaalapparaten
Kollmorgen
Officine Galileo

Ordnance
Bofors
Borletti
Empresa Nacional Bazan
OTO Melara
Oerlikon-Bührle
Snia Viscosa
Vickers

Oropesa sweeps
Sperry Gyroscope

Parts for diesel engines
Blohm & Voss
Bremer Vulkan
CRM
DTCN
Empresa Nacional Bazan
Fincantieri
Hatch & Kirk
Italsider
Korody-Colyer
Paxman Diesels
Rhine-Schelde-Verolme
Vickers

Passenger ships
Ailsa Shipbuilding
Blohm & Voss
Bremer Vulkan
Brooke Marine
Cantiere Navaltecnica
Cantieri Navali Riuniti
Chantiers de la Perriere
Crestitalia
DTCN
Empresa Nacional Bazan
Fincantieri
Howaldtswerke-Deutsche Werft
Italcantieri
Rhine-Schelde-Verolme
SFCN
Vickers

Patrol boats
ARESA
Ailsa Shipbuilding
Brooke Marine
Cantieri Navali Riuniti
De Vries Shipyards
Dravo Steelship
Empresa Nacional Bazan
Fairey Marine
Italcantieri
Italcraft
Nevesbu
Vosper Thornycroft
Yarrow (Shipbuilders)

Patrol boats: launches, tenders and pinnacles
Brooke Marine
Cantiere Navaltecnica
Cantieri Baglietto
Cantieri Navali Riuniti
Chantiers de la Perriere
Chantiers Navals de L'Esterel
Crestitalia
De Vries Shipyards
DTCN
Dubigeon-Normandie
Empresa Nacional Bazan
Fairey Marine
Lürssen Werft
Nevesbu
SFCN
Sillinger
Valtec
Vosper Thornycroft

Penetrators
Graseby Instruments

Periscope fairings
DTCN
Edo Corporation
Kollmorgen
MacTaggart Scott

Periscopes
Barr & Stroud
DTCN
Kollmorgen
Sofrexan

Pipes, copper and brass
Fincantieri
Vickers

Pipes, sea water
Fincantieri
Vickers

Piston heads
Italsider
Korody-Colyer

Pistons, piston rings and gudgeon pins
Hatch & Kirk
Korody-Colyer

Plotting tables
Decca Navigator
Philips Elektronikindustrier
Plessey Radar
SMA
Sofrexan
Thomson CSF

Plugs and sockets
Thomson CSF

Pontoons, self propelled
Bremer Vulkan
Brooke Marine
Chantiers de la Perriere
CNIM
DTCN
Howaldtswerke-Deutsche Werft
SFCN

Portable equipment for aircraft landing
Officine Panerai

Pressure vessels
Bremer Vulkan
Vickers
Yarrow (Shipbuilders)

Propellants
Bofors
Empresa Nacional Bazan
Snia Viscosa

Propeller shaft couplings, flexible
DTCN
Vickers

Propeller shafts and intermediate shafts
Empresa Nacional Bazan
Italsider

Propellers, hovercraft
British Aerospace Dynamics Group

Propellers, ship research
DTCN
Empresa Nacional Bazan
Fincantieri

Propellers, ships
Cantieri Navali Riuniti
DTCN
Empresa Nacional Bazan
Fincantieri
Vickers

Propulsion machinery
AIFO
Avco Lycoming
Blohm & Voss
Bremer Vulkan
Cantieri Navali Riuniti
Castoldi
DTCN
Empresa Nacional Bazan
Fincantieri
Garrett Corporation
Korody-Colyer
MTU
Paxman Diesels
Rhine-Schelde-Verolme
SACM
Vickers

Publishers
DMS
Macdonald & Jane's
Sea Power

Pumps
AIFO
CIT Alcatel
DTCN
Empresa Nacional Bazan
Fincantieri
Garrett Corporation
MacTaggart Scott
Termomeccanica
Thomson CSF
Vickers

CLASSIFIED LIST OF ADVERTISERS

Radar aerials
British Aerospace Dynamics Group
Decca Navigator
DTCN
Hollandse Signaalapparaten
Marconi
Philips Elektronikindustrier
Plessey Radar
Raytheon
Selenia
SMA
Thomson CSF

Radar countermeasures
Hycor
Raytheon
Trieste Club

Radar for fire control
DTCN
ELSAG
Ferranti
Hollandse Signaalapparaten
MSDS
Oerlikon-Bührle
Philips Elektronikindustrier
Plessey Radar
Raytheon
Selenia
SMA
Sperry Gyroscope
Thomson CSF
Trieste Club

Radar for harbour supervision
Decca Navigator
DTCN
Hollandse Signaalapparaten
Plessey Radar
Raytheon
SMA
Thomson CSF
Trieste Club

Radar for navigation warning interception
AEG-Telefunken
Decca Navigator
DTCN
Hollandse Signaalapparaten
Philips Elektronikindustrier
Plessey Radar
Raytheon
Selenia
SMA
Thomson CSF
Trieste Club

Radar transponders
DTCN
Plessey Radar
Raytheon
Thomson CSF
Trieste Club

Radio, air
Decca Navigator
Thomson CSF

Radio, direction finding
Marconi

Radio equipment
Montedel
Montedison Group
Redifon
Thomson CSF

Radio navigation equipment
Elmer Montedel

Radio transmitters and receivers
Ferranti
Elmer Montedel
Montedison Group
Philips Elektronikindustrier
Redifon
Thomson CSF

Radomes
British Aerospace Dynamics Group
British Hovercraft Corporation
DTCN
Hollandse Signaalapparaten
Kollmorgen
Lürssen Werft
Plessey Radar
Raytheon
Thomson CSF
Vickers

Ramjets
Aérospatiale

Rangefinders
Barr & Stroud
Officine Galileo
SMA
Thomson CSF

Relocalisation device
CIT Alcatel
DTCN

Remote controls
CSEE
ELSAG
Oerlikon-Bührle
Officine Galileo
OTO Melara
SEPA
Thomson CSF
Vosper Thornycroft

Remote level indicator equipment for submarine trim tanks
DTCN
Officine Panerai

Remote power control systems
Breda Meccanica
Garrett Corporation

Replacement parts for diesel engines
Blohm & Voss
Bremer Vulkan
CRM
DTCN
Fincantieri
MacTaggart Scott
Vickers

Research ships
Bremer Vulkan
Brooke Marine
Cantieri Navali Riuniti
Chantiers de la Perriere
DTCN
Dubigeon-Normandie
Empresa Nacional Bazan
Fincantieri
Halter Marine
Lürssen Werft
Nevesbu
Rhine-Schelde-Verolme
SFCN
Sillinger
Vickers

Reverse reduction gears, oil operated
Isotta Fraschini
Vickers

Reversing gears
Empresa Nacional Bazan
Isotta Fraschini
Korody-Colyer
Vickers

Rocket launchers
Bofors
Breda Meccanica
CNIM
DTCN
Empresa Nacional Bazan
Oerlikon-Bührle
OTO Melara
Snia Viscosa
Vickers

Roll damping fins
Blohm & Voss
Howaldtswerke-Deutsche Werft
Vickers
Vosper Thornycroft

Rudders
Ailsa Shipbuilding
Bremer Vulkan
Empresa Nacional Bazan
Fincantieri
Howaldtswerke-Deutsche Werft
Italsider
Rhine-Schelde-Verolme
Vosper Thornycroft

Rudderstocks
Howaldtswerke-Deutsche Werft
Italsider
Rhine-Schelde-Verolme

Running gears/forgings
Italsider

Salvage vessels
Ailsa Shipbuilding
Brooke Marine
Crestitalia
De Vries Shipyards
Empresa Nacional Bazan
Fincantieri
Halter Marine
INMA
SFCN

Salvage and boom vessels
Ailsa Shipbuilding
Brooke Marine
Cantiere Navaltecnica
Crestitalia
De Vries Shipyards
Fincantieri
Halter Marine
Nevesbu

Scientific instruments
DTCN
Ferranti
Thomson CSF
Vickers

Vickers make another addition to their submarine fleet.

Piranha

500 class*

1100 class*

Vickers have made another important addition to their range of smaller submarines – the Piranha Class Coastal Submarine.

The Piranha, with a submerged displacement of about 140 tonnes, is small – only a tenth of the size of the Type 1100, but it is large in attacking power. It has a tactical range of up to 1,000 miles from base and has the capacity to release divers or carry landing parties. Its normal complement of 7 can be augmented with about 10 other personnel, and its armament can include 6 mines plus limpet mines, 2 torpedoes plus limpet mines, or two 2-man chariots.

Vickers patrol submarines also include the Type 500 with an advanced design and construction which enable it to carry extremely powerful armament, sonars and batteries for its size, and the 1100 with even greater range, speed and diving depth.

All these designs incorporate advanced technology of the kind derived from the Vickers 'Polaris' pedigree.

For more information on these submarines and their related weapon systems contact the Vickers Shipbuilding Group.

*In association with Ingenieurkontor Lubeck and Howaldtswerke Deutsche Werft A.G.

Vickers Shipbuilding Group Limited, Barrow-in-Furness, Cumbria, England.
Telephone: 0229 20351. Telex: 65171 VICVSB G
A member company of British Shipbuilders.

CLASSIFIED LIST OF ADVERTISERS

Screen wipers
Decca Navigator

Self homing torpedo guidance head
MSDS
Selenia

Ship defence systems
Breda Meccanica
Hycor
MSDS
Snia Viscosa

Ship and submarine design
Cantieri Navali Riuniti
DTCN
Dubigeon-Normandie
Empresa Nacional Bazan
Fincantieri
Halter Marine
Howaldtswerke-Deutsche Werft
Ingenieurkontor Lübeck
Italcantieri
Nevesbu
Rhine-Schelde-Verolme
Vickers
Vosper Thornycroft

Ship machinery
Alsthom Atlantique
Blohm & Voss
Bremer Vulkan
DTCN
Empresa Nacional Bazan
Fincantieri
Garrett Corporation
MTU
Paxman Diesels
Rhine-Schelde-Verolme
Vickers
Yarrow (Shipbuilders)

Ship stabilisers
Blohm & Voss
Cantieri Navali Riuniti
DTCN
Fincantieri
Howaldtswerke-Deutsche Werft
Vickers
Vosper Thornycroft

Ship systems engineering
Bremer Vulkan
British Aerospace Dynamics Group
Cantiere Navaltecnica
Cantieri Navali Riuniti
DTCN
Lips
Nevesbu
Vickers
Vosper Thornycroft
Yarrow (Shipbuilders)

Shipboard air-conditioning and ventilating plant
Aerimpianti
Garrett Corporation
Vitroselenia

Ship brass foundry for sonar and radar
DTCN
Trieste Club

Shipbuilders
Yarrow (Shipbuilders)

Shipbuilders and ship repairers
Ailsa Shipbuilding
Blohm & Voss
Brooke Marine
Cantiere Navaltecnica
Cantieri Navali Riuniti
Chantiers de la Perriere
DTCN
Dubigeon-Normandie
Empresa Nacional Bazan
Fairey Marine
Fincantieri
Halter Marine
Howaldtswerke-Deutsche Werft
Italcantieri
Lürssen Werft
Nevesbu
Rhine-Schelde-Verolme
SFCN
Sofrexan
Vickers
Vosper Singapore
Vosper Thornycroft

Ships magnetic compass test tables
Barr & Stroud
DTCN

Signals
Hycor

Simulators
Decca Navigator
DTCN
ELSAG
Ferranti
Howaldtswerke-Deutsche Werft
Ingenieurkontor Lübeck
Philips Elektronikindustrier
SEPA
Trieste Club
Vickers

Smoke indicators
Barr & Stroud

Sonar equipment
CIT Alcatel
DTCN
Edo Corporation
Ferranti
Graseby Instruments
Hollandse Signaalapparaten
Plessey Marine
Raytheon
Safare-Crouzet
Selenia
Sippican Corporation
Thomson CSF
Trieste Club
USEA

Sonar equipment (passive active-intercept)
CIT Alcatel
DTCN
Edo Corporation
Graseby Instruments
Hollandse Signaalapparaten
Plessey Marine
Raytheon
Safare-Crouzet
Selenia
Thomson CSF
Trieste Club
USEA

Sonar equipment, hull fittings and hydraulics
CIT Alcatel
DTCN
Edo Corporation
Graseby Instruments
Hollandse Signaalapparaten
Plessey Marine
Safare-Crouzet
Thomson CSF
Trieste Club
USEA

Sonar interceptor, direct finder
Safare-Crouzet
Trieste Club

Sonar ranges (design and installation)
DTCN
Graseby Instruments
Raytheon
Safare-Crouzet
Thomson CSF
Trieste Club

Sonobouys
Misar

Spare parts for diesel engines
Blohm & Voss
Bremer Vulkan
CRM
Empresa Nacional Bazan
Hatch & Kirk
Vickers

Speed boats
ARESA
Cantieri Baglietto
Chantiers Navals de L'Esterel
Crestitalia
De Vries Shipyards
DTCN
Empresa Nacional Bazan
Fairey Marine
Halter Marine
SFCN
Sillinger
Vosper Thornycroft

Stabilising equipment
Blohm & Voss
British Aerospace Dynamics Group
Cantieri Navali Riuniti
DTCN
Ferranti
Hollandse Signaalapparaten
Vickers
Vosper Thornycroft

Stabilising equipment for fire control
DTCN
Ferranti
Kollmorgen
Sperry Gyroscope
Vickers

Steam-raising plant, conventional
Blohm & Voss
Empresa Nacional Bazan

Steam-raising plant, nuclear
DTCN
Vickers
Yarrow (Shipbuilders)

CLASSIFIED LIST OF ADVERTISERS

Steam turbines
Blohm & Voss
Bremer Vulkan
Cantieri Navali Riuniti
DTCN
Empresa Nacional Bazan
Fincantieri
Howaldtswerke-Deutsche Werft

Steel-alloy and special steel forgings, plates and sections, stampings
Bofors
DTCN

Steel manganese, wear-resisting
Bofors

Steering gear
Cantieri Navali Riuniti
Decca Navigator
Vickers
Vosper Thornycroft

Sternframes
Howaldstwerke-Deutsche Werft
Italsider

Stress relieving
Bremer Vulkan
Fincantieri
Vickers
Yarrow (Shipbuilders)

Submarine batteries
Accumulatorenfabriken Wilhelm Hagen

Submarine distress buoy
Barr & Stroud
DTCN
Safare-Crouzet
Sofrexan
Thomson CSF
Trieste Club

Submarine fire control
CIT Alcatel
DTCN
Ferranti
Hollandse Signaalapparaten
Philips Elektronikindustrier
Sperry Gyroscope
Trieste Club
Vickers

Submarine-launched buoy systems
Sippican Corporation
Trieste Club

Submarine periscopes
Barr & Stroud
DTCN
Kollmorgen
Thomson CSF
Trieste Club

Submarine propulsion batteries
Accumulatorenfabriken Wilhelm Hagen

Submarines
Accumulatorenfabriken Wilhelm Hagen
DTCN
Empresa Nacional Bazan
Fincantieri
Howaldtswerke-Deutsche Werft
Ingenieurkontor Lübeck
Italcantieri
Nevesbu
Rhine-Schelde Verolme
Trieste Club
Vickers

Submarines, conventional
DTCN
Dubigeon-Normandie
Empresa Nacional Bazan
Fincantieri
Howaldtswerke-Deutsche Werft
Ingenieurkontor Lübeck
Italcantieri
Nevesbu
Rhine-Schelde-Verolme
Trieste Club
Vickers

Submarines, wet
DTCN
Howaldstwerke-Deutsche Werft
Ingenieurkontor Lübeck
Rhine-Schelde-Verolme
Vickers

Submarines, unmanned submersibles
British Aerospace Dynamics Group
Ingenieurkontor Lübeck
SEPA
Trieste Club

Superheaters
Bremer Vulkan
DTCN
Empresa Nacional Bazan
Fincantieri

Superstructure and cavitation noise detector
Safare-Crouzet

Support services
Blohm & Voss
Brooke Marine
Cantieri Navali Riuniti
Decca Navigator
DTCN
Fairey Marine
Fincantieri
Halter Marine
SEPA
Vickers
Vosper Singapore
Vosper Thornycroft

Support service vessels
Chantiers de la Perriere
Empresa Nacional Bazan
Howaldstwerke-Deutsche Werft

Survey equipment
DTCN
MSDS
Sillinger

Surveys/market intellingence
DMS

Switchboards
Blohm & Voss
Lürssen Werft
Thomson CSF
Vosper Singapore
Vosper Thornycroft
Whipp & Bourne

Switchboards and switchgear
Lürssen Werft
Thomson CSF
Vitroselenia
Vosper Singapore
Vosper Thornycroft
Whipp & Bourne

Tactical training simulators
British Aerospace Dynamics Group
British Hovercraft Corporation
CSEE
DTCN
Ferranti
Oerlikon-Bührle
Selenia
SEPA
Sofrexan
Thomson CSF
Vickers

Tankers
Blohm & Voss
Bremer Vulkan
Cantieri Navali Riuniti
DTCN
Empresa Nacional Bazan
Fincantieri
Howaldtswerke-Deutsche Werft
Italcantieri
Nevesbu
SFCN
Vickers

Tankers, small
Bremer Vulkan
Cantieri Navali Riuniti
DTCN
Dubigeon-Normandie
Empresa Nacional Bazan
Fincantieri
Halter Marine
Italcantieri
Lürssen Werft
Yarrow (Shipbuilders)

Tanks, oil and water storage
Bremer Vulkan
DTCN
Howaldtswerke-Deutsche Werft
Sillinger

Technical publications
Vickers
Vosper Thornycroft

Telecommunication equipment
CIT Alcatel
Ferranti
Marconi
Montedison Group
Redifon
Safare-Crouzet
Thomson CSF
Trieste Club

Telegraph systems
Montedel
Thomson CSF

Telemotors
MacTaggart Scott

Tenders
Blohm & Voss
Bremer Vulkan
Empresa Nacional Bazan
Fairey Marine
Halter Marine
Howaldtswerke-Deutsche Werft
Nevesbu
Sillinger

Test equipment for fire control systems
Aérospatiale
CIT Alcatel
DTCN
Hollandse Signaalapparaten
MSDS
Philips Elektronikindustrier
Selenia
Thomson CSF

Textile fibres
DTCN

Thermal imaging systems
Barr & Stroud
Kollmorgen
MSDS

Throughwater communications
Graseby Instruments

Timers
Borletti

CLASSIFIED LIST OF ADVERTISERS

Torpedo control systems
CIT Alcatel
DTCN
ELSAG
Ferranti
Gould Systems
Hollandse Signaalapparaten
MSDS
Philips Elektronikindustrier
Plessey Marine
SEPA
Sperry Gyroscope
Thomson CSF
Trieste Club
Vickers

Torpedo decoys
Graseby Instruments
Trieste Club

Torpedo depth and roll recorders
DTCN
Trieste Club

Torpedo order and reflection control
CIT Alcatel
DTCN
Trieste Club
Vickers

Torpedo side-launchers
Crestitalia
DTCN

Torpedoes and torpedo tubes
CIT Alcatel
DTCN
Empresa Nacional Bazan
MSDS
Plessey Marine
Trieste Club
Vickers

Training equipment
ABMTM
CIT Alcatel
CSEE
Decca Navigator
DTCN
Ferranti
Graseby Instruments
Howaldstwerke-Deutsche Werft
MSDS
Oerlikon-Bührle
Philips Elektronikindustrier
SEPA
Sillinger
Vickers

Training programmes
ABMTM
Decca Navigator
Empresa Nacional Bazan
Howaldstwerke-Deutsche Werft
Vosper Thornycroft

Training services
Decca Navigator
Empresa Nacional Bazan
Fairey Marine
Howaldstwerke-Deutsche Werft
MSDS
SEPA
Vosper Thornycroft

Transmitting magnetic compasses
Decca Navigator

Trawlers
Crestitalia
Dubigeon-Normandie
Empresa Nacional Bazan
Fincantieri
Halter Marine
Howaldtswerke-Deutsche Werft
SFCN

Tugs
Ailsa Shipbuilding
Ameeco (Hydrospace)
Brooke Marine
Cantieri Navali Riuniti
Crestitalia
De Vries Shipyards
Dubigeon-Normandie
Empresa Nacional Bazan
Fincantieri
Halter Marine
SFCN

Turbine gears
Bremer Vulkan
Cantieri Navali Riuniti
CIT Alcatel
DTCN
Empresa Nacional Bazan
Fiat
Fincantieri
Vickers

Turbines
Blohm & Voss
Bremer Vulkan
Cantieri Navali Riuniti
DTCN
Empresa Nacional Bazan
Fiat
Fincantieri
Hatch & Kirk
Howaldtswerke-Deutsche Werft
Rhine-Schelde-Verolme
SACM
Yarrow (Shipbuilders)

Turbines, exhaust
Avco Lycoming
Cantieri Navali Riuniti
DTCN
Fincantieri

Turbines, gas marine
Avco Lycoming
DTCN
Fiat
Garrett Corporation
SACM

Turbines, steam marine
Blohm & Voss
Bremer Vulkan
Cantieri Navali Riuniti
DTCN
Empresa Nacional Bazan
Fincantieri

Underwater acoustic systems
MSDS
Trieste Club

Underwater communication
MSDS
Trieste Club

Underwater lights
DTCN
Officine Panerai
Trieste Club

Underwater television equipment
DTCN
Edo Corporation
Kollmorgen
Sofrexan
Thomson CSF
Trieste Club

Valves and cocks
Riva Calzoni

Valves and cocks, hydraulic
MacTaggart Scott
Riva Calzoni
Trieste Club

Valves: automatic plate or disc
Trieste Club

Voltage regulators, automatic
Ferranti

Warship repairers
Bremer Vulkan
Brooke Marine
Cantieri Navali Riuniti
DTCN
Empresa Nacional Bazan
Fincantieri
Howaldtswerke-Deutsche Werft
Lürssen Werft
Nevesbu
Plessey Radar
Rhine-Schelde-Verolme
Vosper Singapore
Vosper Thornycroft

Warships
Blohm & Voss
Bremer Vulkan
Brooke Marine
Cantieri Navali Riuniti
DTCN
Dubigeon-Normandie
Empresa Nacional Bazan
Fincantieri
Halter Marine
Howaldtswerke-Deutsche Werft
Italcantieri
Lürssen Werft
Nevesbu
Rhine-Schelde-Verolme
SFCN
Sofrexan
Vosper Singapore
Vosper Thornycroft
Yarrow (Shipbuilders)

Water tube boilers
Bremer Vulkan
Cantieri Navali Riuniti
DTCN
Empresa Nacional Bazan
Fincantieri
Howaldtswerke-Deutsche Werft
Rhine-Schelde-Verolme
Yarrow (Shipbuilders)

Weapon control systems
CSEE
ELSAG
SEPA
Trieste Club
Vosper Thornycroft

DECCA ELECTRONICS
The choice of the world's navies

Standard marine radar for navigational and tactical roles–Special displays–Navigation and Action Information Systems–EW Systems–Marine automation systems–Coastal surveillance and harbour radar.

The Decca Navigator Company Limited, Decca Radar Limited   9 Albert Embankment London SE1 7SW

CLASSIFIED LIST OF ADVERTISERS

Weapon systems
Aérospatiale
Bofors
British Aerospace Aircraft Group
British Aerospace Dynamics Group
CNIM
DTCN
ELSAG
Ferranti
Gould Systems
Montedison Group
MSDS
Misar
Oerlikon-Bührle
Officine Galileo
OTO Melara
Philips Elektronikindustrier
Plessey Marine
Plessey Radar
Raytheon
Selenia
SEPA
Sippican Corporation
Sistel-Sistemi
Snia Viscosa
Sofrexan
Sperry Gyroscope
Thomson CSF
Trieste Club
Vickers
Vosper Singapore
Vosper Thornycroft

Weapon systems, sonar components
CIT Alcatel
DTCN
Edo Corporation
Graseby Instruments
Oerlikon-Bührle
Plessey Marine
Raytheon
Selenia
Thomson CSF
Trieste Club
Vitroselenia

Welding: arc, argon arc or gas
Ailsa Shipbuilding
Bremer Vulkan
Chantiers de la Perriere
DTCN
Empresa Nacional Bazan
Lürssen Werft
Rhine-Schelde-Verolme
Vickers

Winches
DTCN
Rhine-Schelde-Verolme
Vickers

Wrist compasses and depth meters for underwater operators
DTCN
Officine Panerai

X-ray work
Bremer Vulkan
DTCN
Empresa Nacional Bazan
Lürssen Werft
Vickers

Yachts, powered
Ailsa Shipbuilding
ARESA
Cantiere Navaltecnica
Cantieri Baglietto
Chantiers Navals de L'Esterel
Crestitalia
DTCN
Dubigeon-Normandie
Empresa Nacional Bazan
Fairey Marine
Halter Marine
Lürssen Werft

IAI HAS THE KEY TO SEA DEFENSE

Israel Aircraft Industries — a name synonymous with total Seaward Defense. IAI has proven expertise ready to assist you as you modernize your navy. Systems and services to help you create a formidable deterrent force to keep your waters secure. IAI supplies the navies of Israel and many other countries with effective, reliable, combat-proven systems. Gabriel weapon systems for missiles and guns. Electronic Warfare systems, including ECM and ESM. Shipborne, airborne and landbased, naval radar and communications systems. Light naval craft like the Dvora multi-mission missiles patrol boat. Sea Scan and Arava aircraft for multiple marine missions: Search & Rescue, reconnaissance, patrol.

Perhaps most important, IAI provides the ancillary services that make naval systems go: Infrastructure. Maintenance. After-sales support. Operational and maintenance training, including simulators and other equipment. Services and systems that can lead to a truly independent, self-sufficient navy.

Israel Aircraft Industries: a single, dependable source for naval systems. Your navy — and your nation — can rely on IAI. Ours do.

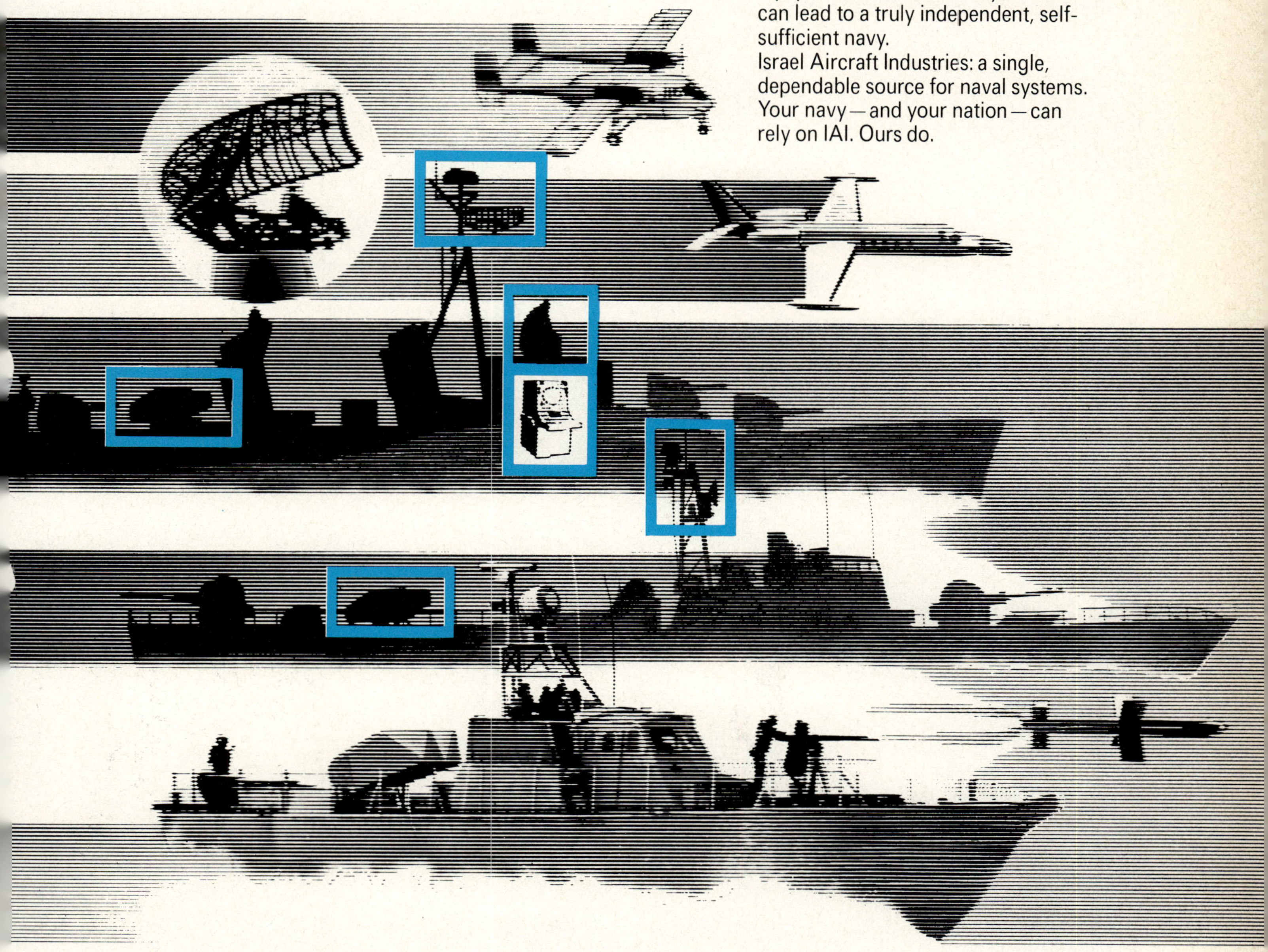

Ben Gurion International Airport, Israel.
Tel: 973111. Telex: ISRAVIA 031114.
Cables: ISRAELAVIA.
New York: Israel Aircraft Industries International Inc., 50 West 23rd Street, N.Y. 10010.
Tel: (212) 6204400. Telex: ISRAIR 125180.
Brussels: c/o Embassy of Israel, 50 Ave. des Arts.
Tel: 5131455. Telex: 62718 ISRAVIb.

IAI ISRAEL AIRCRAFT INDUSTRIES LTD
Naval Systems and Missiles Marketing

Fire Control Systems

The Officine Galileo technical level and long experience in scientific research permit today the production of a vast range of fire control systems for naval, terrestrial and air defence. Great reliability, accuracy, integrability, the shortest reaction time are some of the most qualifying features of these systems entirely designed and produced in Italy.

MONTEDISON GROUP
montedison sistemi

OFFICINE GALILEO
Divisione Sistemi
I - 50134 Firenze - Via Carlo Bini, 44
Tel. (055) 47961 - Telex 570126 GALILE

---

30 of the world's navies use Safare-Crouzet equipment

Naval Equipment

- Underwater detection
- Echo sounding
- Underwater telephony
- Electro-acoustic transducers

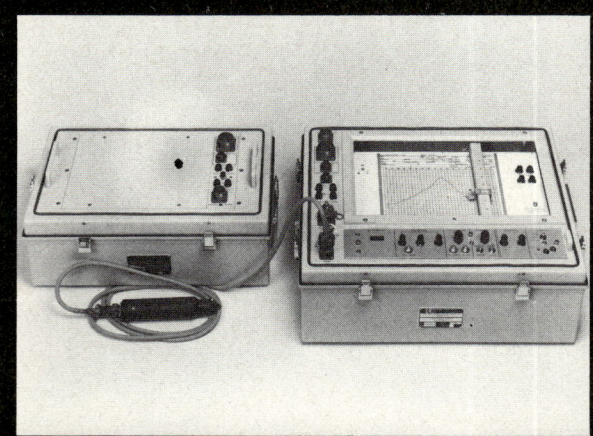

Sonar Noise Recorder DEBB-1

Oceanographic Equipment

- Wave and tide measurement
- Oceanographic and meteorological telemetering buoys
- Buoys of G.A.R.P. experiment - Argos program with satellites

Meteorological Drifting Buoy

 **SAFARE-CROUZET**

Tel. (93) 84.72.79   B.P. 171
Telex 460.813   F - 06005 Nice Cedex France

SEAPOWER

Reliable, maintainable, precise 400 Hertz shipboard power will be ready for the fleets of the 1980's. The Navy Standard Family of Frequency Changers comes in eight different unit sizes: 10KW, 16KW, 25KW, 40KW, 63KW, 100KW, 160KW, and 250KW. Units may be paralleled for split or common bus operation with linear, non-linear, and pulsating loads. Parallel operation includes automatic synchronization of unit oscillators, ten percent load sharing, and faulty unit rejection. All units have short circuit and overload protection by current limiting. Local and centralized fault isolation is built into the equipment to assist in maintenance.

VARO

VARO, INC., POWER SYSTEMS DIVISION, 555 N. FIFTH ST., P.O. BOX 401267, GARLAND, TEXAS 75040 (214) 276-6141 (TWX) 910-860-5093

DEFENCE AND SPACE DIVISION

00187 ROMA, V. SICILIA 162
TEL. 4680 - TX. 61114

CONVENTIONAL AMMUNITION

■ COMPLETE ROUNDS FOR ARTILLERY & MORTARS ■ CARTRIDGES FOR SMALL ARMS ■ PROPELLING POWDERS AND BURSTING EXPLOSIVES

ADVANCED AMMUNITION

■ AIR TO GROUND ROCKETS ■ SURFACE TO SURFACE ROCKETS ■ FIELD SATURATION ROCKETS ■ ROCKET AND MISSILE WARHEADS ■ SOLID PROPELLANT MOTORS ■ DOUBLE BASE AND COMPOSITE PROPELLANTS

SPACE ACTIVITIES

■ APOGEE MOTORS ■ STAGE SEPARATION MOTORS ■ ORBITAL TRANSFER SYSTEMS ■ SPACE LAUNCH VEHICLE MOTORS

RESEARCH AND DEVELOPMENT

■ ANALYSIS AND DEVELOPMENT OF DEFENCE SYSTEMS ■ DEVELOPMENT OF NEW WEAPON SYSTEMS ■ TECHNICAL ASSISTANCE AND TRAINING FOR PLANTS INSTALLATION ■ « TURN KEY » PLANTS OPERATION

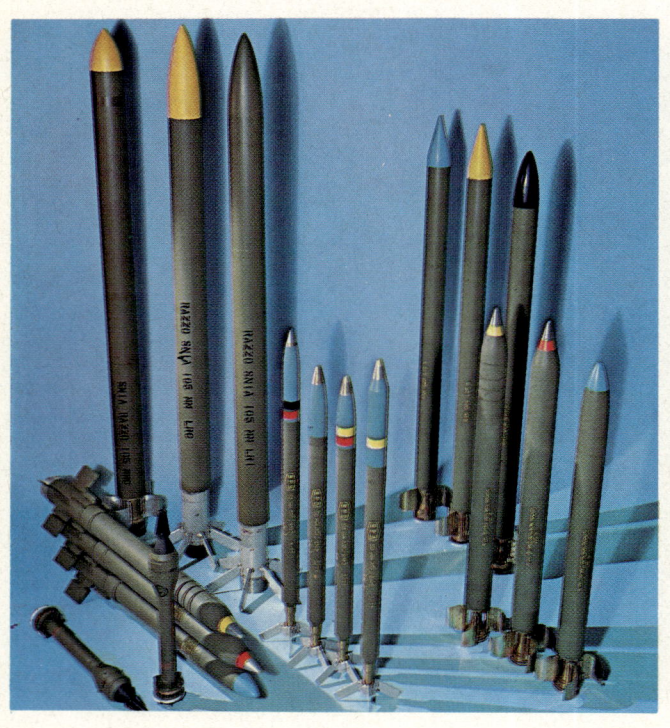

FAST PATROL BOATS

- Design and construction.
- Logistics and documentation.
- Transfer of know-how.
- Builders of the "Storm" class and the "Hauk" class to the Norwegian Navy.
- Builders of the "Hugin" class to the Swedish Navy.

COAST GUARD SHIPS

- Design and construction.
- Design of the Coast Guard Ships for the Norwegian Navy.
- Building of Coast Guard Ships for the Norwegian Navy.

A.S BERGENS MEKANISKE VERKSTEDER
AKER GROUP

P.O.BOX 858 · 5001 BERGEN · NORWAY · PHONE (475) 29 80 40 · TELEX 42133 · CABLE ADRESS: «BERGENYARD»

Italy is surrounded by sea. And of the sea, we are the most important experts in Italy.

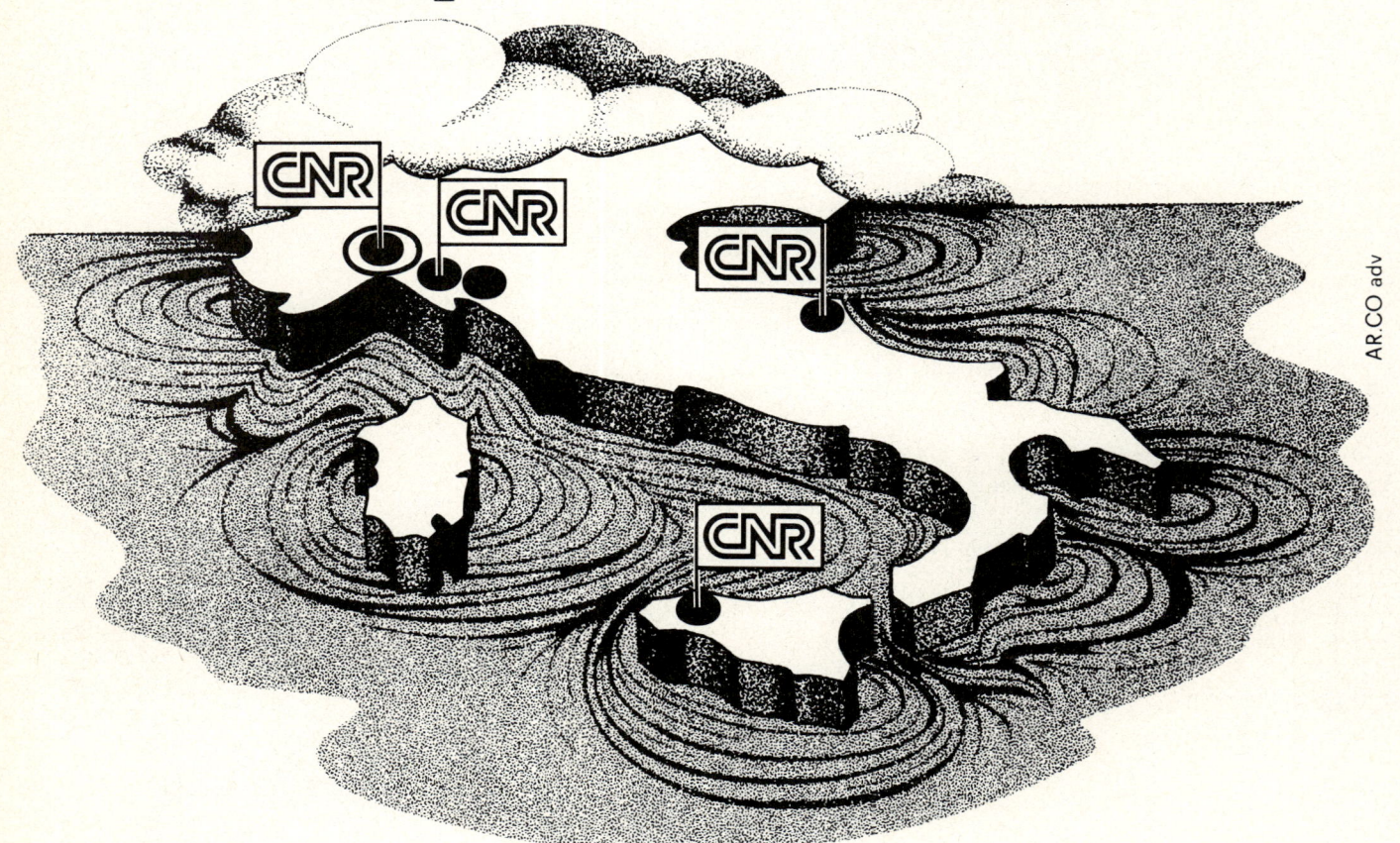

CNR CANTIERI NAVALI RIUNITI GROUP
NAVAL SHIPBUILDERS & REFITTERS

- DESTROYERS
- FRIGATES
- CORVETTES
- FAST PATROL BOATS
- HYDROFOILS
- AUXILIARY SHIPS
- SUPPORT VESSELS
- TRAINING SHIPS
- HYDROGRAPHIC RESEARCH SHIPS
- LANDING CRAFTS

P420
IS OUR PRIDE, THE LATEST OF A LONG SERIES.

The P 420 is a second generation hydrofoil with exceptional technological and operating characteristics.

Its speed of 50 knots, stability in any kind of sea, perfect manoeuvrability, join in highlighting its versatility, whether as a fighting ship, a short or long range coastal survey vessel, or as a unit for fast action in emergencies.

It's our pride, but not the only one and certainly not the last.

CNR CANTIERI NAVALI RIUNITI
FINCANTIERI GROUP

HEAD OFFICE: GENOA (Italy) ☐ Via Cipro 11 ☐ Tel 59951 ☐ Tx 270168 CANT GE
SHIPYARDS: Riva Trigoso ☐ Ancona ☐ Palermo ☐ La Spezia ☐ Genoa

Brooke Mar

An International reputation for the Design and Constructio

H.M.A.S. Fremantle, 42 metre Fast Patrol Craft for the Royal Australian Navy

Lowestoft · Suffolk · England

TELEPHONE: LOWESTOFT (0502) 65221 : TELEX 97145 : CABLES BROOKCRAFT LOWESTOFT

A Member of British Shipbuilders

ine Limited
Established 1874
of Corvettes, Fast Patrol Craft and Naval Support Ships

**S.N.V. Al Mansur,
37.5 metre Fast Patrol
Craft re-armed and refitted
for the Sultanate of Oman**

**S.N.V. Al Munassir
Landing Command Ship
for the Sultanate of Oman**

**H.M.A.V. Arakan,
Landing Craft Logistic
for the British Ministry
of Defence (Army)**

THE MARINE PROPULSION OF THE MODERN AGE

FOR MORE SAFETY, MANOEUVERABILITY, EFFICIENCY, PRACTICALITY AND ECONOMY RUN.

WATER-JET UNITS

JET 04 — 20 - 110 HP
JET 05 — 30 - 200 HP
JET 06 — 100 - 500 HP

MARINE JET ENGINES

900/04 - 46 HP   1600/04 - 89 HP   2000/05 - 108 HP   3000/05 - 141 HP   2400-D/05 - 62 HP   3500-D/05 - 93 HP

CASTOLDI S.p.A. - Viale Mazzini, 161 - 20081 ABBIATEGRASSO-MILANO-ITALIA
Telefono (02) 949341 (8 linee) - Telex 330236 CAST I

The large and small of fire-control systems.

For big jobs, there's the Mk 86. This Lockheed system is now aboard or designated for five classes of US Navy ships: CGNs, LHAs, Spruance destroyers, the lead Aegis ship, and retrofitted DDG-2s. By the end of 1979, the Mk 86 will be in operation on 35 Navy vessels and Mk 86 orders will total 64 systems.

For the US Navy, the Mk 86 is controlling the new 5"/54 lightweight Mk 45 gun. But it can do far more. It can control other weapons – guns ranging up to 8," surface-to-surface and surface-to-air missiles – or a mix of such weapons. And the versatile Mk 86 also handles incoming threats by tracking numbers of targets simultaneously and computing their trajectories.

For smaller weapons, there's the Sharpshooter, the first low-cost digital fire-control system. Now in production at Lockheed, this fast, accurate system controls 20mm to 40mm guns.

There are three versions of the Sharpshooter: on-mount, off-mount, and optical angle tracking.

Both the Mk 86 and the Sharpshooter are modular. They can be tailored to meet precise requirements. And they have something else in common: the reliability and worldwide product support that comes from Lockheed's 30 years of weapon and fire-control experience.

For more information, write to Director of Government Marketing, Lockheed Electronics, Plainfield, NJ 07061.

Cruiser

Frigate

Patrol Boat

Lockheed Electronics

Photo : E.C.P. Armées

Alarm!

Against low-flying attacks:
THOMSON-CSF proximity fuzes for navy shells
are available in all calibres.

Unaffected by weather conditions.

THOMSON-CSF

DIVISION ÉQUIPEMENTS AVIONIQUES
178, BD GABRIEL PERI / 92240 MALAKOFF / FRANCE
TÉL. (1) 655 44.22

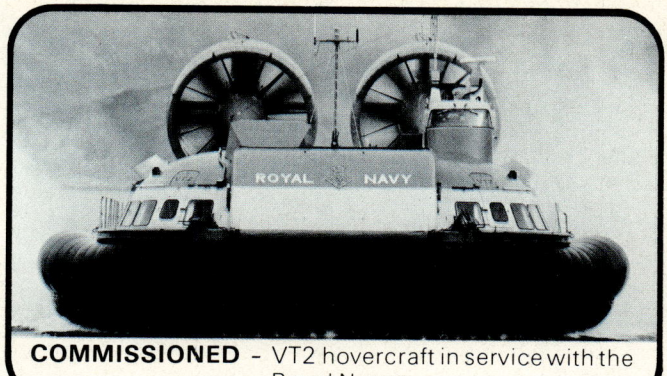

COMMISSIONED – VT2 hovercraft in service with the Royal Navy

ON TRIALS – The first of the Mark 9 corvettes for the Nigerian Navy

NEW DEVELOPMENT – Portchester Shipyard showing the recently completed covered building berth and the new wet dock and the ship lift under construction

UNDER CONSTRUCTION – The second Type 42 destroyer for the Royal Navy

FITTING OUT – *HMS Brecon* the first of the Royal Navy's new Hunt-class mine countermeasures vessels

POST ACCEPTANCE TRIALS – Helicopter landing trials in *Liberal,* the fourth Mark 10 frigate for the Brazilian Navy

Vosper Thornycroft today

Significant among the recent activities is the construction of the third mine countermeasures vessel of the Hunt-class and a new order for a third Type 42 destroyer for the Royal Navy. Also an award by Boeing Marine Systems of a contract to fit out the Royal Navy's new patrol hydrofoil **HMS Speedy**

VOSPER THORNYCROFT

Vosper Thornycroft (UK) Limited, Southampton Road, Paulsgrove, Portsmouth PO6 4QA.
Telephone: Cosham 79481. Telex: 86115. Cables: Repsov, Portsmouth.

A Member of British Shipbuilders

DIESEL SERVICE
our specialty

Our long experience in serving the free world's Navies, operating U.S.-made Diesel Equipment, is at your complete disposal, including:

- Supply of Spares
- Technical Assistance
- Instruction and Parts Book Library
- Special Tools and Test Equipment
- Preserving, Packaging and Packing to U.S. Navy Specifications
- Yearly Maintenance Contracts
- Complete Replacement and Exchange Engines, Transmissions and other Major Components
- Cut-Away Instruction Models

SERVING THE NAVIES OF THE FREE WORLD

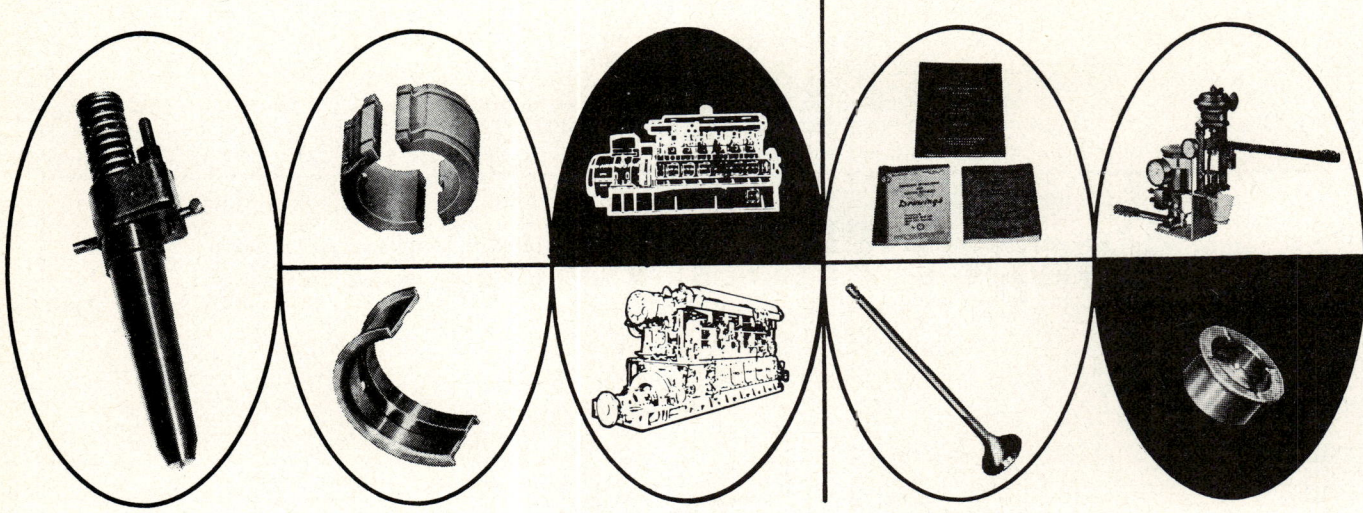

WESTERN EUROPEAN BRANCH WAREHOUSE AT HAVAM, HERUNGERWEG, VENLO, HOLLAND

ADDRESS ALL CORRESPONDENCE TO:

 **KORODY-COLYER CORPORATION**
112 NORTH AVALON BOULEVARD, WILMINGTON, CALIFORNIA
TELEPHONE (213) 830-0330.   CABLE: KORODIESEL

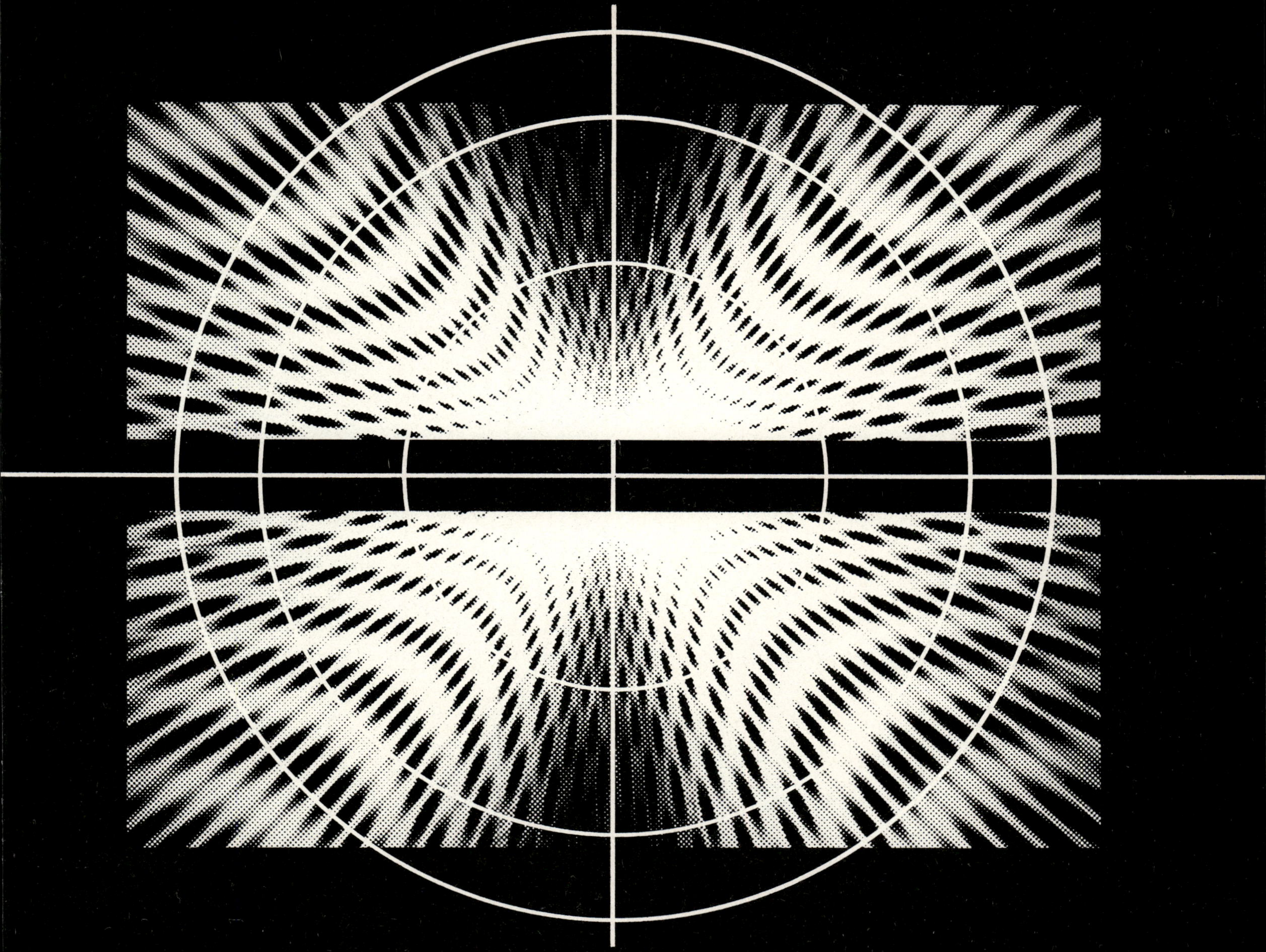

confidence through ELMER radiocommunication systems

The most comprehensive range of multi-purpose radiocommunication equipment integrated in very advanced radiocommunication systems

MONTEDISON GROUP
MONTEDISON SISTEMI

ELMER
DIVISION OF **MONTEDEL**
Viale dell'Industria, 4-00040 Pomezia (Italy)
P.O. Box 189-Telex 610112 ELMER I

CALZONI

Special oil hydro-mechanical devices and complete systems for submarines and other warships

- extra noiseless pumps
- steering and diving gears
- antenna and periscope hoisting devices
- m.t.b. flood and vent valve controls
- remotely controlled hull valves
- windlass and capstan gears
- torpedo handling systems
- trim manifold (remote controlled)
- induction and exhaust snorkel
- etc.

- **noiseless**
- **compact**
- **tailor-made**
- **high shock resistant devices**

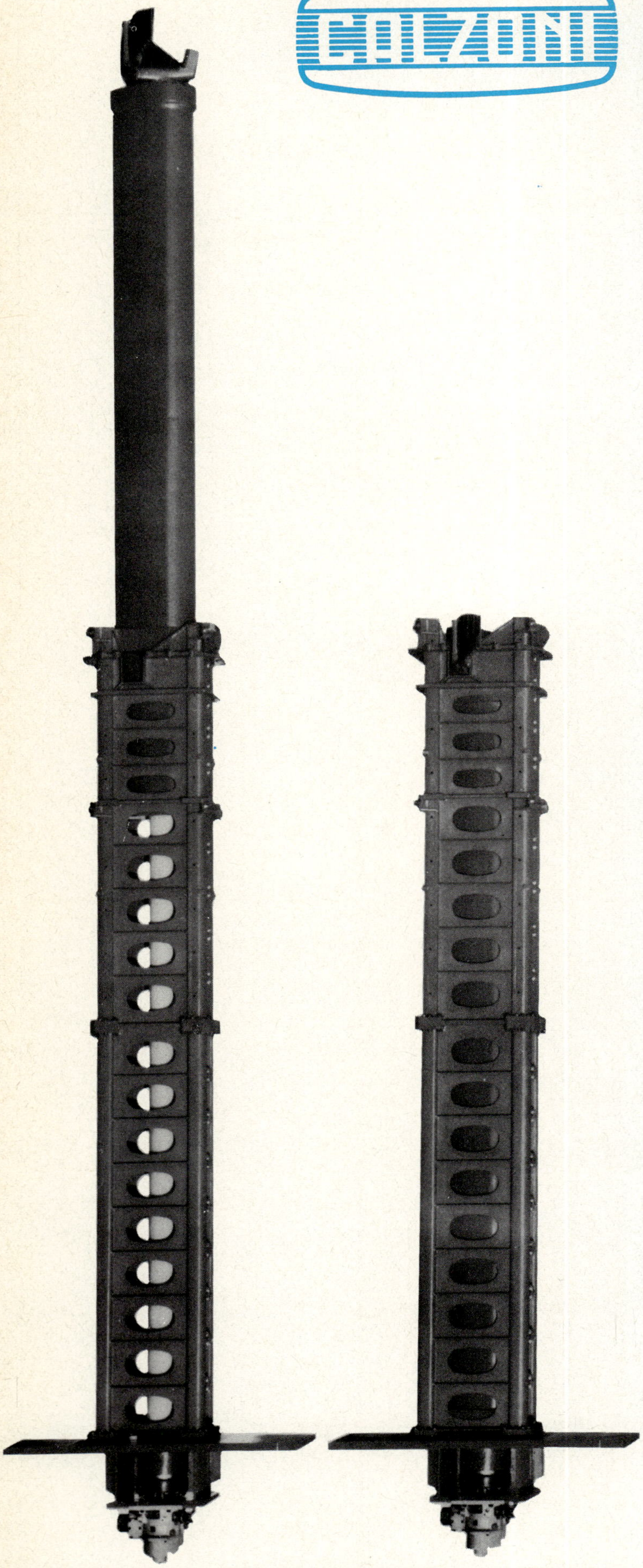

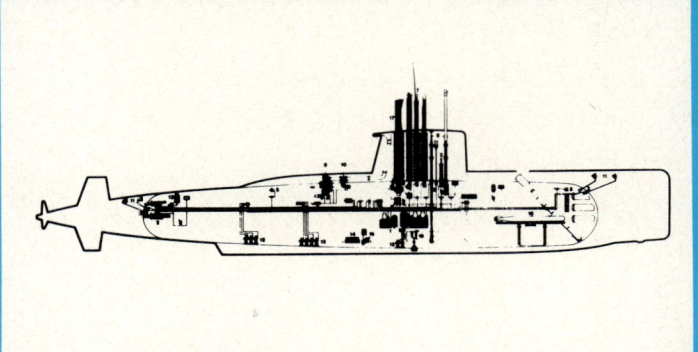

RADAR HOISTING DEVICE FOR SUBMARINES
RAISED   LOWERED

The device, as the other hoisting devices (ECM, VHF), is extremely compact and does not pass through the control room.

RIVA CALZONI S.p.A. — Via Emilia POnente, 72 - Bologna - Italy - Telex 510156

WATERWINGS.

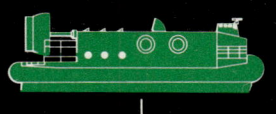

Amphibious Assault Landing Craft (AALC): Under test and evaluation by the U.S. Navy. Each craft shown above and below has six Lycoming Marine Turbines, Model TF40, for both lift and propulsive power.

Coastal Patrol Hovercraft: Fast, maneuverable patrol in shallow waters. Powered by a single TF25. Destined for service in the Middle East.

High speed luxury yacht. Powered by two TF25 Lycoming Marine Turbines.

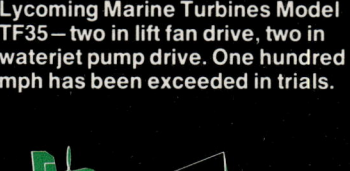

Surface Effect Ship (SES100A): One of the test vessels for tomorrow's "100 knot Navy." Four Lycoming Marine Turbines Model TF35—two in lift fan drive, two in waterjet pump drive. One hundred mph has been exceeded in trials.

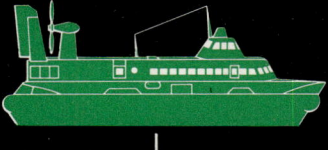

Japanese Hovercraft: Two TF25 Marine Turbines, each driving one lift fan and one airscrew, provide power to a fleet of these 155 passenger, 60 knot air cushion vehicles. Three craft to date.

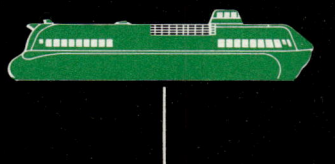

British Hovercraft: Two shaftlines, each powered by a single Lycoming TF25, driving one lift fan and one drive prop. Up to 10 vehicles, 184 passengers at 40 knots—even in rough seas. Three craft to date.

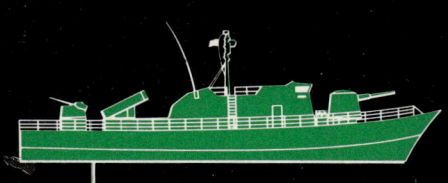

Patrol Ship Multi Mission (PSMM): Semi-planing hull offered in two configurations: 6 TF35 or 3 TF40 Lycoming Marine Turbines. Each engine can be brought on or taken off to save fuel or increase speed as mission demands. Ten craft to date.

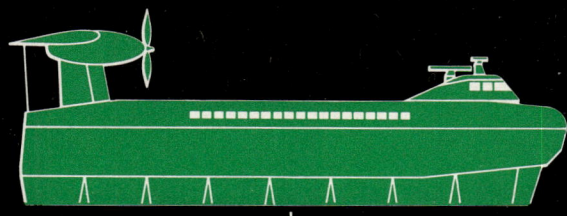

French Hovercraft: Currently the world's largest, they are powered by 5 Avco Lycoming Marine Turbines Model TF40. In the mixed traffic version, the 280-ton craft, carrying 400 passengers and 45 cars, cruises comfortably at 58 knots in 5 foot seas. Two craft to date.

Coastal Patrol and Interdiction Craft (CPIC): Gets its high dash and chase speed from TF25 turbines driving three separate shaftlines, with diesels for routine patrol and slow speed maneuvering.

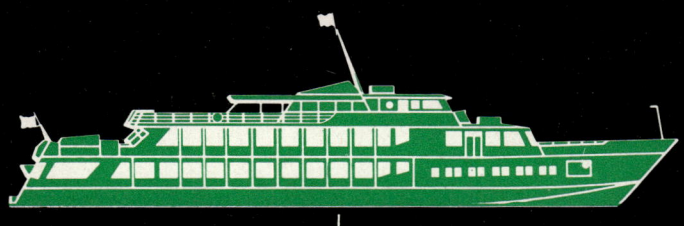

Commuter Ferry for San Francisco Bay. Three Lycoming Marine Turbines Model TF35, driving waterjets. Up to 750 passengers at 25 knots. Three craft to date.

Norwegian Ferry: Dubbed the Westamaran, this twin hull class leader can carry 200 passengers in comfort at up to 40 knots. Two TF40 marine turbines.

Waterwings. Avco Lycoming Gas Turbines and varied drive systems. Single engine shaftlines of 2,000 to 4,600 shaft hp and multiple engine configurations to 18,400 hp per shaftline. For more information write for the new "Super TF" series brochure.

AVCO LYCOMING DIVISION
STRATFORD, CONNECTICUT 06497

[49]

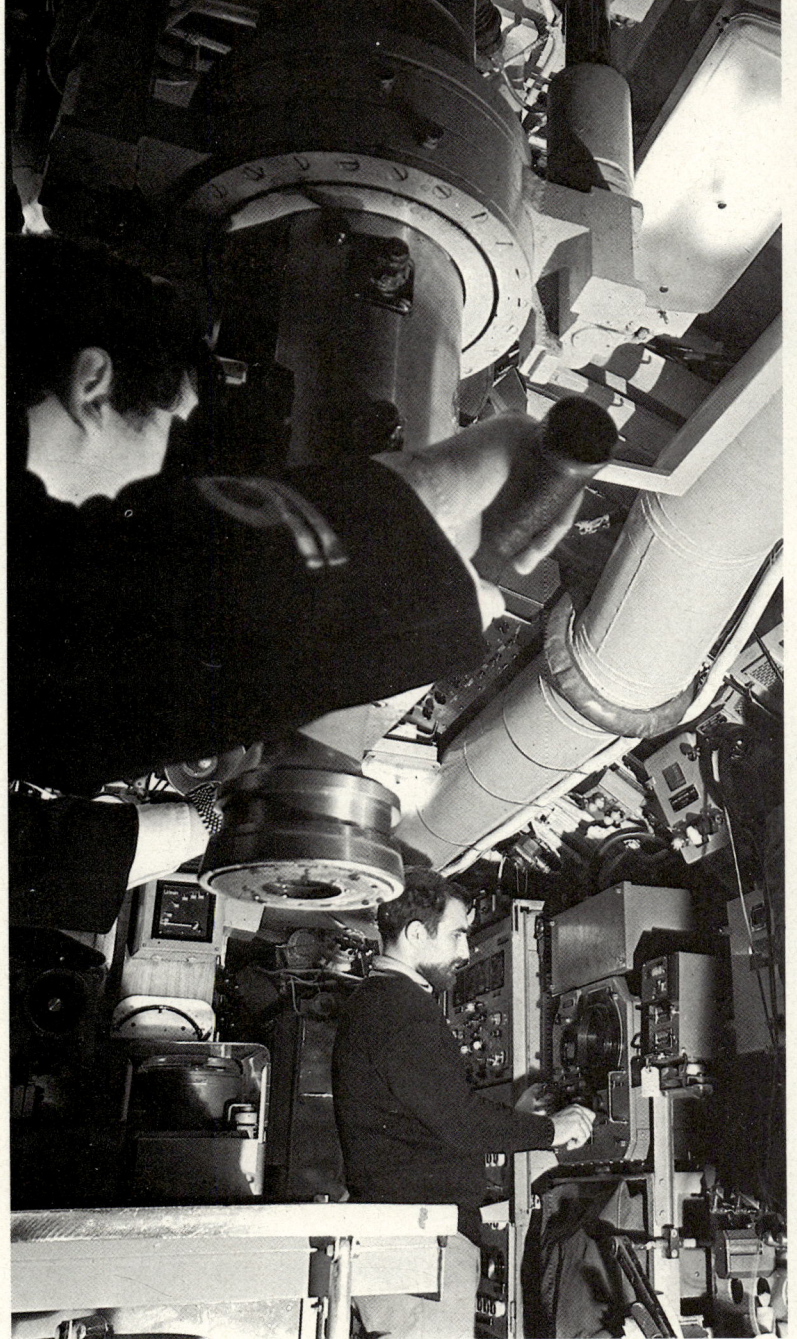

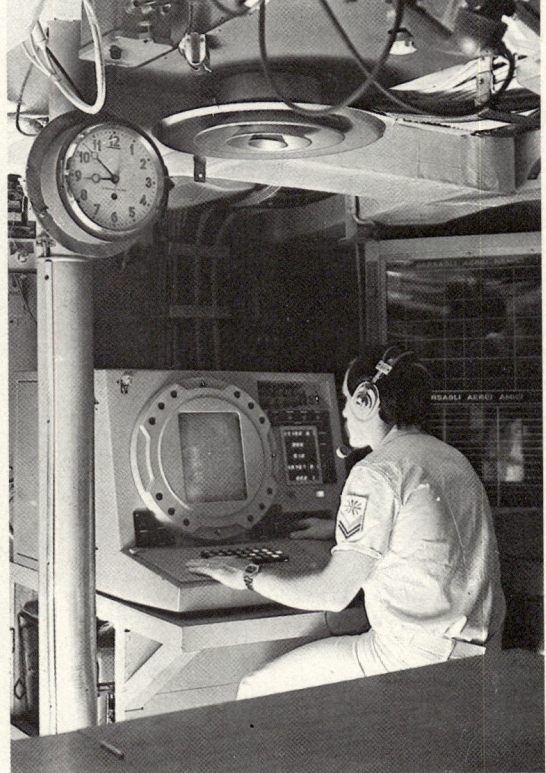

selenia is experience and reliability

The Electronic Warfare system is one of the real assets available to a Warship to ensure mission fulfillment and ship survival. The most advanced hardware and software are necessary to achieve proper operation and performances in the harsh ship environment.

High sensitivity receivers, computer based signal analysis and identification and a variety of ECM techniques, including power management, are the keys to the success of Selenia's shipborne E.W. advanced systems with several Navies.

Selenia's wide experience with development and production of various ground and airborne E.W. systems as well as of radars and Weapons systems is the necessary background and complement to its achievements in the field of shipborne Electronic Warfare.

INDUSTRIE ELETTRONICHE
ASSOCIATE S.p.A.
SPECIAL EQUIPMENT AND SYSTEMS DIVISION
Via dei Castelli Romani, 2
00040 POMEZIA (Rome, ITALY)
P.O. Box 7083, 00100 Rome

SELENIA IS EXPERIENCE IN EW NAVAL SYSTEMS

cantiere navale breda

construction of: tankers up to 250.000 tdw; ore-oil carriers and bulkcarriers up to 175.000 tdw; ore-bulk-oil carriers, completely double-skinned, up to 150.000 tdw; product carriers up to 80.000 tdw; liquid gas carriers up to 80.000 tdw; container-ships of all types and dimensions; general dry cargo and multipurpose vessels of all types and dimensions; merchant and/or passenger/merchant ferry boats.

missile fast strike crafts, minesweepers, support ships, landing ships, corvettes, landing and assault crafts, special crafts, minisubmarines

3000 T
Rescue ship
Italian Navy

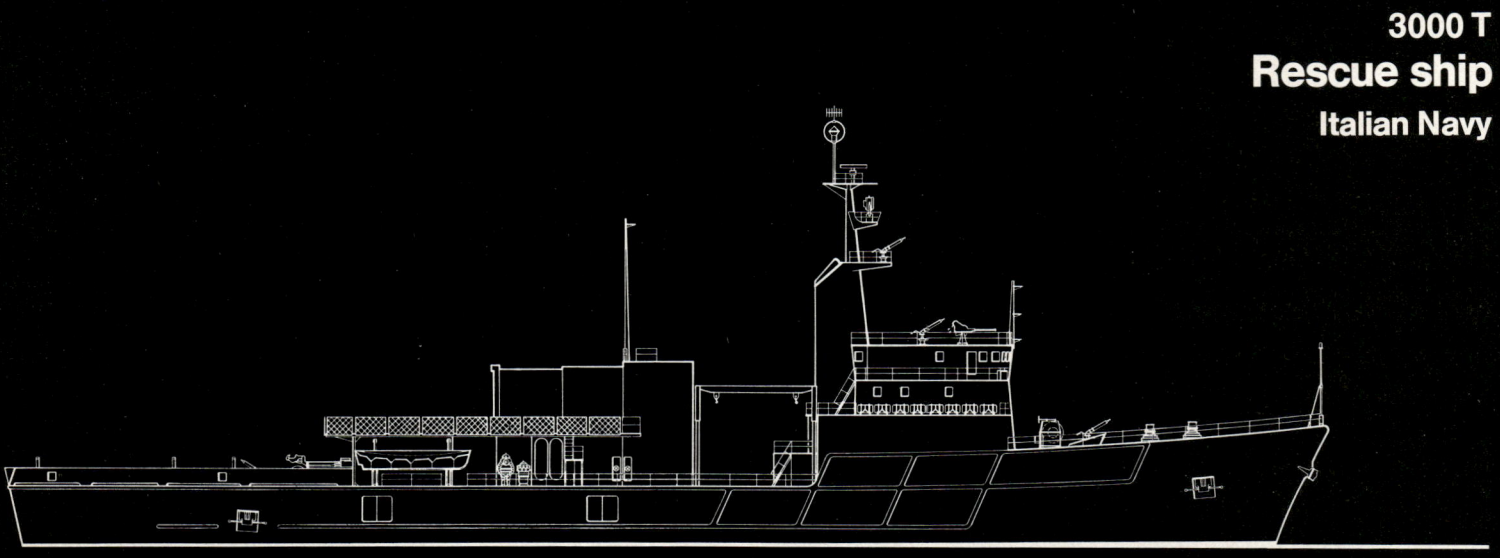

MV 400
Missiles fast strike craft

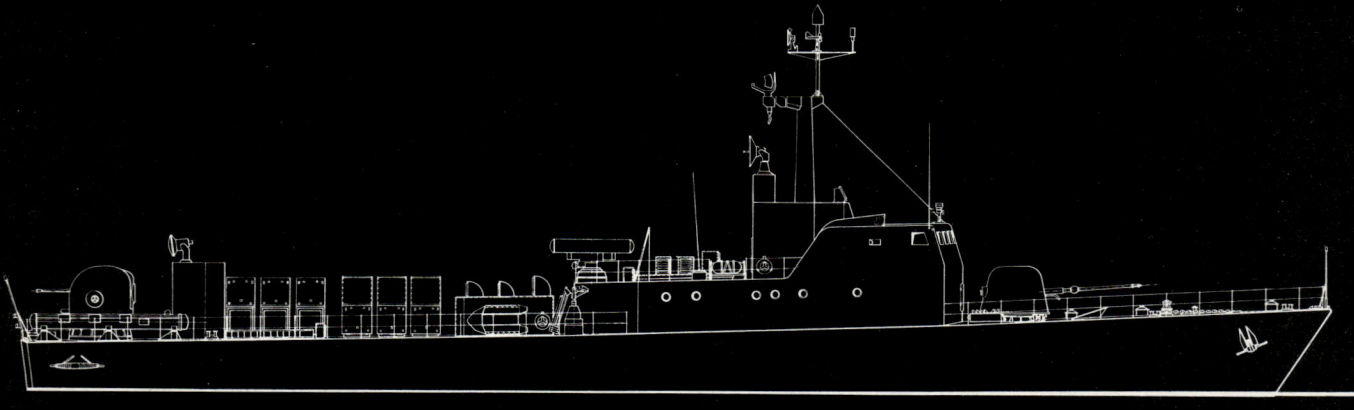

MV 400 H
Missiles fast strike craft helicopter carrier

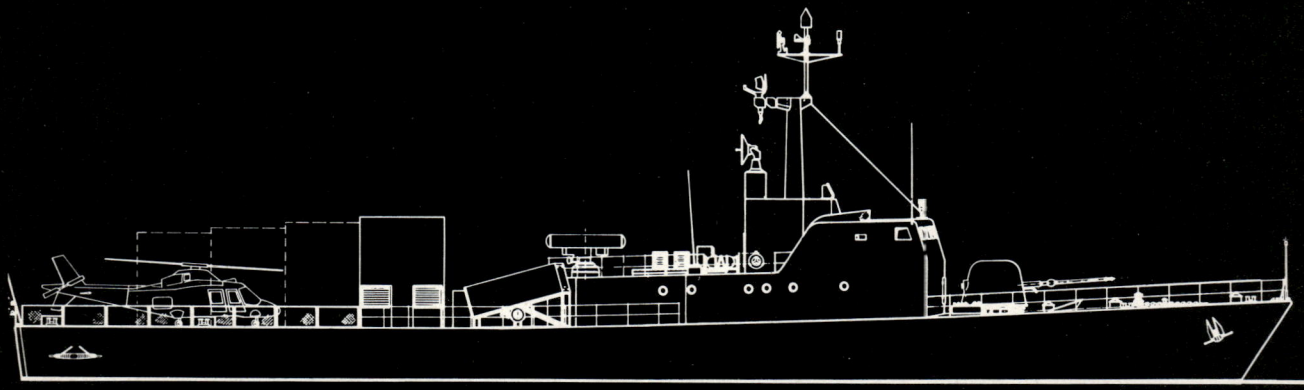

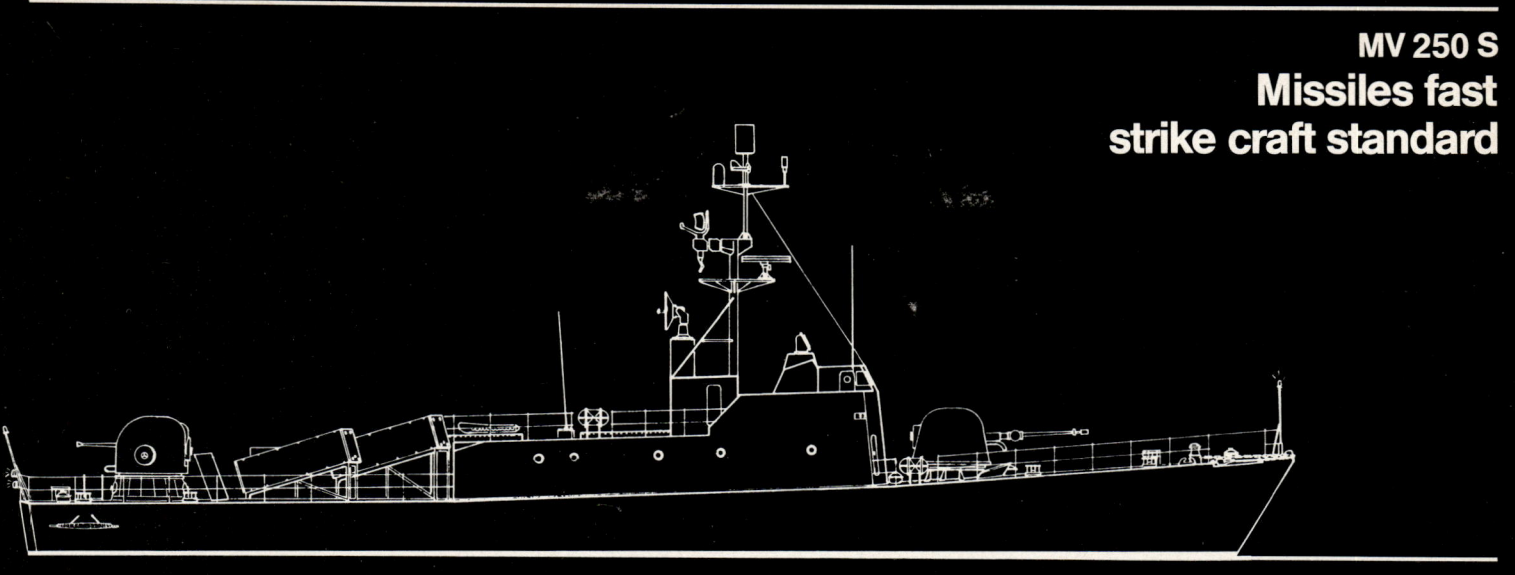

MV 250 S
Missiles fast
strike craft standard

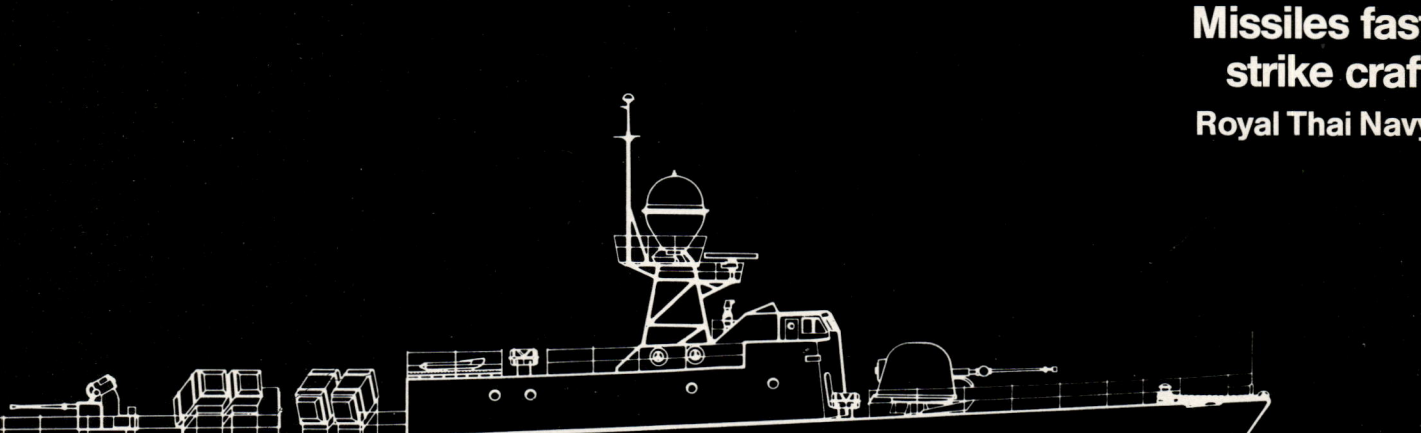

MV 250 T
Missiles fast
strike craft
Royal Thai Navy

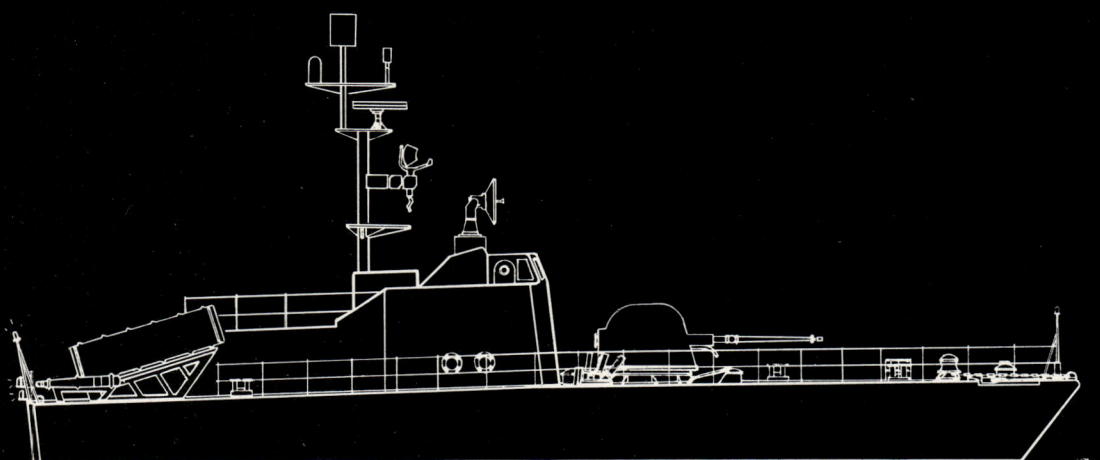

MV 150
Missiles fast
strike craft

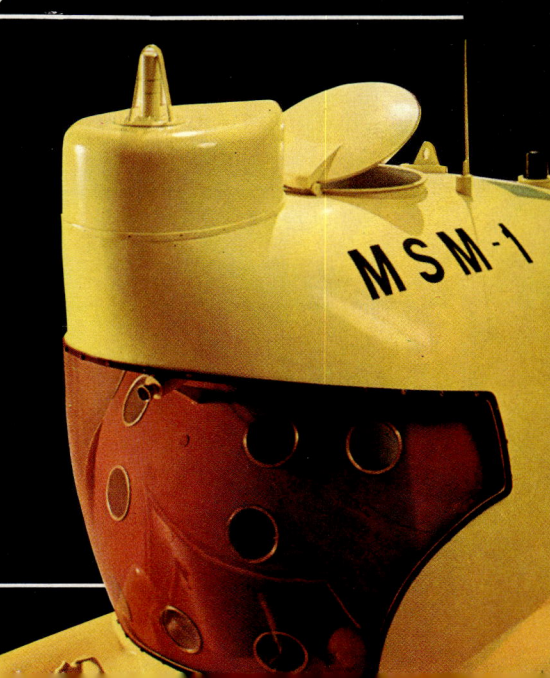

cantiere
navale breda spa

venice marghera italy   postal address
via delle industrie, 18   p.o.b. 1043 (succ. 1) 30170 mestre
phone (041) 59860   capit. soc. 5.000.000.000 int. vers.
telex 41106 bredanav   iscritta al n. 5181 trib. di venezia
cables cantbreda venice iscritta al n. 49929 cciaa venezia

Philips Usfa B.V.

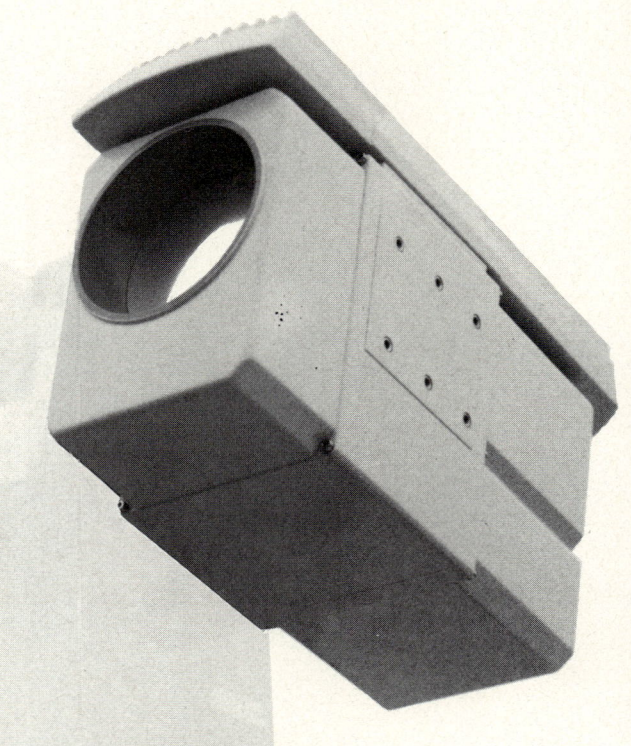

INFRARED CAMERA TYPE UA 9053 FOR PASSIVE TARGET TRACKING

- **LONG LIFE MILITARY STIRLING COOLER TYPE UA 7011**
- **8-12 MICRON WINDOW**
- **CCIR COMPATIBLE VIDEO OUTPUT**
- **IN PRODUCTION**

AND ALSO
- **THERMAL TANK SIGHTS**
- **HANDHELD BIOCULAR NIGHTSIGHT**
- **INDIVIDUAL WEAPON SIGHT**
- **NIGHT DRIVING PERISCOPES**
- **AIMING AND OBSERVATION DAY/NIGHT SIGHT**

DEFENCE EQUIPMENT AND SYSTEMS SINCE 1954
Philips Usfa B.V.
Meerenakkerweg 1
5600 MD Eindhoven
The Netherlands
Telex: 51732 USFAE NL

PHILIPS

ITALCRAFT also means... FAST PATROL CRAFT

Fast attack Commando Anti Smuggling Configuration
Max speed 55 knots with 2 diesel engines
Length o.a. 43 feet (13,30 m)

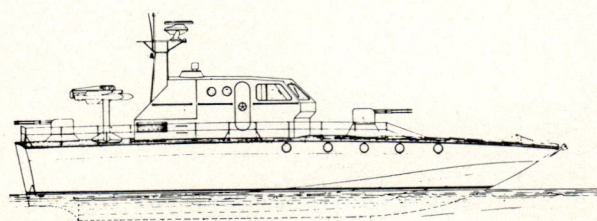

60 feet (18,30 m) Fast Attack Craft
Missile or Patrol - GRP construction
Max speed over 50 knots

One of 66 feet (20,20 m) Fast Patrol Boat built for Guardia di Finanza (Italian Military Custom Force)
Max speed over 36 knots

Rescue Boat "SEPPIETTA"
Self-straightening and unsinkable craft - any sea condition -
Length 28 feet (8,30 m)
Draft 9 feet (2,60 m)
1 diesel engine x 110 H.P.
Max speed 13 knots
Continuous speed 11 knots
Range at continuous speed 200 n.m.
Construction material: G.R.P.
Carrying capacity: 2 Crew + 10 persons

Cantieri Navali Italcraft
Head Office: Via Paolo Frisi 9, 00197 Rome (Italy)
Ph. (06) 802701 875377 870981 - Telex: 613054 ITCRAF I
Yards: Gaeta - Bracciano - Fiumicino

How we t[urned the] Harrier into

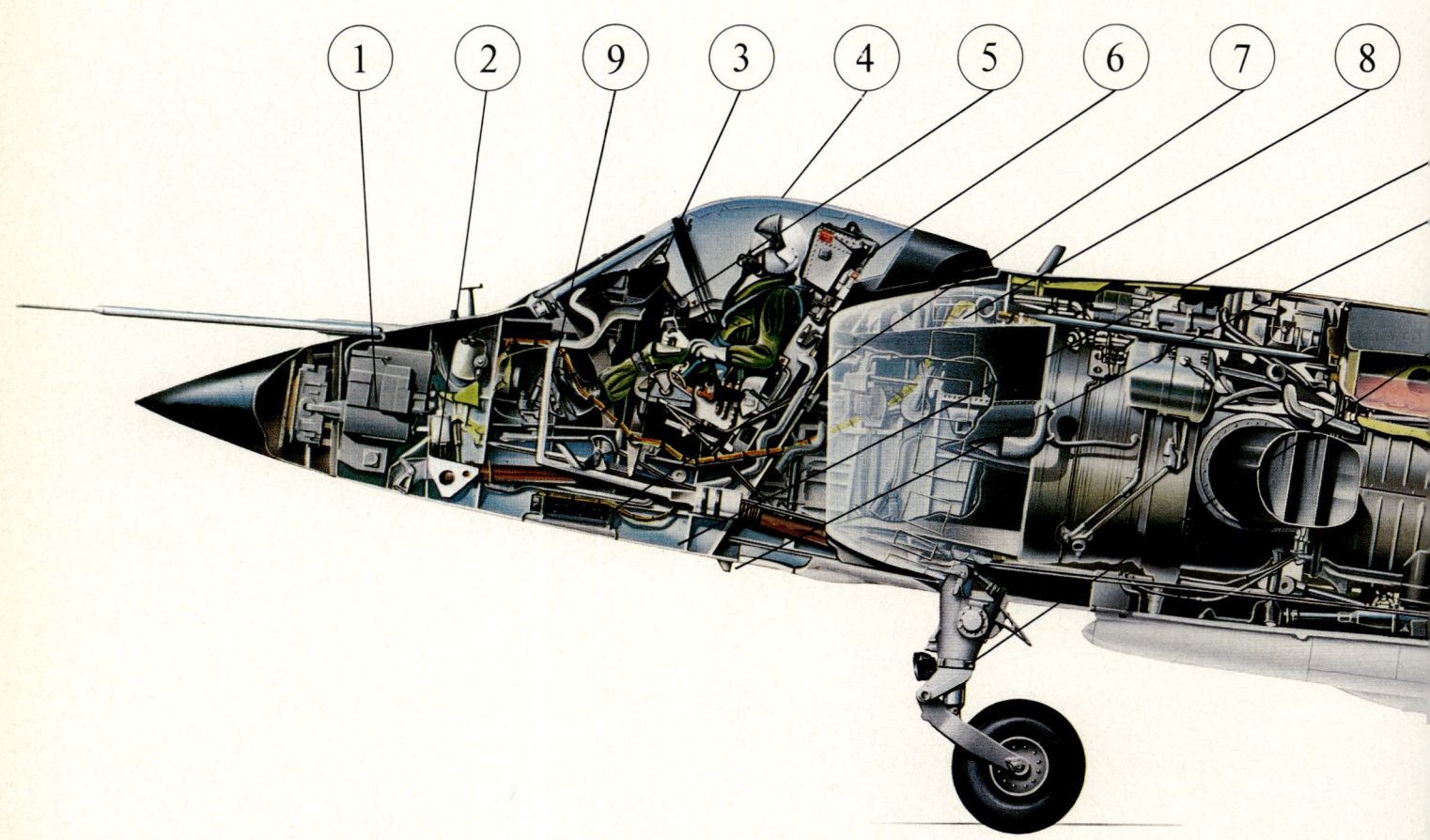

1. We installed Blue Fox multi-mode radar.
2. We fitted a folding nose for hangar stowage.
3. We gave the pilot's HUD a larger field of view.
4. We raised the cockpit.
5. We improved the cockpit layout.
6. We fitted a Mk 10H Ejection Seat.
7. We fitted Doppler Radar.
8. We redesigned the wiring, introducing lightweight cables, digital data highways and advanced EMC-immunity.
9. We ensured easier maintainability.
10. We added an I Band Transponder.
11. We built in storm lashing points.
12. We provided independent emergency brakes.
13. We installed digital navigation and weapon aiming computers.

rned a basic a Sea Harrier.

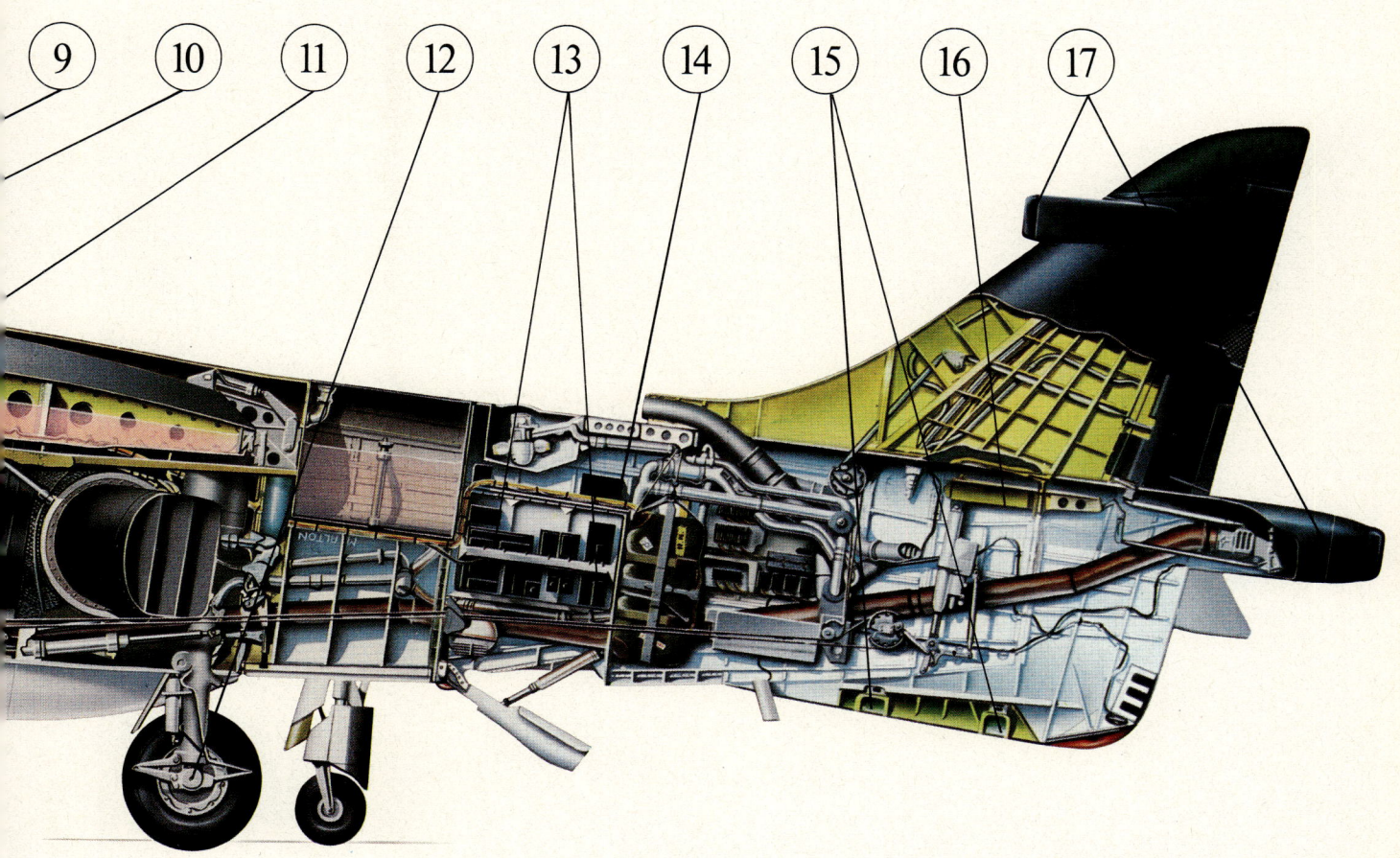

14. We introduced an autopilot.
15. We fitted a radar altimeter.
16. We increased the tailplane authority.
17. We added a radar warning system.

In addition, we improved corrosion pro-
ection throughout, particularly in the engine.

We replaced magnesium alloys.

We catered for air to air and air to surface
missiles.

We strengthened the weapons stations.

All because a basic Harrier on a deck full time is, literally, out of its element.

Getting the best out of V/STOL at sea takes a whole new Harrier. This one.

SEAHARRIER
BRITISH AEROSPACE
unequalled in its range of aerospace programmes
Richmond Road, Kingston upon Thames, Surrey KT2 5QS.

THOMSON-CSF

has what it takes for defense at sea and the exploitation of ocean resources

Antisubmarine Warfare
- Seeker heads and electronics for torpedoes.
- Active sonars for surface ships.
- Active/passive sonars and sonar transmission interceptors for submarines.
- ASW operations room simulators.
- Airborne ASW detection systems.
- Acoustic measurement stations, course plotters and sonar target responders.
- Ancillary equipment: underwater telephony, sound field plotters, sound velocity bathymeters, distress beacons.

Mine Warfare
- Mine detection and destruction sonar systems.
- Practice and live mines.
- Ship degaussing systems.
- Fixed or mobile stations for checking and measuring magnetic fields of ships and their equipment.
- Doppler navigation sonars.
- Acoustic and magnetic equipment for divers.

Oceanography and Offshore Oil Exploration
- Dynamic positioning equipment.
- Underwater location and navigation systems.
- Underwater remote-control and transmission equipment.
- High-definition sonars and re-entry sonars.
- Underwater television cameras.
- Oceanographic instruments: Doppler current-meters, depth sounders, etc.

THOMSON-CSF
DIVISION ACTIVITÉS SOUS-MARINES
B.P. 53 / 06802 CAGNES-SUR-MER / FRANCE / TÉL. : (93) 20 01 40

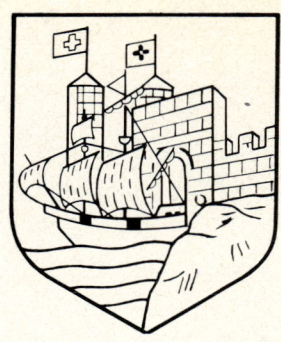

CANTIERI NAVALI DI PISA

56100 PISA - VIA AURELIA KM. 334 DARSENA PISANA - TEL. (050) 22072 - 22073
TELEGRAMMI: CNIPAM - PISA TELEX **590044 CANTPI I**

TWO OF OUR FAST PATROL BOATS IN SERVICE

- **FAST PATROL BOAT of m. 46**
  - Equipped with 3 engines MTU type MB20V538TB91 (HP 4500 x 3) knots 40

- **COAST-GUARD of m. 27 - 32**
  - Equipped with 2 engines MTU type MB20V672TY (HP 3500 x 2) knots 42-40
  - Equipped with 3 engines MTU type MB12V331TC92 (HP 1600 x 3) knots 32-30

- **COAST-GUARD of m. 23**
  - Equipped with 3 engines MTU type MB12V331TC92 (HP 1600 x 3) knots 38
  - Equipped with 2 engines MTU type MB12V331TC92 (HP 1600 x 2) knots 32

- **COAST-GUARD of m. 20**
  - Equipped with 2 engines MTU type MB8V331TC92 (HP 1065 x 2) knots 33
  - Equipped with 2 engines G.M. type 12V71TI (HP 675 x 2) knots 27

- **COAST-GUARD of m. 14,00**
  - Equipped with 2 engines G.M. type 8V71N (HP 350 x 2) knots 25
  - Equipped with 2 engines G.M. type 8V71TI (HP 435 x 2) knots 30
  - Equipped with 2 engines G.M. type 12V71TI (HP 675 x 2) knots 38

Maintenance 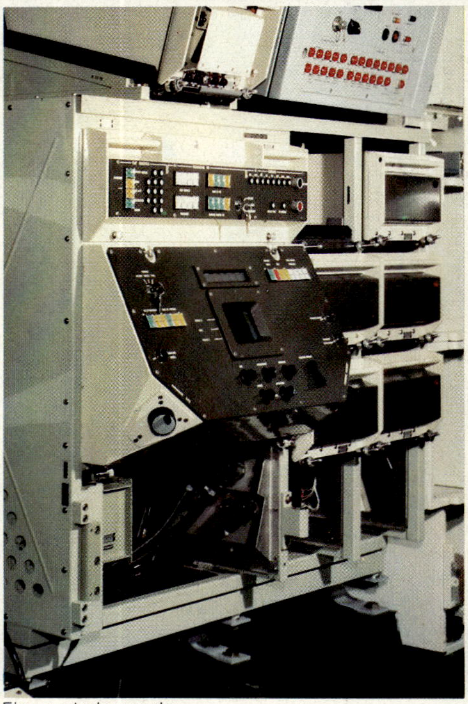 — Fire control console 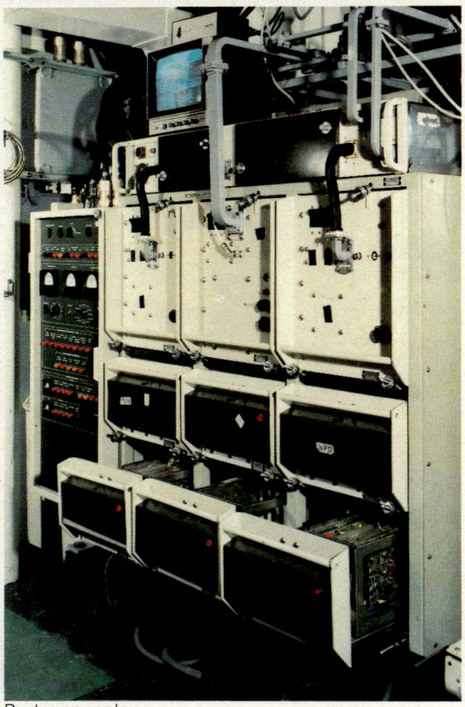 — Radar console

CROTALE NAVAL
the low-altitude, all-weather air defense system

THOMSON-CSF
DIVISION SYSTÈMES ÉLECTRONIQUES
1, RUE DES MATHURINS / B.P. 10 / 92222 BAGNEUX / TÉL : (1) 657 13.65

BORLETTI FOR DEFENCE

Designer and Manufacturer of most comprehensive range of

FUZES

● Point Detonating ● Mechanical Time ● Proximity
for: guns - mortars - rockets - howitzers

FB

BORLETTI DEFENCE DIVISION - Via Washington, 70 - 20146 Milano - PH 43.89 - TLX 332067 BORMI - ITALY

Tomorrow we'll be facing a different sea.

Our image of the sea may change any moment. This requires alertness and possibly action, which means a need of new ships. Here we come in to help find the best solution.

The first step is to produce the design and specifications, to make a contract for the delivery of ships and their main systems.

The next step is to provide the drawings for the actual construction, assembly and outfitting as well as the technical preparations for the purchase of materials and components.

And finally we can advise on supervision, training of personnel and logistic support.

Don't hesitate to contact Nevesbu when you want to anticipate at new naval tasks. We have a briefing team available at short notice.

Nevesbu

P.O. Box 289 – 2501 CG – The Hague – The Netherlands
Telephone (+31 70) 602813 – Telex 31640 genuf nl.

SHIPBOARD AIRCONDITIONING

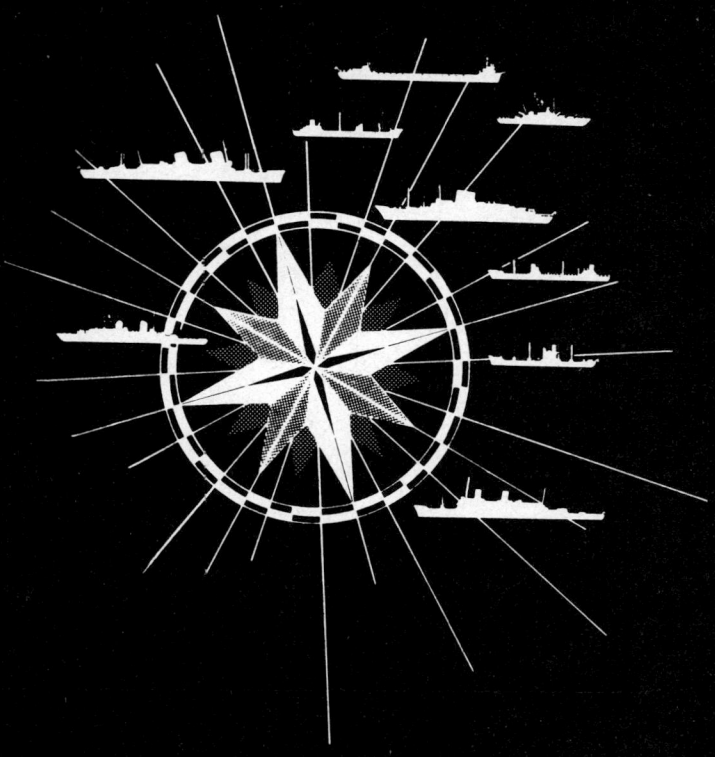

AERIMPIANTI

THE HIGHEST STANDARD IN EQUIPMENTS – DESIGN – ERECTION
TECHNICAL ASSISTANCE IN THE SHIPYARD AND DURING NAVIGATION

Address
20135 Milano—Italy ■ Via Bergamo, 21 ■ Tel. (02) 5497
Telex 312211 AERIMP ■ 61593 AERIMPRO ■ 77123 AERIMPNA
Milan   Rome   Naples

It took a deep commitment to reach new heights in undersea weaponry

Mission: Ocean control

The Mk 48 torpedo — the world's most advanced underwater weapon — designed, manufactured and delivered on schedule and under budget by the Ocean Systems Division of Gould Government Systems.

The Mk 48 program is a prime example of the effectiveness of the Gould total systems responsibility concept. A careful blend of managerial, scientific and technical talents, this total approach combined innovative technology with imaginative program management to produce this superior undersea weapon. It is an approach honed and ready to produce the advanced systems of the future.

Ocean control — making sure that our side stays on top at minimum cost — is a commitment shared by the Navy and Gould's Ocean Systems Division. It is the underlying motivation for Gould's commitment to advanced deepwater systems and the total systems responsibility concept that assures their success.

Gould's deep commitment to the advancement of technology requires the services of talented and dedicated people who desire above-average opportunities and career growth. If you are an electronic, mechanical or systems engineer and would like to join a group on the move, contact Gould Inc., Ocean Systems Division, 18901 Euclid Avenue, Cleveland, Ohio 44117. Or call collect, 216/486-8300. Gould Inc., is an equal opportunity employer.

CHESAPEAKE INSTRUMENT • INFORMATION IDENTIFICATION • NAVCOM SYSTEMS • OCEAN SYSTEMS • SIMULATION SYSTEMS

Gould Government Systems: where total systems responsibility means everything

GOULD
An Electrical/Electronics Company

Providing expertise in every aspect of marine projects

Field Studies – Designs – Specifications – Construction – Commissioning – Training – Servicing – Maintenance – Project Management

ABMTM Marine Division

backed by the 60 years of home and export engineering experience of the ABMTM Group, is at the service of international government and commercial organisations.

ABMTM Ltd., 20 Park Street, London, W1Y 4NA
Tel.: 01-492 1161 / 6. Telex: 21611. Cables: Britoolmak, London W1

italsider
steel forgings and castings for the marine industry

crankshafts of semi built-up and solid types, also continuous grain forged; running gear forgings and castings, hull castings, shaftings and rudder stocks

Italsider produces largest crankshafts required in the world with weights in excess of 220 tons

Sales office
ITALSIDER s.p.a.
piazza Dante 7
16121 GENOVA Italy
phone (10) 59.99
telex 27.06.90 Itasid I

SIDERIUS INC.
Head office
1301 Avenue of the Americas
NEW YORK, N. Y. 10019
phone (212) 489-7470
telex 12-5116 Siderius NYK
TWX 710-581-6221

ANNOUNCEMENT
Hatch & Kirk Inc.
ANNOUNCES THE PURCHASE OF THE ASSETS OF THE
CLEVELAND DIESEL ENGINE DIVISION
FROM THE ELECTRO–MOTIVE DIVISION OF GENERAL MOTORS CORPORATION

ALL TOOLING, ENGINEERING PRINTS, AND PARTS INVENTORIES
HAVE BEEN MOVED TO OUR SEATTLE, WASHINGTON, FACILITIES
TO PROVIDE EFFICIENT, DEPENDABLE SERVICE AT PRACTICAL PRICES.

YOUR CONTINUING SOURCE

IN ORDER TO SUPPORT THE CLEVELAND DIESEL ENGINES OPERATING WORLDWIDE, HATCH & KIRK INC. HAS A COMPREHENSIVE PARTS MANUFACTURING PROGRAM TO ASSURE THE CLEVELAND DIESEL ENGINE OWNERS OF A CONTINUING, RELIABLE SOURCE OF PARTS AT PRACTICAL PRICES. OUR CLEVELAND DIESEL ENGINE PARTS ARE MANUFACTURED IN STRICT ACCORDANCE WITH THE UP-DATED CLEVELAND TECHNICAL PRINTS INSURING A HIGH QUALITY CONTROLLED PRODUCT.

IN ADDITION, HATCH & KIRK INC. MAINTAINS THE LARGEST INVENTORY OF DIESEL ENGINE PARTS IN THE USA FOR:

ALCO 539 · BALDWIN VO · COOPER BESSEMER · HENDY-HILL · HERCULES · SUPERIOR GDB · ENTERPRISE G · AND OTHER U.S. MANUFACTURED DIESEL ENGINES AND ASSOCIATED EQUIPMENT.
WRITE FOR OUR BROCHURE.

Hatch & Kirk Inc.
5111 LEARY AVENUE N.W. · SEATTLE, WASHINGTON 98107
PHONE (206) 783-2766 · TELEX 32-8714

**Whatever the type of ship,
there exists a VEGA system
that befits her.**

THOMSON-CSF
DIVISION DRS-TVT
1, RUE DES MATHURINS / B.P. 10 / 92222 BAGNEUX / FRANCE
TEL : (1) 657 11.65

32 M (105') STEEL PATROL BOAT

for navy, police and customs patrol duties in open sea and coastal waters

cruising range 1000 naut. miles

2 diesel engines of 2600 hp each, speed 29 knots

accomodation for a crew of 19

De Vries: We, as shipbuilders, fulfil your every demand!

We have for seven decades been specializing in building all types and kinds of special purpose vessels, made of steel or aluminium, with lengths ranging from 40 to 200 feet. Quite a record for a small yard.

The de Vries building range includes a series of "customized" vessels, such as patrol and police boats, customs and harbour launches, pilot boats, crew and utility boats, inspection vessels, fire fighting boats. You can deal directly with one of the five members, of our Management team, who are all called de Vries, shipbuilders since 1907.

You can rely on them to provide the solution for your specific demands and requirements. Without any loss of time, without excessive costs, without any misunderstanding.

For details about the vessel you wish to buy contact:

de vries shipyards
DE VRIES SHIPYARDS, P.O. BOX 258, AALSMEER/HOLLAND. TELEPHONE: (02977) 21551. CABLES: VRIESYARDS, TELEX: 14256.

Shockproof Electrical Systems and Components to MIL-C-2212D (Ships) and S-901 For Naval Shipboard Use

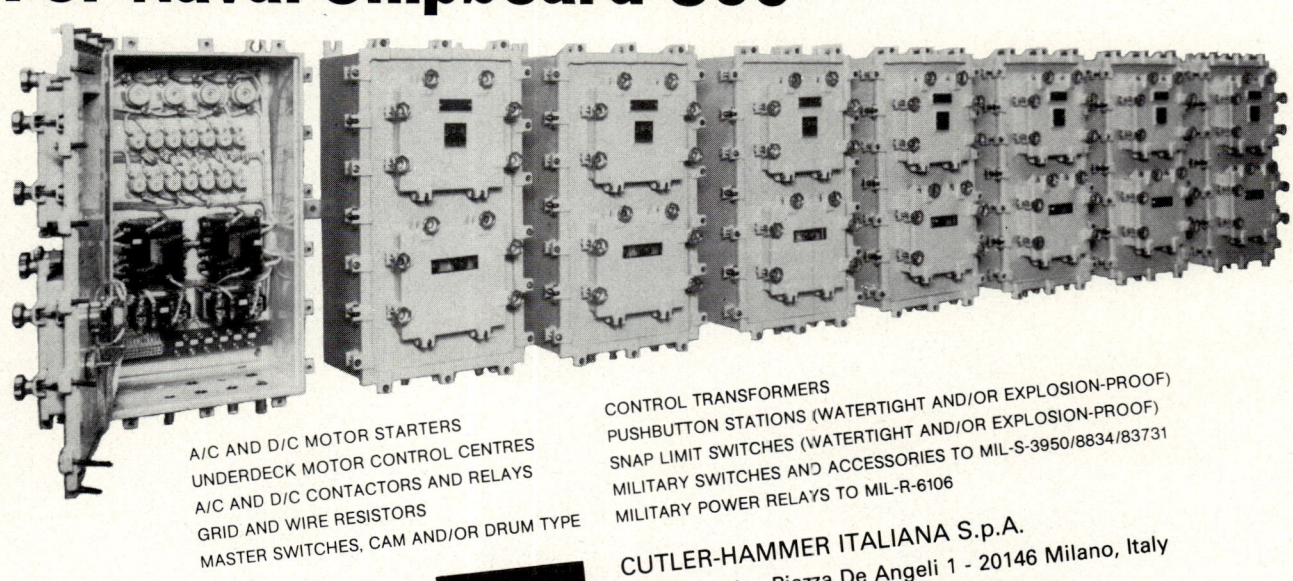

A/C AND D/C MOTOR STARTERS
UNDERDECK MOTOR CONTROL CENTRES
A/C AND D/C CONTACTORS AND RELAYS
GRID AND WIRE RESISTORS
MASTER SWITCHES, CAM AND/OR DRUM TYPE
CONTROL TRANSFORMERS
PUSHBUTTON STATIONS (WATERTIGHT AND/OR EXPLOSION-PROOF)
SNAP LIMIT SWITCHES (WATERTIGHT AND/OR EXPLOSION-PROOF)
MILITARY SWITCHES AND ACCESSORIES TO MIL-S-3950/8834/83731
MILITARY POWER RELAYS TO MIL-R-6106

CUTLER-HAMMER ITALIANA S.p.A.
Hqs & Works: Piazza De Angeli 1 - 20146 Milano, Italy
Telex: 332083 CHITAL - Phone (02) 46.97.838/40
Cables: Cutlerit Milano

SUPPLIERS OF SHIPBOARD AND SHORE INSTALLATIONS

 TRACKING RADARS  SEARCH RADARS

INTEGRATED SHIPBORNE SYSTEM

WEAPON CONTROL SYSTEMS

ANTI-AIRCRAFT AND ANTI-MISSILE SYSTEMS

SELENIA

Elsag
ELETTRONICA SAN GIORGIO

NAVAL SYSTEMS DIVISION

SELENIA
INDUSTRIE ELETTRONICHE ASSOCIATE S.p.A.
via Tiburtina km 12,400
00131 ROMA (Italy)

ELETTRONICA SAN GIORGIO
ELSAG   S.p.A.
via Hermada, 6
16154 GENOVA-SESTRI

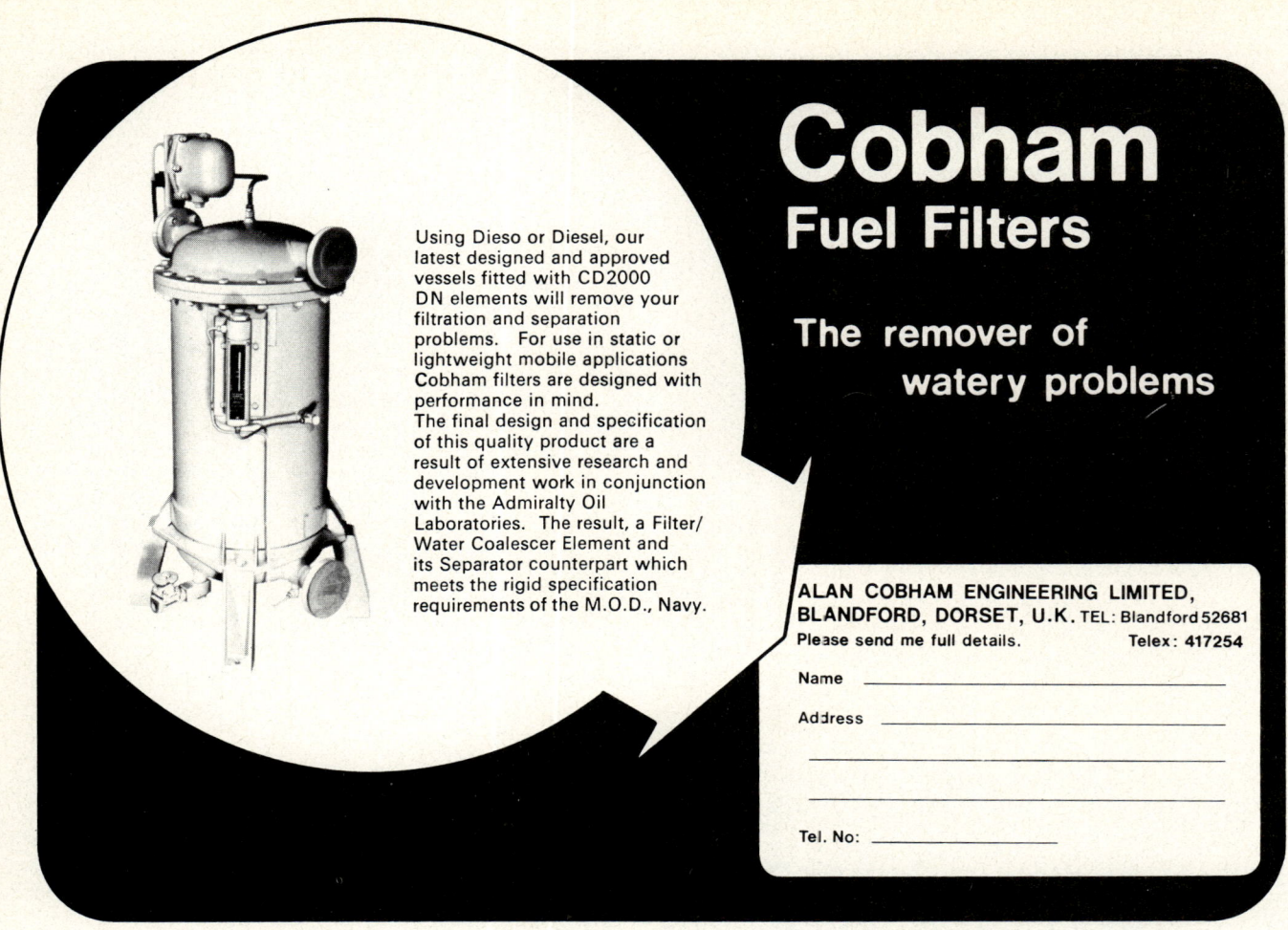

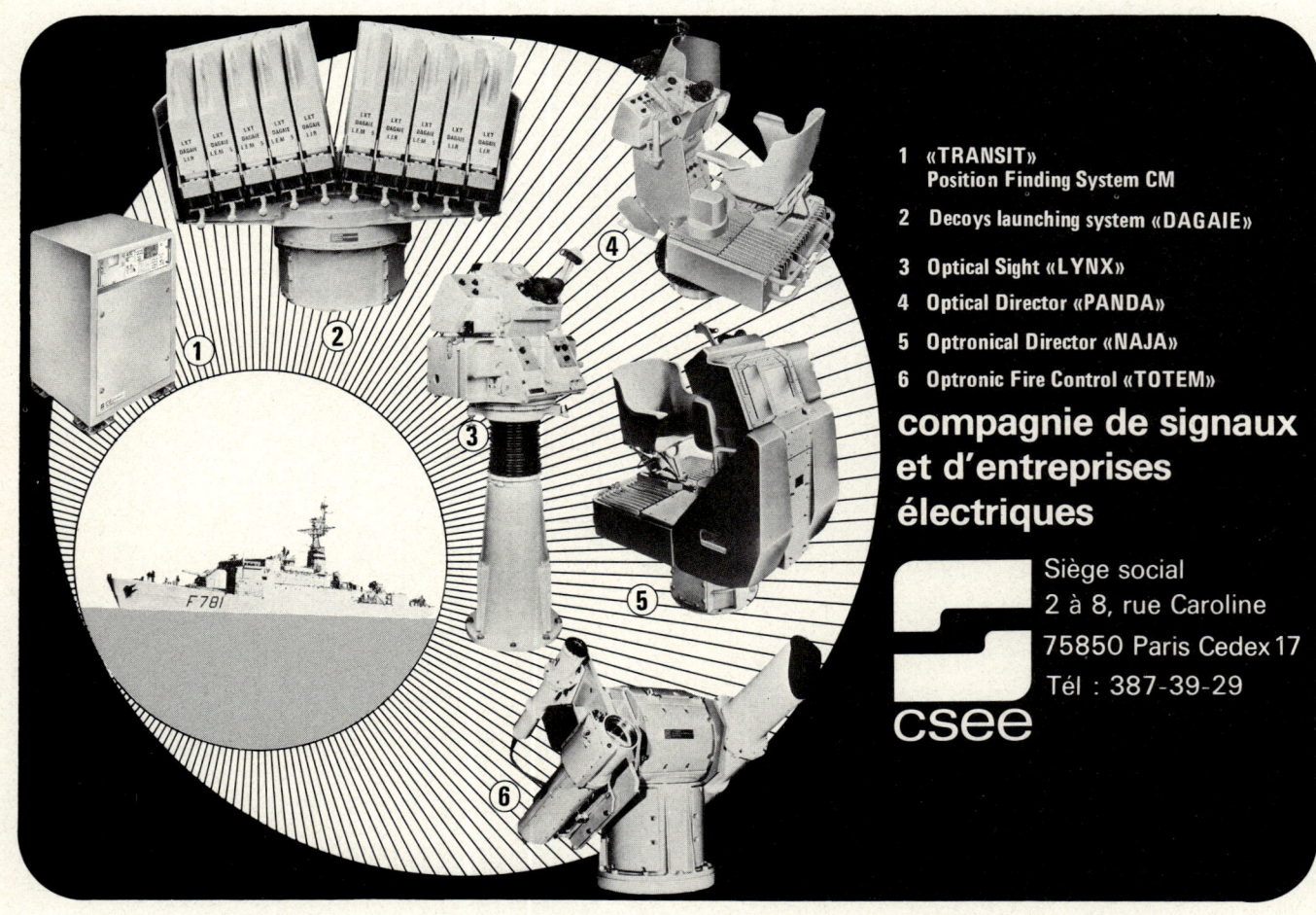

 means mines

SEA MINE MR-80

The newest general purpose ground influence mine presently produced.

It can be laid by surface vessels, by submarines and it is launchable from aircrafts by parachute.
The MR-80 is equipped with the devices for the processing and the combination of the following target signals: pressure, magnetic, low frequency acoustic, audiofrequency acoustic.
It is laid at a variable depth between 8 and 300 meters and it remains effective in water also for over two years.
It can be remote-controlled.
The MR-80 is available in three war versions containing different quantity of explosive and in one drill version with possibility to record on land the working of the mine and of every influence channel.

MISAR S.p.A. ENTERTAINS POSSIBILITY TO MANUFACTURE SEA MINES WITH DIFFERENT CHARACTERISTICS ACCORDING TO THE CLIENT'S REQUIREMENTS.

Via Gavardo 6 - 25016 GHEDI (Brescia) Italy
Tel. 030/901864-901865 - Telex 300489

9 LV 200 Mk 2 Director
THE solution for any size warship

The general purpose multi-sensor
9 LV 200 Mk 2 Director features:

- Broad-band frequency agile, monopulse tracking radar in Ku-band. Circular polarization available as an option.
- High performance TV with associated automatic tracking circuits.
- Available as an option is an advanced, automatic IR-tracker of the thermal imaging type equipped with a unique closed-cycle cooler.
- Another option is a high-prf Laser Rangefinder for optronic ranging against air, surface and land targets.
- Special direct drive hydraulic motors with integrated hydrostatic bearings.
- Special shock absorption and vibration isolation mount.

Present and future installations include:

- 150 - 260 ton heavily armed FPB's
- 1 000 - 2 000 ton Corvettes and Coast Guard vessels
- 1 000 - 2 500 ton Mine Layer — Training Ships
- 3 400 ton Destroyers

Guns controlled in these installations range in calibers from 40 mm to 120 mm. The number of individually controlled guns range from 1 to 5.

Numerous trials have verified an accuracy hitherto achieved only in large and heavy systems. This accuracy and the multi-sensor versatility is now available for small as well as large warships.

Associated parts of complete 9 LV 200 Mk 2 installations control the Penguin, Harpoon, Exocet MM 38 and MM 40 surface-to-surface missiles.

**Philips
Elektronikindustrier AB**
Defence Electronics
S- 175 88 JÄRFÄLLA, Sweden
Tel.Nat. 0758/100 00
Tel.Int. +46758100 00
Telex: 115 05 peab S

Defence Electronics

PHILIPS

Peab-D 045 7811

Landing ship for tanks   Motorised pontoon bridge

Multiple rocket launcher   Multi-purpose logistic support ship

CONSTRUCTIONS NAVALES ET INDUSTRIELLES DE LA MEDITERRANEE

SIEGE SOCIAL
50, Avenue des champs Elysées, Paris 8°
Téléphone : (1) 225.74.23 + 225.86.57 +
TELEX N° 280 119 VASCO - PARIS   CABLE VASCO - PARIS

DIRECTION GENERALE,
CHANTIERS ET ATELIERS :
83501 - La Seyne-sur-Mer - FRANCE.

ARESA

ARENYS DE MAR
BARCELONA - SPAIN

TEL: BARCELONA (93) 792.12.40
SPAIN

ONE OF THE 20 UNITS OF 53' LONG COAST PATROL LAUNCHES,
DESIGNED AND CONSTRUCTED BY **ARESA** FOR THE SPANISH NAVY.

21 METRES HIGH-SPEED PATROL BOAT

CRESTITALIA builds a wide selection of G.R.R. fast patrol boats ranging from 7 to 30 metres.

The high speed patrol boat shown above is one of the most modern, efficient and rational boats yet built in the field of open sea planing hulls.

The main features of the vessel are the hydrodynamic hull shape, the strength of the hull and its proportions as well as the proportions and the reliability of the essential equipment (in particular the power plant and the control equipment) the stability, the safety, the manoeuvrability and, finally, the combination of the logistic, styling and functional characteristics.

To the same family belong also the M/V 55' 16,50 mts and the SENECA 11 mts high speed patrol boats.

Open sea tests carried out on the prototype only served to confirm the parameters characteristic of this series and high-lighted the low advance resistance, the very best performance in heavy seas even at low speed and when in a displacement condition, the excellent qualities of manoeuvrability and directional stability.

MAIN SPECIFICATION

Loa	mts.	21,18
Boa	mts.	5,30
Max displacement, unloaded and dry	tons.	32,60
Max speed, at full power with half load plus four (4) persons, in still water and calm air over	knots	37
Cruising speed over	knots	30
Engines	HP	2 x 1475

This boat can be equipped with a wide range of high speed diesel engine to suit specific requirements.

CRESTITALIA S.p.A. - Head office: 20151 Milano - via Gallarate 26 - tel. 3271873 - telegr. Crestitalia-Milano
Yard: 19031 Ameglia (La Spezia) tel. 65746-65583-65584 - telex: Savid 380201

FR. LÜRSSEN WERFT

FED. REPUBLIC OF GERMANY

2820 BREMEN 70
P.O. BOX 70 00 30
TELEPHONE 04 21 / 6 60 41
TELEX 02 44 484

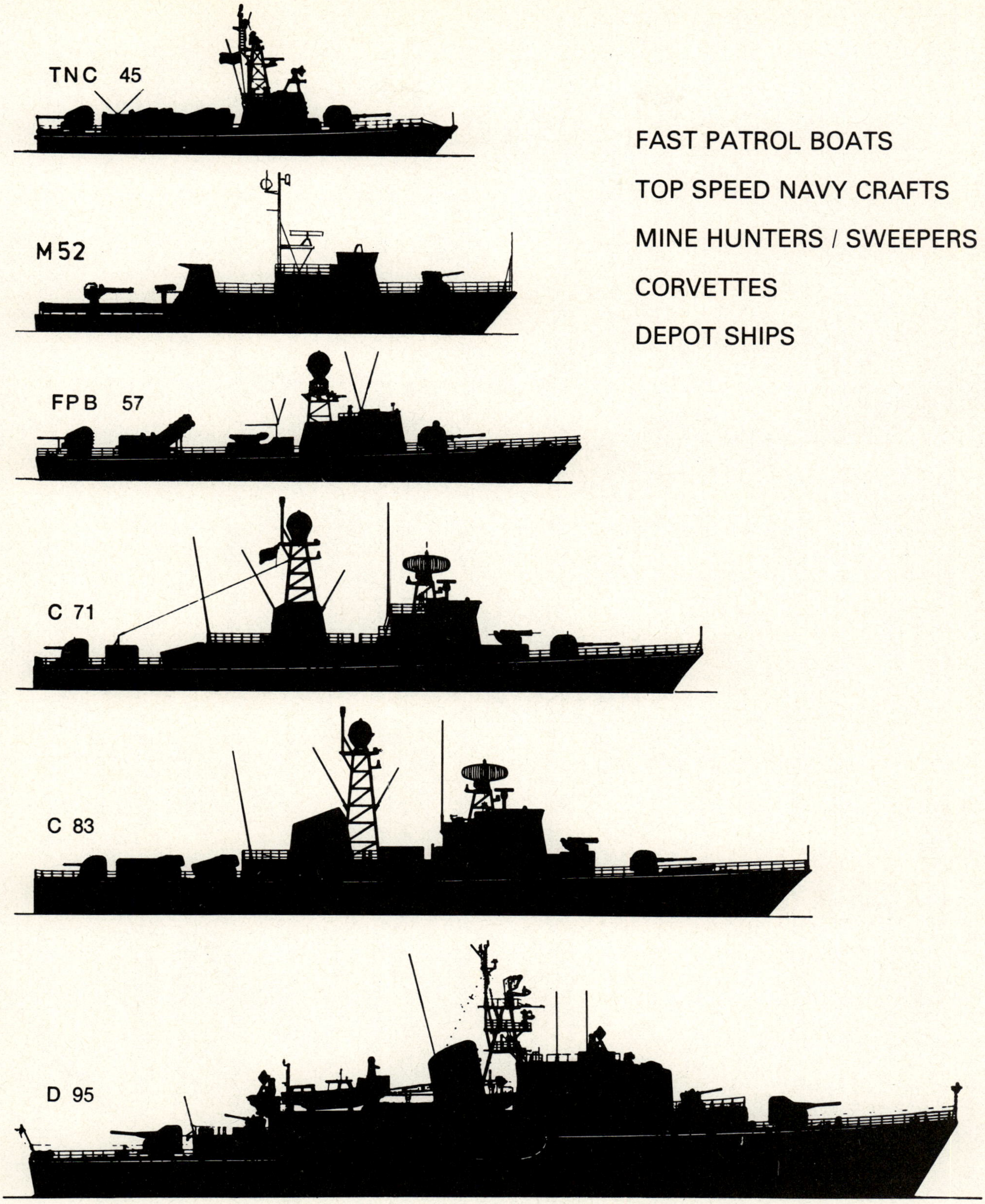

TNC 45

M 52

FPB 57

C 71

C 83

D 95

FAST PATROL BOATS
TOP SPEED NAVY CRAFTS
MINE HUNTERS / SWEEPERS
CORVETTES
DEPOT SHIPS

**DESIGNERS & BUILDERS
OF SOPHISTICATED
NAVAL CRAFT**

Vitroselenia

Via Tiburtina 1020 - 00156 Rome, ITALY
P.O. Box 7119 - 00162 Rome
Phone: 4126641 - 4125251
Cables: VITROSELENIA ROMA
Telex: 611309 VITROSEL

VITROSELENIA USUAL REFITTING ACTIVITIES IN THE NAVAL ELECTRONICS AND SYSTEM ENGINEERING:

- INSTALLATION OF TERRIER, TARTAR, ASROC AND SEA SPARROW MISSILE SYSTEM EQUIPMENT
- SEARCH AND NAVAL RADAR SYSTEM (SIOC) INSTALLATION
- FUNCTIONAL TEST AND ELECTRICAL ALIGNMENTS
- INSTALLATION OF FIRE CONTROL SYSTEMS
- DESIGN, SUPPLY AND INSTALLATION OF AUXILIARY SYSTEMS AND INTEGRATION THEREOF
- DESIGN, SUPPLY AND INSTALLATION OF WEAPON SYSTEM INTERFACE EQUIPMENT
- CABLING AND WIRING OF ALL EQUIPMENT MENTIONED ABOVE
- DESIGN, SUPPLY AND INSTALLATION OF WAVEGUIDES AND EQUIPMENT FOR PRESSURIZATION AND REFRIGERATION
- PREPARATION AND SUPPLY OF TECHNICAL DOCUMENTATION

AS PERFORMED ON ITALIAN AND FOREIGN NAVIES UNITS.

NEW ENGINES FOR NEW NAVAL REQUIREMENTS
propulsion and on-board generating sets

Engines from 90 to 6200 kW (120 to 8400 hp)
DIESEL POYAUD 135 and 150 mm bore / **DIESEL SACM** 175, 195 and 240 mm bore

1	2	3
4	5	6

1. 2 X 2200 hp SACM main engines
2. 4 X 3300 hp SACM main engines
   3 X 140 kW POYAUD generating sets
3. 3 X 4000 hp SACM main engines
   (40 knot patrol boat)
4. 2 X 1800 hp SACM main engines
   2 X 180 kW POYAUD generating sets
5. 3 X 480 kW SACM generating sets
6. 6 X 480 kW SACM generating sets

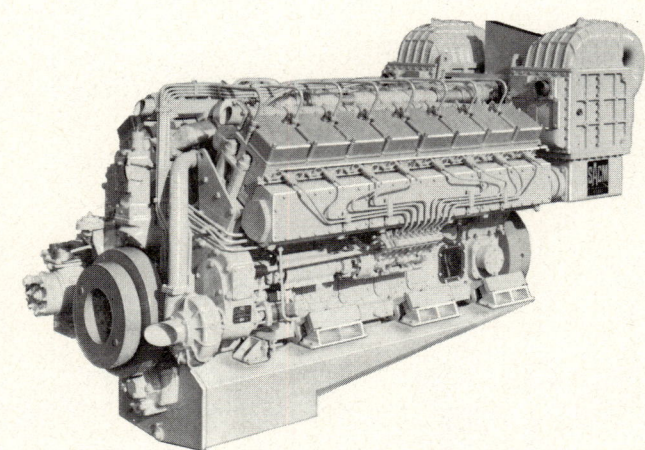

Photos : SACM - SKYFOTO - MARIUS BAR.

SALES OFFICE FOR ENGINES UP TO 1000 kW : **SOCIETE grossol**
14, RUE CHAPTAL – BP 104 – F 92303 LEVALLOIS CEDEX
TEL. : (1) 757.82.90 - TELEX : GROSSOL LVALL 620207 F

SALES OFFICE FOR ENGINES OVER 1000 kW:
SOCIÉTÉ ALSACIENNE DE CONSTRUCTIONS MÉCANIQUES DE MULHOUSE
157, AVENUE CHARLES DE GAULLE – F 92521 NEUILLY SUR SEINE
CEDEX – TEL: 33 (1) 747 51 00 - TELEX: GROSSOL 620207 F

INMA

INDUSTRIE NAVALI MECCANICHE AFFINI

technical, administrative and commercial
management and shipyard
362, viale S. Bartolomeo 19100 La Spezia
p.o. box 346 telephone (0187) 504000
telex 270297 **INMA**
telegraphic add. INMA La Spezia

CONSTRUCTIONS OF:
training ship
landing ship
fleet support ship

fast patrol boats	up to 230	tons
fast missile boats	225	tons
vedette escorteur	130	tons
fast patrol craft	27,90	tons
fast corvette	690	tons
fast strike craft	290	tons
missile boat	153	tons

Better ships and better delivery times:

you'd better come to RSV

You know us

RSV is the largest shipbuilding group in The Netherlands, with over one hundred years' experience in the construction of naval vessels. Yards for naval shipbuilding in RSV are:

Royal Schelde Vlissingen
Wilton Fijenoord Schiedam
Rotterdam Dockyard Company Rotterdam

Naval shipbuilding is our business

Frigate, corvette, submarine, replenishment ship, fast attack craft, any type of naval vessel - you name it, we'll make it. Standard or custom-made. Task and mission taken into account, the result will be not just a ship but a comprehensive, integrated system of platform, sensors, weapons, communication and navigation equipment, together with all follow-up support services. Recent orders for the Royal Netherlands Navy and other navies include ships of the Tromp, Kortenaer, Zwaardvis and Zuiderkruis classes.

What's your problem?

If your naval program calls for new vessels to meet specific operational requirements - consult RSV. A specialized briefing team will be pleased to discuss possibilities. Excellent yard facilities are also available for repairs, conversions and modernisations.
And, count on it, delivery time means delivery time. That's our way at RSV. We invite you to contact us for further information.

RSV/ Naval Engineering

P.O. Box 1425 - Rotterdam - Holland
Telephone: (+31 10) 14 28 11 -
Telex: 23652

**Rhine-Schelde-Verolme
Engineers and Shipbuilders/The Netherlands**

One of eleven vessels of a twenty one vessel programme of Fast Patrol Craft for the Federal Mexican Government built by Ailsa Shipbuilding Co. Ltd.

At the Ailsa yard at Troon on the Clyde Estuary facilities exist to design and build defence craft up to 114 metres overall. The yard has wide experience to British Ministry of Defence standards and considerable familiarity with high speed machinery. Fabrication in non-ferrous materials and close liaison with armament suppliers plus easy access to open water give this Scottish yard considerable advantages in the international defence markets.

AILSA

AILSA SHIPBUILDING CO. LTD. · Harbour Road · Troon · Ayrshire · Tel: 0292 311311 · Telex 778027

THE POWER OF YOUR SUBMARINE

highest energy density
reliable in service
long service life

Supplier of submarine batteries all over the world

ACCUMULATORENFABRIKEN WILHELM HAGEN AG
SOEST · KASSEL · BERLIN
Thomästr. 27 / 28 · P.O.B. 5 · 4770 Soest · Telephone 0 29 21 / 10 21 · Telex 08 4 313 wh - d

P.166-DL3: the versatile round-the-clock performer

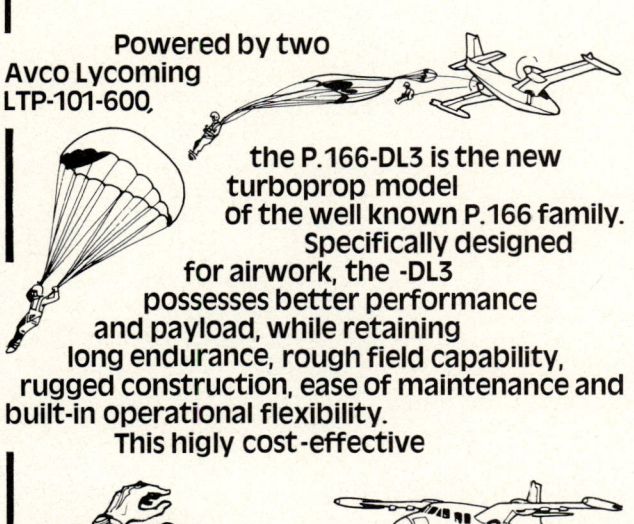

Powered by two Avco Lycoming LTP-101-600, the P.166-DL3 is the new turboprop model of the well known P.166 family. Specifically designed for airwork, the -DL3 possesses better performance and payload, while retaining long endurance, rough field capability, rugged construction, ease of maintenance and built-in operational flexibility. This higly cost-effective

and reliable aircraft is an ideal tool for a variety of military and commercial missions. Maritime patrol SAR, light tactical transport, air command post, paratroop-dropping and ambulance

are just a few of the various tasks which have been field-proven by the P.166 family and which will be even better performed by this new turboprop.

RINALDO PIAGGIO
Via Brigata Bisagno 14 - Genova - Italy - Telex 270695

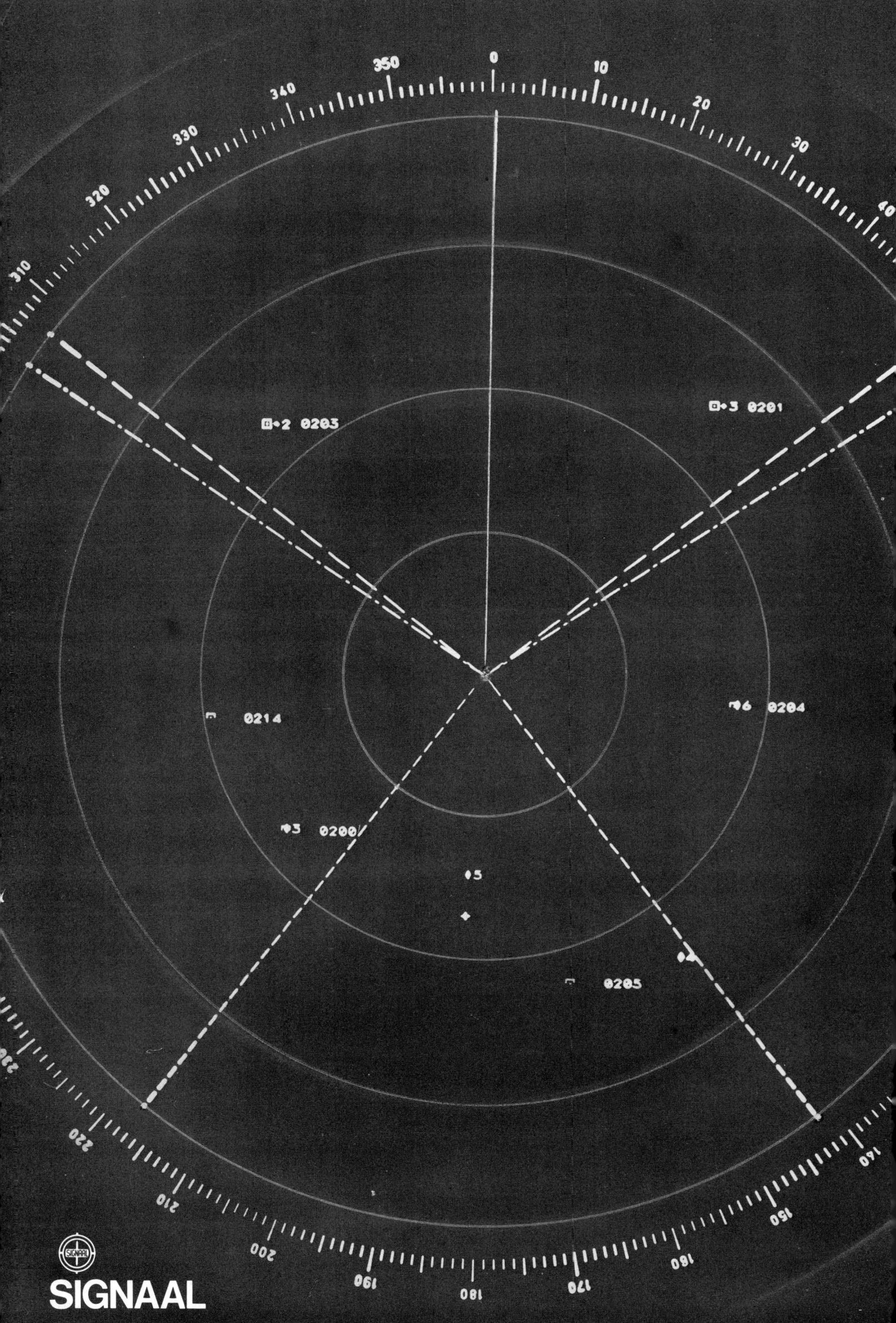

Tactical display Signaal M-20 mini combat systems.

A bright picture generates bright ideas.

To make a series of correct decisions in a very short timespan requires instant information of the highest quality. Signaal's tactical display and the M-20 mini combat system offer you that extra bit of insight that generates bright ideas for the right decisions. Result: tactical superiority and combat supremacy.
This tactical display is the centre of co-ordination of command and control functions, an essential element of combat systems to counter to-day's threat.

Characteristics of the M-20 mini combat systems.

Standard building blocks are used to design tailor-made systems capable of controlling a wide range of weapons:
— dual purpose guns
— surface-to-surface missiles
— surface-to-air missiles
— anti-submarine rockets
— guided and unguided torpedoes.
Advanced radar, display and digital computer techniques are employed to give the systems all the necessary technical and operational features to ensure tactical superiority:
— continuous 360° surface and air surveillance
— freedom of manoeuvring during engagements

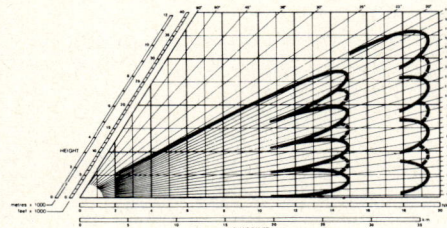
M-20 radar coverage diagram

Mini combat systems, specially for FBS's

— comprehensive display of required tactical data
— computer-assisted threat evaluation and weapon assignment
— automatic target tracking for weapon control

Weapon control console

— computer assistance for tactical manoeuvring and navigation
— extensive ECCM provisions.
Extensive integration and solid-state design allow these mini combat systems to be installed in all classes of ships.

Even with FPB's a hitting power is achieved not normally found in such small ships.

Innovative, alert, flexible.

Signaal can help you counter the growing threat in three ways:
— by keeping abreast of the latest developments in technology, Signaal continuously innovates its designs, realising tactical applications of these technologies
— by being alert to the changing threat scenario, Signaal achieves very short reaction times in developing effective counters to new threats

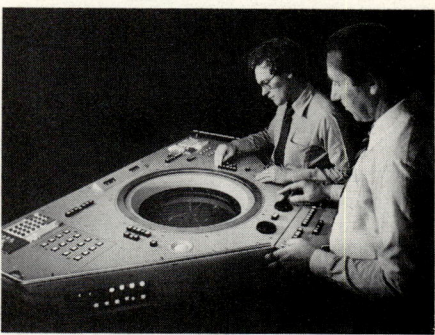
Tactical display console

— by staying flexible in its approach to non-standard requirements and the exigencies typical of military equipment, Signaal is capable to find a solution for each assignment, making use of a vast experience.

Hollandse Signaalapparaten B.V. - P.O.Box 42 - 7550 GD Hengelo - The Netherlands - Tel. 05400 - 88111 - Telex 44310.
Radar, Combat Information and Weapon Control Systems.

Bright ideas generate a bright picture.

M-20 Tactical Display S 24 E

HOWALDTSWERKE-DEUTSCHE WERFT
AKTIENGESELLSCHAFT HAMBURG UND KIEL
A Company of the Salzgitter Group

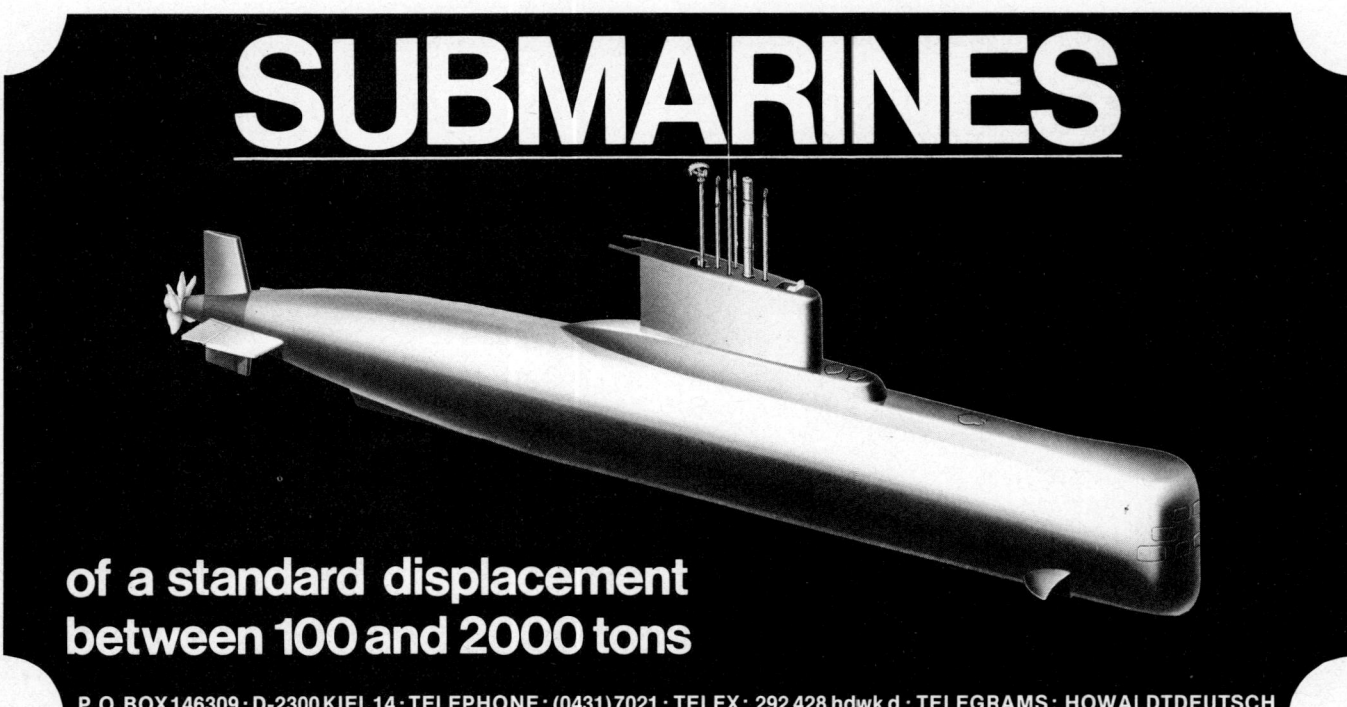

SUBMARINES

of a standard displacement between 100 and 2000 tons

P.O.BOX 146309 · D-2300 KIEL 14 · TELEPHONE: (0431) 7021 · TELEX: 292 428 hdwk d · TELEGRAMS: HOWALDTDEUTSCH

All submarines built in the Federal Republic of Germany after World War II and delivered to the Federal German Navy as well as to foreign navies, were designed by INGENIEURKONTOR LÜBECK

In compliance with our drawings the following submarines were built and/or ordered till 1978:

- 3 Submarines class 201
- 2 Submarines class 202
- 5 Submarines class 205
- 8 Submarines class 205 mod.
- 18 Submarines class 206
- 15 Submarines class 207
- 34 Submarines class 209
- 3 Submarines type 540
- 2 Complete conversions
- 2 Work submersibles TOURS

Totally 92 Submarines for 15 countries

Our program comprises:

- Type 100
- Type 450
- Type 540
- Type 740
- Type 1000 with variants
- Type 2000

We are working at the enlargement of our program for our navy and foreign ones

INGENIEURKONTOR LÜBECK
Prof. Gabler Nachfolger GmbH

P.O. Box 1690 · Niels-Bohr-Ring 5
D-2400 Lübeck 1

Telephone 0451/3107-1, Telex 26 768

 **Aermarelli**

engineers and contractors for fighting ships

1. systems for civil buildings
   - educational centers
   - medical centers
   - business centers
   - residential centers
   - airports

2. industrial air conditioning
   - textile industry
   - chemical pharmaceutical industry
   - food industry
   - manufacturing industry
   - nuclear plants
   - services

3. marine air conditioning and special military systems
   - passengers ships
   - cargo ships
   - drilling ships
   - navy vessels
   - special military systems

4. refrigeration systems
   - cold storages
   - food industry
   - chemical industry
   - sports facilities

The Italian Navy's new Sauro class submarines are fitted with high performance and reliable AERMARELLI air conditioning equipment and systems

'Nazario Sauro'   launched 9 oct. 76

'Fecia di Cossato'   launched 16 nov. 77

The air filtration and ventilation so as two indipendent air conditioning systems including a special refrigerating station are of AERMARELLI original design and make with changeover facility

Machineries and equipment have the Italian Navy antishock "A class" homologation

 Ercole Marelli Group

 **Aermarelli**
Viale V. Lancetti, 43 - 20158 Milan - Italy
Tel. (02) 6998 - Telex: Aermarel 360004

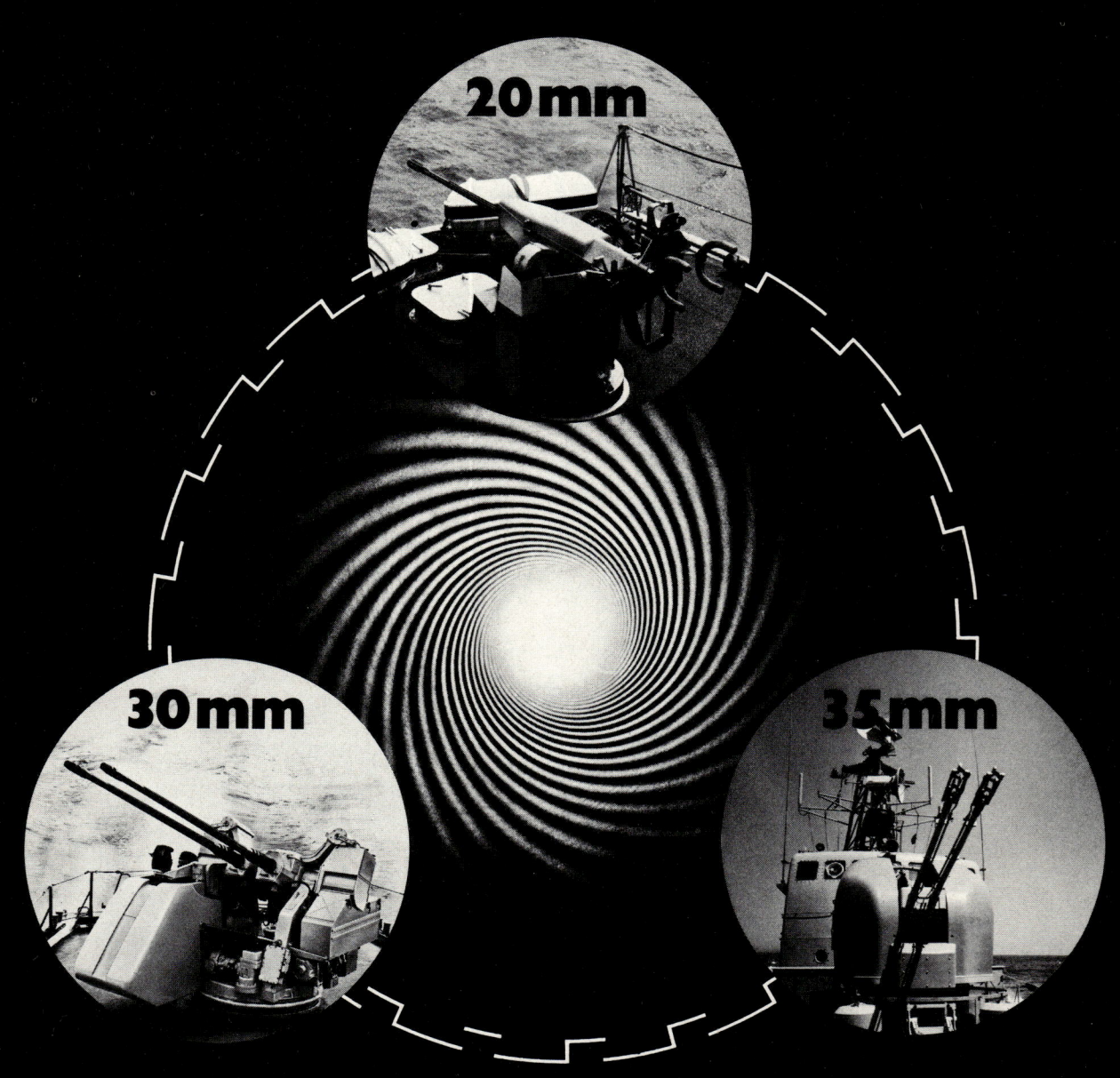

PICCHIOTTI

20m Panther 30 knots

A new generation of Fast Patrol Craft from a modernised traditional yard with over 350 years of experience

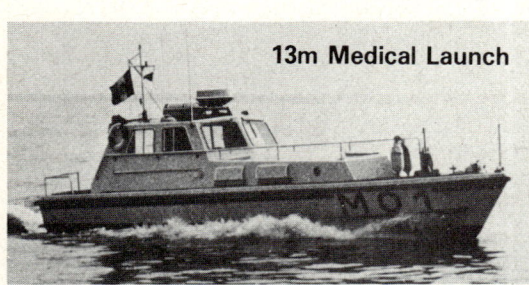
13m Medical Launch

11m Puma 29 knots

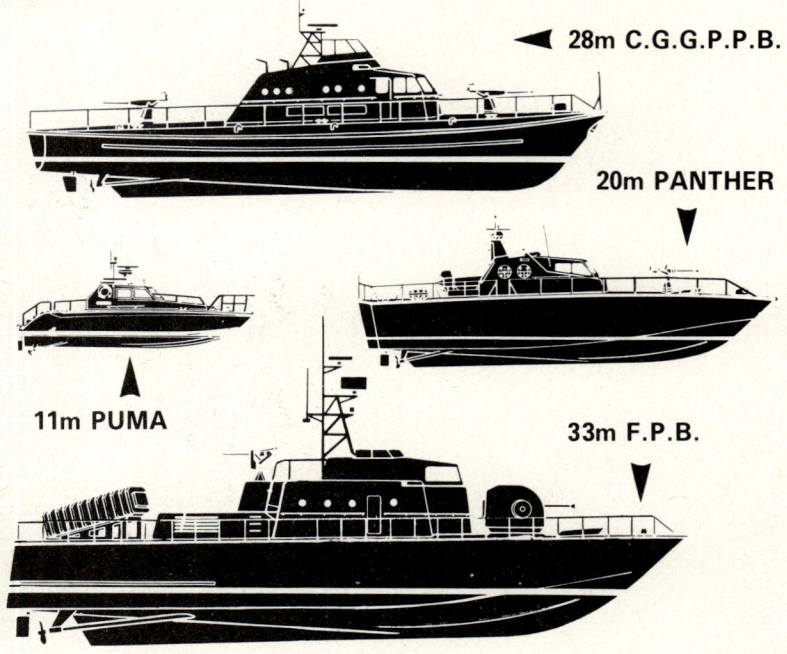
28m C.G.G.P.P.B.
20m PANTHER
11m PUMA
33m F.P.B.

Sales and Marketing:
Picchiotti Commercial Ltd.
P.O. Box 4, Sarisbury Green, Southampton, SO3 6YW, England.

Telephone: (0703) 37838
Telex: 477465 Piccom G.

Production:
Picchiotti S.P.A.
Cantiere Navale, Viareggio 55049, Italy.

Telephone: (584) 45345
Telex: 500328 Piccht I.

350 years of experience in designing and building Fast Naval Vessels, Commercial Craft and Luxury Yachts.

EXOCET

a family of long range missiles
FOR SEA POWER

The MM 38 uses the full detection range of the launcher's radars.

The AM 39 can be launched at all altitudes.

Quadruple launcher MM 40.
MM 40 has an over-the-horizon capability.

- ☐ They can be:
  - Surface-launched (MM 38 - MM 40) from ships of all tonnages, or from fixed or mobile coastal batteries.
  - Air-launched (AM 39) from helicopters, strike aircraft or maritime patrol aircraft.
  - Sub-launched (under development).
- ☐ They have basically the same principle of operation and the same maintenance equipment.
- ☐ They are FIRE AND FORGET and SEA SKIMMING, which makes them practically INVULNERABLE to all enemy defences.
- ☐ They provide SUPERIORITY in anti-surface warfare to those countries which adopt them, owing to their range, speed, accuracy and killing power.

22 countries have chosen the EXOCET.
More than 1.150 EXOCET missiles have been ordered.

aerospatiale
division engins tactiques
2, rue Béranger - Châtillon 92320 FRANCE

AEROSPATIALE MISSILES Ltd.,
178 Piccadilly, LONDON W1V OBA

Range of Activity in electronic defence field:

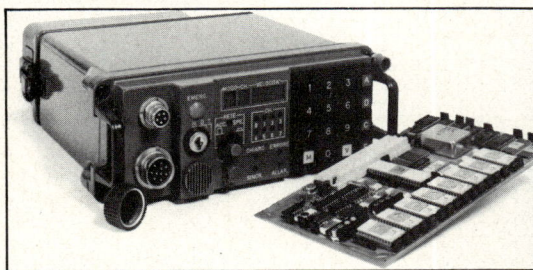
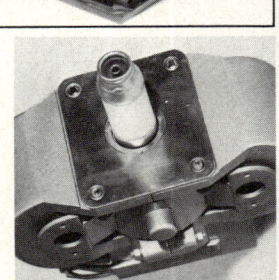

IFF System and equipment
- Interrogator
- Transponder
- Decoder

Encryption System
- Secure Voice Equipment
- Secure Telegraph Equipment
- Secure Data Equipment

Microwave Tubes
- Magnetron
- Klystron

Travelling wave tube

UHF Emergency transceiver

ITALTEL
SOCIETA' ITALIANA TELECOMUNICAZIONI
20149 Milan (Italy) - 12, Piazzale Zavattari - phone (+ 39.2) 4388.1

The new wave in FPB power is here!

Whatever your Fast Patrol Boat design idea—propeller or water jet, high-speed hull or hydrofoil—look first at Garrett's ME990, the new totally marinized gas turbine.

Built under U.S. Navy contract specifically for sea duty, the ME990 uses less engine room space and weighs approximately 25% of the highest-performance comparable diesel propulsion engines.

The 5,000-6,000 shaft horsepower ME990 has the design simplicity and rugged construction—plus the corrosion-resistant materials and coatings—that promise a life expectancy equal to that of the ship it powers. No scheduled major maintenance is required. And because of its modular construction and in-place servicing features, there is no need to pull the entire engine for repair or overhaul. Also, the Garrett ME990 requires no ancillary systems, is complete and ready to fit neatly into your design.

The Garrett ME990 is ready now to serve as primary propulsion for Fast Patrol Boats, as cruise power for DE-class ships, or as a generator set drive for larger craft.

For complete information write or call the Sales Manager, Marine Gas Turbines, AiResearch Manufacturing Company of Arizona, P.O. Box 5217, Phoenix, AZ 85010. (602) 267-3011.

GARRETT ME990 MARINE GAS TURBINE

The Garrett Corporation  **The wave of the future**
One of The Signal Companies

Detect ... Track ... and furnish visual display of radar threats for analysis.

They're the new advanced "Sea Sentry" passive electronic surveillance systems, designed and built by Kollmorgen. "Sea Sentry", a family of cost-effective, completely automatic ESM systems, featuring modular design, 100% probability of detection through omni-directional coverage, simultaneous display of entire threat band, and detection of pulsed or CW signals. It also performs automatic direction finding to better than 10° RMS, modulation analysis of received threat signals, and CRT display of threat identification, bearing and range information.

There are 3 versions of the Sea Sentry System:
    Sea Sentry I — for fast patrol boats
    Sea Sentry II — for surface ships
    Sea Sentry III — for submarines

All this, combined with outstanding performance at a minimum of cost through the use of existing hardware, make it more suitable for a greater variety of defense programs than any other surveillance system available today.

If you want better DF accuracy, increased sensitivity, wider frequency coverage, and interface provisions for other onboard systems, Kollmorgen can provide a "Sea Sentry" system to fit your application.

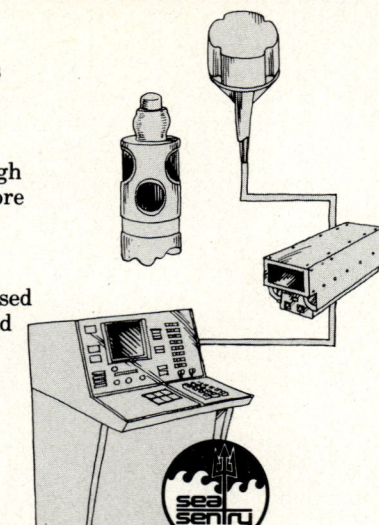

sea sentry

Radar threat detection & analysis system for surface vessels & submarines

KOLLMORGEN
CORPORATION
Northampton, Massachusetts 01060
Telephone (413) 586-2330 TWX: 510-290-2001

Electro-Optical Division

Tomorrow's insight into today's problems

EMPRESA NACIONAL BAZAN

CONSTRUCTION OF ALL TYPES OF NAVAL AND MERCHANT VESSELS. GENERAL SHIP REPAIR WORKS.

- STEAM TURBINES AND DIESEL MOTORS FOR PROPULSION. TURBINES FOR CONVENTIONAL AND NUCLEAR POWER STATIONS
- MARINE AND LAND BASED BOILERS

- NAVAL ORDNANCE AND AMMUNITIONS
- AUXILIARY MACHINERY, MARINE CRAFTS, MOBILE CRANES, PROPELLERS, CASTINGS, AGRICULTURAL MACHINERY, ETC.

SHIPYARDS AT:
    EL FERROL DEL CAUDILLO
    CARTAGENA
    SAN FERNANDO (CADIZ)

ORDNANCE FACTORIES AT:
    SAN FERNANDO (CADIZ)
    CARTAGENA

DRY AND FLOATING DOCKS

HEAD OFFICE:
65 CASTELLANA, MADRID-1 - SPAIN
PHONE 4415100 TELEX 27480
CABLE ADDRESS: BAZAN

LM 2500:
Facts - not a fisherman's tale

From the pathways of the sky to the routes of the oceans. Jointly built by Fiat and General Electric, the LM 2500 is the only turbine of the new generation to have been developed from aircraft engines with technical specifications ensuring its safe use in the propulsion of ships, namely low size-to-power and weight-to-power ratios, a high standard of performance permitting a low level of fuel consumption, and power outputs ranging from 16,000 to 27,000 horsepower. In the wake of the success enjoyed by the LM 2500 on the U.S.S. Callaghan, the U.S. Navy has made provision for the adoption of more than 300 such units as the standard power plant of her new ships. And the Navies of Italy, West Germany, Peru, Venezuela, Australia, Iran, Indonesia, and Saudi Arabia have followed suit by choosing this outstanding turbine for carrying their latest ships over the seven seas. Of great interest is also the possibility of using the LM 2500 on merchant vessels, especially container ships and liquid oil tankers. This is sound technological fact - not a fisherman's tale.

FIAT AVIAZIONE

OFFICINE PANERAI SRL

has elaborated for over a century an activity of research, design and production of optical, mechanical and electronic equipment, apparatus and devices.

Panerai precision devices, such as compasses, pressure gauges, depth-meters, watches, depth-recorders and watertight flashlights were used underwater by the first frog-men, honour and pride of the Italian Navy.

The main headline of this activity has always been the quality of produced materials, made in small and medium series for special uses. Herein are some characteristic items of the present, non-classified production of the company, in use by the Italian Armed Forces:
- Equipment for helicopters night deck landing
- Portable equipment for aircraft landing
- Remote level indicator equipment for submarines trim tanks
- High level water (or liquid in general) alarm systems
- Electronic engine room telegraph
- Fixed and portable optical apparatus, for naval and land uses
- Wrist compasses and depth-meters for underwater operators.

The production and studies of the company include also the field of weapons, devices and fixtures for special troops, which, owing to their top secret nature, cannot be disclosed to the public, but for which the company may give direct and exact information to parties concerned, except when, in very particular productions, the release of these information requires the permission of the Italian Navy.

The accurate performance and high reliability of Panerai production have always obtained the widest acknowledgement and also the personal and warm thanks of many Commanders for whom the availability of Panerai equipment, at the right place and time, has been the resolutive factor in the aims achievement.

OFFICINE PANERAI S.R.L.
2 Piazza G. Ferraris
50131 FIRENZE

Phone: 055/579304
Cable: PANERAI FIRENZE

We are specialists in the design, production and installation of underwater and marine equipment.

The Company's products include the following:-

Cable Penetrators and Connectors for Pressure Hull and Equipment Applications

Umbilical Cable Terminations

Cable Jointing Equipment

Hydrophones

Towed Seismic Arrays

Torsionmeters for propulsion Shafts

Complete Underwater Electrical and Electroacoustic Systems

Designed and manufactured to the highest standards of reliability for all underwater and marine applications.

ameeco
(Hydrospace Limited)

Bilton Road, Erith, Kent
Telephone: Erith STD Code (03224) 46821
Telex: 896230

USEA

STUDY AND DESIGN IN THE AREA OF UNDERWATER ACOUSTIC SUBMARINE DETECTION EQUIPMENTS AND ELECTROMECHANIC AND ELECTRONIC AUXILIARIES

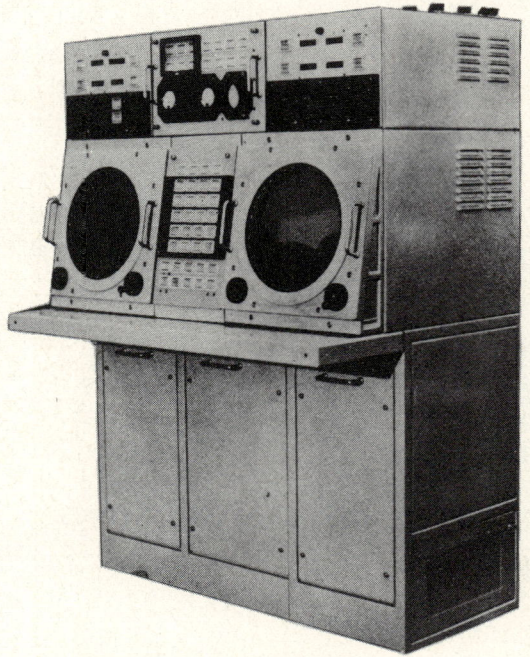

HEAD OFFICE AND RESEARCH LABORATORY
19C30 Pugliola di Lerici (LA SPEZIA) - Italy - via G. Matteotti, 63
Tel (0187) 967.125 / 968.605   Telex 571216 USEA/1

REGISTERED OFFICE
00197 ROMA - Italy - viale Maresciallo Pilsudski, 92
Tel (06) 874.450

100 Years Blohm+Voss

1892	Small Cruiser "Condor"
to	3 Cruisers
1918	9 Heavy Cruisers and Battle Ships a. o. "Goeben", "Seydlitz", "Derfflinger"
	6 Torpedo Boats
	100 Submarines
1918	3 Training Sail Ships and 1 Aviso
to	6 Frigates and Destroyers
1945	1 Heavy Cruiser "Admiral Hipper"
	1 Battle Ship "Bismarck"
	230 Submarines

80 Years Naval Construction

1958	1 Training Sail Ship
to	4 Destroyers of the "Hamburg Class"
1971	6 Frigates of the "Köln Class"
	3 Escorts
	3 Supply Ships and 2 Mine Carriers
	2 Landing Craft
	3 Corvettes
1972 to 1977	Modernisation of the "Hamburg Class" destroyers
1977	1 Frigate for Nigeria (Prime Contractor for G.P. MEKO 360)
1978	2 Repeats Frigate F 122 for the German Federal Navy
	2 Frigates for Argentine (Prime Contractor for MEKO 360 and 4 repeats in Argentine)

Blohm+Voss AG · P.O. Box 10 07 20 · D-2000 Hamburg 1 · Phone 40-3061

a.s.w.

CIT-ALCATEL
DIVISION MARINE

Anti-submarine warfare
French specialist

systems • equipment • armaments
for surface ships • submarines
and aircrafts

GROUPE CGE

SINTRA - Département D.S.M. :
1 av. Aristide-Briand 94117 Arcueil (France)
tél. : (1) 657.11.70 - Télex : 250 675 F.

One in ten of the world's helicopters is made in Italy, by Agusta.

In size, the Agusta Group is now one of world's major aerospace enterprises. It exports to 67 countries.

But size and volume is not the only story. Agusta is now also the most diversified helicopter manufacturer.

Production at Agusta this year includes twelve models, civil and military, some of Agusta original design, some under licence from Bell, Sikorsky, and Boeing-Vertol. Product support is extensive and thorough.

For anyone considering helicopter purchases, Agusta is truly an attractive source.

AGUSTA
Milan, Italy - Telex 333280

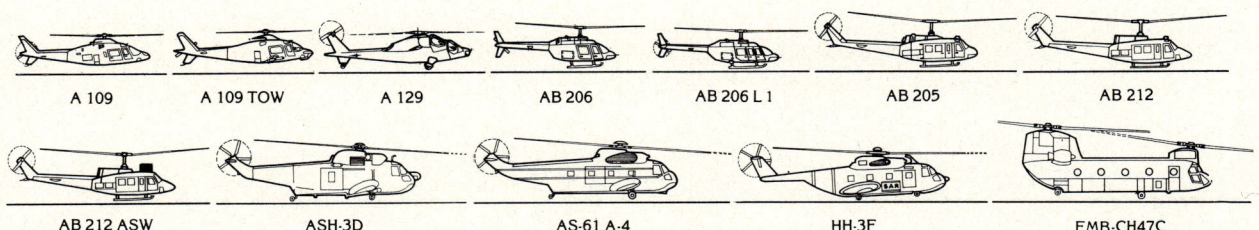

BAGL

MANGUSTA 30 OFFSHORE PATROL CRAFT

20 GC COASTAL PATROL CRAFT

ETTO
SINCE 1854

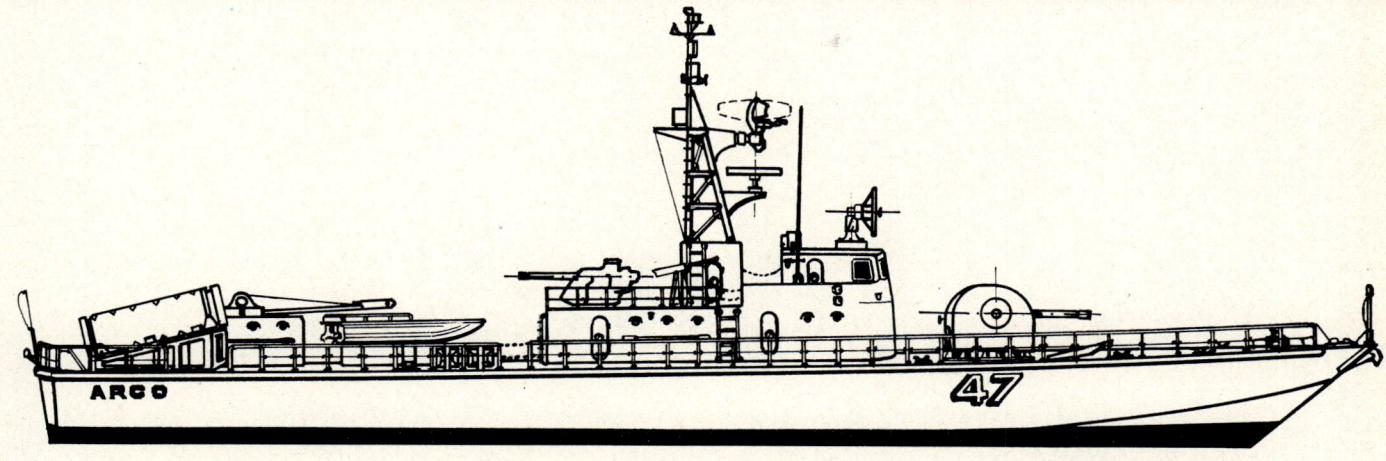

ARGO 47
OFFSHORE PATROL CRAFT

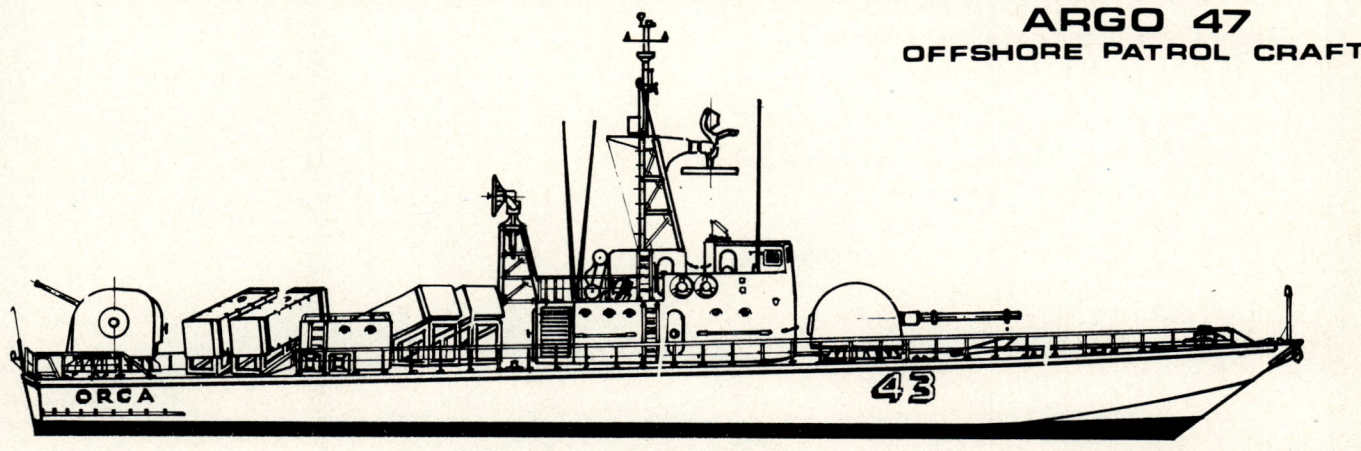

ORCA 43
FAST STRIKE CRAFT

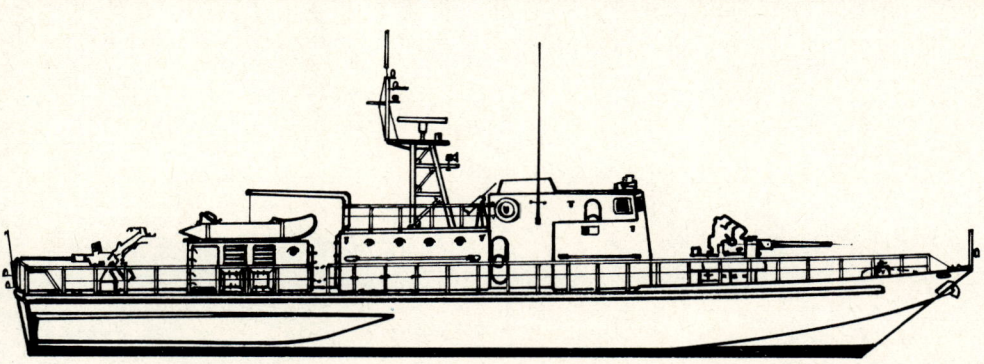

BARRACUDA 32
OFFSHORE PATROL CRAFT

PIRANHA 18
HIGH SPEED INTERCEPTOR

CANTIERI BAGLIETTO S.p.A.
17019 VARAZZE ITALY

(019) 95901 — 95902 — 95903
TLX 271214 CABAG I

Hydraulic Deck Machinery

Complete Systems for all class of ships
Motors · Pumps · Winches · Capstans
Anchor Gear · Boat Davits · R.A.S. Masts
Helicopter Handling · Lifts

MacTaggart Scott
P.O. Box No 1, Hunter Avenue, Loanhead,
Midlothian · EH20 9SP · Scotland.
Tele · 031·440·0311   Telex 72478

PROBLEMS WITH YOUR 200 MILE LIMIT?

Model of type M 600 for Surface-Oriented-Missions.

WE'VE GOT THE ANSWER!

Navaltecnica builds a range of high-speed, reliable, seaworthy hydrofoil craft for coastal patrol, protection of off-shore waters, fisheries surveillance, policing water traffic, search-and-rescue missions, fast attack, hit-and-run missions, customs duties, S.O.M., A.S.W., ...

Cruising speeds are maintained in sea states 5/6.

Behind each Navaltecnica Hydrofoil is more than twenty years of experience in building stable, versatile, cost-effective, high-performance and stabilized hydrofoils ...with over 125 vessels delivered worldwide.

Our military hydrofoil production includes 7 models ranging in size from 22 metres to 35 metres.
The larger units have a heli-pad for landing choppers.

For complete information, please write or call us.
Cantiere Navaltecnica SpA - 22 Via S. Raineri - 98100 Messina - Italy
Tel. (090) 774862 - Cable: Navaltecnica Messina - Telex: 980030 Rodrik I

isotta fraschini
marine diesel

propulsion units for military or civil crafts, pleasure boats
from **200** up to **2000** hp

if you are looking for a dependable marine diesel engine...

f.a. isotta fraschini e motori breda s.p.a.
21047 saronno (va), italy, via milano 7
phone (02) 960.3251/2/3 - cable brif. - telex 332403 BRIF I

A mark of ASW superiority...

A mark of engineering excellence...

SQR-18...a new dimension in Surface Navy ASW. Its long range detection provides the Surface/Sub/Air Team with the tactical means to meet the modern submarine threat...a capability critical to national defense.

From conceptual in-house research and development to the fleet in only four years. That's just what the Navy-EDO SQR-18 team accomplished.

Record performance...in record time. It's one reason that EDO Sonar equipment is seen in more and more navies all over the free world.

For more information on Sonar Systems contact:
Mr. John Devine
President
EDO International Division
14-04 111th Street
College Point, New York 11356
(212) 445-6000/Telex 423094

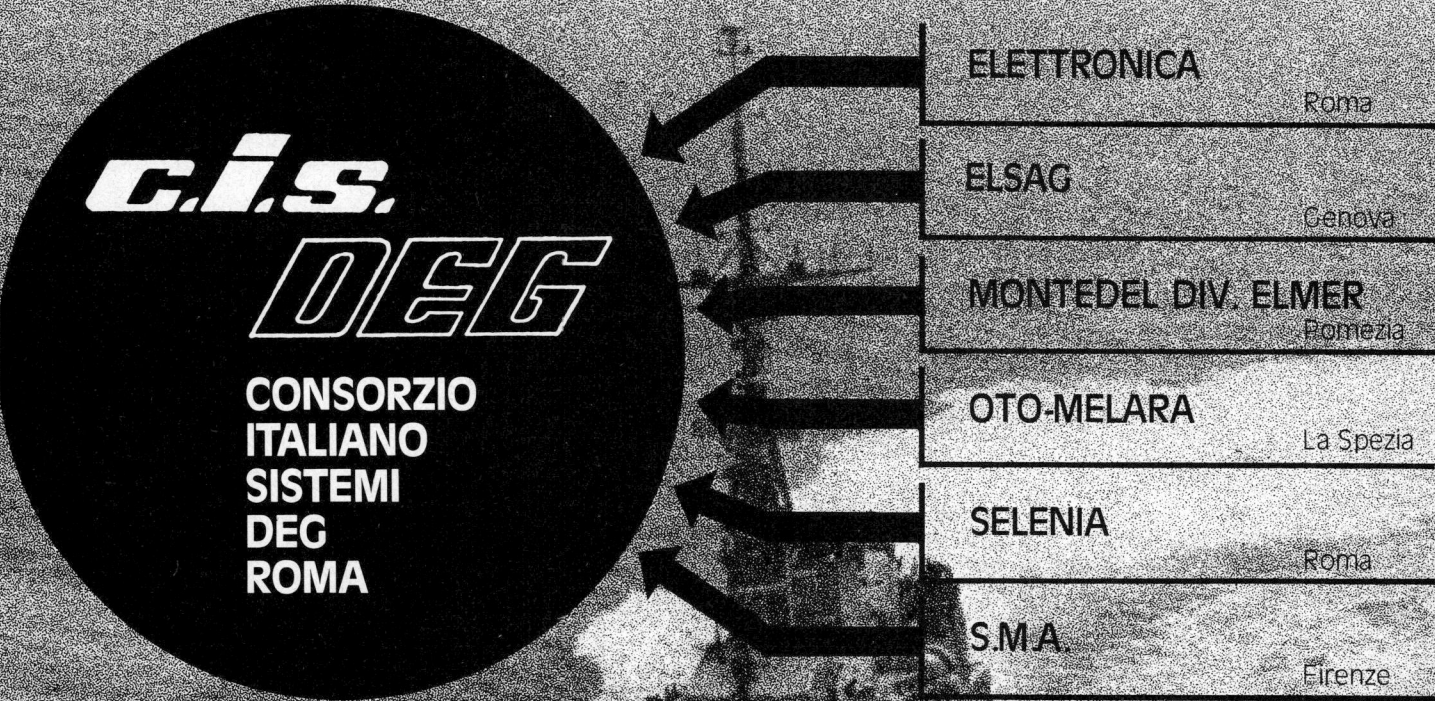

c.i.s. DEG

CONSORZIO ITALIANO SISTEMI DEG ROMA

- ELETTRONICA — Roma
- ELSAG — Genova
- MONTEDEL DIV. ELMER — Pomezia
- OTO-MELARA — La Spezia
- SELENIA — Roma
- S.M.A. — Firenze

- ■ COMBAT SYSTEM ENGINEERING
- ● SYSTEM ANALYSIS
- ● INTERFACE DEFINITION
- ● INSTALLATION DESIGN
- ● SYSTEM INSTALLATION
- ● SUBSYSTEM & SYSTEM TEST
- ● SYSTEM DOCUMENTATION
- ● SYSTEM COURSES

- ■ PRESENT ACTIVITIES OF THE CONSORTIUM:
- ● FRIGATES 'LUPO' CLASS
- ● A/S FRIGATES 'MAESTRALE' CLASS
- ● HYDROFOILS 'SPARVIERO' CLASS
- ● REPLENISHMENT SHIP 'VESUVIO'

Via G.B. Morgagni 30/E 00161 Roma – Telef. 853304-859372 –

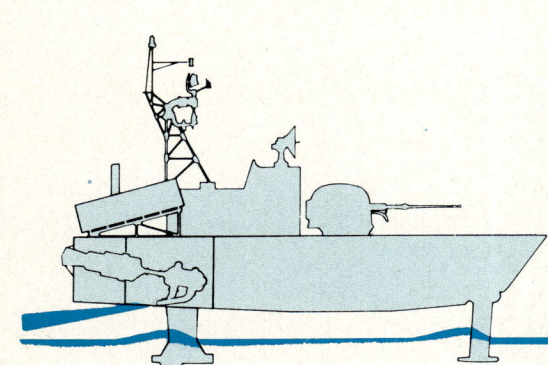

idrogetti per propulsione navale

marine propulsion water jets

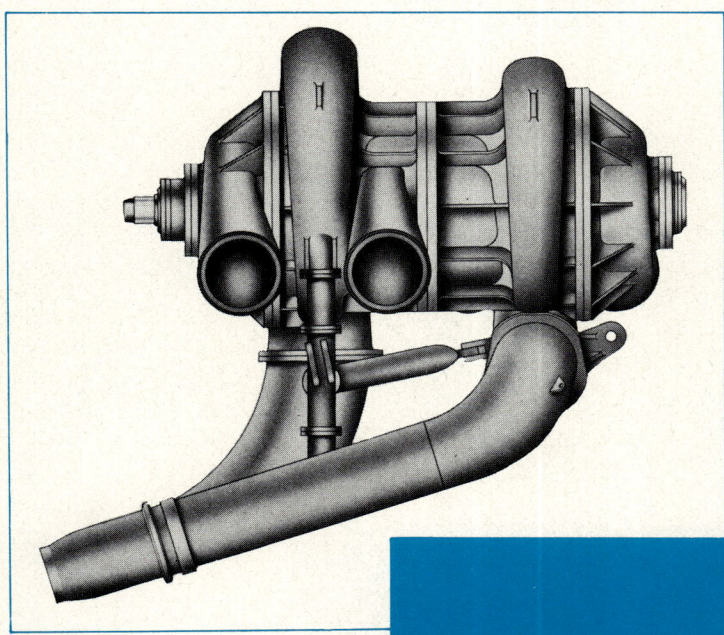

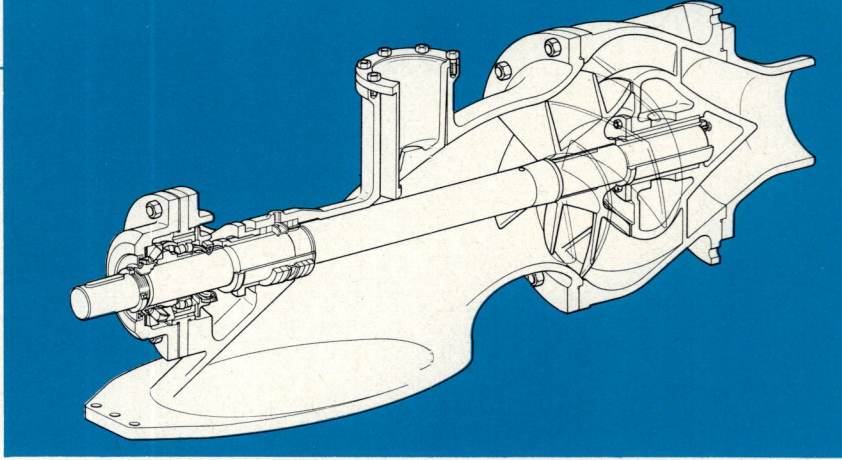

S.P.A. TERMOMECCANICA ITALIANA
ITALY - 19100 LA SPEZIA - VIA DEL MOLO, 1
P.O. BOX 341 - TEL. (0187) 503151 - TX 270171 TMI SPI

ANSALDO
TODAY MEANS
SHIP AUTOMATION

or the past ANSALDO
roduced power genera-
ors electric motors
witchboards and con-
erters for marine use

TODAY
AUTOMATION DIVISION
supply systems for ship
automation

ANSALDO
Società Generale Elettromeccanica s.p.a.

DIVISIONE AUTOMAZIONE * Via N. Lorenzi, 8
16152 * GENOVA CORNIGLIANO * ITALIA
Tel. 010 - 4105 * Telex 270098 ANSALDO

A FRIGATE FIRE POWER AT 36 KNOTS....

"RESHEF" MISSILE-BOAT, COMBAT-PROVEN.

THE NEW DIMENSION, 850 AND 1000 TYPES

ISRAEL SHIPYARDS LTD

P.O.B 1282   HAIFA   tel   9724 749111

tx 45132   yardil   cable israyard

Marine diesel engines Fiat-Aifo

Marine engine 8361 SRM 200 kW

Propulsion
37 ÷ 404 kW

Generating sets
50 Hz 15 ÷ 250 kVA
60 Hz 18 ÷ 290 kVA
400 Hz 15 ÷ 300 kVA

Pumping sets for
– fire fighting – fuel transfert
– stripping

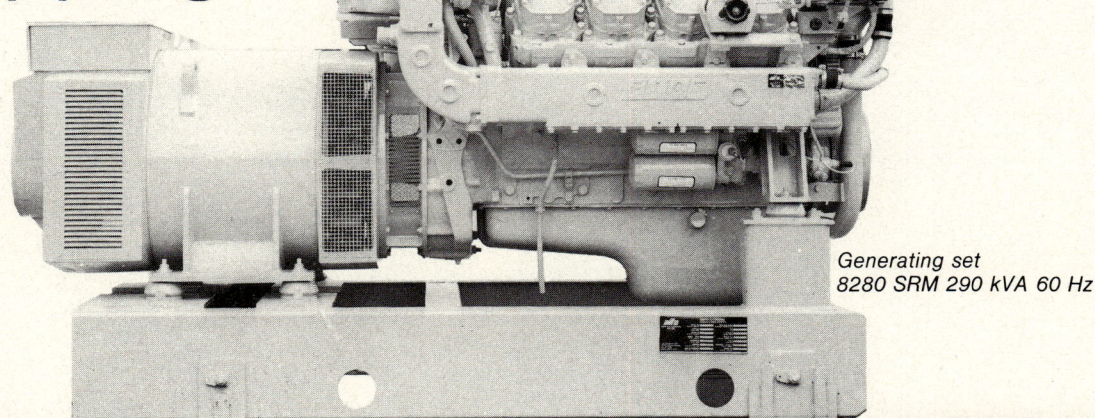

Generating set 8280 SRM 290 kVA 60 Hz

aifo A Fiat subsidiary company   diesel **FIAT**

Aifo S.p.A. - 20123 Milano via Carducci, 29 - tel. (0039-2) 8058351/877006/8058344 - telex 311531 I AIFO

MELARA CLUB

	CANTIERI NAVALI RIUNITI
	GRANDI MOTORI TRIESTE
FIAT	FIAT AVIAZIONE SEPA
	OTO MELARA
	BREDA MECCANICA BRESCIANA
	SELENIA ELETTRONICA SAN GIORGIO NAVAL SYSTEMS DIVISION
	ELETTRONICA
 MONTEDEL ELMER division	MONTEDEL ELMER DIVISION

-MELARA CLUB- MAY BE IDENTIFIED AS A GROUP OF FIRMS FORMING THE BACKBONE OF THE ITALIAN SHIPBUILDING INDUSTRY FOR THE NAVY.

WITH THE DIRECT POSITIVE AID OF THE ITALIAN NAVY, THIS GROUP CAN, ON A WORLDWIDE SCALE, PROVIDE FOR COMPLETE SHIPS, ITALIAN-MADE THROUGHOUT, AS WELL AS REFITTING PROJECTS AND CONNECTED LOGISTIC SUPPORT

sea power

The official magazine of the Navy League of the United States
(Founded 1902)

Writing about and reporting on:

- The United States Navy, Marine Corps, Coast Guard, and Merchant Marine

- National and global defense

- Maritime and oceanic affairs

- Political actions affecting national security

- Books of interest on sea power and related subjects

James D. Hessman, *Editor in Chief*

SEA POWER is published monthly from Washington, D.C. Circulation includes government, military and industry representatives, both U.S. and foreign, news media, academic institutions, and all members of the Navy League of the United States.

For editorial, advertising and circulation information, write:

sea power

Navy League of the United States
818 18th Street, N.W.
Washington, D.C. 20006

(202) 298-9282

FINCANTIERI

more than 2000 naval vessels built by the largest shipbuilding and shiprepairing group in the mediterranean

"Turn Key" production:

- helicopter carriers
- cruisers
- destroyers
- frigates
- corvettes

- submarines
- fast patrol boats
- hydrofoils
- support vessels
- survey vessels

ITALCANTIERI Trieste
CANTIERI NAVALI RIUNITI - C.N.R. Genova
CANTIERE NAVALE MUGGIANO La Spezia
CANTIERE NAVALE LUIGI ORLANDO - C.N.L.O. Livorno

ARSENALE TRIESTINO SAN MARCO Trieste
OFFICINE ALLESTIMENTO E RIPARAZIONI NAVI - O.A.R.N. Genova
SOCIETÀ ESERCIZIO BACINI NAPOLETANI - S.E.B.N. Napoli
STABILIMENTI NAVALI TARANTO Taranto
CANTIERI NAVALI E OFFICINE MECCANICHE DI VENEZIA - C.N.O.M.V. Venezia
GRANDI MOTORI TRIESTE - G.M.T. Trieste
LIPS ITALIANA Livorno
CENTRO STUDI DI TECNICA NAVALE - CE.TE.NA. Genova

FINCANTIERI

Società Finanziaria Cantieri Navali — Roma, via Sardegna 40 — Phone 482.241 — Telex 610180 FINC I — Cables Fincantieri

The USS *Oliver Hazard Perry*—first of the Navy's new FFG-7 class of guided missile frigates—is built for rugged action. And versatility. Three major systems from Raytheon will help the *Oliver Hazard Perry*—and the more than 60 frigates to follow—carry out a wide range of escort missions.

• AN/SPS-49. This long-range, air-search radar —developed and now being produced by Raytheon— acquires fast targets at all altitudes in clutter, bad weather, and in the presence of active and passive countermeasures. The radar features solid-state electronics, digital design, and an antenna stabilized to the horizon.

• AN/SQS-56. This Raytheon-developed sonar provides directional as well as omni-directional active and passive detection, and determines precise range and bearing for weapons control and guidance.

• AN/SLQ-32(V). This just-developed, advanced shipboard EW system—to be installed on the *Oliver Hazard Perry*—utilizes Raytheon's unique, lens-fed, multiple beam array. AN/SLQ-32(V) will provide rapid signal intercept, analysis, identification, ECM response, and alerting signals to other shipboard weapons.

In addition, Raytheon-produced continuous-wave illuminators and signal data converters contribute to the speed and reliability of the *Oliver Hazard Perry*'s missile fire control system.

These systems on board the *Oliver Hazard Perry* typify Raytheon's capabilities in shipboard defense. Other examples include the systems ma

Fast, versatile—and loaded with electronics fron

gement and production of the NATO Seasparrow
urface Missile System, supplying the computer
nd guidance electronics for the TRIDENT mis-
le, and production of the TARTAR-D shipboard
re control system.

For more specific information on the
N/SPS-49 radar, the AN/SQS-56 surface sonar,
r the AN/SLQ-32(V) EW system, please write
aytheon Company, Government Marketing,
41 Spring Street, Lexington, Massachusetts 02173.

Raytheon.

SOFREXAN
30, rue d'Astorg - 75008 Paris
Tél. 742.26.34 - Télex 640670 F

Can one DMS service possibly outweigh all of your current marketing information?

Yes, it can!

Since 1959, DMS has built a worldwide reputation among leading defence and aerospace market planners by carefully reviewing mountains of raw data on the defence industry, and accurately distilling this information into our specialized monthly Market Intelligence Reports®.

DMS also publishes its renowned WORLD AIRCRAFT FORECAST

DMS Market Studies include:
* Military Aircraft
* Gas Turbine Engines
* Electronic Systems
* "AN" Equipment
* Airline Intelligence Reports

Each MARKET INTELLIGENCE REPORT® is backed by a free inquiry service in which DMS editors respond immediately to questions from individual clients.

DMS
Suite 31
100 Northfield Street
Greenwich, CT, U.S.A. 06830

Market planners are invited to contact DMS for further information.

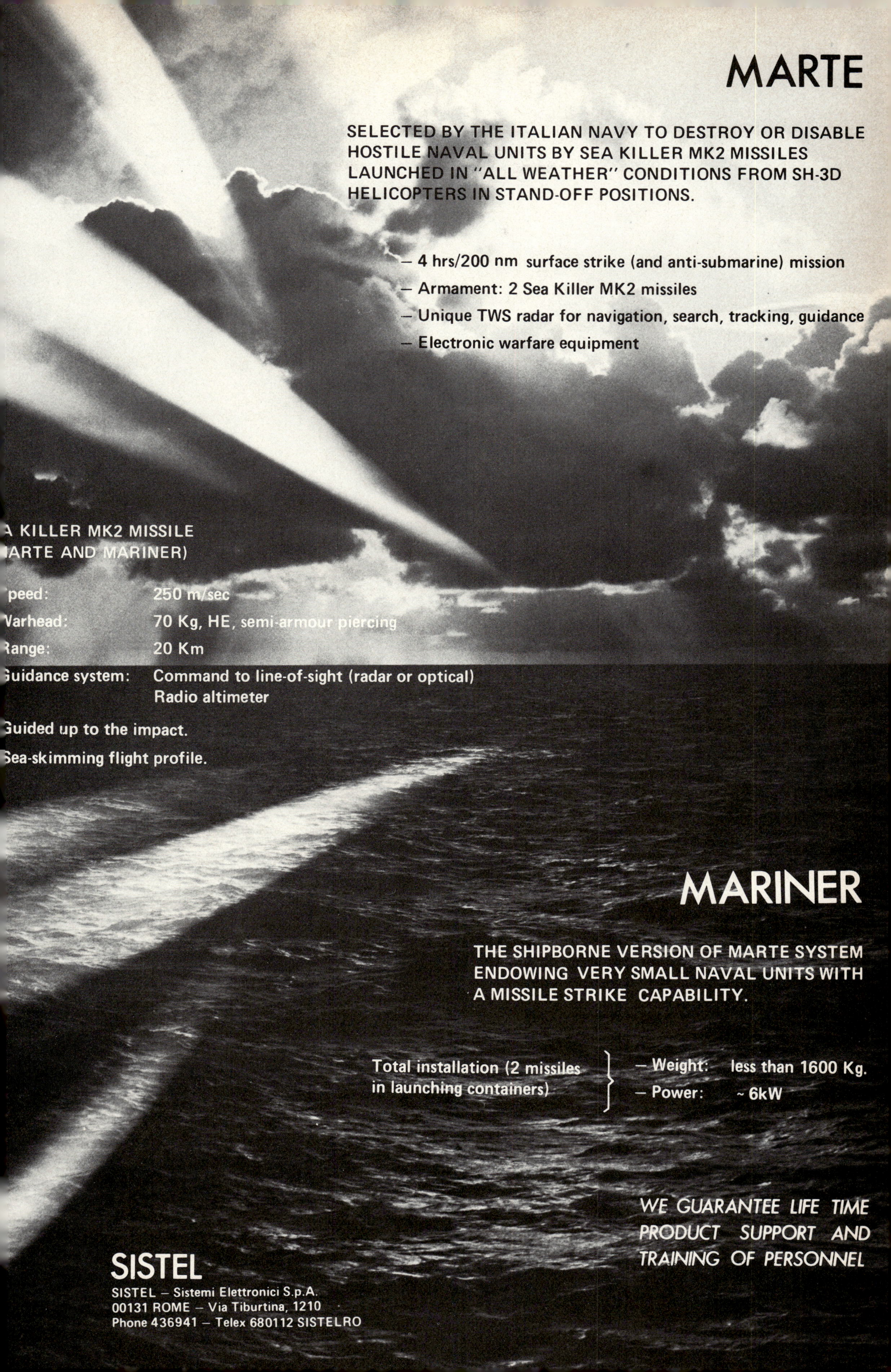

MARTE

SELECTED BY THE ITALIAN NAVY TO DESTROY OR DISABLE HOSTILE NAVAL UNITS BY SEA KILLER MK2 MISSILES LAUNCHED IN "ALL WEATHER" CONDITIONS FROM SH-3D HELICOPTERS IN STAND-OFF POSITIONS.

- 4 hrs/200 nm surface strike (and anti-submarine) mission
- Armament: 2 Sea Killer MK2 missiles
- Unique TWS radar for navigation, search, tracking, guidance
- Electronic warfare equipment

SEA KILLER MK2 MISSILE
(MARTE AND MARINER)

Speed:	250 m/sec
Warhead:	70 Kg, HE, semi-armour piercing
Range:	20 Km
Guidance system:	Command to line-of-sight (radar or optical)
	Radio altimeter

Guided up to the impact.
Sea-skimming flight profile.

MARINER

THE SHIPBORNE VERSION OF MARTE SYSTEM ENDOWING VERY SMALL NAVAL UNITS WITH A MISSILE STRIKE CAPABILITY.

Total installation (2 missiles in launching containers)
- Weight: less than 1600 Kg.
- Power: ~ 6kW

WE GUARANTEE LIFE TIME PRODUCT SUPPORT AND TRAINING OF PERSONNEL

SISTEL

SISTEL — Sistemi Elettronici S.p.A.
00131 ROME — Via Tiburtina, 1210
Phone 436941 — Telex 680112 SISTELRO

make your way sure

MINE HUNTING OPERATIONS

PAP 104 SYSTEM

DUBM 21 A SONAR TRANSDUCERS

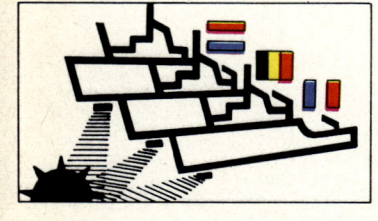

Koningin Elisabeth kwartier
Everestraat
1140 BRUSSEL
BELGIUM

2, rue Royale
Boîte Postale N° 1
75200 PARIS NAVAL
FRANCE

Torenstraat 172
Den HAAG
THE NETHERLANDS

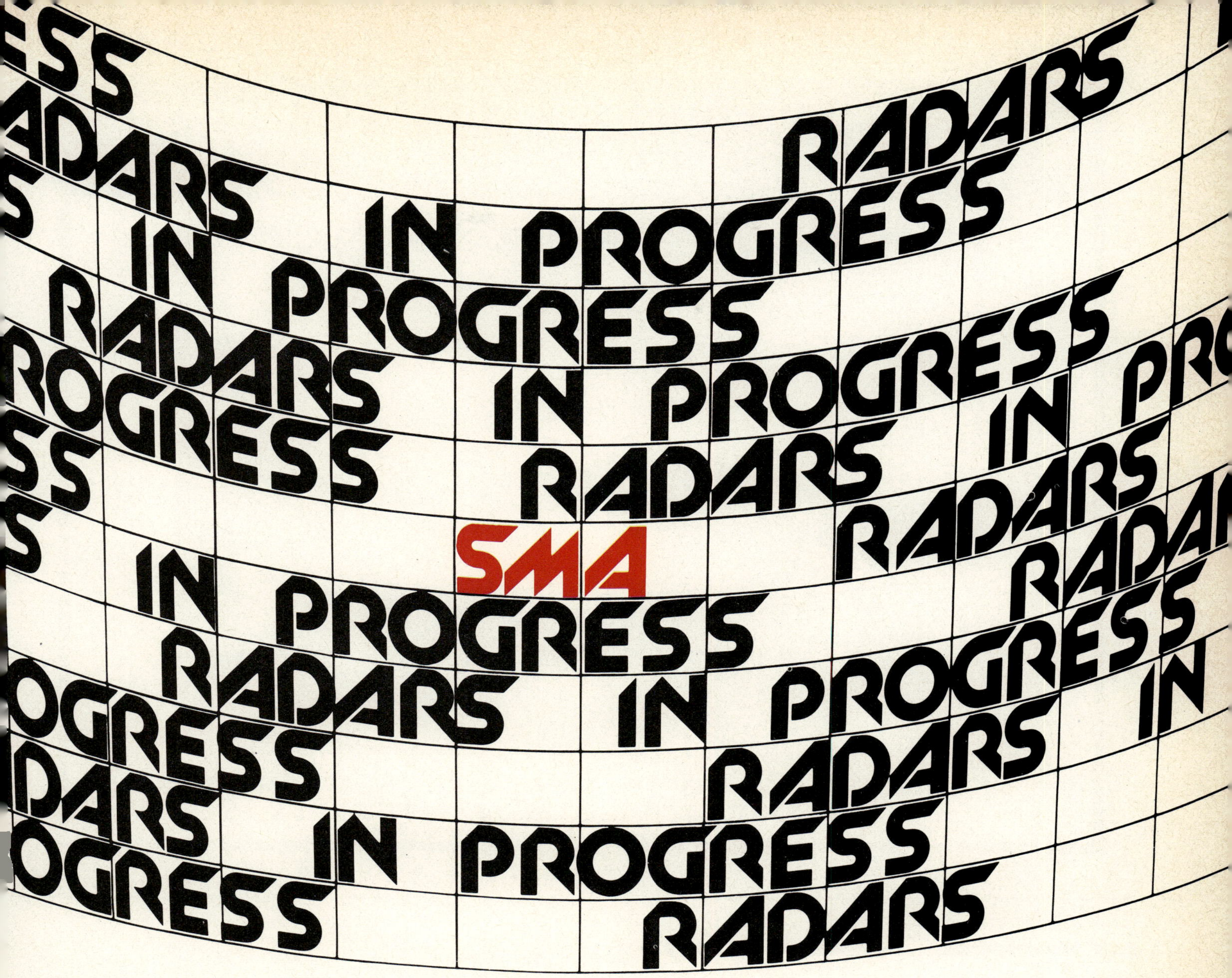

SMA
SEGNALAMENTO MARITTIMO ED AEREO

Radar systems for ships, helicopters and ground stations.
Radars for navigation, air and naval search.
Displays and missile assignment consolles. Homing radars.
Signal processing and data handling techniques. System engineering.
For all information concerning our production, please write to the Sales Manager
of SMA, P.O. Box 200 - Firenze (Italia).
Firenze (Italia) Telephone (055) 705651 - Telex Smaradar 570622 - Cable: SMA Firenze.

Sté NOUVELLE DES ATELIERS & CHANTIERS DU HAVRE
30 Rue J. J. Rousseau – 76090 – LE HAVRE, France
Tél (35) 26 81 77 Télex 190322

ANTI-ROLL STABILIZER FINS TYPE "SAFARI". FRENCH NAVY CORVETTES C 70 ARE FITTED WITH THIS TYPE OF STABILIZER FINS

We are specialists in the design, production and installation of underwater and marine equipment.

The Company's products include the following:-

Cable Penetrators and Connectors for Pressure Hull and Equipment Applications

Umbilical Cable Terminations

Cable Jointing Equipment

Hydrophones

Towed Seismic Arrays

Torsionmeters for propulsion Shafts

Complete Underwater Electrical and Electroacoustic Systems

Designed and manufactured to the highest standards of reliability for all underwater and marine applications.

ameeco
(Hydrospace Limited)

Bilton Road, Erith, Kent
Telephone: Erith STD Code (03224) 46821
Telex: 896230

The Navy's after us...

... so are the Marines, the Customs and the Coastguards. who can blame them? Because Dravo SteelShip make toughest, fastest and most advanced military craft in the wo From a 36ft. assault craft to a 185ft. missile-launching pa vessel. And everything in between.
Want a standard vessel modified? Dravo SteelShip can do too. Or custom design a craft for a specific military operat Dravo SteelShip Corporation. The name with a world-w reputation for quality, delivery and price.

Dravo SteelShip Corporation
Route 4, Box 167, Pine Bluff,
Arkansas 71602 TWX 910-729-2919
Tel: 501-536-0362

Sepa for naval defence

GARIBALDI

LUPO
SAGITTARIO
PERSEO
ORSA

RATCHARIT
WITTHAYAKHOM
UDOMDET

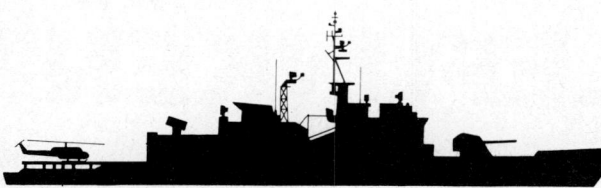

CARVAJAL
VILLAVICENCIO
CNR N° 306
CNR N° 307

NAZARIO SAURO
LEONARDO DA VINCI
FECIA DI COSSATO
GUGLIELMO MARCONI

SUCRE
BRION
URDANETA
SOUBLETTE
SALOM
FELIX RIBAS

TOTI
DANDOLO
MOCENIGO
BAGNOLINI

MAESTRALE
GRECALE
LIBECCIO
SCIROCCO
ALISEO
EURO

NIBBIO
FALCONE
ASTORE
GRIFONE
GHEPPIO
CONDOR

SEPA S.P.A. - Società di Elettronica per l'Automazione - is a firm of the Fiat group and is actively involved in the field of underwater weapons, ship machinery automation systems for both military and merchant navies, computers and industrial automation.

Its activities cover research, system design, manufacturing, test, installation and commissioning, customer training, world wide technical assistance and maintenance.

Its products are characterized by the original design highest quality standards and use of the latest technologies.

The above units are all equipped with Sepa systems including:

- [ ] Cogag computerized bridge control system for **GARIBALDI** class.
- [ ] Codog computerized bridge control systems for **LUPO, CARVAJAL, SUCRE** and **MAESTRALE** classes.
- [ ] Electrical plant control and monitoring for the **RATCHARIT** class.
- [ ] Wire guidance and home electronics for the Whitehead-Moto Fides A 184 weapon system mounted on **MAESTRALE, TOTI** and **SAURO** classes.
- [ ] Attitude control automation for **NIBBIO** class.

Società di Elettronica per l'Automazione S.p.A.
Lungo Stura Lazio 45 - 10156 Torino (Italy)
Tel. (011) 262.3333 (5 linee r.a.) - Telex 221527 Sepa I

User size electronics

AEG-TELEFUNKEN

When modern defence systems are needed...:

On land, in the water and in the air –

Systems Technology by AEG-TELEFUNKEN

AEG-TELEFUNKEN solves defence problems in
- electrical engineering and electronics
- communications and data handling
- radar and navigation
- equipment for missiles, aircraft, vehicles and ships

AEG-TELEFUNKEN undertakes
- management and integration
- concept and definition
- installation and setting-to-work

AEG-TELEFUNKEN is experienced in the management of large-scale projects

Detailed information may be obtained from:
AEG-TELEFUNKEN
Nachrichten- und Verkehrstechnik
Lyoner Straße 26
6000 Frankfurt 71
W. Germany
Tel.: (0611) 6690-1
Telex: 416686
Cables: elektronub

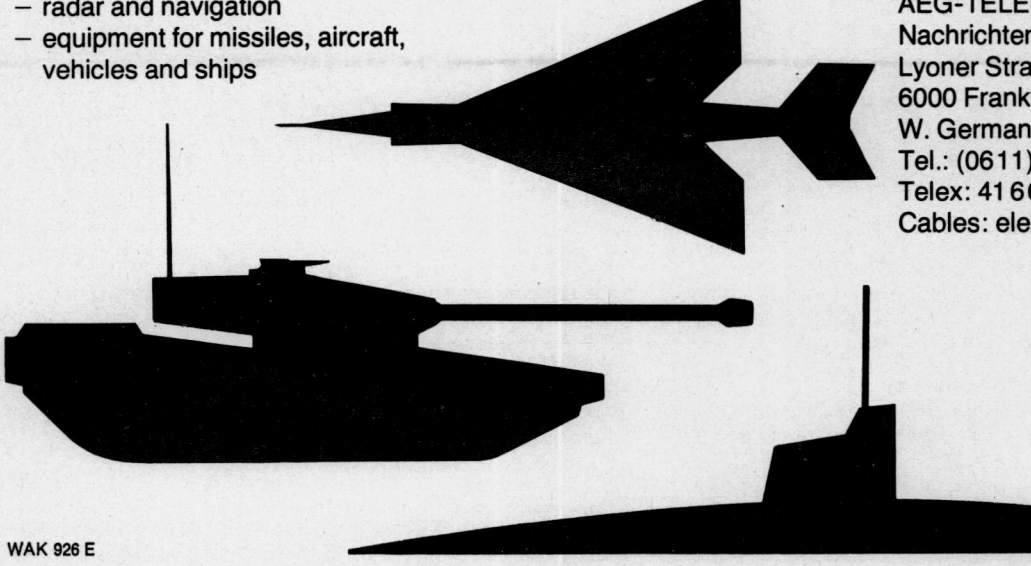

WAK 926 E

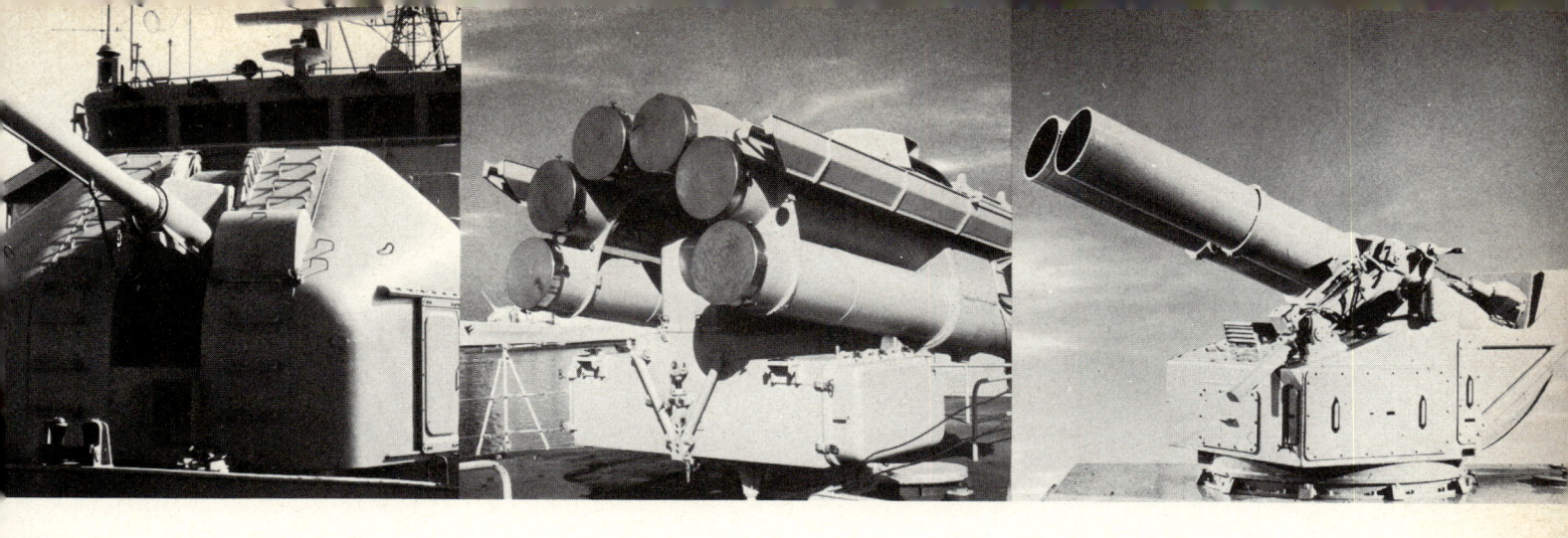

Creusot-Loire draws on many years of research experience in the fields which interest you:
– design studies and general contract work on complete systems for surface ships,
– main and secondary gun armament,
– anti-submarine weapons,
– submarine armament and equipment,
– handling gear,
– parts and plates for hull and armour,
– hydrographic equipment.
To increase your effectiveness even further, Creusot-Loire offers its new 100 mm Compact gun mount currently under development:

the 100 mm COMPACT

A multi-purpose gun mount optimised for anti-missile use. Advance technology makes for high performance and low weight.

CREUSOT-LOIRE
DIVISION DE LA MÉCANIQUE SPÉCIALISÉE
15, rue Pasquier, 75383 PARIS CEDEX 08
Tél.: 260.36.72 - Télex Motoy 650 309 F

Progress bases on experience.

A bow view of the USS **Constitution** Shortly after firing a cannon

USN (PHC Milton Butnam)

JANE'S FIGHTING SHIPS

FOUNDED IN 1897 BY FRED T. JANE

EDITED BY
Captain JOHN MOORE RN, FRGS

1979-80

ISBN 0 531 03913 7

JANE'S YEARBOOKS

FRANKLIN WATTS INC, NEW YORK

"Jane's" is a registered trade mark

Copyright © 1979 by Jane's Publishing Company, Macdonald and Jane's Publishers Limited, 8 Shepherdess Walk, London N1 7LW, England

First published in the United Kingdom 1979 by Jane's Yearbooks
First American publication 1979 by Franklin Watts Inc.

For copyright reasons this edition is available for sale only in Canada, the Philippines and the USA and its dependencies

MSDS—
weapons for the 1980s and beyond

Marconi Space and Defence Systems is the nominated prime contractor for all current torpedo programmes in the United Kingdom, for both submarine-launched and air-launched weapons.

To meet defence needs in the 1980s and beyond, the MSDS Tigerfish wire-guided and acoustic-homing torpedo is in full production for the Royal Navy; and the new and very advanced MSDS Sting Ray lightweight torpedo, which can be launched from aircraft, surface ships or pilotless carriers, is in the late stages of development.

MSDS capability and experience in underwater weapons covers every aspect of research, development, manufacture and in-service support, including torpedo handling and ATE equipment, ancillary instrumentation packages and pre-setters, complex instrumentation systems for underwater test ranges, acoustic targets and facsimile weapons for exercise use.

Marconi Space and Defence Systems Limited
A GEC-Marconi Electronics Company
Marketing Department, The Grove, Warren Lane,
Stanmore, Middlesex HA7 4LY, England
Telephone: 01-954 2311 Telex: 22616
Telegrams: SPADEF Stanmore

underwater weapons
TECHNOLOGY IN DEPTH

CONTENTS

Alphabetical List of Advertisers	[2]
Classified List of Advertisers	[8]
Foreword	[135]
Major Matters	[145]
Acknowledgements	[149]
Glossary	[151]
Ship Designations	[151]
Major Surface Ships Pennant List	[143]
Recognition Silhouettes	1
Ship Reference Section	17
Albania	18
Algeria	20
Angola	22
Anguilla	23
Argentina	24
Australia	35
Austria	49
Bahamas	49
Bahrain	50
Bangladesh	51
Barbados	52
Belgium	53
Belize	57
Benin	57
Bermuda	57
Bolivia	57
Brazil	58
Brunei	69
Bulgaria	70
Burma	73
Cambodia see Kampuchea	
Cameroon	76
Canada, Navy	77
Coast Guard	87
Chile	94
China, People's Republic	103
Colombia	115
Comoro Islands	119
Congo	120
Costa Rica	120
Cuba	120
Cyprus	123
Czechoslovakia	123
Denmark	124
Djibouti	133
Dominican Republic	133
Ecuador	137
Egypt	141
El Salvador	147
Equatorial Guinea	147
Ethiopia	148
Fiji	149
Finland	150
France	156
Gabon	191
Gambia	192
Germany (Democratic Republic)	193
Germany (Federal Republic)	198
Ghana	213
Greece	215
Grenada	225
Guatemala	225
Guinea	227
Guinea Bissau	227
Guyana	228
Haiti	228
Honduras	229
Hong Kong	229
Hungary	231
Iceland	232
India	233
Indonesia	243
Iran	253
Iraq	260
Ireland	262
Israel	264
Italy	268
Ivory Coast	287
Jamaica	288
Japan, Maritime Defence Force	289
Maritime Safety Agency	304
Jordan	314
Kampuchea	315
Kenya	316
Korea, Democratic People's Republic (North)	317
Korea, Republic (South)	322
Kuwait	329
Laos	330
Lebanon	330
Liberia	331
Libya	332
Madagascar	336
Malawi	336
Malaysia	337, 419
Maldives	340
Mali	340
Malta	341
Mauritania	342
Mauritius	343
Mexico	344
Montserrat	348
Morocco	349
Mozambique	351
Netherlands	352
New Zealand	362
Nicaragua	364
Nigeria	365
Norway	368
Oman	376
Pakistan	378
Panama	383
Papua New Guinea	384
Paraguay	385
Peru	387
Philippines	397
Poland	405
Portugal	410
Qatar	415
Romania	416
Sabah	419
St. Kitts	419
St. Lucia	419
St. Vincent	419
Saudi Arabia	420
Senegal	422
Seychelles	423
Sierra Leone	423
Singapore	424
Solomon Islands	425
Somalia	426
South Africa	427
Spain	431
Sri Lanka	447
Sudan	449
Surinam	450
Sweden	451
Switzerland	463
Syria	463
Taiwan	465
Tanzania	474, 781
Thailand	475
Togo	481
Tonga	482
Trinidad & Tobago	482
Tunisia	484
Turkey	486
Union of Soviet Socialist Republics	499
United Arab Emirates	581
United Kingdom	583
United States of America, Navy	630
Coast Guard	749
Uruguay	760
Venezuela	764
Viet-Nam	770
Virgin Islands	773
Yemen Arab Republic (North)	773
Yemen, People's Democratic Republic (South)	774
Yugoslavia	775
Zaïre	781
Zanzibar	781
Appendices	783
Naval Strengths	783
Naval Equipment	787
Aircraft	788
Guns	800
Missiles	804
Radar	808
Sonar	812
Torpedoes	814
Addenda	817
Indexes	819
Named Ships	819
Classes	833

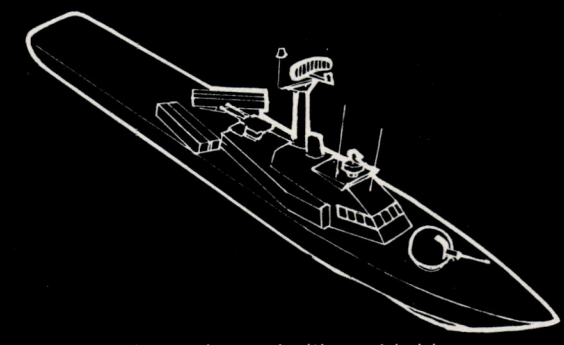
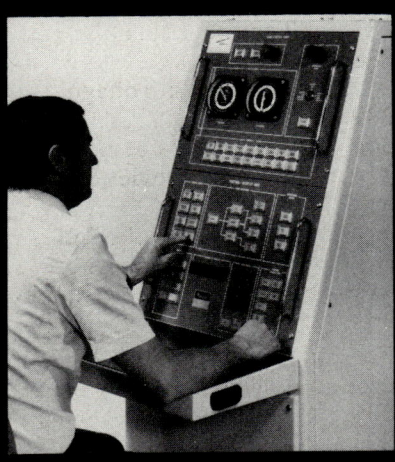

SEA-ARCHER
FOR EFFECTIVE GUNNERY

The SEA ARCHER digital fire control system now proven in service and with worldwide orders maintains earlier Sperry achievements in the field of advanced technology naval systems. Computer prediction ensures high accuracy fire against air, surface or shore targets, and gives the improved weapon performance which until now has only been available with radar fire control systems.

- ☐ EASE OF INSTALLATION, OPERATION AND MAINTENANCE
- ☐ HIGH RELIABILITY ☐ COMPACT AND LIGHTWEIGHT EQUIPMENTS
- ☐ HIGH EFFECTIVENESS FOR LOW-COST
- ☐ A CHOICE OF IR, TV, RADAR AND LASER SENSORS

SPERRY
GYROSCOPE
DOWNSHIRE WAY BRACKNELL
BERKSHIRE ENGLAND RG12 1QL
TELEPHONE: BRACKNELL 0344 3222
TELEX: No. 848129

SPERRY GYROSCOPE IS A DIVISION OF SPERRY RAND LIMITED

FOREWORD

Henry Ford reckoned that 'History is bunk'. He had his reasons, the reasons of a genius. Today we are surrounded by people who, having no spark of the genius or courage of Ford, are prepared by their actions to sidestep the lessons of the past. It is, therefore, more than ever incumbent on the average citizen, whose existence is threatened by the advance of the dictators, to give deep consideration to the proper understanding of history, both of long-past eras and of recent making. It is only within an historical framework and with the appreciation of political motives that we can understand our present and look to our future. The most simple appreciation of the last thousand years will show that mankind's story has been continually influenced by the sea, sometimes to a lesser, sometimes to a greater extent and that those who have ignored this fact have brought about their own downfall and that of their country.

On the periphery of many of today's trouble spots lie the ships, those concerned with the carriage of goods and those whose task is the protection of the sea-lanes or their disruption. Modern methods and instruments have increased the capabilities of both and, in the centenary of the visionary genius Einstein, it is no bad thing to consider how modern technology is affecting the exercise of sea-power.

In the twenty years before World War II the advance of naval science and technology was slow and halting. Ideas were there for development but only a very few ships were at sea with any form of surface detection other than the human eye, while underwater sensors were limited and inaccurate. Six years later all this had changed. Radar and sonar had outstripped the capabilities of the weapons they controlled. The dived speed of submarines had doubled and aircraft were operating with a speed and endurance which had improved beyond all expectations. Mines could be detonated by magnetic, sound and pressure signatures. On the beaches around the world the hulks of a multitude of landing-craft designs were the monuments to a successful campaign to land men on hostile coasts. Under the impulse of necessity, men's minds had kept abreast of these technical advances but on 6 August 1945 the explosion of an atomic bomb over Hiroshima brought untold problems, the resolution of which are still beyond men's ability. Matters were getting out of hand, stretching well beyond the power of politicians and sailors to understand, much less control them. Heavy-footed bureaucracy was not designed to cope with the rapid changes which were lying in the future and today we are in a position where the swift development and introduction of new ideas may easily swing the balance in a quite unexpected way. Such will never be the case unless the training of those involved includes not only the technical aspects of their trade but also the mental discipline needed to appreciate the probable impact of new discoveries. While decision-taking is inhibited by complex committee work and untrained political minds fail to grasp the importance of the rapidly changing technical scene chances will be lost, money wasted and security imperilled.

For many years the inventory of surface ships of any navy has consisted almost entirely of vessels with displacement hulls: 'normal' ships obeying Archimedes' law. It is this very normality which has meant that other forms of hull design have been classified as unconventional: the hydrofoil, hovercraft, Sea Knife and the like. While these have aroused scant enthusiasm among the more traditionally minded, the displacement hull ships have also suffered from lack of imagination. The financially impelled reduction of hull size in order to save materials and money coupled with the desire to include as many weapon systems as possible has resulted in cramped ships such as the British Type 42 and the Italian 'Lupo' class. With these and several other designs expansion has become necessary at increased cost in drawing office time and production outlays. At the same time failure to appreciate how modern design can overcome outmoded shibboleths has meant the construction of ships too large for the task intended: 'no ship under 1,200 tons can carry a helicopter' has long been a popular watchword. Now that a 500-ton ship of broad beam can do just this it is a test of nerve to accept the fact. Part of the problem is the assumption that only the larger ship can provide a stable platform in a heavy sea-way. Thirty-four years of being sea-sick in everything from a battleship to a fast attack craft suggest that stability is relative. To provide the smallest practicable hull for the job is clearly a desirable economy, provided the performance of the sensors and weapon systems remains adequate.

Other factors concerning economy must also be borne in mind. The bigger the ship and the more grandiose the weapon systems embarked the more men are required to run it. As the bill for an average Western navy ship from laying down to break-up includes over 50 per cent for the pay of the ship's company any reduction in the complement is a notable saving. For the Soviet Navy where the average sailor's pay is about an eighth to a tenth that of his Western counterpart this is less of a problem, particularly as Admiral Gorshkov has only retention problems to worry about, not those of recruiting. He has a far larger slice of his budget to spend on ships. If the Western complements are to be reduced maximum automation is required. At the same time automation requires power and the use of the least power-demanding equipment is therefore necessary.

The first requirement in any ship of war is to detect the enemy, then to track him and, finally, to engage him. The age-old method of detection has been the look-out. He is un-jammable and requires little maintenance other than his victuals. In modern naval warfare such attributes are of slight use when dealing with aircraft and missiles travelling at more than Mach 2 and submarines moving at 30 knots well below the surface. Reaction time is necessarily short and any target information must be converted and relayed without delay as a firing solution to the chosen weapon system. Some form of computer is necessary and here we meet again the need for the adoption of modern technology if not only efficiency and speed are to be served but also if reduction of space and power requirements are to be achieved. A comparison of the current fits in the Royal and US Navies is germane. The British FM1600 series computers, which are now standard fit, are big fellows: six feet of hard-wire logic and core storage working on 24-bit words, needing at least 1kW to drive them, cooling water to keep them within limits of $\pm 1°C$ and several kW for their external operation. The American AN/UYK20, which has been standard US Navy fitting for at least five years, is a cube of less than two foot sides, works on 4-, 8- or 16-bit words, is cooled by a fan and requires radically less power for its drive. In the case of the Royal Navy its system of procurement has shackled it to an out-dated computer for years to come while the US Navy, with a long history of micro-processor techniques, is advancing far more rapidly. The weapon system embarked in the US F14 Tomcat aircraft, which has been under development since 1960, incorporates the Hughes AWG-9 fire-control and weapon system with the Phoenix AIM-54A missile and is capable of engaging six targets simultaneously. Under the control of one man a similar system seems an ideal weapon fit for a small ship in which reduction of size and manpower are primary aims.

If new ideas in ship design and new methods of construction and armament are likely to produce smaller ships the overall question of how to propel them applies as much to them as it does to their larger sisters. Although much has been written and said about future sources of energy for land vehicles and domestic services and with aircraft already airborne on liquid hydrogen fuel, little has been published on marine propulsion. Despite the discovery of new oil-bearing areas such as those in Mexico, the fact is that, with a steeply rising consumption rate, oil fuel as we know it today will become scarce in the first quarter of the next century. Alternative fuels must be sought and new engines designed if we are to keep commerce moving on the seas and if navies are to remain mobile in its defence. Warships which are now in the design stage will still be at sea in the period 2015-20. The life of a merchant ship is shorter than that of a naval vessel and the crisis less imminent for them as a result.

The most obvious alternative, on the few occasions in which this matter is discussed in public, is nuclear power. This approach is often the result of ignorance of other methods and frequently fails to take account of the problems of nuclear propulsion. Firstly the cost of the installation, training the operators and provision of support facilities is beyond the resources of many countries. Secondly the power to weight/volume ratio is low and, lastly, the rupture of the containment by missile or mining attack would pose major pollution problems, although this is much less likely in larger ships such as the American CVNs.

Other alternatives are the closed-cycle gas turbines using argon/xenon/helium for energy transference (already under development in the USA with power outputs up to 40 000 hp) and the Brayton Cycle which operates a two-stage turbine by the expansion of an operating fluid, using the same elements as the closed-cycle gas turbine. The heat sources required for these systems are potentially numerous—materials such as carbon blocks with high heat capacity, phase-change systems storing thermal energy as latent heat or reversibe chemical reactions. None is yet in a sufficiently advanced stage for current naval application but all offer development potential. Coal in several forms and combinations is a possible contender: liquefied coal, coal in suspension and other more exotic fashions. But, despite huge deposits, coal is a finite asset and estimates of its availability may not take into account the

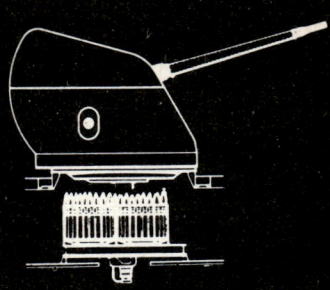
OTO 127/54 COMPACT
MOUNTING (5-INCH)

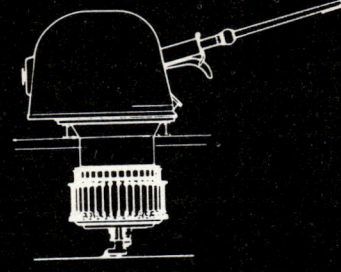
OTO 76/62 COMPACT
MOUNTING (3-INCH)

35 mm OE/OTO
TWIN MOUNTING

OTOMAT ANTI-SHIP
MISSILE SYSTEM

WORLD LEADER FOR NAVAL GUNS AND MISSILE SYSTEMS

OTO MELARA S.p.a.

19100 La Spezia, Italy
15, via Valdilocchi
Tel. 530111
Tx. 270368 OTO I

huge demands of the future.

The rechargeable lead-acid battery used for 80 years in submarines offers no solution for general propulsion needs but other primary batteries show a marked increase in efficiency. Unfortunately the Lithium Thionyl Chloride battery provides a ten-fold increase in energy availability at a cost some 200 times greater than the lead-acid cell. However, the zinc-air (oxygen) battery in which the anode of a conventional battery is combined with the cathode of a fuel-cell and which yields a higher performance when oxygen is used in place of air is already in commercial production and would seem to offer considerable possibilities for naval propulsion.

Next in this very brief survey is the fuel-cell, an electro-chemical system for the direct conversion of the energy of non-fossil fuels and oxidants to electrical power. The practical conversion rate is high, in the region of 50 to 65 per cent, and the principle has been used and is being further developed in the USA, Canada, France, West Germany, Japan and Sweden. Although the United Kingdom had developed a practical fuel-cell 15 years ago no interest in it has been advertised by the British Energy Department. Meanwhile there is every possibility that West Germany will have a submarine at sea under fuel-cell power by the early 1990s with a continuous speed capability of 22 knots. With no recourse to the atmosphere, minimal maintenance, no exhaust other than water and a significantly quieter operation than any current nuclear plant the fuel-cell, if, as it probably will be, successful, will render all submarine diesel-electric propulsion obsolete. There is no apparent reason why this form of propulsion should not be enlarged and improved for surface-ship operation, giving a wide range of efficiency at all speeds, provide immediate reversal and provide the required power without any exhaust-heat to offer a target to infra-red missiles. Its fuels and oxidants: hydrogen, oxygen, hydrazine, hydrogen peroxide, ammonia and many others, are capable of large-scale industrial production without recourse to the vanishing fossil fuels. The NATO nations spend $17,000 million a year on research and development for defence purposes. It would be a sad story if those concerned overlooked the need for prime-movers suitable for the 21st century until it is too late.

The motto 'Find, fix and strike' is as true today as it was when first coined but the means have changed out of all recognition and are still in a stage of rapid development. For finding surface ships, submarines and other aircraft, the aeroplane still has a major role to play. At present satellites provide valuable information and their performance may well be refined over the next ten years. Missiles with "smart" heads of many kinds can carry out their set tasks at high speeds with control up to the moment of impact or explosion. But neither the satellite nor the missile has the flexibility provided by the piloted aircraft. The American F-14 Tomcat has already been cited as an advanced flying weapon system while the F/A-18 Hornets, the first of which recently carried out initial flight tests in the USA, incorporates many advanced techniques. The disadvantage of these machines is that they need an aircraft carrier of considerable dimensions if they are to operate with the fleet and very few navies currently operate fixed-wing carriers, and only the US Navy possesses ships capable of dealing with these very modern machines. The alternative is the Vertical/Short Take-off and Landing (V/STOL) aircraft of which the only Western version is the Harrier (AV-8), which first flew in 1966. Although it requires a highly competent pilot with at least 25 hours additional rigorous tuition the resulting fusion of man and technology provides a means of carrying fixed-wing aircraft in comparatively small ships with significant advantages in heavy weather. Now major advances in technology have allowed further improvements. The result is the AV8-B in which new wing design and changes in the engine and certain of the flight controls have doubled the Harrier's range or its payload. The hardware is available, the pilots are to hand: all that is needed is forethought and decision-making to provide another major factor for the sea-going deterrent. Similar decisions are needed if the air component of the anti-submarine forces is to receive adequate reinforcement. The high flying, long-range maritime patrol aircraft is an essential link in all three tasks of finding, fixing and striking.

Improved electronics are providing greater capability in smaller spaces but the firms which provide the imagination and expertise for such advances can exist only if they receive orders. Small firms with great potential can be killed off very rapidly by the inertia of the bureaucratic process. Rapid decisions are also needed if Western navies are to be adequately supplied with the other airborne member of the anti-submarine team: the helicopter. Potent and deadly it can be but a single helicopter has only a restricted availability—maintenance is required and even the Sea King has a range of little over 500 miles. More are needed at sea. Every available platform must have its air component and only now is the Royal Navy providing new carriers and additional helicopters in frigates and the Royal Fleet Auxiliaries and the US Navy allowing for two helicopters in the new destroyer and frigate designs.

In this very cursory look at the fringes of the vast field of naval technology one salient point emerges throughout: the Western navies can tap an unrivalled technical capability for their support and improvement. What is holding them back from achieving a condition in which they could form a potent deterrent at sea is one fact: decisions on their future are motivated more by internal prejudices and disagreements than by an objective analysis of the need for protecting the interests of the countries concerned. It is, therefore, necessary to consider just what these interests are, how they could be put in jeopardy and how the navies of the world are organising their resources in these circumstances.

The Super-powers

The reactions of the two super-powers at the end of World War II were clearly conditioned by the impact of that war on their people and their economies. The USA had suffered 414 000 killed but no civilians had been threatened in their own homes and the economy was at an unnatural peak. The total Soviet casualties are hard to assess but reports range up to 20 million killed and certainly at least a third of the economy had been shattered. The Americans were in a position to aid the battered world while the USSR was determined to prevent the recurrence of such a catastrophe.

The naval strength of the USA was pre-eminent, that of the USSR at a low ebb. While the former discarded hundreds of ships the latter began a building programme which, at its inception, was apparently designed as a defensive force. At the same time the policies of the two countries were totally at variance. From a base of economic power the USA was planning to aid those who needed and asked for help, while maintaining adequate forces to ensure the safe and timely arrival of the ships and raw materials on which such aid depended. Opposition to colonial policies was made clear to the allies of the USA and, as the great empires were dismembered, so the Soviet intention to replace previous influences with their own became clear. Today this plan is made even more evident by actions world-wide—support for 'Wars of National Liberation' is a corner-stone of the Moscow Kremlin's actions.

The planned size of the original 'defensive' navy of the USSR was apparently out of keeping with any current threat. The USA showed no signs of bellicose intentions or any desire for expansion abroad but, from 1945, plans were laid for action against the Soviet Union should she embark on invasion and external aggression. These, of which Plan Dropshot was probably the most complete, were no doubt rapidly relayed to Moscow, providing a source of deep concern. Under these circumstances the Soviet programme of 1200 submarines in 15 years agreed in 1948 would have had some relevance. Since then the steady increase in Soviet forces as Western numbers have declined dramatically has remained far beyond the needs of defence and, although the overall total of ships available has decreased in recent years, this has been more than compensated for by the size and capabilities of ships now being completed. With the second aircraft-carrier operating East of Suez, two more at least may be expected in the next three years. The task of these ships as the centre of a group in any peacetime confrontation and as the core of an anti-submarine force in war is fairly clear. What is not apparent is the role of the new 'Sovietsky Soyuz' class being built at Leningrad. This monster of some 32 000 tons and her sisters bristle with missiles and guns, can carry aircraft and can best be described by the old-fashioned title 'battle-cruiser'. An interesting comparison can be made with the now-defunct plans for the US Navy's strike-cruiser (CSGN). Both classes were designed with guns, missiles, aircraft and anti-submarine weapons, both with nuclear propulsion. The US ships were planned as screening ships for nuclear-propelled aircraft-carriers in high threat areas as well as being capable of independent operations. But so far the USSR has no nuclear carriers and so the second task is the more likely. But her size, almost twice the tonnage of the CSGN, makes her unique and her employment in support of amphibious operations would be one of a number of possibilities. Reports of the planned class of twelve, if correct, would mean that these huge ships would be completing until the 1990s.

Long-range operations are also foreshadowed by the arrival of two more classes, both of which show a sudden and marked increase in size, the Landing Platform Dock (LPD) of the 'Ivan Rogov' class and the support ship *Berezina*. The first of these can carry a battalion of naval infantry, helicopters, hovercraft and supporting armour on 13 000 tons. This is certainly not a ship designed for the Baltic and, with the class in series production, provides a long-range, long endurance capability. Endurance is a commodity built into the second ship, *Berezina,* which may well be the lead ship of a class of four or more. On 36 000 tons she carries a surface gun armament, SAM missiles and anti-submarine launchers which, from their site, could provide anti-torpedo protection. With two storing gantries, a liquid fuel gantry and five cranes this is probably a specialised support ship for aircraft-carriers during long endurance operations.

With the 'Kirov' class of cruiser under construction as a follow-on to the 'Kresta II' class and the continuation of 'Kara' and 'Krivak' building, a pattern for surface ship operations is emerging. The missiles carried at present include the long-range SS-N-12 cruise missile in the 'Kiev' class, the A/S SS-N-14 in the 'Kresta II', 'Kara', and 'Krivak' classes and the long-range SAM SA-N-3 in the later cruisers, combined with the short-range SA-N-4 which is also mounted in the 'Krivaks'. A new generation of SAM is now at sea in the later 'Karas' and the question that immediately comes to mind is 'what surface-to-surface capability do these ships have?' It seems inconceivable that they should have none so the answer is probably that either or both SS-N-14 and SA-N-3 has or have a dual function. The SS-N-14 carries a torpedo—could this be of similar performance to the US Mark 48 with an anti-ship as well as an anti-submarine capability, thus being impervious to close-in weapon systems? Could the SA-N-3 launcher have a second surface-to-surface weapon available or the Goblet missile have a dual capability? Whatever the answer, it is well-nigh certain that the Soviet fleet does not rely entirely on guns for surface action.

In the anti-submarine field the existence of hull-mounted, variable depth and helicopter sonars working in low and medium frequencies provides a fair range of sensors and may be backed up before long by towed passive arrays.

JANE'S

FOR INTERNATIONAL REFERENCE

Established over three quarters of a century, **JANE'S** is a name synonymous with accuracy and authority throughout the world. Free of bias and opinion with every fact checked and re-checked, the ten **Jane's Yearbooks** are the recognised reference works on Defence, Transport, Finance and Ocean Technology.

JANE'S ALL THE WORLD'S AIRCRAFT
Edited by John W.R. Taylor
Fellow, Royal Historical Society,
Member, Royal Aeronautical Society.

JANE'S FIGHTING SHIPS
Edited by Captain J.E. Moore, Royal Navy

JANE'S WEAPON SYSTEMS
Edited by Ronald Pretty

JANE'S INFANTRY WEAPONS
Edited by Colonel John Weeks

JANE'S SURFACE SKIMMERS
Edited by Roy McLeavy

JANE'S OCEAN TECHNOLOGY
Edited by Robert L. Trillo

JANE'S FREIGHT CONTAINERS
Edited by Patrick Finlay

JANE'S WORLD RAILWAYS
Edited by Paul Goldsack

JANE'S MAJOR COMPANIES OF EUROPE
Edited by Jonathan Love

JANE'S COMBAT SUPPORT EQUIPMENT
Edited by Christopher Foss

Published in the United States and Canada by
Franklin Watts, Inc.
730 Fifth Avenue New York, N.Y. 10019
212-757-4050 *Telex:* 236537 *Cable:* FRAWATTS, NEW YORK

For weapons, reliance is placed on the various MBUs with a maximum range of 2500 yards, and on two missiles. Of these FRAS 1 ranges out to about 15 miles with a torpedo or nuclear bomb cargo and the SS-N-14 carries a torpedo to 20 miles. In addition many ships carry anti-submarine torpedoes of both 533 and 400 mm. In concept this arrangement is no better and no worse than Western armaments although the efficacy of the weapons is not known. The number of MBUs carried is of interest, possibly as the result of a somewhat outmoded plan of close anti-submarine action or possibly retained as an anti-torpedo area weapon. What is of greater interest perhaps is the change of certain Type names which took place in 1977-78. In several instances the Anti-Submarine tag has been replaced by Rocket Cruiser, Rocket Ship or Escort Ship. In some cases these changes reflect modfications involving the addition of SS-N-2(C) missiles in ships such as the 'Kashin' class but the changes in the 'Krivaks' is unexplained and could be the result of experience.

Anti-air defences centre on the SA-N-3 and -4 missile systems supplemented by the new SA-N-10, with close-in weapons of the Gatling type now being provided in profusion, accompanied by their own Bass Tilt radars. When added to the conventional gun armament and modern radars fitted in the newer ships it is fairly obvious that operations in a hostile air-environment are expected—a reasonable deduction considering the existence of the fixed-wing carriers of the USA. At the same time such an armament would be needed during operations within range of opposing shore air-fields, there being no aircraft in the Soviet Naval Air Force capable of acting as effective close air support against high performance fixed-wing aircraft.

This air force is, however, capable of a number of operations in support of the fleet. The 80 heavy and 530 medium bombers are equipped to carry out strikes with stand-off weapons, reconnaissance and air-to-air refuelling. In the anti-submarine role 100 amphibians and 50 maritime patrol aircraft are backed by 200 helicopters of which an increasing number are now embarked in ships, although even the larger cruisers carry only one machine. In the 'Kiev' class a mix of helicopters and VTOL 'Forgers' is embarked, the latter probably armed with air-to-air or air-to-surface missiles as an alternative to anti-submarine weapons and reconnaissance equipment.

The final assessment shows a whole range of naval capability but the question is what is the purpose of this impressive fleet? Its Commander-in Chief has frequently written of the need to protect submarines with air and surface forces: the failure to do so cost the Germans the Battle of the Atlantic in World War II. If matters should reach a state of tension or hostilities this navy, with a higher proportion of its ships in the Northern Fleet than elsewhere but with an increasing force in the Pacific, would be well placed and armed to act as cover for the deployment of attack submarines through the narrow defiles of the North Atlantic and North-West Pacific and as protection for the ballistic missile submarines (SSBNs) lying off their home ports. As the long-range of the SS-N-8 and -18 missiles allow their launch from close into the Soviet shore the only anti-submarine measures currently open to the opposition are the use of attack submarines or a barrage of nuclear missiles. As the latter would be a pre-emptive strike it must be considered most unlikely and the infiltration of attack submarines the only feasible course of action. In this case the deployment of strong Soviet anti-submarine forces would be necessary and, with enemy surface and air forces not far distant, the various forms of Soviet armament make sense. This use of the available ships appears more logical than having little packets of ships searching for American SSBNs deployed in areas becoming more and more remote as missile range increases. These would more probably be the target for Soviet nuclear attack submarines escorted from their bases by the surface and air forces. However, the current state of Soviet sonar technology would probably make such a search a long, tedious operation, yielding little result. The final conclusion is that the seaborne ballistic missile forces of both super-powers have two advantages over their shore-based counterparts—relative invulnerability and deployment away from the homeland, arguments which most cogently recommend the diversion of funds from shore-based weapons to new and improved sea-borne missiles.

Considerations of anti-submarine defence do not affect the US Navy in the same way as the USSR. Free access to the oceans provides for easier deployment and the gathering of information on hostile deployments by shore-based systems and naval patrols makes for safer passages for the American SSBNs. But this is the ultimate deterrent and the launching of the ballistic missiles will indicate with a terrifying finality the failure of that hope. This outcome could be the result of miscalculation but many other less horrific results could stem from a similar source. Failure to offer any protest to Soviet moves into countries in which there can be no reason for their presence other than plans for expansion and eventual control is presenting the Soviet Navy with a series of bases and safe havens which are remarkably similar in their geographical location to those available to the United Kingdom 80 years ago. Indecision and miscalculation by many non-Communist powers have resulted in a position where insufficient ships are available for surveillance of the Soviet Fleet, much less inter-position. By dropping the shield of maritime security the Western leaders have so weakened their own position that they are moving towards a position of vulnerability to blackmail. The results of the blackmail? Deprivation of raw materials, markets and the freedom of those friends who are not strong enough to guarantee their own security are some of them.

In the USA this position appears to stem from a lack of unity in decision-making. The professional advice of the Pentagon is interpreted so very differently by the Executive and Congress that the naval programmes are not only suffering from suspension between two stools but also a continual fluctuation of views from those two supports, which should be the foundations of a long-term strategy and security policy. As a result, we find in this year's section on the US Navy divisive plans on the future of the carrier force, reductions in submarine building, differences over the destroyer programme and reductions in planned modernisation. The current situation shows the Executive standing firm on a new design carrier, the CVV, in place of an additional 'John F. Kennedy' class or a CVN. The cost of the CVV is currently quoted as $1,617 million, that of a new 'John F. Kennedy' as $1,760 million. This saving of $143 million will be offset by the CVV carrying only some 60 aircraft compared with the 'John F. Kennedy's' 87 to 95 and the inevitable stores problems of the 'one-off' venture. Life cycle savings of notable dimensions are quoted for the CVV—hardly surprising in view of its lack of aircraft capacity. Other attempts to save a proportion of the budget are resulting in further cuts and if this tendency continues the decline from 535 active combatant ships on 30 September 1979 (976 at the peak of the Viet-Nam war where there was little naval opposition) to 528 on 30 September 1980 will accelerate. By the end of the century the US Navy might well be below the 400 mark, a situation which could place the USA in an inferior position to the United Kingdom and other Western powers when considered as a balance of ships to population. With the steadily mounting call for imports, particularly of raw materials, freedom of access to the sources of those raw materials and their uninterrupted passage across the seas is of paramount importance. The US Navy is more than competent to do the job, given the tools.

The Rest of NATO and the Mediterranean

Similar problems of decision-making have also been evident in Canada where the life expectancy of a portion of the frigate force is now to be extended and new ships ordered. Where these are to be built and to what design seems inconclusive at the time of writing, with various consortiums in Canada and Italian shipbuilders vying for award of the contract. Time passes and ships grow older.

Across the Atlantic, the United Kingdom has continued with a programme of the Type 22 and Type 42 destroyers, culminating with a pre-election flourish of orders which may have bought a few votes. These new ships will be expanded versions of their predecessors and one cannot help remembering Winston Churchill's remark about 'the hunters becoming the hunted.' At £95 million a piece the Type 22 has become an expensive quarry and the argument of 'a 5 per cent decrease in capability for a 30 per cent decrease in price' must have attractions with a strained budget. There are hopeful signs—minesweepers much less expensive than the £15 million 'Hunt' class are being ordered (though for different purposes), a new class of off-shore patrol ship is forecast and a new hydrofoil and a new hovercraft have been acquired. In the more distant future lies the appearance of a new design of non-nuclear submarine. Whether this will follow the trend of 'big is beautiful' remains to be seen. Or perhaps the example of other NATO countries with far more recent experience in non-nuclear submarine construction and fuel-cell propulsion will be needed. One thing remains fairly certain in all British ship construction unless there is a radical change of approach—delays will occur and money be wasted as a result.

Such is certainly not the case in the Netherlands where the 'Kortenaer' class of frigates is running at about three and a half years in the yard, an imaginative programme made possible by the high level of co-operation between the builders and the navy. Concurrently with this construction programme the modernisation of the 'Van Speijk' class of 'Leander' frigates is well in hand. An interesting comparison with the British 'Leander' modernisation shows that the Netherlands' ships have managed to retain a gun armament while carrying twice as many Exocet launchers as their British counterparts.

Two more new construction programmes are also under way. In December 1978 the first of 15 Tripartite minehunters was laid down, part of a co-operative venture with the French and Belgians, while, in the same month, the first of the new class of 'Improved Zwaardvis' submarines was also begun. With a steady replacement programme the Royal Netherlands Navy is well up to its announced schedule.

In neighbouring West Germany 1978 also saw the start of the new Type 122 frigates, close cousins of the Dutch 'Kortenaer', the ordering of ten more fast missile craft and two minehunting programmes for the 'Lindau' class, the straight minehunter conversion and the Troika conversion of six ships. As might be expected extensive work on submarines is going ahead at IKL—not only are new and larger designs available but by 1990 it is hoped to have the first fuel-cell submarine at sea, a milestone in submarine development. Among the considerable log of foreign orders in West German yards is one of particular interest, the contracted delivery in 38 months of the first Meko 360 destroyer to Argentina by Blohm and Voss.

German influence remains strong to the north where Norway and Denmark are involved with IKL in new submarine designs. Both these NATO partners have new fast attack craft designs—the 'Willemoes' class have commissioned in Denmark and the Norwegian 'Hauks' are coming into service. But despite new construction these are both little more than coast-defence navies despite their large and widely dispersed merchant fleets.

Belgium, having completed her frigate programme, is now embarked on the Tripartite minehunter plan and this is also true in France where the first hull *Eridan*, is now afloat. Once again, financial problems have held back Plan Bleu but with nuclear submarines, destroyers and frigates on the slips and the

Leading european builder of surface ships

Landing ships for the transport of personnel and vehicles.

Fast attack craft of the 130 t PATRA class.

Minehunters.

5090 t guided missile frigates.

"Aviso" 1200 t for ASW and the protection of offshore zones of economic areas.

Fast attack craft designed for interception missions at sea and long endurance maritime surveillance.

Design and construction
of surface ships, submarines and weapons systems.

**Shipyards at Cherbourg, Brest, Lorient, Toulon, Dakar, Papeete.
Offices at Paris, Indret, Ruelle, St-Tropez.**

Direction Technique des Constructions Navales - 2, rue Royale 75200 Paris Naval - tél. 260.33.30

second aircraft-carrier under conversion for the nuclear-capable Super-Etendard the realistic approach of the French to maritime problems continues. With the flagship and four ships in the Indian Ocean, detachments at Papeete, Noumea and the Antilles as well as fleets in the Atlantic and Mediterranean, this is truly a world-wide navy. With a programme that now includes a third new fleet support ship France is achieving a well balanced navy capable of deployment a tous horizons provided her man-power problems are resolved.

In Italy the eight major companies of the Melara Club form a virile organisation which, with the backing of the navy, has, without nationalisation, combined to produce new and interesting designs without recourse to foreign industry. This may not be in the best interests of NATO compatibility but, until that problem is agreed and solved in a sensible manner, Italy will be providing a well-balanced fleet in a vital NATO area.

How vital this part of the Mediterranean is to NATO's plans has been underlined by three factors. The longevity of President Tito of Yugoslavia has been a delight to his adherents but he is not eternal. His departure could being sinister upheavals as the emigré groups move back across the borders of the Warsaw Pact. With the Greek navy building its strength, particularly in the Aegean, internecine problems with her NATO neighbour, Turkey, bedevil productive co-operation on this fragile flank. After a lengthy period when American politics caused a rupture in friendly relations with Turkey, financial problems and a crisis in internal relations have together produced a grave situation. The future might well bring a similar upheaval to that in Iran and a further crumbling of an important NATO outpost. Once again doctrinaire attitudes have imperilled security for, despite a growing and efficient navy, so far provided from within NATO, Turkey's attitudes and operations depend on the temper of those who rule in Ankara.

The uneasy peace on Turkey's southern flank has come as reinforcements continue to the navies of Syria, Israel and Egypt—nothing spectacular, although if the Israeli corvette programme continues as forecast that fleet will have a much enhanced capability and be in a far better position to operate its Harpoon missiles. And, further west, Colonel Qaddafi of Libya is building up a fleet of considerable proportions, lying on the flank of the narrowest area of the central Mediterranean. With Malta independent and Qaddafi a busy if tactless friend of Premier Mintoff, this area presents dubious and challenging problems. If the Soviet Mediterranean fleet comes to rest in Libyan ports the present incompetence of the Colonel's sailors could be overcome by further training and the US Sixth Fleet outflanked.

The Maghreb to the west presents a load of minor problems. The fleets increase, politics keep matters simmering but nothing here is as threatening as in the Malta-Libya zone. Spain is supplying Morocco's needs, probably as a precursor to her entry into the world-wide naval market. With her own fleet being reinforced from the yards of Bazan and her interest in becoming a member of both the EEC and NATO, her much improved navy could become a valuable reinforcement in both the Mediterranean and the Atlantic. The bases in Portugal are available to the Alliance—her ships are in considerable need of refurbishing and reinforcement, and cannot be considered a major contribution to any anti-submarine effort. But this improvement is in hand and if the navy can obtain funds for new construction, possibly British Type 21 frigates, from the sale of her surplus ships a major advance could result.

The Baltic

Although apparently dominated by the Soviet Baltic Fleet there are several points of naval interest in this sea other than those already mentioned. Finland has become the world's greatest builder of icebreakers and now is extending her own designs to other naval shipping. But without the icebreaker orders Finnish shipbuilders would be in a poor position, probably not unlike that of her neighbour Sweden. The nationalisation of the latter's shipyards has come at a time when the larger ships of this distinguished navy are being laid up, apparently giving preference to submarines and fast missile craft. Already possessing strong mine warfare and amphibious forces this is a fleet run on a very tight budget and designed for coast defence.

Across the water Poland and East Germany provide not only handy navies for Warsaw Pact reinforcement but also considerable building effort. Although only supposition, the fact that Poland has placed orders for merchant ships in Britain strongly suggests a busy naval construction programme which is certainly providing amphibious ships and craft for the Warsaw Pact, Iraq, India and others. It seems likely that the British-built ships will be to normal merchant standards unlike many other Warsaw Pact vessels which are built to high naval standards of shock-proofing, pre-wetting and other forms of protection. The reason for including a number of civilian manned Soviet ships in this book is to point out the fact that in their merchant and fishing fleets the Warsaw Pact possesses huge naval reserves capable of amphibious operations with roll-on/roll-off ships, transports, tankers, command ships and reconnaissance vessels.

The Cape Route

If ever political dogmatism and subsequent indecision have put a strategic issue at risk it is on the oil route around South Africa. Despite the withdrawal of Iranian supplies this remains a nodal area on the long haul from the Gulf States. This sea-lane is vital to the Western nations and, irrespective of Mexican, North Sea and, possibly, Moroccan sources, will remain so for many years. The Soviets are well placed to interfere from Nacala in Mozambique,
the Angolan ports and West African havens should they wish. The Western countries have neither a base nor a safe haven on the African coast in the same area. With South Africa spurned and constantly criticised the only remaining chance of retaining a suitable centre for ships and aircraft lacking the range to operate in this area without massive sea support has been thrown away. The double-stance of many Western politicians has seriously threatened a major life-line.

East Africa and the Arabian Peninsula

The Tanzanian-Uganda offensive against Idi Amin has removed a potential threat to the states surrounding Uganda. Kenya and Tanzania could well have been faced by Soviet-supported Libyans in their back-yards but now their main interest remains the sea. As Somalia decides whether to return to the Soviet fold the Ethiopan/Libyan squeeze on the Sudan will continue and the Soviets will consolidate their position in the Dhalek Islands, only 400 miles from the growing Saudi base in Jeddah. Aden remains the key to the Red Sea while Saudi Arabia builds up her American-designed navy and South Yemen sucks in more Soviet-built ships. To the north-east the Sultan of Oman is acquiring a steadily increasing naval force although his neighbour across the Straits of Hormuz, the new and confused government of Iran, is rapidly opting out of all defence commitments at a time when the CENTO treaty has been summarily interred. The United Arab Emirates and other Gulf states which lack Soviet affiliation must rely on Oman to guard their gates— Iran could easily pass under the control of the Moscow-backed Tudeh party. Another stronghold may well be lost for Western maritime power as the result of indecision and incompetence.

The Indian Ocean and the Tasman Sea

At the time of writing it is reported that a US Fifth Fleet is to be based at Diego Garcia. If this comes to pass this fleet will share with the French at Djibouti in representing Western influence, while Pakistan, India, Sri Lanka, Burma, Indonesia and Australia hold the ring. Of these, Burma is ineffective, Sri Lanka concerned with coastal problems, Pakistan has internal dilemmas, the worry of a Soviet-backed Afghanistan and a comparatively small navy, while Indonesia's economy allows for little more than a coast-defence force. India, meanwhile, is building a solid, competent naval force. Destroyers, frigates, minesweepers and amphibious craft from the USSR are melded with British-designed 'Leanders' and will, in the future, join Indian-built frigates and submarines. There is little doubt that new air-capable ships will follow the old *Vikrant* and the Indian Navy is set for maritime supremacy in this area. The Australian Navy, which is still making up its mind as to its replacement for the elderly *Melbourne,* has some 7000 miles of coastline to watch, facing all points of the compass. With a small population, a comparable budget and national political divisions it seems unlikely that this fleet can be anything but sparse in its deployments. The arguments appear strong for greater numbers of smaller air-capable ships to act with submarines as an outer ring for the patrol craft and mine warfare vessels now under construction or consideration. With a small fleet of large ships Australia could well lose control of her own coasts. The same problem faces New Zealand. A small country, many say, but to those who have sailed around the two islands it is no surprise to find that they total over 3000 miles of very varied terrain. All harbours are mine-able but New Zealand has no mine warfare forces—in fact she runs insufficient ships to keep watch on her ten main ports, much less their approaches. This has been the case for many years and, once again, a long coastline is matched with a small budget.

South-east Asia and the North-west Pacific

So much has been written about this area in the past year that a few brief comments should suffice. The ASEAN navies have a capability, with their missile craft, to cause mayhem in the narrow defiles leading to and from the South China Sea. The naval forces of Viet-Nam and Kampuchea are at present in no state to affect affairs in the area. Poorly trained, badly maintained and lacking fuel they are of little current value, although the arrival of the Soviet Navy in Cam-Ranh Bay could well alter this.

Taiwan bristles with guns and missiles: their fleet is proud and, by local standards, efficient. The two Koreas growl unceasingly while building up their own ship-building industries. War is never far away.

Lastly, the two partners to the October 1978 Pact, Japan and China. The naval forces of the former are increasingly efficient while the pact has shown the possibility of a huge reduction in Japan's vulnerable oil routes. Soviet bases to the north and west lie uncomfortably close to both partners, with the added disadvantage to the Chinese of a 4000-mile land border with the USSR. As the Soviet Pacific Fleet has increased steadily over the last year it is hardly surprising that the Chinese have continued a major building programme, though all their ships have little capability beyond home defence. The Chinese fleet includes the third largest submarine force and the largest group of light forces in the world, and this is a navy which may well show interest in foreign designs from destroyers downwards.

Latin America

'Big Brother' remains Brazil with all the adjacent countries, despite their local problems, concerned with that country's future moves. At present Brazil has transferred her submarine building future to West Germany from the United Kingdom. The future may see a rapid home-based expansion but

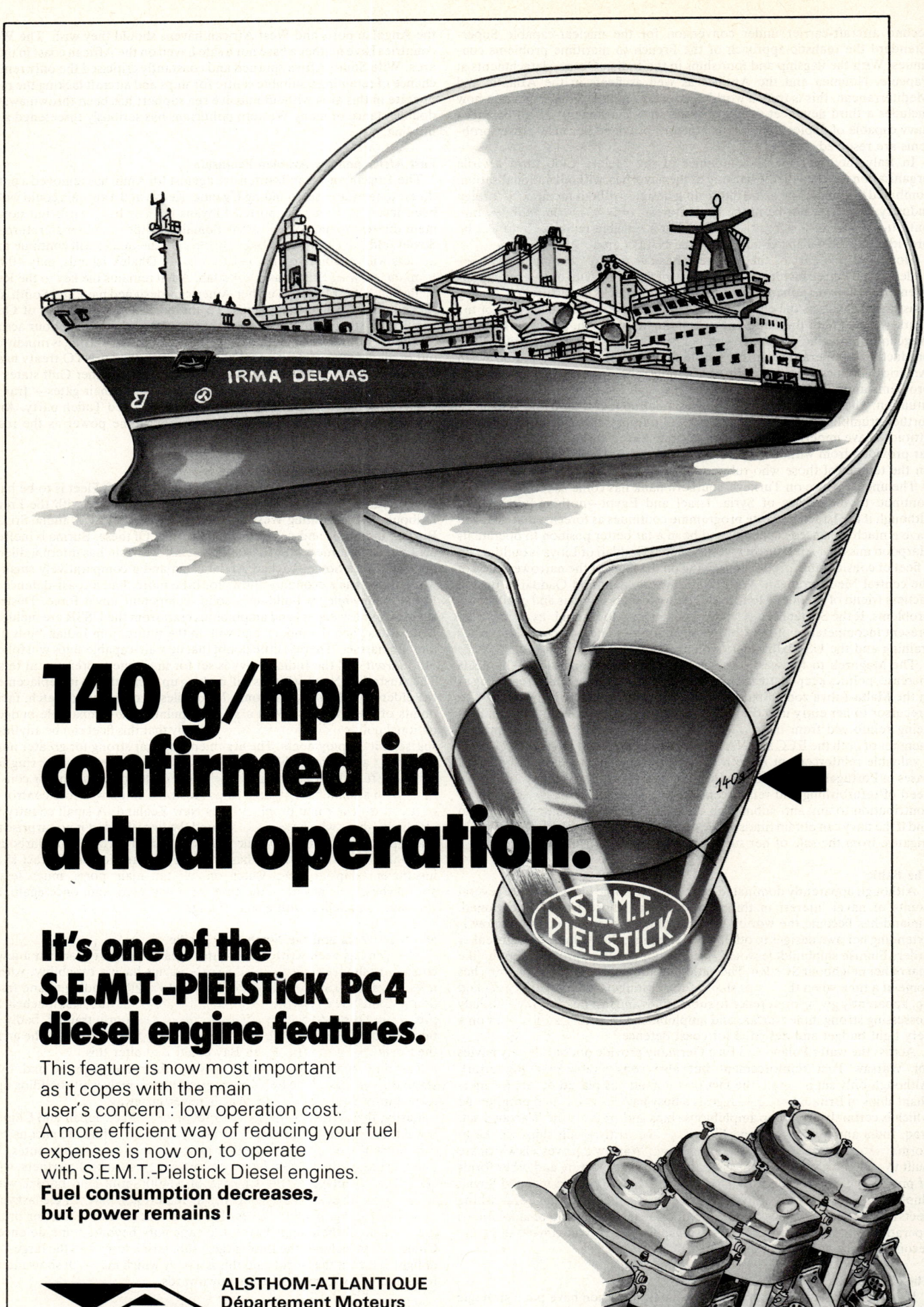

Argentina, with four Nordseewerke submarines and six new West German destroyers on order as well as fast attack craft from Israel, has stolen the limelight. Chile, by contrast, has made no new moves and the delivery of the first 'Lupo' class is reported as stalled because of financial problems. Ecuador has six Italian corvettes on order, Colombia may have cash problems and Venezuela, with considerable oil assets, awaits her European reinforcements of two Type 209 submarines and six Italian 'Lupo' class frigates. How oil wealth will affect Mexico in the future depends on her political situation but there is no doubt of Cuba's state. It is unusual for this country to come last in any estimate but this position in no way reflects her growing naval stature. With her first 'Foxtrot' submarine, 'Turya' class hydrofoils, more 'Osa' class missile craft, more 'Zhuk' patrol craft, two minesweepers and two diving ships from the USSR Cuba has, in the last year, stepped into a new naval league. It is not easy to divine the tasks for such an assembly—it cannot be only to keep up with her southern and western neighbours.

Conclusion

The technology currently available to navies has, in certain cases, apparently out-stripped the ability to profit from it. It is impossible to forecast the applications to which these new ideas may be put during the next decade but we are on the threshold of new and revolutionary improvements. Those fleets which are allowed by their politicians to take advantage of imagination and innovation may well be in a position to provide improved capability on less size at reduced cost. This does not seem to be the Soviet philosophy as their fleet is reinforced by ever larger ships with greater fire-power and range and dependent on an uniquely large slice of the national budget. The West remains dependent on world-wide sea routes but has surrendered a large part of its capability to defend and watch over them. The inability of many Western governments to appreciate their dilemma and the consequent indecision in their approach to solutions has put in jeopardy the peace which NATO has procured over the last thirty years.

J. E. MOORE
May 1979

YARROW
Naval Shipbuilders to the World for over 100 years

1. HMS 'ARDENT'—Completed 1977. One of five Type 21 Frigates built for the British Royal Navy.
2. LOGISTIC SUPPORT SHIP—Capable of beach landing heavy military vehicles and troops and fitted with extensive Helicopter facilities.
3. Typical CORVETTE/LIGHT FRIGATE—Armed with an extensive range of Weapon and Sensor equipments.
4. Typical PATROL VESSEL—Armed with medium and small calibre guns and surface to surface missiles.

Yarrow design and build most types of surface Naval Ships including Fast Attack Craft, Patrol Vessels, Corvettes, Frigates, Survey Ships and Support Ships.

YARROW
SHIPBUILDERS LTD

SCOTSTOUN, GLASGOW G14 0XN, SCOTLAND
Tel: 041-959 1207. Telex: 77357

A member of British Shipbuilders

MAJOR MATTERS

Algeria
Transfer of five "Osa II" class missile craft from USSR. Increased Coast Guard with Italian built "Baglietto" class.

Angola
Transfer of "Shershen" class torpedo craft—up to three now reported.

Argentina
Contract for four patrol submarines signed with Nordseewerke, Bremen—one to be built in Germany, remainder in Buenos Aires.
Contract signed with Thyssen Rheinstahl/Blohm and Voss for construction of six "Meko 360" type frigates (3600 tons), two to be built in Germany, with a delivery time of 38 months for the first, and the other four at Rio Santiago.
Purchase of two "type A69" frigates (ex-South African) from France.
Delivery of new Wärtsila icebreaker. Second ordered.

Australia
The decision on replacement aircraft-carrier(s) not yet available.
Construction of first Brooke Marine "PCF 420" craft in hand.
Modernisation of fire-control, sonar and radar under way in "Oberon" class submarines.
New underway replenishment ship of "Durance" class to be built in France or Australia.
New minehunter designs being progressed for service in mid-1980s.
Acquisition of US Mark 48 submarine torpedoes in hand—Harpoon and Exocet planned.
Modernisation of destroyers and frigates in hand.

Belgium
All four "Wielingen" class frigates commissioned.
Ten, and possibly five more, Tripartite minehunters planned, to be laid down between 1980 and 1984.

Benin
Naval force of unknown size planned.

Brazil
Plans in hand for the purchase of a number of Type 209 submarines, the first to be built in Germany and the remainder in Rio de Janeiro.
Seventh "Niteroi" class ordered from Navyard, Rio de Janeiro. All the original six now in commission.

Brunei
Three "Waspada" class missile craft delivered by Vosper Singapore in 1978/79.

Bulgaria
One "Osa II" class transferred by USSR (addenda).
Two "Vydra" class LCTs transferred by USSR (addenda).
Four "Yevgenya" class minesweepers transferred by USSR (addenda).
Additional ships added in text.

Burma
Six "Carpentaria" class patrol craft ordered from De Havilland Marine, Australia.

Canada
Examination of designs for new class of 3500 ton destroyers/frigates continues. At least six reported as the target although programme may have been under-funded.
New diving support ship commissioned.
Coast Guard has completed two 3600 ton diesel icebreakers and is planning a 33 000 ton nuclear icebreaker.

China
Continuing programme of submarines and fast attack craft with frigates coming slowly. Interest being shown in foreign designs of destroyers, frigates, submarines, MCM vessels and hovercraft.

Colombia
The planned transfer of four frigates from Portugal did not take place, nor did the transfer of two "Asheville" class large patrol craft from the USA.

Cuba
Transfer of one "Foxtrot" class submarine (addenda), four "Osa II" (text and addenda), two "Yevgenya" class minesweepers, three "Zhuk" class patrol craft.
Two "Turya" class hydrofoils (addenda), one "K 8" class minesweeper (addenda) and two diving ships (addenda) from USSR.

Denmark
Plans for new submarines.
First "Niels Juel" class trials—July 1979.
All "Willemoes" class completed.
New "Osprey" class on trials for Fishery Protection.

Dominican Republic
Deletion of two ex-US "Tacoma" class frigates and two ex-Canadian "Flower" class corvettes (addenda).

Ecuador
Both "Type 209" submarines in commission.
Six 650 ton corvettes ordered in Italy.

Egypt
Order for two "Agosta" class submarines from France reported.
Al Zaffer ("Skory" class) fitted with two SS-N-2 missiles.
Order for two "Lupo" class frigates from Italy reported.
Six fast attack craft of "Ramadan" class underway in UK.
Refits of "October" class missile craft underway in UK.
(Note: Withdrawal of Saudi Arabian funds may affect French and Italian orders).

Ethiopia
Transfer of four "Osa II" class and two "Mol" class torpedo craft from USSR.

Finland
New minelayer/training ship completed by Wärtsila.

France
The sixth SSBN is to be laid down in 1980 to a new design.
The first SSN to be launched in 1979 and the second is also under construction.
The nuclear aircraft-carrier PA75 is planned for laying down in 1981.
"Georges Leygues" to commission October 1979, *Dupleix* launched and two more under construction.
Two more "A69" frigates commissioned.
Eridan, first of the fifteen Tripartite minehunters launched.
Second new replenishment tanker *(Meuse)* launched and third laid down.

Gabon
Ngolo, the largest high-speed GRP hull, in commission.

Germany (DDR)
Transfer of one "Koni" class frigate from USSR.
Replacement of "Iltis" class torpedo craft by "Libelle" class.
Replacement of "Robbe" class LSTs by "Frösch" class.

Germany (FDR)
Submarine development continues ("Type 210" and fuel-cells) (foreword).
Construction of six "Type 122" frigates in hand with six more planned.
Ten "Type 143A" missile craft ordered in place of the cancelled Boeing hydrofoil order.
Minehunter conversions of twelve "Lindau" class (to be fitted with PAP) and conversion of six "Lindau" class as Troika guidance ships is well under way.

Ghana
Two fast attack craft completing in 1979 with two larger craft under construction.

Greece
Last two of eight "Type 209" submarines due to commission.
Plans to modernise "Gearing" class apparently shelved.
A busy native construction programme includes six "La Combattante III (modified)", ten 86 ton fast attack craft, a survey ship, a training ship, tankers, tugs and water-boats.

Guatemala
Five new patrol craft and two troop-carriers in commission.

Guinea
Two "Shershen" class transferred from USSR (addenda).

Guinea Bissau
Two "T4" landing craft transferred from USSR (addenda).

India
A programme of Indian-built submarines is planned.
Aircraft-carrier *Vikrant* to embark Sea Harriers after 1979 refit.
Two (at least) "Kashin" class destroyers under construction in USSR.
Frigate programme: reported that approaches have been made to the Netherlands for the construction of gas-turbine frigates. Meanwhile the last two "Leander" class are being followed by an enlarged and modified "Leander" design of Indian origin the first having been laid down.
The third "Nanuchka 2" class has been delivered by USSR as have two "Natya" class minesweepers.
First three "SDB Mark 2" class completed by Garden Reach Dockyard with more to follow. The same yard has completed a new survey ship with two more under construction.
Several tugs, tankers and landing craft under construction.

Indonesia
First two "Type 209" submarines to complete in Germany in 1980 with possible order for second pair.
Three frigates completing in the Netherlands, the last carrying a helicopter. More to be ordered (addenda).
Four missile craft completing in Korea.

Iran
In a confused picture all that seems certain is that four "Spruance" class destroyers, an order for German "Type 209" submarines, the transfer of two US "Tang" class submarines and two British LCLs have been cancelled.

Ireland
Although the full extent of the programme is not clear additional "P21" class corvettes are apparently to be followed by 2000 ton frigates.

Israel
The new 850 ton corvettes are reported under construction as well as another four "Reshef" class.
Orders placed for US "Flagstaff" hydrofoils.
Continuing programme of "Dabur" class patrol craft although it is not clear whether the missile variant "Dvora" is to be ordered.

Italy
Financial strictures have delayed the ordering of two DDGs, two more "Maestrale" frigates and six minehunters.
Two "Sauro" class submarines commissioned with two more building.
Light aircraft-carrier laid down 1979.
First of six "Maestrale" class (an improved "Lupo") frigates to commission in 1980, soon after the last of the four "Lupos" commissions.
The remainder of the seven "Sparviero" class hydrofoils to commission in early 1981.
First four minehunters ordered January 1978.
Second new replenishment tanker commissioned as well as a new salvage ship.

Ivory Coast
Two new French 32 knot patrol craft commissioned.

Japan
With the last of the "Uzushio" submarines commissioning and the "Yuushio" submarines due at one per year from March 1980 the "Fuyushio" class is being paid off.
The first of the "Shirane" helicopter destroyers (3 A/S helos) is due in service in March 1980 and the first of the "DD 122" class two years later.
The "DE 226" class of frigates is well under way the first to commission in March 1981 and the remainder, to improved designs, starting two years later.
The first two 500 ton LSMs are to laid down in 1980.
The first "Hatsushima" class minesweeper commissioned in March 1979, the remainder following at three per year.
A new fleet support ship, a cable layer and two new surveying ships are also in the programme.

[145]

BOFORS

SAK 57 All-purpose gun

The Bofors 57 mm all-purpose gun has a close-range anti-aircraft capacity comparable to that of the extreme anti-aircraft weapons.

Through the use of a special type of surface target shell, this gun system also has a naval target capacity comparable to that of guns of considerably larger calibres.

AB BOFORS Ordnance Division
Box 500, S-690 20 BOFORS, Sweden
Telephone: (0)586-360.00 • Cables: Boforsco, Bofors • Telex: 73210 bofors s

The Japanese Maritime Safety Agency (Coast Guard) is building two 3750 ton patrol ships, a number of coastal patrol craft and fire-fighting vessels.
Kenya
Understood to be rearming with Gabriel missiles.
Korea (North)
Continuing submarine and fast attack craft building programme. No further news of frigates.
Korea (South)
Have now started own frigate building at Hayundai.
Libya
Soviet "Foxtrot" submarines delivered.
First pair of Italian corvettes completed.
"Combattante IIG" class of ten building at Cherbourg.
Two Soviet "Polnochniy" class LCTs arrived.
Malaysia
Four "Spica-M" class building in Sweden.
Mexico
Plans for up to twelve 450 ton patrol craft.
Morocco
One "Descubierta" class frigate and four fast attack craft building in Spain.
Mozambique
Number of patrol craft transferred. Condition doubtful.
Netherlands
Two new submarines building.
First two "Kortenaer" class frigates at sea-programme on schedule.
Modernisation of "Van Speijk" class proceeding.
First of fifteen "Alkmaar" (Tripartite) minehunters laid down for completion in 1981.
Nigeria
One Blohm and Voss "Meko 360" frigate on order for delivery 1981.
Two Vosper Mark 9 Corvettes completed.
Six fast attack craft on order.
Two LSTs and two LCTs delivered.
Norway
Discussions continue with FDR over replacement submarines.
Construction of fourteen "Hauk" class missile craft continues.
New depot ship commissioned.
First three of seven new Coast Guard ships ordered.
Oman
Retrofitting of Exocet in patrol craft completed.
New Logistic Ship delivered by Brooke Marine.
Five new LCUs delivered.
Fifth patrol craft delivered to Royal Oman Police.
Pakistan
Two ex-South African "Agosta" class submarines purchased.
Two "Gearing" class destroyers purchased and refitted in USA.
Peru
Construction of last four "Type 209" submarines continues in Germany.
One ex-Netherlands destroyer taken over.
First pair of "Lupo" class frigates completed in Italy—financial problems.
Philippines
Construction of De Havilland "9209 Type" understood to be continuing.
Portugal
Programme for frigate modernisation planned.
Saudi Arabia
First of four new corvettes to commission August 1980.
First two of four new MSCs completed.
First of nine missile craft to commission April 1980.
Soloman Islands
One "Carpentaria" class patrol craft purchased in Australia.
South Africa
Plans reported to build Israeli corvettes.
Conversion of MSCs to minehunters.
Spain
Four "Agosta" class submarines to complete 1980-83.
One light aircraft-carrier to be laid down in 1980.
Three "FFG7" frigates ordered June 1977—not yet laid down.
Four "Descubierta" class frigates completed—four to come.
Ten 300 ton patrol craft ordered.
Twenty-nine coastal patrol craft completed.
Sweden
Reported that all destroyers and frigates are to be paid off for sale (?) as emphasis is placed on submarines and fast attack craft.
Three "Näken" class submarines completing.
Design contract for new "A17" submarine class awarded.
Ten of seventeen "Hugin" class missile craft completed.
Plans for eighteen "Spica T131-121" classes to be fitted with missiles.
New minelayer to commission 1980.
Syria
Two "Osa II" class transferred from USSR.
Taiwan
Construction of locally designed fast attack craft in progress.
Thailand
Three Italian missile craft delivered.

Trinidad
Two "Spica" (Type CG40) to be delivered by Sweden in 1980.
Tunisia
Two "Shanghai II" class received from China.
Turkey
Two "Type 209" submarines building at Gölcük.
Two of four missile craft completing at Taşkizak.
"Girne" completed but project for series cancelled.
Construction of "SAR 33" Type continuing at Taşkizak after successful trials by Abeking and Rasmussen.
New "Çakabey" class LSTs building at Taşkizak.
USSR
New SSBN—"Typhoon" class (of about 20 000 tons) under construction.
"Delta" class SSBNs programme continues.
Construction of "Charlie II" (SSGN), "Victor II" (SSN) and "Tango" (SS) classes continues.
Second "Kiev" class aircraft-carrier (*Minsk*) commissioned—two more to follow.
First "Sovietsky Soyuz" class nuclear-propelled battle-cruiser completing at Leningrad—first of continuing class.
Follow-on "Kresta II" ("Kirov") class cruisers completing at Leningrad.
Two new "Kara" class cruisers completed.
"Krivak I" and "II" classes continue.
"Koni" class frigates building.
New "Matka", "Sarancha", "Bobochka" classes building (FAC and hydrofoils).
New "Olya" and "Andryusha" classes of minesweepers building.
New "Ivan Rogov" class (landing ship-dock with accommodation for helicopters and hovercraft)—one built, more to come.
New fleet supply-ship *Berezina* in service, apparently designed for aircraft-carrier support.
New 80 000 ton floating dock in place at Vladivostok.
UK
New "Trafalgar" class SSNs—first two laid down, third ordered.
Plans for new SSK class in preparation.
Fifth "Swiftsure" class SSN commissioned.
Ark Royal paid off, *Invincible* started sea trials.
Illustrious launched, new *Ark Royal* laid down.
Bulwark recommissioned.
Broadsword commissioned with three more Type 22 building and two more ordered. Fifth ship to be "stretched."
Four more Type 42 destroyers commissioned—six more building, two more ordered. The eleventh and subsequent ships of this class to be lengthened by 53 feet and with two feet more beam.
"Leander" class conversions continue.
One "Hunt" class MCMV commissioned—five more building.
New "EDATS" deep-water minesweepers to be ordered.
New diving support ship ("sea-bed operations vessel") ordered.
Two more "Island" class patrol ships built.
VT2 hovercraft acquired.
Boeing "Jetfoil" hydrofoil purchased.
Two new fleet replenishment ships completed.
Two new tankers to be built.
USA
Building rate of "Ohio" class SSBNs reduced in March 1978.
Trident conversion schedule published.
"Los Angeles" class SSN construction continues at one per year instead of two per year.
Although the VSTOL programme is under constant pressure the administration is forcing through a CVV programme which may have no advanced VSTOL to embark.
The "Modified Virginia" class of CGN has been cancelled.
Third "Virginia" class commissioned.
Belknap due to complete repair and modernisation in August 1980.
First of DDG 47 (Aegis) ordered.
Request for four "Improved Spruance" class (DDG) to be taken over from Iran after cancellation of order.
Modernisation of "Charles F. Adams" class DDGs to begin in FY 1980.
Five more "Oliver Hazard Perry" class FFGs commissioned.
Five more "Pegasus" class PHMs ordered or building.
Last of "Tarawa" class LHAs to commission mid-1980.
New deep-sweeping MCMVs planned—first in FY 1981.
New destroyer tenders (AD), oilers (AO), submarine tenders (AS), fleet ocean tugs (ATF) and ocean surveillance ships (AGOS) under construction.
Uruguay
Three large patrol craft ordered.
Venezuela
First "Lupo" class frigate commissioned.
Viet-Nam
Two "Petya" class frigates and three "Zhuk" class patrol craft transferred by USSR.
Yemen (North)
Two "Zhuk" class patrol craft transferred by USSR.
Yemen (South)
One "T58" class ocean minesweeper transferred by USSR.
One Fairey Marine "Tracker" commissioned.
Yugoslavia
First "Sava" class submarine commissioned.
Two more "Rade Koncar" missile craft commissioned.

BREDA

anti-missile and anti-aircraft
BREDA 40 L 70 TWIN COMPACT
already selected by 12 Navies....

frigates; in 28 ships for 5 navies
- C.N.R. – MAESTRALE CLASS
- BLOHM & VOSS – MAKO 300
- C.N.R. – LUPO CLASS
- C.N.R. – CARVAJAL CLASS
- C.N.R. – MAR. SUCRE CLASS

helicopter carrier
- ITALCANTIERI – GARIBALDI CLASS

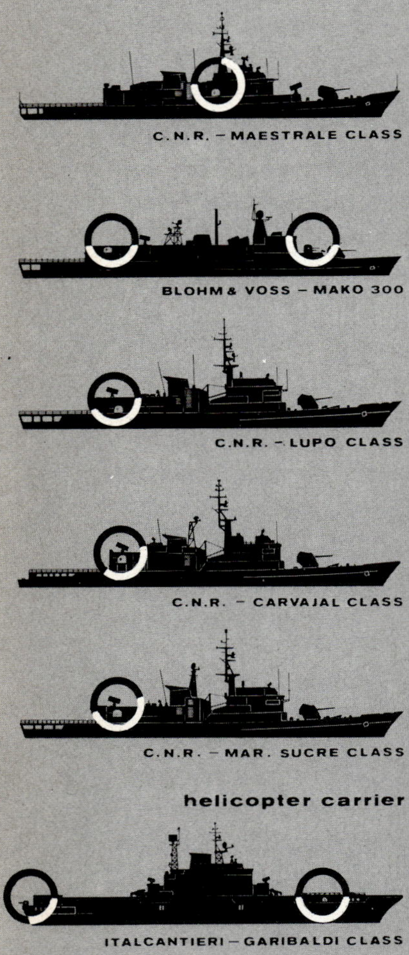

fast patrol boats; in 37 crafts for 7 navies
- C.M.N. – COMBATTANTE
- LÜRSSEN – TOP SPEED NAVY
- S.F.C.N. –
- BROOKE MARINE – 37,5 M.
- VOSPER – 52 M.

landing
- C.N.I.M. –

....and currently proposed for the most
advanced naval weapon systems

BREDA MECCANICA BRESCIANA S.P.A.
Via Lunga, 2 - 25100 BRESCIA (Italy) - tel. 030/314061 - Telex 300056 BREDAR

ACKNOWLEDGEMENTS

The considerable amount of new information, amendments and improved photography and line drawings in this edition is due in great measure to the ready response to my enquiries from an increasing band of correspondents round the world. Of the regular consultants Captain F. de Blocq van Kuffeler stands as the senior member, ably backed by Mr Graeme Andrews for the Australian and New Zealand sections and Dr Robert Scheina. Mr Samuel L. Morison has again been responsible for the information in the USA section in which he must have been delighted to include the new FFG 13 named after his grandfather, that uniquely distinguished naval historian Rear-Admiral and Professor Samuel E. Morison. Of the multitude of others, certain names must be mentioned: Contre-Admiral M. J. Adam CVO CBE, Dr Ian Buxton, Mr D. Dervissis, Mr Adrian English, Commander Aldo Fraccaroli, Lieutenant Commander A. Hague, V.R.D., Mr G. K. Jacobs, Mr R. Jones, Mr John Mortimer, Mr A. J. R. Risseuw, Mr C. W. E. Richardson, Senor X. Taibo, and Mr John Young. With illustrations as a vital part of the book my thanks are very much due to Dr Giorgio Arra, Mr Robert Carlisle, Mr R. Forrest of Wright and Logan, Commander Gerhard Koop, Mr Michael Lennon, Monsieur Y. Robert, Mr and Mrs (C. and S.) Taylor and Mr Leo van Ginderen. The line drawings are being steadily improved and for this I thank Mr A. D. Baker III, Lieutenant Commander Erminio Baguasco, Herr Siegfried Breyer, Sub-Lieutenants James Goldrick and Peter Jones, Mr Ian Sturton and the team of Mr Jack Wood and Mr Euslin Bruce.

To the authors and editors of the other major naval reference books I send my thanks for the part they have played: *Almanacco Navale* edited by Dr Giorgio Giorgerini and Signor Augusto Nani, *Weyer's Flottentaschenbuch* edited by Herr Gerhard Albrecht, *Flottes de Combat,* edited by Monsieur J. Labayle-Couhat, *Marinkalender* edited by Captain Allan Kull and *Die Sowjetische Kriegsmarine* by Commander Ulrich Schulz-Torge and published by Wehr and Wissen.

Apart from the great assistance given by all those mentioned above the Ministry of Defence in London and many governments and their naval or defence attachés have been of the greatest help with both facts and photographs. It would be invidious to list all the "good guys" because it would imply criticism of those, who for various reasons, have chosen to ignore my requests. To all those who came to my aid, my sincere thanks.

Throughout the preparation of the book I have had invaluable technical advice from Dr Ian Buxton, Commander Roy Corlett, Dr Robert Scheina, Señor X. Taibo and Mr Geoffrey Wood. My grateful thanks to them and to Mr Robert Abernethy and his staff for their assistance with the silhouettes as well as to Mr John Taylor, editor of *Jane's All the World's Aircraft,* who not only prepared the copy but checked the galleys of the naval aircraft section.

In the USA section, however, there have been many who have done much to help Mr Samuel L. Morison in his task of improving that section and in particular he wishes to thank the following for their invaluable assistance: Rear-Admiral David M. Cooney, USN, Chief, Office of Naval Information; Captain Robert Lewis, Assistant Chief of Naval Information for Operations; Commander James P. Matthews, Director, Public Information Division, Office of Chief of Naval Information; Mr Robert Carlisle and Lieutenant Commander James J. Harness of his staff; Captain William Blanchard, Public Affairs Office, Department of Defense; Lieutenant Commander Bruce B. Bade, Security Assistance Division, Office of Chief of Naval Operations; Captain R. E. Groder, Captain David Dellinger, Lieutenant F. R. Robbins and Mr Walter Dailey of the Ships Maintenance and Logistics Division, Office of Chief of Naval Operations; Mr Stanley Krol, Navy Shipbuilding and Scheduling Office, Naval Sea Systems Command; Mr Christopher Wright, Naval Systems Division, Pentagon; Mrs Jeanne Koontz, Miss Barbara Gilmore and Mr Charles Haberlain of the Naval Historical Center; and Dr Robert L. Scheina, US Coast Guard Historian. Mr Morison would particularly like to acknowledge the following people whose contributions were especially noteworthy: Captain William Test and Captain Gerard M. Sturm, Jr., Ships maintenance and Logistics Division; Yeomen First Class Nicholas Goodpaster, Office of the Chief of Naval Information; Mr Larry Manning, Legislative/Public Affairs Officer, Military Sealift Command and Miss Delia E. Stoehr, Naval Ship Systems Analyst, Department of the Navy.

The preparation of this book moves in a series of stages and in the arrangement of the original copy and the subsequent checking of the galleys and page proofs my wife has, as always, given me the greatest encouragement and assistance. Jean and David Parsons have put in long hours, particularly on the thankless task of indexing while at the publishers the production team under Ken Harris and the editorial team run by Valerie Passmore have given me unstinted help. Susan Walby has kept a hawk-eye on all aspects of the book and Glynis Long has shown her customary initiative in pasting-up the pages. The imperturbable efficiency of the printers at Netherwood Dalton in Huddersfield has kept the whole process moving swiftly without a word of protest at the many last minute changes—at least none has yet reached me. Lastly my thanks must go to Mr Sidney Jackson the Publishing Director for allowing me complete freedom in the preparation of what we all hope will be a book of use and value.

To ensure that the next edition may provide as accurate a reflection of what is a rapidly changing naval scene may I once more ask my many friends and advisers to let me have their contributions by mid-November if possible? I realise that this cannot always be done but the insertion of material at later stages increases costs which are already seriously affected by inflation. The new edition is already under way and it would greatly assist if letters could be sent directly to me at this address:

Captain J. E. Moore, RN
Elmhurst,
Rickney,
Hailsham,
Sussex BN27 1SF
England

Please remember that any assessment is only as good as its input and the least little fragment will help in building the whole. Thank you.

Note: No illustration from this book may be reproduced without the publishers' permission but the Press may reproduce information and governmental photographs provided *Jane's Fighting Ships* is acknowledged as the source. Photographs credited to other than official organisations must not be reproduced without permission from the originator.

GLOSSARY

AA	Anti-aircraft.
ARM	Anti-radiation missile.
A/S ASW	Anti-submarine (warfare).
ASM	Air to surface missile.
BPDMS	Basic point defence missile system.
Cal	Calibre—the diameter of a gun barrel; also used for measuring length of the barrel e.g. A 6-inch gun 50 calibres long (6 in/50) would be 25 feet long.
CIWS	Close in weapon system eg. US 20 mm Phalanx.
CODAG, CODOG, COGAG, COGOG, COSAG	Descriptions of mixed propulsion systems—Combined diesel and/or gas turbine, diesel or gas turbine, gas turbine and/or gas turbine, gas turbine or gas turbine, steam and/or gas turbine.
DC	Depth charge.
DCT	Depth charge thrower.
DP	Dual purpose (gun) for surface or AA use.
Displacement	Basically the weight of water displaced by a ship's hull when floating: (a) Light: without fuel, water or ammunition. (b) Normal: used for Japanese MSA ships. Similar to "standard". (c) Standard: as defined by Washington Naval Conference 1922—fully manned and stored but without fuel or reserve feed-water. (d) Full load: fully laden with all stores, ammunition, fuel and water.
ECM	Electronic counter measures e.g. jamming.
ELINT	Electronic intelligence e.g. recording radar, W/T etc.
FRAM	US Navy's "Fleet rehabilitation and modernisation" programme.
Hedgehog	Spigot mortar for firing anti-submarine bombs.
Horsepower	Power developed or applied: (a) bhp: brake horsepower = power available at the crankshaft. (b) shp: shaft horsepower = power delivered to the propeller shaft. (c) ihp: indicated horsepower = power produced by expansion of gases in the cylinders of reciprocating steam engines. N.B. If the type of horsepower is not known hp is used instead.
Length	Expressed in various ways: (a) oa: overall = length between extremities. (b) pp: between perpendiculars = between fore side of the stem and after side of the rudderpost. (c) wl: water-line = between extremities on the water-line.
MAD	Magnetic Anomaly Detector—for anti-submarine detection identifying a steel body in the earth's magnetic field.
MAP	US Military Aid Programme.
Mousetrap	Ahead throwing spigot A/S mortar for small ships.
MSC	US Military Sealift Command.
NTDS	Naval tactical data system.
rpm	Revolutions per minute of engines, propellers, radar aerials etc.
SAM	Surface to air missile.
SLBM	Submarine launched ballistic missile.
SLEP	US Service Life Extension Programme for aircraft carriers.
SSBN	Nuclear-powered ballistic missile submarine.
SSM	Surface to surface missile.
Tonnage	Measurement tons, computed on capacity of a ship's hull rather than its displacement (q.v.): (a) Gross: the internal volume of all spaces within the hull and all permanently enclosed spaces above decks that are available for cargo, stores and accommodation. The result in cubic feet divided by 100 = gross tonnage. (b) Net: gross minus all those spaces used for machinery, accommodation etc. ("non-earning" spaces). (c) Dead-weight (dwt): the amount of cargo, bunkers, stores etc. that a ship can carry at her load draught.
VDS	Variable depth sonar which is lowered to best listening depth. Known as dunking sonar in helicopters.

SHIP DESIGNATIONS

In an effort to standardise the type designations in the various navies, despite somewhat idiosyncratic listing in some fleets, a regular formula has been used wherever possible in the majority of sections. This has caused some queries and comments, therefore a list is given below.

SUBMARINES
Strategic Missile	Nuclear propelled and conventionally propelled
Cruise Missile	Nuclear propelled and conventionally propelled
Fleet Submarines	Nuclear propelled—torpedo attack
Patrol Submarines	Conventionally propelled—torpedo attack

AIRCRAFT CARRIERS
Attack Aircraft Carriers (Nuclear)	(US) "Nimitz" and "Enterprise" classes
Attack Aircraft Carriers	
ASW Aircraft Carriers	
Light Aircraft Carriers	"Invincible" class, "Moskva" class

MAJOR SURFACE SHIPS
Cruisers	Over 10 000 tons, including missile conversions
Light Cruisers	5 000 tons to 10 000 tons
Destroyers	3 000 to 5 000 tons, plus original conventional destroyers
Frigates	1 100 to 3 000 tons
Corvettes	500 to 1 100 tons

LIGHT FORCES
Fast Attack Craft (FAC) (25 knots and above)	FAC (Missile) FAC (Gun) FAC (Torpedo) FAC (Patrol)
Patrol Craft (below 25 knots)	Large Patrol Craft (100 to 500 tons) Coastal Patrol Craft (below 100 tons)

AMPHIBIOUS FORCES
- Command Ships
- Assault Ships
- Landing Ships
- Landing Craft
- Transports

MINE WARFARE FORCES
- Minelayers
- MCM Support Ships
- Mine Sweepers (Ocean)
- Mine Hunters
- Mine Sweepers (Coastal)
- Mine Sweepers (Inshore)
- Mine Sweeping Boats

SURVEYING VESSELS
- Surveying Ships
- Coastal Surveying Craft
- Inshore Surveying Craft

GENOA May 1980

ITALIAN NAVAL EXHIBITION

Shipbuilding - Propulsion systems
Electrical and auxiliary engines - Electronics
Weapon systems and ammunition
Aircraft for naval uses
Shipborne equipment for naval defence

Organisation: E. P. I. N. Ente Promozione Industria per la difesa Navale
00187 Roma - via Sardegna, 40 - phone (06) 482241 - telex 610180 Fincant

Enquiries to: FIERA INTERNAZIONALE DI GENOVA - CONSORNAUTICA
16129 Genova · Italia - P.le J F Kennedy 1 - phone (010) 589371 - telex: 271248 Conaut !

MAJOR SURFACE SHIPS PENNANT LIST

Alb	Albania	Gra	Grenada	Plp	Philippines		
Alg	Algeria	Gre	Greece	PNG	Papua New Guinea		
Ana	Anguilla	Gua	Guatemala	Pol	Poland		
Ang	Angola	Guy	Guyana	Por	Portugal		
Arg	Argentina	Hai	Haiti	Qat	Qatar		
Aus	Austria	HK	Hong Kong	RoC	Taiwan		
Aust	Australia	Hon	Honduras	RoK	Korea, Republic (South)		
Ban	Bangladesh	Hun	Hungary	Rom	Romania		
Bar	Barbados	IC	Ivory Coast	SA	South Africa		
Bel	Belgium	Ice	Iceland	SAr	Saudi Arabia		
Ben	Benin	Ind	India	Sen	Senegal		
Bhm	Bahamas	Indo	Indonesia	Sey	Seychelles		
Bhr	Bahrain	Iran	Iran	Sin	Singapore		
Blz	Belize	Iraq	Iraq	SL	Sierra Leone		
Bol	Bolivia	Ire	Ireland	Sol	Solomon Islands		
Bru	Brunei	Isr	Israel	Som	Somalia		
Brz	Brazil	Ita	Italy	Spn	Spain		
Bul	Bulgaria	Jam	Jamaica	Sri	Sri Lanka		
Bur	Burma	Jap	Japan	StK	St Kitts		
Cam	Cameroon	Jor	Jordan	StL	St Lucia		
Can	Canada	Kam	Kampuchea	StV	St Vincent		
Chi	Chile	Ken	Kenya	Sud	Sudan		
Col	Colombia	Kwt	Kuwait	Sur	Surinam		
Com	Comoro Islands	Lao	Laos	Swe	Sweden		
Con	Congo	Lbr	Liberia	Syr	Syria		
CPR	China, People's Republic	Lby	Libya	Tan	Tanzania		
CR	Costa Rica	Leb	Lebanon	Tld	Thailand		
Cub	Cuba	Mad	Madagascar	Tog	Togo		
Cyp	Cyprus	Mex	Mexico	Ton	Tonga		
Cz	Czechoslovakia	Mlt	Malta	TT	Trinidad and Tobago		
Den	Denmark	Mlw	Malawi	Tun	Tunisia		
DPRK	Korea, Democratic People's Republic (North)	Mly	Malaysia	Tur	Turkey		
DR	Dominican Republic	Mnt	Montserrat	UAE	United Arab Emirates		
Ecu	Ecuador	Mor	Morocco	Uga	Uganda		
Egy	Egypt	Moz	Mozambique	UK	United Kingdom		
EIS	El Salvador	Mrt	Mauritius	Uru	Uruguay		
EqG	Equatorial Guinea	Mtn	Mauritania	USA	United States of America		
Eth	Ethiopia	Nic	Nicaragua	USSR	Union of Soviet Socialist Republics		
Fij	Fiji	Nig	Nigeria	Ven	Venezuela		
Fin	Finland	Nld	Netherlands	VI	Virgin Islands		
Fra	France	Nor	Norway	Vtn	Viet-Nam		
Gab	Gabon	NZ	New Zealand	YAR	Yemen Arab Republic (North)		
Gam	Gambia	Omn	Oman	YPDR	Yemen, People's Democratic Republic (South)		
GB	Guinea Bissau	Pak	Pakistan	Yug	Yugoslavia		
GDR	Germany, Democratic Republic	Pan	Panama	Zai	Zaire		
GFR	Germany, Federal Republic	Par	Paraguay	Zam	Zambia		
Gha	Ghana	Per	Peru	Zan	Zanzibar		
Gn	Guinea						

Pennant numbers of major surface ships in numerical order.

Number	Ship's Name	Type	Country	Number	Ship's Name	Type	Country
1	Tahchin	FF	Tld	3	Pin Klao	FF	Tld
1	Brooke	FFG	USA	3	Schofield	FFG	USA
1	Glover	AGFF	USA	3	John King	DDG	USA
1	Raleigh	LPD	USA	3	Belleau Wood	LHA	USA
1	Tarawa	LHA	USA	3	Okinawa	LPH	USA
B 1	Durango	FF	Mex	CAH 3	Ark Royal	CGH	UK
CAH 1	Invincible	CGH	UK	D 3	Pres. Velasco Ibarra	FF	Ecu
D 1	Hercules	DD	Arg	DD 3	Hua Yang	DD	RoC
DD 1	Hsiang Yang	DD	RoC	DE 3	18 De Julio	FF	Uru
D 1	25 De Julio	FF	Ecu	LHA3	Belleau Wood	LHA	USA
DE 1	Uruguay	FF	Uru	03	Prat	CL	Chi
PF 1	Montevideo	PF	Uru	D 03	Santander	DD	Col
A 01	Ethiopia	FF	Eth	D 03	Presidente Velasco Ibarra	FF	Ecu
01	Aetos	FF	Gre	4	General Belgrano	CL	Arg
01	Adelaide	FFG	Aust	4	Nassau	LHA	USA
D 01	Moran Valverde	FF	Ecu	4	Austin	LPD	USA
F 01	Dat Assawari	FFG	Lby	4	Talbot	FFG	USA
IE 01	Cuauthemoc	DD	Mex	4	Lawrence	DDG	USA
PA 01	Dedalo	CVH	Spn	PS 4	Rajah Lakandula	FF	Plp
2	Prasae	FF	Tld	04	Latorre	CL	Chi
2	Ramsey	FFG	USA	5	Nueve de Julio	CL	Arg
2	Charles F. Adams	DDG	USA	5	Tapi	FF	Tld
2	Iwo Jima	LPH	USA	5	Pelelieu	LHA	USA
2	Vancouver	LPD	USA	5	Ogden	LPD	USA
2	Saipan	LHA	USA	5	Richard L. Page	FFG	USA
CAH 2	Illustrious	CGH	UK	5	Claude V. Ricketts	DDG	USA
D 2	Santissima Trinidad	DD	Arg	5	Oklahoma City	CG	USA
DD 2	Heng Yang	DD	RoC	D 5	Artemiz	DDGS	Iran
V 2	25 De Mayo	CVS	Arg	DD 5	Yuen Yang	DD	RoC
D 2	Presidente Alfaro	FF	Ecu	05	Veinte De Julio	DD	Col
DE 2	Artigas	FF	Uru	IB 05	Tehuantepec	FF	Mex
02	Canberra	FFG	Aust	6	Khirirat	FF	Tld
D 02	Presidente Alfaro	FF	Ecu	6	Duluth	LPD	USA
02	O'Higgins	CL	Chi	6	Julius A. Furer	FFG	USA
D 02	Caldas	DD	Col	6	Barney	DDG	USA
D 02	Devonshire	DLGH	UK	DD 6	Huei Yang	DD	RoC
IB 02	Coahuila	PF	Mex	06	Condell	FFG	Chi
IE 02	Cuitlahuac	DD	Mex	06	Siete De Agosto	DD	Col

PENNANT LIST

Number	Ship's Name	Type	Country	Number	Ship's Name	Type	Country
06	Aspis	DD	Gre	16	Joseph Strauss	DDG	USA
IB 06	Usumacinta	FF	Mex	16	Lexington	AVT	USA
IA 06	Como Manuel Azueta	FF	Mex	16	Leahy	CG	USA
7	Makut Rajakumarn	FF	Tld	D 16	London	DLGH	UK
7	Cleveland	LPD	USA	DE 16	Boyaca	FF	Col
7	Henry B. Wilson	DDG	USA	F 16	Diomede	FFGH	UK
7	Guadalcanal	LPH	USA	F 16	Umar Farooq	FF	Ban
7	Oliver Hazard Perry	FFG	USA	F 16	Oland	FF	Swe
DD 7	Fu Yang	DD	RoC	17	Ministero Portales	DD	Chi
E 7	President Bourguiba	FF	Tur	17	Conyngham	DDG	USA
PS 7	Andres Bonifacio	FF	Plp	17	Harry E. Yarnell	CG	USA
O7	Lynch	FFG	Chi	DD 17	Nan Yang	DD	RoC
8	McInerney	FFG	USA	F 17	Uppland	FF	Swe
8	Dubuque	LPD	USA	18	Almirante Riveros	DDG	Chi
8	Lynde McCormick	DDG	USA	18	Semmes	DDG	USA
DD 8	Kwei Yang	DD	RoC	18	Worden	CG	USA
IB 08	Chihuahua	FF	Mex	D 18	Antrim	DLGH	UK
PS 8	Gregorio de Pilar	FF	Plp	DD 18	An Yang	DD	RoC
R 08	Bulwark	LPH	UK	F 18	Galatea	FFGH	UK
08	Vendetta	DD	Aust	J 18	Halland	DD	Swe
9	Guam	LPH	USA	19	Almirante Williams	DDG	Chi
9	Denver	LPD	USA	19	Blue Ridge	LCC	USA
9	Towers	DDG	USA	19	Tattnall	DDG	USA
9	Wadsworth	FFG	USA	19	Dale	CG	USA
9	Long Beach	CGN	USA	D 19	Glamorgan	DLGH	UK
DD 9	Chiang Yang	DD	RoC	DD 19	Kuen Yang	DD	RoC
PS 9	Diego Silang	FF	Plp	J 19	Småland	DD	Swe
10	Albany	CG	USA	20	Almirante Brown	DD	Arg
10	Juneau	LPD	USA	20	Bennington	CVS	USA
10	Sampson	DDG	USA	20	Mount Whitney	LCC	USA
10	Duncan	FFG	USA	20	Goldsborough	DDG	USA
10	Tripoli	LPH	USA	20	Antrim	FFG	USA
DD 10	Po Yang	DD	RoC	20	Richmond K. Turner	CG	USA
F 10	Aurora	FFGH	UK	C 20	Tiger	CL	UK
L 10	Fearless	LPD	UK	D 20	Almirante Brown	DD	Arg
PS 10	Francisco Dagahoy	FF	Plp	DD 20	Lao Yang	DD	RoC
11	Vampire	DD	Aust	D 20	Fife	DLGH	UK
11	Port Said	FF	Egy	J 20	Ostergotland	DD	Swe
11	Intrepid	CVS	USA	21	Espora	DD	Arg
11	Chicago	CG	USA	21	Melbourne	CVS	Aust
11	Coronado	LPD	USA	21	Cochrane	DDG	USA
11	Sellers	DDG	USA	21	Gridley	CG	USA
11	Clark	FFG	USA	D 21	Espora	DD	Arg
11	New Orleans	LPH	USA	D 21	Inhauma	DD	Brz
11	Split	DD	Yug	D 21	Lepanto	DD	Spn
A 11	Minas Gerais	CVS	Brz	D 21	Norfolk	DLGH	UK
D 11	Nueva Esparta	DD	Ven	D 21	Falcon	DD	Ven
DD 11	Dang Yang	DD	RoC	D 21	Carabobo	DD	Ven
F 11	Jamuna	FF (survey)	Ind	DD 21	Liao Yang	DD	RoC
F 11	Visby	DD	Swe	J 21	Södermanland	DD	Swe
F 11	Almirante Clemente	FF	Ven	22	Rosales	DD	Arg
L 11	Intrepid	LPD	UK	22	Benjamin Stoddert	DDG	USA
R 11	Vikrant	CVS	Ind	22	England	CG	USA
12	Shreveport	LPD	USA	D 22	Rosales	DD	Arg
12	Robison	DDG	USA	D 22	Jaceguay	DD	Brz
12	George Philip	FFG	USA	D 22	Almirante Ferrandiz	DD	Spn
12	Inchon	LPH	USA	D 22	Falcon	DD	Ven
12	Hornet	CVS	USA	J 22	Gästrikland	DD	Swe
D 12	Kent	DLGH	UK	23	Almirante Domecq Garcia	DD	Arg
D 12	Zulia	DD	Ven	23	Richard E. Byrd	DDG	USA
DD 12	Chien Yang	DD	RoC	23	Halsey	CG	USA
F 12	Sundsval	DD	Swe	D 23	Almirante Domecq Garcia	DD	Arg
F 12	Achilles	FFGH	UK	D 23	Frontin	DD	Brz
F 12	Gen. José Trinidad Moran	FF	Ven	D 23	Almirante Valdes	DD	Spn
R 12	Hermes	LPH	UK	D 23	Bristol	DLG	UK
13	Nashville	LPD	USA	J 23	Halsingland	DD	Swe
13	Hoel	DDG	USA	24	Almirante Storni	DD	Arg
13	Samuel E. Morison	FFG	USA	24	Waddell	DDG	USA
D 13	Gen. Juan Jose Flores	FF	Ven	24	Reeves	CG	USA
F 13	Halsingborg	FF	Swe	D 24	Almirante Storni	DD	Arg
14	Blanco Encalada	DD	Chi	D 24	Alcala Galiano	DD	Spn
14	Trenton	LPD	USA	F 24	Rahmat	FF	Mly
14	Buchanan	DDG	USA	25	Bainbridge	CGN	USA
14	Sides	FFG	USA	D 25	Segui	DD	Arg
DD 14	Lo Yang	DD	RoC	D 25	Marcilio Diaz	DD	Brz
F 14	Kalmar	FF	Swe	D 25	Jorge Juan	DD	Spn
F 14	Leopard	FF	UK	F 25	Bayandor	PF	Iran
F 14	Almirante Brion	FF	Ven	26	Bouchard	DD	Arg
15	Cochrane	DD	Chi	26	Serrano	PF	Chi
15	Cordoba	DT	Col	26	Belknap	CG	USA
15	Ponce	LPD	USA	D 26	Bouchard	DD	Arg
15	Berkeley	DDG	USA	D 26	Mariz E. Barros	DD	Brz
DD 15	Lao Yang	DD	RoC	F 26	Naghdi	PF	Iran
DT 15	Cordoba	FF	Col	27	Orella	PF	Chi
F 15	Euryalus	FFGH	UK	27	Josephus Daniels	CG	USA
16	Ministero Zenteno	DD	Chi	D 27	Py	DD	Arg
16	Boyaca	FF	Col	D 27	Para	DD	Brz
16	Velos	DD	Gre	F 27	Lynx	FF	UK

PENNANT LIST

Number	Ship's Name	Type	Country	Number	Ship's Name	Type	Country
PF 27	Tai Yuan	DD	RoC	41	Midway	CV	USA
28	Thyella	DD	Gre	D 41	Oquendo	DD	Spn
28	Wainwright	CG	USA	F 41	Defensora	DDH	Brz
28	Thomaston	LSD	USA	F 41	Vincent Yanez Pinzon	FF	Spn
D 28	Paraiba	DD	Brz	42	Mahan	DDG	USA
F 28	Kahnamuie	PF	Iran	D 42	Roger De Lauria	DD	Spn
F 28	Cleopatra	FFGH	UK	F 42	Constituiçào	DDH	Brz
29	Uribe	PF	Chi	F 42	Legazpi	FF	Spn
29	Jouett	CG	USA	F 42	Phoebe	FFGH	UK
29	Plymouth Rock	LSD	USA	PF 42	Kang Shan	FF	RoC
D 29	Buena Piedra	DD	Arg	43	Rashid	FF	Egy
D 29	Parana	DD	Brz	43	Dahlgren	DDG	USA
30	Horne	CG	USA	43	Coral Sea	CV	USA
30	Fort Snelling	LSD	USA	D 43	Marques De La Ensenada	DD	Spn
D 30	Pernambuco	DD	Brz	F 43	Liberal	DDH	Brz
31	Ierax	FF	Gre	F 43	Torquay	FF	UK
31	Galicia	LSD	Spn	PF 43	Chung Shan	FF	RoC
31	Bon Homme Richard	CVA	USA	44	William V. Pratt	DDG	USA
31	Sterett	CG	USA	F 44	Independencia	DDH	Brz
31	Decatur	DDG	USA	45	Yarra	FF	Aust
31	Point Defiance	LSD	USA	45	Dewey	DDG	USA
D 31	Piaui	DD	Brz	F 45	Uniào	DDH	Brz
F 31	Descubierta	FF	Spn	F 45	Minerva	FFGH	UK
F 31	Brahamaputra	FF	Ind	46	Parramatta	FF	Aust
D 32	Santa Catarina	DD	Brz	46	Preble	DDG	USA
32	William H. Standley	CG	USA	F 46	Kistna	FF	Ind
32	John Paul Jones	DDG	USA	F 47	Danae	FFGH	UK
32	Spiegel Grove	LSD	USA	48	Stuart	FF	Aust
D 32	General Jose De Austria	FF	Ven	49	Derwent	FF	Aust
F 32	Nilgiri	FF	Ind	50	Swan	FF	Aust
F 32	Diana	FF	Spn	51	Artemiz	DD	Iran
F 32	Salisbury	FF	UK	51	Meliton Carvajal	FF	Per
PF 32	Yu Shan	FF	RoC	D 51	Liniers	DD	Spn
33	Fox	CG	USA	D 52	Alava	DD	Spn
33	Parsons	DDG	USA	F 52	Juno	FFGH	UK
33	Alamo	LSD	USA	53	Torrens	FF	Aust
D 33	Maranhao	DD	Brz	54	Leon	FF	Gre
D 33	Almirante Jose Garcia	FF	Ven	F 54	Hardy	FF	UK
F 33	Himgiri	FF	Ind	F 55	Waikato	FFGH	NZ
F 33	Infanta Elena	FF	Spn	56	Lonchi	DD	Gre
PF 33	Hua Shau	FF	RoC	F 56	Argonaut	FFGH	UK
34	Biddle	CG	USA	F 57	Andromeda	FFGH	UK
34	Somers	DDG	USA	F 58	Hermione	FFGH	UK
34	Oriskany	CV	USA	59	Forrestal	CV	USA
34	Hermitage	LSD	USA	A 59	Deutschland	CLT	GFR
D 34	Mato Grosso	DD	Brz	F 59	Chichester	FF	UK
F 34	Udaygiri	FF	Ind	60	Saratoga	CV	USA
F 34	Infanta Cristina	FF	Spn	C 60	Mysore	CL	Ind
F 34	Wen Shan	FF	RoC	F 60	Jupiter	FFGH	UK
35	Monticello	LSD	USA	61	Castilla	FF	Per
35	Truxtun	CGN	USA	61	Iowa	BB	USA
D 35	Alagoas	DD	Brz	61	Ranger	CV	USA
D 36	Sergipe	DD	Brz	61	Babr	DDG	Iran
F 35	Dunagiri	FF	Ind	D 61	Churruca	DD	Spn
PF 35	Fu Shan	FF	RoC	F 61	Atrevida	FF	Spn
36	Anchorage	LSD	USA	62	Independence	CV	USA
36	California	CGN	USA	62	New Jersey	BB	USA
F 36	Taragiri	FF	Ind	62	Palang	DDG	Iran
F 36	Whitby	FF	UK	D 62	Gravina	DD	Spn
PF 36	Lu Shan	FF	RoC	F 62	Princesa	FF	Spn
37	Portland	LSD	USA	63	Navarinon	DD	Gre
37	South Carolina	CGN	USA	63	Rodriquez	FF	Per
37	Farragut	DDG	USA	63	Kitty Hawk	CV	USA
D 37	Rio Grande Do Norte	DD	Brz	63	Missouri	BB	USA
F 37	Vindhyagiri	FF	Ind	D 63	Mendez Nuñez	DD	Spn
F 37	Jaguar	FF	UK	64	Constellation	CV	USA
PF 37	Shoa Shan	FF	RoC	64	Wisconsin	BB	USA
38	Perth	DDG	Aust	D 64	Langara	DD	Spn
38	Shangri-La	CVS	USA	F 64	Nautilus	FF	Spn
38	Pensacola	LSD	USA	65	Enterprise	CVN	USA
38	Luce	DDG	USA	D 65	Blas De Lezo	DD	Spn
38	Virginia	CGN	USA	F 65	Villa Bilbao	FF	Spn
D 38	Espirito Santo	DD	Brz	66	America	CV	USA
D 38	Intrepido	FF	Spn	67	Panthir	FF	Gre
F 38	Arethusa	FFGH	UK	67	John F. Kennedy	CV	USA
PF 38	Tai Shan	FF	RoC	68	Nimitz	CVN	USA
39	Hobart	DDG	Aust	P 68	Arnala	FFL	Ind
39	Mount Vernon	LSD	USA	69	Dwight D. Eisenhower	CVN	USA
39	Macdonough	DDG	USA	F 69	Bacchante	FFGH	UK
39	Texas	CGN	USA	P 69	Androth	FFL	Ind
F 39	Naiad	FFGH	UK	70	Carl Vinson	CVN	USA
40	Fort Fisher	LSD	USA	F 70	Apollo	FFGH	UK
40	Coontz	DDG	USA	71	Villar	DD	Per
40	Mississippi	CGN	USA	71	Saam	FF	Iran
F 40	Niteroi	DDH	Brz	F 71	Baleares	FFG	Spn
F 40	Sirius	FFGH	UK	F 71	Scylla	FFGH	UK
41	Brisbane	DDG	Aust	72	Zaal	FF	Iran
41	Arkansas	CGN	USA	72	Guise	DD	Per
41	King	DDG	USA	F 72	Andalucia	FFG	Spn

PENNANT LIST

Number	Ship's Name	Type	Country	Number	Ship's Name	Type	Country
F 72	Ariadne	FFGH	UK	D 118	Coventry	DDGH	UK
73	Rostam	FF	Iran	119	Aokumo	DD	Jap
73	Chung Nam	FF	RoK	F 119	Eskimo	FFH	UK
73	Palacios	DDGS	Per	120	Akigumo	DD	Jap
F 73	Cataluña	FFG	Spn	F 122	Gurkha	FFH	UK
P 73	Anjadip	FFL	Ind	F 124	Zulu	FFH	UK
74	Ferré	DDGS	Per	F 125	Mohawk	FFH	UK
74	Faramaz	FF	Iran	F 126	Plymouth	FFH	UK
C 74	Delhi	CL	Ind	F 127	Penelope	FFGH	UK
F 74	Asturias	FFG	Spn	F 129	Rhyl	FFH	UK
P 74	Andaman	FFL	Ind	F 131	Nubian	FFH	UK
F 75	Extremadura	FFG	Spn	F 133	Tartar	FFH	UK
F 75	Charybdis	FFGH	UK	134	Des Moines	CA	USA
P 75	Amini	FFL	Ind	F 137	Beas	FF	Ind
76	Datu Kalantiaw	FF	Plp	139	Salem	CA	USA
F 76	Hang Tuah	FF	Mly	F 139	Betwa	FF	Ind
D 80	Sheffield	DDGH	UK	F 140	Talwar	FF	Ind
81	Kyong Nam	PF	RoK	141	Haruna	DDH	Jap
81	Almirante Grau	CL	Per	142	Hiei	DDH	Jap
F 81	Descubierta	FF	Spn	143	Shirane	DDH	Jap
82	Ah San	PF	RoK	F 143	Trishul	FF	Ind
82	Coronel Bolognesi	CL	Per	F 144	Kirpan	FF	Ind
83	Ung Po	PF	RoK	F 145	President	FF	SA
83	Capitan Quiñones	CL	Per	F 146	Kuthar	FF	Ind
84	Babur	CL	Pak	F 147	President Steyn	FF	SA
84	Aguirre	CL	Per	F 148	Taranaki	FF	NZ
85	Sfendoni	DD	Gre	F 150	President Kruger	FF	SA
85	Kyong Puk	PF	RoK	L 153	Nafkratoussa	LSD	Gre
F 85	Keppel	FF	UK	160	Alamgir	DD	Pak
86	Jonnam	PF	RoK	161	Akizuki	DD	Jap
D 86	Birmingham	DDGH	UK	161	Badr	DD	Pak
87	Chi Ju	PF	RoK	162	Teruzuki	DD	Jap
D 87	Newcastle	DDGH	UK	162	Jahangir	DD	Pak
F 87	Nigeria	FF	Nig	163	Amatsukaze	DDG	Jap
F 88	Broadsword	FFG	UK	164	Takatsuki	DD	Jap
D 88	Glasgow	DDGH	UK	164	Shah Jahan	DD	Pak
F 89	Battleaxe	FFG	UK	165	Kikuzuki	DD	Jap
90	Kwang Ju	DD	RoK	D 165	Tariq	DD	Pak
F 90	Brilliant	FFG	UK	166	Mochizuki	DD	Jap
91	Chung Mu	DD	RoK	D 166	Taimur	DD	Pak
D 91	Nottingham	DDGH	UK	167	Nagatsuki	DD	Jap
F 91	Brazen	FFG	UK	168	Tachikaze	DDG	Jap
92	Seoul	DD	RoK	169	Asakaze	DDG	Jap
D 92	Godavari	FF	Ind	F 169	Amazon	FFGH	UK
D 92	Liverpool	DDGH	UK	F 170	Antelope	FFGH	UK
93	Pusan	DD	RoK	D 171	Z 2	DD	GFR
95	Chung Buk	DD	RoK	F 171	Active	FFGH	UK
F 95	Sutlej	FF (survey)	Ind	D 172	Z 3	DD	GFR
96	Jeong Buk	DD	RoK	F 172	Ambuscade	FFGH	UK
97	Dae Gu	DD	RoK	F 173	Arrow	FFGH	UK
R 97	Jeanne D'Arc	CHV	Fra	F 174	Alacrity	FFGH	UK
98	In Cheon	DD	RoK	F 176	Avenger	FFGH	UK
R 98	Clemenceau	CVS	Fra	P 177	Kamorta	FF	Ind
99	Taejon	DD	RoK	D 178	Z 4	DD	GFR
C 99	Blake	CL	UK	P 178	Kadmath	FF	Ind
F 99	Lincoln	FF	UK	D 179	Z 5	DD	GFR
R 99	Foch	CVS	Fra	P 179	Kiltan	FF	Ind
F 101	Yarmouth	FFH	UK	P 180	Kavaratti	FF	Ind
101	Harukaze	DD	Jap	D 181	Hamburg	DD	GFR
102	Yukikaze	DD	Jap	P 181	Katchal	FF	Ind
103	Ayanami	DD	Jap	D 182	Schleswig Holstein	DD	GFR
F 103	Lowestoft	FFH	UK	D 183	Bayern	DD	GFR
104	Isonami	DD	Jap	D 184	Hessen	DD	GFR
F 104	Dido	FFGH	UK	F 184	Ardent	FFGH	UK
105	Uranami	DD	Jap	D 185	Lütjens	DDG	GFR
106	Shikinami	DD	Jap	F 185	Avenger	FFGH	UK
F 106	Brighton	FFH	UK	D 186	Mölders	DDG	GFR
107	Murasame	DD	Jap	D 187	Rommel	DDG	GFR
F 107	Rothesay	FFH	UK	202	Ikazuchi	FF	Jap
108	Yudachi	DD	Jap	203	Inazuma	FF	Jap
D 108	Cardiff	DDGH	UK	204	"Riga" class	FF	CPR
F 108	Londonderry	FFH	UK	205	"Riga" class	FF	CPR
109	Harusame	DD	Jap	205	St. Laurent	DDH	Can
F 109	Leander	FFGH	UK	206	"Riga" class	FF	CPR
110	Takanami	DD	Jap	206	Saguenay	DDH	Can
F 110	Kaveri	FF	Ind	207	"Riga" class	FF	CPR
111	Oonami	DD	Jap	207	Skeena	DDH	Can
F 111	Otago	FF	NZ	209	Kiangnan	FF	CPR
112	Makinami	DD	Jap	210	Themistocles	DD	Gre
113	Yamagumo	DD	Jap	211	Miaoulis	DD	Gre
F 113	Falmouth	FFH	UK	211	Isuzu	FF	Jap
114	Makigumo	DD	Jap	212	Kanaris	DD	Gre
F 114	Ajax	FFGH	UK	212	Mogami	FF	Jap
115	Asagumo	DD	Jap	213	Kontouriotis	DD	Gre
F 115	Berwick	FFH	UK	213	Kitakami	FF	Jap
116	Minegumo	DD	Jap	214	Sachtouris	DD	Gre
117	Natsugumo	DD	Jap	214	Ooi	FF	Jap
F 117	Ashanti	FFH	UK	215	Chikugo	FF	Jap
118	Murakumo	DD	Jap	APD 215	Tien Shan	FF	RoC

PENNANT LIST

Number	Ship's Name	Type	Country	Number	Ship's Name	Type	Country
216	Ayase	FF	Jap	D 358	Berk	FF	Tur
217	Mikuma	FF	Jap	D 359	Peyk	FF	Tur
F 217	Milanian	PF	Iran	360	Nuku	FF	Indo
218	Tokachi	FF	Jap	F 421	Canterbury	FFGH	NZ
219	Iwase	FF	Jap	451	Mella	FF	DR
220	Chitose	FF	Jap	452	Gregorio Luperon	FF	DR
F 220	Köln	FF	GFR	453	Pedro Santana	FF	DR
221	Niyodo	FF	Jap	462	Hayase	AM	Jap
F 221	Emden	FF	GFR	F 471	Antonio Enes	FF	Por
222	Teshio	FF	Jap	F 472	Alm Pereira Da Silva	FF	Por
F 222	Augsburg	FF	GFR	F 473	Alm Gago Coutinho	FF	Por
223	Yoshino	FF	Jap	F 474	Alm Magalhaes Correia	FF	Por
F 223	Karlsrühe	FF	GFR	F 475	Joao Coutinho	FF	Por
224	Kumano	FF	Jap	F 476	Jacinto Candido	FF	Por
F 224	Lübek	FF	GFR	F 477	Gen. Pereira D'Eca	FF	Por
225	Noshiro	FF	Jap	F 480	Com Joao Belo	FF	Por
F 225	Braunschweig	FF	GFR	F 481	Com Hermenegildo Capelo	FF	Por
229	Ottawa	DDH	Can	F 482	Com Roberto Ivens	FF	Por
230	Margaree	DDH	Can	F 483	Com Sacadura Cabral	FF	Por
231	"Kiangnan" class	FF	CPR	F 484	Augusto De Castilho	FF	Por
232	"Kiangnan" class	FF	CPR	F 485	Honorio Barreto	FF	Por
233	"Kiangnan" class	FF	CPR	F 486	Baptiste de Andrade	FF	Por
233	Fraser	DDH	Can	F 487	Joao Roby	FF	Por
F 233	Nilgiri	FFGH	Ind	F 488	Afonso Cerqueira	FF	Por
234	Assiniboine	DDH	Can	F 489	Oliveira E Carmo	FF	Por
F 234	Himgiri	FFGH	Ind	511	Rashid	FF	Egy
236	Gatineau	DD	Can	525	Port Said	FF	Egy
240-246	"Luta" class	DD	CPR	F 540	Pietro De Cristofaro	PF	Ita
250	Iman Bondjol	PF	Indo	F 541	Umberto Grosso	PF	Ita
251	Surapati	PF	Indo	F 542	Aquila	PF	Ita
252	Pattimura	PF	Indo	F 543	Albatros	PF	Ita
253	Sultan Hasanudin	PF	Indo	F 544	Alcione	PF	Ita
257	Restigouche	DD	Can	F 545	Airone	PF	Ita
258	Kootenay	DD	Can	F 546	Licio Visintini	PF	Ita
259	Terra Nova	DD	Can	C 550	Vittorio Veneto	CGH	Ita
260	Tippu Sultan	FF	Pak	D 550	Ardito	DDG	Ita
261	Mackenzie	DD	Can	D 551	Audace	DDG	Ita
261.	Tughril	FF	Pak	F 551	Canopo	FF	Ita
262	Saskatchewan	DD	Can	C 553	Andrea Doria	DLGH	Ita
263	Yukon	DD	Can	F 553	Castore	FF	Ita
264	Qu'Appelle	DD	Can	C 554	Caio Duilio	DLGH	Ita
265	Annapolis	DDH	Can	F 554	Centauro	FF	Ita
266	Nipigon	DDH	Can	555	Tariq	FF	Egy
275	Warszawa	DDG	Pol	D 555	Geniere	DD	Ita
D 278	Jan Van Riebeeck	FF	SA	F 555	Cigno	FF	Ita
280	Iroquois	DDH	Can	D 558	Impetuoso	DD	Ita
281	Huron	DDH	Can	D 559	Indomito	DD	Ita
282	Athabaskan	DDH	Can	D 562	San Giorgio	DD	Ita
283	Algonquin	DDH	Can	F 564	Lupo	FF	Ita
F 300	Oslo	FF	Nor	F 565	Sagittario	FF	Ita
F 301	Bergen	FF	Nor	F 566	Perseo	FF	Ita
F 302	Trondheim	FF	Nor	F 567	Orsa	FF	Ita
F 303	Stavanger	FF	Nor	D 570	Impavido	DDG	Ita
F 304	Narvik	FF	Nor	F 570	Maestrale	FF	Ita
F 310	Sleipner	FF	Nor	D 571	Intrepido	DDG	Ita
F 311	Aeger	FF	Nor	F 571	Grecale	FF	Ita
D 340	Istanbul	DD	Tur	F 572	Libeccio	FF	Ita
F 340	Beskytteren	FFH	Den	F 573	Scirocco	FF	Ita
341	Samadikun	FF	Indo	F 574	Alisco	FF	Ita
D 341	Izmir	DD	Tur	F 575	Euro	FF	Ita
342	Martadinata	FF	Indo	F 580	Alpino	FF	Ita
D 342	Izmit	DD	Tur	F 581	Carabiniere	FF	Ita
343	Ngurah Rai	FF	Indo	F 590	Aldebaran	FF	Ita
D 343	Iskenderun	DD	Tur	F 593	Carlo Bergamini	FF	Ita
344	Monginsidi	FF	Indo	F 594	Virginio Fasan	FF	Ita
D 344	Içel	DD	Tur	F 595	Carlo Margottini	FF	Ita
F 344	Bellona	PF	Den	F 596	Luigi Rizzo	FF	Ita
F 345	Diana	PF	Den	D 602	Suffren	DLG	Fra
F 346	Flora	PF	Den	D 603	Duquesne	DLG	Fra
F 347	Triton	PF	Den	D 609	Aconit	DD	Fra
F 348	Hvidbjornen	FFH	Den	D 610	Tourville	DDG	Fra
F 349	Vaedderen	FFH	Den	C 611	Colbert	CLG	Fra
F 350	Ingolf	FFH	Den	D 611	Duguay-Trouin	DDG	Fra
351	Jos Sudarso	FF	Indo	D 612	De Grasse	DDG	Fra
F 351	Fylla	FFH	Den	D 622	Kersaint	DDG	Fra
D 352	Gayret	DD	Tur	D 624	Bouvet	DDG	Fra
F 352	Peder Skram	FF	Den	D 625	Dupetit Thouars	DDG	Fra
D 353	Adatepe	DD	RoC	D 627	Maille Brezé	DDG	Fra
F 353	Herluf Trolle	FF	Den	D 628	Vauquelin	DDG	Fra
D 354	Kocatepe	DD	Tur	D 629	D'Estrées	DDG	Fra
F 354	Niels Juel	FF	Den	D 630	Du Chayla	DDG	Fra
355	Iman Bondjol	FF	Indo	D 631	Casablanca	DDG	Fra
D 355	Tinaztepe	DD	Tur	D 632	Guépratte	DDG	Fra
F 355	Olfert Fischer	FF	Den	D 633	Duperré	DDG	Fra
356	Surapati	FF	Indo	D 634	La Bourdonnais	DDG	Fra
D 356	Zafer	DD	Tur	D 635	Forbin	DDG	Fra
F 356	Peter Tordenskjold	FF	Den	D 636	Tartu	DDG	Fra
357	Lambung Makurat	FF	Indo	D 638	La Galissonière	DD	Fra
D 357	Muavenet	DD	Tur	D 640	Georges Leygues	DDGH	Fra

PENNANT LIST

Number	Ship's Name	Type	Country	Number	Ship's Name	Type	Country
D 641	Dupleix	DDGH	Fra	886	Orleck	DD	USA
D 642	Montcalm	DDGH	Fra	888	Al Nasser	DD	Egy
D 643	Jean de Vienne	DDGH	Fra	890	Meredith	DD	USA
666	6 October	DD	Egy	F 910	Wielingen	FF	Bel
718	Hamner	DD	USA	F 911	Westdiep	FF	Bel
F 725	Victor Schoelcher	FF	Fra	F 912	Wanderlaar	FF	Bel
F 726	Commandant Bory	FF	Fra	F 913	Westhinder	FF	Bel
F 727	Admiral Charner	FF	Fra	931	Forrest Sherman	DD	USA
F 728	Doudart de Lagrée	FF	Fra	933	Barry	DD	USA
F 729	Balny	FF	Fra	937	George F. Davis	DD	USA
F 733	Commandant Riviére	FF	Fra	938	Jonas Ingram	DD	USA
F 740	Commandant Bourdais	FF	Fra	940	Manley	DD	USA
743	Southerland	DD	USA	941	Du Pont	DD	USA
F 748	Protet	FF	Fra	942	Bigelow	DD	USA
F 749	Enseigne de Vaisseau Henry	FF	Fra	943	Blandy	DD	USA
763	William C. Lawe	DD	USA	944	Mullinnix	DD	USA
F 763	Le Boulonnais	FF	Fra	945	Hull	DD	USA
F 765	Le Normand	FF	Fra	946	Edson	DD	USA
F 766	Le Picard	FF	Fra	948	Morton	DD	USA
F 767	Le Gascon	FF	Fra	950	Richard S. Edwards	DD	USA
F 771	Le Savoyard	FF	Fra	951	Turner Joy	DD	USA
F 773	Le Basque	FF	Fra	951	Souya	ML	Jap
F 774	L'Agenais	FF	Fra	963	Spruance	DD	USA
F 775	Le Béarnais	FF	Fra	964	Paul F. Foster	DD	USA
F 776	L'Alsacien	FF	Fra	965	Kincaid	DD	USA
F 777	Le Provencal	FF	Fra	966	Hewitt	DD	USA
F 778	Le Vendeen	FF	Fra	967	Elliott	DD	USA
F 781	D'Estienne D'Orves	FF	Fra	968	Arthur W. Radford	DD	USA
F 782	Amyot D'Inville	FF	Fra	969	Peterson	DD	USA
F 783	Drogou	FF	Fra	970	Caron	DD	USA
784	McKean	DD	USA	971	David R. Ray	DD	USA
F 784	Detroyat	FF	Fra	972	Oldendorf	DD	USA
785	Henderson	DD	USA	973	John Young	DD	USA
F 785	Jean Moulin	FF	Fra	974	Comte De Grasse	DD	USA
F 786	Quartier Maitre Anquetil	FF	Fra	975	O'Brien	DD	USA
F 787	Commandant De Pimodan	FF	Fra	976	Merrill	DD	USA
788	Hollister	DD	USA	977	Brisco	DD	USA
F 788	Seconde Maitre Le Bihan	FF	Fra	978	Stump	DD	USA
F 790	Lieutenant de Vaisseau Lavallée	FF	Fra	979	Connolly	DD	USA
				980	Moosburgger	DD	USA
F 792	Premier Maitre L'Her	FF	Fra	981	John Hancock	DD	USA
F 793	Commandant Blaison	FF	Fra	982	Nicholson	DD	USA
F 794	Enseigne de Vaisseau Jacoubet	FF	Fra	983	John Rogers	DD	USA
				984	Leftwich	DD	USA
801	Pattimura	FF	Indo	985	Cushing	DD	USA
F 801	Tromp	DDG	Nld	986	Harry W. Hill	DD	USA
802	Sultan Hasanudin	FF	Indo	987	O'Bannon	DD	USA
F 802	Van Speijk	FFGH	Nld	988	Thorn	DD	USA
F 803	Van Galen	FFGH	Nld	989	Deyo	DD	USA
F 804	Tjerk Hiddes	FFGH	Nld	990	Ingersoll	DD	USA
F 805	Van Nes	FFGH	Nld	991	Fife	DD	USA
806	Higbee	DD	USA	992	Fletcher	DD	USA
F 806	De Ruyter	DDG	Nld	1037	Bronstein	FF	USA
F 807	Kortenaer	FFGH	Nld	1038	McCloy	FF	USA
D 808	Holland	DDH	Nld	1040	Garcia	FF	USA
F 808	Callenburgh	FFGH	Nld	1041	Bradley	FF	USA
D 809	Zeeland	DDH	Nld	1043	Edward McDonnell	FF	USA
F 809	Van Kinsbergen	FFGH	Nld	1044	Brumby	FF	USA
D 812	Friesland	DD	Nld	1045	Davidson	FF	USA
D 813	Gröningen	DD	Nld	1047	Voge	FF	USA
D 814	Limburg	DD	Nld	1048	Sample	FF	USA
F 814	Isaac Sweers	FFGH	Nld	1049	Koelsch	FF	USA
D 815	Overijssel	DD	Nld	1050	Albert David	FF	USA
F 815	Evertsen	FFGH	Nld	1051	O'Callahan	FF	USA
D 816	Drenthe	DD	Nld	1052	Knox	FF	USA
817	Corry	DD	USA	1053	Roark	FF	USA
D 817	Utrecht	DD	Nld	1054	Gray	FF	USA
D 818	Rotterdam	DD	Nld	1055	Hepburn	FF	USA
D 819	Amsterdam	DD	Nld	1056	Connole	FF	USA
821	Johnston	DD	USA	1057	Rathburne	FF	USA
822	Robert H. McCard	DD	USA	1058	Meyerkord	FF	USA
822	Al Zaffer	DD	Egy	1059	W. S. Sims	FF	USA
825	Carpenter	DD	USA	1060	Lang	FF	USA
827	Robert A. Owens	DD	USA	1061	Patterson	FF	USA
829	Myles C. Fox	DD	USA	1062	Whipple	FF	USA
833	El Fateh	DD	Egy	1063	Reasoner	FF	USA
835	Charles P. Cecil	DD	USA	1064	Lockwood	FF	USA
842	Fiske	DD	USA	1065	Stein	FF	USA
844	Damiette	DD	Egy	1066	Marvin Shields	FF	USA
862	Vogelgesang	DD	USA	1067	Francis Hammond	FF	USA
863	Steinaker	DD	USA	1068	Vreeland	FF	USA
864	Harold J. Ellison	DD	USA	1069	Bagley	FF	USA
866	Cone	DD	USA	1070	Downes	FF	USA
871	Damato	DD	USA	1071	Badger	FF	USA
873	Hawkins	DD	USA	1072	Blakely	FF	USA
876	Rogers	DD	USA	1073	Robert E. Peary	FF	USA
880	Dyess	DD	USA	1074	Harold E. Holt	FF	USA
883	Newman K. Perry	DD	USA	1075	Trippe	FF	USA
885	John R. Craig	DD	USA	1076	Fanning	FF	USA

PENNANT LIST

Number	Ship's Name	Type	Country	Number	Ship's Name	Type	Country
1077	Ouellet	FF	USA	1178	Wood County	LST	USA
1078	Joseph Hewes	FF	USA	1179	Newport	LST	USA
1079	Bowen	FF	USA	1180	Manitowoc	LST	USA
1080	Paul	FF	USA	1181	Sumter	LST	USA
1081	Aylwin	FF	USA	1182	Fresno	LST	USA
1082	Elmer Montgomery	FF	USA	1183	Peoria	LST	USA
1083	Cook	FF	USA	1184	Frederick	LST	USA
1084	McCandless	FF	USA	1185	Schenectady	LST	USA
1085	Donald B. Beary	FF	USA	1186	Cayuga	LST	USA
1086	Brewton	FF	USA	1187	Tuscaloosa	LST	USA
1087	Kirk	FF	USA	1188	Saginaw	LST	USA
1088	Barbey	FF	USA	1189	San Bernardino	LST	USA
1089	Jesse L. Brown	FF	USA	1190	Boulder	LST	USA
1090	Ainsworth	FF	USA	1191	Racine	LST	USA
1091	Miller	FF	USA	1192	Spartanburg County	LST	USA
1092	Thomas S. Hart	FF	USA	1193	Fairfax County	LST	USA
1093	Capodanno	FF	USA	1194	La Moure County	LST	USA
1094	Pharris	FF	USA	1195	Barbour County	LST	USA
1095	Truett	FF	USA	1196	Harlan County	LST	USA
1096	Valdez	FF	USA	1197	Barnstable County	LST	USA
1097	Moinester	FF	USA	1198	Bristol County	LST	USA
1173	Suffolk County	LST	USA	3501	Katori	AGDE	Jap
1177	Lorain County	LST	USA	4201	Azuma	ATS	Jap

SHIP REFERENCE SECTION

ABU DHABI
(see United Arab Emirates)

ALBANIA

Ministerial

Minister of Defence:
Mehmet Shehu

Personnel

(a) 1979: Total 3 000 including 300 coastal frontier guards.
(b) Ratings on 3 years military service.

Bases

Durazzo (Durresi) and Valona (Vlora)

General

Since the break with USSR the remaining Soviet craft must have been decreasing in efficiency due to lack of spares. The transfer of Chinese craft since 1965 (including missile craft in 1976) has provided a small nucleus of new and effective vessels, although the current strained relations between the two countries may have affected the supply of spare parts. Future needs—probably submarines and MCM vessels.

Strength of the Fleet

Submarines	3
Large Patrol Craft	4
Fast Attack Craft (Missile)	4
Fast Attack Craft (Torpedo)	39
Fast Attack Craft (Gun)	6
Minesweepers—Ocean	2
Minesweepers—Inshore	6
MSB	11
Tankers	4
Small Auxiliaries	approx 20

Mercantile Marine

Lloyd's Register of Shipping:
20 vessels of 55 870 tons gross.

DELETIONS

Submarine

1976   1 "Whiskey" class

Light Forces

1976   6 "P 4" class
1977   2 "P 4" class

SUBMARINES

3 Ex-SOVIET "WHISKEY" CLASS

Displacement, tons: 1 030 surfaced; 1 350 dived
Length, feet (metres): 249.3 *(76)*
Beam, feet (metres): 20.6 *(6.3)*
Draught, feet (metres): 16.4 *(5.0)*
Torpedo tubes: 6—21 in (4 bow, 2 stern); 14 torpedoes or 40 mines
Main machinery: Diesels; 4 000 bhp; 2 shafts = 17 knots surfaced; electric motors; 2 500 hp = 15 knots dived
Range, miles: 13 000 at 8 knots surfaced
Complement: 60

Two of these are operational and one is now used as a harbour training boat. All are based at Vlora. Two were transferred from the USSR in 1960, and two others were reportedly seized from the USSR in mid-1961 upon the withdrawal of Soviet ships from their Albanian base. One deleted in 1976.

Radar: Snoop Plate.

"WHISKEY" Class

LIGHT FORCES

4 Ex-SOVIET "KRONSHTADT" CLASS (LARGE PATROL CRAFT)

150   151   340   341

Displacement, tons: 298 standard; 330 full load
Dimensions, feet (metres): 170.6 × 21.5 × 7.2 *(52.0 × 6.5 × 2.2)*
Guns: 1—3.5 in *(85 mm)*; 2—37 mm (single); 6—12.7 MG (3 vertical twin)
A/S weapons: 2 depth charge projectors; 2 DC rails; 2—5-tube rocket launchers
Main engines: 3 diesels; 3 shafts; 3 300 bhp = 21 knots
Range, miles: 1 500 at 12 knots
Complement: 50

Equipped for minelaying; two rails; about eight mines. Four were transferred from the USSR in 1958. Albania sent two for A/S updating in 1960 and two others in 1961.

Radar: Surface search: Ball Gun.
Navigation: Neptun.
IFF: High Pole.

"KRONSHTADT" Class

4 Ex-CHINESE "HOKU" CLASS (FAST ATTACK CRAFT—MISSILE)

Displacement, tons: 70 standard; 80 full load
Dimensions, feet (metres): 83.7 × 19.8 × 5 *(25.5 × 6 × 1.5)*
Missiles: 2 SSM SS-N-2, single launchers
Guns: 2—25 mm (twin, fwd)
Main engines: 2 diesels; 2 shafts; 4 800 bhp = 40 knots
Range, miles: 400 at 30 knots
Complement: 20

Transferred by China 1976-77. Steel hulls.

"KOMAR" Class ("HOKU" similar but with pole mast and launchers further inboard)   1970, USN

ALBANIA / Light forces — Tankers

35 Ex-CHINESE "HU CHWAN" CLASS
(FAST ATTACK HYDROFOIL—TORPEDO)

Displacement, tons: 45
Dimensions, feet (metres): 71 × 14·5 × 3·1 (21·8 × 4·5 × 0·9)
Guns: 2—14·5 mm (twin vertical)
Torpedo tubes: 2—21 in (533 mm)
Main engines: 3 M50 diesels; 3 shafts; 3 600 hp = 55 knots

Built in Shanghai and transferred as follows; six in 1968, fifteen in 1969, two in 1970, seven in 1971, two in June 1974 and three later.

Construction: Have foils forward while the stern planes on the surface.

Radar: Skin Head.

HU CHWAN   1972

6 Ex-CHINESE "SHANGHAI II" CLASS (FAST ATTACK CRAFT—GUN)

Displacement, tons: 120 standard; 155 full load
Dimensions, feet (metres): 128 × 18 × 5·6 (39 × 5·5 × 1·7)
Guns: 4—37 mm (twins); 4—25 mm (twins)
A/S armament: 8 DCs
Mines: Minerails can be fitted; probably only 10 mines
Main engines: 4 diesels; 4 800 bhp = 30 knots
Complement: 25

Four transferred in mid-1974 and two in 1975.

Radar: Pot Head.

"SHANGHAI II" Class

4 Ex-CHINESE "P 4" CLASS (FAST ATTACK CRAFT—TORPEDO)

111   115   304   +1

Displacement, tons: 22·4 full load
Dimensions, feet (metres): 63·3 × 12·1 × 3·3 (19·3 × 3·7 × 1·0)
Guns: (See notes)
Torpedo tubes: 2—18 in (450 mm)
Main engines: 2 M50 diesels; 2 shafts; 2 200 bhp = 55 knots
Range, miles: 400 at 30 knots
Complement: 12

Six were transferred from the USSR in 1956 (with radar and two-12·7 mm MG) and six from China, three in April 1965 and three in September 1965, without radar and with four—12·7 mm MG (2 twin). Radar now fitted. The ex-Soviet craft and two Chinese now believed deleted.

MINE WARFARE FORCES

2 Ex-SOVIET "T 43" CLASS (MINESWEEPERS—OCEAN)

152   342

Displacement, tons: 490 standard; 560 full load
Dimensions, feet (metres): 190·2 × 28·2 × 7·0 (58·0 × 8·6 × 2·3)
Guns: 4—37 mm (2 twin); 8—12·7 mm MG
A/S weapons: 2 DCT
Main engines: 2 Type 9D diesels; 2 shafts; 2 200 bhp = 14 knots
Range, miles: 3 000 at 10 knots
Complement: 40

Transferred in August 1960.

"T 43" Class

6 Ex-SOVIET "T 301" CLASS (MINESWEEPERS—INSHORE)

343   344   +4

Displacement, tons: 146 standard; 160 full load
Dimensions, feet (metres): 124·7 × 16·7 × 5·2 (38·0 × 5·1 × 1·6)
Guns: 2—37 mm; 4—12·7 mm (twins)
Main engines: 3 diesels; 3 shafts; 1 440 bhp = 9 knots
Range, miles: 2 200 at 9 knots
Complement: 25

Transferred from USSR—two in 1957, two in 1959 and two in 1960.

11 Ex-SOVIET "PO 2" CLASS (MSB)

Displacement, tons: 50 standard; 56 full load
Dimensions, feet (metres): 70·6 × 12·5 × 3·3 (21·6 × 3·8 × 1·0)
Gun: 1—12·7 mm MG
Main engine: Diesel; 1 shaft; 300 hp = 12 knots

There are reports of some 11 "PO 2" class in service and possibly three ex-Italian "MS 501" class. The "PO 2" class, though primarily minesweeping boats, are also general utility craft. They were transferred as follows: three in 1957, three in 1958-59, five in 1960.

TANKERS

2 Ex-SOVIET "KHOBI" CLASS (PETROL TANKERS)

PATOS   SEMANI

Displacement, tons: 800 light; 1 500 full load
Measurement, tons: 1 600 deadweight; 1 500 oil
Dimensions, feet (metres): 207·0 × 12·0 × 6·6 (63·0 × 3·8 × 2·0)
Main engines: 2 diesels; 1 600 bhp = 12·5 knots

Launched in 1956. Transferred from the USSR in September 1958 and February 1959. Semani may be ex-Soviet M/V Linda.

Radar: Neptun.

1 Ex-SOVIET "TOPLIVO 3" CLASS (YARD TANKER)

Displacement, tons: 425

Transferred from the USSR in 1960. Generally similar to "Toplivo 1" class.

1 Ex-SOVIET "TOPLIVO 1" CLASS (YARD TANKER)

Displacement, tons: 425
Dimensions, feet (metres): 115 × 22 × 9·6 (34·5 × 6·5 × 3)
Main engine: 1 diesel; 1 shaft = 10 knots
Range, miles: 400 at 7 knots
Complement: 16

Transferred from the USSR in March 1960. Similar to "Khobi" class in appearance though smaller. Oil fuel capacity about 200 tons.

ALBANIA / Tugs — ALGERIA / Light forces

TUGS

Four or more small tugs are employed in local duties or harbour service.

AUXILIARIES

1 Ex-SOVIET "SEKSTAN" CLASS (DEGAUSSING SHIP)

354

Dimensions, feet (metres): 134·0 × 31·2 × 14·0 *(40·8 × 9·5 × 4·3)*
Main engines: Diesels; 400 bhp = 10 knots
Complement: 35

Built in Finland in 1956. Transferred from the USSR in 1960.

2 Ex-SOVIET "POLUCHAT 1" CLASS

SKENDERBEU A641   +1

Displacement, tons: 81 standard; 91 full load
Dimensions, feet (metres): 96·8 × 19·0 × 5·2 *(29·5 × 5·8 × 1·6)*
Guns: 2—14·5 mm
Main engines: 2 M50 diesels; 2 shafts; 2 400 bhp = 18 knots
Range, miles: 460 at 17 knots
Complement: 16

Probably used for torpedo recovery. Transferred in 1958.

2 Ex-SOVIET "NYRYAT" CLASS (DIVING TENDERS)

Displacement, tons: 145
Dimensions, feet (metres): 93 × 18·0 × 5·5 *(28·4 × 5·5 × 1·7)*
Main engine: Diesel; 1 shaft; 450 hp = 12·5 knots
Range, miles: 1 500 at 10 knots
Complement: 15

Built about 1955.

Note: There are reported to be a dozen or so harbour and port tenders including a water carrier and two small transports. The "Atrek" class submarine tender transferred from USSR in 1961 as a depot ship was converted into a merchant ship. With large lakes on both the Yugoslav and Greek borders a number of small patrol craft is stationed on these lakes.

ALGERIA

Ministerial

Minister of Defence:

General

Although up to now Algeria has relied on Soviet support, which is still continuing, the Italian order with Baglietto suggests a diversification which could be important with her patrol and fast attack craft and her minesweepers reaching well into the second half of their lives.

Personnel

(a) 1979: Total 3 800 (300 officers and cadets and 3 500 men)
(b) Voluntary service

Bases

Algiers, Annaba, Mers el Kebir

Mercantile Marine

Lloyd's Register of Shipping:
121 vessels of 1 152 086 tons gross

Strength of the Fleet

Large Patrol Craft	6
Fast Attack Craft (Missile)	17
Fast Attack Craft (Torpedo)	4
Minesweepers—Ocean	2
LCT	1
Miscellaneous	7
Coast Guard	20

Aircraft

12 Fokker F27 are operated by the Algerian Air Force (AAF) in a maritime role.

Deletions

1975   2 "P6" Class
1976   *Sidi Fradj* (training ship)

LIGHT FORCES

6 Ex-SOVIET "SO I" CLASS (LARGE PATROL CRAFT)

P651-656

Displacement, tons: 190 light; 215 full load
Dimensions, feet (metres): 137·8 × 20·0 × 5·9 *(42·0 × 6·1 × 1·8)*
Guns: 4—25 mm (2 twin mounts)
Torpedo tubes: 2—21 in *(533 mm)* (in three craft)
A/S weapons: 4 MBU 1800 rocket launchers
Main engines: 3 diesels; 7 500 bhp = 28 knots
Range, miles: 1 100 at 13 knots
Complement: 31

Delivered by USSR between October 1965 and 8 October 1967. The torpedo tubes used were removed from P6 Fast Attack Craft. Can lay 20 mines.

"SO I" Class

8 Ex-SOVIET "OSA II" AND 3 "OSA I" CLASS (FAST ATTACK CRAFT—MISSILE)

R167   R267   R367   +8

Displacement, tons: 165 standard; 200 full load
Dimensions, feet (metres): 128·7 × 25·1 × 5·9 *(39·3 × 7·7 × 1·8)*
Missiles: SSM—4 SS-N-2 (single launchers)
Guns: 4—30 mm (2 twin)
Main engines: 3 M503 diesels; 12 000, (Osa I) 15 000, (Osa II) bhp = 36 knots
Range, miles: 800 at 25 knots
Complement: 30

One Osa I was delivered by USSR on 7 October 1967. Two others transferred later in same year. Osa IIs transferred 1976-77 (3) and 1978 (5).
All to be re-engined with MTU diesels.

"OSA I" Class

6 Ex-SOVIET "KOMAR" CLASS (FAST ATTACK CRAFT—MISSILE)

671-676

Displacement, tons: 68 standard; 81 full load
Dimensions, feet (metres): 84·2 × 21·1 × 5·0 *(25·7 × 6·4 × 1·5)*
Missiles: SSM—2 SS-N-2 (single launchers)
Guns: 2—25 mm (twin)
Main engines: 4 diesels, 4 shafts, 4 800 bhp = 40 knots
Range, miles: 400 at 30 knots
Complement: 19

Acquired in 1966 from USSR. To be re-engined with MTU diesels.

4 Ex-SOVIET "P6" CLASS (FAST ATTACK CRAFT—TORPEDO)

631-634

Displacement, tons: 66 standard; 75 full load
Dimensions, feet (metres): 84·2 × 20·0 × 5·0 *(25·7 × 6·1 × 1·5)*
Guns: 4—25 mm (twins)
Torpedo tubes: 2—21 in (or mines or depth charges) (see notes)
Main engines: 4 diesels, 4 shafts, 4 800 bhp = 43 knots
Range, miles: 450 at 30 knots
Complement: 20

Acquired from the USSR between 1963 and 1968. Four of the original twelve retain their original armament whilst two, with tubes removed, are used for coast guard duties. Two others have been disarmed and are used for training while the last two are hulks. Two deleted 1975.

AMPHIBIOUS FORCES

1 Ex-SOVIET "POLNOCHNIY" CLASS (LCT)

Displacement, tons: 870 standard; 1 000 full load
Dimensions, feet (metres): 239·4 × 29·5 × 9·8 *(75 × 9 × 3)*
Guns: 2—30 mm
Main engines: 2 diesels; 5 000 bhp = 18 knots
Complement: 40

Transferred in August 1976.

"POLNOCHNIY" Class

MINE WARFARE FORCES

2 Ex-SOVIET "T 43" CLASS (MINESWEEPERS—OCEAN)

M221 M222

Displacement, tons: 490 standard; 560 full load
Dimensions, feet (metres): 190·2 × 28·2 × 6·9 *(58·0 × 8·6 × 2·1)*
Guns: 4—37 mm (twins); 8—12·7 mm (twins)
A/S weapons: 2 DCT
Main engines: 2 Type 9D diesels; 2 shafts; 2 200 bhp = 14 knots
Range, miles: 3 000 at 10 knots
Complement: 40

Transferred in 1968. M221 in reserve since 1974.

MISCELLANEOUS

1 Ex-SOVIET "POLUCHAT" CLASS

A641

Operates as TRV.

2 Ex-SOVIET "P6" CLASS

Used for training. Disarmed. See previous page.

1 Ex-SOVIET "SEKSTAN" CLASS

VASOUYA A640

Transferred in 1964. Was used as survey ship. Now probably a hulk.

1 Ex-SOVIET "NYRYAT" CLASS

YAVDEZAN VP650

Displacement, tons: 145
Dimensions, feet (metres): 93 × 18 × 5·5 *(28·4 × 5·5 × 1·7)*
Main engine: Diesel; 1 shaft; 450 hp = 12·5 knots
Range, miles: 1 500 at 10 knots
Complement: 15

Transferred in 1965. Used as diving tender.

6 FISHERY PROTECTION CRAFT

JEBEL ANTAR   JEBEL HONDA   +4

COAST GUARD

2 Ex-SOVIET "P6" CLASS

Torpedo Tubes removed. See previous page for details.

6 BAGLIETTO "TYPE GEMINI 36"

OMBRINE GC 223   REQUIN GC 331   MARSOUIN GC 333
DORADE GC 224   ESPADON GC 332   MURÈNE GC 334

Displacement, tons: 174
Dimensions, feet (metres): 118·7 × 22·9 × 10·2 *(36·2 × 7 × 3·1)*
Guns: Can carry 40 mm Breda Bofors
Main engines: 2 MTU diesels; 9 000 shp = 37 knots
Range, miles: 500 cruising
Complement: 14

First delivered early 1977 by Baglietto, Varazze, Italy.

10 BAGLIETTO TYPE 20 GC

GC 100   GC 113   GC 221   GC 235   GC 237
GC 112   GC 114   GC 222   GC 236   GC 325

Displacement, tons: 44 full load
Dimensions, feet (metres): 66·9 × 17·1 × 5·5 *(20·4 × 5·2 × 1·7)*
Gun: 1—20 mm
Main engines: 2 CRM 18DS diesels; 2 660 bhp = 35 knots
Range, miles: 245 at 20 knots
Complement: 11

The first pair delivered by Baglietto, Varazze in August 1976 and the remainder in pairs at two monthly intervals. Fitted with three radar sets.

Baglietto GC craft   1978, Baglietto

ANGOLA

Ministerial

Minister of Defence:
  Major Enrique Carreira

Senior Officer
Commander of the Navy:
  Commandant Fnu Ervedoso

General

A number of Portuguese ships were transferred at independence in 1975, and it is reported that these have been reinforced by ex-Soviet landing craft and ships taken up from trade. Angolan names are not known—the details given are in all cases Portuguese. In the confused state of affairs existing in Angola it is impossible to assess the availability of the craft listed.
There is a critical shortage of trained personnel. There are minor repair facilities at Luanda and Lobito—maintenance depends largely on Soviet and Cuban technicians.

Personnel

(a) 1979: 1 500
(b) Voluntary service

Training

A certain amount of training was carried out by the Portuguese before independence. At present some officers are trained in the USSR, a small Portuguese team remains, and a Nigerian team is co-operating with Cuban and Soviet advisers.

Ports and Bases

Luanda, Lobito, Moçamedes. (A number of other good harbours is available on the 1 000 mile coastline.) Naval HQ at Luanda on Ila de Luanda which is being fortified.

Strength of the Fleet

Fast Attack Craft (Torpedo)	1
Large Patrol Craft	5
Coastal Patrol Craft	7
LCTs	2
LCUs etc	5 + ?9
Auxiliaries	?8

Mercantile Marine

Lloyd's Register of Shipping:
  21 vessels of 21 820 tons gross.

LIGHT FORCES

1 Ex-SOVIET "SHERSHEN" CLASS (FAST ATTACK CRAFT—TORPEDO)

Displacement, tons: 150 standard; 160 full load
Dimensions, feet (metres): 115·5 × 23·1 × 5·0 *(35·2 × 7 × 1·5)*
Guns: 4—30 mm (2 twin)
Torpedo Tubes: 4—21 in (single)
A/S weapons: 12 DC
Main engines: 3 diesels; 3 shafts; 12 000 bhp = 38 knots
Complement: 35

Built in late 1960s. Reported as transferred December 1977, possibly with more to follow.

Radar: Search: Pot Drum.
Fire control: Drum Tilt.
IFF: High Pole and Square Head.

"SHERSHEN" Class   1977

5 Ex-PORTUGUESE "ARGOS" CLASS (LARGE PATROL CRAFT)

Name	No.	Builders	Commissioned (Portugal)
Ex-**LIRA**	P 361	Estaleiros Navais de Viano do Castelo	1963
Ex-**ORION**	P 362	Estaleiros Navais de Viano do Castelo	1964
Ex-**ESCORPIAO**	P 375	Arsenal do Alfeite, Lisbon	1964
Ex-**PEGASO**	P 379	Estaleiros Navais de Viano do Castelo	1963
Ex-**CENTAURO**	P1130	Arsenal do Alfeite, Lisbon	1965

Displacement, tons: 180 standard; 210 full load
Dimensions, feet (metres): 136·8 × 20·5 × 7 *(41·6 × 6·2 × 2·2)*
Guns: 2—40 mm
Main engines: 2 Maybach (MTU) diesels; 1 200 bhp = 17 knots
Oil fuel, tons: 16
Complement: 24 (2 officers, 22 men)

"ARGOS" Class   *Portuguese Navy*

Argos and *Dragao* of same class transferred, reportedly, for spares.

1 + ? Ex-SOVIET "ZHUK" CLASS (COASTAL PATROL CRAFT)

Displacement, tons: 50 standard; 60 full load
Dimensions, feet (metres): 85·3 × 16 × 5 *(26 × 4·9 × 1·5)*
Guns: 4—14·5 mm (twin)
Main engines: 2 M50 diesels; 2 shafts; 2 400 hp = 30 knots
Complement: 18 (?)

First transferred February 1977.

"ZHUK" Class (on transport)

1 Ex-PORTUGUESE "JUPITER" CLASS (COASTAL PATROL CRAFT)

Name	No.	Builders	Commissioned (Portugal)
Ex-**JUPITER**	P 1132	Estaleiros Navais do Mondego	1964
Ex-**VENUS**	P 1133	Estaleiros Navais do Mondego	1965

Displacement, tons: 32 standard; 43·5 full load
Dimensions, feet (metres): 69 × 16·5 × 4·3 *(21 × 5 × 1·3)*
Gun: 1—20 mm Oerlikon
Main engines: 2 Cummins diesels; 1 270 bhp = 20 knots
Complement: 8

Existence of Ex-*Jupiter* doubtful—probably cannibalized.

Ex-JUPITER *Portuguese Navy*

5 Ex-PORTUGUESE "BELLATRIX" CLASS (COASTAL PATROL CRAFT)

Name	No.	Builders	Commissioned (Portugal)
Ex-**ESPIGA**	P 366	Beyerische Schiffbaugesellschaft	1961
Ex-**FOMALHAUT**	P 367	Beyerische Schiffbaugesellschaft	1961
Ex-**POLLUX**	P 368	Beyerische Schiffbaugesellschaft	1961
Ex-**ALTAIR**	P 377	Beyerische Schiffbaugesellschaft	1962
Ex-**RIGEL**	P 378	Beyerische Schiffbaugesellschaft	1962

Displacement, tons: 23 standard; 27·6 full load
Dimensions, feet (metres): 68 × 16·2 × 4 *(20·7 × 5·1 × 1·2)*
Gun: 1—20 mm Oerlikon
Main engines: 2 Cummins diesels; 470 bhp = 15 knots
Complement: 7 (1 officer, 6 men)

"BELLATRIX" Class *Portuguese Navy*

AMPHIBIOUS FORCES

Note: In addition to those below five ex-Soviet "T-4" class LCMs reported transferred in 1976 and up to nine ex-Portuguese LCMs and LCVPs reported although these may be in a poor state.

1 Ex-SOVIET "POLNOCHNIY" CLASS (LCT)

One reported as transferred November 1977—Type unknown although probably Type I. See USSR section for details.

1 Ex-PORTUGUESE "ALFANGE" CLASS (LCT)

Name	No.	Builders	Commissioned (Portugal)
Ex-**ALFANGE**	LDG 101	Estaleiros Navais do Mondego	1965

Displacement, tons: 500
Dimensions, feet (metres): 187 × 39 × 6·2 *(57 × 12 × 1·9)*
Main engines: 2 diesels; 1 000 bhp = 11 knots
Complement: 20

Ex-ALFANGE *Portuguese Navy*

MISCELLANEOUS

Also reported that up to eight merchant ships have been acquired from local shipping.

ANGUILLA

General

Since 1971 Anguilla has been administered by a British Commissioner separately from the Associated State of St Christopher—Nevis—Anguilla and since 1976 has had its own separate constitution like a British dependent territory.

Mercantile Marine

Lloyd's Register of Shipping:
 1 vessel of 399 tons gross.

1 FAIREY MARINE "HUNTSMAN" CLASS

LAPWING

A 28 ft launch supplied in 1974. She is unarmed and used for fishery protection, anti-smuggling operations, police work and for Air-Sea Rescue.

ARGENTINA

Headquarters Appointments

Commander of the Navy and Chief of Naval Operations:
  Rear-Admiral E. E. Massera
Chief of Naval Staff:
  Rear-Admiral A. Lambruschini

Diplomatic Representation

Head of Argentine Naval Mission Asunción, Paraguay:
  Captain Federico L. A. Roussillion
Naval Attaché in Asuncion, Paraguay:
  Captain Juan Alberto Iglesias
Naval Attaché in Bogota:
  Captain Jose Antonio Morales
Naval Attaché in Brasilia:
  Captain Jose Julio Sarcona
Naval Attaché in Cape Town:
  Captain Enrique A. Garret
Naval Attaché in Caracas:
  Captain Norman Rubi Azcoitia
Naval Attaché in La Paz:
  Captain Jose Atilio Stortini
Head of Naval Mission, La Paz:
  Captain Guillermo M. Obiglio
Naval Attaché in London and The Hague and Head of the Argentine Naval Mission in Europe:
  Vice-Admiral Horacio Gonzalez Llanos
Naval Attaché in Lima:
  Captain Francisco Guillermo Cobos
Naval Attaché in Madrid:
  Captain Osvaldo Ruben Casal
Naval Attaché in Montevideo:
  Captain Alberto Jose Valdez
Naval Attaché in Paris:
  Captain Eduardo M. Girling
Naval Attaché in Quito:
  Captain Ernesto M. Lopez Fabre
Naval Attaché in Rome:
  Captain Carlos Emilli Barilli
Naval Attaché in Santiago:
  Captain Jorge C. G. Vallarino
Naval Attaché in Tokyo:
  Captain Enrique F. Piattini
Naval Attaché in Washington:
  Rear-Admiral Juan Jose Lombardo

Personnel

(a) 1979: 32 900 (2 890 officers, 18 010 petty officers and ratings and 12 000 conscripts)
   Marine Corps: 6 000 officers and men
(b) Volunteers plus 14 months national service

Note: Cuerpo de Infanteria de Marina (Marine Corps)
1st Marine Force: 2 Infantry Battalions
1st Marine Brigade: 2 Infantry Battalions; 1 Field Artillery Battalion; 1 Service Battalion; 1 Command Battalion.
Amphibious Support Force: 1 Air Defence Battalion; 1 Communications Battalion; Amphibious craft units.
Based at or near naval bases and installations. Equipped with 20 LVTP-7, 15 LARC-5, 10 "Tigercat" SAM, 105 mm how., "Bantam" A-T missiles, 88 mm AA guns, 106 and 120 mm mortars, 75 mm and 105 mm recoilless rifles.

Naval Bases

Buenos Aires (Darsena Norte): Dockyard, 2 Dry Docks, 3 Floating Docks, 1 Floating Crane, Schools.
Rio Santiago (La Plata): Naval Base, Schools, Naval shipbuilding yard (AFNE), New dockyard, 1 Slipway, 1 Floating Crane.
Mar de Plata: Submarine base with slipway, 1 Floating Crane.
Puerto Belgrano: Main Naval Base, Schools, 2 Dry Docks, 1 Floating Dock, 1 Floating Crane.
Ushaia: Small naval base.

Naval Aviation

14 A-4Q Skyhawk*
12 Aermacchi MB 326 GB
10 S-2A/S-2E Tracker*
 8 SP-SE/P-2H Neptune
 9 Alouette III Helicopter*
 6 Bell 47 (Sioux) (2 with PNA)*
 6 Hughes 500M (Cayuse) (PNA)*
 4 Sikorsky S-61D (Sea King)*
 2 Sikorsky S-61 NR*
 3 Sea Lynx*
 3 Fokker F28-3000
 8 C-47 Dakota/Skytrain
 1 FMA IA 50 GII
 1 HS 125 Srs. 400A
 3 Lockheed L-188 Electra
 5 Short Skyvan (PNA)
30 T-28 Fennec
 1 DHC-6 Twin Otter
 8 Beech Super King Air 200
 5 Beech B80 Queen Air
15 Beech T-34 C-1
 3 Fairchild-Hiller Porter
*Ship-based.

Naval Air Bases

Punta Indio, Puerto Belgrano, Commandante Espora, Ezeiza (Buenos Aires), Trelew, Ushuaia.

Missiles

Argentina has acquired a number of Exocet missiles now fitted in "Allen M. Sumner" and "Gearing" classes.

General

With their one carrier over 30 years old, both cruisers of pre-war vintage, eight destroyers with a hull life of 32 or years more and all their corvettes over 30 years old, the reported frigate programme presents no surprise. The production of more submarines, a new Harrier-Carrier programme and a new class of offshore patrol craft would seem sensible additions to the new construction plans.
Plans exist for 30 to 40 new ships and craft including six patrol craft. Five corvettes of 900 tons and three Large Patrol Craft of 130 tons ordered from Bazán. Cost $60 million.

Prefectura Naval Argentina (PNA)

PNA is responsible for coast Guard and rescue duties. It also administers the Merchant Navy School at Buenos Aires.

Prefix to Ships' Names

ARA

Strength of the Fleet

Type	Active	Building
Patrol Submarines	4	1 (3)
Attack Carrier (Medium)	1	—
Cruisers	2	—
Destroyers	8	1 (6)
Frigates	2	(6)
Patrol Ships	10	—
Landing Ships (Tank)	5	—
Landing Craft (Tank)	1	—
Minor Landing Craft	23	—
Fast Attack Craft (Gun)	2	—
Fast Attack Craft (Torpedo)	2	—
Large Patrol Craft	8*	—
Minesweepers (Coastal)	4	—
Minehunters	2	—
Survey/Oceanographic Ships	7	—
Survey Launches	2	—
Transports	4	1
Tankers (Fleet Support)	3	—
Icebreaker	2	—
Training Ship	1	—
Tugs	16	—
Floating Docks	4	—

*In addition the PNA operates another 28 patrol craft.

Mercantile Marine

Lloyd's Register of Shipping:
  432 vessels of 2 000 879 tons gross.

DELETIONS

Submarines

1972 *Santa Fe (ex-Lamprey) Santiago del Estero (ex-Macabi)*, scrapped for spares

Cruiser

1973 *La Argentina*

Destroyers

1973 *Entre Rios, San Juan, Santa Cruz*
1977 *Espora*
1977 *Almirante Brown*

Frigates

1973 *Juan B Azopardo* (**PNA**), *Piedrabuena, Azopardo*

Corvette

1976 *Commandante General Zapiola* grounded and lost (Nov)

Amphibious Forces

1971 *BDI 1, BDI 15, BDM 1, Cabo San Bartolome*
1973 *EDVP 4, 5, 6, 11, 20, 22, 27*
1978 *Cabo San Isidro*

Survey Ships

1972 *Capitan Canepa* (scrap)
1973 *Ushuia* sunk in collision

Transports

1973 *Bahia Thetis*
1975 *San Julian*

Salvage Ship

1974 *Guardiamarina Zicari*

Tug

1974 *Mataco*

PENNANT LIST

Submarines

S21	Santa Fe
S22	Santiago del Estero
S31	Salta
S32	San Luis

Aircraft Carrier

V2	Veinticinco de Mayo

Cruisers

C4	Belgrano
C5	Nueve de Julio

Destroyers

D1	Hercules
D2	Santisima Trinidad
D22	Rosales
D23	Almirante Domecq Garcia
D24	Almirante Storni
D25	Segui
D26	Bouchard
D27	Comodoro Py
D29	Piedra Buena

Patrol Ships

A1	Com. G. Irigoyen
A3	Francisco de Gurruchaga
A4	Thompson
A5	Diaguita
A6	Yamana
A7	Chiriguano
A8	Sanavirón
A9	Alferez Sobral
A10	Comodoro Somellera
GC12	Spiro
P20	Murature
P21	King

Amphibious Forces

Q42	Cabo San Antonio
Q43	Candido De Lasala
Q44	Cabo San Gonzalo
Q50	Cabo San Pio
Q53	Cabo San Vicente
Q57	BDI 4

Light Forces

ELPR1	Intrepida
ELPR2	Indomita
GC13	Delfin
GC21	Lynch
GC22	Toll
GC23	Erezcano
GC31	—
GC46	Pacu
GC47	Tonini
P55	Surubi
P82	Alakush
P84	Towara

Mine Warfare Forces

M1	Neuquen
M2	Rio Negro
M3	Chubut
M4	Tierra del Fuego
M5	Chaco
M6	Formosa

Miscellaneous

A7	Chiriguano
A8	Sanaviron
B2	Bahia Aguirre
B6	Bahia Buen Suceso
B12	Punta Alta
B16	Punta Delgada
B18	Punta Médanos
Q2	Libertad
Q4	General San Martin
Q5	Almirante Irizar
Q7	El Austral
Q9	Islas Orcadas
Q11	Comodoro Rivadavia
Q15	Cormoran
Q17	Goyena
Q—	Puerto Deseado
Q—	Alvaro Alberto
R3	Mataco
R4	Toba
R5	Mocovi
R6	Calchaqui
R10	Chulupi
R12	Huarpe
R16	Capayan
R18	Chiquillan
R19	Morcoyan
R29	Pehuenche
R30	Tonocote
R32	Quilmes
R33	Guaycuru

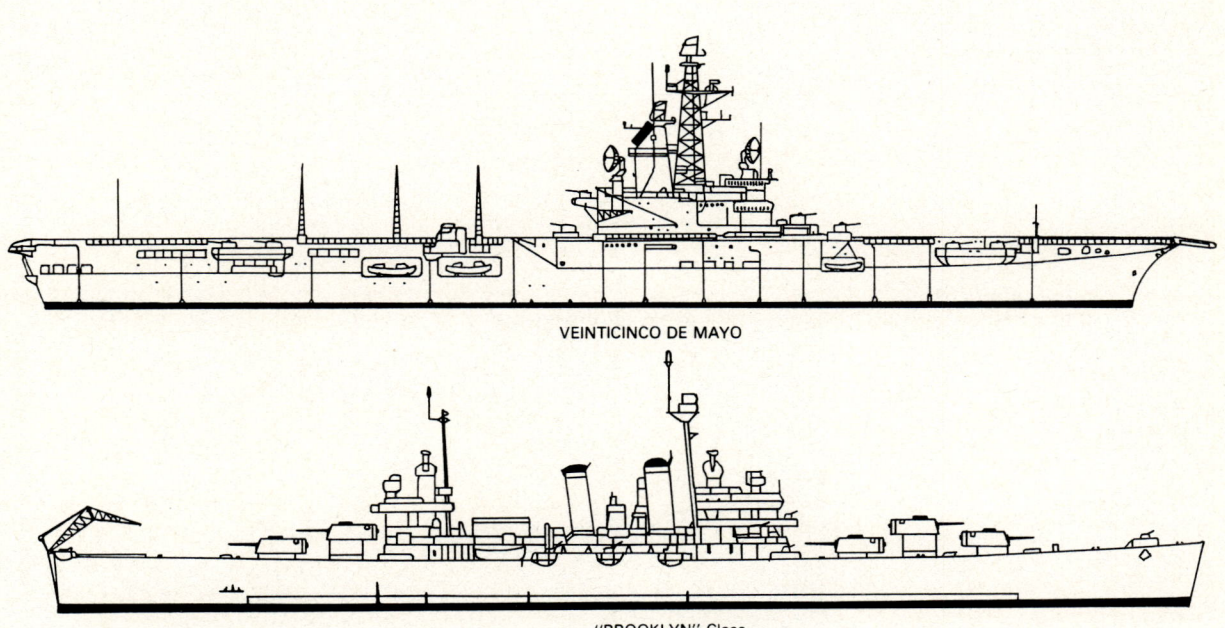

VEINTICINCO DE MAYO

"BROOKLYN" Class

ARGENTINA / Submarines — Aircraft carrier

SUBMARINES

0 +4 NORDSEEWERKE TYPE

Displacement, tons: 1 700

Contract signed 30 November 1977 for one submarine to be built at Emden with parts and overseeing for three more boats to be built in Argentina by Tandanor, Buenos Aires. The Government of the FDR has financially guaranteed the project.

2 "SALTA" CLASS (TYPE 209)

Name	No.	Builders	Laid down	Launched	Commissioned
SALTA	S 31	Howaldtswerke, Kiel	—	22 Nov 1972	7 Mar 1974
SAN LUIS	S 32	Howaldtswerke, Kiel	—	2 May 1973	24 May 1974

Displacement, tons: 1 180 surfaced; 1 285 dived
Length, feet (metres): 183·4 (55·9)
Beam, feet (metres): 20·5 (6·25)
Draught, feet (metres): 17·9 (5·5)
Torpedo tubes: 8—21 in; bow tubes (with reloads)
Main machinery: Diesel-electric; MTU diesels, 4 generators; 1 shaft; 5 000 hp
Speed knots: 10 surfaced, 22 dived
Complement: 32

Built in sections by Howaldtswerke Deutsche Werft AG, Kiel from the IK 68 design of Ingenieurkontor, Lübeck. Sections were shipped to Argentina for assembly at Tandanor, Buenos Aires.

SALTA 1973, Argentine Navy

2 "GUPPY (IA and II)" CLASS

Name	No.	Builders	Laid down	Launched	Commissioned
SANTE FE (ex-USS *Catfish* SS 339)	S 21	Electric Boat Co	6 Jan 1944	19 Nov 1944	19 Mar 1945
SANTIAGO DEL ESTERO (ex-USS *Chivo* SS 341)	S 22	Electric Boat Co	21 Feb 1944	14 Jan 1945	28 Apr 1945

Displacement, tons: 1 870 surfaced; 2 420 (Santa Fe); 2 540 (Santiago) dived
Length, feet (metres): 307·5 (93·7)
Beam, feet (metres): 27·2 (8·3)
Draught, feet (metres): 18·0 (5·5) (Santa Fe); 17·0 (5·2) (Santiago)
Torpedo tubes: 10—21 in (533 mm); 6 fwd, 4 aft
Main machinery: 3 diesels; 4 800 shp; 2 electric motors; 5 400 shp; 2 shafts
Speed, knots: 18 surfaced; 15 dived
Oil fuel, tons: 300
Range, miles: 12 000 at 10 knots
Complement: 82-84

Both of the "Balao" class. *Catfish* was modified under the Guppy II programme (1948-50) and *Chivo* under the Guppy 1A programme (1951). Both transferred to Argentina at Mare Island on 7 January 1971 by sale.

SANTIAGO DEL ESTERO 1978, Argentine Navy

AIRCRAFT CARRIER

1 Ex-BRITISH "COLOSSUS" CLASS

Name	No.	Builders	Laid down	Launched	Commissioned
VEINTICINCO DE MAYO (ex-HNMS *Karel Doorman*, ex-HMS *Venerable*)	V 2	Cammell Laird & Co Ltd, Birkenhead	3 Dec 1942	30 Dec 1943	17 Jan 1945

Displacement, tons: 15 892 standard; 19 896 full load
Length, feet (metres): 630 (192·0) pp; 693·2 (211·3) oa
Beam, feet (metres): 80 (24·4)
Draught, feet (metres): 25 (7·6)
Width, feet (metres): 138·4 (42·2) oa
Hangar:
  Length, feet (metres): 455 (138·7)
  Width, feet (metres): 52 (15·8)
  Height, feet (metres): 17·5 (5·3)
Aircraft: Operates with variable complement of 10 S-2A Trackers, up to 14 A-4Q Skyhawks, S-61D Sea King ASW helicopters and A103 Alouette helicopters
Guns: 10—40 mm/70 (single Bofors L90)
Main engines: Parsons geared turbines; 40 000 shp; 2 shafts
Boilers: Four 3-drum; working pressure 400 psi (28·1 kg/cm²); Superheat 700°F (371°C)
Speed, knots: 24·25
Oil fuel, tons: 3 200
Range, miles: 12 000 at 14 knots, 6 200 at 23 knots
Complement: 1 000

Purchased from the UK on 1 April 1948 and commissioned in the Royal Netherlands Navy on 28 May 1948. Damaged by boiler fire on 29 April 1968. Sold to Argentina on 15 October 1968 and refitted at Rotterdam by N. V. Dok en Werf Mij Wilton Fijenoord. Commissioned in the Argentine Navy on 12 March 1969. Completed refit on 22 August 1969 and sailed for Argentina on 1 September 1969. With modified island superstructure and bridge lattice tripod radar mast, and tall raked funnel, she differs considerably from her former appearance and from her original sister ships in the British, Australian, Brazilian and Indian navies.

Electronics: Fitted with Ferranti CAAIS with Plessey SuperCAAIS displays. The system has been modified to provide control of carrier based aircraft and will be capable of direct computer-to-computer radio data links with the new Type 42 destroyers.

Engineering: The turbine sets and boilers are arranged en echelon, the two propelling-machinery spaces having two boilers and one set of turbines in each space, on the unit system. She was reboilered in 1965-1966 with boilers removed from HMS *Leviathan*. During refit for Argentina in 1968-1969 she received new turbines, also from HMS *Leviathan*.

VEINTICINCO DE MAYO 1978, Dr. Robert Scheina

Radar: Air surveillance: One LW-01, one LW-02.
Height finders: Two VI.
Target indicator and tactical: One DA-02.
Surface warning and navigation: One ZW-01.

Reconstruction: Underwent extensive refit modernisation in 1955-1958 including angled flight deck and steam catapult, rebuilt island, mirror sight landing system, and new anti-aircraft battery of ten 40 mm guns, at the Wilton-Fijenoord Shipyard, at a cost of 25 million guilders. Conversion completed in July 1958.

ARGENTINA / Cruisers — Destroyers 27

CRUISERS

2 Ex-US "BROOKLYN" CLASS

Name	No.	Builders	Laid down	Launched	Commissioned
GENERAL BELGRANO (ex-*17 de Octubre*, ex-*Phoenix*, CL 46)	C 4	New York S.B. Corporation, Camden	15 Apr 1935	12 Mar 1938	18 Mar 1939
NUEVE DE JULIO (ex-*Boise*, CL 47)	C 5	Newport News S.B. & D.D. Co	1 Apr 1935	3 Dec 1936	1 Feb 1939

Displacement, tons: *Gen. Belgrano:* 10 800 standard; 13 645 full load. *Nueve de Julio:* 10 500 standard; 13 645 full load
Length, feet (metres): 608·3 *(185·4)*
Beam, feet (metres): 69 *(21·0)*
Draught, feet (metres): 24 *(7·3)*
Aircraft: 2 helicopters
Missiles: Estimated 70 SAM Seacat—2 quad launchers
Guns: *Gen. Belgrano:* 15—6 in *(153 mm)* 47 cal; 8—5 in *(127 mm)* 25 cal; 2 twin—40 mm; 4—47 mm (saluting)
Nueve de Julio: 15—6 *(153 mm)* 47 cal; 6—5 in *(127 mm)* 25 cal; 4 twin—40 mm; 4—47 mm (saluting)
Armour:
  Belt 4 in—1½ in *(102–38 mm)*
  Decks 3 in—2 in *(76–51 mm)*
  Turrets 5 in—3 in *(127–76 mm)*
  Conning Tower 8 in *(203 mm)*
Main engines: Parsons geared turbines; 100 000 shp; 4 shafts
Boilers: 8 Babcock & Wilcox Express type
Speed, knots: 32·5 (when new)
Range, miles: 7 600 at 15 knots
Oil fuel, tons: 2 200
Complement: 1 000

GENERAL BELGRANO 1978, Argentine Navy

Superstructure was reduced, bulges added, beam increased, and mainmast derricks and catapults removed before transfer. Purchased from the USA in 1951 at a cost of $7·8 million and transferred to the Argentine Navy on 12 April 1951. *General Belgrano* was commissioned under the name *17 de Octubre* at Philadelphia on 17 October 1951. *9 de Julio* was commissioned into the Argentine Navy at Philadelphia on 11 March 1952. *9 de Julio* refers to 9 July 1816, when the Argentine provinces signed the Declaration of Independence. *17 de Octubre* was renamed *General Belgrano* in 1956 following the overthrow of President Peron the year before.

Gunnery: FCS 33 (2) (1 in *Belgrano*), FCS 34 (1), FCS 57 (2), FCS 63 (2), FCS NA9-D1 (1 in *Belgrano*), TDS (1)

Hangar: The hangar in the hull right aft accommodates two helicopters together with engine spares and duplicate parts, though four aircraft was the original complement.

Radar: Search: LWO and DA Series (Signaal).

DESTROYERS

0 + 2 + 4 MEKO 360 TYPE

Displacement, tons: 3 600
Dimensions, feet (metres): 400·3 × 47·9 × 19·3 *(122·0 × 14·6 × 4·4)*
Main engines: 2 Gas turbines; 2 diesels
Speed, knots: 30
Range, miles: 6 500 at economical speed
Complement: 200

On 11 December 1978 the Argentine Navy signed an agreement with Thyssen Rheinstahl/Blohm and Voss for two of this class to be built in Germany and four more at AFNE, Rio Santiago. The first ship is to be delivered in 38 months.

Armament: These ships are of modular construction and can carry a variety of armament. Common features of all variants include eight SSMs, SAM system, helicopter capability, two guns (76 or 100 mm), and A/S equipment.

1 + 1 BRITISH TYPE 42

Name	No.	Builders	Laid down	Launched	Commissioned
HERCULES	D 1 (ex 28)	Vickers, Barrow	16 June 1971	24 Oct 1972	12 July 1976
SANTISIMA TRINIDAD	D 2	AFNE, Rio Santiago	11 Oct 1971	9 Nov 1974	?1982

Displacement, tons: 3 150 standard; 3 650 full load
Length, feet (metres): 392·0 *(119·5)* wl; 410·0 *(125·0)* oa
Beam, feet (metres): 48 *(14·6)*
Draught, feet (metres): 17 *(5·2)*
Missile launchers: 22 SAM Sea Dart—1 twin launcher
Aircraft: 1 Lynx helicopter
Guns: 1—4·5 in/55 Vickers Mk 8; 2—20 mm Oerlikon mk 7
A/S weapons: 6—Mk 32 (2 triple) torpedo tubes
Main engines: Rolls-Royce Olympus gas turbines for full power; Rolls-Royce Tyne gas turbines for cruising; 2 shafts; 50 000 shp
Speed, knots: 30
Range, miles: 4 000 at 18 knots
Complement: 300

These two destroyers are of the British Type 42. On 18 May 1970 the signing of a contract between the Argentine Government and Vickers Ltd, Barrow-in-Furness was announced. This provided for the construction of these two ships, one to be built at Barrow-in-Furness and the second at Rio Santiago with British assistance and overseeing. *Santisima Trinidad* was sabotaged on 22 August 1975 whilst fitting-out and subsequently placed in floating-dock at AFNE. Completion date remains uncertain. *Hercules* was completed 10 May 1976 and arrived in Argentina 20 August 1977 after trials and work-up in the UK.

Electronics: ADAWS-4 for co-ordination of action information by Plessey-Ferranti.

Radar: Search: One Type 965 with double AKE2 array and IFF
Surveillance and target indication: One Type 992Q
Sea Dart fire control: Two Type 909.
Navigation, HDWS and helicopter control: One Type 1006.

Sonar: Type 184 hull-mounted. Type 162 classification.

HERCULES 1978, Argentine Navy

HERCULES 6/1977, Dr. Giorgio Arra

28 ARGENTINA / Destroyers

3 Ex-US "FLETCHER" CLASS

Name	No.	Builders	Laid down	Launched	Commissioned
ROSALES (ex-USS *Stembel*, DD 644)	D 22	Bath Iron Works Corporation, Bath, Maine	21 Dec 1942	8 May 1943	16 July 1943
ALMIRANTE DOMECQ GARCIA (ex-USS *Braine*, DD 630)	D 23	Bath Iron Works Corporation, Bath, Maine	12 Oct 1942	7 Mar 1943	11 May 1943
ALMIRANTE STORNI (ex-USS *Cowell*, DD 547)	D 24	Bethlehem Steel Co, San Pedro	7 Sep 1942	18 Mar 1943	23 Aug 1943

Displacement, tons: 2 050 standard; 3 050 full load
Length, feet (metres): 376·5 *(114·8)*
Beam, feet (metres): 39·5 *(12·0)*
Draught, feet (metres): 18 *(5·5)*
Guns: 4—5 in *(127 mm)*/38 (single Mk 30); 6—3 in *(76 mm)*/50
Torpedo tubes: 4—21 in *(533 mm)* quad (D22)
A/S weapons: 2 fixed Hedgehogs; 1 DC rack (Mk 3);
  6 (2 triple) Mk 32 torpedo tubes;
  2 side-launching torpedo racks (D22)
Main engines: 2 sets GE or AC geared turbines 60 000 shp;
  2 shafts
Boilers: 4 Babcock & Wilcox
Speed, knots: 35
Range, miles: 6 000 at 15 knots
Oil fuel, tons: 650
Complement: 300

First transferred on loan to the Argentine Navy on 1 August 1961 and purchased 14 January 1977. Last pair transferred 17 August 1971. *Almirante Brown* D20 paid off 13 December 1977 for disposal (transferred originally with *Rosales*).

A/S: All fitted with Mk 105 FCS.

Radar: Search: SPS 6.
Tactical: SPS 10.
Fire control: Mk 37 director with Mk 25 radar; Mk 56 director with Mk 35 radar; Mk 63 director with Mk 34 radar (40 mm).
Sonar: One SQS 4.

ROSALES   1978, Argentine Navy

3 Ex-US "ALLEN M. SUMNER" CLASS (FRAM II)

Name	No.	Builders	Laid down	Launched	Commissioned
SEGUI (ex-USS *Hank* DD 702)	D 25	Federal S.B. & D.D. Co	17 Jan 1944	21 May 1944	28 Aug 1944
BOUCHARD (ex-USS *Borie* DD 704)	D 26	Federal S.B. & D.D. Co	29 Feb 1944	4 July 1944	21 Sep 1944
PIEDRA BUENA (ex-USS *Collett* DD 730)	D 29	Bath Iron Works Corporation, Bath, Maine	11 Oct 1943	5 Mar 1944	16 May 1944

Displacement, tons: 2 200 standard; 3 320 full load
Length, feet (metres): 376·5 *(114·8)*
Beam, feet (metres): 40·9 *(12·5)*
Draught, feet (metres): 19 *(5·8)*
Missiles: MM 38 Exocet
Guns: 6—5 in *(127 mm)*/38 (twin Mk 38); 4—3 in *(76 mm)*/50 (twin Mk 33) *(Segui* only)
A/S weapons: 6—(2 triple) Mk 32 torpedo tubes; 2 ahead-firing Hedgehogs; Facilities for small helicopter
Main engines: 2 geared turbines; 60 000 shp; 2 shafts
Boilers: 4
Speed, knots: 34
Range, miles: 4 600 at 15 knots; 990 at 31 knots
Complement: *Bouchard* 291; *Segui* 331

First pair transferred to Argentina 1 July 1972. *Bouchard* has been modernised with VDS, helicopter facilities and hangar. Two units, ex-USS *Mansfield* DD 728 and ex-USS *Collet* DD 730, transferred June 1974 and April 1974 respectively for spares. DD 730 was recommissioned in 1977 as *Piedra Buena* to replace *Espora* D 21 when she was scrapped. DD 728 sold for scrap in 1978.

A/S: Fitted with Mk 105 FCS.

Radar: Search: SPS 6 *(Segui)*; SPS 40 (Others).
Tactical: SPS 10.
Fire control: Mk 37 director with Mk 25 radar. Mk 56 director with Mk 35 radar *(Segui)*.

Sonar: *(Bouchard* and *Piedra Buena)*. SQS 30, SQA 10 (VDS). *(Segui)* SQS 30.

SEGUI   1978, Argentine Navy

1 Ex-US "GEARING" CLASS (FRAM II)

Name	No.	Builders	Laid down	Launched	Commissioned
COMODORO PY (ex-USS *Perkins* DD 877)	D 27	Consolidated Steel Corporation	7 Dec 1944	Mar 1945	5 Apr 1945

Displacement, tons: 2 425 standard; approx 3 500 full load
Length, feet (metres): 390·5 *(119·0)*
Beam, feet (metres): 40·9 *(12·5)*
Draught, feet (metres): 19·0 *(5·8)*
Missiles: MM 38 Exocet
Guns: 6—5 in *(127 mm)*/38 (twin Mk 38)
A/S weapons: 2 fixed Hedgehogs; 6 (2 triple) Mk 32 torpedo tubes; Facilities for small helicopter
Main engines: 2 geared Westinghouse turbines
Boilers: 4 Babcock & Wilcox
Speed, knots: 31·5
Range, miles: 6 150 at 11 knots; 1 475 at 30 knots
Complement: 275

Transferred by sale 15 January 1973.

A/S: Fitted with Mk 105 FCS.

Gunnery: Mk 37 GFCS.

Radar: SPS 37.

Sonar: SQS 29.

COMODORO PY (as USS PERKINS)

ARGENTINA / Frigates — Patrol ships

FRIGATES

A design contract was signed with Vosper Thornycroft on 19 May 1975 which has subsequently been terminated. It is reported that a new contract has been initialled with Blöhm and Voss although Rhine-Scheldt-Verolme with Nevesbu and CNR Riva Trigoso are also understood to have been asked for quotations. Total of Blöhm and Voss order reported as six with one to be built in Germany and remainder by AFNE.

2 FRENCH TYPE A 69

Name	No.	Builders	Laid down	Launched	Completed
(ex-*Good Hope*, ex-*Lieutenant de Vaisseau le Hénaff* F 789)	—	Lorient Naval Dockyard	12 Mar 1976	Mar 1977	Mar 1978
(ex-*Transvaal*, ex-*Commandant l'Herminier* F 791)	—	Lorient Naval Dockyard	1 Oct 1976	Sep 1977	Nov 1978

Displacement, tons: 950 standard; 1 170 full load
Length, feet (metres): 262·5 *(80·0)*
Beam, feet (metres): 33·8 *(10·3)*
Draught, feet (metres): 9·8 *(3·0)*
Missiles: 2—MM 38 Exocet
Guns: 1—3·9 in *(100 mm)*; 2—20 mm
A/S weapons: 1—375 mm Mk 54 Rocket launcher; 4 fixed tubes for A/S torpedoes.
Main engines: 2 SEMT-Pielstick PC2V diesels; 2 shafts; cp propellers; 11 000 bhp.
Speed, knots: 24
Range, miles: 4 500 at 15 knots; 3 000 at 18 knots
Endurance, days: 15
Complement: 79 (5 officers, 74 men)

TYPE A 69   9/1976, Dr. Giorgio Arra

Originally built for the French Navy, sold to the South African Navy in 1976 whilst under construction. As a result of a UN embargo on arms sales to South Africa this sale was cancelled. Purchased by Argentina in autumn 1978 for transfer about December 1978.

Radar: Surface/Air search: one DRBV 51
Fire control: one DRBC 32E
Navigation: one Decca Type 202; One DRBN 32
Sonar: One hull-mounted DUBA 25

PATROL SHIPS

2 Ex-US "CHEROKEE" CLASS

Name	No.	Builders	Commissioned
COMMANDANTE GENERAL IRIGOYEN (ex-USS *Cahuilla* ATF 152)	A 1	Charleston S.B. and D.D. Co	10 Mar 1945
FRANCISCO DE GURRUCHAGA (ex-USS *Luiseno* ATF 156)	A 3	Charleston S.B. and D.D. Co	16 June 1945

Displacement, tons: 1 235 standard; 1 675 full load
Dimensions, feet (metres): 195 wl; 205 oa × 38·2 × 15·3 *(62·5 × 11·6 × 4·7)*
Guns: 6—40/60 mm (2 twin; 2 single)
Main engines: 4 sets diesels with electric drive; 3 000 bhp = 16 knots
Complement: 85

Fitted with powerful pumps and other salvage equipment. *Commandante General Irigoyen* transferred to Argentina at San Diego, California, in 1961. Classified as a tug until 1966 when she was re-rated as patrol vessel. *Francisco De Gurruchaga* transferred 1 July 1975 by sale.

Loss: *Commandante General Zapiola* ran aground in November 1976 off Falkland Islands and was lost.

FRANCISCO DE GURRUCHAGA (as LUISENO)   USN

2 "KING" CLASS

Name	No.	Builders	Commissioned
MURATURE	P 20	Base Nav. Rio Santiago	Apr 1945
KING	P 21	Base Nav. Rio Santiago	Nov 1946

Displacement, tons: 913 standard; 1 000 normal; 1 032 full load
Length, feet (metres): 252·7 *(77·0)*
Beam, feet (metres): 29 *(8·8)*
Draught, feet (metres): 7·5 *(2·3)*
Guns: 4—40 mm Bofors; 5—MG
Main engines: 2—Werkspoor 4-stroke diesels; 2 500 bhp; 2 shafts
Speed, knots: 18
Oil fuel (tons): 90
Range, miles: 6 000 at 12 knots
Complement: 100

Named after Captain John King, an Irish follower of Admiral Brown, who distinguished himself in the war with Brazil, 1826-28; and Captain Murature, who performed conspicuous service against the Paraguayans at the Battle of Cuevas on August 6 1865. Used for cadet training. *King* laid down June 1938, launched November 1943. *Murature* laid down March 1940, launched July 1943.

MURATURE   1974, Argentine Navy

4 Ex-US "SOTOYOMO" CLASS

Name	No.	Builders	Commissioned
DIAGUITA (ex-US ATA 124)	A 5	Levingstone S.B. Co, Orange	24 July 1943
YAMANA (ex-USS *Maricopa* ATA 146)	A 6	Levingstone S.B. Co, Orange	20 Jan 1943
ALFEREZ SOBRAL (ex-USS *Catawba*, ATA 210)	A 9	Levingstone S.B. Co, Orange	18 Apr 1945
COMODORO SOMELLERA (ex-USS *Salish* ATA 187)	A 10	Levingstone S.B. Co, Orange	7 Dec 1944

Displacement, tons: 689 standard; 800 full load
Dimensions, feet (metres): 134·5 wl; 143 oa × 34 × 12 *(43·6 × 10·4 × 3·7)*
Guns: 2—20 mm (twin)
Main engines: Diesel-electric; 1 500 bhp = 12·5 knots
Oil fuel (tons): 154
Range, miles: 16 500 at 8 knots
Complement: 49

Former US auxiliary ocean tugs. A 5 and A 6 are fitted as rescue ships and were acquired in 1947. They bear names of South American Indian tribes. Classified as ocean salvage tugs until 1966 when they were re-rated as patrol vessels. A 9 and A 10 were transferred on 10 February 1972.

Reclassification: *Chiriguano* (ex-US ATA 227) and *Sanaviron* (ex-US ATA 228) now operate as tugs.

YAMANA   1969, Argentine Navy

30 ARGENTINA / Patrol ships — Amphibious forces

1 "BOUCHARD" CLASS

Name	No.	Builders	Commissioned
SPIRO	GC 12	Rio Santiago	1938

Displacement, tons: 560 normal; 650 full load
Dimensions, feet (metres): 197 × 24 × 11·5 (60·0 × 7·3 × 3·5)
Guns: 4—40 mm/60 (twin) Bofors
Main engines: 2 MAN diesels; 2 000 bhp = 13 knots
Range, miles: 3 000 at 10 knots
Complement: 77

Former minesweeper of the "Bouchard" class, now operated by the Prefectura Naval Argentina. Sister ships *Bouchard, Py, Parker* and *Seaver* were transferred to the Paraguayan Navy in 1964-67. This class, originally of nine, were the first warships built in Argentine yards.

SPIRO   1969, Argentine Navy

AMPHIBIOUS FORCES

1 Ex-US LANDING SHIP (DOCK)

Name	No.	Builders	Commissioned
CANDIDO DE LASALA (ex-USS *Gunston Hall* LSD 5)	Q 43	Moor Dry Dock Co, Oakland	10 Nov 1943

Displacement, tons: 5 480 standard; 9 375 full load
Dimensions, feet (metres): 457·8 × 72·2 × 18·0 (139·6 × 22 × 5·5)
Guns: 12—40 mm
Main engines: 2 Skinner Unaflow; 2 shafts; 7 400 shp = 15·4 knots
Boilers: Two 2-drum
Range, miles: 8 000 at 15 knots
Complement: Accommodation for 326 (17 officers and 309 men)

Arcticized in 1948/9. Transferred from the US Navy on 1 May 1970. Carries 14 LCA and has helicopter facilities. Used as light forces tender.

CANDIDO DE LASALA (Type TNC 45 in well)   1976, Michael D. J. Lennon

1 LANDING SHIP (TANK)

Name	No.	Builders	Commissioned
CABO SAN ANTONIO	Q 42	AFNE, Rio Santiago	1977

Displacement, tons: 4 300 light; 8 000 full load
Dimensions, feet (metres): 445 × 62 × 16·5 (135·6 × 18·9 × 5)
Guns: 12—40/60 mm (3 quad)
Main engines: Diesels; 2 shafts; 13 700 bhp = 16 knots
Complement: 124

Designed to carry a helicopter and two landing craft. Launched 1968. Completion delayed. Completed ex-trials 12 January 1977. Modified US "De Soto County" Class—principal difference being the fitting of Stülcken heavy-lift gear and different armament.

Radar: Plessey AWS-1.

CABO SAN ANTONIO   1978, Argentine Navy

3 Ex-US LSTs

Name	No.	Builders	Commissioned
CABO SAN GONZALO (ex-USS LST 872)	Q 44	Jefferson B & M Co, Indiana, USA	22 Jan 1945
CABO SAN PIO (ex-USS LST 1044)	Q 50	Dravo Corporation, Neville Is, Pa, USA	2 Mar 1945
CABO SAN VINCENTE (ex-USS LST 1108)	Q 53	—	1945

Displacement, tons: 2 366 beaching; 4 080 full load
Dimensions, feet (metres): 328 × 50 × 14 (100 × 15·3 × 4·3)
Main engines: 2 diesels; 2 shafts; 1 800 bhp = 11 knots
Oil fuel, tons: 700
Range, miles: 9 500 at 9 knots
Complement: 80

Transferred 1946-47. Being used commercially. Q 46 deleted in 1978, remainder to be deleted in 1979.

1 Ex-US LSIL

BDI-4 (ex-USS LSIL 606) Q 57

Displacement, tons: 230 light; 387 full load
Dimensions, feet (metres): 159 × 23·2 × 5 (48·5 × 7·1 × 1·5)
Guns: 2—20 mm
Main engines: 8 sets diesels; 3 200 bhp; two reversible propellers = 14 knots
Oil fuel, tons: 110
Range, miles: 6 000 at 12 knots
Complement: 30

Used for training.

4 Ex-US LCMs

EDM 1, 2, 3, 4

Displacement, tons: 28
Dimensions, feet (metres): 56 × 14 × ?
Main engines: 2 Gray diesels; 450 bhp = 11 knots

Acquired in USA June 1971.

8 Ex-US LCVPs

Dimensions, feet (metres): 63 × 14·1 × —(19·2 × 4·3 ×—)
Main engine: 1 diesel; approx 250 hp

Incorporated in May 1970. Numbers not known.

15 Ex-US LCVPs

EDVP 1, 3, 7, 8, 9, 10, 12, 13, 17, 19, 21, 24, 28, 29, 30

Displacement, tons: 12
Dimensions, feet (metres): 39·5 × 10·5 × 5·5 (12·1 × 3·2 × 1·7)
Main engines: Diesels, 9 knots

Transferred 1946.

ARGENTINA / Light forces — Mine warfare forces

LIGHT FORCES

2 TYPE TNC 45 (FAST ATTACK CRAFT—GUN)

Name	No.	Builders	Commissioned
INTREPIDA	ELPR 1	Lürssen, Bremen	20 July 1974
INDOMITA	ELPR 2	Lürssen, Bremen	Dec 1974

Displacement, tons: 268 full load
Dimensions, feet (metres): 149 × 24·3 × 7·5 (45·4 × 7·4 × 2·3)
Guns: 1—76 mm (3 in)/62 OTO Melara Compact; 2—40 mm/70 Bofors L70
Rocket launcher: 2 Oerlikon 81 mm
Torpedo tubes: 2—21 in for wire-guided torpedoes
Main engines: 4 diesels; 4 shafts; 12 000 hp = 40 knots
Range, miles: 1 450 at 20 knots
Complement: 35

These two vessels were ordered in 1970. *Intrepida* launched 12 December 1973, *Indomita* 8 April 1974.

Radar: Fire control: Hollandse Signaal WM20 for guns; M11 for torpedoes.

INTREPIDA 1978, Argentine Navy

4 Ex-Israel "DABUR" CLASS (COASTAL PATROL CRAFT)

Displacement, tons: 35
Dimensions, feet (metres): 64·9 × 19 × 2·6 (19·8 × 5·8 × 0·8)
Guns: 2—20 mm; 2MG
Main engines: 2 diesels; 960 hp; 2 shafts = 25 knots
Range, miles: 1 200 at 17 knots
Complement: 9

Transferred 1978. There is also a report of the transfer by Israel of two "Dvora" class fast attack craft missile armed with two Gabriel Missiles although this is a little dubious as their small size would make them vulnerable to the high seas in Argentine waters.

3 "LYNCH" CLASS (LARGE PATROL CRAFT)

Name	No.	Builders	Commissioned
LYNCH	GC 21	AFNE, Rio Santiago	1964
TOLL	GC 22	AFNE, Rio Santiago	1965
EREZCANO	GC 23	AFNE, Rio Santiago	1967

Displacement, tons: 100 normal; 117 full load
Dimensions, feet (metres): 90 × 19 × 6 (27·4 × 5·8 × 1·8)
Gun: 1—20 mm
Main engines: 2 Maybach diesels; 2 700 bhp = 22 knots
Complement: 16

Patrol craft operated by the Prefectura Naval Argentina.

LYNCH 1969, Argentine Navy

1 LARGE PATROL CRAFT

Name	No.	Builders	Commissioned
SURUBI	P 55	Ast. Nav. del Estero	1951

Displacement, tons: 100
Guns: 2—20 mm
Speed, knots: 20

1 Ex-US 63 ft AVR (LARGE PATROL CRAFT)

GC 31

Dimensions as for US 63 ft AVR class but of slightly different silhouette.

1 LARGE PATROL CRAFT

Name	No.	Builders	Commissioned
DELFIN	GC 13	—	1957

Measurement, tons: 518 gross
Dimensions, feet (metres): 196·8 × 29·5 × 15·4 (60 × 9 × 4·7)
Main engines: 2 300 hp = 15 knots
Complement: 32

Trawler type acquired for PNA in 1970.

EX-US "HIGGINS" CLASS (FAST ATTACK CRAFT—TORPEDO)

Name	No.	Builders	Commissioned
ALAKUSH	P 82	New Orleans S.B.	1946
TOWARA	P 84	New Orleans S.B.	1946

Displacement, tons: 45 standard; 50 full load
Dimensions, feet (metres): 78·7 × 9·8 × 4·6 (24 × 3 × 1·4)
Guns: 2—40/60 mm; 4—MG
Rocket launchers: 2 octuple sets 12·7 cm
Main engines: 3 Packard (petrol); 4 500 hp = 42 knots
Range, miles: 1 000 at 20 knots
Complement: 12

The last of a class of nine. Given names in 1972.

1 LARGE PATROL CRAFT

Name	No.	Builders	Commissioned
TONINA	GC 47	Sanym SA. San Fernando	21 Oct 1977

Displacement, tons: 200 full load
Dimensions, feet (metres): 83·8 × 10·1 × — (25·5 × 3·3 × —)
Main engines: 500 hp
Range, miles: 3 400
Complement: 11

Note: In addition the following are listed as operated by PNA: *Robalo, Mandubi, Adhara, Albatross, Dorado,* LT 1 and 8, PAV 1, 2 and 3. PAM 1, 2 and 3, V 2 and 6, GN 1, 4, 38 and 42, PF 17, P 2, 5, 13, 22, 26, 39 and 41. A further craft *Pacu* GC 46 is listed.

MINE WARFARE FORCES

6 Ex-BRITISH "TON" CLASS
(MINESWEEPERS—COASTAL and MINEHUNTERS)

Name	No.	Builders	Launched
NEUQUEN (ex-HMS *Hickleton*)	M 1	Thornycroft	26 Jan 1955
RIO NEGRO (ex-HMS *Tarlton*)	M 2	Doig	10 Nov 1954
CHUBUT (ex-HMS *Santon*)	M 3	Fleetlands	18 Aug 1955
TIERRA DEL FUEGO (ex- HMS *Bevington*)	M 4	Whites	17 Mar 1953
CHACO (ex-HMS *Rennington*)	M 5	Richards	27 Nov 1958
FORMOSA (ex-HMS *Ilmington*)	M 6	Camper, Nicholson	8 Mar 1954

Displacement, tons: 360 standard; 425 full load
Dimensions, feet (metres): 140 pp; 153 oa × 28·8 × 8·2 (46·3 × 8·8 × 2·5)
Gun: 1—40/60 mm
Main engines: 2 diesels; 2 shafts; 3 000 bhp = 15 knots
Oil fuel, tons: 45
Range, miles: 2 300 at 13 knots; 3 000 at 8 knots
Complement: Minesweepers 27; Minehunters 36

Former British coastal minesweepers of the "Ton" class. Of composite wooden and non-magnetic metal construction. Purchased in 1967. In 1968 *Chaco* and *Formosa* were converted into minehunters in HM Dockyard, Portsmouth, and the other four were refitted and modernised as minesweepers by the Vosper Thornycroft Group with Vosper activated-fin stabiliser equipment.

TIERRA DEL FUEGO 1978, Argentine Navy

SURVEY AND OCEANOGRAPHIC SHIPS

2 "PUERTO DESEADO" CLASS

Name	No.	Builders	Commissioned
PUERTO DESEADO	—	Astarsa, San Fernando	1977
ALVARO ALBERTO	—	Alianza, Avellaneda	1978

Displacement, tons: 2 133 standard
Dimensions, feet (metres): 251·9 × 51·8 × 21·3 *(76·8 × 15·8 × 6·5)*
Main engine: 2 Fiat diesels; 1 shaft; 3 600 hp = 15 knots
Range, miles: 12 000 at 12 knots
Complement: 61

Puerto Deseado laid down in 1974 for Consejo Nacional de Investigaciones Tecnicas y Scientificas. Civilian manned. Launched 4 December 1976. Second of class ordered 1976, laid down 17 March 1976, launched December 1977.

2 Ex-US TYPE V4 TUGS

Name	No.	Builders	Commissioned
GOYENA (ex-USS *Dry Tortuga*)	Q 17 (ex-A 3)	Pendleton S.Y. New Orleans	1943
THOMPSON (ex-USS *Sombrero Key*)	A 4	Pendleton S.Y. New Orleans	1943

Displacement, tons: 1 863 full load
Dimensions, feet (metres): 191·3 × 37 × 18 *(58·3 × 11·3 × 5·5)*
Guns: 2—40 mm Bofors (twin); 2—20 mm (single)
Main engines: 2 Enterprise diesels; 2 250 bhp = 12 knots
Oil fuel, tons: 532
Complement: 62

Leased to Argentina in 1965. Q 17 used as survey ship. A 4 reported as in use as patrol ship and for oceanographic research.

THOMPSON — 1973, Argentine Navy

Name	No.	Builders	Commissioned
ISLAS ORCADAS (ex-USS *Eltanin*, T-AGOR 8—AK 270)	Q 9	Avondale, New Orleans	2 Aug 1957

Displacement, tons: 2 036 light; 4 942 full load
Dimensions, feet (metres): 262·2 × 51·5 × 18·7 *(80 × 15·7 × 5·7)*
Main engines: Diesel-electric; 3 200 bhp; 2 shafts = 12 knots
Complement: 12 officers, 36 men, 38 scientists

Converted for Antarctic Research 1961. Operated in conjunction by Argentine Navy, US National Science Foundation and Argentine National Directorate of the Antarctic. Transferred 15 November 1972.

Name	No.	Builders	Commissioned
COMODORO RIVADAVIA	Q 11	Mestrina, Tigre	6 Dec 1974

Displacement, tons: 609 standard; 667 full load
Dimensions, feet (metres): 171·2 × 28·9 × 8·5 *(52·2 × 8·8 × 2·6)*
Main engines: 2 Werkspoor Stork RHO-218K diesels; 1 160 hp = 12 knots
Range, miles: 6 000 at 12 knots
Complement: 27

Laid down 17 July 1971, launched 2 December 1972.

CORMORAN   Q 15

Coastal survey launch of 102 tons with complement of 19, built in 1963. Speed 13 knots. Commissioned February 1964.

PETREL

Coastal survey launch of 50 tons with complement of nine, built in 1965.

1 AUXILIARY SAILING SHIP

Name	No.	Builders	Commissioned
EL AUSTRAL (ex-*Atlantis*)	Q 7	Burmeister and Wain, Copenhagen	1931

Displacement, tons: 571
Dimensions, feet (metres): 110 pp; 141 oa × 27 × 20 *(33·5; 43 × 8·2 × 6·1)*
Main engines: Diesels; 400 bhp
Oil fuel, tons: 22
Complement: 19

Incorporated into the Argentine Navy on 30 April, 1966. Acquired from USA. (Wood's Hole Institute).

TRANSPORTS

Name	No.	Builders	Commissioned
BAHIA AGUIRRE	B 2	Canadian Vickers, Halifax	1950
BAHIA BUEN SUCESO	B 6	Canadian Vickers, Halifax	June 1950

Displacement, tons: 3 100 standard; 5 000 full load
Dimensions, feet (metres): 334·7 × 47 × 13·8 *(102 × 14·3 × 4·2)*
Main engines: 2 sets Nordberg diesels; 2 shafts; 3 750 bhp = 16 knots
Oil fuel, tons: 442 (B 6); 355 (B 2)
Complement: 100

Survivors of class of three.

BAHIA AGUIRRE (new satellite aerial on stern) — 8/1978, Michael D. J. Lennon

3 "COSTA SUR" CLASS

Name	No.	Builders	Commissioned
CANAL BEAGLE	—	A. P. Menghi y Penco	29 Apr 1978
BAHIA SAN BLAS	—	A. P. Menghi y Penco	1978
BAHIA CAMARONES	—	A. P. Menghi y Penco	1979

Measurement, tons: 4 600 gross; 5 800 deadweight
Dimensions, feet (metres): 390·3 × 57·4 × 21 *(119 × 17·5 × 6·4)*
Main engines: 2 diesels; 6 400 hp = 15 knots

Ordered December 1975 from Ast. Principe Menghi y Penco Ga, Avellaneda. To replace three ex-US LSTs *(Cabo San Gonzalo, San Vicente* and *San Pio)*,. To be used commercially. First two laid down on 10 January 1977 and 11 April 1977.

ARGENTINA / Tankers — Icebreakers 33

TANKERS

1 LARGE FLEET TANKER (FLEET SUPPORT)

Name	No.	Builders	Commissioned
PUNTA MEDANOS	B 18	Swan Hunter	10 Oct 1950

Displacement, tons: 14 352 standard; 16 331 full load
Measurement, tons: 8 250 deadweight
Dimensions, feet (metres): 470 pp; 502 oa × 62 × 28·5 (143·4; 153·1 × 18·9 × 8·7)
Main engines: Double reduction geared turbines. 2 shafts; 9 500 shp = 18 knots
Boilers: 2 Babcock & Wilcox 2-drum integral furnace water-tube
Oil fuel, tons: 1 500
Range, miles: 13 700 at 15 knots
Complement: 99

Available as a training vessel. Boilers built under licence by the Wallsend Slipway & Engineering Company. Steam conditions of 400 psi pressure and 750°F.

PUNTA MEDANOS   1978, Argentine Navy

1 Ex-US "KLICKITAT" CLASS (FLEET SUPPORT)

Name	No.	Builders	Commissioned
PUNTA DELGADA (ex-SS Sugarland, ex-Nanticoke AOG 66)	B 16	St. Johns River S.B. Jacksonville	1945

Displacement, tons: 5 930 standard; 6 090 full load
Dimensions, feet (metres): 325 × 48·2 × 20 (99·1 × 14·7 × 6·1)
Main engines: Westinghouse diesel; 1 shaft; 1 400 bhp = 11·5 knots
Oil fuel, tons: 150
Range, miles: 9 000 at 11 knots
Complement: 72

USMS type T1-M-BT1. Launched on 7 April 1945. Used commercially.

1 TANKER (FLEET SUPPORT)

Name	No.	Builder	Commissioned
PUNTA ALTA	B 12	Puerto Belgrano	1938

Displacement, tons: 1 600 standard; 1 900 full load
Measurement, tons: 800 deadweight
Dimensions, feet (metres): 210 × 33·8 × 12·5 (64 × 10·3 × 3·8)
Main engines: Diesel; 1 shaft; 1 850 bhp = 8 knots
Oil fuel, tons: 146
Complement: 40

TRAINING SHIP

Name	No.	Builders	Commissioned
LIBERTAD	Q 2	AFNE, Rio Santiago	1962

Displacement, tons: 3 025 standard; 3 765 full load
Dimensions, feet (metres): 262 wl; 301 oa × 47 × 21·8 (79·9, 91·7 × 14·3 × 6·6)
Guns: 1—3 in; 4—40 mm; 4—47 mm saluting
Main engines: 2 Sulzer diesels; 2 400 bhp = 13·5 knots
Complement: 370 (crew) plus 150 cadets

Launched on 20 June 1956. She is the largest sail training ship in the world and set up the fastest crossing of the North Atlantic under sail in 1966, a record which still stands.

LIBERTAD   1978, Reinhard Nerlich

ICEBREAKERS

1 WÄRTSILA TYPE

Name	No.	Builders	Commissioned
ALMIRANTE IRIZAR	Q 5	Wärtsila (Helsinki)	15 Dec 1978

Displacement, tons: 11 811
Dimensions, feet (metres): 392 × 82 × 31·2 (119·3 × 25 × 9·5)
Main engines: Diesel-electric; 16 200 shp (4 Wärtsila-SEMT-Pielstick 8PC2·5L diesels); 2 shafts
Speed, knots: 16·5
Complement: 133 ship's company; 100 passengers

Contract signed on 17 December 1975. The ship is designed for Antarctic support operations and will be able to remain in the polar regions throughout the winter with 210 people aboard. Fitted for helicopters and landing craft with two 16 ton cranes. Fin stabilisers, Wärtsila bubbling system and a 60 ton towing winch. Laid down 4 July 1977, launched 3 February 1978. Painted with red hull and white upperworks with red funnel and black top. Cost $61·5 million.

Radar: Search: AWS-2.
Navigation: Two Decca.

ALMIRANTE IRIZAR   1978, Wärtsila

34 ARGENTINA / Icebreakers — Army watercraft

Name	No.	Builders	Commissioned
GENERAL SAN MARTIN	Q 4	Seebeck Yd-Weser AG	Oct 1954

Displacement, tons: 4 854 standard; 5 301 full load
Measurement, tons: 1 600 deadweight
Dimensions, feet (metres): 279 × 61 × 21 (85·1 × 18·6 × 6·4)
Aircraft: 1 reconnaissance aircraft and 1 helicopter
Guns: 2—40 mm Bofors
Main engines: 4 diesel-electric; 2 shafts; 7 100 hp = 16 knots
Oil fuel, tons: 1 100
Range, miles: 35 000 at 10 knots
Complement: 160

Launched on 24 June 1954. Fitted for research. New second radar mast fitted on after end of the hangar in late 1972. To be relieved by *Almirante Irizar* in 1979.

GENERAL SAN MARTIN 1970, Argentine Navy
(2nd radar mast now fitted and 4 in gun removed)

TUGS

2 Ex-US "SOTOYOMO" CLASS

Name	No.	Builders	Commissioned
CHIRIGUANO (ex-US ATA 227)	A 7	Levingstone S.B. Co	1945
SANAVIRON (ex-US ATA 228)	A 8	Levingstone S.B. Co	1945

Details as for "Sotoyomo" class under "Patrol Ships" except that gun has been removed.

2 "QUILMES" CLASS

Name	No.	Builders	Commissioned
QUILMES	R 32	Rio Santiago	30 Mar 1960
GUAYCURU	R 33	Rio Santiago	29 July 1960

Displacement, tons: 368 full load
Dimensions, feet (metres): 107·2 × 24·4 × 12·5 (32·7 × 7·4 × 3·8)
Main engines: Skinner Unaflow engines; 645 hp = 9 knots
Boilers: Cylindrical
Oil fuel, tons: 52
Range, miles: 2 200 at 7 knots
Complement: 14

Laid down on 23 August and 15 March 1956 respectively, launched on 27 December 1956 and 8 July 1957.

Name	No.	Builders	Commissioned
PEHUENCHE	R 29	Rio Santiago	1954
TONOCOTE	R 30	Rio Santiago	1954

Displacement, tons: 330
Dimensions, feet (metres): 105 × 24·7 × 12·5 (32 × 7·5 × 3·8)
Main engines: Triple expansion; 600 ihp = 11 knots
Boilers: 2
Oil fuel, tons: 36
Range, miles: 1 200 at 9 knots
Complement: 13

Name	No.	Builders	Commissioned
TOBA	R 4	Hawthorn Leslie Ltd	Mar 1928

Displacement, tons: 600
Measurement, tons: 339 gross
Dimensions, feet (metres): 139 oa × 28.5 × 11·5 (42·4 × 8·7 × 3·5)
Main engines: Triple expansion; 2 shafts; 1 200 ihp = 12 knots
Boilers: 2
Oil fuel, tons: 95
Range, miles: 3 900 at 10 knots
Complement: 34

Launched on 23 December 1927.

Name	No.	Builders	Commissioned
QUERANDI	—	Ast. Vicente Forte, Buenos Aires	July 1978
TEHUELCHE	—	Ast. Vicente Forte, Buenos Aires	Nov 1978

Displacement, tons: 270
Dimensions, feet (metres): 110·2 × 27·6 × 9·8 (33·6 × 8·4 × 3·0)
Main engines: 2 MAN diesels; 2 640 bhp = 12 knots
Range, miles: 1 100 at 12 knots
Complement: 30

Ordered 10 March 1977. Laid down 1 May 1977.

Name	No.	Builders	Commissioned
HUARPE	R 12	Howaldtwerke, Kiel	1927

Displacement, tons: 370
Dimensions, feet (metres): 107 × 27·2 × 12 (32·6 × 8·3 × 3·7)
Main engines: Triple expansion; 800 ihp
Boiler: 1 cylindrical (Howaldtwerke)
Oil fuel, tons: 58
Complement: 13

Entered service in the Argentine Navy in 1942.

MOCOVI	R 5 (ex-US YTL 441)	CAPAYAN	R 16 (ex-US YTL 443)
CALCHAQUI	R 6 (ex-US YTL 445)	CHIQUILLAN	R 18 (ex-US YTL 444)
CHULUPI	R 10 (ex-US YTL 426)	MORCOYAN	R 19 (ex-US YTL 448)

Displacement, tons: 70
Dimensions, feet (metres): 67 × 14 × 13 (20·4 × 4·3 × 4)
Main engines: Diesel; 310 bhp = 10 knots
Oil fuel, tons: 8·7
Complement: 5

YTL Type built in USA and transferred on lease in March 1965 (R 16, 18, 19), remainder in March 1969. All purchased 16 June 1977.

FLOATING DOCKS

Number	Dimensions, feet (metres)	Capacity, tons
Y 1 (ex-ARD 23)	492 × 88·6 × 56 (150 × 27 × 17·1)	3 500
2	300·1 × 60 × 41 (91·5 × 18·3 × 12·5)	1 000
ASD 40	215·8 × 46 × 45·5 (65·8 × 14 × 13·7)	750
—	215·8 × 46 × 45·5 (65·8 × 14 × 13·7)	750

First three are at Darsena Norte, Buenos Aires and the fourth at Puerto Belgrano.

AUXILIARIES

Two naval sail-training ships, *Fortuna I* and *Fortuna II* built by Tandanor, Buenos Aires. Two auxiliaries *E 6,* and *Itati* listed.
The ex-training ship *Presidente Sarmiento* is retained at Buenos Aires as a museum ship, as also is the 1874 Corvette *Uruguay.*
Auxiliary EM6 launched by T.A.R. in 1976.

FLOATING CRANES

At least four—at Darsena Norte, Rio Santiago, Mar de Plata and Puerto Belgrano.

ARMY WATERCRAFT

Several LCPs (BDPs) are operated. Built by Ast. Vicente Forte. Ferries for crossing Rio Pirana include two built in 1969.

AUSTRALIA

Administration

Minister for Defence (and Navy):
  Hon D. J. Killen, MP

Chief of Defence Force Staff:
  Admiral A. M. Synnot, AO, CBE, RAN

Headquarters Appointments

Chief of Naval Staff:
  Vice-Admiral G. J. Willis AO, RAN
Deputy Chief of the Naval Staff:
  Rear-Admiral N. E. McDonald, AO, RAN
Chief of Naval Personnel:
  Rear-Admiral J. D. Stevens, RAN
Chief of Naval Technical Services:
  Rear-Admiral G. A. Bennett, OBE, RAN
Chief of Naval Materiel:
  Rear-Admiral W. J. Rourke, OBE, RAN
Chief of Naval Operational Requirements and Plans:
  Rear-Admiral A. A. Willis, OBE, RAN

Senior Appointments

Flag Officer Commanding Australian Fleet:
  Rear-Admiral D. W. Leech, CBE, MVO, RAN
Flag Officer Support Command:
  Rear-Admiral G. R. Griffiths, DSO, DSC, RAN

Diplomatic Representation

Naval Attaché in Jakarta:
  Act/Captain H. A. Josephs, RAN
Naval Representative in London:
  Commodore I. H. Richards, RAN
Naval Attaché in Paris:
  Captain F. McL. Crawford, RAN
Naval Attaché in Tokyo:
  Captain P. E. M. Holloway, RAN
Naval Attaché in Washington:
  Commodore J. A. O'Farrell, AM, RAN
Head of Australian Defence Liaison Staff, Washington:
  Rear-Admiral J. Davidson, RAN

Personnel

1 January 1975: 15 811 officers and sailors
1 January 1976: 15 909 officers and sailors
1 January 1977: 16 390 officers and sailors (app)
  (including 850 WRANS)
30 June 1978: 16 380 officers and ratings
  (target strength including 900 WRANS)
30 June 1979: 16 330 officers and ratings
  (target strength including 900 WRANS)

Navy Estimates

$A
1972-73: 293 094 000*
1973-74: 319 694 000*
1974-75: 375 014 000
1975-76: 428 879 000
1976-77: 539 808 000
1977-78: 565 172 000
1978-79: 691 376 000
(*Includes US Credits)

Naval Bases

FOCEA—Sydney and Jervis Bay
NOC Queensland—Brisbane and Cairns (PCs and LCHs)
NOC Northern Australia—Darwin (PCs)
NOC W. Australia—HMAS *Stirling* Cockburn Sound (commissioned 28 July 1978)

Naval Shipyards

Building at Williamstown (Melbourne) and Cockatoo Island (Sydney). Refits at both and Garden Island (Sydney). Garden Island Yard is to be renovated.

Fleet Air Arm

Squadron	Aircraft
HC-723	Iroquois, Wessex 31B (Utility) and Bell 206B-1 helos (Utility, SAR and FRU)
VC-724	A4G and TA4G Skyhawks, Macchi Trainers (Training, FRU and Trials)
VF-805	A4G Skyhawks (Front line fighter/strike)
VS-816	S2G Trackers (Front line A/S)
HS-817	Sea King Mk 50 helos (Front line A/S)
VC-851	S2G/S2E Trackers, HS 748 (Training, communications and FRU)

Note: The Royal Australian Air Force (RAAF) has 21 P3C (Orion) maritime patrol aircraft with 2 more ordered late 1976. Four F111C are being fitted with reconnaissance pallets.

Prefix to Ships' Names

HMAS. Her Majesty's Australian Ship

Strength of the Fleet

Type	Active	Building
Patrol Submarines	6	—
Attack Carrier (Medium)	1	—
Destroyers	5 (3DDG)	—
Frigates (GM)		3
Frigates	6	—
MCM Vessels	3	(2)
Large Patrol Craft	13	3 (11)
Oceanographic Survey Ships	4	1
Fleet Tanker	1	—
Destroyer Tender	1	—
Training Ship	1	—
Landing Craft (Heavy)	6	—
Landing Ship (Heavy)	—	1
Miscellaneous	42	3 (1)
Tugs	5	—
Army Craft	20	—
RAAF Craft	3	—

Note: *Vendetta* due to pay off mid-1979 and *Labuan* in 1979-80.

Naval Procurement and Modernisation

In February 1976 the Australian Government accepted a letter of offer from the US Navy for two guided missile frigates of the "Oliver Hazard Perry" (FFG7) class. These ships will enter service in the Royal Australian Navy (RAN) in 1981. In November 1977 the government announced its decision to acquire a third ship of this class. The acquisition of this ship will raise the strength of the destroyer fleet from 11 to 12. The White Paper also stated that investigations were being made into the concepts, characteristics, and cost of "follow-on" destroyers, preferably for construction in Australia. These investigations would be in conjunction with those of missile armed patrol boats.

In September 1977 the Defence Minister announced that an invitation would be issued to Australian and overseas companies to register interest in investigating possible aircraft carrier designs for the RAN. Studies of alternative capabilities which might possibly meet Australia's requirements on the retirement of HMAS *Melbourne* would continue concurrently. The Invitation to Register Interest (ITR) lists five "illustrative ship options" as a guide to interested organisations. These range from 10 000 tonne helicopter-only ship to a ship of 25 000 tonnes or more operating V/STOL aircraft and helicopters. A decision on whether to proceed to a funded investigation will be made on completion of examination of responses to ITR.

A decision to acquire 15 Brooke Marine PCF420 patrol craft also was announced in September 1977. The lead craft is being built in the UK, and the remainder in Australia by North Queensland Engineers and Agents Pty Ltd of Cairns.

In November 1977 a contract was let to Carrington Slipways Pty Ltd for construction of a new Amphibious Heavy Lift Ship, to be named HMAS *Tobruk*.

The RAN plans to replace HMAS *Supply* with a new underway replenishment ship. Investigations are under way to establish whether a ship of the "Durance" class should be built in Australia or France.

Plans to acquire a purpose-built training ship were dropped after the acquisition of the former roll-on roll-off ship MV *Australian Trader* in 1977. The ship is now commissioned as HMAS *Jervis Bay*.

The RAN is proceeding with initial prototype design and acquisition of long-lead items for two prototype mine-hunters. These ships, which will be the first of a class intended to replace the ageing "Ton" class ships now in service, will feature a GRP catamaran hull. The new class is due to enter service in the first half of the 1980s.

A new oceanographic ship, HMAS *Cook*, is being constructed to replace HMAS *Diamantina*, and a new trials and research ship to replace HMAS *Kimbla* in the mid 1980s is also contemplated. The 1976 Defence White Paper announced an intention to construct a further two hydrographic ships and six large survey launches. The new ships probably would be similar to HMAS *Flinders*.

Two new "Oberon" class submarines, HMAS *Orion* and HMAS *Otama*, were commissioned in the UK in 1977 and early 1978 respectively. The RAN's submarine squadron is being modernised by the fitting of new attack sonar and an advanced fire control system. Fitting of a new passive range-finding sonar is proceeding. The acquisition of an initial outfit of Mk 48 torpedoes from the USA was announced in October 1977.

Other procurement and modernisation plans include:
limited acquisition of anti-shipping missiles (e.g. Harpoon, Exocet) for submarines and destroyers.

"Perth" class DDGs are being progressively modernised by installation of new gun mounts, naval combat data systems, and "Standard" SAM systems.

Three of the older "River" class DEs will be modernised, and a fourth, HMAS *Yarra* completed a half-life refit in 1977. When this work is completed in 1982 it is planned to start modernisation of HMAS *Swan* and HMAS *Torrens*.

The useful life of the Macchi jet trainer aircraft will be extended by an equipment and structural refurbishment programme to be carried out within the Australian aircraft industry.

A contract to supply twenty two 12 m aluminium workboats to the RAN and the Army was announced in September 1977.

Other Service Craft

(a) Australian Army
  11 Ex-US LCM (8)
  6 LCVPs
  2 Coastal Tugs
  1 Cargo Lighter
(b) RAAF:
  1 76 ft ASR (Townsville)
  2 63 ft ASR (Newcastle)

Mercantile Marine

Lloyd's Register of Shipping:
  426 vessels of 1 531 739 tons gross

DELETIONS

Ex-Carrier

Sydney	For disposal 20.7.73. Left Sydney for South Korean breakers 23.12.75

Destroyers

Arunta	Sank under tow to breaker 13.2.69
Tobruk	Left Sydney for Taiwan 10.4.72
Anzac	Left Sydney for Hong Kong 30.12.74
Duchess	Decommissioned 24.10.77 At Athol Bight. For disposal.

Frigates

Barcoo	Left Sydney for Taiwan 17.3.72
Culgoa	Left Sydney for Taiwan 17.3.72
Quickmatch	Left Sydney for Japan 10.4.72
Quiberon	Left Sydney for Japan 6.7.72
Gascoyne	Left Sydney for Taiwan 6.7.72
Queenborough	Left Sydney for Hong Kong 12.5.75

Landing Craft (Heavy)

Buna	To Papua New Guinea
Salamaua	Defence Force 14.11.74

MCM Vessels

Hawk	Sold 1975. Removed 1977
Gull	Sold 1975—Rebuilding as private rescue ship.
Teal	Sold 1978 for conversion to trawler.

Large Patrol Craft

Archer and *Bandolier*	To Indonesia 21.10.74 & 16.11.73
Arrow	Sunk Darwin (Cyclone Tracy) 25.12.74
Aitape, Ladava, Lae, Madang, Samarai	To Papua New Guinea Defence Force 16.9.75

Miscellaneous

SDB 1321	1972
Kara Kara	Base Ship sunk as target 30.1.73
Paluma	Sold Commercial 1974
Otter	Sold as fishing boat 1974
Tortoise and *Turtle*	Sold Commercial 1975
Bronzewing (tug)	Sold Commercial 3.6.77
Tug 503	To PNGDF 1974

AUSTRALIA / Introduction

PENNANT LIST

Submarines

S57	Oxley
S59	Otway
S60	Onslow
S61	Orion
S62	Otama
S70	Ovens

Aircraft Carrier

R21	Melbourne

Destroyers

D08	Vendetta
D11	Vampire
D38	Perth
D39	Hobart
D41	Brisbane

Frigates

F01	Adelaide
F02	Canberra
F03	—
D45	Yarra
D46	Parramatta
D48	Stuart
D49	Derwent
D50	Swan
D53	Torrens

Minehunters

M1102	Snipe
M1121	Curlew

Minesweeper (Coastal)

M1183	Ibis

Training Ship

AGT 203	Jervis Bay

Large Patrol Craft

P81	Acute
P82	Adroit
P83	Advance
P87	Ardent
P89	Assail
P90	Attack
P91	Aware
P97	Barbette
P98	Barricade
P99	Bombard
P100	Buccaneer
P101	Bayonet
P203	Fremantle

Amphibious Heavy Lift Ship

L50	Tobruk

Landing Craft

L126	Balikpapan
L127	Brunei
L128	Labuan
L129	Tarakan
L130	Wewak
L133	Betano

Survey Ships

A219	Cook
A266	Diamantina
AGOR314	Kimbla
A73	Moresby
A312	Flinders

Fleet Tanker

AO195	Supply

Destroyer Tender

A215	Stalwart

General Purpose Ships

AG244	Banks
AG247	Bass

Diving Tenders

DTV1001	Seal
DTV1002	Porpoise

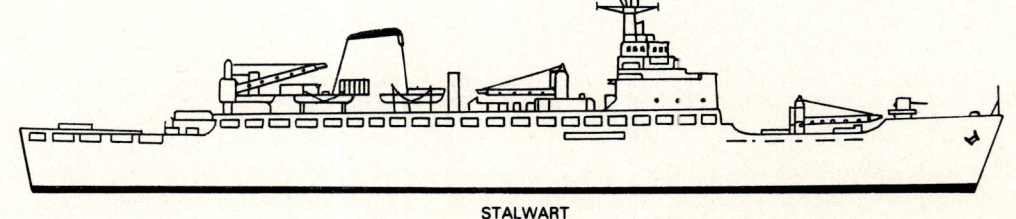

MELBOURNE

"PERTH" Class

VAMPIRE and VENDETTA

PARRAMATTA and YARRA

SWAN and TORRENS

MORESBY

STALWART

AUSTRALIA / Introduction 37

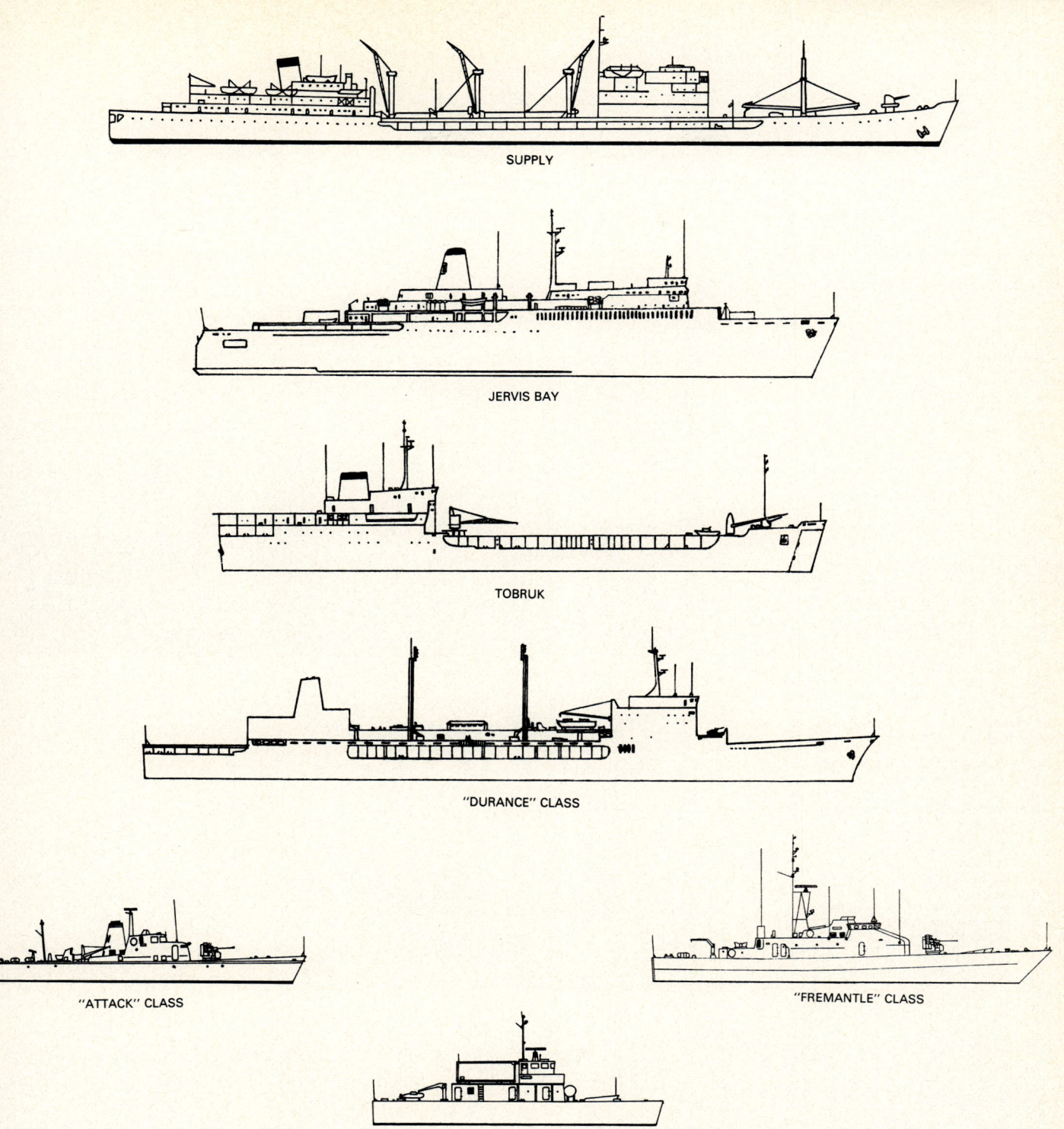

SUPPLY

JERVIS BAY

TOBRUK

"DURANCE" CLASS

"ATTACK" CLASS

"FREMANTLE" CLASS

"MHCAT"

Last six drawings by James Goldrick

AUSTRALIA / Submarines

SUBMARINES

Note: There is no deep diving support ship in service (other than *Seal* and *Porpoise*) or currently planned.

6 "OXLEY" CLASS (BRITISH "OBERON" CLASS)

Name	No.	Builders	Laid down	Launched	Commissioned
OXLEY	S 57	Scotts' Shipbuilding & Eng Co Ltd, Greenock	2 July 1964	24 Sep 1965	18 Apr 1967
OTWAY	S 59	Scotts' Shipbuilding & Eng Co Ltd, Greenock	29 June 1965	29 Nov 1966	23 Apr 1968
ONSLOW	S 60	Scotts' Shipbuilding & Eng Co Ltd, Greenock	4 Dec 1967	3 Dec 1968	22 Dec 1969
ORION	S 61	Scotts' Shipbuilding & Eng Co Ltd, Greenock	6 Oct 1972	16 Sep 1974	15 June 1977
OTAMA	S 62	Scotts' Shipbuilding & Eng Co Ltd, Greenock	25 May 1973	3 Dec 1975	27 Apr 1978
OVENS	S 70	Scotts' Shipbuilding & Eng Co Ltd, Greenock	17 June 1966	4 Dec 1967	18 Apr 1969

Displacement, tons: 1 610 standard; 2 196 surfaced; 2 417 dived
Length, feet (metres): 241 *(73.5)* pp; 295.5 *(90.1)* oa
Beam, feet (metres): 26.5 *(8.1)*
Draught, feet (metres): 18 *(5.5)*
Torpedo tubes: 8—21 in *(533 mm)* (6 bow, 2 stern)
Main machinery: 2 Admiralty Standard Range diesels; 3 600 bhp; 2 shafts; 2 electric motors; 6 000 shp; electric drive
Speed, knots: 16 surfaced; 18 dived; 11 snort
Oil fuel, tons: 300
Range, miles: 12 000 at 10 knots
Complement: 62 (7 officers, 55 sailors)

It was announced by the Minister for the Navy on 22 January 1963 that four submarines of the "Oberon" class were to be built in British shipyards under Admiralty supervision at an overall cost of £A5 million each. These were to constitute the 1st Submarine Squadron RAN based at HMAS Platypus, Neutral Bay, Sydney. Subsequently two more were ordered in October 1971 for delivery in 1975-76 later extended to 1977.

Dock: Slave Dock (Sydney) was first used in 1974, allowing submarine dockings to be carried out without occupying graving docks.

Modernisation: All submarines are being fitted with a new attack sonar from Krupp Atlas of Germany and an advanced fire control system being developed with Singer-Librascope Corporation. They are also being fitted with a new passive ranging sonar (Micropuff) built by Sperry Corporation. Mk 48 Mod 8 torpedoes are being acquired from the USA. In September 1978 the Minister for Defence stated that the fitting of Harpoon in submarines is being studied as also is the feasibility of using submarine-laid mines.

Names: *Oxley* and *Otway* are named after two earlier RAN submarines, completed in 1927. *Otama* is the Queensland aboriginal word for Dolphin, *Onslow* is a town in Western Australia, *Ovens* was an early explorer and *Orion* is named after the constellation.

Radar: Type 1006

Sonar: Attack: Type 187C
Intercept: Type 197.
Torpedo warning: Type 719—being removed
Long range passive search: Type 2007
Passive range finding: AN/BQG

ORION (first arrival in Sydney)   3/7/1978, Ron Wright

OVENS   2/1978, John Mortimer

OTWAY   1976, John Mortimer

AIRCRAFT CARRIER

1 MODIFIED "MAJESTIC" CLASS

Name	No.	Builders	Laid down	Launched	Commissioned
MELBOURNE (ex-*Majestic*)	R 21	Vickers, Barrow	15 Apr 1943	28 Feb 1945	28 Oct 1955

Displacement, tons: 16 000 standard; 19 966 full load
Length, feet (metres): 650·0 *(198·1)* wl; 701·5 *(213·8)* oa
Beam, feet (metres): 80·2 *(24·4)* hull
Draught, feet (metres): 25·5 *(7·8)*
Width, feet (metres): 80·0 *(24·4)* flight deck
  126·0 *(38·4)* oa including 6 degree angled deck and mirrors
Hangar, feet (metres): 444 × 52 × 17·5 *(135·3 × 15·8 × 5·3)*
Aircraft: A mix of A4G Skyhawk jet fighters, S2E Tracker A/S aircraft and Sea King Mk 50 A/S helicopters (see *Aircraft* notes)
Guns: 12—40 mm (4 twin, 4 single) Bofors
Boilers: 4 Admiralty 3-drum type
Main engines: Parsons single reduction geared turbines; 2 shafts; 42 000 shp
Speed, knots: 23
Range, miles: 12 000 at 14 knots; 6 200 at 23 knots
Complement: 1 335 (includes 347 Carrier Air Group personnel); 1 070 (75 officers and 995 sailors) as Flagship

At the end of the Second World War, when she was still incomplete, work on this ship was brought to a standstill pending a decision as to future naval requirements. When full-scale work was resumed during 1949-55, and after her design had been re-cast several times, she underwent reconstruction and modernisation in the UK, including the fitting of the angled deck, steam catapult and mirror deck landing sights, and was transferred to the RAN on completion. She was commissioned and renamed at Barrow-in-Furness on 28 October 1955, sailed from Portsmouth on 5 March 1956, and arrived at Fremantle, Australia, on 23 April 1956. She became flagship of the Royal Australian Navy at Sydney on 14 May 1956. She cost £A8 309 000.

Aircraft: The aircraft complement formerly comprised eight Sea Venom Mk 53 jet fighters, 16 Gannet Mk 1 turbo-prop A/S aircraft and two Sycamore helicopters. The complement changed twice before 1967 to ten Sea Venoms, ten Gannets, two Sycamores and finally four Sea Venoms, six Gannets and ten Wessex Mk 31 A/S helicopters. 14 S2E Tracker A/S aircraft, eight A4G Skyhawk fighter/strike aircraft and two TA4G Skyhawk trainer aircraft were delivered from the USA in 1967 at a cost of about $A46,000,000. Squadrons first embarked in *Melbourne* in 1969. Another eight A4G and two TA4G Skyhawk aircraft were delivered in 1971. HS-817 Squadron recommissioned in February 1976 with Sea King Mk 50 A/S helicopters. A general purpose complement embarked in *Melbourne* is eight Skyhawks, four Trackers and five Sea Kings which can be varied to meet various other roles.
Following a hangar fire at NAS Nowra in December 1976 in which all but three S2E Trackers were destroyed 16 ex-US Navy S2G Trackers were purchased and delivered in April 1977.

Electronics: Plessey tactical displays. URN-20 Tacan pod on masthead; Electronic intercept fitted.

Modernisation: *Melbourne* completed her extended refit during 1969 at a cost of over $A8 750 000 to enable her to operate with S2E Tracker and A4G Skyhawk aircraft, and to improve habitability. In 1971 the catapult was rebuilt and a bridle-catcher fitted, and the flight deck was strengthened. Under refit from November 1972 to July 1973.
On completion of a major refit in 1976 it was announced that *Melbourne* could remain operational until 1985.

Radar: Air surveillance: LW-04 (Type 944/954 IFF Mk 10 integrated).
Surface search: Type 293.
Carrier-controlled approach: SPN-35.
Navigation: Type 978.

MELBOURNE 2/1978, John Mortimer

MELBOURNE 2/1978, John Mortimer

Replacement: 16 designs from France, Italy, Spain, UK and USA have been submitted. A decision must be forthcoming soon if the ship (or ships) are to be ready by 1985.

MELBOURNE (with 63 ft RAAF launch) 10/1977, John Mortimer

40 AUSTRALIA / Destroyers

DESTROYERS

3 "PERTH" CLASS (DDGs)

Name	No.	Builders	Laid down	Launched	Commissioned
PERTH	D 38	Defoe Shipbuilding Co, Bay City, Mich.	21 Sep 1962	26 Sep 1963	17 July 1965
HOBART	D 39	Defoe Shipbuilding Co, Bay City, Mich.	26 Oct 1962	9 Jan 1964	18 Dec 1965
BRISBANE	D 41	Defoe Shipbuilding Co, Bay City, Mich.	15 Feb 1965	5 May 1966	16 Dec 1967

Displacement, tons: 3 370 standard; 4 618 full load
Length, feet (metres): 440·8 *(134·3)*
Beam, feet (metres): 47·1 *(14·3)*
Draught, feet (metres): 20·1 *(6·1)*
Missiles: 40 SAM for Tartar; 1 single launcher (see *Modernisation* note)
Guns: 2—5 in *(127 mm)* 54 cal. Mk 42 mod 10, single-mount
A/S weapons: 2 single launchers for Ikara system
Torpedo tubes: 6 (2 triple) Mk 32 mod 5 for A/S torpedoes
Main engines: 2 GE double reduction turbines, 2 shafts; 70 000 shp
Boilers: 4 Foster-Wheeler "D" type, 1 200 psi; 950°F
Speed, knots: 30+
Range, miles: 4 500 at 15 knots; 2 000 at 30 knots
Complement: 333 (21 officers, 312 sailors)

On 6 January 1962, in Washington, US defence representatives and Australian military officials (on behalf of the Royal Australian Navy) and executives of the Defoe Shipbuilding Company, of Bay City, Michigan, signed a $A25 726 700·contract for the construction of two guided-missile destroyers (shipbuilding cost only). On 22 January 1963 it was announced by the Navy Minister in Canberra, Australia, that a third guided-missile destroyer was to be built in USA for Australia. The first of their kind for the Australian Navy, they constitute the 1st Destroyer Squadron, RAN. All three ships saw action off Viet-Nam where they served with the US 7th fleet.
Hobart is 1st DS leader.

Cost: Original estimate $A12·8 million to $A14 million each (with missiles and electronics $A40 million each). The total cost of *Perth* was reported to be $A50 million.

Design: Generally similar to the US "Charles F. Adams" class, but they differ by the addition of a broad deckhouse between the funnels enclosing the Ikara anti-submarine torpedo-carrying missile system.

Electronics: URN-20 Tacan pod; intercept equipment fitted; URD-4, UHFD/F; Enhanced JPTDS combat data system with UYK-7 computer and Link 11 exchange equipment.

Fire Control: Gunnery: GFCS Mk 68 with SPG53A radar.
Missiles: Mk 74 with SPG51C radar and single Mk 13 launcher.

Modernisation: *Perth* started a modernisation at the Long Beach Naval Shipyard on 3 September 1974, completing 2 January 1975. The work included the installation of a Naval Combat Data System, updating of the Tartar missile fire control system, replacing 5-in gun mounts and modernising radars. *Hobart* completed her modernisation at Garden Island Dockyard in April 1978, and *Brisbane's* started late 1977 and will complete in 1979. *Hobart's* gun mounts were replaced in the USA in 1972 and *Brisbane's* replacement was completed at Garden Island in October 1976. This gunnery alteration includes deletion of local surface fire control with increased reliability.

BRISBANE (at Antwerp)   7/1977, Leo van Ginderen

HOBART   1976, John Mortimer

Radar: Three dimensional: SPS 52.
Air search: SPS 40.
Surface search: SPS 10.
Navigation: Type 975.

Sonar: SQS 23F; AN/UQC 1D; UQN 1.

PERTH   9/1978, John Mortimer

AUSTRALIA / Destroyers

2 "DARING" CLASS (DD)

Name	No.	Builders	Laid down	Launched	Commissioned
VENDETTA	D 08	HMA Naval Dockyard, Williamstown	4 July 1949	3 May 1954	26 Nov 1958
VAMPIRE	D 11	Cockatoo Island Dockyard, Sydney	1 July 1952	27 Oct 1956	23 June 1959

Displacement, tons: 2 800 standard; 3 600 full load
Length, feet (metres): 366 (111·6) pp; 388·5 (118·4) oa
Beam, feet (metres): 43 (13·1)
Draught, feet (metres): 12·8 (3·9)
Guns: 6—4·5 in (115 mm)/45 (twin Mk 6); 6—40 mm/60 (single Mk 9)
A/S weapons: 1—3-barrelled Limbo mortar (see Design note)
Main engines: English Electric geared turbines; 2 shafts; 54 000 shp
Boilers: 2 Foster-Wheeler; 650 psi; 850°F
Speed, knots: 30·5
Range, miles: 3 700 at 20 knots
Oil fuel, tons: 584
Complement: 320 (14 officers, 306 sailors)

Vampire and *Vendetta*, constitute the 2nd Destroyer Squadron, RAN, and are the largest destroyers ever built in Australia. They were ordered in 1946. Their sister ship, *Voyager*, the prototype of the class, collided with the aircraft carrier *Melbourne* and sank off the southern coast of New South Wales on the night of 10 February 1964. She was replaced by the British destroyer *Duchess*, lent to Australia by the UK for four years on 8 May 1964, later extended to 1971, purchased by RAN in 1972 and decommissioned in 1977.

Four large destroyers of this type were originally projected, to have been named after the RAN's famous "Scrap Iron Flotilla" of destroyers during the Second World War, but *Waterhen* was cancelled in 1954. *Vampire* is 2nd DS leader.

Vendetta, who would otherwise require an additional refit, is to pay off late June 1979 to provide manpower for *Adelaide*, probably being put at three months notice with reduced crew at Cockburn Sound.

Design: *Vampire* and *Vendetta* were of similar design, including all welded construction, to that of the "Daring" class, built in the UK, but were modified to suit Australian conditions and have Limbo instead of Squid anti-submarine mortars. The superstructure is of light alloy, instead of steel, to reduce weight.

Modernisation: *Vampire* completed in December 1971. *Vendetta* completed May 1973. The $A20 million programme for both ships included new Mk 22 fire control systems, new LW-02 air-warning and navigation radars, new action-information centre, modernised communications, fitting modernised turrets, improved habitability, the fitting of an enclosed bridge and new funnels. The work was carried out by Williamstown Dockyard. These alterations afford an interesting comparison with the Peruvian "Darings" (ex-*Decoy* and *Diana*) with their eight Exocet SSMs, rebuilt forefunnel and radar and helicopter deck.

Radar: Air surveillance: LW-02.
Surface-search, target indication and fire-control: M22 series.
Surface-search and navigation: 8GR-301A.

Sonar: Types 162, 170, 174 and 185.

VENDETTA 9/1977, Dr. Giorgio Arra

VAMPIRE 9/1978, John Mortimer

VAMPIRE 10/1977, John Mortimer

VENDETTA 2/1978, John Mortimer

42 AUSTRALIA / Frigates

FRIGATES
6 "RIVER" CLASS

Name	No.	Builders	Laid down	Launched	Commissioned
YARRA	D 45	HMA Naval Dockyard, Melbourne	9 Apr 1957	30 Sep 1958	27 July 1961
PARRAMATTA	D 46	Cockatoo Island Dockyard, Sydney	3 Jan 1957	31 Jan 1959	4 July 1961
STUART	D 48	Cockatoo Island Dockyard, Sydney	20 Mar 1959	8 Apr 1961	28 June 1963
DERWENT	D 49	HMA Naval Dockyard, Melbourne	16 June 1958	17 Apr 1961	30 Apr 1964
SWAN	D 50	HMA Naval Dockyard, Melbourne	18 Aug 1965	16 Dec 1967	20 Jan 1970
TORRENS	D 53	Cockatoo Island Dockyard, Sydney	18 Aug 1965	28 Sep 1968	19 Jan 1971

Displacement, tons: 2 100 standard; 2 700 full load
Length, feet (metres): 360·0 *(109·7)* pp; 370·0 *(112·8)* oa
Beam, feet (metres): 41·0 *(12·5)*
Draught, feet (metres): 17·3 *(5·3)*
Missile launchers: 1 quad for Seacat
Guns: 2—4·5 in *(115 mm)*/45 (twin Mk 6)
A/S weapons: 1 launcher for Ikara system; 1 Australian Mk 10 3-barrelled DC mortar (not *Yarra*)
Main engines: 2 double reduction geared turbines; 2 shafts; 30 000 shp
Boilers: 2 Babcock & Wilcox; 550 psi; 850°F
Speed, knots: 30
Range, miles: 3 400 at 12 knots
Complement: 247 (13 officers, 234 sailors) in *Swan* and *Torrens*; 250 (13 officers, 237 sailors) in other four ships

The design of the first four is basically similar to that of British "Type 12", the last pair to that of the "Leander" frigates. All are modified by the RAN to incorporate improvements in equipment and habitability. *Stuart* was the first ship fitted with the Ikara anti-submarine guided missile; (trial ship for the system). *Derwent* was the first RAN ship to be fitted with Seacat. The variable depth sonar has been removed from *Derwent* and *Stuart*. Note difference in sihouette between *Swan* and *Torrens* and the earlier ships of the class, the former pair having a straight-run upper deck. *Torrens* is leader for the frigate squadron.

Modernisation: *Parramatta*, *Stuart* and *Derwent* will undergo half-life modernisation at Williamstown; work on *Parramatta* began in June 1977 (paid off 10 May). This programme includes improved accommodation consequent on reduction in complement, installation of M22 gunnery direction system, the fitting of Australian Mulloka sonar (provided the set goes into production), the conversion of the boilers to burn diesel fuel, installation of Mk 32 torpedo tubes in lieu of Limbo mortar and new navigation radar. *Yarra* has been fitted with Mulloka sonar, trials beginning in April 1975. In October 1976 she started a half-life refit at Cockatoo Island Dockyard and rejoined the Fleet in December 1977. Her Mk 10 mortar was removed during refit. The VDS in *Derwent* was removed during 1977 refit and her stern now resembles that of *Yarra* and *Parramatta*. The whole of the above modernisation programme is due to be completed by 1981 and that of *Swan* and *Torrens* is due to start in 1982.

Radar: Air surveillance: LW-02 (all ships) (with Type 944/954 IFF Mk 10).
Surface search: Type 293 (first four).
Navigation: Type 978 (first four).
Surface search, target indication and fire control: M22 (last pair).
Surface search and navigation: 8GR-301 (last pair).

Note: Type 293 to be replaced by SPS 55 at half-life modernisation and Type 293 and MRS3 by M22 at same time.

Sonar: Types 162, 170, 177M, 185.

YARRA (after half-life refit)   4/1978, Royal Australian Navy

STUART (DERWENT has now had stern altered)   10/1977, Dr. Giorgio Arra

TORRENS (SWAN similar)   2/1978, John Mortimer

AUSTRALIA / Frigates — Light forces 43

0 + 2 + 1 US "FFG 7" CLASS

Name	No.	Builders	Laid down	Launched	Commissioned
ADELAIDE	F 01	Todd Pacific Shipyard Corporation, USA	29 July 1977	21 June 1978	July 1980
CANBERRA	F 02	Todd Pacific Shipyard Corporation, USA	1 Mar 1978	1 Dec 1978	Nov 1981*
—	F 03	Todd Pacific Shipyard Corporation, USA	21 Jan 1980*	26 Sep 1980*	Nov 1982*

*planned dates

Displacement, tons: 3 605 full load
Length, feet (metres): 445 *(135·6)*
Beam, feet (metres): 45 *(13·7)*
Draught, feet (metres): 24·5 *(7·5)*
Aircraft: 2 helicopters (type to be decided)
Missiles: Est. 30 total SAM Standard and SSM Harpoon; 1 single Mk 13 Mod 4 launcher
Gun: 1—3 in *(76 mm)*/62 (single Mk 75) (see note); provision for point defence weapon system
A/S weapons: 6 (2 triple) Mk 32 torpedo tubes
Main engines: 2 GE LM 2 500 gas turbines; 40 000 shp; 1 shaft (cp propeller)
Speed: 28+
Range, miles: 4 500 at 20 knots
Complement: 186

"FFG 7" Class   1977, Royal Australian Navy Model

Two ordered from USA in February 1976 for delivery 1980-81. Third ordered November 1977 for delivery in 1982. Space and weight reserved for CIWS. US Numbers—*Adelaide*, FFG-17; *Canberra*, FFG-18; F03, FFG-35.

Financial: $414 million for *Adelaide* and *Canberra* (January 1977 price). F03 to cost $186 million (August 1977 price).

Fire Control: Mk 92/STIR gun and missile control.

Gunnery: The Mk 75 is an OTO-Melara Compact manufactured in USA under licence.

Radar: Long range air search and early warning: AN SPS 49. Search and navigation: AN SPS 55.

Sonar: SQS 56.

MINE WARFARE SHIPS

Note: The RAN is examining a new concept in minehunting vessels which should provide a more flexible and effective minehunting capability. This envisages an Australian-designed and developed glass-reinforced plastic catamaran (MHCAT) fitted with modern minehunting and mine disposal equipment of 98·4 ft *(30 m)* oa and 106 tonnes. The Government has decided to proceed with the initial prototype design and acquisition of long lead items for two prototype vessels. The objective is to have new operational minehunting craft entering service during the first half of the 1980s.

Studies are to be undertaken for the provision of new MCMVs for the RAN in addition to the catamaran design. Approval for the construction of these later ships has not been given although some long-lead items have been ordered.

3 BRITISH "TON" CLASS (MODIFIED)

Name	No.	Builders	Laid down	Launched	Commissioned
SNIPE (ex-HMS *Alcaston*)	M 1102	Thornycroft	1952	5 Jan 1953	1953
CURLEW (ex-HMS *Chediston*)	M 1121	Montrose S.Y.	1952	6 Oct 1953	1954
IBIS (ex-HMS *Singleton*)	M 1183	Montrose S.Y.	1952	23 Nov 1955	1956

Displacement, tons: 375 standard; 445 full load
Dimensions, feet (metres): 140 pp; 153 oa × 28·8 × 8·2 *(42·7; 46·6 × 8·8 × 2·5)*
Guns: *Ibis* 2—40 mm; *Curlew* and *Snipe* 1—40 mm
Main engines: Napier Deltic diesels; 2 shafts; 3 000 bhp = 14 knots
Range, miles: 2 300 at 13 knots; 3 500 at 8 knots
Complement: *Ibis* 34 (4 officers; 30 sailors); *Curlew* and *Snipe* 38 (3 officers, 35 sailors)

"Ton" class coastal minesweepers. Six purchased from the UK in 1961, and modified in British Dockyards to suit Australian conditions. Turned over to the RAN, commissioned and renamed on 21 August, 7 September and 11 September 1962, respectively. Mirlees diesels were replaced by Napier Deltic, and ships air-conditioned and fitted with stabilisers. Sailed from Portsmouth to Australia on 1 October 1962. Constitute the 1st Mine Countermeasures Squadron. *Curlew* and *Snipe* have been converted into minehunters—*Curlew* 26 June 1967 to 13 December 1968 and *Snipe* 10 April 1969 to 18 December 1970.

Radar: Type 975 I-band.

Sonar: Type 193 (except *Ibis*)

CURLEW   11/1978, John Mortimer

LIGHT FORCES

Note: A Defence Committee has recommended a class of Second Degree patrol boats for detailed coastal inspection. No further action reported.

1 + 14 "FREMANTLE" CLASS (LARGE PATROL CRAFT)

Name	No.	Builders	Laid down	Launched	Commissioned
FREMANTLE	P 203	Brooke Marine, Lowestoft	Oct 1977	Feb 1979	July 1979
WARRNAMBOOL	—	North Queensland Eng. and Agents. Cairns	30 Sep 1978	—	—

To be laid down mid 1980-1985 at Cairns:-
TOWNSVILLE, WOLLONGONG, LAUNCESTON, WHYALLA, IPSWICH, CESSNOCK, BENDIGO, GAWLER, GERALDTON, DUBBO, GEELONG, GLADSTONE, BUNBURY.

Displacement, tons: 220
Dimensions, feet (metres): 137·8 × 23·3 × 5·9 *(42 × 7·1 × 1·8)*
Main engines: 2 MTU Series 538 diesels; 3 200 hp = approx 36 knots
Complement: 22

The decision to buy these new "PCF 420" class patrol craft was announced in September 1977. The design is by Brooke Marine Ltd, Lowestoft who will build the lead ship, the remainder being built by North Queensland Engineers and Agents Pty Ltd, Cairns. Delivery of lead ship planned for June 1979.

Armament: Temporarily 40/60 Bofors in lead ship.

Names: Are derived from the "Bathurst" class of minesweepers of World War II.

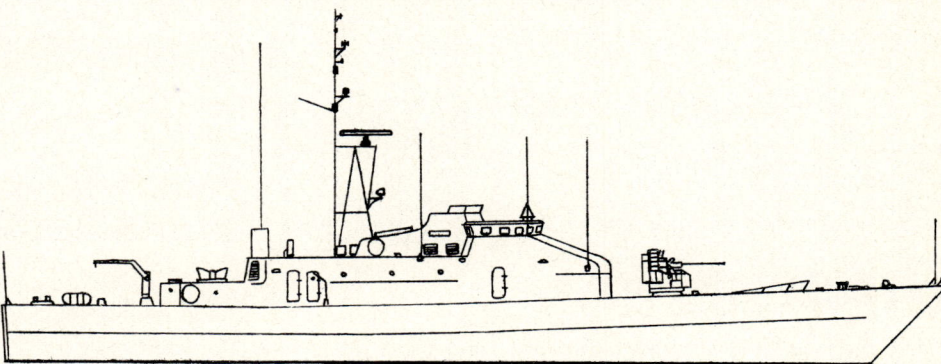

FREMANTLE   1978, James Goldrick

44 AUSTRALIA / Light forces — Oceanographic and survey ships

12 "ATTACK" CLASS (LARGE PATROL CRAFT)

Name	No.	Builders	Laid down	Launched	Commissioned
ACUTE	P 81	Evans Deakin Ltd	Apr 1967	26 Aug 1967	26 Apr 1968
ADROIT	P 82	Evans Deakin Ltd	Aug 1967	3 Feb 1968	17 Aug 1968
ADVANCE	P 83	Walkers Ltd, Maryborough, Queensland	Mar 1967	16 Aug 1967	24 Jan 1968
ARDENT	P 87	Evans Deakin Ltd	Oct 1967	27 Apr 1968	26 Oct 1968
ASSAIL	P 89	Evans Deakin Ltd	Aug 1967	18 Nov 1967	12 July 1968
ATTACK	P 90	Evans Deakin Ltd	Sep 1966	8 Apr 1967	17 Nov 1967
AWARE	P 91	Evans Deakin Ltd	July 1967	7 Oct 1967	21 June 1968
BARBETTE	P 97	Walkers Ltd, Maryborough, Queensland	Nov 1967	10 Apr 1968	16 Aug 1968
BARRICADE	P 98	Evans Deakin Ltd	Dec 1967	29 June 1968	26 Oct 1968
BOMBARD	P 99	Walkers Ltd, Maryborough, Queensland	Apr 1968	6 July 1968	5 Nov 1968
BUCCANEER	P 100	Evans Deakin Ltd	June 1968	14 Sep 1968	11 Jan 1969
BAYONET	P 101	Walkers Ltd, Maryborough, Queensland	Oct 1968	6 Nov 1968	22 Feb 1969

Displacement, tons: 146 full load
Dimensions, feet (metres): 107·5 × 20 × 7·3 *(32·8 × 6·1 × 2·2)*
Guns: 1—40 mm/70 (single Mk 7); 2 medium MG
Main engines: Paxman 16 YJCM diesels; 3 500 hp; 2 shafts = 21-24 knots
Range, miles: 1 220 at 13 knots
Complement: 19 (3 officers, 16 sailors)

Steel construction. Ordered in November 1965. First vessel was originally scheduled for delivery in August 1966, but was not launched until March 1967. Cost $A800 000 each. All have been employed in fishery protection and search and rescue off North Australia.

Disposals: *Bandolier* transferred to Indonesia after refit 16 November 1973. *Archer* transferred 21 October 1974. *Aitape, Ladava, Lae, Madang, Samarai* transferred to Papua New Guinea Defence Force 16 September 1975.

Darwin Cyclone: On 25 December 1974 *Arrow* was lost during Cyclone Tracy at Darwin. *Attack* was beached and badly damaged at the same time but was salved and towed to Cairns for repairs.

Radar: Type RM 916

ADVANCE *3/1978, John Mortimer*

OCEANOGRAPHIC AND SURVEY SHIPS

Note: The 1976 Defence White Paper stated plans to build two more survey ships and six large survey launches although no orders have yet been placed. One of the ships will probably be of the "Flinders" class.

Name	No.	Builders	Laid down	Launched	Commissioned
COOK	A 219	HMA Naval Dockyard, Williamstown	30 Sep 1974	27 Aug 1977	mid-1980

Displacement, tons: 1 900 standard; 2 450 full load
Length, feet (metres): 316·7 *(96·6)*
Beam, feet (metres): 44·0 *(13·4)*
Draught, feet (metres): 15·1 *(4·6)*
Main engines: Diesels; 2 shafts; 3 400 bhp
Speed, knots: 17
Oil fuel, tons: 640
Range, miles: 11 000 at 14 knots
Complement: 150 including 13 scientists

Intended to replace HMAS *Diamantina*. She will have dual hydrographic and oceanographic roles. The after part of the ship will contain research equipment and facilities. Accommodation for 13 scientists. One survey launch. Specialised oceanographic gear will include a data logger, three oceanographic winches, wet laboratory, dry laboratory, magnetometer and gravimeter. No helicopter.

Armament: In wartime could mount 2 twin 30 mm and 4 MG.

Radar: TM 829.

Sonar: Simrad SU2.

Surveying Equipment: Hi-Fix 6; Mini-Ranger MRS3; Atlas Deso 10 and Harris Narrow-Beam echo-sounders.

COOK on launching *8/1977, Royal Australian Navy*

Name	No.	Builders	Laid down	Launched	Commissioned
MORESBY	A 73	State Dockyard, Newcastle, NSW	June 1961	7 Sep 1963	6 Mar 1964

Displacement, tons: 1 714 standard; 2 351 full load
Length, feet (metres): 284·5 *(86·7)* pp; 314·0 *(95·7)* oa
Beam, feet (metres): 42·0 *(12·8)*
Draught, feet (metres): 15·0 *(4·6)*
Aircraft: 1 Bell 206B-1 (Kiowa) helicopter
Guns: 2—40 mm Bofors (single) (removed)
Main engines: Diesel-electric; 3 diesels; 3 990 bhp; 2 electric motors; 2 shafts = 19 knots
Complement: 135

The RAN's first specifically designed survey ship. Built at a cost of £A2 million ($A4 million). Guns are not currently embarked.

Deployment: Based on HMAS *Stirling* (Cockburn Sound W.A.).

Refit: During refit from 13 August 1973 to 18 January 1974 *Moresby's* funnel was heightened, her 40 mm guns removed and an exhaust outlet fitted on her forecastle.

Radar: TM 829.

Sonar: Simrad SU2.

MORESBY *1977, Royal Australian Navy*

AUSTRALIA / Oceanographic and survey ships

Name	No.	Builders	Laid down	Launched	Commissioned
DIAMANTINA	A 266 (ex-F 377)	Walkers Ltd, Maryborough, Queensland	12 Apr 1943	6 Apr 1944	27 Apr 1945

Displacement, tons: 1 340 standard; 2 127 full load
Length, feet (metres): 283 *(86·3)* pp; 301·3 *(91·8)* oa
Beam, feet (metres): 36·7 *(11·2)*
Draught, feet (metres): 12·5 *(3·8)*
Gun: 1—40 mm
Main engines: Triple expansion 5 500 ihp; 2 shafts
Boilers: 2 Admiralty 3-drum
Speed, knots: 19·5
Range, miles: 7 700 at 12 knots
Complement: 125 (6 officers, 119 sailors)

Frigate converted in 1959-60 for survey and completed conversion for oceanographic research in June 1969. The conversion included the provision of special laboratories. Sister ship *Lachlan* was sold to the Royal New Zealand Navy (RNZN), and was finally paid off in 1975. *Diamantina* is to be replaced by *Cook* who is due to commission in 1980.

Armament: The two 4-in guns and two Squid A/S mortars in "B" position were removed.

Deployment: Based on HMAS *Stirling* (Cockburn Sound W.A.).

Radar: Type 975

Sonar: Type 144

DIAMANTINA   8/1978, John Mortimer

Name	No.	Builders	Laid down	Launched	Commissioned
FLINDERS	A 312	HMA Naval Dockyard, Williamstown	11 June 1971	29 July 1972	27 Apr 1973

Displacement, tons: 750
Dimensions, feet (metres): 161 × 33 × 12 *(49·1 × 10 × 3·7)*
Main engines: 2 Paxman Ventura diesels; 1 680 bhp
Speed, knots: 13·5
Range, miles: 5 000 at 9 knots
Complement: 38 (4 officers, 34 sailors)

Similar in design to *Atyimba* built for the Philippines. *Flinders* is based at Cairns, with her primary responsibility in the Barrier Reef area.

Radar: TM 829.

Sonar: Simrad SU2.

FLINDERS   1976, Royal Australian Navy

Name	No.	Builders	Laid down	Launched	Commissioned
KIMBLA	AGOR 314	Walkers Ltd, Maryborough, Queensland	4 Nov 1953	23 Mar 1955	26 Mar 1956

Displacement, tons: 762 standard; 1 021 full load
Dimensions, feet (metres): 150 pp; 179 oa × 32 × 12 *(45·7; 54·6 × 9·8 × 3·7)*
Main engines: Triple expansion; 1 shaft; 350 ihp
Speed, knots: 9·5
Complement: 40 (4 officers, 36 sailors)

Built as a boom defence vessel. Converted to trials vessel in 1959. Guns were removed (one 40 mm; two 20 mm). She is due for replacement about 1980.

Appearance: Enclosed bridge fitted mid-1977.

Radar: Type 975.

Sonar: Simrad SU2.

KIMBLA   8/1977, Royal Australian Navy

AUSTRALIA / Service forces

SERVICE FORCES

1 DESTROYER TENDER

Name	No.	Builders	Laid down	Launched	Commissioned
STALWART	A 215	Cockatoo Island D.Y., Sydney	June 1964	7 Oct 1966	9 Feb 1968

Displacement, tons: 10 000 standard; 15 500 full load
Length, feet (metres): 515·5 *(157·1)*
Beam, feet (metres): 67·5 *(20·6)*
Draught, feet (metres): 29·5 *(9·0)*
Aircraft: One helicopter (normally Wessex 31B)—capacity for 2
Missiles: Provision for Seacat
Guns: 4—40 mm (2 twin)
Main engines: 2 Scott-Sulzer 6-cyl diesels, 2 shafts; 14 400 bhp
Speed, knots: 20+
Range, miles: 12 000 at 12 knots
Complement: 396 (23 officers and 373 sailors)

Largest naval vessel designed and built in Australia. Ordered on 11 September 1963. Designed to maintain destroyers and frigates, and advanced weapons systems, including guided missiles. She has a helicopter flight deck and a hangar, being capable of operating two Wessex 31B or two Sea King Mk 50 helicopters. High standard of habitability. Formerly rated as Escort Maintenance Ship. Redesignated Destroyer Tender in 1968. Cost officially estimated at just under $A15 million.

STALWART   1977, Royal Australian Navy

1 "TIDE" CLASS (FLEET TANKER)

Name	No.	Builders	Laid down	Launched	Commissioned
SUPPLY (ex-*Tide Austral*)	AO 195	Harland and Wolff, Belfast	5 Aug 1952	1 Sep 1954	Mar 1955

Displacement, tons: 15 000 standard; 25 941 full load
Measurement, tons: 17 600 deadweight; 11 200 gross
Dimensions, feet (metres): 550 pp; 583 oa × 71 × 32
(167·6; 177·8 × 21·7 × 9·8)
Guns: 6—40 mm (2 twin, 2 single)
Main engines: Double reduction geared turbines; 15 000 shp
Speed, knots: 17·25
Range, miles: 8 500 at 13 knots
Complement: 205

British "Tide" Class. Lent to the UK until 1 September 1962, when *Tide Austral* was re-named HMAS *Supply* and commissioned in the RAN at Portsmouth 15 August 1962. Sailed for Australia 1 October 1962. Bridge was rebuilt in 1973-74.

Radar: Type 975 (to be replaced by RM 16).

Replacement: An underway replenishment ship of a new class is planned. Investigations are under way to determine whether a replacement ship of the "Durance" class should be built in Australia or France. Decision expected September 1979.

SUPPLY   10/1977, Graeme Andrews

TRAINING SHIP

Name	No.	Builders	Laid down	Launched	Commissioned
JERVIS BAY (ex-*Australian Trader*)	AGT 203	State Dockyard, Newcastle, NSW	18 Aug 1967	17 Feb 1969	17 June 1969 (completion)

Displacement, tons: 8 770; 8 915 full load
Length, feet (metres): 445·1 *(135·7)*
Beam, feet (metres): 70·6 *(21·5)*
Draught, feet (metres): 20·1 *(6·1)*
Main engines: 2—16PC 2V 400 Crossley Pielstick diesels; 2 shafts; 13 000 bhp
Speed, knots: 19·5
Fuel: 820·3 tons *(833·5 tonnes)*
Complement: 108 plus 40+ trainees

The former roll-on roll-off ship MV *Australian Trader* was purchased 28 January 1977 for $A5·07 million from the Australian National Line and commissioned in the RAN on 25 August 1977. A contract for $A720,000 for conversion of the ship to its new role was let to the Sydney firm of Storey and Keers (Ship Repairs) Pty Ltd in October 1977. Conversion work included the construction of a navigation training bridge on top of the existing bridge, and conversion of some cabins into a classroom. Fitted with bow thruster. *Jervis Bay* made her first cruise as a training ship in February 1978. The ship's primary role is navigation training for the RAN, although her vehicle and cargo carrying capability have been retained.

JERVIS BAY   3/1978, D. N. Brigham

AUSTRALIA / Amphibious forces — Tugs 47

AMPHIBIOUS FORCES

0 + 1 HEAVY LIFT SHIP

Name	No.	Builders	Laid down	Launched	Commissioned
TOBRUK	L 50	Carrington Slipways Pty Ltd	Dec 1978	1979	1980

Displacement, tonnes: 5 800
Dimensions, feet (metres): 425 × 60 × — (129·6 × 18·3 × —)
Aircraft: Wessex 31B helicopters
Landing craft: 2 LCVP at davits; 2 LCM8 can be carried on deck
Guns: 2—40 mm
Main engines: 2 diesels = 17 knots (?)
Complement: 130
Troops: 350-550

A contract to build an Amphibious Heavy Lift Ship in Australia was let in November 1977. The design is an update of the British "Sir Bedivere" class and will provide facilities for the operation of helicopters, landing craft, amphibians or side carried pontoons for ship-to-shore movement. A special feature will be the ship's heavy lift derrick system for handling heavy loads. The LSH will be able to embark a squadron of Leopard tanks plus a number of wheeled vehicles and artillery in addition to its troop lift. A comprehensive communication fit and minor hospital facilities will also be provided.

TOBRUK *1976, Royal Australian Navy Drawing*

6 LANDING CRAFT (HEAVY) (LCH)

Name	No.	Builders	Laid down	Launched	Commissioned
BALIKPAPAN	L 126	Walkers Ltd, Maryland, Queensland	May 1971	15 Aug 1971	8 Dec 1971
BRUNEI	L 127	Walkers Ltd, Maryland, Queensland	July 1971	15 Oct 1971	5 Jan 1973
LABUAN	L 128	Walkers Ltd, Maryland, Queensland	Oct 1971	29 Dec 1971	9 Mar 1973
TARAKAN	L 129	Walkers Ltd, Maryland, Queensland	Dec 1971	16 Mar 1972	15 June 1973
WEWAK	L 130	Walkers Ltd, Maryland, Queensland	Mar 1972	18 May 1972	10 Aug 1973
BETANO	L 133	Walkers Ltd, Maryland, Queensland	Sep 1972	5 Dec 1972	8 Feb 1974

Displacement, tons: 310 light; 503 full load
Dimensions, feet (metres): 146 × 33 × 6·5 (44·5 × 10·1 × 2)
Guns: 2—0·5 in MG
Main engines: 2 General Motors diesels; twin screw = 10 knots
Range, miles: 3 000 at 10 knots
Complement: 16

Originally this class was ordered for the Army with whom *Balikpapan* remained until June 1974 being commissioned for naval service on 27 September 1974. All now transferred to RAN. Can carry three medium tanks.
Labuan due to pay off in 1979-80 to provide manpower for *Tobruk*. She is planned to be used for reserve training at HMAS *Moreton* after those dates.

PNGDF: *Buna* and *Salamaua* transferred to Papua New Guinea Defence Force in November 1974.

Radar: Decca 101 (to be replaced by RM 916).

BALIKPAPAN *1978, Graeme Andrews*

GENERAL PURPOSE VESSELS

Name	No.	Builders	Commissioned
BANKS	AG 244	Walkers, Maryborough, Queensland	16 Feb 1960
BASS	AG 247	Walkers, Maryborough, Queensland	25 May 1960

Displacement, tons: 207 standard; 255 and 260 full load respectively
Dimensions, feet (metres): 90 pp; 101 oa × 22 × 8 (27·5; 30·8 × 6·7 × 2·4)
Main engines: Diesels; speed = 10 knots
Complement: 14 (2 officers, 12 sailors)

"Explorer" class. Of all steel construction. *Banks* was fitted for fishery surveillance and *Bass* for surveying, but both are used for other duties, including reserve training. *Banks* based in Port Adelaide, *Bass* in Hobart. Minor differences—*Bass* has a higher flying bridge with consequent raising of her radar pedestal. Ventilators differ.

GPV 958

75 ft (22·9 m) General purpose vessel based at HMAS *Stirling*, W.A.

SDB 1324

80 ft (24·4 m) Seaward defence boat based at HMAS *Lonsdale*, Victoria.

SDB 1325

80 ft (24·4 m) Seaward defence boat based at HMAS *Stirling*, W.A.

BANKS *1977, Graeme Andrews*

TUGS

501 502 504

Displacement, tons: 47·5
Dimensions, feet (metres): 50 × 15 × — (15·2 × 4·6 × —)
Main engines: 2 General Motors diesels; 340 bhp = 8-9 knots
Complement: 3

First pair with bipod mast funnel built by Stannard Bros, Sydney in 1969 and second pair (including 503) with conventional funnel by Perrin Engineering, Brisbane in 1972.

Transfer: Tug 503 transferred to Papua New Guinea in 1974.

2 Ex-US ARMY TYPE

SARDIUS TB9 — TB1536

Of 29 tons GRT (approx 60 tons, full load), 45 ft long with 240 hp Hercules diesel, capable of 10 knots. Complement 4. *Sardius* employed in Sydney as ammunition-lighter tug, TB1536 at HMAS *Cerberus* (Victoria). Wooden hulled.

48 AUSTRALIA / Diving tenders — RAAF

DIVING TENDERS

Name	No.	Builders	Launched
SEAL (ex-HMS *Wintringham*)	DTV 1001	White, Cowes	24 May 1955
PORPOISE (ex-HMS *Neasham*)	DTV 1002	White, Cowes	14 Mar 1956

Displacement, tons: 120 standard; 159 full load
Dimensions, feet (metres): 100 pp × 22 × 5·8 *(30·5 × 6·7 × 1·8)*
Main engines: 2 Paxman diesels; 1 100 bhp = 14 knots
Range, miles: 2 000 at 9 knots; 1 500 at 12 knots
Complement: 7 (can accommodate 14 divers)

Purchased from the Royal Navy in 1966-67, these ex-inshore Minesweepers were converted to Diving Tenders and attached to the Diving School at Sydney. HMS *Popham* (Vospers, launched 11 January 1955) also purchased and renamed *Otter* but not converted and was sold in 1974. Carry recompression chambers.

Status: *Seal* entered service in December 1968 and *Porpoise* in 1973. Neither is a commissioned ship but both are tenders to HMAS *Penguin*, Sydney, working from there as operational diving training vessels.

SEAL 3/1977, John Mortimer

TORPEDO RECOVERY VESSELS

TRV 801 802 803

Displacement, tons: 91·6
Dimensions, feet (metres): 88·5 × 20·9 × 4·5 *(27 × 6·4 × 1·4)*
Main engines: 3 General Motors diesels; 890 hp; triple screws = 13 knots.
Complement: 9 (1 officer, 8 men)

All built at Williamstown—completed between January 1970 and April 1971. TRV 802 used as diving tender.

TRV 803 11/1976, Graeme Andrews

AUXILIARIES

3 + 1 SELF-PROPELLED LIGHTERS

Displacement, tonnes: 1 100 (load)
Length, feet (metres): 124·6 *(38)*

First three were laid down at Williamstown in 1978. The fourth, for HMAS *Stirling*, has not yet been ordered. Total cost $A7 million. To be used for water/fuel transport. Steel hulls with twin swivelling outboard propellers. To replace 50 year old craft now in service.

1 TANK CLEANING VESSEL

Name	No.	Builders	Launched
COLAC	—	Mort's Dock, Sydney	13 Aug 1941

Originally 1 025 ton "Bathurst" class minesweeper. Now a dumb craft, painted black, based in Sydney. Sister ship *Castlemaine*, given by Dept. of Defence as museum ship to Melbourne in 1973.

1 AIR SEA RESCUE CRAFT

Name	No.	Builders	Commissioned
AIR SPRITE	Y 256	Halvorsen, Sydney	1960

Displacement, tons: 23·5 standard
Dimensions, feet (metres): 63 × 15·5 × 3·3 *(19·2 × 4·7 × 1)*
Main engines: 2 Scott Hall Defender (Petrol) = 25 knots
Complement: Up to 8

Used as reserve training and general purpose vessel in Sydney. Other similar craft are operated by the RAAF.

4 MOTOR WATER LIGHTERS

GAYUNDAH (MRL 253), MWL 254, 256, 257

Displacement, tons: 300 standard; 600 (app) full load.
Dimensions, feet (metres): 120 × 24 × — *(36·6 × 7·3 × —)*.
Main engines: 2 Ruston and Hornsby diesels; 440 bhp = 9·5 knots

Sisters of the earlier survey ship *Paluma*; used for carrying water and stores. *Gayundah* used for reserve training at Brisbane.

1 AIRCRAFT LIGHTER—CATAMARAN

AWL 304

Dimensions, feet (metres): 77·8 × 32 × 6·6 *(23·7 × 9·8 × 2)*

Built at Cockatoo Dockyard 1967-68. Coastal craft. Capacity one S2E Tracker or two A4G Skyhawks.

3 CRANE STORES LIGHTERS

CSL 01   02   03

Based on design of AWL 304 but with crane and after superstructure. Built from 1972.

2 Ex-ASR CRAFT

38101   38102

38 ft Bertram craft of little value except in harbour.

WORK BOATS

AM 400-415 +5?

More than 20 are in use all built to a basic 40 ft *(12·2 m)* design.

ARMY WATERCRAFT

11 Ex-US LCM(8) CLASS

AB 1050-1053   1055-1061

Displacement, tons: 116 full load
Dimensions, feet (metres): 73·5 × 21 × 3·3 *(22·4 × 6·4 × 1)*
Main engines: 2 General Motors diesels; 600 hp = 9 knots
Range, miles: 140 at 9 knots

Can carry 60 tons of cargo.

AB 1051 10/1977, Graeme Andrews

6 LCVP

AB 751   752   755   756   758   759

Of 56 ft. Can carry 120 people.

2 TUGS

JOE MANN   THE LUKE

Built in 1964. Of 60 tons with a range of 700 miles and fitted for firefighting, the first at Sydney the second at Brisbane.

1 CARGO LIGHTER

LERIDA AS 3050

Of 22 tons with wooden hull. 66 × 17 ft, capable of 8 knots.

RAAF

One 76 ft ASR at Townsville.
Two 63 ft ASR at Newcastle.

AUSTRIA

Commanding Officer

Major Walter Slovacek

Diplomatic Representation

Defence Attaché in London:
Colonel L. Brosch-Fohraheim

Personnel

(a) 1979: 1 officer, 13 NCOs, 13 ratings (cadre personnel and national service), plus a small shipyard unit
(b) 6 months national service plus 2 months a year for 12 years

Base

Marinekaserne Tegetthof, Wien-Kuchelau (under command of Austrian School of Military Engineering)

Mercantile Marine

Lloyd's Register of Shipping:
10 vessels of 46 148 tons gross

RIVER PATROL CRAFT

Name	No.	Builders	Commissioned
NIEDERÖSTERREICH	A 604	Korneuberg Werft AG	Apr 1970

Displacement, tons: 75
Dimensions, feet (metres): 96·8 × 17·8 × 3·6 *(29·4 × 5·4 × 1·1)*
Guns: 1—20 mm SPz Mk 66 Oerlikon in a turret; 1—12·7 mm MG; 1—Mk 42 MG; 2—8·4 cm PAR 66 "Carl Gustav" AT rifles
Main engines: 2 V16 diesels (turbo engines); 1 600 hp = 22 knots
Complement: 9

Fully welded. Only one built of a projected class of twelve. Engines by MWM, Munich.

NIEDERÖSTERREICH *1975, Austrian Government*

Name	No.	Builders	Commissioned
OBERST BRECHT	A 601	Korneuberg Werft AG	—

Displacement, tons: 10
Dimensions, feet (metres): 40·3 × 8·2 × 2·5 *(12·3 × 2·5 × 0·75)*
Gun: 1—12·7 mm MG
Main engines: 2 diesels; 214 bhp = 10 knots
Complement: 5

Welded hull. Engines by Gräf and Stift, Vienna.

OBERST BRECHT *1974, Heeres Film*

10 Ex-US "M3" PATROL CRAFT

	No.	Builders	Commissioned
4 M3B Type	—	Highway Products and Marine Corporation USA	1965
6 M3D Type	—	Aluminium Co of America	1976

Displacement, tons: 2·9
Dimensions, feet (metres): 27·2 × 8·2 × 6·5 *(8·3 × 2·5 × 2)*
Main engines: M3B—2 Gray Patrol (petrol); 204 hp = 18 knots
M3D—2 General Motors diesels; 184 hp = 18 knots

Unarmed, they form part of the military floating bridge equipment.

"M3" Class *1976, Heeres Film*

BAHAMAS

Senior Officers

Assistant Commissioner:
L. W. Major
Deputy Superintendent:
Leon L. Smith
Assistant Superintendent:
E. K. Andrews

Base

Bay Shore Marina, Nassau

Mercantile Marine

Lloyd's Register of Shipping:
93 vessels of 84 269 tons gross

PATROL CRAFT

2 "103 ft" VOSPER THORNYCROFT

Name	No.	Builders	Commissioned
MARLIN	P01	Vosper Thornycroft	23 May 1978
FLAMINGO	P02	Vosper Thornycroft	23 May 1978

Displacement, tons: 96 standard; 109 full load
Dimensions, feet (metres): 103 × 19·8 × 5·5 *(31·4 × 6 × 1·7)*
Guns: 1—20 mm; 2 MG
Main engines: 2 Paxman 12-cyl Ventura diesels; 3 500 bhp = 27 knots
Range, miles: 2 000 at 13 knots
Complement: 19 (3 officers, 16 men)

Marlin laid down 22 November 1976, launched 20 June 1977. *Flamingo* laid down 6 April 1977. Part of a £5 million order placed in 1975 which also included three 60 ft craft below.

MARLIN *5/1978, C. and S. Taylor*

50 BAHAMAS / Patrol craft — BAHRAIN / Amphibious craft

7 "60 ft" GRP TYPE

Name	No.	Builders	Commissioned
ACKLINS	4	Vosper Thornycroft	5 Mar 1971
ANDROS	—	Vosper Thornycroft	5 Mar 1971
ELEVTHERA	—	Vosper Thornycroft	5 Mar 1971
SAN SALVADOR	—	Vosper Thornycroft	5 Mar 1971
EXUMA	P 25	Vosper Thornycroft	1978
ABACO	P 26	Vosper Thornycroft	1978
INAGUA	P 27	Vosper Thornycroft	1978

Displacement, tons: 30 standard
Dimensions, feet (metres): 62·0 × 15·8 × 4·6 (18·9 × 4·8 × 1·4)
Guns: 1—20 mm fwd; 2 LMG on bridge (first four); 2—20 mm (next three)
Main engines: 2 Caterpillar diesels = 20 knots (total hp 950—last three)
Range, miles: 650 at 16 knots
Complement: 11

INAGUA 10/1977, Michael D. Lennon

"60 ft" Keith Nelson patrol craft in GRP—the first four were the original units of the Bahamas Police Marine Division. With air-conditioned living spaces, these craft are designed for patrol amongst the many islands of the Bahamas Group. The foredeck is specially strengthened for a 20 mm MG with light MGs in sockets either side of the bridge.

BAHRAIN

Ministerial

Minister of the Interior:
Shaikh Mohamad Bin Khalifa Al Khalifa

Personnel

(a) 1979: About 200.
(b) Voluntary service.

Coast Guard

This unit is under the direction of the Ministry of the Interior and not Defence.

Mercantile Marine

Lloyd's Register of Shipping:
32 vessels of 7 161 tons

LIGHT FORCES

1 "TRACKER" CLASS

Name	No.	Builders	Commissioned
BAHRAIN I	—	Fairey Marine Ltd	1975

Displacement, tons: 26
Dimensions, feet (metres): 64 × 16 × 5 (19·5 × 4·9 × 1·5)
Gun: 1—20 mm
Main engines: 2 diesels; 1 120 bhp = 28 knots

Purchased 1974.

2 "SPEAR" CLASS

Name	No.	Builders	Commissioned
SAHAM	4	Fairey Marine Ltd	1975
KHATAF	5	Fairey Marine Ltd	1975

Dimensions, feet (metres): 29·8 × 9·2 × 2·6 (9·1 × 2·8 × 0·8)
Guns: 2 MG
Main engines: 2 Perkins diesels, 290 hp = 26 knots
Complement: 3

Purchased 1974.

2 PATROL CRAFT

JIDA 2   HOWAR 3

Displacement, tons: 15
Dimensions, feet (metres): 45·5 × 12 × 3 (13·9 × 3·7 × 0·9)
Main engines: 2 diesels; 1 080 bhp = 23 knots

Completed February 1974 by Thornycroft, (Singapore).

1 "50 ft" CHEVERTON TYPE (COASTAL PATROL CRAFT)

Name	No.	Builders	Commissioned
MASHTAN	6	Cheverton Ltd, Isle of Wight	1976

Displacement, tonnes: 17·3
Dimensions, feet (metres): 50 × 14·7 × 4·5 (15·2 × 4·5 × 1·4)
Main engines: 2 Detroit GM 8V1TI diesels = 22 knots
Range, miles: 660 at 12 knots

GRP hull.

3 "27 ft" CHEVERTON TYPE (COASTAL PATROL CRAFT)

Name	No.	Builders	Commissioned
NOON	15	Cheverton Ltd, Isle of Wight	1977
ASKAR	16	Cheverton Ltd, Isle of Wight	1977
SUWAD	17	Cheverton Ltd, Isle of Wight	1977

Displacement, tons: 3·5
Dimensions, feet (metres): 27 × 9 × 2·8 (8·2 × 2·7 × 0·8)
Main engines: Twin diesels = 15 knots

Purchased 1976. In addition ten Dhows are used for patrol duties.

AMPHIBIOUS CRAFT

1 60 ft "LOADMASTER"

Name	No.	Builders	Commissioned
SAFRA	7	Cheverton Ltd, Isle of Wight	1976

Measurement, tons: 60 deadweight
Dimensions, feet (metres): 60 oa × 20 × 3·5 (18·3 × 6·1 × 1·1)
Main engines: 2 diesels; 348 hp = 9 knots
Range, miles: 600
Complement: 13
Load: 45 tonnes

SAFRA 1976, Cheverton Ltd

Note: In addition to the above are:

1 Hovercraft from Tropimire Ltd (UK) (1977);
1 60 ft Landing Craft from H.N. Development (Singapore) (1977);
2 56 ft launches from Vosper, (Singapore) (1977);
3 36 ft launches from Vosper, (Singapore) (1977).

BANGLADESH

Headquarters Appointments

Chief of Naval Staff:
  Rear-Admiral Musharraf Husain Khan BN, psn
Assistant Chief of Naval Staff (Ops) and Administrative Authority, Dacca:
  Commodore Mahbub Ali Khan BN, psn
Assistant Chief of Naval Staff (Material):
  Commodore K. M. J. Akbar BN
Assistant Chief of Naval Staff (Logistics):
  Captain M. Rahman BN

Senior Appointments

Commodore Commanding Chittagong:
  Commodore Sultan Ahmad BN
NOIC Khulna:
  Captain F. Ahmed BN

Naval Bases

Chittagong (BNS *Issa Khan* and Naval Academy), Dacca (BNS *Haji Mohsin*), Khulna (BNS *Titumir*), Kaptai (BNS *Shaheed Moazzam*)

General

The personnel of Bangladesh Navy is composed of repatriated Pakistan Navy Personnel and the service was not as such formed afresh with the inception of Bangladesh. The Navy went into action as an organised body with some of the escapees from Pakistan on 10 December 1971; the day is celebrated as the Navy Day in Bangladesh. In the absence of any senior officer of any branch, the Bangladesh Government on 16 December 1971, asked Captain M.K.I. Choudhury of Bangladesh Army to take charge of the Naval contingent in Chittagong—a small shore Establishment called Pakistan Navy Ship *Bakhtiyar*. This Establishment has now been enlarged and commissioned as B.N.S. *Issa Khan*. Lieut. Commander Nurul Huq, an Engineer Officer of the Pakistan Navy escaped from Pakistan in April 1972 and was appointed on Temporary Acting basis Chief of the Naval Staff until the repatriation of remaining naval personnel took place in November 1973. Rear-Admiral (then Captain) M. H. Khan took over on 7 November 1973.

Personnel:

(a) 1979: 5 250 (250 officers, 5 000 ratings)
(b) Voluntary service

Strength of the Fleet

Frigates	2
Large Patrol Craft	4
Riverine Patrol Craft	5
Training Ship	1

Prefix to Ships' Names

BNS

Mercantile Marine

Lloyd's Register of Shipping:
  141 vessels of 284 496 tons gross

FRIGATES

1 Ex-BRITISH "SALISBURY" CLASS (TYPE 61)

Name	No.	Builders	Laid down	Launched	Commissioned
UMAR FAROOQ (ex- HMS *Llandaff*)	F 16	Hawthorn Leslie Ltd	27 Aug 1953	30 Nov 1955	11 Apr 1958

Displacement, tons: 2 170 standard; 2 408 full load
Length, feet (metres): 320 *(97·5)* pp; 339·8 *(103·6)* oa
Beam, feet (metres): 40 *(12·2)*
Draught, feet (metres): 15·5 *(4·7)*
Guns: 2—4·5 in *(115 mm)*/45 (twin Mk 6); 2—40 mm/60 (single Mk 9)
A/S weapons: 1 Squid triple-barrelled DC mortar
Main engines: 8 ASR 1 diesels in three engine rooms; 2 shafts (each with 4 engines); 14 400 bhp
Speed, knots: 24
Oil fuel, tons: 230
Range, miles: 2 300 at full power; 7 500 at 16 knots
Complement: 237 (14 officers, 223 ratings)

Ordered by RN on 28 June 1951. All welded. Transferred to Bangladesh at Royal Albert Dock, London on 10 December 1976 for work-up and passage.

Radar: Long range surveillance: One Type 965 with double AKE 2 array.
Combined warning: One Type 993.
Height finder: One Type 278M.
Warning and Air direction: One Type 986.
Fire control: Mk 6M director with Type 275.
Navigation: One Type 978.

Sonar: Types 174 and 164B.

UMAR FAROOQ   1977, Michael D. J. Lennon

1 Ex-BRITISH "LEOPARD" CLASS (TYPE 41)

Name	No.	Builders	Laid down	Launched	Commissioned
ALI HAIDER (ex-HMS *Jaguar*)	F 17	Wm. Denny & Bros Ltd, Dumbarton	2 Nov 1953	30 July 1957	12 Dec 1959

Displacement, tons: 2 300 standard; 2 520 full load
Length, feet (metres): 320 *(97·5)* pp; 330 *(100·6)* wl; 339·8 *(103·6)* oa
Beam, feet (metres): 40 *(12·2)*
Draught, feet (metres): 16 *(4·9)*
Guns: 4—4·5 in *(115 mm)*/45 (twin Mk 6); 1—40 mm/60 (single Mk 9)
A/S weapons: 1 Squid triple-barrelled DC mortar
Main engines: 8 ASR 1 diesels in three engine rooms; 14 400 bhp; 2 shafts (each with 4 engines)
Speed, knots: 24
Oil fuel, tons: 220
Range, miles: 2 300 at full power; 7 500 at 16 knots
Complement: 235 (15 officers, 220 ratings)

Designed primarily for anti-aircraft protection. All welded. Ordered on 28 June 1951. Fitted with stabilisers. Transferred 16 July 1978. Cost £2 million on transfer. Cost new £3·7 million.

Electronics: ECM and D/F.

Engineering: Fitted with cp propellers, 12 ft diameter 200 rpm. The fuel tanks have a compensating system.

Radar: Air search: One Type 965 with single AKE 1 array and IFF.
Fire control: Mk 6 M I-band. Type 275.
Navigation: One Type 975.

Reconstruction: Refitted in 1966-7 with new mainmast. Refitted at Vosper Thornycroft August-October 1978.

Sonar: Types 164 and 174.

Transfer: Another ship of this class, *Panther,* was transferred to India while building and renamed *Brahmaputra*.

ALI HAIDER   10/1978, Michael D. J. Lennon

52 BANGLADESH / Light forces — BARBADOS / Introduction

LIGHT FORCES

2 Ex-YUGOSLAV "KRALJEVICA" CLASS (LARGE PATROL CRAFT)

Name	No.	Builders	Commissioned
KARNAPHULI (ex-*PBR 502*)	P 301	Yugoslavia	1956
TISTA (ex-*PBR 505*)	P 302	Yugoslavia	1956

Displacement, tons: 190 standard; 202 full load
Dimensions, feet (metres): 134·5 × 20·7 × 7·2 *(41 × 6·3 × 2·2)*
Guns: 2—128 mm rocket launcher; 2—40/60 mm
Main engines: MAN W8V 30/38 diesels; 2 shafts; 3 300 bhp = 18 knots
Range, miles: 1 000 at 12 knots
Complement: 44 (4 officers, 40 ratings)

Transferred and commissioned on 6 June 1975.

Radar: Decca 45.

Sonar: QCU 2.

TISTA 1976, A. G. Burgoyne

2 Ex-INDIAN "AKSHAY" CLASS (LARGE PATROL CRAFT)

Name	No.	Builders	Commissioned
PADMA (ex-*INS Akshay*)	P 201	Hooghly D & E Co, Calcutta	1962
SURMA (ex-*INS Ajay*)	P 202	Hooghly D & E Co, Calcutta	1962

Displacement, tons: 120 standard; 150 full load
Dimensions, feet (metres): 117·2 × 20 × 5·5 *(35·7 × 6·1 × 1·7)*
Gun: 1—40/60 mm
Main engines: 2 Paxman Deltic diesels = 12·5 knots
Range, miles: 5 000 at 10 knots
Complement: 35 (3 officers, 32 ratings)

Generally similar to Royal Navy's "Ford" class. Transferred and commissioned on 12 April 1973 and 26 July 1974 respectively.

SURMA 1977, Bangladesh Navy

5 "PABNA" CLASS (RIVERINE PATROL CRAFT)

Name	No.	Builders	Commissioned
PABNA	P101	DEW Narayangonj, Dacca	12 June 1972
NOAKHALI	P102	DEW Narayangonj, Dacca	8 July 1972
PATUAKHALI	P103	DEW Narayangonj, Dacca	7 Nov 1974
BOGRA	P104	DEW Narayangonj, Dacca	15 July 1977
RANGAMATI	P105	DEW Narayangonj, Dacca	11 Feb 1977

Displacement, tons: 69·5
Dimensions, feet (metres): 75 × 20 × 3·5 *(22·9 × 6·1 × 1·1)*
Gun: 1—40/60 Bofors
Main engine: Cummins diesel = 10·8 knots
Range, miles: 700
Complement: 33 (3 officers, 30 ratings)

The first indigenous naval craft built in Bangladesh. No further plans for any more craft of this class.

Radar: Decca Navigational.

PATUAKHALI 1975, Bangladesh Navy

TRAINING SHIP

SHAHEED RUHUL AMIN (ex-*MV Anticosti*)

Displacement, tons: 710 full load
Dimensions, feet (metres): 155·8 × 36·5 × 10 *(47·5 × 11·1 × 3·1)*
Gun: 1—40/60 mm Bofors
Main engine: Caterpillar diesel; 1 shaft = 11·5 knots
Range, miles: 4 000
Complement: 80 (8 officers, 72 ratings)

Built by Atlantic Shipbuilding Co, Montreal. Laid down 1956, completed March 1957. Sold to India as MV *Anticosti*.
After use in relief work was handed over to BN in 1972, modified at Khulna and commissioned 10 December 1974.

SHAHEED RUHUL AMIN 1976, Bangladesh Navy

BARBADOS

Senior Officer

CO Barbados Coast Guard:
  Major C. A. McConney

Personnel

(a) 1979: 61 (4 officers, 57 other ranks).
(b) Voluntary service

Coast Guard

This was formed early in 1973. A considerable increase in the size of this force is forecast.

Base

Christ Church, Barbados

Prefix to Ships' Names

BCGS

Mercantile Marine

Lloyd's Register of Shipping:
33 vessels of 4 448 tons gross

1 "20 Metre GUARDIAN" CLASS (COASTAL PATROL CRAFT)

Name	No.	Builders	Commissioned
GEORGE FERGUSON	CG 601	Halmatic/Aquarius UK	Dec 1974

Displacement, tons: 30
Dimensions, feet (metres): 65·6 × 17·4 × 4·3 (20 × 5·3 × 1·3)
Guns: 2—·76 mm MG (provision for—not fitted)
Main engines: 2 General Motors 12V 71 Tl diesels; 1 300 hp = 24 knots
Range, miles: 560 at 18 knots
Complement: 10

GRP hull. Air conditioned and designed for Coast Guard/SAR duties. Launched 16 October 1974 for delivery in December.

3 "12 Metre GUARDIAN" CLASS (COASTAL PATROL CRAFT)

Name	No.	Builders	Commissioned
COMMANDER MARSHALL	CG 402	Halmatic/Aquarius UK	Dec 1973
J. T. C. RAMSEY	CG 404	Halmatic/Aquarius UK	Nov 1974
T. T. LEWIS	CG 403	Halmatic/Aquarius UK	Feb 1974

Displacement, tons: 11
Dimensions, feet (metres): 41 × 12·1 × 3·3 (12·5 × 3·7 × 1)
Gun: 1—·76 mm MG (Provision for—not fitted)
Main engines: 2 Caterpillar diesels; 580 hp = 24 knots
Complement: 4

GRP Hulls. Designed for coastal patrol/SAR duties.

MISCELLANEOUS

The ex-US LST *Kemper County* was transferred to Barbadian commerical interests 6 January 1976.

BELGIUM

Headquarters Appointment

Chief of Naval Staff:
Vice-Admiral J. P. L. van Dyck

Diplomatic Representation

Naval, Military and Air Attaché in Bonn:
Colonel AF Derille (Army)
Naval, Military and Air Attaché in The Hague:
Lieutenant-Colonel de Brouchoven de Bergeyck
Naval, Military and Air Attaché in London:
Colonel K. De Wulf (Army)
Naval, Military and Air Attaché in Paris:
Colonel J. A. L. Joseph (Air Force)
Naval, Military and Air Attaché in Washington:
Brigadier-General CA de Wilde

Personnel

(a) 1979: 4 220 (520 National Service)
(b) 10 months national service

Note: 70% of junior ratings are regular.

General

The Belgian Navy has now moved its interests further to sea with its new frigates but the replacement programme of MCMVs listed below will probably absorb the majority of its new construction budget for several years to come.

Strength of the Fleet

Type	Active	Building
Frigates	4	—
Minehunters (Ocean)	7	10 (5)
Minehunters (Coastal)	2	—
Minesweepers (Coastal)	4	—
Minesweepers (Inshore)	14	—
Support Ships	2	—
River Patrol Boats	8	—
Research Ships	2	—
Auxiliary and Service Craft	14	—

Deletion

1976 *Knokke* (MSC)

Naval Aviation

3 Alouette III helicopters
1 Sikorsky S58 helicopter

Bases

Ostend (Main Base): 1 MSO Squadron, 1 MSC Squadron.
Kallo: River patrol boats, 1 MSI Squadron, reserve MSIs.
Zeebrugge: Frigates, command and support ships. (New Main Base started in 1966 for completion in 1985.)
Koksijde: Naval aviation.
Antwerp.

Note: Base at Nieuwpoort paid off in 1976.

Mercantile Marine

Lloyd's Register of Shipping:
268 vessels of 1 684 692 tons gross

PENNANT LIST

Frigates

F 910	Wielingen
F 911	Westdiep
F 912	Wandelaar
F 913	Westhinder

Mine Warfare Forces

M 471	Hasselt
M 472	Kortrijk
M 473	Lokeren
M 474	Turnhout
M 475	Tongeren
M 476	Merksem
M 477	Oudenaarde
M 478	Herstal
M 479	Huy
M 480	Seraing
M 482	Vise
M 483	Ougrée
M 484	Dinant
M 485	Andenne
M 902	Haverbeke
M 903	Dufour
M 904	De Brouwer
M 906	Breydel
M 907	Artevelde
M 908	Truffaut
M 909	Bovesse
M 928	Stavelot
M 930	Rochefort
M 932	Nieuwport
M 933	Koksijde
M 934	Verviers
M 935	Veurne

Support Ships and Auxiliaries

A 950	Valcke
A 951	Hommel
A 952	Wesp
A 953	Bij
A 956	Krekel
A 958	Zenobe Gramme
A 959	Mier
A 960	Godetia
A 961	Zinnia
A 962	Mechelen
A 963	Spa
A 964	Heist

River Patrol Boats

P 901	Leie
P 902	Liberation
P 903	Meuse
P 904	Sambre
P 905	Schelde
P 906	Semois
P 907	Rupel
P 908	Ourthe

FRIGATES
4 "WIELINGEN" CLASS (E-71)

Name	No.	Builders	Laid down	Launched	Commissioned
WIELINGEN	F 910	Boelwerf, Temse	5 Mar 1974	30 Mar 1976	20 Jan 1978
WESTDIEP	F 911	Cockerill, Hoboken	2 Sep 1974	8 Dec 1975	20 Jan 1978
WANDELAAR	F 912	Boelwerf, Temse	1 Apr 1975	21 June 1977	1978
WESTHINDER	F 913	Cockerill, Hoboken	8 Dec 1975	1 Mar 1977	1978

Displacement, tons: 1 880 light; 2 283 full load
Length, feet (metres): 349 (106·4)
Beam, feet (metres): 40·3 (12·3)
Draught, feet (metres): 18·4 (5·6)
Missiles: 8 SAM Sea Sparrow, 1—8 cell launcher; 4 SSM Exocet, 4 launchers
Guns: 1—3·9 in (100 mm)/55 Mod 1968 3; 1 CIWS
Torpedo launchers: 2 for L-5 torpedoes
A/S rocket launchers: 1—6-barrelled 375 mm Le Creuzot-Laire with Bofors rockets
Rocket launchers: 2—8-barrelled Corvus dual-purpose Chaff/flare launchers
Main engines: CODOG—1 Rolls-Royce Olympus TM38 gas turbine; 28 000 bhp; 2 Cockerill CO-240 V12 diesels; 6 000 bhp. Twin cp propellers
Speed, knots: 29 (15 on 1 diesel, 20 on 2 diesels)
Range, miles: 4 500 at 18 knots; 6 000 at 16 knots
Complement: 160 (15 officers; 145 men)

This compact, well-armed class of frigate is the first class fully designed by the Belgian Navy and built in Belgian yards. All to be fitted with hull-mounted sonar and fin stabilisers. Fully air-conditioned.
The programme was approved 23 June 1971 and design studies completed July 1973. A firm order was placed in October 1973 and *Wielingen* was laid down on time.

CIWS: The Belgian Navy is awaiting a decision on which system the Netherlands are to use—a similar system will then probably be fitted on after deck-house.

Decoys: Two Super RBOC and ASW decoy Nixie.

Electrical: 440 volts; 4—500 kW diesel alternators.

Electronics: Fully integrated and automated weapons command and control system of HSA (SEWACO 4). Radar search receiver—ELCOS I.

Missiles: Sea Sparrow RIM 7H-2. Exocet MM 38.

Radar: Air/surface surveillance and tracking: HSA WM-25.
Air/surface surveillance: HSA DA-05.
Navigation: Raytheon TM 1645/9X.
IFF: Mk 10A SIF; AN/UPX-25.

Sonar: SQS 505A (Westinghouse).

WESTHINDER
8/1978, Michael D. J. Lennon

WANDELAAR
1978, M. Voss

54 BELGIUM / Mine warfare forces

MINE WARFARE FORCES

0 + 10 (+ ?5) TRIPARTITE MINEHUNTERS

Name	No.	Builders	Laid down	Launched	Commission
—	—	Polyship	1980-84	—	1982-86

Displacement, tons: 510
Dimensions, feet (metres): 154·5 × 29·2 × 8·2 (47 × 8·9 × 2·6)
Gun: 1—20 mm
Minehunting: 2 PAP 104 systems (39 charges)
Minesweeping: Mechanical sweep gear (medium depth)
Main engine: 1 Werkspoor diesel: 1 860 hp = 15 knots; single axial propeller
Auxiliary propulsion: 2 motors; 170 kw = 7 knots
Range, miles: 3 000 at 12 knots
Endurance: 15 days
Complement: 48 (6 officers, 42 ratings) max

This design, developed in co-operation with the navies of France and the Netherlands, is being built in all three countries. Belgium is building ten with an option on a further five. The hull is of GRP and is fitted with active tank stabilization, full NBC protection and air-conditioning. Has automatic pilot and buoy tracking. Carry six divers when minehunting.

Radar: Navigational set

Sonar: One DUBM 21A

Tasks: A 5 ton container can be carried, stored for varying tasks—HQ support, research, patrol, extended driving, drone control. The ship's company varies from 29-48 depending on the assigned task.

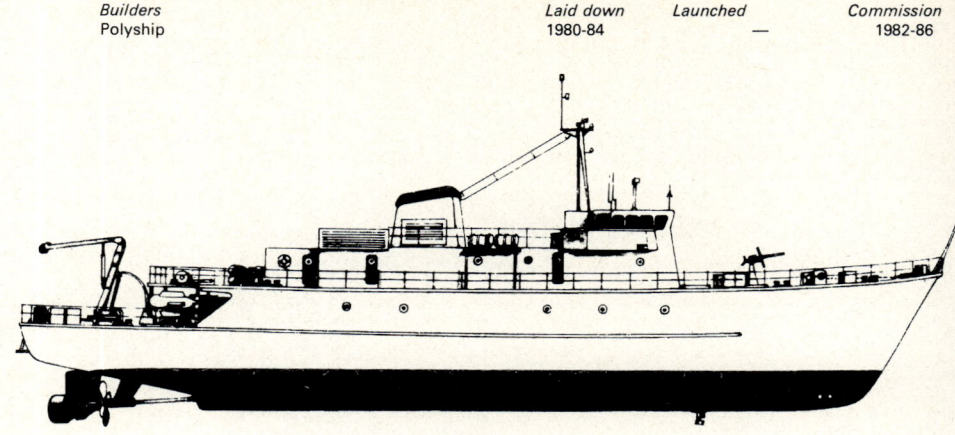
TRIPARTITE minehunter

7 Ex-US "AGGRESSIVE" CLASS (MINEHUNTERS)

Name	No.	Builders	Laid down	Launched	Commissioned
J. E. VAN HAVERBEKE (ex-MSO 522)	M 902	Peterson Builders Inc, Sturgeon Bay, Wisc.	2 Mar 1959	25 Oct 1959	7 Nov 1960
A. F. DUFOUR (ex-*Lagen* M 950, ex-MSO 498, ex-AM 498)	M 903	Bellingham Shipyard Inc, Wash.	11 Feb 1954	13 Aug 1954	27 Sep 1955
DE BROUWER (ex-*Nansen*, M 951, ex-MSO 499, ex-AM 499)	M 904	Bellingham Shipyard Inc, Wash.	25 Apr 1954	15 Oct 1954	1 Nov 1955
BREYDEL (ex-MSO 504, ex-AM 504)	M 906	Tacoma Boatbuilding Co, Tacoma, Wash.	25 Nov 1954	25 Mar 1955	24 Jan 1956
ARTEVELDE (ex-MSO 503, ex-AM 503)	M 907	Tacoma Boatbuilding Co, Tacoma, Wash.	15 Oct 1953	19 June 1954	15 Dec 1955
G. TRUFFAUT (ex-MSO 515, ex-AM 515)	M 908	Tampa Shipbuilding Co, Inc, Tampa, Fla.	1 Feb 1955	1 Nov 1955	21 Sep 1956
F. BOVESSE (ex-MSO 516, ex-AM 516)	M 909	Tampa Shipbuilding Co, Inc. Tampa, Fla.	1 Apr 1954	8 Feb 1956	21 Dec 1956

Displacement, tons: 720 standard; 780 full load
Length, feet (metres): 165·0 (50·3) wl; 172·5 (52·6) oa
Beam, feet (metres): 35·0 (10·7)
Draught, feet (metres): 11·0 (3·4)
Gun: 1—40 mm (only *Artevelde*)
Main engines: 2 General Motors diesels; 2 shafts; 1 600 bhp
Speed, knots: 14
Oil fuel, tons: 50
Range, miles: 2 400 at 12 knots; 3 000 at 10 knots
Complement: 72 (5 officers, 67 men)

Wooden hulls and non-magnetic structure. Capable of sweeping mines of all types. Diesels of non-magnetic stainless steel alloy. Cp propellers.

Dufour and *De Brouwer* originally served in Royal Norwegian Navy (1955-66). *Artevelde* converted to Diving Vessel in 1972 but retains minehunting capability. 1974 fitted with Siebe Gorman recompression chamber.

Sonar: SQQ 14 (GE) (except *Artevelde*).

Transfer dates: M902 9 Dec 1960, M903 14 Apr 1966, M904 14 Apr 1966, M906 15 Feb 1956, M907 16 Dec 1955, M908 12 Oct 1956, M909 25 Jan 1957.

G. TRUFFAUT 11/1978, Leo van Ginderen

6 US "ADJUTANT" CLASS (ex-AMS)
(MINESWEEPERS/HUNTERS—COASTAL)

Name	No.	Builders	Commissioned
STAVELOT	M 928	Boel and Zonen, Temse	21 Feb 1956
ROCHEFORT	M 930	Beliard, Ostend	28 Nov 1955
NIEUWPOORT	M 932	Beliard, Ostend	9 Jan 1956
KOKSIJDE	M 933	Beliard, Ostend	29 Nov 1955
VERVIERS (ex-*MSC 259*)	M 934	Boston, USA	19 June 1956
VEURNE (ex-*MSC 260*)	M 935	Boston, USA	7 Sep 1956

Displacement, tons: 330 light; 390 full load
Dimensions, feet (metres): 139 pp; 144 oa × 27·9 × 8 (42·6; 43·9 × 8·5 × 2·4)
Gun: 1—40 mm
Main engines: 2 General Motors diesels; 2 shafts (Voigt-Schneider propellers); 880 bhp = 13·5 knots
Oil fuel, tons: 28
Range, miles: 3 000 at economical speed (10·5 knots)
Complement: 39

Wooden hulls and constructed throughout of materials with the lowest possible magnetic signature. M 934 and 935 were built the in USA, under MDAP, the others were built in Belgium with machinery and equipment from USA. M 934 (ex-*MSC 259*) transferred 19 June 1956, M 935 (ex-*MSC 260*) was transferred on 7 September 1956. *Verviers* (in 1972) and *Veurne* (in 1969) converted to minehunters with Voith-Schneider propellers. *Veurne* used for survey work since October 1970.

Reclassification: *Mechelen*, A 926 (ex-M 926): research ship since 1964.
Spa A 963 (ex-M 927): conversion to ammunition transport ship started in 1978.
Heist A 964 (ex-M 929): conversion to degaussing ship started in 1978.

STAVELOT 9/1978, Leo van Ginderen

Sonar: Type 193 (Plessey).

Transfers: 3 MSC to Norway—1966; 5 MSC to Greece—1969; 8 MSC to Taiwan—1969.

BELGIUM / Mine warfare forces — River patrol boats 55

14 "HERSTAL" CLASS (MINESWEEPERS—INSHORE)

Name	No.	Builders	Commissioned
HASSELT	M 471	Mercantile Marine Yard, Kruibeke	24 Apr 1958
KORTRYK	M 472	Mercantile Marine Yard, Kruibeke	13 June1958
LOKEREN	M 473	Mercantile Marine Yard, Kruibeke	8 Aug 1958
TURNHOUT	M 474	Mercantile Marine Yard, Kruibeke	29 Sep 1958
TONGEREN	M 475	Mercantile Marine Yard, Kruibeke	9 Dec 1958
MERKSEM	M 476	Mercantile Marine Yard, Kruibeke	6 Feb 1959
OUDENAARDE	M 477	Mercantile Marine Yard, Kruibeke	25 Apr 1959
HERSTAL	M 478 (ex-MSI 90)	Mercantile Marine Yard, Kruibeke	14 Oct 1957
HUY	M 479 (ex-MSI 91)	Mercantile Marine Yard, Kruibeke	24 Mar 1958
SERAING	M 480 (ex-MSI 92)	Mercantile Marine Yard, Kruibeke	3 June1958
VISE	M 482 (ex-MSI 94)	Mercantile Marine Yard, Kruibeke	11 Sep 1958
OUGREE	M 483 (ex-MSI 95)	Mercantile Marine Yard, Kruibeke	10 Nov 1958
DINANT	M 484 (ex-MSI 96)	Mercantile Marine Yard, Kruibeke	14 Jan 1959
ANDENNE	M 485 (ex-MSI 97)	Mercantile Marine Yard, Kruibeke	20 Apr 1959

Displacement, tons: 160 light; 190 full load
Dimensions, feet (metres): 106·7 pp; 113·2 oa × 22·3 × 6 *(32·5; 34·5 × 6·8 × 1·8)*
Guns: 2—0·5 (twin)
Main engines: 2 diesels; 2 shafts; 1 260 bhp = 15 knots
Oil fuel, tons: 18
Range, miles: 2 300 at 10 knots
Complement: 17

Modified AMI "100-foot" class. Originally a class of sixteen.
The first group of eight (M 470 to 477) was financed under the Belgian Navy Estimates, the remaining eight (M 478 to 485) being a US "off-shore" order.

Transfers: 2 MSI to Korea(S)—1970.

TURNHOUT 9/1978, Leo van Ginderen

SUPPORT SHIPS

Name	No.	Builders	Commissioned
ZINNIA	A 961	Cockerill, Hoboken	5 Sep 1967

Displacement, tons: 1 705 light; 2 685 full load
Dimensions, feet (metres): 309 wl; 326·4 oa × 49·9 × 11·8 *(94·2; 99·5 × 15·2 × 3·6)*
Guns: 3—40 mm (single)
Aircraft: 1 helicopter
Main engines: 2 Cockerill V 12 RT 240 CO diesels; 5 000 bhp; 1 shaft
Speed, knots: 20
Oil fuel, tons: 500
Range, miles: 14 000 at 12·5 knots
Complement: 125

Laid down 8 November 1966, launched on 6 May 1967. Cp propeller. Design includes a platform and a retractable hangar for one light liaison-helicopter normally carried on board. Rated as Command and Logistic Support Ship.

ZINNIA 6/1977, Dr. Giorgio Arra

Name	No.	Builders	Commissioned
GODETIA	A 960	Boelwerf, Temse	23 May 1966

Displacement, tons: 1 700 light; 2 500 full load
Dimensions, feet (metres): 289 wl; 301 oa × 46 × 11·5 *(88·0; 91·8 × 14 × 3·5)*
Guns: 2—40 mm (twin)
Main engines: 4 ACEC—MAN diesels; 2 shafts; 5 400 bhp = 19 knots
Oil fuel, tons: 294
Range, miles: 8 700 at 12·5 knots
Complement: 100 plus 35 spare billets

Laid down on 15 February 1965, launched on 7 December 1965. Cp propellers. Provided with a platform which can take a light liaison-helicopter. Rated as Command and Logistic Support Ship.

GODETIA 5/1978, John G. Callis

8 RIVER PATROL BOATS

Name	No.	Builders	Commissioned
LEIE	P 901	Hitzler, Regensburg	1953
LIBERATION	P 902	Hitzler, Regensburg	1954
MEUSE	P 903	Hitzler, Regensburg	1953
SAMBRE	P 904	Hitzler, Regensburg	1953
SCHELDE	P 905	Hitzler, Regensburg	1953
SEMOIS	P 906	Hitzler, Regensburg	1953
RUPEL	P 907/V7	Hitzler, Regensburg	1953
(Tresignies B 30 1964-74)			
OURTHE	P 908/V8	Hitzler, Regensburg	1953
(L39 1964-74)			

Displacement, tons: 25 light; 27·5 full load
Dimensions, feet (metres): 75·5 pp; 82 oa × 12·5 × 3 *(23·0; 25·0 × 3·8 × 0·9)*
  Liberation 85·5 × 13·1 × 3·2 *(26·0 × 4·0 × 1·0)*
Guns: 2—13 mm MG
Main engines: 2 diesels; 2 shafts; 440 bhp = 19 knots
Complement: 7

Rupel and *Ourthe* were loaned to the Marine Cadets, Belgian Navy from 1964-74 at Brussels and Liège respectively but are now operating with the navy again although loaned to the Marine Cadets during the summer using V7, V8 pendant numbers. *Semois* has been used as a diving vessel since 1965.

SAMBRE 7/1978, Leo van Ginderen

56 BELGIUM / Auxiliaries — Miscellaneous

AUXILIARIES

Name	No.	Builders	Commissioned
SPA	A 963 (ex-M 927 1953-77)	Boel and Zonen, Temse	1 Jan 1956
HEIST	A 964 (ex-M 929 1954-77)	Boel and Zonen, Temse	4 Apr 1956

Ex-MSCs (details under *Mechelen* in Research Ships) converted in 1978 to Ammunition Transport and Degaussing Ship respectively. Both named in 1958—previously known by their M pendant numbers.

Harbour craft: There are three tanker barges, namely **FN 4, FN 5** and **FN 6**, displacement 300 tons, length 105 ft, built by Plaquet, Peronne-lez-Antoing in 1957; the ammunition ship *Ekster*, displacement 140 tons, length 118 ft, built at Niel (Germany) in 1953; a diving cutter **ZM 4**, displacement 8 tons, length 33 ft, built by Panesi at Ostend in 1954; and the harbour transport cutter *Spin*, displacement 32 tons, length 47·8 ft, with 250 bhp diesels = 8 knots and Voith-Schneider propeller, built in the Netherlands in 1958.

RESEARCH SHIPS

Name	No.	Builders	Commissioned
ZENOBE GRAMME	A 958	Boel and Zonen, Temse	1962

Displacement, tons: 149
Dimensions, feet (metres): 92 × 22·5 × 7 *(28·0 × 6·8 × 2·1)*
Main engines: 1 MWM diesel; 1 shaft; 200 bhp = 10 knots
Complement: 14

Auxiliary sail ketch. Laid down 17 October 1960, launched 23 October 1961. Designed for scientific research.

ZENOBE GRAMME 1978, Royal Belgian Navy

Name	No.	Builders	Commissioned
MECHELEN	A 962 (ex-M 926 1954-66)	Boel and Zonen, Temse	2 Dec 1954

Displacement, tons: 330 light; 390 full load
Dimensions, feet (metres): 139 pp; 144 oa × 27·9 × 7·5 *(42·4; 44·0 × 8·5 × 2·6)*
Main engines: 2 General Motors diesels; 2 shafts; 880 bhp = 13·5 knots
Oil fuel, tons: 28
Range, miles: 3 000 at economical speed (10·5 knots)
Complement: 26

Former coastal minesweeper of Type 60. Used as a research ship since 1964 being renumbered as A 962 in 1966. Similar to photograph under Mine Warfare Forces with longer bridge and additional deck house by mainmast. First named in 1958.

TUGS

BIJ A 953   **KREKEL** A 956

Harbour tugs with fire-fighting facilities. Of 71 tons and twin shafts; 400 hp with Voith-Schneider propellers. *Bij* built by Akerboom, Lisse 1959, *Krekel* by Ch. Navals de Rupelmonde 1961.

BIJ 12/1978, Leo van Ginderen

HOMMEL A 951   **WESP** A 952

Harbour tugs of 22 tons, 300 bhp diesels with Voith-Schneider propellers. Both built by Voith, Heidenheim in 1953.

HOMMEL 4/1978, Leo van Ginderen

MIER A 959

Harbour tug of 17·5 tons with 90 bhp diesel. Built Liége 1962.

O/Lt VALCKE (ex-AT 1 1953-55) A 950

Displacement, tons: 110
Dimensions, feet (metres): 78·8 pp; 95 oa × 21 × 5·5 *(24·0; 29·0 × 6·4 × 1·7)*
Main engine: 1 diesel; 1 shaft; 600 bhp = 12 knots
Complement: 14

Built by Holland Nautic NV, Haarlem, Netherlands in 1951 and served as Dutch mercantile tug *Elis* until purchased by Belgian Navy in 1953 and renamed. Serves as diving tender.

O/LT VALCKE 11/1978, Leo van Ginderen

MISCELLANEOUS

EKSTER

Ammunition barge built by Niel in 1953.

SPIN

Harbour launch built in Netherlands 1958.

FN 4, 5 and 6

Tanker barges built by Ch. Naval J. and F. Plaquet' Peronnes-les-Antoing in 1957.

ZM 4

Diving Cutter built by Chantier Panesi, Ostend. Completed 5 April 1954.

BELIZE

Personnel

(a) 50 approx
(b) Voluntary service

Base

Belize

Mercantile Marine

Lloyd's Register of Shipping:
3 vessels of 620 tons gross

2 COASTAL PATROL CRAFT

Name	No.	Builders	Commissioned
BELIZE	PBM 01	Brooke Marine, Lowestoft	1972
BELMOPAN	PBM 02	Brooke Marine, Lowestoft	1972

Displacement, tons: 15
Dimensions, feet (metres): 40 × 12 × 2 *(12.2 × 3.6 × 0.6)*
Guns: 3 MG
Main engines: 2 diesels; 370 hp × 22 knots

BENIN

A decision was taken in 1978 to provide a naval branch within the armed forces. At present no details of orders are availble although with only 75 miles of coastline this will be a modest form of Coast Guard.

Mercantile Marine
Lloyd's Register of Shipping:
8 vessels of 1 074 tons gross

BERMUDA

Royal Navy

The Royal Navy retains a base facility in Bermuda.

Base

Hamilton.

Mercantile Marine

Lloyd's Register of Shipping:
99 vessels of 1 814 455 tons gross

Several 20ft coastal patrol craft are operated by the Bermuda Police.

BOLIVIA

Headquarters Appointment

Commander-in-Chief:
Rear-Admiral Gutemberg Barroso Hurtado

Personnel

(a) 1979: 1 500 officers and men (including marines)
(b) 12 months selective military service

A small navy used for patrolling Lake Titicaca and the Beni-Mamore River systems. Most of the training of officers and senior ratings is carried out in Argentina. The junior ratings are almost entirely converted soldiers. The upkeep of some of the craft is certainly below normal standards.

Bases

San Juan de Tiquina.
Loma Suarez (building yard)
Puerto Horquilla (military port)

Prefix to Ships' Names

FNB

TRANSPORT

Name	No.	Builder	Commissioned
SIMON BOLIVAR	—	Fairfield, UK	1951 (see note)

Measurement, tons: 4 214 gross; 6 390 deadweight
Dimensions, feet (metres): 421.1 × 55 × 22.9 *(128.4 × 16.8 × 6.9)*
Main engine: 1 Fairfield-Droxford diesel; 4 600 hp = 16 knots

A gift from Venezuela to Bolivia in 1977. Commissioned 23 March 1978 with a military crew. Used for commercial purposes between Rosario/Nueva Palinira (Bolivian free zones in Argentina and Uruguay) and the USA.

LAKE PATROL CRAFT

Name	No.	Tonnage	Dimensions, feet (metres)	Notes
ALMIRANTE GRAU	M 01	52	44.3 × 10.5 × 4.8 *(13.5 × 3.2 × 1.5)*	Training and Transport. Diesel.
NICOLAS SUAREZ	M 02	26.5	57.6 × 11.2 × 6.4 *(18 × 3.5 × 2)*	Built 1963. Iron hull. Diesel.
MARISCAL SANTA CRUZ	M 03	52	44.3 × 10.5 × 4.8 *(13.5 × 3.5 × 2)*	Training and Transport. Diesel.
PRESIDENTE BUSCH	M 04	52	60.8 × 11.2 × 4.2 *(19 × 3.5 × 1.3)*	Wooden hull. Diesel.
COMANDANTE ARANDIA	M 05	82	72.3 × 12.8 × 4.5 *(22.6 × 4 × 1.4)*	Iron hull. Diesel. Rebuilt 1970.
TOPATER	M 06	—		
BRUNO RACUA	M 07	17	57.6 × 13.1 × 3.8 *(18 × 4.1 × 1.2)*	Wooden hull. Diesel.
CORONEL EDUARDO AVAROA	M 08	82	80 × 27.8 × 4.8 *(25 × 8.7 × 1.5)*	Built 1965.
PRESIDENTE KENNEDY	—	12	38.4 × 11.4 × 3.3 *(12 × 3.5 × 1)*	Wooden hull. Diesel. Ex-US PB Mk 1. Survivor of three transferred 1963.

YACUMA A-3-02, ITENEZ A-3-03, MADERA A-3-04, IBARE A-3-05, CHAPARE A-3-06, ICHILO A-3-07, MUCHULA A-3-08, TORIBIO A-3-09, LITORAL A-3-10, INDEPENDENCIA, MAYTA KAPAC, LADISLAO CABRERA, MAPIRI, TAHUAMANU V-01 are all borne on the nominal list although details are not available.

In addition one river craft of 112 tons (built in Bolivia 1970), one of 55 tons (built in Bolivia in 1971-72), eight smaller river craft (built in Bolivia 1973-76), two ex-US PBR Mark II of 8.5 tons (transferred April 1974) and one Lake Patrol Boat of 12 tons are in service although details, names and pennant number are not available.

BRAZIL

Headquarters Appointments

Chief of Naval Staff:
  Admiral Eddy Sampaio Espellet
Chief of Naval Operations:
  Admiral Roberto Andersen Cavalcanti
Chief of Naval Materiel:
  Admiral Maximiano Eduardo da Silva Fonesca
Chief of Naval Personnel:
  Admiral Carlos Henrique Rezende de Noronha

Diplomatic Representation

Naval Attaché in Asunción:
  Captain Jeronimo de Xerez Sobral
Naval and Defence Attaché in Athens:
  Captain Gerson Fleischauer
Naval Attaché in Bonn and the Hague:
  Captain Oswaldo Mucio Vasconcelos Magalhães Lima
Naval and Defence Attaché in Buenos Aires:
  Captain Paulo Afonso da Rocha
Naval Attaché in La Paz:
  Captain Hugo Lessa Rodrigues
Naval and Defence Attaché in Lima:
  Captain Fernando Hollanda
Naval and Air Attaché in Lisbon and Madrid:
  Captain Almir Motta de Oliveira
Naval and Army Attaché in London, Oslo and Stockholm:
  Captain Lysias Ruland Kerr
Naval Attaché in Montevideo:
  Captain Nauro Monteiro Campos
Naval Attaché in Paris and Rome:
  Captain Roberto Osborne Manso da Costa
Naval and Defence Attaché in Santiago:
  Captain Sergio Roberto Castro Oliviera Queiroz
Naval and Defence Attaché in Tokyo and Seoul:
  Captain José Lauria Sobral Moraes
Naval Attaché in Washington and Ottawa:
  Captain Carlos de Oliveira Froes
Head of the Brazilian Naval Commission in Europe:
  Rear-Admiral E. O. Rodriguez

General

With a coastline of 4 655 miles Brazil has a considerable problem even to patrol the more important areas in peacetime. The "Niteroi" class has brought a considerable addition to the present strength which includes an aircraft-carrier, twelve destroyers and five submarines of World War II construction. While the patrol and river forces are probably adequate a considerable programme of replacement is needed amongst the larger ships.

Personnel

(a)
  1973: 44 337 (3 591 officers and 40 746 men)
  1974: 49 600 (3 887 officers and 45 713 men)
  1975: 43 100 (3 800 officers and 39 300 men)
  1976: 45 300 (3 800 officers and 41 500 men)
  1977: 45 300 (3 800 officers and 41 500 men)
  1978: 45 500 (3 900 officers and 41 600 men)
  1979: 45 500 (3 900 officers and 41 600 men)
Figures include marines and auxiliary corps

(b) 1 years national service

Naval Bases

Rio de Janeiro (main base with 3 dry docks and 1 floating dock)
Aratu (Bahia) (major naval yard with 1 dry dock and 1 floating dock)
Belém (naval base and repair yard with 1 dry dock)
Natal (small naval base and repair yard with 1 floating dock — being rebuilt as major base)
Ladario (river base of *Mato Grosso* flotilla)
Sao Pedro (naval air station)

Maritime Aviation

A Fleet Air Arm was formed on 26 January 1965.

Navy

  4 Sikorsky SH-3D
  3 Westland Whirlwind (UH-5)
  5 Westland Wasp HAS-1 (UH-2)
  18 Bell 206B Jetrangers
  9 Westland Lynx WG 13 to be provided for "Niteroi" class
Note: 3 Wasp HAS-1 planned

Air Force (Comando Costeira)

  8 Grumman S-2E Trackers (ASW)
  12 Grumman HU-16A Albatross (SAR)
  5 Grumman S-2A Trackers (Transport and Training)
  3 Lockheed RC-130E Hercules (SAR/PR)
  6 Convair PBY-5A Catalinas (Transport)
  12 EMB-111 (LRMP)
  6 EMB-110B (PR)
  15 Neiva T25 Universal I (liaison)
  5 Bell SH-1D (SAR helicopters)
  2 Bell 47G (SAR helicopters)

Prefix to Ships' Names

These vary, indicating the type of ship e.g. N Ae L = Aircraft Carrier; CT = Destroyer.

Strength of the Fleet

Type	Active	Building
Submarines (Patrol)	8	—
Attack Carrier (medium)	1	—
Destroyers	12	—
Frigates	6	(1)
Patrol Ships	10	—
Landing Ships	2	—
Landing Craft	48	—
Monitor	1	—
River Patrol Ships	5	—
Large Patrol Craft	6	—
River Patrol Craft	10	—
Minesweepers (Coastal)	6	—
Survey Ships	8	—
Survey Launches	6	—
Light Tenders	5	—
S/M Rescue Ships	1	—
Repair and Support ships	2	(1)
Large Tanker	1	—
Small Tankers	2	—
Transports	15	—
Tugs	17	—
Floating Docks	4	—
Auxiliaries	22	—

New Construction

Forty nine ships are planned including a carrier, submarines, missile cruisers, frigates and amphibious ships.

Mercantile Marine

Lloyd's Register of Shipping:
  565 vessels of 3 701 731 tons gross

DELETIONS

Cruisers

1973 Barroso
1975 Tamandaré offered for auction (Sep)
      (both ex-US "St Louis" class)

Destroyers

1973 Amazonas, Mariz E. Barros
1974 Acre, Araguaia, Araguari—(auction July for scrap)
      (All Brazilian built 1949-51)
1978 Para, Paraiba

Frigates

1973 Baependi, Bracui
1975 Benevente, Bocaina (auction Feb for scrap)
      (All ex-US "Cannon" class)

Submarines

1972 Rio Grande do Sul (ex-Sandlance) sold for scrap June 1975
      Bahia (ex-Plaice) sold to Brazilian Museum of Naval Technology, Santos by USA as a memorial
1978 Rio de Janeiro (ex-Odax)
      Rio Grande do Sul (ex-Grampus)

Mine Warfare Forces

1974 Jutai, Juruena (paid off in Aug)

Patrol Forces

1971 Piraju, Piranha
1972 Paraguaçu
1973 Pirague

Auxiliaries

1976 Javari and Jurua
1977 Faroleiro Santana

PENNANT LIST

Submarines

S10	Guanabara
S12	Bahia
S14	Ceara
S15	Goiaz
S16	Amazonas
S20	Humaita
S21	Tonelero
S22	Riachuelo

Aircraft Carrier

A11	Minas Gerais

Destroyers

D25	Marcilio Dias
D26	Mariz E. Barros
D29	Parana
D30	Pernambuco
D31	Piaui
D32	Santa Catarina
D33	Maranhão
D34	Mato Grosso
D35	Sergipe
D36	Alagoas
D37	Rio Grande do Norte
D38	Espirito Santo

Frigates

F40	Niteroi
F41	Defensora
F42	Constituição
F43	Liberal
F44	Independencia
F45	União

Amphibious Forces

G26	Duque De Caxias
G28	Garcia D'Avila

Patrol Forces

P20	Pedro Teixeira
P21	Raposo Tavares
P30	Roraima
P31	Rondonia
P32	Amapa
U17	Parnaiba
V15	Imperial Marinheiro
V16	Iguatemi
V17	Ipiranga
V18	Forte De Coimbra
V19	Cabocla
V20	Angostura
V21	Baiana
V22	Mearim
V23	Purus
V24	Solimoes

Light Forces

P10	Piratini
P11	Piraja
P12	Pampeiro
P13	Parati
P14	Penedo
P15	Poti
R54	Anchova
R55	Arenque
R56	Atum
R57	Acara
R58	Agulha
R59	Aruana

Mine Warfare Forces

M15	Aratu
M16	Anhatomirim
M17	Atalaia
M18	Aracatuba
M19	Abrolhos
M20	Albardão

Survey Vessels and Tenders

H10	Almirante Saldanha
H11	Paraibano
H12	Rio Branco
H13	Mestre João dos Santos
H14	Nogueira da Gama
H15	Itacurussa
H16	Camocim
H17	Caravelas
H21	Sirius
H22	Canopus
H24	Castelhanos
H25	Faroleiro Nascimento
H27	Faroleiro Areas
H31	Argus
H32	Orion
H33	Taurus
H34	Graça Aranha
H41	Almirante Camara

Miscellaneous

G15	Paraguassu
G16	Barroso Pereira
G17	Potengi
G21	Ary Parreiras
G22	Soares Dutra
G24	Belmonte
G25	Afonso Pena
G26	Am. Jeronimo Gonçalves
G27	Marajó
K10	Gastao Moutinho
R11	Martins De Oliveira
R21	Tritão
R22	Tridente
R23	Triunfo
U20	Rio Doce
U21	Rio das Contas
U22	Rio Formoso
U23	Rio Real
U24	Rio Turvo
U25	Rio Verde
U26	Custodio de Mello
U28	Bauru
U40	Rio Pardo
U41	Rio Negro
U42	Rio Chui
U43	Rio Oiapoque

BRAZIL / Introduction

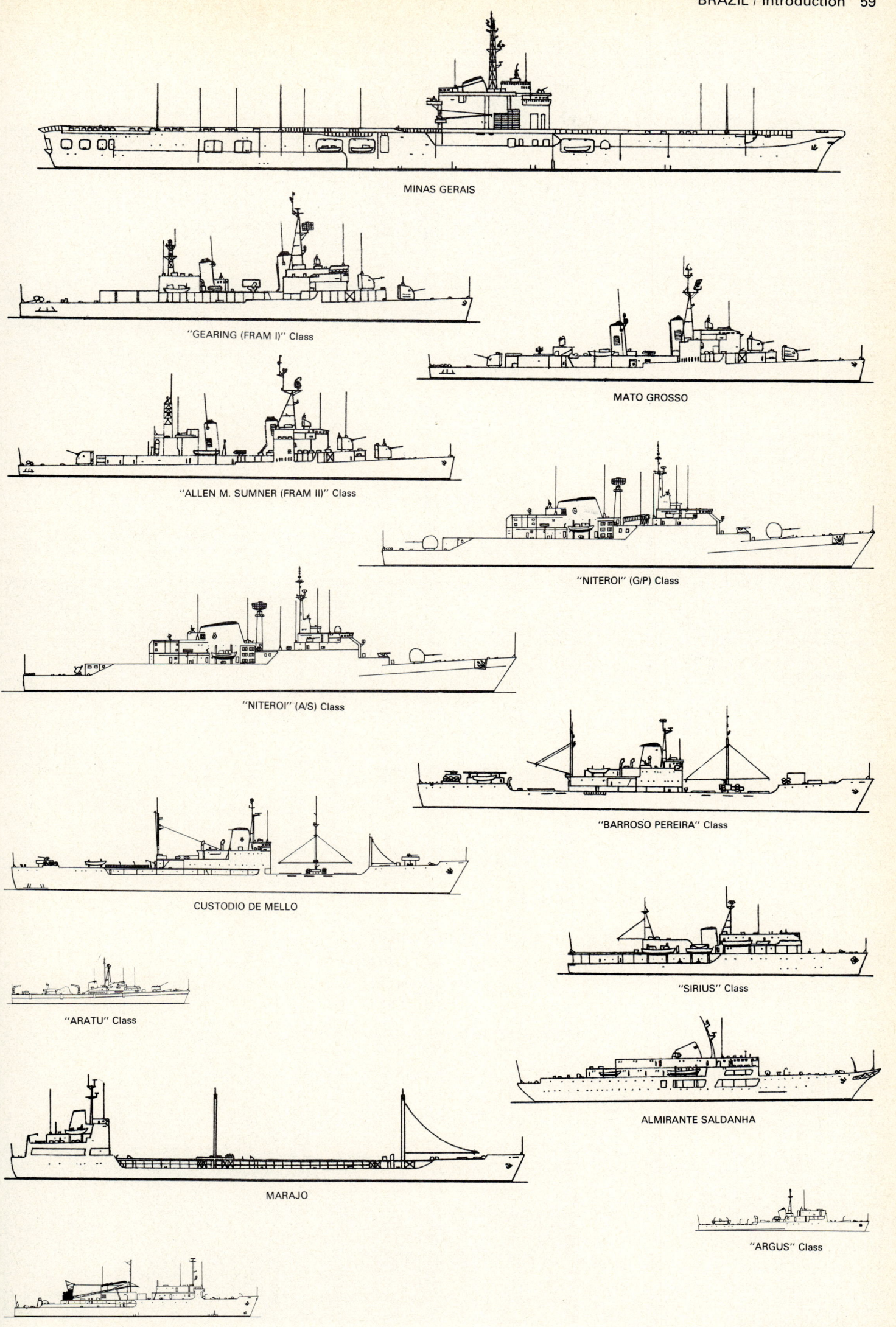

(Drawings by Peter Jones)

60 BRAZIL / Submarines

SUBMARINES

Note: It is reported that plans are in hand for the ordering of a number of Type 209 submarines from Howaldtswerke, Kiel. It is reported that the first will be built in West Germany and the remainder at Navyard, Rio de Janeiro. The production of a considerable amount of the equipment will be made in Brazil.

3 BRITISH "OBERON" CLASS

Name	No.	Builders	Laid down	Launched	Commissioned
HUMAITA	S 20	Vickers, Barrow	3 Nov 1970	5 Oct 1971	18 June 1973
TONELERO	S 21	Vickers, Barrow	18 Nov 1971	22 Nov 1972	10 Dec 1977
RIACHUELO	S 22	Vickers, Barrow	26 May 1973	6 Sep 1975	12 Mar 1977

Displacement, tons: 1 610 standard; 2 030 surfaced; 2 410 dived
Length, feet (metres): 295·5 (90·1)
Beam, feet (metres): 26·5 (8·1)
Draught, feet (metres): 18·0 (5·5)
Torpedo Tubes: 8—21 in (533 mm) (6 bow and 2 stern)
Main machinery: 2 Admiralty Standard Range 1 16-cyl diesels; 3 680 bhp; 2 electric motors; 6 000 shp; 2 shafts
Speed, knots: 12 surfaced, 17 dived
Complement: 70 (6 officers and 64 men)

In 1969 it was announced that two submarines of the British "Oberon" class were ordered from Vickers, Barrow. The third boat was ordered in 1972. Completion of *Tonelero* was much delayed by a serious fire on board originating in the cabling. She spent a period in Chatham Dockyard, having been towed from Barrow, returning in January 1976. She sailed from UK 12 February 1978. It was this fire which resulted in re-cabling of all "Oberons" under construction. Whilst in Chatham the centre 60 ft was replaced. Diesels by Vickers Shipbuilding Group. Electric motors by AEI-English Electric. Sonar, modern navigational aids and provision for modern fire control system developed by Vickers.

RIACHUELO *1977, Michael D. J. Lennon*

2 Ex-US GUPPY III TYPE

Name	No.	Builders	Laid down	Launched	Commissioned
GOIÁZ (ex-USS *Trumpetfish* SS 425)	S 15	Cramp S.B. Co	23 Aug 1943	13 May 1945	29 Jan 1946
AMAZONAS (ex-USS *Greenfish* SS 351)	S 16	Electric Boat Co	29 June 1944	21 Dec 1945	7 June 1946

Displacement, tons: 1 975 standard; 2 450 dived
Length, feet (metres): 326·5 (99·5)
Beam, feet (metres): 27 (8·2)
Draught, feet (metres): 17 (5·2)
Torpedo tubes: 10—21 in; 6 bow 4 stern
Main machinery: 4 diesels; 6 400 hp; 2 electric motors; 5 400 hp; 2 shafts
Speed, knots: 20 surfaced; 15 dived
Complement: 85

Converted in 1960-62. *Goiáz* transferred by sale 15 October 1973 and *Amazonas* by sale 19 December 1973.

Sonar: BQR-2 array, BQG-4 (PUFFS) fire control sonar (fins on casing).

AMAZONAS *1977, Brazilian Navy*

3 Ex-US GUPPY II TYPE

Name	No.	Builders	Laid down	Launched	Commissioned
GUANABARA (ex-USS *Dogfish* SS 350)	S 10	Electric Boat Co	22 June 1944	27 Oct 1945	29 Apr 1946
BAHIA (ex-USS *Sea Leopard* SS 483)	S 12	Portsmouth Navy Yard	7 Nov 1944	2 Mar 1945	11 June 1945
CEARÁ (ex-USS *Amberjack* SS 522)	S 14	Boston Navy Yard	8 Feb 1944	15 Dec 1944	4 Mar 1946

Displacement, tons: 1 870 standard; 2 420 dived
Length, feet (metres): 307·5 (93·7)
Beam, feet (metres): 27·2 (8·3)
Draught, feet (metres): 18 (5·5)
Torpedo tubes: 10—21 in (6 bow, 4 stern)
Main machinery: 3 diesels, 4 800 shp; 2 motors; 5 400 shp; 2 shafts
Speed, knots: 18 surfaced; 15 dived
Range, miles: 12 000 at 10 knots (surfaced)
Complement: 82

Modernised under Guppy II programme 1948-50. Transferred 28 July 1972 *(Guanabara)*, 27 March 1973 *(Bahia)*, 17 October 1973 *(Ceara)*. All by sale.

GUPPY II TYPE *1977, Brazilian Navy*

AIRCRAFT CARRIER

1 Ex-BRITISH "COLOSSUS" CLASS

Name	No.	Builders	Laid down	Launched	Commissioned
MINAS GERAIS (ex-HMS *Vengeance*)	A 11	Swan, Hunter & Wigham Richardson, Ltd, Wallsend on Tyne	16 Nov 1942	23 Feb 1944	15 Jan 1945

Displacement, tons: 15 890 standard; 17 500 normal; 19 890 full load (see *Displacement* note)
Length, feet (metres): 630 *(192·0)* pp; 695 *(211·8)* oa
Beam, feet (metres): 80 *(24·4)*
Draught, feet (metres): 24·5 *(7·5)*
Flight deck,
   Length, feet (metres): 690 *(210·3)*
   Width, feet (metres): 121 *(37·0)* oa as reconstructed
   Height, feet (metres): 39 *(11·9)* above water line
Catapults: 1 steam
Aircraft: 20 aircraft including 7 S2A Trackers, 4 Sea Kings
Guns: 10—40 mm/60 (2 quad Mk2, 1 twin Mk 1), 2—47 mm (saluting)
Main engines: Parsons geared turbines; 2 shafts; 40 000 shp
Boilers: 4 Admiralty 3-drum type; Working pressure 400 psi *(28 kg/cm²)*; max superheat 700°F *(371°C)*
Speed, knots: 24; 25·3 on trials after reconstruction
Oil fuel, tons: 3 200
Range, miles: 12 000 at 14 knots; 6 200 at 23 knots
Complement: 1 000 (1 300 with air group)

MINAS GERAIS   *1971, Brazilian Navy*

Served in the Royal Navy from 1945 onwards. Fitted out in late 1948 to early 1949 for experimental cruise to the Arctic. Lent to the RAN early in 1953, returned to the Royal Navy in August 1955. Purchased by the Brazilian Government on 14 December 1956. Reconstructed at Verolme Dock, Rotterdam from summer 1957 to December 1960. The conversion and overhaul included the installation of the angled deck, steam catapult, mirror-sight deck landing system, armament fire control and radar equipment. The ship was purchased for $9 million and the reconstruction cost $27 million. Commissioned in the Brazilian Navy at Rotterdam on 6 December 1960. Left Rotterdam for Rio de Janeiro on 13 January 1961. Used primarily for anti-submarine aircraft and helicopters. Currently under refit 1976-79, the length of the refit, which has apparently been extended by a year, underlining its necessity. A replacement carrier is being considered.

Displacement: Before reconstruction: 13 190 tons standard; 18 010 tons full load.

Engineering: The two units each have one set of turbines and two boilers installed side by side. Maximum speed at 220 rpm. Steam capacity was increased when the boilers were retubed during reconstruction in 1957-60.

Electrical: During reconstruction an alternating current system was installed with a total of 2 500 kW supplied by four turbo-generators and one diesel generator.

Hangar: Dimensions: length, 445 ft; width, 52 ft; clear depth, 17·5 ft. Aircraft lifts: 45 × 34 ft. During reconstruction in 1957-60 new lifts replaced the original units.

Operational: Single track catapult for launching, and arrester wires for recovering, 30 000 lb aircraft at 60 knots. Catapult accelerator gear port side forward.

Radar: Air surveillance: SPS 12.
Surface search: SPS 4.
Fighter direction: SPS 8B.
Air control: SPS 8A.
Fire control: SPG 34.
Navigation: MP 1402.

MINAS GERAIS   *9/1972, USN*

MINAS GERAIS   *1972, Brazilian Navy*

BRAZIL / Destroyers

DESTROYERS

2 Ex-US "GEARING" (FRAM I) CLASS

No.	Builders	Laid down	Launched	Commissioned
D 25	Consolidated Steel	1944	8 Nov 1944	12 Mar 1945
D 26	Consolidated Steel	1944	26 May 1945	1 Oct 1945

Name
MARCILIO DIAS (ex-USS *Henry W. Tucker* DD 875)
MARIZ E. BARROS (ex-USS *Brinkley Bass* DD 887)

Displacement, tons: 2 425 standard; 3 500 full load
Length, feet (metres): 390·5 *(119·0)*
Beam, feet (metres): 40·9 *(12·4)*
Draught, feet (metres): 19 *(5·8)*
Guns: 4—5 in *(127 mm)*/38 (twin Mk 38)
A/S weapons: 1 Asroc 8-tube launcher; 2 triple Mk 32 torpedo launchers; facilities for small helicopter (Wasp)
Main engines: 2 GE geared turbines; 60 000 shp; 2 shafts
Boilers: 4 Babcock & Wilcox
Speed, knots: 32
Range, miles: 5 800 at 15 knots
Complement: 274 (14 officers, 260 men)

Enlarged "Allen M. Sumner" class—14 ft longer. Transferred 3 December 1973.

Radar: SPS 10 and SPS 40.

Sonar: SQS 23.

MARIZ E. BARROS   1977, Brazilian Navy

5 Ex-US "FLETCHER" CLASS

Name	No.	Builders	Laid down	Launched	Commissioned
PARAÑA (ex-USS *Cushing*, DD 797)	D 29	Bethlehem Steel Co (Staten Island)	3 May 1943	30 Sep 1943	17 Jan 1944
PERNAMBUCO (ex-USS *Hailey*, DD 556)	D 30	Seattle-Tacoma S.B. Corp, (Seattle)	1 Apr 1942	9 Mar 1943	30 Sep 1943
PIAUI (ex-USS *Lewis Hancock*, DD 675)	D 31	Federal S.B. and D.D. Co	31 Mar 1943	1 Aug 1943	29 Sep 1943
SANTA CATARINA (ex-USS *Irwin*, DD 794)	D 32	Bethlehem Steel Co (San Pedro)	2 May 1943	31 Oct 1943	14 Feb 1944
MARANHAO (ex-USS *Shields*, DD 596)	D 33	Puget Sound Navy Yard	10 Aug 1943	25 Sep 1944	8 Feb 1945

Displacement, tons: 2 050 standard; 3 050 full load
Length, feet (metres): 376·5 *(114·8)*
Beam, feet (metres): 39·3 *(12·0)*
Draught, feet (metres): 18 *(5·5)*
Missiles: 1 quad Seacat *(Maranhao only)*
Guns: 5—5 in *(127 mm)*/38 (except *Pernambuco:* 4—5 in); 10—40 mm (2 quad, 1 twin) *(Paraña and Santa Caterina)*;
Torpedo tubes: 5—21 in *(533 mm)* (not in *Maranhao*)
A/S weapons: 2 Hedgehogs; 1 DC rack; 2 side launching torpedo racks *(Paraña and Pernambuco)*; 2 triple Mk 32 torpedo tubes (remainder)
Main engines: 2 GE geared turbines; 2 shafts; 60 000 shp
Boilers: 4 Babcock & Wilcox
Speed, knots: 35
Oil fuel, tons: 650
Range, miles: 5 000 at 15 knots; 1 260 at 30 knots
Complement: 260

Paraña transferred on loan 20 July 1961 and subsequently by sale 8 January 1973; *Pernambuco* on loan 20 July 1961 and *Maranhao* by sale 1 July 1972. *Piaui* was transferred on loan 2 August 1967 whilst *Santa Catarina* was transferred on loan 10 May 1968, and both by sale 11 April 1973.

PIAUI   1977, Brazilian Navy

Radar: Search: SPS 6.
Tactical: SPS 10.
Fire control: I Band.

1 Ex-US "ALLEN M. SUMNER" and 4 Ex-US "ALLEN M. SUMNER" (FRAM II) CLASSES

Name	No.	Builders	Laid down	Launched	Commissioned
MATO GROSSO (ex-USS *Compton*, DD 705)	D 34	Federal S.B. & D.D. Co.	28 Mar 1944	17 Sep 1944	4 Nov 1944
SERGIPE (ex-USS *James C. Owens* DD 776)	D 35	Bethlehem Steel Co (San Francisco)	9 Apr 1944	1 Oct 1944	17 Feb 1945
ALAGOAS (ex-USS *Buck* DD 761)	D 36	Bethlehem Steel Co (San Francisco)	1 Feb 1944	11 Mar 1945	28 June 1946
RIO GRANDE DO NORTE (ex-USS *Strong* DD 758)	D 37	Bethlehem Steel Co (San Francisco)	25 July 1943	23 Apr 1944	8 Mar 1945
ESPIRITO SANTO (ex-USS *Lowry* DD 770)	D 38	Bethlehem Steel Co (San Pedro)	1 Aug 1943	6 Feb 1944	23 July 1944

Displacement, tons: 2 200 standard; 3 320 full load
Length, feet (metres): 376·5 *(114·8)*
Beam, feet (metres): 40·9 *(12·5)*
Draught, feet (metres): 19 *(5·8)*
Missiles: Sea Cat system *(Mato Grosso only)*
Guns: 6—5 in *(127 mm)*/38 (twin Mk 38)
A/S weapons: 2 triple torpedo launchers; 2 ahead-firing Hedgehogs; facilities for small helicopter (Fram II) (Wasp) Depth charges *(Mato Grosso)*
Main engines: 2 geared turbines; 60 000 shp; 2 shafts
Boilers: 4
Speed, knots: 34
Range, miles: 4 600 at 15 knots, 1 260 at 30 knots
Complement: 274

Transferred to Brazil as follows: *Mato Grosso* 27 September 1972, *Sergipe* and *Alagoas* 16 July 1973, *Espirito Santo* 29 October 1973, *Rio Grande do Norte* 31 October 1973, the last four being FRAM II conversions, *Mato Grosso* being of the original "Sumner" class.

Gunnery: 3 in guns in *Mato Grosso* removed before transfer.

Missiles: Sea Cat system transferred to *Mato Grosso* from deleted *Mariz E Barros* of previous "Marcilio Dias" class.

Radar: SPS 6 and 10 and Mk 20 director *(Mato Grosso)*. SPS 10 and 37 *(Espirito Santo)*. SPS 10 and 40 (remainder).

MATO GROSSO   1977, Brazilian Navy

Sonar: SQS 31 *(Mato Grosso)*. SQA 10 and SQS 40 (remainder).

BRAZIL / Frigates 63

FRIGATES

6 (+ 1) "NITEROI" CLASS

Name	No.	Builders	Laid down	Launched	Commissioned
NITEROI	F 40	Vosper Thornycroft Ltd	8 June 1972	8 Feb 1974	20 Nov 1976
DEFENSORA	F 41	Vosper Thornycroft Ltd	14 Dec 1972	27 Mar 1975	5 Mar 1977
CONSTITUIÇÃO	F 42	Vosper Thornycroft Ltd	13 Mar 1974	15 Apr 1976	31 Mar 1978
LIBERAL	F 43	Vosper Thornycroft Ltd	2 May 1975	7 Feb 1977	end 1978
INDEPENDENCIA	F 44	Navyard, Rio de Janeiro	11 June 1972	2 Sep 1974	Mar 1978
UNIÃO	F 45	Navyard, Rio de Janeiro	11 June 1972	14 Mar 1975	Oct 1978

Displacement, tons: 3 200 standard; 3 800 full load
Length, feet (metres): 400 *(121·9)* wl; 424 *(129·2)* oa
Beam, feet (metres): 44·2 *(13·5)*
Draught, feet (metres): 18·2 *(5·5)*
Aircraft: 1 WG 13 Lynx helicopter
Missiles: Both versions: Est. 60 SAM Seacat (2 triple launchers); GP version: 4—SSM Exocet (2 twin launchers); A/S version: 10 Ikara (1 single launcher)
Guns: GP version: 2—4·5 in *(117 mm)*/55 Vickers Mk 8; A/S version: 1—4·5 in/55 Vickers Mk 8; 2—40 mm/70
A/S weapons: 1 Bofors 375 mm twin tube A/S rocket launcher; 2 Plessey STWS1 triple torpedo tube mountings; 1 DC rail
Main engines: CODOG system; 2 Rolls-Royce Olympus gas turbines = 56 000 bhp; 4 MTU diesels = 18 000 shp
Speed, knots: 30 on gas turbines; 22 on diesels
Range, miles: 5 300 at 17 knots (2 diesels); 4 200 at 19 knots (4 diesels); 1 300 at 28 knots (gas turbine)
Endurance: 45 days stores; 60 days provisions
Complement: 200 (21 officers, 179 men)

A very interesting design of handsome appearance—Vosper Thornycroft Mark 10. The moulded depth is 28·5 ft *(8·8 m)*. Exceptionally economical in personnel, amounting to a 50 per cent reduction of manpower in relation to previous warships of this size and complexity. Require 100 fewer men than the British Type 42 of approximately similar characteristics. *Niteroi* started trials in January 1976. *Defensora* started trials October 1976.
Seventh ship with differing armament ordered from Navyard, Rio de Janeiro—to be used as training ship.

Class: F 40, 41, 44 and 45 are of the A/S configuration. F 42 and 43 are General Purpose design.

Contract: A contract announced on 29 September 1970, valued at about £100 million, was signed between the Brazilian Government and Vosper Thornycroft Ltd, England for the design and building of these six Vosper Thornycroft Mark 10 frigates comparable with the British Type 42 guided missile destroyers being built for the Royal Navy.

Construction: Materials, equipment and lead-yard services supplied by Vosper Thornycroft at Navyard, Rio de Janeiro.

Electronics: CAAIS equipment by Ferranti (FM 1600B computers). ECM by Decca.

Radar: Air warning: 1 Plessey AWS-2 with Mk 10 IFF.
Surface warning: 1 Signaal ZW-06.
Weapon control and tracking: 2 Selenia RTN-10X.
Ikara tracker: 1 set in A/S ships only.

Sonar: 1 EDO 610E medium range.
1 EDO 700E VDS (A/S ships only).

Trials: *Constituição*, Oct 1977; *Liberal,* July 1978.

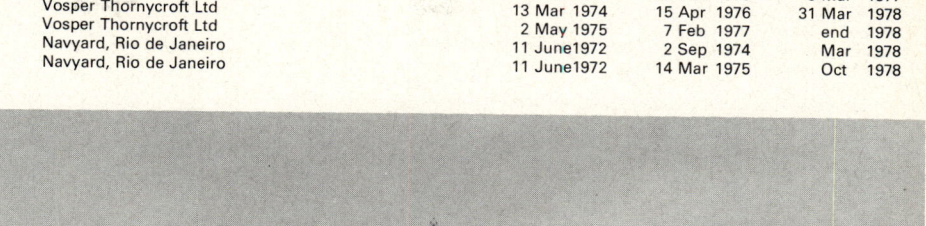

DEFENSORA *9/1977, Wright and Logan*

CONSTITUIÇÃO *1/1978, Vosper Thornycroft*

LIBERAL *11/1978, Michael D. J. Lennon*

64   BRAZIL / Amphibious forces — Patrol forces

AMPHIBIOUS FORCES

1 Ex-US "511-1152" CLASS (LST)

Name	No.	Builders	Commissioned
GARCIA D'AVILA (ex-USS *Outagamie County* LST 1073)	G 28	Bethlehem Steel Co Higham, Mass	17 Apr 1945

Displacement, tons: 1 653 standard; 2 366 beaching; 4 080 full load
Dimensions, feet (metres): 328 × 50 × 14 *(100 × 15·3 × 4·3)*
Guns: 8—40 mm (2 twin, 4 single)
Main engines: General Motors diesels; 2 shafts; 1 700 bhp = 11·6 knots
Complement: 119
Troops: 147

Transferred on loan to Brazil by US Navy 21 May 1971, purchased 1 December 1973.

GARCIA D'AVILA   1977, Brazilian Navy

1 Ex-US "DE SOTO COUNTY" CLASS (LST)

Name	No.	Builders	Commissioned
DUQUE DE CAXAIS (ex-USS *Grant County* LST 1174)	G 26	Avondale, New Orleans	8 Nov 1957

Displacement, tons: 3 828 light; 7 804 full load
Dimensions, feet (metres): 445 × 62 × 16·9 *(135·7 × 18·9 × 5·2)*
Guns: 2—3 in/50 (twin)
Main engines: Diesels; 2 shafts; cp propellers; 13 700 shp = 17·2 knots
Complement: 175 (11 officers, 164 men)
Troops: App. 575

Launched 12 October 1956 and transferred 15 January 1973, purchased December 1977. Now has Stülcken heavy-lift gear fitted.

28 EDVP

Built in Japan 1959-60. Some, including EDVP 3, in Mato Grosso flotilla.

7 EDVP

Fitted with Saab-Scania Diesels of 153 hp. 37 ft long and with GRP hulls. Built in Brazil in 1971-73. Can carry 36 men or equivalent amount of equipment.

4 US "LCU 1610" TYPE

| CAMBORIÁ | GUARAPARI | TIMBAN | TRAMANDAI |

Built in Rio de Janeiro 1974-75 by Arsenal de Marinha.

9 LCM (6)

Also reported but not confirmed.

PATROL FORCES

10 "IMPERIAL MARINHEIRO" CLASS

Name	No.	Builders	Commissioned
IMPERIAL MARINHEIRO	V 15	Netherlands	8 June 1955
IGUATEMI	V 16	Netherlands	17 Sep 1955
IPIRANGA	V 17	Netherlands	22 Sep 1955
FORTE DE COIMBRA	V 18	Netherlands	26 July 1955
CABOCLA	V 19	Netherlands	Apr 1954
ANGOSTURA	V 20	Netherlands	1955
BAIANA	V 21	Netherlands	27 June 1955
MEARIM	V 22	Netherlands	3 Aug 1955
PURUS	V 23	Netherlands	Apr 1955
SOLIMOES	V 24	Netherlands	1955

Displacement, tons: 911 standard
Dimensions, feet (metres): 184 × 30·5 × 11·7 *(56 × 9·3 × 3·6)*
Guns: 1—3 in/50; 4—20 mm
Main engines: 2 Sulzer diesels; 2 160 bhp = 16 knots
Oil fuel, tons: 135
Complement: 60

Actually fleet tugs classed as corvettes. Equipped for fire fighting. *Imperial Marinheiro* employed as submarine support ship.

IGUATEMI   1977, Brazilian Navy

2 "PEDRO TEIXEIRA" CLASS (RIVER PATROL SHIPS)

Name	No.	Builders	Commissioned
PEDRO TEIXEIRA	P 20	Arsenal de Marinha, Rio de Janeiro	17 Dec 1973
RAPOSO TAVARES	P 21	Arsenal de Marinha, Rio de Janeiro	17 Dec 1973

Displacement, tons: 700 standard
Dimensions, feet (metres): 203·4 × 30·7 × 6·3 *(62 × 9·4 × 1·9)*
Guns: 1—40 mm; 2—81 mm mortars 6—0·50 cal MG
Main engines: 4 diesels; 2 shafts = 16 knots

Helicopter platform and hangar fitted. Carry two LCVPs. *Pedro Teixeira* launched 14 October 1970—*Raposo Tavares* 11 June 1972. Belong to Amazon Flotilla.

PEDRO TEIXEIRA   1974, Brazilian Navy

1 THORNYCROFT TYPE (RIVER MONITOR)

Name	No.	Builders	Commissioned
PARNAIBA	U 17 (ex-P 2)	Arsenal de Marinha, Rio de Janeiro	Nov 1937

Displacement, tons: 620 standard; 720 full load
Dimensions, feet (metres): 180·5 × 33·3 × 5·1 *(55 × 10·1 × 1·6)*
Guns: 1—30 in/50; 2—47 mm; 2—40 mm; 6—20 mm
Armour: 3 in side and partial deck protection
Main engines: 2 Thornycroft triple expansion; 2 shafts; 1 300 ihp = 12 knots
Boilers: Two 3-drum type, working pressure 250 psi
Oil fuel, tons: 70
Range, miles: 1 350 at 10 knots
Complement: 90

Laid down on 11 June 1936. Launched on 2 September 1937. In Mato Grosso Flotilla. Rearmed with the above guns in 1960.

PARNAIBA   1971, Brazilian Nav

BRAZIL / Patrol forces — Survey ships

3 "RORAIMA" CLASS (RIVER PATROL SHIPS)

Name	No.	Builders	Commissioned
RORAIMA	P 30	Maclaren, Niteroi	Mar 1974
RONDONIA	P 31	Maclaren, Niteroi	1974
AMAPA	P 32	Maclaren, Niteroi	Jan 1976

Displacement, tons: 340 standard; 365 full load
Dimensions, feet (metres): 147·6 × 27·7 × 4·2 (45 × 8·4 × 1·3)
Guns: 1—40 mm; 2—81 mm mortars; 6—0·50 cal MGs
Main engines: Diesels; 2 shafts; 1 814 shp = 14·5 knots
Complement: 54

Rondonia launched 10 January 1973, *Amapa* 9 March 1973. Carry two LCVPs. Belong to Amazon Flotilla.

RONDONIA   1977, Brazilian Navy

LIGHT FORCES
Note: A new class of Fast Attack Craft is projected.

6 "PIRATINI" CLASS (LARGE PATROL CRAFT)

Name	No.	Builders	Commissioned
PIRATINI (ex-PGM 109)	P 10	Arsenal de Marinha, Rio de Janeiro	Nov 1970
PIRAJA (ex-PGM 110)	P 11	Arsenal de Marinha, Rio de Janeiro	Mar 1971
PAMPEIRO (ex-PGM 118)	P 12	Arsenal de Marinha, Rio de Janeiro	May 1971
PARATI (ex-PGM 119)	P 13	Arsenal de Marinha, Rio de Janeiro	July 1971
PENEDO (ex-PGM 120)	P 14	Arsenal de Marinha, Rio de Janeiro	Sep 1971
POTI (ex-PGM 121)	P 15	Arsenal de Marinha, Rio de Janeiro	Oct 1971

Displacement, tons: 105 standard
Dimensions, feet (metres): 95 × 19 × 6·5 (29 × 5·8 × 2)
Guns: 3—0·50 cal MG; 1—81 mm mortar
Main engines: 4 diesels; 1 100 bhp = 17 knots
Range, miles: 1 700 at 12 knots
Complement: 15 officers and men

Built under offshore agreement with the USA.

PIRAJA   1977, Brazilian Navy

6 "ANCHOVA" CLASS (RIVER PATROL CRAFT)

Name	No.	Builders	Commissioned
ANCHOVA	R 54	Brazil	1965
ARENQUE	R 55	Brazil	1965
ATUM	R 56	Brazil	1966
ACARA	R 57	Brazil	1966
AGULHA	R 58	Brazil	1967
ARUANA	R 59	Brazil	1967

Displacement, tons: 11
Dimensions, feet (metres): 42·6 × 12·5 × 3·9 (13 × 3·8 ×1·2)
Main engines: 2 diesels; 280 hp = 25 knots
Range, miles: 400 at 20 knots
Complement: 3 plus 12 passengers

4 RIVER PATROL CRAFT

Built in 1968. Of about 30 tons and 45 ft (13·7 m) in length. Capable of 17 knots and with a range of 1 400 miles at 10 knots. Operate on the Upper Amazon.

MINE WARFARE FORCES

6 "SCHÜTZE" CLASS (MINESWEEPERS—COASTAL)

Name	No.	Builders	Commissioned
ARATU	M 15	Abeking and Rasmussen	5 May 1971
ANHATOMIRIM	M 16	Abeking and Rasmussen	30 Nov 1971
ATALAIA	M 17	Abeking and Rasmussen	13 Dec 1972
ARACATUBA	M 18	Abeking and Rasmussen	13 Dec 1972
ABROLHOS	M 19	Abeking and Rasmussen	16 Apr 1975
ALBARDÃO	M 20	Abeking and Rasmussen	21 July 1975

Displacement, tons: 230 standard; 280 full load
Dimensions, feet (metres): 154·9 × 23·6 × 6·9 (47·2 × 7·2 × 2·1)
Gun: 1—40 mm
Main engines: 4 Maybach diesels; 2 shafts; 4 500 bhp = 24 knots
Range, miles: 710 at 20 knots
Complement: 39

Wooden hulled. First four ordered in April 1969 and another pair in November 1973. Same design as West German "Schütze" class.

ARATU   1977, Brazilian Navy

SURVEY SHIPS

ALVARO ALBERTO

Dimensions, feet (metres): 196·8 × 39·3 × 14·1 (60 × 12 × 4·3)
Speed, knots: 13
Complement: 26 plus 17 scientists

An oceanographic research ship ordered in 1973.

66 BRAZIL / Survey ships — Survey launches

1 Ex-US "ROBERT D. CONRAD" CLASS

Name	No.	Builders	Commissioned
ALMIRANTE CÀMARA	H 41	Marietta Co, Point Pleasant West Va.	8 Feb 1965
(ex-USNS *Sands* T-AGOR 6)			

Displacement, tons: 1 200 standard; 1 380 full load
Dimensions, feet (metres): 208·9 × 37·4 × 15·3 *(63·7 × 11·4 × 4·7)*
Main engines: Diesel-electric; Caterpillar Tractor Co diesels; 10 000 bhp; 1 shaft = 13·5 knots
Range, miles: 12 000 at 12 knots
Complement: 26 (+15 scientists)

Built specifically for oceanographic research. Equipped for gravimetric, magnetic and geological research. Has bow thruster, 10 ton crane and 620 hp gas turbine for providing "quiet power". Transferred 1 July 1974.

ALMIRANTE CÀMARA (as USNS *Sands*)   USN

2 "SIRIUS" CLASS

Name	No.	Builders	Commissioned
SIRIUS	H 21	Ishikawajima Co Ltd, Tokyo	1 Jan 1958
CANOPUS	H 22	Ishikawajima Co Ltd, Tokyo	15 Mar 1958

Displacement, tons: 1 463 standard; 1 800 full load
Dimensions, feet (metres): 255·7 × 39·3 × 12·2 *(78 × 12·1 × 3·7)*
Guns: 1—3 in; 4—20 mm MG
Main engines: 2 Sulzer diesels; 2 shafts; 2 700 bhp = 15·75 knots
Range, miles: 12 000 at cruising speed of 11 knots
Complement: 116

Laid down 1955-56. Helicopter platform aft. Special surveying apparatus, echo sounders, Raydist equipment, sounding machines installed, and helicopter, landing craft (LCVP), jeep, and survey launches carried. All living and working spaces are air-conditioned. Cp propellers.

CANOPUS   1977, Brazilian Navy

3 "ARGUS" CLASS

Name	No.	Builders	Commissioned
ARGUS	H 31	Arsenal da Marinha, Rio de Janeiro	29 Jan 1959
ORION	H 32	Arsenal da Marinha, Rio de Janeiro	11 June 1959
TAURUS	H 33	Arsenal da Marinha, Rio de Janeiro	23 Apr 1959

Displacement, tons: 250 standard; 343 full load
Dimensions, feet (metres): 147·7 × 20 × 6·6 *(45 × 6·1 × 2)*
Guns: 2—20 mm
Main engines: 2 diesels coupled to two shafts; 1 200 bhp = 15 knots
Oil fuel, tons: 35
Range, miles: 1 200 at 15 knots
Complement: 42

All laid down in 1955 and launched December 1957—February 1958.

ORION   1977, Brazilian Navy

Name	No.	Builders	Launched
ALMIRANTE SALDANHA	H 10 (ex-U 10, ex-NE 1)	Vickers, Barrow	19 Dec 1933

Displacement, tons: 3 325 standard; 3 825 full load
Dimensions, feet (metres): 307·2 × 52 × 19·2 *(93·6 × 15·8 × 45·5)*
Main engine: Diesel; 1 400 bhp = 11 knots
Range, miles: 12 000 at 10 knots
Complement: 218

Former training ship with a total sail area of 25 990 sq ft and armed with four 4 in guns, one 3 in gun and four 3-pounders. Cost £314 500. Instructional minelaying gear was included in equipment. The single 21 in torpedo tube was removed. Re-classified as an Oceanographic Ship (NOc) August 1959, and completely remodelled by 1964. A photograph as sailing ship appears in the 1952-53 to 1959-60 editions.

ALMIRANTE SALDANHA (Old pennant number)   1977, Brazilian Navy

SURVEY LAUNCHES

PARAIBANO	H 11	ITACURUSSA	H 15
RIO BRANCO	H 12	CAMOCIM	H 16
NOGUEIRA DA GAMA (ex-*Jaceguai*)	H 14	CARAVELAS	H 17

Displacement, tons: 32 standard; 50 full load
Dimensions, feet (metres): 52·5 × 15·1 × 4·3 *(16 × 4·6 × 1·3)*
Main engine: 1 diesel; 165 bhp = 11 knots
Range, miles: 600 at 11 knots
Complement: 11

First pair launched 1968—last pair in 1972. Built by Bormann, Rio de Janeiro.

CARAVELAS   1977, Brazilian Navy

1 LIGHTHOUSE TENDER

Name	No.	Builders	Commissioned
GRAÇA ARANHA	H 34	Elbin, Niteroi	9 Sep 1976

Displacement, tons: 2 300
Dimensions, feet (metres): 247·6 × 42·6 × 12·1 *(75·5 × 13 × 3·7)*
Aircraft: 1 helicopter
Main engine: 1 diesel; 2 000 hp; 1 shaft = 14 knots
Complement: 95

Laid down in 1971 and launched 23 May 1974. Fitted with collapsible helo-hangar.

4 BUOY TENDERS

MESTRE JOÃO DOS SANTOS	H 13	FAROLEIRO NASCIMENTO	H 25
CASTELHANOS	H 24	FAROLEIRO AREAS	H 27

Taken over 1973.

BRAZIL / Submarine rescue ship — Transports

SUBMARINE RESCUE SHIP

Name	No.	Builders	Launched
GASTÃO MOUTINHO (ex-USS *Skylark* ASR 20)	K 10	Charleston S.B. & D.D. Co	19 Mar 1946

Displacement, tons: 1 235 standard; 1 740 full load
Dimensions, feet (metres): 205 × 38·5 × 15·3 *(62·5 × 11·7 × 4·7)*
Main engines: Diesel-electric; 1 shaft; 3 000 bhp = 14 knots
Complement: 85

Converted to present form in 1947. Fitted with special pumps, compressors and submarine rescue chamber. Fitted for oxy-helium diving. Transferred 30 June 1973.

GASTÃO MOUTINHO   1975, Brazilian Navy

REPAIR AND SUPPORT SHIPS

Name	No.	Builders	Commissioned
BELMONTE (ex-USS *Helios* ARB 12, ex-LST 1127)	G 24	Maryland D.D. Co, Baltimore	26 Feb 1945

Displacement, tons: 1 625 light; 2 030 standard; 4 100 full load
Dimensions, feet (metres): 328 × 50 × 11 *(100 × 15·2 × 3·4)*
Guns: 8—40 mm
Main engines: General Motors diesels; 2 shafts; 1 700 bhp = 11·6 knots
Oil fuel, tons: 1 000
Range, miles: 6 000 at 9 knots

Former US battle damage repair ship (ex-LST). Laid down on 23 November 1944. Launched on 4 February 1945. Loaned to Brazil by USA in January 1962 under MAP and by purchase 28 December 1977.

BAURU (ex-USS *McAnn* DE 179) U 28

An ex-US "Cannon" class DE, last of eight transferred in 1944. Of 1 900 tons full load used as support vessel in Guanabara Bay.

1 NEW CONSTRUCTION

Projected river support ship. No further details.

TANKERS

Name	No.	Builders	Commissioned
MARAJO	G 27	Ishikawajima do Brasil-Estaleiros SA	22 Oct 1968

Measurements, tons: 10 500 deadweight
Dimensions, feet (metres): 440·7 × 63·3 × 24 *(134·4 × 19·3 × 7·3)*
Main engine: Diesel; 1 shaft = 13·6 knots
Capacity, (cu metres): 14 200
Range, miles: 9 200 at 13 knots
Complement: 80

Laid down on 13 December 1966 and launched on 31 January 1968.

MARAJÓ   1975, Brazilian Navy

Name	No.	Builders	Launched
POTENGI	G 17	Papendrecht, Netherlands	16 Mar 1938

Displacement, tons: 600
Dimensions, feet (metres): 178·8 × 24·5 × 6 *(54·5 × 7·5 × 1·8)*
Main engines: Diesels; 2 shafts; 550 bhp = 10 knots
Oil fuel, tons: 450
Complement: 19

Employed in the Mato Grosso Flotilla on river service.

MARTINS DE OLIVEIRA (ex-*Gastao Moutinho*) R 11

Displacement, tons: 588
Dimensions, feet (metres): 162 × 23·1 × 7·9 *(49·4 × 7 × 2·4)*
Speed, knots: 10·3

Taken over 1973.

TRANSPORTS

Note: A new Training Ship is projected—to have helicopter and hangar.

4 "BARROSO PEREIRA" CLASS

Name	No.	Builders	Commissioned
BARROSO PEREIRA	G 16	Ishikawajima Co Ltd, Tokyo	1 Dec 1954
ARY PARREIRAS	G 21	Ishikawajima Co Ltd, Tokyo	29 Dec 1956
SOARES DUTRA	G 22	Ishikawajima Co Ltd, Tokyo	23 Mar 1957
CUSTÓDIO DE MELLO	U 26	Ishikawajima Co Ltd, Tokyo	30 Dec 1954

Displacement, tons: 4 800 standard; 7 300 full load
Measurement, tons: 4 200 deadweight; 4 879 gross (Panama)
Dimensions, feet (metres): 362 pp; 391·8 oa × 52·5 × 20·5 *(110·4; 119·5 × 16 × 6·3)*
Guns: 4—3 in (U 26); 2—3 in (others); 2/4—20 mm
Main engines: Ishikawajima double reduction geared turbines; 2 shafts; 4 800 shp = 17·67 knots (sea speed 15 knots)
Boilers: 2 Ishikawajima 2-drum water tube type, oil fuel
Complement: 127 (Troop capacity 497)

Transports and cargo vessels. Helicopter landing platform aft except in U26. Troop carrying capacity for 497, with commensurate medical, hospital and dental facilities. Working and living quarters are mechanically ventilated with partial air conditioning. Refrigerated cargo space 5 500 cubic ft. Can carry 4 000 tons of cargo. *Custódio de Mello* has been classified as a training ship since July 1961 with additional deckhouses. The other three operate commercially from time to time.

ARY PARREIRAS   1977, Michael D. J. Lennon

68 BRAZIL / Transports — Auxiliaries

6 "RIO DOCE" CLASS (HARBOUR TRANSPORTS)

Name	No.	Builders	Commissioned
RIO DOCE	U 20	Netherlands	1954
RIO DAS CONTAS	U 21	Netherlands	1954
RIO FORMOSO	U 22	Netherlands	1954
RIO REAL	U 23	Netherlands	1955
RIO TURVO	U 24	Netherlands	1955
RIO VERDE	U 25	Netherlands	1955

Displacement, tons: 150
Dimensions, feet (metres): 120 oa × 21·3 × 6·2 *(36·6 oa × 6·5 × 1·9)*
Main engines: 2 Sulzer 6-TD24; 900 bhp = 14 knots

Can carry 600 passengers.

PARAGUASSU (ex-*Guarapunava*) G 15 (RIVER TRANSPORT)

Displacement, tons: 285
Dimensions, feet (metres): 131·2 × 23 × 3·9 *(40 × 7 × 1·2)*
Speed knots: 12
Range, miles: 2 500 at 10 knots

Acquired 1971. In Mato Grosso flotilla.

4 "RIO PARDO" (HARBOUR TRANSPORTS)

RIO PARDO U 40 **RIO NEGRO** U 41 **RIO CHUI** U 42 **RIO OIAPOQUE** U 43

Displacement, tons: 150
Dimensions, feet (metres): 116·8 × 21·3 × 6·2 *(35·6 × 6·5 × 1·9)*
Main engines: 2 diesels = 14 knots

Capable of carrying 600 passengers. Completed by Inconav de Niteroi 1975-76.

TUGS

Note: One fleet tug projected.

3 Ex-US "SOTOYOMO" CLASS

TRITÃO (ex-ATA 234) R 21   **TRIDENTE** (ex-ATA 235) R 22   **TRIUNFO** (ex-ATA 236) R 23

Displacement, tons: 534 standard; 835 full load
Dimensions, feet (metres): 143 × 33 × 13·2 *(43·6 × 10 × 4)*
Guns: 2—20 mm
Main engines: General Motors diesel-electric; 1 500 hp = 13 knots

All built by Gulfport Boiler & Welding Works, Inc, Port Arthur, Texas, and launched in 1944. R 21 completed 11 December 1945, R 22 on 3 December 1945. Sold to Brazil 26 March 1947 (R 21 and 22) and 22 April 1947 (R 23).

ISLAS DE NORONHA

Of 200 tons. Built 1972.

2 COASTAL TUGS

DNOG   **LAHMEYER**

Of 100 tons and 105 ft long, built in Brazil in 1972. Based at Aratu.

LAURINDO PITTA R 14

514 tons. Vickers 1910. Reconstructed 1969.

WANDENKOLK R 20

350 tons. UK 1910.

AUDAZ R 31	**LAMEGO** R 34
CENTAURO R 32	**PASSO da PATRIA** R 35
GUARANI R 33	**VOLUNTARIO** R 36

Displacement, tons: 130 tons
Dimensions, feet (metres): 90·5 oa × 23·6 × 10·2 *(27·6 × 7·2 × 3·1)*
Main engine: Womag diesel of 765 hp = 11 knots
Complement: 12

Built by Holland Nautic Yard, Netherlands in 1953.

RAIMUNDO NONATO   **ETCHBARNE** R 28   **GRUMETE** (1961)

TANKER

ANITA GARIBALDI

WATER BOATS

ITAPURA R 42   **PAULO AFONSO** R 43

Displacement, tons: 485·3
Dimensions, feet (metres): 140·5 × 23 × 8 *(42·8 × 7 × 2·5)*
Main engines: Diesel

Capacity 389 tons. Launched 1957.

STORE TRANSPORTS

TENENTE FABIO   **TENENTE RAUL**

Displacement, tons: 55 tons
Dimensions, feet (metres): 66·6 × 16·7 × 3·9 *(20·3 × 5·1 × 1·2)*
Main engines: Diesel; 135 hp = 10 knots

1969. 2 ton derrick.

MUNITIONS TRANSPORTS

SAN FRANCISCO DOS SANTOS

1964.

UBIRAJARA DOS SANTOS   **OPERARIO LUIS LEAL**

1968.

TORPEDO TRANSPORTS

MIGUEL DOS SANTOS   **APRENDIZ LEDIO CONCEIÇAO**

1968.

FLOATING DOCKS

CIDADE DE NATAL (ex-AFDL 39)

Displacement, tons: 7 600
Length, feet (metres): 390·3 *(119)*
Beam, feet (metres): 86·9 *(26·5)*
Capacity, tons: 2 800

Concrete floating dock loaned to Brazil by US Navy, 10 November 1966. Purchased 28 December 1977.

ALMIRANTE JERONIMO GONÇALVES (ex-*Goiaz* AFDL 4) ex-G 26

Displacement, tons: 3 000
Length, feet (metres): 200 *(61)*
Beam, feet (metres): 44 *(13·4)*
Capacity, tons: 1 000

Steel floating dock loaned to Brazil by US Navy, 10 November 1966. Purchased 28 December 1977.

AFONSO PENA (ex-*Ceara*, ex-ARD 14) G 25

Displacement, tons: 5 200
Dimensions, feet (metres): 402·0 × 81·0 *(122·6 × 24·7)*

Transferred from the US Navy to the Brazilian Navy in 1963. Purchased 28 December 197

—(ex-US ARD 12)

Transferred on loan—purchased with attendant craft on 28 December 1977.

FLOATING CRANES

At least two in service at Rio de Janeiro—one of 100 tons capacity, one of 30 tons.

AUXILIARIES

ALMIRANTE BRASIL R 13	**IGUASSU** R 41
ARGENTINA	**MARIA QUITERIA** R 44
A. BARBOSA R 27	**MARISCO**
DR. GONDIM R 38	**TENENTE CLAUDIO**
GUAIRIA R 40	**DHN-225**

BRUNEI

(Askar Melayu Diraja Brunei (Royal Brunei Malay Regiment) Flotilla)

Commanding Officer:
Commander David Wright RN

Personnel
(a) 1979: 350 (25 officers and 325 ratings)
(b) Voluntary service

Base
Muara Marine Base

Prefix to Ships' Names
KDB (Kapal Di-Raja Brunei)

Mercantile Marine
Lloyd's Register of Shipping:
2 vessels of 899 tons gross

Deletion
1977 Pahlawan

3 "WASPADA" CLASS (FAST ATTACK CRAFT-MISSILE)

Name	No.	Builder	Commissioned
WASPADA	P 02	Vosper Singapore	1978
—	P 03	Vosper Singapore	1979
SETERIA	P 04	Vosper Singapore	1979

Displacement, tons: 150 full load
Dimensions, feet (metres): 121 × 23·5 × 6 (36·9 × 7·2 × 1·8)
Missiles: SSM MM 38 Exocet (two single launchers)
Guns: 2—30 mm Oerlikon GCM-B01 (twin); 2 MG
Main engines: 2 MTO 538TB 91 diesels; 9 000 bhp; 2 shafts = 32 knots
Range, miles: 1 200 at 14 knots
Complement: 24 (4 officers, 20 ratings)

Welded steel hull.

Flares: Two MOD(N) 2 in flare launchers

Gunnery: Optical fire director with Decca ranging radar and Sperry 1412A digital computer.

Missiles: Sea Archer system with Sperry Co-ordinate Calculator.

Radar: Decca AC 1629.

WASPADA   *1978, Vosper, Singapore*

3 "PERWIRA" CLASS (COASTAL PATROL CRAFT)

Name	No.	Builders	Commissioned
PERWIRA	P 14	Vosper Thornycroft (Singapore)	9 Sep 1974
PEMBURU	P 15	Vosper Thornycroft (Singapore)	17 June 1975
PENYARANG	P 16	Vosper Thornycroft (Singapore)	24 June 1975

Displacement, tons: 30
Dimensions, feet (metres): 71 × 20 × 5 (21·7 × 6·1 × 1·2)
Guns: 2—20 mm Hispano Suiza; 2—7·62 MG
Main engines: 2 MTU MB 12V 331 TC81 diesels; 2 450 bhp = 32 knots
Range, miles: 600 at 22 knots; 1 000 at 16 knots
Complement: 12

Perwira launched 9 May 1974. Other two ordered June 1974. Of all wooden construction on laminated frames. Fitted with enclosed bridges—modified July 1976. Decca 916 radar.

PERWIRA   *1974, Royal Brunei Malay Regiment*

3 COASTAL PATROL CRAFT

Name	No.	Builders	Commissioned
SALEHA	P 11	Vosper Thornycroft (Singapore)	1972
MASNA	P 12	Vosper Thornycroft (Singapore)	1972
NORAIN	P 13	Vosper Thornycroft (Singapore)	Aug 1972

Displacement, tons: 25
Dimensions, feet (metres): 62·0 × 16·0 × 4·5 (18·9 × 4·8 × 1·4)
Guns: 2—20 mm Hispano-Suiza; 2 MG
Main engines: 2 General Motors 71 16-cyl diesels; 1 250 bhp = 26 knots
Range, miles: 600 at 23 knots
Complement: 8

Fitted with Decca 202 radar. Named after Brunei princesses.

NORAIN   *1974, Royal Brunei Malay Regiment*

3 RIVER PATROL CRAFT

Name	No.	Conversion
BENDAHARA	P 21	1974
MAHARAJALELA	P 22	1975
MEMAINDERA	P 23	1975

Displacement, tons: 10
Dimensions, feet (metres): 47·0 × 12·0 × 3·0 (14·3 × 3·6 × 0·9)
Guns: 2 twin MG 42, 7·62 cal
Main engines: 2 General Motors diesels; 334 bhp = 20 knots
Range, miles: 200
Complement: 6

Fitted with Decca 202 radar.

BENDAHARA   *1976, Royal Brunei Malay Regiment*

70 BRUNEI / Amphibious forces — BULGARIA / Frigates

AMPHIBIOUS FORCES

2 CHEVERTON "LOADMASTERS"

Name	No.	Builders	Commissioned
DAMUAN	L 31	Cheverton Ltd, Isle of Wight	May 1976
PUNI	L 32	Cheverton Ltd, Isle of Wight	Feb 1977

Displacement, tons: 60 (64—*Puni*)
Dimensions, feet (metres): 65 × 20 × 3·6 *(19·8 × 6·1 × 1·1)* (length 74·8 *(22·8) Puni*)
Main engines: 2 General Motors V 71 6-cyl diesels = 9 knots
Range, miles: 1 000
Complement: 18

Radar: Decca RM 1216.

DAMUAN
1976, Royal Brunei Malay Regiment

24 FAST ASSAULT BOATS

Rigid Raider type with one MG and two 50 hp outboards.

2 POLICE PATROL CRAFT

Seven metre craft for delivery in 1979.

BULGARIA

Ministerial

Minister of National Defence:
General Dobri Dzhurov

Headquarters Appointment

Commander-in-Chief, Navy:
Vice-Admiral VG Yanakiev

Diplomatic Representation

Naval, Military and Air Attaché in London:
Colonel Dimitar Toskov

Personnel

(a) 1979: 10 000 officers and ratings
(b) 3 years national service (6 000)

Bases

Varna, Burgas, Sozopol

Naval Aviation

2 Mi1 helicopters
6 Mi4 (Hound) helicopters

Strength of the Fleet

No building programme available

Type	Active
Patrol Submarines	2
Frigates	2
Corvettes	3
Fast Attack Craft (Missile)	4
Fast Attack Craft (Torpedo)	10
Large Patrol Craft	6
Minesweepers (Ocean)	2
Minesweepers (Coastal)	4
Minesweeping Boats	12
Landing Craft	20
Surveying Ships	3
Tugs	8
Tankers Small	3
Salvage Craft	2
Auxiliaries	app 28

Mercantile Marine

Lloyd's Register of Shipping:
189 vessels of 1 082 477 tons gross

DELETIONS

Submarines

1972 2 "Whiskey" class (names transferred to "Romeo" class)

Light Forces

1975 2 "Kronshstadt" class (numbers transferred to "Poti" class)
1975 4 "P4" class

Mine Warfare Forces

1974 3 "T 301" class
1975 1 "T 301" class
1976 12 "P 02" class

SUBMARINES (PATROL)

2 Ex-SOVIET "ROMEO" CLASS

POBEDA	SLAVA

Displacement, tons: 1 400 surfaced; 1 800 dived
Length, feet (metres): 252 *(76·8)*
Beam, feet (metres): 23 *(7)*
Draught, feet (metres): 18 *(5·5)*
Torpedo tubes: 8—21 in *(533 mm)* (6 bow; 2 stern)
Main machinery: 2 diesels; 4 000 hp; 2 main motors; 4 000 hp; 2 shafts
Speed, knots: 17 surfaced, 14 dived
Range, miles: 16 000 at 10 knots (surfaced)
Complement: 54

Transferred in 1972-73 as replacements for "Whiskey" class, whose names they took over.

Radar. Snoop Plate.

"ROMEO" Class

FRIGATES

2 Ex-SOVIET "RIGA" CLASS

DRUZKI 31	SMELI 32

Displacement, tons: 1 000 standard; 1 320 full load
Length, feet (metres): 298·8 *(91·0)*
Beam, feet (metres): 33·7 *(10·2)*
Draught, feet (metres): 11·0 *(3·4)*
Guns: 3—3·9 in *(100 mm)*; 4—37 mm
A/S Weapons: 4 MBU 1 800 (5 tubed), 4 DCT
Torpedo tubes: 3—21 in *(533 mm)*
Mines: 50
Main engines: Geared turbines; 2 shafts; 20 000 shp
Speed, knots: 28
Range, miles: 2 500 at 15 knots
Complement: 175

Transferred from USSR in 1957-58.

Radar: Search: Slim Net.
Navigation: Neptun.

SMELI

IFF: High Pole, Square Head.
Fire control: Wasp Head/Sun Visor B.

BULGARIA / Corvettes — Light forces 71

CORVETTES

3 Ex-SOVIET "POTI" CLASS

33   34   35

Displacement, tons: 500 standard; 580 full load
Dimensions, feet (metres): 200·1 × 26·2 × 9·2 *(61 × 8 × 2·8)*
Guns: 2—57 mm (twin)
Torpedo tubes: 4—16 in *(406 mm)* A/S
A/S weapons: 2 MBU 2 500 A
Main engines: 2 gas turbines; 32 000 hp; 2 M503A diesels; 8 000 shp; 4 shafts; = 36 knots
Complement: 80

Transferred December 1975. Built 1961-68.

Radar: Strut Curve, Muff Cob and Spin Trough.

Sonar: One hull-mounted.

Soviet "POTI" Class   *1975*

LIGHT FORCES

Note: It is reported, but not confirmed, that three Ex-Soviet "Stenka" class have been transferred.

6 Ex-SOVIET "SO 1" CLASS (LARGE PATROL CRAFT)

41 to 46

Displacement, tons: 170 light; 215 full load
Length, feet (metres): 138·6 *(42·3)*
Beam, feet (metres): 20 *(6·1)*
Draught, feet (metres): 5·9 *(1·8)*
Guns: 4—25 mm (2 twin)
A/S weapons: Four 5-barrelled MBU 1800 launchers; DCs
Main engines: 3 diesels; 7 500 bhp = 28 knots
Range, miles: 1 100 at 13 knots
Complement: 31

Steel hulled vessels transferred from USSR in 1963.

Radar: Pot Head.
IFF: High Pole A and Dead Duck.

"SO 1" Class   *1978*

4 Ex-SOVIET "OSA I" CLASS (FAST ATTACK CRAFT—MISSILE)

210   220   230   245

Displacement, tons: 165 standard; 200 full load
Dimensions, feet (metres): 128·7 × 25·1 × 5·9 *(39·3 × 7·7 × 1·8)*
Missiles: 4 SSM SS-N-2 (single launchers)
Guns: 4—30 mm (2 twin, 1 fwd, 1 aft)
Main engines: 3 M503 diesels; 12 000 bhp = 36 knots
Range, miles: 800 at 25 knots
Complement: 30

Reported to have been transferred from USSR in 1970-71.

Radar: Drum Tilt and Square Tie.

"OSA 1" Class   *1978*

6 Ex-SOVIET "SHERSHEN" CLASS (FAST ATTACK CRAFT—TORPEDO)

27   28   29   30   +2

Displacement, tons: 145 standard; 160 full load
Dimensions, feet (metres): 115·5 × 25·3 × 5·0 *(35·2 × 7·7 × 1·5)*
Guns: 4—30 mm (2 twin)
Torpedo tubes: 4—21 in (single)
A/S armament: 12 DCs
Main engines: 3 diesels; 3 shafts; 13 200 bhp = 41 knots
Range, miles: 700 at 20 knots
Complement: 16

Transferred from USSR in 1970.

Radar: Pot Drum, Drum Tilt.
IFF: High Pole A and Square Head.

4 Ex-SOVIET "P 4" CLASS (FAST ATTACK CRAFT—TORPEDO)

Displacement, tons: 22·4 full load
Dimensions, feet (metres): 63·3 × 12·1 × 3·3 *(19·3 × 3·7 × 1·0)*
Guns: 2—14·7 mm
Torpedo tubes: 2—18 in
Main engines: 2 M50 diesels; 2 shafts; 2 200 bhp = 55 knots
Range, miles: 400 at 30 knots
Complement: 12

Transferred from USSR in 1956. Will soon be deleted.

"P 4" Class   *1978*

72 BULGARIA / Mine warfare forces — Amphibious forces

MINE WARFARE FORCES

2 Ex-SOVIET "T 43" CLASS (MINESWEEPERS—OCEAN)

38   48

Displacement, tons: 490 standard; 560 full load
Dimensions, feet (metres): 190·2 × 28·2 × 7·0 *(58·0 × 8·6 × 2·3)*
Guns: 4—37 mm (twins); 4—12·7 mm (twins)
Main engines: 2 diesels; 2 shafts; 2 200 hp = 14 knots
Range, miles: 3 000 at 10 knots
Complement: 40

Three were transferred from USSR in 1953—one scrapped for spares. These are the only short-hulled, low bridge, tripod mast "T43s" in existance.

"T 43" Class   1977

4 Ex-SOVIET "VANYA" CLASS (MINESWEEPERS—COASTAL)

36   37   38   39

Displacement, tons: 200 standard; 245 full load
Dimensions, feet (metres): 130·7 × 24 × 6·9 *(39·9 × 7·3 × 2·1)*
Guns: 2—30 mm (twin)
Main engines: 2 diesels; 2 200 bhp = 18 knots
Complement: 30

Transferred from USSR—two in 1970 and two in 1971.

Radar: Don 2.

"VANYA" Class   1977

12 "PO 2" CLASS (MSB)

Built in Bulgaria—first units completed in early 1950s and last in early 1960s. Originally a class of 24—some reports suggest there may be only four remaining.

AMPHIBIOUS FORCES

10 Ex-SOVIET "VYDRA" CLASS

421-428 + 2

Displacement, tons: 425 standard; 600 full load
Dimensions, feet (metres): 179·7 × 26·6 × 6·6 *(54·8 × 8·1 × 2·0)*
Main engines: 2 diesels; 2 shafts; 800 bhp = 11 knots

Transferred from USSR in 1970.

Radar: Spin Trough

"VYDRA" Class   1974

10 MFP D-3 TYPE

Dimensions, feet (metres): 164·0 × 20·0 × 6·6 *(50 × 6·1 × 2·0)*
Gun: 1—37 mm or none

Built in Bulgaria in 1954. Based on a German Second World War MFP design.

BULGARIA / Miscellaneous — BURMA / Frigates 73

MISCELLANEOUS

2 SURVEY SHIPS

VLADIMIR ZAIMOV 350 + 1

"Varna" class survey ships built in Bulgaria in 1959.

1 "MOMA" CLASS (SURVEY SHIP)

Transferred by USSR.

2 TRAINING SHIPS

VAPCAROV

Approx 130 ft *(39·6 m)* with clipper bow.

VAPCAROV

VESSLETZ

Auxiliary schooner with bridge amidships.

2 DEGAUSSING SHIPS

324, 441

Transferred by USSR in 1958 and 1962.

3 COASTAL TANKERS

2 SALVAGE CRAFT

1 EAST GERMAN "700" CLASS (FLEET TUG)

JUPITER

Of 1 800 tons and 12 knots.

JUPITER

7 COASTAL TUGS

Ten or more other auxiliaries probably including diving craft and water boats.

6 BARRACK SHIPS

2 DIVING VESSELS

BURMA

Ministerial

Minister of Defence:
Kyaw Htin

Headquarters Appointment

Vice-Chief of Staff, Defence Services (Navy):
Commodore Thaung Tin

Diplomatic Representation

Naval, Military and Air Attaché in London:
Lieutenant-Colonel Than Lwin

Naval, Military and Air Attaché in Washington:
Colonel Tin Htut

Strength of the Fleet

Type	Active	Building
Frigates	2	—
Corvettes	4	—
Coastal Patrol Craft	—	6
River Patrol Craft	35	—
Gunboats	36	—
Survey Vessels	2	—
Auxiliaries	10	—

Aircraft

The Air Force operates a number of Alouette III, Husky and Sioux helicopters which work with the navy when needed.

Bases

Bassein, Mergui, Moulmein, Seikyi, Sinmalaik, Sittwo.

General

This is an ageing fleet in dire need of replacements which, under the present financial circumstances seems unlikely.

Personnel

(a) 1979: 6 300 including 800 marines
(b) Voluntary service

Mercantile Marine

Lloyd's Register of Shipping:
73 vessels of 70 848 tons gross

DELETIONS

Light Forces

1975   T201-205—Saunders-Roe convertibles

Gunboat

1976   *Indaw* sold commercially.

Transport

1971   *Pyi Daw Aye* scrapped.

FRIGATES

1 Ex-BRITISH "RIVER" CLASS

Name	No.	Builders	Laid down	Launched	Commissioned
MAYU (ex-HMS *Fal*)	—	Smiths Dock Co Ltd, South Bank-on-Tees, Middlesbrough, England	20 May 1942	9 Nov 1942	2 July 1943

Displacement, tons: 1 460 standard; 2 170 full load
Length, feet (metres): 283 *(86·3)* pp; 301·3 *(91·8)* oa
Beam, feet (metres): 36·7 *(11·2)*
Draught, feet (metres): 12 *(3·7)*
Guns: 1—4 in *(102 mm)*; 4—40 mm
Main engines: Triple expansion 5 500 ihp; 2 shafts
Boilers: Two 3-drum type
Speed, knots: 19
Oil fuel, tons: 440
Range, miles: 4 200 at 12 knots
Complement: 140

"River" class frigate. Acquired from the UK and renamed in March 1948.

Radar: British Type 974.

MAYU   *Burmese Navy*

74 BURMA / Frigates — Gunboats

1 Ex-BRITISH "ALGERINE" CLASS

Name	No.	Builders	Laid down	Launched	Commissioned
YAN MYO AUNG (ex-HMS *Mariner*, ex-*Kincardine*)	—	Port Arthur Shipyards, Canada	26 Aug 1943	9 May 1944	23 May 1945

Displacement, tons: 1 040 standard; 1 335 full load
Length, feet (metres): 225 *(68·6)* pp; 235 *(71·6)* oa
Beam, feet (metres): 35·5 *(10·8)*
Draught, feet (metres): 11·5 *(3·5)*
Guns: 1—4 in *(102 mm)*; 4—40 mm
Main engines: Triple expansion; 2 000 ihp; 2 shafts
Boilers: Two 3-drum type
Speed, knots: 16·5
Range, miles: 4 000 at 12 knots
Complement: 140

Former ocean minesweeper in the Royal Navy, used as escort vessel. Handed over to Burma in London and renamed *Yan Myo Aung*, on 18 April 1958. Fitted for minelaying and can carry 16 mines, eight on each side.

Radar: Decca Type 202.

Sonar: British Type 144.

YAN MYO AUNG *1964, Burmese Navy*

CORVETTES

1 Ex-US "PCE 827" CLASS

Name	No.	Builders	Commissioned
YAN TAING AUNG (ex-USS *Farmington* PCE 894)	PCE 41	Willamette Iron & Steel Co, Portland, Oregon	10 Aug 1943

Displacement, tons: 640 standard; 903 full load
Dimensions, feet (metres): 180 wl; 184 oa × 33 × 9·5 *(56 × 10·1 × 2·9)*
Guns: 1—30 in/50; 2—40 mm (1 twin); 8—20 mm (4 twin)
A/S weapons: 1 Hedgehog; 2 DCT; 2 DC racks
Main engines: General Motors diesels; 2 shafts; 1 800 bhp = 15 knots

Laid down on 7 December 1942, launched on 15 May 1943. Transferred on 18 June 1965.

YAN TAING AUNG

1 Ex-US "ADMIRABLE" CLASS

Name	No.	Builders	Commissioned
YAN GYI AUNG (ex-USS *Creddock* MSF 356)	PCE 42	Willamette Iron & Steel Co, Portland, Oregon	1944

Displacement, tons: 650 standard; 945 full load
Dimensions, feet (metres): 180 wl; 184·5 oa × 33 × 9·8 *(56·2 × 10·1 × 3·0)*
Guns: 1—3 in 50 cal single fwd; 4—40 mm (2 twin); 4—20 mm (2 twin)
A/S weapons: 1 US Hedgehog; 2 DCT; 2 DC Racks
Main engines: Diesels; 2 shafts; 1 710 shp = 14·8 knots
Range, miles: 4 300 at 10 knots

Laid down on 10 November 1943 and launched on 22 July 1944. Transferred at San Diego on 31 March 1967. Minesweeping gear removed.

2 "NAWARAT" CLASS

Name	No.	Builders	Commissioned
NAGAKYAY	—	Government Dockyard, Dawbon, Rangoon	3 Dec 1960
NAWARAT	—	Government Dockyard, Dawbon, Rangoon	26 Apr 1960

Displacement, tons: 400 standard; 450 full load
Dimensions, feet (metres): 163 × 26·8 × 5·8 *(49·7 × 8·2 × 1·8)*
Guns: 2—25 pdr QF; 2—40 mm
Main engines: 2 Paxman-Ricardo turbo-charged diesels; 2 shafts; 1 160 bhp = 12 knots
Complement: 43

NAWARAT

LIGHT FORCES

6 "CARPENTARIA" CLASS (COASTAL PATROL CRAFT)

Length, feet (metres): 52·5 *(16)*

Ordered from De Havilland Marine, Australia in 1978.

25 YUGOSLAV-BUILT RIVER PATROL CRAFT

Small craft, 52 ft long, acquired from Yugoslavia in 1965.

10 BURMESE-BUILT RIVER PATROL CRAFT

Small craft, 50 ft long, built in Burma in 1951-52.

GUNBOATS

3 Ex-BRITISH LCG (M) TYPE

INLAY   INMA   INYA

Displacement, tons: 381
Dimensions, feet (metres): 154 oa × 22·5 × 7·8 *(46·9 × 6·9 × 2·4)*
Guns: 2—25 pdr; 2—2 pdr
Main engines: Paxman Ricardo diesels; 2 shafts; 1 000 bhp = 13 knots
Complement: 39

Former British Landing craft, gun (medium) LCG (M). Employed as gunboats.

Radar: British Type 974.

2 IMPROVED "Y 301" CLASS

Y 311   Y 312

Guns: 2—40 mm (single); 4—20 mm (single).

Dimensions approximately as "Y 301" class. Built in Burma 1969.

BURMA / Gunboats — Transports 75

10 "Y 301" CLASS

Y 301 Y 302 Y 303 Y 304 Y 305 Y 306 Y 307 Y 308 Y 309 Y 310

Displacement, tons: 120
Dimensions, feet (metres): 100 pp; 104·8 oa × 24 × 3 *(32 × 7·3 × 0·9)*
Guns: 2—40 mm; 1—2 pdr
Main engines: 2 Mercedes-Benz (MTU) diesels; 2 shafts; 1 000 bhp = 13 knots
Complement: 29

All ten of these boats were completed in 1958 at the Uljanik Shipyard, Pula, Yugoslavia.

6 Ex-US PGM TYPE

PGM 401 PGM 402 PGM 403 PGM 404 PGM 405 PGM 406

Displacement, tons: 141
Dimensions, feet (metres): 101 × 21·1 × 7·5 *(30·8 × 6·4 × 2·3)*
Guns: 2—40 mm; 2—20 mm (twin); 2—0·50 Cal MG
Main engines: 8 General Motors 6-71 diesels; 2 shafts; 2 040 bhp = 17 knots
Range, miles: 1 000 cruising
Complement: 17

Built by the Marinette Marine Corporation, USA. Ex-US PGM 43-46, 51 and 52 respectively. Machinery comprises 2-stroke, 6-cyl, tandem geared twin diesel propulsion unit—1 LH and 1 RH; 500 bhp per unit.

Radar: Raytheon 1 500 in PGM 405-6; EDO 320 in PGM 401-4.

PGM 405

8 GUNBOATS (Ex-TRANSPORTS)

SABAN   SEINDA   SETYAHAT   SHWETHIDA
SAGU   SETKAYA   SHWEPAZUN   SINMIN

Displacement, tons: 98
Dimensions, feet (metres): 94·5 × 22 × 4·5 *(28·8 × 6·7 × 1·4)*
Guns: 1—40 mm, 3—20 mm
Main engine: Crossley ERL—6 diesel; 160 bhp = 12 knots
Complement: 32

7 Ex-US CGC TYPE

MGB 101 MGB 102 MGB 104 MGB 105 MGB 106 MGB 108 MGB 110

Displacement, tons: 49 standard; 66 full load
Dimensions, feet (metres): 78 pp; 83 oa × 16 × 5·5 *(25·3 × 4·9 × 1·7)*
Guns: 1—40 mm; 1—20 mm
Main engines: 4 General Motors diesels; 2 shafts; 800 bhp = 11 knots
Complement: 16

Ex-USCG 83-ft type cutters with new hulls built in Burma. Completed in 1960. Three of this class are reported to have been sunk.

MGB 110

SURVEY VESSELS

1 OCEAN SURVEY SHIP

Name	No.	Builders	Commissioned
THU TAY THI	—	Brodogradiliste "Tito", Belgrade, Yugoslavia	1965

Displacement, tons: 1 059
Length, feet (metres): 204 *(62·2)*
Complement: 99

Fitted with helicopter platform.

THU TAY THI

1 COASTAL SURVEY SHIP

Name	No.	Builders	Commissioned
YAY BO	UBHL 807	Netherlands	1957

Displacement, tons: 108
Complement: 25

YAY BO

SUPPORT SHIP

YAN LON AUNG

Light forces support diving ship of 520 tons, acquired from Japan in 1967.

YAN LON AUNG

TRANSPORTS

8 Ex-US LCM 3 TYPE

LCM 701 LCM 702 LCM 703 LCM 704 LCM 705 LCM 706 LCM 707 LCM 708

Displacement, tons: 52 tons full load
Dimensions, feet (metres): 50 × 14 × 4 *(15·2 × 4·3 × 1·2)*
Guns: 2—20 mm single
Main engines: 2 Gray Marine diesels; 450 bhp = 9 knots

US-built LCM type landing craft. Used as local transports for stores and personnel. Cargo capacity 30 tons.

1 Ex-US LCU TYPE

AIYAR LULIN (ex-USS LCU 1626) 603

Displacement, tons: 200 light; 342 full load
Dimensions, feet (metres): 135·2 × 29 × 5·5 *(41·2 × 8·8 × 1·7)*
Main engines: 4 General Motors 12007 T diesels; 2 shafts (Kort nozzles); 1 000 bhp = 11 knots

US type utility landing craft 603 completed in Rangoon 1966. Used as transport. Cargo capacity 168 tons.

CAMEROON

Ministerial

Minister of Armed Forces:
Daoudou Sadou

Senior Officer:
Lieutenant de Vaisseau Ndangang

Personnel

1979: 600 officers and men

Base

Douala (a new base is to be built by Messrs Continental, Illinois Ltd at a cost of $9 million)

Mercantile Marine

Lloyd's Register of Shipping:
29 vessels of 83 777 tons gross

DELETIONS

1975 French VC Type—*Vigilant* (ex-VC 6), *Audacieux* (ex VC-8)

LIGHT FORCES

2 Ex-CHINESE "SHANGHAI" CLASS (FAST ATTACK CRAFT—GUN)

101 102

Displacement, tons: 120 standard; 155 full load
Dimensions, feet (metres): 115 × 18 × 5·5 *(35·1 × 5·5 × 1·7)*
Guns: 1—57 mm; 2—37 mm
A/S weapons: 8 DC
Minerals: Can be fitted for up to 10 mines
Main engines: 4 diesels; 4 800 bhp = 28 knots
Complement: 25

Transferred July 1976.

Radar: Skin Head.

"SHANGHAI II" Class (with 75 mm forward)

1 PR 48 TYPE (LARGE PATROL CRAFT)

Name	No.	Builders	Commissioned
L'AUDACIEUX	—	Soc Français de Construction Naval	11 May 1976

Displacement, tons: 250 full load
Dimensions, feet (metres): 157·5 × 23·3 × 7·5 *(48 × 7·1 × 2·3)*
Missiles: Fitted for 8 SS-12
Guns: 2—40 mm
Main engines: 2 MGO diesels; 2 400 hp = 22 knots
Range, miles: 2 000 at 15 knots
Complement: 25

Ordered in September 1974. Laid down 10 February 1975, launched 31 October 1975. Similar to "Bizerte" class in Tunisia.

PR 48 Type

Name	No.	Builders	Commissioned
QUARTIER MAÎTRE ALFRED MOTTO	—	At. et Ch. de l'Afrique Equatoriale Libreville, Gabon	1974

Displacement, tons: 96
Dimensions, feet (metres): 95·4 × 20·3 × 6·3 *(29·1 × 6·2 × 1·9)*
Guns: 2—20 mm; 2 MG
Main engines: 2 Baudoin diesels; 1 290 bhp = 15·5 knots
Complement: 17

Name	No.	Builders	Commissioned
BRIGADIER M'BONGA TOUNDA	—	Ch. Navals de l'Esterel	1967

Displacement, tons: 20 full load
Dimensions, feet (metres): 59·7 × 13·5 × 4 *(18·2 × 4·1 × 1·2)*
Gun: 1—12·7 mm MG
Main engines: 2 Caterpillar diesels; 2 shafts; 540 bhp = 22·5 knots
Complement: 8

Customs duties. Sister of Mauritanian *Im Raq Ni*.

Name	No.	Builders	Commissioned
LE VALEUREUX	—	Ch. Navals de l'Esterel	1970

Displacement, tons: 45 full load
Dimensions, feet (metres): 88 × 16·3 × 5·1 *(26·8 × 5·0 × 1·5)*
Gun: 1—20 mm
Main engines: 2 General Motors diesels; 2 shafts; 960 hp = 25 knots
Complement: 11

LE VALEUREUX   1970, Ch navals de l'Esterel

6 COASTAL PATROL CRAFT

First three (Type 800) delivered August 1977 by Chantiers Plascoa, Cannes, second three (Type 650) in 1979. For Customs duties.

MISCELLANEOUS

1 FAIREY MARINE "INTERCEPTOR" CLASS

25 ft *(7·6 m)* craft with catamaran hull. Can carry a platoon of soldiers or eight life-rafts. Twin 135 hp outboard motors = 30 knots. Delivered 1 December 1976.

2 HARBOUR LAUNCHES

SANAGA   BIMBIA

Of 10 tons.

1 LCM

BAKASI

Built by Carena, Abidjan, Ivory Coast. Of 57 tons and 56 ft long. 9 knots on two Baudoin diesels.

5 LCVP

INDÉPENDANCE   REUNIFICATION   SOUELLABA   MACHTIGAL   MANOKA

Built by Ateliers et Chantiers de l'Afrique Equatoriale, Libreville, Gabon except *Souellabe* at A.C.R.E., Libreville, Gabon. Of 11 tons and 10 knots.

AUXILIARIES

Tornade and *Ouragan*—built in 1966. *St. Sylvestre*—built in 1967.
Four small outboard craft.
Mungo operated by Transport Ministry. *Dr. Jamot* operated by Health Ministry.

CANADA

Ministerial

Minister of National Defence:
Hon. Barney Danson, MP

Headquarters Appointments

Chief of Defense Staff:
Admiral R. H. Falls, CMM, CD
Chief of Maritime Doctrine and Operations:
Rear-Admiral D. N. Mainguy CD
Director General Maritime Doctrine and Operations:
Commodore N. D. Brodeur, CD

Senior Appointments

Commander, Maritime Command:
Vice-Admiral A. L. Collier, CMM, DSC, CD
Commander, Maritime Forces, Pacific:
Rear-Admiral M. A. Martin, CD

Diplomatic Representation

Senior Liaison Officer (Maritime) London:
Captain (N) H. O. Arnsdorf, CD
Canadian Forces Attaché and Maritime Liaison Officer, Washington:
Commodore R. D. Yanow, CD
Canadian Forces Attaché (Naval) Moscow:
Commander (N) M. Tait, CD

General

In December 1977, the Government of Canada approved the first stage of a ship programme to replace the "St. Laurent" Class destroyers on a one-for-one basis. The vessel being specified is a helicopter carrying frigate capable of meeting Canadian sovereignty needs as well as fulfilling the role of a NATO escort. It is anticipated that the first of these replacement vessels will enter service in 1985. A life extension programme that will enable the older classes of ships to remain operational until their eventual replacement is being considered.

Personnel

(a) 1971: 16 906 (2 379 officers, 14 527 men and women)
    1972: 15 223 (2 590 officers, 12 633 men and women)
    1973: 16 003 (1 985 officers, 14 018 men and women)
    1974: 14 000 (2 000 officers, 12 000 men and women)

Note: Canada no longer accounts for separate services in a unified command. Total armed forces 78 000

(b) Voluntary service

Defence Estimates (Naval)

1971-72: $348 000 000
1972-73: $363 000 000
1973-74: $394 300 000
1975-76: $472 268 000
1976-77: $712 000 000

Note: Canada no longer accounts for separate services in a unified command.

Bases

Halifax and Esquimalt

Air Arm

In an integrated force there is no specific Fleet Air Arm, but two squadrons of Sea King helicopters provide for ships' needs. The Argus maritime patrol aircraft are due to be replaced by Auroras, a special Canadian version of the Lockheed Orion.

Prefix to Ships' Names

HMCS

Establishment

The Royal Canadian Navy (RCN) was officially established on 4 May 1910, when Royal Assent was given to the Naval Service Act. On 1 February 1968 the Canadian Forces Reorganisation Act unified the three branches of the Canadian Forces and the title "Royal Canadian Navy" was dropped.

Strength of the Fleet

Type	Active	Building
Patrol Submarines	3	—
Destroyers (DDH)	4	—
Frigates (some with helicopters)	16	—
Replenishment Ships	3	—
Maintenance Ship	1	—
Small Tankers	2	—
Patrol Escorts (Small)	7	—
Patrol Craft	6	—
Research Ships	4	—
Diving Support Ship and Tenders	3	—
Gate Vessels	5	—
Training Ships	6	—
Tugs: Ocean	3	—
Harbour	19	—
Auxiliaries	3	—

Reserve (Cat. C)

Frigates

1974 *Columbia, St. Croix, Chaudiere*

Hydrofoil

1971 *Bras D'Or*

Mercantile Marine

Lloyd's Register of Shipping:
1 289 vessels of 2 954 499 tons gross

DELETIONS

Frigates

1974 *Granby*
1975 *St. Laurent.* Break-up at Halifax

Submarine

1976 *Rainbow* broken up at Esquimalt

Patrol Escorts (Small)

1973 *Fort Steele* from RCMP to DND
1975 *PBs 191, 192, 193, 194, 195* from RCMP to DND
1976 *PB 196* from RCMP to DND

Maintenance Ships

1972 *Cape Breton* decommissioned but in alongside service
1977 *Cape Scott* sold for scrap

Research Vessels

1972 *Fort Frances* scrapped in Spain
1976 *Kapuskasing*
1977 *Laymore* on sales list

TRANSFERS

Gate Vessels

1974 *Porte Dauphine* from MOT to DND

Tugs

1975 *Glendyne* sunk for diver training, *Heatherton* transferred to DPW (Canada)
1976 *Clifton, Glenbrook, Glenlivet, Mannville, Parksville, Merrickville*

PENNANT NUMBERS

Submarines

72	Ojibwa
73	Onondaga
74	Okanagan

Destroyers

280	Iroquois
281	Huron
282	Athabaskan
283	Algonquin

Frigates

206	Saguenay
207	Skeena
229	Ottawa
230	Margaree
233	Fraser
234	Assiniboine
235	*Chaudiere
236	Gatineau
256	*St. Croix
257	Restigouche
258	Kootenay
259	Terra Nova
260	*Columbia
261	Mackenzie
262	Saskatchewan
263	Yukon
264	Qu'Appelle
265	Annapolis
266	Nipigon

*Cat. C Reserve 1974.

Replenishment Ships

AOR 508	Provider
AOR 509	Protecteur
AOR 510	Preserver
AOTL 501	Dundalk
AOTL 502	Dundurn

Research Vessels

AGOR 113	Sackville
AGOR 114	Bluethroat
AGOR 171	Endeavour
AGOR 172	Quest

Diving Support Ship

| ASXL 20 | Cormorant |

Patrol Escorts

PF 140	Fort Steele
PF 159	Fundy
PF 160	Chignecto
PF 161	Thunder
PF 162	Cowichan
PF 163	Miramichi
PF 164	Chaleur
PH 400	*Bras d'Or

Gate Vessels

180	Porte St. Jean
183	Porte St. Louis
184	Porte de la Reine
185	Porte Quebec
186	Porte Dauphine

Patrol Craft (ex-RCMP)

PB191	Adversus
PB192	Detector
PB193	Captor
PB194	Acadian
PB195	Sidney
PB196	Nicholson

Tugs

ATA 528	Riverton
ATA 531	St. Anthony
ATA 533	St. Charles
YTB 640	Glendyne
YTB 641	Glendale
YTB 642	Glenevis
YTB 643	Glenbrook
YTB 644	Glenside
YTL 550	Eastwood
YTL 553	Wildwood
YTL 582	Burrard
YTL 583	Beamsville
YTL 584	Cree
YTL 586	Queensville
YTL 587	Plainsville
YTL 588	Youville
YTL 589	Loganville
YTL 590	Lawrenceville
YTL 591	Parksville
YTL 592	Listerville
YTL 593	Merrickville
YTL 594	Marysville

CANADA (Navy) / Introduction

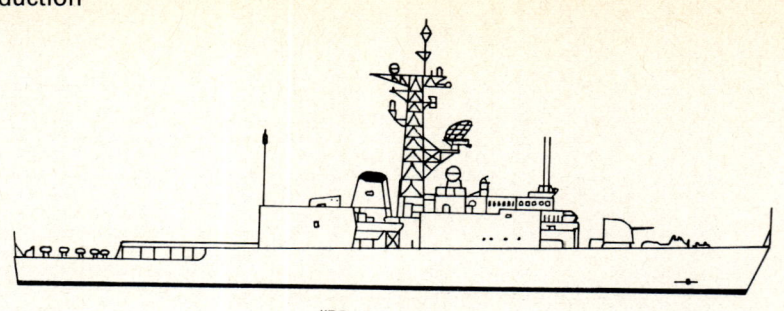
"DD 280" Class

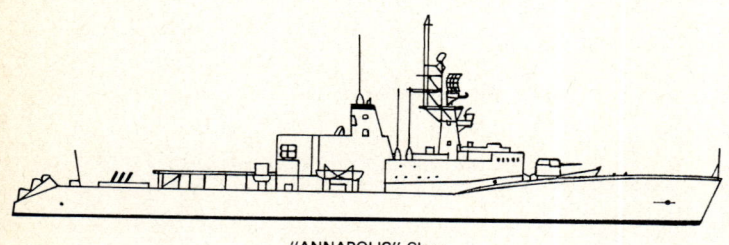
"ANNAPOLIS" Class

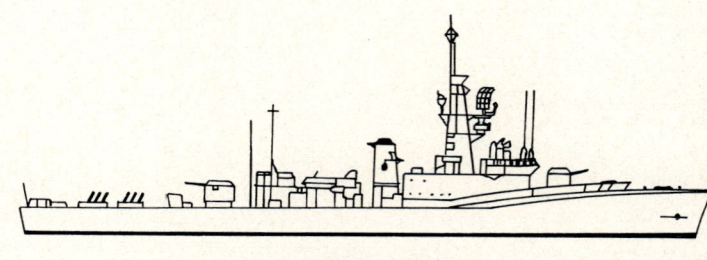
"MACKENZIE" Class

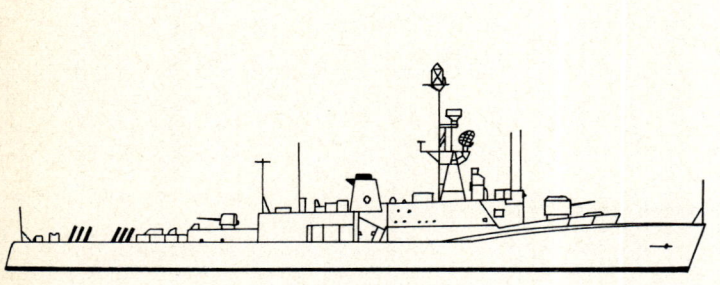
"RESTIGOUCHE" Class

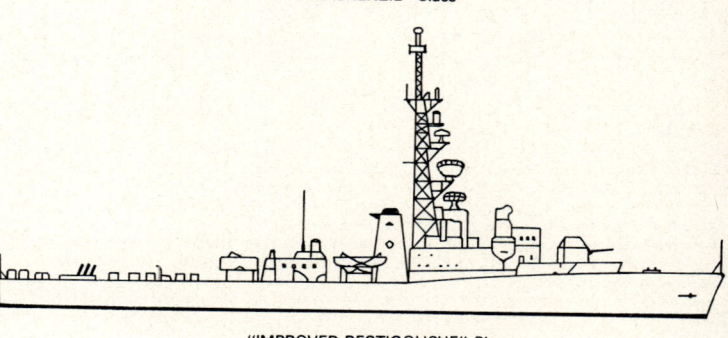
"IMPROVED RESTIGOUCHE" Class

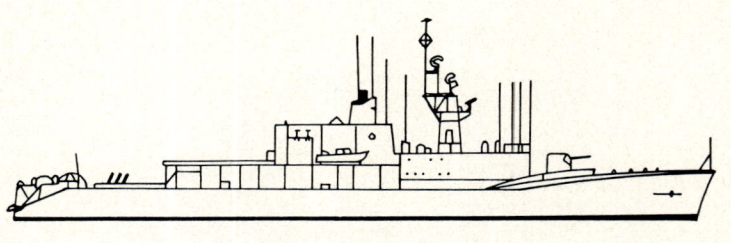
"ST. LAURENT" Class (except FRASER)

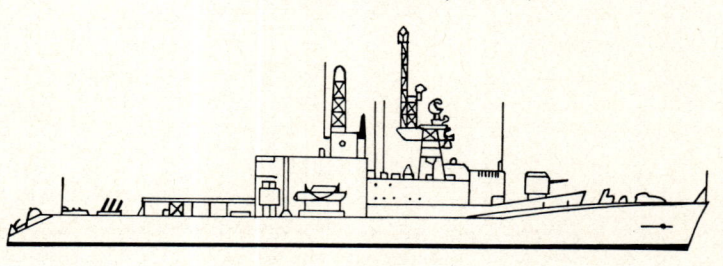
FRASER

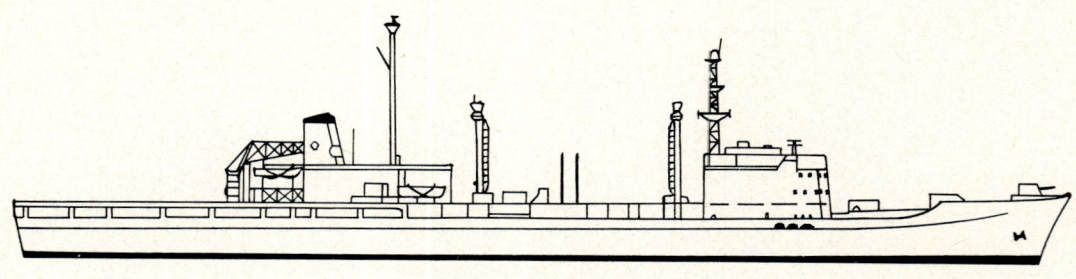
PROTECTEUR, PRESERVER

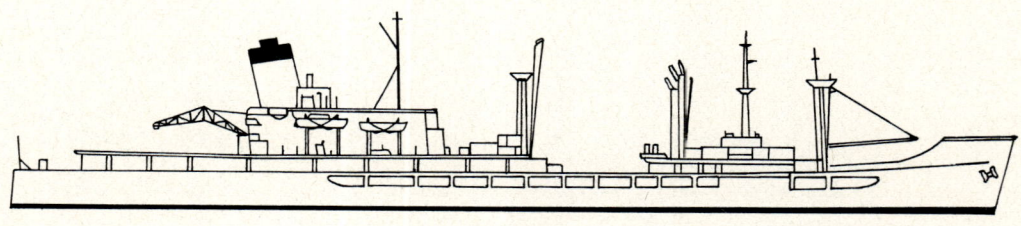
PROVIDER

SUBMARINES

3 "OBERON" CLASS (PATROL SUBMARINES)

Name	No.	Builders	Laid down	Launched	Commissioned
OJIBWA (ex-*Onyx*)	72	HM Dockyard, Chatham	27 Sep 1962	29 Feb 1964	23 Sep 1965
ONONDAGA	73	HM Dockyard, Chatham	18 June 1964	25 Sep 1965	22 June 1967
OKANAGAN	74	HM Dockyard, Chatham	25 Mar 1965	17 Sep 1966	22 June 1968

Displacement, tons: 2 060 full bouyancy surface; 2 200 normal surfaced; 2 420 dived
Length, feet (metres): 294·2 *(89·7)*
Beam, feet (metres): 26·5 *(8·1)*
Draught, feet (metres): 18 *(5·5)*
Torpedo tubes: 8—21 in *(533 mm)*, 6 bow and 2 stern
Main machinery: 2 Admiralty Standard Range diesels; 3 680 bhp; 2 shafts; 2 electric motors; 6 000 hp
Speed, knots: 12 surfaced; 17 dived
Complement: 65 (7 officers, 58 ratings)

On 11 April 1962 the Ministry of National Defence announced that Canada was to buy three "Oberon" class submarines in the UK. The first of these patrol submarines was obtained by the Canadian Government from the Royal Navy construction programme. She was laid down as *Onyx* but launched as *Ojibwa*. The other two were specific Canadian orders. There were some design changes to meet specific new needs including installation of RCN communications equipment and increase of air-conditioning capacity to meet the wide extremes of climate encountered in Canadian operating areas.

Nomenclature: The name *Ojibwa* is that of a tribe of North American Indians now widely dispersed in Canada and the USA and one of the largest remnants of aboriginal population. *Okanagan* and *Onondaga* are also Canadian Indian tribes.

Radar: Type 1006.

Sonar: Attack: Type 187.
Intercept: Type 197.
Torpedo warning: Type 719
Long range passive search: Type 2007.

Torpedoes: Carry Mk 37C ASW torpedoes only.

OJIBWA 5/1978, *Wright and Logan*

OJIBWA 10/1975, *Dr. Giorgio Arra*

OKANAGAN 1976, *Michael D. J. Lennon*

CANADA (Navy) / Destroyers

DESTROYERS

NEW CONSTRUCTION

Displacement, tons: 3 500 approx
Aircraft: 2 Sea King helicopters
Missiles: Harpoon and Sea Sparrow
Gun: 1—76 mm OTO Melara
Main engines: COGOG; Pratt and Whitney FT4; 25 000 hp each; Pratt and Whitney FT12; 3 370 hp each
Speed, knots: 28-30 app
Complement: 175

Early in 1978 $63 million was approved for a project definition of this new class to replace the "St. Laurent" class and in August 1978 tenders were invited, the first ship to be laid down in 1980 for completion 1985. A first order of six has been mentioned although a one-for-one replacement of the "St. Laurents" would require seven, the name of the ship of this class having already been deleted.

4 "DD 280" CLASS (DDH)

Name	No.	Builders	Laid down	Launched	Commissioned
IROQUOIS	280	Marine Industries Ltd, Sorel	15 Jan 1969	28 Nov 1970	29 July 1972
HURON	281	Marine Industries Ltd, Sorel	15 Jan 1969	3 Apr 1971	16 Dec 1972
ATHABASKAN	282	Davie S.B. Co, Lauzon	1 June 1969	27 Nov 1970	30 Nov 1972
ALGONQUIN	283	Davie S.B. Co, Lauzon	1 Sep 1969	23 Apr 1971	30 Sep 1973

Displacement, tons: 4 700 full load
Length, feet (metres): 398 (121·3) pp; 426 (129·8)
Beam, feet (metres): 50 (15·2)
Draught, feet (metres): 14·5 (4·4)
Aircraft: 2 Sea King CHSS-2 A/S helicopters
Missiles: Est. 32 SAM Sea Sparrow, 2 quad launchers (see note)
Gun: 1—5 in (127 mm)/54 OTO-Melara Compact
A/S weapons: 1 Mk 10 Limbo; 2 triple Mk 32 torpedo tubes
Main engines: Gas turbine; 2 Pratt & Whitney FT4A2 50 000 shp; 2 Pratt & Whitney FT12AH3 7 400 shp for cruising; 2 shafts
Speed, knots: 29 +
Range, miles: 4 500 at 20 knots
Complement: 245 (20 officers, 225 men) plus air unit, (7 officers + 33 men)

These ships have the same hull design, dimensions and basic characteristics as the large general purpose frigates cancelled at the end of 1963 (see particulars and illustration in the 1963-64 edition). Designed as anti-submarine ships, they are fitted with variable depth and hull sonar, landing deck equipped with double hauldown and Beartrap, flume type anti-rolling tanks to stabilise the ships at low speed, pre-wetting system to counter radio-active fallout, enclosed citadel, and bridge control of machinery.

Engineering: The gas turbines feed through a Swiss double reduction gearbox to two five-bladed cp propellers.

Electronics: Mk 22 Weapon System Control by Hollandse Signaal. CCS 280 by Litton.

Missiles: Launch system (GMLS) by Raytheon for Mk III Sea Sparrow missiles. Two quadruple launchers in forward end of the superstructure, retracting into deck-house.

Radar: Surface warning and navigation; SPQ 2D.
Long range warning; LW-02.
Fire control; M 22.

Sonar: Hull-mounted; SQS 505 in 14 ft dome.
VDS; SQS 505, 18 ft towed body aft.
Bottomed target classification; SQS 501.

Torpedoes: The Mk 32 tubes are to be used with Mk 46 torpedoes.

IROQUOIS 5/1978, Wright and Logan

ALGONQUIN 10/1978, J. L. M. van der Burg

HURON 8/1978

CANADA (Navy) / Frigates 81

FRIGATES

2 "ANNAPOLIS" CLASS

Name	No.	Builders	Laid down	Launched	Commissioned
ANNAPOLIS	265	Halifax Shipyards Ltd, Halifax	July 1960	27 Apr 1963	19 Dec 1964
NIPIGON	266	Marine Industries Ltd, Sorel	Apr 1960	10 Dec 1961	30 May 1964

Displacement, tons: 2 400 standard; 3 000 full load
Length, feet (metres): 371·0 *(113·1)*
Beam, feet (metres): 42·0 *(12·8)*
Draught, feet (metres): 14·4 *(4·4)*
Aircraft: 1 CHSS-2 Sea King helicopter
Guns: 2—3 in *(76 mm)*/50 US Mk 33 (twin)
A/S weapons: 1 Mk 10 Limbo in after well; 6 (2 triple) Mk 32 A/S torpedo tubes
Main engines: Geared turbines; 2 shafts; 30 000 shp
Boilers: 2 water tube
Speed, knots: 28 (30 on trials)
Range, miles: 4 570 at 14 knots
Complement: 210 (11 Officers, 199 ratings)

These two ships represented the logical development of the original "St. Laurent" class, through the "Restigouche" and "Mackenzie" designs. Due to the erection of a helicopter hangar and flight deck, and Variable Depth Sonar only one Limbo mounting could be installed. Also the 50 cal 3-in mounting had to be moved forward to replace the 70 cal mounting in the original design.

Classification: Officially classified as DDH.

Construction: As these are largely prefabricated no firm laying down date is officially given. Work on hull units started under cover long before components were laid on the slip.

Electronics: Tacan (AN/URN-22) aerial fitted above funnel. CCS-280 data system by Litton.

Radar: Search: SPS 12.
Tactical: SPS 10.
Fire control: SPG 48.

Refit: *Nipigon* underwent major refit 1977-78. *Annapolis* undergoing major refit 1978-79 at Canadian Vickers Ltd, Montreal.

Sonar: Types 501, 502, 503, 504, SQS 10/11.

ANNAPOLIS *1978, Canadian Armed Forces*

4 "MACKENZIE" CLASS

Name	No.	Builders	Laid down	Launched	Commissioned
MACKENZIE	261	Canadian Vickers Ltd, Montreal	15 Dec 1958	25 May 1961	6 Oct 1962
*SASKATCHEWAN	262	Victoria Machinery (and Yarrow)	16 July 1959	1 Feb 1961	16 Feb 1963
YUKON	263	Burrard D.D. & Shipbuilding	25 Oct 1959	27 July 1961	25 May 1963
QU'APPELLE	264	Davie Shipbuilding & Repairing	14 Jan 1960	2 May 1962	14 Sep 1963

Displacement, tons: 2 380 standard; 2 880 full load
Length, feet (metres): 366·0 *(111·6)*
Beam, feet (metres): 42·0 *(12·8)*
Draught, feet (metres): 13·5 *(4·1)*
Guns: 4—3 in *(76 mm)* (1 twin Mk 6 fwd 1 twin Mk 33 aft); (*Qu'Appelle*; 2—3 in *(76 mm)*/50 (twin Mk 33))
A/S weapons: 2 Mk 10 Limbo in well aft; side launchers for Mk 43 torpedoes
Main engines: Geared turbines; 2 shafts; 30 000 shp
Boilers: 2 water tube
Speed, knots: 28
Range, miles: 4 750 at 14 knots
Complement: 210 (11 officers, 199 ratings)

Classification: Officially classified as DD.

Fire Control: GFCS Mk 69.

Radar: Search: SPS 12.
Tactical: SPS 10.
Fire control: I Band.

Sonar: 501, 502, 503, SQS 10/11.

Saskatchewan was launched by Victoria Machinery Depot Co Ltd, but completed by Yarrow's Ltd.

SASKATCHEWAN *10/1977, Dr. Giorgio Arra*

3 "RESTIGOUCHE" CLASS

Name	No.	Builders	Laid down	Launched	Commissioned
CHAUDIERE	235	Halifax Shipyards Ltd	30 July 1953	13 Nov 1957	14 Nov 1959
ST. CROIX	256	Marine Industries Ltd, Sorel	15 Oct 1954	17 Nov 1957	4 Oct 1958
COLUMBIA	260	Burrard D.D. and Shipbuilding	11 June 1953	1 Nov 1956	7 Nov 1959

Displacement, tons: 2 370 standard; 2 880 full load
Length, feet (metres): 366·0 *(111·6)*
Beam, feet (metres): 42·0 *(12·8)*
Draught, feet (metres): 13·5 *(4·1)*
Guns: 4—3 in *(76 mm)*/70, twin Mk 6
A/S weapons: 2 Mk 10 Limbo in well aft; side launchers for Mk 43 torpedoes
Main engines: Geared turbines; 2 shafts; 30 000 shp
Boilers: 2 water tube
Speed, knots: 28
Range, miles: 4 750 at 14 knots
Complement: 248 (12 officers, 236 ratings)

All three paid off into Category C Reserve in 1974.

Classification: Officially classified as DD.

Radar: Search: SPS 12.
Tactical: SPS 10.
Fire control: SPG 48.

CHAUDIERE *1970, Canadian Forces*

Sonar: 501, 502, 503, SQS 10/11.

82 CANADA (Navy) / Frigates

4 "IMPROVED RESTIGOUCHE"

Name	No.	Builders	Laid down	Launched	Commissioned
GATINEAU	236	Davie Shipbuilding & Repairing	30 Apr 1953	3 June 1957	17 Feb 1959
RESTIGOUCHE	257	Canadian Vickers, Montreal	15 July 1953	22 Nov 1954	7 June 1958
KOOTENAY	258	Burrard D.D. & Shipbuilding	21 Aug 1952	15 June 1954	7 Mar 1959
TERRA NOVA	259	Victoria Machinery Depot Co	14 Nov 1952	21 June 1955	6 June 1959

Displacement, tons: 2 390 standard; 2 900 full load
Length, feet (metres): 371·0 (113·1)
Beam, feet (metres): 42·0 (12·8)
Draught, feet (metres): 14·1 (4·3)
Missiles: Sea Sparrow
Guns: 2—3 in (76 mm)/70 (twin Mk 6)
A/S weapons: ASROC aft and 1 Mk 10 Limbo in after well
Main engines: Geared turbines; 2 shafts; 30 000 shp
Boilers: 2 water tube
Speed, knots: 28 plus
Range, miles: 4 750 at 14 knots
Complement: 214 (13 officers, 201 ratings)

Classification: Officially classified as DD.

Conversion: These four ships were refitted with ASROC aft and lattice foremast. Work included removing the after 3 in 50 cal twin gun mounting and one Limbo A/S Mk 10 triple mortar, to make way for ASROC and Variable Depth Sonar. Dates of refits Terra Nova was completed on 18 October 1968: Gatineau completed in 1972 and Kootenay and Restigouche in 1973. Refit also included improvements to communications fit and fitting of Sea Sparrow.

Radar: Search: SPS 12.
Tactical: SPS 10.
Fire control: SPG 48.
Navigation: Sperry Mk II.

GATINEAU *1972, Canadian Forces*

Sonar: 501, 505, 505 VDS.

6 "ST. LAURENT" CLASS

Name	No.	Builders	Laid down	Launched	Commissioned
SAGUENAY	206	Halifax Shipyards Ltd, Halifax	4 Apr 1951	30 July 1953	15 Dec 1956
SKEENA	207	Burrard Dry Dock & Shipbuilding	1 June 1951	19 Aug 1952	30 Mar 1957
OTTAWA	229	Canadian Vickers Ltd, Montreal	8 June 1951	29 Apr 1953	10 Nov 1956
MARGAREE	230	Halifax Shipyards Ltd, Halifax	12 Sep 1951	29 Mar 1956	5 Oct 1957
*FRASER	233	Yarrows Ltd, Esquimalt, BC	11 Dec 1951	19 Feb 1953	28 June 1957
ASSINIBOINE	234	Marine Industries Ltd, Sorel, Quebec	19 May 1952	12 Feb 1954	16 Aug 1956

Displacement, tons: 2 260 standard; 3 051 full load (after version)
Length, feet (metres): 366·0 (111·6)
Beam, feet (metres): 42·0 (12·8)
Draught, feet (metres): 13·2 (4·0)
Aircraft: 1 CHSS-2 Sea King helicopter
Guns: 2—3 in (76 mm)/50 cal (twin Mk 33)
A/S weapons: 1 Mk 10 Limbo in after well; 2 triple Mk 32 torpedo tubes
Main engines: English Electric geared turbines; 2 shafts; 30 000 shp
Boilers: 2 water tube
Speed, knots: 28·5
Range, miles: 4 570 at 12 knots
Complement: 213 (16 officers, 197 ratings) (plus air unit of 7 officers and 13 ratings)

The first major warships to be designed in Canada. In design, much assistance was received from the Royal Navy (propelling machinery of British design) and the US Navy.
St. Laurent declared surplus in 1974.

*Fraser was launched by Burrard Dry Dock & Shipbuilding but completed by Yarrows Ltd.

Classification: Officially classified as DDH.

Gunnery: Original armament was 4—3 in, 50 cal (2 twin), 2—40 mm (single), and 2 Limbo mortars.

Radar: Search: SPS 12.
Tactical: SPS 10.
Navigation: Sperry Mk II.
Fire control: SPG 48.

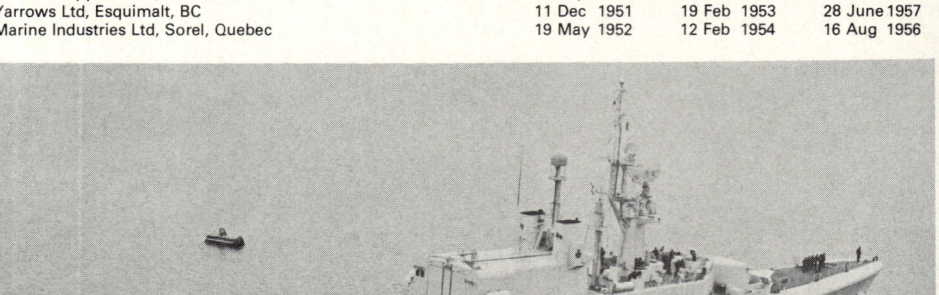

MARGAREE *1976, Canadian Armed Forces*

Reconstruction: All have helicopter platforms and VDS. Twin funnels were fitted to permit forward extension of the helicopter hangar.
Gunhouses are of glass fibre. In providing helicopter platforms and hangars it was possible to retain only one 3-barrelled Limbo mortar and only one twin 3 in gun mounting. Two steam turbo alternators and three diesel generators; total 1 500 kWs. Dates of recommissioning after conversion: Assiniboine 28 June 1963, St. Laurent 4 October 1963, Ottawa 21 October 1964, Saguenay 14 May 1965, Skeena 15 August 1965, Margaree 15 October 1965, Fraser 14 October 1966.

Fraser has lattice radar-mast between the funnels for Tacan aerial. All other ships have this aerial on a pole mast.

Refits: Fraser, Ottawa and Skeena underwent major refit 1977-78. Second three undergoing major refit 1978-79 at Canadian Vickers Ltd, Montreal.

Sonar: 501, 502, SQS 502, 503, 504.

ASSINIBOINE *1977, Canadian Armed Forces*

CANADA (Navy) / Replenishment ships — Maintenance ship 83

REPLENISHMENT SHIPS

Name	No.	Builders	Laid down	Launched	Commissioned
PROTECTEUR	AOR 509	St. John Dry Dock Co Ltd, NB	17 Oct 1967	18 July 1968	30 Aug 1969
PRESERVER	AOR 510	St. John Dry Dock Co Ltd, NB	17 Oct 1967	29 May 1969	30 July 1970

Displacement, tons: 8 380 light; 24 700 full load
Measurement, tons: 22 100 gross; 13 250 deadweight
Length, feet (metres): 564 *(171·9)*
Beam, feet (metres): 76 *(23·2)*
Draught, feet (metres): 30 *(9·1)*
Aircraft: 3 CHSS-2 Sea King helicopters
Guns: 2—3 in *(76 mm)*/50 (twin Mk 33)
Main engines: Geared turbine; 21 000 shp; 1 shaft
Boilers: 2 forced draught water tube
Speed, knots: 21
Range, miles: 4 100 at 20, 7 500 at 11·5 knots
Complement: 290 (28 officers, 262 ratings)

Contract price $47·5 million for both ships. In design they are an improvement on that of the prototype *Provider*. They can carry spare anti-submarine helicopters, military vehicles and bulk equipment for sealift purposes. 13 100 tons FFO, 600 tons diesel, 400 tons aviation fuel, 1 048 tons dry cargo and 1 250 tons of ammunition.

Electronics: Tacan aerial.

Radar: Decca 969, Sperry Mk II.

Sonar: SQS 505.

PROTECTEUR *1978, Wright and Logan*

Name	No.	Builders	Laid down	Launched	Commissioned
PROVIDER	AOR 508	Davie Shipbuilding Ltd, Lauzon	1 May 1961	5 July 1962	28 Sep 1963

Displacement, tons: 7 300 light; 22 000 full load
Measurement, tons: 20 000 gross; 14 700 deadweight
Length, feet (metres): 523 *(159·4)* pp; 555 *(169·2)* oa
Beam, feet (metres): 76 *(23·2)*
Draught, feet (metres): 32 *(9·8)*
Aircraft: 3 CHSS-2 Sea King helicopters
Main engines: Double reduction geared turbine 21 000 shp; 1 shaft
Boilers: 2 water tube
Speed, knots: 20
Oil fuel, tons: 12 000
Range, miles: 3 600 at 20 knots
Complement: 166 (15 officers, 151 ratings)

Preliminary construction work was begun in September 1960. Cost $15·7 million.
The helicopter flight deck is aft with the hangar at the same level and immediately below the funnel. The flight deck can receive the largest and heaviest helicopters. A total of 20 electro-hydraulic winches are fitted on deck for ship-to-ship movements of cargo and supplies, as well as shore-to-ship requirements when alongside.

PROVIDER *1975, Canadian Armed Forces*

2 "DUN" CLASS TANKERS

DUNDALK AOTL 501 **DUNDURN** AOTL 502

Displacement, tons: 950
Dimensions, feet (metres): 178·8 × 32·2 × 13 *(54·5 × 9·8 × 3·9)*
Main engine: Diesel; 700 bhp = 10 knots
Complement: 24.

Small tankers, classed as fleet auxiliaries.

DUNDALK *1977, Canadian Armed Forces*

MAINTENANCE SHIP

1 "CAPE" CLASS

Name	No.	Builders	Laid down	Launched	Commissioned
CAPE BRETON	100	Burrard Dry Dock Co, Vancouver, BC	5 July 1944	7 Oct 1944	25 Apr 1945

Displacement, tons: 8 580 standard; 10 000 full load
Dimensions, feet (metres): 441·5 × 57 × 20 *(134·7 × 17·4 × 6·1)*

Alongside Base Ship for FMUs in Esquimalt. The last ship of a large class which was originally built in Canada for the Royal Navy. Purchased back 1951.

84 CANADA (Navy) / Research vessels — Patrol craft

RESEARCH VESSELS

Name	No.	Builders	Commissioned
BLUETHROAT	AGOR 114	Geo. T. Davie & Sons Ltd, Lauzon	28 Nov 1955

Displacement, tons: 785 standard; 870 full load
Dimensions, feet (metres): 157 × 33 × 10 *(47 × 9·9 × 3)*
Main engines: Diesel; 2 shafts; 1 200 bhp = 13 knots

Authorised under 1951 Programme. Laid down on 31 October 1952. Launched on 15 September 1955. Completed on 28 November 1955 as Mine and Loop Layer. In 1957 she was rated Controlled Minelayer, NPC 114. Redesignated as Cable Layer (ALC) in 1959, and as Research Vessel (AGOR) and GP craft in 1964.

BLUETHROAT 1975, Canadian Armed Forces

Name	No.	Builders	Commissioned
SACKVILLE	AGOR 113	St John Dry Dock Co	30 Dec 1941

Displacement, tons: 1 085 standard; 1 350 full load
Dimensions, feet (metres): 205 × 33 × 14·5 *(62·5 × 10·1 × 6·4)*
Main engines: Triple expansion; 2 750 ihp = 16 knots
Boilers: 2 SE

Ex-"Flower" class corvette completed 30 December 1941. Later converted to loop layer. Designated AN 113—rated cable layer in 1959 (ALC). Redesignated as research vessel 1964. Employed by Naval Research Laboratories for oceanographic work.

SACKVILLE 1976, Michael D. J. Lennon

Name	No.	Builders	Commissioned
QUEST	AGOR 172	Burrard Dry Dock Co, Vancouver	21 Aug 1969

Displacement, tons: 2 130
Dimensions, feet (metres): 235 × 42 × 15·5 *(77·2 × 12·8 × 4·6)*
Aircraft: Light helicopter
Main engines: Diesel-electric; 2 shafts; 2 950 shp = 16 knots; bow thruster propeller
Range, miles: 10 000 at 12 knots
Complement: 55

Built for the Naval Research Establishment of the Defence Research Board for acoustic, hydrographic and general oceanographic work. Capable of operating in heavy ice in the company of an icebreaker. Construction began in 1967. Launched on 9 July 1968. Based at Halifax.

QUEST 1972, Canadian Maritime Command

Name	No.	Builders	Commissioned
ENDEAVOUR	AGOR 171	Yarrows Ltd, Esquimalt, BC	9 Mar 1965

Displacement, tons: 1 560
Dimensions, feet (metres): 236 × 38·5 × 13 *(71·9 × 11·7 × 4)*
Aircraft: 1 light helicopter
Main engines: Diesel-electric; 2 shafts; 2 960 shp = 16 knots
Range, miles: 10 000 at 12 knots
Complement: 50 (10 officers, 13 scientists, 25 ratings plus helicopter pilot and engineer)

A naval research ship designed primarily for anti-submarine research. Flight deck 48 by 31 ft. Stiffened for operating in ice-covered areas. She is able to turn in 2·5 times her own length. Two 9 ton Austin-Weston telescopic cranes are fitted. There are two oceanographical winches each holding 5 000 fathoms of wire, two bathythermograph winches and a deep-sea anchoring and coring winch. She has acoustic insulation in her machinery spaces.

ENDEAVOUR 1970, Canadian Maritime Command

1 ANTI-SUBMARINE HYDROFOIL (PH)

Name	No.	Builders	Commissioned
BRAS D'OR	PH 400	Marine Industries, Sorel	1969 (trials)

Displacement, tons: 180 standard; 237 full load
Dimensions, feet (metres): 150·8 × 21·5 × 15 (hull depth) *(46 × 6·6 × 5·1)*; *(7·5 (2·3)* (60 knots) draught on foils) Foil base 90
Main engines: Pratt & Whitney FT4A-2 gas turbine on foils; 22 000 shp = 50-60 knots
 Davey Paxman diesel when hull borne; 2 000 shp = 12-15 knots
 Pratt and Whitney ST 6A gas-turbine for hull-borne boost and foil-borne auxiliary power— 390 shp

A prototype craft designed by De Havilland Aircraft (Canada) and laid down in July 1968. After very successful trials she was laid up in Category C reserve, ashore at Halifax in 1971 for five years, a period now extended.

BRAS D'OR 1971, Canadian Armed Forces

PATROL CRAFT

ADVERSUS	PB 191	ACADIAN	PB 194
DETECTOR	PB 192	NICHOLSON	PB 195
CAPTOR	PB 193	SIDNEY	PB 196

All transferred from RCMP in 1975, except *Nicholson* (75 ft) in 1976.

CANADA (Navy) / Training ships — Diving ship   85

TRAINING SHIPS

6 "BAY" CLASS Ex-MSC (PF)

Name	No.	Builders	Commissioned
FUNDY	159	Davie Shipbuilding Co, Lauzon	27 Nov 1956
CHIGNECTO	160	Davie Shipbuilding Co, Lauzon	1 Aug 1957
THUNDER	161	Port Arthur S.B. Co	3 Oct 1957
COWICHAN	162	Yarrows Ltd, Esquimalt	19 Dec 1957
MIRAMICHI	163	Victoria Machinery Depot Co	28 Oct 1957
CHALEUR	164	Marine Industries Ltd, Sorel	12 Sep 1957

Displacement, tons: 390 standard; 464 full load
Dimensions, feet (metres): 152·0 × 28·0 × 7·0 (50 × 9·2 × 2·8)
Main engines: 2 General Motors V-12 diesels; 2 shafts; 2 400 bhp = 16 knots
Oil fuel, tons: 52
Range, miles: 3 290 at 12 knots
Complement: 18+ (2 officers, 16 ratings + trainees)

Extensively built of aluminium, including frames and decks. There were originally 20 vessels of this class of which six were transferred to France, four to Turkey and four sold commercially. Named after Canadian straits and bays. Designation changed from AMC to MCB in 1954. They were redesignated as Patrol Escorts (small) (PF) in 1972 being used as training ships.

THUNDER   1976, Canadian Armed Forces

1 "FORT" CLASS PATROL VESSEL (PF)

Name	No.	Builders	Commissioned
FORT STEELE	140	Canadian S.B. and Eng. Co	Nov 1955

Displacement, tons: 85
Dimensions, feet (metres): 118 × 21 × 7 (36 × 6·4 × 2·1)
Main engines: 2 Paxman Ventura 12 YJCM diesels; 2 shafts; Kamewa cp propellers; 2 800 bhp = 18 knots
Complement: 16

Steel hull aluminium superstructure. Twin rudders. Acquired by DND in 1973 from RCMP—acts as Reserve Training ship based on Halifax.

FORT STEELE   1975, Canadian Armed Forces

5 "PORTE" CLASS (GATE VESSELS)

Name	No.	Builders	Commissioned
PORTE ST. JEAN	180	Geo T. Davie	4 June 1952
PORTE ST. LOUIS	183	Geo T. Davie	28 Aug 1952
PORTE DE LA REINE	184	Victoria Machinery	19 Sep 1952
PORTE QUEBEC	185	Burrard Dry Dock	7 Oct 1952
PORTE DAUPHINE	186	Ferguson Ind.	12 Dec 1952

Displacement, tons: 429 full load
Dimensions, feet (metres): 125·5 × 26·3 × 13 (38·3 × 8·0 × 4·0)
Main engines: Diesel; AC electric; 1 shaft; 600 bhp = 11 knots
Complement: 23 (3 officers, 20 ratings)

Of trawler design. Multi-purpose vessels used for operating gates in A/S booms, fleet auxiliaries, anti-submarine netlayers for entrances to defended harbours. Can be fitted for minesweeping. Designation changed from YNG to YMG in 1954. First four used during summer for training Reserves. *Porte Dauphine* was reacquired from MOT in 1974 and employed in Reserve Training in Great Lakes area.

Note: Ex-Diving Tender YMT2 of 46 ft is used for sea-cadet training and the yacht *Oriole* QW3 has been used for officer cadet training since 1953.

PORTE QUEBEC   1977, Canadian Armed Forces

DIVING SHIP

1 FLEET DIVING SUPPORT SHIP

Name	No.	Builder	Commissioned
CORMORANT (ex-*Aspa Quarto*)	ASXL 20	Italy	10 Nov 1978 (CAF)

Displacement, tons: 2 350
Dimensions, feet (metres): 245 × 39 × 16·5 (74·7 × 11·9 × 5)
Main engines: Diesel-electric = 14 knots
Complement: 65

Italian stern trawler bought in 1975 which underwent maintenance and design modification until 1977. She was then taken in hand for conversion by Davie Shipbuilding Ltd, Lauzon, Qe returning to Halifax a year later to commission. She carries two SDL-1 submersibles in a heated hangar. The SDL-1 is a manned untethered craft capable of operations to 2 000 ft with a lock-out compartment for divers.

CORMORANT   1977, Canadian Armed Forces

86 CANADA (Navy) / Diving tenders — Sailing ketch

2 DIVING TENDERS

Name	No.	Builders	Commissioned
YDT 11	—	Ferguson, Pictou, NS	Jan 1962
YDT 12	—	Ferguson, Pictou, NS	7 Aug 1963

Displacement, tons: 110
Main engines: General Motors diesels; 228 bhp = 10·75 knots
Complement: 23 (3 officers, 20 ratings)

Can operate four divers at a time to 250 ft. Recompression chamber.

2 TORPEDO RECOVERY VESSELS

Name	No.	Builders	Commissioned
SONGHEE	YPT 1	Falconer Marine	1944
NIMPKISH	YPT 120	Falconer Marine	1944

Displacement, tons: 162
Length, feet (metres): 94·5 (22·8)
Main engines: 400 bhp
Complement: 7

TUGS

2 "SAINT" CLASS

Name	No.	Builders	Commissioned
SAINT ANTHONY	ATA 531	St. John Dry Dock Co	22 Feb 1957
SAINT CHARLES	ATA 533	St. John Dry Dock Co	7 June 1957

Displacement, tons: 840 full load
Dimensions, feet (metres): 151·5 × 33 × 17 (46·2 × 10 × 5·2)
Main engine: Diesel; 1 shaft; 1 920 bhp = 14 knots
Complement: 21

Ocean tugs. Authorised under the 1951 Programme. Originally class of three.

1 "NORTON" CLASS

Name	No.	Builders	Commissioned
RIVERTON	ATA 528	—	Late 1944

Displacement, tons: 462
Dimensions, feet (metres): 111·2 × 28 × 11 (33·9 × 8·5 × 3·4)
Main engine: Dominion Sulzer diesel; 1 000 bhp = 11 knots
Complement: 17

Ocean tug.

5 "GLEN" CLASS (HARBOUR/COASTAL)

Name	No.	Builders	Commissioned
GLENDYNE	YTB 640	Yarrows, Esquimalt	1975
GLENDALE	YTB 641	Yarrows, Esquimalt	1975
GLENEVIS	YTB 642	Georgetown Sy. PEI	1976
GLENBROOK	YTB 643	Georgetown Sy. PEI	16 Dec 1976
GLENSIDE	YTB 644	Georgetown Sy. PEI	1977

Displacement, tons: 255
Dimensions, feet (metres): 92·5 × 28 × 14·5 (28·2 × 8·5 × 4·4)
Main engines: 2 diesels with Voith-Schneider propellers; 1 300 hp = 11·5 knots
Complement: 6

GLENDYNE — 1977, Canadian Armed Forces

5 "VILLE" CLASS (NEW)

Name	No.	Builders	Commissioned
LAWRENCEVILLE	YTL 590	Vito Steel & Barge Co	1974
PARKSVILLE	YTL 591	Vito Steel & Barge Co	1974
LISTERVILLE	YTL 592	Georgetown S.Y. PEI	1974
MERRICKVILLE	YTL 593	Georgetown S.Y. PEI	1974
MARYSVILLE	YTL 594	Georgetown S.Y. PEI	1974

Dimensions, feet (metres): 64 × 15·5 × 9 (19·5 × 4·7 × 2·7)
Main engine: Diesel; 1 shaft; 365 bhp = 9·8 knots

Small harbour tugs employed at Esquimalt and Halifax.

Other medium harbour tugs are:
FT1, FT2. Employed as fire tugs, hull numbers YMT 556 and 557 respectively.

7 "VILLE" CLASS (OLD)

Name	No.	Builders	Commissioned
BURRARD (ex-Lawrenceville)	YTL 582	Russell Bros	1944
BEAMSVILLE	YTL 583	Russell Bros	1944
CREE (ex-Adamsville)	YTL 584	Russell Bros	1944
QUEENSVILLE	YTL 586	Russell Bros	1944
PLAINSVILLE	YTL 587	Russell Bros	1944
YOUVILLE	YTL 588	Russell Bros	1944
LOGANVILLE	YTL 589	Russell Bros	1944

Dimensions, feet (metres): 40 × 10·5 × 4·8 (12·2 × 3·2 × 1·5)
Main engine: Diesel; 1 shaft; 150 bhp

Small harbour tugs now used for Reserve training.

There are small diving tenders YMT 6, YMT 8, YMT 9 and YMT 10, 70 tons, 75 × 18·5 × 8·5 ft, 2 diesels 165 bhp. YMT 1 (46 ft) was transferred to the Naval Research Establishment as a yard craft. Two new diving tenders, YSD 1 and YSD 2, entered service in 1965.

2 "WOOD" CLASS

Name	No.	Builders	Commissioned
EASTWOOD	YTL 550	Le Blanc S.B.	1944
WILDWOOD	YTL 553	Falconer Marine	1944

Displacement, tons: 65
Dimensions, feet (metres): 60 × 16 × 5 (18·3 × 4·9 × 1·5)
Main engine: Diesel; 250 hp = 10 knots
Complement: 3

Medium harbour tugs. Used as A/S Target Towing Vessels.

EASTWOOD — 1976, Canadian Armed Forces

1 SAILING KETCH

ORIOLE

Based on Esquimalt.

Canadian ASW Hunting Group — 1977, Canadian Armed Forces

CANADIAN COAST GUARD

Administration

Minister of Transport:
  Hon Otto Lang PC, MP
Deputy Minister of Transport:
  Mr. Sylvain Cloutier
Administrator, Marine Transportation Administration:
  Mr. G. M. Sinclair
Commissioner Canadian Coast Guard:
  Mr. W. A. O'Neil

Ships

The Canadian Coast Guard comprises 150 ships and craft of all types. They operate in Canadian waters from the Great Lakes to the northernmost reaches of the Arctic Archipelago.
There are heavy icebreakers, medium icebreakers, buoys tenders and lighthouse re-supply vessels, marine survey craft, weather-oceanographic ships, and many specialised vessels for tasks such as search and rescue, cable lifting and repair, marine research and shallow-draft operations in areas such as the Mackenzie River system and other areas of the Arctic.
The principal bases for the ships are at— St. John's, Newfoundland; Dartmouth, N.S; Saint John, N.B; Charlottetown, P.E.I; Quebec, Sorel and Montreal, Que; Prescott, Amherstburg, Parry Sound, Sault Ste-Marie and Thunder Bay, Ont; Victoria and Prince Rupert, B.C; and at Hay River, on Great Slave Lake.

Establishment

In January 1962 all ships owned and operated by the Federal Department of Transport with the exception of pilotage and canal craft, were amalgamated into the Canadian Coast Guard, a civilian service.

Flag

The Canadian Coast Guard has its own distinctive jack, a red maple leaf on a white ground at the hoist and two gold dolphins on a blue ground at the fly.
Canadian Coast Guard vessels have white funnels with a red band at the top and the red maple leaf against the white.

Missions

The Canadian Coast Guard carries out the following missions:
1. Icebreaking and Escort. Icebreaking is carried out in the Gulf of St. Lawrence and River St. Lawrence and the Great Lakes in winter to assist shipping and for flood control, and in Arctic waters in summer.
2. Icebreaker-Aids to Navigation Tenders. Installation, supply and maintenance of fixed and floating aids-to-navigation in Canadian waters.
3. Organise and provide icebreaker support and some cargo vessels for the annual Northern sealift which supplies bases and settlements in the Canadian Arctic and Hudson Bay.
4. Provide and operate special patrol cutters and lifeboats for marine search and rescue.
5. Provide and operate survey and sounding vessels for the St. Lawrence River Ship Channel.
6. Provide and operate weatherships for Ocean Station "Papa" in the Pacific.
7. Provide and operate vessel for the repairing of undersea cables.
8. Provide and operate vessel for Marine Traffic Control on the St. Lawrence river.
9. Operate a small fleet of aircraft primarily for aids to navigation, ice reconnaissance, and pollution control work.

Fleet Strength

Heavy Icebreakers	8
Heavy Icebreaker/Cable Ship	1
Medium Icebreaker/Navaids Tenders	7
Light Icebreaker/Navaids Tender	6
Ice Strengthened Navaids Tenders	6
Non-Ice Strengthened Navaids Tenders	13
Northern Supply/Navaids Tender	1
Ocean Weather Ships	2
Offshore Search and Rescue Patrol Vessels	3
Inshore Search and Rescue Patrol Vessels	6
Great Lakes Search and Rescue Patrol Cutters	3
Shorebased Search and Rescue Self-Righting Lifeboats	14
Shorebased Search and Rescue Launches	6
Shorebased Inflatable Rescue Boats	14
Cadet Training Vessel	1
Sounding Vessels	3
Base Work Boats	18
Auxiliary: Landing Craft, Dumb Barges	22
Oil Slicklickers	16
Total	**150**

Aircraft

Fixed wing	1
Helicopters	34

DELETIONS
1978 *Ernest Lapointe, Eider, Mink, Detector*

OCEAN WEATHER SHIPS

Name	No.	Builders	Commissioned
QUADRA	—	Burrard Dry Dock Co Ltd	Mar 1967
VANCOUVER	—	Burrard Dry Dock Co Ltd	4 July 1966

Displacement, tons: 5 600 full load
Dimensions, feet (metres): 404·2 × 50 × 17·5 *(123·2 × 15·2 × 5·3)*
Aircraft: 1 helicopter
Main engines: Turbo-electric; 2 shafts; 7 500 shp = 18 knots
Boilers: 2 automatic Babcock & Wilcox D type
Range, miles: 10 400 at 14 knots
Complement: 96

Turbo-electric twin screw weather and oceanographic vessels for Pacific Ocean service. *Quadra* laid down February 1965, launched 4 July 1966. *Vancouver* laid down March 1964, launched 29 June 1965. They have bow water jet reaction system to assist steering at slow speeds. Flume stabilisation systems are fitted. They are turbo-electric powered, with oil-fired boilers to provide the quiet operation needed for vessels housing much scientific equipment. Their complement includes 15 technical officers such as meteorologists, oceanographers and electronics technicians.

VANCOUVER

1975, Canadian Ministry of Transport

88 CANADA (Coast guard) / Icebreakers

ICEBREAKERS

0 + 1 CANADIAN CLASS 10 (NUCLEAR ICEBREAKER)

On 3 January 1979 it was announced that a 33 000 ton nuclear propelled icebreaker (630 × 150·5 × 40 ft) capable of 20 knots on 90 000 hp and able to deal with 7 ft ice was being ordered. Complement 118 plus 56 extra billets. Due for completion 1985 at a cost of £150 million.

Name	No.	Builders	Commissioned
PIERRE RADISSON	—	Burrard D.D. Co Ltd, Vancouver	June 1978
FRANKLIN	—	Burrard D.D. Co Ltd, Vancouver	1979

Displacement, tons: 6 400 standard; 7 594 full load
Dimensions, feet (metres): 322 × 64 × 23·5 (98·1 × 19·5 × 7·2)
Aircraft: 1 helicopter
Main engines: Diesel-electric; 13 600 hp; 2 shafts = 16 knots
Oil fuel, tons: 2 240
Range, miles: 20 000
Complement: 64 (11 spare billets)

Ordered 1 May 1975. *Pierre Radisson* laid down 16 February 1976 and launched 3 June 1977. *Franklin* laid down 4 January 1977, launched 10 March 1978.

PIERRE RADISSON 1978, Canadian Coast Guard

Name	No.	Builders	Commissioned
LOUIS ST. LAURENT	—	Canadian Vickers Ltd, Montreal	Oct 1969

Displacement, tons: 13 800 full load
Dimensions, feet (metres): 366·5 × 80 × 31 (111·7 × 24·4 × 9·5)
Aircraft: 2 helicopters
Main engines: Turbo-electric; 3 shafts; 24 000 shp = 17·75 knots
Range, miles: 16 000 miles at 13 knots cruising speed
Complement: Total accommodation for 216

She is larger than any of the former Coast Guard icebreakers. She has a helicopter hangar below the flight deck, with an elevator to raise the two helicopters to the deck when required. She was launched on 3 December 1966. She is officially rated as a heavy icebreaker.

LOUIS ST. LAURENT 1971, Canadian Coast Guard

Name	No.	Builders	Commissioned
NORMAN McLEOD ROGERS	—	Canadian Vickers Ltd, Montreal	Oct 1969

Displacement, tons: 6 320 full load
Dimensions, feet (metres): 295 × 62·5 × 20 (90 × 19·1 × 6·1)
Aircraft: 1 helicopter
Landing craft: 2
Main engines: 4 diesels and 2 gas turbines powering 2 electric motors; 2 shafts; 12 000 shp = 15 knots
Complement: 55

Built for use in the Gulf of St. Lawrence and East Coast waters. This is the world's first application of gas turbine/electric propulsion in an icebreaker. Officially rated as a heavy icebreaker.

NORMAN McLEOD ROGERS 1975, Canadian Coast Guard

Name	No.	Builders	Commissioned
JOHN CABOT	—	Canadian Vickers Ltd, Montreal	July 1965

Displacement, tons: 6 375 full load
Dimensions, feet (metres): 313·3 × 60 × 21·5 (95·6 × 18·3 × 6·6)
Aircraft: 1 helicopter
Main engines: Diesel-electric; 2 shafts; 9 000 shp = 15 knots
Range, miles: 10 000 at 12 knots
Complement: 85 officers and men

Laid down May 1963 and launched 15 April 1964. Combination cable repair ship and icebreaker. Designed to repair and lay cable over the bow only. For use in East Coast and Arctic waters. Bow water jet reaction manoeuvring system, heeling tanks and Flume stabilisation system. Three circular storage holds handle a total of 400 miles of submarine cable. Personnel include technicians and helicopter pilots.

JOHN CABOT 1975, Canadian Coast Guard

Name	No.	Builders	Commissioned
JOHN A. MACDONALD	—	Davie Shipbuilding Ltd, Lauzon	Sep 1960

Displacement, tons: 9 160 full load
Measurement, tons: 6 186 gross
Dimensions, feet (metres): 315 × 70 × 28 (96 × 21·3 × 8·5)
Aircraft: 2 helicopters
Main engines: Diesel-electric; 15 000 shp = 15·5 knots

Officially rated as a heavy icebreaker. Launched 3 October 1959.

JOHN A. MACDONALD 1975, Canadian Coast Guard

CANADA (Coast guard) / Icebreakers — Aid to navigation vessels

Name	No.	Builders	Commissioned
LABRADOR	—	Marine Industries Ltd, Sorel	8 July 1954

Displacement, tons: 6 490 full load
Measurement, tons: 3 823 gross
Dimensions, feet (metres): 290·0 × 63·5 × 29·0 (88·4 × 19·4 × 8·8)
Aircraft: 2 helicopters
Main engines: Diesel-electric; 10 000 shp = 16 knots

Ordered in February 1949, laid down on 18 November 1949, launched on 14 December 1951 and completed for the Royal Canadian Navy but transferred to the Department of Transport in February 1958. Officially rated as a Heavy Icebreaker. She was the first naval vessel to traverse the North West passage and circumnavigate North America.

LABRADOR　　1975, Canadian Coast Guard

Name	No.	Builders	Commissioned
d'IBERVILLE	—	Davie Shipbuilding Ltd, Lauzon	May 1953

Displacement, tons: 9 930 full load
Measurement, tons: 5 678 gross
Dimensions, feet (metres): 310 × 66·5 × 30·2 (94·5 × 20·3 × 9·2)
Aircraft: 1 helicopter
Main engines: Steam reciprocating; 10 800 ihp = 15 knots

Officially rated as a Heavy Icebreaker.

d'IBERVILLE　　1975, Canadian Coast Guard

AID TO NAVIGATION VESSELS

Name	No.	Builders	Commissioned
GRIFFON	—	Davie Shipbuilding Ltd, Lauzon	Dec 1970

Displacement, tons: 3 096
Dimensions, feet (metres): 234 × 49 × 15·5 (71·4 × 14·9 × 4·7)
Aircraft: 1 helicopter
Main engines: Diesel; 4 000 bhp; 13·5 knots

Officially rated as Medium Icebreaking Aid to Navigation Vessel.

GRIFFON　　1975, Canadian Coast Guard

Name	No.	Builders	Commissioned
J. E. BERNIER	—	Davie Shipbuilding Ltd, Lauzon	Aug 1967

Displacement, tons: 3 096
Dimensions, feet (metres): 231 × 49 × 16 (70·5 × 14·9 × 4·9)
Aircraft: 1 helicopter
Main engines: Diesel-electric; 4 250 bhp = 13·5 knots (trial speed)

Officially rated as Medium Icebreaking Aid to Navigation Vessel.

J. E. BERNIER　　1975, Canadian Coast Guard

Name	No.	Builders	Commissioned
CAMSELL	—	Burrard Dry Dock Co Ltd	Oct 1959

Displacement, tons: 3 072 full load
Measurement, tons: 2 020 gross
Dimensions, feet (metres): 223·5 × 48 × 16 (68·2 × 14·6 × 4·9)
Aircraft: 1 helicopter
Main engines: Diesel-electric; 4 250 shp = 13 knots

Launched 17 February 1959. Officially rated as Medium Icebreaking Aid to Navigation Vessel.

CAMSELL　　1975, Canadian Coast Guard

90 CANADA (Coast guard) / Aid to navigation vessels

Name	No.	Builders	Commissioned
MONTCALM	—	Davie Shipbuilding Ltd, Lauzon	June 1957
WOLFE	—	Canadian Vickers Ltd, Montreal	Nov 1959

Displacement, tons: 2 017 full load *(Montcalm)*; 2 995 *(Wolfe)*
Dimensions, feet (metres): 220 × 48 × 16 *(67·2 × 14·7 × 5·0) (Montcalm)*; 252 × 48·3 × 16·3 *(76·9 × 14·7 ×5) (Wolfe)*
Aircraft: 1 helicopter
Main engines: Steam reciprocating; 4 000 ihp = 13 knots

Montcalm launched 23 October 1956. Officially rated as Medium Icebreaking Aid to Navigation Vessels. *Wolfe* has a modified bow section.

WOLFE   *1975, Canadian Coast Guard*

Name	No.	Builders	Commissioned
ALEXANDER HENRY	—	Port Arthur S.B. Ltd	July 1959

Displacement, tons: 2 497 full load
Measurements, tons: 1 647 gross
Dimensions, feet (metres): 210 × 43·5 × 16 *(64 × 13·3 × 4·9)*
Main engines: Diesel; 3 550 bhp = 13 knots

Launched 18 July 1958. Officially rated as a Medium Icebreaking Aid to Navigation Vessel.

ALEXANDER HENRY   *1978, Canadian Coast Guard*

Name	No.	Builders	Commissioned
SIR HUMPHREY GILBERT	—	Davie Shipbuilding Ltd, Lauzon	June 1959

Displacement, tons: 3 000 full load
Measurement, tons: 1 930 gross
Dimensions, feet (metres): 220 × 48 × 16·3 *(67 × 14·6 × 5·0)*
Aircraft: 1 helicopter
Main engines: Diesel-electric; 4 250 shp = 13 knots

Officially rated as Medium Icebreaking Aid to Navigation Vessel.

SIR HUMPHREY GILBERT   *1970, Canadian Coast Guard*

Name	No.	Builders	Commissioned
SIR WILLIAM ALEXANDER	—	Halifax Shipyards Ltd	June 1959

Displacement, tons: 3 555 full load
Measurements, tons: 2 153 gross
Dimensions, feet (metres): 227·5 × 45 × 17·5 *(69·4 × 13·7 × 5·3)*
Main engines: Diesel-electric; 4 250 shp = 15 knots

Launched 13 December 1958. Equipped with Flume Stabilisation System. Officially rated as a Medium Icebreaking Aid to Navigation Vessel.

SIR WILLIAM ALEXANDER   *1975, Canadian Coast Guard*

Name	No.	Builders	Commissioned
TRACY	—	Port Weller Drydocks	1968

Displacement, tons: 1 300
Dimensions, feet (metres): 251·5 × 42 × 12 *(76·7 × 12·8 × 3·7)*
Main engines: Diesel; 2 000 bhp = 11 knots

Officially rated as Light Icebreaking Aid to Navigation Vessel.

Name	No.	Builders	Commissioned
NARWHAL	—	Canadian Vickers Ltd, Montreal	July 1963

Measurement, tons: 2 064 gross
Dimensions, feet (metres): 251·5 × 42·0 × 12·0 *(76·7 × 12·8 × 3·7)*
Main engines: Diesel; 2 000 bhp
Range, miles: 9 200 cruising
Complement: 32

Originally rated as Sealift Stevedore Depot Vessel, now re-rated as Light Icebreaking Aid to Navigation Vessel.

Name	No.	Builders	Commissioned
N. B. McLEAN	—	Halifax S.Y. Ltd	1930

Displacement, tons: 5 034 full load
Measurements, tons: 3 254 gross
Dimensions, feet (metres): 277 × 60·5 × 24·0 *(90 × 19·5 × 6·1)*
Main engines: Steam reciprocating; 6 500 ihp = 13 knots

Officially rated as Medium Icebreaker.

NARWHAL   *1975, Canadian Coast Guard*

CANADA (Coast guard) / Aid to navigation vessels

Name	No.	Builders	Commissioned
SIMON FRASER	—	Burrard D. Y. Co Ltd	Feb 1960
TUPPER	—	Marine Industries Ltd	Dec 1959

Displacement, tons: 1 876 full load
Measurements, tons: 1 357 gross
Dimensions, feet (metres): 204·5 × 42 × 14 *(62·4 × 12·8 × 4·3)*
Main engines: Diesel-electric; 2 900 shp = 13·5 knots

Simon Fraser was launched 18 August 1959. Both officially rated as Light Icebreaking Aid to Navigation Vessels.

SIMON FRASER   1978, Canadian Coast Guard

Name	No.	Builders	Commissioned
THOMAS CARLETON	—	St. John Dry Dock Ltd	1960

Displacement, tons: 1 532 full load
Dimensions, feet (metres): 180 × 42 × 13 *(54·9 × 12·8 × 4)*
Main engines: Diesel; 2 000 bhp = 12 knots

Officially rated as Light Icebreaking Aid to Navigation Vessel.

Name	No.	Builders	Commissioned
WALTER E. FOSTER	—	Canadian Vickers Ltd, Montreal	Dec 1954

Displacement, tons: 2 715 full load
Measurement, tons: 1 672 gross
Dimensions, feet (metres): 229·2 × 42·5 × 16 *(69·9 × 12·9 × 4·9)*
Main engines: Steam reciprocating; 2 000 ihp = 12·5 knots

Officially rated as a Light Icebreaking Aid to Navigation Vessel.

WALTER E. FOSTER   1975, Canadian Coast Guard

Name	No.	Builder	Commissioned
EDWARD CORNWALLIS	—	Canadian Vickers Ltd, Montreal	Dec 1949

Displacement, tons: 3 700 full load
Measurement, tons: 1 965 gross
Dimensions, feet (metres): 259 × 43·5 × 18 *(79 × 13·3 × 5·5)*
Main engines: Steam reciprocating; 2 800 ihp = 13·5 knots

Launched 5 August 1949. In reserve. Officially rated as a Light Icebreaking Aid to Navigation Vessel.

EDWARD CORNWALLIS   1971, Canadian Coast Guard

Name	No.	Builders	Commissioned
BARTLETT	—	—	1970
PROVO WALLIS	—	—	1970

Displacement, tons: 1 620
Dimensions, feet (metres): 189·3 × 42·5 × 12·5 *(57·7 × 13 × 3·8)*
Main engines: Diesel; 1 760 bhp = 12 knots

Classed as Ice Strengthened Aid to Navigation Vessels.

BARTLETT   1975, Canadian Coast Guard

Name	No.	Builders	Commissioned
SIMCOE	—	Canadian Vickers Ltd, Montreal	1962

Displacement, tons: 1 300 full load
Dimensions, feet (metres): 179·5 × 38 × 12 *(54·7 × 11·6 × 3·7)*
Main engines: Diesel-electric; 2 000 shp = 12 knots

Officially rated as Ice Strengthened Aid to Navigation Vessel.

Name	No.	Builders	Commissioned
MONTMORENCY	—	Davie Shipbuilding Ltd, Lauzon	Aug 1957

Displacement, tons: 1 006 full load
Measurement, tons: 750 gross
Dimensions, feet (metres): 163 × 34 × 11 *(49·7 × 10·2 × 3·4)*
Main engines: Diesel; 1 200 bhp

Officially rated as an Ice Strengthened Aid to Navigation Vessel.

MONTMORENCY   1975, Canadian Coast Guard

92 CANADA (Coast guard) / Aid to navigation vessels — Patrol cutters

Name	No.	Builders	Commissioned
SKIDEGATE	—	Burrard Dry Dock Co	?

Displacement, tons: 360
Dimensions, feet (metres): 101 × 26·6 × 7·8 (30·8 × 8·1 × 2·4)
Main engines: Diesel; 640 bhp = 11 knots

Modified 1977. Small Aid to Navigation Tender.

Name	No.	Builders	Commissioned
NAMAO	—	Riverton Boat Works, Manitoba	1975

Displacement, tons: 380
Dimensions, feet (metres): 110 × 28 × 7 (33·5 × 8·5 × 2·1)
Main engines: 2 diesels; 1 350 shp = 11·5 knots
Range, miles: 2 000 at 11 knots

Buoy tender for Lake Winnipeg.

Name	No.	Builders	Commissioned
VERENDRYE	—	Davie Shipbuilding Ltd, Lauzon	Oct 1959

Displacement, tons: 400 full load
Dimensions, feet (metres): 125·0 × 26·0 × 7·0 (38·1 × 7·9 × 2·1)
Main engines: Diesel; 760 bhp

Officially rated as Aid to Navigation Tender.

Name	No.	Builders	Commissioned
ALEXANDER MACKENZIE	—	Burrard Dry Dock Ltd	1950
SIR JAMES DOUGLAS	—	Burrard Dry Dock Ltd	Nov 1956

Displacement, tons: 720 full load
Dimensions, feet (metres): 150·0 × 30·0 × 10·3 (45·7 × 9 × 3·1)
Main engines: Diesel; 1 000 bhp

Officially rated as Aid to Navigation Tenders.

Name	No.	Builders	Commissioned
ROBERT FOULIS	—	St. John Drydock	1969

Displacement, tons: 260
Dimensions, feet (metres): 104 × 25 × 7 (31·7 × 7·6 × 2·1)
Main engines: Diesel; 960 bhp = 10 knots

Officially rated as Aid to Navigation Tender.

Name	No.	Builders	Commissioned
MONTMAGNY	—	Russel Bros, Owen Sound	May 1963

Displacement, tons: 565 full load
Dimensions, feet (metres): 148·0 × 29·0 × 8·0 (45·1 × 10·2 × 2·4)
Main engines: Diesel; 1 000 bhp

Officially rated as Aid to Navigation Tender.

KENOKI

Displacement, tons: 270
Dimensions, feet (metres): 108 × 36 × 5 (32·9 × 11 × 1·5)
Main engines: Diesel; 940 bhp = 10 knots

Officially rated as Aid to Navigation Tender.

NOKOMIS

Displacement, tons: 64
Dimensions, feet (metres): 66 × 17 × 7 (20·1 × 5·2 × 2·1)
Main engines: Diese ; 120 bhp

Officially rated as Aid to Navigation Tender.

PATROL CUTTERS

3 NEW CONSTRUCTION

Name	No.	Builders	Commissioned
CAPE —	—	Breton Industrial and Marine	Feb 1977
CAPE HARRISON	—	Breton Industrial and Marine	1977
CAPE LOUISBURG	—	Breton Industrial and Marine	1978

Displacement, tons: 120
Length, feet (metres): 125 × 26 × 8·3 (38·1 × 7·9 × 2·5)
Main engines: 2 diesels; 4 500 shp(?) = 20 knots

Built at Port Hawkesbury. *Cape Harrison* launched 28 August 1976 and *Cape Louisburg* on 17 July 1977.

Name	No.	Builders	Commissioned
ALERT	—	Davie Shipbuilding Ltd, Lauzon	Dec 1969

Displacement, tons: 2 025
Dimensions, feet (metres): 234·3 × 39·9 × 15·1 (71·4 × 12·2 × 4·6)
Aircraft: 1 helicopter
Main engines: Diesel-electric; 7 716 hp = 18·75 knots
Range, miles: 6 000

Officially rated as Offshore Patrol Cutter.

Name	No.	Builders	Commissioned
DARING (ex-*Wood*, MP 17)	—	Davie Shipbuilding Ltd, Lauzon	July 1958

Displacement, tons: 600 standard
Dimensions, feet (metres): 178 × 29 × 9·8 (54·3 × 8·8 × 3·0)
Main engines: 2 Fairbanks-Morse diesels; 2 shafts; 2 660 bhp = 16 knots

Used for patrol on the east coast of Canada, this ship is built of steel, strengthened against ice, with aluminium superstructure. Transferred from the Royal Canadian Mounted Police Marine Division to the Ministry of Transport in 1971, and renamed *Daring*. Offshore Patrol Cutter.

DARING (as *Wood*)   1966, Director of Marine Services

Name	No.	Builders	Commissioned
GRENFELL	—	Bel-Aire S.Y. Vancouver	1973

Dimensions, feet (metres): 170·3 × 45 × 16·5 (51·9 × 13·7 × 5)
Main engines: Diesel; 6 000 hp

Name	No.	Builders	Commissioned
CAPE ROGERS	—	Ferguson (Pictou)	25 Aug 1977

Displacement, tons: 1 400
Dimensions, feet (metres): 205 × 40 × 13·3 (62·5 × 12·2 × 4·1)
Main engines: 2 diesels, 2 200 hp; 1 shaft = 16·5 knots
Range, miles: 7 000 at 13 knots
Complement: 42

Laid down 13 November 1975, launched 12 June 1976. Fishery protection vessel.

Name	No.	Builders	Commissioned
RACER	—	Yarrows Ltd, Esquimalt	1963
RALLY	—	Davie Shipbuilding Ltd	1963
RAPID	—	Ferguson Industries, Picton	1963
READY	—	Burrard Dry Dock	1963
RELAY	—	Kingston Shipyard	1963
RIDER	—	—	1963

Measurement, tons: 153 gross
Dimensions, feet (metres): 95·2 × 20 × 6·5 (29 × 6·1 × 2)
Main engines: Diesel; 2 400 bhp = 20 knots designed

Rider, completed for the Department of Fisheries, was taken over by the Coast Guard in March 1969. *Relay* rerated as St. Lawrence River Marine Traffic Control Vessel.

Name	No.	Builders	Commissioned
SPINDRIFT	—	Cliff Richardson Ltd, Meaford	1963
SPRAY	—	J. J. Taylor & Sons Ltd, Toronto	1963
SPUME	—	Grew Ltd, Penetanguishene	1964

Measurement, tons: 57 gross
Dimensions, feet (metres): 70 × 16·8 × 4·7 (21·4 × 5·1 × 1·4)
Main engines: 2 diesels; 1 050 bhp = 19 knots

Employed on Great Lakes Patrol.

Note. For search and rescue and patrol duties: six launches (*Mallard, Moorhen*, CG 110-113) and one Hovercraft (CG 021).

CANADA (Coast guard) / Northern supply vessel — Fisheries and Environment Dept

NORTHERN SUPPLY VESSEL

1 FORMER TANK LANDING CRAFT (LCT 8)

Name	No.	Builders	Commissioned
SKUA	—	Harland & Wolff	1946

Measurement, tons: 1 083 to 1 104 gross
Dimensions, feet (metres): 231·2 × 38 × 7 *(70·5 × 11·6 × 2·1)*
Main engines: Diesel; 1 000 shp = 9 knots

Converted LCT (8), acquired from the UK in 1961.

SHORE-BASED CRAFT

| DUMIT | ECKALOO | MISKANAW | TEMBAH | NAHIDIK |

Assist navigation in Mackenzie River operations. Small buoy tender type.

TEMBAH   *1978, Canadian Coast Guard*

CG 101-109   CG 114-118

Displacement, tons: 18
Dimensions, feet (metres): 44 × 12 × 3 *(13·4 × 3·7 × 0·9)*
Main engines: Diesel; 294 bhp = 14 knots
Range, miles: 150

Lifeboats shore-based at Coast Guard Stations on both coasts.

1 HOVERCRAFT

One BH-6H-9009 was completed at Cowes by BHC Ltd on 3 March 1977.

TRAINING SHIP

MIKULA

Displacement, tons: 617
Dimensions, feet (metres): 128 × 30 × 11 *(39 × 9·2 × 3·4)*
Main engines: Diesel; 150 bhp = 9 knots

Converted Light Vessel.

MIKULA   *1978, Canadian Coast Guard*

SURVEY AND SOUNDING VESSELS

BEAUPORT

Displacement, tons: 767 full load
Dimensions, feet (metres): 167·5 × 24·0 × 9·0 *(51·1 × 7·3 × 2·7)*
Main engines: Diesels; 1 280 bhp

Completed in 1960.

BEAUPORT   *1978, Canadian Coast Guard*

NICOLET

Displacement, tons: 935 full load
Dimensions, feet (metres): 166·5 × 35·0 × 9·6 *(50·8 × 10·7 × 2·9)*
Main engines: Diesels; 1 350 bhp

NICOLET   *1978, Canadian Coast Guard*

VILLE MARIE

Displacement, tons: 493 full load
Dimensions, feet (metres): 134·0 × 28·0 × 9·5 *(40·9 × 8·5 × 2·9)*
Main engines: Diesel-electric; 1 000 hp

Completed in 1960.

There are also two smaller vessels *Glendada* and *Jean Bourdon* for the St. Lawrence Ship Channel.

FISHERIES AND ENVIRONMENT DEPARTMENT (SHIP BRANCH)

Director: Mr D. R. Saxon

Name	Displacement	Date launched	Officers	Crew
HUDSON	4 800	1963	13	49
BAFFIN	3 700	1957	13	55
DAWSON	1 787	1967	9	23
PARIZEAU	1 787	1967	9	23
WM. J. STEWART	1 500	1932	9	55
LIMNOS	609	1968	6	10
VECTOR	520	1967	6	11
MAXWELL	330	1961	4	13
BAYFIELD	234	1960	3	6
RICHARDSON	100	1961	2	4
ADVENT	50	1972	2	1

CHILE

Ministerial

Minister of National Defence:
  Major General H. J. Brady Roche

Headquarters Appointments

Commander-in-Chief of the Navy:
  Admiral José Toribio Merino Castro
Chief of the Naval Staff:
  Vice-Admiral Carlos A. Le May Délano

Diplomatic Representation

Naval Attaché in Brasilia:
  Captain Reinaldo Rivas
Naval Attaché in Buenos Aires, Montevideo and Asunción:
  Captain Fernando Camus
Naval Attaché in Lima:
  Captain Jorge Contreras
Naval Attaché in London, Paris, The Hague and Stockholm:
  Captain Osvaldo Schwartzenberg
Naval Attaché in Madrid:
  Captain Pedro Romero
Naval Attaché in Quito and Bogota:
  Captain Franklin Gonzalez
Naval Attaché in Tokyo:
  Commander Enrique La Luz
Naval Attaché in Washington:
  Rear-Admiral Jorge Hess

Personnel

(a) 1979: 23 000 (1 320 officers, 19 000 ratings, 3 680 marines)
(b) 1 years national service

Naval Bases

Talcahuano. Main Naval Base, Schools, major repair yard, (2 dry docks, 3 floating docks) 2 floating cranes.
Valparaiso. Naval Base, Schools, major repair yard, 1 floating dock.
Puerto Montt. Small naval base.
Punta Arenas. Small naval base. Repair yard with slipway.
Puerto Williams. Small naval base.

Maritime Air

Personnel—500

      4 Bell 206 A JetRangers
     12 Bell 47
      5 Grumman HU-16B Albatross
      6 EMB-111
      1 Piper PA-31-310 Navajo
      6 Beech T-34B Mentor
      3 EMB-110 Bandeirante
      2 Sikorsky S-58
      2 Casa 212 Aviocar
      4 Lockheed SP-2E Neptune
      6 Alouette III
      3 PBY-6A Catalina

General

Except for the two "Leander" Class, the two "Oberon" Class, one LPC and four "Lürssen" FAC the main units of the fleet are all reaching advanced age, even the "Almirante" Class, being 17 years old. With the remainder having hull-lives of 30-40 years a replacement programme is clearly needed if the 4 000 miles of coastline is to be patrolled to a 200 mile limit. The current problems of acquiring US vessels must make any future purchases more likely to be of European construction.

Infanteria de Marina

1 Brigade and Coast Defence units (2 680 marines).
Four bases at Iquique, Punta Arenas, Talcahuano and Valparaiso in addition to an embarked battalion.

Strength of the Fleet

Type	Active	Building
Patrol Submarines	2	—
Cruisers	3	—
Destroyers	6	—
Frigates	5	—
Patrol Ships	3	—
Landing Ships (Tank)	4	—
Landing Craft	7	—
Fast Attack Craft (Torpedo)	4	—
Large Patrol Craft	3	—
Coastal Patrol Craft	12	—
Survey Ship	1	—
Sail Training Ship	1	—
Transports	6	—
Tankers	2	—
Floating Docks	3	—
Tugs	4	—

Mercantile Marine

Lloyd's Register of Shipping:
  146 vessels of 466 319 tons gross

DELETIONS

Submarine

1973 *Thomson* (ex-US "Balao" Class)

Frigate

1973 *Riquelme* (ex-US "Charles Lawrence" Class)

Landing Craft

1973 *Grumete Tellez* (withdrawn from service)
1977 *Aspirante Morel, Grumete Diaz, Comandante Toro,* (ran aground, beyond repair)

Light Forces

1977 *Contramaestre Ortiz*

Tanker

1977 *Jorge Montt*

Tugs

1977 *S. Aldea*
1978 *Ancud, Caupolican, Monreal*

PENNANT LIST

Submarines

21 Simpson
22 O'Brien
23 Hyatt

Cruisers

02 O'Higgins
03 Prat
04 Latorre

Destroyers/Frigates

06 Condell
07 Lynch
14 Blanco Encalada
15 Cochrane
16 Ministero Zenteno
17 Ministero Portales
18 Almirante Riveros
19 Almirante Williams
26 Serrano
27 Orella
29 Uribe

Patrol Forces

60 Lientul
62 Lautaro
63 Sergento Aldea

Light Forces

37 Papudo
75 Marinero Fuentealba
76 Cabo Odger
80 Guacolda
81 Fresia
82 Quidora
83 Tegualda

Survey Ship

64 Yelcho

Training Ship

43 Esmeralda

Amphibious Forces

86 Valdivia
88 Comandante Hemmerdinger
89 Comandante Araya
90 Elicura
91 Aguila
94 Orompello

Transports

45 Piloto Pardo
47 Aquiles
70 Angamos
110 Meteoro
111 Cirujano Videla
112 Grumete Perez

Tankers

53 Araucano
54 Beagle

Tugs

73 Colocolo
120 Reyes
128 Cortez

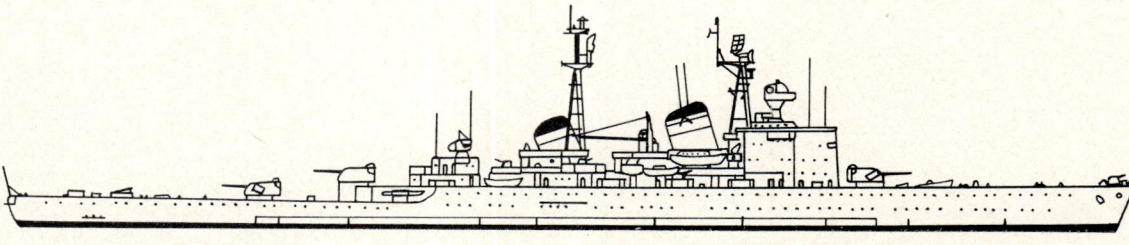

LATORRE

CHILE / Introduction — Submarines   95

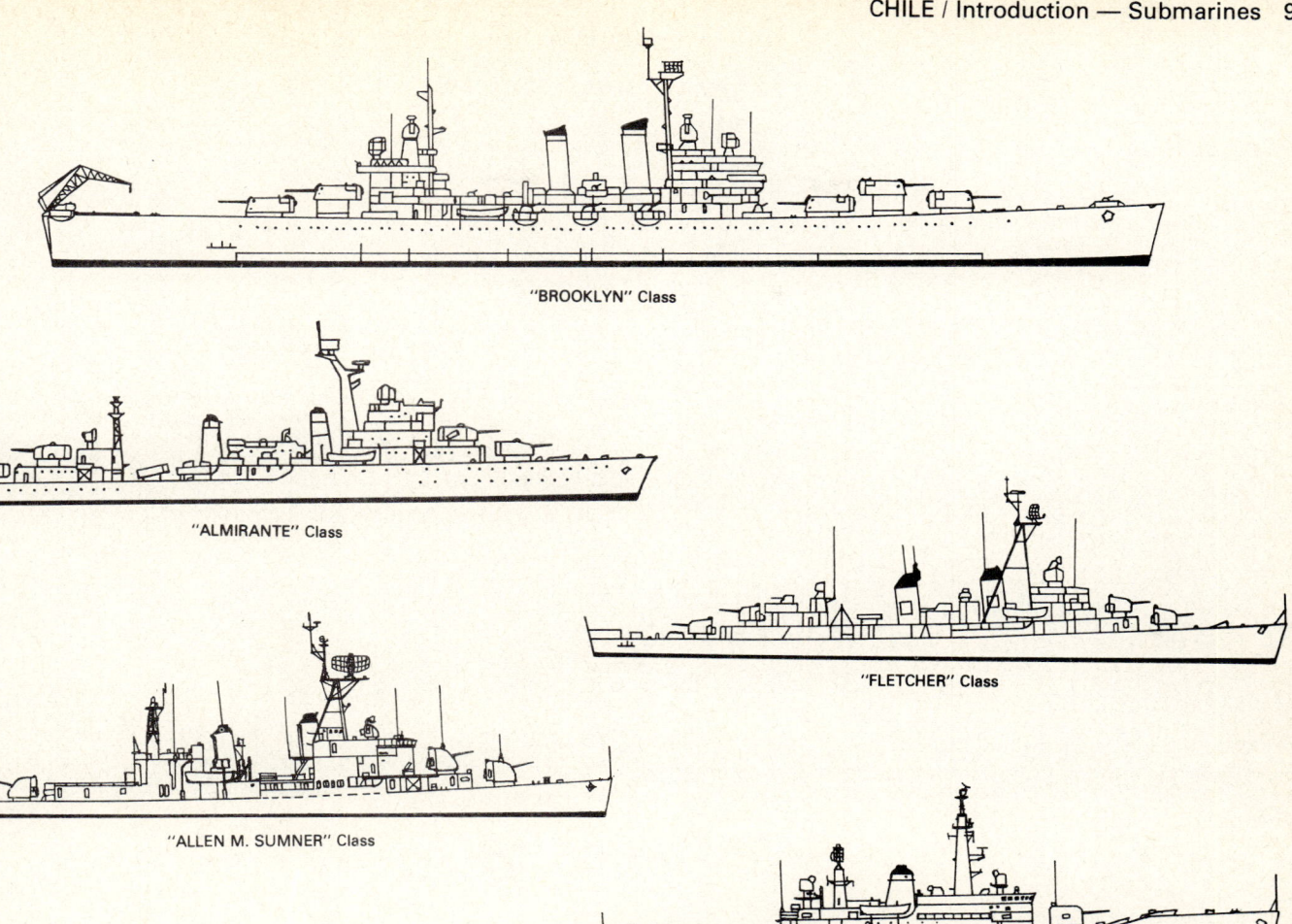

"BROOKLYN" Class

"ALMIRANTE" Class

"FLETCHER" Class

"ALLEN M. SUMNER" Class

"LEANDER" Class

SUBMARINES

2 BRITISH "OBERON" CLASS

Name	No.	Builders	Laid down	Launched	Commissioned
O'BRIEN	22	Scott-Lithgow	17 Jan 1971	21 Dec 1972	Apr 1976
HYATT (ex-*Condell*)	23	Scott-Lithgow	10 Jan 1972	26 Sep 1973	27 Sep 1976

Displacement, tons: 1 610 standard; 2 030 surfaced; 2 410 dived
Length, feet (metres): 241·0 *(73·5)* pp; 295·2 *(90·0)* oa
Beam, feet (metres): 26·5 *(8·1)*
Draught, feet (metres): 18·1 *(5·5)*
Torpedo tubes: 8—21 in *(533 mm)*
Main machinery: 2 diesels; 3 680 bhp; 2 electric motors; 6 000 shp; 2 shafts
Speed, knots: 12 surfaced; 17 dived

Ordered from Scott's Shipbuilding & Engineering Co Ltd, Greenock, late 1969. Both suffered delays in fitting out due to re-cabling and a minor explosion in *Hyatt* in January 1976. Original completion was due in July 1974 and April 1975 (see new commissioning dates above). *O'Brien* arrived in Chile July 1976, *Hyatt* February 1977. *Hyatt* completed 31 August 1976.

O'BRIEN   1976, Chilean Navy

1 Ex-US "BALAO" CLASS

Name	No.	Builders	Laid down	Launched	Commissioned
SIMPSON (ex-USS *Spot*, SS 413)	21	Mare Island Navy Yard	1943	20 May 1944	3 Aug 1944

Displacement, tons: 1 816 surfaced; 2 425 dived
Length, feet (metres): 311·6 *(95)*
Beam, feet (metres): 27 *(8·2)*
Draught, feet (metres): 17 *(5·2)*
Torpedo tubes: 10—21 in *(533 mm)* (6 bow, 4 stern)
Gun: 1—5 in/25
Main machinery: 4 General Motors diesels; 6 500 hp; 2 electric motors; 4 610 bhp
Speed, knots: 20 surfaced; 10 dived
Complement: 80

Transferred end of 1961. Paid off 1975. Reactivated 1977 after a major refit.

SIMPSON   1977, Chilean Navy

96 CHILE / Cruisers — Destroyers

CRUISERS
1 Ex-SWEDISH "GOTA LEJON" CLASS

Name	No.	Builders	Laid down	Launched	Commissioned
LATORRE (ex-Göta Lejon)	04	Eriksberg Mekaniska Verkstad, Göteborg	27 Sep 1943	17 Nov 1945	15 Dec 1947

Displacement, tons: 8 200 standard; 9 200 full load
Length, feet (metres): 590·5 (180·0) wl; 597 (182·0) oa
Beam, feet (metres): 54 (16·5)
Draught, feet (metres): 21·5 (6·6)
Guns: 7—6 in (150 mm)/53 (1 triple fwd, 2 twin aft) 4—57 mm; 11—40 mm
Torpedo tubes: 6—21 in
Armour: 3 in—5 in (75—125 mm)
Main engines: 2 sets De Laval geared turbines; 100 000 shp; 2 shafts
Boilers: 4 Swedish 4-drum type
Speed, knots: 33
Complement: 610

Radar control arrangements were installed for 6 in guns. Fitted for minelaying with a capacity of 120 mines. Reconstructed in 1951-52, modernised in 1958, with new radar, 57 mm guns etc.

Gunnery: The 6-in guns are automatic weapons with an elevation of 70 degrees. Originally ordered for R. Neth. Navy "De Zeven Provincien" class in 1938.

Radar: Search: LW-03, Type 227.
Tactical: Type 293.
Fire control: I band.

Transfer: Purchased by Chile from Sweden July 1971. Commissioned in Chilean Navy 18 September 1971.

LATORRE   1975, Chilean Navy

2 Ex-US "BROOKLYN" CLASS

Name	No.	Builders	Laid down	Launched	Commissioned
O'HIGGINS (ex-USS Brooklyn CL 40)	02	New York Navy Yard	12 Mar 1935	30 Nov 1936	18 July 1938
PRAT (ex-USS Nashville CL 43)	03	New York S.B. Corporation	24 Jan 1935	2 Oct 1937	25 Nov 1938

Displacement, tons: 10 000 standard; 13 500 full load
Length, feet (metres): 608·3 (185·4)
Beam, feet (metres): 69 (21·0)
Draught, feet (metres): 24 (7·3)
Aircraft: 1 Bell helicopter
Guns: 15—6 in (152 mm)/47, triple Mk 16; 8—5 in (127 mm)/25, single Mk 27; 28—40 mm/60, (4 quad and 6 twin Mk 2 and Mk 1); 24—20 mm/80 (single and twin)
Armour, inches (mm):
  Belt 4—1½ (102—38);
  Decks 3—2 (76—51);
  Turrets 5—3 (127—76);
  C.T. 8 in (203)
Main engines: Parsons geared turbines 100 000 shp; 4 shafts
Boilers: 8 Babcock & Wilcox Express type
Oil fuel, tons: 2 100
Speed, knots: 32·5
Range, miles: 14 500 at 15 knots
Complement: 888 to 975 (peace)

Former cruisers of the US "Brooklyn" Class. Purchased from the USA in 1951 at a price representing 10 per cent of original cost ($37 million) plus the expense of reconditioning. Again refitted in USA 1957-58.

Class: O'Higgins (ex-USS Brooklyn) was damaged by grounding 12 August 1974. She was subsequently used as an alongside accommodation ship and was no longer considered operational. However, after a very expensive refit in 1977/78 she has been recommissioned.

PRAT   1974, Chilean Navy

Hangar: The hangar in the hull right aft could accommodate six aircraft if necessary together with engine spares and duplicate parts, though four aircraft was the normal capacity. Above the hangar two catapults were mounted as far outboard as possible, and a revolving crane was placed at the stern extremity overhanging the aircraft hatch.

Radar: Search: SPS 12.
Tactical: SPS 10.

DESTROYERS
2 Ex-US "FLETCHER" CLASS

Name	No.	Builders	Laid down	Launched	Commissioned
BLANCO ENCALADA (ex-USS Wadleigh DD 689)	14	Bath Iron Works Corporation, Bath, Maine	Mar 1943	7 Aug 1943	19 Oct 1943
COCHRANE (ex-USS Rooks DD 804)	15	Todd Pacific Shipyards	Jan 1944	6 June 1944	2 Sep 1944

Displacement, tons: 2 100 standard; 2 750 full load
Length, feet (metres): 376·5 (110·5)
Beam, feet (metres): 39·5 (12·0)
Draught, feet (metres): 18 (5·5)
Guns: 4—5 in (127 mm)/38 single Mk 30; 6—3 in (76 mm)/50 twin Mk 33
Torpedo tubes: 5—21 in (533 mm) (quin)
A/S weapons: 2 Hedgehogs; 2 side launching torpedo racks; 1 DC rack; 6 "K" DCT
Main engines: 2 Westinghouse geared turbines; 60 000 shp; 2 shafts
Boilers: 4 Babcock & Wilcox
Speed, knots: 35
Oil fuel, tons: 650
Range, miles: 5 000 at 15 knots; 1 260 at 30 knots
Complement: 250 (14 officers, 236 men). Accommodation for 324 (24 officers, 300 men)

Transferred to Chile under the Military Aid Programme in 1963. Three more destroyers were scheduled for transfer from the US Navy to the Chilean Navy under a new transfer law signed by the President of the USA in 1966. The ships were to have been refitted and modernised and adapted to Chilean requirements before transfer to the new flag, but the four frigates of the US "Charles Lawrence" Class were transferred instead.

COCHRANE   1978, Chilean Navy

Radar: Search: SPS 6.
Tactical: SPS 10.
Fire control: I Band.

CHILE / Destroyers 97

2 "ALMIRANTE" CLASS

Name	No.	Builders	Laid down	Launched	Commissioned
ALMIRANTE RIVEROS	18	Vickers-Armstrong Ltd, Barrow	12 Apr 1957	12 Dec 1958	31 Dec 1960
ALMIRANTE WILLIAMS	19	Vickers-Armstrong Ltd, Barrow	20 June 1956	5 May 1958	26 Mar 1960

Displacement, tons: 2 730 standard; 3 300 full load
Length, feet (metres): 402 *(122·5)*
Beam, feet (metres): 43 *(13·1)*
Draught, feet (metres): 13·3 *(4·0)*
Missiles: 4 SSM Exocet (single cells);
  Est 16 SAM Sea Cat (2 quad launchers)
Guns: 4—4 in *(102 mm)*/60 (single Mk(N)R);
  4—40 mm/70 single Bofors L70
A/S weapons: 2 Squid 3-barrelled DC mortars;
  6 (2 triple) Mk 32 torpedo tubes (Mk 44 torpedoes)
Main engines: Parsons Pametrada geared turbines;
  54 000 shp; 2 shafts
Boilers: 2 Babcock & Wilcox
Speed, knots: 34·5
Range, miles: 6 000 at 16 knots
Complement: 266

Ordered in May 1955. Layout and general arrangements are conventional. Bunks fitted for entire crew. Both modernised by Swan Hunter, *Almirante Williams* in 1971-74 and *Almirante Riveros* in 1973-75.

Electrical: The electrical system is on alternating current. Galleys are all electric. There is widespread use of fluorescent lighting. Degaussing cables are fitted.

Gunnery: The 4 in guns are in four single mountings, two superimposed forward and two aft. These mountings are unique. They are automatic with a range of 12 500 yards *(11 400 metres)* and an elevation of 75 degrees.

Missiles: British Seacat surface-to-air installations were fitted at the Chilean Navy Yard at Talcahuano in 1964. Exocet MM 38 fitted during modernisations.

Operational: The operations room and similar spaces are air-conditioned. Twin rudders. Ventilation and heating system designed to suit Chilean conditions, extending from the tropics to the Antarctic.

Radar: Plessey AWS-I and Target Indication radar with AIO autonomous displays being fitted at refits.

ALMIRANTE RIVEROS   1976, Swan Hunter

ALMIRANTE WILLIAMS   1977, Chilean Navy

2 Ex-US "ALLEN M. SUMNER" (FRAM II) CLASS

Name	No.	Builders	Laid down	Launched	Commissioned
MINISTRO ZENTENO (ex-USS *Charles S. Sperry*, DD 697)	16	Todd (Pacific) Shipyards	1944	30 Sep 1944	26 Dec 1944
MINISTRO PORTALES (ex-USS *Douglas H. Fox*, DD 779)	17	Federal S.B. and D.D. Co	1943	13 Mar 1944	17 May 1944

Displacement, tons: 2 200 standard; 3 320 full load
Length, feet (metres): 376·5 *(114·8)*
Beam, feet (metres): 40·9 *(12·4)*
Draught, feet (metres): 19 *(5·8)*
Aircraft: 1 helicopter
Guns: 6—5 in *(127 mm)*/38 twin Mk 38
A/S weapons: 2 triple Mk 32 launchers; 2 Hedgehogs
Main engines: 2 geared turbines; 60 000 shp; 2 shafts
Boilers: 4
Speed, knots: 34
Range, miles: 4 600 at 15 knots
Complement: 274

Transferred 8 January 1974 by sale.

Radar: Search; SPS 37 *(Zenteno)*, SPS 40 *(Portales)*.
Tactical; SPS 10.

Sonar: SQS 40. VDS.

MINISTRO ZENTENO   1976, Chilean Navy

MINISTRO PORTALES   1978, Chilean Navy

FRIGATES

2 BRITISH "LEANDER" CLASS

Name	No.	Builders	Laid down	Launched	Commissioned
CONDELL	06	Yarrow & Co Ltd	5 June 1971	12 June 1972	21 Dec 1973
ALMIRANTE LYNCH	07	Yarrow & Co Ltd	6 Dec 1971	6 Dec 1972	25 May 1974

Displacement, tons: 2 500 standard; 2 962 full load
Length, feet (metres): 360·0 *(109·7)* wl; 372·0 *(113·4)* oa
Beam, feet (metres): 43·0 *(13·1)*
Draught, feet (metres): 18·0 *(5·5)*
Aircraft: 1 light helicopter
Missiles: 4 SSM Exocet (single cells);
　Est. 16 SAM Sea Cat (1 quad launcher)
Guns: 2—4·5 in *(115 mm)*/45 twin Mk 6; 2—20 mm/70
A/S weapons: 6 (2 triple) Mk 32 torpedo tubes
Main engines: 2 geared turbines; 30 000 shp
Boilers: 2
Speed, knots: 30
Range, miles: 4 500 at 12 knots
Complement: 263

Ordered from Yarrow & Co Ltd, Scotstoun in the modernisation programme of the Chilean Navy. Until the Swedish cruiser was acquired, *Condell,* laid down on 5 June 1971, was to have been named *Latorre*. Renamed 1971. Both arrived in Chilean waters by February 1975.

Appearance: Have slightly taller foremasts than British "Leanders". No Limbo or VDS.

Missiles: The Exocet launchers are placed on the quarter-deck thus, as opposed to the British conversion, allowing the retention of the 4·5 in turret.

Radar: Surveillance, target indication: Type 992Q.
Air search: Type 965.
Navigation: Type 975.
Sea Cat/Gunnery: GWS 22/MRS3.

ALMIRANTE LYNCH　　　　　　　　　　　　　　　　　　　1978, Chilean Navy

Sonar: Type 162, 170 and 177.

3 Ex-US "CHARLES LAWRENCE" CLASS

Name	No.	Builders	Laid down	Launched	Commissioned
SERRANO (ex-USS *Odum,* APD 71, ex-DE 670)	26	Consolidated Steel, Orange	15 Oct 1943	19 Jan 1944	12 Jan 1945
ORELLA (ex-USS *Jack C. Robinson,* APD 72, ex-DE 671)	27	Consolidated Steel, Orange	10 Nov 1943	8 Jan 1944	2 Feb 1945
URIBE (ex-USS *Daniel Griffin,* APD 38, ex-DE 54)	29	Bethlehem, Hingham	7 Sep 1942	25 Feb 1943	9 June 1943

Displacement, tons: 1 400 standard; 2 130 full load
Length, feet (metres): 300·0 *(91·4)* wl; 306·0 *(93·3)* oa
Beam, feet (metres): 37·0 *(11·3)*
Draught, feet (metres): 12·6 *(3·8)*
Guns: 1—5 in *(127 mm)*/38 (single Mk 30);
　6—40 mm/60 (twins Mk 1)
A/S weapons: 2 Hedgehogs (some); 2 DC racks
Main engines: GE turbo-electric; 2 shafts; 12 000 shp = 23·6 knots; 2 turbines 6 000 hp each; 2 generators 4 500 kW each
Boilers: 2 Foster Wheeler "D" type
Range, miles: 5 000 at 15 knots; 2 000 at 23 knots
Complement: 209

These former high speed transports (APD) were purchased from the USA, transferred at Orange, Texas 25 November 1966 (first two) and Norfolk Va 1 December 1966 *(Uribe)*. They have been modernised, *Riquelme* was also transferred but was used for provision of spare parts. Deleted 1973. Carry two LCUs.

Radar: Combined search: AN/SPS-4.
Navigation: commercial (no gunnery control by radar).

ORELLA　　　　　　　　　　　　　　　　　　　　　　　　1976, Chilean Navy

PATROL FORCES

2 Ex-US "SOTOYOMO" CLASS

Name	No.	Builders	Commissioned
LIENTUR (ex-USS *ATA 177*)	60	Levingstone S.B. Co, Orange	2 Sep 1944
LAUTARO (ex-USS *ATA 122*)	62	Levingstone S.B. Co, Orange	10 June 1943

Displacement, tons: 534 standard; 835 full load
Dimensions, feet (metres): 134·5 wl; 143 oa × 33 × 13·2 *(43·6 × 10·1 × 4)*
Guns: 1—3 in *(76 mm)*/50; 2—20 mm
Main engines: General Motors diesel-electric; 1 500 shp = 12·5 knots
Oil fuel, tons: 187
Complement: 33

Launched—*Lautaro* 27 November 1942, *Lientur* 5 June 1944. Originally ocean rescue tugs (ATRs), transferred to the Chilean Navy and reclassified as patrol vessels.

LAUTARO　　　　　　　　　　　　　　　　　　　　　　　1970, Chilean Navy

CHILE / Patrol forces — Light forces 99

1 Ex-US "CHEROKEE" CLASS

Name	No.	Builders	Commissioned
SERGENTO ALDEA (ex-USS *Arikara*, ATF 98)	63	Charleston S.B. & D.D. Co	5 Jan 1944

Displacement, tons: 1 235 standard; 1 675 full load
Dimensions, feet (metres): 195·0 wl; 205·0 oa × 38·5 × 15·5 *(62·5 × 11·7 × 4·7)*
Gun: 1—3 in *(76 mm)*/50
Main engines: Diesel-electric; 1 shaft; 3 000 bhp = 15 knots
Complement: 85

Launched on 22 June 1943. Transferred on 1 July 1971 by lease.

SERGENTO ALDEA   *1976, Chilean Navy*

LIGHT FORCES

4 LÜRSSEN TYPE (FAST ATTACK CRAFT—TORPEDO)

Name	No.	Builders	Commissioned
GUACOLDA	80	Bazan, Cadiz	30 July 1965
FRESIA	81	Bazan, Cadiz	9 Dec 1965
QUIDORA	82	Bazan, Cadiz	1966
TEGUALDA	83	Bazan, Cadiz	1966

Displacement, tons: 134
Dimensions, feet (metres): 118·1 × 18·4 × 7·2 *(36 × 5·6 × 2·2)*
Guns: 2—40 mm
Torpedo tubes: 4—21 in *(533 mm)*
Main engines: Diesels; 2 shafts; 4 800 bhp = 32 knots
Range, miles: 1 500 at 15 knots
Complement: 20

Built to German Lürssen design.

QUIDORA (*Tegualda* and *Guacolda* behind)   *1976, Chilean Navy*

1 US "PC-1638" CLASS (LARGE PATROL CRAFT)

Name	No.	Builders	Commissioned
PAPUDO (ex-US PC 1646)	37	Asmar, Talcahuano	27 Nov 1971

Displacement, tons: 450 full load
Dimensions, feet (metres): 173·0 × 23·0 × 10·2 *(52·7 × 7 × 3·1)*
Guns: 1—40 mm; 4—20 mm (twins)
A/S weapons: 1 Mk 15 Trainable Hedgehog; 2 "K" DCT; 4 DC racks
Main engines: 2 diesels; 2 shafts; 2 800 bhp = 19 knots
Complement: 69 (4 officers, 65 men)

Of similar design to the Turkish "Hisar" class built to the US PC plan.

PAPUDO   *1976, Chilean Navy*

2 LARGE PATROL CRAFT

Name	No.	Builders	Commissioned
MARINERO FUENTEALBA	75	Asmar, Talcahuano	22 July 1966
CABO ODGER	76	Asmar, Talcahuano	21 Apr 1967

Displacement, tons: 215
Dimensions, feet (metres): 80 × 21 × 9 *(24·4 × 6·4 × 2·7)*
Guns: 1—20 mm; 3—12·7 mm MG
Main engines: 1 Cummins diesel 340 hp = 9 knots
Range, miles: 2 600 at 9 knots
Complement: 19

MARINERO FUENTEALBA   *1972, Chilean Navy*

10 COASTAL PATROL CRAFT

Of 61 ft *(18·6 m)* built by Maclaren, Niteroi, Brazil. Ordered 1977.

2 COASTAL PATROL CRAFT

Two 32 ft Equity Standard Craft delivered in 1968. Diesel; 400 hp = 35 knots.

100 CHILE / Amphibious forces — Training ship

AMPHIBIOUS FORCES

3 Ex-US "511-1152" CLASS (LSTs)

Name	No.	Builders	Commissioned
COMANDANTE HEMMERDINGER (ex-USS New London County, LST 1066)	88	Bethlehem Steel, Hingham, Mass	20 Mar 1945
COMANDANTE ARAYA (ex-USS Nye County, LST 1067)	89	Bethlehem Steel, Hingham, Mass	24 Mar 1945
AGUILA (ex-USS Aventinus ARVE 3, ex-LST 1092)	91	American Bridge Co, Ambridge	19 May 1945

Displacement, tons: 1 653 standard; 4 080 full load
Dimensions, feet (metres): 328 × 50 × 14 (100 × 15.3 × 4.3)
Guns: Fitted for 8—40 mm
Main engines: General Motors diesels; 1 700 shp; 2 shafts = 11.6 knots
Complement: approx 110

Nos 88 and 89 transferred 29 August 1973. No 91 was a conversion to Aircraft Repair Ship and was transferred to Chile in 1963 under MAP. After various employments all are now available for amphibious duties.

"511-1152" Class LST — USN

1 Ex-US LCM

VALDIVIA 86

Survivor of three transferred in 1960 (*Pisagua* 85 and *Junin* 87 deleted).

6 Ex-US LCVPs

Transferred in 1960.

2 CHILEAN LANDING CRAFT

Name	No.	Builders	Commissioned
ELICURA	90	Talcahuano	10 Dec 1968
OROMPELLO	94	Dade Dry Dock Co, Miami	15 Sep 1964

Displacement, tons: 290 light; 750 full load
Dimensions, feet (metres): 138 wl; 145 oa × 34 × 12.8 (44.2 × 10.4 × 3.9)
Guns: 3—20 mm (*Elicura*)
Main engines: Diesels; 2 shafts; 900 bhp = 10.5 knots
Oil fuel (tons): 77
Range, miles: 2 900 at 9 knots
Complement: 20

Orompello was built for the Chilean Government in Miami, *Elicura* was launched on 21 April 1967. Two of similar class operated by Chilean Shipping Co.

OROMPELLO — 1971, Chilean Navy

SURVEY SHIP

1 Ex-US "CHEROKEE" CLASS

Name	No.	Builders	Commissioned
YELCHO (ex-USS Tekesta, ATF 93)	64	Commercial Iron Works, Portland, Oregon	16 Aug 1943

Displacement, tons: 1 235 standard; 1 675 full load
Dimensions, feet (metres): 195 wl; 205 oa × 38.5 × 15.5 (62.5 × 11.7 × 4.7)
Guns: 2—40 mm
Main engines: 4 diesels/diesel-electric; 1 shaft; 3 000 bhp = 15 knots
Complement: 85

Fitted with powerful pumps and other salvage equipment. *Yelcho* was laid down on 7 September 1942, launched on 20 March 1943 and loaned to Chile by the USA on 15 May 1960, having since been employed as Antarctic research ship and surveying vessel.

YELCHO — 1972, Chilean Navy

TRAINING SHIP

Name	No.	Builders	Commissioned
ESMERALDA (ex-*Don John de Austria*)	43	Echevarietta, Cadiz	1952

Displacement, tons: 3 040 standard; 3 673 full load
Dimensions, feet (metres): 308.8 × 43 × 23 (94.1 × 13.1 × 7)
Guns: 2—57 mm (saluting)
Sail area: Total 26 910 sq ft
Main engine: 1 Fiat auxiliary diesel; 1 shaft; 1 400 bhp = 11 knots
Range, miles: 8 000 at 8 knots
Complement: 271 plus 80 cadets

Four-masted schooner originally intended for the Spanish Navy. Transferred to Chile on 12 May 1953. Near sister ship of *Juan Sebastian de Elcano* in the Spanish Navy. Replaced transport *Presidente Pinto* as training ship. Refitted Saldanha Bay, South Africa, 1977.

ESMERALDA — 1977, Chilean Navy

CHILE / Transports — Tankers 101

TRANSPORTS

Name	No.	Builders	Commissioned
ANGAMOS (ex-M/V *Puerto Montt*, ex-M/V *Kobenhavn*)	70	Orenst & Koppel, Germany	1966

Measurement, tons: 4 616 gross
Dimensions, feet (metres): 308·2 × 53·2 × 13·6 *(93·92 × 16·20 × 4·15)*
Main engines: 2 Lind-Pielstick diesels; 6 500 hp = 17 knots

Acquired from Chilean state shipping company early 1977 for conversion to transport. Former Chilean and Danish ferryboat.

Name	No.	Builders	Commissioned
AQUILES (ex-*Tjaldur*)	47	Aalborg Vaerft, Denmark	1953

Measurement, tons: 2 660 registered; 1 462 net; 1 395 deadweight
Dimensions, feet (metres): 288 × 44 × 17 *(87·8 × 13·4 × 5·2)*
Gun: 1—40 mm
Main engine: 1 Burmeister & Wain diesel; 3 600 bhp = 16 knots
Range, miles: 5 500 at 16 knots
Complement: 60 crew plus 447 troops

Ex-Danish M/V *Tjaldur* bought by Chile in 1967.

AQUILES   1976, Chilean Navy

Name	No.	Builders	Commissioned
PILOTO PARDO	45	Haarlemsche Scheepsbouw, Netherlands	1959

Displacement, tons: 1 250 light; 2 000 standard; 3 000 full load
Dimensions, feet (metres): 269 × 39 × 15 *(82 × 11·9 × 4·6)*
Aircraft: 1 helicopter
Guns: 1—101 mm/50; 2—20 mm
Main engines: 2 diesel-electric; 2 000 hp = 14 knots
Range, miles: 6 000 at 10 knots
Complement: 44 (plus 24 passengers)

Antarctic patrol ship, transport and research vessel with reinforced hull to navigate in ice. Launched 11 June 1958.

PILOTO PARDO   1974, Chilean Navy

Name	No.	Builders	Commissioned	Name	No.	Builders	Commissioned
METEORO	110	Asmar, Talcahuano	1967	CIRUJANO VIDELA	111	Asmar, Talcahuano	1964
GRUMETE PEREZ	112	Asmar, Talcahuano	1975				

Displacement, tons: 205
Main engine: Diesel = 8 knots

Ferry—capacity 220.

Displacement, tons: 140
Dimensions, feet (metres): 101·7 × 21·3 × 6·6 *(31 × 6·5 × 2)*
Main engine: Diesel; 700 hp = 14 knots

Hospital and dental facilities are fitted. A modified version of US PGM 59 design with larger superstructure and less power.

TANKERS

Name	No.	Builders	Commissioned
ARAUCANO	53	Burmeister & Wain, Copenhagen	10 Jan 1967

Displacement, tons: 17 300
Measurement, tons: 18 030 deadweight
Dimensions, feet (metres): 497·6 × 74·9 × 28·8 *(151·7 × 22·8 × 8·8)*
Guns: 8—40 mm (twins)
Main engines: Babcock & Wilcox diesels; 10 800 bhp = 15·5 knots (17 on trial)
Range, miles: 12 000 at 15·5 knots

Launched on 21 June 1966.

ARAUCANO   1974, Chilean Navy

1 Ex-US "PATAPSCO" CLASS

Name	No.	Builders	Commissioned
BEAGLE (ex-USS *Genesee*, AOG 8)	54	Cargill Inc, Savage, Minn.	27 May 1944

Displacement, tons: 4 240 standard
Dimensions, feet (metres): 310 × 48·7 × 16 *(94·5 × 14·9 × 4·9)*
Guns: 2—3 in/50; 4—20 mm
Range, miles: 6 690 at 10 knots

Transferred on loan 5 July 1972.

BEAGLE   1976, Chilean Navy

TUGS

Name	No.	Builders	Commissioned
COLOCOLO	73	Bow, McLachlan & Co, Paisley	1930

Displacement, tons: 790
Dimensions, feet (metres): 126·5 × 27·0 × 12·0 *(38·6 × 8·2 × 3·7)*
Main engines: Triple expansion; 1 050 ihp = 11 knots
Oil fuel, tons: 155

Formerly classed as Coast Guard vessel. Rebuilt in 1962-63. Last of class of five.

Name	No.	Builders	Commissioned
GALVEZ	—	Southern Shipbuilders Ltd, Faversham, England	June 1975

Measurement, tons: 112 gross
Dimensions, feet (metres): 83·6 × 24 × 9·2 *(25·5 × 7·3 × 2·8)*

Dockyard tug in Talcahuano.

REYES 120   **CORTEZ** 128

FLOATING DOCKS

2 Ex-US ARD

INGENIERO MERY (ex-US *ARD 25*) 131
MUTILLA (ex-US *ARD 32*) 132

Displacement, tons: 5 200
Capacity, tons: 3 000
Dimensions, feet (metres): 492 × 84 × 5·7 to 33·2 *(150·0 × 25·6 × 1·7 to 10·1)*

Mutilla leased to Chile 15 December 1960. *Ingeniero Mery* transferred 20 August 1973. Both at ASMAR yard, Talcahuano.

1 Ex-COMMERCIAL DOCK

Capacity, tons: 4 500
Dimensions, feet (metres): 365 × 64 × 21·6 *(110·2 × 19·5 × 6·5)*

Built for commercial firm 1924. taken over by ASMAR Valparaiso 1 January 1978.

MANTEROLA

Capacity, tons: 500 (originally 1 000)
Dimensions, feet (metres): 216 × 42 × 15 *(66 × 12·8 × 4·6)*

Built by ASMAR yard, Talcahuano before World War I.

Two Floating Cranes of 30 and 180 tons lift are at Talcahuano.

Notes: (a) *Huascar,* completed 1865, previously Peruvian, now harbour flagship at Talcahuano.
(b) *Castor* and *Sobenes,* also listed.

CHINA (People's Republic)

Administration

Minister of National Defence:
  Yeh Chien-ying

Headquarters Appointments

Commander-in-Chief of the Navy:
  Hsiao Ching Kuang
Deputy Commander-in-Chief and 1st Political Commissar:
  Su Chen-Hua
2nd Political Commissar:
  Wang Hung-K'un
Chief of Staff:
  P'an Yen
Vice Chief Naval Staff:
  Lin Zhen

Fleet Commanders

North Sea Fleet:
  Ma Chung-Ch'uan
East Sea Fleet:
  Mei Chia-Sheng
South Sea Fleet:
  Kuei Shao-Pin

Diplomatic Representation

Defence and Naval Attaché in London:
  Fang Wen

Personnel

(a) 1979: 192 000 officers and men, plus 30 000 naval air force and 28 000 marines.
(b) 6 years national service.

Training

Carried out at following schools/academies:
Shanghai:
  Officer Training School
  Naval Aviation School
  Coastal Artillery School
  Supply School
  Radar School
  School of Naval Architecture
  Fleet Training Centre (Ratings)
Dairen:
  Naval Academy
  Mining School
Nanking:
  War College
  Ratings Training School
Tsingtao:
  Naval Aviation School
  Main Ratings Training School
  Submarine School
Lushua:
  Submarine School
Yulin:
  Submarine School

Minor ratings' schools at 'Wei Hai Wei, An' Ching, Foochow. Chusan and Hangchow.

Bases

North Sea Fleet: Tsingtao (HQ), Lu Shun, Wei Hai Hui, Ching San, Luta, Hu Lu Tao, Hsiao Ping Tao
East Sea Fleet: Shanghai (HQ), Chusan, Tai Shan, Ta Hsieh Tao, Hsia Men, Wen Chou, Hai Men, Ma Wei, Fu Chou
South Sea Fleet: Chan Chiang (HQ), Yu Lin, Hai Kou, Huang Pu/Canton, Shan Tou, Pei Hai
(The fleet is split with the main emphasis on the North Sea Fleet).

Strength of the Fleet

Type	Active	Building
Fleet Submarines	1	?
Missile Firing Submarine	1	—
Patrol Submarines	79	6
Destroyers (DDG)	11	—
Frigates	14	4?
Fast Attack Craft (Missile)	172	20
Fast Attack Craft (Gun)	404	10?
Fast Attack Craft (Torpedo)	200	10?
Fast Attack Craft (Patrol)	23	4
Large Patrol Craft	21	—
Coastal Patrol Craft	100+	?
Minesweepers (Ocean)	17	—
Landing Ships (LST)	15	—
LSMs	14	—
LSILs	15	—
LCTs	17	—
LCMs—LCUs	450	—
Survey & Research Ships	20	—
Supply Ships	24 (+12?)	—
Tankers (small)	18	—
Boom Defence Vessels	6	—
Escorts (old)	15	—
Repair Ship	1	—
Misc. Small Craft	375	—

General

While studying this section it must be remembered that not only is there a steady building programme of all classes in the modernised Chinese Yards but also the Chinese have an advanced nuclear and missile capability. This combination will make the Chinese navy, already more than twice as strong in manpower as the Royal Navy, an important element in the future balance of power East of Suez.

Recently there has been evidence of delays in all the new building programmes except Submarines and Light Forces. Whether this is due to problems of weapon production, faults discovered in new construction ships or a straight political decision is not known. It is of interest that these delays appear to date from 1972, shortly after the flight and death of Lin Piao, the Defence Minister under whom the programmes were presumably generated. This may be coincidence but the plain fact is that the main emphasis today is on defensive units rather than the long-range forces whose design must have started in the mid or early 1960s.

Recent changes in government policy on foreign purchases have been reflected in interest being shown in European and US markets. This is believed to include equipment for ships of up to 10 000 tons.

Naval Air Force

With 30 000 officers and men and over 600 aircraft, this is a considerable land-based naval air force. Equipped with about 200-300 MIG 17 and 19 (and possibly MIG 21) fighter aircraft and SA2-SAM, with 150 IL 28 Torpedo bombers, Tu-2 bombers, Madge flying boats, Hound M14 helicopters and transport and communication aircraft this is primarily a defensive force.

Mercantile Marine

Lloyd's Register of Shipping:
  713 vessels of 5 168 898 tons gross

Naval Radars

Code Name	Frequency	Function	Fitting
Ball End	E/F	Surface Warning	Kaibokan and other escorts
Ball Gun	E/F	Surface Warning	Kronshtadt, T 43, Kiangnan
Cross Bird	G	Early Warning	Gordy
Cross Slot		Early Warning	Luta, Chang Ch'iang
Decca 707	I	Surface Search	Corvettes, Light Forces
Drum Tilt	I	Armament Control	Osa
High Pole A	G	IFF	General
Mina	I	Fire Control	Gordy 130mm
Neptun	I	Navigation	General
Post Lamp	I	Fire Control	Luta
Pot Head	I	Surface Search	Hai Nan, Kronshtadt, Light Forces
Skinhead	I	Surface Search	Light Forces
Ski Pole	G	IFF	Gordy
Slim Net	E/F	Surface Warning	Riga
Square Tie	I	Fire Control	Gordy, Luta, Riga, Osa
Sun Visor	I	Fire Control	Riga
Wok Won	I	Fire Control	Kiangnan

DELETIONS

1976 10 "P4" class, 1 "Shantung" class, 10 "Swatow" class, 5 "Whampoa" class, 4 ex-US YMS, 2 ex-Japanese AMS.
1977 20 "P4" class, 10 "Swatow" class, 10 "Whampoa" class.
1978 10 "Shanghai I" class, 5 "P4" class, 5 "Swatow" class, 5 "Whampoa" class.
(Where other alterations of numbers occur this is as a result of more up-to-date information).

"LUTA" Class

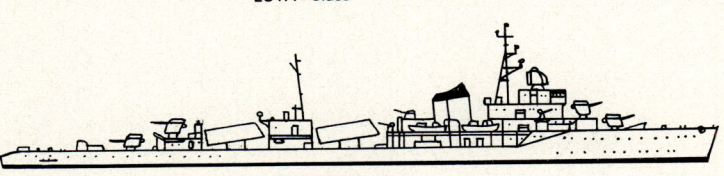
"ANSHAN" Class

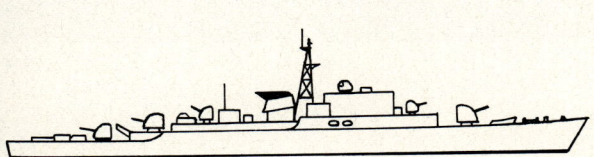
"KIANG NAN" Class

"CH'ENG TU" Class

"KRONSHTADT" Class

SUBMARINES

Reports suggest the construction of at least one nuclear submarine. This combined with the known Chinese capability to build liquid-fuelled rockets of the MRBM, IRBM and ICBM types and the completion of a solid-propellant factory, suggests that the forecast of a Chinese ballistic-missile nuclear submarine in the early 1980s may not be out of the question.

1 "HAN" CLASS

This is the first possible Chinese nuclear submarine. With an Albacore hull the first of this class was probably laid down in 1971-72. Her construction may have been delayed if problems were encountered with the power plant, but she appears to have run trials in 1974. Existence of second "Han" class is reported but not confirmed. Built at Luta.

2 "MING" CLASS

Displacement, tons: Possibly about 1 500 standard
Length, feet: Possibly about 250
Armament: Possibly 6—21 in (533 mm) torpedo tubes
Main machinery: Probably diesels and main motors

First believed to have been laid down in 1971-72 which would give an operational date around late 1974 or 1975.

1 SOVIET "GOLF" CLASS (BALLISTIC MISSILE TYPE)

Displacement, tons: 2 350 surfaced; 2 800 dived
Length, feet (metres): 320·0 (97·5)
Beam, feet (metres): 27·9 (8·5)
Draught, feet (metres): 22·0 (6·7)
Missile launchers: 3 vertical tubes
Torpedo tubes: 10—21 in (533 mm) 6 bow, 4 stern (22 torpedoes)
Main machinery: 3 diesels, total 6 000 hp; 3 shafts
3 electric motors, total 6 000 hp
Speed, knots: 17 surfaced; 14 dived
Range, miles: 22 700 surfaced; cruising
Complement: 86 (1 officers, 74 men)

Ballistic missile submarine similar to the Soviet "Golf" class. Built at Dairen in 1964. The missile tubes are fitted in the conning tower. It is not known whether this boat has been fitted with missiles, although it is possible in the future and well within Chinese technical capability (see note above concerning SLBMs).

"GOLF" Class — 1972

57 Ex-SOVIET AND CHINESE "ROMEO" CLASS (PATROL TYPE)

Displacement, tons: 1 400 surfaced; 1 800 dived
Length, feet (metres): 251·9 (76·8)
Beam, feet (metres): 24 (7·3)
Draught, feet (metres): 18 (5·5)
Torpedo tubes: 6—21 in (533 mm) (bow); 2—21 in (stern) (18 torpedoes or 36 mines)
Main machinery: 2 diesels; total 4 000 hp; 2 electric motors; total 4 000 hp; 2 shafts
Speed, knots: 17 surfaced; 16 dived
Complement: 65

The Chinese continue to build their own Soviet designed "Romeo" class submarines possibly at a rate of six a year at Kuang Chou/Canton, Kiangnan/Shanghai and Wu Chang.

"ROMEO" Class — 1975

21 SOVIET "WHISKEY" CLASS (PATROL TYPE)

Displacement, tons: 1 080 surfaced; 1 350 dived
Length, feet (metres): 249·3 (76·0)
Beam, feet (metres): 22 (6·7)
Draught, feet (metres): 15 (4·6)
Guns: 2—25 mm (twin) in some at base of fin
Torpedo tubes: 6—21 in (533 mm); 4 bow, 2 stern (20 torpedoes or 40 mines)
Main machinery: Diesel-electric; 2 shafts; 4 000 bhp diesels; 2 500 hp electric motors
Speed, knots: 17 surfaced; 15 dived
Range, miles: 13 000 at 8 knots surfaced
Complement: 60

Equipped with snort. Early boats assembled from Soviet components in Chinese yards between 1956 and 1964—remainder built in China, probably at Chiang Nan S.Y. near Shanghai.

"WHISKEY" Class — 1974

1 Ex-SOVIET "S-1" CLASS (PATROL TYPE)

Displacement, tons: 840 surfaced; 1 050 dived
Torpedo tubes: 6—21 in (533 mm)
Main machinery: 4 200 hp diesels; 2 200 hp electric motors

Launched in 1939. Transferred from the USSR in 1955.
One deleted. Last of class now harbour training boat.

CHINA / Destroyers 105

DESTROYERS

7 "LUTA" CLASS (DDG)

Name	No.	Builders	Laid down	Launched	Commissioned
—	240	Hungchi, Talien	—	—	1971
—	241	Hungchi, Talien	—	—	1972
—	242	Hungchi, Talien	—	—	1972
—	243	Hungchi, Talien	—	—	1973
—	244	Hungchi, Talien	—	—	1974
—	245	Hungchi, Talien	—	—	1974
—	246	Hungchi, Talien	—	—	1975

Displacement, tons: 3 250 standard; 3 750 full load
Dimensions, feet (metres): 430 × 45 × 15 *(131 × 13·7 × 4·6)*
Missiles: SSM—Six SS-N-2 type (two triple launchers)
Guns: 4—130 mm (2 twins) 4—57 mm; 8—25 mm
A/S weapons: 2—A/S rocket launchers
Main engines: Geared turbines; 45 000 shp; 2 shafts
Speed: 32+
Range, miles (estimated): 4 000 at 15 knots
Complement (approx): 200

The first Chinese-designed destroyers of such a capability to be built. Of similarity to Soviet "Kotlin" class. The programme has been much retarded since 1971 which, possibly coincidentally, marked the death of Lin Piao. Although capable of foreign deployment none so far reported. Three of this class serve in the South Sea Fleet.

Radar: Air search: Cross Slot.
Fire control, guns: Wasp Head, Post Lamp.
Fire control, missiles: Square Tie.
Navigation: Neptun.

"LUTA" Class   *1972, Chinese*

"LUTA" Class

"LUTA" Class   *1973*

4 "ANSHAN" (Ex-SOVIET "GORDY") CLASS

Name	No.	Builders	Laid down	Launched	Commissioned
ANSHAN (ex-*Razyaschy*)	—	Nikolayev-Dalzavod, USSR	1935	1938	1940
CHANG CHUN (ex-*Reshitelny*)	—	Nikolayev-Dalzavod, USSR	1936	1939	1941
CHI LIN (ex-*Retivy*)	—	Nikolayev-Komsomolsk, USSR	1936	1940	1941
FU CHUN (ex-*Rezky*)	—	Nikolayev-Komsomolsk, USSR	1935	1939	1941

Displacement, tons: 1 657 standard; 2 040 full load
Length, feet (metres): 357·7 *(109·0)* pp; 370 *(112·8)* oa
Beam, feet (metres): 33·5 *(10·2)*
Draught, feet (metres): 13 *(4·0)*
Missiles: SSM—Four SS-N-2 type (two twin launchers)
Guns: 4—5·1 in *(130 mm)*; 8—37 mm (twins)
A/S weapons: 2 DC racks
Main engines: Tosi geared turbines; 48 000 shp; 2 shafts
Boilers: 3-drum type
Speed, knots: 32
Oil fuel, tons: 540
Range, miles: 2 600 at 19 knots
Complement: 200

Gordy Type 7 of Odero-Terni-Orlando design. Fitted for minelaying. Two transferred in December 1954 and two in July 1955. Probably reaching the end of their useful lives.

Conversion: All converted between 1971 and 1974. The alterations consist of the replacement of the torpedo tubes by a pair of twin SS-N-2 launchers and the fitting of twin 37 mm mounts in place of the original singles.

Radar: Air search: Cross Bird.
Fire control: Square Tie.
Navigation: Neptun.
IFF: Ski Pole.

CHANG CHUN (before conversion)   *Hajime Fukaya*

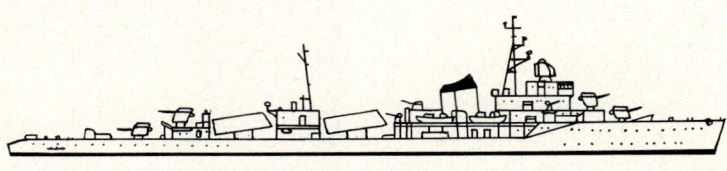
"ANSHAN" Class (after conversion)

106 CHINA / Frigates

FRIGATES

3 + 2 "KIANG HU" CLASS

Builders	Laid down	Launched	Commissioned
Shanghai	1974	1975	1976
Shanghai	1974	1975	1976
Shanghai	1975	1976	1977

Name	No.
—	521
—	525
—	—

Displacement, tons: 1 800 standard; 2 200 full load
Dimensions, feet (metres): 337·8 × 39·4 × 13·1 (103 × 12 × 4)
Missiles: SSM—Four SS-N-2 type (two twin launchers)
Guns: 2—3·9 in (100 mm); 8—37 mm
A/S weapons: 2—MBU 1800; 2 DCT
Main engines: 2 diesels; 2 shafts; 24 000 shp = 28 knots

Appears to be a modification of "Kiang Tung" class with SSM in place of SAM.

Two others reported under construction.

"KIANG HU" Class

2 + 2(?) "KIANG TUNG" CLASS

Builders	Laid down	Launched	Commissioned
Hutung, Shanghai	1971	1973	1977
Hutung, Shanghai	1972	1974	?

Name	No.
CHUNG TUNG	—
—	—

Displacement, tons: 1 800 tons standard; 2 200 full load
Dimensions, feet (metres): 337·8 × 39·4 × 13·1 (103 × 12 × 4)
Missiles: 2 twin SAM
Guns: 4—3·9 in (100 mm) (twin); 8—37 mm (twins)
A/S weapons: 2 MBU 1 800; 2 DCT
Main engines: 2 diesels; 2 shafts; 24 000 shp = 28 knots

There have apparently been no further additions to this class—further evidence of the delays in new construction of major surface ships. First SAM armed Chinese ships, a missile which apparently caused problems when first introduced and is probably still doing so.
Two may be under construction.

"KIANG TUNG" Class

5 "KIANG NAN" CLASS

Builders	Laid down	Launched	Commissioned
Kiang Nan, Shanghai	1965	Jan 1966	1967
Kiang Nan, Shanghai	1965	—	1967
Kiang Nan, Shanghai	1966	—	1968
Chiang Nan, Canton	1966	—	1968
Chiang Nan, Canton	1967	—	1969

Name	No.
—	209
—	214
—	231
—	232
—	233

Displacement, tons: 1 350 standard; 1 600 full load
Length, feet (metres): 288·6 (88)
Beam, feet (metres): 33·0 (10)
Draught, feet (metres): 12·8 (3·9)
Guns: 3—3·9 in (100 mm)/56, 1 fwd, 2 aft;
8—37 mm (twins); 4—12·7 mm (twins)
A/S weapons: 2 MBU 1 800; 4 DCT; 2 DC racks
Main engines: 4 diesels; 24 000 shp; 2 shafts
Speed, knots: 28
Complement: 175

The Chinese Navy embarked on a new building programme in 1965 of which this class was the first. One of this class was reported as engaged with South Viet-Nam forces 19-20 January 1974. Similar to Soviet "Riga" class.

Mines: Reported to have a minelaying capability.

"KIANG NAN" Class

Radar: Surface warning: Ball Gun.
Fire control: Wok Won.
Navigation: Neptun.

4 "CH'ENG TU" (Ex-SOVIET "RIGA") CLASS

Builders	Laid down	Launched	Commissioned
Chiang Nan, Canton	1955	1957	1959
Hutung, Shanghai	—	26 Sep 1956	1958
Chiang Nan, Canton	—	1957	1959
Hutung, Shanghai	1955	28 Apr 1956	1958

Name	No.
KUEI LIN	204
KUEI YANG	205
K'UN MING	206
CH'ENG TU	207

Displacement, tons: 1 200 standard; 1 600 full load
Length, feet (metres): 298·8 (91)
Beam, feet (metres): 33·7 (10·2)
Draught, feet (metres): 10 (3·0)
Missiles: SSM—Two SS-N-2 type (twin launcher)
Guns: 3—3·9 in (100 mm) (single); 4—37 mm
A/S weapons: 4 DC projectors
Mines: 50 capacity, fitted with rails
Main engines: Geared turbines; 2 shafts; 25 000 shp
Boilers: 2
Speed, knots: 28
Oil fuel, tons: 300
Range, miles: 2 000 at 10 knots
Complement: 150

Assembled from Soviet components.
All had light tripod mast and high superstructure, but later converted with heavier mast and larger bridge. Similar to the Soviet "Riga" class frigates. Two were redesigned with modified superstructure.

Conversion: Two started conversion in 1971 for the replacement of the torpedo tubes by a twin SS-N-2 launcher. All now converted.

Radar: Surface warning: Slim Net.
Fire control: Sun Visor for Guns, Square Tie for missiles.
Navigation: Neptun.

"RIGA" Class (before conversion)   1971

ESCORTS

Note: It is reported that the majority of these escorts are, in fact, not only still in commission but have been refitted and rearmed.

Class	Total	Names	No.	Displacement tons, standard	Speed (knots)	Guns	Launched	Range, miles	Complement
Ex-Japanese "Kamishima"	1	—	391	766	16	2—3 in 6—37 mm	1945	2 400 at 11 knots	130 (est)
Ex-Japanese "Ukuru"	1	HUI AN (ex-*Shisaka*)	218	940	19·5	3—3·9 in 6—37 mm	1943	5 000 at 16 knots	—
Ex-Japanese "Etorofu"	1	CHANG PI (ex-*Oki*)	—	870	19	3—3·9 in 3—37 mm	1942	8 000 at 16 knots	—
Ex-Japanese "Hashidate"	1	NAN CHANG (ex-*Uji II*)	—	999	19·5	2—5·1 in 6—37 mm	1940	3 460 at 14 knots	—
Ex-Japanese "C"/Kaibokan I	2	— (ex-*Shen Yang*) — (ex-*Chi-An*)	— —	745	15·5	2—3·9 in 6—37 mm (single) 4/8—25 mm	1945	6 500 at 14 knots	145
Ex-Japanese "D"/Kaibokan II	5	TUNG AN (ex-*Jap 192*) CHIANG SHA (ex-*Chieh 12*) CHI NAN (ex-*Chieh 6*) HSI AN (ex-*Chieh 14*) WU CHANG (ex-*Chieh 5*)	215 216 217 219 220	740	17·5	2—3 in or 8—37 mm (single) 4/8—25 mm	1944 to 1945	4 500 at 14 knots	145
Ex-British "Castle"	1	KUANG CHOU (ex-HMS *Hever Castle*, ex-HMCS *Koppercliff*)	602	1 100	16·5	2—3·9 in 10—37 mm	1944	5 400 at 9·5 knots	120
Ex-British "Flower"	1	LIN I (ex-HMS *Heliotrope*)	213	1 020	16	2—3·9 in 4—37 mm	1941	—	—
Ex-Australian "Bathurst"	1	LOYANG (ex-HMAS *Bendigo*)	—	815	15	2—3·9 in 4—37 mm	1941	4 300 at 10 knots	100
—	1	CHANG CHIANG (ex-*Hsien Nin*)	53/219	418	16	4—37 mm (twin)	1928	—	50?

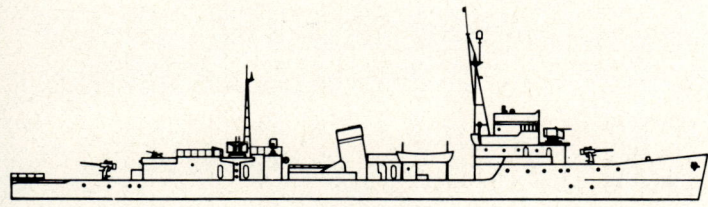

Ex "KAMISHIMA" Class

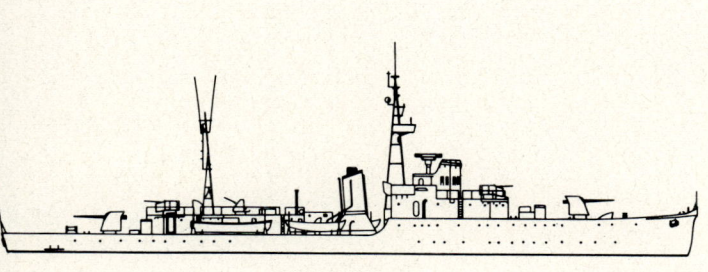

NAN CHANG

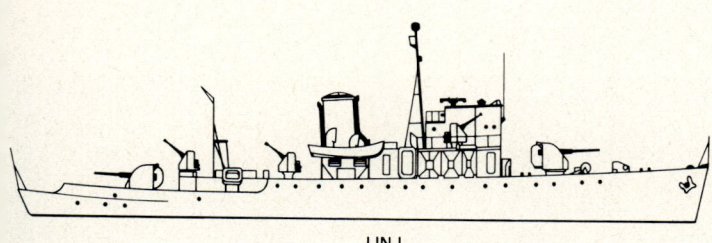

LIN I

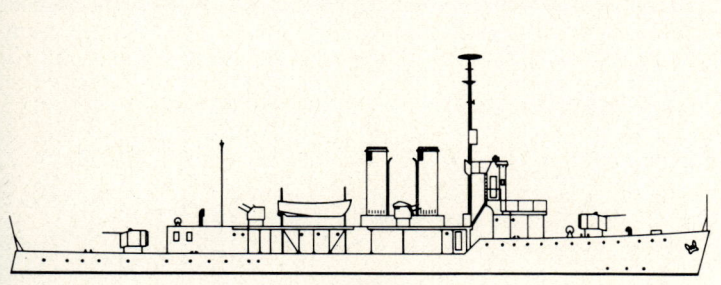

CHANG CHIANG

CHANG PI

KUANG CHOU

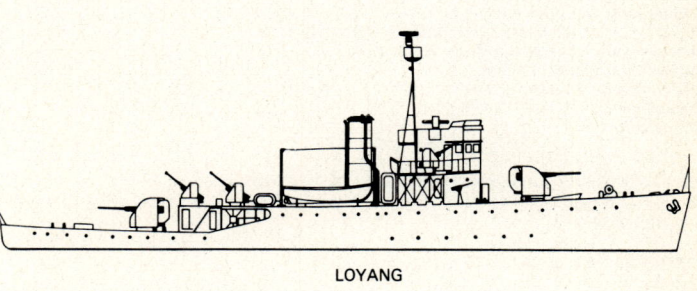

LOYANG

LIGHT FORCES

?2 "HAI DAU" CLASS

Displacement, tons: 300(?)
Dimensions, feet (metres): 155 × 23 × 6·5 *(47 × 7 × 2)*
Missiles: SSM—Six SS-N-2 type (single launchers)
Guns: 4—57 mm (twins)
Main engines: Possibly 1 gas turbine and 2 diesels; 3 shafts = ?35 knots
Complement: Possibly 40

First seen in a film sequence. Has an air intake some 15 ft high as well as radar, EW and communication aerials. If this is a new design, rather than an experimental class or film prop it is a radical departure and might have top-weight problems.

HAI DAU   1975

90 SOVIET and CHINESE "OSA" CLASS + 1 "HOLA" CLASS
(FAST ATTACK CRAFT—MISSILE)

Displacement, tons: 165 standard; 200 full load
Dimensions, feet (metres): 128·7 × 25·1 × 5·9 *(39·3 × 7·7 × 1·8)*
Missiles: SSM—Four SS-N-2 type (single launchers)
Guns: 4—25 mm (2 twin, 1 fwd and 1 aft) (30 mm in first four)
Main engines: 3 diesels; 13 000 bhp = 32 knots
Range, miles: 800 at 25 knots
Complement: 25

It was reported in January 1965 that one "Osa" class guided missile patrol boat had joined the Navy from the USSR. Four more were acquired in 1966-67, and two in 1968. A building programme of ten boats a year in China is assumed. The only boat of the "Hola" class, a Chinese variant of the "Osa", has a radome aft, (this may be a prototype for new missile guidance radar), no guns, slightly larger dimensions, and a folding mast.

Radar: Square Tie and Drum Tilt in "Osas".

"OSA" Class   1972

4 + 86 SOVIET "KOMAR" and CHINESE "HOKU" CLASS + 1 "HOMA" CLASS
(FAST ATTACK CRAFT—MISSILE)

Displacement, tons: 70 standard; 80 full load
Dimensions, feet (metres): 83·7 × 19·8 × 5 *(25·5 × 6 × 1·5)*
  (26·8 m—"Hoku"; 28·6 m—"Homa")
Missiles: SSM—Two SS-N-2 type (single launchers)
Guns: 2—25 mm (1 twin fwd) (4—25 mm (twins) in "Homa")
Main engines: Diesels; 4 shafts; 4 800 bhp = 40 knots
Range, miles: 400 at 30 knots
Complement: 11

One "Komar" class was reported as joining the fleet from the USSR in 1965. Two or three more were delivered in 1967. A building programme of ten a year is assumed of the "Hoku" class a Chinese variant of the "Komar" with a steel hull instead of wooden. The chief external difference is the siting of the launchers clear of the bridge and further inboard, eliminating sponsons and use of pole instead of lattice mast. A hydrofoil variant, the "Homa" class, has a semi-submerged foil forward.

Transfers: Four to Albania, 1976.

"KOMAR" Class   1972

20 "KRONSHTADT" CLASS (LARGE PATROL CRAFT)

Nos 251 252 253 261 262 263 264 265 266 286 + 10

Displacement, tons: 300 standard; 330 full load
Dimensions, feet (metres): 170·6 × 21·5 × 9 *(52 × 6·5 × 2·7)*
Guns: 1—3·5 in *(85 mm)*; 2—37 mm; 6—14·5 mm (triples)
A/S weapons: 2 rocket launchers; 2 DC racks
Mines: 2 rails for 8-10 mines
Main engines: 3 Diesels; 3 shafts; 3 300 shp = 24 knots
Range, miles: 1 500 at 12 knots
Complement: 65

Six built in 1950-53 were received from USSR in 1956-57. Remainder were built at Shanghai and Canton, with 12 completed in 1956. The last was completed in 1957. A number of these may now be non-operational.

Radar: Ball Gun.

"KRONSHTADT" Class firing Rocket Launchers   1972

25 "HAINAN" CLASS (FAST ATTACK CRAFT—PATROL)

Nos 267—285 +8

Displacement, tons: 360 standard, 400 full load
Dimensions, feet (metres): 197 × 24 × 6·1 *(60 × 7·40 × 2·1)*
Guns: 4—57 mm (twins); 4—25 mm (twins)
A/S weapons: 4—MBU 1 800; 2 DCT; 2 DC racks
Mines: Rails fitted
Main engines: 4 Diesels; 4 shafts; 8 000 shp
Speed, knots: 24
Range, miles: 1 000 at 10 knots (est)
Complement: 60 (est)

Chinese built version of Soviet "SO1". Low freeboard. The 25 mm guns are abaft the bridge. Programme started 1963-64 and continues—probably four per year in Shanghai.

Radar: Pot Head in most ships, Skin Head in others.
Fire control and navigation sets.

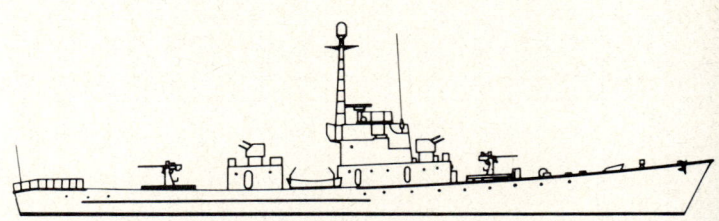

"HAINAN" Class

CHINA / Light forces 109

1 Ex-US 173 ft TYPE (LARGE PATROL CRAFT)

Displacement, tons: 280 standard; 450 full load
Dimensions, feet (metres): 173.5 × 23 × 10.8 (52.9 × 7 × 3.3)
Guns: 2—3 in (76 mm) (single); 3—37 mm (single)
A/S weapons: 2 DC racks; 1 DC rail
Main engines: 2 diesels; 2 880 bhp; 2 shafts = 20 knots
Range, miles: 3 000 at 15 knots
Complement: 70

Transferred 1947. Partially rearmed in 1950s. Used for training in South Sea Fleet.

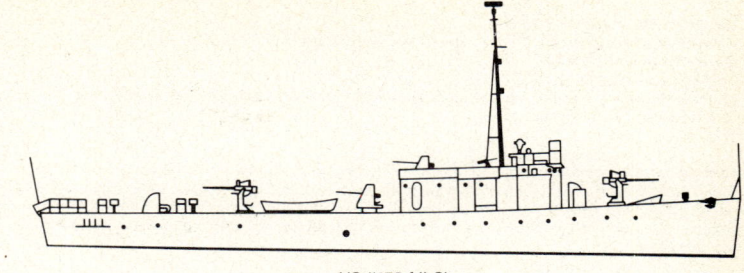

ex-US "173 ft" Class

15 "SHANGHAI" CLASS TYPE I (FAST ATTACK CRAFT—GUN)

Displacement, tons: 100 full load
Dimensions, feet (metres): 115 × 18 × 5.5 (35.1 × 5.5 × 1.7)
Guns: 2—57 mm (twin fwd)
Torpedo tubes: Twin 18 in (originally in some—now removed)
A/S armament: 8 DCs
Mines: Minerails can be fitted
Main engines: 4 diesels; 4 800 bhp = 28 knots
Complement: 25

The prototype of these boats appeared in 1959. Main difference from successors is lack of midships guns.

Radar: Skin Head.

Sonar: Hull-mounted

350 "SHANGHAI" CLASS TYPE II (FAST ATTACK CRAFT—GUN)

Displacement, tons: 120 standard; 155 full load
Dimensions, feet (metres): 128 × 18 × 5.6 (39 × 5.5 × 1.7)
Guns: 4—37 mm (twin); 4—25 mm (twin)
  Note: In some boats a twin 75 mm recoilless rifle is mounted forward
A/S weapons: 8 DCs
Mines: Minerails can be fitted but probably for no more than 10 mines
Main engines: 4 diesels; 4 800 bhp = 30 knots
Complement: 25

Construction continues at Shanghai and other yards at rate of about ten a year.

Appearance: The three versions vary slightly in the outline of their bridges.

Radar: Skin Head.

Sonar: It is reported that a hull-mounted set is fitted with VDS in some.

Transfers: 6 to Albania, 2 to Cameroon in 1976, 3 to Congo, 4 to Guinea, 15 to North Korea, 12 to Pakistan, 5 to Sri Lanka in 1972, 2 to Sierra Leone in 1973, 6 to Tanzania in 1970-71, 4 to North Viet-Nam in May 1966. + Romanian craft of indigenous Construction.

"SHANGHAI II" Class   1970

6 "HAI KOU" CLASS (FAST ATTACK CRAFT—GUN)

Displacement, tons: 160 standard; 175 full load (est)
Dimensions, feet (metres): 150 × 21 × 7 (est) (45.7 × 6.4 × 2.1)
Guns: 4—37 mm (twins); 4—25 mm (twin, vertical)
Main engines: 4 Diesels = 30 knots
Range, miles: 850 at 20 knots (est)

Believed built in 1960s on enlarged "Shanghai" hull.

"HAI KOU" Class   1976

25 "SWATOW" CLASS (FAST ATTACK CRAFT—GUN)

Displacement, tons: 80 full load
Dimensions, feet (metres): 83.5 × 19 × 6.5 (25.5 × 5.8 × 2)
Guns: 4—37 mm, in twin mountings; 2—12.7 mm (some boats mount a twin 75 mm recoilless rifle fwd)
A/S weapons: 8 DCs
Main engines: 4 diesels = 30 knots (?)
Range, miles: 500 at 28 knots; 750 at 15 knots
Complement: 17

From 1958 constructed at Dairen, Canton, and Shanghai. A steel-hulled version of Soviet "P 6". Now obsolescent and being deleted.

Transfers: 8 to North Korea, 12 to North Viet-Nam.

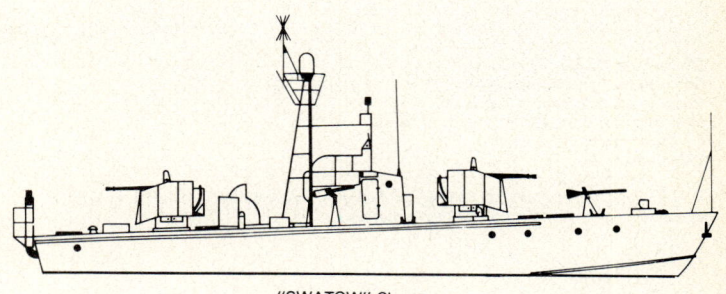

"SWATOW" Class

110 CHINA / Light forces

130 "HU CHWAN" CLASS (FAST ATTACK CRAFT—TORPEDO)

Displacement, tons: 39 full load
Dimensions, feet (metres): 71·5 × 16·6 oa × 3·3 (hullborne) *(21·8 × 5 × 1·0)*
Guns: 2—14·5 mm (twin)
Torpedo tubes: 2—21 in *(533 mm)*
Main engines: 3 M50 12-cyl diesels; 2 shafts; 3 600 hp = 50+ knots in calm conditions
Range, miles: 500 cruising

Hydrofoils designed and built by China, in the Hutang yard, Shanghai. Construction started in 1956. At least 25 hydrofoils were reported to be in the South China Fleet in 1968. Of all-metal construction with a bridge well forward and a low super-structure extending aft. Forward pair of foils can apparently be withdrawn into recesses in the hull. A continuing programme at possibly ten per year.

Radar: Skin Head.

Transfers: 32 to Albania, 4 to Pakistan, 4 to Tanzania + Romanian craft of indigenous construction.

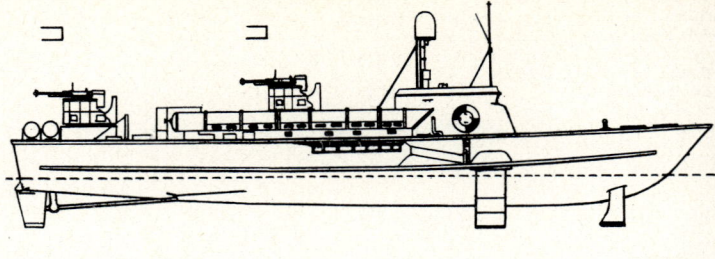
"HU CHWAN" Class S. Breyer

70 "P 6" CLASS (FAST ATTACK CRAFT—TORPEDO)

Displacement, tons: 66 standard; 75 full load
Dimensions, feet (metres): 84 × 20 × 6 *(25·7 × 6·1 × 1·8)*
Guns: 4—25 mm (twins)
Torpedo tubes: 2—21 in *(533 mm)* (or mines or 12 DCs)
Main engines: 4 M50 diesels; 4 800 bhp = 43 knots
Range, miles: 450 at 30 knots
Complement: 12

This class has wooden hulls. Some were constructed in Chinese yards largely at Shanghai. Most built prior to 1966.

Radar: Skin Head plus navigation and fire-control sets.

Transfers: 6 to North Viet-Nam in 1967.

"P 6" Class J. Meister

25 "P 4" CLASS (FAST ATTACK CRAFT—TORPEDO)

Displacement, tons: 22·5 full load
Dimensions, feet (metres): 62·7 × 11·6 × 5·6 *(19·1 × 3·5 × 1·7)*
Guns: 2—14·5 mm
Torpedo tubes: 2—18 in *(457 mm)*
Main engines: 2 M50 diesels; 2 400 bhp; 2 shafts = 40 knots

This class has aluminium hulls. Numbers decreasing.

"P 4" Class J. Meister

2 "SHANTUNG" CLASS (FAST ATTACK HYDROFOIL—GUN)

Displacement, tons: 80
Dimensions, feet (metres): 83·5 × 19·0 × 6·5 *(25·5 × 5·8 × 2·0)*
Guns: 4—37 mm (twins); 1 recoilless rifle
Speed, knots: 40

An unsuccessful hydrofoil variant of the "Swatow" class. Numbers decreasing.

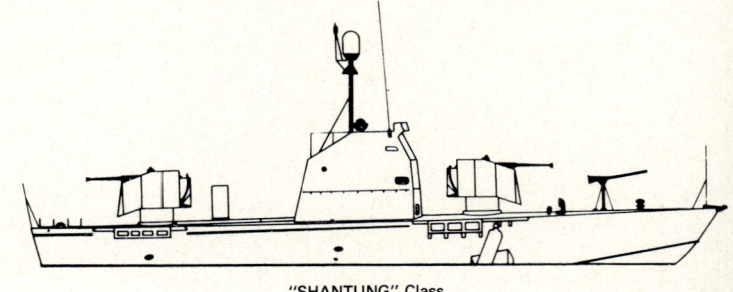
"SHANTUNG" Class

20 "WHAMPOA" CLASS (RIVER PATROL CRAFT)

Displacement, tons: 42 standard; 50 full load
Dimensions, feet (metres): 88·6 × 13 × 5 *(27·0 × 4 × 1·5)*
Guns: 4—25 mm (twins) (rearmed)
Main engines: 2 diesels; 600 hp = 14 knots
Range, miles: 400 at 9 knots
Complement: 25

Built in Canton and Shanghai 1950-55 probably for riverine duties. Underpowered with low freeboard. Now probably decreasing in numbers.

"WHAMPOA" Class 1975

CHINA / Light forces — Mine warfare forces 111

40 "YU LIN" CLASS (COASTAL PATROL CRAFT)

Displacement, tons: 10
Dimensions, feet (metres): 40 × 9·5 × 3·5 *(12·2 × 2·9 × 1·1)*
Guns: 2—14·5 mm (twin); 2—12·7 mm
Main engine: 1 diesel; 300 bhp; 1 shaft = 20-24 knots
Complement: 10

Built in Shanghai 1964-68.

Transfers: 4 to Congo (1966), 3 to Khmer, 4 to Tanzania.

"YU LIN" Class   1975

"FUKIEN" CLASS (COASTAL PATROL CRAFT)

Length, feet (metres): 65 *(20)* app.
Guns: 2—12·7 mm (single); 1 MG.

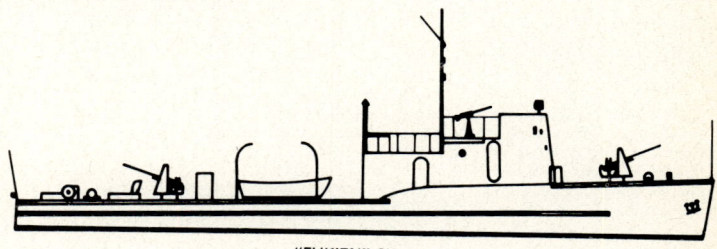
"FUKIEN" Class

"YING KOU" CLASS (COASTAL PATROL CRAFT)

Displacement, tons: 30 (est)
Dimensions, feet (metres): 70 × 12 × 3 *(21·3 × 3·7 × 0·8)*
Guns: 2—12·7 mm (single)
Main engine: 1 diesel; 300 bhp; 1 shaft = 16 knots

Built in early 1960s.

"YING KOU" Class

4 "TAI SHAN" CLASS (COASTAL PATROL CRAFT)

30 "PEI HAI" CLASS (COASTAL PATROL CRAFT)

Displacement, tons: 50 app.
Length, feet (metres): 90 *(27·5)* app.
Guns: 4—25 mm (twin)

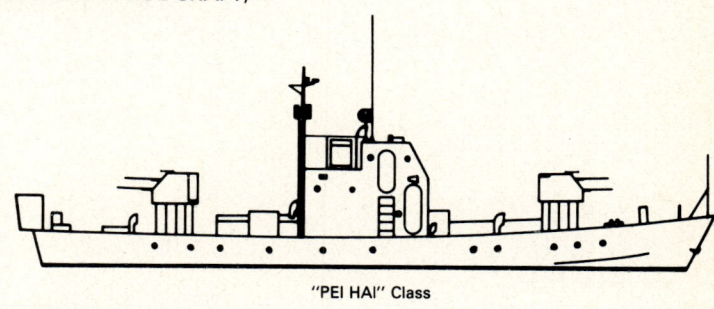
"PEI HAI" Class

MINE WARFARE FORCES

Note: (a) One ship of "Wu Sung" class (MSC) built in 1970-72. Apparently unsuccessful. Reported transferred to North Viet-Nam 1974.
(b) There are also some 60 auxiliary minesweepers of various types including trawlers.
(c) 20 MSC of "Fushun" class also reported.

17 SOVIET "T 43" CLASS (MINESWEEPERS—OCEAN)

Nos 377, 386, 396 + 14

Displacement, tons: 500 standard; 610 full load
Dimensions, feet (metres): 196·8 × 28·2 × 6·9 *(60 × 8·6 × 2·1)*
Guns: 4—37 mm (2 twins); 4—25 mm (2 twins); 4—14·5 mm (twins—in most ships)
A/S weapons: 2 DCT
Main engines: 2 diesels; 2 shafts; 2 200 bhp = 14 knots
Range, miles: 1 600 at 10 knots
Complement: 77

Four were acquired from USSR in 1954-55. Two being returned 1960. 21 more were built in Chinese shipyards, the first two in 1956. The construction of "T 43" class fleet minesweepers was stopped at Wuchang, but continued at Canton. Three converted for surveying three transferred as civilian research ships. Most of the Chinese variant are of the 60 m "Long hull" design.

Radar: Ball Gun and navigation set.

"T 43" Class   1972

AMPHIBIOUS WARFARE FORCES

13 Ex-US LSM TYPE

Ex-**HUA 201** (ex-US *LSM 112*)	Ex-**HUA 211**
Ex-**HUA 202** (ex-US *LSM 248*)	Ex-**HUA 212**
Ex-**HUA 204** (ex-US *LSM 430*)	Ex-**CHUAN SHIH SHUI**
Ex-**HUA 205** (ex-US *LSM 336*)	Ex-**HUAI HO** (ex-Chinese *Wan Fu*)
Ex-**HUA 207** (ex-US *LSM 282*)	Ex-**HUANG HO** (ex-Chinese *Mei Sheng*
Ex-**HUA 208** (ex-US *LSM 42*)	ex-US *LSM 433*)
Ex-**HUA 209** (ex-US *LSM 153*)	Ex-**YUN HO** (ex-Chinese *Wang Chung*)

Displacement, tons: 743 beaching; 1 095 full load
Dimensions, feet (metres): 196.5 wl; 203.5 oa × 34.5 × 8.8 *(59.9; 62.1 × 10.5 × 2.7)*
Guns: 4—37 mm (twins)
Main engines: 2 diesels; 2 shafts; 2 800 hp = 12 knots
Range, miles: 2 500 at 12 knots

Built in USA in 1944-45. Some were converted for minelaying and as support ships. Armament varies. Up to ten of these may be transferred temporarily to commercial operations.

15 Ex-US "511-1152" CLASS (LSTs)

CHANG PAI SHAN	Ex-**CHUNG 102**
CH'ING KANG SHAN	Ex-**CHUNG 107** (ex-US *LST 1027*)
I MENG SHAN (ex-*Chung 106,* ex-US *LST 589*)	Ex-**CHUNG 110**
TA PIEH SHAN	Ex-**CHUNG 111** (ex-US *LST 805*)
TAI HSING SHAN	Ex-**CHUNG 116** (ex-US *LST 406*)
SZU CH'ING SHAN	Ex-**CHUNG 122** (ex-*Ch'ing Ling*)
Ex-**CHUNG 100** (ex-US *LST 355*)	Ex-**CHUNG 125**
Ex-**CHUNG 101** (ex-US *LST 804*)	

Displacement, tons: 1 653 standard; 4 080 full load
Dimensions, feet (metres): 328 × 50 × 14.4 *(100 × 15.3 × 4.4)*
Guns: 2/3—76.2 mm; 6/8—40 mm
Mines: All capable of minelaying
Main engines: 2 diesels; 2 shafts; 1 700 bhp = 11 knots
Troops: 165

Two transferred to North Viet-Nam as tankers. Some other ex-US LSTs are in the merchant service. Some armed with rocket launchers.

US LST   1968, USN

15 Ex-US LSIL TYPE

MIN 301	306	312	319	
303	311	313	321	+7

Displacement, tons: 230 light; 387 full load
Dimensions, feet (metres): 159 × 23.7 × 5.7 *(48.5 × 7.2 × 1.7)*
Guns: 4—20 or 25 mm
Main engines: 2 diesels; 2 shafts; 1 320 bhp = 14 knots

Built in USA in 1943-45. Reported to be fitted with rocket launchers. Some are fitted as minesweepers. Armament varies.

2 "YU LING" CLASS (LSM)

250 ft *(76.3 m)*—1 500 ton LSM built in China since 1971. Continuing programme.

300 "YUNNAN" CLASS (LCUs)

Built in China 1968-72.

17 Ex-US or BRITISH LCU (ex-LCT) TYPE

Displacement, tons: 160 light; 320 full load
Dimensions, feet (metres): 119 × 33 × 5 *(36.3 × 10 × 1.5)*
Guns: Vary
Main engines: Diesels; 3 shafts; 475 bhp = 10 knots
Oil fuel (tons): 80

Former Tank Landing Craft later reclassified as Utility Landing Craft. There are reported to be eleven utility landing craft comprising two of the ex-British LCT (3) class and eight of the ex-US LCT (5) and LCT (6) class. Used for logistic support and carry auxiliary pennants.

About 150 Ex-BRITISH/US LCMs

SUBMARINE SUPPORT SHIP

TA CHIH

Displacement, tons: 5 to 6 000
Dimensions, feet (metres): 350 × 50 × 20 *(106.7 × 15.3 × 6.1)*
Guns: 4—37 mm (twins); 4—25 mm (twins)

Reported in 1973.

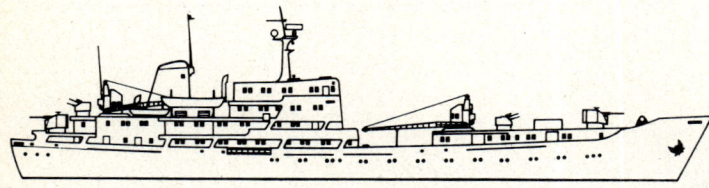

TA CHIH

REPAIR SHIP

TAKU SHAN (ex-*Hsing An,* ex-USS *Achilles,* ARL 41, ex-*LST 455*)

Displacement, tons: 1 625 light; 4 100 full load
Dimensions, feet (metres): 328 × 50 × 11 *(100 × 15.3 × 3.4)*
Guns: 12—37 mm (twins)
Main engines: Diesel-electric; 2 shafts; 1 800 bhp = 11 knots

Launched on 17 October 1942. Burned and grounded in 1949, salvaged and refitted. Reportedly operates from Shanghai.

SURVEY AND RESEARCH SHIPS

2 "SHIH JIAN" CLASS (AGOR)

SHIH JIAN   **TUNG FAN HUNG 02**

Displacement, tons: 3 750
Dimensions, feet (metres): 311.6 × 46 × 16.4 *(95 × 14 × 5)*
Guns: 8—14.5 mm (twins)
Main engines: Diesels; 2 shafts
Range, miles: 8 000
Complement: 125 approx

Completed August 1968.

Radar: Decca 707.

SHIH JIAN   1973

1 "YEN HSI" CLASS

HSIANG YANG HUNG WU

Displacement, tons: 14 000
Dimensions, feet (metres): 500 × 64 × 28·9 (152·5 × 19·5 × 8·8)
Main engines: 2 diesels; 7 250 shp = 16 knots
Range, miles: 12-15 000

Built as Polish B41 Type (*Francesco Nullo*) in 1967. Purchased by China and rebuilt 1970-72 at Kuanchou (Canton). Stationed at Canton. Possibly civilian manned. Acts as environmental research ship. Four sister ships in Chinese mercantile fleet.

HSIANG YANG HUNG WU   1976, USN

HSIANG YANG HUNG SAN +2 others, maybe more

These ships, of varying tonnage but all of an ocean-going size, operate in conjunction with the Academy of Science.

2 "HA T'SE" CLASS (AGS)

HAI SHENG 701   **HAI SHENG** 702

Displacement, tons: 400 standard
Dimensions, feet (metres): 125 × 25 × 11 (est) (38 × 7·6 × 3·4)
Guns: 4—25 mm (vertical twins)
Main engine: 1 diesel; 4 600 bhp = 12 knots (est)

Possibly built in 1960s. Certainly operational in 1971 off Paraul Islands.

1 "YEN LUN" CLASS (AGOR)

YEN LUN

Completed in 1965, possibly at Shanghai. Similar to Soviet 3 000-ton "Zubov" class.

1 Ex-JAPANESE "KAIBOKAN" CLASS (AGS)

Displacement, tons: 740
Speed, knots: 17·5

Believed built in 1945.

3 "SHU KUANG" CLASS (ex T-43) (AGOR)

SHU KUANG 1, 2 and 3   Nos 377, 386, 396

For details see under Mine Warfare Forces. Converted from Minesweepers in late 1960s. All painted white.

2-3 "YEN LAI" CLASS (AGS)

HAI T'SE 629   — 512   —

Displacement, tons: 1 100
Dimensions, feet (metres): 229·6 × 32·1 × 9·7 (70 × 9·8 × 3)
Guns: 4—37 mm (twins)
Main engine: Probably diesel; 1 shaft = 16 knots
Range, miles: 2 000 approx
Complement: 100

Probably built in Shanghai in early 1970s. Prominent square bridge and funnel amidships.

1 "KAN-CHU" CLASS (AGS)

K 420

Displacement, tons: 1 000
Dimensions, feet (metres): 213·2 × 29·5 × 9·7 (65 × 9 × 3)
Guns: 4—37 mm (twins); 4—25 mm (twins)
Main engines: Diesel; approx 5 000 shp = 20 knots
Complement: 125 (est)

Built at Changchou (Canton) 1971-73. Frigate-type bridge. Prominent raked funnel. Worked in Hong Kong area 1975.

1 Ex-BRITISH "FLOWER" CLASS (AGS)

KAI FENG (ex-*Clover*)

Displacement, tons: 1 160
Main engines: Steam reciprocating, 2 750 ihp

Built by Fleming and Ferguson in 1941. Sold commercially and acquired by China. Served as escort and reported as disarmed for survey duties in 1974-75.

1 COASTAL SURVEY CRAFT

Ex-CHUNG NING (ex-Japanese *Takebu Maru*)

Displacement, tons: 200 standard
Dimensions, feet (metres): 115 × 16 × 6 (35 × 4·9 × 1·8)
Speed, knots: 10

Former Japanese. Employed for hydrographic and general purpose duties.

1 COASTAL SURVEY CRAFT

Ex-FUTING

Displacement, tons: 160 standard
Dimensions, feet (metres): 90 × 20 × 8 (27 × 6·1 × 2·4)
Speed, knots: 11

BOOM DEFENCE VESSELS

Note: Probably now used as service vessels.

1 Ex-BRITISH "BAR" CLASS

— (Ex-Japanese No 101, ex-HMS *Barlight*)

Displacement, tons: 750 standard; 1 000 full load
Dimensions, feet (metres): 173·8 × 32·2 × 9·5 (53 × 9·8 × 2·9)
Guns: 1—3 in; 6 MG
Main engines: Triple expansion; 850 ihp = 11·75 knots
Boilers: 2 single-ended

Built by Lobnitz & Co Ltd, Renfrew. Launched on 10 September 1938. Captured by Japanese in 1941. Acquired by China in 1945.

5 Ex-US "TREE" CLASS

Displacement, tons: 560 standard; 805 full load
Dimensions, feet (metres): 163 × 30·5 × 11·8 (49·7 × 9·3 × 3·6)
Gun: 1—3 in
Main engines: Diesel-electric; 800 bhp = 13 knots

SUPPLY SHIPS

5 Ex-US ARMY FS 330 TYPE

Ex-US Army FS 146 (ex-*Clover*)
Ex-US Army FS 155 (ex-*Violet*)   +3

Displacement, tons: 1 000 standard
Dimensions, feet (metres): 175 × 32 × 10 (53·4 × 9·9 × 2)
Main engines: General Motors diesels; 1 000 bhp = 12 knots

Built in USA in 1944-45. Two are reported to be employed as support ships for fast attack craft.

2 "GALATI" CLASS (AK)

HAI YUN 318   **HAI CHIU** 600

Displacement, tons: 5 300
Dimensions, feet (metres): 328 × 47·9 × 21·6 (100 × 14 × 6·6)
Main engine: Diesel; 1 shaft = 12·5 knots
Oil fuel: 250 tons
Range, miles: 4—5 000
Complement: 50

Built at Santierial Shipyard, Calati, Romania in 1960s. Nine ships purchased of which these two were converted to AKs in early 1970s. Cargo capacity approx 3 750 tons with ten crane/booms for handling. Both reported operating in South Sea Fleet.

1 "CHAN TOU" CLASS (AK)

Displacement, tons: 4 500
Dimensions, feet (metres): 311·6 × 41 × 18 (95 × 12·5 × 5·5)
Main engine: 1 diesel; 1 shaft = 12·5 knots approx
Range, miles: 3—4 000
Complement: 50 approx

A class of 15-20 merchant ships was built in Shanghai 1959-65 of which one or maybe more transferred to the navy. Have prominent bridge and funnel aft.

1 "AN TUNG" CLASS (AF)

Chinese built.

114 CHINA / Supply ships — Tugs

2 or 3 "TAN LIN" CLASS (AK)

Displacement, tons: 1 500

There may be another 12 coastal merchant ships operating under naval control.

5 "LEI CHOU" CLASS (AOTL)

Displacement, tons: 900
Dimensions, feet (metres): 157·4 × 28·9 × 9·7 (48 × 8·8 × 3)
Main engine: Diesel; 1 shaft = 10-12 knots
Range, miles: 1 200
Complement: 25-30

Built in late 1960s probably at Ching Tao or Wutung.

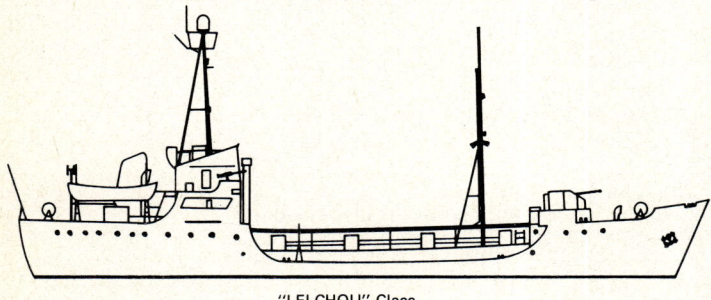

"LEI CHOU" Class

3-4 "LEI CHOU" CLASS (WTL)
Details as above.

4-5 "FU CHOU" CLASS (WTL)

FU CHOU   +3 or 4

Large water carriers of 1 100 tons. Details under same class in Tankers section.

TANKERS

14 + "FU CHOU" CLASS

Displacement, tons: 1 100
Dimensions, feet (metres): 164 × 29·5 × 11·5 (50 × 9 × 3·5)
Main engine: 1 diesel; 1 shaft = 12 knots
Range, miles: 1 500
Complement: 30-35

Reported as built in Shanghai 1964-70. Some may carry twin 25 mm or 37 mm mounts. Cargo capacity 650-700 tons. Prominent bridge and funnel aft.

2 Ex-US "MATTAWEE" CLASS (AOG)

Originally petrol tankers.

1 Ex-JAPANESE "TM" CLASS (AO)

HAI YU 401

Displacement, tons: 4 500
Dimensions, feet (metres): 308·3 × 44·3 × 19 (94 × 13·5 × 5·8)
Main engines: Turbo-electric; 1 shaft = 11 knots
Fuel: 250 tons
Range, miles: 3 750 at 7·5 knots
Complement: 35 (est)

Cargo capacity 3 750 tons FFO. Bridge and funnel aft. An emergency Japanese class handed to USSR in 1945 and to China in Shanghai 1945. Modernisation in 1960s changed appearance somewhat.

ICEBREAKERS

2 "HAI PING" CLASS

101   102

Displacement, tons: 3 000
Dimensions, feet (metres): 275 × 50 × 16 (83·8 × 15·3 × 4·9)
Guns: 8—37 mm (twins)
Main engine: 3 000 hp; 1 shaft = 15 knots

Built in 1969-73 at Shanghai. Employed as icebreaking tugs in Po Hai Gulf for port clearance.

REPAIR SHIPS

1 Ex-US ARL TYPE

TAKU SHAN

1 "GALATI" CLASS

Converted AK.

SERVICE CRAFT

There are also reported to be 125 armed motor junks, 100 armed motor launches and 150 service craft and miscellaneous boats.

TUGS

16 "GROMOVOY" CLASS (ARS)

Chinese built.

3 "TING HAI" CLASS (ARS)

4 "YEN TENG" CLASS (ARS)

1 Ex-SOVIET "ROSLAVL" CLASS (ARS)
3 CHINESE "ROSLAVL" CLASS (ARS)

Displacement, tons: 670 full load
Dimensions, feet (metres): 145 × 31 × 11·4 (44·2 × 9·5 × 3·5)
Main engine: Diesel; 1 shaft; 1 500 shp = 12 knots
Fuel: 100 tons
Range, miles: 6 000 at 11 knots
Complement: 28

First ship transferred by USSR late 1950s. Remainder built in China in mid-1960s.

2 Ex-US 149' ATA

2 Ex-US 143' ATA

5 Ex-US ARMY 75' YTL

3 FT-14 CLASS (ARS)

COLOMBIA

Ministerial

Minister of National Defence:
  General Abraham Varon Valencia

Headquarters Appointments

Fleet Commander:
  Admiral Jaime Barrera Larrarte
Chief of Naval Operations:
  Vice-Admiral Alfonso Diaz Osorio
Chief of Naval Staff:
  Rear-Admiral Héctor Calderón Salazar

Diplomatic Representative

Naval Attaché in Washington:
  Captain Rafael Grau Arano

Personnel

(a) 1979: 700 officers and 6 500 men and 1 500 marines
(b) 2 years national service

Destroyers

1973 Antioquia ("Fletcher" class) (paid off 20 Dec)
1977 Caldes ("Allen M. Sumner" class)

Frigates

1972 Almirante Brion (ex-US APD type)
1973 Almirante Padilla (ex-US APD type)
1977 Almirante Tono (ex-US APD type)

Bases

Cartagena. Main naval base (floating dock, 1 slipway) synchrolift, schools.
Buenaventura. Small Pacific base.

Maritime Air Force

The Colombian Air Force with 50 helicopters and a number of attack/reconnaissance aircraft provides any support required by the navy.

Naval Infantry

Corpo de Infanteria de Marina is one battalion based at Cartagena, Buenaventura and Barranquilla.

Prefix to Ships' Names

ARC (Armada Republica de Colombia)

DELETIONS

Light Forces

1974 Gen. Rafael Reyes, Alberto Restrepo, Independiente, Palace, Tormentosa, Triunfante, Valerosa, Voladora

Survey Ship

1974 Bocas de Ceniza

Strength of the Fleet

Type	Active	Building
Patrol Submarines	2 + 4 (70 tons)	—
Destroyers	3	—
Frigates	2	—
Patrol Ships	3	—
Coastal Patrol Craft	10	—
Customs Craft	9	—
Gunboats	4	—
Survey Vessels	3	—
Tanker	1	—
Transports	4	—
Repair Ship	1	—
Training Ship	1	—
Tugs	12	—
Floating Docks	3	—
Floating Workshop	1	—
Repair Craft	1	—

Customs Service

AN numbered Patrol Craft belong to this force which carries out certain Coast Guard duties and also operates some aircraft.

Mercantile Marine

Lloyd's Register of Shipping:
  61 vessels of 271 953 tons gross

Transport

1974 Bell Salter, Rafael Martinez

Tankers

1974 Covenas, Mamonal, Sancho Jimeno

Tugs

1975 Bahia Honda (grounded 13 Feb and scrapped)
1977 Abadia Mendez

SUBMARINES

2 TYPE 209 PATROL SUBMARINES

Name	No.	Builders	Commissioned
PIJAO	SS 28	Howaldtswerke, Kiel	17 Apr 1975
TAYRONA	SS 29	Howaldtswerke, Kiel	18 July 1975

Displacement, tons: 1 180 surfaced; 1 285 dived
Length, feet (metres): 183·4 (55·9)
Beam, feet (metres): 20·5 (6·25)
Draught, feet (metres): 17·9 (5·4)
Torpedo tubes: 8—21 in bow with reloads
Main machinery: Diesel-electric; 4 MTU diesel-generators; 1 shaft; 5 000 hp
Speed, knots: 22 dived

Ordered in 1971.

PIJAO　　　　　　　　　　　　　　　　　　1975, Dhr. J. van der Woude

4 TYPE SX-506 SUBMARINES

Name	No.	Builders	Commissioned
INTREPIDO	SS 20	Cosmos Livorno	1972
INDOMABLE	SS 21	Cosmos Livorno	1972
RONCADOR	SS 23	Cosmos Livorno	1974
QUITA SUENO	SS 24	Cosmos Livorno	1974

Displacement, tons: 58 surfaced; 70 dived
Dimensions, feet (metres): 75·4 × 6·6 × 13·2 (23 × 2 × 4)
Main machinery: Diesel-electric; 300 bhp
Speed, knots: 8 surfaced; 6 dived; 7 snorting
Range, miles: 1 200 at 7 knots
Complement: 5

Delivered in sections for assembly in Cartagena. Can carry eight attack swimmers with 2 tons of explosives, as well as two swimmer-delivery-vehicles (SDVs). Diving depth 330 ft (100 m). It has been reported that SS23 and 24 have been taken out of service.

116 COLOMBIA / Destroyers — Frigates

DESTROYERS

2 MODIFIED "HALLAND" CLASS

Name	No.	Builders	Laid down	Launched	Commissioned
VEINTE DE JULIO	D 05	Kockums Mek Verkstads A/B, Malmo	Oct 1955	26 June 1956	15 June 1958
SIETE DE AGOSTO	D 06	Götaverken, Göteborg	Nov 1955	19 June 1956	31 Oct 1958

Displacement, tons: 2 650 standard; 3 300 full load
Length, feet (metres): 380·5 *(116·0)* pp; 397·2 *(121·1)* oa
Beam, feet (metres): 40·7 *(12·4)*
Draught, feet (metres): 15·4 *(4·7)*
Guns: 6—4·7 in *(120 mm)* (3 twin turrets); 4—40 mm (single)
Torpedo tubes: 4—21 in *(533 mm)*
A/S weapons: 1 Bofors 375 mm A/S rocket launcher
Main engines: De Laval double reduction geared turbines; 2 shafts; 55 000 shp
Boilers: 2 Penhöet-Motala-Verkstad; 568 psi; 840°F
Speed, knots: 25 (16 economical); 32 *(Siete de Agosto)*
Oil fuel, tons: 524
Range, miles: 445 at full power
Complement: 248 (21 officers, 227 men)

Ordered in 1954. The hull and machinery are similar to the Swedish class but they have different armament (six 4·7 in instead of four, no 57 mm guns, four 40 mm guns instead of six, and four torpedo tubes instead of eight) and different accommodation arrangements. They have an anti-submarine rocket projector, more radar and communication equipment, and air-conditioned living spaces, having been designed for the tropics. It is reported that *Veinte de Julio* is in reserve.

Engineering: Although the designed speed was 35 knots, it is officially stated that the maximum sustained speed does not exceed 25 knots.

Radar: Search: HSA LW-03/SGR 114.
Tactical: HSA DA-02/SGR 105.
Fire control: I band, probably HSA M20 series (6 sets).

Refit: *Siete de Agosto* returned to Colombia in 1975 after a lengthy refit in USA during which her engines were extensively overhauled.

VEINTE DE JULIO   1975, Dhr. J. van der Woude

SIETE DE AGOSTO   1975, Dhr. J. van der Woude

1 Ex-US "ALLEN M. SUMNER (FRAM II)" CLASS

Name	No.	Builders	Laid down	Launched	Commissioned
SANTANDER (ex-USS *Waldron*, DD 699)	D 03	Federal S.B. Co	16 Nov 1943	26 Mar 1944	8 June 1944

Displacement, tons: 2 200 standard; 3 320 full load
Length, feet (metres): 376 *(114·6)*
Beam, feet (metres): 40·9 *(12·5)*
Draught, feet (metres): 19 *(5·8)*
Guns: 6—5 in *(127 mm)*/38 (twins)
A/S weapons: 2 fixed Hedgehogs; 2 triple torpedo tubes (Mk 32); Facilities for small helicopter
Main engines: 2 geared turbines; 2 shafts; 60 000 shp
Boilers: 4 Babcock & Wilcox
Speed, knots: 30
Range, miles: 2 400 at 25 knots; 4 600 at 15 knots
Complement: 274

Santander was modernised under the Fram II programme and transferred by sale on 30 October 1973.

Fire control: Mk 37 director with Mk 25 radar.

Radar: Search: SPS 10 and 40.

Sonar: SQS 30. VDS removed before transfer.

SANTANDER   1975, Dhr. J. van der Woude

FRIGATES

Note: The expected transfer of four "Joao Coutinho" class frigates from Portugal (reported in 1978-79 edition) did not take place.

1 Ex-US "CROSLEY" CLASS

Name	No.	Builders	Commissioned
CORDOBA (ex-USS *Ruchamkin* LPR 89, ex-*APD 89*, ex-*DE 228*)	DT 15	Philadelphia Navy Yard	June 1945

Displacement, tons: 1 400 standard; 2 130 full load
Dimensions, feet (metres): 306 × 37 × 15·4 *(93·3 × 11·3 × 4·7)*
Guns: 1—5 in *(127 mm)*/38 (single Mk 30); 4—40 mm/50
A/S weapons: 6 Mk 32 torpedo tubes (triple); 1 DC rack
Main engines: GEC turbines with electric drive; 2 shafts; 12 000 shp = 23 knots
Boilers: 2 "D" Express
Range, miles: 5 500 at 15 knots
Complement: 204 (plus accommodation for 162 troops)

Cordoba was laid down on 14 February 1944, launched on 15 June 1944 and transferred on 24 November 1969. Purchased 31 March 1978. Modernised to Fram II standards.

CORDOBA   197

COLOMBIA / Frigates — Light forces 117

1 Ex-US "COURTNEY" CLASS

Name	No.	Builders	Commissioned
BOYACA (ex-USS *Hartley* DE 1029)	DE 16	New York S.B. Corporation	26 Jan 1957

Displacement, tons: 1 450 standard; 1 914 full load
Dimensions, feet (metres): 314·5 × 36·8 × 13·6 *(95·9 × 11·2 × 4·1)*
Guns: 2—3 in *(76 mm)*/50 (twin Mk 33)
A/S weapons: 6 Mk 32 torpedo tubes (triple); 1 DC rack
Main engines: 1 De Laval geared turbine; 20 000 shp; 1 shaft
Boilers: 2 Foster-Wheeler
Speed, knots: 25
Range, miles: 4 500 at 15 knots
Complement: 161 (11 officers, 150 men)

Transferred 8 July 1972, by sale. Helicopter platform in X position.

Radar: SPS 6 and 10.

Sonar: SQS 23.

BOYACA   1974

PATROL SHIPS

3 Ex-US "CHEROKEE" CLASS

Name	No.	Builders	Commissioned
— (ex-USS *Carib*, ATF 82)	—	Charleston S.B. and D.D. Co	24 July 1943
— (ex-USS *Hidatsa*, ATF 102)	—	Charleston S.B. and D.D. Co	25 Apr 1944
— (ex-USS *Jicarilla*, ATF 104)	—	Charleston S.B. and D.D. Co	26 June 1944

Displacement, tons: 1 235 standard; 1 640 full load
Dimensions, feet (metres): 205 × 38·5 × 15·5 *(62·5 × 11·7 × 4·7)*
Gun: 1—3 in *(76 mm)*/50 (single Mk 22)
Main engines: Diesel-electric; 1 shaft; 3 000 bhp = 15 knots
Complement: 75

Built as fleet tugs. Launched 7 February 1943, 29 December 1943 and 25 February 1944 respectively. All three placed in reserve in USA July 1963. Transferred in 1978 for duties as patrol ships.

LIGHT FORCES

Note: The transfer of two "Asheville" class PGs from the USA (reported in 1978-79 edition) did not take place.

3 "ARAUCA" CLASS GUNBOATS

Name	No.	Builders	Commissioned
RIOHACHE	CF 35	Union Industrial de Barranquilla	1956
LETICIA	CF 36	Union Industrial de Barranquilla	1956
ARAUCA	CF 37	Union Industrial de Barranquilla	1956

Displacement, tons: 184 full load
Dimensions, feet (metres): 163·5 × 23·5 × 2·8 *(49·9 × 7·2 × 0·9)*
Guns: 2—3 in *(76 mm)*/50; 4—20 mm
Main engines: 2 Caterpillar diesels; 916 bhp = 14 knots
Range, miles: 1 890 at 14 knots
Complement: 43 (*Leticia* 39 and 6 orderlies)

Launched in 1955. *Leticia* has been equipped as a hospital ship with six beds—reported as disarmed.

RIOHACHE   1966, Colombian Navy

1 "BARRANQUILLA" CLASS GUNBOAT

Name	No.	Builders	Commissioned
CARTAGENA	CF 33	Yarrow & Co Ltd, Scotstoun	1930

Displacement, tons: 142
Dimensions, feet (metres): 137·8 × 23·5 × 2·8 *(42 × 7·2 × 0·9)*
Guns: 2—3 in *(76 mm)*; 1—20 mm; 4 MG
Main engines: 2 Gardner semi-diesels; 2 shafts working in tunnels; 600 hp = 15·5 knots
Oil fuel (tons): 24
Complement: 39

Launched on 22 March 1930.

CARTAGENA   1971, Colombian Navy

1 COASTAL PATROL CRAFT

Name	No.	Builders	Commissioned
ESPARTANA	GC 100	Ast. Naval, Cartagena	1950

Displacement, tons: 50
Dimensions, feet (metres): 96 × 13·5 × 4 *(29·3 × 4·1 × 1·2)*
Gun: 1—20 mm
Main engines: 2 diesels; 300 bhp = 13·5 knots

1 COASTAL PATROL CRAFT

Name	No.	Builders	Commissioned
CAPITAN R. D. BINNEY	GC 101	Ast. Naval, Cartagena	1947

Displacement, tons: 23
Dimensions, feet (metres): 67 × 10·7 × 3·5 *(20·4 × 3·3 × 1·1)*
Main engines: Diesels; 115 bhp = 13 knots

Buoy and lighthouse inspection boat. Named after first head of Colombian Naval Academy, Lt-Commander Ralph Douglas Binney, RN.

1 COASTAL PATROL CRAFT

CALIBIO LR 127

5 COASTAL PATROL CRAFT

Name	No.	Builders	Commissioned
JUAN LUCIO	LR 122	Ast. Naval, Cartagena	1953
ALFONSO VARGAS	LR 123	Ast. Naval, Cartagena	1952
FRITZ HAGALE	LR 124	Ast. Naval, Cartagena	1952
HUMBERTO CORTES	LR 126	Ast. Naval, Cartagena	1953
CARLOS GALINDO	LR 128	Ast. Naval, Cartagena	1954

Displacement, tons: 33
Dimensions, feet (metres): 76 × 12 × 2·8 *(23·2 × 3·7 × 0·8)*
Guns: 1—20 mm; 4 Mortars
Main engines: 2 General Motors diesels; 280 bhp = 13 knots
Complement: 10

Designed for operations on rivers. Named after naval officers.

2 COASTAL PATROL CRAFT

Name	No.	Builders	Commissioned
DILIGENTE	LR 138	Ast. Naval, Cartagena	1952
VENGADORA	LR 139	Ast. Naval, Cartagena	1954

Originally a class of eight.

CUSTOMS SERVICE

Name	No.	Builders	Commissioned
RODRIGUEZ	AN 1	—	—

40 ft CGB.

Name	No.	Builders	Commissioned
OLAYA HERRERA	AN 203	Ast. Magdalena Barranquilla	1960

Displacement, tons: 40
Dimensions, feet (metres): 68·8 pp × 12·8 × 3·5 (21 × 3·9 × 1·1)
Gun: 1—0·50 mm Browning
Main engines: 2 Merbens diesels; 570 bhp = 20 knots

Name	No.	Builders	Commissioned
PEDRO GUAL	AN 204	Schurenstedt KG Barden Fleth	1964
ESTEBAN JARAMILLO	AN 205	Schurenstedt KG Barden Fleth	1964
CARLOS E. RESTREPO	AN 206	Schurenstedt KG Barden Fleth	1964

Displacement, tons: 85
Dimensions, feet (metres): 107·8 pp × 18 × 6 (32·9 × 5·5 × 1·8)
Gun: 1—20 mm
Main engines: 2 Maybach (MTU) diesels; 2 450 bhp = 26 knots

Name	No.	Builders	Commissioned
JORGE SOTO DEL CORVAL	AN 207	Finland	1971
CARLOS ALBAN	AN 208	Finland	1971
NITO RESTREPO	AN 209	Finland	1971

Displacement, tons: 100
Dimensions, feet (metres): 108 × 18 × 6 (33 × 5·5 × 1·8)
Guns: 2—20 mm
Main engines: 2 (MTU) diesels; 2 450 bhp = 17 knots

Near sisters to Finnish "Ruissalo" class.

Name	No.	Builders	Commissioned
GENERAL VASQUES COBO	AN 202	Lürssen	1955

Displacement, tons: 146
Dimensions, feet (metres): 124·7 × 23 × 5 (38 × 7 × 1·5)
Gun: 1—40 mm
Main engines: 2 Maybach (MTU) diesels; 2 500 bhp = 18 knots
Complement: 20

Launched on 27 September 1955.

PEDRO GUAL — 1965, Colombian Navy

CARLOS ALBAN — 1971, Colombian Navy

AMPHIBIOUS SHIP
1 Ex-US '511-1152 SERIES" (LST)

Name	No.	Builders	Commissioned
—(ex-USS Duval County, LST 758)	—	—	19 Aug 1944

Displacement, tons: 1 653 standard; 4 080 full load
Dimensions, feet (metres): 328 × 50 × 14 (100 × 15·2 × 4·3)
Guns: 6—40 mm
Main engines: 2 General Motors diesels; 2 shafts; 1 700 bhp = 11·6 knots
Complement: 119
Troops: 147

Transferred 1977. She was the last World War II LST serving in the US Navy.

SURVEY VESSELS

Name	No.	Builders	Commissioned
SAN ANDRES (ex-USS Rockville, PCER 851)	BO 151	Pullman Standard Car Co, Chicago	15 May 1944

Displacement, tons: 674 standard; 968 full load
Dimensions, feet (metres): 184·5 × 33·6 × 7·0 (56·2 × 10·2 × 2·1)
Main engines: 2 diesels; 2 shafts; 1 800 bhp = 15 knots
Complement: 50

Former US patrol rescue escort vessel converted for surveying duties. Laid down on 18 October 1943, launched on 22 February 1944. Acquired on 5 June 1969.

Name	No.	Builders	Commissioned
QUINDIO (ex-US YFR 443)	RM 153	Niagara S.B. Corporation	11 Nov 1943

Displacement, tons: 380 light; 600 full load
Dimensions, feet (metres): 131 × 29·8 × 9 (40 × 9·1 × 2·7)
Main engines: 2 diesels; 300 hp = 10 knots
Complement: 17

Transferred by lease July 1964 and by sale 31 March 1978.

Name	No.	Builders	Commissioned
GORGONA	FB 161	Lidingoverken, Sweden	1955

Displacement, tons: 574
Dimensions, feet (metres): 135 × 29·5 × 9·3 (41·2 × 9 × 2·8)
Main engines: 2 Nohab diesels; 910 bhp = 13 knots
Complement: 45

Formerly classified as a tender.

TANKER
1 Ex-US "PATAPSCO" CLASS (AOG)

Name	No.	Builders	Commissioned
TUMACO (ex-USS Chewaucan, AOG 50)	BT 67	Cargill Inc, Savage, Minn.	19 Feb 1945

Displacement, tons: 1 850 light; 4 570
Dimensions, feet (metres): 310·8 × 48·5 × 16 (94·8 × 14·8 × 4·9)
Guns: 2—3 in (76 mm)
Main engines: Diesel-electric; 2 shafts; 3 840 bhp = 15 knots
Range, miles: 4 740 at 15 knots; 8 350 at 11·5 knots
Complement: 95

Transferred 1 July 1975 by sale.

TUMACO (As USS Chewaucan) — 1970, A. and J. Pavia

COLOMBIA / Repair ship — COMORO ISLANDS 119

REPAIR SHIP

1 Ex-US "ARISTAEUS" CLASS

Name	No.	Builders	Commissioned
— (ex-USS *Midas*, ARB 5)	—	Chicago Bridge and Iron Co	23 May 1944

Displacement, tons: 1 625 standard; 3 455 full load
Dimensions, feet (metres): 328 × 50 × 11 *(100 × 15·2 × 4·3)*
Guns: 8—40 mm
Main engines: Diesels; 1 800 bhp; 2 shafts = 11·6 knots
Complement: 190

Converted from LST hull. Transferred 1978.

"ARISTAEUS" Class

TRANSPORTS

Name	No.	Builders	Commissioned
CIUDAD DE QUIBDO (ex-*Shamrock*)	TM 43	Gebr Sander Deltzijl	1953 (see note)

Displacement, tons: 633
Dimensions, feet (metres): 165 × 23·5 × 9 *(50·3 × 7·2 × 2·7)*
Main engines: 1 MAN diesel; 1 shaft; 390 bhp = 11 knots
Oil fuel, tons: 32
Complement: 12

Ex-Dutch coaster *Shamrock* sold to Colombia by commercial firm in March 1953.

Name	No.	Builders	Commissioned
MARIO SERPA	TF 51	Ast. Naval, Cartagena	1954
HERNANDO GUTIERREZ	TF 52	Ast. Naval, Cartagena	1955
SOCORRO (ex-*Alberto Gomez*)	BD 33	Ast. Naval, Cartagena	1956

Displacement, tons: 70
Dimensions, feet (metres): 82 × 18 × 2·8 *(25 × 5·5 × 0·9)*
Main engines: 2 General Motors diesels; 260 bhp = 9 knots
Oil fuel, tons: 4
Range, miles: 650 at 9 knots
Complement: 12 (berths for 48 troops and medical staff)

River transports. Named after Army officers. *Socorro* was converted in July 1967 into a floating surgery. *Hernando Gutierrez* and *Mario Serpa* were converted into dispensary ships in 1970.

FLOATING DOCK

MAYOR ARIAS

Displacement, tons: 700
Capacity, tons: 165
Length, feet (metres): 140 *(42·7)*

Note: It is reported that the 6 700 ton *Rodriguez Zamora* (ex-ARD 28), the small floating dock *Manuel Lara*, the floating workshop *Mantilla* (ex-YR 66) and the repair craft *Victor Cubillos* (ex USS YFND 6) purchased 31 March 1978, are probably under civil contract.

Also listed:- *Sabogal*

TUGS

PEDRO DE HEREDIA (ex-USS *Choctaw*, ATF 70) RM 72

Displacement, tons: 1 235 standard; 1 764 full load
Dimensions, feet (metres): 205 × 38·5 × 15·5 *(62·5 × 11·7 × 4·7)*
Main engines: 4 diesels; electric drive; 3 000 bhp = 15 knots
Complement: 75

Former United States ocean tug of the "Cherokee" class. Launched on 18 October 1942 and commissioned 21 April 1943.
Transferred 1961 and by sale 31 March 1978.

BAHIA UTRIA (ex-USS *Kalmia* ATA 184) RM 75

Displacement, tons: 534 standard; 858 full load
Dimensions, feet (metres): 143·0 × 33·9 × 8·0 *(43·6 × 10·3 × 2·4)*
Gun: 1—3 in
Main engines: 2 General Motors diesel-electric; 1 shaft; 1 500 bhp = 13 knots
Complement: 45

Launched 29 August 1944 and commissioned 6 November 1944. Transferred from the US Navy on 1 July 1971 on lease and by purchase 31 March 1978.

ANDAGOYA RM 71

Measurement, tons: 117 gross
Dimensions, feet (metres): 92·6 × 20 × 10 *(28·2 × 6·1 × 3·05)*
Main engines: Caterpillar diesel; 400 bhp = 10 knots

Launched in 1928. Re-engined in 1955.

CAPITAN CASTRO RR 81
CANDIDO LEGUIZAMO RR 82
CAPITAN ALVARO RUIZ RR 84
CAPITAN RIGOBERTO GIRALDO RR 86
CAPITAN VLADIMIR VALEK RR 87
TENIENTE LUIS BERNAL RR 88
JOVES FIALLO RR 90

Displacement, tons: 50
Dimensions, feet (metres): 63 × 14 × 2·5 *(19·2 × 4·3 × 0·8)*
Main engines: 2 General Motors diesels; 260 bhp = 9 knots

TENIENTE SORZANO RM 73

Displacement, tons: 54
Dimensions, feet (metres): 65·7 oa × 17·5 × 9 *(20 × 5·3 × 2·7)*
Main engines: 6-cyl diesel; 240 bhp

Former US tug.

TENIENTE MIGUEL SILVA RR 89

Dimensions, feet (metres): 73·3 × 17·5 × 3 *(22·4 × 5·3 × 0·9)*
Main engines: 2 diesels; 260 hp = 9 knots

River tug built by Union Industrial (UNIMAL), Barranquilla

TRAINING SHIP

Name	No.	Builders	Commissioned
GLORIA	—	Bilbao	1968

Displacement, tons: 1 300
Dimensions, feet (metres): 212 × 34·8 × 21·7 *(64·7 × 10·6 × 6·6)*
Main engines: Auxiliary diesel; 500 bhp = 10·5 knots
Sail training ship. Barque rigged. Hull is entirely welded.
Sail area: 1 675 sq yards *(1 400 sq metres)*.

GLORIA 7/1976, USN

COMORO ISLANDS

Three of the four islands of this group joined in a unilateral declaration of independence in July 1975. The only port of any pretensions is Moroni.

Mercantile Marine

Lloyd's Register of Shipping:
3 vessels of 765 tons gross

Ex-LCT 9061 (ex-HMS *Buttress*, 4099)

Displacement, tons: 657 standard; 1 000 full load
Dimensions, feet (metres): 231·2 × 39 × 5·9 *(70·5 × 11·9 × 1·8)*
Guns: 2—20 mm; 1—120 mm mortar
Main engines: 4 Paxman diesels; 2 shafts; 1 840 bhp = 9 knots
Complement: 29

1 Ex-BRITISH LCT(8)

Bought by France in July 1965. Transferred 1976. Built in the UK in 1945.

CONGO

The People's Republic of Congo, which became independent on 15 August 1960, formed a naval service, but the patrol vessel *Reine N' Galifourou* (ex-French P 754) which was transferred 16 November 1962 was returned to France on 18 February 1965 and then re-transferred to Senegal as *Siné Saloum*.

Ministerial

Minister of Defence:
   Major Marien N'gouabi

Personnel

(a) 1979: 200 officers and men
(b) Voluntary service

Base

Pointe-Noire.

Mercantile Marine

Lloyd's Register of Shipping:
   16 vessels of 6 942 tons gross

3 Ex-CHINESE "SHANGHAI" CLASS

Displacement, tons: 120 standard; 155 full load
Dimensions, feet (metres): 128 × 18 × 5·6 *(39 × 5·5 × 1·7)*
Guns: 4—37 mm (twins); 4—25 mm (twins)
A/S armament: 8 DCs (may be removed)
Mines: Mine rails can be fitted for up to 10 mines
Main engines: 4 diesels; 4 800 hp = 30 knots
Complement: 25

Probably transferred in 1974.

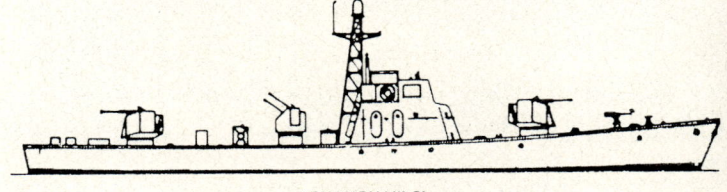

"SHANGHAI" Class

4 "YU LIN" CLASS (RIVER PATROL CRAFT)

Reported as about 10 tons, transferred by China.

MISCELLANEOUS

It is reported that up to 12 small craft with outboard motors are employed on river patrol.

COSTA RICA

Personnel

(a) 1979: 50 officers and men
(b) Voluntary service

Ports

Limon, Golfito, Puntarenas, Puerto Simon

Mercantile Marine

Lloyd's Register of Shipping:
   19 vessels of 10 462 tons gross

3 COASTAL PATROL CRAFT

401   402   403

Displacement, tons: 10
Dimensions, feet (metres): 41 × 10 × 2·3 *(12·5 × 3·1 × 0·7)*
Gun: 1 MG

Built in mid-1950s. Of US Coast Guard 40 ft type.

An armed tug is also reported.

CUBA

Ministerial

Minister of the Revolutionary Armed Forces:
   Raul Castro Ruz

Senior Appointment

Commander-in-Chief:
   Commodore Aldo Santamaria

Personnel

(a) 1979: 6 000 (380 officers, 220 petty officers and 5 400 men)
(b) 3 years national service

Standard of Efficiency

Cuba has the highest estimated annual defence expenditure in Central America and the Caribbean at about £120 million, a fair proportion of this being on Soviet aid. The navy is the smallest of the three services but, with an adequate budget and Soviet assistance in training, must be assessed as having a reasonable level of tactical and material efficiency.

Naval Establishments

Naval Academy:
   At Mariel, for officers and cadets

Naval School:
   At Morro Castle, for petty officers and men

Naval Bases:
   Cabanas, Cienfuegos, Havana, Mariel, Varadero plus at least four more in preparation.

Maritime Airforce

A helicopter force of 25 Mi-4 (Hound) and 30 Mi-1 (Hare) from USSR is in existence although these are probably all operated by the Air Force.

Strength of the Fleet

	Active	Building or (Reserve)
Frigates	—	(1)
Large Patrol Craft	18	—
Fast Attack Craft (Missile)	27	—
Fast Attack Craft (Torpedo)	24	—
Fast Attack Craft (Patrol)	5	—
Coastal Patrol Craft	12	—
Minesweepers	2	—
LCMs	7	—
Survey Vessels	12	—
Miscellaneous	8	—
Frontier Guard	14	—

Mercantile Marine

Lloyd's Register of Shipping:
   331 vessels of 779 187 tons gross

DELETIONS

Cruiser (so called)

1972 *Cuba* (built 1911—of 2 000 tons)

Frigates

1975 *Antonio Maceo, Jose Marti* (ex-US PF Type) sunk as targets.

Corvettes

1973 *Sibony* (ex-US PCER)
1976 *Caribe* (ex-US PCER)

Light Forces

1973 *Donotivo, Matanzas*
1976 *Habana, Las Villas, Oriente, Pinar del Rio, Leoncio, Prado, GC 32, GC 33, GC 34, GC 11, GC 13, GC 14, R 41, R 42*

Tug

1976 *Diez de Octubre*

FRIGATES

One of the three ex-US frigates of the PF type—believed to be *Maximo Gomez*—which was completed in 1944 and acquired in 1947 is still in existence as harbour hulk but has no operational value.

LIGHT FORCES
12 Ex-SOVIET "SO I" CLASS (LARGE PATROL CRAFT)

Displacement, tons: 170 standard; 215 full load
Dimensions, feet (metres): 137·8 × 19·7 × 5·9 (42 × 6 × 1·8)
Guns: 4—25 mm (2 twin)
A/S weapons: Four 5-barrelled rocket launchers; DC rails
Main engines: 3 diesels; 7 500 bhp = 28 knots
Range, miles: 1 100 at 13 knots
Complement: 31

Six were transferred from the USSR by September 1964, and six more in 1967.

"SO I" Class 1970, USN

6 Ex-SOVIET "KRONSHTADT" CLASS (LARGE PATROL CRAFT)

Displacement, tons: 310 standard; 380 full load
Dimensions, feet (metres): 170·6 × 21·3 × 7 (52·0 × 6·5 × 2·1)
Guns: 1—3·5 in; 2—37 mm; 6—12·7 mm (twins)
A/S weapons: 2 MBU 1800A; 2 DCT; 2 DC racks
Mines: 6 on two racks at the stern
Main engines: 3 diesels; 3 shafts; 3 300 hp = 24 knots
Range, miles: 1 500 at 12 knots
Complement: 40

Transferred from the USSR in 1962. Two reported as probably paid off.

Radar: Surface: Ball End.
Navigation: Don.
IFF: High Pole A, Dead Duck.

Soviet "KRONSHTADT" Class

6 Ex-SOVIET "OSA I" AND 3 "OSA II" CLASS
(FAST ATTACK CRAFT—MISSILE)

Displacement, tons: 160 standard; 210 full load
Dimensions, feet (metres): 128·7 × 26·6 × 5·9 (39·3 × 8·1 × 1·8)
Missiles: 4 SSM SS-N-2 (singles)
Guns: 4—30 mm (2 twin, 1 fwd, 1 aft)
Main engines: 3 M503 (Osa I) M504 (Osa II) diesels; 13 000 bhp (Osa I), 15 000 (Osa II) = 36 knots
Range, miles: 800 at 25 knots
Complement: 30

Two boats of this class were transferred to Cuba from the USSR in January 1972 and three in 1973. These were followed by one "Osa I" and one "Osa II" in mid 1976, one "Osa II" in December 1976 and one "Osa II" in mid-1978. With the obvious rundown of the ex-US Navy ships in the Cuban Navy and the determination of the Cuban Government to maintain an independent Naval presence in the Caribbean, these could be the forerunners of further reinforcements. With the "Komar" class units there are now 27 hulls mounting 72 of the proven and effective Styx missiles in a highly sensitive area.

Radar: Surveillance; Square Tie.
Fire control: Drum Tilt.
IFF: Square Head, High Pole A (I), High Pole B (II)

"OSA I" Class

18 Ex-SOVIET "KOMAR" CLASS (FAST ATTACK CRAFT—MISSILE)

Displacement, tons: 68 standard; 75 full load
Dimensions, feet (metres): 87·9 × 21·1 × 5·0 (26·8 × 6·4 × 1·5)
Missiles: 2 SSM SS-N-2 (singles)
Guns: 2—25 mm
Main engines: 4 M50 diesels; 4 shafts; 4 800 bhp = 40 knots
Range, miles: 400 at 30 knots
Complement: 19

First twelve transferred in 1962. Last pair arrived in December 1966.

Radar: Surveillance: Square Tie
IF: Dead Duck, High Pole A

"KOMAR" Class 1970, USN

122 CUBA / Light forces — Amphibious forces

12 Ex-SOVIET "P 6" CLASS (FAST ATTACK CRAFT—TORPEDO)

Nos. 81-92

Displacement, tons: 64 standard; 73 full load
Dimensions, feet (metres): 83·4 × 20 × 6 *(25·4 × 6·1 × 1·9)*
Guns: 4—25 mm (2 twin)
Torpedo tubes: 2—21 in *(533 mm)* (two single)
Main engines: 4 M50 diesels; 4 shafts; 4 800 hp = 41 knots
Range, miles: 450 at 30 knots
Complement: 20

Transferred in 1962. Can carry mines or depth charges in place of torpedo tubes.

Radar: Skin Head.

"P 6" Class 1970, USN

12 Ex-SOVIET "P 4" CLASS (FAST ATTACK CRAFT—TORPEDO)

Displacement, tons: 22 standard; 25 full load
Dimensions, feet (metres): 62·7 × 11·6 × 3·3 *(19·1 × 3·5 × 1·0)*
Guns: 2—25 mm
Torpedo tubes: 2—18 in
Main engines: 2 M50 diesels; 2 400 bhp; 2 shafts = 50 knots
Complement: 12

Transferred from the USSR in 1962-64.

Radar: Skin Head

"P 4" Class 1971

12 Ex-SOVIET "ZHUK" CLASS (FAST ATTACK CRAFT—PATROL)

Displacement, tons: 60 full load
Dimensions, feet (metres): 85·3 × 16 × 5 *(26 × 4·9 × 1·5)*
Guns: 4—14·5 mm (twins)
Main engines: 2 M50 diesels; 2 shafts; 2 400 hp = 34 knots
Complement: 18?

Transferred 1975-76.

"ZHUK" Class

6 COASTAL PATROL CRAFT

| SV 7 | SV 8 | SV 9 | SV 10 | SV 12 | SV 14 |

Length, feet (metres): 40 *(12·2)*
Gun: 1—50 cal MG
Main engines: 2 General Motors diesels = 25 knots

Later boats of the SV type equipped with radar. Completed 1958.

6 COASTAL PATROL CRAFT

| SV 1 | SV 2 | SV 3 | SV 4 | SV 5 | SV 6 |

Displacement, tons: 6·15
Dimensions, feet (metres): 32 × 10 × 2·8 *(9·8 × 3·1 × 0·8)*
Main engines: 2 Chrysler Crown, 230 bhp = 18 knots

Auxiliary patrol boats for port patrol, launched in 1953.

MINE WARFARE FORCES

2 Ex-SOVIET "YEVGENYA" CLASS (MSI)

Displacement, tons: 70 standard; 80 full load
Dimensions, feet (metres): 85·6 × 19·0 × 3·9 *(26·1 × 5·8 × 1·2)*
Main engine: One M50 diesel; 1 200 hp = 16 knots
Complement: 12

Transferred mid-1978 with more reported to follow.

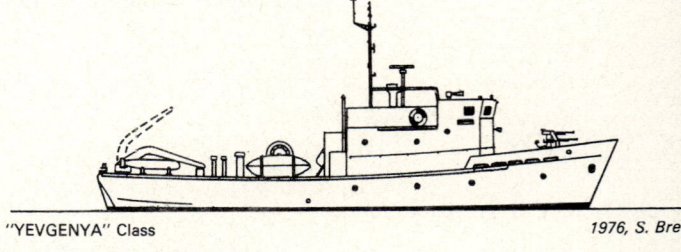

"YEVGENYA" Class 1976, S. Breye

AMPHIBIOUS FORCES

7 "T 4" CLASS LCMs

Displacement, tons: 94
Main engines: 2 diesels; 2 shafts; 400 hp = 9 knots

Obtained 1967-74. Mainly employed as Harbour Craft.

CUBA / Survey vessels — CZECHOSLOVAKIA

H 101

Measurement, tons: 530

An ex-fishing trawler/buoy tender also used for cadet training.

5 MOTOR LAUNCHES

No details available but all used for surveying.

2 LIGHTHOUSE TENDERS

ENRIQUE COLLAZO (ex-*Joaquin Godoy*)

Displacement, tons: 815
Dimensions, feet (metres): 211 × 24 × 9 *(64.3 × 7.3 × 2.7)*
Main engines: Triple expansion; 2 shafts; 672 ihp = 8 knots

Built at Paisley, Scotland. Launched in 1906. Acquired in 1950 from Cuban Mercantile Marine.

BERTHA SF 10

Displacement, tons: 98
Dimensions, feet (metres): 104 × 19 × 11 *(31.7 × 5.8 × 3.4)*
Main engines: 2 Gray Marine diesels; 450 bhp = 10 knots

Launched in 1944.

1 Ex-SOVIET "OKHTENSKY" CLASS (OCEAN TUG)

CARIBE

Displacement, tons: 835 standard; 992 full load
Dimensions, feet (metres): 155.1 × 32.8 × 13.4 *(47.3 × 10.0 × 4.1)*
Guns: 1—3 in *(76 mm)*; 2—20 mm.
Main engines: 2 BM diesels; 2 electric motors; 2 shafts; 2 000 bhp = 13 knots
Oil fuel, tons: 187
Complement: 34

Transferred in 1976 to replace *Diez de Octubre*. Name taken from deleted corvette.

GRANMA A 11

Yacht which reached Cuba on 2 December 1956 with Dr Fidel Castro and the men who began the liberation war. Historic vessel incorporated into the Navy as an Auxiliary.

SURVEY VESSELS

6 Ex-SOVIET "NYRYAT 1" CLASS

| H 91 | H 92 | H 93 | H 94 | H 95 | H 96 |

Displacement, tons: 125
Dimensions, feet (metres): 95.1 × 16.4 × 5.6 *(29 × 5 × 1.7)*
Main engines: Diesel = 12 knots
Range, miles: 1 600 at 10 knots
Complement: 15

MISCELLANEOUS

3 HARBOUR AUXILIARIES

| A1 | A2 | A3 |

Displacement, tons: 58
Dimensions, feet (metres): 74 × 15 × 5 *(22.6 × 4.6 × 1.5)*
Gun: 1 MG
Main engines: 2 Gray Marine diesels; 2 shafts; 225 hp

Built in USA 1949.

FRONTIER GUARD

A number of small craft operate under the direction of the Ministry of the Interior. Pennant numbers painted in red.

| GF 101 | GF 102 | GF 107 |

Similar to US Coast Guard 70 ft craft.

| GF 528 | GF 720 | GF 725 | GF 825 |

Similar to US Coast Guard 40 ft craft.

GUANABACOA

Of 22 knots, built in Cadiz.

CAMILO CIENFUEGOS	CUARTEL MONCADA
ESCAMBRAY	FINLAY
MACEO	MARTI

Six fast craft built in Spain 1971-72.

CYPRUS

General

For a considerable period six ex-Soviet "P 4" class and two ex-German "R" boats served in Cypriot waters. However the majority were sunk during the Turkish operations of July 1974 and one was stranded and lost. There is therefore no craft to be listed this year.

Mercantile Marine

Lloyd's Register of Shipping:
 793 vessels of 2 599 529 tons gross

New Construction

Two Fast Attack Craft (Missile) ordered from Chantiers Navals de l'Esterel were not taken up and were transferred to Greece as *Kelefstis Stamou* and *Diopos Antonio*.

CZECHOSLOVAKIA

Although a navy as such does not exist there is a river patrol force, the personnel of which wear naval-type uniforms. About 1 200 strong with some 20 river patrol craft.

Mercantile Marine

Lloyd's Register of Shipping:
 15 vessels of 150 770 tons gross

DENMARK

Ministerial

Minister of Defence:
P. Søgaard

Headquarters Appointment

Commander-in-Chief:
Vice-Admiral S. Thostrup
Flag Officer Denmark:
Rear-Admiral F. C. Heisterberg-Andersen

Diplomatic Representation

Defence Attaché, Bonn
Colonel H. A. Bjørnsholt
Defence Attaché, London:
Colonel H. H. Prince Georg of Denmark, KCVO
Assistant Defence Attaché, London:
Commander B. O. Sørensen
Defence Attaché, Washington:
Captain H. Nielsen (N)

Personnel
(a) 1979: 1 345 officers, 3 345 regular ratings,
1380 Nat Service ratings.
2 490 civilians.
Reserves: 13 640
Naval Home Guard: 5 000.
(b) 9 months national service

Navy Estimates

1973-74: 583 600 000 Kr.
1974-75: 638 500 000 Kr.
1975-76: 729 900 000 Kr.
1976-77: 846 300 000 Kr.
1977-78: 775 700 000 Kr (Apr 1976 level).

Naval Bases

Copenhagen, Korsør, Frederikshavn, Århus (NHQ)
Grønnedal (Greenland)
Thorshavn (Faeroes)

Naval Air Arm

7 Lynx helicopters (ordered 1978)
8 Alouette III helicopters
Air Force; LRMP aircraft

Prefix to Ships' Names

HDMS

Coast Defence

There are forts at Steves and Langeland (on Southern approaches to Sound and Great Belt) armed with 150 mm and 40 mm guns. Six radar stations and a number of coast watching stations in the area.

Command and Control

It was originally the intention to have all government vessels under The Directorate of Waters (Farvandsdirektoratet). However the Ministry of Trade and Shipping now run the icebreakers and some training ships (the icebreakers are maintained by the navy and are based at Frederikshavn in the summer) while the Ministry of the Environment (Miljøministeriet) control two new Pollution Control Ships (with another under construction) based at Copenhagen and Korsør (both manned and maintained by the navy). Survey ships are run by the Kongelike Søkortarkiv (Chart Archives) under the Directorate of Waters and the Ministry of Fisheries have four rescue vessels and a new "Osprey" class.

Strength of the Fleet

Type	Active	Building or (Projected)
Submarines (Patrol)	6	—
Frigates	7	3
Corvettes	2	—
Fast Attack Craft (Missile)	10	—
Fast Attack Craft (Torpedo)	6	—
Large Patrol Craft	22	(1)
Coastal Patrol Craft	8	—
Minelayers	7	—
Minesweepers (Coastal)	8	—
Tankers (Small)	2	—
Icebreakers	3	1
Royal Yacht	1	—
Naval Home Guard	33	—
Survey Ship and craft (see Icebreakers)	7	—

Appearance

All ships are light grey with the exception of Fast Attack Craft, "Daphne" class and tankers which are olive green, the Royal Yacht which has a white hull and yellow superstructure and the icebreakers which have black hulls and yellow superstructure.

Mercantile Marine

Lloyd's Register of Shipping:
1 397 vessels of 5 530 408 tons gross

DELETIONS

Corvettes

1974 *Diana* ("Triton" class)
1978 *Flora* ("Triton" class)

Fast Attack Craft

1974 6 "Flyvefisken" Class (scrapped May 1976)
1977 4 "Falken" Class (in reserve)

Large Patrol Craft

1972 *Alholm*
1978 *Havmanden, Tejsten*

Coastal Patrol Craft

1975 Y 354, Y 359, *Ertholm, Lindholm*
1976 *Faeno*

Mine Warfare Forces

1974 2 "Lougen" Class Minelayers
4 "Vig" Class Inshore Minesweepers

Tenders

1973 *Hjaelperen* (sold for scrap October 1976)
1974 *Henrik Gerner* (sold for scrap in July 1976)

Icebreakers

1972 *Lillebjørn*
1975 *Storebjørn*

PENNANT LIST

Submarines

S 320	Narhvalen
S 321	Nordkaperen
S 326	Delfinen
S 327	Spaekhuggeren
S 328	Tumleren
S 329	Springeren

Frigates and Corvettes

F 340	Beskytteren
F 344	Bellona
F 347	Triton
F 348	Hvidbjørnen
F 349	Vaedderen
F 350	Ingolf
F 351	Fylla
F 352	Peder Skram
F 353	Herluf Trolle
F 354	Niels Juel
F 355	Olfert Fischer
F 356	Peter Tordenskjold

Light Forces

P 510	Søløven
P 511	Søridderen
P 512	Søbjørnen
P 513	Søhesten
P 514	Søhunden
P 515	Søulven
P 530	Daphne
P 531	Dryaden
P 533	Havfruen
P 534	Najaden
P 535	Nymfen
P 536	Neptun
P 537	Ran
P 538	Rota
P 540	Bille
P 541	Bredal
P 542	Hammer
P 543	Huitfeldt
P 544	Krieger
P 545	Norby
P 546	Rodsteen
P 547	Sehested
P 548	Suenson
P 549	Willemoes
Y 300	Barsø
Y 301	Drejø
Y 302	Romsø
Y 303	Samsø
Y 304	Thurø
Y 305	Vejrø
Y 306	Farø
Y 307	Laesø
Y 308	Rømø
Y 384	Maagen
Y 385	Mallemukken
Y 386	Agdleq
Y 387	Agpa
Y 388	Tulugaq
Y 389	—

Mine Warfare Forces

N 42	Langeland
N 43	Lindormen
N 44	Lossen
N 80	Falster
N 81	Fyen
N 82	Møen
N 83	Sjaelland
M 571	Aarøsund
M 572	Alssund
M 573	Egernsund
M 574	Grønsund
M 575	Guldborgsund
M 576	Omøsund
M 577	Ulvsund
M 578	Vilsund

Auxiliaries

A 540	Dannebrog
A 568	Rimfaxe
A 569	Skinfaxe

Naval Home Guard

MHV 1	
MHV 51	
MHV 54	
MHV 55	
MHV 57	
MHV 60	
MHV 62	
MHV 63	
MHV 65	
MHV 67	
MHV 68	
MHV 70	
MHV 71	
MHV 72	
MHV 74	
MHV 75	
MHV 81	Askø
MHV 82	Enø
MHV 83	Manø
MHV 84	Baagø
MHV 85	Hjortø
MHV 86	Lyø
MHV 90	
MHV 91	
MHV 92	
MHV 93	
MHV 94	
MHV 95	

"PEDER SKRAM" Class

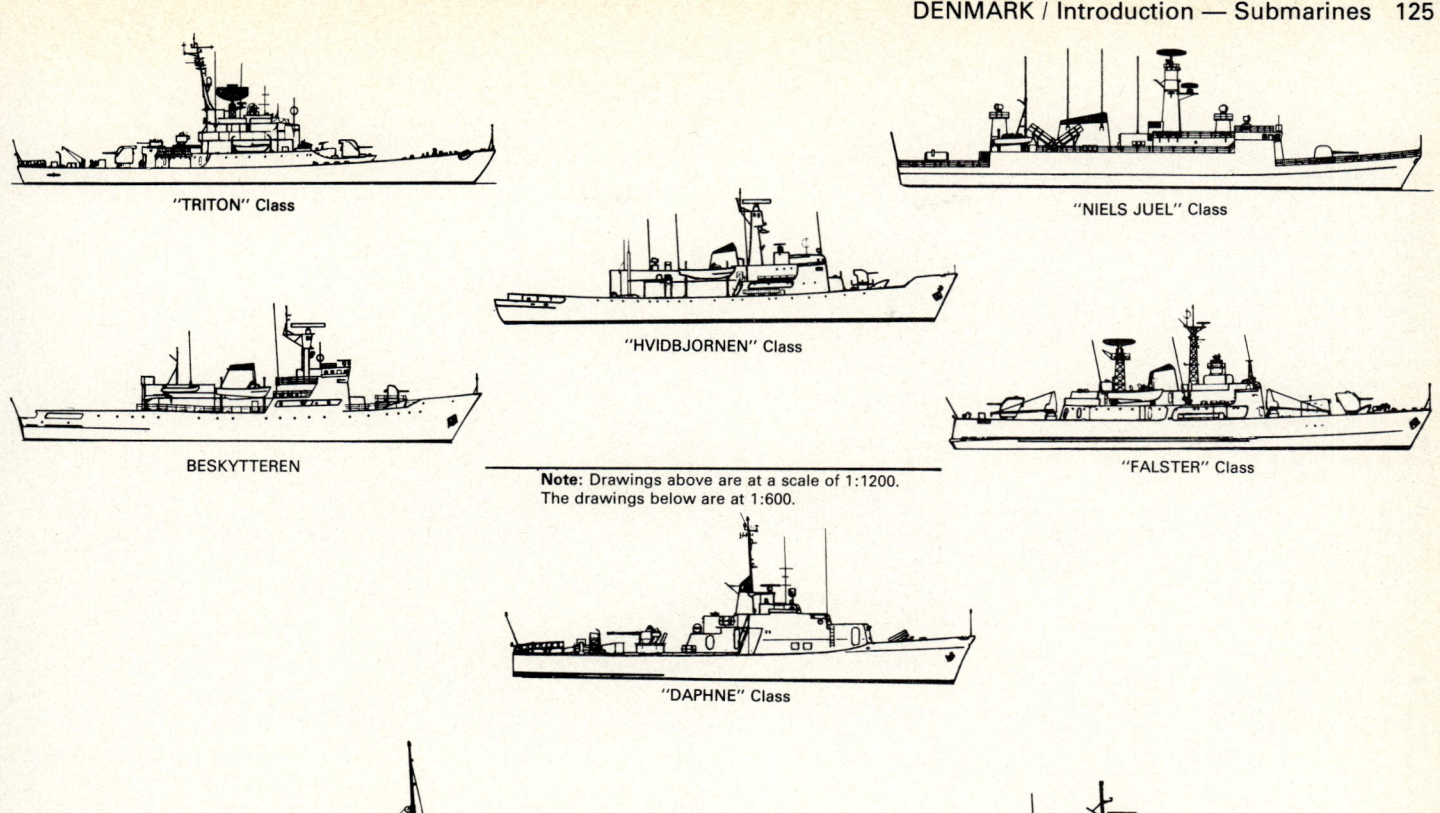

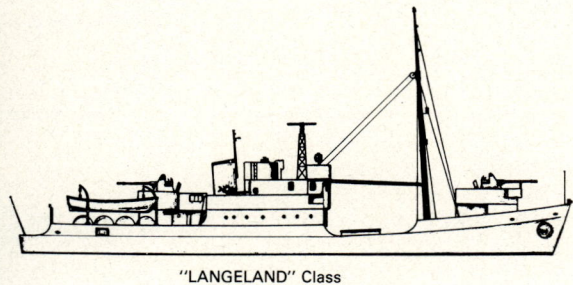

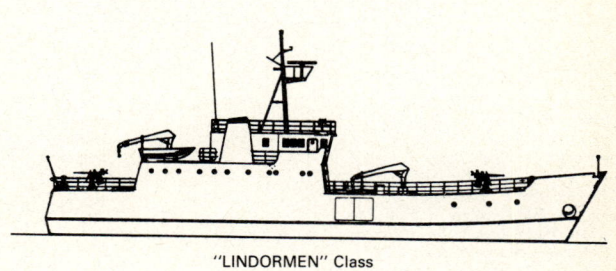

Note: Drawings above are at a scale of 1:1200. The drawings below are at 1:600.

SUBMARINES

Note: Denmark is planning to build six new submarines. It is likely that these will eventually be of the same design as the German/Norwegian Type 210 of about 750 tons.

2 "NARHVALEN" CLASS

Name	No.	Builders	Laid down	Launched	Commissioned
NARHVALEN	S 320	Royal Dockyard, Copenhagen	16 Feb 1965	10 Sep 1968	27 Feb 1970
NORDKAPEREN	S 321	Royal Dockyard, Copenhagen	20 Jan 1966	18 Dec 1969	22 Dec 1970

Displacement, tons: 370 surfaced; 450 dived
Length, feet (metres): 144·4 (44·0)
Beam, feet (metres): 15 (4·6)
Draught, feet (metres): 12·5 (3·8)
Torpedo tubes: 8—21 in (533 mm) bow
Main machinery: 2 MB diesels; 1 500 bhp surfaced; 2 electric motors; 1 500 bhp dived
Speed, knots: 12 surfaced; 17 dived
Complement: 22

These coastal submarines are similar to the German Improved Type 205 and were built under licence at the Royal Dockyard, Copenhagen with modifications for Danish needs. Active and passive sonar.

NORDKAPEREN   1978, Royal Danish Navy

4 "DELFINEN" CLASS

Name	No.	Builders	Laid down	Launched	Commissioned
DELFINEN	S 326	Royal Dockyard, Copenhagen	1 July 1954	4 May 1956	16 Sep 1958
SPAEKHUGGEREN	S 327	Royal Dockyard, Copenhagen	1 Dec 1954	20 Feb 1957	27 June 1959
TUMLEREN	S 328	Royal Dockyard, Copenhagen	22 May 1956	22 May 1958	15 Jan 1960
SPRINGEREN	S 329	Royal Dockyard, Copenhagen	3 Jan 1961	26 Apr 1963	22 Oct 1964

Displacement, tons: 550 standard; 595 surfaced; 643 dived
Length, feet (metres): 177·2 (54·0)
Beam, feet (metres): 15·4 (4·7)
Draught, feet (metres): 13·1 (4·0)
Torpedo tubes: 4—21 in (533 mm)
Main machinery: 2 Burmeister & Wain diesels; 1 200 bhp surfaced; electric motors; 1 200 hp dived
Speed, knots: 15 surfaced and dived
Range, miles: 4 000 at 8 knots
Complement: 33

Active and passive sonar. Now reaching the end of their hull lives.

TUMLEREN   1975, Royal Danish Navy

126 DENMARK / Frigates

FRIGATES

2 "PEDER SKRAM" CLASS

Name	No.	Builders	Laid down	Launched	Commissioned
PEDER SKRAM	F 352	Helsingörs J. & M.	25 Sep 1964	20 May 1965	30 June 1966
HERLUF TROLLE	F 353	Helsingörs J. & M.	18 Dec 1964	8 Sep 1965	16 Apr 1967

Displacement, tons: 2 030 standard; 2 720 full load
Length, feet (metres): 354·3 *(108)* pp; 396·5 *(112·6)* oa
Beam, feet (metres): 39·5 *(12)*
Draught, feet (metres): 11·8 *(3·6)*
Missiles: 8 SSM Harpoon (two 4-cell launchers); Est. 16 SAM Sea Sparrow (one 4-cell launcher)
Guns: 2—5 in *(127 mm)*/38 (twin Mk 38); 4—40 mm/60
Torpedo tubes: 4—21 in for wire-guided and A/S torpedoes
A/S weapons: DCs
Main engines: CODOG:—2 General Motors 16-567 D diesels; 4 800 hp; 2 Pratt & Whitney PWA GG 4A-3 gas turbines; 44 000 hp total output; 2 shafts
Speed, knots: 30, 18 economical
Complement: 180

Danish design. In addition to other armament they were originally designed for three 21 in torpedo tubes and the Terne anti-submarine weapon. But the latter has been dropped in favour of Sea Sparrow and two twin 21 in mountings fitted on the beams.

Conversion: Mid-life conversion in 1977-78. *Peder Skram Herluf Trolle* 1976-77.

Radar: Combined warning: Two CWS 3.
Fire control: Three CGS 1.
Tactical: One NWS 1.
Navigation: One NWS 2.

Sonar: PMS 26.

HERLUF TROLLE   10/1978, J. L. M. van der Burg

3 "NIELS JUEL" CLASS

Name	No.	Builders	Laid down	Launched	Commissioned
NIELS JUEL	F 354	Aalborg Vaerft	20 Oct 1976	27 Sep 1978	June 1980
OLFERT FISCHER	F 355	Aalborg Vaerft	1977	—	?1980
PETER TORDENSKJOLD	F 356	Aalborg Vaerft	1977	—	1981

Displacement, tons: 1 320 full load
Length, feet (metres): 275 oa *(84)*
Beam, feet (metres): 32·8 *(10)*
Draught, feet (metres): 13·2 *(4)*
Missiles: 8 SSM Harpoon (two 4-cell launchers); 8 SAM Sea Sparrow (8-cell launcher)
Gun: 1—76 mm/62 (Compact)
A/S weapons: 6—Mk 32 Torpedo tubes (triple)
Mines: Have laying capability
Rocket Projectors: 2 for illumination, Chaff and HE rockets
Main engines: CODOG General-Electric LM 2 500 gas turbine; 26 600 shp; 2 MTU 20 V—956 diesels; 4 800 hp at 1 500 revs, 6 000 for short periods; SSS clutches; GEC gearbox; 2 shafts.
Speed, knots: 28
Complement: 90

First of a class which is planned eventually to reach a total of six. Designed to replace "Triton" class and, possibly, "Peder Skram" class.
YARD Glasgow designed the class to Danish order. Three Danish shipyards were asked to tender in early 1975 (Helsingør, Lindø and Aalborg). On 5 December 1975 announced that first three would be built by Aalborg Vaerft. Delivery date for trials of *Niels Juel*—September 1978; *Olfert Fischer*—Spring 1980; *Peter Tordenskjold*—Spring 1981.
Programme for *Niels Juel* announced March 1978—installation of armament, December 1978—June 1979; full trials, July 1979—November 1979; Completion, December 1979—June 1980.

Radar: Plessey AWS 5.

NIELS JUEL   1978, Royal Danish Navy

1 MODIFIED "HVIDBJØRNEN" CLASS

Name	No.	Builders	Laid down	Launched	Commissioned
BESKYTTEREN	F 340	Aalborg Vaerft	15 Dec 1974	27 May 1975	27 Feb 1976

Displacement, tons: 1 970 full load
Length, feet (metres): 244 *(74·4)* oa
Beam, feet (metres): 39·4 *(12)*
Draught, feet (metres): 15·4 *(5)*
Aircraft: 1 Alouette III helicopter
Gun: 1—3 in *(76 mm)*
Main engines: 3 B and W Alpha diesels; 7 440 bhp; 1 shaft
Speed, knots: 18
Range, miles: 4 500 at 16 knots on 2 engines; 6 000 at 13 knots on 1 engine
Complement: 59

Cost approximately £5 million. Strengthened for navigation in ice. Designed for similar duties as *Hvidbjørnen*.

Radar: Search: One AWS 1/CWS 2.
Tactical: One NWS 1.
Navigation: One NWS 2.

Sonar: PMS 26.

BESKYTTEREN   7/1977, Leo van Ginderen

DENMARK / Frigates — Light forces 127

4 "HVIDBJØRNEN" CLASS

Name	No.	Builders	Laid down	Launched	Commissioned
HVIDBJØRNEN	F 348	Aarhus Flydedok	4 June 1961	23 Nov 1961	15 Dec 1962
VAEDDEREN	F 349	Aalborg Vaerft	30 Oct 1961	6 Apr 1962	19 Mar 1963
INGOLF	F 350	Svendborg Vaerft	5 Dec 1961	27 July 1962	27 July 1963
FYLLA	F 351	Aalborg Vaerft	27 June 1962	18 Dec 1962	10 July 1963

Displacement, tons: 1 345 standard; 1 650 full load
Length, feet (metres): 219·8 *(67·0)* pp; 238·2 *(72·6)* oa
Beam, feet (metres): 38·0 *(11·6)*
Draught, feet (metres): 16 *(4·9)*
Aircraft: 1 Alouette III helicopter
Gun: 1—3 in *(76 mm)*
A/S weapons: DCs
Main engines: 4 General Motors 16—567C diesels; 6 400 bhp; 1 shaft
Speed, knots: 18
Range, miles: 6 000 at 13 knots
Complement: 73

Ordered in 1960-61. Of frigate type for fishery protection and surveying duties in the North Sea, Faroe Islands and Greenland waters. They are equipped with a helicopter platform aft.

Radar: Search: One AWS 1/CWS 2.
Tactical: One NWS 1.

Sonar: PMS 26.

Surveying: *Hvidbjørnen* can act as a survey ship with a complement of ten officers and 75 ratings.

HVIDBJØRNEN 1978, Royal Danish Navy

CORVETTES

2 "TRITON" CLASS

Name	No.	Builders	Laid down	Launched	Commissioned
BELLONA	F 344	Naval Meccanica, Castellammare	1954	9 Jan 1955	31 Jan 1957
TRITON	F 347	Cantiere Navali di Taranto	1953	12 Sep 1954	10 Aug 1955

Displacement, tons: 760 standard; 873 full load
Length, feet (metres): 242·8 *(74·0)* pp; 250·3 *(76·3)* oa
Beam, feet (metres): 31·5 *(9·6)*
Draught, feet (metres): 9 *(2·7)*
Guns: 2—3 in *(76 mm)*; 1—40 mm
A/S: 2 Hedgehogs; 4 DCT
Main engines: 2 Ansaldo Fiat 409T diesels, 4 400 bhp; 2 shafts
Speed, knots: 20
Range, miles: 3 000 at 18 knots
Complement: 110

These were built in Italy for the Danish Navy under the US "offshore" account. Sisters of the Italian "Albatros" class. Originally class of four. *Triton* in reserve.

Classification: Officially classified as corvettes in 1954, but have "F" pennant numbers.

Radar: Search: Plessey AWS 1.
Navigation: E Band.

Sonar: QCU-2.

TRITON 2/1978 J. L. M. van der Burg

LIGHT FORCES

10 "WILLEMOES" CLASS (FAST ATTACK CRAFT—MISSILE)

Name	No.	Builders	Commissioned
BILLE	P 540	Frederikshavn V and F	Oct 1976
BREDAL	P 541	Frederikshavn V and F	21 Jan 1977
HAMMER	P 542	Frederikshavn V and F	1 Apr 1977
HUITFELD	P 543	Frederikshavn V and F	15 June 1977
KRIEGER	P 544	Frederikshavn V and F	22 Sep 1977
NORBY	P 545	Frederikshavn V and F	22 Nov 1977
RODSTEEN	P 546	Frederikshavn V and F	16 Feb 1978
SEHESTED	P 547	Frederikshavn V and F	Mar 1978
SUENSON	P 548	Frederikshavn V and F	June 1978
WILLEMOES	P 549	Frederikshavn V and F	June 1976 (trials)

Displacement, tons: 260 full load
Dimensions, feet (metres): 151 × 24 × 8 *(46 × 7·4 × 2·4)*
Missiles: 8 Harpoon (in place of after torpedo tubes) (see *Armament* note)
Gun: 1—76 mm/62 (Compact)
Torpedo tubes: 2 or 4—21 in (see notes)
Main engines: CODOG 3 Rolls-Royce Proteus gas turbines; 12 750 bhp; 3 General Motors V 71 diesels for cruising on wing shafts; 800 bhp; cp propellers.
Speed, knots: 38 (12 on diesels).
Complement: 25 (6 officers, 19 ratings).

Designed by Lürssen to Danish order. Very similar to Swedish "Spica II" class (also Lürssen). Original order to Frederikshavn for four boats, increased to eight and finally ten.
Building dates: *Willemoes* (prototype) laid down 20 July 1974, launched 5 October 1974 and completed for trials (with four torpedo tubes and no missiles) in 7 October 1975. Series production with *Bille* in 1974. She was launched 26 March 1976. Further boats laid down 2 October 1974, 14 December 1974 and 17 February 1975. *Suenson* (last boat) launched 4 February 1978.

Cost: 50 million Danish kronen (equipped).

Armament: From the 6th boat all are fitted with two torpedo tubes and Harpoon. The rest are to be similarly retrofitted. It is possible that there may be variations in the armament—eight Harpoon and no torpedo tubes or four Harpoon and two torpedo tubes or no Harpoon and four torpedo tubes.

Fire control: Phillips 9LV200.

Radar: Warning combined: One.
Fire control: One.
Navigation: One NWS 3.

NORBY 1978, Royal Danish Navy

128   DENMARK / Light forces

6 "SØLØVEN" CLASS (FAST ATTACK CRAFT—TORPEDO)

Name	No.	Builders	Commissioned
SØLØVEN	P 510	Vosper	12 Feb 1965
SØRIDDEREN	P 511	Vosper	10 Feb 1965
SØBJORNEN	P 512	R. Dockyard, Copenhagen	Sep 1965
SØHESTEN	P 513	R. Dockyard, Copenhagen	June 1966
SØHUNDEN	P 514	R. Dockyard, Copenhagen	Dec 1966
SØULVEN	P 515	R. Dockyard, Copenhagen	Mar 1967

Displacement, tons: 95 standard; 120 full load
Dimensions, feet (metres): 99 × 26·2 × 8·2 *(30·3 × 8·0 × 2·5)*
Guns: 2—40 mm Bofors
Torpedo tubes: 4—21 in *(533 mm)*
Main engines: 3 Bristol Siddeley Proteus gas turbines; 3 shafts; 12 750 bhp = 54 knots
General Motors diesels on wing shafts for cruising = 10 knots
Range, miles: 400 at 46 knots
Complement: 29

The design is a combination of the Vosper "Brave" class hull form and "Ferocity" type construction. *Søløven* and *Søridderen* were both completed in June 1964 and handed over to the RDN after six month's trials.

Radar: One NWS 1.

SØULVEN — 1978, Royal Danish Navy

8 "DAPHNE" CLASS (LARGE PATROL CRAFT)

Name	No.	Builders	Commissioned
DAPHNE	P 530	R. Dockyard, Copenhagen	19 Dec 1961
DRYADEN	P 531	R. Dockyard, Copenhagen	4 Apr 1962
HAVFRUEN	P 533	R. Dockyard, Copenhagen	20 Dec 1962
NAJADEN	P 534	R. Dockyard, Copenhagen	26 Apr 1963
NYMFEN	P 535	R. Dockyard, Copenhagen	4 Oct 1963
NEPTUN	P 536	R. Dockyard, Copenhagen	18 Dec 1963
RAN	P 537	R. Dockyard, Copenhagen	15 May 1964
ROTA	P 538	R. Dockyard, Copenhagen	20 Jan 1965

Displacement, tons: 170
Dimensions, feet (metres): 121·3 × 20 × 8·5 *(37 × 6·8 × 2·6)* (P 530-533)
Gun: 1—40 mm plus 2—51 mm flare launchers
A/S weapons: DCs
Main engines: Two 12-cyl Maybach diesels; 2 shafts; 2 600 bhp = 20 knots (plus 1 cruising 6-cyl Foden diesel; 100 bhp)
Complement: 23

Four were built under US offshore programme. Some have been disarmed.

Design: P 530-533 have a rounded stern and P 534-538 have a straight stern.

Radar: One NWS 3.

Sonar: PMS 26.

DAPHNE — 1978, Royal Danish Navy

3 + 1 "AGDLEQ" CLASS (LARGE PATROL CRAFT)

Name	No.	Builders	Commissioned
AGDLEQ	Y 386	Svendborg Vaerft	12 Mar 1974
AGPA	Y 387	Svendborg Vaerft	14 May 1974
TULAGAQ	Y 388	Svendborg Vaerft	1979
—	Y 389	—	—

Displacement, tons: 300
Dimensions, feet (metres): 101·7 × 26·2 × 11·5 *(31 × 8 × 3·5)*
Guns: 2—20 mm
Speed, knots: 12
Complement: 14

Designed for service off Greenland. A slightly larger ship, *Tulagaq*, of 330 tons ordered from same builders in 1977 for delivery 1979 to replace *Tijsten*. Main engine—1 BLW Alpha diesel for 14 knots (800 bhp). Cost 11·4 million Danish kronen.

Radar: Navigation: Two NWS 3.

AGDLEQ — 1974, Royal Danish Navy

2 "MAAGEN" CLASS (LARGE PATROL CRAFT)

Name	No.	Builders	Commissioned
MAAGEN	Y 384	Helsingør Dockyard	May 1960
MALLEMUKKEN	Y 385	Helsingør Dockyard	May 1960

Displacement, tons: 190
Dimensions, feet (metres): 88·5 × 22·9 × 9·5 *(27 × 7·0 × 2·9)*
Guns: 2—20 mm
Main engine: 385 hp; 1 shaft = 10 knots
Complement: 14

Of steel construction. Laid down 15 January 1960.

Radar: Two NWS 3.

MAAGEN — 1976, Royal Danish Navy

DENMARK / Light forces 129

9 "BARSØ" CLASS (LARGE PATROL CRAFT)

Name	No.	Builders	Commissioned
BARSØ	Y 300	Svendborg Vaerft	1969
DREJØ	Y 301	Svendborg Vaerft	1969
ROMSØ	Y 302	Svendborg Vaerft	1969
SAMSØ	Y 303	Svendborg Vaerft	1969
THURØ	Y 304	Svendborg Vaerft	1969
VEJRØ	Y 305	Svendborg Vaerft	1969
FARØ	Y 306	Svendborg Vaerft	1972
LAESØ	Y 307	Svendborg Vaerft	1973
ROMØ	Y 308	Svendborg Vaerft	1973

Displacement, tons: 155
Dimensions, feet (metres): 82·0 × 19·7 × 9·8 *(25·0 × 6 × 2·8)*
Guns: 2—20 mm
Speed: 11 knots
Complement: 12

Rated as patrol cutters.

Radar: One NWS 3.

BARSØ   *1978, Royal Danish Navy*

2 LARGE BOTVED TYPE (COASTAL PATROL CRAFT)

Y 375   Y 376

Displacement, tons: 12
Dimensions, feet (metres): 42·9 × 14·8 × 3·7 *(13·1 × 4·5 × 1·1)*
Main engines: Diesel; 2 shafts; 680 hp = 26 knots

Built in 1974 by Botved Boats

Radar: One NWS 3.

Y 376   *1978, Royal Danish Navy*

3 SMALL BOTVED TYPE (COASTAL PATROL CRAFT)

Y 377   Y 378   Y 379

Displacement, tons: 9
Dimensions, feet (metres): 32·1 × 10·4 × 3·1 *(9·8 × 3·3 × 0·9)*
Main engines: Diesels; 2 shafts; 500 hp = 27 knots

Built in 1975 by Botved Boats.

Radar: One NWS 3.

Small BOTVED Type   *1975, Royal Danish Navy*

3 Y TYPE (COASTAL PATROL CRAFT)

Y 338   Y 339   Y 343

Miscellaneous patrol cutters (ex-fishing vessels) all built in 1944-45.

6 "MHV 90" CLASS (COASTAL PATROL CRAFT)

MHV 90   MHV 91   MHV 92   MHV 93   MHV 94   MHV 95

Displacement, tons: 90
Dimensions, feet (metres): 64·9 × 18·7 × 8·2 *(19·8 × 5·7 × 2·5)*
Gun: 1—20 mm
Main engine: Diesel; 1 shaft = 10 knots

Built in 1975. Manned by Naval Home Guard.

Radar: One NWS 3.

MHV 93   *1975, Royal Danish Navy*

130 DENMARK / Light forces — Mine warfare forces

6 "MHV 80" CLASS (COASTAL PATROL CRAFT)

Name	No.	Builders	Commissioned
ASKØ (ex-Y 386, ex-M 560, ex-MS 2)	MHV 81	Denmark	1941
ENØ (ex-Y 388, ex-M 562, ex-MS 5)	MHV 82	Denmark	1941
MANØ (ex-Y 391, ex-M 566, ex-MS 9)	MHV 83	Denmark	1941
BAAGØ (ex-Y 387, ex-M 561, ex-MS 3)	MHV 84	Denmark	1941
HJORTØ (ex-Y 389, ex-M 564, ex- MS 7)	MHV 85	Denmark	1941
LYØ (ex-Y 390, ex-M 565, ex-MS 8)	MHV 86	Denmark	1941

Displacement, tons: 74
Dimensions, feet (metres): 78·8 × 21 × 5 *(24·0 × 6·4 × 1·5)*
Gun: 1—20 mm
Main engine: Diesel; 1 shaft; 350 bhp = 11 knots

Of wooden construction. All launched in 1941. Former inshore minesweepers. Manned by the Naval Home Guard.

Radar: One NWS. 3.

HJORTØ   1978, Royal Danish Navy

3 "MHV 70" CLASS (COASTAL PATROL CRAFT)

Name	No.	Builders	Commissioned
MHV 70	—	R. Dockyard, Copenhagen	1958
MHV 71	—	R. Dockyard, Copenhagen	1958
MHV 72	—	R. Dockyard, Copenhagen	1958

Displacement, tons: 76
Dimensions, feet (metres): 65·9 × 16·7 × 8·2 *(20·1 × 5·1 × 2·5)*
Gun: 1—20 mm
Main engine: 200 bhp = 10 knots

Patrol boats and training craft for the Naval Home Guard. Formerly designated DMH, but allocated MHV numbers in 1969.

Radar: One NWS 3.

MHV 71   1974, Royal Danish Navy

5 "MHV 20" CLASS (COASTAL PATROL CRAFT)

Dimensions, feet (metres): 54·1 × 13·8 × 6·6 *(16·5 × 4·2 × 2)*
Gun: 1 MG
Main engines: 2 Mercedes diesels; 2 shafts; 500 bhp = 15 knots
Complement: 9

Built by Eyvinds Plastik Både Vaerft, Svendborg of GRP. For use of Naval Home Guard. Cost approximately 2 million kroner.

Note: In addition there is a number of small vessels of the trawler and other types used by the Naval Home Guard—MHVs 1, 51, 54, 55, 57, 60, 62, 63, 65, 67, 68, 74, 75 and some other fishing craft types.

MHV 20   1978

MINE WARFARE FORCES

4 "FALSTER" CLASS (MINELAYERS)

Name	No.	Builders	Commissioned
FALSTER	N 80	Nakskov Skibsvaerft	7 Nov 1963
FYEN	N 81	Frederikshavn Vaerft	18 Sep 1963
MØEN	N 82	Frederikshavn Vaerft	29 Apr 1964
SJAELLAND	N 83	Nakskov Skibsvaerft	7 July 1964

Displacement, tons: 1 900 full load
Length, feet (metres): 238 *(72·5)* pp; 252·6 *(77·0)* oa
Beam, feet (metres): 42·6 *(13)*
Draught, feet (metres): 13·1 *(4)*
Missiles: Sea Sparrow
Guns: 4—3 in *(76 mm)*, (twin US Mk 35)
Mines: 400
Main engines: 2 General Motors—567D 3 diesels; 4 800 shp; 2 shafts
Speed, knots: 17
Complement: 120

Ordered in 1960-61 and launched 1962-63. All are named after Danish islands. The steel hull is flush-decked with a raking stem, a full stern and a prominent knuckle forward. The hull has been specially strengthened for ice navigation. Similar to Turkish *Nusret*. *Møen* employed on midshipmen's training.

Conversion: *Sjaelland* converted in 1976 to act as depôt ship for submarines and FAC in place of *Henrik Gerner*.

Fire control: Contraves.

MØEN   8/1978, Leo van Ginderen

Gunnery: All mountings now fitted with shields.

Radar: Warning combined: One CWS 2.
Fire control: One CGS 1.
Tactical: One NWS 1.
Navigation: One NWS 2.

DENMARK / Mine warfare forces — Tankers 131

2 "LINDORMEN" CLASS (MINELAYERS)

Name	No.	Builders	Commissioned
LINDORMEN	N 43	Svendborg Vaerft	Nov 1977
LOSSEN	N 44	Svendborg Vaerft	1978

Displacement, tons: 570
Dimensions, feet (metres): 147·6 × 29·5 × 8·0 *(45 × 9 × 2·5)*
Guns: 2—20 mm
Mines: 50-60 (Depending on type)
Main engines: Diesels; 1 600 hp = 14 knots
Complement: 27

Replacements for "Lougen" Class. Controlled Minelayers. *Lindormen* laid down January 1977, launched 9 September 1977 and *Lossen* laid down in February 1977, launched 16 December 1977.

LINDORMEN   *1978, Royal Danish Navy*

1 "LANGELAND" CLASS (COASTAL MINELAYER)

Name	No.	Builders	Commissioned
LANGELAND	N 42	Royal Dockyard, Copenhagen	1951

Displacement, tons: 310 standard; 332 full load
Dimensions, feet (metres): 144·3 × 23·7 × 7·2 *(44·0 × 7·2 × 2·1)*
Guns: 2—40 mm; 2—20 mm Madsen
Main engines: Diesels; 2 shafts; 770 bhp = 11·6 knots
Complement: 37

Laid down in 1950. Launched on 17 May 1950.

LANGELAND   *1978, Royal Danish Navy*

8 Ex-US MSC "ADJUTANT" CLASS (Ex-AMS) (MINESWEEPERS—COASTAL)

AARØSUND (ex-*MSC* 127) M 571	**GULDBORGSUND** (ex-*MSC* 257) M 575
ALSSUND (ex-*MSC* 128) M 572	**OMØSUND** (ex-*MSC* 221) M 576
EGERNSUND (ex-*MSC* 129) M 573	**ULVSUND** (ex-*MSC* 263) M 577
GRØNSUND (ex-*MSC* 256) M 574	**VILSUND** (ex-*MSC* 264) M 578

Displacement, tons: 350 standard; 376 full load
Dimensions, feet (metres): 138 pp; 144 oa × 27·9 × 8·5 *(42·1; 43·9 × 8·5 × 2·6)*
Gun: 1—40 mm
Main engines: Diesels; 2 shafts; 1 200 bhp = 12 knots
Range, miles: 2 500 at 10 knots
Complement: 35

"MSC (ex-AMS) 60" class NATO coastal minesweepers all built in USA. Completed in 1954-56. *Aarøsund* was transferred on 24 January 1955, *Alssund* on 5 April 1955, *Egernsund* on 3 August 1955, *Grønsund* on 21 September 1956, *Guldborgsund* on 11 November 1956, *Omøsund* on 20 June 1956, *Ulvsund* on 20 September 1956 and *Vilsund* on 15 November 1956. *Guldborgsund* has been fitted with a charthouse between bridge and funnel and is employed on surveying duties.

Radar: One NWS 3.

VILSUND   *1978, Royal Danish Navy*

SLEIPNER A 558

A 200 ton torpedo recovery/transporter.

SERVICE FORCES

Note: There is a road-borne support unit (MOBA) for the Fast Attack Craft with two sections. The first, of eight vehicles with radar, W/T and control offices is MOBA (Ops) and the second, of 25 vehicles for stores, fuel, provisions, torpedoes and workshops in MOBA (Log).

TANKERS

2 Ex-US "YO 65" CLASS

Name	No.	Builders	Commissioned
RIMFAXE (ex-US *YO 226*)	A 568	Jefferson Bridge & Machine Co, USA	2 Nov 1945
SKINFAXE (ex-US *YO 229*)	A 569	Jefferson Bridge & Machine Co, USA	7 Dec 1945

Displacement, tons: 422 light; 1 390 full load
Dimensions, feet (metres): 174 × 32 × 13·2 *(53·1 × 9·8 × 4)*
Main engine: 1 General Motors diesel; 560 bhp = 10 knots
Complement: 23

Transferred to the RDN from the USA on 2 August 1962.

RIMFAXE   *1971, Royal Danish Navy*

132 DENMARK / Icebreakers — Fishery protection

ICEBREAKERS

Note: Icebreakers are controlled by the Ministry of Trade and Shipping, but are maintained by RDN at Frederikshavn in summer.

Name	No	Builders	Commissioned
—	—	Lindø Vaerft, Odense	—

Displacement, tons:
Dimensions, feet (metres): 221·4 × 50·2 × 15·4 (67·5 × 15·3 × 4·7)
Main engines: 6 800 hp; 2 shafts = 16·5 knots

No bow thruster. Side rolling tanks. To be fitted for surveying duties in non-ice periods. Cost 65 million Danish kronen.

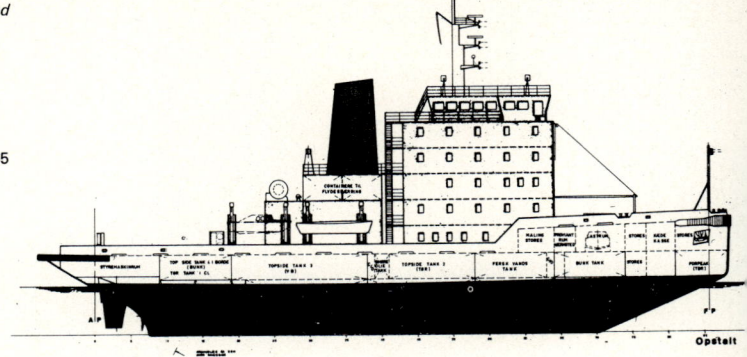
New Icebreaker   1978

Name	No.	Builders	Commissioned
DANBJØRN	—	Lindø Vaerft, Odense	1965
ISBJØRN	—	Lindø Vaerft, Odense	1966

Displacement, tons: 3 685
Dimensions, feet (metres): 252 × 56 × 20 (76·8 × 17·1 × 6·1)
Main engines: Diesel-electric; 10 500 shp = 14 knots
Complement: 34

DANBJØRN   1976, Royal Danish Navy

Name	No.	Builders	Commissioned
ELBJØRN	—	Frederikshavn Vaerft	1966

Displacement, tons: 893 standard; 1 400 full load
Dimensions, feet (metres): 156·5 × 40·3 × 14·5 (47 × 12·1 × 4·4)
Main engines: Diesel-electric; 3 600 bhp = 12 knots

Used by RDN for surveying in summer.

ROYAL YACHT

Name	No.	Builders	Commissioned
DANNEBROG	A 540	R. Dockyard, Copenhagen	1932

Displacement, tons: 1 130
Dimensions, feet (metres): 246 × 34 × 11·2 (75 × 10·4 × 3·4)
Guns: 2—37 mm
Main engines: 2 sets Burmeister & Wain 8-cyl 2 cycle diesels; 1 800 bhp = 14 knots
Complement: 57

Launched on 10 October 1931.

DANNEBROG   1976, Royal Danish Navy

FISHERY PROTECTION

4 RESCUE VESSELS

1 "OSPREY" CLASS

An adaptation of the much publicised craft which has now been adopted by the Danish Fishery Protection department. Provided with one Lynx helicopter.

"OSPREY" class (model)   1978, Peter Thornycroft

SURVEY VESSELS

(See *Hvidbjornen*)

SUND

Of 376 tons; launched 1954, completed 1956; complement 35.

SKA 3 4 5 6 7 8

Of 27 tons standard; built 1958-68; complement 6. SKA7 and 8 are stationed in Denmark, the remainder in Greenland.

6 LAUNCHES

SKA7   1978

ENVIRONMENT CRAFT

2 POLLUTION CONTROL CRAFT

MILSØ 101 and 102

Displacement, tons: 18·3
Dimensions, feet (metres): 53·8 × 14·4 × 7·1 *(16·4 × 4·4 × 2·2)*
Main engine: 1 MWM diesel; 454 hp = 15 knots
Range, miles: 350 at 8 knots
Complement: 4

Built by Ejvinds Plastikbodevarft-Svendborg. Carry derricks and booms for framing oil slicks and dispersant fluids.

MILSØ 102   1978

DJIBOUTI

After the declaration of independence in 1977 the nucleus of a naval force was formed with the commissioning of one Tecimar 30 ton coastal patrol craft, capable of 25 knots and carrying two MGs.

DOMINICAN REPUBLIC

Ministerial

Minister of the Armed Forces:
  Juan Rene Beauchamps Javier

Headquarters Appointments

Chief of Naval Staff:
  Vice-Admiral Francisco J. Rivera Caminero
Vice-Chief of Naval Staff:
  Captain Francisco A. Marte Victoria

Personnel

(a) 1979: 4 050 officers and men
(b) Selective military service

Maritime Air
(All operated by Dominican Air Force)

2 PBY-5A Catalinas
3 Alouette II/III helicopters
2 H-19 Chickasaws
7 OH-6A Cayuse
2 Hiller 12-E Ravens

Naval Bases

"27 de Febrero", Santo Domingo Naval, Staff HQ.
"Las Calderas": Las Calderas, Bani. Naval dockyard and Training centre. 900 ton synchrolift.

Strength of the Fleet

Type	Active (Reserve)
Frigates	1 (2)
Corvettes	5 (2)
Large Patrol Craft	2 (3)
Coastal Patrol Craft	9
LSM	1
LCUs	2
Survey Vessels	3
Tankers (Small)	2
Tugs (Large)	2
Tugs (Harbour)	6
Training Ship	1

Note: Although listed as "Active" several of the major units are reported as non-operational.

Mercantile Marine

Lloyd's Register of Shipping:
  21 vessels of 18 313 tons gross

DELETIONS

Destroyer

1972 *Duarte* (ex-HMS *Hotspur*)

Corvettes

1972 *Gerardo Jansen, Juan Bautista Cambiaso, Juan Bautista Maggiola* (all ex-Canadian "Flower" class)

Light Forces

1975 *Maymyon, Puerto Hemosa*
1977 *Albacora, Bonito*

Amphibious Craft

1975 *Enriquillo*

Survey Craft

1972 *Caonobo*

Tugs

1975 *Consuelo, Haina, Santana*

DOMINICAN REPUBLIC / Frigates — Corvettes

FRIGATES
1 Ex-CANADIAN "RIVER" CLASS

Name	No.	Builders	Laid down	Launched	Commissioned
MELLA (ex-*Presidente Trujillo*, ex-HMCS *Carlplace*)	451	Davies S.B. & Repairing Co, Lauzon, Canada	—	6 July 1944	1944

Displacement, tons: 1 400 standard; 2 125 full load
Length, feet (metres): 301·5 *(91·9)*
Beam, feet (metres): 36·7 *(11·2)*
Draught, feet (metres): 12·0 *(3·7)*
Guns: 1—100 mm/45 (single Mk 23); 2—47mm/60;
 1—40 mm/60; 4—20 mm/70 (single)
Main engines: Triple expansion; 2 shafts; 5 500 ihp
Boilers: 2 of 3-drum type
Speed, knots: 20
Oil fuel, tons: 645
Range, miles: 4 200 at 12 knots
Complement: 195 (15 officers, 130 ratings, 50 midshipmen)

Transferred to the Dominican Navy in 1946. Modified for use as Presidential yacht with extra accommodation and deck-houses built up aft. Pennant number as a frigate was F 101, but as the Presidential yacht it was no longer worn. Now carries pennant number 451 as flagship of Dominican naval forces. Used by the staff in naval operations. Renamed *Mella* in 1962.

MELLA   *1972, Dominican Navy*

2 Ex-US "TACOMA" CLASS

Name	No.	Builders	Laid down	Launched	Commissioned
GREGORIO LUPERÓN (ex-*Presidente Troncoso*, ex-USS *Pueblo*, PF 13)	452 (ex-F 103)	Leatham D. Smith S.B. Co, Wis.	15 Apr 1943	10 July 1943	29 Apr 1944
CAPITAN GENERAL PEDRO SANTANA (ex-*Presidente Peynado*, ex-USS *Knoxville*, PF 64)	453 (ex-F 104)	Kaiser S.Y. Richmond, Cal.	14 Nov 1943	20 Jan 1944	27 May 1944

Displacement, tons: 1 430 standard; 2 415 full load
Length, feet (metres): 298·0 *(90·8)* wl; 304·0 *(92·7)* oa
Beam, feet (metres): 37·5 *(11·4)*
Draught, feet (metres): 13·7 *(4·2)*
Guns: 3—3 in *(76 mm)*/50 (singles, Mk 22);
 4—40 mm/60 (twins Mk 1)
Main engines: Triple expansion; 2 shafts; 5 500 ihp
Boilers: 2 of 3-drum type
Speed, knots: 19
Oil fuel, tons: 760
Range, miles: 9 500 at 12 knots
Complement: 140

Formerly US patrol frigates, PF of the "Tacoma" class similar to the contemporary British frigates of the "River" class. Transferred from the US Navy to the Dominican Republic Navy in July 1946 (453) and September 1947 (452). Renamed in 1962. Both in reserve.

GREGORIO LUPERON   *1972, Dominican Navy*

CORVETTES
3 Ex-US "COHOES" CLASS

Name	No.	Builders	Commissioned
CAMBIASO (ex-USS *Etlah*, AN 79)	P 207	Marietta Manufacturing Co, Point Pleasant	16 Apr 1945
SEPARACION (ex-USS *Passaconaway*, AN 86)	P 208	Marine S.B. Co	27 Apr 1945
CALDERAS (ex-USS *Passaic*, AN 87)	P 209	Leatham D Smith S.B. Co	6 Mar 1945

Displacement, tons: 650 standard; 785 full load
Dimensions, feet (metres): 168·5 × 33 × 10·8 *(51·4 × 10 × 3·3)*
Guns: 1—3 in *(76 mm)*; 3—20 mm
Main engines: Busch Sulzer diesel-electric;
 1 200 shp = 12 knots
Complement: 48

Ex-netlayers in reserve in USA since 1963. Transferred by sale 29 September 1976. Now used for patrol duties.

SEPARACION   *1977, Dominican Navy*

2 Ex-US "ADMIRABLE" CLASS

Name	No.	Builders	Commissioned
PRESTOL BOTELLO (ex-*Separacion*, ex-USS *Skirmish*, MSF 303)	BM 454	Associated S.B.	16 Aug 1943
TORTUGUERO (ex-USS *Signet*, MSF 302)	BM 455	Associated S.B.	16 Aug 1943

Displacement, tons: 650 standard; 900 full load
Dimensions, feet (metres): 180·0 wl; 184·5 oa × 33·0 × 14·5 *(56·3 × 9·9 × 4·4)*
Guns: 1—3 in; 2—40 mm; 6—20 mm
A/S weapons: 1 Hedgehog
Main engines: 2 diesels; 2 shafts; 1 710 bhp = 14 knots
Range, miles: 5 600 at 9 knots
Complement: 90 (8 officers, 82 men)

Former US fleet minesweepers. Purchased on 13 January 1965. *Prestol Botello* renamed early 1976. Sweep-gear removed.

PRESTOL BOTELLO   *7/1976, Norman Friedman*

DOMINICAN REPUBLIC / Corvettes — Light forces

2 Ex-CANADIAN "FLOWER" CLASS

Name	No.	Builders	Laid down	Launched	Commissioned
CRISTÓBAL COLÓN (ex-HMCS *Lachute*)	401 (ex-C 101)	Morton Ltd, Quebec City	—	9 June 1944	24 Oct 1944
JUAN ALEJANDRO ACOSTA (ex-HMCS *Louisburg*)	402 (ex-C 102)	Morton Ltd, Quebec City	—	13 July 1943	13 Dec 1943

Displacement, tons: 1 060 standard; 1 350 full load
Length, feet (metres): 193·0 *(58·8)* pp; 208·0 *(63·4)* oa
Beam, feet (metres): 33·0 *(10·0)*
Draught, feet (metres): 13·3 *(4·0)*
Guns: 1—4 in *(102 mm)*
C. Colon: 1—40 mm; 6—20 mm; 4—·5 in MG (2 twin)
J. A. Acosta: 1—40 mm; 6—20 mm; 2—·5 in MG
Main engines: Triple expansion; 2 750 ihp
Boilers: 2 of 3-drum type
Speed, knots: 16
Oil fuel, tons: 282
Range, miles: 2 900 at 15 knots
Complement: 53

Built in Canadian shipyards under the emergency construction programme during the Second World War. Five were transferred to the Dominican Navy in 1947. Pennant numbers were changed in 1968. Both in reserve and now in line for deletion.

JUAN ALEJANDRO ACOSTA   1972, Dominican Navy

LIGHT FORCES

3 Ex-USCG "ARGO" CLASS (LARGE PATROL CRAFT)

Name	No.	Builders	Commissioned
INDEPENDENCIA (ex-USCGC *Icarus*)	204 (ex-P 105)	Bath Ironworks	1932
LIBERTAD (ex-*Rafael Atoa*, ex-USCGC *Thetis*)	205 (ex-P 106)	—	—
RESTAURACION (ex-USCGC *Galathea*)	206 (ex-P 104)	John H. Machis & Co, Camden, NJ	1933

Displacement, tons: 337 standard
Dimensions, feet (metres): 165·0 × 25·2 × 9·5 *(50·3 × 7·7 × 2·9)*
Guns: 1—3 in; 1—40 mm; 1—20 mm
Main engines: 2 diesels; 1 280 bhp = 15 knots
Range, miles: 1 300 at 15 knots
Complement: 49 (5 officers, 44 men)

Ex-US Coast Guard Cutters. Rebuilt in 1975. In reserve.

RESTAURACION   1977, Dominican Navy

1 US "PGM 71" CLASS (LARGE PATROL CRAFT)

Name	No.	Builders	Commissioned
BETELGEUSE (ex-US *PGM* 77)	GC 102	Peterson, USA	1966

Displacement, tons: 130 standard; 145·5 full load
Dimensions, feet (metres): 101·5 × 21·0 × 5·0 *(30·9 × 6·4 × 1·5)*
Guns: 1—40 mm; 4—20 mm (singles); 2—·5 in 50 cal MG
Main engines: 8 General Motors 6-71 diesels; 2 shafts; 2 200 bhp = 21 knots
Range, miles: 1 500 at 10 knots
Complement: 20

Built in the USA and transferred to the Dominican Republic under the Military Aid Programme on 14 January 1966.

BETELGEUSE   1972, Dominican Navy

1 LARGE PATROL CRAFT

Name	No.	Builders	Commissioned
CAPITAN ALSINA (ex-*RL 101*)	GC 105	—	1944

Displacement, tons: 100 standard
Dimensions, feet (metres): 92·0 wl; 104·8 oa × 19·2 × 5·8 *(32 × 5·9 × 1·8)*
Guns: 2—20 mm
Main engines: 2 General Motors diesels; 2 shafts; 1 000 hp = 17 knots
Complement: 20

Of wooden construction. Launched in 1944. Named as above in 1957. Rebuilt 1977.

CAPITAN ALSINA

4 "BELLATRIX" CLASS (COASTAL PATROL CRAFT)

Name	No.	Builders	Commissioned
PROCION	GC 103	Sewart Seacraft Inc, Berwick, La.	1967
ALDEBARÁN	GC 104	Sewart Seacraft Inc, Berwick, La.	1972
BELLATRIX	GC 106	Sewart Seacraft Inc, Berwick, La.	1967
CAPELLA	GC 107	Sewart Seacraft Inc, Berwick, La.	1968

Displacement, tons: 60
Dimensions, feet (metres): 85 × 18 × 5 *(25·9 × 5·5 × 1·5)*
Guns: 3—·5 MG
Main engines: 2 General Motors diesels; 500 bhp = 18·7 knots
Complement: 12

Transferred to the Dominican Navy by USA, *Bellatrix* on 18 August 1967, *Procion* on 1 May 1967, *Capella* on 15 October 1968 and *Aldebarán* in May 1972.

BELLATRIX   1970, Dominican Navy

136 DOMINICAN REPUBLIC / Light forces — Tugs

1 COASTAL PATROL CRAFT

Name	No.	Builders	Commissioned
RIGEL (ex-US AVR)	GC 101	—	1953

Displacement, tons: 27 standard; 32·2 full load
Dimensions, feet (metres): 63·0 × 15·5 × 5·0 (19·2 × 4·7 × 1·5)
Guns: 2—50 cal MG
Main engines: General Motors V8—71 diesels = 18·5 knots
Complement: 9

Originally built in 1953 as aircraft rescue launch. Reconditioned by NAUSTA, Key West, USA. Rebuilt 1976.

4 COASTAL PATROL CRAFT

Name	No.	Builders	Commissioned
CARITE	BA 3	Ast. Navales Dominicanos	1975
ATÚN	BA 6	Ast. Navales Dominicanos	1975
PICÚA	BA 9	Ast. Navales Dominicanas	1975
JUREL	BA 15	Ast. Navales Dominicanos	1975

Displacement, tons: 24
Dimensions, feet (metres): 45 × 13 × 6·6 (13·7 × 4 × 1·9)
Gun: 1—MG
Main engine: 1 General Motors diesel; 101 hp = 9 knots
Complement: 4

Auxiliary sailing craft with a sail area of 750 sq ft and a cargo capacity of 7 tons. *Mero* previously listed apparently deleted.

AMPHIBIOUS FORCES

1 LCU

Name	No.	Builders	Commissioned
SAMANA (ex-LA 2)	LDM 302	Ast. Navales Dominicanos	1958

Displacement, tons: 150 standard; 310 full load
Dimensions, feet (metres): 105 wl; 119·5 oa × 36 × 3 (36·4 × 11 × 0·9)
Guns: 1—·5 cal MG
Main engines: 3 General Motors diesels; 441 bhp = 8 knots
Oil fuel, tons: 80
Complement: 17

Similar characteristics to US LCT 5 Type although slightly larger.

SAMANA   1972, Dominican Navy

1 LCU

Name	No.	Builders	Commissioned
OCOA	LDM 303	Ast. Navales Dominicanos	1976

Displacement, tons: 36·8
Dimensions, feet (metres): 56·2 × 14 × 3·9 (17·1 × 4·3 × 1·2)
Main engines: 2—6-cyl diesels; 225 bhp = 6 knots
Complement: 5

Capacity about 30 tons.

SURVEY VESSELS

Name	No.	Builders	Commissioned
CAPOTILLO (ex-Camillia)	FB 101	—	—

Displacement, tons: 337
Dimensions, feet (metres): 117 × 24 × 7·8 (35·7 × 7·3 × 2·4)
Main engines: 2 diesels; 880 bhp = 10 knots
Complement: 29 (3 officers, 26 men)

Built in the USA in 1911. Acquired from the US Coast Guard in 1949. Underwent a major refit in Dominican Republic in 1970. Buoy Tender.

Name	No.	Builders	Commissioned
NEPTUNO (ex-Toro)	BA 10	John H. Mathis Co, New Jersey	Feb 1954

Displacement, tons: 72·2
Dimensions, feet (metres): 64 × 18·1 × 8 (19·5 × 5·7 × 2·4)
Main engines: 1 General Motors diesel = 10 knots
Complement: 7

NEPTUNO   1975, Dominican Navy

ESPLORA (probably ex-*Atlantida*) of 63 ft

AUXILIARY

1 Ex-US "LSM I" CLASS

Name	No.	Builders	Commissioned
SIRIO (ex-US LSM 483)	BDM 301 (ex-BA 104)	Brown S.B. Co, Houston	13 Apr 1945

Displacement, tons: 734 standard; 1 100 full load
Dimensions, feet (metres): 203·5 × 34 × 10 (61·9 × 10·4 × 3·1)
Main engines: 2 General Motors diesels; 2 shafts; 1 800 bhp = 14 knots
Oil fuel, tons: 164
Complement: 30

Laid down on 17 February 1945, launched on 10 March 1945. Transferred to the Dominican Navy in March 1958. Refitted in Dominican Republic in 1970. Now decked over and used for commercial logistic service. Included because of capability in emergency.

TANKERS

2 Ex-US OIL BARGES

Name	No.	Builders	Commissioned
CAPITAN W. ARVELO (ex-US YO 213)	BT 4	Ira S. Bushey Inc, Brooklyn	8 Nov 1945
CAPITAN BEOTEGUI (ex-US YO 215)	BT 5	Ira S. Bushey Inc, Brooklyn	17 Dec 1945

Displacement, tons: 370 light; 1 076 full load
Dimensions, feet (metres): 156·1 × 32 × 13·0 (47·6 × 9·8 × 4)
Gun: 1—20 mm
Main engines: 2 Union diesels; 525 hp = 8 knots
Capacity: 6 570 barrels
Complement: 25

Former US self-propelled fuel oil barges. Lent by the USA in April 1964.

CAPITAN W. ARVELO   1977, Dominican Navy

TUGS

4 HARBOUR TUGS

MAGUANA (ex-*R 10*) RP 14   CALDERAS RP 19
BOHECHIO RP 16   ISABELA (ex-*R 1*) RP 20

Small tugs for harbour and coastal use. Not all of uniform type and dimensions. *Bohechio* of US YTL 600 type, transferred January 1971.

DOMINICAN REPUBLIC / Tugs — ECUADOR / Introduction   137

1 Ex-US "CHEROKEE" CLASS

Name	No.	Builders	Commissioned
MACORIX (ex-USS *Kiowa* ATF 72)	RM 21	Charleston S.B. and D.D. Co	7 June 1943

Displacement, tons: 1 235 standard; 1 675 full load
Dimensions, feet (metres): 205 × 38·5 × 15·5 *(62·5 × 11·7 × 4·7)*
Gun: 1—3 in/50 *(76 mm)*
Main engines: Diesel-electric; 1 shaft; 3 000 bhp = 15 knots
Complement: 85

Carries additional salvage equipment. Transferred 16 October 1972.

Radar: SPS 5D.

1 Ex-US "SOTOYOMO" CLASS

Name	No.	Builders	Commissioned
CAONABO (ex-USS *Sagamore* ATA 208)	RM 18	Gulfport Boiler and Welding Works	19 Mar 1945

Displacement, tons: 534 standard; 835 full load
Dimensions, feet (metres): 143 × 33·9 × 13 *(43·6 × 10·3 × 4)*
Main engines: 2 General Motors diesel-electric; 1 shaft; 1 500 bhp = 13 knots

Transferred 1 February 1972.

Radar: SPS 5D.

MACORIX   1975, Dominican Navy

CAONABO   1975, Dominican Navy

2 "HERCULES" CLASS

Name	No.	Builders	Commissioned
HERCULES (ex-*R 2*)	RP 12	Ast. Navales Dominicanos	1960
GUACANAGARIX (ex-*R 5*)	RP 13	Ast. Navales Dominicanos	1960

Displacement, tons: 200 (approx)
Dimensions, feet (metres): 70·0 × 15·6 × 9·0 *(21·4 × 4·8 × 2·7)*
Main engine: 1 Caterpillar motor; 500 hp; 1 225 rpm
Complement: 8

TRAINING SHIP

DUARTE

Displacement, tons: 60
Dimensions, feet (metres): 75 × 18 × 7 *(22·9 × 5·7 × 2·1)*
Main engine: General Motors diesel; 325 hp; 1 shaft
Complement: 30

DUBAI

(see United Arab Emirates)

ECUADOR

Ministerial

Minister of Defence:
  General Andres Arrata Macias

Headquarters Appointment

Commander-in-Chief of the Navy:
  Vice-Admiral Alfredo Poveda Burbano

Diplomatic Representation

Naval Attaché in Bonn:
  Captain Ethiel Rodriguez
Naval and Air Attaché in London:
  Colonel Alfonso Villagomez
Naval Attaché in Washington:
  Captain Fausto Cevallos

Personnel

(a) 1979. Total 3 800 (300 officers and 3 500 men)
(b) Two years selective national service

Naval Bases

Guayaquil (main naval base).
San Lorenzo and Galapagos Island (small bases).

Establishments

The Naval Academy is in Guayaquil

Maritime Air

Air Force planes working with the Navy.

2 Alouette III helicopters
1 IAI Arava
1 Cessna 320E
1 Cessna 177
2 Cessna T 337 F/G
2 Cessna T-41D/172H

Naval Infantry

A small force of naval infantry (700 men) exists of which a detachment is based on the Galapagos Islands and in the Eastern area.

Prefix to Ships' Names

BAE

Strength of the Fleet

Type	Active	Building (Projected)
Patrol Submarines	2	—
Destroyer	1	—
Frigate	1	—
Corvettes	2	(6)
Fast Attack Craft (Missile)	3	—
Fast Attack Craft (Torpedo)	3	—
Large Patrol Craft	2	—
Coastal Patrol Craft	5	—
LST	1	—
LSMs	2	—
Survey Vessels	2	—
Tugs	5	—
Supply Ship (Small)	1	—
Floating Dock	1	—
Sail Training Ship	1	—
Miscellaneous	5	—

New Construction

The Ecuadorian Navy, has ordered six 650 ton corvettes from CNR, Riva Trigoso, Italy.

Mercantile Marine

Lloyd's Register of Shipping:
  59 vessels of 201 244 tons gross

DELETIONS

Frigates

1972   *Guayas* (ex-US PF Type)
1978   *Presidente Alfaro*
       Presidente Velasco Ibarra (5 May)

Light Forces

1976   LSP 4, 5 and 6

PENNANT LIST

Submarines

| S 11 | Shiri |
| S 12 | Huancavilca |

Frigate

| D 01 | Morán Valverde |

Corvettes

| P 22 | Esmeraldas |
| P 23 | Manabi |

Light Forces

LC 61	24 De Mayo
LC 62	25 De Julio
LM 31	Quito
LM 32	Guayaquil
LM 33	Cuenca
LP 81	10 De Agosto
LP 82	9 De Octubre
LP 83	3 De Noviembre
LT 41	Manta
LT 42	Tulcan
LT 43	Nuevo Rocafuerte

Amphibious Forces

| T 51 | Jambeli |
| T 52 | Tarqui |

Survey Vessels

| O 111 | Orion |
| O 112 | Rigel |

Tugs

R 101	Cayambe
R 102	Sangay
R 103	Cotopaxi
R 104	Antizana
R 105	Chimborazo

Miscellaneous

BE 01	Guayas
BT 123	Putumayo
DF 121	Amazonas
T 53	Calicuchima
T 62	Atahualpa
UT 111	Isla de la Plata
UT 112	Isla Puná

138 ECUADOR / Submarines — Corvettes

SUBMARINES

2 TYPE 209

Name	No.	Builders	Laid down	Launched	Commissioned
SHYRI	S 11	Howaldtswerke, Kiel	1975	8 Oct 1976	16 Mar 1978
HUANCAVILCA	S 12	Howaldtswerke, Kiel	1975	18 Mar 1977	1 June 1978

Displacement, tons: 1 260 surfaced; 1 390 dived
Dimensions, feet (metres): 195·1 × 20·5 × 17·9 *(59·5 × 6·3 × 5·4)*
Torpedo tubes: 8—21 in (bow) with reloads
Main machinery: Diesel-electric; MTU diesels; 4 generators; 1 shaft; 5 000 shp
Speed, knots: 10 surfaced; 22 dived
Complement: 32

Ordered in 1974.

HUANCAVILCA   6/1978, Howaldtswerke

DESTROYER

1 Ex-US "GEARING (FRAM I)" CLASS

Name	No.	Builders	Laid down	Launched	Commissioned
PRESIDENTE ELOY ALFARO (ex-USS *Holder*, DD 819)	—	Consolidated Steel Corporation	1945	25 Aug 1945	18 May 1946

Displacement, tons: 2 425 standard; 3 425 full load
Dimensions, feet (metres): 390·5 × 40·9 × 19 *(119 × 12·4 × 5·8)*
Guns: 4—5 in *(127 mm)*/38
A/S weapons: 2 triple Mk 32 torpedo tubes
Main engines: 2 geared turbines; 60 000 shp; 2 shafts = 34 knots
Boilers: 4
Complement: 274

An enlarged version of the "Allen M. Sumner" class. Served in the Naval Reserve Force until transferred on 1 September 1978 by sale. Overhauled in USA 1978-79.

FRIGATE

1 Ex-US "CHARLES LAWRENCE" CLASS

Name	No.	Builders	Laid down	Launched	Commissioned
MORAN VALVERDE (ex-*Veinticinco de Julio*, ex-USS *Enright*, APD 66, ex-*DE 216*)	D 01 (ex-E 12)	Philadelphia Navy Yard	22 Feb 1943	29 May 1943	21 Sep 1943

Displacement, tons: 1 400 standard; 2 130 full load
Dimensions, feet (metres): 306·0 × 37·0 × 12·6 *(93·3 × 11·3 × 3·8)*
Guns: 1—5 in *(127 mm)*/38 (Mk 30); 4—40 mm/60 (twins, Mk 1)
A/S weapons: DC racks
Main engines: GE geared turbines with electric drive; 2 shafts; 12 000 shp = 23 knots
Boilers: 2 "D" Express
Range, miles: 2 000 at 23 knots
Complement: 204

Former US high speed transport (APD, modified destroyer escort). Transferred to Ecuador on 14 July 1967 under MAP. Purchased 30 August 1978. Can carry 162 troops. Now has small helicopter deck aft.

Radar: SPS 6 and SPS 10.

MORAN VALVERDE (Now D 01) (Now has small helicopter deck aft)   1968, Ecuadorian Navy

CORVETTES

Note: Six 650 ton corvettes have been ordered from CNR Italy. Generally similar to the design being used for Libya.

2 Ex-US "PCE 827" CLASS

Name	No.	Builders	Laid down	Launched	Commissioned
ESMERALDAS (ex-USS *Eunice*, PCE 846)	P 22 (ex-E 22, ex-E 03)	Pullman Standard Car Co, USA	10 Aug 1943	20 Dec 1943	4 Mar 1944
MANABI (ex-USS *Pascagoula*, PCE 874)	P 23 (ex-E 23, ex-E 02)	Albina Engine and Machine Co, USA	1 Mar 1943	11 May 1943	31 Dec 1943

Displacement, tons: 640 standard; 903 full load
Dimensions, feet (metres): 184·5 × 33 × 9·5 *(56·3 × 10 × 2·9)*
Guns: 1—3 in; 6—40 mm (twins)
A/S weapons: 4 DCT; 2 DC Racks; Hedgehog
Main engines: General Motors diesels; 2 shafts; 1 800 bhp = 15·4 knots
Range, miles: 4 300 at 10 knots
Complement: 100 officers and men

Former US patrol vessels (180 ft Escorts). Transferred on 29 November and 5 December 1960 respectively and by purchase 30 August 1978.

MANABI   1974

ECUADOR / Light forces — Amphibious ships   139

LIGHT FORCES

2 US "PGM-71" CLASS (LARGE PATROL CRAFT)

Name	No.	Builders	Commissioned
25 DE JULIO (ex-*Quito*, ex-US PGM 75)	LC 61	Peterson, USA	1965
24 DE MAYO (ex-*Guayaquil*, ex-US PGM 76)	LC 62	Peterson, USA	1965

Displacement, tons: 130 standard; 145·5 full load
Dimensions, feet (metres): 101·5 × 21 × 5 *(30·9 × 6·4 × 1·5)*
Guns: 1—40 mm; 4—20 mm (twin) 2—·5 cal MGs
Main engines: 4 Mercedes-Benz diesels; 2 shafts; 2 200 bhp = 21 knots
Range, miles: 1 000 at 12 knots
Complement: 15

VEINTECINCO DE JULIO (old Pennant number)   1967, Ecuadorian Navy

Transferred to the Ecuadorian Navy under MAP on 30 November 1965. Original names transferred to missile craft.

3 LÜRSSEN TYPE (FAST ATTACK CRAFT—MISSILE)

Name	No.	Builders	Commissioned
QUITO	LM 31	Lürssen, Vegesack	13 July 1976
GUAYAQUIL	LM 32	Lürssen, Vegesack	early 1977
CUENCA	LM 33	Lürssen, Vegesack	July 1977

Displacement, tons: 255
Dimensions, feet (metres): 147·6 × 23 × 12·8 *(45 × 7 × 3·9)*
Missiles: 4 SSM Exocet (single cells)
Guns: 1—76 mm/62 (Compact); 2—35 mm/90 (twin Oerlikon)
Main engines: 4 MTU diesels; 14 000 hp; 4 shafts = 40 knots
Range, miles: 700 at 40 knots; 1 800 at 16 knots
Complement: 35

Launched—*Quito,* 20 November 1975; *Guayaquil* 5 April 1976. *Cuenca* December 1976. *Cuenca* started trials in July 1977.

Radar: Thomson-CSF Triton and Pollux with Vega system.

QUITO   1976, Lürssen wertt

3 "MANTA" CLASS (FAST ATTACK CRAFT—TORPEDO)

Name	No.	Builders	Commissioned
MANTA	LT 41 (ex-LT 91)	Lürssen, Vegesack	11 June 1971
TULCAN	LT 42 (ex-LT 92)	Lürssen, Vegesack	2 Apr 1971
NUEVO ROCAFUERTE	LT 43 (ex-LT 93)	Lürssen, Vegesack	23 June 1971

Displacement, tons: 119 standard; 134 full load
Dimensions, feet (metres): 119·4 × 19·1 × 6·0 *(36·4 × 5·8 × 1·8)*
Guns: 1—40 mm; 1—twin Oerlikon unguided rocket launcher
Torpedo tubes: 2—21 in
Main engines: 3 MTU diesels; 3 shafts; 9 000 bhp = 35 knots
Range, miles: 700 at 30 knots; 1 500 at 15 knots
Complement: 19

Similar design to the Chilean "Guacoida" Class with an extra diesel—3 knots faster. *Manta* launched 8 September 1970.

MANTA (old Pennant number)   1972, Ecuadorian Navy

3 COASTAL PATROL CRAFT

Name	No.	Builders	Commissioned
10 DE AGOSTO	LP 81	Schurenstedt, Bardenfleth	Aug 1954
9 DE OCTUBRE	LP 82	Schurenstedt, Bardenfleth	Aug 1954
3 DE NOVIEMBRE	LP 83	Schurenstedt, Bardenfleth	1955

Displacement, tons: 45 standard; 64 full load
Dimensions, feet (metres): 76·8 × 13·5 × 6·3 *(23·4 × 4·6 × 1·8)*
Guns: Light MGs
Main engines: 2 Bohn & Kähler diesels; 2 shafts; 1 200 bhp = 22 knots
Range, miles: 550 at 16 knots
Complement: 9

LP Class   1963, Ecuadorian Navy

Ordered in 1954.

1 US 65 ft COASTAL PATROL CRAFT

Built by Halter Marine, New Orleans. Delivered 1976.

1 US 40 ft COASTAL PATROL CRAFT

Transferred 1971.

AMPHIBIOUS SHIPS

1 Ex-US "512-1152 SERIES" (LST)

Name	No.	Builders	Commissioned
HUALCOPO (ex-USS *Summit County*, LST 1148)	T 55	Chicago Bridge and Iron Co	9 June 1945

Displacement, tons: 1 653 standard; 4 080 full load
Dimensions, feet (metres): 328 × 50 × 14 *(100 × 16·1 × 4·3)*
Guns: 8—40 mm
Main engines: 2 General Motors diesels; 1 700 bhp; 2 shafts = 11·6 knots
Complement: 119
Troops: 147

Purchased 14 February 1977. Commissioned November 1977 after extensive refit.

140 ECUADOR / Amphibious ships — Floating dock

2 Ex-US "LSM-1" CLASS

Name	No.	Builders	Commissioned
JAMBELI (ex-USS *LSM 539* ex-T 31)	T 51	Brown S.B. Co, Houston	1945
TARQUI (ex-USS *LSM 555* ex-T 32)	T 52	Charleston Navy Yard	1945

Displacement, tons: 743 beaching; 1 095 full load
Dimensions, feet (metres): 196·5 wl; 203·0 oa × 34·0 × 7·9 *(61·9 × 10·3 × 2·4)*
Guns: 2—40 mm
Main engines: Diesels; 2 shafts; 2 800 bhp = 12·5 knots
Range, miles: 2 500 at 12 knots

Jambeli was laid down on 10 May 1945, *Tarqui* was laid down on 3 March 1945 and launched on 22 March 1945. Transferred to the Ecuadorian Navy at Green Cove Springs, Florida in November 1958.

JAMBELI (old Pennant number)   1967, Ecuadorian Navy

SURVEY VESSELS

1 Ex-US "ALOE" CLASS

Name	No.	Builders	Commissioned
ORION (ex-USS *Mulberry*, AN 27)	O 111 (ex-A 101)	American S.B. Co, Cleveland, Ohio	Nov 1941

Displacement, tons: 560 standard; 805 full load
Dimensions, feet (metres): 163 × 30·5 × 11·8 *(49·7 × 9·3 × 3·6)*
Gun: 1—3 in *(76 mm)*
Main engines: Diesel-electric; 800 bhp = 13 knots
Complement: 35

Former US netlayer. Launched on 26 March 1941. Transferred to Ecuador in November 1965 as loan and by purchase August 30 1978.

RIGEL O 112

Of 50 tons, launched in Ecuador in 1975. Complement ten.

TUGS

1 Ex-US "CHEROKEE" CLASS

Name	No.	Builders	Commissioned
CAYAMBE (ex-USS *Cusabo*, ATF 155)	R 101 (ex-R 51, ex-R 01)	Charleston S.B. & D.D. Co	28 Apr 1945
CHIMBORAZO (ex-USS *Chowanoc* ATF 100)	R 105	—	21 Feb 1945

Displacement, tons: 1 235 standard; 1 675 full load
Dimensions, feet (metres): 205 × 38·5 × 15·5 *(62·5 × 11·7 × 4·7)*
Guns: 1—3 in; 2—40 mm; 2—20 mm
Main engines: 4 diesels with electric drive; 3 000 bhp = 16·5 knots
Complement: 85

Cayambe launched on 26 February 1945. Fitted with powerful pumps and other salvage equipment. Transferred to Ecuador by lease on 2 November 1960 and renamed *Los Rios*. Again renamed *Cayambe* in 1966 and purchased 30 August 1978. *Chimborazo* transferred 1 October 1977.

CAYAMBE (old Pennant number)   1970, Ecuadorian Navy

Name	No.	Builders	Commissioned
SANGAY (ex-*Loja*)	R 102 (ex-R 53)	—	1952

Displacement, tons: 295 light; 390 full load
Dimensions, feet (metres): 107 × 26 × 14 *(32·6 × 7·9 × 4·3)*
Main engine: Fairbanks-Morse diesel; speed = 12 knots

Acquired in 1964. Renamed in 1966.

Name	No.	Builders	Commissioned
COTOPAXI (ex-USS *R. T. Ellis*)	R 103 (ex-R 52)	Equitable Building Corporation	1945

Displacement, tons: 150
Dimensions, feet (metres): 82 × 21 × 8 *(25 × 6·4 × 2·4)*
Main engine: Diesel; 1 shaft; 650 bhp = 9 knots

Purchased from the USA in 1947.

ANTIZANA R 104

MISCELLANEOUS

In addition unidentified *Pintac* reported.

TRAINING SHIP

Name	No.	Builders	Commissioned
GUAYAS	BE 01	Ast. Celaya, Spain	23 July 1977

Measurement, tons: 934 gross; 234 deadweight
Dimensions, feet (metres): 264 × 33·5 × 13·4 *(80 × 10·2 × 4·2)*
Main engine: 1 General Motors 12V-149 diesel; 700 bhp = 11·3 knots
Accommodation: 180

Three masted sail training ship. Launched 23 September 1976.

1 Ex-US SUPPLY SHIP

Name	No.	Builders	Commissioned
CALICUCHIMA (ex-US *FS 525*)	T 53 (ex-T 34, ex-T 42)	USA	1944

Displacement, tons: 650 light; 950 full load
Dimensions, feet (metres): 176 × 32 × 14 *(53·7 × 9·8 × 4·3)*
Main engines: Diesels; 2 shafts; 500 bhp = 11 knots

Former US small cargo ship of the Army FS type. Leased to Ecuador on 8 April 1963 and purchased on 30 August 1978. Provides service to the Galapagos Islands.

2 Ex-US YP TYPE

Name	No.	Builders	Commissioned
ISLA DE LA PLATA	UT 111	SA	—
ISLA PUNA	UT 112	USA	—

Dimensions, feet (metres): 42 *(12·8)*
Main engine: 1 diesel

Transferred 1962. Coast Guard utility boats.

1 Ex-US YR TYPE

Name	No.	Builders	Commissioned
PUTUMAYO (ex-US *YR 34*)	BT 123 (ex-BT 62)	New York Navy Yard	—

Repair barge leased July 1962. Purchased 30 August 1978.

1 Ex-US "YW" CLASS WATER CARRIER

Name	No.	Builders	Commissioned
ATAHUALPA (ex-US *YW 131*)	T 62 (ex-T 33, ex-T 41, ex-A 01)	Leatham D. Smith S.B. Co.	1945

Displacement, tons: 415 light; 1 235 full load
Dimensions, feet (metres): 174·0 × 32·0 × 15·0 *(53·1 × 9·8 × 4·6)*
Main engines: General Motors diesels; 750 bhp = 11·5 knots

Acquired by the Ecuadorian Navy on 2 May 1963. Purchased 30 August 1978.

1 Ex-US "ARD 12" CLASS FLOATING DOCK

Name	No.	Builders	Commissioned
AMAZONAS (ex-US *ARD 17*)	DF 121	USA	1944

Measurement, tons: 3 500 lifting capacity
Dimensions, feet (metres): 491·7 oa × 81·0 oa × 32·9 *(149·9 × 24·7 × 10)*

Transferred on loan on 7 January 1961. Suitable for docking destroyers and landing ships. Dry dock companion craft YFND 20 was leased on 2 November 1961.

EGYPT

Ministerial

Minister of Defence:
  General Kamal Hussein Ali

Administrative

Armed Forces Chief of Staff:
  General Ahmad Badawi

Headquarters Appointment

Commander of Naval Forces:
  Rear-Admiral Mohamed Ali Mohamed

Diplomatic Representation

Defence Attaché in London:
  Brigadier M. Lotfy Abou el Kheir

Light Forces

1975 4 "P 6" Class
      4 "108" Class

Strength of the Fleet

Type	Active	Building (Projected)
Destroyers	5	—
Frigates	3	(2)
Submarines (Patrol)	12	(2)
Fast Attack Craft (Missile)	21	—
Fast Attack Craft (Torpedo)	26	—
Fast Attack Craft (Gun)	4	(6)
Large Patrol Craft	15	—
Coastal Patrol Craft	6	—
LCTs	3	—
LCUs	14	—
Minesweepers (Ocean)	10	—
Minesweepers (Inshore)	4	—
Training Ships	2	—
Tugs	2	—
Hovercraft	3	—
Miscellaneous	5	—

New Construction and Refits

The rupture of relations with the USSR has meant a greater reliance by Egypt on Western shipbuilders and repairers. So far reported—although not officially confirmed either in Egypt or by the contractors—are the following:
(a) Construction of 6—52 metre Fast Attack Craft by Vosper Thornycroft ("Ramadan" class).
(b) Construction of 2 "Agosta" class submarines in France.
(c) Construction of 2 "Lupo" class frigates in Italy.

DELETIONS

Auxiliary

1972(?) *Nasr* (ex-HMS *Bude*) sunk as Styx target

Personnel

(a) 1979: 17 500 officers and men, including the Coast Guard. (Reserves of about 12 000)
(b) 3 years national service

Bases

Alexandria, Port Said, Mersa Matru, Port Tewfik, Hurghada and Safaqa on the Red Sea.
Naval Academy; Abu Quir.

Coastal Defences

The Samlet missiles employed for Coastal Defence are Naval-manned.

Mercantile Marine

Lloyd's Register of Shipping:
  205 vessels of 456 291 tons gross

SUBMARINES

Note: See New Construction section at head of entry.

6 Ex-SOVIET "ROMEO" CLASS

711   722   733   744   755   766

Displacement, tons: 1 000 surfaced; 1 600 dived
Length, feet (metres): 251·9 *(76·8)*
Beam, feet (metres): 24·0 *(7·3)*
Draught, feet (metres): 18 *(5·5)*
Torpedo tubes: 6—21 in *(533 mm)* (bow); 2—21 in (stern)
Main machinery: 2 diesels; 4 000 bhp; 2 electric motors; 4 000 hp; 2 shafts
Speed, knots: 17 surfaced; 16 dived
Range, miles: 16 000 at 10 knots surfaced
Complement: 54

One "Romeo" was transferred to Egypt in February 1966. Two more replaced "Whiskeys" in May 1966 and another pair was delivered later that year. The sixth boat joined in 1969. Unconfirmed reports suggest two of this class have been used for spares.

"ROMEO" Class No. 766   1978

6 Ex-SOVIET "WHISKEY" CLASS

415   418   421   432   455   477

Displacement, tons: 1 080 surface; 1 350 dived
Length, feet (metres): 249·6 *(76)*
Beam, feet (metres): 22 *(6·7)*
Draught, feet (metres): 15·1 *(4·9)*
Torpedo tubes: 6—21 in *(533 mm)*; 4 bow, 2 stern; 18 torpedoes or 40 mines
Main machinery: 2 diesels; 4 000 bhp; 2 electric motors; 2 500 hp
Speed, knots: 18 surfaced; 15 dived
Range, miles: 13 000 at 8 knots surfaced
Complement: 54

The first four "Whiskey" class were transferred from the Soviet Navy to the Egyptian Navy in June 1957. Three more arrived at Alexandria on 24 January 1958. Another was transferred to Egypt at Alexandria in January 1962. Two were replaced by "Romeos" in February 1966.
Two "Whiskey" class sailed from Alexandria to Leningrad in late 1971 under escort, being replaced the following year.
455 is non-operational.

"WHISKEY" Class No 418   1974

142 EGYPT / Destroyers — Frigates

DESTROYERS

4 Ex-SOVIET "SKORY" CLASS

6 OCTOBER (ex *Suez*) 666	**DIAMIETTE** 844
AL ZAFFER 822	**AL NASSER** 888

Displacement, tons: 2 240 standard; 3 080 full load
Length, feet (metres): 395·2 *(120·5)*
Beam, feet (metres): 38·7 *(11·8)*
Draught, feet (metres): 15·1 *(4·6)*
Missiles: SSM; 2 SS-N-2 (*Al Zaffer* only)
Guns: 4—5·1 in *(130 mm)*/50; 2—3·4 in *(88 mm)*;
    8—37 mm; 4—25 mm (twins) (unmodified);
    4—57 mm (quad); 4—37 mm (twins);
    4—25 mm (twins) (modified)
A/S weapons: 2 DCT; 2 DC racks (unmodified)
    2—12-barrelled RBU 2500;
    2 DCT; 2 DC racks (modified)
Torpedo tubes: 10—21 in *(533 mm)* (quins)
Mines: 80 can be carried
Main engines: Geared turbines; 2 shafts; 60 000 shp
Boilers: 3
Speed, knots: 35
Range, miles: 4 000 at 15 knots
Complement: 272

Launched in 1951. *Al Nasser* and *Al Zaffer* were delivered to the Egyptian Navy on 11 June 1956 at Alexandria. *Damiette* and *Suez* were delivered at Alexandria in January 1962. In April 1967 the original *Al Nasser* and *Damiette* were exchanged for ships with modified secondary and A/S armament which took the same names. *Suez* was later renamed *6 October* to commemorate the Egyptian crossing of the Suez Canal in the 1973 Israeli war.

Radar: Search: High Sieve; Cross Bird.
Navigation: Don.
Fire control: Top Bow, Half Bow or Post Lamp.

AL ZAFFER (with SS-N-2)   1978

AL ZAFFER (Before modernisation)   1977

1 Ex-BRITISH "Z" CLASS

Name	No.	Builders	Laid down	Launched	Commissioned
EL FATEH (ex-HMS *Zenith*)	833	Wm. Denny & Bros, Dumbarton	19 May 1942	5 June 1944	22 Dec 1944

Displacement, tons: 1 730 standard; 2 575 full load
Length, feet (metres): 350 *(106·8)* wl; 362·8 *(110·6)* oa
Beam, feet (metres): 35·7 *(10·9)*
Draught, feet (metres): 17·1 *(5·2)*
Guns: 4—4·5 in *(115 mm)*/45 (singles); 6—40 mm/60
A/S weapons: 4 DCT
Main engines: Parsons geared turbines; 2 shafts; 40 000 shp
Boilers: 2 Admiralty 3-drum
Speed, knots: 31
Oil fuel, tons: 580
Range, miles: 2 800 at 20 knots
Complement: 250

Purchased from the UK in 1955. Before being taken over by Egypt, *El Fateh* was refitted by John I. Thornycroft & Co Ltd, Woolston, Southampton in July 1956, subsequently modernised by J. S. White & Co Ltd, Cowes, completing July 1964.

Radar: Search: Type 960 Metric wavelength.
Tactical: Type 293. E/F Band.
Fire control: I Band.

EL FATEH   11/1977

FRIGATES

Note: See New Construction section at head of entry.

1 Ex-BRITISH "BLACK SWAN" CLASS

Name	No.	Builders	Laid down	Launched	Commissioned
TARIQ (ex-*Malek Farouq*, ex-HMS *Whimbrel*)	555 (ex-42)	Yarrow & Co Ltd, Glasgow	31 Oct 1941	25 Aug 1942	13 Jan 1943

Displacement, tons: 1 490 standard; 1 925 full load
Length, feet (metres): 283 *(86·3)* pp; 299·5 *(91·3)* oa
Beam, feet (metres): 38·5 *(11·7)*
Draught, feet (metres): 14·0 *(4·3)*
Guns: 6—4 in *(102 mm)*/45 (twins Mk 19); 4—40 mm/60;
    2—20 mm
A/S weapons: 4 DCT; DC racks
Main engines: Geared turbines; 2 shafts; 4 300 shp
Boilers: two 3-drum type
Speed, knots: 19·75
Oil fuel, tons: 370
Range, miles: 4 500 at 12 knots
Complement: 180

Transferred from the UK in November 1949. Was recently to have been converted as a submarine tender—decision deferred.

TARIQ   1978

EGYPT / Frigates — Light forces 143

1 Ex-BRITISH "RIVER" CLASS

Name	No.	Builders	Laid down	Launched	Commissioned
RASHID (ex-HMS *Spey*)	511 (ex-43)	Smith's Dock Co Ltd	18 July 1941	10 Dec 1941	19 May 1942

Displacement, tons: 1 490 standard; 2 216 full load
Length, feet (metres): 283 *(86.3)* pp; 301.5 *(91.9)* oa
Beam, feet (metres): 36.7 *(11.2)*
Draught, feet (metres): 14.1 *(4.3)*
Guns: 1—4 in *(102 mm)*/45; 2—40 mm/60 (twin Mk 5); 6—20 mm/70
A/S weapons: 4 DCT
Main engines: Triple expansion; 2 shafts; 5 500 ihp
Boilers: 2 Admiralty 3-drum type
Speed, knots: 18
Oil fuel, tons: 640
Range, miles: 7 700 at 12 knots
Complement: 180

Purchased in December 1949. Has been operated as Submarine Support Ship.

Appearance: Was fitted with large deck-house aft.

RASHID   1978

1 Ex-BRITISH "HUNT" CLASS

Name	No.	Builders	Laid down	Launched	Commissioned
PORT SAID (ex-*Mohamed Ali*, ex-*Ibrahim el Awal*, ex-HMS *Cottesmore*)	525 (ex-11)	Yarrow & Co Ltd, Glasgow	12 Dec 1939	5 Sep 1940	29 Dec 1940

Displacement, tons: 1 000 standard; 1 490 full load
Length, feet (metres): 273 *(83.2)* wl; 280 *(85.3)* oa
Beam, feet (metres): 29 *(8.8)*
Draught, feet (metres): 14.1 *(4.3)*
Guns: 4—4 in *(103 mm)*/45 (single); 2—37 mm; 2—25 mm (twin)
A/S weapons: 2DCT
Main engines: Parsons geared turbines; 2 shafts; 19 000 shp
Boilers: two 3-drum type
Speed, knots: 25
Oil fuel, tons: 280
Range, miles: 2 000 at 12 knots
Complement: 146

Transferred from the Royal Navy to the Egyptian Navy in July 1950: sailed for Egypt in April 1951, after a nine months refit by J. Samuel White & Co Ltd, Cowes.

PORT SAID   1978

LIGHT FORCES

Note: See New Construction section at head of entry.

8 Ex-SOVIET "OSA I" CLASS (FAST ATTACK CRAFT—MISSILE)

301 312 323 341 356 378 389 390

Displacement, tons: 160 standard; 210 full load
Dimensions, feet (metres): 127.9 × 26.6 × 5.9 *(39 × 8.1 × 1.8)*
Missiles: SSM; 4 SS-N-2 (singles) (see notes)
Guns: 4—30 mm (2 twin, 1 fwd, 1 aft) (+2 MG in refitted craft)
Main engines: 3 diesels (MTU in refitted boats); 12 000 bhp = 36 knots
Complement: 30

Ten reported to have been delivered to Egypt by the Soviet Navy in 1966. Some reported sunk during the Israeli War October 1973. At least four have been refitted as above.

Missiles: All carry SA-7 Grail.
Radar: Recently refitted craft carry a new Kelvin Hughes 1006 surveillance radar and a Decca navigation radar.
Before refit: Search: Square Tie.
Fire control: Drum Tilt.
IF: High Pole and Square Head.

"OSA I" Class   1974, USN

4 Ex-SOVIET "KOMAR" CLASS (FAST ATTACK CRAFT—MISSILE)

Displacement, tons: 68 standard; 75 full load
Dimensions, feet (metres): 87.9 × 20.3 × 4.9 *(26.8 × 6.2 × 1.5)*
Missiles: SSM; 2 SS-N-2 (singles)
Guns: 2—25 mm (twin); 2—7.62 mm (single)
Main engines: 4 diesels; 4 shafts; 4 800 hp = 40 knots
Range, miles: 400 at 30 knots
Complement: 19

Transferred from the USSR in 1962 to 1967. One of this type was sunk by Israeli jets on 16 May 1970. Two reported sunk in Israeli War October 1973.

Radar: Search: Square Tie.
IF: High Pole and Dead Duck.

"KOMAR" Class   1966, Colonel Bjorn Borg

144 EGYPT / Light forces

9 + ? EGYPTIAN "OCTOBER" CLASS (FAST ATTACK CRAFT—MISSILE)

Displacement, tons: 80 full load
Dimensions, feet (metres): 84 × 20 × 5 (25·6 × 6 × 1·5)
Missiles: Otomat (French version)
Guns: 2—30 mm British A 32
Main engines: 4 diesels; 4 shafts; 4 800 hp = 40 knots
Range, miles: 400 at 30 knots
Complement: ? 20

Built in Alexandria 1975—76. Hull of same design as Soviet "Komar" class and fitted with Soviet diesels although now reported that these have been replaced with MTU. The armament is of West European manufacture including British electronics.
Six being refitted by Vosper Thornycraft, first to complete 1979. Up to three other craft built but being fitted out in Egypt.

"OCTOBER" Class   1978, Michael D. J. Lennon

6 Ex-SOVIET "SHERSHEN" CLASS
(2 FAST ATTACK CRAFT—TORPEDO, 4 FAST ATTACK CRAFT—GUN)

310   321   332   343   354   365

Displacement, tons: 145 standard; 160 full load
Dimensions, feet (metres): 118·1 × 25·3 × 4·9 (36 × 7·7 × 1·5)
Guns: 4—30 mm (2 twin)
Rocket launchers: 40 tube; (122 mm) (see notes)
Torpedo tubes: 4—21 in (533 mm) (single)
A/S weapons: 12 DC
Main engines: 3 diesels; 3 shafts; 13 200 hp = 41 knots
Complement: 16

One delivered from USSR in February 1967, two more in October 1967, and three since. Four have had their guns removed to make way for multiple BM21 rocket-launchers and one SA-7 Grail.

Radar: Search: Pot Drum.
Fire Control: Drum Tilt.
IFF: High Pole.

"SHERSHEN" Class   1974, USN

20 Ex-SOVIET "P 6" CLASS (FAST ATTACK CRAFT—TORPEDO)

Displacement, tons: 64 standard; 73 full load
Dimensions, feet (metres): 85·3 × 20 × 4·9 (26 × 6·1 × 1·5)
Guns: 2 or 4—25 mm (12 have forward guns replaced by 122 mm 8-barrelled rocket launcher)
Torpedo tubes: 2—21 in (4—21 in in two boats)
A/S weapons: 12 DCs
Main engines: 4 diesels; 4 shafts; 4 800 hp = 41 knots
Range, miles: 450 at 30 knots
Complement: 20

The first twelve boats arrived at Alexandria on 19 April 1956, 6 more in 1960. Two were destroyed by British naval aircraft on 4 November 1956, two were sunk by the Israeli destroyer *Elath* off Sinai on 12 July 1967, two by Israeli MTBs off Sinai coast on 11 July 1967, two by Israeli air attacks in 1969, and two in the Red Sea on 22 January 1970.
Further reinforcements have been sent by USSR—none since October 1973. Several have been built at Alexandria.

Radar: Decca in most craft.
Rockets: Twelve fitted with BM21 rocket launchers

"P 6" Class   1978

4 Ex-SOVIET/SYRIAN "P 4" CLASS (FAST ATTACK CRAFT—TORPEDO)

Transferred by Syria in 1970. Now armed with 8 barrelled 122 mm rocket launcher forward and twin 14·5 mm aft as well as two torpedo tubes. Decca radar is now fitted.

"P 4" Class with 8-barrelled rocket launcher   10/197

12 Ex-SOVIET "SO I" CLASS (LARGE PATROL CRAFT)

211 217 222 228 230 233 239 244 251 255 262 266

Displacement, tons: 170 light; 215 full load
Dimensions, feet (metres): 137·8 × 19·7 × 5·9 (42 × 6 × 1·8)
Guns: 4—25 mm (2 twin mountings)
A/S weapons: four 5-barrelled MBU 1800
Mines: Can carry 20
Main engines: 3 diesel; 7 500 bhp = 28 knots
Range, miles: 1 100 at 13 knots
Complement: 31

Eight reported to have been transferred by the USSR to Egypt in 1962 to 1967 and four others later.
Some craft carry SA-7 Grail missiles and others two—21 in torpedo tubes. Six are fitted with BM21 rocket launchers.

222   19

EGYPT / Light forces — Mine warfare forces 145

3 LARGE PATROL CRAFT

NISR   NIMR   THAR

Displacement, tons: 110
Gun: 1—20 mm

Built by Castro, Port Said and launched in May 1963.

6 BERTRAM TYPE (COASTAL PATROL CRAFT)

Displacement, tons: 8 approx
Length, feet (metres): 28 (8·5)
Guns: 2—12·7 mm MG
Rocket launchers: 4—122 mm

GRP hulls. Built in Miami, Florida

Now in service probably with the Coast Guard.

BERTRAM Type   10/1974

AMPHIBIOUS FORCES

3 Ex-SOVIET "POLNOCHNIY" CLASS (LCT)

915   +2

Displacement, tons: 1 000 full load
Dimensions, feet (metres): 239·4 × 29·5 × 5·9 (73 × 9 × 1·8)
Guns: 2—25 mm (twin)
Rocket launchers: 2—18-barrelled 140 mm launchers
Main engines: 2 diesels; 5 000 bhp = 18 knots
Complement: 40

Can carry six tanks. Transferred early 1970s.

915   1978

10 Ex-SOVIET "VYDRA" CLASS (LCU)

681   +9

Displacement, tons: 425 standard; 600 full load
Dimensions, feet (metres): 179·7 × 26·6 × 6·6 (54·8 × 8·1 × 2)
Main engines: Two 3D 12 diesels; 2 shafts; 800 bhp = 11 knots

Can carry and land up to 250 tons of military equipment and stores. For a period after the "October War" several were fitted with rocket launchers and two 37 or 40 mm guns all of which have now been removed.

4 Ex-SOVIET "SMB 1" CLASS (LCU)

Displacement, tons: 200 standard; 420 full load
Dimensions, feet (metres): 157·5 × 21·3 × 5·6 (48 × 6·5 × 1·7)
Main engines: 2 diesels; 400 hp = 11 knots

Delivered to the Egyptian Navy in 1965. Can carry 150 tons of military equipment.

10 LCMs

Generally used as harbour-craft.

MINE WARFARE FORCES

6 Ex-SOVIET "T 43" CLASS (MINESWEEPERS—OCEAN)

ASSIUT   CHARKIEH   GHARBIA
BAHAIRA   DAKHLA   SINAI

Displacement, tons: 500 standard; 580 full load
Dimensions, feet (metres): 190·2 × 27·6 × 6·9 (58 × 8·4 × 2·1)
Guns: 4—37 mm (twins); 2—25 mm (twins)
A/S weapons: 2 DCT
Main engines: 2 diesels; 2 shafts; 2 200 hp = 14 knots
Range, miles: 3 200 at 10 knots
Complement: 65

Three were transferred from the Soviet Navy and delivered to Egypt 1956-59, and three since 1970. *Miniya* was sunk by Israeli air attack in the Gulf of Suez on 6 February 1970 but was later replaced.

Pennant numbers: Include 650, 659, 672.
Radar: Ball End and Neptun.

"T 43" Class   1978

4 Ex-SOVIET "YURKA" CLASS (MINESWEEPERS—OCEAN)

GIZA 690   ASWAN 695   QENA 696   SOHAG 699

Displacement, tons: 400 standard; 460 full load
Dimensions, feet (metres): 172 × 31 × 6·6 (52·5 × 9·5 × 2)
Guns: 4—30 mm (2 twin)
Mines: Can lay 20
Main engines: 2 diesels; 4 000 bhp = 18 knots
Complement: 45

Steel-hulled minesweepers transferred from USSR 1970-71.

Appearance: Egyptian "Yurka" class do not carry Drum Tilt radar and have a number of ship's-side scuttles.

Radar: Navigation: Don

ASWAN   1978

146 EGYPT / Mine warfare forces — Miscellaneous

2 Ex-SOVIET "T 301" CLASS (MINESWEEPERS—INSHORE)

EL FAYOUD 708   **EL MANUFIEH**

Displacement, tons: 140 standard; 160 full load
Dimensions, feet (metres): 121·6 × 19·7 × 4·9 *(38·1 × 5·5 × 1·5)*
Guns: 2—37 mm; 2—MG
Main engines: 2 diesels; 2 shafts; 1 440 hp = 13 knots
Complement: 20

Reported to have been transferred by the USSR to Egypt in 1962; a third ship may have been transferred later.

Radar: IFF; Dead Duck and High Pole A.

EL FAYOUD   1978

2 Ex-SOVIET "K 8" CLASS (MINESWEEPERS—INSHORE)

618 + 1

Displacement, tons: 20 standard; 26 full load
Dimensions, feet (metres): 55·4 × 10·5 × 3·9 *(16·9 × 3·2 × 1·2)*
Guns: 2—14·5 mm
Main engines: 2 diesels; 700 shp = 18 knots
Complement: 6

Several transferred but survivors used mainly as harbour-craft.

"K8" Class   1978

SURVEY CRAFT

SAFAGA   **ABU EL GHOSON**

Of 20 tons, launched in 1968 with complement of four officers and 14 men.

MISCELLANEOUS

3 WINCHESTER (SR.N6) HOVERCRAFT

Displacement, tons: 10 normal gross weight
Dimensions, feet (metres): 48·4 × 25·3 × 15·9 (height) *(14·8 × 7·7 × 4·8)*
Guns: MGs
Main engine: 1 Gnome Model 1050 gas turbine = 58 knots

Purchased in 1975 as refitted second-hand craft. Reportedly converted into minelayers

2 Ex-YUGOSLAVIAN "108" CLASS (FAST TARGET CRAFT)

Displacement, tons: 55 standard; 60 full load
Dimensions, feet (metres): 69 pp; 78 oa × 21·3 × 7·8 *(23·8 oa × 6·5 × 2·4)*
Main engines: 3 Packard motors; 3 shafts; 5 000 bhp = 36 knots
Complement: 14

Purchased from Yugoslavia in 1956. Similar to the boats of the US "Higgins" class. Originally a class of six. Remaining pair now fitted with reflectors and used as targets.

2 Ex-SOVIET "NYRYAT" CLASS

Diving support ships transferred in 1964.

2 Ex-SOVIET "POLUCHAT II" CLASS

Torpedo recovery craft.

2 Ex-SOVIET "OKHTENSKY" CLASS TUGS

AL MAKAS   **ANTAR**

Two transferred to the Egyptian Navy in 1966—assembled in Egypt.

1 Ex-SOVIET "SEKSTAN" CLASS

160

Used as cadet training ship.

2 TRAINING SHIPS

EL HORRIYA (ex-*Mahroussa*)

Of 4 560 tons, built by Sanuda, Poplar in 1865 and once the Egyptian Royal Yacht, has been completely refitted and is used as a training ship.

EL HORRIYA   1976, USN

INTISHAT
A smaller training ship.

SWIMMER DELIVERY VEHICLES

There is a strong underwater team in the Egyptian navy who use, amongst other equipment, the two-man SDVs shown here. Range could be four hours at 3-4 knots.

SDV   10/1974

EL SALVADOR

Personnel
(a) 1979: 130 officers and men
(b) Voluntary service

Ports
Acajutla, La Libertad, La Union

Mercantile Marine
Lloyd's Register of Shipping:
2 vessels of 1 987 tons gross

DELETION

1975 GC 1

PATROL BOATS

1 Ex-BRITISH HDML

Name	No.	Builders	Commissioned
GC 2 (ex-*Nohaba*)	—	UK	1942

Displacement, tons: 46
Dimensions, feet (metres): 72 × 16 × 5·5 *(21·9 × 4·9 × 1·7)*
Gun: 1—20 mm
Main engines: 2 diesels; 2 shafts = 12 knots
Complement: 16

Purchased from commercial sources in 1959.

2 Ex-US CG TYPE

Name	No.	Builders	Commissioned
GC 3	—	USA	1950
GC 4	—	USA	1950

Displacement, tons: 10·6
Dimensions, feet (metres): 40·3 × 11·2 × 3·3 *(12·3 × 3·4 × 1·0)*
Gun: 1—12·7 mm
Main engines: 2 diesels; 2 shafts; 400 hp = 18 knots
Range, miles: 160 at 18 knots

1 SEWART 65 ft TYPE

Name	No.	Builders	Commissioned
GC 5	—	Sewart, USA	1967

Displacement, tons: 33
Dimensions, feet (metres): 65 × 16·3 × 5·0 *(19·8 × 4·9 × 1·5)*
Guns: 3 MG
Main engines: General Motors diesels; 1 600 hp = 25 knots

Transferred September 1967.

3 CAMCRAFT 100 ft TYPE

GC 6, GC 7, GC 8

100 ft *(30·5 m)* craft ordered in 1976.

Miscellaneous: 25 launches with outboard engines are also held.

EQUATORIAL GUINEA

Ministerial
President and Minister of People's Armed Forces:
Francisco Macias Nguema

Personnel
1979: 100 officers and men

Ports
Malabo, Bata (Rio Muni).

Mercantile Marine
Lloyd's Register of Shipping:
1 vessel of 3 070 tons gross

LIGHT FORCES

1 Ex-SOVIET "P6" CLASS (FAST ATTACK CRAFT—TORPEDO)

Displacement, tons: 64 standard; 73 full load
Dimensions, feet (metres): 84·2 × 20 × 4·9 *(25·7 × 6·1 × 1·5)*
Guns: 4—25 mm
Torpedo tubes: 2—21 in *(533 mm)*
A/S Weapons: 8 DCs
Main engines: 4 M50 diesels; 4 shafts; 4 800 hp = 41 knots
Range, miles: 450 at 30 knots
Complement: 20

Doubtful if the torpedo armament is operational.

Radar: Skin Head.

1 Ex-SOVIET "POLUCHAT" CLASS

Displacement, tons: 70 standard; 91 full load
Dimensions, feet (metres): 97·1 × 19·0 × 4·8 *(29·6 × 5·8 × 1·5)*
Guns: 2—14·5 mm (twin)
Main engines: 2 diesels; 2 shafts; 2 400 bhp = 20 knots
Range, miles: 460 at 17 knots
Complement: 16

Miscellaneous: 2 small patrol craft.

ETHIOPIA

Personnel
(a) 1979: 2 000 officers and men
(b) Voluntary service ?

Naval Establishments
Massawa: Naval Base and College, established in 1956.
Embaticalla: Marine Commando Training School.
Assab: Naval Base, expanding to include a ship repair facility.

Mercantile Marine
Lloyd's Register of Shipping:
17 vessels of 23 490 tons gross

DELETION

1977   PC 12 sunk

FRIGATE
1 Ex-US "BARNEGAT" CLASS

Name	No.	Builders	Commissioned
ETHIOPIA (ex-USS *Orca*, AVP 49)	A 01	Lake Washington S.Y.	23 Jan 1944

Displacement, tons: 1 766 standard; 2 800 full load
Dimensions, feet (metres): 310·8 × 41 × 13·5 *(94·7 × 12·5 × 3·7)*
Guns: 1—5 in/38; 5—40 mm
Main engines: 2 sets diesels; 2 shafts; 6 080 bhp = 18·2 knots
Complement: 215

Former US small seaplane tender of "Barnegat" class. Laid down 13 July 1942, launched on 4 October 1942. Transferred from the US Navy in January 1962.

ETHIOPIA   1972, Imperial Ethiopian Navy

EX-MINESWEEPER (COASTAL)
1 Ex-NETHERLANDS "WILDERVANK" CLASS

Name	No.	Builders	Commissioned
MS 41 (ex-*Elst*, M 829)	—	Netherlands	1956

Displacement, tons: 373 standard; 417 full load
Dimensions, feet (metres): 149·8 × 28·0 × 7·5 *(45·7 × 8·5 × 2·3)*
Guns: 2—40 mm
Main engines: 2 Werkspoor diesels; 2 shafts; 2 500 bhp = 14 knots
Oil fuel, tons: 25 tons
Range, miles: 2 500 at 10 knots
Complement: 38

Launched 21 March 1956. Purchased by Ethiopia and transferred from the Royal Netherlands Navy in 1971.

Missiles: It has been reported that MS 41 has been fitted for launching SS-12 missiles.

MS 41 (as *Elst*)

LIGHT FORCES

4 EX-SOVIET "OSA II" CLASS (FAST ATTACK CRAFT—MISSILE)

Displacement, tons: 165 standard; 210 full-load
Dimensions, feet (metres): 127·9 × 26·6 × 5·9 *(39 × 8·1 × 1·8)*
Missiles: SSM; 4 SS-N-2 (single launchers)
Guns: 4—30 mm (twin)
Main engines: 3 M504 diesels; 15 000 hp; 3 shafts = 36 knots
Range, miles: 800 at 25 knots
Complement: 30

First delivered spring 1978 the remainder in autumn 1978 with possibly more to follow. Because of Ethiopian naval inexperience with such craft and missiles it is presumed that Soviet "advisers" will remain embarked. The presence of these craft in the Dahlak Islands, where the navigable Red Sea is only 60 miles wide, could pose a threat to shipping not oriented to Ethiopia or the USSR.

Radar: Surveillance: Square Tie
Fire control: Drum Tilt
IFF: Square Head and High Pole B.

"Osa II" Class

2 EX-SOVIET "MOL" CLASS (FAST ATTACK CRAFT — TORPEDO)

Displacement, tons: 160 standard; 210 full load
Dimensions, feet (metres): 127·9 × 26·6 × 5·9 *(39 × 8·1 × 1·8)*
Guns: 4—30 mm (twins)
Torpedo tubes: 4—21 in (533 mm)
A/S weapons: 12 DCs
Main engines: 3 diesels; 3 shafts; 13 500 hp = 36 knots
Complement: 30

Transferred spring 1978. It is not certain whether the torpedo tubes are shipped.

Radar: Surveillance: Pot Drum
Fire control: Drum Tilt
IFF: Square Head, High Pole B.

"MOL" Class (without torpedo tubes)

4 SEWART "105 ft" TYPE (LARGE PATROL CRAFT)

P 201   P 202   P 203   P 204

Displacement, tons: 118
Dimensions, feet (metres): 105 × 20 × 6·5 *(32 × 6·1 × 2)*
Guns: 4 Emerlec 30 mm (twins); 1—20 mm
Main engines: 2 diesels = 30 knots
Complement: 21

Eight ordered in 1976 of which four were delivered in April 1977 before the cessation of US arms sales with Ethiopia.

ETHIOPIA / Light forces — FIJI

4 "PGM 53" AND USCG "CAPE" CLASSES (LARGE PATROL CRAFT)

Name	No.	Builders	Commissioned
PC 11 (ex-US CG WVP 95304)	—	Peterson, USA	1958
PC 13 (ex-USN PGM 53)	—	Peterson, USA	1961
PC 14 (ex-USN PGM 54)	—	Peterson, USA	1961
PC 15 (ex-USN PGM 58)	—	Peterson, USA	1962

Displacement, tons: 145·5 full load
Dimensions, feet (metres): 95 × 19 × 5·2 (29·0 × 5·8 × 1·6)
Guns: 1—40 mm; 1—50 cal MG
A/S weapons: 1 Mousetrap
Main engines: 4 diesels; 2 shafts; 2 200 bhp = 21 knots
Range, miles: 1 500 at cruising speed
Complement: 20

Loss: PC 12 sunk by Ethiopian Air Force in 1977 while trying to defect.

"PGM 53" Class 1970, Imperial Ethiopian Navy

1 Ex-YUGOSLAV "KRALJEVICA" CLASS (LARGE PATROL CRAFT)

Name	No.	Builders	Commissioned
— (ex-507)	—	Yugoslavia	1953

Displacement, tons: 190·5 standard; 202 full load
Dimensions, feet (metres): 134·5 × 20·7 × 7·2 (41 × 6·3 × 2·2)
Guns: 1—3 in; 1—40 mm; 4—20 mm
A/S weapons: DCs
Main engines: 2 MAN diesels; 2 shafts; 3 300 bhp = 18 knots

Transferred 1975.

4 "SEWART" CLASS (COASTAL PATROL CRAFT)

Name	No.	Builders	Commissioned
GB 21	—	Sewart Inc, Berwick	1966
GB 22	—	Sewart Inc, Berwick	1966
GB 23	—	Sewart Inc, Berwick	1967
GB 24	—	Sewart Inc, Berwick	1967

Displacement, tons: 15
Length, feet (metres): 40 (12·2)
Guns: 2—50 cal/MG
Speed, knots: 20
Complement: 7

GB 21 1970, Imperial Ethiopian Navy

LANDING CRAFT

There are two of the US LCM type and two of the US LCVP type. Two were bought in 1962 and two in 1971.

FIJI

On 12 June 1974 the Royal Fiji Military Forces were authorised to raise a Naval Squadron to carry out Fishery Protection, Surveillance, Hydrographic Surveying and Coast Guard duties. The RFMF is under the authority of the Minister for Home Affairs.

Commanding Officers

RFMF:
  Colonel P. F. Manueli OBE

Naval Squadron:
  Commander S. B. Brown MBE VRD

Personnel

1979: 160 (20 officers, 140 sailors)

Ministerial

Minister for Home Affairs:
  Ratu Sir Penaia Ganilau KBE CMG CVO DSO

Base

HMFS Viti, Suva.

Prefix to Ships' Names

HMFS.

Mercantile Marine

Lloyd's Register of Shipping:
  37 vessels of 10 023 tons gross

3 Ex-US "REDWING" CLASS (MINESWEEPERS—COASTAL)

Name	No.	Builders	Commissioned
KIKAU (ex-USS Woodpecker, MSC 209)	204	Bellingham SY, USA	3 Feb 1956
KULA (ex-USS Vireo, MSC 205)	205	Bellingham SY, USA	7 June 1955
KIRO (ex-USS Warbler, MSC 206)	206	Bellingham SY, USA	23 July 1955

Displacement, tons: 370 full load
Dimensions, feet (metres): 144 oa × 28 × 8·5 (43·9 × 8·5 × 2·6)
Guns: 1—20 mm; 2—5 MG
Main engines: 2 General Motors diesels; 2 shafts; 880 bhp = 13 knots
Range, miles: 2 500 at 10 knots
Complement: 39

First pair transferred 14 October 1975 and the third in June 1976. Kiro and Kula have been refitted for removal of magnetic MS equipment.

KIRO 1976, RFMF

RUVE (ex-Volasiga, ex-Marinetta)

Displacement, tons: 100
Dimensions, feet (metres): 94 × 17·5 × 7·5 (28·7 × 5·3 × 2·3)
Complement: 14

Transferred from Fiji Marine Department, June 1976. Used for Surveying.
Built in 1929. Replacement of 30 metres length, laid down at Suva April 1978 for completion April 1979.

150 FINLAND / Introduction — Frigates

FINLAND

Headquarters Appointment

Commander-in-Chief Finnish Navy:
Rear-Admiral Jorma Haapkylä

Diplomatic Representation

Naval Attaché in London:
Lieutenant-Colonel Pertti E. Nykänen

Naval Attaché in Moscow:
Colonel Kalevi Markkula

Naval Attaché in Paris:
Lieutenant-Colonel Sami Sihvo

Naval Attaché in Washington:
Colonel Veikko Hietamies

Treaty Limitations

The Finnish Navy is limited by the Treaty of Paris (1947) to 10 000 tons of ships and 4 500 personnel. Submarines and torpedo boats are prohibited.

Personnel

(a) 1975: 2 500 (200 officers and 2 300 ratings)
    1976: 2 500 (200 officers and 2 300 ratings)
    1977: 2 500 (200 officers and 2 300 ratings)
    1978: 2 500 (200 officers and 2 300 ratings)
    1979: 2 500 (200 officers and 2 300 ratings)
(b) 8-11 months national service

Hydrographic Department

This office and the survey ships come under the Ministry of Trade and Industry.

Frontier Guard

All Frontier Guard vessels come under the Ministry of the Interior.

Icebreakers

All these ships work for the Board of Navigation.

Mercantile Marine

Lloyd's Register of Shipping:
337 vessels of 2 262 095 tons gross

Strength of the Fleet

Type	Active	Building (Planned)
Frigates	2	—
Corvettes	2	—
Fast Attack Craft (Missile)	4+1	(1)
Fast Attack Craft (Gun)	14	(1)
Large Patrol Craft	5	—
Minelayers	2	—
Minesweepers, Inshore	6	(8)
HQ Ships	2	—
Transports (LCUs)	13	—
Tugs	3	—
Support Ships	6	—
Transport Craft	12	—
Cable Ship	1	—
Icebreakers	9	—

Frontier Guard

Large Patrol Craft	5	—
Training Ship	1	—
Coastal Patrol Craft	45	—

New Construction

Staff studies have begun on designs for a Fast Attack Craft and a Large Patrol Craft. New minelayer to commission in 1979—also to act as training ship.

DELETIONS

Frigate
1975 *Matti Kurki* (ex-British "Bay" Class)

Light Forces
1975 *Tursas* (Large Patrol Craft)
1977 *Vasama I* (Fast Attack Craft)

Mine Warfare Forces
1975 *Ruotsinsalmi*

Coast Guard Vessels
1970 VMV 11, 13, 19 and 20
1971 *Aura*

PENNANT LIST

Frigates
01 Uusimaa
02 Hämeenmaa

Corvettes
03 Turunmaa
04 Karjala

Light Forces
11 Tuima
12 Tuisku
14 Tuuli
15 Tyrsky
16 Isku
31-43 "Nuoli" class
? Vasama 2
51 Rihtniemi
52 Rymattyla
53 Ruissalo
54 Raisio
55 Roytta

Mine Warfare Forces
? Ruotsinsalmi
05 Keihässalmi
21-26 "Kuha" class

Miscellaneous
90 Louhi
96 Pikkala
120 Pyhtää
220 Pellinki

"UUSIMAA" Class

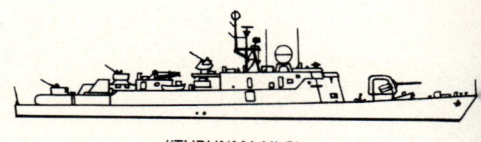

"TURUNMAA" Class

FRIGATES

2 Ex-SOVIET "RIGA" CLASS

UUSIMAA 01   HÄMEENMAA 02

Displacement, tons: 1 000 standard; 1 320 full load
Length, feet (metres): 298·8 *(91)*
Beam, feet (metres): 33·7 *(10·2)*
Draught, feet (metres): 11 *(3·4)*
Guns: 3—3·9 in *(100 mm)* single; 2—40 mm; 2—30 mm (twin) (in bow)
A/S weapons: 1 Hedgehog; 4 DC projectors
Torpedo tubes: 3—21 in *(533 mm)*
Mines: 50 (capacity)
Main engines: Geared turbines; 2 shafts; 20 000 shp
Speed, knots: 28
Boilers: 2
Range, miles: 2 000 at 15 knots
Complement: 175

Built in USSR—*Uusimaa* in 1955 and *Hämeenmaa* in 1957. Purchased from the USSR and transferred to the Finnish Navy on 29 April 1964 and 14 May 1964, respectively. Armament modified in 1971 with extra 30 mm.
Hämeenmaa in reserve, due for deletion.

Radar: Search: Slim Net.
Fire control: Sun Visor A (with Wasphead fire control system).
Navigation: Decca.
IFF: High Pole and Square Head.

Sonar: Hull-mounted.

UUSIMAA   1978, Finnish Navy

FINLAND / Corvettes — Light forces 151

CORVETTES

2 "TURUNMAA" CLASS

Name	No.	Builders	Laid down	Launched	Commissioned
TURUNMAA	03	Wärtsilä, Helsinki	Mar 1967	11 July 1967	29 Aug 1968
KARJALA	04	Wärtsilä, Helsinki	Mar 1967	16 Aug 1967	21 Oct 1968

Displacement, tons: 660 standard; 770 full load
Dimensions, feet (metres): 243.1 × 25.6 × 7.9 *(74.1 × 7.8 × 2.4)*
Guns: 1—4.7 in *(120 mm)* Bofors fwd;
  2—40 mm; 2—30 mm (1 twin aft)
A/S weapons: 2 DCT; 2 DC racks
Main engines: CODOG. 3 Mercedes-Benz (MTU) diesels; 3 000 bhp; 1 Rolls-Royce Olympus gas turbine; 22 000 hp = 35 knots. On diesels = 17 knots
Complement: 70

Ordered on 18 February 1965 from Wärtsilä, Helsinki. Flush decked. Rocket flare guide rails on sides of 4.7 in turret. Fitted with Vosper Thornycroft fin stabiliser equipment. Due for modification, possibly with SAM.

Radar: Search and Tactical: M20 Series (HSA).

KARJALA   1978, Finnish Navy

LIGHT FORCES

4 "TUIMA" CLASS (FAST ATTACK CRAFT—MISSILE)

TUIMA 11 **TUISKU** 12 **TUULI** 14 **TYRSKY** 15

Displacement, tons: 165 standard; 210 full load
Dimensions, feet (metres): 127.9 × 26.6 × 5.9 *(39.0 × 8.1 × 1.8)*
Missiles: SSM; 4 SS-N-2 (singles)
Guns: 4—30 mm (twins)
Main engines: Three M504 diesels; 15 000 hp
Speed, knots: 36
Range, miles: 800 at 25 knots
Complement: 30

Ex-Soviet "Osa II" class purchased from USSR 1974—75. New construction but with Finnish electronics.

TUULI   1978, Finnish Navy

1 EXPERIMENTAL CRAFT—MISSILE

Name	No.	Builders	Commissioned
ISKU	16	Reposaaron, Konepaja	1970

Displacement, tons: 140 full load
Dimensions, feet (metres): 86.5 × 28.6 × 6.4 *(26.4 × 8.7 × 1.8)*
Missiles: SSM; 4 SS-N-2 (singles)
Guns: 2—30 mm (1 twin)
Main engines: 4 Soviet M50 diesels; 3 600 bhp = 15 knots
Complement: 25

Guided missile craft of novel design built for training and experimental work. The construction combines a missile boat armament on a landing craft hull. Laid down November 1968 and launched 4 December 1969.

ISKU   1976, Finnish Navy

13 "NUOLI" CLASS (FAST ATTACK CRAFT—GUN)

Name	No.	Builders	Commissioned
NUOLI 1—13	31—43	Laivateollisuus, Turku	1961—6

Displacement, tons: 40 standard
Dimensions, feet (metres): 72.2 × 21.7 × 5.0 *(22 × 6.6 × 1.5)*
Guns: 1—40 mm; 1—20 mm
A/S weapons: 4 DCs
Main engines: 3 Soviet M50 diesels; 2 700 bhp = 40 knots
Complement: 15

Designed by Laivateollisuus, Turku. Delivery dates—14 September 1961, 19 October 1961, 1 November 1961, 21 November 1961, 6 July 1962, 3 August 1962, 22 August 1962, 10 October 1962, 27 October 1963, 5 May 1964, 5 May 1964, 30 November 1964, 12 October 1966. This class is split into two: Nuoli 1 (1-9) and Nuoli 2 (10-13). The main difference is a lower superstructure in Nuoli 2.

Radar: I-band Decca.

NUOLI 8   1978, Finnish Navy

152 FINLAND / Light forces — Mine warfare forces

1 "VASAMA" CLASS (FAST ATTACK CRAFT—GUN)

Name	No.	Builders	Commissioned
VASAMA 2	—	Saunders Roe (Anglesey) Ltd	1 May 1957

Displacement, tons: 50 standard; 70 full load
Dimensions, feet (metres): 67·0 pp; 71·5 oa × 19·8 × 6·1 *(21·8 oa × 5·9 × 1·8)*
Guns: 2—40 mm
A/S weapons: 4 Depth Charges
Main engines: 2 Napier Deltic diesels; 5 000 bhp = 40 knots
Complement: 20

British "Dark" class.

VASAMA 2   *1976, Finnish Navy*

3 "RUISSALO" CLASS (LARGE PATROL CRAFT)

Name	No.	Builders	Commissioned
RUISSALO	53	Laivateollisuus, Turku	11 Aug 1959
RAISIO	54	Laivateollisuus, Turku	12 Sep 1959
RÖYTTA	55	Laivateollisuus, Turku	14 Oct 1959

Displacement, tons: 110 standard; 130 full load
Dimensions, feet (metres): 111·5 × 19·8 × 5·9 *(34 × 6 × 1·8)*
Guns: 1—40 mm; 1—20 mm; 2 MG (4—23 mm (twins) in *Ruissalo*)
A/S weapons: 1 Squid mortar (2 DCT in *Ruissalo*)
Mines: Can lay mines
Main engines: 2 Mercedes-Benz (MTU) diesels; 2 500 bhp = 18 knots
Complement: 20

Ordered in January 1958. Launched on 16 June, 2 July and 2 June 1959. *Ruissalo* was modernised in 1976.

Radar: Decca.

Sonar: 1 hull-mounted.

RAISIO   *1975, Finnish Navy*

2 "RIHTNIEMI" CLASS (LARGE PATROL CRAFT)

Name	No.	Builders	Commissioned
RIHTNIEMI	51	Rauma-Repola, Rauma	21 Feb 1957
RYMÄTTYLÄ	52	Rauma-Repola, Rauma	20 May 1957

Displacement, tons: 90 standard; 110 full load
Dimensions, feet (metres): 101·7 × 18·7 × 5·9 *(31 × 5·6 × 1·8)*
Guns: 1—40 mm; 1—20 mm; 2 MG
A/S weapons: 2—RBU 1200
Mines: Can lay mines
Main engines: 2 Mercedes-Benz (MTU) diesels; 2 500 bhp = 18 knots
Complement: 20

Ordered in June 1955, launched in 1956. Cp propellers. Both modernised for A/S work.

RIHTNIEMI   *1976, Finnish Navy*

MINE WARFARE FORCES

1 MINELAYER

Name	No.	Builders	Commissioned
RUOTSINSALMI	—	Wärtsila, Helsinki	May 1979

Displacement, tons: 1 000 standard; 1 100 full load
Dimensions, feet (metres): 255·8 × 37·7 × 9·8 *(78·2 × 11·6 × 3·0)*
Guns: 1—120 mm Bofors (fwd); 2—40 mm; 4—23 mm (twins)
A/S weapons: 2 DCT
Mines: ?
Main engines: 2 Wärtsila Vasa 16V22B diesels; 5 850 bhp; 2 shafts (cp propellers) = 20 knots
Complement: 77

Design completed 1976. Also to serve as training ship. Will carry 56 trainees in place of mines. Helicopter pad on stern but no hangar. Ordered late 1977. Laid down May 1978. Launched 28 August 1978.

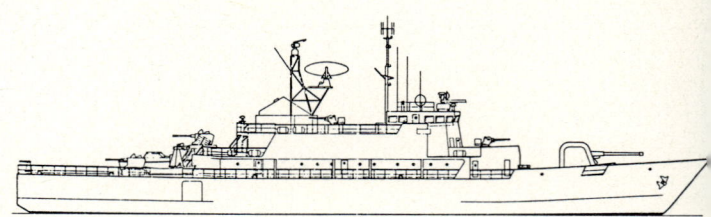
RUOTSINSALMI   *1978*

1 MINELAYER

Name	No.	Builders	Commissioned
KEIHÄSSALMI	05	Valmet, Helsinki	1957

Displacement, tons: 360
Dimensions, feet (metres): 168 × 23 × 6 *(51·2 × 7 × 1·8)*
Guns: 4—30 mm (twins); 2—20 mm
Mines: Up to 100 capacity
Main engines: 2 Wärtsilä diesels; 2 shafts; 2 000 bhp = 15 knots
Complement: 60

Contract dated June 1955. Launched on 16 March 1957. Armament modified in 1972.

Radar: Search and Tactical; I band. Decca.

KEIHÄSSALMI   *1974, Finnish Navy*

FINLAND / Mine warfare forces — Icebreakers

6 "KUHA" CLASS (MINESWEEPERS—INSHORE)

Name	No.	Builders	Commissioned
KUHA 21—26	21—26	Laivatteollisuus, Turku	1974—75

Displacement, tons: 90
Dimensions, feet (metres): 87·2 × 23 × 6·6 (26·6 × 7 × 2)
Guns: 2—23 mm (twin); 1—20 mm
Main engines: 2 diesels; 600 shp; 1 shaft (cp) = 12 knots
Complement: 15

All ordered 1972. Fitted for magnetic, acoustic and pressure-mine sweeping. Have active rudders.
Kuha 21 completed 28 June 1974. *Kuha 26* in late 1975. Hulls are of GRP. Funds for further eight craft provided.

Radar: Decca.

KUHA 22   1974, Finnish Navy—SA Kuva

ICEBREAKERS
(Controlled by Board of Navigation)

Note: There is also the West German owned, Finnish manned, icebreaker *Hansa,* of the "Karhu" class, completed on 25 November 1966, which operates off Germany in winter and off Finland at other times.

2 "URHO" CLASS

Name	No.	Builders	Commissioned
URHO	—	Wärtsilä, Helsinki	5 Mar 1975
SISU	—	Wärtsilä, Helsinki	28 Jan 1976

Displacement, tons: 7 800 *(Urho);* 7 900 *(Sisu)* standard; 9 500 full load
Dimensions, feet (metres): 343·1 × 78·1 × 23·9 *(104·6 × 23·8 × 8·3)*
Aircraft: 1 helicopter
Main engines: Diesel-electric; 5 Wärtsilä-SEMT Pielstick diesels 25 000 bhp. electric motors; 22 000 shp; 2 shafts fwd, 2 aft; = 18 knots
Complement: 57

Ordered on 11 December 1970 and 10 May 1971 respectively. Fitted with two screws aft, taking 60 per cent of available power and two forward, taking the remainder. Sisters to Swedish "Atle" class.

SISU   1977, Wärtsila

3 "TARMO" CLASS

Name	No.	Builders	Commissioned
TARMO	—	Wärtsilä, Helsinki	1963
VARMA	—	Wärtsilä, Helsinki	1968
APU	—	Wärtsilä, Helsinki	25 Nov 1970

Displacement, tons: 4 890
Dimensions, feet (metres): 281·0 × 71·0 × 22·5 *(85·7 × 21·7 × 6·8)*
Aircraft: 1 helicopter
Main engines: Wärtsilä-Sulzer diesels; electric drive; 4 shafts (2 screws fwd 2 screws aft); 12 000 shp = 17 knots

APU   1977, Finnish Navy

3 "KARHU" CLASS

Name	No.	Builders	Commissioned
KARHU	—	Wärtsilä, Helsinki	Dec 1958
MURTAJA	—	Wärtsilä, Helsinki	1959
SAMPO	—	Wärtsilä, Helsinki	1960

Displacement, tons: 3 540
Dimensions, feet (metres): 243·2 × 57 × 21 *(74·2 × 17·4 × 6·4)*
Main engines: Diesel-electric; 4 shafts; 7 500 bhp = 16 knots

Karhu was launched on 22 October 1957, *Murtaja* was launched on 23 September 1958. Both these ships have tripod foremasts.

MURTAJA   1978, Finnish Navy

1 "VOIMA" CLASS

Name	No.	Builders	Commissioned
VOIMA	—	Wärtsilä, Helsinki	1954

Displacement, tons: 4 415
Dimensions, feet (metres): 274 × 63·7 × 22·5 *(83·6 × 19·4 × 6·8)*
Main engines: Diesels with electric drive; 4 shafts; 12 840 kW = 16·5 knots
Oil fuel, tons: 740

Launched in 1953. Two propellers forward and aft. Engine room rebuilt in 1978-79.

VOIMA   1975, Finnish Navy

154 FINLAND / Miscellaneous — Transport craft

MISCELLANEOUS
(Under Naval control)

1 Ex-ICEBREAKER (HQ SHIP)

Name	No.	Builders	Commissioned
LOUHI (ex-*Sisu*)	90	Wärtsilä, Helsinki	1939

Displacement, tons: 2 075
Dimensions, feet (metres): 210·2 × 46·5 × 16·8 *(64·1 × 14·2 × 5·1)*
Guns: 4—40 mm
Main engines: 2 sets Atlas Polar diesels with electric drive; 2 shafts and a bow propeller; 4 000 hp = 16 knots
Complement: 28

Launched on 24 September 1938. Used as submarine depot ship 1939—45. Converted 1975 to be HQ and Logistics ship for fast attack craft.

LOUHI   1978, Finnish Navy

1 HEADQUARTERS SHIP

KORSHOLM (ex-*Korsholm III*, ex-*Öland*)

Displacement, tons: 650
Dimensions, feet (metres): 157·4 × 27·9 × 9·5 *(48 × 8·5 × 2·9)*
Guns: 2—20 mm
Main engines: Steam; 865 hp = 11 knots

Converted car ferry. Built in 1931 in Sweden. Bought by Rederi Ab Vaasa-Umea in 1958. Sold to Navy in 1967.

2 "KAMPELA" CLASS (LCU TRANSPORTS)

Name	No.	Builders	Commissioned
KAMPELA 1	—	Enso Gutzeitoj	July 1977
KAMPELA 2	—	Enso Gutzeitoj	Oct 1977

Displacement, tons: 90
Dimensions, feet (metres): 106·6 × 26·2 × 4·9 *(32·5 × 8·0 × 1·5)*
Guns: 2—20 mm
Mines: ?
Main engines: 2 Scania diesels; 460 bhp = 9 knots
Complement: 10

Can be used as amphibious craft, transports, minelayers or for shore support. Armament can be changed to suit role.

"KAMPELA" Class   1977, Finnish Navy

6 "KALA" CLASS (LCU TRANSPORTS)

KALA 1—6

Displacement, tons: 60
Dimensions, feet (metres): 88·6 × 26·2 × 6 *(27 × 8 × 1·8)*
Gun: 1—20 mm
Mines: 34
Main engines: 2 Valmet diesels; 360 bhp = 9 knots
Complement: 10

Completed between 20 June 1956 (*Kala 1*) and 4 December 1959 (*Kala 6*). Can be used as transports, amphibious craft, minelayers or for shore support. Armament can be changed to suit role.

5 "KAVE" CLASS (LCU TRANSPORTS)

KAVE 1—4 and 6

Displacement, tons: 27
Dimensions, feet (metres): 59 × 16·4 × 4·3 *(18 × 5 × 1·3)*
Gun: 1—20 mm
Main engines: 2 Valmet diesels; 360 hp = 9 knots
Complement: 3

Completed between 16 November 1956 (*Kave 1*) and 1960 (*Kave 6* on 19 December 1960). Built by Haminan Konepaja Oy (*Kave 1*) remainder by F. W. Hollming, Rauma. *Kave 5* lost in tow 15 December 1960.

KAVE 4   1961, Finnish Navy

3 TRANSPORTS

PIKKALA 96 **PYHTÄÄ** 120
PELLINKI 220

3 "PUKKIO" CLASS (SUPPORT SHIPS)

PANSIO   **PORKKALA**   **PUKKIO**

Displacement, tons: 162 standard
Dimensions, feet (metres): 93·4 × 19·2 × 9·0 *(28·5 × 6·0 × 2·7)*
Guns: 1—40 mm; 1—20 mm
Mines: 20
Main engines: Diesels; 300 bhp = 9 knots

Built by Valmet, Turku. Delivered 25 May 1947, 1940 and 1939 respectively. Vessels of the tug type used as transports, minesweeping tenders, minelayers and patrol vessels.

3 "PIRTTISAARI" CLASS

PIRTTISAARI (ex-DR 7)   **PURHA** (ex-DR 10)   **PYHTÄÄ** (ex-DR 2)

Displacement, tons: 150
Dimensions, feet (metres): 69 × 20 × 8·5 *(21 × 6·1 × 2·6)*
Gun: 1—20 mm
Main engine: 1 diesel; 400 bhp = 8 knots
Complement: 10

Former US Army Tugs. Launched in 1943-44. General purpose vessels used as minesweepers, minelayers, patrol vessels, tenders, tugs or personnel transports. *Pyhtää* belongs to the Coast Artillery.

PIRTTISAARI   1970, Finnish Navy

PUTSAARI (CABLE SHIP)

Displacement, tons: 430
Dimensions, feet (metres): 149·2 × 29·2 × 7·5 *(45·5 × 8·9 × 2·3)*
Main engine: 1 Wärtsilä diesel; 450 bhp = 10 knots
Complement: 10

Built by Rauma Repola, Rauma. Ordered 11 November 1963. Launched in December 1965. Fitted with bow-thruster and active rudder, two 10 ton cable winches and accommodation for 20. Strengthened for ice operations.

TRANSPORT CRAFT

Class	Total	Tonnage	Speed	Commissioned
Hauki	3	30	12	1978
H	6	34	10	1960

FRONTIER GUARD

(Controlled by Ministry of the Interior)

1 TRAINING SHIP

Name	No.	Builders	Commissioned
ECKERO	—	Kone and Silta	1954

Displacement, tons: 55
Dimensions, feet (metres): 70·2 × 13·1 × 6·2 *(21·4 × 4 × 1·9)*
Main engine: Mercedes-Benz diesel; 445 hp = 10 knots

Former customs vessel now used for Coast Guard training.

1 LARGE PATROL CRAFT

Name	No.	Builders	Commissioned
VALPAS	—	Laivateollisuus, Turku	21 July 1971

Displacement, tons: 545
Dimensions, feet (metres): 159·1 × 27·9 × 12·5 *(48·5 × 8·5 × 3·8)*
Gun: 1—20 mm
Main engine: 1 Werkspoor diesel; 2 000 bhp = 15 knots
Complement: 22

An improvement on the *Silmä* design. Ordered 14 July 1969, launched 22 December 1970. First frontier guard ship with sonar. Ice strengthened.

Sonar: Hull-mounted set.

VALPAS 1975, Finnish Navy

1 LARGE PATROL CRAFT

Name	No.	Builders	Commissioned
TURVA	—	Laivateollisuus, Turku	15 Dec 1977

Displacement, tons: 550
Dimensions, feet (metres): 159·1 × 28 × 14 *(48·5 × 8·6 × 3·9)*
Gun: 1—20 mm
Main engines: 2 Wärtsila diesels; one shaft; 2 000 shp = 16 knots

Ordered 24 June 1975. Improved "Valpas" design.

TURVA 1978, Finnish Navy

1 LARGE PATROL CRAFT

Name	No.	Builders	Commissioned
SILMÄ	—	Laivateollisuus, Turku	19 Aug 1963

Displacement, tons: 530
Dimensions, feet (metres): 158·5 × 27·2 × 14·1 *(48·3 × 8·3 × 4·3)*
Gun: 1—20 mm
Main engine: 1 Werkspoor diesel; 1 800 hp = 15 knots
Complement: 22

Improved *Uisko* design. Ordered 21 February 1962, launched 25 March 1963.

SILMÄ 1975, Finnish Navy

1 LARGE PATROL CRAFT

Name	No.	Builders	Commissioned
UISKO	—	Valmet, Helsinki	1959

Displacement, tons: 370
Dimensions, feet (metres): 141 × 24 × 12·8 *(43 × 7·3 × 3·9)*
Gun: 1—20 mm
Main engine: 1 Werkspoor diesel; 1 800 hp = 15 knots
Complement: 21

Launched in 1958.

UISKO 1975, Finnish Navy

1 LARGE PATROL CRAFT

Name	No.	Builders	Commissioned
VIIMA	—	Laivateollisuus, Turku	1964

Displacement, tons: 135
Dimensions, feet (metres): 118·1 × 21·7 × 7·5 *(36 × 6·6 × 2·3)*
Gun: 1—20 mm
Main engines: 3 Mercedes-Benz diesels; 4 050 bhp = 25 knots
Complement: 13

Launched 20 July 1964.

8 "TELKKA/KOSKELO" CLASS (COASTAL PATROL CRAFT)

KAAKKURI*	KOSKELO*	KUIKKA*	TAVI*
KIISLA*	KUOVI*	KURKI*	TELKKA

(*"Koskelo" class)

Displacement, tons: 92 *(Telkka)*; 95 *(Koskelo)* full load
Dimensions, feet (metres): 95·1 × 16·4 × 4·9 *(29 × 5 × 1·5)*
Gun: 1—20 mm (see notes)
Main engines: 2 Mercedes-Benz (MTU) diesels; 2 shafts; 2 700 bhp = 23 knots (modified).
Complement: 9 *(Telkka)*, 11 *(Koskelo)*

Built of steel. Between 1955 *(Koskelo)* and 1960 *(Tavi)*. Originally of much lower horsepower. *Telkka* modernised in 1970 and "Koskelo"s in 1972-74 by Laivateollisuus. New internal arrangements, new decking and new engines increasing their speed by 8 knots. Can all mount a 40 mm on quarter-deck.

3 COASTAL PATROL CRAFT

Dimensions, feet (metres): 46·9 × 11·8 × 5·2 *(14·3 × 3·6 × 1·6)*
Main engine: 1 Mercedes-Benz diesel; 1 shaft; 1 300 bhp = 12 knots

Built by Hollming Oy, Rauma. Two completed January 1978 and the third 1 September 1978. For patrol, towing and salvage.

COASTAL PATROL CRAFT

Class	Nos.	Tonnage	Speed	Commissioned
RV 4	4 & 5	12	9	1951
RV 8	8	10	10	1958
RV 9	9-17	12	10	1959-60
RV 10	18-28	18	10	1961-63
RV 30	30-36	19	10	1973-74
RV 37	37-39	20	10	1978
RV 41	41	17	10	1965

RV 38 1978, Finnish Navy

FRANCE / Introduction

Ministerial

Minister of Defence:
M. Yvon Bourges

Headquarters Appointments

Conseil Supérieur de la Marine:
Amiraux Lannuzel, Tardy
Vice-Amiraux d'Escadre Wacrenier,
Sabatier, Cassere
Vice-Amiraux Chaperon, Accary

Senior Appointments

Préfet Maritime de la Première Région (PREMAR UN):
Vice-Amiral d'Escadre Wacrenier
C in C Atlantic Theatre (CECLANT) and Préfet Maritime de la Deuxième Région (PREMAR DEUX):
Vice-Amiral d'Escadre Coulondres
C in C Mediterranean Theatre (CECMED) and Préfet Maritime de la Troisième Région (PREMAR TROIS):
Vice-Amiral Accary
C in C French Naval Forces, Polynesia:
Contre-Amiral Leenhart
C in C Atlantic Fleet:
Contre-Amiral Brac de la Perriere
C in C Mediterranean Fleet:
Vice-Amiral de Bigault de Cazanove

Diplomatic Representation

Naval Attaché in Algiers:
Capitaine de Frégate Travot Cussac
Naval Attaché in Bonn:
Capitaine de Frégate Ragugt
Naval Attaché in Brasilia:
Capitaine de Corvette de Gentile Duquesne
Naval Attaché in the Hague:
Capitaine de Vaisseau Stoever
Naval Attaché in Lisbon:
Capitaine de Vaisseau Rambourg
Naval Attaché in London (& Defence Attaché):
Contre-Amiral Francis de Queylar
Naval Attaché in Madrid:
Capitaine de Vaisseau Raterre
Naval Attaché in Moscow:
Capitaine de Vaisseau Gagelin
Naval Attaché in Oslo:
Capitaine de Vaisseau Euzen
Naval Attaché in Rome:
Capitaine de Vaisseau de Seynes
Naval Attaché in Santiago:
Capitaine de Frégate Tourrel
Naval Attaché in Tokyo:
Capitaine de Vaisseau Gayno
Naval Attaché in Washington:
Contre-Amiral Menetrier
Naval Attaché in Wellington:
Capitaine de Frégate Bouvet

Personnel

(a) 1974: 67 700 (4 500 officers, 63 200 ratings)
    1975: 68 000 (4 550 officers, 63 450 ratings)
    1976: 68 315 (4 550 officers, 63 765 ratings)
    1977: 68 285 (including 17 438 national service)
    1978: 68 230 (4 230 officers, 64 000 ratings of whom 18 412 national service)

(personnel to be increased by 5 000 under the 15-year re-equipment plan)

(b) National service, 12 months

FRANCE

Bases

Cherbourg: Channel Fleet base. Prémar Un
Brest: Main Atlantic base. SSBN base. Prémar Deux
Lorient: Atlantic submarine base
Toulon: Main Mediterranean Fleet base. Prémar Trois

Fleet Dispositions

Mediterranean Fleet: *Colbert* (Flag), 2 aircraft carriers, 12 submarines, 6 destroyers, 7 frigates, 4 large patrol craft, 6 MCM vessels, 3 survey ships, 4 support ships.
Atlantic Fleet: 11 destroyers, 4 frigates, 4 SSBNs, 6 submarines, 1 tanker.
Indian Ocean: *La Charente* (Flag), 1 destroyer, 4 frigates, 5 patrol craft, 3 support ships.
West Indies: 2 ships.
Training Squadron: *Jeanne d'Arc, Forbin.*

Strength of the Fleet

Type	Active (Reserve)	Building or (Projected)
Submarines (Strat Missile)	4	1 (1)
	1 (Diesel powered)	
Submarines (Fleet)	—	2 (4)
Submarines (Patrol)	23	—
Attack Carriers (Medium)	2	—
Helicopter VSTOL Carrier (Nuclear)	—	(1)
Helicopter Carrier	1	—
Cruiser	1	—
Destroyers	20	3 (5)
Frigates	23	4 (1)
Fast Attack Craft (Missile)	5	— (6)
Large Patrol Craft	22	—
Coastal Patrol Craft	5	—
LPD	2	—
LST	7	(2)
LCT	12	—
LCM	36	—
Minesweepers (Ocean)	4	—
Minesweepers (Coastal)	22	—
Minehunters	12	1 (14)
Surveying Ships	5	—
Coastal Survey Ships	3	—
Inshore Survey Craft	1	—
Tankers (UR)	4	1 (1)
Tankers (Support)	5	—
Maintenance Ships	1	—
Depot Ships	5	—
Repair Ships (ex-LCT)	1	—
Trials Ships	9	—
Boom Defence Vessels	11	—
Torpedo Recovery Vessels	3	—
Victualling Stores Ship	1	—
Stores Ship	1	—
Supply Tenders	5	—
Small Transports	13	—
Tenders	17	—
Tugs	87	10
Training Ships	8	—

Naval Air Stations

St. Raphael, Lann Bihoue, Nimes Poulmic, Dax, Aspretto, Landvisiau, Hyères, St. Mandrier.

Shipyards (Naval)

Cherbourg: Submarines and Fast Attack Craft
Brest: Major warships and refitting
Lorient: Destroyers, frigates and avisos

Submarine Service

Known as Force Océanique Stratégique (FOST) with HQ at Houilles near Paris. SSBN *(SNLE)* force based at Ile Longue Brest with a training base at Roche-Douvres and VLFW/T station at Rosay. Patrol submarines are based at Lorient and Toulon. Plans for nuclear fleet submarines are included in the 15-year plan, with the first being laid down in 1976 and the second in 1978.

15-Year Re-equipment Plan

Note: All submarines laid down after 1976 are nuclear-powered.

This programme ("Plan Bleu") was approved by l'Assemblé on 29 February 1972 and provided for the following fleet by 1985 and reduced to figures in brackets in June 1977:

2 Aircraft Carriers
2 Helicopter Carriers } (total 3)
30 Frigates or Corvettes
35 Avisos (27 Avisos)
6 SSBN
20 Patrol Submarines (or Fleet) (12 Fleet submarines)
30 Fast Attack Craft
36 MHC and MSC
5 Replenishment Tankers
Logistic Support and Maintenance Ships (total of 85 000 tons)
2 Assault Ships
Landing Ships and Craft
Transports
50 LRMP aircraft
Carrier borne aircraft
Helicopters

In November 1978 it was announced by the Minister of Defence (M. Bourges) that the aim of the naval programme was to provide 109 warships and 26 support ships by 1990.

1971-75 New Construction Plan

Financial problems have necessitated the addition of an extra year to this plan. Financial allowance made for construction of ships listed below although this Plan and the 1977-81 Plan combined will not achieve the Plan Bleu strength.

1 Helicopter Carrier (PH 75) (postponed to next Plan)
3 Guided Missile Destroyers ("Corvettes") "C 70" Type
3 Guided Missile Destroyers ("Corvettes") "C 67" Type
14 Escorts (officially rated as *Avisos*) "A 69" Type (one delayed)
3 Nuclear Powered Ballistic Missile Submarines (one delayed)
4 Patrol Submarines
4 Patrol Boats (for overseas service)
1 Fleet Support & Repair Ship (major conversion)
1 Fleet Replenishment Ship (one added—total two)
2 Medium Landing Ships (Transports)
1 Fleet Submarine added
1 Minehunter added

1977-81 New Construction Plan

This plan allowed for:

1 Nuclear-propelled carrier (PA 75) (to be laid down 1981)
3 "C 70" ASM destroyers ("Georges Leygues" class)
3 "C 70" AA destroyers ("Georges Leygues" class) (at end of period)
4 SSN Fleet submarines (3 sisters to SNA 72 and 1 advanced type)
1 SSBN *(L'Inflexible)* postponed until 1982
12 Minehunters (in collaboration with Belgium and Netherlands) (for total of 13—2 more to follow later)
6 Large Patrol Vessels (250-350 tons)
1 Fleet Replenishment ship added

Mercantile Marine

Lloyd's Register of Shipping:
1 317 vessels of 12 197 354 tons gross

DELETIONS

Helicopter Carrier
1974 *Arromanches*

Destroyers
1975 *Chevalier Paul*
1976 *Cassard, Guichen*
1977 *Jaureguiberry, La Bourdonnais*

Frigates
1975 *Le Bordelais, Le Brestois, Le Champenois, Le Corse*
1976 *Aventure, Le Bourguignon, Le Lorrain*
1977 *Le Boulonnais, Le Gascon*

Light Forces
1974 *M 691, P 9785, P 9786, VC 2, VC 10*
1975 *L'Agile, Le Fougeux, L'Opiniatre*
1976 *La Bayonnaise, P 753*
1977 *L'Alerte, Le Frondeur, Le Hardi, L'Intrepide*
1978 *L'Attentif, L'Effronté, L'Enjoué, L'Etourdi, Oiseau des Iles*

Mine Warfare Forces
1974 *Begonia, Glaieul; Aries* (to Morocco); *Ajonc* as diving training ship
1975 *Bellatrix, Dénébola, Pégase; Gardenia, Liseron* and *Magnolia* reclassified as diving base ships, *Jacinthe* as minelayer
1977 *Bleuet* and *Chrysanthéme* (deleted for spares); *Algol, Cassiopée, Giroflée*
1978 *Autan, Colmar; Marjolaine* (to Tunisia). *Antares*

Amphibious Forces
1974 LCT 9099; LCT 9095 (to Senegal)
1975 LCT 9061 (to Comoro Islands)
1976 LCT 9071, 9081

Survey Ships
1975 *La Découverte* (as target)
1977 *Alidade, La Pérouse*

BDVs
1974 *Scorpion, Locuste*
1976 *Persistante, Victorieuse*
1977 *Araignée, Commandant Robert Giraud*

Service Forces
1974 *Oasis* (Water Carrier)
1975 *Maurienne* (Fleet Support Ship), *Cataracte* (Water Carrier), *Belouga* (Tender)
1976 *La Seine* (Tanker), *Déluge, Mirage* (Water Carriers), *Trébéron* (Transport)
1977 *Fontaine* (Water Carrier), *Falleron* (Transport)
1978 *Moselle* (Maintenance Ship)

Miscellaneous
1974 M 691 (ex-*SC 525*), FNRS 3

Tugs
1975 *Charaa, Hippocampe, Kasserine, Pont de Fahs, Poulpé, Rascasse, Rossignol*
1976 *Anfa, Belier, Canari, Coolie, Gillies, Grive, Hanneton, Hirondelle, Moule, Oursin*
1977 *Délange, Fontaine, Forméne, Giens, Infatigable, Jean Claude, Jonque, Marronier, Murène, Ondeé, Tupa*
1978 *Bambou, Haut Barr*

PENNANT LIST

Submarines

S 610	Le Foudroyant	
S 611	Le Redoutable	
S 612	Le Terrible	
S 613	L'Indomptable	
S 614	Le Tonnant	
S 616	SNA 72	
S 620	Agosta	
S 621	Bévéziers	
S 622	La Praya	
S 623	Ouessant	
S 631	Narval	
S 632	Marsouin	
S 633	Dauphin	
S 634	Requin	
S 635	Aréthuse	
S 636	Argonaute	
S 637	Espadon	
S 638	Morse	
S 639	Amazone	
S 640	Ariane	
S 641	Daphné	
S 642	Diane	
S 643	Doris	
S 645	Flore	
S 646	Galatée	
S 648	Junon	
S 649	Venus	
S 650	Psyche	
S 651	Sirène	
S 655	Gymnote	

Aircraft and Helicopter Carriers

R 97	Jeanne d'Arc	
R 98	Clemenceau	
R 99	Foch	

Cruiser

C 611	Colbert	

Destroyers

D 602	Suffren	
D 603	Duquesne	
D 609	Aconit	
D 610	Tourville	
D 611	Duguay-Trouin	
D 612	De Grasse	
D 622	Kersaint	
D 624	Bouvet	
D 625	Dupetit Thouars	
D 627	Maillé Brézé	
D 628	Vauquelin	
D 629	D'Estrées	
D 630	Du Chayla	
D 631	Casabianca	
D 632	Guépratte	
D 633	Duperré	
D 635	Forbin	
D 636	Tartu	
D 638	La Galissonnière	
D 640	Georges Leygues	
D 641	Dupleix	
D 642	Montcalm	
D 643	—	

Frigates and Corvettes

F 725	Victor Schoelcher	
F 726	Commandant Bory	
F 727	Amiral Charner	
F 728	Doudart de Lagrée	
F 729	Balny	
F 733	Commandant Rivière	
F 740	Commandant Bourdais	
F 748	Protet	
F 749	Enseigne de Vaisseau Henry	
F 765	Le Normand	
F 766	Le Picard	
F 771	Le Savoyard	
F 773	Le Basque	
F 774	L'Agenais	
F 775	Le Béarnais	
F 776	L'Alsacien	
F 777	Le Provençal	
F 778	Le Vendéen	
F 781	D'Estienne d'Orves	
F 782	Amyot d'Inville	
F 783	Drogou	
F 784	Detroyat	
F 785	Jean Moulin	
F 786	Quartier Maitre Anquetil	
F 787	Commandant de Pimodan	
F 788	Seconde Maitre Le Bihan	
F 790	Lieutenant de Vaisseau Lavallée	
F 792	Premier Maitre l'Her	
F 793	Commandant Blaison	
F 794	Enseigne de Vaisseau Jacoubet	

Mine Warfare Forces

M 610	Ouistreham
M 612	Alençon
M 613	Berneval
M 615	Cantho
M 616	Dompaire
M 617	Garigliano
M 618	Mytho
M 619	Vinh Long
M 620	Berlaimont
M 623	Baccarat
M 632	Pervenche
M 633	Pivoine
M 635	Réséda
M 638	Acacia
M 639	Acanthe
M 641	Eridan
M 668	Azalée
M 671	Camélia
M 674	Cyclamen
M 675	Eglantine
M 679	Glycine
M 680	Jacinthe
M 681	Laurier
M 682	Lilas
M 684	Lobelia
M 687	Mimosa
M 688	Muguet
M 712	Cybele
M 713	Calliope
M 714	Clio
M 715	Circe
M 716	Ceres
M 737	Capricorne
M 749	Phénix
M 755	Capella
M 756	Céphée
M 757	Verseau
M 765	Mercure

Light Forces

P 635	L'Ardent
P 640	Le Fringant
P 644	L'Adroit
P 650	Arcturus
P 652	La Lorientaise
P 653	La Dunkerquoise
P 655	La Dieppoise
P 656	Altair
P 657	La Paimpolaise
P 658	Croix du Sud
P 659	Canopus
P 660	Etoile Polaire
P 661	Jasmin
P 662	Petunia
P 670	Trident
P 671	Glaive
P 672	Epée
P 673	Pertuisane
P 707	Vega
P 730	La Combattante
P 741	Aldebaran
P 743	Sagittaire
P 759	Lyre
P 770	PB
P 771	PB
P 772	PB
P 774	PB
P 784	Geranium
P 787	Jonquille
P 789	Paquerette

Amphibious Forces

L 9003	Argens
L 9004	Bidassoa
L 9007	Trieux
L 9008	Dives
L 9009	Blavet
L 9021	Ouragan
L 9022	Orage
L 9030	Champlain
L 9031	Francis Garnier
L 9070	LCT
L 9072	LCT
L 9073	LCT
L 9074	LCT
L 9082	LCT
L 9083	LCT
L 9084	Workshop
L 9091	LCT
L 9092	LCT
L 9093	LCT
L 9094	LCT
L 9096	LCT
(CTM	LCMs 1-16)

Auxiliaries Survey and Support Ships

A 603	Henry Poincaré
A 607	Meuse
A 610	Ile d'Oléron
A 615	Loire
A 617	Garonne
A 618	Rance
A 619	Aber Wrach
A 620	Jules Verne
A 621	Rhin
A 622	Rhône
A 625	Papenoo
A 626	La Charente
A 628	La Saône
A 629	Durance
A 630	Lac Tonlé Sap
A 632	Punaruu
A 638	Sahel
A 640	Origny
A 643	Aunis
A 644	Berry
A 646	Triton
A 648	Archimède
A 649	L'Etoile
A 650	La Belle Poule
A 652	Mutin
A 653	La Grande Hermine
A 660	Hippopotame
A 664	Malabar
A 665	Goliath
A 666	Eléphant
A 667	Hercule
A 668	Rhinocéros
A 669	Tenace
A 671	Le Fort
A 672	Utile
A 673	Lutteur
A 674	Centaure
A 675	Isère
A 683	Octant
A 685	Robuste
A 686	Actif
A 687	Laborieux
A 688	Valeureux
A 692	Travailleur
A 693	Acharné
A 694	Efficace
A 698	Petrel
A 699	Pelican
A 701	Ajonc
A 702	Girelle
A 706	Courageux
A 710	Myosotis
A 711	Gardénia
A 714	Tourmaline
A 722	Poseidon
A 723	Liseron
A 730	Libellule
A 731	Tianée
A 733	Saintonge
A 734	Issole
A 735	Hibiscus
A 736	Dahlia
A 737	Tulipe
A 738	Capucine
A 739	Oeillet
A 740	Hortensia
A 741	Armoise
A 742	Violette
A 747	Betelgeuse
A 756	Espérance
A 757	D'Entrecasteaux
A 758	La Recherche
A 759	Gustav Zedé
A 760	Cigale
A 761	Criquet
A 762	Fourmi
A 763	Grillon
A 764	Scarabée
A 766	Estafette
A 767	Chamois
A 768	Elan
A 769	Narvik
A 770	Magnolia
A 772	Engageante
A 773	Vigilante
A 774	Chevreuil
A 775	Gazelle
A 776	Isard
A 777	Luciole
A 780	L'Astrolabe
A 781	Boussole
A 789	L'Archéonaute
A 794	Corail

Auxiliaries

Y 601	Acajou
Y 602	Aigrette
Y 604	Ariel
Y 607	Balsa
Y 611	Bengali
Y 612	Bouleau
Y 613	Faune
Y 617	Mouette
Y 618	Cascade
Y 620	Chataigner
Y 621	Mésange
Y 623	Charme
Y 624	Chêne
Y 625	Cigogne
Y 628	Colibri
Y 629	Cormier
Y 630	Bonite
Y 632	Cygne
Y 634	Rouget
Y 635	Equeurdibille
Y 636	Martinet
Y 637	Fauvette
Y 638	Maronnier
Y 643	Tourterelle
Y 644	Frêne
Y 645	Gave
Y 646	Geyser
Y 648	Goeland
Y 653	Heron
Y 654	Hêtre
Y 655	Hévéa
Y 661	Korrigan
Y 662	Dryade
Y 663	Latanier
Y 664	Lutin
Y 666	Manguier
Y 668	Méléze
Y 669	Merisier
Y 670	Merle
Y 671	Morgane
Y 673	Moineau
Y 675	Martin Pecheur
Y 682	Okoume
Y 684	Oued
Y 686	Palétuvier
Y 687	Passereau
Y 688	Calmar
Y 689	Pin
Y 690	Pingouin
Y 691	Pinson
Y 694	Pivert
Y 695	Platana
Y 696	Alphée
Y 704	Sycomore
Y 706	Chimère
Y 708	Saule
Y 710	Sylphe
Y 711	Farfadet
Y 717	Ébene
Y 718	Erable
Y 719	Olivier
Y 720	Santal
Y 721	Alouette
Y 722	Vauneau
Y 723	Engoulevent
Y 724	Sarcelle
Y 725	Marabout
Y 726	Toucan
Y 727	Macreuse
Y 728	Grand Duc
Y 729	Eider
Y 730	Ara
Y 735	Merlin
Y 736	Mélusine
Y 739	Noyer
Y 740	Papayer
Y 741	Elfe
Y 743	Palangrin
Y 745	Aiguière
Y 746	Embrun
Y 747	Loriot
Y 748	Gelinotte
Y 749	La Prudente
Y 750	La Persévérante
Y 751	La Fidèle

158 FRANCE / Introduction

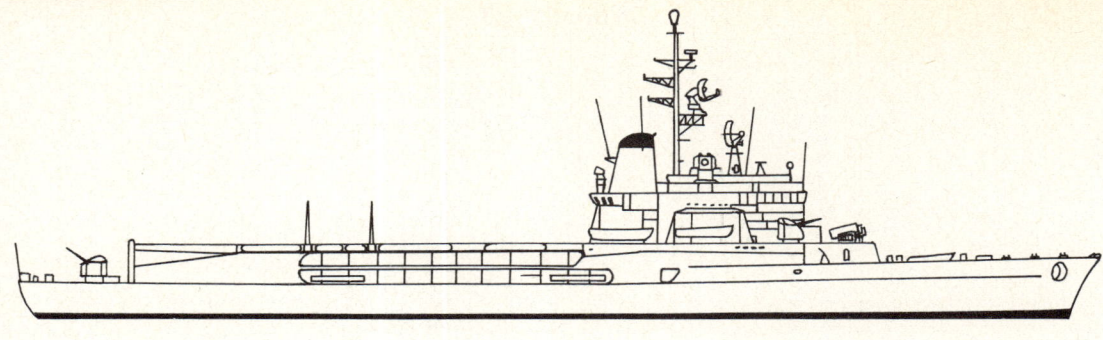

JEANNE D'ARC

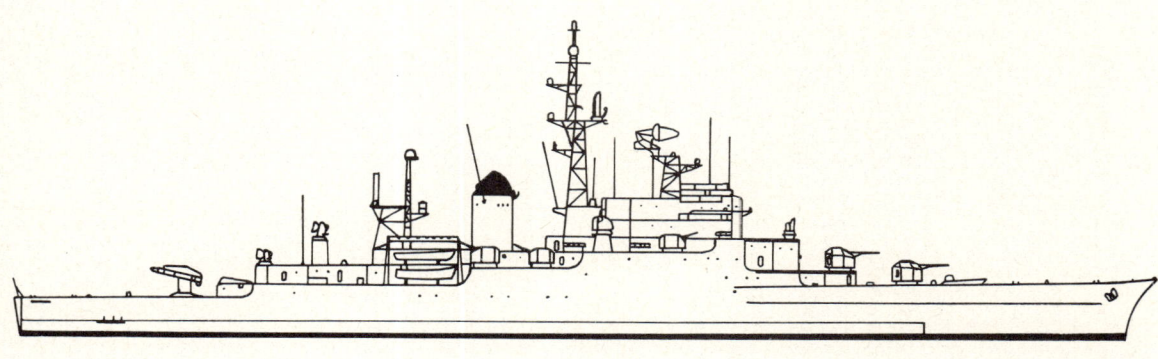

COLBERT

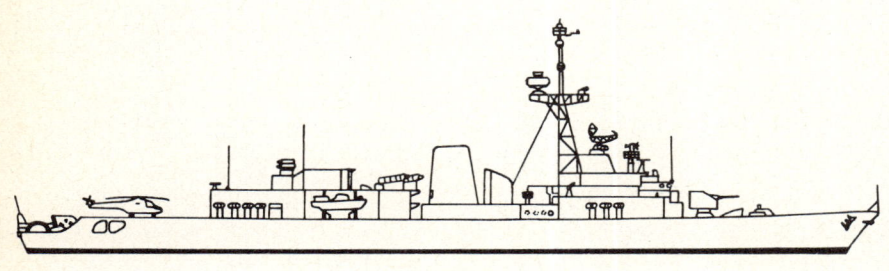

TYPE C70 (A/S)

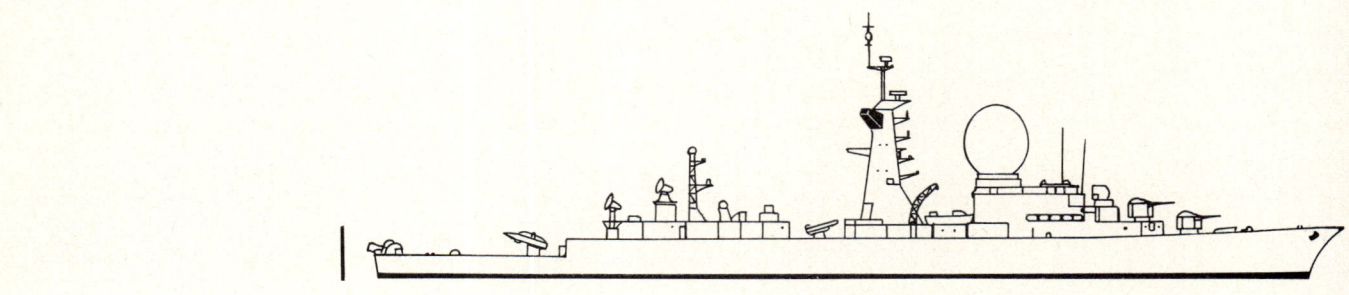

"SUFFREN" Class

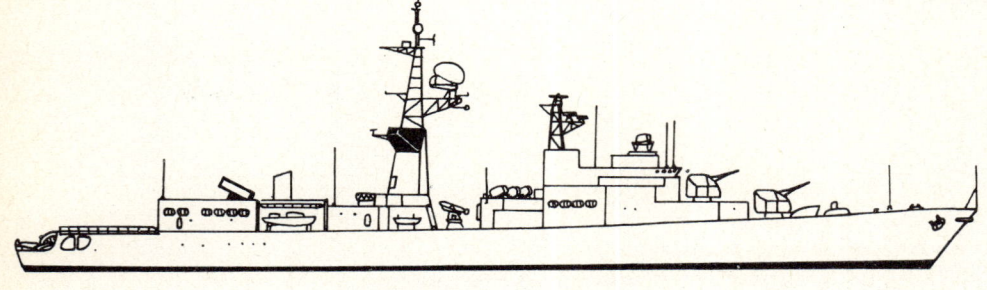

TYPE F67

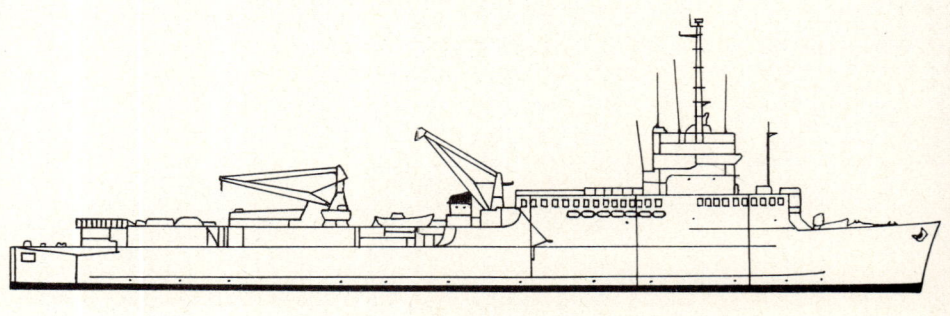

OURAGAN and ORAGE

FRANCE / Introduction 159

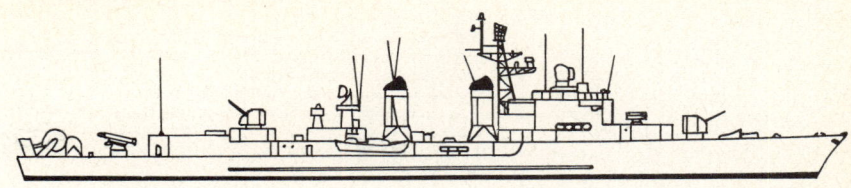
TYPE 47 (DDG)

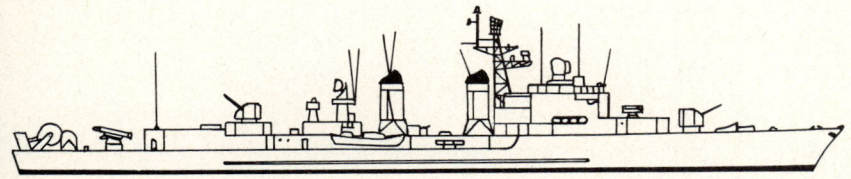
TYPE 47 (ASW)

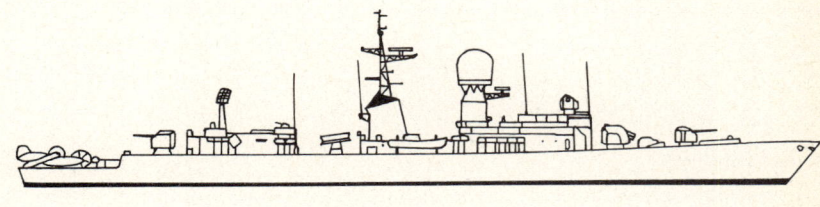
ACONIT

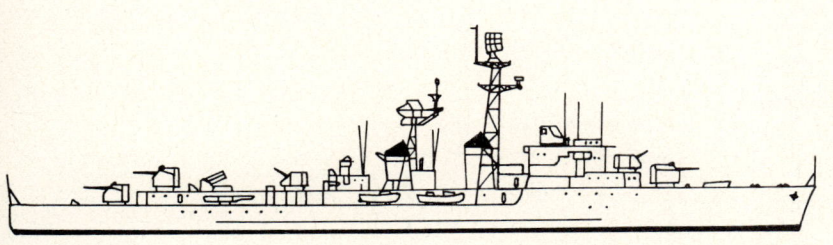
TYPE 53

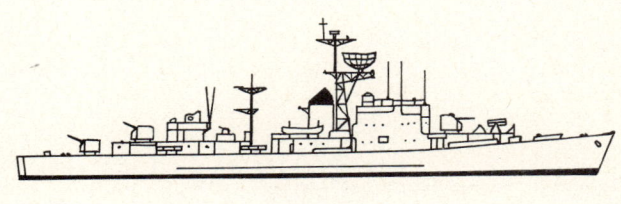
E52 TYPE

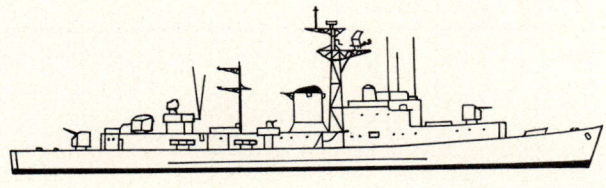
E52B TYPE

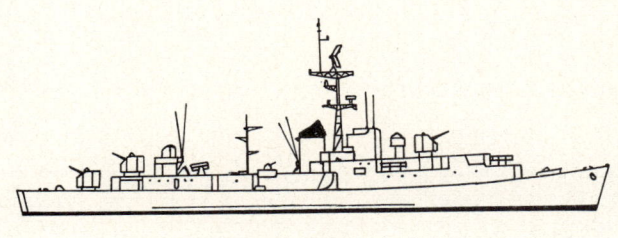
E50 TYPE

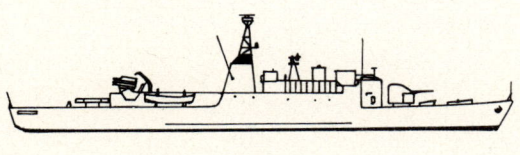
A69 TYPE

NAVAL AIR ARM

1978 Strength: 233 fixed-wing aircraft, 86 helicopters.
Embarked Aircraft: 25—Alizé; 24—Etendard IV M; 8—Etendard IV P; 20—Crusader; 23—HSS; 12—Super Frelon; 8—Alouette III.
MP Aircraft: 28—Atlantic; 11—Neptune P2H.
Support Aircraft: 4—Neptune P2H; 1—DC6, 1—C54, 4—C47; 10—Nord 262; 1—N2504; 8—MS760; 3—Alizé; 3—Falcon; 14—PA31; 11—MS880 Rallye.
Training Aircraft: 19—C47; 8—N262; 12—CM175; 5—Etendard IV P; 8—Alizé; 5—MS880; 4—Alouette II.

Notes: (a) On 1 January 1979 Squadron 11F received the first 17 Super Etendard in place of Etendard IV M. During 1979 Squadron 14F will be supplied with Super Etendard in place of Crusader F8E which will be transferred to Squadron 12F.
(b) All 71 Super Etendard are due to be delivered by 1981.

NAVAL AIR ARM

Squadron Number	Base	Aircraft	Task
Embarked Squadrons			
4F	Lann Bihoue	BR1050 "Alize"	Patrol & A/S
6F	Nimes Garons	BR1050 "Alize"	Patrol & A/S
11F	Landivisiau	Super Etendard	Strike Fighter
12F	Landivisiau	F8E "Crusader"	Interceptors
14F	Landivisiau	Super Etendard	Strike Fighter
16F	Landivisiau	ETD IV P	Reconnaissance
17F	Hyeres	ETD IV M	Fighter Bomber
31F	St. Mandrier	HSS 1	A/S
32F	Lanveoc Poulmic	Super-Frelon	A/S
33F	St. Mandrier	HSS 1	Assault
J. d'Arc	J. d'Arc or St. Mandrier	HSS 1	Training
SRL	Landivisiau	MS 760 "Paris"	Support
Support Squadrons			
2S	Lann Bihoue	Navajo, Nord 262	Support 1st & 2nd Region
3S	Hyeres	Navajo, Nord 262	Support 3rd Region
10S	St. Raphael	Nord 2504, BR1050 Navajo, MS 733	Trials CEPA
20S	St. Raphael	AL 11, AL 111 AL 111 ASM HSS 1, Super Frelon	Trials CEPA
22S	Lanveoc Poulmic	AL 11, AL 111 AL 111 VSV	Support 2nd Region SAR
23S	St. Mandrier	AL 11, AL 111	Support 3rd Region, SAR
SSD	Dugny	C 54, Nord 262 Navajo	Support
Maritime Patrol Squadrons			
21F	Nimes Garons	BR 1150 "Atlantic"	MP
22F	Nimes Garons	BR 1150 "Atlantic"	MP
23F	Lann Bihoue	BR 1150 "Atlantic"	MP
24F	Lann Bihoue	BR 1150 "Atlantic"	MP
25F	Lann Bihoue	Neptune P2H	MP
Training Squadrons			
55S	Aspretto	Nord 262, SNB 5	Twin-engine conversion
56S	Nimes Garons	C 47	Flying School
59S	Hyeres	ET IV, BR 1050 CM 175 "Zephyr"	Fighter School
SVS	Lanveoc Poulmic	MS 733	Naval School Recreational
Esalat Dax	Dax	AL 11	Helicopter School
Overseas Detachments			
New Caledonia	Tontouta	C 54, C 47	Support and Liaison
Malagasy	Diego Suarez	C 47	Support and Liaison
CEP Formations			
Sectal Pac.	Hao	AL 111	Support
27S	Hao	Super-Frelon	Support
12S	Papeete	Neptune P2H	MP

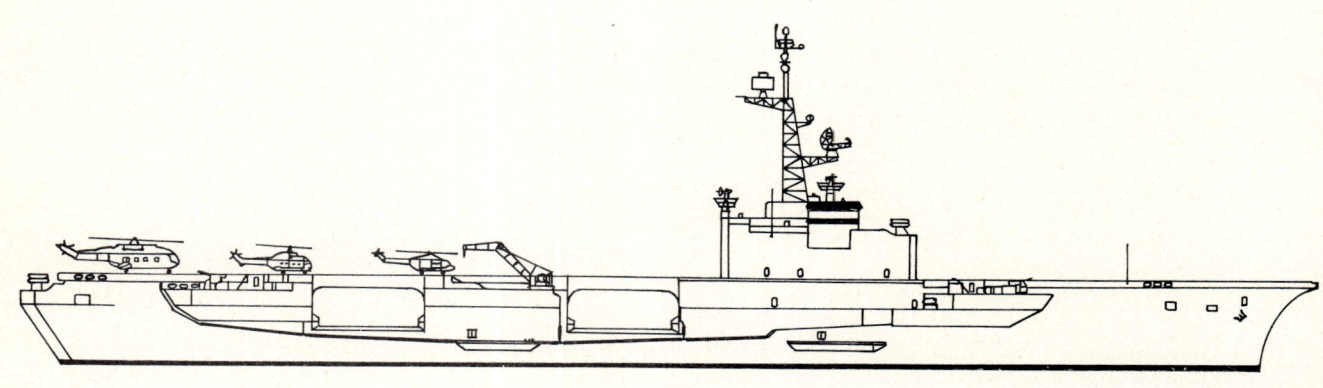

PA 75

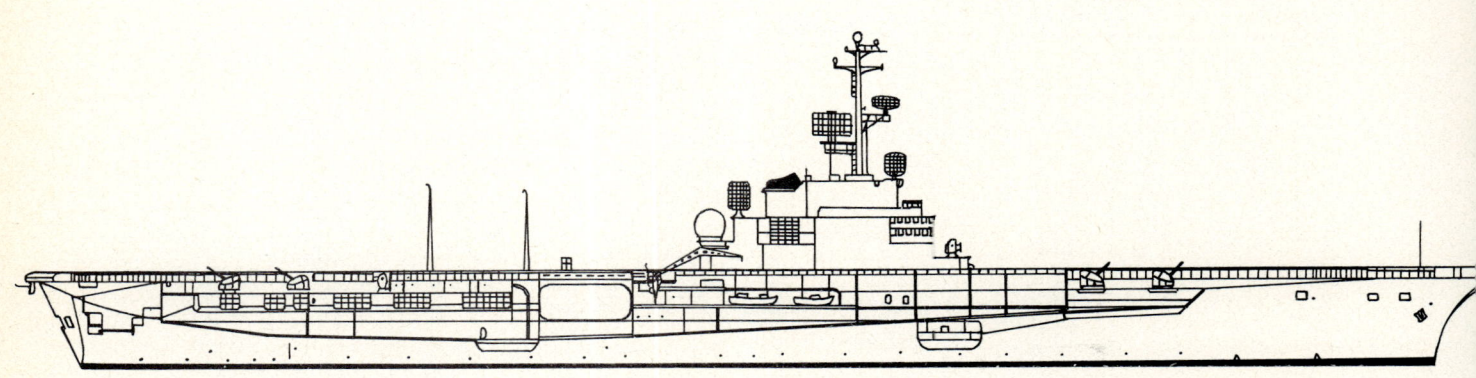

"CLEMENCEAU" Class

FRANCE / Submarines

SUBMARINES

1 NUCLEAR POWERED BALLISTIC MISSILE TYPE (SNLE)

Name	No.	Builders	Laid down	Launched	Trials	Operational
L'INFLEXIBLE	—	Cherbourg Naval Dockyard	early 1980	mid-1982	—	1985

In September 1978 a decision was taken by President Giscard D'Estaing to proceed with the construction of a sixth SNLE to be of an intermediate type between her predecessors and a new class planned for 1990-2000. Her cost will be about 2 milliard francs. The reasoning behind this order is that in order to have three submarines continuously available, of which two are on patrol, six hulls are required. If the ordering of this boat had not been delayed in December 1975 she would have been built with the M-20 missile system instead of the M4 system which will soon be operational. Having accepted the fact that France would need six, if not seven, SNLE operational by 2000 the logic of having the most up-to-date missile system is clear. The M-4 with a range of some 2 500-3 000 miles and carrying seven 150 kT MIRV heads will combine with improved inertial navigation systems, sonar, diving depth, reactor and armament to provide a submarine "qui utilisera les techniques des années 80" as M. Bourges described it. Preliminary construction started April 1979.

4 + 1 NUCLEAR POWERED BALLISTIC MISSILE TYPE (SNLE)

Name	No.	Builders	Laid down	Launched	Trials	Operational
LE FOUDROYANT	S 610	Cherbourg Naval Dockyard	12 Dec 1969	4 Dec 1971	May 1973	6 July 1974
LE REDOUTABLE	S 611	Cherbourg Naval Dockyard	30 Mar 1964	29 Mar 1967	July 1969	1 Dec 1971
LE TERRIBLE	S 612	Cherbourg Naval Dockyard	24 June 1967	12 Dec 1969	1971	1 Jan 1973
L'INDOMPTABLE	S 613	Cherbourg Naval Dockyard	4 Dec 1971	17 Aug 1974	Dec 1975	23 Dec 1976
LE TONNANT	S 614	Cherbourg Naval Dockyard	Oct 1974	17 Sep 1977	Apr 1979	May 1980

Displacement, tons: 7 500 surfaced; 9 000 dived
Length, feet (metres): 420 *(128·0)*
Beam, feet (metres): 34·8 *(10·6)*
Draught, feet (metres): 32·8 *(10·0)*
Missile launchers: 16 tubes amidships for MSBS M-2 (M-20 in *L'Indomptable, Le Terrible*)
Torpedo tubes: 4—21·7 in *(550 mm)* (18 torpedoes)
Nuclear reactor: 1 pressurised water-cooled
Main machinery: 2 turbo-alternators; 1 electric motor; 15 000 hp; 1 shaft
Auxiliary propulsion: 1 diesel; 2 670 hp; fuel for 5 000 miles
Speed, knots: 20 surfaced; 25 dived
Complement: 2 alternating crews each of 135 (15 officers, 120 men)
Diving depth: Over 900 ft *(300 m)*

Le Redoutable was the first French nuclear-powered, ballistic missile armed submarine and the prototype of the *"Force de dissuasion"*. The decision to build a fourth unit of this class was announced on 7 December 1967, the fifth in February 1972 and the sixth on 30 April 1974. (see *L'Inflexible* above)

Missiles: Originally armed with MSBS M-1 of 18 tons launch weight. Subsequently MSBS M-2 of 19·9 tons with a 1 300 n. mile range and a 500 KT head was shipped, the first submarine with this outfit being *Le Redoutable* at her 1976 refit. The 1 500 n. mile M-20 missiles with a megaton reinforced head have now been shipped in *Le Terrible* and *L'Indomptable*, are being fitted in *Le Foudroyant* and *Le Tonnant* and will probably be provided later in *Le Redoutable* which still carries M-2. All submarines will be fitted with M-4 missiles after 1985.

Radar: *Le Redoutable* is equipped with Calypso I Band radar for navigation and attack. Has passive ECM and DF systems.

Reactor: The reactor is a natural-water-cooled type running on enriched uranium, feeding twin turbines and two turbo-alternators.

Subroc: Possibility of acquisition being investigated.

LE REDOUTABLE *1975, French Navy*

LE REDOUTABLE, LE TERRIBLE, LE FOUDROYANT *1973, French Navy*

162 FRANCE / Submarines

1 EXPERIMENTAL MISSILE TYPE

Name	No.	Builders	Laid down	Launched	Commissioned
GYMNOTE	S 655	Cherbourg Naval Dockyard	17 Mar 1963 (see *Hull* Note)	17 Mar 1964	17 Oct 1966

Displacement, tons: 3 000 surfaced; 3 250 dived
Length, feet (metres): 275·6 *(84·0)*
Beam, feet (metres): 34·7 *(10·6)*
Draught, feet (metres): 25 *(7·6)*
Missile launchers: 2 tubes for MSBS
Main machinery: 4 sets 620 kW diesel-electric; 2 electric motors; 2 shafts; 2 600 hp
Speed, knots: 11 surfaced; 10 dived
Complement: 78 (8 officers, 70 men)

An experimental submarine for testing ballistic missiles for the French nuclear-powered SSBNs, and for use as an underwater laboratory to prove equipment and arms for nuclear-powered submarines.
Started conversion in early 1977 (completion January 1979) for trial firings of M-4 Missiles. These require tubes of greater diameter. First M-4 trials February 1979.

Hull: *Gymnote* was the hull laid down in 1958 as the nuclear-powered submarine Q 244 which was cancelled in 1959. The hull was still available when a trials vessel for the French MSBS type missiles was required and was completed as *Gymnote*. Has fixed bow-planes.

GYMNOTE 1970, French Navy

FLEET SUBMARINES

0 + 2 + 4 TYPE SNA 72

Name	No.	Builders	Laid down	Launched	Commissioned
— (Q 265)	S 616	Cherbourg Naval Dockyard	10 Dec 1976	1979	early 1982
— (Q 266)	—	Cherbourg Naval Dockyard	1978	—	1984

Displacement, tons: 2 385 surfaced; 2 670 dived
Dimensions, feet (metres): 236·5 × 24·9 × 21 *(72·1 × 7·6 × 6·4)*
Torpedo tubes: 4—21 in *(533 mm)* (14 torpedoes or mines)
Missiles: Tube-launched SM 39 (see note)
Main machinery: 1 nuclear reactor; 48 MW; 2 turbo alternators; 1 main motor; 1 shaft with emergency electric motor
Speed, knots: 25
Complement: 66 (9 officers, 35 petty officers, 22 junior ratings)

A new class of fleet-submarines with the first included in the 1974 programme. The armament, sonar and fire control equipment will be similar to the "Agosta" class. Three of this class and one of an improved type are included in the 1977-82 building programme. Second boat ordered 1977. Funds for third boat approved in 1979.
Hull of S 616 completed December 1978 and the second hull is nearing completion. S 616 to start trials mid-1980.

Future: Two squadrons of these submarines are forecast, one to be stationed at Brest and the other at Toulon.

Machinery: Studies of the machinery are continuing at Cadarache. As this is the smallest class of SSNs ever designed except for the 400 ton NR-1 of the US Navy there has clearly been a great reduction in the size of the reactor compared with that of the "Le Redoutable" class.

Missiles: The SM 39, an adaptation of the MM 38 Exocet, will have a range of about 50 km.

Name: The well-known name *Rubis* has been mentioned as a possible choice for S 616.

Trials: Anticipated date for start of S 616 trials is October 1980.

PATROL SUBMARINES

4 "AGOSTA" CLASS

Name	No.	Builders	Laid down (see note)	Launched	Commissioned
AGOSTA	S 620	Cherbourg Naval Dockyard	1 Nov 1972	19 Oct 1974	28 July 1977
BÉVÉZIERS	S 621	Cherbourg Naval Dockyard	17 May 1973	14 June 1975	27 Sep 1977
LA PRAYA	S 622	Cherbourg Naval Dockyard	1974	15 May 1976	9 Mar 1978
OUESSANT	S 623	Cherbourg Naval Dockyard	1974	23 Oct 1976	27 July 1978

Displacement, tons: 1 200 standard; 1 450 surfaced; 1 725 dived
Length, feet (metres): 221·7 *(67·6)*
Beam, feet (metres): 22·3 *(6·8)*
Draught, feet (metres): 17·7 *(5·4)*
Torpedo tubes: 4—21·7 in *(550 mm)* (bow) (20 torpedoes)
Main machinery: Diesel-electric; 2 SEMT-Pielstick 16 PA4 diesels 3 600 hp; 1 main motor (3 500 kW) 4 600 hp; 1 cruising motor (23 kW); 1 shaft
Speed, knots: 12 surfaced; 20 dived
Range, miles: 8 500 at 9 knots (snorting); 350 at 3·5 knots (dived)
Endurance: 45 days
Complement: 54 (7 officers, 47 men)

Building of this class was announced in 1970 under the third five-year new construction plan 1971-75. Considerable efforts have been made to improve the silencing of this class, including a clean casing and the damping of internal noise.
All in the Mediterranean.

Laid down dates: Those given are for the placing of the first prefabricated section in the building dock. Prefabrication of *Agosta* started 7 February 1972 and of *Beveziers* December 1972.

Radar: Possibly I Band Calypso Th D 1030 or 1031 for search/navigation.

Sonar: DUUA 2 active sonar with transducers forward and aft; DSUV passive sonar with 36 hydrophones; passive ranging; intercept set.

Trials: *Bévéziers* October 1976, *La Praya* April 1977, *Ouessant* October 1977.

Torpedo tubes: A new design allowing for torpedo discharge at all speeds and down to full diving depth. Rapid reloading fitted.

Foreign orders: Four being built at Cartagena for Spanish Navy and two for Pakistan by Dubigeon.

AGOSTA 1977, French Navy

FRANCE / Submarines   163

9 "DAPHNÉ" CLASS

Name	No.	Builders	Laid down	Launched	Commissioned
DAPHNÉ	S 641	Dubigeon	Mar 1958	20 June 1959	1 June 1964
DIANE	S 642	Dubigeon	July 1958	4 Oct 1960	20 June 1964
DORIS	S 643	Cherbourg Naval Dockyard	Sep 1958	14 May 1960	26 Aug 1964
FLORE	S 645	Cherbourg Naval Dockyard	Sep 1958	21 Dec 1960	21 May 1964
GALATÉE	S 646	Cherbourg Naval Dockyard	Sep 1958	22 Sep 1961	25 July 1964
JUNON	S 648	Cherbourg Naval Dockyard	July 1961	11 May 1964	25 Feb 1966
VENUS	S 649	Cherbourg Naval Dockyard	Aug 1961	24 Sep 1964	1 Jan 1966
PSYCHÉ	S 650	Brest Naval Dockyard	May 1965	28 June 1967	1 July 1969
SIRÈNE	S 651	Brest Naval Dockyard	May 1965	28 June 1967	1 Mar 1970

Displacement, tons: 869 surfaced; 1 043 dived
Length, feet (metres): 189·6 *(57·8)*
Beam, feet (metres): 22·3 *(6·8)*
Draught, feet (metres): 15·1 *(4·6)*
Torpedo tubes: 12—21·7 in *(550 mm)* 8 bow 4 stern
Main machinery: SEMT-Pielstick diesel-electric;
  1 300 bhp surfaced; 1 600 bhp motors dived; 2 shafts
Range, miles: 2 700 at 12·5 knots (surfaced); 4 500 at 5 knots (snorting); 3000 at 7 knots (snorting)
Speed, knots: 13·5 surfaced; 16 dived
Complement: 45 (6 officers, 39 men)

Improved "Aréthuse" class with diving depth about 1 000 ft *(300 m)*. Siréne sank at Lorient in 1972, and was subsequently salved.
All in the Mediterranean.

Diving depth: About 900 ft *(300 m)*

Radar: I Band Calypso II for search/navigation.

Sonar: DUUA 2 active sonar with transducers forward and aft; passive ranging; intercept set.

Foreign orders: South Africa (1967) (3), Pakistan (1966) (3), Portugal (1964) (4), (1 to Pakistan later), Spain (built in Spain) (1965) (4).

DAPHNÉ   7/1976, Dr. Giorgio Arra

SIRÈNE   10/1977, Leo van Ginderen

4 "ARÉTHUSE" CLASS

Name	No.	Builders	Laid down	Launched	Commissioned
ARÉTHUSE	S 635	Cherbourg Naval Dockyard	Mar 1955	9 Nov 1957	23 Oct 1958
ARGONAUTE	S 636	Cherbourg Naval Dockyard	Mar 1955	29 June1957	11 Feb 1959
AMAZONE	S 639	Cherbourg Naval Dockyard	Dec 1955	3 Apr 1958	1 July 1959
ARIANE	S 640	Cherbourg Naval Dockyard	Dec 1955	12 Sep 1958	16 Mar 1960

Displacement, tons: 400 standard; 543 surfaced; 669 dived
Length, feet (metres): 162·7 *(49·6)*
Beam, feet (metres): 19 *(5·8)*
Draught, feet (metres): 13·1 *(4·0)*
Torpedo tubes: 4—21·7 in *(550 mm)* bow, 4 reloads
Main machinery: 12-cyl SEMT-Pielstick diesel-electric;
  1 060 bhp surfaced; 1 300 hp motors dived; 1 shaft
Speed, knots: 12·5 surfaced; 16 dived
Complement: 40 (6 officers, 34 men)

An excellent class of small submarines with a minimum number of ballast tanks and a diving depth of about 600 ft *(182·8 m)*.
All in the Mediterranean.

Sonar: DUUA 2.

ARÈTHUSE   6/1976, Dr. Giorgio Arra

6 "NARVAL" CLASS

Name	No.	Builders	Laid down	Launched	Commissioned
NARVAL	S 631	Cherbourg Naval Dockyard	June 1951	11 Dec 1954	1 Dec 1957
MARSOUIN	S 632	Cherbourg Naval Dockyard	Sep 1951	21 May 1955	1 Oct 1957
DAUPHIN	S 633	Cherbourg Naval Dockyard	May 1952	17 Sep 1955	1 Aug 1958
REQUIN	S 634	Cherbourg Naval Dockyard	June 1952	3 Dec 1955	1 Aug 1958
ESPADON	S 637	Normand	Dec 1955	15 Sep 1958	2 Apr 1960
MORSE	S 638	Seine Maritime	Feb 1956	10 Dec 1958	2 May 1960

Displacement, tons: 1 320 standard; 1 635 surfaced; 1 910 dived
Length, feet (metres): 254·6 *(77·6)*
Beam, feet (metres): 25·6 *(7·8)*
Draught, feet (metres): 17·7 *(5·4)*
Torpedo tubes: 6—21·7 in *(550 mm)* bow; 14 reload torpedoes; capable of minelaying
Main machinery: Diesel-electric, three 12-cyl SEMT-Pielstick diesels; two 2 400 hp electric motors; 2 shafts
Speed, knots: 15 surfaced; 18 dived
Range, miles: 15 000 at 8 knots (snorting)
Endurance: 45 days
Complement: 63 (7 officers, 56 men)

Improved versions based on the German Type XXI. *Dauphin, Marsouin, Narval* and *Requin* were built in seven prefabricated parts each of 10 metres in length.
All in the Atlantic.

Engineering: New main propelling machinery installed on reconstruction during 1965 to 1970 includes diesel-electric drive on the surface with SEMT-Pielstick diesels. The original main machinery was Schneider 4 000 bhp 7-cyl 2 stroke diesels for surface propulsion and 5 000 hp electric motors dived.

Reconstruction: During a five-year reconstruction programme, announced in 1965 and completed by the end of 1970, these submarines, *Requin* in spring 1967 and *Espadon* and *Morse* in succession at Lorient followed by the other three were given new weapon and detection equipment.

Sonar: DUUA 1.

MORSE   1978, Michael D. J. Lennon

FRANCE / Aircraft carriers

AIRCRAFT CARRIERS

2 "CLEMENCEAU" CLASS

Name	No.	Builders	Laid down	Launched	Commissioned
CLEMENCEAU	R 98	Brest Naval Dockyard	Nov 1955	21 Dec 1957	22 Nov 1961
FOCH	R 99	Chantiers de l'Atlantique	Feb 1957	28 July 1960	15 July 1963

Displacement, tons: 27 307 normal; 32 780 full load
Length, feet (metres): 780·8 *(238·0)* pp; 869·4 *(265·0)* oa
Beam, feet (metres): 104·1 *(31·7)* hull (with bulges)
Width, feet (metres): 168·0 *(51·2)* oa (flight deck and sponsons)
Draught, feet (metres): 28·2 *(8·6)*
Aircraft: Capacity 40 (3 Flights)
   2 of Super Etendard *(Clemenceau),*
   1 of Breguet Alizé (see Aircraft note)
Catapults: 2 Mitchell-Brown steam, Mk BS 5
Guns: 8—3·9 in *(100 mm)* automatic in single turrets
Armour Flight deck, island superstructure and bridges, hull (over machinery spaces and magazines)
Main engines: 2 sets Parsons geared turbines; 2 shafts; 126 000 shp
Boilers: 6; steam pressure 640 psi *(45 kg/cm²),* superheat 842°F *(450°C)*
Speed, knots: 32
Oil fuel, tons: 3 720
Range, miles: 7 500 at 18 knots; 4 800 at 24 knots; 3 500 at full power
Complement: 1 338 (64 officers, 1 274 men) (fixed wing)
   984 (45 officers, 939 men) (helo)

CLEMENCEAU   7/1976, Dr. Giorgio Arra

First aircraft carriers designed as such and built from the keel to be completed in France. Authorised in 1953 and 1955, respectively. *Clemenceau* ordered from Brest Dockyard on 28 May 1954 and begun in November 1955. *Foch* begun at Chantiers de l'Atlantique at St. Nazaire, Penhoet-Loire, in a special dry dock (contract provided for the construction of the hull and propelling machinery) and completed by Brest Dockyard.
Clemenceau refitted in 1978 to accommodate Super Etendard aircraft and tactical nuclear weapons. Post-refit trials started on 12 November 1978.
Foch will have a four month maintenance period in 1979 and a similar refit to *Clemenceau's* in 1980-81. Until this is done she will operate as a helicopter carrier.

Aircraft: Each flight has ten aircraft. In addition two Super Frelon and two Alouette III helicopters are carried. As a peacetime economy only *Clemenceau* operates fixed wing aircraft, *Foch* carrying out A/S duties with a reduced complement, all helicopters. See "Complement" for resultant changes.

Bulges: *Foch* was completed with bulges. These having proved successful, *Clemenceau* was modified similarly on first refit, increasing her beam by 6 ft *(1·83 m).*

Electronics: Comprehensive DF and ECM equipment. *Clemenceau* fitted with SENIT 2 Tactical data automation system after refit.

Flight Deck: Angled deck, two lifts, measuring 52·5 × 36 ft *(16·00 × 10·97 m),* one on the starboard deck edge, two steam catapults and two mirror landing aids. The flight deck measures 543 × 96·8 ft *(165·50 × 29·50 m)* and is angled at 8 degrees. Flight deck letters: F = *Foch,* U = *Clemenceau.*

Gunnery: Originally to have been armed with 24—2·25 in *(57 mm)* guns in twin mountings, but the armament was revised to 12—3·9 in *(100 mm)* in 1956 and to 8—3·9 in *(100 mm)* in 1958. Rate of fire 60 rounds per minute.

Hangar: Dimensions of the hangar are 590·6 × 78·7 × 23·0 ft *(180 × 24 × 7 m).*

Radar: Surveillance: One DRBV 50.
Air surveillance: One DRBV 23B.
Warning: One DRBV 20C.
Fire control: One DRBC 31.
Height finders: Two DRBI 10.

Sonar: One SQS 505.

FOCH   1974, Dr. Giorgio Arra

CLEMENCEAU   7/1976, Dr. Giorgio Arra

FRANCE / Aircraft carriers

1 PA 75 (NUCLEAR-PROPELLED AIRCRAFT CARRIER)

Name	No.	Builders	Laid down	Launched	Commissioned
—	PA 75	DCAN, Brest	1981	—	—

Displacement, tons: 16 400 trials; 18 400 full load
Length, feet (metres): 682·2 *(208)*
Length, feet (metres): 662·6 flight deck *(202)*
Beam, feet (metres): 86·6 wl *(26·4)*
Beam, feet (metres): 157·4 flight deck *(46)*
Draught, feet (metres): 21·3 *(6·5)*
Aircraft: 25 WG 13 Lynx or 10 Super Frelon or 15 Puma helicopters
Missiles: 2 Crotale SAM systems; 4 SAM systems with a sea-skimming capability for anti-missile defence are eventually to replace the guns
Guns: 2—100 mm (singles—fwd); 2—40 mm Breda-Bofors
Main engines: 1—CAS 230 reactor to two turbines; 65 000 bhp; 2 emergency AGO diesels
Speed, knots: 28
Range, miles: Unlimited on reactor; 3 000 at 18 knots (diesels)
Endurance: Stores for 45 days; 30 days for passengers
Complement: 890 (840 ship, 50 staff) plus 1 500 passengers

Coming at a time of financial stringency, this is a bold design showing the French Navy's appreciation of the great and universal value of helicopters in both peace and war. While her wartime role in a force composed of both A/S and AA ships is clear, she has been designed with an intervention role in mind as well. For peacetime duties in the event of natural disasters, her large passenger and hospital capacity will be of immense value. Although the original plan allowed for her completion in 1980 the new 1977-81 plan states that she will not be laid down until 1981. This date is subject to considerable modification and reports of her new title vary from PA 78 to PA 82 and PA 88, probably reflecting the uncertainty as to her start date. Other reports have placed her full load displacement as high as 20 000 tons.

Accommodation: A crew of 840 plus 50 staff and Ground Intervention Staff is provided for. Passenger accommodation is available for 1 000, with more austere conditions on portable bunks for an extra 500 in the garage (forward of the hangar).

Aircraft: Although designed primarily for helicopter operations the possibility of VTOL operations was also taken into account.

Electrical supply: A total of 9 400 kW from two turbines each driving a pair of 1 500 kW alternators and four diesel alternators of 850 kW each.

Flight deck: The flight deck, 662 ft *(201·77 m)* long, is 157 ft *(47·85 m)* wide at its maximum and 102 ft *(31·09 m)* at the island. Four spots are provided for Super Frelon helicopters and eight for Lynx or Puma.

Hangar: One hangar, 275 × 69 × 21 ft *(83·82 × 21·03 × 6·40 m)*, is provided with two lateral lifts to starboard at the rear of the island. Storage for 1 000 cubic metres of TR5 fuel in tanks is available. One fixed crane and one mobile crane are provided.

Hospital: Three main wards, one X-ray ward, one intensive care ward, one infectious diseases ward, two dental surgeries and a laboratory.

Main engines: The CAS 230 reactor of 230 megawatts is being constructed under the supervision of l'Establissement des Constructions et Armes Navales d'Indret.

Operations rooms: Normal Operations Room, ASW centre and Communication Offices are supplemented by an Operations Centre with facilities for Ground Intervention Forces and Air Intervention Forces. These include a Warfare Coordinating Centre, an Air Intervention Command Centre and a Helicopter Command Station.

Radar: Air search: One DRBV 26
Combined search: One DRBV 51C
Missile guidance: One DRBC 32
Navigation: Two Decca

Replenishment: 1 250 tons of fuel is carried for replenishment of Escorts.

Type: Although originally classified as PH (Porte helicoptères) this has been changed to PA (Porte aeronefs) signifying her V/STOL capability.

Sonar: One DUBA 25.

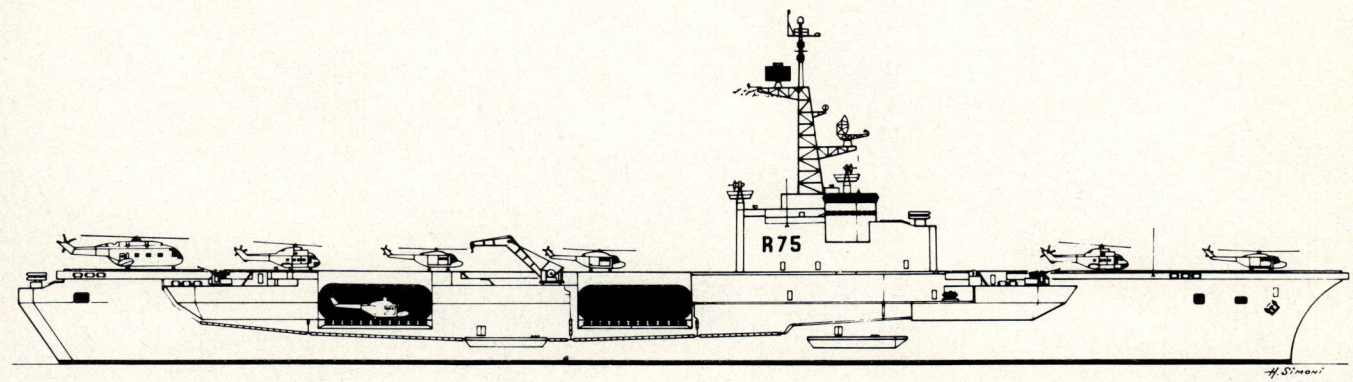

PA 75   1974, French Navy

166 FRANCE / Helicopter carrier

HELICOPTER CARRIER

Name	No.	Builders	Laid down	Launched	Commissioned
JEANNE D'ARC (ex-*La Résolue*)	R 97	Brest Naval Dockyard	7 July 1960	30 Sep 1961	1 July 1963 (trials) 30 June 1964 (service)

Displacement, tons: 10 000 standard; 12 365 full load
Length, feet (metres): 564·2 *(172)* pp; 597·1 *(182·0)* oa
Beam, feet (metres): 78·7 *(24·0)* hull
Draught, feet (metres): 24·0 *(7·3)*
Flight deck, feet (metres): 203·4 × 68·9 *(62·0 × 21·0)*
Aircraft: Heavy helicopters (4 in peace-time as training ship; 8 in wartime)
Missiles: SSM; 6 Exocet (single cells)
Guns: 4—3·9 in *(100 mm)* single
Main engines: Rateau-Bretagne geared turbines; 2 shafts; 40 000 shp
Boilers: 4; working pressure 640 psi *(45 kg/cm²)*; 842°F *(450°C)*
Speed, knots: 26·5
Oil fuel, tons: 1 360
Range, miles: 6 000 at 15 knots
Complement: 809 (30 officers, 587 ratings and 192 cadets)

Authorised under the 1957 estimates. Used for training officer cadets in peacetime. In wartime, after rapid modification, she would be used as a commando ship, helicopter carrier or troop transport with commando equipment and a battalion of 700 men. The lift has a capacity of 12 tons. The ship is almost entirely air-conditioned.
Operates with the Training Squadron.

Electronics: 2 Syllex systems.

Missiles: Due to be fitted with Crotale.

Modifications: Between first steaming trials and completion for operational service the ship was modified with a taller funnel to clear the superstructure and prevent the smoke and exhaust gases swirling on to the bridges.

Radar: One DRBV 22D; one DRBV 50; one DRBN 32 one DRBI 10.

Sonar: One SQS 503.

JEANNE D'ARC *3/1977, Dr. Giorgio Arra*

JEANNE D'ARC *3/1977, Dr. Giorgio Arra*

JEANNE D'ARC *1/1978, Chris G*

FRANCE / Cruiser

CRUISER

Name	No.	Builders	Laid down	Launched	Commissioned
COLBERT	C 611	Brest Dockyard	Dec 1953	24 Mar 1956 (floated out of dry dock)	5 May 1959 (trials late 1957)

Displacement, tons: 8 500 standard; 11 300 full load
Length, feet (metres): 593·2 *(180·8)*
Beam, feet (metres): 66·1 *(20·2)*
Draught, feet (metres): 25·2 *(7·7)*
Missile launchers: SSM; 4 Exocet MM38 (singles);
  SAM; 48 Masurca (1 twin launcher)
Guns: 2—3·9 in *(100 mm)* single automatic;
  12—57 mm in 6 twin mountings, 3 on each side
Armour: 50—80 mm belt and 50 mm deck
Main engines: 2 sets CEM-Parsons geared turbines; 2 shafts;
  86 000 shp
Boilers: 4 Indret multitubular; 640 psi *(45 kg/cm²); 842°F (450°C)*
Speed, knots: 31·5
Oil fuel, tons: 1 492
Range, miles: 4 000 at 25 knots
Complement: 560 (24 officers, 536 men)

She was equipped as command ship and for radar control of air strikes. Serves as Flagship of the Mediterranean Fleet.

Electronics: SENIT data automation system; radar intercept equipment; wireless intercept equipment; two Knebworth Corvus dual-purpose launchers for CHAFF. 2 Syllex.

Gunnery: Prior to April 1970 the armament comprised 16 5 in *(127 mm)* dual purpose guns in 8 twin mountings, and 20 57 mm Bofors anti-aircraft guns in 10 twin mountings.

Missiles: *Colbert* carries Mk 2 Mod 3 semi-active radar homing version missiles for Masurca. Crotale to be fitted at later refit.

Radar: Surveillance: One DRBV 50.
Air surveillance: One DRBV 23C
Warning: One DRBV 20.
Fire control: Two DRBR 51; one DRBR 32C; two DRBC 31.
Height finder: One DRBI 10D.
Navigation: One Decca RM 416.

Reconstruction: Between April 1970 and October 1972 she underwent a complete reconstruction and rearmament. The gunnery systems were altered to those given above, the Masurca surface-to-air missile system was fitted and helicopter facilities were installed on the quarter-deck. Reductions in the original armament schedule saved 80 million francs from the original refit cost of 350 million francs.

Sonar: Hull-mounted set.

COLBERT 1978, Ulrich Schimmel

COLBERT 3/1976, Reinhard Nerlich

COLBERT 7/1976, Dr. Giorgio Arra

FRANCE / Destroyers

DESTROYERS

1 + 3 + 5 TYPE C 70

Name	No.	Builders	Laid down	Launched	Commissioned
GEORGES LEYGUES	D 640	Brest Naval Dockyard	June 1974	17 Dec 1975	Oct 1979
DUPLEIX	D 641	Brest Naval Dockyard	17 Oct 1975	2 Dec 1978	early 1981
MONTCALM	D 642	Brest Naval Dockyard	Dec 1975	—	late 1982
—	D 643	Brest Naval Dockyard	1978-79	—	—
—	—	—	—	—	—

Displacement, tons: 3 800 standard; 4 100 full load
Length, feet (metres): 455·9 *(139)*
Beam, feet (metres): 45·9 *(14)*
Draught, feet (metres): 18·7 *(5·7)*
Aircraft: Two WG 13 Lynx helicopters with Mk 44 or 46 torpedoes
Missiles: A/S Version; SSM; 4 Exocet; SAM; 1 Crotale
A/A Version; SSM; 4 Exocet; SAM; 40 SM2
Guns: 1—3·9 in *(100 mm)*; 2—20 mm (A/S version)
2—3·9 in *(100 mm)*; 2—20 mm (A/A version)
Torpedo tubes: 10 tubes in 2 mountings for Mk L5
Main engines: CODOG; 2 Rolls-Royce Olympus gas turbines 42 000 bhp; 2 SEMT-Pielstick 16PA6 diesels 10 000 bhp; 2 shafts; cp screws
Speed, knots: 29·75 (19·5 on diesels) *(Georges Leygues 31 on trials)*
Range, miles: 9 500 at 18 knots on diesels
Complement: 271 (21 officers, 250 men) (billets)

A new C 70 type of so-called "corvette".
A total of nine is planned, six of an A/S version like *Georges Leygues* and three of an A/A version. Fourth ship ready for laying down. Funds for fifth ship (A/A) version allotted in 1978 and for the sixth (A/A) version in 1979.

Electronics: Senit action data automation system. Two Dagaie systems. Fitted with Thomson-CSF Vega system.

Helicopter: The Lynx, as well as its A/S role, can have an anti-surface role when armed with four AS 12 missiles.

Missiles: A/A version to carry Standard SM2 system.

Radar: Surface/air surveillance: One DRBV 51
Air search: One DRBV 26
Fire control: One DRBC 32
Navigation: Two Decca 1226 (A/S version).
One DRBV 26; one DRBJ 11; two SPG 51C (A/A version).

Sonar: One DUBV 23 (hull-mounted); one DUBV 43 (VDS) (A/S version).
One DUBV 25 or 26 (A/A version).

Trials: *Georges Leygues* began trials on 23 July 1977 and is expected to complete in July 1979.

GEORGES LEYGUES 10/1978

GEORGES LEYGUES 10/1978

FRANCE / Destroyers 169

2 "SUFFREN" CLASS

Name	No.	Builders	Laid down	Launched	Commissioned
SUFFREN	D 602	Lorient Naval Dockyard	Dec 1962	15 May 1965	July 1967
DUQUESNE	D 603	Brest Naval Dockyard	Nov 1964	12 Feb 1966	Apr 1970

Displacement, tons: 5 090 standard; 6 090 full load
Length, feet (metres): 517·1 *(157·6)*
Beam, feet (metres): 50·9 *(15·5)*
Draught, feet (metres): 20·0 *(6·1)*
Missiles: SSM; 4 Exocet (single launchers);
 SAM; Masurca (twin launchers)
Guns: 2—3·9 in *(100 mm)* (automatic, single)
 2—20 mm (single)
A/S weapons: Malafon single launcher with 13 missiles;
 4 launchers (2 each side) for L5 A/S homing torpedoes
Main engines: Double reduction Rateau geared turbines;
 2 shafts; 72 500 shp
Boilers: 4 automatic; working pressure 640 psi *(45 kg/cm²)*;
 superheat 842°F *(450°C)*
Speed, knots: 34
Range, miles: 5 100 at 18 knots; 2 400 at 29 knots
Complement: 355 (23 officers, 332 men)

Ordered under the 1960 Programme. Equipped with gyro controlled stabilisers controlling three pairs of non-retractable fins. Air-conditioning of accommodation and operational areas. Excellent sea-boats and weapon platforms.
Both in the Mediterranean.

Electronics: SENIT I action data automatic system. Two Syllex.

Missiles: Carry 48 Masurca missiles, a mix of Mk 2 Mod 2 beam riders and Mk 2 Mod 3 semi-active homers. During their 1977-78 refit four Exocet launchers replaced the 30 mm gun mountings. *Duquesne* completed February 1977. *Suffren* 1979.

Radar: Search and navigation: One DRBN 32.
Air surveillance and target designator (radome): One DRBI 23.
Surface surveillance: One DRBV 50.
Masurca fire-control: Two DRBR 51.
Gun fire-control: One DRBC 32A.

Sonar: One DUBV 23 hull-mounted set and one DUBV 43 VDS.

SUFFREN 7/1978, J. Y. Robert

SUFFREN 1978, Ulrich Schimmel

DUQUESNE 6/1977, C. and S. Taylor

170 FRANCE / Destroyers

3 TYPE F 67 (ex-C-67A)

Name	No.	Builders	Laid down	Launched	Commissioned
TOURVILLE	D 610	Lorient Naval Dockyard	16 Mar 1970	13 May 1972	21 June 1974
DUGUAY-TROUIN	D 611	Lorient Naval Dockyard	25 Feb 1971	1 June 1973	17 Sep 1975
DE GRASSE	D 612	Lorient Naval Dockyard	1972	30 Nov 1974	1 Oct 1977

Displacement, tons: 4 580 standard; 5 745 full load
Length, feet (metres): 501·3 *(152·8)*
Beam, feet (metres): 50·2 *(15·3)*
Draught, feet (metres): 18·7 *(5·7)*
Aircraft: Two WG 13 Lynx ASW helicopters
Missiles: SSM; 6 Exocet (single launchers); SAM; Crotale (see note)
Guns: 2—3·9 in *(100 mm)*
A/S weapons: 1 Malafon rocket/homing torpedo (13 missiles); 2 mountings for Mk L5 torpedoes
Main engines: Rateau geared turbines; 2 shafts; 54 400 shp
Boilers: 4 automatic
Speed, knots: 31
Range, miles: 5 000 at 18 knots
Complement: 303 (25 officers, 278 men)

Developed from the "Aconit" design. Originally rated as "Corvettes" but reclassified as "Frigates" on 8 July 1971 and given "D" pennant numbers like destroyers.
All in the Atlantic, *De Grasse* being the flagship.

Electronics: SENIT action data automatic system. Fitted with Thomson-CSF Vega system. Two Syllex.

Missiles: Octuple Crotale fit in place of after 100 mm gun. *Douguay-Trouin,* January 1979, *Tourville* in 1980 and *De Grasse* 1981.

Radar: Surface/air surveillance: One DRBV 51
Fire control: One DRBC 32D
Navigation: Two Decca type 1226
Air search: One DRBV 26

Sonars: One DUBV 23 hull-mounted; one DUBV 43 VDS.

TOURVILLE (see *Missile* note) 7/1976, Dr. Giorgio Arra

DUGUAY-TROUIN 10/1977, C. and S. Taylor

1 TYPE T 56

Name	No.	Builders	Laid down	Launched	Commissioned
LA GALISSONNIÈRE	D 638	Lorient Naval Dockyard	Nov 1958	12 Mar 1960	July 1962

Displacement, tons: 2 750 standard; 3 740 full load
Length, feet (metres): 435·7 *(132·8)*
Beam, feet (metres): 41·7 *(12·7)*
Draught, feet (metres): 21·4 *(6·3)*
Aircraft: One A/S helicopter
A/S weapons: 1 Malafon rocket/homing torpedo launcher
Guns: 2—3·9 in *(100 mm)* automatic, single
Torpedo tubes: 6—21·7 in *(550 mm)* (2 triple for Mks K2 and L3)
Main engines: 2 sets Rateau geared turbines; 2 shafts; 63 000 shp
Boilers: 4 A & C de B Indret; 500 psi *(35 kg/cm²)*; 617°F *(380°C)*
Speed, knots: 32
Oil fuel, tons: 800
Range, miles: 5 000 at 18 knots
Complement: 270 (15 officers, 255 men)

Same characteristics as regards hull and machinery as T 47 and T 53 types, but different armament. She has a hangar which hinges outwards and a platform for landing a helicopter. When first commissioned she was used as an experimental ship for new sonars and anti-submarine weapons.
Serves in the Mediterranean.

Armament: First French combatant ship to be armed with Malafon. This is the reason for the two 3·9 in *(100 mm)* guns instead of the three or four previously planned. France's first operational guided missile ship.

Electronics: Tacan beacon and full DF and ECM fit.

Radar: Surface/air surveillance: One DRBV 50
Navigation: One DRBN 32
Air search: One DRBV 22
Gun fire control: One DRBC 32A

LA GALISSONNIÈRE 7/1976, Dr. Giorgio Arra

Sonar: One hull-mounted DUBV 23; one DUBV 43 VDS.

FRANCE / Destroyers 171

1 TYPE T 53 (MODIFIED—ASW)

Name	No.	Builders	Laid down	Launched	Commissioned
DUPERRÉ	D 633	Lorient Naval Dockyard	Nov 1954	23 June 1956	8 Oct 1957

Displacement, tons: 2 800 standard; 3 900 full load
Length, feet (metres): 435·7 *(132·8)*
Beam, feet (metres): 41·7 *(12·7)*
Draught, feet (metres): 20 *(6·1)*
Aircraft: One WG 13 Lynx helicopter
Missiles: SSM; 4 Exocet (single launchers)
Gun: 1—3·9 in *(100 mm)*
A/S weapons: Launcher for 8 torpedoes (Mk L5)
Main engines: 2 sets Rateau geared turbines; 2 shafts; 63 000 shp
Boilers: 4 A & C de B Indret; 500 psi *(35 kg/cm²)*; 617°F *(380°C)*
Speed, knots: 32
Oil fuel, tons: 800
Range, miles: 5 000 at 18 knots
Complement: 272 (15 officers, 257 men)

Originally built as Type T 53.
After serving as trial ship from 1967-71, she was converted at Brest to her present state in 1972-74. Recommissioned 21 May 1974 and served as flagship Atlantic Fleet. On Friday 13 January 1978 she grounded heavily off Brest and was severely damaged. Taken to Brest Navy Yard for repairs—completion expected mid-1979.

Electronics: One SENIT automatic data system. Thomson-CSF Vega system. Two Syllex.

Gunnery: Appears to lack radar fire control for 100 mm gun.

Radar: Air search: One DRBV 22A
Surface/air surveillance: One DRBV 51
Fire control: One DRBC 32E
Navigation: One Decca
Helicopter control: One Decca

Sonar: DUBV 23 hull-mounted; DUBV 43 VDS.

DUPERRÉ 6/1975, Dr. Giorgio Arra

2 TYPE T 53

Name	No.	Builders	Laid down	Launched	Commissioned
FORBIN	D 635	Brest Naval Dockyard	Aug 1954	15 Oct 1955	1 Feb 1958
TARTU	D 636	At. Chantiers de Bretagne	Nov 1954	2 Dec 1955	5 Feb 1958

Displacement, tons: 2 750 standard; 3 740 full load
Length, feet (metres): 421·9 *(128·6)*
Beam, feet (metres): 41·7 *(12·7)*
Draught, feet (metres): 18·0 *(5·5)*
Guns: 5 in *(127 mm)* (twins); *(Forbin* 4—5 in*);*
  6—57 mm (twins) *(Tartu)*, 4—57 mm (twins) *(Forbin);*
  2—20 mm
A/S weapons: 2 triple mountings *(550 mm)* for Mk K2 and L3; 375 mm Mk 54 projector
Main engines: 2 geared turbines; 63 000 shp; 2 shafts
Boilers: 4 A & C de B Indret
Speed, knots: 32
Oil fuel, tons: 800
Range, miles: 5 000 at 18 knots
Complement: 276 (15 officers, 261 men)

Air-direction ships—*Forbin* has helicopter platform aft in place of Y mount.
Forbin acts as a training ship for l'École d'Application des Enseignes de Vaisseau, being part of the *Jeanne d'Arc* group. *Tartu* in the Mediterranean.

Electronics: SENIT automatic data system.
Tacan Beacon.

Radar: Three dimensional air search: DRBI 10A
Air search: DRBV 22A
Navigation: DRBV 31

Sonar: One DUBA 1; one DUBV 24.

TARTU 7/1976, Dr. Giorgio Arra

FORBIN 2/1978, Chris Gee

172 FRANCE / Destroyers

4 TYPE T 47 (DDG)

Name	No.	Builders	Laid down	Launched	Commissioned
KERSAINT	D 622	Lorient Naval Dockyard	June 1951	3 Oct 1953	20 Mar 1956
BOUVET	D 624	Lorient Naval Dockyard	Nov 1951	3 Oct 1953	13 May 1956
DUPETIT THOUARS	D 625	Brest Naval Dockyard	Mar 1952	4 Mar 1954	15 Sep 1956
DU CHAYLA	D 630	Brest Naval Dockyard	July 1953	27 Nov 1954	4 June 1957

Displacement, tons: 2 750 standard; 3 740 full load
Length, feet (metres): 421·9 *(128·6)*
Beam, feet (metres): 41·7 *(12·7)*
Draught, feet (metres): 21·4 *(6·3)*
Missiles: SAM; 40 Tartar SMI or SMIA (single Mk 13 launcher)
Guns: 6—57 mm (twins)
A/S weapons: 2 triple mountings *(550 mm)* for Mk K2 and L3;
  1—375 mm Mk 54 projector
Main engines: 2 geared turbines; 63 000 shp; 2 shafts
Boilers: 4 A & C de B Indret
Speed, knots: 32
Oil fuel, tons: 800
Range, miles: 5 000 at 18 knots
Complement: 277 (17 officers, 260 men) (peace); 320 (war)

Originally built as destroyers with six—5 in guns. Converted into DDGs 1961-65. All in the Atlantic.

Electronics: SENIT automatic data system.

Radar: Air-search: One DRBV 20 A
Tartar search (3D): One SPS 39A or B
Tartar control: Two SPG 51B
Navigation: One DRBV 31

Sonars: One DUBA 1; one DUBV 24.

KERSAINT — 1976, Michael D. J. Lennon

BOUVET — 7/1978, Wright and Logan

5 TYPE T 47 (ASW)

Name	No.	Builders	Laid down	Launched	Commissioned
MAILLE BRÉZÉ	D 627	Lorient Naval Dockyard	Oct 1953	26 Sep 1954	4 May 1957
VAUQUELIN	D 628	Lorient Naval Dockyard	Mar 1953	26 Sep 1954	3 Nov 1956
D'ESTRÉES	D 629	Brest Naval Dockyard	May 1953	27 Nov 1954	19 Mar 1957
CASABIANCA	D 631	F. C. Gironde	Oct 1953	13 Nov 1954	4 May 1957
GUÉPRATTE	D 632	A. C. Bretagne	Aug 1953	8 Nov 1954	6 June 1957

Displacement, tons: 2 750 standard; 3 900 full load
Length, feet (metres): 434·6 *(132·5)*
Beam, feet (metres): 41·7 *(12·7)*
Draught, feet (metres): 21·4 *(6·3)*
Guns: 2—3·9 in *(100 mm)* (singles); 2—20 mm
A/S weapons: 1 Malafon; 1—375 mm Mk 54 projector;
  2 triple mountings *(550 mm)* for Mk K2 and L3
Main engines: 2 geared turbines; 63 000 shp; 2 shafts
Boilers: 4 A & C de B Indret
Speed, knots: 32
Oil fuel, tons: 800
Range, miles: 5 000 at 18 knots
Complement: 260 (15 officers, 245 men)

Originally with six 5 in guns.
Converted between 1968-71 including air-conditioning of living spaces, replacement of electronic equipment and updating of damage control equipment.
Maille Brézé, Vauquelin and *Casabianca* in the Atlantic, the others in the Mediterranean.

Electronics: SENIT data handling.

Radar: Navigation: One DRBN 32
Air surveillance: One DRBV 23A
Air/surface search: One DRBV 50
Gun fire control: Two DRBC 32A

Sonars: One DUBV 23 hull-mounted; one DUBV 43 VDS.

MAILLE BRÉZÉ — 1978, Michael D. J. Lennon

MAILLE BRÉZÉ — 1978, Reinhard Nerlich

FRANCE / Destroyers — Frigates 173

1 TYPE C 65

Name	No.	Builders	Laid down	Launched	Commissioned
ACONIT	D 609 (ex-F 703)	Lorient Naval Dockyard	Jan 1966	7 Mar 1970	30 Mar 1973 (trials 15 May 1971)

Displacement, tons: 3 500 standard; 3 900 full load
Length, feet (metres): 416·7 *(127·0)*
Beam, feet (metres): 44·0 *(13·4)*
Draught, feet (metres): 18·9 *(5·8)*
Missiles: SSM; 4 Exocet (single cells)
Guns: 2—3·9 in *(100 mm)*
A/S weapons: 1 Malafon launcher;
 1 quad 12 in *(305 mm)* mortar;
 2 launchers for Mk L5 torpedoes
Main engines: 1 Rateau geared turbine; 1 shaft; 28 650 shp
Boilers: 2 automatic (450°C)
Speed, knots: 27
Range, miles: 5 000 at 18 knots
Complement: 228 (15 officers, 213 men)

Forerunner of the F67 Type. A one-off class ordered under 1965 programme. In the Atlantic Fleet.

Electronics: An early form of centralised data analysis. Two Syllex.

Radar: Pulse Doppler (E/F band surveillance): One DRBV 13
Air surveillance: One DRBV 22A.
100 mm guns fire control: One DRBC 32B
Navigation: One DRBN 32

Refit: 1 July 1977—1 April 1978 including the fitting of Exocet.

Sonar: One hull-mounted DUBV 23; one DUBV 43 VDS.

ACONIT 2/1977, Michael D. J. Lennon

FRIGATES

9 "COMMANDANT RIVIÈRE" CLASS

Name	No.	Builders	Laid down	Launched	Commissioned
VICTOR SCHOELCHER	F 725	Lorient Naval Dockyard	Oct 1957	Oct 1958	Dec 1962
COMMANDANT BORY	F 726	Lorient Naval Dockyard	Mar 1958	Oct 1958	Mar 1964
AMIRAL CHARNER	F 727	Lorient Naval Dockyard	Nov 1958	Mar 1960	Dec 1962
DOUDART DE LAGRÉE	F 728	Lorient Naval Dockyard	Mar 1960	Apr 1961	Mar 1963
BALNY	F 729	Lorient Naval Dockyard	Mar 1960	Mar 1962	Feb 1971
COMMANDANT RIVIÈRE	F 733	Lorient Naval Dockyard	Apr 1957	Oct 1958	Dec 1962
COMMANDANT BOURDAIS	F 740	Lorient Naval Dockyard	Apr 1959	Apr 1961	Mar 1963
PROTET	F 748	Lorient Naval Dockyard	Sep 1961	Dec 1962	May 1964
ENSEIGNE DE VAISSEAU HENRY	F 749	Lorient Naval Dockyard	Sep 1962	Dec 1963	Jan 1965

Displacement, tons: 1 750 standard; 2 250 full load
 (Balny 1 650 standard; 1 950 full load)
Length, feet (metres): 340·3 *(103·7)*
Beam, feet (metres): 38·4 *(11·7)*
Draught, feet (metres): 15·7 *(4·8)*
Aircraft: 1 light helicopter can land aft
Missiles: SSM; 4 Exocet (single cells) (except *Balny)*
Guns: 2—3·9 in *(100 mm)* automatic, singles; 2—30 mm
A/S weapons: 1—12 in *(305 mm)* quad mortar;
 6—21 in *(533 mm)* (triple) for Mk K2 and L3
Main engines: 4—SEMT-Pielstick diesels; 16 000 bhp; 2 shafts;
 (except *Balny:* CODAG; 2 diesels (16-cyl); one TG Turboméca M38; 1 shaft; vp screw)
Speed, knots: 25
Range, miles: 7 500 at 15 knots *(Balny* 8 000 at 12 knots*)*
Complement: 167 (10 officers, 157 men)

Built for world-wide operations—air-conditioned. *Commandant Bory, Doudart De Lagrée, Commandant Rivière* and *Protet* are stationed in the Indian Ocean, the remainder operating on Fishery Protection from Cherbourg or in the Pacific.

Accommodation: Can carry a senior officer and staff. If necessary a force of 80 soldiers can be carried as well as two 30 ft *(9 m)* LCPs with a capacity of 25 men at 11 knots.

Engines: Experimental CODAG arrangement in *Balny. Commandant Bory* was fitted with experimental machinery which was replaced with SEMT-Pielstick diesels in 1974-75.

Helicopter: In 1973 *Amiral Charner, Commandant Bourdais* and *Enseigne Henry* were fitted with a helicopter platform. All these platforms now removed to make way for Exocet. (See *Missiles* note).

Missiles: All of this class except *Balny* have been fitted with four MM 38 Exocet in place of X gun. *Bory* was the first to be fitted followed by *Doudart de Lagrée*. At the same time the 100 mm gun is replaced in Y position.

Radar: Navigation: One DRBN 32
Fire control: One DRBC 32A
Air search: One DRBV 22A
Surface/air search: One DRBV 50
Exocet ships: One DRBC 32C.

Sonar: One DUBA 3; one SQS 17.

COMMANDANT RIVIÈRE 4/1978, Michael D. J. Lennon

COMMANDANT RIVIÈRE 4/1978, Michael D. J. Lennon

6 TYPE E 52 and 3 TYPE E 52B

Name	No.	Builders	Laid down	Launched	Commissioned
LE NORMAND	F 765	F. Ch. de la Mediterranée	July 1953	13 Feb 1954	3 Nov 1956
LE PICARD	F 766	A. C. Loire	Nov 1953	31 May 1954	20 Sep 1956
LE SAVOYARD	F 771	F. Ch. de la Mediterranée	Nov 1953	7 May 1955	14 June 1956
LE BASQUE	F 773	Lorient Naval Dockyard	Dec 1954	25 Feb 1956	18 Oct 1957
L'AGENAIS	F 774	Lorient Naval Dockyard	Aug 1955	23 June 1956	14 May 1958
LE BÉARNAIS	F 775	Lorient Naval Dockyard	Dec 1955	23 June 1956	18 Oct 1958
L'ALSACIEN	F 776	Lorient Naval Dockyard	July 1956	26 Jan 1957	27 Aug 1960
LE PROVENÇAL	F 777	Lorient Naval Dockyard	Feb 1957	5 Oct 1957	6 Nov 1959
LE VENDÉEN	F 778	F. Ch. de la Mediterranée	Mar 1957	27 July 1957	1 Oct 1960

Displacement, tons: 1 250 standard; 1 702 full load
Length, feet (metres): 311·7 *(95·0)* pp; 327·4 *(99·8)* oa
Beam, feet (metres): 33·8 *(10·3)*
Draught, feet (metres): 13·5 *(4·1)*
Guns: 6—2·25 in *(57 mm)* in twin mountings (4 only in F 771 and 773); 2—20 mm
A/S weapons: Sextuple Bofors ASM mortar fwd (except F 776, 777, 778 with 1—12 in *(305 mm)* quad mortar); 2 DC mortars; 1 DC rack; 12 tubes (4 triple mountings aft) for Mk K2 and L3
Main engines: Parsons or Rateau geared turbines; 20 000 shp
Boilers: 2 Indret; pressure 500 psi *(35·2 kg/cm²)*; superheat 725°F *(385°C)*
Speed, knots: 27
Range, miles: 4 500 at 15 knots
Oil fuel, tons: 310
Complement: 205 (13 officers, 192 men)

L'Agenais, L'Alsacien, Le Basque, Le Béarnais, Le Provençal and *Le Vendéen* have a different arrangement of bridges from the remainder. *L'Alsacien, Le Provencal* and *Le Vendéen* are of the E 52B type and have the Strombos-Velensi modified funnel cap.

Class: *L'Agenais* and *Le Picard* to reserve in 1977 for disposal.

Radar: Navigation: One DRBV 31
Air search: One DRBV 22A
Fire control: One DRBC 31

Sonar: One DUBV 24; (one DUBV 1 in 771 and 773); one DUBA 1

Trials: *Le Basque* carries experimental fire-control equipment in place of third mounting and is due to be fitted with OTOMAT for trials in 1979.
Le Savoyard carries large electronic missile guidance equipment in place of after gun-mounting.

LE SAVOYARD   1978, Michael D. J. Lennon

L'ALSACIEN   9/1976, Dr. Giorgio Arra

FRANCE / Frigates

8 + 4 + (1) TYPE A 69

Name	No.	Builders	Laid down	Launched	Commissioned
D'ESTIENNE D'ORVES*	F 781	Lorient Naval Dockyard	1 Sep 1972	1 June 1973	10 Sep 1976
AMYOT D'INVILLE	F 782	Lorient Naval Dockyard	Sep 1973	30 Nov 1974	13 Oct 1976
DROGOU*	F 783	Lorient Naval Dockyard	1 Oct 1973	30 Nov 1974	30 Sep 1976
DÉTROYAT	F 784	Lorient Naval Dockyard	15 Dec 1974	31 Jan 1976	4 May 1977
JEAN MOULIN	F 785	Lorient Naval Dockyard	15 Jan 1975	31 Jan 1976	11 May 1977
QUARTIER MAITRE ANQUETIL	F 786	Lorient Naval Dockyard	1 Aug 1975	7 Aug 1976	4 Feb 1978
COMMANDANT DE PIMODAN*	F 787	Lorient Naval Dockyard	1 Sep 1975	7 Aug 1976	20 May 1978
SECOND MAITRE LE BIHAN	F 788	Lorient Naval Dockyard	15 Feb 1976	5 Mar 1977	Apr 1979
LIEUTENANT DE VAISSEAU LAVALLÉE	F 790	Lorient Naval Dockyard	1 Sep 1976	13 Aug 1977	Dec 1979
PREMIER MAITRE L'HER	F 792	Lorient Naval Dockyard	July 1978	Dec 1979	Oct 1980
COMMANDANT BLAISON	F 793	Lorient Naval Dockyard	Sep 1978	Dec 1979	Apr 1982
ENSEIGNE DE VAISSEAU JACOUBET	F 794	Lorient Naval Dockyard	Apr 1979	June 1980	June 1982

*Exocet fitted

Displacement, tons: 950 standard; 1 170 full load
Length, feet (metres): 262·5 (80·0)
Beam, feet (metres): 33·8 (10·3)
Draught, feet (metres): 9·8 (3·0)
Missiles: SSM; 2 Exocet (single launchers) (see *Missiles* note)
Guns: 1—3·9 in (100 mm); 2—20 mm
A/S weapons: 1—375 mm Mk 54 Rocket launcher; 4 fixed tubes for Mk L3 and L5 torpedoes
Main engines: 2 SEMT-Pielstick PC2V diesels; 2 shafts; cp propellers; 11 000 bhp
Speed, knots: 24
Range, miles: 4 500 at 15 knots
Endurance, days: 15
Complement: 79 (5 officers, 74 men)

Primarily intended for coastal A/S operations—officially classified as "Avisos". Also available for overseas patrols and can carry an extra detachment of one officer and 17 men. *D'Estienne d'Orves* commissioned for trials 26 October 1974. *Commandant Blaison* and *Enseigne Jacoubet* will be fitted to receive a platform and light helicopter. Another ship of this class, to be similar to F 793 and 794, ordered under 1978 budget.

Appearance: *Jean Moulin* F 785 has a modified funnel, a feature in all ships in due course. All masts are being replaced.

Deployment: Mediterranean—F 781, 782, 783, 787.
Atlantic—F 784, 785, 786, 788.

Electronics: Thomson-CSF Vega system.

Missiles: Two MM 38 Exocet fitted in those ships earmarked for the Mediterranean—either side of the funnel. The remainder will be fitted "for but not with". By mid-1978 Exocet fitted in F 781, 783 and 787.

Radar: Surface/air search: One DRBV 51
Fire control: One DRBC 32
Navigation: One Decca Type 202; one DRBN 32

Sonar: One hull-mounted sonar DUBA 25.

Trials: *Second Maitre Le Bihan* F 788 ready for trials September 1978.

Transfers: *Lieutenant de Vaisseau Le Henaff* (F 789) and *Commandant l'Herminier* (F 791) sold to South Africa in 1976 whilst under construction. As a result of the UN embargo on arms sales to South Africa, they were sold to Argentina in September 1978.

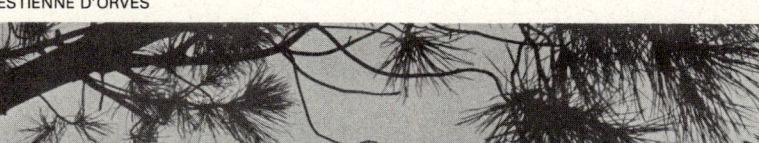

D'ESTIENNE D'ORVES 7/1978, J. Y. Robert

DROGOU 9/1978, J. Y. Robert

AMYOT D'INVILLE 10/1978, Leo van Ginderen

NEW CONSTRUCTION TYPE A 70

Although this was originally planned as a separate class with missiles the fitting of Exocet in type A 69 has removed the major difference.

176 FRANCE / Amphibious forces

AMPHIBIOUS FORCES

2 LANDING SHIPS (DOCK) (TCD)

Name	No.	Builders	Laid down	Launched	Commissioned
OURAGAN	L 9021	Brest Naval Dockyard	June 1962	9 Nov 1963	June 1965
ORAGE	L 9022	Brest Naval Dockyard	June 1966	22 Apr 1967	Mar 1968

Displacement, tons: 5 800 light; 8 500 full load; 15 000 when fully docked down
Length, feet (metres): 488·9 (149·0)
Beam, feet (metres): 75·4 (23)
Draught, feet (metres): 17·7 (5·4); 28·5 (8·7) (flooded)
Aircraft: Main helo deck; 3 Super Frelon or 10 Alouette helicopters. Portable platform; 1 Super Frelon or 3 Alouette helicopters.
Guns: 2—4·7 in (120 mm) mortars; 6—30 mm
Main engines: 2 diesels; 2 shafts; (cp propellers); 8 600 bhp
Speed, knots: 17
Range, miles: 9 000 at 15 knots
Complement: 238; 343 troops; 129 passengers (short haul)

Ouragan was completed for trials in 1964. Bridge is on the starboard side. Fitted with a platform for helicopters and portable platform aft. Able to carry two EDICs loaded with eleven light tanks each, or 18 loaded LCMs Type VI. In the logistic role 1 500 tons of material and equipment can be carried and handled by two 35 ton cranes. *Orage* is allocated to the Pacific Nuclear Experimental Centre. Have command facilities for directing amphibious and helicopter operations. Carry three LCVPs.

Docking: Can dock a 400 ton ship.

Loading: Typical loads—18 Super Frelon or 80 Alouette helicopters or 120 AMX 13 tanks or 84 DUKWs or 340 Jeeps or 12—50 ton barges.

Radar: Navigational set.

Repair Facilities: Carry main, hull, engine, carpenters, electrical and ordnance workshops.

Sonar: One SQS-17 in *Ouragan*.

OURAGAN 1975, Wright and Logan

ORAGE 1969, French Navy

2 + (2) BATRAL TYPE (LIGHT TRANSPORTS)

Name	No.	Builders	Commissioned
CHAMPLAIN	L 9030	Brest Naval Dockyard	5 Oct 1974
FRANCIS GARNIER	L 9031	Brest Naval Dockyard	21 June 1974

Displacement, tons: 750 standard; 1 409 full load
Dimensions, feet (metres): 262·4 × 42·6 × 7·9 (80 × 13 × 2·4)
Guns: 2—40 mm; 1—81 mm mortar
Main engines: 2 diesels; 2 shafts; (cp propellers); 3 600 hp = 16 knots
Range, miles: 4 500 at 13 knots
Complement: 47

Fitted with bow doors, and stowage for vehicles above and below decks. Helicopter landing platform. Can carry a landing company (Guépard) of four officers and 175 men with 12 vehicles. Both launched 17 November 1973. Two more ordered 1979.
Total load 380 tons. One LCVP carried and one LCPS. 10 ton derrick fitted.

Radar: Decca navigation.

Sonar: Two hull-mounted.

CHAMPLAIN 8/1977, J. Y. Robert

5 LANDING SHIPS (TANK) (BDC)

Name	No.	Builders	Commissioned
ARGENS	L 9003	Ch. de Bretagne	1960
BIDASSOA	L 9004	Ch. Seine Maritime	1961
TRIEUX	L 9007	Ch. de Bretagne	1960
DIVES	L 9008	Ch. Seine Maritime	1961
BLAVET	L 9009	Ch. de Bretagne	1960

Displacement, tons: 1 400 standard; 1 765 normal; 4 225 full load
Dimensions, feet (metres): 335 × 50·9 × 10·5 (102·1 × 15·5 × 3·2)
Guns: 3—40 mm; 1—20 mm; 1—4·7 in (120 mm) mortar
Main engines: SEMT-Pielstick diesels; 2 shafts; 2 000 bhp = 11 knots
Range, miles: 18 500 at 10 knots
Complement: 75 (6 officers and 69 men) . Plus 170 troops (normal)

Launched on 7 April 1959, 30 December 1960, 15 January 1960, 29 June 1960 and 6 December 1958, respectively. Can carry: four LCVPs, 1 800 tons of freight, 335 troops under austere conditions (up to 807 in a brief emergency). *Blavet* and *Trieux* are fitted as light helicopter carriers with a hangar before the bridge and can carry two Alouette III.

ARGENS 11/1975, Dr. Giorgio Arra

FRANCE / Amphibious forces — Light forces 177

11 LANDING CRAFT (TANK) (EDIC)

L 9070 (30 Mar 1967)	L 9082 (1964)	L 9092 (2 Dec 1958)
L 9072 (1968)	L 9083 (1964)	L 9093 (17 Apr 1958)
L 9073 (1968)	L 9091 (7 Jan 1958)	L 9094 (24 July 1958)
L 9074 (22 July 1969)		L 9096 (11 Oct 1958)

Displacement, tons: 250 standard; 670 full load
Dimensions, feet (metres): 193·5 × 39·2 × 4·5 *(59 × 12 × 1·3)*
Guns: 2—20 mm
Main engines: MGO diesels; 2 shafts; 1 000 bhp = 8 knots
Range, miles: 1 800 at 8 knots
Complement: 16 (1 officer, and 15 men)

Seven were built by C. N. Franco Belges, three by Toulon Dockyard, two by La Perrière. Launch dates above. Can carry eleven lorries or five Light Fighting Vehicles. L 9084 in Service Forces as Repair Ship.

Transfer: L 9095 transferred to Senegal 1 July 1974 as *La Falence*.

EDIC L 9092   *1973, Dr. Giorgio Arra*

ISSOLE A 734

Displacement, tons: 610 full load
Dimensions, feet (metres): 160·8 × 32 × 7·2 *(49 × 9·7 × 2·2)*
Main engines: 2 diesels; 1 000 bhp = 12 knots

Built at Toulon in 1957-58. LCT type with bow doors and ramp.

ISSOLE   *1974, Michael D. J. Lennon*

16 LCMs

CTM 1 to 16

Displacement, tons: 56 standard; 150 full load
Dimensions, feet (metres): 92·8 × 21 × 3·9 *(28·3 × 6·4 × 1·2)*
Main engines: Hispano diesels; 2 shafts; 225 hp = 9·5 knots
Complement: 6

Can carry up to 90 tons in coastal or protected waters. Built 1966-67. Bow ramp.

20 LCMs

Of varying displacements between 26 and 52 tons.

LIGHT FORCES

4 "TRIDENT" CLASS (FAST ATTACK CRAFT—MISSILE)

Note: Six more of a larger class (250-350 tons) to be built under 1977-81 programme.

Name	No.	Builders	Commissioned
TRIDENT	P 670	Auroux, Arcachon	17 Dec 1976
GLAIVE	P 671	Auroux, Arcachon	2 Apr 1977
EPÉE	P 672	C.M.N. Cherbourg	9 Oct 1976
PERTUISANE	P 673	C.M.N. Cherbourg	20 Jan 1977

Displacement, tons: 115 standard; 130 full load
Dimensions, feet (metres): 121·4 × 18 × 5·2 *(37 × 5·5 × 1·6)*
Missiles: 6—SS 12
Guns: 1—40 mm; 1—12·7 mm
Main engines: 2 AGO diesels; 2 shafts (cp propellers); 4 000 hp = 26 knots
Range, miles: 1 750 at 10 knots; 750 at 20 knots
Complement: 18 (1 officer and 17 men)

Trident laid down 3 December 1974, launched 31 May 1975; *Glaive*, 16 January 1975 and 27 August 1976; *Epée* 10 April 1975, 31 March 1976; *Pertuisane*, 26 August 1975 and 2 June 1976. These were intended as lead boats for a class of 30 in "Plan Bleu" of which 16 were to be adapted for overseas service.
Like other craft of similar size they have proved too small for their intended role.
Trials for *Trident* started 1 October 1975.

GLAIVE   *8/1978, Michael D. J. Lennon*

1 "LA COMBATTANTE I" TYPE (FAST ATTACK CRAFT—MISSILE)

Name	No.	Builders	Commissioned
LA COMBATTANTE	P 730	C.M.N. Cherbourg	1 Mar 1964

Displacement, tons: 180 standard; 202 full load
Dimensions, feet (metres): 147·8 × 24·2 × 6·5 *(45 × 7·4 × 2·5)*
Missiles: 1 quad launcher for SS 11
Guns: 2—40 mm
Main engines: 2 SEMT-Pielstick diesels; 2 shafts; cp propellers; 3 200 bhp = 23 knots
Range, miles: 2 000 at 12 knots
Complement: 25 (3 officers, 22 men)

Authorised under the 1960 Programme. Laid down in April 1962, launched on 20 June 1963. Of wooden and plastic laminated non-magnetic construction. Can carry a raiding force of 80 for a very short run. Now based at Cherbourg.

Gunnery: Flare launcher aft replaced by 40 mm Mk 3 gun before she left for Indian Ocean in 1975.

LA COMBATTANTE   *1974, Dr. Giorgio Arra*

178 FRANCE / Light forces

9 "SIRIUS" CLASS (LARGE PATROL CRAFT)

Name	No	Builder	Commissioned
ARCTURUS	P 650	C.N. Caen	1954
ALTAIR	P 656	C.M.N.	1956
CROIX DU SUD	P 658	Seine Maritime	1956
CANOPUS	P 659	Normand	1956
ÉTOILE POLAIRE	P 660	Seine Maritime	1957
VEGA	P 707	Penhoët	1953
ALDEBARAN (ex-*Eridan*)	P 741	Penhoët	1955
SAGITTAIRE	P 743	Seine Maritime	1955
LYRE	P 759	Penhoët	1956

All of "Sirius" class minesweepers (see *Mine Warfare* section for details) transferred to coastal patrol operations 1973. Minesweeping gear removed. P 707, 741, 743 in reserve.
Aldebaran renamed in 1977 to free *Eridan* for new construction minehunter.

CANOPUS   1975, J. van der Woude

3 "LE FOUGUEUX" CLASS (LARGE PATROL CRAFT)

Name	No	Builder	Commissioned
L'ARDENT	P 635	Normand	1959
LE FRINGANT	P 640	F. C. Mediterranée	1960
L'ADROIT	P 644	Lorient	1958

Displacement, tons: 325 standard; 400 full load
Dimensions, feet (metres): 173·9 × 24 × 10·2 *(53 × 7·3 × 3·1)*
Guns: 2—40 mm Bofors
A/S weapons: 1—120 mm A/S mortar; 2 DC mortars; 2 DC racks
Main engines: 4 SEMT-Pielstick diesel engines coupled 2 by 2; 3 240 bhp = 18·6 knots
Range, miles: 3 000 at 12 knots; 2 000 at 15 knots
Complement: 46 (4 officers, 42 men)

Originally class of 17.

Radar: One Decca.

Sonar: One QCU2.

Similar ships: One in Yugoslavia, one in Tunisia.

LE FRINGANT   1978, Michael D. J. Lennon

4 Ex-CANADIAN "LA DUNKERQUOISE" CLASS (LARGE PATROL CRAFT)

Name	No.	Builders	Commissioned
LA LORIENTAISE (ex-HMCS *Miramichi*)	P 652	St John D.D.	1953
LA DUNKERQUOISE (ex-HMCS *Fundy*)	P 653	St John D.D.	1952
LA DIEPPOISE (ex-HMCS *Chaleur*)	P 655	P. Arthur S.Y.	1952
LA PAIMPOLAISE (ex-HMCS *Thunder*)	P 657	Vickers	1953

Displacement, tons: 370 full load; 470 standard
Dimensions, feet (metres): 164 × 30·2 × 9·2 *(50 × 9·2 × 2·8)*
Gun: 1—40 mm
Main engines: General Motors diesels; 2 shafts; 2 500 bhp = 15 knots
Oil fuel, tons: 52
Range, miles: 4 500 at 11 knots
Complement: 35 (4 officers, 31 men)

La Paimpolaise (launched 17 July 1953) transferred to the French flag at Halifax on 1 April 1954, *La Dunkerquoise* (launched 17 July 1953) on 30 April 1954, and *La Dieppoise* (launched 21 June 1952) on 30 April 1954 and *La Lorientaise* (launched in 1953) on 10 October 1954. All similar to the "Bay" class in the Canadian Forces. All transferred from minesweeping to overseas patrol operations 1973. They have been air conditioned.

LA DIEPPOISE (old pennant number)   1971, French Navy

5 Ex-BRITISH "HAM" CLASS (LARGE PATROL CRAFT)

Name	No.	Builders	Commissioned
JASMIN (ex-HMS *Stedham*, ex-M 776)	P 661	Blackmore, Bideford	1955
PETUNIA (ex-HMS *Pineham*, ex-M 789)	P 662	McLean, Renfrew	1956
GÉRANIUM (ex-HMS *Tibenham* ex-M 784)	P 784	McGruer	1955
JONQUILLE (ex-HMS *Sulham*, ex-M 787)	P 787	Fairlie Yacht Co	1955
PAQUERETTE (ex-HMS *Kingham*, ex-M 775)	P 789	J. S. White	1955

Displacement, tons: 140 standard; 170 full load
Dimensions, feet (metres): 100 pp; 106·5 oa × 21·2 × 5·5 *(32·4 × 6·5 × 1·7)*
Gun: 1—20 mm Oerlikon forward
Main engines: 2 Paxman diesels; 550 bhp = 14 knots
Oil fuel, tons: 15
Complement: 12 (2 officers, 10 men)

Former British inshore minesweepers of the "Ham" class transferred to France under the US "off-shore" procurement programme in 1955. Now used as patrol craft, *Geranium, Jonquille* and *Paquerette* by Gendarmerie Maritime. *Violette* replaced by *Paquerette* A 742 in 1976, taking her place as a tender and assuming her number.

PETUNIA   9/1978, Michael D. J. Lennon

4 TECIMAR TYPE (COASTAL PATROL CRAFT)

P 770   P 771   P 772   P 774

Displacement, tons: 30
Dimensions, feet (metres): 43·6 × 13·4 × 3·5 *(13·3 × 4·1 × 1·1)*
Guns: 1—12·7 mm MG; 1—7·5 mm MG
Main engines: 2 General Motors diesels; 480 bhp = 25 knots

Hulls of moulded polyester. Built for gendarmerie in 1974.

1 COASTAL PATROL CRAFT

TOURMALINE A 714

Displacement, tons: 45
Dimensions, feet (metres): 88 × 16·8 × 4·8 *(26·8 × 5·1 × 1·5)*
Gun: 1—20 mm
Main engines: 2 diesels; 1 120 hp = 27 knots
Complement: 9

Completed 1974 by Chantiers Navals de L'Esterel for training duties.

FRANCE / Mine warfare forces 179

MINE WARFARE FORCES

1 + 14 "ERIDAN" ("TRIPARTITE") CLASS (MINEHUNTERS)

Name	No.	Builders	Laid down	Launched	Commissioned
ERIDAN	M 641	Lorient	20 Dec 1977	2 Feb 1979	Jan 1981

Displacement, tons: 510 standard; 544 full load
Dimensions, feet (metres): 161 × 29·2 × 8·2 *(49·1 × 8·9 × 2·5)*
Gun: 1—20mm
Main engines: 1 Werkspoor diesel; 1 shaft (single anti-clockwise cp screw by Lips); 2 280 bhp: 2 active rudders
Speed, knots: 15
Range, miles: 3 000 at 12 knots
Complement: 22 to 45 (see note)

Belgium, France and the Netherlands have agreed to build 15 of this design each with a joint bureau de programme in Paris. Each country will build its own GRP hulls to a central design. Belgium will provide all the electrical installations, France all the minehunting gear and some electronics and the Netherlands the propulsion systems.
The second and third ships are on order and funds for two more are to be provided in 1979.

Complement: For simple tasks a crew of 22 will be adequate, increasing to 45 for major minehunting operations.

Electronics and Navigation: Auto pilot and hovering; automatic radar navigation; Nav-aids by Loran and Syledis; Evec data system.

Minehunting and sweeping: 2 French PAP 104; Medium depth mechanical sweep gear.

Propulsion: Bow thruster and auxiliary system of 2-88 kw Wullocks = 7 knots.

Radar: One Decca 1229.

Sonar: One DUBM 21A

Tasks: Minehunting, minesweeping, patrol, training, directing ship for unmanned mine sweeping, HQ ship for diving operations and pollution control. Pre-packed 5 ton modules of equipment to be embarked for separate tasks.

"ERIDAN" Class   1979, French Navy

5 "CIRCÉ" CLASS (MINEHUNTERS)

Name	No.	Builders	Commissioned
CYBÈLE	M 712	C.M. de Normandie	28 Sep 1972
CALLIOPE	M 713	C.M. de Normandie	28 Sep 1972
CLIO	M 714	C.M. de Normandie	18 May 1972
CIRCÉ	M 715	C.M. de Normandie	18 May 1972
CERES	M 716	C.M. de Normandie	8 Mar 1973

Displacement, tons: 460 standard; 495 normal; 510 full load
Dimensions, feet (metres): 167 × 29·2 × 11·15 *(50·9 × 8·9 × 3·4)*
Gun: 1—20 mm
Main engines: 1 MTU diesel; single axial screw; 1 800 bhp = 15 knots (2 active rudders)
Range, miles: 3 000 at 12 knots
Complement: 48 (4 officers, 44 men)

Ordered in 1968. *Circé* launched 15 December 1970; *Clio* launched 10 June 1971; *Calliope* launched 21 November 1971; *Cybèle* launched January 1972; *Ceres* launched 10 August 1972.

Minehunting: All ships are fitted with DUBM 20 minehunting sonar. The 9 ft *(2·74 m)* long PAP is propelled by two electric motors at 6 knots and is wire-guided to a maximum range of 500 metres. Fitted with a television camera, this machine detects the mine and lays its 100 kgm charge nearby. This is then detonated by an ultra-sonic signal.

Minesweeping: These ships carry no normal minesweeping equipment.

CYBELE   2/1978, Michael D. J. Lennon

11 Ex-US "AGGRESSIVE" CLASS
(MINESWEEPERS—OCEAN and MINEHUNTERS)

NARVIK (ex-*MSO 512*, ex-*M 609*) A 769	GARIGLIANO (ex-*MSO 452*) M 617	
OUISTREHAM (ex-*MSO 513*) M 610	MYTHO (ex-*MSO 475*) M 618	
LENCON (ex-*MSO 453*) M 612	VINH LONG (ex-*MSO 477*) M 619	
BERNEVAL (ex-*MSO 450*) M 613	BERLAIMONT (ex-*MSO 500*) M 620	
CANTHO (ex-*MSO 476*) M 615	BACCARAT (ex-*MSO 505*) M 623	
DOMPAIRE (ex-*MSO 454*) M 616		

Displacement, tons: 700 standard; 780 full load
Dimensions, feet (metres): 165 wl; 171 oa × 35 × 10·3 *(50·3; 52·1 × 10·7 × 3·2)*
Gun: 1—40 mm
Main engines: 2 General Motors diesels; 2 shafts; vp propellers; 1 600 bhp = 13·5 knots
Oil fuel, tons: 47
Range, miles: 3 000 at 10 knots
Complement: 58 (5 officers, 53 men)

The USA transferred these MSOs to France in three batches during 1953. *Bir Hacheim* M 614 (ex-*MSO 451*) was returned to the US Navy at Brest on 4 September 1970 and transferred to Uruguayan navy, being renamed *Maldonado*. *Origny* converted for survey duties in 1960.

Appearance: *Baccarat*, *Berlaimont*, *Narvik* and *Ouistreham* have a taller funnel.

Minehunters: *Cantho, Dompaire, Garigliano, Mytho* and *Vinh Long* converted for minehunting between 1975 and 1979. *Dompaire* commissioned as minehunter 14 April 1977, *Mytho* on 1 April 1978 and *Vinh Long* on 10 April 1978. *Baccarat, Berlaimont, Alençon, Berneva* and *Ouistreham* being converted to complete between 1979 and 1981. Considerable change in appearance results.

Trials: *Narvik* engaged in trials of AP 4 sweep and lenticular sonar with changed pennant number.

MYTHO (squat funnel)   9/1978, Michael D. J. Lennon

180 FRANCE / Mine warfare forces — Oceanographic and survey ships

6 "SIRIUS" CLASS (MINESWEEPERS—COASTAL)

CAPRICORNE (8 Aug 1956) M 737		CAPELLA (6 Sep 1955) M 755	
BETELGEUSE (12 July 1954) A 747		CÉPHÉE (3 Jan 1956) M 756	
PHÉNIX (23 May 1955) M 749		VERSEAU (26 Apr 1956) M 757	

Displacement, tons: 400 standard; 440 full load
Dimensions, feet (metres): 140 pp; 152 oa × 28 × 8·2 (42·7; 46·4 × 8·6 × 2·5)
Guns: 1—40 mm Bofors; 1—20 mm Oerlikon (several have 2—20 mm)
Main engines: SEMT-Pielstick 16-cyl diesels; 2 shafts; 2 000 bhp = 15 knots (11·5 knots when sweeping)
Oil fuel, tons: 48
Range, miles: 3 000 at 10 knots
Complement: 38 (3 officers, 35 men)

Of wooden and aluminium alloy construction. Of same general characteristics as the British "Ton" class. Launch dates above. Built by CMN, Cherbourg.

Class: *Bételgeuse* employed as experimental ship since May 1977 with new A pennant number.

Reserve: *Lyre, Eridan* (now *Aldebaran*), *Sagittaire* and *Vega* to reserve as patrol craft 1977.

Transfers: Three of this class, built in France and originally numbered D 25, 26 and 27 (now called *Hrabri, Smeli* and *Slobodni*), were joined by *Snazni* (built in Yugoslavia) after their transfer to Yugoslavia in 1957. *Fomalhaut, Orion, Pollux* and *Procyon* were returned to the US Navy in 1970, *Achernar* and *Centaure* in 1971. *Aries* (M 758) loaned to Morocco in 1974.

PHENIX 9/1978, Michael D. J. Lennon

15 Ex-US "ADJUTANT" CLASS (MINESWEEPERS—COASTAL)

PERVENCHE (ex-*MSC 141*) M 632	EGLANTINE (ex-*MSC 117*) M 675*
PIVOINE (ex-*MSC 125*) M 633	GLYCINE (ex-*MSC 118*) M 679
RÉSÉDA (ex-*MSC 126*) M 635*	LAURIER (ex-*MSC 86*) M 681
ACACIA (ex-*MSC 69*) M 638*	LILAS (ex-*MSC 93*) M 682
ACANTHE (ex-*MSC 70*) M 639	LOBÉLIA (ex-*MSC 96*) M 684*
AZALÉE (ex-*MSC 67*) M 668*	MIMOSA (ex-*MSC 99*) M 687
CAMÉLIA (ex-*MSC 68*) M 671	MUGUET (ex-*MSC 97*) M 688
CYCLAMEN (ex-*MSC 119*) M 674*	

*See Status note

Displacement, tons: 300 standard; 372 full load
Dimensions, feet (metres): 136·2 pp; 141 oa × 26 × 8·3 (43 × 8 × 2·6)
Guns: 2—20 mm
Main engines: 2 General Motors diesels; 2 shafts; 1 200 bhp = 13 knots (8 sweeping)
Oil fuel, tons: 40
Range, miles: 2 500 at 10 knots
Complement: 38 (3 officers, 35 men)

The USA agreed in September 1952 to allocate to France in 1953, 36 new AMS (later redesignated MSC) under the Mutual Defence Assistance Programme, but only 30 were finally transferred to France in 1953.

Deletions:
Bleuet and *Chrysanthème* cannibalized for spares—1976 onwards.

Status: *Acacia, Azalée, Cyclamen, Eglantine, Lobelia, Réséda* in reserve and no longer maintained in anti-magnetic state.

Transfers:
(a) Six of the class were not taken up by France—two (MSC 139 and 143) to Spain; two to Japan (MSC 95, 144) and two retained by USA.
(b) *Marguerite* (ex-*MSC 94*) M 686 returned to USA and transferred to Uruguay as *Rio Negro* 10 November 1969.
(c) *Pavot* (ex-*MSC 124*) M 631 and *Renoncule* (ex-*MSC 142*) M 634 returned to USA and transferred to Turkey on 24 March 1970 and 19 November 1970 respectively.
(d) *Coquelicot* (ex-*MSC 84*) M 673 to Tunisia in 1973.
(e) *Bégonia* (ex-*MSC 83*) M 669 and *Glaieul* (ex-*MSC 120*) M 678 returned to USA 1974.
(f) *Marjolaine* to Tunisia 26 July 1977.

Change of Task:
(a) *Ajonc* (ex-*M 667*) A 701 to diving training ship—1974.
(b) *Magnolia* M 685, *Liseron* (ex-*M 683*) A 723 and *Gardénia* (ex-*M 676*) A 711 to clearance-diving base ship.
(c) *Jacinthe* M 680 to minelaying duties in 1968.
(d) *Acacia* M 638, *Azalée* M 668 and *Lobélia* M 684 to reserve 1976.
(e) *Cyclamen* M 674, *Eglantine* M 675 and *Réséda* M 635 to reserve 1977.

LAURIER 4/1978, J. Y. Robert

1 SPECIAL TYPE DB 1 (MINESWEEPER—COASTAL)

Name	No.	Builders	Commissioned
MERCURE	M 765	Mecaniques de Normandie	Dec 1958

Displacement, tons: 333 light; 365 normal; 400 full load
Dimensions, feet (metres): 137·8 pp; 145·5 oa × 27 × 8·5 (44·4 × 8·3 × 4)
Guns: 2—20 mm
Main engines: 2 Mercedes-Benz (MTU) diesels; 2 shafts; Kamewa vp propellers; 4 000 bhp = 15 knots
Oil fuel, tons: 48
Range, miles: 3 000 at 15 knots
Complement: 48

Ordered in France under the "off-shore" programme. Laid down in January 1955. Launched on 21 December 1957. Will be fitted as fishery protection vessel 1979-80. Currently in reserve.

Foreign sales: Six built for West Germany, five of which were later transferred to Turkey, the sixth now being a research ship.

MERCURE 1968, French Navy

OCEANOGRAPHIC AND SURVEY SHIPS

Note: (a) These ships are painted white.
(b) A total of 20 officers and 74 technicians with oceanographic and hydrographic training is employed in addition to the ships' companies listed here. They occupy the extra billets marked as "scientists".

Name	No.	Builders	Commissioned
D'ENTRECASTEAUX	A 757	Brest Naval Dockyard	10 Oct 1970

Displacement, tons: 2 400 full load
Dimensions, feet (metres): 292 × 42·7 × 14·4 (89 × 13 × 4·4)
Main engines: 2 diesel-electric; 1 000 kW; 2 cp propellers; speed: 15 knots
Auxiliary engines: 2 Schottel trainable and retractable
Aircraft: 1 helicopter
Range, miles: 10 000 at 12 knots
Complement: 79 (6 officers, 73 men plus 38 scientific staff)

This ship was specially designed for oceanographic surveys capable of working to 6 000 metres. Hangar for Alouette II helicopter. Carries one LCPS and three survey launches.

Radar: Two sets.
Sonar: Two sets.

D'ENTRECASTEAUX 1975, Wright and Logan

FRANCE / Oceanographic and survey ships 181

Name	No.	Builders	Commissioned
ESPÉRANCE (ex-*Jacques Coeur*)	A 756	Gdynia	see note
ESTAFETTE (ex-*Jacques Cartier*)	A 766	Gdynia	see note

Displacement, tons: 956 standard; 1 360 full load
Dimensions, feet (metres): 208·3 × 32·1 × 19·4 *(63·5 × 9·8 × 5·9)*
Main engines: MAN diesels; 1 850 bhp = 15 knots
Range, miles: 7 500 at 13 knots
Complement: 32 (3 officers, 29 men plus scientists)

Former trawlers built in 1962 at Gdynia and purchased in 1968-69. Adapted as survey ships commissioning in 1969 and 1972. Can carry 14 scientists.

ESPÉRANCE　　　　　　　　　　　　　　　　　　　　　　　　　　　　　11/1978, Wright and Logan

Name	No.	Builders	Commissioned
LA RECHERCHE (ex-*Guyane*)	A 758	Chantiers Ziegler, Dunkirk	see note

Displacement, tons: 810 standard; 910 full load
Dimensions, feet (metres): 221·5 × 34·2 × 13 *(67·5 × 10·4 × 4·5)*
Main engines: 1 Werkspoor diesel; 1 535 bhp = 13·5 knots
Range, miles: 3 100 at 10 knots
Complement: 23 (2 officers, 21 men) (plus 43 scientists)

Former passenger motor vessel. Launched in April 1951. Purchased in 1960 and converted by Cherbourg Dockyard into a surveying ship. Commissioned into the French Navy in March 1961 and her name changed from *Guyane* to *La Recherche*. To improve stability she was fitted with bulges. Now comes under the Ministry for Overseas Affairs.

LA RECHERCHE　　　　　　　　　　　　　　　　　　　　　　　　　　　　　1975, Dr. Giorgio Arra

ORIGNY A 640

Displacement, tons: 700 standard; 780 full load
Dimensions, feet (metres): 171 × 35 × 10·5 *(52·2 × 10·7 × 3·2)*
Gun: 1—40 mm
Main engines: 2 General Motors diesels; 2 shafts; 1 600 bhp = 13·5 knots
Range, miles: 3 000 at 10 knots
Complement: 52

Launched February 1955 as a Minesweeper—Ocean of "Berneval" class. Converted for Oceanographic research 1961-62.

ORIGNY　　　　　　　　　　　　　　　　　　　　　　　　　　　　　1974, Wright and Logan

Name	No.	Builders	Commissioned
L'ASTROLABE	A 780	Chantiers de la Seine Maritime, Le Trait	1964
BOUSSOLE	A 781	Chantiers de la Seine Maritime, Le Trait	1964

Displacement, tons: 330 standard; 440 full load
Dimensions, feet (metres): 140 × 27·9 × 9·5 *(42·7 × 8·5 × 2·9)*
Guns: 1—40 mm; 2 MG *(L'Astrolabe* only)
Main engines: 2 Baudoin DV.8 diesels; 1 shaft; vp propeller; 800 bhp = 13 knots
Range, miles: 4 000 at 12 knots
Complement: 33 (1 officer, 32 men)

Authorised under the 1961 Programme. Specially designed for surveys in tropical waters. Laid down in 1962, launched on 27 May and 11 April 1963 respectively. Each ship carries a crane on either side of the funnel and has two 4·5 ton wireless-equipped survey craft.

L'ASTROLABE　　　　　　　　　　　　　　　　　　　　　　　　　　　　　11/1978, Wright and Logan

OCTANT (ex-*Michel Marie*) A 683

Displacement, tons: 128 standard; 133 full load
Dimensions, feet (metres): 78·7 × 20 × 10·5 *(24 × 6·1 × 3·2)*
Main engines: 2 diesels; 1 shaft; vp propeller; 200 bhp = 9 knots
Range, miles: 2 000 at 7 knots
Endurance: 12 days
Complement: 13 (12 men)

Small fishing trawler purchased by the Navy and converted into survey craft by the Constructions Mécaniques de Normandie at Cherbourg as tender to *La Recherche*. Wooden hull and steel upperworks. Conversion completed on 20 December 1962. Commissioned in 1963. Sister *Alidade* deleted April 1977.

OCTANT　　　　　　　　　　　　　　　　　　　　　　　　　　　　　6/1975, Dr. Giorgio Arra

182 FRANCE / Oceanographic and survey ships — Service forces

1 INSHORE SURVEY CRAFT

Name	No.	Builders	Commissioned
CORAIL (ex-*Marc Joly*)	A 794	Thuin, Belgium	1967

Displacement, tons: 54·8 light
Dimensions, feet (metres): 58·4 × 16·1 × 5·9 *(17·8 × 4·9 × 1·8)*
Main engine: 1 Caterpillar diesel; 250 bhp = 10·3 knots
Complement: 7

Operating in New Caledonia from 1974.

SERVICE FORCES

2 + 1 "DURANCE" CLASS
(UNDERWAY REPLENISHMENT TANKERS)

Name	No.	Builders	Commissioned
MEUSE	A 607	Brest Naval Dockyard	1 Aug 1980
DURANCE	A 629	Brest Naval Dockyard	1 Dec 1976
—	—	Brest Naval Dockyard	—

Displacement, tons: 17 800 full load
Dimensions, feet (metres): 515·9 × 69·5 × 28·5 *(157·3 × 21·2 × 8·7)*
Aircraft: 1 WG 13 Lynx helicopter
Guns: 2—40 mm
Main engines: 2 diesels SEMT-Pielstick 16 PC 2·5; 2 shafts; vp propellers 20 000 hp = 19 knots
Oil fuel, tons: 750
Range, miles: 9 000 at 15 knots
Complement: 150 (45 passengers)

Durance laid down 1973, launched 6 September 1975. Helicopter hangar. Classed as PRE (Pétrolier Ravitaileur d'Escadre). *Meuse* laid down 2 June 1977, launched 2 December 1978, when a third ship, ordered in October 1977, was laid down.

Capacity: *Durance* can carry a total of 10 000 tonnes (7 500 FFO, 1 500 diesel, 500 TR5 Avcat, 130 distilled water, 170 victuals, 150 munitions, 50 naval stores). *Meuse* to carry 5 000 FFO, 3 200 diesel, 1 800 TR5 Avcat and the rest as in *Durance*.

Transfer: Four beam positions and one astern, two of the beam positions having heavy transfer capability.

DURANCE   1976, French Navy

1 UNDERWAY REPLENISHMENT TANKER and COMMAND SHIP

Name	No.	Builders	Commissioned
LA CHARENTE (ex-*Beaufort*)	A 626	Holdens Mek Verksted, Tönsberg	1957

Displacement, tons: 7 440 light; 26 000 full load
Dimensions, feet (metres): 587·2 × 72 × 34·1 *(179 × 21·9 × 10·4)*
Guns: 4—40 mm
Main engine: 1 General Electric geared turbine; 1 shaft = 17·5 knots
Boilers: 2
Complement: 100 (6 officers, 94 men)

Former Norwegian tanker. Purchased by the French Navy in May 1964. Now converted for service as flagship of the Flag Officer commanding Indian Ocean forces. Fitted with helicopter platform and hangar and carries LCVP. Stern transfer position.

LA CHARENTE (after conversion)   1974, French Navy

1 UNDERWAY REPLENISHMENT TANKER

Name	No.	Builders	Commissioned
ISÈRE	A 675	Ch. Seine Maritime	see note
(ex-*La Mayenne*, ex-*Caltex Strasbourg*)			

Displacement, tons: 7 440 standard; 26 700 full load
Dimensions, feet (metres): 559 × 71·2 × 30·3 *(170·4 × 21·7 × 9·3)*
Main engine: 1 single geared Parsons turbine; 8 260 shp = 16 knots
Boilers: 2
Complement: 92 (6 officers, 86 men)

Launched on 22 June 1959. Former French tanker. Purchased in 1965. Fitted for two beam fuelling positions as well as stern rig. Due for replacement by third ship of "Durance" class.

ISÈRE   4/1978, J. Y. Rober

1 UNDERWAY REPLENISHMENT TANKER

Name	No.	Builders	Commissioned
LA SAÔNE	A 628	A. C. France	1948

Displacement, tons: 8 550 light; 24 200 full load
Dimensions, feet (metres): 525 × 72·5 × 33 *(160 × 22·1 × 10)*
Guns: 3—40 mm
Main engines: Parsons geared turbines; 2 shafts; 15 800 shp = 18 knots
Boilers: 3 Penhoet
Complement: 177 (9 officers, 168 men)

Ordered as fleet tanker. Completed as merchant tanker in 1948. Returned to the French Navy from charter company in September 1953. *La Saône* was fitted as a fleet replenishment ship in 1961. Carries 9 100 tons of fuel, 730 tons of diesel fuel, 200 tons of fresh provisions and wine tanks holding 82 000 litres. Fitted with automatic tensioning. Two heavy transfer positions abeam and two positions aft.
La Seine paid off 13 October 1976. *La Saône* due for replacement 1980 by *Meuse*.

LA SAÔNE   3/1976, Reinhard Nerli

FRANCE / Service forces   183

1 SUPPORT TANKER

Name	No.	Builders	Commissioned
ABER WRACH (ex-CA 1)	A 619	Cherbourg	1966

Displacement, tons: 1 220 standard; 3 500 full load
Dimensions, feet (metres): 284 × 40 × 19 (86·6 × 12·2 × 5·8)
Gun: 1—40 mm
Main engine: 1 diesel; vp propeller; 3 000 bhp = 12 knots
Range, miles: 5 000 at 12 knots
Complement: 48 (3 officers, 45 men)

Authorised in 1956. Ordered in 1959. Laid down in 1961. The after part with engine room was launched on 24 April 1963. The fore part was built on the vacated slip, launched and welded to the after part. Complete hull floated up on 21 November 1963. Carries white oil, lubricating oil and petrol—2 220 tons.

ABER WRACH   2/1978, Michael D. J. Lennon

2 SUPPORT TANKERS

PAPENOO (ex-Norwegian *Bow Queen*) A 625
PUNARUU (ex-Norwegian *Bow Cecil*) A 632

Displacement, tons: 1 195 standard; 2 927 full load
Dimensions, feet (metres): 272·2 × 45·6 × 19·0 (83 × 13·9 × 5·8)
Main engines: 2 diesels; 1 vp screw; 2 050 hp = 12 knots (bow screw in addition)

Two small Norwegian built tankers added to the navy in late 1969. Capacity 2 500 cubic metres (ten tanks). Have replenishment at sea facility astern.

PUNARUU   1975, French Navy

1 SUPPORT TANKER

LAC TONLÉ SAP A 630

Displacement, tons: 800 light; 2 700 full load
Dimensions, feet (metres): 235 × 37 × 15·8 (71·7 × 11·3 × 4·8)
Guns: 3—20 mm
Main engines: 2 Fairbanks-Morse diesels; 1 150 bhp = 11 knots
Range, miles: 6 300 at 11 knots
Complement: 37 (2 officers, 35 men)

Ex-US Oil Barge acquired in 1945. Due to stay in service until 1981. Has replenishment at sea facility abeam.

LAC TONLÉ SAP   1973, French Navy

1 SUPPORT TANKER

Name	No.	Builders	Commissioned
SAHEL	A 638	Chantiers Naval de Caen	Aug 1951

Displacement, tons: 630 light; 1 450 full load
Measurement, tons: 650 deadweight
Dimensions, feet (metres): 176·2 × 29·5 × 14·5 (53·7 × 9 × 4·5)
Guns: 2—20 mm
Main engines: 2 diesels; 1 400 bhp = 12 knots

SAHEL   1972, Dr. Giorgio Arra

5 "RHIN" CLASS (DEPOT SHIPS)

Name	No.	Builders	Commissioned
LOIRE	A 615	Lorient Naval Dockyard	10 Oct 1967
GARONNE	A 617	Lorient Naval Dockyard	1 Sep 1965
RANCE	A 618	Lorient Naval Dockyard	5 Feb 1966
RHIN	A 621	Lorient Naval Dockyard	1 Mar 1964
RHÔNE	A 622	Lorient Naval Dockyard	1 Dec 1964

Displacement, tons: 2 075 standard; 2 445 full load (*Rhin, Rance* and *Rhône*)
  2 320 standard (*Garonne* and *Loire*)
Dimensions, feet (metres): 302·0 pp; 331·5 oa × 43·0 × 12·1 (92·1; 101·1 × 13·1 × 3·7)
Guns: 3—40 mm; 1—40 mm (*Garonne*)
Aircraft: 1 to 3 Alouette helicopters (except *Garonne* and *Loire*)
Landing craft: 2 LCP
Main engines: 2 SEMT-Pielstick diesels (16PA2V in *Rhin* and *Rhône*, 12PA4 in *Rance, Loire* and *Garonne*); 1 shaft; 3 300 bhp = 16·5 knots
Range, miles: 13 000 at 13 knots
Complement: *Rhin* and *Rhône* 148 (6 officers, 142 men); *Rance* 150 (10 officers, 140 men) and about 118 passengers; *Garonne* 221 (10 officers, 211 men); *Loire* 140 (9 officers, 131 men)

LOIRE (RHIN and RHÔNE similar)   10/1977, Michael D. J. Lennon

Designed for supporting various classes of ships. Have a 5 ton crane, carry two LCPs and have a helicopter platform (except *Garonne*). *Rhin* has a hangar and carries an Alouette helicopter. *Rance* carries three in her hangar. *Garonne* is designed as a Repair Workshop, *Loire* for minesweeper support, *Rance* for laboratory and radiological experimental services, *Rhin* for electronic maintenance and *Rhône* for submarines.

Radar: One DRBV 50; DRBV 22C in *Rance* in addition.

RANCE   10/1978, Michael D. J. Lennon

184 FRANCE / Service forces — Trials/Research ships

1 MAINTENANCE and REPAIR SHIP

Name	No.	Builders	Commissioned
JULES VERNE (ex-*Achéron*)	A 620	Brest Naval Dockyard	1 June 1976

Displacement, tons: 6 485 standard; 10 250 full load
Dimensions, feet (metres): 482·2 × 70·5 × 21·3 *(147 × 21·5 × 6·5)*
Aircraft: 2 helicopters
Guns: 2—40 mm
Main engines: 2 diesels SEMT-Pielstick; 1 shaft; 21 500 hp = 18 knots
Range, miles: 9 500 at 18 knots
Complement: 323 (20 officers, 303 men)

Ordered in 1961 budget, originally as an Armament Supply Ship. Role and design changed whilst building—now rated as Engineering and Electrical Maintenance Ship. Launched 30 May 1970. Currently serving in Indian Ocean. Carries stocks of torpedoes and ammunition.

JULES VERNE 3/1976, J. van der Woude

1 REPAIR SHIP (Ex-LCT)

L 9084

Displacement, tons: 310 standard; 685 full load
Dimensions, feet (metres): 193·5 × 39 × 5 *(59 × 11·9 × 1·6)*
Main engines: 2 diesels MGO; 1 000 bhp = 8 knots
Range, miles: 1 800 at 8 knots
Complement: 15

Built in 1964-65 by Chantiers Navals Franco-Belge. Repair facilities grafted onto LCT hull. Primarily an electrical stores ship.

Ex-LCT 1972, Dr. Giorgio Arra

5 SUPPLY TENDERS

Name	No.	Builders	Commissioned
CHAMOIS	A 767	La Perrière, Lorient	24 Sep 1976
ELAN	A 768	La Perrière, Lorient	7 Apr 1978
CHEVREUIL	A 774	La Perrière, Lorient	7 Oct 1977
GAZELLE	A 775	La Perrière, Lorient	13 Jan 1978
ISARD	A 776	La Perrière, Lorient	15 Dec 1978

Displacement, tons: 495 full load
Dimensions, feet (metres): 136·1 × 24·6 × 10·5 *(41·5 × 7·5 × 3·2)*
Main engines: 2 diesels SACM AGO V-16; 2 vp propellers; 2 200 hp = 15 knots
Complement: 10 (10 spare berths)

Similar to the standard FISH oil rig support ships. Fitted with one 30 ton crane and one hydraulic crane (5·6 tons at 5 metres). Can act as tugs, oil pollution vessels, salvage craft (two 30 ton and two 5 ton winches), coastal and harbour controlled minelaying, torpedo recovery, diving tenders and a variety of other tasks. Bow thruster of 80 hp and twin rudders. Can carry 100 tons of stores on deck or 125 tons of fuel and 40 tons of water or 65 tons of fuel and 120 tons of water. Four more planned.
Elan laid down 16 March 1977, launched 28 July 1977; *Chevreuil* laid down 15 September 1976, launched 4 March 1977; *Gazelle* laid down 30 December 1976, launched 7 June 1977; *Isard* laid down 2 November 1977, launched 2 May 1978.

CHAMOIS 5/1978, Leo van Ginderen

1 VICTUALLING STORES SHIP

SAINTONGE (ex-*Santa Maria*) A 733

Measurement, tons: 300 standard; 990 full load
Dimensions, feet (metres): 177 × 28 × 10·5 *(54 × 8·5 × 3·2)*
Main engine: 1 diesel; 1 shaft; 760 bhp = 10 knots
Complement: 15

Built by Chantiers Duchesne et Bossière, Le Havre, for a Norwegian owner under the name of *Sven Germa*. Launched on 12 July 1956. Purchased in April 1965 from the firm of H. Beal & Co, Fort de France for the Pacific Nuclear Experimental Centre. Now serves in Indian Ocean.

TRIALS/RESEARCH SHIPS

Note: A research ship was ordered from Méchanique Cherbourg in December 1976. No further details known.

Name	No.	Builders	Commissioned
HENRI POINCARÉ (ex-*Maina Marasso*)	A 603	Cantieri Riuniti de Adriaticos, Monfalcone	1967

Displacement, tons: 24 000 full load
Dimensions, feet (metres): 565·0 pp; 590·6 oa × 72·8 × 28·9 *(180 × 22·2 × 9·4)*
Guns: 2—20 mm
Main engine: 1 Parsons geared turbine; 1 shaft; 10 000 shp = 15 knots
Boilers: 2 Foster-Wheeler high pressure water tube
Range, miles: 11 800 at 13·5 knots
Complement: 214 + 9 (11 officers, 9 civilians, 203 men)

Launched in October 1960. Former Italian tanker. Purchased in September 1964. Converted in Brest dockyard from 1 October 1964 to 1967. To work with the experimental guided missile station in the Landes (SW France). Named after the mathematician and scientist.

Aircraft: Can land heavy helicopters and has space for two large or five light helicopters in her hangar.

Operations: She is primarily a missile-range-ship and acts as Flagship of Force M, the trials squadron of the French Navy. To enable her to plot the trajectory etc of missiles fired from land or sea she is equipped with three tracking radars, a telemetry station, transit nav-aid, cinetheodolite, infra-red tracking as well as an up-to-date fit of hull-mounted sonar, meteorological and oceanographic equipment.

Radar: One Savoie, two Bearn, one DRBV 22D.

HENRI POINCARÉ 7/1976, Michael D. J. Lennon

FRANCE / Trials/Research ships

ILE D'OLÉRON (ex-*Munchen*, ex-*Mur*) A 610

Displacement, tons: 5 500 standard; 6 500 full load
Dimensions, feet (metres): 378 × 50·0 × 21·3 *(115·2 × 15·2 × 6·5)*
Main engines: MAN 6-cyl diesels; 1 shaft; 3 500 bhp
Speed, knots: 14·5
Oil fuel, tons: 340
Range, miles: 7 200 at 12 knots
Complement: 195 (12 officers, 183 men)

Launched in Germany in 1939. Taken as a war prize. Formerly rated as a transport. Converted to experimental guided missile ship in 1957-58 by Chantiers de Provence and l'Arsenal de Toulon. Commissioned early in 1959. Equipped with stabilisers.

Experimental: When converted, was designed for experiments with two launchers for ship-to-air missiles, the medium range Masurca and the long range Masalca, and one launcher for ship to shore missiles, the Malaface. Latterly fitted with one launcher for target planes. Now fitted for trials on MM 38 Exocet and for Crotale trials from 1977.

Radar: One DRBV 22C; one DRBV 50; one DRBI 10.
The missile system tracking radar operates in G band.

ILE D'OLÉRON   9/1976, Dr. Giorgio Arra

1 TRIALS SHIP

Name	No.	Builders	Commissioned
AUNIS (ex-*Regina Pacis*)	A 643	Roland Werft, Bremen	see note

Displacement, tons: 2 900 full load
Dimensions, feet (metres): 283·8 × 38 × 15 *(86·5 × 11·6 × 4·6)*
Main engines: MAN diesels geared to 1 shaft; 2 400 bhp = 12 knots
Range, miles: 4 500 at 12 knots

Launched on 3 July 1956. Purchased in November 1966 from Scotto Ambrosino & Pugliese and converted in Toulon 1972-73. Employed as trials ship in Operation Cormoran with deep sonar. Sonar transferred from *Duperré*.

AUNIS   1975, Wright and Logan

1 TRIALS SHIP

BERRY (ex-M/S *Médoc*) A 644

Displacement, tons: 1 148 standard; 2 700 full load
Dimensions, feet (metres): 284·5 × 38 × 15 *(86·7 × 11·6 × 4·6)*
Main engines: 2 MWM diesels coupled on one shaft; 2 400 bhp = 15 knots
Range, miles: 7 000 at 15 knots

Built by Roland Werft, Bremen. Launched on 10 May 1958. Purchased in October 1964 and refitted in 1964-66. In 1976-77 converted at Toulon from victualling stores ship to Mediterranean electronic trials ship. Recommissioned February 1977.

BERRY   9/1978, J. Y. Robert

1 TRIALS SHIP

Name	No.	Builders	Commissioned
TRITON	A 646	Lorient	1972

Displacement, tons: 1 410 standard; 1 510 full load
Dimensions, feet (metres): 242·7 × 38·9 × 12 *(74 × 11·8 × 3·7)*
Main engines: 2 MGO V diesels driving a Voith Schneider screw aft; 2 electric motors driving a Voith Schneider fwd
Speed, knots: 13
Range, miles: 4 000 at 13 knots
Complement: 65 (4 officers, 44 men + 5 officers and 12 men for diving)

Under sea recovery and trials ship. Equipped with a helicopter platform. Launched on 7 March 1970. Support ship for the two-man submarine *Griffon*. Painted white.

Operations: Operated by GISMER (Groupe d'Intervention sous la Mer) for trials of submarines and deep-sea diving equipment. Underwater TV, recompression chamber, four-man diving bell of 13·5 tons and laboratories are fitted. Available as submarine rescue ship. Also carries a number of diving saucers.

Radar: Navigational.

Sonar: Special equipment for deep operations.

Submarine: The submarine *Griffon* is carried amidships on the starboard side of *Triton*. She is 25 ft *(7·8 m)* long, displaces 16 tons and is driven by an electric motor. Her diving depth is 2 000 ft *(600 m)* and her endurance 24 miles at 4 knots. Can be used for deep recovery operations. Fitted with manipulating arm.

TRITON (with *Griffon* amidships)   6/1975, Dr. Giorgio Arra

186 FRANCE / Trials/Research ships — Boom and mooring vessels

1 TRIALS SHIP

Name	No.	Builders	Commissioned
GUSTAV ZEDÉ (ex-*Marcel Le Bihan*, ex-*Grief*)	A 759	Stettiner Oderwerke AG	1937

Displacement, tons: 800 standard; 1 250 full load
Dimensions, feet (metres): 236·2 × 34·8 × 10·5 *(72 × 10·6 × 3·2)*
Guns: 4—20 mm (twins)
Main engines: 2 General Motors diesels; 2 shafts; 4 400 bhp = 13 knots
Range, miles: 2 500 at 13 knots
Complement: 50 (3 officers, 47 men), accommodation for 22 extra hands

Former German aircraft tender. Launched in 1936. Transferred by USA in February 1948. 4·1 in gun and two 40 mm removed. Tender for DSV *Archimède*. Renamed 1977 to avoid confusion with Type A 69 frigate.

GUSTAV ZEDÉ 3/1978, *Michael D. J. Lennon*

1 DEEP SUBMERGENCE VEHICLE

ARCHIMÈDE A 648

Built in Toulon. 68·9 ft *(20·39 m)* long with surface displacement of 60 tons. Diving depth 36 000 ft *(11 000 m)*. *Gustav Zedé* acts as tender.

ARCHIMÈDE 1974, *Wright and Logan*

1 ARCHAEOLOGICAL RESEARCH CRAFT

L'ARCHÉONAUTE A 789

Built by Auroux, Arcachon August 1967. 120 tons full load and 96 ft long *(29·3 m)* with two Baudoin diesels; 600 hp; twin vp propellers; 12 knots. For underwater archaeological research carries a complement of two officers, four men, three archaeologists and six divers.

L'ARCHÉONAUTE 1975, *Wright and Logan*

1 RADIOLOGICAL RESEARCH CRAFT

PALANGRIN Y 743

Acquired 1969. Of 44 tons with single diesel of 220 hp.

BOOM AND MOORING VESSELS

Name	No.	Builders	Commissioned
LA PRUDENTE	Y 749	AC Manche	1969
LA PERSÉVÉRANTE	Y 750	AC La Rochelle	1969
LA FIDÈLE	Y 751	AC Manche	1969

Displacement, tons: 446 standard; 626 full load
Dimensions, feet (metres): 142·8 × 32·8 × 9·2 *(43·5 × 10 × 2·8)*
Main engines: 2 Baudoin diesels; diesel-electric; 1 shaft; 620 bhp=10 knots
Range, miles: 4 000 at 10 knots
Complement: 30 (1 officer, 29 men)

Net layers and tenders. Launched on 26 August 1968 *(La Fidèle)*, 14 May 1968 *(La Persévérante)* and 13 May 1968 *(La Prudente)*. 25 ton lift.

LA PERSÉVÉRANTE 2/1977, *J. A. Verhoog*

FRANCE / Boom and mooring vessels — Torpedo recovery vessels

Name	No.	Builders	Commissioned
TIANÉE	A 731	Brest	1975

Displacement, tons: 842 standard; 905 full load
Dimensions, feet (metres): 178·1 × 34·8 (54·3 × 10·6)
Main engines: Diesel-electric; 2 diesels; 1 shaft = 12 knots
Range, miles: 5 200 at 12 knots
Complement: 37 (1 officer, 36 men)

Launched 17 November 1973. For service in the Pacific. Fitted with lateral screws in bow tunnel.

TIANÉE　　　　　　　　　　　　　　　　　　1974, French Navy

Name	No.	Builders	Commissioned
CIGALE	A 760	CN La Pallice	1955
CRIQUET	A 761	AC Seine Maritime	1955
FOURMI	A 762	AC Seine Maritime	1955
GRILLON	A 763	Penhoët	1955
SCARABÉE	A 764	Penhoët	1954

Displacement, tons: 770 standard; 850 full load
Dimensions, feet (metres): 151·9 × 33·5 × 10·5 (46·3 × 10·2 × 3·2)
Guns: 1—40 mm Bofors; 4—20 mm
Main engines: two 4-stroke diesels, electric drive, 1 shaft; 1 600 bhp = 12 knots
Range, miles: 5 200 at 12 knots
Complement: 37 (1 officer, 36 men)

US off-shore order. Sister ship G 6 was allocated to Spain. *Criquet* was launched on 3 June 1954, *Cigale* on 23 September 1954, *Fourmi* on 6 July 1954, *Grillon* on 18 February 1954 and *Scarabée* on 21 November 1953.
Scarabée has square upper bridge.

FOURMI　　　　　　　　　　　　　　　　　　6/1975, Dr. Giorgio Arra

2 Ex-US AN TYPE NETLAYERS

LIBELLULE (ex-*Rosewood*)	A 730
LUCIOLE (ex-*Sandalwood*)	A 777

Displacement, tons: 560 standard, 850 full load
Dimensions, feet (metres): 163·0 × 30·5 × 11·7 (50 × 9·3 × 4·8)
Guns: 1—3 in (76 mm); some MG
Main engines: 2 General Motors diesels; diesel-electric; 1 shaft; 1,300 bhp = 13 knots
Range, miles: 7,200 at 12 knots
Complement: 39 (2 officers, 37 men)

Launched on 1 April 1941, 6 March 1941 respectively. *Luciole* was purchased in 1967. *Libellule* in 1969.

LUCIOLE　　　　　　　　　　　　　　　　　1974, Wright and Logan

2 MOORING VESSELS

TUPA Y 667

292 tons with 210 hp diesel.

CALMAR Y 688

270 tons full load with Baudoin diesel = 9·5 knots. Complement 11.
Converted for raising moorings.

TORPEDO RECOVERY VESSELS

PÉLICAN (ex-*Kerfany*) A 699

Displacement, tons: 362 standard; 425 full load
Dimensions, feet (metres): 121·4 × 28·0 × 13·1 (37 × 8·6 × 4)
Torpedo tube: 1
Main engine: 1 Burmeister & Wain diesel; 1 shaft; 650 bhp = 11 knots
Complement: 19

Built in USA in 1951. Purchased in 1965 and converted from tunny fisher into torpedo recovery craft in 1966.

PÉLICAN　　　　　　　　　　　　　　　　11/1975, Dr. Giorgio Arra

188 FRANCE / Torpedo recovery vessels — Diving tenders

PÊTREL (ex-*Cap Lopez*, ex-*Yvon Loic II*) A 698

Displacement, tons: 277 standard; 318 full load
Dimensions, feet (metres): 98·4 × 25·6 × 11·5 *(30 × 7·8 × 3·5)*
Main engines: 2 Baudoin diesels; 1 vp screw; 600 bhp = 10 knots
Complement: 19

Built by Dubigeon 1960. Purchased 1965 and converted from tunny fisher to torpedo recovery craft.

PÉGASE

Catamaran TRV with two 440 hp diesels completed by SFCN in 1975.

TRANSPORTS

8 SMALL TRANSPORTS

ARIEL Y 604	**DRYADE** Y 662	**NEREIDE** Y —
FAUNE Y 613	**ALPHÉE** Y 696	**ONDINE** Y —
KORRIGAN Y 661	**ELFE** Y 741	

Displacement, tons: 195 standard; 225 full load
Dimensions, feet (metres): 132·8 × 24·5 × 10·8 *(40·5 × 7·5 × 3·3)*
Main engines: 2 MGO or Poyaud diesels; 2 shafts; 1 640 bhp/1 730 bhp = 15 knots
Complement: 9

Ariel was launched on 27 April 1964. *Korrigan* on 6 March 1964. *Alphée* on 10 June 1969. *Elfe* on 14 April 1970, *Faune* on 8 September 1971, *Dryade* in 1973 and *Nereide* on 17 February 1977. All built by Societe Française de Construction Naval (ex-Franco-Belge) except for *Nereide* and *Ondine* by DCAN Brest. Can carry 400 passengers (250 seated).

ARIEL   1976, Dr Giorgio Arra

5 SMALL TRANSPORTS

SYLPHE Y 710

Displacement, tons: 171 standard; 189 full load
Dimensions, feet (metres): 126·5 × 22·7 × 8·2 *(38·5 × 6·9 × 2·5)*
Main engine: 1 MGO diesel; 1 shaft; 425 bhp = 12 knots
Complement: 9

Small transport for passengers, built by Chantiers Franco-Belge in 1959-60. Based at Toulon.

LUTIN (ex-*Georges Clemenceau*) Y 664

Displacement, tons: 68
Main engines: 400 hp = 10 knots

Purchased in 1965. Ex-vedette. Detection school, Toulon.

MORGANE Y 671	**MERLIN** Y 735	**MÉLUSINE** Y 736

Displacement, tons: 170
Dimensions, feet (metres): 103·3 × 23·2 × 7·9 *(31·5 × 7·1 × 2·4)*
Main engines: MGO diesels; 2 shafts; 960 bhp = 11 knots

Small transports for 400 passengers built by Chantiers Navals Franco-Belge at Chalon sur Saône (*Mélusine* and *Merlin*) and Ars. de Mourillon *(Morgane)*. Laid down in December 1966 and accepted June 1968. Their home port is Toulon.

MORGANE   1975, Wright and Logan

DIVING TENDERS

4 Ex-US "ADJUTANT" CLASS (MSC)

AJONC (ex-*M 667*) A 701
GARDÉNIA (ex-*M 676*) A 711
LISERON (ex-*M683*) A 723
MAGNOLIA (ex-*M 685*) A 770

Details as in same class under Mine Warfare Forces except for complement, now 11. *Ajonc* employed as diving training ship, remainder as clearance-diving base ships. *Magnolia* transferred 1976.

LISERON   9/1977, Wright and Logan

FRANCE / Diving tenders — Tugs

1 Ex-BRITISH "HAM" CLASS (MSI)

MYOSOTIS (ex-*M 788*) A 710

Details as in same class under Light Forces. Employed as diving-tender.

TENDERS

8 Ex-BRITISH "HAM" CLASS (MSI)

HIBISCUS (ex-HMS *Sparham*, ex-M 785) A 735
DAHLIA (ex-HMS *Whippingham*, ex-M 786) A 736
TULIPE (ex-HMS *Frettenham*, ex-M 771) A 737
CAPUCINE (ex-HMS *Petersham*, ex-M 782) A 738
OEILLET (ex-HMS *Isham*, ex-M 774) A 739
HORTENSIA (ex-HMS *Mileham*, ex-M 783) A 740
ARMOISE (ex-HMS *Vexham*, ex-M 772) A 741
VIOLETTE (ex-HMS *Mersham*, ex-M 773) A 742

Details as in same class under Light Forces. Now general purpose tenders. *Violette* exchanged duties with *Paquerette* (in Light Forces) assuming her pennant number.

HORTENSIA 6/1978, John G. Callis

JACINTHE M 680

Minelaying tender. Details in Mine Warfare Forces—"Adjutant" class.

POSEIDON A 722

Displacement, tons: 220
Dimensions, feet (metres): 132.9 × 23.6 × 7.3 *(40.5 × 7.2 × 2.2)*
Main engine: 1 diesel; 600 bhp = 13 knots
Endurance: 8 days
Complement: 42

Base ships for assault swimmers. Completed 6 August 1975.

POSEIDON 1975, French Navy

GIRELLE A 702

Patrol launch with twin davits aft.

TRAINING SHIPS

CHIMÈRE Y 706   **FARFADET** Y 711

Displacement, tons: 100
Main engine: 1 diesel; 200 hp = 11 knots

Auxiliary sail training ships built at Bayonne in 1971. Tenders to the Naval School.

LA GRANDE HERMINE (ex-*La Route Est Belle*, ex-*Ménestral*) A 653

Ex-sailing fishing boat built in 1932. Purchased in 1964 as the Navigation School (E.O.R.) training ship. Length 46 ft *(14.02 m)*.

ENGAGEANTE (ex-*Cayolle*) A 772   **VIGILANTE** (ex-*Iseran*) A 773

Displacement, tons: 286
Dimensions, feet (metres): 98.4 × 22 × 12.5 *(30 × 6.7 × 3.8)*
Main engine: 1 Deutz diesel; 560 hp; 1 shaft = 11 knots

Ex-motor trawlers built by At. et Ch. de la Rochelle-Pallice in 1964. Bought in 1975 for conversion as training ships for the Petty Officers Navigation School. Decca radar.

L'ÉTOILE A 649   **LA BELLE POULE** A 650

Displacement, tons: 227
Dimensions, feet (metres): 128 × 23.7 × 11.8 *(32.3 × 7 × 3.2)*
Main engines: Sulzer diesels; 125 bhp = 6 knots

Auxiliary sail vessels. Built by Chantiers de Normandie (Fécamp) in 1932. Accommodation for three officers, 30 cadets, five petty officers, 12 men. Attached to Naval School.

MUTIN A 652

A 57 ton coastal tender built in 1927 by Chaffeteau, Les Sables. Auxiliary diesel and sails. Attached to the Navigation School.

TUGS

3 OCEAN TUGS

MALABAR A 664   **TENACE** A 669   **CENTAURE** A 674

Displacement, tons: 1 080 light; 1 454 full load
Dimensions, feet (metres): 167.3 × 37.8 × 18.6 *(51 × 11.5 × 5.7)*
Main engines: 2 diesels; Kort engines 4 600 hp; 1 shaft = 15 knots
Range, miles: 9 500 at 15 knots
Complement: 42

Malabar and *Tenace* built by J. Oelkers, Hamburg, *Centaure* built at La Pallice 1972-74. *Malabar* commissioned 7 October 1975.

TENACE 1973, Reiner Nerlich

190 FRANCE / Tugs — Government maritime forces

1 OCEAN TUG

ÉLÉPHANT (ex-*Bar*) A 666

Displacement, tons: 880 standard; 1 180 full load
Main engines: Triple expansion; 2 000 ihp = 11 knots

3 OCEAN TUGS

HIPPOPOTAME (ex-*Utrecht*) A 660   **RHINOCEROS** A 668

Displacement, tons: 640 standard; 940 full load
Main engines: Diesel-electric; 1 850 shp = 12 knots

Hippopotame built as USN ATA of "Sotoyomo" class. Former Netherlands civilian ocean tug. Built in 1943. Purchased by the French Navy in January 1964 to be used at the Experimental Base in the Pacific. *Rhinoceros* purchased direct from US Navy.

ABEILLE NORMANDIE

Civilian ocean tug on charter 1979-82.

RHINOCEROS   7/1976, Dr. Giorgio Arra

1 COASTAL TUG

GOLIATH A 665

Displacement, tons: 380
Main engines: 900 hp

In special reserve.

12 COASTAL TUGS

HERCULE A 667	**ROBUSTE** A 685	**TRAVAILLEUR** A 692
LE FORT A 671	**ACTIF** A 686	**ACHARNÉ** A 693
UTILE A 672	**LABORIEUX** A 687	**EFFICACE** A 694
LUTTEUR A 673	**VALEUREUX** A 688	**COURAGEUX** A 706

Displacement, tons: 230
Dimensions, feet (metres): 92 × 26 × 13 *(28·1 × 7·9 × 4)*
Main engine: 1 MGO diesel; 1 050 bhp = 11 knots
Range, miles: 2 400
Complement: 15

Courageux, Hercule, Robuste and *Valeureux* were completed in 1960, four more in 1962-63, two more in late 1960s and *Acharné* and *Efficace* in 1974.

LUTTEUR   9/1978, Leo van Ginderen

61 HARBOUR TUGS

28 "105 TON" TYPE

Acajou Y601, *Balsa* Y607, *Bouleau* Y612, *Chataigner* Y620, *Charme* Y623, *Chene* Y624, *Cormier* Y629, *Equeurdeville* Y635, *Maronnier* Y638, *Frene* Y644, *Hêtre* Y654, *Hevea* Y655, *Latanier* Y663, *Manquier* Y666, *Meleze* Y668, *Merisier* Y669, *Okoume* Y682, *Paletuvier* Y686, *Pin* Y689, *Platana* Y695, *Sycomore* Y704, *Saule* Y708, *Ebène* Y717, *Erable* Y718, *Olivier* Y719, *Santal* Y720, *Noyer* Y739, *Papayer* Y740.

Of 105 tons. 10 ton bollard pull with 700 bhp diesel and max speed of 11 knots.

2 "93 TON" TYPE

BONITE Y630   **ROUGET** Y634

Of 93 tons. 7 ton bollard pull with 380 bhp and max speed of 10 knots.

31 "56 TON" TYPE

Aigrette Y602, *Bengali* Y611, *Mouette* Y617, *Mesange* Y621, *Cigogne* Y625, *Colibri* Y628, *Cygne* Y632, *Martinet* Y636, *Fauvette* Y637, *Tourterelle* Y643, *Goeland* Y648, *Héron* Y653, *Merle* Y670, *Moineau* Y673, *Martin Pecheur* Y675, *Passereau* Y687, *Pingouin* Y690, *Pinson* Y691, *Pivert* Y694, *Alouette* Y721, *Vanneau* Y722, *Engoulevent* Y723, *Sarcelle* Y724, *Marabout* Y725, *Toucan* Y726, *Macreuse* Y727, *Grand Duc* Y728, *Eider* Y729, *Ara* Y730, *Loriot* Y747, *Gelinotte* Y748.

Of 56 tons 3·5 ton bollard pull with 250 bhp diesel and max speed of 9 knots. *Ibis* Y 658 loaned to Senegal.

Note: Reported that ten Water Tractors are under construction.
One additional Tug *Murene* Y 680 listed.

CHENE   1978, W. S. Kerkhoven

6 PUMP-TUGS

Cascade Y 618, *Gave* Y 645, *Geyser* Y 646, *Oued* Y 684, *Aiguière* Y 745, *Embrun* Y 746.

GOVERNMENT MARITIME FORCES

LA DOUANE

The French customs service has a number of tasks not normally associated with such an organisation. In addition to the usual duties of dealing with ships entering either their coastal area or ports La Douane also has certain responsibilities for rescue at sea, control of navigation, fishery protection and pollution protection. For these purposes 650 officers and men operate a number of craft of various dimensions; Class I of 30 metres, 24 knots and a range of 1 200 miles—Class II of 27 metres, 24 knots and with a range of 900 miles—Class III of 17-20 metres, 24 knots and a range of 400 miles—Class IV of 12-17 metres, 24 knots and a range of 400 miles. In addition La Douane operates a number of helicopters and fixed wing aircraft.

GENDARMERIE

A number of naval vessels and others are operated by the Gendarmerie.

GABON

Ministerial

Minister of National Defence:
President Albert Bernard Bongo

Bases

Libreville, Port Gentil

Personnel

(a) 1979: 200+ officers and men
(b) Voluntary service

Mercantile Marine

Lloyd's Register of Shipping:
15 vessels of 77 520 tons gross

DELETION

1975 *Bouet-Willaumez* (ex-HDML 102)

LIGHT FORCES

1 FAST ATTACK CRAFT (MISSILE)

Name	No.	Builders	Commissioned
PRESIDENT EL HADJ OMAR BONGO	P 10	Chantiers Navals de l'Esterel	7 Aug 1978

Displacement, tons: 155
Dimensions, feet (metres): 138 × 25·7 × 6·5 *(42 × 7·8 × 1·9)*
Missiles: 4—SS12M
Guns: 1—40 mm; 1—20 mm
Main engines: 3 MTU 20V 672 TY90 diesels; 3 shafts; 9 450 hp = 38·5 knots
Range, miles: 1 500 at 15 knots
Complement: 13

Trials: On trials achieved 10 500 bhp giving 40 knots.

PRESIDENT EL HADJ OMAR BONGO   1978, Chantiers Navals de l'Esterel

1 FAST ATTACK CRAFT (GUN)

Name	No.	Builders	Commissioned
NGOLO	GC 04	Intermarine, Sarzana, Italy	1977

Displacement, tonnes: 85 full load
Dimensions, feet (metres): 79·4 × 22·3 × 5·4 *(24·2 × 6·8 × 2·1)*
Guns: 1—40 mm Bofors; 1—20 mm
Main engines: 2 MTU diesels; 7 000 hp = 36 knots
Range, miles: 600 at 36 knots
Complement: 12

Laid down June 1976. Launched December 1976. Currently the largest high-speed GRP hull in commission.

Trials: On measured distance trials in Italy each engine developed 3 480 bhp at a speed of 43·8 knots. Contractual trials at tropical ratings resulted in 3 120 bhp per engine giving a max speed 40·15 knots and a continuous run giving 2 600 bhp per engine for a speed of 36·4 knots. Ranges at tropical ratings 1 260 miles at 14 knots and 1 020 miles at 20 knots. In Force 5-7, sea state 4, a four hour run gave an average of 35·2 knots.

NGOLO   1978

1 LARGE PATROL CRAFT

Name	No.	Builders	Commissioned
PRESIDENT ALBERT BERNARD BONGO	GC 02	Chantiers Navals de l'Esterel	Mar 1972

Displacement, tons: 80 full load
Dimensions, feet (metres): 105 × 19 × 5·3 *(32 × 5·8 × 1·6)*
Guns: 2—20 mm
Main engines: 2 MTU diesels; 5 400 hp = 30 knots
Range, miles: 1 500 at 15 knots
Complement: 17 (3 officers, 14 ratings)

Fitted with radar and echo sounder.

PRESIDENT ALBERT BERNARD BONGO   1978, Chantiers Navals de l'Esterel

2 LARGE PATROL CRAFT

Name	No.	Builders	Commissioned	Name	No.	Builders	Commissioned
PRESIDENT LEON M'BA	GC 01	Gabon	1968	N'GUENE	GC 03	Swiftships, USA	Apr 1975

Displacement, tons: 85 standard
Dimensions, feet (metres): 92 × 20·5 × 5 *(28 × 6·3 × 1·5)*
Guns: 1—75 mm; 1—12·7 mm MG
Main engines: Diesel = 12·5 knots
Complement: 16

Launched on 16 January 1968.

Displacement, tons: 118
Dimensions, feet (metres): 105·6 × — × 7·5 *(32·2 × — × 2·3)*
Guns: 2—40 mm (twin); 2—20 mm (twin); 2—12·7 mm MG
Main engines: 3 diesels; 3 shafts = 27 knots
Range, miles: 825 at 25 knots
Complement: 21

192 GABON / Coast guard — GAMBIA / Light forces

COAST GUARD

6 ARCOA COASTAL PATROL CRAFT

Capable of 15 knots.

2 COASTAL PATROL CRAFT

NDJOLE   OMBOUF

Dimensions, feet (metres): 40 × 12·3 × 3 (12·2 × 3·8 × 0·9)
Main engine: 1 diesel; 1 shaft; 171 hp = 10 knots

Ordered from La Manche October 1976, launched September 1977, completed 24 November 1977.

1 ARCOA 960 COASTAL PATROL CRAFT

Capable of 25 knots.

1 LAUNCH

N'GOMBE

Dimensions, feet (metres): 56·3 × 14·8 × 4·3 (17·2 × 4·5 × 1·3)
Main engine: 1 diesel; 1 shaft; 215 hp = 10 knots

Ordered from La Manche October 1976, completed 24 November 1977. For buoy servicing.

THE GAMBIA

Mercantile Marine

Lloyd's Register of Shipping:
8 vessels of 4 224 tons

Port

Banjul

LIGHT FORCES

1 COASTAL PATROL CRAFT

MANSA KILA IV

Displacement, tons: 40
Dimensions, feet (metres): 74·5 × 19·7 × 5·0 (22·7 × 6·0 × 1·5)
Main engines: 2 Cummins diesels; 750 bhp = 20 knots

Built by Camper and Nicholson Ltd. Gosport, England to Keith Nelson 75 ft design for a private order—eventually purchased by The Gambia in 1974.

1 FAIREY "TRACKER 2" CLASS (COASTAL PATROL CRAFT)

Name	No.	Builders	Commissioned
JATO	P 2	Fairey Marine, UK	1978

Displacement, tons: 31
Dimensions, feet (metres): 63·1 × 16·3 × 4·8 (19·3 × 5 × 1·5)
Gun: 1—20 mm
Main engines: 2 General Motors 12V 71T1 diesels; 2 shafts; 1 290 bhp = 24 knots
Range, miles: 650 at 20 knots
Complement: 11

Hull and superstructure of GRP. Air conditioned accommodation. One navigational radar.

JATO   1978, Fairey Marine

1 FAIREY MARINE "LANCE" CLASS (COASTAL PATROL CRAFT)

Name	No.	Builders	Commissioned
SEA DOG	P 1	Fairey Marine, UK	28 Oct 1976

Displacement, tons: 17
Dimensions, feet (metres): 48·7 × 15·3 × 4·3 (14·8 × 4·7 × 1·3)
Guns: 1—20 mm; 2 MG
Main engines: 2 General Motors 8V 71T1; 850 hp = 23 knots
Complement: 9

Delivered 28 October 1976 for the Customs service.

SEA DOG   1976, Fairey Marine

GERMANY (Democratic Republic)

Ministerial

Minister of National Defence:
 General Heinz Hoffmann

Headquarters Appointments

Commander-in-Chief, Volksmarine:
 Vice-Admiral Willi Ehm
Chief of Naval Staff:
 Rear-Admiral Gustav Hesse

Personnel

(a) 1974: 1 750 officers and 15 300 men (including GBK)
    1975: 1 800 officers and 15 500 men (including GBK)
    1976: 1 850 officers and 16 000 men (including GBK)
    1977: 1 800 officers and 15 200 men (including GBK)
    1978: 1 800 officers and 15 200 men (including GBK)
    1979: 1 800 officers and 15 200 men (including GBK)

(b) 18 months national service

Frigate

1976 Karl Marx ("Riga" Class)

Bases

Rostock/Gehlsdorf: Navy Headquarters;
Peenemunde: HQ 1st Flotilla;
Warnemunde: HQ 4th Flotilla;
Dranske-Bug: HQ 6th Flotilla;
Sassnitz: Minor base;
Wolgast: Minor base;
Tarnewitz: Minor base.

Naval Air

1 squadron with 8 Mi-4 helicopters

Grenzbrigade Kuste (GBK)

The seaborne branch of the Frontier Guards, this is a force of about 3 000 men. Their various craft are difficult to disentangle from those of the Navy, many being taken from that list. Where possible, mention of this is made in the notes.

Mercantile Marine

Lloyd's Register of Shipping:
 452 vessels of 1 539 994 tons gross

Strength of the Fleet

Type	Active	Building
Frigates	2	—
Large Patrol Craft	14	—
Fast Attack Craft—Missile	15	—
Fast Attack Craft—Torpedo	61	—
Coastal Patrol Craft	18	—
Landing Ships and Craft	14	1
Minesweepers—Coastal	51	—
Intelligence Ships	3	—
Survey Ships	23	—
Supply Ships	4	—
Support Tankers	4	—
Buoy Tenders	17	—
Ice Breakers	3	—
Tugs	13	—
Tenders	4	—
Training Ships and Craft	11	—
Cable Layer	1	—
Torpedo Recovery Vessels	2	—
State Yacht	1	—

DELETIONS

Light Forces

1978 4 "SO 1" Class, 25 "Iltis" Class, 4 "P6" Class

Amphibious Forces

1978 7 "Robbe" Class, 10 "Labo" Class

FRIGATES

1 SOVIET "KONI" CLASS

Name	No.	Builders	Commissioned
ROSTOCK	142	Leningrad	25 July 1978

Displacement, tons: 1 700 standard; 2 100 full load
Dimensions, feet (metres): 306·7 × 37·1 × 11 *(93·5 × 11·3 × 3·4)*
Missiles: One twin SA-N-4
Guns: 4—3 in (76 mm) (twins); 2 Gatlings
A/S weapons: 2—12-barrel MBUs
Main engines: CODAG; 2 diesels (outer shafts); 1 200 shp; 1 gas turbine (centre shaft); 30 000 shp
Speed, knots: 32 (gas); 22 (diesel)
Complement: 130

Second to be transferred 1979. More may follow.

"KONI" Class (Soviet pennant number—on tow)   1978

1 Ex-SOVIET "RIGA" CLASS

ERNST THÄLMANN 141

Displacement, tons: 1 000 standard; 1 320 full load
Dimensions, feet (metres): 298·8 × 33·7 × 11 *(91 × 10·2 × 3·4)*
Guns: 3—3·9 in 100 mm (single); 2—37 mm (twin); 2—25mm (twin)
Torpedo tubes: 3—21 in *(533 mm)* (twin)
A/S weapons: 2 RBU 1800; 2 DCT
Mines: Can carry 50
Main engines: Geared turbines; 2 shafts; 20 000 shp = 28 knots
Oil fuel, tons: 300
Range, miles: 2 500 at 15 knots
Complement: 175

Sister ships *Friedrich Engels* 124 and *Karl Liebknecht* 123 were paid off in 1971. A fifth ship of this type was burnt out at the end of 1959 and became a total wreck. Two of these hulks are beached at Warnemünde. *Karl Marx* 142 deleted late 1976.

Radar: Search: Slim Net.
Fire control: Sun Visor.
Navigation: Neptun.

"RIGA" Class   1965, Werner Kähling

LIGHT FORCES

14 "HAI" CLASS (LARGE PATROL CRAFT)

BAD DOBERAN	LÜBZ	RIBNITZ-DAMGARTEN
BÜTZOW	LUDWIGSLUST	STERNBERG
DIRNA	PARCHIM	TETEROW
GADEBUSCH	PERLEBERG	WISMAR + 1
GRAVESMÜHLEN		

Displacement, tons: 300 standard; 370 full load
Dimensions, feet (metres): 187 × 19 × 10 *(57 × 5·8 × 3·1)*
Guns: 4—30 mm (2 twin)
A/S weapons: 4 RBU 1 800 five barrelled launchers; 2 DC racks
Main engines: 2 gas turbines; diesels; 8 000 bhp = 25 knots
Complement: 45

Built by Peenewerft, Wolgast. The prototype vessel was completed in 1963. All were in service by the end of 1969, and the programme is now completed.

"HAI" Class   9/1977, Gerhard Koop

194 GERMANY (DEMOCRATIC) / Light forces

12 Ex-SOVIET "OSA I" CLASS — 3 "OSA II" CLASS (FAST ATTACK CRAFT—MISSILE)

ALAIN KOBIS
ALBERT GAST
ARVID HARNACK
AUGUST LUTTGENS
FRIEDRICH SCHULZE
FRITZ GAST
HEINRICH DORRENBACH
JOSEF SCHARES
KARL MESEBERG
MAX REICHPIETSCH
OTTO TOST
PAUL EISENSCHNEIDER
PAUL WIECZOREK
RICHARD SORGE
RUDOLF EGELHOFER

Displacement, tons: 160 standard; 210 full load
Dimensions, feet (metres): 127·9 × 26·6 × 5·9 (39·1 × 8·1 × 1·8)
Missiles: SSM; 4 SS-N-2 (single launchers)
Guns: 4—30 mm (2 twin, 1 fwd, 1 aft)
Main engines: 3 diesels; 12 000/15 000 hp = 36 knots
Complement: 30

Pennant numbers: 531, 711-714, 731-734, 751-754. 3 "Osa II" transferred 1976.

"OSA I" Class   1965, Reinecke

18 Ex-SOVIET "SHERSHEN" CLASS (FAST ATTACK CRAFT—TORPEDO)

ADAM KUCKHOFF
ANTON SAEFKOW
ARTHUR BECKER
BERNARD BÄSTLEIN
BRUNO KÜHN
EDGAR ANDRÉ
ERNST GRUBE
ERNST SCHNELLER
FIETE SCHULZE
FRITZ BEHN
FRITZ HECKERT
HANS COPPI
HEINZ KAPELLE
RUDOLF BREITSCHEID
WILLI BANSCH
+3

Displacement, tons: 145 standard; 160 full load
Dimensions, feet (metres): 118·1 × 25·3 × 5 (36 × 7·7 × 1·5)
Guns: 4—30 mm (2 twin)
A/S weapons: 12 DC
Torpedo tubes: 4—21 in (single)
Main engines: 3 diesels; 13 200 bhp; 3 shafts = 41 knots
Complement: 16

Acquired from the USSR. Four were delivered in 1968-69, the first installment of a flotilla. The last three transferred 1976. They do not differ from the Soviet boats of the class.
Pennant numbers 831-5, 842, 844, 845, 851-5, 861-5.

"SHERSHEN" Class   6/1978

28 "LIBELLE" CLASS (FAST ATTACK CRAFT—TORPEDO)

Displacement, tons: 30
Dimensions, feet (metres): 59 × 16·4 × 6·6 (18 × 5 × 2)
Guns: 2—23 mm (twin)
Torpedo tubes: 2—21 in (stern launching)
Main engines: 3 diesels; 3 shafts; 3 600 hp = 50 knots

A class first reported in 1975. An improved "Iltis" class. Can be used for minelaying and commando operations. Conversion for new tasks is a speedy job. In series production. Pennant numbers 931, 955, 992, 993 and 995 known.

"LIBELLE" Class   1978

15 "ILTIS" CLASS (FAST ATTACK CRAFT—TORPEDO)

Displacement, tons: 20
Dimensions, feet (metres): 55·8 × 10·5 × 2·5 (17 × 3·2 × 0·8)
Torpedo tubes: 2—21 in (torpedoes fired over stern). Some have 3 tubes (Type 3).
   Mines can be carried in place of torpedo tubes
Main engines: Diesels; 3 000 bhp = 30 knots

No guns. Several different types of this class exist, varying in hull material and silhouette, eg Type 1 are flush-decked and Type 2 have a raised forecastle. With the torpedo tubes removed these boats are used to land frogmen and raiding parties. Displacement and dimensions given are for Type 2. Others vary slightly. Built by Mitteldeutschland, starting in 1962.
Some pennant numbers 912, 914, 915, 916 and in 970, 980, 990 series.
All are probably in reserve having been relieved by the "Libelle" class, a considerable proportion of "Iltis" being deleted.

"ILTIS" Class   1971

18 "KB 123" CLASS (COASTAL PATROL CRAFT)

Displacement, tons: about 25
Dimensions, feet (metres): 74 × 16·4 × — (23 × 5 × —)
Guns: 2—14·5 mm (twin)
Main engines: 2 diesels = 14 knots

This class (total uncertain) was introduced in 1971 for operations on rivers and inland waterways by the GBK. Reported as "Bremse" class.
Pennant number WS 3 known.

"KB 123" Class (unarmed)   1972

GERMANY (DEMOCRATIC) / Amphibious forces — Mine warfare forces 195

AMPHIBIOUS FORCES

9 +1 "FRÖSCH" CLASS (LST)

Displacement, tons: 1 950
Length, feet (metres): 298·4 × 38·7 × 9·2 (91 × 11·8 × 2·8)
Guns: 4—57 mm (twins); 4—30 mm (twins)
Main engines: 2 diesels; 2 shafts = 18 knots

A class similar but not identical to Soviet "Ropuchka" class. Building by Peenewerft, Wolgast. First seen in Baltic in 1976. Can carry 900-1 000 tons. Continuing programme. Pennant numbers in early 600 series.

Armament: Space provided for rocket launcher between forward 57 mm mounting and bridge. Not yet fitted. Fitted for minelaying with stern ports.

Radar: Search: Square Head; Strut Curve.
Fire control: Muff Cob.
IFF: High Pole.

"FRÖSCH" Class   1978

3 "ROBBE" CLASS (LST)

EBERSWALDE   GRIMMEN   LÜBBEN

Displacement, tons: 600 standard; 800 full load
Dimensions, feet (metres): 196·8 × 32·8 × 6·6 (60 × 10 × 2·0)
Guns: 2—57 mm (1 twin); 4—25 mm (2 twin)
Main engines: Diesels = 12 knots

Launched in 1962-64 by Peenewerft, Wolgast. Can carry 500 tons stores and vehicles. Pennant numbers 614-616. Originally a class of ten now being replaced by "Frösch" class.

"ROBBE" Class   1971, S. Breyer

2 "LABO" CLASS (LCT)

GERHARD PRENZLER   ROLF PETERS

Displacement, tons: 150 standard; 200 full load
Dimensions, feet (metres): 131·2 × 27·9 × 5·9 (40·0 × 8·5 × 1·8)
Guns: 4—25 mm (2 twin)
Main engines: Diesels = 10 knots

Built by Peenewerft, Wolgast. Launched in 1961-63. Being deleted.
Pennant numbers: 606, 607.

"LABO" Class   1969, S. Breyer

MINE WARFARE FORCES

51 "KONDOR I" and "II" CLASS (MINESWEEPERS—COASTAL)

AHRENSHOOP	GUBEN	ROSSLAU
ALTENTREPTOW	GREIFSWALD	SCHÖNEBECK
ALTENBURG	JÜTERBOG	SÖMMERA
BANSIN	KAMENZ	STRALSUND
BERGEN	KLÜTZ	STRASBURG
BITTERFELD	KUHLUNGSBORN	TANGERHÜTTE
BERNAU	KYRITZ	TEMPLIN
BOLTENHAGEN	NEURUPPIN	UCKERMÜNDE
DEMMIN	NEUSTRELITZ	VITTE
DESSAU	ORANIENBURG	WARNEMÜNDE
EILENBURG	PREROW	WEISSWASSER
EISLEBEN	PASEWALK	WILHELM PIECKSTADT
GENTHIN	PRITZWALK	WITTSTOCK
GRAAL-MÜRITZ	RATHENOW	WOLGAST
GRANSEE	RIESA	ZEITZ
GRIMMA	ROBEL	ZERBST
		ZINGST
		+2

Displacement, tons: 245 standard; 280 full load
Dimensions, feet (metres): 154·2 × 23·0 × 6·6 (47 × 7 × 2) ("Kondor II" plus 2 metres)
Guns: 2—25 mm ("Kondor I"); 6—25 mm (twins) ("Kondor II")
Main engines: 2 diesels; 2 shafts; 4 000 bhp = 21 knots
Complement: 20-24

Built by Peenewerft, Wolgast. Five units of "Kondor I" class were operational in 1970 and 15 by the end of 1971. They replace the small minesweepers of the "Schwalbe" class. Type II has additional length and extra MGs. First appeared in 1971. Production continues.

PENNANT NUMBERS

These have been changed with some frequency. At present the following is as near as can be offered:

Type I (Total 23)   Prototype-V31. S24-26. Attached to GBK; G11-16. G21-26. G41-46.
Conversion for torpedo recovery—B73 and B74.
Conversion to AGIs *Meteor* and *Komet*.
Conversion to state yacht *Ostseeland*.

Type II (Total 28)   Prototype—V32. Active minesweepers 311-316, 321-326, 331-336, 341-346. V383 (ex-327), V382 (ex-347), V381, V32.

"KONDOR I" Class   9/1976

"KONDOR II" Class   9/1976

GERMANY (DEMOCRATIC) / Intelligence ships — Service forces

INTELLIGENCE SHIPS

2 "KONDOR I" CLASS

METEOR **KOMET**

Displacement, tons: 245 standard; 280 full load
Dimensions, feet (metres): 154·2 × 23·0 × 6·6 (47 × 7 × 2)
Guns: 2—25 mm
Main engines: 2 diesels; 2 shafts; 4 000 bhp
Speed, knots: 21

Conversions from standard "Kondor I" class Coastal Minesweepers with sweepgear removed and deckhouse fitted aft. *Komet* has no black funnel cap.

METEOR 5/1977, Gerhard Koop

HYDROGRAPH

Displacement, tons: 500 standard
Dimensions, feet (metres): 167 × 28·8 × 11·2 (50·9 × 8·7 × 3·4)
Main engine: 1 diesel; 540 hp = 11 knots
Range, miles: 8 000 at 11 knots
Complement: 32

Built in 1960 by Volkswerft, Stralsund to Soviet "Okean" trawler design.

SURVEY SHIPS

KARL F. GAUSS **ALFRED MERZ**

Built on 280 ton "Kondor" hull. Unarmed. Carry four small survey launches. Naval manned.

PROFESSOR KRÜMMEL

Built in 1954. Of 135 tons and 10 knots.
Civilian Research Ship.

HELMUT JUST **JOHAN KRUGER**

Built 1951-52 of 420 tons and 9 knots.

JORDAN **MAGNETOLOGE**

Of 83 tons and 9 knots.

FLAGGTIEF

Built in 1953. Of 50 tons and 8 knots.

D 01-14

Built in 1955. Of 50 tons and 15 knots.

HUGO ECKENER U 33

Research Ship.

HUGO ECKENER 5/1977, Gerhard Koop

SERVICE FORCES

1 "BASKUNCHAK" CLASS (SUPPLY SHIP)

USEDOM

Displacement, tons: 2 500
Dimensions, feet (metres): 227 × 29 × 12·3 (70 × 8·9 × 3·8)
Speed, knots: 13

Tanker converted to act as supply ship.

USEDOM 1973, S. Breyer

3 TYPE 600 (SUPPORT TANKERS)

C 37 (ex-*Hiddensee*) **C 76** (ex-*Riems*) **C —** (ex-*Poel*)

Displacement, tons: 1 000
Dimensions, feet (metres): 195 × 29·5 × 12·5 (59·5 × 9·0 × 3·8)
Guns: 4—25 mm (twins)
Main engines: 2 diesels; 2 800 bhp = 14 knots
Complement: 26

Built by Peenewerft, Wolgast, in 1960-61. Civilian manned. Oil capacity 645 tons.

Ex-POEL 1971, S. Breyer

3 "KUMO" CLASS

RUDEN E 18 **FREUNDSCHAFT** (ex-*Rugen*) V 71 **VILM** E 44

Displacement, tons: 550
Dimensions, feet (metres): 118 × 24 × 8·9 (36 × 7·3 × 2·7)
Main engines: Diesel = 10 knots

Built in mid-1950s by Mathias Thesen, Wismar. *Freundschaft* is a training ship since 1977, *Vilm* a tanker and *Ruden* employed as Supply Ship.

1 Ex-SOVIET "KAMENKA" CLASS (BUOY LAYER)

BUK

Displacement, tons: 1 000 standard
Dimensions, feet (metres): 180·5 × 31·2 × 11·5 (55 × 9·5 × 3·4)
Main engines: Diesels = 16 knots

BUK

1 CABLE LAYER

DORNBUSCH

Cable layer of 700 tons with bow rollers.

DORNBUSCH 1967

1 SALVAGE SHIP

Name	No	Builders	Commissioned
OTTO VON GUERICKE	—	Danzig North	1977

Displacement, tons: 1 560 standard; 1 732 full load
Dimensions, feet (metres): 240 × 32·8 × 13·1 *(73·2 × 10 × 4)*
Guns: 8—25 mm (4 twin)
Main engines: 2 diesels; 3 800 bhp; 2 shafts = 16·5 knots
Range, miles: 3 000 at 12 knots.

Basically a "Moma" class hull; sister to Polish "Piast" class. Carries extensive towing and fire-fighting equipment as well as a bargee diving-bell stowed on port side forward of bridge.

2 "KONDOR I" CLASS (TRVs)

B 73   B 74

Details under Mine Warfare Forces. Converted for Torpedo Recovery.

B 74   9/1978, Gerhard Koop

1 STATE YACHT

OSTSEELAND

Converted "Kondor I" Class. Details under Mine Warfare Forces.

LUMME

Small diving tender. Tug type.

FREESENDORF

Built in 1963. Buoy-layer.

4 "TAUCHER" CLASS (DIVING TENDERS)

SATZHAFF (?) +3

Displacement, tons: 310 full load
Dimensions, feet (metres): 98·4 × 21·3 × 9 *(30 × 6·5 × 3)*
Main engines: 2 diesels = 12 knots

Small diving tenders with recompression chamber.

8 BUOY TENDERS

BREITLING	GOLWITZ	LANDTIEFF	RAMZOW
ESPER ORT	GRASS ORT	PALMER ORT	ROSEN ORT

Displacement, tons: 158 standard; 320 full load
Dimensions, feet (metres): 97 × 20·3 × 6·2 *(29·6 × 6·2 × 1·9)*
Main engine: 1 diesel; 580 hp = 11·5 knots

Delivered 1970-72. Civilian manned under the Naval Hydrographic Service.

BREITLING   1972

3 BUOY TENDERS

ARKONA   DASSER ORT   STUBBENKAMMER

Built in 1956. Of 55 tons and 10 knots.

TRAINING SHIPS

Name	No.	Builders	Commissioned
WILHELM PIECK	561	Naval Yard, Gdynia	6 July 1976

Displacement, tons: 2 000
Dimensions, feet (metres): 239·4 × 39·4 × — *(73 × 12 × —)*
Guns: 2—30 mm (twin); 4—25 mm (twins)
Main engines: 2 diesels = 17 knots
Complement: 100

Cadets' training ship. Sister ship to Polish "Wodnik" class training ships.

NEW CONSTRUCTION

A new sailing ship is under consideration. USSR discussing such a programme with Blohm and Voss, Hamburg but it is not known if such an approach covers this ship.

7 "KONDOR I" CLASS

Details in Mine Warfare Forces. Ex-*Anklam* transferred for training duties at Greifswald Shore Establishment.

3 "KRAKE" CLASS (ex-MINESWEEPERS—OCEAN)

BERLIN   POTSDAM   ROSTOCK

Displacement, tons: 650 standard
Dimensions, feet (metres): 229·7 × 26·5 × 12·2 *(70 × 8·1 × 3·7)*
Guns: 1—3·4 in; 10—25 mm (vertical twins)
A/S weapons: 4 DCT
Mines: Can carry 30
Main engines: Diesels; 2 shafts; 3 400 bhp = 18 knots
Complement: 90

Built in 1956-58 by Peenewerft, Wolgast. Of the original ten, four completed in 1958, were originally for Poland. Appearance is different compared with the first type, the squat wide funnel being close to the bridge with lattice mast and radar. Fitted for minelaying. On 1 May 1961 they were given the names of the capitals of districts etc of East Germany. Pennant numbers are S11-13. All used for training and will probably be deleted before long.

"KRAKE" Class   1970, Niels Gartig

FISHERY PROTECTION SHIPS

ERNS HAECKEL   ROBERT KOCH

Built in 1962 and 1955. Of 1 108 tons (grt) and 13 knots. Built by Neptun, Rostock.

ICEBREAKERS

STEPHAN JANTZEN

Of 2 500 tons and 13 knots built in 1965. Of Soviet "Dobrynya Nikitch" class. Civilian manned.

EISBAR   EISVOGEL

Of 550 tons and 12 knots built in 1957. Civilian manned.

TUGS

A 14

Of 800 tons and 12 knots.

WISMAR

Of 700 tons and 14 knots. Possibly civilian manned.

11 HARBOUR TUGS

Of varying classes.

Note: Gesellschaft für Sport und Technik (GST) (Association for Sport and Technical Science) controls several training ships—*Ernst Thälman*, a retired "Habicht I" Class minesweeper; *Ernst Schneller*, "Tummler" class; *Partisan*, and *Pionier* of 80 tons; *Freundschaft* of 200 tons; *F. L. Jahn* of 100 tons; and the sail training ships *Seid Bereil*, *Jonny Scheer*, *Max Reichpietsch II* and *Knechtsand II*.

GERMANY (Federal Republic)

Headquarters Appointment

Chief of Naval Staff, Federal German Navy:
Vice-Admiral Günter Luther

Senior Appointment

Commander-in-Chief of the Fleet:
Vice-Admiral Günther Fromm

Diplomatic Representation

Naval Attaché in The Hague:
Commander H. Grande
Defence Attaché in Lisbon:
Commander J. Ullmann
Naval Attaché in London:
Captain K. Reichert
Naval Attaché in Oslo (and Stockholm):
Commander G. Dietze
Naval Attaché in Paris:
Captain G. Ving
Naval Attaché in Rome:
Commander W. D. Fischer-Mühlen
Naval Attaché in Washington:
Captain D. Erhardt

Personnel

(a) 1973: 36 000 (4 550 officers, 31 450 men)
    1974: 36 000 (4 550 officers, 31 450 men)
    1975: 35 900 (4 775 officers, 31 125 men)
    1976: 35 900 (5 100 officers, 30 800 men)
    1977: 38 275 (5 600 officers, 32 675 men)
    1978: 38 394 (5 600 officers, 32 794 men)

(Includes Naval Air Arm)

(b) 15 months national service

Bases

Gluecksburg (C in C Fleet), Flensburg, Wilhelmshaven, Kiel, Olpenitz.
The administration of these bases is vested in the Naval Support Command at Wilhelmshaven.

Naval Air Arm

(See Future Developments)

6 000 men total
1 LRMP squadron (14 Breguet Atlantic), MFG 3
2 Fighter bomber squadrons (60 F104G—conversion to Tornados to start May 1981), MFG 1 and 2
1 Helicopter squadron (re-equipping with 22 Sea King Mk 41 for SAR.) from Kiel, Westerland and Borkum, MFG 5
20 Liaison aircraft (DO28), MFG 5
(MFG = Marine Flieger Geschwader)

Prefix to Ships' Names

Not normally used but in British waters prefix FGS is used.

Future Development and Acquisitions

Interest is being shown by the Naval Staff in various and varied projects.
(a) Development of more powerful ship-to-ship missiles.
(b) Development of SAMs and ASMs with the Franco German Kormoran ASM
(c) New frigates of 2 500 tons standard, 3 800 tons full load with guided weapons to replace "Köln" Class—12 are planned, first batch similar to Netherlands "Kortenaer" class. Six ordered.
(d) Replacement of F104G aircraft by MRCA—Tornados ordered.
(e) Modernisation of Breguet Atlantics preferred to replacement (mid-1978). Conversions to complete—April 1981 to spring 1983.
(f) Mine Warfare forces to be improved by conversion of 12 MSCs to Minehunters and replacement of "Schütze" class by six other MSCs being modified to operate remotely controlled unmanned systems. (Troika)
(g) Development of new 750 ton submarine.
(h) Ordering of 10 new FACs.
(i) On 28 September 1978 decision taken to acquire Lynx helicopters for new frigates.

Hydrographic Service

This service is under the direction of the Ministry of Transport, is civilian manned with HQ at Hamburg. Survey ships are listed at the end of the section.

Strength of the Fleet

Type	Active	Building (Projected)
Submarines—Patrol	24	—
Destroyers	11	—
Frigates	6	2 (10)
Corvettes	5	—
Fast Attack Craft (Missile)	30	(10)
Fast Attack Craft (Torpedo)	10	—
LCUs	22	—
LCMs	28	—
Minesweepers— Coastal and Minehunter	40	—
Minesweepers—Inshore	19	—
Depot Ships	11	—
Repair Ships	2 (1 small)	—
Replenishment Tankers	5	—
Support Tankers	5	—
Support Ships	8	—
Ammunition Transports	2	—
Mine Transports	2	—
Training Ship	1	—
Sail Training Ships	2	—
TRVs	13	—
SAR Launch	1	—
Coastal Patrol Craft	8	—
Auxiliaries (some non-naval)	28	—
Tugs—Ocean	8	—
Tugs—Harbour/Coastal	17	—
Icebreakers	2+1*	—
*Coast Guard Craft	8+	—
*Survey Ships	9	—
*Fishery Protection Ships	8	—

*Non-naval

Mercantile Marine

Lloyd's Register of Shipping:
1 999 vessels of 9 736 667 tons gross

DELETIONS

Submarines

1974 U4, 5, 6, 7, 8, (Type 205)

Fast Attack Craft (Torpedo)

1973 Jaguar, Kranich, Leopard, Luchs, Panther
1974 Dommel, Elster
1975 20 "Jaguar" class transferred (Alk, Fuchs, Häher, Löwe, Pelikan, Pinguin, Reiher, Storch, Tiger and Wolf to Turkey and Albatros, Bussard, Falke, Geier, Greif, Habicht, Kondor, Seeadler and Sperber to Greece).
1977 Kormoran, to Greece

Coastal Patrol Craft

1974 TM 1, KW 2, KW 8, FW 2, FW 3

Minesweepers Coastal

1973 Capella, Krebs, Mira, Orion, Pegasus, Steinbock, Uranus ("Schütze" class) (5 to Greece)
1975 Vegesack, Hampeln, Siegen, Detmold, Worms ("Vegesack" class) (transferred to Turkey, Sep)

Depot Ships

1975 Weser (transferred to Greece)
1976 Ruhr (transferred to Turkey)

Supply Ships

1974 Schwarzwald
1976 Dithmarschen (transferred to Turkey)
1977 Frankenland, Emsland, Münsterland, Bodensee (last to Turkey)

Auxiliaries

1975 Karl Kolls (sold), FL 11, Herman von Helmoltz
1978 Ems, Eider, Pellworm

PENNANT LIST

Submarines

S 170	U 21		
S 171	U 22		
S 172	U 23		
S 173	U 24		
S 174	U 25		
S 175	U 26		
S 176	U 27		
S 177	U 28		
S 178	U 29		
S 179	U 30		
S 180	U 1		
S 181	U 2		
S 188	U 9		
S 189	U 10		
S 190	U 11		
S 191	U 12		
S 192	U 13		
S 193	U 14		
S 194	U 15		
S 195	U 16		
S 196	U 17		
S 197	U 18		
S 198	U 19		
S 199	U 20		

Destroyers

D 171	Z 2
D 172	Z 3
D 178	Z 4
D 179	Z 5
D 181	Hamburg
D 182	Schleswig-Holstein
D 183	Bayern
D 184	Hessen
D 185	Lütjens
D 186	Mölders
D 187	Rommel

Frigates

F 220	Köln
F 221	Emden
F 222	Augsburg
F 223	Karlsruhe
F 224	Lübeck
F 225	Braunschweig

Light Forces

P 6092	Zobel
P 6093	Wiesel
P 6094	Dachs
P 6095	Hermelin
P 6096	Nerz
P 6097	Puma
P 6098	Gepard
P 6099	Hyäne
P 6100	Frettchen
P 6101	Ozelot
P 6111	S 61
P 6112	S 62
P 6113	S 63
P 6114	S 64
P 6115	S 65
P 6116	S 66
P 6117	S 67
P 6118	S 68
P 6119	S 69
P 6120	S 70
P 6141	S 41
P 6142	S 42
P 6143	S 43
P 6144	S 44
P 6145	S 45
P 6146	S 46
P 6147	S 47
P 6148	S 48
P 6149	S 49
P 6150	S 50
P 6151	S 51
P 6152	S 52
P 6153	S 53
P 6154	S 54
P 6155	S 55
P 6156	S 56
P 6157	S 57
P 6158	S 58
P 6159	S 59
P 6160	S 60

Mine Warfare Forces

M 1051	Castor
M 1054	Pollux
M 1055	Sirius
M 1056	Rigel
M 1057	Regulus
M 1058	Mars
M 1059	Spika
M 1060	Skorpion
M 1062	Schütze
M 1063	Waage
M 1064	Deneb
M 1065	Jupiter
M 1067	Atair
M 1069	Wega
M 1070	Göttingen
M 1071	Koblenz
M 1072	Lindau
M 1073	Schleswig
M 1074	Tübingen
M 1075	Wetzlar
M 1076	Paderborn
M 1077	Weilheim
M 1078	Cuxhaven
M 1079	Düren
M 1080	Marburg
M 1081	Konstanz
M 1082	Wolfsburg
M 1083	Ulm
M 1084	Flensburg
M 1085	Minden
M 1086	Fulda
M 1087	Völklingen
M 1090	Perseus
M 1092	Pluto
M 1093	Neptun

GERMANY (FEDERAL) / Introduction

Mine Warfare Forces

M 1094	Widder
M 1095	Herkules
M 1096	Fische
M 1097	Gemma
M 1099	Uranus
M 2650	Ariadne
M 2651	Freya
M 2652	Vineta
M 2653	Hertha
M 2654	Nymphe
M 2655	Nixe
M 2656	Amazone
M 2657	Gazelle
M 2658	Frauenlob
M 2659	Nautilus
M 2660	Gefion
M 2661	Medusa
M 2662	Undine
M 2663	Minerva
M 2664	Diana
M 2665	Loreley
M 2666	Atlantis
M 2667	Acheron

Corvettes

P 6052	Thetis
P 6053	Hermes
P 6054	Najade
P 6055	Triton
P 6056	Theseus

Amphibious Forces

L 760	Flunder
L 761	Karpfen
L 762	Lachs
L 763	Plötze
L 764	Rochen
L 765	Schlei
L 766	Stör
L 767	Tümmler
L 768	Wels
L 769	Zander
L 788	Butt
L 789	Brasse
L 790	Barbe
L 791	Delphin
L 792	Dorsch
L 793	Felchen
L 794	Forelle
L 795	Inger
L 796	Makrele
L 797	Muräne
L 798	Renke
L 799	Salm

Support Ships and Auxiliaries

A 50	Alster
A 52	Oste
A 53	Oker
A 54	Isar
A 55	Lahn
A 56	Lech
A 58	Rhein
A 59	Deutschland
A 60	Gorch Fock
A 61	Elbe
A 63	Main
A 65	Saar
A 66	Neckar
A 67	Mosel
A 68	Werra
A 69	Donau
A 512	Odin
A 513	Wotan
A 1401	Eisvogel
A 1402	Eisbär
A 1407	Wittensee
A 1411	Lüneburg
A 1412	Coburg
A 1413	Freiburg
A 1414	Glücksburg
A 1415	Saarburg
A 1416	Nienburg
A 1417	Offenburg
A 1418	Meersburg
A 1424	Walchensee
A 1425	Ammersee
A 1426	Tegernsee
A 1427	Westensee
A 1428	Harz
A 1429	Eifel
A 1435	Westerwald
A 1436	Odenwald
A 1437	Sachsenwald
A 1438	Steigerwald
A 1439	Rhön
A 1442	Spessart
A 1449	Hans Bürkner
A 1450	Planet
A 1451	Wangerooge
A 1452	Spiekeroog
A 1453	Langeoog
A 1454	Baltrum
A 1455	Norderney
A 1457	Helgoland
A 1458	Fehmarn
Y 805	Memmert
Y 806	Hansa
Y 809	Arcona
Y 811	Knurrhahn
Y 812	Lütje Hörn
Y 813	Mellum
Y 814	Knechtsand
Y 815	Scharhörn
Y 816	Vogelsand
Y 817	Nordstrant
Y 818	Trischen
Y 819	Langeness
Y 820	Sylt
Y 821	Föhr
Y 822	Amrum
Y 823	Neuwerk
Y 827	KW 15
Y 829	KW 3
Y 830	KW 16
Y 832	KW 18
Y 833	KW 19
Y 834	Nordwind
Y 835	TF 105
Y 836	Holnis
Y 837	SP 1
Y 838	Wilhelm Pullwer
Y 841	Walther von Ledebur
Y 844	Barbara
Y 845	KW 17
Y 846	KW 20
Y 849	Stier
Y 851	TF 1
Y 852	TF 2
Y 853	TF 3
Y 854	TF 4
Y 855	TF 5
Y 856	TF 6
Y 857-859	FL 5-7
Y 862	FL 10
Y 863	FL 11
Y 864	FW 1
Y 867	FW 4
Y 868	FW 5
Y 869	FW 6
Y 871	Heinz Roggenkamp
Y 872	TF 106
Y 873	TF 107
Y 874	TF 108
Y 875	Hiev
Y 876	Griep
Y 877	H.C. Oersted
Y 880	Wilhelm Bauer
Y 881	Adolf Bestelmeyer
Y 882	Otto Meycke
Y 883	TF 101
Y 884	TF 102
Y 886	TF 104
Y 888	Friedrich Voge
Y 889	Rudolf Diesel
Y 1641	Förde
Y 1642	Jade
Y 1643	Niobe
Y 1661	Baltrum
Y 1664	Juist
Y 1678	TB 1

Coast Guard

BG 5	Rettin
BG 11	Neustadt
BG 12	Bad Bramstedt
BG 13	Uelzen
BG 14	Duderstadt
BG 15	Eschwege
BG 16	Alsfeld
BG 17	Bayreuth
BG 18	Rosenheim

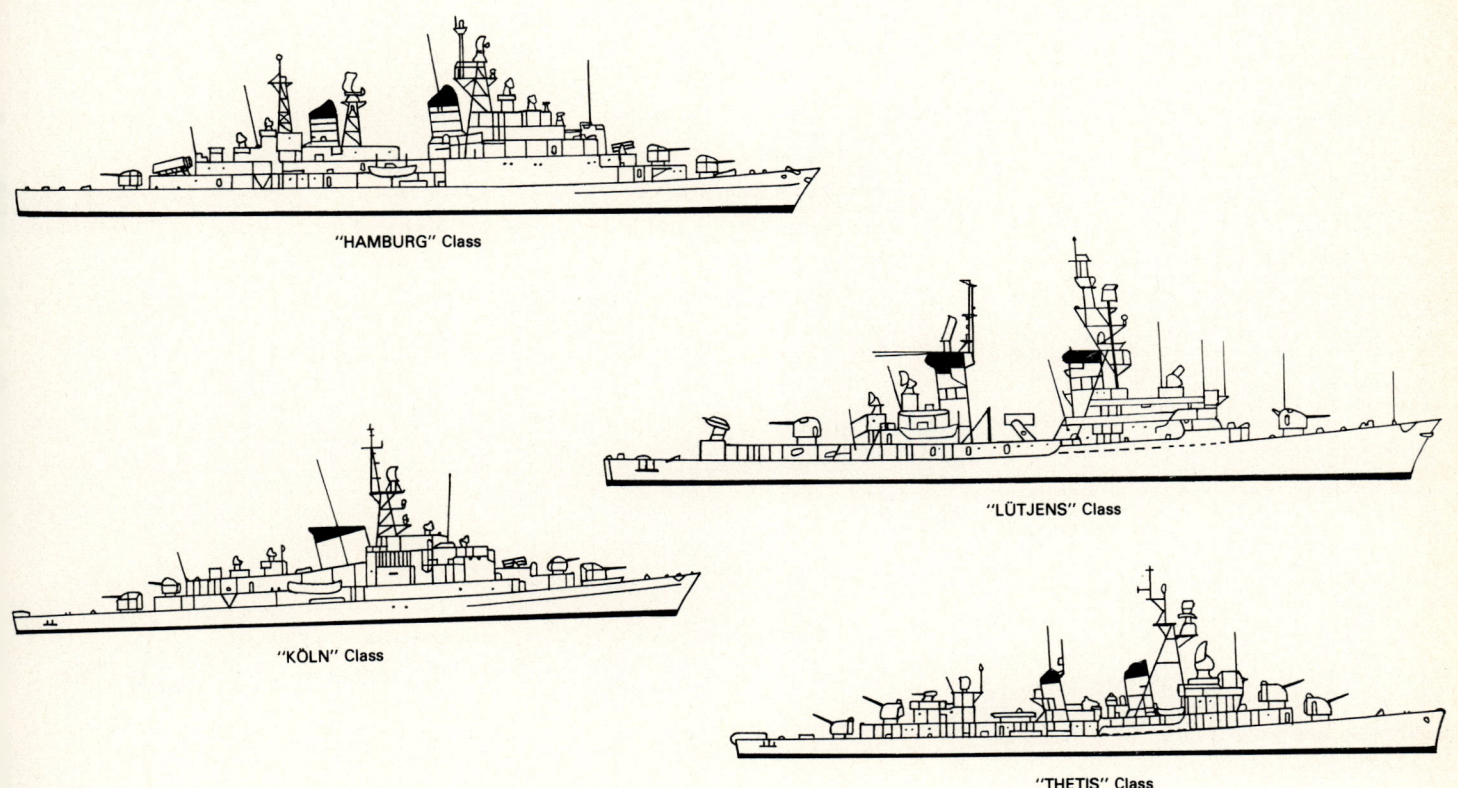

"HAMBURG" Class

"LÜTJENS" Class

"KÖLN" Class

"THETIS" Class

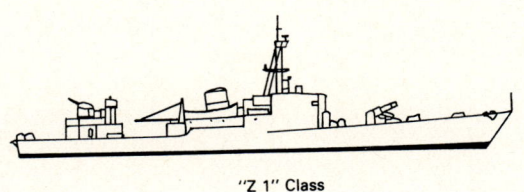

"Z 1" Class

GERMANY (FEDERAL) / Submarines

SUBMARINES
TYPE 210

The development project between Norway and the FDR noted last year has now been changed to allow for different operating requirements. Norway with Project 28 and the FDR with Type 210 submarines will achieve about 90 per cent commonality and both designs will incorporate the pressure tight bulk head and Gabler escape capsule. Development due to complete early 1980s. By 1984 the shore prototype for fuel-cell propulsion will be completed and the first Type 208 with this system is expected at sea in 1986.

18 TYPE 206

Name	No.	Builders	Laid down	Launched	Commissioned
U 13	S 192	Howaldtswerke, Kiel	24 Nov 1969	28 Sep 1971	19 Apr 1973
U 14	S 193	Reinstahl Nordseewerke, Emden	10 Sep 1970	1 Feb 1972	19 Apr 1973
U 15	S 194	Howaldtswerke, Kiel	29 May 1970	15 June 1972	17 Apr 1974
U 16	S 195	Reinstahl Nordseewerke, Emden	22 Apr 1971	29 Aug 1972	9 Nov 1973
U 17	S 196	Howaldtswerke, Kiel	19 Oct 1970	10 Oct 1972	28 Nov 1973
U 18	S 197	Reinstahl Nordseewerke, Emden	28 July 1971	31 Oct 1972	19 Dec 1973
U 19	S 198	Howaldtswerke, Kiel	14 Jan 1971	15 Dec 1972	9 Nov 1973
U 20	S 199	Reinstahl Nordseewerke, Emden	15 Feb 1972	16 Jan 1973	24 May 1974
U 21	S 170	Howaldtswerke, Kiel	14 Apr 1971	9 Mar 1973	16 Aug 1974
U 22	S 171	Reinstahl Nordseewerke, Emden	3 May 1972	27 Mar 1973	26 July 1974
U 23	S 172	Reinstahl Nordseewerke, Emden	21 Aug 1972	22 May 1973	2 May 1975
U 24	S 173	Reinstahl Nordseewerke, Emden	10 July 1972	26 June 1973	16 Oct 1974
U 25	S 174	Howaldtswerke, Kiel	6 Oct 1971	23 May 1973	14 June 1974
U 26	S 175	Reinstahl Nordseewerke, Emden	17 Nov 1972	20 Nov 1973	13 Mar 1975
U 27	S 176	Howaldtswerke, Kiel	11 Jan 1972	21 Aug 1973	16 Oct 1974
U 28	S 177	Reinstahl Nordseewerke, Emden	26 Jan 1972	22 Jan 1974	18 Dec 1974
U 29	S 178	Howaldtswerke, Kiel	29 Feb 1972	5 Nov 1973	27 Nov 1974
U 30	S 179	Reinstahl Nordseewerke, Emden	27 Apr 1973	26 Mar 1974	13 Mar 1975

Displacement, tons: 450 surfaced; 498 dived
Length, feet (metres): 159·4 (48·6)
Beam, feet (metres): 15·1 (4·6)
Draught, feet (metres): 14·1 (4·3)
Torpedo tubes: 8—21 in (533 mm) (bow)
Main machinery: MTU diesel-electric; Diesels; 1 500 hp; main motors 1 800 hp; 1 shaft
Speed, knots: 10 surfaced; 17 dived
Range, miles: 4 500 at 5 knots (surfaced)
Complement: 22

Authorised on 7 June 1969 from Howaldtswerke Deutsche Werft (8) and Rheinstahl Nordseewerke, Emden (10).

Hull: The Type 206 hulls are built of high-tensile non-magnetic steel. In this the FDR submarines are unique.

Mines: A system has been developed by Ingenieurkontor, Lübeck and tested by the navy which consists of a GRP container secured outside the hull on each side. Each container holds 12 mines and can be carried in addition to the normal torpedo armament.

Squadrons: First: U 25-30 U 1 and 2, 9-12. Third: U 13-24.

U 29
6/1978, Wright and Logan

6 TYPE 205

Name	No.	Builders	Laid down	Launched	Commissioned
U 1	S 180	Howaldtswerke, Kiel	8 June 1960	21 Oct 1961	20 Mar 1962
U 2	S 181	Howaldtswerke, Kiel	1 Sep 1960	25 Jan 1962	3 May 1962
U 9	S 188	Howaldtswerke, Kiel	10 Dec 1964	20 Oct 1966	11 Apr 1967
U 10	S 189	Howaldtswerke, Kiel	15 July 1965	5 June 1967	28 Nov 1967
U 11	S 190	Howaldtswerke, Kiel	1 Apr 1966	9 Feb 1968	21 June 1968
U 12	S 191	Howaldtswerke, Kiel	1 Sep 1966	10 Sep 1968	14 Jan 1969

Displacement, tons: 370 surfaced; 450 dived
Length, feet (metres): 142·7 (43·5)
Beam, feet (metres): 15·1 (4·6)
Draught, feet (metres): 12·8 (3·8)
Torpedo tubes: 8—21 in (533 mm) (bow)
Main machinery: 2 Maybach (MTU) diesels; total 1 200 bhp; 2 Siemens electric motors; total 1 500 bhp; single screw
Speed, knots: 10 surfaced; 17 dived
Complement: 21

All built in floating docks. Fitted with snort mast. First submarines designed and built by Germany since the end of the Second World War. U 4-12 were built to a heavier and improved design. U 1 and U 2 were modified accordingly and refloated on 17 February 1967 and 15 July 1966 respectively. U 1 was reconstructed late 1963 to 4 March 1965. (See original appearance in the 1962-63 and 1963-64 editions). U 9-12 have hulls of different steel alloys of non-magnetic properties. U 3 of this class lent to Norway on 10 July 1962 and temporarily named *Kobben* (S 310), was returned to Germany in 1964 and decommissioned on 15 September 1967 for disposal.

Radar: French Thomson-CSF Calypso, nav/attack set. Passive DF.

Torpedo equipment: The boats are trimmed by the stern to load through the bow caps. Also fitted for minelaying. Fire control by Hollandse Signaal Mk 8.

U 9
1975, Reinhard Nerlich

1 CONVERTED TYPE XXI

Name	No.	Builders	Laid down	Launched	Commissioned
WILHELM BAUER (ex-*U 2540*)	Y 880	Blohm and Voss, Hamburg	29 Oct 1944	13 Jan 1945	24 Feb 1943

Displacement, tons: 1 620 surfaced; 1 820 dived
Length, feet (metres): 252·7 (77·0) pp
Beam, feet (metres): 21·7 (6·6)
Draught, feet (metres): 20·3 (6·2)
Torpedo tubes: 4—21 in (533 mm) (bow)
Main machinery: MTU diesel-electric drive; 2 diesels total 4 200 bhp; 2 electric motors total 5 000 hp
Speed, knots: 15·5 surfaced; 17·5 dived

Scuttled after air attack off Flensburg on 4 May 1945. Raised in 1957. Rebuilt in 1958-59 at Howaldtswerke, Kiel. Commissioned on 1 September 1960. Used for experiments on submarine equipment. Conning tower was modified.

WILHELM BAUER
1973, Howaldtswerke, Kiel

GERMANY (FEDERAL) / Destroyers 201

DESTROYERS

3 US "MODIFIED CHARLES F. ADAMS" CLASS (DDGs)

Name	No.	Builders	Laid down	Launched	Commissioned
LÜTJENS (ex-US *DDG 28*)	D 185	Bath Iron Works Corporation	1 Mar 1966	11 Aug 1967	12 Mar 1969
MÖLDERS (ex-US *DDG 29*)	D 186	Bath Iron Works Corporation	12 Apr 1966	13 Apr 1968	12 Sep 1969
ROMMEL (ex-US *DDG 30*)	D 187	Bath Iron Works Corporation	22 Aug 1967	1 Feb 1969	24 Apr 1970

Displacement, tons: 3 370 standard; 4 717 full load
Length, feet (metres): 431 *(131·4)* wl; 440·6 *(134·3)* oa
Beam, feet (metres): 47 *(14·3)*
Draught, feet (metres): 15·2 *(4·6)*
Missiles: SAM; 40 Tartar (single Mk 13) (see notes)
Guns: 2—5 in *(127 mm)*/54 (single Mk 42)
A/S weapons: 8 A/S Asroc rockets (octuple launcher); 6 Mk 32 torpedo tubes (triples); 1 DCT
Main engines: Geared steam turbines 70 000 shp; 2 shafts
Boilers: 4 Combustion Engineering; 1 200 psi *(84·4 kg/cm²)*
Speed, knots: 35
Oil fuel, tons: 900
Range, miles: 4 500 at 20 knots
Complement: 337 (19 officers, 318 men)

Modified to suit Federal German requirements and practice. 1965 contract.
Cost $43 754 000 each.

Appearance: Some differences from "Charles F Adams" in W/T aerials and general outline, particularly the funnels.

Electronics: SATIR I (similar to SENIT 2) automatic data system. TACAN beacon.

Modernisation: Work now in hand includes:
a. Replacement of after 5 in *(127 mm)* gun by 2 twin Harpoon launchers.
b. Improved Tartar and 5 in fire control with digital in place of analog computers.
c. Sundry minor modifications.

Radar: Three dimensional air search and target designator: One SPS 52 (after funnel)
Air surveillance: One SPS 40 (main-mast)
Tartar fire control: Two SPG 51 (abaft after funnel)
Surface warning: One SPS 10.
Gun fire control: One GFCS 68.

Sonar: One SQS 23.

LÜTJENS 11/1976, Michael D. J. Lennon

LÜTJENS 10/1978, J. L. M. van der Burg

LÜTJENS 1976, Michael D. J. Lennon

202 GERMANY (FEDERAL) / Destroyers

4 "HAMBURG" CLASS

Name	No.	Builders	Laid down	Launched	Commissioned
HAMBURG	D 181	H. C. Stülcken Sohn, Hamburg	29 Jan 1959	26 Mar 1960	23 May 1964
SCHLESWIG-HOLSTEIN	D 182	H. C. Stülcken Sohn, Hamburg	20 Aug 1959	20 Aug 1960	12 Oct 1964
BAYERN	D 183	H. C. Stülcken Sohn, Hamburg	14 Sep 1960	14 Aug 1962	6 July 1965
HESSEN	D 184	H. C. Stülcken Sohn, Hamburg	15 Feb 1961	4 May 1963	8 Oct 1968

Displacement, tons: 3 340 standard; 4 692 full load
Length, feet (metres): 420 *(128)* wl; 439·7 *(134·0)* oa
Beam, feet (metres): 44 *(13·4)*
Draught, feet (metres): 15·7 *(4·8)*
Missiles: SSM; 4 Exocet (single cells)
Guns: 3—3·9 in *(100 mm)*/55 (single Mod 1954);
  8—40 mm (4 twin)
A/S weapons: 2 Bofors 4-barrel DC mortars; 1 DCT;
  4—21 in torpedo tubes for A/S torpedoes
Main engines: 2 Wahodag dr geared turbines; 68 000 shp;
  2 shafts
Boilers: 4 Wahodag; 910 psi *(64 kg/cm²)*, 860°F *(460°C)*
Speed, knots: 34; 18 economical
Range, miles: 6 000 at 13 knots; 920 at 34 knots
Complement: 268 (19 officers, 249 men)

All named after countries of the German Federal Republic. Capable of minelaying. Carry one 20-barrelled SCLAR launcher.

Electronics: FCS for Bofors A/S launcher, torpedoes and DC from Hollandse Signaalapparaten. ECM fitted.

Modernisation: Replacement of 100 mm in X position by four MM 38 Exocet, replacement of 40 mm Bofors by Bredas and addition of two extra A/S torpedo tubes. Modernisation started in 1975 with *Hessen* followed by *Hamburg, Schleswig-Holstein* and *Bayern*. *Hessen* completed November 1975. Hamburg taken in hand by Blohm and Voss 18 August 1975 completed mid-1976. *Schleswig-Holstein* taken in hand April 1976 completed February 1977. *Bayern* started early in 1977 completed 24 November 1977.
During later refits bridges have been partially re-modelled.

HAMBURG
10/1977, C. and S. Taylor

Radar: All by Hollandse Signaalapparaten.
Air warning: One LW-02.
Target designator: One DAO 2
Navigation/surface warning: Decca
100 mm fire control: Two M 45 series
40 mm fire control: Two M 45 series

Sonar: One ELAC 1BV hull-mounted.

BAYERN
10/1978, Michael D. J. Lennon

4 Ex-US "FLETCHER" CLASS

Name	No.	Builders	Laid down	Launched	Commissioned
Z 2 (ex-USS *Ringgold*, DD 500)	D 171	Federal S.B. & D.D. Co, Port Newark	25 June 1942	11 Nov 1942	24 Dec 1942
Z 3 (ex-USS *Wadsworth*, DD 516)	D 172	Bath Iron Works Corporation, Maine	18 Aug 1942	10 Jan 1943	16 Mar 1943
Z 4 (ex-USS *Claxton*, DD 571)	D 178	Consolidated Steel Corporation, Orange	25 June 1941	1 Apr 1942	8 Dec 1942
Z 5 (ex-USS *Dyson*, DD 572)	D 179	Consolidated Steel Corporation, Orange	25 June 1941	15 Apr 1942	30 Dec 1942

Displacement, tons: 2 100 standard; 2 750 full load
Length, feet (metres): 368·4 *(112·3)* wl; 376·5 *(114·8)* oa
Beam, feet (metres): 39·5 *(12)*
Draught, feet (metres): 18 *(5·5)*
Guns: 4—5 in *(127 mm)*/38 (single Mk 30)
  6—3 in *(76 mm)*/50 (twins Mk 33) (Z 4; 4—3 in)
A/S weapons: 2 Hedgehogs; 1 DC rack
  2 single 21 in *(533 mm)* torpedo tubes
Torpedo tubes: 5—21 in *(533 mm)* (quins)
Main engines: 2 sets GE geared turbines; 60 000 shp; 2 shafts
Boilers: 4 Babcock & Wilcox, 569 psi *(40 kg/cm²)*; 851°F *(455°C)*
Speed, knots: 32; 17 economical
Oil fuel, tons: 540
Range, miles: 3 450 at 15 knots (as modified)
Complement: 250

Former US "Fletcher" class destroyers. The original loan from the US of a class of five for five years was extended. First ship arrived at Bremerhaven on 14 April 1958. Commissioned in FGN as follows: Z 2, 14 July 1959; Z 3, 6 October 1959; Z 4, 15 December 1959; Z 5, 23 February 1960. Purchased 7 March 1977. Capable of minelaying. Form 3rd Destroyer squadron. To be paid off from 1979.

Gunnery: Z 4 carried out trials of a containerised 3 in *(76 mm)* OTO Melara gun in 1975 in place of after 3 in mounting. On completion of trials OTO Melara mounting was removed but original twin 3 in was not replaced.

Z 3
11/1978, Leo van Ginderen

Radar: Air and surface search: One SPS 6
Surface surveillance: One SPS 10
Fire control: One GFCS 56 and 68.

Sonar: SQS 29.

GERMANY (FEDERAL) / Frigates — Corvettes 203

FRIGATES

0 + 6 + 6 TYPE 122

Name	No.	Builders	Laid down	Launched	Commissioned
—	F 226	Bremer Vulkan	1978	—	July 1981
—	F 227	AG Weser, Bremen	1978	—	Apr 1982
—	F 228	Blohm und Voss	—	—	—
—	F 229	Nordseewerke, Emden	—	—	—
—	F 230	Blohm und Voss	—	—	—
—	F 231	Howaldtswerke, Kiel	—	—	1984

Displacement, tons: 3 800 full load (approx)
Dimensions, feet (metres): 419·8 × 48·5 × 19·7 (128 × 14·4 × 4·2)
Aircraft: 2 Lynx helicopters
Missiles: 8 Harpoon; 1—8 cell Sea Sparrow; 2 multiple Stinger launchers
Guns: 1—76 mm/62; Breda 105 mm 20 tube rocket launcher
A/S weapons: 6 Mk 32 torpedo tubes (triples)
Main engines: 2 GE-LM 2500 gas turbines; 53 200 hp; 2 MTU 20V-956-TB92 diesels; 10 400 hp; 2 shafts
Speed, knots: 30
Range, miles: 4 000 at 18 knots
Complement: 203

Approval given in early 1976 for six of this class, a modification of the Netherlands "Kortenaer" class. Six more planned. To replace "Fletcher", and "Köln" classes. First six to be completed by 1984. Consideration being given to a request for two more ships.

Radar: HSA DW-08; HSA WM-25; SMA 3RM 20; HSA Stir.

Sonar: Active/Passive DSQS-21 BZ.

TYPE 122 1976, Federal German Navy

6 "KÖLN" CLASS

Name	No.	Builders	Laid down	Launched	Commissioned
KÖLN	F 220	H. C. Stülcken Sohn, Hamburg	21 Dec 1957	6 Dec 1958	15 Apr 1961
EMDEN	F 221	H. C. Stülcken Sohn, Hamburg	15 Apr 1958	21 Mar 1959	24 Oct 1961
AUGSBURG	F 222	H. C. Stülcken Sohn, Hamburg	29 Oct 1958	15 Aug 1959	7 Apr 1962
KARLSRUHE	F 223	H. C. Stülcken Sohn, Hamburg	15 Dec 1958	24 Oct 1959	15 Dec 1962
LÜBECK	F 224	H. C. Stülcken Sohn, Hamburg	28 Oct 1959	23 July 1960	6 July 1963
BRAUNSCHWEIG	F 225	H. C. Stülcken Sohn, Hamburg	28 July 1960	3 Feb 1962	16 June1964

Displacement, tons: 2 100 standard; 2 550 full load
Length, feet (metres): 360·9 (110)
Beam, feet (metres): 36·1 (11·0)
Draught, feet (metres): 11·2 (3·4)
Guns: 2—3·9 in (100 mm)/55 (single mod 1954); 6—40 mm (2 twin and 2 single)
A/S weapons: 2 Bofors 4-barrel DC mortars (72 charges); 4—21 in (533 mm) (singles) for A/S torpedoes
Mines: Can carry 80
Main engines: Combined diesel and gas turbine plant; 4 MAN 16-cyl diesels; total 12 000 bhp; 2 Brown Boveri gas turbines, 24 000 bhp; total 36 000 bhp; 2 shafts
Speed, knots: 32; 23 economical
Oil fuel, tons: 333
Range, miles: 920 at 32 knots
Complement: 200

Ordered in Mar 1957. All ships of this class are named after towns of West Germany. Form 2nd Frigate Squadron.

Electronics: Hollandse Signaalapparaten FCS for Bofors A/S launchers. M9 torpedo fire control.

Engineering: Each of the two shafts is driven by two diesels coupled and geared to one BBC gas turbine. Controllable pitch propellers. A speed of 32 knots is reported to have been attained on full power trials.

KÖLN 1978, Reinhard Nerlich

Radar: All by Hollandse Signaalapparaten.
Navigation/surface search: One set.
Target designator: One DA 02.
Fire control (100 mm): Two M 45 series.
Fire control (40 mm): Two M 45 series.

Sonar: One PAE/CWE M/F set, hull-mounted.

CORVETTES

5 "THETIS" CLASS

Name	No.	Builders	Commissioned
THETIS	P 6052	Rolandwerft, Bremen	1 July 1961
HERMES	P 6053	Rolandwerft, Bremen	16 Dec 1961
NAJADE	P 6054	Rolandwerft, Bremen	12 May 1962
TRITON	P 6055	Rolandwerft, Bremen	10 Nov 1962
THESEUS	P 6056	Rolandwerft, Bremen	15 Aug 1963

Displacement, tons: 564 standard; 650 full load
Dimensions, feet (metres): 229·7 × 27 × 14 (70 × 8·5 × 4·2)
Guns: 2—Breda 40 mm L 70 (twin mounting). (To be replaced by 1—3 in OTO Melara)
A/S weapons: Bofors DC mortar (4-barrelled)
Torpedo tubes: 4—21 in (533 mm)
Main engines: 2 MAN diesels; 2 shafts; 6 800 bhp = 24 knots
Complement: 48

Najade has computer house before bridge. Form Flotten Dienst Geschwäder with *Hans Bürckner*.

Electronics: HSA M9 series torpedo control.

Radar: Nav/surface warning; KH14; TRS-N.

Sonar: ELAC 1BV.

THESEUS 6/1978, Stefan Terzibaschitsch

204 GERMANY (FEDERAL) / Corvettes — Light forces

Name	No.	Builders	Commissioned
HANS BÜRKNER	A 1449	Atlaswerke, Bremen	18 May 1963

Displacement, tons: 950 standard; 1 000 full load
Dimensions, feet (metres): 265·2 × 30·8 × 10 *(81 × 9·4 × 2·8)*
A/S weapons: 1 DC mortar (4-barrelled); 2 DC racks;
2—21 in *(533 mm)* torpedo tubes
Main engines: 4 MAN diesels; 2 shafts; 13 600 shp = 24 knots
Complement: 50

Launched on 16 July 1961. Named after designer of German First World War battleships (1909-18). General purpose utility vessel.

Radar: TRS-N; K-H14.

Sonar: Has small VDS aft.

HANS BÜRKNER *1975, Federal German Navy*

LIGHT FORCES

0 + 10 TYPE 143 A (FAST ATTACK CRAFT—MISSILE)

Displacement, tons: 390 full load
Dimensions, feet (metres): 188·9 × 25·6 × 7·2 *(57·6 × 7·8 × 2·2)*
Missiles: SSM; 4 Exocet; SAM; SATCP system
Gun: 1—76 mm OTO Melara
Main engines: 4 MTU diesels; 4 shafts; 16 000 hp = 38 knots
Complement: 34

Ordered mid-1978 from AEG Telefunken with sub-contracting to Lürssen (7 hulls) and Kröger (3 hulls). To be built of steel instead of wood. Completion 1982-84.

10 TYPE 143 (FAST ATTACK CRAFT—MISSILE)

Name	No.	Builders	Commissioned
S 61	P 6111	Lürssen, Vegesack	1 Nov 1976
S 62	P 6112	Lürssen, Vegesack	14 Apr 1976
S 63	P 6113	Lürssen, Vegesack	2 June 1976
S 64	P 6114	Lürssen, Vegesack	14 Aug 1976
S 65	P 6115	Kröger, Rendsburg	27 Sep 1976
S 66	P 6116	Lürssen, Vegesack	25 Nov 1976
S 67	P 6117	Kröger, Rendsburg	17 Dec 1976
S 68	P 6118	Lürssen, Vegesack	28 Mar 1977
S 69	P 6119	Kröger, Rendsburg	23 Dec 1977
S 70	P 6120	Lürssen, Vegesack	18 July 1977

Displacement, tons: 295 nominal, 390 full load
Dimensions, feet (metres): 188·9 × 24·6 × 7·2 *(57·6 × 7·8 × 2·2)*
Missiles: SSM; 4 Exocet MM 38
Guns: 2—76 mm OTO Melara
Torpedoes: 2—21 in *(533 mm)* wire guided aft
Main engines: 4 MTU diesels; 16 000 hp; 4 shafts = 38 knots
Range, miles: 1 300 at 30 knots
Complement: 40

AEG Telefunken main contractor with construction by sub-contractors.
Ordered in 1972 as replacements for last ten boats of the "Jaguar" class from 1976 onwards. Final funds allocated 13 July 1972. First laid down late 1972. The first boat, S 61, started trials in Dec 1974. Wooden hulled craft. Launch dates—S 61, 22 Oct 1973; S 62, 21 Mar 1974; S 63, 18 Sep 1974; S 64, 10 Dec 1974; S 65, 10 Dec 1974; S 66, 5 Sep 1975; S 67, 6 Mar 1975; S 68, 17 Nov 1975; S 69, 5 June 1975; S 70, 14 Apr 1976. Now form 2nd S Boat Squadron.

Electronics: Fully automatic data processing Command and fire-control system.

S 62 *1978, Federal German Navy*

Minelaying: To be fitted for minelaying in early 1980s when "Zobel" class is deleted.

Radar: All by Hollandse Signaal. WM 27 in radome for Exocet, gun and torpedo control.

20 TYPE 148 (FAST ATTACK CRAFT—MISSILE)

Name	No.	Builders (see note re Lürssen)	Commissioned
S 41	P 6141	C. M. de Normandie, Cherbourg	30 Oct 1972
S 42	P 6142	C. M. de Normandie, Cherbourg	8 Jan 1973
S 43	P 6143	C. M. de Normandie, Cherbourg	9 Apr 1973
S 44	P 6144	C. M. de Normandie, Cherbourg	14 June 1973
S 45	P 6145	C. M. de Normandie, Cherbourg	21 Aug 1973
S 46	P 6146	C. M. de Normandie, Cherbourg	17 Oct 1973
S 47	P 6147	C. M. de Normandie, Cherbourg	13 Nov 1973
S 48	P 6148	C. M. de Normandie, Cherbourg	9 Jan 1974
S 49	P 6149	C. M. de Normandie, Cherbourg	26 Feb 1974
S 50	P 6150	C. M. de Normandie, Cherbourg	27 Mar 1974
S 51	P 6151	C. M. de Normandie, Cherbourg	12 June 1974
S 52	P 6152	C. M. de Normandie, Cherbourg	17 July 1974
S 53	P 6153	C. M. de Normandie, Cherbourg	24 Sep 1974
S 54	P 6154	C. M. de Normandie, Cherbourg	27 Nov 1974
S 55	P 6155	C. M. de Normandie, Cherbourg	7 Jan 1975
S 56	P 6156	C. M. de Normandie, Cherbourg	12 Feb 1975
S 57	P 6157	C. M. de Normandie, Cherbourg	3 Apr 1975
S 58	P 6158	C. M. de Normandie, Cherbourg	22 May 1975
S 59	P 6159	C. M. de Normandie, Cherbourg	24 June 1975
S 60	P 6160	C. M. de Normandie, Cherbourg	6 Aug 1975

Displacement, tons: 234 standard; 265 full load
Dimensions, feet (metres): 154·2 × 23·0 × 5·9 *(47 × 7 × 2)*
Missiles: SSM; 4 Exocet MM 38
Guns: 1—76 mm OTO Melara; 1—40 mm (Bofors)
Main engines: 4 MTU diesels; 4 shafts; 12 000 bhp = 33·5 knots
Oil fuel, tons: 39
Range, miles: 600 at 30 knots
Complement: 30 (4 officers, 26 men)

S 60 *6/1976, Reinhard Nerlich*

Ordered in October 1970. For completion from 1973 onwards to replace the first 20 of the "Jaguar" class. Eight hulls contracted to Lürssen (S 46, S 48, S 50, S 52, S 54, S 56, S 58, S 60) but all fitted out in France. Steel-hulled craft.
Launch dates: S 41, 27 Sep 1972; S 42, 12 Dec 1972; S 43, 7 Mar 1973; S 44, 5 May 1973; S 45, 3 July 1973; S 46, 21 May 1973; S 47, 20 Sep 1973; S 48, 10 Sep 1973; S 49 11 Jan 1974; S 50, 10 Dec 1973; S 51, 11 June 1974; S 52, 25 May 1974; S 53, 4 July 1974; S 54, 8 July 1974; S 55, 15 Nov 1974; S 56, 30 Oct 1974; S 57, 18 Feb 1975; S 58, 26 Feb 1975; S 59, 15 May 1975; S 60, 28 May 1975.

Electronics: Thomson-CSF, Vega-Pollux PCET control system, controlling missiles, torpedoes and guns.

Radar: Navigation: Three RM 20.
Air and surface search/target designator: Triton G-band
Tracking: Pollux I band.

Squadrons: Third: S 41-50. Fifth: S 51-60.

S 48 *1977, Michael D, J. Lennon*

GERMANY (FEDERAL) / Light forces — Mine warfare forces 205

10 "ZOBEL" CLASS (TYPE 142 FAST ATTACK CRAFT—TORPEDO)

Name	No.	Builders	Commissioned
ZOBEL	P 6092	Lürssen, Vegesack	12 Dec 1961
WIESEL	P 6093	Lürssen, Vegesack	25 June 1962
DACHS	P 6094	Lürssen, Vegesack	25 Sep 1962
HERMELIN	P 6095	Kröger, Rendsburg	28 Nov 1962
NERZ	P 6096	Lürssen, Vegesack	11 Jan 1963
PUMA	P 6097	Kröger, Rendsburg	21 Dec 1962
GEPARD	P 6098	Lürssen, Vegesack	18 Apr 1963
HYANE	P 6099	Kröger, Rendsburg	10 May 1963
FRETTCHEN	P 6100	Lürssen, Vegesack	26 June 1963
OZELOT	P 6101	Lürssen, Vegesack	25 Oct 1963

Displacement, tons: 225 full load
Dimensions, feet (metres): 139·4 × 23·4 × 7·9 (42·5 × 7·2 × 2·4)
Guns: 2—40 mm Bofors L 70 (single)
Torpedo tubes: 2—21 in (533 mm) for Seal wire-guided torpedoes
Main engines: 4 Mercedes-Benz (MTU) 20-cyl diesels; 4 shafts; 12 000 bhp = 40·5 knots
Complement: 39

Originally units of the "Jaguar" class, but, after conversion, known as the "Zobel" class. Form 7th Squadron.

Radar: Fire control: Two M 20 series in radome

DACHS 1978, Reinhard Nerlich

AMPHIBIOUS FORCES

22 TYPE 520 (LCUs)

FLUNDER L 760	SCHLEI L 765	BUTT L 788	FORELLE L 794
KARPFEN L 761	STÖR L 766	BRASSE L 789	INGER L 795
LACHS L 762	TÜMMLER L 767	BARBE L 790	MAKRELE L 796
PLOTZE L 763	WELS L 768	DELPHIN L 791	MURÄNE L 797
ROCHEN L 764	ZANDER L 769	DORSCH L 792	RENKE L 798
		FELCHEN L 793	SALM L 799

Displacement, tons: 200 light; 403 full load
Dimensions, feet (metres): 136·5 × 28·9 × 6·9 (41·6 × 8·8 × 2·1)
Guns: 2—20 mm (see Gunnery notes)
Main engines: General Motors diesels; 2 shafts; 1 380 bhp = 12 knots
Complement: 17

Similar to the US LCU (Landing Craft Utility) type. Provided with bow and stern ramp. Built by Howaldtswerke, Hamburg, 1965-66. Can carry 160 tons load. *Inger* employed for seamanship training. *Renke* and *Salm* in reserve.

Gunnery: Have been rearmed with two modern 20 mm (twin).

DELPHIN 1976, J. A. Verhoog

28 LCM TYPE 521

LCM 1-28

Displacement, tons: 116 standard; 140 full load
Dimensions, feet (metres): 77·3 × 21 × 4·3 (23·5 × 6·4 × 1·3)
Main engines: 2 diesels; 1 320 hp = 10 knots

Similar to US LCM 8 type. Built by Blohm and Voss and Rheinwerft 1965-67. Can carry 50 tons.

MINE WARFARE FORCES

18 "LINDAU" CLASS (TYPE 320)
(MINESWEEPERS—COASTAL and MINEHUNTERS)

Name	No.	Builders	Commissioned
GÖTTINGEN	M 1070	Burmester, Bremen	31 May 1958
KOBLENZ	M 1071	Burmester, Bremen	8 July 1958
LINDAU	M 1072	Burmester, Bremen	24 Apr 1958
SCHLESWIG	M 1073	Burmester, Bremen	30 Oct 1958
TÜBINGEN	M 1074	Burmester, Bremen	25 Sep 1958
WETZLAR	M 1075	Burmester, Bremen	20 Aug 1958
PADERBORN	M 1076	Burmester, Bremen	16 Dec 1958
WEILHEIM	M 1077	Burmester, Bremen	28 Jan 1959
CUXHAVEN	M 1078	Burmester, Bremen	11 Mar 1959
DÜREN	M 1079	Burmester, Bremen	22 Apr 1959
MARBURG	M 1080	Burmester, Bremen	11 June 1959
KONSTANZ	M 1081	Burmester, Bremen	23 July 1959
WOLFSBURG	M 1082	Burmester, Bremen	8 Oct 1959
ULM	M 1083	Burmester, Bremen	7 Nov 1959
FLENSBURG	M 1084	Burmester, Bremen	3 Dec 1959
MINDEN	M 1085	Burmester, Bremen	22 Jan 1960
FULDA	M 1086	Burmester, Bremen	5 Mar 1960
VÖLKLINGEN	M 1087	Burmester, Bremen	21 May 1960

Displacement, tons: 370 standard; 420 full load
Dimensions, feet (metres): 142·7 pp; 156·5 oa × 27·2 × 8·5 (47·7 × 8·3 × 2·5)
Guns: 1—40 mm; 2—20 mm
Main engines: Maybach (MTU) diesels; 2 shafts; 4 000 bhp = 16·5 knots
Range, miles: 850 at 16·5 knots
Complement: 46

KOBLENZ 1978, J. A. Verhoog

PADERBORN 1/1979, Leo van Ginderen

Lindau, first German built vessel for the Federal German Navy since the Second World War, launched on 16 February 1957. Basically of NATO WU type but modified for German requirements. The hull is of wooden construction, laminated with plastic glue. The engines are of non-magnetic materials. The first six, *Göttingen, Koblenz, Lindau, Schleswig, Tubingen* and *Wetzlar*, were modified with lower bridges in 1958-59. *Schleswig* was lengthened by 6·8 ft (2·07 m) in 1960—all others in 1960-64. *Fulda* and *Flensburg* were converted into minehunters in 1968-69 as part of a total of 12 ships to be so converted, with the second group started in 1975, *Lindau, Tübingen Minden, Koblenz, Wetzlar, Göttingen, Weilheim, Völkingen, Cuxhaven* and *Marburg* in that order. Owing to industrial problems delays caused all ten ships to be in the yards at the same time. *Lindau* eventually completed February 1978 and *Marburg* is hoped to complete in 1980.
These are being fitted with Plessey sonar and French PAP exploders.

Minehunter Conversions: *Koblenz* completed 21 June 1978, *Lindau* 10 February 1978, *Tubingen* 20 March 1978, *Flensburg* 1969, *Minden* 31 May 1978, *Fulda* 1969.

Troika Conversion: The six ships (*Düren, Konstanz, Paderborn, Ulm, Schleswig* and *Wolfsburg*) not being converted to minehunters are being converted as guidance ships for Troika. Each will carry three of these unmanned minesweeping vehicles. The whole of this programme will replace the surviving "Schütze" class. *Ulm* paid off 28 July 1978 as first conversion. Eighteen Troika vehicles ordered in 1978 from MAK Kiel, each of 95-100 tons 24·8 × 4·5 metres with diesel hydraulic propulsion.

Squadrons: All operational ships belong to MCM Squadron North Sea.

GERMANY (FEDERAL) / Mine warfare forces

22 "SCHÜTZE" CLASS (TYPE 340-341) (MINESWEEPERS—COASTAL (FAST))

Name	No.	Builders	Commissioned
CASTOR	M 1051	Abeking and Rasmussen	1962
POLLUX	M 1054	Abeking and Rasmussen	1961
SIRIUS	M 1055	Abeking and Rasmussen	1961
RIGEL	M 1056	Abeking and Rasmussen	1962
REGULUS	M 1057	Abeking and Rasmussen	1962
MARS	M 1058	Abeking and Rasmussen	1960
SPICA	M 1059	Abeking and Rasmussen	1961
SKORPION	M 1060	Abeking and Rasmussen	1963
SCHÜTZE	M 1062	Abeking and Rasmussen	1959
WAAGE	M 1063	Abeking and Rasmussen	1962
DENEB	M 1064	Schürenstedt	1961
JUPITER	M 1065	Schürenstedt	1961
ATAIR	M 1067	Schlichting, Travemünde	1961
WEGA	M 1069	Abeking and Rasmussen	1963
PERSEUS	M 1090	Schlichting, Travemünde	1961
PLUTO	M 1092	Schürenstedt	1960
NEPTUN	M 1093	Schlichting, Travemünde	1960
WIDDER	M 1094	Schürenstedt	1960
HERKULES	M 1095	Schlichting, Travemünde	1960
FISCHE	M 1096	Abeking and Rasmussen	1960
GEMMA	M 1097	Abeking and Rasmussen	1960
STIER	Y 849	Abeking and Rasmussen	1961

Displacement, tons: 230 standard; 280 full load
Dimensions, feet (metres): 155 × 23·5 × 7·2 *(47·2 × 7·2 × 2·2)*
Gun: 1—40 mm (except *Stier*)
Main engines: MTU diesels; 4 500 bhp = 24 knots
Range, miles: 2 000 at 13 knots
Complement: 31

HERKULES   1976, Reinhard Nerlich

30 originally built between 1959 and 1964. (Ex-*Uranus* is now German Navy League ship in Trier). The design is a development of the "R" boats of World War II. *Stier*, former number M 1061, carries no weapons, but has a recompression chamber, being a clearance diving vessel. Formerly classified as inshore minesweepers, but re-rated as fast minesweepers in 1966. Form the 1st and 5th MCM Squadrons. All to be replaced by Troika fitted "Lindau" class in early 1980s.

Radar: TRS-N.

Transfer: Five transferred to Greece, deleted in 1974.

STIER (with recompression chamber)   1975, Federal German Navy

10 "FRAUENLOB" CLASS (TYPE 394) (MINESWEEPERS—INSHORE)

Name	No.	Builders	Commissioned
FRAUENLOB	M 2658	Krögerwerft, Rendsburg	1966
NAUTILUS	M 2659	Krögerwerft, Rendsburg	1966
GEFION	M 2660	Krögerwerft, Rendsberg	1967
MEDUSA	M 2661	Krögerwerft, Rendsburg	1967
UNDINE	M 2662	Krögerwerft, Rendsburg	1967
MINERVA	M 2663	Krögerwerft, Rendsburg	1967
DIANA	M 2664	Krögerwerft, Rendsburg	1967
LORELEY	M 2665	Krögerwerft, Rendsburg	1968
ATLANTIS	M 2666	Krögerwerft, Rendsburg	1968
ACHERON	M 2667	Krögerwerft, Rendsburg	1969

Displacement, tons: 204 standard; 230 full load
Dimensions, feet (metres): 124·7 × 27 × 6·6 *(38 × 8·2 × 2)*
Gun: 1—40 mm
Mines: Laying capability
Main engines: Maybach (MTU) diesels; 2 shafts; Escher Wyss propellers; 2 000 bhp = 14 knots
Complement: 24

Launched in 1965-67. Originally designed coastguard boats with "W" numbers. Rated as inshore minesweepers in 1968 with the "M" numbers. All subsequently allocated Y numbers and later reallocated M numbers. 7th MCM Squadron.

MINERVA   1977, J. A. Verhoog

8 "ARIADNE" CLASS (TYPE 393) (MINESWEEPERS—INSHORE)

Name	No.	Builders	Commissioned
ARIADNE	M 2650	Krögerwerft, Rendsburg	1961
FREYA	M 2651	Krögerwerft, Rendsburg	1962
VINETA	M 2652	Krögerwerft, Rendsburg	1962
HERTHA	M 2653	Krögerwerft, Rendsburg	1962
NYMPHE	M 2654	Krögerwerft, Rendsburg	1963
NIXE	M 2655	Krögerwerft, Rendsburg	1963
AMAZONE	M 2656	Krögerwerft, Rendsburg	1963
GAZELLE	M 2657	Krögerwerft, Rendsburg	1963

Displacement, tons: 184 standard; 210 full load
Dimensions, feet (metres): 124·3 × 27·2 × 6·6 *(37·9 × 8·3 × 2)*
Gun: 1—40 mm
Mines: Laying capability
Main engines: 2 Mercedes-Benz (MTU) diesels; 2 shafts; 2 000 bhp = 14 knots
Range, miles: 740 at 14 knots
Complement: 23

All launched from April 1960 *(Ariadne)*. All named after cruisers of 1897-1900. Formerly classified as patrol boats but re-rated as inshore minesweepers in 1966, and given new M numbers in January 1968, Y numbers in 1970, and M numbers once more in 1974. 3rd MCM Squadron.

VINETA   11/1976, Stefan Terzibaschitsch

GERMANY (FEDERAL) / Mine warfare forces — Service forces 207

1 TRIALS MINESWEEPER

Name	No.	Builders	Commissioned
HOLNIS	Y 836 (ex-M 2651)	Abeking and Rasmussen	1966

Displacement, tons: 180
Dimensions, feet (metres): 116·8 × 24·3 × 6·9 (35·6 × 7·4 × 2·1)
Gun: 1—20 mm
Main engines: 2 Mercedes-Benz (MTU) diesels; 2 shafts; 2 000 bhp = 14·5 knots
Complement: 21

Now serving for trials and evaluation. *Holnis* was launched on 22 May 1965 as the prototype of a new design projected as a class of 20 such vessels but she is the only unit of this type, the other 19 boats having been cancelled. Hull number changed from M 2651 to Y 836 in 1970.

HOLNIS   1975, Federal German Navy

2 "NIOBE" CLASS (MINESWEEPERS—INSHORE)

Name	No.	Builders	Commissioned
HANSA	Y 806	Krögerwerft, Rendsburg	1958
NIOBE	Y 1643	Krögerwerft, Rendsburg	1958

Displacement, tons: 150 standard; 180 full load
Dimensions, feet (metres): 115·2 × 21·3 × 5·6 (35·1 × 6·5 × 1·7)
Gun: 1—40 mm
Mines: Laying capability
Main engines: *Hansa:* 1 Mercedes-Benz (MTU) diesel; 1 shaft; 950 bhp = 14 knots
Niobe: 2 Mercedes-Benz (MTU) diesels; 2 shafts; 1 900 bhp = 16 knots
Range, miles: 1 100 at max speed
Complement: *Hansa* 19; *Niobe* 22

Hansa serves as support ship for clearance divers. *Niobe* is test and trials ship for Troika system.

HANSA   1975, Federal German Navy

SERVICE FORCES

11 "RHEIN" CLASS (DEPOT SHIPS)

Name	No.	Builders	Commissioned
ISAR	A 54	Blohm and Voss	25 Jan 1964
LAHN	A 55	Flender, Lübeck	24 Mar 1964
LECH	A 56	Flender, Lübeck	8 Dec 1964
RHEIN	A 58	Schliekerwerft, Hamburg	6 Nov 1961
ELBE	A 61	Schliekerwerft, Hamburg	17 Apr 1962
MAIN	A 63	Lindenau, Kiel	29 June 1963
SAAR	A 65	Norderwerft, Hamburg	11 May 1963
NECKAR	A 66	Lürssen, Vegesack	7 Dec 1963
MOSEL	A 67	Schliekerwerft, Hamburg	8 June 1963
WERRA	A 68	Lindenau, Kiel	2 Sep 1964
DONAU	A 69	Schlichting, Travemünde	23 May 1964

Displacement, tons: 2 370 standard; 2 540 full load
except *Lahn* and *Lech* 2 460 standard; 2 680 full load
Length, feet (metres): 304·5 (92·8) wl; 323·5 (99) oa
Beam, feet (metres): 38·8 (11·8)
Draught, feet (metres): 12·8 (3·9)
Guns: 2—3·9 in (100 mm); none in *Lahn, Lech;* 4—40 mm
Main engines: 6 Maybach or Daimler (MTU) diesels; diesel-electric drive in *Isar, Lahn, Lech, Mosel, Saar* 11 400 bhp; 2 shafts
Speed, knots: 20·5, 15 economical
Range, miles: 1 625 at 15 knots
Oil fuel, tons: 334
Complement: 110 (accommodation for 200); 198 *(Lahn* and *Lech)*

Originally a class of 13. Rated as depot ships for minesweepers *(Isar, Mosel, Saar)*, submarines *(Lahn, Lech)*, and fast attack craft (others) but these ships with their 3·9 in *(100 mm)* guns could obviously be used in lieu of frigates.

Conversion: *Lahn* major conversion in 1975.

Launch dates: *Donau* 26 Nov 1960, *Elbe* 5 May 1960, *Isar* 14 July 1962, *Lahn* 21 Nov 1961, *Lech* May 1962, *Main* 23 July 1960, *Mosel* 15 Dec 1960, *Neckar* 26 June 1961, *Rhein* 10 Feb 1959, *Saar* 1 Mar 1961, *Werra* 26 Mar 1963.

SAAR   10/1978, Wright and Logan

Operation: *Saar,* 1st MCM Squadron; *Isar,* MCM Squadron; *Mosel,* 5th MCM Squadron; *Elbe,* 2nd FPB Squadron; *Rhein,* 3rd FPB Squadron; *Main,* 5th FPB Squadron; *Neckar* and *Werra,* 7th FPB Squadron; *Lahn,* 1st Submarine Squadron; *Lech,* 3rd Submarine Squadron.

Radar: All by Hollandse Signaal. Search: HSA DA 02.
Fire control: Two HSA M 45 for 100 mm and 40 mm.

Status: Five of these comparatively new ships, namely *Donau, Isar, Lahn, Lech* and *Weser* (now deleted) were placed in reserve by July 1968. This was part of the economy programme announced by the Federal German Navy in September 1967 but all have subsequently been recommissioned or transferred.

Transfer: *Wester* to Greece 1975. *Ruhr* to Turkey 1976.

2 Ex-US "ARISTAEUS" CLASS (REPAIR SHIPS)

ODIN (ex-USS *Ulysses,* ARB 9, ex-*LST 967*) A 512
WOTAN (ex-USS *Diomedes,* ARB 11, ex-*LST 1119*) A 513

Displacement, tons: 1 625 light; 3 455 full load
Dimensions, feet (metres): 328 × 50 × 9·2 (100 × 15·2 × 2·8)
Guns: 4—20 mm
Main engines: 2 General Motors diesels, 2 shafts; 1 800 bhp = 11·6 knots
Oil fuel, tons: 600
Range, miles: 2 000 at 9 knots
Complement: 187

Repair ships. Transferred under MAP in June 1961.
Odin commissioned in January 1966 and *Wotan* on 2 December 1965. *Wotan* now civilian-manned.

WOTAN   1975, Federal German Navy

MEMMERT Y 805

The small repair ship *Memmert* Y 805 (ex-USN *106,* ex-*India,* ex-*BP 34*), 165 tons and 8 knots, rated as torpedo repair ship, salvage vessel with a derrick.

208 GERMANY (FEDERAL) / Service forces

2 "704" CLASS (FLEET REPLENISHMENT SHIPS)

Name	No	Builder	Commissioned
SPESSART (ex-*Okapi*)	A 1442	Kröger, Rendsburg	1974
RHÖN (ex-*Okene*)	A 1443	Kröger, Rendsburg	1974

Displacement, tons: 17 590 full load
Measurement, tons: 6 103 grt; 10 800 deadweight
Length, feet (metres): 426·7 *(130·1)*
Beam, feet (metres): 64·3 *(19·6)*
Draught, feet (metres): 26·9 *(8·2)*
Main engines: 8 000 hp = 16 knots
Complement: 42

Completed for Terkol Group as Tankers. Acquired in 1976 for conversion which started in January 1977. (*Spessart* at Bremerhaven, *Rhön* at Kröger). The former commissioned for naval service on 5 September 1977 and the latter on 23 September 1977. Unarmed and civilian manned.

RHÖN   1978, Federal German Navy

1 "BODENSEE" CLASS (REPLENISHMENT TANKER)

Name	No.	Builders	Commissioned
WITTENSEE (ex-*Sioux*)	A 1407	Lindenau, Kiel	26 Mar 1959

Displacement, tons: 1 970 full load
Measurement, tons: 1 238 deadweight; 985 gross
Dimensions, feet (metres): 221 × 32·5 × 15 *(67·5 × 9·8 × 4·3)*
Main engines: Diesels; 1 050—1 250 bhp = 12 knots
Complement: 21

Launched on 23 September 1958.

WITTENSEE   11/1976, Stefan Terzibaschitsch

1 REPLENISHMENT TANKER

Name	No.	Builders	Commissioned
EIFEL (ex-*Friedrich Jung*)	A 1429	Norderwerft, Hamburg	27 May 1963

Displacement, tons: 4 720
Dimensions, feet (metres): 334 × 47·2 × 23·3 *(102 × 14·4 × 7·1)*
Main engines: 3 360 hp = 13 knots

Launched on 29 March 1958. Purchased in 1963 for service in the Federal German Navy.

EIFEL   1970, Federal German Navy

4 "WALCHENSEE" CLASS (TYPE 703) (SUPPORT TANKERS)

Name	No.	Builders	Commissioned
WALCHENSEE	A 1424	Lindenau, Kiel	29 June 1966
AMMERSEE	A 1425	Lindenau, Kiel	2 Mar 1967
TEGERNSEE	A 1426	Lindenau, Kiel	23 Mar 1967
WESTENSEE	A 1427	Lindenau, Kiel	6 Oct 1967

Displacement, tons: 2 174
Dimensions, feet (metres): 233 × 36·7 × 13·5 *(74·2 × 11·2 × 4·1)*
Main engines: Diesels; 2 shafts; 1 400 bhp = 12·6 knots

Launched on 22 September 1966, 22 October 1966, 10 July 1965 and 25 February 1966 respectively.

WALCHENSEE   1975, Reiner Nerlich

1 SUPPORT TANKER

Name	No.	Builders	Commissioned
HARZ (ex-*Claere Jung*)	A 1428	Norderwerft, Hamburg	1953 (see note)

Displacement, tons: 3 696 deadweight
Dimensions, feet (metres): 303·2 × 43·5 × 21·7 *(92·4 × 13·2 × 6·6)*
Main engines: 2 520 hp = 12 knots
Complement: 42

Built in 1953 and purchased in 1963 for service as a tanker, commissioning on 27 May.

HARZ   1978, J. A. Verhoe

GERMANY (FEDERAL) / Service forces 209

8 "LÜNEBURG" CLASS (SUPPORT SHIPS)

Name	No.	Builders	Commissioned
LÜNEBURG*	A 1411	Flensburger, Schiffbau	9 July 1968
COBURG	A 1412	Flensburger Schiffbau	9 July 1968
FREIBURG	A 1413	Blohm and Voss	27 May 1968
GLÜCKSBURG*	A 1414	Flensburger, Schiffbau	9 July 1968
SAARBURG*	A 1415	Blohm and Voss	30 July 1968
NIENBURG	A 1416	Vulkan, Bremen	1 Aug 1968
OFFENBURG	A 1417	Blohm and Voss	27 May 1968
MEERSBURG*	A 1418	Vulkan, Bremen	25 June 1968

*conversions

Displacement, tons: 3 254
Dimensions, feet (metres): 341·2 × 43·3 × 13·8 (104 × 13·2 × 4·2) (379 ft—115·5 m for lengthened ships)
Guns: 4—40 mm (cocooned)
Main engines: 2 Maybach (MTU) diesels; 2 shafts; 5 600 bhp = 17 knots
Complement: 103

Modernisation: Four of this class have been lengthened by 37·8 ft (11·52 m) and modernised to serve the missile installations of the new classes of Fast Attack Craft and converted destroyers, including MM 38 Exocet maintenance. *Saarburg* completed 1975—*Lüneburg* 1976—*Meersburg* 1976—*Glücksburg* 1977.

COBURG 1978, Reinhard Nerlich

2 "WESTERWALD" CLASS (AMMUNITION TRANSPORTS)

Name	No.	Builders	Commissioned
WESTERWALD	A 1435	Lübecker, Masch	1 Feb 1967
ODENWALD	A 1436	Lübecker, Masch	23 Mar 1967

Displacement, tons: 3 460
Dimensions, feet (metres): 347·8 × 46 × 12·2 (106 × 14 × 3·7)
Guns: 4—40 mm (twins)
Main engines: MTU diesels; 5 600 bhp = 17 knots
Complement: 60

Odenwald was launched on 5 May 1966 and *Westerwald* was launched on 25 February 1966.

WESTERWALD 4/1976, Dr. Giorgio Arra

2 "SACHSENWALD" CLASS (MINE TRANSPORTS)

Name	No.	Builders	Commissioned
SACHSENWALD	A 1437	Blohm and Voss, Hamburg	20 Aug 1969
STEIGERWALD	A 1438	Blohm and Voss, Hamburg	20 Aug 1969

Displacement, tons: 3 850 full load
Dimensions, feet (metres): 363·5 × 45·6 × 11·2 (111 × 13·9 × 3·4)
Guns: 4—40 mm (2 twin mountings)
Mines: Laying capacity
Main engines: 2 MTU diesels; 2 shafts; 5 600 hp = 17 knots
Range, miles: 3 500
Complement: 65

Built as mine transports. Laid down on 1 August 1966 and 9 May 1966. Launched on 20 December 1966 and 10 March 1967. Have mine ports in the stern and can be used as minelayers.

SACHSENWALD 1976, German Federal Navy

4 "FW" CLASS (WATER BOATS)

FW 1 Y 864 **FW 4** Y 867 **FW 5** Y 868 **FW 6** Y 869

Measurement, tons: 350 deadweight
Dimensions, feet (metres): 144·4 × 25·6 × 8·2 (44·1 × 7·8 × 2·5)
Main engine: MWM diesel, 230 bhp = 9·5 knots

Originally class of six built in pairs by Schiffbarges, Unterweser, Bremerhaven; H. Rancke, Hamburg and Jadewerft, Wilhelmshaven, in 1963-64.

FW 5 8/1975, Stefan Terzibaschitsch

GERMANY (FEDERAL) / Training ships — Miscellaneous

TRAINING SHIPS

1 "DEUTSCHLAND" CLASS

Name	No.	Builders	Commissioned
DEUTSCHLAND	A 59	Nobiskrug, Rendsburg	25 May 1963

Displacement, tons: 4 880 normal; 5 400 full load
Length, feet (metres): 452·8 *(138·0)* pp; 475·8 *(145·0)* oa
Beam, feet (metres): 59 *(18)*
Draught, feet (metres): 15·7 *(4·8)*
Guns: 4—3·9 in *(100 mm)*/55 (single Mod 1954); 6—40 mm (2 twin, 2 single)
A/S weapons: 2 Bofors 4-barrel rocket launchers; 4—21 in *(533 mm)* torpedo tubes
Torpedo tubes: 2—21 in *(533 mm)* (surface targets)
Mines: Laying capacity
Main engines: 6 800 bhp MTU diesels (2 Daimler-Benz and 2 Maybach); 2 shafts with vp propellers; 8 000 shp double reduction MAN geared turbines; 1 shaft
Boilers: 2 Wahodag; 768 psi *(54 km/cm²)*; 870°F *(465°C)*
Speed, knots: 22 (3 shafts); 17 (2 shafts) 14 economical (1 shaft)
Oil fuel, tons: 230 furnace; 410 diesel
Range, miles: 6 000 at 17 knots
Complement: 554 (33 officers, 271 men, 250 cadets)

DEUTSCHLAND   6/1974, USN

Electronics: HSA fire control for Bofors A/S launchers and torpedoes.

Radar: All by Hollandse Signaalapparaten.
Navigation/surface warning: SGR 103, 105, 114.
Air warning: One LW-02/3
Target designator: One DA 02.
Fire control: Two M 45 series (M2/2; M4).

Sonar: One ELAC 1BV hull-mounted set.

First West German naval ship to exceed the post-war limit of 3 000 tons. Designed with armament and machinery of different types for training purposes. The name originally planned for this ship was *Berlin*. Ordered in 1956. Laid down in 1959 and launched 5 November 1960. Carried out her first machinery sea trials on 15 January 1963.

SAIL TRAINING SHIPS

Name	No.	Builders	Commissioned
GORCH FOCK	A 60	Blöhm and Voss, Hamburg	17 Dec 1958

Displacement, tons: 1 760 standard; 1 870 full load
Dimensions, feet (metres): 257 × 39·2 × 15·8 *(81·3 × 12 × 4·8)*
Main engine: Auxiliary MAN diesel; 880 bhp = 11 knots
Sail area, sq ft: 21 141
Range, miles: 1 990 on auxiliary diesel
Complement: 206 (10 officers, 56 ratings, 140 cadets)

Sail training ship of the improved "Horst Wessel" type. Barque rig. Launched on 23 August 1958.

GORCH FOCK   11/1978, Reinhard Nerlich

Name	No.	Builders	Commissioned
NORDWIND	Y 834	—	1944

Displacement, tons: 110
Dimensions, feet (metres): 78·8 × 22 × 9 *(24 × 6·4 × 2·5)*
Main engine: Diesel; 150 bhp = 8 knots (sail area 2 037·5 sq ft)

Ketch rigged.

There are over 70 other sailing vessels of various types serving for sail training and recreational purposes. *Achat, Alarich, Amsel, Argonaut, Borasco, Brigant, Dankwart, Diamont, Dietrich, Dompfaff, Drossel, Fafnir, Fink, Flibustier, Freibeuter, Geiserich, Gernot, Geuse, Giselher, Go¨dicke, Gunnar, Gunter, Hadubrand, Hagen, Hartnaut, Hilderbrand, Horand, Hunding, Jaspis, Kaper, Klipper, Korsar, Kuchkuch, Lerche, Likendeeler, Magellan, Meise, Michel, Mime, Mistral, Monsun, Nachtigall, Ortwin, Ostwind, Pampero, Pirol, Ruediger, Samum, Saphir, Schirocco, Seeteufel, Siegfried, Siegmund, Siegura, Smaragd, Star, Stieglitz, Storetbecker, Taifun, Teja, Topas, Tornadon, Totila, Vitalienbrüder, Volker, Walter, Wate, Westwind, Wiking, Wittigo, Zeisig.*

---

7 COASTAL PATROL CRAFT

KW 15 Y 827		KW 19 Y 833	
KW 16 Y 830		KW 17 Y 845	
KW 18 Y 832		KW 20 Y 846	

Displacement, tons: 45 standard; 60 full load
Dimensions, feet (metres): 93·5 × 15·5 × 4·0 *(28·9 × 4·9 × 1·5)*
Main engines: 2 Mercedes-Benz (MTU) diesels; 2 000 bhp = 25 knots
Complement: 14

Built in 1951-53.

MISCELLANEOUS

13 TORPEDO RECOVERY VESSELS

TF 1-6 (Y 851-856)	TF 101-102 (Y 883-884)	TF 104 (Y 886)
TF 105 (Y 835)	TF 106 (Y 872)	TF 107-108 (Y873-874)

All of approximately 30-40 tons. TF 1-6 and 106-108 built in 1966, the remainder a deal older.

KW 18   5/1975, Reiner Nerlich

KW 3 Y 829. Of 112 tons and 8 knots built in 1943.

TF 2   1978, Reinhard Nerlich

TUGS

2 SALVAGE TUGS

Name	No.	Builders	Commissioned
HELGOLAND	A 1457	Unterweser, Bremerhaven	8 Mar 1966
FEHMARN	A 1458	Unterweser, Bremerhaven	1 Feb 1967

Displacement, tons: 1 310 standard; 1 643 full load
Dimensions, feet (metres): 223·1 × 41·7 × 14·4 (68·0 × 12·7 × 4·4)
Guns: 2—40 mm (removed in Helgoland)
Main engines: Diesel-electric; 4 MWM diesels; 2 shafts; 3 800 hp = 17 knots
Range, miles: 6 000 at 10 knots
Complement: 36-45

Launched on 25 November 1965 and 8 April 1965. Carry firefighting equipment.

FEHMARN   1974, Federal German Navy—Marineamt

6 SALVAGE TUGS

Name	No.	Builders	Commissioned
WANGEROOGE	A 1451	Schichau, Bremerhaven	9 Apr 1968
SPIEKEROOG	A 1452	Schichau, Bremerhaven	14 Aug 1968
LANGEOOG	?	Schichau, Bremerhaven	14 Aug 1968
NORDERNEY	?	Schichau, Bremerhaven	15 Oct 1970
JUIST	Y 1664	Schichau, Bremerhaven	1 Oct 1971
BALTRUM	Y 1661	Schichau, Bremerhaven	8 Oct 1968

Displacement, tons: 854 standard; 1 024 full load
Dimensions, feet (metres): 170·6 × 39·4 × 12·8 (52·0 × 12·1 × 3·9)
Gun: 1—40 mm (removed in Wangerooge)
Main engines: Diesel-electric; 2 shafts; 2 400 hp = 14 knots
Range, miles: 5 000 at 10 knots
Complement: 24-35

Wangerooge, prototype salvage tug, was launched on 4 July 1966, Baltrum on 8 October 1968. Pennant numbers of training ships changed in late 1976.

Duties: Baltrum diving training ship (1974). Norderney, Juist and Langeoog converted and employed as diving training ships 1976-78. (last two completed 1978.)

BALTRUM   1978, J. A. Verhoog

4 HARBOUR TUGS

Name	No.	Builders	Commissioned
SYLT	Y 820	Schichau, Bremerhaven	1962
FÖHR	Y 821	Schichau, Bremerhaven	1962
AMRUM	Y 822	Schichau, Bremerhaven	1963
NEUWERK	Y 823	Schichau, Bremerhaven	1963

Displacement, tons: 266 standard
Dimensions, feet (metres): 100·7 × 25·2 (30·6 × 7·5)
Main engine: 1 Deutz diesel; 800 bhp = 12 knots
Complement: 10

Launched in 1961.

3 HARBOUR TUGS

Name	No.	Builders	Commissioned
NEUENDE	Y 1680	Schichau, Bremerhaven	1971
HEPPENS	Y 1681	Schichau, Bremerhaven	1971
ELLERBEK	Y 1682	Schichau, Bremerhaven	1971

Displacement, tons: 122
Dimensions, feet (metres): 87·2 × 24·3 × 8·5 (26·6 × 7·4 × 2·6)
Main engine: 1 MWM diesel; 1 shaft; 800 hp
Speed, knots: 12
Complement: 6

ELLERBEK   6/1978, Stefan Terzibaschitsch

Harbour Type: There are also nine small harbour tugs all completed in 1958-60:—Knechtsand Y 814, Langeness Y 819, Lütjie Hörn Y 812, Mellum Y 813, Nordstrand Y 817, Plon Y 802, Scharhörn Y 815, Trischen Y 818 and Vogelsand Y 816.

ICEBREAKERS

Name	No.	Builders	Commissioned
HANSE	—	Wärtsilä, Helsinki	13 Dec 1966

Displacement, tons: 2 771
Dimensions, feet (metres): 226·6 × 57 × 28·9 (69·1 × 17·4 × 8·8)
Main engines: Diesel-electric; 4 shafts; 7 500 bhp = 16 knots

Laid down on 12 January 1965. Launched on 17 October 1966. Completed on 25 November 1966. Although owned by West Germany she sails under the Finnish flag, manned by a Finnish crew. Only when the winter is so severe that icebreakers are needed in the southern Baltic will she be transferred under the German flag and command. She is of improved "Karhu" class. She does not belong to the Bundesmarine.

Name	No.	Builders	Commissioned
EISVOGEL	A 1401	J. G. Hitzler, Lauenburg	11 Mar 1961
EISBAR	A 1402	J. G. Hitzler, Lauenburg	1 Nov 1961

Displacement, tons: 560 standard
Dimensions, feet (metres): 125·3 × 31·2 × 15·1 (38·2 × 9·5 × 4·6)
Gun: 1—40 mm
Main engines: 2 Maybach diesels; 2 shafts; 2 000 bhp = 14 knots

Launched on 28 April and 9 June 1960 respectively.

EISBAR   1978, J. A. Verhoog

GERMANY (FEDERAL) / Auxiliary ships

AUXILIARY SHIPS

1 RADAR TRIALS SHIP

Name	No.	Builders	Commissioned
OSTE (ex-*Puddefjord*, ex-*USN 101*)	A 52	Akers Mekaniske V, Oslo	1943

Displacement, tons: 567 gross
Dimensions, feet (metres): 160 × 29.7 × 17 *(48.8 × 9 × 5.2)*
Main engine: 1 Akers diesel; 1 shaft; 1 600 bhp = 12 knots

Taken over from the US Navy. Converted in 1968.

OSTE 8/1976, P. Crichton

2 RADAR TRIALS SHIPS

Name	No.	Builders	Commissioned
ALSTE (ex-*Mellum*)	A 50	Unterweser, Bremen	1972
OKER (ex-*Hoheweg*)	A 53	Unterweser, Bremen	1972

Measurement, tons: 1 187
Dimensions, feet (metres): 237.8 × 34.4 × 16.1 *(72.5 × 10.5 × 4.9)*
Main engines: Diesel-electric; 1 shaft = 15 knots
Complement: 30

OKER 2/1977, Michael D. J. Lennon

1 TRIALS SHIP

Name	No.	Builders	Commissioned
WALTHER VON LEDEBUR	Y 841	Burmester, Bremen	1966

Displacement, tons: 725
Dimensions, feet (metres): 219.8 × 34.8 × 8.9 *(63 × 10.6 × 2.7)*
Main engines: Maybach (MTU) diesels; 2 shafts; 5 000 bhp = 19 knots
Complement: 11 + 10

Wooden hulled vessel. Trials ship. Launched on 30 June 1966.

WALTHER VON LEDEBUR 10/1975, Reinhard Nerlich

3 Ex-COASTAL MINESWEEPERS

H.C. OERSTED (ex-*Vinstra*, ex-*NYMS 247*) Y 877
ADOLF BESTELMEYER (ex-*BYMS 2213*) Y 881
RUDOLF DIESEL (ex-*BYMS 2279*) Y 889

Displacement, tons: 270 standard; 350 full load
Dimensions, feet (metres): 136 × 24.5 × 8 *(41.5 × 7.5 × 2.4)*
Main engines: 2 MTU diesels; 2 shafts; 1 000 bhp = 15 knots

Of US YMS type. Built in 1943. *Adolf Bestelmeyer* and *Rudolf Diesel* are used for gunnery trials. *H. C. Oersted* was acquired from the Royal Norwegian Navy and used as degaussing ship.

RUDOLF DIESEL 2/1976, Reinhard Nerlich

PLANET A 1450. Of 1 943 tons and 13.5 knots. Built in 1965. Weapons research ship.

WILHELM PULLWER Y 838, **SP 1** Y 837. Of 160 tons and 12.5 knots. Built in 1966. Trials ships.

HEINZ ROGGENKAMP Y 871. Of 785 tons and 12 knots. Built in 1952. Trials ship.

HEINZ ROGGENKAMP 1978, Reinhard Nerlich

FRIEDRICH VOGE Y 888. Of 179 tons. Trials ship.

FRIEDRICH VOGE 1978, Reinhard Nerlich

OTTO MEYCKE Y 882 Diving Trials.

TB 1 Y 1678. Of 70 tons and 14 knots. Diving boat built in 1972.

LP 1, 2 and **3**. Battery workshop craft of 180 tons built in 1963-73.

FÖRDE Y 1641   **JADE** Y 1642

Tank cleaning vessels. Of 600 tons, completed in 1967.

FÖRDE 8/1975, Stefan Terzibaschitsch

ARCONA (ex-*Royal Prince*) Y 809
KNURRHAHN Y 811 of 261 tons.

Both accommodation ships. *Arcona* ex-liner.

BARBARA Y 844, lifting ship of 3 500 tons.
HIEV Y 875, **GRIEP** Y 876, Floating cranes.

GERMANY (FEDERAL) / Coast guard vessels — GHANA / Corvettes 213

COAST GUARD VESSELS
(BUNDESGRENZSCHUTZ—SEE)

Note: This paramilitary force consists of about 1 000 men who operate the craft below as well as helicopters.

1 ICEBREAKING TUG

Name	No	Builders	Commissioned
RETTIN	BG 5	Mützelfeldwerft	3 Dec 1976

Measurement, tons: 120 brt
Dimensions, feet (metres): 73·8 × 21·7 × 9·5 (22·5 × 6·6 × 2·9)
Main engines: 2 diesels; 590 hp = 9 knots
Complement: 4

Launched 29 October 1976.

8 LARGE PATROL CRAFT

NEUSTADT BG 11	ESCHWEGE BG 15
BAD BRAMSTEDT BG 12	ALSFELD BG 16
UELTZEN BG 13	BAYREUTH BG 17
DUDERSTADT BG 14	ROSENHEIM BG 18

Displacement, tons: 203
Length, feet (metres): 127·1 (38·5)
Guns: 2—40 mm
Main engines: 3 MTU diesels; 4 500 hp = 30 knots
Complement: 24

All built between 1969 and late 1970—BG 13 by Schlichting, Travemünde, the remainder by Lürssen, Vegesack. Form two flotillas: BG 11-14 the 1st and BG 15-18 the 2nd. A third flotilla of smaller craft has been formed.

FISHERY PROTECTION SHIPS

Operated by Ministry of Agriculture and Fisheries.

ANTON DOHRN of 1 950 tons and 15 knots.
FRITHJOF of 2 150 tons and 15 knots.
MEERKATZE of 2 250 tons and 14 knots. Completed 1977.
MINDEN of 973 tons and 16 knots.
ROTERSAND of 1 000 tons. Built in 1974.
SOLEA of 340 tons and 12 knots.
UTHÖRN of 110 tons and 9 knots.
WALTHER HERTWIG of 2 500 tons and 15 knots.

Previous *Meerkatze* sold in 1976 and *Nordenham* returned to her owners in 1977.

SURVEY SHIPS

The following ships operate for the Deutsches Hydrographisches Institut, under the Ministry of Transport.
A new ship for hydrographic and fishery research duties was ordered in 1978 from the Schlichting Yard. She is to be of 1 370 tons. speed 13·5 knots and due for completion in March 1980.

METEOR (research ship) 3 085 tons, launched 1964, complement 53
KOMET (survey and research) 1 595 tons, launched 1969, complement 42
GAUSS (survey and research) 1 074 tons, launched 1949, complement 31
SÜDEROOG (survey ship) 211 tons, launched 1956, complement 17
ATAIR (survey and wrecks) 148 tons, launched 1962, complement 12
WEGA (survey and wrecks) 148 tons, launched 1962, complement 12
POSEIDON (survey) 1 266 tons, launched 1976, complement 28
VICTOR HENSEN (survey) 1 266 tons, launched 1976, complement 28
SENCKENBURG (research) 165 tons, launched 1976, complement 5

GAUSS 1974, Reiner Nerlich

UELTZEN 1978, Reinhard Nerlich

GHANA

Administration
Commander of the Navy:
Commodore C. K. Dzang

Personnel
(a) 1979: 2 000
(b) Voluntary service

General
The new orders with Lürssen may replace the four craft of the original order from Ruthof Werft. However, after a short fling with Soviet craft, it is notable that orders are now being directed to Western Europe. A programme for patrol craft to replace the aged British minesweepers would not be unreasonable as the new FACs seem an expensive way of patrolling off-shore limits.

Deletions
1973: 3 ex-Soviet "Poluchat I" Class Patrol Craft
1977: *Yogaga, Afadzato* ("Ham" class)

Naval Bases
Sekondi (Western Naval Command)
Tema, near Accra (Eastern Naval Command)

Mercantile Marine
Lloyd's Register of Shipping:
85 vessels of 186 079 tons gross

CORVETTES

2 "KROMANTSE" CLASS (VOSPER MARK I TYPE)

Name	No.	Builders	Commissioned
KROMANTSE	F 17	Vosper Ltd.	27 July 1964
KETA	F 18	Vickers Ltd (Tyne)	18 May 1965

Displacement, tons: 380 light; 440 standard; 500 full load
Dimensions, feet (metres): 162 wl; 177 oa × 28·5 × 13 (49·4, 54 × 8·7 × 4)
Guns: 1—4 in; 1—40 mm (see notes)
A/S weapons: 1 Squid triple-barrelled depth charge mortar
Main engines: 2 Bristol Siddeley Maybach (MTU) diesels; 2 shafts; 390 rpm; 7 100 bhp = 20 knots
Oil fuel, tons: 60
Range, miles: 2 000 at 16 knots; 2 900 at 14 knots
Complement: 54 (6 + 3 officers, 45 ratings)

Designed by Vosper Ltd, Portsmouth, a joint venture with Vickers-Armstrong's Ltd, one ship being built by each company. Vosper roll damping fins, and air conditioning throughout excepting machinery spaces. Generators 360 kW. The electrical power supply is 440 volts, 60 cycles ac. A very interesting patrol vessel design, an example of what can be achieved on a comparatively small platform to produce an inexpensive and quickly built anti-submarine vessel. *Kromantse* was launched at the Camber Shipyard, Portsmouth, on 5 September 1963. *Keta* was launched at Newcastle on 18 January 1965.

Radar: Search: Plessey AWS 1.

Refit: Both were fully refitted by Vosper Thornycroft Ltd (a £1·2 million contract) in 1974-75—*Keta* completed in April 1975 and *Kromantse* in September 1975.

Sonar: Both fitted with hull-mounted set.

KROMANTSE 9/1975, Vosper Thornycroft

KETA 1978, Ghana Navy

214 GHANA / Light forces — Service craft

LIGHT FORCES

2 TYPE 45 (FAST ATTACK CRAFT—GUN)

Name	No.	Builders	Commissioned
DZATO	P 26	Lürssen, Vegesack	2 Dec 1978
SEBO	P 27	Lürssen, Vegesack	Jan 1979

Displacement, tons: 255
Dimensions, feet (metres): 147·6 × 23 × 7·5 (45 × 7 × 2·3)
Guns: 1—76 mm OTO Melara; 1—40 mm
Main engines: 2 MTU diesels; 6 000 hp; 2 shafts = 27 knots
Range, miles: 700 at 40 knots; 1 800 at 16 knots
Complement: 30

Ordered in 1976. *Dzato* laid down 16 January 1978.

SEBO   1978, Lürssen Werft

2 PB 57 TYPE (FAST ATTACK CRAFT—GUN)

Displacement, tons: 410
Dimensions, feet (metres): 190·6 × 25 × 8·8 (58·1 × 7·6 × 2·7)
Guns: 1—76 mm OTO Melara; 1—40 mm
Main engines: 3 MTU diesels; 9 000 hp; 3 shafts = 32 knots
Range, miles: 700 at 35 knots.
Complement: ? 40

Ordered from Lürssen, Vegesack in 1977.

2 LARGE PATROL CRAFT

Name	No.	Builders	Commissioned
DELA	P 24	Ruthof Werft, Mainz	1974
SAHENE	P 25	Ruthof Werft, Mainz	1974

Displacement, tons: 160
Dimensions, feet (metres): 115·5 × 21·3 × 5·9 (35·2 × 6·5 × 1·8)
Guns: 2—40 mm

Ordered from Ruthof, Werft (Mainz) BRG in 1973 as part of a class of six. Only these two had been delivered when the builders went bankrupt in 1975.

SAHENE   1978, Ghana Navy

2 "FORD" CLASS (LARGE PATROL CRAFT)

Name	No.	Builders	Commissioned
ELMINA	P 13	Yarrow, Scotstoun	1962
KOMENDA	P 14	Yarrow, Scotstoun	Dec 1962

Displacement, tons: 120 standard; 142 full load
Dimensions, feet (metres): 117·5 × 20 × 7 (35·8 × 6·1 × 2·1)
Gun: 1—40 mm, 60 cal Bofors
A/S weapons: Depth charge throwers
Main engines: 2 MTU (Maybach) diesels; type MD 16 V 53 87 B 90;
   2 shafts = 3 000 hp at 1 790 rpm = 18 knots
Range, miles: 1 000 at 13 knots
Complement: 32 (3 officers, 29 ratings)

KOMENDA   1969, Ghana Navy

4 "SPEAR 2" CLASS (COASTAL PATROL CRAFT)

Displacement, tons: 4·5
Dimensions, feet (metres): 30 × 9·5 × 2·8 (9·1 × 2·9 × 0·8)
Guns: 3—0·30 in MG
Main engines: 2 diesels; 2 shafts; 360 hp = 29 knots
Range, miles: 250 at 26 knots
Complement: 3

Supplied by Fairey Marine, UK in 1978.

MINE WARFARE FORCES

1 Ex-BRITISH "TON" CLASS (MINESWEEPER—COASTAL)

Name	No.	Builders	Commissioned
EJURA (ex-HMS *Aldington*)	M 16	Camper and Nicholson	1955

Displacement, tons: 360 standard; 425 full load
Dimensions, feet (metres): 153 × 28·8 × 8·2 (46·7 × 8·6 × 2·4)
Guns: 1—40 mm fwd; 2—20 mm aft
Main engines: Deltic diesels; 2 shafts; 3 000 bhp = 15 knots
Oil fuel, tons: 45
Range, miles: 2 300 at 13 knots
Complement: 27

Lent to Ghana by the UK in 1964. Acquired outright in 1974.

EJURA   1978, Ghana Navy

SERVICE CRAFT

ASUANTSI (ex-*MRC* 1122)

Displacement, tons: 657
Dimensions, feet (metres): 225 pp; 231·3 oa × 39 × 5 (68·6; 70·5 × 11·9 × 1·5)
Main engines: 4 Paxman diesels; 1 840 bhp = 9 knots cruising

Acquired from the UK in 1965 and arrived in Ghana waters in July 1965. Used as a base workshop at Tema Naval Base. Is kept operational, and does a fair amount of seatime in general training and exercise tasks. Converted LCT.

GREECE

Ministerial

Minister of National Defence:
Evangelos Averof

Headquarters Appointments

Chief Hellenic Navy:
Vice-Admiral S. Konofaos
Deputy Chief:
Rear-Admiral J. Vassiliadis

Fleet Command

Commander of the Fleet:
Vice-Admiral T. Deyiannis

Senior Appointments

Deputy Chief National Defence General Staff
Vice-Admiral A. Damiralis
Commander, Navy Training Command
Rear-Admiral S. Hasiotis
Commander, Navy Logistics Command
Rear-Admiral I. Fakidis

Diplomatic Representation

Naval Attaché in Ankara:
Captain M. Danilidis
Naval Attaché in Bonn:
Captain P. Bekyros
Naval Attaché in Cairo:
Captain J. Karras
Naval Attaché in London:
Captain Nikolaos Pappas
Naval Attaché in Washington:
Captain A. Triantafillidis

Personnel

(a) 1978: 19 500 (2 500 officers and 17 000 ratings)
(b) 2 years national service

Naval Bases

Patra, Salamis, Thessaloniki, Suda Bay and Volos (marines).

Naval Commands

Commander of the fleet has under his flag all combatant ships. Navy Logistic Command is responsible for the bases at Salamis and Suda Bay, the Supply Centre and all auxiliary ships. Navy Training Command is in charge of the Naval Officers' Academy, three Petty Officers' Schools, two training centres and a training ship.

Naval Districts: Aegean, Ionian and Northern Greece.

Naval Aviation

1 Squadron Alouette III helicopters with naval crews (4).
14—HU-16B Albatross are operated under naval command by mixed Air Force and Navy crews.
8—AB 212 ASW helicopters (further helicopters to be ordered).

Harbour Corps

This force is equipped with coastal patrol craft and charged with harbour policing and coast guard duties.

Prefix to Ships' Names

H.S. (Hellenic Ship)

Strength of the Fleet

Type	Active	Building
Patrol Submarines	9	2
Destroyers	12	—
Frigates	4	—
Corvettes	5	—
Fast Attack Craft—Missile	10	6
Fast Attack Craft—Torpedo	14	—
Large Patrol Craft	3	—
Fast Attack Craft—Patrol	4	—
Coastal Patrol Craft	5	—
Landing Ships	16	—
LCUs	6	—
Minor Landing Craft	61	—
Minelayers—Coastal	2	—
Minesweepers—Coastal	14	—
Survey Vessels	6	—
Depot Ship	1	—
Training Ships	2	1
Support Tankers	2	—
Harbour Tankers	6	—
Salvage Ship	2	—
Lighthouse Tenders	2	—
Tugs	17	—
Netlayers	1	1
Water Boats	6	—
Auxiliary Transports	2	—

New Construction

Four Type 209 submarines, six Combattante III and ten coastal patrol craft for customs and coast guard duties.

Mercantile Marine

Lloyd's Register of Shipping:
3 666 vessels of 33 956 093 tons gross

DELETIONS

Submarine

1975 *Poseidon*

Light Forces

1976 *Plotarkhis Maridakis, Plotarkhis Vlachavas*

Minesweepers—Coastal

1973 *Afroessa, Kalymnos, Karteria, Kerkyra, Paralos, Zakynthos*

Survey Vessel

1973 *Ariadne*

Minesweeper Depot Ship

1973 *Hermes* (sunk as target)

Harbour Tanker

1976 *Prometheus* (target)

Light House Tenders

1976 *St. Lykoudis, Skyros*

PENNANT NUMBERS

Submarines

S 86	Triaina	
S 110	Glavkos	
S 111	Nereus	
S 112	Triton	
S 113	Proteus	
S 114	Papanikolis	
S 115	Katsonis	
S —	Possidon	
S —	Amphitriti	
S —	Okeanos	
S —	Pontos	

Destroyers and Frigates

D 01	Aetos
D 06	Aspis
D 16	Velos
D 28	Thyella
D 31	Ierax
D 54	Leon
D 56	Lonchi
D 63	Navarinon
D 67	Panthir
D 85	Sfendoni
D 210	Themistocles
D 211	Miaoulis
D 212	Kanaris
D 213	Kountouriotis
D 214	Sachtouris
D 215	Tompazis

Minelayers

N 04	Aktion
N 05	Amvrakia

Minesweepers

M 12	Armatolos
M 58	Mahitis
M 64	Navmachos
M 74	Polemistis
M 202	Atalanti
M 205	Antiopi
M 206	Faedra
M 210	Thalia
M 211	Alkyon
M 213	Klio
M 214	Avra
M 240	Pleias
M 241	Kichli
M 242	Kissa
M 246	Aigli
M 247	Dafni
M 248	Aedon
M 254	Niovi

Light Forces

P 14	Arsianoglou
P 20	Astrapi
P 21	Andromeda
P 22	N. I. Goulandris I
P 23	Kastor
P 24	Kyknos
P 25	Pigassos
P 26	Toxotis
P 28	Kelefstis Stamou
P 29	Diopos Antoniou
P 50	Antihliarpos Laskos
P 51	Plotarhis Blessas
P 52	Ipoploiarhos Troupakis
P 53	Ipoploiarhos Konidis
P 54	Ipoploiarhos Batsis
P 55	Ipoploiarhos Arliotis
P 56	Anthipoploiarhos Anninos
P 57	Ipoploiarhos Mikonios
P 61	E. Panagopoulos
P 70	A. Pezopoulos
P 96	P. Chadzikonstandis
P 196	Esperos
P 197	Kataigis
P 198	Kentavros
P 199	Kyklon
P 225	Skorpios
P 228	Laelaps
P 230	Tyfon
P 267	Dilos
P 268	Lindos
P 269	Knossos
P 286	Adamidis
P 288	Stassis
P 290	N. I. Goulandris II

Amphibious Forces

L 104	Inousse
L 116	Kos
L 144	Syros
L 145	Kassos
L 146	Karpathos
L 147	Kimolos
L 148	Kea
L 149	Kithos
L 150	Sifnos
L 151	Skopelos
L 152	Skiathos
L 153	Nafkratoyssa
L 154	Ikaria
L 157	Rodos
L 158	Limnos
L 161	I. Grigoropoulos
L 162	I. Tournas
L 163	I. Daniolos
L 164	I. Roussen
L 165	I. Krystallidis
L 171	Kriti
L 172	Lesbos
L 179	Samos
L 185	Kithira
L 189	Milos
L 195	Chios

Service Forces

A 03	Aegeon
A 245	Doris
A 307	Thetis
A 329	Sakipis
A 372	Zeus
A 373	Kronos
A 374	Promitheus
A 375	Sirios
A 377	Arethousa
A 407	Antaios
A 409	Achilleus
A 410	Atromitos
A 411	Adamastos
A 412	Aias
A 413	Hephestos
A 414	Ariadni
A 415	Evros
A 416	Ouranos
A 417	Hyperion
A 418	Romaleus
A 419	Pandora
A 420	Pandrosos
A 421	Minotavros
A 423	Heraklis
A 424	Iason
A 425	Odisseus
A 426	Kiklops
A 428	Atlas
A 430	Samson
A 431	Titan
A 432	Gigas
A 443	Kerkini
A 464	Prespe
A 467	Volvi
A 468	Kalliroe
A 470	Kastoria
A 471	Vivies
A 474	Iliki
A 476	Maliopoulos
A 478	Naftilos
A 479	Karavoyianos-Theophilopoulos
A 481	St. Likoudis

216 GREECE / Introduction — Submarines

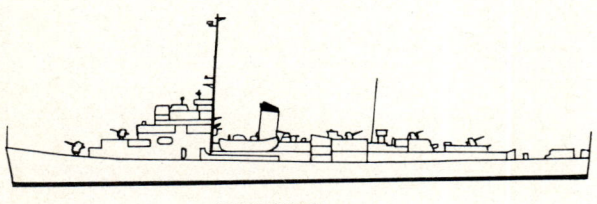
"GEARING FRAM I" Class

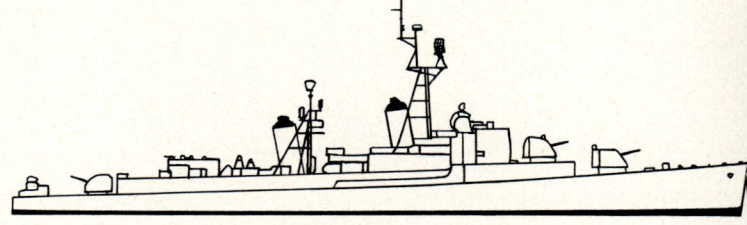
"GEARING FRAM II" Class

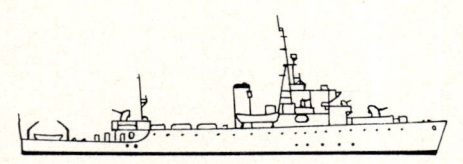
"CANNON" Class

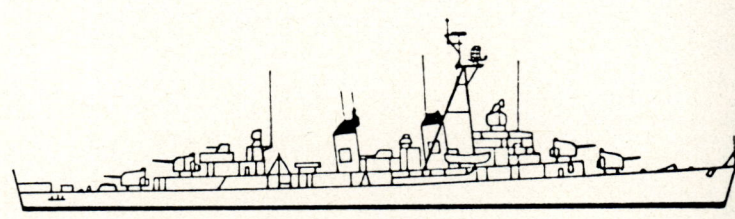
"FLETCHER" Class (4 Guns)

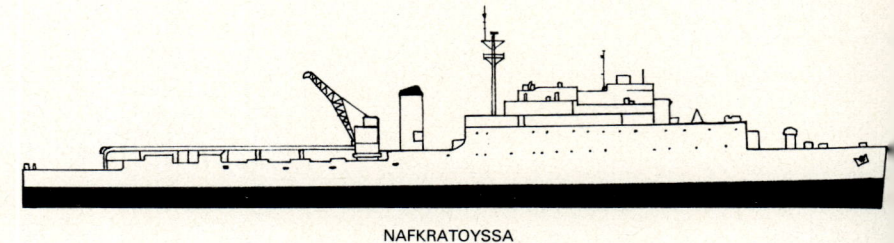
"ALGERINE" Class

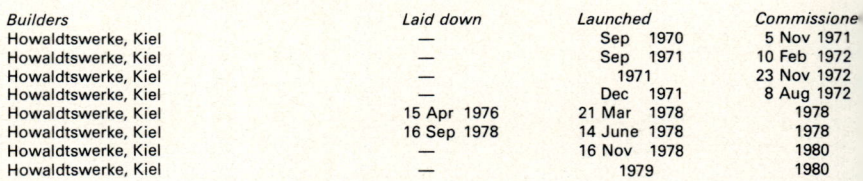
NAFKRATOYSSA

SUBMARINES

6 + 2 TYPE 209 "GLAVKOS" CLASS

Name	No.	Builders	Laid down	Launched	Commissioned
GLAVKOS	S 110	Howaldtswerke, Kiel	—	Sep 1970	5 Nov 1971
NEREUS	S 111	Howaldtswerke, Kiel	—	Sep 1971	10 Feb 1972
TRITON	S 112	Howaldtswerke, Kiel	—	1971	23 Nov 1972
PROTEUS	S 113	Howaldtswerke, Kiel	—	Dec 1971	8 Aug 1972
POSSIDON	—	Howaldtswerke, Kiel	15 Apr 1976	21 Mar 1978	1978
AMPHITRITI	—	Howaldtswerke, Kiel	16 Sep 1978	14 June 1978	1978
OKEANOS	—	Howaldtswerke, Kiel	—	16 Nov 1978	1980
PONTOS	—	Howaldtswerke, Kiel	—	1979	1980

Displacement, tons: 1 100 surfaced; 1 210 dived
Length, feet (metres): 177·1 (54·1)
Beam, feet (metres): 20·3 (6·2)
Draught, feet (metres): 17·9 (5·5)
Torpedo tubes: 8—21 in (with reloads) bow
Main machinery: Diesel-electric; 4 MTU; Siemens diesel-generators; 1 Siemens electric motor; 1 shaft
Speed, knots: 10 surfaced; 22 dived
Endurance: 50 days
Complement: 31

Designed by Ingenieurkontor, Lübeck for construction by Howaldtswerke, Kiel and sale by Ferrostaal Essen all acting as a consortium. Second four ordered 1975-76.
A single-hull design with two ballast tanks and forward and after trim tanks. Fitted with snort and remote machinery control. The single screw is slow revving. Very high capacity batteries with GRP lead-acid cells and battery cooling—by Wilh. Hagen and VARTA. Active and passive sonar, sonar detection equipment, sound ranging and underwater telephone. Fitted with two periscopes, radar and Omega receiver.

TRITON 1973, Hellenic Nav

GREECE / Submarines — Destroyers 217

1 Ex-US "GUPPY III" CLASS

Name	No.	Builders	Laid down	Launched	Commissioned
KATSONIS (ex-USS *Remora*, SS 487)	S 115	Portsmouth Navy Yard	5 Mar 1945	12 July 1945	3 Jan 1946

Displacement, tons: 1 975 standard; 2 450 dived
Dimensions, feet (metres): 326 × 27 × 17 *(99·4 × 8·2 × 5·2)*
Torpedo tubes: 10—21 in; 6 bow, 4 stern
Main machinery: 4 diesels; 6 400 hp;
  2 electric motors; 5 400 shp; 2 shafts
Speed, knots: 20 surfaced; 15 dived
Range, miles: 12 000 at 10 knots (surfaced)
Complement: 85

Originally of the wartime "Tench" class, subsequently converted under the Guppy II programme and, in 1961-62 to Guppy III. Amongst other modifications this involved the fitting of BQG-4 Sonar (Puffs) for dived fire-control, in addition to the BQR-2 array sonar. Transferred 29 October 1973 by sale.

KATSONIS 1978, D. Dervissis

1 Ex-US "GUPPY IIA" CLASS

Name	No.	Builders	Laid down	Launched	Commissioned
PAPANIKOLIS (ex-USS *Hardhead*, SS 365)	S 114	Manitowoc S.B. Co	7 July 1943	12 Dec 1943	Apr 1944

Displacement, tons: 1 840 standard; 2 445 dived
Length, feet (metres): 306 *(93·2)*
Beam, feet (metres): 27 *(8·3)*
Draught, feet (metres): 17 *(5·2)*
Torpedo tubes: 10—21 in; 6 bow, 4 stern
Main machinery: 3 diesels; 4 800 shp;
  2 motors, 5 400 shp; 2 shafts
Speed, knots: 17 surfaced; 15 dived
Range, miles: 12 000 at 10 knots (surfaced)
Complement: 84

Transferred 26 July 1972 by sale.

PAPANIKOLIS 1973, Hellenic Navy

1 Ex-US "BALAO" CLASS

Name	No.	Builders	Laid down	Launched	Commissioned
TRIAINA (ex-USS *Scabbard Fish* SS 397)	S 86	Portsmouth Navy Yard	1943	27 Jan 1944	29 Apr 1944

Displacement, tons: 1 816 surfaced; 2 425 dived
Length, feet (metres): 311·5 *(94·9)*
Beam, feet (metres): 27·0 *(8·2)*
Draught, feet (metres): 17·0 *(5·2)*
Torpedo tubes: 10—21 in *(533 mm)*, 6 bow, 4 stern
Main machinery: 4 diesels; 6 400 hp;
  2 electric motors; 5 400 hp; 2 shafts
Speed, knots: 20 surfaced, 10 dived
Range, miles: 12 000 at 10 knots (surfaced)
Complement: 85

Originally one of the wartime "Balao" class later having a streamlined fin fitted. Transferred 26 February 1965 and by sale in April 1976.

Spares: USS *Lapon* (SS 260) transferred by sale April 1976 for scrapping for spares.

TRIAINA 1978, D. Dervissis

DESTROYERS

1 Ex-US "ALLEN M. SUMNER" CLASS

Name	No.	Builders	Laid down	Launched	Commissioned
MIAOULIS (ex-USS *Ingraham*, DD 694)	211	Federal S.B. & D.D. Co	4 Aug 1943	16 Jan 1944	10 Mar 1944

Displacement, tons: 2 200 standard; 3 320 full load
Length, feet (metres): 376·5 *(114·8)*
Beam, feet (metres): 40·9 *(12·4)*
Draught, feet (metres): 19·0 *(5·8)*
Guns: 6—5 in *(127 mm)*/38 (twins Mk 38)
A/S weapons: 2 triple torpedo launchers, Mk 32;
  2 ahead throwing Hedgehogs
Main engines: 2 geared turbines; 2 shafts; 60 000 shp
Boilers: 4
Speed, knots: 34
Range, miles: 4 600 at 15 knots
Complement: 269 (16 officers, 94 POs, 159 men)

Former fleet destroyer of the "Allen M. Sumner" class which had been modernised under the FRAM II programme. Transferred by USA July 1971.

MIAOULIS 1973, Hellenic Navy

218 GREECE / Destroyers

1 Ex-US "GEARING FRAM II" CLASS
4 Ex-US "GEARING FRAM I" CLASS

Name	No.	Builders	Laid down	Launched	Commissioned
THEMISTOCLES (ex-USS *Frank Knox*, DD 742)	210	Bath Iron Works	8 May 1944	17 Sep 1944	11 Dec 1944
KANARIS (ex-USS *Stickell*, DD 888)	212	Consolidated Steel Corporation	5 Jan 1945	16 June 1945	26 Sep 1945
KOUNTOURIOTIS (ex-USS *Rupertus*, DD 851)	213	Bethlehem (Quincy)	2 May 1945	21 Sep 1945	8 Mar 1946
SACHTOURIS (ex-USS *Arnold J. Isbell*, DD 869)	214	Bethlehem (Staten Island)	14 Mar 1945	6 Aug 1945	5 Jan 1946
TOMPAZIS (ex-USS *Gurke*, DD 783)	215	Todd Pacific Shipyards	Oct 1944	15 Feb 1945	12 May 1945

Displacement, tons: 2 425 standard; 3 500 full load
Length, feet (metres): 390·5 *(119·0)*
Beam, feet (metres): 40·9 *(12·4)*
Draught, feet (metres): 19·0 *(5·8)*
Aircraft: 1 helicopter (see *Alteration* note)
Guns: 6—5 in (*127 mm*)/38 (twins Mk 38) (210); 4—5 in (*127 mm*)/38 (twins Mk 38) (remainder); 1—76 mm OTO Melara Compact (aft); 1—40 mm (fwd)
A/S weapons: 2 fixed Hedgehogs, (*Themistocles*); 1 ASROC 8-barrelled launcher and facilities for small helicopter in remainder
Torpedo tubes: 2 triple (Mk 32)
Main engines: 2 Westinghouse geared turbines; 2 shafts; 60 000 shp
Boilers: 4 Babcock & Wilcox
Speed, knots: 34
Range, miles: 4 800 at 15 knots
Complement: 269 (16 officers, 253 men)

Themistocles was a FRAM II Radar Picket conversion, remainder are FRAM I DD conversions.

Alterations: The modernisation to ships of this class planned to be carried out by CNR, Italy has apparently been shelved. The 76 mm Compact is now mounted on the Helicopter deck so it is unlikely that helo-operations are now possible. This is a little surprising as *Kontouriotis* has an enlarged hangar for an Alouette III helicopter.

Fire control: Mk 37 director with Mk 25 or 28 radar.

Radar: Search: SPS 10.
Fire control: SPS 37 or 40.

Sonar: SQS 23.

Transfers: From USA: *Sachtouris*, 4 Dec 1973 (sold 11 July 1978); *Kanaris*, 1 July 1972; *Kountouriotis*, 10 July 1973 (sold 11 July 1978); *Themistocles* 30 Jan 1971; *Tombazis* by sale 17 Mar 1977, commissioned 20 Mar 1977.

THEMISTOCLES (FRAM II)   *1978, D. Dervissis*

KOUNTOURIOTIS   *1978, D. Dervissis*

6 Ex-US "FLETCHER" CLASS

Name	No.	Builders	Laid down	Launched	Commissioned
ASPIS (ex-USS *Conner*, DD 582)	06	Boston Navy Yard	16 Apr 1942	18 July 1942	8 June 1943
VELOS (ex-USS *Charette*, DD 581)	16	Boston Navy Yard	20 Feb 1941	3 June 1942	18 May 1943
THYELLA (ex-USS *Bradford*, DD 545)	28	Bethlehem (S. Pedro)	28 Apr 1942	12 Dec 1942	12 June 1943
LONCHI ((ex-USS *Hall*, DD 583)	56	Boston Navy Yard	16 Apr 1942	18 July 1942	6 July 1943
NAVARINON (ex-USS *Brown*, DD 546)	63	Bethlehem (S. Pedro)	27 June 1942	22 Feb 1943	10 July 1943
SFENDONI (ex-USS *Aulick*, DD 569)	85	Consolidated Steel Corporation, Texas	14 May 1941	2 Mar 1942	27 Oct 1942

Displacement, tons: 2 100 standard; 3 050 full load
Length, feet (metres): 376·5 *(114·7)*
Beam, feet (metres): 39·5 *(12·0)*
Draught, feet (metres): 18 *(5·5)*
Guns: 4—5 in (*127 mm*)/38 in *Aspis, Lonchi, Sfendoni* and *Velos,* 5—5 in *Navarinon* and *Thyella*
6—3 in (*76 mm*)/55 (twin Mk 33), in *Aspis, Lonchi, Sfendoni* and *Velos.* 10—40 mm/60 (2 quad, 1 twin) in *Navarinon* and *Thyella*
A/S weapons: Hedgehogs; DCs
Torpedo tubes: 5—21 in (*533 mm*), (quin), in *Aspis, Lonchi, Sfendoni* and *Velos,* none in *Navarinon* and *Thyella*
Torpedo racks: Side-launching for A/S torpedoes
Main engines: 2 sets GE geared turbines; 2 shafts; 60 000 shp
Boilers: 4 Babcock & Wilcox; 615 psi *(43·5 km/cm²)* 800°F *(427°C)*
Speed, knots: 32
Range, miles: 6 000 at 15 knots; 1 260 at full power
Oil fuel, tons: 506
Complement: 250

Transferred from USA, *Aspis, Lonchi* and *Velos* at Long Beach, Cal, on 15 September 1959, 9 February 1960 and 15 June 1959, respectively, *Sfendoni* at Philadelphia on 21 August 1959, *Navarinon* and *Thyella* at Seattle, Wash, on 27 September 1962. All purchased 25 April 1977.

Electronics: Reported that whole class has received extensive electronic modernisation.

Fire control: Single Mk 37 director with Mk 25 or 28 radar for 5-in guns. Two Mk 63 directors with SPG-34 radar and one Mk 56 director with Mk 35 radar for 3 in guns. Mk 51 directors for 40 mm guns.

Radar: Search: SPS 6, SPS 10.

Sonar: SQS 23.

VELOS   *1973, Dr. Giorgia Arra*

GREECE / Frigates — Light forces 219

FRIGATES

Note: Depot ship *Aegeon* currently employed on frigate duties.

4 Ex-US "CANNON" CLASS

Name	No.	Builders	Laid down	Launched	Commissioned
AETOS (ex-USS *Slater*, DE 766)	01	Tampa S.B. Co	9 Mar 1943	13 Feb 1944	1 May 1944
IERAX (ex-USS *Elbert*, DE 768)	31	Tampa S.B. Co	1 Apr 1943	23 May 1944	12 July 1944
LEON (ex-USS *Eldridge*, DE 173)	54	Federal S.B. & D.D. Co	22 Feb 1943	25 June 1943	27 Aug 1943
PANTHIR (ex-USS *Garfield Thomas*, DE 193)	67	Federal S.B. & D.D. Co	23 Sep 1943	12 Dec 1943	24 Jan 1944

Displacement, tons: 1 240 standard; 1 900 full load
Length, feet (metres): 306 *(93·3)*
Beam, feet (metres): 36·7 *(11·2)*
Draught, feet (metres): 14 *(4·3)*
Guns: 3—3 in *(76 mm)*/50 (single Mk 22);
　6—40 mm/60 (3 twin Mk 1);
　14—20 mm/70 (twins)
A/S weapons: Hedgehog; 8 DCT; 1 DC rack
Torpedo racks: Side launching for A/S torpedoes
Main engines: 4 sets General Motors diesel-electric;
　6 000 bhp; 2 shafts
Speed, knots: 19·25
Oil fuel, tons: 316
Range, miles: 9 000 at 12 knots
Complement: 220

Aetos and *Ierax* were transferred on 15 March 1951 and *Leon* and *Panthir* on 15 January 1951. Their three—21 in torpedo tubes in a triple mount were removed.

PANTHIR　　　　　　　　　　　　　　　　　　　　　　1977, Michael D. J. Lennon

LIGHT FORCES

4 + 6 "LA COMBATTANTE III" CLASS (FAST ATTACK CRAFT—MISSILE)

Name	No.	Builders	Commissioned
ANTIPLOIARHOS LASKOS	P 50	Construction M. de Normandie	20 Apr 1977
PLOTARHIS BLESSAS	P 51	Construction M. de Normandie	7 July 1977
IPOPLOIARHOS TROUPAKIS	P 52	Construction M. de Normandie	8 Nov 1977
IPOPLOIARHOS MIKONIOS	P 53	Construction M. de Normandie	10 Feb 1978
—	—	Hellenic Shipyards, Skaramanga	1980
—	—	Hellenic Shipyards, Skaramanga	1980
—	—	Hellenic Shipyards, Skaramanga	1980
—	—	Hellenic Shipyards, Skaramanga	1981
—	—	Hellenic Shipyards, Skaramanga	1981
—	—	Hellenic Shipyards, Skaramanga	1981

Displacement, tons: 385 standard; 425 full load (first four); 329 standard; 429 full load (second group)
Dimensions, feet (metres): 184 × 23·7 × 7 *(56·2 × 7·4 × 2·1)*
Missiles: SSM; 4 Exocet (single cells) (first four); SSM; 6 Penguin II (second group)
Guns: 2—76 mm/62 (single Compact); 4—30 mm Emerlec (twins) (first four);
　1—76 mm/62 (single Compact); 2—40 mm (twins) (second group)
Torpedo tubes: 2—21 in *(533 mm)*
Main engines: 4 MTU MD20V-538-TB-91 diesels; 18 000 bhp;
　4 shafts (cp propellers) = 35·7 knots
Range, miles: 700 at 32·6 knots; 2 000 at 15 knots
Complement: 42

IPOPLOIARHOS TROUPAKIS　　　　　　　　　　　6/1977, John Mortimer

First four ordered in September 1974. *A. Laskos* laid down 28 June 1975, launched 6 July 1976; *P. Blessas* laid down 28 October 1975, launched 10 November 1976; *I. Troupakis* laid down 27 January 1976, launched 25 January 1977, *I. Mikonios* laid down 7 April 1976, launched 5 May 1977. Second group of six ordered 1978, first pair laid down mid-1978.

Electronics: Thomson-CSF Vega II system.
Radar: Surveillance and navigation: One Triton
Fire control: I band

4 "LA COMBATTANTE II" CLASS
(FAST ATTACK CRAFT—MISSILE)

Name	No.	Builders	Commissioned
POPLOIARHOS KONIDIS (ex-*Kymothoi*)	P 53	C. M. de Normandie, Cherbourg	July 1972
IPOPLOIARHOS BATSIS (ex-*Calypso*)	P 54	C. M. de Normandie, Cherbourg	Dec 1971
POPLOIARHOS ARLIOTIS (ex-*Evniki*)	P 55	C. M. de Normandie, Cherbourg	Apr 1972
ANTHIIPLOIARHOS ANNINOS (ex-*Navsithoi*)	P 56	C. M. de Normandie, Cherbourg	June 1972

Displacement, tons: 234 standard; 255 full load
Dimensions, feet (metres): 154·2 × 23·3 × 8·2 *(47 × 7·1 × 2·5)*
Missiles: SSM; 4 Exocet (single cells)
Guns: 4—35 mm/90 (twin Oerlikon)
Torpedo tubes: 2 aft for wire-guided torpedoes
Main engines: 4 MTU diesels; 4 shafts; 12 000 bhp = 36·5 knots
Oil fuel, tons: 39
Range, miles: 850 at 25 knots
Complement: 40 (4 officers, and 36 men)

IPOPLOIARHOS KONIDIS　　　　　　　　　　　　　1973, Hellenic Navy

Ordered in 1969. Fitted with Thomson CSF Triton radar and Plessey IFF Mk 10. *I. Arliotis* launched 26 April 1971. *I. Anninos* launched 8 September 1971. *I. Batsis* launched 26 January 1971. *I. Konidis* launched 20 December 1971.

220 GREECE / Light forces

2 FAST ATTACK CRAFT (MISSILE)

Name	No.	Builders	Commissioned
KELEFSTIS STAMOU	P 28	Ch. N. de l'Esterel	1975
DIOMO ANTONIOU	P 29	Ch. N. de l'Esterel	1975

Displacement, tons: 80
Dimensions, feet (metres): 105 × 19 × 5·3 *(32 × 5·8 × 1·6)*
Missiles: 4—SS 12
Guns: 1—40 mm Bofors; 1—20 mm
Main engines: 2 MTU 12V 331 TC81 diesels; 2 720 hp = 30 knots
Range, miles: 1 500 at 15 knots
Complement: 17

Wooden hulls. Originally ordered for Cyprus; later transferred to Greece.

KELEFSTIS STAMOU *1976, Chantiers Navals de l'Esterel*

5 "NASTY" CLASS (FAST ATTACK CRAFT—TORPEDO)

Name	No.	Builders	Commissioned
ANDROMEDA	P 21	Mandal, Norway	Feb 1967
KASTOR	P 23	Mandal, Norway	1967
KYKNOS	P 24	Mandal, Norway	1967
PIGASSOS	P 25	Mandal, Norway	1967
TOXOTIS	P 26	Mandal, Norway	1967

Displacement, tons: 69 standard; 76 full load
Dimensions, feet (metres): 80·4 × 24·6 × 6·9 *(24·5 × 7·5 × 2·1)*
Torpedo tubes: 4—21 in *(533 mm)*
Guns: 2—40 mm
Main engines: 2 Napier Deltic T 18-37 K diesels; 3 100 bhp = 43 knots
Complement: 22

Andromeda and *Iniohos* (deleted 1972) were taken over in February 1967 from Mandal, Norway. *Kastor* and *Kyknos,* and the third pair, *Pigassos* and *Toxotis,* were delivered in succession in 1967.

ANDROMEDA *1974, Hellenic Navy*

7 Ex-GERMAN "JAGUAR" CLASS (FAST ATTACK CRAFT—TORPEDO)

Name	No.	Builders	Commissioned
HESPEROS (ex-*Seeadler* P 6068)	P 196	FDR	1958
KATAIGIS (ex-*Falke* P 6072)	P 197	FDR	1958
KENTAUROS (ex-*Habricht* P 6075)	P 198	FDR	1958
KYKLON (ex-*Grief* P 6071)	P 199	FDR	1958
LELAPS (ex-*Kondor* P 6070)	P 228	FDR	1958
SCORPIOS (ex-*Kormoran* P 6077)	P 229	FDR	1958
TYFON (ex-*Geier* P 6073)	P 230	FDR	1958

Displacement, tons: 160 standard; 190 full load
Dimensions, feet (metres): 139·4 × 23·4 × 7·9 *(42·5 × 7·2 × 2·4)*
Guns: 2—40 mm Bofors L70 (single)
Torpedo tubes: 4—21 in *(533 mm)*
Main engines: 4 diesels; 4 shafts; 12 000 bhp—42 knots
Complement: 39

Transferred 1976-77. *Kataigis, Kyklon, Tyfon* commissioned in Hellenic Navy 12 December 1976. *Hesperos* and *Lelaps* on 24 March 1977 and *Kentauros* and *Scorpios* on 22 May 1977. Three others (ex-*Albatros*, ex-*Bussard* and ex-*Sperber*) transferred at same time for spares. Built by Lürssen Vegesack or Kroger Rendsburg.

TYFON (before transfer) *1975, Reiner Nerlich*

1 VOSPER "BRAVE" CLASS (FAST ATTACK CRAFT—TORPEDO)

Name	No.	Builders	Commissioned
ASTRAPI (ex-*Strahl* P 6194)	P 20	Vosper, Portsmouth	21 Nov 1962

Displacement, tons: 95 standard; 110 full load
Dimensions, feet (metres): 99 × 25 × 7 *(30·2 × 7·6 × 2·1)*
Torpedo chutes: 4—21 in side launching
Guns: 2—40 mm
Main engines: 3 Bristol Siddeley Marine Proteus gas turbines; 3 shafts; 12 750 bhp = 55·5 knots

Launched on 10 January 1962. Commissioned in Federal German Navy on 21 November 1962. Transferred to Hellenic Navy in April 1967. Refitted by Vosper in 1968. Of similar design to British "Brave" class.

ASTRAPI *1972, Hellenic Navy*

1 VOSPER "FEROCITY" CLASS (FAST ATTACK CRAFT—TORPEDO)

Name	No.	Builders	Commissioned
AIOLOS (ex-*Pfeil* P 6193)	P 19	Vosper, Portsmouth	27 June 1962

Displacement, tons: 75 standard; 80 full load
Dimensions, feet (metres): 95 × 23·9 × 6·5 *(29 × 7·3 × 2)*
Torpedo chutes: 4—21 in side launching
Guns: 2—40 mm
Main engines: 2 Bristol Siddeley Marine Proteus gas turbines; 2 shafts; 8 500 bhp = 50 knots

Launched on 26 October 1961. Commissioned in German Navy on 27 June 1962. Transferred to Hellenic Navy in April 1967. Refitted by Vosper in 1968. Based on design of Vosper prototype *Ferocity*.

AIOLOS *1972, Hellenic Navy*

GREECE / Light forces — Amphibious forces

4 + 3 + 3 FAST ATTACK CRAFT—PATROL/TORPEDO

Displacement, tons: 74·5 standard; 86 full load
Dimensions, feet (metres): 95·1 × 16·2 × 5·6 *(29 × 5 × 1·7)*
Torpedo tubes: 2—21 in *(533 mm)* (naval version)
Main engines: 2 MTU 12V-331-TO-81 diesels; 2 shafts; 2 720 = 27 knots
Complement: 15

Ordered from Hellenic Shipyards, Skaramanga in May 1976 to a design by Abeking and Rasmussen. The first was launched in November 1977 and completed January 1978 for the Coast Guard. Two more are building for the Coast Guard, three for the Customs Service and four for the navy.

3 Ex-US "PGM-9" CLASS (LARGE PATROL CRAFT)

PLOIARHOS ARSLANOGLOU (ex-*PGM 25*, ex-*PC 1565*) P 14
ANTIPLOIARHOS PEZOPOULOS (ex-*PGM 21*, ex-*PC 1552*) P 70
PLOIARHOS CHADZIKONSTANDIS (ex-*PGM 29*, ex-*PC 1565*) P 96

Displacement, tons: 335 standard; 439 full load
Dimensions, feet (metres): 174·7 × 23 × 10·8 *(53·8 × 7 × 3·3)*
Guns: 1—3 in; 6—20 mm
A/S weapons: Hedgehog; side launching torpedo racks; depth charges
Main engines: 2 General Motors diesels; 2 shafts; 3 600 bhp = 19 knots

All launched in 1943-44. Acquired from USA in August 1947. The two 40 mm guns were removed and a Hedgehog was installed in 1963.

ANTHIPLOIARHOS PEZOPOULOS *Hellenic Navy*

3 + ? COASTAL PATROL CRAFT

Name	No.	Builders	Commissioned
N. I. GOULANDRIS I	P 22	Syros Shipyard	25 June 1975
E. PANAGOPOULOS	P 61	Syros Shipyard	23 June 1976
N. I. GOULANDRIS II	P 290	Syros Shipyard	6 June 1977

Displacement, tons: 38·5
Dimensions, feet (metres): 78·7 × 20·3 × 3·4 *(24 × 6·2 × 1·1)*
Main engines: 2 diesels; 2 700 hp = 30 knots
Range, miles: 1 600 at cruising speed

The first of these craft was donated to the Hellenic Navy by the wealthy shipowner after whom she is named. She is lead craft of a number of the same type, most of them donated by Greek shipowners. P 290 launched and commissioned on 6 June 1977.

2 Ex-FDR "KW" CLASS

ARHIKELEFSTIS STASSIS   **ARHIKELEFSTIS MALIOPOULOS**

Transferred 1976.

AMPHIBIOUS FORCES

1 Ex-US "CABILDO" CLASS (LSD)

Name	No.	Builders	Commissioned
NAFKRATOUSSA	L 153	Boston Navy Yard	31 Oct 1945
(ex-USS *Fort Mandan*, LSD 21)			

Displacement, tons: 4 790 light; 9 357 full load
Dimensions, feet (metres): 457·8 × 72·2 × 18 *(139·6 × 22 × 5·5)*
Guns: 8—40 mm
Main engines: Geared turbines; 2 shafts; 7 000 shp = 15·4 knots
Boilers: 2

Laid down on 2 January 1945. Launched on 22 May 1945. Taken over from USA in 1971 replacing the previous *Nafkratoussa* (ex-*Hyperion*, ex-LSD 9) out of service in 1971 as Headquarters ship of Captain, Landing Forces.

NAFKRATOUSSA *1973, Hellenic Navy*

2 Ex-US "TERREBONNE PARISH" CLASS (LSTs)

Name	No.	Builders	Commissioned
INOUSE (ex-USS *Terrell County*, LST 1157)	L 104	Bath Iron Works Corporation	19 Mar 1953
KOS (ex-USS *Whitfield County*, LST 1169)	L 116	Christy Corporation	14 Sep 1954

Displacement, tons: 2 590 light; 5 800 full load
Dimensions, feet (metres): 384 × 55 × 17 *(117·1 × 16·7 × 5·2)*
Guns: 6—3 in/50
Main engines: 4 General Motors diesels; 6 000 bhp; 2 shafts (cp propellers) = 15 knots
Complement: 115
Troops: 395

Part of class of fifteen—Transferred 17 March 1977 by sale. Towed to Greece for reactivation and modernisation.

KOS *1978, D. Dervissis*

8 Ex-US "511—1152" (2) and "1—510" (6) CLASSES (LSTs)

511—1152 Series
IKARIA (ex-USS *Potter County*, LST 1086) L 154
KRITI (ex-USS *Page County*, LST 1076) L 171

1—510 Series
SYROS (ex-USS *LST 325*) L 144
RODOS (ex-USS *Bowman County*, LST 391) L 157
LIMNOS (ex-USS *LST 36*) L 158
LESBOS (ex-USS *Boone County*, LST 389) L 172
SAMOS (ex-USS *LST 33*) L 179
CHIOS (ex-USS *LST 35*) L 195

Displacement, tons: 1 653 standard; 2 366 beaching; 4 080 full load
Dimensions, feet (metres): 328 × 50 × 14 *(100 × 15·3 × 2·9)*
Guns: 8—40 mm; 6—20 mm (*Rodos* 10—40 mm)
Main engines: 2 General Motors diesels; 2 shafts; 1 700 bhp = 11·6 knots
Range, miles: 9 500 at 9 knots
Complement: 93 (8 officers, 85 men)

KRITI *1978, D. Dervissis*

Former US tank landing ships. Cargo capacity 2 100 tons. *Ikaria*, *Lesbos* and *Rodos* were transferred to the Hellenic Navy on 9 August 1960. *Syros* was transferred on 29 May 1964 at Portsmouth, Virginia, under MAP. *Kriti* was transferred in March 1971 and sold 11 July 1978, the others being provided under lease-lend in 1943.

222 GREECE / Amphibious forces — Mine warfare forces

5 Ex-US "LSM 1" CLASS

IPOPLOIARHOS GRIGOROPOULOS (ex-USS *LSM 45*) L 161
IPOPLOIARHOS TOURNAS (ex-USS *LSM 102*) L 162
IPOPLOIARHOS DANIOLOS (ex-USS *LSM 227*) L 163
IPOPLOIARHOS ROUSSEN (ex-USS *LSM 399*) L 164
IPOPLOIARHOS KRISTALIDIS (ex-USS *LSM 541*) L 165

Displacement, tons: 743 beaching; 1 095 full load
Dimensions, feet (metres): 203·5 × 34·2 × 8·3 *(62·1 × 10·4 × 2·5)*
Guns: 2—40 mm; 8—20 mm
Main engines: Diesel direct drive; 2 shafts; 3 600 bhp = 13 knots

LSM 541 was handed over to Greece at Salamis on 30 October 1958 and *LSM 45*, *LSM 102*, *LSM 227* and *LSM 399* at Portsmouth, Virginia on 3 November 1958. All were renamed after naval heroes killed during World War 2.

IPOPLOIARHOS KRISTALIDIS   *1974, Hellenic Navy*

6 Ex-US "LCU 501" CLASS (Ex-LCT 6)

Name	No.	Builders	Commissioned
KASSOS (ex-*LCU 1382*)	L 145	Mare Island Naval Yard	30 Nov 1944
KARPATHOS (ex-*LCU 1379*)	L 146	Mare Island Naval Yard	17 Nov 1944
KIMOLOS (ex-*LCU 971*)	L 147	Mare Island Naval Yard	1 Feb 1944
KITHNOS (ex-*LCU 763*)	L 149	Missouri Valley Bridge and Iron Co	24 Dec 1944
SIFNOS (ex-*LCU 677*)	L 150	Pidgeon-Thomas Iron Co	11 Mar 1944
SKIATHOS (ex-*LCU 827*)	L 152	Kansas City Steel	10 Apr 1944

Displacement, tons: 143 standard; 309 full load
Dimensions, feet (metres): 119 × 32·7 × 5 *(36·3 × 10 × 1·5)*
Guns: 2—20 mm
Main engines: Diesels; 3 shafts; 440 bhp = 8 knots
Complement: 13

Former US Utility Landing Craft of the *LCU* (ex-*LCT 6*) type. *Skiathos* acquired in 1959. *Kithnos* and *Sifnos* were transferred from USA in 1961, and *Karpathos*, *Kassos* and *Kimolos* in 1962.

KITHNOS   *1971, Hellenic Navy*

13 Ex-US LCMs

Transferred from USA.

14 LCPs

Ordered from Greek shipyards in 1977.

34 Ex-US LCVPs

Transferred from USA.

MINE WARFARE FORCES

2 COASTAL MINELAYERS

Name	No.	Builders	Commissioned
AKTION (ex-*LSM 301*, ex-*MMC 6*)	N 04	Charleston Naval Shipyard	1 Jan 1945
AMVRAKIA (ex-*LSM 303*, ex-*MMC 7*)	N 05	Charleston Naval Shipyard	6 Jan 1945

Displacement, tons: 720 standard; 1 100 full load
Dimensions, feet (metres): 203·5 × 34·5 × 8·3 *(62·1 × 10·5 × 2·5)*
Guns: 8—40 mm (4 twin); 6—20 mm (single)
Mines: Capacity 100 to 130
Main engines: 2 diesels; 2 shafts; 3 600 bhp = 12·5 knots
Range, miles: 3 000 at 12 knots
Complement: 65

Former US "LSM 1" Class. *Aktion* was launched on 1 January 1945 and *Amvrakia* on 14 November 1944. Converted in the USA into minelayers for the Hellenic Navy. Underwent extensive rebuilding from the deck up. Twin rudders. Transferred on 1 December 1953.

AMVRAKIA   *1974, Hellenic Navy*

9 US "MSC 294" CLASS (MINESWEEPERS—COASTAL)

Name	No.	Builders	Commissioned
ALKYON (ex-*MSC 319*)	M 211	Peterson Builders	3 Dec 1968
ARGO (ex-*MSC 317*)	M 213	Peterson Builders	7 Aug 1968
AVRA (ex-*MSC 318*)	M 214	Peterson Builders	3 Oct 1968
PLEIAS (ex-*MSC 314*)	M 240	Peterson Builders	22 June 1967
KICHLI (ex-*MSC 308*)	M 241	Peterson Builders	14 July 1964
KISSA (ex-*MSC 309*)	M 242	Peterson Builders	1 Sep 1964
AIGLI (ex-*MSC 299*)	M 246	Tacoma, California	4 Jan 1965
DAFNI (ex-*MSC 307*)	M 247	Peterson Builders	23 Sep 1964
AEDON (ex-*MSC 310*)	M 248	Peterson Builders	13 Oct 1964

Displacement, tons: 320 standard; 370 full load
Dimensions, feet (metres): 144 × 28 × 8·2 *(43·3 × 8·5 × 2·5)*
Guns: 2—20 mm (twin)
Main engines: 2 General Motors diesels; 2 shafts; 880 bhp = 13 knots
Complement: 39

Built in USA for Greece. Wooden hulls.

AVRA   *1974, Hellenic Navy*

5 Ex-US "ADJUTANT" CLASS (MINESWEEPERS—COASTAL)

ATALANTI (ex-Belgian *St. Truiden*, M 919, ex-USS *MSC 169*) M 202
ANTIOPI (ex-Belgian *Herve*, M 921, ex-USS *MSC 153*) M 205
FAEDRA (ex-Belgian *Malmedy*, M 922, ex-USS *MSC 154*) M 206
THALIA (ex-Belgian *Blankenberge*, M 923, ex-USS *MSC 170*) M 210
NIOVI (ex-Belgian *Laroche*, M 924, ex-USS *MSC 171*) M 254

Displacement, tons: 330 standard; 402 full load
Dimensions, feet (metres): 145·0 × 27·9 × 8·0 *(44·2 × 8·5 × 2·4)*
Guns: 2—20 mm Oerlikon (1 twin)
Main engines: 2 General Motors diesels; 2 shafts; 900 bhp = 14 knots
Complement: 38 officers and men

Originally supplied to Belgium under MDAP. Subsequently returned to USA and simultaneously transferred to Greece as follows: 29 July 1969 (*Herve* and *St. Truiden*) and 26 September 1969 (*Laroche*, *Malmedy* and *Blankenberge*). *Atalanti* employed on surveying duties.

ANTIOPI   *1973, Dr. Giorgio Arra*

GREECE / Survey and research vessels — Service forces 223

SURVEY AND RESEARCH VESSELS

Name	No.	Builders	Commissioned
NAFTILOS	A 478	Annastadiades Tsortanides (Perama)	3 Apr 1976

Displacement, tons: 1 400
Dimensions, feet (metres): 207 × 38 × 13·3 (63·1 × 11·6 × 4·2)
Main engine: 1 Babcock & Wilcox diesel; 2 640 hp = 15 knots
Complement: 74 (8 officers, 66 men)

Launched 19 November 1975. Trials February 1976.

MALIOPOULOS A 476

DORIS A 245

Transferred from minesweeping duties. Details as for "MSC 294" class. Built by Tacoma, USA and commissioned on 9 November 1964. Complement three officers and 32 men.

ATALANTI M 202

Of "Adjutant" class MSCs. For details see Mine Warfare Forces.

1 Ex-US "BARNEGAT" CLASS

Name	No.	Builders	Commissioned
HEPHESTOS (ex-USNS *Josiah Willard Gibbs*, T-AGOR 1, ex-USS *San Carlos*, AVP 51)	A 413	Lake Washington Shipyard, Houghton, Wash.	21 Mar 1944

Displacement, tons: 1 750 standard; 2 800 full load
Dimensions, feet (metres): 310·8 × 41·2 × 13·5 (94·8 × 12·6 × 4·1)
Main engines: 2 Fairbanks-Morse diesels; 2 shafts; 6 080 bhp = 18 knots
Range, miles: 10 000 at 14 knots
Endurance: 30 days
Complement: 82 (8 officers and 74 men)

Former US seaplane tender converted for oceanographic research. Laid down on 7 September 1942, launched on 20 December 1942. Transferred to the Hellenic Navy on 7 December 1971. Purchased 15 February 1977. In reserve.

HEPHESTOS 1974, Hellenic Navy

1 SURVEYING LAUNCH

Of 25 tons, launched in 1940. Complement nine.

SERVICE FORCES

1 NEW CONSTRUCTION TRAINING SHIP

ARIS

Displacement, tons: 4 500
Length, feet (metres): 310·8 (94·8)
Main engines: 2 MAK diesels; 2 shafts; 10 000 hp = 20 knots
Complement: 500 (officers and cadets)

Laid down October 1976 at Salamis. Launched 4 October 1978. To be fitted with helicopter facilities.

1 Ex-FDR DEPOT SHIP

Name	No.	Builders	Commissioned
AEGEON (ex-*Weser* A 62)	A 03	Elsflether Werft	1960

Displacement, tons: 2 370
Dimensions, feet (metres): 323·5 × 38·8 × 11·2 (99 × 11·8 × 3·4)
Guns: 2—3·9 in (100 mm); 4—40 mm
Main engines: 6 diesels; 12 000 hp
Speed, knots: 20·5
Range, miles: 1 625 at 15 knots (economical)
Complement: 110

Transferred July 1975. Currently employed on frigate duties and as FAC support ship.

AEGEON (Old Pennant number) 7/1976, Roland Wiegran

2 Ex-US "PATAPSCO" CLASS (SUPPORT TANKERS)

Name	No.	Builders	Commissioned
ARETHOUSA (ex-USS *Natchaug*, AOG 54)	A 377	Cargill Inc, Savage, Minn.	11 June 1945
ARIADNI (ex-USS *Tombigbee*, AOG 11)	A 414	Cargill Inc, Savage, Minn.	12 July 1944

Displacement, tons: 1 850 light; 4 335 full load
Measurement, tons: 2 575 deadweight; cargo capacity 2 040
Dimensions, feet (metres): 310·8 × 48·5 × 15·7 (93·2 × 14·8 × 4·8)
Guns: 4—3 in/50
Main engines: General Motors diesels; 2 shafts; 3 300 bhp = 14 knots
Complement: 43 (6 officers, 37 men)

Former US petrol carriers. *Arethousa* laid down on 15 August 1944. Launched on 16 December 1944. Transferred from the USA to Greece under the Mutual Defense Assistance Program in July 1959 and *Ariadni* transferred 7 July 1972 (sold 11 July 1978), both at Pearl Harbor.

ARIADNI 10/1978, D. Dervissis

1 AMMUNITION SHIP

Name	No.	Builders	Commissioned
EVROS (ex-FDR *Schwarzwald* A1400, ex-*Amalthee*)	A 415	Ch. Dubigeon Nantes	1957

Measurement, tons: 1 667 gross
Dimensions, feet (metres): 263·1 × 39 × 15·1 (80·2 × 11·9 × 4·6)
Guns: 4—40 mm Bofors
Main engines: Sulzer diesel; 3 000 bhp = 15 knots

Bought by FDR from Societé Navale Caënnaise in February 1960. Transferred to Greece 6 June 1976.

EVROS (as *Schwarzwald*) 1971

224   GREECE / Service forces — Floating cranes

2 HARBOUR TANKERS

Name	No.	Builders	Commissioned
OURANOS	A 416	Greece	Feb 1977
HYPERION	A 417	Greece	Feb 1977

Displacement, tons: 1 200

Order announced 24 June 1976.

1 HARBOUR TANKER

SIRIOS (ex-*Poseidon*, ex-*Empire Faun*) A 345

Formerly on loan from the UK, but purchased outright in 1962. This ship was renamed *Sirios* when the name *Poseidon* was given to the submarine *Lapon* acquired from the USA in 1958. Capacity 850 tons.

1 HARBOUR TANKER

VIVIES A 471

Originally a water carrier. Capacity 687 tons.

1 PETROL CARRIER

ZEUS (ex-YOG 98) A 372

Dimensions, feet (metres): 165 × 35 × 10 *(50·3 × 10·2 × 3·2)*

Former US yard petrol carrier. Launched in 1944. Capacity 900 tons.

1 HARBOUR TANKER

KRONOS (ex-*Islay*, ex-*Dresden*) A 373

Displacement, tons: 311
Capacity: 110 tons

CORVETTES

2 Ex-BRITISH "ALGERINE" CLASS (TRAINING SHIPS)

Name	No.	Builders	Commissioned
PYRPOLITIS (ex-HMS *Arcturus*)	A 476	Redfern Construction Co	23 Oct 1943
POLEMISTIS (ex-HMS *Gozo*)	M 74	Redfern Construction Co	29 Sep 1943

Displacement, tons: 1 030 standard; 1 325 full load
Length, feet (metres): 225 *(68·6)*
Beam, feet (metres): 35·5 *(10·8)*
Draught, feet (metres): 11·5 *(3·5)*
Guns: 1—3 in *(76 mm)* (US Mark 21) (none in *Polemistis*); 4—20 mm (US), 2 MG
A/S weapons: 2 to 4 DCT
Main engines: 2 triple expansion, 2 shafts; 2 700 ihp
Speed, knots: 16
Boilers: 2 Yarrow, 250 psi *(17·6 kg cm²)*
Oil fuel, tons: 235
Range, miles: 5 000 at 10 knots; 2 270 at 14·5 knots
Complement: 85

Former British ocean minesweepers. Acquired from the Executive Committee of Surplus Allied Material.

Class: *Armatolos* sunk as target for Exocet on 25 May 1977. *Mahitis* and *Navmachos* deleted in 1976 one being sunk as a target.

Duties: Now employed variously as training ships and personnel transports. *Pyrpolitis* normally operates for the Petty officers' School at Poros.

MISCELLANEOUS

4 YACHTS

THESEUS

Ex-Royal Yacht used for VIP visits.

CHRISTINA (ex-HMCS *Stormont*)

Presented by Miss Christina Onassis and commissioned on 12 July 1978. Originally RCN "River" class frigate of 1 445 tons standard built by Vickers Montreal in 1943. Sold 1947—renamed *Christina* in 1951.

ARGO

KERAVNOS

1 + 1 NETLAYERS

Name	No.	Builders	Commissioned
THETIS (ex-USS AN 103)	A 307	Kröger, Rendsburg	Apr 1960
—	—	Kröger, Randsburg	1979

Displacement, tons: 680 standard; 805 full load
Dimensions, feet (metres): 169·5 × 33·5 × 11·8 *(51·7 × 10·2 × 3·6)*
Guns: 1—40 mm; 4—20 mm
Main engines: MAN diesels; 1 shaft; 1 400 bhp = 12 knots
Complement: 48

US offshore order. *Thetis* launched in 1959. Second ordered 1977.

4 SEA-AIR RESCUE LAUNCHES

DILOS P 267   KNOSSOS P 269
LINDOS P 268   ADAMIDIS P 286

Belong to the Air Force SAR Centre but are manned and maintained by the Navy.

2 AUXILIARY TRANSPORTS

Name	No.	Builders	Commissioned
PANDORA	A 419	Perama Shipyard	1973
PANDROSOS	A 420	Perama Shipyard	1974

Displacement, tons: 350
Length, feet (metres): 212·2 *(64·6)*
Speed, knots: 13

Launched 1972 and 1973. Transport capacity for 500 people.

2 LIGHTHOUSE TENDERS

ST. LIKOUDIS A 481
I. KARAVOYIANNOS THEOPHILOPOULOS A 479

Displacement, tons: 1 350
Length, feet (metres): 207·3 *(63·2)*
Main engine: 1 diesel; 2 400 hp = 15 knots
Complement: 40

Built at Perama Shipyard 1976-77. Have facilities for small helicopter.

3 NEW CONSTRUCTION TUGS

Of 345 tons laid down 1977 at Perama Shipyard. 98·5 × 26 × 11·3 ft with one MWM diesel. 12 kts launched 29 December 1977, March 1978 and 8 April 1978.

14 TUGS

ANTAIOS (ex-USS *Busy*, YTM 2012) A 407   HERAKLIS A 423
ATLAS (ex-*F 5*) A 428   IASON A 424
ACCHILEUS (ex-USS *Confident*) A 409   ODISSEUS A 425
ATROMITOS A 410   KILKLOPS A 426
AIAS (ex-USS *Ankachak*, YTM 767) A 412   SAMSON (ex-*F 16*) A 430
ROMALEUS A 418   TITAN A 431
MINOTAUROS (ex-*Theseus*, ex-*ST 539*) A 421   GIGAS A 432

Aias transferred on lease 1972 and sold 11 July 1978.

6 WATER BOATS

KERKINI (ex-FDR FW) A 443   KALLIROE A 468
PRESPA A 464   KASTORIA A 470
VOLVI A 467   ILIKI A 474

Capacity: *Iliki* 120 tons, *Volvi* 350 tons, *Kastoria* 520 tons. *Kerkini*, of 350 ton DWT transferred by FDR 1976. *Kalliroe* and *Prespa* completed at Perama Shipyard on 13 December 1976. (600 tons).

Doirani of 450 tons, built in 1976, reported as taken over from another Government Department.

5 FLOATING CRANES

Built in Greece.

ADAMIDIS   1978, D. Dervissis

GREECE / Miscellaneous — GUATEMALA / Coastal patrol craft 225

1 Ex-CRUISER

AVEROF

No excuse is needed for including this ship, which is now classified as a National Monument and moored at Poros. Laid down by Orlando, Italy in 1907 and armed with four 9·2 in guns she served during World War I in the Dardanelles campaign and in World War II in the Mediterranean and Indian Ocean.

AVEROF   1977, P. D. Greenish

GRENADA

Grenada was granted self-government, in association with the UK (who was responsible for her defence) on 3 March 1967.
Independence was achieved in February 1973.

Mercantile Marine

Lloyd's Register of Shipping:
2 vessels of 226 tons gross

1 COASTAL PATROL CRAFT

Displacement, tons: 15
Dimensions, feet (metres): 40 × 12 × 2 *(12·2 × 3·7 × 0·6)*
Guns: 3 MG
Main engines: 2 diesels; 370 hp = 22 knots

Delivered by Brooke Marine, Lowestoft early in 1972.

GUATEMALA

On 5 January 1959 Guatemala announced the establishment of a navy for coastguard work. Subsequently the navy was assigned missions of search and rescue and the support of amphibious operations. The commissioning of a Marine Elevator (Synchrolift) at Santo Tomás on 23 June 1973 (230 ton lift) has greatly improved this navy's repair facilities.

Ministerial

Minister of National Defence:
General D. F. Rubio Coronado

Personnel

(a) 1979: 600 (100 officers and 500 men, including 10 officers and 200 men of the Marines)
(b) 2 years national service

Bases

Santo Tomás de Castillas (Atlantic); Sipacate (Pacific)

Mercantile Marine

Lloyd's Register of Shipping:
7 vessels of 11 645 tons gross

3 "BROADSWORD" CLASS (COASTAL PATROL CRAFT)

Name	No.	Builder	Commissioned
KUKOLKAN	P 1051	Halter Marine	4 Aug 1976
—	P 1052	Halter Marine	22 Oct 1976
—	P 1053	Halter Marine	1977

Displacement, tons: 90·5 standard; 110 full load
Dimensions, feet (metres): 105 × 20·4 × 6·3 *(32 × 6·2 × 1·9)*
Guns: 1—75 mm recoilless; 1—81 mm mortar; 2—30 mm (twin); 4 MG (quad)
Main engines: 2 General Motors 16V-149TI diesels; 2 shafts; 3 200 hp = 32 knots
Complement: 20 (5 officers, 15 men)

KUKOLKAN   1978

2 85 ft COASTAL PATROL CRAFT

Name	No.	Builders	Commissioned
ATATLAN	P 851	Sewart, Louisiana	May 1967
SUBTENIENTE USORIO SARAVIA	P 852	Sewart, Louisiana	1972

Displacement, tons: 60
Dimensions, feet (metres): 85 × 18·7 × 3 *(25·9 × 5·7 × 0·9)*
Guns: 2 MG
Main engines: 2 General Motors diesels; 2 200 bhp = 23 knots
Range, miles: 400 at 12 knots
Complement: 12 (2 officers, 10 ratings)

Built to "Commercial Cruiser" design.

2 Ex-US AVR (COASTAL PATROL CRAFT)

Name	No.	Builders	Commissioned
CABRAKAN	P 631	USA	1945
HUNAHPU	P 632	USA	1945

Displacement, tons: 32
Dimensions, feet (metres): 63·3 × 15·4 × 3 *(19·3 × 4·7 × 0·9)*
Guns: 2 MG
Main engines: 2 General Motors 8V71 diesels = 25 knots
Complement: 10 (2 officers, 8 men)

Transferred—*Hunahpu,* 1964; *Cabrakan,* 1965.

226 GUATEMALA / Coastal patrol craft — Tug

2 "STRIKECRAFT" (COASTAL PATROL CRAFT)

XUCUXUY P 281   CAMALOTE P 282

Displacement, tons: 6·5
Length, feet (metres): 28·2 (8·6)
Gun: 1 MG
Main engine: 1 General Motors 6-53 diesel = 30 knots

Transferred in 1961.

5 US "CUTLASS" CLASS (COASTAL PATROL CRAFT)

Name	No.	Builders	Commissioned
TECUNUMAN	P 651	Halter Marine	1972
KAIBILBALAM	P 652	Halter Marine	1972
AZUMANCHE	P 653	Halter Marine	1972
TZACOL	P 654	Halter Marine	10 Mar 1976
BITOL	P 655	Halter Marine	4 Aug 1976

Displacement, tons: 32 full load
Dimensions, feet (metres): 64·5 × 17 × 3 (19·7 × 5·2 × 0·9)
Guns: 1—12·7 mm; 3—7·6 mm MG (triple)
Main engines: 2 General Motors diesels; 2 shafts; 960 hp = 25 knots
Complement: 10 (2 officers, 8 ratings)

2 "MACHETE" CLASS TROOP CARRIERS

Name	No.	Builder	Commissioned
PICUDA	P 361	Halter Marine	4 Aug 1976
BARRACUDA	P 362	Halter Marine	4 Aug 1976

Displacement, tons: 8·3 full load
Dimensions, feet (metres): 36 × 12·5 × 2 (11 × 3·8 × 0·6)
Main engines: 2 General Motors 6V-53PI; 2 water jets; 540 hp = 36 knots
Complement: 2 + 20 troops

Armoured, open deck, aluminium craft.

2 Ex-USCG 40 ft UTILITY BOATS MK IV

TIKAL P 401   IXINCHE P 402

Transferred August 1963.

1 Ex-US LCM (6)

CHINALTENANGO 561

Transferred December 1965.

1 Ex-US REPAIR BARGE

Ex-US YR 40. Transferred in 1952.

BITOL   1978

6 MOTOR LAUNCHES

Procured in late 1960s. Reported as inboard/outboard craft.

1 TUG

Note: Three other names listed—*Escuintla, Mazatenango, Retalhuleu*—in addition to two yachts—*Mendieta* and one other.

GUINEA

Personnel
(a) 1979: 400 officers and men
(b) Conscript service—2 years

Bases
Conakry, Kakanda

Mercantile Marine
Lloyd's Register of Shipping:
13 vessels of 15 041 tons gross

LIGHT FORCES

6 Ex-CHINESE "SHANGHAI II" CLASS (FAST ATTACK CRAFT—GUN)

P 733   P 734   P 735   P 736   +2

Displacement, tons: 120 standard; 155 full load
Dimensions, feet (metres): 128 × 18 × 5·6 *(39 × 5·5 × 1·7)*
Guns: 4—37 mm (twins); 4—25 mm (twins)
A/S weapons: 8 DCs
Main engines: 4 diesels; 4 shafts; 3 600 hp = 28 knots
Complement: 25

Transferred 1973-74 (first four) and 1976.

"SHANGHAI" Class

4 Ex-SOVIET "P 6" CLASS (FAST ATTACK CRAFT—TORPEDO)

Displacement, tons: 64 standard; 73 full load
Dimensions, feet (metres): 84·2 × 20·0 × 6·0 *(25·7 × 6·1 × 1·8)*
Guns: 4—25 mm
Torpedo tubes: 2—21 in (or mines or depth charges)
Main engines: 4 diesels; 4 shafts; 4 800 bhp = 41 knots
Range, miles: 450 at 20 knots
Complement: 20

It seems unlikely that the torpedo armament is operational.

Radar: Skin Head.

3 Ex-SOVIET "POLUCHAT I" CLASS (COASTAL PATROL CRAFT)

Displacement, tons: 70 standard; 91 full load
Dimensions, feet (metres): 97·1 × 19·0 × 4·8 *(29·6 × 5·8 × 1·5)*
Guns: 2—14·5 mm (1 twin)
Main engines: 2 diesels; 2 shafts; 2 400 bhp = 20 knots
Oil fuel, tons: 9·25
Range, miles: 460 at 17 knots
Complement: 16 (2 officers, 14 ratings)

Radar: One navigation set.

2 Ex-SOVIET "MO VI" CLASS (COASTAL PATROL CRAFT)

Displacement, tons: 50 standard; 66 full load
Dimensions, feet (metres): 83·6 × 19·7 × 4·0 *(25·5 × 6 × 1·2)*
Guns: 4—25 mm (twin)
A/S weapons: DC mortars and racks
Main engines: 4 diesels; 4 shafts; 4 800 hp = 38 knots
Complement: 12

Transferred 1972-73.

Radar: Skin Head.

LANDING CRAFT

2 SMALL UTILITY TYPE

Recent visits by considerable numbers of Soviet ships may have increased these numbers.

GUINEA BISSAU

Personnel
(a) 1979: 100 officers and men
(b) Voluntary service

Base
Bissau.

Aircraft
Purchase of patrol aircraft for offshore surveillance is projected.

Mercantile Marine
Lloyd's Register of Shipping:
2 vessels of 370 tons gross

1 Ex-SOVIET "P 6" CLASS (FAST ATTACK CRAFT—TORPEDO)

Details as in Guinea section. Reported 1977.

2 COASTAL PATROL CRAFT

CABO ROXO   ILHA DE POILÃO

Of French construction.

Several river craft and some small LCU type are reported in service.

GUYANA

Ministerial
Premier and Minister of National Security:
L. F. S. Burnham

Personnel
(a) 1979: Approximately 150 members of Guyana Defence Force
(b) Voluntary

Bases
Georgetown, New Amsterdam

Prefix to Ships' Names
GDFS

Mercantile Marine
Lloyd's Register of Shipping:
72 vessels of 16 773 tons gross

---

1 VOSPER THORNYCROFT "103 ft TYPE" (LARGE PATROL CRAFT)

Name	No.	Builders	Commissioned
PECCARI	DF 1010	Vosper Thornycroft	26 Jan 1977

Displacement, tons: 96 standard; 109 full load
Dimensions, feet (metres): 103 × 19·8 × 5·5 *(31·4 × 6·0 × 1·6)*
Guns: 2—20 mm
Main engines: 2—12-cyl Paxman Ventura diesels; 3 500 hp = 27 knots
Range, miles: 1 400 at 14 knots
Complement: 22

Launched 26 March 1976. Trials started 25 November 1976.

PECCARI *1977, Michael D. J. Lennon*

3 VOSPER "12·2 METRE" TYPE (COASTAL PATROL CRAFT)

Name	No.	Builders	Commissioned
JAGUAR	—	Vosper's	28 Apr 1971
MARGAY	—	Vosper's	21 May 1971
OCELOT	—	Vosper's	22 June 1971

Displacement, tons: 10
Dimensions, feet (metres): 40 × 12 × 3·5 *(12·2 × 3·7 × 1·1)*
Gun: 1—7·62 mm MG
Main engines: 2 Cummins diesels; 370 hp = 19 knots
Range, miles: 150 at 12 knots
Complement: 6

They have glass fibre hulls with aluminium superstructures.

JAGUAR *1971, C. and S. Taylor*

3 Ex-US "45 ft" CLASS (COASTAL PATROL CRAFT)

CAMOUDIE   LABANA   RATTLER

1 TUG

— (ex-*YTM 190*)

Transferred from USA 1975.

1 LIGHTER

— (ex-*YFN 960*)

Transferred from USA 1 August 1975.

HAITI

Ministerial
Secretary for Interior and National Defence:
Pierre Biamby

Personnel
(a) 1979: Total 300 (40 officers and 260 men)
(b) Voluntary service

Base
Port Au Prince

Mercantile Marine
Lloyd's Register of Shipping:
1 vessel of 394 tons gross

DELETIONS

1977 *Jean Jacques Dessalines* ("Cohoes" class) returned to USA. *Admiral Killick, Seize Août 1946, Savannah, Artibonite, Sans Souci,* 6-83 ft cutters.

COAST GUARD VESSELS

2 Ex-USCG "CAPE" CLASS

Name	No.	Builders	Commissioned
LA CRETE A PIERROT (ex-USCG *95315*)	MH 8	US Coast Guard Yard, Curtiss Bay, Maryland	—
VERTIERES	MH 9	—	—

Displacement, tons: 100
Dimensions, feet (metres): 95 × 19 × 5 *(29 × 5·8 × 1·5)*
Guns: 3—20 mm
Main engines: 4 Cummins diesels; 2 shafts; 2 200 bhp = 21 knots
Range, miles: 1 500
Complement: 15

Former US Coast Guard steel cutters. Acquired on 26 February 1956 (MH 8), and in 1960 (MH 9).

3 COASTAL PATROL CRAFT

MH 21, MH 22, MH 23.

Displacement, tons: 33 full load
Dimensions, feet (metres): 69·9 × 17·1 × 3·3 *(21·3 × 5·2 × 1·0)*
Guns: 2—12·7 mm
Main engines: 3 General Motors 8 V 71 diesels; 3 shafts; 1 590 hp = 25 knots

Built by Sewart, Louisiana in 1976.

2 COASTAL PATROL CRAFT

MH 5, MH 6

31 ft *(9·5 m)* Bertram "Enforcer" Class with inboard/outboard motor.

Other craft listed—*Citadelle Henry, Haiti Cherie* and *22 Juin.*

Also reported, though not confirmed, that *Sans Souci* has been retained as a Presidential yacht.

HONDURAS

Ministerial

Minister of Defence:
Brigadier General M. E. Chinchilla Carcamao

Personnel

(a) 1979: 50
(b) 8 months conscript service

Base

Puerto Cortes

Mercantile Marine

Lloyd's Register of Shipping:
70 vessels of 130 831 tons gross

1 "SWIFT 105 FT" CLASS (FAST PATROL CRAFT)

Displacement, tons: 103
Dimensions, feet (metres): 105 × 24 × 5 *(32 × 7·3 × 1·5)*
Main engines: 2 MTU diesels; 7 000 hp = 32 knots
Range, miles: 1 200 at 18 knots
Complement: 16

Delivered by Swiftships, Morgan City in April 1977.

1 HYDROGRAPHIC LAUNCH

Of 56 ft, transferred from USA 1976.

4 "SWIFT 65 FT" CLASS (COASTAL PATROL CRAFT)

Name	No	Builder	Commissioned
GRAL	GC 6501	Swiftships	Dec 1973
GEN J. T. CABANAS	GC 6502	Swiftships	Jan 1974
+2			

Displacement, tons: 36·3 full load
Dimensions, feet (metres): 65·3 × 18·4 × 5·2 *(19·9 × 5·6 × 1·6)*
Main engines: 3 General Motors diesels; 3 shafts; 1 590 hp = 27 knots
Range, miles: 2 000 at 22 knots
Complement: 5

Originally built by Swiftships, Morgan City for Haiti. Contract cancelled and Honduras bought the two completed boats. No armament. Delivered in 1977. Further two with MTU diesels (= 36 knots).

HONG KONG

All the following craft are operated by the Marine District of the Royal Hong Kong Police Force.

Senior officers

District Police Commander:
Sze-to Che-yan CPM JP

Assistant Commissioner:
R. J. L. MacDonald

Personnel

(a) 1979: 71 officers, 330 NCOs, 890 constables
(b) Voluntary service

Mercantile Marine

Lloyd's Register of Shipping:
150 vessels of 874 850 tons gross

DELETIONS

1975: Logistic Craft No 24
45 ft Patrol Craft No 5 and 8

POLICE CRAFT

2 COMMAND VESSELS

No. 1   No. 2

Displacement, tons: 222·5
Dimensions, feet (metres): 111·3 × 24 × 10·5 *(33·9 × 7·3 × 3·2)*
Main engines: 2 diesels of 337 bhp = 11·8 knots
Range, miles: 5 200 at 11·8 knots
Complement: 25

Built at Taikoo 1965 (now Hong Kong United Dockyard). Can carry two platoons in addition to complement. Cost $HK 1 778 550.

POLICE LAUNCH No. 2   1974, RHKP

7 "78 ft" PATROL CRAFT

Nos. 50-56

Displacement, tons: 82
Dimensions, feet (metres): 78·5 × 17·2 × 5·6 *(23·9 × 5·2 × 1·7)*
Gun: 1—·50 cal MG
Main engines: 2 Cummins diesels; 1 500 hp = 20·7 knots
Range, miles: 4 000 at 20 knots
Complement: 16

Steel hulled craft built by Thornycroft, Singapore. Delivered May 1972 to May 1973 to the Royal Hong Kong Police. Can carry an extra Platoon. Cost $HK 1 873 800.

POLICE LAUNCH No. 51   1974, RHKP

1 "78 ft" PATROL CRAFT

No. 4

Displacement, tons: 72
Dimensions, feet (metres): 78 × 15 × 4·5 *(22·8 × 4·6 × 1·4)*
Main engines: 3 diesels; 690 hp = 15·5 knots
Range, miles: 600 at 15·5 knots
Complement: 21

Built by Thornycroft, Singapore in 1958.

HONG KONG / Police craft

9 "70 ft" PATROL CRAFT

Nos. 26-34

Displacement, tons: 52
Dimensions, feet (metres): 70 × 17 × 5·2 (24·5 × 5·2 × 1·6)
Main engines: 2 diesels; 215 bhp = 10 knots
Range, miles: 1 600 at 10 knots
Complement: 12

Built by Hong Kong S.Y. (26-28) in 1954 and Choy Lee S.Y. (29-34 in 1955).

POLICE LAUNCH No. 26   1978, Dr. Giorgio Arra

1 "65 ft" PATROL CRAFT

No. 6

Displacement, tons: 48
Dimensions, feet (metres): 65 × 14·5 × 5·5 (19·8 × 4·4 × 1·8)
Main engine: 1 diesel; 152 bhp = 10·5 knots
Range, miles: 1 400 at 9 knots
Complement: 11

8 "45 ft" PATROL CRAFT

Nos. 9-16

Displacement, tons: 27·7
Dimensions, feet (metres): 45 × 15 × 7 (13·7 × 4·6 × 2·1)
Main engine: 1 diesel; 144 bhp = 9 knots
Range, miles: 1 700 at 8 knots
Complement: 5

Built by Australian Ministry of Munitions in 1946.

POLICE LAUNCH No. 12   1976, RHKP

3 "40 ft" PATROL CRAFT

Nos. 20-22

Displacement, tons: 17
Dimensions, feet (metres): 40·3 × 11·6 × 2 (12·3 × 3·5 × 0·6)
Main engines: 2 diesels; 370 bhp = 24 knots
Range, miles: 380 at 24 knots
Complement: 5

Built in Choy Lee in 1971.

POLICE LAUNCH No. 22   1974, RHKP

1 "58 ft" LOGISTIC CRAFT

No. 3

Of 37 tons and 16 knots with a range of 240 miles at 15 knots. Complement eight. Built by Thornycroft Singapore in 1958.

POLICE LAUNCH No. 3   1976, RHKP

1 LOGISTIC CRAFT

No. 7

Displacement, tons: 18·5
Main engines: 2 diesels; 700 hp = 23·5 knots
Range, miles: 300+ at 20 knots
Complement: 6 plus 19 passengers

Built by Hip Hing Cheung shipyard in 1975.

POLICE LAUNCH No. 7   1977, Hip Hing Cheung Shipyard

11 "22 ft" LAUNCHES

Nos. 35-45

Of 4·8 tons and 20 knots with a range of 160 miles at full speed. Built by Choy Lee S.Y. in 1970.

POLICE LAUNCH No. 38   9/1977, Dr. Giorgio Arra

HUNGARY

Ministerial

Minister of Defence:
Lazos Czinege

Diplomatic Representation

Military and Air Attaché London:
Colonel Imry Mózsik

Personnel

(a) 1979: 500 officers and men
(b) 2 years national service

Mercantile Marine

Lloyd's Register of Shipping:
23 vessels of 77 738 tons gross

The Navy was dissolved by 1968 but a maritime wing of the Army is still very active on the Danube. The total number of craft operated is about 45.

LIGHT FORCES

10 "100 ton" PATROL CRAFT

Displacement, tons: 100
Gun: 1—14·7 mm
Main engines: 2 diesels

MINE WARFARE FORCES

Several riverine MCM vessels.

SERVICE FORCES

Several troop transports of up to 1 000 tons.
Five small LCUs.
A number of tugs.
Several river icebreakers.
Transport barges which can double as landing craft or bridging element.

ICELAND

Ministerial

Minister of Justice:
Olafur Johannesson

Senior Officer

Director of Coast Guard:
Pétur Sigurdsson

Personnel

1979: 160 officers and men

Duties

The Coast Guard Service (Landhelgisgaezlan) deals with fishery protection, salvage, rescue, hydrographic research, surveying and lighthouse duties. All ships have at least double the number of berths required for the complement.

Base

Reykjavik

Deletion

1978 *Albert*

Aircraft

2 Bell helicopter
1 Hughes helicopter
2 Fokker Friendship

Research Ships

A number of Government Research Ships bearing RE pennant numbers operate off Iceland.

Mercantile Marine

Lloyd's Register of Shipping:
383 vessels of 175 097 tons gross

COAST GUARD PATROL VESSELS

Name	No.	Builders	Commissioned
AEGIR	—	Aalborg Vaerft, Denmark	1968
TYR	—	Dannebrog Vaerft, Denmark	15 Mar 1975

Displacement, tons: 1 200 *(Tyr* 1 300*)*
Dimensions, feet (metres): 204 × 33 × 14·8 *(62·2 × 10 × 4·6)* Aegir
 (Tyr 205 ft *62·5 m)*
Gun: 1—57 mm
Main engines: 2 MAN diesels; 2 shafts; 8 000 bhp = 19 knots
Complement: 22

Aegir was the first new construction patrol vessel for the Icelandic Coast Guard Service for about eight years. Projected in February 1965. Laid down in May 1967. *Tyr*, basically similar to *Aegir*, but a slightly improved design with higher speed was launched by Aarhus Flyedock AS, Denmark on 10 October 1974. Both have helicopter deck and hangar.

Radar: Three search sets.

Sonar: One hull-mounted.

AEGIR *1969, Icelandic Coast Guard*

Name	No.	Builders	Commissioned
ODINN	—	Aalborg Vaerft, Denmark	Jan 1960

Displacement, tons: 1 000
Dimensions, feet (metres): 187 pp × 33 × 13 *(57 × 10 × 4)*
Gun: 1—57 mm
Main engines: 2 Burmester & Wain diesels; 2 shafts; 5 050 bhp = 18 knots
Complement: 22

Laid down in January 1959. Launched in September 1959. Refitted in Denmark by Aarhus Flyedock late 1975, with twin funnels and helicopter hangar.

Radar: Two search sets.

Sonar: One hull-mounted.

ODINN *1976, Icelandic Coast Guard*

Name	No.	Builders	Commissioned
THOR	—	Aalborg Vaerft, Denmark	late 1951

Displacement, tons: 900
Dimensions, feet (metres): 206 × 31·2 × 13 *(62·8 × 9·5 × 4)*
Gun: 1—57 mm
Main engines: 2—6-cyl MWM diesels; 3 200 bhp = 17 knots
Complement: 22

Launched in 1951. Fitted with helicopter platform during refit in 1972. Now has twin funnels and hangar.

Radar: Two search sets.

Sonar: One hull-mounted set.

THOR *1975, Icelandic Coast Guard*

Name	No.	Builders	Commissioned
ARVAKUR	—	Bodewes, Netherlands	1962

Displacement, tons: 700
Dimensions, feet (metres): 109·2 × 33 × 13 *(33·3 × 10 × 4)*
Gun: 1 MG
Main engine: 1 Deutz diesel; 1 000 bhp = 12 knots
Complement: 14

Built as a lighthouse tender in the Netherlands. Acquired by Iceland and converted for duty in the Coast Guard Service in 1969.

Radar: Two search sets.

HVALORG (ex-*Tyr*)

Reported that the ex-whaler *Tyr* built in 1952 was acquired in December 1977. Of 631 tons.

"21 SS SMUGGLER" CRAFT

A number of these craft fitted with Italian Castoldi jets (157 hp) and capable of 36 knots has recently been delivered by Smuggler Boats Trading AS Norway.

SURVEY CRAFT

Reported that another *Tyr* of 34 tons built in 1956 with a crew of six is used for surveying duties, probably not by the Coast Guard.

INDIA

Ministerial

Minister of Defence:
  Mr Jagjivan Ram

Headquarters Appointment

Chief of the Naval Staff:
  Admiral R. L. Pereira

Senior Appointments

Flag Officer C in C, Western Naval Command:
  Rear-Admiral V. E. C. Barboza
Flag Officer Commanding Western Fleet:

Flag Officer C in C Eastern Naval Command:
  Vice-Admiral M. R. Schunker
Flag Officer Commanding Eastern Fleet:
  Rear-Admiral D. S. Paintal
Flag Officer, Southern Naval Area:
  Rear-Admiral O. S. Dawson

Diplomatic Representation

Naval Attaché in Bonn:
  Commodore H. Johnson
Naval Adviser, Dacca:
  Captain R. B. Mukherjee
Naval Attaché in Jakarta:
  Captain R. V. Singh
Naval Adviser in London:
  Commodore K. N. Dubash
Naval Attaché in Moscow:
  Commodore I. J. S. Khurana
Defence Attaché in Washington:
  Brigadier Srendra Singh MC

Naval Bases and Establishments

Bombay (C in C Western Fleet, barracks and main Dockyard);
Vishakapatnam (C in C Eastern Command, submarine base, dockyard and barracks);
Cochin (FO Southern Area Naval Air Station, barracks and professional schools);
Lonavala and Jamnagar (professional schools);
Calcutta, Goa and Port Blair (small bases only);
New Delhi (HQ)

Personnel

(a) 1978: 46 000 officers and ratings (including Naval Air Arm)
(b) Voluntary service

Naval Air Arm

Squadron No.	Aircraft	Role
300	Seahawk FGA6 (25)	Strike
310	Alize 1050 (10)	ASW
312	5 Super Constellations	MR
	3 Ilyushin IL38 May	
321	Alouette III (7)	SAR
330	Sea Kings (12)	ASW
331	Alouette III (7)	ASW
550	Alize, Alouette	Training
561	2 Devon	Training
	4 Hughes 300,	
	4 Vampire T-55,	
	7 HJT 16-Kiran	

Note: Five Britten-Norman Defenders ordered in 1976.

Prefix to Ships' Names

IS (Indian Ship)

Strength of the Fleet

Type	Active	Building
Patrol Submarines	8	(?)
Attack Carrier (Medium)	1	—
Cruiser	1	—
Destroyer	1	—
Frigates	29	2
Corvettes	4	(4)
Fast Attack Craft—Missile	16	—
Fast Attack Craft—Patrol	3	7
Large Patrol Craft	1	—
Coastal Patrol Craft	7	—
Landing Ship	1	—
Landing Craft	6	—
LCUs	3	?
Minesweepers—Ocean	2	3
Minesweepers—Coastal	4	—
Minesweepers—Inshore	4	—
Survey Ships	4	2
Submarine Tender	1	—
Submarine Rescue Ship	1	—
Replenishment Tankers	2	—
Support Tankers	2	—
Repair Ship	1	—
Ocean Tugs	3	—
Harbour Craft	9	—

COAST GUARD

Administration

Director General:
  Vice-Admiral V. A. Kamath, PVSM (Retd)
Deputy Director General:
  Commodore M. S. Ratra, AVSM, VSM

An Interim Coast Guard Force started operations as a part of the Indian Navy on 1 February 1977. It was constituted as an independent para-military service on 19 August 1978 with the passing of the Coast Guard Act, 1978 by the Indian Parliament.

Its responsibilities include:—
(a) Ensuring the safety and protection of artificial islands, offshore terminals and other installations in the Maritime Zones.
(b) Measures for the safety of life and property at sea including assistance to mariners in distress.
(c) Measures to preserve and protect the marine environment and control marine pollution.
(d) Assisting the Customs and other authorities in anti-smuggling operations.
(e) Enforcing the provisions of enactments in force in the Maritime Zones.

The Headquarters of the Coast Guard is located in Delhi with Regional Headquarters in Bombay, Madras and Port Blair. The present force consists of two Frigates and five Patrol Boats transferred from the Navy at the time of setting up the Interim Coast Guard.
There are plans for strengthening the Coast Guard with new ships and aircraft. In the short term it is intended to equip the Coast Guard with a number of Inshore and Offshore Patrol Vessels, the latter equipped with a light helicopter on board, and light twin-engined coastal surveillance aircraft based ashore. The long term plan envisages larger patrol vessels, medium range surveiilance aircraft, and long range rescue helicopters.

Mercantile Marine

Lloyd's Register of Shipping:
  591 vessels of 5 759 224 tons gross

DELETIONS

Cruiser

1978 *Delhi* (May)

Destroyers

1976 *Rana, Rajput* (British "R" Class)

Frigates

1971 *Khukri* sunk in war with Pakistan (9 Dec)
1975 *Ganga* and *Gomati* ("Hunt" Class) paid off

Survey Ship

1975 *Investigator* ("River" class) paid off

Light Forces

1974 *Ajay* and *Akshay* to Bangladesh, *Amar* to Mauritius (Apr).
1975 *Savitri, Sharayu, Subhadra, Suvarna* paid off

Mine Warfare Forces

1973 *Konkan* (last of 6 "Bangor" class) paid off

Harbour Tankers

1976 *Chilka, Sambhar*

PENNANT LIST

Submarines

S 20	Kursura
S 21	Karanj
S 22	Kanderi
S 23	Kalvari
S 40	Vela
S 41	Vagir
S 42	Vagli
S 43	Vagsheer

Aircraft Carrier

| R 11 | Vikrant |

Cruiser

| C 60 | Mysore |

Destroyer

| D 141 | Ranjit |

Frigates

D 92	Godavari
F 11	Jamuna (Survey)
F 31	Brahmaputra
F 32	Himgiri
F 33	Nilgiri
F 34	Dunagiri
F 35	Udaygiri
F 36	Taragiri
F 37	Beas
F 38	Vindhyagiri
F 39	Betwa
F 40	Talwar
F 43	Trishul
F 46	Kistna
F 95	Sutlej (Survey)
F 110	Kaveri
F 256	Tir
CG	Kirpan
CG	Kuthar

Corvettes

K 71	Vijay Durg
K 72	Sinhu Durg
K 73	Hos Durg
K 74	Nanuchka No 4

Light Forces
(including "Petya" class with P numbers)

K 82	Veer
K 83	Vidyut
K 84	Vijeta
K 85	Vinash
K 86	Nipat
K 87	Nashat
K 88	Nirbhik
K 89	Nirghat
K 90	Prachand
K 91	Pralaya
K 92	Pratap
K 93	Prabal
K 94	Chapal
K 95	Chapmak
K 96	Chatak
K 97	Charag
P 68	Arnala
P 69	Androth
P 73	Anjadip
P 74	Andaman
P 75	Amini
P 77	Kamorta
P 78	Kadmath
P 79	Kiltan
P 80	Kavaratti
P 81	Katchal
P 82	Kanjar
P 83	Amindivi
T 35	Abhay
CG	Panvel
CG	Pamban
CG	Puri
CG	Panaji
CG	Pulicat
T 51	SDB Mk 2
T 52	SDB Mk 2
T 53	SDB Mk 2
SPB 3132	Sukanya
SPB 3133	Sharada

Mine Warfare Forces

M 61	Pondicherry
M 62	Porbandar
M 88	Bhaktal
M 89	Bulsar
M 90	Cuddalore
M 91	Cannamore
M 92	Karwar
M 93	Kakinada
M 2705	Bimlipitan
M 2707	Bassein

Amphibious Forces

L 11	Magar
L 12	Gharial
L 13	Guldar
L 14	Ghorpad
L 15	Kesari
L 16	Shardul
L 17	Sharab

Service Forces

A 14	Amba
A 15	Nistar
A 50	Deepak
A 57	Shakti
A 139	Darshak
A 306	Dharini
A 1751	Gaj

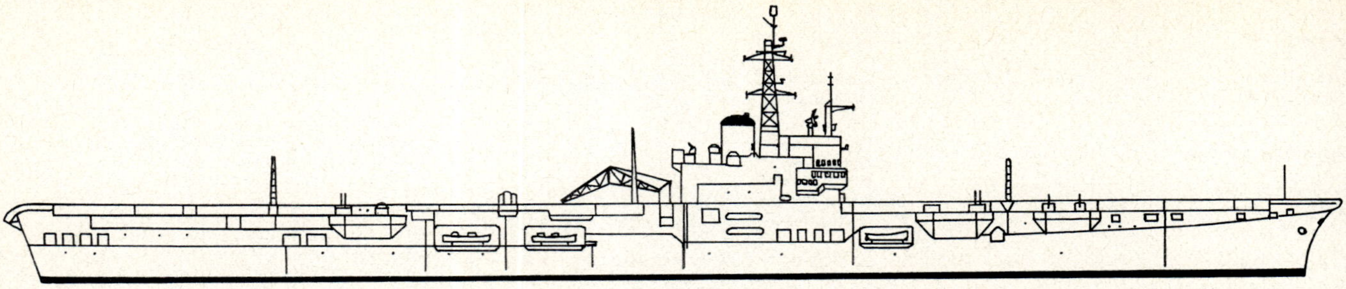

INDIA / Introduction

VIKRANT

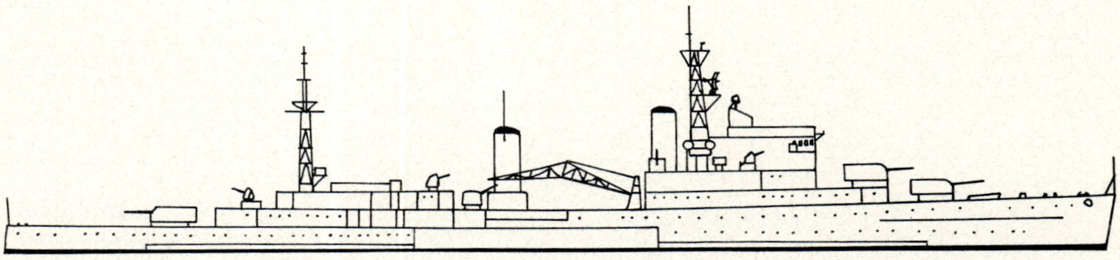

MYSORE

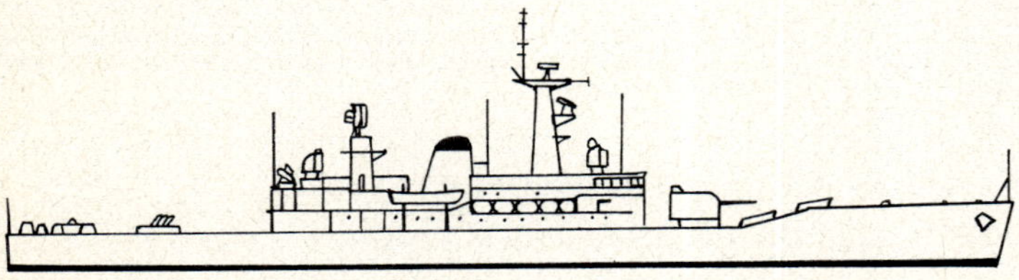

"LEANDER" Class

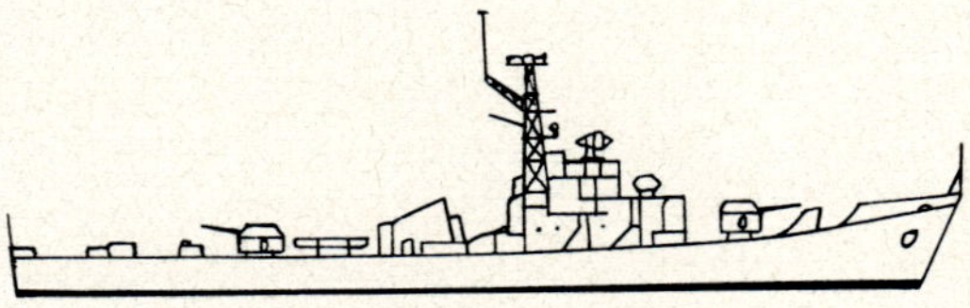

"PETYA" Class

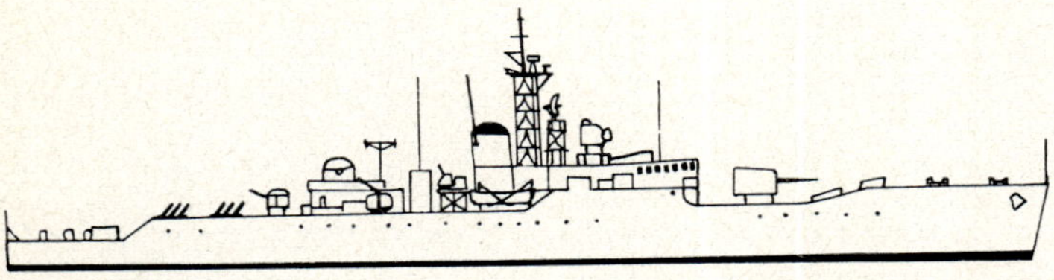

TRISHUL

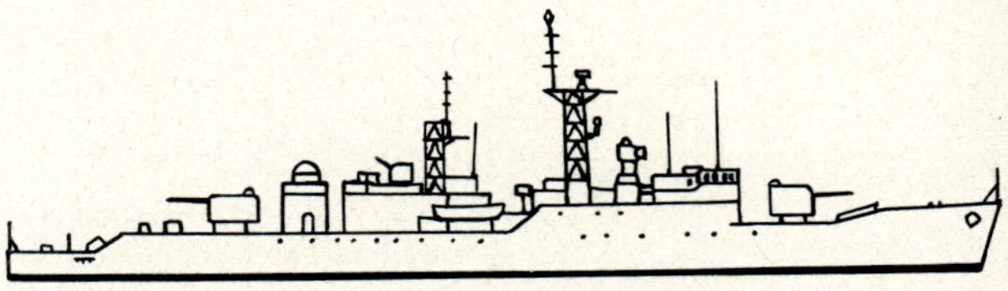

BEAS, BETWA, BRAHMAPUTRA

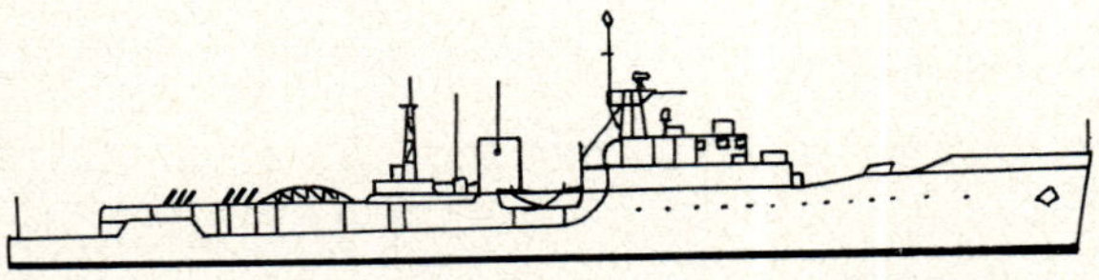

KIRPAN, KUTHAR (CG)

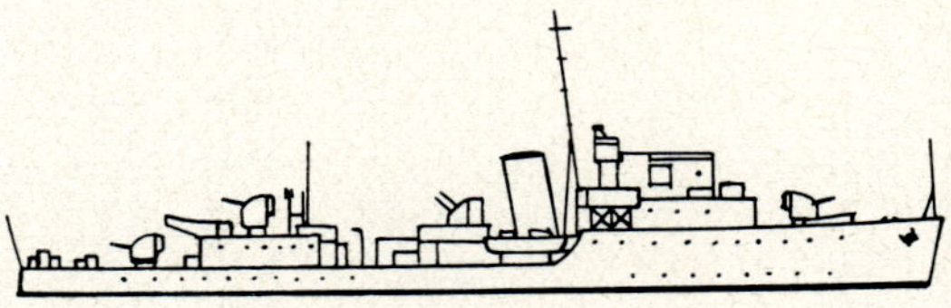

"HUNT" Class

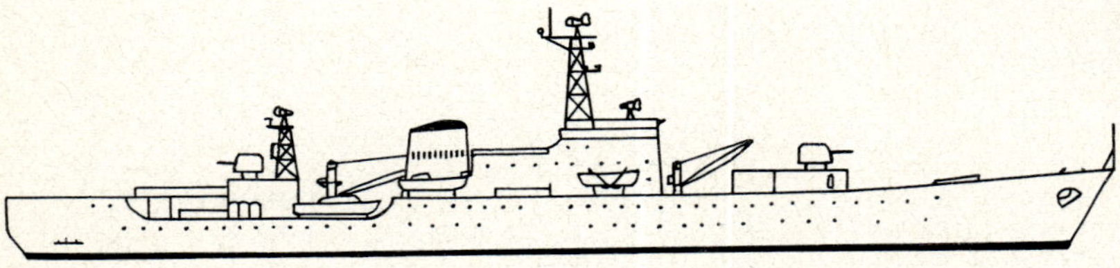

AMBA

INDIA / Submarines — Cruisers 235

SUBMARINES

Note: Plans are proceeding for the construction of submarines in India, possibly at Vishakapatnam. It seems likely that these will be of about 1 500 tons and may be of the IKL Type 1500 with integral bulkhead/escape capsule. If this is the case the first two would be built in the home yard and the remainder in India. It is reported that the target total is twenty submarines of this class.

8 Ex-SOVIET "FOXTROT" CLASS

KURSURA S 20	**VELA** S 40
KARANJ S 21	**VAGIR** S 41
KANDERI S 22	**VAGLI** S 42
KALVARI S 23	**VAGSHEER** S 43

Displacement, tons: 2 000 surfaced; 2 300 dived
Length, feet (metres): 296·8 (90·5)
Beam, feet (metres): 42·1 (7·3)
Draught, feet (metres): 19·0 (5·8)
Torpedo tubes: 10—21 in (20 torpedoes carried)
Main machinery: 3 diesels; 3 shafts; 6 000 bhp; 3 electric motors; 6 000 hp
Speed, knots: 20 surfaced; 15 dived
Complement: 70

KARANJ   1/1978

Kalvari arrived in India on 16 July 1968, *Kanderi* in January 1969. *Karanj* in October 1970 and *Kursura* in December 1970. *Vela* November 1973, *Vagir* December 1973, *Vagli* September 1974, *Vagsheer* May 1975.

Additions: There are reports, so far unconfirmed, that a further pair may be transferred later.

AIRCRAFT CARRIER

1 Ex-BRITISH "MAJESTIC" CLASS

Name	No.	Builders	Laid down	Launched	Commissioned
VIKRANT (ex-HMS *Hercules*)	R 11	Vickers-Armstrong Ltd, Tyne	14 Oct 1943	22 Sep 1945	4 Mar 1961

Displacement, tons: 16 000 standard; 19 500 full load
Length, feet (metres): 630 (192·0) pp; 700 (213·4) oa
Beam, feet (metres): 80 (24·4) hull
Width, feet (metres): 128 (39·0)
Draught, feet (metres): 24 (7·3)
Aircraft: 22 capacity (18 Sea Hawk, 4 Alize)
Guns: 15—40 mm/60 (4 twin, 7 single)
Main engines: Parsons single reduction geared turbines; 40 000 shp; 2 shafts
Boilers: 4 Admiralty 3-drum; 400 psi; 700°F
Speed, knots: 24·5
Oil fuel, tons: 3 200
Range, miles: 12 000 at 14 knots; 6 200 at 23 knots
Complement: 1 075 (peace); 1 345 (war)

Acquired from the UK in January 1957 after having been suspended in May 1946 when structurally almost complete and 75 per cent fitted out. Taken in hand by Harland & Wolff Ltd, Belfast, in April 1957 for completion in 1961. Commissioned on 4 March 1961 and renamed *Vikrant*. Completed extensive overhaul—1973 to August 1974.

Aircraft: Still equipped with Sea Hawks. Harrier trials in mid-1972 showed promise. First batch of Sea-Harriers ordered 1978, more to follow. Will be replacement for Sea Hawks after 1979 refit.

Engineering: One set of turbines and two boilers are installed side by side in each of the two propelling machinery spaces, on the unit system, so that the starboard propeller shaft is longer than the port.

Flight deck: The aircraft, including strike and anti-submarine aircraft, operate from an angled deck with steam catapult, landing sights and two electrically operated lifts.

Habitability: Partially air-conditioned and insulated for tropical service, the ship's sides being sprayed with asbestos cement instead of being lagged. Separate messes and dining halls.

Radar: Search: Type 960, Type 277.
Tactical: Type 293.
Miscellaneous: Type 963 Carrier Controlled Approach.

Refit: Major refit planned mid-1979. (see *Aircraft* note)

VIKRANT   1971, John G. Callis

CRUISER

1 Ex-BRITISH "FIJI" CLASS

Name	No.	Builders	Laid down	Launched	Commissioned
MYSORE (ex-HMS *Nigeria*)	C 60	Vickers-Armstrong Ltd, Tyne	8 Feb 1938	18 July 1939	23 Sep 1940

Displacement, tons: 8 700 standard; 11 040 full load
Length, feet (metres): 538·0 (164·0) pp; 549·0 (167·3) wl; 555·5 (169·3) oa
Beam, feet (metres): 62·0 (18·9)
Draught, feet (metres): 21·0 (6·4)
Guns: 9—6 in (152 mm)/50 (triple Vickers); 8—4 in (102 mm), (twin Mk 19); 12—40 mm/60 (5 twin, 2 single)
Armour: Side 3½ in (89 mm); Deck 2 in (51 mm); Conning tower 4 in (102 mm); Turrets 2 in (51 mm)
Main engines: Parsons geared turbines; 4 shafts; 72 500 shp
Boilers: 4 Admiralty 3-drum type
Speed, knots: 31·5 (designed)
Oil fuel, tons: 1 700
Range, miles: 4 500 at 20 knots
Complement: 800

Flagship at the Battle of Porsanger Fjord September 1941. Purchased from the UK on 8 April 1954 for £300 000. Extensively refitted and reconstructed by Cammell Laird & Co Ltd, Birkenhead, before commissioning. Formally handed over to the Indian Navy at Birkenhead and renamed *Mysore* on 29 August 1957. Involved in two serious collisions, the second in late 1972 with *Beas*, resulting in two months of repairs. Flagship of training squadron in place of *Delhi* May 1978.

Radar: Search: Type 960, Type 277.
Tactical: Type 293.
Fire control: Type 274 for 6 in guns; Type 275 for 4 in guns.

MYSORE (*Vijay Durg* alongside)   8/1977

Reconstruction: Ship formerly had tripod masts. During reconstruction the triple 6 in turret in "X" position and the six 21 in torpedo tubes (tripled) were removed, the bridge was modified, two lattice masts were stepped, all electrical equipment was replaced and the engine room and other parts of the ship were refitted.

236　INDIA / Destroyers — Frigates

DESTROYERS

3 Ex-SOVIET "KASHIN" CLASS

"MODIFIED KASHIN" Class

Displacement, tons: 3 950 standard; 4 950 full load
Dimensions, feet (metres): 478·9 × 51·8 × 15·7 *(146·0 × 15·8 × 4·8)*
Missiles: SSM; 4 SS-N-2B; SAM; 4 SA-N-1 (2 twin)
Guns: 2—76 mm L59; 4—23 mm gatling
A/S weapons: 2—MBU 2500
Torpedo tubes: 5—21 in *(533 mm)* (quin)
Main engines: 8 gas turbines; 96 000 shp; 2 shafts = 35 knots
Range, miles: 4 500 at 18 knots
Complement: 320

Reported as due to be transferred in 1979. One report states that a Hormone helicopter is to be embarked although it is difficult to see where this aircraft could be accommodated.

Radar: Surveillance: Two Head Net A or Head Net C and Big Net A.
Missile control: Two Peel Group.
Fire control: Two Owl Screech; Two Bass Tilt.
Navigation; Two Don Kay.
IFF: High Pole B.

Sonar: Hull-mounted and VDS.

1 Ex-BRITISH "R" CLASS

Name	No.	Builders	Laid down	Launched	Commissioned
RANJIT (ex-HMS *Redoubt*)	D 141	John Brown & Co Ltd, Clydebank	19 June 1941	2 May 1942	1 Oct 1942

Displacement, tons: 1 725 standard; 2 424 full load
Length, feet (metres): 339·5 *(103·5)* wl; 362·0 *(110·3)* oa
Beam, feet (metres): 35·7 *(10·9)*
Draught, feet (metres): 17·1 *(5·2)*
Guns: 4—4·7 in *(120 mm)* (singles); 4—40 mm
A/S weapons: 4 DCT
Main engines: Parsons geared turbines; 2 shafts; 40 000 shp
Boilers: 2 Admiralty 3-drum type
Oil fuel, tons: 490
Speed, knots: 32
Range, miles: 2 500 at 20 knots
Complement: 240

Transferred 4 July 1949.

Radar: Type 293.

"R" Class

FRIGATES

Note: It is reported that India has approached the Netherlands for assistance in designing a new class of frigate with gas turbines to be built as successors to the "Modified Leander" Class.

0 + 1 + ? "MODIFIED LEANDER" CLASS

Name	No.	Builders	Laid down	Launched	Commissioned
—	—	Mazagon Docks Ltd, Bombay	2 June 1978	—	—

Displacement, tons: 3 850 full load
Dimensions, feet (metres): 420? × 48 × 16·4 *(128? × 14·6 × 5)*
Aircraft: 2 Sea King helicopters
Missiles: SSM; 2 SS-N-2B (single cells);
　SAM; 1 SA-N-4 (mid-line)
Guns: 1—? 76 mm (possibly of Indian design); 2—?Gatlings
Main engines: ? 2 geared turbines; 2 shafts = 30 knots
Range, miles: ? 4 500 at 12 knots
Complement: ? 250

A further modification of the original "Leander" design, although this is the first truly hybrid Soviet/British ship to be built, apparently including both nationalities of radar (as well as Dutch), Soviet missiles and a pair of British helicopters. As the last two of the previous 'Leander" programme are reported to carry the Canadian Bear-Trap haul-down gear it is possible that this may be included in these ships. If the dimensions are correct as reported what is particularly noteworthy is the embarkation of two Sea Kings (width overall app. 16 ft) on a smaller beam than the Canadian "DDH 280" Class.

Radar: Surface-air search: ? Head Net C and HSA LW-05.
Missile control: Pop Group.
Gun control: ? Drum Tilt.
Navigation/helo control: ? Type 978.

Sonar: ? Type 184 as in "Leander" class.

Torpedoes: Reported that A/S torpedoes are to be fitted.

"MODIFIED LEANDER" Class

INDIA / Frigates

6 BRITISH "LEANDER" CLASS

Name	No.	Builders	Laid down	Launched	Commissioned
HIMGIRI	F 32	Mazagon Docks Ltd, Bombay	1967	6 May 1970	23 Nov 1974
NILGIRI	F 33	Mazagon Docks Ltd, Bombay	Oct 1966	23 Oct 1968	3 June 1972
UDAYGIRI	F 34	Mazagon Docks Ltd, Bombay	Jan 1973	9 Mar 1974	1 Feb 1977
DUNAGIRI	F 35	Mazagon Docks Ltd, Bombay	14 Sep 1970	24 Oct 1972	18 Feb 1976
TARAGIRI	F 36	Mazagon Docks Ltd, Bombay	1974	25 Oct 1976	?1979
VINDHYAGIRI	F 38	Mazagon Docks Ltd, Bombay	1975	12 Nov 1977	?1979

Displacement, tons: 2 450 standard; 2 800 full load
Length, feet (metres): 360 (109·7) wl; 372 (113·4) oa
Beam, feet (metres): 43 (13·1)
Draught, feet (metres): 18 (5·5)
Aircraft: 1 Alouette III helicopter in first four; 1 Sea King in F 36 and 38
Missiles: SAM; Sea Cat (est 32, 2 quad launchers) (all but *Nilgiri*—one launcher)
Guns: 2—4·5 in (115 mm)/45 (twin Mk 6); 2—20 mm/70
A/S weapons: 1 Limbo 3-barrelled DC mortar (except in F 36 and 38); A/S torpedo tubes (F 36 and 38)
Main engines: 2 geared turbines; 30 000 shp
Boilers: 2
Oil fuel, tons: 460
Speed, knots: 30
Range, miles: 4 500 at 12 knots
Complement: 267 (17 officers and 250 ratings)

The first major warships built in Indian yards. Of similar design to the "Broad-beam Leanders" but with several differences. In the first four the hangar was lengthened to take the Alouette III helicopter while in the last pair, a much-changed design, the Limbo has been removed as well as VDS and the aircraft space increased to make way for a Sea King helicopter with Canadian Bear-Trap haul-down gear. After the first ship Dutch radar was adopted.

Missiles: *Nilgiri* has one Sea Cat launcher with UK GWS22 control. Remainder have two Sea Cat launchers with two Dutch M4 directors.

UDAYGIRI   6/1977, C. and S. Taylor

Radar: Air surveillance: One Type 965 *Nilgiri*.
Remainder: HSA LW-05.

Sonar: VDS in first three ships only.
All carry Type 184.

Squadron: Form 14th Frigate Squadron.

NILGIRI   6/1977

12 Ex-SOVIET "PETYA II" CLASS

ARNALA P 68
ANDROTH P 69
ANJADIP P 73
ANDAMAN P 74
AMINI P 75
KAMORTA P 77
KADMATH P 78
KILTAN P 79
KAVARATTI P 80
KATCHAL P 81
KANJAR P 82
AMINDIVI P 83

Displacement, tons: 950 standard; 1 150 full load
Length, feet (metres): 250·0 (76·2) wl; 270 (82·3) oa
Beam, feet (metres): 29·9 (9·1)
Draught, feet (metres): 10·5 (3·2)
Guns: 4—3 in (76 mm) (2 twin)
A/S weapons: 4 MBU 2 500 (16-barrelled rocket launchers); 2 internal DC racks
Torpedo tubes: 3—21 in (533 mm)
Mines: Have minerails
Main engines: 2 gas turbines; 30 000 hp; 2 diesels; 2 shafts; 6 000 hp
Speed, knots: 30
Complement: 98

Transferred to the Indian Navy since 1969. *Andaman* delivered March 1974, *Amini* late 1974. All are of an export version of "Petya II" class with simplified communications.
Form 32nd Frigate Squadron

Radar: Surface search: Slim Net.
Fire control: Hawk Screech
Navigation: Don 2

Sonar: One Hercules.

ANDAMAN   6/1977

238   INDIA / Frigates

2 Ex-BRITISH "WHITBY" CLASS

Name	No.	Builders	Laid down	Launched	Commissioned
TALWAR	F 40	Cammell Laird & Co Ltd, Birkenhead	1957	18 July 1958	1960
TRISHUL	F 43	Harland & Wolff Ltd, Belfast	1957	18 June 1959	1960

Displacement, tons: 2 144 standard;
  2 545 full load *(Talwar),* 2 557 *(Trishul)*
Length, feet (metres): 360 *(109·7)* pp; 369·8 *(112·7)* oa
Beam, feet (metres): 41 *(12·5)*
Draught, feet (metres): 17·8 *(5·4)*
Missiles: see note
Guns: 2—4·5 in *(115 mm)*/45 (twin Mk 6)
  (see *Missile* note)
  4—40 mm (1 twin before Limbos, 2 singles abaft funnel)
A/S weapons: 2 Limbo 3-barrelled DC mortars
Main engines: 2 sets geared turbines; 30 000 shp; 2 shafts
Boilers: 2 Babcock & Wilcox
Oil fuel, tons: 400
Speed, knots: 30
Range, miles: 4 500 at 12 knots
Complement: 231 (11 officers, 220 men)

Generally similar to the British frigates of the "Whitby" class, but slightly modified to suit Indian conditions. *Trishul* acts as Squadron commander of 15th Frigate Squadron.

Missiles: In late 1975 *Talwar* was fitted with three SS-N-2 missile launchers from an "Osa" class in place of the 4·5 in turret.

Radar: Tactical: Type 293 and 277.
  Fire control: I Band. (FPS 6 director).
  Missile control *(Talwar)*: Square Tie.

TALWAR (after SS-N-2 Mod)   1976

3 Ex-BRITISH "LEOPARD" CLASS

Name	No.	Builders	Laid down	Launched	Commissioned
BRAHMAPUTRA (ex-*Panther*)	F 31	John Brown & Co Ltd, Clydebank	1956	15 Mar 1957	28 Mar 1958
BEAS	F 37	Vickers-Armstrong Ltd, Tyne	1957	9 Oct 1958	24 May 1960
BETWA	F 39	Vickers-Armstrong Ltd, Tyne	1957	15 Sep 1959	8 Dec 1960

Displacement, tons: 2 251 standard; 2 515 full load
Length, feet (metres): 320·0 *(97·5)* pp; 330·0 *(100·6)* wl; 339·8 *(103·6)* oa
Beam, feet (metres): 40·0 *(12·2)*
Draught, feet (metres): 16·0 *(4·9)*
Guns: 4—4·5 in *(114 mm)*/45 (twin Mk 6); (2 in *Brahmaputra*)
  2—40 mm/60
A/S weapons: 1 Squid 3-barrelled DC motar
Main engines: Admiralty standard range diesels 2 shafts; 14 400 bhp
Speed, knots: 24
Range, miles: 7 500 at 16 knots
Complement: 210

Brahmaputra, orignally ordered as *Panther* for the Royal Navy on 28 June 1951, was the first major warship to be built in the UK for the Indian Navy since India became independent. All three ships are generally similar to the British frigates of the "Leopard" class, but modified to suit Indian conditions. Form 16th Frigate Squadron.

Radar: Search: Type 960.
  Tactical: Type 293.
  Fire control: Type 275.

BRAHMAPUTRA (with deckhouse in place of after turret)   1978

2 Ex-BRITISH "BLACKWOOD" CLASS (COAST GUARD)

Name	No.	Builders	Laid down	Launched	Commissioned
KIRPAN	Coast Guard	Alex Stephen & Sons Ltd, Govan, Glasgow	1957	19 Aug 1958	July 1959
KUTHAR	Coast Guard	J. Samuel White & Co Ltd, Cowes, Isle of Wight	1957	14 Oct 1958	1959

Displacement, tons: 1 180 standard; 1 456 full load
Length, feet (metres): 300 *(91·4)* pp; 310 *(94·5)* oa
Beam, feet (metres): 33 *(10·0)*
Draught, feet (metres): 15·5 *(4·7)*
Guns: 3—40 mm (single)
A/S weapons: 2 Limbo 3-barrelled DC mortars
Main engines: 1 set geared turbines; 15 000 shp; 1 shaft
Boilers: Babcock & Wilcox
Speed, knots: 27·8
Oil fuel, tons: 300
Range, miles: 4 000 at 12 knots
Complement: 150

Generally similar to the British frigates of the "Blackwood" class, but slightly modified to suit Indian requirements. *Khukri* of this class was sunk in the Pakistan war on 9 December 1971.

Radar: Fitted with E Band air and surface surveillance radar.

KIRPAN   1978, Rajiv Nair

INDIA / Frigates — Corvettes 239

1 Ex-BRITISH "HUNT" CLASS TYPE II

Name	No.	Builders	Laid down	Launched	Commissioned
GODAVARI (ex-HMS *Bedale*, ex-ORP *Slazak*, ex-HMS *Bedale*)	D 92	R. & W. Hawthorn, Leslie & Co Ltd, Hebburn	25 May 1940	23 July 1941	9 May 1942

Displacement, tons: 1 050 standard; 1 610 full load
Length, feet (metres): 264·2 *(80·5)* pp; 280·0 *(85·3)* oa
Beam, feet (metres): 31·5 *(9·6)*
Draught, feet (metres): 14·0 *(4·3)*
Guns: 6—4 in *(102 mm)* (twins); 4—20 mm; quad Pom-pom
Main engines: Parsons geared turbines; 2 shafts; 19 000 shp
Boilers: 2 Admiralty 3-drum
Oil fuel, tons: 280
Speed, knots: 25
Range, miles: 3 700 at 14 knots
Complement: 150

Lent to Poland April 1942—November 1946. Transferred from the UK in May 1953. Lent to the Indian Navy for three years, subject to extension by agreement. Now used for training. Ran aground in Maldives 1976—subsequently salvaged but may soon be deleted.

GANGA (*Godavari* similar)   *A. & J. Pavia*

2 Ex-BRITISH "BLACK SWAN" CLASS

Name	No.	Builders	Laid down	Launched	Commissioned
KISTNA	F 46	Yarrow & Co Ltd, Scotstoun, Glasgow	14 July 1942	22 Apr 1943	23 Aug 1943
KAVERI	F 110	Yarrow & Co Ltd, Scotstoun, Glasgow	28 Oct 1942	15 June 1943	21 Oct 1943

Displacement, tons: 1 470 standard; 1 925 full load
Length, feet (metres): 283·0 *(86·3)* pp; 295·5 *(90·1)* wl; 299·5 *(91·3)* oa
Beam, feet (metres): 38·5 *(11·7)*
Draught, feet (metres): 11·2 *(3·4)*
Guns: 4—4 in *(102 mm)*; 4—40 mm
A/S weapons: 2 DCT
Main engines: Parsons geared turbines; 2 shafts; 4 300 shp
Boilers: Two 3-drum type
Speed, knots: 19
Oil fuel, tons: 370
Range, miles: 4 500 at 12 knots
Complement: 210

Former sloops of the British "Black Swan" class built for India and modified to suit Indian conditions.
Cauvery was renamed *Kaveri* in 1968.

Radar: Fitted with E band air and surface surveillance radar and ranging radar for the gunfire control systems.

KISTNA

1 Ex-BRITISH "RIVER" CLASS

Name	No.	Builders	Laid down	Launched	Commissioned
TIR (ex-HMS *Bann*)	F 256	Charles Hill & Sons Ltd, Bristol	18 June 1942	29 Dec 1942	7 May 1943

Displacement, tons: 1 463 standard; 1 934 full load
Length, feet (metres): 283·0 *(86·3)* pp; 303 *(92·4)* oa
Beam, feet (metres): 37·6 *(11·2)*
Draught, feet (metres): 14·5 *(4·4)*
Guns: 1—4 in *(102 mm)*; 1—40 mm; 2—20 mm
Main engines: Triple expansion; 2 shafts; 5 500 ihp
Boilers: 2 Admiralty 3-drum type
Speed, knots: 18
Oil fuel, tons: 385
Range, miles: 4 200 at 12 knots
Complement: 120

Transferred on 3 December 1945. Converted to a Midshipman's Training Frigate by Bombay Dockyard in 1948.

TIR   *Indian Navy*

CORVETTES

4 + (?2) Ex-SOVIET "NANUCHKA" CLASS

VIJAY DURG	K 71	HOS DURG	K 73
SINHU DURG	K 72	—	K 74

Displacement, tons: 850 full load
Length, feet (metres): 196·8 *(60)*
Beam, feet (metres): 39·6 *(12)*
Draught, feet (metres): 9·9 *(3)*
Missiles: SSM; 4—SS-N-2B (single cells); SAM; 1—SA-N-4
Guns: 2—57 mm (twin)
Main engines: 6 diesels; 30 000 shp; 3 shafts
Speed, knots: 34
Range, miles: 3 600 at 15 knots
Complement: 70

A notable addition to Indian capabilities.
Vijay Durg delivered March 1977.
Reported that a total of eight is to be delivered.

Radar: Search; Band Stand.
Fire control: Pop Group, Muff Cob.
Navigation: Don.

The Band Stand radar is mounted lower than in Soviet ships of this class due to the absence of Fish Bowl with the use of SS-N-2 missiles in place of SS-N-9.

VIJAY DURG   *6/1977*

240 INDIA / Light forces — Amphibious forces

LIGHT FORCES

16 Ex-SOVIET "OSA I and II" CLASS (FAST ATTACK CRAFT—MISSILE)

VEER K 82	NASHAT K 87	*PRATAP K 92
VIDYUT K 83	NIRBHIK K 88	*PRABAL K 93
VIJETA K 84	NIRGHAT K 89	CHAPAL K 94
VINASH K 85	*PRACHAND K 90	*CHAMAK K 95
NIPAT K 86	*PRALAYA K 91	*CHATAK K 96
		*CHARAG K 97

*Osa II

Displacement, tons: 165 standard ("Osa II"); 200 full load
Dimensions, feet (metres): 127·9 × 26·6 × 5·9 (39 × 8·1 × 1·8)
Missiles: SSM; 4—SS-N-2 (single cells)
Guns: 4—30 mm L65 (2 twin)
Main engines: 3 (M503A, Osa I; M504, Osa II) diesels; 3 shafts; 12 000 bhp (Osa I), 15 000 bhp (Osa II) = 36 knots
Range, miles: 800 at 25 knots
Complement: 30

INDIAN "OSA" Class   6/1977

Some of these craft took part in a night attack with Styx off Karachi on 4-5 December 1971. They sank the PNS *Khaibar*, damaged *Badr* and a CMS as well as one Panamanian m/s without damage to themselves.
Further eight delivered February-October 1976. ("Osa II" class). Three others reported sunk in Indo-Pakistani War 1971.

Missiles: *Vijeta* had three SS-N-2 launchers transferred to I. S. *Talwar* in late 1975.
Radar: Search: Square Tie.
Fire control: Drum Tilt.
IFF: High Pole and Square Head.

3 + ?7 "SDB MARK 2" CLASS (FAST ATTACK CRAFT—PATROL)

T 51   T 52   T 53

Displacement, tons: 203 full load
Dimensions, feet (metres): 123 × 24·6 × 5·9 (37·5 × 7·5 × 1·8)
Gun: 1—40/60 mm Bofors
A/S weapons: 18—Mk 7 DCs; 10—Mk 12 DCs
Main engines: 2 Paxman Deltic diesels; 2 shafts; 6 880 bhp = 29 knots
Auxiliary propulsion: 1—Kirloskar-Cummins diesel on centre shaft; 165 bhp = 4 knots
Range, miles: 1 400 at 14 knots

First launched 16 July 1976, started trials September 1977. T 53 launched spring 1978. All building by Garden Reach S.Y., Calcutta. Indian Customs Service to purchase a number of this class—"for but not with" armament.

5 Ex-SOVIET "POLUCHAT" CLASS (COAST GUARD PATROL CRAFT)

PANVEL	PURI	PULICAT
PAMBAN	PANAJI	

Displacement, tons: 86 standard; 91 full load
Dimensions, feet (metres): 98 × 15 × 4·8 (29·9 × 4·6 × 1·5)
Guns: 2—14·5 mm (twin)
Main engines: 2 diesels; 2 shafts; 2 400 bhp = 18 knots
Range, miles: 460 at 17 knots
Complement: 16

One transferred to Bangladesh in 1973 but returned. Originally operated by the Home Department—now transferred to the Coast Guard.

"POLUCHAT" Class   1978

1 "ABHAY" CLASS (LARGE PATROL CRAFT)

Name	No.	Builders	Commissioned
ABHAY	T 35	Hoogly Docking & Engineering Co Ltd, Calcutta	13 Nov 1961

Displacement, tons: 120 standard; 151 full load
Dimensions, feet (metres): 117·2 × 20 × 5 (35·7 × 6·1 × 1·5)
Gun: 1—40 mm
Main engines: 2 diesels; speed = 18 knots

Generally similar to the "Ford" class in the Royal Navy. Originally a class of six. *Ajay* and *Akshay* transferred to Bangladesh 1974, *Amar* to Mauritius April 1974.

2 "SHARADA" CLASS (COASTAL PATROL CRAFT)

Name	No.	Builders	Commissioned
SUKANYA	SPB 3132	Yugoslavia	5 Dec 1959
SHARADA	SPB 3133	Yugoslavia	5 Dec 1959

Displacement, tons: 83 standard; 100 full load
Dimensions, feet (metres): 98·4 × 19·7 × 4·9 (30 × 6 × 1·5)
Guns: Small arms
Main engines: 2 Mercedes-Benz diesels; 1 900 hp = 18 knots
Complement: 16

Probably now laid up.

AMPHIBIOUS FORCES

6 Ex-SOVIET "POLNOCHNIY" CLASS (LCT)

GHARIAL L 12	GHORPAD L 14	SHARDUL L 16
GULDAR L 13	KESARI L 15	SHARAB L 17

Displacement, tons: 780 standard; 1 000 full load (L 12 and L 13); 1 100 full load (remainder)
Dimensions, feet (metres): 239 × 29·5 × 6·6 (72·9 × 9 × 2) (L 12 and L 13); Remainder length 265 ft (80·8), beam 31 ft (9·5)
Guns: 2—25 mm (twin) (L 12 and L 13); 4—30 mm (twins) (remainder); 2—140 mm rocket launchers (18 tubes)
Main engines: 2 diesels; 5 000 bhp (P III class); 4 000 bhp (P I class) = 18 knots
Complement: 40

First pair (Polnochniy I class) transferred from USSR in 1966, *Ghorpad* in 1975, *Kesari* September 1975, *Shardul* December 1975 and *Sharab* March 1976. 350 ton cargo in P III class, 200 in P I class. Last four of Polnochniy III class.

Radar: Drum Tilt not fitted.
Navigation: Don 2.

1 Ex-BRITISH LST (3)

MAGAR (ex-HMS *Avenger*) L 11

Displacement, tons: 2 256 light; 4 980 full load
Dimensions, feet (metres): 347·5 × 55·2 × 11·2 (106 × 16·8 × 3·4)
Guns: 2—40 mm; 6—20 mm; (2 twin, 2 single)
Main engines: Triple expansion; 2 shafts; 5 500 ihp = 13 knots

3 INDIAN LANDING CRAFT UTILITY

A new design, of which three have been laid down at Goa S.Y. (subsidiary of Mazagon Docks Ltd)—two in 1977 and one in 1978. The draught is less than 4 ft with a capacity of 125 men or 25 tons.

There is also LCT 4294 (ex-1294), yard craft of 200 tons, speed 9·5 knots.

INDIA / Mine warfare forces — Survey ships

MINE WARFARE FORCES

2 + 3 Ex-SOVIET "NATYA" CLASS (MINESWEEPERS—OCEAN)

PONDICHERRY M 61 **PORBANDAR** M 62

Displacement, tons: 650 standard; 750 full load
Dimensions, feet (metres): 200.1 × 31.5 × 7.5 *(61 × 9.6 × 2.3)*
Guns: 4—30 mm L65 (twins); 4—25 mm L70 (twins)
Main engines: 2 diesels; 2 shafts; 8 000 shp = 20 knots
Complement: 70

Transferred early-1978 with three more to follow.

Radar: Fire control: Drum Tilt.
Navigation: Don 2.

SOVIET "NATYA" Class

4 Ex-BRITISH "TON" CLASS (MINESWEEPERS—COASTAL)

Name	No.	Builders	Commissioned
CUDDALORE (ex-HMS *Wennington*)	M 90	J. S. Doig Ltd, Grimsby	1955
CANNAMORE (ex-HMS *Whitton*)	M 91	Fleetlands Shipyard Ltd, Gosport	1956
KARWAR (ex-HMS *Overton*)	M 92	Camper & Nicholson Ltd, Gosport	1956
KAKINADA (ex-HMS *Durweston*)	M 93	Dorset Yacht Co Ltd, Hamworthy	1955

Displacement, tons: 360 standard; 425 full load
Dimensions, feet (metres): 153.0 × 28.8 × 8.2 *(46.7 × 8.8 × 2.5)*
Guns: 2—20 mm
Main engines: Napier Deltic diesels; 2 shafts; 1 250 bhp = 15 knots
Oil fuel, tons: 45
Range, miles: 3 000 at 8 knots
Complement: 40

KAKINADA 1977

"Ton" class coastal minesweepers of wooden construction built for the Royal Navy, but transferred from the UK to the Indian Navy in 1956. *Cannamore* was launched 30 January 1956, *Karwar* was launched 30 January 1956. *Cuddalore* and *Kakinada* were taken over in August 1956, and sailed for India in November-December 1956. Named after minor ports in India. Constitute the 18th Mine Counter Measures Squadron, together with the inshore minesweepers.

4 "HAM" CLASS (MINESWEEPERS—INSHORE)

Name	No.	Builders	Commissioned
BHAKTAL	M 88	Mazagon Docks Ltd, Bombay	1968
BULSAR	M 89	Mazagon Docks Ltd, Bombay	1970
BIMLIPITAN (ex-HMS *Hildersham*)	M 2705	Vosper Ltd, Portsmouth	1954
BASSEIN (ex-HMS *Littleham*)	M 2707	Brooke Marine Ltd, Oulton Broad, Lowestoft	1954

Displacement, tons: 120 standard; 170 full load
Dimensions, feet (metres): 107.0 × 22.0 × 6.7 *(32.6 × 6.7 × 1.6)*
Gun: 1—20 mm
Main engines: 2 Paxman diesels; 550 bhp = 14 knots (9 knots sweeping)
Oil fuel, tons: 15
Complement: 16

BASSEIN 1971, A. & J. Pavia

Of wooden construction two of which were built for the Royal Navy but transferred from the UK to the Indian Navy in 1955. *Bassein* was launched on 4 May 1954; *Bimlipitan* was launched on 5 February 1954. *Bhaktal* was launched in April 1967, and *Bulsar* on 17 May 1969.

SURVEY SHIPS

Name	No.	Builders	Commissioned
DARSHAK	A 139	Hindustan Shipyard, Vishakapatnam	28 Dec 1964

Displacement, tons: 2 790
Length, feet (metres): 319 *(97.2)*
Beam, feet (metres): 49 *(14.9)*
Draught, feet (metres): 28.8 *(8.8)*
Main engines: 2 diesel-electric units; 3 000 bhp
Speed, knots: 16
Complement: 150

First ship built by Hindustan Shipyard for the Navy. Launched on 2 November 1959. Provision was made to operate a helicopter. The ship is all welded.

DARSHAK 1967

1 + 2 "SANDHAYAK" CLASS

Name	No.	Builders	Commissioned
SANDHAYAK	—	Garden Reach D.Y. Calcutta	1979
—	—	Garden Reach D.Y. Calcutta	1980?
—	—	Garden Reach D.Y. Calcutta	1981?

Displacement, tons: 1 830 full load
Dimensions, feet (metres): 281.3 × 42 × 11.0 *(85.8 × 12.8 × 3.3)*
Aircraft: 1—Alouette III helicopter
Guns: 2—40 mm Bofors
Main engines: 2 GRSE/MAN diesels; 3 920 bhp; 2 shafts
Speed, knots: 16.8
Range, miles: 6 000 at 14 knots

Sandhayak launched 6 April 1977. Second laid down 15 November 1976 and third on 18 June 1977.

242 INDIA / Survey ships — Service forces

2 "SUTLEJ" CLASS

Name	No.	Builders	Laid down	Launched	Commissioned
JAMUNA (ex-*Jumna*)	F 11	Wm. Denny & Bros Ltd, Dumbarton	20 Feb 1940	16 Nov 1940	13 May 1941
SUTLEJ	F 95	Wm. Denny & Bros Ltd, Dumbarton	4 Jan 1940	10 Oct 1940	23 Apr 1941

Displacement, tons: 1 300 standard; 1 750 full load
Length, feet (metres): 276 *(84·1)* wl; 292·5 *(89·2)* oa
Beam, feet (metres): 37·5 *(11·4)*
Draught, feet (metres): 11·5 *(3·5)*
Gun: 1—40 mm
Main engines: Parsons geared turbines 3 600 shp; 2 shafts
Boilers: 2 Admiralty 3-drum
Speed, knots: 18
Oil fuel, tons: 370
Range, miles: 5 600 at 12 knots
Complement: 150

Former frigates employed as survey ships since 1957 and 1955 respectively. Both ships are generally similar to the former British frigates of the "Egret" class.

JAMUNA 11/1975, P. Elliott

SERVICE FORCES

1 Ex-SOVIET "UGRA" CLASS (SUBMARINE TENDER)

AMBA A 14

Displacement, tons: 6 000 light; 9 000 full load
Length, feet (metres): 463·8 × 58·1 × 21·3 *(141·4 × 17·7 × 6·5)*
Guns: 4—3 in *(76 mm)* (twins)
Main engines: Diesels; 2 shafts; 7 000 bhp = 17 knots

Acquired from the USSR in 1968. Provision for helicopter. Can accommodate 750. Two cranes, one of 6 tons and one of 10 tons.

Radar: Search: One Strut Curve.
Fire control: One Don 2.
Navigation: Two Muff Cob.

AMBA 1977

1 Ex-SOVIET "T58" (Mod.) CLASS (SUBMARINE RESCUE SHIP)

NISTAR A 15

Displacement, tons: 790 standard; 900 full load
Dimensions, feet (metres): 229·6 × 29·5 × 7·9 *(70 × 9·1 × 2·3)*
Main engines: 2 diesels; 2 shafts; 4 000 bhp = 18 knots
Complement: 80

Converted from a fleet minesweeper to a submarine rescue ship and transferred from USSR late 1971. Carries diving-bell, recompression chamber and two rescue chambers aft.

Radar: Navigation: One Don 2.

1 REPAIR SHIP

DHARINI (ex- *La Petite Hermine*) A 306

Displacement, tons: 6 000 (oil capacity 1 000)
Dimensions, feet (metres): 324·7 × 45·6 × 13·3 *(99 × 13·9 × 4)*
Main engines: Triple expansion; 809 ihp = 9 knots
Oil fuel, tons: 621

Cargo ship built by Foundation Maritime Ltd, Canada as *Ketowna Park*. Launched 25 July 1944. Sold to India for commercial use in 1953. Transferred to navy in 1957. Converted and commissioned in May 1960.

DHARINI 1964, Indian Navy

2 REPLENISHMENT TANKERS

Name	No.	Builders	Commissioned
DEEPAK	A 50	Bremer-Vulkan	1967
SHAKTI	A 57	Bremer-Vulkan	31 Dec 1975

Displacement, tons: 15 828
Measurement, tons: 12 690·6 GRT
Dimensions, feet (metres): 552·6 × 75·5 × 30 *(168·4 × 23 × 9·2)*
Guns: 3—40 mm; 2—20 mm
Main engine: 1 BV/BBC steam turbine; 16 500 bhp = 18·5 knots
Boiler: 1 Babcock and Wilcox
Range, miles: 5 500
Complement: 169

SHAKTI 1/197

On charter to Indian Navy from Mogul Lines. Fitted with a helicopter landing platform aft and hangar. Automatic tensioning fitted to replenishment gear. Heavy and light jackstays. Stern fuelling as well as alongside.
Shakti launched September 1975.

Capacity: 1 280 tons diesel; 12 624 FFO; 1 495 tons avcat; 812 tons FW.

Equipment: DG fitted; NBCD fitted.

1 SUPPORT TANKER

LOK ADHAR (ex-*Hooghly*)

Displacement, tons: 9 231

Formerly *Baqir* of Gulf Shipping Corp Ltd. Acquired in 1972.

2 + 1 SUPPORT TANKERS

PRADHAYAK **PURAN** +1

Displacement, tons: 376
Dimensions, feet (metres): 149.5 × — × 9.8 *(49.7 × — × 3.0)*
Main engine: 1 Diesel; 560 hp = 9 knots

Built at Rajabagan Yard, Bombay. *Puran* completed 3 June 1977 and *Pradhayak* February 1978. Third reported building.

1 SUPPORT TANKER

DESH DEEP

Measurement, tons: 11 000 deadweight

Launched in 1932.

Ex-Japanese merchant tanker taken over in 1972.

1 TUG (OCEAN)

MATANGA

Displacement, tons: 1 600 full load
Dimensions, feet (metres): 226.4 × 40.4 × — *(66 × 11.6 × —)*
Main engines: 2 GRSE/MAN diesels; 2 shafts; 3 920 bhp = 15 knots
Range, miles: 8 000 at 12 knots.

Built by Garden Reach S.Y. Laid down 11 February 1976, launched 29 October 1977. The largest tug so far built in India with a bollard pull of 40 tons and capable of towing a 20 000 ton ship at 8 knots.

1 TUG (OCEAN)

GAJ A 1751

Displacement, tons: 1 465 full load
Dimensions, feet (metres): 196.9 × 37.7 × 13.1 *(60 × 11.5 × 4)*
Main engines: 2 GRSE/MAN G7V diesels; 2 shafts; cp propellers; 2 970 bhp = 15 knots

Built by Garden Reach S.Y. in 1973-74. Bollard pull 40 tons. Fitted for salvage.

1 TUG (OCEAN)

Name	No.	Builders	Commissioned
HATHI	—	Taikoo Dock & Engineering Company, Hong Kong	1933

Displacement, tons: 668
Dimensions, feet (metres): 147.5 × 23.7 × 15 *(45 × 7.2 × 4.6)*
Main engines: Triple expansion; speed = 13 knots

Launched in 1932.

4 Ex-BRITISH HDML TYPE

SPC 3110 (ex-*HDML 1110*)   SPC 3117 (ex-*HDML 1117*)
SPC 3112 (ex-*HDML 1112*)   SPC 3118 (ex-*HDML 1118*)

Displacement, tons: 48 standard; 54 full load
Dimensions, feet (metres): 72 × 16 × 4.7 *(22 × 4.9 × 1.4)*
Guns: 2—20 mm
Main engines: Diesels; 2 shafts; 320 bhp = 12 knots
Complement: 14

Used as harbour-craft.

1 + 2 WATER CARRIERS

Displacement, tons: 200
Dimensions, feet (metres): 108.3 × — × 8 *(32 × — × 2.4)*

First laid down Rajabagan Yard 18 January 1977. Second pair under construction at Mazagon Docks Ltd, Bombay.

0 + 4 TRANSPORTS (PERSONNEL)

Building at Peoples' Engineering Yard.

0 + 3 DIVING TENDERS

Building at Cleback Yard.

1 TARGET PONTOON

Of 78 tons launched at Cleback Yard 26 September 1976. Completed March 1977.

Barq (ex-*MMS 132*), *MMS 130* and *MMS 154*, former British motor minesweepers of the "105 ft" type of wooden construction, transferred from the UK, are employed as yard craft. *MMS 1632* and *MMS 1654* are yard craft in Bombay.

INDONESIA

Ministerial

Minister of Defence and Security:
  General Maraden Panggabean

Administration

Chief of the Naval Staff:
  Admiral Waluyo Sugito
Deputy Chief of the Naval Staff:
  Rear-Admiral Mustopo
Inspector General of the Navy:
  Rear-Admiral Toto
Chief for Naval Material:
  Commodore Mohammad Suud
Chief for Naval Personnel:
  Commodore M. Hatta
Commander of Navy Marine Corps:
  Brigadier General Kahpi Suriediredja

Fleet Command

Commandar Military Sea Lift Command:
  Rear-Admiral Suparno
Commander-in-Chief Indonesian Fleet:
  Rear-Admiral Prasojo Mahdi

Diplomatic Representation

Naval Attaché in Bangkok:
  Lieutenant Colonel Purnomo
Naval Attaché in Canberra:
  Colonel Eddy Tumengkol
Naval Attaché in Delhi:
  Colonel B. Sumitro
Naval Attaché and Naval Attaché for Air in London:
  Lieut. Colonel Z. A. Maulani
Naval Attaché in Moscow:
  Colonel Priyonggo
Naval Attaché in Tokyo:
  Colonel Agus Subroto
Naval Attaché and Naval Attaché for Air in Washington:
  Colonel Ariffin Roesady

Personnel

(a) 1979: 40 000 including 5 000 Marine Commando Corps and 1 000 Naval Air Arm
(b) Selective national service

Bases

Gorontalo, Kemajaran (Jakarta), Surabaja

Strength of the Fleet

Type	Active	Building
Patrol Submarines	3	2 (2)
Frigates	9	3
Fast Attack Craft—Missile	9	4
Fast Attack Craft—Torpedo	4	—
Large Patrol Craft	22	—
Coastal Patrol Craft	8	—
LSTs	9	—
Amphibious Craft	41+	—
Minesweepers—Ocean	5	—
Minesweepers—Coastal	2	—
Survey Ships	4	—
Submarine Tenders	2	—
Destroyer Depot Ship	1	—
Repair Ship	1	—
Replenishment Tanker	1	—
Support Tankers	2	—
Harbour Tankers	3	—
Cable Ship	1	—
Tugs	9	—
Training Ships	1	1
Customs	24+	14
Army	16	—
Air Force	6	—

Ex-Soviet Ships

Indonesia obtained 104 ships from the USSR. Of these half have now been deleted and all will have gone in the near future.

Future Plans

It is planned, over the next 20 years, to provide a Navy of some 25 000 seamen and 5 000 marines to man a Fleet including four fast A/S Frigates, some Submarines, Light Forces of Fast Attack Craft—Missile and—Torpedo, Minelayers, Minesweepers, a fast HQ ship and a fast Supply Ship. Three Corvettes/Frigates are being built by the Netherlands, two submarines in West Germany and four fast attack craft in South Korea.

Naval Air Arm

6—GAF Nomad (MR)
5—HU 16B Albatross (SAR)
6—C 47
3—Alouette II helicopters
3—Alouette III helicopters
4—Bell 47G helicopters
3—Commander

Prefix to Ships' Names

KRI (Kapal di Republik Indonesia)

Mercantile Marine

Lloyd's Register of Shipping:
  1 093 vessels of 1 272 387 tons gross

244 INDONESIA / Introduction

DELETIONS

Submarines

1974 *Alugoro, Hendradjala, Nagarangsang, Tjandrasa, Tjundmani, Trisula, Widjajadanu* (all "Whiskey" class)

Cruiser

1972 *Irian*

Destroyers

1973 *Brawidjaja, Sandjaja, Sultan Babarudin*

Frigates

1973 *Kakiali, Slamet Rijadi*
1974 *Ngurah Rai* ("Riga" class)
1978 *Iman Bondjol, Surapati*

Amphibious Forces

1974 3 ex-Yugoslav LCTs, *Tandjung Nusanive* (ex-US LST); 3 ex-US LCI Type

Mine Warfare Forces

1974 4 ex-Dutch CMS, 5 "R" class
1976 *Pulau Rondo* ("T 43" class), *Rau, Rindja, Rusa* ("R" class), *Pulau Alor, Pulau Anjer, Pulau Antang, Pulau Aru, Pulah Aruan, Pulau Impalasa* ("Falcon" class)

Light Forces

1970 *310, 314, 315, 316* (Kraljevica), *Dorang, Lajang, Rubara*
1974 2 "Jaguar" class, 25 HDMLs, 10 Motor Launches, *Palu, Tenggiri*
1975 14 "P 6" class, 18 "BK" class, *Landjuru, Lapai, Lumba Lumba, Madidihang, Tongkol, Tjutjut* ("Kronshtadt" class)
1976 *Katula, Momare* ("Kronshtadt" class), *Krapu* ("Kraljevica" class), *Katjabola, Tritusta* ("Komar" class)
1977 *Serigala* ("TNC 45" class)

Survey Ships

1972 *Hidral*
1973 *Dewa Kembar*

Auxiliaries

1974 2 Transports, 1 Salvage Vessel, 1 Tug, 37 Patrol Craft
1976 *Thamrin* ("Atrek" class), *Pangkalin Brandan, Wono Kromo* ("Uda" class)

PENNANT LIST

Submarines

401 Cakra
402 Candrasa
403 Naga Banda
410 Pasopati
412 Bramastra

Frigates

341 Samadikun
342 Martadinata
343 Mongisidi
344 Ngurah Rai
351 Jos Sudarso
357 Lambung Makurat
360 Nuku
361 Fata Hilla
362 Mala Hayati
363 Nala
801 Pattimura
802 Sultan Hasanudin

Light Forces

570 Bentang Kalungkang
571 Bentang Waitatire
572 Bentang Silunkang
601 Kelaplintah
602 Kalamisani
603 Sarpawasesa
604 Pulang Geni
605 Kalanada
608 Surotama
609 Sarpamina
611 Naga Pasa
612 Guawidjaja
652 Beruang
653 Matjan Kumbang
654 Harimau
655 Anoa
805 Hiu
806 Torani
807 Kakalang
808 Kelabang
809 Kompas
810 Kala Hitam
814 Pandorong
815 Sura
816 Kakap
817 Barakuda
818 Sembilang
819 Layang
820 Lemadang
821 Krapu
822 Dorang
823 Todak
846 Silinan
847 Sibarau

Mine Warfare Forces

701 Pulau Rani
702 Pulau Ratewo
703 Pulau Roon
704 Pulau Rorbas
705 Pulau Raja
707 Pulau Rengat
708 Pulau Rapat

Amphibious Forces

501 Teluk Langsa
502 Teluk Bajur
503 Teluk Amboina
504 Teluk Kau
505 Teluk Manado
508 Teluk Tomini
509 Teluk Ratai
510 Teluk Saleh
511 Teluk Bone

Support Ships

561 Multatuli
562 Dumai
4101 Ratulangi

Service Forces

906 Sungai Jerong
911 Sorong
921 Jaya Wijaya
925 Banggai
928 Rakata
934 Lampo Batang
935 Tambora
936 Bromo
952 Nura Telu
960 Pakan Baru

Survey Ships

1002 Burdjamhal
1005 Jalanidhi
1006 Burudjulasad
1008 Aries

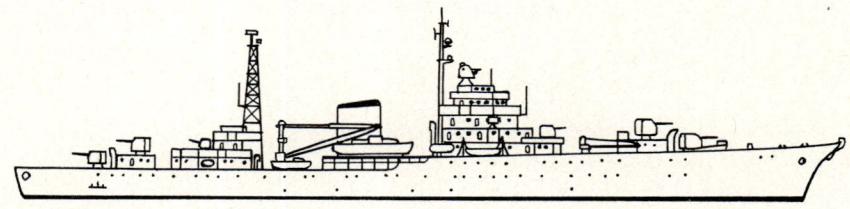

RATULANGI

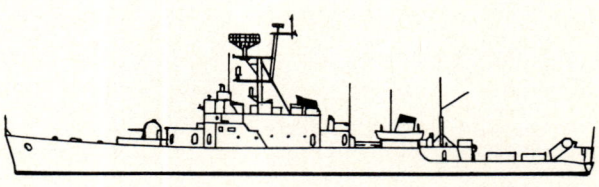

"CLAUD JONES" Class

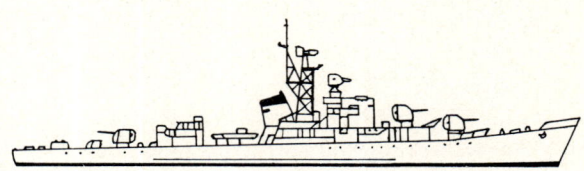

"RIGA" Class

INDONESIA / Submarines — Frigates 245

SUBMARINES
2 + (2) TYPE 209

Name	No.	Builders	Laid down	Launched	Commissioned
CAKRA	401	Howaldtswerke, Kiel	1977	1979	1980
CANDRASA	402	Howaldtswerke, Kiel	1977	1979	1980

Displacement, tons: 1 260 surfaced; 1 390 dived
Dimensions, feet (metres): 195·2 × 20·3 × 16·4 *(59·5 × 6·2 × 5)*
Torpedo Tubes: 8—21 in *(533 mm)* bow with reloads
Main machinery: Diesel electric; 4 MTU-Siemens diesel generators; 1 Siemens electric motor; 5 000 shp; 1 shaft
Speed, knots: 10 surfaced; 22 dived
Endurance: 50 days
Complement: 31

Ordered on 2 April 1977. Negotiations in hand for second pair.

Type 209

3 Ex-SOVIET "WHISKEY" CLASS

NAGA BANDA 403 BRAMASTRA 412
PASOPATI 410

Displacement, tons: 1 030 surfaced; 1 350 dived
Length, feet (metres): 249·3 *(76)*
Beam, feet (metres): 22 *(6·7)*
Draught, feet (metres): 15 *(4·6)*
Torpedo tubes: 6—21 in *(533 mm)* 4 fwd, 2 aft; 18 torpedoes carried
Guns: 2—25 mm (403)
Mines: 40 in lieu of torpedoes
Main machinery: 4 000 bhp diesels; 2 500 hp electric motors, diesel-electric drive; 2 shafts
Speed, knots: 17 surfaced; 15 dived
Range, miles: 13 000 at 8 knots surfaced
Complement: 60

The four Soviet submarines of the "Whiskey" class, which arrived in Indonesia on 28 June 1962, brought the total number of this class transferred to Indonesia to 14 units, but it was reported that only six would be maintained operational, while six would be kept in reserve and two used for spare parts. Now reduced to three operational boats of which two have been refitted and have received new batteries from UK. *Naga Banda* refitted 1978.

PASOPATI 1978, Indonesian Navy

FRIGATES

Name	No.	Builders	Laid down	Launched	Commissioned
FATA HILLA	361	Wilton Fijenoord, Netherlands	31 Jan 1977	22 Dec 1977	mid-1979
MALA HAYATI	362	Wilton Fijenoord, Netherlands	28 July 1977	19 June 1978	end 1979
NALA	363	Wilton Fijenoord, Netherlands	27 Jan 1978	Dec 1978	mid-1980

Displacement, tons: 1 200 standard
Dimensions, feet (metres): 276 × 36 × 10·7 *(84 × 11 × 3·3)*
Missiles: SSM; 4 Exocet
Guns: 1—76 mm/62 (single Compact); 2—40 mm (twin Bofors)
A/S weapons: Bofors 375 mm rocket projector
Main engines: CODOG; 1 General Electric LM2500 gas turbine 28 000 hp; 2 MTU diesels; 6 000 hp; 2 shafts
Speed, knots: 30

Ordered August 1975. Officially rated as "Corvettes".

Helicopter: *Nala* is being fitted with a telescopic hangar/landing deck for one helicopter; makers Machinefabriek Oldenzaal BV, Netherlands.

Radar: HSA—LW series and possibly WM 27.

NEW CONSTRUCTION FRIGATE (not *Nala*) 1976, Wilton Fijenoord

246 INDONESIA / Frigates

4 Ex-US "CLAUD JONES" CLASS

Name	No.	Builders	Laid down	Launched	Commissioned
SAMADIKUN (ex-USS *John R. Perry* DE 1034)	341	Avondale Marine Ways	1 Oct 1957	29 July 1958	5 May 1959
MARTADINATA (ex-USS *Charles Berry* DE 1035)	342	American S.B. Co, Toledo, Ohio	29 Oct 1958	17 Mar 1959	25 Nov 1959
MONGISIDI (ex-USS *Claud Jones* DE 1033)	343	Avondale Marine Ways	1 June 1957	27 May 1958	10 Feb 1959
NGURAH RAI (ex-USS *McMorris* DE 1036)	344	American S.B. Co, Toledo, Ohio	5 Nov 1958	26 May 1959	4 Mar 1960

Displacement, tons: 1 450 standard; 1 750 full load
Length, feet (metres): 310 *(95)*
Beam, feet (metres): 37 *(11·3)*
Draught, feet (metres): 18 *(5·5)*
Guns: 1—3 in *(76 mm)*/50 (single Mk 34) (see note);
  2—37 mm (twin); 2—25 mm (twin) (341-342);
  2—3 in *(76 mm)* (single); 2—25 mm (twin) (343-344)
A/S weapons: 2 triple torpedo tubes (Mk 32); 2 Hedgehogs
Main engines: 4 diesels; 9 200 hp; 1 shaft
Speed, knots: 22
Complement: 175

Samadikun served as fleet flagship—relieved by *Multatuli*.

Electronics: ECM/ESM gear removed

Gunnery: Fire control system Mk 70 for 3 in.
Secondary armament is ex-Soviet.

Radar: Search: SPS 6.
Fire control: SPS 10.

Sonar: SQS 29-32 series.

Transfer: *Samadikun*, 20 February 1973; *Martadinata*, 31 January 1974; *Mongisidi* and *Ngurah Rai* 16 December 1974.

SAMADIKUN *1975, Indonesian Navy*

3 Ex-SOVIET "RIGA" CLASS

JOS SUDARSO 351   NUKU 360
LAMBUNG MANGKURAT 357

Displacement, tons: 1 200 standard; 1 600 full load
Length, feet (metres): 298·8 *(91)*
Beam, feet (metres): 33·7 *(10·2)*
Draught, feet (metres): 11 *(3·4)*
Guns: 3—3·9 in *(100 mm)* (single); 4—37 mm
A/S weapons: 4 DC projectors
Torpedo tubes: 3—21 in *(533 mm)*
Mines: Fitted with mine rails
Main engines: Geared steam turbines; 2 shafts; 25 000 shp
Boilers: 2
Speed, knots: 28
Range, miles: 2 500 at 15 knots
Complement: 150

Built 1955-57.
Transferred in 1964.

Radar: Search and warning: Slim Net.
Fire control: Sun Visor A with Wasp Head director.
Navigation: Neptun.
IFF: High Pole A.

JOS SUDARSO *1974, John Mortimer*

2 "PATTIMURA" CLASS

Name	No.	Builders	Laid down	Launched	Commissioned
PATTIMURA	801	Ansaldo, Leghorn	8 Jan 1956	1 July 1956	28 Jan 1958
SULTAN HASANUDIN	802	Ansaldo, Leghorn	8 Jan 1957	24 Mar 1957	8 Mar 1958

Displacement, tons: 950 standard; 1 200 full load
Length, feet (metres): 246 *(75·0)* pp; 270·2 *(82·4)* oa
Beam, feet (metres): 34 *(10·4)*
Draught, feet (metres): 9 *(2·7)*
Guns: 2—3 in *(76 mm)*/40; 2—30 mm/70 (twin)
A/S weapons: 2 Hedgehogs; 4 DCT
Main engines: 3 Ansaldo-Fiat diesels; 3 shafts; 6 900 bhp
Speed, knots: 22
Range, miles: 2 400 at 18 knots
Oil fuel, tons: 100
Complement: 110

Similar to Italian "Albatros" class.
Sultan Hasanudin in reserve.

PATTIMURA *Dr.Ing Luigi Accorsi*

LIGHT FORCES

6 Ex-SOVIET "KRONSHTADT" CLASS (LARGE PATROL CRAFT)

PANDORONG 814	KAKAP 816	SEMBILANG 818
SURA 815	BARAKUDA 817	TOHOK

Displacement, tons: 310 standard; 380 full load
Dimensions, feet (metres): 170·6 × 21·5 × 9 *(52·0 × 6·5 × 2·7)*
Guns: 1—3·5 in *(85 mm)*; 2—37 mm; 6—12·7 mm
A/S weapons: 2 DCT; 2 RBU 1800; 2 dc racks
Mines: 2 mine rails for 10 mines
Main engines: 3 diesels; 3 shafts; 3 300 bhp = 19 knots
Oil fuel, tons: 20
Range, miles: 1 500 at 12 knots
Complement: 65

Built in 1951-54. Transferred to the Indonesian Navy on 30 December 1958. *Kakap* in reserve.

Radar: Ball Gun or Don 2.
IFF: High Pole A

"KRONSHTADT" Class

3 Ex-US "PC-461" CLASS (LARGE PATROL CRAFT)

HIU (ex-USS *Malvern*, PC 580) 805
TORANI (ex-USS *Manville*, PC 581) 806
KAKALANG (ex-USS *Pierre*, PC 1141) 807

Displacement, tons: 280 standard; 450 full load
Dimensions, feet (metres): 173·7 × 23 × 10·8 *(55·7; 53 × 7 × 3·3)*
Guns: 1—37 mm; 4—25 mm (twin)
A/S weapons: 4 DCT
Main engines: 2 General Motors diesels; 2 shafts; 2 880 bhp = 20 knots
Oil fuel, tons: 60
Range, miles: 5 000 at 10 knots
Complement: 54 (4 officers, 50 men)

Gunnery: Original armament of 1—3 in *(76 mm)*; 1—40 mm; 2—20 mm has been replaced in most ships by armament shown from deleted ex-Soviet ships.

Built in 1942-43. *Kakalang* transferred from the US Navy at Pearl Harbor, Hawaii in October 1958 and *Hui* and *Torani* in March 1960. *Kakalang* and *Torani* in reserve.

"PC-461" Class   *1966, Indonesian Navy*

4 PSMM Mark 5 (FAST ATTACK CRAFT—MISSILE)

Displacement, tons: 290 full load
Dimensions, feet (metres): 165 × 24 × 9·5 *(50·3 × 7·3 × 2·9)*
Missiles: SSM; 4 Exocet (single cells)
Guns: 1—57 mm; 1—40 mm
Main engines: 1 General Electric LM 2500 gas turbine; 2 MTU diesels; 2 shafts (cp propellers) = 45 knots (gas) 17 knots (diesels)
Complement: 32

Ordered from Korea-Tacoma Boatbuilding Co, Washington for delivery April, May, July, September 1979.
Building in South Korea.

Fire control: HSA.

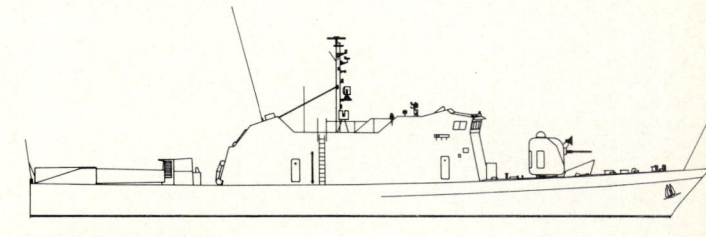
BASIC PSMM Mk 5 DESIGN   *1976*

9 Ex-SOVIET "KOMAR" CLASS (FAST ATTACK CRAFT—MISSILE)

KELAPLINTAH 601	PULANG GENI 604	SARPAMINA 609
KALAMISANI 602	KALANADA 605	NAGA PASA 611
SARPAWASESA 603	SUROTAMA 608	GUAWIDJAJA 612

Displacement, tons: 68 standard; 75 full load
Dimensions, feet (metres): 87·9 × 19·8 × 5 *(26·8 × 6·0 × 1·8)*
Guns: 2—35 mm (1 twin)
Missiles: SSM; 2-SS-N-2 (single cells) (See note)
Main engines: 4 diesels; 4 shafts; 4 800 hp = 40 knots
Range, miles: 400 at 30 knots
Complement: 19

Six were transferred to Indonesia in 1961-63, four more in September 1964 and two in 1965. Missiles probably of doubtful capability. *Guawidjaya* and *Naga Pasa* in reserve. All for deletion 1979.

Hardadali of this class sank early 1976 after hitting an underwater obstacle.

Radar: Square Tie.

SARPAMINA   *1967*

4 "LURSSEN TNC-45" CLASS (FAST ATTACK CRAFT—TORPEDO)

Name	No.	Builders	Commissioned
BERUANG	652	Lürssen, Vegesack	1959
MATJAN KUMBANG	653	Lürssen, Vegesack	1960
HARIMAU	654	Lürssen, Vegesack	1960
ANOA	655	Lürssen, Vegesack	1959

Displacement, tons: 160 standard; 190 full load
Dimensions, feet (metres): 138 × 22 × 7·5 *(42·1 × 6·7 × 2·3)*
Guns: 2—40 mm (single)
Torpedo tubes: 4—21 in
Main engines: 4 Daimler-Benz (MTU) diesels; 4 shafts; 12 000 bhp = 42 knots
Complement: 39

Steel hulled—of the original eight, four had wooden hulls. Similar to German "Jaguar" class.

HARIMAU   *Indonesia*

248 INDONESIA / Light forces

5 Ex-YUGOSLAV "KRALJEVICA" CLASS (LARGE PATROL CRAFT)

LAYANG (ex-*PBR 515*) 819	**DORANG** (ex-*PBR 514*) 822
LEMADANG (ex-*PBR 517*) 820	**TODAK** (ex-*PBR 518*) 823
KRAPU (ex-*PBR 513*) 821	

Displacement, tons: 190 standard; 245 full load
Dimensions, feet (metres): 134·5 × 20·8 × 7 *(41 × 6·3 × 2·1)*
Guns: 1—3 in; 1—40 mm; 6—20 mm
A/S weapons: DC
Main engines: 2 MAN diesels; 2 shafts; 3 300 bhp = 20 knots
Oil fuel, tons: 15
Range, miles: 1 500 at 12 knots
Complement: 54

Purchased and transferred on 27th December 1958.

DORANG   *1968, Indonesian Navy*

3 "KELABANG" CLASS (LARGE PATROL CRAFT)

KELABANG 808   **KOMPAS** 809   **KALA HITAM** 810

Displacement, tons: 147
Gun: 1—40 mm/60; 4—12·7 mm MG (twins)
Main engines: 2 MAN diesels = 21 knots

Built in Indonesia in 1966-70. *Kompas* in reserve.

KALA HITAM   *1968, Indonesian Navy*

2 Ex-AUSTRALIAN "ATTACK" CLASS (LARGE PATROL CRAFT)

Name	No.	Builders	Commissioned
SILINAN (ex-HMAS *Archer*)	846	Australia	1968
SIBARAU (ex-HMAS *Bandolier*)	847	Australia	1968

Displacement, tons: 146 full load
Dimensions, feet (metres): 107·5 × 20 × 7·3 *(32·8 × 6·1 × 2·2)*
Gun: 1—40 mm/60; 4—12·7 mm MG (twins)
Main engines: 2 Paxman diesels; 2 shafts = 21 knots
Complement: 19 (3 officers, 16 men)

Transferred from RAN after refit—*Bandolier* 16 November 1973, *Archer* in 1974.

SIBARAU (old number)   *1973, Graeme Andrews*

3 Ex-US "PGM 39" CLASS (LARGE PATROL CRAFT)

BENTANG KALUNGKANG (ex-*PGM 57*) 570
BENTANG WAITATIRE (ex-*PGM 56*) 571
BENTANG SILUNGKANG (ex-*PGM 55*) 572

Displacement, tons: 122 full load
Dimensions, feet (metres): 100 × 21 × 8·5 *(30·5 × 6·4 × 2·6)*
Guns: 2—20 mm; 2 MG
Main engines: 2 Mercedes-Benz MB 820 dB diesels; 2 shafts = 17 knots

Originally intended as Amphibious Control Craft. Now used for normal patrol duties.
All transferred January 1962.

Gunnery: Original armament four 12·7 mm MG (twin).

6 AUSTRALIAN DE HAVILLAND TYPE (COASTAL PATROL CRAFT)

Name	No.	Builders	Commissioned
SAMADAR	—	Hawker-De Havilland Aust	Aug 1976
SASILA	—	Hawker-De Havilland Aust	Sep 1976
SABOLA	—	Hawker-De Havilland Aust	Oct 1976
SADARIN	—	Hawker-De Havilland Aust	Nov 1976
SAWANGI	—	Hawker-De Havilland Aust	—
SALMANETI	—	Hawker-De Havilland Aust	—

Displacement, tons: 27 full load
Dimensions, feet (metres): 52·5 × 16·4 × 3·9 *(16 × 5 × 1·2)*
Guns: 2 MGs
Main engines: 2 MTU diesels; 1 400 bhp = 30 knots
Range, miles: 950 at 18 knots
Endurance: 4/5 days
Complement: 10

First delivered June 1976. Numbers 851—856.

DE HAVILLAND SERIES 9311   *10/1977, Graeme Andrews*

2 FAIREY MARINE "SPEAR" CLASS (COASTAL PATROL CRAFT)

Dimensions, feet (metres): 29·8 × 9·2 × 2·6 *(9·1 × 2·8 × 0·8)*
Main engines: 2 diesels; 360 hp
Speed, knots: 30
Range, miles: 200 at 26 knots

Purchased in 1973-74.

AMPHIBIOUS FORCES

8 Ex-US "LST 1-511" and "512-1152" CLASSES

Name	No.	Builders	Commissioned
TELUK LANGSA (ex-USS *LST 1128*)	501	—	—
TELUK BAJUR (ex-USS *LST 616*)	502	—	—
TELUK KAU (ex-USS *LST 652*)	504	—	—
TELUK MANADO (ex-USS *LST 657*)	505	—	—
TELUK TOMINI (ex MV; ex-USS *Bledsoe County, LST 356*)	508	—	—
TELUK RATAI (ex-Liberian *Inagua Shipper*)	509	—	—
TELUK SALEH (ex-USS *Clark County, LST 601*)	510	—	—
TELUK BONE (ex-USS *Iredell County, LST 839*)	511	—	—

Displacement, tons: 1 653 standard; 4 080 full load
Dimensions, feet (metres): 328 × 50 × 14 *(100 × 15·3 × 4·3)*
Guns: 7—40 mm; 2—20 mm (some); 6—37 mm (remainder)
Main engines: General Motors diesels; 2 shafts; 1 700 bhp = 11·6 knots
Oil fuel, tons: 600
Range, miles: 7 200 at 10 knots
Cargo capacity: 2 100 tons
Complement: 119 (accommodation for 266)

Gunnery: Older units and previously unarmed ships now fitted with ex-Soviet 37 mm guns.

Transfers: 505 in March 1960, 502, 510 and 511 in June 1961. 504 and 501 in July 1970.

1 JAPANESE TYPE LST

Name	No.	Builders	Commissioned
TELUK AMBOINA	503	Sasebo, Japan	1961

Displacement, tons: 2 200 standard; 4 200 full load
Dimensions, feet (metres): 327 × 50 × 15 *(99·7 × 15·3 × 4·6)*
Guns: 4—40 mm; 1—37 mm
Main engines: MAN diesels; 2 shafts; 3 000 bhp = 13·1 knots
Oil fuel, tons: 1 200
Range, miles: 4 000 at 13·1 knots
Complement: 88 (accommodation for 300)

Launched on 17 March 1961 and transferred in June 1961. A copy of US "LST 511" class.

3 LCU TYPE

AMURANG   BANTEN   DORE

Displacement, tons: 182 standard; 275 full load
Dimensions, feet (metres): 125·7 × 32·8 × 5·9 *(38·3 × 10 × 1·8)*
Main engines: Diesels; 210 hp = 8 knots
Complement: 17

Built in Austria.

13 INDONESIAN LCMs

First three completed in 1976.

25 + LCM TYPES

Possibly 25 ex-UK LCM 7.
Possibly two LCM 6.

20 + LCVP TYPE

Ex-US Craft, possibly with Indonesian Army Transportation Corps (See end of section).

MINE WARFARE FORCES

5 Ex-SOVIET "T 43" CLASS (MINESWEEPERS—OCEAN)

PULAU RANI 701   PULAU ROON 703   PULAU RAJA 705
PULAU RATEWO 702 PULAU RORBAS 704

Displacement, tons: 500 standard; 610 full load
Dimensions, feet (metres): 190·2 × 28·2 × 6·9 *(58 × 8·6 × 2·1)*
Guns: 4—37 mm (twins); 8—12·7 mm (twins)
A/S weapons: 2 DCT
Main engines: 2 diesels; 2 shafts; 2 000 bhp = 17 knots
Range, miles: 1 600 at 10 knots
Complement: 40

Transferred to Indonesia by the USSR, four in 1962 and two in 1964.

PULAU RANI   1978, Indonesian Navy

2 "R" CLASS (MINESWEEPERS—COASTAL)

Name	No.	Builders	Commissioned
PULAU RENGAT	707	Abeking & Rasmussen, Lemwerder	—
PULAU RAPAT	708	Abeking & Rasmussen, Lemwerder	—

Displacement, tons: 139·4 standard
Dimensions, feet (metres): 129 × 18·7 × 5 *(39·3 × 5·7 × 1·5)*
Guns: 1—40 mm; 2—20 mm
Main engines: 2 MAN 12-cyl diesels; 2 800 bhp = 24·6 knots
Complement: 26

Originally a class of ten. These boats have a framework of light metal covered with wood. Both in reserve.

"R" Class   Indonesian Navy

SURVEY SHIPS

Name	No.	Builders	Commissioned
BURUDJULASAD	1006	—	1967

Displacement, tons: 2 150 full load
Dimensions, feet (metres): 269·5 × 37·4 × 11·5 *(82·2 × 11·4 × 3·5)*
Main engines: 4 MAN diesels; 2 shafts; 6 850 bhp = 19·1 knots
Complement: 113

Burudjulasad was launched in 1966; her equipment includes laboratories for oceanic and meteorological research, a cartographic room, and a helicopter.

BURUDJULASAD   1978, Indonesian Navy

250 INDONESIA / Survey ships — Service forces

Name	No.	Builders	Commissioned
BURDJAMHAL	1002	Scheepswerf De Waal, Zaltbommel	6 July 1953

Displacement, tons: 1 500 full load
Dimensions, feet (metres): 211·7 × 33·2 × 10 (64·6 × 10·1 × 3·3)
Main engines: 2 Werkspoor diesels; 1 160 bhp = 10 knots
Complement: 90

Launched on 6 September 1952.

JALANIDHI 1005

Displacement, tons: 985
Dimensions, feet (metres): 159·1 × 31·2 × 14·1 (48·5 × 9·5 × 4·3)
Speed, knots: 11·5
Complement: 58

Launched in 1962. Oceanographic Research ship.

ARIES 1008

Displacement, tons: 95
Dimensions, feet (metres): 82 × 16·7 × 5·6 (25 × 5·1 × 1·7)
Main engines: 2 diesels; 450 bhp
Complement: 13

Launched 1960. Ex-Soviet "PO 2" class.

COMMAND AND SUPPORT SHIPS

1 Ex-SOVIET "DON" CLASS (SUBMARINE TENDER)

RATULANGI (ex-*Kartasov*) 4101

Displacement, tons: 6 700 standard; 9 000 full load
Dimensions, feet (metres): 458·9 × 57·7 × 22·3 (140 × 17·6 × 6·8)
Guns: 4—3·9 in; 8—57 mm; 8—25 mm (twins)
Main engines: Diesels; 14 000 bhp = 21 knots
Complement: 300

A submarine support ship, escort vessel and maintenance tender transferred from the USSR to Indonesia in 1962, arriving in Indonesia in July. Fitted with Slim Net search and warning radar and with fire control radar.

RATULANGI — 1968, Indonesian Navy

1 SUBMARINE TENDER

Name	No.	Builders	Commissioned
MULTATULI	561	Ishikawajima-Harima Heavy Industries Co Ltd	Aug 1961

Displacement, tons: 3 220
Dimensions, feet (metres): 365·3 × 52·5 × 23 (111·4 × 16 × 7)
Guns: 8—37 mm (2 twin, 4 single); 4—MG
Aircraft: 1 Alouette II helicopter
Main engines: Burmester Wain diesel; 5 500 bhp = 18·5 knots
Oil fuel, tons: 1 400
Range, miles: 6 000 at 16 knots cruising speed
Complement: 134

Built as a submarine tender. Launched on 15 May 1961. Delivered to Indonesia August 1961. Flush decker. Capacity for replenishment at sea (fuel oil, fresh water, provisions, ammunition, naval stores and personnel). Medical and hospital facilities. Equipment for supplying compressed air, electric power and distilled water to submarines. Air-conditioning and mechanical ventilation arrangements for all living and working quarters. Now used as fleet flagship.

Reconstruction: After 76 mm mounting replaced by helicopter deck.

MULTATULI — 1978, Indonesian Navy

SERVICE FORCES

1 Ex-US "ACHELOUS" CLASS (REPAIR SHIP)

JAYA WIJAYA (ex-USS *Askari* 9109, ex-*ARL 30*, ex-*LST 1131*) 921

Displacement, tons: 1 625 light; 4 100 full load
Dimensions, feet (metres): 328·0 × 50·0 × 11·0 (100 × 15·3 × 3·4)
Guns: 8—40 mm (2 quad)
Main engines: General Motors diesels; 2 shafts; 1 800 bhp = 11·6 knots
Complement: 280

Of wartime construction this ship was in reserve from 1956-66. She was recommissioned and reached Viet-Nam in 1967 to support River Assault Flotilla One. She was used by the US Navy and Vietnamese Navy working up the Mekong in support of the Cambodian operations in May 1970. Transferred on lease to Indonesia at Guam on 31 August 1971.

JAYA WIJAYA — 1978, Indonesian Navy

INDONESIA / Service forces — Tenders 251

1 Ex-US "SHENANDOAH" CLASS (DESTROYER DEPOT SHIP)

DUMAI (ex-USS *Tidewater* AD31) 562

Displacement, tons: 8 165 standard; 16 635 full load
Dimensions, feet (metres): 492 × 69·5 × 27·2 *(150·1 × 21·2 × 8·3)*
Gun: 1—5 in *(127 mm)*/38
Main engines: Geared turbines; 1 shaft; 8 500 shp = 18·4 knots
Boilers: 2 Babcock & Wilcox
Complement: 778

Transferred February 1971 as destroyer depot ship. No longer operational with most of equipment removed and used as accommodation ship for oil-field personnel.

DUMAI   1978, Indonesian Navy

1 REPLENISHMENT TANKER

SORONG 911

Measurement, tons: 5 100 deadweight
Dimensions, feet (metres): 367·4 × 50·5 × 21·6 *(112 × 15·4 × 6·6)*
Guns: 8—12·7 mm (twins)
Speed, knots: 15 (10 economical)

Built in Yugoslavia in 1965. Has underway replenishment facilities. Capacity 3 000 tons fuel and 300 tons water.

SORONG   1974, John Mortimer

1 Ex-SOVIET "UDA" CLASS (SUPPORT TANKER)

BALIKPAPAN

Displacement, tons: 5 500 standard; 7 200 full load
Dimensions, feet (metres): 400·3 × 51·8 × 20·3 *(122·1 × 15·8 × 6·2)*
Guns: 6—25 mm (twins)
Main engines: 2 diesels; 2 shafts; 8 000 bhp = 17 knots

Survivor of three transferred in 1962.

1 SUPPORT TANKER

SUNGAI GERONG 906

Displacement, tons: 1 300 deadweight
Guns: 4—14·5 mm (twins)
Main engine: Diesel; 1 shaft = 13 knots

Soviet built. Transferred 1964.

1 Ex-SOVIET "KHOBI" CLASS (HARBOUR TANKER)

PAKAN BARU 960

Displacement, tons: 1 500 full load
Dimensions, feet (metres): 63 × 11·5 × 4·5 *(19·2 × 3·5 × 1·2)*
Main engines: Diesels; 2 shafts; 800 bhp = 11 knots

2 HARBOUR TANKERS

TARAKAN   BULA

Displacement, tons: 1 340 full load
Dimensions, feet (metres): 352·0 × 37·7 × 14·8 *(107·4 × 11·5 × 4·5)*
Main engines: Diesels; 1 shaft; 1 500 bhp = 13 knots

MISCELLANEOUS

5 "TISZA" CLASS (AKL) (Army)

KARIMATA, KARIMUDJAWA, MENTAWAI, NATUNA, TALAUD

Built in Hungary and transferred 1962 by USSR.

1 TRAINING SHIP

Name	No.	Builders	Commissioned
DEWARUTJI	—	H. C. Stülcken & Sohn, Hamburg	9 July 1953

Displacement, tons: 810 standard; 1 500 full load
Dimensions, feet (metres): 136·2 pp; 191·2 oa; × 31·2 × 13·9 *(41·5; 58·3 × 9·5 × 4·2)*
Main engines: MAN diesels; 600 bhp = 10·5 knots
Complement: 110 (32 + 78 midshipmen)

Barquentine of steel construction. Sail area, 1 305 sq yards *(1 091 sq metres)*. Launched on 24 January 1953.

1 TRAINING SHIP

Displacement, tons: 1 820 full load
Dimensions, feet (metres): 317·3 × 36·8 × 11·8 *(96·7 × 11·1 × 3·5)*
Main engines: CODOG; 1 Olympus gas turbine; 22 300 hp; 2 MTU16V956/T1391 diesels; 7 500 hp = 26/20 knots
Complement: 93+100 trainees.

Ordered 14 March 1978 from Yugoslavia where the hull is to be built and engines fitted. Armament and electronics to be fitted in the Netherlands or Indonesia. For eventual completion in 1980.

1 CABLE SHIP

Name	No.	Builders	Commissioned
BIDUK	1003	J & K Smit, Kinderijk	30 July 1952

Displacement, tons: 1 250 standard
Dimensions, feet (metres): 213·2 × 39·5 × 11·5 *(65 × 12 × 3·5)*
Main engine: 1 triple expansion engine; 1 600 ihp = 12 knots
Complement: 66

Cable layer, lighthouse tender, and multi-purpose naval auxiliary. Launched on 30 October 1951.

TENDERS

2 SMALL TRANSPORTS

BANGGAI (ex-*Biscaya*) 925
NUSA TELU (ex-*Casablanca*) 952

Of 750 tons.

1 Ex-SOVIET "PODZHARNY" CLASS

Firefloat.

2 "105 ft" WATER BOATS

DEWARUTJI   1978, Reinhard Nerlich

252 INDONESIA / Tenders — Police craft

1 Ex-SOVIET "CHAYKA" CLASS

Patrol Launch.

4 "35 ft" PATROL LAUNCHES

FLOATING DOCKS

There are three large floating docks in Surabaya which are used for naval purposes.

TUGS

1 Ex-US "CHEROKEE" CLASS

RAKATA (ex-USS *Menominee,* ATF 73) 928

Displacement, tons: 1 235 standard; 1 675 full load
Dimensions, feet (metres): 205 × 38·5 × 15·5 *(62·5 × 11·7 × 4·7)*
Guns: 1—3 in *(76 mm);* 2—40 mm; 4—25 mm (twins)
Main engines: 4 diesels with electric drive; 3 000 bhp = 16·5 knots
Complement: 85

Launched on 14 February 1942. Transferred at San Diego in March 1961. Civilian manned

1 Ex-SOVIET "OKHTENSKY" CLASS

TAMRAU (ex-*Maraim*) (Army)

Displacement, tons: 835
Dimensions, feet (metres): 143 × 34 × 15 *(43·6 × 10·4 × 4·6)*
Guns: 1—3 in *(76 mm);* 2—20 mm
Main engines: 2 BM diesels; 2 electric motors; 2 shafts; 1 875 bhp = 14 knots
Complement: 34

Ocean tug.

Name	No.	Builders	Commissioned
LAMPO BATANG	934	Japan	Nov 1961

Displacement, tons: 250
Dimensions, feet (metres): 92·3 × 23·2 × 11·3 *(28·2 × 7·1 × 3·4)*
Main engines: 2 diesels; 1 200 bhp = 11 knots
Oil fuel, tons: 18
Range, miles: 1 000 at 11 knots
Complement: 43

Ocean tug. Launched in April 1961.

Name	No.	Builders	Commissioned
TAMBORA (Army)	935	Japan	June 1961
BROMO	936	Japan	Aug 1961

Displacement, tons: 150
Dimensions, feet (metres): 79 × 21·7 × 9·7 *(24·1 × 6·6 × 3)*
Main engines: 2 MAN diesels; 2 shafts; 600 bhp = 10·5 knots
Oil fuel, tons: 9
Range, miles: 690 at 10·5 knots
Complement: 15

Harbour tugs.

2 Ex-SOVIET "TUGUR" CLASS

DEMPO   MUTIS

Harbour Tugs.

2 Ex-SOVIET "SITHOLE" CLASS

Harbour Tugs.

CUSTOMS PATROL CRAFT

A very large force of which the following are examples.

3 COASTAL PATROL CRAFT

Name	No.	Builders	Commissioned
—	BC 1001	Ch. Navals de l'Esterel	11 Apr 1975
—	BC 1002	Ch. Navals de l'Esterel	23 June 1975
—	BC 1003	Ch. Navals de l'Esterel	25 Sep 1975

Displacement, tons: 55
Dimensions, feet (metres): 91·8 × 17·1 × 5·2 *(28 × 5·2 × 1·6)*
Gun: 1—20 mm or several MGs
Main engines: 2 MTU 12V 331 TC 81; 2 700 hp = 35 knots
Range, miles: 750 at 15 knots
Complement: 9

14 more ordered summer 1978, order to be shared between CN d l'Esterel and CMN.

BC 1002   *1976, Ch. N de l'Esterel*

15 DKN TYPE

Name	No.	Builders	Commissioned
—	DKN 901	Lürssen, Vegesack	1958
—	DKN 902	Lürssen, Vegesack	1958
—	DKN 903	Abeking & Rasmussen, Lemwerder	1958
—	DKN 904	Lürssen, Vegesack	1959
—	DKN 905	Abeking & Rasmussen, Lemwerder	1959
—	DKN 907	Italy	1959
—	DKN 908	Italy	1960
—	DKN 909	Italy	1960
—	DKN 910	Italy	1960
—	DKN 911	Italy	1960
—	DKN 912	Italy	1960
—	DKN 913	Italy	1960
—	DKN 914	Italy	1960
—	DKN 915	Italy	1960
—	DKN 916	Italy	1960

Displacement, tons: 140
Dimensions, feet (metres): 128 × 19 × 5·2 *(39 × 5·8 × 1·6)*
Guns: 4—20 mm
Main engines: Maybach diesels; 2 shafts; 3 000 bhp = 24·5 knots

In addition are DKN 504-13.

6 "PAT" CLASS

PAT 01	PAT 02	PAT 03	PAT 04	PAT 05	PAT 06

Dimensions, feet (metres): 100 × 17 × 6 *(30·5 × 5·2 × 1·8)*
Main engines: 2 Caterpillar diesels; 340 bhp

ARMY CRAFT

A.D.R.I. operate fourteen 6-8000 GRT transports and two ex-US LSTs in addition to ships shown above.

AIR FORCE CRAFT

A.U.R.I. operates six cargo ships (all with bow doors).

POLICE CRAFT

The police operate a number of craft of varying sizes including 14 "Bango" class of 194 tons.

IRAN

Ministerial

Minister of War:

Headquarters Appointments

Commander-in-Chief Imperial Iranian Navy:
  Vice-Admiral K. M. Habibollahi
Deputy Commander-in-Chief:
  Vice-Admiral A. Mohsenzadeh

Fleet Command

Commander Fleet
  Rear-Admiral K. H. Azadhi

Diplomatic Representation

Naval Attaché in London, Brussels and The Hague:
  Captain M. Garachorlou
Naval Attaché in Rome and Paris:
  Captain H. Keshvardoost
Naval Attaché in Washington and Ottawa:
  Captain S. Bahrmast

Personnel

(a) 1979: 22 000 officers and men
(b) 2 years national service

Note: A Marine Battalion is being formed.

Bases

Persian Gulf
  Bandar Abbas (MHQ)
  Booshehr
  Kharg Island
  Khorramshar (Light Forces)
Indian Ocean
  Chah Bahar (under construction)
Caspian Sea
  Bandar—Pahlavi (Training)

Naval Air

7 Sikorsky SH-3D (Sea King) (11 on order)
7 Bell AB-212
2 Lockheed P-3C Orions (Maritime Patrol)
4 Fokker F-27 Mk 400 M (Transport)
4 Aero Commanders (Flag officers)
6 RH.53D helicopters (3 on order)
4 Falcon F20

Prefix to Ships' Names

IIS

Current Plans

There is no information available at present as to what government will eventually assume power and no changes of orders or deployment can therefore be made.

Strength of the Fleet

Type	Active	Building (Planned)
Submarines	1	(?)
Destroyers	3	2
Frigates	4	—
Corvettes	4	—
Fast Attack Craft (Missile)	—	12
Large Patrol Craft	7	—
Hovercraft	14	—
Landing Ships (L)	2	1 (2 ?)
Landing Craft (U)	1	—
Minesweepers—Coastal	3	—
Minesweepers—Inshore	2	—
Replenishment Tanker	—	1
Supply Ships	2	1
Repair Ship	1	—
Harbour Tanker	1	—
Water Boat	1	—
Tugs	3	—
Yachts	2	—
Floating Dock	1	—
Survey Craft	3	—
Customs Craft	2	—
Coast Guard (Coastal Patrol Craft)	30	—

Mercantile Marine

Lloyd's Register of Shipping:
  208 vessels of 1 194 675 tons

DELETIONS

Mine Warfare Forces

1974 *Shahbaz* (ex-US *MSC*) after collision damage.

Service Forces

1974 *Sohrab* (ex-US *ARL 36*) sunk as A/S target.

Coast Guard

1975 *Gohar, Shahpar, Shahram* (to Sudan)

PENNANT NUMBERS

Submarines

101	Kusseh
102	Nahang
103	Dolfin

Destroyers

51	Artemiz
61	Babr
62	Palang

Frigates

71	Saam
72	Zaal
73	Rostam
74	Faramarz

Corvettes

81	Bayandor
82	Naghdi
83	Milanian
84	Khanamuie

Light Forces

01-08	"Winchester" class hovercraft
101-106	"Wellington" class hovercraft
201	Kaivan
202	Tiran
203	Mehran
204	Mahan
211	Parvin
212	Bahram
213	Nahid
P 221	Kaman
P 222	Zoubin
P 223	Khadang
P 224	Peykan
P 225	Joshan
P 226	Falakhon
P 227	Shamshir
P 228	Gorz
P 229	Gardouneh
P 230	Khanjar
P 231	Neyzeh
P 232	Tabarzin

Mine Warfare Forces

301	Shahrokh
302	Simorgh
303	Karkas
311	Harischi
312	Riazi

Service and Auxiliary Forces

45	Bahmanshir
98	Kharg
401	Lengeh
402	Hormuz
421	Bandar Abbas
422	Booshehr
441	Chahbahar
501	Quesham
511	Hengam
512	Lerak

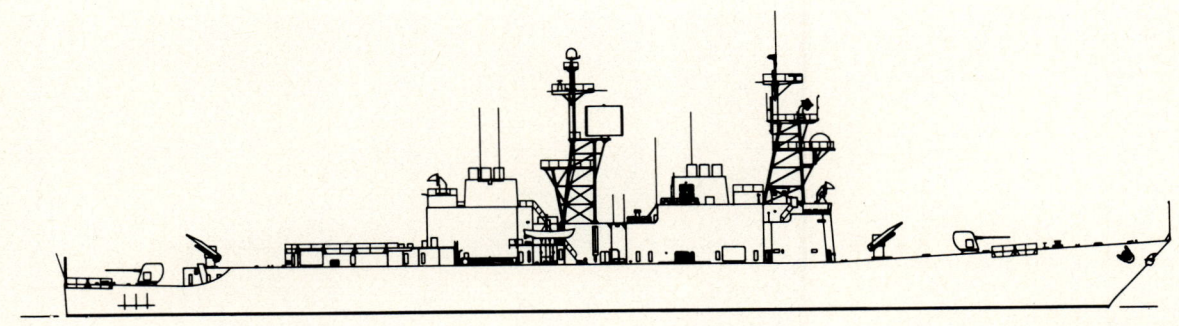

"DD 993" Class

1976, A. D. Baker III

254 IRAN / Introduction — Destroyers

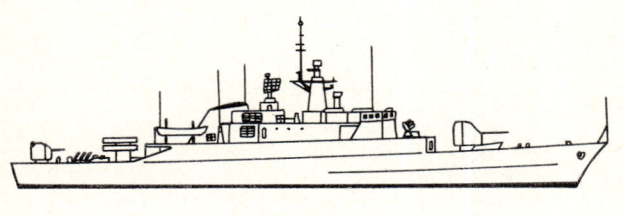
BABR and PALANG

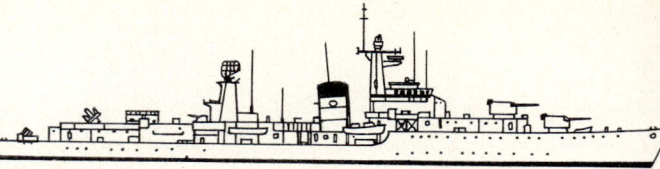
ARTEMIZ

"SAAM" Class

"BAYANDOR" Class

SUBMARINES

TYPE 209

Six submarines had been ordered from Howaldtswerke, Kiel although it is reported that this order has now been cancelled.

(3) Ex-US "TANG" CLASS (PATROL SUBMARINES)

Name	No.	Builders	Laid down	Launched	Commissioned
KUSSEH (ex-USS *Trout*, SS 566)	101	Electric Boat Co, Groton	1 Dec 1949	21 Aug 1951	27 June 1952
NAHANG (ex-USS *Wahoo*, SS 565)	102	Portsmouth Navy Yard	24 Oct 1949	16 Oct 1951	30 May 1952
DOLFIN (ex-USS *Tang*, SS 563)	103	Portsmouth Navy Yard	18 Apr 1949	Apr 1951	25 Oct 1951

Displacement, tons: 2 100 surfaced; 2 700 dived
Dimensions, feet (metres): 287 × 27·3 × 19 *(87·4 × 8·3 × 6·2)*
Torpedo tubes: 8—21 in *(533 mm)* (6 fwd, 2 aft)
Main machinery: 3 diesels; 4 500 bhp;
  2 electric motors; 5 600 shp; 2 shafts
Speed, knots: 16 surfaced; 16 dived
Complement: 87 (8 officers, 79 men)

Agreement on transfer from US Navy reached in 1975 to provide training for the establishment of a large submarine force although this is now very much in the balance. It is reported that one has been taken over but not whether the other two will follow.

Names: *Kusseh* (shark), *Nahang* (whale).

Transfer: *Kusseh* Aug 1978; *Nahang* 1979; *Dolfin* 1979-80.

"TANG" Class   *1970, USN*

DESTROYERS

2 US "MODIFIED SPRUANCE" CLASS

Name	No.	Builders	Laid down	Launched	Commissioned
KOUROOSH (ex-US DD 993)	11	Ingalls S.B. Division, Litton Industries, USA	26 June 1978	—	—
DARYUSH (ex-US DD 994)	12	Ingalls S.B. Division, Litton Industries, USA	8 Jan 1979	—	—

Displacement, tons: approx 8 500 full load
Dimensions, feet (metres): 563·3 × 55 × 29 *(171·1 × 17·6 × 8·8)*
Aircraft: 1 helicopter (Sea King)
Missiles: 2 twin Tartar-D launchers for Standard-MR SAM (Mk 26)
Guns: 2—5 in *(127 mm)*/54 (single Mk 45)
A/S weapons: 2 triple Mk 32 torpedo tubes
Main engines: 4 GE-LM 2500 gas turbines; 80 000 shp; 2 shafts
Speed, knots: 30+
Range, miles: 6 000 at 20 knots
Complement: approx 290

Ordered from Litton Industries, USA, in 1974, first to be delivered in 1980. Original order was for six ships, reduced June 1976 with cancellation of *Shapour* and *Ardeshir*. Two more cancelled in February 1979 to be taken over by US Navy. They are modifications of the "Spruance" design with improved AA capability, better radars, and more powerful air-conditioning.

Classification: Classed as CG by IIN.

Names: Called after ancient kings.

Radar: Radome: SPQ 9.
Search: SPG 60.
3-D: SPS 48.
Fire control radars.

Sonar: SQS 53 (mod) bow-mounted.

"MODIFIED SPRUANCE" Class   *1975, Imperial Iranian Navy*

IRAN / Destroyers — Frigates 255

1 Ex-BRITISH "BATTLE" CLASS

Name	No.	Builders	Laid down	Launched	Commissioned
ARTEMIZ (ex-HMS Sluys, D 60)	51	Cammell Laird & Co Ltd, Birkenhead	24 Nov 1943	28 Feb 1945	30 Sep 1946

Displacement, tons: 2 325 standard; 3 360 full load
Length, feet (metres): 355·0 *(108·2)* pp; 379·0 *(115·5)* oa
Beam, feet (metres): 40·5 *(12·3)*
Draught, feet (metres): 17·5 *(5·2)*
Missiles: SSM; Standard (8 with quad launcher);
  SAM; Sea Cat; (est 16 with quad launcher)
Guns: 4—4·5 in *(115 mm)* (twin, fwd);
  2—40 mm/60 (single)
A/S weapons: 1 Squid 3-barrelled DC mortar
Main engines: Parsons geared turbines; 2 shafts; 50 000 shp
Boilers: 2 Admiralty 3-drum type
Speed, knots: 35·5
Oil fuel, tons: 680
Range, miles: 3 000 at 20 knots
Complement: 270

Transferred to Iran at Southampton on 26 January 1967, and handed over to the Imperial Iranian Navy after a three-year modernisation refit by the Vosper Thornycroft Group.

Radar: Search: Plessey AWS 1.
Air surveillance with on-mounted IFF.
Fire control: Contraves Sea-Hunter.
Radar intercept: Decca RDL 1.
Racal DF equipment.

Refit: At Cape Town 1975-76.

ARTEMIZ   1978, Chris Gee

2 Ex-US "ALLEN M. SUMNER" CLASS (FRAM II)

Name	No.	Builders	Laid down	Launched	Commissioned
BABR (ex-USS Zellers, DD 777)	61	Todd Pacific Shipyards	24 Dec 1943	19 July 1944	25 Oct 1944
PALANG (ex-USS Stormes, DD 780)	62	Todd Pacific Shipyards	15 Dec 1944	4 Nov 1944	27 Jan 1945

Displacement, tons: 2 200 standard; 3 320 full load
Length, feet (metres): 376·5 *(114·8)*
Beam, feet (metres): 40·9 *(12·4)*
Draught, feet (metres): 19 *(5·8)*
Aircraft: 1 A/S helicopter
Missiles: SSM; Standard (8 with 4 launchers)
Guns: 4—5 in *(127 mm)*/38 (twin Mk 38)
A/S weapons: 2 fixed Hedgehogs;
  2 triple torpedo launchers (Mk 32)
Main engines: 2 geared turbines; 60 000 shp; 2 shafts
Boilers: 4
Speed, knots: 34
Complement: 274 (14 officers, 260 ratings)

Two "FRAM II" conversion destroyers of the "Allen M. Sumner" class nominally transferred to Iran from the US Navy in March 1971 for delivery in 1972.

Conversion: Both ships received a full refit as well as conversion at Philadelphia NSY before sailing for Iran. This included a much-improved air-conditioning layout, the removal of B gun-mount with its magazine, altered accommodation, the fitting of a Canadian telescopic hangar, the siting of the four Standard missile launchers athwartships beside the new torpedo stowage between the funnels, the rigging of VDS and fitting of Hedgehogs in B position.

Electronics: Extensive intercept and jamming (ULQ/6) arrays fitted.

Names: Babr (Tiger), Palang (Leopard).

PALANG (old pennant number)   1975, Imperial Iranian Navy

Radar: Search: SPS 10
Air-surveillance: SPS 37 with on-mounted IFF.
Gun fire control system Mk 37 with radar Mk 25 on director.
Navigational: One on bridge.

Sonar: SQS 29 series; VDS *(Babr)*.

Spares: USS *Gainard* (DD 706) was to have been taken over in March 1971, but, being beyond repair, was replaced by USS *Stormes* (DD 780). Ex-USS *Kenneth D. Bailey* (DD 713) ("Gearing" class) purchased 13 January 1975 and ex-USS *Bordelon* (DD 881) on 1 February 1977 for spares.

FRIGATES

4 "SAAM" CLASS

Name	No.	Builders	Laid down	Launched	Commissioned
SAAM	71	Vosper Thornycroft, Woolston	22 May 1967	25 July 1968	20 May 1971
ZAAL	72	Vickers, Barrow	3 Mar 1968	4 Mar 1969	1 Mar 1971
ROSTAM	73	Vickers, Newcastle & Barrow	10 Dec 1967	4 Mar 1969	June 1972
FARAMARZ	74	Vosper Thornycroft, Woolston	25 July 1968	30 July 1969	28 Feb 1972

Displacement, tons: 1 110 standard; 1 290 full load
Length, feet (metres): 310·0 *(94·4)*
Beam, feet (metres): 34·0 *(10·4)*
Draught, feet (metres): 11·2 *(3·4)*
Missiles: SSM; 5 Sea Killer (quin launcher);
  SAM; Sea Cat (est 9, triple launcher)
Guns: 1—4·5 in *(115 mm)*/55 (Mk 8)
  2—35 mm/90 Oerlikon (1 twin)
A/S weapons: 1 Limbo 3-barrelled DC mortar
Main engines: 2 Rolls-Royce "Olympus" gas turbines;
  46 000 shp; 2 Paxman 16-cyl Ventura diesels; 3 800 shp;
  2 shafts
Speed, knots: 40
Complement: 125 (accommodation for 146)

It was announced on 25 August 1966 that Vosper Ltd, Portsmouth had received an order for four vessels for the Iranian Navy. Air-conditioned throughout. Fitted with Vosper stabilisers. *Rostam* was towed to Barrow for completion.

Names: All heroes of the Shah Nameh, the national epic.

Radar: Air surveillance Plessey AWS 1 with on-mounted IFF. Two Contraves Seahunter systems for control of 35 mm, Sea Killers and Sea Cats. Decca RDL 1 passive DF equipment.

Refit: *Saam* and *Zaal* taken in hand by HM Dockyard Devonport July/August 1975 for major refit including replacement of Mk 5 4·5 in gun by Mk 8. Completed 1977.

ROSTAM   1978, Chris Gee

256   IRAN / Corvettes — Light forces

CORVETTES

4 Ex-US "PF 103" CLASS

Name	No.
BAYANDOR (ex-US *PF 103*)	81
NAGHDI (ex-US *PF 104*)	82
MILANIAN (ex-US *PF 105*)	83
KAHNAMUIE (ex-US *PF 106*)	84

Builders	Laid down	Launched	Commissioned
Levingstone Shipbuilding Co, Orange, Texas	20 Aug 1962	7 July 1963	18 May 1964
Levingstone Shipbuilding Co, Orange, Texas	12 Sep 1962	10 Oct 1963	22 July 1964
Levingstone Shipbuilding Co, Orange, Texas	1 May 1967	4 Jan 1968	13 Feb 1969
Levingstone Shipbuilding Co, Orange, Texas	12 June 1967	4 Apr 1968	13 Feb 1969

Displacement, tons: 900 standard; 1 135 full load
Length, feet (metres): 275·0 *(83·8)*
Beam, feet (metres): 33·0 *(10·0)*
Draught, feet (metres): 10·2 *(3·1)*
Guns: 2—3 in *(76 mm)*/50 (single); 2—40 mm/60 (twin); 2—23 mm (twin)
A/S weapons: 4 DCT; 2 DC racks
Main engines: F-M diesels; 2 shafts; 6 000 bhp
Speed, knots: 20
Complement: 140

Built as two pairs, five years apart. Transferred from the USA to Iran under the Mutual Assistance programme in 1964 *(Bayandor* and *Naghdi)* and 1969 *(Kahnamuie* and *Milanian).*

Conversion: Mid-life conversion planned to include 76 mm OTO Melara guns.

Gunnery: The 23 mm guns were purchased from the Soviet army and replace the Hedgehog.

Names: Naval officers killed in the engagement with the British in 1941.

Radar: Search: SPS 6.
Navigation: Raytheon.
Fire control: SPG 34 on forward 76 mm (Mk 33) mount.
Mk 63 for 76 mm. Mk 51 for 40 mm.

BAYANDOR (old pennant number)   1975, Imperial Iranian Navy

LIGHT FORCES

12 "KAMAN" CLASS (FAST ATTACK CRAFT—MISSILE)

Name	No.	Builders	Commissioned
KAMAN	P 221	Construction de Mécanique, Normandie	1977
ZOUBIN	P 222	Construction de Mécanique, Normandie	1977
KHADANG	P 223	Construction de Mécanique, Normandie	1977
PEYKAN	P 224	Construction de Mécanique, Normandie	1977
JOSHAN	P 225	Construction de Mécanique, Normandie	1978
FALAKHON	P 226	Construction de Mécanique, Normandie	1978
SHAMSHIR	P 227	Construction de Mécanique, Normandie	1978
GORZ	P 228	Construction de Mécanique, Normandie	1978
GARDOUNEH	P 229	Construction de Mécanique, Normandie	1978
KHANJAR	P 230	Construction de Mécanique, Normandie	1978
NEYZEH	P 231	Construction de Mécanique, Normandie	1978
TABARZIN	P 232	Construction de Mécanique, Normandie	1978

Displacement, tons: 249 standard; 275 full load
Dimensions, feet (metres): 154·2 × 23·3 × 6·4 *(47 × 7·1 × 1·9)*
Missiles: SSM; 4 Harpoon (single cells)
Guns: 1—76 mm/62 (single Compact); 1—40 mm/70 Bofors
Main engines: 4 MTU diesels; 4 shafts; 14 400 bhp = 36 knots
Oil fuel, tons: 41
Range, miles: 700 at 30+ knots
Complement: 30

Of La Combattante II design. Ordered in February 1974. For completion by April 1979. *Kaman* laid down 5 February 1975, launched 8 January 1976; *Zoubin* laid down 4 April 1975, launched 31 March 1976; *Khadang* laid down 20 June 1975, launched 15 July 1976; *Peykan* laid down 15 October 1975, launched 12 October 1976. *Joshan* laid down 5 January 1976, launched 21 February 1977; *Falakhon* laid down 15 March 1976, launched 2 June 1977; *Shamshir* laid down 15 May 1976; *Gorz* laid down 5 August 1976; *Gardouneh* laid down 18 October 1976; *Khanjar* laid down 17 January 1977; *Neyzeh* laid down 12 April 1977; *Tabarzin* laid down 24 June 1977.

GORZ   5/1978, C. and S. Taylor

Names: *Kaman* (bow), *Zoubin* (javelin), *Khadang* (arrowhead), *Peykan* (arrow), *Joshan* (boiling oil), *Falakhon* (sling), *Shamshir* (scimitar), *Gorz* (mace), *Gardouneh* (roulette), *Khanjar* (dagger) *Neyzeh* (spear), *Tabarzin* (battleaxe).

Radar: Tactical and fire control: WM 28 (Hollandse Signaalapparaten).

3 IMPROVED "PGM-71" CLASS (LARGE PATROL CRAFT)

Name	No.	Builders	Commissioned
PARVIN (ex-US *PGM 103*)	211	Peterson Builders Inc	1967
BAHRAM (ex-US *PGM 112*)	212	Peterson Builders Inc	1969
NAHID (ex-US *PGM 122*)	213	Peterson Builders Inc	1970

Displacement, tons: 105 standard; 146 full load
Dimensions, feet (metres): 100 × 22 × 10 *(30·5 × 6·7 × 3·1)*
Guns: 1—40 mm; 2—20 mm; 2—50 cal MG
Main engines: 8 General Motors diesels; 2 000 bhp = 15 knots

Names: *Parvin* (Mercury), *Bahram* (Mars), *Nahid* (Venus).

PARVIN (original number)   197

4 US COAST GUARD "CAPE" CLASS (LARGE PATROL CRAFT)

Name	No.	Builders	Commissioned
KAIVAN	201	USA	14 Jan 1956
TIRAN	202	US Coast Guard, Curtis Bay, Maryland	1957
MEHRAN	203	USA	1959
MAHAN	204	USA	1959

Displacement, tons: 85 standard; 107 full load
Dimensions, feet (metres): 95 × 20·2 × 6·8 *(28·9 × 6·2 × 2)*
Gun: 1—40 mm
A/S weapons: 8-barrelled 7·2 in projector, 8—300 lb depth charges
Main engines: 4 Cummins diesels; 2 shafts; 2 200 bhp = 20 knots
Range, miles: 1 500 cruising
Complement: 15

Names: All islands in the Gulf.

MAHAN (old pennant number)   1975, Imperial Iranian Navy

IRAN / Light forces — Mine warfare forces 257

20 + 50 US "64 ft Mk III" CLASS (COASTAL PATROL CRAFT)

Displacement, tons: 28·6
Dimensions, feet (metres): 64·9 × 18·4 × 6·6 (19·8 × 5·6 × 2·0)
Guns: 3—20 mm; 1—12·7 mm
Main engines: 3 General Motors 8V71-TI diesels; 3 shafts; 2 050 hp = 30 knots
Range, miles: 500 at 30 knots
Complement: 5

20 ordered from Peterson, USA in 1973 and 50 in 1976. 20 are listed under Coast Guard on later page.

40 BERTRAM ENFORCER TYPE

31 ft and 20 ft harbour patrol craft.

20 US "50 ft Mk II" CLASS

Displacement, tons: 22
Dimensions, feet (metres): 50·2 × 15·7 × 6·2 (15·3 × 4·8 × 1·9)
Guns: 4—12·7 mm (twins)
Main engines: 2 General Motors 12V71 diesels; 2 shafts; 900 hp = 26 knots
Complement: 6

Ordered from Peterson, USA in 1976-77.

6 "WELLINGTON" (BH.7) CLASS (HOVERCRAFT)

Name	No.	Builders	Commissioned
—	101	British Hovercraft Corporation	Nov 1970
—	102	British Hovercraft Corporation	Mar 1971
—	103	British Hovercraft Corporation	mid-1974
—	104	British Hovercraft Corporation	mid-1974
—	105	British Hovercraft Corporation	late 1974
—	106	British Hovercraft Corporation	early 1975

Weight, tons: 50 max; 33 empty
Dimensions, feet (metres): 76 × 45 ×42 (23·2 × 13·7 × 12·8)
Missiles: SSMs in last four (see note)
Guns: 2 Browning MG
Main engine: 1 Proteus 15 M/541 gas turbine = 60 knots
Oil fuel, tons: 10

First pair are BH 7 Mk 4 and the next four are Mk 5 craft. Mk 5 craft fitted for, but not with, surface-to-surface missiles.

"Wellington" Hovercraft 101   1975, Imperial Iranian Navy

8 "WINCHESTER" (SR.N6) CLASS (HOVERCRAFT)

Name	No.	Builders	Commissioned
—	01	British Hovercraft Corporation	1973
—	02	British Hovercraft Corporation	1973
—	03	British Hovercraft Corporation	1973
—	04	British Hovercraft Corporation	1974
—	05	British Hovercraft Corporation	1974
—	06	British Hovercraft Corporation	1975
—	07	British Hovercraft Corporation	1975
—	08	British Hovercraft Corporation	1975

Weight, tons: 10 normal gross (basic weight 14 200 lb; disposable load 8 200 lb)
Dimensions, feet (metres): 48·4 × 25·3 × 15·9 (height) (14·8 × 7·7 × 4·8)
Guns: 1 or 2—50 cal MGs
Main engines: 1 Gnome Model 1050 gas turbine = 58 knots
  1 Peters diesel as auxiliary power unit

Ordered 1970-72. The Imperial Iranian Navy has the world's largest fully operational hovercraft squadron, which is used for coastal defence and logistic duties.

"Winchester" Hovercraft 03   1971

LANDING CRAFT

QESHM (ex-US LCU 1431) 501

Displacement, tons: 160 light; 320 full load
Dimensions, feet (metres): 119 × 32 × 5·7 (36·3 × 9·8 × 1·7)
Guns: 2—20 mm
Main engines: Diesels; 675 bhp = 10 knots
Complement: 14

LCU 1431 was transferred to Iran by USA in September 1964 under the Military Aid Programme. Named after an island in the Gulf.

QESHM   1971

MINE WARFARE FORCES

3 Ex-US "MSC 292 and 268" CLASS (MINESWEEPERS—COASTAL)

Name	No.	Builders	Commissioned
SHAHROKH (ex-USS MSC 276)	301	Bellingham Shipyards Co	1960
SIMORGH (ex-USS MSC 291)	302	Tacoma Boatbuilding Co	1962
KARKAS (ex-USS MSC 292)	303	Peterson Builders Inc	1959

Displacement, tons: 320 light; 378 full load
Dimensions, feet (metres): 145·8 × 28 × 8·3 (44·5 × 8·5 × 2·5)
Gun: 1—20 mm (double-barrelled)
Main engines: 2 General Motors diesels; 2 shafts; 890 bhp = 12·8 knots
Oil fuel, tons: 27
Range, miles: 2 400 at 11 knots
Complement: 40 (4 officers, 2 midshipmen, 34 men)

Originally class of four. Of wooden construction. Launched in 1958-61 and transferred from USA to Iran under MAP in 1959-62. Shahrokh now in the Caspian Sea.

Names: Shahrokh (an ancient king), Simorgh (a fabled bird), Karkas (vulture).

SIMORGH (old pennant number)   1975, Imperial Iranian Navy

258 IRAN / Mine warfare forces — Service forces

2 US "CAPE" CLASS (MINESWEEPERS—INSHORE)

Name	No.	Builders	Commissioned
HARISCHI (ex-*Kahnamuie*, ex-*MSI 14*)	311	Tacoma Boatbuilding Co	3 Sep 1964
RIAZI (ex-*MSI 13*)	312	Tacoma Boatbuilding Co	15 Oct 1964

Displacement, tons: 180 standard; 235 full load
Dimensions, feet (metres): 111 × 23 × 6 *(33.9 × 7.0 × 1.8)*
Gun: 1—50 cal MG
Main engines: Diesels; 650 bhp = 13 knots
Oil fuel, tons: 20
Range, miles: 1 000 at 9 knots
Complement: 23 (5 officers, 18 men)

Delivered to Iran under MAP. Laid down on 22 June 1962 and 1 February 1963, and transferred at Seattle, Washington, on 3 September 1964 and 15 October 1964, respectively. In August 1967 *Kahnamuie* was renamed *Harischi* as the name was required for one of the new US PFs (see Corvettes).

RIAZI (old pennant number)   1975, Imperial Iranian Navy

SERVICE FORCES

1 REPLENISHMENT SHIP

Name	No.	Builders	Commissioned
KHARG	431	Swan Hunter Ltd, Wallsend	1978

Displacement, tonnes: 10 890 light; 33 014 full load
Measurement, tons: 20 100 deadweight; 21 100 gross
Dimensions, feet (metres): 680 × 87 × 30 *(207.2 × 26.5 × 9.1)*
Aircraft: 3 helicopters
Guns: 1—76 mm OTO Melara; 4—40 mm (twin)
Main engine: Westinghouse geared turbine; 26 870 shp; 1 shaft
Boilers: 2 Babcock & Wilcox, 2-drum high pressure
Speed, knots: 21.5
Complement: 248

KHARG   1978, Swan Hunter Ltd

Ordered October 1974. Laid down January 1976. Launched 3 February 1977.
A design incorporating some of the features of the British "Ol" class but carrying ammunition and dry stores in addition to fuel.

4 LANDING SHIPS (LOGISTIC)

Name	No.	Builders	Commissioned
HENGAM	511	Yarrow (Shipbuilders) Ltd, Clyde	12 Aug 1974
LARAK	512	Yarrow (Shipbuilders) Ltd, Clyde	12 Nov 1974
LAVAN	513	Yarrow (Shipbuilders) Ltd, Clyde	1979
TONB	514	Yarrow (Shipbuilders) Ltd, Clyde	1979

Displacement, tons: 2 500
Dimensions, feet (metres): 305 × 49 × 7.3 *(93 × 15 × 2.4)*
Guns: 4—40 mm (single)
Main engines: 4 Paxman 12 YJCM diesels; 2 shafts; 5 600 bhp
Speed, knots: 14.5
Complement: 80 plus 227 embarked troops

Smaller than British *Sir Lancelot* design with no through tank deck. Carry up to nine tanks depending on size (one Chieftain abreast or two T54/55). Ordered 25 July 1972. *Hengam* laid down late 1972, launched 27 September 1973. *Larak* laid down 1973, launched 7 May 1974. Two more were under construction but were cancelled in February 1979.

Names: Islands in the Gulf.

LARAK (old pennant number)   5/1975, C. and S. Taylor

2 FLEET SUPPLY SHIPS

Name	No.	Builders	Commissioned
BANDAR ABBAS	421	C. Lühring Yard, Brake, W. Germany	Apr 1974
BOOSEHR	422	C. Lühring Yard, Brake, W. Germany	Nov 1974

Measurement, tons: 3 250 deadweight
Dimensions, feet (metres): 354.2 × 54.4 × 14.8 *(108 × 16.6 × 4.5)*
Aircraft: 1 helicopter
Guns: 2—40 mm
Main engines: 2 MAN (MTU) diesels; 2 shafts; 6 000 bhp
Speed, knots: 16
Complement: 60

Combined tankers and store-ships carrying victualling, armament and general stores. *Bandar Abbas* launched 11 August 1973, *Bushehr* launched 23 March 1974.

BOOSEHR   2/1978, Chris Gee

1 Ex-US "AMPHION" CLASS (REPAIR SHIP)

Name	No.	Builders	Commissioned
CHAHBAHAR (ex-USS *Amphion*, ex-*AR 13*)	441	Tampa Shipbuilding Co	30 Jan 1946

Displacement, tons: 7 826 standard; 14 490 full load
Dimensions, feet (metres): 492.0 × 70.0 × 27.5 *(150.1 × 21.4 × 8.4)*
Guns: 2—3 in 50 cal
Main engines: Westinghouse turbines; 1 shaft; 8 500 shp = 16.5 knots
Boilers: 2 Foster-Wheeler
Complement: Accommodation for 921

Launched on 15 May 1945. Transferred to IIN on 1 October 1971. Based at Bandar Abbas as permanent repair facility, although she does go to sea occasionally.

CHAHBAHAR (old pennant number)   1972, Imperial Iranian Navy

IRAN / Service forces — Customs vessels

1 SUBMARINE RESCUE SHIP
— (ex-USS *Tringa* ASR 16)

Commissioned 1956

1 HARBOUR TANKER

Name	No.	Builders
HORMUZ (ex-YO 247)	401	Cantiere Castellammàre

Displacement, tons: 1 250 standard; 1 700 full load
Dimensions, feet (metres): 178·3 × 32·2 × 14 *(54·4 × 9·8 × 4·3)*
Guns: 2—20 mm
Main engine: 1 Ansaldo Q 370, 4-cyl diesel
Oil fuel, tons: 25

Cargo oil capacity: 5 000 to 6 000 barrels.

HORMUZ *1970, Imperial Iranian Navy*

2 WATER TANKERS

KANGAN   TAHERI

Displacement, tons: 9 430
Dimensions, feet (metres): 460 pp × 70·5 × 16·5 *(139 × 21·2 × 5)*
Main engine: MAN diesel; 7 385 hp = 15 knots

First launched 24 March 1977.
Both built at Mazagon Docks, Bombay, completing in 1978 and 1979.

2 Ex-ITALIAN LINERS

RAFFELLO   MICHELANGELO

Purchased as barracks ships at Chahbahar and Bandar Abbas. Retain Italian names.
Of 42 000 tons and originally 29 knots.

1 TUG

BAHMANSHIR 451

Harbour tug (ex-US Army *ST 1002*), 150 tons, transferred in 1962.

1 Ex-US "YW-83" CLASS (WATER TANKER)

LENGEH (ex-US YW 88) 402

Displacement, tons: 1 250 standard
Dimensions, feet (metres): 178·3 × 32·2 × 14 *(54·4 × 9·8 × 4·3)*
Main engines: Diesels; speed = 10 knots

Transferred to Iran by USA in 1964. Similar to tanker *Hormuz*.

2 HARBOUR TUGS

No. 1 (ex-German *Karl*)   **No. 2** (ex-German *Ise*)

Sister ships of 134 tons taken over from West Germany 17 June 1974. Both built 1962-63.

26 BARGES

Built in Pakistan 1976-77 the largest being a 260 ft self-propelled lighter.

FLOATING DOCK

400 (ex-US *ARD 28*, ex- *FD 4*)

Lift: 3 000 tons

Transferred on loan September 1971. Of steel construction. Purchased 1 March 1977.

IMPERIAL YACHTS

Name	No.	Builders	Commissioned
SHAHSAVAR	—	N.V. Boele, Bolnes, Netherlands	1936

Displacement, tons: 530
Dimensions, feet (metres): 176 × 25·3 × 10·5 *(53·7 × 7·7 × 3·2)*
Main engines: 2 Stork diesels; 1 300 bhp

Launched in 1936. In the Caspian Sea.

Name	No.	Builders	Commissioned
KISH	—	Burmester, Germany	1970

Displacement, tons: 178
Dimensions, feet (metres): 122 × 25 × 7 *(37·2 × 7·6 × 2·1)*
Main engines: 2 MTU diesels; 2 920 hp

A smaller and more modern Imperial Yacht. In the Persian Gulf.

COAST GUARD

20 "65 ft" TYPE (COASTAL PATROL CRAFT)

1201-1220

Built by Peterson Builders, Wisconsin 1975-76. Armed with three 20 mm and two ·50 MG.

6 "40 ft" SEWART TYPE (COASTAL PATROL CRAFT)

MAHNAVI-HAMRAZ   MAHNAVI-VAHEDI   MORVARID
MAHNAVI-TAHERI   MARDJAN   SADAF

Displacement, tons: 10 standard
Dimensions, feet (metres): 40·0 × 11·0 × 3·7 *(12·2 × 3·4 × 1·1)*
Guns: Light MG
Main engines: 2 General Motors diesels = 30 knots

Small launches for port duties of Sewart (USA) standard 40 ft type. All transferred June 1953.
Pennant numbers 5001 and above. Some serve in the Caspian Sea.

SURVEY VESSELS

(Operated by the Ministry of Finance except for *Abnegar*)

MEHR

Of 422 tons. Launched in 1964. Complement 22.

ABNEGAR

50 ton wooden oceanographic vessel built in Ireland. Operated by IIN.

HYDROGRAPH SHAHPOUR

Of 9 tons. Launched in 1965.

HYDROGRAPH PAHLAVI

Of 9 tons. Launched in 1966.

CUSTOMS VESSELS

TOUFAN   TOUSAN

Built by CN Inmar, La Spezia in 1954-55. Of 65 tons with twin diesels. 22 knots.

IRAQ

Ministerial

Minister of Defence:
  Ahmad Hasan al-Bakr

Administration

Commander-in-Chief:
  Rear-Admiral Abd Al Diri
Chief of Staff:
  Commander Samad Sat Al Mufti

Personnel

(a) 1979: 3 000 officers and men
(b) 2 years national service

Mercantile Marine

Lloyd's Register of Shipping:
  110 vessels of 1 135 245 tons gross

Bases

Basra, Umm Qasr

SOVIET-IRAQI TREATIES

Under the treaty, signed in April 1972, the Soviet fleet would have access to the Iraqi base of Umm Qasr, in return for Soviet assistance to strengthen Iraq's defences. This resulted in the acquisition by Iraq of 14 "Osa" class.
A further treaty signed in August 1976 has been kept secret but it is reported that, from the naval point of view, it includes provision for the Soviet occupation of Umm Qasr in return for the provision of "ten missile frigates" to Iraq. Whether these will be similar to the "Nanuchka" class sent to India remains to be seen.

AMPHIBIOUS FORCES

3 Ex-SOVIET "POLNOCHNIY" CLASS LCTs

ATIKA   GANDA   +1

Displacement, tons: 890 standard: 1 100 full load
Dimensions, feet (metres): 239·4 × 29·5 × 5·9 *(75 × 9 × 1·8)*
Guns: 4—30 mm (twins); 2 rocket launchers
Main engines: 2 diesels; 5 000 bhp = 18 knots
Complement: 40

Built in Poland and transferred in 1977. Of original hull design but with a new type of deck-structure amidships. This would appear to be a form of helicopter platform were it not for the swimming-pool sized hole in the middle.

Iraqi "POLNOCHNIY" Class   5/1977, MOD

LIGHT FORCES

6 Ex-SOVIET "OSA I" and 8 "OSA II" CLASSES (FAST ATTACK CRAFT—MISSILE)

EL TAMI   HAZRAN NAUNI   NISAN   TAMUZ   +10

Displacement, tons: 160/165 standard; 200 full load
Dimensions, feet (metres): 127·9 × 26·6 × 5·9 *(39·0 × 8·1 × 1·8)*
Missiles: SSM; 4—SS-N-2 (single launchers)
Guns: 4—30 mm (twins)
Main engines: 3 diesels; 13 000 hp (Osa I), 15 000 (Osa II) = 36 knots
Range, miles: 800 at 25 knots
Complement: 30

A combination of six "Osa I" delivered 1972-74 and 8 "Osa II" classes delivered in pairs in 1974, 1975 and 1976.

Names: Some of those reported are very similar to Arabic names of the months and may, therefore, be suspect.

Radar: Search: Square Tie.
Fire control: Drum Tilt.

"OSA I" Class

3 Ex-SOVIET "SO I" CLASS

210, 211, 212

Displacement, tons: 170 light; 215 full load
Dimensions, feet (metres): 138·6 × 20 × 5·9 *(42·3 × 6·1 × 1·8)*
Guns: 4—25 mm
A/S weapons: 4—MBU 1800
Mines: 20
Main engines: 3 diesels; 7 500 bhp = 29 knots
Complement: 30

Delivered by the USSR to Iraq in 1962.

Radar: Search: Pot Head.

Sonar: One hull-mounted.

"SO I" Class   1970, USN

10 Ex-SOVIET "P 6" CLASS (FAST ATTACK CRAFT—TORPEDO)

AL ADRISI	LAMAKI
AL SHAAB	RAMADAN
AL TAMI	SHULAB
ALEF	TAMUR
IBN SAID	TAREQ BEN ZAID

Displacement, tons: 66 standard; 75 full load
Dimensions, feet (metres): 84.2 × 20 × 6 (25.7 × 6.1 × 1.8)
Guns: 4—25 mm
Torpedo tubes: 2—21 in (533 mm)
Main engines: 4 diesels; 4 shafts; 4 800 bhp = 41 knots
Complement: 20

Transferred from the USSR. Two were received in 1959, four in November 1960, and six in January 1961. Two deleted 1977.

"P 6" Class 1970, USN

2 Ex-SOVIET "POLUCHAT I" CLASS (LARGE PATROL CRAFT)

Displacement, tons: 90 standard
Dimensions, feet (metres): 97.1 × 19.0 × 4.8 (29.6 × 5.8 × 1.5)
Guns: 2—14.5 mm
Main engines: 2 diesels; 2 400 hp = 20 knots
Complement: 15

Transferred by USSR in late 1960s. Also used for torpedo recovery.

"POLUCHAT I" Class 10/1975, MOD

4 COASTAL PATROL CRAFT

Name	No.	Builders	Commissioned
ABD AL RAHMAN	1	John I. Thornycroft & Co Ltd, Woolston, Southampton	1937
AL GHAZI	2	John I. Thornycroft & Co Ltd, Woolston, Southampton	1937
DAT AL DIYARI	3	John I. Thornycroft & Co Ltd, Woolston, Southampton	1937
JANNADA	4	John I. Thornycroft & Co Ltd, Woolston, Southampton	1937

Displacement, tons: 67
Dimensions, feet (metres): 100 × 17 × 3 (30.5 × 5.2 × 0.9)
Guns: 1—3.7 in howitzer; 2—3 in mortars; 4 MG
Main engines: 2 Thornycroft diesels; 2 shafts; 280 bhp = 12 knots

Protected by bullet-proof plating. All launched, completed and delivered in 1937.

4 Ex-SOVIET "ZHUK" CLASS (COASTAL PATROL CRAFT)

Displacement, tons: 50 standard; 60 full load
Dimensions, feet (metres): 85.3 × 16 × 5 (26 × 4.9 × 1.5)
Guns: 4—14.5 mm MG (twins)
Main engines: 2 M 50 diesels; 2 shafts; 2 400 hp
Speed, knots: 30
Complement: 18

Transferred in 1975.

"ZHUK" Class

4 Ex-SOVIET "NYRYAT II" CLASS (COASTAL PATROL CRAFT)

Displacement, tons: 125
Dimensions, feet (metres): 95.1 × 16.4 × 5.6 (29 × 5 × 1.7)
Main engine: 1 diesel = 12 knots
Range, miles: 1 600 at 10 knots
Complement: 15

Similar in appearance to "PO 2" class without bulwarks. Multi-purpose craft probably used as diving craft.

2 Ex-SOVIET "PO 2" CLASS (COASTAL PATROL CRAFT)

Displacement, tons: 95 full load
Dimensions, feet (metres): 82 × 16.7 × 5.6 (25 × 5.1 × 1.7)
Guns: 2—25 mm or 2—12.7 mm
Main engines: 2 diesels = 30 knots

8 THORNYCROFT "36 ft" TYPE

Length, feet (metres): 36 *(11·0)*
Main engine: 1 diesel; 125 bhp

Patrol boats built by John I. Thornycroft & Co for the Iraqi Ports Administration.

4 THORNYCROFT "21 ft" TYPE

Length, feet (metres): 21 *(6·4)*
Main engine: 1 diesel; 40 bhp

Pilot despatch launches built by John I. Thornycroft & Co for the Iraqi Ports Administration.

MINE WARFARE FORCES

2 Ex-SOVIET "T 43" CLASS (MINESWEEPERS—OCEAN)

AL YARMOUK 465   AL KADISIA 467

Displacement, tons: 580 full load
Dimensions, feet (metres): 190·2 × 27·6 × 6·9 *(58·0 × 8·4 × 2·1)*
Guns: 4—37 mm L63 (twins); 4—25 mm L70 (twins); 8—12·7 mm (quads)
A/S weapons: 2 DCT
Mines: 30
Main engines: 2 diesels; 2 shafts; 2 200 hp = 14 knots
Range, miles: 3 200 at 10 knots
Complement: 65

Transferred early 1970s.

Radar: Search: Ball End.
Navigation: Neptun.

"T 43" Class

3 Ex-SOVIET "YEVGENYA" CLASS (MINESWEEPERS—INSHORE)

Displacement, tons: 80 full load
Dimensions, feet (metres): 85·6 × 19 × 3·9 *(26·1 × 5·8 × 1·2)*
Guns: 2—25 mm (twin)
Main engines: 2 diesels; 2 shafts; 600 hp = 16 knots
Complement: 10

GRP hulls. Delivered in 1975 under cover-name of "oceanographic craft".

Radar: Don 2

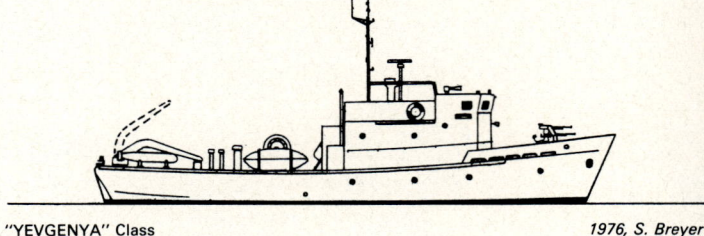
"YEVGENYA" Class   1976, S. Breyer

HARBOUR AUTHORITY CRAFT

AL THAWRA (ex-*Malike Aliye*)

Displacement, tons: 746
Main engines: Diesels; 2 shafts; 1 800 shp = 14 knots

Royal Yacht before assassination of King Faisal II in 1958, after which she was renamed *Al Thawra (The Revolution)* instead of *Malike Aliye (Queen Aliyah)*.

AL THAWRA   1966, Aldo Fraccaroli

MISCELLANEOUS

A number of customs craft and a large Dutch-built dredger of the Harbour Authority are also listed.

IRELAND

Minister for Defence:
  Mr. R. M. Molloy
Commanding Officer and Director Naval Service:
  Captain P. Kavanagh, NS

Naval Base

Haulbowline Island (Cork), HQ' naval base and dockyard, naval school, sea-going replacement section, ship support and maintenance section.

Future Plans

In March 1977 the Minister of Defence stated that a total of fifteen sea-going and ten coastal patrol ships with a strength of 2 000 men would be necessary to patrol Ireland's portion of the expanded EEC fishing zone. How far this is in line with the later statements that eight of the "P21" class are planned with a manpower target of 1 200 is not clear. However it is obvious that Ireland's naval strength will be notably increased by the 1980s.

Personnel

(a) 1979: Approximately 800 officers and men
(b) Voluntary service

Prefix to Ships' Names

L.É.

Mercantile Marine

Lloyd's Register of Shipping:
  110 vessels of 212 143 tons gross

DELETIONS

Cliona (ex-HMS *Bellwort*) and *Macha* (ex-HMS *Borage*), both built by George Brown, & Co (Marine) Ltd, Greenock, were sold for breaking up in 1970-71. *Maev* (ex-HMS *Oxlip*) deleted 1972. Tender *Wyndham* sold in 1968 and *General McHardy* in 1971.

IRELAND / Frigate — Miscellaneous 263

FRIGATE

Plans are reported for the next new construction ship to be of about 235 ft and 2 000 tons with a helicopter. The design will probably be similar to the 72 m ship illustrated.

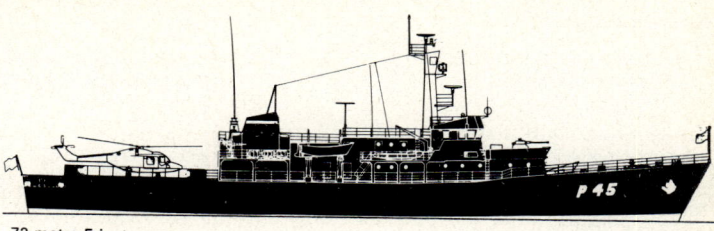

72 metre Frigate   1978, Verolme, Cork

CORVETTES

3 + 1 "P 21" and "DEIRDRE" CLASSES

Name	No.	Builders	Commissioned
DEIRDRE	P 20	Verolme, Cork	May 1972
EMER	P 21	Verolme, Cork	9 Jan 1978
AOIF	P 22	Verolme, Cork	mid-1979
—	P 23	Verolme, Cork	1980

Displacement, tons: 972 (Deirdre); 1 019·5 (Emer)
Dimensions, feet (metres): 184·3 pp × 34·1 × 14·4 (56·2 × 10·4 × 4·4) (Deirdre); 213·7 × 34·4 × 14·1 (65·2 × 10·5 × 4·3) (Emer)
Guns: 1—40 mm Bofors; 2—20 mm Oerlikon (not Deirdre)
Main engines: 2 British Polar diesels (Deirdre), 2 SEMT-Pielstick (Emer) coupled to 1 shaft; cp propeller 4 200 bhp (Deirdre), 4 800 (Emer) = 18 knots
Oil fuel, tons: 170
Range, miles: 4 500 at 18 knots; 6 750 at 12 knots
Complement: 46 (5 officers, 41 men)

Stabilisers fitted. *Deirdre* was the first vessel ever built for the Naval Service in the Republic of Ireland. Launched on 29 December 1971. The port after boat has been deleted in *Emer* and subsequent ships. In December 1977 a contract for a third of this class was placed with Verolme, Cork at a cost of £5 million and in early 1979 both this and a fourth ship were under construction.

Class: In January 1978 the Minister of Defence stated that it was intended to continue construction at the rate of one per year. It is further reported that the target total is eight ships including *Deirdre*, *Emer* and *Aoif*.

Electronics: Decca navigator; full communications UHF to MF; satellite navigation in P22 and 23.

Radar: Two Decca sets.

Sonar: Simrad bottom and sidescanning.

EMER   2/1978, A. J. English

COASTAL MINESWEEPERS

3 Ex-BRITISH "TON" CLASS

Name	No.	Builders	Commissioned
GRÁINNE (ex-HMS *Oulston*, M 1129)	CM 10	Thornycroft	1955
BANBA (ex-HMS *Alverton*, M 1104)	CM 11	Camper and Nicholson Ltd, Gosport	1953
FÓLA (ex-HMS *Blaxton*, M 1132)	CM 12	Thornycroft	1956

Displacement, tons: 360 standard; 425 full load
Dimensions, feet (metres): 153·0 × 28·8 × 8·2 (46·7 × 8·8 × 2·5)
Guns: 1—40 mm; 2—20 mm
Main engines: 2 diesels; 2 shafts; 3 000 bhp = 15 knots
Oil fuel, tons: 45
Range, miles: 2 300 at 13 knots
Complement: 33

Former British "Ton" class coastal minesweepers. Double mahogany hulls and otherwise constructed of aluminium alloy and other materials with the lowest possible magnetic signature. Purchased from the UK in 1971 for fishery protection duties as replacements for previous corvettes.

GRÁINNE   5/1974, Irish Naval Service

TRAINING SHIP

Name	No.	Builders	Commissioned
SETANTA (ex-*Isolda*)	A 15	Liffey D.Y., Dublin	1953

Displacement, tons: 1 173
Dimensions, feet (metres): 208 pp × 38 × 13 (63·5 × 11·6 × 4)
Guns: 2—20 mm Oerlikon
Main engines: Steam recip: 1 500 ihp; 2 shafts = 11·5 knots
Oil fuel, tons: 276
Range, miles: 3 500 at 10 knots
Complement: 44

Acquired from the Commissioners of Irish Lights in 1976

SETANTA   10/1977, Irish Naval Service

MISCELLANEOUS

Name	No.	Builders	Commissioned
JOHN ADAMS	—	Richard Dunston, Thorne, Yorks.	1934

Measurement, tons: 94 gross
Dimensions, feet (metres): 85 × 18·5 × 7 (25·9 × 5·6 × 2·1)
Main engine: Diesel; 216 bhp = 10 knots

Employed on harbour duties. New engine fitted in 1976. Civilian manned for harbour duties.

COLLEEN

Service launch of 35 ft, built in Wales in 1930. Single 30 hp diesel.

CHOWL

Oil barge of 100 tons with single 50 hp diesel.

SIR CECIL   **RAVEN**   **JACKDAW**

Civilian manned passenger transports based at Cork. Taken over 1938.

ISRAEL

Headquarters Appointment

Commander in Chief of the Israeli Navy:
  Commodore Zeev Almog

Diplomatic Representation

Defence Attaché in London:
  Brigadier General R. Sivron
Naval Attaché in Rome:
  Captain P. Pinchasi
Naval Attaché in Washington:
  Captain M. Tabak

Personnel

(a) 1979: 6 600 (800 officers and 5 800 men, of whom 3 500 are conscripts. Includes a Naval Commando)
(b) 3 years national service for Jews and Druses
Note (An additional 5 000 Reserves available on mobilisation).

Submarines

1975 Leviathan (ex-T class)
1977 Dolphin (ex-T class)

Bases

Haifa, Ashdod, Sharm-el-Sheikh
A repair base has been built at Eilat where a synchro-lift is installed.

Prefix to Ships' Names

INS (Israeli Naval Ship)

Deployment

At Sharm-el-Sheikh there are normally 4 "Reshef" class, 2 "Saar" class, 6 "Dabur" class, some tugs, landing craft and a depot ship.

Missiles

The re-equipment with Gabriel 2 (with double the range of Gabriel 1) will take a considerable time. Until this is achieved a mixed-bag of Gabriel 1 and 2 and Harpoon will be in use.

DELETIONS

Light Forces

1975 12 Bertram Type; 14 Swift Type
1976 Yarkon

Strength of the Fleet

Type	Active	Building
Patrol Submarines	3	—
Corvettes	—	2 (?6)
Fast Attack Craft (Missile)	20	4
Hydrofoils	—	2 (10)
Hovercraft	2	—
Coastal Patrol Craft	38	2
"Firefish"	1	—
LSMs	3	—
LCTs	6	—
LCMs	3	—
Transports	2	—
Support Ship	1	—
Training Ship	1	—

Mercantile Marine

Lloyd's Register of Shipping:
  55 vessels of 420 433 tons gross

SUBMARINES

3 IKL/VICKERS TYPE 206

Name	No.	Builders	Laid down	Launched	Commissioned
GAL	—	Vickers Ltd, Barrow	1973	2 Dec 1975	Jan 1977
TANIN	—	Vickers Ltd, Barrow	1974	25 Oct 1976	1977
RAHAV	—	Vickers Ltd, Barrow	—	—	Dec 1977

Displacement, tons: 420 surfaced; 600 dived
Dimensions, feet (metres): 146·7 × 15·4 × 12 *(45·0 × 4·7 × 3·7)*
Torpedo tubes: 8—21 in bow
Main machinery: Diesels; 2 000 hp; electric motor; 1 800 hp; 1 shaft; diesel-electric
Speed, knots: 11 surfaced; 17 dived
Complement: 22

A contract was signed for the building of these boats by Vickers in April 1972.
Incorporated in the fin is the British SLAM missile launcher for Blowpipe missiles.

TANIN   1976

CORVETTES

0 + 2 + ?6 NEW CONSTRUCTION

Displacement, tons: 850
Dimensions, feet (metres): 253·2 × 30·2 × 10·8 *(77·2 × 9·2 × 3·3)*
Aircraft: 1 helicopter
Missiles: SSM; 4—Gabriel 2 (single launchers) (see note)
Guns: 2—76 mm OTO Melara; 4—30 mm (twins)
A/S weapons: 1 triple Bofors 375 mm rocket launcher
Main engines: Codag; 1 General Motors LM2500 gas turbine; 24 000 bhp; 2 MTU diesels; 4 000 hp; 2 shafts (cp propellers)
Speed, knots: 40-42
Range, miles: 4 500 on diesels
Complement: 45

A new design (QU-09-35) being built by Israel Shipyards Haifa. Will probably have a mix of Harpoon and Gabriel. Two building. These ships may well be intended for target acquisition for Harpoon fitted "Reshefs" with command and control facilities.

ISRAEL / Light forces 265

LIGHT FORCES

8 + 4 "RESHEF" CLASS (FAST ATTACK CRAFT—MISSILE)

Name	No.	Builders	Commissioned
RESHEF	—	Haifa Shipyard	Apr 1973
KESHET	—	Haifa Shipyard	Oct 1973
ROMAH	—	Haifa Shipyard	Mar 1974
KIDON	—	Haifa Shipyard	Sep 1974
TARSHISH	—	Haifa Shipyard	Mar 1975
YAFFO	—	Haifa Shipyard	Apr 1975
MITZAHON	—	Haifa Shipyard	Dec 1978
—	—	Haifa Shipyard	mid-1979
—	—	Haifa Shipyard	end 1979
—	—	Haifa Shipyard	mid-1980
—	—	Haifa Shipyard	end 1980
—	—	Haifa Shipyard	mid-1981

Displacement, tons: 415 standard
Dimensions, feet (metres): 190·6 × 25 × 8 *(58 × 7·8 × 2·4)*
Missiles: SSM; 4 Harpoon, 5 Gabriel (single launchers)
Guns: 2—76 mm/62 (single Compact); 2—20 mm Oerlikon (see *Gunnery* note)
Engines: 4 Maybach (MTU) diesels; 2 670 hp each; 2 shafts
Speed, knots: 32
Range, miles: 1 650 at 30 knots; 4 000 at 17·5 knots
Complement: 45

RESHEF
1974, Michael D. J. Lennon

These steel-hulled boats carry US missiles, Israeli-made missiles and electronics as well as chaff launchers.

Reshef was launched on 19 February 1973; *Keshet* 2 August 1973.
This very interesting class has an extremely long range at cruising speed, two pairs having made the passage from Israel to the Red Sea via the Strait of Gibraltar and Cape of Good Hope, relying entirely on refuelling at sea. This is a great tribute not only to their endurance but also to their sea-keeping qualities. A further illustration of this was the appearance of two "Reshefs" in New York July 1976.

The first pair was successfully engaged in the Arab-Israeli War, October 1973. The whole class will eventually be equipped with the new 22 mile range Gabriel missiles.
An expansion of the building slips at Haifa Dockyard is allowing the more rapid construction of the next six boats ordered in January 1975. These are slightly larger with an overall length of 202·6 ft *(61·7 m)* and may have increased speed of 36 knots. Numbers may be reduced with construction of new corvettes. *Mitzahon* launched 10 July 1978.
It is now reported, but not confirmed, that a further six ships have been ordered for a total of eighteen.

Aircraft: *Tarshish* has had her after 76 mm gun removed to make way for a helicopter platform.

Deployment: *Tarshish* and *Yaffo* in Mediterranean. Other four of first six in Red Sea.

Gunnery: *Mitzahon* fitted with 40 mm forward and 76 mm aft.

Missiles: Fitted with 4 Harpoon from Jan-Feb 1978 in addition to Gabriel.

Sonar: Fitted in ships deployed in the Red Sea. (ELAC).

Transfers: Six of this class built for South Africa in Haifa and Durban.

6 "SAAR 1 and 2" and 6 "SAAR 3" CLASSES (FAST ATTACK CRAFT—MISSILE)

Name	No.	Builders	Commissioned
"Saar 1/2"			
MIVTACH	311	Ch. de Normandie	1968
MIZNACH	312	Ch. de Normandie	1968
MISGAV	313	Ch. de Normandie	1968
EILAT	321	Ch. de Normandie	1968
HAIFA	322	Ch. de Normandie	1968
ACCO	323	Ch. de Normandie	1968
"Saar 3"			
SAAR	331	Ch. de Normandie	1969
SOUFA	332	Ch. de Normandie	1969
GAASH	333	Ch. de Normandie	1969
HEREV	341	Ch. de Normandie	1969
HANIT	342	Ch. de Normandie	1969
HETZ	343	Ch. de Normandie	1969

Displacement, tons: 220 standard; 250 full load
Dimensions, feet (metres): 147·6 × 23·0 × 8·2 *(45·0 × 7·0 × 2·5)*
Missiles: SSM; Gabriel (see notes)
Guns: 40 mm or 76 mm (see notes)
Main engines: 4 Maybach (MTU) diesels; 13 500 bhp; 4 shafts = 40+ knots
Oil fuel, tons: 30
Range, miles: 2 500 at 15 knots; 1 600 at 20 knots; 1 000 at 30 knots
Complement: 35 to 40

"SAAR" Class with 76mm and six Gabriel missiles
1973

Built from designs by Lürssen Werft of Bremen. Political problems caused their building in France instead of Germany—a political embargo kept the last five in France until their journey to Israel began on Christmas Eve 1969. Two batches were built, the first six (1 and 2) being fitted originally with three 40 mm guns and ordered in 1965. The second six (3) were ordered in 1966 and fitted with 76 mm OTO Melara guns. Five of these ships were delivered to Israel and two *(Acco* and *Saar)* made the journey on completion of local trials after the 1969 French arms embargo. The last five arrived off Haifa in January 1970 after a much-publicised passage which proved the remarkable endurance of this class.
The first batch was fitted for sonar but this was omitted from the 76 mm gun fitted group. After their arrival in Israel provision of Gabriel surface to surface missiles progressed. The first group can mount an armament varying from one 40 mm gun and eight Gabriel missiles (two single fixed mounts forward and two triple trainable mounts amidships) to three 40 mm guns. The second group can mount the two triple Gabriel launchers amidships as well as the 76 mm OTO Melara gun forward.
The Gabriel missile system is controlled by radar and optical sights and launches a low-altitude missile with a 150 lb HE head to a range of 12·5 miles in the first configuration and 22 miles in the later versions.

Sonar: ELAC sonar in "Saar 1 and 2".

Torpedoes: "Saar 1 and 2" designed for four torpedo tubes for Mk 46 torpedoes.

"SAAR" Class with three 40 mm and torpedo tubes
1974

HANIT with one 40 mm and eight Gabriel missiles
1971, Israeli Navy

"SAAR" Class with 40 mm guns and torpedo tubes (see note)
1974

ISRAEL / Light forces

0 + 2 + 10 US "FLAGSTAFF 2" CLASS (HYDROFOILS)

Displacement, tons: 91·5
Dimensions, feet (metres): 96·4 × 21·3 × — (29·4 × 6·5 × —)
Missiles: SSM; 4 Gabriel
Guns: 2—30 mm (twin)
Speed, knots: 52

The first pair has been ordered in the USA from Grumman with possibly ten more to be built in Israel. Probably to replace the "Saar" class.

? "DVORA" CLASS (FAST ATTACK CRAFT—MISSILE)

Displacement, tons: 47
Dimensions, feet (metres): 75 × ? × ? (23 × ? × ?)
Missiles: SSM; 2 Gabriel (single launchers)
Guns: 2—20 mm (singles)
Main engines: 2 MTU diesels = 36 knots
Range, miles: 700 at 27 knots

A private design of Israel Shipyards Ltd which is basically an improved "Dabur" class. The smallest missile craft so far built. First trials December 1977—it is still uncertain whether the small size of this craft will make it acceptable to the Israeli Navy.

"DVORA" Class　　　　　　　　　　　　　　　　1978, Israeli Shipyards

35 "DABUR" CLASS (COASTAL PATROL CRAFT)

Displacement, tons: 35 full load
Dimensions, feet (metres): 64·9 × 19 × 2·6 (19·8 × 5·8 × 0·8)
Guns: 2—20 mm; 2 twin 50 cal MGs (see note)
Main engines: 2 geared diesels; 960 shp; 2 shafts = 25 knots
Range, miles: 1 200 at 17 knots
Complement: 6/9 depending on armament

Twelve built in USA and remainder by Israel Aircraft Industry. Aluminium hull. There are several variations in their armament. Deployed in the Mediterranean and Red Seas, this being facilitated as these craft have been designed for overland transport. Good rough weather performance. A continuing programme in hand at the IAI plant at Ramta.

Missiles: There are reports that some may carry missiles of an unspecified type.

Transfer: Four to Argentina in 1978.

"DABUR" Class　　　　　　　　　　　　　　　　1978, Israeli Shipyards

3 Ex-US PBR TYPE (COASTAL PATROL CRAFT)

Dimensions, feet (metres): 32 × 11 × 2·6 (9·8 × 3·4 × 0·8)
Guns: 2—12·7 mm MG
Main engines: 2 geared diesels; waterjets = 25 knots
Complement: 5

Purchased 1974 and subsequently. GRP Hulls.

PBR Type　　　　　　　　　　　　　　　　　　　1976, Israeli Navy

1 FIREFISH MODEL III

Displacement, tons: 6
Dimensions, feet (metres): 28 × 7·5 (8·5 × 2·3)
Main engines: 2 Mercruiser V-8; 430 hp
Speed, knots: 52
Range, miles: 250 cruising; 150 max speed

Built by Sandaire, San Diego. Glass fibre craft, can carry five men. Capable of being radio-controlled for attack missions or minesweeping under ship or aircraft control.

FIREFISH III　　　　　　　　　　　　　　　　　　1976, Israeli Navy

AMPHIBIOUS FORCES

3 Ex-US "LSM 1" CLASS

Displacement, tons: 1 095 full load
Dimensions, feet (metres): 203·5 × 34·5 × 7·3 (62·1 × 10·5 × 2·2)
Guns: 2—40 mm; 4—20 mm
Main engines: Diesels; 2 800 bhp; 2 shafts = 12·5 knots
Complement: 70

Purchased in 1972 from commercial sources.

"LSM 1" Class   1976, Israeli Navy

3 "ASH" CLASS (LCT)

Name	No.	Builders	Commissioned
ASHDOD	61	Israel Shipyards, Haifa	1966
ASHKELON	63	Israel Shipyards, Haifa	1967
ACHZIV	65	Israel Shipyards, Haifa	1967

Displacement, tons: 400 standard; 730 full load
Dimensions, feet (metres): 205·5 × 32·8 × 5·8 (62·7 × 10·0 × 1·8)
Guns: 2—20 mm
Main engines: 3 MWM diesels; 3 shafts; 1 900 bhp = 10·5 knots
Oil fuel, tons: 37
Complement: 20

"ASH" Class (being fitted with helicopter deck aft)   1976, Israeli Navy

3 LC TYPE (LCT)

Name	No.	Builders	Commissioned
ETZION GUEBER	51	Israel Shipyards, Haifa	1965
SHIQMONA	53	Israel Shipyards, Haifa	1965
KESSARAYA	55	Israel Shipyards, Haifa	1965

Displacement, tons: 182 standard; 230 full load
Dimensions, feet (metres): 120·0 × 23·2 × 4·7 (Etzion Geuber of only 90 ft (27·5) length) (36·6 × 7·1 × 1·4)
Guns: 2—20 mm
Main engines: 2 diesels; 2 shafts; 1 280 bhp = 10 knots
Complement: 12

LC Type   1976, Israeli Navy

3 Ex-US LCM TYPE

Displacement, tons: 22 tons standard; 60 full load
Dimensions, feet (metres): 50 × 14 × 3·2 (15·3 × 4·3 × 1)
Main engines: 2 diesels; 450 bhp = 11 knots

2 SEALAND Mark III HOVERCRAFT

Purchased in UK in 1978.

SUPPORT SHIPS

Note: Training ship 'Nogah' converted from 500 ton coaster.

Name	No.	Builders	Commissioned
MA'OZ	—	Todd Marine, Washington	1976

Displacement, tons: 4 000?

Oil-rig tender for use as Light Forces Support ship.

1 "BAT SHEVA" CLASS (TRANSPORT)

Name	No.	Builders	Commissioned
BAT SHEVA	—	Netherlands	1967

Displacement, tons: 900
Dimensions, feet (metres): 311·7 × 36·7 × 26·9 (95·1 × 11·2 × 8·2)
Guns: 4—20 mm
Main engines: Diesels; speed = 10 knots
Complement: 26

Purchased from South Africa in 1968.

1 "BAT YAM" CLASS (TRANSPORT)

Name	No.	Builders	Commissioned
BAT YAM	T 82	Netherlands	—

A small armed merchant ship of 1 200 tons used as a transport. Bought from Netherlands in 1967.

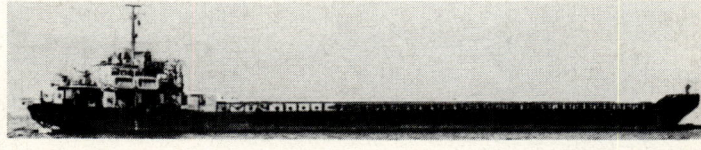

BAT SHEVA   1971, Israeli Navy

AUXILIARIES

1 "YAR" CLASS (TRAINING CRAFT)

Name	No.	Builders	Commissioned
YARDEN	42	Burmester, Germany	1958

Displacement, tons: 96 standard; 109 full load
Dimensions, feet (metres): 100 × 20 × 6 (30·5 × 6·1 × 1·8)
Guns: 2—20 mm
Main engines: MTU diesels; 2 shafts; speed 22 knots
Complement: 16

Has become non-naval training craft.

4 "KEDMA" CLASS (COASTAL PATROL CRAFT)

Name	No.	Builders	Commissioned
KEDMA	46	Japan	1968
YAMA	48	Japan	1968
NEGBA	52	Japan	1968
ZAFONA	60	Japan	1968

Displacement, tons: 32
Dimensions, feet (metres): 67·0 × 15·0 × 4·8 (20·4 × 4·6 × 1·5)
Guns: 2—20 mm
Main engines: 2 diesels; 2 shafts; 1 540 bhp = 25 knots
Complement: 10

Used for Coast Guard and police work in peace time.

ITALY

Headquarters Appointments

Chief of Naval Staff:
  Admiral Giovanni Torrisi
Chief of Naval Personnel:
  Vice-Admiral Vittorio Gioncada

Principal Commands

Commander, Allied Naval Forces, Southern Europe (Naples) and Commander-in-Chief Dipartimento Basso Tirreno:
  Admiral Aldo Baldini
Commander-in-Chief of Fleet (and Comedcent):
  Admiral Angelo Monassi
Commander-in-Chief Dipartimento Alto Tirreno:
  Admiral Luigi Cacioppo
Commander-in-Chief Dipartimento Adriatico:
  Vice-Admiral Enzo Consolo
Commander-in-Chief Dipartimento dello Jonio e Canale d'Otranto:
  Vice-Admiral Vittorio Marulli
Commander Sicilian Naval Area:
  Rear-Admiral Luigi de Ferrante
Commander Submarine Force:
  Rear-Admiral R. A. Emanuele Calori

Diplomatic Representation

Naval Attaché in Bonn:
  Captain Pietro Scagliusi
Naval Attaché in London:
  Rear-Admiral Giulio Benini
Naval Attaché in Moscow:
  Captain Armando Vigliano
Naval Attaché in Paris:
  Captain Roberto Falciai
Naval Attaché in Washington:
  Commander Antonio Cenciarelli

Personnel

(a) 1979: 41 900 (including Naval Air Arm and San Marco Battalion, (Force of Marines))
(b) 1½ years national service

Bases

Main—La Spezia (Alto Tirreno), Taranto (Jonio e Canale d'Otranto), Ancona (Adriatico)
Secondary—Brindisi, Augusta, Messina, La Maddalena, Cagliari, Naples, Venice

Naval Air Arm

2 LRMP Squadrons—18 Breguet Atlantics (BR 1150) (increasing to 32)
2 Shore-based helicopter squadrons (24 SH 3D)
3 Ship-borne helicopter squadrons (27 AB 204, 28 AB 212) (26 more on order)

Note: Atlantics operated by Navy with Air Force support and maintenance.

Strength of the Fleet

Type	Active	Building (Ordered)
Submarines	10	2
Light Aircraft Carriers	1	1
Cruisers	2	—
Destroyers	7	—
Frigates	14	1 (5)
Corvettes	8	—
Hydrofoil—Missile	3	4
Fast Attack Craft	7	—
LSTs	2	—
Minehunters	3	4
Minesweepers—Ocean	4	—
Minesweepers—Coastal	27	—
Minesweepers—Inshore	10	—
Survey/Research Vessels	4	—
Replenishment Tankers	2	—
Transport	1	—
Fleet Support Ship	1	—
Coastal Transports	9	—
Transports (LCM)	19	—
Transports (LCVP)	37	—
Sail Training Ships	4	—
Netlayer	1	—
Lighthouse Tenders	3	—
Salvage Ships	2	—
Repair Craft	7	—
Water Carriers	13	—
Tugs—Large	10	—
Tugs—Small	48	—

Shipbuilding and Conversion Programme

In 1975 a law (Legge Navale) was approved which provided 1 000 000 million lire for the next ten years (1975-84), for the provision of new ships and helicopters over and above the normal annual expenditure.
The tentative new-construction programme under the Legge Navale is as follows:
  1   Light Anti-Submarine Cruiser
 (2)   Guided Missile Destroyers
  6 (2)   Frigates "Maestrale" classes
  2   Submarines "Sauro" class
  6   "Sparviero" Hydrofoils
  4 (6)   Minehunters
 (1)   LPD
  1   Salvage ship
  1   Replenishment Tanker; sister to *Stromboli*
 27 (9)   AB212 helicopters
Figures in brackets indicate ships not yet definitely decided upon or not ordered.

Current budget:
  4   "Lupo" class frigates
  3   "Sparviero" class hydrofoils
  2   "Sauro" class submarines
  4   Ocean Tugs
  8   Coastal Tugs
 12   SH3D helicopters

All ships in service to be modernised.

Conversion programme (1977-80)
 10   MSCs to MSHs

Mercantile Marine

Lloyd's Register of Shipping:
1 694 vessels of 11 491 873 tons gross

DELETIONS

Submarines
1973 Leonardo da Vinci, Enrico Tazzoli
1975 Francesco Morosini ("Balao" Class) (15 Nov)
1976 Evangelista Torricelli
1977 Alfredo Cappellini ("Balao" Class)

Destroyers
1975 Geniere
1977 Fanté

Frigates
1975 Aviere (target)
1976 Aldebaran (ex-US "Cannon" class)

Corvettes
1976-77 Sfinge, Bombarda, Chimera ("Ape" class)
1977   Vedetta (ex-US PC)

Minesweepers (Coastal)
1974 Rovere, Acacia, Betulla, Ciliegio
1977 Abete

Minesweepers (Inshore)
1974 Arsella, Attinia, Calamaro, Conchiglia, Dromia, Ostrica, Paguro, Seppia, Tellina, Totano

Amphibious Forces
1974 Anteo, MTM 9903, 9904, 9906, 9921. MTP 9701, 9702, 9704-6, 9709, 9712, 9717, 9718, 9721, 9722, 9724, 9731
1976 MTP 9713, 9726. MTM 9908

Light Forces
1974 MS 472 (ex-813)
1975 MS 452 (ex-852) MS 473 (ex-813)
1977 Folgore
1978 MS 453, 474, 481

Miscellaneous
1974 Po, Flegetonte, Isonzo, Sesia, Metauro, Arno, Leno and Sprugola (water carriers). 24 tugs
1975 Sterope (repl. tanker), Frigido (water carrier), MTM 9916-7, Porto Vecchio (tug)
1976 Volturno, Tevere (water carriers)
1977 Filicudi, Rampino

PENNANT NUMBERS

Submarines
S 501	Primo Longobardo
S 502	Gianfranco Gazzana Priaroggia
S 505	Attilio Bagnolini
S 506	Enrico Toti
S 513	Enrico Dandolo
S 514	Lazzaro Mocenigo
S 515	Livio Piomarta
S 516	Romeo Romei
S 518	Nazario Sauro
S 519	Carlo Fecia di Cossato
S 520	Leonardo Da Vinci
S 521	Guglielmo Marconi

Light Aircraft Carriers
C 550	Vittorio Veneto
C 551	Giuseppe Garibaldi

Cruisers
C 553	Andrea Dorea
C 554	Caio Duilio

Destroyers
D 550	Ardito
D 551	Audace
D 558	Impetuoso
D 559	Indomito
D 562	San Giorgio
D 570	Impavido
D 571	Intrepido

Frigates
F 551	Canopo
F 553	Castore
F 554	Centauro
F 555	Cigno
F 564	Lupo
F 565	Sagittario
F 566	Perseo
F 567	Orsa
F 570	Maestrale
F 571	Grecale
F 572	Libeccio
F 573	Scirocco
F 574	Aliseo
F 575	Euro
F 580	Alpino
F 581	Carabiniere
F 593	Carlo Bergamini
F 594	Virginio Fasan
F 595	Carlo Margottini
F 596	Luigi Rizzo

Corvettes
F 540	Pietro De Cristofaro
F 541	Umberto Grosso
F 542	Aquila
F 543	Albatros
F 544	Alcione
F 545	Airone
F 546	Licio Visintini
F 550	Salvatore Todaro

ITALY / Introduction 269

Light Forces

P 420	Sparviero
P 421	Nibbio
P 422	Falcone
P 423	Astore
P 424	Grifone
P 425	Gheppio
P 426	Condor
P 491	Lampo
P 492	Baleno
P 493	Freccia
P 494	Saetta
—	MS 441
—	MS 443

Minesweepers

M 5430	Salmone
M 5431	Storione
M 5432	Sgombro
M 5433	Squalo
M 5450	Aragosta
M 5452	Astice
M 5457	Gambero
M 5458	Granchio
M 5459	Mitilo
M 5462	Pinna
M 5463	Polipo
M 5464	Porpora
M 5465	Riccio
M 5466	Scampo
M 5504	Castagno
M 5505	Cedro
M 5507	Faggio
M 5508	Frassino
M 5509	Gelso
M 5510	Larice
M 5511	Noce
M 5512	Olmo
M 5513	Ontano

Minesweepers

M 5514	Pino
M 5516	Platano
M 5517	Quercia
M 5519	Mandorlo (hunter)
M 5521	Bambù
M 5522	Ebano
M 5523	Mango
M 5524	Mogano
M 5525	Palma
M 5527	Sandalo
M 5531	Agave
M 5532	Alloro
M 5533	Edera
M 5534	Gaggia
M 5535	Gelsomino
M 5536	Giaggiolo
M 5537	Glicine
M 5538	Loto
M 5540	Timo
M 5541	Trifoglio
M 5542	Vischio

Amphibious Forces

L 9871	Andrea Bafile
L 9890	Grado
L 9891	Caorle

Service Forces

A 5301	Pietro Cavezzale
A 5303	Ammiraglio Magnaghi
A 5304	Alicudi
A 5306	Mirto
A 5307	Pioppo
A 5309	Anteo
A 5310	Proteo
A 5311	Palinuro

Service Forces

A 5312	Amerigo Vespucci
A 5313	Stella Polare
A 5314	Quarto
A 5315	Barbara
A 5316	Corsaro II
A 5317	Atlante
A 5318	Prometeo
A 5319	Ciclope
A 5320	Colosso
A 5321	Forte
A 5322	Gagliardo
A 5323	Robusto
A 5326	S. Giusto
A 5327	Stromboli
A 5328	Ape
A 5329	Vesuvio
A 5331-5338	MOC 1201-1208
A 5354	Piave
A 5356	Basento
A 5357	Bradano
A 5358	Brenta
A 5359	Bormida
A 5361-5363	MTF 1301-1303
A 5369	Adige
A 5374	Mincio
A 5376	Tanaro
A 5377	Ticino
Y 418	Caprera
Y 424	Favignana
Y 425	Levanzo
Y 432	Pantelleria
Y 434	Pianosa
Y 436	Porto d'Ischia
Y 438	Porto Pisano
Y 441	Porto Recanati
Y 443	Riva Trigoso
Y 445	Salvore
Y 447	Tino
Y 448	Ustica
Y 451	Vigoroso

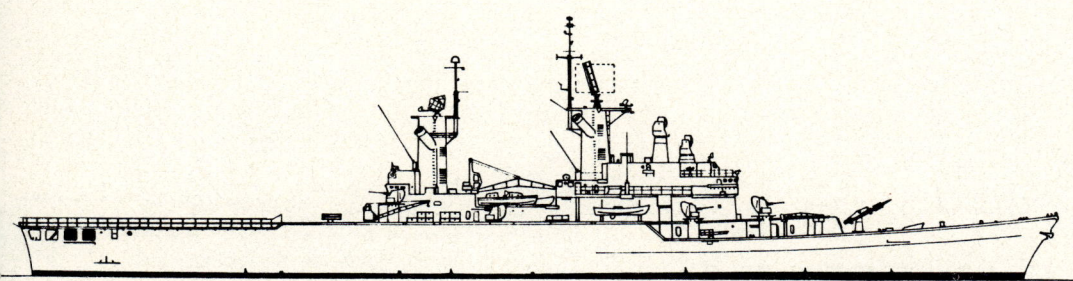

VITTORIO VENETO

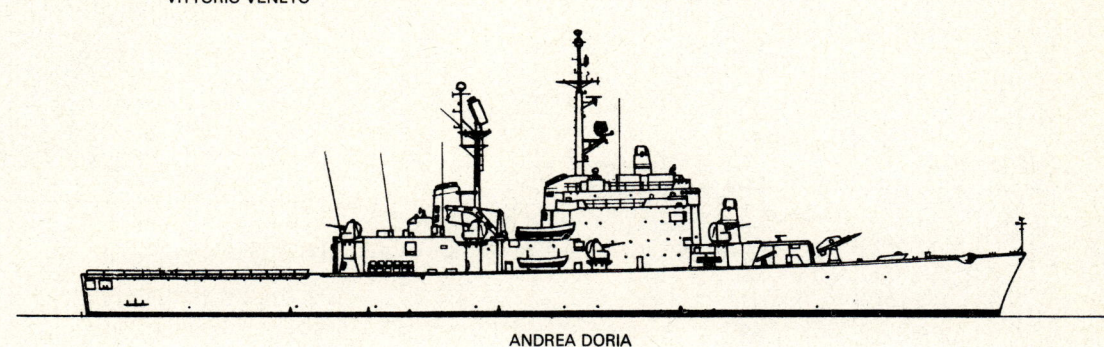

ANDREA DORIA

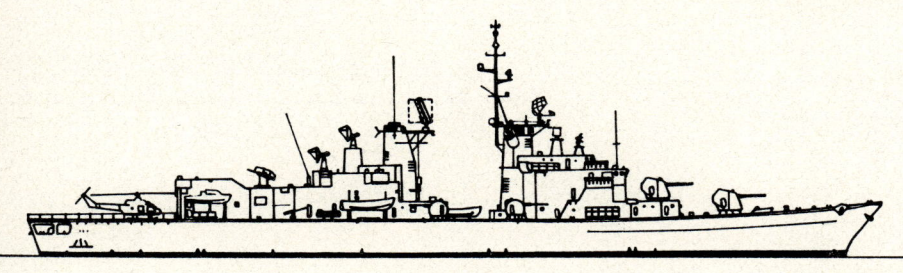

AUDACE

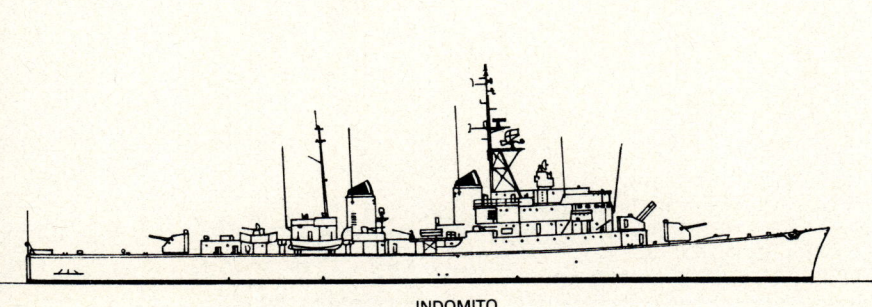

INDOMITO

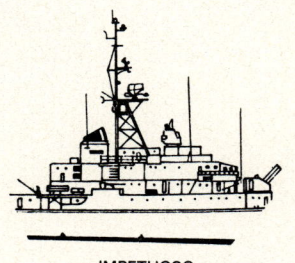

IMPETUOSO

270 ITALY / Introduction

Drawings, Lieutenant-Commander Erminio Bagnasco

SUBMARINES

4 "SAURO" CLASS (1081 TYPE)

Name	No.	Builders	Laid down	Launched	Commissioned
NAZARIO SAURO	S 518	Italcantieri, Monfalcone	15 July 1974	9 Oct 1976	1979
FECIA DI COSSATO	S 519	Italcantieri, Monfalcone	15 Nov 1975	16 Nov 1977	1979
LEONARDO DA VINCI	S 520	Italcantieri, Monfalcone	early 1979	early 1981	1982
GUGLIELMO MARCONI	S 521	Italcantieri, Monfalcone	early 1980	early 1982	1983

Displacement, tons: 1 456 surfaced; 1 631 dived
Length, feet (metres): 210 *(63·9)*
Beam, feet (metres): 22·5 *(6·8)*
Draught, feet (metres): 18·9 *(5·7)*
Torpedo tubes: 6—21 in (bow) (6 reloads)
Main machinery: 3 diesel generators; 3 210 bhp; 1 electric motor; 3 650 hp; 1 shaft
Speed, knots: 11 surfaced; 20 dived; 12 (snorting)
Range, miles: 7 000 miles surfaced; 12 500 snorting at 4 knots; 400 miles dived at 4 knots; 20 miles dived at 20 knots
Endurance: 45 days
Complement: 45

Two of this class were originally ordered in 1967 but were cancelled in the following year. Reinstated in the building programme in 1972. Second pair provided for in Legge Navale and ordered 12 February 1976.

Diving depth: 985 ft *(300 m)*

Electronics: ECM; IFF, full communications fit.

Radar: One search/navigation set. 3 RM20/SMG.

Sonar: Active and passive: Velox.
Passive ranging: Acoustic ESM.

NAZARIO SAURO   *1978, Italcantieri*

4 "TOTI" CLASS (1075 TYPE)

Name	No.	Builders	Laid down	Launched	Commissioned
ATTILIO BAGNOLINI	S 505	Italcantieri, Monfalcone	15 Apr 1965	26 Aug 1967	16 June 1968
ENRICO TOTI	S 506	Italcantieri, Monfalcone	15 Apr 1965	12 Mar 1967	22 Jan 1968
ENRICO DANDOLO	S 513	Italcantieri, Monfalcone	10 Mar 1967	16 Dec 1967	25 Sep 1968
LAZZARO MOCENIGO	S 514	Italcantieri, Monfalcone	12 June 1967	20 Apr 1968	11 Jan 1969

Displacement, tons: 460 standard; 524 surfaced; 582 dived
Length, feet (metres): 151·5 *(46·2)*
Beam, feet (metres): 15·4 *(4·7)*
Draught, feet (metres): 13·1 *(4·0)*
Torpedo tubes: 4—21 in
Main machinery: 2 Fiat MB 820 N/I diesels, 1 electric motor, diesel-electric drive; 2 200 hp; 1 shaft
Speed, knots: 14 surfaced; 15 dived
Range, miles: 3 000 at 5 knots (surfaced)
Complement: 26 (4 officers, 22 men)

Italy's first indigenously-built submarines since the Second World War. The design was recast several times.

Diving depth: 600 ft *(180 m)*.

Electronics: WT, HF, UHF and VLF equipment. Computer based fire control.

Radar: Search/navigation set. 3 RM20/SMG.
IFF, ECM.

Sonar: Passive set in stem.
Active set in bow dome.
Passive range finding.
Ray path analyzer.

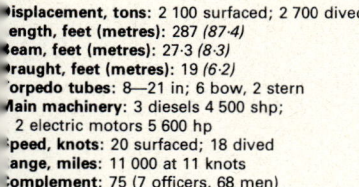
LAZZARO MOCENIGO   *6/1978, Commander Aldo Fraccaroli*

2 Ex-US "TANG" CLASS

Name	No.	Builders	Laid down	Launched	Commissioned
LIVIO PIOMARTA (ex-USS *Trigger*, SS 564)	S 515	General Dynamics (Electric Boat Div)	24 Feb 1949	3 Dec 1951	19 Aug 1952
ROMEO ROMEI (ex-USS *Harder*, SS 568)	S 516	General Dynamics (Electric Boat Div)	30 June 1950	14 June 1951	31 Mar 1952

Displacement, tons: 2 100 surfaced; 2 700 dived
Length, feet (metres): 287 *(87·4)*
Beam, feet (metres): 27·3 *(8·3)*
Draught, feet (metres): 19 *(6·2)*
Torpedo tubes: 8—21 in; 6 bow, 2 stern
Main machinery: 3 diesels 4 500 shp; 2 electric motors 5 600 hp
Speed, knots: 20 surfaced; 18 dived
Range, miles: 11 000 at 11 knots
Complement: 75 (7 officers, 68 men)

Transferred as follows: Romeo Romei 20 February 1974, Livio Piomarta 10 July 1973. Subsequently refitted at Philadelphia Navy Yard.

Radar: BPS-12.

ROMEO ROMEI   *11/1978, Commander Aldo Fraccaroli*

272   ITALY / Submarines — Light aircraft carriers

2 Ex-US "GUPPY III" CLASS

Name	No.	Builders	Laid down	Launched	Commissioned
PRIMO LONGOBARDO (ex-USS *Volador*, SS 490)	S 501	Portsmouth Navy Yard	15 June 1945	17 Jan 1946	10 Jan 1948
GIANFRANCO GAZZANA PRIAROGGIA (ex-USS *Pickerel*, SS 524)	S 502	Boston Navy Yard	8 Feb 1944	15 Dec 1944	4 Apr 1949

Displacement, tons: 1 975 standard; 2 450 dived
Length, feet (metres): 326·5 *(99·4)*
Beam, feet (metres): 27 *(8·2)*
Draught, feet (metres): 17 *(5·2)*
Torpedo tubes: 10—21 in; 6 bow, 4 stern
Main machinery: 4 diesels, 6 400 bhp;
    2 electric motors; 5 400 shp; 2 shafts
Speed, knots: 20 surfaced; 15 dived
Oil fuel, tons: 300
Range, miles: 12 000 at 10 knots (surfaced)
Complement: 85 (10 officers, 75 men)

Both transferred 18 August 1972.

PRIMO LONGOBARDO   *1975, Wright and Logan*

LIGHT AIRCRAFT CARRIERS

1 NEW CONSTRUCTION

Name	No.	Builders	Laid down	Launched	Commissioned
GIUSEPPE GARIBALDI	—	Italcantieri, Monfalcone	1979	1981	1982

Displacement, tons: 12 000 standard; 13 250 full load
Dimensions, feet (metres): 590·4 × 98 × 22 *(180 × 30 × 6·7)*
Flight Deck, feet (metres): 570·7 × 99·7 *(174 × 30·4)*
Aircraft: 18 Sea King helicopters or 16 Sea Harriers plus one helo
Missiles: SSM; 4 "Teseo" launchers for Otomat; SAM; 2 "Albatros" systems with Aspide missiles.
Guns: 6—40/70 mm guns (3 twins) with Dardo control system
A/S weapons: 6 A/S torpedo tubes (2 triple)
Main engines: 4 Fiat/GE LM2 500 gas turbines; 80 000 hp
Speed, knots: 29·5
Range, miles: 7 000 at 20 knots
Complement: 550 (accommodation 825)

The design has already changed considerably to replace *Andrea Doria* and *Duilio*.

Aircraft: VSTOL may also be included in the complement.

Electronics: System I PN 10 for data processing.

Radar: Long range surveillance: RAN 3L.
Air surveillance: RAN 10S.
Combined search: SPQ 2D.
Fire control: NA 10.

Rocket launcher: One SCLAR.

Sonar: One, possibly SQS 23.

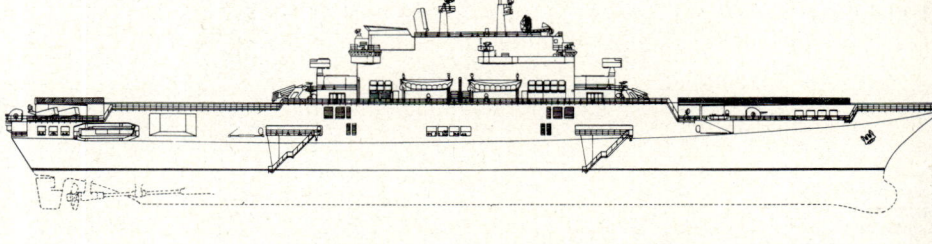

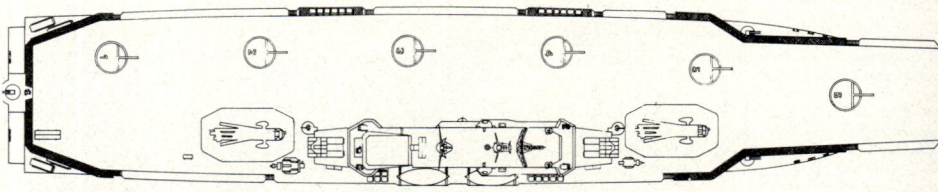

GIUSEPPE GARIBALDI   *1979, Italcantieri*

Name	No.	Builders	Laid down	Launched	Commissioned
VITTORIO VENETO	C 550	Italcantieri, Castellammare	10 June 1965	5 Feb 1967	12 July 1969

Displacement, tons: 7 500 standard; 8 850 full load
Length, feet (metres): 589 *(179·6)*
Beam, feet (metres): 63·6 *(19·4)*
Draught, feet (metres): 19·7 *(6)*
Aircraft: 9 AB-204B or AB-212 helicopters
Missiles: SAM; Terrier (est 40; twin launcher Mk 10; Aster system)
Guns: 8—3 in *(76 mm)*/62 (MMK single)
A/S weapons: 2 triple US Mk 32 for A/S torpedoes; helicopter torpedoes
Main engines: 2 Tosi double reduction geared turbines; 73 000 shp; 2 shafts
Boilers: 4 Foster-Wheeler type (Ansaldo); 711 psi *(50 kg/cm²)*; 842°F *(450°C)*

Speed, knots: 32
Oil fuel, tons: 1 200
Range, miles: 6 000 at 20 knots
Complement: 550 (50 officers, 500 men)

Developed from the "Andrea Doria" class but with much larger helicopter squadron and improved facilities for anti-submarine operations. Projected under the 1959-60 New Construction Programme, but her design was recast several times. Started trials 30 April 1969. Flagship of C-in-C Fleet. Fitted with two sets of stabilisers.

Electronics: Tacan URN-20 fitted.

Radar: Air search and target designator (3D on fore funnel): One SPS 52.
Long range search (after funnel): One SPS 40.
Search: One SMA/SPQ 2.
Terrier fire control: Two SPG 55B.
Gun fire control: Four Orion radars in Argo/Elsag NA9 systems.
Navigation: Three RM7.

SCLAR: Fitted with control and launchers for SCLAR rockets—range 7 miles; fitted with HE heads, flares or chaff.

Sonar: One SQS 23.

VITTORIO VENETO   *1973, Dr. Giorgio Arra*

CRUISERS

2 "ANDREA DORIA" CLASS

Name	No.	Builders	Laid down	Launched	Commissioned
ANDREA DORIA	C 553	Cantieri del Tirreno, Riva Trigoso	11 May 1958	27 Feb 1963	23 Feb 1964
CAIO DUILIO	C 554	Navalmeccanica	16 May 1958	22 Dec 1962	30 Nov 1964

Displacement, tons: 5 000 standard; 6 500 full load
Length, feet (metres): 489·8 *(149·3)*
Beam, feet (metres): 56·4 *(17·2)*
Draught, feet (metres): 16·4 *(5·0)*
Aircraft: 4 AB-204B or AB-212 helicopters
Missiles: SAM; Terrier (est 32; twin launcher) (see *Refit* note)
Guns: 8—3 in *(76 mm)*/62 (single MMK)
A/S weapons: 2 triple US Mk 32 torpedo tubes; helicopter torpedoes
Main engines: 2 double reduction geared turbines 60 000 shp (*Doria*, CNR; *Duilio*, Ansaldo); 2 shafts
Boilers: 4 Foster-Wheeler 711 psi *(50 kg/cm²)* Ansaldo, *Duilio*; CNR, *Doria*); 842°F *(450°C)*
Speed, knots: 31
Range, miles: 6 000 at 20 knots
Oil fuel, tons: 1 100
Complement: 470 (45 officers, 425 men)

Escort cruisers of novel design with a good helicopter capacity in relation to their size. *Enrico Dandolo* was the name originally allocated to *Andrea Doria*. Both to be replaced in mid-1980s by *Giuseppi Garibaldi*.

Electronics: ECM and DF. Tacan beacon (URN-20).

Gunnery: The anti-aircraft battery includes eight 3 in fully automatic guns, disposed in single turrets, four on each side amidships abreast the funnels and the bridge.

Helicopter platform: Helicopters operate from a platform aft measuring 98·5 ft by 52·5 ft *(30 m by 16 m)*.

Roll damping: Both ships have Gyrofin-Salmoiraghi stabilisers.

Radar: Air surveillance and target designator (3D on mainmast): One SPS 52 (*Doria*—SPS 76B).
Long range search: One SPS 40.
Navigation: One SPQ 2.
Terrier fire control: Two SPG 55A (*Andrea Doria*—SPG 55C).
Gun fire control: Four Orion radars in Argo/Elsag NA9 systems.

Refit: *Andrea Doria* modernised 1976-78. SAM updated for Standard ER and improved electronics fitted.

SCLAR: Fitted with control and launchers for SCLAR rockets—range 7 miles; fitted with HE heads, flares or chaff.

Sonar: One SQS 23 (*Doria*); One SQS 39 (*Duilio*).

ANDREA DORIA   6/1978, Commander Aldo Fraccaroli

ANDREA DORIA   6/1978, Commander Aldo Fraccaroli

CAIO DUILIO   1978, Michael D. J. Lennon

ITALY / Destroyers

DESTROYERS

Note: Two "Improved Audace" class with COGOG or CODOG machinery to be built under Legge Navale as replacements for "Impetuoso" class. At present this order has been postponed.

2 "AUDACE" CLASS (DDG)

Name	No.	Builders	Laid down	Launched	Commissioned
ARDITO	D 550	Italcantieri, Castellammare	19 July 1968	27 Nov 1971	5 Dec 1973
AUDACE	D 551	Cantieri del Tirreno, Riva Trigoso	27 Apr 1968	2 Oct 1971	16 Nov 1972

Displacement, tons: 3 600 standard; 4 400 full load
Length, feet (metres): 446·4 *(136·6)*
Beam, feet (metres): 47·1 *(14·5)*
Draught, feet (metres): 15 *(4·6)*
Aircraft: 2 AB-204B or AB-212 helicopters
Missiles: SAM; Tartar/Standard (est 36; single launcher Mk 13)
Guns: 2—5 in *(127 mm)*/54 (single Compact);
4—3 in *(76 mm)*/62 (single Compact)
A/S weapons: 2 triple US Mk 32 torpedo tubes; helicopter torpedoes
Main engines: 2 double reduction geared turbines (*Audace*—CNR, *Ardito*—Ansaldo); 73 000 shp; 2 shafts
Boilers: 4 Foster-Wheeler type
Speed, knots: 33
Complement: 380 (30 officers, 350 men)

It was announced in April 1966 that two new guided missile destroyers would be built. They are basically similar to, but an improvement in design on that of the "Impavido" class. Both fitted with stabilisers.

Aircraft: Originally planned to carry two AB-204B helicopters carrying two A/S torpedoes. These may be replaced by two Sea King SH3Ds.

Radar: Air surveillance (3D on after funnel): One SPS 52.
Tracking and missile guidance: Two SPG 51.
Air search: One SPS 12.
Surface search: SPQ 2.
Gun fire control: Three Orion RTN 10X for Argo 10/Elsag NA 10 systems.

Sonar: One CWE 610.

SCLAR: Fitted with SCLAR control and launch units for 105 mm rockets which can be fitted with chaff dispensers, flares or HE heads and have a range of 7 miles.

Torpedo tubes: The two triple Mk 32 launchers for Mk 44 torpedoes are on either beam amidships.

AUDACE
6/1976, Commander Aldo Fraccaroli

ARDITO
6/1978, Commander Aldo Fraccaroli

ARDITO
6/1978, Commander Aldo Fraccaroli

ITALY / Destroyers 275

2 "IMPAVIDO" CLASS (DDG)

Name	No.	Builders	Laid down	Launched	Commissioned
IMPAVIDO	D 570	Cantieri del Tirreno, Riva Trigoso	10 June 1957	25 May 1962	16 Nov 1963
INTREPIDO	D 571	Ansaldo, Leghorn	16 May 1959	21 Oct 1962	28 July 1964

Displacement, tons: 3 201 standard; 3 851 full load
Length, feet (metres): 429·5 (131·3)
Beam, feet (metres): 44·7 (13·6)
Draught, feet (metres): 14·8 (4·5)
Missiles: SAM; Tartar/Standard (est 36; single launcher Mk 13)
Guns: 2—5 in (127 mm)/38 (twin Mk 38);
4—3 in (76 mm)/62 (single MMI)
A/S weapons: 2 triple US Mk 32 torpedo tubes
Boilers: 4 Foster-Wheeler; 711 psi (50 kg/cm²); 842°F (450°C)
Main engines: 2 double reduction geared turbines 70 000 shp; 2 shafts
Speed, knots: 33
Range, miles: 3 300 at 20 knots; 2 900 at 25 knots; 1 500 at 30 knots
Oil fuel, tons: 650
Complement: 340 (23 officers, 317 men)

Built under the 1956-57 and 1958-59 programmes respectively. Both ships have stabilisers.

Engineering; On first full power trials *Impavido*, at light displacement, reached 34·5 knots (33 knots at normal load).

Modernisation: In 1974-75 *Intrepido* underwent modernisation which included the improvement of the missile system and the replacement of the original gun fire control system by Argo 10/Elsag NA 10 system. Same modifications carried out in *Impavido* 1976-77.

Radar: Search: SPS 12, SPS 39 (3-D) and SPQ 2.
Fire control: SPG 51 for Tartar (2); 3 Orion RTN 10X, Argo 10, Elsag NA 10 for guns.

SCLAR: Fitted with SCLAR control and launchers—for details see *Vittorio Veneto*.

Sonar: One SQS 23.

IMPAVIDO
1975, Michael D. J. Lennon

INTREPIDO
6/1975, Dr. Giorgio Arra

1 "SAN GIORGIO" CLASS (DD)

Name	No.	Builders	Laid down	Launched	Commissioned
SAN GIORGIO (ex-*Pompeo Magno*)	D 562	Cantieri N. Riuniti Ancona	23 Sep 1939	28 Aug 1941	24 June 1943

Displacement, tons: 3 950 standard; 4 350 full load
Length, feet (metres): 455·2 (138·8) wl; 466·5 (142·3) oa
Beam, feet (metres): 47·2 (14·4)
Draught, feet (metres): 21·0 (4·5)
Guns: 4—5 in (127 mm)/38 (twin Mk 38);
3—3 in (76 mm)/62 (single MMI)
A/S weapons: One 3-barrelled mortar (MENON);
2 triple torpedo tubes
Main engines: 2 Tosi Metrovick gas turbines; 15 000 bhp;
4 Fiat diesels; 16 600 hp; 2 shafts
Speed, knots: 20 (diesels), 28 (diesel and gas)
Range, miles: 4 800 at 20 knots
Oil fuel, tons: 500 (diesel oil)
Complement: 295 (20 officers, 275 men) plus 130 cadets

Converted into fleet destroyer in 1951 by Cantieri del Tirreno, Genoa, being completed 1 July 1955. Underwent complete re-construction at the Naval Dockyard, La Spezia, in 1963-65. The modernisation included her adaptation as a Training Ship for 130 cadets of the Accademia Navale. Changes were made in the armament and new machinery was fitted, gas turbines and diesels replacing steam turbines and boilers. To be replaced eventually by new training ship whose construction has been postponed

Gunnery: 5 in control—US Mk 37 with Mk 25 radar.

Radar: Search: SPS 6, SPQ 2.
Fire control: One US Mk 25 for Mk 37 FCS; one Orion 3 for Contraves A3 FCS; two Orion 3 for OG3 FCS.
Navigation: Three RM7.

Sonar: One SQS 11.

SAN GIORGIO
6/1978, Commander Aldo Fraccaroli

276 ITALY / Destroyers — Frigates

Name	No.
IMPETUOSO	D 558
INDOMITO	D 559

2 "IMPETUOSO" CLASS

Builders	Laid down	Launched	Commissioned
Cantieri del Tirreno, Riva Trigosa	7 May 1952	16 Sep 1956	25 Jan 1958
Ansaldo, Leghorn (formerly OTO)	24 Apr 1952	7 Aug 1955	23 Feb 1958

Displacement, tons: 2 755 standard; 3 800 full load
Length, feet (metres): 405 *(123·4)* pp; 418·7 *(127·6)* oa
Beam, feet (metres): 43·5 *(13·3)*
Draught, feet (metres): 17·5 *(4·5)*
Guns: 4—5 in *(127 mm)*/38 (twin Mk 38);
  16—40 mm/56 (twin and quad, Mk 1 and Mk 4)
A/S weapons: 2 triple US Mk 32 torpedo tubes; one 3-barrelled mortar; 4 DCT; 1 DC rack
Main engines: 2 double reduction geared turbines; 2 shafts; 65 000 shp
Boilers: 4 Foster-Wheeler; 711 psi *(50 kg/cm²)* working pressure; 842°F *(450°C)* superheat temperature
Speed, knots: 34 (see *Engineering* notes)
Oil fuel, tons: 650
Range, miles: 3 400 at 20 knots
Complement: 315 (15 officers, 300 men)

Italy's first destroyers built since Second World War. To be relieved in mid-1980s by "Improved Audace" class which have been postponed.

Engineering: On their initial sea trials these ships attained a speed of 35 knots at full load.

Gunnery: For 5 in—US Mk 37 director with Mk 25 radar.
For 40 mm—four mounts have US Mk 34 radars. In addition six US Mk 51 directors.

Radar: Search: SPS 6 and SPQ 2.
Fire control: one US Mk 25 for Mk 37 FCS; four SPG 34 for Mk 63 FCS.

Sonar: One SQS 11.

INDOMITO *1975, Commander Aldo Fraccaroli*

IMPETUOSO *1978, Commander Aldo Fraccaroli*

FRIGATES
0 + 6 "MAESTRALE" CLASS

Name	No.	Builders	Laid down	Launched	Commissioned
MAESTRALE	F 570	Cantieri Navali Riuniti	8 Mar 1978	Feb 1980	Aug 1980
GRECALE	F 571	Cantieri Navali Riuniti	—	Oct 1980	Apr 1981
LIBECCIO	F 572	Cantieri Navali Riuniti	—	Apr 1981	Oct 1981
SCIROCCO	F 573	Cantieri Navali Riuniti	—	Sep 1981	Mar 1982
ALISEO	F 574	Cantieri Navali Riuniti	—	Feb 1982	Aug 1982
EURO	F 575	Cantieri Navali Riuniti	—	July 1982	Jan 1983

Displacement, tons: 2 500 standard; 3 040 full load
Dimensions, feet (metres): 405 × 42·5 × 13·4 *(122·7 ×12·9 × 4·1)*
Aircraft: 2 AB 212 helicopters
Missiles: SSM; 4 Otomat Mk 2 with Teseo system;
  SAM; 4 Albatros with Aspide missiles (quad launcher)
Guns: 1—5 in *(127 mm)*/54 (Compact);
  4—40 mm/70 (Breda Compact—twin)
A/S weapons: 2 triple US Mk 32 torpedo tubes
Torpedo tubes: 2 for A 184 torpedoes
Main engines: CODOG; 2 Fiat LM 2 500 gas turbines; 50 000 shp; 2 diesels GMT 2 320; 11 000 hp; 2 shafts (cp propellers)
Speed, knots: 30 (32·5 Trials)
Range, miles: 5 500 at 16 knots
Complement: 226 (23 officers, 203 ratings)

An improved "Lupo" class design provided for in Legge Navale. There has been a notable increase of 50 feet in length and 5 ft in beam over the "Lupo" class, probably providing more comfortable accommodation and better handling facilities. First six ordered December 1976. First ship due for trials February 1980. Fitted with stabilisers. Improved A/S capability and an integrated gun/missile control system.

Class: *Espero* F 576 and *Zeffiro* F 577 have been postponed.

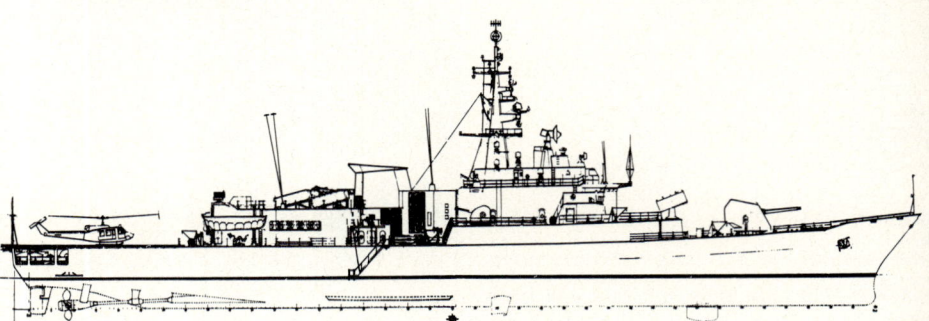

"MAESTRALE" Class *1977, Italian Navy*

Radar: Air search: RAN 10S.
Surface search: MM/SPS 702.
Navigation: MM/SPS 703.
Fire control: One Orion for Albatros; two Orion 20 for Dardo gun control system.

Rocket launchers: Fitted with SCLAR.

Sonar: One Raytheon DE 1164 hull-mounted: one VDS.

ITALY / Frigates 277

4 "LUPO" CLASS

Name	No.	Builders	Laid down	Launched	Commissioned
LUPO	F 564	Cantieri del Tirreno, Riva Trigoso	11 Oct 1974	29 July 1976	12 Sep 1977
SAGITTARIO	F 565	Cantieri del Tirreno, Riva Trigoso	4 Feb 1976	22 June 1977	18 Nov 1978
PERSEO	F 566	Cantieri del Tirreno, Riva Trigoso	28 Feb 1977	12 July 1978	May 1979
ORSA	F 567	Cantieri del Tirreno, Riva Trigoso	1 Aug 1977	1 Mar 1979	Jan 1980

Displacement, tons: 2 208 standard; 2 500 full load
Length, feet (metres): 371·3 *(113·2)*
Beam, feet (metres): 37·1 *(11·3)*
Draught, feet (metres): 12·1 *(3·7)*
Aircraft: AB 204B or 212 helicopter (see *Aircraft* note)
Missiles: SSM: 8 Otomat Mk 2 (single cells);
 SAM; Nato Sea Sparrow (8 cell launcher) (see *Missile* note)
Guns: 1—5 in *(127 mm)*/54 (Compact);
 4—40 mm/70 (twin Breda) (twin Dardo systems)
A/S weapons: 6 (2 triple) US Mk 32 torpedo tubes for Mk 46 torpedoes; helicopter torpedoes
Main engines: CODOG—2 Fiat LM 2 500 gas turbines; 50 000 hp; 2 GMT diesels; 7 800 hp; 2 shafts (cp propellers)
Speed, knots: 35 on turbines; 21 on diesels
Range, miles: 5 500 at 16 knots (diesels)
Complement: 185 (16 officers, 169 ratings)

LUPO   5/1978, Commander Aldo Fraccaroli

First of class named after the most famous Italian torpedo-boat of Second World War. Fitted with stabilisers.
The decision to build the "Maestrale" Class which is 50 ft longer and 5 ft more in the beam suggests that the "Lupo" design was too tight and cramped, a defect to be found in other navies with the same problem of money saving.

Aircraft: Although two helicopters can be carried there is a telescopic hangar space for only one and normally only one will be carried.

Construction: 14 watertight compartments; fixed-fin stabilisers; 90 days endurance.

Electronics: Automatic command and control system IPN 10 (Selenia); ECM System (Elettronica); Telecommunications System (Elmer).

Foreign sales: Similar ships being built for Peru and Venezuela.

Missiles: Budget permitting, all ships are planned eventually to receive Albatros SAM system for Aspide missiles.

Radar: Air search: One MM/SPS 774.
Combined search: One RAN 10S system (Selenia).
Gun fire control: Orion 10X for each Dardo system.

SCLAR: Fitted with control and two launchers for SCLAR rockets; for details see *Vittorio Veneto*.

Sonar: One DE 1160B (Raytheon) hull-mounted set.

ORSA   3/1979, Commander Aldo Fraccaroli

2 "ALPINO" CLASS

Name	No.	Builders	Laid down	Launched	Commissioned
ALPINO (ex-*Circe*)	F 580	Cantieri del Tirreno, Riva Trigoso	27 Feb 1963	10 June 1967	14 Jan 1968
CARABINIERE (ex-*Climene*)	F 581	Cantieri del Tirreno, Riva Trigoso	9 Jan 1965	30 Sep 1967	28 Apr 1968

Displacement, tons: 2 700 full load
Length, feet (metres): 371·7 *(113·3)*
Beam, feet (metres): 43·6 *(13·3)*
Draught, feet (metres): 12·7 *(3·9)*
Aircraft: 2 AB-204B or AB-212 helicopters
Guns: 6—3 in *(76 mm)*/62 (single MMI)
A/S weapons: 1 single semi-automatic depth charge mortar K 113; 6 (2 triple) Mk 32 A/S torpedo tubes; helicopter torpedoes
Main engines: 4 Tosi diesels; 16 800 hp; 2 Tosi Metrovick gas turbines; 16 000 hp; 2 shafts
Speed, knots: 22 (diesel), 29 (diesel and gas)
Oil fuel, tons: 275
Range, miles: 4 200 at 18 knots
Complement: 163 (13 officers, 150 men)

The design is an improved version of that of the "Centauro" class combined with that of the "Bergamini" class. Fitted with stabilisers.

Gunnery: MAD gunfire control aerial fitted in *Alpino* 1975.

Radar: Combined search: One SPS 12.
Air/surface search/navigation: One SPQ2.
Fire control: Three Orion radars in Elsag/Argo "O" control systems.
Radar intercept: MM/SPR A.

SCLAR: Fitted with control and launchers for SCLAR rockets; for details see *Vittorio Veneto*.

Sonar: One SQS 43, one SQA 10, VDS.

ALPINO   6/1977, Commander Aldo Faccaroli

278 ITALY / Frigates — Corvettes

4 "BERGAMINI" CLASS

Name	No.	Builders	Laid down	Launched	Commissioned
CARLO BERGAMINI	F 593	San Marco, CRDA Trieste	19 May 1959	16 June 1960	23 June 1962
VIRGINIO FASAN	F 594	Navalmeccanica, Castellammare	6 Mar 1960	9 Oct 1960	10 Oct 1962
CARLO MARGOTTINI	F 595	Navalmeccanica, Castellammare	26 May 1957	12 June 1960	5 May 1962
LUIGI RIZZO	F 596	Navalmeccanica, Castellammare	26 May 1957	6 Mar 1960	15 Dec 1961

Displacement, tons: 1 650 full load
Length, feet (metres): 311·7 *(95·0)*
Beam, feet (metres): 37·4 *(11·4)*
Draught, feet (metres): 10·5 *(3·2)*
Aircraft: 1 AB-204B helicopter
Guns: 2—3 in *(76 mm)*/62 (single)
A/S weapons: 1 single semi-automatic depth charge mortar K 113; 2 triple US Mk 32 for A/S torpedoes
Main engines: 4 diesels (Fiat in *Fasan* and *Margottini,* Tosi in others); 2 shafts; 16 000 bhp
Speed, knots: 24·5
Range, miles: 4 000 at 18 knots
Complement: 163 (13 officers, 150 men)

Modernisation: A slightly enlarged helicopter platform was fitted and a telescopic hangar shipped to allow for embarkation of one AB-204B helicopter. The after 3 in gun was removed. *Carlo Margottini,* 1968; *Virginio Fasan,* 1969; *Carlo Bergamini,* 1970; *Luigi Rizzo,* 1971.

Radar: Combined search: One SPS 12.
Air/surface search/navigation: One SPQ 2.
Fire control: One Orion 3 for OG3 FCS.
Radar intercept: MM/SPR A.

CARLO BERGAMINI 5/1974, Commander Aldo Fraccaroli

Roll damping: Two Denny-Brown stabilisers reduce inclination in heavy seas from 20 to 5 degrees.
Sonar: One SQS 40.

4 "CENTAURO" CLASS

Name	No.	Builders	Laid down	Launched	Commissioned
CANOPO	F 551 (ex-*D 570*)	Cantieri Navali di Taranto	15 May 1952	20 Feb 1955	1 Apr 1958
CASTORE	F 553 (ex-*D 573*)	Cantieri Navali di Taranto	14 Mar 1955	8 July 1956	14 July 1957
CENTAURO	F 554 (ex-*D 571*)	Ansaldo, Leghorn	31 May 1952	4 Apr 1954	5 May 1957
CIGNO	F 555 (ex-*D 572*)	Cantieri Navali di Taranto	10 Feb 1954	20 Mar 1955	7 Mar 1957

Displacement, tons: 1 807 standard; 2 250 full load
Length, feet (metres): 308·4 *(94)* pp; 338·4 *(103·1)* oa
Beam, feet (metres): 39·5 *(12)*
Draught, feet (metres): 12·6 *(3·8)*
Guns: 3—3 in *(76 mm)*/62 (single MMI)
A/S weapons: 1—3-barrelled depth charge mortar; 2 triple US Mk 32 A/S torpedo tubes
Main engines: 2 double reduction geared turbines 2 shafts; 22 000 shp
Boilers: 2 Foster-Wheeler (Ansaldo); 626 psi *(44 kg/cm²)* working pressure; 842°F *(450°C)* superheat temperature
Speed, knots: 25
Oil fuel, tons: 360
Range, miles: 3 660 at 20 knots
Complement: 207 (12 officers, 195 men)

Built to Italian plans and specifications under the US off-shore programme.

Conversion: Carried out as follows: *Castore*—1966-67, *Canopo*—1968-69, *Centauro*—1970-71, *Cigno*—1972-73. This provided the new 3 in *(76 mm)* armament.

Radar: Search: One SPS 6.
Combined search and navigation: One SMA/SPQ 2.
Fire control: One Orion 3 for OG3 FCS.
Radar Intercept: MM/SPR A.

Sonar: One SQS 11; one SQS 36.

CANOPO 6/1978, Commander Aldo Faccarol

CORVETTES

4 "DE CRISTOFARO" CLASS

Name	No.	Builders	Laid down	Launched	Commissioned
PIETRO DE CRISTOFARO	F 540	Cantiere de Tirreno, Riva Trigoso	30 Apr 1963	29 May 1965	19 Dec 1965
UMBERTO GROSSO	F 541	Cantiere Ansaldo, Leghorn	21 Oct 1962	12 Dec 1964	25 Apr 1966
LICIO VISINTINI	F 546	CRDA Monfalcone	30 Sep 1963	30 May 1965	25 Aug 1966
SALVATORE TODARO	F 550	Cantiere Ansaldo, Leghorn	21 Oct 1962	24 Oct 1964	25 Apr 1966

Displacement, tons: 850 standard; 1 020 full load
Length, feet (metres): 246 *(75·0)* pp; 263·2 *(80·2)* oa
Beam, feet (metres): 33·7 *(10·3)*
Draught, feet (metres): 9 *(2·7)*
Guns: 2—3 in *(76 mm)*/62 (single MMI)
A/S weapons: 1 single semi automatic DC mortar; 2 triple US Mk 32 A/S torpedo tubes
Main engines: 2 diesels = 8 400 bhp; 2 shafts
Speed, knots: 23·5
Oil fuel, tons: 100
Range, miles: 4 000 at 18 knots
Complement: 131 (8 officers, 123 men)

The design is an improved version of the "Albatros" class.

Radar: Combined search: One SMA/SPQ 2.
Fire control: One Orion 3 for OG3 FCS.

Sonar: ELSAG DLB-1 fire control system.
SQS 36 (hull-mounted and VDS)

LICIO VISINTINI 6/1975, Dr. Giorgio Arr

ITALY / Corvettes — Light forces 279

4 "ALBATROS" CLASS

Name	No.	Builders	Laid down	Launched	Commissioned
AQUILA	F 542	Breda Marghera, Mestre, Venice	25 July 1953	31 July 1954	2 Oct 1956
ALBATROS	F 543	Navalmeccanica, Castellammare	1953	18 July 1954	1 June 1955
ALCIONE	F 544	Navalmeccanica, Castellammare	1953	19 Sep 1954	23 Oct 1955
AIRONE	F 545	Navalmeccanica, Castellammare	1953	21 Nov 1954	29 Dec 1955

Displacement, tons: 800 standard; 950 full load
Length, feet (metres): 250·3 *(76·3)*
Beam, feet (metres): 31·5 *(9·6)*
Draught, feet (metres): 9·2 *(2·8)*
Guns: 2—40 mm/70 Bofors (see *Gunnery*)
A/S weapons: 2 Hedgehogs Mk II; 2 DCT; 1 DC rack; 6 (2 triple) US Mk 32 A/S torpedo tubes
Main engines: 2 Fiat diesels; 2 shafts; 5 200 bhp
Speed, knots: 19
Oil fuel, tons: 100
Range, miles: 3 000 at 18 knots
Complement: 99

Eight ships of this class were built in Italy under US offshore MDAP orders; three for Italy, four for Denmark and one for the Netherlands. *Aquila*, laid down on 25 July 1953, was transferred to the Italian Navy on 18 October 1961 at Den Helder.

Gunnery: The two 3 in *(76 mm)* guns originally mounted, one forward and one aft, were temporarily replaced by two 40 mm guns in 1963. The ultimate armament was planned to include two 3 in *(76 mm)* OTO Melara guns.

Radar: Combined search and navigation: One SMA/SPQ 2.   **Sonar:** One QCU 2.

ALBATROS   *1974, Dr. Giorgio Arra*

1 "APE" CLASS

Name	No.	Builders	Laid down	Launched	Commissioned
APE	A 5328	Navalmeccanica, Castellammare	1942	1942	1943

Displacement, tons: 670 standard; 771 full load
Length, feet (metres): 192·8 *(58·8)* wl; 212·6 *(64·8)* oa
Beam, feet (metres): 28·5 *(8·7)*
Draught, feet (metres): 8·9 *(2·7)*
Guns: 2—40 mm/56
Main engines: 2 Fiat diesels; 2 shafts; 3 500 bhp
Speed, knots: 15
Oil fuel, tons: 64
Range, miles: 2 450 at 15 knots
Complement: 66 (6 officers, 60 men)

Originally fitted for minesweeping. Modified with navigating bridge. Now support ship for frogmen and commandos.

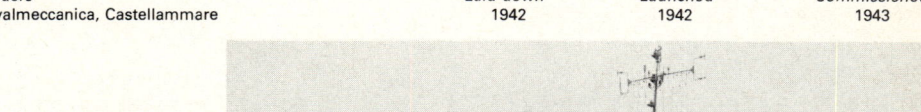
APE (Diving support ship)   *6/1976, Dr. Giorgio Arra*

LIGHT FORCES

3 + 4 "SPARVIERO" CLASS (HYDROFOIL—MISSILE)

Name	No.	Builders	Commissioned
SPARVIERO	P 420	Alinavi, La Spezia	15 July 1974
NIBBIO	—	Cantieri Navale Riuniti	Apr 1979
FALCONE	—	Cantieri Navale Riuniti	Aug 1979
ASTORE	—	Cantieri Navale Riuniti	Feb 1980
GRIFONE	—	Cantieri Navale Riuniti	June 1980
GHEPPIO	—	Cantieri Navale Riuniti	Oct 1980
CONDOR	—	Cantieri Navale Riuniti	Feb 1981

Displacement, tons: 62·5
Dimensions, feet (metres): 80·7 × 39·7 × 14·4 *(24·6 × 12·1 × 4·4)* (length and beam foils extended, draught hullborne); 75·4 × 22·9 × 5·2 *(23 × 7 × 1·6)* (hull size)
Missiles: SSM; Otomat 2 (single cells); *(Sparviero)*; Otomat Mk 2 with Teseo system (remainder)
Gun: 1—76 mm/62 (Compact)
Main engines: Proteus gas turbine driving waterjet pump; 4 500 bhp; diesel and retractable propeller unit for hullborne propulsion
Speed, knots: 50 max, 42 cruising (sea state 4)
Range, miles: 400 at 45 knots; 1 200 at 8 knots
Complement: 10 (2 officers, 8 men)

Sparviero completed for trials 9 May 1973. *Falcone* laid down May 1977. Missiles made by OTO Melara/Matra. Fitted with Elsag NA-10 Mod 1 fire control system with Orion RTN-10X radar.

SPARVIERO   *1974, Italian Navy*

Delivered to the Navy as class prototype on 15 July 1974. Eight more hydrofoils planned of this class although only six so far ordered. Four planned hydrofoils of US "Pegasus" design now cancelled. Alinavi, La Spezia transferred to CNR.

2 "FRECCIA" CLASS (FAST ATTACK CRAFT—CONVERTIBLE)

Name	No.	Builders	Commissioned
FRECCIA (ex-*MC 590*)	P 493	Cantiere del Tirreno, Riva Trigoso	6 July 1965
SAETTA (ex-*MC 591*)	P 494	CRDA, Monfalcone	25 Apr 1966

Displacement, tons: 188 standard; 205 full load
Dimensions, feet (metres): 150 × 23·8 × 5·5 *(45·8 × 7·3 × 1·7)*
Guns: As Gunboat: 3—40 mm/70 or 2—40 mm/70. As Fast Minelayer: 1—40 mm with 8 mines. As Torpedo Boat: 2—40 mm/70
Torpedo tubes: As Torpedo Boat: 2—21 in *(533 mm)*
Main engines: 2 diesels; 7 600 bhp; 1 Bristol Siddeley Proteus gas turbine, 4 250 shp; cp propellers = 40 knots
Complement: 37 (4 officers, 33 men)

Freccia was laid down on 30 April 1963 and launched on 9 January 1965. *Saetta* was laid down on 11 June 1963, launched on 11 April 1965. Can be converted in 24 hours to gunboat, torpedo boat, fast minelayer, or missile boat. Fitted with E band navigation and tactical radar. *Saetta* has been armed with Sea Killer Mk 1 system with 5 tube trainable launcher.

Fire control: *Freccia:* US Mk 51 optical FCS. *Saetta:* RTN 150 radar with TV camera on top for Contraves GFCS.

SAETTA experimentally armed with five Sea Killer 1 missiles   *1970, Italian Navy*

FRECCIA   *1974, Italian Navy*

280 ITALY / Light forces — Amphibious forces

2 "LAMPO" CLASS (FAST ATTACK CRAFT—CONVERTIBLE)

Name	No.	Builders	Commissioned
LAMPO (ex-MC 491)	P 491	Arsenale MM, Taranto	July 1963
BALENO (ex-MC 492)	P 492	Arsenale MM, Taranto	16 July 1965

Displacement, tons: 170 standard; 196 full load
Dimensions, feet (metres): 131·5 × 21 × 5 (40·1 × 6·4 × 1·5)
Guns: As Gunboat: 3—40 mm/70 or 2—40 mm/70; As Torpedo Boat: 2—40 mm/70
Torpedo tubes: As Torpedo Boat: 2—21 in (533 mm)
Main engines: 2 MTU 518-D diesels; 1 Metrovick gas turbine; 3 shafts; total 11 700 hp = 39 knots
Complement: 33 (5 officers, 28 men)

Convertible gunboats. Lampo was laid down on 4 January 1958 and launched on 22 November 1960. Baleno was laid-down on the same slip on 22 November 1960, launched on 10 May 1964. She has been converted to an improved design. Both fitted with new diesels in 1976.

Fire control: US Mk 51 optical for 40/70 guns.

Radar: 3 ST 7-250.

LAMPO — 6/1975, Dr. Giorgio Arra

3 Ex-US "HIGGINS" CLASS (FAST PATROL CRAFT)

MS 441 (ex-GIS 841)   MS 443 (ex-GIS 843)   MS 453 (ex-GIS 853)

Displacement, tons: 64 full load
Dimensions, feet (metres): 78 × 20 × 6 (23·8 × 6·1 × 1·8)
Guns: 2—20 mm/70
Main engines: 3 CRM ASM 185 petrol motors; 3 shafts; 4 500 bhp = 34 knots
Range, miles: 1 000 at 20 knots
Complement: 11 (1 officer, 10 men)

Commissioned March 1948.
MS 441 and 453 converted for frogmen support with after weapons removed. Refitted in Italy in 1949-53.

Radar: One SPS 21.

M 453 (modified for frogmen support) — 6/1975, Dr. Giorgio Arra

---

AMPHIBIOUS FORCES

Note: A new 6 000 ton LPD is to be built under Legge Navale to act as training ship in place of San Giorgio in addition to amphibious duties. Postponed for time being.

2 Ex-US "DE SOTO COUNTY" CLASS (LSTs)

Name	No.	Builders	Commissioned
GRADO (ex-USS De Soto County, LST 1171)	L 9890	Avondale, New Orleans	1957
CAORLE (ex-USS York County, LST 1175)	L 9891	Newport News S.B. & D.D. Co	1957

Displacement, tons: 4 164 light; 8 000 full load
Dimensions, feet (metres): 444 × 62 × 16·5 (133·4 × 18·9 × 5)
Guns: 6—3 in (76 mm)
Main engines: 6 Fairbanks-Morse diesels; 14 400 shp; 2 shafts; (cp propellers) = 17·5 knots
Range, miles: 16 500 at 13 knots
Complement: 165 (10 officers, 155 men)
Troops: Approx 575

Both completed 1957 and transferred 17 July 1972.

Radar: One 3 RM 20.

GRADO — 1978, Michael D. J. Lennon

1 Ex-US "KENNETH WHITING" CLASS (TRANSPORT)

Name	No.	Builders	Commissioned
ANDREA BAFILE (ex-USS St. George, AV 16)	L 9871 (ex-A5314)	Todd Pacific SY	24 July 1944

Displacement, tons: 8 510 standard; 14 000 full load
Dimensions, feet (metres): 492 × 69·5 × 26 (163 × 23 × 8·5)
Aircraft: 1 or 2 helicopters
Guns: 2—5 in/38
Main engines: Allis-Chalmers geared turbines; 1 shaft; 8 500 shp = 17 knots
Boilers: 2 Foster-Wheeler
Range, miles: 13 400 at 13 knots
Complement: 58 (10 officers, 48 men)

Former US Navy seaplane tender, launched on 14 February 1944. Purchased and commissioned in the Italian Navy on 11 December 1968 and modified. Depot ship for "Special Forces". In reserve at Taranto since 1976.

ANDREA BAFILE — 1974, Italian Navy

ITALY / Mine warfare forces 281

MINE WARFARE FORCES

0 + 4 + (6) NEW CONSTRUCTION (MINEHUNTERS/SWEEPERS)

LERICE	SAPRI	MILAZZO	VIESTE
GAETA	TERMOLI	ALGHERO	NUMANA
CROTONE	VIAREGGIO		

Displacement, tons: 470
Dimensions, feet (metres): 163·7 × 30·8 × 8·2 (49·9 × 9·4 × 2·5)
Gun: 1—40 mm
Main engines: Passage—1 GMT 230B 8-cyl diesel; 1 840 hp = 15 knots;
 Hunting—Hydraulic thrust jets = 0 to 7 knots
Range, miles: 2 500 at 12 knots
Endurance: 10 days
Complement: 39

First four ordered 7 January 1978 under Legge Navale from Intermarine, Sazana. Next six currently postponed.

Construction: Of GRP throughout hull, decks and bulkheads.

Electrics: 440 volt, 60 cycle 3 phase AC.

Engineering: All machinery is mounted on vibration dampers.

Minehunting: CGE-Fiart SQQ 14 minehunting sonar; SMA navigation system with data processing; 2 underwater detection/destruction vehicles; diving equipment and recompression chamber.

NEW CONSTRUCTION 1976, Intermarine

Minesweeping: Oropesa wire sweep.

Radar: SMA.

Sonar: CGE-Fiart SQQ 14 VDS (lowered from keel forward of bridge).

4 Ex-US "AGGRESSIVE" CLASS (MINESWEEPERS—OCEAN)

Name	No.	Builders	Commissioned
SALMONE (ex-*MSO 507*)	M 5430	Martinolich S.B. Co	15 June 1956
STORIONE (ex-*MSO 506*)	M 5431	Martinolich S.B. Co	23 Feb 1956
SGOMBRO (ex-*MSO 517*)	M 5432	Tampa Marine Co	12 May 1957
SQUALO (ex-*MSO 518*)	M 5433	Tampa Marine Co	20 June 1957

Displacement, tons: 665 standard; 750 full load
Dimensions, feet (metres): 173 × 35 × 13·6 (52·7 × 10·7 × 4)
Gun: 1—40 mm/56
Main engines: 2 General Motors 8-278 ANW diesels; 2 shafts; 1 600 bhp = 14 knots
Oil fuel, tons: 46
Range, miles: 3 000 at 10 knots
Complement: 51 (7 officers, 44 men)

Wooden hulls and non-magnetic diesels of stainless steel alloy. Cp propellers. *Storione,* launched on 13 November 1954, *Salmone,* launched on 19 February 1955 transferred at San Diego, on 17 June 1956.

Radar: One 3 ST 7/DG.

STORIONE 6/1976, Dr. Giorgio Arra

13 Ex-US "ADJUTANT" CLASS
(MINESWEEPERS/HUNTERS—COASTAL)

CASTAGNO M 5504	LARICE M 5510	PINO M 5514
CEDRO M 5505	NOCE M 5511	PLATANO M 5516
FAGGIO M 5507	OLMO M 5512	QUERCIA M 5517
FRASSINO M 5508	ONTANO M 5513	MANDORLO M 5519
GELSO M 5509		

Displacement, tons: 378 standard; (*Mandorlo* 360); 405 full load
Dimensions, feet (metres): 144 × 26·9 × 8·5 (43·9 × 8·2 × 2·6)
Guns: 2—20 mm (twin)
Main engines: 2 diesels; 2 shafts; 1 200 bhp = 13·5 knots
Oil fuel, tons: 25
Range, miles: 2 500 at 10 knots
Complement: 31 (2 officers, 29 men)

Wooden hulled and constructed throughout of anti-magnetic materials. All commissioned August 1953-December 1954 and transferred by the USA in 1953-54. Originally class of 18. *Pioppo* used for surveying.

Minehunting conversion: *Mandorlo* completed 1978, *Platano* in November 1978. Five more of this class and the "Agave" class are to be similarly converted—all to complete by end 1981.

Builders: *Castagno* (Grebe, Chicago), *Cedro* (Berg S.Y.), *Faggio* (Lake Union Co, Seattle), *Frassino* (Blaine), *Gelso* (Grebe, Chicago), *Larice* (Lake Union Co), *Noce* (Bellingham S.Y.), *Olmo* (Bellingham S.Y.), *Ontano* (Grebe, Chicago), *Pino, Platano* and *Quercia* (Bellingham S.Y.).

CEDRO 6/1978, Commander Aldo Fraccaroli

17 "AGAVE" CLASS (MINESWEEPERS—COASTAL)

BAMBU M 5521	AGAVE M 5531	GLICINE M 5537
EBANO M 5522	ALLORO M 5532	LOTO M 5538
MANGO M 5523	EDERA M 5533	TIMO M 5540
MOGANO M 5524	GAGGIA M 5534	TRIFOGLIO M 5541
PALMA M 5525	GELSOMINO M 5535	VISCHIO M 5542
SANDALO M 5527	GIAGGIOLO M 5536	

Displacement, tons: 375 standard; 405 full load
Dimensions, feet (metres): 144 × 25·6 × 8·5 (43 × 8 × 2·6)
Guns: 2—20 mm/70 (twin)
Main engines: 2 diesels; 2 shafts; 1 200 bhp = 13·5 knots
Oil fuel, tons: 25
Range, miles: 2 500 at 10 knots
Complement: 38 (5 officers, 33 men)

Non-magnetic minesweepers of composite wooden and alloy construction similar to those transferred from the USA but built in Italian yards; all completed November 1956-April 1957. Originally class of 19. *Mirto* now used for surveying.

Minehunting conversion: *Loto* completed March 1979. (See similar note for "Adjutant" class above.)

Builders: CRDA Monfalcone: *Agave, Alloro, Edera, Bambu, Ebano, Mango, Mogano, Palma, Sandalo.* Baglietto, Varazze: *Gaggia, Gelsomino.* Picchiotti, Viareggio: *Giaggiolo, Glicine.* Celli, Venezia: *Loto.* Costaguta, Voltri: *Timo.* CN, Taranto: *Trifoglio.* Cant. Mediterraneo: *Vischio.*

ALLORO 11/1978, Commander Aldo Fraccaroli

Radar: 3 ST 7/DG.

282 ITALY / Mine warfare forces — Service forces

10 "ARAGOSTA" CLASS (MINESWEEPERS—INSHORE)

ARAGOSTA M 5450	GRANCHIO M 5458	POLIPO M 5463
ASTICE M 5452	MITILO M 5459	PORPORA M 5464
GAMBERO M 5457	PINNA M 5462	RICCIO M 5465
		SCAMPO M 5466

Displacement, tons: 188 full load
Dimensions, feet (metres): 106 × 21 × 6 *(32·5 × 6·4 × 1·8)*
Main engines: 2 diesels; 1 000 bhp = 14 knots
Oil fuel, tons: 15
Range, miles: 2 000 at 9 knots
Complement: 16 (4 officers, 12 men)

Similar to the British "Ham" class. All constructed to the order of NATO in 1955-57. All names of small sea creatures. Designed armament of one 20 mm gun not mounted. Originally class of 20. *Aragosta* has large deck-house aft as support ship for frogmen.

Builders: CRDA Monfalcone: *Aragosta, Astice.* Picchiotti, Viareggio: *Gambero, Granchio, Mitilo.* Costaguta, Voltri: *Pinna, Polipo, Porpora.* Apuano, Marina di Currara: *Riccio, Scampo.*

GAMBERO   *1978, Commander Aldo Fraccaroli*

SURVEY VESSELS

Name	No.	Builders	Commissioned
AMMIRAGLIO MAGNAGHI	A 5303	Cantieri Navali di Tirreno é Riuniti	2 May 1975

Displacement, tons: 1 700
Dimensions, feet (metres): 271·3 × 44·9 × 11·5 *(82·7 × 13·7 × 3·5)*
Aircraft: 1—AB 204 helicopter
Gun: 1—40 mm
Main engines: 2 General Motors B 306 SS diesels = 3 000 hp; 1 shaft (cp propeller); auxiliary electric motor—240 hp = 4 knots
Speed, knots: 16
Range, miles: 6 000 at 12 knots (1 diesel); 4 200 at 16 knots (2 diesels)
Complement: 148 (14 officers, 15 scientists, 119 men)

Ordered under 1972 programme. Laid down 13 June 1973. Launched 11 October 1974. Fitted with flight-deck and hangar, bow thruster, full air-conditioning, bridge engine controls, flume-type stabilisers and fully equipped for oceanographical studies.

Radar: Two RM 20.

AMMIRAGLIO MAGNAGHI   *5/1978, Commander Aldo Fraccaroli*

Name	No.	Builders	Commissioned
MIRTO	A 5306	Breda, Porta Marghera	4 Aug 1956
PIOPPO	A 5307	Bellingham S.Y., Seattle	31 July 1954

Mirto of the "Agave" class and *Pioppo* of the "Adjutant" class (see Mine Warfare section for details) have been converted for surveying duties with complement of four officers and thirty six men.

PIOPPO   *1978, Commander Aldo Fraccaroli*

SERVICE FORCES

2 REPLENISHMENT TANKERS

Name	No.	Builders	Commissioned
STROMBOLI	A 5327	Cantiere Navali Riuniti, Riva Trigoso	20 Nov 1975
VESUVIO	A 5329	Cantiere del Muggiano	18 Nov 1978

Displacement, tons: 3 556 light; 8 706 full load
Dimensions, feet (metres): 403·4 × 59 × 21·3 *(123 × 18 × 6·5)*
Guns: 1—76 mm/62 (Compact); 2—40 mm
Main engines: 2 Fiat diesels C428 SS; 11 400 hp; 1 shaft; 4-bladed LIPS propeller
Speed, knots: 20
Complement: 115 (9 officers, 106 men)

Stromboli laid down on 1 October 1973. Launched 20 February 1975. *Vesuvio* ordered August 1976 and launched 4 June 1977. *Vesuvio* is the first large ship to be built at Muggiano (near La Spezia) since the war and the first with funds under Legge Navale 1975.

Aircraft: Helicopter flight deck but no hangar.

Capacity: 3 000 tons FFO; 1 000 tons dieso, 400 tons lub oil, 100 tons other stores.

Radar/Fire control: One Orion RTN 10X for Argo 10/Elsag NA 10 FCS.

STROMBOLI   *1978, Italian Navy*

2 EXPERIMENTAL SHIPS

Name	No.	Builders	Commissioned
QUARTO	A 5314	Taranto Naval Shipyard	1967

Displacement, tons: 764 standard; 980 full load
Dimensions, feet (metres): 226·4 × 31·3 × 6 *(69·1 × 9·5 × 1·8)*
Guns: 4—40 mm (2 twin)
Main engines: 3 diesels; 2 300 bhp = 13 knots
Range, miles: 1 300 at 13 knots

Laid down on 19 March 1966 and launched on 18 March 1967. The design is intermediate between that of LSM and LCT. She is now being used as experimental ship for new weapon-systems trials and evaluation. Currently employed on Otomat trials with two launchers forward and requisite aerials on mast and bridge.

QUARTO (fitted for missile trials)   6/1975, Commander Aldo Fraccaroli

BARBARA

Displacement, tons: 195
Dimensions, feet (metres): 98·4 × 20·7 × 4·9 *(30 × 6·3 × 1·5)*
Main engines: 2 diesels; 600 hp = 12 knots

A fishing vessel purchased and converted for research work in 1975.
Built by Castracani, Ancona.

1 Ex-US "BARNEGAT" CLASS (SUPPORT SHIP)

Name	No.	Builders	Commissioned
PIETRO CAVEZZALE (ex-USS Oyster Bay, ex-AGP 6, AVP 28)	A 5301	Lake Washington Shipyard	1943

Displacement, tons: 1 766 standard; 2 800 full load
Dimensions, feet (metres): 311·8 × 41 × 13·5 *(95 × 12·5 × 3·7)*
Guns: 1—76 mm; 2—40 mm/56
Main engines: 2 sets Fairbanks-Morse 38 D8 1/8 diesels; 2 shafts; 6 080 bhp = 16 knots
Oil fuel, tons: 300
Range, miles: 10 000 at 11 knots
Complement: 114 (7 officers, 107 men)

Former US seaplane tender (previously motor torpedo boat tender). Launched on 7 September 1942. Transferred to the Italian Navy on 23 October 1957 and renamed.

Radar: SPS 6 and Jason.

PIETRO CAVEZZALE   11/1978, Commander Aldo Fraccaroli

9 Ex-GERMAN MFP TYPE (COASTAL TRANSPORTS)

MTC 1004	MTC 1006	MTC 1008	MTC 1010
MTC 1005	MTC 1007	MTC 1009	MTC 1101
			MTC 1102

Displacement, tons: 240 standard
Dimensions, feet (metres): 164 × 21·3 × 5·7 *(50 × 6·5 × 1·7)*
Guns: 2 or 3—20 or 37 mm
Main engines: 2 or 3 diesels; 500 bhp = 10 knots
Complement: 19 (1 officer, 18 men)

Moti-Trasporti Costieri, MTC 1004 to 1010 are Italian MZ *(Motozattere).* MTC 1101 and 1102 ex-German built in Italy.

MTC 1006   1974, Italian Navy

19 Ex-US LCM TYPE

MTM 9901	MTM 9909	MTM 9914	MTM 9920	MTM 9925
MTM 9902	MTM 9911	MTM 9915	MTM 9922	MTM 9926
MTM 9905	MTM 9912	MTM 9918	MTM 9923	MTM 9927
	MTM 9913	MTM 9919	MTM 9924	MTM 9928

Displacement, tons: 20 standard
Dimensions, feet (metres): 49·5 × 14·8 × 4·2 *(15·1 × 4·5 × 1·3)*
Guns: 2—20 mm
Main engines: Diesels; speed 11 knots

Built in 1943-44. Transferred 1952-53.

37 US LCVP TYPE

MTP 9703	MTP 9715	MTP 9730	MTP 9739	MTP 9747
MTP 9707	MTP 9719	MTP 9732	MTP 9740	MTP 9748
MYP 9708	MTP 9720	MTP 9733	MTP 9741	MTP 9749
MTP 9710	MTP 9723	MTP 9734	MTP 9742	MTP 9750
MTP 9711	MTP 9727	MTP 9735	MTP 9743	MTP 9751
MTP 9714	MTP 9728	MTP 9736	MTP 9744	MTP 9752
	MTP 9729	MTP 9737	MTP 9745	MTP 9753
		MTP 9738	MTP 9746	MTP 9754

Displacement, tons: 8 standard
Dimensions, feet (metres): 36·5 × 10·8 × 3 *(11·1 × 3·3 × 0·9)*
Guns: 2 MG
Main engines: Diesels; speed 12 knots

MTP 9703 to 9723 are former US landing craft of the LCVP type. Transferred 1952, 1956, 1965, 1970, 1972. MTP 9727 and following craft of similar characteristics are of Italian construction.

1 HOVERCRAFT

HC 9801

SR N6 hovercraft from UK in service since 1968.

284   ITALY / Training ships — Salvage ships

MISCELLANEOUS

TRAINING SHIPS

Name	No.	Builders	Commissioned
AMERIGO VESPUCCI	A 5312	Castellammare	15 May 1931

Displacement, tons: 3 543 standard; 4 146 full load
Dimensions, feet (metres): 229·5 pp; 270 oa hull; 330 oa bowsprit × 51 × 22 (70 × 82·4; 100 × 15·5 × 7)
Guns: 4—3 in/50; 1—20 mm
Main engines: 2 Fiat diesels with electric drive to 2 Marelli motors, 1 shaft; 2 000 hp = 10 knots
Sail area: 22 604 sq ft
Endurance: 5 450 miles at 6·5 knots
Complement: 243 (13 officers, 230 men)

Launched on 22 March 1930. Hull, masts and yards are of steel. Extensively refitted at La Spezia Naval Dockyard in 1964.

AMERIGO VESPUCCI   1974, Wright and Logan

Name	No.	Builders	Commissioned
PALINURO (ex-*Commandant Louis Richard*)	A 5311	Ch. Dubigeon, Nantes	1934

Displacement, tons: 1 042 standard; 1 450 full load
Measurement, tons: 858 gross
Dimensions, feet (metres): 193·5 × 32·8 × 15·7 (59 × 10 × 4·8)
Main engine: 1 diesel; 1 shaft; 450 bhp = 7·5 knots
Endurance, miles: 5 390 at 7·5 knots
Sail area: 1 152 sq ft
Complement: 47

Barquentine launched in 1934. Purchased in 1951. Rebuilt in 1954-55 and commissioned in Italian Navy on 1 July 1955. She was one of the last two French Grand Bank cod-fishing Barquentines. Owned by the Armement Glâtre she was based at St Malo until bought by Italy.

PALINURO   6/1978, Commander Aldo Fraccaroli

Name	No.	Builders	Commissioned
CORSARO II	A 5316	Costaguta Yard, Voltri	6 Jan 1961

Measurement, tons: 47
Dimensions, feet (metres): 69 × 15·4 × 9·8 (21 × 4·7 × 3)
Sail area: 2 200 sq ft
Complement: 14 (12 officers, 2 men)

Special yacht for sail training and oceanic navigation. RORC class.

Name	No.	Builders	Commissioned
STELLA POLARE	A 5313	Sangermani, Chiavari	7 Oct 1965

Measurement, tons: 41
Dimensions, feet (metres): 68·6 × 15·4 × 9·5 (20·9 × 4·7 × 2·9)
Auxiliary engine: 1 Mercedes-Benz diesel, 96 bhp
Sail area: 2 117 sq ft
Complement: 14 (8 officers, 6 men)

Yawl rigged built as a sail training vessel for the Italian Navy.

NETLAYER

1 "ALICUDI" CLASS

Name	No.	Builders	Commissioned
ALICUDI (ex-USS *AN 99*)	A 5304	Ansaldo, Leghorn	1955

Displacement, tons: 680 standard; 834 full load
Dimensions, feet (metres): 165·3 × 33·5 × 10·5 (46·3 × 10·2 × 3·2)
Guns: 1—40 mm/70; 4—20 mm/70
Main engines: Diesel-electric; 1 200 shp = 12 knots
Complement: 51 (5 officers, 46 men)

Built to the order of NATO. Laid down on 22 April 1954 and launched on 11 July 1954.

ALICUDI   11/1977, Commander Aldo Fraccaroli

LIGHTHOUSE TENDERS

3 Ex-BRITISH LCT (3) TYPE

MTF 1301 A 5361   **MTF 1302** A 5362   **MTF 1303** A 5363

Displacement, tons: 296 light; 700 full load
Dimensions, feet (metres): 192 × 31 × 7 (58·6 × 9·5 × 2·1)
Guns: 1—40 mm/56; 2—20 mm/70
Main engine: Diesel; 1 shaft = 8 knots
Complement: 23 (3 officers, 20 men)

Converted to lighthouse stores transports.

MTF 1301   1968, Italian Navy

SALVAGE SHIPS

Name	No.	Builders	Commissioned
ANTEO	A 5309	C.N. Breda-Mestre	Apr 1979

Displacement, tons: 3 200
Dimensions, feet (metres): 324·7 × 47 × 16·7 (98·4 × 15·8 × 5·1)
Aircraft: 1 helicopter
Guns: 2—20 mm
Main engines: Diesel-electric; 3 Fiat GMT A-230 diesels; 8 100 hp; 1 electric motor; 4 000 hp
Speed, knots: 19
Range, miles: 4 000 at 14 knots
Complement: 121 (including salvage staff)

Comprehensively fitted with flight deck and hangar, extensive salvage gear, one DSRV to starboard, two LCVPs to port, two lifeboats under helicopter deck and one in chute aft. Three fire-fighting systems. Bow thruster. Full towing equipment. Designed to carry midget submarine of 13·2 tons dived with dimensions 26·2 × 6·2 × 8·9 (8 × 1·9 × 2·7). Speed 5 knots and carries two men.
Ordered mid-1977, launched 11 November 1978.

Name	No.	Builders	Commissioned
PROTEO (ex-*Perseo*)	A 5310	Cantieri Navali Riuniti, Ancona	24 Aug 1951

Displacement, tons: 1 865 standard; 2 147 full load
Dimensions, feet (metres): 248 × 38 × 21 *(67·3; 75·6 × 11·6 × 6·4)*
Guns: 3—20 mm
Main engines: 2 diesels; 4 800 bhp; single shaft = 16 knots
Range, miles: 7 500 at 13 knots
Complement: 130 (10 officers, 120 men)

Laid down at Cantieri Navali Riuniti, Ancona, in 1943. Suspended in 1944. Seized by Germans and transferred to Trieste. Construction re-started at Cantieri Navali Riuniti, Ancona, in 1949. Formerly mounted one 3·9 in gun and two 20 mm. To be relieved by *Anteo*.

PROTEO (with lengthened funnel)   11/1978, Commander Aldo Fraccaroli

REPAIR CRAFT

7 Ex-BRITISH LCT 3s

MOC 1201 A 5331	MOC 1203 A 5333	MOC 1205 A 5335	MOC 1208 A 5338
MOC 1202 A 5332	MOC 1204 A 5334	MOC 1207 A 5337	

Displacement, tons: 350 standard; 640 full load
Dimensions, feet (metres): 192 × 31 × 7 *(58·6 × 9·5 × 2·1)*
Guns: 2—40 mm; 2—20 mm (2 ships have 2—40 mm and 1 ship has 3—20 mm)
Main engines: Diesel = 8 knots
Complement: 24 (3 officers, 21 men)

Originally converted as repair craft. Other duties have been taken over—MOC 1207 and 1208 are ammunition transports and MOC 1201 is used for torpedo trials.

MOC 1201 (with torpedo tube)   6/1978, Commander Aldo Fraccaroli

WATER CARRIERS

(Guns not mounted in peacetime)

PIAVE A 5354

973 tons full load—launched 1971 by Orlando (Livorno) and commissioned 23 May 1973. Complement 55 (7 officers, 48 men).

Guns: 4—40 mm (twins).

PIAVE   1977, J. A. Verhoog

Name	No.	Builders	Commissioned
BASENTO	A 5356	Inma di La Spezia	1970
PADANO	A 5357	Inma di La Spezia	1971
BRENTA	A 5358	Inma di La Spezia	1972

914 tons. Laid down in 1969-70. Main engines, 2 Fiat diesels 1 730 hp = 13 knots. Complement 24 (3 officers, 21 men)

Guns: 2—20 mm

BASENTO   6/1976, Dr. Giorgio Arra

ADIGE (ex-*YW 92*) A 5369   **TICINO** (ex-*YW 79*) A 5377
TANARO (ex-*YW 99*) A 5376

Ex-US Army YW type. 1 470 tons full load. Complement 35 (4 officers, 31 men).

Guns: 3—20 mm.

Builders: *Adige* and *Tanaro*, Rochester NY; *Ticino*, Bethlehem, New Orleans.

TANARO   6/1976, Dr. Giorgio Arra

MINCIO A 5374

645 tons. Launched in 1929. Complement 19 (1 officer, 18 men).

BORMIDA A 5359

Complement 11 (1 officer, 10 men)

TIMAVO

645 tons. Built by COMI, Venezia, 1926.

OFANTO

250 tons. Built 1913-14.

SIMETO   **STURA**

Small water carriers of 167 and 126 tons displacement, respectively.

TUGS

CICLOPE A 5319

Displacement, tons: 1 200
Dimensions, feet (metres): 157·5 × 32·5 × 13 *(48 × 9·8 × 4)*
Main engine: Triple expansion; 1 shaft; 1 000 ihp = 8 knots

Commissioned 1947.

Name	No.	Builders	Commissioned
ATLANTE	A 5317	Visentini-Donada	14 Aug 1975
PROMETEO	A 5318	Visentini-Donada	14 Aug 1975

Displacement, tons: 750 full load
Dimensions, feet (metres): 116·7 × 28·8 × 14·8 *(39 × 9·6 × 4·1)*
Main engine: Diesel; 1 shaft; cp propeller; 2 670 hp = 13·5 knots

Both launched 1974.

ATLANTE   1975, Dr. Luigi Accorsi

286 ITALY / Tugs — Government maritime forces

COLOSSO (ex-*LT 214*) A 5320   **FORTE** (ex-*LT 159*) A 5321

Displacement, tons: 525 standard; 835 full load
Dimensions, feet (metres): 142·8 × 32·8 × 11 *(43·6 × 10 × 3·4)*
Main engines: 2 diesel-electric; 690 hp = 11 knots

Ex-US Army. Built in 1943-44. Transferred 1948.

COLOSSO   6/1976, Dr. Giorgio Arra

SAN GIUSTO A 5326

Displacement, tons: 486 standard
Main engines: 900 hp = 12 knots

Built in 1952 by CNR, Palermo.

GAGLIARDO A 5322 (1938)   **ERCOLE** A 5388 (1971)
ROBUSTO A 5323 (1939)   **VIGOROSO** Y 451 (1971)

Displacement, tons: 389 standard; 506 full load
Main engines: 1 000 ihp = 8 knots

PORTO D'ISCHIA Y 436   **RIVA TRIGOSO** Y 443

Displacement, tons: 296 full load
Dimensions, feet (metres): 83·7 × 23·3 × 10·8 *(27·3 × 7·1 × 3·3)*
Main engine: Diesel; 1 shaft; 850 bhp = 12·1 knots

Both launched in September 1969 by CNR Riva Trigoso. Cp propeller.
Porto d'Ischia commissioned 1970, *Riva Trigosa*, 1969.

MISENO   **MONTE CRISTO**

Displacement, tons: 285
Main engine: 1 diesel GM 8/567, 700 shp.

Former US Navy harbour tugs. Both commissioned 1 July 1948.

CAPRERA Y 418 (1972)   **PANTELLERIA** Y 432 (1972)
FAVIGNANA Y 424 (1973)   **PIANOSA** Y 434 (1974)
LEVANZO Y 426 (1973)   **USTICA** Y 448 (1973)

Displacement, tons: 270 standard
Dimensions, feet (metres): 114·8 × 29·5 × 13 *(35 × 9 × 4)*
Main engine: Triple expansion; 1 shaft; 1 200 hp = 13 knots

AUSONIA   **PANARIA**

Displacement, tons: 240

Both launched in 1945. Coastal tugs for general duties.

PORTO PISANO Y 438 (1937)   **SALVORE** Y 445 (1927)
PORTO RECANATI Y 441 (1937) **TINO** Y 447 (1930)

Displacement, tons: 230
Dimensions, feet (metres): 88·8 × 22 × 10 *(27·1 × 6·7 × 3·1)*
Main engines: 600 ihp = 9 knots

Principally employed as harbour tugs.

VENTIMIGLIA

Displacement, tons: 230 standard
Dimensions, feet (metres): 108·2 × 23 × 7·2 *(33 × 7 × 2·2)*
Main engines: 550 hp = 10 knots

Commissioned January 1940.

CIRCEO Y 433 (1956)   **PASSERO** Y 439 (1934)   **RIZZUTO** Y 473 (1956)

Principally employed as ferry tugs.

ALBENGA Y 412 (1973)   **LINARO** Y 430 (1913)
ARZACHENA Y 414 (1931)   **MESCO** Y 435 (1933)
ASINARA Y 415 (1934)   **NISIDA** Y 437 (1943)
LAMPEDUSA Y 416 (1972)   **PIOMBINO** Y 440 (1969)
BOEO Y 417 (1943)   **SAN BENEDETTO** Y 446 (1941)
CARBONARA Y 419 (1936)   **SPERONE** Y 454 (1965)
CHIOGGIA Y 421 (1919)   **No 78** Y 469 (1965)
POZZI Y 422 (1912)   **No 96** Y 474 (1962)

Small tugs for harbour duties.

RP 101 Y 403 (1972)   **RP 105** Y 408 (1974)   **RP 109** Y 456 (1975)
RP 102 Y 404 (1972)   **RP 106** Y 410 (1974)   **RP 110** Y 458 (1975)
RP 103 Y 406 (1974)   **RP 107** Y 413 (1974)   **RP 111** Y 460 (1975)
RP 104 Y 407 (1974)   **RP 108** Y 452 (1975)   **RP 112** Y 462 (1975)

Displacement, tons: 75 full load
Dimensions, feet (metres): 61·6 × 14·6 × 5·9 *(18·8 × 4·5 × 1·8)*
Main engines: 1 diesel; 431 hp = 12 knots

Built by Cantiere Navale Visentini-Loreo.

GOVERNMENT MARITIME FORCES

CORPO DELLE CAPITANERIE DI PORTO (CAPTAINS OF THE PORTS)

A considerable Corps of the naval service.

GUARDIA DI FINANZA DI MARE

Deploys considerable number of craft of differing sizes many of which are armed.

IVORY COAST

Ministerial

Minister of Marine:
Kouadio Fadika

Senior Officer
Lieut Commander Timite

Bases

Use made of ports at Abidjan, Sassandra, Tabou and San Pedro

Personnel

1979: 280 officers and men

Future Plans

Eventually it is intended to organise the navy into two coastal patrol squadrons with the addition of further craft of the "Patra" design.

Mercantile Marine

Lloyd's Register of Shipping:
65 vessels of 156 749 tons gross

LIGHT FORCES

2 FRANCO-BELGE TYPE

Name	No.	Builders	Commissioned
LE VIGILANT	—	SFCN	1968
LE VALEUREUX	—	SFCN	25 Sep 1976

Displacement, tons: 235 standard (250 *Valeureux*)
Dimensions, feet (metres): 155·8 × 23·6 × 8·2 *(47·5 × 7 × 2·6)* *(Valeureux 157·5 ft (48 m))*
Missiles: 8—SS12
Guns: 2—40 mm
Main engines: 2 AGO diesels; 2 shafts; 4 220 bhp = 18·5 knots *(Valeureux 22 knots)*
Range, miles: 2 000 at 15 knots
Complement: 25 (3 officers, and 22 men)

Vigilant laid down in February 1967. Launched on 23 May 1967. Sister ship to *Malaika* of Malagasy Navy and to *Saint Louis* and *Popenguine* of Senegal and similar craft in Tunisia and Cameroons.
Le Valeureux ordered October 1974, laid down 20 October 1975, launched 8 March 1976.

2 "PATRA" CLASS (LARGE PATROL CRAFT)

Name	No.	Builders	Commissioned
L'ARDENT	—	Chartier Auroux, d'Arcachon	6 Oct 1978
L'INTREPIDE	—	Chartier Auroux, d'Arcachon	6 Oct 1978

Displacement, tons: 115 standard; 148 full load
Dimensions, feet (metres): 133·5 × 19·4 × 5·2 *(40·7 × 5·9 × 1·6)*
Missiles: 6—SS-12
Guns: 1—40 mm; 1—20 mm
Main engines: 2 SACM diesels; 2 shafts (cp propellers); 4 400 shp = 32·6 knots
Range, miles: 1 500 cruising
Endurance: 10 days
Complement: 19 (3 officers, 16 ratings)

Of similar design to French "Patra" class. Laid down 7 July 1977.

1 Ex-FRENCH VC TYPE

Name	No.	Builders	Commissioned
PERSEVERANCE (ex-*VC 9, P 759*)	—	Constructions Mécaniques de Normandie, Cherbourg	25 Feb 1958

Displacement, tons: 75 standard; 82 full load
Dimensions, feet (metres): 104·5 × 15·5 × 5·5 *(31·8 × 4·7 × 1·7)*
Guns: 2—20 mm
Main engines: 2 Mercedes-Benz (MTU) diesels; 2 shafts; 2 700 bhp = 28 knots
Oil fuel, tons: 10
Range, miles: 1 100 at 16·5 knots; 800 at 21 knots
Complement: 15

Former French seaward defence motor launch. Transferred from France to Ivory Coast 26 April 1963. Recently reported as unserviceable.

PERSEVERANCE *1964, Ivory Coast Armed Forces*

5 RIVER PATROL CRAFT

Of varying sizes from 24—34 ft. Used for river and lake patrols.

LANDING CRAFT

1 BATRAL TYPE (LIGHT TRANSPORT)

Name	No.	Builders	Commissioned
LEPHANT	—	Dubigeon/Normandy Nantes	2 Feb 1977

Displacement, tons: 750 standard; 1 380 full load
Dimensions, feet (metres): 262·4 × 42·6 × 7·5 *(80 × 13 × 2·3)*
Guns: 2—40 mm; 2—81 mm mortars
Main engines: 2 diesels; 2 shafts; cp propellers; 3 600 hp = 16 knots
Range, miles: 3 500 at 13 knots
Complement: 47

Ordered 20 August 1974. Laid down 1975. Fitted with helicopter deck

2 LCVP

Displacement, tons: 7
Guns: 2 MG
Main engines: Mercedes diesels
Speed, knots: 9

Built in Abidjan in 1970.

MISCELLANEOUS

OKODJO

Displacement, tons: 450

Now used as a training and supply ship. Built in West Germany in 1953 and purchased in 1970. Trawler type.

1 SMALL TRANSPORT

Capable of carrying 25 men.

JAMAICA

Defence Force Coast Guard

Jamaica, which became independent within the Commonwealth on 6 August 1962, formed the Coast Guard as the Maritime Arm of the Defence Force. This is based at HMJS Cagway, Port Royal.

Administration

Commanding Officer Jamaica Defence Force Coast Guard:
Commander L. E. Scott

Personnel

1979: 18 officers, 115 petty officers and ratings *(Coast Guard Reserve:* 16 officers, 30 men*)*

Training

a) Officers: BRNC Dartmouth and other RN Establishments, RCN and US Search and Rescue School.
b) Ratings: JMF Training depot, RN, RCN, US Search and Rescue School and MTU Engineering Germany.

Mercantile Marine

Lloyd's Register of Shipping:
7 vessels of 10 430 tons gross.

LIGHT FORCES

Name	No.	Builders	Commissioned
FORT CHARLES	P 7	Sewart Seacraft Inc, Berwick, La, USA	1974

Displacement, tons: 103
Dimensions, feet (metres): 105 × 22 × 7 *(31·5 × 6·6 × 2·1)*
Guns: 1—20 mm; 2—·50 cal MG
Main engines: 2 Maybach (MTU) MB 16V 538 TB90 diesels; 7 000 shp = 32 knots
Range, miles: 1 200 at 18 knots
Complement: 16 (3 officers, 13 ratings)

Of all aluminium construction launched July 1974. Navigation equipment includes Omega Navigator.
Accommodation for 24 soldiers and may be used as 24 bed mobile hospital in an emergency.

FORT CHARLES   1975, Jamaican CG

Name	No.	Builders	Commissioned
DISCOVERY BAY	P 4	Sewart Seacraft Inc, Berwick, La, USA	3 Nov 1966
HOLLAND BAY	P 5	Sewart Seacraft Inc, Berwick, La, USA	4 Apr 1967
MANATEE BAY	P 6	Sewart Seacraft Inc, Berwick, La, USA	9 Aug 1967

Displacement, tons: 60
Dimensions, feet (metres): 85 × 18 × 6·0 *(25·9 × 5·7 × 1·8)*
Guns: 3—·50 cal Browning
Main engines: 3 MTU 8V 331 TC81 diesels, 3 shafts; 3 000 shp = 30 knots
Oil fuel, tons: 13
Range, miles: 800 at 20 knots
Complement: 11 (2 officers, 9 ratings)

All aluminium construction. *Discovery Bay,* the prototype was launched in August 1966. *Holland Bay* and *Manatee Bay* were supplied under the US Military Assistance programme. All three boats were extensively refitted and modified in 1972-73 by the builders with General Motors 12V 71 Turbo-injected engines to give greater range, speed and operational flexibility. They were again re-engined and refitted at Swift Ship Inc, Louisiana, USA—*Discovery Bay* in late 1975, *Holland Bay* in mid-1977 and *Manatee Bay* in late 1977.

DISCOVERY BAY   1973, Jamaican CG

1 "110 ft" PATROL CRAFT

With three Cummins V-8 diesels and a crew of five.

1 "40 ft" INSHORE PATROL CRAFT

With two Caterpillar V-8 diesels and a crew of three.

JAPAN

Naval Board

Chief of the Maritime Staff, Defence Agency:
  Admiral Ryohei Oga
Commander-in-Chief, Self-Defence Fleet:
  Vice-Admiral Tsugio Yata
Chief, Administration Division, Maritime Staff Office:
  Vice-Admiral Tsuruo Koga

Diplomatic Representation

Defence (Naval) Attaché in London:
  Captain Y. Imaizumi
Naval Attaché in Moscow:
  Captain Masamichi Oga
Defence Attaché in Paris:
  Colonel Yoshiaki Murata
Defence (Naval) Attaché in Washington:
  Captain Yutaka Tamura

Personnel

1976: 39 000 (including Naval Air)
1977: 41 388 (including Naval Air)
1978: 42 278 (including Naval Air)
  plus 4 389 civilians

Bases

Naval—Yokosuka, Kure, Sasebo, Maizuru, Oominato
Naval Air—Atsugi, Hachinohe, Iwakuni, Kanoya, Komatsujima, Okinawa, Ozuki, Oominato, Oomura, Shimofusa, Tateyama, Tokushima

Fleet Air Arm

14 Air ASW Sqns, P2-J, P2V-7, PS-1, S2F-1, HSS-2
4 Air Training Sqns, P2-J, P2V-7, YS-11, B-65, KM-2, Mentor, Bell-47, OH-6, HSS-2
1 Transport Sqn, YS-11
1 MCM Sqn

Note: Eight Orion LRMP aircraft have been requested with an eventual target of forty five.

Names

The practice of painting the ships' names on the broadsides of the hulls was discontinued in 1970. For submarines the painting of pennant numbers on the fins was stopped in September 1976.

Mercantile Marine

Lloyd's Register of Shipping:
  9 321 vessels of 39 182 079 tons gross

Defence Plan—New Construction

If programmes are agreed in period 1977-81 the fleet in 1982 will consist of: 60 DD, 16 SS, 40-45 MSC/MSB, 25-30 others, 15 supply ships, LST and special duty ships and 220 aircraft. (White Paper of 30 October 1976). Manpower 40 000.
The Fourth Defence Plan (1 April 1972-31 March 1977) has had certain problems but will be completed as agreed in the next year or two. The Fifth Defence Plan (1 April 1977-31 March 1982) requires a continuing reinforcement of the MSDF although the requests put forward each year are often reduced by the government.

Strength of the Fleet

Type	Active	Building (Projected)
Submarines—Patrol	13	2 (2)
Destroyers	32	3 (5)
Frigates	15	1 (2)
Corvettes	12	—
Fast Attack Craft—Torpedo	5	—
Patrol Craft—Coastal	10	—
LSTs	6	—
LSU	—	— (2)
M/S Support Ships	2	—
Minesweepers—Coastal	31	3 (3)
MSBs	6	—
Training Ship	1	—
S/M Rescue Vessels	2	—
Support Tanker	2	—
Icebreaker	1	(1)
Auxiliaries	21	—
Survey Ships	7	(1)
Cable Layer	1	1
Training Support Ship	1	—
Experimental Ship	—	1

New Construction Programme

1975 1 DDH, 1 SS, 3 MSC, 1 LST
1976 1 DDH, 1 MSC, 1 AGS, 1 AOE
1977 1 DD, 1 DE, 1 SS, 2 MSC, 1 ARC (a reduction of 1 DDG and 2 MSC)
1978 1 DDG, 1 DD, 1 SS, 1 MSC (a reduction of 1 DE, 2 MSC, 1 PHM and 1 AS)
1979 33—2 900 ton DD, 1—1 400 ton DE, 1—2 200 ton SS, 2—440 ton MSC, 2—500 ton LSU, 1—1 100 ton AGS

Naval Shipbuilders

Due to amalgamation the names of many Japanese shipyards have changed over the last twenty years and a number have been listed with their Japanese titles—Jyuko = Heavy Industries Co; Zoosen = Shipbuilders. The current situation is as follows:

Present name	Incorporating	Building
1. Mitsubishi Heavy Industries	Mitsubishi Shipbuilders, Nagasaki; Shin-Mitsubishi Heavy Industries, Kobe; Mitsubishi-Nippon Heavy Industries, Yokohama	DDG and DD at Nagasaki. ARC and ASR at Yokohama. PT and ASH at Shimonoseki and Hiroshima. DD and Submarines at Kobe.
2. Ishikawajima Harima Heavy Industries	Ishikawajima Heavy Industries, Tokyo; Kure Shipbuilders; Harima Shipbuilders	DDH, DD, DE and LST at Tokyo 1 and 2 (Yokohama) YF at Isogo, PC at Kure.
3. Hitachi Shipbuilders	Hitachi Shipbuilders; Maizuru Heavy Industries (originally Iino Heavy Industries, Maizuru)	MSC and MSB at Maizuru and Kanagawa.
4. Sumitomo Heavy Industries	Uraga Heavy Industries (originally Uraga Dock Co); Sumitomo Machine Ltd	DDK, DD and ASR.
5. Sasebo Heavy Industries	Originally Sasebo Senpak Kabushiki Kaishiya	LST, PC and ASU.
6. Mitsui Shipbuilders, Tamano	—	DD, DDE.
7. Kawasaki Heavy Industries, Kobe	—	Submarines and DD.
8. Nippon Steel Tube Co	—	Earlier MSC, MSB, AG at Tsurumi. Later MSC at Isogo.

DELETIONS

Note: A number of ships on removal from the active list are classified as YAC (Harbour accommodation ship). As these have no operational value they are included as deletions marked *.

Submarines

1976 *Oyashio* (scrap list 30 Sep)
1977 *Hayashio* (July)
1978 *Natsushio* (20 Mar), *Wakashio* (23 Mar)

Destroyers

1974 *Ariake, Yugure* (Transferred to South Korea for spares in 1976—scrapped).

Frigates

1972 *Bura, Kashi, Moni, Tochi, Ume, Maki, Matsu, Nata, Sakura,* (all ex-US PFs). *Wakaba*
1975 *Asahi* and *Hatsuhi* (ex-"Cannon" class) returned to USA for disposal
1976 *Ikazuchi**, *Akebono**, *Kusu**
1977 *Inazuma**, *Nire* (sunk as target 21 Aug), *Keyaki* (scrapped)
1978 *Kaya* (missile target)

Corvettes

1977 *Kari, Kiji, Taka, Washi, Tsubame* (14 May), *Kamome* and *Misago* (1 Dec)

Light Forces

1972 PT 7, 9; PB 4, 11, 13-16, 18
1973 PB 1, 3, 12, 17; *Kosoku* 3
1974 PT 8; *Kosoku* 2, 4 and 5
1975 PT 10

LSTs

1972 *Hayatomo*
1974 *Oosumi*
1975 *Shimokita*
1976 *Shiretoko* (returned to USA in Mar and passed to Philippines)

LSM

1974 3001

Mine Warfare Forces

1972 MSB 01, 02
1974 MSB 03, 04, 05, 06 deleted
1975 5 MSC converted
1976 1 MSC converted

Tenders

1973 YAS 49 (ex-PT 2), YAS 52 (ex-PT 3), YAS 53 (ex-PT 4)
1974 YAS 48 (ex-PT 1), YAS 54 (ex-PT 5), YAS 55 (ex-PT 6), YAS 45 (*Suma*, ex-US YTL 749), YAS 59 (*Minho*, ex-US FS 524)
1976 YAS 51 (*Nasami* ex-US FS 409), YAS 3 (ex-US YTL 750), YAS 47 (ex-MSC 652 ex-US AMS 595)
1978 YAS 46, 57, 60 and 61

JAPAN (MDF) / Introduction

PENNANT LIST

Submarines—Patrol

SS	524	Fuyushio
	561	Ooshio
	562	Asashio
	563	Harushio
	564	Michishio
	565	Arashio
	566	Uzushio
	567	Makishio
	568	Isoshio
	569	Narushio
	570	Kuroshio
	571	Takashio
	572	Yaeshio
	573	Yuushio
	574	New Construction
	575	New Construction
	576	New Construction

Destroyers

DD	101	Harukaze
	102	Yukikaze
	103	Ayanami
	104	Isonami
	105	Uranami
	106	Shikinami
	107	Murasame
	108	Yudachi
	109	Harusame
	110	Takanami
	111	Oonami
	112	Makinami
	113	Yamagumo
	114	Makigumo
	115	Asagumo
	116	Minegumo
	117	Natsugumo
	118	Murakumo
	119	Aokumo
	120	Akigumo
	121	Yuugumo
	122	New Construction
	123	New Construction
	141	Haruna
	142	Hiei
	143	Shirane
	144	New Construction
	161	Akizuki
	162	Teruzuki
	163	Amatsukaze
	164	Takatsuki
	165	Kikuzuki
	166	Mochizuki
	167	Nagatsuki
	168	Tachikaze
	169	Asakaze
	170	New Construction

Frigates

DE	211	Isuzu
	212	Mogami
	213	Kitakami
	214	Ooi
	215	Chikugo
	216	Ayase
	217	Mikuma
	218	Tokachi
	219	Iwase
	220	Chitose
	221	Niyodo
	222	Teshio
	223	Yoshino
	224	Kumano
	225	Noshiro
	226	New Construction
	227	New Construction

Light Forces

PC	305	Kamome
	306	Tsubame
	307	Misago
	309	Umitaka
	310	Otaka
	311	Mizutori
	312	Yamadori
	313	Otori
	314	Kasasagi
	315	Hatsukari
	316	Umidori
	317	Wakataka
	318	Kumataka
	319	Shiratori
	320	Hiyodori
	811-815	PT 11-15
	919-927	PB 19-27
	06	Kosoku 6

Minesweepers—Coastal

MSC	619	Mutsure
	620	Chiburi
	621	Ootsu
	622	Kudako
	623	Rishiri
	624	Rebun
	625	Amami
	626	Urume
	627	Minase
	628	Ibuki
	629	Katsura
	630	Takami
	631	Iou
	632	Miyake
	633	Utone
	634	Awaji
	635	Toushi
	636	Teuri
	637	Murotsu
	638	Tashiro
	639	Miyato
	640	Takane
	641	Muzuki
	642	Yokose
	643	Sakate
	644	Oumi
	645	Fukue
	646	Okitsu
	647	Hashira
	648	Iwai
	649	Hatsushima
	650	New Construction
	651	New Construction
	652	New Construction
	653	New Construction
	654	New Construction
	655	New Construction

Minesweeping Boats

707	Nana-go
708	Hachi-go
709	Kyuu-go
710	Jyuu-go
711	Jyuu-Ichi-go
712	Jyuu-Ni-go

Minesweeper Tender

MST	473	Kouzu

MSC Support Ships

MMC	951	Souya
MST	462	Hayase

Amphibious Forces

LST	4101	Atsumi
	4102	Motobu
	4103	Nemuro
	4151	Miura
	4152	Ozika
	4153	Satsuma

Salvage Vessel

YE	41	Shobo

Submarine Rescue Ships

ASR	401	Chihaya
	402	Fusimi

Tanker

AO	411	Hamana

Fleet Support Ship

AOE	4011	New Construction

Training Ship

TV	3501	Katori

Training Support Ship

ATS	4201	Azuma

Cable Layers

ARC	481	Tsugaru
	482	New Construction

Icebreaker

AGB	5001	Fuji

Surveying Ships

AGS	5101	Akashi
	5102	Futami
	5111	Ichi-Go
	5112	Ni-Go
	5113	San-Go
	5114	Yon-Go
	5115	Go-Go
	5116	Roku-Go

Tugs

YT	55
YT	56
YT	57
YT	58

Tenders

ASH	81-85	
ASY	91	Hayabusa
YAS	56	Atada
	58	Yashiro
	62	Shisaka
	63	Koshiki
	64	Sakito
	65	Kanawa
	66	Tsukumi
	67	Mikura
	68	Shikine
	69	Erimo
	70	Hotaka
	71	Karato

"HARUNA" Class

"TAKATSUKI" Class

"YAMAGUMO" Class

"MINEGUMO" Class

AMATSUKAZE

JAPAN (MDF) / Introduction 291

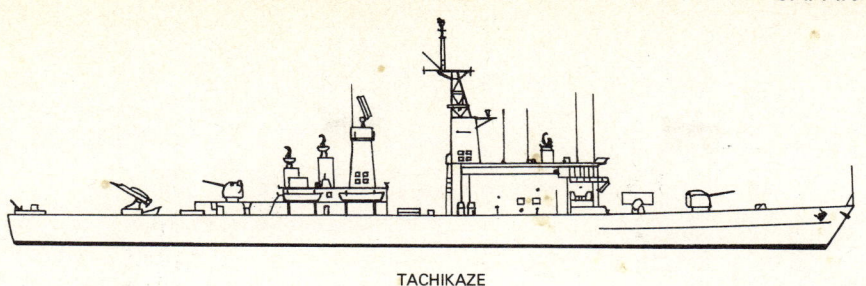
TACHIKAZE

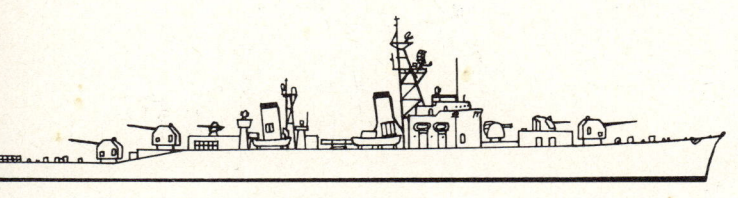
"AKIZUKI" Class

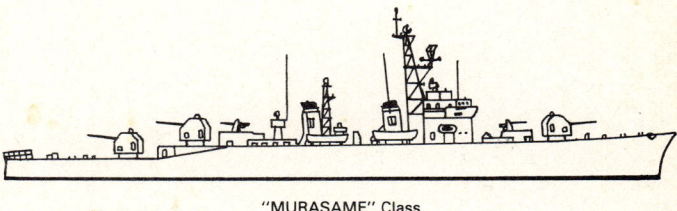
"MURASAME" Class

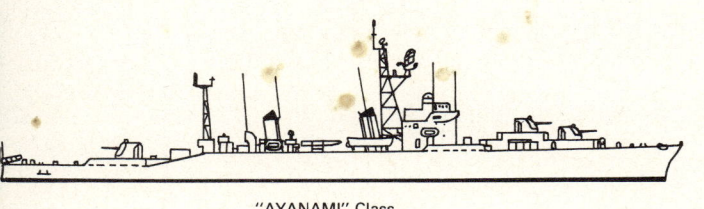
"AYANAMI" Class

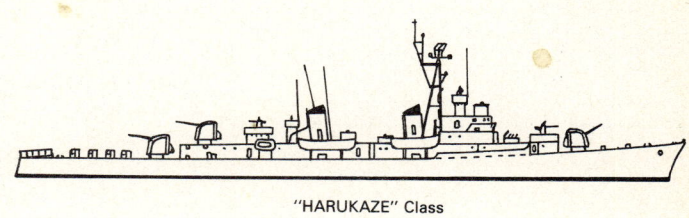
"HARUKAZE" Class

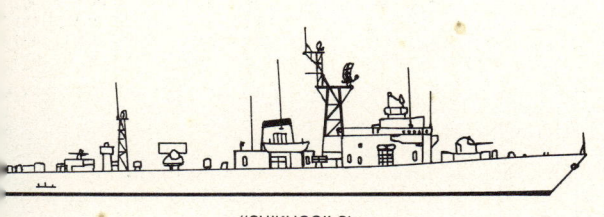
"CHIKUGO" Class

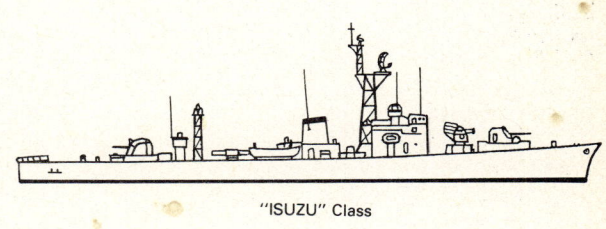
"ISUZU" Class

"MIZUTORI" Class

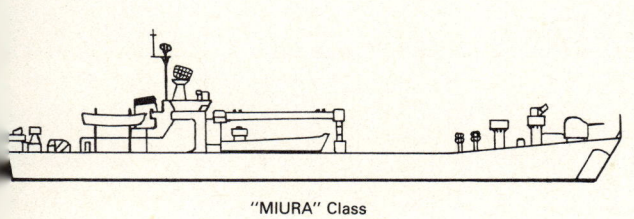
"MIURA" Class

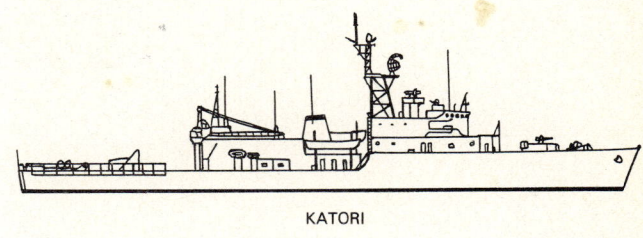
KATORI

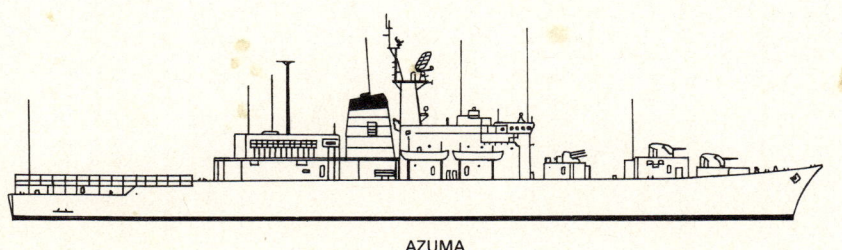
AZUMA

SUBMARINES

0 + 3 + 1 "YUUSHIO" CLASS

Name	No.	Builders	Laid down	Launched	Commissioned
YUUSHIO	SS 573	Mitsubishi, Kobe	3 Dec 1976	29 Mar 1979	Mar 1980
—	SS 574	Kawasaki, Kobe	28 Apr 1978	Apr 1980	Mar 1981
—	SS 575	Mitsubishi, Kobe	Apr 1979	Feb 1981	Mar 1982
—	SS 576	Kawasaki, Kobe	Apr 1980	Feb 1982	Mar 1983

Displacement, tons: 2 200
Dimensions, feet (metres): 249·3 × 32·5 × 24·6 *(76 × 9·9 × 7·5)*
Torpedo tubes: 6—21 in *(533 mm)* bow
Main machinery: 2 Kawasaki MAN diesels; 4 200 bhp; 1 shaft; 1 electric motor; 7 200 bhp
Speed, knots: 13 surfaced; 20 dived
Complement: 80

An enlarged version of the "Uzushio" class with improved diving depth and fitted with Mascar. SS 574 approved in FY 1977, 575 in FY 1978, 576 requested in FY 1979.

7 "UZUSHIO" CLASS

Name	No.	Builders	Laid down	Launched	Commissioned
UZUSHIO	SS 566	Kawasaki, Kobe	25 Sep 1968	11 Mar 1970	21 Jan 1971
MAKISHIO	SS 567	Mitsubishi, Kobe	21 June 1969	27 Jan 1971	2 Feb 1972
ISOSHIO	SS 568	Kawasaki, Kobe	9 July 1970	18 Mar 1972	25 Nov 1972
NARUSHIO	SS 569	Mitsubishi, Kobe	8 May 1971	22 Nov 1972	28 Sep 1973
KUROSHIO	SS 570	Kawasaki, Kobe	5 July 1972	22 Feb 1974	27 Nov 1974
TAKASHIO	SS 571	Mitsubishi, Kobe	6 July 1973	30 June 1975	30 Jan 1976
YAESHIO	SS 572	Kawasaki, Kobe	14 Apr 1975	19 May 1977	7 Mar 1978

Displacement, tons: 1 850 standard
Length, feet (metres): 236·2 *(72·0)*
Beam, feet (metres): 29·5 *(9·0)*
Draught, feet (metres): 24·6 *(7·5)*
Torpedo tubes: 6—21 in *(533 mm)*; amidships
Main machinery: 2 Kawasaki MAN diesels; 3 400 bhp; 1 shaft; 1 electric motor; 7 200 hp
Speed, knots: 12 surfaced; 20 dived
Complement: 80

Of double-hull construction and "tear-drop" form, built of HT steel to increase diving depth to 650 ft *(200 m)*. New bow sonar fitted.

MAKISHIO   *1976, Japanese Maritime Self-Defence Force*

5 "OOSHIO" CLASS

Name	No.	Builders	Laid down	Launched	Commissioned
OOSHIO	SS 561	Mitsubishi, Kobe	29 June 1963	30 Apr 1964	31 Mar 1965
ASASHIO	SS 562	Kawasaki, Kobe	5 Oct 1964	27 Nov 1965	13 Oct 1966
HARUSHIO	SS 563	Mitsubishi, Kobe	12 Oct 1965	25 Feb 1967	1 Dec 1967
MICHISHIO	SS 564	Kawasaki, Kobe	26 July 1966	5 Dec 1967	29 Aug 1968
ARASHIO	SS 565	Mitsubishi, Kobe	5 July 1967	24 Oct 1968	25 July 1969

Displacement, tons: 1 650 standard; *Ooshio* 1 600
Length, feet (metres): 288·7 *(88·0)*
Beam, feet (metres): 26·9 *(8·2)*
Draught, feet (metres): 16·2 *(4·9) Ooshio* 15·4 *(4·7)*
Torpedo tubes: 6—21 in *(533 mm)* (bow); 2—12·7 in A/S torpedoes in swim-out tubes (stern)
Main machinery: 2 diesels; 2 900 bhp; 2 shafts; 2 electric motors; 6 300 hp
Speed, knots: 14 surfaced; 18 dived
Complement: 80

Double-hulled boats. A bigger design to obtain improved seaworthiness, a larger torpedo capacity and more comprehensive sonar and electronic devices. *Ooshio* was built under the 1961 programme, *Asashio* 1963.
Ooshio is specially equipped for training duties.

ASASHIO   *1976, Japanese Maritime Self-Defence Force*

1 "FUYUSHIO" CLASS

Name	No.	Builders	Laid down	Launched	Commissioned
FUYUSHIO	SS 524	Kawasaki, Kobe	6 Dec 1961	14 Dec 1962	17 Sep 1963

Displacement, tons: 790 standard
Length, feet (metres): 200·1 *(61·0)*
Beam, feet (metres): 21·3 *(6·5)*
Draught, feet (metres): 13·5 *(4·1)*
Torpedo tubes: 3—21 in *(533 mm)* (bow)
Main machinery: 2 diesels; total 900 hp; 2 shafts; 2 electric motors, total 2 300 hp
Speed, knots: 11 surfaced; 15 dived
Complement: 40

Very handy and successful class of its time, with a large safety factor, complete air-conditioning and good habitability. Originally class of four. Probably turned out to be too small for the heavy seas encountered around Japan.

JAPAN (MDF) / Destroyers   293

DESTROYERS

0 + 2 "SHIRANE" CLASS

Name	No.	Builders	Laid down	Launched	Commissioned
SHIRANE	DD 143	Ishikawajima Harima, Tokyo	25 Feb 1977	18 Sep 1978	20 Mar 1980
—	DD 144	Ishikawajima Harima, Tokyo	17 Feb 1978	Sep 1979	Mar 1981

Displacement, tons: 5 250
Length, feet (metres): 521·5 *(159·0)*
Beam, feet (metres): 57·5 *(17·5)*
Draught, feet (metres): 17·5 *(5·3)*
Aircraft: 3 anti-submarine helicopters
Missiles: 1 Sea Sparrow launcher
Guns: 2—5 in *(127 mm)*/54 (single Mk 42); 2—35 mm/90
A/S weapons: US Mk 16 Octuple Asroc launcher; 6 (2 triple) US Mk 32 torpedo tubes
Main engines: 2 turbines; 70 000 shp; 2 shafts
Speed, knots: 32
Complement: 350

One in 1975 programme and one in 1976 programme. To be twin funnelled. Contract for DD 144 signed 31 March 1977. Fitted with Vosper Thornycroft fin stabilisers. The fore funnel is offset slightly to port, the after funnel to starboard. The crane is set on the starboard after corner of the hangar.

Gunnery: Mk 2 GFCS.

Radar: Air search: SPS 52B; OPS 28.

Sonar: OQS 101 (hull-mounted); SQS 35(J) (VDS).

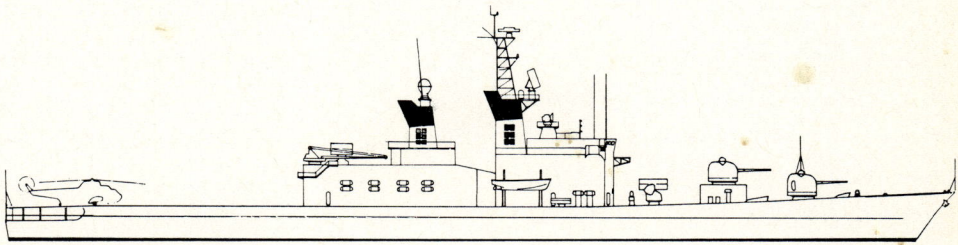
SHIRANE   1979

2 "HARUNA" CLASS

Name	No.	Builders	Laid down	Launched	Commissioned
HARUNA	DD 141	Mitsubishi, Nagasaki	19 Mar 1970	1 Feb 1972	22 Feb 1973
HIEI	DD 142	Ishikawajima, Tokyo	8 Mar 1972	13 Aug 1973	27 Nov 1974

Displacement, tons: 4 700
Length, feet (metres): 502·0 *(153·0)*
Beam, feet (metres): 57·4 *(17·5)*
Draught, feet (metres): 16·7 *(5·1)*
Aircraft: 3 anti-submarine helicopters
Guns: 2—5 in *(127 mm)*/54 (single Mk 42)
A/S weapons: US Mk 16 Octuple Asroc launcher; 6 (2 triple) US Mk 32 torpedo tubes
Main engines: 2 turbines; 70 000 shp; 2 shafts
Speed, knots: 32
Complement: 364

Ordered under the third five-year defence programme (from 1967-71).
The enclosed bridge has an area of 100 sq metres compared with *Takatsuki's* 70 sq metres. The funnel is offset slightly to port. Fitted with fin stabilisers.

Aircraft: Fitted with Canadian Beartrap haul down gear.

Gunnery: Mk 1 GFCS.

Radar: Air search: OPS 11.
Surface search: OPS 17.

Sonar: OQS 3 (hull-mounted).

HIEI   5/1976

0 + 2 + 3 NEW CONSTRUCTION

Name	No.	Builders	Laid down	Launched	Commissioned
—	DD 122	Sumitomo, Uraga	Mar 1979	Nov 1980	Mar 1982
—	DD 123	Hitachi, Maizuru	Jan 1980	Aug 1981	Feb 1983
—	DD 124		Aug 1981	—	Jan 1984
—	DD 125		Aug 1981	—	Jan 1984
—	DD 126		Aug 1981	—	Jan 1984

Displacement, tons: 2 950
Dimensions, feet (metres): 413·3 × 44·6 × 27·9 *(126 × 13·6 × 8·5)*
Aircraft: 1 HSS-2 A/S helicopter
Missiles: SSM; 8 Harpoon (2 quad launchers); SAM; 1 Sea Sparrow
Gun: 1—76 mm/62 (single Compact); 2 Phalanx CIWS (later ships)
A/S weapons: 1 Asroc; 2 triple US Mk 32 torpedo tubes
Main engines: COGOG; 2 Olympus TM3B; 45 000 shp; 2 Tyne RM1C; 2 shafts; 10 680 shp; (cp propellers)
Speed, knots: 30

DD 122 approved in 1977 estimates and DD 123 in 1978 estimates. Fitted with fin stabilisers.

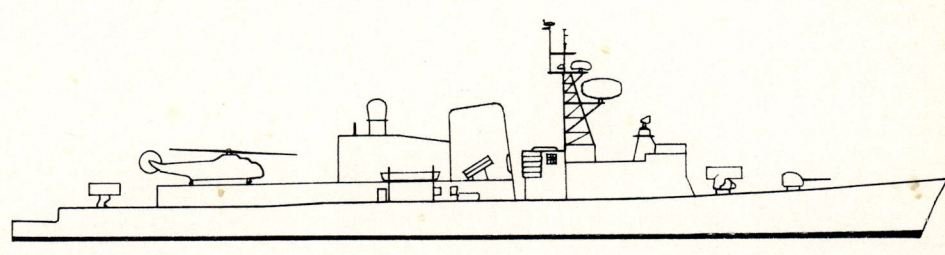
DD 122   1978

2 + 1 "TACHIKAZE" CLASS

Name	No.	Builders	Laid down	Launched	Commissioned
TACHIKAZE	DD 168	Mitsubishi, Nagasaki	19 June 1973	7 Dec 1974	26 Mar 1976
ASAKAZE	DD 169	Mitsubishi, Nagasaki	27 May 1976	15 Oct 1977	27 Mar 1979
—	DD 170	Mitsubishi, Nagasaki	Sep 1979	Apr 1981	Mar 1983

Displacement, tons: 3 900; 3 850 *(Asakaze)*
Dimensions, feet (metres): 443 × 47 × 15 *(135 × 14·3 × 4·6)* Length; 469 *(143) (Asakaze)*
Missiles: SAM; 1 Tartar D launcher Mk 13 Mod 3 for Standard RIM 60A
Guns: 2—5 in *(127 mm)*/54 (single Mk 42)
A/S weapons: US Mk 16 Octuple Asroc launcher; 6 (2 triple) US Mk 32 torpedo tubes
Main engines: 2 turbines; 2 shafts; 60 000 hp
Speed, knots: 33 (32, *Asakaze*)
Complement: 260 (250, *Asakaze*)

Asakaze ordered 3 March 1975. DD 170 approved in 1978 estimates.

Gunnery: Mk 1 GFCS.

Radar: 3D search: SPS 52.
Surface search: OPS 17.
Missile control: SPG 51.

TACHIKAZE   1978

Sonar: OQS 3 (hull-mounted).

294 JAPAN (MDF) / Destroyers

4 "TAKATSUKI" CLASS

Name	No.	Builders	Laid down	Launched	Commissioned
TAKATSUKI	DD 164	Ishikawajima Harima, Tokyo	8 Oct 1964	7 Jan 1966	15 Mar 1967
KIKUZUKI	DD 165	Mitsubishi, Nagasaki	15 Mar 1966	25 Mar 1967	27 Mar 1968
MOCHIZUKI	DD 166	Ishikawajima Harima, Tokyo	25 Nov 1966	15 Mar 1968	25 Mar 1969
NAGATSUKI	DD 167	Mitsubishi, Nagasaki	2 Mar 1968	19 Mar 1969	12 Feb 1970

Displacement, tons: 3 100
Length, feet (metres): 446·2 *(136·0)*
Beam, feet (metres): 44·0 *(13·4)*
Draught, feet (metres): 14·5 *(4·4)*
Aircraft: 2 Dash helicopters (see *Modifications* note)
Missiles: (see *Modifications* note)
Guns: 2—5 in *(127 mm)*/54 (single Mk 42) (see *Modifications* note)
A/S weapons: 1 US Mk 16 Octuple Asroc launcher; 1 four-barrelled rocket launcher; 6 (2 triple) Mk 32 torpedo tubes
Main engines: 2 Mitsubishi WH geared turbines; 60 000 shp; 2 shafts
Boilers: 2 Mitsubishi CE
Speed, knots: 32
Range, miles: 7 000 at 20 knots
Complement: 270

Takatsuki was provided under the 1963 programme. Equipped with helicopter hangar.

Gunnery: US Mk 56 GFCS.

Modifications: In 1980 *Takatsuki* to be taken in hand for modifications to include removal of after 5 in gun and Dash helicopters, fitting of SSM Harpoon SAM Sea Sparrow and CIWS 20 mm MG. The remainder of the class will be similarly modified in the future.

NAGATSUKI 7/1976, USN

Radar: Air search: OPS 11.
Surface search: OPS 17.
Fire control: US Mk 35.

Sonar: VDS; SQS 35(J); *Takatsuki* (1970), *Kikuzuki* (1972). Remainder not so fitted though planned.
Hull: SQS 23 (164-165); OQS 3 (166-167).

6 "YAMAGUMO" CLASS

Name	No.	Builders	Laid down	Launched	Commissioned
YAMAGUMO	DD 113	Mitsui, Tamano	23 Mar 1964	27 Feb 1965	29 Jan 1966
MAKIGUMO	DD 114	Uraga	10 June 1964	26 July 1965	19 Mar 1966
ASAGUMO	DD 115	Maizuru	24 June 1965	25 Nov 1966	29 Aug 1967
AOKUMO	DD 119	Sumitomo, Uraga	2 Oct 1970	30 Mar 1972	25 Nov 1972
AKIGUMO	DD 120	Sumitomo, Uraga	7 July 1972	23 Oct 1973	24 July 1974
YUUGUMO	DD 121	Sumitomo, Uraga	4 Feb 1976	31 May 1977	24 Mar 1978

Displacement, tons: 2 150
Length, feet (metres): 377 *(114·9)*
Beam, feet (metres): 38·7 *(11·8)*
Draught, feet (metres): 13·1 *(4)*
Guns: 4—3 in *(76 mm)*/50 (twin Mk 33)
A/S weapons: 1 US Mk 16 Octuple Asroc launcher; one 4-barrelled rocket launcher; 6 (2 triple) Mk 32 torpedo tubes
Main engines: 6 diesels; 26 500 bhp; 2 shafts
Speed, knots: 27
Range, miles: 7 000 at 20 knots
Complement: 210

Class: DD 121 was to have been lead ship of an improved class—slightly larger with CODOG machinery giving possibly up to 32 knots. This plan has been replaced by the new "DD 122" class of 2 950 tons.

Gunnery: 3 in guns to be replaced by OTO Melara 76 mm at refits.
US Mk 56 GFCS; US Mk 63 GFCS.

Radar: Air search: OPS 11.
Surface search: OPS 17.
Fire control: US Mk 35.

Sonar: Hull-mounted: SQS 23 (113-115); OQS 3 (119-121).
VDS: SQS 35(J) (113, 114, 120, 121.)

AOKUMO 1976, Michael D. J. Lennon

3 "MINEGUMO" CLASS

Name	No.	Builders	Laid down	Launched	Commissioned
MINEGUMO	DD 116	Mitsui, Tamano	14 Mar 1967	16 Dec 1967	21 Aug 1968
NATSUGUMO	DD 117	Uraga	26 June 1967	25 July 1968	25 Apr 1969
MURAKUMO	DD 118	Maizuru	19 Oct 1968	15 Nov 1969	21 Aug 1970

All data as for "Yamagumo" class.
Note difference in silhouettes between this and the "Yamagumo" class.

Aircraft: 2 Dash helicopter in place of Asroc although this will be reversed.

Gunnery: US Mk 56 GFCS; US Mk 63 GFCS.

Guns: In 1978 *Murakumo* had Y turret removed and replaced by an OTO Melara 76 mm Compact for trials.

Radar: Air search: OPS 11.
Surface search: OPS 17.
Fire control: US Mk 35.

Refit: *Murakumo* refitted in 1978 to replace Dash with Asroc. Remainder to be similarly altered.

Sonar: Hull-mounted: OQS 3.
VDS: SQS 35(J) *(Murakumo).*

NATSUGUMO 1978

JAPAN (MDF) / Destroyers 295

1 "AMATSUKAZE" CLASS

Name	No.	Builders	Laid down	Launched	Commissioned
AMATSUKAZE	DD 163	Mitsubishi, Nagasaki	29 Nov 1962	5 Oct 1963	15 Feb 1965

Displacement, tons: 3 050 standard; 4 000 full load
Length, feet (metres): 429·8 (131·0)
Beam, feet (metres): 44 (13·4)
Draught, feet (metres): 13·8 (4·2)
Missiles: SAM; Standard ASM-12 (single launcher)
Guns: 4—3 in (76 mm)/50 (twin Mk 33)
A/S weapons: 1 US Mk 16 Octuple Asroc launcher;
  2 Hedgehogs Mk 15; 6 (2 triple) Mk 32 torpedo tubes
Main engines: 2 Ishikawajima GE geared turbines 2 shafts;
  60 000 shp
Boilers: 2 Ishikawajima Foster-Wheeler
Speed, knots: 33
Oil fuel, tons: 900
Range, miles: 7 000 at 18 knots
Complement: 290

Ordered under the 1960 programme. Refitted in 1967 when A/S tubes and new sonar were fitted. In 1968 equipped with Asroc launcher between funnels.

Gunnery: US Mk 63 GFCS.

Guns: 3 in guns to be replaced by OTO Melara 76 mm at next refit.

Missiles: In 1978 Tartar was replaced by Standard ASM-12.

Radar: 3D search: SPS 52.
Air search: SPS 29.
Surface search: OPS 16.
Missile control: SPG 51C.

Sonar: SQS 23.

AMATSUKAZE   1975, Japanese Maritime Self-Defence Force

2 "AKIZUKI" CLASS

Name	No.	Builders	Laid down	Launched	Commissioned
AKIZUKI	DD 161	Mitsubishi, Nagasaki	31 July 1958	26 June 1959	13 Feb 1960
TERUZUKI	DD 162	Shin Mitsubishi, Kobe	15 Aug 1958	24 June 1959	29 Feb 1960

Displacement, tons: 2 350 standard; 2 890 full load
Length, feet (metres): 387·2 (118·0)
Beam, feet (metres): 39·4 (12·0)
Draught, feet (metres): 13·1 (4·0)
Guns: 3—5 in (127 mm)/54 (single Mk 39)
  4—3 in (76 mm)/50 (twin Mk 33)
A/S weapons: 6 (2 triple) Type 68 torpedo tubes; one
  4-barrelled Bofors 375 mm rocket launcher (Teruzuki) (see
  note)
Torpedo tubes: 4—21 in (533 mm) Type 65 (quad)
Main engines: 2 geared turbines: Akizuki: Mitsubishi/Escher-
  Weiss. Teruzuki: Westinghouse 45 000 shp, 2 shafts
Boilers: 2 Mitsubishi CE type
Speed, knots: 32
Complement: 330

Built under the 1957 Military Aid Programme.

A/S weapons: Teruzuki rearmed September 1976-January 1977, Akizuki in 1978.

Gunnery: US Mk 57 GFCS; US Mk 63 GFCS.

Guns: The 5 in Mk 39 were originally mounted in the US "Midway" class. With a disappointingly low rate of fire it is hoped they may be replaced by 76 mm OTO Melara.

TERUZUKI   1978

Radar: Air search: OPS 1.
Surface search: OPS 15.
Fire control: US Mk 34.

Sonar: Hull-mounted: SQS 29.
VDS: OQA 1 (Akizuki (1968)—Teruzuki (1967)).

3 "MURASAME" CLASS

Name	No.	Builders	Laid down	Launched	Commissioned
MURASAME	DD 107	Mitsubishi, Nagasaki	17 Dec 1957	31 July 1958	28 Feb 1959
YUDACHI	DD 108	Ishikawajima, Tokyo	16 Dec 1957	29 July 1958	25 Mar 1959
HARUSAME	DD 109	Uraga	17 June 1958	18 June 1959	15 Dec 1959

Displacement, tons: 1 800 standard; 2 500 full load
Length, feet (metres): 354·3 (108·0)
Beam, feet (metres): 36 (11·0)
Draught, feet (metres): 12·2 (3·7)
Guns: 3—5 in (127 mm)/54 (single Mk 39);
  4—3 in (76 mm)/50 (twin Mk 33)
A/S weapons: 2 Mk 4 torpedo launchers; 1 Hedgehog;
  1 DC rack; 1 Y-gun (see note)
Main engines: 2 sets geared turbines; 30 000 shp; 2 shafts
Boilers: 2 (see Engineering notes)
Speed, knots: 30
Range, miles: 6 000 at 18 knots
Complement: 250

Murasame and Yudachi were built under the 1956 Programme, Harusame 1957 Programme.

A/S weapons: Murasame fitted September 1975 with two Type 68 triple torpedo tubes in place of the Mk 4 above. DC rack and Y-gun removed.
Harusame will be similarly fitted in 1979.

Engineering: Murasame has Mitsubishi Jyuko turbines and Mitsubishi CE boilers; and the other two have Ishikawajima Harima Jyuko turbines and Ishikawajima FW-D boilers.

Gunnery: US Mk 57 and 63 GFCS.

Guns: As in the "Akizuki" class the 5 in guns were originally mounted in the US "Midway" class.

HARUSAME   1975, Japanese Maritime Self-Defence Force

Radar: Air search: OPS 1.
Surface search: OPS 15.
Fire control: US Mk 34.

Sonar: Hull-mounted: SQS 29.
VDS: OQA 1 (Harusame (1968)).

296　JAPAN (MDF) / Destroyers — Frigates

7 "AYANAMI" CLASS

Name	No.	Builders	Laid down	Launched	Commissioned
AYANAMI	DD 103	Mitsubishi, Nagasaki	20 Nov 1956	1 June 1957	12 Feb 1958
ISONAMI	DD 104	Shin Mitsubishi, Kobe	14 Dec 1956	30 Sep 1957	14 Mar 1958
URANAMI	DD 105	Kawasaki, Tokyo	1 Feb 1957	29 Aug 1957	27 Feb 1958
SHIKINAMI	DD 106	Mitsui, Tamano	24 Dec 1956	25 Sep 1957	15 Mar 1958
TAKANAMI	DD 110	Mitsui, Tamano	8 Nov 1958	8 Aug 1959	30 Jan 1960
OONAMI	DD 111	Ishikawajima, Tokyo	20 Mar 1959	13 Feb 1960	29 Aug 1960
MAKINAMI	DD 112	Iino, Maizuru	20 Mar 1959	25 Apr 1960	30 Oct 1960

Displacement, tons: 1 700 standard; 2 500 full load
Length, feet (metres): 357·6 (109·0)
Beam, feet (metres): 35·1 (10·7)
Draught, feet (metres): 12 (3·7)
Guns: 6—3 in (76 mm)/50 (twin Mk 33)
A/S weapons: 6 (2 triple) Mk 4 torpedo launchers (103, 104, 105, 106, 112); 2 Mk 4 torpedo launchers (110, 111);
　2 US Mk 15 Hedgehogs
Torpedo tubes: 4—21 in (533 mm) Type 65 (quad) (103, 105, 110, 111, 112) (see *Training Ships* notes)
Main engines: 2 Mitsubishi/Escher-Weiss geared turbines;
　2 shafts; 35 000 shp
Boilers: 2 (see *Engineering* notes)
Speed, knots: 32
Range, miles: 6 000 at 18 knots
Complement: 230

A/S weapons: Trainable Hedgehogs forward of the bridge.

Engineering: Types of boilers installed are as follows:
Mitsubishi CE in *Ayanami*, *Isonami*, and *Uranami*. Hitachi, Babcock & Wilcox in *Oonami*, *Shikinami* and *Takanami*. Kawasaki Jyuko BD in *Makinami*.

Gunnery: US Mk 57 and 63 GFCS.

Guns: Gunshields are of Japanese design and manufacture.

Radar: Air search: OPS 1 or 2.
Surface search: OPS 15 or 16.
Fire control: US Mk 34.

SHIKINAMI　　　　　　　　　　　　　　　　　　　　　　　　　　1978

Sonar: Hull-mounted: OQS 12.
VDS: OQA 1 (103, 104, 110)

Training Ships: *Isonami* and *Shikinami* converted 1975-76 to training ships in place of *Asahi* and *Hatsuhi*. 21 in torpedo tubes removed and lecture hall built in the space.

2 "HARUKAZE" CLASS

Name	No.	Builders	Laid down	Launched	Commissioned
HARUKAZE	DD 101	Mitsubishi, Nagasaki	15 Dec 1954	20 Sep 1955	26 Apr 1956
YUKIKAZE	DD 102	Shin Mitsubishi, Kobe	17 Dec 1954	20 Aug 1955	31 July 1956

Displacement, tons: 1 700 standard; 2 340 full load
Length, feet (metres): 347·8 (106·0) wl; 358·5 (109·3) oa
Beam, feet (metres): 34·5 (10·5)
Draught, feet (metres): 12·0 (3·7)
Guns: 3—5 in (127 mm)/38 (single Mk 38);
　8—40 mm (quad Mk 2)
A/S weapons: 2 Mk 4 torpedo launchers; 2 Hedgehogs;
　4 K-guns; 1 DC rack (see note)
Main engines: 2 sets geared turbines;
　Harukaze; 2 Mitsubishi Escher Weiss;
　Yukikaze; 2 Westinghouse; 2 shafts; 30 000 shp
Boilers: *Harukaze*: 2 Hitachi-Babcock; *Yukikaze*: 2 Combustion Engineering
Speed, knots: 30
Range, miles: 6 000 at 18 knots
Oil fuel, tons: 557
Complement: 240

Authorised under the 1953 programme. First destroyer hulled vessels built in Japan after the Second World War. Electric welding was extensively used in hull construction; development of weldable high tension steel in main hull and light alloy in superstructure were also new.
Nearly all the armament was supplied from the USA under the MSA clause.

Gunnery: US Mk 57 and 63 GFCS.
Experimental Contraves GFCS in *Harukaze*.

Modifications: *Yukikaze* has been modified for experimental duties. One 5 in (Y gun), four K-guns and one DC rack removed to make way for towed passive sonar array in 1975.

Radar: Air search: SPS 6.
Surface search: OPS 37.
Fire control: US Mk 26 and 34.

HARUKAZE　　　　　　　　　　　　　　　1975, Japanese Maritime Self-Defence Force

YUKIKAZE (before modification)　　　　　　　　　　　　　　　　1972

Sonar: SQS 30J.

FRIGATES

0 + 1 + 2 "DE 226" CLASS

Name	No.	Builders	Laid down	Launched	Commissioned
—	DE 226	Mitsui, Tamano	Apr 1978	Mar 1980	Mar 1981
—	DE 227	—	Mar 1981	Mar 1982	Mar 1983

Displacement, tons: 1 250 (see note)
Dimensions, feet (metres): 275·5 × 34·7 × 19·2
　(84 × 10·6 × 5·9) (see note)
Missiles: Quad Harpoon
Gun: 1—76 mm OTO Melara Compact (see note)
A/S weapons: Quad Bofors launcher;
　6 (2 triple) Type 68 torpedo tubes.
Main engines: CODOG; 1 Olympus TM3B; 22 500 shp;
　one 6 DRV diesel; 4 700 shp; 2 shafts (cp propellers)
Speed, knots: 25

DE 226 approved in 1977 estimates. Two further ships requested in 1979 estimates.
DE 226 will be the prototype for a large class. The design of succeeding ships may well depart considerably from the data given here — tonnage may be increased, armament siting altered, engine-room improvements to be made, possibly COGOG arrangement giving a higher speed.
The design of DE 227 is already an improvement on that of 226 (illustrated last year) with a tonnage increased to 1 400 on an enlarged hull giving improved accommodation, speed and sea-keeping qualities. A Phalanx 20 mm CIWS has been included on the quarter-deck.

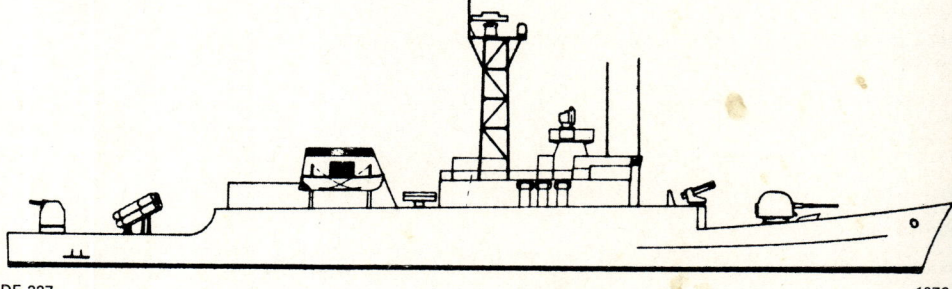

DE 227　　　　　　　　　　　　　　　　　　　　　　　　　　　1978

JAPAN (MDF) / Frigates — Light forces 297

11 "CHIKUGO" CLASS

Name	No.	Builders	Laid down	Launched	Commissioned
CHIKUGO	DE 215	Mitsui, Tamano	9 Dec 1968	13 Jan 1970	31 July 1970
AYASE	DE 216	Ishikawajima Harima	5 Dec 1969	16 Sep 1970	20 May 1971
MIKUMA	DE 217	Mitsui, Tamano	17 Mar 1970	16 Feb 1971	26 Aug 1971
TOKACHI	DE 218	Mitsui, Tamano	11 Dec 1970	25 Nov 1971	17 May 1972
IWASE	DE 219	Mitsui, Tamano	6 Aug 1971	29 June 1972	12 Dec 1972
CHITOSE	DE 220	Hitachi, Maizuru	7 Oct 1971	25 Jan 1973	31 Aug 1973
NIYODO	DE 221	Mitsui, Tamano	20 Sep 1972	28 Aug 1973	8 Feb 1974
TESHIO	DE 222	Hitachi, Maizuru	11 July 1973	29 May 1974	10 Jan 1975
YOSHINO	DE 223	Mitsui, Tamano	28 Sep 1973	22 Aug 1974	6 Feb 1975
KUMANO	DE 224	Hitachi, Maizuru	29 May 1974	24 Feb 1975	19 Nov 1975
NOSHIRO	DE 225	Mitsui, Tamano	27 Jan 1976	23 Dec 1976	31 Aug 1977

Displacement, tons: 1 470 (216, 217-219,221); 1 480 (215, 220); 1 500 (222 onwards)
Length, feet (metres): 305·5 *(93·1)*
Beam, feet (metres): 35·5 *(10·8)*
Draught, feet (metres): 11·5 *(3·5)*
Guns: 2—3 in *(76 mm)*/50 (twin Mk 33); 2—40 mm/60 (twin Mk 1)
A/S weapons: 1 US Mk 16 Octuple Asroc launcher; 6 (2 triple) Mk 32 torpedo tubes
Main engines: 4 Mitsui Babcock & Wilcox diesels (215, 217, 218, 219, 221, 223, 225); 4 Mitsubishi UEV 30/40 N diesels (remainder); 2 shafts; 16 000 shp
Speed, knots: 25
Complement: 165

These are the smallest warships in the world to mount Asroc.

Gunnery: Mk 1 GFCS.

Radar: Air search: OPS 14.
Surface search: OPS 17.
Fire control: Mk 33.

Sonar: Hull-mounted: OQS 3.
VDS: SPS 35(J).

NOSHIRO   1978

4 "ISUZU" CLASS

Name	No.	Builders	Laid down	Launched	Commissioned
ISUZU	DE 211	Mitsui, Tamano	16 Apr 1960	17 Jan 1961	29 July 1961
MOGAMI	DE 212	Mitsubishi, Nagasaki	4 Aug 1960	7 Mar 1961	28 Oct 1961
KITAKAMI	DE 213	Ishikawajima Harima, Tokyo	7 June 1962	21 June 1963	27 Feb 1964
OOI	DE 214	Maizuru	10 June 1962	15 June 1963	22 Jan 1964

Displacement, tons: 1 490 standard; 1 700 full load
Length, feet (metres): 309·5 *(94·3)*
Beam, feet (metres): 34·2 *(10·4)*
Draught, feet (metres): 11·5 *(3·5)*
Guns: 4—3 in *(76 mm)*/50 (twin Mk 33)
A/S weapons: 4-barrelled Bofors rocket launcher; 6 (2 triple) Type 68 torpedo tubes; 1 Y-gun; 1 DC rack *(Ooi and Isuzu)*
Torpedo tubes: 4—21 in *(533 mm)* (quad)
Main engines: 4 diesels, Mitsui in *Ooi, Isuzu,* Mitsubishi in *Kitakami, Mogami,* 16 000 hp; 2 shafts
Speed, knots: 25
Complement: 180

Modernisation: In 1966 *(Mogami)* and 1968 *(Kitakami)* one Y-gun and DC racks removed for VDS. *Isuzu* (1974-75) and *Mogami* (1974) modified for new Bofors rocket launcher.

Gunnery: US Mk 63 GFCS.

Radar: Air search: OPS 1.
Surface search: OPS 16.
Fire control: US Mk 34.

Sonar: Hull-mounted: SQS 29.
VDS: OQA 1 (212-213).

OOI   1975

LIGHT FORCES

8 "MIZUTORI" CLASS (LARGE PATROL CRAFT)

Name	No.	Builders	Laid down	Launched	Commissioned
MIZUTORI	311	Kawasaki, Kobe	13 Mar 1959	22 Sep 1959	27 Feb 1960
YAMADORI	312	Fujinagata, Osaka	14 Mar 1959	22 Oct 1959	15 Mar 1960
OTORI	313	Kure Shipyard	16 Dec 1959	27 May 1960	13 Oct 1960
HAYABUSA	314	Fujinagata, Osaka	18 Dec 1959	31 May 1960	31 Oct 1960
KASASAGI	315	Sasebo	25 Jan 1960	24 June 1960	15 Nov 1960
UMIDORI	316	Sasebo	15 Feb 1962	15 Oct 1962	30 Mar 1963
SHIRATORI	319	Sasebo	29 Feb 1964	8 Oct 1964	26 Feb 1965
HIYODORI	320	Sasebo	26 Feb 1965	25 Sep 1965	28 Feb 1966

Displacement, tons: 420 to 440 standard
Dimensions, feet (metres): 197·0 × 23·3 × 7·5 *(60·0 × 7·1 × 2·3)*
Guns: 2—40 mm/60 (twin Mk 1)
A/S weapons: 1 Hedgehog; 1 DC rack; 6 (2 triple) Mk 32 torpedo tubes (316, 319, 320); 2 Mk 4 torpedo launchers (remainder)
Main engines: 2 MAN diesels; 2 shafts; 3 800 bhp = 20 knots
Range, miles: 2 000 at 12 knots
Complement: 80

Gunnery: Mk 63 GFCS.

Radar: Surface search: OPS 35 (311-312); OPS 36 (313-316); OPS 16 (319-320).

Sonar: SQS 11A.

OTORI (with two Mk 4 torpedo launchers)   1978

JAPAN (MDF) / Light forces — Amphibious forces

4 "UMITAKA" CLASS (LARGE PATROL CRAFT)

Name	No.	Builders	Laid down	Launched	Commissioned
UMITAKA	309	Kawasaki, Kobe	13 Mar 1959	25 July 1959	30 Nov 1959
OTAKA	310	Kure Shipyard	18 Mar 1959	3 Sep 1959	14 Jan 1960
WAKATAKA	317	Kure Shipyard	5 Mar 1962	13 Nov 1962	30 Mar 1963
KUMATAKA	318	Fujinagata, Osaka	20 Mar 1963	21 Oct 1963	25 Mar 1964

Displacement, tons: 440 to 460 standard
Dimensions, feet (metres): 197·0 × 23·3 × 8·0 *(60·0 × 7·1 × 2·4)*
Guns: 2—40 mm/60 (twin Mk 1)
A/S weapons: 1 Hedgehog, 1 DC rack; 6 (2 triple) Mk 32 torpedo tubes (317, 318); 2 Mk 32 torpedo launchers (309, 310)
Main engines: 2 Babcock & Wilcox diesels; 2 shafts; 4 000 bhp = 20 knots
Range, miles: 3 000 at 12 knots
Complement: 80

Gunnery: Mk 63 GFCS.

Radar: Surface search: OPS 35 (309-310); OPS 36 (317); OPS 16 (318)

Sonar: SQS 11A.

WAKATAKA — *1976, Japanese Maritime Self-Defence Force*

5 FAST ATTACK CRAFT—TORPEDO

Name	No.	Builders	Commissioned
PT 11	811	Mitsubishi, Shimonoseki	27 Mar 1971
PT 12	812	Mitsubishi, Shimonoseki	28 Mar 1972
PT 13	813	Mitsubishi, Shimonoseki	16 Dec 1972
PT 14	814	Mitsubishi, Shimonoseki	15 Feb 1974
PT 15	815	Mitsubishi, Shimonoseki	10 July 1975

Displacement, tons: 135
Dimensions, feet (metres): 116·4 × 30·2 × 3·9 *(35·5 × 9·2 × 1·2)*
Guns: 2—40 mm (single Mk 3)
Torpedo tubes: 4—21 in
Main engines: CODAG; 2 Mitsubishi diesels; 2 IHI gas turbines; 3 shafts; 11 000 hp (PT 11; 10 500 hp) = 50 knots
Complement: 26-28

Laid down on 17 March 1970, 22 April 1971, 28 March 1972, 23 March 1973, and 23 April 1974 respectively.

Radar: OPS 13.

PT 14 — *1976, Japanese Maritime Self-Defence Force*

9 COASTAL PATROL CRAFT

Name	No.	Builders	Commissioned
PB 19	919	Ishikawajima, Yokohama	31 Mar 1971
PB 20	920	Ishikawajima, Yokohama	31 Mar 1971
PB 21	921	Ishikawajima, Yokohama	31 Mar 1971
PB 22	922	Ishikawajima, Yokohama	31 Mar 1971
PB 23	923	Ishikawajima, Yokohama	31 Mar 1972
PB 24	924	Ishikawajima, Yokohama	31 Mar 1972
PB 25	925	Ishikawajima, Yokohama	29 Mar 1973
PB 26	926	Ishikawajima, Yokohama	29 Mar 1973
PB 27	927	Ishikawajima, Yokohama	29 Mar 1973

Displacement, tons: 18
Dimensions, feet (metres): 55·8 × 14·1 × 2·7 *(17 × 4·3 × 0·8)*
Gun: 1—20 mm
Main engines: 2 diesels; 760 hp = 20 knots
Complement: 6

GRP hulls.

Radar: OPS 29.

PB 22 — *11/1975*

Name	No.	Builders	Commissioned
KOSOKU 6	06	Mitsubishi, Shimonoseki	20 Mar 1967

Displacement, tons: 40
Dimensions, feet (metres): 75·9 × 18·2 × 3·3 *(23·1 × 5·6 × 1)*
Main engines: 3 diesels; 2 800 bhp = 30 knots

Of aluminium construction. Laid down on 28 June 1966 under the 1965 programme. Launched 22 November 1966.

Radar: OPS 4C.

KOSOKU 6 — *1974, Japanese Maritime Self-Defence Force*

AMPHIBIOUS FORCES

Note: New construction 1980/82 of four to five 500 ton LSMs. First two to be laid down May 1980.

3 "MIURA" CLASS (LST)

Name	No.	Builders	Commissioned
MIURA	4151	Ishikawajima Harima, Tokyo	29 Jan 1975
OJIKA	4152	Ishikawajima Harima, Tokyo	22 Mar 1976
SATSUMA	4153	Ishikawajima Harima, Tokyo	17 Feb 1977

Displacement, tons: 2 000
Dimensions, feet (metres): 321·4 × 45·9 × 9·8 *(98 × 14 × 3)*
Guns: 2—3 in *(76 mm)* (twin); 2—40 mm (twin)
Main engines: 2 Kawasaki/MAN V8V 22/30 ATL diesels; 2 shafts; 4 400 hp = 14 knots
Complement: 115

Miura laid down 26 November 1973, launched 13 August 1974. *Ojika* laid down 10 June 1974, launched 2 September 1975. *Satsuma* laid down 26 May 1975, launched 12 May 1976. Carry two LCMs and two LCVPs, ten type 74 tanks. Accommodation for 200 troops.

Radar: OPS 14; OPS 18.

MIURA — *1976, Japanese Maritime Self-Defence Force*

JAPAN (MDF) / Amphibious forces — Mine warfare forces 299

3 "ATSUMI" CLASS (LST)

Name	No.	Builders	Commissioned
ATSUMI	4101	Sasebo Heavy Industries	27 Nov 1972
MOTOBU	4102	Sasebo Heavy Industries	21 Dec 1973
NEMURO	4103	Sasebo Heavy Industries	27 Oct 1977

Displacement, tons: 1 480 (Atsumi); 1 550 (Motobu); 1 500 (Nemuro)
Dimensions, feet (metres): 291·9 × 42·6 × 8·5 (89 × 13 × 2·6)
Guns: 4—40 mm (twins)
Main engines: 2 diesels; 4 400 hp = 13 knots (Motobu) = 14 knots (Atsumi)
Complement: 100 (Atsumi); 95 (Motobu)

Atsumi laid down 7 December 1971, launched 13 June 1972. Motobu laid down 23 April 1973, launched 3 August 1973. Nemuro laid down 18 November 1976; launched 16 June 1977. Accommodation for 130 troops.

Radar: OPS 9.

MOTOBU 1974, Japanese Maritime Self-Defence Force

MINE WARFARE FORCES

1 "SOUYA" CLASS (MINESWEEPER SUPPORT SHIP)

Name	No.	Builders	Laid down	Launched	Commissioned
SOUYA	951	Hitachi, Maizuru	9 July 1970	31 Mar 1971	30 Sep 1971

Displacement, tons: 2 150 standard; 3 050 full load
Length, feet (metres): 324·8 (99·0)
Beam, feet (metres): 49·5 (15·0)
Draught, feet (metres): 13·9 (4·2)
Guns: 2—3 in (76 mm)/50 (twin Mk 33); 2—20 mm
A/S weapons: 6 (2 triple) Mk 32 A/S torpedo tubes
Main engines: 4 diesels; 4 000 bhp; 2 shafts
Speed, knots: 18
Complement: 185

With twin rails can carry 200 buoyant mines. Has helicopter platform aft and acts at times as command ship for MCM forces.

Fire control: GFCS Mk 1.
Radar: OPS 14; OPS 16.
Sonar: SQS 11A.

SOUYA 1974, Japanese Maritime Self-Defence Force

1 "HAYASE" CLASS (MINESWEEPER SUPPORT SHIP)

Name	No.	Builders	Commissioned
HAYASE	462	Ishikawajima, Haruna	6 Nov 1971

Displacement, tons: 2 000 standard
Length, feet (metres): 324·8 (99·0)
Beam, feet (metres): 42·7 (13·0)
Draught, feet (metres): 12·5 (3·8)
Guns: 2—3 in (76 mm)/50 (twin Mk 33); 2—20 mm
A/S weapons: 6 (2 triple) Mk 32 A/S torpedo tubes
Main engines: 2 diesels; 4 000 bhp; 2 shafts
Speed, knots: 18
Complement: 180

Laid down 16 September 1970, launched 21 June 1971. Has helicopter platform aft.

Radar: OPS 14; OPS 16.
Sonar: SQS 11A.

HAYASE 1978

1 + 4 + 2 "HATSUSHIMA" CLASS (MINESWEEPERS—COASTAL)

Name	No.	Builders	Commissioned
HATSUSHIMA	MSC 649	Nippon Steel Tube Co (Isogo)	Mar 1979
—	MSC 650	Hitachi, Kanagawa	Jan 1980
—	MSC 651	Nippon Steel Tube Co (Isogo)	Jan 1980
—	MSC 652	Nippon Steel Tube Co (Isogo)	Feb 1981
—	MSC 653	Hitachi, Kanagawa	Nov 1980
—	MSC 654	—	Nov 1981
—	MSC 655	—	Nov 1981

Displacement, tons: 440 standard
Dimensions, feet (metres): 180·4 × 30·8 × 13·8 (55 × 9·4 × 4·2)
Gun: 1—20 mm Oerlikon (1—Phalanx CIWS in later ships)
Main engines: 2 diesels; 2 shafts; 1 440 bhp = 14 knots
Complement: 45

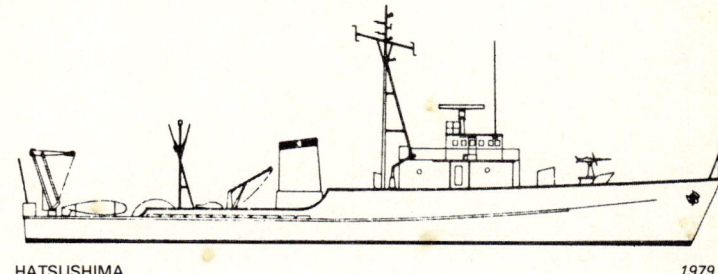

HATSUSHIMA 1979

To be fitted with new S4 mine detonating equipment, a remote-controlled counter-mine charge. First of class ordered under 1976 programme. Contract for 649 signed 31 March 1977. Laid down 6 December 1977 (649), 8 May 1978 (650), 8 November 1978 (651), October 1979 (652), March 1979 (653), August 1980 (654, 655). Launch dates, 30 October 1978 (649), July 1979 (650), September 1979 (651), August 1980 (652), June 1980 (653), June 1981 (654, 655). MSC 652 and 653 approved in 1978 estimates, 654 and 655 requested in 1979 estimates.

300 JAPAN (MDF) / Mine warfare forces

19 "TAKAMI" CLASS (MINESWEEPERS—COASTAL)

Name	No.	Builders	Commissioned
TAKAMI	MSC 630	Hitachi, Kanagawa	15 Dec 1969
IOU	MSC 631	Nippon Steel Tube Co	22 Jan 1970
MIYAKE	MSC 632	Hitachi, Kanagawa	19 Nov 1970
UTONE	MSC 633	Nippon Steel Tube Co	3 Sep 1970
AWAJI	MSC 634	Hitachi, Kanagawa	29 Mar 1971
TOUSHI	MSC 635	Nippon Steel Tube Co	18 Mar 1971
TEURI	MSC 636	Hitachi, Kanagawa	10 Mar 1972
MUROTSU	MSC 637	Nippon Steel Tube Co	3 Mar 1972
TASHIRO	MSC 638	Hitachi, Kanagawa	30 July 1973
MIYATO	MSC 639	Nippon Steel Tube Co	24 Aug 1973
TAKANE	MSC 640	Hitachi, Kanagawa	28 Aug 1974
MUZUKI	MSC 641	Nippon Steel Tube Co	28 Aug 1974
YOKOSE	MSC 642	Hitachi, Kanagawa	15 Dec 1975
SAKATE	MSC 643	Nippon Steel Tube Co	17 Dec 1975
OUMI	MSC 644	Hitachi, Kanagawa	18 Nov 1976
FUKUE	MSC 645	Nippon Steel Tube Co	18 Nov 1976
OKITSU	MSC 646	Hitachi, Kanagawa	20 Sep 1977
HASHIRA	MSC 647	Nippon Steel Tube Co (Isogo)	28 Mar 1978
IWAI	MSC 648	Hitachi, Kanagawa	28 Mar 1978

Of similar dimensions to "Kasado" class below but of slightly different construction and with a displacement of 380 tons.
As minehunters fitted with mine-detecting sonar and carry four clearance divers.
Laid down—*Okitsu* 26 April 1976, *Hashira* 22 February 1977; *Iwai* 20 July 1976. Launch dates—*Okitsu* 4 March 1977, *Hashira* 8 November 1977, *Iwai* 24 November 1977.

Radar: OPS 9.

Sonar: ZQS 2.

SAKATE *1976, Japanese Maritime Self-Defence Force*

11 "KASADO" CLASS (MINESWEEPERS—COASTAL)

Name	No.	Builders	Commissioned
MUTSURE	MSC 619	Nippon Steel Tube Co	24 Mar 1964
CHIBURI	MSC 620	Hitachi, Kanagawa	25 Mar 1964
OOTSU	MSC 621	Nippon Steel Tube Co	24 Feb 1965
KUDAKO	MSC 622	Hitachi, Kanagawa	24 Mar 1965
RISHIRI	MSC 623	Nippon Steel Tube Co	5 Mar 1966
REBUN	MSC 624	Hitachi, Kanagawa	24 Mar 1966
AMAMI	MSC 625	Nippon Steel Tube Co	6 Mar 1967
URUME	MSC 626	Hitachi, Kanagawa	30 Jan 1967
MINASE	MSC 627	Nippon Steel Tube Co	25 Mar 1967
IBUKI	MSC 628	Hitachi, Kanagawa	27 Feb 1968
KATSURA	MSC 629	Nippon Steel Tube Co	15 Feb 1968

Displacement, tons: 330 standard; (380 later ships); 448 full load (later ships)
Dimensions, feet (metres): 150·9 × 28 × 7·5 *(46 × 8·5 × 2·3)*; 171·6 × 28·9 × 7·9 *(52·3 × 8·8 × 2·4)* later ships
Gun: 1—20 mm
Main engines: 2 diesels; 2 shafts; 1 200 bhp (1 440 later ships) = 14 knots
Complement: 43 (47 in later ships)

Originally a class of 29 ships. Hull is of wooden construction. Otherwise built of non-magnetic materials. 16 of this class converted as MCM support ship (1), survey craft (5), E.O.D. (diving tenders) (4) and tenders (8).

Radar: OPS 9 or OPS 4.

IBUKI *1976, Japanese Maritime Self-Defence Force*

1 "KOUZU" CLASS (MCM SUPPORT SHIP)

KOUZU MST 473 (ex-*MSC 609*)

Similar to "Kasado" class but has had minesweeping gear removed and was fitted as MCM command ship in June 1972. Used as tender for "Nana-Go" class MSBs.

KOUZU

6 "NANA-GO" CLASS (MSBs)

Name	No.	Builders	Commissioned
NANA-GO	707	Hitachi, Kanagawa	30 Mar 1973
HACHI-GO	708	Nippon Steel Tube Co	27 Mar 1973
KYUU-GO	709	Hitachi, Kanagawa	28 Mar 1974
JYUU-GO	710	Nippon Steel Tube Co	29 Mar 1974
JYUU-ICHI-GO	711	Hitachi, Kanagawa	10 May 1975
JYUU-NI-GO	712	Nippon Steel Tube Co	22 Apr 1975

Displacement, tons: 53
Dimensions, feet (metres): 73·8 × 17·7 × 3·3 *(22·5 × 5·4 × 1)*
Main engines: 2 Mitsubishi diesels; 2 shafts; 480 hp = 11 knots
Complement: 10

Laid down 26 May 1972, 3 August 1972, 5 July 1973, 7 June 1973, 2 July 1974, respectively. 712 launched 27 January 1975. No radar.

JYUU-GO *3/1974*

SERVICE FORCES

1 TRAINING SUPPORT SHIP

Name	No.	Builders	Commissioned
AZUMA	ATS 4201	Maizuru	26 Nov 1969

Displacement, tons: 1 950 standard; 2 500 full load
Length, feet (metres): 323·4 (98·6)
Beam, feet (metres): 42·7 (13·0)
Draught, feet (metres): 12·5 (3·8)
Aircraft: 1 helicopter, 3 jetdrones, 10 propeller drones
Gun: 1—3 in (76 mm)/50
A/S weapons: 2 A/S Mk 4 torpedo launchers
Main engines: 2 diesels; 2 shafts; 4 000 bhp
Speed, knots: 18
Complement: 140

Laid down on 15 July 1968, launched on 14 April 1969. Has drone hangar amidships and catapult on flight deck. Can operate towed target. Training Support Ship for AA gunnery.

AZUMA   1974, Japanese Maritime Self-Defence Force

Radar: OPS 16; SPS 40
Sonar: SQS 11A

1 TRAINING SHIP

Name	No.	Builders	Commissioned
KATORI	3501	Ishikawajima Harima, Tokyo	10 Sep 1969

Displacement, tons: 3 350 standard; 4 000 full load
Length, feet (metres): 422·4 (128·7)
Beam, feet (metres): 49·5 (15·5)
Draught, feet (metres): 14·6 (4·5)
Guns: 4—3 in (76 mm)/50 (single)
A/S weapons: One 4-barrelled rocket launcher; 6 (2 triple) Type 68 torpedo tubes
Main engines: Geared turbines; 2 shafts; 20 000 shp
Range, miles: 7 000 at 18 knots
Speed, knots: 25
Complement: 460 (295 ship's company and 165 trainees)

Laid down 8 December 1967, launched on 19 November 1968. Provided with a landing deck aft of 30 × 13 metres for a helicopter and large auditorium for trainees amidships. Used for training midshipmen.

KATORI   8/1977, John Mortimer

Radar: Search: OPS 17. Tactical: SPS 12.
Sonar: SQS 4.

1 E.O.D. TENDER

Name	No.	Builders	Commissioned
ERIMO	YAS 69 (ex-AMC 491)	Uraga	28 Dec 1955

Displacement, tons: 630 standard
Dimensions, feet (metres): 210 × 26 × 8 (64·0 × 7·9 × 2·4)
Guns: 2—40 mm; 2—20 mm
A/S weapons: 1 Hedgehog; 2 K-guns; 2 DC racks
Main engines: Diesel; 2 shafts; 2 500 bhp = 18 knots
Complement: 80

Conversion to tender for E.O.D. (Mine Hunting Diver) completed March 1976.

ERIMO   1978

6 E.O.D. TENDERS

SHISAKA (ex-MSC 605) YAS 62
SAKITO (ex-MSC 607) YAS 64
TSUKUMI (ex-MSC 611) YAS 66
SHIKINE (ex-MSC 613) YAS 68
HOTAKA (ex-MSC 616) YAS 70
KARATO (ex-MSC 617) YAS 71

Of "Kasado" class (see Mine Warfare section for details) transferred after conversion to E.O.D. (Mine Hunting Diver) duties which includes removal of minesweeping gear to provide for divers room and equipment.

SHISAKA   1978

1 SUBMARINE RESCUE SHIP

Name	No.	Builders	Commissioned
FUSIMI	ASR 402	Sumitomo, Uraga	10 Feb 1970

Displacement, tons: 1 430 standard
Dimensions, feet (metres): 249·5 × 41 × 12 (76·0 × 12·5 × 3·7)
Main engines: 2 diesels; 1 shaft; 3 000 bhp = 16 knots
Complement: 100

Laid down on 5 November 1968, launched 10 September 1969. Has a rescue chamber and two recompression chambers.

Radar: OPS 9.
Sonar: SQS 11A

FUSIMI   1976, Japanese Maritime Self-Defence Force

JAPAN (MDF) / Service forces

1 SUBMARINE RESCUE SHIP

Name	No.	Builders	Commissioned
CHIHAYA	ASR 401	Mitsubishi Nippon, Yokohama	15 Mar 1961

Displacement, tons: 1 340 standard
Dimensions, feet (metres): 239·5 × 39·3 × 12·7 *(73 × 12 × 3·9)*
Main engines: Diesels; 2 700 bhp = 15 knots
Complement: 90

Authorised under the 1959 programme. The first vessel of her kind to be built in Japan. Laid down on 15 March 1960. Launched on 4 October 1960. Has rescue chamber, two recompression chambers, four-point mooring equipment and a 12 ton derrick.

Radar: OPS 4.

Sonar: SQS 11A.

CHIHAYA *1976, Japanese Maritime Self-Defence Force*

1 FLEET SUPPORT SHIP

Name	No.	Builders	Commissioned
SAGAMI	AOE 421	Hitachi, Maizuru	31 Mar 1979

Displacement, tons: 5 000
Dimensions, feet (metres): 478·9 × 62·3 × 35·4 *(146 × 19 × 10·8)*
Main engines: 2 diesels; 2 shafts; 20 000 bhp
Speed, knots: 22
Range, miles: 9 500 at 20 knots
Complement: 130

Merchant type hull. Included in 1976 estimates. Ordered December 1976. Laid down 28 September 1977, launched 4 September 1978. Has six re-supply stations each side. No armament but can be fitted. Helicopter platform but no hangar.

SAGAMI *1979*

1 SUPPORT TANKER

Name	No.	Builders	Commissioned
HAMANA	AO 411	Uraga	10 Mar 1962

Displacement, tons: 2 900 light; 7 550 full load
Dimensions, feet (metres): 420 × 51·5 × 20·5 *(128·0 × 15·7 × 6·3)*
Guns: 2—40 mm
Main engine: 1 diesel; 5 000 bhp; 1 shaft = 16 knots
Complement: 100

Built under the 1960 programme. Laid down on 17 April 1961, launched on 24 October 1961.

1 SALVAGE VESSEL

Name	No.	Builders	Commissioned
SHOBO	YE 41	Azumo, Yokosuka	28 Feb 1964

Displacement, tons: 45
Dimensions, feet (metres): 75 × 18 × 3·3 *(22·9 × 5·5 × 1)*
Main engines: Diesels; 3 shafts; speed = 19 knots
Complement: 8

Four fixed fire hoses fitted. Now on auxiliary list. Used as rescue and salvage ship for A/S Flying Boats.

1 NEW CONSTRUCTION CABLE LAYER

Name	No.	Builders	Commissioned
—	ARC 482	Mitsubishi, Shimonoseki	Mar 1980

Displacement, tons: 4 500

To replace *Tsugaru*. Ocean survey capability. Laid down 28 November 1978, launched July 1979.

ARC 482 *1979*

1 CABLE LAYER

Name	No.	Builders	Commissioned
TSUGARU	ARC 481	Yokohama Shipyard	15 Dec 1955

Displacement, tons: 2 150 standard
Dimensions, feet (metres): 337·8 × 40·7 × 16 *(103 × 12·4 × 4·9)*
Guns: 2—20 mm
Main engines: 2 diesels; 2 shafts; 3 200 bhp = 13 knots
Complement: 103

Dual purpose cable layer and coastal minelayer. Built under the 1953 programme. Laid down on 18 December 1954. Launched on 19 July 1955. Converted to cable-layer 10 July 1969-30 April 1970 by Nippon Steel Tube Co.

TSUGARU *1972, Toshio Tamura*

1 HARBOUR TANKER

Name	No.	Builder	Commissioned
—	YOG 8	Usuki Tekko	29 Mar 1977

Displacement, tons: 270
Dimensions, feet (metres): 120·5 × 8·5 × — *(36·7 × 2·5 × —)*
Main engine: 1 diesel; 370 hp = 9 knots

Laid down 15 November 1976.

SURVEYING SHIPS

1 + (1) "FUTAMI" CLASS (AGS)

Name	No.	Builders	Commissioned
FUTAMI	AGS 5102	Mitsubishi, Shimonoseki	Mar 1979

Displacement, tons: 2 050
Dimensions, feet (metres): 317·5 × 49·2 × 24·9 *(96·8 × 15·0 × 7·6)*
Main engines: 2 diesels; 2 shafts; 4 400 hp = 16 knots
Range, miles: 14 000 at 14 knots
Complement: 105

Ordered 26 December 1976. Laid down 20 January 1978. Launched 9 August 1978. Built to merchant marine design. Bow-thruster. Second ship requested in FY 1979.

Radar: OPS 18.

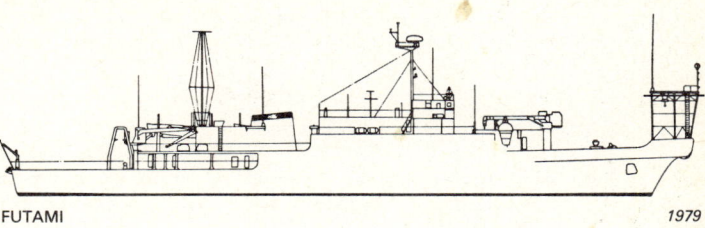
FUTAMI 1979

1 "AKASHI" CLASS (AGS)

Name	No.	Builders	Commissioned
AKASHI	AGS 5101	Nippon Steel Tube Co	25 Oct 1969

Displacement, tons: 1 420
Dimensions, feet (metres): 244·2 × 42·2 × 14·2 *(74·0 × 13·0 × 4·3)*
Main engines: 2 diesels; 2 shafts; 3 200 bhp
Speed, knots: 16
Range, miles: 16 500 at 14 knots
Complement: 65

Laid down 21 September 1968. Launched 30 May 1969.

Radar: OPS 9.

AKASHI 1974, Japanese Maritime Self-Defence Force

5 Ex-"KASADO" CLASS (AGS)

Name	No.
CHI-GO (ex-*Kasado* MSC 604)	5111
NI-GO (ex-*Habushi* MSC 608)	5112
SAN-GO (ex-*Tatara* MSC 610)	5113
YON-GO (ex-*Hirado* MSC 614)	5114
GO-GO (ex-*AMS*)	5115
ROKU-GO (ex-*Hario*)	5116

Displacement, tons: 340
Dimensions, feet (metres): 150·9 × 28 × 7·5 *(46 × 8·5 × 2·3)*
Main engines: 2 diesels; 2 shafts; 1 200 bhp = 14 knots

SAN-GO 1978

TENDERS

5 "500 TON" CLASS

Name	Laid down	Launched	Commissioned
ASU 81	10 Oct 1967	18 Jan 1968	30 Mar 1968
ASU 82	25 Sep 1968	20 Dec 1968	31 Mar 1969
ASU 83	2 Apr 1971	24 May 1971	30 Sep 1971
ASU 84	4 Feb 1972	15 June 1972	13 Sep 1972
ASU 85	20 Feb 1973	16 July 1973	19 Sep 1973

Displacement, tons: 500
Dimensions, feet (metres): 171·6 × 33·0 × 8·3 *(52·3 × 10·1 × 2·5)*
Main engines: 2 diesels; 2 shafts; 1 600 bhp = 14 knots

Training support and rescue.

Radar: OPS 19 (85); OPS 29 (84); OPS 10 (remainder).

ASU 84 1978

1 "HAYABUSA" CLASS

Name	No.	Builders	Laid down	Launched	Commissioned
HAYABUSA	ASY 91	Mitsubishi, Nagasaki	23 May 1956	20 Nov 1956	10 June 1957

Displacement, tons: 380 standard
Dimensions, feet (metres): 190·2 × 25·7 × 7 *(58 × 7·8 × 2·1)*
Main engines: 2 diesels; 4 000 bhp; 2 shafts = 20 knots
Range, miles: 3 000 at 12 knots
Complement: 75

Built under the 1954 fiscal year programme.
A gas turbine was installed in March 1962 and removed in 1970. Reconstructed as ASY (Auxiliary Special Service Yacht) beginning 1 October 1977.

Radar: Surface search: OPS 37.
Sonar: SQS 11A.

HAYABUSA (old pennant number) 1974, Japanese Maritime Self-Defence Force

6 Ex-"KASADO" CLASS

Name	No.	Builders	Commissioned
ATADA (ex-MSC 601)	YAS 56	Hitachi, Kanagawa	30 Apr 1956
YASHIRO (ex-MSC 603)	YAS 58	Nippon Steel Tube Co	10 July 1956
SHISAKA (ex-MSC 605)	YAS 62	Nippon Steel Tube Co	16 Aug 1958
KOSHIKI (ex-MSC 615)	YAS 63	Nippon Steel Tube Co	29 Jan 1962
KANAWA (ex-MSC 606)	YAS 65	Hitachi, Kanagawa	24 July 1959
MIKURA (ex-MSC 612)	YAS 67	Nippon Steel Tube Co	27 May 1960

Details as for "Kasado" class under Mine Warfare Forces.

ICEBREAKER

Name	No.	Builders	Commissioned
FUJI	5001	Nippon Steel Tube Co	15 July 1965

Displacement, tons: 5 250 standard; 7 760 normal; 8 566 full load
Dimensions, feet (metres): 328 × 72·2 × 29 *(100 × 22 × 8·8)*
Aircraft: 3 helicopters
Main engines: 4 diesel-electric; 2 shafts; 12 000 bhp = 17 knots
Oil fuel, tons: 1 900
Range, miles: 15 000 at 15 knots
Complement: 200 plus 35 scientists and observers

Antarctic Support Ship. Laid down on 28 August 1964, launched on 18 March 1965. Hangar and flight deck aft. Can cope with ice up to 8·5 ft *(2·5 m)*.

Radar: OPS 4; OPS 16.

Sonar: SQS 11A.

FUJI *1975, Japanese Maritime Self-Defence Force*

4 TUGS

YT 55, YT 56, YT 57, YT 58

Displacement, tons: 195
Dimensions, feet (metres): 84·8 × 23 × 7·5 *(25·8 × 7 × 2·3)*
Main engines: 2 diesels; 500 hp = 11 knots
Complement: 15

YT 55 entered service on 22 August 1975, YT 56 on 13 July 1976, YT 57 in 1977, YT 58 in 1978.

MARITIME SAFETY AGENCY
(KAIJO HOANCHO)

Establishment

Established in May 1948 as an external organisation of the Ministry of Transport to carry out patrol and rescue duties as well as hydrographic and navigation aids services.

Over the last 30 years a very considerable organisation with HQ in Tokyo has been built up. The Academy for the Agency is in Kure and the School in Maizuru.
The main operational branches are the Guard and Rescue Dept, the Hydrographic Dept and the Navigation Aids Dept. Regional Maritime Safety offices control the 11 Districts with their location as follows (air bases in brackets): RMS 1—Otaru (Chitose, Hakodate, Kushiro); 2—Shiogama (Sendai); 3—Yokohama (Haneda); 4—Nagoya (Ise); 5—Kobe (Yao); 6—Hiroshima (Hiroshima); 7—Kitakyushu (Fukuoka); 8—Maizuru (Miho); 9—Niigata (Niigata); 10—Kagoshima (Kagoshima); 11—Naha (Naha, Ishigaki). This organisation includes, as well as the RMS HQ, 65 MS officers, 51 MS Bases, 25 MS Detachments, 4 Control Communication Centres, 1 Traffic Advisory Centre, 5 Hydrographic Observatories and 140 Navigation Aids offices.

Commandant: Hisao Takahashi

Personnel

1978: 11 188
1979: 11 452

New Construction

Under FY 1977 programme following are to be acquired:
1—3 800 ton PL, 4 "Bihoro" class PM, 1—350 ton PM, 1 "Hiryu" class FL, 2—30 m PC, 1 "Akizuki" class PC, 2 "Chiyokaze" class CL, 1 FM, 5 SS, 2 OR.

Future Programme

The 1977-80 programme allowed for four PL (with helicopters), thirty-four 1 000 ton PLs or PMs, nineteen 30 metre PCs, seven long-range aircraft, twelve medium-range aircraft, twenty helicopters and an increase of complement from 11 200 to 12 700.

Budget

FY 1977: 76 843 million yen
FY 1978: 99 776 million yen

Strength of the Fleet

GUARD AND RESCUE SERVICE
Patrol Vessels:
    Large (PL) — 15
    Medium (PM) — 62
    Small (PS) — 19
    Fire Fighting Vessels (FL) — 5
Patrol Craft:
    Patrol Craft (PC) — 50
    Patrol Craft (CL) — 155
    Patrol Craft (CS) — 8
    Fire Fighting Craft (FM) — 8
Special Service Craft:
    Monitoring Craft (MS) — 3
    Surveillance Craft (SS) — 30
    Oil Recovery Craft (OR) — 5
    Oil Skimming Craft (OS) — 3
    Oil Boom Craft (OX) — 19
    Miscellaneous Craft (NO) — 6

HYDROGRAPHIC SERVICE
Surveying Vessels:
    Large (HL) — 3
    Medium (HM) — 3
    Small (HS) — 18

NAVIGATION AIDS SERVICE
Navigation Aids Research Vessel (LL) — 1
Buoy Tenders:
    Large (LL) — 3
    Medium (LM) — 1
Navigation Aids Tenders:
    Medium (LM) — 11
    Small (LS) — 79

AIRCRAFT
Fixed Wing:
    NAMC YS-11A — 5
    Short Skyvan — 2
    Beechcraft E 18S, G 18S and H 18 — 11
    Cessna U206G — 1
Helicopters:
    Mit-Sikorsky S 62A — 1
    Bell 212 — 14
    Bell 206B — 4
    Kaw-Bell 47G3B-KH4 — 6
    Kaw-Hughes 369HS — 2

DELETIONS

1975: *Abukuma, Fuji, Ishikari, Isuzu, Kikuchi, Kuzuryu, Oyodo, Tenryu* ("Fuji", later "Sagami" class small patrol vessels)
Suzunami, Hayanami, Hatagumo, Makigumo, Tatsugumo (patrol craft)
CS 57, 58, 115 (harbour patrol craft)
FS 01, 02, 04, 05, 06 (salvage craft)

1976: *Sagami, Yoshino, Noshiro, Kiso, Nagara, Tone* (small patrol vessels)
Yaegumo (patrol craft)
CS 105, 117 (harbour patrol craft). FS 03 (salvage craft). M 601, 611, 616, 801, 802

1977: *Mogami, Wakakusa, Shinano, Chikugo, Kumano, Kitakami, Asagumo* and *Shinkai*.
PC 34 and 35, CL 301 and 303, FS 07, M 618 and 902

1978: *Soya* (PL 107), *Genkai, Hanayuki, Mineyuki*, all CS 100 series, *Minoo, Sokai*, numerous navigation tenders.

GUARD AND RESCUE SERVICE
LARGE PATROL VESSELS
1 + 2 "SOYA" CLASS

Name	No.	Builders	Commissioned
SOYA	PL 01	Nippon Kokan, Tsurumi	Nov 1978
—	—	—	1979
—	—	—	1979

Displacement, tons: 3 750 normal
Dimensions, feet (metres): 323·4 × 51·2 × 17·1 (98·6 × 15·6 × 5·2)
Aircraft: 1 Bell 212 helicopter with hangar
Guns: 1—40 mm; 1—20 mm
Main engines: 2 diesels; 15 600 bhp; 2 shafts
Speed, knots: 20
Range, miles: 5 500 at 18 knots
Endurance: 25 days
Complement: 71

Soya (replacement for the previous ship of the same name) ordered under the FY 1977 programme laid down 12 September 1977 and launched 3 July 1978. Soya has an icebreaking capability while the two later ships are ice strengthened.

Radar: Two navigation sets.
One helicopter control set.

SOYA   1978, Maritime Safety Agency

2 "IZU" CLASS

Name	No.	Builders	Commissioned
IZU	PL 31	Hitachi Mukai Shima	July 1967
MIURA	PL 32	Maizuru	Mar 1969

Displacement, tons: 2 081 normal
Dimensions, feet (metres): 313·3 × 38 × 12·8 (95·6 × 11·6 × 3·9)
Gun: 1—40 mm
Main engines: 2 diesels; 2 shafts; 10 400 bhp = 21·6 knots
Range, miles: 14 500 at 12·7 knots; 5 000 at 21 knots
Complement: 72

Izu was laid down in August 1966, launched in January 1967. Miura was laid down in May 1968, launched in October 1968. Employed in long range rescue and patrol duties. Equipped with various types of marine instruments. Ice strengthened hull.

Radar: One navigation set.

Station: Yokohama.

IZU   1978, Maritime Safety Agency

5 "SHIRETOKO" CLASS

Name	No.	Builders	Commissioned
SHIRETOKO	PL 101	Mitsui Tamano	8 Nov 1978
ESAN	PL 102	Sumitomo	16 Nov 1978
WAKASA	PL 103	Kawaju Kobe	29 Nov 1978
YAHIKO	PL 104	Mitsubishi Shimonoseki	16 Nov 1978
MOTOBU	PL 105	Sasebo	29 Nov 1978

Displacement, tons: 1 290 normal
Dimensions, feet (metres): 255·8 × 31·5 × 10·5 (78·0 × 9·6 × 3·2)
Gun: 1—40 mm
Main engines: 2 diesels; 7 000 bhp; 2 shafts
Speed, knots: 20
Range, miles: 5 200 at 16 knots
Endurance: 25 days
Complement: 41

SHIRETOKO   1978, Maritime Safety Agency

4 "ERIMO" AND "DAIO" CLASSES

Name	No.	Builders	Commissioned
ERIMO	PL 13	Hitachi	30 Nov 1965
SATSUMA	PL 14	Hitachi	30 July 1966
DAIO	PL 15	Hitachi Maizuru	28 Sep 1973
MUROTO	PL 16	Naikai	30 Nov 1974

Displacement, tons: 1 009 normal (1 194 Daio)
Dimensions, feet (metres): 251·3 × 30·2 × 9·9 (76·6 × 9·2 × 3)
(Daio and Muroto; 251·3 × 31·5 × 10·7 (76·6 × 9·6 × 3·3))
Guns: 1—3 in/50; 1—20 mm (1—40 mm; 1—20 mm Daio and Muroto)
Main engines: Diesels; 2 shafts; 4 800 bhp = 19·78 knots
(7 000 bhp; cp propellers = 20 knots, Daio and Muroto)
Range, miles: 5 000 at 17 knots
Complement: 72

Erimo was laid down on 29 March 1965 and launched on 14 August 1965. Her structure is strengthened against ice. Employed as a patrol vessel off northern Japan. Satsuma, is assigned to guard and rescue south of Japan. Daio was laid down 18 October 1972 and launched 19 June 1973. Muroto was laid down 15 March 1974 and launched 5 August 1974.

Stations: PL 13—Kushiro; 14—Kagoshima; 15—Kushiro; 16—Kagoshima.

Radar: One navigation set.

SATSUMA   5/1977, Yoshifumi Mayama

306 JAPAN (MSA) / Guard and rescue service

1 "KOJIMA" CLASS

Name	No.	Builders	Commissioned
KOJIMA	PL 21	Kure	21 May 1964

Displacement, tons: 1 201
Dimensions, feet (metres): 228·3 × 33·8 × 10·5 (69·6 × 10·3 × 3·2)
Guns: 1—3 in; 1—40 mm; 1—20 mm
Main engines: Diesels; 2 600 hp = 17 knots
Range, miles: 6 000 at 13 knots
Complement: 17 officers, 42 men, 47 cadets

Maritime Safety Agency training ship at Kure Academy.

Radar: Two navigation sets.

KOJIMA 5/1977, Yoshifumi Mayama

2 "NOJIMA" CLASS

Name	No.	Builders	Commissioned
NOJIMA	PL 11	Uraga	30 Apr 1962
OJIKA	PL 12	Uraga	10 June 1963

Displacement, tons: 950 standard; 1 009 normal; 1 113 full load
Dimensions, feet (metres): 226·5 × 30·2 × 10·5 (69·1 × 9·2 × 3·2)
Main engines: 2 diesels; 3 000 bhp = 17·5 knots
Range, miles: 9 270 at 17 knots
Complement: 51

Nojima laid down on 27 October 1961, launched on 12 February 1962. Both employed as patrol vessels and weather ships.

Radar: One navigation set.

Stations: PL 11—Yokohama; 12—Shiogama.

OJIKA 2/1977, Yoshifumi Mayama

MEDIUM PATROL VESSELS

20 "BIHORO" CLASS

Name	No.	Builders	Commissioned
BIHORO	PM 73	Tohoku	28 Feb 1974
KUMA	PM 74	Usuki	28 Feb 1974
FUJI	PM 75	Usuki	7 Feb 1975
KABASHIMA	PM 76	Usuki	25 Mar 1975
SADO	PM 77	Tohoku	1 Feb 1975
ISHIKARI	PM 78	Tohoku	13 Mar 1976
ABUKUMA	PM 79	Tohoku	30 Jan 1976
ISUZU	PM 80	Naikai	10 Mar 1976
KIKUCHI	PM 81	Usuki	6 Feb 1976
KUZURYU	PM 82	Usuki	18 Mar 1976
HOROBUTSU	PM 83	Tohoku	27 Jan 1977
SHIRAKAMI	PM 84	Tohoku	24 Mar 1977
SAGAMI	PM 85	Naikai	30 Nov 1976
TONE	PM 86	Usuki	30 Nov 1976
YOSHINO	PM 87	Usuki	28 Jan 1977
KUROBE	PM 88	Shikoku	15 Feb 1977
CHIKUGO	PM 90	Naikai	27 Jan 1978
YAMAKUNI	PM 91	Usuki	26 Jan 1978
KATSURA	PM 92	Shikoku	15 Feb 1978
SHINANO	PM 93	Tohoku	23 Feb 1978

Displacement, tons: 636 normal
Dimensions, feet (metres): 208 × 25·6 × 8·3 (63·4 × 7·8 × 2·5)
Gun: 1—20 mm
Main engines: 2 diesels; 2 shafts; 3 000 hp = 18 knots
Range, miles: 3 200 at 18 knots
Complement: 34

Radar: Two navigation sets.

KIKUCHI 5/1976, Yoshifuma Mayama

2 "TAKATORI" CLASS

Name	No.	Builders	Commissioned
TAKATORI	PM 89	Naikai	24 Mar 1978
KUMANO	PM 94	Namura	23 Feb 1979

Displacement, tons: 634 normal
Dimensions, feet (metres): 149·9 × 30·2 × 9·3 (45·7 × 9·2 × 2·9)
Main engines: 2 diesels; 3 000 bhp; 2 shafts
Speed, knots: 15·7
Range, miles: 750 miles at 15 knots
Complement: 29

TAKATORI 1978, Japanese Maritime Safety Agency

JAPAN (MSA) / Guard and rescue service 307

7 "KUNASHIRI" CLASS

Name	No.	Builders	Commissioned
KUNASHIRI	PM 65	Maizuru	28 Mar 1969
MINABE	PM 66	Maizuru	28 Mar 1970
SAROBETSU	PM 67	Maizuru	30 Mar 1971
KAMISHIMA	PM 68	Usuki	31 Jan 1972
MIYAKE	PM 70	Tohoku	25 Jan 1973
AWAJI	PM 71	Usuki	25 Jan 1973
YAEYAMA	PM 72	Usuki	20 Dec 1972

Displacement, tons: 498 normal
Dimensions, feet: 190.4 × 24.2 × 7.9 (58.1 × 7.4 × 2.4)
Gun: 1—20 mm
Main engines: 2 diesels; 2 600 bhp = 17.6 knots
Range, miles: 3 000 at 16.9 knots
Complement: 40

Kunashiri was laid down in October 1968 and launched in December 1968. *Minabe* was laid down in October 1969.

Radar: One navigation set.

MIYAKE   10/1974, Yoshifumi Mayama

5 "MATSUURA" CLASS

Name	No.	Builders	Commissioned
MATSUURA	PM 60	Osaka	18 Mar 1961
SENDAI	PM 61	Osaka	14 Apr 1962
AMAMI	PM 62	Hitachi	29 Mar 1965
NATORI	PM 63	Hitachi	20 Jan 1966
KARATSU	PM 64	Hitachi	21 Mar 1967

Displacement, tons: 425 normal
Dimensions, feet (metres): 181.5 × 23 × 7.5 (55.4 × 7 × 2.3)
Gun: 1—20 mm
Main engines: 2 diesels; 1 400 bhp = 16.5 knots (*Matsuura, Sendai*); 1 800 bhp = 16.8 knots (*Amami, Natori*); 2 600 bhp (*Karatsu*) = 17 knots
Range, miles: 3 500 at 12 knots
Complement: 37

Matsuura was laid down on 16 October 1960, launched on 24 December 1960. *Sendai* was laid down on 23 August 1961, launched on 18 January 1962.

Radar: One navigation set.

NATORI   12/1974, Yoshifumi Mayama

7 "YAHAGI" CLASS

Name	No.	Builders	Commissioned
YAHAGI	PM 54	Niigata	31 July 1956
SUMIDA	PM 55	Niigata	30 June 1957
CHITOSE	PM 56	Niigata	30 Apr 1958
SORACHI	PM 57	Niigata	1 Mar 1959
YUBARI	PM 58	Niigata	15 Mar 1960
HORONAI	PM 59	Niigata	4 Feb 1961
OKINAWA	PM 69	Usuki	1 Oct 1970

Displacement, tons: 375.7 normal
Dimensions, feet (metres): 164.9 × 24 × 7.4 (50.3 × 7.3 × 2.3)
Gun: 1—40 mm
Main engines: 2 diesels; 1 400 bhp = 15.5 knots
Range, miles: 3 500 at 12 knots
Complement: 37

Yahagi was laid down on 9 December 1955, launched on 19 May 1956. *Chitose* was laid down on 20 September 1957, launched on 24 February 1958.
Okinawa transferred to MSA in 1972.

Radar: One navigation set.

OKINAWA   5/1976, Yoshifumi Mayama

1 "TESHIO" CLASS

Name	No.	Builders	Commissioned
TESHIO	PM 53	Uraga	19 Mar 1955

Displacement, tons: 421.5 normal
Dimensions, feet (metres): 165 × 23 × 8.2 (50.3 × 7 × 2.5)
Gun: 1—40 mm
Main engines: 2 diesels; 1 400 bhp = 15.71 knots
Range, miles: 3 800 at 12 knots
Complement: 37

Laid down on 15 September 1954, launched on 12 January 1955.

Radar: One navigation set.

TESHIO   1975, Japanese Maritime Safety Agency

2 "TOKACHI" CLASS

Name	No.	Builders	Commissioned
TOKACHI	PM 51	Harima Dockyard, Kure	31 July 1954
TATSUTA	PM 52	Harima Dockyard, Kure	10 Sep 1954

Displacement, tons: 336 standard; 381 normal (*Tokachi*) 324 standard; 369 normal (*Tatsuta*)
Dimensions, feet (metres): 170 × 21.9 × 11.2 (51.9 × 6.7 × 3.4)
Gun: 1—40 mm
Main engines: 2—4-cycle single acting diesels; 1 500 bhp = 16 knots (*Tokachi*); 1 400 bhp = 15 knots (*Tatsuta*)
Range, miles: 3 800 at 12 knots
Complement: 37

Tokachi was laid down on 14 November 1953, launched on 8 May 1954.

Radar: One navigation set.

TOKACHI   1975, Japanese Maritime Safety Agency

308 JAPAN (MSA) / Guard and rescue service

5 "CHIFURI" CLASS

Name	No.	Builders	Commissioned
CHIFURI	PM 18	Nihonkai	30 Apr 1952
KUROKAMI	PM 19	Nihonkai	31 Mar 1952
KOZU	PM 20	Niigata	9 Dec 1951
SHIKINE	PM 21	Niigata	9 Jan 1952
DAITO	PM 22	Niigata	25 Feb 1952

Displacement, tons: 465 standard; 483 normal
Dimensions, feet (metres): 182·7 × 25·2 × 8·5 (55·9 × 7·7 × 2·6)
Guns: 1—3 in/50; 1—20 mm
Main engines: 2 diesels; 1 300 bhp = 15·8 knots
Range, miles: 3 000 at 12 knots
Complement: 45

Radar: One navigation set.

DAITO 5/1977, Yoshifumi Mayama

13 "REBUN" CLASS

Name	No.	Builders	Commissioned
REBUN	PM 04	Hitachi	28 Feb 1951
IKI	PM 05	Hitachi	5 Apr 1951
OKI	PM 06	Mitsui Tamano	19 Feb 1951
HACHIJO	PM 08	Nakanihon	6 Mar 1951
AMAKUSA	PM 09	Nakanihon	8 Mar 1951
OKUSHIRI	PM 10	Hitachi	27 June 1951
KUSAKAKI	PM 11	Hitachi	30 July 1951
RISHIRI	PM 12	Fujinagata	30 June 1951
NOTO	PM 13	Fujinagata	25 Aug 1951
HEKURA	PM 14	Harima	30 June 1951
MIKURA	PM 15	Harima	19 July 1951
KOSHIKI	PM 16	Nishinihon	31 Aug 1951
HIRADO	PM 17	Nishinihon	4 Sep 1951

Displacement, tons: 450 standard; 495 normal
Dimensions, feet (metres): 171·9 × 26·5 × 8·5 (52·4 × 8·1 × 2·6)
Guns: 1—3 in/50; 1—20 mm (2—20 mm only in some)
Main engines: 2 diesels; 1 300 bhp = 15 knots
Range, miles: 3 000 at 12 knots
Complement: 45

A development of the original "Awaji" class design all of which are now scrapped. *Kusakaki* due for disposal.

Radar: One navigation set.

REBUN 1975, Japanese Maritime Safety Agency

SMALL PATROL VESSELS

14 "HIDAKA" CLASS

Name	No.	Builders	Commissioned
HIDAKA	PS 32	Azuma	23 Apr 1962
HIYAMA	PS 33	Hitachi	13 Mar 1963
TSURUGI	PS 34	Mukaijima	13 Mar 1963
ROKKO	PS 35	Shikoku	31 Jan 1964
TAKANAWA	PS 36	Hayashikane	27 Jan 1964
AKIYOSHI	PS 37	Hashihama	29 Feb 1964
KUNIMI	PS 38	Hayashikane	15 Feb 1965
TAKATSUKI	PS 39	Kurashima	30 Mar 1965
KAMUI	PS 41	Hayashikane	15 Feb 1966
ASHITAKA	PS 43	Usuki	10 Feb 1967
KURAMA	PS 44	Usuki	28 Feb 1967
IBUKI	PS 45	Usuki	5 Mar 1968
TOUMI	PS 46	Usuki	20 Feb 1968
NOBARU	PS 49	Mukaijima	10 Dec 1968

Displacement, tons: 166·2 to 164·4 standard; 169·4 normal
Dimensions, feet (metres): 111 × 20·8 × 5·5 (33·8 × 6·3 × 1·7)
Main engine: 1 diesel; 1 shaft; 690 to 700 bhp = 13·5 knots
Range, miles: 1 200 at 12 knots
Complement: 17

Hidaka was laid down on 4 October 1961, launched on 2 March 1962. *Kunimi* was built under the 1964 programme, laid down on 15 November 1964, launched on 19 December 1964.

Radar: One navigation set.

ASHITAKA 1975, Japanese Maritime Safety Agency

1 "TSUKUBA" CLASS

Name	No.	Builders	Commissioned
TSUKUBA	PS 31	Kanagawa	30 Mar 1962

Displacement, tons: 63 normal
Dimensions, feet (metres): 80·5 × 21·5 × 3·7 (24·6 × 6·6 × 1·1)
Main engines: 2 Niigata diesels; 1 800 bhp = 18 knots
Range, miles: 230 at 15 knots
Complement: 19

Radar: One navigation set.

TSUKUBA 1974, Japanese Maritime Safety Agency

JAPAN (MSA) / Guard and rescue service — Coastal patrol craft 309

3 "BIZAN" CLASS

Name	No.	Builders	Commissioned
BIZAN	PS 42	Shimonoseki	28 Mar 1966
ASAMA	PS 47	Shimonoseki	31 Jan 1969
SHIRAMINE	PS 48	Shimonoseki	15 Dec 1969

Displacement, tons: 40 normal; *Shiramine* 48 normal
Dimensions, feet (metres): 85·3 × 18·3 × 2·8 *(26 × 5·6 × 0·9)*
Gun: 1 MG aft
Main engines: 2 Mitsubishi diesels; 1 140 bhp = 21·6 knots.
Shiramine, 2 Benz (MTU) diesels; 2 200 bhp = 25 knots
Range, miles: 400 at 18 knots; *Shiramine* 250 at 25 knots
Complement: 14

Of light metal construction.

Radar: One navigation set.

BIZAN   1974, Japanese Maritime Safety Agency

1 "AKAGI" CLASS

Name	No.	Builders	Commissioned
AKAGI	PS 40	Kanagawa	24 Mar 1965

Displacement, tons: 42 normal
Dimensions, feet (metres): 78·8 × 17·8 × 3·2 *(24·0 × 5·4 × 1)*
Main engines: 2 Mercedes-Benz diesels; 2 200 bhp = 28 knots
Range, miles: 350 at 21 knots
Complement: 19

Radar: One navigation set.

AKAGI   1974, Japanese Maritime Safety Agency

COASTAL PATROL CRAFT

8 "MURAKUMO" CLASS

Name	No.	Builders	Commissioned
MURAKUMO	PC 201	Mitsubishi Shimonoseki	24 Mar 1978
KITAGUMO	PC 202	Hitachi Kanagawa	17 Mar 1978
YUKIGUMO	PC 203	Hitachi Kanagawa	27 Sep 1978
ASAGUMO	PC 204	Mitsubishi Shimonoseki	21 Sep 1978
HAYAGUMO	PC 205	Mitsubishi Shimonoseki	30 Jan 1979
AKIGUMO	PC 206	Hitachi Kanagawa	28 Feb 1979
YAEGUMO	PC 207	Mitsubishi Shimonoseki	16 Mar 1979
NATSUGUMO	PC 208	Hitachi Kanagawa	22 Mar 1979

Displacement, tons: 88
Dimensions, feet (metres): 101·7 × 20·7 × 10·8 *(31 × 6·3 × 3·3)*
Gun: 1—13 mm
Main engines: 2 MTU diesels; 2 shafts; 4 800 bhp
Speed, knots: 32
Range, miles: 350 at 28 knots
Complement: 10

MURAKUMO   1978, Japanese Maritime Safety Agency

10 "AKIZUKI" CLASS

Name	No.	Builders	Commissioned
AKIZUKI	PC 64	Mitsubishi	28 Feb 1974
SHINONOME	PC 65	Mitsubishi	25 Feb 1974
URAYUKI	PC 72	Mitsubishi	31 May 1975
SEYUKI	PC 73	Mitsubishi	31 July 1975
MAKIGUMO	PC 75	Mitsubishi	19 Mar 1976
HATAGUMO	PC 76	Mitsubishi	21 Feb 1976
HAMAZUKI	PC 77	Mitsubishi	29 Nov 1976
SOZUKI	PC 78	Mitsubishi	18 Mar 1977
SHIMANAMI	PC 79	Mitsubishi	23 Dec 1977
YUZUKI	PC 80	Mitsubishi	22 Mar 1979

Displacement, tons: 74 normal
Dimensions, feet (metres): 83·5 × 20·7 × 9·8 *(26 × 6·3 × 3)*
Main engines: 3 Mitsubishi diesels; 3 000 bhp = 22·1 knots
Range, miles: 220 at 22 knots
Complement: 10

Shimanami laid down 29 June 1977.

Radar: One navigation set.

MAKIGUMO   5/1977, Yoshifumi Mayama

310   JAPAN (MSA) / Coastal patrol craft

17 "SHIKINAMI" CLASS

Name	No.	Builders	Commissioned
SHIKINAMI	PC 54	Mitsubishi, Shimonoseki	25 Feb 1971
TOMONAMI	PC 55	Mitsubishi, Shimonoseki	30 Mar 1971
WAKANAMI	PC 56	Mitsubishi, Shimonoseki	30 Oct 1971
ISENAMI	PC 57	Hitachi, Kanagawa	29 Feb 1972
TAKANAMI	PC 58	Mitsubishi, Shimonoseki	30 Nov 1971
MUTSUKI	PC 59	Hitachi, Kanagawa	18 Dec 1972
MOCHIZUKI	PC 60	Hitachi, Kanagawa	18 Dec 1972
HARUZUKI	PC 61	Mitsubishi, Shimonoseki	30 Nov 1972
KIYOZUKI	PC 62	Mitsubishi, Shimonoseki	18 Dec 1972
URAZUKI	PC 63	Hitachi, Kanagawa	30 Jan 1973
URANAMI	PC 66	Hitachi, Kanagawa	22 Dec 1973
TAMANAMI	PC 67	Mitsubishi, Shimonoseki	25 Dec 1973
MINEGUMO	PC 68	Mitsubishi, Shimonoseki	30 Nov 1973
KIYONAMI	PC 69	Mitsubishi, Shimonoseki	30 Oct 1973
OKINAMI	PC 70	Hitachi, Kanagawa	8 Feb 1974
WAKAGUMO	PC 71	Hitachi, Kanagawa	25 Mar 1974
ASOYUKI	PC 74	Hitachi, Kanagawa	16 June 1975

Displacement, tons: 44 normal
Dimensions, feet (metres): 69 × 17·4 × 3·2 *(21 × 5·3 × 1)*
Main engines: 2 Mercedes-Benz (MTU) diesels; 2 200 bhp = 26·5 knots
Range, miles: 280 miles at near maximum speed
Complement: 10

Built completely of light alloy.

Radar: One navigation set.

KIYONAMI   1973, Japanese Maritime Safety Agency

14 "MATSUYUKI" CLASS

Name	No.	Builders	Commissioned
MATSUYUKI	PC 40	Hitachi, Kanagawa	28 Mar 1964
SHIMAYUKI	PC 41	Hitachi, Kanagawa	31 Jan 1966
TAMAYUKI	PC 42	Hitachi, Kanagawa	7 Feb 1966
HAMAYUKI	PC 43	Hitachi, Kanagawa	24 Mar 1966
YAMAYUKI	PC 44	Hitachi, Kanagawa	15 Mar 1967
KOMAYUKI	PC 45	Hitachi, Kanagawa	15 Mar 1967
UMIGIRI	PC 46	Hitachi, Kanagawa	15 Mar 1968
ASAGIRI	PC 47	Hitachi, Kanagawa	15 Mar 1968
HAMAGIRI	PC 48	Sumidagawa	19 Mar 1970
SAGIRI	PC 49	Hitachi, Kanagawa	31 Mar 1970
SETOGIRI	PC 50	Hitachi, Kanagawa	5 Mar 1970
HAYAGIRI	PC 51	Hitachi, Kanagawa	5 Mar 1970
HAMANAMI	PC 52	Sumidagawa	22 Mar 1971
MATSUNAMI	PC 53	Hitachi, Kanagawa	30 Mar 1971

Displacement, tons: 38 normal
Dimensions, feet (metres): 69 × 16·6 × 3·2 *(21 × 5·1 × 1)* (see note)
Gun: 1—13 mm
Main engines: 2 Mercedes-Benz (MTU) diesels; 2 200 bhp = 26·3 knots;
   PC 48 1 140 bhp = 14·6 knots; PC 52 = 21·8 knots; PC 53 = 20·8 knots
Range, miles: About 300 miles at near maximum speed
Complement: 10

Class: PCs 40-47 and 49-52 were built of light alloy frames with wooden hulls. PCs 48 and 52 were built of steel. PC 53 was built completely of light alloy and is sometimes classified as a separate class having larger dimensions (25 × 6 × 2·8 metres).

Radar: One navigation set.

MATSUYUKI   1975, Japanese Maritime Safety Agency

1 "ISOYUKI" CLASS

Name	No.	Builders	Commissioned
ISOYUKI	PC 39	Sumidagawa	Feb 1960

Displacement, tons: 46
Dimensions, feet (metres): 72 × 17·6 × 3·2 *(22 × 5·4 × 1)*
Main engines: 2 diesels; 1 800 bhp = 21·3 knots
Complement: 13

Light wooden hull.

Radar: One navigation set.

155 "15 METRE" TYPE

CL 21-156, 201-204, 304, 306-319

Displacement, tons: 20·2 full load
Dimensions, feet (metres): 49·2 × 13·5 × 3·1 *(15 × 4·1 × 1)*
Main engines: 2 diesels; 2 shafts; 520 bhp = 19 knots
Range, miles: 160 at 15 knots
Complement: 6

For coastal patrol and rescue duties. Built of high tensile steel.

Classes: This total includes six different classes of similar characteristics— "Yukikaze" (6) "Yakaze" (31), "Chiyokaze" (96), "Nogekaze" (4), "Hamakaze" (8), "Asashimo" (10).

Completions: 1962—2; 1963—2; 1964—3; 1965—3; 1966—6; 1967—6; 1968—6; 1969—9; 1970—13; 1971—26; 1972—21; 1973—21; 1974—4; 1975—7; 1976—5. Nineteen others of similar characteristics but built between 1948-53 were transferred to MSA by other ministries 1965-70.

Names: All but 24 of these craft have names. For convenience these have not been listed but are available.

Radar: One navigation set.

CL 201—YAMAYURI   1978, Japanese Maritime Safety Agency

FIRE FIGHTING VESSELS AND CRAFT

5 "HIRYU" CLASS

Name	No.	Builders	Commissioned
HIRYU	FL 01	Asano Dockyard	4 Mar 1969
SHORYU	FL 02	Asano Dockyard	4 Mar 1970
NANRYU	FL 03	Asano Dockyard	4 Mar 1971
KAIRYU	FL 04	Asano Dockyard	18 Mar 1977
SUIRYU	FL 05	Asano Dockyard	24 Mar 1978

Displacement, tons: 251 normal
Dimensions, feet (metres): 90·2 × 34·1 × 7·2 *(27·5 × 10·4 × 2·2)*
Main engines: 2 sets diesels; 2 200 bhp = 13·5 knots
Range, miles: 395 at 13·4 knots
Complement: 14

Hiryu, a catamaran type fire boat, was laid down in October 1968, launched 21 January 1969. Designed and built for fire fighting services to large tankers. *Shoryu* was launched on 18 January 1970, *Nanryu* on 16 January 1971, and *Kairyu* on 18 January 1977. *Suiryu* was ordered 7 June 1976.

Radar: One navigation set.

HIRYU   5/1976, Yoshifumi Mayama

8 "NUNOBIKI" CLASS

Name	No.	Builders	Commissioned
NUNOBIKI	FM 01	Yokohama Yacht Co Ltd	25 Feb 1974
YODO	FM 02	Yokohama Yacht Co Ltd	30 Mar 1975
OTOWA	FM 03	Sumidagawa	25 Dec 1974
SHIRAITO	FM 04	Yokohama Yacht Co Ltd	25 Feb 1975
KOTOBIKI	FM 05	Yokohama Yacht Co Ltd	31 Jan 1976
NACHI	FM 06	Sumidagawa	14 Feb 1976
KEGON	FM 07	Yokohama Yacht Co Ltd	29 Jan 1977
MINOO	FM 08	Sumidagawa	27 Jan 1978

Displacement, tons: 87
Dimensions, feet (metres): 75·4 × 19·7 × 10·5 *(23 × 6 × 3·2)*
Main engines: 1 Mercedes-Benz (MTU) diesel plus 2 Nissan diesels; 1 100 bhp + 500 bhp = 14 knots
Range, miles: 1 800 at 14 knots
Complement: 12

Radar: One navigation set.

OTOWA   5/1976, Yoshifumi Mayama

HYDROGRAPHIC SERVICE

Name	No.	Builders	Commissioned
SHOYO	HL 01	Hitachi, Maizuru	26 Feb 1972

Displacement, tons: 2 044 normal
Dimensions, feet (metres): 262·4 × 40·3 × 13·8 *(80 × 12·3 × 4·2)*
Main engines: 2 Fuji V-12 diesels; 4 800 hp; 1 shaft = 17·4 knots
Range, miles: 8 340 at 16 knots
Complement: 44

Launched 18 September 1971. Fully equipped for all types of hydrographic and oceanographic work. Based at Tokyo.

Radar: Two navigation sets.

SHOYO   1973, Japanese Maritime Safety Agency

Name	No.	Builders	Commissioned
TAKUYO	HL 02	Niigata	12 Mar 1957

Displacement, tons: 853 normal
Dimensions, feet (metres): 204·7 × 31·2 × 10·7 *(62·4 × 9·5 × 3·3)*
Main engines: 2 diesels; 1 300 bhp = 14 knots
Range, miles: 8 000 at 12 knots
Complement: 36

Laid down on 19 May 1956, launched on 19 December 1956. Based at Tokyo.

Radar: One navigation set.

TAKUYO   1975, Japanese Maritime Safety Agency

Name	No.	Builders	Commissioned
MEIYO	HL 03	Nagoya	15 Mar 1963

Displacement, tons: 486 normal
Measurement, tons: 360 gross
Dimensions, feet (metres): 146 × 26·5 × 9·5 *(44·5 × 8·1 × 2·9)*
Main engine: 1 diesel; 700 bhp = 12 knots
Range, miles: 5 000 at 11 knots
Complement: 25

Laid down on 14 September 1962, launched 22 December 1962. Cp propeller. Based at Tokyo.

Radar: One navigation set.

MEIYO   1975, Japanese Maritime Safety Agency

312 JAPAN (MSA) / Hydrographic service — Navigation aids service

Name	No.	Builders	Commissioned
KAIYO	HM 06	Nagoya	14 Mar 1964

Displacement, tons: 378 normal
Dimensions, feet (metres): 146 × 26·5 × 7·8 (44·5 × 8·1 × 2·4)
Main engine: 1 diesel; 450 bhp = 12 knots
Range, miles: 6 100 at 11 knots
Complement: 23

Cp propeller.

Radar: One navigation set.

KAIYO   2/1976, Yoshifumi Mayama

Name	No.	Builders	Commissioned
TENYO	HM 05	Yokohama Yacht Co	30 Mar 1961

Displacement, tons: 171 normal
Dimensions, feet (metres): 99·1 × 19·2 × 9·2 (30·2 × 5·9 × 2·8)
Main engines: Diesels; 230 bhp = 10 knots
Range, miles: 3 160 at 10 knots
Complement: 16

Radar: One navigation set.

TENYO   1975, Japanese Maritime Safety Agency

Name	No.	Builders	Commissioned
HEIYO	HM 04	Shimuzu Dockyard	22 Mar 1955

Displacement, tons: 77 normal
Dimensions, feet (metres): 76·5 × 14·5 × 8 (23·3 × 4·4 × 2·4)
Main engine: 1 diesel; 150 bhp = 9 knots
Range, miles: 670 at 9 knots
Complement: 9

Radar: One navigation set.

HEIYO   1975, Japanese Maritime Safety Agency

SURVEYING CRAFT

11 "HAMASHIO" CLASS

HS 01-11

Completed 1969-72. Of 10 metres.

1 "HASHIMA" CLASS

HS 17

Completed 1951 by Yamanishi. Of 10 metres.

2 "FUKAE" CLASS

HS 20 and 21

Completed 1951. Of 12 metres.

5 "AKASHI" CLASS

HS 31-35

Completed 1973-75. Of 15 metres.

NAVIGATION AIDS SERVICE

Name	No.	Builders	Commissioned
TSUSHIMA	LL 01	Mitsui, Tamano	9 Sep 1977

Displacement, tons: 1 834 normal
Dimensions, feet (metres): 246·0 × 41 × 13·8 (75 × 12·5 × 4·2)
Main engine: 1 diesel; 4 000 shp; 1 shaft = 15·5 knots
Range, miles: 10 000 at 15 knots
Endurance: 30 days
Complement: 54

Built under FY 1975 programme. Laid down 10 June 1976, launched 7 April 1977. Replacement for *Wakakusa* as Lighthouse Supply Ship, taking her pennant number. Fitted with bow thruster and tank stabilisers. Equipped with modern electronic instruments for carrying out research on electronic aids to navigation.

Armament: Can ship one 76 mm and two 40 mm.

TSUSHIMA   1978, Japanese Maritime Safety Agency

JAPAN (MSA) / Navigation aids service   313

Name	No.	Builders	Commissioned
—	LL—	Sasebo	1979

Displacement, tons: 800 normal
Dimensions, feet (metres): 180·4 × 34·8 × 8·7 *(55 × 10·6 × 2·7)*
Main engines: 2 diesels; 2 shafts; 1 300 bhp
Range, miles: 3 000 at 13 knots
Complement: 31

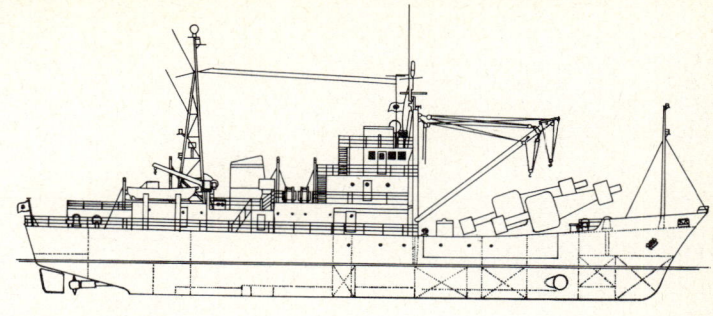

NEW CONSTRUCTION LL   1978

Name	No.	Builders	Commissioned
KAIO	LL 13	Namura	24 Mar 1955

Displacement, tons: 730
Dimensions, feet (metres): 165 × 33·2 × 8·3 *(50·2 × 10·1 × 2·5)*
Main engines: 2 diesels; 2 shafts; 560 hp = 11·6 knots
Range, miles: 6 730 at 10 knots
Complement: 28

KAIO   1978, Japanese Maritime Safety Agency

Name	No.	Builders	Commissioned
GINGA	LL 12	Osaka	30 June 1954

Displacement, tons: 500 normal
Dimensions, feet (metres): 135·5 × 30·8 × 8·5 *(41·3 × 9·4 × 2·6)*
Main engines: 2 diesels; 420 bhp = 11·26 knots
Range, miles: 2 800 at 10 knots
Complement: 38

Ginga was laid down on 11 November 1953 and launched on 6 May 1954. Equipped with 15 ton derrick for laying buoys. Rated as Navigation Aid Vessel (Buoy Tender).

Radar: One navigation set.

GINGA   1971, Japanese Maritime Safety Agency

Name	No.	Builders	Commissioned
HOKUTO	LL 11	Kawasaki	12 Mar 1952

Displacement, tons: 616 standard
Dimensions, feet (metres): 153·8 × 33·8 × 8·9 *(46·9 × 10·3 × 2·7)*
Main engines: Recip; 400 ihp = 10·4 knots
Range, miles: 1 821
Complement: 38

HOKUTO   9/1975, Yoshifumi Mayama

Name	No.	Builders	Commissioned
MYOJO	LM 11	Asano	25 Mar 1974

Displacement, tons: 303 normal
Dimensions, feet (metres): 88·6 × 39·4 × 8·8 *(27 × 12 × 2·7)*
Main engines: 2 diesels; 600 bhp = 11·1 knots
Range, miles: 1 360 at 10 knots
Complement: 49

Completed in March 1974 to replace an identical ship of the same name, completed in 1967, which was lost in collision April 1972. Catamaran type buoy tender, propelled by cp propellers, this ship is employed in maintenance and position adjustment service to floating aids to navigation.

MYOJO   5/1976, Yoshifumi Mayama

NAVIGATION AIDS TENDERS

Name	No.	Builders	Commissioned
ZUIUN	LM 101	Nihonkai	Nov 1962
REIUN	LM 102	Kanto Kogyo	Nov 1971
SEKIUN	LM 105	Usuki	Mar 1970
HAKUUN	LM 106	Sumidagawa	Feb 1978
TOUN	LM 107	Sumidagawa	Mar 1959
REIMEI	LM 108	Shikoku	Mar 1966
SHOUN	LM 109	Usuki	Mar 1966
SEIUN	LM 110	Yokohama Yacht	Mar 1968
HOUN	LM 111	Usuki	Mar 1970
AYABANE	LM 112	Shimoda	Dec 1972
GENUN	LM 113	Izumi	Mar 1973

HAKUUN　　　　　　　　　　　　　　　　　1978, Japanese Maritime Safety Agency

MISCELLANEOUS

MONITORING CRAFT

KINUGASA FS 01　　**SAIKAI** FS 02　　**KATUREN** FS 03

First two 10 metre catamaran craft, 03 of 16 metres.

SURVEILLANCE CRAFT

SS 01, 02, 04, 05-22

6 metre craft completed between 1972-1976.

OIL SKIMMERS

OS 01-03

Completed 1974-75 by Lockheed.

OIL BOOM CRAFT

M 101-119

20 metre dumb barges completed 1974-76.

UTILITY CRAFT

M 603, 615, 618, 804

Of varying sizes about 6 metres. M 803 renamed *Wakaba* operates for MSA Academy at Kure.

OIL RECOVERY CRAFT

SHIRASAGI　OR 01

Displacement, tons: 140
Dimensions, feet (metres): 72·3 × 21 × 2·8 *(22·0 × 6·4 × 0·8)*
Main engines: 2 diesels; 780 bhp = 10 knots
Complement: 6

Completed 31 January 1977 by Sumidagawa.

SHIRASAGI　　　　　　　　　　　　　　　　　5/1977, Yoshifumi Mayama

JORDAN

Ministerial

Minister of Defence:
　Mudar Badran (Premier)

Diplomatic Representation

Defence Attaché in London:
　Brigadier Mohammad Hussein

Coastal Guard

It was officially stated in 1969 that Jordan had no naval force known as such, but the Jordan Coastal Guard, sometimes called the Jordan Sea Force, took orders directly from the Director of Operations at General Headquarters. There is no longer a flotilla in the Dead Sea.

Base

Aqaba

Personnel

(a) 1979: 300 officers and men
(b) Voluntary service

Mercantile Marine

Lloyd's Register of Shipping:
　3 vessels of 2 295 tons gross

LIGHT FORCES

HUSSEIN ABDALLAH

Wooden hulled of 40 ft *(12 m)* acquired in August 1974.

1 BERTRAM TYPE (COASTAL PATROL CRAFT)

Displacement, tons: 7
Dimensions, feet (metres): 30·4 × 10·8 × 1·6 *(9·2 × 3·3 × 0·5)*
Guns: 1—12·7 mm; 1—7·2 mm
Main engines: Diesels = 24 knots
Complement: 8

Glass fibre hull.

4 "25 ft" TYPE (COASTAL PATROL CRAFT)

Aluminium hulls.

4 PATROL CRAFT

Wooden hulled craft of about 18 ft—unarmed.

KAMPUCHEA (CAMBODIA)

The Marine Royale Khmer was established on 1 March 1954 and became Marine Nationale Khmer on 9 October 1970. With the imminent victory of the forces of Khmer Rouge in April-May 1975, several ships (listed in Deletions section) escaped from Khmer waters.
Originally Cambodia, became known as the Khmer Republic and is now officially called Democratic Kampuchea.

Note: The facts of this force are very uncertain. There is no postal link with Kampuchea now and what follows is probably "the worst possible case". It is probable that less than a third of the craft listed is operational, although the new links with Viet-Nam may have provided some much-needed spares. Nevertheless neither navy has much operational value.

Personnel
(a) 1975: 11 000 officers and men including Marine Corps (4 000 officers and men) (current situation not known)
(b) 18 months national service

Mercantile Marine
Lloyd's Register of Shipping:
3 vessels of 3 558 tons gross

DELETIONS

Large Patrol Craft
1975 E 311 to Thailand (16 May), E 312 to Subic Bay, Philippines (2 May) P111 and P112 to Subic Bay (17 April) and to Philippine Navy

Light Forces
1975 VR1 and VR2 (ex-Yugoslav "101" class) believed sunk by US aircraft during *Mayaguez* incident (13 May)

LIGHT FORCES

17 Ex-US "SWIFT" CLASS (COASTAL PATROL CRAFT)
Displacement, tons: 22·5
Dimensions, feet (metres): 50 × 13 × 3·5 *(15 × 4 × 1·1)*
Guns: 1—81 mm mortar; 3—50 cal MG
Main engines: 2 diesels; 960 hp; 2 shafts = 28 knots
Complement: 6

Transferred in 1972-73.

2 Ex-US AVR TYPE (COASTAL PATROL CRAFT)
VR 3   VR 4

Displacement, tons: 30
Dimensions, feet (metres): 63 × 13 × 4·6 *(19·1 × 4 × 1·4)*
Guns: 4—12·7 mm MG
Main engines: General Motors diesel; 500 bhp = 15 knots
Complement: 12

65 Ex-US PBR MARK 1 and II (RIVER PATROL CRAFT)
Displacement, tons: 8
Dimensions, feet (metres): 32 × 11 × 2·6 *(9·8 × 3·4 × 0·8)*
Guns: 3—50 MG; 1 grenade launcher
Main engines: 2 geared diesels; water jets = 25 knots
Complement: 5

Transferred 1973-74.

3 Ex-CHINESE "YU-LIN" CLASS (COASTAL PATROL CRAFT)
VP 1   VP 2   VP 3

Displacement, tons: 7·7 standard; 9·7 full load
Dimensions, feet (metres): 40 × 9·5 × 3·5 *(13 × 2·9 × 1·1)*
Guns: 2—14·5 mm; 2—12·7 mm
Main engine: Diesel; 300 bhp = 24 knots
Complement: 10

Transferred from the People's Republic of China in January 1968. Built in Shanghai.

1 Ex-HDML TYPE (COASTAL PATROL CRAFT)
VP 212 (ex-*VP 748*, ex-*HDML 1223*)

Displacement, tons: 46 standard; 54 full load
Dimensions, feet (metres): 72 × 16 × 5·5 *(22 × 4·9 × 1·7)*
Guns: 2—20 mm; 4—7·5 mm MG
Main engines: 2 diesels; 2 shafts; 300 bhp = 10 knots
Complement: 8

Former British harbour defence motor launch of the HDML type. Transferred from the British Navy to the French Navy in 1950 and again transferred from the French Navy to the MNK in 1956.

AMPHIBIOUS VESSELS

2 Ex-US "LCU 1466" CLASS
T 917 (ex-US *YFU*, ex-*LCU 1577*)
SKILAK T 920 (ex-US *YFU 73*)

Displacement, tons: 320 full load
Dimensions, feet (metres): 119 × 32·7 × 5 *(36·3 × 10 × 1·5)*
Guns: 2—20 mm
Main engines: Diesels; 675 bhp; 3 shafts = 10 knots
Complement: 13

T 917 transferred October 1969. T 920 in November 1973.

1 EDIC TYPE
T 916 (ex-*EDIC 606*)

Displacement, tons: 292 standard; 650 full load
Dimensions, feet (metres): 193·5 × 39·2 × 4·5 *(59 × 12 × 1·4)*
Guns: 1—81 mm mortar; 2—12·7 mm MG
Main engines: 2 MGO diesels; 2 shafts; 1 000 bhp = 10 knots
Complement: 16 (1 officer, 15 men)

Completed and transferred from the French Government in August 1969.

4 Ex-US "LCU 501" CLASS
T 914 (ex-US *LCU 783*)   T 918 (ex-US *LCU 646*)
T 915 (ex-US *LCU 1421*)   T 919 (ex-US *LCU 1385*)

Displacement, tons: 180 standard; 360 full load
Dimensions, feet (metres): 119 × 34 × 6 *(36·3 × 10·4 × 1·8)*
Guns: 2—20 mm
Main engines: 3 diesels; 3 shafts; 675 bhp = 8 knots
Complement: 12

LCU 783 and LCU 1421 were transferred on 31 May 1962. T919 (ex-US *LCU 1577*) was sunk by a mine on 5 May 1970, her number being taken by new T919 transferred in November 1972 at same time as T918. Both these had operated as YFU—68 and 56 respectively.

MISCELLANEOUS

1 TUG
KINGOUIE R 911 (ex-US *YTL 556*)

2 FLOATING DOCKS
One of 350 tons from France in 1955.
One of 1 000 tons from USA in 1972.

3 SURVEYING CRAFT
Craft of 14, 15 and 16 tons.

316 KENYA / Introduction — Light forces

KENYA

Ministerial

Minister of Defence:
  James Samuel Gichuru

Establishment

The Kenya Navy was inaugurated on 12 December 1964, the first anniversary of Kenya's independence.

Administration

Commander, Kenya Navy:
  Lieutenant Colonel E. S. Mbilu

General

With a coastline of only 350 miles the present force is probably adequate for coastal patrol duties. With a 200 mile limit to think about and with the three 31 metre craft probably well into the second half of their lives the possibility of some type of corvette replacement must be on the cards. Something of at least 500 tons would be necessary for offshore work, particularly in the NE Monsoon season.
The Mombasa dry dock with a capacity of 18 000 tons was opened in March 1978.

Personnel

(a) 1979: 350 officers and men
(b) Voluntary service

Prefix to Ships' Names

KNS

Base

Mombasa

Mercantile Marine

Lloyd's Register of Shipping:
  20 vessels of 15 224 tons gross

LIGHT FORCES

3 BROOKE MARINE 32·6 metre TYPE (LARGE PATROL CRAFT)

Name	No.	Builders	Commissioned
MADARAKA	P 3121	Brooke Marine, Lowestoft	16 June 1975
JAMHURI	P 3122	Brooke Marine, Lowestoft	16 June 1975
HARAMBEE	P 3123	Brooke Marine, Lowestoft	22 Aug 1975

Displacement, tons: 120 standard; 145 full load
Dimensions, feet (metres): 107 × 20 × 5·6 *(32·6 × 6·1 × 1·7)*
Missiles: See note
Guns: 2—40 mm
Main engines: 2 Paxman 16-cyl Valenta diesels; 5 400 bhp; 2 shafts = 25·5 knots
Range, miles: 2 500 at 12 knots
Complement: 21 (3 officers, 18 men)

Ordered 10 May 1973. *Madaraka* launched 28 January 1975, *Jamhuri* 14 March 1975, *Harambee* 2 May 1975.

Missiles: It is reported that these craft are being fitted with Gabriel missiles.

HARAMBEE   7/1976, Michael D. J. Lennon

BROOKE MARINE 37·5 metre TYPE (LARGE PATROL CRAFT)

Name	No.	Builders	Commissioned
MAMBA	P 3100	Brooke Marine, Lowestoft	7 Feb 1974

Displacement, tons: 125 standard; 160 full load
Dimensions, feet (metres): 123 × 22·5 × 5·2 *(37·5 × 6·9 × 1·6)*
Missiles: See note
Guns: 2—40 mm Bofors
Main engines: 2 Paxman 16-cyl Ventura diesels; 4 000 hp = 25 knots
Range, miles: 3 300 at 13 knots
Complement: 25 (3 officers, 22 men)

Laid down 17 February 1972.

Missiles: It is reported that *Mamba* is being fitted with Gabriel missiles.

MAMBA   1974

3 VOSPER 31 metre TYPE (LARGE PATROL CRAFT)

Name	No.	Builders	Commissioned
SIMBA	P 3110	Vosper Ltd, Portsmouth	23 May 1966
CHUI	P 3112	Vosper Ltd, Portsmouth	7 July 1966
NDOVU	P 3117	Vosper Ltd, Portsmouth	27 July 1966

Displacement, tons: 96 standard; 109 full load
Dimensions, feet (metres): 103 × 19·8 × 5·8 *(31·4 × 6 × 1·8)*
Guns: 2—40 mm Bofors
Main engines: 2 Paxman Ventura diesels; 2 800 bhp = 24 knots
Range, miles: 1 500 at 16 knots
Complement: 23 (3 officers and 20 ratings)

The first ships specially built for the Kenya Navy. Ordered on 28 October 1964. *Simba* was launched on 9 September 1965. All three left Portsmouth on 22 August 1966 and arrived at their base in Mombasa on 4 October 1966. Air-conditioned. Fitted with roll damping fins.

SIMBA   1973, Kenyan Navy

KOREA—North
(Democratic People's Republic)

Ministerial

Minister of Peoples Armed Forces:
O Chin-u

Administration

Commander of the Navy:
Rear-Admiral Yu Chang Kwon

Personnel

a) 1979: 30 300 officers and men (40 000 reserves)
b) 5 years national service

Bases

Main: Wonsan (East), Nampo (West)
Minor: Ch'ongjin, Haeju, Najin (Naval Academy), Munchon, Pipa-got, Cha-ho, Mayang Do, Sagon-ni, Kimchaek, Kosong, Songjon Pando, Yoko Ri, Chodo, Kwangyang Ni.

Mercantile Marine

Lloyd's Register of Shipping:
21 vessels of 90 078 tons gross

Strength of the Fleet

Type	Active	Building
Submarines—Patrol	16	2
Frigates	4	—
Fast Attack Craft—Missile	18	—
Fast Attack Craft—Torpedo	165	2
Fast Attack Craft—Gun	134	4
Large Patrol Craft	26	—
Coastal Patrol Craft	30	—
LCAs (Large)	70	—
Trawlers etc.	105	—

SUBMARINES

Note: Up to five midget submarines reported as built in North Korea since 1974.

12 + 2 Ex-CHINESE "ROMEO" CLASS (PATROL TYPE)

Displacement, tons: 1 400 surfaced; 1 800 dived
Dimensions, feet (metres): 251·9 × 23·9 × 18 *(76·8 × 7·3 × 5·5)*
Torpedo tubes: 6—21 in *(533 mm)* (bow); 2—21 in *(533 mm)* (stern); 18 torpedoes
Main machinery: 2 diesels; 4 000 bhp; 2 electric motors; 4 000 hp; 2 shafts
Speed, knots: 17 surfaced; 16 dived
Range, miles: 16 000 at 10 knots (surfaced)
Complement: 54

Two transferred from China 1973, two in 1974 and two in 1975. Local building at Mayang Do provided two more in 1976. Continuing programme with slightly different dimensions etc. Stationed on West coast (Yellow Sea).

Radar: Snoop Plate.

Sonar: Hercules.

"ROMEO" Class

4 Ex-SOVIET "WHISKEY" CLASS (PATROL TYPE)

Displacement, tons: 1 080 surfaced; 1 350 dived
Dimensions, feet (metres): 249·3 × 22 × 15 *(76 × 6·7 × 4·6)*
Torpedo tubes: 6—21 in (4 bow, 2 stern); 18 torpedoes carried normally (or up to 40 mines)
Main machinery: 2 diesels; 4 000 bhp; 2 electric motors; 2 700 hp; 2 shafts
Speed, knots: 17 surfaced; 15 dived
Range, miles: 13 000 at 8 knots (surfaced)
Complement: 54

Stationed on East Coast (Sea of Japan).

"WHISKEY" Class

FRIGATES

4 "NAJIN" CLASS

025 3026 3027 +1

Displacement, tons: 1 500
Dimensions, feet (metres): 328 × 32·8 × 8·9 *(100 × 10 × 2·7)*
Guns: 2—3·9 in *(100 mm)*/56 (single); 4—57 mm (twin); 4—25 mm (twin vertical); 8—14·5 mm (twins)
A/S weapons: 2—MBU 1800; 2 DC racks; 2 A/S mortars
Torpedo tubes: 3—21 in *(533 mm)*
Mines: 30 (estimated)
Main engines: 2 diesels; 15 000 bhp; 3 shafts
Speed, knots: 26
Range, miles: 4 000 at 14 knots
Complement: 180

Built in North Korea. First laid down 1971, completed 1973; second completed 1975; third completed 1976; fourth laid down 1976.

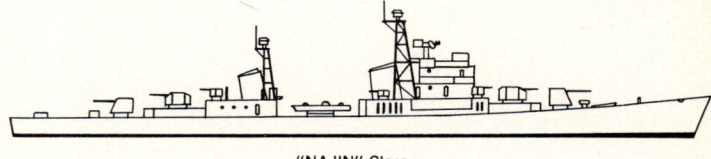

"NAJIN" Class

Radar: Surface search: Skin Head, Pot Head.
IFF: Ski Pole.

Sonar: Hull-mounted and VDS.

LIGHT FORCES

8 Ex-SOVIET "OSA 1" CLASS (FAST ATTACK CRAFT—MISSILE)

Displacement, tons: 165 standard; 200 full load
Dimensions, feet (metres): 127·9 × 26·6 × 5·9 *(39·0 × 8·1 × 1·8)*
Missiles: SSM; 4-SS-N-2 (single cells)
Guns: 4—30 mm (1 twin fwd, and aft)
Main engines: 3 diesels; 12 000 bhp = 36 knots
Range, miles: 800 at 25
Complement: 30

The combination of the "Osa" flotilla and the "Komar" units both armed with the very potent 23 mile range Styx missile, provides a powerful striking force on the South Korean border and within 250 miles of Japan.

Radar: Fire control: Square Tie, Drum Tilt.
IFF: High Pole and Square Head.

"OSA 1" Class

10 Ex-SOVIET "KOMAR" CLASS (FAST ATTACK CRAFT—MISSILE)

Displacement, tons: 68 standard; 75 full load
Dimensions, feet (metres): 87·9 × 20·3 × 4·9 *(26·8 × 6·2 × 1·5)*
Missiles: SSM; 2-SS-N-2 (single cells)
Guns: 2—25 mm (1 twin fwd)
Main engines: 4 diesels; 4 shafts; 4 800 bhp = 40 knots
Range, miles: 400 at 30 knots
Complement: 19

See note under "Osa" class above. Another class, "Sohung", may be a North Korean version of the "Komar".

Radar: Fire control: Square Tie.
IFF: High Pole and Dead Duck.

"KOMAR" Class

2 Ex-SOVIET "TRAL" CLASS (LARGE PATROL CRAFT)

Displacement, tons: 475
Dimensions, feet (metres): 203·5 pp × 23·8 × 7·8 *(62 × 7·2 × 2·4)*
Guns: 1—3·9 in *(100 mm)*/56; 3—37 mm (singles); 4—12·7 mm MG
A/S weapons: 2 DC racks
Mines: 30
Main engines: 2 diesels; 2 800 hp; 2 shafts
Speed, knots: 18
Complement: 52

An elderly class of Fleet Minesweepers of which eight were transferred by USSR in mid-1950s. Used for escort purposes.
All originally commissioned in 1938. One (ex-*Strela*, ex-T 1) was transferred to Soviet Pacific Fleet via Panama Canal in 1939 and another (ex-*Paravan* ex-T 5) at the same time via Suez.

Radar: Surface search: Skin Head.
IFF: Yard Rake.

Sonar: Hull-mounted and VDS.

"TRAL" Class

3 "SARIWAN" CLASS (LARGE PATROL CRAFT)

725   726   727(?)

Displacement, tons: 475
Dimensions, feet (metres): 203·7 × 23·9 × 7·8 *(62·1 × 7·3 × 2·4)*
Guns: 1—85 mm; 2—57 mm (twin); 12/16—14·5 mm (quad—poss. ZPU-4 type)
A/S weapons: DC rails
Mines: 30
Main engines: 2 diesels; 3 000 bhp; 2 shafts
Speed, knots: 21 (estimated)
Complement: 65-70

Built in North Korea in the mid-1960s.

Radar: Surface search: Skin Head.
Navigation: Don 2.
IFF: Ski Pole or Yard Rake.

Sonar: Hull-mounted.

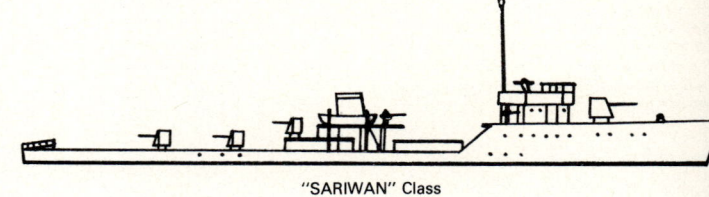

"SARIWAN" Class

4 Ex-CHINESE "HAI NAN" CLASS (LARGE PATROL CRAFT)

Displacement, tons: 360 standard; 400 full load
Dimensions, feet (metres): 197 × 24 × 6·1 *(60 × 7·4 × 2·1)*
Guns: 2—3 in *(76 mm)*; 4—25 mm (twins)
A/S weapons: 4 MBU 1800; 2 DCT; 2 DC racks
Main engines: Diesels; 8 000 shp = 28 knots
Range, miles: 1 000 at 10 knots (est)
Complement: 60

Transferred in 1975 (2), 1976 (2).

"HAI NAN" Class

KOREA (DPR) / Light forces 319

15 SOVIET and KOREAN "SO 1" CLASS (LARGE PATROL CRAFT)

Displacement, tons: 170 light; 215 normal
Dimensions, feet (metres): 138·6 × 20·0 × 5·9 *(42·3 × 6·1 × 1·8)*
Guns: 1—85 mm; 2—37 mm (twin); 4—14·5 mm MG (Korean version);
  4—25 mm L 70 (Soviet version)
Main engines: 3 diesels; 7 500 bhp = 28 knots
Range, miles: 1 100 at 13 knots
Complement: 31

Six transferred by USSR in 1957-61. Remainder built in North Korea—of modified form.

Radar: Fire control: Pot Head.
Navigation: Don 2.
IFF: Ski Pole.

Soviet "SO 1" Class (guns differ in Korean version) 1972

1 or 2 Ex-SOVIET "ARTILLERIST" CLASS (LARGE PATROL CRAFT)

Displacement, tons: 240
Dimensions, feet (metres): 160·8 × 19 × 6·5 *(49 × 5·8 × 2)*
Guns: 1—3·9 in *(100 mm)*; 2—37 mm (singles); 4/6—25 mm (twin, vertical)
Main engines: 2 diesels; 3 300 bhp; 2 shafts
Speed, knots: 25
Complement: 30

Transferred in 1950s.

8 Ex-CHINESE "SHANGHAI" CLASS (FAST ATTACK CRAFT—GUN)

Displacement, tons: 120 standard; 155 full load
Dimensions, feet (metres): 128 × 18 × 5·6 *(39 × 5·5 × 1·7)*
Guns: 4—37 mm (twin); 4—25 mm (abaft bridge);
  2—3 in *(75 mm)* recoilless rifles (bow)
A/S weapons: 8 DC
Main engines: 4 diesels; 4 800 bhp = 30 knots
Mines: Rails can be fitted for 10 mines
Range, miles: 800 at 17 knots
Complement: 25

Acquired from China since 1967.

Radar: Surface search: Skin Head.

"SHANGHAI" Class

4 "CHODO" CLASS (FAST ATTACK CRAFT—GUN)

Displacement, tons: 130 (estimated)
Dimensions, feet (metres): 140 × 19 × 8·5 *(42·7 × 5·8 × 2·6)*
Guns: 4—37 mm (single); 4—25 mm (twin, vertical)
Main engines: Diesels; 2 shafts; 6 000 bhp
Speed, knots: 25
Range, miles: 2 000 at 10 knots
Complement: 40

Built in North Korea in mid-1960s.

Radar: Surface search: Skin Head.
Navigation: Don.

"CHODO" Class

8 Ex-CHINESE "SWATOW" CLASS (FAST ATTACK CRAFT—GUN)

Displacement, tons: 80
Dimensions, feet (metres): 83·5 × 19 × 6·6 *(25·5 × 5·8 × 2)*
Guns: 4—37 mm (twins); 4—12·7 mm (twins) or 2—76 mm recoilless rifles (twin)
A/S weapons: 8 DC
Main engines: 4 diesels; 3 000 bhp = 28 knots
Range, miles: 500 at 28 knots
Complement: 17

Transferred from China in 1968.

Radar: Surface search: Skin Head.
Navigation: Don.

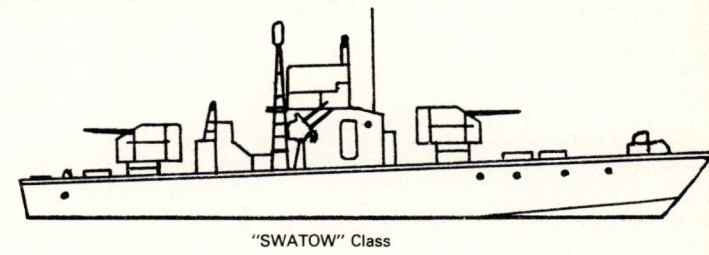

"SWATOW" Class

4 "K-48" CLASS (FAST ATTACK CRAFT—GUN)

Displacement, tons: 110 (estimated)
Dimensions, feet (metres): 125 × 18 × 4·9 *(38·1 × 5·5 × 1·5)*
Guns: 1—3 in *(76 mm)*/50 (fwd); 3—37 mm (single);
  4/6—14·5 mm MG (twin)
Main engines: 2 diesels; 4/5 000 bhp; 2 shafts
Speed, knots: 24 (estimated)

May have been built in North Korea in mid-1950s.

Radar: Surface search: Skin Head.

"K-48" Class

320 KOREA (DPR) / Light forces

20 Ex-SOVIET "MO IV" CLASS (FAST ATTACK CRAFT—GUN)

Displacement, tons: 56
Dimensions, feet (metres): 88·5 × 13·1 × 4·9 *(27 × 4 × 1·5)*
Guns: 1—37 mm; 1/2—14·5 mm MG
Main engines: 2 Skoda diesels; 2 600 hp = 25 knots
Complement: 20

Transferred in 1950s. Built in 1945-47. Wooden hulls.

Radar: One navigation set.

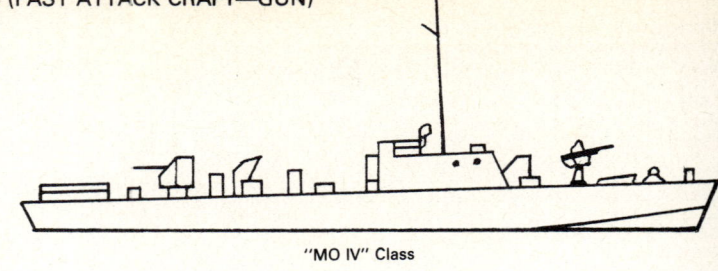
"MO IV" Class

60 "CHAHO" CLASS (FAST ATTACK CRAFT—GUN)

Displacement, tons: 80 full load
Dimensions, feet (metres): 90·9 × 20 × 5·9 *(27·7 × 6·1 × 1·8)*
Guns: 8—200 mm; 40 tube rocket launchers; 4—14·5 mm
Main engines: 4 diesels; 4 800 shp = 38-40 knots
Complement: 10-12 (est)

Reported as building in North Korea since 1974. Based on "P 6" hull.

Radar: One navigation set.

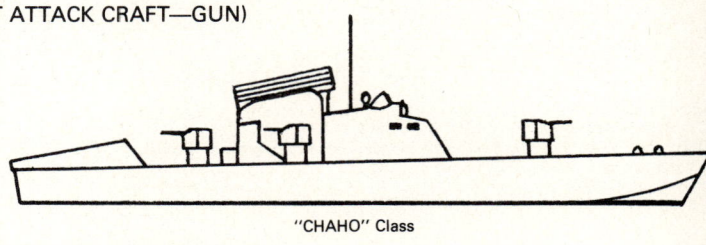
"CHAHO" Class

30 "CHONG-JIN" CLASS (FAST ATTACK CRAFT—GUN)

Particulars similar to "Chaho" class of which this is an improved version. Building began about 1975.

4 Ex-SOVIET "SHERSHEN" CLASS (FAST ATTACK CRAFT—TORPEDO)

Displacement, tons: 145 standard; 160 full load
Dimensions, feet (metres): 118·1 × 25·3 × 4·9 *(36 × 7·7 × 1·5)*
Guns: 4—30 mm (2 twins)
Torpedo tubes: 4—21 *(533 m)* (single)
A/S weapons: 12 DC
Main engines: 3 diesels; 3 shafts; 13 000 bhp = 41 knots
Complement: 16

Transferred in 1973-74.

Radar: Search/Navigation: Pot Drum.
Fire control: Drum Tilt.
IFF: High Pole and Square Head.

Soviet "SHERSHEN" Class   1970

62 Ex-SOVIET "P 6" CLASS and 6 "SINPO" CLASS (FAST ATTACK CRAFT—TORPEDO)

Displacement, tons: 64 standard; 73 full load
Dimensions, feet (metres): 85·3 × 20 × 4·9 *(26 × 6·1 × 1·5)*
Guns: 4—25 mm (original); 2—37 mm (in some in addition)
Torpedo tubes: 2—21 in (or mines or DC)
Main engines: 4 diesels; 4 800 hp; 4 shafts = 41 knots
Range, miles: 450 at 30 knots
Complement: 20

There is a growing number of these craft in North Korea with local building programme in hand of a modified form. Some transferred originally by USSR and China. A further development, the six boats of the "Sinpo" class are reported to carry six 14·5 mm MG.

Radar: Surface search: Pot Head or Skin Head.
Navigation: One set.

"P 6" Class   1972

"MODIFIED P 6" Class

KOREA (DPR) / Light forces — Service forces 321

12 Ex-SOVIET "P 4" CLASS (FAST ATTACK CRAFT—TORPEDO)

Displacement, tons: 25
Dimensions, feet (metres): 62·3 × 10·8 × 3·3 *(19 × 3·3 × 1)*
Guns: 2—MG
Torpedo tubes: 2—18 in
Main engines: 2 diesels; 2 200 bhp = 50 knots.
Range, miles: 400 at 13 knots
Complement: 12

Built in 1951-57. Aluminium hulls.

Radar: Surface search: Skin Head.
Navigation: One set.

"P 4" Class   1971

15 "IWON" CLASS (FAST ATTACK CRAFT—TORPEDO)

Displacement, tons: 40
Dimensions, feet (metres): 63 × 12 × 5 *(19·2 × 3·7 × 1·5)*
Guns: 4—25 mm (twin, vertical)
Torpedo tubes: 2—21 in *(533 mm)*

Built in North Korea in late 1950s. Similar to older Soviet "P 2" class design.

Radar: Surface search: Skin Head.
Navigation: One set.

"IWON" Class

6 "AN JU" CLASS (FAST ATTACK CRAFT—TORPEDO)

Displacement, tons: 35
Dimensions, feet (metres): 65 × 12 × 6 *(19·8 × 3·7 × 1·8)*
Guns: 2—25 mm (twin, vertical)
Torpedo tubes: 2—21 in *(533 mm)*
Main engines: Diesels; 4 shafts
Range, miles: 1 300 at 20 knots
Complement: 20

Built in North Korea in 1960s.

Radar: One navigation set.

"AN JU" Class

10 SOVIET "KM 4" CLASS (COASTAL PATROL CRAFT)

Displacement, tons: 10
Dimensions, feet (metres): 46 × 10·5 × 3 *(14 × 3·2 × 0·9)*
Guns: 1—36 mm; 1—14·5 mm MG
Main engines: Petrol; 146 shp; 2 shafts
Complement: 10

Built in North Korea to Soviet design.

20 LIGHT GUNBOATS

Believed to be for inshore patrols. Locally built.

60 "KU SONG" CLASS
(FAST ATTACK CRAFT—TORPEDO)

Displacement, tons: 35
Dimensions, feet (metres): 60 × 11 × 5·5 *(18·3 × 3·4 × 1·7)*
Guns: 2—14·5 mm (twin)
Torpedo tubes: 2—18 in or 2—21 in

Built in North Korea mid-1950s to 1970. Frequently operated on South Korean border. All resemble the Soviet "D-3" class of 25 years ago.

Radar: One navigation set.

AMPHIBIOUS FORCES

Note: 5-10 LCU and 15 LCM now in service with others building in North Korea. Used on South Korean border.

70 "NAMPO" CLASS

Displacement, tons: 82
Dimensions, feet (metres): 84·2 × 20 × 6 *(27·7 × 6·1 × 1·8)*
Guns: 6—14·7 mm MG
Main engines: Diesels; 4 shafts; 4 800 bhp = 40 knots
Range, miles: 375 at 40 knots
Complement: 19

A class of assault landing craft based on a "P 6" hull. Building began about 1975. Have a retractable ramp in bows.

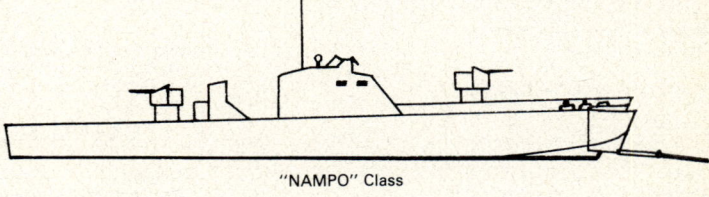

"NAMPO" Class

5 "HANCHON" CLASS (LCUs)

SERVICE FORCES

Five to ten Large Trawlers and small cargo vessels used as store ships. Some of the trawlers operate on the South Korean border where several have been sunk in the last few years. Some 100 craft in all of various types are employed as support craft with a secondary mission of coastal patrol.

KOREA, Republic (South)

Ministerial

Minister of National Defence:
So Chong-Ch'ol

Senior Flag Officers

Chief of Naval Operations:
Vice-Admiral Kim Kyu-Sup
Commander-in-Chief of Fleet:
Rear-Admiral Chong-Yon Hwang

Diplomatic Representation

Naval Attaché in London:
Commander Tae Hong Chi
Naval Attaché in Paris:
Colonel Ock-Sup Yoon (Army)
Naval Attaché in Washington:
Captain Choong Hah Choi

Personnel

a) 1979: 20 000 (approx) Navy, 20 000 (approx) Marine Corps.
b) 3 years (Navy), national service with a proportion of ratings and all marines being volunteers.

Frigates

1977 *Kang Won* (28 Oct), *Kyong Ki* (28 Dec) (ex-US "Cannon" class)

Bases

Major: Chinhae (Fleet HQ).
Minor: Cheju, Mokpo, Mukho, Pohang, Inchon, Pusan.

Marine Corps

Over 20 000 organised into one division and one brigade plus smaller and support units. Since October 1973 the ROK Marine Force has been placed directly under the ROK Navy command with a Vice Chief of Naval Operations for Marine Affairs replacing the Commandant of Marine Corps.

Naval Aviation

The ROK Navy operates 23 S-2 A/F Tracker anti-submarine aircraft. Approximately ten utility aircraft and several helicopters are operated by the ROK Marine Corps. Additional Tracker aircraft are being acquired.
Base: Kimhae.

Pennant Numbers

All pennant numbers were changed in June 1978. New numbers have been shown where known.

DELETIONS

Corvettes

1977 *Han San, Ok Po* (15 Sep), *Ro Ryang, Myong Ryang* (28 Dec) (ex-US "PCE 827" class)

Strength of the Fleet

Type	Active	Building (Proposed)
Destroyers	10	—
Frigates	7	1 (3?)
Corvettes	6	—
Fast Attack Craft—Missile	8	—
Fast Attack Craft—Patrol	1	4
Large Patrol Craft	10	—
Coastal Patrol Craft	23+	—
MSCs	8	—
MSB	1	—
LSTs	8	—
LSMs	12	—
LCU	1	—
Repair Ship	1	—
Supply Ships	6	—
Tankers	4	—
Tugs	2	—
Survey Ships and Craft	6	—

Mercantile Marine

Lloyd's Register of Shipping:
1 148 vessels of 2 975 389 tons gross

Mine Warfare Forces

1977 *Kim Po, Ko Chang, Kum Hwa* (15 Sep) (ex-US "Albatross" class)

DESTROYERS

5 Ex-US "GEARING" CLASS (FRAM I and II)

Name	No.	Builders	Laid down	Launched	Commissioned
KWANG JU (ex-USS *Richard E. Kraus*, DD 849)	DD 90	Bath Iron Works Corporation, Bath, Maine	31 July 1945	2 Mar 1946	23 May 1946
CHUNG BUK (ex-USS *Chevalier*, DD 805)	DD 954	Bath Iron Works Corporation, Bath, Maine	12 June 1944	29 Oct 1944	9 Jan 1945
JEONG BUK (ex-USS *Everett F. Larson*, DD 830)	DD 96	Bath Iron Works Corporation, Bath, Maine	4 Sep 1944	28 Jan 1945	6 Apr 1945
TAEJON (ex-USS *New*, DD 818)	DD 99	Consolidated Steel Corporation	14 Apr 1945	18 Aug 1945	5 Apr 1946
KANG WON (ex-USS *William R. Rush*, DD 714)	DD —	Federal S.B. and D.D. Co, Newark	19 Oct 1944	8 July 1945	21 Sep 1945

Displacement, tons: 2 425 standard; approx 3 500 full load
Length, feet (metres): 383 *(116.7)* wl; 390.5 *(119.0)* oa
Beam, feet (metres): 40.9 *(12.4)*
Draught, feet (metres): 19 *(5.8)*
Guns: 6—5 in *(127 mm)*/38 (twin) (Mk 38);
1—20 mm Vulcan Gatling *(Chung Buk* and *Jeong Buk)*;
2—30 mm (twin Emerlak) *(Jeong Buk* only)
A/S weapons: 6 (2 triple) Mk 32 A/S torpedo tubes;
2 fixed Hedgehogs (Mk 11)
Main engines: 2 General Electric geared turbines;
60 000 shp; 2 shafts
Boilers: 4 Babcock & Wilcox
Speed, knots: 34
Complement: 280

Chung Buk and *Jeong Buk* were converted to radar picket destroyers (DDR) in 1949; subsequently modernised under the US Navy's Fleet Rehabilitation and Modernisation programme—first pair to Fram II standards, second pair Fram I. Fitted with small helicopter hangar and flight deck. Anti-ship torpedo tubes have been removed.

Aircraft: All to be converted to carry Alouette III helicopter.

A/S weapons: 15 in Mk 32 torpedo tubes are fitted with liners to reduce them to 12.75 in.

Guns: Vulcan Gatlings installed on after hangar deck in 1976.

Radar: Surface search: SPS 10.
Air search: SPS 40.

Sonar: SQS 29 (hull-mounted).

JEONG BUK   1973

Transfers: First pair on loan on 5 July 1972 and 30 October 1972 respectively and by purchase 31 January 1977. Second pair 23 February 1977 by sale. *Kang Won* by sale 1 July 1978.

3 Ex-US "FLETCHER" CLASS

Name	No.	Builders	Laid down	Launched	Commissioned
CHUNG MU (ex-USS *Erben*, DD 631)	DD 91	Bath Iron Works Corporation, Bath, Maine	28 Oct 1942	21 Mar 1943	28 May 1943
SEOUL (ex-USS *Halsey Powell*, DD 686)	DD 92	Bethlehem Steel, Staten Island, New York	1943	30 June 1943	25 Oct 1943
PUSAN (ex-USS *Hickox*, DD 673)	DD 93	Federal S.B. & D.D. Co, Kearny, New Jersey	1943	4 July 1943	10 Sep 1943

Displacement, tons: 2 050 standard; 3 050 full load
Length, feet (metres): 361.8 *(110.3)* wl; 376.5 *(114.8)* oa
Beam, feet (metres): 39.6 *(12.0)*
Draught, feet (metres): 18 *(5.5)*
Guns: 5—5 in *(127 mm)*/38 (single) (Mk 30); 6-10—40 mm/60 (2 quad, 1 twin Mk 1 and 2) except *Seoul* (none)
A/S weapons: 6 (2 triple) Mk 32 A/S torpedo tubes;
2 Hedgehogs (Mk 10/11); depth charges
Main engines: General Electric geared turbines; 60 000 shp; 2 shafts
Boilers: 4 Babcock & Wilcox
Speed, knots: 35
Range, miles: 600 at 15 knots
Complement: 350

Radar: Surface search: SPS 10.
Air search: SPS 6.
Plus fire control (2) and navigation (1).

Sonar: SQS 20 (hull-mounted).

Transfers: DD 91, 1 May 1963; DD 92, 27 April 1968; DD 93, 15 November 1968 on loan. All purchased 31 January 1977.

SEOUL   1968, USN

KOREA (REPUBLIC) / Destroyers — Frigates 323

2 Ex-US "ALLEN M. SUMNER" CLASS (FRAM II)

Name	No.	Builders	Laid down	Launched	Commissioned
DAE GU (ex-USS *Wallace L. Lind*, DD 703)	DD 97	Bath Iron Works Corporation, Bath, Maine	Apr 1944	14 June 1944	8 Sep 1944
IN CHEON (ex-USS *De Haven*, DD 727)	DD 981	Federal S.B. & D.D. Co, Kearney, New Jersey	Oct 1943	9 Jan 1944	31 Mar 1944

Displacement, tons: 2 200 standard; 3 320 full load
Length, feet (metres): 376·5 *(114·8)*
Beam, feet (metres): 40·9 *(12·4)*
Draught, feet (metres): 19 *(5·8)*
Guns: 6—5 in *(127 mm)*/38 (twin) (Mk 38);
  1—20 mm Vulcan Gatling
A/S weapons: 6 (2 triple) Mk 32 A/S torpedo tubes;
  2 fixed Hedgehogs (Mk 11)
Main engines: 2 General Electric geared turbines
  60 000 shp; 2 shafts
Boilers: 4 Babcock & Wilcox
Speed, knots: 34
Complement: 235

Both ships were modernised under the US Navy's Fleet Rehabilitation and Modernisation (FRAM II) programme. Fitted with small helicopter deck and hangar.

Radar: Surface search: SPS 10.
Air search: SPS 37 *(In Cheon).*
SPS 40 *(Dae Gu).*
Sonar: SQS 29 (hull-mounted).
SQA 10 (VDS).

Transfers: December 1973 and by sale—*Dae Gu* 4 December 1977, *In Cheon* 5 December 1977.

IN CHEON (*Chung Buk* alongside) 7/1978, Michael D. J. Lennon

FRIGATES

1 + ?3 NEW CONSTRUCTION

A new frigate of approximately 1 600 tons with twin screws and CODAG driven is under construction at Hayundai SY, Mipo Bay, Ulsan. It is reported that three more may be ordered. Armament reported as one 5 in gun and SSM.

1 Ex-US "RUDDEROW" CLASS

Name	No.	Builders	Laid down	Launched	Commissioned
CHUNG NAM (ex-USS *Holt*, DE 706)	DE 73	Defoe Shipbuilding Co, Bay City, Michigan	Oct 1943	15 Dec 1943	9 June 1944

Displacement, tons: 1 450 standard; 1 890 full load
Length, feet (metres): 300 *(91·5)* wl; 306 *(83·2)* oa
Beam, feet (metres): 37 *(11·3)*
Draught, feet (metres): 14 *(4·3)*
Guns: 2—5 in *(127 mm)*/38 (single Mk 30);
  4—40 mm/60 (twin Mk 1)
A/S weapons: 6 (2 triple) Mk 32 A/S torpedo tubes;
  1 Hedgehog; depth charges
Main engines: Turbo-electric drive (General Electric geared turbines); 12 000 shp; 2 shafts
Boilers: 2 (Combustion Engineering)
Speed, knots: 24
Range, miles: 5 000 at 15 knots
Complement: 210

Former US destroyer escort of the TEV design.

Radar: Surface search: SPS 5.
Air search: SPS 6.

Sonar: Hull-mounted set.

Transfer: 19 June 1963 on loan and by purchase on 15 November 1974.

CHUNG NAM 1971, Korean Navy

6 Ex-US "CHARLES LAWRENCE" and "CROSLEY" CLASSES

Name	No.	Builders	Launched	Commissioned	Transferred
KYONG NAM (ex-USS *Cavallaro*, APD 128)	APD 81	Defoe Shipbuilding Co, Bay City, Michigan	15 June 1944	13 Mar 1945	Oct 1959
AH SAN (ex-USS *Harry L. Corl*, APD 108)	APD 82	Bethlehem Shipbuilding Co, Higham, Mass	1 Mar 1944	5 June 1945	June 1966
UNG PO (ex-USS *Julius A. Raven*, APD 110)	APD 83	Bethlehem Shipbuilding Co, Higham, Mass	3 Mar 1944	28 June 1945	June 1966
KYONG PUK (ex-USS *Kephart*, APD 61)	APD 85	Charleston Navy Yard, South Carolina	6 Sep 1943	7 Jan 1944	Aug 1967
ONNAM (ex-USS *Hayter*, APD 80)	APD 86	Charleston Navy Yard, South Carolina	11 Nov 1943	16 Mar 1944	Aug 1967
CHR JU (ex-USS *William M. Hobby*, APD 95)	APD 87	Charleston Navy Yard, South Carolina	11 Feb 1944	4 Apr 1945	Aug 1967

Displacement, tons: 1 400 standard; 2 130 full load
Length, feet (metres): 299·8 *(91·4)* wl; 306 *(93·3)* oa
Beam, feet (metres): 37 *(11·3)*
Draught, feet (metres): 10·5 *(3·2)*
Guns: 1—5 in *(127 mm)*/38; 6—40 mm (twin)
A/S weapons: depth charges
Main engines: Turbo-electric (General Electric turbines); 12 000 shp; 2 shafts
Boilers: 2 (Foster-Wheeler "D" Express)
Speed, knots: 23·6
Range, miles: 5 500 at 15 knots
Complement: 200
Troop capacity: 160

All begun as destroyers escorts (DE), but converted during construction to high-speed transports (APD).
In Korean service four latter ships originally rated as gunboats (PG); changed in 1972 to APD. All are fitted to carry approximately 160 troops. Can carry four LCVPs.
Two different configurations; "Charles Lawrence (APD 37)" class with high bridge and lattice mast supporting 10 ton capacity boom; "Crosley (APD 87)" class with low bridge and tripod mast supporting 10 ton capacity boom.
All purchased by South Korea 15 November 1974.

KYONG NAM

CORVETTES

3 Ex-US "AUK" CLASS

Name	No.	Builders	Launched
SHIN SONG (ex-USS Ptarmigan, MSF 376)	PCE 1001	Savannah Machine & Foundry Co, Savannah, Georgia	15 Jan 1944
SUNCHON (ex-USS Speed, MSF 116)	PCE 1002	American S.B. Co, Lorain, Ohio	15 Oct 1942
KOJE (ex-USS Dextrous, MSF 341)	PCE 1003	Gulf S.B. Corporation, Madisonville, Texas	8 Sep 1943

Displacement, tons: 890 standard; 1 250 full load
Dimensions, feet (metres): 221·2 × 32·2 × 10·8 (67·4 × 9·8 × 3·1)
Guns: 2—3 in (76 mm)/50 (single); 4—40 mm (twin); 4—20 mm (twin)
A/S weapons: 3 (1 triple) Mk 32 A/S torpedo tubes; 1 Hedgehog; depth charges
Main engines: Diesel-electric (General Motors diesels); 3 532 bhp; 2 shafts = 18 knots
Complement: approx 110

Former US Navy minesweepers (originally designated AM). PCE 1001 transferred to ROK Navy in July 1963, PCE 1002 in November 1967, and PCE 1003 in December 1967. The minesweeping gear was removed prior to transfer and a second 3 in gun fitted aft; additional anti-submarine weapons also fitted.

A/S weapons: Mk 32 tubes fitted with 12·75 in liners.

Radar: Surface search and navigation.

Sonar: One hull-mounted set.

SHIN SONG

3 Ex-US "PCE 827" CLASS

Name	No.	Builders	Commissioned
PYOK PA (ex-USS Dania, PCE 870)	PCE 57	Albina Works, Portland Oreg.	5 Oct 1943
RYUL PO (ex-USS Somerset, PCE 892)	PCE 58	Willamette Corporation, Portland, Oreg.	8 July 1943
SA CHON (ex-USS Batesburg, PCE 903)	PCE 59	Willamette Corporation, Portland, Oreg.	16 May 1943

Displacement, tons: 640 standard; 950 full load
Dimensions, feet (metres): 184·5 × 33 × 9·5 (56·2 × 10·1 × 2·9)
Guns: 1—3 in (76 mm)/50; 6—40 mm (twin); 4 or 8—20 mm (single or twin)
A/S weapons: 1 Hedgehog; depth charges
Main engines: Diesels (General Motors); 2 000 bhp; 2 shafts = 15 knots
Complement: 100

Original class of seven transferred on loan December 1961 and by sale 15 November 1974.

"PCE 827" Class   1969

LIGHT FORCES

7 TACOMA PSMM 5 TYPE (FAST ATTACK CRAFT—MISSILE)

Name	No.	Builders	Commissioned
PAEK KU 12	102	Tacoma Boatbuilding Co, Tacoma, Wash.	14 Mar 1975
PAEK KU 13	103	Tacoma Boatbuilding Co, Tacoma, Wash.	14 Mar 1975
PAEK KU 15	105	Tacoma Boatbuilding Co, Tacoma, Wash.	1 Feb 1976
PAEK KU 16	106	Tacoma Boatbuilding Co, Tacoma, Wash.	1 Feb 1976
PAEK KU 17	107	Korea—Tacoma International	1976-77
PAEK KU 18	108	Korea—Tacoma International	1976-77
PAEK KU 19	109	Korea—Tacoma International	1976-77

Displacement, tons: approx 250 full load
Dimensions, feet (metres): 165 oa × 24 × 9·5 (50·3 × 7·3 × 2·9)
Missile launchers: 4 launchers for Standard missiles (1 reload each) (Harpoon planned)
Guns: 1—3 in (76 mm)/50 (single Mk 34)
   1—40 mm (aft; may have been removed with missile installation)
   2—50 cal MG
Main engines: 6 TF 35 gas turbines (Avco Lycoming); 16 800 hp;
   2 shafts (cp propellers) = 40+ knots
Range, miles: 2 400 at 18 knots
Complement: 32 (5 officers, 27 enlisted men)

Aluminium hulls. Based on the US Navy's *Asheville* (PG 84) design. Tacoma design designation was PSMM for multi-mission patrol ship. The Korean designation *Paek Ku* means seagull. *Paek Ku 12* launched 17 February 1975.

Engineering: The six TF 35 gas turbines turn two propeller shafts; the "Asheville" class ships have combination gas turbine-diesel power plants. In the Korean units one, two, or three turbines can be selected to provide each shaft with a variety of power settings.

PAEK KU 12 (old pennant number)   1975, Alfred W. Harri

1 Ex-US "ASHEVILLE" CLASS (FAST ATTACK CRAFT—MISSILE)

Name	No.	Builders	Commissioned
PAEK KU 11 (ex-USS Benicia, PG 96)	PGM 101 (ex-PGM 11)	Tacoma Boatbuilding Co, Tacoma, Wash.	25 Apr 1970

Displacement, tons: 225 standard; 245 full load
Dimensions, feet (metres): 164·5 oa × 23·8 × 9·5 (50·1 × 7·3 × 2·9)
Missiles: Launchers for Standard SSM
Guns: 1—3 in (76 mm)/50 (single Mk 34); 1—40 mm/60 (single Mk 3); 4—·50 MG (twin)
Main engines: CODAG; 2 diesels (Cummins); 1 450 bhp; 2 shafts = 16 knots;
   1 gas turbine (General Electric); 13 300 shp; 2 shafts = 40+ knots
Range, miles: 1 700 at 16 knots
Complement: 25

Former US "Asheville" class patrol gunboat. Launched 20 December 1969; transferred to ROK Navy on 15 October 1971 and arrived in Korea in January 1972. No anti-submarine sensors or weapons are fitted.

Missiles: During 1971, while in US Navy service, this ship was fitted experimentally with one launcher for the Standard surface-to-surface missile. The box-like container/launcher held two missiles. Launchers fitted in South Korea 1975-76.

PAEK KU 11 (old pennant number)   197

KOREA (REPUBLIC) / Light forces 325

1 + 4 CPIC TYPE (FAST ATTACK CRAFT—PATROL)

Name	No.	Builders	Commissioned
GIREOGI	PKM 123	Tacoma Boatbuilding Co, Tacoma, Wash.	1975

Displacement, tons: 71·25 full load
Dimensions, feet (metres): 100 × 18·5 × 6 (30·5 × 5·6 × 1·8)
Guns: 2—30 mm MG (twin) (Mk 74); 1—20 mm
Main engines: 3 gas turbines (Avco Lycoming); 6 750 shp; 3 shafts = 45 knots;
  2 auxiliary diesels (Volvo); 500 bhp
Complement: 11 (varies with armament)

Transferred on 1 August 1975. A further seven were to be built in South Korea (PKM 125-131) but this order has been reduced to four—launched 1978.

Missiles: SSM may be fitted.

CPIC on trials   1974, USN

8 Ex-US COAST GUARD "CAPE" CLASS (LARGE PATROL CRAFT)

PB 3 (ex-USCGC *Cape Rosier*, WPB 95333)
PB 5 (ex-USCGC *Cape Sable*, WPB 95334)
PB 6 (ex-USCGC *Cape Providence*, WPB 95335)
PB 8 (ex-USCGC *Cape Porpoise*, WPB 95327)
PB 9 (ex-USCGC *Cape Falcon*, WPB 95330)
PB 10 (ex-USCGC *Cape Trinity*, WPB 95331)
PB 11 (ex-USCGC *Cape Darby*, WPB 95323)
PB 12 (ex-USCGC *Cape Kiwanda*, WPB 95329)

Displacement, tons: 98 full load
Dimensions, feet (metres): 95 × 19 × 6 (28·9 × 5·8 × 1·8)
Guns: 1—50 cal MG; 1—81 mm mortar; several ·30 cal MG
Main engines: 4 diesels (Cummins); 2 200 bhp; 2 shafts = 20 knots
Range, miles: 1 500 at 18 knots
Complement: 13

Former US Coast Guard steel hulled patrol craft. Built in 1958-1959. Nine units transferred to South Korea in September 1968.
Combination machinegun/mortar mount is forward; single light machineguns are mounted aft.
See US Coast Guard listings for additional details.

PB 11

2 "100-ft" PATROL TYPE (LARGE PATROL CRAFT)

PK 10   PK 11

Displacement, tons: 120
Dimensions, feet (metres): 100 (30·5)
Guns: 1—40 mm; 1—20 mm
Main engines: Diesels (Mercedes-Benz-MTU); 10 200 bhp; 3 shafts = 35 knots

Two patrol craft reported built in Korea in 1971-72.

10-20 "SCHOOLBOY" CLASS (COASTAL PATROL CRAFT)

Displacement, tons: 30
Dimensions, feet (metres): 72 × 11·5 × 3·6 (21·9 × 3·5 × 1·2)
Guns: 2—20 mm (single)
Main engines: 2 MTU diesels; 1 600 bhp; 2 shafts

At least 10 and possibly as many as 20 patrol craft of this type have been built in Korea, with the first units completed in 1973. Believed to be designated in the PB series.

9 US 65-ft SEWART TYPE (COASTAL PATROL CRAFT)

FB 1	FB 3	FB 6	FB 8	FB 10
FB 2	FB 5	FB 7	FB 9	

Displacement, tons: 33 full load
Dimensions, feet (metres): 65 × 16 (19·8 × 4·9)
Guns: 2—20 mm (single); 3 MG
Main engines: 3 diesels (General Motors); 1 590 bhp; 3 shafts = 25 knots
Range, miles: 1 200 at 17 knots
Complement: 5

These craft were built in the USA by Sewart. The design is adapted from a commercial 65 ft craft. Referred to as "Toksuuri" No. 1 etc. by the South Koreans.
Transferred to South Korea in August 1967.

FB 10 on marine railway

4 US 40-ft SEWART TYPE (COASTAL PATROL CRAFT)

SB 1   SB 2   SB 3   SB 5

Displacement, tons: 9·25 full load
Dimensions, feet (metres): 40 × 12 × 3 (12·2 × 3·7 × 0·9)
Guns: 1—50 cal MG; 2—30 cal MG
Main engines: 2 diesels (General Motors); 500 bhp; 2 shafts = 31 knots
Complement: 7

These are aluminium hulled craft built in the USA by Sewart.
Transferred to South Korea in 1964.

326 KOREA (REPUBLIC) / Mine warfare forces — Amphibious forces

MINE WARFARE FORCES

Note: *Pung To* ("LSM-1" Class) serves as mine force flagship. See under Amphibious Forces.

8 Ex-US "MSC 268" and "294" CLASSES (MINESWEEPERS COASTAL)

Name	No.	Builders	Commissioned
KUM SAN (ex-US *MSC 284*)	MSC 522	Peterson Builders, Wisconsin	1959
KO HUNG (ex-US *MSC 285*)	MSC 523	Peterson Builders, Wisconsin	1959
KUM KOK (ex-US *MSC 286*)	MSC 525	Peterson Builders, Wisconsin	1959
NAM YANG (ex-US *MSC 295*)	MSC 526	Peterson Builders, Wisconsin	1963
NA DONG (ex-US *MSC 296*)	MSC 527	Peterson Builders, Wisconsin	1963
SAM CHOK (ex-US *MSC 316*)	MSC 528	Peterson Builders, Wisconsin	1968
YONG DONG (ex-US *MSC 320*)	MSC 529	Peterson Builders, Wisconsin	1975
OK CHEON (ex-US *MSC 321*)	MSC 530	Peterson Builders, Wisconsin	1975

Displacement, tons: 320 light; 370 full load
Dimensions, feet (metres): 141 × 26·2 × 8·5 *(43·0 × 8 × 2·6)*
Guns: 2—20 mm
Main engines: Diesels; 1 200 bhp; 2 shafts = 14 knots
Complement: approx 40

Built by the USA specifically for transfer under the Military Aid Programme. Wood hulled with non-magnetic metal fittings.
Kum San transferred to South Korea in June 1959, *Ko Hung* in September 1959, *Kum Kok* in November 1959, *Nam Yang* in September 1963, *Na Dong* in November 1963, *Sam Chok* in July 1968, *Yong Dong* and *Ok Cheon* on 2 October 1975.

KUM KOK

1 Ex-US MSB

Name	No.
PI BONG (ex-US *MSB 2*)	MSB 1

Displacement, tons: 30 light; 39 full load
Dimensions, feet (metres): 57·2 × 15·3 × 4 *(17·4 × 4·7 × 1·2)*
Guns: Machine guns
Main engines: 2 geared diesels (Packard); 600 bhp; 2 shafts = 12 knots

Transferred on 1 December 1961 and by sale on 2 July 1975. Wood hulled.

PI BONG   1969, Korean Navy

AMPHIBIOUS FORCES

8 Ex-US "1-510" and "511-1152" CLASSES (LST)

Name	No.	Commissioned
UN PONG (ex-USS *LST 1010*)	LST 807	25 Apr 1944
DUK BONG (ex-USS *LST 227*)	LST 808	14 Oct 1943
BI BONG (ex-USS *LST 218*)	LST 809	12 Aug 1943
KAE BONG (ex-USS *Berkshire County*, LST 288)	LST 810	20 Dec 1943
WEE BONG (ex-USS *Johnson County*, LST 849)	LST 812	16 Jan 1945
SU YONG (ex-USS *Kane County*, LST 853)	LST 813	11 Dec 1945
BUK HAN (ex-USS *Lynn County*, LST 900)	LST 815	28 Dec 1944
HWA SAN (ex-USS *Pender County*, LST 1080)	LST 816	29 May 1945

Displacement, tons: 1 653 standard; 2 366 beaching; 4 080 full load
Dimensions, feet (metres): 328 × 50 × 14 *(100 × 15·2 × 4·3)*
Guns: 6 or 8—40 mm
Main engines: Diesels; 1 700 bhp; 2 shafts = 11·6 knots
Complement: 110

DUK BONG

Former US Navy tank landing ships. Cargo capacity 2 100 tons. Carry two LCVP and twenty tanks. *Un Bong* transferred to South Korea in February 1955, *Duk Bong* in March 1955, *Bi Bong* in May 1955, *Kae Bong* in March 1956, *Wee Bong* in January 1959, *Su Yong* and *Buk Han* in December 1958, and *Hwa San* in October 1958. All purchased 15 November 1974.

Launch dates: 807, 29 Mar 1944; 808, 21 Sep 1943; 809, 20 July 1943; 810, 7 Nov 1943; 812, 30 Dec 1944; 813, 17 Nov 1944; 815, 9 Dec 1944; 816, 2 May 1945.

1 Ex-US "ELK RIVER" CLASS (LSMR)

Name	No.	Builders
SI HUNG (ex-USS *St Joseph River* LSMR 527)	LSMR 311	Brown S.B. Co, Houston, Texas

Displacement, tons: 944 standard; 1 084 full load
Dimensions, feet (metres): 206·2 × 34·5 × 10 *(62·9 × 10·5 × 3)*
Guns: 1—5 in *(127 mm)*/38; 2—40 mm; 4—20 mm
Rocket launchers: 8 twin Mk 105 launchers for 5 in rockets
Main engines: 2 diesels (General Motors); 2 800 bhp; 2 shafts = 12·6 knots
Complement: approx 140

SI HUNG   1967, Korean Navy

Former US Navy landing ship completed as a rocket-firing ship to support amphibious landing operations. Launched on 19 May 1945, transferred to South Korea on 15 September 1960 and purchased 15 November 1974. Configuration differs from conventional LSM type with "island" bridge structure and 5 in gun aft; no bow doors.

KOREA (REPUBLIC) / Amphibious forces — Service forces 327

11 Ex-US "LSM-1" CLASS

Name	No.
TAE CHO (ex-USS *LSM 546*)	LSM 601
TYO TO (ex-USS *LSM 268*)	LSM 602
KA TOK (ex-USS *LSM 462*)	LSM 605
KO MUN (ex-USS *LSM 30*)	LSM 606
PIAN (ex-USS *LSM 96*)	LSM 607
PUNG TO (ex-USS *LSM 54*)	LSM 608 (LSML)
WOL MI (ex-USS *LSM 57*)	LSM 609
KI RIN (ex-USS *LSM 19*)	LSM 610
NUNG RA (ex-USS *LSM 84*)	LSM 611
SIN MI (ex-USS *LSM 316*)	LSM 612
UL RUNG (ex-USS *LSM 17*)	LSM 613

Displacement, tons: 743 beaching; 1 095 full load
Dimensions, feet (metres): 203·5 × 34·6 × 8·5 *(62 × 10·5 × 2·6)*
Guns: 2—40 mm (twin); several 20 mm
Main engines: 2 diesels (direct drive; Fairbanks-Morse except *Tyo To* General Motors); 2 800 bhp; 2 shafts = 12·5 knots
Complement: approx 60

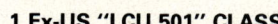
TYO TO   1969

Former US Navy medium landing ships. Built 1944-45. LSM 601, 602, and 605 transferred to South Korea in 1955; others in 1956. *Sin Mi* served in Indochina as French L 9014 and *Ul Rung* as French L 9017 during 1954-55; returned to USA in October 1955 and retransferred to South Korea in autumn 1956. All purchased 15 November 1974.
Pung To serves as mine force flagship fitted with mine-laying rails and designated LSML. Arrangement of 20 mm guns differs; some ships have two single mounts adjacent to forward 40 mm mount on forecastle; other 20 mm guns along sides of cargo well.

1 Ex-US "LCU 501" CLASS

LCU 1 (ex-USS *LCU 531*)

Displacement, tons: 309 full load
Dimensions, feet (metres): 119·1 × 32·7 × 5 *(36·3 × 9·9 × 1·5)*
Main engines: Diesels (Gray Marine); 675 bhp; 3 shafts = 10 knots

Former US Navy utility landing craft. Built in 1943 as LCT(6) 531. Transferred to South Korea in December 1960. No name assigned.

SERVICE FORCES

1 Ex-US "ACHELOUS" CLASS (LIGHT REPAIR SHIP)

Name	No.	Builders	Commissioned
DUK SU (ex-USS *Minotaur*, ARL 15, ex-*LST 645*)	ARL 1	Chicago Bridge & Iron Co, Seneca, Illinois	30 Sep 1944

Displacement, tons: 2 366 standard; 3 640 full load
Dimensions, feet (metres): 328 × 50 × 11·2 *(100 × 15·2 × 3·4)*
Guns: 2—40 mm; 6—20 mm
Main engines: Diesels (General Motors); 1 800 bhp; 2 shafts = 11·6 knots
Complement: approx 250

DUK SU

Former US Navy landing craft repair ship. Converted during construction from an LST. Launched on 20 September 1944, transferred to South Korea in October 1955 on loan and purchased 31 January 1977.

6 Ex-US ARMY FS TYPE (SUPPLY SHIPS)

Name	No.	Builders
IN CHON (ex-US Army *FS 198*)	AKL 902	Higgins Industries
CHI NAM PO (ex-US Army *FS 356*)	AKL 905	J. K. Welding
MOK PO (ex-USCGC *Trillium*, WAK 170, ex-US Army *FS 397*)	AKL 907	Ingalls, Decatur, Alabama
KU SAN (ex-USS *Sharps*, AKL 10, ex-*AG 139*, ex-US Army *FS 385*)	AKL 908	Ingalls, Decatur, Alabama
MA SAN (ex-USS *AKL 35*, ex-US Army *FS 383*)	AKL 909	Ingalls, Decatur, Alabama
UL SAN (ex-USS *Brule*, AKL 28, ex-US Army *FS 370*)	AKL 910	Sturgeon Bay

Displacement, tons: approx 700
Dimensions, feet (metres): 176·5 × 32·8 × 10 *(53·8 × 10 × 3·1)*
Guns: 2—20 mm (single) in most ships
Main engine: Diesel; 1 000 bhp; 1 shaft = 10 knots
Complement: approx 20

MA SAN   1957

Originally US Army freight and supply ships built in World War II for coastal operation. *In Chon* and *Chin Nam Po* transferred to South Korea in 1951; *Mok Po, Ku San,* and *Ma San* in 1956; *Ul San* on 1 November 1971.
Many subsequently served in US Navy and Military Sea Transportation Service (later Military Sealift Command). Details and configurations differ.

1 Ex-NORWEGIAN TANKER

Name	No.	Builders	Launched
CHUN JI (ex-*Birk*)	AO 2	A/S Berken Mek Verks, Bergen	1951

Displacement, tons: 1 400 standard; 4 160 full load
Dimensions, feet (metres): 319·8 × 47·9 × 19·3 *(97·5 × 14·6 × 5·9)*
Guns: 1—40 mm; 2—20 mm
Main engines: 2 diesels; 1 800 bhp; 1 shaft = 12 knots
Complement: approx 70

Transferred to South Korea in September 1953.

CHUN JI   1969

KOREA (REPUBLIC) / Service forces — Coast guard

1 Ex-US 235-ft YO TYPE (HARBOUR TANKER)

Name	No.
HWA CHON (ex-*Paek Yeon* AO 5, ex-USS *Derrick* YO 59)	AO 5

Displacement, tons: 890 standard; 2 700 full load
Dimensions, feet (metres): 235 × 37 × 15 *(71·6 × 11·3 × 4·6)*
Guns: Several 20 mm
Main engine: Diesel (Fairbanks-Morse); 1 150 bhp; 1 shaft = 10·5 knots
Complement: approx 45

Former US Navy self-propelled fuel barge. Transferred to South Korea on 14 October 1955. Capacity 10 000 barrels petroleum. The ship has been laid up in reserve since 1974, although purchased on 2 July 1975.

HWA CHON   1969

2 Ex-US 174-ft YO TYPE (HARBOUR TANKERS)

KU YONG (ex-USS *YO 118*) YO 1 — (ex-USS *YO 179*) YO 6

Displacement, tons: 1 400 full load
Dimensions, feet (metres): 174 × 32 *(53 × 9·8)*
Guns: Several 20 mm
Main engine: Diesel (Union); 500 bhp; 1 shaft = 7 knots
Complement: approx 35

Former US Navy self-propelled fuel barges. Transferred to South Korea on 3 December 1946 and 13 September 1971, respectively. Cargo capacity 6 570-barrels.

2 Ex-US "SOTOYOMO" CLASS (TUGS)

Name	No.	Builders	Launched
YONG MUN (ex-USS *Keosanqua*, ATA 198)	ATA 2	Levingston S.B. Co, Orange, Texas	17 Jan 1945
DO BONG (ex-USS *Pinola*, ATA 206)	ATA (S) 3	Gulfport Boiler & Welding Works, Port Arthur, Texas	14 Dec 1944

Displacement, tons: 538 standard; 835 full load
Dimensions, feet (metres): 143 × 33·8 *(43·6 × 10·3)*
Guns: 1—3 in *(76 mm)*/50; 4—20 mm
Main engine: Diesel (General Motors); 1 500 bhp; 1 shaft = 13 knots
Complement: 45

Former US Navy auxiliary ocean tugs. Both transferred to South Korea in February 1962. *Do Bong* modified for salvage work.

The South Korean Navy also operates nine small harbour tugs (designated YTL). These include one ex-US Navy craft (YTL 550) and five ex-US Army craft.

SERVICE CRAFT

The South Korean Navy operates approximately 35 small service craft in addition to the YO-type tankers listed above and the harbour tugs noted above. These craft include open lighters, floating cranes, diving tenders, dredgers, ferries, non-self-propelled fuel barges, pontoon barges, and sludge removal barges. Most are former US Navy craft.

HYDROGRAPHIC SERVICE

The following craft are operated by the Korean Hydrographic Service which is responsible to the Ministry of Transport.

2 Ex-BELGIAN MSI TYPE

SURO 5 (ex-Belgian *Temse*, ex-US *MSI 470*)
SURO 6 (ex-Belgian *Tournai*, ex-US *MSI 481*)

Displacement, tons: 143
Dimensions, feet (metres): 113·2 × 22·3 × 6 *(34·5 × 6·8 × 1·8)*
Main engines: Diesels; 1 260 bhp; 2 shafts = 15 knots
Complement: 16 (6); 18 (5)

Former Belgian inshore minesweepers. Built in Belgium, the *Tournai* being financed by USA. Launched on 6 August 1956 and 18 May 1957, respectively. Transferred to South Korea in March 1970.

1 Ex-US "YMS-1" CLASS

SURO 3 (ex-USC&GS *Hodgson*)

Displacement, tons: 264 full load
Dimensions, feet (metres): 136 × 24·5 × 9·3 *(41·4 × 7·5 × 2·8)*
Main engines: Diesels; 1 000 bhp; 2 shafts = 15 knots
Complement: 31

YMS type transferred to South Korea from US Coast & Geodetic Survey in 1968. Launched in 1943.

SURO 2

Of 145 tons launched in 1942. Complement 12.

SURO 7   SURO 8

Of 30 tons with complement of six.

COAST GUARD

The Korean Coast Guard operates about 25 small ships and craft including several tugs and rescue craft.

KUWAIT

Ministerial

Minister of Defence:
  Sa'd al Abdallah al-Sabah

Personnel

(a) 1979: 500 (Coast Guard) Administered by Ministry of the Interior
(b) Voluntary service

Future Plans

A contract was awarded to a Japanese firm in mid-1977 for the construction of a base. This will be necessary with the planned expansion of this force.

Mercantile Marine

Lloyd's Register of Shipping:
  251 vessels of 2 240 030 tons gross

LIGHT FORCES

Note: As a result of enquiries at the 1979 London Boat Show a considerable expansion of this force may be expected.

10 THORNYCROFT 78 ft TYPE (COASTAL PATROL CRAFT)

AL SALEMI	AMAN	MASHHOOR	MURSHED
AL SHURTI	INTISAR	MAYMOON	WATHAH
AL MUBARAKI	MARZOOK		

Displacement, tons: 40
Dimensions, feet (metres): 78 × 15.5 × 4.5 *(23.8 × 4.7 × 1.4)*
Gun: 1 MG
Main engines: 2 Rolls-Royce V8 marine diesels; 1 340 shp at 1 800 rpm; 1 116 shp at 1 700 rpm = 20 knots
Range, miles: 700 at 15 knots
Complement: 12 (5 officers, 7 men)

Two were built by Thornycroft before the merger and eight by Vosper Thornycroft afterwards. *Al Salemi* and *Al Mubaraki* were shipped to Kuwait on 8 September 1966 and the last pair *Al Shurti* and *Intisar* in 1972.
Hulls are of welded steel construction, with superstructures of aluminium alloy. Twin hydraulically operated rudders, Decca type D 202 radar. The later boats are slightly different in appearance with modified superstructure and no funnel, see photograph of *Intisar*.

INTISAR   1972, Vosper Thornycroft

4 VOSPER THORNYCROFT 56 ft TYPE (COASTAL PATROL CRAFT)

Name	No.	Builders	Commissioned
DASTOOR	—	Vosper Thornycroft Private Ltd, Singapore	June 1974
KASAR	—	Vosper Thornycroft Private Ltd, Singapore	June 1974
—	—	Vosper, Singapore	1977
—	—	Vosper, Singapore	1978

Displacement, tons: 25
Dimensions, feet (metres): 56 × 16 × 3.8 *(17.1 × 4.9 × 1.2)*
Guns: 1—20 mm; 2 MG
Main engines: 2 MTU MB6 V.331 diesels; 1 350 hp = 26 knots (30 knots in second pair)
Range, miles: 320 at 20 knots
Complement: 8 (2 officers, 6 men)

First two ordered September 1973. Both laid down 31 October 1973. Steel hulls and aluminium superstructure. Two more ordered in 1976.

KASAR (guns not fitted)   1974, Vosper Thornycroft

7 THORNYCROFT 50 ft TYPE (COASTAL PATROL CRAFT)

Built by the Singapore Yard of Thornycroft (Malaysia) Limited, now the Tanjong Rhu, Singapore Yard of Vosper Thornycroft Private Ltd.

1 VOSPER THORNYCROFT 46 ft TYPE (COASTAL PATROL CRAFT)

Name	No.	Builders	Commissioned
MAHROOS	—	Vosper Thornycroft Private Ltd, Singapore	Jan 1976

Length, feet (metres): 46 *(14)*
Guns: Can mount 2—20 mm
Main engines: 2 Rolls-Royce C8M-410 diesels; 780 hp = 21+ knots
Complement: 5

Ordered in October 1974. Hull is of welded steel construction with aluminium superstructure.

MAHROOS (guns not fitted)   1975, Singapore Hilton

11 VOSPER THORNYCROFT 35 ft TYPE (COASTAL PATROL CRAFT)

Displacement, tons: 6.3
Dimensions, feet (metres): 36 × 10 × 2 *(10.9 × 3.0 × 0.6)*
Guns: 2 MG
Main engines: 2 turbocharged Perkins diesels; 420 hp = 25 knots
Complement: 4

Ordered July 1972 from Vosper Thornycroft Private Ltd, Singapore. Built of double-skinned teak with Cascover sheathing. First four delivered late 1972, second four in May 1973, last three on 2 December 1977.

7 MAGNUM SEDAN (COASTAL PATROL CRAFT)

Dimensions, feet (metres): 27·3 × 7·9 × 2·4 *(8·3 × 2·4 × 0·7)*
Main engines: Twin Mercruiser; 660 hp = 60 knots
Range, miles: 200

First three delivered 1977, one in 1978 and three in 1979 by Magnum Marine, USA.

MAGNUM SEDAN 1978, Magnum Marine

3 VOSPER 12 metre TYPE (COASTAL PATROL CRAFT)

Of 39·4 ft *(12 m)* completed in 1978.

LANDING CRAFT

3 + 2 VOSPER THORNYCROFT 88 ft TYPE

Name	No.	Builders	Commissioned
WAHEED	—	Vosper Thornycroft Private Ltd, Singapore	May 1971
FAREED	—	Vosper Thornycroft Private Ltd, Singapore	May 1971
REGGA	—	Vosper Thornycroft Private Ltd, Singapore	Nov 1975

Dimensions, feet (metres): 88 × 22·6 × 4·3 *(27 × 6·9 × 1·3)*
Main engines: 2 Rolls-Royce C8M-410 diesels; 752 bhp = 10 knots
Complement: 9 (can carry 8 passengers)

First pair ordered in 1970 and third in October 1974 by Kuwait Ministry of the Interior. Can carry 6 400 gallons oil-fuel, 9 400 gallons water and 40 tons deck cargo, the last being handled by a 2·5 ton derrick. Used to support landing-parties working on Kuwait's off-shore islands. Two slightly larger craft ordered in 1978 will have stern ramp.

WAHEED 1974, Vosper Thornycroft

LAOS

The situation in this force is very uncertain.

Ministerial

Minister of National Defence:
Khamtai Siphandon

Personnel

(a) 1979: 550 officers and men approx
(b) 18 months national service

RIVER PATROL CRAFT

7	LCM (6) Type	28 tons	4 in commission, 3 in reserve
6	Cabin Type	21 tons	2 in commission, 4 in reserve
2	Chris Craft Type	15 tons	2 in commission
12	11 metre Type	10 tons	5 in commission, 7 in reserve
8	8 metre Type	6 tons	8 in reserve
7	Cargo Transport	50 tons	1 in commission, 6 in reserve

LEBANON

Senior Officer

Naval Commander:
Major Munir Joseph Ruhayim

Diplomatic Representation

Naval Military and Air Attaché in London:
Colonel F. El Hussami

Personnel

1979: 250 officers and men

Base

Jounieh

Mercantile Marine

Lloyd's Register of Shipping:
189 vessels of 277 846 tons gross

DELETION

1975 Djounieh (ex-*Fairmile B. ML*)

LIGHT FORCES

2 LARGE PATROL CRAFT

Name	No.	Builders	Commissioned
JIHAD	—	Hamelin S.Y.	Jan 1978
SALAMI	—	Hamelin S.Y.	Jan 1978

Displacement, tons: 135
Dimensions, feet (metres): 121·4 × 20·3 × — *(37 × 6·2 × —)*
Guns: 2—30 mm
Speed, knots: 29

Despite previous reports these two, of an order for three, were delivered.

LEBANON / Light forces — LIBERIA / Light forces 331

1 LARGE PATROL CRAFT

Name	No.	Builders	Commissioned
TARABLOUS	31	Ch. Navals de l'Estérel	1959

Displacement, tons: 90
Dimensions, feet (metres): 124·7 × 18 × 5·8 (38 × 5·6 × 1·8)
Guns: 2—40 mm; 2—12·7 mm
Main engines: 2 MTU diesels; 2 shafts; 2 700 bhp = 27 knots
Range, miles: 1 500 at 15 knots
Complement: 19 (3 officers, 16 men)

Laid down in June 1958. Launched in June 1959. Completed in 1959.

TARABLOUS   1975, Chantiers Navals de l'Estérel

3 "BYBLOS" CLASS (COASTAL PATROL CRAFT)

Name	No.	Builders	Commissioned
BYBLOS	11	France	1955
SIDON	12	France	1955
BEYROUTH (ex-Tir)	13	France	1955

Displacement, tons: 28 standard
Dimensions, feet (metres): 66 × 13·5 × 4 (20·1 × 4·1 × 1·2)
Guns: 1—20 mm; 2 MG
Main engines: General Motors diesels; 2 shafts; 530 bhp = 18·5 knots

French built ML type craft. Launched in 1954-55.

LANDING CRAFT

1 Ex-US "LCU 1466" CLASS

SOUR (ex-LCU 1474)

Displacement, tons: 180 standard; 360 full load
Dimensions, feet (metres): 115 × 34 × 6 (35·1 × 10·4 × 1·8)
Guns: 2—20 mm
Main engines: 3 diesels; 3 shafts; 675 bhp = 10 knots

Built in 1957, transferred in November 1958.

LIBERIA

Ministerial

Minister of National Defence:
   Hon E. Jonathan Goodridge
Assistant Minister of Defence:
   Hon W. R. Davis Jr

Personnel

(a) 1979: 225 officers and men
(b) Voluntary service

Presidential Yacht

1976 Liberian

Command

This Coast Guard force is controlled by a Coast Guard Commandant who is responsible to the Minister of National Defence.

Commandant LNCG:
   Commander W. Kelly Garnett
Deputy Commandant LNCG:
   Lieutenant-Commander S. Weaka Peters

DELETIONS

Patrol Craft

1976 ML 4001, ML 4002 (40 ft USCG)

Base

Elijah Johnson CG Base, Monrovia.

Mercantile Marine

Lloyd's Register of Shipping:
   2 523 vessels of 80 191 329 tons gross

LIGHT FORCES

1 US "PGM 71" CLASS

Name	No.	Builders	Commissioned
ALERT (ex-US PGM 102)	102	Peterson Ltd, Sturgeon Bay, USA	2 Dec 1966

Displacement, tons: 100
Dimensions, feet (metres): 100 × 19 × 5 (30·5 × 5·8 × 1·5)
Guns: 1—40 mm; 5—50 cal MGs
Main engines: 4—8-6-71 diesels; 2 shafts; 2 200 bhp = 21 knots
Complement: 15 (2 officers, 13 ratings)

PGM 102 (US number) was built in the USA for transfer under the Military Aid Programme. She was commissioned by the late President William V. S. Tubman. Similar to *Betelgeuse* in the Dominican Republic.

2 COASTAL PATROL CRAFT

Name	No.	Builders	Commissioned
CAVILLA	—	Swiftships Inc, Louisiana, USA	22 July 1976
MANO	—	Swiftships Inc, Louisiana, USA	22 July 1976

Displacement, tons: 38 full load
Dimensions, feet (metres): 65 × 19 × 2·6 (19·8 × 5·8 × 0·8)
Guns: 2—M-60 MGs (bridge); 1—81 mm mortar; 1—50 cal MG
Main engines: 2 V12-71 turbocharged diesels; 2 shafts; 1 920 shp = 24 knots
Range, miles: 600 at 21·5 knots
Complement: 20 (2 officers, 18 ratings)

Similar to US Sewart 65 ft type in use in many other navies. Aluminium hulls.

MANO   1976

1 COASTAL PATROL CRAFT

Name	No.	Builders	Commissioned
ST. PAUL	—	Swiftships Inc, Louisiana, USA	22 July 1976

Displacement, tons: 11
Dimensions, feet (metres): 42 × 12 × 1·5 (12·8 × 3·7 × 0·5)
Guns: 2—M60 MGs (bridge)
Main engines: 2—V8-71 turbocharged diesels; 870 bhp = 20 knots
Complement: 4

LIBYA

Establishment

The Libyan Navy was established in November 1962 when a British Naval Mission was formed and first recruits were trained at HMS *St. Angelo*, Malta. Cadets were also trained at the Britannia Royal Navy College, Dartmouth, and technical ratings at HMS *Sultan*, Gosport, and HMS *Collingwood*, Fareham, England.

Headquarters Appointment

Senior Officer, Libyan Navy:
Commander A. Shaksuki

Mining Capability

Although few of the listed Libyan ships are credited with a mining capability the fact that, in June 1973, two minefields were laid off Tripoli harbour, some eight miles out and the ability of several ships to lay mines suggests that a stock of mines is available.

Personnel

(a) 1979: Total 3 000 officers and ratings, including Coast Guard
(b) Voluntary service

Bases

Tripoli. Operating Ports at Benghazi, Darna, Tobruk.
New bases are either under construction or on order in several localities. The main centre will probably be to the south of Benghazi.

Future programmes

In a manner reminiscent of some other countries, such as India, Libya is obtaining naval supplies from both West and East. The final result if all programmes are fulfilled (four missile corvettes (Italian), ten missile craft (French) and reportedly twelve missile craft (Soviet) plus up to six submarines (Soviet)) will be a large and up-to-date fleet at a crucial position in the Mediterranean. While the training task to man this fleet must be formidable the Libyans are also showing keen interest in the procurement of GRP minehunters/sweepers.
An expansion of this magnitude will clearly call for a large increase in the training programme which may well cause considerable problems.

Strength of the Fleet

Type	Active	Building (Planned)
Submarines	3	?3
Frigate	1	—
LSD	1	—
LSTs	2	—
LCTs	2	1
Corvettes	3	2
Fast Attack Craft—Missile	11	14
Large Patrol Craft	10	—
Coastal Patrol Craft	1	—
MRC	1	—
Tugs	4	—

Mercantile Marine

Lloyd's Register of Shipping:
75 vessels of 885 362 tons gross

DELETIONS

Inshore Minesweepers

1973 *Brak* and *Zura* ("Ham" Class)

SUBMARINES

3 + ?3 Ex-SOVIET "FOXTROT" CLASS

AL BADR 312   AL FATEH
AL AHAD

Displacement, tons: 1 950 surfaced; 2 400 dived
Dimensions, feet (metres): 300·1 × 24·6 × 20 *(91·5 × 7·5 × 6·1)*
Torpedo tubes: 10—21 in (6 bow, 4 stern) 22 torpedoes
Main machinery: 3 diesels; 3 shafts; 6 000 bhp; 3 electric motors; 5 000 hp
Speed, knots: 18 surfaced; 17 dived
Range, miles: 20 000 surfaced
Complement: 70

Coming from a re-activated building line in Leningrad. *Al Badr* arrived in Tripoli 27 December 1976; the second boat in late 1977, the third in early 1978. Three more on order and building while Libyan crews continue training in USSR and Soviet officers (up to 12 in each boat) are attached to each submarine to ensure some measure of safety. In Egypt's case this surveillance continued for several years.

Radar: Snoop Tray.

Sonar: Hercules.

AL BADR   *6/1978, Michael D. J. Lennon*

FRIGATE

1 VOSPER THORNYCROFT MARK 7

Name	No.	Builders	Laid down	Launched	Commissioned
DAT ASSAWARI	F 01	Vosper Thornycroft	27 Sep 1968	Sep 1969	1 Feb 1973

Displacement, tons: 1 325 standard; 1 625 full load
Length, feet (metres): 310·0 *(94·5)* pp; 330·0 *(100·6)* oa
Beam, feet (metres): 36·0 *(11·0)*
Draught, feet (metres): 11·2 *(3·4)*
Missiles: SAM; Est 18 Sea Cat (two triple launchers)
Guns: 1—4·5 in *(114 mm)*/55 (single Mk 8); 2—40 mm/70 (single L/70); 2—35 mm/90 (twin Oerlikon)
A/S weapons: 1 Mortar Mk 10
Main engines: CODOG arrangement; 2 shafts; with Kamewa cp propellers; 2 Rolls-Royce Olympus gas turbines; 46 400 shp = 37·5 knots; 2 Paxman 16-cyl Ventura diesels; 3 500 bhp = 17 knots economical cruising speed
Range, miles: 5 700 at 17 knots

Mark 7 Frigate ordered from Vosper Thornycroft on 6 February 1968. Generally similar in design to the two Iranian Mark 5s built by this firm, but larger and with different armament. After trials she carried out work-up at Portland, England, reaching Tripoli autumn 1973.

Radar: Air surveillance AWS-1.
Fire control radar and RDL-1 radar direction finder.

Refit: Due to failure of generators a refit was planned in UK in 1978. However, possibly because of the length of the passage involved, this refit was transferred to CNR, Italy.

DAT ASSAWARI   *1973, John G. Callis*

LIBYA / Logistic support ship — Light forces 333

LOGISTIC SUPPORT SHIP

1 LSD TYPE

Name	No.	Builders	Laid down	Launched	Commissioned
ZELTIN	—	Vosper Thornycroft, Woolston	1967	29 Feb 1968	23 Jan 1969

Displacement, tons: 2 200 standard; 2 470 full load
Length, feet (metres): 300·0 *(91·4)* wl; 324·0 *(98·8)* oa
Beam, feet (metres): 48·0 *(14·6)*
Draught, feet (metres): 10·2 *(3·1)*; 19·0 *(5·8)* aft when flooded
Dock:
Length, feet (metres): 135·0 *(41·1)*
Width, feet (metres): 40·0 *(12·2)*
Guns: 2—40 mm
Main engines: 2 Paxman 16-cyl Ventura diesels; 3 500 bhp; 2 shafts
Speed, knots: 15
Fuel, tons: 350
Range, miles: 3 000 at 14 knots
Complement: As Senior Officer Ship: 101 (15 officers and 86 ratings)

ZELTIN 1969

The ship provides full logistic support, including mobile docking maintenance and repair facilities for the Libyan fleet. Craft up to 120 ft can be docked. Used as tender for Light Forces. The Vosper Thornycroft Group received the order for this ship in January 1967 for delivery in late 1968.

Fitted with accommodation for a flag officer or a senior officer and staff. Operational and administrative base of the squadron. Workshops with a total area of approx 4 500 sq ft are situated amidships with ready access to the dock, and there is a 3 ton travelling gantry fitted with outriggers to cover ships berthed alongside up to 200 ft long.

Radar: Thomson-CSF Triton for Vega system.

CORVETTES

2 + 2 "550 TON" MISSILE CORVETTES

Name	No.	Builders	Laid down	Launched	Commissioned
WADI M'RAGH	412	Cantieré del Muggiano, La Spezia	—	29 Sep 1977	mid-1978
WADI MAJER	—	Cantieré del Muggiano, La Spezia	—	20 Apr 1978	1979
—	—	Cantieré del Muggiano, La Spezia	—	—	—
—	—	Cantieré del Muggiano, La Spezia	—	—	—

Displacement, tons: 630 full load
Dimensions, feet (metres): 202·4 × 30·5 × 7·2 *(61·7 × 9·3 × 2·2)*
Missiles: SSM; 4 Otomat (single cells)
Guns: 1—76mm/62 (single Compact); 2—35 mm/90 (twin Oerlikon)
A/S weapons: 6 (2 triple) Mk 32 A/S torpedo tubes
Mines: Can lay 16 mines
Main engines: 4 MTU MA 16 V956 TB91 diesels; 18 000 hp; 4 shafts = 33 knots
Range, miles: 4 400 at 14 knots
Complement: 56

Ordered in 1974. As these corvettes can be provided with two, three or four diesels, the performance is very variable. The data given above is basic information for the missile variant (schedule 1).
Wadi M'ragh started trials spring 1978.

Electronics: ECM equipment; ELMER telecommunications system.

Radar: Air and surface search: Selenia RAN 11 LX
Navigation: Decca TM 1226.
Fire control: Elsag NA 10.

Sonar: Diodon from Thomson CSF.

WADI M'RAGH 5/1978, Commander Aldo Fraccaroli

Name	No.	Builders	Commissioned
TOBRUK	C 01	Vosper Ltd, Portsmouth and Vickers Ltd	20 Apr 1966

Displacement, tons: 440 standard; 500 full load
Dimensions, feet (metres): 177 × 28·5 × 13 *(54 × 8·7 × 4)*
Guns: 1—4 in; 4—40 mm (twin)
Main engines: 2 Paxman Ventura 16 YJCM diesels; 2 shafts; 3 800 bhp = 18 knots
Range, miles: 2 900 at 14 knots
Complement: 63 (5 officers and 58 ratings)

Launched on 29 July 1965, completed on 30 March 1966, commissioned for service at Portsmouth on 20 April 1966, and arrived in Tripoli on 15 June 1966. Fitted with surface warning radar, Vosper roll damping fins and air-conditioning. A suite of State apartments is included in the accommodation.

TOBRUK 1971, A. & J. Pavia

LIGHT FORCES

2 + 8 "COMBATTANTE II G" CLASS (FAST ATTACK CRAFT—MISSILE)

Displacement, tons: 311
Dimensions, feet (metres): 160·7 × 24·9 × 7·9 *(49 × 7·6 × 2·4)*
Missiles: SSM; 4 Otomat (single cells)
Guns: 1—76 mm/62 (single Compact); 2—40 mm/70 (twin Compact)
Main engines: 4 diesels; 20 000 bhp; 4 shafts = 40 knots
Range, miles: 1 600 at 15 knots
Complement: 31

Steel hull with alloy superstructure. Ordered from CMN Cherbourg in May 1977. First pair laid down early spring 1978 and 19 June 1978. Delivery likely 1979-82.

Radar: Thomson-CSF Triton and Castor radars for Vega system.

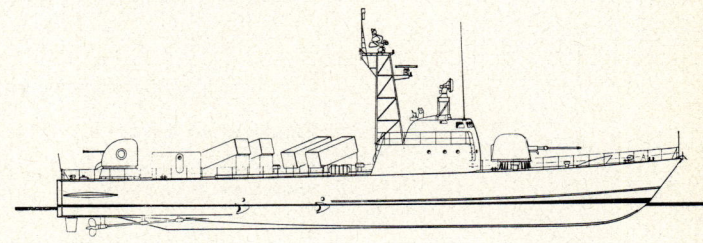

"COMBATTANTE II G" 1976, CMN Cherbourg

334   LIBYA / Light forces

6 + ? Ex-SOVIET "OSA II" CLASS (FAST ATTACK CRAFT—MISSILE)

205 + 5

Displacement, tons: 165 standard; 210 full load
Dimensions, feet (metres): 128·7 × 25·1 × 5·9 *(39·3 × 7·7 × 1·8)*
Missile launchers: SSM; 4 SS-N-2 (single cells)
Guns: 4—30 mm (2 twins)
Main engines: 3 diesels; 12 000 bhp = 32 knots
Range, miles: 800 at 25 knots
Complement: 30

The first craft arrived in October 1976, two more in early 1977, two more later in 1977 and a sixth in 1978. In November 1975 the Libyan government said that 24 of this class were to be acquired—subsequent reports suggest this may have been reduced to 12.

"OSA II" Class   1970

3 "SUSA" CLASS (FAST ATTACK CRAFT—MISSILE)

Name	No.	Builders	Commissioned
SUSA	P 01	Vosper Ltd, Portsmouth	23 Jan 1969
SIRTE	P 02	Vosper Ltd, Portsmouth	23 Jan 1969
SEBHA (ex-*Sokna*)	P 03	Vosper Ltd, Portsmouth	1969

Displacement, tons: 95 standard; 114 full load
Dimensions, feet (metres): 100·0 × 25·5 × 7·0 *(30·5 × 7·8 × 2·1)*
Missiles: 8—SS 12
Guns: 2—40 mm (single)
Main engines: 3 Bristol Siddeley "Proteus" gas turbines; 3 shafts; 12 750 bhp = 54 knots
Complement: 20

SEBHA (now carry pennant numbers)   1969, Wright and Logan

The order for these three fast patrol boats was announced on 12 October 1966. They are generally similar to the "Soloven" class designed and built by Vosper for the Royal Danish Navy. Fitted with air-conditioning and modern radar and radio equipment. *Suza* was launched on 31 August 1967, *Sirte* on 10 January 1968 and *Sokna* (renamed *Sebha*) on 29 February 1968. First operational vessels in the world to be armed with Nord-Aviation SS 12(M) guided weapons with sighting turret installation and other equipment developed jointly by Vosper and Nord. All three overhauled in Italy in 1977. Two are probably to be transferred to Malta—dates and names unknown.

4 "GARIAN" CLASS (LARGE PATROL CRAFT)

Name	No.	Builders	Commissioned
KHAWLAN	—	Brooke Marine, Lowestoft	30 Aug 1969
MERAWA	—	Brooke Marine, Lowestoft	early 1970
SABRATHA	—	Brooke Marine, Lowestoft	early 1970
GARIAN	—	Brooke Marine, Lowestoft	30 Aug 1969

Displacement, tons: 120 standard; 159 full load
Dimensions, feet (metres): 106 × 21·2 × 5·5 *(32·3 × 6·5 × 1·7)*
Guns: 1—40 mm; 1—20 mm
Main engines: 2 Paxman 12-cyl Ventura diesels; 2 200 bhp = 24 knots
Range, miles: 1 500 at 12 knots
Complement: 15 to 22

Launched on 21 April, 29 May, 25 October and 30 September 1969, respectively.

KHAWLAN   1970, Brooke Marine

6 THORNYCROFT TYPE (LARGE PATROL CRAFT)

Name	No.	Builders	Commissioned
AKRAMA	—	Vosper Thornycroft	early 1969
AR RAKIB	—	John I. Thornycroft, Woolston	4 May 1967
BENINA	—	Vosper Thornycroft	29 Aug 1968
FARWA	—	John I. Thornycroft, Woolston	4 May 1967
HOMS	—	Vosper Thornycroft	early 1969
MISURATA	—	Vosper Thornycroft	29 Aug 1968

Displacement, tons: 100
Dimensions, feet (metres): 100 × 21 × 5·5 *(30·5 × 6·4 × 1·7)*
Gun: 1—20 mm
Main engines: 3 Rolls-Royce DV8TLM diesels; 1 740 bhp = 18 knots
Range, miles: 1 800 at 14 knots

Welded steel construction. Slight difference in silhouette between first pair and the remainder.

FARWA   1969, Thornycroft

1 THORNYCROFT TYPE (COASTAL PATROL CRAFT)

Dimensions, feet (metres): 78 × 15 × 4·5 *(23·8 × 4·6 × 1·4)*
Gun: 1 MG
Main engines: 3 Rolls-Royce diesels; 3 shafts; 945 bhp = 22·5 knots
Range, miles: 400 at 15 knots

Built by John I. Thornycroft, Singapore in 1962. Two similar but smaller boats transferred to Malta in 1974.

AMPHIBIOUS FORCES

2 "PS 700" CLASS (LST)

Name	No.	Builders	Commissioned
IBN OUF	130	CNI de la Mediterranée	11 Mar 1977
IBN HARITHA	131	CNI de la Mediterranée	10 Mar 1978

Displacement, tons: 2 800 full load
Dimensions, feet (metres): 326·4 × 51·2 × 8·2 *(99·5 × 15·6 × 2·4)*
Aircraft: Deck for Alouette III
Guns: 6—40 mm (twin turrets) Breda Bofors; 1—81 mm mortar
Main engines: 2 SEMT-Pielstick diesels; 5 340 hp; 2 shafts (cp propellers) = 15·4 knots
Range, miles: 4 000 at 14 knots
Complement: 35

Can carry 240 troops under normal conditions. Have bow doors and ramp for the 11 tanks carried. Helicopter platform.
Ibn Ouf laid down 1 April 1976 and launched 22 October 1976; *Ibn Haritha* laid down 18 April 1977, launched 18 October 1977.

IBN OUF   *1977, Marius Bar, Toulon*

2 + ?1 Ex-SOVIET "POLNOCHNIY" CLASS (LCT)

AL EMLAKA
IBN AL HADRAMI   112
+ 1?

Displacement, tons: 1 000 full load
Dimensions, feet (metres): 239·4 × 29·5 × 9·8 *(75 × 9 × 3)*
Guns: 4—30 mm; 2 rocket launchers
Main engines: 2 diesels; 5 000 hp = 18 knots
Complement: 40

The first to be transferred arrived in December 1977. *Ibn Al Hadrami* visited Malta in June 1978. On 14 September 1978 *Ibn Qis* was totally burned out during a landing exercise and must be considered a total loss. *Al Emlaka* arrived 5 November 1978.

IBN AL HADRAMI   *6/1978, Michael D. J. Lennon*

MAINTENANCE REPAIR CRAFT

ZLEITEN (ex-*MRC 1013*, ex-*LCT*)

Displacement, tons: 657 standard; 900 approx full load
Dimensions, feet (metres): 231·3 × 39·0 × 5·0 *(70·5 × 11·9 × 1·5)*
Main engines: 4 Paxman diesels; 2 shafts; 1 840 bhp = 9 knots cruising

Built in 1944-45. Purchased from UK on 5 September 1966. Now a hulk.

TUGS

4 COASTAL TYPE

Name	No.	Builders	Commissioned
RAS EL-HELAL	—	Mondego, Portugal	22 Oct 1976
AL SHWEIRIF	—	Mondego, Portugal	17 Feb 1977
AL KERIAT	—	Mondego, Portugal	1 July 1977
TABKAH	—	Argibay, Lisbon	29 July 1978

Measurement, tons: 200 gross
Dimensions, feet (metres): 114 × 29·5 × 13 *(34·8 × 9 × 4)*
Main engines: 2 diesels, 2 300 hp = 14 knots

Laid down—*Ras El-Helal,* 5 February 1976; *Al Shweirif* 23 March 1976; *Al Keriat,* 23 March 1976.

MADAGASCAR

Ministerial

Minister of Defence:
Lieutenant-Colonel Mampila Jaona

Personnel

(a) 1979: 600 officers and men (including Marine Company)
(b) 18 months national service

Mercantile Marine

Lloyd's Register of Shipping:
45 vessels of 40 303 tons gross

Bases and Ports

Diego Suarez, Tamatave, Majunga, Tulear, Nossi-Be, Fort Dauphin, Manakara.

DELETION

1976 *Jasmine* (Tender)

LIGHT FORCES

1 TYPE 48 (LARGE PATROL CRAFT)

Name	No.	Builders	Commissioned
MALAIKA	—	Chantiers Navals Franco-Belges (SFCN)	Dec 1967

Displacement, tons: 235 light
Dimensions, feet (metres): 155·8 × 23·6 × 8·2 *(47·5 × 7·1 × 2·5)*
Guns: 2—40 mm
Main engines: 2 MGO diesels; 2 shafts; 2 400 bhp = 18·5 knots
Range, miles: 2 000 at 15 knots
Complement: 25

Ordered by the French Navy for delivery to Madagascar. Laid down in November 1966 launched on 22 March 1967.

5 PATROL BOATS

Displacement, tons: 46
Length, feet (metres): 78·7 *(24)*
Gun: 1—40 mm
Main engines: 2 diesels = 22 knots

Used by the Maritime Police. Built in 1962.

AMPHIBIOUS FORCE

1 "BATRAM" CLASS

Name	No.	Builders	Commissioned
TOKY	—	Arsenal de Diego Suarez	Oct 1974

Displacement, tons: 810
Dimensions, feet (metres): 217·8 × 41 × 6·2 *(66·4 × 12·5 × 1·9)*
Missiles: 8—SS 12
Guns: 2—40 mm
Main engines: 2 MGO diesels; 2 400 hp; 2 shafts = 13 knots
Complement: 27
Range, miles: 3 000 at 12 knots

Can carry 250 tons stores and 30 passengers or 120 troops over short distances. Paid for by the French Government as military assistance.
Fitted with a bow ramp and similar to, though larger, than the French EDIC.

TRAINING SHIP

Name	No.	Builders	Commissioned
FANANTENANA (ex-*Richelieu*)	—	A. G. Weser, Bremen, Germany	1959

Displacement, tons: 1 040 standard; 1 200 full load
Dimensions, feet (metres): 206·4 × 30 × 14·8 *(62·9 × 9·2 × 4·5)*
Guns: 2—40 mm
Main engines: 2 Deutz diesels; 1 shaft; 1 560 bhp = 12 knots

Trawler purchased and converted in 1966-67 to Coast Guard and training ship. 691 tons gross.

MALAWI

1 FAIREY MARINE "SPEAR" CLASS

Dimensions, feet (metres): 29·8 × 9·2 × 2·6 *(9·1 × 2·8 × ·8)*
Guns: 2—7·62 mm MG
Main engines: 2 Perkins diesels of 290 hp = 25 knots
Complement: 3

Acquired late 1976.

Three other small patrol-boats are deployed on Lake Nyasa (L. Malawi). The first was bought in 1968.

MALAYSIA
(see also Sabah)

Administration

Minister of Defence:
Hon. Dato Hussein bin Onn

Headquarters Appointments

Chief of the Naval Staff:
Rear-Admiral Dato Mohd. Zain bin Mohd. Salleh, DPMJ, KMN
Deputy Chief of the Naval Staff:
Commodore Abdul Wahab bin Haji Nawi, KMN, SMJ

Senior Commands

Commander Naval Area 1:
Commodore P. K. Nettur, KMN
Commander Naval Area 2:
Commodore Aris Fadzillah bin Alang Ahmad

Diplomatic Representation

Services Adviser (Navy) in London:
Major Ahmad Kamal

Personnel

(a) 1979: 6 000 officers and ratings (Reserves about 1 000)
(b) Voluntary service

Bases

KD *Malaya*, Johore Straits; Labuan. (KD *Sri Labuan, Sri Tawau, Sri Rejang*).

Prefix to Ships' Names

The names of Malaysian warships are prefixed by KD, (Kapal Diraja).

Mercantile Marine

Lloyd's Register of Shipping:
182 vessels of 552 456 tons gross

Strength of the Fleet

Type	Active	Building
Frigates	2	—
Fast Attack Craft—Missile	4	4
Fast Attack Craft—Gun	6	
Large Patrol Craft	22	—
Minesweepers—Coastal	5	
Diving Tender	1	
Survey Vessels	1	—
LSTs	3	—
Police Launches	30	—

DELETIONS

Frigate
1977 Hang Tuah ("Loch" Class)

Light Forces
1976 Sri Kedah, Sri Pahang
1977 Gempita, Handalan, Penderkar, Perkase

Mine Warfare Forces
1977 Jerai ("Ton" Class)

Survey Ship
1979 Perantau

PENNANT LIST

Frigates
| F 24 | Rahmat |
| F 76 | Hang Tuah |

Light Forces
P 34	Kris
P 36	Sundang
P 37	Badek
P 38	Renchong
P 39	Tombak
P 40	Lembing
P 41	Serampang
P 42	Panah
P 43	Kerambit
P 44	Beledau
P 45	Kelewang
P 46	Rentaka
P 47	Sri Perlis
P 49	Sri Johor
P 3139	Sri Selangor
P 3140	Sri Perak
P 3142	Sri Kelantan
P 3143	Sri Trengganu
P 3144	Sri Sabah
P 3145	Sri Sarawak
P 3146	Sri Negri Sembilan
P 3147	Sri Melaka
P 3501	Perdana
P 3502	Serang
P 3503	Ganas
P 3504	Ganyang
P 3505	Jerong
P 3506	Todak
P 3507	Paus
P 3508	Yu
P 3509	Baung
P 3510	Pari

Mine Warfare Forces
M 1127	Mahamiru
M 1134	Kinabalu
M 1143	Ledang
M 1163	Tahan
M 1172	Brinchang

Support Forces
A 152	Mutiara
A 1109	Duyong
A 1500	Sri Langkawi
A 1501	Sri Banggi
A 1502	Rajah Jarom

Police Craft
| PX 1-30 | Coastal Patrol Craft |

FRIGATES

1 YARROW TYPE

Name	No.	Builders	Laid down	Launched	Commissioned
RAHMAT (ex-*Hang Jebat*)	F 24	Yarrow Shipbuilders & Co Ltd	Feb 1966	18 Dec 1967	Mar 1971

Displacement, tons: 1 250 standard; 1 600 full load
Length, feet (metres): 300·0 *(91·44)* pp; 308 *(93·9)* oa
Beam, feet (metres): 34·1 *(10·4)*
Draught, feet (metres): 14·8 *(4·5)*
Aircraft: Can land helo. on MacGregor hatch on Limbo well
Missiles: SAM; Est 8 Sea Cat (one quad launcher)
Guns: 1—4·5 in *(114 mm)*/45 (single); 2—40 mm (singles)
A/S weapon: 1 Limbo 3-barrelled mortar
Main engines: 1 Bristol Siddeley Olympus gas turbine; 19 500 shp; Crosley Pielstick diesel; 3 850 bhp; 2 shafts
Speed, knots: 26 boosted by gas turbine; 16 on diesel alone
Range, miles: 6 000 at 16 knots; 1 000 at 26 knots
Complement: 140

Fully automatic with saving in complement. Ordered on 1 February 1966.

Radar: Air surveillance: HSA LW 02.
Fire control: M 20 with radar in spherical radome for guns; M 44 for Sea cat.

RAHMAT   1972, Wright and Logan

1 UK TYPE 41/61

Name	No.	Builders	Laid down	Launched	Commissioned
HANG TUAH (ex-HMS *Mermaid*)	F 76	Yarrow Shipbuilders & Co Ltd	1965	29 Dec 1966	16 May 1973 (see notes)

Displacement, tons: 2 300 standard; 2 520 full load
Dimensions, feet (metres): 339·3 × 40 × 12 *(103·5 × 12·2 × 3·7)*
Guns: 2—4 in (twin); 2—40 mm (singles)
A/S weapons: 1—3-barrelled Limbo mortar
Main engines: 8 diesels; 14 400 shp; 2 shafts; 2 cp propellers = 24 knots
Oil fuel, tons: 230
Range, miles: 4 800 at 15 knots

Similar in hull and machinery to "Leopard" and "Salisbury" classes. Originally built for Ghana as a display ship for ex-president Nkrumah at a cost of £5m but put up for sale after his departure. She was launched without ceremony on December 1966 and completed in 1968. She was transferred Portsmouth Dockyard in April 1972 being acquired by the Royal Navy. Refit started October 1972 at Chatham. Commissioned in Royal Navy 16 May 1973. She was based at Singapore 1974-75 returning to UK early 1976.

Transfer: To Malaysia May 1977 as replacement for the previous Hang Tuah. She was refitted by Vosper Thornycroft and commissioned on 22 July 1977 sailing for Malaysia in August.

HANG TUAH   8/1977, Michael D. J. Lennon

MALAYSIA / Light forces

LIGHT FORCES

0 + 4 "SPICA-M" CLASS (FAST ATTACK CRAFT—MISSILE)

Displacement, tons: 240
Dimensions, feet (metres): 142·6 × 23·3 × 7·4 *(43·6 × 7·1 × 2·4)*
Missiles: SSM; 4 MM38 Exocet (single cells); 1 Blowpipe (8 tubes)
Guns: 1—57 mm; 1—40 mm
Main engines: 3 MTU diesels; 3 shafts; 10 800 hp = 34·5 knots
Range, miles: 1 850 at 14 knots

Bridge further forward than in Swedish class to accommodate Exocet.
Ordered from Karlskrona Shipyard 15 October 1976 for delivery in 1979. First laid down 24 May 1977, second 27 June 1977, third 15 July 1977, fourth 21 October 1977.

4 "PERDANA" CLASS (FAST ATTACK CRAFT—MISSILE)

Name	No.	Builders	Commissioned
PERDANA	P 3501	Constructions Mécaniques de Normandie	Dec 1972
SERANG	P 3502	Constructions Mécaniques de Normandie	31 Jan 1973
GANAS	P 3503	Constructions Mécaniques de Normandie	28 Feb 1973
GANYANG	P 3504	Constructions Mécaniques de Normandie	20 Mar 1973

Displacement, tons: 234 standard; 265 full load
Dimensions, feet (metres): 154·2 × 23·1 × 12·8 *(47·0 × 7·0 × 3·9)*
Missiles: SSM; 2 MM 38 Exocet (single cells)
Guns: 1—57 mm Bofors; 1—40 mm/70 Bofors
Main engines: 4 MTU diesels; 4 shafts; 14 000 bhp = 36·5 knots
Range, miles: 800 at 25 knots

Perdana launched 31 May 1972 and *Ganas* launched 26 October 1972, *Serang* launched 22 December 1971, and *Ganyang* launched 16 March 1972. All of basic "La Combattante II" design. Left Cherbourg for Malaysia 2 May 1973.

Radar: Thomson-CSF Triton and Pollux radars for Vega system.

PERDANA   1976, A. G. Burgoyne

6 "JERONG" CLASS (FAST ATTACK CRAFT—GUN)

Name	No.	Builders	Commissioned
JERONG	3505	Hong-Leong-Lürssen, Butterworth	27 Mar 1976
TODAK	3506	Hong-Leong-Lürssen, Butterworth	16 June 1976
PAUS	3507	Hong-Leong-Lürssen, Butterworth	16 Aug 1976
YU	3508	Hong-Leong-Lürssen, Butterworth	15 Nov 1976
BAUNG	3509	Hong-Leong-Lürssen, Butterworth	11 Jan 1977
PARI	3510	Hong-Leong-Lürssen, Butterworth	23 Mar 1977

Displacement, tons: 254 full load
Dimensions, feet (metres): 147·3 × 23 × 8·3 *(44·9 × 7 × 2·5)*
Guns: 1—57 mm; 1—40 mm
Main engines: 3 Maybach Mercedes-Benz diesels; 9 900 bhp = 32 knots
Range, miles: 2 000 at 15 knots
Complement: 41

Launch dates: *Jerong*, 28 July 1975; *Todak*, 15 March 1976; *Paus*, 3 June 1976; *Yu*, 17 July 1976; *Baung*, 5 October 1976; *Pari*, January 1977.

JERONG   1976, Royal Malaysian Navy

4 "KEDAH" CLASS (LARGE PATROL CRAFT)

Name	No.	Builders	Commissioned
SRI SELANGOR	P 3139	Vosper Ltd, Portsmouth	25 Mar 1963
SRI PERAK	P 3140	Vosper Ltd, Portsmouth	June 1963
SRI KELANTAN	P 3142	Vosper Ltd, Portsmouth	12 Nov 1963
SRI TRENGGANU	P 3143	Vosper Ltd, Portsmouth	16 Dec 1963

4 "SABAH" CLASS (LARGE PATROL CRAFT)

Name	No.	Builders	Commissioned
SRI SABAH	P 3144	Vosper Ltd, Portsmouth	2 Sep 1964
SRI SARAWAK	P 3145	Vosper Ltd, Portsmouth	30 Sep 1964
SRI NEGRI SEMBILAN	P 3146	Vosper Ltd, Portsmouth	28 Sep 1964
SRI MELAKA	P 3147	Vosper Ltd, Portsmouth	2 Nov 1964

14 "KRIS" CLASS (LARGE PATROL CRAFT)

Name	No.	Builders	Commissioned
KRIS	P 34	Vosper Ltd, Portsmouth	1 Jan 1966
SUNDANG	P 36	Vosper Ltd, Portsmouth	29 Nov 1966
BADEK	P 37	Vosper Ltd, Portsmouth	15 Dec 1966
RENCHONG	P 38	Vosper Ltd, Portsmouth	17 Jan 1967
TOMBAK	P 39	Vosper Ltd, Portsmouth	2 Mar 1967
LEMBING	P 40	Vosper Ltd, Portsmouth	12 Apr 1967
SERAMPANG	P 41	Vosper Ltd, Portsmouth	19 May 1967
PANAH	P 42	Vosper Ltd, Portsmouth	27 July 1967
KERAMBIT	P 43	Vosper Ltd, Portsmouth	28 July 1967
BELEDAU	P 44	Vosper Ltd, Portsmouth	12 Sep 1967
KELEWANG	P 45	Vosper Ltd, Portsmouth	4 Oct 1967
RENTAKA	P 46	Vosper Ltd, Portsmouth	22 Sep 1967
SRI PERLIS	P 47	Vosper Ltd, Portsmouth	24 Jan 1968
SRI JOHOR	P 49	Vosper Ltd, Portsmouth	14 Feb 1968

Displacement, tons: 96 standard; 109 full load
Dimensions, feet (metres): 103 × 19·8 × 5·5 *(31·4 × 6 × 1·7)*
Guns: 2—40 mm/70
Main engines: 2 Bristol Siddeley/Maybach (MTU) MD 655/18 diesels; 3 500 bhp = 27 knots
Range, miles: 1 400 (*Sabah* class 1 660) at 14 knots
Complement: 22 (3 officers, 19 ratings)

The first six boats, constituting the "Kedah" class were ordered in 1961 for delivery in 1963. The four boats of the "Sabah" class were ordered in 1963 for delivery in 1964. The remaining 14

SRI SABAH ("Sabah" Class)   1976, A. G. Burgoyne

boats of the "Kris" class were ordered in 1965 for delivery between 1966 and 1968. All are of prefabricated steel construction and are fitted with Decca radar, air-conditioning and Vosper roll damping equipment. The differences between the three classes are minor, the later ones having improved radar, communications, evaporators and engines of Maybach (MTU), as opposed to Bristol Siddeley construction. *Sri Johor*, the last of the 14 boats of the "Kris" class, was launched on 22 June 1967.

MALAYSIA / Mine warfare forces — Tug 339

MINE WARFARE FORCES

5 Ex-BRITISH "TON" CLASS (MINESWEEPERS—COASTAL)

Name	No.	Builders	Commissioned
MAHAMIRU (ex-HMS *Darlaston*)	M 1127	Cook, Welton and Gemmell	1954
KINABALU (ex-HMS *Essington*)	M 1134	Camper and Nicholson	1955
LEDANG (ex-HMS *Hexton*)	M 1143	Cook, Welton and Gemmell	1954
TAHAN (ex-HMS *Lullington*)	M 1163	Harland and Wolff	1956
BRINCHANG (ex-HMS *Thankerton*)	M 1172	Camper and Nicholson	1957

Displacement, tons: 360 standard; 425 full load
Dimensions, feet (metres): 152 × 28·8 × 8·2 *(46·4 × 8·8 × 2·5)*
Guns: 1—40 mm (fwd); 2—20 mm (aft)
Main engines: 2 Deltic diesels; 2 shafts; 2 500 bhp = 15 knots
Oil fuel, tons: 45
Range, miles: 2 300 at 13 knots
Complement: 39

Mahamiru transferred from the Royal Navy on May 1960. *Ledang*, refitted at Chatham Dockyard before transfer, commissioned for Malaysia in October 1963. *Jerai* and *Kinabalu*, refitted in Great Britain, arrived in Malaysia summer 1964. *Brinchang* and *Tahan*, refitted in Singapore, transferred to Malaysian Navy in May and April 1966, respectively. All six underwent a nine month refit by Vosper Thornycroft, Singapore during 1972-73 which will extend their availability by some years.

KINABALU 1976, A. G. Burgoyne

AMPHIBIOUS FORCES

Note: Two landing craft, *Melaban* and *Jerijih*, of unknown size and ownership completed in 1978.

3 Ex-US "511-1152" CLASS (LSTs)

SRI LANGKAWI (ex-USS *Hunterdon County*, AGP 838 ex-*LST 838*) A 1500
SRI BANGGI (ex-USS *Henry County LST 824*) A 1501
RAJAH JAROM (ex-USS *Sedgewick County LST 1123*) A 1502

Displacement, tons: 1 653 standard; 2 366 beaching; 4 080 full load
Dimensions, feet (metres): 328·0 × 50·0 × 14·0 *(100 × 15·3 × 4·3)*
Guns: 8—40 mm (2 twin, 4 single)
Main engines: General Motors diesels; 2 shafts; 1 700 bhp = 11·6 knots
Complement: 138 (11 officers, 127 ratings)

Built in 1945. *Sri Langkawi* transferred on loan from the US Navy and commissioned in the Royal Malaysian Navy on 1 July 1971. Sold 1 August 1974. Other two transferred by sale 7 October 1976 and used as cargo support ships. Cargo capacity 2 100 tons. *Sri Langkawi* operates as a tender to Light Forces.

SRI LANGKAWI 1976, A. G. Burgoyne

SURVEY VESSEL

Name	No.	Builders	Commissioned
MUTIARA	A 152	Hong-Leong-Lürssen, Butterworth	12 Jan 1978

Displacement, tons: 1 905
Dimensions, feet (metres): 232·9 × 42·6 × 13·1 *(71 × 13 × 4)*
Guns: 2—20 mm
Main engines: 2 Deutz diesels; 4 000 hp = 16 knots
Range, miles: 4 500 at 16 knots
Complement: 156 (13 officers, 143 ratings)

Ordered in early 1975.

MUTIARA 1978, Royal Malaysian Navy

DIVING TENDER

Name	No.	Builders	Commissioned
DUYONG	A 1109	Kall Teck (Pte) Ltd, Singapore	5 Jan 1971

Displacement, tons: 120 standard; 140 full load
Dimensions, feet (metres): 110·0 × 21·0 × 5·8 *(33·6 × 6·4 × 1·8)*
Gun: 1—20 mm
Main engines: 2 Cummins diesels; 1 900 rpm; 500 bhp = 10 knots
Complement: 23

Launched on 18 August 1970 as TRV.

DUYONG 1976, A. G. Burgoyne

TUG

TUNDA SATU

Of 150 tons. 85·3 ft with one Cummins diesel. Built by Ironwood (Malaysia). Laid down 1 March 1977, launched 24 February 1978.

ROYAL MALAYSIAN POLICE

18 PX CLASS

MAHKOTA PX 1	BENTARA PX 7	PEKAN PX 13
TEMENGGONG PX 2	PERWIRA PX 8	KELANG PX 14
HULUBALANG PX 3	PERTANDA PX 9	KUALA KANGSAR PX 15
MAHARAJASETIA PX 4	SHAHBANDAR PX 10	ARAU PX 16
MAHARAJALELA PX 5	SANGSETIA PX 11	SRI GUMANTONG PX 17
PAHLAWAN PX 6	LAKSAMANA PX 12	SRI LABUAN PX 18

Displacement, tons: 85
Dimensions, feet (metres): 87·5 × 19 × 4·8 (26·7 × 5·8 × 1·5)
Guns: 2—20 mm
Main engines: 2 Mercedes-Benz (MTU) diesels; 2 shafts; 2 700 hp = 25 knots
Range, miles: 700 at 15 knots
Complement: 15

6 IMPROVED PX CLASS

ALOR STAR PX 19	KUALA TRENGGANU PX 21	SRI MENANTI PX 23
KOTA BAHRU PX 20	JOHORE BAHRU PX 22	KUCHING PX 24

Displacement, tons: 92
Dimensions, feet (metres): 91 (27·8)
Guns: 2—20 mm
Main engines: 2 (MTU) diesels; 2 460 hp = 25 knots
Range, miles: 750 at 15 knots
Complement: 18

All 24 boats built by Vosper Thornycroft Private, Singapore; PX class between 1963 and 1970, Improved PX class 1972-73. *Sri Gumantong* and *Sri Labuan* operated by Sabah Government, remainder by Royal Malaysian Police.

SRI MENANTI — 1972, Yam Photos, Singapore

6 LÜRSSEN PATROL CRAFT

SRI — PX 25	SRI KUDAT PX 26	SRI TAWAU PX 27	+ 3

Of 62·5 tons and 25 knots with one 20 mm gun. First three completed mid-1973.

MALDIVES

A series of widely separated atolls where fishing has been interrupted by foreign craft and the small communities can be reached only by sea.

Mercantile Marine

Lloyd's Register of Shipping:
41 vessels of 76 218 tons gross.

---

1 Ex-BRITISH TARGET TOWING LAUNCH

Displacement, tons: 34·6
Dimensions, feet (metres): 68 × 19 × 6 (20·7 × 5·8 × 1·8)
Main engines: 2 Rolls-Royce Sea Griffon diesels; 1 100 bhp = 30 knots
Complement: 9

Transferred by RAF after their evacuation of Gan in 1976.

1 Ex-BRITISH PINNACE

Displacement, tons: 28·3
Dimensions, feet (metres): 63 × 15·5 × 5 (19·2 × 4·9 × 1·5)
Main engines: 2 Rolls-Royce C6 diesels; 190 bhp = 13 knots
Complement: 5

5 tons cargo capacity. Transferred by RAF in 1976.

4 Ex-BRITISH LANDING CRAFT

64 ft General Purpose craft transferred by RAF in 1976.

3 Ex-TAIWANESE TRAWLERS

Confiscated for illegal fishing. Fitted with one twin 25 mm (Soviet) gun on foc's'le.

1 FAIREY MARINE 45 ft TYPE

Provided for patrol and intercommunication duties in 1975.

MALI

Personnel

1979: 50 officers and men

Patrol Craft

A small river patrol service with three craft operating on headwaters of the Niger with bases Bamako, Segou, Mopti and Timbuktu.

MALTA

A coastal patrol force of small craft was formed in 1973. It is manned by the Maltese Regiment and primarily employed as a Coast Guard. It is reported that two of the Libyan "Susa" class are to be handed over to Malta.

Mercantile Marine

Lloyd's Register of Shipping:
47 vessels of 101 541 tons gross

1 CUSTOMS LAUNCH

C 21

Displacement, tons: 25
Dimensions, feet (metres): 54·1 × 12·8 × 4·9 *(16·5 × 3·9 × 1·5)*
Main engines: 2 Fiat 521 3M diesels
Complement: 6

Built by Malta Drydocks 1960 and purchased 1973.

2 Ex-US "SWIFT" CLASS

C 23 (ex-US C 6823)   **C 24** (ex-US C 6824)

Displacement, tons: 22·5
Dimensions, feet (metres): 50 × 13 × 4·9 *(15·6 × 4 × 1·5)*
Guns: 3—·50 cal Browning M2 MG; 81 mm mortars
Main engines: 2 General Motors 12V-71N diesels = 25 knots
Endurance: 24 hours
Complement: 6

Built by Sewart Seacraft Ltd in 1967. Bought in February 1971.

C 23   1977, Michael D. J. Lennon

2 Ex-LIBYAN CUSTOMS LAUNCHES

C 25   **C 26**

Displacement, tons: 86·2
Dimensions, feet (metres): 103 × 16·1 × 4·9 *(31·4 × 4·9 × 1·5)*
Gun: 1—·50 cal Browning M2
Main engines: 2 Mercedes-Benz MB 820B diesels; 2 shafts; 630 bhp = 21 knots
Complement: 12

First transferred 16 January 1974.

C 26   1976, Michael D. J. Lennon

3 Ex-GERMAN CUSTOMS LAUNCHES

C 27 (ex-*Brunsbuttel*)

Displacement, tons: 105
Dimensions, feet (metres): 96·8 × 17·1 × 5·2 *(29·5 × 5·2 × 1·6)*
Gun: 1—·50 cal Browning M2
Main engines: 2 Motoren Werke TRM 134S diesels
Complement: 9

Built in 1953 by Buschmann, Hamburg.

C 27   1976, Michael D. J. Lennon

C 28 (ex-*Geier*)

Displacement, tons: 125
Dimensions, feet (metres): 91·8 × 17·4 × 6·6 *(28 × 5·3 × 2)*
Main engines: 2 Mercedes-Benz diesel MB 846 AB—electric drive
Complement: 7

Built in 1955 by Bremen Burg. No guns.

C 28   1978, Michael D. J. Lennon

342   MALTA / Customs launches — MAURITANIA / Light forces

C 29 (ex-*Kondor*)

Displacement, tons: 100
Dimensions, feet (metres): 90·5 × 17·1 × 6·2 *(28 × 5·3 × 2)*
Gun: 1—·50 cal Browning M2
Main engines: 1 Deutz R.T. 8M 233 diesel
Complement: 9

Built in 1953 by Lürssen, Bremen.

C 29   1975, D. Batema

MAURITANIA

Ministerial

Minister of National Defence:
  Abdullahi Ould Bah

Personnel

(a) 1979: 300 officers and men
(b) Voluntary service

Base

Port Etienne

Mercantile Marine

Lloyd's Register of Shipping:
  3 vessels of 489 tons gross

CORVETTES

2 Ex-SOVIET "MIRNY" CLASS

Name	No.	Builders	Commissioned
BOULANOUAR	—	Nikolaev	1956
IDINI	—	Nikolaev	1956

Displacement, tons: 850
Dimensions, feet (metres): 208 × 31·2 × 13·8 *(63·4 × 9·5 × 4·2)*
Guns: 2—30 mm; 1 MG
Main engines: Diesel-electric; 1 shaft = 17 knots

Ex-Whale-catchers converted for use as patrol craft and for support of Light Forces. Similar to Soviet AGIs.

"MIRNY" Class   19

LIGHT FORCES

2 SPANISH "BARCELO" CLASS

Name	No.	Builders	Commissioned
—	—	Bazan-La Carraca	Apr 1978
—	—	Bazan-La Carraca	May 1978

Displacement, tons: 139
Dimensions, feet (metres): 118·7 × 18·9 × 8·2 *(36·2 × 5·8 × 2·5)*
Guns: 1—40 mm; 2—20 mm
Main engines: 2 MTU MD-16 TB-90 diesels; 6 000 shp = 40 knots
Range, miles: 1 200 at 17 knots
Complement: 19 (3 officers, 16 ratings)

The original Spanish *Barcelo* was built by Lürssen to their design, Bazan building the remainder.
Ordered 21 July 1976.

BARCELO   3/1976, E. N. Baz

2 Ex-SPANISH LARGE PATROL CRAFT

Name	No.	Builders	Commissioned
TICHITT	—	Chantiers Navals de l'Estérel	Apr 1969
DAR EL BARKA	—	Chantiers Navals de l'Estérel	June 1969

Displacement, tons: 75 standard; 80 full load
Dimensions, feet (metres): 105 × 18·9 × 5·2 *(31·4 × 5·8 × 1·6)*
Guns: 2—20 mm
Main engines: 2 Mercedes Maybach (MTU) 12V 331 TC81 diesels; 2 shafts; 2 700 bhp = 30 knots
Range, miles: 1 500 at 15 knots
Complement: 17

DAR EL BARKA   Chantiers Navals de l'Este

MAURITANIA / Light forces — MAURITIUS   343

Name	No.	Builders	Commissioned
— (ex-*Centinela* W 33)	—	Bazan, Ferrol	1953
— (ex-*Serviola* W 34)	—	Bazan, Ferrol	1953

Displacement, tons: 255 standard; 282 full load
Dimensions, feet (metres): 117·5 × 22·5 × 9·8 *(35·8 × 6·9 × 3)*
Guns: 2—37 mm
Main engine: 1 diesel; 430 bhp = 12 knots

Used as fishery protection ships in Spain. Transferred 5 March 1977.

SERVIOLA   1974, Spanish Navy

Name	No.	Builders	Commissioned
IM RAQ NI	—	Chantiers Navals de l'Estérel	Nov 1965
SLOUGHI	—	Chantiers Navals de l'Estérel	May 1968

CHINGUETTI

Small patrol craft reaching the end of her life.

Displacement, tons: 20
Dimensions, feet (metres): 59 × 13·5 × 3·8 *(18 × 4·1 × 1·2)*
Gun: 1—12·7 mm
Main engines: 2 General Motors 671M diesels; 512 bhp = 22·5 knots
Range, miles: 860 at 12 knots; 400 at 15 knots
Complement: 6

MAURITIUS

Ministerial

Minister of National Defence:
Sir Seewoosagur Ramgoolam (Premier)

Mercantile Marine

Lloyd's Register of Shipping:
18 vessels of 40 732 tons gross

---

1 Ex-INDIAN "ABHAY" CLASS (LARGE PATROL CRAFT)

AMAR

Displacement, tons: 120 standard; 151 full load
Dimensions, feet (metres): 117·2 × 20 × 5 *(35·7 × 6·1 × 1·5)*
Gun: 1—40 mm
Main engines: 2 diesels = 18 knots

Built by Hooghly D & E Co, Calcutta 1961. Transferred April 1974. Retained original name.

AMAR   1976

MEXICO

344 MEXICO / Introduction — Frigates

Ministerial

Secretary of National Defence:
  General Hermenegildo Cuenca Diaz

Headquarters Appointments

Secretary of the Navy:
  Admiral C. G. Demn. Luis M. Bravo Carrera
Under-Secretary of the Navy:
  Rear-Admiral Ing M. N. Ricardo Chazaro Lara
Commander-in-Chief of the Navy:
  Vice-Admiral C. G. Demn. Humberto Uribe Escandon
Chief of the Naval Staff:
  Rear-Admiral C. G. Demn. Miguel A. Gomez Ortega
Director Naval Air Services:
  Rear-Admiral Blanco Peyrefitte
Director of Services:
  Rear-Admiral C. G. Demn. Mario Artigas Fernandez

Diplomatic Representation

Naval Attaché in London:
  Rear-Admiral Fernandes Oleire
Naval Attaché in Washington:
  Vice-Admiral Miguel Manzarraga

Personnel

(a) 1979: Total 11 000 officers and men (including Naval Air Force and 1 300 Marines)
(b) Voluntary service

Naval Bases

The Naval Command is split between the Pacific and Gulf areas and each subdivided into Naval Zones and, subsequently, Naval Sectors.

Gulf Command: (odd numbered zones):
  Veracruz (HQ 3rd Naval Zone and Command HQ)
  Tampico (1st Naval Zone)
  Ciudad del Carmen (5th Naval Zone)
  Isla Mujeres (7th Naval Zone)
  Tuxpan, Coatzacoalcos, Progreso, Chetumal (Naval Sector HQs)

Pacific Command: (even numbered zones):
  Acapulco (HQ 8th Naval Zone and Command HQ)
  Puerto Cortes (2nd Naval Zone)
  Guaymas (4th Naval Zone)
  Manzanillo (6th Naval Zone)
  Ensenada, La Paz, Mazatlan, Salina Cruz (Naval Sector HQs)

Strength of the Fleet

Type	Active	Building
Destroyers	2	—
Frigates	5	—
Corvettes	34	—
Large Patrol Craft	22	9
Survey Vessels	2	—
Coastal and River Patrol Craft	14	—
Transport	1	—
LSTs (1 repair ship)	3	—
Tankers-Harbour	2	—
Tugs	6	—
Floating Docks	4	—
Floating Cranes	7	—

Naval Air Force

Naval air bases at Mexico City, Las Bajadas, Puerto Cortes, Isla Mujeres, Ensenada.

4 Hu-16 Albatros
2 Bell 47G helicopters
1 Bell 47J helicopter
4 Alouette III helicopters
5 Hughes 269A
4 DC 3 (Dakota)
1 Riley Turbo-Rocket
1 Cessna 402B
3 Beechcraft C45H
4 Cessna 150
1 Cessna 180-D
1 Cessna 337
1 Cessna 402B
1 Stearman
3 Mentor T-43B
1 Beech B-55 Baron
2 Beech F-33A Bonanza
1 Learjet 24D

General

One of the persistent problems facing the Mexican Navy is the incursion of foreign fishery poachers, frequently highly organised groups working from the USA. This explains the considerable emphasis which has been put on aircraft and medium sized patrol craft.

Mercantile Marine

Lloyd's Register of Shipping:
  336 vessels of 727 201 tons gross

DELETIONS

Frigates

1972 Potosi, Queretaro ("Guanajato" class). California (APD standard type) (16 Jan)
1975 Guanajato
1976 Papaloapan (ex-US APD)
1978 Durango

Survey Ships

1973 Sotavento
1975 Virgilio Uribe

Tugs

1974 R4
1978 R2

DESTROYERS

2 Ex-US "FLETCHER" CLASS

Name	No.	Builders	Laid down	Launched	Commissioned
CUAUTHEMOC (ex-USS Harrison, DD 573)	IE 01 (ex-F 1)	Consolidated Steel Corporation	25 July 1941	7 May 1942	25 Jan 1943
CUITLAHUAC (ex-USS John Rodgers, DD 574)	IE 02 (ex-F 2)	Consolidated Steel Corporation	25 July 1941	7 May 1942	9 Feb 1943

Displacement, tons: 2 100 standard; 3 050 full load
Length, feet (metres): 376·5 (114·7)
Beam, feet (metres): 39·5 (12·0)
Draught, feet (metres): 18·0 (5·5)
Guns: 5—5 in (127 mm)/38 (single Mk 30);
  10—40 mm/60 (twin Mk 2)
Torpedo tubes: 5—21 in (533 mm) (quin)
Main engines: 2 geared turbines; 2 shafts; 60 000 shp
Boilers: 4
Speed, knots: 36; 14 economical
Oil fuel, tons: 650
Range, miles: 5 000 at 14 knots
Complement: 197

Former US destroyers of the original "Fletcher" class. Transferred to the Mexican Navy in August 1970.

Radar and Fire control:
Mk 12 radar for Mk 37 director: SC and SG1 radars; 1 modern commercial radar; 5—Mk 51 GFCS for 40 mm.

CUAUTHEMOC (old pennant number)   1972, Mexican Navy

FRIGATES

Note: Reported that Mexico may be considering the order of two "Lupo" class in Italy. This would not be a surprising move in view of the age of Como Manuel Azeta and the deletion of Durango.

1 Ex-US "EDSALL" CLASS

Name	No.	Builders	Laid down	Launched	Commissioned
COMO MANUEL AZUETA (ex-USS Hurst, DE 250)	A 06	Brown S.B. Co, Houston, Texas	27 Jan 1943	14 Apr 1943	30 Aug 1943

Displacement, tons: 1 200 standard; 1 850 full load
Dimensions, feet (metres): 302·7 × 36·6 × 13 (92·3 × 11·3 × 4)
Guns: 3—3 in (76 mm)/50 (single Mk 22);
  8—40 mm/60 (1 quad, 2 twins) (Mk 2 and Mk 1)
Main engines: 4 Fairbanks-Morse 38D8 10-cyl diesels;
  6 000 shp; 2 shafts
Speed, knots: 20; 12 economical
Range, miles: 13 000 at 12 knots
Complement: 216 (15 officers, 201 ratings)

Transferred to Mexico 1 October 1973. Employed as training ship with Gulf Fleet command. A/S weapons removed.

Radar: One Kelvin Hughes Type 14;
One Kelvin Hughes Type 17.

Sonar: QCS 1.

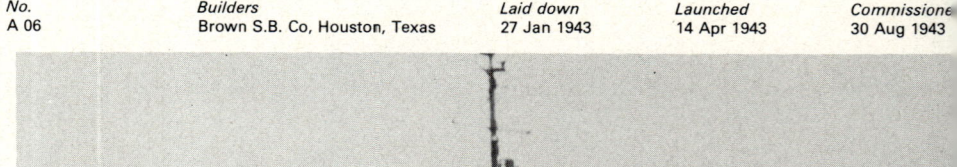

COMO MANUEL AZUETA   1975, Mexican Navy

MEXICO / Frigates — Patrol ships 345

4 Ex-US "CHARLES LAWRENCE" and "CROSLEY" CLASSES

Name	No.	Builders	Laid down	Launched	Commissioned
COAHUILA (ex-USS *Rednour*, APD 102, ex-*DE 592*)	IB-02	Bethlehem S.B. Co, Hingham, Mass	9 Jan 1944	1 Mar 1944	15 Mar 1945
TEHUANTEPEC (ex-USS *Joseph M. Auman*, APD 117, ex-*DE 674*)	IB-05 (ex-H 5)	Consolidated Steel Corporation	8 Nov 1943	5 Feb 1944	25 Apr 1945
USUMACINTA (ex-USS *Don O. Woods*, APD 118, ex-*DE 721*)	IB-06 (ex-H 6)	Consolidated Steel Corporation	1 Dec 1943	19 Feb 1944	28 May 1945
CHIHUAHUA (ex-USS *Barber*, APD 57, ex-*DE 161*)	IB-08	Norfolk Navy Yard, Norfolk, Va	27 Apr 1943	20 May 1943	10 Oct 1943

Displacement, tons: 1 400 standard; 2 130 full load
Length, feet (metres): 300·0 *(91·5)* wl; 306·0 *(93·3)* oa
Beam, feet (metres): 37·0 *(11·3)*
Draught, feet (metres): 11·3 *(3·4)*
Guns: 1—5 in *(127 mm)*/38 (single Mk 30);
  6—40 mm/60 (3 twin Mk 1); 6—20 mm/80 (single)
Main engines: GE turbo-electric; 2 shafts; 12 000 shp
Speed, knots: 20; 13 economical
Boilers: 2 Foster-Wheeler "D" with superheater
Range, miles: 5 000 at 15 knots
Oil fuel, tons: 350
Complement: 204 plus 162 troops

IB 05-06 were purchased by Mexico in December 1963 and IB 08 on 17 February 1969. *California* (ex-USS *Belet* APD 109) stranded and lost 16 January 1972 on Bahia Peninsula.

Fire control: 5 in: local control.
40 mm: 3—Mk 51 GFCS.
Radar: Combined search: SC.
Navigation: Commercial.

CHIHUAHUA   *1976, Mexican Navy*

PATROL SHIPS

3 Ex-US "ABNAKI" CLASS (PF)

Name	No.	Builder	Commissioned
YAGUI (ex-USS *Abnaki* ATF 96)	A 18	Charleston S.B. and D.D. Co	15 Nov 1943
SERI (ex-USS *Cocopa* ATF 101)	A 19	Charleston S.B. and D.D. Co	25 Mar 1944
CORA (ex-USS *Hitchin* ATF 103)	A 20	Charleston S.B. and D.D. Co	27 May 1944

Displacement, tons: 1 675 full load
Dimensions, feet (metres): 205 × 38·5 × 15·5 *(62·5 × 11·7 × 4·7)*
Gun: 1—3 in (76 mm)
Main engines: Diesel-electric; 3 000 bhp; 1 shaft = 15 knots
Complement: 75

Transferred 1978. Tugs used as patrol ships.

"ABNAKI" Class   *1/1977, Dr Giorgio Arra*

18 Ex-US "AUK" Class

Name	No.
LEANDRO VALLE (ex-USS *Pioneer*, MSF 105)	IG-01
GUILLERMO PRIETO (ex-USS *Symbol*, MSF 123)	IG-02
MARIANO ESCOBEDO (ex-USS *Champion*, MSF 314)	IG-03
PONCIANO ARRIAGA (ex-USS *Competent*, MSF 316)	IG-04
MANUAL DOBLADO (ex-USS *Defense*, MSF 317)	IG-05
SEBASTIAN L. DE TEJADA (ex-USS *Devastator*, MSF 318)	IG-06
SANTOS DEGOLLADO (ex-USS *Gladiator*, MSF 319)	IG-07
IGNACIO DE LA LLAVE (ex-USS *Spear*, MSF 322)	IG-08
JUAN N. ALVARES (ex-USS *Ardent*, MSF 340)	IG-09
MELCHOR OCAMPO (ex-USS *Roselle*, MSF 379)	IG-10
VALENTIN G. FARIAS (ex-USS *Starling*, MSF 64)	IG-11
IGNACIO ALTAMIRANO (ex-USS *Sway*, MSF 120)	IG-12
FRANCISCO ZARCO (ex-USS *Threat*, MSF 124)	IG-13
IGNACIO L. VALLARTA (ex-USS *Velocity*, MSF 128)	IG-14
JESUS G. ORTEGA (ex-USS *Chief*, MSF 315)	IG-15
GUTIERRIEZ ZAMORA (ex-USS *Scoter*, MSF 381)	IG-16
JUAN ALDAMA (ex-USS *Pilot*, MSF 104)	IG-18
HERMENEGILDO GALENA (ex-USS *Sage*, MSF 111)	IG-19

Displacement, tons: 890 standard; 1 250 full load
Dimensions, feet (metres): 221·2 × 32·2 × 10·8 *(67·5 × 10 × 3·3)*
Guns: 1—3 in/50; 4—40 mm (twins); 8—20 mm (twins)
Main engines: Diesel-electric; 2 shafts; 3 500 bhp
Speed, knots: 17; 10 economical
Complement: 9 officers and 96 ratings

Transferred—6 in February 1973, 4 in April 1973, 9 in September 1973. Employed on patrol duties—*Mariano Matamoros* of this class employed on surveying duties with after armament replaced by large deck-house. (see Survey Vessels—later)

IGNACIO L. VALLARTA   *2/1976*

Appearance: Variations are visible in the mid-ships section where some have a bulwark running from the break of the fo'c'sle to the quarter-deck.

Radar: SO13 and commercial navigation set.

346 MEXICO / Patrol ships — Light forces

16 Ex-US "ADMIRABLE" CLASS

Name	No.
DM 01 (ex-USS *Jubilant* AM 255)	ID-01
DM 02 (ex-USS *Hilarity* AM 241)	ID-02
DM 03 (ex-USS *Execute* AM 232)	ID-03
DM 04 (ex-USS *Specter* AM 306)	ID-04
DM 05 (ex-USS *Scuffle* AM 298)	ID-05
DM 06 (ex-USS *Eager* AM 224)	ID-06
DM 10 (ex-USS *Instill* AM 252)	ID-10
DM 11 (ex-USS *Device* AM 220)	ID-11
DM 12 (ex-USS *Ransom* AM 283)	ID-12
DM 13 (ex-USS *Knave* AM 256)	ID-13
DM 14 (ex-USS *Rebel* AM 284)	ID-14
DM 15 (ex-USS *Crag* AM 214)	ID-15
DM 16 (ex-USS *Dour* AM 223)	ID-16
DM 17 (ex-USS *Diploma* AM 221)	ID-17
DM 18 (ex-USS *Invade* AM 254)	ID-18
DM 19 (ex-USS *Intrigue* AM 253)	ID-19

Displacement, tons: 650 standard; 945 full load
Dimensions, feet (metres): 184.6 × 33 × 9 *(56.3 × 10.1 × 2.7)*
Guns: 1—3 in/50; 4—40 mm; 6/8—20 mm (see note)
Main engines: 2 diesels; 2 shafts; 1 710 bhp = 15 knots
Range, miles: 4 300 at 10 knots
Complement: 104

DM 18   1976, Mexican Navy

Former US steel hulled fleet minesweepers. All completed in 1943-44. DM 20 now fitted for surveying (see *Survey Vessels*—later).

Gunnery: 20 mm armament varies from six (2 twin, 2 single) to eight (4 twin).

LIGHT FORCES

Note: It is reported that the navy is planning to order twelve fast attack craft of 450 tons of at least 30 knots and at least 4 000 miles range. Responses are believed to have been made by firms in Denmark, France, Germany (FDR), Italy, Spain and UK.

22 + 9 "AZTECA" CLASS (LARGE PATROL CRAFT)

Name	No.	Builders	Commissioned
ANDRES QUINTANA ROOS	P 01	Ailsa Shipbuilding Co Ltd	1 Nov 1974
MATIAS DE CORDOVA	P 02	Scott & Sons, Bowling	22 Oct 1974
MIGUEL RAMOS ARIZPE	P 03	Ailsa Shipbuilding Co Ltd	23 Dec 1974
JOSE MARIA IZAZGU	P 04	Ailsa Shipbuilding Co Ltd	19 Dec 1974
JUAN BAUTISTA MORALES	P 05	Scott & Sons, Bowling	19 Dec 1974
IGNACIO LOPEZ RAYON	P 06	Ailsa Shipbuilding Co Ltd	19 Dec 1974
MANUEL CRECENCIO REJON	P 07	Ailsa Shipbuilding Co Ltd	4 July 1975
ANTONIO DE LA FUENTE	P 08	Ailsa Shipbuilding Co Ltd	4 July 1975
LEON GUZMAN	P 09	Scott & Sons, Bowling	7 Apr 1975
IGNACIO RAMIREZ	P 10	Ailsa Shipbuilding Co Ltd	17 July 1975
IGNACIO MARISCAL	P 11	Ailsa Shipbuilding Co Ltd	23 Sep 1975
HERIBERTO JARA CORONA	P 12	Ailsa Shipbuilding Co Ltd	7 Nov 1975
JOSE MARIA MAJA	P 13	J. Lamont & Co Ltd	13 Oct 1975
FELIX ROMERO	P 14	Scott & Sons, Bowling	23 June 1975
FERNANDO LIZARDI	P 15	Ailsa Shipbuilding Co Ltd	24 Dec 1975
FRANCISCO J. MUJICA	P 16	Ailsa Shipbuilding Co Ltd	21 Nov 1975
PASTOR ROUAIX	P 17	Scott & Sons, Bowling	7 Nov 1975
JOSE MARIA DEL CASTILLO VELASCO	P 18	Lamont & Co Ltd	14 Jan 1975
LUIS MANUEL ROJAS	P 19	Lamont & Co Ltd	3 Apr 1976
JOSE NATIVIDAD MACIAS	P 20	Lamont & Co Ltd	2 Sep 1976
ESTEBAN BACA CALDERON	P 21	Lamont & Co Ltd	18 June 1976
IGNACIO ZARAGOZA	P 22	Vera Cruz	1 June 1976

Displacement, tons: 130
Dimensions, feet (metres): 111.8 × 28.1 × 6.8 *(34.1 × 8.6 × 2.0)*
Guns: 1—40 mm; 1—20 mm
Main engines: 2—12-cyl Paxman Ventura diesels; 3 600 bhp = 24 knots
Range, miles: 2 500 at 12 knots
Complement: 24

Ordered by Mexico, for Fishery Protection duties, on 27 March 1973 from Associated British Machine Tool Makers Ltd.

JOSE MARIA IZAZGU   1975, Mexican Navy

HM Queen Elizabeth II went to sea in *Andres Quintana Roos* during her visit to Mexico in March 1975—an intent on to place further orders for this class was announced shortly afterwards. Ten have been ordered for building in Mexican yards with ABMTM assistance (seven at Vera Cruz, three at Salina Cruz) and a final total of 80 is planned.

4 "POLIMAR" CLASS (COASTAL PATROL CRAFT)

Name	No.	Builders	Commissioned
POLIMAR 1	IF 01 (ex-G 1)	Astilleros de Tampico	1 Oct 1962
POLIMAR 2	IF 02 (ex-G 2)	Icacas Shipyard, Guerrero	1966
POLIMAR 3	IF 03 (ex-G 3)	Icacas Shipyard, Guerrero	1966
POLIMAR 4	IF 04 (ex-G 4)	Astilleros de Tampico	1968

Displacement, tons: 37 standard; 57 full load
Dimensions, feet (metres): 67.2 × 14.8 × 4.3 *(20.1 × 4.5 × 1.3)*
Gun: 1—20 mm
Main engines: 2 diesels; 456 bhp = 11 knots

Of steel construction.

POLIMAR 3   1972, Mexican Navy

2 "AZUETA" CLASS (COASTAL PATROL CRAFT)

Name	No.	Builders	Commissioned
AZUETA	IF 06 (ex-G 9)	Astilleros de Tampico	1959
VILLAPANDO	IF 07 (ex-G 6)	Astilleros de Tampico	1960

Displacement, tons: 80 standard; 85 full load
Dimensions, feet (metres): 85.3 × 16.4 × 7.0 *(26 × 5 × 2.1)*
Guns: 2—13.2 mm (1 twin)
Main engines: Superior diesels; 600 bhp = 12 knots

Of all steel construction.

8 RIVER TYPE (RIVER PATROL CRAFT)

Name	No.	Builders	Commissioned
AM 1	IF 11	Tampico	1960
AM 2	IF 12	Vera Cruz	1960
AM 3	IF 13	Tampico	1961
AM 4	IF 14	Vera Cruz	1961
AM 5	IF 15	Tampico	1961
AM 6	IF 16	Vera Cruz	1962
AM 7	IF 17	Tampico	1962
AM 8	IF 18	Vera Cruz	1962

Displacement, tons: 37
Dimensions, feet (metres): 56.1 × 16.4 × 8.2 *(17.1 × 5 × 2.5)*
Main engines: Diesel; speed = 6 knots

Of steel construction.

MEXICO / Survey vessels — Service forces 347

SURVEY VESSELS

1 Ex-US "ADMIRABLE" CLASS

OCEANOGRAFICO (ex-*DM 20,* ex-USS *Harlequin* AM 365) H 2 (ex-ID-20)

Details given in "Admirable" class under Corvettes. Now unarmed.

1 Ex-US "AUK" CLASS

MARIANO METAMOROS (ex-USS *Herald,* MSF 101) H 1 (ex-IG 17)

Details given in "Auk" class under Corvettes. Took over surveying duties from *Virgilio Uribe.* After guns replaced by large deck-house.

MARIANO METAMOROS　　　　　　　　　　　　　　　　10/1977, Dr Giorgio Arra

SERVICE FORCES

2 Ex-US "511-1152" CLASS (LSTs)

Name	No.	Builders	Commissioned
RIO PANUCO (ex-USS *Park County,* LST 1077)	IA 01	Bethlehem Steel Co, Hingham, Mass	8 May 1945
MANZANILLO (ex-USS *Clearwater County,* LST 602)	IA 02	Chicago Bridge and Iron Co, Seneca, Illinois	31 Mar 1944

Displacement, tons: 1 653 standard; 2 366 beaching; 4 080 full load
Dimensions, feet (metres): 328 × 50 × 14 *(100 × 15·3 × 4·3)*
Guns: 6—40 mm (1 twin; 4 singles)
Main engines: 2 General Motors diesels; 2 shafts; 1 700 bhp = 10·5 knots
Range, miles: 6 000 at 11 knots
Complement: 130
Troop capacity: 147

Transferred to Mexico on 20 September 1971 and 25 May 1972 respectively. Both employed as rescue ships.

RIO PANUCO　　　　　　　　　　　　　　　　1976, Mexican Navy

1 Ex-US "FABIUS" CLASS (LIGHT FORCES TENDER)

Name	No.	Builders	Commissioned
GENERAL VINCENTE GUERRERO (ex-USS *Megara,* ARVA-6)	IA 05	American Bridge Co, Ambridge, Penn	27 June 1945

Displacement, tons: 1 625 light; 4 100 full load
Dimensions, feet (metres): 328 × 50 × 14 *(100 × 15·3 × 4·3)*
Guns: 8—40 mm
Main engines: 2 General Motors diesels; 2 shafts; 1 800 bhp = 14·6 knots
Range, miles: 10 000 at 10 knots
Complement: 250

Ex-aircraft repair ship sold to Mexico 1 October 1973.

GENERAL VINCENTE GUERRERO　　　　　　　　　1976, Mexican Navy

Name	No.	Builders	Commissioned
ZACATECAS	B 2	Ulua Shipyard, Vera Cruz	1960

Displacement, tons: 785 standard
Dimensions, feet (metres): 158 × 27·2 × 10 *(48·2 × 8·3 × 2·7)*
Guns: 1—40 mm; 2—20 mm (single)
Main engine: 1 MAN diesel; 560 hp = 8 knots
Complement: 50 (13 officers and 37 men)

Launched in 1959. Cargo ship type. The hull is of welded steel construction. Cargo capacity 400 tons. Now employed as a transport.

2 Ex-US YOG/YO TYPE (HARBOUR TANKERS)

Name	No.	Builders	Commissioned
AGUASCALIENTES (ex-*YOG 6*)	A 5	Geo H. Mathis Co Ltd, Camden, N.J.	1943
TLAXCALA (ex-*YO 107*)	A 6	Geo Lawley & Son, Neponset, Mass	1943

Displacement, tons: 440 light; 1 480 full load
Dimensions, feet (metres): 159·2 × 30 × 8·2 *(48·6 × 9·2 × 2·5)*
Gun: 1—20 mm
Main engine: Fairbanks-Morse diesel; 1 shaft; 500 bhp = 8 knots
Capacity: 6 570 barrels
Complement: 26 (5 officers and 21 ratings)

Former US self-propelled fuel oil barges. Purchased in August 1964. Entered service in November 1964.

AGUASCALIENTES　　　　　　　　　　　　　　1975, Mexican Navy

348 MEXICO / Auxiliaries — MONTSERRAT

AUXILIARIES

1 Ex-US "ABNAKI" CLASS (TUG)

— (ex-USS *Molala,* ATF 106) R 7

4 Ex-US MARITIME ADMINISTRATION "V 4" CLASS (TUGS)

R-1 (ex-*Farallon*) A 11
R-3 (ex-*Point Vicente*) A 13
R-5 (ex-*Burnt Island*) A 15
R-6 (ex-*Aegeon Point*) A 16

Measurement, tons: 786 deadweight; 1 117 gross
Dimensions, feet (metres): 185·6 × 37·7 × 18·7 *(56·6 × 11·5 × 5·7)*
Guns: 1—76 mm; 2—20 mm
Main engines: 2 Nat Supply 8-cyl diesels; 1 Kort nozzle = 14 knots
Range, miles: 19 000 at 14 knots

Part of a large class built 1943-45 by US Maritime Administration for civilian use. Not a successful design; most were laid up on completion. In 1968 six were taken from reserve and transferred by sale in June 1969. Of the class R2 was paid off 1978 and R4 sank in 1973. All originally unarmed—guns fitted in Mexico. R1 and 5—Gulf Fleet; R3 and 6—Pacific Fleet.

Radar: Kelvin Hughes.

PRAGMAR   PATRON

Tugs acquired in 1973.

4 FLOATING DOCKS

Ex-US ARD 2   Ex-US ARD 11   Ex-US ARD 15

ARD 2 (150 × 24·7 m) transferred August 1963 and ARD 11 (same size) in June 1974. Lift 3 550 tonnes. Two 10 ton cranes and 1 100 kW generator. ARD 15 has the same capacity and facilities—transferred April 1971.

Ex-US AFDL 28

Lift capacity of 1 000 tons. Built of steel. (61 × 19·5 m).
Built in 1944 and transferred in January 1973 and by purchase July 1978.

7 FLOATING CRANES

Ex-US YDs 156, 157, 179, 180, 183, 194 and 203, transferred September 1964 to July 1971. All, except 179 and 194 purchased July 1978.

1 PILE DRIVER

Ex-US YPD 43 leased August 1968.

1 DREDGER

Ex-US YM. Date of transfer not known.

MONTSERRAT

Senior Officers

Commissioner of Police:
  Mr Galton B St John
CO Base:
  Cpl. Angus Prospere

Marine Police

The following craft is employed on general patrol duties under control of Montserrat Police Force.

Base

Plymouth

Mercantile Marine

Lloyd's Register of Shipping:
  3 vessels of 1 248 tons gross

1 BROOKE MARINE 12 metre TYPE

EMERALD STAR

Displacement, tons: 15
Length, feet (metres): 40 *(12)*
Guns: Can mount 3 MGs
Main engines: 2 diesels; 370 hp = 22 knots
Complement: 4

Purchased in 1971.

EMERALD STAR   *1975, Montserrat Government*

MOROCCO

Diplomatic Representation

Defence Attaché in London:
Colonel Benomar Sbay

Personnel

(a) 1979: 1 800 officers and ratings (including 500 Marines)
(b) 18 months national service

Bases

Casablanca, Safi, Agadir, Kenitra, Tangier

Strength of the Fleet

Type	Active	Building (Projected)
Frigate	—	1
Fast Attack Craft (Gun)	2	4
Large Patrol Craft	4	—
Coastal Patrol Craft	9	(6)
Landing Craft	4	—
Customs Craft	12	—

General

At a time of tension in the Maghreb the increase in new construction is significant particularly with the increase from Soviet sources not only of the neighbouring Algerian force but also the long range capabilities, including submarines, of Libya. Frigates with an A/S capability are logical reinforcements and the choice of Spanish yards may also be a pointer.

Mercantile Marine

Lloyd's Register of Shipping:
117 vessels of 341 410 tons gross

DELETION

Frigate

1975 *Al Maouna*

FRIGATE

0 + 1 MODIFIED "DESCUBIERTA" CLASS

Displacement, tons: 1 200 standard; 1 497 full load
Dimensions, feet (metres): 291·3 × 34 × 11·5 *(88·8 × 10·5 × 3·5)*
Missiles: To be fitted with SAM Crotale. (see note)
Guns: 1—76 mm/62 (single Compact);
   2—40 mm/70 (single L70)
A/S weapons: 1—375 mm Bofors twin launcher;
   6 (2 triple) Mk 32 torpedo tubes
Main engines: 4 MTU-Bazan 16V956 diesels; 16 000 bhp;
   2 shafts; cp propellers
Speed, knots: 26
Range, miles: 4 000 cruising
Complement: 100

One ordered 14 June 1977 from Bazán, Cartagena, Spain. Above data is for the Spanish ships of this class.

Missiles: It is not known if SSMs will be fitted but SAM Crotale is reported.

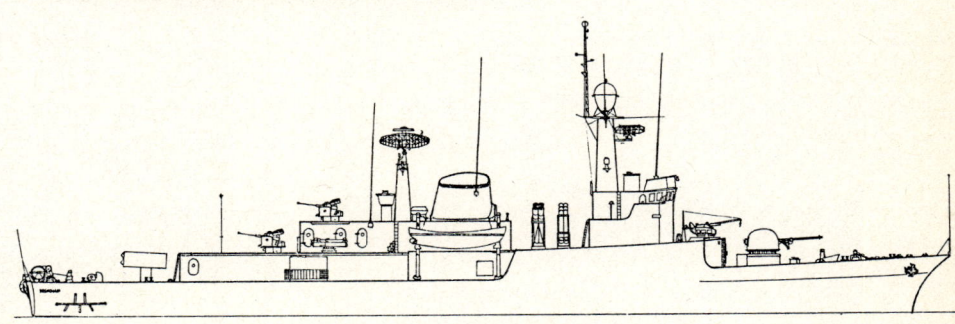

"DESCUBIERTA" Class (Spanish version)

LIGHT FORCES

2 FRENCH PR 72 TYPE (FAST ATTACK CRAFT—GUN)

Name	No.	Builders	Commissioned
OKBA	—	Soc. Francaise de Construction Navale	16 Dec 1976
TRIKI	—	Soc. Francaise de Construction Navale	Feb 1977

Displacement, tons: 375 standard; 445 full load
Dimensions, feet (metres): 188·8 × 25 × 7·1 *(57·5 × 7·6 × 2·1)*
Guns: 1—76 mm/72 (single Compact); 1—40 mm/70 (single Breda Bofors L70)
Main engines: 4 AGO V16 diesels; 4 shafts; 11 040 hp
Speed, knots: 28
Range, miles: 2 500 at 16 knots
Complement: 53 (5 officers; 48 ratings)

Ordered June 1973. This type can be fitted with Exocet—as the Vega control system will be installed this would be a simple operation. *Okba* launched 10 October 1975, *Triki* 1 February 1976. Two more in the New Construction Programme.

0 + 4 MODIFIED "LAZAGA" CLASS (FAST ATTACK CRAFT—GUN)

Displacement, tons: 420 full load
Dimensions, feet (metres): 190·2 × 24·9 × 8·5 *(58 × 7·6 × 2·6)*
Guns: 1—76 mm/72 (single Compact); 1—40 mm/70 (L70); 2—20 mm
A/S weapons: 2 DC racks; possibly triple Mk 32 torpedo tubes
Main engines: 2 MTU-Bazan TB 91 diesels; 8 000 bhp
Speed, knots: 28
Range, miles: 6 100 at 17 knots
Complement: 30

Ordered from Bazan, Spain 14 June 1977.

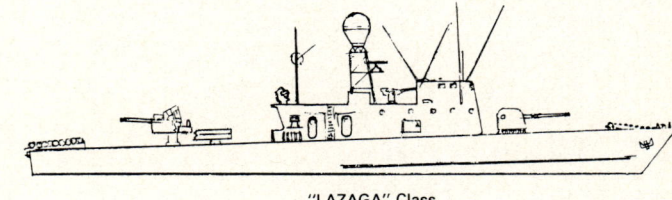

"LAZAGA" Class

1 FRENCH "SIRIUS" CLASS (LARGE PATROL CRAFT)

TAWFIC (ex-*Aries M 758*)

Displacement, tons: 365 standard; 424 full load
Dimensions, feet (metres): 152 × 28 × 8·2 *(46·3 × 8·5 × 2·1)*
Guns: 1—40 mm; 1—20 mm
Main engines: 2 diesels; 2 shafts; 2 000 bhp = 15 knots
Range, miles: 3 000 at 15 knots
Complement: 38

Launched 31 March 1956. Transferred on loan by France on 28 November. Ex-minesweeper used for patrol duties.

"SIRIUS" Class   1975, Dhr. J. van der Woude

350 MOROCCO / Light forces

1 LARGE PATROL CRAFT

Name	No.	Builders	Commissioned
LIEUTENANT RIFFI	32	Constructions Mécaniques de Normandie, Cherbourg	May 1964

Displacement, tons: 311 standard; 374 full load
Dimensions, feet (metres): 174 × 23 × 6·6 (53 × 7 × 2)
Guns: 1—76 mm; 2—40 mm
A/S weapons: 2—A/S mortars
Main engines: 2 SEMT-Pielstick diesels; 2 cp propellers; 3 600 bhp = 19 knots
Range, miles: 3 000 at 12 knots
Complement: 49

Of modified "Fougeux" design. Laid down May 1963.

LIEUTENANT RIFFI *CMN*

1 LARGE PATROL CRAFT

Name	No.	Builders	Commissioned
AL BACHIR	22 (ex-12)	Constructions Mécaniques de Normandie, Cherbourg	30 Mar 1967

Displacement, tons: 125 light; 154 full load
Dimensions, feet (metres): 133·2 × 20·8 × 4·7 (40·6 × 6·4 × 1·4)
Guns: 2—40 mm; 2—MG
Main engines: 2 SEMT-Pielstick diesels; 2 shafts; 3 600 bhp = 25 knots
Oil fuel, tons: 21
Range, miles: 2 000 at 15 knots
Complement: 23

Ordered in 1964. Launched 25 February 1967.

AL BACHIR *CMN*

1 Ex-FRENCH VC TYPE (LARGE PATROL CRAFT)

Name	No.	Builders	Commissioned
EL SABIQ (ex-P 762, VC 12)	11	Chantiers Navals de l'Estérel	1957

Displacement, tons: 60 standard; 80 full load
Dimensions, feet (metres): 103·5 × 19 × 5·3 (31·5 × 5·8 × 1·6)
Missiles: Fitted for SS-12
Guns: 2—20 mm
Main engines: 2 MTU diesels; 2 shafts; 2 700 bhp = 30 knots
Range, miles: 1 500 at 15 knots
Complement: 17

Former French seaward defence motor launch. Launched on 13 August 1957. Transferred from the French Navy to the Moroccan Navy on 15 November 1960 and renamed *El Sabiq*.

VC type (under French colours) *1960, C. N. de l'Esterel*

6 + (6) P 32 TYPE (COASTAL PATROL CRAFT)

Name	No.	Builders	Commissioned
EL WACIL	—	Constructions Mécaniques de Normandie, Cherbourg	9 Oct 1975
EL JAIL	—	Constructions Mécaniques de Normandie, Cherbourg	3 Dec 1975
EL MIKDAM	—	Constructions Mécaniques de Normandie, Cherbourg	30 Jan 1976
EL HARIS	—	Constructions Mécaniques de Normandie, Cherbourg	30 June 1976
EL KHAFIR	—	Constructions Mécaniques de Normandie, Cherbourg	16 Apr 1976
ESSAHIR	—	Constructions Mécaniques de Normandie, Cherbourg	16 July 1976

Displacement, tons: 90
Dimensions, feet (metres): 105 × 17·6 × 9·8 (32 × 5·3 × 2·9)
Guns: 2—20 mm
Main engines: 2 MGO-12V BZSHR diesels; 2 700 bhp; 2 shafts = 29 knots
Range, miles: 1 500 at 15 knots
Complement: 17

Wooden hull sheathed in plastic.
The first six of these patrol craft were ordered in February 1974. Launch dates—*El Wacil* 12 June 1975, *El Jail* 10 October 1975, *El Mikdam* 26 November 1975, *El Haris* 3 March 1976, *El Khafir* 1 January 1976, *Essahir* 2 June 1976. Six more in the New Construction Programme.

Radar: One set Decca.

EL WACIL *1976, CMN*

3 COASTAL PATROL CRAFT

"Arcor 31" type of 24 knots built by C. N. Arcor, Bordeaux.

AMPHIBIOUS FORCES

3 BATRAL TYPE

Name	No.	Builders	Commissioned
DAOUD BEN AICHA	—	Dubigeon, Normandie	28 May 1977
AHMED ES SAKALI	—	Dubigeon, Normandie	Sep 1977
ABOU ABDALLAH EL AYACHI	—	Dubigeon, Normandie	Mar 1978

Displacement, tons: 750 standard; 1 250 full load
Dimensions, feet (metres): 262·4 × 42·6 × 7·5 *(80 × 13 × 2·3)*
Guns: 2—40 mm; 2—81 mm mortars
Main engines: 2 diesels; 2 shafts; 3 600 hp = 16 knots
Range, miles: 3 500 at 13 knots
Complement: 47

Fitted with helicopter landing platform and with vehicle-stowage above and below decks. Can carry an extra 140 men and 12 vehicles. Two ordered on 12 March 1975. Third ordered 19 August 1975. Of same class as the French *Champlain*.

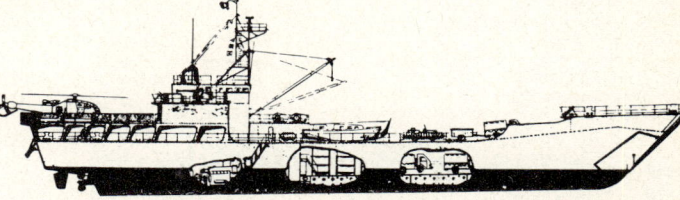

BATRAL TYPE *1974, French Navy*

Name	No.	Builders	Commissioned
LIEUTENANT MALGHAGH	21	Chantiers Navals Franco-Belges	1965

Displacement, tons: 292 standard; 642 full load
Dimensions, feet (metres): 193·6 × 39·2 × 4·3 *(59 × 12 × 1·3)*
Guns: 2—20 mm; 1—120 mm mortar
Main engines: 2 MGO diesels; 2 shafts; 1 000 bhp = 8 knots
Complement: 16 (1 officer, 15 men)

Ordered early in 1963. Similar to the French landing craft of the EDIC type built at the same yard.

LIEUTENANT MALGHAGH *1971, Royal Moroccan Navy*

There are also the yacht *Essaouira*, 60 tons, from Italy in 1967, used as a training vessel for watchkeepers; and 12 customs boats, four of 40 tons, 82 ft, diesels 940 bhp = 23 knots, and eight 42·7 ft; all built in 1963. The *Murene*, Coast Guard Cutter, has also been reported.

MOZAMBIQUE

Senior Appointment

Commander of the Navy:
Isaac Musakua

Personnel

(a) 700
(b) Voluntary

Training

Training has been provided by Tanzania and certain key personnel have been sent to the USSR.

Bases

Maputo (Naval HQ); Nacala; Beira; Pemba (Porto Amelia); Metangula (Lake Nyassa).

Mercantile Marine

Lloyd's Register of Shipping:
70 vessels of 36 169 tons gross

LIGHT FORCES

1 Ex-SOVIET "POLUCHAT" CLASS (COASTAL PATROL CRAFT)

Displacement, tons: 90 tons full load
Dimensions, feet (metres): 97 × 19 × 4·8 *(29·6 × 5·8 × 1·5)*
Guns: 2—14·5 mm (twin)
Main engines: 2 diesels; 2 400 hp = 20 knots
Complement: 15

Reported transferred by USSR in 1977.

2 Ex-PORTUGUESE "BELLATRIX" CLASS (COASTAL PATROL CRAFT)

Displacement, tons: 23 light; 27·6 full load
Dimensions, feet (metres): 68·0 × 15·2 × 4·0 *(20·7 × 4·6 × 1·2)*
Gun: 1—20 mm
Main engines: 2 Cummins diesels; 450 bhp = 15 knots
Complement: 7

3 Ex-PORTUGUESE "JUPITER" CLASS (COASTAL PATROL CRAFT)

Displacement, tons: 32 standard; 43·5 full load
Dimensions, feet (metres): 69 × 16·5 × 4·3 *(21 × 5 × 1·3)*
Guns: 2—20 mm (twin)
Main engines: 2 Cummins diesels; 1 270 bhp = 20 knots
Complement: 8

1 Ex-PORTUGUESE PATROL CRAFT

(ex-*Antares* P 360)

Displacement, tons: 18
Dimensions, feet (metres): 56·0 × 15·2 × 4 *(17·1 × 4·6 × 1·2)*
Gun: 1—20 mm
Main engines: 2 Cummins diesels; 460 bhp = 18·2 knots
Complement: 7

SURVEY SHIP

1 Ex-BRITISH "BANGOR" CLASS

(ex-*Almirante Lacerda* (ex-HMS *Caraquet*))

Displacement, tons: 830 full load
Dimensions, feet (metres): 180 × 28·5 × 9·5 *(54·8 × 8·6 × 2·8)*
Guns: 1—3 in *(76 mm)*; 2—20 mm
Main engines: Triple expansion; 2 shafts; 2 400iph = 16 knots (originally)
Boilers: Two 3-drum small-tube
Complement: 49

Built in Canada in 1941. Transferred by the Portuguese Navy in 1975. Alongside in Maputo—has some crew but apparently, little capacity for movement.

AMPHIBIOUS CRAFT

(ex-*Ariete* LDG 102)

Displacement, tons: 500
Length, feet (metres): 187 *(56·9)*
Main engines: 2 diesels; 1 000 bhp
Complement: 20

Transferred by Portuguese Navy 1975. May have been wrecked subsequently.

NETHERLANDS

Administration

Minister of Defence:
  Mr. W. Scholten
State Secretary of Defence (Personnel):
  C. L. J. van Lent
State Secretary of Defence (Equipment):
  Dr. W. F. van Eekelen
Chief of the Defence Staff:
  General A. J. W. Wijting RNAF

Headquarters Appointments

Chief of the Naval Staff:
  Vice-Admiral H. L. van Beek
Flag Officer Naval Personnel:
  Rear-Admiral R. H. Post
Flag Officer Naval Material:
  Rear-Admiral R. P. J. M. Stoltz

Commands

Admiral Netherlands Home Command:
  Rear-Admiral J. H. B. Hulshof
Commander Netherlands Task Group:
  Rear-Admiral J. H. Scheuer
Commandant General Royal Netherlands Marine Corps:
  Major-General A. J. Romijn
Flag Officer Netherlands Antilles:
  Commodore H. C. van der Lee

Diplomatic Representation

Naval Attaché in Bonn:
  Captain J. A. C. Hartogh
Naval Attaché in London:
  Captain J. R. Roele
Naval Attaché in Paris:
  Captain C. J. van Westenbrugge
Naval Attaché in Washington and NLR SACLANT:
  Rear-Admiral J. J. Binnendijk

Personnel

(a) 1 January 1979: 16 900 officers and ratings (including the Navy Air Service, Royal Netherlands Marine Corps and about 360 officers and women of the W.R.NI.NS.)
(b) 14-17 months national service
Note: The 1979 Estimates state that previously planned reductions in personnel would not now take place and the total would remain at about 16 900.

Bases

Main Base: Den Helder
Minor Bases: Flushing and Curacao
Fleet Air Arm: NAS Valkenburgh (main), NAS De Kooy (helicopters)
R. Neth. Marines: Rotterdam, Doorn and Texel
Training Base: Amsterdam

Naval Air Force

Personnel: 1 700

Squadron	Aircraft	Task
3	—	LRMP work-up
7	6 Lynx (UH 14A)	Utility and Transport
320	15 Neptunes	LRMP
321	7 Atlantics	LRMP
860	10 Wasp helicopters	Embarked

Notes:
(a) On 9 Dec 1978 announced that 13 Orion P3C had been ordered for delivery from 1981 to replace Neptunes.
(b) 8 Lynx-SH14B helicopters with dunking sonar ordered for delivery 1979-80.
(c) 10 Lynx-SH14C helicopters with towed MAD ordered in 1978 for delivery 1980-81.
(d) Total of Lynx helicopters to be 40 including Wasp replacements.

Prefix to Ships' Names

Hr Ms

Strength of the Fleet

	Active	Building (Projected)
Submarines (Patrol)	6	2
Destroyers	10	—
Frigates	8	10 (1)
Corvettes	6	—
MCM Support Ships	3	—
Mine Hunters	4	15
Minesweepers—Coastal	11	—
Diving Ships	3	—
Minesweepers—Inshore	16	—
Large Patrol Craft	5	—
LCAs	10	—
Surveying Vessels	3	—
Combat Support Ships	2	—
Training Ships	2	—
Tugs	13	—
Miscellaneous	33	—

Future New Construction Programme (1979-83)

2 Submarines (2 more in 1982-3)
1 Frigate (Command and Air Defence)
12 Frigates (ASW)
18 Lynx helicopters
15 Minehunters
13 Orion aircraft

Strength of the Fleet 1983.

6 Submarines
2 Tromp class
1 DDG
12 "Kortenaer" class
6 "Van Speyck" class
2 "Zuiderkruis" class
2 "Wolf" class
8 "Dokkum" class
7 "Alkmaar" class
16 MSI
3 AGS
13 Orion LRMP aircraft
34 helicopters
2 RM. Commando Units +1 Cold Weather Company

Future New Construction Programme (1983-88)

4 Frigates (replacing "Wolf" class)
Replacements for "Van Speyck" class, SS, MSIs and Wasp helicopters.
Midlife conversions.

Planned Deployment in 1980s

2 ASW Groups each of 6 ASW frigates, 1 DLG, 1 Support Ship (helicopters in all ships) to operate in Eastlant Area
1 ASW Group of 6 ASW frigates and 1 DLG to operate in Channel Approaches (helicopters in all ships)
1 ASW Group of 4 frigates to operate in Channel Command
6 Patrol Submarines
21 LRMP Aircraft in 3 squadrons (1 training)
2 MCM Groups of 12 ships each operating off Dutch ports
1 MCM Group of 7 ships for Channel command
2 R. Neth Marine Commando Groups and 1 Cold Weather Reinforced Company

Mercantile Marine

Lloyd's Register of Shipping:
  1 238 vessels of 5 180 392 tons gross

DELETIONS

Cruisers

1972 De Ruyter to Peru as Almirante Grau (Oct)
1976 De Zeven Provincien to Peru as Aguirre (Aug)

Destroyers

1973 Gelderland for harbour training
1974 Noord Brabant (after collision 9 Jan 1974)
1978 Holland (to Peru, Feb), Zeeland (29 Sep)

Admin. Escort

1976 Onversaagd (returned to USA)

Minesweepers

1972 Onvermoeid, Bolsward, Breukelen, Bruinisse returned to US Navy
1973 Grijpskerk for harbour training
1974 Wildervank, Meppel, Goes, Brummen, Brouwershaven to disposal
  Axel, Aalsmeer to Oman
1975 Waalwijk, Leersum ("Wildervank" class) Beemster, Bedum, Beilen, Borculo, Borne, Blaricum, Brielle, Breskens, Boxtel ("Beemster" class MSC)

Survey Ships

1972 Luymes to disposal
1973 Snellius as accommodation ship and
1977 for disposal by sale

Amphibious Forces

1975 L 9521
1978 L 9526

Storeships

1972 Woendi
1973 Pelikaan

PENNANT NUMBERS

Submarines

S 804	Potvis
S 805	Tonijn
S 806	Zwaardvis
S 807	Tijgerhaai
S 808	Dolfijn
S 809	Zeehond
—	Walrus

Destroyers

F 801	Tromp
F 806	De Ruyter
D 812	Friesland
D 813	Groningen
D 814	Limburg
D 815	Overijssel
D 816	Drenthe
D 817	Utrecht
D 818	Rotterdam
D 819	Amsterdam

Frigates

F 802	Van Speijk
F 803	Van Galen
F 804	Tjerk Hiddes
F 805	Van Nes
F 807	Kortenaer
F 808	Callenburgh
F 809	Van Kinsbergen
F 810	Banckert
F 811	Piet Heyn
F 812	Pieter Floresz
F 813	Witte de With
F 814	Isaac Sweers
F 815	Evertsen
F 816	Abraham Crijnssen
F 823	Philips van Almonde
F 824	Blois van Treslong
F 825	Jan van Brakel
F 826	Willem van der Zaan

Corvettes

F 817	Wolf
F 818	Fret
F 819	Hermelijn
F 820	Vos
F 821	Panter
F 822	Jaguar

MCM Command/Support Ships

A 855	Onbevreesd
A 858	Onvervaard
A 859	Onverdroten

Mine Hunters

M 801	Dokkum
M 818	Drunen
M 828	Staphorst
M 842	Veere
M 850	Alkmaar
M 851	Delfjije
M 852	Dordrecht
M 853	Haarlem
M 854	Harlingen
M 855	Hellevoetsluis
M 856	Maassluis
M 857	Makkum
M 858	Middelburg
M 859	Scheveningen
M 860	Schiedam
M 861	Urk
M 862	Veere
M 863	Vlaarnigen
M 864	Willemstad

NETHERLANDS / Introduction

Diving Vessels

M 806	Roermond
M 820	Woerden
M 844	Rhenen

Coastal Minesweepers

M 802	Hoogezand
M 809	Naaldwijk
M 810	Abcoude
M 812	Drachten
M 813	Ommen
M 815	Giethoorn
M 817	Venlo
M 823	Naarden
M 827	Hoogeveen
M 830	Sittard
M 841	Gemert

Inshore Minesweepers

M 868	Alblas
M 869	Bussemaker
M 870	Lacomblé
M 871	Van Hamel
M 872	Van Straelen
M 873	Van Moppes

Inshore Minesweepers

M 874	Chömpff
M 875	Van Well-Groeneveld
M 876	Schuiling
M 877	Van Versendaal
M 878	Van Der Wel
M 879	Van 't Hoff
M 880	Mahu
M 881	Staverman
M 882	Houtepen
M 883	Zomer

Large Patrol Craft

P 802	Balder
P 803	Bulgia
P 804	Freijer
P 805	Hadda
P 806	Hefring

Amphibious Forces

L 9510-15	
L 9517-18	
L 9520	
L 9522	

Auxiliary Ships

A 832	Zuiderkruis
A 835	Poolster
A 847	Argus
A 848	Triton
A 849	Nautilus
A 850	Hydra
A 856	Mercuur
A 870	Wamandai
A 871	Wambrau
A 872	Westgat
A 873	Wielingen
A 903	Zeefakkel
A 904	Buyskes
A 905	Blommendal
A 906	Tydeman
A 920	Dreg IV
A 923	Van Bochove
Y 8014	Harbour Tug
Y 8016	Harbour Tug
Y 8017	Harbour Tug
Y 8022	Harbour Tug
Y 8028	Harbour Tug
Y 8037	Berkel
Y 8038	Dintel
Y 8039	Dommel
Y 8040	Ijssel
Y 8050	Urania
Y 8536	Patria

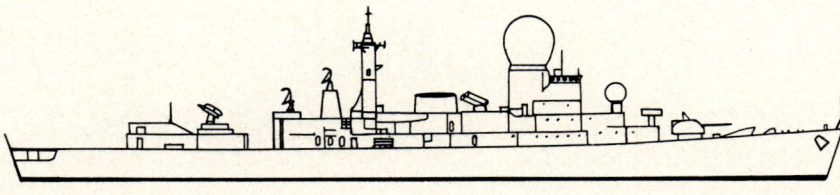
"TROMP" Class

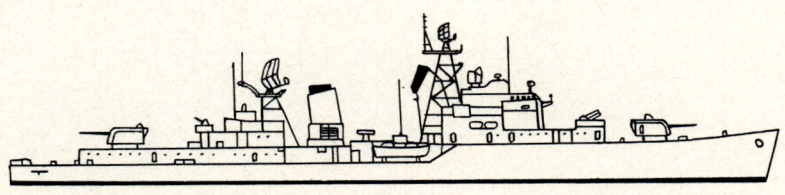
"FRIESLAND" Class

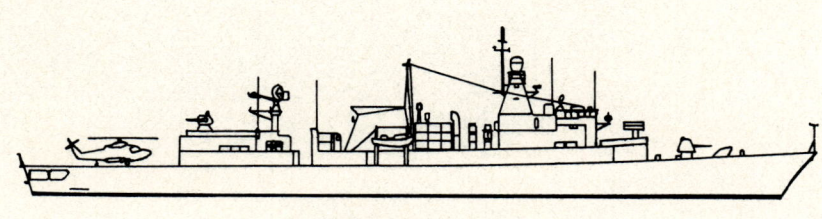
"KORTENAER" Class

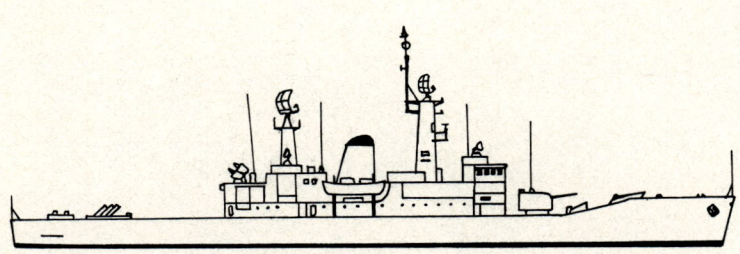
"VAN SPEIJK" Class (unmodified)

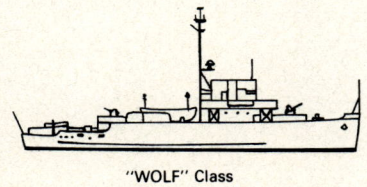
"WOLF" Class

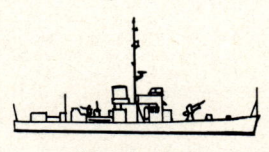
"BALDER" Class

354 NETHERLANDS / Submarines

SUBMARINES

2 NEW CONSTRUCTION

Name	No.	Builders	Laid down	Launched	Commissioned
WALRUS ?	—	Rotterdam Drydock (Rhine-Scheldt-Verolme)	Dec 1978	—	1982
ZEEHOND ?	—	Rotterdam Drydock (Rhine-Scheldt-Verolme)	—	—	1983

Displacement, tons: 1 900
Dimensions, feet (metres): 220 × 28·6 × — (67 × 8·5 × —)
Torpedo tubes: ?6—21 in (533 mm)
Main machinery: 3 SEMT-Pielstick diesels; 1 electric motor
Speed, knots: ?
Complement: 49

In the 1975 Estimates money was set aside for design work on this class and a contract for the building of the first was signed 19 June 1978 with and undertaking that the second would be ordered in 1979.

These will be an improvement on the "Zwaardvis" class with similar dimensions and identical silhouette.. Use of new French "Marel" HT steel will increase the diving depth by some fifty per cent. A new fire control and electronic command system called Gipsy will be fitted and automation will reduce the crew from 67 to 49.

Cost: The cost of app. 212·5 million guilders each will be spread across 1978-84. The increase over original 150 million g. caused by inflation and use of "Marel" steel.

Future: Two more of this class are planned to continue the building stream.

2 "ZWAARDVIS" CLASS

Name	No.	Builders	Laid down	Launched	Commissioned
ZWAARDVIS	S 806	Rotterdamse Droogdok Mij, Rotterdam	14 July 1966	2 July 1970	18 Aug 1972
TIJGERHAAI	S 807	Rotterdamse Droogdok Mij, Rotterdam	14 July 1966	25 May 1971	20 Oct 1972

Displacement, tons: 2 350 surfaced; 2 640 dived
Length, feet (metres): 217·2 (66·2)
Beam, feet (metres): 33·8 (10·3)
Draught, feet (metres): 23·3 (7·1)
Torpedo tubes: 6—21 in (533 mm)
Main machinery: Diesel-electric; 3 diesel generators; 1 shaft
Speed, knots: 13 surfaced; 20 dived
Complement: 67

In the 1964 Navy Estimates a first instalment was approved for the construction of two conventionally powered submarines of tear-drop design. HSA M8 Fire control.

Radar: Type 1001.

TIJGERHAAI 4/1977, Wright and Logan

2 "POTVIS" CLASS
2 "DOLFIJN" CLASS

Name	No.	Builders	Laid down	Launched	Commissioned
POTVIS	S 804	Wilton-Fijenoord, Schiedam	17 Sep 1962	12 Jan 1965	2 Nov 1965
TONIJN	S 805	Wilton-Fijenoord, Schiedam	27 Nov 1962	14 June 1965	24 Feb 1966
DOLFIJN	S 808	Rotterdamse Droogdok Mij, Rotterdam	30 Dec 1954	20 May 1959	16 Dec 1960
ZEEHOND	S 809	Rotterdamse Droogdok Mij, Rotterdam	30 Dec 1954	20 Feb 1960	16 Mar 1961

Displacement, tons: 1 140 standard; 1 494 surfaced; 1 826 dived
Length, feet (metres): 260·9 (79·5)
Beam, feet (metres): 25·8 (7·8)
Draught, feet (metres): 16·4 (5·0)
Torpedo tubes: 8—21 in (533 mm) (4 bow, 4 stern)
Main machinery: 2 MAN diesels; 3 100 bhp; electric motors; 4 200 hp; 2 shafts
Speed, knots: 14·5 surfaced; 17 dived
Complement: 64

These submarines are of a triple-hull design, giving a diving depth 980 ft (300 m). Potvis and Tonijn, originally voted for in 1949 with the other pair, but suspended for some years, had several modifications compared with Dolfijn and Zeehond and were officially considered to be a separate class; but modernisation of both classes has been completed, and all four boats are now almost identical. HSA M8 Fire control.

Construction: The hull consists of three cylinders arranged in a triangular shape. The upper cylinder accommodates the crew, navigational equipment and armament. The lower two cylinders house the propulsion machinery comprising diesel engines, batteries and electric motors, as well as store-rooms.

Engineering: Main engines to be replaced by SEMT-Pielstick diesels.

Radar: Type 1001.

ZEEHOND 3/1976, Wright and Logan

DESTROYERS

2 "TROMP" CLASS

Name	No.	Builders	Laid down	Launched	Commissioned
TROMP	F 801	Koninklijke Maatschappij De Schelde, Flushing	4 Sep 1971	4 June 1973	3 Oct 1975
DE RUYTER	F 806	Koninklijke Maatschappij De Schelde, Flushing	22 Dec 1971	9 Mar 1974	3 June 1976

Displacement, tons: 4 300 standard; 5 400 full load
Length, feet (metres): 429·5 *(130·9)* pp; 454·1 *(138·4)* oa
Beam, feet (metres): 48·6 *(14·8)*
Draught, feet (metres): 15·1 *(4·6)*
Aircraft: 1 Lynx helicopter
Missiles: SSM; 16 Harpoon (eight single cells);
  SAM; 40 Tartar (single Mk 13 launcher);
  SAM; 16 Sea Sparrow (two quad launchers)
Guns: 2—4·7 in *(120 mm)*/50 (twin Bofors)
A/S weapons: 6 (2 triple) Mk 32 ASW torpedo tubes
Main engines: 2 Olympus gas turbines; 50 000 hp;
  2 Tyne cruising gas turbines, 8 000 hp
Speed, knots: 30
Complement: 306 (275 peace)

First design allowance was voted for in 1967 estimates. Ordered (announced on 27 July 1970) for laying down in 1971. Hangar and helicopter landing platform aft. Fitted as flagships.

ECM: 2 Knebworth Corvus Chaff projectors (and illuminators).

Electronics: Sewaco I automated AIO.

Engineering: Each ship carries 4-1 000 kW diesel generators by Ruston Paxman, England.

Gunnery: Turrets from old destroyer *Gelderland* with considerable modifications. Including full automation.

Midlife Conversions: Scheduled for 1983-88.

Radar: Search and designator: One HSA 3D in radome.
Search, tracker and fire control for Sea Sparrow and 4·7 in guns: one HSA WM 25.
Tartar control: Two SPG-51.
Navigation: Two Decca.

Sonar: One CWE 610.

DE RUYTER 8/1978, J. L. van der Burg

DE RUYTER 8/1978, Michael D. J. Lennon

TROMP 6/1977, C. and S. Taylor

356 NETHERLANDS / Destroyers — Frigates

8 "FRIESLAND" CLASS

Name	No.	Builders	Laid down	Launched	Commissioned
FRIESLAND	D 812	Nederlandse Dok en Scheepsbouw Mij, Amsterdam	17 Dec 1951	21 Feb 1953	22 Mar 1956
GRONINGEN	D 813	Nederlandse Dok en Scheepsbouw Mij, Amsterdam	21 Feb 1952	9 Jan 1954	12 Sep 1956
LIMBURG	D 814	Koninklijke Maatschappij De Schelde, Flushing	28 Nov 1953	5 Sep 1955	31 Oct 1956
OVERIJSSEL	D 815	Dok-en-Werfmaatschappij Wilton-Fijenoord	15 Oct 1953	8 Aug 1955	4 Oct 1957
DRENTHE	D 816	Nederlandse Dok en Scheepsbouw Mij, Amsterdam	9 Jan 1954	26 Mar 1955	1 Aug 1957
UTRECHT	D 817	Koninklijke Maatschappij De Schelde, Flushing	15 Feb 1954	2 June 1956	1 Oct 1957
ROTTERDAM	D 818	Rotterdamse Droogdok Mij, Rotterdam	7 Jan 1954	26 Jan 1956	28 Feb 1957
AMSTERDAM	D 819	Nederlandse Dok en Scheepsbouw Mij, Amsterdam	26 Mar 1955	25 Aug 1956	10 Aug 1958

Displacement, tons: 2 497 standard; 3 070 full load
Length, feet (metres): 380·5 *(116·0)*
Beam, feet (metres): 38·5 *(11·7)*
Draught, feet (metres): 17 *(5·2)*
Guns: 4—4·7 in *(120 mm)*/50 (twin Bofors);
4—40 mm/70 (single L70)
A/S weapons: Two 4-barrelled 375 mm. Bofors rocket launchers; 2 DC racks
Main engines: 2 Werkspoor geared turbines, 60 000 shp; 2 shafts
Boilers: 4 Babcock & Wilcox
Speed, knots: 36
Complement: 284 (war)

These ships have side armour as well as deck protection. Twin rudders. Propellers 370 rpm. Named after provinces of the Netherlands, and the two principal cities. To be replaced by "Kortenaer" class of frigates.

Gunnery: The 4·7 in guns are fully automatic with a rate of fire of 42 rounds per minute. All guns are radar controlled. Originally six 40 mm guns were mounted.

Radar: Search: LW 03.
Tactical: DA 05.
Fire control: HSA M 45 for 4·7 in.
HSA fire control for 40 mm and A/S rockets.

AMSTERDAM   5/1978, J. L. M. van der Burg

Torpedo tubes: *Utrecht* was equipped with eight 21 in A/S torpedo tubes (single, four on each side) in 1960 and *Overijssel* in 1961, and the others were to have been, but the project was dropped and tubes already fitted were removed.

FRIGATES

2 + 10 "KORTENAER" CLASS

Name	No.	Builders	Laid down	Launched	Commissioned
KORTENAER	F 807	Koninklijke Maatschappij De Schelde, Flushing	8 Apr 1975	18 Dec 1976	26 Oct 1978
CALLENBURGH	F 808	Koninklijke Maatschappij De Schelde, Flushing	30 June 1975	12 Mar 1977	Summer 1979
VAN KINSBERGEN	F 809	Koninklijke Maatschappij De Schelde, Flushing	2 Sep 1975	16 Apr 1977	early 1980
BANCKERT	F 810	Koninklijke Maatschappij De Schelde, Flushing	25 Feb 1976	1 July 1978	late 1980
PIET HEYN	F 811	Koninklijke Maatschappij De Schelde, Flushing	28 Apr 1977	1 June 1978	Summer 1981
PIETER FLORESZ	F 812	Koninklijke Maatschappij De Schelde, Flushing	1 July 1977	1979	early 1982
WITTE DE WITH	F 813	Koninklijke Maatschappij De Schelde, Flushing	13 June 1978	1979	late Summer 1982
ABRAHAM CRIJNSSEN	F 816	Koninklijke Maatschappij De Schelde, Flushing	25 Oct 1978	—	early 1983
PHILIPS VAN ALMONDE	F 823	Dok en Werfmaatschappij Wilton, Fijenoord	3 Oct 1977	1979	Spring 1982
BLOIS VAN TRESLONG	F 824	Dok en Werfmaatschappij Wilton, Fijenoord	27 Apr 1978	—	Spring 1983
JAN VAN BRAKEL	F 825	Koninklijke Maatschappij De Schelde, Flushing	Nov 1979	—	Autumn 1983
WILLEM VAN DER ZAAN	F 826	Koninklijke Maatschappij De Schelde, Flushing	Jan 1980	—	late 1983

Displacement, tons: 3 500
Dimensions, feet (metres): 419·8 × 47·2 × 14·3 *(128 × 14·4 × 4·4)*
Aircraft: 1 Lynx helicopter (see note)
Missiles: 8 Harpoon surface-to-surface; NATO Sea Sparrow PDMS
Guns: 2—76 mm/62 (single Compact) (see notes)
A/S weapons: 4 (2 double) Mk 32 torpedo tubes for Mk 46 in after deckhouse
Main engines: 2 Rolls-Royce Olympus gas turbines = 50 000 shp; 2 Rolls-Royce Tyne gas turbines = 8 000 shp; 2 variable pitch propellers
Speed, knots: 30
Range, miles: 4 000 on Tyne cruising turbines
Complement: 176

First four of class ordered 31 August 1974; second four 28 November 1974; third four 29 December 1976 (two to built by same constructors as rest of class, two by Wilton-Fijenoord). The thirteenth of class (SAM version) is to have different armament (see note below) for trials 1 April 1978. *Callenburgh* ready for trials February 1979 and to commission in Summer 1979 and thereafter ships will follow at approximately six monthly intervals. These ships are to replace the "Holland" and "Friesland" classes. Cost at 1974 prices £37 m.

Air Defence Ship/Flagship: Expected to be ordered in 1979. Hull and engines same as remainder of "Kortenaer" class but with AA armament. Name not yet announced but *Heemskerck* is suggested.

Building area: Covered area at No 6 repair dock at Wilton, Fijenoord now reaching completion. Two covered building docks and covered slipway at De Schelde.

Complement: Reduced to 176 by adoption of large amount of automation.

Electronics: Sewaco system.

Gunnery: Twin 35 mm/90 is to be mounted on top of hangar when system becomes available. Until then second 76 mm will be mounted in lieu on first four ships and 40 mm on remainder.

Helicopters: Although only one Lynx is carried in peacetime there is hangar accommodation for two.

Radar: Surface search: One DO.
Fire-control: One LWO 8; one WW 25 system.
Navigation: One ZWO 6.

Rocket launchers: Two Knebworth Corvus launchers.

Sonar: SQS 505.

KORTENAER   1978, Royal Netherlands Navy

CALLENBURGH   3/1979, Michael D. J. Lennon

NETHERLANDS / Frigates — Corvettes 357

6 "VAN SPEIJK" CLASS

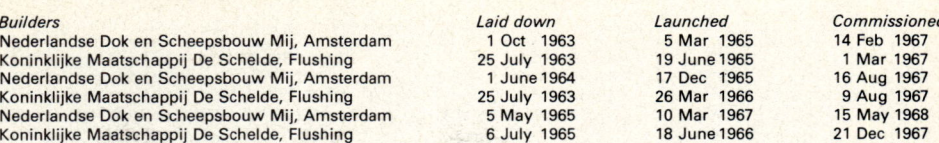

Name	No.	Builders	Laid down	Launched	Commissioned
VAN SPEIJK	F 802	Nederlandse Dok en Scheepsbouw Mij, Amsterdam	1 Oct 1963	5 Mar 1965	14 Feb 1967
VAN GALEN	F 803	Koninklijke Maatschappij De Schelde, Flushing	25 July 1963	19 June 1965	1 Mar 1967
TJERK HIDDES	F 804	Nederlandse Dok en Scheepsbouw Mij, Amsterdam	1 June 1964	17 Dec 1965	16 Aug 1967
VAN NES	F 805	Koninklijke Maatschappij De Schelde, Flushing	25 July 1963	26 Mar 1966	9 Aug 1967
ISAAC SWEERS	F 814	Nederlandse Dok en Scheepsbouw Mij, Amsterdam	5 May 1965	10 Mar 1967	15 May 1968
EVERTSEN	F 815	Koninklijke Maatschappij De Schelde, Flushing	6 July 1965	18 June 1966	21 Dec 1967

Displacement, tons: 2 200 standard; 2 850 full load
Dimensions, feet (metres): 372 × 41 × 18
  (113·4 × 12·5 × 5·8)
Aircraft: 1 Lynx helicopter
Missiles: SSM; 8—MM38 Exocet (single cells);
  SAM; Sea Cat (2 quad launchers)
Gun: 1—76 mm/62 (single Compact)
A/S weapons: 6 (2 triple) Mk 32 torpedo tubes
Main engines: 2 double reduction geared turbines; 2 shafts;
  30 000 shp (to be modernised)
Boilers: 2 Babcock & Wilcox (fully automated)
Speed, knots: 30
Complement: 254 (after modernisation 231)

Four ships were ordered in October 1962 and two in 1964.

Design: Although in general these ships are based on the design of the British Improved Type 12 ("Leander" class), there are a number of modifications to suit the requirements of the Royal Netherlands Navy. As far as possible equipment of Netherlands manufacture was installed. This resulted in a number of changes in the ship's superstructure compared with the British "Leander" class. To avoid delay these ships were in some cases fitted with equipment already available, instead of going through long development stages.

Electronics: Sewaco I integration system and Daisy data-processing.

EVERTSEN   10/1977, C. and S. Taylor

Modernisation: This class is undergoing mid-life modernisation at Rykswerf Den Helder. This will take two years, one ship being accepted every eight months from January 1977 when *Van Speijk* was taken in hand (completion early 1979). This includes new electronics and electrics, updating of Ops. Room, improved communications, extensive automation with reduction in complement, enlarged hangar for Lynx and improved habitability. *Van Galen* is the second in hand (completion mid-1979), *Van Nes* the third, *Tjerk Hiddes* the fourth, *Evertsen* the fifth, *Isaac Sweers* the sixth.

Electronics: ECM equipment.

Radar: (new radar systems being fitted and integrated with Daisy during modernisation)
LW 02 air surveillance on mainmast
DA 05 target indicator on foremast
Kelvin-Hughes Surface-warning/nav set on foremast (to be replaced by new nav/helo control set)
One M45 for 4·5 in guns
Two M44 for Sea Cat

Sonar: Hull-mounted and VDS.

VAN SPEIJK (after modernisation)   11/1978, Leo van Ginderen

CORVETTES

6 "WOLF" CLASS

Name	No.	Builders	Commissioned
WOLF (ex-*PCE 1607*)	F 817	Avondale Marine Ways, Inc, New Orleans, La	26 Mar 1954
FRET (ex-*PCE 1604*)	F 818	General Shipbuilding and Engineering Works, Boston	4 May 1954
HERMELIJN (ex-*PCE 1605*)	F 819	General Shipbuilding and Engineering Works, Boston	5 Aug 1954
VOS (ex-*PCE 1606*)	F 820	General Shipbuilding and Engineering Works, Boston	2 Dec 1954
PANTER (ex-*PCE 1608*)	F 821	Avondale Marine Ways, Inc, New Orleans, La	11 June 1954
JAGUAR (ex-*PCE 1609*)	F 822	Avondale Marine Ways, Inc, New Orleans, La	11 June 1954

Displacement, tons: 870 standard; 975 full load
Dimensions, feet (metres): 184·5 × 33 × 14·5 *(56·2 × 10 × 4·4)*
Guns: 1—3 in *(76 mm)*; 6—40 mm *(Jaguar, Panter:* 4—40 mm*)*; 8—20 mm (not mounted)
A/S weapons: 1 Hedgehog; 2 DCT *(Jaguar, Panter:* 4 DCT*)*; 2 DC racks
Main engines: 2 General Motors diesels; 1 800 bhp; 2 shafts
Speed, knots: 15
Range, miles: 4 300 at 10 knots
Complement: 96

FRET   8/1978, Michael D. J. Lennon

Built as part of the US "off-shore" agreement—all laid down 1952-53. 20 mm guns not fitted in peacetime.

Radar: Kelvin Hughes navigation set.

Replacement: Now become aged but funds for replacements are unlikely to be available before 1983. Thus two "Friesland" class destroyers will be kept over-age to bridge the gap. The design of the "M" class frigates (smaller than the "Kortenaers" but similar in many ways and including a single helicopter) is under way for a replacement programme for the corvettes.

Sonar: One hull-mounted set.

358 NETHERLANDS / Light forces — Mine warfare forces

LIGHT FORCES

5 "BALDER" CLASS (LARGE PATROL CRAFT)

Name	No.	Builders	Commissioned
BALDER	P 802	Rijkswerf Willemsoord	6 Aug 1954
BULGIA	P 803	Rijkswerf Willemsoord	9 Aug 1954
FREYR	P 804	Rijkswerf Willemsoord	1 Dec 1954
HADDA	P 805	Rijkswerf Willemsoord	3 Feb 1955
HEFRING	P 806	Rijkswerf Willemsoord	23 Mar 1955

Displacement, tons: 169 standard; 225 full load
Dimensions, feet (metres): 119·1 × 20·2 × 5·9 (36·3 × 6·2 × 1·8)
Guns: 1—40 mm; 3—20 mm
A/S weapons: Mousetrap; depth charges
Main engines: Diesels; 2 shafts; 1 300 shp = 15·5 knots
Range, miles: 1 000 at 13 knots
Complement: 27

Built on US "off-shore" account.

Radar: Decca navigation set.

Sonar: One hull-mounted.

HADDA   11/1978, Leo van Ginderen

MINE WARFARE FORCES

0 + 15 "ALKMAAR" CLASS (TRIPARTITE TYPE) (MINEHUNTERS)

Name	No.	Builders	Commissioned
ALKMAAR	850	Van der Giessen-de Noord-Alblasserdam	1981
DELFZIJL	851	Van der Giessen-de Noord-Alblasserdam	1981
DORDRECHT	852	Van der Giessen-de Noord-Alblasserdam	1982
HAARLEM	853	Van der Giessen-de Noord-Alblasserdam	1982
HARLINGEN	854	Van der Giessen-de Noord-Alblasserdam	1982
HELLEVOETSLUIS	855	Van der Giessen-de Noord-Alblasserdam	1983
MAASSLUIS	856	Van der Giessen-de Noord-Alblasserdam	1983
MAKKUM	857	Van der Giessen-de Noord-Alblasserdam	1983
MIDDELBURG	858	Van der Giessen-de Noord-Alblasserdam	1984
SCHEVENINGEN	859	Van der Giessen-de Noord-Alblasserdam	1984
SCHIEDAM	860	Van der Giessen-de Noord-Alblasserdam	1984
URK	861	Van der Giessen-de Noord-Alblasserdam	1985
VEERE	862	Van der Giessen-de Noord-Alblasserdam	1985
VLAARDINGEN	863	Van der Giessen-de Noord-Alblasserdam	1985
WILLEMSTAD	864	Van der Giessen-de Noord-Alblasserdam	1986

Displacement, tons: 510
Dimensions, feet (metres): 154·5 pp × 29·2 × 8·2 (47·1 × 8·9 × 2·5)
Gun: 1—20 mm (an additional short range missile system may be added for patrol duties)
Minehunting: 2 PAP systems
Minesweeping: Mechanical sweep gear
Main engine: 1 Werkspoor diesel; single axial propeller; 2 280 hp = 15 knots
Auxiliary propulsion: 2—88 kW motors = 7 knots
Range, miles: 3 000 at 12 knots
Endurance: 15 days
Complement: From 22-45 depending on task

"ALKMAAR" Class   1978, Royal Netherlands Navy

This class is the Netherlands part of a cooperative plan with Belgium and France for GRP hulled minehunters. The whole class will be built in a specially constructed "ship-factory" (472 × 141 ft) which was completed December 1978. First two ships ordered June 1977. 850 laid down 15 December 1978, four currently ordered and remainder at two per year.

Electronics: Automatic radar navigation system; automatic data processing and display; EVEC automatic pilot; automatic hovering.

Sonar: DUBM-21A.

Tasks: A 5 ton container can be shipped, stored for varying tasks—HQ-support; research; patrol; extended diving; drone control.

3 Ex-US "AGGRESSIVE" CLASS (MCM SUPPORT SHIPS)

Name	No.	Builders	Commissioned
ONBEVREESD (ex-*AM 481*)	A 855 (ex-*M 885*)	Astoria Marine Construction Co	21 Sep 1954
ONVERVAARD (ex-*AM 482*)	A 858 (ex-*M 888*)	Astoria Marine Construction Co	31 Mar 1955
ONVERDROTEN (ex-*AM 485*)	A 859 (ex-*M 889*)	Peterson Builders, Wisconsin	22 Nov 1954

Displacement, tons: 735 standard; 790 full load
Dimensions, feet (metres): 172·0 × 36·0 × 10·6 (52·5 × 11 × 3·2)
Gun: 1—40 mm
A/S weapons: 2 DC
Main engines: Diesels; 1 600 bhp = 15·5 knots
Oil fuel, tons: 46
Range, miles: 2 400 at 12 knots
Complement: 70

Built in USA for the Netherlands. Of wooden and non-magnetic construction. Originally designed as Minesweepers—Ocean—reclassified in 1966 and in 1972. *Onbevreesd, Onverdroten* and *Onvervaard* are MCM Command/Support Ships. *Mercuur* (ex-*Onverschrokken*) was converted into a Tender and Torpedo Trials Ship in 1972.

ONBEVREESD   1976, Michael D. J. Lennon

NETHERLANDS / Mine warfare forces — Amphibious forces 359

18 "DOKKUM" CLASS (MINESWEEPERS, COASTAL and MINEHUNTERS)

DOKKUM M 801 (H)	**OMMEN** M 813	**HOOGEVEEN** M 827
HOOGEZAND M 802	**GIETHOORN** M 815	**STAPHORST** M 828 (H)
ROERMOND M 806 (D)	**VENLO** M 817	**SITTARD** M 830
NAALDWIJK M 809	**DRUNEN** M 818 (H)	**GEMERT** M 841
ABCOUDE M 810	**WOERDEN** M 820 (D)	**VEERE** M 842 (H)
DRACHTEN M 812	**NAARDEN** M 823	**RHENEN** M 844 (D)

Displacement, tons: 373 standard; 453 full load
Dimensions, feet (metres): 149·8 × 28 × 6·5 (45·7 × 8·5 × 2)
Guns: 2—40 mm
Main engines: 2 diesels; Fijenoord MAN; 2 500 bhp = 16 knots
Range, miles: 2 500 at 10 knots
Complement: 38

Of 32 Western Union type coastal minesweepers built in the Netherlands, 18 were under offshore procurement as the "Dokkum" class, with MAN engines, and 14 on Netherlands account as the "Wildervank" class, with Werkspoor diesels. All launched in 1954-56 and completed in 1955-56.
Of the "Dokkum" class four have been converted to minehunters (H), (1968-73) and three to diving vessels (D) (1962-68). The remaining eleven minesweepers and diving vessels of this class were subject to a fleet rehabilitation and modernisation programme completed by 1977. All "Wildervank" class deleted by 1976. "Dokkum" class to be replaced by "Alkmaar" class.

Sonar: Type 193 in hunters.

DOKKUM (Hunter)   12/1978, Leo van Ginderen

ABCOUDE (Sweeper)   9/1978, Michael D. J. Lennon

16 "VAN STRAELEN" CLASS (MINESWEEPERS—INSHORE)

Name	No.	Builders	Commissioned
ALBLAS	M 868	Werf de Noord, Albasserdam	12 Mar 1960
BUSSEMAKER	M 869	G. de Vries Lentsch Jr, Amsterdam	1960
LACOMBLE	M 870	N.V. de Arnhemse Scheepsbouw Maatschappij	1960
VAN HAMEL	M 871	G. de Vries Lentsch Jr, Amsterdam	1960
VAN STRAELEN	M 872	N.V. de Arnhemse Scheepsbouw Maatschappij	1960
VAN MOPPES	M 873	Werf de Noord, Albasserdam	1960
CHÖMPFF	M 874	Werf de Noord, Albasserdam	1961
VAN WELL GROENVELD	M 875	N.V. de Arnhemse Scheepsbouw Maatschappij	1961
SCHUILING	M 876	G. de Vries Lentsch Jr, Amsterdam	1961
VAN VERSENDAAL	M 877	Werf de Noord, Albasserdam	1961
VAN DER WEL	M 878	G. de Vries Lentsch Jr, Amsterdam	1961
VAN 'T HOFF	M 879	Werf de Noord, Albasserdam	1961
MAHU	M 880	Werf de Noord, Albasserdam	1962
STAVERMAN	M 881	G. de Vries Lentsch Jr, Amsterdam	1962
HOUTEPEN	M 882	N.V. de Arnhemse Scheepsbouw Maatschappij	1962
ZOMER	M 883	N.V. de Arnhemse Scheepsbouw Maatschappij	1962

CHÖMPFF   12/1978, Leo van Ginderen

Displacement, tons: 151 light; 169 full load
Dimensions, feet (metres): 99·3 × 18·2 ×5·2 (30·3 × 5·6 × 1·6)
Gun: 1—20 mm
Main engines: Werkspoor diesels; 2 shafts; 1 100 bhp = 13 knots
Complement: 14

Eight were built under the offshore procurement programme, with MDAP funds, and the remaining eight were paid for by Netherlands. All ordered in mid-1957. Built of non-magnetic materials. *Alblas*, the first, was laid down on 26 February 1958, launched on 29 June 1959, started trials on 15 January1960. To be replaced after 1983.

AMPHIBIOUS FORCES

L 9510	L 9512	L 9514	L 9517	L 9520
L 9511	L 9513	L 9515	L 9518	L 9522

Displacement, tons: 13·6
Dimensions, feet (metres): 46·2 × 11·5 × 6 (14·1 × 3·5 × 1·8)
Main engine: Rolls-Royce diesel; Schottel propeller; 200 bhp = 12 knots
Complement: 3

Landing craft made of polyester, all commissioned in 1962-63, except L 9520 in 1964. Built by "Le Conte".

L 9518   8/1978, Leo van Ginderen

360 NETHERLANDS / Survey ships — Service forces

SURVEY SHIPS

1 "TYDEMAN" CLASS (HYDROGRAPHIC/OCEANOGRAPHIC SHIP)

Name	No.	Builders	Commissioned
TYDEMAN	A 906	Scheepswerf en Machine Fabriek "de Merwede"	10 Nov 1976

Displacement, tons: 2 977
Dimensions, feet (metres): 295 × 47·2 × 15·7 (90 × 14·4 × 4·8)
Aircraft: Helicopter deck
Main engines: Diesel-electric: 3 Stork-Werkspoor diesels; 3 690 shp;
   1 Paxman V diesel; 485 shp; 1 electric motor; 2 730 shp; 1 shaft
Speed, knots: 15
Range, miles: 15 700 at 10·3 knots; 10 300 at 13·5 knots
Complement: 58 plus 15 scientists

Ordered in October 1974. Laid down 29 April 1975, launched 18 December 1975. Fitted with bow thruster (450 shp) and active rudder (300 shp). Passive stabilisation tank. Normally operates in North Atlantic.

Cost: £6·7 million (1974).

Technical equipment: Able to operate Oceanographic cables down to 7 000 m. Has six laboratories and two container spaces each for 20 ft standard container. Has forward working-deck with wet-hall, midships and after working decks, one 10 ton crane, one 4 ton crane and frames. Diving facilities. Two automation systems, HYDRAUT and OCEANLOG data logging systems.

TYDEMAN   12/1976, Royal Netherlands Navy

2 "BUYSKES" CLASS

Name	No.	Builders	Commissioned
BUYSKES	A 904	Boele's Scheepswerven en Machinefabriek BV, Bolnes	9 Mar 1973
BLOMMENDAL	A 905	Boele's Scheepswerven en Machinefabriek BV, Bolnes	22 May 1973

Displacement, tons: 967 standard; 1 033 full load
Dimensions, feet (metres): 196·6 × 36·4 × 12 (60 × 11·1 × 3·7)
Main engines: Diesel-electric; 3 Paxman diesels; 2 100 hp = 13·5 knots
Range, miles: 3 000 at 11·5 knots
Complement: 43

Both designed primarily for hydrographic work but have also limited oceanographic and meteorological capability. They will operate mainly in the North Sea. A data logging system is installed as part of the automatic handling of hydrographic data. They carry two 22 feet survey launches capable of 15 knots and two work-boats normally used for sweeping.

Sonar: Side-scanning and wreck-search.

Technical equipment: HYDRAUT logging system; wire-drags, normal echo-sounders.

BLOMMENDAL   5/1978, J. L. M. van der Burg

SERVICE FORCES

2 "POOLSTER" CLASS (FAST COMBAT SUPPORT SHIPS)

Name	No.	Builders	Commissioned
ZUIDERKRUIS	A 832	Verolme Shipyards, Albasserdam	27 June 1975
POOLSTER	A 835	Rotterdamse Droogdok Mij	10 Sep 1964

Displacement, tons: 16 800 full load; 16 900 (Zuiderkruis)
Measurement, tons: 10 000 deadweight
Dimensions, feet (metres): 556 × 66·7 × 27 (169·6 × 20·3 × 8·2)
   (Zuiderkruis 561 (171·1))
Aircraft: Capacity: 5 helicopters
Guns: 2—40 mm in *Poolster*; 2—20 mm in *Zuiderkruis*
Main engines: 2 turbines; 22 000 shp = 21 knots (*Poolster*)
   2 Werkspoor diesels; 21 000 hp = 21 knots (*Zuiderkruis*)
Complement: 200

Poolster laid down on 18 September 1962. Launched on 16 October 1963. Trials mid-1964. Helicopter deck aft. Funnel heightened by 4·5 m. *Zuiderkruis* ordered October 1972. Laid down 16 July 1973, launched 15 October 1974.
Both carry A/S weapons for helicopters.

Radar: Kelvin Hughes navigation set.

Sonar: Hull-mounted set.

POOLSTER   10/1978, Michael D. J. Lennon

ZUIDERKRUIS   7/1978, Wright and Logan

TRAINING SHIPS

Name	No.	Builders	Commissioned
ZEEFAKKEL	A 903	J. & K. Smit, Kinderdijk	22 May 1951

Displacement, tons: 355 standard; 384 full load
Dimensions, feet (metres): 149 × 24·7 × 6·9 (45·4 × 7·6 × 2·1)
Guns: 1—3 in; 1—40 mm
Main engines: 2 Smit/MAN 8-cyl diesels; 2 shafts; 640 bhp = 12 knots
Complement: 29

Laid down September 1949, launched 21 July 1950. Former surveying vessel. Now used as local training ship at Den Helder.

Name	No.	Builders	Commissioned
URANIA (ex-*Tromp*)	Y 8050	—	23 Apr 1938

Displacement, tons: 38
Dimensions, feet (metres): 72 × 16·3 × 10 (22 × 5 × 3·1)
Main engine: Diesel; 65 hp
Complement: 15

Schooner used for training in seamanship.

Note: *Gelderland* (ex-destroyer) and *Grypskerk* (ex-minesweeper) are used at Amsterdam as harbour training and accommodation ships for the Technical Training establishment. *Soemba* (ex-sloop) used at Den Oever as harbour training and accommodation ship for divers and underwater-swimmers—to be replaced by a shore barracks in 1979-80.

TUGS

Name	No.	Builders	Commissioned
WESTGAT	A 872	Rijkswerf, Willemsoord	10 Jan 1968
WIELINGEN	A 873	Rijkswerf, Willemsoord	4 Apr 1968

Displacement, tons: 185
Dimensions, feet (metres): 90·6 × 22·7 × 7·7 (27·6 × 6·9 × 2·3)
Guns: 2—20 mm
Main engine: Bolnes diesel; 750 bhp = 12 knots

Launched on 22 August 1967 and 6 January 1968, respectively. Equipped with salvage pumps and fire fighting equipment. Stationed at Den Helder.

WESTGAT   11/1978 Leo van Ginderen

Name	No.	Builders	Commissioned
WAMANDAI	A 870 (ex-Y 8035)	Rijkswerf, Willemsoord	1960

Displacement, tons: 159 standard; 201 full load
Dimensions, feet (metres): 89·2 × 21·3 × 7·5 (27·2 × 6·5 × 2·3)
Guns: 2—20 mm
Main engine: Diesel; 500 bhp = 11 knots

Launched on 28 May 1960. Equipped with salvage pumps and fire fighting equipment. In the Netherlands Antilles since 1964.

Name	No.	Builders	Commissioned
WAMBRAU	A 871	Rijkswerf, Willemsoord	8 Jan 1957

Displacement, tons: 154 standard; 179 full load
Dimensions, feet (metres): 86·5 × 20·7 × 7·5 (26·4 × 6·3 × 2·3)
Guns: 2—20 mm
Main engine: Werkspoor diesel and Kort nozzle; 500 bhp = 10·8 knots

Launched on 27 August 1956. Equipped with salvage pumps and fire fighting equipment. Stationed at Den Helder.

Name	No.	Builders	Commissioned
BERKEL	Y 8037	H. H. Bodewes, Millingen	1956
DINTEL	Y 8038	H. H. Bodewes, Millingen	1956
DOMMEL	Y 8039	H. H. Bodewes, Millingen	1957
IJSSEL	Y 8040	H. H. Bodewes, Millingen	1957

Displacement, tons: 139 standard; 163 full load
Dimensions, feet (metres): 82 × 20·5 × 7·3 (25 × 6·3 × 2·2)
Main engine: Werkspoor diesel and Kort nozzle; 500 bhp

Harbour tugs specially designed for use at Den Helder.

There are also five small harbour tugs—Y 8014, Y 8016, Y 8017, Y 8022, Y 8028—of 75 tons, (8014) 43 tons, (8016 and 8017) and 70 tons (last pair).

ACCOMMODATION SHIPS

(See note under Training Ships)

Cornelis Drebbel is the name of the "Boatel"—775 tons, length 206·7 ft, beam 38·7 ft, draught 3·6 ft, complement 200, cost 3m guilders. Ordered in 1969 from Scheepswerf Voorwaarts at Hoogezand, launched on 19 November 1970 and completed in 1971. Serves as accommodation vessel for crews of ships refitting at private yards in the Rotterdam area.

AUXILIARIES

1 TORPEDO TENDER

Name	No.	Builders	Commissioned
MERCUUR (ex-*Onvers-chrokken*, ex-AM 483)	A 856 (ex-M 886)	Peterson Builders, Wisconsin	22 July 1954

Of Ex-US "Aggressive" class. Details in Mine Warfare section.

1 TORPEDO TRIALS SHIP

Name	No.	Builders	Commissioned
VAN BOCHOVE	A 923	Zaanlandse Scheepsbouw Mij, Zaandam	Aug 1962

Displacement, tons: 140
Dimensions, feet (metres): 97·2 × 18·2 × 6 (29·6 × 5·6 × 1·8)
Main engine: Kromhout diesel; Schottel propeller; 140 bhp = 8 knots
Complement: 8

Ordered October 1961. Launched on 20 July 1962. Has two 21 in (533 mm) torpedo tubes.

4 DIVING TENDERS

Name	No.	Builders	Commissioned
ARGUS	A 847	Rijkswerf, Willemsoord	1939
TRITON	A 848	Rijkswerf, Willemsoord	4 Apr 1964
NAUTILUS	A 849	Rijkswerf, Willemsoord	20 Apr 1965
HYDRA	A 850	Rijkswerf, Willemsoord	20 Apr 1965

Displacement, tons: 44 (*Argus*); 67 (remainder)
Dimensions, feet (metres): 75·4 × 15·4 × 3·3 (23 × 4·7 × 1) (*Argus*);
76 × 16·4 × 4·6 (23·2 × 5 × 1·4) (remainder)
Main engine: Diesel; 144 hp = 8 knots (*Argus*)
Diesel, 117 hp = 9 knots (remainder)
Complement: 8

DREG IV A 920

Displacement, tons: 46 standard; 48 full load
Dimensions, feet (metres): 65·7 × 15·1 × 4·9 (20 × 4·6 × 1·5)
Main engine: 120 hp = 9·5 knots
Complement: 10

Former survey launch used for communication duties in Rotterdam area.

1 FUEL OIL LIGHTER

PATRIA Y 8536

Dimensions, feet (metres): 202·2 × 26·5 × — (61·6 × 8·1 × —)
Main engine: Bolnes diesel; 300 hp
Capacity, tons: 827

Built in 1963 by H. H. Bodewes, Mallingen a/d Rijen. Based at Den Helder and used for transport from Rotterdam and bunkering. Purchased 1978.

2 FUEL LIGHTERS

Y 8335   Y 8538

Built 1952 and 1955 respectively.

1 WATER CARRIER

Y 8480

Built in 1950.

2 SMALL TRANSPORTS (CARGO)

Y 8500   Y 8501

Built in 1953 and 1951 respectively.

1 TORPEDO TRANSPORT

Y 8512

Built in 1947.

2 SMALL FLOATING DOCKS

Y 8678

Of 131·3 × 29·6 × 12·4 ft. Built in 1949.

Y 8679

Of 131·3 × 34·9 × 13 ft. Built in 1960.

1 FLOATING POWER STATION

Y 8676

Built in 1962. Self-propelled.

In addition non-self-propelled craft include Y 8514, floating crane built in 1974 and about 40 others including tank-cleaning vessels, barges etc.

NEW ZEALAND

Headquarters Appointments

Chief of Naval Staff:
  Rear-Admiral N. D. Anderson, CBE
Deputy Chief of Naval Staff:
  Commodore R. H. Humby

The three New Zealand Service Boards were formally abolished in 1971 as part of the Defence Headquarters reorganisation. The former three Service Headquarters and Defence Office have been reorganised into functional branches and offices.
On 1 June 1970 the command and control of the three New Zealand Services was vested in the Chief of Defence Staff who exercises this authority through the three Service Chiefs of Staff.

Diplomatic Representation

Head of New Zealand Defence Liaison Staff, London and Senior Naval Liaison Officer:
  Commodore F. H. Bland, OBE
Deputy Head of New Zealand Defence Staff, Washington and Naval Attaché:
  Captain E. R. Ellison, OBE

Personnel

(a) January 1974: 2 730 officers and ratings
    January 1975: 2 690 officers and ratings
    January 1976: 2 800 officers and ratings
    January 1977: 2 648 officers and ratings
    January 1978: 2 757 officers and ratings
    January 1979: 2 825 officers and ratings
(b) Voluntary service
    Reserve; 347 RNZNVR

Base

Auckland (HMNZS *Philomel*)

Prefix to Ships' Names

HMNZS

Mercantile Marine

Lloyd's Register of Shipping:
  109 vessels of 211 112 tons gross

Strength of the Fleet

Type	Active	Building
Frigates	4	—
Large Patrol Craft	4	—
Survey Ship	1	—
Survey Craft	2	2
Research Vessel	1	—
Tender	1	—
Tug	1	—
Reserve Training HDMLs	5	—

DELETIONS

Corvettes

1976 *Inverell, Kiama* (Sep)

Patrol Craft

1972 *Maroro* (HDML)
1975 *Kahawai, Mako, Parore, Tamure* (HDMLs)

Survey Ship

1974 *Lachlan* (Dec)

Tug

1979 *Manawanui*

PENNANT LIST

Frigates

F 55	Waikato
F 111	Otago
F 148	Taranaki
F 421	Canterbury

Light Forces

P 3552	Paea
P 3563	Kuparu
P 3564	Koura
P 3565	Haku
P 3567	Manga
P 3568	Pukaki
P 3569	Rotoiti
P 3570	Taupo
P 3571	Hawea

Surveying Vessels

A 06	Monowai
P 3556	Takapu
P 3566	Tarapunga

Research Vessel

A 2	Tui

FRIGATES

1 "LEANDER" and 1 "BROAD-BEAMED LEANDER" CLASSES

Name	No.	Builders	Laid down	Launched	Commissioned
WAIKATO	F 55	Harland & Wolff Ltd, Belfast	10 Jan 1964	18 Feb 1965	16 Sep 1966
CANTERBURY	F 421	Yarrow Ltd, Clyde	12 Apr 1969	6 May 1970	22 Oct 1971

Displacement, tons: 2 450 standard; 2 860 full load *Waikato*;
  2 470 standard; 2 990 full load *Canterbury*
Length, feet (metres): 360·0 *(109·7)* pp; 372·0 *(113·4) Waikato*;
  370·0 *(112·8)* pp *Canterbury*
Beam, feet (metres): 41·0 *(12·5) Waikato*;
  43·0 *(13·1) Canterbury*
Draught, feet (metres): 18 *(5·5)*
Aircraft: 1 Wasp helicopter
Missiles: SAM; Est. 12 Sea Cat (one quad launcher)
Guns: 2—4·5 in *(115 mm)*/45 (twin Mk 6);
  2—20 mm/70 (single L70)
A/S weapons: 2 triple Mk 32 Mod 5 A/S torpedo tubes
Main engines: 2 sets dr geared turbines; 2 shafts; 30 000 shp
Boilers: 2 Babcock & Wilcox
Speed, knots: 30 *Waikato*; 28 *Canterbury*
Complement: 248 (14 officers, 234 ratings) *Waikato*;
  243 (14 officers, 229 ratings) *Canterbury*

Waikato, ordered on 14 June 1963. Commissioned on 16 September 1966, trials in the UK until spring 1967, arrived in New Zealand waters in May 1967. *Canterbury* was ordered in August 1968, arrived in New Zealand in August 1972. *Canterbury* has extensions fitted to her funnel uptakes. *Waikato* completed long refit and modernisation July 1977.

Aircraft: Hangar has been enlarged to take Lynx although that aircraft has not yet been ordered.

Radar: Search: Type 965.
Tactical: Type 993.
Fire control: MRS 3 System and I Band.

WAIKATO (with enlarged helicopter deck and hangar) 1978, J. Fam

NEW ZEALAND / Frigates — Light forces 363

2 "WHITBY" CLASS (TYPE 12)

Name	No.	Builders	Laid down	Launched	Commissioned
OTAGO (ex-HMS *Hastings*)	F 111	J. I. Thornycroft & Co Ltd, Woolston, Southampton	1957	11 Dec 1958	22 June 1960
TARANAKI	F 148	J. Samuel White & Co Ltd, Isle of Wight	1958	19 Aug 1959	28 Mar 1961

Displacement, tons: 2 144 standard; 2 557 full load
Length, feet (metres): 360·0 *(109·7)* pp; 370·0 *(112·8)*
Beam, feet (metres): 41·0 *(12·5)*
Draught, feet (metres): 17·3 *(5·3)*
Missiles: SAM; Est. 12 Sea Cat (quad launcher) (see *Class* note)
Guns: 2—4·5 in *(115 mm)*/45 (twin Mk 6);
 2—20 mm/70 (*Taranaki* only)
A/S weapons: 6 (2 triple) Mk 32 Mod 5 A/S torpedo tubes (see *Class* note)
Main engines: 2 sets dr geared turbines; 2 shafts; 30 000 shp
Boilers: 2 Babcock & Wilcox
Speed, knots: 30
Complement: 240 (13 officers, 227 ratings) (see *Class* note)

Taranaki was ordered direct (announced by J. Samuel White & Co on 22 February 1957). For *Otago* New Zealand took over the contract (officially stated on 26 February 1957) for *Hastings* originally ordered from John I. Thornycroft & Co in February 1956 for the Royal Navy. Both vessels are generally similar to the "Whitby" class in the Royal Navy, but were modified to suit New Zealand conditions and have had the most necessary "Rothesay" class alterations and additions. *Otago* has had enclosed foremast since 1967 refit; *Taranaki* was similarly fitted during 1969.

Class: *Taranaki* refitted 1978-79 and reduced to "Resources Protection and Sea Training" role. Limbo and Sea Cat removed and ships company reduced to about 100.

OTAGO　　　　　　　　　　　　　　　　　　　　　　　　　　　　　　1977, *Royal New Zealand Navy*

Radar: Search: Type 993 and Type 277.
Fire control: Type 275.

Torpedo tubes: The original twelve 21 in *(533 mm)* A/S torpedo tubes (eight single and two twin) were removed.

SURVEY VESSELS

Name	No.	Builders	Laid down	Launched	Commissioned
MONOWAI (ex-*Moana Roa*)	A 06	Grangemouth D.Y.	—	—	Aug 1960

Displacement, tons: 3 800
Measurement, tons: 2 893 gross; 1 318 net
Dimensions, feet (metres): 298 × 46 × 17 *(90·8 × 14 × 5·2)*
Aircraft: 1 helicopter
Main engines: 2 Sulzer 7-cyl diesels; 3 640 hp = 14 knots
Oil fuel, tons: 300
Range, miles: 12 000 cruising
Complement: 126 (11 officers, 115 ratings)

Previously employed on the Cook Islands service. Taken over 1974—put out to tender in early 1975 for conversion which included an up-rating of the engines, provision of a helicopter deck and hangar and fitting of cp propellers and a bow thruster. Conversion undertaken by Scott Lithgow Drydocks Ltd. Commissioned 4 October 1977.
May be used for training when available.

MONOWAI　　　　　　　　　　　　　　　　　　　　　　　　　　　　　　1978, *D. N. Brigham*

2 HDML TYPE

TAKAPU P 3556 (ex-*Q 1188*)
TARAPUNGA P 3566 (ex-*Q 1387*)

Similar description as those listed under Light Forces. To be deleted late 1979 when new construction survey craft will take over their names.

2 NEW CONSTRUCTION

Name	No.	Builders	Commissioned
(TAKAPU)	—	Whangarei Engineering Ltd	mid-1979
(TARAPUNGA)	—	Whangarei Engineering Ltd	late 1979

On 30 November 1977 the NZ Cabinet approved the construction of two 88·6 ft *(27 m)* survey craft with hull and machinery similar to those of the new diving tender *Manawanui*. Their equipment has been specifically designed to work with *Monowai*. They will replace *Takapu* and *Tarapunga* taking over their names.

LIGHT FORCES

4 "LAKE" CLASS (LARGE PATROL CRAFT)

Name	No.	Builders	Commissioned
PUKAKI	P 3568	Brooke Marine, Lowestoft, England	24 Feb 1975
ROTOITI	P 3569	Brooke Marine, Lowestoft, England	24 Feb 1975
TAUPO	P 3570	Brooke Marine, Lowestoft, England	29 July 1975
HAWEA	P 3571	Brooke Marine, Lowestoft, England	29 July 1975

Displacement, tons: 105 standard; 134 full load
Dimensions, feet (metres): 107 × 20 × 11·8 *(32·8 × 6·1 × 3·6)*
Guns: 2—12·7 mm (·50 cal) M2 MGs (fwd); 1—81 mm mortar/·50 cal MG combination (aft)
Main engines: 2 Paxman 12YJCM diesels; 3 000 bhp = 25 knots
Complement: 21 (3 officers, 18 ratings)

The first to complete, *Pukaki*, was finished on 20 July 1974. She and *Rotoiti* were shipped to New Zealand in November 1974. Launch dates—*Hawea*, 9 September 1974; *Pukaki*, 1 March 1974; *Rotoiti*, 8 March 1974; *Taupo*, 25 July 1974.

PUKAKI　　　　　　　　　　　　　　　　　　　　　　　　　　　　　　1976, *Royal New Zealand Navy*

364 NEW ZEALAND / Light forces — NICARAGUA / Patrol craft

5 HDML TYPE

PAEA (ex-Q 1184) P 3552
KUPARU (ex-*Pegasus,* ex-Q 1349) P 3563
KOURA (ex-*Toroa,* ex-Q 1350) P 3564
HAKU (ex-*Wakefield,* ex-Q 1197) P 3565
MANGA (ex-Q 1185) P 3567

Displacement, tons: 46 standard; 54 full load
Dimensions, feet (metres): 72 × 16 × 5·5 *(22 × 4·9 × 1·7)*
Guns: Armament removed
Main engines: 2 diesels; 2 shafts; 320 bhp = 12 knots
Complement: 9

All built in various yards in the USA and Canada and shipped to New Zealand. All have been converted with lattice masts surmounted by a radar aerial. *Manga* refitting 1979.
Attached to RNZNVR divisions;
 Auckland: *Haku.*
 Canterbury: *Kuparu.*
 Otago: *Koura.*
 Wellington: *Paea.*

HAKU   1973, Royal New Zealand Navy

TUG

ARATAKI

Dimensions, feet (metres): Length: 75 *(22·9)*
Main engine: Diesel; 1 shaft; 320 hp

Steel tug used for dockyard work. Built by Steel Ships Ltd, Auckland in 1947.

RESEARCH VESSEL

Name	No.	Builders	Commissioned
TUI (ex-USS *Charles H. Davis,* T-AGOR 5)	A 2	Christy Corporation, Sturgeon Bay, Wis.	25 Jan 1963

Displacement, tons: 1 200 standard; 1 380 full load
Dimensions, feet (metres): 208·9 × 37·4 × 15·3 *(63·7 × 11·3 × 4·7)*
Main engine: Diesel-electric; 1 shaft; 10 000 hp = 12 knots
Complement: 8 officers, 16 ratings, 15 scientists

Oceanographic research ship. Laid down on 15 June 1961, launched on 30 June 1962. On loan from USA since 28 July 1970 for five years. Commissioned in the RNZN on 11 September 1970. Announced that she will remain in RNZN until at least 1980. Operates for NZ Defence Research Establishment on acoustic research. Bow propeller 175 hp.

Appearance: Port after gallows removed—new gallows at stern—cable reels on quarterdeck and amidships—light cable-laying gear over bow.

TUI   4/1978, John Mortimer

1 DIVING TENDER

Name	No.	Builders	Commissioned
MANAWANUI	—	Whangarei Engineering Ltd	Jan 1979

Length, feet (metres): 88·6 *(27)*

NICARAGUA

Ministerial

Minister of Defence:
 Heberto Sanchez

Personnel

1979: 200 officers and men

All craft operated by Marine Section of the Guardia Naçional

Ports

Carinto, Puerto Cabezas, Puerto Somaza, San Juan del Sur

Mercantile Marine

Lloyd's Register of Shipping:
 30 vessels of 34 588 tons gross

PATROL CRAFT

1 SEWART TYPE

RIO KURINGWAS GC 7

Displacement, tons: 60
Dimensions, feet (metres): 85 × 18·8 × 5·9 *(25·9 × 5·6 × 1·8)*
Guns: 3—7·62 mm MG
Main engines: 3 General Motors diesels; 3 shafts; 2 000 shp = 26·5 knots
Range, miles: 1 000 at 20 knots
Complement: 10

Delivered July 1972.

RIO CRUTA

Dimensions, feet (metres): Length: 85 *(25·9)*
Gun: 1—20 mm (bow)
Main engines: Diesels; speed = 9 knots
Complement: 11

Wooden hulled.

4 "90 ft" LARGE PATROL CRAFT

Wooden hulled (27·5 metres).

2 "80 ft" LARGE PATROL CRAFT

Wooden hulled (24·4 metres).

1 "75 ft" LARGE PATROL CRAFT

Built in 1925 so present existence doubtful. Was used for training. (22·9 metres).

1 "40 ft" UTILITY CRAFT

Acquired in 1962.

1 "26 ft" COASTAL PATROL CRAFT

Armed with a 20 mm gun, capable of 25 knots and with a crew of six. (7·9 metres).

1 Ex-US LCM 6

Acquired in 1970.

NIGERIA

Headquarters Appointments

Chief of the Naval Staff:
  Rear-Admiral Michael Ayinde Adelanwa
Chief of Operations:
  Captain Denis Eresecohima Okujagu

Commands

Flotilla Command:
  Commodore Akintunde Akinyoye Aduwo
Western Naval Command:
  Commodore Hussaini Abdullahi
Eastern Naval Command:
  Captain Muftau Adeguke Babatunde Elegbede

Diplomatic Representation

Naval Adviser in Delhi:
  Captain Raheem Adisa Oladipo Adegbite
Naval Adviser in London:
  Commander P. A. Hemben

Personnel

(a) 1979: 408 officers and 2 915 ratings
(b) Voluntary service

Bases

Apapa—Lagos:
  Western Naval Command
  Dockyard Training Schools
  New dockyard under construction
Calabar:
  Eastern Naval Command

Prefix to Ships' Names

NNS

Strength of the Fleet

Type	Active	Building
Frigates	1	1
Corvettes	4	—
Fast Attack Craft (Missile)	0	6
Large Patrol Craft	12	—
Coastal Patrol Craft	0	15
Landing Ships	1	1
LCTs	0	2
Survey Ship	1	—
Training Ship	1	—
Tugs	2	—
Police Craft	8	—

Mercantile Marine

Lloyd's Register of Shipping:
  101 vessels of 324 024 tons gross

DELETIONS

Light Forces

1975 3 ex-Soviet "P6" class; *Kaduna, Ibadan II* ("Ford" class)

Survey Ships

1975 *Pathfinder*
1977 *Penelope*

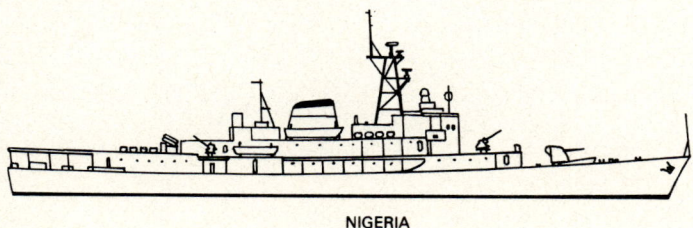

NIGERIA   LANA

FRIGATES

1 BLOHM AND VOSS MEKO TYPE 360

Displacement, tons: 3 700
Dimensions, feet (metres): 400·3 × 47·9 × 15 *(122 × 14·6 × 4·4)*
Aircraft: 1 helicopter
Missiles: SSM and SAM
Guns: 2—76 mm Compact
A/S weapons: A/S torpedoes and DCs
Torpedo Tubes: 2—21 in *(533 mm)*
Main engines: CODOG; 2 gas turbines; 2 diesels
Speed, knots: 30
Range, miles: 6 500 cruising
Complement: 200

Ordered from Blohm and Voss, Hamburg in 1979 for completion 1981. The weapon fit is not yet published—the above is the Blohm and Voss multi-role version.

Radar: Search: One set.
Search/fire control: One set.
Navigation: One set.
IFF/SIF: Two sets.

All the above by Hollandse Signaal Apparaten.

Sonar: One hull-mounted.

MEKO TYPE 360   *1978, Blohm and Voss*

Name	No.	Builders	Laid down	Launched	Commissioned
NIGERIA	F 87	Wilton-Fijenoord NV, Netherlands	9 Apr 1964	12 Apr 1965	16 Sep 1965

Displacement, tons: 1 724 standard; 2 000 full load
Length, feet (metres): 341·2 *(104·0)* pp; 360·2 *(109·8)*
Beam, feet (metres): 37·0 *(11·3)*
Draught, feet (metres): 11·5 *(3·5)*
Guns: 2—4 in *(102 mm)* (1 twin); 4—40 mm (single)
A/S weapons: 1—triple-barrelled Squid mortar
Main engines: 4 MAN diesels; 2 shafts; 16 000 bhp
Speed, knots: 26
Range, miles: 3 500 at 15 knots
Complement: 216

Original cost £3·5 million. Helicopter platform aft. Refitted at Birkenhead, 1973. Suffered a serious fire on return from refit. Further refit completed at Schiedam October 1977.

Radar: Type 293/AWS 4

Sonar: Removed.

NIGERIA   *10/1977, Michael D. J. Lennon*

NIGERIA / Corvettes — Light forces

CORVETTES

2 Mk 9 VOSPER THORNYCROFT TYPE

Name	No.	Builders	Commissioned
ERIN'MI	F 83	Vosper Thornycroft Ltd	1979
ENYIMIRI	F 84	Vosper Thornycroft Ltd	1980

Displacement, tons: 850 full load
Dimensions, feet (metres): 226 × 31·5 × 9·8 (69 × 9·6 × 3)
Missiles: SAM; Est. 12 Sea Cat (triple launcher)
Guns: 1—76 mm/62 Mod 6 Compact; 1—40 mm L70 Bofors; 2—20 mm Oerlikon
A/S weapons: 1 Bofors rocket launcher (twin)
Main engines: 4 MTU 20V 956 TB 92 diesels; 17 600 shp
Speed, knots: 28
Range, miles: 2 200 at 14 knots
Complement: 90 (including flag officer)

Ordered from Vosper Thornycroft 22 April 1975. *Erin'mi* laid down 14 October 1975 and launched 20 January 1977. *Enyimiri* laid down 11 February 1977 and launched 9 February 1978.

Radar: Search: Plessey AWS 2.
Fire control: HSA WM 24.
Navigation: Decca TM 1226.

Sonar: Plessey PMS 26.

ERIN'MI   11/1978, Michael D. J. Lennon

2 Mk 3 VOSPER THORNYCROFT TYPE

Name	No.	Builders	Commissioned
DORINA	F 81	Vosper Thornycroft	June 1972
OTOBO	F 82	Vosper Thornycroft	Nov 1972

Displacement, tons: 500 standard; 650 full load
Dimensions, feet (metres): 202 × 31 × 11·33 (61·6 × 9·5 × 3·5)
Guns: 2—4 in (1 twin) UK Mk 19; 2—40 mm Bofors (single) 2—20 mm
Main engines: 2 MAN diesels; 8 000 bhp; 2 shafts = 22 knots
Range, miles: 3 000 at 14 knots
Complement: 67 (8 officers and 59 ratings)

Ordered on 28 March 1968. *Dorina* laid down 26 January 1970, launched 16 September 1970, *Otobo* laid down 28 September 1970, launched 25 May 1971. Both refitted by Vosper Thornycroft 1975.

Radar: Air search: Plessey AWS 1.
Fire control: HSA M22.
Navigation: Decca TM626.

Sonar: Plessey MS 22.

DORINA   9/1976, Wright and Logan

LIGHT FORCES

0 + 3 LÜRSSEN S-143 CLASS (FAST ATTACK CRAFT—MISSILE)

Displacement, tons: 295 standard; 378 full load
Dimensions, feet (metres): 200 × 24·6 × 8·5 (57 × 7·8 × 2·4)
Missiles: 4 launchers for OTOmat
Guns: 2—76 mm
Torpedo tubes: 2—21 in (533 mm) aft
Main engines: 4 MTU diesels; 16 000 shp; 4 shafts = 38 knots
Range, miles: 1 300 at 30 knots
Complement: 40

Ordered from Lürssen, Vegesack late 1977. The above data is that of the West German S143 class with a change to OTOmat missiles. It is possible that, as in the following Combattante III class, the after 76 mm may be changed for a 40 mm and the torpedo tubes dispensed with. To carry HSA WM 28 fire control.

Type 143   Reinhard Nerlich

0 + 3 COMBATTANTE IIIB CLASS (FAST ATTACK CRAFT—MISSILE)

Displacement, tons: 385 standard; 425 full load
Dimensions, feet (metres): 184 × 26 × 7 (56·2 × 8 × 2·1)
Missiles: 4 launchers for MM 38 Exocet
Guns: 1—76 mm OTO Melara Compact; 1—40 mm Breda; 4—30 mm (twins) Emerlec (bridge)
Main engines: 4 16-cyl MTU diesels; 20 000 shp; 4 shafts = 37 knots
Range, miles: 2 000 at 15 knots
Complement: 42

A 50 million franc order placed with CMN, Cherbourg in late 1977. Thomson CSF fire control.

COMBATTANTE III Class (with 2—76 mm)   CMN

4 BROOKE MARINE TYPE (LARGE PATROL CRAFT)

Name	No.	Builders	Commissioned
MAKURDI	P 167	Brooke Marine, Lowestoft	14 Aug 1974
HADEJIA	P 168	Brooke Marine, Lowestoft	14 Aug 1974
JEBBA	P 171	Brooke Marine, Lowestoft	29 Apr 1977
OGUTA	P 172	Brooke Marine, Lowestoft	29 Apr 1977

Displacement, tons: 115 standard; 143 full load
Dimensions, feet (metres): 107 × 20 × 11·5 (32·6 × 6·1 × 3·5)
Guns: 2—40 mm; 2 Rocket flare launchers (to be fitted with twin 30 mm Emerlac in place of 40 mm)
Main engines: 2 Paxman 12-cyl Ventura diesels; 3 000 bhp; 2 shafts = 20·5 knots
Complement: 21

First pair ordered in 1971. Second pair ordered 30 October 1974, laid down 20 January 1975. Launch dates—*Hadejia*, 25 May 1974; *Makurdi*, 21 March 1974; *Jebba*, 1 December 1976; *Oguta* 17 January 1977. Completion dates for second pair 11 February 1977 and 18 March 1977 respectively.

HADEJIA   9/1974, C. and S. Taylor

NIGERIA / Light forces — Police craft 367

4 Ex-BRITISH "FORD" CLASS (LARGE PATROL CRAFT)

Name	No.	Builders	Commissioned
BENIN (ex-HMS *Hinksford*)	P 03	Richards, Lowestoft	1955
BONNY (ex-HMS *Gifford*)	P 04	Scarr, Hessle	1954
ENUGU	P 05	Camper & Nicholson's, Gosport	14 Dec 1961
SAPELE (ex-HMS *Dubford*)	P 09	J. Samuel White, Cowes	1953

Displacement, tons: 120 standard; 160 full load
Dimensions, feet (metres): 117·2 × 20 × 5 *(35·7 × 6·1 × 1·5)*
Guns: 1—40 mm Bofors; 2—20 mm Oerlikon
Main engines: Davey Paxman diesels; Foden engine on centre shaft; 1 100 bhp = 18 knots
Complement: 26

Enugu was the first warship built for the Nigerian Navy. Ordered in 1960. Sailed from Portsmouth for Nigeria on 10 April 1962. Fitted with Vosper roll damping fins. *Hinksford* purchased from the UK on 1 July 1966 and transferred at Devonport on 9 September 1966. *Dubford* and *Gifford* were purchased from the UK during 1967-68.

BENIN   1970, Nigerian Navy

4 ABEKING AND RASMUSSEN TYPE (LARGE PATROL CRAFT)

Name	No.	Builders	Commissioned
ARGUNGU	P 165	Abeking & Rasmussen	Aug 1973
YOLA	P 166	Abeking & Rasmussen	Aug 1973
BRAS	P 169	Abeking & Rasmussen	Mar 1976
EPE	P 170	Abeking & Rasmussen	Mar 1976

Displacement, tons: 90
Dimensions, feet (metres): 95·1 × 18·0 × 5·2 *(29 × 5·5 × 1·6)*
Guns: 4—30 mm Emerlac (twins)
Main engines: 2 Paxman 8-cyl Ventura diesels; 2 200 hp; 2 shafts = 20 knots
Complement: 25

Launch dates—*Argungu*, 9 July 1973. *Yola*, 12 June 1973; *Bras*, 12 January 1976; *Epe*, 9 February 1976. Rearmed in 1978.

YOLA (old armament)   10/1974, Michael D. J. Lennon

15 COASTAL PATROL CRAFT

Of 59·7 ft *(18·2 m)* ordered from Intermarine, Italy for delivery in 1979-80.

SURVEY SHIP

Name	No.	Builders	Commissioned
LANA	—	Brooke Marine, Lowestoft	15 July 1976

Displacement, tons: 800 standard; 1 100 full load
Dimensions, feet (metres): 189 × 37·5 × 12 *(57·8 × 11·4 × 3·7)*
Main engines: 4 Paxman 6-cyl Ventura diesels; 2 shafts; 3 000 bhp = 16 knots
Range, miles: 4 500 at 12 knots
Complement: 52

Ordered in late 1973, laid down 5 April 1974, launched 4 March 1976. Sister to Royal Navy "Bulldog" Class.

LANA   10/1976, Wright and Logan

SERVICE FORCES

2 GERMAN (FDR) TYPE RORD 1300 (LSTs)

Name	No.	Builders	Commissioned
AMBE	—	Howaldtswerke, Kiel	Feb 1979
—	—	Howaldtswerke, Kiel	—

Displacement, tons: 1 750 full load
Dimensions, feet (metres): 285·4 × 45·9 × 7·5 *(87 × 14 × 2·3)*
Speed, knots: 17

Ordered late 1977. Built to a design prepared for the FGN. *Ambe* laid down 3 March 1978 and launched 15 September 1978. Second probably laid down 1979.

0 + 2 FRENCH LCTs

Dimensions, feet (metres): 196·8 × 41·3 × 6 *(60 × 12·6 × 1·8)*
Main engines: 2 diesels; 800 hp = 9 knots

Ordered from La Manche, Dieppe June 1977. First laid down 23 September 1977 and second on 7 October 1977.

2 TUGS

Name	No.	Builders	Commissioned
RIBADU	A 486	Oelkers, Hamburg	19 May 1973

Displacement, tons: 147
Dimensions, feet (metres): 93·5 × 23·6 × 12·1 *(28·5 × 7·2 × 3·7)*
Main engines: Diesel; 800 shp = 12 knots

Fitted for firefighting and salvage work.

Name	No.	Builders	Commissioned
AIN JI-DAM	—	De Hoop S.Y. Hardinxveld, Netherlands	1978

Of 90 tons gross. Launched 15 November 1977.

1 TRAINING SHIP

Name	No.	Builders	Commissioned
RUWAN YARO (ex-*Ogina Brereton*)	A 497	Van Lent, Netherlands	1976

Displacement, tons: 400
Dimensions, feet (metres): 144·6 × 26·2 × 12·8 *(44·2 × 8 × 3·9)*
Main engines: 2 Deutz diesels; 3 000 hp = 17 knots
Range, miles: 3 000 at 15 knots
Complement: 42

Originally built in 1975 as a yacht. Used as navigational training vessel. Acquired 1976.

RUWAN YARO   12/1976, Michael D. J. Lennon

1 LAUNCH

MURTALA MUHAMED

Of 12·8 tons. Launched 14 August 1976 by Akerboom, Netherlands. Completed 28 September 1976.

POLICE CRAFT

8 VOSPER THORNYCROFT TYPE (COASTAL PATROL CRAFT)

Displacement, tons: 15
Dimensions, feet (metres): 34 × 10 × 2·8 *(10·4 × 3·1 × 0·9)*
Gun: 1 MG
Main engines: 2 diesels; 290 hp = 19 knots
Complement: 6

Ordered for Nigerian Police March 1971, completed 1971-72. GRP hulls.

NORWAY

Ministerial

Minister of Defence:
 Rolf Hansen

Headquarters Appointments

Inspector General Sea Defence Forces:
 Rear-Admiral C. O. Herlofson
Commander Naval Logistics Services:
 Rear-Admiral R. Helfseth
Commodore Sea Training:
 Commodore Rolf Henningsen
Coast Guard Inspector:
 Commodore N. Tiltnes
Coast Artillery Inspector:
 Commodore R. Eichinger

Diplomatic Representation

Defence Attaché in Bonn:
 Lieutenant Colonel L. Tvilde
Defence Attaché in Helsinki:
 Lieutenant Colonel G. J. Jervaas
Defence Attaché in London:
 Commodore B. Eia
Defence Attaché in Moscow:
 Lieutenant Colonel T. Dypedal
Defence Attaché in Ottawa:
 Lieutenant Colonel O. Ravneberg
Defence Attaché in Paris:
 Lieutenant Colonel E. C. Klykken
Defence Attaché in Stockholm:
 Lieutenant Colonel A. Riegels
Defence Attaché in Vienna:
 Colonel B. Gåsekjølen
Defence Attaché in Washington (for USA and Canada):
 Lieutenant General E. Tufte Johnsen

Personnel

(a) 1974: 8 400 officers and ratings
    1975: 8 400 officers and ratings
    1976: 8 000 officers and ratings
    1977: 8 400 officers and ratings
    1978: 8 400 officers and ratings
    1979: 8 500 officers and ratings
    (All above figures include 1 600 Coast Artillery)
(b) 12-15 months national service

Naval Bases

Karl Johans Vern (Horten), Haakonsvern (Bergen), Ramsund (Harstad) and Olavsvern (Tromsø)

Prefix to Ships' Names

KNM (Naval)
K/V (Coast Guard)

Coast Artillery

Man numerous coastal ports—all with guns and some with torpedo tubes and/or controlled minefields.

Coast Guard

Founded April 1977 with operational control held by Norwegian Defence Command.

Strength of the Fleet

Type	Active	Building
Submarines—Coastal	15	—
Frigates	5	—
Corvettes	3	—
Fast Attack Craft—Missile	28	12
Fast Attack Craft—Torpedo	17	—
Minelayers	3	—
Minesweepers—Coastal	10	—
LCTs	7	—
Depot Ship	1	—
Auxiliaries	14	—
Coast Guard Vessels	14	3

Air Forces

5 Orion Maritime Patrol a/c (Air Force) 10 Sea King helicopters (Air Force SAR). On order—4 Lynx (with option on two more for Coast Guard) and 2 Orion.
Note: The Coast Guard will have three Maritime Patrol a/c and six helicopters.

Mercantile Marine

Lloyd's Register of Shipping:
 2 646 vessels of 26 128 428 tons gross

DELETIONS

Light Forces

1978 *Skarv*
1979 *Teist, Lom*

Training Ship

1974 *Haakon VII*

LCT

1975 *Tjeldsund*

Minelayers

1976 *Gor, Tyr*
1978 *Brage, Uller*

Depot Ship

1977 *Valkyrien*

PENNANT LIST

Submarines

S 300	Ula
S 301	Utsira
S 302	Utstein
S 303	Utvaer
S 304	Uthaug
S 305	Sklinna
S 306	Skolpen
S 307	Stadt
S 308	Stord
S 309	Svenner
S 315	Kaura
S 316	Kinn
S 317	Kya
S 318	Kobben
S 319	Kunna

Frigates and Corvettes

F 300	Oslo
F 301	Bergen
F 302	Trondheim
F 303	Stavanger
F 304	Narvik
F 310	Sleipner
F 311	Aeger

Minesweepers

M 311	Sauda
M 312	Sira
M 313	Tana
M 314	Alta
M 315	Ogna
M 316	Vosso
M 317	Glomma
M 331	Tista
M 332	Kvina
M 334	Utla

Minelayers

N 51	Borgen
N 52	Vidar
N 53	Vale

Light Forces

P 340	Vadsø
P 343	Tjeld
P 346	Jo
P 348	Stegg
P 349	—
P 350	Falk
P 357	Ravn
P 380	Skrei
P 381	Hai
P 382	Sel
P 383	Hval
P 384	Laks
P 385	Knurr
P 386	Delfin
P 387	Lyr
P 388	Gribb
P 389	Geir
P 390	Erle
P 960	Storm
P 961	Blink
P 962	Glimt
P 963	Skjold
P 964	Trygg
P 965	Kjekk
P 966	Djerv
P 967	Skudd
P 968	Arg
P 969	Steil
P 970	Brann
P 971	Tross
P 972	Hvass
P 973	Traust
P 974	Brott
P 975	Odd
P 976	Pil
P 977	Brask
P 978	Rokk
P 979	Gnist
P 980	Snögg
P 981	Rapp
P 982	Snar
P 983	Rask
P 984	Kvikk
P 985	Kjapp
P 986	Hauk
P 987	Ørn
P 988-999	New Construction

Amphibious Forces

F 4500	Kvalsund
F 4501	Raftsund
F 4502	Reinsöysund
F 4503	Söröysund
F 4504	Maursund
F 4506	Rotsund
F 4507	Borgsund

Auxiliaries

A 530	Horten
A 533	Norge
HSD 15	Krøttøy
NSD 35	Rotvaer
OSD 2	Wisting
RSD 23	Fjøløy
TRSD 4	Karlsøy
TSD 5	Tautra
VSD 1	Vernøy
VSD 2	Marsteinen
VSD 4	Torpen
VSD 6	Kvarven

Coast Guard

K/V 300	Nornen
K/V 301	Farm
K/V 302	Heimdal
K/V 303	Andenes
K/V 304	Senja
K/V 305	Nordkapp
K/V 311	Kr. Tønder
K/V 312	Sørfold
K/V 313	Møgsterfjord
K/V 314	Stålbas
K/V 315	Norviking
K/V 316	Volstad Jr.
K/V 317	Rig Tugger

SUBMARINES

PROJECT 28

A design contract for a new class of 750/900 ton patrol submarines has been placed with IKL (Lübeck).

15 TYPE 207

Name	No.	Builders	Laid down	Launched	Commissioned
ULA	S 300	Rheinstahl-Nordseewerke, Emden, West Germany	1962	19 Dec 1964	7 May 1965
UTSIRA	S 301	Rheinstahl-Nordseewerke, Emden, West Germany	1963	11 Mar 1965	1 July 1965
UTSTEIN	S 302	Rheinstahl-Nordseewerke, Emden, West Germany	1962	19 May 1965	9 Sep 1965
UTVAER	S 303	Rheinstahl-Nordseewerke, Emden, West Germany	1962	30 June 1965	1 Dec 1965
UTHAUG	S 304	Rheinstahl-Nordseewerke, Emden, West Germany	1962	8 Oct 1965	16 Feb 1966
SKLINNA	S 305	Rheinstahl-Nordseewerke, Emden, West Germany	1963	21 Jan 1966	27 May 1966
SKOLPEN	S 306	Rheinstahl-Nordseewerke, Emden, West Germany	1963	24 Mar 1966	17 Aug 1966
STADT	S 307	Rheinstahl-Nordseewerke, Emden, West Germany	1963	10 June 1966	15 Nov 1966
STORD	S 308	Rheinstahl-Nordseewerke, Emden, West Germany	1964	2 Sep 1966	9 Feb 1967
SVENNER	S 309	Rheinstahl-Nordseewerke, Emden, West Germany	1965	27 Jan 1967	1 July 1967
KAURA	S 315	Rheinstahl-Nordseewerke, Emden, West Germany	1961	16 Oct 1964	5 Feb 1965
KINN	S 316	Rheinstahl-Nordseewerke, Emden, West Germany	1960	30 Nov 1963	8 Apr 1964
KYA	S 317	Rheinstahl-Nordseewerke, Emden, West Germany	1961	20 Feb 1964	15 June 1964
KOBBEN	S 318	Rheinstahl-Nordseewerke, Emden, West Germany	1961	25 Apr 1964	17 Aug 1964
KUNNA	S 319	Rheinstahl-Nordseewerke, Emden, West Germany	1961	16 July 1964	1 Oct 1964

Displacement, tons: 370 standard; 435 dived
Length, feet (metres): 149 *(45·2)*
Beam, feet (metres): 15 *(4·6)*
Draught, feet (metres): 14 *(4·3)*
Torpedo tubes: 8—21 in *(533 mm)* (bow)
Main machinery: 2 MB 820 Maybach-Mercedes-Benz (MTU) diesels; 1 200 bhp; electric drive; 1 200 hp; 1 shaft
Speed, knots: 10 surfaced; 17 dived
Complement: 18 (5 officers, 13 men)

It was announced in July 1959 that the USA and Norway would share equally the cost of these submarines. These are a development of IKL Type 205 (West German U4-U8) with increased diving depth. *Svenner* has a second periscope for COs training operations—a metre longer.

Names: *Kobben* was the name of the first submarine in the Royal Norwegian Navy. Commissioned on 28 November 1909.

Sonar: Small dome fitted forward.

KOBBEN 1976, Michael D. J. Lennon

FRIGATES

5 "OSLO" CLASS

Name	No.	Builders	Laid down	Launched	Commissioned
OSLO	F 300	Marinens Hovedverft, Horten	1963	17 Jan 1964	29 Jan 1966
BERGEN	F 301	Marinens Hovedverft, Horten	1964	23 Aug 1965	15 June 1967
TRONDHEIM	F 302	Marinens Hovedverft, Horten	1963	4 Sep 1964	2 June 1966
STAVANGER	F 303	Marinens Hovedverft, Horten	1965	4 Feb 1966	1 Dec 1967
NARVIK	F 304	Marinens Hovedverft, Horten	1964	8 Jan 1965	30 Nov 1966

Displacement, tons: 1 450 standard; 1 745 full load
Length, feet (metres): 308 *(93·9)* pp; 317 *(96·6)*
Beam, feet (metres): 36·7 *(11·2)*
Draught, feet (metres): 17·4 *(5·3)*
Missiles: 6 Penguin, Octuple Sea Sparrow
Guns: 4—3 in *(76 mm)* (2 twin mounts US Mk 33)
A/S weapons: Terne system; 6 (2 triple) Mk 32 A/S torpedo tubes
Main engines: 1 set De Laval Ljungstrom double reduction geared turbines; 1 shaft; 20 000 shp
Boilers: 2 Babcock & Wilcox
Speed, knots: 25
Complement: 151 (11 officers, 140 ratings)

Built under the five-year naval construction programme approved by the Norwegian *Storting* (Parliament) late in 1960. Although all the ships of this class were constructed in the Norwegian Naval Dockyard, half the cost was borne by Norway and the other half by the USA. The design of these ships is based on that of the "Dealey" class destroyer escorts of the US Navy, but considerably modified to suit Norwegian requirements.

Engineering: The main turbines and auxiliary machinery were all built by De`Laval Ljungstrom, Sweden at the company's works in Stockholm-Nacka.

Radar: Search: DRBV 22.
Tactical and fire control: HSA M 24 system.

Sonar: One Terne III Mk 3; one SQS 36.

NARVIK 10/1978, Michael D. J. Lennon

TRONDHEIM 6/1978, Michael D. J. Lennon

CORVETTES

2 "SLEIPNER" CLASS

Name	No.	Builders	Laid down	Launched	Commissioned
SLEIPNER	F 310	Nylands Verksted Shipyard	1963	9 Nov 1963	29 Apr 1965
AEGER	F 311	Akers, Oslo	1964	24 Sep 1965	31 Mar 1967

Displacement, tons: 600 standard; 780 full load
Dimensions, feet (metres): 227·8 × 26·2 × 8·2 *(69 × 8 × 2·4)*
Guns: 1—3 in *(76 mm)* (US Mk 34 mount); 1—40 mm
A/S weapons: Terne ASW system; 6 (2 triple) Mk 32 A/S torpedo tubes
Main engines: 4 Maybach (MTU) diesels; 2 shafts; 9 000 bhp = over 20 knots
Complement: 62

Under the five-year programme only two instead of the originally planned five new corvettes were built.

Radar and Fire Control: US Mk 63 GFCS with Mk 34 radar.

Sonar: One Terne III Mk 3; one SQS 36.

AEGER 1977, J. L. M. van der Burg

1 "VADSØ" CLASS

Name	No.	Builders	Laid down	Launched	Commissioned
VADSØ	P 340	A/S Stord Verft	1950	1951	1951

Displacement, tons: 631
Dimensions, feet (metres): 169·3 × 29·5 × 18 *(51 × 9 × 5·5)*
Gun: 1—40 mm
Main engine: 1 MAK 8M451 diesel
Complement: 20

Built as a whaler and rebuilt in 1976.

VADSØ 1977, Royal Norwegian Navy

LIGHT FORCES

2 + 12 "HAUK" CLASS (FAST ATTACK CRAFT—MISSILE)

Name	No.	Builders	Commissioned
HAUK	P 986	Bergens Mek. Verksteder	17 Aug 1977
ØRN	P 987	Bergens Mek. Verksteder	Jan 1979
—	P 988-999	See notes	—

Displacement, tons: 120 standard; 150 full load
Dimensions, feet (metres): 119·7 × 20·3 × 5·5 *(36·5 × 6·2 × 1·6)*
Missiles: SSM; 6 Penguin Mk 2 (single launchers)
Guns: 1—40 mm; 1—20 mm
Torpedo tubes: 4—21 in *(533 mm)*
Main engines: 2 MTU diesels; 7 000 hp = 34 knots
Range, miles: 440 at 34 knots
Complement: 22

Ordered 12 June 1975—ten from Bergens Mek. Verksteder (Lakeseväg) and four from Westermöen (Alta). Very similar to "Snögg" class with improved fire control. *Hauk* laid down May 1976 and launched 21 February 1977. *Ørn* laid down June 1977, 988 laid down October 1977.

Control system: Weapon control by MSI-80S developed by Kongsberg Våpenfabrikk.

Missiles: Of a longer range version developed in collaboration with the Royal Swedish Navy.

HAUK (not fully armed) 1977, Royal Norwegian Navy

NORWAY / Light forces — Mine warfare forces 371

20 "STORM" CLASS (FAST ATTACK CRAFT—MISSILE)

Name	No.	Builders	Commissioned
STORM	P 960	Bergens MV	1968
BLINK	P 961	Bergens MV	18 Dec 1965
GLIMT	P 962	Bergens MV	1966
SKJOLD	P 963	Westermoen, Mandal	1966
TRYGG	P 964	Bergens MV	1966
KJEKK	P 965	Bergens MV	1966
DJERV	P 966	Westermoen, Mandal	1966
SKUDD	P 967	Bergens MV	1966
ARG	P 968	Bergens MV	1966
STEIL	P 969	Westermoen, Mandal	1967
BRANN	P 970	Bergens MV	1967
TROSS	P 971	Bergens MV	1967
HVASS	P 972	Westermoen, Mandal	1967
TRAUST	P 973	Bergens MV	1967
BROTT	P 974	Bergens MV	1967
ODD	P 975	Westermoen, Mandal	1967
PIL	P 976	Bergens MV	1967
BRASK	P 977	Bergens MV	1967
ROKK	P 978	Westermoen, Mandal	1968
GNIST	P 979	Bergens MV	1968

Displacement, tons: 100 standard; 125 full load
Dimensions, feet (metres): 120·0 × 20·5 × 5·0 (36·5 × 6·2 × 1·5)
Missiles: SSM; 6 Penguin (single launchers)
Guns: 1—3 in (76 mm); 1—40 mm
Main engines: 2 Maybach (MTU) diesels; 2 shafts; 7 200 bhp = 32 knots

TROSS   1978, Reinhard Nerlich

The first of 20 (instead of the 23 originally planned) gunboats of a new design built under the five-year programme was *Storm,* launched on 8 February 1963, and completed on 31 May 1963, but this prototype was eventually scrapped and replaced by a new series construction boat as the last of the class. The first of the production boats was *Blink,* launched on 28 June 1965 and completed on 18 December 1965. The introduction of Penguin surface-to-surface guided missile launchers started in 1970, in addition to originally designed armament.

6 "SNÖGG" CLASS (FAST ATTACK CRAFT—MISSILE)

Name	No.	Builders	Commissioned
SNÖGG (ex-*Lyr*)	P 980	Båtservice, Mandal	1970
RAPP	P 981	Båtservice, Mandal	1970
SNAR	P 982	Båtservice, Mandal	1970
RASK	P 983	Båtservice, Mandal	1971
KVIKK	P 984	Båtservice, Mandal	1971
KJAPP	P 985	Båtservice, Mandal	1971

Displacement, tons: 100 standard; 125 full load
Dimensions, feet (metres): 120·0 × 20·5 × 5·0 (36·5 × 6·2 × 1·3)
Missiles: SSM; 4 Penguin (single launchers)
Gun: 1—40 mm
Torpedo tubes: 4—21 in (533 mm)
Main engines: 2 Maybach (MTU) diesels; 2 shafts; 7 200 bhp = 32 knots
Complement: 18

Steel hulled fast attack craft, started coming into service in 1970. Hulls are similar to those of the "Storm" class gunboats.

RASK   1978, Royal Norwegian Navy

17 "TJELD" CLASS (FAST ATTACK CRAFT—TORPEDO)

Name	No.	Builders	Commissioned
TJELD	P 343	Båtservice, Mandal	June 1960
LO	P 346	Båtservice, Mandal	Feb 1961
STEGG	P 348	Båtservice, Mandal	June 1961
—	P 349	Båtservice, Mandal	Aug 1961
FALK	P 350	Båtservice, Mandal	Sep 1961
RAVN	P 357	Båtservice, Mandal	Dec 1961
SKREI	P 380	Båtservice, Mandal	1962
HAI	P 381	Båtservice, Mandal	July 1964
SEL	P 382	Båtservice, Mandal	May 1963
HVAL	P 383	Båtservice, Mandal	Mar 1964
LAKS	P 384	Båtservice, Mandal	May 1964
KNURR	P 385	Båtservice, Mandal	1965
DELFIN	P 386	Båtservice, Mandal	20 May 1966
LYR	P 387	Båtservice, Mandal	1966
GRIBB	P 388	Båtservice, Mandal	Mar 1962
GEIR	P 389	Båtservice, Mandal	Aug 1962
ERLE	P 390	Båtservice, Mandal	June 1962

Displacement, tons: 70 standard; 82 full load
Dimensions, feet (metres): 80·3 × 24·5 × 6·8 (24·5 × 7·5 × 2·1)
Guns: 1—40 mm; 1—20 mm

"TJELD" Class   1973, Royal Norwegian Navy

Torpedo tubes: 4—21 in (533 mm)
Main engines: 2 Napier Deltic Turboblown diesels; 2 shafts; 6 200 bhp = 45 knots
Range, miles: 450 at 40 knots; 600 at 25 knots
Complement: 18

Built of mahogany to Båtservice design, known generally as "Nasty" class.

Transfers: Two to Turkey via West Germany, two to USA and six to Greece.

MINE WARFARE FORCES
2 COASTAL MINELAYERS

Name	No.	Builders	Commissioned
VIDAR	N 52	Mjellem and Karlsen, Bergen	21 Oct 1977
VALE	N 53	Mjellem and Karlsen, Bergen	10 Feb 1978

Displacement, tons: 1 500 standard; 1 673 full load
Dimensions, feet (metres): 212·6 × 39·4 × 13·1 (64·8 × 12 × 4)
Guns: 2—40 mm
Mines: See note
Main engines: 2 Wichmann 7AX diesels; 4 200 bhp; 2 shafts = 15 knots
Complement: 50

Ordered 11 June 1975. Laid down—*Vale* (by Skaaluren, Rosendal), 1 February 1976. *Vidar,* March 1976. Launched—18 March 1977 and 5 August 1977 respectively. *Vale* towed to Bergen for completion. One used for training duties originally carried out by *Haakon VII* and then by *Geipner* and *Aeger.*

Mines: Carry 300-400 (dependent on type) on three decks with an automatic lift between. Loaded through hatches forward and aft each served by two cranes.

VIDAR   1977, Royal Norwegian Navy

372 NORWAY / Mine warfare forces — Depot ship

1 CONTROLLED MINELAYER

Name	No.	Builders	Commissioned
BORGEN	N 51	Marinens Hovedverft, Horten	1961

Displacement, tons: 282 standard
Dimensions, feet (metres): 102·5 × 26·2 × 11 *(31·2 × 8 × 3·4)*
Main engines: 2 General Motors diesels; 2 Voith-Schneider propellers; 330 bhp = 9 knots

Launched 29 April 1960.

BORGEN　　　　　　　　　　　　　　　　　　1977, Royal Norwegian Navy

10 Ex-US "ADJUTANT"/"SAUDA" CLASS (MSC 60) (MINESWEEPERS—COASTAL)

Name	No.	Builders	Commissioned
SAUDA (ex-USS *MSC 102*)	M 311	Hodgeson Bros, Gowdy & Stevens, Maine	25 Aug 1953
SIRA (ex-USS *MSC 132*)	M 312	Hodgeson Bros, Gowdy & Stevens, Maine	28 Nov 1955
TANA (ex-*Roeselaere*, M 914, ex-*MSC 103*)	M 313	Hodgeson Bros, Gowdy & Stevens, Maine	1954
ALTA (ex-*Arlon* M 915, ex-*MSC 104*)	M 314	Hodgeson Bros, Gowdy & Stevens, Maine	1954
OGNA	M 315	Båtservice, Mandal	5 Mar 1955
VOSSO	M 316	Skaaluren Skibsbyggeri, Rosendal	16 Mar 1955
GLOMMA (ex-*Bastogne*, M 916, ex-*MSC 151*)	M 317	Hodgeson Bros, Gowdy & Stevens, Maine	1954
TISTA	M 331	Forende Batbyggeriex, Risör	27 Apr 1955
KVINA	M 332	Båtservice, Mandal	12 July 1955
UTLA	M 334	Båtservice, Mandal	15 Nov 1955

Displacement, tons: 333 standard; 384 full load
Dimensions, feet (metres): 144 × 28 × 8·5 *(44 × 8·5 × 2·6)*
Guns: 1—50 cal MG (2—20 mm in *Tana*)
Main engines: General Motors diesels; 880 bhp = 13·5 knots
Oil fuel, tons: 25
Complement: 38 (39 in *Tana*)

TISTA　　　　　　　　　　　　　　　　　　7/1975, J. L. M. van der Burg

Hull of wooden construction. Five coastal minesweepers were built in Norway with US engines. *Alta, Glomma* and *Tana* were taken over from the Royal Belgian Navy in May, September and March 1966, respectively, having been exchanged for two Norwegian ocean minesweepers of the US MSO type, *Lagen* (ex-*MSO 498*) and *Nansen* (ex-*MSO 499*).

Minehunter: *Tana* converted as a minehunter in 1977—recommissioned 1 September 1977.

TANA　　　　　　　　　　　　　　　　　　1977, Royal Norwegian Navy

AMPHIBIOUS FORCES

5 "REINØYSUND" CLASS (LCT)

Name	No.	Builders	Commissioned
REINØYSUND	F 4502	Mjellem & Karlsen, Bergen	Jan 1972
SØRØYSUND	F 4503	Mjellem & Karlsen, Bergen	June 1972
MAURSUND	F 4504	Mjellem & Karlsen, Bergen	Sep 1972
ROTSUND	F 4505	Mjellem & Karlsen, Bergen	1973
BORGSUND	F 4506	Mjellem & Karlsen, Bergen	1973

Displacement, tons: 590 ("Reinøysund" class 596)
Dimensions, feet (metres): 167·3 × 39·4 × 5·9 *(50 × 11·9 × 1·8)*
Guns: 2—20 mm (3 in "Reinøysund" class)
Speed, knots: 11

All capable of carrying seven tanks. Both classes of same dimensions.

2 "KVALSUND" CLASS (LCT)

Name	No.	Builders	Commissioned
KVALSUND	F 4500	Mjellem & Karlsen, Bergen	1970
RAFTSUND	F 4501	Mjellem & Karlsen, Bergen	1970

KVALSUND (old pennant number)　　　　　　1976, Royal Norwegian Navy

DEPOT SHIP

Name	No.	Builders	Commissioned
HORTEN	A 530	A/S Horten Verft	Apr 1978

Displacement, tons: 2 500
Dimensions, feet (metres): 285·5 × 42·6 × 23 *(87 × 13 × 7)*
Aircraft: 1 helicopter on deck
Guns: 2—40 mm
Main engines: 2 Wichmann diesels; 2 shafts = 16·5 knots
Complement: 85

Contract signed 30 March 1976. Laid down 28 January 1977; launched 12 August 1977. Cost approx £8 million. To serve both submarines and fast attack craft. Quarters for 60 extra and can cater for 190 extra.

HORTEN　　　　　　　　　　　　　　　　　1978, Royal Norwegian Navy

NORWAY / Diving tenders — Research ship 373

2 DIVING TENDERS

Name	No.	Builders	Commissioned
DRAUG	SKV 11	Nielsen, Harstad	1972
SARPEN	—	Nielsen, Harstad	1972

Small depot ships of 250 tons for frogmen and divers.

2 TRAINING VESSELS

Name	No.	Builders	Delivered
MARSTEINEN	VSD 2	Fjellstrand Aluminium Yachts, Omastrand	Jan 1978
KVARVEN	VSD 6	Fjellstrand Aluminium Yachts, Omastrand	July 1978

Displacement, tons: 39
Dimensions, feet (metres): 77 × 16·4 × 3·5 (23·5 × 5·0 × 1·1)
Gun: 1 MG, Browning 12·7 mm
Main engines: 2 General Motors diesels; 2 shafts = over 20 knots
Complement: 5
Berths: 18

The vessels are designed for training students at the Royal Norwegian Naval Academy in navigation, manoeuvring and seamanship. All-welded aluminium hulls. Also equipped with an open bridge and a blind pilotage position below deck.

DRAUG   1977, Royal Norwegian Navy

MARSTEINEN   1978, Royal Norwegian Navy

7 "WISTING" CLASS (COASTAL TRANSPORTS)

Name	No.	Builders	Delivered
TORPEN	VSD 4	Båtservice Verft, Mandal	Dec 1977
WISTING	ØSD 2	Voldnes Skipsverft, Fosnavåg	Jan 1978
TAUTRA	TSD 5	Båtservice Verft, Mandal	Feb 1978
ROTVAER	NSD 35	Båtservice Verft, Mandal	Mar 1978
FJØLØY	RSD 23	Voldnes Skipsverft, Fosnavåg	Apr 1978
KRØTTØY	HSD 15	Voldnes Skipsverft, Fosnavåg	June 1978
KARLSØY	TRSD 4	P Høivolds Mek Verksted, Kr.s and S	July 1978

Displacement, tons: 300 full load
Dimensions, feet (metres): 95·1 × 21·6 × 10 (29 × 6·7 × 3·2)
Gun: 1 MG, Browning 12·7 mm
Main engine: 1 MWM TBD 601-6K diesel = 11 knots
Complement: 5

ROYAL YACHT

Name	No.	Builders	Commissioned
NORGE (ex-*Philante*)	A 533	Camper & Nicholson's Ltd, Gosport, England	1937

Measurement, tons: 1 686 (Thames yacht measurement)
Dimensions, feet (metres): 263 × 28 × 15·2 (80·2 × 8·5 × 4·6)
Main engines: 8-cyl diesels; 2 shafts; 3 000 bhp = 17 knots

Built to the order of Mr. T. O. M. Sopwith as an escort and store vessel for the yachts *Endeavour I* and *Endeavour II*. Launched on 17 February 1937. Served in the Royal Navy as an anti-submarine escort during the Second World War, after which she was purchased by the Norwegian people for King Haakon at a cost of nearly £250 000 and reconditioned as a Royal Yacht at Southampton. Can accommodate about 50 people in addition to crew.

FJØLØY   1978, Royal Norwegian Navy

1 TORPEDO RECOVERY VESSEL

Name	No.	Builders	Delivered
VERNØY	VSD 1	Fjellstrand Aluminium Yachts, Omastrand	Oct 1978

Displacement, tons: 100
Dimensions, feet (metres): 102·9 × 22·5 × 6·5 (31·3 × 6·8 × 2·0)
Main engines: 2 MWM diesels; 2 Schottel rudder-propeller = over 10 knots
Complement: 5

The vessel is fitted with equipment for oil pollution operations and fire-fighting. All-welded aluminium hull.

NORGE   1971, Royal Norwegian Navy

RESEARCH SHIP

Name	No.	Builders	Commissioned
H. U. SVERDRUP	—	Orens Mekaniske Verkstad, Trondheim	1960

Displacement, tons: 400
Measurement, tons: 295 gross
Dimensions, feet (metres): 127·7 × 25 × 13 (38·9 × 7·6 × 4)
Main engines: Wichmann diesel; 600 bhp = 11·5 knots
Oil fuel, tons: 65
Range, miles: 5 000 at 10 knots cruising speed
Complement: 10 crew; 9 scientists

Operates for Norwegian Defence Research Establishment. Trawler hull.

VERNØY   1978, Royal Norwegian Navy

NORWAY / Coast guard

COAST GUARD

Set up in April 1977 for combined duties of Fishery Protection and Oil Rig Patrol. The base for this force is Sortland.

Name	No.	Builders	Commissioned
NORNEN	W 300	Mjellem & Karlsen, Bergen	1963

Measurement, tons: 1 030 gross
Dimensions, feet (metres): 201·8 × 32·8 × 15·8 (61·5 × 10 × 4·8)
Gun: 1—3 in (76 mm)
Main engines: 4 diesels; 3 500 bhp = 17 knots
Complement: 32

Launched 20 August 1962. Modernisation in 1978 with increased tonnage.

NORNEN   1978, Royal Norwegian Navy

Name	No.	Builders	Commissioned
ANDENES	W 303	Netherlands	1957
SENJA	W 304	Netherlands	1957
NORDKAPP	W 305	Netherlands	1957

Measurement, tons: 500 gross
Dimensions, feet (metres): 186 × 31 × 16 (56·7 × 9·5 × 4·9)
Gun: 1—3 in (76 mm)
Main engine: MAN diesel; 2 300 bhp = 16 knots
Complement: 29

All three built in 1957 as whalers of varying appearance. Acquired by Norway in 1965 and converted into Fishery Protection Ships.

NORDKAPP   1978, Royal Norwegian Navy

Name	No.	Builders	Commissioned
FARM	W 301	Ankerlokken Verft	1962
HEIMDAL	W 302	Bolsones Verft, Molde	1962

Measurement, tons: 600 gross
Dimensions, feet (metres): 177 × 26·2 × 16·5 (54·3 × 8·2 × 4·9)
Gun: 1—3 in (76 mm)
Main engines: 2 diesels; 2 700 bhp = 16 knots
Complement: 29

Farm launched 22 February 1962 and *Heimdal* 7 March 1962.

FARM   1978, Royal Norwegian Navy

7 TRAWLER TYPE

Name	No.	Tonnage	Completion
KR. TØNDER	W 311	984	1962
SØRFOLD	W 312	827	1951
MØGSTERFJORD	W 313	762	1975
STÅLBAS	W 314	498	1955
NORVIKING	W 315	1311	1965
VOLSTAD JR.	W 316	598	1950
RIG TUGGER	W 317	497	1973

Chartered in 1977 to fill the gap until completion of new construction patrol vessels. All armed with one 40 mm gun.

KR. TØNDER   1978, Royal Norwegian Navy

SØRFOLD   1978, Royal Norwegian Navy

MØGSTERFJORD   1978, Royal Norwegian Navy

NORWAY / Coast guard — Survey vessels 375

0 + 3 + 4 NEW CONSTRUCTION PATROL VESSELS

Displacement, tons: 2 800
Dimensions, feet (metres): 319·8 pp × 47·9 × 15·1 *(97·5 pp × 14·6 × 4·6)*
Aircraft: 1 Lynx helicopter
Guns: 1—57 mm Bofors; 2—20 mm Rheinmetall
A/S weapons: Possibly 2 Mk 32 mountings
Main engines: 4 Wichmann diesels; 14 000 bhp

Put to tender November 1976. Contract signed 1978. Three to commission in 1981. Strengthened for ice, some A/S capacity, mention of (possibly) Penguin missiles. To be fitted for fire-fighting, anti-pollution work, all with two motor cutters and a Gemini-type dinghy. In November 1977 the Coast Guard Budget was cut from 2 000 million Kroner to 1 400 million resulting in a reduction of the immediate building programme from seven to three ships. It is presumed that the above data will remain correct despite a past tendency for this design to swell.

Radar: Possibly DRBV 22.

STÅLBAS 1978, Royal Norwegian Navy

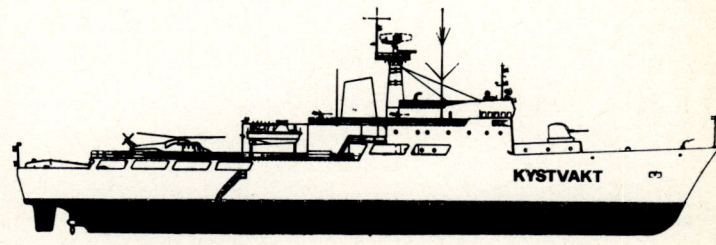

COAST GUARD PATROL VESSEL

NORVIKING 1977, Royal Norwegian Navy

VOLSTAD JR. 1977, Royal Norwegian Navy

RIG TUGGER 1977, Royal Norwegian Navy

SURVEY VESSELS

Under control of Ministry of Environment

Name	Displacement	Launched	Officers	Crew
HYDROGRAF	300	1967	3	15
SJØVERN	215	1948	3	12
SJØMALEREN	80	1942	2	9
SJØFALK	70	1937	1	4
SJØSKVETT	80	1964	1	4
SJØROKK	75	1964	1	4
SJØDREV	80	1973	1	4
SJØTROLL	80	1976	1	4
SJØDRAG	94	1958	1	4
OLJEVERN 02	156	1978	1	4
OLJEVERN 03	156	1978	1	4
OLJEVERN 04	156	1978	1	4

376 OMAN / Introduction — Light forces

OMAN

Personnel
(a) 1979: 600 officers and men
(b) Voluntary service

Senior Officers
Commander Sultan of Oman's Navy:
  Commodore H. Mucklow
Deputy Commander:
  Commander D. M. Connell

Bases
Qa'Adat Sultan Bin Ahmed Al Bahryya, Muscat (Main base and slipway). Raysut (advanced naval base)

Prefix to Ships' Names
SNV (Sultanate Naval Vessel)

Mercantile Marine
11 vessels of 5 630 tons gross

DELETION

1978 Al Bushra (Lost in Biscay storm 28 December)

CORVETTES

Name	No.	Builders	Commissioned
AL SAID	—	Brooke Marine, Lowestoft	1971

Displacement, tons: 900
Dimensions, feet (metres): 203·4 × 35·1 × 9·8 *(62 × 10·7 × 3)*
Gun: 1—40 mm
Main engines: 2 Paxman Ventura 12-cyl diesels; 2 shafts; 2 470 bhp
Complement: 32 + 7 staff + 32 troops

Built by Brooke Marine, Lowestoft. Launched 7 April 1970 as a yacht for the Sultan of Muscat and Oman, she was converted for a dual purpose role with a gun on her forecastle as flagship of the Sultanate Navy. Carried on board is one Fairey Marine Spear patrol craft. Helicopter deck added in last refit.

Radar: Decca TM 626.

AL SAID   1971, Brooke Marine

2 Ex-NETHERLANDS "WILDERVANK" CLASS

Name	No.	Builders	Commissioned
AL NASIRI (ex-*Aalsmeer*, M 811)	P 1	Netherlands	1955
AL SALIHI (ex-*Axel*, M 808)	P 2	Netherlands	1955

Displacement, tons: 373 standard; 417 full load
Dimensions, feet (metres): 149·8 × 28 × 6·5 *(46·6 × 8·8 × 2)*
Guns: 3—40 mm
Main engines: 2 Werkspoor diesels; 2 500 bhp
Speed, knots: 16
Range, miles: 2 500 at 10 knots
Complement: 38

Acquired in March 1974 and converted for patrol duties at Van der Giessen/de Noord in 1974-75.

Radar: Decca TM 916.

AL SALIHI   1976, Omani Dept. of Defence

LIGHT FORCES

6 BROOKE MARINE 37·5 metre TYPE (LARGE PATROL CRAFT)

Name	No.	Builders	Commissioned
AL MANSUR	B 2	Brooke Marine, Lowestoft	26 Mar 1973
AL NEJAH	B 3	Brooke Marine, Lowestoft	13 May 1973
AL WAFI	B 4	Brooke Marine, Lowestoft	Mar 1977
AL FULK	B 5	Brooke Marine, Lowestoft	24 Mar 1977
AL MUJAHID	B 6	Brooke Marine, Lowestoft	20 July 1977
AL JABBAR	B 7	Brooke Marine, Lowestoft	6 Oct 1977

Displacement, tons: 135 standard; 153 full load
Dimensions, feet (metres): 123 × 22·5 × 5·5 *(37·5 × 6·9 × 1·7)*
Missiles: SSM; 2 Exocet (single cells)
Guns: 2—40 mm (B 2-3); 1—76 mm/62 OTO Melara Compact; 1—20 mm (B 4-7)
Main engines: 2 Paxman Ventura diesels; 4 800 bhp = 29 knots
Range, miles: 3 300 at 15 knots
Complement: 27 (3 officers, 24 ratings)

First three ordered 5 January 1971.
Four more (B 4-7) ordered from Brooke Marine 26 April 1974.

Gunnery: Lawrence-Scott optical director in B 4-7.

Loss: *Al Bushra* (B 1) lost overboard from transport in hurricane force winds in the Bay of Biscay December 1978 while being shipped home after refit.

Radar: Decca TM 916.

Refits: B 1-3 refitted November 1977-November 1978 by Brooke Marine with addition of twin Exocet with Sea Archer fire control.

AL MANSUR   4/1978, Brooke Marine

AL FULK   1978, Sperr

3 "27 ft" CHEVERTON TYPE (COASTAL PATROL CRAFT)

W 1   W 2   W 3

Displacement, tons: 3·5
Dimensions, feet (metres): 27 × 9 × 2·8 *(8·2 × 2·7 × 0·8)*
Main engines: Twin diesels = 25 knots

Purchased April 1975.

OMAN / Amphibious forces — Royal Oman Police   377

AMPHIBIOUS FORCES

1 LOGISTIC SHIP

Name	No.	Builders	Commissioned
AL MUNASSIR	L 1	Brooke Marine, Lowestoft	31 Jan 1979

Displacement, tons: 2 000
Dimensions, feet (metres): 276 × 49 × ? *(84·1 × 14·9 × ?)*
Guns: 1—76 mm; 2—20 mm
Main engines: 2 Mirrlees Blackstone diesels; 2 440 bhp = 12 knots
Complement: 47 plus 188 troops

Ordered 1 March 1977. Bow ramp. Full naval command facilities. Capable of carrying tanks, guns and troops. Carry two Rotork landing craft. Helicopter deck suitable for large aircraft. Laid down 4 July 1977. Launched 25 May 1978.

AL MUNASSIR   1/1979, Michael D. J. Lennon

2 "60 ft" CHEVERTON "LOADMASTERS"

Name	No.	Builders	Commissioned
AL SANSOOR	—	Cheverton Ltd, Isle of Wight	Jan 1975
KINZEER AL BAHR	—	Cheverton Ltd, Isle of Wight	Jan 1975

Measurement, tons: 60 deadweight
Dimensions, feet (metres): 60 × 20 × 3·5 *(18·3 × 6·1 × 1·1)*
Main engines: 2 diesels; 240 hp = 8·5 knots

AL SANSOOR   1975, Roger Smith

1 "45 ft" CHEVERTON "LOADMASTER"

Name	No.	Builders	Commissioned
SULHAFA AL BAHR	—	Cheverton Ltd, Isle of Wight	1975

Measurement, tons: 45
Dimensions, feet (metres): 45 × 15 × 3 *(13·7 × 4·6 × 0·9)*
Main engines: Twin Perkins diesels = 8·5 knots

5 LCU

Name	No.	Builders	Commissioned
KHASAB	—	Impala Marine, Twickenham, UK	Nov 1977
—	—	Impala Marine, Twickenham, UK	1978
—	—	Impala Marine, Twickenham, UK	—
—	—	Impala Marine, Twickenham, UK	—
—	—	Impala Marine, Twickenham, UK	—

Measurement, tons: 117 deadweight
Dimensions, feet (metres): 84 × 25 × 6 *(25·6 × 7·6 × 1·8)*
Main engines: 2 Caterpillar diesels; 2 shafts; 520 bhp = 9 knots

---

MISCELLANEOUS

Name	No.	Builders	Commissioned
AL SULTANA	—	Conoship, Groningen	4 June 1975

Measurement, tons: 1 380 deadweight
Dimensions, feet (metres): 214·3 × 35 × 13·5 *(65·4 × 10·7 × 4·2)*
Main engines: Mirrlees Blackstone diesel; 1 150 bhp = 11 knots
Complement: 12

Launched 18 May 1975.

2 TRAINING SHIPS

DHOFAR

Displacement, tons: 1 500 full load
Dimensions, feet (metres): 219 × 34 × 13 *(66·8 × 10·4 × 4)*
Main engines: MAK diesel; 1 500 bhp = 10·5 knots
Complement: 22

Ex-Logistic ship now used for new entry training.

AL SULTANA   1975, Dick van der Heijde Jnr.

DHOFAR   1974, Omani Dept. of Defence

1 CHEVERTON LAUNCH

Of 9 tons, 39 ft and 10 knots—completed April 1975.

YOUTH OF OMAN (ex-*Captain Scott*)

Sail training schooner taken over from Dulverton Trust in 1978.

ROYAL OMAN POLICE

5 VOSPER THORNYCROFT 75 ft TYPE (COASTAL PATROL CRAFT)

HARAS 1-5

Displacement, tons: 45
Dimensions, feet (metres): 75 × 19·5 × 5 *(22·9 × 6 × 1·5)*
Guns: 2—20 mm
Main engines: 2 Caterpillar diesels; 1 840 hp = 24·5 knots
Range, miles: 600 at 20 knots; 1 000 at 11 knots
Complement: 11

Completed 22 December 1975 by Vosper Thornycroft. GRP hulls. *Haras 5* commissioned November 1978.

HARAS 5   11/1978, Royal Oman Police

PAKISTAN

Ministerial

Minister of Defence:
Mr. Ali Ahmed Talpur

Headquarters Appointments

Chief of the Naval Staff:
Admiral M. Shariff NI(M), HJ

Command Appointment

Commander Pakistan Fleet:
Rear-Admiral A. Zamir SJ

Diplomatic Representation

Naval Attaché in London:
Captain I. A. Sirohey
Naval Attaché in Paris:
Captain A. Tasnim SJ
Naval Attaché in Teheran:
Captain A. H. Khan
Naval Attaché in Washington:
Captain N. S. Khan

Personnel

(a) 1979: 11 000 (950 officers; 10 050 ratings)
(b) Voluntary service

Naval Base and Dockyard

Karachi

Naval Air Arm

3 Breguet Atlantic BR 1150
6 Sea King helicopters
4 Alouette III helicopters
2 Cessna

Prefix to Ships' Names

PNS

Strength of the Fleet

Type	Active	Building
Submarines—Patrol	4	2
Submarines—40 tons	6	—
Cruiser	1	—
Destroyers	6	—
Frigate	1	—
Fast Attack Craft—Gun	14	—
Fast Attack Craft—Torpedo	4	—
Large Patrol Craft	3	—
Minesweepers—Coastal	7	—
Survey Ship	1	—
Tankers	2	—
Tugs—Ocean	2	—
Tugs—Harbour	2	—
Water-barge	1	—
Floating Docks	2	—

Mercantile Marine

Lloyd's Register of Shipping:
80 vessels of 442 401 tons gross

DELETION

Frigate

1977 Tughril

PENNANT LIST

Submarines

S 131	Hangor
S 132	Shushuk
S 133	Mangro
S 134	Ghazi

Cruiser

| C 84 | Babur |

Destroyers

D 160	Alamgir
D 161	Badr
D 162	Jahangir
D 164	Shah Jahan
D 165	Tariq
D 166	Taimur

Frigate

| F 260 | Tippu Sultan |

Minesweepers

M 160	Mahmood
M 161	Momin
M 162	Mubarak
M 164	Mujahid
M 165	Mukhtar
M 166	Munsif
M 167	Moshal

Survey Ship

| A 262 | Zulfiquar |

Light Forces

HDF 01-04	"Hu Chwan" Class
P 140	Rajshahi
P 141	Lahore
P 142	Multan
P 143	Gilgit
P 144	Sehwan
P 145	Pishin
P 146	Kalat
P 147	Sukkur
P 148	Quetta
P 149	Sahiwal
P 150	Bannu
P 151	Larkana
P 152	Bahawalpur
P 153	Mardan
P 154	—
P 301	Sind
P 302	Baluchistan

Service Forces

A 40	Attock
A 41	Dacca
A 42	Madadgar
YW 15	Zum Zum

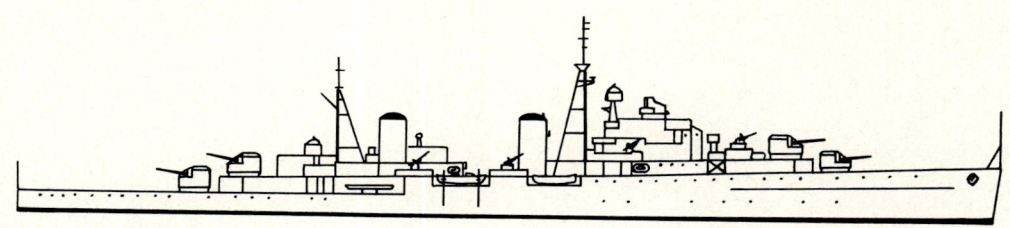

BABUR

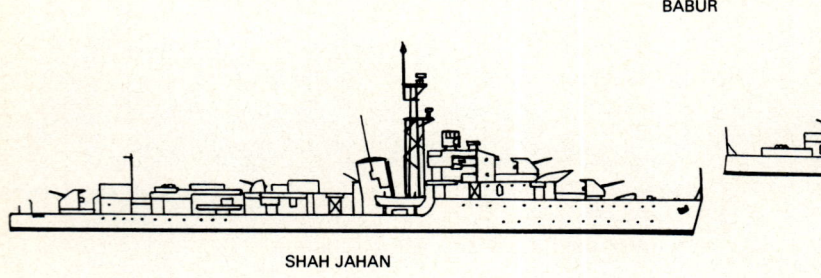

SHAH JAHAN

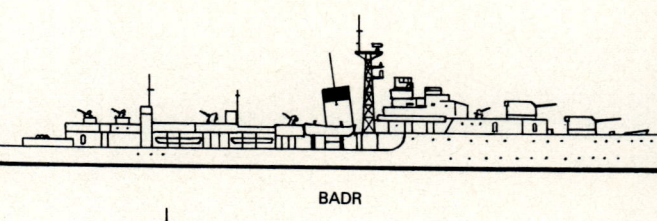

BADR

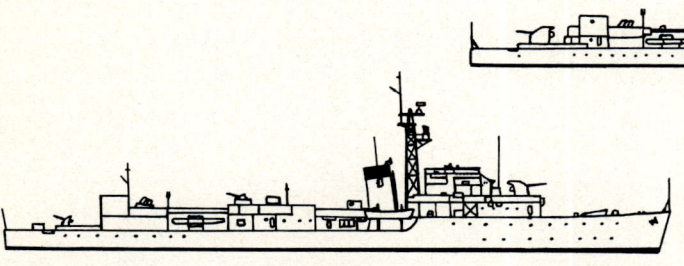

TIPPU SULTAN

ALAMGIR and JAHANGIR

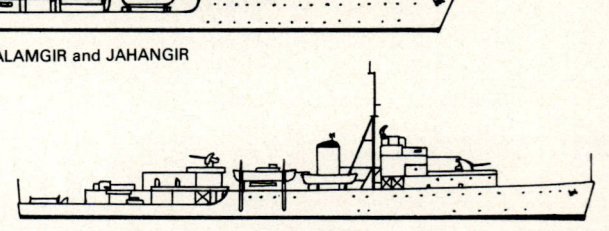

ZULFIQUAR

SUBMARINES

2 FRENCH "AGOSTA" CLASS

Name	No.	Builders	Laid down	Launched	Commissioned
— (ex-SAS *Astrant*)	—	Dubigeon—Normandie (Nantes)	15 Sep 1976	14 Dec 1977	?
— (ex-SAS *Adventurous*)	—	Dubigeon—Normandie (Nantes)	—	—	?

Displacement, tons: 1 200 standard; 1 450 surfaced; 1 725 dived
Length, feet (metres): 221·7 *(67·6)*
Beam, feet (metres): 22·3 *(6·8)*
Draught, feet (metres): 17·7 *(5·4)*
Torpedo tubes: 4—21·7 in *(550 mm)* (20 reload torpedoes)

Main machinery: Diesel-electric; 2 SEMT-Pielstick 16 PA4 diesels 3 600 hp; 1 main motor (3 500 kW) 4 600 hp; 1 cruising motor (23 kW); 1 shaft
Speed, knots: 12 surfaced; 20 dived
Range, miles: 8 500 at 9 knots (snorting); 350 at 3·5 knots (dived)

Endurance: 45 days
Complement: 54 (7 officers, 47 men)

Purchased in mid-1978 after United Nations' ban on arms sales to South Africa.

4 FRENCH "DAPHNE" CLASS

Name	No.	Builders	Laid down	Launched	Commissioned
HANGOR	S 131	Arsenal de Brest	1 Dec 1967	28 June 1969	12 Jan 1970
SHUSHUK	S 132	C. N. Ciotat (Le Trait)	1 Dec 1967	30 July 1969	12 Jan 1970
MANGRO	S 133	C. N. Ciotat (Le Trait)	8 July 1968	7 Feb 1970	8 Aug 1970
GHAZI (ex-*Cachalote*)	S 134	Dubigeon, Normandie	12 May 1967	23 Sep 1968	1 Oct 1969

Displacement, tons: 700 standard; 869 surfaced; 1 043 dived
Length, feet (metres): 189·6 *(57·8)*
Beam, feet (metres): 22·3 *(6·8)*
Draught, feet (metres): 15·1 *(4·6)*
Torpedo tubes: 12—21·7 in *(550 mm)* 8 bow, 4 stern (external)
Main machinery: Diesel-electric; 1 300 bhp (surfaced); electric motors 1 600 hp (dived); 2 shafts
Speed, knots: 13 surfaced; 15·5 dived
Complement: 45

MANGRO *1971, Contre Amiral M. J. Adam*

The first three are the first submarines built for the Pakistan Navy. They are basically of the French "Daphne" class design, but slightly modified internally to suit Pakistan requirements and naval conditions. They are broadly similar to the submarines built in France for Portugal and South Africa and the submarines constructed to the "Daphne" design in Spain.

Transfer: The Portuguese "Daphne" class *Cachalote* was bought by Pakistan in December 1975.

SHUSHUK *1972*

6 "SX 404" CLASS

Displacement, tons: 40
Dimensions, feet (metres): 52·4 × 6·6 × — *(16 × 2 × —)*
Speed, knots: 11 surfaced; 6·5 dived
Range, miles: 1 200 surfaced; 60 dived
Complement: 4

Purchased 1972-73 from Cosmos, Livorno. With a diving depth of 330 ft *(100 m)* and capable of carrying 12 passengers these submarines are valuable craft for clandestine raids, reconnaissance and a multitude of shallow-water tasks.

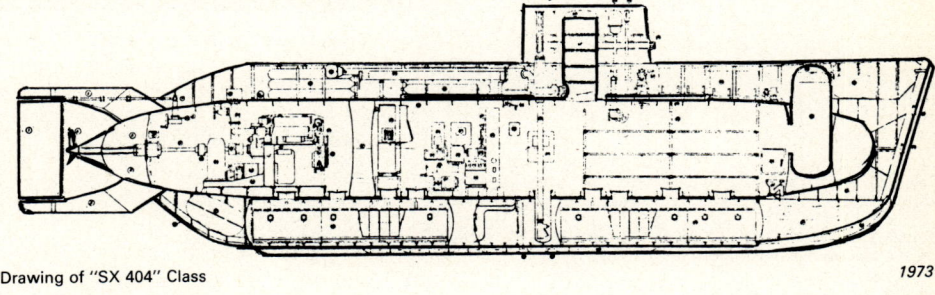
Drawing of "SX 404" Class *1973*

CRUISER

1 Ex-BRITISH "MODIFIED DIDO" CLASS

Name	No.	Builders	Laid down	Launched	Commissioned
BABUR (ex-HMS *Diadem*)	C 84	R. & W. Hawthorn Leslie & Co Ltd, Hebburn-on-Tyne	15 Nov 1939	26 Aug 1942	6 Jan 1944

Displacement, tons: 5 900 standard; 7 560 full load
Length, feet (metres): 485 *(147·9)* pp; 512 *(156·1)*
Beam, feet (metres): 52·0 *(15·8)*
Draught, feet (metres): 18·5 *(5·6)*
Guns: 8—5·25 in *(133 mm)* (4 twin); 14—40 mm
Torpedo tubes: 6—21 in *(533 mm)* (2 triple)
Armour: 3 in *(76 mm)* sides; 2 in *(51 mm)* decks and turrets
Main engines: Parsons sr geared turbines; 4 shafts; 62 000 shp
Boilers: 4 Admiralty 3-drum
Speed, knots: 30
Oil fuel, tons: 1 100
Range, miles: 4 000 at 18 knots
Complement: 588

Purchased on 29 February 1956. Refitted at HM Dockyard, Portsmouth and there transferred to Pakistan and renamed *Babur* on 5 July, 1957.

Radar: Search: Type 960, Type 293.
Fire control: Type 284/285.

BABUR *1976, Pakistan Navy*

PAKISTAN / Destroyers

DESTROYERS

2 Ex-US "GEARING" (FRAM 1) CLASS

Name	No.	Builders	Laid down	Launched	Commissioned
TARIQ (ex-USS *Wiltsie*, DD 716)	D 165	Federal S.B. & D.D. Co	13 Mar 1945	31 Aug 1945	12 Jan 1946
TAIMUR (ex-USS *Epperson*, DD 719)	D 166	Todd Pacific Shipyards	20 June 1945	29 Dec 1945	19 Mar 1949

Displacement, tons: 2 425 standard; 3 500 full load
Length, feet (metres): 390·5 *(119)*
Beam, feet (metres): 40·9 *(12·4)*
Draught, feet (metres): 19 *(5·8)*
Guns: 4—5 in *(127 mm)*/38 (twins)
A/S weapons: 6 (2 triple) Mk 32 A/S torpedo tubes; facilities for small helicopter; ASROC
Main engines: 2 geared turbines; 60 000 shp; 2 shafts
Boilers: 4 Babcock & Wilcox
Speed, knots: 30
Complement: 274

Transfer by purchase 29 April 1977. Reactivated and overhauled in USA during 1977-78 by Campbell Industries, San Diego at cost of $7·43 million.

Radar: SPS 10 and 40.

Sonar: SQS 23.

TAIMUR (refitting in San Diego)   2/1978, Dr. Giorgio Arra

1 Ex-BRITISH "BATTLE" CLASS

Name	No.	Builders	Laid down	Launched	Commissioned
BADR (ex-HMS *Gabbard*, D 47)	D 161	Swan, Hunter & Wigham Richardson Ltd, Wallsend-on-Tyne	2 Feb 1944	16 Mar 1945	10 Dec 1946

Displacement, tons: 2 325 standard; 3 361 full load
Length, feet (metres): 355·0 *(108·2)* pp; 379·0 *(115·5)*
Beam, feet (metres): 40·2 *(12·3)*
Draught, feet (metres): 17·0 *(5·2)*
Guns: 4—4·5 in *(115 mm)*; 7—40 mm (2 twin; 3 single)
A/S weapons: Squid triple DC mortar
Torpedo tubes: 4—21 in *(533 mm)* (quad)
Main engines: Parsons geared turbines; 2 shafts; 50 000 shp
Boilers: 2 Admiralty 3-drum type
Speed, knots: 35·75
Oil fuel, tons: 680
Range, miles: 6 000 at 20 knots
Complement: 270

Purchased from Britain on 29 February 1956. Modernised with US funds under MDAP. Refitted at Palmers Hebburn, Yarrow, transferred to Pakistan on 24 January 1957 and sailed from Portsmouth for Karachi on 17 February 1957.

Radar: Search: Type 293. One Marconi set.
Fire control: Type 275.

BADR   1977, Pakistan Navy

PAKISTAN / Destroyers — Light forces

3 Ex-BRITISH "CH" and "CR" CLASSES

Name	No.	Builders	Laid down	Launched	Commissioned
ALAMGIR (ex-HMS *Creole*, D 82)	D 160	J. Samuel White & Co Ltd, Cowes	3 Aug 1944	22 Nov 1945	14 Oct 1946
JAHANGIR (ex-HMS *Crispin*, ex-*Craccher*, D 168)	D 162	J. Samuel White & Co Ltd, Cowes	1 Feb 1944	23 June 1945	10 July 1946
SHAH JAHAN (ex-HMS *Charity*, D 29)	D 164	John I. Thornycroft Co Ltd, Woolston	9 July 1943	30 Nov 1944	19 Nov 1945

Displacement, tons: 1 710 standard; 2 545 full load
Length, feet (metres): 362·7 *(110·5)*
Beam, feet (metres): 35·7 *(10·9)*
Draught, feet (metres): 17·0 *(5·2)*
Guns: 3—4·5 in *(115 mm)*; 6—40 mm
A/S weapons: 2 Squid triple DC mortars
Torpedo tubes: 4—21 in *(533 mm)* (quad)
Main engines: Parsons geared turbines; 2 shafts; 40 000 shp
Boilers: 2 Admiralty 3-drum type
Speed, knots: 36·75
Range, miles: 5 600 at 20 knots
Complement: 200

Shah Jahan purchased by USA and handed over to Pakistan on 16 December 1958, under MDAP, at yard of J. Samuel White & Co Ltd, Cowes, who refitted her. Sister ship *Taimur* (ex-HMS *Chivalrous*) was returned to the Royal Navy and scrapped in 1960-61.
Alamgir and *Jahangir* purchased by Pakistan in February 1956. Refitted and modernised in the UK by John I. Thornycroft & Co Ltd, Woolston, Southampton, in 1957-58 with US funds under MDAP. Turned over to the Pakistan Navy at Southampton in 1958 (*Crispin* on 18 March and *Creole* 20 June) and renamed.

Radar: Search: Type 293.
Fire control: Type 275.

Sonar: Types 170 and 174.

JAHANGIR   1977, Pakistan Navy

FRIGATE

1 Ex-BRITISH TYPE 16

Name	No.	Builders	Laid down	Launched	Commissioned
TIPPU SULTAN (ex-HMS *Onslow*, ex-*Pakenham*, F 249)	F 260	John Brown & Co Ltd, Clydebank	1 July 1940	31 Mar 1941	8 Oct 1941

Displacement, tons: 1 800 standard; 2 300 full load
Length, feet (metres): 328·7 *(100·2)* pp; 345·0 *(104·5)*
Beam, feet (metres): 35·0 *(10·7)*
Draught, feet (metres): 15·7 *(4·8)*
Guns: 2—4 in *(102 mm)*; 5—40 mm
A/S weapons: 2 Squid triple DC mortars
Torpedo tubes: 4—21 in *(533 mm)*
Main engines: Parsons geared turbines; 2 shafts; 40 000 shp
Boilers: 2 Admiralty 3-drum type
Speed, knots: 34
Complement: 170

Originally three "O" class destroyers were acquired from the UK, *Tippu Sultan* being handed over on 30 September 1949; *Tariq* on 3 November 1949; and *Tughril* on 6 March 1951. An agreement was signed in London between the UK and USA for refit and conversion in the UK of *Tippu Sultan* and *Tughril* (announced 29 April 1957) with US funds. All three ships were scheduled for conversion into fast anti-submarine frigates. *Tippu Sultan* and *Tughril* were converted at Liverpool by Grayson Rolls & Clover Docks Ltd, Birkenhead, and C. & H. Crighton Ltd, respectively. *Tariq* disposed of 1959 and *Tughril* in 1977.

Radar: Search: Type 293.

TIPPU SULTAN   1977, Pakistan Navy

LIGHT FORCES

2 Ex-CHINESE "HAI NAN" CLASS (LARGE PATROL CRAFT)

SIND P 301   BALUCHISTAN P 302

Displacement, tons: 360 standard; 400 full load
Dimensions, feet (metres): 197 × 24 × 6·1 *(60 × 7·4 × 2·1)*
Guns: 2—3 in; 4—25 mm (twins)
A/S weapons: 4—MBU 1 800; 2 DCT; 2 DC Racks
Mines: Rails fitted
Main engines: Diesels; 8 000 shp
Speed, knots: 28
Range, miles: 1 000 at 10 knots
Complement: 60

First pair transferred mid-1976.

Radar: Pot Head

BALUCHISTAN   1976

382 PAKISTAN / Light forces — Survey ship

14 Ex-CHINESE "SHANGHAI II" CLASS (FAST ATTACK CRAFT—GUN)

LAHORE P 141	KALAT P 146	LARKANA P 151
MULTAN P 142	SUKKUR P 147	BAHAWALPUR P 152
GILGIT P 143	QUETTA P 148	MARDAN P 153
SEHWAN P 144	SAHIWAL P 149	— P —
PISHIN P 145	BANNU P 150	

Displacement, tons: 120 standard; 155 full load
Dimensions, feet (metres): 128 × 18 × 5·6 (39·1 × 5·5 × 1·7)
Guns: 4—37 mm (twin); 4—25 mm (twin)
Mines: Fitted with minerails for approx 10 mines
Main engines: 4 diesels; 3 000 bhp = 27 knots
Complement: 25

Transferred between 1972 and 1976.

Radar: Pot Head.

"SHANGHAI II" Class   1977, Pakistan Navy

4 Ex-CHINESE "HU CHWAN" CLASS (FAST ATTACK HYDROFOIL—TORPEDO)

HDF 01, 02, 03, 04

Displacement, tons: 45
Dimensions, feet (metres): 70 × 16·5 × 3·1 (21·4 × 5·0 × 0·9)
Torpedo tubes: 2—21 in (533 mm)
Guns: 4—14·5 mm (twins)
Main engines: 2—12-cyl diesels; 2 shafts; 2 200 hp = 55 knots (calm)

Hydrofoil craft transferred by China in 1973.

PAKISTAN "HU CHWAN" Class   1973, Pakistan Navy

1 "TOWN" CLASS (LARGE PATROL CRAFT)

Name	No.	Builders	Commissioned
RAJSHAHI	P 140	Brooke Marine	1965

Displacement, tons: 115 standard; 143 full load
Dimensions, feet (metres): 107 × 20 × 11 (32·6 × 6·1 × 3·4)
Guns: 2—40 mm; 70 cal Bofors
Main engines: 2 MTU 12V 538 diesels; 3 400 bhp = 24 knots
Complement: 19

The last survivor of a class of four built by Brooke Marine in 1965 (see *Deletions*). Steel hull and aluminium superstructure.

RAJSHAHI   1973, Pakistan Navy

MINE WARFARE FORCES

7 "ADJUTANT" and "MSC 268" CLASSES (MINESWEEPERS—COASTAL)

MAHMOOD (ex-*MSC 267*) M 160	MUKHTAR (ex-*MSC 274*) M 165
MOMIN (ex-*MSC 293*) M 161	MUNSIF (ex-*MSC 273*) M 166
MUBARAK (ex-*MSC 262*) M 162	MOSHAL (ex-*MSC 294*) M 167
MUJAHID (ex-*MSC 261*) M 164	

Displacement, tons: 335 light; 375 full load
Dimensions, feet (metres): 144 × 27 × 8·5 (43·9 × 8·2 × 2·6)
Guns: 2—20 mm
Main engines: General Motors diesels; 2 shafts; 880 bhp = 14 knots
Complement: 39

Transferred to Pakistan by the USA under MAP. *Mukhtar* and *Munsif* on 25 June 1959, *Mujahid* in November 1956, *Mahmood* in May 1957, *Mubarak* in 1957, *Momin* in August 1962 and *Moshal* on 13 July 1963.

MUNSIF   1972, Pakistan Navy

SURVEY SHIP

Name	No.	Builders	Commissioned
ZULFIQUAR (ex-*Dhanush*, ex-*Deveron* F 265)	A 262	Smith's Dock Co Ltd, South Bank-on-Tees	2 Mar 1943

Displacement, tons: 1 370 standard; 2 100 full load
Dimensions, feet (metres): 301·5 × 36·7 × 12·5 (91·9 × 11·2 × 3·8)
Guns: 1—4 in (102 mm); 2—40 mm
Main engines: Triple expansion; 5 500 ihp
Boilers: 2 Admiralty 3-drum type
Speed, knots: 20
Range, miles: 6 000 at 12 knots
Complement: 150

ZULFIQUAR   1972, Pakistan Navy

Former British frigate of the "River" class converted into a survey ship, additional charthouse aft. She has strengthened davits and carries survey motor boats. The after 4 in gun was removed.

TANKERS

1 Ex-US "MISSION" CLASS (UNDERWAY REPLENISHMENT TANKER)

DACCA (ex-USNS *Mission Santa Cruz*, AO 132) A 41

Displacement, tons: 5 730 light; 22 380 full load
Dimensions, feet (metres): 523·5 × 68 × 30·9 *(159·7 × 20·7 × 9·4)*
Guns: 3—40 mm
Main engines: Turbo-electric; 6 000 shp = 15 knots
Boilers: 2 Babcock & Wilcox
Oil capacity: 20 000 tons
Complement: 160 (15 officers and 145 men)

Transferred on loan to Pakistan under MDAP. Handed over from the USA on 17 January 1963 after being refitted for under-way replenishment. Purchased 31 May 1974.

DACCA

1 Ex-US YO TYPE

Name	No.	Builders	Commissioned
ATTOCK (ex-USS *YO 249*)	A 40	Trieste	1960

Displacement, tons: 600 standard; 1 255 full load
Dimensions, feet (metres): 177·2 × 32 × 15 *(54 × 9·8 × 4·6)*
Main engines: Direct coupled diesel; speed 8·5 knots
Complement: 26

A harbour oiler of 6 500 barrels capacity built for the Pakistan Navy. Transferred under the Mutual Defence Assistance Programme of USA.

RESCUE SHIP

Ex-US "CHEROKEE" CLASS

Name	No.	Builders	Commissioned
MADADGAR (ex-USS *Yuma*, ATF 94)	A 42	Commercial Iron Works, Portland, Oregon	31 Aug 1943

Displacement, tons: 1 235 standard; 1 675 full load
Dimensions, feet (metres): 205 × 38·5 × 15·3 *(62·5 × 11·7 × 4·7)*
Guns: 1—3 in *(76 mm)*; 2—40 mm
Main engines: 4 General Motors diesels; electric drive; 1 shaft; 3 000 bhp = 16·5 knots
Complement: 85

Ocean-going salvage tug. Laid down on 13 February 1943. Launched on 17 July 1943. Transferred from the US Navy to the Pakistan Navy on 25 March 1959 under MDAP. Fitted with powerful pumps and other salvage equipment.

MADADGAR 1976

TUGS

RUSTOM

Dimensions, feet (metres): 105 × 30 × 11 *(32 × 9·1 × 3·3)*
Main engines: Crossley diesel; 1 000 bhp = 9·5 knots
Range, miles: 3 000 at economic speed
Complement: 21

General purpose tug for the Pakistan Navy originally ordered from Werf-Zeeland at Hansweert, Netherlands, in August 1952, but after the liquidation of this yard the order was transferred to Worst & Dutmer at Meppel. Launched on 29 November 1955.

Name	No.	Builders	Commissioned
GAMA (ex-US *YTL 754*)	—	Costaguta-Voltz	Sep 1958
BHOLU (ex-US *YTL 755*)	—	Costaguta-Voltz	Sep 1958

Small harbour tugs built under an "off-shore" order.

AUXILIARIES

1 WATER BARGE

ZUM ZUM YW 15

Built in Italy under MDA programme.

2 FLOATING DOCKS

PESHAWAR (ex-US *ARD 6*)

Transferred June 1961. 3 000 tons lift.

FD II

Built 1974. 1 200 tons lift.

PANAMA

Personnel
1979: approx 300
Voluntary service

Coast Guard service split between both coasts.

Mercantile Marine
Lloyd's Register of Shipping:
3 640 ships of 20 748 679 tons gross

LIGHT FORCES

2 VOSPER TYPE (LARGE PATROL CRAFT)

Name	No.	Builders	Commissioned
PANQUIACO	GC 10	Vospers, Porchester, Portsmouth	Mar 1971
LIGIA ELENA	GC 11	Vospers, Porchester, Portsmouth	Mar 1971

Displacement, tons: 96 standard; 123 full load
Dimensions, feet (metres): 103·0 × 18·9 × 5·8 *(31·4 × 5·8 × 1·8)*
Guns: 2—20 mm
Main engines: 2 Paxman Ventura 12-cyl diesels; 2 800 bhp = 24 knots
Complement: 23

Hull of welded mild steel and upperworks of welded or buck-bolted aluminium alloy. Vosper fin stabiliser equipment. *Panquiaco* was launched on 22 July 1970 and *Ligia Elena* on 25 August 1970.

PANAMA / Light forces — PAPUA NEW GUINEA / Light forces

2 Ex-US 63 ft AVR CLASS (COASTAL PATROL CRAFT)

Name	No.	Builders	Commissioned
AYANASI	GC 12	USA	1943
ZARTI	GC 13	USA	1943

Displacement, tons: 35
Dimensions, feet (metres): 63·3 × 15·3 × 3·3 (19·3 × 4·7 × 1)
Guns: 2—12·7 mm MGs
Main engines: 2 General Motors 8V-71 diesels; 2 shafts = 22·5 knots
Complement: 8

Transferred to Panama 1965 (*Ayanasi*) and 1966. Wooden hulls with glass fibre sheathing.
Radar: Raytheon 1500B.

2 Ex-USCG 40 ft UTILITY TYPE (COASTAL PATROL CRAFT)

Name	No.	Builders	Commissioned
MARTI	GC 14	USA	1950
JUPITER	GC 15	USA	1950

Displacement, tons: 13
Dimensions, feet (metres): 40·3 × 11·2 × 3·3 (12·3 × 3·4 × 1)
Gun: 1—12·7 mm MG
Main engines: 2 General Motors 6-71 diesels = 18 knots
Range, miles: 160 at 18 knots
Complement: 4

Transferred under MAP in 1962. Steel hulled Mk 1 Type. No radar—magnetic compass only.

AMPHIBIOUS FORCES

1 Ex-US MODIFIED "ELK RIVER" CLASS

TIBURON (ex-USS *Smokey Hill River*) GN 9

Displacement, tons: 944 standard; 1 084 full load
Dimensions, feet (metres): 206·2 × 34·5 × 10 (67·6 × 11·3 × 3·3)
Guns: 1—5 in (127 mm); 2—40 mm; 4—20 mm
Main engines: 2 General Motors diesels; 2 800 bhp = 12 knots
Complement: 140

Purchased 14 March 1975 from commercial sources. Armament may be removed. With a door cut in the bow she is used for logistic support. Originally a US Navy LSM Type completed as a rocket support ship with no bow doors—probably in 1945.

3 Ex-US "LCM 8" CLASS

GN 1, 2 and 3

Displacement, tons: 118 full load
Dimensions, feet (metres): 73·5 × 21 × 5·2 (22·4 × 6·4 × 1·6)
Main engines: 4 General Motors 6-71 diesels; 2 shafts = 10 knots
Complement: 6

Used for patrol and logistic duties with wheelhouse replaced by two deckhouses giving increased berthing thereby extending endurance. Unarmed. Transferred 1972.

MISCELLANEOUS

1 Ex-US YF-852 CLASS

— (ex-*YF 886*)

Displacement, tons: 590 full load
Dimensions, feet (metres): 132·9 × 29·9 × 8·9 (40·5 × 9·1 × 2·7)
Main engines: 2 General Motors diesels = 11 knots
Complement: 11

Built by Defoe S.B. Co in 1945. Acquired May 1975. Logistic support ship.

1 "65 ft" TRAWLER

— GN 8

Existence doubtful.

1 "65 ft" SHRIMP BOAT

Bought in 1976. Steel hulled. Single diesel = 11 knots. Can carry 150 troops on short hauls.

PAPUA NEW GUINEA

The Australian base at Manus in the Admiralty Islands, HMAS *Tarangau*, was de-commissioned on 14 November 1974 and handed over to the PNG Defence Force. It is now the PNGDF Patrol Boat Base Lombrun. The following ships were handed over to the PNGDF by the RAN.

Senior Officer
Brigadier E. R. Diro OBE (Commander PNGDF)

Bases
Port Moresby (HQ PNGDF); Lombrun

Mercantile Marine
Lloyd's Register of Shipping:
67 vessels of 16 718 tons gross

LIGHT FORCES

5 "ATTACK" CLASS (LARGE PATROL CRAFT)

Name	No.	Builders	Commissioned
AITAPE	84	Walkers Ltd, Maryborough	13 Nov 1967
SAMARAI	85	Evans Deakin & Co, Queensland	1 Mar 1968
LADAVA	92	Walkers Ltd, Maryborough	21 Oct 1968
LAE	93	Evans Deakin & Co, Queensland	3 Apr 1968
MADANG	94	Evans Deakin & Co, Queensland	28 Nov 1968

Displacement, tons: 146 full load
Dimensions, feet (metres): 107·5 × 20 × 7·3 (32·8 × 6·1 × 2·2)
Guns: 1—40 mm; 2 MG
Main engines: 2 Paxman 16 YJCM diesels; 2 shafts; 3 500 bhp = 24 knots
Complement: 18

Steel hulls with aluminium superstructure. Can lay mines.

LAE 1976, PNGDF

PAPUA NEW GUINEA / Amphibious forces — PARAGUAY / Corvettes 385

AMPHIBIOUS FORCES

2 LANDING CRAFT (LCH)

Name	No.	Builders	Commissioned
SALAMAUA	131	Walkers Ltd, Maryborough	1973
BUNA	132	Walkers Ltd, Maryborough	1973

Displacement, tons: 310 light; 503 full load
Dimensions, feet (metres): 146 × 33 × 6·5 (44·5 × 10·1 × 1·9)
Guns: 2—·5 in MG
Main engines: 2 V12 General Motors diesels; twin screw = 10 knots
Complement: 13

BUNA 1974, John Mortimer

1 TUG

— (ex- RAN 503)

Displacement, tons: 47·5
Dimensions, feet (metres): 50 × 15 × — (15·2 × 4·6 × —)
Main engines: 2 General Motors diesels; 340 bhp = 8·9 knots
Complement: 3

Built by Perrin Engineering, Brisbane 1972.
Transferred 1974.

PARAGUAY

Ministerial

Minister of National Defence:
Major Gen. Marcial Samaniego

Personnel

(a) 1979: 2 000 officers and men including Coast Guard and 500 marines (25% conscripts)
(b) 2 years national service

Bases

Puerto Sajonia (Asunción) (main base, dockyard with one dry dock, one floating dock and one slipway, arsenal, marine barracks and helicopter station)
Chaco I (opposite Asunción) (naval air base and minor craft base)
Bahia Negra (on upper Paraguay River—secondary base)

Naval Air Arm

H-13 Sioux helicopters
North American AT-6 (Trainers)
Cessna U-206
Cessna 150M

General

Accepting the fact that river water keeps circulating systems cleaner than does sea-water, thus extending machinery life, the age of some of these ships must be causing concern. On the whole their hulls have not had the wearing effect of wave-action but seventy-one years is a long time for any ship to be running. A replacement programme must be fairly close ahead.

Training

(a) Officers—Basic training at National Military College, Asunción. Specialist and sea training in Argentina.
(b) Technical Ratings—at Naval School, Puerto Sajonia.

Coast Guard

Two distinct groups under naval control:
(a) Prefectura de Puertos (Harbour guard)
(b) Cuerpo de Defensa Fluvial (River guard)

Prefix to Ships' Names

Type designators only used

Mercantile Marine

Lloyd's Register of Shipping:
26 vessels of 21 930 tons gross

Strength of the Fleet

2 River Defence Vessels
3 Corvettes
1 Large Patrol Craft
8 Coastal Patrol Craft
2 Tugs
1 Tender
2 LCUs
1 Floating Dock
7 Service Craft
6 Survey Vessels

RIVER DEFENCE VESSELS

2 "HUMAITA" CLASS

Name	No.	Builders	Commissioned
PARAGUAY (ex-Commodor Meza)	C 1	Odero, Genoa	May 1931
HUMAITA (ex-Capitan Cabral)	C 2	Odero, Genoa	May 1931

Displacement, tons: 636 standard; 865 full load
Dimensions, feet (metres): 231 × 35 × 5·3 (70 × 10·7 × 1·7)
Guns: 4—4·7 in; 3—3 in; 2—40 mm; 2—20 mm (Paraguay only)
Mines: 6
Armour: ·5 in side amidships; ·3 in deck; ·8 in CT
Main engines: Parsons geared turbines; 2 shafts; 3 800 shp = 17 knots
Boilers: 2
Oil fuel, tons: 150
Range, miles: 1 700 at 16 knots
Complement: 86

Both refitted in 1975.

Radar: One navigation set (Paraguay).

PARAGUAY 1974, A. J. English

CORVETTES

3 "BOUCHARD" CLASS

Name	No.	Builders	Commissioned
NANAWA (ex-Seaver M 12)	M 1	Hansen and Puccini, San Fernando	20 May 1939
CAPITAN MEZA (ex-Bouchard M 7)	M 2	Rio Santiago Naval Yard	16 May 1937
TENIENTE FARINA (ex-Py M 10)	M 3	Rio Santiago Naval Yard	1 July 1939

Displacement, tons: 450 standard; 620 normal; 650 full load
Dimensions, feet (metres): 197 × 24 × 8·5 (60 × 7·3 × 2·6)
Guns: 4—40 mm Bofors; 2 MG
Main engines: 2 sets MAN 2-cycle diesels; 2 000 bhp = 16 knots
Oil fuel, tons: 50
Range, miles: 6 000 at 12 knots
Complement: 70

Former Argentinian minesweepers of the "Bouchard" class.
Launched on 24 August 1938, 20 March 1936, 31 March 1938 respectively. Can carry mines.
Transferred from the Argentinian Navy to the Paraguayan Navy; Capitan Meza, February 1964; Teniente Farina, and Nanawa, 5 March 1968.

NANAWA 11/1975, A. J. English

PARAGUAY / Light forces — Tugs

LIGHT FORCES

1 LARGE PATROL CRAFT

Name	No.	Builders	Commissioned
CAPITAN CABRAL (ex-*Triunfo*)	A 1	Werf-Conrad, Haarlem	1908

Displacement, tons: 180 standard; 206 full load
Dimensions, feet (metres): 107·2 × 23·5 × 9·8 *(32·7 × 7·2 × 3)*
Guns: 1—3 in Vickers; 2—37 mm Vickers; 4 MG
Main engines: Triple expansion; 1 shaft; 300 ihp = 9 knots
Complement: 47

Former tug. Launched in 1907. Of wooden construction. Stationed on Upper Paraña River.

2 CG TYPE (COASTAL PATROL CRAFT)

P1 (ex-USCGC 20417)   P2 (ex-USCGC 20418)

Displacement, tons: 16
Dimensions, feet (metres): 45·5 × 13·5 × 3·5 *(13·9 × 4·1 × 1·1)*
Guns: 2—20 mm
Main engines: 2 petrol motors; 2 shafts; 190 hp = 20 knots
Complement: 10

Of wooden construction. Built in the USA in 1944. Acquired from the United States Coast Guard in 1944. Existence now doubtful.

6 "701" CLASS (COASTAL PATROL CRAFT)

P 101   102   103   104   105   106

Patrol craft of 40 ft and 10 tons with 2—20 mm guns transferred by USA—two in December 1967, three in September 1970 and one in March 1971.

"701" Class   11/1975, A. J. English

TENDER

Ex-US LSM-1 CLASS (CONVERTED)

Name	No.	Builders	Commissioned
TENIENTE PRATTS GIL (ex-Argentine *Corrientes*, ex-US *LSM 86*)	PH 1	Brown S.B. Co, Houston	13 Oct 1944

Displacement, tons: 1 095 full load
Dimensions, feet (metres): 203·5 × 33·8 × 8 *(62·0 × 10·3 × 2·4)*
Guns: 4—40 mm
Main engines: 2 diesels; 2 shafts; 2 800 hp = 13 knots
Range, miles: 4 100 at 12 knots
Complement: 66

Transferred as a gift from Argentina 13 January 1972. Light Forces Tender with helicopter deck added aft. Officially classified as "helicopter-carrier" but whether she can carry one or two helicopters is not known—two might be a crowd. Converted at Navyard, Buenos Aires during 1968.

TENIENTE PRATTS GIL   11/1975, A. J. English

SURVEY VESSELS

Name	Displacement	Date launched	Officers	Crew
REPULSOR (Rp. 1)	107	1908	1	27
DRAGA (D. 1)	140	1908	2	28
BALIZADOR (B. 1)	30	—	2	10
GRÚA FLOTANTE	—	—	1	8
DRAGA (D. 2)	110	1957	2	17
LANCHA ECOGRAFA	50	1957	1	6

TUGS

2 Ex-US YTL TYPE

Name	No.	Builders	Commissioned
— (ex-US *YTL 211*)	R 5	Everett Pacific S.B. & D.D. Co, Wash	1945
— (ex-US *YTL 567*)	R 11	Everett Pacific S.B. & D.D. Co, Wash	1945

Displacement, tons: 82 full load
Dimensions, feet (metres): 66·2 × 17 × 8·5 *(20·2 × 5·2 × 2·6)*
Main engine: 1 diesel; 300 bhp
Complement: 5

Small harbour tugs transferred to Paraguay by the USA under the Military Aid Programme in March 1967 (YTL 211) and April 1974 (YTL 567). By sale both on 11 February 1977.

1 FLOATING DOCK

DF 1 (Ex-US *AFDL 26*)

Built 1944, leased June 1965. Purchased 11 February 1977. Lift 1 000 tons.

1 FLOATING WORKSHOP

— (Ex-US *YR 37*)

Built in 1942. Transferred March 1963 and by sale 11 February 1977. No engines.

1 DREDGER

TENIENTE O CARRERAS SAGUIER

1 RIVER TRANSPORT

PRESIDENTE STROESSNER T 1

Possibly ex-*Adolfo Riquelene* of 150 tons. Ex-yacht built in 1901 and reconstructed in 1973-75 10 knots. No armament.

4 STORE CARRIERS

No details available.

2 Ex-US "LCU 501" CLASS

BT 1 (ex-US *YFB 82*)   **BT 2** (ex-US *YFB 86*)

Built in 1945 and converted in 1960.
Leased by USA in June 1970 and by sale 11 February 1977. Used as ferries.

PERU

Headquarters Appointments

Minister of Marine and Chief of Naval Operations:
Vice-Admiral Carlos Tirado Alcorta
Chief of Naval Staff:
Vice-Admiral Juan Egusquiza Babilonia

Command

Commander-in-Chief of the Fleet:
Vice-Admiral José Montoya Carcelen

Diplomatic Representation

Naval Attaché in London and Paris:
Rear-Admiral Edmundo Masias Scheelje
Naval Attaché in Washington:
Vice-Admiral Julio Guinand Hturne

Personnel

(a) 1979: 20 500 (2 000 officers, 18 500 men) (including Naval Air Arm)
(b) 2 years national service

Bases

Callao—Main naval base; dockyard with ship-building capacity, 1 dry dock, 2 floating docks, 1 floating crane; training schools
Iquitos—River base for Amazon flotilla; small building yard, repair facilities, floating dock
La Punta (naval academy), San Lorenzo (submarine base), Talara, Puno (Lake Titicaca), Madre de Dios (river base)

Naval Air Arm

4 SH-3D Sea Kings (for *Aguirre*)
6 Bell AB 212 (on order for "Lupos")
2 Fokker 27 FPA MP aircraft
2 Alouette III helicopters
4 Bell 47G
9 Grumman S-2E (ASW)
2 Douglas C-47 (Transport)
1 Douglas DC-3
2 Cessna 150
6 Beech T-34-C (Training)

Following operated in maritime role by Peruvian Air Force;
4 Grumman HU-16B Albatros (ASW/SAR)

Marines

There is one battalion of 1 400 men, additionally armed with amphibious vehicles (twin Oerlikon, 81 mm rocket launchers) and armoured cars.

Coast Guard

A separate service set up in 1975 with a number of light forces transferred from the navy.

Prefix to Ships' Names

BAP (Buque Armada Peruana)

Strength of the Fleet

Type	Active	Building (Planned)
Submarines—Patrol	8	4
Cruisers	4	—
Destroyers	5	—
Frigates	2	(2)
Fast Attack Craft (Missile)	—	6
River Patrol Craft	3	—
Coastal Patrol Craft	—	6
River Gunboats	5	—
Lake Gunboats	2	—
Landing Ships	4	—
Transports	2	—
Tankers	8	—
Survey Vessels	2	—
Floating Docks	3	1
Tugs	5	—
Water Carriers	3	—
Floating Workshop	1	—
Hospital Craft	2	1
S/M Accommodation Ship	1	—

Coast Guard

Corvettes	2	—
Large Patrol Craft	9	—
Minor Patrol Craft	11	—

Mercantile Marine

Lloyd's Register of Shipping:
686 vessels of 574 718 tons gross

DELETIONS

Frigate

1974 *Aguirre* (target for Exocet tests)

Mine Warfare Forces

1974 *Bondy, San Martin* (ex-YMS)

Transports

Sep 1972 *Callao*
1973 *Rimac* (transferred to mercantile use on bare boat charter)

Amphibious Forces

1975 3 LCUs, 10 LCAs

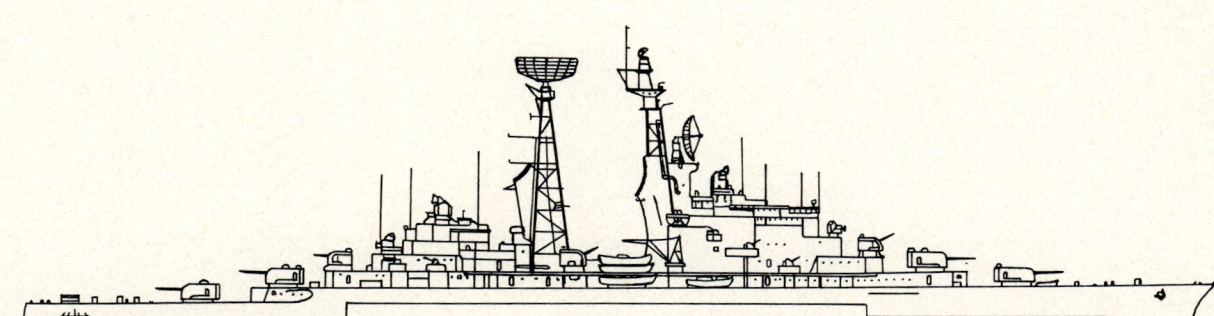

ALMIRANTE GRAU

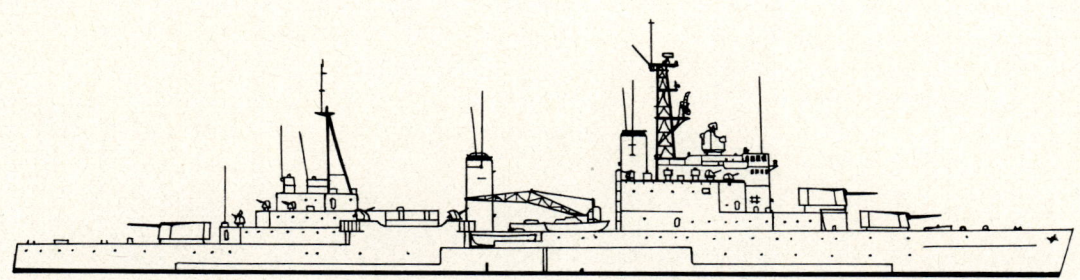

CORONEL BOLOGNESI *(Capitan Quiñones* differs)

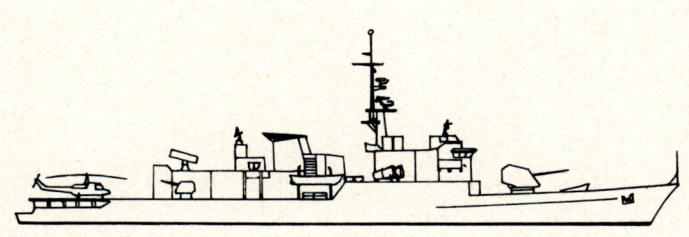

"LUPO" Class

388 PERU / Submarines

SUBMARINES

2 + 2 + 2 TYPE 209

Name	No.	Builders	Laid down	Launched	Commissioned
ISLAY	S 45	Howaldtswerke, Kiel	1971	1973	28 Aug 1974
ARICA	S 46	Howaldtswerke, Kiel	1972	17 Apr 1974	21 Jan 1975
—	—	Howaldtswerke, Kiel	—	—	—
—	—	Howaldtswerke, Kiel	—	—	—

Displacement, tons: 1 180 surfaced; 1 290 dived
Length, feet (metres): 177·1 *(54·0)*
Beam, feet (metres): 20·3 *(6·2)*
Torpedo tubes: 8—21 in (with reloads)
Main machinery: Diesel-electric; 4 MTU Siemens diesel-generators; 1 Siemens electric motor; 3 600 hp; 1 shaft
Speed, knots: 10 surfaced; 22 dived
Range: 50 days
Complement: 31

Designed by Ingenieurkontor, Lübeck for construction by Howaldtswerke, Kiel and sale by Ferrostaal Essen all acting as a consortium.
A single-hull design with two ballast tanks and forward and after trim tanks. Fitted with snort and remote machinery control. The single screw is slow revving, very high capacity batteries with GRP lead-acid cells and battery cooling—by Wilh. Hagen and VARTTA. Active and passive sonar, sonar detection equipment, sound ranging gear and underwater telephone. Fitted with two periscopes, radar and Omega receiver. Foreplanes retract.
Islay ran trials in June 1974.
Two further boats ordered 12 August 1976 and two more ordered in March 1977.

ARICA   *1975, Peruvian Navy*

2 Ex-US "GUPPY 1A" CLASS

Name	No.	Builders	Laid down	Launched	Commissioned
LA PEDRERA (ex-*Pabellon de Pica*, ex-USS *Sea Poacher* SS 406)	S 49	Portsmouth Navy Yard, USA	23 Feb 1944	20 May 1944	31 July 1944
PACOCHA (ex-USS *Atule* SS 403)	S 48	Portsmouth Navy Yard, USA	2 Dec 1943	6 Mar 1944	21 June 1944

Displacement, tons: 1 870 standard; 2 440 dived
Dimensions, feet (metres): 308 × 27 × 17 *(93·8 × 8·2 × 5·2)*
Torpedo tubes: 10—21 in; 6 fwd, 4 aft
Main machinery: 3 diesels; 4 800 hp; 2 electric motors; 5 400 shp; 2 shafts
Speed, knots: 18 surfaced; 15 dived
Complement: 85

Modernised under the 1951 Guppy programme. Purchased by Peru—*La Pedrera* on 1 July 1974, *Pacocha* on 31 July 1974. The name of *La Pedrera* was changed a fortnight after purchase. Both became operational in 1975 after refit. Ex-USS *Tench* (SS 417) purchased for spares 16 September 1976.

LA PEDRERA (as *Sea Poacher*)   *1966, Dr. Giorgio Arra*

4 "ABTAO" CLASS

Name	No.	Builders	Laid down	Launched	Commissioned
DOS DE MAYO (ex-*Lobo*)	S 41	General Dynamics (Electric Boat), Groton, Connecticut	12 May 1952	6 Feb 1954	14 June 1954
ABTAO (ex-*Tiburon*)	S 42	General Dynamics (Electric Boat), Groton, Connecticut	12 May 1952	27 Oct 1953	20 Feb 1954
ANGAMOS (ex-*Atun*)	S 43	General Dynamics (Electric Boat), Groton, Connecticut	27 Oct 1955	5 Feb 1957	1 July 1957
IQUIQUE (ex-*Merlin*)	S 44	General Dynamics (Electric Boat), Groton, Connecticut	27 Oct 1955	5 Feb 1957	1 Oct 1957

Displacement, tons: 825 standard; 1 400 dived
Length, feet (metres): 243 *(74·1)*
Beam, feet (metres): 22 *(6·7)*
Draught, feet (metres): 14 *(4·3)*
Gun: 1—5 in *(127 mm)*/25 (*Abtao* and *Dos de Mayo*)
Torpedo tubes: 6—21 in *(533 mm);* 4 bow, 2 stern
Main machinery: 2 General Motors 278A diesels; 2 400 bhp; electric motors; 2 shafts
Speed, knots: 16 surfaced, 10 dived
Oil fuel, tons: 45
Range, miles: 5 000 at 10 knots (surfaced)
Complement: 40

They are of modified US "Mackerel" class. Refitted at Groton as follows—*Dos de Mayo* and *Abtao* in 1965, other pair in 1968.

ABTAO   *1975, Peruvian Navy*

PERU / Cruisers 389

CRUISERS

2 Ex-NETHERLANDS "DE RUYTER" CLASS

Name	No.	Builders	Laid down	Launched	Commissioned
ALMIRANTE GRAU (ex-KMS *De Ruyter*)	CL 81 (ex-83)	Wilton-Fijenoord, Schiedam	5 Sep 1939	24 Dec 1944	18 Nov 1953
AGUIRRE (ex-KMS *De Zeven Provincien*)	CL 84	Rotterdamse Droogdok Maatschappij	19 May 1939	22 Aug 1950	17 Dec 1953

Displacement, tons: 9 529 standard; 12 165 full load *(Grau)*; 9 850 and 12 250 *(Aguirre)*
Dimensions, feet (metres): 609 × 56·7 × 22 *(185·6 × 17·3 × 6·7)*
Aircraft: 3 helicopters *(Aguirre)*
Guns: 8—6 in *(150 mm)*/53 (twin); 8—57 mm/60 (twin); 8—40 mm/70 *(Almirante Grau)*
4—6 in *(150 mm)*/53 (twin); 6—57 mm/60 (twin); 4—40 mm/70 *(Aguirre)*
Main engines: 2 De Schelde-Parsons geared turbines; 85 000 shp; 2 shafts
Boilers: 4 Werkspoor-Yarrow
Speed, knots: 32
Complement: 953 (49 officers, 904 ratings)

Almirante Grau transferred by purchase 7 March 1973 and *Aguirre* bought August 1976.
Almirante Grau commissioned in Peruvian Navy 23 May 1973 and sailed for Peru 18 June 1973.

Aircraft: Three Sea Kings to be carried aboard *Aguirre* with spare ashore. Hangar measures 67 × 54 ft and the flight deck 115 × 56 ft.

Reconstruction: After sale *Aguirre* was taken in hand by her original builders for conversion to a helicopter cruiser. The Terrier missile system has been returned to USA and a helicopter flight deck with a hangar has been built from midships to the stern. Conversion completed 31 October 1977. Sailed March 1978.

Radar: Search: LW-01 *(Grau)*; LW-02 *(Aguirre)*.
Heightfinder: SGR 104 *(Grau)*.
Tactical: DA 02.
Fire control: HSA M25 for 6 in guns and M45 for secondary battery.
Navigation: ZW-01.

AGUIRRE   1978, Bewapeningswerkplaatsen

ALMIRANTE GRAU   1976, Dr. Robert Scheina

AGUIRRE   1978, H. W. van Boeijen

2 Ex-BRITISH "CEYLON" CLASS

Name	No.	Builders	Laid down	Launched	Commissioned
CORONEL BOLOGNESI (ex-HMS *Ceylon*)	CL 82	Alexander Stephen & Sons Ltd, Govan, Glasgow	27 Apr 1939	30 July 1942	13 July 1943
CAPITAN QUIÑONES (ex-*Almirante Grau*, ex-HMS *Newfoundland*)	CL 83	Swan, Hunter & Wigham Richardson Ltd, Wallsend-on-Tyne	9 Nov 1939	19 Dec 1941	31 Dec 1942

Displacement, tons:
Capitan Quiñones: 8 800 standard; 11 090 full load
Col. Bolognesi: 8 781 standard; 11 110 full load
Length, feet (metres): 555·5 *(169·3)*
Beam, feet (metres): 62·0 *(18·9)*
Draught, feet (metres): 20·5 *(6·2)*
Guns: 9—6 in *(152 mm)*/50 (triple Mk 23);
8—4 in *(102 mm)*/45 (twin Mk 19)
12—40 mm/60 *(Capitan Quiñones)*
18—40 mm/60 *(Col. Bolognesi)*
Armour: 3½ in *(89 mm)* sides and CT; 2 in *(51 mm)* turrets and deck
Main engines: Parsons sr geared turbines; 72 500 shp; 4 shafts
Boilers: 4 Admiralty 3-drum; 400 psi *(28 kg/cm²)*; 720°F *(382°C)*
Speed, knots: 31·5
Oil fuel, tons: 1 620
Range, miles: 6 000 at 13 knots; 2 000 at full power
Complement: *Capitan Quiñones:* 743; *Col. Bolognesi:* 766

83 was transferred as *Almirante Grau* in December 1959, being renamed *Capitan Quiñones* on 15 May 1973. 82 was transferred as *Coronel Bolognesi* on 9 February 1960.

Radar: Search: Types 960, 277 and 293.
Fire control: Types 284, 275.

CAPITAN QUIÑONES   1976, Dr. Robert Scheina

Reconstruction: 83 was reconstructed in 1951-53 at HM Dockyard, Devonport, with two lattice masts, new bridge and improved AA armaments, her torpedo tubes being removed. 82 was modified in 1955-56 with lattice foremast and covered bridge, her torpedo tubes being removed.

Reserve: *Capitan Quiñones* reported as in reserve (1978) pending disposal.

DESTROYERS

2 Ex-BRITISH "DARING" CLASS

Name	No.	Builders	Laid down	Launched	Commissioned
PALACIOS (ex-HMS *Diana*)	DD 73	Yarrow Co Ltd, Scotstoun	3 Apr 1947	8 May 1952	29 Mar 1954
FERRÉ (ex-HMS *Decoy*)	DD 74	Yarrow Co Ltd, Scotstoun	22 Sep 1946	29 Mar 1949	28 Apr 1953

Displacement, tons: 2 800 standard; 3 600 full load
Length, feet (metres): 366 *(111·7)* pp; 390 *(118·9)*
Beam, feet (metres): 43 *(13·1)*
Draught, feet (metres): 18 *(5·5)*
Missiles: SSM; 8 Exocet (single cells)
Guns: 4—4·5 in *(115 mm)*/45 (twin Mk 6); 4—40 mm/60 (twin Mk 5)
Main engines: English Electric dr geared turbines; 2 shafts
Boilers: 2 Foster-Wheeler; pressure 650 psi *(45·7 kg/cm²)*; superheat 850°F *(454°C)*
Oil fuel, tons: 580
Speed, knots: 32
Range, miles: 3 000 at 20 knots
Complement: 297

Purchased by Peru in 1969 and refitted by Cammel Laird (Ship Repairers) Ltd, Birkenhead, for further service.

Reconstruction: The first major reconstruction was carried out in 1970-73. The main points of this refit were the reconstructed and enclosed foremast carrying Plessey AWS-1 radar and the Exocet launcher positions in place of the Close Range Blind Fire Director forward of X Turret.
Commissioned after refit—*Palacios* February 1973. *Ferré* April 1973.
The next major change took place 1975-76 when the Squid was removed to make way for a helicopter landing deck.
The third reconstruction was in 1977-78 when X-turret was removed to allow for a larger helicopter deck. The two 40 mm guns were replaced by two twin 40 mm Breda-Bofors L70 Compact. The bridge was enclosed, the after funnel remodelled and new fire control system fitted. A drawing of this reconstruction is at the head of this section.

Radar: Fire control: TSF on fore-funnel.
Search: Plessey AWS 1.

FERRÉ (after first reconstruction) 1975, Michael D. J. Lennon

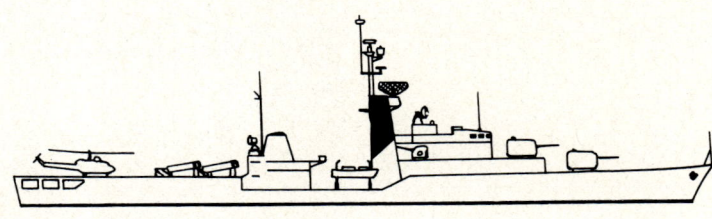
"DARING" Class after third reconstruction

PALACIOS (after second reconstruction) 1976, Dr. Robert L. Scheina

1 Ex-NETHERLANDS "HOLLAND" CLASS

Name	No.	Builders	Laid down	Launched	Commissioned
GARCIA y GARCIA (ex-*Holland*)	75 (ex-D 808)	Rotterdamse Droogdok Mij, Rotterdam	21 Apr 1950	11 Apr 1953	31 Dec 1954

Displacement, tons: 2 215 standard; 2 765 full load
Length, feet (metres): 371·1 *(113·1)*
Beam, feet (metres): 37·5 *(11·4)*
Draught, feet (metres): 16·8 *(5·1)*
Guns: 4—4·7 in *(120 mm)*; 1—40 mm
A/S weapons: Two 4-barrelled 375 mm, Bofors rocket launchers; 2 DC racks
Main engines: Werkspoor Parsons geared turbines; 2 shafts; 45 000 shp
Boilers: 4 Babcock & Wilcox
Speed, knots: 32
Complement: 247

Sold to Peru on 2 January 1978 and re-commissioned 20 January 1978.

Gunnery: The 4·7 in guns are fully automatic with a rate of fire of 42 rounds per minute. All guns are radar controlled.

Radar: Search: LW 03.
Tactical: DA 02.
Fire control: HSA M 45 for 4·7 in.
HSA fire control for A/S rocket launcher.

GARCIA y GARCIA 2/1978, H. W. van Boeijen

PERU / Destroyers — Light forces 391

2 Ex-US "FLETCHER" CLASS

Name	No.	Builders	Laid down	Launched	Commissioned
VILLAR (ex-USS *Benham*, DD 796)	DD 71	Bethlehem Steel Co, Staten Island	Jan 1943	29 Aug 1943	20 Dec 1943
GUISE (ex-USS *Isherwood*, DD 520)	DD 72	Bethlehem Steel Co, Staten Island	12 May 1942	24 Nov 1942	10 Apr 1943

Displacement, tons: 2 120 standard; 3 050 full load
Length, feet (metres): 376·2 *(114·7)*
Beam, feet (metres): 39·7 *(12·1)*
Draught, feet (metres): 18 *(5·5)*
Guns: 4—5 in *(127 mm)*/38 (single Mk 30);
6—3 in *(76 mm)*/50 (twin Mk 33)
A/S weapons: 2 fixed Hedgehogs;
2 side-racks for A/S torpedoes
Torpedo tubes: 5—21 in *(533 mm)* (quin)
Main engines: 2 GE impulse reaction geared turbines;
60 000 shp; 2 shafts
Boilers: 4 Babcock & Wilcox; 600 psi *(42 kg/cm²)*; 850°F *(455°C)*
Speed, knots: 34
Oil fuel, tons: 650
Range, miles: 5 000 at 15 knots; 900 at full power
Complement: 245 (15 officers and 230 men)

GUISE (Note helo deck on stern (VILLAR same))   *1976, Dr. Robert Scheina*

Former US destroyers of the later "Fletcher" class *(Villar)* and "Fletcher" class *(Guise)*.
Two other "Fletcher" class, ex-USS *La Vallette* (DD 448) and *Terry* (DD 513) were transferred for spares in July 1974.

Helicopter: A helicopter deck without hangar or fuelling facilities was fitted on the quarter-deck in 1975-76.

Radar: Search: SPS 6, SPS 10.
Fire control: GFCS 68 system forward, GFCS 56 system aft.

Transfer: Transferred from the US Navy to the Peruvian Navy at Boston, Massachusetts, on 8 October 1961, and at San Diego, California, on 15 December 1960 respectively.

FRIGATES

2 + 2 ITALIAN "MODIFIED LUPO" CLASS

Name	No.	Builders	Laid down	Launched	Completed
MELITON CARVAJAL	51	CNR Riva Trigoso	8 Aug 1974	17 Nov 1976	mid-1978
MANUEL VILLAVICENCIO	52	CNR Riva Trigoso	6 Oct 1976	Nov 1977	Oct 1978
—	—	SIM Callao	—	—	—
—	—	SIM Callao	—	—	—

Displacement, tons: 2 208 standard; 2 500 full load
Dimensions, feet (metres): 347·7 × 39·5 × 12 *(106 × 12 × 3·7)*
Aircraft: 1 helicopter
Missiles: SSM; 8 Otomat (twin cells);
SAM; 8 Albatros/Aspide (octuple launcher)
Guns: 1—5 in *(127 mm)*/54 (single Compact);
4—40 mm/70 (twin Compact)
Rocket launchers: 2—105 mm Breda ELSAG multi-purpose 20-barrelled launchers
A/S weapons: 6 (2 triple) Mk 32 A/S torpedo tubes (port and starboard)
Main engines: CODOG with 2 GE Fiat LM 2500 gas turbines;
50 000 hp; 2 Fiat 20-cyl A 230 diesels; 7 800 hp
Speed, knots: 35

In the design for the pair to be built in Callao a main mast is to be added, the hangar is to be fixed instead of telescopic, there are only two 40 mm (mounted higher), the Otomats are reduced to four to accommodate the hangar and reloading of the Albatros is by hand not power.

Commissioning: That of 51 and 52 reported as delayed due to financial queries.

MANUEL VILLAVICENCIO   *11/1978, Commander Aldo Fraccaroli*

LIGHT FORCES

0 + 6 PR-72P CLASS (FAST ATTACK CRAFT—MISSILE)

Displacement, tons: 465 standard; 536 full load
Dimensions, feet (metres): 188·8 × 25 × 8·4 *(57·5 × 7·6 × 2·5)*
Missiles: SSM; 4 Exocet (single cell)
Guns: 1—76/62 mm OTO Melara; 2—40/70 Breda/Bofors; 2—20 mm Oerlikon
Main engines: 4 SACM AGO 240V16 diesels; 20 000 shp; 4 shafts = 37 knots
Range, miles: 700 at 30 knots; 2 000 at 16 knots
Complement: 45

Ordered late 1976 from SFCN, France. Three hulls sub-contracted to Lorient Naval Yard.

Radar: Search: Thomson-CSF Triton.
Fire control: Thomson-CSF Vega/Pollux.
Navigation: Decca.

2 "MARAÑON" CLASS (RIVER GUNBOATS)

Name	No.	Builders	Commissioned
MARAÑON	CF 13	John I. Thornycroft & Co Ltd	July 1951
UCAYALI	CF 14	John I. Thornycroft & Co Ltd	June 1951

Displacement, tons: 365 full load
Dimensions, feet (metres): 154·8 wl × 32 × 4 *(47·2 × 9·7 × 1·2)*
Guns: 2—3 in/50; 1—40 mm; 4—20 mm (twins)
Main engines: British Polar M 441 diesels; 800 bhp = 12 knots
Range, miles: 6 000 at 10 knots
Complement: 40

Ordered early in 1950 and both laid down in early 1951. Employed on police duties in Upper Amazon. Superstructure of aluminium alloy. Based at Iquitos.

UCAYALI   *1975, Peruvian Navy*

392 PERU / Light forces — Amphibious forces

2 "LORETO" CLASS (RIVER GUNBOATS)

Name	No.	Builders	Commissioned
AMAZONAS	CF 11	Electric Boat Co, Groton	1935
LORETO	CF 12	Electric Boat Co, Groton	1935

Displacement, tons: 250 standard
Dimensions, feet (metres): 145 × 22 × 4 *(44·2 × 6·7 × 1·2)*
Guns: 2—3 in; 2—40 mm; 2—20 mm
Main engines: Diesel; 750 bhp = 15 knots
Range, miles: 4 000 at 10 knots
Complement: 35

Launched in 1934. In upper Amazon flotilla.

LORETO   *1973, Peruvian Navy*

1 RIVER GUNBOAT

Name	No.	Builders	Commissioned
AMERICA	CF 15	Tranmere Bay Development Co Ltd, Birkenhead	1904

Displacement, tons: 240
Dimensions, feet (metres): 133 × 19·5 × 4·5 *(40·6 × 5·9 × 1·4)*
Guns: 2—40 mm; 4—20 mm
Main engines: Triple expansion; 350 ihp = 14 knots
Complement: 26

Built of steel. Converted from coal to oil fuel burning. In the Upper Amazon Flotilla. The river gunboat *Iquitos* was discarded in 1967 and after 92 years service.

AMERICA   *Peruvian Navy*

3 RIVER PATROL CRAFT

Name	No.	Builders	Commissioned
RIO ZARUMILLA	PL 250 (ex-*01*)	Viareggio, Italy	5 Sep 1960
RIO TUMBES	PL 251 (ex-*02*)	Viareggio, Italy	5 Sep 1960
RIO PIURA	PL 252 (ex-*04*)	Viareggio, Italy	5 Sep 1960

Displacement, tons: 37 full load
Dimensions, feet (metres): 65·7 × 17 × 3·2 *(20 × 5·2 × 1)*
Guns: 2—40 mm
Main engines: 2 General Motors diesels; 2 shafts; 1 200 bhp = 18 knots

Ordered in 1959 as a class of four laid down on 15 July 1959. Stationed at El Salto on Ecuadorian border.

RIO PIURA   *1975, Peruvian Navy*

0 + 6 COASTAL/LAKE PATROL CRAFT

Of unknown characteristics reported as ordered from McLaren, Niteroi, Brazil; possibly in 1977.

2 LAKE GUNBOATS

RÍO RAMIS PL 290   **RÍO ILLAVE** PL 291

Of 12 tons with light MGs. Complement four.

Patrol craft on Lake Titicaca   *1973, Peruvian Navy*

AMPHIBIOUS FORCES

1 Ex-US "LST 1" CLASS

Name	No.	Builders	Commissioned
CHIMBOTE (ex-M/S *Rawhiti*, ex-US *LST 283*)	142	American Bridge Co Ambridge, Penn	18 Nov 1943

Displacement, tons: 1 625 standard; 4 050 full load
Dimensions, feet (metres): 328 × 50 × 14·1 *(100 × 15·3 × 4·3)*
Gun: 1—3 in
Main engines: General Motors diesels; 2 shafts; 1 700 bhp = 10 knots
Oil fuel, tons: 600 oil tanks; 1 100 ballast tanks
Range, miles: 9 500 at 9 knots
Complement: Accommodation for 16 officers and 130 men

Laid down on 2 August 1943, launched on 10 October 1943. Sold to Peru by a British firm in March 1947. Served commercially until 1951 when she was transferred to the Peruvian Navy.

PERU / Amphibious forces — Service forces 393

1 Ex-US "LST 511" CLASS

Name	No.	Builders	Commissioned
PAITA (ex-USS Burnett County, LST 512)	141 (ex-AT 4)	Chicago Bridge & Iron Co	8 Jan 1944

Displacement, tons: 1 653 standard; 4 080 full load
Dimensions, feet (metres): 328 × 50 × 14·5 (100 × 15·3 × 4·4)
Guns: 6—20 mm
Main engines: General Motors diesels; 2 shafts; 1 700 bhp = 10 knots
Range, miles: 9 500 at 9 knots
Complement: 13 officers, 106 men

Laid down on 29 July 1943. Launched on 10 December 1943. Purchased by Peru in September 1957. Unique deck-house forward of bridge. Helicopters are operated from upper deck amidships.

PAITA (old pennant number) 1976, Dr. Robert Scheina

2 Ex-US "LSM-1" CLASS

Name	No.	Builders	Commissioned
LOMAS (ex-US LSM 396)	145	Charleston Navy Yard	23 Mar 1945
ATICO (ex-US LSM 554)	146	Charleston Navy Yard	14 Sep 1945

Displacement, tons: 513 standard; 913 full load
Dimensions, feet (metres): 203·5 × 34·5 × 7 (62·1 × 10·5 × 2·1)
Guns: 2—40 mm; 4—20 mm
Main engines: Diesels; 800 rpm; 2 shafts; 3 600 bhp = 12 knots
Range, miles: 5 000 at 7 knots
Complement: Accommodation for 116 (10 officers and 106 men)

Purchased in 1959.

LOMAS (old pennant number) 1975, Peruvian Navy

SURVEY VESSELS

1 Ex-US "SOTOYOMO" CLASS

Name	No.	Builders	Commissioned
UNANUE (ex-USS Wateree, ATA 174)	170	Levingston S.B. Co, Orange, Texas	20 July 1944

Displacement, tons: 534 standard; 852 full load
Dimensions, feet (metres): 143 × 33·9 × 13·2 (43·6 × 10·3 × 4)
Main engines: General Motors diesel-electric; 1 500 bhp = 13 knots
Complement: 39

Former US auxiliary ocean tug. Laid down on 5 October 1943, launched on 18 November 1943. Purchased from the USA in November 1961 under MAP.

CARDENAS (ex-US YP 99) 171

Of 19 tons, launched in 1950, with a complement of 11. Transferred November 1958.

1 RESEARCH CRAFT

Of 77 ft (23·5 m) with accommodation for 16 operated on the Amazona by El Instituto del Mar (Ministry of Marine). Commissioned May 1976.

SERVICE FORCES

1 Ex-US "BELLATRIX" CLASS (TRANSPORT)

Name	No.	Builders	Commissioned
INDEPENDENCIA (ex-USS Bellatrix, AKA 3, ex-Raven, AK 20)	130 (ex-21)	Tampa Shipbuilding Co, Tampa, Florida	1941

Displacement, tons: 6 194 light
Dimensions, feet (metres): 459 × 63 × 26·5 (140 × 19·2 × 8·1)
Guns: 1—5 in/38; 3—3 in/50; 10—20 mm
Main engine: 1 Nordberg diesel; 1 shaft; 6 000 bhp = 16·5 knots

Former US attack cargo ship. Transferred to Peru at Bremerton, Washington on 20 July 1963 under the Military Aid Programme. Training ship for the Peruvian Naval Academy.

INDEPENDENCIA 1977, Michael D. J. Lennon

1 "ILO" CLASS (TRANSPORT)

Name	No.	Builders	Commissioned
ILO	131	Servicio Industrial de la Marina, Callao	Dec 1971

Displacement, tons: 18 400 full load
Measurement, tons: 13 000 deadweight
Dimensions, feet (metres): 507·7 × 67·3 × 27·2 (154·8 × 20·5 × 8·3)
Main engines: Diesels
Speed, knots: 15·6

The Ilo is used from time to time for commercial purposes. Her sister ship Rimac was launched at the same yard on 12 December 1971 and transferred from the navy for commercial use by State Shipping Company (CPV) on "bare-boat charter" in 1973.

ILO 1976, Michael D. J. Lennon

394 PERU / Service forces — Tugs

2 "TALARA" CLASS (REPLENISHMENT TANKERS)

Name	No.	Builders	Commissioned
TALARA	152	Servicio Industrial de la Marina, Callao	23 Jan 1978
BAYOVAR	153	Servicio Industrial de la Marina, Callao	1978

Measurement, tons: 25 000 deadweight
Dimensions, feet (metres): 561·5 × 82 × 31·2 (171·2 × 25 × 9·5)
Main engines: Diesels; 12 000 hp
Speed, knots: 15·5

Cargo space 35 662 cu metres. *Talara* laid down 1975, launched 9 July 1976. *Bayovar* laid down 9 July 1976, launched 18 July 1977 having been originally ordered by Petroperu and transferred to navy while building. A third, *Trompeteros*, of this class has been built for Petroperu.

2 "PARINAS" CLASS (REPLENISHMENT TANKERS)

Name	No.	Builders	Commissioned
PARINAS	155	Servicio Industrial de la Marina, Callao	13 June 1968
PIMENTEL	156	Servicio Industrial de la Marina, Callao	27 June 1969

Displacement, tons: 3 434 light; 13 600 full load
Measurement, tons: 10 000 deadweight
Dimensions, feet (metres): 410·9 × 63·1 × 26 (125·3 × 19·2 × 7·9)
Main engine: Burmeister & Wain Type 750 diesel; 5 400 bhp = 14·5 knots

All tankers may be used for commercial purposes if not required for naval use by Petroperu (State Oil Company).

PARINAS 1975, Peruvian Navy

2 "SECHURA" CLASS (SUPPORT TANKERS)

Name	No.	Builders	Commissioned
ZORRITOS	158	Servicio Industrial de la Marina, Callao	1959
LOBITOS	159	Servicio Industrial de la Marina, Callao	1966

Displacement, tons: 8 700 full load
Measurement, tons: 4 300 gross; 6 000 deadweight
Dimensions, feet (metres): 385·0 × 52·0 × 21·2 (117·4 × 15·9 × 6·4)
Main engines: Burmeister & Wain diesels; 2 400 bhp = 12 knots
Boilers: 2 Scotch with Thornycroft oil burners for cargo tank cleaning

Zorritos launched 8 October 1958, *Lobitos* May 1965.

LOBITOS 1975, Peruvian Navy

1 SUPPORT TANKER

Name	No.	Builders	Commissioned
MOLLENDO (ex-*Amalienborg*)	151	Japan	Sep 1962

Displacement, tons: 6 084 standard; 25 670 full load
Dimensions, feet (metres): 534·8 × 72·2 × 30 (164·3 × 22 × 9·2)
Main engines: 674-VTFS-160 diesels; 7 500 bhp = 14·5 knots

This Japanese built tanker, completed September 1962, was acquired by Peru in April 1967. Used in commercial work when not required by navy.

MOLLENDO 1975, Peruvian Navy

1 HARBOUR TANKER

— (Ex-US *YO 221*)

Transferred to Peru February 1975.

SUBMARINE ACCOMMODATION SHIP

1 Ex-US "CANNON" CLASS

Name	No.	Builders	Commissioned
RODRIQUEZ (ex-USS *Weaver*, DE 741)	DE 163	Western Pipe & Steel Co, San Pedro, California	30 Nov 1943

Displacement, tons: 1 240 standard; 1 900 full load
Dimensions, feet (metres): 306 × 36·9 × 14·1 (93·3 × 11·2 × 4·3)
Guns: 3—3 in (76 mm)/50 (single Mk 22); 6—40 mm/60 (twin Mk 1); 10—20 mm
A/S weapons: 1 Mk 10 Hedgehog; 8 K mortars; 2 DC racks aft
Main engines: 4 General Motors diesel-electric sets 6 000 hp; 2 shafts
Speed, knots: 21
Range, miles: 10 500 at 12 knots
Complement: 172 (12 officers and 160 men)

Transferred to Peru on 26 October 1951, under the Mutual Defence Assistance Programme. Reconditioned and modernised at Green Cove Springs and Jacksonville, Florida. Arrived in Peru on 24 May 1952.
Used as submarine accommodation ship.

TUGS

1 Ex-US "CHEROKEE" CLASS

Name	No.	Builders	Commissioned
GUARDIAN RIOS (ex-USS *Pinto*, ATF 90)	123	USA	1943

Displacement, tons: 1 235 standard; 1 675 full load
Dimensions, feet (metres): 205 × 38·5 × 15·5 (62·5 × 11·7 × 4·7)
Main engines: 4 General Motors diesel-electric; 3 000 bhp = 16·5 knots

Launched on 5 January 1943. Transferred to Peru in 1960 and delivered in January 1961. Fitted with powerful pumps and other salvage equipment.

CONTROMESTRE NAVARRO 184

50 ton tug for Amazon flotilla built in Peru in 1973.

PERU / Tugs — Coast guard   395

Name	No.	Builders	Commissioned
OLAYA	128	Ruhrorter, SW. Duisburg	1967
GELENDON	129	Ruhrorter, SW. Duisburg	1967

Measurement, tons: 80 gross
Dimensions, feet (metres): 61·3 × 20·3 × 7·4 (18·7 × 6·2 × 2·3)
Main engines: 600 hp = 10 knots

Name	No.	Builders	Commissioned
RANCO (ex-USS Iwana, YTM2)	124	City Point Iron Works, Boston, USA	1892

Displacement, tons: 192
Dimensions, feet (metres): 92·6 pp × 20·1 × 8 (28·2 × 6·4 × 2·4)

Laid down April 1891. Transferred March 1946.

RIVER HOSPITAL CRAFT

Name	No.	Builders	Commissioned
MORONA	302	SIMAI, Iquitos	1976
—	—	SIMAI, Iquitos	1977
—	—	SIMAI, Iquitos	1979

Displacement, tons: 150
Dimensions, feet (metres): 98·4 × 19·6 × 1·5 (30 × 6 × 0·6)

For service on Peruvian Rivers.

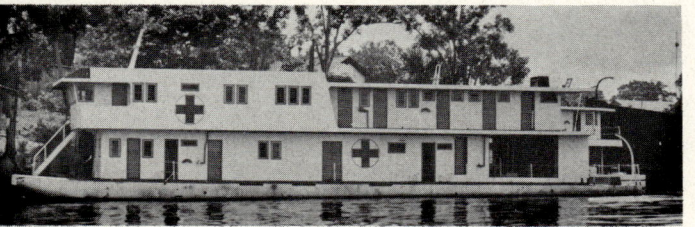

MORONA   1976, Dr. Robert Scheina

+ 1 FLOATING DOCK

Displacement, tons: 15 000
Dimensions, feet (metres): 639·7 × 137·7 × 55·7 (195 × 42 × 17)

Ordered in West Germany 13 February 1978. Can be extended to 225 metres and 18 000 tons displacement.

FLOATING DOCK

FD 111 (ex-WY 19, ex-US AFDL 33)

Displacement, tons: 1 900
Dimensions, feet (metres): 288 × 64 × 8·2/31·5 (92·2 × 19·5 × 2·5/9·6)

Launched in October 1944. Transferred July 1959.

FLOATING DOCK

FD 112 (ex-WY 20, ex-US ARD 8)

Displacement, tons: 5 200
Dimensions, feet (metres): 492 × 84 × 5·7/33·2 (150·1 × 25·6 × 1·7/10·1)

Transferred February 1961.

SMALL FLOATING DOCK

FD 108

Dimensions, feet (metres): 194 × 61·3 × ? (59·2 × 18·7 × ?)
Lift: 600 tons

Built by John I. Thornycroft, Southampton in 1951. Based at Iquitos.

FD 108 (with Amazonas)   1976, Dr. Robert Scheina

1 FLOATING WORKSHOP

105 (ex-US YR 59)

Transferred 8 August 1961.

1 FLOATING CRANE

At Callao; of 120 tons capacity.

Other names of unidentified types: Duenas, Noguera, Neptuno, Corrillo.

3 WATER CARRIERS

Name	No.	Builders	Commissioned
MANTILLA (ex-US YW 22)	110 (ex-141)	Henry C. Grebe & Co Inc, Chicago, Illinois	1945

Displacement, tons: 1 235 full load
Dimensions, feet (metres): 174 × 32 × — (52·3 × 9·8 × —)
Gun: 1 MG fwd
Speed, knots: 8
Capacity, gallons: 200 000

Former US water barge. Lent to Peru in July 1963.

ABA 091

Built in Peru 1972. Attached to Amazon Flotilla. Capacity 800 tons water.

ABA 113

Of 300 tons. Built in Peru 1972.

COAST GUARD

Note: In addition to the ships listed below there are eleven minor patrol craft with the Coast Guard.

2 Ex-US "AUK" CLASS

Name	No.	Builders	Commissioned
GALVEZ (ex-USS Ruddy, MSF 380)	220 (ex-68)	Gulf Shipbuilding Corporation	28 Apr 1945
DIEZ CANSECO (ex-USS Shoveller, MSF 382)	221 (ex-69)	Gulf Shipbuilding Corporation	28 June 1945

Displacement, tons: 890 standard; 1 250 full load
Dimensions, feet (metres): 221·2 × 32·2 × 11 (67·5 × 9·8 × 3·4)
Guns: 1—3 in/50; 2—40 mm
A/S weapons: 1 Hedgehog
Main engines: Diesel-electric; 2 shafts; 3 532 bhp = 18 knots
Range, miles: 4 300 at 10 knots
Complement: 100

Recommissioned at San Diego, California, and transferred to the Peruvian Navy under the Mutual Defence Assistance Programme on 1 November 1960. Sonar equipment was fitted so that they could be used as patrol vessels. Both purchased by Peru in 1974. Transferred to the Coast Guard Service in 1975. Both still capable of minesweeping.

1 LARGE PATROL CRAFT

Name	No.	Builders	Commissioned
RIO CANETE	234	SIMA, Peru, Callao	1 Apr 1976

Displacement, tons: 298 full load
Dimensions, feet (metres): 166·8 × 24·8 × 5·6 (50·6 × 7·4 × 1·7)
Gun: 1—40 mm
Main engines: 4—MTU diesels; 5 640 hp; 2 shafts = 22 knots
Complement: 39

Launched 8 August 1974.

6 VOSPER TYPE (LARGE PATROL CRAFT)

Name	No.	Builders	Commissioned
RIO CHICAMA	224	Vosper Ltd, Portsmouth	1965
RIO PATIVILCA	225	Vosper Ltd, Portsmouth	1965
RIO HUAURA	226	Vosper Ltd, Portsmouth	1965
RIO LOCUMBA	227	Vosper Ltd, Portsmouth	1965
RIO ICA	228	Vosper Ltd, Portsmouth	1965
RIO VITOR	229	Vosper Ltd, Portsmouth	1965

Displacement, tons: 100 standard; 130 full load
Dimensions, feet (metres): 109·7 × 21 × 5·7 (33·5 × 6·4 × 1·7)
Guns: 2—20 mm
A/S weapons: DC racks
Main engines: 2 Napier Deltic 18-cyl, turbocharged diesels; 6 200 bhp = 30 knots
Range, miles: 1 100 at 15 knots
Complement: 25 (4 officers and 21 ratings)

Of all-welded steel construction with aluminium upperworks. Equipped with Vosper roll damping fins, Decca Type 707 true motion radar, comprehensive radio, up-to-date navigation aids, sonar, and air-conditioning. The first boat, 229, was launched on 10 July 1964, the last, 227, on 18 February 1965. Last arrived Callao 1 December 1965. Can be armed as gunboat, torpedo boat (four side-launched torpedoes) or minelayer. A twin rocket projector can be fitted forward instead of gun. All transferred to the Coast Guard Service in 1975 and renamed.

RIO LOCUMBA   *1971, Peruvian Navy*

2 US "PGM 71" CLASS (LARGE PATROL CRAFT)

Name	No.	Builders	Commissioned
RÍO SAMA (ex-US *PGM 78*)	222 (ex-*PC 11*)	Peterson Builders, USA	Sep 1966
RÍO CHIRA	223 (ex-*PC 12*)	SIMA, Callao	1972

Displacement, tons: 130 standard; 147 full load
Dimensions, feet (metres): 101 × 21 × 6 (30·8 × 6·4 × 1·8)
Guns: 1—40 mm; 4—20 mm; 2—·5 cal MG
Main engines: 2 diesels; 2 shafts; 1 800 hp = 18·5 knots
Range, miles: 1 500 at 10 knots
Complement: 15

Rio Sama completed under the US Military Aid Programme. Transferred to the Coast Guard Service in 1975.

RIO SAMA   *1971, Peruvian Navy*

PHILIPPINES

Ministerial

Minister of National Defence:
Juan Ponce Enrile

Senior Officers

Flag Officer in Command:
Rear-Admiral Hilario M. Ruiz
Commander, Naval Operating Forces:
Captain Simeon M. Alejandro

Diplomatic Representation

Armed Forces Attaché London:
Captain Artemio A. Tadiar, Jr (Navy)
Naval Attaché Washington:
Commander Ernesto M. Arzaga

Personnel

1979: approx 2 000 officers and 15 000 enlisted men

Prefix to Ships' Names

RPS for Republic of Philippines Ship

Marine Corps

Commandant: Captain Rodolfo Punsalang
Personnel: 500 officers and 5 000 men (organised into a single brigade)

Coast Guard

Commandant: Commodore Ernesto R. Ogbinar
Personnel: 300 officers and 1 700 men

Naval Base

Sangley Point

Strength of the Fleet

	Active	Building
Frigates	8	—
Corvettes	11	—
Fast Attack Craft, Missile	0	3
Large Patrol Craft	11	5
Hydrofoils	4	—
Coastal Patrol Craft	62	?
Minesweepers (Coastal)	2	—
LSTs	23	—
LSMs	4	—
LSSLs	4	—
LSILs	4	—
Landing Craft	71	—
Repair Ships	3	—
Tankers	4	—
Tugs	8	—
Floating Docks	5	—
Survey Ships	4	—
Miscellaneous	5	—
Coast Guard Craft	?	—

Mercantile Marine

Lloyd's Register of Shipping:
577 vessels of 1 264 995 tons gross

DELETIONS

Light Forces

1976 3 "Swift" Mk 1
1977 Nueva Ecija (ex-US "PC 461" class)

Frigates

1976 ex-Yukutat, ex-Cook Inlet ("Casco" class USCG)

Corvettes

1976 2 MSO Type 4 (to US for disposal 1977) (Davao del Norte, Davao del Sur)
1977 Datu Tupas (ex-US "Admirable" class)

Amphibious Forces

1978 Bulacan, Albay, Misamis Oriental, Cambanga del Sur

Coast and Geodetic Survey

1976 Samar

FRIGATES

1 Ex-US "SAVAGE" CLASS

Name	No.	Builders	Laid down	Launched	Commissioned
RAJAH LAKANDULA (ex-Tran Hung Dao, ex-USS Camp, DER 251)	PS 4	Brown S.B. & Co, Houston	27 Jan 1943	16 Apr 1943	16 Sep 1943

Displacement, tons: 1 590 standard; 1 850 full load
Length, feet (metres): 306 (93.3)
Beam, feet (metres): 36.6 (11.2)
Draught, feet (metres): 14 (4.3)
Guns: 2—3 in (76 mm)/50 (single Mk 34)
A/S weapons: 6 (2 triple) Mk 32 torpedo tubes; 1 trainable Hedgehog (Mk 15); depth charge rack
Main engines: Diesel (Fairbanks-Morse); 6 000 bhp; 2 shafts
Speed, knots: 19
Complement: approx 170

Former US Navy destroyer escort, of the FMR design group. After World War II this ship was extensively converted to radar picket configuration to serve as seaward extension of US aircraft attack warning system; redesignated DER with original hull number. Subsequently employed during 1960s in Indochina for coastal patrol and interdiction by US Navy Operation MARKET TIME. Transferred to South Vietnamese Navy 6 February 1971. Acquired by the Philippines in 1975 and formally transferred on 5 April 1976.

Fire control: Mk 63 (fwd) SPG 34 on gun mount. Mk 51 (aft).

Radar: SPS 28 and SPS 10 search radars on forward tripod mast. Apparently most electronic warfare equipment was removed prior to transfer. (See Fire control).

Sonar: SQS 31.

RAJAH LAKANDULA

6/1977, Dr. Giorgio Arra

398 PHILIPPINES / Frigates — Corvettes

4 Ex-US "CASCO" CLASS COAST GUARD CUTTERS

Name	No.	Builders	Laid down	Launched	Commissioned
ANDRES BONIFACIO (ex-*Ly Thoung Kiet*, ex-USCGC *Chincoteague*, WHEC 375, ex-*AVP 24*)	PS 7	Lake Washington S.Y.	23 July 1941	15 Apr 1942	12 Apr 1942
GREGORIO DE PILAR (ex-*Ngo Kuyen*, ex-USCGC *McCulloch*, WHEC 386, ex-USS *Wachapreague*, AGP 8, AVP 56)	PS 8	Lake Washington S.Y.	1 Feb 1943	10 July 1943	17 May 1944
DIEGO SILANG (ex-*Tran Quang Khai*, ex-USCGC *Bering Strait*, WHEC 382, ex-*AVP 34*)	PS 9	Lake Washington S.Y.	7 June 1943	15 Jan 1944	19 July 1944
FRANCISCO DAGAHOY (ex-*Tran Binh Trong*, ex-USCGC *Castle Rock*, WHEC 383, ex-*AVP 35*)	PS 10	Lake Washington S.Y.	12 July 1943	11 Mar 1944	8 Oct 1944

Displacement, tons: 1 766 standard; 2 800 full load
Length, feet (metres): 310·8 *(94·5)*
Beam, feet (metres): 41·1 *(12·5)*
Draught, feet (metres): 13·5 *(4·1)*
Guns: 1—5 in *(127 mm)*/38 (single Mk 30); 1 or 2—81 mm mortars in some ships; most have 2 or 3—40 mm aft; several MG
Main engines: Diesels (Fairbanks-Morse); 6 080 bhp; 2 shafts
Speed, knots: approx 18
Complement: approx 200

Built as seaplane tenders of the "Barnegat" class for the US Navy.
All transferred to US Coast Guard in 1946-48, initially on loan designated WAVP and then on permanent transfer except ex-*McCulloch* transferred outright from US Navy to Coast Guard; subsequently redesignated as high endurance cutters (WHEC).

Appearance: These ships are distinguished from the former US Navy radar picket frigate of similar size by their pole masts forward, open side passages amidships, and radar antenna on second mast. Note combination ·50 cal MG/81 mm mortar forward of bridge in "B" position.

Aircraft: All are to be fitted with helo deck aft but not with support facilities.

Fire control: Mk 52 with Mk 26 radar for 5 in gun.

Radar: SPN 21 (foremast); SPS 29 (mainmast).

Transfers: Transferred from US Coast Guard to South Vietnamese Navy in 1971-72. Acquired by the Philippines in 1975 and formally transferred on 5 April 1976.
Ex-USCGC *Yukutat* and *Cook Inlet* transferred for spares 5 April 1976.

DIEGO SILANG   1971, Vietnamese Navy

3 Ex-US "CANNON" CLASS

Name	No.	Builders	Laid down	Launched	Commissioned
DATU KALANTIAW (ex-USS *Booth*, DE 170)	PS 76	Norfolk Navy Yard, Portsmouth Va.	30 Jan 1943	21 June 1943	19 Aug 1943
— (ex-*Asahi*, DE 262, ex-USS *Amick*, DE 168)	—	Federal Shipbuilding & Dry Dock Co, Newark, New Jersey	30 Nov 1942	27 May 1943	26 July 1943
— (ex-*Hatsuhi*, DE 263, ex-USS *Atherton*, DE 169)	—	Norfolk Navy Yard, Portsmouth Va.	14 Jan 1943	27 May 1943	29 Aug 1943

Displacement, tons: 1 220 standard; 1 620 full load
Length, feet (metres): 306 *(93·3)*
Beam, feet (metres): 36·6 *(11·2)*
Draught, feet (metres): 14 *(4·3)*
Guns: 3—3 in *(76 mm)*/50 (single Mk 22); 6—40 mm (twin); 2—20 mm (single) (6—20 mm in ex-Japanese)
A/S weapons: 1 Hedgehog; 6 (2 triple) Mk 32 torpedo tubes; depth charges (PS 76);
1 Hedgehog; 6 K-guns; 2 DC racks (ex-Japanese)
Main engines: Diesel-electric drive (General Motors diesels); 6 000 bhp; 2 shafts
Speed, knots: 21
Complement: approx 165

Appearance: Ex-Japanese ships have pole foremast.

Fire control: Mk 52 GFCS with Mk 51 rangefinder and Mk 26 radar for 3 in gun; 3—Mk 51 Mod 2 GFCS for 40 mm.

Radar: The *Datu Kalantiaw* has been refitted with SPS 5 and SPS 6 radars with antennae mounted on tripod mast.

Transfers: PS 76 to Philippines 15 December 1967. Stricken in USN 15 July 1978 and sold 31 August 1978. Ex-Japanese ships *Asahi* and *Hatsuhi* originally transferred 14 June 1955 and were paid off June 1975. Transferred to Philippines 13 September 1976.

DATU KALANTIAW   Philippine Navy

CORVETTES

2 Ex-US "AUK" CLASS MSF TYPE

Name	No.	Builders	Commissioned
RIZAL (ex-USS *Murrelet*, MSF 372)	PS 69	Savannah Machine & Foundry Co, Georgia	21 Aug 1945
QUEZON (ex-USS *Vigilance*, MSF 324)	PS 70	Associated Shipbuilders, Seattle, Washington	28 Feb 1944

Displacement, tons: 890 standard; 1 250 full load
Dimensions, feet (metres): 221·2 × 32·2 × 10·8 *(67·4 × 9·8 × 3·3)*
Guns: 2—3 in *(76 mm)*/50 (single); 4—40 mm (twin); 4—20 mm (twin)
A/S weapons: 3 (1 triple) Mk 32 torpedo tubes; 1 Hedgehog; depth charges
Main engines: Diesel-electric (General Motors diesels); 3 532 bhp; 2 shafts = 18 knots
Complement: approx 100

Upon transfer the minesweeping gear was removed and a second 3 in gun fitted aft; additional anti-submarine weapons also fitted. *Quezon* has bulwarks on iron-deck to end of superstructure which *Rizal* does not have.

Radar: SPS 5.

Transfers: PS 69 transferred to the Philippines on 18 June 1965 and PS 70 on 19 August 1967.

QUEZON   1976, Michael D. J. Lennon

PHILIPPINES / Corvettes — Light forces 399

8 Ex-US "PCE 827" CLASS

Name	No.	Builders	Commissioned
MIGUEL MALVAR (ex-*Ngoc Hoi* ex-USS *Brattleboro*, EPCER 852)	PS 19	Pullman Standard Car Co, Chicago	26 May 1944
SULTAN KUDARAT (ex-*Dong Da II* ex-USS *Crestview*, PCE 895)	PS 22	Willamette Iron & Steel Corporation, Portland	30 Oct 1943
DATU MARIKUDO (ex-*Van Kiep II* ex-USS *Amherst*, PCER 853)	PS 23	Pullman Standard Car Co, Chicago	16 June 1944
CEBU (ex-USS *PCE 881*)	PS 28	Albina E and M Works, Portland, Oregon	31 July 1944
NEGROS OCCIDENTAL (ex-USS *PCE 884*)	PS 29	Albina E and M Works, Portland, Oregon	30 Mar 1944
LEYTE (ex-USS *PCE 885*)	PS 30	Albina E and M Works, Portland, Oregon	30 Apr 1945
PANGASINAN (ex-USS *PCE 891*)	PS 31	Willamette Iron & Steel Corporation, Portland	15 June 1944
ILOILO (ex-USS *PCE 897*)	PS 32	Willamette Iron & Steel Corporation, Portland	6 Jan 1945

Displacement, tons: 640 standard; 850 full load
Dimensions, feet (metres): 184·5 × 33·1 × 9·5 *(56·3 × 10·1 × 2·9)*
Guns: 1—3 in *(76 mm)*/50; 3 or 6—40 mm (single or twin) (28-32); 2—40 mm (single) (remainder); 4—20 mm (single) (28-32); 8—20 mm (twin) (remainder)
Main engines: Diesels (General Motors); 2 000 bhp; 2 shafts = 15 knots
Complement: approx 90-100

Two originally were fitted as rescue ships (PCER).

Transfers: Five units transferred to the Philippines in July 1948; PS 22 to South Viet-Nam on 29 November 1961, PS 19 on 11 July 1966, and PS 23 in June 1970. PS 19 and 22 to Philippines November 1975 and PS 23 5 April 1976.

LEYTE *10/1977, Dr. Giorgio Arra*

1 Ex-US "ADMIRABLE" CLASS

Name	No.	Builders	Commissioned
MAGAT SALAMAT (ex-*Chi Lang II*, ex-USS *Gayety*, MSF 239)	PS 20	Winslow Marine Railway & S.B. Co, Seattle, Wash	1944

Displacement, tons: 650 standard; 945 full load
Dimensions, feet (metres): 184·5 × 33 × 9·8 *(56·3 × 10·1 × 3·0)*
Guns: 1—3 in *(76 mm)*/50; 2—40 mm (single); up to 8—20 mm (twin)
Main engines: 2 Cooper-Bessemer diesels; 1 710 bhp; 2 shafts = 14 knots
Complement: approx 80

Launched 19 March 1944. Minesweeping equipment has been removed. Believed to have two 20 mm twin mounts at after end of bridge and one or two 20 mm twin mounts on quarter-deck.

Transfer: *Magat Salamat* transferred to South Viet-Nam in April 1962. To Philippines November 1975.

MAGAT SALAMAT (old name) *1962, Vietnamese Navy*

LIGHT FORCES

1 + 5 LARGE PATROL CRAFT

Displacement, tons: 135
Dimensions, feet (metres): 118·1 × 20·3 × 5·6 *(36 × 6·2 × 1·7)*
Guns: 2—30 mm
Main engines: 2 MTU diesels; 5 000 hp; 2 shafts = 29 knots

Ordered from Hamelin S.Y. FDR. First delivery 11 October 1978. Reported that another 14 are to be built locally.

4 Ex-US "PC 461" CLASS (LARGE PATROL CRAFT)

Name	No.	Builders	Commissioned
BATANGAS (ex-USS *PC 1134*)	PS 24	Defoe S.B. Corporation	11 Sep 1943
CAPIZ (ex-USS *PC 1564*)	PS 27	Leathem D. Smith S.B. Co	4 Aug 1944
NEGROS ORIENTAL (ex-*E 312*, ex-*L'Inconstant*, P 636, ex-USS *PC 1171*)	PS 29	Leathem D. Smith S.B. Co	15 May 1943
NUEVA VISCAYA (ex-USAF *Altus*, ex-USS *PC 568*)	PS 80	Brown S.B. Co	13 July 1942

Displacement, tons: 280 standard; 450 full load
Dimensions, feet (metres): 173·7 × 23 × 10·8 *(52·9 × 7·0 × 3·3)*
Guns: 1—3 in *(76 mm)*/50; 1—40 mm; several—20 mm (single or twin)
A/S weapons: Depth charges (except *Negros Oriental*)
Main engines: Diesels (General Motors); 2 800 bhp; 2 shafts = 20 knots
Complement: approx 70

Ordered September 1977.

Transfers: PS 24 and 27 transferred July 1948 and PS 80 (which had served with USAF 1963-68) in March 1968. PS 29 to France in 1951, Khmer Republic 1956 and, after transferring to Philippines in 1975 bought December 1976.

CAPIZ *Philippine Navy*

1 "140 ft" LARGE PATROL CRAFT

Completed in 1977 by Sumi Dagawa S.Y., Tokyo. No further details available.

5 US "PGM-39" and "71" CLASSES (LARGE PATROL CRAFT)

Name	No.	Builders	Commissioned
BASILAN (ex-*PGM 83*, ex-*Hon Troc*)	PG 60	Peterson Builders, Wisconsin	—
AGUSAN (ex-*PGM 39*)	PG 61	Tacoma Boatbuilding Co, Washington	Mar 1960
CATANDUANES (ex-*PGM 40*)	PG 62	Tacoma Boatbuilding Co, Washington	Mar 1960
ROMBLON (ex-*PGM 41*)	PG 63	Tacoma Boatbuilding Co, Washington	June 1960
PALAWAN (ex-*PGM 42*)	PG 64	Tacoma Boatbuilding Co, Washington	June 1960

Displacement, tons: 122 full load
Dimensions, feet (metres): 100·3 × 21·1 × 6·9 *(30·6 × 6·4 × 2·1)*
Guns: 1—40 mm; 4—20 mm (twins); 4—·50 cal MGs (except 2 only in *Basilan*)
Main engines: 2 Mercedes-Benz diesels; 1 900 bhp; 2 shafts = 17 knots
 (*Basilan* 8 General Motors 6—71 diesels)
Complement: approx 15

Steel-hulled craft built under US military assistance programmes; PG 61-64 for the Philippines, PG 60 for South Viet-Nam. Assigned US PGM-series numbers while under construction. Transferred upon completion. *Basilan* transferred to South Viet-Nam in April 1967 and acquired by the Philippines December 1975.
These craft are lengthened versions of the US Coast Guard 95 ft "Cape" class patrol boat design. PG 62 serves with the Coast Guard.

CATANDUANES   *10/1977, Dr. Giorgio Arra*

2 ITALIAN DESIGN (HYDROFOIL PATROL CRAFT)

Name	No.	Builders	Commissioned
SIQUIJOR	HB 76	Cantiere Navaltecnica, Messina	Apr 1965
CAMIGUIN	HB 77	Cantiere Navaltecnica, Messina	Apr 1965

Displacement, tons: 28
Dimensions, feet (metres): 15·3 *(24·3 over foils) (4·7 (7·4))* × 3·8 *(8·9 foilborne) (1·2 (2·7))*
Guns: MG
Main engines: 2 diesels (Mercedes-Benz-MTU); 1 250 bhp; 2 shafts = 38 knots
Complement: 9

Laid down on 26 May and 28 October 1964. For military and police patrol.

CAMIGUIN   *Philippine Navy*

2 HITACHI PT 32 DESIGN (HYDROFOIL PATROL CRAFT)

Name	No.	Builders	Commissioned
BONTOC	HB 74	Hitachi, Kanagawa	Dec 1966
BALER	HB 75	Hitachi, Kanagawa	Dec 1966

Displacement, tons: 32 full load
Dimensions, feet (metres): 68·9 × 15·7 (24·6 over foils) *(21 × 4·8, 7·5)*
Guns: MG can be mounted fore and aft; normally unarmed
Main engines: Ikegai-Mercedes-Benz (MTU) diesel; 3 200 bhp = 37·8 knots (32 cruising). Also auxiliary engine
Complement: 14

For smuggling prevention. Also used as inter-island ferries. Based on Schertel-Sachsenburg foil system.

BALER on foils   *Philippine Navy*

31 + ? De HAVILLAND SERIES 9209 (COASTAL PATROL CRAFT)

PC 326-331 + 25

Displacement, tons: 16·5 full load
Dimensions, feet (metres): 45·9 × 15·1 × 3·3 *(14 × 4·6 × 1)*
Guns: 2—·5 in MGs
Main engines: 2 Cummins diesels; 740 hp = 25 knots
Range, miles: 500 at 12 knots
Complement: 8

GRP hulls. First six built by De Havilland Marine, Sydney NSW. Completed between 20 November 1974 and 8 February 1975. In August 1975 80 further craft of this design were reported ordered from Marcelo Yard, Manila to be delivered 1976-78 at the rate of two per month. By the end of 1976, 25 more had been completed but a serious fire in the shipyard destroyed 14 new hulls and halted production temporarily.

De HAVILLAND CPC   *1977, De Havilland*

PHILIPPINES / Light forces — Amphibious forces 401

15 SWIFT (Mk 1 and 2) TYPE (COASTAL PATROL CRAFT)

PCF 300	PCF 308	PCF 313
PCF 301	PCF 309	PCF 314
PCF 303	PCF 310	PCF 315
PCF 306	PCF 311	PCF 316
PCF 307	PCF 312	PCF 317

Displacement, tons: 22·5 full load
Dimensions, feet (metres): 50 × 13·6 × 4 *(15·2 × 4·1 × 1·2)* (Mk 1 300-303)
51·3 ft *(15·6)* (Mk 2 306-317)
Guns: 2—·50 cal MG (twin)
Main engines: 2 geared diesels (General Motors); 860 bhp; 2 shafts = 28 knots

Most built in the USA. PCF 303 served in US Navy prior to transfer to the Philippines; others built for US military assistance programmes. PCF 300 and 301 transferred to Philippines in March 1966, PCF 303 in August 1966, PCF 306-313 in February 1968, PCF 314-316 in July 1970. PCF 317 built in 1970 in the Philippines (ferro concrete) with enlarged superstructure used as yacht for Señora Marcos.

PCF 308   10/1977, Dr. Giorgio Arra

13 IMPROVED SWIFT TYPE (COASTAL PATROL CRAFT)

PCF 318	PCF 323	PCF 337
PCF 319	PCF 333	PCF 338
PCF 320	PCF 334	PCF 339
PCF 321	PCF 336	PCF 340
PCF 322		

Displacement, tons: 33 full load
Dimensions, feet (metres): 65 × 16 × 3·4 *(19·8 × 4·9 × 1·0)*
Guns: 2—·50 cal MG (twin); 2—·30 cal MG (single)
Main engines: 3 diesels (General Motors); 1 590 bhp; 3 shafts = 25 knots
Complement: 8

Improved Swift type inshore patrol boats built by Sewart for the Philippine Navy. First six delivered January-June 1972, 333 and 334 in April 1975, 337 and 338 in July 1975, 336 in November 1975 and 339 and 340 in December 1976.

2 COASTAL PATROL CRAFT

Name	No.
ABRA	FB 83
BUKINDON	FB 84

Displacement, tons: 40 standard
Dimensions, feet (metres): 87·5 × 19 × 4·8 *(26·7 × 5·8 × 1·5)*
Guns: 2—20 mm
Main engines: Diesels (Mercedes-Benz/MTU); 2 460 bhp; 2 shafts = approx 25 knots
Complement: 15 (3 officers, 12 men)

Abra built Singapore. Completed 8 January 1970. *Bukindon* completed Cavite 1970-71. Wood hulls and aluminium superstructure.

MINE WARFARE FORCES

2 Ex-US "MSC 218" CLASS (MINESWEEPERS—COASTAL)

Name	No.	Builders	Commissioned
ZAMBALES (ex-USS *MSC 218*)	PM 55	Bellingham Shipyard, Washington	7 Mar 1956
ZAMBOANGA DEL NORTE (ex-USS *MSC 219*)	PM 56	Bellingham Shipyard, Washington	23 Apr 1956

Displacement, tons: 320 light; 385 full load
Dimensions, feet (metres): 144 × 28 × 8·2 *(43·9 × 8·5 × 2·5)*
Guns: 2—20 mm (twin)
Main engines: 2 diesels; 880 bhp; 2 shafts = 12 knots
Complement: approx 40

Built by the USA specifically for transfer under the military aid programme. Wood hull with non-magnetic metal fittings.

ZAMBALES

AMPHIBIOUS FORCES

23 Ex-US "1-511" and "512-1152" CLASSES (LSTs)

Name	No.	Commissioned
MINDORO OCCIDENTAL (ex-USNS *T-LST 222*)	LT 93	1944
SURIGAO DEL NORTE (ex-USNS *T-LST 488*)	LT 94	1944
SURIGAO DEL SUR (ex-USNS *T-LST 546*)	LT 95	1942
— (ex-*Thi Nai*, ex-USS *Cayuga County*, LST 529)	(ex-HQ 502)	1944
MAQUINDANAO (ex-USS *Caddo Parish*, LST 515)	LT 96	1944
CAGAYAN (ex-USS *Hickman County*, LST 825)	LT 97	1945
ILOCOS NORTE (ex-USS *Madera County*, LST 905)	LT 98	1945
— (ex-*Nha Trang*, ex-USS *Jerome County*, LST 848)	(ex-HQ 505)	1943
— (ex-USNS *T-LST 47*)		1943
LAGUNA (ex-USNS *T-LST 230*)	(ex-LT 501)	1944
— (ex-USNS *T-LST 287*)		1944
— (ex-USNS *T-LST 491*)		1943
LANAO DEL NORTE (ex-USNS *T-LST 566*)	(ex-LT 504)	1944
— (ex-USNS *T-LST 607*)		Mar 1944
— (ex-USNS *Daggett County*, T-LST 689)		1944
— (ex-USNS *Davies County*, T-LST 692)		1944
— (ex-*Can Tho*, ex-USS *Garrett County*, AGP 786, ex-LST 786)		1944
DUMAGAT (ex-*My Tho*, ex-USS *Harnett County*, AGP 821, ex-LST 821)	(ex-A 57)	1944
AURORA (ex-USS *Harris County*, T-LST 822)	(ex-LT 508)	1945
— (ex-USNS *Hillsdale County*, LST 835)		1944
— (ex-USNS *Nansemond County*, T-LST 1064)		1945
— (ex-USNS *Orleans Parish*, T-LST 1069, ex-*MSC 6*, LST 1069)		1945
TAWI-TAWI (ex-USNS *T-LST 1072*)	(ex-LT 512)	1945

Displacement, tons: 1 620 standard; 2 366 beaching; 4 080 full load
Dimensions, feet (metres): 328 × 50 × 14 *(100 × 15·2 × 4·3)*
Guns: 7 or 8—40 mm (1 or 2 twin, 4 or 5 single); several 20 mm in former Vietnamese ships; former USNS ships are unarmed.
Main engines: Diesels (General Motors); 1 700 bhp; 2 shafts = 11·6 knots
Complement: varies; approx 60 to 110 (depending upon employment)

Ex-NHA TRANG (tripod mast)

Cargo capacity 2 100 tons. Many of these ships served as cargo ships in the Western Pacific under the US Military Sealift Command (USNS/T-LST); they were civilian manned by Korean and Japanese crews.
The ex-HQ 505 and some of the later USNS ships have tripod masts; others have pole masts. The USNS ships lack troop accommodations and other amphibious warfare features. Many of these ships are used for general cargo work in Philippine service.

Transfers: LT 96-98 on 29 November 1969; LT 93-95 on 15 July 1972; 502, 505 transferred from US Navy to South Korean Navy in April 1962 and December 1963 and acquired by the Philippines in 1976. Ex-US 689, 835 and 1064 were transferred to Japan in April 1961 and thence to Philippines in 1975—remainder transferred from US Navy in 1976 with exception of ex-*My Tho* and ex-*Can Tho* which were used as light craft repair ships in South Viet-Nam and have retained amphibious capability (transferred to Viet-Nam 1970 and to Philippines 1976 acquired by purchase 13 September 1977). Ex-US 529 and 975 transferred (grant aid) 17 November 1975. Ex-US 1064 acquired by purchase 24 September 1977. Several of these ships are undergoing major refit including replacement of frames and plating as well as engines and electrics.

402 PHILIPPINES / Amphibious forces — Service forces

4 Ex-US "LSM-1" CLASS

Name	No.	Commissioned
ISABELA (ex-USS *LSM 463*)	LP 41	1 Mar 1945
BATANES (ex-*Huong Giang*, ex-USS *Oceanside*, LSM 175)	LP 65	25 Sep 1944
WESTERN SAMAR (ex-*Hat Giang*, ex-*LSM 9011*, ex-USS *LSM 335*)	LP 66	9 Dec 1944
ORIENTAL MINDORO (ex-USS *LSM 320*)	LP 68	19 Aug 1944

Displacement, tons: 743 beaching; 1 095 full load
Dimensions, feet (metres): 203·5 × 34·5 × 8·5 *(62 × 10·5 × 2·6)*
Guns: 2—40 mm (twin); several 20 mm
Main engines: Diesels; 2 800 bhp; 2 shafts = 11·6 knots
Complement: approx 70

LP 41 transferred to the Philippines in March 1961 and LP 68 in April 1962; LP 66 originally transferred from US Navy to French Navy for use in Indochina in January 1954; subsequently transferred to South Viet-Nam in December 1955; LP 65 transferred from US Navy to South Viet-Nam on 1 August 1961. Acquired by the Philippines 17 November 1975.
LP 66 was fitted as hospital ship (LSM-H) for treating casualties retaining her armament. Has deck houses in and above well-deck.
LSM 110 (ex-Viet-Nam (S)) transferred 17 November 1975 for spares and scrap.

WESTERN SAMAR (old pennant number) *Vietnamese Navy*

4 Ex-US "LSSL-1" CLASS

Name	No.	Commissioned
CAMARINES SUR (ex-*Niguyen Duc Bong*, ex-US *LSSL 129*)	LS 48	31 Dec 1944
SULU (ex-*LSSL 96*)	LS 49	23 Jan 1945
— (ex-Japanese, ex-US *LSSL 68*)	—	15 Jan 1945
— (ex-Japanese, ex-US *LSSL 87*)	—	18 Dec 1944

Displacement, tons: 227 standard; 383 full load
Dimensions, feet (metres): 158 × 23·7 × 5·7 *(48·2 × 7·2 × 1·7)*
Guns: 1—3 in; 4—40 mm; 4—20 mm; 4 MG
Main engines: 2 diesels; 1 600 bhp; 2 shafts = 14 knots
Complement: 60

Former US Navy landing ships support; designed to provide close-in-fire support for amphibious assaults, but suitable for general gunfire missions.
Ex-*Doan Ngoc Tang* (ex-US *LSSL 9*) was transferred to France in 1951 *(Hallebarde* L. 9023) transferred to Japan 1956-64; returned and transferred to South Viet-Nam in 1965 for spares. Acquired by Philippines for spares 1975 as was ex-*Lulu Phu Tho* (ex-US *LSSL 101*). LS 48 and 49 and ex-US *LSSL 68* transferred 17 November 1975. Ex-US *LSSL 87* transferred September 1976.

CAMARINES SUR (old pennant number) *Vietnamese Navy*

4 Ex-US "LSIL 351" CLASS

Name	No.	Commissioned
MARINDUQUE (ex-US *LSIL 875*)	LS 36	1944
SORSOGON (ex-*Thien Kich* ex-*L 9038*, ex-US *LSIL 872*)	LS 37	1944
CAMARINES NORTE (ex-*Loi Cong* ex-*L 9034*, ex-US *LSIL 699*)	LS 52	1944
MISAMIS OCCIDENTAL (ex-*Tam Set* ex-*L 9033*, ex-US *LSIL 871*)	LS 53	1944

Displacement, tons: 227 standard; 383 full load
Dimensions, feet (metres): 158 × 22·7 × 5·3 *(48·2 × 6·9 × 1·6)*
Guns: 1—3 in; 1—40 mm; 2—20 mm; 4 MG; and up to 4 army mortars (2—81 mm; 2—60 mm)
Main engines: Diesel; 1 600 bhp; 2 shafts = 14·4 knots
Complement: 55

Designed to carry 200 troops. LS 53 originally transferred to France in 1951 and others in 1953 for use in Indochina; subsequently retransferred in 1956 to South Viet-Nam. All acquired by the Philippines 17 November 1975. Ex-US *LSIL 476* transferred for spares at same time.

SORSOGON (old pennant number)

11 Ex-US "LCM-8" CLASS

TKM 90-1, TKM 90-2, LCM 257, 258, 260-266.

TKMs transferred March 1972, 257 and 258 June 1973, remainder June 1975.

50 Ex-US "LCM-6" CLASS

LCM 224-227, 229, 231-234, 237, 239, 240, 249, 255, 256, 259 + 34

One transferred in 1955, 13 in 1971-73, 24 in November 1975, remaining dozen 1973-75.

7 Ex-US "LCVP" CLASS

LCVP 175, 181 + 5

Five to be scrapped or sold in FY 1977. Two transferred in 1955-56, one in 1965, two in 1971 and 175 and 181 in June 1973.

3 Ex-US "LCU" CLASS

Ex US-LCU 1603, 1604, 1606

Transferred from Japan November 17 1975.

SERVICE FORCES

3 Ex-US "ACHELOUS" CLASS (REPAIR SHIPS)

Name	No.	Commissioned
KAMAGONG (ex-*Aklan*, ex-USS *Romulus*, ARL 22, ex-*LST 926*)	AR 67	9 Dec 1944
NARRA (ex-USS *Krishna*, ARL, 38, ex-*LST 1149*)	AR 88	3 Dec 1945
YAKAL (ex-USS *Satyr*, ARL 23, ex-*LST 852*)	—	20 Nov 1944

Displacement, tons: 4 100 full load
Dimensions, feet (metres): 328 × 50 × 14 *(100 × 15·2 × 4·3)*
Guns: 8—40 mm (2 quad)
Main engines: Diesels (General Motors); 1 700 bhp; 2 shafts = 11·6 knots
Complement: approx 220

Converted during construction. Extensive machine shop, spare parts stowage, supplies, etc.

Transfers: AR 67 transferred to the Philippines in November 1961, AR 88 on 31 October 1971 and third on 24 January 1977.

KAMAGONG *1968, Philippine Navy*

PHILIPPINES / Miscellaneous 403

MISCELLANEOUS

1 PRESIDENTIAL YACHT

Name	No.	Builders	Commissioned
ANG PANGULO	TP 777	Ishikawajima, Japan	1959
(ex-*The President*, ex-*Roxas*, ex-*Lapu-Lapu*)			

Dimensions, feet (metres): 275 × 42·6 × 21 (83·8 × 13·0 × 6·4)
Guns: 2—20 mm
Main engines: Diesels; 5 000 bhp; 2 shafts = 18 knots
Complement: approx 90

Built as war reparation; launched in 1958. Used as presidential yacht and command ship. Originally named *Lapu-Lapu* after the chief who killed Magellan; renamed *Roxas* on 9 October 1962 after the late Manuel Roxas, the first President of the Philippines Republic, renamed *The President* in 1967 and *Ang Pangulo* in 1975.

ANG PANGULO　　　　　　　　　　　　　　　　11/1976, Dr. Giorgio Arra

1 Ex-US "ADMIRABLE" CLASS (PRESIDENTIAL YACHT)

Name	No.	Builders	Commissioned
MOUNT SAMAT (ex-*Pagasa*, ex-*Santa Maria*, ex-*Pagasa*, ex-*APO 21*, ex-USS *Quest*, AM 281)	TK 21	Gulf Shipbuilding Corporation	25 Oct 1944

Displacement, tons: 650 standard; 945 full load
Dimensions, feet (metres): 183·5 × 33 × 9·8 (56·3 × 10·1 × 3·0)
Guns: 2—20 mm
Main engines: Diesels (Cooper Bessemer); 1 710 bhp; 2 shafts = 14·8 knots
Complement: approx 60

Former US Navy minesweeper (AM). Commissioned on 25 October 1944. Transferred to the Philippines in July 1948. Used as presidential yacht and command ship.

MOUNT SAMAT　　　　　　　　　　　　　　　　10/1977, Dr. Giorgio Arra

YACHT

Name	No.	Builders	Commissioned
—	—	Vosper Thornycroft, Singapore	Dec 1975

Dimensions, feet (metres): 212·3 × 38 × 6 (64·7 × 11·6 × 1·8)
Main engines: 2 diesels; 7 500 hp = 28·5 knots

Used as a Command Ship.

Ex-US YON TYPE (FUEL BARGE)

— (Ex-US YON 279)

Transferred December 1975.

Ex-US YW TYPE (WATER CARRIERS)

LAKE LANAO (ex-US YW 125)	YW 42	
LAKE BULUAN (ex-US YW 111)	YW 33	
LAKE PAOAY (ex-US YW 130)	YW 34	

Displacement, tons: 1 235 full load
Dimensions, feet (metres): 174 × 32 × 15 (53 × 9·8 × 4·6)
Guns: 2—20 mm
Main engine: Diesel, 560 bhp; 1 shaft = 8 knots

Basically similar to YOG type but adapted to carry fresh water. Cargo capacity 200 000 gallons. Lake Lanao transferred to the Philippines in July 1948; others on 16 July 1975—YW 103 for spare parts and scrap.

3 Ex-US YO/YOG TYPE (TANKERS)

Name	No.	Commissioned
LAKE MAINIT (ex-US YO 116)	YO 35	1943
LAKE NAUJAN (ex-US YO 173)	YO 43	1943
LAKE BUHI (ex-US YO 73)	YO 78	1944

Displacement, tons: 520 standard; approx 1 400 full load
Dimensions, feet (metres): 174 × 32 × 15 (53 × 9·8 × 4·6)
Guns: several 20 mm
Main engine: Diesel; 560 bhp; 1 shaft = 8 knots

Former US Navy harbour oiler (YO) and gasoline tankers (YOG). Cargo capacity 6 570 barrels. YO 43 carries fuel oil and the YO 78 gasoline and diesel oil.

Deletions: Two craft from South Viet-Nam ex-*YOG 33* and ex-*YOG 80* accepted for scrapping and spare parts 17 November 1975.

Transfers: YO 43 transferred to the Philippines in July 1948 YO 78 in July 1967 and YO 35 in July 1975. Ex-*YO 115* and *YOG 61* transferred from US Navy to the Philippines on 16 July 1975 for spare parts and scrap.

LAKE NAUJAN　　　　　　　　　　　　　　　　10/1977, Dr. Giorgio Arra

1 Ex-US C1-M-AV1 TYPE (SUPPORT SHIP)

Name	No.	Builders	Commissioned
MACTAN (ex-USCGC *Kukui*, WAK 186, ex-USS *Colquitt*, AK 174)	TK 90	Froemming Brothers, Milwaukee	22 Sep 1945

Displacement, tons: 4 900 light; 5 636 full load
Dimensions, feet (metres): 338·5 × 50 × 18 (103·2 × 15·2 × 5·5)
Guns: 2—20 mm
Main engine: Diesel (Nordberg); 1 750 bhp; 1 shaft = 11·5 knots

Commissioned in US Navy on 22 September 1945; transferred to the US Coast Guard two days later. Subsequently served as Coast Guard supply ship in Pacific until transferred to Philippines on 1 March 1972. Used to supply military posts and lighthouses in the Philippine archipelago.

1 LIGHTHOUSE TENDER

PEARL BANK (ex-US Army LO 4, ex-Australian *MSL*)

Displacement, tons: 160 standard; 300 full load
Dimensions, feet (metres): 120 × 24·5 × 8 (36·6 × 7·5 × 2·4)
Main engines: Diesels (Fairbanks-Morse); 240 bhp; 2 shafts = 7 knots

Originally an Australian motor stores lighter; subsequently transferred to the US Army and then to the Philippines. Employed as a lighthouse tender.

4 Ex-US ARMY FS TYPE (BUOY TENDERS)

Name	No.
LAUIS LEDGE (ex-US Army FS 185)	TK 45
BOJEADOR (ex-US Army FS 203)	TK 46
LIMASAWA (ex-USCGC *Nettle* WAK 129, ex-US Army FS 169)	TK 79
— (ex-Japanese, ex-US Army FS 408)	—

Displacement, tons: 470 standard; 811 full load
Dimensions, feet (metres): 180 × 23 × 10 (54·9 × 7 × 3)
Main engine: Diesel; 1 000 shp; 1 shaft = 11 knots

Former US Army freight and supply ships. Employed as tenders for buoys and lighthouses. Ex-*FS 408* transferred 24 September 1976 by sale. *Limasawa* acquired by sale 31 August 1978.

LAUIS LEDGE　　　　　　　　　　　　　　　　1969, Philippine Navy

404 PHILIPPINES / Miscellaneous — Coast guard

1 TUG Ex-US ATR TYPE

Name	No.	Launched
IFUGAO (ex-HMS *Emphatic*, ex-US *ATR 96*)	AQ 44	27 Jan 1944

Displacement, tons: 783 full load
Dimensions, feet (metres): 143 × 33·8 × 13·5 *(43·6 × 10·3 × 4·1)*
Guns: 1—3 in *(76 mm)*/50; 2—20 mm
Main engine: Diesel; 1 500 bhp; 1 shaft = 13 knots

US-built rescue tug transferred to Royal Navy upon launching; subsequently returned to US Navy and retransferred to the Philippines in July 1948.

IFUGAO

1 TUG Ex-US ARMY

TIBOLI (ex-US Army *LT 1976*) YQ 58

Transferred March 1976.

6 TUGS Ex-US "YTL 422" CLASS

IGOROT (ex-*YTL 572*) YQ 222   ILONGOT (ex-*YTL 427*) YQ 225
TAGBANUA (ex-*YTL 429*) YQ 223   TASADAY (ex-*YTL 425*) YQ 226
— (ex-*YTL 750*) —   — (ex-*YTL 748*) —

Former US Navy 66 ft harbour tugs.

Ex-748 and 750 transferred from Japan—17 November 1975 and 24 September 1976 by sale respectively.

5 FLOATING DOCKS

YD 200 (ex-*AFDL 24*)   YD 203 (ex-*AFDL 3682*)   YD 205 (ex-*ADFL 44*)
YD 201 (ex-*AFDL 3681*)   YD 204 (ex-*AFDL 20*)

Floating dry docks built in the USA; three are former US Navy units with YD 200 transferred in July 1948, YD 204 in October 1961, and YD 205 in September 1969; two other units built specifically for Philippine service were completed in May 1952 and August 1955, respectively.

2 FLOATING CRANES

YU 206 (ex-US *YD 163*)   YU 207 (ex-US *YD 191*)

SURVEY SHIPS

Operated by Coast and Geodetic Survey of Ministry of National Defence.

Name	No.	Builders	Commissioned
PATHFINDER	—	—	1909

Displacement, tons: 1 057
Guns: 2—20 mm
Complement: 69

Ex-US Coast Guard vessel. Date of transfer unknown.

Name	No.	Builders	Commissioned
ALUNYA	—	Walkers, Maryborough, Australia	1964
ARINYA	—	Walkers, Maryborough, Australia	1962

Displacement, tons: 245 full load
Dimensions, feet (metres): 90 pp × 22 × 10·5 *(27·4 × 6·7 × 3·2)*
Main engines: 2 diesels; 336 bhp = 10 knots
Complement: 33 (6 officers, 27 ratings)

Coaster type with raised quarter-deck.

1 SURVEY SHIP

Name	No.	Builders	Commissioned
ATYIMBA	—	Walkers, Maryborough, Australia	1969

Displacement, tons: 611 standard; 686 full load
Dimensions, feet (metres): 161 × 33 × 12 *(49·1 × 10 × 3·7)*
Guns: 2—20 mm
Main engines: 2 Paxman diesels; 726 bhp = 11 knots
Range, miles: 5 000 at 8 knots
Complement: 54

Similar to HMAS *Flinders* with differences in displacement and use of davits aft instead of cranes.

ATYIMBA   1976, Dr. Giorgio Arra

COAST GUARD

The Coast Guard operates a number of Coastal Patrol Craft numbered from 90 upwards plus P 62. Of these the majority are of US construction although several come from foreign builders.

1 Ex-US COAST GUARD "BALSAM" CLASS (TENDER)

Name	No.	Builders	Commissioned
KALINGA (ex-USCGC *Redbud*, WAGL 398, ex-USNS *Redbud*, T-AKL 398)	TK 89	Marine Iron & Shipbuilding Co, Duluth	11 Sep 1943

Displacement, tons: 935 standard
Dimensions, feet (metres): 180 × 37 × 13 *(54·8 × 11·3 × 4·0)*
Guns: Unarmed
Main engines: Diesel-electric; 1 200 bhp; 1 shaft = 13 knots

Originally US Coast Guard buoy tender (WAGL 398). Transferred to US Navy on 25 March 1949 as AG 398; redesignated AKL 398 on 31 March 1949; transferred to Military Sea Transportation Service on 20 February 1952 (T-AKL 398); reacquired by Coast Guard on 20 November 1970 transferred to Philippines 17 May 1972.

KALINGA   10/1977, Dr. Giorgio Arr

POLAND

Headquarters Appointments

Commander-in-Chief of the Polish Navy:
  Vice-Admiral Ludwik Janczyszyn

Chief of the Naval Staff:
  Rear-Admiral Henryk Pietraszkiewicz

Diplomatic Representation

Naval, Military and Air Attaché in London:
  Colonel A. Wasilewski
Naval, Military and Air Attaché in Washington:
  Colonel Henryk Nowaczyk
Naval, Military and Air Attaché in Moscow:
  Brigadier General Waclaw Jagas
Naval, Military and Air Attaché in Paris:
  Colonel Marian Bugaj

Personnel

(a) 1979: 25 000 (2 800 officers and 22 200 men)
(b) 3 years national service

Bases

Gdynia, Hel, Swinoujscie.

Naval Aviation

There is a Fleet Air Arm of about 50 fixed-wing aircraft (mainly MiG-17 and IL-28) and helicopters.

Prefix to Ships' Names

ORP, standing for *Okret Polskiej Rzeczpospolitej*

Mercantile Marine

Lloyd's Register of Shipping:
  796 vessels of 3 490 587 tons gross

Strength of the Fleet

Including WOP (Coast Guard)

Type	Active
Submarines—Patrol	4
Destroyer	1
Fast Attack Craft—Missile	12
Fast Attack Craft—Torpedo	21
	(some as targets)
Large Patrol Craft	26
Coastal Patrol Craft	5
Minesweepers—Ocean	24
Minesweeping Boats	20
LCTs	23
LCPs	15+
Surveying Vessel	1
AGI	1
Training Ships	7
Salvage Ships	2
Tankers	8
TRVs	2+
Tugs	20
DGVs	3
Miscellaneous	40

DELETIONS

Destroyers

1974 *Blyskawica* (museum ship in Gdynia in place of *Burza*)
1975 *Grom* and *Wicher* (ex-"Skory" class) now immobile AA batteries at Gdynia.

Corvettes

1973 *Czuiny, Wytrwaly, Zawziety, Zrezczny, Zwinny, Zwrotny*
1974 *Grozny, Nieugiety* ("Kronshtadt" class)

Fast Attack Craft—Torpedo

1973 3 "P 6" class
1974 6 "P 6" class
1975 4 "P 6" class

SUBMARINES

4 Ex-SOVIET "WHISKEY" CLASS

ORZEL 292	**KONDOR** 294
SOKOL 293	**BIELIK** 295

Displacement, tons: 1 080 surfaced; 1 350 dived
Length, feet (metres): 249·6 *(76)*
Beam, feet (metres): 22 *(6·7)*
Draught, feet (metres): 15·1 *(4·9)*
Torpedo tubes: 6—21 in *(533 mm)*, (4 bow, 2 stern)
  12 torpedoes carried
Mines: 40 mines in lieu of torpedoes
Main machinery: Diesel-electric; 2 diesels; 4 000 hp; 2 shafts;
  Electric motors; 2 500 hp
Speed, knots: 18 surfaced; 15 dived
Range, miles: 13 000 at 8 knots (surfaced)
Complement: 54

Built in the USSR and transferred to the Polish Navy.

Radar: Snoop Plate.

SOKOL   *1971, Polish Navy*

KONDOR   *1972*

DESTROYER

1 Ex-SOVIET "SAM KOTLIN" CLASS

WARSZAWA (ex-*Spravedlivy*) 275

Displacement, tons: 2 900 standard; 3 950 full load
Length, feet (metres): 418·2 *(127·5)*
Beam, feet (metres): 42·3 *(12·9)*
Draught, feet (metres): 15·1 *(4·6)*
Missiles: SAM. Est. 20 SA-N-1 (twin launcher)
Guns: 2—5·1 in *(130 mm)* (1 twin); 4—45 mm (quad);
  8—30 mm (twin)
A/S weapons: 2—16-barrelled MBU 2500A
Torpedo tubes: 5—21 in *(533 mm)* (quin)
Main engines: Geared turbines; 2 shafts; 72 000 shp
Oil fuel, tons: 800
Range, miles: 5 500 at 16 knots
Speed, knots: 36
Complement: 285

Transferred from the USSR to the Polish Navy in 1970.

Radar: Air search: Head Net A.
Fire control: Peel Group (SA-N-1);
Wasp Head/Sun Visor B (main armament), Hawk Screech.
IFF: High Pole B.

WARSZAWA   *5/1975, C. and S. Taylor*

LIGHT FORCES

12 Ex-SOVIET "OSA" CLASS (FAST ATTACK CRAFT—MISSILE)

Displacement, tons: 160 standard; 210 full load
Dimensions, feet (metres): 127·9 × 26·6 × 5·9 *(39·0 × 8·1 × 1·8)*
Missiles: SSM; 4 SS-N-2 (single launchers)
Guns: 4—30 mm (2 twin, 1 forward, 1 aft)
Main engines: 3 M503A diesels; 12 000 bhp = 36 knots
Range, miles: 800 at 25 knots
Complement: 30

Most pennant numbers are in the 140-170 series as well as 084 and 136 and are carried on side-boards on the bridge.

Radar: Search: Square Tie.
Fire control: Drum Tilt.

"OSA" Class   1969

15 "WISLA" CLASS (FAST ATTACK CRAFT—TORPEDO)

Displacement, tons: 70 full load
Dimensions, feet (metres): 82·0 × 18·0 × 6·0 *(25 × 5·5 × 1·8)*
Guns: 2—30 mm (twin)
Torpedo tubes: 4—21 in *(533 mm)*
Main engines: Diesels; speed 30 knots

Polish built in a continuing programme since early 1970s. Most pennant numbers in 490 series but include 463.

"WISLA" Class   1975, S. Breyer

6 Ex-SOVIET "P 6" CLASS (FAST ATTACK CRAFT—TORPEDO)

Displacement, tons: 64 standard; 73 full load
Dimensions, feet (metres): 85·3 × 20 × 4·9 *(26·0 × 6·1 × 1·5)*
Guns: 4—25 mm; 8 DC
Torpedo tubes: 2—21 in *(533 mm)*
Main engines: 4 diesels; 4 800 bhp = 41 knots
Complement: 20

Acquired from the USSR in 1957-58. Torpedo tubes removed in some. At least two have been converted to target craft with reflectors similar to East German variant.

Radar: Surface search: Pot Head.
IFF: High Pole A and Dead Duck.

"P 6" Class   1971, Polish Navy

5 "OBLUZE" CLASS (LARGE PATROL CRAFT)

Note: All Polish-built Large Patrol Craft based on German R-boat design with modified superstructure and deck-houses.

Name	No.	Builders	Commissioned
—	349	Oksywie Shipyard	1965
—	350	Oksywie Shipyard	1965
—	351	Oksywie Shipyard	1965
—	352	Oksywie Shipyard	1966
—	353	Oksywie Shipyard	1966

Displacement, tons: 170
Dimensions, feet (metres): 143·0 × 19·0 × 7·0 *(43·6 × 6 × 2·1)*
Guns: 4—30 mm (2 twins)
A/S weapons: 2 internal DC racks
Main engines: 2 diesels = 20 knots

Some belong to WOP (Coast Guard).

Radar: Search: Tamirio RN 231.
Fire control: Drum Tilt (not WOP craft).

"OBLUZE" Class   1970

8 "MODIFIED OBLUZE" CLASS (LARGE PATROL CRAFT)

301   302   303   304   305   306   307   308

Displacement, tons: 150
Dimensions, feet (metres): 137·8 × 19 × 6·6 *(42 × 5·8 × 2)*
Guns: 4—30 mm
A/S weapons: 2 internal DC racks
Main engines: 2 diesels = 20 knots

Slightly smaller than original "Obluze" class. Built late 1960s.

Radar: Search: Tamirio RN 231.
Fire control: Drum Tilt.

"MODIFIED OBLUZE" Class   1972, S. Breyer

POLAND / Light forces — Mine warfare forces 407

4 "OKSYWIE" CLASS (LARGE PATROL CRAFT)

336   337   338   339

Displacement, tons: 170 standard
Dimensions, feet (metres): 134·5 × 19·0 × 6·9 (41 × 5·8 × 2·1)
Guns: 2—37 mm; 4—12·7 mm
A/S weapons: 2 DC racks
Main engines: Diesels; speed = 20 knots

Some serve with WOP (Coast Guard). Built 1962-64.

Sonar: Tamirio.

"OKSYWIE" Class (old pennant number)   1972

9 "GDANSK" CLASS (LARGE PATROL CRAFT)

340-348

Displacement, tons: 120
Dimensions, feet (metres): 124·7 × 19·2 × 5·0 (38 × 5·9 × 1·5)
Guns: 2—37 mm; 2—12·7 mm (twin)
A/S weapons: DC rails
Main engines: Diesels = 20 knots

Built in Poland in 1960. Belong to WOP (Coast Guard).

Sonar: Tamirio.

"GDANSK" Class (old pennant number)   1970

5 "PILICA" CLASS (COASTAL PATROL CRAFT)

701   702   703   704   705

Displacement, tons: 100 (approx)
Guns: 2—25 mm (twin)
Main engines: 2 diesels = 15 knots

Built in Poland since 1973. Belong to WOP (Coast Guard).

MINE WARFARE FORCES

12 "KROGULEC" CLASS (MINESWEEPERS—OCEAN)

Name	No.	Builders	Commissioned
ORLIK	643	Stocznia, Gdynia	1964
KROGULEC	644	Stocznia, Gdynia	1963
JASTRAB	645	Stocznia, Gdynia	1964
KORMORAN	646	Stocznia, Gdynia	1963
CZAJKA	647	Stocznia, Gdynia	1964
ALBATROS	648	Stocznia, Gdynia	1965
PELIKAN	649	Stocznia, Gdynia	1965
TUKAN	650	Stocznia, Gdynia	1966
KANIA	651	Stocznia, Gdynia	1966
JASKOLKA	652	Stocznia, Gdynia	1966
ZURAW	653	Stocznia, Gdynia	1967
CZALPA	654	Stocznia, Gdynia	1967

Displacement, tons: 500
Dimensions, feet (metres): 190·3 × 24·6 × 8·2 (58 × 7·5 × 2·5)
Guns: 6—25 mm (twins)
Main engines: Diesels = 16 knots

PELIKAN (old pennant number)   5/1975, C. and S. Taylor

12 SOVIET "T 43" CLASS (MINESWEEPERS—OCEAN)

Name	No.	Builders	Commissioned
ZUBR*	631	Stocznia, Gdynia	1957
TUR*	632	Stocznia, Gdynia	1957
LOS*	633	Stocznia, Gdynia	1957
DZIK*	634	Stocznia, Gdynia	1958
BIZON	635	Stocznia, Gdynia	1958
BOBR	636	Stocznia, Gydnia	1959
ROZMAK	637	Stocznia, Gdynia	1959
DELFIN	638	Stocznia, Gdynia	1960
FOKA	639	Stocznia, Gdynia	1960
MORS	640	Stocznia, Gdynia	1961
RYS	641	Stocznia, Gdynia	1961
ZBIK	642	Stocznia, Gdynia	1962

* 58 metre class.

Displacement, tons: 500 standard; 610 full load (*); 630 (remainder)
Dimensions, feet (metres): 190·2 × 28·2 × 6·9 (58 × 8·6 × 2·1) (*) 197 (60) (remainder)
Guns: 4—37 mm (twins); 4—25 mm (twins); 4—14·5 mm (twins)
A/S weapons: 2 DC throwers
Minelaying: Can lay mines
Main engines: 2 diesels; 2 shafts; 2 000 hp = 17 knots
Range, miles: 1 600 at 10 knots
Complement: 40

DELFIN (old pennant number)   1969, Polish Navy

20 "K 8" CLASS (MINESWEEPING BOATS)

Displacement, tons: 20 standard; 26 full load
Dimensions, feet (metres): 55·4 × 10·5 × 3·9 (16·9 × 3·2 × 1·2)
Guns: 2—14·5 mm (twin); 2 MG (twin)
Mines: Can lay mines
Main engines: 2 diesels; 2 shafts; 700 hp = 18 knots
Complement: 6

Now obsolescent and due for deletion.

AMPHIBIOUS FORCES

23 "POLNOCHNIY" CLASS (LCT)

BALAS	JANOW	NARWIK	
GRUNWALD 811	LENIN	WARTA	+ 17

Displacement, tons: 780 standard; 1 000 full load
Dimensions, feet (metres): 240·1 × 29·2 × 5·9 *(73·2 × 8·9 × 1·8)*
Guns: 4—30 mm (twin); 2—18-barrelled 140 mm rocket launchers
Main engines: 2 diesels; 5 000 bhp = 18 knots

Polish built in Gdansk, but same as the Soviet "Polnochniy" class—can carry six tanks. Of various types including Polish variations. Pennant numbers—811/832 and 851.

Radar: Fire control: Drum Tilt.
Navigation: Don 2.
IFF: Square Head and High Pole.

"POLNOCHNIY" Class   1978

15 + LCPs

Length, feet (metres): 70 *(21·3)* approx
Gun: 1—30 mm

Pennant numbers in 500 series. Introduced 1975. Reported as "Marabut" and "Eichstaden" classes.

LCP   8/1975

INTELLIGENCE VESSEL

1 "B 10" TYPE

BALTYK

Displacement, tons: 1 200
Measurements, tons: 658 gross; 450 deadweight
Dimensions, feet (metres): 194·3 × 29·5 × 14 *(59·2 × 9·0 × 4·3)*
Main engines: Steam; 1 000 hp = 11 knots

Trawler of B-10 type. Built in 1954 in Gdansk. Converted and structure altered.

BALTYK   9/1978, G. Koop

SURVEYING VESSEL

1 "MOMA" CLASS

KOPERNIK

Displacement, tons: 1 240 standard; 1 800 full load
Dimensions, feet (metres): 240 × 32·8 × 13·2 *(73·2 × 10 × 4)*
Main engines: Diesels = 16 knots

TRAINING SHIPS

NAVIGATOR

Details as for *Kopernik* above. Commissioned June 1975. Navigational training ship. Much altered in the upperworks and unrecognisable as a "Moma".

NAVIGATOR   9/1977, G. Koop

Note: New three masted sailing ship Dar Molodiezy to be built.

1 SAIL TRAINING SHIP

Name	No.	Builders	Commissioned
ISKRA (ex-*Pigmy*, ex-*Iskra*, ex-*St. Blanc*, ex-*Vlissingen*)	—	Muller, Foxhol	1917

Displacement, tons: 560
Dimensions, feet (metres): 128 × 25 × 10 *(39 × 7·6 × 3·0)*
Main engines: Diesels; 250 bhp = 7·5 knots
Complement: 30, plus 40 cadets

A three masted schooner with auxiliary engines. Launched in 1917. Cadet training ship. Now used for harbour training.

— (ex-*Gryf*, ex-*Zetempowiec*, ex-*Opplem*, ex-*Omsk*, ex-*Empire Contees*, ex-*Irene Oldendorf*)

Apart from holding the record in this book for name changes this 1 959 ton ship launched in 1944, is now an alongside—accommodation ship for cadets. Due for deletion.

2 "WODNIK" CLASS

WODNIK	GRYF

Displacement, tons: 1 800
Dimensions, feet (metres): 239·4 × 39·4 × ?16·4 *(73 × 12 × ?5)*
Guns: 4—30 mm (twin); 2—25 mm (twin)
Main engines: Diesel = 17 knots

Built at Gdynia. *Wodnik* launched November 1975, *Gryf* March 1976. Sisters to East German *Wilhelm Pieck*.

"WODNIK" Class   9/1976, MOD

3 "BRYZA" CLASS (TRAINING SHIPS)

ELEW   KADET   PODCHORAZY

Displacement, tons: 150
Dimensions, feet (metres): 98·4 × 9·8 × 6·4 (30 × 7 × 2)
Main engines: Diesels = 10 knots
Complement: 11 plus 26 cadets

Podchorazy commissioned 30 November 1974, Elew 5 March 1975 and Kadet July 1975.

ELEW   6/1977

TANKERS
3 "MOSKIT" CLASS

KRAB Z 1   MEDUSA Z 2   SLIMAK Z 3

Displacement, tons: approx 700
Guns: 2—30 mm (twin)

SLIMAK   1974

5 "TYPE 5"

Z 5   Z 6   Z 7   Z 8   Z 9

Lighters of 300 tons gross with diesels, converted into tankers for coastal service.

Z 7   1974

TORPEDO RECOVERY VESSELS

2 + "PAJAK" CLASS

Some of this class, including K 11, have been reported.

POLAND / Training ships — Auxiliaries

TUGS

H 1-9, DP 51, HERCULES, NATEK, NEPTUNIA, POSEIDON, SMOK, SWAROZYC, SWIATOWID + 3

"MOTYL" Class   1973

DEGAUSSING VESSELS

3 "MROWKA" CLASS

SD 11/13

Dimensions, feet (metres): 200 × 30 × 12 (61 × 9·1 × 3·6)

A class of DGVs. First completed in 1972. Unarmed.

"MROWKA" Class   1978

SALVAGE SHIPS

Name	No.	Builders	Commissioned
PIAST	—	Stocznia, Gdansk	26 Jan 1974
LECH	—	Stocznia, Gdansk	30 Nov 1974

Displacement, tons: 1 560 standard; 1 732 full load
Dimensions, feet (metres): 240 × 32·8 × 13·1 (73·2 × 10 × 4)
Guns: 8—25 mm (twins)
Main engines: 2 ZGODA diesels; 3 800 shp; 2 shafts
Speed, knots: 16·5
Range, miles: 3 000 at 12 knots

Carry a diving bell. Basically a "Moma" class hull.

"PIAST" Class   1977

AUXILIARIES

Ex-AGI Kompas now used as a barrack ship. Some 18 small diving craft, four 180 ton salvage craft.
Hydrograf and Kontroller, of 30 and 80 tons are civilian-operated survey craft.
Icebreaker Perkun of 800 is civilian-operated but available for naval use.
Some 15 other tenders.

PORTUGAL

Headquarters Appointment

Chief of Naval Staff:
  Admiral E. Sousa Leitaõ

Diplomatic Representation

Naval Attaché in Bonn:
  Captain Rogério F. Tavares Simoẽs
Defence Attaché in Brasilia:
  Colonel (PAF) João M. C. Viegas Polina
Naval Attaché in London:
  Captain I. M. Serpa Gouveia
Naval Attaché in Paris:
  Captain Antonio L. Estacio dos Reis
Naval Attaché in Washington:
  Captain Jose M. Niny dos Santos

Personnel

(a) 1979: 14 000 including 2 000 marines
(b) 2 years national service

Naval Bases

Main Base: Lisbon—Alfeite
Dockyard: Arsenal do Alfeite

Maritime Reconnaissance Aircraft

Whilst there are no aircraft belonging to the Navy, P2V Neptunes of the Portuguese Air Force are placed under naval operational control for specific maritime operations.

Prefix to Ships' Names

NRP

Strength of the Fleet

Type	Active	Building
Submarines (Patrol)	3	—
Frigates	17	—
Large Patrol Craft	10	—
Coastal Patrol Craft	17	—
Minesweepers (Coastal)	4	—
LCT	2	—
LCMs	12	1
LCA	1	—
Survey Ships and Craft	4	—
Replenishment Tanker	1	—
Sail Training Ship	1	—
Ocean Tug	1	—
Harbour Tugs	2	—
Harbour Tanker	1	—

Mercantile Marine

Lloyd's Register of Shipping:
  342 vessels of 1 239 963 tons gross

DELETIONS
(see ANGOLA section)

Frigate

1975 *Pero Escobar*

Submarine

1975 *Cachalote* ("Daphne" class) (to Pakistan)

Amphibious Forces

1975 *Alfanage, Ariete, Cimitarra* ("Alfange" class LCTs)
      LDM 401-411, 413-417 ("400" class LCMs)
      LDM 304, 309 ("300" class LCMs)
      LDM 204 ("200" class LCM)
      LDM 101, 102, 105-118 ("100" class LCMs)
      LDP 301-303, 201, 203-217, 107, 108 (21 LCAs)
1976 *Montanee, Bacamarte* ("Alfange" class)
1978 LDM 419

Large Patrol Craft

1973 *Porto Sante, Fogo, Maio* ("Maio" class)
1975 *Boavista, Brava, Santa Luzia* ("Maio" class)
1976 *Sao Nicolau*

Light Forces

1975 *Cassiopeia, Escorpião, Lira, Orion, Pegaso* ("Argos" class)
      Sabre (River patrol craft)
      Albufeira, Aljezur, Alvor ("Alvor" class)
      Aldebaran, Altair, Arcturus, Bellatrix, Espiga, Fomalhaut, Pollux, Procion, Rigel, Sirius and *Vega* ("Bellatrix" class)
      Jupiter, Marte, Mercurio, Saturno, Urano and *Venus* ("Jupiter" class)
      Antares (Coastal patrol craft)
      Azevia, Corvina, Dourada ("Azevia" class)
1976 *Argos, Centauro, Dragao, Hidra, Sagitario* ("Argos" class) (some to Angola)
      Castor, Regulus, Bicuda ("Azevia" class)

Survey Ships

1975 *Almirante Lacerda, Cavalho Araujo, Cruzeiro do Sul*
1976 *Pedro Nunes*

Service Forces

1975 *Sam Bras* (Fleet Supply Ship) (now used as accommodation ship), *Santo André*
1976 *São Rafael*

Minesweepers

1973 *Angra do Heroismo, Ponta Delgada, S. Pedro* (MSC)
      Corvo, Pico, Graciosa, S. Jorge (MSO)
1975 *Lajes, Santa Cruz* (MSC)
1976 *Horta, Velas, Vila do Porto*

PENNANT LIST

Submarines

S 163	Albacora
S 164	Barracuda
S 166	Delfin

Frigates

F 471	Antonio Enes
F 472	Almirante Pereira Da Silva
F 473	Almirante Gago Coutinho
F 474	Almirante Magalhaes Correia
F 475	João Coutinho
F 476	Jacinto Candido
F 477	Gen. Pereira d'Eca
F 480	Comandante João Belo
F 481	Comandante Hermenegildo Capelo
F 482	Comandante Roberto Ivens
F 483	Comandante Sacadura Cabral
F 484	Augusto de Castilho
F 485	Honorio Barreto
F 486	Baptiste de Andrade
F 487	João Roby
F 488	Afonso Cerqueira
F 489	Oliveira E. Carmo

Light Forces

P 370	Rio Minho
P 1140	Cacine
P 1141	Cunene
P 1142	Mandovi
P 1143	Rovuma
P 1144	Cuanza
P 1145	Geba
P 1146	Zaire
P 1147	Zambeze
P 1148	Dom Aleixo
P 1149	Dom Jeremias
P 1160	Limpopo
P 1161	Save
P 1162	Albatroz
P 1163	Acor
P 1164	Andorinha
P 1165	Aguia
P 1167	Cisne

Mine Warfare Forces

M 401	Sao Roque
M 402	Ribeira Grande
M 403	Lagoa
M 404	Rosario

Amphibious Forces

LDG 201	Bombarda
LDG 202	Alabarda
LDM 119-121	
LDM 406	
LDM 414	
LDM 418 and 420-424	
LDP 216	

Service Forces

A 520	Sagres
A 521	Schultz Xavier
A 526	Afonso de Albuquerque
A 527	Almeida Carvalho
A 5200	Mira
A 5206	São Gabriel

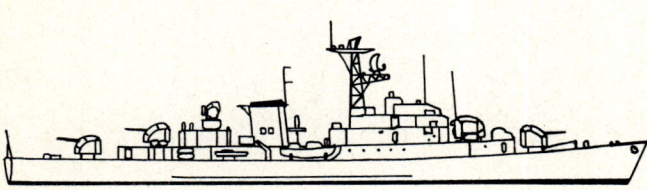
"COMANDANTE JOÃO BELO" Class

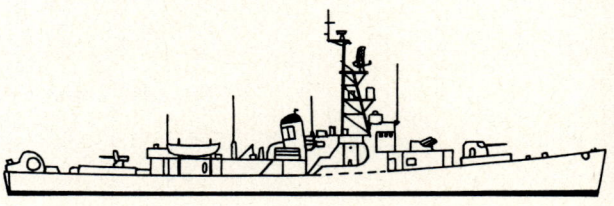
"ALMIRANTE PEREIRA DA SILVA" Class

"JOAO COUTINHO" Class

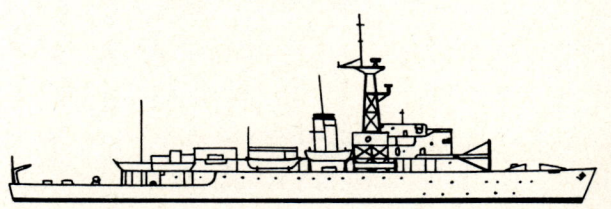
AFONSO DE ALBUQUERQUE

SUBMARINES

3 FRENCH "DAPHNE" CLASS

Name	No.	Builders	Laid down	Launched	Commissioned
ALBACORA	S 163	Dubigeon-Normandie	6 Sep 1965	13 Oct 1966	1 Oct 1967
BARRACUDA	S 164	Dubigeon-Normandie	19 Oct 1965	24 Apr 1967	4 May 1968
DELFIM	S 166	Dubigeon-Normandie	14 May 1967	23 Sep 1968	1 Oct 1969

Displacement, tons: 700 standard; 869 surfaced; 1 043 dived
Length, feet (metres): 189·6 *(57·8)*
Beam, feet (metres): 22·3 *(6·8)*
Draught, feet (metres): 15·1 *(4·6)*
Torpedo tubes: 12—21·7 in *(550 mm);* (8 bow, 4 stern)
Main machinery: SEMT-Pielstick diesels, 1 300 bhp; electric motors; 450 kW, 1 600 hp; 2 shafts
Speed, knots: 13·2 surfaced; 16 dived
Oil fuel, tons: 90
Range, miles: 2 710 at 12·5 knots surfaced; 2 130 at 10 knots snorting
Complement: 50 (5 officers; 45 men)

The prefabricated construction of these submarines was begun between 1 October 1964 and 6 September 1965 at the Dubigeon-Normandie Shipyard. They are basically similar to the French "Daphne" type, but slightly modified to suit Portuguese requirements.

Transfer: *Cachalote* transferred to Pakistan as *Ghazi* 1975.

BARRACUDA   1978, Portuguese Navy

FRIGATES

4 "COMANDANTE JOÃO BELO" CLASS

Name	No.	Builders	Laid down	Launched	Commissioned
COMANDANTE JOÃO BELO	F 480	At et Ch de Nantes	6 Sep 1965	22 Mar 1966	1 July 1967
COMANDANTE HERMENEGILDO CAPELO	F 481	At et Ch de Nantes	13 May 1966	29 Nov 1966	26 Apr 1968
COMANDANTE ROBERTO IVENS	F 482	At et Ch de Nantes	13 Dec 1966	8 Aug 1967	23 Nov 1968
COMANDANTE SACADURA CABRAL	F 483	At et Ch de Nantes	18 Aug 1967	15 Mar 1968	25 July 1969

Displacement, tons: 1 990 standard; 2 230 full load
Length, feet (metres): 321·5 *(98)* pp; 338 *(103·0)*
Beam, feet (metres): 37·7 *(11·5)*
Draught, feet (metres): 14·5 *(4·42)*
Guns: 3—3·9 in *(100 mm)*/55 (single Mod 1953); 2—40 mm/70
A/S weapons: 1—12 in quad mortar
Torpedo tubes: 6—21·7 in *(550 mm)* A/S (triple)
Main engines: SEMT-Pielstick diesels; 2 shafts; 18 760 bhp
Speed, knots: 25
Range, miles: 4 500 at 15 knots; 2 300 at 25 knots
Complement: 200 (14 officers, 186 men)

Designed for tropical service.

Construction: The prefabricated construction of these frigates was begun on 1 October 1964.

Conversion: Programme in hand for modernisation including provision of helicopter.

Design: They are similar to the French "Commandant Rivière" class except for the 30 mm guns which were replaced by 40 mm guns.

Radar: Search: DRBV 22A.
Tactical: DRBV 50.
Fire control: DRBC 31D.
Navigation: Decca RM 316.

Sonar: Search: SQS 17A.
Attack: DUBA-3A.

COMANDANTE JOÃO BELO   1978, Portuguese Navy

412 PORTUGAL / Frigates

3 "ALMIRANTE PEREIRA DA SILVA" CLASS

Name	No.	Builders	Laid down	Launched	Commissioned
ALMIRANTE PEREIRA DA SILVA	F 472 (ex-US *DE 1039*)	Estaleiros Navais (Lisnave), Lisbon	14 June 1962	2 Dec 1963	20 Dec 1966
ALMIRANTE GAGO COUTINHO	F 473 (ex-US *DE 1042*)	Estaleiros Navais (Lisnave), Lisbon	2 Dec 1963	13 Aug 1965	29 Nov 1967
ALMIRANTE MAGALHÃES CORREA	F 474 (ex-US *DE 1046*)	Estaleiros Navais de Viana do Castelo	30 Aug 1965	26 Apr 1966	4 Nov 1968

Displacement, tons: 1 450 standard; 1 914 full load
Length, feet (metres): 314·6 *(95·9)*
Beam, feet (metres): 36·68 *(11·18)*
Draught, feet (metres): 17·5 *(5·33)*
Guns: 4—3 in *(76 mm)*/50 (twin Mk 33)
A/S weapons: 2 Bofors 4-barrelled 375 mm rocket launchers; 6 (2 triple) Mk 32 A/S torpedo tubes
Main engines: De Laval dr geared turbines; 1 shaft; 20 000 shp
Boilers: 2 Foster-Wheeler, 300 psi, 850°F
Speed, knots: 27
Oil fuel, tons: 400
Range, miles: 3 220 at 15 knots
Complement: 166 (12 officers, 154 men)

After over ten years service there are certain maintenance problems with this class. A Life Extension Programme for all three is planned.

Construction: The prefabrication of *Almirante Pereira da Silva* and *Almirante Gago Coutinho* was begun in 1961 at Lisnave (formerly Navais Shipyard, Lisbon) and of *Almirante Magalhães Correa* in 1962.

Design: Similar to the US destroyer escorts of the "Dealey" class, but modified to suit Portuguese requirements.

Radar: Search: MLA-1b.
Fire control: SPG 34 (on 3 in mounts).
Navigational: Decca RM 316P.
Tactical: Type 978.
Extensive EW.

Sonar: Search: SQS 30-32A. SQA 10A (VDS).
Attack: DUBA-3A.

ALMIRANTE PEREIRA DA SILVA *10/1978, J. L. M. van der Burg*

4 "BAPTISTA DE ANDRADE" CLASS

Name	No.	Builders	Laid down	Launched	Commissioned
BAPTISTE DE ANDRADE	F 486	Empresa Nacional Bazán, Spain	1972	Mar 1973	19 Nov 1974
JOAO ROBY	F 487	Empresa Nacional Bazán, Spain	1972	3 June 1973	18 Mar 1975
AFONSO CERQUEIRA	F 488	Empresa Nacional Bazán, Spain	1973	6 Oct 1973	26 June 1975
OLIVEIRA E. CARMO	F 489	Empresa Nacional Bazán, Spain	1972	Feb 1974	Feb 1975

Displacement, tons: 1 250 standard; 1 380 full load
Dimensions, feet (metres): 277·5 × 33·8 × 11·8 *(84·6 × 10·3 × 3·6)*
Guns: 1—3·9 in *(100 mm)*/55 (single Mod. 1968); 2—40 mm /70 Bofors (single L70)
A/S weapons: 2 triple Mk 32 torpedo tubes
Main engines: 2 OEW 12-cyl Pielstick diesels; 11 000 bhp = 23·5 knots
Range, miles: 5 900 at 18 knots
Complement: 107, plus marine detachment

All four of this class were to be sold to Colombia in 1977. However this transfer did not take place.

Radar: Air search: Plessey AWS 2.
Navigation: Decca TM 626.
Fire control: Thomson SCF Pollux.

Sonar: Diodon.

OLIVEIRA E. CARMO *1978, Portuguese Navy*

6 "JOÃO COUTINHO" CLASS

Name	No.	Builders	Laid down	Launched	Commissioned
ANTONIO ENES	F 471	Empresa Nacional Bazán, Spain	Apr 1968	16 Aug 1969	18 June 1971
JOÃO COUTINHO	F 475	Blohm and Voss AG, Hamburg, Germany	Sep 1968	2 May 1969	7 Mar 1970
JACINTO CANDIDO	F 476	Blohm and Voss AG, Hamburg, Germany	Apr 1968	16 June 1969	16 June 1970
GENERAL PEREIRA D'ECA	F 477	Blohm and Voss AG, Hamburg, Germany	Oct 1968	26 July 1969	10 Oct 1970
AUGUSTO DE CASTILHO	F 484	Empresa Nacional Bazán, Spain	Aug 1968	4 July 1969	14 Nov 1970
HONORIO BARRETO	F 485	Empresa Nacional Bazán, Spain	July 1968	11 Apr 1970	15 Apr 1971

Displacement, tons: 1 203 standard; 1 380 full load
Length, feet (metres): 227·5 *(84·6)*
Beam, feet (metres): 33·8 *(10·3)*
Draught, feet (metres): 11·8 *(3·6)*
Guns: 2—3 in *(76 mm)*/50 (twin Mk 34); 2—40 mm/70
A/S weapons: 1 Hedgehog; 2 DC throwers; 2 DC racks
Main engines: 2 OEW 12-cyl Pielstick diesels; 10 560 bhp
Speed, knots: 24·4
Range, miles: 5 900 at 18 knots
Complement: 100 (9 officers, 91 men) plus marine detachment of 34

Modernisation: A programme for this class is planned.

Fire control: 40 m Mk 51 GFCS (first six).

Radar: Air search: MLA-1B.
Navigation: Decca TM 626.
Main guns: On-mounted radar SPG 34 (Mk 63 GFCS).

JACINTO CANDIDO *1978, Portuguese Navy*

PORTUGAL / Light forces — Mine warfare forces

LIGHT FORCES

10 "CACINE" CLASS (LARGE PATROL CRAFT)

Name	No.	Builders	Commissioned
CACINE	P 1140	Arsenal do Alfeite	1969
CUNENE	P 1141	Arsenal do Alfeite	1969
MANDOVI	P 1142	Arsenal do Alfeite	1969
ROVUMA	P 1143	Arsenal do Alfeite	1969
CUANZA	P 1144	Estaleiros Navais do Mendogo	May 1969
GEBA	P 1145	Estaleiros Navais do Mendogo	May 1969
ZAIRE	P 1146	Estaleiros Navais do Mendogo	Nov 1970
ZAMBEZE	P 1147	Estaleiros Navais do Mendogo	1971
LIMPOPO	P 1160	Arsenal do Alfeite	Apr 1973
SAVE	P 1161	Arsenal do Alfeite	May 1973

Displacement, tons: 292·5 standard; 310 full load
Dimensions, feet (metres): 144·0 × 25·2 × 7·1 *(44 × 7·7 × 2·2)*
Guns: 2—40 mm; 1—32-barrelled rocket launcher 37 mm
Main engines: 2 MTU 12V 538 Maybach (MTU) diesels; 4 000 bhp = 20 knots
Range, miles: 4 400 at 12 knots
Complement: 33 (3 officers, 30 men)

Radar: KH 975.

CACINE 1978, Portuguese Navy

2 "DOM ALEIXO" CLASS (COASTAL PATROL CRAFT)

Name	No.	Builders	Commissioned
DOM ALEIXO	P 1148	S. Jacintho Aveiro	7 Dec 1967
DOM JEREMIAS	P 1149	S. Jacintho Aveiro	22 Dec 1967

Displacement, tons: 62·6 standard; 67·7 full load
Dimensions, feet (metres): 82·1 × 17·0 × 5·2 *(25 × 5·2 × 1·6)*
Gun: 1—20 mm
Main engines: 2 Cummins diesels; 1 270 bhp = 16 knots
Complement: 10 (2 officers, 8 men)

Dom Jeremias in use as survey craft.

Radar: Decca 303.

DOM JEREMIAS 1973, Portuguese Navy

14 "ALBATROZ" CLASS (COASTAL PATROL CRAFT)

Name	No.	Builders	Commissioned
ALBATROZ	P 1162	Arsenal do Alfeite	1974
ACOR	P 1163	Arsenal do Alfeite	1974
ANDORINHA	P 1164	Arsenal do Alfeite	1975
AGUIA	P 1165	Arsenal do Alfeite	1975
CONDOR	P 1166	Arsenal do Alfeite	1974
CISNE	P 1167	Arsenal do Alfeite	1974
+ 8			

Displacement, tons: 45
Dimensions, feet (metres): 72 × 17 × 5 *(23·6 × 5·6 × 1·6)*
Guns: 1—20 mm; 2—50 cal MGs
Main engines: 2 Cummins diesels; 1 100 hp
Speed, knots: 20
Range, miles: 2 500 at 12 knots
Complement: 8 (1 officer, 7 men)

An increasing class of which eight more than those listed above have been reported.

Radar: Decca RM 316P.

ANDORINHA 1978, Portuguese Navy

1 COASTAL PATROL CRAFT

Name	No.	Builders	Commissioned
RIO MINHO	P 370	Arsenal do Alfeite	1957

Displacement, tons: 14
Dimensions, feet (metres): 49·2 × 10·5 × 2·3 *(15 × 3·2 × 0·7)*
Guns: 2 light MG
Main engines: 2 Alfa Romeo diesels; 130 bhp = 9 knots
Complement: 7

Built for the River Minho on the Spanish border.

RIO MINHO 1978, Portuguese Navy

MINE WARFARE FORCES

4 "SAO ROQUE" CLASS (MINESWEEPERS—COASTAL)

Name	No.	Builders	Commissioned
SAO ROQUE	M 401	CUF Shipyard, Lisbon	6 June 1956
RIBEIRA GRANDE	M 402	CUF Shipyard, Lisbon	8 Feb 1957
LAGOA	M 403	CUF Shipyard, Lisbon	10 Aug 1956
ROSARIO	M 404	CUF Shipyard, Lisbon	8 Feb 1956

Displacement, tons: 394·4 standard; 451·9 full load
Dimensions, feet (metres): 152·0 × 28·8 × 7·0 *(46·3 × 8·8 × 2·3)*
Guns: 2—20 mm (twin)
Main engines: 2 Mirrlees diesels; 2 shafts; 2 500 bhp = 15 knots
Complement: 47 (4 officers, 43 men)

Similar to British "Ton" class coastal minesweepers, laid down on 7 September 1954, under the OSP-MAP. *Lagoa* and *Sao Roque* were financed by USA and other two by Portugal. 40 mm gun removed 1972.

LAGOA (before change of armament) 1972, Portuguese Navy

414 PORTUGAL / Amphibious forces — Service forces

AMPHIBIOUS FORCES

Note: One small landing craft under construction.

2 "BOMBARDA" CLASS LDG (LCT)

Name	No.	Builders	Commissioned
BOMBARDA	LDG 201	Estaleiros Navais do Mondego	1969
ALABARDA	LDG 202	Estaleiros Navais do Mondego	1970

Displacement, tons: 510 standard; 652 full load
Dimensions, feet (metres): 184·3 × 38·7 × 6·2 *(56·2 × 11·8 × 1·9)*
Main engines: 2 Maybach-Mercedes-Benz (MTU) diesels; 910 hp = 9·5 knots
Range, miles: 2 600 at 9·5 knots
Complement: 20 (2 officers, 18 men)

Radar: Decca RM 316.

BOMBARDA   1978, Portuguese Navy

8 "LDM 400" CLASS (LCM)

LDM 406	LDM 418	LDM 421	LDM 423
LDM 414	LDM 420	LDM 422	LDM 424

Displacement, tons: 48 full load
Dimensions, feet (metres): 58·3 × 15·8 × 3·3 *(17·3 × 4·8 × 1)*
Main engines: 2 Cummins diesels; 400 hp = 10 knots

1 "LDP 200" (Ex-LD) CLASS (LCA)

Name	No.	Builders	Commissioned
—	LDP 216	Estaleiros Navais do Mondego	5 Feb 1969

Displacement, tons: 12 light; 18 full load
Length, feet (metres): 46 *(14)*
Main engines: 2 diesels; 187 bhp

3 "LDM 100" CLASS (LCM)

LDM 119	LDM 120	LDM 121

Displacement, tons: 50 full load
Dimensions, feet (metres): Length: 50 *(15·25)*
Main engines: 2 diesels; 450 bhp

All built at the Estaleiros Navais do Mondego in 1965.

SURVEY SHIPS

1 Ex-BRITISH "BAY" CLASS

Name	No.	Builders	Commissioned
AFONSO DE ALBUQUERQUE (ex-HMS *Dalrymple*, ex-HMS *Luce Bay*)	A 526	Wm. Pickersgill & Sons Ltd, Sunderland and completed by HM Dockyard, Devonport	10 Feb 1949

Displacement, tons: 1 590 standard; 2 230 full load
Length, feet (metres): 286·0 *(87·2)* pp; 307·0 *(93·6)*
Beam, feet (metres): 38·5 *(11·7)*
Draught, feet (metres): 14·2 *(4·3)*
Main engines: 4-cyl triple expansion; 2 shafts; 5 500 ihp
Boilers: 2 Admiralty 3-drum type
Speed, knots: 19·5
Range, miles: 7 055 at 9·1 knots
Complement: 109 (9 officers, 100 men)

Modified "Bay" class frigate. Laid down on 29 April 1944. Launched on 12 April 1945. Purchased from the UK in April 1966.

AFONSO DE ALBUQUERQUE   1978, Portuguese Navy

1 Ex-US "KELLAR" CLASS

Name	No.	Builders	Commissioned
ALMEIDA CARVALHO (ex-USNS *Kellar*, T-AGS 25)	A 527	Marietta Shipbuilding Co	31 Jan 1969

Displacement, tons: 1 200 standard; 1 400 full load
Dimensions, feet (metres): 190 × 39·0 × 15·0 *(58 × 11·7 × 4·5)*
Main engines: Diesel-electric; 1 shaft; 1 200 hp = 15 knots
Complement: 30 (5 officers, 25 men)

Laid down on 20 November 1962, launched on 30 July 1964. On loan from the US Navy since 21 January 1972.

Radar: One RCA CRM-N2A-30.
One Decca TM 829.

DOM JEREMIAS

See *Light Forces* section for details.

MIRA (ex-*Fomalhaut*, ex-*Arrabida*) A 5200

Displacement, tons: 30 standard
Dimensions, feet (metres): 62·9 × 15·2 × 4 *(19·2 × 4·6 × 1·2)*
Main engines: 3 Perkins diesels; 300 bhp = 15 knots
Range, miles: 650 at 8 knots (economical speed)
Complement: 6

Launched 1961. No radar.

SERVICE FORCES

1 REPLENISHMENT TANKER

Name	No.	Builders	Commissioned
SÃO GABRIEL	A 5206	Estaleiros de Viana do Castelo	27 Mar 1963

Displacement, tons: 9 000 standard; 14 200 full load
Measurement, tons: 9 854 gross; 9 000 deadweight
Dimensions, feet (metres): 479·0 × 59·8 × 26·2 *(146 × 18·2 × 8)*
Main engine: 1 Pametrada-geared turbine; 1 shaft; 9 500 shp = 17 knots
Boilers: 2
Range, miles: 6 000 at 15 knots
Complement: 98 (10 officers, 88 men)

Radar: Search: SPS 6C.
Navigation: KH 975.

SÃO GABRIEL   1978, Portuguese Navy

PORTUGAL / Service forces — QATAR / Light forces 415

1 TRAINING SHIP

Name	No.	Builders	Commissioned
SAGRES (ex-*Guanabara*, ex-*Albert Leo Schlageter*)	A 520	Blohm & Voss, Hamburg	1 Feb 1938

Displacement, tons: 1 725 standard; 1 869 full load
Dimensions, feet (metres): 293·5 × 39·3 × 17·0 *(89·5 × 12 × 4·6)*
Main engines: 2 MAN auxiliary diesels; 1 shaft; 750 bhp = 10 knots
Oil fuel, tons: 52
Range, miles: 3 500 at 6·5 knots
Complement: 153 (10 officers, 143 men)

Former German sail training ship. Built by Blohm & Voss, Hamburg. Launched in June 1937 and completed on 1 February 1938. Sister of US Coast Guard training ship *Eagle* (ex-German *Horst Wessel*) and Soviet *Tovarisch*. Taken by USA as a reparation after the Second World War in 1945 and sold to Brazil in 1948. Purchased from Brazil and commissioned in the Portuguese Navy on 2 February 1972 at Rio de Janeiro and renamed *Sagres*.
Sail area 20 793 sq ft. Height of main-mast 142 ft.

SAGRES   1973, Portuguese Navy

TUGS

1 OCEAN TUG

Name	No.	Builders	Commissioned
SCHULTZ XAVIER	A 521	Alfeite Naval Yard	14 July 1972

Displacement, tons: 900
Main engines: 2 diesels; 2 shafts; 2 400 hp = 14·5 knots
Range, miles: 3 000 at 12·5 knots

A dual purpose ocean tug and buoy/lighthouse tender ordered late in 1968.

SCHULTZ XAVIER   1978, Portuguese Navy

2 HARBOUR TUGS

RB 1 (ex-*ST 1994*)   **RB 2** (ex-*ST 1996*)

Transferred from US Navy—RB 1 December 1961, RB 2 March 1962.

1 HARBOUR TANKER

BC 3 (ex-US *YO 194*)

Transferred April 1962.

QATAR

Now possesses an expanding Marine Police Division of the Qatar Police Force. The geographical position of the state, dividing the Persian Gulf and covering Bahrain, gives this force added importance. The main oil-terminal is at Umm-Said.

Senior Officer
Commander Naval Force:
Colonel Salah Eddin Azab Saleem

Personnel
(a) 1979: 400 officers and men
(b) Voluntary service

Base
Doha

Mercantile Marine
Lloyd's Register of Shipping:
28 vessels of 87 767 tons gross

LIGHT FORCES

6 VOSPER THORNYCROFT 103 ft TYPE (LARGE PATROL CRAFT)

Name	No.	Builders	Commissioned
BARZAN	Q 11	Vosper Thornycroft Ltd	13 Jan 1975
HWAR	Q 12	Vosper Thornycroft Ltd	30 Apr 1975
THAT ASSUARI	Q 13	Vosper Thornycroft Ltd	3 Oct 1975
AL WUSAAIL	Q 14	Vosper Thornycroft Ltd	28 Oct 1975
FATEH-AL-KHAIR	Q 15	Vosper Thornycroft Ltd	22 Jan 1976
TARIQ	Q 16	Vosper Thornycroft Ltd	1 Mar 1976

Displacement, tons: 120
Dimensions, feet (metres): 110 × 21 × 5·5 *(33·5 × 6·3 × 1·6)*
Guns: 2—20 mm
Main engines: 2 Paxman 16-cyl Valenta diesels; 6 250 hp = 27 knots
Complement: 25

Ordered in 1972-73. All laid down between September 1973 and November 1974.

AL WUSAAIL   12/1974, C. and S. Taylor

2 "75 ft" COASTAL PATROL CRAFT

Length, feet (metres): 75 *(22·5)*
Guns: 2—20 mm
Main engines: 2 diesels; 1 420 hp

Built by Whittingham and Mitchell, Chertsey 1969.

2 KEITH NELSON "45 ft" TYPE (COASTAL PATROL CRAFT)

Displacement, tons: 13
Dimensions, feet (metres): 44 × 12·3 × 3·8 *(13·5 × 3·8 × 1·1)*
Guns: 1—12·7 mm; 2—7·62 mm (singles)
Main engines: 2 Caterpillar diesels; 800 hp = 26 knots
Complement: 6

The third vessel of this group has been converted into a pilot cutter.

25 FAIREY MARINE "SPEAR" CLASS (COASTAL PATROL CRAFT)

71-95

Displacement, tons: 4·3
Dimensions, feet (metres): 29·8 × 9 × 2·8 *(9·1 × 2·8 × 0·8)*
Guns: 3—7·62 mm
Main engines: 2 diesels; 290 hp; 2 shafts = 26 knots
Complement: 4

First seven ordered early 1974. Delivered 19 June 1974, 16 September 1974, 18 September 1974, 2 November 1974, December 1974, January 1975, February 1975. Contract for further five signed December 1975. Third contract for three fulfilled with delivery of two on 30 June 1975 and one on 14 July 1975. Fourth order for ten (4 Mk 1—6 Mk 2) received October 1976 and delivery effected April 1977.

FAIREY MARINE "SPEARS" *1974, Fairey Marine*

2 FAIREY MARINE "INTERCEPTOR" CLASS (FAST ASSAULT/RESCUE CRAFT)

Displacement, tons: 1·25
Dimensions, feet (metres): 25 × 8 × 2·5 *(7·9 × 2·4 × 0·8)*
Main engines: 2 Johnson outboard motors; 270 bhp = 35 knots
Range, miles: 150 at 30 knots
Complement: 3

In assault role can carry 10 troops. In rescue role carry number of life rafts. GRP catamaran hull. Delivered 28 November 1975.

RAS AL KHAIMAH
(see United Arab Emirates)

ROMANIA

Headquarters Appointment

Commander in Chief of the Navy:
 Vice-Admiral Sebastian Ulmeanu

Diplomatic Representation

Defence Attaché in London:
 Colonel Cornel Popa

Bases

Mangalia, Constanta, Tulcea (Danube base)

Personnel

(a) 1979: 10 000 officers and ratings
 (including 2 000 Coastal Defence)
(b) 2 years national service

Mercantile Marine

Lloyd's Register of Shipping:
 239 vessels of 1 428 041 tons gross

Strength of the Fleet

(No details of building programme available)

Type	Active
Corvettes	3
Large Patrol Craft	3
Fast Attack Craft (Missile)	5
Fast Attack Craft (Gun and Patrol)	18
Fast Attack Craft (Torpedo)	23
River Patrol Craft	28
Minesweepers (Coastal)	4
Minesweepers (Inshore)	10
MSBs	8
Training Ships	1 + 1
Tugs	2

(Other unconfirmed vessels listed at end of section).

CORVETTES

3 Ex-SOVIET "POTI" CLASS

V 31   V 32   V 83

Displacement, tons: 550 standard; 600 full load
Dimensions, feet (metres): 193·5 × 26·2 × 9·2 *(59 × 8 × 2·8)*
Guns: 2—57 mm (twin)
Torpedo tubes: 2—21 in *(533 mm)*
A/S weapons: 2—16-barrelled MBU 2 500
Main engines: 2 gas turbines; 2 diesels; 2 shafts; total 20 000 hp = 28 knots
Complement: 50

Transferred from the USSR in 1970.

Radar: Don, Strut Curve, Muff Cob.

"POTI" Class

LIGHT FORCES

3 Ex-SOVIET "KRONSHTADT" CLASS (LARGE PATROL CRAFT)

V-1   V-2   V-3

Displacement, tons: 310 standard; 380 full load
Dimensions, feet (metres): 170·6 × 21·5 × 9 *(52 × 6·5 × 2·7)*
Guns: 1—3·4 in; 2—37 mm (single); 6—12·7 mm (twins)
A/S weapons: 2 DC throwers; 2 depth charge racks
Main engines: 3 diesels; 3 shafts; 3 300 bhp = 24 knots
Range, miles: 1 500 at 12 knots
Complement: 65

Transferred by USSR in 1956.

Radar: Ball End.

"KRONSHTADT" Class

ROMANIA / Light forces 417

18 Ex-CHINESE "SHANGHAI" CLASS (FAST ATTACK CRAFT—GUN and PATROL)

VP 20-29   VP 31   VS 41-46   VS 52

Displacement, tons: 120 standard; 155 full load
Dimensions, feet (metres): 128 × 18 × 5·6 *(39 × 5·5 × 1·7)*
Guns: VP type: 1—57 mm; 2—37 mm (twin). VS type: 1—37 mm; 4—14·5 mm MG
A/S weapons: VS type: two 5-barrelled MBU 1200; 2 DC racks
Main engines: 4 diesels; 4 800 bhp = 30 knots
Complement: 25

Two variants of the "Shanghai" class of which the VS type (patrol A/S) is a new departure.
Built at Mangalia since 1973 in a continuing programme.

"SHANGHAI" Class—VS Type   8/1974

5 Ex-SOVIET "OSA" CLASS (FAST ATTACK CRAFT—MISSILE)

194 to 198

Displacement, tons: 160 standard; 210 full load
Dimensions, feet (metres): 127·9 × 26·6 × 5·9 *(39·0 × 8·1 × 5·9)*
Missiles: SSM; 4 SS-N-2 (single cells)
Guns: 4—30 mm (2 twin, 1 fwd, 1 aft)
Main engines: 3 M503A diesels; 12 000 bhp = 36 knots
Range, miles: 800 at 25 knots
Complement: 30

Transferred by USSR in 1964.

Radar: Search: Square Tie.
Fire control: Drum Tilt.
IFF: High Pole and Square Head.

"OSA I" Class

10 CHINESE "HU CHWAN" CLASS (FAST ATTACK CRAFT—TORPEDO)

VT 51-53 + 7

Displacement, tons: 45
Dimensions, feet (metres): 70 × 16·5 × 3·1 *(21·4 × 5 × 1)*
Guns: 4—14·5 mm (twins)
Torpedo tubes: 2—21 in *(533 mp)*
Main engines: 2 diesels; 2 200 hp = 55 knots (foilborne in calm conditions)
Range, miles: 500 cruising

Hydrofoils of the same class as the Chinese which were started in 1956.
Three with unknown pennant numbers imported from China. Further three (VT 51-53) locally
built in a continuing programme which started 1973-74.

"HU CHWAN" Class   8/1974

13 Ex-SOVIET "P 4" CLASS (FAST ATTACK CRAFT—TORPEDO)

87 to 92 + 7

Displacement, tons: 22 standard; 25 full load
Dimensions, feet (metres): 62·7 × 11·6 × 3·3 *(19·1 × 3·5 × 1·0)*
Guns: 2—14·5 mm (twin)
Torpedo tubes: 2—18 in *(457 mm)*
Main engines: 2 diesels; 2 200 bhp = 50 knots
Complement: 12

Built in 1955-56. Becoming obsolescent and ready for deletion. One has had guns removed.

Radar: Search: Skin Head.
IFF: High Pole and Dead Duck.

"P 4" Class   1971

418 ROMANIA / Light forces — Auxiliaries

9 RIVER PATROL CRAFT

VB 76-82 + 2

Dimensions, feet (metres): 105 × 16 × 3 *(32 × 4·8 × 0·9)*
Guns: 1—85 mm; 4—25 mm (twins); 2—81 mm mortars
Complement: about 25

Built in Romania from 1973 in continuing programme. Belong to Danube Flotilla.

RIVER PATROL CRAFT 8/1974

10 "VG" CLASS (RIVER PATROL CRAFT)

Displacement, tons: 40
Dimensions, feet (metres): 52·5 × 14·4 × 4 *(16 × 4·4 × 1·2)*
Guns: 2 MG
Main engines: 2 diesels; 600 hp = 18 knots
Complement: 10

Steel-hulled craft built at Galata in 1954. Obsolescent. Belong to Danube Flotilla.

9 "SM 165" CLASS (RIVER PATROL CRAFT)

SM 161-169

Locally built from 1954-56. Belong to Danube Flotilla.

MINE WARFARE FORCES

4 Ex-GERMAN "M 40" CLASS (MINESWEEPERS—COASTAL)

DESCATUSARIA DB 13   **DEMOCRATIA** DB 15
DESROBIREA DB 14   **DREPTATEA** DB 16

Displacement, tons: 543 standard; 775 full load
Dimensions, feet (metres): 206·5 × 28 × 7·5 *(62·3 × 8·5 × 2·6)*
Guns: 6—37 mm (twin); 3—20 mm (singles)
A/S weapons: 2 DCT
Main engines: Triple expansion; 2 shafts; 2 400 ihp = 17 knots
Boilers: Two 3-drum water tube
Range, miles: 1 200 at 17 knots
Complement: 80

German "M Boote" design—designed as coal-burning minesweepers. Built at Galati. Converted to oil in 1951.

DEMOCRATIA and DREPTATEA 1968

10 Ex-SOVIET "T 301" CLASS (MINESWEEPERS—INSHORE)

DR 19, 21-29

Displacement, tons: 150 standard; 180 full load
Dimensions, feet (metres): 128 × 18 × 4·9 *(39 × 5·5 × 1·5)*
Guns: 2—37 mm; 4—12·7 mm MG (twins)
Main engines: 2 diesels; 1 440 bhp; 2 shafts = 17 knots
Complement: 30

Transferred to Romania by the USSR in 1956-60. Probably half of these are non-operational. Two deleted 1975.

8 Ex-POLISH "TR-40" CLASS (MSBs)

VD-241 VD-242 VD-243 VD-244 VD-245 VD-246 VD-247 VD-248

Displacement, tons: 50 standard; 70 full load
Dimensions, feet (metres): 92 × 13·6 × 2·5 *(28 × 4·1 × 0·7)*
Guns: 2 MG (twin)
Main engines: 2 diesels; 2 shafts = 14 knots
Complement: 18

Employed on shallow water and river duties. These were originally a Polish class begun in 1955 but completed in Romania in late 1950s.

TRAINING SHIPS

Name	No.	Builders	Commissioned
MIRCEA	—	Blohm & Voss, Hamburg	29 Mar 1939

Displacement, tons: 1 604
Dimensions, feet (metres): 239·5 oa; 267·3 (with bowsprit) × 39·3 × 16·5 *(73; 81·5 × 12 × 5)*
Sail area: 18 830 sq ft
Main engines: Auxiliary MAN 6-cyl diesel; 500 bhp = 9·5 knots
Complement: 83 + 140 midshipmen for training

Laid down on 30 April 1938. Launched on 22 September 1938. Refitted at Hamburg in 1966.

1 TRAINING SHIP

Name	No.	Builders	Commissioned
NEPTUN	—	Szczecin	1976

Of 5 600 tons and launched 29 April 1976.

TUGS

4 "ROSLAVL" CLASS

VITEAZUL RM 101   **VOINICUL** —   **+ 2**

Displacement, tons: 450
Dimensions, feet (metres): 135 × 29·3 × 11·8 *(41·2 × 8·9 × 3·6)*
Main engines: Diesels; 1 250 hp = 12·5 knots
Complement: 28

Built in Galata shipyard 1953-54.

AUXILIARIES

Although details are not available the following have been reported—two survey craft, three tankers, ten transports and twelve "Braila" class LCUs.

MIRCEA 1970, Michael D. J. Lennon

SABAH
(see also Malaysia)

Base

Labuan

2 "91 ft" PATROL BOATS

Name	No.	Builders	Commissioned
SRI GUMANTONG	—	Vosper Thornycroft Ltd, Singapore	8 Apr 1970
SRI LABUAN	—	Vosper Thornycroft Ltd, Singapore	6 Apr 1970

Sri Gumantong launched 18 August 1969. On detachment from Royal Malaysian Police (see Malaysian section for details).

1 YACHT

Name	No.	Builders	Commissioned
PUTRI SABAH	—	Vosper Thornycroft Ltd, Singapore	11 July 1971

Displacement, tons: 117
Dimensions, feet (metres): 91 × 19 × 5·5 *(27·8 × 5·8 × 1·7)*
Main engine: 1 diesel = 12 knots
Complement: 22

2 "55 ft" PATROL BOATS

Name	No.	Builders	Commissioned
SRI SEMPORNA	—	Chevertons, Isle of Wight	Feb 1975
SRI BANGJI	—	Chevertons, Isle of Wight	Feb 1975

Displacement, tons: 50
Dimensions, feet (metres): 55 × 15 × 3 *(16·8 × 4·6 × 0·9)*
Gun: 1—MG
Main engines: Diesels; 1 200 hp = 20 knots
Range, miles: 300 at 15 knots
Complement: 11

ST. KITTS

Senior Appointment

Chief of Police:
O. A. Hector

Base

Basseterre

Mercantile Marine

Lloyd's Register of Shipping:
1 vessel of 256 tons

1 FAIREY MARINE "SPEAR" CLASS

Displacement, tons: 4·3
Dimensions, feet (metres): 29·8 × 9 × 2·8 *(9·1 × 2·8 × 0·8)*
Guns: Mountings for 2—7·62 mm
Main engines: 2 diesels; 360 hp = 30 knots
Complement: 2

Ordered for the Police in June 1974—delivered 10 September 1974.

ST. LUCIA

Mercantile Marine

Lloyd's Register of Shipping:
3 vessels of 928 tons gross

1 BROOKE MARINE PATROL CRAFT

HELEN

Displacement, tons: 14
Dimensions, feet (metres): 40 × 11·7 × 4 *(12·2 × 3·4 × 1·3)*
Main engines: 2 Cummins V8 diesels; 2 shafts = 21 knots (12 at present)

Completed 20 July 1970.

ST. VINCENT

Senior Appointment

Commissioner of Police:
R. J. O'Garro

Base

Kingstown

Mercantile Marine

Lloyd's Register of Shipping:
25 vessels of 8 428 tons gross

1 BROOKE MARINE PATROL CRAFT

CHATOYER

Displacement, tons: 15
Dimensions, feet (metres): 45 × 13 × 3·8 *(13·7 × 4 × 1·2)*
Guns: 3 MG
Main engines: 2 Cummins diesels; 370 hp; 2 shafts = 21 knots

CHATOYER 1976, St. Vincent Police

SAUDI ARABIA

Ministerial

Minister of Defence:
Amir Sultan ibn 'Abd al-'Aziz

Diplomatic Representation

Defence Attaché in London:
Colonel A. Ismail

Personnel

(a) 1979: 2 200 officers and men
(b) Voluntary service

Bases

Jiddah, Al Qatif/Jubail, Ras Tanura, Dammam, Yanbo, Ras al-Mishab.

Coast Guard Bases

Haqi, Ash Sharmah, Qizan.

Strength of the Fleet

	Active	Building
Corvettes—Missile	—	4
Minesweepers	4	—
Fast Attack Craft—Missile	—	9
Fast Attack Craft—Torpedo	3	—
Large Patrol Craft	1	—
Coastal Patrol Craft and Patrol Boats	115	—
Hovercraft	8	—
MSCs	2	2
LCUs	4	—
Tugs	2	—
Royal Yacht	1	—

New Construction

In January 1972 an agreement was signed with the USA for a ten-year programme to provide si[x] corvettes, four MSC, two coastal patrol craft, four LCTs, three training ships and two tugs. I[n] addition orders have been placed in France, Germany and the UK.
To man a proportion of these a considerable training programme is under way in the USA[.]

Mercantile Marine

Lloyd's Register of Shipping:
154 vessels of 1 246 112 tons gross

CORVETTES

4 NEW CONSTRUCTION

Name	No.	Builders	Commissioned
BADR	612	Tacoma Boatbuilding Co, Washington, USA	Aug 1980
AL YARMOUK	614	Tacoma Boatbuilding Co, Washington, USA	Jan 1981
HITTEEN	616	Tacoma Boatbuilding Co, Washington, USA	Apr 1981
TABUK	618	Tacoma Boatbuilding Co, Washington, USA	July 1981

Displacement, tons: 720
Dimensions, feet (metres): 234·5 × 27·6 × 8·8 *(71·4 × 8·4 × 2·7)*
Missiles: SSM; 8 Harpoon (single cells)
Guns: 1—76 mm (Compact); 1—81 mm mortar; 2—40 mm mortars; 2—20 mm
A/S weapons: 6 (2 triple) Mk 32 A/S torpedo tubes
Main engines: CODOG; 1 General Electric gas turbine; 16 500 hp; 2 diesels; 3 000 hp
Speed, knots: 30 on gas turbines; 20 on diesels
Complement: 53 (5 officers, 48 ratings)

Ordered 30 August 1977. Laid down dates December 1978, July 1979, October 197[9] January 1980.

Radar: Surface warning: SPS 60.
Air warning: SPS 40B.
Fire control system: Mk 92.

Sonar: SQS 56.

MINE WARFARE FORCES

4 "MSC 322" CLASS (MINESWEEPERS—COASTAL)

Name	No.	Builders	Commissioned
ADDRIYAH	MSC 412	Peterson Builders, Wisconsin	1978
AL-QUYSUMAH	MSC 414	Peterson Builders, Wisconsin	1978
AL-WADEEAH	MSC 416	Peterson Builders, Wisconsin	1979
SAFWA	MSC 418	Peterson Builders, Wisconsin	1979

Displacement, tons: 320 standard; 375 full load
Dimensions, feet (metres): 144 × 27 × 8·3 *(43·9 × 8·2 × 2·5)*
Guns: 2—20 mm (twin)
Main engines: 2 Wankesha L1616 diesels; 1 200 hp; 2 shafts = 14 knots

Ordered on 30 September 1975 under the International Logistics Programme.
Laid down—412, 12 May 1976; 414, 24 August 1976; 416, 28 December 1976; 418 March 1977[.]
412 launched 20 December 1976, 418 on 7 December 1977.

LIGHT FORCES

9 FAST ATTACK CRAFT (MISSILE)

Name	No.	Builders	Commissioned
AS SADDIQ	511	Peterson Builders, Wisconsin	Apr 1980
AL FAROUQ	513	Peterson Builders, Wisconsin	Aug 1980
ABDUL AZIZ	515	Peterson Builders, Wisconsin	Nov 1980
FAISAL	517	Peterson Builders, Wisconsin	Apr 1981
KAHLID	519	Peterson Builders, Wisconsin	May 1981
AMYR	521	Peterson Builders, Wisconsin	July 1981
TARIQ	523	Peterson Builders, Wisconsin	Oct 1981
OQBAH	525	Peterson Builders, Wisconsin	Jan 1982
ABU OBAIDAH	527	Peterson Builders, Wisconsin	Apr 1982

Displacement, tons: 320
Dimensions, feet (metres): 184·4 × 25 × 5·8 *(56·2 × 7·6 × 1·8)*
Missiles: 2 twin Harpoon launchers
Guns: 1—76 mm OTO Melara; 1—81 mm mortar; 2—40 mm mortars; 2—20 mm
Main engines: CODOG; 1 GE gas turbine; 16 500 hp; 2 diesels; 1 500 hp
Speed, knots: 38 (gas turbine); 18 (diesel)
Complement: 35

Ordered 16 February 1977. First craft (511) laid down November 1977. Last (527) to be laid dow[n] May 1980. First launch June 1979—last, August 1981.

3 GERMAN "JAGUAR" CLASS (FAST ATTACK CRAFT—TORPEDO)

Name	No.	Builders	Commissioned
DAMMAM	—	Lürssen, Vegesack	1969
KHABAR	—	Lürssen, Vegesack	1969
MACCAH	—	Lürssen, Vegesack	1969

Displacement, tons: 160 standard; 190 full load
Dimensions, feet (metres): 139·4 × 23·4 × 7·9 *(42·5 × 7 × 2·4)*
Guns: 2—40 mm
Torpedo tubes: 4—21 in *(533 mm)*
Main engines: 4 MTU diesels; 12 000 bhp = 42 knots
Complement: 33 (3 officers, 30 men)

Refitted in Germany 1976.

"JAGUAR" Class   1974, Reiner Nerli

SAUDI ARABIA / Light forces

1 USCG TYPE (LARGE PATROL CRAFT)

RYADH

Displacement, tons: 100 standard
Dimensions, feet (metres): 95·0 × 19·0 × 6·0 (29 × 5·8 × 1·9)
Gun: 1—40 mm
Main engines: 4 diesels; 2 shafts; 2 200 bhp = 21 knots
Complement: 15

Steel hulled patrol boat transferred to Saudi Arabia in 1960.

8 "P 32 TYPE" (COASTAL PATROL CRAFT)

Displacement, tons: 90
Dimensions, feet (metres): 105 × 17·6 × 9·8 (32 × 5·3 × 2·9)
Guns: 2—20 mm
Main engines: 2 MGO 12V diesels; 2 700 bhp; 2 shafts = 29 knots
Range, miles: 1 500 at 15 knots
Complement: 17

Wooden hulls sheathed with GRP. Sisters to Moroccan "El Wacil" class. Ordered from CMN (Cherbourg) January 1976.

P 32 Type 1976, CMN

12 "RAPIER" CLASS (COASTAL PATROL CRAFT)

Length, feet (metres): 50 (15·2)
Guns: 2 MG
Main engines: 2 diesels; 1 300 bhp = 28 knots
Complement: 9

Three completed 1976, remainder in 1977 by Halter Marine, New Orleans.

20 "45 ft" COASTAL PATROL CRAFT

Built by Whittingham and Mitchell, Chertsey, England. Armed with one ·5 cal MG and powered with two 362 hp diesels.

2 Ex-US "40 ft" UTILITY BOATS

Transferred late 1960s.

43 "C-80" CLASS (COASTAL PATROL CRAFT)

Displacement, tons: 2·8
Dimensions, feet (metres): 29·3 × 9·3 × 1·5 (8·9 × 2·9 × 0·6)
Main engines: 1 Caterpillar diesel; 210 bhp; Castoldi pump jet unit = 20 knots
Gun: 1 MG

All delivered 1975 to Saudi Coast Guard. Built by Northshore Yacht Yards under sub-contract to Planning Associates Ltd (London). Contract 1974.

"C-80" Class 1975, Northshore

10 "23 ft HUNTRESS" PATROL BOATS

Built by Fairey Marine, Hamble, England. Capable of 20 knots with a cruising range of 150 miles and a complement of four.

20 "20 ft" PATROL BOATS

Smaller editions of the 45 ft craft above, built by Whittingham and Mitchell.

8 SRN-6 HOVERCRAFT

50   051   +6

Displacement, tons: 10 normal (load 8 200 lbs)
Dimensions, feet (metres): 48·4 × 25·3 × 15·9 (height) (14·8 × 7·7 × 4·8)
Main engine: 1 Gnome model 1050 gas turbine.
Speed, knots: 58

Acquired from British Hovercraft Corporation Ltd, between February and December 1970.

SRN-6 hovercraft 1971

SERVICE FORCES

1 TRAINING SHIP

Name	No.	Builders	Commissioned
TEBUK	—	Bayerischen Schiffbau, Erlenbach, FDR	Dec 1977

Displacement, tons: 350
Dimensions, feet (metres): 196·8 × 32·8 × 5·8 *(60 × 10 × 1·8)*
Main engines: 2 MTU diesels; 5 260 bhp = 20 knots
Complement: 60

Ordered 1976.

1 SALVAGE TUG

JEDDAH 13

Displacement, tons: 350
Length, feet (metres): 112·8 *(34·4)*
Main engines: 2 diesels; 800 hp = 12 knots

Built at Hayashikane, Shimonoseki. Laid down 19 August 1977.

2 Ex-US YTB TYPE (HARBOUR TUGS)

TUWAIG (ex-*YTB 837*) EN 111   DAREEN (ex-*YTB 838*) EN 112

Displacement, tons: 350 full load
Dimensions, feet (metres): 109 × 30 × 13·8 *(31·1 × 9·8 × 4·5)*
Main engines: 2 diesels; 2 000 bhp; 2 shafts
Complement: 12

Transferred by US Navy 15 October 1975.

4 Ex-US LCUs

AL QIAQ (ex-*SA 310*) 212
AS SULAYEL (ex-*SA 311*) 214
AL ULA (ex-*SA 312*) 216
AFIF (ex-*SA 313*) 218

Transferred June/July 1976.

1 ROYAL YACHT

Name	No.	Builders	Commissioned
AL RIYADH	—	Van Lent (de Kaag), Netherlands	1978

Displacement, tons: 650
Dimensions, feet (metres): 212 × 32 × 10 *(69·5 × 10·5 × 3·3)*
Main engines: 2 diesels; 6 300 hp = 26 knots
Complement: 26 (accommodation for 24 passengers)

Ordered 12 December 1975. Laid down 6 May 1976. Launched 17 December 1977. Cost £7 million.

Fittings: Helicopter pad, sauna, swimming pool, hospital with intensive care unit.

2 AIR SEA-RESCUE LAUNCHES

ASR 1   ASR 2

With two diesels of 1 230 hp and capable of 25 knots. Belong to Ministry of Transportation.

SENEGAL

Ministerial

Minister of Armed Forces:
Amadu Sall

Personnel

(a) 1979: approx 350 officers and men
(b) 2 years conscript service

Base

Dakar

Mercantile Marine

Lloyd's Register of Shipping:
80 vessels of 29 404 tons gross

DELETION

Light Forces

1974 *Sénégal*

LIGHT FORCES

3 "P 48" CLASS (LARGE PATROL CRAFT)

Name	No.	Builders	Commissioned
SAINT LOUIS	—	Ch. Navales Franco-Belges	1 Mar 1971
POPENGUINE	—	Soc. Français de Constructions Navales	10 Aug 1974
PODOR	—	Soc. Français de Constructions Navales	13 July 1977

Displacement, tons: 250 full load
Dimensions, feet (metres): 156 × 23·3 × 8·1 *(47·5 × 7·1 × 2·5)*
Guns: 2—40 mm
Main engines: 2 MGO diesels; 1 shaft; 2 400 bhp = 23 knots
Range, miles: 2 000 at 18 knots
Complement: 33

Saint Louis laid down on 20 April 1970, launched on 5 August 1970. *Popenguine* laid down in December 1973, launched 22 March 1974. Sisters to *Malaika* of Malagasy, *Vigilant* and *Le Valereux* of Ivory Coast and "Bizerte" Class of Tunisian Navy. *Podor* ordered August 1975, laid down December 1975, launched 20 July 1976.

"P 48" Class   1972

2 Ex-FRENCH VC TYPE

Name	No.	Builders	Commissioned
CASAMANCE (ex-*VC 5*, ex-*P 755*)	—	Constructions Mécaniques de Normandie, Cherbourg	1958
SINE-SALOUM (ex-*Reine N'Galifourou*, ex-*VC 4*, ex-*P 754*)	—	Constructions Mécaniques de Normandie, Cherbourg	1958

Displacement, tons: 75 standard; 82 full load
Dimensions, feet (metres): 104·5 × 15·5 × 5·5 *(31·8 × 4·7 × 1·7)*
Guns: 2—20 mm
Main engines: 2 Mercedes-Benz (MTU) diesels; 2 shafts; 2 700 bhp = 28 knots
Complement: 15

Former French patrol craft (Vedettes de Surveillance Côtière). *Casamance* was transferred from France to Senegal in 1963. *Sine-Saloum* was given to Senegal on 24 August 1965 after having been returned to France by the Congo in February 1965.

SINE-SALOUM   1967, Senegalese Navy

SENEGAL / Light forces — SIERRA LEONE

1 TRAWLER TYPE

LES ALMADIES

Used previously on fishery protection.

12 VOSPER 45 ft TYPE

Dimensions, feet (metres): 45 × 13·2 × 3·5 (13·7 × 4 × 1·1)
Guns: 1—12·7 mm; 2—7·62 mm
Main engines: 2 diesels; 920 hp = 25 knots
Complement: 6

1 FAIREY MARINE "LANCE" CLASS (COASTAL PATROL CRAFT)

Displacement, tons: 15·7 light
Dimensions, feet (metres): 48·7 × 15·3 × 4·3 (14·8 × 4·7 × 1·3)
Guns: 2—7·62 mm
Main engines: 2 General Motors 8 V 71 T1; 850 hp = 24 knots
Complement: 7

Completed June 1977 for customs service. Has capacity for boarding party of 12. Air conditioned.

"LANCE" Class   1977, Fairey Marine

1 FAIREY MARINE "SPEAR" CLASS
(COASTAL PATROL CRAFT)

Displacement, tons: 4·3
Dimensions, feet (metres): 29·8 × 9 × 2·8 (9·1 × 2·8 × 0·8)
Guns: 1—12·7 mm; 2—7·62 mm
Main engines: 2 diesels; 360 hp = 30 knots
Complement: 4

Completed 28 February 1974 for Senegal Customs.

2 FAIREY MARINE "HUNTRESS" CLASS
(COASTAL PATROL CRAFT)

Dimensions, feet (metres): 23·2 × 8·8 × 2·8 (7·1 × 2·7 × 0·8)
Main engine: 1 diesel; 180 hp; 29 knots
Complement: 2

Completed March 1974 for Senegal Customs.

AMPHIBIOUS FORCES

1 Ex-FRENCH EDIC

LA FALENCE (ex-9095) (LCT)

Displacement, tons: 250 standard; 670 full load
Dimensions, feet (metres): 193·5 × 39·2 × 4·5 (59 × 12 × 1·3)
Guns: 2—20 mm
Main engines: 2 MGO diesels; 2 shafts; 1 000 bhp = 8 knots
Complement: 6

Launched 7 April 1958. Transferred 1 July 1974.

2 Ex-US "LCM 6" CLASS

DIOU LOULOU (ex-6723)   **DIOMBOS** (ex-6733)

Transferred July 1968. Of 26 tons.

1 TENDER

CRAME JEAN

18 ton fishing boat used as training craft.

SEYCHELLES

Mercantile Marine

Lloyd's Register of Shipping:
10 vessels of 53 646 tons gross

1 LANDING CRAFT (TANK)

Name	No.	Builders	Commissioned
CINQ JUIN	—	La Perrière, France	1979

Displacement, tons: 350
Dimensions, feet (metres): 186·8 × 38 × 6 (56·9 × 11·6 × 1·9)
Main engines: 2 Poyaud diesels; 880 hp = 9 knots

Ordered 12 December 1977. Although government owned this ship may be commercially operated.

SHARJAH
(see United Arab Emirates)

SIERRA LEONE

Personnel

(a) 1979: 150 officers and men
(b) Voluntary service

Base

Freetown

Mercantile Marine

Lloyd's Register of Shipping:
11 vessels of 4 689 tons gross

3 Ex-CHINESE "SHANGHAI II" CLASS (FAST ATTACK CRAFT—GUN)

001   002   003

Displacement, tons: 120 standard; 155 full load
Dimensions, feet (metres): 127·3 × 17·7 × 5·2 (38·8 × 5·4 × 1·6)
Guns: 4—37 mm; 4—25 mm
A/S weapons: 8 DCs
Mines: Mine rails can be fitted
Main engines: 4 diesels; 4 800 hp = 30 knots
Complement: 25

Transferred by China June 1973.
Radar: Skin Head.

"SHANGHAI" Class

424 SINGAPORE / Introduction — Mine warfare forces

SINGAPORE

Ministerial

Minister of Defence:
  Howe Yoon Chong

Headquarters Appointment

Commander of the Republic of Singapore Navy:
  Colonel Khoo Eng An

Personnel

(a) 1979: 3 000 officers and men
(b) 2-3 years national service and regular volunteers

Prefix to Ships' Names

RSS

Mercantile Marine

Lloyd's Register of Shipping:
  954 vessels of 7 489 205 tons gross

LIGHT FORCES

6 + 2 LÜRSSEN "TNC 45" CLASS (FAST ATTACK CRAFT—MISSILE)

Name	No.	Builders	Commissioned
SEA WOLF	P 76	Lürssen Werft, Vegesack	1972
SEA LION	P 77	Lürssen Werft, Vegesack	1972
SEA DRAGON	P 78	Singapore Shipbuilding & Engineering Co	1974
SEA TIGER	P 79	Singapore Shipbuilding & Engineering Co	1974
SEA HAWK	P 80	Singapore Shipbuilding & Engineering Co	1975
SEA SCORPION	P 81	Singapore Shipbuilding & Engineering Co	1975

Displacement, tons: 230
Dimensions, feet (metres): 147·3 × 23 × 7·5 *(44·9 × 7 × 2·3)*
Missiles: SSM; 5 Gabriel (single cells)
Guns: 1—57 mm; 1—40 mm
Main engines: 4 MTU diesels; 4 shafts; 14 400 hp = 38 knots
Complement: 40

Designed by Lürssen Werft who built the first pair, *Sea Wolf* and *Sea Lion,* which arrived autumn 1972. Another pair ordered from Singapore S and E Co in 1977.

Fire control: Hollandse Signaal WM28.

SEA DRAGON Lürssen Werft

6 VOSPER THORNYCROFT DESIGN 3 "TYPE A" (FAST ATTACK CRAFT—GUN)

Name	No.	Builders	Commissioned
INDEPENDENCE	P 69	Vosper Thornycroft Ltd, UK	8 July 1970
FREEDOM	P 70	Vosper Thornycroft Private Ltd, Singapore	11 Jan 1971
JUSTICE	P 72	Vosper Thornycroft Private Ltd, Singapore	23 Apr 1971

Displacement, tons: 100 standard
Dimensions, feet (metres): 109·6 × 21·0 × 5·6 *(33·5 × 6·4 × 1·8)*
Guns: 1—40 mm (fwd); 1—20 mm (aft)
Main engines: 2 Maybach (MTU 16 V538) diesels; 7 200 bhp = 32 knots
Range, miles: 1 100 at 15 knots
Complement: 19 to 22

On 21 May 1968 the Vosper Thornycroft Group announced the receipt of an order for six of their 110 ft fast patrol boats for the Republic of Singapore. Two sub-types, the first of each *(Independence* and *Sovereignty)* built in UK, the remainder in Singapore. *Independence* was launched 15 July 1969. *Freedom* 18 November 1969 and *Justice* 20 June 1970.

INDEPENDENCE 1971, Vosper Thornycroft

3 "TYPE B" (FAST ATTACK CRAFT—GUN)

Name	No.	Builders	Commissioned
SOVEREIGNTY	P 71	Vosper Thornycroft Ltd, Portsmouth, England	Feb 1971
DARING	P 73	Vosper Thornycroft Private Ltd, Singapore	18 Sep 1971
DAUNTLESS	P 74	Vosper Thornycroft Private Ltd, Singapore	1971

Displacement, tons: 100 standard; 130 full load
Dimensions, feet (metres): 109·6 × 21·0 × 5·6 *(33·5 × 6·4 × 1·8)*
Guns: 1—76 mm Bofors; 1—20 mm Oerlikon
Main engines: 2 Maybach (MTU 16 V538) diesels; 7 200 bhp = 32 knots
Range, miles: 1 100 at 15 knots
Complement: 19 (3 officers, 16 ratings)

Sovereignty was launched 25 November 1969. *Dauntless* launched 6 May 1971. Steel hulls of round bilge form. Aluminium alloy superstructure.

Fire control: Hollandse Signaal M26.

DARING 1976, A. G. Burgoyne

MINE WARFARE FORCES

2 Ex-US "REDWING" CLASS (MINESWEEPERS—COASTAL)

JUPITER (ex-USS *Thrasher* MSC 203)	M 101
MERCURY (ex-USS *Whippoorwill* MSC 207)	M 102

Displacement, tons: 370 full load
Dimensions, feet (metres): 144 × 28 × 8·2 *(43·9 × 8·5 × 2·5)*
Gun: 1—20 mm
Main engines: 2 General Motors diesels; 1 760 bhp; 2 shafts = 12 knots
Range, miles: 2 500 at 10 knots
Complement: 39

Transferred by sale 5 December 1975.

MERCURY 1976, Singapore Navy

SINGAPORE / Training ships — SOLOMON ISLANDS 425

TRAINING SHIPS

1 "FORD" CLASS (LARGE PATROL CRAFT)

Name	No.	Builders	Commissioned
PANGLIMA	P 68	United Engineers, Singapore	May 1956

Displacement, tons: 119 standard; 134 full load
Dimensions, feet (metres): 117·0 × 20·0 × 6·0 (35·7 × 6·1 × 1·8)
Guns: 1—40 mm/60; 1—20 mm
Main engines: Paxman YHAXM supercharged B 12 diesels = 14 knots
Oil fuel, tons: 15
Complement: 15 officers and men

Laid down in 1954. Launched on 14 January 1956. Similar to the British seaward defence boats of the "Ford" class. Transferred to the Royal Malaysian Navy on the formation of Malaysia. Transferred to the Republic of Singapore in 1967.

PANGLIMA   1975, Singapore Navy

Name	No.	Builders	Commissioned
ENDEAVOUR	P 75	Shiffswerft Oberwinter, Germany	30 Sep 1970

Displacement, tons: 250
Dimensions, feet (metres): 135 × 25 × 8 (40·9 × 7·6 × 2·4)
Guns: 2—20 mm
Main engines: 2 Maybach diesels; 2 600 bhp
Range, miles: 800 at 8 knots
Complement: 24

ENDEAVOUR   1976, Singapore Navy

AMPHIBIOUS FORCES

6 Ex-US "511-1152" CLASS (LSTs)

Name	No.	Builders	Commissioned
ENDURANCE (ex-USS Holmes County, LST 836)	L 201 (ex-A81)	American Bridge Co	25 Nov 1944
EXCELLENCE (ex-US LST 629)	L 202 (ex-A82)	Chicago Bridge & Iron Co	28 July 1944
INTREPID (ex-US LST 579)	L 203 (ex-A83)	Missouri Valley B and I Co	21 June 1944
RESOLUTION (ex-US LST 649)	L 204 (ex-A84)	Chicago Bridge & Iron Co	26 Oct 1944
PERSISTENCE (ex-US LST 613)	L 205 (ex-A85)	Chicago Bridge & Iron Co	19 May 1944
PERSEVERANCE (ex-US LST 623)	L 206 (ex-A86)	Chicago Bridge & Iron Co	21 June 1944

Displacement, tons: 1 653 light; 4 080 full load
Dimensions, feet (metres): 328·0 × 50·0 × 14·0 (100 × 15·2 × 4·3)
Guns: 8—40 mm (4 twin) (see note)
Main engines: General Motors diesels; 2 shafts; 1 700 bhp = 11·6 knots
Complement: 120

ENDURANCE   1978, D. N. Brigham

Endurance loaned from the US Navy on 1 July 1971 and sold on 5 December 1975. Remainder transferred 4 June 1976. *Endurance* leased commercially in 1976; *Excellence* and *Intrepid* active; *Resolution*, *Persistence* and *Perseverance* in reserve. Carry two LCUs on davits.

Appearance: *Excellence* underwent a conversion in 1977 in which a goal-post derrick was added forward of the bridge and the lattice mast was replaced by a pole mast.

Guns: *Excellence* does not mount a twin 40 mm in the bow, having no gun-tub.

6 LANDING CRAFT (RPL)

BRANI, BERLAYER + 4

Of 30-50 tons—all ex-Australian.

SURVEY CRAFT
(Operated by Singapore Port Authority)

MATA IKAN	UTARA	GEMA
Of 125 tons. Launched 1967.	Of 23 tons. Launched 1965.	Of 5 tons. Launched 1966.

POLICE PATROL CRAFT

4 VOSPER THORNYCROFT TYPE

Name	No.	Builders	Commissioned
—	PX 10	Vosper Thornycroft Ltd, Portsmouth, England	1969
—	PX 11	Vosper Thornycroft Ltd, Portsmouth, England	1969
—	PX 12	Vosper Thornycroft Ltd, Portsmouth, England	1969
—	PX 13	Vosper Thornycroft Ltd, Portsmouth, England	1969

Displacement, tons: 40 standard
Length, feet (metres): 87·0 (26·5)
Guns: 2—20 mm

Built for marine police duties.

SOLOMON ISLANDS

Mercantile Marine

Lloyd's Register of Shipping:
10 vessels of 2 018 tons gross

1 "CARPENTARIA" CLASS

Displacement, tons: 27 full load
Dimensions, feet (metres): 52·5 × 16·4 × 3·9 (16 × 5 × 1·2)
Guns: 2 MGs
Main engines: 2 MTU diesels; 1 400 bhp = 30 knots

Built by De Havilland Marine, Homebush Bay, Australia. Launched December 1978.

SOMALIA

Personnel
(a) 1979: 350 officers and men
(b) Voluntary service

General
With the withdrawal of the Soviet element from Somalia and the cessation of imports of equipment and spares the state of this navy will deteriorate unless replacements and refits are arranged outside the Soviet bloc.

Bases
Berbera, Mogadishu and Kismayu

Mercantile Marine
Lloyd's Register of Shipping:
  19 vessels of 72 961 tons gross

LIGHT FORCES

3 Ex-SOVIET "OSA II" CLASS (FAST ATTACK CRAFT—MISSILE)

Displacement, tons: 165 standard; 210 full load
Dimensions, feet (metres): 127·9 × 26·6 × 5·9 *(39 × 8·1 × 1·8)*
Missiles: SSM; 4—SS-N-2 (single launchers)
Guns: 4—30 mm (twins)
Main engines: 3 M504 diesels; 15 000 bhp = 36 knots
Range, miles: 800 at 25 knots
Complement: 30

Transferred in December 1975.

"OSA II" Class

4 Ex-SOVIET "MOL" CLASS (FAST ATTACK CRAFT—TORPEDO/PATROL)

Displacement, tons: 240 full load
Dimensions, feet (metres): 127·9 × 26·6 × 5·9 *(39 × 8·1 × 1·8)*
Guns: 4—30 mm (twins)
Torpedo tubes: 4—21 in *(533 mm)* can be mounted on sponsons
Main engines: 3 M503 diesels; 13 000 bhp; 3 shafts = 40 knots
Complement: 25

Transferred 1976. Some do not carry torpedo tubes.

"MOL" Class   *1976*

4 Ex-SOVIET "P6" CLASS (FAST ATTACK CRAFT—TORPEDO)

Displacement, tons: 66 standard; 75 full load
Dimensions, feet (metres): 85·3 × 20·0 × 4·9 *(26 × 6·1 × 1·5)*
Guns: 4—25 mm
Torpedo tubes: 2—21 in *(533 mm)*
Main engines: 4 diesels; 4 shafts; 4 800 hp = 41 knots
Range, miles: 450 at 30 knots
Complement: 20

Transferred in 1968.

5 Ex-SOVIET "POLUCHAT I" CLASS (LARGE PATROL CRAFT)

Displacement, tons: 100 standard; 120 full load
Dimensions, feet (metres): 97·1 × 19 × 4·8 *(29·6 × 5·8 × 1·5)*
Guns: 2—14·5 mm
Main engines: 2 diesels; 2 400 hp = 20 knots
Complement: 15

Transferred two in 1965, three in 1966.

AMPHIBIOUS FORCES

1 Ex-SOVIET "POLNOCHNIY" CLASS (LCT)

Displacement, tons: 1 000 full load
Dimensions, feet (metres): 239·4 × 29·5 × 5·9 *(73 × 9 × 1·8)*
Guns: 2—14·5 mm (twin)
Rocket launchers: 2—18-barrelled 140 mm launchers
Main engines: 2 diesels; 5 000 bhp = 18 knots

Can carry six tanks. Transferred December 1976.

Soviet "POLNOCHNIY" Class

4 Ex-SOVIET "T4" CLASS (LCM)

Displacement, tons: 70
Dimensions, feet (metres): 62·3 × 14·1 × 3·3 *(19 × 4·3 × 1)*
Main engines: 2 diesels; 2 shafts = 10 knots

Transferred 1968-69.

SOUTH AFRICA

Ministerial

Minister of Defence:
Mr. P. W. Botha (Prime Minister)

Headquarters Appointments

Chief of South African Defence Force:
General M. A. de M. Malan, SSA, SM
Chief of the Navy:
Vice-Admiral J. C. Walters, SM
Chief of Naval Staff (Operations):
Rear-Admiral G. N. Green

Diplomatic Representation

Defence Attaché in Bonn:
Captain P. E. Blitzker
Armed Forces Attaché in Buenos Aires:
Captain W. H. Kelly, SM
Naval Attaché in London:
Captain P. R. Le Roux
Naval Attaché in Paris:
Commander T. J. Honiball SM
Defence Attaché in Washington:
Commodore W. N. Du Plessis

Personnel

(a) 1974: Total 4 204 (475 officers, 2 329 ratings and 1 400 national service ratings)
1975: Total 4 250 (475 officers, 2 375 ratings and 1 400 national service ratings)
1976: Total 4 700 (500 officers, 2 800 ratings and 1 400 national service ratings)
1977: Total 4 800 (500 officers, 2 900 ratings and 1 400 national service ratings)
1978: Total 3 960 (560 officers, 2 000 ratings and 1 400 national service ratings)
(b) Voluntary service plus 18 months national service

Naval Bases

HM Dockyard at Simonstown was transferred to the Republic of South Africa on 2 April 1957. The new submarine base at Simonstown, SAS *Drommedaris*, incorporating offices, accommodation and operations centre alongside a Synchrolift marine elevator, capable of docking all South African ships except the *Tafelberg*, was opened in July 1972.
A new Maritime Headquarters was opened in March 1973 at Silvermine on the Cape Peninsula.

Air Sea Rescue Base

The SAAF Maritime Group base at Langebaan was transferred to the South African Navy on 1 November 1969, becoming SAN Sea Rescue Base (SAS *Flamingo*). The ASR launches were given Naval Coastal Forces numbers to replace SAAF "R" numbers.

Maritime Air

The SAAF operates an MP group consisting of 18 Piaggio P166s and 7 Shackleton MR 3. In addition 11 Wasp helicopters are available for embarkation in the frigates.

Prefix to Ships' Names

SAS (Suid Afrikaanse Skip)

Strength of the Fleet

Type	Active	Building
Submarines (Patrol)	3	—
Frigates	3	—
Fast Attack Craft—Missile	6	6
Large Patrol Craft	4	—
Minesweepers (Coastal) (see note)	10	—
Survey Ships	3	—
Fleet Replenishment Ship	1	—
BDV	1	—
TRV	1	—
Training Ship	1	—
Tugs	2	—
SAR Launches	4	—

Note: (a) Two MSCs converted for minehunting and two for patrol duties.
(b) It is reported that the RSA is planning to acquire one or more Israeli-designed corvettes (see Israeli section for details).

Mercantile Marine

Lloyd's Register of Shipping:
295 vessels of 660 735 tons gross

DELETIONS

Destroyers

1976 *Simon van der Stel*
1978 *Jan van Riebeeck*

Frigates

1976 *Vrystaat* (sunk as target in Apr)
Good Hope, Transvaal,
Pietermaritzburg (shore accommodation ship)

Survey Ship

1972 *Natal* (sunk as target Sep)

Training Ship

1975 HDML 1204

PENNANT LIST

Submarines

S 97	Maria Van Riebeeck
S 98	Emily Hobhouse
S 99	Johanna Van der Merwe

Frigates

F 145	President Pretorius
F 147	President Steyn
F 150	President Krüger

Mine Warfare Forces

M 291	Pietermaritzburg
M 1207	Johannesburg
M 1210	Kimberley
M 1212	Port Elizabeth
M 1213	Mosselbaai
M 1214	Walvisbaai
M 1215	East London
M 1498	Windhoek
M 1499	Durban

Service Forces

A 243	Tafelberg
A 324	Protea
—	Agulhas

Light Forces

P 285	Somerset (BDV)
P 1556	Pretoria
P 1557	Kaapstad
P 3105	Gelderland
P 3120	Nautilus
P 3125	Rijger
P 3126	Haerlem
P 3127	Oosterland
P 3148	Fleur (TRV)

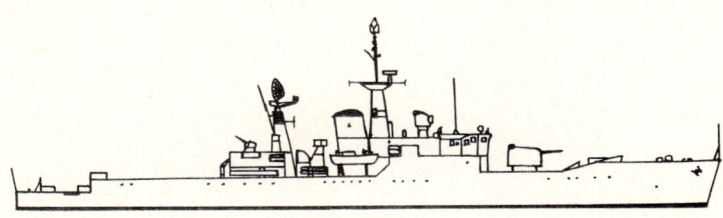

"PRESIDENT" Class

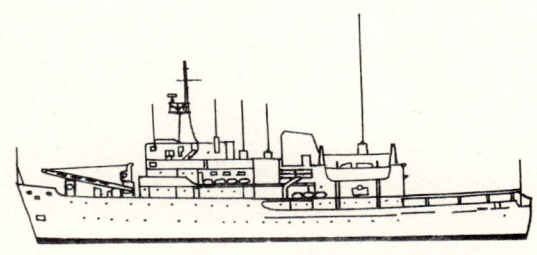

PROTEA

SUBMARINES

3 FRENCH "DAPHNE" CLASS

Name	No.	Builders	Laid down	Launched	Commissioned
MARIA VAN RIEBEECK	S 97	Dubigeon—Normandie, Nantes-Chantenay	14 Mar 1968	18 Mar 1969	22 June 1970
EMILY HOBHOUSE	S 98	Dubigeon—Normandie, Nantes-Chantenay	18 Nov 1968	24 Oct 1969	25 Jan 1971
JOHANNA VAN DER MERWE	S 99	Dubigeon—Normandie, Nantes-Chantenay	24 Apr 1969	21 July 1970	21 July 1971

Displacement, tons: 850 surfaced; 1 040 dived
Length, feet (metres): 190·3 *(58)*
Beam, feet (metres): 22·3 *(6·8)*
Draught, feet (metres): 15·4 *(4·7)*
Torpedo tubes: 12—21·7 in *(550 mm)* (8 bow, 4 stern)
Main machinery: SEMT-Pielstick diesel electric;
  2 diesels; 1 300 bhp; 2 electric motors; 1 600 hp; 2 shafts
Speed, knots: 16 surfaced and dived
Range, miles: 4 500 at 5 knots (snorting)
Complement: 47 (6 officers, 41 men)

First submarines ordered for the South African Navy. They are of the French "Daphne" design, similar to those built in France for that country, Pakistan and Portugal and also built in Spain.

EMILY HOBHOUSE   *1973, South African Navy*

FRIGATES

3 "PRESIDENT" CLASS

Name	No.	Builders	Laid down	Launched	Commissioned
PRESIDENT PRETORIUS	F 145	Yarrow & Co, Scotstoun	21 Nov 1960	28 Sep 1962	4 Mar 1964
PRESIDENT STEYN	F 147	Alex Stephen & Sons, Govan	20 May 1960	23 Nov 1961	25 Apr 1963
PRESIDENT KRUGER	F 150	Yarrow & Co, Scotstoun	6 Apr 1959	20 Oct 1960	1 Oct 1962

Displacement, tons: 2 250 standard; 2 800 full load
Dimensions, feet (metres): 370 × 41·1 × 17·1 *(112·8 × 12·5 × 5·2)*
Aircraft: 1 Wasp helicopter
Guns: 2—4·5 in *(115 mm)*/(twin Mk 6); 2—40/70 mm Bofors; 4—3 pdr (saluting)
A/S weapons: 6 (2 triple) Mk 32 torpedo tubes; 1 Limbo 3-barrel DC mortar
Main engines: 2 sets dr geared turbines; 2 shafts; 30 000 shp
Boilers: 2 Babcock & Wilcox 550 psi; 850°F
Speed, knots: 30
Oil fuel, tons: 430
Range, miles: 4 500 at 12 knots
Complement: 203 (13 officers, 190 men)

PRESIDENT STEYN *(President Pretorius similar)*   *12/1976, South African Navy*

Originally "Rothesay" Type 12 frigates, *President Kruger* arrived in South Africa on 27 March 1963.

Modernisation: Refitted to carry a Wasp A/S helicopter, with hangar and landing deck. To accommodate this, one Limbo A/S mortar was removed and the two single 40 mm remounted on the hangar roof. *President Kruger* completed refit and recommissioned on 5 August 1969, *President Steyn* completed refit in 1971, when *President Pretorius* was taken in hand although delayed to take advantage gained from the previous conversions. Refit completed 12 July 1977. The refits were carried out at S.A. Naval Dockyard, Simonstown and included replacement of the lattice foremast by a truncated pyramid tower. *Kruger* completed further modernisation in 1979. Small differences exist between all three ships.

Radar: Surveillance: Thomson CSF Jupiter.
Air/Surface search: Type 293.
Fire control: Elsag NA9C.

PRESIDENT KRUGER *(before modernisation)*   *7/1976, USN*

LIGHT FORCES

6 + 6 "RESHEF" CLASS (FAST ATTACK CRAFT—MISSILE)

Displacement, tons: 430 full load
Dimensions, feet (metres): 204 × 25 × 8 *(62·2 × 7·8 × 2·4)*
Missiles: SSM; 6 Gabriel (single cells)
Guns: 2—76 mm/62 (single Compact)
Main engines: 4 Maybach diesels; 2 shafts; 5 340 hp = 32 knots
Range, miles: ? 1 500 at 30 knots; 4 000+ at economical speed
Complement: 45

Contract signed with Israel in late 1974. Three built in Haifa and reached South Africa in July 1978. First to be built in Durban was completed late 1978 and last pair soon after. Further six ordered in a contract signed 15 November 1977. These to be built at Durban.

"RESHEF" Class   *1974, Michael D. J. Lennon*

5 BRITISH "FORD" CLASS (LARGE PATROL CRAFT)

Name	No.	Builders	Commissioned
GELDERLAND (ex-*Brayford*)	P 3105	A. & J. Inglis Ltd, Glasgow	30 Aug 1954
NAUTILUS (ex-*Glassford*)	P 3120	Dunston, Thorne	23 Aug 1955
RIJGER	P 3125	Vosper Ltd, Portsmouth	1958
HAERLEM	P 3126	Vosper Ltd, Portsmouth	1959
OOSTERLAND	P 3127	Vosper Ltd, Portsmouth	1959

Displacement, tons: 120 standard; 160 full load
Dimensions, feet (metres): 117·2 × 20·0 × 7 *(35·7 × 6·1 × 2·1)*
Gun: 1—40 mm
A/S weapons: 2 DCT in *Oosterland* and *Rijger*
Main engines: 2 Davey Paxman diesels; Foden engine on centre shaft; 1 100 bhp = 18 knots
Complement: 19

Gelderland was purchased from Britain, and handed over to South Africa at Portsmouth on 30 August 1954. Second ship, *Nautilus* was handed over 23 August 1955, *Rijger* was launched on 6 February 1958, *Haerlem* on 18 June 1958, *Oosterland* on 27 January 1959. All three of these later ships are fitted with Vosper roll damping fins. *Haerlem* had a charthouse added aft as an inshore survey craft.

RIJGER   *12/1976, South African Navy*

SOUTH AFRICA / Mine warfare forces — Torpedo recovery vessel

MINE WARFARE FORCES

10 BRITISH "TON" CLASS (MINESWEEPERS—COASTAL and MINEHUNTERS)

Name	No.	Builders	Commissioned
JOHANNESBURG (ex-HMS *Castleton*)	M 1207	White, Southampton	1958
KIMBERLEY (ex-HMS *Stratton*)	M 1210	Dorset Yacht Co	1958
PORT ELIZABETH (ex-HMS *Dumbleton*)	M 1212	Harland & Wolff, Belfast	1958
MOSSELBAAI (ex-HMS *Oakington*)	M 1213	Harland & Wolff, Belfast	1959
WALVISBAAI (ex-HMS *Packington*)	M 1214	Harland & Wolff, Belfast	1959
EAST LONDON (ex-HMS *Chilton*)	M 1215	Cook Welton and Gemmell	1958
WINDHOEK	M 1498	Thornycroft, Southampton	1959
DURBAN	M 1499	Camper & Nicholson, Gosport	1957
PRETORIA (ex-HMS *Dunkerton*)	P 1556	Goole Shipbuilding Co	1954
KAAPSTAD (ex-HMS *Hazleton*)	P 1557	Cook Welton and Gemmell	1954

Displacement, tons: 360 standard; 425 full load
Dimensions, feet (metres): 152·0 × 28·8 × 8·2 *(49·8 × 9·4 × 2·7)*
Guns: 1—40 mm Bofors; 2—20 mm
Main engines: Mirrlees diesels in *Kaapstad* and *Pretoria*, 2 500 bhp; Deltic diesels in remainder; 3 000 bhp = 15 knots
Range, miles: 2 300 at 13 knots

KAAPSTAD (as Patrol Craft)   1977, Michael D. J. Lennon

Kaapstad and *Pretoria*, open bridge and lattice mast, were purchased in 1955 and converted with enclosed bridge and lattice mast in 1973. *Windhoek*, enclosed bridge and tripod mast, was launched by Thornycroft, Southampton, on 27 June 1957. *Durban*, enclosed bridge and tripod mast, was launched at Camper & Nicholson, Gosport, on 12 June 1957. *East London* and *Port Elizabeth*, transferred from the Royal Navy at Hythe on 27 October 1958, sailed for South Africa in November 1958. *Johannesburg*, *Kimberley* and *Mosselbaai* were delivered in 1959. *Walvisbaai* was launched by Harland & Wolff, Belfast on 3 July 1958 and delivered in 1959.

Minehunters: *Kimberley* converted to minehunter 1977-78—second undergoing conversion.

Patrol Craft: Some now used on patrol duties. (Note change of pennant numbers for *Kaapstad* and *Pretoria*).

EAST LONDON   1977, Michael D. J. Lennon

SURVEY SHIPS

Name	No.	Builders	Commissioned
PROTEA	A 324	Yarrow (Shipbuilders) Ltd	23 May 1972

Displacement, tons: 1 930 standard; 2 750 full load
Length, feet (metres): 260·1 *(79·3)*
Beam, feet (metres): 49·1 *(15·0)*
Draught, feet (metres): 15·1 *(4·6)*
Aircraft: 1 helicopter
Main engines: 4 Paxman/Ventura diesels geared to 1 shaft and cp propeller; 4 880 bhp
Speed, knots: 16
Range, miles: 12 000 at 11 knots
Oil fuel, tons: 560
Complement: Total 121 (10 officers, 104 ratings plus 7 scientists)

An order was placed with Yarrow (Shipbuilders) Ltd, for a "Hecla" class survey ship on 7 November 1969. Equipped for hydrographic survey with limited facilities for the collection of oceanographical data and for this purpose fitted with special communications equipment, naval surveying gear, survey launches and facilities for helicopter operations. Hull strengthened for navigation in ice and fitted with a transverse bow thrust unit and passive roll stabilisation system. Laid down 20 July 1970. Launched 14 July 1971.

PROTEA   1973, South African Navy

HAERLEM P 3126

Converted July 1963 from "Ford" class for survey duties. Complement 23. See Light Forces section for details.

FLEET REPLENISHMENT SHIP

Name	No.	Builders	Commissioned
TAFELBERG (ex-*Annam*)	A 243	Nakskovs Skibsvaert, Denmark	1959

Measurement, tons: 12 500 gross; 18 980 deadweight
Dimensions, feet (metres): 559·8 × 72·1 × 30·2 *(170·6 × 21·9 × 9·2)*
Main engines: Burmester and Wain diesels; 8 420 bhp = 15·5 knots
Complement: 100

Built as Danish East Asiatic Co tanker. Launched on 20 June 1958. Purchased by the Navy in 1965. Accommodation rehabilitated by Barens Shipbuilding & Engineering Co, Durban with extra accommodation, air conditioning, re-wiring for additional equipment, new upper RAS (replenishment at sea) deck to contain gantries, re-fuelling pipes. Remainder of conversion by Jowies, Brown & Hamer, Durban. A helicopter flight-deck was added aft during refit in 1975.

TAFELBERG   1977, Michael D. J. Lennon

TORPEDO RECOVERY VESSEL

Name	No.	Builders	Commissioned
FLEUR	P 3148	Dorman Long (Africa) Ltd	3 Dec 1969

Displacement, tons: 220 standard; 257 full load
Dimensions, feet (metres): 121·5 × 27·5 × 11·1 *(39·8 × 9·0 × 3·6)*
Main engines: 2 Paxman Ventura diesels; 1 400 bhp
Complement: 22 (4 officers, 18 ratings)

Combined Torpedo Recovery Vessel and Diving Tender.

FLEUR   1973, South African Navy

430 SOUTH AFRICA / Boom defence vessel — Department of Transport

BOOM DEFENCE VESSEL

Name	No.	Builders	Commissioned
SOMERSET (ex-HMS *Barcross*)	P 285	Blyth Dry Dock & S.B. Co Ltd	14 Apr 1942

Displacement, tons: 750 standard; 960 full load
Dimensions, feet (metres): 182·0 × 32·2 × 11·5 *(59 × 10·5 × 3·8)*
Main engines: Triple expansion; 850 hp = 11 knots
Boilers: 2 single ended
Oil fuel, tons: 186

Originally two in the class. Laid down on 15 April 1941, launched on 21 October 1941. Engined by Swan, Hunter & Wigham Richardson Ltd, Tyne.

SOMERSET 12/1976, South African Navy

TRAINING VESSEL

Name	No.	Builders	Commissioned
NAVIGATOR	—	Fred Nicholls (Pty) Ltd, Durban	1964

Navigational Training Vessel. 75 tons displacement; 63 × 20 ft; two Foden diesels, 200 bhp = 9·5 knots. Based at Naval College, Gordon's Bay. Round bilge fishing boat wooden hull.

AIR SEA RESCUE LAUNCHES

2 FAIREY MARINE "TRACKER" CLASS

Name	No.	Builders	Commissioned
—	P 1554	Groves and Gutteridge, Cowes	1973
—	P 1555	Groves and Gutteridge, Cowes	1973

Displacement, tons: 26
Dimensions, feet (metres): 64 × 16 × 5 *(19·5 × 4·9 × 1·5)*
Main engines: 2 diesels; 1 120 bhp = 28 knots

Built by subsidiary of Fairey Marine.

P 1554 1973, South African Navy

2 KROGERWERFT TYPE

Name	No.	Builders	Commissioned
—	P 1551 (ex-*R 31*)	Krogerwerft, Rendsburg	1962
—	P 1552 (ex-*R 30*)	Krogerwerft, Rendsburg	1961

Displacement, tons: 87
Dimensions, feet (metres): 96 × 19 × 4 *(29·3 × 5·8 × 1·2)*
Main engines: 2 diesels; 4 480 bhp = 30 knots

P 1552 1977, Michael D. J. Lennon

There are also two 24 ft Tenders.

TUGS

Name	No.	Builders	Commissioned
DE NEYS	—	Globe Engineering Works Ltd, Cape Town	23 July 1969
DE NOORDE	—	Globe Engineering Works Ltd, Cape Town	Dec 1961

Displacement, tons: 180 and 170 respectively
Dimensions, feet (metres): 94·0 × 26·5 × 15·75 and 104·5 × 25·0 × 15·0 *(30·8 × 8·7 × 5·2; 34·2 × 8·2 × 4·9)*
Main engines: 2 Lister-Blackstone diesels; 2 shafts; 608 bhp = 9 knots
Complement: 10

De Neys fitted with Voith-Schneider screws.

DE NOORDE 12/1976, South African Navy

DEPARTMENT OF TRANSPORT

1 ANTARCTIC SURVEY AND SUPPLY VESSEL

Name	No.	Builders	Commissioned
AGULHAS	—	Mitsubishi, Shimonoseki	31 Jan 1978

Measurement, tons: 3 050 deadweight
Dimensions, feet (metres): 358·3 × 59 × 19 *(109·2 × 18 × 5·8)*
Aircraft: 2 helicopters
Main engines: 2 Mirrlees-Blackstone diesels; 6 000 shp; 1 shaft = 14 knots
Range, miles: 8 200 at 14 knots
Complement: 40 (92 spare berths)

Ordered 11 August 1976. Laid down 14 June 1977. Launched 30 September 1977.

AGULHAS 1978, Michael D. J. Lennon

SPAIN

Ministerial

First Deputy Premier for Security Affairs and National Defence:
  Lieutenant-General Manuel Gutierrez Mellado
Defence Minister:
  Senor Agustin Rodriguez Sahagun

Headquarters Appointments

(In 1977 all three Service Ministries were combined in a single Ministry of Defence)

Chief of the Naval Staff:
  Admiral Excmo Sr Don Antonio Arevalo Pelluz
Chief of Fleet Support:
  Admiral Excmo Sr Don Miguel Romero Moreno
Vice Chief of the Naval Staff:
  Vice-Admiral Excmo Sr Don Manuel Manso Quijano

Commands

Commander-in-Chief of the Fleet:
  Vice-Admiral Excmo Sr Don José R. Caamano Fernandez
Captain General, Cantabrian Zone:
  Admiral Excmo Sr Don José Maria de la Guardia y Oya
Captain General, Straits Zone:
  Admiral Excmo Sr Don Vicente Alberto y Lloveres
Captain General, Mediterranean Zone:
  Admiral Excmo Sr Don Juan Carlos Muñoz Delgado y Pinto
Commandant General, Marines:
  Lieutenant-General Excmo Sr Don Jose Rincon Dominguez

Diplomatic Representation

Naval Attaché in London:
  Captain Don J. M. Gonzalez-Aldama
Naval Attaché in Washington:
  Captain Sr Don Obrador Sierra

Personnel

a) 1979: Total 44 800 (4 085 officers, 32 669 ratings, 8 046 civil branch)
   Infanteria de Marina 10 614 (614 officers, 10 000 marines)
b) 18 months national service

Bases

Ferrol: Cantabrian Zone HQ—Ferrol arsenal, support centre at Graña, naval school at Marín, Pontevedra, electronics school at Rios, Vigo
Cadiz: Straits Zone HQ—La Carraca arsenal, naval air base at Rota, amphibious base at Puntales, Tarifa small ships' base
Cartagena: Mediterranean Zone HQ—Cartagena arsenal, support station at La Algameca, support base at Mahón, Minorca, Palma arsenal, Majorca, submarine weapons school at Sóller, Majorca
Canaries: Las Palmas arsenal (new base planned)

Naval Air Service

- 5 Harrier AV-8A (Matador) (5 on order for delivery 1980)
- 2 Harrier TAV-8A (Matador)
- 11 Bell 47G (and derivatives) helicopters
- 6 AB 212 (with AS-12 missiles) (6 more may be ordered)
- 4 AB 204B
- 10 Sikorsky SH-3D Sea King (with AS-12 missiles) (6 more may be ordered)
- 12 Hughes 500 M(ASW)
- 4 Bell AH-1G "Hueycobra"
- 1 Sikorsky S-55 (phasing out)
- 2 Piper Comanche
- 2 Twin Comanche

New Aircraft: It is planned to provide;
- 12 Hughes 316HM Cayuse (ASW version)
- 5 Matador (Harrier)

Infanteria de Marina: This Marine Corps consists of four "Tercios" (intermediate between a regiment and a brigade) based in Ferrol, Cadiz, Cartagena and Puntales (Cadiz). The first three are for base defence while the fourth, Tercio de Armada, is a brigade-sized assault force. This last has a landing battalion, a support fighting group and a logistic group and is provided with LVTP-7, M-48 tanks (to be replaced by AMX30), SP artillery including M-52 (105 mm), M-56 (90 mm), Panhard M-3 and AML-245 with 60 mm mortars, and towed OTO Melara 105 mm guns. Infantry support weapons include 106 mm M-40 recoilless rifles, 120, 81 and 60 mm ECIA mortars and Rasura radar. The Pegaso 3550 3 ton amphibious truck is now being introduced.

Strength of the Fleet

Type	Active	Building
Submarines—Patrol	8	4
Aircraft Carriers	1	1
Destroyers	11	—
Frigates	17	6
Fast Attack Craft (Patrol)	12	—
Large Patrol Craft	0	10
Coastal Patrol Craft	36	—
Inshore Patrol Craft	42	—
LSD	1	—
Attack Transports	2	—
LSTs	3	—
LCTs	7	—
Minor Landing Craft	26	—
Minesweepers—Ocean	4	—
Minesweepers—Coastal	12	—
Survey Ships	6	—
Replenishment Tanker	1	—
Harbour Tankers	13	2
Training Ship	1	—
Tugs (Ocean, Coastal and Harbour)	27	4
Miscellaneous	52	—

New Construction

Because of financial considerations the current programme has been cut to the following; one aircraft carrier; three FFG-7 class frigates; eight corvettes and four "Agosta" class submarines.

Fleet Deployment

1. Flota
   (a) Grupo Aeronaval: (based at Rota)
       Dédalo with appropriate escorts
   (b) Mando de Escoltas: (HQ at Ferrol)
       11th Squadron; 5 "Gearing" Class, 2 "Roger de Lauria" Class (based at Ferrol)
       21st Squadron; 4 "Fletcher" Class, *Descubierta* (based at Cartagena)
       31st Squadron; 5 "Baleares" class (based at Ferrol)
   (c) Mando Anfibio: (based at Puntales, Cádiz)
       All Amphibious Forces
   (d) Mando de Medidas contra Minado: (HQ at Palma de Mallorca)
       MSCs 21,25,27,29 (based at Graña/Ferrol)
       MSO 41 (based at Rota)
       All remaining MCM forces (based at Palma)
   (e) Flotilla de Submarinos: (based at Cartagena)
       All submarines
2. Support units, Cantabrian Zone:
   2 Frigates, 7 Patrol Craft, 8 Tugs, 2 Water Boats
   16 Service Craft (Ferrol)
   6 Service Craft (Graña)
   2 Frigates, 1 Yacht, 7 Service Craft (Marín)
   1 MSC, 4 Patrol Craft (Coruña, Vigo, Tuy, Villagarcia)
3. Support units, Straits Zone:
   3 Frigates, 8 Patrol Craft, all Survey Vessels
   6 Tugs, 1 Water-Boat, 18 Service Craft
4. Support units, Mediterranean Zone:
   1 Tanker, 3 Patrol Craft, 8 Diving Support Vessels
   7 Tugs, 1 Water-Boat, 9 Service Craft (Cartagena)
   2 Patrol Craft (La Algameca)
   3 Service Craft (Mahón)
   6 Patrol Craft (Barcelona, San Pedro de Pinatar, Castelló de la Plana)
5. Support units, Canaries:
   3 Patrol Craft, 4 LCTs, 2 Tugs, 1 Water-Boat, 5 Service Craft (Las Palmas)

Mercantile Marine

Lloyd's Register of Shipping:
  2 753 vessels of 8 056 080 tons gross

DELETIONS

Corvette
1973 *Diana* ("Atrevida" Class)

Mine Warfare Forces
1972 *Bidasoa, Nervion, Segura, Tambre, Ter* ("Bidasoa" Class)
1976 *Tinto* ("Guardiaro" Class) (31 Jan)
1977 *Eume* (1 Sep); *Guardiaro* (15 May) *Almanzora* ("Guardiaro" Class)
1978 *Guadalhorce, Eo* ("Guardiaro" Class) (2 Nov)
1979 *Navia* ("Guardiaro" Class)

Amphibious Forces
1974 LSM 3
1976 LSM 1, LSM 2
1978 BDK 1 (15 Oct)

Light Forces
1973 *Ciés* (Fishery Protection)
1974 V 2, V 12, V 13, V 18, *Candido Pérez*, AR 10 (Coastal Launches)
1977 LT 30, LT 31 (Lürssen Type). RR 19, 20 (20 Apr)
     Centinela and *Serviola* (Fishery Protection—to Mauritania 5 Mar 1977)
1978 V 9

Survey Ships
1975 *Tofiño, Juan de la Cosa* (30 Apr)

Service Forces
1974 PP 1, 3, 4, PB 5, 6, 17 (tankers)
1977 *Almirante Lobo* (30 Apr), A 1 (14 Mar), A 8 (30 Apr), AB 10 (19 May), BL 11 (20 Apr)

Submarines

1977 *SA 51, SA 52* ("Tiburon" Class)
     Narciso Menturiol

Cruiser

1975 *Canarias* (17 Dec)

Destroyers

1978 *Oquendo* ("Oquendo" Class) (2 Nov),
     Almirante Ferrandiz ("Fletcher" Class)

Frigates

1972 *Eolo, Triton* ("Eolo" Class), *Neptuno* ("Jupiter" Class)
1973 *Osado* ("Audaz" Class)
1974 *Audaz, Furor, Rayo* ("Audaz" Class), *Jupiter* ("Jupiter" Class), *Sarmiento de Gamboa* ("Pizarro" Class)
1975 *Meteoro, Relampago, Temerario,* ("Audaz" Class)
1977 *Vulcano* ("Jupiter" Class)
1978 *Alava* ("Alava" Class) (2 Nov),
     Legazpi ("Pizarro" Class) (4 Nov)

PENNANT LIST

Submarines

S 31	Almirante Garcia de los Reyes
S 32	Isaac Peral
S 34	Cosme Garcia
S 35	(no name)
S 61	Delfin
S 62	Tonina
S 63	Marsopa
S 64	Narval
S 71-74	New Construction

Aircraft Carriers

PA 01	Dédalo
PA 11	New Construction

Destroyers

D 21	Lepanto
D 23	Almirante Valdes
D 24	Alcala Galiano
D 25	Jorge Juan
D 42	Roger de Lauria
D 43	Marques de la Ensenada
D 61	Churruca
D 62	Gravina
D 63	Mendez Nuñez
D 64	Langara
D 65	Blas de Lezo

Frigates

D 38	Intrépido
D 51	Liniers
F 31	Descubierta
F 32	Diana
F 33	Infanta Elena
F 34	Infanta Cristina
F 35	Cazadora
F 36	Vencedora
F 37	New Construction
F 38	New Construction
F 41	Vicente Yáñez Pinzon
F 61	Atrevida
F 62	Princesa
F 64	Nautilus
F 65	Villa de Bilbao
F 71	Baleares
F 72	Andalucia

432 SPAIN / Introduction

Frigates

- F 73   Cataluña
- F 74   Asturias
- F 75   Extremadura

Light Forces

- P 01   Lazaga
- P 02   Alsedo
- P 03   Cadarso
- P 04   Villamil
- P 05   Bonifaz
- P 06   Recalde
- P 11   Barceló
- P 12   Laya
- P 13   Javier Quiroga
- P 14   Ordóñez
- P 15   Acevedo
- P 16   Candido Pérez
- LPI 1-5
- LAS 10, 20, 30
- LVC 1-20
- LVE 1-4
- LVI 1-30
- RR 29
- V-1
- V-4   Alcatraz
- V-5
- V-6
- V-10
- V-11
- V-21
- V 22   Cabo Fradera
- V-31
- V-32
- V-33
- V-34
- W 0   Gaviota
- W 32   Salvora

Amphibious Forces

- E 81-86
- K 2-8   BDK 2-8
- L 11   Velasco
- L 12   Martin Alvarez
- L 13   C. de Venadito
- LCU 1-2
- TA 11   Aragon
- TA 21   Castilla
- TA 31   Galicia

Mine Warfare Forces

- M 21   Nalón
- M 22   Llobregat
- M 23   Jucar
- M 24   Ulla
- M 25   Miño
- M 26   Ebro
- M 27   Turia
- M 28   Duero
- M 29   Sil
- M 30   Tajo
- M 31   Genil
- M 32   Odiel
- M 41   Guadalete
- M 42   Guadalmedina
- M 43   Guadalquivir
- M 44   Guadiana

Survey Ships

- A 21   Castor
- A 22   Pollux
- A 23   Antares
- A 24   Rigel
- A 31   Malaspina
- A 32   Tofiño

Service Forces

(The majority of these have no name and are known only by their numbers)

- BP 11   Teide
- BS 1   Poseidon
- WO 1   Azor

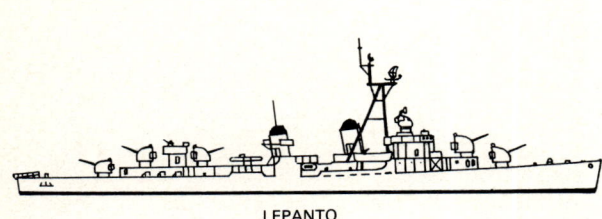

DEDALO

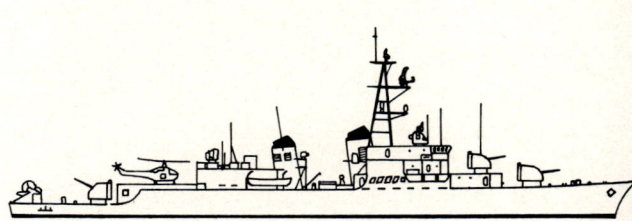

"ROGER DE LAURIA" Class

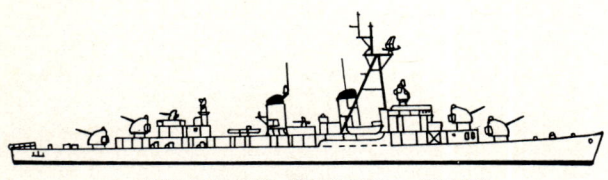

LEPANTO

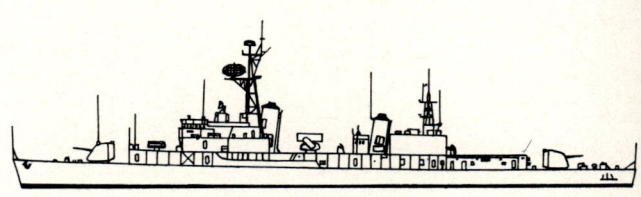

Ex-US "GEARING" ("D 60") Class

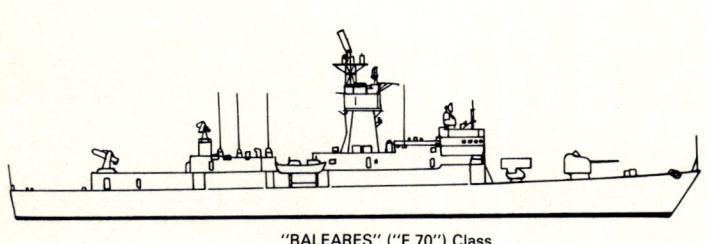

ALCALA GALIANO, JORGE JUAN and VALDES

"DESCUBIERTA" ("F 30") Class

"BALEARES" ("F 70") Class

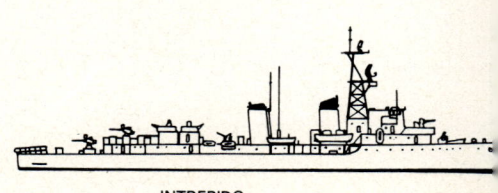

INTREPIDO

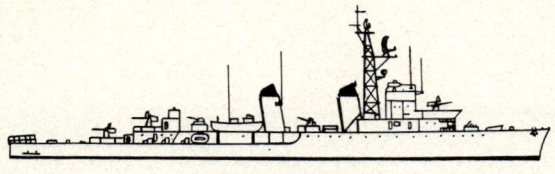
"LINIERS" ("D 50") Class

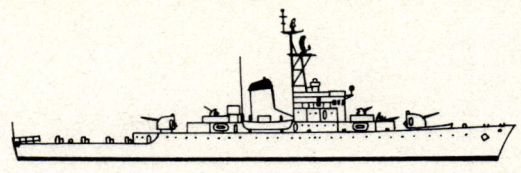
Mod. "PIZARRO" ("F 40") Class

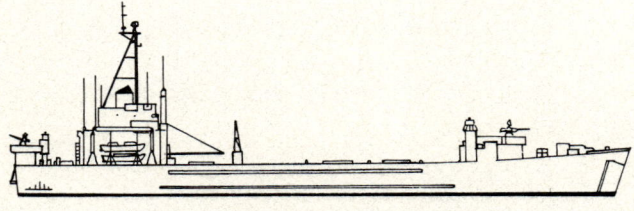
"TERREBONNE PARISH" ("L 10") Class

SUBMARINES

0 + 4 "S 70" CLASS (FRENCH "AGOSTA" CLASS)

Name	No.	Builders	Laid down	Launched	Commissioned
—	S 71	Bazán, Cartagena	1977?	1979	1980
—	S 72	Bazán, Cartagena	1977?	1980	1981
—	S 73	Bazán, Cartagena	—	1981	1982
—	S 74	Bazán, Cartagena	—	1982	1983

Displacement, tons: 1 450 surfaced; 1 725 dived
Dimensions, feet (metres): 221·7 × 22·3 × 17·7
  (67·6 × 6·8 × 5·4)
Torpedo tubes: 4—21·7 in (550 mm) (16 reloads)
Main machinery: Diesel-electric; 2 diesels; 3 600 hp;
  1 main motor; 6 400 hp; 1 cruising motor; 1 shaft
Speed, knots: 12 surfaced; 20 dived
Range, miles: 9 000 at 9 knots (snorting);
  350 at 3·5 knots (dived)
Endurance: 45 days
Complement: 50

First two ordered 9 May 1975 and second pair 29 June 1977. Building with some French advice. About 67 per cent of equipment and structure from Spanish sources.

Cost: Approximately 4 500 million pesetas (1977 prices)

Missiles: Submarine Exocet may be carried.

Radar: Calypso I Band.

Sonar: Two DUUA active; one DSUV passive.

"S 70" Class   1979, Royal Spanish Navy

4 "S 60" CLASS (FRENCH "DAPHNE" CLASS)

Name	No.	Builders	Laid down	Launched	Commissioned
DELFIN	S 61	Bazán, Cartagena	13 Aug 1968	25 Mar 1972	3 May 1973
TONINA	S 62	Bazán, Cartagena	1969	3 Oct 1972	10 July 1973
MARSOPA	S 63	Bazán, Cartagena	19 Mar 1971	15 Mar 1974	12 Apr 1975
NARVAL	S 64	Bazán, Cartagena	1971	14 Dec 1974	22 Nov 1975

Displacement, tons: 870 surfaced; 1 040 dived
Length, feet (metres): 189·6 (57·8)
Beam, feet (metres): 22·3 (6·8)
Draught, feet (metres): 15·1 (4·6)
Torpedo tubes: 12—21·7 in (550 mm) (8 bow, 4 stern)
  (no reloads — mining capability)
Main machinery: SEMT-Pielstick diesel-electric;
  2 600 bhp surfaced; 2 700 hp dived; 2 shafts
Speed, knots: 13·2 surfaced; 15·5 dived
Range, miles: 4 500 at 5 knots (snorting);
  2 710 at 12·5 knots (surfaced)
Complement: 47 (6 officers, 41 men)

Identical to the French "Daphne" class and built with extensive French assistance. First pair ordered 26 December 1966 and second pair in March 1970. S 63 cost 1 040 million pesetas.

Radar: Thompson CSF DRUA-31 plus ECM.

Sonar: Active, DUUA 1; Passive with rangefinding, DSUV. Goniometer; DUUG-1.

TONINA   6/1975, Dr. Giorgia Arra

434 SPAIN / Submarines

3 "S 30" CLASS (Ex-US GUPPY IIA TYPE)

Name	No.	Builders	Laid down	Launched	Commissioned
ISAAC PERAL (ex-USS *Ronquil*, SS 396)	S 32	Portsmouth Navy Yard	9 Sep 1943	27 Jan 1944	22 Apr 1944
COSME GARCIA (ex-USS *Bang*, SS 385)	S 34	Portsmouth Navy Yard	30 Apr 1943	30 Aug 1943	4 Dec 1943
— (ex-USS *Jallao*, SS 385)	S 35	Manitowoc S.B. Corporation	29 Sep 1943	12 Mar 1944	8 July 1944

Displacement, tons: 1 840 surfaced; 2 445 dived
Length, feet (metres): 306·0 *(93·3)*
Beam, feet (metres): 27·0 *(8·2)*
Draught, feet (metres): 17·0 *(5·2)*
Torpedo tubes: 10—21 in *(533 mm)* 6 bow, 4 stern
Main machinery: 3 Fairbanks-Morse diesels; total 4 800 bhp; 2 shafts; 2 Elliot electric motors; 5 400 shp
Speed, knots: 18 surfaced; 14 dived
Oil fuel, tons: 464 (472 in SS 35)
Range, miles: 12 000 at 10 knots
Complement: 74

Transferred to Spain on- 1 July 1971 *(Peral)* 1 October 1972 *(Garcia)* and (ex-*Jallao*) 26 June 1974. *Monturiol* and *Garcia* purchased 18 November 1974 the other pair being transferred by sale. *Narciso Monturiol* deleted, as expected after her mechanical problems of 1975, on 30 April 1977.

Diving Depth: 450 ft *(140 m)*.

Electronics: Mk 106 TDC.

Radar: SS 2.

Sonar: BQS, BQR.

COSME GARCIA   *1973, Royal Spanish Navy*

S-35   *1977, Royal Spanish Navy*

1 Ex-US "BALAO" CLASS

Name	No.	Builders	Laid down	Launched	Commissioned
ALMIRANTE GARCIA DE LOS REYES (ex-USS *Kraken*, SS 370)	S 31	Manitowoc S.B. Co	13 Dec 1943	30 Apr 1944	8 Sep 1944

Displacement, tons: 1 816 surfaced; 2 400 dived
Dimensions, feet (metres): 311·5 × 27·2 × 17·2 *(95 × 8·3 × 5·2)*
Torpedo tubes: 10—(6—21 in *(533 mm)* and 4 for A/S torpedoes)
Main machinery: 4 diesels; 6 400 bhp; 2 main motors; 4 600 shp; 2 shafts
Speed, knots: 18·5 surfaced; 10 dived
Oil fuel, tons: 472
Range, miles: 12 000 at 10 knots (surfaced)
Complement: 80

Transferred 24 October 1959 after modernisation at Pearl Harbor. Although due to be paid off in 1975 retained in service (see note under "S 30" class).

ALMIRANTE GARCIA DE LOS REYES   *1977, Royal Spanish Navy*

SPAIN / Aircraft carriers — Destroyers   435

AIRCRAFT CARRIERS

1 NEW CONSTRUCTION

| Name (See note) | No. PA 11 | Builders Bazán, Ferrol | Laid down 1980 | Launched 1982 | Commissioned 1984 |

Displacement, tons:
Dimensions, feet (metres): 639·9 × 79·4 × 29·8 (195·1 × 24·2 × 9·1)
Flight deck, feet (metres): 574 × 98·4 (175 × 30)
Aircraft: 19 (V/STOL and helicopters)
Guns: 4—Meroka 20 mm (12-barrels) CIWS.
Main engines: 2 LM2500 gas turbines; 40 000 shp
Range, miles: 7 500 at 20 knots
Complement: 780 (including Air Group)

Basically to the US Navy Sea Control Ship design she was ordered on 29 June 1977. Associated US firms are Gibbs and Cox and Dixencast. The design has been offered to Argentina, Australia, France, India and Iran. Building of this ship is apparently to take precedence over the "FFG 7" frigates.

Cost: 18 000 million pesetas (1977 price).

Electronics: Digital command and control system.

Name: Probably Dédalo instead of original Almirante Carrero Blanco.

Radar: Surface search: ?.
Three dimensional: SPS 52 B.

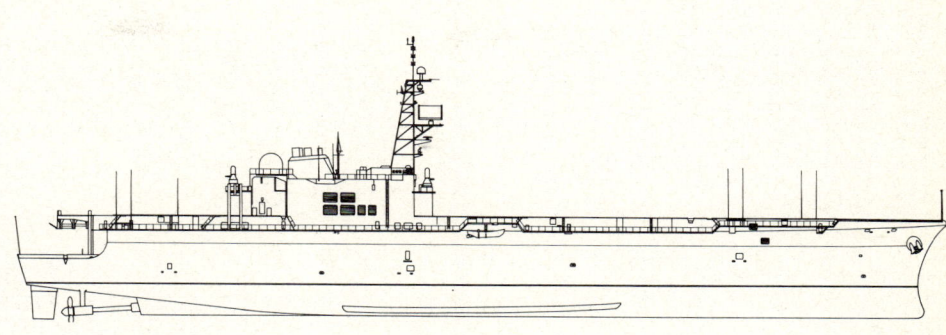

PA 11   1977

1 Ex-US "INDEPENDENCE" CLASS (CVL)

| Name | No. | Builders | Laid down | Launched | Commissioned |
| DÉDALO (ex-USS Cabot, AVT 3, ex-CVL 28, ex-Wilmington, CL 79) | PA 01 | New York Shipbuilding Corporation | 16 Aug 1942 | 4 Apr 1943 | 24 July 1943 |

Displacement, tons: 13 000 standard; 16 416 full load
Length, feet (metres): 623·0 (189·9)
Beam, feet (metres): 71·5 (21·8) hull
Width, feet (metres): 109·0 (33·2)
Draught, feet (metres): 26·0 (7·9)
Aircraft: 7 Harriers (5 AV-8A, 2 TAV-8A) (Matador)
20 helicopters (ASW/Sea Kings—Combat/Huey Cobras—Landings/specially embarked Bell 212s or 204s)
Guns: 26—40 mm/60 (2 quad, 9 twin Mk 2 and Mk 1)
Armour: 2 to 5 in sides; 2 to 3 in deck
Main engines: GE geared turbines; 4 shafts; 100 000 shp
Boilers: 4 Babcock & Wilcox
Speed, knots: 32
Range, miles: 7 200 at 15 knots
Oil fuel, tons: 1 800
Complement: 1 112 (without Air Groups)

Completed as an aircraft carrier from the hull of a "Cleveland" class cruiser. Originally carried over 40 aircraft. Converted with strengthened flight and hangar decks, large port side catapult, revised magazine arrangements, new electronic gear, with stability corrected to offset the added top-weight. Hangar capacity altered to take 20 aircraft. Flight deck: 545 × 108 ft (166·1 × 32·9 m).
Reactivated and modernised at Philadelphia Naval Shipyard, where she was transferred to Spain on 30 August 1967, on loan for five years. Purchased December 1973. Fleet flagship. Rerated "Portaaronaves" on 28 September 1976 with change of flag superior from PH to PA.

Aircraft: Hangar capacity—18 Sea Kings. Six more can be spotted on flight deck.

Electronics: WLR1 ECM; Tacan.

Gunnery: Reported that Meroka 20 mm system is to be shipped.

Radar: Three dimensional: SPS 8 (to be replaced by SPS 52B).
Air search: SPS 6 and SPS 40.
Tactical: SPS 10.
Fire control: Four sets.
Navigation: Two sets.

DÉDALO   1974, Michael D. J. Lennon

DESTROYERS

2 "ROGER DE LAURIA" CLASS

Name	No.	Builders	Laid down	Launched (see note)	Commissioned
ROGER DE LAURIA	D 42	Bazán, Ferrol/Cartagena	4 Sep 1951	12 Nov 1958	30 May 1969
MARQUÉS DE LA ENSENADA	D 43	Bazán, Ferrol/Cartagena	4 Sep 1951	15 July 1959	10 Sep 1970

Displacement, tons: 3 012 standard; 3 785 full load
Length, feet (metres): 391·5 (119·3)
Beam, feet (metres): 42·7 (13·0)
Draught, feet (metres): 18·4 (5·6)
Aircraft: 1 Hughes 369 HM ASW helicopter
Guns: 6—5 in (127 mm)/38 (twin Mk 38)
A/S weapons: 2 triple Mk 32 tubes for Mk 44 A/S torpedoes
Torpedo tubes: 2—21 in (533 mm) fixed single Mk 25 tubes for Mk 37 torpedoes
Main engines: 2 Rateau-Bretagne geared turbines; 2 shafts; 60 000 shp
Boilers: Three 3-drum type
Speed, knots: 28
Oil fuel, tons: 700
Range, miles: 4 500 at 15 knots
Complement: 318 (20 officers, 298 men)

Ordered in 1948. Originally of the same design as Oquendo. Towed to Cartagena for reconstruction to a new design. Roger de Lauria was re-launched after being lengthened and widened on 29 August 1967 and Marqués de la Ensenada on 2 March 1968. Weapons and electronics identical to Gearing Fram II.

Electronics: ESM; WLRI. Torpedo control; ? Mk 114.

Fire control: One Mk 37 director with Mk 25 radar.
One Mk 56 director with Mk 35 radar.

MARQUÉS DE LA ENSENADA   1976, Royal Spanish Navy

Gunnery: To be fitted with Meroka 20 mm system.

Missiles: Recent modernisation has made provision for fitting SAM missiles.

Radar: Search: SPS 40.
Tactical: SPS 10.

Sonar: One hull-mounted, SQS 32C; one VDS, SQA 10.

436 SPAIN / Destroyers

5 Ex-US "GEARING" (FRAM I) CLASS ("D 60" CLASS)

Name	No.	Builders	Laid down	Launched	Commissioned
CHURRUCA (ex-USS *Eugene A. Greene*, DD 711)	D 61	Federal S.B. & D.D. Co	1944	18 Mar 1945	8 June 1945
GRAVINA (ex-USS *Furse*, DD 882)	D 62	Consolidated Steel Corporation	1944	9 Mar 1945	10 July 1945
MENDEZ NUÑEZ (ex-USS *O'Hare*, DD 889)	D 63	Consolidated Steel Corporation	1945	22 June 1945	29 Nov 1945
LANGARA (ex-USS *Leary*, DD 879)	D 64	Consolidated Steel Corporation	1944	20 Jan 1945	7 May 1945
BLAS DE LEZO (ex-USS *Noa*, DD 841)	D 65	Bath Iron Works	1945	30 July 1945	2 Nov 1945

Displacement, tons: 2 425 standard; 3 480 full load
Length, feet (metres): 390·5 *(119·0)*
Beam, feet (metres): 40·9 *(12·4)*
Draught, feet (metres): 19 *(5·8)*
Aircraft: 1 Hughes 500 helicopter
Guns: 4—5 in *(127 mm)*/38 (twin Mk 38)
A/S weapons: 1 Asroc launcher; 2 triple Mk 32 tubes
Main engines: 2 geared turbines (GE or Westinghouse) 60 000 shp; 2 shafts
Boilers: 4 Babcock & Wilcox
Speed, knots: 34
Fuel, tons: 650
Range, miles: 4 800 at 15 knots (economical)
Complement: 274 (17 officers, 257 ratings)

Appearance: Blas de Lezo has two forward gun mounts and torpedo tubes by after funnel.

Electronics: ESM; WLRI.

Fire control: Radar directed Mk 37 Director.

Radar: Air search: D61 and 62, SPS 40—remainder, SPS 37; Surface search: SPS 10.

Refits: The first pair were refitted at El Ferrol on transfer. The remainder arrived at El Ferrol on 23 July 1974 after refit in the USA.

Sonar: SQS 23 (hull-mounted).

Torpedo control: ? Mk 114.

Transfers: D61 and 62—31 Aug 1972; D63-65—31 Oct 1973. (All finally purchased 17 May 1978.)

LANGARA *1975, Spanish Navy*

4 Ex-US "FLETCHER" CLASS ("D 20" CLASS)

Name	No.	Builders	Laid down	Launched	Commissioned
LEPANTO (ex-USS *Capps*, DD 550)	D 21	Gulf S.B. Corporation, Chickasaw, Ala	12 June 1941	31 May 1942	23 June 1943
ALMIRANTE VALDES (ex-USS *Converse*, DD 509)	D 23	Bath Iron Works	23 Feb 1942	30 Aug 1942	8 June 1943
ALCALA GALIANO (ex-USS *Jarvis*, DD 799)	D 24	Todd Pacific Shipyards	7 June 1943	14 Feb 1944	3 June 1944
JORGE JUAN (ex-USS *McGowan*, DD 678)	D 25	Federal S.B. & D.D. Co	May 1943	14 Nov 1943	20 Dec 1943

Displacement, tons: 2 080 standard; 2 750 normal; 3 050 full load
Length, feet (metres): 376·5 *(114·8)*
Beam, feet (metres): 39·5 *(12·0)*
Draught, feet (metres): 18·0 *(5·5)*
Guns: D21: 5—5 in *(127 mm)*/38 (single Mk 30); Others: 4—5 in *(127 mm)* single
D21: 6—40 mm/60 (twin Mk 1); 6—20 mm/70 (single Mk 4); Others: 6—3 in *(76 mm)*/50 (twin Mk 33)
A/S weapons: 6 (2 triple) Mk 32 A/S torpedo tubes (D21, 24 and 25); 2 Mk 11 Hedgehogs; 6 DCT in D21, 4 in D23; 2 DC racks in D21, 1 in others
Torpedo tubes: 3—21 in *(533 mm)* in D23, 24 and 25 only
Torpedo racks: 2 side launching Mk 4 each with 3 Mk 32 A/S torpedoes (to be replaced by torpedo tubes)
Main engines: Geared turbines; (Westinghouse in D21, GE in others); 2 shafts; 60 000 shp
Boilers: 4 Babcock & Wilcox
Speed, knots: 35
Oil fuel, tons: 506
Range, miles: 5 000 at 15 knots
Complement: 290 (17 officers, 273 men)

Lepanto and *Almirante Ferrandiz* (now deleted) were reconditioned at San Francisco, Cal, and there turned over to the Spanish Navy on 15 May 1957, sailing for Spain on 1 July 1957. *Valdes* was transferred at Philadelphia on 1 July 1959, *Jorge Juan* was transferred at Barcelona on 1 December 1960 and *Alcala Galiano* at Philadelphia on 3 November 1960, both being of the later "Fletcher" class. Modernisation of A/S equipment is planned. All purchased from USA on 1 October 1972. *Lepanto* damaged on grounding 16 April 1977.

Electronics: Torpedo director Mk 5. A/S director Mk 105.

Fire control: Radar controlled Mk 37 directors; Mk 56 director with Mk 35 radar (D 23, 24 and 25); Mk 63 director with SPG 34 radar for 3 in *(76 mm)* guns (D 23, 24 and 25).

Radar: Search: SPS 6C.
Tactical: SPS 10.

Sonar: One hull-mounted set. SQS 29 or SQS 4.

ALMIRANTE VALDES *1974, Wright and Logan*

ALCALA GALIANO *1977, X. I. Taibo*

SPAIN / Frigates 437

FRIGATES

0 + 3 US "FFG 7" CLASS (NEW CONSTRUCTION)

Name	No.	Builders	Laid down	Launched	Commissioned
NAVARRA (?)	F—1	Bazán, Ferrol	1980	—	?1981
MURCIA (?)	F—2	Bazán, Ferrol	—	—	—
LEÓN (?)	F—3	Bazán, Ferrol	—	—	—

Displacement, tons: 3 605 full load
Length, feet (metres): 445 (135·6)
Beam, feet (metres): 45 (13·7)
Draught, feet (metres): 24·5 (7·5)
Aircraft: 2 helicopters
Missiles: SSM/SAM; 16 Harpoon/24 Standard (Mk 13 Mod 4)
Guns: 1—76 mm/62 (single Mk 75); 1—Meroka system
A/S weapons: 2 triple torpedo tubes (Mk 32)
Main engines: 2—LM 2500 gas turbines (General Electric); 41 000 shp; 1 shaft (cp propeller)
Speed, knots: 30
Range, miles: 4 500 at 20 knots
Complement: 163 (11 officers, 152 ratings)

Three ordered 29 June 1977.
The execution of this programme has been delayed, although the reason is not clear. It might be due to the emphasis on the carrier building at Ferrol or to some change of plan.

Sonar: DE 1160B or SQS 56 with TACTAS.

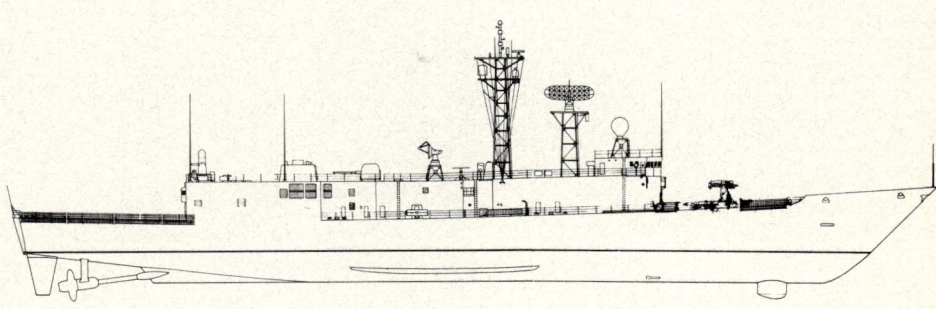

"FFG 7" Class *Drawing, A. D. Baker III*

5 + 3 "F 30" CLASS (NEW CONSTRUCTION)

Name	No.	Builders	Laid down	Launched	Commissioned
DESCUBIERTA	F 31	Bazán, Cartagena	16 Nov 1974	8 July 1975	18 Nov 1978
DIANA	F 32	Bazán, Cartagena	8 July 1975	26 Jan 1976	1978
INFANTA ELENA	F 33	Bazán, Cartagena	26 Jan 1976	14 Sep 1976	1978
INFANTA CRISTINA	F 34	Bazán, Cartagena	14 Sep 1976	25 Apr 1977	1979
CAZADORA	F 35	Bazán, Ferrol	14 Dec 1977	17 Oct 1978	1980
VENCEDORA	F 36	Bazán, Ferrol	May 1978	Mar 1979	—
	F 37	Bazán, Ferrol	31 Oct 1978	June 1979	—
	F 38	Bazán, Ferrol	—	—	—

Displacement, tons: 1 233 standard; 1 479 full load
Dimensions, feet (metres): 291·3 × 34 × 11·1 (88·8 × 10·4 × 3·2)
Missiles: SSM; 8 Harpoon (two 4-cell launchers);
 1 Octuple Sea Sparrow mounting (16 reloads) (see note)
Guns: 1—3 in (76 mm)/62 Oto Melara;
 2—40 mm/70 Breda-Bofors (singles);
 1 Meroka 20 mm/120 (12-barrels non-rotating)
A/S weapons: 1—375 mm Bofors twin-barrelled rocket launcher; 6 (2 triple) Mk 32 for Mk 46 torpedoes
Main engines: 4 MTU-Bazán 16V956 "TB 91" diesels; 16 000 bhp (18 000 bhp supercharged for 2 hours); 2 shafts; cp propellers
Speed, knots: 25·5
Range, miles: 4 000 at 18 knots
Complement: 116; (plus 30 Marine detachment)

Similar to the Portuguese "Improved João Coutinho" class built by Bazán with modifications to the armament and main engines. Officially rated as corvettes. *Diana* (tenth of the name) originates with the galley *Diana* of 1570. Infanta Elena and Cristina are the daughters of King Juan Carlos. Approval for second four ships given on 21 May 1976. First four ordered 7 December 1973 (83 per cent Spanish ship construction components) and four more from Bazán, Ferrol on 25 May 1976.

Appearance: Altered from original design by use of Y-shaped funnel.

Cost: Approximately 4 200 million pesetas.

Design: Original Portuguese "João Coutinho" design by Comodoro de Oliveira PN developed by Blohm and Voss and considerably modified by Bazán.

Electrical: 1 700 kVA—4 diesel alternators with Bazán-MAN RBV 16 TLS of 520 hp and emergency gas turbine alternator of 450 kVA. Normal cruising load from two alternators (one engine room); action state requiring three. Additional power available for modernisation.

Electronics: ECM Elettronica SpA "Beta".

Engineering: Fully automatic computerised engine and alternator control; two independent engine rooms; normal running on two diesels.

Gunnery: 144 ready rounds for 40 mm. Secondary optical director, DME ("CSEE"). In later ships the two single 40 mm/70 guns may be replaced by a twin mounting or the upper 40 mm may make way for a 12-barrelled Meroka 20 mm CIWS.
Missiles: Selenia system (Albatros) for Sea Sparrow. This is built partly in Spain. Harpoon with two 4-cell launchers between bridge and funnel.

Radar: Air/surface search: HSA DA 05/2.
Navigation and helo control: HSA ZW-06.
Fire control: HSA WM 22/41 system.

Sonar: Raytheon 1160B (hull-mounted);
Raytheon 1167 (VDS) (initially only in F 35-38).

Sound reduction: Masker fitted to shafts; propellers (five tested) under trial for four years; auxiliary gas turbine generator fitted on upper deck for use during passive sonar search; all main and auxiliary diesels sound-mounted.

Stabilisers: Space and power provided.

DESCUBIERTA *1979, Royal Spanish Navy*

1 "AUDAZ" CLASS

Name	No.	Builders	Laid down	Launched	Commissioned
INTRÉPIDO	D 38	Bazán, Ferrol	14 July 1945	15 Feb 1961	25 Mar 1965

Displacement, tons: 1 227 standard; 1 550 full load
Length, feet (metres): 295·2 (90·0) pp; 308·2 (94·0) oa
Beam, feet (metres): 30·5 (9·3)
Draught, feet (metres): 17·1 (5·2)
Guns: 2—3 in (76 mm)/50 (twin Mk 34);
 2—40 mm/70 (twin SP 48)
A/S weapons: 2 Mk 11 Hedgehogs; 8 mortars; 2 DC racks; 2 side launching racks for Mk 32 A/S torpedoes (6 torpedoes)
Main engines: 2 Rateau-Bretagne geared turbines; 2 shafts; 28 000 shp (32 500 max)
Boilers: 3 La Seine 3-drum type
Speed, knots: 28
Oil fuel, tons: 290
Range, miles: 3 800 at 14 knots
Complement: 199 (13 officers, 186 men)

Survivor of class of nine based on the pre-war French "Le Fier" design. The long delay between laying down and launch due to a complete re-design. Allocated D Pennant number in 1961.

Engineering: The boilers are in two compartments separated by the engine rooms.

Radar: Surface search, SPS 5B.
Air search: MLA-1B.
Fire control: One Mk 63.

Sonar: One QHBa hull-mounted set.

INTRÉPIDO *1969, Spanish Navy*

438 SPAIN / Frigates

5 "BALEARES (F 70)" CLASS

Name	No.	Builders	Laid down	Launched	Commissioned
BALEARES	F 71	Bazán, Ferrol	31 Oct 1968	20 Aug 1970	24 Sep 1973
ANDALUCIA	F 72	Bazán, Ferrol	2 July 1969	30 Mar 1971	23 May 1974
CATALUÑA	F 73	Bazán, Ferrol	20 Aug 1970	3 Nov 1971	16 Jan 1975
ASTURIAS	F 74	Bazán, Ferrol	30 Mar 1971	13 May 1972	2 Dec 1975
EXTREMADURA	F 75	Bazán, Ferrol	3 Nov 1971	21 Nov 1972	10 Nov 1976

Displacement, tons: 3 015 standard; 4 177 full load
Length, feet (metres): 415·0 *(126·5)* pp; 438·0 *(133·6)* oa
Beam, feet (metres): 46·9 *(14·3)*
Draught, feet (metres): 15·4 *(4·7)*
Missiles: SAM; 16 Tartar/Standard missiles (lightweight Mk 22 launcher)
Gun: 1—5 in *(127 mm)*/54 (single Mk 42)
A/S weapons: 1 8-tube ASROC launcher (8 reloads);
  4 Mk 32 for Mk 46 torpedoes;
  2 Mk 25 for Mk 37 torpedoes (stern)
Main engines: 1 set Westinghouse geared turbines; 1 shaft; 35 000 shp
Boilers: 2 high pressure V2M type; 1 200 psi *(84·4 kg/cm²)*
Speed, knots: 28
Range: 4 500 miles at 20 knots
Complement: 256 (15 officers, 241 men)

This class resulted from a very close co-operation between Spain and the USA. Programme approved 17 November 1964, technical support agreement with USA being signed 31 March 1966. US Navy supplied weapons and sensors. Major hull sections, turbines and gearboxes made at El Ferrol, superstructures at Alicante, boilers, distilling plants and propellers at Cadiz.

Cost: Approximately 4 000 million pesetas.

Design: This class replaced the "Leander" class from the United Kingdom which order was cancelled in 1962 as the result of political insults in that country. Generally similar to US Navy's "Knox" class although they differ in the missile system, hull sonar, Mk 25 torpedo tubes and lack of helicopter facilities. The last is a cause of criticism along with similar criticisms in US Navy of low speed, lack of manoeuvrability (1 screw) and inadequate missile stowage.
The anchor arrangement provides for a 2 ton anchor on the port bow and a 4 ton anchor in the keel aft of the sonar dome.

ASTURIAS   7/1976, Arthur D. Baker III

Fire control: Mk 68 GFCS with SPG 53B radar for guns and missiles; Mk 74 missile control system integrating Mk 73 missile control director and SPG 51C radar. Mk 111 replaced by digital control Mk 152 calculator. Mk 114 torpedo control system.

Gunnery: 600—5 in rounds carried.
Meroka system due to be shipped in 1979.

Missile system: Mk 22 launcher with stowage for 16 missiles. Single director with two lines of fire against different targets with Mk 68 GFCS. To receive SSMs.

Radar: Search: SPS 52A (3D).
Tactical: SPS 10.
Fire control: SPG 51C continuous wave for missiles; Mk 68 with SPG 53B for guns with continuous wave injection for limited use with missiles.

Torpedoes and tubes: All are fitted fixed internally the Mk 32 being angled at 45 degrees. Total of 41 torpedoes carried.

Sonar: SQS 23 bow mounted; SQS 35V VDS below quarterdeck.

CATALUÑA   9/1975, Dr. Giorgio Arra

1 "ALAVA" CLASS

Name	No.	Builders	Laid down	Launched	Commissioned
LINIERS	D 51 (ex-21)	Bazán, Cartagena	1 Jan 1945	1 May 1946	27 Jan 1951

Displacement, tons: 1 842 standard; 2 287 full load
Length, feet (metres): 336·3 *(102·5)*
Beam, feet (metres): 31·5 *(9·6)*
Draught, feet (metres): 19·7 *(6·0)*
Guns: 3—3 in *(76 mm)*/50 (single Mk 34);
  3—40 mm/70 (single SP 48)
A/S weapons: 2 Hedgehogs; 8 DC mortars; 2 DC racks;
  2 side launching racks for A/S torpedoes (6 torpedoes)
Main engines: Parsons geared turbines; 2 shafts; 31 500 shp
Boilers: 4 Yarrow 3-drum type
Speed, knots: 29
Oil fuel, tons: 370
Range, miles: 4 100 at 15 knots
Complement: 222 (15 officers, 207 men)

Ordered in 1936, but construction was held up by the Civil War. After being resumed, was again suspended in 1940, but restarted at Empresa Nacional Bazán. The last of the old "Churruca" class of which 18 were built.
Mid-life conversion in 1962 changed the armament from conventional destroyer outfit.

Fire control: Mk 63 FCS with Mk 34 radar.

Radar: Air search: MLA 1B.
Surface search: SG-6B.
Navigation: Decca TM 626.

Sonar: One SQS 30A hull-mounted set.

"ALAVA" Class   1974, Spanish Navy

SPAIN / Frigates — Light forces 439

1 MODERNISED "PIZARRO" CLASS

Name	No.	Builders	Laid down	Launched	Commissioned
VICENTE YÁÑEZ PINZON	F 41	Bazán, Ferrol	Sep 1943	8 Aug 1945	5 Aug 1949

Displacement, tons: 1 924 standard; 2 228 full load
Length, feet (metres): 279·0 (85·0) pp; 312·5 (95·3) oa
Beam, feet (metres): 39·5 (12·0)
Draught, feet (metres): 17·7 (5·4)
Guns: 2—5 in (127 mm)/38 (twin Mk 30);
4—40 mm/70 (twin SP 48)
A/S weapons: 2 Hedgehogs; 8 mortars; 2 DC racks;
2 side launching racks for A/S torpedoes (6 torpedoes)
Main engines: 2 sets Parsons geared turbines; 2 shafts;
6 000 shp
Boilers: 2 Yarrow type
Speed, knots: 18·5
Range, miles: 3 000 at 15 knots
Oil fuel, tons: 390
Complement: 255 (16 officers, 239 men)

Survivor of a class of eight.
Originally designed to carry 30 mines.

Fire control: GFCS Mk 52 with Mk 29 radar on one director.

Modernisation: Completed 25 March 1960.

Radar: Surface search: SPS 5B.
Air search: MLA-1B.
Navigation: Decca TM 626.

VICENTE YÁÑEZ PINZON 1974, Spanish Navy

4 "ATREVIDA - F 60" CLASS

Name	No.	Builders	Laid down	Launched	Commissioned
ATREVIDA	F 61	Bazán, Cartagena	26 June 1950	2 Dec 1952	19 Aug 1954
PRINCESA	F 62	Bazán, Cartagena	18 Mar 1953	31 Mar 1956	2 Oct 1957
NAUTILUS	F 64	Bazán, Cadiz	27 July 1953	23 Aug 1956	10 Dec 1959
VILLA DE BILBAO	F 65	Bazán, Cadiz	18 Mar 1953	19 Feb 1958	2 Sep 1960

Displacement, tons: 1 031 standard; 1 135 full load
Length, feet (metres): 247·8 (75·5)
Beam, feet (metres): 33·5 (10·2)
Draught, feet (metres): 9·8 (3·0)
Guns: 1—3 in (76 mm)/50 (Mk 22); 3—40 mm/70 (SP 48)
A/S weapons: 2 Hedgehogs; 8 mortars; 2 DC racks
Mines: 20 can be carried
Main engines: Sulzer diesels; 2 shafts; 3 000 bhp
Speed, knots: 18·5
Oil fuel, tons: 105
Range, miles: 8 000 at 10 knots
Complement: 132 (9 officers, 123 men)

Survivors of a class of six.
All have been modernised, F 61 in 1959-60, remainder while
building. No funnel, the diesel exhaust being on the starboard
side waterline. Allocated F pennant numbers in 1961 although
still officially classed as corvettes.
Atrevida and *Villa de Bilbao* due for early deletion.

Aircraft: Although no deck is fitted helicopters can be refuelled
in flight.

Radar: Modified SPS 5B combined air/surface search.

Sonar: One QHBa.

PRINCESA X. I. Taibo

LIGHT FORCES

Note: Two fishery protection vessels at 500 million pesetas each are to be built but it is uncertain
whether these will be Naval-manned. There are reports, so far unconfirmed, of a further thirty
3-ton craft being ordered.

6 "LAZAGA (P-OO)" CLASS (FAST ATTACK CRAFT—PATROL)

Name	No.	Builders	Commissioned
LAZAGA	P 01	Lürssen, Vegesack	16 July 1975
ALSEDO	P 02	Bazán, La Carraca	28 Feb 1977
CADARSO	P 03	Bazán, La Carraca	10 July 1976
VILLAMIL	P 04	Bazán, La Carraca	26 Apr 1977
BONIFAZ	P 05	Bazán, La Carraca	11 July 1977
RECALDE	P 06	Bazán, La Carraca	17 Dec 1977

Displacement, tons: 275 standard; 399 full load
Dimensions, feet (metres): 190·6 × 24·9 × 8·5 (58·1 × 7·6 × 2·6)
Guns: 1—3 in (76 mm)/62 (Compact); 1—40 mm/70 Breda-Bofors 350P;
2—20 mm Oerlikon GK 204 (in some cases original 76 mm L50 Mk 22 has been retained eg.
Cadarso)
A/S weapons: 2 DC racks; provision for 2 triple Mk 32 torpedo tube mountings
Main engines: 2 MTU-Bazán MA15 TB91 diesels; 8 000 bhp
Speed, knots: 30
Range, miles: 6 100 at 17 knots
Complement: 34 (4 officers, 30 ratings)

LAZAGA 1975, Lürssen

Ordered in 1972, primarily for Fishery Protection duties. Although all are operated by the Navy
half the cost is being borne by the Ministry of Commerce. Of similar hull form to Israeli "Reshef"
class and to S-143 class of FDR and of basic Lürssen Type 57 design but with only two engines.
Lazaga was steamed to Spain in April 1975 for equipping and arming.

Building dates: *Lazaga;* May 1974 (laid down), 10 October 1974 (launched).
Alsedo; 10 May 1974, 8 January 1975.
Cadarso; 24 May 1974, 8 January 1975.
Villamil and *Bonifaz;* 8 January 1975, 24 May 1975.
Recalde; 24 May 1975, 9 November 1975.

Cost: 910 231 000 pesetas fully fitted.

Electronics: ECM and IFF.

Fire control: Optical director CSEE (HSM Mk 22).

Gunnery: All guns assembled under licence by Bazán.

Missiles: Provision has been made for fitting surface-to-surface missiles (four Exocet or eight
Harpoon or MM 39), without change of gun armament.

Radar: Surface search and target indication: HSA-M 20 series.
Navigation: Decca TM626.

Sonar: One hull-mounted set (?ELAC).

Note: A modified version of this class, "Cormoran" of 169·2 ft (51·6 m), 355 tons full load,
36 knots, 2 500 miles at 15 knots with 4 Exocet, one 76/62 OTO Melara, one 40/70 mm gun, M-20
series radar and CSEE secondary director is under discussion with foreign purchasers and may
have been bought by Morocco (see Moroccan section where information is given for "Lazaga"
class).

440 SPAIN / Light forces

6 "BARCELO (P 10)" CLASS (FAST ATTACK CRAFT—PATROL)

Name	No.	Builders	Commissioned
BARCELÓ	P 11	Lürssen, Vegesack	20 Mar 1976
LAYA	P 12	Bazán, La Carraca	23 Dec 1976
JAVIER QUIROGA	P 13	Bazán, La Carraca	4 Apr 1977
ORDÓÑEZ	P 14	Bazán, La Carraca	7 June 1977
ACEVEDO	P 15	Bazán, La Carraca	14 July 1977
CÁNDIDO PÉREZ	P 16	Bazán, La Carraca	25 Nov 1977

Displacement, tons: 134 full load
Dimensions, feet (metres): 118·7 × 19 × 6·2 *(36·2 × 5·8 × 1·9)*
Guns: 1—40 mm Breda Bofors 350; 2—20 mm Oerlikon GAM 204; 2—12·7 mm
Torpedo tubes: Provision for 2—21 in *(533 mm)*
Main engines: 2 MTU-Bazán MD-16V TB 90 diesels; 5 760 bhp; 2 shafts
Speed, knots: 36; 20 cruising
Range, miles: 1 200 at 17 knots
Complement: 19

BARCELO   3/1976, E. N. Bazán

Ordered 5 December 1973, the prototype, *Barceló,* being built by Lürssen, Vegesack with MTU engines. All manned by the Navy although the cost is being borne by the Ministry of Commerce. Cost 610 million pesetas (1976) per craft. Of Lürssen TNC 36 design.

Building dates: *Barceló;* 3 March 1975 (laid down), November 1975 (launched).
Laya, J. Quiroga; 9 May 1975, 18 December 1975.
Ordóñez, Acevedo; 9 February 1976, 10 September 1976.
C. Perez; 3 March 1977 (launched).

Fire control: CSEE optical director for 40 mm.

Missiles: Reported as able to take two or four Surface-to-Surface missiles.

0 + 10 LARGE PATROL CRAFT

Displacement, tons: 300 tons
Dimensions, feet (metres): 131·2 × 21·6 × 8·2 *(40 × 6·6 × 2·5)*
Guns: 2—20 mm
Main engine: 1 diesel; 4 300 hp = 20 knots

Ordered from Bazán, Cadiz in 1978. For fishery and EEZ patrol duties.

4 "LVE" CLASS (COASTAL PATROL CRAFT)

LVE 1—4

Displacement, tons: 85
Dimensions, feet (metres): 106·6 × 17·4 × 4·6 *(32·2 × 5·3 × 1·4)*
Main engines: 2 diesels, 2 800 hp = 25 knots
Range, miles: 1 200 (cruising)

A class of 85 ton craft ordered in 1978 under the programme of 13 May 1977, funded jointly by the navy and the Ministry of Commerce. Cost approximately 62·5 million pesetas each. All completed 1978-79 by Bazán, Partagena. Naval manned.

20 "LVC" "CLASS (COASTAL PATROL CRAFT)

LVC 1—20

Displacement, tons: 18·5 standard; 21·2 full load
Dimensions, feet (metres): 52·2 × 14·4 × 4·3 *(15·9 × 4·4 × 1·3)*
Gun: 1—7·62 mm MG
Main engines: 2 Baudoin-Interdiesel DNP-350; 768 hp = 25·7 knots
Range, miles: 430 at 18 knots
Complement: 5

Ordered under the programme agreed 13 May 1977, funded jointly by the navy and the Ministry of Commerce. Built to the Aresa 15 PT 37 design by Aresa, Arenys de Mar, Barcelona. GRP hull and Decca 110 radar. Cost approximately 22 million pesetas each (1977 prices). Naval manned. LVC1 carried out trials in July 1978. All to be completed by end 1979.

5 "LPI-1" CLASS (COASTAL PATROL CRAFT)

Name	No.	Builders	Commissioned
—	LPI-1	Bazán, La Carraca	Feb 1965
—	LPI-2	Bazán, La Carraca	Feb 1965
—	LPI-3	Bazán, La Carraca	Mar 1965
—	LPI-4	Bazán, La Carraca	Mar 1965
—	LPI-5	Bazán, La Carraca	Mar 1965

Displacement, tons: 17·2 standard; 25 full load
Dimensions, feet (metres): 46 × 15·4 × 3·3 *(14 × 4·7 × 1)*
Guns: 2—7·62 mm (twin)
Main engines: 2 Gray Marine diesels; 450 hp = 13 knots
Complement: 8

Laid down 1964 by Bazán, La Carraca. Wooden hulled.

LPI-3   1965, Spanish Navy

1 FISHERY PROTECTION VESSEL

SALVORA (ex-*Virgen de la Almudena,* ex-*Mendi Eder*) W 32

Displacement, tons: 180 standard; 275 full load
Dimensions, feet (metres): 107·0 × 20·5 × 9·0 *(31 × 6·1 × 2·5)*
Gun: 1—20 mm Mk 4/70
Main engine: 1 Sulzer diesel; 1 shaft; 400 bhp = 12 knots
Oil fuel, tons: 25
Complement: 31

Trawler. Built in 1948 by SA Juliana, Gijon. Commissioned 25 September 1954.

Radar: Decca RM 914.

3 USCG "83 ft" TYPE (COASTAL PATROL CRAFT)

Name	No.	Builders	Commissioned
—	LAS 10 (ex-*LAS 1*)	Bazán, Cartagena	26 Apr 1965
—	LAS 20 (ex-*LAS 2*)	Bazán, Cartagena	4 May 1965
—	LAS 30 (ex-*LAS 3*)	Bazán, Cartagena	3 Sep 1965

Displacement, tons: 49 standard; 63 full load
Dimensions, feet (metres): 83·3 × 16·1 × 6·6 *(25·4 × 4·9 × 2)*
Guns: 1—20 mm; 2—7 mm (single)
A/S weapons: 2 Mousetrap Mk 20 (4 rockets each)
Main engines: 800 bhp; 2 shafts = 15 knots
Complement: 15

Of wooden hull construction. All launched 1964.

Radar: Decca 978.

Sonar: QCU 2.

SPAIN / Light forces — Amphibious forces 441

1 PATROL VESSEL

RR 29

Displacement, tons: 364 standard; 498 full load
Dimensions, feet (metres): 124·6 × 27·6 × 9·8 *(38 × 8·4 × 3)*
Guns: 1—1·5 in/85; 1—20 mm
Main engine: Triple expansion; 1 shaft; 800 ihp = 10 knots
Boilers: 1 cylindrical, *(13 kg/cm)*
Fuel, tons: 100 coal
Range, miles: 620 at 10 knots

Former tug launched in 1941. To be retired soon in wake of sisters RR 19-20.

Radar: DK 12.

1 COASTAL PATROL CRAFT

V 31

Displacement, tons: 3·3
Dimensions, feet (metres): 30·7 × 11·5 × 2·7 *(9·1 × 3·2 × 0·8)*
Speed, knots: 27

Built to commercial "Courier" design by Cytra, Darmstadt, Germany in 1977.

2 COASTAL PATROL CRAFT

V 33 **V 34**

Displacement, tons: 25
Gun: 1 MG
Speed, knots: 25

Similar but not identical craft built in 1977; V 33 by Viudes, Barcelona and V 34 by Aresa, Barcelona. V 33 has a Decca 110 radar.

30 LVI CLASS (INSHORE PATROL CRAFT)

LVI 1-30

Displacement, tons: 4·2 full load
Dimensions, feet (metres): 29·2 × 10·2 × 2·3 *(8·9 × 3·1 × 0·7)*
Gun: 1 MG
Main engines: 2 diesels; 240 hp × 18 knots
Range, miles: 120
Complement: 4

A class ordered from Rodman, Vigo under the programme agreed 13 May 1977, funded jointly by the navy and the Ministry of Commerce. Cost approximately 3 million pesetas each. LVI 1 commissioned 4 September 1978. All completed 1978-79. Naval manned.

10 COASTAL/RIVER PATROL LAUNCHES

Name	No.	Builders	Commissioned
—	V 1	Kiel, Germany	1926
ALCATRAZ	V 4	Egaña, Motrico	10 Apr 1947
—	V 5	Arsenal, Cartagena	13 June 1969
—	V 6 (ex-V 22)	—	—
—	V 10	—	—
—	V 11	—	—
—	V 21	UK	—
CABO FRADERA	V 22	Bazán, La Carraca	25 Feb 1963
—	V 32	Re-Al, Barcelona	23 Mar 1974
GAVIOTA	W 0	Germany	1944

Gaviota W 0, 104·2 tons standard, 27·5 × 5·2 × 2 metres, 2 MG, complement 14, ex-smuggler, commissioned in Spanish Navy 26 November 1970; V 1 (ex-Azor) 112 tons, 31·1 × 5·7 × 2·1 metres, complement 16, yacht employed by Naval School, Marin; Alcatraz V 4, 65 tons, 19 × 4·6 × 2·1 metres, speed 8 knots, complement 13; V 5, 5 tons, 8·2 × 2·9 × 1 metres, 5 knots, complement 7; V 6 (ex-V 22), 42 tons standard, 22 × 4·8 × 1·6 metres, 19 knots, complement 7; V 10 (ex-V 19), 30 tons standard, 14·4 × 4·7 × 1·5 metres, 9 knots, complement 7; V 10 and 11, 11·7 tons standard, 14·8 × 3 × 1 metres, 8 knots, complement 7; V 21 (ex-British ML, smuggler taken over April 1961), commissioned 23 July 1962, complement 12; Cabo Fradera V 22, 28 tons, 1—7·62 mm MG, based at Tuy on River Miño for border patrol with Portugal; V 32 of 5 tons. All craft prior to V 31 are probably to be deleted in near future when relieved by new construction.

CABO FRADERA   1976, Royal Spanish Navy

AMPHIBIOUS FORCES

1 Ex-US "HASKELL" CLASS (ATTACK TRANSPORT)

Name	No.	Builders	Commissioned
ARAGÓN (ex-USS Noble, APA 218)	TA 11	USA	1945

Displacement, tons: 6 720 light; 12 450 full load
Dimensions, feet (metres): 455 × 63·5 × 24 *(138·8 × 19·3 × 7·2)*
Guns: 12—40 mm/60 (1 quad, 4 twin)
Main engine: 1 geared turbine; 8 500 shp = 17 knots
Boilers: 2 Babcock & Wilcox
Oil fuel, tons: 1 150
Range, miles: 14 700 at 16 knots
Complement: 357

Former US Attack Transport, transferred at San Francisco on 19 December 1964. Can carry 1 190 men and 680 tons cargo (or 11—2½ ton trucks and 49—¾ ton trucks). 24 landing craft. Amphibious forces flagship.

Radar: Air search: SPS 6.
Surface search: SPS 4.

ARAGÓN   1975, Spanish Navy

1 Ex-US "ANDROMEDA" CLASS (ATTACK CARGO SHIP)

Name	No.	Builders	Commissioned
CASTILLA (ex-USS Achernar, AKA 53)	TA 21	USA	1944

Displacement, tons: 7 430 light; 11 416 full load
Dimensions, feet (metres): 457·8 × 63 × 24 *(139·6 × 19·2 × 7·3)*
Guns: 1—5 in/38; 8—40 mm/60 (twins) (Mk 1)
Main engine: 1 GE geared turbine; 6 000 shp = 16 knots
Boilers: 2 Foster-Wheeler
Oil fuel, tons: 1 400
Range, miles: 18 500 at 12 knots
Complement: 324

Former US Attack Cargo Ship transferred at New York on 2 February 1965. Can carry 98 men, six M 48 tanks, 36—2½ ton trucks and 267 Jeeps. 24 landing craft.

Radar: Surface search: SPS 10

CASTILLA   1975, Spanish Navy

442 SPAIN / Amphibious forces

1 Ex-US "CABILDO" CLASS (LSD)

Name	No.	Builders	Commissioned
GALICIA (ex-USS *San Marcos*, LSD 25)	TA 31	Philadelphia Navy Yard	15 Apr 1945

Displacement, tons: 4 790 standard; 9 375 full load
Dimensions, feet (metres): 475·4 × 72·6 × 18·0 *(139 × 21·9 × 4·9)*
Guns: 12—40 mm/60 (2 quad, 2 twin) (see note)
Main engines: Geared turbines; 2 shafts; 7 000 shp = 15·4 knots
Boilers: Two 3-drum cylindrical
Oil fuel, tons: 1 727
Range, miles: 8 000 at 15 knots
Complement: 301 (18 officers, 283 men)

Transferred to Spain on 1 July 1971 and by sale August 1974. Fitted with helicopter platform. Can carry three LCUs or 18 LCMs. 1 347 tons of cargo or 100—2½ ton trucks or 27—M 48 tanks or 11 heavy helicopters. Accommodation for 137 troops (overnight) or 500 for short haul.

Fire control: GFCS with Mk 51 radar.

Guns: It is reported that the two twin 40 mm are being replaced by two ex-destroyer single 3 in *(76 mm)* guns.

Radar: Surface search: SPS 10.
Navigation: One set.

GALICIA   1975, Spanish Navy

3 Ex-US "TERREBONNE PARISH" CLASS (LST)

Name	No.	Builders	Commissioned
VELASCO (ex-USS *Terrebonne Parish*, LST 1156)	L 11	Bath Iron Works	21 Nov 1952
MARTIN ALVAREZ (ex-USS *Wexford County*, LST 1168)	L 12	Christy Corporation	15 June 1954
CONDE DE VENADITO (ex-USS *Tom Green County*, LST 1159)	L 13	Bath Iron Works	12 Sep 1953

Displacement, tons: 2 590 standard; 5 800 full load
Dimensions, feet (metres): 384·0 × 55·0 × 17·0 *(117·4 × 16·7 × 3·7)*
Guns: 6—3 in/50 (3 twin, 2 fwd, 1 aft)
Main engines: 4 General Motors diesels; 2 shafts; 6 000 bhp = 15 knots
Range, miles: 15 000 at 9 knots
Complement: 116 (troops 395)

LST 1156 and 1168 transferred on 29 October 1971, LST 1159 on 5 January 1972. Can carry 395 men, ten M-48 tanks or 17 LVTP. Four landing craft. Purchase approved 5 August 1976 and carried out 1 November 1976.

Fire control: 2 Mk 63 GFCS with SPG 34 radar.

Radar: Surface search: SPS 10.

MARTIN ALVAREZ   5/1976, P. Crichton

1 Ex-BRITISH LCT (4)

BDK 2   K 2

Displacement, tons: 440 standard; 868 full load
Dimensions, feet (metres): 185·3 × 38·7 × 6·2 *(56·5 × 11·8 × 1·9)*
Guns: 2—20 mm (single)
Main engines: 2 Paxman diesels; 2 shafts; 920 bhp = 9 knots
Range, miles: 1 100 at 8 knots

Can carry 350 tons or 500 men. Both laid down 1945 and commissioned 11 November 1948.

3 EDIC TYPE (LCT)

Name	No.	Builders	Commissioned
BDK 6	K 6	Bazán, La Carraca	6 Dec 1966
BDK 7	K 7	Bazán, La Carraca	30 Dec 1966
BDK 8	K 8	Bazán, La Carraca	30 Dec 1966

Displacement, tons: 279 standard; 665 full load
Dimensions, feet (metres): 193·5 × 39·0 × 5·0 *(59 × 11·9 × 1·3)*
Guns: 2—12·7 mm MG; 1—81 mm mortar
Main engines: 2 diesels; 2 shafts; 1 040 bhp = 9·5 knots
Range, miles: 1 500 at 9 knots
Complement: 17

Landing craft of the French EDIC type.

Radar: One navigation set.

BDK 6   1976, Royal Spanish Navy

3 SPANISH BUILT LCTs

Name	No.	Builders	Commissioned
BDK 3	K 3	Bazán, Ferrol	15 June 1959
BDK 4	K 4	Bazán, Ferrol	15 June 1959
BDK 5	K 5	Bazán, Ferrol	15 June 1959

Displacement, tons: 902 full load
Dimensions, feet (metres): 186 × 38·4 × 6 *(56·6 × 11·6 × 1·7)*
Guns: 2—20 mm (singles)
Main engines: 2 M60 V8 AS diesels; 2 shafts; 1 000 hp = 8·5 knots
Range, miles: 1 000 at 7 knots
Complement: Complement 20 (1 officer, 19 men)

All laid down 1958. Can carry 300 tons or 400 men.

BDK 5   1971, Spanish Navy

2 Ex-US LCUs

LCU 1 (ex-*LCU 1471*)
LCU 2 (ex-*LCU 1491*)

Displacement, tons: 360
Dimensions, feet (metres): 119·7 × 31·5 × 5·2 *(36·5 × 9·6 × 1·6)*
Speed, knots: 7·6
Complement: 13

Transferred June 1972. Sold August 1976.

SPAIN / Amphibious forces — Mine warfare forces 443

6 US LCM (8)

| E 81 | E 82 | E 83 | E 84 | E 85 | E 86 |

Displacement, tons: 115 full load
Dimensions, feet (metres): 74·5 × 21·7 × 5·9 *(22·7 × 6·6 × 1·8)*
Speed, knots: 9
Complement: 5

This new class was ordered from Oxnard, California in 1974. Assembled in Spain. All commissioned in July-September 1975.

Note: Total of landing craft (including those attached to *Aragón, Castilla,* and LSTs):
2 LCU; 12 LCM (3) and (6); 6 LCM (8); 16 LCP (L); 1 LCP (R); 49 LCVP.
All of US origin except 8 LCP (L), built at Cartagena.

MINE WARFARE FORCES

4 Ex-US "AGGRESSIVE" CLASS (MINESWEEPERS—OCEAN)

Name	No.	Builders	Commissioned
GUADALETE (ex-USS *Dynamic*, MSO 432)	M 41	Colbert BW, Stockton, Calif	15 Dec 1953
GUADALMEDINA (ex-USS *Pivot*, MSO 463)	M 42	Wilmington BW, Calif	12 July 1954
GUADALQUIVIR (ex-USS *Persistant*, MSO 491)	M 43	Tacoma, Washington	3 Feb 1956
GUADIANA (ex-USS *Vigor*, MSO 473)	M 44	Burgess Boat Co, Manitowoc	8 Nov 1954

Displacement, tons: 665 standard; 750 full load
Dimensions, feet (metres): 172·0 × 36·0 × 13·6 *(52·3 × 10·4 × 4·2)*
Guns: 2—20 mm (twin)
Main engines: 4 Packard diesels; 2 shafts; cp propellers; 2 280 bhp = 15·5 knots
Oil fuel, tons: 46
Range, miles: 3 000 at 10 knots
Complement: 74 (6 officers, 68 men)

The first three were transferred and commissioned on 1 July 1971. The fourth ship was delivered 4 April 1972. All purchased August 1974.

Minehunting: Although these ships have a mine classification capability they remain as "dragaminas" having no PAP or diving facilities.

Radar: Surface search: SPS 5C.
Navigation: One set.

Sonar: SQQ 14 (VDS) with mine classification capability.

GUADALETE   *1973, X. I. Taibo*

12 Ex-US "ADJUTANT", "REDWING" and "MSC 268" CLASSES ("NALON" (M 20) CLASS)
(MINESWEEPERS—COASTAL)

Name	No.	Builders	Commissioned
NALÓN (ex-*MSC 139*)	M 21	S. Coast S.Y., Calif	Feb 1954
LLOBREGAT (ex-*MSC 143*)	M 22	S. Coast S.Y., Calif	Nov 1954
JUCAR (ex-*MSC 220*)	M 23	Bellingham S.Y.	June 1956
ULLA (ex-*MSC 265*)	M 24	Adams Y.Y., Mass	July 1958
MIÑO (ex-*MSC 266*)	M 25	Adams Y.Y., Mass	Oct 1956
EBRO (ex-*MSC 269*)	M 26	Bellingham S.Y.	Dec 1958
TURIA (ex-*MSC 130*)	M 27	Hildebrand D.D., NY	Jan 1955
DUERO (ex-*Spoonbill*, MSC 202)	M 28	Tampa Marine Corporation	Jan 1959
SIL (ex-*Redwing*, MSC 200)	M 29	Tampa Marine Corporation	Jan 1959
TAJO (ex-*MSC 287*)	M 30	Tampa Marine Corporation	July 1959
GENIL (ex-*MSC 279*)	M 31	Tacoma, Seattle	Sep 1959
ODIEL (ex-*MSC 288*)	M 32	Tampa Marine Corporation	Oct 1959

Displacement, tons: 355 standard; 384 full load
Dimensions, feet (metres): 144·0 × 27·2 × 8·0 *(43 × 8 × 2·6)*
Guns: 2—20 mm (1 twin)
Main engines: 2 diesels; 2 shafts; 900 bhp = 14 knots
Oil fuel, tons: 30
Range, miles: 2 700 at 10 knots
Complement: 39

Wooden hulled.
Two sub-types: (a) with derrick on mainmast: M 21, 22, 23, 24, 25, 27, 28, 29, (b) with no mainmast but crane abreast the funnel: M 26, 30, 31, 32.

Tasks: *Llobregat* and *Ulla* have been allocated to coastal patrol duties.

Radar: Decca TM 626 or RM 914.

Sonar: UQS 1.

DUERO, Class A, with mainmast   *1975, Wright and Logan*

EBRO, Class B, small crane   *1974, Dr. Giorgio Arra*

444   SPAIN / Survey ships — Service forces

SURVEY SHIPS

4 "CASTOR" (A 20) CLASS

Name	No.	Builders	Commissioned
CASTOR	A 21 (ex-*H 4*)	Bazán, La Carraca	10 Nov 1966
POLLUX	A 22 (ex-*H 5*)	Bazán, La Carraca	6 Dec 1966
ANTARES	A 23	Bazán, La Carraca	21 Nov 1974
RIGEL	A 24	Bazán, La Carraca	21 Nov 1974

Displacement, tons: 327 standard; 383 full load
Dimensions, feet (metres): 125·9 × 24·9 × 8·9 *(38·4 × 7·6 × 2·8)*
Main engine: 1 Sulzer 4TD-36 diesel; 720 hp = 11·7 knots
Range, miles: 3 620 at 8 knots
Complement: 39 (A 23 and 24) 37 (A 21 and 22)

Antares and *Rigel* ordered summer 1972, launched 1973. Fitted with Raydist, Omega and digital presentation of data. Cost of later ships 105 million pesetas.

Appearance: A 21 and 22 have gaps in the gunwhale aft for Oropesa sweep. In A 23 and 24 this is a full run to the stern.

Radar: Raytheon.

CASTOR   1974, Spanish Navy

2 "MALASPINA" (A 30) CLASS (OCEANOGRAPHIC SHIPS)

Name	No.	Builders	Commissioned
MALASPINA	A 31	Bazán, La Carraca	21 Feb 1975
TOFIÑO	A 32	Bazán, La Carraca	23 Apr 1975

Displacement, tons: 820 standard; 1 090 full load
Dimensions, feet (metres): 188·9 × 38·4 × 11·8 *(57·6 × 11·7 × 3·6)*
Guns: 2—20 mm (single)
Main engines: 2 San Carlos MWM TbRHS-345-61 diesels; 3 600 bhp; 2 vp propellers = 15·3 knots
Range, miles: 4 000 at 12 knots; 3 140 at 14·5 knots
Complement: 63 (9 officers, 54 men)

Ordered mid-1972.
Malaspina laid down early 1973, launched 15 August 1973. *Tofiño* laid down 15 August 1973, launched 22 December 1973. Both named after their immediate predecessors. Of similar design to British "Bulldog" class costing 380 million pesetas each.

Electrical: Three 250 kVA alternators and one emergency 30 kVA.

Equipment: Fitted with Atlas Echograph *(4 500 metres)*, Raydist and Transit, Hewlett Packard 2100A computer inserted into Magnavox Transit satellite navigation system, active rudder with fixed pitch auxiliary propeller.

TOFIÑO   1976, Royal Spanish Navy

SERVICE FORCES

1 REPLENISHMENT TANKER

Name	No.	Builders	Commissioned
TEIDE	BP 11	Bazán, Cartagena	20 Oct 1956

Displacement, tons: 2 747 light; 8 030 full load
Oil capacity: 5 350 cu m
Dimensions, feet (metres): 385·5 × 48·5 × 20·3 *(117·5 × 14·8 × 6·2)*
Gun: 1—4·1 in (not mounted)
Main engines: 2 diesels; 3 360 bhp = 12 knots
Complement: *98

Ordered in December 1952. Laid down on 11 November 1954. Launched on 20 June 1955. Modernised in 1962 with refuelling at sea equipment (300 tons/hr).

Radar: Navigation: Decca TM 626.

TEIDE   1976, Royal Spanish Navy

1 HARBOUR TANKER

PP 1

Displacement, tons: 470
Dimensions, feet (metres): 147·5 × 25 × 9·5 *(45 × 7·6 × 2·9)*
Main engine: Deutz diesel; 220 bhp = 10 knots
Complement: 12

Built at Santander and launched in 1939.

O + 1 HARBOUR TANKER

PP —

Displacement, tons: 535
Dimensions, feet (metres): 111·5 × 22·9 × 9·8 *(34 × 7 × 3)*
Main engine: 1 diesel; 600 hp = 10·8 knots

Building by Bazán, Cartagena.

3 HARBOUR TANKERS

PP 3   PP 4   PP 5

Displacement, tons: 510
Dimensions, feet (metres): 121·4 × 22·3 × 9·8 *(37 × 6·8 × 3)*

9 HARBOUR TANKERS

PB 1, 2, 3, 4, 5, 6, 20, 21, 22

Displacement, tons: 200
Dimensions, feet (metres): 111·5 × 19·7 × 8·9 *(34 × 6 × 2·7)*

Small harbour tankers with capacity; 1-3, 100 tons; 4-6, 300 tons; 20-22, 193 tons (of similar construction to water carriers AB 1-3). All built by Bazán between 1960 and 1965. Dimensions and displacement given refer to PB 20-22.

SPAIN / Service forces — Boom defence vessels 445

0 + 1 HARBOUR TANKER

PB —

Displacement, tons: 214
Dimensions, feet (metres): 78·7 × 18 × 7·2 *(24 × 5·5 × 2·2)*
Main engine: 1 diesel; 400 hp = 10·7 knots

Building by Bazán, Cadiz. Capacity 100 tons.

1 SAIL TRAINING SHIP

Name	No.	Builders	Commissioned
JUAN SEBASTIAN DE ELCANO	—	Echevarrieta, Cadiz	28 Feb 1928

Displacement, tons: 3 420 standard; 3 754 full load
Dimensions, feet (metres): 269·2 pp; 308·5 oa × 43 × 23 *(94·1 × 13·6 × 7)*
Guns: 2—37 mm
Main engine: 1 Sulzer diesel; 1 shaft; 1 500 bhp = 9·5 knots
Oil fuel, tons: 230
Range, miles: 10 000 at 9·5 knots
Complement: 292 + 80 cadets

Four masted top-sail schooner—near sister of Chilean *Esmeralda*. Named after the first circumnavigator of the world (1519-26) who succeeded to the command of the expedition led by Magellanes after the latter's death. Laid down 24 November 1925. Launched on 5 March 1927.

Radar: Two Decca TM 626.

JUAN SEBASTIAN DE ELCANO and friends 7/1976, USN

ROYAL YACHT

Name	No.	Builders	Commissioned
AZOR	W0 1	Bazán, Ferrol	20 July 1949

Displacement, tons: 442 standard; 486 full load
Dimensions, feet (metres): 153·0 × 25·2 × 10·9 *(47 × 7·7 × 3·3)*
Main engines: 2 diesels; 1 200 bhp = 13·3 knots
Range, miles: 4 000
Complement: 47

Built as the Caudillo's yacht. Launched on 9 June 1949. Underwent an extensive refit in 1960, her hull being cut to admit an extension in length. Now painted royal blue with a buff funnel.

Radar: Decca TM 626.

AZOR 1970, X. I. Taibo

BOOM DEFENCE VESSELS

Name	No.	Builders	Commissioned
—	CR 1 (ex-G 6)	Penhoët, France	29 July 1955

Displacement, tons: 630 standard; 831 full load
Dimensions, feet (metres): 165·5 × 34 × 10·5 *(50·5 × 10·2 × 3·2)*
Guns: 1—40 mm; 4—20 mm (single)/70
Main engines: 2 diesels; electric drive; 1 shaft; 1 500 bhp = 12 knots
Oil fuel, tons: 126
Range, miles: 5 200 at 12 knots
Complement: 40

US off-shore order. Launched on 28 September 1954. Transferred from the USA in 1955 under MDAP. Sister ship of French "Cigale" class. Based at Cartagena.

Radar: One navigation set.

PBP 1, 2 and 3

Dimensions, feet (metres): 73·1 × 28·5 × 2·6 *(22·3 × 8·7 × 0·8)*

Gate Vessels.
Delivered 1959-60.

CR 1 1976, Royal Spanish Navy

PR 1-5

Dimensions, feet (metres): 72·2 × 28·5 × 4·3 *(22 × 8·7 × 4·3)*

Net laying barges.
Delivered 1959-60.

PRA 1-8

Dimensions, feet (metres): 91·8 × 27·9 × 2·3 *(28 × 8·5 × 0·7)*

Tugs for PBPs and PRs.
Delivered 1959-60.

446 SPAIN / Ocean tugs — Research craft

2 OCEAN TUGS

Name	No.	Builders	Commissioned
—	RA 1	Bazán, Cartagena	9 July 1955
—	RA 2	Bazán, Cartagena	12 Sep 1955

Displacement, tons: 757 standard; 1 039 full load
Dimensions, feet (metres): 184 × 33·5 × 12 *(56·1 × 10·1 × 3·9)*
Guns: 2—20 mm (singles)
Mines: Can lay 24
Main engines: 2 Sulzer diesels; 3 200 bhp; 1 shaft; cp propeller = 15 knots
Oil fuel, tons: 142
Range, miles: 5 500 at 15 knots
Complement: 49

Originally known as "Valen" class.

Radar: Decca 12.

RA 2   1974, Reiner Nerlich

1 OCEAN TUG

Name	No.	Builders	Commissioned
— (ex-*Metinda III*, ex-*Empire Jean*)	RA 3	Clelands, England	Apr 1945

Displacement, tons: 762 standard; 1 080 full load
Dimensions, feet (metres): 143 × 33·1 × 15·5 *(43·6 × 10·1 × 4·5)*
Main engines: Triple expansion; 3 200 ihp = 10 knots
Complement: 44

Purchased by Spain 26 May 1961.

Radar: Decca.

RA 3   1976, Royal Spanish Navy

3 OCEAN TUGS

Name	No.	Builders	Commissioned
POSEIDÓN	BS 1 (ex-*RA 6*)	Bazán, La Carraca	8 Aug 1964
—	RA 4	Bazán, La Carraca	25 Mar 1964
—	RA 5	Bazán, La Carraca	11 Apr 1964

Displacement, tons: 951 standard; 1 069 full load
Dimensions, feet (metres): 183·5 × 32·8 × 13·1 *(55·9 × 10 × 4)*
Main engines: 2 Sulzer diesels; 3 200 bhp = 15 knots
Range, miles: 4 640
Complement: 49 *(Poseidón 60)*

RA 6 was renumbered BS 1 when she became a frogman support ship, known as *Poseidón*. She carries a 300 metre/6 hour bathyscope.

Radar: Decca TM 626.

POSEIDÓN   1973, Dr. Giorgio Arra

COASTAL TUGS

RR —, RR —

Displacement, tons: 422
Dimensions, feet (metres): 91·8 × 26·2 × 12·5 *(28 × 8 × 3·8)*
Main engine: 1 diesel; 1 600 hp = 12·4 knots

Building by Bazán, Ferrol.

Name	No.	Builders	Commissioned
—	RR 50	Bazán, Cartagena	1963
—	RR 51	Bazán, Cartagena	1963
—	RR 52	Bazán, Cartagena	1963
—	RR 53	Bazán, Cartagena	1967
—	RR 54	Bazán, Cartagena	1967
—	RR 55	Bazán, Cartagena	1967

Displacement, tons: 205 (RR 50-52); 227 (RR 53-55) standard; 320 full load
Dimensions, feet (metres): 91·2 × 23 × 8·2 *(27·8 × 7 × 2·6)*
Main engines: Diesels; 1 shaft; 1 400 bhp (53 to 55), 800 bhp (50 to 52)
Complement: 13

Radar: Pilot 7D 20 in RR 50, 51 and 52.

RR 16

88·6 ft *(27 m)* long with complement of ten.
Built by Bazán, La Carraca. Commissioned 26 April 1962.

HARBOUR TUGS

RP —, RP —

Displacement, tons: 229
Dimensions, feet (metres): 91·8 × 24·6 × 11·2 *(28 × 7·5 × 3·4)*
Main engine: 1 diesel; 950 hp = 11 knots

Building by Bazán, Cartagena.

RP 1-12

Dimensions, feet (metres): 60·7 × 15·5 × — *(18·5 × 4·7 × —)*

Of 65 tons and 200 bhp (diesel). Commissioned 1965-67.

RP 40

Dimensions, feet (metres): 69·7 × 19·4 × — *(21·3 × 5·9 × —)*
Complement: 8

Of 150 tons and 600 bhp (diesel). Commissioned 27 December 1961.

RP 18

Displacement, tons: 160 standard
Dimensions, feet (metres): 81·0 × 17·7 × 7·9 *(24·7 × 5·4 × 2·4)*
Main engine: Triple expansion; 1 shaft (Kort nozzle)
Fuel: Coal

Laid down 1946 at Cartagena. Commissioned 1952.

Note: Five tug-launches of less than 50 tons—LR 47, 51, 67, 68, 69.

9 TORPEDO RECOVERY CRAFT

BTM 1-6

Built by Bazán 1961-63 of 60-190 tons. To carry torpedoes and mines and, in emergency, can act as minelayers. Complement eight.

ST 5

Torpedo tracking craft on range at Alcudia, Majorca. 36 ft *(11 m)* long.

LRT 3 and 4

TRVs built in 1956. 58·2 tons—58·1 × 6·6 × — *(17·7 × 2·2 × —)*. Can carry six torpedoes. Have stern ramp and crane. Based at submarine base, Cartagena.

RESEARCH CRAFT

An unpropelled underwater research base under construction 1976 by Bazán Cartagena. Can accommodate four. Dimensions: 40·7 × 20·7 *(12·4 × 6·3)* Hull diameter 11·8 *(3·6)*

WATER CARRIERS

A 2

Built in 1936. Of 1 785 tons full load with 1 000 tons capacity. Ocean going.

A 6

Displacement, tons: 1 785
Dimensions, feet (metres): 200 × 31·5 × 14·1 *(61 × 9·6 × 4·3)*
Main engine: Triple expansion; 1 shaft; 800 ihp = 9 knots
Complement: 27

Commissioned 30 January 1952.

A 7   A 9   A 10   A 11

Displacement, tons: 610 full load (A 7-8; 706 full load)
Dimensions, feet (metres): 146·9 × 24·9 × 9·8 *(44·8 × 7·6 × 3)*
Main engine: 1 shaft = 9 knots
Range, miles: 1 000
Complement: 16

All built at Bazán, La Carraca. A 7 commissioned 1952. A 9-11, 24 January 1963. All oceangoing.

Radar: Pilot 7 D20 (A 9-11).

A 11   *1973, Spanish Navy*

A —

Displacement, tons: 895 full load
Dimensions, feet (metres): 160·1 × 24·6 × 11·2 *(48·8 × 7·5 × 3·4)*
Main engine: 1 diesel; 700 hp = 10·8 knots
Capacity, tons: 600

Building by Bazán, Cadiz

A —

Displacement, tons: 535 full load
Dimensions, feet (metres): 111·5 × 22·9 × 9·8 *(34 × 7 × 3)*
Main engine: 1 diesel; 600 hp = 10·8 knots
Capacity: 300

Building by Bazán, Cadiz.

AB 1, 2, 3, 17, 18

All of less than 400 tons. Harbour water boats with 200 tons (AB 1-3) capacity.

5 DIVING CRAFT

BZL 1, 3, 9   NEREIDA (BZL 10)

Small self-propelled craft of less than 50 tons.

BL 13

Dumb barge for diving.

8 FLOATING CRANES

SANSÓN GRI (100 tons lift)
GR 3, 4 and 5 (30 tons lift)
GR 6, 7, 8, 9 (15 tons lift)

Based at Cartagena, Ferrol, La Carraca and Mahon.

CUSTOMS SERVICE

3 "AGUILUCHO" CLASS (COASTAL PATROL CRAFT)

Name	No.	Builders	Commissioned
AGUILUCHO	—	J. Roberto Rodriguez e Hijos, Vigo	1973
GAVILAN I	—	J. Roberto Rodriguez e Hijos, Vigo	1975
GAVILAN II	—	J. Roberto Rodriguez e Hijos, Vigo	1976

Displacement, tons: 45
Dimensions, feet (metres): 85·5 × 16·7 × 4·3 *(26·1 × 5·1 × 1·3)*
Gun: 1 MG
Main engines: Diesels; 2 shafts; 2 750 bhp = 30 knots
Range, miles: 750 at 30 knots

Aguilucho launched 19 February 1973 for Customs duties. *Gavilan I* launched 22 July 1975.

3 Ex-FRENCH "VC" CLASS

Name	No.	Builders	Commissioned
ALBATROS	—	CMN Cherbourg	1958
ALBATROS II	—	CMN Cherbourg	1968
ALBATROS III	—	CMN Cherbourg	1968

Displacement, tons: 82 full load
Dimensions, feet (metres): 104·5 × 15·5 × 5·5 *(31·8 × 4·7 × 1·7)*
Gun: 1—20 mm
Main engines: 2 diesels; 2 shafts; 2 700 bhp = 28 knots
Complement: 15

ALBATROS   *CMN*

In addition a number of other craft, some of wartime British and German classes, operate for the Finance ministry. Some named *Milano, Sacre, Nebli, Basanta Silva, Sangual.*

ARMY CRAFT

The Spanish Army operates a number of small cargo ships, the most recent acquisition being *Capitán Parra* (ex-smuggler *Lady Anastasia*), commissioned on 22 September 1978.

SRI LANKA

Formation

The Royal Ceylon Navy was formed on 9 December 1950 when the Navy Act was proclaimed. Called the Sri Lanka Navy since Republic Day 22 May 1972.

Headquarters Appointment

Commander of the Navy:
Rear-Admiral D. B. Goonesekera

General

Emphasis now being placed on local building of Coastal Patrol Craft although a 200 mile EEZ will call for larger craft than the Shanghais, more suitable craft than the "MOL" and, therefore, some ship or ships to replace *Gajabahu*, probably foreign built.

Personnel

(a) 1979: 2 600 (230 officers and 2 370 sailors)
(b) Voluntary service
(c) SLNR; 550 (50 officers, 500 sailors)

Strength of the Fleet

Type	Active	Building
Fast Attack Craft—Gun	6	—
Coastal Patrol Craft	29	—
Survey Craft	4	—

Naval Bases

A Naval Base established at Trincomalee, which was a British base from 1795 until 1957.
Minor bases at Karainagar, Colombo, Welisara, Tangale, Kalpitiya and Talaimannar.

Prefix to Ships' Names

SLNS

Mercantile Marine

Lloyd's Register of Shipping:
37 vessels of 92 528 tons gross

DELETIONS

1974 Short hydrofoil and 1 Thornycroft Patrol Craft (101)
1975 Tug *Aliya*
1978 *Gajabahu*

LIGHT FORCES

5 "SOORAYA" CLASS (Ex-CHINESE "SHANGHAI II") (FAST ATTACK CRAFT—GUN)

BALAWATHA   SOORAYA
DAKSAYA   WEERAYA
RAMAKAMI

Displacement, tons: 155 full load
Dimensions, feet (metres): 127·3 × 17·7 × 5·2 *(38·8 × 5·4 × 1·6)*
Guns: 4—37 mm (2 twin); 4—25 mm (2 twin abaft the bridge)
A/S weapons: 8 DCs
Main engines: 4 diesels; 4 800 bhp; 4 shafts = 30 knots
Range, miles: 800 at 17 knots
Complement: 25

The first pair was transferred by China in February 1972, the second pair in July 1972 and the last in December 1972. In monsoonal conditions off the coast of Sri Lanka these boats are lively and uncomfortable.

Radar: Skin Head.

SOORAYA   *1974, Sri Lanka Navy*

1 Ex-SOVIET "MOL" CLASS (FAST ATTACK CRAFT—GUN)

Name	No.	Builders	Commissioned
SAMUDRA DEVI	—	USSR	31 Dec 1975

Displacement, tons: 170 standard; 210 full load
Dimensions, feet (metres): 127·9 × 26·6 × 5·9 *(39·0 × 8·1 × 1·8)*
Guns: 4—30 mm (twin)
Main engines: 3 M 504 diesels; 12 000 bhp; 3 shafts
Speed, knots: 40
Complement: 25

Built 1975. Has certain variations from standard Soviet craft although the hull is a basic "Osa" type. The after radar pedestal mounts only a Kolonka optical sight and the torpedo tubes have been unshipped although the sponsons remain. An additional section of superstructure has been added abaft the after pedestal.

Radar: Don and High Pole IFF.

SAMUDRA DEVI   *12/1975, Sri Lanka Navy*

3 COASTAL PATROL CRAFT

Name	No.	Builders	Commissioned
PRADEEPA	—	Colombo D.Y. Ltd	1976
—	—	Colombo D.Y. Ltd	1977
—	—	Colombo D.Y. Ltd	1978

Displacement, tons: 44
Dimensions, feet (metres): 62 × 18 × 7 *(18·9 × 5·5 × 2·1)*
Guns: 2—20 mm
Main engines: 2 General Motors 8V 71-TI diesels; 1 240 hp; 2 shafts = 19 knots
Range, miles: 1 200 at 14 knots
Complement: 12

Ordered June 1976 (first pair) and November 1976.

2 COASTAL PATROL CRAFT

Name	No.	Builders	Commissioned
HANSAYA	—	Korody Marine Corporation, Venice	1956
LIHINIYA	—	Korody Marine Corporation, Venice	1956

Displacement, tons: 36
Dimensions, feet (metres): 66 × 14 × 4 *(20·1 × 4·3 × 1·2)*
Main engines: 2 General Motors diesels; 900 bhp = 16 knots

5 COASTAL PATROL CRAFT

Name	No.	Builders	Commissioned
BELIKAWA	421	Cheverton Workboats (UK)	Apr 1977
DIYAKAWA	422	Cheverton Workboats (UK)	June 1977
KORAWAKKA	423	Cheverton Workboats (UK)	July 1977
SERUWA	424	Cheverton Workboats (UK)	Sep 1977
TARAWA	425	Cheverton Workboats (UK)	Oct 1977

Displacement, tons: 22
Dimensions, feet (metres): 55·9 × 14·8 × 3·9 *(17 × 4·5 × 1·2)*
Guns: 3 MG
Main engines: Twin diesels; 640 hp = 23 knots
Range, miles: 1 000 at 12 knots
Complement: 7

Decca Navigation radar. Originally provided for the Customs service but used for general patrol duties.

BELIKAWA   *1977, Cheverton Workboats*

1 COASTAL PATROL CRAFT

Name	No.	Builders	Commissioned
—	—	Colombo D.Y. Ltd	1976

Displacement, tons: 15
Dimensions, feet (metres): 45 × 12 × 3 *(13·7 × 3·6 × 0·9)*
Gun: 1 MG
Main engines: 2 General Motors 6-71M diesels; 530 hp; 2 shafts = 16 knots
Range, miles: 250 at 16 knots
Complement: 8

18 (+ 2 SURVEY CRAFT) THORNYCROFT TYPE (COASTAL PATROL CRAFT)

Name	No.	Builders	Commissioned
—	102	Thornycroft (Malaysia) Ltd, Singapore	1966
—	103	Thornycroft (Malaysia) Ltd, Singapore	1966
—	104	Thornycroft (Malaysia) Ltd, Singapore	1967
—	105	Thornycroft (Malaysia) Ltd, Singapore	1967
—	106	Thornycroft (Malaysia) Ltd, Singapore	1967
—	107	Thornycroft (Malaysia) Ltd, Singapore	1967
—	108	Thornycroft (Malaysia) Ltd, Singapore	1967
—	109	Thornycroft (Malaysia) Ltd, Singapore	1967
—	110	Thornycroft (Malaysia) Ltd, Singapore	1967
—	201	Thornycroft (Malaysia) Ltd, Singapore	1967
—	202	Thornycroft (Malaysia) Ltd, Singapore	1967
—	203	Thornycroft (Malaysia) Ltd, Singapore	1968
—	204	Thornycroft (Malaysia) Ltd, Singapore	1968
—	205	Thornycroft (Malaysia) Ltd, Singapore	1968
—	206	Thornycroft (Malaysia) Ltd, Singapore	1968
—	207	Thornycroft (Malaysia) Ltd, Singapore	1968
—	208	Thornycroft (Malaysia) Ltd, Singapore	1968
—	209	Thornycroft (Malaysia) Ltd, Singapore	1968
—	210	Thornycroft (Malaysia) Ltd, Singapore	1968
—	211	Thornycroft (Malaysia) Ltd, Singapore	1968

Displacement, tons: 13
Dimensions, feet (metres): 45·5 × 12 × 3 *(14·9 × 3·9 × 0·9)*
Main engines: 102: Thornycroft K6SMI engines; 500 bhp; 2 shafts = 25 knots
  Remainder: General Motors 6 71-Series; 500 bhp; 2 shafts = 25 knots

The hulls are of hard chine type with double skin teak planking. Equipped with radar, radio, searchlight etc. Two ordered in 1965. Seven ordered in 1966. Assembled in Sri Lanka and completed by September 1968. Originally 21 boats.
They are based, as two squadrons, at Kalpitiya and Karainagar. Two (pennant numbers not known) employed as surveying craft HV 11 and 12 (see below).

SURVEY CRAFT

Name	No.	Builders	Commissioned
SERUWA	—	Italy	1955
TARAWA	—	Italy	1955

Of 13 tons and 15 knots with two Foden diesels.

HV 11   HV 12

Thornycroft type of coastal patrol craft converted to survey craft, 1977.

SUDAN

Establishment

The navy was established in 1962 to operate on the Red Sea coast and on the River Nile. The original training staff was from Yugoslav Navy, but this staff left in 1972.

Diplomatic Representation

Naval, Military and Air Attaché in London:
  Colonel A. El-Tayeb El-Mihaina

Personnel

(a) 1979: 600 officers and men
(b) Voluntary service

Bases

Port Sudan for Red Sea operations with a separate riverine unit on the Nile based at Khartoum.

General

The overall standard of operational efficiency has apparently suffered from lack of maintenance and spare parts.

Mercantile Marine

Lloyd's Register of Shipping:
  13 vessels of 43 375 tons gross

LIGHT FORCES

2 Ex-YUGOSLAV "KRALJEVICA" CLASS (LARGE PATROL CRAFT)

Name	No.	Builders	Commissioned
EL FASHER	522	Yugoslavia	1954
EL KHARTOUM	523	Yugoslavia	1955

Displacement, tons: 190 standard; 245 full load
Dimensions, feet (metres): 134·5 × 20·7 × 7·2 *(41 × 6·3 × 2·2)*
Guns: 2—40 mm; 2—20 mm
Main engines: Diesel; 2 shafts; 3 300 bhp = 20 knots
Range, miles: 1 500 at 12 knots

Transferred from the Yugoslav Navy during 1969.

"KRALJEVICA" Class

6 Ex-YUGOSLAV "101" CLASS (FAST ATTACK CRAFT—GUN)

Displacement, tons: 55 standard; 60 full load
Dimensions, feet (metres): 78 × 21·3 × 7·8 *(23·8 × 6·5 × 2·4)*
Guns: 2—40 mm; 2—20 mm (single)
Main engines: 3 Packard petrol motors; 3 shafts; 5 000 bhp = 36 knots
Complement: 14

Transferred in this "Gun" version of the class in 1970. Same characteristics as US "Higgins" class.

"101" Class

3 Ex-IRANIAN COASTAL PATROL CRAFT

Name	No.	Builders	Commissioned
— (ex-*Gohar*)	—	Abeking and Rasmussen	1970
— (ex-*Shahpar*)	—	Abeking and Rasmussen	1970
— (ex-*Shahram*)	—	Abeking and Rasmussen	1970

Displacement, tons: 70
Dimensions, feet (metres): 75·2 × 16·5 × 6 *(22·9 × 5 × 1·8)*
Main engines: 2 diesels; 2 shafts; 2 200 hp = 27 knots
Complement: 19

Built for Iran. Transferred to Iranian Coast Guard 1975 and to Sudan later that year.

450   SUDAN / Light forces — SURINAM / Light forces

4 Ex-YUGOSLAV PBR TYPE (LARGE PATROL CRAFT)

Name	No.	Builders	Commissioned
GIHAD	PB 1	Mosor Shipyard, Trogir, Yugoslavia	1961
HORRIYA	PB 2	Mosor Shipyard, Trogir, Yugoslavia	1961
ISTIQLAL	PB 3	Mosor Shipyard, Trogir, Yugoslavia	1962
SHAAB	PB 4	Mosor Shipyard, Trogir, Yugoslavia	1962

Displacement, tons: 100
Dimensions, feet (metres): 115 × 16·5 × 5·2 *(35 × 5 × 1·7)*
Guns: 1—40 mm; 1—20 mm; 2—7·6 mm MG
Main engines: Mercedes-Benz (MTU 12V 493) diesels; 2 shafts; 1 800 bhp = 20 knots
Range, miles: 1 400 at 12 knots
Complement: 20

Of steel construction. First craft acquired by the newly established Sudanese Navy.

GIHAD

AMPHIBIOUS FORCES

2 Ex-YUGOSLAV "DTK 221" CLASS (LCTs)

SOBAT   DINDER

Displacement, tons: 410
Dimensions, feet (metres): 144·3 × 19·7 × 7 *(44 × 6 × 2·1)*
Guns: 1—20 mm; 2—12·7 mm
Speed, knots: 10
Complement: 15

Transferred during 1969.

"DTK 221" Class

1 Ex-YUGOSLAV "DTM 231" CLASS (LCU)

Transferred by Yugoslavia 1970—of 40 tons.

SERVICE FORCES

1 SUPPORT TANKER

FASHODA (ex-PN 17)

Displacement, tons: 420 standard; 650 full load
Dimensions, feet (metres): 141·5 × 22·8 × 13·6 *(43·2 × 7 × 4·2)*
Main engines: 300 bhp = 7 knots

Former Yugoslav Tanker rehabilitated and transferred to the Sudanese Navy in 1969.

1 SURVEY SHIP

TIENGA

A small vessel, converted into a hydrographic ship, acquired from Yugoslavia in 1969.

1 WATER BOAT

BARAKA (ex-PV 6)

A small water carrier, transferred from Yugoslavia to the Sudanese Navy in 1969.

SURINAM

Formerly Dutch Guiana—granted independence in 1975.

Ministerial

Prime Minister and Minister of Internal Affairs:
  Henck Arron

Base

Paramaribo

Mercantile Marine

Lloyd's Register of Shipping:
  21 vessels of 8 847 tons gross

LIGHT FORCES

3 LARGE PATROL CRAFT

Name	No.	Builders	Commissioned
—	S 401	De Vries, Aalsmeer, Netherlands	16 Nov 1976
—	S 402	De Vries, Aalsmeer, Netherlands	3 May 1977
—	S 403	De Vries, Aalsmeer, Netherlands	1 Nov 1977

Displacement, tons: 127
Dimensions, feet (metres): 105 × 21·3 × 5·5 *(32 × 6·5 × 1·7)*
Guns: 2—40 mm
Main engines: 2 Paxman 12 YHCM diesels; 2 110 hp = 17·5 knots
Range, miles: 1 200 at 13·5 knots
Complement: 15

This design has far greater speed and armament potential but Surinam apparently opted for the scaled-down version.

1 COASTAL PATROL CRAFT

Length, feet (metres): 32·8 *(10)*
Main engine: 1 Dorman 8 JT; 280 hp

Ordered December 1974 from Schottel, Netherlands. Delivered August 1975.

3 COASTAL PATROL CRAFT

Length, feet (metres): 72·2 *(22)*
Gun: 1—40 mm Bofors
Main engines: 2 Paxman 12 YHCM diesels; 2 110 hp; 2 shafts

Ordered April 1975 from Schottel, Netherlands. Delivered 1976.

3 COASTAL PATROL CRAFT

Length, feet (metres): 41·4 *(12·6)*
Main engine: 1 Dorman 8 JT; 280 hp

Ordered December 1974 from Schottel, Netherlands. Delivered August 1975.

SWEDEN

Headquarters Appointments

Commander-in-Chief:
 Vice-Admiral Per Rudberg
Chief of Naval Material Department:
 Rear-Admiral Gunnar Grandin
Chief of Naval Staff:
 Major-General Bo Varenius (Coastal Artillery)

Senior Command

Commander-in-Chief of Coastal Fleet:
 Rear-Admiral Bengt Rasin

Diplomatic Representation

Defence and Naval Attaché in London:
 Rear-Admiral Rolf Rheborg
Naval Attaché in Washington:
 Captain Åke Johnson

Personnel

a) 1979: 14 900 officers and men of Navy and Coast Artillery made up of 4 800 regulars, 3 100 Reservists and 7 000 National Servicemen. In addition 8 000 conscripts receive annual training
b) 7½-15 months national service

Bases

Stockholm, Karlskrona, Göteborg
Minor base at Härnösand

Composition of the Navy

In addition to seagoing personnel the Navy includes the Coastal Artillery, manning 20 mobile and 45 coastal batteries of both major guns and SSMs. A number of amphibious and patrol craft are also controlled by the Coastal Artillery.

Naval Air Arm

 5 Alouette II helicopters (training)
10 Jet Ranger helicopters
10 Vertol 107 (Hkp-4B)

Mercantile Marine

Lloyd's Register of Shipping:
 696 vessels of 6 508 255 tons gross

Strength of the Fleet

Type	Active (Reserve)	Building (Planned)
Submarines—Patrol	11	3 (4)
Destroyers	1 (5)	—
Frigates	— (2)	—
Fast Attack Craft—Missile	10	7
Fast Attack Craft—Torpedo	25	—
Large Patrol Craft	7	—
Coastal Patrol Craft	31	—
Minelayers	3	1
Minelayers—Coastal	9	—
Minelayers—Small	36	—
Minesweepers—Coastal	12	—
Minesweepers—Inshore	18	—
LCMs	9	—
LCUs	81	—
LCAs	54	—
Mine Transports	2	—
Survey Ships	6	—
Tanker—Support	1	—
Supply Ship	1	—
Tugs	20	—
Salvage Ship	1	—
Sail Training Ships	2	—
Icebreakers	8	—
TRVs	3	—
Tenders	10	—
Water Boats	2	—

Note: It is reported that all destroyers and frigates will be put up for disposal in the near future.

DELETIONS

Submarines

1975 Gäddan, Siken ("Abborren" Class)
1976 Abborren, Laxen, Makrillen ("Abborren" Class)
1978 Bävern, Hajen, Illern, Sälen, Uttern, Valen

Frigates

1974 Karlskrona
1978 Hälsingborg, Kalmar, Öland, Uppland

Light Forces

1973 T 101
1975 T 38, 39, 40
1976 T 102-106
1977 T 108-109, T 111
1978 T 46-52

Mine Warfare Forces

1977 Orust, Tjörn

Surveying Vessels

1972 Johen Nordenankar, Petter Gedda
1973 Anden
1975 Ledaren

Depot Ships

1972 Patricia
1976 Marieholm

Miscellaneous

1973 Gälnan (water carrier)
1974 Ymer (icebreaker)
1975 Urd (experimental ship)

PENNANT LIST

Submarines

Del	Delfinen
Dra	Draken
Gri	Gripen
Näc	Näcken
Naj	Najad
Nep	Neptun
Nor	Nordkaparen
Sbj	Sjöbjörnen
Shu	Sjöhunden
Shä	Sjöhästen
Sle	Sjölejonet
Sor	Sjöormen
Spr	Springaren
Vgn	Vargen

Destroyers

J 18	Halland
J 19	Smaaland
J 20	Östergötland
J 21	Södermanland
J 22	Gästrikland
J 23	Hälsingland

Frigates

F 11	Visby
F 12	Sundsvall

Light Forces

P 150	Jägaren
P 151	Hugin
P 152	Munin
P 153	Magne
P 154	Mode
P 155	Vale
P 156	Vidar
P 157	Mjölner
P 158	Mysing
P 159	Kaparen
P 160	Väktaren
P 161	Snapphanen
P 162	Spejaren
P 163	Styrbjörn
P 164	Starkodder
P 165	Tordón
P 166	Tirfing
T 53-56	"T 42" class
T 107	Aldebaran
T 110	Arcturus
T 112	Astrea
T 121	Spica
T 122	Sirius
T 123	Capella
T 124	Castor
T 125	Vega
T 126	Virgo
T 131	Norrköping
T 132	Nynäshamn
T 133	Norrtälje
T 134	Varberg
T 135	Västeräs
T 136	Västervik
T 137	Umea
T 138	Pitea
T 139	Lulea
T 140	Halmstad
T 141	Strömstad
T 142	Ystad
V 01	Skanór
V 02	Smyge
V 03	Arild
V 04	Viken

Amphibious Forces

A 324	Ane
A 325	Balder
A 326	Loke
A 327	Ring
A 333	Skagul
A 335	Sleipner
201-276	LCUs
280-284	LCUs
301 on	LCAs

Mine Warfare Forces

M 01	Älvsnabben
M 02	Älvsborg
M 03	Visborg
M 04	Karlskrona
M 15-16, 21-26	MSI
M 31	Gåssten
M 32	Norsten
M 33	Viksten
M 43	Hisingen
M 44	Blackan
M 45	Dämman
M 46	Galten
M 47	Gillöga
M 48	Rödlöga
M 49	Svartlöga
M 51	Hanö
M 52	Tärnö
M 53	Tjurkö
M 54	Sturkö
M 55	Ornö
M 56	Utö
M 57	Arkö
M 58	Spårö
M 59	Karlsö
M 60	Iggö
M 61	Styrsö
M 62	Skaftö
M 63	Aspö
M 64	Hasslö
M 65	Vinö
M 66	Vållö
M 67	Nämdö
M 68	Blidö
MUL 11-19	Coastal Minelayers
501-536	Small Minelayers

Service Forces

A 211	Belos
A 216	Unden
A 217	Fryken
A 221	Freja
A 228	Brännaren
A 231	Lommen
A 232	Spoven
A 236	Fållaren
A 237	Minören
A 242	Skuld
A 246	Hagern
A 247	Pelikanen
A 248	Pingvinen
A 251	Achilles
A 252	Ajax
A 253	Hermes
A 256	Sigrun
A 321	Hector
A 322	Heros
A 323	Hercules
A 324	Hera
A 326	Hebe
A 327	Passop
A 328	Ran
A 329	Henrik
A 330	Atlas
A 332	Mársgarn
A 336	Vitsgarn
A 341	ATB 1
A 342	ATB 2
A 343	ATB 3
A 345	Granaten
A 347	Edda
A 349	Gerda
L 51-55	LCUs
S 01	Gladan
S 02	Falken

452 SWEDEN / Introduction — Submarines

"ÖSTERGÖTLAND" Class

"HALLAND" Class

"ÖLAND" Class

"VISBY" Class

"ÄLVSBORG" Class

KARLSKRONA

SUBMARINES

Notes: (a) Submarines do not have pennant numbers on fin but carry distinctive letters in their place.
(b) A rescue vehicle, *Urf,* of 52 tons with a diving depth of 1 500 ft *(460 m)* was launched 17 April 1978. Similar to US Navy DSRV she has a capacity for 25 men on each dive.

NEW CONSTRUCTION "A 17" CLASS

Design contract for four boats awarded to Kockums, Malmö on 17 April 1978.

3 "NÄCKEN" CLASS (A 14)

Name	No.	Builders	Laid down	Launched	Commissioned
NÄCKEN	Näk	Kockums, Malmö	Nov 1972	17 Apr 1978	1979
NAJAD	Naj	Karlskrona Varvet	Sep 1973	—	1979
NEPTUN	Nep	Kockums, Malmö	Mar 1974	—	1979

Displacement, tons: 980 surfaced; 1 125 dived
Length, feet (metres): 135 *(41)*
Beam, feet (metres): 20·0 *(6·1)*
Draught, feet (metres): 13·4 *(4·1)*
Torpedo tubes: 6—21 in *(533 mm)*
Mines: Minelaying capability
Main machinery: Diesels; electric motors; 1 shaft with large 5-bladed propeller
Speed, knots: 20 surfaced and dived
Complement: 19

The very high beam to length ratio is notable in this Albacore hull design. Have large bow mounted sonar. Main accommodation space is abaft the control room with machinery spaces right aft. A central computer provides both attack information and date on main machinery. Single periscope.

Future: It is possible that two more of this class may be built before the "A 17" class.

NÄCKEN
1979, Royal Swedish Navy

5 "SJÖORMEN" CLASS (A 11B)

Name	No.	Builders	Laid down	Launched	Commissioned
SJÖORMEN	Sor	Kockums, Malmö	1965	25 Jan 1967	31 July 1967
SJÖLEJONET	Sle	Kockums, Malmö	1966	29 June 1967	16 Dec 1968
SJÖHUNDEN	Shu	Kockums, Malmö	1966	21 Mar 1968	25 June 1969
SJÖBJÖRNEN	Sbj	Karlskrona Varvet	1967	6 Aug 1968	28 Feb 1969
SJÖHÄSTEN	Shä	Karlskrona Varvet	1966	9 Jan 1968	15 Sep 1969

Displacement, tons: 1 125 standard; 1 400 dived
Length, feet (metres): 167·3 *(50·5)*
Beam, feet (metres): 20·0 *(6·1)*
Draught, feet (metres): 16·7 *(5·1)*
Torpedo tubes: 4—21 in *(533 mm)* bow; 2 A/S tubes
Main machinery: 2 Pielstick diesels; 1 large 5-bladed propeller; 2 200 bhp; 1 electric motor
Speed, knots: 15 surfaced; 20 dived
Endurance: 3 weeks
Complement: 23

Albacore hull. Twin-decked. Diving depth 500 ft.

SJÖHÄSTEN
5/1976, Reinhard Nerlich

SWEDEN / Submarines — Destroyers 453

6 "DRAKEN" CLASS (A 11)

Name	No.	Builders	Laid down	Launched	Commissioned
DELFINEN	Del	Karlskrona Varvet	1959	7 Mar 1961	7 June 1962
DRAKEN	Dra	Kockums, Malmö	1958	1 Apr 1960	4 Apr 1962
GRIPEN	Gri	Karlskrona Varvet	1959	31 May 1960	28 Apr 1962
NORDKAPAREN	Nor	Kockums, Malmö	1959	8 Mar 1961	4 Apr 1962
SPRINGAREN	Spr	Kockums, Malmö	1960	31 Aug 1961	7 Nov 1962
VARGEN	Vgn	Kockums, Malmö	1958	20 May 1960	15 Nov 1961

Displacement, tons: 770 standard; 835 surfaced; 1 110 dived
Length, feet (metres): 226·4 *(69·0)*
Beam, feet (metres): 16·7 *(5·1)*
Draught, feet (metres): 16·4 *(5·0)*
Torpedo tubes: 4—21 in *(533 mm)* bow
Main machinery: 2 Pielstick diesels; 1 660 bhp; 1 large 5-bladed propeller; 1 electric motor
Speed, knots: 17 surfaced; 20 dived
Complement: 36

DELFINEN 5/1976, Reinhard Nerlich

DESTROYERS

4 "SÖDERMANLAND" CLASS

Name	No.	Builders	Laid down	Launched	Commissioned
ÖSTERGÖTLAND	J 20	Götaverken, Göteborg	1 Sep 1955	8 May 1956	3 Mar 1958
SÖDERMANLAND	J 21	Eriksberg Mek Verkstads	1 June 1955	28 May 1956	27 June 1958
GÄSTRIKLAND	J 22	Götaverken, Göteborg	1 Oct 1955	6 June 1956	14 Jan 1959
HÄLSINGLAND	J 23	Kockums Mek Verkstads A/B	1 Oct 1955	14 Jan 1957	17 June 1959

Displacement, tons: 2 150 standard; 2 600 full load
Length, feet (metres): 367·5 *(112·0)*
Beam, feet (metres): 36·8 *(11·2)*
Draught, feet (metres): 12·0 *(3·7)*
Missiles: SSM; RB 08A (Mk 20 launcher)
SAM; Sea Cat (RB 07) (1 quad launcher)
Guns: 4—4·7 in *(120 mm)*/50 (twin); 4—40 mm/70 (single)
A/S weapons: 1 triple-barrelled Squid
Torpedo tubes: 6—21 in *(533 mm)* (1 mount)
Mines: 60 can be carried
Main engines: De Laval turbines; 2 shafts; 47 000 bhp

Boilers: 2 Babcock & Wilcox
Speed, knots: 35
Oil fuel, tons: 330
Range, miles: 2 200 at 20 knots
Complement: 244 (18 officers, 226 men)

Modernisation: *Gästrikland* in 1965, *Södermanland* in 1967, *Hälsingland* in 1968, *Östergötland* in 1969.

Radar: Search and target designator: Thomson CSF Saturn.
Fire control: HSA M 44 for Sea Cat—M 45 series for guns.

All four in reserve. Although there are reports of their possible conversion to frigates it is possible that all will be scrapped in 1982 unless previously sold.

SÖDERMANLAND 1977, Royal Swedish Navy

2 "HALLAND" CLASS

Name	No.	Builders	Laid down	Launched	Commissioned
HALLAND	J 18	Götaverken, Göteborg	1951	16 July 1952	8 June 1955
SMÅLAND	J 19	Eriksberg Mek Verkstads	1951	23 Oct 1952	12 Jan 1956

Displacement, tons: 2 800 standard; 3 400 full load
Length, feet (metres): 397·2 *(121·0)*
Beam, feet (metres): 41·3 *(12·6)*
Draught, feet (metres): 14·8 *(4·5)*
Missiles: SSM; RB 08A (Mk 20 launcher)
Guns: 4—4·7 in *(120 mm)*/50 (twin); 2—57 mm/60 (twin); 6—40 mm/70
A/S weapons: Two 4-barrelled rocket-launcher (Bofors)
Torpedo tubes: 8—21 in *(533 mm)* (1 quin, 1 triple)
Mines: Can be fitted for minelaying
Main engines: De Laval double reduction geared turbines; 2 shafts; 58 000 bhp
Boilers: 2 Penhöet
Speed, knots: 35
Oil fuel, tons: 500
Range, miles: 3 000 at 20 knots
Complement: 290 (18 officers, 272 men)

Both ordered in 1948. The first Swedish destroyers of post-war design. Fully automatic gun turrets forward and aft. Both modernised in 1962. *Halland* in reserve.

Missiles: Being re-equipped with missiles 1977-78.

Radar: Search and target designator: Thomson CSF Saturn (foremast).
Air warning: LW-02 (mainmast).
Fire control, search and tracking: M 22 and associated sets (radome).
ECM.

HALLAND 1978, Michael D. J. Lennon

454 SWEDEN / Frigates — Light forces

FRIGATES

2 "VISBY" CLASS

Name	No.	Builders	Laid down	Launched	Commissioned
VISBY	F 11	Götaverken, Göteborg	1941	16 Oct 1942	10 Aug 1943
SUNDSVALL	F 12	Eriksberg Mek Verkstads	1941	20 Oct 1942	17 Sep 1943

Displacement, tons: 1 150 standard; 1 320 full load
Length, feet (metres): 321·5 *(98·0)*
Beam, feet (metres): 30 *(9·1)*
Draught, feet (metres): 12·5 *(3·8)*
Aircraft: 1 helicopter platform
Guns: 2—57 mm
A/S weapons: 1—375 mm Bofors 4-tube rocket launcher
Main engines: 2 De Laval geared turbines; 2 shafts; 36 000 shp
Boilers: Three 3-drum type
Speed, knots: 39
Range, miles: 1 600 at 20 knots
Oil fuel, tons: 150
Complement: 140

SUNDSVALL   1972, Royal Swedish Navy

All of the class of four were originally fitted for minelaying. Both in reserve.

Radar: Thorpson CSF Saturn S-band long-range search and target designator.

M 24 fire control systems with co-mounted radars for search and tracking for guns.

Armament: Before conversion to frigates: Mounted 3—47 in *(120 mm)*; 2—57 mm and 3—40 mm.

LIGHT FORCES

10 + 7 "HUGIN" (Ex-"JÄGAREN") CLASS (FAST ATTACK CRAFT—MISSILE)

Name	No.	Builders	Commissioned
JÄGAREN	P 150	Norway	8 June 1972
HUGIN	P 151	Norway	3 June 1977
MUNIN	P 152	Norway	1 Apr 1978
MAGNE	P 153	Norway	15 June 1978
MODE	P 154	Norway	9 Jan 1978
VALE	P 155	Norway	8 Aug 1978
VIDAR	P 156	Norway	11 Nov 1978
MJÖLNER	P 157	Norway	3 Feb 1979
MYSING	P 158	Norway	May 1979
KAPAREN	P 159	Norway	Aug 1979
VÄKTAREN	P 160	Norway	—
SNAPPHANEN	P 161	Norway	—
SPEJAREN	P 162	Norway	—
STYRBJÖRN	P 163	Norway	—
STARKODDER	P 164	Norway	—
TORDÖN	P 165	Norway	—
TIRFING	P 166	Norway	—

Displacement, tons: 140
Dimensions, feet (metres): 118 × 20·3 × 4·9 *(36 × 6·2 × 1·5)*
Missiles: SSM; 6 Penguin Mark 2 (single cells)
Gun: 1—57 mm/70 Bofors
Main engines: 2 MTU MB20V 672 TY90 diesels; 2 shafts; 7 000 bhp = 35 knots
Complement: 19

HUGIN   1978, Royal Swedish Navy

Instead of the motor gunboats projected for several years a choice was made of fast attack craft similar to the Norwegian "Hauk" class armed with Penguin missiles. They can be fitted for minelaying at the expense of missiles or torpedoes.
Jägaren underwent extensive trials and, on 15 May 1975, an order for a further 11 was placed with Bergens Mekaniske Verksted, Norway and five from Westermoen. *Hugin* and *Munin* reached Sweden on 6 July 1978. *Magne* was launched 9 January 1978, *Mode* on 8 August 1978. Guns and electronics are being provided from Sweden. Fitted for alternative minelaying capability aft.
An extra deck-mounting ring is fitted amidships though now blanked by Penguin mounts.

12 "SPICA T 131" CLASS (FAST ATTACK CRAFT—TORPEDO)

Name	No.	Builders	Commissioned
NORRKÖPING	T 131	Karlskrona Varvet	1 Mar 1973
NYNÄSHAMN	T 132	Karlskrona Varvet	8 Sep 1973
NORRTÄLJE	T 133	Karlskrona Varvet	1 Feb 1974
VARBERG	T 134	Karlskrona Varvet	13 June 1974
VÄSTERÅS	T 135	Karlskrona Varvet	25 Oct 1974
VÄSTERVIK	T 136	Karlskrona Varvet	15 Jan 1975
UMEÅ	T 137	Karlskrona Varvet	15 May 1975
PITEÅ	T 138	Karlskrona Varvet	13 Sep 1975
LULEÅ	T 139	Karlskrona Varvet	28 Nov 1975
HALMSTAD	T 140	Karlskrona Varvet	9 Apr 1976
STRÖMSTAD	T 141	Karlskrona Varvet	13 Sep 1976
YSTAD	T 142	Karlskrona Varvet	10 Jan 1976

Displacement, tons: 230
Dimensions, feet (metres): 134·5 × 23·3 × 5·2 *(41 × 7·1 × 1·6)*
Gun: 1—57 mm/70 Bofors
Rocket launchers: 8 for 57 mm flare rockets
Torpedo tubes: 6—21 in *(533 mm)* for wire-guided torpedoes
Main engines: 3 Rolls-Royce Proteus gas turbines; 3 shafts; 12 900 bhp = 40·5 knots
Complement: 27

VÄSTERVIK   1975, Kapten Goran Frisk

Similar to the original "Spica" class from which they were developed. Launched—*Norrköping* 16 November 1972, *Nynäshamn* 24 April 1973, *Norrtalje* 18 September 1973, *Varberg* 2 February 1974, *Västerås* 15 May 1974, *Västervik* 2 September 1974, *Umea* 13 January 1975, *Pitea* 12 May 1975. Laid down—*Luleå* 6 September 1974, *Halmstad* 7 February 1975.

Missiles: Plans exist for the fitting of two twin missile launchers aft in place of after pair of torpedo tubes. These may be Penguin II in some boats and Harpoon in others. A number of the latter has been ordered from the USA.

Radar: Philips Teleindustrie 9 LV 200-simultaneous air and surface search in I band with tracking in separate band.

6 "SPICA T 121" CLASS (FAST ATTACK CRAFT—TORPEDO)

Name	No.	Builders	Commissioned
SPICA	T 121	Götaverken, Göteborg	1966
SIRIUS	T 122	Götaverken, Göteborg	1966
CAPELLA	T 123	Götaverken, Göteborg	1966
CASTOR	T 124	Karlskrona Varvet	1967
VEGA	T 125	Karlskrona Varvet	1967
VIRGO	T 126	Karlskrona Varvet	1967

Displacement, tons: 200 standard; 230 full load
Dimensions, feet (metres): 134·5 × 23·3 × 5·2 *(41 × 7·1 × 1·6)*
Gun: 1—57 mm/70 Bofors
Torpedo tubes: 6—21 in *(533 mm)* (single, fixed)
Rocket launchers: 6—57 mm flare rockets; 4—103 mm flare rockets
Main engines: 3 Bristol Siddeley Proteus gas turbines; 3 shafts; 12 720 shp = 40 knots
Complement: 28 (7 officers, 21 ratings)

The 57 mm gun is in a power operated turret controlled by a radar equipped director.

Missiles: Plans exist for the fitting of two twin missile launchers aft in place of after pair of torpedo tubes (post 1978).

Radar: M 22 fire control system with co-mounted radars in radome for guns and torpedoes.

SPICA   1977, Royal Swedish Navy

3 "PLEJAD" CLASS (FAST ATTACK CRAFT—TORPEDO)

Name	No.	Builders	Commissioned
ALDEBARAN	T 107	Lürssen, Vegesack	1956
ARCTURUS	T 110	Lürssen, Vegesack	1957
ASTREA	T 112	Lürssen, Vegesack	1956

Displacement, tons: 155 standard; 170 full load
Dimensions, feet (metres): 147·6 × 19 × 5·2 (45 × 5·8 × 1·6)
Guns: 2—40 mm/70 Bofors (single)
Rocket launchers: 4—103 mm flare rockets; 1—12 rail 57 mm flare launcher
Torpedo tubes: 6—21 in (533 mm)
Main engines: 3 Mercedes-Benz (MTU 20 V 672) diesels; 3 shafts; 9 000 bhp = 37·5 knots
Range, miles: 600 at 30 knots
Complement: 33

Launched between 1954 and 1957. Due for deletion. Survivors of a class of twelve.

"PLEJAD" Class 1975, Royal Swedish Navy

4 "T 42" CLASS (FAST ATTACK CRAFT—TORPEDO)

Name	No.	Builders	Commissioned
—	T 53	Naval Dockyard, Stockholm	1958
—	T 54	Naval Dockyard, Stockholm	1959
—	T 55	Naval Dockyard, Stockholm	1959
—	T 56	Naval Dockyard, Stockholm	1959

Displacement, tons: 40 standard
Dimensions, feet (metres): 75·5 × 19·4 × 4·6 (23 × 5·9 × 1·4)
Gun: 1—40 mm Bofors
Rocket launchers: 1—12 rail 57 mm flare launcher
Torpedo tubes: 2—21 in (533 mm)
Main engines: 3 Isotta Fraschini petrol engines; 4 500 bhp = 45 knots

T 42-45 converted to "V 01" class.

T 56 1975, Royal Swedish Navy

6 "HANÖ" CLASS (LARGE PATROL CRAFT)

Name	No.	Builders	Commissioned
HANÖ	M 51	Karlskrona Varvet	1954
TÄRNÖ	M 52	Karlskrona Varvet	1954
TJURKÖ	M 53	Karlskrona Varvet	1954
STURKÖ	M 54	Karlskrona Varvet	1954
ORNÖ	M 55	Karlskrona Varvet	1954
UTÖ	M 56	Karlskrona Varvet	1954

Displacement, tons: 275 standard
Dimensions, feet (metres): 131·2 × 23 × 8 (40 × 7 × 2·4)
Guns: 2—40 mm/70 (except Utö; 1—40mm) (single)
Main engines: 2 Nohab diesels; 2 shafts; 910 bhp = 14·5 knots

Steel hulls. Converted for patrol duties—reclassified 1 January 1979.

TJURKÖ 1975, Royal Swedish Navy

1 LARGE PATROL CRAFT

V 57

Displacement, tons: 115 standard
Dimensions, feet (metres): 98 × 17·3 × 7·5 (30 × 5·3 × 2·3)
Gun: 1—20 mm
Main engine: Diesel; 500 bhp = 13·5 knots
Complement: 12

Built at Stockholm. Launched in 1953. Fitted for minelaying. Attached to Coastal Artillery.

5 COASTAL PATROL CRAFT

SVK 1   SVK 2   SVK 3   SVK 4   SVK 5

Displacement, tons: 19 standard
Dimensions, feet (metres): 52·5 × 12·1 × 3·9 (16 × 3·7 × 1·2)
Gun: 1—20 mm
Main engine: Diesel; 100 to 135 bhp = 10 knots
Complement: 12

Patrol craft of the Sjövarnskarens (RNVR). All launched in 1944.

17 COASTAL PATROL CRAFT

61-77

Displacement, tons: 28 standard
Dimensions, feet (metres): 69 × 15 × 5 (21 × 4·6 × 1·5)
Gun: 1—20 mm
Main engine: Diesel; speed = 18 knots

These are attached to the Coastal Artillery. "60" series launched in 1960-61 and "70" series in 1966-67.
Radar: One navigation set.

PATROL CRAFT 66 1975, Royal Swedish Navy

456 SWEDEN / Light forces — Mine warfare forces

4 "V 01" CLASS (COASTAL PATROL CRAFT)

Name	No.	Builders	Commissioned (after reconstruction)
SKANÖR	V 01	Kockums, Malmö	Dec 1976
SMYGE	V 02	Kockums, Malmö	1977
ARILD	V 03	Kockums, Malmö	1977
VIKEN	V 04	Kockums, Malmö	1977

Displacement, tons: 40 standard
Dimensions, feet (metres): 75·5 × 19·4 × 4·6 *(23 × 5·9 × 1·4)*
Gun: 1—40 mm Bofors
Rocket launcher: 1—12 rail 57 mm
Main engines: 3 diesels

These four craft were originally of the "T-42" class (T42-45) which commissioned in 1957. They were reconstructed at Karlskrona having their torpedo tubes removed and their petrol engines replaced by diesels.

SKANÖR   1976, Royal Swedish Navy

5 COAST GUARD PATROL CRAFT

TV 103-107

Displacement, tons: 50
Dimensions, feet (metres): 87·6 × 16·5 × 3·6 *(26·7 × 5·2 × 1·1)*
Main engines: 2 diesels; 1 800 hp; 2 shafts = 25 knots
Range, miles: 1 000
Complement: 8 (accommodation for 16)

All welded aluminium hull and upperworks. Twin rudders. Equipped for salvage divers. Built since 1969 at Karlskrona.

Radar: One Navigational radar.

Sonar: One hull-mounted.

MINE WARFARE FORCES

Note: The class of GRP minesweepers mentioned in previous editions has not yet been ordered.

1 NEW CONSTRUCTION

Name	No.	Builders	Commissioned
KARLSKRONA	M 04	Karlskrona Varvet	1980?

Displacement, tons: 3 200
Dimensions, feet (metres): 344·4 × 49·2 × — *(105 × 15 × —)*
Guns: 2—57 mm (single); 2—40 mm (single)
Mines: Can lay 105
Main engines: 2 diesels; 10 560 hp = 20 knots
Complement: 95 plus 185 trainees

Ordered 25 November 1977, laid down in 1978 and to be launched in 1980 at the same time as Karlskrona celebrates its tercentenary. When completed is planned to relieve *Alvsnabben* as Cadet Training Ship as well as serving as a minelayer. Fitted with helicopter deck.

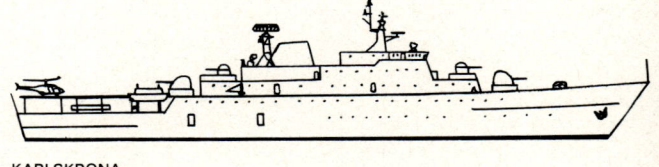

KARLSKRONA

2 "ALVSBORG" CLASS (MINELAYERS)

Name	No.	Builders	Commissioned
ÄLVSBORG	M 02	Karlskrona Varvet	10 Apr 1971
VISBORG	M 03	Karlskrona Varvet	6 Feb 1976

Displacement, tons: 2 660 (M 02); 2 540 (M 03)
Length, feet (metres): 301·8 *(92)*
Beam, feet (metres): 48·2 *(14·7)*
Draught, feet (metres): 13·2 *(4·0)*
Aircraft: 1 helicopter
Guns: 3—40 mm Bofors
Main engines: 2 Nohab-Polar 12-cyl diesels; 1 shaft; 4 200 bhp
Speed, knots: 16
Complement: 95 (accommodation for 205 submariners in M 02—158 admiral's staff in M 03)

Älvsborg was ordered in 1968 and launched on 11 November 1969. She replaced the submarine depot ship *Patricia* which was sold in 1972.
Visborg, laid down on 16 October 1973 and launched 22 January 1975 has succeeded *Marieholm* as Command Ship for C-in-C Coastal Fleet.

Fire control: M 20 Series.

ÄLVSBORG   1975, Royal Swedish Navy

SWEDEN / Mine warfare forces 457

1 MINELAYER/TRAINING SHIP

Name	No.	Builders	Commissioned
ÄLVSNABBEN	M 01	Eriksberg Mek Verkstads	8 May 1943

Displacement, tons: 4 250 standard
Length, feet (metres): 334·7 *(102·0)*
Beam, feet (metres): 44·6 *(13·6)*
Draught, feet (metres): 16·4 *(5·0)*
Guns: 2—6 in *(152 mm)*; 2—57 mm Bofors;
 2—40 mm; 4—37 mm saluting
Main engines: Diesels; 1 shaft; 3 000 bhp
Speed, knots: 14
Complement: 255 (63 cadets)

Built on a mercantile hull. Laid down on 31 October 1942, launched on 19 January 1943. Employed as a training ship during 1953-58. Relieved the anti-aircraft cruiser *Gotland* as Cadets' Seagoing Training Ship in 1959. Re-armed in 1961. Formerly carried four 6 in, eight 40 mm, six 20 mm.

Radar: Search and target designator: Thomson CSF Saturn.
Fire control: M45 series.

ÄLVSNABBEN *1978, Commander Aldo Fraccaroli*

Note: A new construction coastal minelayer MUL 20 projected for Coast Artillery.

8 COASTAL MINELAYERS

| MUL 12 (1952) | MUL 14 (1953) | MUL 16 (1956) | MUL 18 (1956) |
| MUL 13 (1952) | MUL 15 (1953) | MUL 17 (1956) | MUL 19 (1956) |

Displacement, tons: 245 full load
Dimensions, feet (metres): 95·1 × 24·3 × 10·2 *(29 × 7·4 × 3·1)*
Gun: 1—40 mm
Main engines: 2 Nohab diesel-electric; 460 bhp = 10·5 knots

Launch dates in brackets. All completed by 1957. Operated by Coast Artillery.

Radar: One navigation set.

MUL 12 *1975, Royal Swedish Navy*

1 COASTAL MINELAYER

MUL 11

Displacement, tons: 200 full load
Dimensions, feet (metres): 88·6 × 23·6 × 11·8 *(27 × 7·2 × 3·6)*
Guns: 2—20 mm
Main engines: 2 Atlas diesels; 300 bhp = 10 knots

Launched in 1946. Operated by Coast Artillery.

Radar: One navigation set.

MUL 11 *1976, Royal Swedish Navy*

36 SMALL MINELAYERS

501-536

Ordered in 1969. Of 15 tons and 14 knots with diesel engines. Mines are laid from single traps on either beam. Nine more projected.

Radar: One navigation set.

SMALL MINELAYER 502 *1975, Royal Swedish Navy*

SWEDEN / Mine warfare forces

12 "ARKÖ" CLASS (MINESWEEPERS—COASTAL)

Name	No.	Builders	Commissioned
ARKÖ	M 57	Karlskrona Varvet	1958
SPÄRÖ	M 58	Hälsingborg	1958
KARLSÖ	M 59	Karlskrona Varvet	1958
IGGÖ	M 60	Hälsingborg	1961
STYRSÖ	M 61	Karlskrona Varvet	1962
SKAFTÖ	M 62	Hälsingborg	1962
ASPÖ	M 63	Karlskrona Varvet	1962
HASSLÖ	M 64	Hälsingborg	1962
VINÖ	M 65	Karlskrona Varvet	1962
VÄLLÖ	M 66	Hälsingborg	1963
NÄMDÖ	M 67	Karlskrona Varvet	1964
BLIDÖ	M 68	Hälsingborg	1964

Displacement, tons: 285 standard; 300 full load
Dimensions, feet (metres): 137·7 × 24·6 × 7·9 *(42 × 7·5 × 2·4)*
Gun: 1—40 mm/70
Main engines: 2 Mercedes-Benz (MTU 12V 493) diesels; 2 shafts; 1 600 bhp = 14·5 knots

Of wooden construction. There is a small difference in the deck-line between M 57-59 and M 60-68. *Arkö* was launched on 21 January 1957.

ASPÖ 1975, Royal Swedish Navy

3 "M 47" CLASS (MINESWEEPERS—INSHORE)

GILLÖGA M 47   RÖDLÖGA M 48   SVARTLÖGA M 49

Details same as "M 43" class. Built in 1964. Trawler type.

RÖDLÖGA 1976, Royal Swedish Navy

4 "M 43" CLASS (MINESWEEPERS—INSHORE)

HISINGEN M 43   DÄMMAN M 45
BLACKAN M 44   GALTEN M 46

Displacement, tons: 140
Dimensions, feet (metres): 72·2 × 21 × 11·2 *(22 × 6·4 × 3·4)*
Gun: 1—40 mm
Main engine: 1 diesel; 380 bhp = 9 knots

Built in 1960. Trawler type.

3 "M 31" CLASS (MINESWEEPERS—INSHORE)

Name	No.	Builders	Commissioned
GÅSSTEN	M 31	Knippla Skeppsvarv	16 Nov 1973
NORSTEN	M 32	Hellevikstrands Skeppsvarv	12 Oct 1973
VIKSTEN	M 33	Karlskrona Varvet	1 July 1974

Displacement, tons: 120 standard; 135 full load
Dimensions, feet (metres): 79 × 21·7 × 12·2 *(24 × 6·6 × 3·7)*
Gun: 1—40 mm
Main engine: 1 diesel; 460 bhp = 11 knots

Ordered 1972. *Viksten*, built of GRP, as a forerunner to new minehunters to be built at Karlskrona. Others have wooden hulls. *Gåssten* launched November 1972. *Norsten* April 1973, *Viksten* April 1974.

VIKSTEN 1975, Royal Swedish Navy

SWEDEN / Mine warfare forces — Amphibious forces 459

8 "M 15" CLASS (MINESWEEPERS—INSHORE)

M 15   M 16   M 21   M 22   M 23   M 24   M 25   M 26

Displacement, tons: 70 standard
Dimensions, feet (metres): 85·3 × 16·5 × 4·5 *(26 × 5 × 1·4)*
Gun: 1—20 mm
Main engines: 2 diesels; 320-430 bhp = 12-13 knots

All launched in 1941. M 17, M 18 and M 20 of this class were re-rated as tenders and renamed *Lommen, Spoven* and *Skuld* respectively: see later page.

M 25   1975, Royal Swedish Navy

2 MINE TRANSPORTS

FÄLLAREN A 236   MINÖREN A 237

Displacement, tons: 165 standard
Dimensions, feet (metres): 97 × 19 × 6·7 *(31·8 × 6·2 × 2·2)*
Main engines: 2 diesels; 1 shaft; 240 bhp = 9 knots

Launched in 1941 and 1940 respectively.

AMPHIBIOUS FORCES

3 LCM

Name	No.	Builders	Commissioned
BORE	—	Åsigeverken	1967
GRIM	—	Åsigeverken	1962
HEIMDAL	—	Åsigeverken	1967

Displacement, tons: 340 full load
Dimensions, feet (metres): 118·1 × 27·9 × 8·5 *(36 × 8·5 × 2·6)*
Guns: 2—20 mm
Main engines: Diesels; 800 bhp = 12 knots

Launched in 1961 *(Grim)* and other two in 1966. Attached to Coastal Artillery.

BORE   1969, Royal Swedish Navy

2 LCM

Name	No.	Builders	Commissioned
SKAGUL	A 333	—	1960
SLEIPNER	A 335	—	1960

Displacement, tons: 335 standard
Dimensions, feet (metres): 114·8 × 27·9 × 9·5 *(35 × 8·5 × 2·9)*
Main engines: Diesels; 640 bhp = 10 knots

Sleipner was launched in 1959 and *Skagul* in 1960. Attached to Coastal Artillery.

4 "ANE" CLASS (LCM)

ANE 324   BALDER 325   LOKE 326   RING 327

Displacement, tons: 135 standard
Dimensions, feet (metres): 91·9 × 26·2 × 6·0 *(28 × 8 × 1·2)*
Guns: 1—20 mm; 1 or 2 MG
Main engines: Speed = 8·5 knots

Built in 1943-45. Attached to Coastal Artillery.

81 LCUs

Nos. 201-276 and 280-284

Displacement, tons: 31
Dimensions, feet (metres): 69 × 13·8 × 4·2 *(20 × 4·2 × 1·3)*
Guns: 2—6·5 mm MG
Main engines: Diesels; 600 hp = 17 knots

"201" class (201-241) launched 1957-60. "242" class (242-255) built in 1971-73; "256" class (256-276); 256-263 completed 1975; 264-269 and 274-276 completed 1976; 270-273 completed 1977; "280" class (280-284) completed 1976-77.

LCU 227 ("201" Class)   1975, Royal Swedish Navy

54 LCAs

337-354 of 6 tons and 21 knots. Built 1970-73.
332-336 of 5·4 tons and 25 knots. Built in 1967.
331 of 6 tons and 20 knots. Built in 1965.
301-330 of 4 tons and 9·5 knots. Built in 1956-59.

460 SWEDEN / Icebreakers — Survey ships

ICEBREAKERS

3 FINNISH "URHO" CLASS

Name	No.	Builders	Commissioned
ATLE	—	Wärtsilä, Helsinki	21 Oct 1974
FREJ	—	Wärtsilä, Helsinki	30 Sep 1975
YMER	—	Wärtsilä, Helsinki	25 Oct 1977

Displacement, tons: 7 900
Dimensions, feet (metres): 337·8 × 77·1 × 24·6 (104·6 × 23·8 × 7·3)
Aircraft: 1 helicopter
Main engines: 5 Wärtsilä-Pielstick diesels of 25 000 bhp; 4 Stromberg electric motors; 4 shafts (2 fwd, 2 aft); 22 000 shp = 18 knots
Complement: 54 (16 officers, 38 men)

Atle laid down 10 May 1973, launched 27 November 1973. *Frej* launched 3 June 1974. *Ymer* ordered 24 March 1975, laid down 12 February 1976 and launched 3 September 1976. Sister ships of Finnish "Urho" class.

YMER   1977, Wärtsilä

Name	No.	Builders	Commissioned
NJORD	—	Wärtsilä, Helsinki	Dec 1969

Displacement, tons: 5 150 standard; 5 686 full load
Dimensions, feet (metres): 283·8 × 69·6 × 20·3 (86·5 × 20·5 × 6·2)
Main engines: Wärtsilä diesel-electric; 4 shafts, (2 fwd, 2 aft); 12 000 hp = 18 knots

Launched on 20 October 1968. Near sister ship of *Tor*.
Has deck-rings for four 40 mm guns.

NJORD   1971, Royal Swedish Navy

Name	No.	Builders	Commissioned
TOR	—	Wärtsilä, Crichton-Vulcan Yard, Turku	31 Jan 1964

Displacement, tons: 4 980 standard; 5 290 full load
Dimensions, feet (metres): 277·2 × 69·6 × 20·3 (84·5 × 20·5 × 6·2)
Main engines: Wärtsilä-Sulzer diesel-electric; 4 shafts; (2 fwd; 2 aft); 12 000 hp = 18 knots

Launched on 25 May 1963. Towed to Sandvikens Skeppsdocka, Helsingfors, for completion. Larger but generally similar to *Oden,* and a near sister to *Tarmo* built for Finland.
Has deck-rings for four 40 mm guns

TOR   1972, Royal Swedish Navy

Name	No.	Builders	Commissioned
ALE	—	Wärtsilä, Helsinki	19 Dec 1973

Displacement, tons: 1 488
Dimensions, feet (metres): 150·9 × 42·6 × 16·4 (46 × 13 × 5)
Main engines: Diesels; 4 750 hp; 2 shafts = 14 knots
Complement: 28

Built for operations on Lake Vänern. Launched 1 June 1973. Also used for surveying.

Name	No.	Builders	Commissioned
THULE	—	Naval Dockyard, Karlskrona	1953

Displacement, tons: 2 200 standard; 2 280 full load
Dimensions, feet (metres): 204·2 × 52·8 × 19·4 (57 × 16·1 × 5·9)
Main engines: Diesel-electric; 3 shafts (1 fwd); 4 800 bhp = 14 knots
Complement: 43

Launched in October 1951.

Name	No.	Builders	Commissioned
ODEN	—	Sandviken, Helsingfors	1958

Displacement, tons: 4 950 standard; 5 220 full load
Dimensions, feet (metres): 273·5 × 63·7 × 22·7 (78 × 19·4 × 6·9)
Main engines: Diesel-electric; 4 shafts (2 fwd); 10 500 shp = 16 knots
Oil fuel, tons: 740
Complement: 75

Similar to the Finnish *Voima* and three Soviet icebreakers. Launched on 16 October 1956.

ODEN   1972, Royal Swedish Navy

SURVEY SHIPS

(Owned by Ministry of Transport but manned and operated by the navy).

Note: See *Ale* in Icebreakers section.

1 NEW CONSTRUCTION

—

Dimensions, feet (metres): 211·6 × 42·6 × 11·5 (64·5 × 13 × 3·5)
Main engines: 2 diesels; 4 000 hp; 1 shaft = 14 knots
Complement: 59

Ordered and laid down 1977. Completion 1 January 1979.

RAN

Displacement, tons: 285 standard
Dimensions, feet (metres): 98·4 × 23·0 × 8·5 (30 × 7 × 2·6)
Main engines: Diesels; 260 bhp = 9 knots
Complement: 37

Ran was launched and commissioned in 1946.

JOHAN MÅNSSON

Displacement, tons: 977 standard; 1 030 full load
Dimensions, feet (metres): 183·7 × 36·1 × 11·5 *(56 × 11 × 3·5)*
Main engines: Diesels; 3 300 bhp = 15 knots
Complement: 85

Launched on 14 January 1966. Her surveying launches are lowered and recovered over a stern ramp.

JOHAN MÅNSSON   1975, Royal Swedish Navy

GUSTAF AF KLINT

Displacement, tons: 750 standard
Dimensions, feet (metres): 170·6 × 36·2 × 15·4 *(52 × 11 × 4·7)*
Main engines: Diesels; 640 bhp = 10 knots
Complement: 66

Launched in 1941. Reconstructed in 1963. She formerly displaced 650 tons with a length of 154 ft *(47 m)*.

GUSTAV AF KLINT   1976, Royal Swedish Navy

NILS STRÖMCRONA

Displacement, tons: 140 standard
Dimensions, feet (metres): 88·6 × 17·0 × 8·2 *(27 × 5·2 × 2·5)*
Guns: None in peacetime
Main engines: Diesels; 300 bhp = 9 knots
Complement: 14

Launched in 1894 and reconstructed in 1952.

NILS STRÖMCRONA   1976, Royal Swedish Navy

SWEDEN / Survey ships — Service forces   461

ANDERS BURE (ex-*Rali*)

Displacement, tons: 54
Dimensions, feet (metres): 82·0 × 19·4 × 6·9 *(25 × 5·9 × 2·1)*
Main engines: Diesels = 15 knots
Complement: 11

Built in 1968 as *Rali*. She was purchased in 1971 and renamed.

ANDERS BURE   1976, Royal Swedish Navy

SERVICE FORCES

1 SUPPLY SHIP

Name	No.	Builders	Commissioned
FREJA	A 221	Kroger, Rendsburg	1954

Displacement, tons: 415 standard; 465 full load
Dimensions, feet (metres): 160·8 × 27·9 × 12·1 *(49 × 8·5 × 3·7)*
Main engines: Diesels; 600 bhp = 11 knots

Launched in 1953. Employed as a provision ship.

1 SUPPORT TANKER

BRÄNNAREN A 228

Displacement, tons: 857
Dimensions, feet (metres): 203·4 × 28·2 × 12·1 *(62 × 8·6 × 3·7)*
Speed, knots: 11

Ex-German merchant tanker *Indio* purchased early 1972. Built 1965.

BRÄNNAREN   1978, Reinhard Nerlich

1 SALVAGE SHIP

Name	No.	Builders	Commissioned
BELOS	A 211	—	29 May 1963

Displacement, tons: 1 000 standard
Dimensions, feet (metres): 204·4 × 37·0 × 12·0 *(58 × 11·2 × 3·8)*
Aircraft: 1 helicopter
Main engines: Diesels; 2 shafts; 1 200 bhp = 13 knots

Launched on 15 November 1961. Equipped with decompression chamber.

BELOS   1970, Royal Swedish Navy

462 SWEDEN / Service forces — Tugs

2 SAIL TRAINING SHIPS

Name	No.	Builders	Commissioned
GLADAN	S 01	—	1947
FALKEN	S 02	—	1948

Displacement, tons: 220 standard
Dimensions, feet (metres): 129·5 × 23·5 × 13·5 *(42·5 × 7·7 × 4·4)*
Main engine: Auxiliary diesel; 120 bhp

Sail training ships. Two masted schooners. Launched 1947 and 1946 respectively. Sail area 5 511 sq ft *(512 sq m)*.

GLADAN   1977, Royal Swedish Navy

TENDERS

3 TRVs

Name	No.	Builders	Commissioned
PINGVINEN	A 248	Lundevarv-Ooverkstads AB, Kramfors	Mar 1975

Displacement, tons: 191
Dimensions, feet (metres): 108·2 × 20 × 6 *(33 × 6·1 × 1·8)*
Main engines: 2 diesels; 1 100 hp = 13 knots

Ordered 1972. Torpedo recovery and rocket trials ship. Launched 26 September 1973.

PINGVINEN   1976, Royal Swedish Navy

Name	No.	Builders	Commissioned
PELIKANEN	A 247	—	26 Sep 1963

Displacement, tons: 130 standard
Dimensions, feet (metres): 108·2 × 19·0 × 6·0 *(33 × 5·8 × 1·8)*
Main engines: 2 Mercedes-Benz diesels; 1 040 bhp = 15 knots

Torpedo recovery and rocket trials vessel.

HÄGERN A 246

Displacement, tons: 50 standard
Dimensions, feet (metres): 88·6 × 16·4 × 4·9 *(29 × 5·4 × 1·6)*
Main engines: 2 diesels; 240 bhp = 10 knots

Launched in 1951.

5 "L 51" CLASS (LCU)

| L 51 | L 52 | L 53 | L 54 | L 55 |

Displacement, tons: 32 standard
Dimensions, feet (metres): 50·8 × 16 × 3·2 *(14 × 4·8 × 1)*
Main engine: Diesel; 140 bhp = 7 knots

Launched in 1947-48.

5 TENDERS

SIGRUN A 256

Displacement, tons: 250 standard
Dimensions, feet (metres): 105·0 × 22·3 × 11·8 *(32 × 6·8 × 3·6)*
Main engines: Diesels: 320 bhp = 11 knots

Launched in 1961. Laundry ship.

URD (ex-*Capella*) A 241

Displacement, tons: 63 standard; 90 full load
Dimensions, feet (metres): 72·1 × 18·3 × 9·2 *(22 × 5·6 × 2·8)*
Main engines: Diesels; 200 bhp = 8 knots

Experimental vessel added to the official list in 1970. Launched in 1969.

LOMMEN (ex-*M 17*) A 231   **SKULD** (ex-*M 20*) A 242
SPOVEN (ex-*M 18*) A 232

Displacement, tons: 70 standard
Dimensions, feet (metres): 85·3 × 16·5 × 4·5 *(26 × 5 × 1·4)*
Main engines: 2 diesels; 410 bhp = 13 knots

Former inshore minesweepers of the "M 15" Class. All launched in 1941.

TUGS

HERMES A 253   **HECTOR** A 321   **HEROS** A 322

Displacement, tons: 185 standard
Dimensions, feet (metres): 80·5 × 24·6 × 11·3 *(24·5 × 7·4 × 3·6)*
Main engines: Diesels; 600 bhp = 11 knots

Launched 1953-57. Icebreaking tugs.

HERCULES A 323   **HERA** A 324

Displacement, tons: 127 tons
Dimensions, feet (metres): 70·4 × 22·5 × 13·5 *(21·4 × 6·9 × 4·1)*
Main engines: Diesels; 615 bhp = 11·5 knots

Launched 1969 and 1971. Icebreaking tugs.

ACHILLES A 251   **AJAX** A 252

Displacement, tons: 450
Dimensions, feet (metres): 116·6 × 31·4 × 12·8 *(35·5 × 9·5 × 3·9)*
Main engine: Diesel; 1 650 bhp = 12 knots

Achilles was launched in 1962 and *Ajax* in 1963. Both are icebreaking tugs.

AJAX   5/1976, Reinhard Nerlich

Also listed:
HEBE A326; **PASSOP** A327; **RAN** A328; **HENRIK** A329; **ATLAS** A330; **MÄRSGARN** A332; **VITSGARN** A336.

ATB 1 A341; **ATB 2** A342; **ATB 3** A343.

GRANATEN A345; **EDDA** A347; **GERDA** A349.

SWEDEN / Water carriers — SYRIA / Frigates 463

WATER CARRIERS

INDEN A 216

Displacement, tons: 540 standard
Dimensions, feet (metres): 130·8 × 24·6 × 1·4 (39·8 × 7·6 × 3·2)
Main engines: Steam reciprocating; 225 ihp = 9 knots

Launched in 1946.

FRYKEN A 217

Displacement, tons: 307 standard
Dimensions, feet (metres): 113 × 20·2 × 9 (34·4 × 6·1 × 2·9)
Main engines: Diesels; 370 bhp = 10 knots

A naval construction water carrier. Launched in 1959 and completed in 1960.

FRYKEN   1976, Royal Swedish Navy

SWITZERLAND

Diplomatic Representation

Defence Attaché in London:
Colonel W. Dudli

Mercantile Marine

Lloyd's Register of Shipping:
27 vessels of 230 762 tons gross

3 + ? PATROL CRAFT

Displacement, tons: 4·3
Dimensions, feet (metres): 32·8 × 11·2 × — (10 × 3·4 × —)
Main engines: 2 Volvo diesels; 510 hp = 27 knots

A new class under construction by Müller AG of Spiez for operation by the Swiss Army. These are to replace the ten elderly craft now being phased out which were built about 1942, one of which is illustrated here. The new craft have radio and radar equipment.

In addition to the above there are also water-transport detachments and other detachments with smaller patrol craft.

SWISS PATROL CRAFT   1966, Swiss Army

SYRIA

Ministerial

Minister of Defence:
Major General Mustafa Tlass

Headquarters Appointments

Commander-in-Chief Navy:
Commodore Fadl Husayn
Chief of Staff:
Commodore Mustafa Tayyare
Director of Naval Operations:
Commodore Muhammad Hamud

Personnel

(a) 1979: 2 500 officers and men
(b) 18 months national service

Naval Aviation

6-10 Ka25 Hormone helicopters

Bases

Latakia, Baniyas, Tartous, Al-Mina-al-Bayda

Mercantile Marine

Lloyd's Register of Shipping:
41 vessels of 26 518 tons gross

FRIGATES

2 Ex-SOVIET "PETYA I" CLASS

Displacement, tons: 950 standard; 1 150 full load
Dimensions, feet (metres): 270 × 29·8 × 10·5 (82·3 × 9·1 × 3·2)
Guns: 4—3 in (76 mm) (twin)
A/S weapons: 4—16-barrelled MBU 2500
Torpedo tubes: 5—21 in (533 mm)
Main engines: 1 diesel; 6 000 hp; 2 gas-turbines; 30 000 hp; 3 shafts
Speed, knots: 30
Complement: 98

Transferred by USSR in 1975-76.

Radar: Search: Slim Net.
Fire control: Hawk Screech.
Navigation: Don.
IFF: High Pole B and Square Head.

Sonar: One hull-mounted.

"PETYA I" Class   3/1975, MOD

464 SYRIA / Light forces — Miscellaneous

LIGHT FORCES

6 Ex-SOVIET "OSA I" and 2 "OSA II" CLASSES (FAST ATTACK CRAFT—MISSILE)

Displacement, tons: 160/165 standard; 210 full load
Dimensions, feet (metres): 127·9 × 26·6 × 5·9 *(39 × 8·1 × 1·8)*
Missiles: SSM; 4 SS-N-2 (single launchers)
Guns: 4—30 mm (twins) (1 fwd, 1 aft)
Main engines: 3 M503A/504 diesels; 12 000/15 000 bhp = 36 knots
Range, miles: 800 at 25 knots
Complement: 30

Original pair sunk in October 1973 war. Two "Osa II" class transferred in 1978, possibly with more to follow.

Radar: Search: Square Tie.
Fire control: Drum Tilt.
IFF: Square Head and High Pole.

Syrian "OSA" Class   12/197

6 Ex-SOVIET "KOMAR" CLASS (FAST ATTACK CRAFT—MISSILE)

Displacement, tons: 68 standard; 75 full load
Dimensions, feet (metres): 87·9 × 20·3 × 4·9 *(26·8 × 6·2 × 1·5)*
Missiles: SSM; 2 SS-N-2 (single launchers)
Guns: 2—25 mm (twin)
Main engines: 4 M50 diesels; 4 shafts; 4 800 bhp = 40 knots
Range, miles: 400 at 30 knots
Complement: 19

Transferred between 1963 and 1966. Three reported lost in Israeli War October 1973, but were replaced.

Radar: Search: Square Tie.
IFF: Dead Duck and High Pole A.

"KOMAR" Class

8 Ex-SOVIET "P 4" CLASS (FAST ATTACK CRAFT—TORPEDO)

Displacement, tons: 22 standard; 25 full load
Dimensions, feet (metres): 62·3 × 10·8 × 3·3 *(19 × 3·3 × 1)*
Torpedo tubes: 2—18 in *(457 mm)*
Guns: 2—14·5 mm MG (twin)
Main engines: 2 diesels; 2 200 bhp; 2 shafts = 50 knots
Range, miles: 400 at 13 knots
Complement: 12

Five torpedo boats were transferred from the USSR at Latakia on 7 February 1957, and at lea 12 subsequently. One reported lost in Israeli War October 1973. Four transferred to Egypt 1970. Only eight of the remainder considered operational out of remaining 12.

3 Ex-FRENCH CH TYPE (LARGE PATROL CRAFT)

| ABABEH IBN NEFEH | ABDULLAH IBN ARISSI | TAREK IBN ZAYED |

Displacement, tons: 107 standard; 131 full load
Dimensions, feet (metres): 121·8 × 17·5 × 6·5 *(39·9 × 5·7 × 2·1)*
Guns: 2—20 mm
A/S weapons: Depth charges
Main engines: MAN diesels; 2 shafts; 1 130 bhp = 16 knots
Oil fuel, tons: 50
Range, miles: 1 200 at 8 knots; 680 at 13 knots
Complement: 28

All built in France, the first by AC de France and second pair by Seine Maritime. Completed in 1940. Rebuilt in 1955-56 when the funnels were removed. These were transferred in 1962 to form the nucleus of the Syrian Navy. Two of these ships are probably non-operational.

CH Type   M Henri Le Masso

MINE WARFARE FORCES

1 Ex-SOVIET "T 43" CLASS (MINESWEEPER—OCEAN)

YARMOUK

Displacement, tons: 500 standard; 580 full load
Dimensions, feet (metres): 190·2 × 27·6 × 6·9 *(58 × 8·4 × 2·1)*
Guns: 4—37 mm (twins); 4—25mm (twins); 8—14·5 mm (twins)
Mines: Can carry 30
Main engines: 2 diesels; 2 shafts; 2 200 hp = 14 knots
Range, miles: 1 600 at 10 knots
Complement: 40

Reported in 1962 to have been transferred from the Soviet Navy. The second of this class was sunk in the Israeli War October 1973.

Radar: Search: Ball End.
Navigation: Neptun.
IFF: Square Head and High Pole.

2 Ex-SOVIET "VANYA" CLASS (MINESWEEPERS—COASTAL)

Displacement, tons: 200 standard; 245 full load
Dimensions, feet (metres): 130·7 × 24 × 5·9 *(39·9 × 7·3 × 1·8)*
Guns: 2—30 mm (twin)
Main engines: 2 diesels; 2 200 bhp = 18 knots
Complement: 30

Transferred December 1972.

Radar: Navigation: Don 2.
IFF: Square Head and High Pole.

MISCELLANEOUS

1 Ex-SOVIET "POLUCHAT" CLASS

Displacement, tons: 70 standard; 90 full load
Dimensions, feet (metres): 97·1 × 19·0 × 4·8 *(29·6 × 5·8 × 1·5)*
Guns: 2—14·5 mm (twin)
Main engines: 2 diesels; 2 200 hp = 20 knots
Complement: 15

Used as divers' base-ship.

TAIWAN

Ministerial

Minister of National Defence:
 Kao K'uei-yuan

Senior Flag Officers

Chief of the General Staff:
 Admiral Soong Chang-chih
Commander-in-Chief:
 Admiral Tsou Chien
Deputy Commanders-in-Chief:
 Vice-Admiral Yang Sung-chuan
 Vice-Admiral Liu Ho-chien
Chief of Staff:
 Vice-Admiral Chih-shen Lin
Commander, Fleet Command:
 Vice-Admiral Chen Tung-hai
Commandant of Marine Corps:
 Lieutenant-General Kung Lin-cheng

Personnel

(a) 1979; 7 100 officers and 28 000 men in Navy, 3 000 officers and 26 000 men in Marine Corps (2 divisions with armour, APCs and heavy artillery)
(b) 3 years conscript service

Bases

Tsoying: HQ First Naval District (Southern Taiwan, Pratas and Spratly) Main Base, HQ of Fleet Command and Marine Corps. Officers and ratings training. Naval Shipyard.
Kaohsiung; Naval Shipyard.
Makung (Pescadores): HQ Second Naval District (Pescadores, Quemoy and Wu Ch'iu) Naval Shipyard and Training facilities.
Keelung: HQ Third Naval District (Northern Taiwan and Matsu group). Naval Shipyard.

Commands

C in C Fleet commands the Surface Force (TF62) which consists of four Task Groups, the northern and southern patrols and the northern and southern transport groups, the Mine Warfare Squadron, the Service Squadron and the Fleet Training Command.

Naval Aviation

One squadron of ten Air Force S-2A tracker ASW aircraft is under Navy operational control.
The Marine Corps operates several observation aircraft and helicopters.

Pennant Numbers

A major revision of warship pennant numbers took place in 1976. In the following text revisions have been made where known but many gaps remain.

Missiles

A missile called Hsiung Feng is used in the Taiwan navy. This appears to be either a Gabriel missile renamed or a Taiwanese version of that missile.

Strength of the Fleet

Type	Active	Building
Destroyers	22	—
Frigates	11	—
Corvettes	3	—
Submarines (Patrol)	2	—
Fast Attack Craft (Missile)	1	1
Fast Attack Craft (Torpedo)	9	—
Coastal Patrol Craft	14	—
Coastal Minesweepers	14	—
Minesweeping Boats	8	—
LSDs	2	—
Landing Ships	27	—
Utility Landing Craft	22	—
Repair Ship	1	—
Transports	2	—
Survey Ships	4	—
Support Tankers	7	—
Cargo Ship	1	—
Tugs	9	—
Floating Docks	5	—
Service Craft	25	—
Customs	7+	—

General

The most modern of the major combatants of this navy is *Dang Yang*, a "Gearing" Class destroyer which was first commissioned in 1947. With thirty five ships and submarines in this bracket of antiquity it must be very soon that, if the Taiwanese fleet is to retain any credibility, replacements are put in hand. As this is not a navy with long-range commitments the ordering of corvettes with missile and helicopter facilities would seem logical. How such a programme will be affected by the December 1978 agreements between the USA and the PRC in Peking remains to be seen.

Mercantile Marine

Lloyd's Register of Shipping:
 443 vessels of 1 558 713 tons gross

DELETIONS

Submarines

1974-75 3 SX404 small submarines

Destroyers

1975 *Lo Yang, Han Yang, Nan Yang* (ex-US "Benson" class)
 (all names transferred to later ships)
1976 *Hsien Yang* (sunk for film unit)

Frigates

1972 *Tai Kang*
1972-73 *Tai Cho, Tai Chong, Tai* (ex-US "Cannon" class)
1975 *Tai Hu* (ex-US "Cannon" class)
1976 *Heng Shan, Lung Shan* (APDs)
1978 *Kang Shan* (APD)

LST

1978 *Chung Chie*

Repair Ship

1974 *Tien Tai*

Survey Ship

1976 *Yang Ming*

Tankers

1972 *Tai Yun*
1975 *Kuichi*

Tugs

1975-76 YTLs 3, 8 and 10

Customs

1974 PC122

SUBMARINES

2 Ex-US GUPPY II TYPE

Name	No.	Builders	Launched	Commissioned
HAI SHIH (ex-USS *Cutlass*, SS 478)	736 (ex-SS 91)	Portsmouth Navy Yard	5 Nov 1944	17 Mar 1945
HAI PAO (ex-USS *Tusk*, SS 426)	794 (ex-SS 92)	Federal S.B. & D.D. Co, Kearney, New Jersey	8 July 1945	11 Apr 1946

Displacement, tons: 1 870 standard; 2 420 dived
Length, feet (metres): 307·5 *(93·6)*
Beam, feet (metres): 27·2 *(8·3)*
Draught, feet (metres): 18 *(5·5)*
Torpedo tubes: 10—21 in *(533 mm)*; (6 fwd; 4 aft)
Main machinery: 3 diesels (Fairbanks-Morse); 4 800 bhp; 2 electric motors (Elliott); 5 400 shp; 2 shafts
Speed, knots: 18 surfaced; 15 dived
Complement: 81 (11 officers, 70 ratings)

Originally fleet-type submarines of the US Navy's "Tench" class; extensively modernised under the GUPPY II programme. These submarines each have four 126-cell electric batteries; fitted with snorkel.
Taiwan is the only nation in the Western Pacific currently to operate former US Navy submarines.

Torpedoes: A number of Italian torpedoes suitable for submarine operations were sold to Taiwan in 1976. The submarine torpedo-tubes, "sealed" by the US Navy, must, therefore, have been "unsealed" in Taiwan and these submarines must be considered operational.

Transfers: 91, 12 Apr 1973; 92, 18 Oct 1973.

HAI SHIH *1972, USN*

DESTROYERS

9 Ex-US "GEARING" CLASS (FRAM I and II)

Name	No.	Builders	Laid down	Launched	Commissioned
DANG YANG (ex-USS *Lloyd Thomas*, DD 764) (FRAM II)	966 (ex-DD 11)	Bethlehem Steel, San Francisco	1945	5 Oct 1945	21 Mar 1947
CHIEN YANG (ex-USS *James E. Kyes*, DD 787)	921 (ex-DD 12)	Todd Pacific S.Y., Seattle, Wash	1945	4 Aug 1945	8 Feb 1946
HAN YANG (ex-USS *Herbert J. Thomas*, DD 833)	978 (ex-DD 15)	Bath Iron Works Corporation	1944	25 Mar 1945	29 May 1945
LAO YANG (ex-USS *Shelton*, DD 790)	— (ex-DD 20)	Todd Pacific S.Y., Seattle, Wash	1945	8 Mar 1946	21 June 1946
LIAO YANG (ex-USS *Hanson*, DD 832)	938 (ex-DD 21)	Bath Iron Works Corporation	1944	11 Mar 1945	11 May 1945
KAI YANG (ex-USS *Richard B. Anderson*, DD 786)	—	Todd Pacific S.Y., Seattle, Wash	1945	7 July 1945	26 Oct 1945
TE YANG (ex-USS *Sarsfield*, DD 837)	925	Bath Iron Works Corporation	1945	27 May 1945	31 July 1945
SHEN YANG (ex-USS *Power*, DD 839)	932	Bath Iron Works Corporation	1945	30 June 1945	13 Sep 1945
LAI YANG (ex-USS *Leonard F. Mason*, DD 852)	981	Bethlehem (Quincy)	1945	4 Jan 1946	28 June 1946

Displacement, tons: 2 425 standard; approx 3 500 full load
Length, feet (metres): 390·5 *(119·0)*
Beam, feet (metres): 40·9 *(12·4)*
Draught, feet (metres): 19 *(5·8)*
Aircraft: 1 helicopter and hangar
Missiles: 3 Gabriel *(Dang Yang)*
Guns: 4—5 in *(127 mm)*/38 (twin) (Mk 38); 4—40 mm (twins) *(Han Yang* only); several ·50 cal MG fitted in some ships
A/S weapons: ASROC 8-tube launcher except in *Dang Yang* and *Kai Yang; Dang Yang* has trainable Hedgehog (Mk 15); 6—(2 triple) Mk 32 A/S torpedo tubes
Main engines: 2 geared turbines (General Electric); 60 000 shp; 2 shafts
Boilers: 4
Speed, knots: 34
Complement: approx 275

Dang Yang was modified to a special anti-submarine configuration and reclassified as an escort destroyer (DDE) in 1950; changed again to "straight" DD upon modernisation in 1962. Armament listed above was at time of transfer. *Lao Yang* has twin 5 in gun mounts in "A" and "B" positions with A/S torpedo tubes alongside second funnel; other ships have the "A" and "Y" gun mounts with torpedo tubes in "B" position except *Dang Yang* has torpedo tubes between funnels.

In 1963-64 *Herbert J. Thomas* was modified for protection against biological, chemical, and atomic attack; the ship could be fully sealed with enclosed lookout and control positions, special air-conditioning. Upon transfer to Taiwan *Herbert J. Thomas*, originally transferred for spares but re-activated, assumed name and pennant number of an ex-US "Benson" class destroyer in Taiwan service.

Three of the FRAM I ships were initially scheduled for transfer to Spain; however, they were declined by Spain and allocated to Taiwan.

Deletions: *Chao Yang* (ex-USS *Rowan* DD 782) (sold 10 June 1977) ran aground 22 August 1977 while in tow to Taiwan. Beyond salvage—being stripped for spares.

Electronics: Most have ULQ-6 ECM and WLR-1 and WLR-3 passive warning receivers.

Radar: At time of transfer three of these ships had SPS 37 and SPS 10 search radar antennae on their tripod mast; *Dang Yang* had older SPS 6 and SPS 10 antennae; *Chien Yang* had SPS 40 and SPS 10. *Lao Yang* now has SPS 10 and SPS 29. Navigation: Mk 5 (TDS).

Sonar: SQS 23 except *Dang Yang* with SQS 29 series.

Transfers: *Dang Yang*, 12 Oct 1972; *Chien Yang*, 18 Apr 1973; *Han Yang*, 6 May 1974; *Lao Yang*, 18 Apr 1973; *Liao Yang*, 18 Apr 1973; *Kai Yang*, 10 June 1977 by sale; *Te Yang* and *Shen Yang*, 1 Oct 1977 by sale; *Lai Yang*, Jan 1978.

DANG YANG (as USS *Lloyd Thomas*)   1970, USN

LIAO YANG (as USS *Hanson*)   1971, USN

1 Ex-US "GEARING" CLASS RADAR PICKET (FRAM II)

Name	No.	Builders	Laid down	Launched	Commissioned
FU YANG (ex-USS *Ernest G. Small*, DD 838)	963 (ex-DD 7)	Bath Iron Works Corporation	1945	14 June 1945	21 Aug 1945

Displacement, tons: 2 425 standard; approx 3 500 full load
Length, feet (metres): 390·5 *(119·0)*
Beam, feet (metres): 40·8 *(12·4)*
Draught, feet (metres): 19 *(5·8)*
Missiles: 3 Gabriels
Guns: 6—5 in *(127 mm)*/38 (twin Mk 38); 8—40 mm (twin); 4—50 cal MG (single)
A/S weapons: 6 (2 triple) torpedo tubes (Mk 32); 2 fixed Hedgehogs
Main engines: 2 geared turbines; (General Electric); 60 000 shp; 2 shafts
Boilers: 4 Babcock & Wilcox
Speed, knots: 34
Complement: approx 275

Converted to a radar picket destroyer (DDR) during 1952 and subsequently modernised under the FRAM II programme; redesignated as a "straight" destroyer (DD), but retained specialised electronic equipment. Not fitted with helicopter flight deck or hangar. The 40 mm guns were installed after transfer to Taiwan.

Fire control: US Mk 25 and Mk 37; Taiwan built Mk 51 (adapted from F86 aircraft).

Radar: At time of transfer *Fu Yang* had SPS 37 and SPS 10 search radars on forward tripod mast, and large TACAN antenna on second tripod mast. Navigation: Mk 5 (TDS).

Sonar: SQS 29 (hull-mounted); SQS 10 (VDS).

Transfer: Feb 1971.

FU YANG (Old pennant number)

TAIWAN / Destroyers 467

8 Ex-US "ALLEN M. SUMNER" CLASS

Name	No.	Builders	Laid down	Launched	Commissioned
HSIANG YANG (ex-USS *Brush*, DD 745)	986 (ex-DD 1)	Bethlehem Steel, Staten Island	1943	28 Dec 1943	17 Apr 1944
HENG YANG (ex-USS *Samuel N. Moore*, DD 747)	976 (ex-DD 2)	Bethlehem Steel, Staten Island	1943	23 Feb 1944	24 June 1944
HUA YANG (ex-USS *Bristol*, DD 857)	988 (ex-DD 3)	Bethlehem Steel, San Pedro	1944	29 Oct 1944	17 Mar 1945
YUEN YANG (ex-USS *Haynsworth*, DD 700)	944 (ex-DD 5)	Federal S.B. & D.D. Co	1943	15 Apr 1944	22 June 1944
HUEI YANG (ex-USS *English*, DD 696)	972 (ex-DD 6)	Federal S.B. & D.D. Co	1943	27 Feb 1944	4 May 1944
LO YANG (ex-USS *Maddox*, DD 731)	928 (ex-DD 10)	Bath Iron Works Corporation	1943	19 Mar 1944	2 June 1944
PO YANG (ex-USS *Taussig*, DD 746)	949 (ex-DD 14)	Bethlehem Steel, Staten Island	1943	25 Jan 1944	20 May 1944
NAN YANG (ex-USS *John W. Thomason*, DD 760)	954 (ex-DD 17)	Bethlehem Steel, San Francisco	1944	30 Sep 1944	11 Oct 1945

Displacement, tons: 2 200 standard; 3 320 full load
Length, feet (metres): 376·5 *(114·8)*
Beam, feet (metres): 40·9 *(12·4)*
Draught, feet (metres): 19 *(5·8)*
Missiles: 7 Gabriels (1 triple, 2 twin) in DD 1, 3 and 5
Guns: 6—5 in *(127 mm)*/38 (twin Mk 38); 4—3 in *(76 mm)*/50 (2 twin); some including *Heng Yang* and *Yuen Yang*, have 8—40 mm (1 quad, 2 twin); several ·50 cal MG (single) in most ships
A/S weapons: 6 (2 triple) A/S torpedo tubes (Mk 32); 2 fixed Hedgehogs; depth charges in some ships
Main engines: 2 geared turbines (General Electric or Westinghouse); 60 000 shp; 2 shafts
Boilers: 4 Babcock & Wilcox
Speed, knots: 34
Complement: approx 275

These ships have not been modernised under the FRAM programmes, but retain their original configurations with removal of original torpedo tubes, and 40 mm and 20 mm guns, and installation of improved electronic equipment. Secondary gun battery now varies; during the 1950s most of these ships were rearmed with six 3 in guns (two single alongside forward funnel and two twin amidships); number retained apparently varies from ship to ship, with some ships retaining original 40 mm guns. Tripod mast fitted.

Po Yang and *Nan Yang* have names and numbers previously assigned to now deleted ex-US destroyers.

Fire control: US Mk 25, 37 and 51.

Radar: Surface search: SPS 6 and SPS 10 (*Po Yang* has SPS 40 and SPS 10, *Nan Yang* has SPS 37 and SPS 10 and *Lo Yang* has SPS 10 and SPS 29).
Navigation: Mk 5 (TDS).

Transfers: *Hsiang Yang,* 9 Dec 1969; *Heng Yang,* Feb 1970; *Hua Yang,* 9 Dec 1969; *Yuen Yang,* 12 May 1970; *Huei Yang,* Sep 1970; *Po Yang,* 6 July 1972; *Lo Yang,* 6 May 1974; *Nan Yang,* 6 May 1974.

HSIANG YANG (old pennant number) 1971, USN

HENG YANG (old pennant number) "Ships of the World"

4 Ex-US "FLETCHER" CLASS

Name	No.	Builders	Laid down	Launched	Commissioned
WEI YANG (ex-USS *Twining*, DD 540)	956 (ex-DD 8)	Bethlehem Steel, San Francisco	1943	11 July 1943	1 Dec 1943
CHING YANG (ex-USS *Mullany*, DD 528)	947 (ex-DD 9)	Bethlehem Steel, San Francisco	1942	12 Oct 1942	23 Apr 1943
AN YANG (ex-USS *Kimberly*, DD 521)	997 (ex-DD 18)	Bethlehem Steel, Staten Island	1942	4 Feb 1943	22 May 1943
KUN YANG (ex-USS *Yarnall*, DD 541)	934 (ex-DD 19)	Bethlehem Steel, San Francisco	1943	25 July 1943	30 Dec 1943

Displacement, tons: 2 100 standard; 3 050 full load
Length, feet (metres): 376·5 *(114·7)*
Beam, feet (metres): 35·9 *(11·9)*
Draught, feet (metres): 18 *(5·5)*
Missiles: SAM; Sea Chaparral launcher above "X" 5 in mount
Guns: 5—5 in *(127 mm)*/38 (single) except 4 guns in *Ching Yang* (Mk 30); 5—3 in *(76 mm)*/50 in *Kwei Yang* and *Ching Yang*; 6—40 mm (twin) in *An Yang* and *Kun Yang*
A/S weapons: 6 (2 triple) A/S torpedo tubes (Mk 32) in *Kwei Yang* and *Ching Yang*; 2 fixed Hedgehogs and depth charges in some ships
Torpedo tubes: 5—21 in *(533mm)* (quin) in *Kun Yang*
Main engines: 2 geared turbines (General Electric in *An Yang*, Allis Chalmers in *Kun Yang*, Westinghouse in others); 60 000 shp; 2 shafts
Boilers: 4 Babcock & Wilcox
Speed, knots: 36
Complement: approx 250

All now have tripod mast. Only *Kun Yang* retains anti-ship torpedo tubes installed between second funnel and third 5 in gun mount. Reportedly, the ship has been fitted for minelaying.

Electronics: BLR 1 or SLR 2 passive detection.

Fire control: US Mk 25 and 37.

Radar: SPS 6 and 10 (ex-DD 8, 9, 19); SPS 10 and 12 (ex-DD 18).
Navigation: Mk 5 (TDS).

Transfers: *Kwei Yang,* 6 Oct 1971 (sale); *Ching Yang,* 6 Oct 1971 (sale); *An Yang,* 2 June 1967; *Kun Yang,* 10 June 1968. Last pair purchased Jan 1974.

KUN YANG (5 main guns) (old pennant number) C. B. Mulholland

468 TAIWAN / Frigates — Corvettes

FRIGATES

9 Ex-US "CHARLES LAWRENCE" and "CROSLEY" CLASSES

Name	No.	Builders	Laid down	Launched	Commissioned
YU SHAN (ex-USS *Kinzer*, APD 91/DE 232)	— (ex-PF 32)	Charleston Navy Yard, South Carolina	1943	9 Dec 1943	1 Nov 1944
HUA SHAN (ex-USS *Donald W. Wolf*, APD 129/DE 713)	854 (ex-PF 33)	Defoe S.B. Co, Bay City, Michigan	1944	22 July 1944	13 Apr 1945
WEN SHAN (ex-USS *Gantner*, APD 42/DE 60)	834 (ex-PF 34)	Bethlehem S.B. Co, Higham, Mass	1942	17 Apr 1943	23 July 1943
FU SHAN (ex-USS *Truxton*, APD 98/DE 282)	838 (ex-PF 35)	Charleston Navy Yard, South Carolina	1943	9 Mar 1944	9 July 1944
LU SHAN (ex-USS *Bull*, APD 78/DE 693)	821 (ex-PF 36)	Defoe S.B. Co, Bay City, Michigan	1942	25 Mar 1943	12 Aug 1943
SHOU SHAN (ex-USS *Kline*, APD 120/DE 687)	893 (ex-PF 37)	Bethlehem, Quincy, Mass	1944	27 June 1944	18 Oct 1944
TAI SHAN (ex-USS *Register*, APD 92/DE 233)	878 (ex-PF 38)	Charleston Navy Yard, South Carolina	1943	20 Jan 1944	11 Jan 1945
CHUNG SHAN (ex-USS *Blessman*, APD 48/DE 69)	845 (ex-PF 43)	Bethlehem S.B. Co, Higham, Mass	1943	19 June 1943	19 Sep 1943
TIEN SHAN (ex-USS *Kleinsmith*, APD 134/DE 718)	615 (ex-APD 315)	Defoe S.B. Co, Bay City, Michigan	1944	27 Jan 1945	12 June 1945

Displacement, tons: 1 400 standard; 2 130 full load
Length, feet (metres): 306 *(93·3)*
Beam, feet (metres): 37 *(11·3)*
Draught, feet (metres): 12·6 *(3·2)*
Guns: 2—5 in *(127 mm)*/38; 6—40 mm (twin); 4—20 mm (single) except *Hua Shan* and possibly others have 8 guns (twin mounts)
A/S weapons: 6—12·75 in *(324 mm)* torpedo tubes (Mk 32 triple) except some have two Hedgehogs; depth charges
Main engines: Geared turbines (General Electric) with electric drive; 12 000 shp; 2 shafts
Boilers: 2 Foster-Wheeler
Speed, knots: 23·6
Range, miles: 5 000 at 15 knots
Complement: 200

All begun as destroyer escorts (DE), but converted during construction or after completion to high speed transports carrying 160 troops, commandoes, or frogmen.
The ex-USS *Walter B Cobb* (APD 106/DE 596) transferred to Taiwan in 1966 was lost at sea while under tow to Taiwan; replaced by ex-USS *Bull*.

Appearance: "Charles Lawrence" class has high bridge; "Crosley" class has low bridge. Radars and fire control equipment vary. Davits amidships can hold four LCVP-type landing craft but ships usually carry only one each.

Fire control: Most have US Mk 26 Mod 4.

Gunnery: All ships are now believed to have been refitted with a second 5 in gun aft. One twin 40 mm gun mount is forward of bridge and two twin mounts are amidships.

Radar: Most have SPS 5. Some have Decca 707 in addition.

Transfers: Ex-PF 32, Apr 1962; 33, May 1965; 34, May 1966; 35, Mar 1966; 36, Aug 1966; 37, Mar 1966; 38, Oct 1966; 42, July 1967; 43, July 1967; APD 215, June 1967.

HUA SHAN (old pennant number)   *C. B. Mulholland*

1 Ex-US "RUDDERLOW" CLASS

Name	No.	Builders	Laid down	Launched	Commissioned
TAI YUAN (ex-USS *Riley*, DE 579)	959 (ex-PF 27)	Bethlehem Steel Co, Higham, Mass	1943	29 Dec 1943	13 Mar 1944

Displacement, tons: 1 450 standard; approx 2 000 full load
Length, feet (metres): 306 *(93·3)*
Beam, feet (metres): 37 *(11·3)*
Draught, feet (metres): 14 *(4·3)*
Guns: 2—5 in *(127 mm)*/38 (single); 4—40 mm (twin); 4—20 mm (single)
A/S weapons: 6—(2 triple) A/S torpedo tubes (Mk 32); 1 Hedgehog; depth charges
Main engines: Geared turbines (General Electric) with electric drive; 12 000 shp; 2 shafts
Boilers: 2 Foster-Wheeler
Speed, knots: 24
Range, miles: 5 000 at 15 knots
Complement: approx 200

Refitted with tripod mast and platforms before bridge for 20 mm guns. (Hedgehog is on main deck, behind forward 5 in mount). Fitted for minelaying.
Designation changed from DE to PF in 1975.

Radar: SPS 6 and 10.

Transfer: 10 July 1968; sale Mar 1974.

TAI YUAN (old pennant number)   *C. B. Mulholland*

CORVETTES

3 Ex-US "AUK" CLASS

Name	No.	Builders	Commissioned
WU SHENG (ex-USS *Redstart*, MSF 378)	884 (ex-PCE 66)	Savannah Machine & Foundry Co, Georgia	4 Apr 1945
CHU YUNG (ex-USS *Waxwing*, MSF 389)	896 (ex-PCE 67)	American S.B. Co, Cleveland, Ohio	6 Aug 1945
PING JIN (ex-USS *Steady*, MSF 118)	867 (ex-PCE 70)	American S.B. Co, Cleveland, Ohio	16 Nov 1942

Displacement, tons: 890 standard; 1 250 full load
Dimensions, feet (metres): 221·1 × 32·1 × 10·8 *(61·4 × 10·5 × 3·5)*
Guns: 2—3 in *(76 mm)*/50 (single); 4—40 mm (twin)
A/S weapons: 1 Hedgehog; 3—12·75 in *(324 mm)* torpedo tubes (Mk 32 triple); depth charges
Mines: Mine-rails fitted in *Chu Yung* (1975)
Main engines: Diesel-electric (General Motors diesels); 7 060 bhp; 2 shafts = 18 knots
Complement: 80

Minesweeping equipment removed and second 3 in gun fitted aft in Taiwan service. One fitted for minelaying.

Transfers: 66, July 1965; 67, Nov 1965; 70, Mar 1968.

WU SHENG (old pennant number)

TAIWAN / Light forces

LIGHT FORCES

1 + 1 FAST ATTACK CRAFT (MISSILE)

LUNG CHIANG PGG 581   — PGG 582

Displacement, tons: 240 standard; 270 full load
Dimensions, feet (metres): 164·5 × 23·i × 7·5 *(50·2 × 7·3 × 2·3)*
Missiles: SSM; 4 Hsiung Feng (single launchers) (see note)
Guns: 1—76 mm OTO Melara; 2—30 mm (Emerson) (twin); 2—0·50 cal MG
Main engines: CODAG; 3 Avco Lycoming gas turbines; 13 800 shp (15 000 max); 3 diesels; 2 880 shp; 3 shafts (cp propellers)
Speed, knots: 20 knots (diesels); 40 knots (gas turbines)
Range, miles: 2 700 at 12 knots (1 diesel); 1 900 at 20 knots (3 diesels); 700 at 40 knots (3 gas turbines)
Complement: 34 (5 officers, 29 ratings)

Ordered from Tacoma Boatbuilding Co Inc, Washington, USA. The first built at Tacoma, the second in Taiwan. Designated Patrol Ship Multi-Mission Mk 5 (PSMM Mk 5). Originally to be a class of 15 but 13 cancelled and to be replaced by Taiwan-designed Patrol Craft. This cancellation is reported as due to non-availability of American or Italian missiles.

Fire control: NA 10 Mod 0 GFCS with Selenia RAN 11 L/X and IPN 10.

Missiles: The Hsiung Feng missile appears to be either a Gabriel renamed or a Taiwanese version of that missile.

PSMM Mk 5

2 "79 ft" TYPE (FAST ATTACK CRAFT—TORPEDO)

Name	No.	Builders	Commissioned
FU KUO	PT 515	Hutchins Yacht Corporation, Jacksonville, Florida	—
TIAN KUO	PT 516	Hutchins Yacht Corporation, Jacksonville, Florida	—

Displacement, tons: 46 light; 53 full load
Dimensions, feet (metres): 79 × 23·25 × 5·5 *(25·9 × 7·6 × 1·8)*
Guns: 1—40 mm; 2—·50 cal MG (single)
Torpedo launchers: 2
Main engines: 3 petrol engines; 3 shafts = 39 knots max; 32 knots cruising
Complement: 12

Transferred to Taiwan on 1 September 1957.

2 "71 ft" TYPE (FAST ATTACK CRAFT—TORPEDO)

Name	No.	Builders	Commissioned
FAN KONG	PT 513	Annapolis Yacht Yard, Annapolis, Maryland	—
SAO TANG	PT 514	Annapolis Yacht Yard, Annapolis, Maryland	—

Displacement, tons: 39 light; 46 full load
Dimensions, feet (metres): 71 × 19 × 5 *(23·3 × 6·3 × 1·6)*
Guns: 1—20 mm; 4—·50 cal MG (twin)
Torpedo launchers: 2 (?)
Main engines: 3 petrol engines; 3 shafts = 42 knots max; 32 knots cruising
Complement: 12

Transferred to Taiwan on 19 August 1957 and 1 November 1957, respectively.

2 JAPANESE TYPE (FAST ATTACK CRAFT—TORPEDO)

Name	No.	Builders	Commissioned
FUH CHOW	—	Mitsubishi S.B. Co	—
HSUEH CHIH	—	Mitsubishi S.B. Co	—

Displacement, tons: 33 light; 40 full load
Dimensions, feet (metres): 69 × 19·9 *(22·6 × 6·5)*
Guns: 1—40 mm; 2—20 mm (twin)
Torpedo launchers: 2—18 in *(457 mm)*
Main engines: 3 petrol engines; 3 shafts = 40 knots max; 27 knots cruising
Complement: 12

Transferred to Taiwan on 1 June 1957 and 6 November 1957, respectively.

Note: At least three additional fast attack craft (torpedo) are known to be in service; details are not available.

FUH CHOW (forward 40 mm unshipped)

10 COASTAL PATROL CRAFT

Displacement, tons: approx 30 tons
Gun: 1—40 mm

Small patrol boats designated PB. Constructed in Taiwan with the first of a reported ten units completed about 1971. These are believed the first warships of indigenous Taiwan construction.

PB 1

470 TAIWAN / Mine warfare forces — Amphibious forces

MINE WARFARE FORCES

Note: Previously reported transfer of ex-USS *Bold* and *Bulwark* ("Agile" class MSOs) did not take place.

14 US "ADJUTANT" and "MSC 268" CLASSES (MINESWEEPERS—COASTAL)

Name	No.	Builders	Commissioned
YUNG PING (ex-US *MSC 140*)	— (ex-MSC 155)	USA	June 1955
YUNG AN (ex-US *MSC 123*)	— (ex-MSC 156)	USA	June 1955
YUNG NIEN (ex-US *MSC 277*)	— (ex-MSC 157)	USA	Dec 1958
YUNG CHOU (ex-US *MSC 278*)	— (ex-MSC 158)	USA	July 1959
YUNG HSIN (ex-US *MSC 302*)	— (ex-MSC 159)	USA	Mar 1965
YUNG JU (ex-US *MSC 300*)	— (ex-MSC 160)	USA	Apr 1965
YUNG LO (ex-US *MSC 306*)	— (ex-MSC 161)	USA	June 1960
YUNG FU (ex-*Diest*, ex-USS *Macaw* MSC 77)	— (ex-MSC 162)	USA	1953
YUNG CHING (ex-*Eekloo*, ex-US *MSC 101*)	— (ex-MSC 163)	USA	1955
YUNG SHAN (ex-*Lier*, ex-US *MSC 63*)	— (ex-MSC 164)	USA	1954
YUNG CHENG (ex-*Maaseick*, ex-US *MSC 78*)	— (ex-MSC 165)	USA	1955
YUNG CHI (ex-*Charleroi*, ex-US *MSC 152*)	— (ex-MSC 166)	USA	1955
YUNG JEN (ex-*St Nicholas*, ex-US *MSC 64*)	— (ex-MSC 167)	USA	1953
YUNG SUI (ex-*Diksmude*, ex-US *MSC 65*)	— (ex-MSC 168)	USA	1954

Displacement, tons: 380 full load
Dimensions, feet (metres): 144 × 28 × 8·5 *(43·9 × 8·5 × 2·6)*
Guns: 2—20 mm (twin)
Main engines: 2 General Motors diesels; 2 shafts = 13·5 knots
Range, miles: 2 500 at 12 knots
Complement: 40 to 50

Non-magnetic, wood-hulled minesweepers built in the USA specifically for transfer to allied navies. First seven units listed above transferred to Taiwan upon completion: MSC 160 in April 1965, and MSC 161 in June 1966.
All are of similar design; the ex-Belgian ships have a small boom aft on a pole mast. They carried a single 40 mm gun forward in Belgian service.

Transfers: Last seven originally built for Belgium and transferred to Taiwan November 1969. *De Panne* (ex-US *MSC 131*) was also transferred but has been stripped for spares.

YUNG SHAN (pole mast aft) (old pennant number)

YUNG CHOU (no pole mast aft) (old pennant number)

1 MINESWEEPING BOAT

MSB 12 (ex-US *MSB 4*)

Dimensions, feet (metres): 57·1 × 15·1 × 3·9 *(17·4 × 4·6 × 1·2)*
Main engines: 2 diesels; 1 200 hp = 12 knots
Complement: 6

Former US Army minesweeping boat; assigned hull number MSB 4 in US Navy and transferred to Taiwan in December 1961. Navigation radar.

8 MINESWEEPING LAUNCHES

MSML 1	MSML 5	MSML 7	MSML 11
MSML 3	MSML 6	MSML 8	MSML 12

50 ft minesweeping launches built in the USA and transferred to Taiwan in March 1961.

AMPHIBIOUS FORCES

1 Ex-US "ASHLAND" CLASS (LSD)

Name	No.	Builders	Commissioned
CHUNG CHENG (ex-*Tung Hai*, ex-USS *White Marsh*, LSD 8)	LSD 639 (ex-LSD 191)	Moore Dry Dock Co, Oakland, California	2 July 1945

Displacement, tons: 4 790 standard; 8 700 full load
Dimensions, feet (metres): 457·8 × 72 × 18 *(139·6 × 21·9 × 5·5)*
Guns: 12—40 mm (2 quad and 2 twin)
Main engines: Skinner Unaflow; 7 400 ihp; 2 shafts = 15 knots
Boilers: 2

Launched on 19 July 1943. Designed to serve as parent ship for landing craft and coastal craft. Transferred from the US Navy to Taiwan on 17 November 1960. Purchased May 1976.

CHUNG CHENG (as LSD 191)

1 Ex-US "CABILDO" CLASS (LSD)

Name	No.	Builders	Commissioned
CHEN HAI (Ex-USS *Fort Marion*, LSD 22)	618	Gulf S.B. Co, Chickasaw, Alabama	29 Jan 1946

Displacement, tons: 4 790 standard; 9 375 full load
Dimensions, feet (metres): 475·4 × 76·2 × 18 *(144·9 × 23·2 × 5·5)*
Guns: 12—40 mm (2 quad and 2 twin)
Main engines: Geared turbines; 7 000 shp; 2 shafts = 15·4 knots
Boilers: 2
Range, miles: 8 000 at 15 knots
Complement: 316

Launched on 22 May 1945 and transferred to Taiwan on 15 April 1977. Docking well is 392 × 44 ft; can accommodate three LCUs or 18 LCMs or 32 LVTs (amphibious tractors) in docking well. Fitted with helicopter platform over well.

Electronics: UPX 12 IFF.

Fire control: US Mk 26 Mod 4.

Radar: SPS 5.

"CABILDO" Class   1965, USN

TAIWAN / Amphibious forces 471

21 Ex-US "LST 1-510" and "511-1152" CLASSES

Name	No.
CHUNG HAI (ex-USS LST 755)	697 (ex-201)
CHUNG TING (ex-USS LST 537)	— (ex-203)
CHUNG HSING (ex-USS LST 557)	— (ex-204)
CHUNG CHIEN (ex-USS LST 716)	— (ex-205)
CHUNG CHI (ex-USS LST 1017)	— (ex-206)
CHUNG SHUN (ex-USS LST 732)	624 (ex-208)
CHUNG LIEN (ex-USS LST 1050)	691 (ex 209)
CHUNG YUNG (ex-USS LST 574)	— (ex-210)
CHUNG KUANG (ex-USS LST 503)	— (ex-216)
CHUNG SUO (ex-USS Bradley County, LST 400)	— (ex-217)
CHUNG CHUAN (ex-LST 1030)	— (ex-221)
CHUNG SHENG (ex-LST 211, ex-USS LSTH 1033)	— (ex-222)
CHUNG FU (ex-USS Iron County, LST 840)	619 (ex-223)
CHUNG CHENG (ex-USS Lafayette County, LST 859)	— (ex-224)
CHUNG CHIANG (ex-USS San Bernardino County, LST 1110)	— (ex-225)
CHUNG CHIH (ex-USS Sagadahoc County, LST 1091)	— (ex-226)
CHUNG MING (ex-USS Sweetwater County, LST 1152)	— (ex-227)
CHUNG SHU (ex-USS LST 520)	— (ex-228)
CHUNG WAN (ex-USS LST 535)	— (ex-229)
CHUNG PANG (ex-USS LST 578)	— (ex-230)
CHUNG YEH (ex-USS Sublette County, LST 1144)	— (ex-231)

Displacement, tons: 1 653 standard; 4 080 full load
Dimensions, feet (metres): 328 × 50 × 14 *(100 × 15·2 × 4·3)*
Guns: Varies; up to 10—40 mm (2 twin, 6 single) with some modernised ships rearmed with 2—3 in (single) and 6—40 mm (twin)
Several 20 mm (twin or single)
Main engines: 2 General Motors diesels; 1 700 bhp; 2 shafts = 11·6 knots
Complement: Varies: 100 to 125 in most ships

Constructed during World War II. These ships have been rebuilt in Taiwan. Hull numbers of LSTs are being changed to 600 series. Including 629 and 654.

Appearance: Some have davits forward and aft.

Electronics: Some have UPX 5 or 12 IFF.

Radar: US SO 1, 2 or 8.

Transfers: 201-208, 1946; 209 and 222, 1947; 228, 1948; 217, 223-230, 1958; 210, 1959; 216 and 218, 1960; 231, 1961.

"LST 1-510" Class (*Ho Shan* alongside) (old pennant number) 1974

CHUNG SHUN (old pennant number)

1 Ex-US "LST 511-1152" CLASS (FLAGSHIP) (AGC)

Name	No.	Builders	Commissioned
KAO HSIUNG (ex-*Chung Hai*, LST 219, AGC 663 ex-USS *Dukes County*, LST 735)		Dravo Corporation, Neville Island, Penn	26 Apr 1944

Displacement, tons: 1 653 standard; 4 080 full load
Dimensions, feet (metres): 328 × 50 × 14 *(100 × 15·2 × 4·3)*
Guns: Several 40 mm (twin)
Main engines: 2 General Motors diesels; 1 700 bhp; 2 shafts = 11·6 knots

Launched on 11 March 1944. Transferred to Taiwan in May 1957 for service as an LST. Converted to a flagship for amphibious operations and renamed and redesignated (AGC) in 1964. Purchased November 1974.
Note latice mast above bridge structure, modified bridge levels, and antenna mountings on main deck.

KAO HSIUNG

4 Ex-US "LSM-1" CLASS

Name	No.
MEI TSENG (ex-USS LSM 431)	649 (ex-LSM 341)
MEI SUNG (ex-USS LSM 457)	694 (ex-LSM 347)
MEI PING (ex-USS LSM 471)	659 (ex-LSM 353)
MEI LO (ex-USS LSM 362)	637 (ex-LSM 356)

Displacement, tons: 1 095 full load
Dimensions, feet (metres): 203·5 × 34·5 × 7·3 *(62 × 10·5 × 2·2)*
Guns: 2—40 mm (twin); 4 or 8—20 mm (4 single or 4 twin)
Main engines: Diesels; 2 800 bhp; 2 shafts = 12·5 knots
Complement: 65 to 75

Constructed during World War II. Originally numbered in the 200-series in Taiwan service. Rebuilt in Taiwan.

Radar: Surface search: SO 8.

Transfers: 341 and 347 1946; 353, 1956; 356, 1962.

MEI PING (old pennant number)

22 Ex-US "LCU 501" and "LCU 1466" CLASSES

Name	No.	Name	No.
HO CHUN (ex-LCU 892)	— (ex-481)	HO SHUN (ex-LCU 1225)	— (ex-494)
HO TSUNG (ex-LCU 1213)	— (ex-482)	HO YUNG (ex-LCU 1271)	— (ex-495)
HO CHUNG (ex-LCU 849)	— (ex-484)	HO CHIEN (ex-LCU 1278)	— (ex-496)
HO CHANG (ex-LCU 512)	— (ex-485)	HO CHI (ex-LCU 1212)	— (ex-401)
HO CHENG (ex-LCU 1145)	— (ex-486)	HO HOEI (ex-LCU 1218)	— (ex-402)
HO SHAN (ex-LCU 1596)	— (ex-488)	HO YAO (ex-LCU 1244)	— (ex-403)
HO CHUAN (ex-LCU 1597)	— (ex-489)	HO DENG (ex-LCU 1367)	— (ex-404)
HO SENG (ex-LCU 1598)	— (ex-490)	HO FENG (ex-LCU 1397)	— (ex-405)
HO MENG (ex-LCU 1599)	— (ex-491)	HO CHAO (ex-LCU 1429)	— (ex-406)
HO MOU (ex-LCU 1600)	— (ex-492)	HO TENG (ex-LCU 1452)	— (ex-407)
HO SHOU (ex-LCU 1601)	— (ex-493)	HO CHIE (ex-LCU 700)	— (ex-SB1)

The LCU 501 series were built in the USA during World War II; initially designated LCT(6) series. The six of LCU 1466 series built by Ishikawajima Heavy Industries Co, Tokyo, Japan, for transfer to Taiwan; completed in March 1955. All originally numbered in 200-series; subsequently changed to 400-series.

Transfers: 401-407: Nov/Dec 1959. SB1, 494-496: Jan/Feb 1958. Remainder: 1946-48.

"LCU 501" Class

Displacement, tons: 158 light; 268 full load
Dimensions, feet (metres): 115·1 × 32 × 4·2 *(35·1 × 9·8 × 1·3)*
Guns: 2—20 mm (single); some units also may have 2—50 cal MG
Main engines: 3 diesels; 675 bhp; 3 shafts = 10 knots
Complement: 10 to 25

"LCU 1466" Class

Displacement, tons: 130 light; 280 full load
Dimensions, feet (metres): 115·1 × 34 × 4·1 *(35·1 × 10·7 × 1·2)*
Guns: 3—20 mm (single); some units may also have 2—50 cal MG
Main engines: 3 diesels; 675 bhp; 3 shafts = 10 knots
Complement: 15 to 25

472 TAIWAN / Survey ships — Service forces

SURVEY SHIPS

1 Ex-US C1-M-AV1 TYPE

Name	No.	Builders	Commissioned
CHIU HUA (ex-USNS *Sgt. George D. Keathley*, T-AGS 35, ex-T-APC 117)	AGS 398	—	—

Displacement, tons: 6 090 tons
Dimensions, feet (metres): 338·8 × 50·3 × 17·5 *(103·3 × 15·3 × 5·3)*
Guns: 1—40 mm; 2—20 mm
Main engine: Diesel; 1 750 bhp; 1 shaft = 11·5 knots
Complement: 72

Built in 1945 as merchant ship; subsequently acquired by US Army for use as transport, but assigned to Navy's Military Sea Transportation Service in 1950 and designated as coastal transport (T-APC 117). Refitted for oceanographic survey work in 1966-67 and redesignated T-AGS 35. Transferred to Taiwan on 29 March 1972 and by sale 19 May 1976.

1 Ex-US "LSIL 351" CLASS

Name	No.	Builders	Commissioned
LIEN CHANG (ex-USS *LSIL 1017*)	AGSC 466	Albina Engineering & Machinery Works, Portland, Oregon	12 Apr 1944

Dimensions, feet (metres): 159 × 23·6 × 5·6 *(48·4 × 7·2 × 1·7)*
Guns: 2—40 mm (twin); several 20 mm
Main engines: 2 General Motors diesels; 2 320 bhp; 2 shafts = 14 knots

Launched on 14 March 1944. Transferred to Taiwan in March 1958. Employed as surveying ship; retains basic LSIL appearance.

1 SURVEY SHIP

WU KANG

Of 907 tons, launched 1943 with complement of 59.

1 Ex-US "SOTOYOMO" CLASS

Name	No.	Builders	Commissioned
CHIU LIEN (ex-USS *Geronimo*, ATA 207)	AGS 563	Gulfport Boiler & Welding Works, Port Arthur, Texas	1 Mar 1945

Displacement, tons: 835
Dimensions, feet (metres): 143 × 33·9 × 13·2 *(43·6 × 10·3 × 4)*
Main engine: Diesel-electric (General Motors); 1 500 bhp; 1 shaft = 13 knots

Former US Navy auxiliary tug. Launched 4 January 1945. Transferred to Taiwan in February 1969 and converted to surveying ship. Currently employed as research ship for the Institute of Oceanology. Civilian manned. Painted white.

CHIU LIEN

SERVICE FORCES

Note: USS *Tappahannock,* AOG 43 is to be transferred.

1 Ex-US "AMPHION" CLASS (REPAIR SHIP)

Name	No.	Builders	Commissioned
YU TAI (ex-USS *Cadmus*, AR 14)	ARG 358	Tampa Shipbuilding Co, Tampa, Florida	23 Apr 1946

Displacement, tons: 7 826 standard; 14 490 full load
Dimensions, feet (metres): 492 × 70 × 27·5 *(150 × 21·3 × 8·4)*
Gun: 1—5 in *(127 mm)*/38
Main engines: Turbines (Westinghouse); 8 500 shp; 1 shaft = 16·5 knots
Boilers: 2 (Foster-Wheeler)

Launched on 5 August 1945. Transferred to Taiwan on 15 January 1974. Replaced *Tien Tai* (ex-USS *Tutuila*, ARG 4).

1 Ex-US "ACHELOUS" CLASS (TRANSPORT)

Name	No.	Builders	Commissioned
WU TAI (ex-*Sung Shan*, ARL 336, ex-USS *Agenor*, ARL 3, ex-*LST 490*)	AP 520	Kaiser Co, Vancouver, Wash	20 Aug 1943

Displacement, tons: 1 625 light; 4 100 full load
Dimensions, feet (metres): 328 × 50 × 11 *(100 × 15·2 × 3·4)*
Guns: 8—40 mm (quad)
Main engines: 2 General Motors diesels; 1 800 bhp; 2 shafts = 11·6 knots
Troops: 600

Begun for the US Navy as a LST completed as a repair ship for landing craft (ARL). Launched on 3 April 1943. Transferred to France in 1951 for service in Indochina; subsequently returned to USA and retransferred to Taiwan on 15 September 1957.
Employed as a repair ship (ARL 336, subsequently ARL 236) until converted in 1973-74 to troop transport.

WU TAI (as repair ship) (old pennant number)

1 TAIWAN TYPE (TRANSPORT)

Name	No.	Builders	Commissioned
LING YUEN	522	Taiwan Shipbuilding Co, Keelung	15 Aug 1975

Measurement, tons: 2 510 deadweight; 3 040 gross
Dimensions, feet (metres): 328·7 × 47·9 × 16·4 *(100·2 × 14·6 × 5)*
Guns: 2—20 mm (single); 2—0·5 in MG (single)
Main engines: Diesel 6-cyl
Complement: 55
Accommodation for troops: 500

Designed by Chinese First Naval Shipyard at Tsoying.
Launched 27 January 1975.

LING YUEN 1975

1 JAPANESE TYPE (SUPPORT TANKER)

Name	No.	Builders	Commissioned
WAN SHOU	AOG 512	Ujina Shipbuilding Co, Hiroshima, Japan	1 Nov 1969

Displacement, tons: 1 049 light; 4 150 full load
Dimensions, feet (metres): 283·8 × 54 × 18 *(86·5 × 16·5 × 5·5)*
Guns: 2—40 mm (single); 2—20 mm
Main engine: Diesel; 2 100 bhp; 1 shaft = 13 knots
Complement: 70
Cargo: 73 600 gallons fuel; 62 000 gallons water

Employed in resupply of offshore islands.

3 Ex-US "PATAPSCO" CLASS (SUPPORT TANKERS)

Name	No.	Builders	Commissioned
CHANG PEI (ex-USS *Pecatonica* AOG 57)	AOG 378	Cargill, Inc, Savage Minnesota	28 Nov 1945
LUNG CHUAN (ex-HMNZS *Endeavour*, ex-USS *Namakagon*, AOG 53)	AOG 342	Cargill, Inc, Savage Minnesota	1945
HSIN LUNG (ex-USS *Elkhorn* AOG 7)	AOG 389	Cargill, Inc, Savage Minnesota	12 Feb 1944

Displacement, tons: 1 850 light; 4 335 full load
Dimensions, feet (metres): 310·8 × 48·5 × 15·7 *(94·8 × 14·8 × 4·8)*
Main engines: 2 General Motors diesels; 3 300 bhp; 2 shafts = 14 knots

Chang Pei was launched on 17 March 1945 and transferred to Taiwan on 24 April 1961. The ex-USS *Namakagon* was launched on 4 November 1944 and transferred to New Zealand on 6 October 1962 for use as an Antarctic resupply ship; stengthened for polar operations and renamed *Endeavour*; returned to the US Navy on 29 June 1971 and retransferred to Taiwan the same date. *Hsin Lung* was launched on 15 May 1943 and was transferred to Taiwan on 1 July 1972.
All three transferred by sale 19 May 1976.

Radar: *Chang Pei* has SPS 21.

CHANG PEI

Ex-US YO TYPE (SUPPORT TANKER)

Name	No.	Builders	Commissioned
WU MING (ex-US *YO 198*)	AOG 504 (ex-AOG 304)	Manitowoc S.B. Co, Manitowoc, Wisconsin	1945

Displacement, tons: 650 light; 1 595 full load
Dimensions, feet (metres): 174 × 32 *(53 × 9·8)*
Guns: 1—40 mm; 5—20 mm (single)
Main engine: 1 Union diesel; 560 bhp; 1 shaft = 10·5 knots
Complement: approx 65

Transferred to Taiwan in December 1949. Reportedly placed in reserve in 1976.

Radar: SO 8.

JAPANESE TYPE (SUPPORT TANKERS)

Also reported to be in service.

Ex-US "DIVER" CLASS (SALVAGE SHIP)

Name	No.	Builders	Commissioned
TA HU (ex-USS *Grapple*)	— (ex-ARS 7)	Basalt Rock Co, Napa, California	16 Dec 1943

Displacement, tons: 1 530 standard; 1 900 full load
Dimensions, feet (metres): 213·5 × 39 × 13 *(65·1 × 11·9 × 4)*
Gun: 1—40 mm
Main engines: Diesel-electric; 2 shafts; 2 440 shp = 14 knots
Complement: 85

Fitted for salvage, towing and compressed-air diving.
Transferred 1 December 1977.

Ex-US "MARK" CLASS (CARGO SHIP)

Name	No.	Builders	Commissioned
LUNG KANG (ex-USS *Mark*, AKL 12, ex-AG 143, ex-US Army *FS 214*)	AKL 359	Higgins	1944

Displacement, tons: approx 700
Dimensions, feet (metres): 176·5 × 32·8 × 10 *(53·8 × 10 × 3)*
Guns: 2—20 mm
Main engine: Diesel; 1 000 bhp; 1 shaft = 10 knots

Built as a small cargo ship (freight and supply) for the US Army. Transferred to US Navy on 30 September 1947; operated in South East Asia from 1963 until transferred to Taiwan on 1 June 1971 and by sale 19 May 1976. Acts as AGI.

TUGS

2 Ex-US "CHEROKEE" CLASS

Name	No.	Builders	Commissioned
TA TUNG (ex-USS *Chickasaw*, ATF 83)	ATF 548	United Engineering Co, Alameda, California	4 Feb 1943
TA WAN (ex-USS *Apache*, ATF 67)	ATF 550	Charleston S.B. & D.D. Co, South Carolina	12 Dec 1942

Displacement, tons: 1 235 standard; 1 675 full load
Dimensions, feet (metres): 205 × 38·5 × 15·5 *(62·5 × 11·7 × 4·7)*
Guns: 1—3 in *(76 mm)*/50; several light MG
Main engines: Diesel-electric; 3 000 bhp; 1 shaft = 15 knots

Launched on 23 July 1942 and 8 May 1942 respectively. *Ta Tung* transferred to Taiwan in January 1966 and by sale 19 May 1976 and *Ta Wan* on 30 June 1974.

3 Ex-US "SOTOYOMO" CLASS

Name	No.	Builders	Commissioned
TA SUEH (ex-USS *Tonkawa*, ATA 176)	ATA 357	Levingston S.B. Co, Orange, Texas	19 Aug 1944
TA TENG (ex-USS *Cahokia*, ATA 186)	ATA 367	Levingston S.B. Co, Orange, Texas	24 Nov 1944
TA PENG (ex-USS *Mohopac*, ATA 196)	ATA 395	Levingston S.B. Co, Orange, Texas	21 Dec 1944

Displacement, tons: 435 standard; 835 full load
Dimensions, feet (metres): 143 × 33·9 × 13 *(43·6 × 10·3 × 4)*
Guns: 1—3 in *(76 mm)*/50; several light MG
Main engine: Diesel-electric (General Motors diesel); 1 500 bhp; 1 shaft = 13 knots

Ta Sueh launched on 1 March 1944 and transferred to Taiwan in April 1962. *Ta Teng* launched on 18 September 1944; assigned briefly to US Air Force in 1971 until transferred to Taiwan on 29 March 1972. *Ta Peng* transferred on 1 July 1971. Latter two by sale 19 May 1976.
A fourth tug of this class serves as a surveying ship.

TA YU (ex-US *LT 310*) ATA 373

Transferred April 1949. Also reported.

1 Ex-US ARMY ST TYPE

YTL 9 (ex-US Army *ST 2004*)

Former US Army 76 ft harbour tug.

3 Ex-US "YLT 422" CLASS

YTL 11 (ex-USN *YTL 454*)   **YTL 14** (ex-USN *YTL 585*)
YTL 12 (ex-USN *YTL 584*)

Former US Navy 66 ft harbour tugs.

5 Ex-US FLOATING DRY DOCKS

Name	No.	Builders	Commissioned
HAY TAN (ex-USN *AFDL 36*)	AFDL 1	—	—
KIM MEN (ex-USN *AFDL 5*)	AFDL 2	—	—
HAN JIH (ex-USN *AFDL 34*)	AFDL 3	—	—
FO WU 5 (ex-USN *ARD 9*)	ARD 5	—	—
FO WU 6 (ex-USS *Windsor*, ARD 22)	ARD 6	—	—

Former US Navy floating dry docks; see USA section for characteristics.

Transfers: AFDL 1 in Mar 1947, AFDL 2 in Jan 1948, AFDL 3 in July 1959, ARD 5 in Oct 1967, ARD 6 in June 1971. ARD 6 by sale 19 May 1976 and ARD 5 on 12 Jan 1977.

SERVICE CRAFT

Approximately 25 non-self-propelled service craft are in use; most are former US Navy service craft.

CUSTOMS SERVICE

Several small ships and small craft as well as the ships listed below are in service with the Customs Service of Taiwan, an agency of the Ministry of Finance.

2 Ex-US "ADMIRABLE" CLASS

Name	No.	Builders	Commissioned
HUNG HSING (ex-USS *Embattle*, AM 226)	A 7	American Shipbuilding Co, Lorain, Ohio	25 Apr 1945
— (ex-USS *Improve*, AM 247)	—	Savannah Machine & Foundry Co, Georgia	29 Feb 1944

Dimensions, feet (metres): 184·5 × 33 × 9·8 *(56·3 × 10·1 × 3)*
Guns: 2—20 mm
Main engines: 2 diesels (Cooper Bessemer); 1 710 bhp; 2 shafts = 14 knots

Former US Navy minesweepers (AM). Launched on 17 September 1944 and 26 September 1943 respectively.

3 Ex-US "PC-461" CLASS

Name	No.	Builders	Commissioned
—Ex-*Tung Kiang* (ex-USS *Placerville*, PC 1087)	PC 119	USA	1943
—Ex-*Hsi Kiang* (ex-USS *Susanville*, PC 1149)	PC 120	USA	1944
—Ex-*Pei Kiang* (ex-USS *Hanford* PC 1142)	PC 122	USA	1943

Displacement, tons: 450 full load
Dimensions, feet (metres): 173·66 × 23 × 10·8 *(56·9 × 7·5 × 3·5)*
Guns: 2—20 mm
Main engines: 2 General Motors diesels; 2 880 bhp; 2 shafts = 20 knots
Range, miles: 5 000 at 10 knots
Complement: 65

Former US Navy steel hulled submarine chasers. Originally transferred to Taiwan for naval use; subsequently allocated to the Customs Service. Transferred in July 1957.
All sold in May 1976.

2 HALTER "78 ft" PATROL CRAFT

Purchased in 1977.

474 TANZANIA / Introduction — Light forces

TANZANIA
(see also Zanzibar)

Ministerial

Minister of Defence:
Rashidi Kawawa

Personnel

(a) 1979: 700 (approx)
(b) Voluntary service

Base

Dar Es Salaam. A base area built under Chinese supervision.

Mercantile Marine

Lloyd's Register of Shipping:
26 vessels of 36 968 tons gross

LIGHT FORCES

7 Ex-CHINESE "SHANGHAI II" CLASS (FAST ATTACK CRAFT—GUN)

JW 9861-7

Displacement, tons: 155 full load
Dimensions, feet (metres): 127·3 × 17·7 × 5·2 (38·8 × 5·4 × 1·6)
Guns: 4—37 mm (twin) 4—25 mm (twin)
Main engines: 4 M50F diesels; 4 800 bhp = 30 knots
Range, miles: 800 at 17 knots
Complement: 25

Transferred by the Chinese People's Republic in 1970-71.

Radar: Search: Skin Head.

"SHANGHAI" Class

4 Ex-CHINESE "HU CHWAN" CLASS
(FAST ATTACK CRAFT—HYDROFOIL (TORPEDO))

Displacement, tons: 39 full load
Dimensions, feet (metres): 70·4 × 24·6 × 1 (21·8 × 7·5 × 0·3) (foilborne)
Guns: 2—14·5 MG (twin)
Torpedo tubes: 2—21 in (533 mm)
Main engines: 3 diesels; 3 600 bhp = 55 knots (calm)
Range, miles: 500 at 20 knots

Transferred 1975.

Radar: Search: Skin Head.
Navigation: Don.

"HU CHWAN" Class

3 Ex-EAST GERMAN "P6" CLASS (FAST ATTACK CRAFT—GUN)

Displacement, tons: 73 full load
Dimensions, feet (metres): 85·3 × 20 × 4·9 (26 × 6·1 × 1·5)
Guns: 4—25 mm
Main engines: 4 diesels; 4 shafts; 4 800 bhp = 41 knots
Range, miles: 450 at 30 knots
Complement: 20

Transferred 1974-75. Torpedo tubes removed.

Radar: Search: Pot Head.

4 Ex-SOVIET "P4" CLASS (FAST ATTACK CRAFT—TORPEDO)

JW 9841-4

Displacement, tons: 22 standard
Dimensions, feet (metres): 62·3 × 10·8 × 3·3 (19·0 × 3·3 × 1·0)
Guns: 2—14·5 mm MG (twin)
Torpedo tubes: 2—18 in (457 mm)
Main engines: 2 diesels; 2 shafts; 2 200 bhp = 50 knots
Complement: 12

Transferred 1970-73 (from USSR and from East Germany). Some have torpedo tubes removed.

Radar: Search: Skin Head.

1 Ex-SOVIET "POLUCHAT" CLASS (LARGE PATROL CRAFT)

Displacement, tons: 90 full load
Dimensions, feet (metres): 97·1 × 19 × 4·8 (29·6 × 5·8 × 1·5)
Guns: 2—14·5 mm (twin)
Main engines: 2 diesels; 2 400 hp = 20 knots
Range, miles: 460 at 17 knots
Complement: 15

2 Ex-EAST GERMAN "SCHWALBE" CLASS
(COASTAL PATROL CRAFT)

ARAKA   SALAAM

Displacement, tons: 70 full load
Dimensions, feet (metres): 85·2 × 14·8 × 4·6 (26 × 4·5 × 1·4)
Guns: 2—25 mm (twin); 2 MG
Main engines: Diesel; 300 hp = 17 knots

Launched 1955-56. Transferred 1966-67.

"SCHWALBE" Class

2 Ex-EAST GERMAN COASTAL PATROL CRAFT

RAFIKI   UHURU

Displacement, tons: 50
Dimensions, feet (metres): 78·7 × 16·4 × 4·3 (24 × 5 × 1·3)
Guns: 1—40 mm; 4 MG

Purchased 1967, via Portugal.

4 Ex-CHINESE "YU LIN" CLASS (COASTAL PATROL CRAFT)

Displacement, tons: 27
Dimensions, feet (metres): 42·6 × 13 × 4·2 (13 × 4 × 1·2)
Gun: 1—12·7 mm MG
Speed, knots: 20
Complement: 10

Transferred late 1966. Based on Victoria Nyanza.

1 SURVEY LAUNCH

Dimensions, feet (metres): 91·8 × 15·7 × 3·3 (28 × 4·8 × 1)
Main engine: 1 Caterpillar diesel; 480 hp = 14 knots

Ordered from Bayerische Schiffbau West Germany for completion end 1978.

2 Ex-CHINESE LCMs

THAILAND

THAILAND / Introduction — Frigates 475

Ministerial

Minister of Defence:
 General Kriangsak Chomanan

Administration

Commander-in-Chief of the Navy:
 Admiral Kawee Sinqha
Deputy Commander-in-Chief:
 Admiral Smut Sahanavin
Chief of Staff (RTN):
 Admiral Udom Pumhiran

Senior Flag Officer

Commander-in-Chief, Fleet:
 Admiral Adul Tulyanon

Diplomatic Representation

Naval Attaché in London:
 Captain Amnuay Iamsuro
Naval Attaché in Washington:
 Captain Vinit Tapasanan

Personnel

(a) 1979: Navy, 20 000 (2 000 officers and 18 000 ratings) including Marine Corps: 7 000 (500 officers and 6 500 men)
(b) 2 years national service

Bases

Bangkok, Sattahip, Songkhla, Paknam. A new base on the West coast has been reported.

Prefix to Ships' Names

HTMS

General

With three Frigates, three Fast Attack Craft (with three building) and a few coastal patrol craft as the only ships of under ten years of age this is an aged fleet. Replacement will presumably take account of the problems of extended off-shore limits and the continued upheavals in the Kampuchea—Viet-Nam area. The navies of the latter pair present no great threat at the moment with lack of fuel and training but intrusions into the offshore areas and the Malaysian border areas suggest a need for fast patrol craft with fairly light armament but considerable range and sea-keeping qualities.

Strength of the Fleet

Type	Active	Building
Frigates	6	—
Fast Attack Craft (Missile)	6	—
Large Patrol Craft	22	—
Coastal Patrol Craft	25	—
Coastal Minelayers	2	—
Coastal Minesweepers	4	—
MCM Support Ship	1	—
MSBs	10	—
LSTs	5	—
LSMs	3	—
LCG	1	—
LSILs	2	—
LCUs	6	—
LCMs	26	—
LCVPs	8	—
Survey Vessels	4	—
Support Tankers	2	—
Harbour Tankers	2	—
Water Boats	2	—
Tugs	4	—
Transports	2	—
Training Ships	3	—

Mercantile Marine

Lloyd's Register of Shipping:
 117 vessels of 335 116 tons gross

DELETIONS

Note: Frigates *Bangpakong*, *Maeklong* and *Phosamton* transferred to training duties.

Large Patrol Craft

1973 SC 7
1976 *Chumporn*, *Phuket* and *Trad*, *Kantang* and *Klongyai*
1978 *Pattani*, *Surasdra*, *Chandhaburi*, *Rayong*, T 85

Coastal Patrol Craft

1973 CGC1 and 11, T 31, 33, 34 and 35
1976 T 93

Harbour Tankers

1975 *Prong* and *Samui*

FRIGATES

1 YARROW TYPE

Name	No.	Builders	Laid down	Launched	Commissioned
MAKUT RAJAKUMARN	7	Yarrow & Co Ltd, Scotstoun	11 Jan 1970	18 Nov 1971	7 May 1973

Displacement, tons: 1 650 standard; 1 900 full load
Length, feet (metres): 320·0 *(97·6)*
Beam, feet (metres): 36·0 *(11·0)*
Draught, feet (metres): 18·1 *(5·5)*
Missile launchers: SAM; 1 quad Sea Cat
Guns: 2—4·5 in Mk 8 *(114 mm)* (single)
 2—40 mm/60 Bofors (single)
A/S weapons: 1 triple-barrelled Limbo mortar; 1 DC rack; 2 depth charge throwers
Main engines: 1 Rolls-Royce Olympus gas turbine; 23 125 shp; 1 Crossley-Pielstick 12 PC2V diesel; 2 shafts; 6 000 bhp
Speed, knots: 26, 18 on diesel
Range, miles: 5 000 at 18 knots (diesel); 1 200 at 26 knots
Complement: 140 (16 officers, 124 ratings)

An order was placed on 21 August 1969 for a general purpose frigate. The ship is largely automated with a consequent saving in complement, and has been most successful in service. Fitted as flagship.

Electronics: HSA CIC system. Racal DF.

Radar: Surveillance: One LW 04 (amidships).
Fire control: One M 22 series (radome).
Sea Cat control: One M 44 Series (aft).
Navigation: One Decca Type 626.
IFF: UK Mk 10.

Sonar: UK Type 170 B, Plessey Type MS 27 and Type 162.

MAKUT RAJAKUMARN   *1978, Royal Thai Navy*

2 US "PF-103" CLASS

Name	No.	Builders	Laid down	Launched	Commissioned
TAPI	5	American S.B. Co, Toledo, Ohio	1 Apr 1970	17 Oct 1970	1 Nov 1971
KHIRIRAT	6	Norfolk S.B. & D.D. Co	18 Feb 1972	2 June 1973	10 Aug 1974

Displacement, tons: 900 standard; 1 135 full load
Length, feet (metres): 275 *(83·8)*
Beam, feet (metres): 33 *(10·0)*
Draught, feet (metres): 10 *(3·0)*
Guns: 2—3 in *(76 mm)*; 2—40 mm (twin)
A/S weapons: Hedgehogs; 6 (2 triple) Mk 32 A/S torpedo tubes
Main engines: 2 FM Diesels; 6 000 bhp
Speed, knots: 20
Complement: 150

Of similar design to the Iranian ships of the "Bayandor" class. *Tapi* was ordered on June 27 1969. *Khirirat* was ordered on 25 June 1971.

Fire control: Mk 63 GFCS (SPG 34). Mk 51 GFCS (40 mm).

Radar: Air search: SPS 6.
Fire control: SPG 34.

TAPI   *1975, Royal Thai Navy*

476 THAILAND / Frigates — Light forces

1 Ex-US "CANNON" CLASS

Name	No.	Builders	Laid down	Launched	Commissioned
PIN KLAO (ex-USS *Hemminger*, DE 746)	3 (ex-1)	Western Pipe & Steel Co	1943	12 Sep 1943	30 May 1944

Displacement, tons: 1 240 standard; 1 900 full load
Length, feet (metres): 306·0 *(93·3)*
Beam, feet (metres): 37·0 *(11·3)*
Draught, feet (metres): 14·1 *(4·3)*
Guns: 3—3 in *(76 mm)*/50; 6—40 mm
A/S weapons: 8 DCT
Torpedo tubes: 6 (2 triple) Mk 32 for A/S torpedoes
Main engines: General Motors diesels with electric drive; 2 shafts; 6 000 bhp
Speed, knots: 20
Oil fuel, tons: 300
Range, miles: 11 500 at 11 knots
Complement: 220

Transferred from US Navy to Royal Thai Navy at New York Navy Shipyard in July 1959 under MDAP and by sale 6 June 1975. The three 21 in torpedo tubes were removed and the four 20 mm guns were replaced by four 40 mm. The six A/S torpedo tubes were fitted in 1966. Finally purchased 6 June 1975.

Radar: SPS 5 and SC.

PIN KLAO   1977, Royal Thai Navy

2 Ex-US "TACOMA" CLASS

Name	No.	Builders	Laid down	Launched	Commissioned
TAHCHIN (ex-USS *Glendale*, PF 36)	1	Consolidated Steel Corporation, Los Angeles	6 Apr 1943	28 May 1943	1 Oct 1943
PRASAE (ex-USS *Gallup*, PF 47)	2	Consolidated Steel Corporation, Los Angeles	18 Aug 1943	17 Sep 1943	29 Feb 1944

Displacement, tons: 1 430 standard; 2 100 full load
Length, feet (metres): 304·0 *(92·7)*
Beam, feet (metres): 37·5 *(11·4)*
Draught, feet (metres): 13·7 *(4·2)*
Guns: 3—3 in *(76 mm)*/50; 2—40 mm; 9—20 mm
A/S weapons: 6 (2 triple) Mk 32 A/S torpedo tubes; 8 DCT
Main engines: Triple expansion; 2 shafts; 5 500 ihp
Boilers: 2 small water tube 3-drum type
Speed, knots: 19
Oil fuel, tons: 685
Range, miles: 7 800 at 12 knots
Complement: 180

Delivered to the Royal Thai Navy on 29 October 1951. *Prasae* partially non-operational after collision in January 1972 and *Tahchin* may also be non-operational.

PRASAE   8/1977, Royal Thai Navy

LIGHT FORCES

3 FAST ATTACK CRAFT—MISSILE

Name	No.	Builders	Commissioned
RATCHARIT	4	C. N. Breda (Venezia)	1979
WITTHAYAKHOM	5	C. N. Breda (Venezia)	1979
UDOMDET	6	C. N. Breda (Venezia)	1979

Displacement, tons: 235 standard; 270 full load
Dimensions, feet (metres): 163·4 × 24·6 × 5·6 *(49·8 × 7·5 × 1·7)*
Missiles: SSM; 4 Exocet (single cells)
Guns: 1—76 mm/62 (single Compact); 2—40 mm Breda Bofors
Main engines: 3 MTU diesels; 13 500 hp = 36 knots
Range: 2 000 at 15 knots
Complement: 45

Ordered June 1976. Standard Breda BMB 230 design.

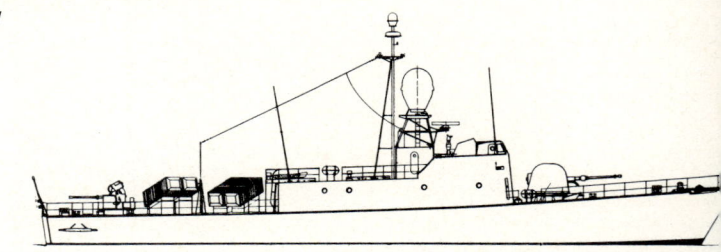

RATCHARIT   1978, Royal Thai Navy

3 LÜRSSEN TNC 45 TYPE (FAST ATTACK CRAFT—MISSILE)

Name	No.	Builders	Commissioned
PRABPARAPAK	1	Singapore Shipbuilding and Engineering Ltd	28 July 1976
HANHAK SATTRU	2	Singapore Shipbuilding and Engineering Ltd	6 Nov 1976
SUPHAIRIN	3	Singapore Shipbuilding and Engineering Ltd	1 Feb 1977

Displacement, tons: 224 standard; 260 full load
Dimensions, feet (metres): 147·3 × 22·9 × 6·9 *(44·9 × 7·0 × 2·1)*
Missiles: SSM; 5 Gabriel (1 triple, 2 single)
Guns: 1—57 mm/70 Bofors (fwd); 1—40 mm/70 Bofors (aft)
Main engines: 4 Maybach (MTU) diesels; 14 400 shp = 34 knots
Range: 2 000 cruising
Complement: 41

Ordered June 1973. Built under licence from Lürssen. Launch dates—*Prabparapak* 29 July 1975, *Hanhak Sattru* 28 October 1975, *Suphairin* 20 February 1976.

PRABPARAPAK   1978, Royal Thai Navy

THAILAND / Light forces 477

7 "LIULOM" CLASS (LARGE PATROL CRAFT)

SARASIN (ex-PC 495) PC 1   TONGPLIU (ex-PC 616) PC 6
THAYANCHON (ex-PC 575) PC 2   LIULOM (ex-PC 1253) PC 7
PHALI (ex-PC 1185) PC 4   LONGLOM (ex-PC 570) PC 8
SUKRIP (ex-PC 1218) PC 5

Displacement, tons: 280 standard; 400 full load
Dimensions, feet (metres): 174 × 23·2 × 6·5 (53 × 7 × 2)
Guns: 1—3 in; 1—40 mm; 5—20 mm
A/S weapons: 2 (single) Mk 32 ASW torpedo tubes (except Sarasin)
Main engines: 2 diesels; 2 shafts; 3 600 bhp = 19 knots
Oil fuel, tons: 60
Range, miles: 6 000 at 10 knots
Complement: 62 to 71

Launched in 1941-43 as US PCs. All transferred between March 1947 and December 1952.

Radar: SPS 25.

LIULOM   1978, Royal Thai Navy

1 "KLONGYAI" CLASS (LARGE PATROL CRAFT)

Name	No.	Builders	Commissioned
SATTAHIP	8	Royal Thai Naval Dockyard, Bangkok	1958

Displacement, tons: 110 standard; 135 full load
Dimensions, feet (metres): 131·5 × 15·5 × 4 (40·1 × 4·7 × 1·2)
Guns: 1—3 in; 1—20 mm
Torpedo tubes: 2—18 in
Main engines: Geared turbines; 2 shafts; 2 000 shp = 19 knots
Boilers: 2 water-tube
Range, miles: 480 at 15 knots
Oil fuel, tons: 18
Complement: 31

Sattahip was laid down on 21 November 1956, launched on 28 October 1957.

10 Ex-US "PGM 71" CLASS (LARGE PATROL CRAFT)

Name	No.	Builders	Commissioned
—	T 11 (ex-US PGM 71)	Peterson Builders Inc	1 Feb 1966
—	T 12 (ex-US PGM 79)	Peterson Builders Inc	1967
—	T 13 (ex-US PGM 107)	Peterson Builders Inc	28 Aug 1967
—	T 14 (ex-US PGM 116)	Peterson Builders Inc	18 Aug 1969
—	T 15 (ex-US PGM 117)	Peterson Builders Inc	18 Aug 1969
—	T 16 (ex-US PGM 115)	Peterson Builders Inc	12 Feb 1970
—	T 17 (ex-US PGM 113)	Peterson Builders Inc	12 Feb 1970
—	T 18 (ex-US PGM 114)	Peterson Builders Inc	12 Feb 1970
—	T 19 (ex-US PGM 123)	Peterson Builders Inc	25 Dec 1970
—	T 110 (ex-US PGM 124)	Peterson Builders Inc	Oct 1970

Displacement, tons: 130 standard; 147 full load
Dimensions, feet (metres): 101·0 × 21·0 × 6·0 (30·8 × 6·4 × 1·9)
Guns: 1—40 mm; 4—20 mm; 2—·50 cal MG
Main engines: Diesels; 2 shafts; 1 800 bhp = 18·5 knots
Range, miles: 1 500 at 10 knots
Complement: 30

T 11 was launched on 5 May 1965.

T 11   8/1976, Dr. Giorgio Arra

4 Ex-US CG "CAPE" CLASS (LARGE PATROL CRAFT)

T 81 (ex-CG 13)   T 83 (ex-CG 15)
T 82 (ex-CG 14)   T 84 (ex-CG 16)

Displacement, tons: 95 standard; 105 full load
Dimensions, feet (metres): 95 × 20·2 × 5 (29 × 5·8 × 1·6)
Gun: 1—20 mm
A/S weapons: 2 DC racks; 2 Mousetraps
Main engines: 2 diesels; 1 900 hp; 2 shafts = 17 knots
Range, miles: 1 500 at 14 knots
Complement: 15

US coast guard cutters transferred in 1954. Similar to those built for US Coast Guard by US Coast Guard Yard, Curtis Bay in 1953. Cost £475 000 each.

T 82 (as CG 14)   Royal Thai Navy

3 THAI BUILT (COASTAL PATROL CRAFT)

Name	No.	Builders	Commissioned
—	T 91	Royal Thai Naval Dockyard, Bangkok	1971
—	T 92	Royal Thai Naval Dockyard, Bangkok	1971
—	T 93	Royal Thai Naval Dockyard, Bangkok	1978

Displacement, tons: 87·5 standard
Dimensions, feet (metres): 104·3 × 17·5 × 5·5 (31·8 × 5·3 × 1·7)
(T 93; 118 × 18·7 × 4·9 (36 × 5·7 × 1·5))
Guns: 1—40 mm; 1—20 mm
Main engines: 2 diesels; 2 shafts; 1 600 bhp = 25 knots
Range, miles: 700 at 21 knots
Complement: 21 (23—T 93)

T 91   1970, Royal Thai Navy

478 THAILAND / Light forces — Mine warfare forces

3 "HALTER 65 ft" TYPE (COASTAL PATROL CRAFT)

651   652   653

Dimensions, feet (metres): 65 × 17 × 8·3 *(19·8 × 5·2 × 2·5)*
Main engines: 2 Detroit 12V7 ITI diesels; 1 020 hp

Delivered by Halter Marine, New Orleans in 1978 for customs duties. Aluminium hulls.

651   1978, Halter Marine

12 Ex-US "SWIFT" CLASS (COASTAL PATROL CRAFT)

| T 27 | T 29 | T 31 | T 33 | T 35 | T 211 |
| T 28 | T 30 | T 32 | T 34 | T 210 | T 212 |

Displacement, tons: 20 standard; 22 full load
Dimensions, feet (metres): 50 × 13 × 3·5 *(15·2 × 4 × 1·1)*
Guns: 2—81 mm mortars; 2—·50 cal (1 twin)
Main engines: Diesels; 2 shafts; 480 bhp = 25 knots
Complement: 5

"Swift" class patrol craft transferred from US Navy; T 28 in August 1968, T 29-31 in February 1970. T 27 in May 1970, T 32 in March 1970, T 33 in April 1970, T 34, 35, 210-212 in 1975.

6 Ex-US RPC TYPE (COASTAL PATROL CRAFT)

T 21   T 22   T 23   T 24   T 25   T 26

Displacement, tons: 10·4 standard; 13·05 full load
Dimensions, feet (metres): 35 × 10 × — *(10·6 × 3 × —)*
Guns: 2—·50 cal (1 twin); 2—·30 cal
Main engines: Diesels; 2 shafts; 225 bhp = 14 knots
Complement: 7

Transferred March 1967.

T 21   8/1976, Dr. Giorgio Arra

1 COASTAL PATROL CRAFT

Dimensions, feet (metres): 16·4 × 6·6 × — *(5 × 2 × —)*
Main engine: 1 Castoldi marine jet engine Mod 3000/05 = 38 knots

Fibreglass trimaran built in Thailand.

There are reports that a patrol of Riverine Craft is maintained on the Upper Mekong although details are not available.

MINE WARFARE FORCES

Note: Transfer of ex-USS *Prime* and *Reaper* ("Agile" class MSOs) was cancelled.

2 "BANGRACHAN" CLASS (COASTAL MINELAYERS)

Name	No.	Builders	Commissioned
BANGRACHAN	MMC 1	Cantiere dell'Adriatico, Monfalcone	1937
NHONG SARHAI	MMC 2	Cantiere dell'Adriatico, Monfalcone	1936

Displacement, tons: 368 standard; 408 full load
Dimensions, feet (metres): 172·9 × 27·9 × 7·9 *(52·7 × 8·5 × 2·4)*
Guns: 2—3 in; 2—20 mm
Mines: 142
Main engines: Burmeister & Wain diesels; 2 shafts; 540 bhp = 12 knots
Oil fuel, tons: 180
Range, miles: 2 700 at 10 knots
Complement: 55

Launched in 1936.

NHONG SARHAI

THAILAND / Mine warfare forces — Amphibious forces   479

4 US "BLUEBIRD" CLASS (MINESWEEPERS—COASTAL)

me	No.	Builders	Commissioned
DYA (ex-US MSC 297)	5	Peterson Builders Inc, Sturgeon Bay, Wisc	14 Dec 1963
NGEKO (ex-US MSC 303)	6	Dorchester S.B. Corporation, Camden	9 July 1965
DINDENG (ex-US MSC 301)	7	Tacoma Boatbuilding Co, Tacoma, Wash	26 Aug 1965
NCHEDI (ex-US MSC 313)	8	Peterson Builders Inc, Sturgeon Bay, Wisc	17 Sep 1965

splacement, tons: 330 standard; 362 full load
mensions, feet (metres): 145·3 × 27 × 8·5 (44·3 × 8·2 × 2·6)
ns: 2—20 mm
ain engines: 4 General Motors diesels; 2 shafts; 1 000 bhp = 13 knots
nge, miles: 2 500 at 10 knots
mplement: 43 (7 officers, and 36 men)

nstructed for Thailand.

TADINDENG   1978, Royal Thai Navy

1 MCM SUPPORT SHIP

me	No.	Builders	Commissioned
NG KWIEN (ex-Umihari Maru)	MSC 11	Mitsubishi Co	1944

splacement, tons: 586 standard
mensions, feet (metres): 162·3 × 31·2 × 13·0 (49 × 9·5 × 4)
ns: 2—20 mm
ain engines: Triple expansion steam; speed = 10 knots

ginally built as a tug. Acquired by Royal Thai Navy on 6 September 1967.

RANG KWIEN   1969, Royal Thai Navy

5 MSB

SML 6-10

ai built. 50 ft, 30 tons with two 20 mm guns.

5 MSB

MSML 1-5

Thai built. 40 ft, 25 tons with two 20 mm guns.

AMPHIBIOUS FORCES

5 Ex-US "1-510" and "511-1152 CLASSES (LST)

me	No.	Builders	Commissioned
GTHONG (ex-USS LST 294)	LST 1	American Bridge Co, Pa.	Jan 1944
ANG (ex-USS Lincoln County, LST 898)	LST 2	Dravo Corporation	29 Dec 1944
NGAN (ex-USS Stark County, LST 1134)	LST 3	Chicago Bridge and Iron Co, Ill.	7 Apr 1945
NTA (ex-USS Stone County, LST 1141)	LST 4	Chicago Bridge and Iron Co, Ill.	7 Apr 1945
ATHONG (ex-USS Dodge County, LST 722)	LST 5	Jefferson B & M Co, Ind.	13 Sep 1944

splacement, tons: 1 625 standard; 4 080 full load
mensions, feet (metres): 328 × 50 × 14 (100 × 15·2 × 4·4)
ns: 6—40 mm; 4—20 mm
in engines: General Motors diesels; 2 shafts; 1 700 bhp = 11 knots
nge, miles: 9 500 at 9 knots
mplement: 80
rgo capacity: 2 100 tons

CHANG   1967, Royal Thai Navy

Angthong is employed as training ship. Chang, transferred to Thailand in 1962, was laid down on 15 October 1944. Pangan was transferred on 16 May 1966, Lanta on 12 March 1970 and Prathong on 17 December 1975.

3 Ex-US "LSM-1" CLASS

me	No.	Builders	Commissioned
T (ex-USS LSM 338)	LSM 1	Pullman Std Car Co, Chicago	16 Jan 1945
AI (ex-USS LSM 333)	LSM 2	Pullman Std Car Co, Chicago	25 Nov 1945
AM (ex-USS LSM 469)	LSM 3	Brown S.B. Co, Houston, Texas	17 Mar 1945

splacement, tons: 743 standard; 1 095 full load
mensions, feet (metres): 203·5 × 34·5 × 8·3 (62 × 10·5 × 2·4)
ns: 2—40 mm
in engines: Diesel direct drive; 2 shafts; 2 800 bhp = 12·5 knots
nge, miles: 2 500 at 12 knots
mplement: 55

mer US landing ships of the LCM, later LSM (Medium Landing Ship) type. Kram was sferred to Thailand under MAP at Seattle, Washington, on 25 May 1962.

PHAI

2 Ex-US "LSIL 351" CLASS

AB (ex-LSIL 670) LSIL 1   SATAKUT (ex-LSIL 739) LSIL 2

splacement, tons: 230 standard; 387 full load
mensions, feet (metres): 157 × 23 × 6 (47·9 × 7 × 1·8)
ns: 2—20 mm
in engines: Diesel; 2 shafts; 1 320 bhp = 14 knots
mplement: 54

b non-operational.

PRAB

480 THAILAND / Amphibious forces — Service forces

1 Ex-US LCG TYPE

NAKHA (ex-USS *LSSL* 102) LSSL 3

Displacement, tons: 233 standard; 287 full load
Dimensions, feet (metres): 158 × 23 × 4·25 *(47·5 × 7 × 1·4)*
Guns: 1—3 in; 4—40 mm; 4—20 mm; 4—81 mm mortars
Main engines: Diesels; 2 shafts; 1 320 bhp = 15 knots
Range, miles: 4 700 at 10 knots

Transferred in 1966. Acquired when Japan returned her to USA.

NAKHA

26 Ex-US LCM 6

14-16, 61-68, 71-78, 81-82, 85-87

First 21 delivered 1969.

8 Ex-US LCVP

1 LCA

Dimensions, feet (metres): 39·4 × 9·8 × — *(12 × 3 × —)*
Main engines: 2 Chrysler diesels; 2 Castoldi Mod 06 jet units = 25 Knots
Capacity: 35 troops

Built in Thailand. Fibreglass hull with bow ramp.

6 Ex-US LCUs

MATAPHON LCU 1	**ARDANG** LCU 3	**KOLUM** LCU 5
RAWI LCU 2	**PHETRA** LCU 4	**TALIBONG** LCU 6

Displacement, tons: 134 standard; 279 full load
Dimensions, feet (metres): 112 × 32 × 4 *(34·1 × 9·8 × 1·2)*
Guns: 2—20 mm
Main engines: 3 diesels; 3 shafts; 675 bhp = 10 knots
Complement: 37

Employed as transport ferries. Originally LCT-6 class.

LCAs

There is also a large but unknown number of Thai-built LCAs.

TRAINING SHIPS

1 Ex-BRITISH "ALGERINE" CLASS

Name	No.	Builders	Commissioned
PHOSAMTON (ex-HMS *Minstrel*)	MSF 1	Redfern Construction Co	1945

Displacement, tons: 1 040 standard; 1 335 full load
Length, feet (metres): 225·0 *(68·6)*
Beam, feet (metres): 35·5 *(10·8)*
Draught, feet (metres): 10·5 *(3·2)*
Guns: 1—4 in *(102 mm)* ; 6—20 mm
A/S weapons: 4 DCT
Main engines: Triple expansion; 2 shafts; 2 000 ihp
Boilers: Two 3-drum type
Speed, knots: 16
Oil fuel, tons: 270
Range, miles: 5 000 at 10 knots
Complement: 103

Transferred in April 1947. The 20 mm guns were increased from three to six, and the DCTs from two to four in 1966. Marginally operational—now used for training.

Name	No.	Builders	Commissioned
MAEKLONG	4	Uraga Dock Co, Japan	June 1937

Displacement, tons: 1 400 standard; 2 000 full load
Length, feet (metres): 269·0 *(82·0)*
Beam, feet (metres): 34·0 *(10·4)*
Draught, feet (metres): 10·5 *(3·2)*
Guns: 4—3 in *(76 mm)*/50 (singles); 3—40 mm; 3—20 mm
Main engines: Triple expansion; 2 shafts; 2 500 ihp
Boilers: 2 water tube
Speed, knots: 14
Oil fuel, tons: 487
Range, miles: 8 000 at 12 knots
Complement: 155 as training ship

Employed as training ship. The four 18 in torpedo tubes were removed.

Armament: Four 4·7 in guns replaced by 3 in guns in 1974.

1 Ex-BRITISH "FLOWER" CLASS

Name	No.	Builders	Commissioned
BANGPAKONG (ex-*Gondwana*, ex-HMS *Burnet*)	P4	Ferguson Bros, Port Glasgow	23 Sep 1943

Displacement, tons: 1 060 standard; 1 350 full load
Dimensions, feet (metres): 203·2 × 33 × 14·5 *(61·9 × 10 × 4·4)*
Guns: 1—3 in *(76 mm)*/50; 1—40 mm; 6—20 mm
A/S weapons: 4 DCT
Main engines: Triple expansion; 2 880 ihp = 16 knots
Boilers: Two 3-drum type
Range, miles: 4 800 at 12 knots
Complement: 100

Served in Indian Navy before transfer to Thailand 15 May 1947. Now used for training.

SURVEY SHIPS

Name	No.	Builders	Commissioned
CHANDHARA	AGS 11	C. Melchers & Co, Bremen, Germany	1961

Displacement, tons: 870 standard; 996 full load
Dimensions, feet (metres): 229·2 × 34·5 × 10 *(71 × 10·5 × 3)*
Gun: 1—20 mm
Main engines: 2 diesels; 2 shafts; 1 000 bhp = 13·25 knots
Range, miles: 10 000 (cruising)
Complement: 72

Laid down on 27 September 1960. Launched on 17 December 1960.

3 OCEANOGRAPHIC CRAFT

Of 90 tons, with a crew of eight launched in 1955.

SERVICE FORCES

2 SUPPORT TANKERS

CHULA AO 2   MATRA AO 3

Displacement, tons: 2 395 standard; 4 744 full load
Dimensions, feet (metres): 328 × 45·2 × 20 *(100 × 14 × 6·1)*
Main engines: Steam turbines

Built in Japan during World War II. Exact sisters *Chula* employed as floating storage, *Matra* freighting and fleet replenishment tanker and naval stores ship.

1 HARBOUR TANKER

Name	No.	Builders	Commissioned
SAMED	YO 11	Royal Thai Naval Dockyard, Bangkok	15 Dec 1970

Displacement, tons: 360 standard; 485 full load
Dimensions, feet (metres): 120 × 20 × 10 *(36·6 × 6·1 × 3)*
Main engine: Diesel; 500 bhp = 9 knots

Launched on 8 July 1966.

1 HARBOUR TANKER

Name	No.	Builders	Commissioned
PROET	YO 9	Royal Thai Naval Dockyard, Bangkok	16 Jan 1970

Displacement, tons: 360
Dimensions, feet (metres): 122·7 × 19·7 × 8·7 *(37·4 × 6 × 2·7)*
Main engines: Diesels; 500 bhp = 9 knots

THAILAND / Service forces — TOGO / Light forces 481

1 TRANSPORT

Name	No.	Builders	Commissioned
SICHANG	AKL 1	Harima Co, Japan	Jan 1938

Displacement, tons: 815 standard
Dimensions, feet (metres): 160 × 28 × 16 (48·8 × 8·5 × 4·9)
Main engines: 2 diesels; 2 shafts; 550 bhp = 16 knots
Complement: 30

Sichang was launched on 10 November 1937. Completed in January 1938.

1 TRANSPORT

KLED KEO AF 7

Displacement, tons: 382 standard; 450 full load
Dimensions, feet (metres): 154·9 × 25·4 × 14 (46 × 7·6 × 4·3)
Guns: 3—20 mm
Main engine: 1 diesel; 600 hp = 12 knots
Complement: 54

Operates with patrol boat squadron.

KLED KAO

2 WATER CARRIERS

Name	No.	Builders	Commissioned
CHUANG	YW 8	Royal Thai Naval Dockyard, Bangkok	1965
CHARN	YW 6	Royal Thai Naval Dockyard, Bangkok	1965

Displacement, tons: 305 standard; 485 full load
Dimensions, feet (metres): 136 × 25 × 10 (42 × 7·5 × 3·1)
Main engine: General Motors diesel; 500 bhp = 11 knots
Complement: 29

Chuang launched on 14 January 1965.

TUGS

Name	No.	Builders	Commissioned
SAMAE SAN (ex-Empire Vincent)	YTM 1	Cochrane & Sons Ltd, Selby, N. Yorks, England	—

Displacement, tons: 503 full load
Dimensions, feet (metres): 105·0 × 26·5 × 13·0 (32 × 8·1 × 4)
Main engine: Triple expansion; 850 ihp = 10·5 knots
Complement: 27

3 Ex-US "YTL 422" CLASS

KLUENG BADEN YTL 2   **RAD** (ex-USN YTL 340) YTL 4
MARN VICHAI YTL 3

Displacement, tons: 63 standard (Rad 52 standard)
Dimensions, feet (metres): 64·7 × 16·5 × 6·0 (19·7 × 5 × 1·8)
Rad 60·7 × 17·5 × 5·0 (18·5 × 5·3 × 1·5)
Main engines: Diesels; speed = 8 knots (Rad 6 knots)

Rad transferred May 1955 from USA, the other pair bought from Canada 1953.

RAD   8/1976, Dr. Giorgio Arra

TOGO

Ministerial
Minister of National Defence:
General Gnassingbe Eyadema (President)

Personnel
(a) 1979: 200
(b) Voluntary service

Base
Lome

Mercantile Marine
Lloyd's Register of Shipping:
4 vessels of 15 498 tons gross

LIGHT FORCES

2 COASTAL PATROL CRAFT

Name	No.	Builders	Commissioned
MONO	—	Chantiers Navals de l'Esterel	1976
KARA	—	Chantiers Navals de l'Esterel	1976

Displacement, tons: 80
Dimensions, feet (metres): 105 × 19 × 5·2 (32 × 5·8 × 1·6)
Missiles: Can carry SS-12
Guns: 1—40 mm (aft); 1—20 mm
Main engines: 2 MTU diesels; 2 700 bhp = 30 knots
Range, miles: 1 400 at 15 knots
Complement: 17

Radar: One navigation set.

Note: Unconfirmed report of 2 other patrol craft.

MONO and KARA   1976, Ch. Navals de l'Esterel

TONGA

On 10 March 1973 King Taufa'ahau Tupou IV commissioned the first craft of Tonga's Maritime Force, a necessary service in a Kingdom of seven main groups of islands spread over 270 square miles.

Mercantile Marine

Lloyd's Register of Shipping:
14 vessels of 20 663 tons gross

LIGHT FORCES
2 COASTAL PATROL CRAFT

Name	No.	Builders	Commissioned
NGAHAU KOULA	P 101	Brooke Marine, Lowestoft	10 Mar 1973
NGAHAU SILIVA	P 102	Brooke Marine, Lowestoft	10 May 1976

Displacement, tons: 15
Dimensions, feet (metres): 45 × 13 × 3·8 (13·7 × 4 × 1·2)
Guns: 2—·50 Browning MG
Main engines: 2 Cummins V8 diesels; 2 shafts = 21 knots
Range, miles: 800 (101), 1 000 (102)
Complement: 7

DF and echo-sounder (Ferrograph). Manned by volunteers from the Maritime Defence Division Tongan Defence Service. *Ngahau Siliva* was completed 2 February 1976 and commissioned by HM Queen Halaevalu Mata'aho in May. Names mean Golden and Silver Arrow respectively.

Radar: Decca 101.

NGAHAU SILIVA   1977, Royal Tongan Defence Service

TRINIDAD AND TOBAGO
COAST GUARD

Ministerial

Minister of National Security:
Senator John Donaldson

Headquarters Appointment

Commanding Officer:
Commander M. O. Williams, MOM

Personnel

(a) 1979: 286 (30 officers, 256 ratings)
(b) Voluntary service

Base

Staubles Bay

Mercantile Marine

Lloyd's Register of Shipping:
39 vessels of 15 890 tons gross

DELETIONS

| 1975-76 | *Sea Hawk* and *Sea Scout* |
| 1976 | CG 6, 7 and 8 |

LIGHT FORCES
0 + 2 TYPE CG 40 (LARGE PATROL CRAFT)

Name	No.	Builders	Commissioned
—	—	Karlskrona Varvet	1980
—	—	Karlskrona Varvet	1980

Displacement, tons: 200
Dimensions, feet (metres): 133·2 × 21·9 × 5·2 (40·6 × 6·7 × 1·6)
Guns: 1—40 mm, 1—20 mm
Main engines: 2 Paxman Valenta 16 RP200 diesels = 31 knots
Range, miles: 2 000 at 15/20 knots
Complement: 22

Ordered in Sweden mid-1978. Construction started late 1978. Fitted with foam-cannon oil pollution equipment and for oceanographic and hydrographic work. Nine spare berths.

2 LATER VOSPER TYPE (LARGE PATROL CRAFT)

Name	No.	Builders	Commissioned
CHAGUARAMUS	CG 3	Vosper Ltd, Portsmouth	18 Mar 1972
BUCCOO REEF	CG 4	Vosper Ltd, Portsmouth	18 Mar 1972

Displacement, tons: 100 standard; 125 full load
Dimensions, feet (metres): 103·0 × 19·8 × 5·8 (31·5 × 5·9 × 1·6)
Gun: 1—20 mm Hispano Suiza
Main engines: 2 Paxman Ventura diesels; 2 900 bhp = 24 knots
Oil fuel, tons: 20
Range, miles: 2 000 at 13 knots
Complement: 19 (3 officers, 16 ratings)

Chaguaramus was laid down on 1 February 1971 and launched on 29 March 1971. Fitted with air-conditioning and roll-damping. Both commissioned at Portsmouth, England.

CHAGUARAMUS   1975, Trinidad and Tobago Coast Guard

TRINIDAD AND TOBAGO / Light forces 483

2 VOSPER TYPE (LARGE PATROL CRAFT)

Name	No.	Builders	Commissioned
TRINITY	CG 1	Vosper Ltd, Portsmouth	20 Feb 1965
COURLAND BAY	CG 2	Vosper Ltd, Portsmouth	20 Feb 1965

Displacement, tons: 96 standard; 123 full load
Dimensions, feet (metres): 102·6 × 19·7 × 5·5 (31·4 × 5·9 × 1·7)
Gun: 1—40 mm Bofors
Main engines: 2 12-cyl Paxman Ventura YJCM turbo-charged diesels; 2 910 bhp = 24·5 knots
Oil fuel, tons: 18
Range, miles: 1 800 at 13·5 knots
Complement: 17 (3 officers, 14 ratings)

Designed by Vosper Limited, Portsmouth. Of steel construction with aluminium alloy superstructure. The boats are air-conditioned throughout except the engine room. Vosper roll-damping equipment is fitted. Laid down October 1963. *Trinity* was launched on 14 April 1964. *Trinity* is named after Trinity Hills, so named by Columbus on making his landfall in 1498, and *Courland Bay* after a bay in Tobago where a settlement was founded by the Duke of Courland in the 17th century. Both commissioned at Portsmouth, England.

TRINITY   1975, Trinidad and Tobago Coast Guard

1 + 1 FAIREY "SWORD" CLASS (COASTAL PATROL CRAFT)

SEA SPRAY

Displacement, tons: 15·5
Dimensions, feet (metres): 44·9 × 13·4 × 4·3 (13·7 × 4·1 × 1·3)
Gun: 1—7·62 mm
Main engines: 2 diesels; 850 hp = 28 knots

First delivered by Fairey Marine, Hamble January 1978. Second on order.

1 COASTAL PATROL CRAFT

Length, feet (metres): 55 (16·7)
Main engines: 2 General Motors diesels
Complement: 6

Built by Tugs and Lighters Ltd in 1977.

1 COASTAL PATROL CRAFT

CG 9

Locally built of glass fibre, 23 ft long with one Caterpillar diesel. Capable of 27 knots. Used for inshore patrol work, mainly in the Gulf of Paria.

1 SAIL TRAINING SHIP

HUMMING BIRD II

40 ft cutter-rigged ketch with three-cylinder Lister auxiliary diesel. Built in Trinidad 1966.

1 COASTAL PATROL CRAFT

Name	No.	Builders	Commissioned
NAPARIMA	—	Tugs and Lighters, Port of Spain	13 Aug 1976

Dimensions, feet (metres): 50 × 16 × 8 (16·4 × 52·5 × 26·2)
Main engines: 2 General Motors 8V 71 diesels; 460 bhp
Complement: 5

SEA SPRAY   1977, Fairey Marine

TUNISIA

Headquarters Appointment

Chief of Naval Staff:
Capitaine Habib Fedhila

Diplomatic Representation

Defence Ataché in Paris (and for London):
Colonel A. El-Fehri

Personnel

(a) 1979: 2 600 officers and men
(b) 1 year national service

Strength of the Fleet

Type	Active	Building
Frigate	1	—
Fast Attack Craft—Gun	2	—
MSCs	2	—
Large Patrol Craft	5	—
Coastal Patrol Craft	12	—
Tugs	3	—

Mercantile Marine

Lloyd's Register of Shipping:
41 vessels of 112 303 tons gross

FRIGATE

1 Ex-US "SAVAGE" CLASS

Name	No.	Builders	Commissioned
PRÉSIDENT BOURGUIBA (ex-USS *Thomas J. Gary* DER 326, ex-DE 326)	E 7	Consolidated Steel Corporation	27 Nov 1943

Displacement, tons: 1 590 standard; 2 100 full load
Dimensions, feet (metres): 306 × 36·6 × 14 *(93·3 × 11·1 × 4·3)*
Guns: 2—3 in *(76 mm)*/50; 2—20 mm
A/S weapon: 6 (2 triple) Mk 32 A/S torpedo tubes
Main engines: 4 diesels; 6 000 bhp; 2 shafts = 19 knots
Range, miles: 11 500 at 11 knots
Complement: 169

Completed as "Edsall" class DE. Converted to Radar Picket "Savage" class in 1958. Transferred 27 October 1973.

Radar: SPS 29 and SPS 10.

PRESIDENT BOURGUIBA   1977, Tunisian Navy

COASTAL MINESWEEPERS

2 Ex-US "ADJUTANT" CLASS

Name	No.	Builders	Commissioned
HANNIBAL (ex-*Coquelicot*, ex-USN *MSC 84*)	—	Stephen Bros, Calif	May 1953
SOUSSE (ex-*Marjolaine*, ex-USN *MSC 66*)	—	Harbor B.B. Co, Calif	Mar 1953

Displacement, tons: 320 standard; 372 full load
Dimensions, feet (metres): 141 × 26 × 8·3 *(43 × 8 × 2·6)*
Guns: 2—20 mm
Main engines: 2 General Motors diesels; 2 shafts; 1 200 bhp = 13 knots
Oil fuel, tons: 40
Range, miles: 2 500 at 10 knots
Complement: 38

Built for France under MDAP *Hannibal* delivered in 1953—to Tunisia in 1973. *Sousse* transferred July 1977. Of French "Acacia" class. Currently in use for patrol duties and fishery protection.

HANNIBAL   1974, Tunisian Navy

LIGHT FORCES

2 Ex-CHINESE "SHANGHAI II" CLASS (FAST ATTACK CRAFT-GUN)

GAFSAH 305   AMILCARE

Displacement, tons: 155
Dimensions, feet (metres): 127·3 × 17·7 × 5·2 *(38·8 × 5·4 × 1·6)*
Guns: 4—37 mm (twin); 4—25 mm (twin)
Main engines: 4 M50F diesels; 4 800 hp; 4 shafts = 30 knots
Range, miles: 800 at 17 knots
Complement: 25

Transferred late 1977.

Radar: Search: Skin Head.

"SHANGHAI II" Class

1 Ex-FRENCH "LE FOUGEUX" CLASS (LARGE PATROL CRAFT)

Name	No.	Builders	Commissioned
SAKIET SIDI YOUSSEF (ex-*UW 12*)	P 303	Dubigeon, Nantes	1956

Displacement, tons: 325 standard; 440 full load
Dimensions, feet (metres): 170 pp × 23 × 6·5 *(53 × 7·3 × 2)*
Guns: 1—40 mm; 2—20 mm
A/S weapons: Mousetrap; 4 DCT; 2 DC racks
Main engines: 4 SEMT-Pielstick diesels; 3 240 bhp = 18·7 knots
Range, miles: 2 000 at 15 knots
Complement: 4 officers, 59 men

Built in France, under US off-shore order. Purchased by West Germany in 1957 and served as A/S trials vessel. Transferred to Tunisia in December 1969.

SAKIET SIDI YOUSSEF   1977, Tunisian Navy

2 VOSPER THORNYCROFT "103 ft" TYPE (FAST ATTACK CRAFT—PATROL)

Name	No.	Builders	Commissioned
TAZARKA	P 205	Vosper Thornycroft	27 Oct 1977
MENZEL BOURGUIBA	P 206	Vosper Thornycroft	27 Oct 1977

Displacement, tons: 120
Dimensions, feet (metres): 103 × 19·5 × 5·5 (31·4 × 5·9 × 1·7)
Guns: 2—20 mm
Main engines: 2 diesels; 4 000 hp = 27 knots
Range, miles: 1 500 cruising
Complement: 24

Ordered 9 September 1975. P205 laid down 23 March 1976 and launched 19 July 1976.

TAZARKA 10/1977 Michael D. J. Lennon

3 "P 48" CLASS (LARGE PATROL CRAFT)

Name	No.	Builders	Commissioned
BIZERTE	P 301	Ch. Franco-Belges (Villeneuve, la Garenne)	10 July 1970
HORRIA (ex-Liberté)	P 302	Ch. Franco-Belges (Villeneuve, la Garenne)	Oct 1970
MONASTIR	P 304	Soc. Francaise Constructions Navale	25 Mar 1975

Displacement, tons: 250
Dimensions, feet (metres): 157·5 × 23·3 × 7 (48 × 7·1 × 2·3)
Missiles: 8—SS 12
Guns: 2—40 mm
Main engines: 2 MTU diesels; 4 800 bhp = 20 knots
Range, miles: 2 000 at 16 knots

First pair ordered in 1968. *Bizerte* was launched on 20 November 1969. *Horria* launched 12 February 1970. *Monastir* ordered in August 1973, laid down January 1974, launched 25 June 1974, completed 20 February 1975 but commissioned on 25 March 1975.

HORRIA 1974, Tunisian Navy

4 "32-metre" COASTAL PATROL CRAFT

Name	No.	Builders	Commissioned
ISTIKLAL (ex-VC 11, P 761)	P 201	Ch. Navals de l'Esterel	1957
JOUMHOURIA	P 202	Ch. Navals de l'Esterel	Jan 1969
AL JALA	P 203	Ch. Navals de l'Esterel	Nov 1963
REMADA	P 204	Ch. Navals de l'Esterel	July 1967

Displacement, tons: 60 standard; 82 full load
Dimensions, feet (metres): 103·3 × 19 × 5·6 (31·5 × 5·8 × 1·7)
Gun: 1—20 mm
Main engines: 2 MTU 12V 493 Mercedes-Benz diesels; 2 shafts; 2 700 bhp = 28 knots
Range, miles: 1 400 at 15 knots
Complement: 17

Istiklal transferred from France March 1959.

ISTIKLAL 1971, Tunisian Navy

6 "25-metre" COASTAL PATROL CRAFT

Name	No.	Builders	Commissioned
—	V 101	Ch. Navals de l'Esterel	1961
—	V 102	Ch. Navals de l'Esterel	1961
—	V 103	Ch. Navals de l'Esterel	1962
—	V 104	Ch. Navals de l'Esterel	1962
—	V 105	Ch. Navals de l'Esterel	1963
—	V 106	Ch. Navals de l'Esterel	1963

Displacement, tons: 38
Dimensions, feet (metres): 83 × 15·6 × 4·1 (25 × 4·8 × 1·3)
Gun: 1—20 mm
Main engines: 2 twin General Motors diesels; 2 400 hp = 23 knots
Range, miles: 900 at 16 knots
Complement: 11

V 104 1970, Tunisian Navy

Two further craft of the same design (V 107 and V 108) but unarmed were supplied to the Fisheries Administration in 1971.

V 105 1974, Tunisian Navy

TUGS

Name	No.	Builders	Commissioned	Name	No.	Builders	Commissioned
RAS ADAR (ex-Zeeland, ex-Pan American, ex-Ocean Pride, ex-HMS Oriana, BAT 1)	—	Gulfport Boilerworks & Eng Co	1942	JAOUEL EL BAHR	T 1	Ch. Navals de l'Esterel	—
				SABBACK EL BAHR	T 2	Ch. Navals de l'Esterel	—

Displacement, tons: 540 standard
Dimensions, feet (metres): 144·4 × 33 × 13·5 (43 × 10 × 4)

Built in 1942 and lend leased to the Royal Navy in that year as BAT 1 HMS *Oriana*, returned and sold in 1946 as *Ocean Pride*, then *Pan America* in 1947, then *Zeeland* in 1956.

TURKEY

Headquarters Appointment

Commander in Chief, Turkish Naval Forces:
Admiral Bülend Ulusu

Senior Command

Fleet Commander:
Vice-Admiral Nejat Tümer

Diplomatic Representation

Naval Attaché in Athens:
Lieutenant-Commander G. Key
Naval Attaché in Bonn:
Lieutenant-Commander T. Dinçer
Naval Attaché in Cairo:
Lieutenant-Commander C. Güngen
Naval Attaché in London:
Lieutenant-Commander E. Doran
Naval Attaché in Moscow:
Captain K. Pulat
Naval Attaché in Oslo:
Captain Ö. Özel
Naval Attaché in Rome:
Lieutenant-Commander A. Kanel
Naval Attaché in Tokyo:
Captain C. Üren
Naval Attaché in Washington:
Captain Aydan Erol

Personnel

(a) 1978: 45 000 officers and ratings
(b) 20 months national service

Naval Bases

Headquarters: Ankara
Main Naval Base: Gölçük
Senior Flag Officers: Istanbul, Izmir
Other Flag Officers: Eregli, Bosphorus, Heybeliada (Training), Dardanelles, Iskenderun
Dockyards: Gölçük, Taşkizak (Istanbul)

Naval Air Arm

4 AB-212 Helicopters
3 AB-204B Helicopters
16 S2E ASW Aircraft

Strength of the Fleet

Type	Active	Building
Submarines—Patrol	12	2 (+7?)
Destroyers	12	—
Frigates	2	—
Fast Attack Craft—Missile	8	—
Fast Attack Craft—Torpedo	13	—
Large Patrol Craft	45	11
Coastal Patrol Craft	4	—
Minelayer—Large	1	—
Minelayers—Coastal	6	—
Minesweepers—Coastal	21	—
Minesweepers—Inshore	4	—
Minehunting Boats	9	—
LSTs	5	?
LCTs	32	—
LCUs	16	—
LCMs	20	—
Support Tankers	5	—
Harbour Tanker	1	—
Water Tankers	3	—
Repair Ships	2	—
Transports	9	—
Submarine Rescue Ships	3	—
BDVs	4	—
Gate Vessels	3	—
Tug—Ocean	5	—
Tugs—Harbour	4	—
Floating Docks	7	—
Training Ship	1	—
Survey Vessels	4	—
Depot Ships	2	—

Mercantile Marine

Lloyd's Register of Shipping:
460 vessels of 1 358 779 tons gross

DELETIONS

Submarines
(Most replaced by submarines of same name).

1973 *Birinci Inönü, Çanakkale, Çerbe, Ikinci Inönü, Piri Reis*
1974 *Gür* (ex-*Chub*), *Sakarya* (ex-*Boarfish*)
1977 *Dumlupinar, Hizir Reis, Turgut Reis*

Destroyers

1973 *Gaziantep, Giresun*
1974 *Kocatepe* (ex-USS *Harwood*) sunk on 22 July. *Gemlik*
1976 *Gelibolu*

Corvettes

1973 *Edremit, Eregli* (ex-MSF)
1974 *Çardak, Çesme, Edincik* (ex-MSF)
1975 *Alanya, Ayvalik*

Fast Attack Craft

1973 *Dogan, Marti* ("Nasty" class), *AB 1-4, 6-7*

Support Tanker

1975 *Akar*

Boom Defence Vessels

1975 *AG 2, AG 3, Kaldaray*

Training Ship

1977 *Savarona*

Survey Craft

1975 *Mesaha 3* and *4*

Tug

1975 *Önder*

PENNANT LIST

Submarines

S 333	Ikinci Inönü	
S 335	Burak Reis	
S 336	Murat Reis	
S 337	Oruc Reis	
S 338	Uluçali Reis	
S 340	Çerbe	
S 341	Çanakkale	
S 345	Preveze	
S 346	Birinci Inönü	
S 347	Atilay	
S 348	Saldiray	
S 349	Batiray	
S 350	Yildiray	
S 351	—	

Destroyers

D 340	Istanbul	
D 341	Izmir	
D 342	Izmit	
D 343	Iskenderun	
D 344	Içel	
D 351	M. Fevzi Çakmak	
D 352	Gayret	
D 353	Adatepe	
D 354	Kocatepe	
D 355	Tinaztepe	
D 356	Zafer	
DM 357	Muavenet	

Frigates

D 358	Berk	
D 359	Peyk	

Amphibious Forces

C 101	LCT	
C 103-133	LCTs	
C 201-216	LCUs	
C 301-320	LCMs	
L 401	Ertugrul	
L 402	Serdar	
L 403	Bayraktar	
L 404	Sancaktar	
L 405	Çakabey	

Mine Warfare Forces (Sweepers)

M 500	Foça
M 501	Fethiye
M 502	Fatsa
M 503	Finike
M 507	Seymen
M 508	Selcuk
M 509	Seyhan
M 510	Samsun
M 511	Sinop
M 512	Sumene
M 513	Seddulbahir
M 514	Silifke
M 515	Saros
M 516	Sigacik
M 517	Sapanca
M 518	Sariyer
M 520	Karamürsel
M 521	Kerempe
M 522	Kilimli
M 523	Kozlu
M 524	Kuşadasi
M 530	Trabzon
M 531	Terme
M 532	Tirebolu
M 533	Tekirdag

Mine Warfare Forces (Layers)

N 101	Mordogan
N 102	Meriç
N 103	Marmaris
N 104	Mersin
N 105	Mürefte
N 110	Nusret
N 115	Mehemetcik

Light Forces

J 12-30	Large Patrol Craft
J 34	Large Patrol Craft
P 111	Sultanhisar
P 112	Demirhisar
P 113	Yarhisar
P 114	Akhisar
P 115	Sivrihisar
P 116	Koçhisar
P 140	Girne
P 301	AG 1 (BDV)
P 304	AG 4 (BDV)
P 305	AG 5 (BDV)
P 306	AG 6 (BDV)
P 311-14	MTB 1-4
P 316-20	MTB 6-10
P 321	Denizkuzu
P 322	Atmaca
P 323	Sahin
P 324	Kartal
P 325	Melten
P 326	Pelikan
P 327	Albatros
P 328	Şimşek
P 329	Kasirga
P 330	Firtina
P 331	Tufan
P 332	Kiliç
P 333	Mizrak
P 334	Yildiz
P 335	Kalkan
P 336	Karayel
P 338	Yildirim
P 339	Bora
P 340	Dogan
P 341	Marti
P 342	Tayfun
P 343	Volkan
P 1209-12	LS 9-12
P 1221-34	AB 21-34
S 61-63	Large Patrol Craft

Service Forces

A 571	Yuzbaşi Tolunay
A 572	Albay Hakki Burak
A 573	Binbaşi Saadettin Gürçan
A 574	Akpina
A 575	Inebolu
A 579	Gazi Hasan Paşa
A 581	Onaran
A 582	Başaran
A 583	Donatan
A 584	Kurtaran
A 585	Akin
A 586	Ülkü
A 587	Gazal
A 588	Umurbey
A 593	Çandarli (survey)
A 594	Çarşamba (survey)
A 599	Erkin
Y 1081-1087	Floating Docks
Y 1117	Sonduren
Y 1118	Akbas
Y 1119	Kepez
Y 1120	Odev
Y 1121	Yedekci
Y 1122	Kuvvet
Y 1123	Öncu
Y 1129	Kudret
Y 1155	Kanaria
Y 1156	Sarköy
Y 1163	Lapseki
Y 1164	Erdek
Y 1165	Eceabad
Y 1166	Kilya
Y 1168	Tuzla
Y 1201-3	Kapi I-III
Y 1204-5	Transports
Y 1207	Gölçuk
Y 1208	Van
Y 1209	Ulabat
Y 1217	Sogut

TURKEY / Introduction — Submarines 487

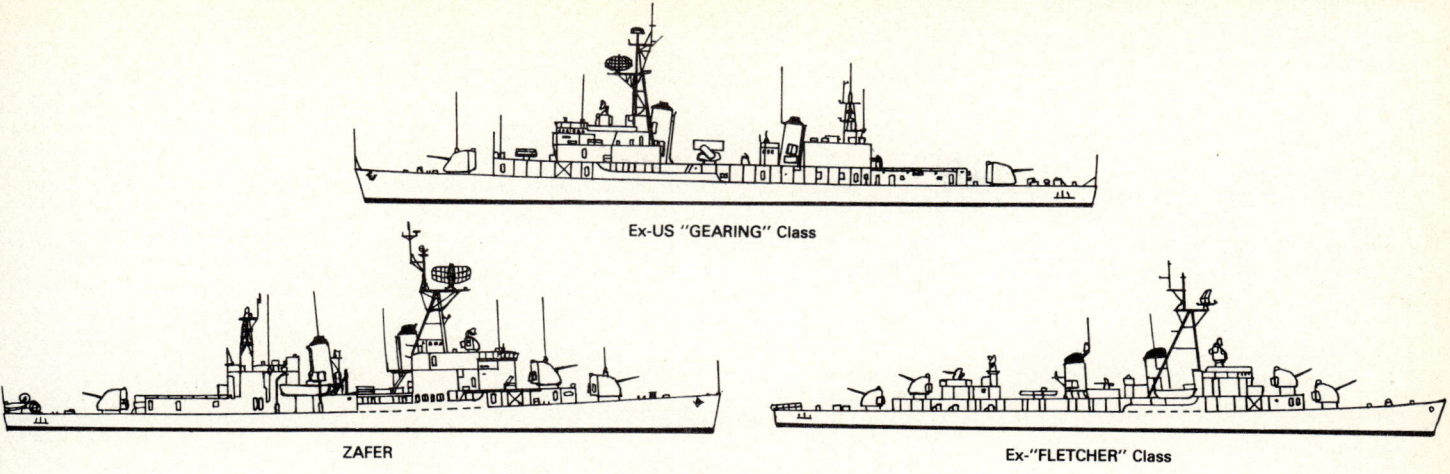

Ex-US "GEARING" Class

ZAFER

Ex-"FLETCHER" Class

SUBMARINES

Note: *Dumlupinar* (deleted 1977) is probably in use at Gölcük as an alongside training hulk.

3 + 2 + (??) TYPE 209 (HOWALDTSWERKE)

Name	No.	Builders	Laid down	Launched	Commissioned
ATILAY	S 347	Howaldtswerke, Kiel	2 Aug 1972	23 Oct 1974	29 July 1975
SALDIRAY	S 348	Howaldtswerke, Kiel	1973	14 Feb 1975	16 Jan 1977
BATIRAY	S 349	Howaldtswerke, Kiel	11 June 1975	1977	20 July 1978
YILDIRAY	S 350	Gölcük	—	—	1980
—	S 351	Gölcük	—	—	1981

Displacement, tons: 990 surfaced; 1 290 dived
Length, feet (metres): 183·7 *(56·0)*
Beam, feet (metres): 20·3 *(6·2)*
Torpedo tubes: 8—21 in (with reloads)
Main machinery: Diesel-electric; 4 MTU Siemens diesel-generators; 1 Siemens electric motor; 1 shaft
Speed, knots: 10 surfaced; 22 dived
Range: 50 days
Complement: 31

Designed by Ingenieurkontor, Lübeck for construction by Howaldtswerke, Kiel and sale by Ferrostaal, Essen all acting as a consortium.
A single-hull design with two ballast tanks and forward and after trim tanks. Fitted with snort and remote machinery control. The single screw is slow revving. Very high capacity batteries with GRP lead-acid cells and battery cooling—by Wilh. Hagen and VARTA. Active and passive sonar, sonar detection equipment, sound ranging gear and underwater telephone.

SALDIRAY 1978, Turkish Navy

Fitted with two periscopes, radar and Omega receiver. Foreplanes retract. *Saldiray* completed 21 October 1975 but was not taken over until January 1977. *Batiray* arrived Turkey 29 September 1978.

Future Construction: Two of this class are the first submarines ever built in Turkey. Up to a total of twelve is planned.

Torpedo Fire Control: Hollandse Signaal M8.

2 Ex-US "GUPPY III" CLASS

Name	No.	Builders	Laid down	Launched	Commissioned
ÇANAKKALE (ex-USS *Cobbler* SS 344)	S 341	Electric Boat Co	3 Apr 1944	1 Apr 1945	8 Aug 1945
IKINCI INONÜ (ex-USS *Corporal* SS 346)	S 333	Electric Boat Co	27 Apr 1944	10 June 1945	9 Nov 1945

Displacement, tons: 1 975 standard; 2 540 dived
Torpedo tubes: 10—21 in *(533 mm)* 6 bow, 4 stern
Main machinery: 4 diesels; 6 400 shp;
 2 electric motors; 5 400 bhp; 2 shafts
Speed: 20 surfaced; 15 dived
Complement: 86

Transferred 21 November 1973.

Future Additions: When the US Congress imposed an arms embargo on exports to Turkey in 1975 arrangements were well-advanced for the transfer of the two "Guppy III" class, *Clamagore* and *Tiru*. It is reported that these will possibly be transferred in 1979.

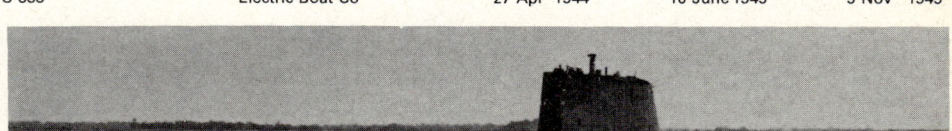

IKINCI INONÜ (ex-US number) Turkish Navy

7 Ex-US "GUPPY II A" CLASS

Name	No.	Builders	Laid down	Launched	Commissioned
BURAK REIS (ex-USS *Seafox*, SS 402)	S 335	Portsmouth Navy Yard	2 Nov 1943	28 Mar 1944	13 June 1944
MURAT REIS (ex-USS *Razorback*, SS 394)	S 336	Portsmouth Navy Yard	9 Sep 1943	27 Jan 1944	3 Apr 1944
ORUC REIS (ex-USS *Pomfret*, SS 391)	S 337	Portsmouth Navy Yard	14 July 1943	27 Oct 1943	19 Feb 1944
ULUÇ ALI REIS (ex-USS *Thornback*, SS 418)	S 338	Portsmouth Navy Yard	5 Apr 1944	7 July 1944	13 Oct 1944
ÇERBE (ex-USS *Trutta*, SS 421)	S 340	Portsmouth Navy Yard	22 Dec 1943	22 May 1944	16 Nov 1944
PREVEZE (ex-USS *Entemedor*, SS 340)	S 345	Electric Boat Co	3 Feb 1944	17 Dec 1944	6 Apr 1945
BIRINCI INÖNÜ (ex-USS *Threadfin*, SS 410)	S 346	Portsmouth Navy Yard	18 Mar 1944	26 June 1944	30 Aug 1944

Displacement, tons: 1 840 standard; 2 445 dived
Dimensions, feet (metres): 306 × 27 × 17 *(93·2 × 8·2 × 5·2)*
Torpedo tubes: 10—21 in *(533 mm)* (6 bow, 4 stern);
 24 torpedoes carried
Main machinery: 3 General Motors diesels; 4 800 hp;
 2 electric motors; 5 400 hp
Speed, knots: 17 surfaced; 15 dived
Range, miles: 12 000 at 10 knots surfaced
Complement: 85

The fact that the same names are used for replacement submarines as for their predecessors can be confusing, eg "Cerbe" was used for both ex-USS *Hammerhead* and now for ex-USS *Trutta*.

Transfers: *Burak Reis* December 1970, *Murat Reis* 17 November 1970, *Oruç Reis* 3 May 1972, *Çerbe*, June 1972, *Preveze, Uluç Ali Reis* 24 August 1973, *Birinci Inönü* 15 August 1973.

BIRINCI INÖNÜ 1978, Turkish Navy

488 TURKEY / Destroyers

DESTROYERS

5 Ex-US "GEARING" CLASS (FRAM I and II)

Name	No.	Builders	Laid down	Launched	Commissioned
M. FEVZI ÇAKMAK (ex-USS *Charles H. Roan*, DD 853)	D 351	Bethlehem Steel Corporation, Quincy	1944	15 May 1945	12 Sep 1946
GAYRET (ex-USS *Eversole*, DD 789)	D 352	Todd Pacific Shipyard	1945	8 Jan 1946	10 July 1946
ADATEPE (ex-USS *Forrest Royal*, DD 872)	D 353	Bethlehem, Staten Island	1945	17 Jan 1946	28 June 1946
KOCATEPE (ex-USS *Norris*, DD 859)	D 354	Bethlehem Steel Corporation, San Pedro	1944	25 Feb 1945	9 June 1945
TINAZTEPE (ex-USS *Keppler*, DD 765)	D 355	Bethlehem Steel Corporation, San Francisco	1944	24 June 1945	23 May 1947

Displacement, tons: 2 425 standard; 3 500 full load
Length, feet (metres): 390·5 *(119·0)*
Beam, feet (metres): 40·9 *(12·5)*
Draught, feet (metres): 19·0 *(5·8)*
Aircraft: Helicopter deck and hangar
Guns: 4—5 in *(127 mm)*/38 (twin Mk 38); 2—40 mm (single)
A/S weapons: FRAM I; 1 Asroc 8-tube launcher; 2 triple torpedo tubes (Mk 32); FRAM II; 1 trainable Hedgehog; 2 triple torpedo tubes (Mk 32)
Main engines: 2 geared turbines; 2 shafts; 60 000 shp
Boilers: 4 Babcock & Wilcox
Speed, knots: 34
Oil fuel, tons: 650
Range, miles: 4 800 at 15 knots; 2 400 at 25 knots
Complement: 275 (15 officers, 260 ratings)

ADATEPE (old armament)   1973, Dr. Giorgio Arra

Adatepe, *Gayret* and *Çakmak* FRAM I conversions and *Kocatepe* and *Tinaztepe* FRAM II. They were transferred to Turkey on 27 March 1971 *(Adatepe)* 30 June 1972 *(Tinaztepe)* 11 July 1973 *(Gayret)* and 21 September 1973 *(Çakmak)*, *Adatepe* purchased 15 February 1973 and *Kocatepe* 7 July 1974, commissioned 24 July 1975.

Fire control: GFCS Mk 37 with Mk 25 radar.

Radar: Long range air search: SPS 40 (FRAM I) SPS 6 (FRAM II). Surface search: SPS 10.

Replacement: The previous *Kocatepe* D 354 was sunk 22 July 1974. USS *Norris* had been purchased for spares on 7 July 1974 and has been re-activated to replace *Kocatepe*.

Sonar: FRAM I, SQS 23. FRAM II, SQS 29 series.

TINAZTEPE   6/1975, Dr. Giorgio Arra

1 Ex-US "ALLEN M. SUMNER (FRAM II)" CLASS

Name	No.	Builders	Laid down	Launched	Commissioned
ZAFER (ex-USS *Hugh Purvis* DD 709)	D 356	Federal S.B. and D.D. Co	1944	17 Dec 1944	1 Mar 1945

Displacement, tons: 2 200 standard; 3 320 full load
Length, feet (metres): 376·5 *(114·8)*
Beam, feet (metres): 40·9 *(12·5)*
Draught, feet (metres): 19·0 *(5·8)*
Guns: 6—5 in/38 (twin Mk 38); 6—40 (2 twin Mk 1, 2 single)
A/S weapons: 6 (2 triple) Mk 32 A/S torpedo tubes; 2 Hedgehogs
Main engines: 2 geared turbines; 2 shafts; 60 000 shp
Boilers: 4 Babcock & Wilcox
Speed, knots: 34
Oil fuel, tons: 650
Range, miles: 4 600 at 15 knots
Complement: 275 (15 officers, 260 ratings)

Zafer is of "Allen M. Sumner" class of modified FRAM II having been used as a US Navy trials ship for planar passive sonar. There is an extra deck-house on the hangar. Purchased 15 February 1972.

Fire control: Mk 51 for 40 mm.

Guns: Six 40 mm added in 1977—two singles aft on Dash deck, two twins amidships.

Radar: Air search: SPS 40.
Surface search: SPS 10.

ZAFER   1978, Turkish Navy

Sonar: SQS 29 series.

1 Ex-US "ROBERT H. SMITH" CLASS

Name	No.	Builders	Laid down	Launched	Commissioned
MUAVENET (ex-USS *Gwin*, ex-MMD 33, ex-DD 772)	DM 357	Bethlehem Steel Corporation, San Pedro	1943	9 Apr 1944	30 Sep 1944

Displacement, tons: 2 250 standard; 3 375 full load
Dimensions, feet (metres): 376·5 × 41 × 19 *(114·8 × 12·5 × 5·8)*
Guns: 6—5 in *(127 mm)*/38 (twin Mk 38);
12—40 mm/60 (2 quad Mk 2, 2 twin Mk 1); 11—20 mm/70
Mines: 80
Main engines: Geared turbines; 60 000 shp; 2 shafts
Boilers: 4 Babcock & Wilcox
Speed, knots: 34
Range, miles: 4 600 at 15 knots
Complement: 274

Modified "Allen M. Sumner" class converted for minelaying. After modernisation at Philadelphia she was transferred on 22 October 1971.

Fire control: GFCS director Mk 37 with Mk 28 radar; Mk 34 director for Mk 51 GFCS for a quad 40 mm.

Radar: Air search: SPS 6.
Surface search: SPS 10

Sonar: QCU or QHB.

MUAVENET   1978, Selçuk Emre

TURKEY / Destroyers — Light forces 489

5 Ex-US "FLETCHER" CLASS

Name	No.	Builders	Laid down	Launched	Commissioned
ISTANBUL (ex-USS *Clarence K. Bronson*, DD 668)	D 340	Federal S.B. & D.D. Co, Newark	1942	18 Apr 1943	11 June 1943
IZMIR (ex-USS *Van Valkenburgh*, DD 656)	D 341	Gulf Shipbuilding Corporation	1943	19 Dec 1943	2 Aug 1944
IZMIT (ex-USS *Cogswell*, DD 651)	D 342	Bath Iron Works, Corporation	1942	5 June 1943	17 Aug 1943
ISKENDERUN (ex-USS *Boyd*, DD 544)	D 343	Bethlehem Steel Corporation, San Pedro	1942	29 Oct 1942	8 May 1943
IÇEL (ex-USS *Preston*, DD 795)	D 344	Bethlehem Steel Corporation, San Pedro	1943	12 Dec 1943	20 Mar 1944

Displacement, tons: 2 050 standard; 3 000 full load
Length, feet (metres): 376·5 *(114·8)*
Beam, feet (metres): 39·5 *(12·1)*
Draught, feet (metres): 18·0 *(5·5)*
Guns: 4—5 in *(127 mm)*/38 (single Mk 30);
  6—3 in *(76 mm)*/50 (twin Mk 33)
A/S weapons: 2 Hedgehogs
Torpedo tubes: 5—21 in *(533 mm)* (quin)
Main engines: GE geared turbines; 2 shafts; 60 000 shp
Boilers: 4 Babcock & Wilcox
Speed, knots: 34
Oil fuel, tons: 650
Range, miles: 5 000 at 15 knots
Complement: 250

Fire control: Mk 37 GFCS forward with Mk 25 radar.
Mk 56 GFCS aft with Mk 35 radar.
Two Mk 51 GFCS amidships.

Radar: Search: SPS 6.
Tactical: SPS 10.

Transfers: Transferred as follows: *Istanbul* 14 January 1967, *Izmir* 28 February 1967, *Iskenderun* and *Izmit* on 1 October 1969, and *Içel* on 15 November 1969.

ISTANBUL 1975, Turkish Navy

FRIGATES

2 "BERK" CLASS

Name	No.	Builders	Laid down	Launched	Commissioned
BERK	D 358	Gölcük Naval Yard	9 Mar 1967	25 June 1971	12 July 1972
PEYK	D 359	Gölcük Naval Yard	18 Jan 1968	7 June 1972	24 July 1975

Displacement, tons: 1 450 standard; 1 950 full load
Length, feet (metres): 311·7 *(95·0)*
Beam, feet (metres): 38·7 *(11·8)*
Draught, feet (metres): 18·1 *(5·5)*
Aircraft: 1 helicopter
Guns: 4—3 in *(76 mm)*/50 (twin Mk 33)
A/S weapons: 6 (2 triple) Mk 32 A/S torpedo tubes; 1 DC rack
Main engines: 4 Fiat diesels; 2 shafts; 24 000 bhp
Speed, knots: 25

First major warships built in Turkey, the start of a most important era in the Eastern Mediterranean. Both are named after famous ships of the Ottoman Navy. Of modified US "Claud Jones" design.

Fire control: Each mounting has GFCS Mk 63.

Radar: SPG 34.
Air search: SPS 40.
Surface search: SPS 10.

BERK 6/1977, Dr. Giorgio Arra

LIGHT FORCES

4 LÜRSSEN TYPE (FAST ATTACK CRAFT—MISSILE)

Name	No.	Builders	Commissioned
DOĞAN	P 340	Lürssen, Vegesack	15 June 1977
MARTI	P 341	Taşkizak Yard, Istanbul	28 July 1978
TAYFUN	P 342	Taşkizak Yard, Istanbul	1978
VOLKAN	P 343	Taşkizak Yard, Istanbul	1979

Displacement, tons: 410
Dimensions, feet (metres): 190·6 × 25 × 8·8 *(58·1 × 7·6 × 2·7)*
Missiles: SSM; 8 Harpoon (2 quad launchers)
Guns: 1—76 mm (Compact); 2—35 mm/90 Oerlikon/Bührle (twin aft)
Main engines: 4—16-cyl MTU diesels; 18 000 hp = 38 knots
Range, miles: 700 at 35 knots

Ordered 3 August 1973. *Dogan* laid down 2 June 1975 (launched 16 June 1976), *Marti* 1 July 1975 (launched 30 June 1977), *Tayfun* 1 December 1975.

Weapon control: Hollandse Signaal WM28.

DOGAN 1977, Selçuk Emre

490 TURKEY / Light forces

9 "KARTAL" CLASS (FAST ATTACK CRAFT—MISSILE/TORPEDO)

Name	No.	Builders	Commissioned
DENIZKUSU	P 321 (ex-P 336)	Lürssen, Vegesack	1967
ATMACA	P 322 (ex-P 335)	Lürssen, Vegesack	1967
SAHIN	P 323 (ex-P 334)	Lürssen, Vegesack	1967
KARTAL	P 324 (ex-P 333)	Lürssen, Vegesack	1967
MELTEM	P 325 (ex-P 330)	Lürssen, Vegesack	1968
PELIKAN	P 326	Lürssen, Vegesack	1968
ALBATROS	P 327 (ex-P 325)	Lürssen, Vegesack	1968
ŞIMŞEK	P 328 (ex-P 332)	Lürssen, Vegesack	1968
KASIRGA	P 329 (ex-P 338)	Lürssen, Vegesack	1967

Displacement, tons: 160 standard; 180 full load
Dimensions, feet (metres): 140·5 × 23·5 × 7·2 (42·8 × 7·1 × 2·2)
Missiles: (see note)
Guns: 2—40 mm/70 (single)
Torpedo tubes: 4—21 in (533 mm)
Main engines: 4 MTU 16V 538 (Maybach) diesels; 4 shafts; 12 000 bhp = 42 knots
Complement: 39

Of the German Jaguar type. Launch dates—*Atmaca* 6 May 1966, *Kartal* 4 November 1965, *Meltem* 28 December 1966.

Missiles: Penguin 2 surface-to-surface missiles embarked in *Albatros, Meltem, Pelikan* and *Şimşek* during 1975.

MELTEM   1978, Selçuk Emre

7 Ex-FDR "JAGUAR" CLASS (FAST ATTACK CRAFT—TORPEDO)

Name	No.	Builders	Commissioned
FIRTINA (ex-FDR Pelikan, P 6086)	P 330	Lürssen, Vegesack	1962
TUFAN (ex-FDR Storch, P 6085)	P 331	Lürssen, Vegesack	1962
KILIÇ (ex-FDR Löwe, P 6065)	P 332	Lürssen, Vegesack	1960
MIZRAK (ex-FDR Hähner, P 6087)	P 333	Lürssen, Vegesack	1962
YILDIZ (ex-FDR Tiger, P 6063)	P 334	Lürssen, Vegesack	1959
KALKAN (ex-FDR Wolf, P 6062)	P 335	Lürssen, Vegesack	1959
KARAYEL (ex-FDR Pinguin, P 6090)	P 336	Lürssen, Vegesack	1962

Displacement, tons: 160 standard; 190 full load
Dimensions, feet (metres): 139·4 × 23·4 × 7·9 (42·5 × 7·2 × 2·4)
Guns: 2—40 mm/70 Bofors (single)
Torpedo tubes: 4—21 in (533 mm) (2 tubes can be removed to embark 4 mines)
Main engines: 4 Maybach (MTU) diesels; 4 shafts; 12 000 bhp = 42 knots
Complement: 39

In late 1975-early 1976 seven "Jaguar" class were transferred by the FDR to Turkey. In addition three more were transferred for spare parts—*Alk* P 6084, *Fuchs* P 6066 and *Reiher* P 6089.

FIRTINA   1976, Reinhard Nerlich

1 "NASTY" CLASS (FAST ATTACK CRAFT—TORPEDO)

Name	No.	Builders	Commissioned
GIRNE	P 140	Taşkizak Naval Yard	1976

Displacement, tons: 63·5 standard; 74·5 full load
Dimensions, feet (metres): 80·4 × 21 × 6·9 (24·5 × 6·4 × 2·1)
Guns: 2—40 mm
Torpedo tubes: 4—21 in (533 mm)
A/S weapons: Mousetrap
Main engines: 2 Deltic diesels; 6 200 hp; 2 shafts = 44 knots
Range, miles: 450 at 38 knots
Complement: 20

Originally first of a series. Project now cancelled.

GIRNE   1978, Selçuk Emre

2 Ex-US "ASHEVILLE" CLASS (LARGE PATROL CRAFT)

Name	No.	Builders	Commissioned
YILDIRIM (ex-USS Defiance, PG 95)	P 338	Petersons, Wisconsin	24 Sep 1969
BORA (ex-USS Surprise, PG 97)	P 339	Petersons, Wisconsin	17 Oct 1969

Displacement, tons: 225 standard; 245 full load
Dimensions, feet (metres): 164·5 × 23·8 × 9·5 (50·1 × 7·3 × 2·9)
Guns: 1—3 in (76m mm)/50 (Mk 34); 1—40 mm/60 (Mk 10); 4—50 cal MG
Main engines: CODAG; 2 Cummins diesels; 1 450 hp = 16 knots;
1 GE gas turbine; 13 300 shp = 40 shp
Complement: 25

These vessels belong to the largest Patrol Type built by the US Navy since World War II and the first of that Navy to have gas turbines. Transferred to Turkey on 11 June 1973 and 28 February 1973 respectively.

BORA (as *Surprise*)   1975, Turkish Navy

10 LARGE PATROL CRAFT

Name	No.	Builders	Commissioned
AB 25	P 1225	Taşkizak Naval Yard	1967
AB 26	P 1226	Taşkizak Naval Yard	1967
AB 27	P 1227	Taşkizak Naval Yard	1967
AB 28	P 1228	Taşkizak Naval Yard	1968
AB 29	P 1229	Taşkizak Naval Yard	1968
AB 30	P 1230	Taşkizak Naval Yard	1969
AB 31	P 1231	Taşkizak Naval Yard	1969
AB 32	P 1232	Taşkizak Naval Yard	1970
AB 33	P 1233	Taşkizak Naval Yard	1970
AB 34	P 1234	Taşkizak Naval Yard	1970

AB 28 (old pennant number)   1970, Turkish Navy

Displacement, tons: 170
Dimensions, feet (metres): 132 × 21 × 5·5 (40·2 × 6·4 × 1·7)
Guns: 2—40 mm (in some)
Speed, knots: 22

First was launched on 9 March 1967. Six similar launches are operated by the Gendarmerie.

TURKEY / Light forces

6 Ex-US "PC 1638" CLASS (LARGE PATROL CRAFT)

Name	No.	Builders	Commissioned
SULTANHISAR (ex-*PC 1638*)	P 111	Gunderson Bros Engineering Co, Portland, Oregon	1943
DEMIRHISAR (ex-*PC 1639*)	P 112	Gunderson Bros Engineering Co, Portland, Oregon	1943
YARHISAR (ex-*PC 1640*)	P 113	Gunderson Bros Engineering Co, Portland, Oregon	1943
AKHISAR (ex-*PC 1641*)	P 114	Gunderson Bros Engineering Co, Portland, Oregon	1943
SIVRIHISAR (ex-*PC 1642*)	P 115	Gunderson Bros Engineering Co, Portland, Oregon	1943
KOÇHISAR (ex-*PC 1643*)	P 116	Gölcük Dockyard, Turkey	1965

Displacement, tons: 280 standard; 412 full load
Dimensions, feet (metres): 173.7 × 23 × 10.2 *(53 × 7 × 3.1)*
Guns: 1—3 in; 1—40 mm
A/S weapons: 4 DCT; 1 Hedgehog (in some in place of 3 in gun)
Main engines: 2 FM diesels; 2 shafts; 2 800 bhp = 19 knots
Range, miles: 6 000 at 10 knots
Complement: 65 (5 officers, and 60 men)

Transferred in May 1964, 22 April 1965, September 1964, 3 December 1964, June 1965 and July 1965 respectively.

DEMIRHISAR   1975, Turkish Navy

4 US "PGM 71" CLASS (LARGE PATROL CRAFT)

Name	No.	Builders	Commissioned
AB 21 (ex-*PGM 104*)	P 1221	Peterson, Sturgeon Bay, USA	Dec 1967
AB 22 (ex-*PGM 105*)	P 1222	Peterson, Sturgeon Bay, USA	Dec 1967
AB 23 (ex-*PGM 106*)	P 1223	Peterson, Sturgeon Bay, USA	Dec 1967
AB 24 (ex-*PGM 108*)	P 1224	Peterson, Sturgeon Bay, USA	Apr 1968

Displacement, tons: 130 standard; 147 full load
Dimensions, feet (metres): 101 × 21 × 7 *(30.8 × 6.4 × 2.1)*
Guns: 1—40 mm; 4—20 mm
Main engines: 2 diesels; 2 shafts; 1 850 hp = 18.5 knots
Range, miles: 1 500 at 10 knots
Complement: 15

AB 23 (old pennant number)   1970, Turkish Navy

20 LARGE PATROL CRAFT

Name	No.	Builders	Commissioned
—	J 12	Schweers, Bardenfleth	1961
—	J 13	Schweers, Bardenfleth	1961
—	J 14	Schweers, Bardenfleth	1961
—	J 15	Schweers, Bardenfleth	1961
—	J 16	Schweers, Bardenfleth	1962
—	J 17	Schweers, Bardenfleth	1962
—	J 18	Schweers, Bardenfleth	1962
—	J 19	Schweers, Bardenfleth	1962
—	J 20	Schweers, Bardenfleth	1962
—	J 21	Gölcük Navy Yard	1968
—	J 22	Gölcük Navy Yard	1968
—	J 23	Taşkizak Naval Yard	1969
—	J 24	Taşkizak Naval Yard	1969
—	J 25	Taşkizak Naval Yard	1969
—	J 26	Taşkizak Naval Yard	1969
—	J 27	Taşkizak Naval Yard	1969
—	J 28	Taşkizak Naval Yard	1970
—	J 29	Taşkizak Naval Yard	1971
—	J 30	Taşkizak Naval Yard	1971
—	J 34	Taşkizak Naval Yard	1977

Displacement, tons: 150
Dimensions, feet (metres): 129.3 × 20.6 × 4.9 *(39.4 × 6.3 × 1.5)*
(J 34; 131.2 × 20 × 4.9 *(40 × 6.5 × 1.5)*
Guns: 2—40 mm
Main engines: 4 MTU 12V 493 diesels; 2 shafts; 3 200 bhp = 22 knots

Some operated by Gendarmerie.

J TYPE   1976, Michael D. J. Lennon

3 + 11 SAR 33 TYPE (LARGE PATROL CRAFT)

S 61   S 62   S 63

Displacement, tons: 170 full load
Dimensions, feet (metres): 108.3 × 28.3 × 9.7 *(33 × 8.6 × 3)*
Guns: 1—40 mm; 2 MG
Main engines: 3 SCAM diesels; 12 000 hp = 40 knots
Range, miles: 450 at 35 knots; 1 000 at economical speed
Complement: 23

Prototype ordered from Abeking and Rasmussen, Lemwerder in May 1976. Laid down October 1976, launched 12 December 1977. The remaining 13 being built at Taşkizak Naval Yard Istanbul. Ordered for Gendarmerie.

Armament: Could carry SSM, 76 mm and 35 mm (twin) but guns shown to be fitted for Gendarmerie.

S 61   1978, Selçuk Emre

4 Ex-US COAST GUARD "83 ft" CLASS (COASTAL PATROL CRAFT)

LS 9	P 1209 (ex-US *A 001*)	LS 11	P 1211 (ex-US *C 001*)
LS 10	P 1210 (ex-US *B 001*)	LS 12	P 1212 (ex-US *D 001*)

Displacement, tons: 63 standard
Dimensions, feet (metres): 83.0 × 14.0 × 5.0 *(25.3 × 4.3 × 1.6)*
Gun: 1—20 mm
A/S weapons: 2 Mousetrap
Main engines: 2 Cummins diesels; 1 100 bhp = 20 knots

Transferred on 25 June 1953.

LS 10   1978, Selçuk Emre

492 TURKEY / Mine warfare forces

MINE WARFARE FORCES

1 MINELAYER

Name	No.	Builders	Commissioned
NUSRET	N 110 (ex-*N 108*)	Frederikshaven Dockyard, Denmark	16 Sep 1964

Displacement, tons: 1 880 standard
Length, feet (metres): 252·7 *(77·0)*
Beam, feet (metres): 41 *(12·6)*
Draught, feet (metres): 11 *(3·4)*
Guns: 4—3 in *(76 mm)* (2 twin)
Mines: 400
Main engines: General Motors diesels; 4 800 hp; 2 shafts
Speed, knots: 18
Complement: 146

Laid down in 1962, launched in 1964. Similar to Danish "Falster" class.

Radar: Search: RAN 7S.
Fire control: I Band.
Navigation radar.

NUSRET   1975, Turkish Navy

5 Ex-US MODIFIED "LSM 1" CLASS (COASTAL MINELAYERS)

Name	No.	Builders	Commissioned
MORDOĞAN (ex-US *LSM 484* ex-*MMC 11*)	N 101	Brown S.B. Co, Texas	15 Apr 1945
MERİÇ (ex-US *LSM 490*, ex-*MMC 12*)	N 102	Brown S.B. Co, Texas	28 Apr 1945
MARMARIS (ex-US *LSM 481*, ex-*MMC 10*)	N 103	Brown S.B. Co, Texas	8 Apr 1945
MERSIN (ex-US *LSM 494*, ex-*MMC 13*)	N 104	Brown S.B. Co, Texas	8 May 1945
MÜREFTE (ex-US *LSM 492*, ex-*MMC 14*)	N 105	Brown S.B. Co, Texas	1 May 1945

Displacement, tons: 743 standard; 1 100 full load
Dimensions, feet (metres): 203·2 × 34·5 × 8·5 *(61·9 × 10·5 × 2·6)*
Guns: 6—40 mm (twins); 2—20 mm
Main engines: Diesels; 2 shafts; 2 880 bhp = 12 knots
Oil fuel, tons: 60
Range, miles: 2 500 at 12 knots
Complement: 89

Ex-US Landing Ships Medium. All launched in 1945, converted into coastal minelayers by the US Navy in 1952 and taken over by the Turkish Navy (LSM 481, 484 and 490) and the Norwegian Navy (LSM 492 and 494) in October 1952 under MAP. LSM 492 *(Vale)* and LSM 494 *(Vidar)* were retransferred to the Turkish Navy on 1 November 1960 at Bergen, Norway.

MÜREFTE   1978, Selçuk Emre

1 Ex-US YMP TYPE (COASTAL MINELAYER)

Name	No.	Builders	Commissioned
MEHMETCIK (ex-US *YMP 3*)	N 115	Higgins Inc, New Orleans	1958

Displacement, tons: 540 full load
Dimensions, feet (metres): 130 × 35 × 6 *(39·6 × 10·7 × 1·9)*
Main engines: Diesels; 2 shafts; 600 bhp = 10 knots
Complement: 22

Former US motor mine planter. Steel hulled. Transferred under MAP in 1958. For harbour defence.

MEHMETCIK   1978, Selçuk Emre

12 Ex-US "ADJUTANT" "MSC 268" and "MSC 294" CLASSES (MINESWEEPERS—COASTAL)

SEYMEN (ex-*MSC 131*) M 507
SELCUK (ex-*MSC 124*) M 508
SEYHAN (ex-*MSC 142*) M 509
SAMSUN (ex-USS *MSC 268*) M 510
SINOP (ex-USS *MSC 270*) M 511
SURMENE (ex-USS *MSC 271*) M 512
SEDDULBAHIR (ex-*MSC 272*) M 513
SILIFKE (ex-USS *MSC 304*) M 514
SAROS (ex-USS *MSC 305*) M 515
SIGACIK (ex-USS *MSC 311*) M 516
SAPANCA (ex-USS *MSC 312*) M 517
SARIYER (ex-USS *MSC 315*) M 518

Displacement, tons: 320 standard; 370 full load
Dimensions, feet (metres): 144·0 × 28·0 × 9·0 *(43·9 × 8·5 × 2·7)*
Guns: 2—20 mm
Main engines: 2 diesels; 2 shafts; 1 200 bhp = 14 knots
Oil fuel, tons: 25
Range, miles: 2 500 at 10 knots
Complement: 38 (4 officers, 34 men)

Transferred on 19 November 1970, 24 March 1970, 24 March 1970, 30 September 1958, February 1959, 27 March 1959, May 1959, September 1965, February 1966, June 1965, 26 July 1965, 8 September 1967, respectively. *Selcuk* and *Seyhan* were transferred from France (via USA) and *Seymen* from Belgium (via USA).

SURMENE   1975, Turkish Navy

4 Ex-CANADIAN MCB TYPE (MINESWEEPERS—COASTAL)

TRABZON (ex-HMCS *Gaspe*) M 530
TERME (ex-HMCS *Trinity*) M 531
TIREBOLU (ex-HMCS *Comax*) M 532
TEKIRDAG (ex-HMCS *Ungava*) M 533

Displacement, tons: 390 standard; 412 full load
Dimensions, feet (metres): 152·0 × 20·8 × 7·0 *(46·3 × 6·3 × 2·1)*
Gun: 1—40 mm
Main engines: Diesels; 2 shafts; 2 400 bhp = 16 knots
Oil fuel, tons: 52
Range, miles: 4 500 at 11 knots
Complement: 44

Sailed from Sydney, Nova Scotia, to Turkey on 19 May 1958. Built by Davie S.B. Co. 1951-53. Of similar type to British "Ton" class.

TIREBOLU   1978, Selçuk Emre

TURKEY / Mine warfare forces — Amphibious forces 493

5 Ex-FDR "VEGESACK" CLASS (MINESWEEPERS—COASTAL)

Name	No.	Builders	Commissioned
KARAMÜRSEL (ex-*Worms* M 1253)	M 520	Amiot, Cherbourg	1960
KEREMPE (ex-*Detmold* M 1252)	M 521	Amiot, Cherbourg	1960
KILIMLI (ex-*Siegen* M 1254)	M 522	Amiot, Cherbourg	1960
KOZLU (ex-*Hameln* M 1251)	M 523	Amiot, Cherbourg	1960
KUŞADASI (ex-*Vegesack* M 1250)	M 524	Amiot, Cherbourg	1960

Displacement, tons: 362 standard; 378 full load
Dimensions, feet (metres): 155·1 × 28·2 × 9·5 *(47·3 × 8·6 × 2·9)*
Guns: 2—20 mm
Main engines: 2 Mercedes-Benz (MTU) diesels; 2 shafts; 1 500 bhp = 15 knots (cp propellers)

Of similar class to French *Mercure*. Transferred by FDR to Turkey late 1975-early 1976.

KARAMÜRSEL   1978, Selçuk Emre

4 Ex-US "CAPE" CLASS (MINESWEEPERS—INSHORE)

Name	No.	Builders	Commissioned
FOÇA (ex-*MSI 15*)	M 500	USA	Aug 1967
FETHIYE (ex-*MSI 16*)	M 501	USA	Aug 1967
FATSA (ex-*MSI 17*)	M 502	USA	Sep 1967
FINIKE (ex-*MSI 18*)	M 503	Peterson Builders Inc	8 Nov 1967

Displacement, tons: 180 standard; 235 full load
Dimensions, feet (metres): 111·9 × 23·5 × 7·9 *(34 × 7·1 × 2·4)*
Gun: 1—·50 cal
Main engines: 4 diesels; 2 shafts; 960 bhp = 13 knots
Complement: 30

Built in USA and transferred under MAP at Boston, Massachusetts, August-December 1967.

FOÇA   1970, Turkish Navy

9 MINEHUNTING BOATS

MTB 1 P 311	MTB 3 P 313	MTB 6 P 316	MTB 8 P 318
MTB 2 P 312	MTB 4 P 314	MTB 7 P 317	MTB 9 P 319
			MTB 10 P 320

Displacement, tons: 70 standard
Dimensions, feet (metres): 71·5 × 13·8 × 8·5 *(21·8 × 4·2 × 2·6)*
Main engines: Diesels; 2 000 bhp = 20 knots

All launched in 1942. Now employed as minehunting base ships.

MTB 10   1972, Turkish Navy

AMPHIBIOUS FORCES

2 Ex-US "TERREBONNE PARISH" CLASS (LSTs)

Name	No.	Builders	Commissioned
ERTUĞRUL (ex-USS *Windham County*, LST 1170)	L 401	Christy Corporation	1954
SERDAR (ex-USS *Westchester County*, LST 1167)	L 402	Christy Corporation	1954

Displacement, tons: 2 590 light; 5 800 full load
Dimensions, feet (metres): 384 × 55 × 17 *(117·1 × 16·8 × 5·2)*
Guns: 6—3 in/50 (twins)
Main engines: 4 General Motors diesels; 2 shafts (cp propellers); 6 000 bhp = 15 knots
Complement: 116
Troops: 395

Transferred by USA June 1973. (L 401) and 27 August 1974 (L 402).

SERDAR   1979, Selçuk Emre

2 Ex-US LST "512-1152" CLASS (LSTs)

Name	No.
BAYRAKTAR (ex-FDR *Bottrop*, ex-USS *Saline County* L 1101)	L 403 (ex-N-111, ex-A 579)
SANCAKTAR (ex-FDR *Bochum*, ex-USS *Rice County* L 1089)	L 404 (ex-N-112, ex-A 580)

Displacement, tons: 1 653 standard; 4 080 full load
Dimensions, feet (metres): 328 × 50 × 14 *(100 × 15·2 × 4·3)*
Guns: 6—40 mm (2 twin, 2 single)
Main engines: 2 General Motors diesels; 2 shafts; 1 700 bhp = 11 knots
Range, miles: 15 000 at 9 knots
Complement: 125

Transferred to West Germany in 1961 and thence to Turkey on 13 December 1972. Converted into minelayers in West Germany 1962-64. Minelaying gear removed 1974-75.

BAYRAKTAR (old pennant number)   1973, Reinhard Nerlich

494 TURKEY / Amphibious forces

1 + ? TURKISH "ÇAKABEY" CLASS (LSTs)

Name	No.	Builders	Commissioned
ÇAKABEY	L 405	Taşkizak Naval Yard	1979

Displacement, tons: 1 600
Dimensions, feet (metres): 253·5 × 39·4 × 7·5 *(77·3 × 12 × 2·3)*
Guns: 2—40 mm; 2—20 mm
Main engines: 3 diesels; 4 320 hp = 14 knots

Of conventional design. *Çakabey* launched 30 June 1977. Helicopter platform amidships. Capacity, ten tanks. Continuing programme reported.

ÇAKABEY   1/1979, Selçuk Emre

5 Ex-BRITISH LCTs

C 101 and 103-106

Displacement, tons: 500 light; 700 full load
Dimensions, feet (metres): 180·9 × 27·7 × 5·4 *(55·2 × 8·4 × 1·6)*
Guns: 2—20 mm
Complement: 15

Built in UK in 1942. Transferred 25 September 1967.

C 104   1975, Turkish Navy

27 TURKISH-BUILT LCTs

C 107-133

Displacement, tons: 400 light; 580 full load
Dimensions, feet (metres): 180·9 × 36·8 × 4·8 *(57 × 12 × 1·4)*
Guns: 2—20 mm
Speed, knots: 10·5
Complement: 15

Built in Turkey 1966-1973. Of French EDIC type.

C 121   1978, Selçuk Emre

12 TURKISH-BUILT LCUs

C 205-216

Displacement, tons: 320 light; 405 full load
Dimensions, feet (metres): 142 × 28 × 5·7 *(43·3 × 8·5 × 1·7)*
Guns: 2—20 mm
Main engines: General Motors diesels; 2 shafts; 600 bhp = 10 knots

Built in Turkey 1965-66. Of US LCU type.

C 207   1975, Turkish Navy

4 Ex-US LCU 501 SERIES

C 201-204 (ex-US *LCU 588, 608, 666* and *667*)

Displacement, tons: 160 light; 320 full load
Dimensions, feet (metres): 119 × 32·7 × 5 *(36·3 × 10 × 1·5)*
Guns: 2—20 mm
Main engines: 3 diesels; 675 bhp = 10 knots
Complement: 13

Transferred from USA July 1967.

C 204   1975, Turkish Navy

20 TURKISH-BUILT LCM 8 TYPE

C 301-320

Displacement, tons: 58 light; 113 full load
Dimensions, feet (metres): 72 × 20·5 × 4·8 *(22 × 6·3 × 1·4)*
Guns: 2—12·7 mm
Main engines: General Motors diesels; 2 shafts; 660 bhp = 9·5 knots
Complement: 9

Built in Turkey in 1965.

TURKEY / Survey ships — Service forces 495

SURVEY SHIPS

2 US "AUK" CLASS

Name	No.	Builder	Commissioned
ÇANDARLI (ex-HMS *Frolic*)	A 593 (ex-AGS-2)	General Engineering and D.D. Co, Alameda USA	1943
ÇARŞAMBA (ex-HMS *Tattoo*)	A 594 (ex-AGS-1)	Associated S.B. Cleveland	1943

Displacement, tons: 1 125 full load
Dimensions, feet (metres): 221 × 32 × 10·8 *(67·4 × 9·8 × 3·3)*
Guns: 1—3 in *(76 mm)*; 2—40 mm
Main engines: Diesel-electric; 2 shafts; 3 500 bhp
Speed, knots: 18
Complement: 98 (8 officers, 90 ratings)

The survivors of a class of seven transferred from the Royal Navy in 1947, having been transferred by the USA during construction.

ÇARŞAMBA 1978, Selçuk Emre

MESAHA 1 and 2

Of 45 tons with a complement of eight—built in 1966.

MESAHA 1 1/1979, Selçuk Emre

SERVICE FORCES

Ex-FDR DEPOT SHIP (TRAINING SHIP)

Name	No.	Builders	Commissioned
CEZAYIRLI GAZI HASAN PAŞA (ex-FDR *Ruhr*)	A 579	Schiekerwerft, Hamburg	2 May 1964

Displacement, tons: 2 370 standard; 2 540 full load
Dimensions, feet (metres): 323·5 × 38·8 × 11·2 *(99 × 11·8 × 3·4)*
Guns: 2—3·9 in *(100 mm)*/55 (single); 4—40 mm (twin)
Main engines: 6 diesels; 11 400 bhp; 2 shafts
Speed, knots: 20·5
Range, miles: 1 625 at 15 knots
Complement: 110 (accommodation for 200)

Used as Training Ship. Commissioned in Turkish Navy 16 January 1977.

Radar: Search: HSA DA 02.
Fire control: Two HSA M 45.

Transfer: 12 July 1975 followed by major refit.

CEZAYIRLI GAZI HASAN PAŞA 1978, Selçuk Emre

1 SUPPORT TANKER

Name	No.	Builders	Commissioned
BINBAŞI SAADETTIN GÜRÇAN	A 573	Taşkizak Naval D.Y., Istanbul	1970

Displacement, tons: 1 505 standard; 4 460 full load
Dimensions, feet (metres): 294·2 × 38·7 × 17·7 *(89·7 × 11·8 × 5·4)*
Main engines: Diesels; 4 400 bhp

Launched 1 July 1969.

1 SUPPORT TANKER

ALBAY HAKKI BURAK A 572

Displacement, tons: 3 800 full load
Dimensions, feet (metres): 274·7 × 40·2 × 18 *(83·7 × 12·3 × 5·5)*
Main engines: 2 General Motors diesels; electric drive; 4 400 bhp = 16 knots
Complement: 88

Built in 1964.

ALBAY HAKKI BURAK 1975, Turkish Navy

1 SUPPORT TANKER

Name	No.	Builders	Commissioned
YUZBAŞI TOLUNAY	A 571	Taşkizak, Naval D.Y., Istanbul	1951

Displacement, tons: 2 500 standard; 3 500 full load
Dimensions, feet (metres): 260 × 41 × 19·5 *(79 × 12·4 × 5·9)*
Main engines: Atlas-Polar diesels; 2 shafts; 1 920 bhp = 14 knots

Launched on 22 August 1950.

YUZBAŞI TOLUNAY 1975, Turkish Navy

1 Ex-US SUPPORT TANKER

Name	No.	Builders	Commissioned
AKPINAR (ex-USS *Chiwankum*, AOG 26)	A 574	East Coast S.Y. Inc, Bayonne	22 July 1944

Displacement, tons: 700 light; 2 700 full load
Measurement, feet (metres): 1 453 deadweight
Dimensions, feet (metres): 220·5 × 37 × 12·8 *(67·3 × 11·3 × 3·9)*
Guns: 1—40 mm; 1—20 mm
Main engine: Diesel; 800 bhp = 10 knots

Laid down on 2 April 1944. Launched on 5 May 1944. Transferred to Turkey in May 1948.

AKPINAR 1975, Turkish Navy

496 TURKEY / Service forces

1 Ex-FDR SUPPORT TANKER

Name	No.	Builders	Commissioned
INEBOLU (ex-*Bodensee*, A 1406, ex-*Unkas*)	A 575	Lindenau, Kiel	26 Mar 1959

Measurement, tons: 985 gross; 1 238 deadweight
Dimensions, feet (metres): 219·8 × 32·1 × 14·1 *(67 × 9·8 × 4·3)*
Main engines: Diesels; 1 050 bhp = 12 knots
Complement: 26

Launched 19 November 1955. Transferred September 1977 at Wilhelmshavn, under West German military aid programme. Has replenishment capability.

"BODENSEE" Class   5/1975, Reinhard Nerlich

1 HARBOUR TANKER

Name	No.	Builders	Commissioned
GÖLCÜK (ex-*A 573*)	Y 1207	Gölcük Dockyard	1954

Displacement, tons: 1 255
Measurement, tons: 750 deadweight
Dimensions, feet (metres): 185 × 31·1 × 10 *(56·4 × 9·5 × 3·1)*
Main engines: Burmester & Wain diesel; 700 bhp = 12·5 knots

Launched on 4 November 1953.

1 Ex-US SUBMARINE TENDER

DONATAN (ex-USS *Anthedon*, AS 24) A 583

Displacement, tons: 8 100 standard
Dimensions, feet (metres): 492 × 69·5 × 26·5 *(150 × 21·8 × 8·1)*
Main engines: Geared turbines; 1 shaft; 8 500 shp = 14·4 knots
Boilers: 2

Former US submarine tender of the "Aegir" class transferred to Turkey on 7 February 1969.

DONATAN   1972, Turkish Navy

2 Ex-US REPAIR SHIPS

Name	No.	Builders	Commissioned
ONARAN (ex-*Alecto*, AGP 14, ex-*LST 558*)	A 581	Missouri Valley Bridge & Iron Co	1945
BAŞARAN (ex-*Patroclus*, ARL 19, ex-*LST 955*)	A 582	Bethlehem Hingham Shipyard	1945

Displacement, tons: 1 625 standard; 4 080 full load
Dimensions, feet (metres): 328 × 50 × 14 *(100 × 15·2 × 4·4)*
Guns: 2—40 mm; 8—20 mm
Main engines: 2 diesels; 2 shafts; 1 700 bhp = 11 knots
Oil fuel, tons: 1 000
Range, miles: 9 000 at 9 knots
Complement: 80

Former US repair ship and MTB tender, respectively, of the LST type. *Başaran* was launched on 22 October 1944, *Onaran* on 14 April 1944. Acquired from the USA in November 1952 and May 1948, respectively.

ONARAN   1973, Dr. Giorgio Arra

1 HQ SHIP (LOGISTICS)

ERKIN (ex-*Trabzon*, ex-*Imperial*) A 599

Dimensions, feet (metres): 441 × 58·5 × 23 *(133 × 17·5 × 7)*
Guns: 2—40 mm
Speed, knots: 16
Complement: 128

Built in 1938. Purchased in 1968 and placed on the Navy list in 1970.

ERKIN   1978, Selçuk Emre

1 Ex-US "CHANTICLEER" CLASS (SUBMARINE RESCUE SHIP)

Name	No.	Builders	Commissioned
AKIN (ex-USS *Greenlet*, ASR 10)	A 585	Moore S.B. & D.D. Co.	29 May 1943

Displacement, tons: 1 770 standard; 2 321 full load
Dimensions, feet (metres): 251·3 × 42·2 × 14·7 *(75·5 × 12·7 × 4·3)*
Guns: 1—40 mm; 2—20 mm (twin)
Main engine: Diesel-electric; 1 shaft; 3 000 bhp = 15 knots
Complement: 85

Akin transferred 12 June 1970 and purchased 15 February 1973.

AKIN   1978, Selçuk Emre

1 SUBMARINE RESCUE SHIP

KURTARAN (ex-USS *Bluebird*, ASR 19, ex-*Yurak* AT 165) A 584

Displacement, tons: 1 294 standard; 1 675 full load
Dimensions, feet (metres): 205·0 × 38·5 × 11·0 *(62·5 × 12·2 × 3·5)*
Guns: 1—3 in; 2—40 mm
Main engines: Diesel-electric; 3 000 bhp = 16 knots

Former salvage tug adapted as a submarine rescue vessel in 1947. Transferred from the US Navy on 15 August 1950.

KURTARAN   1978, Selçuk Emre

2 Ex-FDR "ANGELN" CLASS (DEPOT SHIPS)

Name	No.	Builders	Commissioned
ÜLKÜ (ex-FDR *Angeln*)	A 586	A. C. de Bretagne	1955
UMURBEY (ex-FDR *Dithmarschen*)	A 588	A. C. de Bretagne	1956

Displacement, tons: 2 600 full load
Dimensions, feet (metres): 296·9 × 43·6 × 20·3 *(90·5 × 13·3 × 6·2)*
Main engine: Pielstick diesel; 1 shaft; 3 000 bhp = 17 knots
Complement: 57

Ex-cargo ships bought by FDR in 1959. Transferred 22 March 1972 and December 1975. *Umurbey* employed as submarine depot ship and *Ulku* as Light Forces depot ship.

UMURBEY   1978, Selçuk Emre

4 TRANSPORTS

APSEKI Y 1163   **ERDEK** Y 1164   **KILYA** Y 1166   **TUZLA** Y 1168

Measurement, tons: 700
Dimensions, feet (metres): 183·7 × 37·2 × 8·9 *(56 × 12·2 × 2·7)*
Main engines: Steam; 700 hp = 9·5 knots

Have a minelaying capability. Survivors of a class of 11 car-ferries built in UK 1940-42.

APSEKI   1978, Selçuk Emre

3 SMALL TRANSPORTS

SARKÖY Y 1156   **ECEABAD** Y 1165   **KANARYA** Y 1155

Gun: 1—20 mm

Funnel-aft coaster type.

SARKÖY   1978, Selçuk Emre

2 Ex-US TRANSPORTS

Y 1204 (ex-US *APL 47*)
Y 1205 (ex-US *APL 53*)

Transferred: Y 1204 on October 1972 and Y 1205 on 6 December 1974.

TURKEY / Service forces — Boom defence vessels

1 WATER TANKER

SOGUT (ex-FDR *FW 6*) Y 1217

Measurement, tons: 350 deadweight
Dimensions, feet (metres): 144·4 × 25·6 × 8·2 *(44·1 × 7·8 × 2·5)*
Main engines: MWM diesels; 230 bhp = 9·5 knots

Transferred by West Germany 18 July 1975.

SOGUT   9/1976, Michael D. J. Lennon

2 WATER TANKERS

Name	No.	Builders	Commissioned
VAN	Y 1208	Gölcük Dockyard	1970
ULABAT	Y 1209	Gölcük Dockyard	1969

Displacement, tons: 1 200
Main engines: Designed for a speed of 14·5 knots

Two small tankers for the Turkish Navy built in 1968-70.

BOOM DEFENCE VESSELS

Name	No.	Builders	Commissioned
AG 6 (ex-USS *AN 93*, ex-Netherlands *Cerberus*, A 895)	P 306	Bethlehem Steel Corporation, Staten Island	10 Nov 1952

Displacement, tons: 780 standard; 902 full load
Dimensions, feet (metres): 165·0 × 33·0 × 10·0 *(50·3 × 10·1 × 3)*
Guns: 1—3 in; 4—20 mm
Main engines: Diesel-electric; 1 shaft; 1 500 bhp = 12·8 knots

Netlayer. Launched in May 1952. Transferred from USA to Netherlands in December 1952. Used first as a boom defence vessel and latterly as salvage and diving tender since 1961 but retained her netlaying capacity. Handed back to US Navy on 17 September 1970 but immediately turned over to the Turkish Navy.

AG 6   1975, Turkish Navy

Name	No.	Builders	Commissioned
AG 5 (ex-*AN 104*)	P 305	Kröger, Rendsburg	5 Feb 1961

Displacement, tons: 680 standard; 860 full load
Dimensions, feet (metres): 173·8 × 35·0 × 13·5 *(53 × 10·7 × 4·1)*
Guns: 1—40 mm; 3—20 mm
Main engines: 4 MAN diesels; 2 shafts; 1 450 bhp = 12 knots

Netlayer *AN 104* built in US off-shore programme for Turkey. Launched on 20 October 1960.

AG 5   1/1979, Selçuk Emre

498 TURKEY / Boom defence vessels — Auxiliaries

Name	No.	Builders	Commissioned
AG 4 (ex-USS *Larch*, ex-*AN 21*)	P 304	American S.B. Co, Cleveland	1941

Displacement, tons: 560 standard; 805 full load
Dimensions, feet (metres): 163·0 × 30·5 × 10·5 *(50 × 9·3 × 3·2)*
Gun: 1—3 in
Main engines: Diesel-electric; 800 bhp = 12 knots

Former US netlayer of the "Aloe" class. Laid down in 1940. Launched on 2 July 1941. Acquired in May 1946.

AG 4   *1969*

1 "BAR" CLASS

Name	No.	Builders	Commissioned
AG 1 (ex-HMS *Barbarian*)	P 301	Blyth S.B. Co	1938

Displacement, tons: 750 standard; 1 000 full load
Dimensions, feet (metres): 173·8 × 32·2 × 9·5 *(52·9 × 9·8 × 2·9)*
Gun: 1—3 in
Main engines: Triple expansion; 850 ihp = 11·5 knots
Boilers: 2 SE

Former British boom defence vessel.

3 GATE VESSELS

KAPI I, II, III (Y 1201, 1202, 1203)

Displacement, tons: 360
Dimensions, feet (metres): 102·7 × 34 × 4·7 *(30·8 × 10·2 × 1·3)*

These gate vessels were built by USA for Turkey under MAP. Transferred March 1961.

TUGS

1 Ex-US OCEAN TUG

GAZAL (ex-USS *Sioux* ATF 75) A 587

Displacement, tons: 1 235 standard; 1 675 full load
Dimensions, feet (metres): 205 × 38·5 × 16 *(60·7 × 11·6 × 4·7)*
Gun: 1—3 in
Main engines: Diesel-electric; 3 000 bhp = 16 knots
Complement: 85

Transferred 30 October 1972. Purchased 15 August 1973. Can be used for salvage.

3 Ex-US ARMY "149 ft" CLASS

AKBAS Y 1118   **KEPEZ** Y 1119   **ODEV** Y 1120

Displacement, tons: 971
Dimensions, feet (metres): 149 × 33·9 × 14 *(44·7 × 10·2 × 4·3)*
Speed, knots: 12

1 Ex-US OCEAN TUG

KUVVET (ex-US *ATA*) Y 1122

Displacement, tons: 390
Dimensions, feet (metres): 107 × 26·5 × 12 *(32·1 × 8 × 3·6)*

Transferred February 1962.

2 Ex-US "YTL" TYPE (HARBOUR TUGS)

SONDUREN (ex-US *YTL 751*) Y 1117   **YEDEKCI** (ex-US *YTL 155*) Y 1121

Transferred July 1957 and November 1954.

1 HARBOUR TUG

ÖNCU Y 1123

Displacement, tons: 500
Speed, knots: 12

Transferred under MAP.

1 HARBOUR TUG

KUDRET Y 1129

Displacement, tons: 128
Dimensions, feet (metres): 65 × 19·6 × 9 *(21·3 × 6·4 × 2·9)*

FLOATING DOCKS

Y 1081	Y 1082	Y 1083 (ex-US *AFDL*)
16 000 tons lift.	12 000 tons lift.	2 500 tons lift.
Y 1084	Y 1085	Y 1086
4 500 tons lift.	400 tons lift.	3 000 tons lift.

Y 1087 (ex-US *ARD 12*)
3 500 tons lift.

Transferred November 1971.

AUXILIARIES

Note: Others listed but not identified; *Ersen Bayrak* Y 1134, *L-1 Samandira* Y 1148, *L-2 Samandira* Y 1149.

1 HARBOUR PATROL CRAFT

Y 1223

1 NAVAL DREDGER

TARAK

Of 200 tons.

1 FLOATING CRANE

ALGARNA III Y 1023 (ex-US *YD 185*)

Transferred September 1963.

UNION OF SOVIET SOCIALIST REPUBLICS

Flag Officers Soviet Navy

Commander-in-Chief of the Soviet Navy and Deputy Minister of Defence:
  Admiral of the Fleet of the Soviet Union Sergei Georgiyevich Gorshkov
First Deputy Commander-in-Chief of the Soviet Navy:
  Admiral of the Fleet N. I. Smirnov
Deputy Commander-in-Chief:
  Vice-Admiral A. M. Kosov
Deputy Commander-in-Chief:
  Admiral G. A. Bondarenko
Deputy Commander-in-Chief:
  Admiral V. V. Mikhaylin
Deputy Commander-in-Chief:
  Engineer Admiral P. G. Kotov
Deputy Commander-in-Chief:
  Engineer Admiral V. G. Novikov
Deputy Commander-in-Chief (Rear Services):
  Admiral L. V. Mizin
Commander of Naval Aviation:
  Colonel-General A. A. Mironenko
Chief of the Political Directorate (Naval):
  Admiral V. M. Grishanov
Chief of Main Naval Staff:
  Admiral of the Fleet G. M. Yegorov
1st Deputy Chief of the Main Naval Staff:
  Admiral P. N. Navoytsev
Chief of the Hydrographic Service:
  Admiral A. I. Rassokho

Deputy Chief of General Staff:
  Admiral N. N. Amelko
Deputy Head Main Political Directorate:
  Admiral A. I. Sorokin

Northern Fleet

Commander-in-Chief:
  Admiral V. N. Chernavin
1st Deputy Commander-in-Chief:
  Vice-Admiral V. S. Kruglyakov
Chief of Staff:
  Vice-Admiral L. Matushkin
In Command of the Political Department:
  Vice-Admiral Ju. I. Padorin

Pacific

Commander-in-Chief:
  Admiral V. P. Maslov
1st Deputy Coomander-in-Chief:
  Vice-Admiral E. N. Spiridonov
Chief of Staff:
  Vice-Admiral Ya. M. Kudelkin
In Command of the Political Department:
  Vice-Admiral V. D. Sabaneyev

Black Sea

Commander-in-Chief:
  Admiral N. I. Khovrin
1st Deputy Commander-in-Chief:
  Vice-Admiral V. A. Samoylov
Chief of Staff:
  Vice-Admiral V. I. Akimov
In Command of the Political Department:
  Vice-Admiral P. N. Medvedev

Baltic

Commander-in-Chief:
  Vice-Admiral V. V. Sidorov
1st Deputy Commander-in-Chief:
  Vice-Admiral I. M. Kapitanets
Chief of Staff:
  Vice-Admiral A. M. Kalinin
In Command of the Political Department:
  Vice-Admiral N. I. Shablikov

Caspian Flotilla

Commander-in-Chief:
  Vice-Admiral G. G. Kasumbekov
Chief of Staff:
  Rear-Admiral V. M. Buynov
In Command of the Political Department:
  Rear-Admiral R. N. Likhvonin

Indian Ocean Squadron

  Vice-Admiral N. Y. Yasakov

Mediterranean Fleet

  Rear-Admiral N. I. Ryabinsky

Leningrad Naval Base

Commander:
  Vice-Admiral A. P. Mikhailovskiy
In Command of the Political Department:
  Engineer Vice-Admiral A. A. Plekhanov
Head of the A. A. Grechko Naval Academy:
  Admiral V. S. Sysoyev
Head of Frunze Naval College:
  Vice-Admiral V. V. Platonov

Diplomatic Representation

Naval Attaché in Berlin (DDR):
  Rear-Admiral M. N. Lystshin
Naval Attaché in London:
  Captain I. Ivanov
Naval Attaché in Oslo:
  Rear-Admiral I. G. Smirnov
Naval Attaché in Paris:
  Rear-Admiral W. M. Golitsyn

Personnel

(a) 1979: 525 000 officers and ratings (Afloat, 185 000; Naval Aviation, 50 000; Training, 55 000; Naval Infantry, 12 000; Coastal Defence, 8 000; Shore Support, 130 000; In new construction, 10 000; Civilians, 75 000)
(b) Approximately 18 per cent volunteers (officers and senior ratings)—remainder 3 years national service at sea and 2 if ashore

Main Naval Bases

North: Severomorsk (HQ), Motovskij Gulf, Polyarny, Severodvinsk (building)
Baltic: Leningrad (Kronshtadt), Tallinn, Lepaia, Baltiisk (HQ)
Black Sea: Sevastopol (HQ), Tuapse, Poti, Balaclava, Odessa, Nikolayev (building)
Pacific: Vladivostock (HQ), Sovetskaia Gavan, Magadan, Petropavlovsk

Pennant Numbers

The Soviet Navy has frequent changes of pennant numbers with change of fleet and so these are of little use in identifying individual ships. The last major overall change of numbers took place in 1978. For that reason such a list has been omitted in this section.
It will be noticed that, in some cases, the same ship has different numbers in different photographs.

Deletions and Conversions

Whilst it is not possible to provide an accurate estimate of total deletions and conversions during the last year the following is a guide to those estimates used in this section.

Destroyers
"Kashin" class conversions with SSM appear to be postponed, at least.

Frigates
Conversion of "Petya I/II" class to "Mod Petya I/II" class continues slowly.
Deletion of seven "Riga" class.

Fast Attack Craft
Deletion of more "P6" class.

Service Forces
Conversion of several more tankers for underway replenishment.

Building Programme

The following is an abstract of the programme used in estimating force levels.

Aircraft Carriers
2 "Kiev" class building.

Submarines
"Typhoon" class building. Continuing programme for "Delta III", "Charlie II", "Alfa", "Victor II" and "Tango" classes.

Cruisers
Continuing programme for "Kara" class. New construction of nuclear powered "Kirov" class and follow-on to "Kresta II".

Frigates
Both "Krivak I and II" classes continue. "Koni" class continues. Also provided for export—GDR has one delivered summer 1978.
"Grisha III" class continues.

Light Forces
"Nanuchka", "Sarancha", "Babochka" and "Matka" classes continue.
"Turya" class hydrofoils continue.
"Zhuk" class coastal patrol craft continue.

Mine Warfare Forces
"Sonya" class (MSC) and "Natya" class continue.
New "Olya" class building.

Amphibious Forces
"Rogov" class LSD and "Ropucha" class LST continue.

Air Cushion Vehicles
A large programme.

Support and Depot Ships
"Amur" and "Smolny" (training ships) classes continue.

Service Forces
"Ingul", "Sorum" and "Pamir" class tugs continue.

Several types and classes have been revised from new information, not necessarily as new construction.

Mercantile Marine

Lloyd's Register of Shipping:
  7 991 vessels of 22 261 927 tons gross

Strength of the Fleet

Aircraft Carriers	2 + 2 building	Hydrofoil (Missile)	3 + ? building	Space Associated Ships	7 + 13 (civilian)
Helicopter Carriers	2	Fast Attack Craft (Patrol)	87 + 2 building	Training Ships	3
Submarines (SSBN)	73 + 4 building	Fast Attack Craft (Hydrofoil)	54	Fleet Replenishment Ships	9
Submarines (SSB)	20	Fast Attack Craft (Torpedo)	58	Replenishment Tankers	23
Submarines (SSGN)	45 + 2 building	Large Patrol Craft	65	Coastal Tankers	24
Submarines (SSG)	24	River Patrol Craft	80	Salvage Vessels	25
Submarines (SSN)	46 + ?2 building	Coastal Patrol Craft	20	Rescue Ships	25
Submarines (SS)	*153 + 2 building	Minesweepers—Ocean	173 + 3 building	Lifting Ships	10
Cruiser (CGN)	0 + 1 building	Minehunters	33	Tenders	135 +
Cruisers (CG)	28 + 3 building	Minesweepers—Coastal	78 + 3 building	Icebreakers (Nuclear)	3 + 1 building
Cruisers (Gun)	10	Minesweepers—Inshore	119	Icebreakers	46 + 2 building
Destroyers (DDG)	39	LPD	1 + 1 building	Cable Ships	10 + 1 building
Destroyers (Gun)	53	LSTs	27 + 1 building	Large Tugs	50 +
Frigates (missile)	24 + 3 building	LCTs	70	Transports	77
Frigates	113 + 2 building	LCUs	60	Hovercraft	52
	(a number in reserve)	Depot and Repair Ships	66 + 1 building		
Corvettes (Missile)	50	Intelligence Collectors (AGI)	56		
Corvettes	70 + 2 building	Survey Ships	92 + 38 (civilian)	* plus 100 or more in reserve.	
Fast Attack Craft (Missile)	126	Research Ships	16 + 26 (civilian)		

Approximate Deployments

The following figures do not attempt to give an exact deployment of the Soviet Navy but offer an approximate apportionment of the totals given above. It must be remembered that at any normal time at least some ten per cent of submarines, cruisers, destroyers, frigates, amphibious forces, depot ships and service forces are deployed "out of area" ie in the Mediterranean, Indian Ocean, West Africa etc or on passage. This figure is normally higher for ballistic missile submarines.

Fleets

Type	Northern	Baltic	Black Sea and Caspian	Pacific	Type	Northern	Baltic	Black Sea and Caspian	Pacific
SSBN	49	—	—	24	CL	2	3	2	3
SSB	8	6	—	6	DD**	11	13	12	17
SSGN	28	—	—	17	FF and Corvettes	47	43	44	49
SSG	12	2	4	6	FAC(M) and Missile Corvettes	39	36	39	55
SSN	32	1	—	13	Light Forces	32	140	158	111
SS*	20	51	38	44	MSO/MSC	65	156	80	103
CV	1	—	—	1	LPD	—	—	—	1
CHG	—	—	2	—	LST	2	10	4	9
CG	9	1	11	7	LCT and LCU	11	26	56	46
DDG	8	5	16	10	Depot Ships	25	2	17	21
FFG	5	10	4	7	Service Forces (large)	21	3	14	16
					Hovercraft	—	18	16	18

* In addition about 115 believed in reserve.
** A considerable number of the older destroyers in reserve.

SOVIET NAVAL AVIATION

The Soviet Navy operates some 1 300 fixed-wing aircraft and helicopters in *Voyenno Morskaya Aviatsiya*, the world's second largest naval air arm. The primary combat components are
(1) Long range and medium bombers employed in the maritime reconnaissance role.
(2) Medium bombers mostly equipped with air-to-surface missiles in the anti-ship strike role.
(3) Land based patrol aircraft, amphibians and helicopters in the anti-submarine role.
(4) The "Forger" V/STOL aircraft operating from the "Kiev" class aircraft carriers.

Bombers: The Soviet naval air arm has about 80 heavy and 530 medium bombers in the anti-shipping, strike, tanker and reconnaissance roles. The main strike force comprises almost 300 "Badger" equipped with "Kipper" and "Kelt" air-to-surface missiles as well as an increasing number (now about 30) "Backfire" supersonic bombers first introduced in 1974 and the earlier "Blinder" conventional bombers. The reconnaissance aircraft are about 50 "Bear D" (long range recce); 70 "Badger" and about 40 "Blinders". About 80 "Badgers" are equipped as tankers.

ASW Helicopters: Over 200 anti-submarine helicopters are believed to be in the naval air arm, mostly Ka-25 "Hormone" (a twin-turbine craft) and some of the older Mi-4 "Hound" helicopters which are now being replaced for shore-based ASW by the "Haze" helicopters. The "Hormone" anti-submarine helicopters, armed with torpedoes or other ASW weapons operate from the "Kiev" class and *Moskva* and *Leningrad* which can each operate some 15 to 20 helicopters, servicing them in a hangar below the flight deck. They have also been seen in the "Kara", "Kresta I" and "Kresta II" class cruisers which are the first Soviet ships of this type to be fitted with a helicopter hangar. In some of these ships the radar fitted helicopter ("Hormone B") with a reconnaissance role associated with the surface-to-surface missile system. Other types of helicopter are also used in the transport role ashore. The presence of *Kiev* and, later, her sister notably increases the seaborne helicopter capability.

ASW Patrol Aircraft: The Soviet Union is the only nation other than Japan maintaining modern military flying boats, about 100 Be-12 "Mail" (turboprop) aircraft of this type being operational. The latter aircraft, an amphibian often-photographed on runways, has an advanced anti submarine capability evidenced by a radome extending forward, a Magnetic Anomaly Detector (MAD) boom extending aft and a weapons bay in the rear fuselage.
The "May", of which some 50 are in service, is a militarised version of the four-turboprop commercial air freighter (code name "Coot") in wide commercial service. The patrol/anti submarine version has been lengthened and fitted with a MAD boom as well as other electronic equipment and a weapons capability. Some of these are being transferred to India. There is also another variant of the "Bear" bomber, the "Bear F" engaged in ASW operations in increasing numbers.

Transports/Training Aircraft: There are also about 280 transports, utility, and training fixed wing aircraft and helicopters under Navy control.

Aircraft names are NATO code names; "B" names indicate bombers, "H" names for helicopters, and "M" names for miscellaneous aircraft. Single syllable names are propeller driven and two syllable names are jet-propelled.

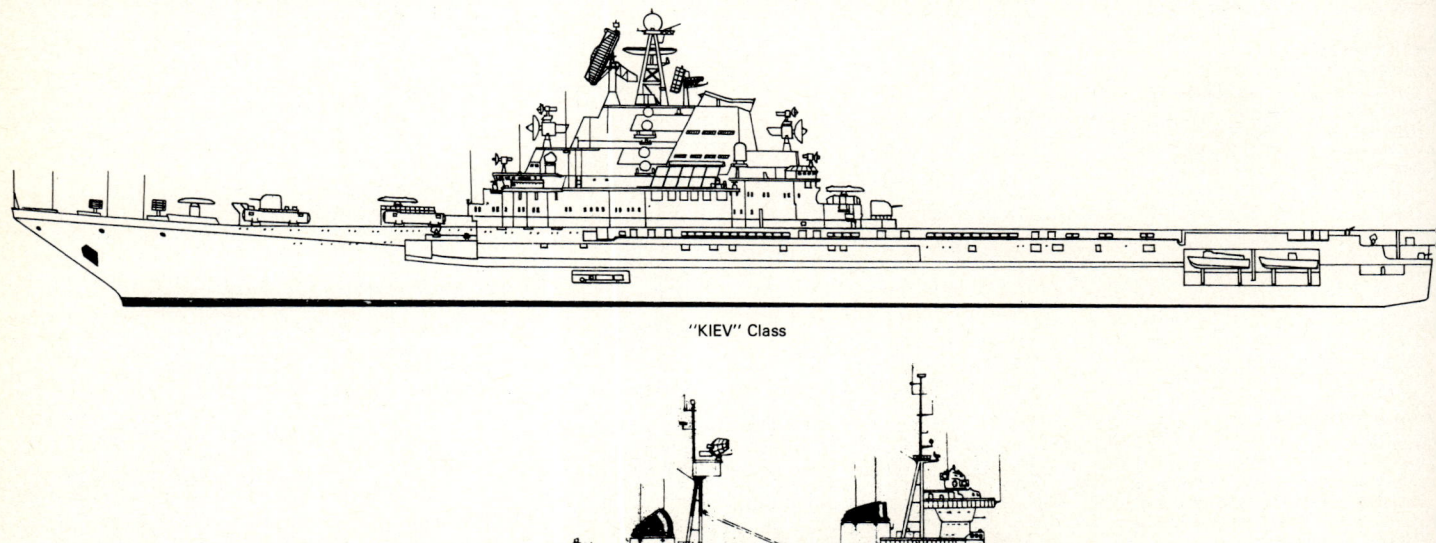

"KIEV" Class

"SVERDLOV" Class

502 USSR / Introduction

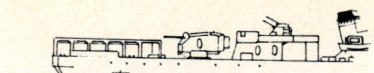

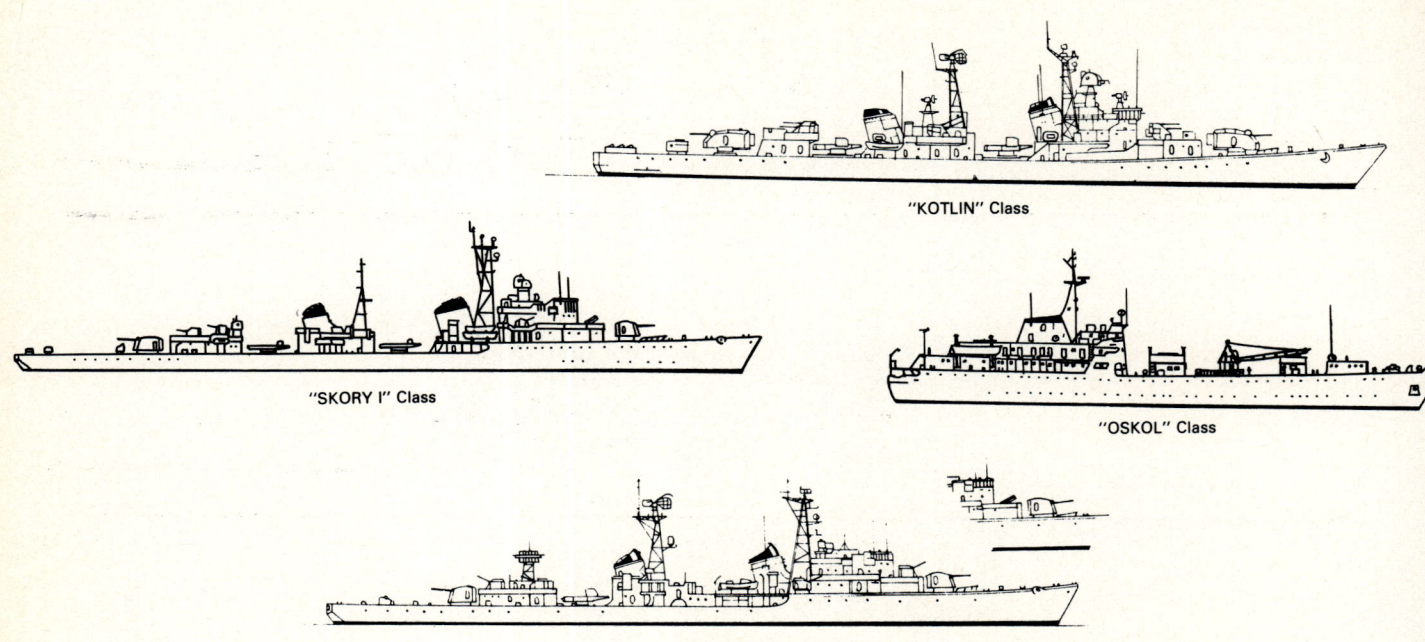

"KOTLIN" Class

"SKORY I" Class

"OSKOL" Class

"SKORY II" Class

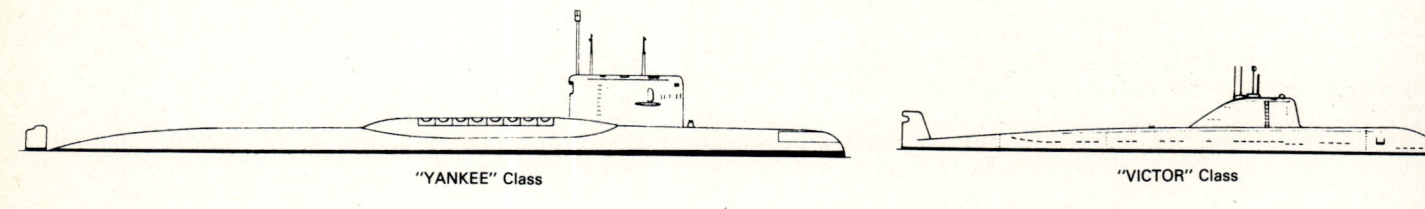

"YANKEE" Class

"VICTOR" Class

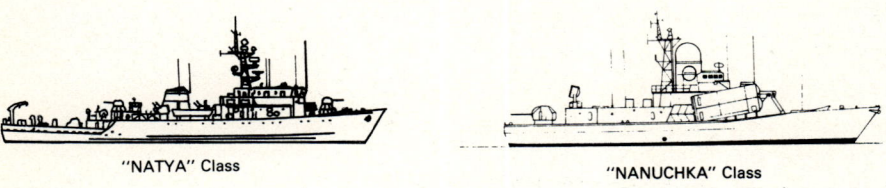

"NATYA" Class

"NANUCHKA" Class

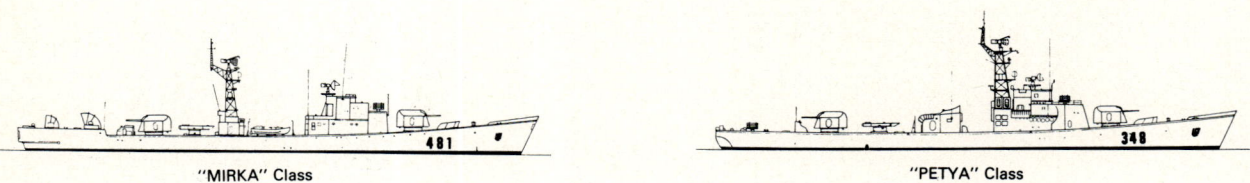

"MIRKA" Class

"PETYA" Class

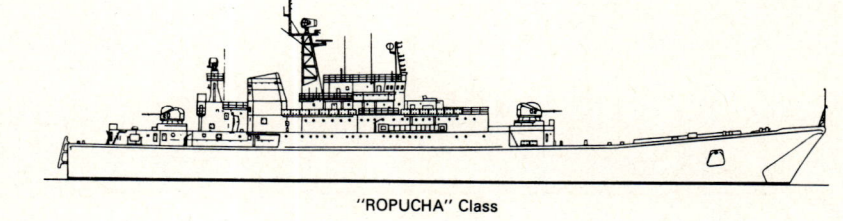

"ROPUCHA" Class

"POLNOCHNIY I and II" Classes

"OSA I" Class

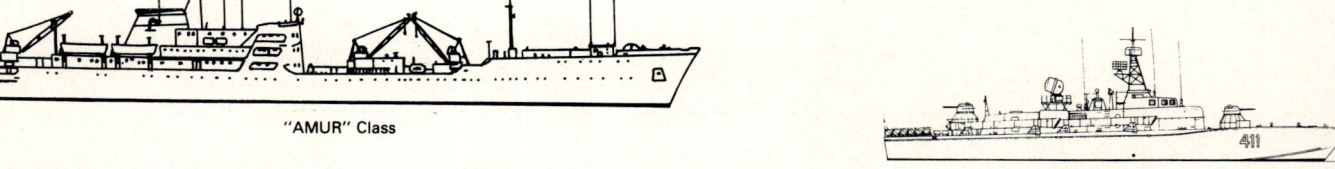

"AMUR" Class

"SHERSHEN" Class

Note: Line drawings by courtesy of Erminio Bagnasco and Siegfried Breyer. Scale is 1 : 1200 except for Osa I and Shershen classes, which are 1 : 600.

SUBMARINES
Ballistic Missile Classes

Note: The development of Soviet submarine launched ballistic missiles dates from early trials with German V2 (A4) missiles. The Lafferentz Project of 1944 was for the launching of V-2 from capsules towed by U-boats. The Soviets probably attempted such operations with the Golem series of missiles without success and then turned to tube launchers.

The deployment of operational missiles dates from the development of the 300 mile surface launched SS-N-4 missile which was first launched in September 1955. The "Zulu V" class was converted to carry this missile in two tubes in the fin. All this class now deleted. In 1958 the diesel-propelled "Golf" class appeared and in 1959 the nuclear "Hotel" class. Both originally carried the SS-N-4 but from 1962 all the "Hotels" and thirteen of the "Golfs" were converted for the 700 mile SS-N-5 which had the added advantage of dived-launch capability. Both the 4 and 5 missiles carried a megaton head and were 42·5 ft long but the apparent lack of an inertial navigation system in the submarines may have presented targetting problems. The SS-N-6 was installed in the "Yankees", with a 1 300 mile range. In 1971 Mk II and III of SS-N-6 with 1 600 mile range and MRV warheads were tested and are now operational. Recently the SS-N-17, with a range of some 1 800 miles and with solid propellant has been noted.

In the late 1960s the SS-N-8 was first tested and this was fitted in the "Delta I" class and subsequently the "Delta II". This is a much larger missile (42·5 ft long) than its predecessors with a range of 4 800 miles and required the increased size of the "Deltas" to house it. The SS-N-18 is now being fitted in the "Delta III" class and has a MIRV capability.

The Soviet navy is now at the SALT I agreed limits which are expected to be maintained with some deletions as new SSBNs are built.

0 + 1 "TYPHOON" CLASS

Displacement, tons: 18 000 dived
Missiles: Possibly 24 for SS-N-18

First of class building at Severodvinsk.

7 + 3 "DELTA III" CLASS (BALLISTIC MISSILE SUBMARINES SSBN)

Similar in dimensions and other data to "Delta II" class (below). Carry 16 tubes for SS-N-18 missiles (5 000 mile range approximately, with MIRV capability). Building at Severodvinsk.

5 "DELTA II" CLASS (BALLISTIC MISSILE SUBMARINES SSBN)

Displacement, tons: 9 350 surfaced; 11 750 dived
Dimensions, feet (metres): 498·6 × 38·7 × 33·5 (152·7 × 11·8 × 10·2)
Missiles: 16—SS-N-8 tubes
Torpedo tubes: 6—21 in (533 mm) (bow)
Main machinery: One nuclear reactor; 2 steam turbines; 60 000 shp; 2 shafts
Speed, knots: 22 surfaced; 28 dived
Complement: 132

First reported November 1973. Building yard—Severodvinsk.

Radar: One Snoop Tray.

19 "DELTA I" CLASS (BALLISTIC MISSILE SUBMARINES SSBN)

Displacement, tons: 8 350 surfaced; 9 300 dived
Dimensions, feet (metres): 446·1 × 38 × 32·8 (136 × 11·6 × 10)
Missiles: 12—SS-N-8 tubes
Torpedo tubes: 6—21 in (533 mm) (bow)
Main machinery: 1 nuclear reactor; 2 steam turbines; 2 shafts; 60 000 shp
Speed, knots: 22 surfaced; 30 dived
Complement: 120

This advance on the "Yankee" class SSBNs was announced at the end of 1972. The missile armament is 12 SS-N-8s with a range of 4 800 miles. As the SS-N-6 has already been tested with MRV warheads, however, it is not unlikely that these missiles will in due course be similarly armed. The longer-range SS-N-8 missiles are of greater length than the SS-N-6s and, as this length cannot be accommodated below the keel, they stand several feet proud of the after-casing. At the same time their presumed greater diameter and the need to compensate for the additional top-weight would seem to be the reasons for the reduction to 12 missiles in this class. Programme probably completed 1973-77.

Radar: One Snoop Tray.

"DELTA I" Class

"DELTA" Class

504 USSR / Submarines (SSBN)

34 "YANKEE" CLASS (BALLISTIC MISSILE SUBMARINES SSBN)

Displacement, tons: 7 800 surfaced; 9 300 dived
Dimensions, feet (metres): 427·8 × 38 × 25·6 *(129·5 × 11·6 × 7·8)*
Missiles: 16 tubes for SS-N-6 missiles (see note)
Torpedo tubes: 6—21 in *(533 mm)*; 18 torpedoes carried
Main machinery: 1 nuclear reactor; 2 steam turbines; 2 shafts; 30 000 shp
Speed, knots: 20 surfaced; 30 dived
Complement: 120

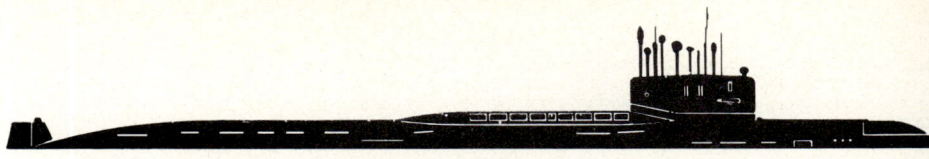

"YANKEE" Class

The vertical launching tubes are arranged in two rows of eight, and the SS-N-6 missiles have a range of 1 300/1 600 n. miles. These missiles have been tested with MRV warheads and these are now operational. At about the time that the USS *George Washington* was laid down (1 November 1957) as the world's first SSBN it is likely that the Soviet Navy embarked on its own major SSBN programme. With experience gained from the diesel-propelled "Golf" class and the nuclear-propelled "Hotel" class, the "Yankee" design was completed. Modelled on the USS "Ethan Allen" design. The first of the class was delivered late 1967 and the programme then accelerated from four boats in 1968 to eight in 1971, the last of the class being completed in 1976. Construction took place at Severodvinsk and Komsomolsk. The original deployment of this class was to the Eastern seaboard of the US giving a coverage at least as far as the Mississippi. Increase in numbers allowed a Pacific patrol to be established off California extending coverage at least as far as the Rockies.

Appearance: Fin mounted fore-planes.

Class: Of the total of 34, twenty are fitted with SS-N-6 Mod 1 (1 300 miles), thirteen with SS-N-6 Mod 3 (1 600 miles) and one with twelve SS-N-17 (2 400 miles—solid propellant).

Engineering: The twin screws and great horsepower give this class a speed advantage over some western counterparts.

Missiles: SS-N-6 Mod 3 has a MRV capability (C3 heads).

Radar: One Snoop Tray.

"YANKEE" Class

"YANKEE" Class

"YANKEE" Class

1 "HOTEL III" CLASS
7 "HOTEL II" CLASS
(BALLISTIC MISSILE SUBMARINES SSBN)

Displacement, tons: 4 750 surfaced; 5 600 dived
Dimensions, feet (metres): 377·2 × 29·8 × 25 *(115·2 × 9·1 × 7·6)*
Missiles: 3—SS-N-5 tubes
Torpedo tubes: 6—21 in *(533 mm)* (bow); 4—15·8 in *(400 mm)* (stern); 22 torpedoes carried
Main machinery: 1 nuclear reactor; 2 steam turbines; 2 shafts; 30 000 shp
Speed, knots: 20 surfaced; 26 dived
Complement: 90

"HOTEL II" Class

Three vertical ballistic missile tubes in the large fin. All this class was completed as "Hotel I" class between 1958 and 1962. Originally fitted with SS-N-4 system with Sark missiles (300 miles). Between 1962 and 1967 this system was replaced by the dived launch SS-N-5 system with Serb missiles capable of over 700 mile range the class then being renamed "Hotel II". A number of these boats was deployed off both coasts of the USA and Canada. As the limitations of SALT are felt the "Hotel IIs" will probably be phased-out to allow the maximum number of "Delta" class to be built. The "Hotel III" is a single unit converted for the test firings of the SS-N-8 (carries 6 missiles). The earlier boats of this class, which was of a similar hull and reactor design to the "Echo" class, will, by the late 1970s, be reaching their twentieth year in service.

Appearance: Of similar hull form to the "November" and "Echo I" class although the huge fin is distinctive.

Naviiation: There has been no evidence that these submarines are fitted with an inertial navigation system.

Radar: One Snoop Tray.

"HOTEL II" Class damaged in North Atlantic *2/1972, USN*

"HOTEL II" Class *1978*

7 "GOLF I" and 13 "GOLF II" CLASS (BALLISTIC MISSILE SUBMARINES SSB)

Displacement, tons: 2 350 surfaced; 2 850 dived (Golf I); 2 300 surfaced; 2 800 dived (Golf II)
Dimensions, feet (metres): 321·4 × 27·9 × 21 *(98 × 8·5 × 6·4)*
Missiles: 3—SS-N-4 (G I); 3—SS-N-5 (G II)
Torpedo tubes: 6—21 in (bow); 4—15·8 in *(400 mm)* (stern); 22 torpedoes carried
Main machinery: 3 diesels; 3 shafts; 6 000 hp; electric motors; 12 000 hp
Speed, knots: 17·6 surfaced; 14 dived
Range, miles: 22 700 surfaced cruising
Complement: 86 (12 officers, 74 men)

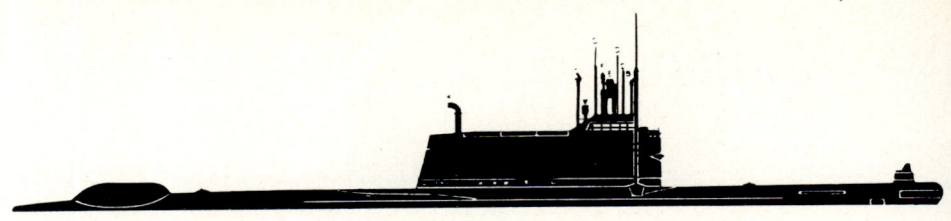

"GOLF II" Class

This class has a very large fin fitted with three vertically mounted tubes and hatches for launching ballistic missiles. Built at Komsomolsk and Severodvinsk. Building started in 1958 and finished in 1961-62. After the missile conversion of the "Hotel" class was completed in 1967 thirteen of this class ("Golf II") were converted to carry the SS-N-5 system with 700 miles Serb missiles in place of the shorter range (300 mile) Sarks. One sank in the Pacific in 1968 and was partially raised by the USA in 1974.
One of this class has been built by China, although apparently lacking missiles.

Class: Two "Golf I" modified to launch SS-N-8 missiles ("Golf III"), one "Golf I" modified for SS-N-6 missiles ("Golf IV") and one modified for test-firing of new type of ballistic missile ("Golf V"). Three more "Golf I" may have had their missiles removed to serve as SS.

Deployment: Six "Golf II" deployed in the Baltic since August-October 1976, the first SSBs to enter that sea.

SALT I: The "Golf" class hulls are not included in the SALT I totals. However if new missiles are embarked these are to be counted in the overall missile total.

Radar: One Snoop Tray or Snoop Plate.

"GOLF II" Class (with VLF buoy abaft fin)   1978

"GOLF I" Class (with four folding HF masts and other aerials)   11/1978, MOD

"GOLF II" Class (with stern VLF buoy)   9/1977, MOD

"GOLF II" Class   1978

USSR / Submarines (SSGN) 507

Cruise Missile Classes

Note: The first appearance of cruise-missiles at sea in Soviet submarines was in the Twin-cylinder variant of the "Whiskey" class in 1958-60. These carried two SS-N-3 missiles with a maximum range of 400 miles against shore targets. A capability against ships appears doubtful in view of the targetting problems. The fact that the US Navy had carried out trials with Loon missiles in the submarines *Cusk* and *Carbonero* in 1948-49 and soon afterwards converted several submarines, some to fire and some to guide the 80 ft Regulus cruise-missile, shows that at this stage the Soviet navy had lagged far behind. In fact in the Fiscal Year 1956 programme the US Navy included the first nuclear-propelled cruise missile submarine *Halibut*, designed to carry five 560 mile Regulus I missiles. By 1965 the cruise-missile programme had been abandoned by the US Navy. Meanwhile the Soviet Navy had gone ahead with the production of the first nuclear-propelled cruise-missile submarine ("Echo I") in the early 1960s to counter the threat of US Navy carriers with nuclear-armed aircraft. The "Echo I" was followed very closely by the "Echo II" nuclears and the conventional "Juliett" class which were building over the same period. By 1968 both production lines had stopped when the first "Charlie" class appeared with underwater launch capability for its 25 mile SS-N-7 missiles. The problem which had faced all the earlier boats, that of having to surface to launch, had been overcome and improvements of the "Charlies", "Charlie II" and "Papa", have been in service for five years.

1 "PAPA" CLASS (CRUISE MISSILE SUBMARINES SSGN)

Displacement, tons (approx): 6 700 surfaced; 7 000 dived
Dimensions, feet (metres): 346·7 × 36·1 × 24·6 *(105·7 × 11 × 7·5)*
Missiles: 10 tubes for SS-N-7 (see note)
Torpedo tubes: 6—21 in *(533 mm)*
Main machinery: 1 nuclear reactor; 2 steam turbines; 2 shafts; 40 000 shp
Speed, knots: 26 surfaced; 30 dived
Complement: 90

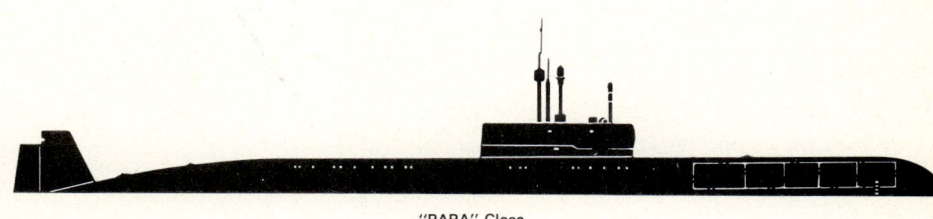
"PAPA" Class

A single member of an SSGN class apparently a development of the "Charlie" class first reported in 1973. The fin is of a much more angular shape than the "Charlies" with a higher casing, a more rounded bow and with the missile tubes having square covers. Whether the missiles are SS-N-7 or a derivative is uncertain.

Radar: One Snoop Tray.

3 "CHARLIE II" CLASS (CRUISE MISSILE SUBMARINES SSGN)

Displacement, tons: 4 300 surfaced; 5 200 dived
Dimensions, feet (metres): 337·5 × 32·5 × 25·6 *(102·9 × 9·9 × 7·8)*
Missiles: 8 tubes for SS-N-7
Torpedo tubes: 8—21 in *(533 mm)* (see note)
Main machinery: 1 nuclear reactor; 2 steam turbines; 30 000 shp; 1 shaft
Speed, knots: 20 surfaced; 33 dived
Complement: 90

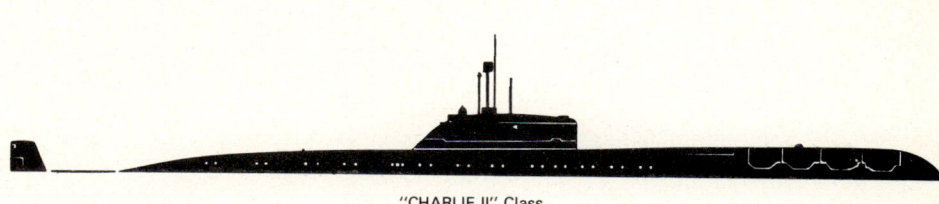
"CHARLIE II" Class

Enlarged "Charlie" class, first reported in 1973 and now in production at Gorky in place of the earlier version. The increase in size may be due to the fitting of equipment for firing the SS-N-15, a Subroc-type weapon, from her torpedo tubes.

Radar: One Snoop Tray.
ECM: One Stop Light.

12 "CHARLIE I" CLASS (CRUISE MISSILE SUBMARINES SSGN)

Displacement, tons: 3 900 surfaced; 4 700 dived
Dimensions, feet (metres): 308 × 32·5 × 24·6 *(93·9 × 9·9 × 7·5)*
Missiles: 8 tubes for SS-N-7 missiles
Torpedo tubes: 6—21 in *(533 mm)* (bow); 18 torpedoes carried
Main machinery: 1 nuclear reactor; 2 steam turbines; 30 000 shp; 1 shaft
Speed, knots: 17 surfaced; 27 dived
Complement: 90

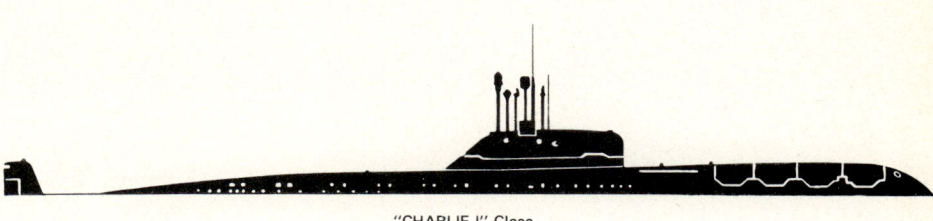
"CHARLIE I" Class

A class of cruise-missile submarines built at Gorky. The first of class was delivered in 1968, representing a very significant advance in the cruise-missile submarine field. With eight missile tubes for the SS-N-7 system (25 n. miles range) which has a dived launch capability, this is a great advance on the "Echo" class. These boats have an improved hull and reactor design and must be assumed to have an organic control for their missile system therefore posing a notable threat to any surface force. Their deployment to the Mediterranean, the area of the US 6th Fleet, is only a part of their general and world-wide operations.

Appearance: Although similar to the "Victor" class the bulge at the bow, the almost vertical drop of the forward end of the fin, a slightly lower after casing and a different arrangement of free-flood holes in the casing give a clear differentiation.

Radar: One Snoop Tray.

Sonar: Fin sonar fitted. This may be of value when tracking for missile firing data, although bound to be speed-limited.

"CHARLIE I" Class — 1974, MOD(N)

"CHARLIE I" Class — 4/1974

508 USSR / Submarines (SSGN)

29 "ECHO II" CLASS (CRUISE MISSILE SUBMARINES SSGN)

Displacement, tons: 4 800 surfaced; 5 800 dived
Dimensions, feet (metres): 384·7 × 30·2 × 25·5 *(117·3 × 9·2 × 7·9)*
Missiles: 8 tubes for SS-N-12/3 (see note)
Torpedo tubes: 6—21 in *(533 mm)* (bow); 4—15·8 in *(400 mm)* (stern)
Main machinery: 1 nuclear reactor; 2 steam turbines; 2 shafts; 30 000 shp
Speed, knots: 20 surfaced; 25 dived
Complement: 100

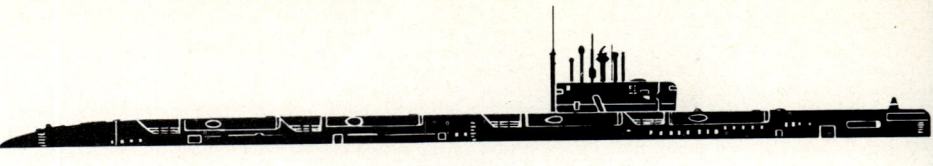
"ECHO II" Class

The decision to produce this class may have been due to the availability of slips because of a break in SSBN production between the "Hotel" and "Yankee" classes in the first half of the 1960s, the development of the SS-N-3 cruise missile with an anti-ship capability and the need to counter the threat from Western strike carriers.
With a slightly lengthened hull over the "Echo I", a fourth pair of launchers was installed and between 1963 and 1967 29 of this class were built. They are now deployed evenly between the Pacific and Northern fleets and still provide a useful group of boats some being deployed to the Mediterranean.
Built at Severodvinsk and Komsomolsk.

Design: This was a new design from the "Echo I", longer and carrying eight launchers instead of six. The "Echo I" was probably a stop-gap and all were stripped of their missile equipment in 1971-74.

Missiles: Approximately 20 have been fitted to launch SS-N-12 missiles (260 miles) in place of SS-N-3.

Radar: Mid-course guidance for SS-N-3; Front Piece and Front Door.
One Snoop Tray.

"ECHO II" Class   1973

"ECHO II" Class   1973, MOD

"ECHO II" Class   6/19

16 "JULIETT" CLASS (CRUISE MISSILE SUBMARINES SSG)

Displacement, tons: 2 800 surfaced; 3 550 dived
Dimensions, feet (metres): 284·4 × 33·1 × 22·9 *(86·7 × 10·1 × 7)*
Missiles: 4 tubes for SS-N-3; 2 before and 2 abaft the fin
Torpedo tubes: 6—21 in *(533 mm)* (bow); 4—15·8 in *(400 mm)* (stern); 22 torpedoes carried
Main machinery: Diesel-electric; 3 diesels; 7 000 bhp; 3 electric motors; 5 000 hp; 2 shafts
Speed, knots: 19 surfaced; 17 dived
Range, miles: 15 000 surfaced cruising
Complement: 79

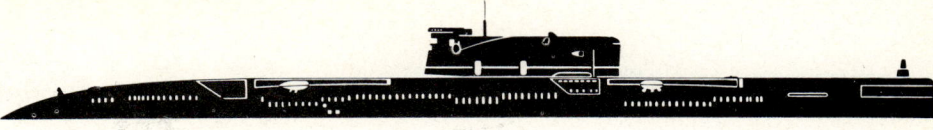
"JULIETT" Class

Completed between 1962 and 1967 at Gorky. Four SS-N-3 launchers, one pair either end of the fin which appears to be comparatively low. This class was the logical continuation of the "Whiskey" class conversions. A number of this class has in the past been deployed to the Mediterranean.

Appearance: The massive casing and fairly low fin make this an unmistakable class.

Radar: Mid-course guidance for SS-N-3; Front Piece and Front Door.
One Snoop Slab.

"JULIETT" Class 7/1973

"JULIETT" Class 1973, MOD(N)

"JULIETT" Class 5/1972, USN

6 "WHISKEY LONG-BIN" CLASS (CRUISE MISSILE SUBMARINES SSG)

Displacement, tons: 1 200 surfaced; 1 500 dived
Dimensions, feet (metres): 274·9 × 25·6 × 16·4 *(83·8 × 7·8 × 5)*
Missiles: 4 tubes for SS-N-3
Torpedo tubes: 6—21 in *(533 mm)* (bow); 12 torpedoes carried
Main machinery: Diesel-electric; 2 diesels; 4 000 bhp; electric motors; 2 700 hp
Speed, knots: 18 surfaced; 14 dived
Range, miles: 13 000 surfaced, cruising
Complement: 60

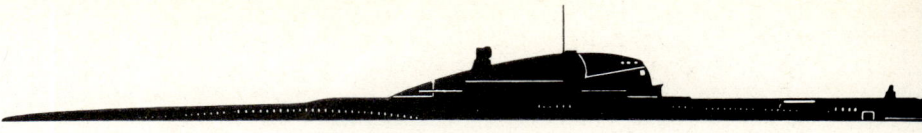
"WHISKEY LONG-BIN" Class

A more efficient modification of the "Whiskey" class than the "Twin-Cylinder" with four SS-N-3 launchers built into a remodelled fin on a hull lengthened by 33 ft. Converted between 1960-63. Has little capability against ship targets. Must be a very noisy boat when dived.
Two or three probably in reserve.

Radar: One Snoop Tray.

"WHISKEY LONG-BIN" Class   1975

2 "WHISKEY TWIN-CYLINDER" CLASS (CRUISE MISSILE SUBMARINES SSG)

Displacement, tons: 1 050 surfaced; 1 600 dived
Dimensions, feet (metres): 249·3 × 24·9 × 16·4 *(76 × 7·6 × 5)*
Missiles: 2 tubes for SS-N-3
Torpedo tubes: 4—21 in *(533 mm)* (bow); 2—15·8 in *(400 mm)* (stern)
Main machinery: Diesel-electric; 2 diesels; 4 000 bhp; electric motors; 2 700 hp
Speed, knots: 18 surfaced; 15 dived
Range, miles: 13 000, surfaced, cruising
Complement: 56

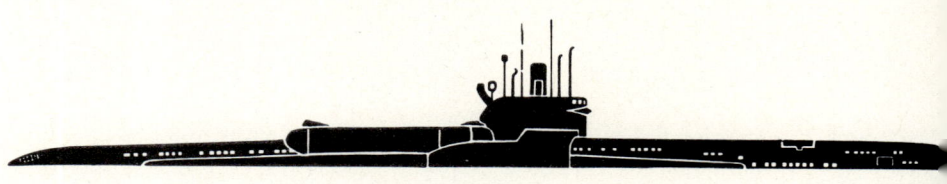
"WHISKEY TWIN-CYLINDER" Class

A 1958-60 modification of the conventional "Whiskey" class design. Probably never truly operational being a thoroughly messy and noisy conversion. The modification consisted of fitting a pair of launchers abaft the fin. Probably now used for training while retaining an operational capability. Five originally modified.

Radar: One Snoop Plate.

"WHISKEY TWIN-CYLINDER" Class   7/1973

Fleet Submarine Classes

Note: The use of nuclear power for marine propulsion was developed from 1950 onwards, the first submarine reactor being put in hand in 1953 probably about the same time as a larger reactor for the icebreaker *Lenin* was under construction. The latter commissioned in September 1959, a year after the first of the "November" class entered service. These submarines, of which 14 were built in about five years had a very long hull, and this long form was also used in the "Hotel" and "Echo I" designs. It was a new concept designed to take full advantage of the available horse-power and, in the "Novembers", was fitted with a small streamlined fin.

Apparently no prototype was produced before series production of the "Novembers" began and this was also true for the "Victors" which followed after a five year pause. Since the early "Novembers" provided sea-experience of this new form of submarine some seven years of redesign was therefore available before the first "Victor" was laid down. The ability to produce hydrodynamically advanced hull forms was further proved by the efficiency of the "Victor" and her near sister the "Charlie". Five years after the first "Victor" came the "Victor II", an enlarged edition whose increase in size may be due to the fitting of the new tube-launched weapon system, SS-N-15, probably similar to the Subroc of the US Navy.

The "Alfa" class now appears to be the new attack submarine class with a length/beam ratio very different from its predecessors and a much improved propulsion plant.

2 + ? "ALFA" CLASS (FLEET SUBMARINES SSN)

Displacement, tons: 2 800 surfaced; 3 300 dived
Dimensions, feet (metres): 260·1 × 32·8 × 24·9 *(79·3 × 10 × 7·6)*
Torpedo tubes: 6—21 in *(533 mm)*
Main machinery: 1 nuclear reactor; steam turbine; 24 000 shp; 1 shaft
Speed, knots: 16 surfaced; 32+ dived
Complement: 50

One unit of this class was completed in 1970 at Sudomekh, Leningrad. The building time was very long and it seems most likely that this was a prototype with some advanced hull material and propulsion aspects. As Sudomekh is particularly associated with propulsion engineering the latter seems most likely. A greater diving depth, possibly well over 2 000 ft *(610 m)* is a probability. Now in slow series production.

"ALFA" Class

6 + ? "VICTOR II" CLASS (FLEET SUBMARINES SSN)

Displacement, tons: 4 600 surfaced; 5 700 dived
Dimensions, feet (metres): 323·1 × 32·8 × 22·3 *(98·5 × 10 × 6·8)*
Torpedo tubes: 8—21 in *(533 mm)* (bow) (see note)
Main machinery: 1 nuclear reactor; 2 steam turbines; 1 shaft; 30 000 shp
Speed, knots: 16 surfaced; 31 dived
Complement: 90

An enlarged "Victor" design, 5·6 metres longer. This additional length may be used to house the equipment needed for firing the tube-launched SS-N-15, a Subroc type weapon of which this class probably can carry ten. First appeared in 1972. In series production.

Radar: One Snoop Tray.

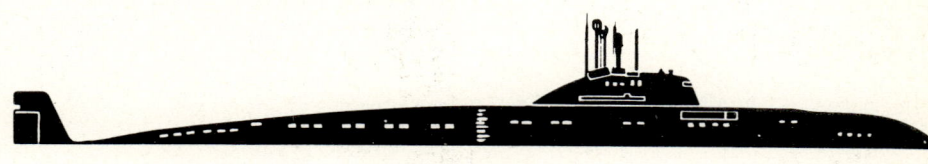

"VICTOR II" Class

"VICTOR II" Class   1978

16 "VICTOR I" CLASS (FLEET SUBMARINES SSN)

Displacement, tons: 4 300 surfaced; 5 100 dived
Dimensions, feet (metres): 307·7 × 32·1 × 23·9 *(93·9 × 9·8 × 7·3)*
Torpedo tubes: 8—21 in *(533 mm)* (bow)
Main machinery: 1 nuclear reactor; 2 steam turbines; 30 000 shp; 1 shaft
Speed, knots: 16 surfaced; 32 dived
Complement: 90

Designed purely as an attack submarine for both A/S and anti-ship roles. The first of class entered service in 1967-68 with a subsequent building rate of about two per year, which now has been superseded by the "Victor II" programme. Built at Admiralty Yard, Leningrad.
The majority is deployed with the Northern Fleet, although some have joined the Pacific Fleet.

Radar: One Snoop Tray.

"VICTOR I" Class

"VICTOR I" Class   4/1974, MOD

512 USSR / Submarines (SSN)

13 "NOVEMBER" CLASS (FLEET SUBMARINES SSN)

Displacement, tons: 4 200 surfaced; 5 000 dived
Dimensions, feet (metres): 359·8 × 29·8 × 21·9
 (109·7 × 9·1 × 6·7)
Torpedo tubes: 8—21 in (533 mm) (bow);
 4—16 in (406 mm) (stern); 36 torpedoes carried
Main machinery: 1 nuclear reactor; 2 steam turbines;
 30 000 shp
Speed, knots: 20 surfaced; 28 dived
Complement: 86

The first class of Soviet nuclear submarines which entered service between 1958 and 1963. Built at Severodvinsk. The hull form with the great number of free-flood holes in the casing suggests a noisy boat. In April 1970 one of this class sank south-west of the UK.

Diving Depth: Reported as 1 650 ft (500 m).

Radar: One Snoop Tray.

"NOVEMBER" Class

"NOVEMBER" Class

"NOVEMBER" Class (in Gulf of Mexico) 7/1969, USI

5 "ECHO" CLASS (FLEET SUBMARINES SSN)

Displacement, tons: 4 600 surfaced; 5 300 dived
Dimensions, feet (metres): 379·8 × 29·8 × 23·9
 (115·8 × 9·1 × 7·3)
Torpedo tubes: 6—21 in (533 mm) (bow);
 4—16 in (406 mm) (stern)
Main machinery: 1 nuclear reactor; 2 steam turbines;
 30 000 shp; 1 shaft
Speed, knots: 20 surfaced; 28 dived
Complement: 92 (12 officers, 80 men)

This class was completed in 1960-62. Originally mounted six SS-N-3 launchers raised from the after casing.
The hull of this class is very similar to the "Hotel"/"November" type and it is probably powered by similar nuclear plant. Only five "Echo Is" were built, being followed immediately by the "Echo IIs". In 1971-74 the "Echo I" class was converted into fleet submarines with the removal of the missile system, a decision which may have been due to the development of the "Echo II" class with its anti-ship cruise missile system. It has been reported that in their original configuration this class carried only two torpedo tubes.

Radar: One Snoop Tray.

"ECHO" Class

"ECHO" Class (as SSN) 8/1975, MO

Patrol Submarine Classes
(see "Golf" class)

Note: When the time came to rebuild the Soviet navy after the Revolution the first major new construction programme was that for submarines. By 1939 this force numbered 185 and by the start of the Great Patriotic War in June 1941, 218 were listed. At the end of the war new German ideas became available to the USSR—new designs, new concepts. This new knowledge was incorporated in a 1948 plan to build 1 200 submarines between 1950 and 1965 at an initial rate of 78 a year, increasing to 100. This programme was probably split into three sections, representing the three zones of defence—200 long-range boats ("Zulu" and, later, "Foxtrot" classes), 900 medium-range boats, ("Whiskey" and, later, "Romeo" classes) and 100 coastal boats of the "Quebec" class, the last being fitted with either Walther turbines or closed-cycle diesels. These last were German designs as were the hull-forms of the submarines, being similar to the German Type XXI.

This plan was largely amended with the post-Stalin readjustments and the successful experiments with nuclear power plants. Of the projected boats only 28 out of 40 "Zulus" were built, 60 out of 160 "Foxtrots", 240 out of 340 "Whiskeys" (albeit in seven years), 20 out of 560 "Romeos" and 40 out of 100 "Quebecs". After the arrival of the nuclears the "Golfs" and "Julietts" were the only other diesel submarines completed until 1968. Then the "Bravos" appeared and set a problem for Western analysts until they were classified as "padded targets". Finally, the "Tangos" joined the fleet in 1973. These last, apparently possessing excellent underwater performance and a considerable fire-power, may be the logical product of the twin facts that the USSR has large areas of shallow water around her coasts in which nuclear submarines cannot develop their full potential and that the diesel-boat is still the quietest listening platform.

10 + ? "TANGO" CLASS (PATROL SUBMARINES SS)

Displacement, tons: 2 100 surfaced; 2 500 dived
Dimensions, feet (metres): 301·8 × 28·9 × 21·3 *(92 × 8·8 × 6·5)*
Torpedo tubes: ? 6—21 in *(533 mm)* see note
Main machinery: 3 diesels; 6 000 shp; 3 electric motors; 6 000 shp; 3 shafts
Speed, knots: 20 surfaced; 16 dived
Complement: 62

This class was first seen at the Sevastopol Review in July 1973. Notable features are the rise in the forecasing and a new shape for the snort exhaust. This class, following five years after the "Bravo", shows a continuing commitment to diesel-propelled boats which is of interest in view of the comparatively slow building programme of nuclear attack submarines. As this is clearly an advanced design it may be intended to cover the large shallow-water areas around the USSR where nuclear submarines would be less efficiently deployed. Continuing programme of two a year at Gorky.

Radar: One Snoop Tray.

Torpedoes: The increase in the bow section suggests that these submarines can launch the SS-N-15 (Subroc type) weapon.

"TANGO" Class

"TANGO" Class   1978

"TANGO" Class   1978, Selçuk Emre

"TANGO" Class   1976

4 "BRAVO" CLASS (PATROL SUBMARINES SS)

Displacement, tons: 2 400 surfaced; 2 900 dived
Dimensions, feet (metres): 229·9 × 32·1 × 23·9 *(70·1 × 9·8 × 7·3)*
Torpedo tubes: 6—21 in *(533 mm)*
Main machinery: Diesel-electric; 2 diesels; 2 500 hp; 2 electric motors; 2 500 hp
Speed, knots: 14 surfaced; 16 dived
Complement: 60

The beam-to-length ratio is larger than normal in a diesel submarine which would account in part for the large displacement for a comparatively short hull.
First completed in 1968. These four submarines are spread over at least three of the four fleets, reinforcing the view that these are "padded targets" for torpedo and A/S firings.

"BRAVO" Class

60 "FOXTROT" CLASS (PATROL SUBMARINES SS)

Displacement, tons: 1 950 surfaced; 2 400 dived
Dimensions, feet (metres): 300·1 × 24·6 × 20 *(91·5 × 7·5 × 6·1)*
Torpedo tubes: 6—21 in *(533 mm)* (bow); 4—16 in *(406 mm)* (stern); 22 torpedoes carried
Main machinery: 3 diesels; 6 000 bhp; 3 electric motors; 6 000 hp; 3 shafts
Speed, knots: 18 surfaced; 18 dived
Range: 20 000 miles surfaced, cruising
Complement: 75

Built since 1958 at Sudomekh although the Soviet naval programme finished in the early 1970s. A follow-on of the "Zulu" class with similar propulsion to the "Golf" class. Only 60 out of a total programme of 160 were completed as the change over to nuclear boats took effect. A most successful class which has been deployed world-wide, forming the bulk of the Soviet submarine force in the Mediterranean. Four transferred to India in 1968-69 with a further four new constructions following. This is a continuing programme for export, now including Libya—one delivered to that country in 1976 and two others in 1978 with more reportedly on order. One to Cuba 7 February 1979.

Radar: One Snoop Tray.

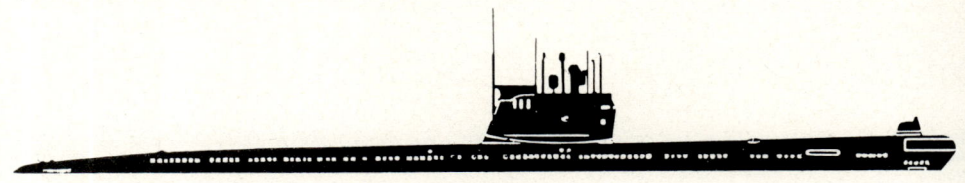
"FOXTROT" Class

"FOXTROT" Class (Indian Ocean) 5/1974, USN

"FOXTROT" Class (Mediterranean—USS *Jonas Ingram* behind) 12/1973, USN

10 + 9 (Reserve) "ZULU IV" CLASS (PATROL SUBMARINES SS)

Displacement, tons: 1 950 surfaced; 2 300 dived
Dimensions, feet (metres): 295·2 × 24·3 × 20 *(90 × 7·4 × 6·1)*
Torpedo tubes: 10—21 in (6 bow, 4 stern);
 (24 torpedoes carried or 40 mines)
Main machinery: 3 diesels; 10 000 bhp;
 3 electric motors; 4 050 hp; 3 shafts
Speed, knots: 17 surfaced; 17 dived
Range, miles: 20 000 surfaced, cruising
Complement: 75

"ZULU IV" Class

The first large post-war patrol submarines built by USSR. 28 completed from late 1951 to 1955 out of an original programme of 40. General appearance is streamlined with a complete row of free-flood holes along the casing. Eighteen were built by Sudomekh Shipyard, Leningrad, in 1952-55 and others at Severodvinsk. The general external similarity to the later German U-boats of World War II is notable. All now appear to be of the "Zulu IV" type. This class is obsolescent and will soon be disposed of.
The six "Zulu V" conversions of this class provided the first Soviet ballistic missile submarines with SS-N-4 systems, the first becoming operational in 1955. The majority of these conversions no longer have a missile capability and have either been scrapped or are used in an auxiliary role such as oceanographic research.

Radar: One Snoop Plate or Snoop Tray.

"ZULU IV" Class *1978*

"ZULU IV" Class *1977, Selçuk Emre*

12 "ROMEO" CLASS (PATROL SUBMARINES SS)

Displacement, tons: 1 400 surfaced; 1 800 dived
Dimensions, feet (metres): 254·9 × 23·9 × 18 *(76·8 × 7·3 × 5·5)*
Torpedo tubes: 8—21 in *(533 mm)* (6 bow, 2 stern);
 18 torpedoes or 36 mines in place of torpedoes
Main machinery: 2 diesels; 4 000 bhp;
 2 electric motors; 4 000 hp; 2 shafts
Speed, knots: 17 surfaced; 16 dived
Range, miles: 16 000 at 10 knots (surfaced)
Complement: 54

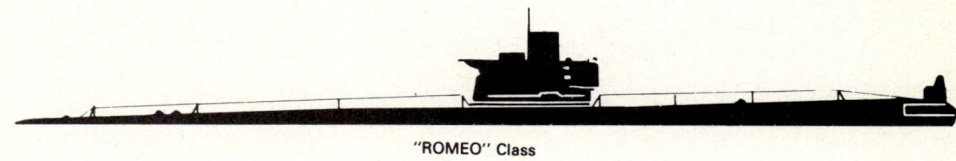
"ROMEO" Class

These are an improved "Whiskey" class design with modernised conning tower, and sonar installation. All built in 1958 to 1961. This was to have been numerically the largest class in the post-war submarine build-up. As their construction period coincided with the successful introduction of nuclear propulsion only about 20 were completed out of the staggering planned total of 560.

Radar: One Snoop Plate.

Transfers: Six to Egypt in 1966-68. Two to Bulgaria in early 1970s. China and North Korea building submarines of similar design.

"ROMEO" Class *1974*

"ROMEO" Class *1970*

516   USSR / Submarines (SS)

50 "WHISKEY" CLASS (see note) (PATROL SUBMARINES SS)

Displacement, tons: 1 080 surfaced; 1 350 dived
Dimensions, feet (metres): 249·6 × 22 × 15·1 *(76 × 6·7 × 4·9)*
Torpedo tubes: 4—21 in *(533 mm)* (bow); 2—16 in *(406 mm)* (stern); 18 torpedoes carried (or 40 mines)
Main machinery: Diesel-electric; 2 shafts
  2 diesels; 4 000 bhp
  2 electric motors; 2 700 hp
Speed, knots: 18 surfaced; 15 dived
Range, miles: 13 000 at 8 knots (surfaced)
Complement: 54

"WHISKEY V" Class

This was the first post-war Soviet design for a medium-range submarine. Like its larger contemporary the "Zulu", this class shows considerable German influence. About 240 of the "Whiskeys" were built between 1951 and 1957 at yards throughout the USSR. Like its successor, the "Romeo", this class was cut back from the original planned total of 340 as nuclear propulsion became established. Built in five types—I and IV had guns forward of the conning tower, II had guns both ends, whilst III and V have no guns. All Soviet "Whiskey" class are now Type V.

Class Total: There may be about 50 operational although decreasing numbers are seen out of area. Some 80 are probably in reserve, a sizeable proportion probably unmaintained.

Conversions: Two of this class, named *Severyanka* and *Slavyanka*, were converted for oceanographic and fishery research and have probably now been scrapped.

Foreign Transfers: Has been the most popular export model, with about 40 in all transferred. Currently in service:—
Albania (4), Bulgaria (2), Egypt (6), Indonesia (3), Korea (N) (4), Poland (4). China has carried out her own building programme.

Radar: One Snoop Plate.

"WHISKEY V" Class   1974, J. D. R. Rawlings

"WHISKEY V" Class   9/1977, MOD

"WHISKEY V" Class   1973

USSR / Submarines (SS) 517

3 "WHISKEY CANVAS BAG" CLASS (RADAR PICKET SUBMARINES SSR)

Displacement, tons: 1 080 surfaced; 1 350 dived
Dimensions, feet (metres): 249·6 × 22 × 15·1 (76 × 6·7 × 4·9)
Torpedo tubes: 4—21 in (533 mm) (bow);
  2—16 in (406 mm) (stern)
Main machinery: Diesel-electric; 2 shafts; 2 diesels; 4 000 bhp;
  2 electric motors; 2 700 hp
Speed, knots: 18 surfaced; 15 dived
Range, miles: 13 000 at 8 knots surfaced
Complement: 54

"WHISKEY CANVAS BAG" Class

Basically of same design as the "Whiskey" class but with long-range Boat-Sail radar aerial mounted on the fin. The coy way in which this was covered prompted the title "Canvas Bag". Converted in 1959 to 1963 as surveillance pickets. The introduction of "Bear" aircraft around 1963 probably rendered this plan redundant and thus very few were converted. Some have, however, remained in service so presumably a task has been found for them.

Radar: One Boat Sail; one Snoop Plate.

"WHISKEY CANVAS BAG" Class (with radar aerial abeam)   1975

4 + 15 (Reserve) "QUEBEC" CLASS (PATROL SUBMARINES SS)

Displacement, tons: 420 surfaced; 510 dived
Dimensions, feet (metres): 185·0 × 18 × 13·4 (56·4 × 5·5 × 4·1)
Torpedo tubes: 4—21 in (533 mm) (bow)
Main machinery: Diesel-electric; 3 shafts; 2 diesels; 2 000 bhp;
  3 electric motors; 3 500 hp
Speed, knots: 16 surfaced; 15 dived
Oil fuel, tons: 50
Range, miles: 7 000 surfaced cruising
Complement: 40

"QUEBEC" Class

Short range, coastal submarines. Built from 1954 to 1957. Thirteen were constructed in 1955 by Sudomekh Shipyard, Leningrad. The original planned total was cut from 100 to at least 22, overtaken by nuclear propulsion and with the failure of the unconventional propulsion in the earlier boats.

Class Total: Four may be still running but most are in reserve and may be deleted in the near future.

Propulsion system: In the late 1930s both closed cycle diesels and a closed cycle turbine were under development in Germany. After initial sea trials both were tried out in the Type XVII and later submarines. Thus when the Soviet Union occupied a large part of Germany at the war's end they had a great deal of knowledge available and experiments continued at Leningrad. The Walther/Kreislof Turbine was certainly put to sea and possibly also closed cycle diesels. The fuels required, high test peroxide for the turbines and liquid oxygen for the diesels, was dangerous to handle, frequently causing fires and explosions. Consequently this class reverted to normal diesel and electric propulsion, losing their title of "Cigarette Lighters".

Radar: One Snoop Plate.

"QUEBEC" Class   1970

"QUEBEC" Class   1970

1 "INDIA" CLASS (RESCUE SUBMARINE)

Displacement, tons: 2 500 approx

This single diesel submarine is in service in the pacific. Designed for rescue work she carries two bells on the after casing.

USSR / Aircraft carriers

AIRCRAFT CARRIERS

2 + 2 "KIEV" CLASS (AIRCRAFT CARRIERS)

Name	Builders	Laid down	Launched	Commissioned
KIEV	Nikolayev South (Nosenko, 444)	Sep 1970	Dec 1972	May 1975
MINSK	Nikolayev South (Nosenko, 444)	Dec 1972	May 1975	Feb 1978
KHARKOV	Nikolayev South (Nosenko, 444)	Oct 1975	Dec 1978	1980
NOVOROSSIISK?	Nikolayev South (Nosenko, 444)	mid-1978	late 1981	1983

Displacement, tons: 32 000 standard; 38 000 full load
Length, feet (metres): 898·7 *(274)*
Beam, feet (metres): 135 *(41·2)* (hull);
  157·4 *(48)* (oa, including flight deck and sponsons)
Draught, feet (metres): 27·2 *(8·3)*
Aircraft (estimated): 43—normal mix, 12 Forger A, 1 Forger B, 27 Hormone A, 3 Hormone B
Missiles: SSM; 4 twin SS-N-12
  SAM; 2 twin SA-N-3; 2 twin SA-N-4
  A/S; 1 twin SUW-N-1
Guns: 4—76 mm (twins); 8 Gatling 30 mm mounts
A/S weapons: 2—12-barrelled MBU 2500A launchers fwd
Torpedo tubes: 10—21 in *(533 mm)* (*Kiev* only) recessed below waterline (may have been removed)
Main engines: 4 steam turbines; 4 shafts (2 rudders); 160 000 shp
Speed, knots: 32
Range, miles: 13 000 at 18 knots; 4 000 at 30 knots
Complement: 1 800 (including air group)

KIEV

KIEV (with "Forgers" on deck and VDS streamed)   8/1976, MOD

After years of argument and indecision the first sign of Soviet acceptance of the need for organic air was the appearance of *Moskva* and *Leningrad* in 1968-69, the first ships built with a flat deck in the post-war years. They carried the embarked helicopter concept a long stage further than the cruisers with a single embarked helicopter. It is most probable that a much larger number was projected and the reason for the cancellation of the remainder might be because of any or all of a number of factors. Two appear to be of considerable importance—the growing Soviet realisation of the important part their navy could play in overseas affairs and the appearance of the prototype of the first Soviet VTOL aircraft, the Yakovlev *Freehand*. This first appeared in public in 1967 and its capabilities were known at least a year before that. This was ten years before *Kiev* became operational, (*Kiev* passed the Turkish Straits on 18 July 1976) a reasonable lead time for Soviet designers and constructors.

The task of this class is probably twofold—an advanced ASW role in wartime and an intervention capability in so-called peacetime with excellent command, control and communication capabilities. The inclusion of the very considerable SSM capability, A/S weapons as well as sonar equipment, and a gun armament as well as both missile and Point Defence Systems shows a continuation of the Soviet plan for multi-purpose ships.

The apparent delay in the appearance of the next two of this class (*Minsk* passed the Turkish Straits on 25 February 1979) suggest that design modifications have resulted from *Kiev's* experience. These are probably all that will be built to this design and a class of larger ships may be expected in the early 1980s.

Aircraft: The complement is a mix of *Hormone* helicopters and *Forger* (Yak 36) VTOL aircraft. The *Forger* comes in two versions—A, a single seater of which about a dozen were embarked in *Kiev* in July-August 1976 and B, a twin-seat trainer of which only one was seen. Some 20 *Hormones*, mostly A but with one or two B, were also carried on the same trip.
The functions of the *Forger* have not been fully revealed and may not yet, in fact, be fully evaluated. It appears to have the potential to carry both air-to-air and air-to-surface missiles as well as A/S weapons. All this, combined with a reconnaissance role, means that a new dimension in Soviet capability has been achieved.
The Hormone A is primarily an A/S aircraft while Hormone B is used for missile guidance (SS-N-12).

ECM: A full fit is carried including Side Globe housings.

Flight Deck: 620 ft *(189 m)* long with a 4 degree angle, 68 ft *(20·7 m)* wide with two lifts, one larger one abaft the island and a smaller one amidships abreast the bridge. Six spots are provided with a seventh at the forward tip of the flight deck. A larger spot amidships aft is apparently for V/STOL.

Missiles: The four twin SSM launchers carry SS-N-12 missiles, an advance on the SS-N-3 with a range of over 250 miles at a speed of Mach 2/3.
The SAM armament is standard.
The A/S missile launcher can presumably launch either SS-N-14 or FRAS-1.

Operations: With a relative wind of up to 15 knots fine on the port bow (sometimes requiring a very slow ship's speed) a maximum of two aircraft is normally launched. A reasonable standard of flying efficiency has now been achieved.

Radar: 3D search: Top Sail.
Search: (Air and Surface); Top Knot
Fire control: Head Light (SA-N-3); Pop Group (SA-N-4); Owl Screech *(76 mm)* Bass Tilt (Gatlings)
Aircraft control: Top Steer and Trap Door.
Navigation: Don Kay, Palm Front.
IFF: High Pole B.

Sonar: LF hull-mounted and MF VDS.

Soviet Type Name: Protivo Lodochny Kreyser meaning anti-submarine cruiser. This is an interesting designation for a ship of this size which, at the time *Kiev* was completed, continued the then Soviet practice of calling nearly all major surface units by an ASW title.
A further reason may have been the apparent prohibition on the movement of aircraft-carriers through the Bosphorous contained in the Montreaux Convention.

MINSK   3/1979, MOD

MINSK   2/1979, Ulrich Schulz-Torge

USSR / Aircraft carriers 519

MINSK — 2/1979, MOD

KIEV — 12/1977, MOD

MINSK — 2/1979, Selçuk Emre

KIEV — 10/1976, USN

520 USSR / Helicopter cruisers

HELICOPTER CRUISERS

2 "MOSKVA" CLASS

Name	Builders	Laid down	Launched	Commissioned
MOSKVA	Nikolayev South	1963	1965	July 1967
LENINGRAD	Nikolayev South	1964	1966	1968

Displacement, tons: 14 500 standard; 18 000 full load
Length, feet (metres): 624·8 *(190·5)*
Beam, feet (metres): 111·5 *(34)* (flight deck);
  85·3 *(26)* (waterline)
Draught, feet (metres): 24·9 *(7·6)*
Aircraft: 18 Hormone A ASW helicopters
Missiles: SAM;2 twin SA-N-3
Guns: 4—57 mm (2 twin mountings)
A/S weapons: 1 twin SUWN-1 A/S missile launcher;
  2—12 tube MBU 2500A on forecastle
Main engines: Geared turbines; 2 shafts; 100 000 shp
Boilers: 4 watertube
Speed, knots: 30
Complement: 840

This class represented a radical change of thought in the Soviet fleet. The design must have been completed while the "November" class submarines were building and the heavy A/S armament and efficient sensors (helicopters and VDS) suggest an awareness of the problem of dealing with nuclear submarines. Alongside what is apparently a primary A/S role these ships have a capability for A/A warning and self-defence as well as a command function. With a full fit of radar and ECM equipment they clearly represent good value for money. Why only two were built is discussed earlier in the notes on the "Kiev" class aircraft carriers.

Air facilities: Hangar, feet (metres): 219·8 × 82 *(67 × 25)*
Deck, feet (metres): 265·7 × 111·5 *(81 × 34)*

Electronics: Six Side Globe ECM.

Modification: In early 1973 *Moskva* was seen with a landing pad on the after end of the flight deck, probably for flight tests of VTOL aircraft. Since removed.

Radar: Search: Top Sail 3-D and Head Net C 3-D.
Fire control: Head Light (2). Muff Cob (2).
Navigation: Don 2 (3).

Sonar: Hull-mounted: One LF.
VDS: One MF.
In addition all helicopters have dunking-sonar.

Soviet Type Name: Protivo Lodochny Kreyser meaning Anti-Submarine Cruiser.

Torpedo tubes:
Originally two quintuple 21 in now removed.

"MOSKVA" Class

MOSKVA   5/1974, USN

LENINGRAD   1977, Selçuk Emre

MOSKVA   1978, Selçuk Emre

CRUISERS

1 + 1 + ? "SOVIETSKY SOYUZ" CLASS

Name	Builders	Laid down	Launched	Commissioned
—	Baltic Yard, Leningrad	1975	Dec 1977	?1980
—	Baltic Yard, Leningrad	1976	—	—

Displacement, tons: 32 000 full load (approx)
Dimensions, feet (metres): 811·9 × 90·1 × 32·8 (247·5 × 27·5 × 10)
Aircraft: Some Forger VTOL and Hormone helicopters
Missiles: Probably 4—SS-N-12; SA-N-3 and 4 (or successors)
Guns: 57-100 mm; 8 Gatling 30 mm
A/S weapons: 2—MBU 2500A
Main engines: Nuclear
Speed, knots: ?32

This class of similar dimensions and speed to the battle-cruisers of the past appears to be a self-contained element coming between the "Kara" and "Kiev" with a much-enhanced range due to nuclear propulsion. The similarity between this design and that of the USN Strike Cruiser is apparent. The tasks of the latter, "Screening ships for carriers in high threat areas but also undertaking independent operations" could also be true of the "Kirovs", of which a long production, possibly up to twelve may be expected. As the focus of a task force including "Karas", "Krivaks" and "Ivan Rogov" class with support from "Berezina" or "Boris Chilikin" classes they would form a formidable intervention force, with VTOL and helicopter aircraft as well as a full outfit of missiles and heavy guns.

Engineering: The first Soviet surface combatant with nuclear propulsion.

Radar: The main surveillance radar appears to be a combination of Top Sail and Big Net. Other radars probably similar to "Kiev" and "Kara" classes.

Sonar: Hull-mounted and VDS.

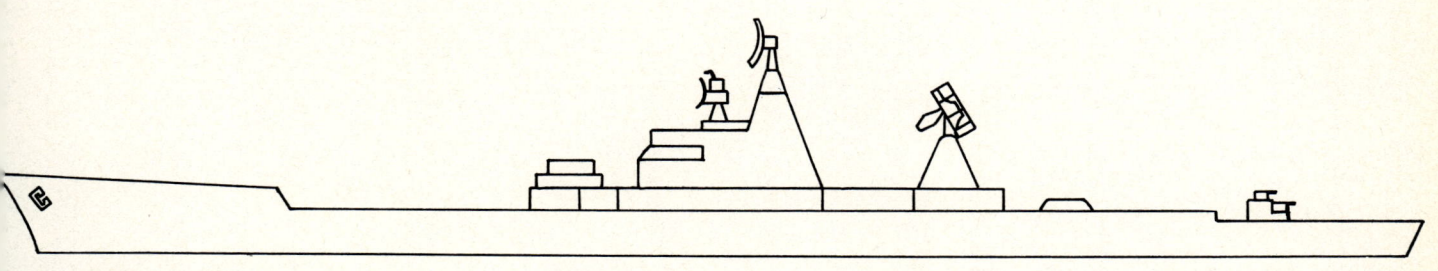

Sketch of "SOVIETSKY SOYUZ" Class   1979

0 + 3 + ? "KIROV" CLASS

Name	Builders	Laid down	Launched	Commissioned
—	Zhdanov Yard, Leningrad	1976	Dec 1978	1980
—	Zhdanov Yard, Leningrad	1977	—	—
—	Zhdanov Yard, Leningrad	1978	—	—

Displacement, tons: 10 000 approx
Dimensions, feet (metres): 550 × 59 × 20 (168 × 18 × 6·2) approx
Missiles: New SAM systems
Guns: Possibly 180 mm main armament
Main engines: Steam turbines

The successors to the "Kresta II" design and built at the same yard.

Missiles: The missile fit is uncertain but it is probable that a new SAM system similar to that fitted in *Azov* or *Provorny* would be shipped.

522 USSR / Cruisers

7 + 3 "KARA" CLASS (CG)

Name	Builders	Laid down	Launched	Commissioned
NIKOLAYEV	Nikolayev South	1969	1971	1973
OCHAKOV (ex-Novorossiisk)	Nikolayev South	1970	1972	1974
KERCH	Nikolayev South	1971	1973	1975
AZOV	Nikolayev South	1972	1974	1976
PETROPAVLOVSK	Nikolayev South	1973	1975	1977
TASHKENT	Nikolayev South	1974	1976	1978
TALLIN	Nikolayev South	1974	1976	1978
—	Nikolayev South	1975	1977	1979
—	Nikolayev South	1976	1978	1980
—	Nikolayev South	1977	1979	1981

Displacement, tons: 8 200 standard; 9 500 full load
Length, feet (metres): 570 (173·8)
Beam, feet (metres): 60 (18·3)
Draught, feet (metres): 20 (6·2)
Aircraft: 1 Hormone A helicopter (Hangar aft)
Missiles: A/S; 8—SS-N-14 (2 quad launchers abreast bridge)
 SAM; SA-N-10 (*Petropavlovsk* and *Tashkent*)
 SAM; 4—SA-N-3 (twins)
 SAM; 4—SA-N-4 (twins either side of mast)
Guns: 4—76 mm (2 twins abaft bridge)
 4—Gatling 23 mm (abreast funnel) (see *Gunnery* note)
A/S weapons: 2—12-barrelled MBU (fwd)
 2—6-barrelled MBU (aft)
Torpedo tubes: 10—21 in (533 mm) (2 quin mountings abaft funnel)
Main engines: 4 gas turbines; 120 000 hp; 2 shafts
Speed, knots: 32
Range, miles: 8 000 at 15 knots
Complement: 550

"KARA" Class

Apart from the specialised "Moskva" class this is the first class of large cruisers to join the Soviet navy since the "Sverdlovs". *Nikolayev* was first seen in public when she entered the Mediterranean from the Black Sea on 2 March 1973. Clearly capable of prolonged operations overseas.
All built or building at Nikolayev. *Azov* is of a modified design but has not yet emerged from the Black Sea (see *Missile* note). Continuing programme of about one a year. The eighth hull, with a redesigned after section, is reported as having a new SAM system with Head Light radar and SA-N-3 replaced.

ECM: A full oufit appears to be housed on the bridge and mast.

Gunnery: The siting of both main and secondary armament on either beams in the waist follows the precedent of both "Kresta" classes, although the weight of the main armament is increased. The single mountings are Gatling.

Missiles: In addition to the "Kresta II" armament of eight tubes for the SS-N-14 A/S system (possibly with a surface-to-surface capability) and the pair of twin launchers for SA-N-3 system with Goblet missiles, "Kara" mounts the SA-N-4 system in two silos, either side of the mast. *Azov* is reported as being the trials ship for the new SAM system designed for the eighth and subsequent ships of this class.
In *Petropavlovsk* and *Tashkent* a new missile system, possibly SA-N-10 and similar to that in the "Kashin" class *Provorny*, is mounted just forward of the bridge. This is reported to be a Mach 6 missile designed to combat cruise-missiles.

Radar: Surveillance: Top Sail, Head Net C and Sheet Curve.
SA-N-3 control: Head Light (2).
SA-N-4 control: Pop Group (2).
76 mm gun control: Owl Screech (2).
Gatling gun control: Bass Tilt (2).
Navigation: Don Kay and Don 2.

Sonar and A/S: VDS is mounted below the helicopter pad and is presumably complementary to a hull-mounted set or sets. The presence of the helicopter with dipping-sonar and an A/S weapon load adds to her long-range capability.

Soviet Type Name: Bolshoy Protivolodochny Korabl, meaning Large Anti-Submarine Ship.

KERCH 2/1976, MC

"KARA" Class 7/19

USSR / Cruisers 523

TASHKENT   2/1979, Ulrich Schulz-Torge

TASHKENT   2/1979, Selçuk Emre

PETROPAVLOVSK   2/1979, Ulrich Schulz-Torge

524 USSR / Cruisers

10 "KRESTA II" CLASS (CG)

Name	Builders	Commissioned
KRONSHTADT	Zhdanov, Leningrad	1970
ADMIRAL ISAKOV	Zhdanov, Leningrad	1971
ADMIRAL NAKHIMOV	Zhdanov, Leningrad	1972
ADMIRAL MAKAROV	Zhdanov, Leningrad	1973
MARSHAL VOROSHILOV	Zhdanov, Leningrad	1973
ADMIRAL OKTYABRSKY	Zhdanov, Leningrad	1974
ADMIRAL ISACHENKOV	Zhdanov, Leningrad	1975
MARSHAL TIMOSHENKO	Zhdanov, Leningrad	1976
VASILIY CHAPAEV	Zhdanov, Leningrad	1977
ADMIRAL YUMASCHEV	Zhdanov, Leningrad	1978

"KRESTA II" Class

Displacement, tons: 6 000 standard; 7 600 full load
Length, feet (metres): 519·9 *(158·5)*
Beam, feet (metres): 55·7 *(17·1)*
Draught, feet (metres): 19·7 *(6·0)*
Aircraft: 1 Hormone A helicopter (hangar aft)
Missiles: A/S; 8—SS-N-14 (two quad launchers)
SAM; 4—SA-N-3 (two twin launchers)
Guns: 4—57 mm (2 twin); 4—Gatling 30 mm
A/S weapons: 2—12-barrelled MBU (fwd);
2—6-barrelled MBU (aft)
Torpedo tubes: 10—21 in *(533 mm)* (2 quin)
Main engines: 2 steam turbines; 2 shafts; 100 000 shp
Boilers: 4 watertube
Speed, knots: 34
Range, miles: 5 500 at 18 knots
Complement: 350

The design was developed from that of the "Kresta I" class, but the layout is more up-to-date. The missile armament shows an advance on the "Kresta I" SAM armament and a complete change of practice in the fitting of the SS-N-14 A/S missile system. The fact that it has subsequently been fitted in the "Kara" and "Krivak" classes and that it must have a very limited anti-surface-ship capability indicates a possible change in tactical thought. The Zhdanov slipways are now in use for the succeeding new class the "Kresta II" programme having been completed.

Electronics: ECM fit with 8 Side Globe.

Radar: 3D search: Top Sail.
Search: Head Net C.
SA-N-3 control: Head Light (2).
57 mm control: Muff Cob (2).
Gatling control: Bass Tilt.
Navigation: Don Kay (2).

Soviet Type Name: Bolshoy Protivolodochny Korabl, meaning Large Anti-Submarine Ship.

ADMIRAL MAKAROV 7/1974, USN

ADMIRAL MAKAROV 9/1978, MOD (L. Air (Phot.) J. Anderson

ADMIRAL OKTYABRSKY 1975, MOD

USSR / Cruisers 525

4 "KRESTA I" CLASS (CG)

Name	Builders	Commissioned
ADMIRAL ZOZULYA	Zhdanov, Leningrad	1967
VLADIVOSTOK	Zhdanov, Leningrad	1968
VICE-ADMIRAL DROZD	Zhdanov, Leningrad	1969
SEVASTOPOL	Zhdanov, Leningrad	1970

Displacement, tons: 6 140 standard; 7 500 full load
Length, feet (metres): 510 *(155·5)*
Beam, feet (metres): 55·7 *(17)*
Draught, feet (metres): 19·7 *(6)*
Aircraft: 1 Hormone B helicopter with hangar aft
Missiles: SSM; 4—SS-N-3 (2 twin launchers);
  SAM; 4—SA-N-1 (2 twin launchers)
Guns: 4—57 mm (2 twins); 4 Gatling 23 mm (*Drozd* only)
A/S weapons: 2—12-barrelled MBU (fwd);
  2—6-barrelled MBU (aft)
Torpedo tubes: 10 (2 quin) 21 in
Main engines: Steam turbines; 2 shafts; 100 000 shp
Boilers: 4 watertube
Speed, knots: 35
Range, miles: 5 500 at 18 knots
Complement: 400

ADMIRAL ZOZULYA

Provided with a helicopter landing deck and hangar aft for the first time in a Soviet ship. This gives an enhanced carried-on-board target-location facility for the 200 mile SS-N-3 system. The "Kresta I" was therefore the first Soviet missile cruiser free to operate alone and distant from own shore-based aircraft. The prototype ship *Admiral Zozulya* was laid down in September 1964, launched in 1965 and carried out sea trials in the Baltic in February 1967. The second ship was launched in 1966 and the others in 1967-68.

ECM: Full kit with eight Side Globe.

Radar: Search: Head Net C, Big Net and Plinth Net (2).
Fire control: Scoop Pair for Shaddock system;
Peel Group (2) for Goa system.
57 mm control: Muff Cob (2).
Gatling control: Bass Tilt (*Drozd* only) (2).
Navigation: Don Kay.
IFF: High Pole B.

Refit: The first ship undergoing a major refit, *Vice-Admiral Drozd*, was completed in 1975 with new Bass Tilt radar and Gatling guns on a new superstructure between the bridge and the tower mast.

Soviet Type Name: Originally Bolshoy Protivolodochny Korabl, meaning Large Anti-Submarine Ship. Changed in 1977-78 to Raketny Kreyser, meaning Rocket Cruiser.

"KRESTA I" Class 4/1977

VLADIVOSTOK 1974, USN

VICE-ADMIRAL DROZD (after 1975 refit) 2/1976, MOD(N)

526 USSR / Cruisers

4 "KYNDA" CLASS (CG)

Name	Builders	Commissioned
GROZNY	Zhdanov, Leningrad	June 1962
ADMIRAL FOKIN	Zhdanov, Leningrad	Aug 1962
ADMIRAL GOLOVKO	Zhdanov, Leningrad	1963
VARYAG	Zhdanov, Leningrad	1964

Displacement, tons: 4 400 standard; 5 700 full load
Length, feet (metres): 465·8 *(142·0)*
Beam, feet (metres): 51·8 *(15·8)*
Draught, feet (metres): 17·4 *(5·3)*
Aircraft: Pad for helicopter on stern
Missiles: SSM; 8—SS-N-3 (quad launchers with one reload per tube);
  SAM; 2—SA-N-1 (twin launcher)
Guns: 4—3 in *(76 mm)* (2 twins)
A/S weapons: 2—12-barrelled MBUs on forecastle
Torpedo tubes: 6—21 in *(533 mm)* (2 triple amidships)
Main engines: 2 sets geared turbines; 2 shafts; 100 000 shp
Boilers: 4 high pressure
Speed, knots: 35
Range, miles: 7 000 at 15 knots
Complement: 390

The first ship of this class, *Grozny,* was laid down in June 1960, launched in April 1961. The second ship was launched in November 1961. Two enclosed towers, instead of masts, are stepped forward of each raked funnel. In this class there is no helicopter embarked, so guidance, for the SS-N-3 system would be more difficult than in later ships. She will therefore be constrained in her operations compared with the later ships with their own helicopters.

Radar: This class showed at an early stage the Soviet ability to match radar availability to weapon capability. The duplicated aerials provide not only a capability for separate target engagement but also provide a reserve in the event of damage.
Search: Head Net A.
Fire control: Scoop Pair (2) for Shaddock systems, Peel Group for Goa systems and Owl Screech for guns.
Navigation: Don 2 (2).
IFF: High Pole B.

Soviet Type Name: Raketny Kreyser meaning Rocket Cruiser.

"KYNDA" Class

ADMIRAL GOLOVKO　　　　　7/1973, MOD

"KYNDA" Class　　　　　1975

ADMIRAL GOLOVKO　　　　　7/1978

"KYNDA" Class　　　　　4/1975, MOD (N)

1 "SVERDLOV" CLASS ((CG)
2 "SVERDLOV" CLASS (CC)
9 "SVERDLOV" CLASS (CL)

ADMIRAL LAZAREV
ADMIRAL SENYAVIN (CC)
ADMIRAL USHAKOV

ALEKSANDR NEVSKI
ALEKSANDR SUVOROV
DMITRI POZHARSKI

DZERZHINSKI (CG)
MIKHAIL KUTUZOV
MURMANSK

OKTYABRSKAYA REVOLUTSIYA
SVERDLOV
ZHDANOV (CC)

Displacement, tons: 16 000 standard; 17 500 full load
Length, feet (metres): 656·2 *(200·0)* pp; 689·0 *(210·0)* oa
Beam, feet (metres): 72·2 *(22·0)*
Draught, feet (metres): 24·5 *(7·5)*
Aircraft: Helicopter pad in *Zhdanov*. Pad and hangar in *Senyavin*
Armour: Belts 3·9—4·9 in *(100—125 mm);* fwd and aft 1·6—2 in *(40—50 mm);* turrets 4·9 in *(125 mm);* C.T. 5·9 in *(150 mm);* decks 1—2 in *(25—50 mm)* and 2—3 in *(50—75 mm)*
Missiles: SAM; 2—SA-N-2 (twin launcher) aft in *Dzerzhinski;* SAM; 2—SA-N-4 in *Zhdanov* and *Senyavin* (twin launcher) see *Conversions)*
Guns: 12—6 in *(152 mm),* (4 triples) (9—6 in in *Dzerzhinski* and *Zhdanov);* 6—6 in in *Senyavin);* 12—3·9 in *(100 mm),* (6 twins), 16—37 mm (twins), 8—30 mm (twin) *(Zhdanov);* 6—30 mm (twins) *Senyavin* and *O. Revolutsiya)*
Mines: 150 capacity—(except *Zhdanov* and *Senyavin)*
Main engines: Geared turbines; 2 shafts; 110 000 shp
Boilers: 6 watertube
Speed, knots: 30
Oil fuel, tons: 3 800
Range, miles: 8 700 at 18 knots
Complement: 1 000 average

Of the 24 cruisers of this class originally projected, 20 keels were laid and 17 hulls were launched from 1951 onwards, but only 14 ships were completed by 1956. There were two slightly different types. *Sverdlov* and sisters had the 37 mm guns near the fore-funnel one deck higher than in later cruisers. All ships except *Zhdanov* and *Senyavin* are fitted for minelaying. Mine stowage is on the second deck. Two ships in reserve.

Builders: Built at Baltisk (Leningrad), Nikolayev or Severodovinsk.

Conversions: *Dzerzhinski* has been fitted with an SA-N-2 launcher aft replacing X-Turret the only ship so fitted—presumably the experiment was not sufficiently successful to extend this item. In 1972 *Admiral Senyavin* returned to service with both X and Y turrets removed and replaced by a helicopter pad and a hangar surmounted by four 30 mm mountings and SA-N-4 mounting. At about the same time *Zhdanov* had only X-turret removed and replaced by a high deckhouse mounting an SA-N-4.
Oktyabrskaya Revolutsiya completed refit in early 1977 which included the extension of her bridge work aft and the fitting of eight mounts with associated four Bass Tilt radars.

Gunnery: The refit of *O. Revolutsiya* with the fitting of Gatlings round the bridge shows an intention to keep this big-gun class in commission.

Names: The ship first named *Molotovsk* was renamed *Oktyabrskaya Revolutsiya* in 1957.

Torpedoes: All torpedo tubes removed by 1960.

Radar: Unmodified ships—
Air search: Big Net or Knife Rest or Top Trough or Hair/Slim Net.
Surface search: Low or High Sieve.
Target indication: Half Bow.
Fire control: Top Bow (152 mm); Egg Cup (152 mm turrets); Sun Visor (100 mm); Drum Tilt *(O. Revolutsiya)*.
Navigation: Don 2 (2) or Neptun.
Dzerzhinski—
Air search: Big Net; Slim Net.
Surface search: Low Sieve.
Missile control: Fan Song E.
Fire control: As in unmod.
Navigation: Neptun.
Senyavin and *Zhdanov*—
Air search: Top Trough.
Surface search, navigation and fire control: As in *Dzerzhinski*.
30 mm control: Drum Tilt.
SA-N-4 control: Pop Group.

Soviet Type Name: Kreyser meaning Cruiser.

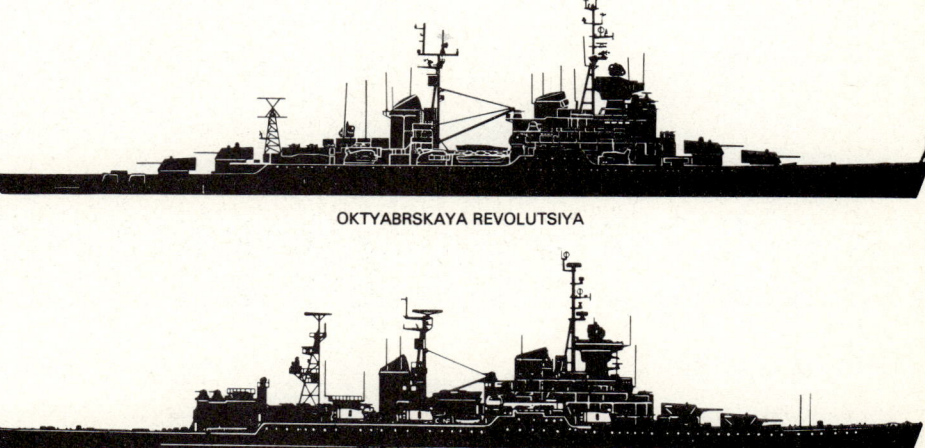
OKTYABRSKAYA REVOLUTSIYA

ADMIRAL SENYAVIN

OKTYABRSKAYA REVOLUTSIYA 1978

SVERDLOV 7/1976, MOD(N)

528 USSR / Cruisers

ZHDANOV 1978, Selçuk Emr

ADMIRAL SENYAVIN 19

1 "CHAPAEV" CLASS (CL)

KOMSOMOLETS (ex-*Chkalov*)

Displacement, tons: 11 300 standard; 15 000 full load
Length, feet (metres): 659·5 *(201·0)* wl; 665 *(202·8)*
Beam, feet (metres): 62 *(18·9)*
Draught, feet (metres): 24 *(7·3)*
Armour: Side 3 in *(75 mm)*; deck 2 in *(50 mm)*; gunhouses 3·9 in *(100 mm)* CT 3 in *(75 mm)*
Guns: 12—6 in *(152 mm)*/57 (4 triple); 8—3·9 in *(100 mm)*/70 (4 twin); 24—37 mm (12 twin)
Mines: 200 capacity; 425 ft rails
Main engines: Geared turbines, with diesels for cruising speeds; 4 shafts; 110 000 shp
Boilers: 6 watertube
Speed, knots: 30
Range, miles: 7 000 at 20 knots
Oil fuel, tons: 2 500
Complement: 900

Originally a class of six ships of which one was never completed—shows signs of both Italian and German influence. Laid down in 1939-40. Launched during 1941-47. All work on these ships was stopped during the war, but was resumed in 1946-47. Completed 1949-50 at Baltisk (Leningrad). Catapults were removed from all ships of this type. Remaining ship serves as training cruiser.

Gunnery: Turret guns fitting allows independent elevation to 45 degrees.

Radar: Air search: Slim Net.
Surface search: Low Sieve.
Fire control: Top Bow (152 mm); Egg Cup (152 mm turret Sun Visor (100 mm).
Navigation: Neptun.
IFF: Square Head and High Pole.

Soviet Type Name: Kreyser meaning Cruiser.

KOMSOMOLETS 11/19

DESTROYERS

13 "KASHIN" and 6 "MODIFIED KASHIN" CLASS (DDG)

KOMSOMOLETS UKRAINY	OGNEVOY* (**)	SLAVNY* (**)	SPOSOBNY
KRASNY-KAVKAZ	PROVORNY*	SMELY*	STEREGUSHCHY (**)
KRASNY-KRIM	SKORY	SMETLIVY	STROGIY
OBRAZTSOVY (**)	RESHITELNY	SMYSHLENY*	STROYNY
ODARENNY (**)	SDERZHANNY*	SOOBRAZITELNY	

* modified (**) Zhdanov built, remainder at Nikolayev

Displacement, tons: 3 750 standard; 4 500 full load (Kashin) 3 950/4 950 (Kashin mod)
Length, feet (metres): 470·9 *(143·3)*/481 *(146·5)* (mod)
Beam, feet (metres): 52·5 *(15·9)*
Draught, feet (metres): 15·4 *(4·7)*
Missiles: SAM; 4—SA-N-1 (twin launchers); SSM; 4—SS-N-2 (C) (singles) (in mod-class)
Guns: 4—3 in *(76 mm)* (2 twin); 4—23 mm Gatlings (mod-class)
A/S weapons: 2—12-barrelled MBU fwd; 2—6-barrelled MBUs aft (unmodified)
Torpedo tubes: 5—21 in *(533 mm)* quin, amidships
Main engines: 4 sets gas turbines; 96 000 hp; 2 shafts
Speed, knots: 35
Range, miles: 4 500 at 18 knots
Complement: 280 (320 mod)

The first class of warships in the world to rely entirely on gas-turbine propulsion giving them the quick getaway and acceleration necessary for modern tactics. These ships were delivered from 1962 onwards from the Zhdanov Yard, Leningrad and the Nosenko Yard, Nikolayev.
As they were built at the same time as "Kynda" class they may originally have been intended as AA support for the latter.

Conversion: In order to bring this class up-to-date with SSM and VDS a conversion programme was started in 1974. This conversion consists of lengthening the hull by 10 ft, shipping four SS-N-2 (mod) launchers (SSM), four Gatling close range weapons, a VDS under a new stern helicopter platform and removing the after MBUs. By 1978 five had been so converted. One of this class, *Provorny*, has a separate and distinctive conversion from the remainder. This consists of the replacement of both SA-N-1 mountings by two new SAM mountings. The forward of these is in a housing while the after is a single-arm launcher. *Provorny* does not carry SS-N-2 and is still under trial in the Black Sea for weapons designed for future classes of ship.

Loss: *Otvazhny* of this class foundered in the Black Sea in September 1974, apparently as the result of an internal explosion followed by a fire which lasted for five hours. Nearly 300 of the ship's company were lost, making this the worst peacetime naval loss for many years.

Radar: Unmodified ships—
Search: Head Net C and Big Net in some ships; Head Net A (2) in others.
Fire control: Peel Group (2) for Goa system and Owl Screech (2) for guns.
Modified ships—
Search: Head Net C and Big Net or 2 Head Net A.
Fire control: As in unmod plus Bass Tilt for Gatlings.
IFF: High Pole B.

Sonar: Hull-mounted plus VDS in modernised ships.

Soviet Type Name: Bolshoy Protivolodochny Korabl, meaning Large Anti-Submarine Ship (unmodified ships). Bolshoy Raketny Korabl meaning Large Rocket Ship (modified ships).

Transfers: Two or three under construction to be transferred to India in 1979-80.

"KASHIN" Class

Modified "KASHIN" Class

SKORY 1978, Selçuk Emre

OBRAZTSOVY at Portsmouth 5/1976, C. and S. Taylor

SLAVNY (modified) 1978, Selçuk Emre

3 "MOD KILDIN" and 1 "KILDIN" CLASS (DDG)

BEDOVY*   **NEULOVIMY***
NEUDERZHIMY   **PROZORLIVY***
* modified

Displacement, tons: 3 000 standard; 3 800 full load
Length, feet (metres): 414·9 *(126·5)*
Beam, feet (metres): 42·6 *(13·0)*
Draught, feet (metres): 16·1 *(4·9)*
Missiles: SSM; 1—SS-N-1 (before conversion);
    SSM; 4 for SS-N—2 (C) (singles) (conversions)
A/S weapons: 2—16-barrelled MBU on forecastle
Guns: 4—76 mm (twins aft) (after conversion);
    16—57 mm (quads—2 fwd, 2 between funnels)
Torpedo tubes: 4—21 in *(533 mm)* (2 twin)
Main engines: Geared turbines: 2 shafts; 72 000 shp
Boilers: 4 high pressure
Speed, knots: 35
Range, miles: 4 000 at 16 knots
Complement: 300 officers and men

Converted "KILDIN" Class

These were the last four "Kotlin" hulls with an SS-N-1 launcher replacing the after turret and the forward turret removed. *Bedovy* built at Nikolaev, *Neuderzhimy* at Komsomolsk, *Neulovimy* at Leningrad and *Prozorlivy* at Nikolaev. All completed in 1958.

Conversion: In 1972 *Neulovimy* was taken in hand for modification. This was completed in mid-1973 and consisted of the replacement of the SS-N-1 on the quarterdeck by two superimposed twin 76 mm turrets, the fitting of four SS-N-2 (Mod) launchers abreast the after funnel and the fitting of new radar. The substitution of the 40 n. mile SS-N-2 (Mod) system (a modified Styx) for the obsolescent SS-N-1 system and the notable increase in gun armament illustrate two trends in Soviet thought. *Bedovy* and *Prozorlivy* have now completed this conversion. The fourth ship *Neuderzhimy*, is unlikely to be modernised due to her age.

Radar: Original ships—
Air search: Slim Net and Flat Spin.
Fire control: Top Bow; Hawk Screech.
Conversions—
Air search: Head Net C (2 Strut Curve in *Bedovy*).
Fire control: Owl Screech (76 mm); Hawk Screech (57 mm).
IFF: Square Head and High Pole A.

Sonar: Hull-mounted.

Soviet Type Name: Originally Bolshoy Protivolodochny Korabl meaning Large Anti-Submarine Ship. Changed in 1977-78 to Bolshoy Raketny Korabl meaning Large Rocket Ship.

"KILDIN" Class (before conversion)   3/1975, USN

NEULOVIMY after conversion   7/1977

NEUDERZHIMY   1978, Selçuk Emre

8 "KANIN" CLASS (DDG)

BOYKY	GNEVNY	GREMYASHCHY	ZHGUCHY
DERZKY	GORDY	UPORNY	ZORKY

Displacement, tons: 3 700 standard; 4 700 full load
Length, feet (metres): 455·9 *(139)*
Beam, feet (metres): 48·2 *(14·7)*
Draught, feet (metres): 16·4 *(5·0)*
Aircraft: Helicopter platform
Missiles: SAM; 2—SA-N-1 (twin launcher aft)
Guns: 8—57 mm (2 quad fwd); 8—30 mm (twin) (by after funnel) (not *Gremyashchy*)
A/S weapons: 3—12-barrelled MBU
Torpedo tubes: 10—21 in *(533 mm)* (2 quin)
Main engines: 2 sets geared steam turbines; 2 shafts; 84 000 shp
Boilers: 4 watertube
Speed, knots: 34
Oil fuel, tons: 900
Range, miles: 4 500 at 16 knots
Complement: 350

All ships of this class have been converted from "Krupnys" at Zhdanov Yard, Leningrad and in the Pacific between 1968 and 1977, being given a SAM capability instead of the latter's SSM armament.

Appearance: As compared with the "Krupny" class these ships have enlarged bridge, converted bow (probably for a new sonar) and larger helicopter platforms.

Gunnery: The four twin 30 mm around the after funnel were a late addition to the armament.

Radar: Search: Head Net C.
Fire control: Peel Group for SA-N-1; Hawk Screech for guns.
Drum Tilt (2) for additional 30 mm guns.
Navigation: Don Kay (2).

Sonar: Hull-mounted.

Soviet Type Name: Bolshoy Protivolodochny Korabl, meaning Large Anti-Submarine Ship.

"KANIN" Class

BOYKY with additional 30 mm guns
10/1973, MOD(N)

ZHGUCHY
1976, Michael D. J. Lennon

"KANIN" Class (in Caribbean)
8/1970, USN

532 USSR / Destroyers

8 "SAM KOTLIN" CLASS (DDG)

BRAVY*	NASTOYCHIVY	SKROMNY	SOZNATELNY**
NAKHODCHIVY	NESOKRUSHIMY**	SKRYTNY**	VOZBUZHDENNY

* Original R and D conversion   ** Modified guns (30 mm)

Displacement, tons: 2 850 standard; 3 600 full load
Dimensions, feet (metres): 418·2 × 42·3 × 15·1
  (127·5 × 12·9 × 4·6)
Missiles: SAM; 2—SA-N-1 (twin launcher)
Guns: 2—5·1 in (130 mm) (1 twin); 4—45 mm (1 quad);
  (12—45 mm in *Bravy*); 8—30 mm (twins) (in three ships)
Torpedo tubes: 5—21 in (533 mm) (quin)
A/S weapons: 2—12-barrelled MBU (2—16-barrelled in *Bravy*
  and *Skromny*)
Main engines: Geared turbines; 2 shafts; 72 000 shp
Boilers: 4 high pressure
Speed, knots: 36
Range, miles: 4 000 at 16 knots
Complement: 360

"SAM KOTLIN" Class

Converted "Kotlin" class destroyers with a surface-to-air missile launcher in place of the main twin turret aft and anti-aircraft guns reduced to one quadruple mounting in all but *Bravy* which still has three quadruple mountings.
The prototype *(Bravy)* was completed in the early 1960s and the others between 1966 and 1972. Three subsequently modified with 30 mm armament and Drum Tilt radar.

Appearance: The prototype SAM "Kotlin" *(Bravy)* has a different after funnel and different radar pedestal from those in the rest of the class.

Radar: Search: Head Net C.
Fire control: Peel Group for SA-N-1;
Sun Visor for 130 mm guns;
Egg Cup in turret;
Hawk Screech for 45 mm guns;
Drum Tilt for 30 mm in modified ships.
IFF: High Pole B.

Transfer: Poland (1).

"BRAVY"   4/1975, USN

"SAM KOTLIN" Class

NASTOYCHIVY   6/1978, W. Admira

18 "KOTLIN" CLASS (DD)

BLAGORODNY
BLESTYASHCHY
BURLIVY
BYVALY
NAPORISTY

PLAMENNY
SPESHNY
DALNEVOSTOCHNY KOMSOMOLETS
MOSKOVSKY KOMSOMOLETS
SPOKOJNY
SVEDUJSCHY

SVETLY
VDOKHNOVENNY
VESKY
VLIJATELNY
VOZMUSHCHENNY
VYDERZHANNY
VYZYVAYUSCHY

Displacement, tons: 2 850 standard; 3 800 full load
Length, feet (metres): 414·9 *(126·5)*
Beam, feet (metres): 42·6 *(13·0)*
Draught, feet (metres): 16·1 *(4·9)*
Guns: 4—5·1 in *(130 mm)* (2 twins); 16—45 mm (4 quads);
 4 or 8—25 mm (twins) (in mod "Kotlins")
A/S weapons: 2—16-barrelled MBU (fwd);
 2—6-barrelled MBU (aft) (mod "Kotlins");
 6—DCT (unmod except *Svetly* which has a helo platform)
Torpedo tubes: 5 (mod) and 10 (unmod) 21 in *(533 mm)* (quin)
Mines: 80 capacity
Main engines: Geared turbines; 2 shafts; 72 000 shp
Boilers: 4 high pressure
Speed, knots: 36
Range, miles: 4 000 at 16 knots
Complement: 285

Built in 1954-57. The last four hulls laid down were completed as "Kildins". Over half now modified. Several now in reserve.

Modifications: (a) Eight converted to "Sam Kotlins" plus one transferred to Poland. (b) *Svetly* only ship now provided with helicopter platform on stern. (c) Modified ships had after torpedo-tubes replaced by a deckhouse. (d) Modified ships had two 16-barrelled MBUs (forward) and two 6-barrelled MBUs (aft) fitted. (e) The latest addition in some ships is the fitting of four or eight 25 mm either side of the after-funnel.

Radar: Search: Slim Net.
Fire control: Sun Visor (130 mm); Egg Cup (130 mm turrets);
Hawk Screech (45 mm); Post Lamp or Top Bow.
Navigation: Don (2) or Neptun.
IFF: High Pole and Square Head.

Sonar: One hull-mounted.

Soviet Type Names: Esminyets meaning Fleet Torpedo Ship.

Modified "KOTLIN" Class

"KOTLIN" Class 1978

SVETLY (North Sea) 7/1976, MOD(N)

Modified "KOTLIN" Class (MBUs on B gun-deck and quarter-deck with deck house in place of after torpedo-tubes) 10/1973, USN

35 "SKORY" CLASS (DD)

BEZUPRECHNIY
BEZUKORIZNENNY
OGNENNY
OSTOROZNY
OTVETSTVENNY

OZHESTOCHENNY
OZHIVLENNIY
SERDITY
SMOTRYASHCHY
SOKRUSHITELNY
SOLIDNY

SOVERSHENNY
STATNY
STEPENNY
STOYKY
STREMITELNY
SUROVY

SVOBODNY
VDUMCHIVY
VEDUSHCHY
VERNY
VNIMATELNY
VRAZUMITELNY + 12

Displacement, tons: 2 240 standard; 3 100 full load
Length, feet (metres): 395·2 *(120·5)*
Beam, feet (metres): 38·9 *(11·8)*
Draught, feet (metres): 15·1 *(4·6)*
Guns: 4—5·1 in *(130 mm)*, (2 twins) (all ships); 2—3·4 in *(86 mm)*, (1 twin) (unmodified); 8—37 mm (4 twin), (unmodified); 4—25 mm (twin) (some unmodified); 5—57 mm (single) (modified)
A/S weapons: 4 DCT (unmodified); 2—16-barrelled MBU (modified)
Torpedo tubes: 10—21 in *(533 mm)* (unmodified); 5—21 in (modified)
Mines: 80 can be carried
Main engines: 2 geared turbines; 2 shafts; 60 000 shp
Boilers: 4 high pressure
Speed, knots: 33
Range, miles: 3 900 at 13 knots
Complement: 280

"SKORY" Class

There were to have been 85 destroyers of this class, but construction beyond 75 units was discontinued in favour of later types of destroyers, and the number has been further reduced to 35 by transfers to other countries, translations to other types and disposals. Further deletions expected in this elderly class.

Appearance: There were three differing types in this class, the anti-aircraft guns varying with twin and single mountings; and two types of foremast, one vertical with all scanners on top and the other with one scanner on top and one on a platform half way.

Modernisation: At least six ships of the "Skory" class were modified from 1959 onwards including extensive alterations to anti-aircraft armament, electronic equipment and anti-submarine weapons. These now have five 57 mm (single) in place of the 86 mm and 37 mm, five torpedo tubes and two 16-barrelled MBU.

Radar: Search: Slim Net (mod); High Sieve, Knife Rest or Cross Bird (unmod).
Fire control: Hawk Screech (mod); Top Bow or Half Bow and Post Lamp (unmod).
Navigation: Don.

Reserve: Nearly 50 per cent of this class now in reserve.

Transfers: Of this class *Skory* and *Smely* were transferred to the Polish Navy in 1957-58, two to the Egyptian Navy in 1956, two in 1959, eight to the Indonesian Navy in 1959-63, and a further two (modernised) to Egypt in 1968 in place of earlier pair.

Soviet Type Name: Esminyets meaning Fleet Torpedo Ship.

SOVERSHENNY   1978, Selçuk Emre

"SKORY" Class (unmodified)   5/1972, MOD(N)

"SKORY" Class (modified)   9/1971, MOD

USSR / Frigates 535

FRIGATES

17 + ? "KRIVAK I" CLASS, 7 + ? "KRIVAK II" CLASS (FFG)

KRIVAK I (Zhdanov, Leningrad/Kaliningrad)
BDITELNY
BODRY
SVIREPY
SILNY
STOROZHEVOY
RAZUMNY
RAZYASCHY
ZHARKI
RETIVY
LENINGRADSKI KOMSOMOLETS
LETUCHKY
PYLKY

KRIVAK I (Kamysch-Burun (Kerch))
DOSTOYNY
DOBLESTNY
DEYATELNY
DRUZHNY
+1

KRIVAK II (Leningrad/Kaliningrad)
REZVY
REZKY
RAZYTELNY
GROZYASHCHY
NEUKROTIMY
BESSMENNY
GROMKY
+2

Displacement, tons: 3 300 standard; 3 600 full load
Length, feet (metres): 404·8 *(123·4)*
Beam, feet (metres): 45·9 *(14·0)*
Draught, feet (metres): 16·4 *(5·0)*
Missiles: A/S; 4—SS-N-14, in A position (quad launcher); SAM; 4—SA-N-4 (twin launchers)
Guns: 4—3 in *(76 mm)* (2 twin) X and Y positions in "Krivak I"; 2—100 mm (singles, aft) in "Krivak II"
A/S weapons: 2—12-barrelled MBU (fwd)
Torpedo tubes: 8—21 in *(533 mm)* (2 quads)
Main engines: 4 sets gas turbines; 2 shafts; 72 000 shp
Speed, knots: 32
Complement: 220

This handsome class, the first ship of which appeared in 1971, incorporates A/S and anti-air capability, a VDS with associated MBUs, two banks of tubes, all in a hull designed for both speed and sea-keeping. The use of gas-turbines gives the "Krivak" class a rapid acceleration and availability. Building continues at about three per year.

Class: "Krivak II" Class has X-gun mounted higher and a larger VDS apart from other variations noted.
Now classified as "missile frigates" by NATO.

Missiles: The missiles of the SS-N-14 system continue the A/S trend of the "Kresta II" class and the "Kara" class. The SA-N-4 SAMs are of the same design which is now mounted also in the "Kiev", "Kara", "Nanuchka", "Grisha" and other classes. The launcher retracts into the mounting for stowage and protection, rising to fire and retracting to reload. The two mountings are forward of the bridge and abaft the funnel.

Radar: Search: Head Net C.
Missile control: Eye Bowl (SS-N-14), Pop Group (SA-N-4) (2).
Gunnery control: Owl Screech.
Navigation: Don Kay (2).

Sonar: One hull-mounted set in bow; 1 VDS.

Soviet Type Name: Originally Bolshoy Protivolodochny Korabl, meaning Large Anti-Submarine Ship. Changed in 1977-78 to Storozhevoy Korabl meaning Escort Ship.

"KRIVAK" Class

"KRIVAK" Class 1978, Selçuk Emre

REZKY ("KRIVAK II" Class) 6/1977, MOD

DEYATELNY 2/1979, Ulrich Schulz-Torge

BDITELNY 9/1978, MOD (Phot. Stewart Kent)

2 + ? "KONI" CLASS

ZELONODOLSK

Displacement, tons: 1 700 standard; 2 300 full load
Dimensions, feet (metres): 311·6 × 39·3 × 13·7 (95 × 12 × 4·2)
Missiles: SAM; 4—SA-N-4 (twin launchers)
Guns: 4—3 in (76 mm) (twins); 4—30 mm (twins)
A/S weapons: 2—12-barrelled MBU (fwd)
Main engines: CODAG; 1 gas turbine (centre shaft); 30 000 shp; 2 diesels (outer shafts); 12 000 shp
Speed, knots: 32 (gas); (22 diesel)
Range, miles: 2 000 at 14 knots
Complement: 110

A new class of frigate first reported in the Black Sea in 1977. The second ship was transferred to GDR in June 1978. How many of this class will be built for the Soviet navy is uncertain. Continuing programme of up to four per year at Zelonodolsk.

Radar: Search: Strut Curve.
Fire control: Hawk Screech; Drum Tilt; Pop Group.

Sonar: Hull-mounted.

Soviet Type Name: Storozhevoy Korabl meaning Escort Ship.

"KONI" Class 1978

20 "MIRKA I and II" CLASS

Displacement, tons: 950 standard; 1 100 full load
Dimensions, feet (metres): 265·6 × 29·9 × 9·8 (81 × 9·1 × 3)
Guns: 4—3 in (76 mm) (2 twin)
A/S weapons: 4—MBU (2 fwd, 2 aft) (I); 2—MBU (fwd) (II); DC racks
Torpedo tubes: 5—16 in (400 mm) A/S (I); 10—16 in (400 mm) A/S (II)
Main engines: 2 diesels; 12 000 hp; 2 gas turbines, 30 000 hp; 2 shafts
Speed, knots: 34
Range, miles: 5 000 at 10 knots
Complement: 98

This class of ships was built in 1964-67 as variation on "Petya" class. The difference between the Mark I and II is that the latter have the after MBU rocket launchers removed and an additional quintuple 16 in torpedo mounting fitted between the bridge and the mast.

Radar: Search: Strut Curve.
Fire control: Hawk Screech.

Sonar: One hull-mounted.
Dipping sonar is also fitted in some units on the transom.

Soviet Type Name: Originally Maly Protivolodochny Korabl meaning Small Anti-Submarine Ship. Changed in 1977-78 to Storozhevoy Korabl meaning Escort Ship.

"MIRKA II" Class

"MIRKA II" Class (with two torpedo mountings) 4/1975, MOD

"MIRKA I" Class 1978

"MIRKA II" Class 1978

USSR / Frigates 537

13 "PETYA I" CLASS
9 "MOD PETYA I" CLASS
25 "PETYA II" CLASS
1 "MOD PETYA II" CLASS

Displacement, tons: 950 standard; 1 100 full load
Dimensions, feet (metres): 268·9 × 29·9 × 10·5 *(82 × 9·1 × 3·2)*
Guns: 4—3 in *(76 mm)* (2 twins)
A/S weapons: 4—MBU (I); 2—MBU (II); internal DC racks
Torpedo tubes: 5—16 in *(400 mm)* (I and mod I);
  10—16 in *(400 mm)* (II)
Main engines: 1 diesel, 6 000 hp;
  2 gas turbines; 30 000 hp; 3 shafts
Speed, knots: 34
Range, miles: 5 000 at 10 knots
Complement: 98

Small freeboard with a low wide funnel. The first ship reported to have been built in 1960-61 at Kaliningrad. Construction continued until about 1972. Fitted with two mine rails. "Petya II" class mount an extra quintuple torpedo tube in place of after MBUs.

Radar: Search: Strut Curve/Slim Net.
Fire control: Hawk Screech.

Sonar: One hull-mounted (see *VDS* note)

Soviet Type Name: Originally Maly Protivolodochny Korabl meaning Small Anti-Submarine Ship. Changed in 1977-78 to Storezhevoy Korabl meaning Escort Ship.

Transfers: 12 to India, two to Syria, two to Viet-Nam December 1978.

VDS: In eight of "Petya I" class a deck-house containing Variable Depth Sonar has replaced the after MBUs and encloses the quarter-deck whilst the prototype has the VDS in the open. This group, part of a continuing programme, is now classified Petya I Mod" class (originally "Petya III"). In 1978 a new modification appeared—a "Petya II" with the after torpedo tubes removed and a deckhouse built abaft the after 76 mm gun to contain the VDS gear.
One ship has different VDS from remainder and deck-house abaft funnel. Possibly a training ship.

"MOD PETYA I" Class

"PETYA II" Class

"MOD PETYA I" Class 2/1976, MOD

"PETYA II" Class 10/1974, USN

"PETYA I" Class 3/1975, MOD

538 USSR / Frigates

BARSUK	KOBCHIK	SHAKAL
BUYVOL	LISA	TURMAN
BYK	MEDVED	VOLK
GEPARD	PANTERA	+36
GIENA		

Displacement, tons: 1 000 standard; 1 420 full load
Dimensions, feet (metres): 298·8 × 33·1 × 10·5 *(91 × 10·1 × 3·2)*
Guns: 3—3·9 in *(100 mm)* (single); 4—37 mm (2 twins); 4—25 mm (twins) in some
A/S weapons: 2—16-barrelled MBU (in some); 2 DC racks, 1 Hedgehog (some); 4 DCT (some)
Torpedo tubes: 2 or 3—21 in *(533 mm)* in some
Mines: 50
Main engines: 2 geared turbines; 2 shafts; 20 000 shp
Boilers: 2
Speed, knots: 28
Range, miles: 2 500 at 15 knots
Complement: 175

Built from 1952 to 1959. Successors to the "Kola" class escorts, of which they are lighter and less heavily armed but improved versions. Fitted with mine rails. At least eight in reserve.

Anti-submarine: The two 12-barrelled MBU rocket launchers are mounted just before the bridge abreast B gun.

Conversion: A small number of this class has been improved. Some have a twin 25 mm gun mounting on either side of the funnel.
One or more now fitted with main mast carrying extensive electronic arrays.

Radar: Search: Slim Net.
Fire control: Sun Visor B; Wasp Head.
Navigation: Don/Neptun.
IFF: Square Head and High Pole.

Sonar: One hull-mounted. HF.

Soviet Type Name: Storozhevoy Korabl meaning Escort Ship.

Transfers: Bulgaria (2), East Germany (4), Finland (2), Indonesia (8), Romania (6).

40 "RIGA" CLASS

"RIGA" Class

"RIGA" Class   1978, Selçuk Emre

"RIGA" Class   1976

3 "KOLA" CLASS

SOVIETSY AZERBAIJAN, SOVIETSKY DAGESTAN, SOVIETSY TURKMENESTAN

Displacement, tons: 1 200 standard; 1 600 full load
Length, feet (metres): 321·4 *(98)*
Beam, feet (metres): 31·2 *(9·5)*
Draught, feet (metres): 10·6 *(3·2)*
Guns: 4—3·9 in *(100 mm)* (single); 4—37 mm; 4—25 mm (twin) (some)
A/S weapons: 4 DC rails
Torpedo tubes: 3—21 in *(533 mm)*
Mines: 30
Main engines: Geared turbines; 2 shafts; 25 000 shp
Boilers: 2
Speed, knots: 30
Range, miles: 3 500 at 12 knots
Complement: 190

Built in 1950-52. In design this class of flushdecked frigates appears to be a combination of the former German "Elbing" class destroyers, with a similar hull form, and of the earlier Soviet "Birds" class escorts. Serving in the Caspian Sea. Last of a class of twelve.

Radar: Surface search: Ball Gun.
Air search: Cross Bird.
Fire control: Sun Visor (100 mm).
IFF: High Pole.

Soviet Type Name: Storozhevoy Korabl meaning Escort Ship.

"KOLA" Class

CORVETTES

2 + ? "TARANTUL" CLASS (MISSILE CORVETTES)

Displacement, tons: 760 full load
Dimensions, feet (metres): 183·7 × 34·4 × 8·1 *(56 × 10·5 × 2·5)*
Missiles: SSM; 4—SS-N-2 C (twins)
Guns: 1—76 mm (fwd); 2—30 mm Gatling (aft, both beams)
Main engines: 3 gas turbines
Speed, knots: 35
Complement: 50

First sighted early 1979. Built at Petrovsky, Leningrad. Laid down early 1977 and launched April 1978. Second laid down early 1978.

Radar: Fire control: Bass Tilt.
IFF: Squaw Head and High Pole.

15 "GRISHA I", 6 "GRISHA II" and 14 "GRISHA III" CLASSES

AMETYST, BRILLANT, IZUMRUD, RUBIN, ZEMCHUG +31

Displacement, tons: 900 standard; 1 000 full load
Dimensions, feet (metres): 236·2 × 32·8 × 11 *(72 × 10 × 3·6)*
Missiles: SAM; 2—SA-N-4 (twin launcher) ("Grisha I" and "III" classes)
Guns: 2—57 mm (1 twin) (4 in "Grisha II" class); Gatling mount aft ("Grisha III")
Torpedo tubes: 4—21 in *(533 mm)* (2 twins)
A/S weapons: 2 MBU; internal DC racks
Mines: Fitted for minelaying
Main engines: 1 gas turbine; 12 000 shp; 2 diesels; 18 000 shp; 3 shafts = 30 knots
Complement: 60

"GRISHA I" Class

"GRISHA III" Class

Reported to have started series production in the late 1969-70 period. Continuing programme of about three a year. SA-N-4 launcher mounted on the forecastle in "Grisha I" and "III" classes. This is replaced by a second twin 57 mm in "Grisha II" class which may be operated by KGB. "Grisha III" class has Muff Cob radar removed, Bass Tilt and Gatling (fitted aft), and Rad-haz-screen removed from abaft funnel.

Radar: Air search: Strut Curve.
Fire control: Pop Group (SA-N-4 "Grisha I" and "III");
Muff Cob (57 mm) (except in "Grisha III");
Bass Tilt (57 mm and Gatlings) ("Grisha III").
Navigation: Don 2.

Sonar: One hull-mounted. Some have a similar VDS to that used in Hormone helicopters.

Soviet Type Name: Maly Protivolodochny Korabl meaning Small Anti-Submarine Ship.

"GRISHA III" Class   1978, Selçuk Emre

"GRISHA II" Class   7/1974, MOD

"GRISHA I" Class   7/1974

540 USSR / Corvettes

16 + ? "NANUCHKA I" and 3 + ? "NANUCHKA III" CLASSES (MISSILE CORVETTES)

GRAD, RADUGA +17

Displacement, tons: 800 standard; 950 full load
Length, feet (metres): 193·5 (59)
Beam, feet (metres): 39·6 (12·0)
Draught, feet (metres): 9·9 (3·0)
Missiles: SSM: 6—SS-N-9 (two triple launchers);
SAM; 2—SA-N-4 (twin launcher);
Guns: 2—57 mm (1 twin) (I); 1—76 mm; 1—30 mm Gatling (III)
Main engines: 6 M503A diesels; 28 000 shp; 3 shafts
Speed, knots: 32
Complement: 60

"NANUCHKA" Class

Probably mainly intended for deployment in coastal waters although several have been deployed in the Mediterranean, North Sea and Pacific. Built from 1969 onwards. Has received many type designations including "Missile Cutter". Built at Petrovsky, Leningrad (continuing programme) and possibly in the Pacific. SS-N-9 has a range of about 60 miles.

New Construction: "Nanuchka III", first seen in 1978, has a 76 mm in place of the twin 57 mm and an added Gatling as in "Grisha III", Bass Tilt radar in place of Muff Cob and a heavier mast structure.

Radar: Air search: Band Stand.
Fire control: Fish Bowl; Muff Cob (Bass Tilt in "Nanuchka III"); Pop Group and SS-N-9 guidance in radome.
Navigation: Don.
IFF: High Pole; Square Head.

Transfers: Three of a modified version ("Nanuchka II") with four SS-N-2 (B) missiles have been supplied to India.

"NANUCHKA I" Class   7/1978

"NANUCHKA I" Class   7/1976, MOD(N)

64 "POTI" CLASS

Displacement, tons: 400 standard; 600 full load
Dimensions, feet (metres): 193·5 × 26·2 × 8 (59 × 8 × 2·4)
Guns: 2—57 mm (1 twin mounting)
Torpedo tubes: 4—16 in (406 mm)
A/S weapons: 2—6-barrelled MBU
Main engines: 2 gas turbines; 24 000 shp; 2 diesels; 8 000 shp; 2 shafts = 34 knots
Complement: 80

This class of ship was under series construction from 1961 to 1968.

Radar: Air search: Strut Curve.
Fire control: Muff Cob.
Navigation: Don.

Soviet Type Name: Maly Protivo Lodochny Korabl meaning Small Anti-Submarine Ship.

Transfers: Three to Bulgaria; three to Romania.

"POTI" Class

"POTI" Class   11/1970, USN

LIGHT FORCES

(Note: All "Komars" now deleted)

3 + ? "SARANCHA" CLASS (FAST ATTACK CRAFT—MISSILE HYDROFOIL)

Displacement, tons: 235 full load
Dimensions, feet (metres): 139·4 × 32·8 × 6·6 *(42·5 × 10 × 2)*
Missiles: SSM; 4—SS-N-9 (twin launchers);
  SAM; 1—SA-N-4 (twin launcher)
Gun: 1—30 mm Gatling
Main engines: 2 gas turbines; 2 diesels; 13 900 hp; 4 shafts = 45 knots
Complement: 35

First reported 1976. Built at Petrovsky, Leningrad—could be "Osa" replacement. Foil system similar to US "PHM".

Radar: Air search: Band Stand.
Fire control: Fish Bowl; Bass Tilt.
IFF: High Pole and Square Head.

SARANCHA 4/1977, Ulrich Schulz-Torge

70 "OSA I" and 50 "OSA II" CLASSES (FAST ATTACK CRAFT—MISSILE)

Displacement, tons: 160 standard; 210 full load ("Osa I"); 165 standard ("Osa II")
Dimensions, feet (metres): 128·7 × 25·1 × 5·9 *(39·3 × 7·7 × 1·8)*
Missiles: SSM; 4—SS-N-2 (single launchers)
Guns: 4—30 mm; (2 twin, 1 fwd, 1 aft)
Main engines: 3 diesels; 12 000 bhp (I); 15 000 bhp (II) = 36 knots
Range, miles: 800 at 25 knots
Complement: 30

Built from 1959 to early 1970s. They have a surface-to-surface missile range of up to 23 miles. Later boats have cylindrical missile launchers, comprising the "Osa II" class.
This class was a revolution in naval shipbuilding. Although confined by their size and range to coastal operations the lethality and accuracy of the Styx missile have already been proved by the sinking of the Israeli destroyer *Eilat* on 21 October 1967 by an Egyptian "Komar". The operations of the Indian "Osas" in the war with Pakistan in December 1971 were equally successful: they sank *Khaibar* (destroyer) and several merchant vessels by night. These operations surely represent a most important lesson in naval operations and, in light of this, the list of transfers should be noted. It must be borne in mind that modern tactics and EW systems have reduced the efficacy of the SS-N-2.

Missiles: A few ships have SA-N-5 (converted Grail SA7) (quad) launchers.

Radar: Search: Square Tie.
Fire control: Drum Tilt.
IFF: High Pole; Square Head (2).

Transfers: Algeria (9), Bulgaria (4), China (17), Cuba (8), Egypt (12), East Germany (15), Finland (4), India (16), Iraq (12), North Korea (8), Libya (6), Poland (13), Romania (5), Somalia (3), Syria (10), Yugoslavia (10).

"OSA II" Class 4/1976

"OSA I" Class 4/1974

"OSA I" Class 1977

"OSA II" Class 1977

542 USSR / Light forces

55 "SO I" CLASS (LARGE PATROL CRAFT)

Displacement, tons: 170 light; 215 full load
Dimensions, feet (metres): 137.8 × 19.7 × 5.9 *(42 × 6 × 1.8)*
Guns: 4—25 mm (2 twin mountings) (see notes)
A/S weapons: 4—MBU 1 800 (5-barrelled); DCT
Torpedo tubes: 2—16 in (some)
Mines: Can carry 20
Main engines: 3 diesels; 7 500 bhp; 3 shafts = 28 knots
Range, miles: 1 100 at 13 knots
Complement: 31

Built between 1957 and late 1960s—total about 150. Steel hulled. Modernised boats of this class have one 45 mm and two 25 mm guns with two 16 in anti-submarine torpedo tubes. Being phased out of service.

Radar: Search: Pot Head.
IFF: High Pole A; Dead Duck.

Soviet Type Name: Maly Protivo Lodochny Korabl meaning Small Anti-Submarine Ship.

Transfers: Algeria (6), Bulgaria (6), Cuba (12), Egypt (12), East Germany (12), Iraq (3), North Korea (12), Viet-Nam (2 or 3), South Yemen (2).

"SO I" Class 1974

"SO I" Class (mod. with torpedo tubes) 8/1974

1 "SLEPEN" CLASS (FAST ATTACK CRAFT—PATROL)

Displacement, tons: 210 full load
Dimensions, feet (metres): 128.7 × 25.1 × 5.9 *(39.3 × 7.7 × 1.8)*
Guns: 1—76 mm; 1—30 mm Gatling
Main engines: 3 M503A diesels; 3 shafts; 12 000 shp = 36 knots
Complement: 30

Built on a "Osa" hull this single craft has the tripod mast mounted further aft and different radar. Originally built at Petrovsky, Leningrad in 1970 with twin 57 mm, 30 mm gatling and prototype Bass Tilt as trials ship for "Grisha III" class. In 1975 the 57 mm replaced by single 76 mm turret as trials ship for "Matka" and "Nanuchka III" classes. Also carried out trials for Chaff launchers for "Krivak" and "Nanuchka" classes.

"SLEPEN" Class (with 57 mm guns) 1974

87 "STENKA" CLASS (FAST ATTACK CRAFT—PATROL)

Displacement, tons: 170 standard; 210 full load
Dimensions, feet (metres): 128.7 × 26.6 × 5.9 *(39.3 × 8.1 × 1.8)*
Guns: 4—30 mm (2 twin)
Torpedo tubes: 4—15.8 in *(400 mm)*
A/S weapons: 2 depth charge racks
Main engines: 3 M503A diesels; 12 000 bhp = 36 knots
Complement: 25

Based on the hull design of the "Osa" class. Built from 1967-68 onwards. Continuing programme of about two a year. A variant of this class, the "Mol", is in production apparently for export. (See *Transfers* below.)

Radar: Search: Pot Drum.
Fire control: Muff Cob.
IFF: High Pole; Square Head (2).

Sonar: Some have Hormone type dipping sonar.

Transfers: "Stenka" class: Bulgaria (3) in 1977.
"Mol" class: Ethiopia (2) in 1978; Somalia (4) in 1976; Sri Lanka (1) in 1975.

"STENKA" Class 9/1974

1 "BABOCHKA" CLASS (FAST ATTACK CRAFT—PATROL HYDROFOIL)

Displacement, tons: 440 full load
Dimensions, feet (metres): 164 × 27·9 × 6·6 (50 × 8·5 × 2)
Guns: 2—Gatlings
A/S weapons: 8 A/S torpedo tubes (quads, fwd)
Main engines: 3 gas turbines; 2 diesels = 45 knots
Complement: 45

This is a much larger hydrofoil than any previously seen. First sighted 1977. Unusual features include a new hydrofoil arrangement, the large gas turbine exhausts aft, the trainable torpedo mountings forward and the large object forward of the first Gatling.

Radar: Bass Tilt.

"BABOCHKA" Class 1978

6 + ? "MATKA" CLASS (FAST ATTACK CRAFT—MISSILE HYDROFOIL)

Displacement, tons: 215 full load
Dimensions, feet (metres): 128·7 × 25·1 × 3·9 (39·3 × 7·7 × 1·8)
Missiles: SSM; 2—SS-N-2 C
Guns: 1—76 mm; 1—30 mm Gatling
Main engines: 3 diesels, 13 500 hp = 42 knots
Complement: 33

In early 1978 the first of class was seen. Built at Izhora Yard, Leningrad. Similar hull to the "Osa" class with similar hydrofoil system to "Turya" class. The combination has produced a better sea-boat than the "Osa" class.

Radar: Fire control: Bass Tilt.
IFF: High Pole and Square Head.

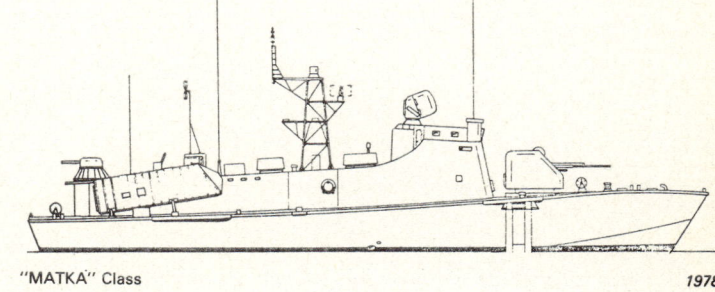

"MATKA" Class 1978

34 "TURYA" CLASS (FAST ATTACK CRAFT—TORPEDO HYDROFOIL)

Displacement, tons: 190 standard; 220 full load
Dimensions, feet (metres): 128·7 × 25·1 × 5·9 (39·3 × 7·7 × 1·8)
Guns: 2—57 mm (twin, aft); 2—25 mm (twin, fwd)
Torpedo tubes: 4—21 in (533 mm)
Main engines: 3 M504 diesels; 15 000 shp; 3 shafts
Speed, knots: 40
Complement: 30

The second class of hydrofoil. Has a naval orientation rather than the earlier "Pchela" class of the KBG. Entered service from 1973—in series production, possibly four-five per year. Basically "Osa" hull.

Radar: Search: Pot Drum.
Fire control: Drum Tilt.
IFF: High Pole and Square Head.

Sonar: A form of VDS is fitted on the transom (similar to Hormone sonar). In view of this the apparent lack of A/S weapons is surprising. Could operate with shore-based helicopters.

Transfer: Two to Cuba 9 February 1979.

"TURYA" Class 1977

20 "PCHELA" CLASS (FAST ATTACK CRAFT—PATROL HYDROFOIL)

Displacement, tons: 70 standard; 83 full load
Dimensions, feet (metres): 83 × 19 × 4·3 (25·3 × 5·8 × 1·3) (without foils)
Guns: 4 MG (2 twins)
A/S weapons: DCs
Main engines: 2 diesels; 4 800 bhp; 2 shafts = 45 knots
Complement: 12

This class of hydrofoil is reported to have been built since 1964-65. Also carry depth charges. Used for frontier guard duties by KGB in Baltic and Black Seas.

Radar: Search: Pot Drum.
IFF: High Pole B.

Sonar: One type of VDS.

"PCHELA" Class 1976

50 "SHERSHEN" CLASS (FAST ATTACK CRAFT—TORPEDO)

Displacement, tons: 145 standard; 160 full load
Dimensions, feet (metres): 118·1 × 25·3 × 4·9 (36 × 7·7 × 1·5)
Guns: 4—30 mm (2 twin)
Torpedo tubes: 4—21 in (533 mm) (single)
A/S weapons: 12 DC
Main engines: 3 M503A diesels; 3 shafts; 12 000 bhp = 38 knots
Range, miles: 450 at 34 knots
Complement: 16

First of class produced in 1963. Programme apparently completed.

Radar: Search: Pot Drum.
Fire control: Drum Tilt.
IFF: High Pole and Square Head.

Transfers: Angola (1), Bulgaria (6), East Germany (15), Egypt (6), Guinea (2), North Korea (5), Yugoslavia (13).

"SHERSHEN" Class 1977

USSR / Light forces — River patrol craft

8 "P 6" CLASS (FAST ATTACK CRAFT—TORPEDO)

Displacement, tons: 66 standard; 75 full load
Dimensions, feet (metres): 84·2 × 20·0 × 6·0 (25·7 × 6·1 × 1·8)
Guns: 4—25 mm (twins)
Torpedo tubes: 2—21 in (533 mm)
A/S weapons: DCs (or mines)
Main engines: 4 diesels; 4 shafts; 4 800 bhp = 43 knots
Range, miles: 450 at 30 knots
Complement: 20

The "P 6" class (Soviet Type 184 originally) was of a standard medium sized type running into series production. Launched during 1951 to 1960. Known as "MO VI" class in the patrol craft version. The later versions, known as the "P 8" and "P 10" classes, were powered with gas-turbines, and had different bridge and funnel; "P 8" boats with hydrofoils. The "P 6" class is now being deleted because of old age; some have been converted to radio-controlled target craft. "P 8" and "P 10" classes are reported to have been completely deleted. Originally 250-300 boats of these classes were built.

Radar: Search: Skin Head or Pot Head.
IFF: High Pole.

Transfers: Algeria (12), China (80, indigenous construction), Cuba (12), Egypt (28), East Germany (18), Guinea (4), Indonesia (14), Iraq (12), North Korea (10), Nigeria (3), Poland (20), North Viet-Nam (6), Somalia (4), Tanzania (3), South Yemen (2).

"P 6" Class

20 "ZHUK" CLASS (COASTAL PATROL—CRAFT)

Displacement, tons: 60
Dimensions, feet (metres): 75 × 16 × 6 (24·6 × 5·2 × 1·9)
Guns: 2—14·5 mm (twin fwd); 1—12·7 mm (aft)
Main engines: 2 M50 diesels; 2 400 hp; 2 shafts = 34 knots
Complement: 17 (?)

First seen in 1976.
Mainly manned by the KGB. Export versions have twin (over/under) 14·5 mm aft.

Radar: One navigation set.

Transfers: Angola, Cuba (twelve in 1975-78), Iraq (four in 1975), Viet-Nam (three in 1978), Yemen (S) (two in 1978).

"ZHUK" Class

RIVER PATROL CRAFT

Attached to Black Sea and Pacific Fleets for operations on the Danube, Amur and Usuri Rivers, and to the Caspian Flotilla.

75 "SHMEL" CLASS

Displacement, tons: 60 full load
Dimensions, feet (metres): 92 × 15·9 × 3·3 (28·1 × 4·3 × 1)
Guns: 1—76 mm/48 (tank turret); 2—25 mm/70 (twin)
Main engines: 2 M50 diesels; 2 400 hp; 2 shafts
Speed, knots: 22
Complement: 8

Some also mount one or two multi-barrelled rocket launchers amidships. Built 1967-74. This class superceded the BK 4 class which have now been deleted. Earlier "Shmels" have an after twin MG mount.

"SHMEL" Class

1 COMMAND SHIP

PS 10

Displacement, tons: 300
Guns: 2—20 mm
Speed, knots: 12

Support ship on the Danube for the river patrols.

PS 10   4/1975, Heinz Stocking

MINE WARFARE FORCES

3 "ALËSHA" CLASS (MINELAYERS)

... 5   083   PRIPYAT

Displacement, tons: 2 300 standard; 2 900 full load
Dimensions, feet (metres): 344·5 × 47·6 × 15·7 (98 × 14·5 × 4·8)
Guns: 4—57 mm (1 quad fwd)
Mines: 400
Main engines: 4 diesels; 2 shafts; 8 000 bhp = 20 knots
Range, miles: 8 000 at 14 knots
Complement: 150

In service since 1965. Fitted with four mine tracks to provide stern launchings. Also have a capability in general support role.

Radar: Search: Strut Curve.
Fire control: Muff Cob.
Navigation: Don 2.
IFF: High Pole.

"ALESHA" Class   1969

34 "NATYA" CLASS (MINESWEEPERS—OCEAN)

ADMIRAL PERSHIN, KONTRE ADMIRAL CHOROSHKIN, MINER, NAVODVHIK, RULEVOY, SIGNALCHIK +28

Displacement, tons: 650 standard; 750 full load
Dimensions, feet (metres): 200·1 × 31·5 × 7·5 (61 × 9·6 × 2·3)
Guns: 4—30 mm (2 twins); 4—25 mm (2 twins)
A/S weapons: 2—MBU 1 800
Mines: Can lay mines
Main engines: 2 diesels; 4 800 bhp; 2 shafts = 18 knots
Complement: 50

First reported in 1971, evidently intended as successors to the "Yurka" class. Steel hulls. Building rate of three a year. Usually operate in home waters but have been deployed to the Mediterranean.

Radar: Fire control: Drum Tilt.
Navigation: Don 2.

Transfers: India (two in 1978).

"NATYA" Class   1976

49 "YURKA" CLASS (MINESWEEPERS—OCEAN)

SAKHALINSKY KOMSOMOLETS, PRIMORSKY KOMSOMOLETS +47

Displacement, tons: 400 standard; 460 full load
Dimensions, feet (metres): 170·6 × 30·5 × 6·6 (52 × 9·3 × 2)
Guns: 4—30 mm (2 twin)
Mines: Can carry 20
Main engines: 2 diesels; 4 000 bhp; 2 shafts = 18 knots
Range, miles: 1 100 at 18 knots
Complement: 45

A class of medium fleet minesweepers with steel hull. Built from 1963 to the late 1960s.

Radar: Fire control: Drum Tilt.
Navigation: Don 2.

Transfer: Four to Egypt.

"YURKA" Class   1974

17 "T 58" CLASS (MINESWEEPERS—OCEAN)

Displacement, tons: 790 standard; 900 full load
Dimensions, feet (metres): 229·9 × 29·5 × 7·9 (70·1 × 9 × 2·4)
Guns: 4—57 mm (2 twin)
A/S weapons: 2—MBU 1800; 2 DCT
Main engines: 2 diesels; 2 shafts; 4 000 bhp = 17 knots
Complement: 82

Built from 1957 to 1964. Steel hulls. Of this class 14 were converted to submarine rescue ships with armament and sweeping gear removed, see later page ("Valdai" class). Frequently deployed to the Indian Ocean. Have minelaying capability. One has been sighted with Big Net Radar.

Radar: Search: Ball End.
Fire control: Muff Cob (in most).
Navigation: Neptun.

Transfer: One to Yemen S (1978).

"T 58" Class   1/1975, MOD

546　USSR / Mine warfare forces

73 "T 43" CLASS (MINESWEEPERS—OCEAN)

Displacement, tons: 500 standard; 580 full load (600 for *60 m* ships)
Dimensions, feet (metres): 190·2 × 28·2 × 6·9 *(58 × 8·6 × 2·1)* (older units)
　(198 *(60 m)* in later ships)
Guns: 2—45 mm (singles); 4—25 mm or 4—8 MGs (not in older units)
A/S weapons: 2 DCT
Mines: Can carry 30
Main engines: 2 diesels; 2 shafts; 2 200 bhp = 14 knots
Range, miles: 1 600 at 10 knots
Complement: 65

Built in 1948-57 in shipyards throughout the Soviet Union. Steel hulls. The later version *(60 m long)* carries the additional 4—25 mm guns. A number of this class were converted into radar pickets (see below). The remainder are gradually being replaced by newer types of fleet minesweepers and at least half are probably in reserve. Of the 200+ hulls built a number were also used as diving ships, tenders etc.

Radar: Search: Ball End.
Navigation: Neptun.

Transfers: Algeria (2), Albania (2), Bulgaria (3), China (20), Egypt (7), Indonesia (6), Iraq (2), Poland (12), Syria (2).

"T 43" Class (60 m version)　　　4/1972

5 "T 43/AGR" CLASS

Displacement, tons: 500 standard; 580 full load
Dimensions, feet (metres): 190·2 × 28·2 × 6·9 *(58 × 8·6 × 2·1)*
Guns: 4—37 mm; 2—25 mm
Main engines: 2 diesels; 2 shafts; 2 200 bhp = 14 knots
Range, miles: 1 600 at 10 knots
Complement: 60

Former fleet minesweepers of the "T 43" class converted into radar pickets with comprehensive electronic equipment. It is reported that there may be a dozen vessels of this type.

Radar: Air search: Big Net or Knife Rest or Squat Eye.
Navigation: Don 2.

"T43-AGR" Class (with Big Net radar)　　　1973, USN

"T43-AGR" Class (with Knife Rest radar)　　　8/1970

"T43-AGR" Class (with Squat Eye radar)　　　7/1977

3 + ? "ANDRYUSHA" CLASS (MINESWEEPERS—SPECIAL)

Displacement, tons: 360 full load
Dimensions, feet (metres): 147·3 × 26·8 × 6·5 *(44·9 × 8·2 × 2)*
Guns: None
Main engines: 2 diesels; 2 200 hp = 15 knots
Range, miles: 3 000 at 10 knots
Complement: 40

First entered service in 1975. Specially designed, possibly with GRP hulls, for deep water magnetic sweeping. Possibly carry a gas turbine generator.

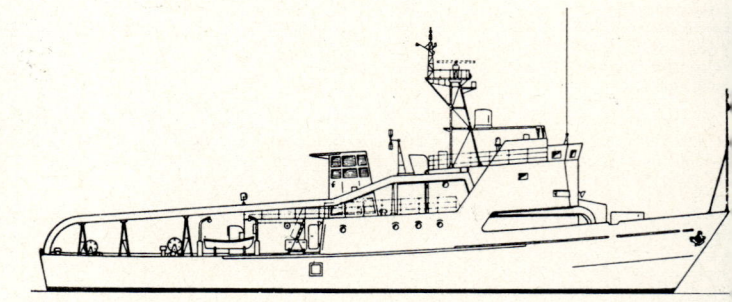
"ANDRYUSHA" Class　　　1978

30 "SONYA" CLASS (MINESWEEPERS/HUNTERS)

Displacement, tons: 350 standard; 400 full load
Dimensions, feet (metres): 159·1 × 23·9 × 6·2 *(48·5 × 7·3 × 1·9)*
Guns: 2—30 mm (twin); 2—25 mm (twin)
Main engines: 2 diesels; 2 400 shp; 2 shafts = 18 knots
Complement: 18

Wooden hull. Minehunter. Now in series production at about three/four a year. First reported 1973.

Radar: Search/navigation: Don 2.
IFF: Square Head and High Pole B.

"SONYA" Class   7/1976

4 "ZHENYA" CLASS (MINESWEEPERS—COASTAL)

Displacement, tons: 220 standard; 300 full load
Dimensions, feet (metres): 141 × 25 × 6 *(43 × 7·6 × 1·8)*
Guns: 2—30 mm (twin)
Main engines: 2 diesels; 2 400 shp; 2 shafts = 18 knots
Complement: 40

Reported to be a trial class for GRP hulls which may not have been successful as the "Sonyas" followed with wooden hulls. First reported 1972.

"ZHENYA" Class   1974

72 "VANYA" CLASS (MINESWEEPERS—COASTAL)

Displacement, tons: 200 standard; 245 full load
Dimensions, feet (metres): 131·2 × 23·9 × 5·9 *(40 × 7·3 × 1·8)*
Guns: 2—30 mm (1 twin); 2—25 mm (twin) in conversions
Main engines: 2 diesels; 2 200 bhp = 18 knots
Range, miles: 1 100 at 18 knots
Complement: 30

A coastal class with wooden hulls of a type suitable for series production built from 1961-73.

Conversion: Three have been converted with superstructure extended forward, with 25 mm mounting on foc's'le in place of 30 mm, lattice mast at break amidships and two boats stowed on quarterdeck. Probably guidance ships for "Ilyusha" class (following).

Transfers: Bulgaria (4), Syria (2).

Radar: Navigation: Don 2; Don Kay in conversions.

"VANYA" Class   1975

10 "SASHA" CLASS (MINESWEEPERS—COASTAL)

Displacement, tons: 250 standard; 280 full load
Dimensions, feet (metres): 147·9 × 20·5 × 6·6 *(45·1 × 6·3 × 2)*
Guns: 1—57 mm; 4—25 mm (2 twins)
Main engines: 2 diesels; 2 200 bhp; 2 shafts = 18 knots
Complement: 25

Of steel construction. Built between 1956-60. Now phasing out.

Radar: Search: Ball End.

"SASHA" Class   1976

35 "YEVGENYA" CLASS (MINESWEEPERS—INSHORE)

Displacement, tons: 80
Dimensions, feet (metres): 85·6 × 19 × 3·9 *(26·1 × 5·8 × 1·2)*
Guns: 2—14·7 mm (twin)
Main engines: 1 or 2 diesels; 600 or 1 200 hp = 16 knots
Range, miles: 1 000 at 9 knots
Complement: 12

GRP hulls. Production started 1972. Can also lay mines.

Radar: Navigation: Don 2.

Transfers: Two to Cuba, three to Iraq.

"YEVGENYA" Class   1976

548 USSR / Mine warfare forces — Amphibious forces

10 "ILYUSHA" CLASS (MINESWEEPERS—INSHORE)

Displacement, tons: 70
Dimensions, feet (metres): 78·7 × 16·4 × 4·3 (24 × 5 × 1·3)
Main engine: 1 diesel; 450 shp = 12 knots
Complement: 10

Large foremast carrying electronic arrays. Probably capable of operating unmanned and radio controlled. (See "Vanya" Class—preceding.)

Radar: One Spin Trough.

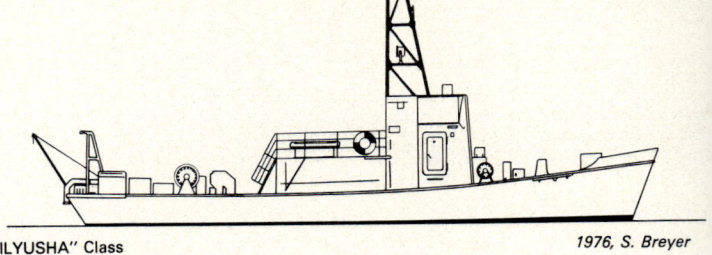

"ILYUSHA" Class 1976, S. Breyer

4 "OLYA" CLASS (MINESWEEPERS—INSHORE)

Displacement, tons: 50 standard; 70 full load
Dimensions, feet (metres): 83·6 × 14·8 × 4·6 (25·5 × 4·5 × 1·4)
Guns: 2—25 mm
Main engines: 2 diesels; 2 200 shp = 15 knots
Complement: 15

Radar: One Spin Trough.

5 "TR 40" CLASS (MINESWEEPING BOATS)

Displacement, tons: 50 standard; 70 full load
Dimensions, feet (metres): 92·0 × 13·5 × 2·3 (28 × 4·1 × 0·7)
Guns: 2 MG (twin); 2—25 mm (twin)
Main engines: 2 diesels; 600 bhp = 16 knots
Complement: 16

55 "K 8" CLASS (MINESWEEPING BOATS)

Displacement, tons: 26 full load
Dimensions, feet (metres): 55·4 × 10·5 × 4·0 (16·9 × 3·2 × 1·2)
Guns: 2 MG (twin)
Main engines: 2 diesels; 700 shp = 18 knots
Complement: 6

Built in Poland between 1954-59. Due for deletion shortly. Over half in reserve.

AMPHIBIOUS FORCES

2 + ? "IVAN ROGOV" CLASS (LPD)

Displacement, tons: 11 000 standard; 13 100 full load
Dimensions, feet (metres): 521·6 × 80·2 × 21·2—27·8 (159 × 24·5 × 6·5—8·5 flooded)
Missiles: SAM; 2—SA-N-4 (twin launcher)
Guns: 2—76 mm (twin); 4—23 mm Gatlings;
 1—Rocket launcher BM-21 (naval) (2 × 20-barrelled)

Main engines: 4 diesels; 20 000 shp = 20 knots
Range, miles: 7 500 at 16 knots
Complement: 400

First appeared in 1978 having been built at Kaliningrad. Second in 1979. Has bow ramp and rear doors opening into a docking bay possibly 220 ft long. A helicopter spot forward has a flying-control station and the after helicopter deck and hangar is similarly fitted. With a capacity for at least a battalion of Naval Infantry, up to 40 tanks as well as supporting vehicles this class provides a long range, long endurance assault capacity of far greater potential than any previous Soviet ship. Can carry up to three ACVs in docking bay.

Radar: Search; Head Net C.
Fire control: Owl Screech, (76 mm); Bass Tilt (Gatlings); Pop Group (SA-N-4).
Navigation: Don Kay.
IFF: High Pole.

IVAN ROGOV 1978

IVAN ROGOV 1978

13 "ROPUCHA" CLASS (LST)

Displacement, tons: 3 450 standard; 4 400 full load
Dimensions, feet (metres): 360 × 49·2 × 11·5 *(110 × 14·5 × 3·6)*
Guns: 4—57 mm (twins)
Main engines: 4 diesels; 10 000 shp; 2 shafts
Speed, knots: 18
Complement: 80

"ROPUCHA" Class

Built at Gdansk, Poland at a rate of about three a year. First completed 1975. A "roll-on-roll-off" design.
These ships have a higher troop-to-vehicle ratio than the "Alligator" class and thus the two provide a distant-ocean assault capability hitherto unavailable in the Soviet navy, now much enhanced by the arrival of the "Ivan Rogov" class.

Modification: The thirteenth and last hull has modified superstructure with rounded corners and other slight changes.

Radar: Search: Strut Curve.
Fire control: Muff Cob.
Navigation: Don 2.
IFF: High Pole B.

"ROPUCHA" Class   *7/1977, MOD(N)*

"ROPUCHA" Class   *10/1975, MOD*

550 USSR / Amphibious forces

14 "ALLIGATOR" CLASS (LST)

ALEKSANDR TORTSEV
DONETSKY SHAKHTER
KRASNAYA PRESNYA
KRYMSKY KOMSOMOLETS
NIKOLAI FILCHENKOV
NIKOLAI OBYEKOV
NIKOLAI VILKOV
PETR ILICHEV
SERGEJ LAZO
TOMSKY KOMSOMOLETS
VORONEZHSKY KOMSOMOLETS
50 LET SHEFTSVA VLKSM
+2

Displacement, tons: 3 400 standard; 4 500 full load
Dimensions, feet (metres): 374 × 50·8 × 14·7 *(114 × 15·5 × 4·5)*
Guns: 2—57 mm (twin); 2 rocket launchers; 2 or 4—25 mm (some); mortars (Type III)
Main engines: 2 diesels; 9 000 bhp; 2 shafts = 18 knots
Range, miles: 6 000 at 16 knots
Complement: 100

First ship built in 1965-66 and commissioned in 1966. These ships have ramps on the bow and stern. Carrying capacity 1 700 tons. There are three variations of rig. In earlier type two or three cranes are carried—later types have only one crane. In the third type the bridge structure has been raised and the forward deck house has been considerably lengthened to accommodate 25 mm guns and mortars. These ships operate regularly off West Africa and in the Mediterranean and the Indian Ocean, usually with Naval Infantry units embarked.

Radar: Don and Muff Cob (in some).

KRYMSKY KOMSOMOLETS (Type I) 10/1974, MOD

"ALLIGATOR III" Class

"ALLIGATOR I" Class

"ALLIGATOR" Class (Type II) 1974, USN

"ALLIGATOR" Class 1972

NIKOLAI VILKOV (Type III) (Hull 14) 4/1976, MOD

"ALLIGATOR" Class (Type II) 4/1973, USN

60 "POLNOCHNIY" CLASS (LCT)

Displacement, tons: Group A: 780 standard; 950 full load
Group B: 890 standard; 1 050 full load
Group C: 700 standard; 920 full load
Group D: 1 000 standard; 1 250 full load
Dimensions, feet (metres): Group A: 239·5 × 29·2 × 5·8 *(73 × 8·9 × 1·8)*
Groups B and C: 249·3 × 29·2 × 5·8 *(76 × 8·9 × 1·8)*
Group D: 269 × 32·8 × 5·8 *(82 × 10 × 1·8)*
Guns: Group A: 2—14·5 mm or 2—25 mm or 2—30 mm; 2—140 mm rocket launchers
Group B: 2 or 4—30 mm (twins); 2—140 mm rocket launchers
Groups C and D: 4—30 mm (twin); 2—140 mm rocket launchers
Main engines: 2 diesels; 5 000 shp = 18 knots (20 Group C)
Complement: 40

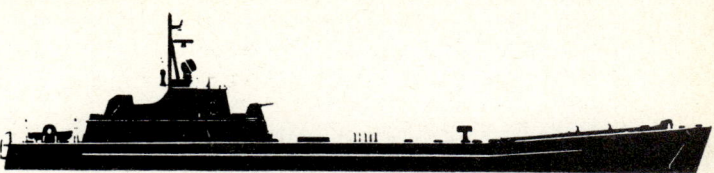
"POLNOCHNIY" Class (Group B)

Carrying capacity 350 tons. Can carry six tanks. Up to nine types of this class have been built. In I to IV the mast and funnel are combined—in V onwards the mast is stepped on the bridge—in VI to VIII there is a redesign of the bow-form—IX is a completely new design of greater length with corresponding increase in tonnage. For convenience these have been put into four groups in the data sections.

Missiles: Some reported with SA-7 Grail.

Radar: Group A: Drum Tilt in some; Don 2 or Spin Trough.
Group B: Drum Tilt; Don 2 or Spin Trough.
Groups C and D: Drum Tilt and Don 2.

Transfers: One to Algeria, six to Egypt, six to India, two to Iraq, three to Libya, one to Somalia, two to South Yemen.

"POLNOCHNIY" Class (Group C)   1974, S. Breyer

"POLNOCHNIY" Class (Group A) with 2—30 mm before bridge

"POLNOCHNIY" Class (Type IX Group D)   1973, USN

10 "MP 4" CLASS (LCTs)

Displacement, tons: 620 standard; 780 full load
Dimensions, feet (metres): 183·7 × 26·2 × 8·9 *(56 × 8 × 2·7)*
Guns: 4—25 mm (2 twin)
Main engine: 1 diesel; 1 100 bhp = 10 knots
Complement: 50

Built in 1956-58. Of the small freighter type in appearance. Two masts, one abaft the bridge and one in the waist. Gun mountings on poop and forecastle. Can carry six to eight tanks. Several ships now serve as transports—remainder in reserve.

Deletions: The other "MP" classes—MP 2, 6, 8 and 10—are now reported as deleted, although some may be used as transports.

Radar: Don.

"MP 4" Class   1973, J. Rowe

25 "VYDRA" CLASS (LCU)

Displacement, tons: 425 standard; 600 full load
Dimensions, feet (metres): 179·7 × 26·6 × 6·6 *(54·8 × 8·1 × 2)*
Main engines: 2 diesels; 2 shafts; 800 hp = 11 knots

Built from 1967-69. No armament. Carrying capacity 250 tons. Fifteen active, ten in reserve.

Transfers: Ten to Bulgaria, ten to Egypt.

"VYDRA" Class   1971

36 "SMB 1" CLASS (LCU)

Displacement, tons: 180 standard; 360 full load
Dimensions, feet (metres): 157·4 × 19·6 × 6·6 *(48 × 6 × 2)*
Main engines: 2 diesels; 600 hp = 10 knots
Complement: 16

Built in 1960-65. Capacity 180 tons. Thirty in reserve.

"SMB 1" Class   1971

552 USSR / Air cushion vehicles

AIR CUSHION VEHICLES

(Fuller details appear in the latest *Jane's Surface Skimmers*).

8 "AIST" CLASS

| 525 | 527 | 529 | +5 |

Operating weight: 220 tons
Dimensions, feet (metres): 150 × 60 *(45·7 × 18·3)*
Guns: 4—30 mm (twin)
Main engines: 2 gas turbines driving four axial lift fans and four propeller units for propulsion
Speed, knots: 70 approx

Currently in production at Leningrad for Naval Infantry. Is the first large Soviet hovercraft for naval use. Similar to British SR.N4.

"AIST" Class (prototype)

"AIST" Class

33 "GUS" CLASS

| 715 | 732 | +31 |

Operating weight: 27 tons
Dimensions, feet (metres): 70 × 24 *(21·4 × 7·3)*
Propulsion: 2—780 hp marine gas turbines (vp and reversible propellers)
Lift: 1—780 hp marine gas turbine
Speed, knots: 58
Range, miles: 230 cruising

This is a naval version of a 50-seat passenger carrying design *(Skate)*. In production for Naval Infantry. Deployed to all four fleets.

"GUS" Class

11 "LEBED" CLASS

Operating weight: 15 tons
Dimensions, feet (metres): 70 × 30 *(21·4 × 9·2)*
Propulsion: 2—350 hp aircraft radial engines
Lift: 1—350 hp aircraft radial with centrifugal fan
Speed, knots: 50

In use in the Soviet Navy since 1967 for tests and evaluation.

"LEBED" Class

EKRANOPLAN CRAFT (WIG)

Dimensions, feet (metres): 400 × 125 (approx wing span) *(122 × 38)*
Propulsion: 10 gas turbines
Speed, knots: 300 approx

An experimental craft, a wing-in-ground-effect machine, with a carrying capacity of about 900 troops and with potential for a number of naval applications such as ASW, minesweeping or patrol. Claimed to be capable of operations in heavy weather as well as crossing marshes, ice and low obstacles. Several other prototypes of unknown characteristics exist.
On take-off the forward engines are temporarily angled down with propulsion from the after pair.

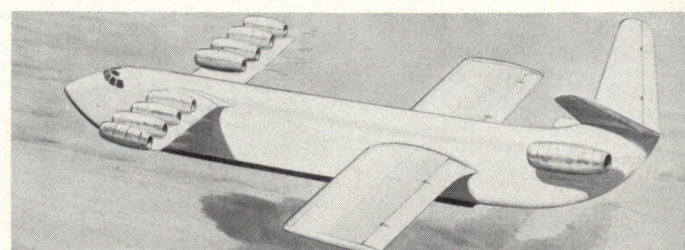

EKRANOPLAN   *Jane's Surface Skimm*

SUPPORT AND DEPOT SHIPS

7 "UGRA" CLASS (SUBMARINE DEPOT SHIPS); 2 (TRAINING SHIPS)

BORODINO*
GANGUT*
IVAN KOLYSHKIN
IVAN KUCHERENKO
IVAN VADREMEEV
TOBOL
VOLGA
+2
*Training

Displacement, tons: 6 750 standard; 9 000 full load
Length, feet (metres): 452·6 *(141)*
Beam, feet (metres): 57·6 *(17·6)*
Draught, feet (metres): 19·8 *(6·0)*
Aircraft: 1 helicopter
Guns: 8—57 mm (twins)
Main engines: 4 diesels; 2 shafts; 14 000 bhp = 20 knots
Range, miles: 10 000 at 12 knots
Complement: 300

Improved versions of the "Don" class. Built from 1961 onwards, all in Nikolayev. Equipped with workshops. Provided with a helicopter platform and, in later versions, a hangar. Has mooring points in hull about 100 ft apart, and has baggage ports possibly for coastal craft and submarines. The last pair of this class *(Borodino* and *Gangut)* mount a large superstructure from the mainmast to quarter-deck and are used for training. Built at Nikolayev from 1962 to 1972.

Aerials: *Volga* and some others have lattice mainmast with Vee-cone HF aerial.

Cranes: No bow lift. Two 10 ton and two 5 ton cranes.

Radar: Search: Strut Curve.
Fire control: Muff Cob.
Navigation: Don 2.
IFF: Square Head and High Pole A.

"UGRA" Class Training Ship

Transfer: A tenth ship, *Amba*, which had four 76 mm guns, was transferred to India.

"UGRA" Class   5/1974, MOD

6 "DON" CLASS (SUBMARINE SUPPORT)

NIKOLAY STOLBOV
DMITRI GALKIN
FEDOR VIDYAEV
KAMCHATSKY KOMSOMOLETS (ex-*Mikhail Tukhachevsky*)
MAGOMED GADZHIEV
VIKTOR KOTELNIKOV

Displacement, tons: 6 800 standard; 9 000 full load
Length, feet (metres): 449·2 *(137)*
Beam, feet (metres): 54·1 *(16·5)*
Draught, feet (metres): 22·3 *(6·8)*
Aircraft: Provision for helicopter in two ships
Guns: 4—3·9 in *(100 mm)*; 8—57 mm (4 twins) (see notes)
Main engines: 4 diesels; 14 000 bhp; 2 shafts
Speed, knots: 21
Range, miles: 10 000 at 12 knots
Complement: 300

"DON" Class

Support ships, all named after officers lost in World War II. Built in 1957 to 1962. Originally seven ships were built, all in Nikolayev. Quarters for about 450 submariners.

Aerials: Some have lattice mainmast with Vee-Cone HF aerials.

Aircraft: In *Viktor Kotelnikov* and possibly one other Y-gun has been removed to provide space for a helicopter platform.

Communications: Vee Cone fitted in three ships for long range communications.

Cranes: Have a 100 ton bow lift and two 10 ton cranes and two 5 ton.

Gunnery: In *Fedor Vidyaev* only two 3·9 in. In *K. Komsomolets* no 3·9 in mounted. In two of class 8—25 mm (twin) are mounted.

Radar: Search: Slim Net; probably Strut Curve in some.
Fire control: Sun Visor; Hawk Screech.
Navigation: Neptun.
IFF: Square Head and High Pole.

Transfers: One to Indonesia in 1962.

FEDOR VIDYAEV with Vee-Cone HF aerial on mainmast   1977, MOD

554 USSR / Support and depot ships

5 "DNEPR" CLASS (SUBMARINE TENDERS)

Displacement, tons: 4 500 standard; 6 000 full load
Dimensions, feet (metres): 370·7 × 54·1 × 14·4 (113 × 16·5 × 4·4)
Main engine: 1 diesel; 2 000 bhp = 11 knots
Range, miles: 6 000 at 8 knots
Complement: 380

Bow lift repair ships for S/M support and maintenance. Built in 1960-64 at Nikolayev and equipped with workshops and servicing facilities. The last two ships of this class with flush-decked hull form the "Dnepr II" Class. All unarmed.

Radar: Navigation: Don or Don 2.

"DNEPR II" Class   1978

6 "LAMA" CLASS (MISSILE SUPPORT)

Displacement, tons: 4 500 standard; 6 000 full load
Dimensions, feet (metres): 370 × 49·2 × 13·7 (112·8 × 15 × 4·4)
Guns: 8—57 mm, (2 quad, 1 on the forecastle; 1 on the break of the quarter deck) (in 2 ships);
4—57 mm (quad) (in one ship);
2—57 mm; 4—25 mm (in two ships);
2—57 mm (in one ship)
Main engines: 2 diesels; 2 shafts; 5 000 shp
Speed, knots: 15
Complement: 250

Built between 1963 and 1972.
The engines are sited aft to allow for a very large and high hangar or hold amidships for carrying missiles or weapons' spares for submarines, surface ships and missile craft. This is about 12 ft high above the main deck. There are doors at the forward end with rails leading in and a raised turntable gantry or 20 ton travelling cranes for armament supply.
There are mooring points along the hull for ships of low freeboard such as submarines to come alongside. The well deck is about 40 ft long, enough for most missiles to fit horizontally before being lifted for loading.
There are several differences in midships superstructure in these ships.

Radar: Search: Slim Net or Strut Curve.
Fire control: Hawk Screech (2), or Muff Cob. Various combinations in different ships.
Navigation: Don 2.
IFF: Square Head and High Pole.

"LAMA" Class   1978

4 "AMGA" CLASS (MISSILE SUPPORT)

AMGA   VETLUGA   +2

Displacement, tons: 4 800 standard; 5 800 full load
Dimensions, feet (metres): 334·5 × 59 × 14·2 (102 × 18 × 4·4)
Guns: 4—25 mm (twins)
Main engines: Diesels; 9 000 hp = 16 knots
Complement: 210

Ships of similar size and duties to the "Lama" class. May be distinguished from those ships by the break at the bridge, giving a lower freeboard than that of the "Lamas". Fitted with a large 50 ton crane forward and thus capable of handling much larger missiles than their predecessors. Probably, therefore, designed for servicing submarines, particularly those armed with SS-N-8 missiles and others of equal size. First appeared in December 1972 and the second in 1976.

Radar: Search: Strut Curve.
Navigation: Don.

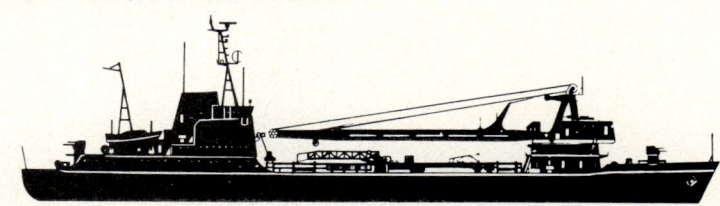
"AMGA" Class

"AMGA" Class   1976

18 + ? "AMUR" CLASS (REPAIR SHIPS)

Displacement, tons: 5 000 standard; 6 400 full load
Dimensions, feet (metres): 377·3 × 57·4 × 18·0 (115 × 17·5 × 5·5)
Main engines: 2 diesels; 10 000 shp; 1 shaft = 18 knots
Complement: 150

General purpose depot ships built since 1968 in Szeczin, Poland. Successors to the "Oskol" class.

Radar: Navigation: Don 2.

"AMUR" Class

"AMUR" Class   1978, Selçuk Emre

"AMUR" Class   1978

USSR / Support and depot ships 555

12 "OSKOL" CLASS (REPAIR SHIPS)

Displacement, tons: 2 500 standard; 3 000 full load
Dimensions, feet (metres): 295·2 × 39·4 × 14·8 *(90 × 12 × 4·5)*
Guns: (See notes)
Main engines: 2 diesels; 2 shafts; speed = 16 knots
Complement: 100

Three series: "Oskol I" class, well-decked hull, no armament; "Oskol II" class, well-decked hull, armed with two 57 mm guns (1 twin) and four 25 mm guns (two twins); "Oskol III" class, flush-decked hull. No armament. General purpose tenders and repair ships. Built from 1963 to 1970 in Poland.

Radar: Fire control: Muff Cob (In "II").
Navigation: Don.

"OSKOL" Class

"OSKOL" Class   1978, Selçuk Emre

"OSKOL" Class   1975

4 "TOMBA" CLASS (SUBMARINE SUPPORT SHIPS)

Displacement, tons: 3 500 standard; 4 900 full load
Dimensions, feet (metres): 316·5 × 50·8 × 16·4 *(96·5 × 15·5 × 5)*
Main engine: 1 diesel; 6 000 shp; 1 shaft = 18 knots
Complement: 180

First completed 1974. Deployed in Northern Fleet and Pacific. After funnel serves propulsion diesel, forefunnel serves the auxiliaries, donkey funnel on f'c's'le. Two 3 ton cranes. In series production.

Radar: Navigation: Don 2.
IFF: High Pole.

"TOMBA" Class

"TOMBA" Class   6/1978, Gerhard Koop

2 "MOD ANDIZHAN" CLASS (SUPPORT SHIPS)

GENUTA   VILYUI

Displacement, tons: 3 500 standard; 4 500 full load
Dimensions, feet (metres): 341·1 × 47·2 × 16·4 *(104 × 14·4 × 5)*
Main engine: 1 diesel; 2 000 shp = 13 knots
Range, miles: 6 000 at 13 knots
Complement: 98

Cargo ships built in late 1950s. Converted to support ships 1974-75. Have one main crane forward, two smaller cranes aft and a helicopter platform.

Radar: Navigation: Don 2.
IFF: Square Head and High Pole.

"MOD ANDIZHAN" Class

INTELLIGENCE COLLECTORS (AGIs)

6 "PRIMORYE" CLASS

PRIMORYE	KRYM	ZAPOROZHIYE
KAVKAZ	ZABAIKALYE	ZAKARPATYE

Displacement, tons: 3 400 standard; 4 500 full load
Dimensions, feet (metres): 274 × 45 × 26·2 (83·6 × 13·7 × 8)
Main engines: 2 diesels; 4 000 shp = 12 knots
Complement: 120

The most modern intelligence collectors in the world, apparently with built-in processing and possibly, analysis capability. Built to the same hull design as the "Mayakovsky" class of stern trawlers.

ZAKARPATYE

2 "NIKOLAI ZUBOV" CLASS

GAVRIL SARYCHEV   KHARITON LAPTEV

Displacement, tons: 2 674 standard; 3 021 full load
Dimensions, feet (metres): 295·2 × 42·7 × 15 (90 × 13 × 4·6)
Main engines: 2 diesels; 5 300 shp; 2 shafts = 18 knots
Range, miles: 11 000 at 14 knots
Complement: 50

Built in Poland. Similar class operate as Survey Ships.

GAVRIL SARYCHEV   1973, Michael D. J. Ler

2 "PAMIR" CLASS

GIDROGRAF   PELENG

Displacement, tons: 1 443 standard; 2 240 full load
Dimensions, feet (metres): 256 × 42 × 13·5 (78 × 12·8 × 4·1)
Main engines: 2—4 stroke diesels; 2 shafts; 4 200 bhp = 17 knots
Range, miles: 21 000 at 12 knots
Complement: 72

Built in Sweden 1959-60. Originally salvage tugs and have higher deckhouse abaft bridge than other ships of class.

PELENG   4/1970,

6 "MOMA" CLASS

ARKHIPELAG	NAKHODKA
ILMEN	PELORUS
YUPITER	SELIGER

Displacement, tons: 1 240 standard; 1 550 full load
Dimensions, feet (metres): 219·8 × 34·4 × 13·1 (67 × 10·5 × 4)
Main engines: 2 Skoda diesels; 3 600 hp; 2 shafts = 16 knots

The modernised version (*Arkhipelag* and *Yupiter*) has a new foremast in the fore well-deck and a new, low superstructure before the bridge. Similar class operate as Survey Ships.

YUPITER   1976, Commander Aldo Fracc

4 "MIRNY" CLASS

BAKAN   VAL
LOTSMAN   VERTIKAL

Displacement, tons: 850 standard; 1 200 full load
Dimensions, feet (metres): 208 × 31·2 × 13·8 (63·4 × 9·5 × 4·2)
Main engines: Diesel-electric; 4 diesels; 3 100 hp; 1 shaft = 18 knots
Range, miles: 18 700 at 11 knots
Complement: 31

Converted from whale-catchers in 1965.

"MIRNY" Class   1978, H. W. van Bo

USSR / Intelligence collectors 557

8 "MAYAK" CLASS

EROID	KURSOGRAF
ORULEVOY	LADOGA
ERSONES	GS 239
RS	GS 242

Displacement, tons: 1 050 full load
Dimensions, feet (metres): 178 × 30·6 × 11·8 *(54·3 × 9·3 × 3·6)*
Main engine: 1 diesel; 1 shaft; 800 hp = 12 knots
Complement: 29

Built in USSR from 1967. Advance on "Okean" class.

KHERSONES   1978

15 "OKEAN" CLASS

DADA	EKHOLOT	REDUKTOR
PERMETR	GIDROFON	REPITER
ROGRAF	KRENOMETR	TEODOLIT
ROMETR	LINZA	TRAVERZ
FLEKTOR	LOTLIN	ZOND

Displacement, tons: 720 full load
Dimensions, feet (metres): 167·3 × 28·9 × 12·1 *(51 × 8·8 × 3·7)*
Main engine: Diesel; 1 shaft; 540 hp = 11 knots
Range, miles: 7 500 at 10 knots
Complement: 32

Built in USSR 1965. Have the same variations in the superstructure with the port side closed in and the starboard side open as in the "Mayak" class, although there are many variations.

ZOND (Modified "OKEAN" Class)   1977

8 "LENTRA" CLASS

MA	KASHA	UFA
LAS	RUZA	UGRA
LGOTA		+1

Displacement, tons: 250 standard; 261 full load
Dimensions, feet (metres): 128·6 × 24·3 × 11·2 *(39·2 × 7·4 × 3·4)*
Main engine: 1 diesel; 400 hp = 10·5 knots
Range, miles: 6 900 at 9 knots

Built in USSR and East Germany 1957-63. Mainly employed in-area.

KASHA   MOD

2 "DNEPR" CLASS

| ERITEL | PROTRAKTOR |

Displacement, tons: 430 standard; 500 full load
Dimensions, feet (metres): 150 × 30 × 8 *(45·8 × 9·2 × 2·4)*
Main engines: 2 Burmeister and Wain diesels; 1 shaft; 1 250 shp = 11 knots
Complement: 70?

Ex Tuna-fishing ships built in Japan. Similar class name to depot ships.
Appearance differs from other AGIs in having the funnel widely separated from the bridge which is block-shaped with an inclined cat-walk up the side.

2 "DALDYN" CLASS

Displacement, tons: 260
Dimensions, feet (metres): 103·6 × 24·3 × 8·4 *(31·7 × 7·3 × 2·8)*
Main engine: 1 diesel; 1 300 shp = 9 knots
Complement: 13

First seen in May 1973. Of "Kareliya" class trawler design with a high bridge.

DALDYN   1973

558　USSR / Naval survey ships

NAVAL SURVEY SHIPS

Note: Two converted "Zulu V" class submarines *Lira* and *Vega* are employed on oceanographical research.

9 "NIKOLAI ZUBOV" CLASS

A. CHIRIKOV	F. LITKE	SEMYEN DEZHNEV
A. VILKITSKY	NIKOLAI ZUBOV	T. BELLINSGAUSEN
BORIS DAVIDOV	S. CHELYUSKIN	V. GOLOVNIN

Displacement, tons: 2 674 standard; 3 021 full load
Dimensions, feet (metres): 295·2 × 42·7 × 15 *(90 × 13 × 4·6)*
Main engines: 2 diesels; 5 280 shp; 2 shafts = 18 knots
Range, miles: 11 000 at 14 knots
Complement: 50

Oceanographic research ships built at Szczecin Shipyard, Poland in 1964. Also employed on navigational, sonar and radar trials. Have nine laboratories and small deck aft for hydromet-balloon work. Carry two to four survey launches.

SEMYEN DEZHNEV　　　　　　　　　　　　　197

"NIKOLAI ZUBOV" Class

23 "MOMA" CLASS (+6 AGIs)

ALTAIR	ASKOLD	KRILON	
ANADIR	BEREZAN	KOLGUEV	RYBACHI
ANDROMEDA	CHELEKEN	LIMAN	SEVER
ANTARES	EKVATOR	MARS	TAYMYR
ANTARKTYDA	ELTON	MORSOVIETS	VEGA
ARTIKA	KILDIN	OKEAN	ZAPOYLARA

Displacement, tons: 1 240 standard; 1 550 full load
Dimensions, feet (metres): 219·8 × 34·4 × 13·1 *(67 × 10·5 × 4)*
Main engines: 2 Skoda diesels; 3 600 shp; 2 shafts = 16 knots

Eight ships of this class were reported to have been built from 1967 to 1970 and the remainder since. Four laboratories. One survey launch and a 5 ton crane.

Radar: Navigation: Don 2 (2).

"MOMA" Class　　　　　　　　　　　　　197

"MOMA" Class

ASKOLD　　　　　　　　　　　　　197

5 "TELNOVSK" CLASS

AYTODOR	SIRENA	STVOR	SVIYAGA	ULYANA GROMOVA

Displacement, tons: 1 200 standard; 1 700 full load
Dimensions, feet (metres): 229·6 × 32·8 × 13·1 *(70 × 10 × 4)*
Main engines: 4 diesels; 1 600 shp = 10 knots
Complement: 50

Formerly coastal freighters. Built in Hungary in 1950s. Refitted and modernised for naval supply and surveying duties. *Stvor* has additional accommodation forward of the bridge and a gantry foremast. One survey launch.

AYTODOR　　　　　　　　　1974, Michael D. J. Lenno

USSR / Naval survey ships   559

15 "SAMARA" CLASS

ZIMUT	GRADUS	TROPIK
EVIATOR	KOLESNIKOV	VAGACH
IGROMETR	KOMPAS	VOSTOK
LUBOMER	PAMYAT MERKURYIA	YUG
ORIZONT	RUMB	ZENIT

Displacement, tons: 800 standard; 1 200 full load
Measurement, tons: 1 276 gross; 1 000 net
Dimensions, feet (metres): 198 × 36·3 × 10·8 (58 × 10·5 × 3·8)
Main engines: 2 Skoda diesels; 3 000 hp; 2 shafts = 15 knots
Range, miles: 6 200 at 11 knots
Complement: 45

Built at Gdansk, Poland 1962-64 for hydrographic surveying and research. Have laboratories and one survey launch. 5 ton crane.

Radar: Don 2.

KOMPAS   5/1977, MOD

12 "BIYA" CLASS

GS 193, 194, 198, 202, 204, 271, 273, 275 +4

Displacement, tons: 750 standard; 1 000 full load
Dimensions, feet (metres): 229·6 × 32·8 × 11·5 (70 × 10 × 3·5)
Main engines: 2 diesels = 16 knots
Range, miles: 4 700+ at 11 knots

With laboratory and one survey launch. Built in Poland 1972-77.

Radar: Don 2.

"BIYA" Class   1976

10 "KAMENKA" CLASS

ELBEK, SIMA, WIERNIER, GS 66, 74, 107, 108, 203, 207 +1

Displacement, tons: 650 standard; 1 000 full load
Dimensions, feet (metres): 180·5 × 31·2 × 11·5 (55·1 × 9·5 × 3·5)
Main engines: 2 diesels; 3 000 shp = 16 knots

Built in Poland 1968-72. 5 ton crane forward.

Radar: Don 2.

"KAMENKA" Class   1974, MOD

10 "LENTRA" CLASS (+8 AGIs)

ISBERG, GIDROSAT, GROT, POLYARNIK, TAIFUN, GS 1, GS 2, GS 54, RKS 4 +1

Displacement, tons: 261 full load
Dimensions, feet (metres): 128·6 × 24·3 × 11·2 (39·2 × 7·4 × 3·4)
Main engine: 1 diesel; 400 hp = 10·5 knots

"LENTRA" Class   MOD

CIVILIAN MANNED SURVEY SHIPS

3 "ONEGA" CLASS

Displacement, tons: 2 150 standard; 2 500 full load
Dimensions, feet (metres): 282·1 × 34·4 × 18 *(86 × 10·5 × 5·5)*
Main engines: Gas turbines = 20 knots
Complement: 45

First seen in September 1973. A heavy looking ship with a high foc's'le running to the mainmast which is alongside the funnel. A low bridge with a high trunked foremast. Helicopter platform but no hangar. Pennant numbers GKS. Probably used as sound research ships. May be naval manned.

18 "DMITRI OVSTYN" CLASS

A. SMIRNOV	PROFESSOR BOGOROV
DMITRI LAPTEV	PROFESSOR KURENTSOV
DMITRI OVSTYN	PROFESSOR VODNANITSKY
DMITRI STERLEGOV	S. KRAKOV*
E. TOLL	STEFAN MALYGIN
FEDOR MATISEN	VALERIAN ALBANOV
IVAN KIREYEV	V. SUKHOTSKY*
N. KOLOMEYTSEV	YAKOV SMIRNITSKY
N. YEVGENOV*	
PAVEL BASHMAKOV	

Displacement, tons: 1 800 full load
Dimensions, feet (metres): 220 × 39 × 15 *(67·1 × 11·9 × 4·6)*
Main engine: 1—6-cyl Deutz diesel; 2 200 bhp = 16 knots
Complement: 52 (including 20 scientists)

Built by Abo at Laivateollisuus, Finland except *P. Bogorov* at Turku, Finland. Fitted with bow thruster and eight laboratories. Employed largely on geological research oceanographic work and survey in the Arctic. Those marked *, completed January-August 1974. *P. Bogorov* launched 11 October 1975, *P. Kurentsov* 17 December 1975, *Professor Vodnanitsky* 3 March 1976, *Fedor Matisen* 6 May 1976, *Paval Bashmakov* 10 December 1976, *Yakov Smirnitsky* 14 February 1977. Last ship, *Ivan Kireyev,* completed 3 November 1977. Average time from launch to completion, seven months.
Owned by Ministry of Merchant Marine.

DMITRI OVSTYN 1974

3 "VALERIAN URYVAEV" CLASS

VALERIAN URYVAEV VSEVOLOD BERYOZKIN YAKOV GAKKEL

Measurement, tons: 350 deadweight; 697 gross; 85 net
Dimensions, feet (metres): 180·1 × 31·2 × 13·1 *(54·9 × 9·5 × 4)*
Main engine: 1 Deutz diesel; 850 bhp = 12 knots

Built at Khabarovsk—1974, *V. Uryvaev;* 1975, other two.
Hydromet ships based at Sakhalin *(V. Uryvaev)*, Murmansk *(V. Beryozkin)*, Odessa *(Y. Gakkel)*. Reports of another and larger ship ordered from Abo, Laivateollisuus, Finland on 26 January 1977 and laid down 30 November 1977 must refer to a single ship of another unknown class.

YAKOV GAKKEL 9/1977, Giorgio Ghiglione

1 "KOLOMNA" CLASS

MIKHAIL LOMONOSOV

Displacement, tons: 5 960 normal
Measurement, tons: 3 897 gross; 1 195 net
Dimensions, feet (metres): 336·0 × 47·2 × 14·0 *(102·5 × 14·4 × 4·3)*
Main engine: 1—4-cyl Liebknecht triple-expansion; 2 450 ihp = 13 knots

Built by Neptun, Rostock, in 1957 from the hull of a freighter of the "Kolomna" class. Operated for the Academy of Sciences by Ukraine Institute of Oceanology, Black Sea. Equipped with 16 laboratories. Carries a helicopter for survey. Civilian manned.

MIKHAIL LOMONOSOV 1970, Michael D. J. Lennon

5 "AKADEMIK L. ORBELI" CLASS

AKADEMIK KOVALEVSKY	AKADEMIK VAVILOV	
AKADEMIK L. ORBELI	PERVENETS	+1

Measurement, tons: 284 gross *(Vavilov 255)*
Dimensions, feet (metres): 126·8 × 23·7 × 11·5 *(38·1 × 7·2 × 3·5);*
 (Vavilov 119·7 × 24·1 × 11·5 *(36·5 × 7·4 × 3·5)*
Main engine: 1 diesel = 10 knots

Built in East Germany in 1949. Oceanographic ships run by Academy of Sciences.

AKADEMIK KOVALEVSKY 1974, Michael D. J. Lennon

3 "MELITOPOL" CLASS

MAYAK, NIVELIR, PRIZMA

Displacement, tons: 775 full load
Dimensions, feet (metres): 189 × 29.5 × 14.1 *(57.6 × 9 × 4.3)*
Main engines: 2 diesels; 2 000 hp = 10 knots
Complement: 21

Built in USSR 1952-55. May be naval manned.

AKADEMIK ARKHANGELSKY   YURIJ GODIN

Measurement, tons: 416 tons gross
Dimensions, feet (metres): 132.9 × 25 × 13 *(40.5 × 7.6 × 4)*
Main engine: 1 diesel = 10 knots

Built in USSR in 1963.

AKADEMIK ARKHANGELSKY   *1974, Michael D. J. Lennon*

MGLA

Measurement, tons: 299 gross
Dimensions, feet (metres): 129.5 × 24.3 × 11.8 *(39.5 × 7.4 × 3.6)*
Main engine: 1 diesel = 8.5 knots

Hydromet research ship.

MGLA   *1974, Michael D. J. Lennon*

ZARYA

Measurement, tons: 333 gross; 71 net

Built in 1952 for geomagnetic survey work. Run by Academy of Sciences.

ZARYA   *1972, Michael D. J. Lennon*

NEREY   NOVATOR

Measurement, tons: 369 gross
Dimensions, feet (metres): 118.1 × 24.7 × 11.5 *(36 × 7.5 × 3.5)*
Main engines: 2 diesels = 11 knots

Built in USSR in 1956 and 1955. Originally fleet tugs. Converted for seismic research. Run by Academy of Sciences.

NEREY   *9/1978, Reinhard Nerlich*

USSR / Civilian manned survey ships — Naval research ships

PETRODVORETS (ex-*Bore II*)

Measurement, tons: 1 965 gross; 985 net
Dimensions, feet (metres): 254·2 × 39·4 × 24·9 *(77·5 × 12 × 7·6)*
Main engine: Diesel = 13·5 knots

Built at Abo, Finland for Finnish owners in 1938. Sold to USSR in 1950 and renamed.

ZVEZDA

Measurement, tons: 348 gross
Dimensions, feet (metres): 129 × 24·2 × 11·4 *(39·3 × 7·4 × 3·5)*
Main engine: Diesel = 10 knots

Built in East Germany in 1957. Carries winches in the chains on the quarters. Sister ships *Zarnitsa* and *Yug* are used for transporting crews to ships building outside the USSR.

ZVEZDA 1974, Ian Brooke

NAVAL RESEARCH SHIPS

8 "VYTEGRALES" CLASS

APSHERON (ex-*Tosnoles*)	DONBASS (ex-*Kirishi*)
BASKUNCHAK (ex-*Vostok 4*)	SEVAN (ex-*Vyborgles*)
DAURIYA (ex-*Suzdal*)	TAMAN (ex-*Vostok 3*)
DIKSON (ex-*Vagales*)	YAMAL (ex-*Svirles*)

Displacement, tons: 4 900 standard; 5 970 full load
Dimensions, feet (metres): 400·3 × 55·1 × 22·3 *(122·1 × 16·8 × 6·8)*
Main engine: One Burmester and Wain diesel; 5 200 hp; 1 shaft = 16 knots
Complement: 46

Standard timber carriers of a class of 27. These eight ships were modified with helicopter flight deck. Built at Zhdanov Yard, Leningrad between 1963 and 1966. Used as missile range ships.

Class name: The first of class, completed in 1962, was originally *Vytegrales,* but this was later changed to *Kosmonaut Pavel Belyayev* and remains a merchant ship. Since these eight and the four others of the same class (but civilian manned) have been taken over for scientific work they have been variously, but incorrectly, called "Vostok", "Baskunchak" etc.

TAMAN 1978, Selcuk Emre

Communications: 2 Vee Cone.

Radar: Don 2 (2).

5 "AKADEMIK KRILOV" CLASS

ADMIRAL VLADIMIRSKY	IVAN KRUZENSTERN	LEONID DYMEEN
AKADEMIK KRILOV	LEONID SOBOLEV	

Displacement, tons: 9 100
Dimensions, feet (metres): 469·1 × 60·7 × 20·3 *(143 × 18·5 × 6·2)*
Main engines: Diesels = 15 knots

A new class of research ships, the fifth built in Stettin.

Radar: Don 2 (2).

"AKADEMIK KRILOV" Class

AKADEMIK KRILOV 7/1976, MOD

4 "ABKHAZIYA" CLASS

ABKHAZIYA	ADZHARIYA	BASHKIRIYA	MOLDAVYA

Displacement, tons: 7 000 full load
Dimensions, feet (metres): 409·2 × 56 × 21·1 *(124·8 × 17·1 × 6·4)*
Aircraft: 1 helicopter
Main engines: 2 MAN diesels; 8 000 bhp = 18·2 knots
Range, miles: 20 000 at 15 knots
Endurance: 60 days

Built by Mathias Thesen Werft at Wismar. Fitted with helicopter platform and hangar aft. Naval manned. Completed; 1971, *Abkhaziya,* 1972, *Adzhariya,* 1973, other two. Some are hydromet reporting ships. Fitted with two bow thrusters.

"ABKHAZIYA" Class

BASHKIRIYA 1/1974

3 "POLYUS" CLASS ("KOVEL" TYPE)

BAIKAL   BALKHASH   POLYUS

Displacement, tons: 6 900 standard
Measurement, tons: 3 897 gross; 1 195 net
Dimensions, feet (metres): 365·8 × 46·2 × 20·7 *(111·6 × 14·1 × 6·3)*
Main engines: Diesel-electric; 1 shaft; 4 000 bhp = 13·5 knots

These ships are a part of the "Andizhan" class of some 45 ships. They were converted whilst building by Schiffswerft Neptun of Rostock. *Polyus* in 1962 and the other two in 1964. Oceanographic research ships.

POLYUS   1970

1 "NEVELSKOY" CLASS

NEVELSKOY

Displacement, tons: 2 350
Dimensions, feet (metres): 272·3 × 49·2 × 11·5 *(83 × 15 × 3·5)*
Main engine: 1 diesel; 2 000 hp = 18 knots
Complement: 45

Was predecessor to "Zubov" class. Serves in the Pacific.

NEVELSKOY   1978, Michael D. J. Lennon

3 "MODIFIED SUSANIN" CLASS

GEORGY SEDOV   PETR PAKHTUSOV   VLADIMIR KAVRAYSKY

Displacement, tons: 2 800 full load
Dimensions, feet (metres): 223·1 × 59·1 × 18·1 *(68 × 18 × 5·5)*
Main engines: 3 shafts = 13·8 knots

Part of a numerous class of icebreakers built at Leningrad in the early 1960s—converted for polar research in 1972 under Ministry of Shipping. First two may be civilian manned.

VLADIMIR KAVRAYSKY   5/1975, MOD

USSR / Civilian research ships

CIVILIAN RESEARCH SHIPS

Note: There are some 180 ships ranging downwards from 3 200 tons engaged on Fishery Research worldwide. The larger ships are of the "Mayakovsky", "Tropik", "Atlantik", "Leskov" and "Luchecorsk" classes of 3 200-2 400 tons. Two of the "Mayakovsky" class carry submersibles.

MIKHAIL SOMOV

Displacement, tons: 7 000

Operates under Arctic and Antarctic Research Institute for research duties and Antarctic support.

7 "AKADEMIK KURCHATOV" CLASS

AKADEMIK KOROLEV	DMITRI MENDELEYEV
AKADEMIK KURCHATOV	PROFESSOR ZUBOV
AKADEMIK SHIRSHOV	PROFESSOR VIZE
AKADEMIK VERNADSKY	

Displacement, tons: 6 681 full load
Measurement, tons: 1 986 deadweight; 5 460 gross; 1 387 net
Dimensions, feet (metres): 400·3 to 406·8 × 56·1 × 15·0 *(122·1 to 124·1 × 17·1 × 4·6)*
Main engines: 2 Halberstadt 6-cyl diesels; 2 shafts; 8 000 bhp = 18 to 20 knots

All built by Mathias Thesen Werft at Wismar, East Germany between 1966 and 1968. All have a hull of the same design as the "Mikhail Kalinin" class of merchant vessels. There are variations in mast and aerial rig. *Professor Vize* is similar to *A. Shirshov* whilst *A. Kurchatov*, *A. Vernadsky* and *D. Mendeleyev* are the same. Two bow thrusters.

Duties: Hydromet (Vladivostock): *A. Korolev, A. Shirshov*.
Inst. Oceanology (Baltic): *A. Kurchatov*.
Inst. Oceanology (Vladivostock): *D. Mendeleyev*.
Ukraine Inst. Oceanology: *A. Vernadsky*.
Hydromet (Baltic): *P. Vize, P. Zubov*.

AKADEMIK KURCHATOV *1973, Michael D. J. Lennon*

VITYAZ (ex-*Mars*, ex-*Empire Forth*, ex-*Equator*)

Displacement, tons: 5 700 standard
Dimensions, feet (metres): 357·5 × 48·9 × 15·5 *(109 × 14·9 × 4·7)*
Main engines: Diesels; 3 000 bhp = 14·5 knots
Range, miles: 18 400 at 14 knots
Complement: 137 officers and men including 73 scientists

The first post-war Soviet oceanographic research ship. Formerly a German freighter built at Wismar in 1939 which was taken over by the British after World War II, transferred to the USSR in 1949. Renamed on conversion in 1957. Equipped with 13 laboratories. Has now steamed over 2 million miles.
Run for Academy of Sciences by Institute of Oceanology, Vladivostock.

VITYAZ *1972, Michael D. J. Lennon*

IZUMRUD

Measurement, tons: 3 862 gross, 465 net
Dimensions, feet (metres): 326 × 46 × 15·5 *(99·4 × 14 × 4·7)*
Main engines: Diesel-electric; 4 generators; 1 shaft = 13·8 knots

A research ship built in 1970 at Nikolaev. Civilian manned for structural and material tests. Owned by Ministry of Shipping. Operated by Naval Institute of Shipbuilding, Black Sea.

IZUMRUD *1972, Michael D. J. Lennon*

9 "PASSAT" CLASS (B 88 TYPE)

ERNST KRENKEL (ex-*Vikhr*)	OKEAN	PRILIV
GEORGI USHAKOV (ex-*Schkval*)	PASSAT	VIKTOR BUGAEV (ex-*Poriv*)
MUSSON	PRIBOI	VOLNA

Measurement, tons: 3 280 gross; 3 311 *(E. Krenkel, V. Bugaev)*
Dimensions, feet (metres): 319 × 45 × 15·5 *(97·1 × 13·9 × 4·7)*;
328 × 48·5 × 15·5 *(100 × 14·8 × 4·7)* *(E. Krenkel, V. Bugaev)*
Main engines: 2 Sulzer 8-cyl Cegielski diesels; 2 shafts; 4 800 bhp = 16 knots

Hydromet ships built at Szczecin, Poland—1968, *Musson, Passat, Volna*; 1969, *Okean, Priboi*; 1970, *Priliv*; 1971, *G. Ushakov, V. Krenkel, V. Bugaev*.

Duties: Based at:
Vladivostock: *Okean, Priboi, Priliv, Volna, Passat*.
Black Sea: Remainder.

GEORGI USHAKOV *1975, Michael D. J. Lennon*

2 "LEBEDEV" CLASS

PETR LEBEDEV	SERGEI VAVILOV

Measurement, tons: 3 642 gross; 1 164 net
Dimensions, feet (metres): 308·3 × 45·9 × 18·4 *(94 × 14 × 5·6)*
Main engine: 1—6-cyl Sulzer diesel; 2 400 hp = 14 knots

Research vessels with comprehensive equipment and accommodation. Both built by Crichton-Vulcan, Finland in 1954.
Run by Hydroacoustic Institute, Baltic. Civilian manned. Freighter conversions.

Radar: One Neptun.

PETR LEBEDEV

2 "MODIFIED MAYAKOVSKY" CLASS

AKADEMIK VOEYKOV, YURI M. SHOKALSKY

Displacement, tons: 3 000

Operated by Hydromet Service, Vladivostock.

2 "TROPIK" CLASS

KALLISTO   PEGAS

Measurement, tons: 1 200 deadweight; 2 345 gross; 1 100 net
Dimensions, feet (metres): 262 × 43 × ? (79·8 × 13·2 × ?)
Main engines: 2—8-cyl Liebknecht diesels; 2 shafts; 1 660 bhp = 12·5 knots

Operated by Scientific Research Institute, Sakhalin. Modified for geological and biological research. Originally stern-trawler factory ships of the 70 strong class built by Volkswerft, Stralsund, East Germany between 1962 and 1966. Nine others converted for fishery research.

VLADIMIR OBRUCHEV

Measurement, tons: 534 gross
Dimensions, feet (metres): 156·5 × 32·2 × 16·4 (47·7 × 9·8 × 5)
Main engines: 2 diesels; = 11 knots

One of the "Gromovoy" class tugs built in Romania in 1959 and subsequently converted for seismic research duties. Civilian manned.

VLADIMIR OBRUCHEV   1972, Michael D. J. Lennon

NAVAL SPACE ASSOCIATED SHIPS

2 "DESNA" CLASS

CHAZHMA (ex-*Dangara*)   **CHUMIKAN** (ex-*Dolgeschtschelje*)

Displacement, tons: 5 300 light; 14 065 full load
Dimensions, feet (metres): 457·7 × 59·0 × 25·9 (139·6 × 18 × 7·9)
Aircraft: 1 helicopter
Main engines: 2—7-cyl diesels; 5 200 hp = 16 knots

Formerly bulk ore-carriers of the "Dshankoy" class (7 265 tons gross). Soviet Range Instrumentation Ships (SRIS). Active since 1963.

Communications: 2 Vee Cone.

Radar: Search: Head Net B; Ship Globe.
Navigation: Don 2.

"DESNA" Class

4 "SIBIR" CLASS

SAKHALIN   SIBIR   SPASSK (ex-*Chukotka*)   **SUCHAN**

Displacement, tons: 3 820 standard; 4 800 full load
Dimensions, feet (metres): 354 × 49·2 × 20 (108 × 15 × 6·1)
Main engines: Compound 4-cyl with LP turbine; 2 500 hp = 12 knots
Range, miles: 3 300 at 12 knots

Converted bulk ore carriers employed as Missile Range Ships in the Pacific. *Sakhalin* and *Sibir* have three radomes forward and aft, and carry helicopters. *Suchan* is also equipped with a helicopter flight deck. Launched in 1957-59. Formerly freighters of the Polish B 31 type ("Donbass" class). Rebuilt in 1958-59 as missile range ships in Leningrad.

Names: Reported that *Suchan* has become *Spassk* although no information on latter's new name.

Refit: One ship (believed to be *Spassk* and possibly renamed) refitted and now has new funnel, mast and electronics.

"SIBIR" Class

566 USSR / Civilian space associated ships

CIVILIAN SPACE ASSOCIATED SHIPS

Note: See "Kazbek" class tankers under Service Forces.

1 "GAGARIN" CLASS

KOSMONAVT YURI GAGARIN

Displacement, tons: 45 000
Measurement, tons: 32 291 gross; 5 247 net
Dimensions, feet (metres): 773·3 × 101·7 × 30·0 (235·9 × 31 × 9·2)
Main engines: 2 geared steam turbines; 1 shaft; 19 000 shp = 17 knots

Design based on the "Sofia" or "Akhtuba" (ex-"Hanoi") class steam tanker. Built at Leningrad by Baltic S.B. & Eng Works in 1970, completed in 1971. Used for investigation into conditions in the upper atmosphere, and the control of space vehicles. She is the largest Soviet research vessel. Has bow and stern thrust units for ease of berthing. With all four aerials vertical and facing forward she experiences a loss in speed of 2 knots. Based in Black Sea.

KOSMONAVT YURI GAGARIN   2/1977

KOSMONAVT YURI GAGARIN   5/1978, S. C. Vessey

1 "KOMAROV" CLASS

KOSMONAVT VLADIMIR KOMAROV (ex-*Genichesk*)

Displacement, tons: 17 500 full load
Measurement, tons: 6 650 deadweight; 13 935 gross; 5 304 net
Dimensions, feet (metres): 510·8 × 75·5 × 29·5 (155·8 × 23 × 9)
Main engine: 1—6-cyl Bryansk diesel; 9 000 bhp
Speed, knots: 17·5

She was launched in 1966 at Kherson as *Genichesk* and operated as a "Poltava" class dry cargo ship in the Black Sea for about six months. Converted to her present role at Leningrad in 1967. The ship is named in honour of the Soviet astronaut who died when his space craft crashed in 1967. Based in Black Sea.

KOSMONAVT VLADIMIR KOMAROV   1977, Selçuk Emre   KOSMONAVT VLADIMIR KOMAROV   2/1977

1 "KOROLEV" CLASS

AKADEMIK SERGEI KOROLEV

Displacement, tons: 21 250
Measurement, tons: 17 114 gross; 2 158 net
Dimensions, feet (metres): 597·1 × 82·0 × 30·0 (182·1 × 25 × 9·2)
Main engine: 1—8-cyl Bryansk diesel; 12 000 shp
Speed, knots: 17

Built at Chernomorsky Shipyard, Nikolayev in 1970, completing in 1971. Equipped with the smaller type radome and two "saucers". Based in Black Sea.

AKADEMIK SERGEI KOROLEV   1972, Michael D. J. Lennon   AKADEMIK SERGEI KOROLEV   1977, MoD

USSR / Civilian space associated ships — Training ships

1 "BEZHITSA" CLASS

BEZHITSA

Measurement, tons: 13 935 gross; 6 650 deadweight
Dimensions, feet (metres): 510·4 × 75·5 × 29·5 *(155·7 × 20·6 × 9)*
Main engine: 1—6-cyl Bryansk diesel; 8 750 bhp = 17·5 knots

Former freighter of "Poltava" class launched at Kherson in 1963, and subsequently converted as a research ship. The Vee-cone horns were fitted in 1971. Directional aerials similar to those in *Ristna* fitted on crane stowage forward of the bridge. Based in Baltic.

BEZHITSA   1972, Michael D. J. Lennon

4 "KOSMONAVT PAVEL BELYAYEV" CLASS

KOSMONAVT VLADKLAV VOLKOV   KOSMONAVT PAVEL BELYAYEV
KOSMONAVT GEORGY DOBROVOLSKY   KOSMONAVT SAYEV

Displacement, tons: 9 000

Former freighters of "Vytegrales" class rebuilt as space associated research ships at Leningrad 1977-78. Reported as replacements for *Ristna, Bezhitsa* and previously deleted *Dolinsk* and *Aksay*.

1 "POVENETS" (Conversion) CLASS

RISTNA

Measurement, tons: 4 200 deadweight; 3 724 gross; 1 819 net
Dimensions, feet (metres): 347·8 × 47·9 × 14·0 *(106·1 × 14·6 × 4·3)*
Main engine: 1—MAN 6-cyl diesel; 3 250 bhp = 15 knots

Converted from a "Povenets" class merchant ship. Built in East Germany at Rostok by Schiffswerft—Neptun in 1963. Painted white. Fitted with directional aerials on top of bridge wings.
Space monitoring ship. Based in Baltic.

RISTNA   1970, Michael D. J. Lennon

4 "VYTEGRALES" CLASS

BOROVICHI (ex-*Svirles*)   KEGOSTROV (ex-*Taimyr*)   MORZHOVETS   NEVEL

Former timber carriers built at Zhdanov Yard, Leningrad in 1965-66 and completely modified with a comprehensive array of tracking, direction finding and directional aerials in 1967. Additional laboratories built above the forward holds. Sister ships to the naval-manned "Vytegrales" class. Based in the Baltic.

NEVEL   1972, Michael D. J. Lennon

KEGOSTROV   1977, J. Pritchard-Gordon

TRAINING SHIPS

Notes: (a) It is reported but unconfirmed that two "Wodnik" class (similar to the East German and Polish training ships) are in commission.
(b) In addition to the naval training ships listed here a considerable fleet of other training ships, mainly mercantile marine, may be encountered. These are mainly in the 300-400 ft bracket. Names: *Equator, Gorizont, Meridian, Professor Anichkov, P. Khlyustin, P. Kudrevich, P. Minyayev, P. Pavlenko, P. Rybaltovsky, P. Shchyogolev, P. Ukhov, P. Yushenko, Zenit.*
(c) For details of two "Ugra" class see *Support and Depot Ships* section.

3 "SMOLNY" CLASS

SMOLNY   PEREKOP   KMASAN

Displacement, tons: 6 500 full load
Dimensions, feet (metres): 452·6 × 59 × 20·3 *(138 × 18 × 6·2)*
Guns: 4—76 mm (twins); 4—30 mm (twins)
A/S weapons: 2—MBU 2500
Main engines: 2 diesels; 2 shafts; 12 000 shp = 20 knots
Range, miles: 20 000 at 15 knots

Built at Stettin, Poland. *Smolny* completed in 1976, *Perekop* in 1977 and *Kmasan* in 1978. Can carry 280 cadets.

Radar: Search: One Head Net C.
Fire control: One Owl Screech.
Navigation/Training: Four Don 2.
Sonar: One hull-mounted.

KMASAN   5/1978, Selçuk Emre

568 USSR / Cable ships — Service forces

CABLE SHIPS

6 "KLASMA" CLASS

DONETZ   INGUL*   TSNA   YANA*   ZEYA   +1
*Type I

Displacement, tons: 6 000 standard; 6 900 full load
Measurement, tons: 3 400 deadweight; 5 786 gross
Dimensions, feet (metres): 427·8 × 52·5 × 19 (130·5 × 16 × 5·8)
Main engines: 5 Wärtsila Sulzer diesels; 5 000 shp = 14 knots
Complement: 110

Ingul and *Yana* were built by Wärtsilä, Helsingforsvarvet, Finland, laid down on 10 October 1961 and 4 May 1962 and launched on 14 April 1962 and 1 November 1962 respectively, *Donetz* and *Tsna* were built at the Wärtsilä, Abovarvet, Abo. *Donetz* was launched on 17 December 1968 and completed 3 July 1969. *Tsna* was completed in summer 1968. *Zeya* was delivered on 20 November 1970. *Donetz*, *Tsna* and *Zeya* are of slightly modified design.

"KLASMA" Class

YANA (Type I—no gantry aft)   3/1976, MOD

TSNA (Type II—with gantry aft)   Wärtsilä

4 + 1 "MOD KLASMA" CLASS

INGURI   KALAR   KATUN   TAVDA   +1

First pair ordered from Wärtsilä in 1972/73 and two more on 16 July 1974. An improved "Klasma" class of similar appearance and the same data. *Kalar* launched on 20 March 1974. *Tavda* laid down 14 April 1976 and launched 21 October 1976—completed 6 October 1977. *Inguri* laid down 21 October 1976 and launched 7 October 1977. A fifth ship ordered from Wärtsilä in early 1978 for completion in 1980.

COMMUNICATIONS RELAY SHIPS

20 "LIBAU" CLASS

Displacement, tons: 310 standard; 380 full load
Dimensions, feet (metres): 170·6 × 21·5 × 9·0 (52 × 6·6 × 2·7)
Main engines: 3 diesels; 3 shafts; 3 300 bhp = 24 knots
Range, miles: 1 500 at 12 knots

Converted "Kronshtadt" class.

SERVICE FORCES

Note: With the Soviet merchant fleet under State control any ships of the merchant service, including tankers, may be diverted to a fleet support role at any time. Over half the Soviet navy's support out-of-area is from merchant tankers.

1 "BEREZINA" CLASS (FLEET REPLENISHMENT SHIP)

BEREZINA

Displacement, tons: 36 000 full load approx
Dimensions, feet (metres): 688·8 × 85·3 × 32·2 (210 × 26 × 10)
Aircraft: 2 Hormone A helicopters
Missiles: SAM; Two SA-N-4 (twin launcher abaft funnel)
Guns: 4—57 mm (twins); 4—30 mm Gatlings
A/S weapons: 2—MBUs 4500A (6-barrelled)
Speed, knots: 22
Range, miles: 15 000 at 16 knots
Complement: 550

Built at Nikolayev (61 Kommuna) and completed in 1977 this very impressive ship is probably the first of a group designed to support the "Kiev" class aircraft carriers. The weight of her armament is notable in comparison with Western practice. This is the first Soviet replenishment ship to be fitted with SAM missiles and Gatling guns as well as carrying helicopters and mounting MBUs. This total gives her a considerable AA capability and, if the helicopters have an A/S as well as VERTREP role, a certain self-sufficiency in anti-submarine operations. The siting of the MBU4500A forward of the bridge is unique in this navy. Laid down 1973, launched 1975.

Radar: Search: Strut Curve.
Fire control: Pop Group (SA-N-4); Muff Cob (57 mm); Bass Tilt (2) (Gatlings).

Replenishment gear: Two storing gantries (apparently with moving high-points); Four 7·5 ton cranes and one other; Liquid fuelling gantry (amidships).

Sonar: One hull-mounted.

BEREZINA   1/1979, MOD

BEREZINA   2/1979, Ulrich Schulz-Torge

USSR / Service forces 569

6 "BORIS CHILIKIN" CLASS (FLEET REPLENISHMENT SHIPS)

BORIS BUTOMA	GENRIK GASANOV
BORIS CHILIKIN	IVAN BUBNOV
DNESTR	VLADIMIR KOLECHITSKY

Displacement, tons: 23 400 full load
Dimensions, feet (metres): 531·5 × 70·2 × 28·1 *(162·1 × 21·4 × 8·6)*
Guns: 4—57 mm (2 twins) (guns removed in all ships)
Main engines: 4 diesels; 9 600 hp; 1 shaft = 19 knots
Range, miles: 10 000 at 16 knots

"BORIS CHILIKIN" Class

Based on the "Veliky Oktyabr" merchant ship tanker design *Boris Chilikin* was built at the Baltic Yard, Leningrad completing in 1971. This is the first Soviet Navy class of purpose built underway fleet replenishment ships for the supply of both liquids and solids, indicating a growing awareness of the need for afloat support for a widely dispersed fleet.
Carry 13 000 tons fuel oil, 400 tons ammunition, 400 tons spares and 400 tons victualling stores.
A continuing programme at the same yard.
The removal of both fire control radar and armament is in contrast to the considerable weight of such items carried in *Berezina*.

Radar: Search: Strut Curve.
Fire control: Muff Cob.
Navigation: Don Kay (2).

DNESTR   9/1974, MOD

2 "MANYCH" CLASS (FLEET REPLENISHMENT SHIPS)

| MANYCH | TAGIL |

Displacement, tons: 8 600 full load
Dimensions, feet (metres): 377·2 × 49·2 × 23·0 *(115 × 15 × 7)*
Guns: 4—57 mm (twins) (see note)
Main engines: 2 diesels; 9 000 shp; 2 shafts = 18 knots
Complement: 100

Completed 1972 and 1976 in Kaliningrad and Vyborg. A smaller edition of the *Boris Chilikin* but showing the new interest in custom-built replenishment ships. The high point on the single gantry is very similar to that on *Boris Chilikin's* third gantry. Both ships reported in use as distilled water-carriers with armament removed—possibly because of problems with her operation as a small replenishment ship.

Radar: Search: Strut Curve.
Fire control: Muff Cob (2).
Navigation: Don Kay.

MANYCH   2/1973

3 + 1 "DUBNA" CLASS (REPLENISHMENT TANKERS)

| DUBNA | IRKUT | PECHENGA | +1 |

Displacement, tons: 12 000
Measurement, tons: 6 800 deadweight; 6 022 gross; 2 990 net
Dimensions, feet (metres): 426·8 × 65·8 × 23·8 *(130 × 21·6 × 7·8)*
Main engine: Diesel; 6 000 hp = 16 knots

"DUBNA" Class

Dubna completed 1974, *Irkut* launched January 1975, completed December 1975 both at Rauma-Repola, Finland. Two more ordered April 1977. *Pechenga* commissioned end 1978.
Normally painted in merchant navy colours.

Replenishment: Carry FFO, dieso, lub-oil, fresh water, spares and victualling stores. Can refuel on either beam and astern.

DUBNA   9/1977, MOD

1 "SOFIA" CLASS (REPLENISHMENT TANKER)

AKHTUBA (ex-*Hanoi*)

Displacement, tons: 62 000 full load
Dimensions, feet (metres): 757·9 × 101·7 × 37·7 *(231·2 × 31 × 11·6)*
Main engine: Steam turbine; 19 000 hp = 17 knots
Range, miles: 21 000 at 17 knots
Complement: 65

Built as the merchant tanker *Hanoi* in 1963 at Leningrad, she was taken over by the Navy in 1969 and renamed *Akhtuba*. The hull type was used in the construction of the space associated ship *Kosmonavt Yuri Gagarin*.

AKHTUBA (as *Hanoi*)   1971, MOD

570 USSR / Service forces

3 "KAZBEK" CLASS (REPLENISHMENT TANKERS)

ALATYR   DESNA   VOLKHOV

Displacement, tons: 16 250 full load
Measurement, tons: 12 000 deadweight; 8 230 gross; 3 942 net
Dimensions, feet (metres): 477·2 × 62·9 × 26·9 (145·5 × 19·2 × 8·2)
Main engines: 2 diesels; single shaft

Former "Leningrad" class merchant fleet tankers taken over by the Navy. Built at Leningrad and Nikolaev from 1951 to 1961. Eight others—*Karl Marx, Kazbek, Dzerzhinsk, Grodno, Cheboksary, Liepaya, Zhitomir* and *Buguzuslan* have acted in support of naval operations. The original class numbered 64. All now modified for alongside replenishment.

Appearance: The naval ships of this class can be distinguished by the A-frame before the bridge, the two forward kingposts and the cat-walks.

Radar: Don 2.

DESNA   1976, MOD

7 "ALTAY" (IMPROVED "OLEKMA") CLASS (SUPPORT TANKERS)

ALTAY   IZHORA   KOLA   PRUT   TARKHANKUT   YEGORLIK   YELNYA

Displacement, tons: 5 500 standard
Dimensions, feet (metres): 348 × 51 × 19·7 (106·2 × 15·5 × 6)
Main engine: 1 Burmester and Wain diesel; 2 900 hp; 1 shaft = 14 knots
Range, miles: 8 600 at 12 knots
Complement: 44

Building from 1967 onwards. Most now modified for alongside replenishment. This class is part of 38 ships, being the third group of Rouma types built in Finland in 1967. Of similar hull to "Olekma/Pevek" classes (following) through with bridge aft.

PRUT   4/1977, MOD

3 "OLEKMA/PEVEK" CLASSES (SUPPORT TANKERS)

IMAN   OLEKMA   ZOLOTOY ROG

Displacement, tons: 4 000 standard; 6 700 full load
Dimensions, feet (metres): 344·5 × 47·9 × 20·0 (105·1 × 14·6 × 6·1)
Main engine: 1 diesel; 2 900 bhp = 14 knots
Range, miles: 8 000 at 13 knots
Complement: 40

Part of the second group of 34 tankers built by Rauma-Repola, Finland between 1960 and 1966. Similar hull to "Altay" class (preceding) though with bridge amidships.

"OLEKMA" Class   1973, Michael D. J. Lennon

1 REPLENISHMENT TANKER

POLYARNIK (ex-*Kärnten*, ex-*Netherlands*)

Displacement, tons: 12 500
Dimensions, feet (metres): 344 × 48 × ? (105 × 14·7 × ?)
Main engines: 2 diesels; 7 000 shp; 2 shafts = 15 knots
Complement: 57

The most senior naval tanker serving. Thought to have been deleted. Sighted in 1977 in Pacific. Was transferred after World War II. Can carry fuels, water and solids.

POLYARNIK   USN

6 "UDA" CLASS (SUPPORT TANKERS)

DUNAY   KOIDA   LENA   SHEKSNA   TEREK   VISHERA

Displacement, tons: 5 500 standard; 7 200 full load
Dimensions, feet (metres): 400·3 × 51·8 × 20·3 (122·1 × 15·8 × 6·2)
Main engines: Diesels; 2 shafts; 8 000 bhp = 17 knots
Complement: 85

All have a beam replenishment capability. Fitted for two quadruple 57 mm guns. Built since 1961.

"UDA" Class

LENA   1/1975, MOD

1 "FEOLENT" CLASS (SUPPORT TANKER)

FEOLENT (ex-*Jeverland*)

Displacement, tons: 5 250
Dimensions, feet (metres): 297·8 × 45·2 × 18·3 *(90·8 × 13·8 × 5·6)*
Main engines: 2 Schichau diesels; 2 shafts; 3 500 shp = 15 knots
Cargo, tons: 2 600
Complement: 65

Built in Denmark 1939-40. Rebuilt for naval service May 1942. Taken from Germany 1946.

5 "KONDA" CLASS (SUPPORT TANKERS)

| KONDA | ORSK | ROSSOSH | SOYANNA | YAKHROMA |

Displacement, tons: 1 178 standard; 1 300 full load
Dimensions, feet (metres): 226·3 × 33 × 14·1 *(69 × 10 × 4·4)*
Main engine: 1 diesel; 1 600 bhp = 13 knots
Complement: 26

Originally of the "Iskra" class of merchant tankers built in 1955.

3 "NERCHA" CLASS (SUPPORT TANKERS)

| KLYASMA | NARA | NERCHA |

Displacement, tons: 1 080 standard; 1 250 full load
Dimensions, feet (metres): 226·3 × 33 × 14·1 *(69 × 10 × 4·3)*
Main engine: One 6-cyl diesel; 1 000 hp = 11 knots
Complement: 25

Built in Finland 1952-55 as part of class of 12. Renamed in naval service.

15 "KHOBI" CLASS (SUPPORT TANKERS)

CHEREMSHAN	METAN	SHACHA	TARTU
INDIGA	MOKSHA	SHELON	TITAN
KHOBI	ORSHA	SOSVA	TUNGUSKA
LOVAT	SEIMA	SYSOLA	

Displacement, tons: 800 light; 2 000 approx full load
Dimensions, feet (metres): 207 × 32·8 × 12 *(63 × 10 × 3·8)*
Main engines: 2 diesels; 1 600 shp = 12 knots
Complement: 29

Built from 1957 to 1959. Part of a class of 25.

LOVAT   1977

1 "URAL" CLASS (NUCLEAR SUPPORT SHIP)

URAL

Displacement, tons: 4 000 (approx)
Dimensions, feet (metres): 340 × 45 × 20 *(103 × 14 × 6)* (approx)
Main engines: Diesel

Radar: Don.

URAL   7/1973

9 "LUZA" CLASS (SPECIAL TANKERS)

ALAMBAI	BARGUZIN	KAMA	SASIGA
ARAGUI	DON	OKA	SELENGA
			YENISEY

Displacement, tons: 3 000 full load
Dimensions, feet (metres): 267·3 × 37·6 × 13·4 *(81·5 × 11·5 × 4·3)*
Main engine: 1 diesel; 2 200 = 12 knots

Used for transporting radiological liquids.

OKA   Siegfried Breyer

572 USSR / Salvage vessels

SALVAGE VESSELS

9 "PRUT" CLASS

ALTAI	BRESHTAU	VLADIMIR TREFOLEV	ZHIGUILI
SS 21	SS 23	SS 26 SS 44	SS 83

Displacement, tons: 2 120 standard; 2 640 full load
Dimensions, feet (metres): 285 × 43·9 × 14·1 (86·9 × 13·4 × 4·3)
Guns: 4—57 mm (quad) (some)
Main engines: 2 diesels; 4 200 bhp = 18 knots
Complement: 42

Large rescue vessels. Built since 1960.

Radar: Search: Strut Curve.
Fire control: Muff Cob (some).
Navigation: Don.

"PRUT" Class

"PRUT" Class   1970, S. Breyer

10 "SURA" CLASS

KIL 1, 2, 21, 22, 27, 29, 31, 32, 33 + 1

Displacement, tons: 2 370 standard; 3 150 full load
Dimensions, feet (metres): 285·4 × 48·6 × 16·4 (87 × 14·8 × 5)
Main engines: Diesel-electric; 2 240 bhp = 13·2 knots
Complement: 73

Heavy lift ships built as mooring and buoy tenders between 1965 and 1972 in East Germany. 65 ton and 5 ton lifts with stern cage.

Names: Apparently names have now been added eg. KIL 33 is *Dioklas*.

"SURA" Class

DIOKLAS   5/1978, Selçuk Emre

15 "NEPTUN" CLASS

Displacement, tons: 700 light; 1 230 standard
Dimensions, feet (metres): 187·9 × 36·6 × 10·8 (57·3 × 11·4 × 3·3)
Main engines: 2 turbines; 2 5000 hp = 12 knots
Complement: 25

Mooring tenders similar to Western boom defence vessels. Built in 1957-60 by Neptun Rostock. Have a crane of 75 tons lifting capacity on the bow. One of this class is now based at Murmansk for the Maritime Fleet. She is acting as a diving vessel for hydrogeologists and construction personnel.

"NEPTUN" Class   1973

USSR / Submarine rescue ships — Transports 573

SUBMARINE RESCUE SHIPS

1 "NEPA" CLASS

KARPATY

Displacement, tons: 3 500 standard; 5 000 full load
Dimensions, feet (metres): 410·1 × 52·5 × 16·4 *(125 × 16 × 5)*
Main engines: 2 diesels; 6 000 shp; 2 shafts = 20 knots
Complement: 270

Submarine rescue and salvage ship of improved design with a special high stern which extends out over the water for rescue manoeuvres with a 600 ton lift. Several other lifting points provided. Has several rescue bells and observation chambers. Completed 1969.

"NEPA" Class

KARPATY 1972, A. Nubert

15 "VALDAY" CLASS (Ex-"T 58" CLASS)

KHAZBEK   KHIBINY   VALDAY   ZANGEZUR   + 11

Displacement, tons: 725 standard; 850 full load
Dimensions, feet (metres): 229·6 × 29·5 × 7·9 *(70 × 9 × 2·4)*
Main engines: 2 diesels; 2 shafts; 4 000 bhp = 18 knots
Complement: 82

Basically of similar design to that of the "T 58" class fleet minesweepers, but they were completed as emergency salvage vessels and submarine rescue ships at Leningrad. Equipped with diving bell, recompression chamber and emergency medical ward. Have stern lift and rescue chamber aft.

Radar: Ball End.

Transfer: One to India *(Nistar)*.

"VALDAY" Class 1973

9 Ex-"T 43" CLASS

Details under Mine Warfare Forces. Carry recompression chambers and diving bells. Stern lift but no rescue chamber.

TRANSPORTS

Note: In addition to the following some forty other cargo ships/transports have naval connections but, as with all such ships of the USSR, it is virtually impossible to tell which side of the naval/merchant fence they lie.

1 "YAVZA" CLASS

YAVZA

Displacement, tons: 13 200
Dimensions, feet (metres): 436 × 62 × 29 *(133 × 19 × 8·6)*
Main engines: Diesel-electric; 9 000 hp = 15 knots

3 "CHULYM" CLASS

CHULYM   INSAR   KUZNETSKY

Displacement, tons: 5 050 full load
Dimensions, feet (metres): 311 × 44·5 × 18·3 *(101·9 × 14·6 × 6)*
Main engines: Compound 4-cyl; 1 650 hp = 14 knots
Range, miles: 5 500 at 11 knots
Complement: 40

Built by Stocznia Szczecinska, Poland from 1953-57. Nineteen others of this B 32 type operate with the merchant navy. *Chulym* original name—others appear to have been renamed.

2 "KAMCHATKA" CLASS

KAMCHATKA   SHILKA

Measurement, tons: 4 300 deadweight; 3 745 gross; 1 800 net
Dimensions, feet (metres): 347 × 48 × ? *(105·8 × 14·6 × ?)*
Main engine: MAN 6-cyl diesel; 3 250 bhp = 13·5 knots

Part of a class of 40 ships built at Rostock 1964-66 by Schiffswerft Neptun. Sister ship *Ristna* converted to space-events ship.

2 "ISHIM" CLASS

ISHIM   MONGOL

Measurement, tons: 2 638 deadweight; 3 560 gross; 1 560 net
Dimensions, feet (metres): 326 × 46 × ? *(99·4 × 14 × ?)*
Main engine: Diesel-electric; 1 shaft = 13·5 knots

Built at Nosenko, Nikolaiev 1964-66 as fish carriers. Funnel and bridge aft, twin-legged foremast. *Ishim* is Coast Guard transport.

1 "BAIKAL" CLASS

OB

Displacement, tons: 12 400 full load
Dimensions, feet (metres): 427 × 61·9 × 29·2 *(130·2 × 18·9 × 8·9)*
Main engines: Diesel-electric; 4 generators; 7 000 shp = 15·5 knots
Range, miles: 13 500 at 15 knots
Complement: 60

Built by Kon. Mij de Schelde, Flushing. Ice-strengthened. *Ob* is operated by Academy of Sciences as Antarctic Transport/Support ship. Five others of the same class come under the Ministry of Merchant Marine.

OB 1973, Michael D. J. Lennon

574 USSR / Transports — Torpedo operating / patrol craft

1 "MIKHAIL KALININ" CLASS

KUBAN (ex-*Nadeshda-Krupskaya*)

Displacement, tons: 6 400 full load
Dimensions, feet (metres): 401 × 52 × 16·5 *(122·2 × 16 × 5)*
Main engines: 2 MAN 6-cyl diesels; 2 shafts; 8 000 bhp = 18 knots
Range, miles: 8 100 at 17 knots

Built in 1963 by Mathias Thesen Werft, Wismar, East Germany. Part of "Mikhail Kalinin" class originally to have been 24 ships of which only 19 were completed 1958-64. Name changed on transfer to naval service.
Employed under naval command as personnel support ship for the Soviet Mediterranean Squadron. Accommodation for 350 passengers and can carry 1 000 tons of stores.

KUBAN   9/1976, Michael D. J. Lennon

9 "KEYLA" CLASS

BEREZINA, ERUSLAN, MEZEN, ONEGA, PONOI, RITSA, TERIBERKA, TULOMA, UNJA

Displacement, tons: 1 400
Dimensions, feet (metres): 258·4 × 34·4 × 15·1 *(78·8 × 10·5 × 4·6)*
Main engine: Diesel = 12 knots

15 "LENTRA" CLASS

Victualling transports. Details under AGIs. Being phased out.

10 "MAYAK" CLASS

Victualling transports. Details under AGIs.

9 "MUNA" CLASS

Torpedo transports.

16 "TELNOVSK" CLASS

Of 1 650 tons. Light freighters.

8 "MP 6" CLASS

2 000 ton ex-amphibious craft.

BIRA—"MP 6" Class   1975

TORPEDO OPERATING/PATROL CRAFT

Note: A number of "Kronshtadt" class has been converted for torpedo recovery.

2 "POTOK" CLASS (TORPEDO EXPERIMENTAL SHIPS)

POTOK   + 1

Length, feet (metres): 220
Torpedo tubes: 4—21 in *(533 mm)* (quad)
Main engines: 2 diesels

Apparently used for torpedo trials in Black Sea.

"POTOK" Class   1976

90 "POLUCHAT I" CLASS

Displacement, tons: 100 standard
Dimensions, feet (metres): 98·4 × 19·7 × 5·9 *(30 × 6 × 1·8)*
Guns: 2 MG (1 twin) (in some)

Employed as specialised or dual purpose torpedo recovery vessels and/or patrol boats. They have a stern slipway. Several exported as patrol craft.

"POLUCHAT I" Class   10/1975, MOD

DIVING TENDERS/PATROL CRAFT

"NYRYAT I" CLASS

Displacement, tons: 145
Dimensions, feet (metres): 93 × 18 × 5·5 *(28·4 × 5·5 × 1·7)*
Gun: 1—12·5 MG (in some)
Main engine: Diesel; 1 shaft; 450 hp = 12·5 knots
Range, miles: 1 500 at 10 knots
Complement: 15

Built from 1955. Can operate as patrol craft.

Transfers: Cuba, Iraq (2), North Yemen.

2 "YELVA" CLASS

Displacement, tons: 295
Dimensions, feet (metres): 132·8 × 26·2 × 6·5 *(40·5 × 8 × 2)*

Diving tenders built in early 1970s with two 1·5 ton cranes.

Radar: One Spin Trough.

Transfers: Two to Cuba 1978, one to Libya 1977.

"YELVA" Class   1973

WATER CARRIERS

14 "VODA" CLASS

Displacement, tons: 2 100 standard
Dimensions, feet (metres): 267·3 × 37·7 × 14 *(81·5 × 11·5 × 4·3)*
Main engines: Diesels; speed = 12 knots

Built in 1956 onwards. No armament.

"VODA" Class   1970

FIRE/PATROL CRAFT

"POZHARNY I" CLASS

Displacement, tons: 180
Dimensions, feet (metres): 114·5 × 20 × 6 *(34·9 × 6·1 × 1·8)*
Guns: 4—12·7 mm or 14·5 mm (in some)
Main engines: 2 diesels; 1 shaft; 1 800 hp = 12·5 knots

Built in USSR in mid-1950s. Harbour fire boats but can be used for patrol duties.

Transfers: Iraq (2), North Yemen.

DEGAUSSING SHIP

1 "KHABAROV" CLASS

KHABAROV

Displacement, tons: 500 full load
Dimensions, feet (metres): 150·3 × 26·5 × 8 *(45·8 × 8·1 × 2·4)*
Main engine: Diesel; 1 shaft; 400 bhp = 10·5 knots
Range, miles: 1 130 at 10 knots
Complement: 30

Steel-hulled. Prominent deckhouse and stern anchors. One of class, *Kilat,* transferred to Indonesia 1961—subsequently disposed of.
Several others known to exist.

ICEBREAKERS

Note: The majority of these ships is operated by Ministry of Merchant Marine—only a small number being naval manned. No excuse is offered for including them here as they are an indispensible part of many operations not only in the Baltic, Northern and Pacific Fleet areas but also on rivers, lakes and canals.

1 PROJECTED LARGE NUCLEAR POWERED

Main engines: Nuclear reactors; steam turbines; 80 000 hp

Reported as in the design stage in October 1974.

2 "ARKTIKA" CLASS

ARKTIKA   SIBIR

Displacement, tons: 19 300 standard; 24 460 full load
Dimensions, feet (metres): 485·4 × 91·8 × 36·1 *(148 × 28 × 11)*
Aircraft: Helicopter with hangar
Main engines: 2 nuclear reactors; steam turbines; 66 000 shp; 3 shafts aft
Speed, knots: 21

Building yard—Leningrad. *Arktika* launched summer 1973, started trials on 30 November 1974 and was operational late 1975. Fitted with new type of reactor, the development of which may have retarded these ships' completion. *Sibir* completed 7 November 1977 and commissioned 28 December 1977. Civilian manned.

SIBIR

"ARKTIKA" Class

1 NUCLEAR POWERED

LENIN

Displacement, tons: 15 300 standard; 19 240 full load
Dimensions, feet (metres): 406·7 × 87·9 × 34·4 *(124 × 26·8 × 10·5)*
Aircraft: 2 helicopters
Main engines: 3 pressurised water-cooled nuclear reactors, 4 steam turbines; 3 shafts; 39 200 shp = 19·7 knots
Complement: 230

The world's first nuclear powered surface ship to put to sea. Reported to have accommodation for 1 000 personnel. Civilian manned.

Construction: Built at the Admiralty Yard, Leningrad. Launched on 5 December 1957. Commissioned on 15 September 1959.

Engineering: The original reactors, prototype submarine variety, were replaced during refit at Murmansk 1966-72. The new reactors presumably have a longer core-life than the 18 months of their predecessors. The turbines were manufactured by the Kirov plant in Leningrad. Three propellers aft, but no forward screw.

Operation: Can maintain a speed of 3-4 knots in 8 ft ice, giving a path of some 100 ft.

LENIN

3 "YERMAK" CLASS

Name	No.	Builders	Commissioned
YERMAK	—	Wärtsilä, Helsinki	30 June 1974
ADMIRAL MAKAROV	—	Wärtsilä, Helsinki	2 June 1975
KRASIN	—	Wärtsilä, Helsinki	Jan 1976

Displacement, tons: 20 241 full load
Dimensions, feet (metres): 442·8 × 85·3 × 36·1 *(135 × 26 × 11)*
Aircraft: 2 helicopters
Main engines: 9 Wärtsilä-Sulzer 12-cyl 12 ZH 40/48 diesels of 4 600 bhp each (total 41 400 hp) with Stromberg Ab generators feeding three Stromberg electric motors of total 36 000 shp; 3 shafts
Speed, knots: 19·5
Range, miles: 40 000 at 15 knots
Complement: 118 plus 28 spare berths

The Soviet Union ordered three large and powerful icebreakers on 29 April 1970 from Wärtsilä Shipyard, Helsinki, for delivery in 1974, 1975 and 1976. Six Wärtsilä auxiliary diesels, 7 200 bhp. Propelling and auxiliary machinery controlled electronically. These are the first vessels to be fitted with Wärtsilä mixed-flow air-bubbling system to decrease friction between hull and ice. *Yermak* launched 7 September 1973. *A. Makarov* laid down 10 September 1973 and launched 26 April 1974. *Krasin* laid down 9 July 1974, launched 18 April 1975. Civilian manned.

ADMIRAL MAKAROV

USSR / Icebreakers 577

5 "MOSKVA" CLASS

VLADIVOSTOCK   KIEV   LENINGRAD   MOSKVA   MURMANSK

Displacement, tons: 13 290 standard; 15 360 full load
Dimensions, feet (metres): 400·7 × 80·3 × 34·5 (122·2 × 24·5 × 10·5)
Aircraft: 2 helicopters
Main engines: 8 Sulzer diesel-electric; 3 shafts; 22 000 shp = 18 knots
Oil fuel, tons: 3 000
Range, miles: 20 000
Complement: 145

Civilian manned.

Construction: Built by Wärtsilä Shipyard, Helsinki. *Moskva* was launched on 10 January 1959 and completed in June 1960. *Leningrad* was laid down in January 1959. Launched on 24 October 1959, and completed in 1962. *Kiev* was completed in 1966. *Murmansk* was launched on 14 July 1967, and *Vladivostock* on 28 May 1968.

Design: Designed to stay at sea for a year without returning to base. The concave embrasure in the ship's stern is a housing for the bow of a following vessel when additional power is required. There is a landing deck for helicopters and hangar space for two aircraft.

Engineering: Eight generating units of 3 250 bhp each comprising eight main diesels of the Wärtsilä-Sulzer 9 MH 51 type which together have an output of 26 000 hp. Four separate machinery compartments. Two engine rooms, four propulsion units in each. Three propellers aft. No forward propeller. Centre propeller driven by electric motors of 11 000 hp and each of the side propellers by motors of 5 500 hp. Two Wärtsilä-Babcock & Wilcox boilers for heating and donkey work.

Operation: *Moskva* has four pumps which can move 480 tonnes of water from one side to the other in two minutes to rock the icebreaker and wrench her free of thick ice.

MOSKVA   1960, Wärtsilä

LENINGRAD   1964

2 "KAPITAN SOROKIN" CLASS

Name	No.	Builders	Commissioned
KAPITAN SOROKIN	—	Wärtsilä, Helsinki	14 July 1977
KAPITAN NIKOLAEV	—	Wärtsilä, Helsinki	31 Jan 1978

Displacement, tons: 14 900
Dimensions, feet (metres): 432·6 × 86·9 × 27·9 (131·9 × 26·5 × 8·5)
Aircraft: 2 helicopters
Main engines: 6 Wärtsilä-Sulzer 9 ZL 40/48 diesels; 24 800 bhp; 6 AC generators; 22 000 shp; 3 shafts with DC motors
Speed, knots: 19
Complement: 76 (16 spare berths)

Shallow draught polar icebreakers fitted with Wärtsilä bubbling system. Fitted with single cabins (except spare berths), sauna, swimming pool, gymnasium, library, cinema and hospital. *K. Sorokin* laid down 5 December 1975, launched 10 December 1976. *K. Nikolaev* laid down 5 December 1976.

KAPITAN SOROKIN   1977, Wärtsilä

2 NEW CONSTRUCTION

Displacement, tons: 15 000 approx
Dimensions, feet (metres): 432·6 × 86·9 × 27·9 (131·9 × 26·5 × 8·5)
Main engines: Diesel-electric; 6 Wärtsilä-Sulzer 9 ZL 40/48 diesels; 24 800 hp; electric motors; 22 000 hp; 2 shafts = 19 knots

Ordered in December 1978, the first ship to be delivered in autumn 1980 the second in summer 1981. A development of the "Kapitan Sorokin" design these ships are planned for North Siberian operations in shallow deltas at ambient temperatures down to −50°C. Fitted with Wärtsilä bubbling equipment.

OTTO SCHMIDT

Displacement, tons: 3 650
Main engines: Diesel-electric; 5 400 shp
Range, miles: 11 000

Built at Admiralty Yard, Leningrad. Icebreaker/polar research ship. Launched 1978. Commissioned January 1979.

1 "PURGA" CLASS

Displacement, tons: 2 250 standard; 3 000 full load
Length, feet (metres): 295·2 (90)
Beam, feet (metres): 44·3 (13·5)
Draught, feet (metres): 17·1 (5·2)
Guns: 4—3·9 in (100 mm) (singles)
Mines: 50 capacity
Main engines: Diesels
Speed, knots: 18
Complement: 250

Laid down in 1939 in Leningrad and completed in 1948. Equipped as icebreaker. Fitted with director similar to those in the "Riga" class frigates. Modernised in 1958-60.

"PURGA" Class

3 "KAPITAN BELOUSOV" CLASS

Name	No.	Builders	Commissioned
KAPITAN BELOUSOV	—	Wärtsilä, Helsinki	1955
KAPITAN MELEKHOV	—	Wärtsilä, Helsinki	1957
KAPITAN VORONIN	—	Wärtsilä, Helsinki	1956

Displacement, tons: 4 375 to 4 415 standard; 5 350 full load
Dimensions, feet (metres): 273 × 63·7 × 23 (83·3 × 19·4 × 7)
Main engines: Diesel-electric; 6 Polar 8-cyl; 10 500 bhp = 14·9 knots
Oil fuel, tons: 740
Complement: 120

The ships have four screws, two forward under the forefoot and two aft. Civilian manned. *K. Belousov* launched 1954, *K. Voronin* 1955 and *K. Melechov* 19 October 1956.

KAPITAN BELOUSOV   1970, Michael D. J. Lennon

USSR / Icebreakers — Armed icebreakers

20 "VASILY PRONCHISHTCHEV" CLASS

AFANASY NIKITIN (ex-*Ledokol 2*)
BURAN
DOBRINYA NIKITCH
FEDOR LITKE
ILIA MUROMETS
IVAN MOSKVITIN
IVAN KRUZENSTERN (ex-*Ledokol 6*)
KHARITON LAPTEV (ex-*Ledokol 3*)
PERESVET
PLUG
SADKO
SEMYEN CHELYUSKIN
SEMYEN DEZHNEV
VASILY POIARKOV (ex-*Ledokol 4*)
VASILY PRONCHISHTCHEV (ex-*Ledokol 1*)
VLADIMIR RUSANOV (ex-*Ledokol 7*)
VYUGA
YEMELYAN PUGATCHEV
YEROFEI KHABAROV (ex-*Ledokol 5*)
YURIK LISYANSKIY (ex-*Ledokol 8*)

Displacement, tons: 2 500 standard (average)
Measurement, tons: 2 305 gross (ships vary)
Dimensions, feet (metres): 223·1 × 26·2 × 19·9 *(68 × 8 × 6·1)*
Guns: 2—57 mm; 2—25 mm *(Peresvet* and *Plug)*
Main engines: 3 shafts (1 bow, 2 stern); 5 400 hp = 13·8 knots

All built at Leningrad between 1961 (first ship, *Vasily Pronchishtchev*) and 1965 (last ship, *Ivan Moskvitin*). Divided between the Baltic, Black Sea and Far East. All civilian manned except *Buran*, *Peresvet* and *Plug*. Last two are armed.

YURIK LISYANSKIY 1972, Michael D. J. Lennon

AFANASY NIKITIN Michael D. J. Lennon

6 "KAPITAN CHECHKIN" CLASS

Name	No.	Builders	Commissioned
KAPITAN CHECHKIN	—	Wärtsilä	6 Nov 1977
KAPITAN PLAHIN	—	Wärtsilä	30 Dec 1977
KAPITAN CHADAEV	—	Wärtsilä	7 Apr 1978
KAPITAN KRUTOV	—	Wärtsilä	6 June 1978
KAPITAN BUKAEV	—	Wärtsilä	29 Sep 1978
KAPITAN ZARUBIN	—	Wärtsilä	10 Nov 1978

Displacement, tons: 2 240
Dimensions, feet (metres): 254·5 × 53·5 × 10·7 *(77·6 × 16·3 × 3·3)*
Main engines: Diesel-electric; Wärtsilä 12V22 diesels; 6 330 hp; 3 shafts; 4 490 hp = 14 knots
Complement: 28

Ordered 16 May 1975. *K. Chechkin* laid down 22 October 1976 and launched 29 April 1977. *K. Plahin* laid down 24 January 1977, launched 8 August 1977. *K. Chadaev* laid down 16 February 1977, launched 13 October 1977. *K. Krutov* laid down 1 July 1977, launched 11 January 1978. *K. Bukaev* laid down 9 September 1977. Designed for service on Volga-Baltic waterways and Siberian rivers. Fitted with three rudders, air-bubbling system and an automatic lowering system for masts, radar and aerials.

KAPITAN CHADAEV (operating bubbling equipment) 1978, Wärtsilä

3 "KAPITAN IZMAYLOV" CLASS

Name	No.	Builders	Commissioned
KAPITAN M. IZMAYLOV	—	Wärtsilä, Helsinki	15 June 1976
KAPITAN KOSOLAPOV	—	Wärtsilä, Helsinki	14 July 1976
KAPITAN A. RADZABOV	—	Wärtsilä, Helsinki	5 Oct 1976

Displacement, tons: 2 045
Dimensions, feet (metres): 185·3 × 51·5 × 13·8 *(56·5 × 15·7 × 4·2)*
Main engines: Diesel-electric; Diesels; 4 100 hp; 2 shafts; 3 400 shp; 2 rudders
Speed, knots: 13

Contract signed with Wärtsilä, Helsinki on 22 March 1974 for the building of these three icebreakers for delivery in 1976. All fitted with Wärtsilä air-bubbler system. Machinery by Wärtsilä Vasa. Electrical machinery by Oy Strömberg Ab.
Laid down: *K. Izmaylov* 12 June 1975 (launched 11 December 1975), *K. Kosolapov* 19 August 1975 (launched 13 February 1976), *K. Radzabov* 17 June 1975 (launched 9 March 1976). Civilian manned.

KAPITAN IZMAYLOV 10/1976, Wärtsilä

ARMED ICEBREAKERS

5 "SUSANIN" CLASS

AISBERG IMENI XXV SVEZDA KPSS IVAN SUSANIN RUSLAN DUNAY

Of similar major characteristics to Icebreakers of "Vasily Pronchishtchev" class but lengthened by 80 ft and modified with new bridge structure, twin 76 mm forward (except *Ruslan*), two 30 mm Gatling guns aft (in all but *Aisberg*) and a helicopter platform. May be operated by KGB.

"SUSANIN" Class

AISBERG 1977

TUGS

2 "INGUL" CLASS

PAMIR   MASHUK

Displacement, tons: 4 050
Dimensions, feet (metres): 295 × 52 × 18 *(92·8 × 15·4 × 5·8)*
Main engines: 2—16-cyl 58D-4R diesels; 9 000 hp = 18·7 knots
Complement: 35 (plus salvage party of 18)

NATO class-name the same as one of the "Klasma" class cable-ships.
Naval manned Arctic salvage and rescue tugs.
Two more civilian manned—one named *Jaguar*. This class has an interesting underwater shape with a large protruding bulb at the forefoot.

Name: Reported that *Pamir* has been renamed *Ingul*.

PAMIR   4/1975, MOD(N)

2 "PAMIR" CLASS

AGATAN   ALDAN

Measurement, tons: 2 032 gross
Dimensions, feet (metres): 256 × 42 × 13·5 *(78 × 12·8 × 4·1)*
Main engines: 2—10-cyl 4 stroke diesels; 2 shafts; 4 200 bhp = 17 knots

Salvage tugs built at AB Gävle Varv, Sweden, in 1959-60. Equipped with strong derricks, powerful pumps, air compressors, diving gear, fire fighting apparatus and electric generators.

ALDAN   4/1975, MOD(N)

9 "SORUM" CLASS

AMUR   KAMCHATKA   SAKHALIN   MB 15   MB 18   MB 105
MB 115   MB 119   +1

Displacement, tons: 1 630
Dimensions, feet (metres): 190·2 × 41·3 × 15·1 *(58 × 12·6 × 4·6)*
Guns: 4—30 mm (twins) (3 twins—*Amur, Kamchatka, Sakhalin*)
Main engines: Diesels; 2 100 hp

A new class of ocean tugs first seen in 1973. All are naval manned and *Amur, Kamchatka* and *Sakhalin*, are KGB operated. Built in Nikolayev and Leningrad.
First completed in 1972, remainder launched in 1976-77 and completed in 1978.
Not all are armed.

KAMCHATKA   5/1976, MOD

50 "OKHTENSKY" CLASS

Displacement, tons: 835
Dimensions, feet (metres): 143 × 34 × 15 *(43·6 × 10·4 × 4·6)*
Guns: 1—3 in; 2—20 mm
Main engines: 2 BM diesels; 2 electric motors; 2 shafts; 1 875 bhp = 14 knots
Oil fuel, tons: 187
Complement: 34

Oceangoing salvage and rescue tugs. Fitted with powerful pumps and other apparatus for salvage. Pennant numbers preceded by MB.

"OKHTENSKY" Class

4 "GORYN" CLASS

BAYKALSK   BEREZINSK   BOLSHEVETSK   BILBINO

Displacement, tons: 1 600 deadweight
Dimensions, feet (metres): 000·0 × 00·0 × 0·0 *(63·5 × 14·5 × 5)*
Main engine: 1 diesel; 3 500 hp = 14 knots
Complement: 40

Built by Nystads S.Y., Finland 1977-78. Rescue tugs fitted with fire fighting gear.

Radar: Two Don 2.

BAYKALSK   1978

5 "OREL" CLASS SALVAGE TUGS

Measurement, tons: 1 070 gross
Dimensions, feet (metres): 201·2 × 39·2 × 18·1 *(61·4 × 12 × 5·5)*
Main engines: 2 diesels = 14 knots

Class of salvage and rescue tugs normally operated by Ministry of Fisheries with the fishing fleets although at least two are naval manned. Built in Finland in late 1950s and early 1960s.

STREMITELNY—"Orel" Class   1972, Michael D. J. Lennon

USSR / Tugs

7 "KATUN" CLASS

Displacement, tons: 950
Length, feet (metres): 210 *(64)*

Built in 1970-71.

"KATUN" Class   1970

FINNISH "530 TON" CLASS

Measurement, tons: 533 gross
Dimensions, feet (metres): 157·1 × 31·3 × 15·5 *(47·9 × 9·5 × 4·7)*
Main engines: Steam = 9·5 knots

Numerous class built in Finland in 1950s.

EAST GERMAN BERTHING TUGS

Measurement, tons: 233 gross
Main engines: Diesels

Numerous class built in 1970 in East Germany.

EAST GERMAN HARBOUR TUGS

Measurement, tons: 132 gross
Dimensions, feet (metres): 94·5 × 21·3 × 9·8 *(28·8 × 6·5 × 3)*
Main engine: 1 diesel = 10 knots

Very numerous class built in East Germany in 1964.

There are a large number of other tugs available in commercial service which could be directed to naval use.

UNITED ARAB EMIRATES

Headquarters Staff

Commander, Naval Forces:
To be named

Deputy Commander, Naval Forces:
Colonel Madwar

General

This federation of the former Trucial States (Abu Dhabi, Ajman, Dubai, Fujairah, Ras al Khaimah, Sharjah, Umm al Qaiwan) was formed under a provisional constitution in 1971 with a new constitution coming into effect on 2 December 1976.
Following a decision of the UAE Supreme Defence Council on 6 May 1976 the armed forces of the member states were unified and the organisation of the UAE Armed Forces was furthered by decisions taken on 1 February 1978. Overall control will be exercised by GHQ (UAE) in Abu Dhabi with a newly appointed Commander, Naval Forces coming under the general direction of that GHQ.

Personnel

(a) 1979: 986 (120 officers, 866 ratings)
(b) Voluntary service

Ports

Mina Zayed (Abu Dhabi).

A 500 ton lift floating dock was delivered to Abu Dhabi in 1977 by Blohm and Voss, Germany.

LIGHT FORCES

4 "P 48 (JAGUAR II)" CLASS

Displacement, tons: 230
Dimensions, feet (metres): 158 × 23 × 7·5 *(48 × 7 × 2·3)*
Missiles: SSM
Guns: 1—57 mm; 1—40 mm
Main engines: 4 MTU diesels; 14 400 hp; 4 shafts = 34 knots
Complement: 40

Ordered in late 1977 from Lürssen, Vegesack.

6 VOSPER THORNYCROFT TYPE (LARGE PATROL CRAFT)

Name	No.	Builders	Commissioned
ARDHANA	P 1101	Vosper Thornycroft	24 June 1975
ZURARA	P 1102	Vosper Thornycroft	14 Aug 1975
MURBAN	P 1103	Vosper Thornycroft	16 Sep 1975
AL GHULLAN	P 1104	Vosper Thornycroft	16 Sep 1975
RADOOM	P 1105	Vosper Thornycroft	1 July 1976
GHANADHAH	P 1106	Vosper Thornycroft	1 July 1976

Displacement, tons: 110 standard; 175 full load
Dimensions, feet (metres): 110 × 21 × 6·6 *(33·5 × 6·4 × 2·0)*
Guns: 2—30 mm A32 (twin); 1—20 mm A41A (carry 2—2 in flare projectors)
Main engines: 2 Paxman Valenta diesels; 5 400 hp = 30 knots
Range, miles: 1 800 at 14 knots
Complement: 26

A class of round bilge steel hull craft. 1101-2 and 1105-6 transported to Abu Dhabi by heavy-lift ships. 1103 and 1104 were sailed out.

Radar: Decca TM 1626.

MURBAN 9/1975, John G. Callis

3 KEITH NELSON TYPE (COASTAL PATROL CRAFT)

Name	No.	Builders	Commissioned
KAWKAB	P 561	Keith Nelson, Bembridge	7 Mar 1969
THOABAN	P 562	Keith Nelson, Bembridge	7 Mar 1969
BANI YAS	P 563	Keith Nelson, Bembridge	27 Dec 1969

Displacement, tons: 32 standard; 38 full load
Dimensions, feet (metres): 57 × 16·5 × 4·5 *(17·4 × 5·0 × 1·4)*
Guns: 2—20 mm (single)
Main engines: 2 Caterpillar diesels. 750 bhp = 19 knots
Range, miles: 445 at 15 knots
Complement: 11 (2 officers, 9 men)

Of glass fibre hull construction. Originally operated by Abu Dhabi.

Radar: Decca TM 1626.

BANI YAS 11/1976, UAE Armed Forces

POLICE CRAFT

(under control of Ministry of Interior)

6 "DHAFEER" CLASS (COASTAL PATROL CRAFT)

Name	No.	Builders	Commissioned
DHAFEER	P 401	Keith Nelson, Bembridge	1 July 1968
GHADUNFAR	P 402	Keith Nelson, Bembridge	1 July 1968
HAZZA	P 403	Keith Nelson, Bembridge	1 July 1968
DURGHAM	P 404	Keith Nelson, Bembridge	7 June 1969
TIMSAH	P 405	Keith Nelson, Bembridge	1 June 1969
MURAYJIB	P 406	Keith Nelson, Bembridge	7 June 1970

Displacement, tons: 10
Dimensions, feet (metres): 40.3 × 11 × 3.5 (12.3 × 3.4 × 1.1)
Guns: 2—7.62 mm MG
Main engines: 2 Cummins diesels; 370 bhp = 19 knots
Range, miles: 350 at 15 knots
Complement: 6 (1 officer, 5 men)

Of glass fibre hull construction. Transferred to Ministry of Interior (Marine Police) (Abu Dhabi) in July 1977.

TIMSAH   11/1976, UAE Armed Forces

2 "50 ft" CHEVERTON TYPE

Name	No.	Builders	Commissioned
AL SHAHEEN	—	Cheverton Ltd, Isle of Wight	Feb 1975
AL AQAB	—	Cheverton Ltd, Isle of Wight	Feb 1975

Displacement, tons: 20
Dimensions, feet (metres): 50 × 14 × 4.5 (15.2 × 4.3 × 1.4)
Gun: 1 MG
Main engines: 2 General Motors diesels; 2 shafts; 850 bhp = 23 knots
Range, miles: 1 000 at 20 knots
Complement: 8

GRP hull. Originally delivered to the Sharjah Marine Police.

AL SHAHEEN   1975, Roger M. Smith

6 FAIREY MARINE "SPEAR" CLASS (COASTAL PATROL CRAFT)

Dimensions, feet (metres): 29.8 × 9.2 × 2.6 (9.1 × 2.8 × 0.8)
Guns: 2—7.62 mm MGs
Main engines: 2 Perkins diesels of 290 hp = 25 knots
Complement: 3

Order placed in February 1974. Craft delivered between July 1974 and January 1975 five to Abu Dhabi, one to Dubai.

2 "27 ft" CHEVERTON TYPE (TENDERS)

A 271   A 272

Displacement, tons: 3.3
Dimensions, feet (metres): 27 × 9 × 2.7 (8.2 × 2.7 × 0.8)
Main engine: 1 Lister RMW3 diesel; 150 hp = 15 knots

Built of GRP. Acquired from Chevertons, Cowes, Isle of Wight in 1975 by Abu Dhabi. A 272 has a 2 ton hoist.

4 "20 ft" COASTAL PATROL CRAFT

Delivered to Sharjah Marine Police in 1977.

1 FAIREY MARINE "INTERCEPTOR" CLASS

25 ft (7.6 m) craft with catamaran hull. Powered by twin 135 hp outboard motors—speed 30 knots. Can carry a platoon of soldiers or eight life-rafts. Originally delivered to Dubai.

"SPEAR" Class   1974, Faireys

UNITED KINGDOM

Admiralty Board

Secretary of State for Defence (Chairman):
  The Right Hon Francis L. Pym, PC, MC, DL
Minister of State: Ministry of Defence (Vice-Chairman) and Minister of State for Defence Procurement:
  The Right Hon Lord Strathcona and Mount Royal
Parliamentary Under-Secretary of State for Defence for the Royal Navy:
  Herbert Keith Speed, MP, RD
Chief of the Defence Staff:
  Admiral Sir Terence Lewin, GCB, MVO, DSC, ADC
Chief of the Naval Staff and First Sea Lord:
  Admiral Sir Henry Leach, GCB
Chief of Naval Personnel and Second Sea Lord:
  Admiral Sir Gordon Tait, KCB, DSC
Controller of the Navy:
  Vice-Admiral J. D. E. Fieldhouse
Chief of Fleet Support:
  Vice-Admiral W. T. Pillar
Vice-Chief of the Naval Staff:
  Vice-Admiral Sir Anthony Morton, KCB

Commanders-in-Chief

Commander-in-Chief, Naval Home Command:
  Admiral Sir Richard Clayton, KCB
Commander-in-Chief, Fleet:
  Admiral Sir James Eberle, KCB

Flag Officers

Flag Officer, Naval Air Command:
  Rear-Admiral E. R. Anson
Flag Officer, Sea Training:
  Rear-Admiral A. J. Whetstone
Flag Officer, Gibraltar:
  Rear-Admiral G. I. Pritchard
Flag Officer, Medway:
  Rear-Admiral C. B. Williams, OBE
Flag Officer, Plymouth:
  Vice-Admiral Sir Peter Berger, KCB, MVO, DSC
Flag Officer, Portsmouth:
  Rear-Admiral P. E. Bass
Flag Officer, Scotland and Northern Ireland:
  Vice-Admiral C. Rusby, MVO (Vice-Admiral T. H. E. Baird from 11/1979)
Hydrographer of the Navy:
  Rear-Admiral D. W. Haslam, OBE

General Officers, Royal Marines

Commandant-General, Royal Marines:
  Lieutenant-General J. C. C. Richards
Chief of Staff to Commandant-General, Royal Marines:
  Major-General Sir Stewart Pringle, Bt
Major-General Training Group, Royal Marines:
  Major-General P. L. Spurgeon
Major-General Commando Forces, Royal Marines:
  Major-General J. J. Moore, OBE, MC, ADC

Diplomatic Representation

British Naval Attaché in Bonn:
  Captain B. R. Outhwaite
British Naval Adviser in Canberra:
  Captain R. F. G. Laughton
British Naval Attaché in Moscow:
  Captain C. J. Ward
British Naval Adviser in Ottawa:
  Commodore J. J. Streatfield-James
British Naval Attaché in Paris:
  Captain W. S. Gueterbock
British Naval Attaché in Rome:
  Captain G. J. Byers
British Naval Attaché in Washington:
  Rear-Admiral R. M. Burgoyne

Personnel (including Royal Marines)

(a) 1975: 72 500 (10 000 officers, 62 500 ratings and ORs) plus 3 700 servicewomen
    1976: 72 300 (9 900 officers, 62 300 ratings and ORs) plus 3 900 servicewomen
    1977: 72 200 (9 800 officers, 62 400 ratings and ORs) plus 4 000 servicewomen
    1978: 71 200 (9 600 officers, 61 600 ratings and ORs) plus 4 000 servicewomen
    1979: 69 600 (9 500 officers, 60 100 ratings and ORs) plus 3 900 servicewomen
(b) Voluntary service
(c) Regular Reserves (1979): 28 700 men; 1 000 women
(d) RNR and RMR (1979): 5 600 men; 900 women

Fleet Disposition

First Flotilla (Rear-Admiral D. J. Hallifax)
Blake (Flag), 2 "County" class, 4 Frigate Squadrons: 1st (*Galatea* + 4 frigates), 2nd (*Apollo* + 4 frigates), 5th (*Hermione* + 1 destroyer and 4 frigates), 6th (*Sirius* + 1 destroyer and 5 frigates)

Second Flotilla (Rear-Admiral T. M. Stanford, MVO)
2 "County" class, 4 Frigate Squadrons: 3rd (*Arethusa* + 1 destroyer and 5 frigates), 4th (*Cleopatra* + 5 frigates), 7th (*Jupiter* + 1 destroyer and 4 frigates), 8th (*Ajax* + 1 destroyer and 3 frigates)

Third Flotilla (Rear-Admiral P. G. M. Herbert, OBE) (Rear-Admiral J. M. H. Cox from 12/1979)
Hermes, Bulwark, Antrim, Bristol, Intrepid.
Submarine Command (Rear-Admiral R. R. Squires) HQ at Northwood
1st Squadron (*Dolphin*, Portsmouth) 7 Patrol Submarines; 2nd Squadron (Devonport) 5 Fleet Submarines, 2 Patrol Submarines; 3rd Squadron (*Neptune*, Faslane) 4 Fleet Submarines, 2 Patrol Submarines; 10th Squadron (*Neptune*, Faslane) 3 SSBN
MCM Commands:
1st Squadron (Rosyth), 2nd Squadron (Portsmouth), 3rd Squadron (Portland), FPS (Rosyth), 10th Squadron (RNR).
Stand-by Squadron:
Lincoln, Lynx, Glasserton as reserve for deployment.

Strength of the Fleet

Type	Active	Building (Projected)	Reserve
SSBNs	3 (+1 refit)	—	—
Submarines—Fleet	10 (+1 refit)	3 (+1)	—
Submarines—Patrol	11 (+5 refit)	—	2
Aircraft Carriers	2	—	—
A/S Carriers	1	2	—
Helicopter Cruisers	1	—	1
Light Cruisers	6 (+1 refit)	—	—
Destroyers	7	13	—
Frigates	42 (+9 refit)	—	3
Assault Ships (LPD)	1	—	1
LSLs	5 (+1 refit)	—	—
LCLs	2	—	—
LCT	1	—	—
LCMs	28	—	—
LCVPs	26	—	—
LCPLs	3	—	—
LPA	—	1 (conversion)	—
Offshore Patrol Craft	7	—	—
Fast Attack Craft—Patrol	1	—	—
Large Patrol Craft	11	—	—
Fast Training Boats	3	—	—
MCM Support Ship	1	—	—
Minehunters	15 (+2 refit)	4	—
Minesweepers—Coastal	15 (+2 refit)	—	—
Minesweepers—Inshore	5	—	—
MSM	2	— (12)	—
Maintenance Ships	3	—	—
Target Ship	1	—	—
Survey Ships	4	—	—
Coastal Survey Ships	4	—	—
Inshore Survey Craft	5	—	—
Ice Patrol Ship	1	—	—
Royal Yacht	1	—	—
Hovercraft	6	—	—
Diving Support Ships	2	—	—
Large Fleet Tankers	5	—	—
Support Tankers	4	(2)	—
Coastal Tanker	1	—	—
Small Fleet Tankers	4 (+1 refit)	—	—
Helicopter Support Ship	1	—	—
Stores Support Ships	3	—	—
Fleet Replenishment Ships	4	1	—
Store Carrier	1	—	—
MSBVs	11	—	—
Trials Ships	6	1	—
TRVs	11	4	—
Cable Ship	1	—	—
Armament Carriers	1	—	2
Water Carriers	8	—	3
Ocean Tugs	11	—	1
Harbour Tugs	55	(4)	3
Tenders	52	—	—
RNXS Craft	10	4	—
DG Vessels	3	2	—
TCVs	4	—	—
Diving Tenders	5	—	—

Fleet Air Arm

Aircraft	Role	Deployment	No. of sqdns or flights	Squadron No.
Sea Harrier	VSTOL	*Hermes*	1 Sqdn	800
Sea Harrier	VSTOL	*Invincible*	1 Sqdn	801
Sea Harrier	VSTOL	*Illustrious*	1 Sqdn	802
Jetstream T2	Observer Training	Culdrose	1 Sqdn	850

Note: 35 Sea Harriers on order.

Helicopters

Aircraft	Role	Deployment	No. of sqdns or flights	Squadron No.
Lynx	Aircrew Training	Yeovilton	1 Sqdn	702
Lynx	ASW	Destroyers and Frigates	13 Flights	702
Sea King	ASW	RFAs	1 Sqdn	824
Sea King	ASW	*Hermes*	1 Sqdn	814
Sea King	ASW	*Bulwark* and *Blake*	2 Sqdns	820, 826
Sea King	ASW	Prestwick	1 Sqdn	819
Sea King	Aircrew Training	Culdrose	1 Sqdn	706
Sea King	ASW	RFAs	2 Flights	706
Wasp	ASW	"Leander" Class		
Wasp	ASW	"Rothesay" Class		
Wasp	ASW	"Tribal" Class	31 Flights	829
Wasp	ASW	Type 21		
Wasp	ASW	Type 42		
Wasp	Aircrew Training	Portland	1 Sqdn	703
Wessex 3	ASW	"County" Class	5 Flights	737
Wessex 3	Aircrew Training	Portland	1 Sqdn	737
Wessex 5	Commando Assault	Yeovilton	2 Sqdns	815, 816
Wessex 5	Aircrew Training	Yeovilton	1 Sqdn	707
Wessex 5	Fleet Requirements	Portland	1 Sqdn	772

Note: (a) 15 Westland Sea King Mk IV on order. On completion 815 and 816 Squadrons will have four Sea King Mk IV and six Wessex. Remainder of Sea King Mk IVs to 707 Squadron for training and SAR. First deliveries late 1979.
(b) New design in progress for helicopter WG 34. This is to be slightly smaller than Sea King with enhanced A/S capability.

Mercantile Marine

Lloyd's Register of Shipping:
  3 359 vessels of 30 896 606 tons gross

DELETIONS
(**Note:** Disposal List following)

Submarines

1972 *Artemis, Acheron, Alderney, Aeneas, Alcide, Alliance*
1976 *Rorqual*
1977 *Andrew* (b.u.—4 May)
1979 *Narwhal* (b.u. Plymouth)

Carriers (of all kinds)

1972 *Centaur* and *Albion*
1978 *Eagle* (b.u. Cairn Ryan)

Cruiser

1975 *Lion* (b.u. Inverkeithing 24 Apr)

Light Cruiser

1976 *Hampshire*

Destroyers

1972 *Crossbow, Defender, Saintes*
1974 *Agincourt* (b.u. Sunderland 27 Oct)
1975 *Corunna* (b.u. Blyth 11 Sep)
1978 *Barrosa* (b.u. Blyth 29 Nov). *Matapan* (b.u. Blyth)

Frigates

1972 *Verulam, Venus*
1974 *Tenby, Scarborough. Whirlwind* (target 28 Oct)
1976 *Blackwood, Puma. Llandaff* (to Bangladesh), *Volage*
1977 *Mermaid* (to Malaysia), *Scarborough* (b.u.)
1978 *Jaguar* (to Bangladesh). *Leopard, Blackpool, Undaunted* (sunk as target Nov), *Malcolm*
1979 *Whitby* (b.u. Queenborough). *Exmouth* (b.u. Britonterry)

Depot Ship

1978 *Maidstone* to Rosyth for b.u. (May)

MCM Vessels

1974 *Woolaston*
1975 *Boulston, Maddiston* (scrapped). *Birdham, Odiham* (for sale)
1976 *Highburton, Woolaston, Arlingham. Fittleton* (sunk in collision Sep b.u. after salvage)
1977 *Ashton* (Aug). *Dufton* (b.u.—10 June). *Chawton* (b.u.—6 Aug)

Fast Attack Craft

1976 *Dark Gladiator* (sunk as target—Portland)

Service Forces

1973 *Moorsman, Foulness*
1974 *Wave Chief, Derwentdale* (returned to owners), *Brown Ranger* (Tankers) *Barmond* (MSBV), *Miner III*
1975 *Dispenser*, (MSBV), *Robert Middleton* (Stores Carrier), *Icewhale* (Trials Ship), *Freshmere* (Water boat), *Bowstring* (Armament Carrier). *Ironbridge, Nordenfeld*
1976 *Tideflow* (to b.u. Bilbao—4 May). *Spalake, Spaburn, Freshpool, Freshpond*
1977 *Tidesurge* (Tanker, b.u.—April). *Barfoot* (MSBV, b.u.—23 Aug) *Reliant* (Airstores Ship, b.u.—23 Aug). *Throsk* (Stores Ship, b.u.—12 June) *Spa Beck, Spa Brook* (water carriers)
1978 *Hebe, Empire Gull, Orangeleaf, Retainer, Coll, Graemsay, Bern*
1979 *Cherryleaf*

Survey Ship

1976 *Vidal* (b.u. Bruges—June)

Tugs

1975 *Diver, Driver, Eminent, Empire Ace, Empire Demon, Empire Fred, Empire Rosa, Fidget, Foremost, Freedom, Frisky, Handmaid, Impetus, Integrity, Prompt, Security, Tampeon, Trunnion, Vagrant, Weasel*
1976 *Reward* (to disposal after salvage 29 Aug)

DISPOSAL LIST

The following ships already deleted from the Navy List are not on the Active or Reserve list and are held in the ports shown pending disposal by sale or scrap in which event they are transferred to Deletions above.

Submarines

Narwhal, Cachalot, Finwhale

Aircraft Carrier

Ark Royal (Plymouth)

Light Cruiser

Devonshire

Destroyer

Caprice (Plymouth)

Frigates

Grenville (Portsmouth)
Keppel (Portsmouth)
Palliser (Portsmouth)
Rapid (Milford Haven—Target)
Chichester, Eastbourne, Dundas, Hardy

Minesweeper—Coastal

Belton (Rosyth)

Minesweepers—Inshore

Bottisham, Chelsham, Pagham, Thakeham, Tongham, Odiham, Puttenham, Birdham

Fast Attack Craft

Brave Borderer (Pembroke Dock)
Brave Swordsman (Pembroke Dock)
Dark Hero (Pembroke Dock)

Submarine Depot Ship

Forth (Devonport)

Service Forces

Tidereach (Portsmouth)

LSTs

Lofoten (Rosyth)
Messina (Plymouth)
Stalker (Rosyth)
Zeebrugge (Plymouth)

Immobile Tenders

Diamond D 35. Attached to *Sultan* for engineering training at Portsmouth
Ulster F 83. Accommodation ship at Plymouth
Russell F 97. Attached to *Sultan/Collingwood*—Portsmouth
Grampus S 04. Harbour Training—*Dolphin*—Portsmouth
Duncan F 80. Attached to *Caledonia*—Rosyth
Eastbourne F 73. Attached to *Caledonia*—Rosyth (approved for disposal 1978)

LIST OF PENNANT NUMBERS

Note: Not displayed on Submarines or RMAS craft.

*Disposal List

Submarines

S 01	Porpoise	
S 03	Narwhal*	
S 04	Grampus*	
S 05	Finwhale*	
S 06	Cachalot*	
S 07	Sealion	
S 08	Walrus	
S 09	Oberon	
S 10	Odin	
S 11	Orpheus	
S 12	Olympus	
S 13	Osiris	
S 14	Onslaught	
S 15	Otter	
S 16	Oracle	
S 17	Ocelot	

Submarines

S 18	Otus	
S 19	Opossum	
S 20	Opportune	
S 21	Onyx	
S 22	Resolution	
S 23	Repulse	
S 26	Renown	
S 27	Revenge	
S 101	Dreadnought	
S 102	Valiant	
S 103	Warspite	
S 104	Churchill	
S 105	Conqueror	
S 106	Courageous	
S 108	Sovereign	
S 109	Superb	

Submarines

S 110	Sceptre	
S 111	Spartan	
S 112	Splendid	
S 113	Trafalgar	
S 114	New Construction	
S 126	Swiftsure	

Aircraft Carriers

R 08	Bulwark	
R 09	Ark Royal	
R 12	Hermes	
CAH 1	Invincible	
CAH 2	Illustrious	
CAH 3	Ark Royal	

Cruisers

C 20	Tiger	
C 99	Blake	

Light Cruisers and Destroyers

D 01	Caprice*	
D 02	Devonshire*	
D 12	Kent	
D 16	London	
D 18	Antrim	
D 19	Glamorgan	
D 20	Fife	
D 21	Norfolk	
D 23	Bristol	

UK / Introduction

Light Cruisers and Destroyers

D 35	Diamond	
D 80	Sheffield	
D 86	Birmingham	
D 87	Newcastle	
D 88	Glasgow	
D 89	Exeter	
D 90	Southampton	
D 91	Nottingham	
D 92	Liverpool	
D 95	Manchester	
D 108	Cardiff	
D 118	Coventry	

Frigates

F 10	Aurora	
F 12	Achilles	
F 15	Euryalus	
F 16	Diomede	
F 18	Galatea	
F 27	Lynx	
F 28	Cleopatra	
F 32	Salisbury	
F 38	Arethusa	
F 39	Naiad	
F 40	Sirius	
F 42	Phoebe	
F 43	Torquay	
F 45	Minerva	
F 47	Danae	
F 52	Juno	
F 54	Hardy	
F 56	Argonaut	
F 57	Andromeda	
F 58	Hermione	
F 59	Chichester	
F 60	Jupiter	
F 69	Bacchante	
F 70	Apollo	
F 71	Scylla	
F 72	Ariadne	
F 75	Charybdis	
F 80	Duncan*	
F 83	Ulster*	
F 85	Keppel*	
F 88	Broadsword	
F 89	Battleaxe	
F 90	Brilliant	
F 91	Brazen	
F 94	Palliser*	
F 97	Russell*	
F 99	Lincoln	
F 101	Yarmouth	
F 103	Lowestoft	
F 104	Dido	
F 106	Brighton	
F 107	Rothesay	
F 108	Londonderry	
F 109	Leander	
F 113	Falmouth	
F 114	Ajax	
F 115	Berwick	
F 117	Ashanti	
F 119	Eskimo	
F 122	Gurkha	
F 124	Zulu	
F 125	Mohawk	
F 126	Plymouth	
F 127	Penelope	
F 129	Rhyl	
F 131	Nubian	
F 133	Tartar	
F 138	Rapid*	
F 169	Amazon	
F 170	Antelope	
F 171	Active	
F 172	Ambuscade	
F 173	Arrow	
F 174	Alacrity	
F 184	Ardent	
F 185	Avenger	
F 197	Grenville*	

Assault Ships

L 10	Fearless
L 11	Intrepid

Logistic Landing Ships and LCTs

L 700-711	LCM 9
L 3004	Sir Bedivere
L 3005	Sir Galahad
L 3027	Sir Geraint
L 3029	Sir Lancelot
L 3036	Sir Percivale
L 3505	Sir Tristram
L 3507-8	LCM 9
L 4001	Ardennes
L 4002	Agheila
L 4003	Arakan

LCMs (RCT)

RPL 01	Avon
RPL 02	Bude
RPL 03	Clyde
RPL 04	Dart
RPL 05	Eden
RPL 06	Forth
RPL 07	Glen
RPL 08	Hamble
RPL 09	Itchen
RPL 10	Kennet
RPL 11	Loddon
RPL 12	Medway

Helicopter Support Ship

K 08	Engadine

Minelayer

N 21	Abdiel

Support Ships and Auxiliaries

A 00	Britannia
A 70	Echo
A 71	Enterprise
A 72	Egeria
A 75	Tidespring
A 76	Tidepool
A 77	Pearleaf
A 78	Plumleaf
A 82	Cherryleaf
A 85	Faithful
A 86	Forceful
A 87	Favourite
A 88	Agile
A 89	Advice
A 90	Accord
A 93	Dexterous
A 94	Director
A 95	Typhoon
A 99	Beaulieu
A 100	Beddgelert
A 101	Bembridge
A 102	Airedale
A 103	Bibury
A 104	Blakeney
A 105	Brodick
A 106	Alsatian
A 108	Triumph
A 111	Cyclone
A 112	Felicity
A 113	Alice
A 116	Agatha
A 117	Audrey
A 121	Agnes
A 122	Olwen
A 123	Olna
A 124	Olmeda
A 126	Cairn
A 127	Torrent
A 128	Torrid
A 129	Dalmatian
A 133	Hecla
A 134	Rame Head
A 137	Hecate
A 138	Herald
A 144	Hydra
A 145	Daisy
A 146	Waterman
A 148	Fiona
A 152	Georgina
A 155	Deerhound
A 156	Daphne
A 157	Loyal Helper
A 158	Supporter
A 159	Loyal Watcher
A 160	Loyal Volunteer
A 161	Loyal Mediator
A 162	Elkhound
A 164	Goosander
A 165	Pochard
A 166	Kathleen
A 168	Labrador
A 170	Kitty
A 171	Endurance
A 172	Lesley
A 173	Dorothy
A 174	Lilah
A 175	Mary
A 177	Edith
A 178	Husky
A 179	Whimbrel
A 180	Mastiff
A 181	Irene
A 182	Saluki
A 183	Isabel
A 188	Pointer
A 189	Setter
A 190	Joan
A 191	Berry Head
A 193	Joyce
A 196	Gwendoline
A 197	Sealyham
A 198	Helen
A 199	Myrtle
A 201	Spaniel
A 202	Nancy
A 205	Norah
A 207	Llandovery
A 208	Lamlash

Support Ships and Auxiliaries

A 210	Charlotte
A 211	Lechlade
A 216	Bee
A 217	Christine
A 220	Loyal Moderator
A 222	Spapool
A 228	Clare
A 229	Cricket
A 230	Cockchafer
A 231	Reclaim
A 232	Kingarth
A 236	Wakeful
A 239	Gnat
A 250	Sheepdog
A 252	Doris
A 253	Ladybird
A 259	St. Margarets
A 261	Eddyfirth
A 263	Cicala
A 268	Green Rover
A 269	Grey Rover
A 270	Blue Rover
A 271	Gold Rover
A 273	Black Rover
A 274	Ettrick
A 277	Elsing
A 280	Resurgent
A 281	Kinbrace
A 288	Sea Giant
A 289	Confiance
A 290	Confident
A 308	Ilchester
A 309	Instow
A 310	Invergordon
A 317	Bulldog
A 318	Ixworth
A 319	Beagle
A 320	Fox
A 322	Betty
A 323	Bridget
A 324	Barbara
A 327	Basset
A 328	Collie
A 330	Corgi
A 332	Caldy
A 335	Fawn
A 336	Lundy
A 338	Skomer
A 339	Lyness
A 341	Fotherby
A 344	Stromness
A 345	Tarbatness
A 346	Switha
A 348	Felsted
A 350	Cartmel
A 351	Cawsand
A 353	Elkstone
A 354	Froxfield
A 355	Epworth
A 361	Roysterer
A 363	Denmead
A 364	Whitehead
A 365	Fulbeck
A 366	Robust
A 367	Newton
A 377	Maxim
A 381	Cricklade
A 382	Vigilant (ex-Loyal Factor)
A 385	Fort Grange
A 386	Fort Austin
A 389	Clovelly
A 391	Criccieth
A 392	Glencoe
A 393	Dunster
A 394	Fintry
A 402	Grasmere
A 404	Bacchus
A 480	Resource
A 482	Kinloss
A 486	Regent
A 488	Cromarty
A 490	Dornoch
A 502	Rollicker
A 507	Uplifter
A 510	Alert (ex-Loyal Governor)
A 1767	Hever
A 1768	Harlech
A 1769	Hambledon
A 1770	Loyal Chancellor
A 1771	Loyal Proctor
A 1772	Holmwood
A 1773	Horning
A 1776	Headcorn

Auxiliaries

Y 10	Aberdovey
Y 11	Abinger
Y 12	Alness
Y 13	Alnmouth
Y 14	Appleby
Y 15	Watercourse
Y 16	Ashcote
Y 17	Waterfall
Y 18	Watershed
Y 19	Waterspout
Y 20	Waterside
Y 21	Oilpress
Y 22	Oilstone
Y 23	Oilwell
Y 24	Oilfield
Y 25	Oilbird
Y 26	Oilman
Y 30	Watercourse
Y 31	Waterfowl

Boom Defence Vessels

P 190	Laymoor
P 192	Mandarin
P 193	Pintail
P 194	Garganey
P 195	Goldeneye

Light Forces

P 260	Kingfisher
P 261	Cygnet
P 262	Peterel
P 263	Sandpiper
P 271	Scimitar
P 274	Cutlass
P 275	Sabre
P 276	Tenacity
P 277	Anglesey
P 278	Alderney
P 295	Jersey
P 297	Guernsey
P 298	Shetland
P 299	Orkney
P 300	Lindisfarne
P 1007	Beachampton
P 1055	Monkton
P 1089	Wasperton
P 1093	Wolverton
P 1096	Yarnton
P 3104	Dee (ex-Beckford)
P 3113	Droxford

Coastal Minesweepers

M 29	Brecon
M 1103	Alfriston
M 1109	Bickington
M 1110	Bildeston
M 1113	Brereton
M 1114	Brinton
M 1115	Bronington
M 1116	Wilton
M 1124	Crichton
M 1125	Cuxton
M 1133	Bossington
M 1140	Gavington
M 1141	Glasserton
M 1146	Hodgeston
M 1147	Hubberston
M 1151	Iveston
M 1153	Kedleston
M 1154	Kellington
M 1157	Kirkliston
M 1158	Laleston
M 1165	Maxton
M 1166	Nurton
M 1167	Repton
M 1173	Pollington
M 1180	Shavington
M 1181	Sheraton
M 1182	Shoulton
M 1187	Upton
M 1188	Walkerton
M 1195	Wotton
M 1199	Belton*
M 1200	Soberton
M 1204	Stubbington
M 1208	Lewiston
M 1216	Crofton

Inshore Minesweepers

M 2002	Aveley
M 2010	Isis (ex-Cradley)
M 2614	Bucklesham TRV
M 2621	Dittisham
M 2622	Downham TRV
M 2626	Everingham TRV
M 2628	Flintham
M 2630	Fritham TRV
M 2635	Haversham TRV
M 2636	Lasham TRV
M 2717	Fordham DGV
M 2720	Waterwitch (ex-Powderham)
M 2726	Shipham RNXS
M 2737	Warmingham DGV
M 2780	Woodlark (ex-Yaxham)
M 2781	Portisham RNXS
M 2790	Thatcham DGV
M 2791	Sandringham
M 2793	Thornham

DGV	=	Degaussing Vessels
RNXS	=	Royal Naval Auxiliary Service
TRV	=	Torpedo Recovery Vessels
R	=	Reserve (ex-RAF)

586 UK / Introduction

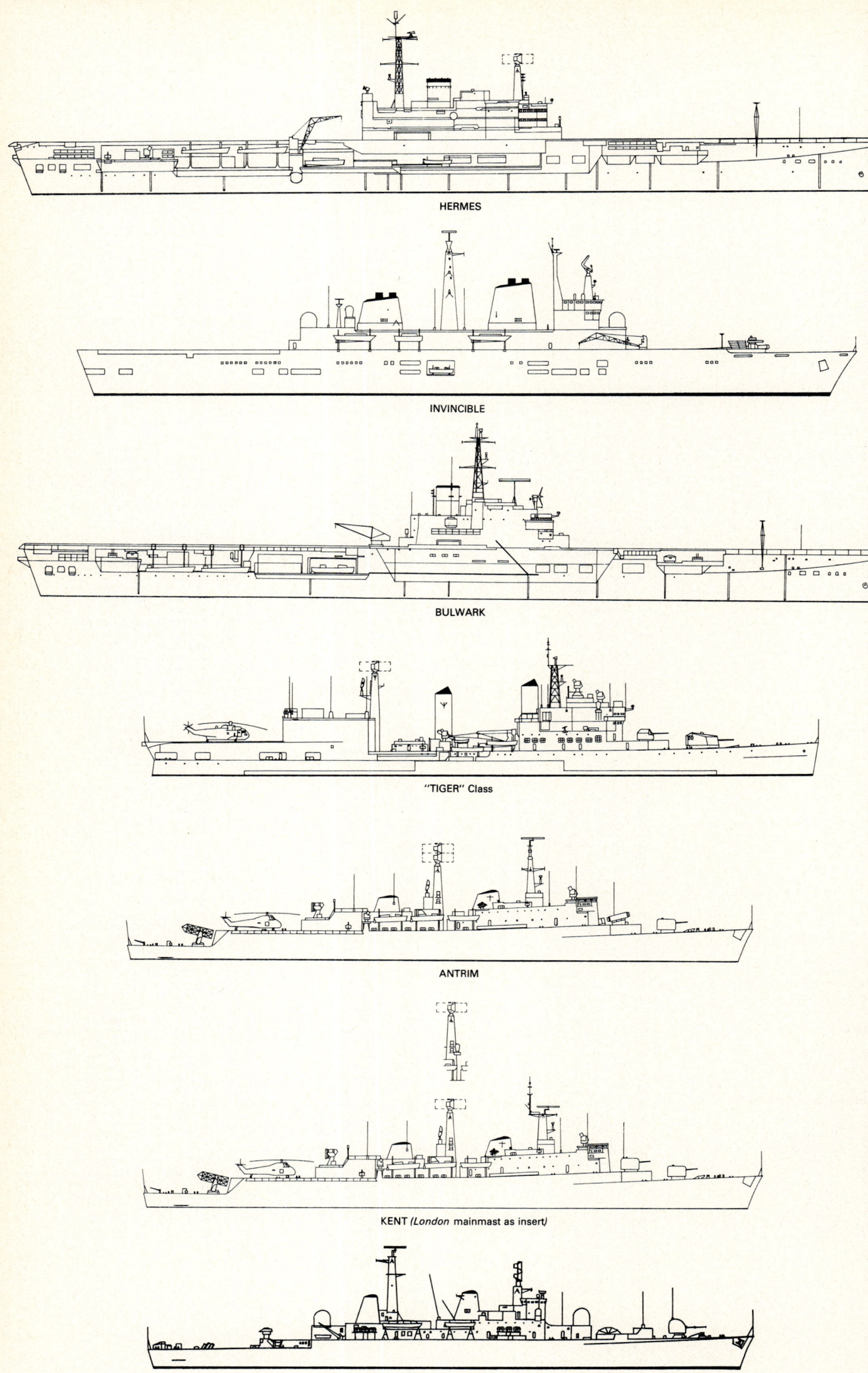

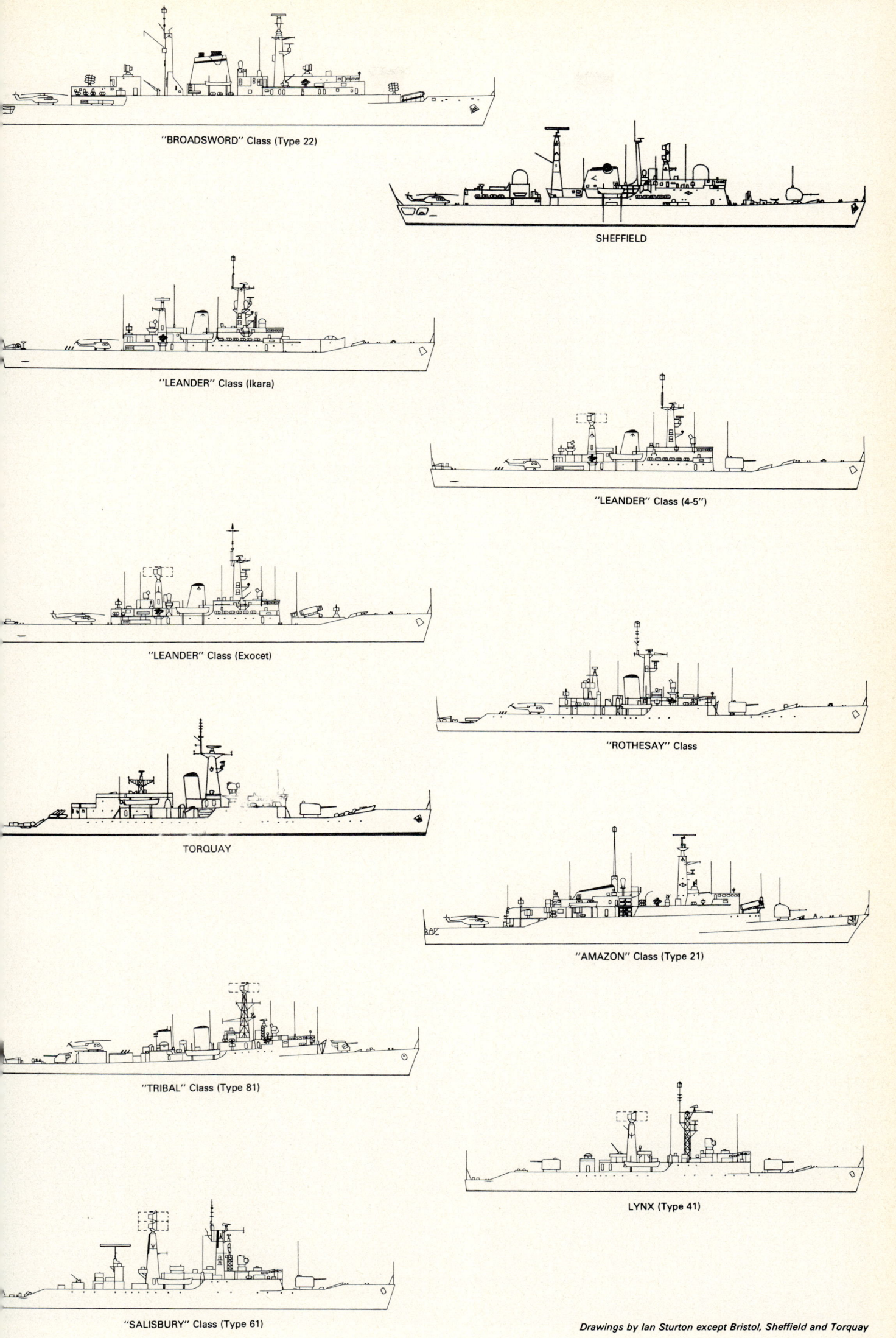

SUBMARINES
Nuclear Powered Ballistic Missile Submarines (SSBN)
4 "RESOLUTION" CLASS

Name	No.	Builders	Laid down	Launched	Commissioned
RESOLUTION	S 22	Vickers (Shipbuilding) Ltd, Barrow-in-Furness	26 Feb 1964	15 Sep 1966	2 Oct 1967
REPULSE	S 23	Vickers (Shipbuilding) Ltd, Barrow-in-Furness	12 Mar 1965	4 Nov 1967	28 Sep 1968
RENOWN*	S 26	Cammell Laird & Co Ltd, Birkenhead	25 June 1964	25 Feb 1967	15 Nov 1968
REVENGE	S 27	Cammell Laird & Co Ltd, Birkenhead	19 May 1965	15 Mar 1968	4 Dec 1969

* Refit

Displacement, tons: 7 500 surfaced; 8 400 dived
Length, feet (metres): 425 *(129·5)*
Beam, feet (metres): 33 *(10·1)*
Draught, feet (metres): 30 *(9·1)*
Missiles, surface: 16 tubes amidships for Polaris A—3 SLBMs
Torpedo tubes: 6—21 in *(533 mm)* (bow)
Nuclear reactors: 1 pressurised water-cooled
Main machinery: Geared steam turbines; 1 shaft
Speed, knots: 20 surfaced; 25 dived
Complement: 143 (13 officers, 130 ratings); 2 crews (see *Personnel*)

In February 1963 it was officially stated that it was intended to order four or five 7 000 ton nuclear powered submarines, each to carry 16 Polaris missiles, and it was planned that the first would be on patrol in 1968. Their hulls and machinery would be of British design. As well as building two submarines Vickers (Shipbuilding) would give lead yard service to the builder of the other two. Four Polaris submarines were in fact ordered in May 1963. The plan to build a fifth Polaris submarine was cancelled on 15 February 1965. Britain's first SSBN, *Resolution,* put to sea on 22 June 1967 and completed six weeks trial in the Firth of Clyde and Atlantic on 17 August 1967.

Cost: *Resolution,* £40·24 million; *Renown,* £39·95 million; *Repulse,* £37·5 million; *Revenge,* £38·6 million; completed ships excluding missiles.

External gear: Hoist gear by MacTaggart, Scott & Co Ltd for: Attack and search periscopes, Radar and EW masts, Snort induction and exhaust, ALP and ALK aerials.

Missiles: Polaris A3 carry ten MIRV heads each of 60 KT.

Personnel: Each submarine, which has accommodation for 19 officers and 135 ratings, is manned on a two-crew basis, in order to get maximum operational time at sea.

Radar: Search: I-band.
Periscope radar.

Sonar: Types 2001 and 2007.

RESOLUTION   1978, MOD(N)

REVENGE   1978, MOD(N)

REPULSE   1978, MOD(N)

UK / Submarines 589

Fleet Submarines

Note: (a) It is planned to provide Sub-Harpoon in all Fleet Submarines from the early 1980s.
(b) Negotiations for supply of Sub-Harpoon in early 1980s completed 1977.

0 + 2 + 1 NEW CONSTRUCTION "TRAFALGAR" CLASS

Name	No.	Builders	Laid down	Launched	Commissioned
TRAFALGAR	S 113	Vickers (Shipbuilding) Ltd, Barrow-in-Furness	1978	—	—
—	S 114	Vickers (Shipbuilding) Ltd, Barrow-in-Furness	1979	—	—

The first of an improved class of Fleet Submarines was ordered in September 1977. S 114 ordered 29 July 1978 with a third to be ordered in 1979. Improvements include equipment, endurance and speed.

5 + 1 "SWIFTSURE" CLASS

Name	No.	Builders	Laid down	Launched	Commissioned
SOVEREIGN	S 108	Vickers (Shipbuilding) Ltd, Barrow-in-Furness	17 Sep 1970	17 Feb 1973	11 July 1974
SUPERB	S 109	Vickers (Shipbuilding) Ltd, Barrow-in-Furness	16 Mar 1972	30 Nov 1974	13 Nov 1976
SCEPTRE	S 110	Vickers (Shipbuilding) Ltd, Barrow-in-Furness	25 Oct 1973	20 Nov 1976	14 Feb 1978
SPARTAN	S 111	Vickers (Shipbuilding) Ltd, Barrow-in-Furness	24 Apr 1976	7 Apr 1978	May 1979
SPLENDID	S 112	Vickers (Shipbuilding) Ltd, Barrow-in-Furness	1 Nov 1977	Oct 1979	? 1981
SWIFTSURE*	S 126	Vickers (Shipbuilding) Ltd, Barrow-in-Furness	15 Apr 1969	7 Sep 1971	17 Apr 1973

*Refit

Displacement, tons: 4 000 light; 4 200 standard; 4 500 dived
Length, feet (metres): 272·0 *(82·9)*
Beam, feet (metres): 32·3 *(9·8)*
Draught, feet (metres): 27 *(8·2)*
Torpedo tubes: 5—21 in *(533 mm)* (20 reloads)
Nuclear reactor: 1 pressurised water-cooled
Main machinery: English Electric geared steam turbines; 15 000 shp; 1 Paxman auxiliary diesel; 4 000 hp; 1 shaft
Speed, knots: 30 dived
Complement: 97 (12 officers, 85 men)

Compared with the "Valiant" class submarines these are slightly shorter with a fuller form, with the fore-planes set further forward, with one less torpedo tube and with a deeper diving depth.
Sovereign visited the North Pole 1976. *Spartan* started sea trials in March 1979.

Costs: Building—*Swiftsure* £37·1 million, *Superb* £41·3 million. Running cost £3·8 million per submarine per year.

Design: The pressure hull in the "Swiftsures" maintains its diameter for much greater length than previously.

Electrical: 112 cell emergency battery.

Engineering: Whilst the basic reactor design remains similar to previous types core-life has probably increased.

External gear: Control gear by MacTaggart, Scott & Co Ltd for: Attack and search periscopes, Snort induction and exhaust, Radar and EW masts, ALR buoy. The forward hydroplanes house within the casing, the only activated housing hydroplanes in any submarine design.

Orders: *Swiftsure*, 3 Nov 1967; *Sovereign*, 16 May 1969; *Superb*, 20 May 1970; *Sceptre*, 1 Nov 1971; *Spartan*, 17 Feb 1973; *Severn*, 26 May 1976.

SWIFTSURE 2/1978, MOD(N) (LA Phot. K. W. Taylor)

Radar: Search: Type 1003.

Sonar: Type 2001 in "chin" position, Types 2007, 197 and 183.

Torpedoes: Individual reloading of torpedoes in 15 seconds. To carry Mk 24 (Modified) with anti-ship capability.

SCEPTRE 10/1978, Michael D. J. Lennon

SUPERB 6/1978, MOD(N) (LA Phot. R. C. H. Hodgson)

590 UK / Submarines

5 "VALIANT" CLASS

Name	No.	Builders	Laid down	Launched	Commissioned
VALIANT*	S 102	Vickers (Shipbuilding) Ltd, Barrow-in-Furness	22 Jan 1962	3 Dec 1963	18 July 1966
WARSPITE	S 103	Vickers (Shipbuilding) Ltd, Barrow-in-Furness	10 Dec 1963	25 Sep 1965	18 Apr 1967
CHURCHILL	S 104	Vickers (Shipbuilding) Ltd, Barrow-in-Furness	30 June 1967	20 Dec 1968	15 July 1970
CONQUEROR	S 105	Cammell Laird & Co Ltd, Birkenhead	5 Dec 1967	28 Aug 1969	9 Nov 1971
COURAGEOUS	S 106	Vickers (Shipbuilding) Ltd, Barrow-in-Furness	15 May 1968	7 Mar 1970	16 Oct 1971

* Refit

Displacement, tons: 4 000 light; 4 400 standard; 4 900 dived
Length, feet (metres): 285 *(86·9)*
Beam, feet (metres): 33·2 *(10·1)*
Draught, feet (metres): 27 *(8·2)*
Torpedo tubes: 6—21 in *(533 mm)* (26 reloads)
Nuclear reactor: 1 pressurised water-cooled
Main machinery: English Electric geared steam turbines; 1 shaft
Speed, knots: 28 dived
Complement: 103 (13 officers, 90 men)

It was announced on 31 August 1960 that the contract for a second nuclear powered submarine *(Valiant)* had been awarded to Vickers Ltd, the principal sub-contractors being Vickers-Armstrong (Engineers) Ltd, for the machinery and its installation, and Rolls-Royce and Associates for the nuclear steam raising plant. The class, of which she is the first, is broadly of the same design as that of *Dreadnought,* but slightly larger. She was originally scheduled to be completed in September 1965, but work was held up by the Polaris programme.

Cost: Varied from £24 million *(Warspite)* to £30 million *(Conqueror).*

Electrical: 112 cell emergency battery.

Endurance: On 25 April 1967 *Valiant* completed the 12 000 mile homeward voyage from Singapore, the record submerged passage by a British submarine, after 28 days non-stop.

Engineering: *Valiant's* reactor core was made in the UK, with machinery of British design and manufacture similar to the shore prototype installed in the Admiralty Reactor Test Establishment at Dounreay. The main steam turbines and condensers were designed and manufactured by the English Electric Company, Rugby, and the electrical propulsion machinery and control gear by Laurence, Scott & Electromotors Ltd.

External gear: Control gear by MacTaggart, Scott & Co Ltd for: Attack and search periscopes, radar, SHFD/F and communication masts, snort induction and exhaust masts and ALK buoy.

Orders: *Valiant,* 31 Aug 1960—*Warspite,* 12 Dec 1962—*Churchill,* 21 Oct 1965—*Conqueror,* 9 Aug 1966—*Courageous,* 1 Mar 1967.

Radar: Search: Type 1003.

Sonar: Type 2001 in "chin" position; Types 2007, 197 and 183.

Torpedoes: Individual reloading in 15 seconds.

VALIANT 6/1977, C. and S. Taylor

CHURCHILL 1978, MOD(N)

1 "DREADNOUGHT" CLASS

Name	No.	Builders	Laid down	Launched	Commissioned
DREADNOUGHT	S 101	Vickers-Armstrong, Barrow-in-Furness	12 June 1959	21 Oct 1960	17 Apr 1963

Displacement, tons: 3 000 standard; 3 500 surfaced; 4 000 dived
Length, feet (metres): 265·8 *(81·0)*
Beam, feet (metres): 32·2 *(9·8)*
Draught, feet (metres): 26 *(7·9)*
Torpedo tubes: 6—21 in *(533 mm)* (bow)
Nuclear reactor: 1 S5W pressurised water-cooled
Main machinery: Geared steam turbines; 15 000 shp; 1 shaft
Speed, knots: 28 dived
Complement: 88 (11 officers, 77 men)

As originally planned *Dreadnought* was to have been fitted with a British designed and built nuclear reactor, but in 1958 an agreement was concluded with the US Government for the purchase of a complete set of propulsion machinery of the type fitted in USS *Skipjack.* This agreement enabled the submarine to be launched far earlier. The supply of this machinery was made under a contract between the Westinghouse Electric Corporation and Rolls-Royce. The latter were also supplied with design and manufacturing details of the reactor and with safety information and set up a factory in this country to manufacture similar cores. *Dreadnought* has a hull of British design both as regards structural strength and hydrodynamic features, although the latter are based on the pioneering work of the US Navy in *Skipjack* and *Albacore.* From about amidships aft, the hull lines closely resemble *Skipjack* to accommodate the propulsion machinery. The forward end is wholly British in concept. In the Control Room and Attack Centre the instruments are fitted into consoles.

The improved water distilling plant for the first time provides unlimited fresh water for shower baths and for washing machines in the fully equipped laundry.

She is fitted with an inertial navigation system and with means of measuring her depth below ice and was the first British submarine to surface at the North Pole, in 1970.

Radar: Search: I-band.

Sonar: Type 2001 in "chin" position; Type 2007.

DREADNOUGHT 6/1977, Wright and Logan

UK / Submarines 591

Patrol Submarines

NEW CONSTRUCTION

It is now policy to build a further class of patrol (non-nuclear) submarines. It is too early to suggest any parameters although it is to be hoped that modern technology will keep their displacement well within 2 000 tons which is proving not only a practicable size but a marketable one.

13 "OBERON" CLASS   3 "PORPOISE" CLASS

"OBERON" CLASS

Name	No.	Builders	Laid down	Launched	Commissioned
OBERON	S 09	HM Dockyard, Chatham	28 Nov 1957	18 July 1959	24 Feb 1961
ODIN	S 10	Cammell Laird & Co Ltd, Birkenhead	27 Apr 1959	4 Nov 1960	3 May 1962
ORPHEUS	S 11	Vickers (Shipbuilding) Ltd, Barrow-in-Furness	16 Apr 1959	17 Nov 1959	25 Nov 1960
OLYMPUS	S 12	Vickers (Shipbuilding) Ltd, Barrow-in-Furness	4 Mar 1960	14 June 1961	7 July 1962
OSIRIS	S 13	Vickers (Shipbuilding) Ltd, Barrow-in-Furness	26 Jan 1962	29 Nov 1962	11 Jan 1964
ONSLAUGHT	S 14	HM Dockyard, Chatham	8 Apr 1959	24 Sep 1960	14 Aug 1962
OTTER*	S 15	Scotts (Shipbuilding) Co Ltd, Greenock	14 Jan 1960	15 May 1961	20 Aug 1962
ORACLE*	S 16	Cammell Laird & Co Ltd, Birkenhead	26 Apr 1960	26 Sep 1961	14 Feb 1963
OCELOT*	S 17	HM Dockyard, Chatham	17 Nov 1960	5 May 1962	31 Jan 1964
OTUS*	S 18	Scotts (Shipbuilding) Co Ltd, Greenock	31 May 1961	17 Oct 1962	5 Oct 1963
OPOSSUM*	S 19	Cammell Laird & Co Ltd, Birkenhead	21 Dec 1961	23 May 1963	5 June 1964
OPPORTUNE	S 20	Scotts (Shipbuilding) Co Ltd, Greenock	26 Oct 1962	14 Feb 1964	29 Dec 1964
ONYX	S 21	Cammell Laird & Co Ltd, Birkenhead	16 Nov 1964	18 Aug 1966	20 Nov 1967

*Refit

"PORPOISE" CLASS

Name	No.	Builders	Laid down	Launched	Commissioned
PORPOISE	S 01	Vickers (Shipbuilding) Ltd, Barrow-in-Furness	15 June 1954	25 Apr 1956	17 Apr 1958
SEALION	S 07	Cammell Laird & Co Ltd, Birkenhead	5 June 1958	31 Dec 1959	25 July 1961
WALRUS	S 08	Scotts (Shipbuilding) Co Ltd, Greenock	12 Feb 1958	22 Sep 1959	10 Feb 1961

Displacement, tons: 1 610 standard; 2 030 surfaced; 2 410 dived
Length, feet (metres): 295·2 (90·0)
Beam, feet (metres): 26·5 (8·1)
Draught, feet (metres): 18 (5·5)
Torpedo tubes: 8—21 in (533 mm) (6 bow, 2 stern); 24 torpedoes carried
Main machinery: 2 Admiralty Standard Range 1, 16 VMS diesels; 3 680 bhp; 2 electric motors; 6 000 shp; 2 shafts
Speed, knots: 12 surfaced; 17 dived
Range, miles: 9 000 surfaced
Complement: 68 (6 officers, 62 men) in "Oberon" class
71 (6 officers, 65 men) in "Porpoise" class

As a result of the 1975 Defence Review the following have been retired some years before the end of hull life:—
Torqual scrapped 1977.
Grampus to reserve 1976.
Narwhal to reserve 1977.
Cachalot to reserve September 1977.
Finwhale to reserve November 1978.

Cost: Running cost, at 1976 prices, £1·1 million per boat per year. Building cost: *Oberon* £2·43 million, *Onyx* £3·6 million.

Construction: For the first time in British submarines plastic was used in the superstructure construction of the "Oberon" class. Before and abaft the bridge the superstructure is mainly of glass fibre laminate in most units of this class. The superstructure of *Orpheus* is of light alloy aluminium.

Diving depth: 800-900 ft.

Engineering: 3-bladed, 7 ft diameter propellers; 400 rpm.

External gear: Control gear by MacTaggart, Scott and Co Ltd or: Search and attack periscopes, radar, communications and HFD/F masts, short induction and exhaust masts.

Gunnery: "O" class submarines serving in the Far East carried a 20 mm Oerlikon gun during Indonesian Confrontation.

Modification: *Oberon* has been modified with deeper casing to house equipment for the initial training of personnel for nuclear powered submarines. Others of this class are currently undergoing modification.

OSIRIS 7/1978, Michael D. J. Lennon

OPOSSUM 9/1978, John G. Callis

Radar: Search: I-band.

Sonar: Types 186 and 187.

Transfer: The submarine of the "Oberon" class laid down on 27 September 1962 at HM Dockyard, Chatham as *Onyx* for the Royal Navy was launched on 29 February 1964 as *Ojibwa* for the Royal Canadian Navy. She was replaced by another "Oberon" class submarine named *Onyx* for the Royal Navy built by Cammell Laird, Birkenhead.

OBERON 8/1978, J. L. M. van der Burg

592 UK / Aircraft carriers

AIRCRAFT CARRIERS

Name	No.	Builders	Laid down	Launched	Commissioned
HERMES	R 12	Vickers (Shipbuilding) Ltd, Barrow-in-Furness	21 June 1944	16 Feb 1953	18 Nov 1959

Displacement, tons: 23 900 standard; 28 700 full load
Length, feet (metres): 744·3 *(226·9)*
Beam, feet (metres): 90·0 *(27·4)* hull
Draught, feet (metres): 28·5 *(8·7)*
Width, feet (metres): 160·0 *(48·8)* oa
Aircraft: A squadron of Sea King, and Wessex 5 helicopters
Armour: Reinforced flight deck (0·75 in); 1—2 in over magazines and machinery spares
Missiles: 2 quad Sea Cat launchers either side abaft the after lift
Main engines: Parsons geared turbines; 2 shafts; 76 000 shp
Boilers: 4 Admiralty 3-drum type
Speed, knots: 28
Oil fuel, tons: 4 200 furnace; 320 diesel
Complement: 1 350 (143 officers, 1 207 ratings). In emergency a Commando can be embarked

Originally name ship of a class including *Albion, Bulwark* and *Centaur*, but design was modified to a more advanced type, incorporating new equipment and improved arrangements, including five post-war developments— angled deck, steam catapult, landing sight, 3D radar, and deck edge-lift. Air-conditioned. Embarked air squadrons and joined the Fleet summer 1960. Long refit 1964 to 1966, costing £10 million.

Aircraft: Current complement (1979): nine Sea Kings and four Wessex 5. From 1980: five Sea Harriers and nine Sea Kings. The armament for the Sea Harriers (the first squadron to form) will be the P3T ASM and Sidewinder AIM9L AAM both controlled by Blue Fox radar. By 1980 all Sea Kings are expected to be modified to the standard of the Mk 2 helicopters now in production. They will all have improved radar and communications, an acoustic processor and sono-buoys to supplement the dunking sonar.

Conversion: *Hermes* was taken in hand for conversion to a Commando Carrier on 1 March 1971, commissioning for this role on 17 August 1973. Fixed wing facilities such as catapults and arrester gear were removed. The whole performance cost over £25 million.
In 1976, as a result of the Defence Review and pressure from other NATO countries, *Hermes'* role was altered to that of A/S carrier with the retention of a capability for commando support. As a result she underwent yet another conversion at Devonport which was completed January 1977. How long she continues in this role depends on how much extra delay is experienced on the "Invincible" class but it seems likely that she will continue to run until at least 1984-85. When the Harriers are eventually in naval service they will fly from this ship amongst others. The first operational squadron is due for embarkation in *Hermes* in 1980.

Electrical: Five turbo and four diesel alternators = 9 000 kW.

Engineering: 15 ft 6 in diameter propellers: 230 rpm.

Flight deck: Angled 6·5 degree off centre line of ship, the biggest angle that could be contrived in an aircraft carrier of this size. Strengthened to take Harrier aircraft. During 1979 refit to be fitted with 7 degree Ski-jump.

Radar: Surveillance: One Type 965 with single AKE-1 array.
Search: One Type 993.
Navigation: One Type 978.
Fire control: Two GWS 22.
Tacan beacon.

Sonar: Type 184.

Turning circle: 800 yards.

HERMES 3/1979, Michael D. J. Lennon

HERMES 3/1979, Michael D. J. Lennon

UK / Aircraft carriers 593

Name	No.	Builders	Laid down	Launched	Commissioned
BULWARK	R 08	Harland & Wolff Ltd, Belfast	10 May 1945	22 June 1948	4 Nov 1954

Displacement, tons: 23 300 standard; 27 705 full load
Length, feet (metres): 737·8 *(224·9)*
Beam, feet (metres): 90 *(27·4)* hull
Draught, feet (metres): 28 *(8·5)*
Width, feet (metres): 123·5 *(37·7)* oa
Aircraft: 20 Sea King and Wessex 5 helicopters
Landing craft: 4 LCVP
Guns: 8—40 mm/70 (twin Mk 5) Bofors
Main engines: Parsons geared turbines; 76 000 shp; 2 shafts
Boilers: 4 Admiralty 3-drum
Speed, knots: 28
Oil fuel, tons: 3 880 furnace; 320 diesel
Complement: 980 plus 750 Royal Marine Commando and troops

Former fixed-wing aircraft carrier. Converted into commando ship in Portsmouth Dockyard, January 1959 to January 1960. Her arrester gear and catapults have been removed. She was placed in reserve in April 1976 as a result of the 1975 Defence Review. In late 1977 it was decided to reactivate *Bulwark* to cover the period after *Ark Royal's* deletion. She recommissioned at Portsmouth after a considerable refit on 23 February 1979 for a five year period. To rejoin the Fleet in mid-1979.

Aircraft: There is no plan to operate Sea Harriers from *Bulwark*.

Flight Deck: This is not angled.

Role: Her dual role is as an ASW/Commando carrier with Sea Kings of 826 Squadron for A/S and SAR duties and Wessex 5s of 846 Squadron for assault, armed close support and medevac duties. LCVPs manned by 7th Assault Squadron, RM.

Radar: Surveillance: Type 993.
Navigation: Type 978.
Aircraft direction: Type 982.

BULWARK 3/1979, MOD(N)

BULWARK 3/1979, Michael D. J. Lennon

BULWARK 3/1979, MOD(N)

UK / Aircraft carriers

1 + 2 LIGHT AIRCRAFT CARRIERS

Name	No.	Builders	Laid down	Launched	Commissioned
INVINCIBLE	CAH 1	Vickers (Shipbuilding) Ltd, Barrow-in-Furness	20 July 1973	3 May 1977	1980
ILLUSTRIOUS	CAH 2	Swan Hunter Ltd, Wallsend	7 Oct 1976	1 Dec 1978	?1982
ARK ROYAL	CAH 3	Swan Hunter Ltd, Wallsend	14 Dec 1978	1981	?1985

Displacement, tons: 16 000 standard; 19 500 full load
Length, feet (metres): 677 *(206·6)*
Beam, feet (metres): 90 *(27·5)* wl; 115 *(35)* deck
Draught, feet (metres): ?24 *(7·3)*
Flight deck length, feet (metres): 550 *(167·8)*
Aircraft: Total of 18: 10 Sea King helicopters and 8 Sea Harriers
Missiles: SAM; Twin Sea Dart (see notes)
Main engines: 4 Olympus gas turbines; 112 000 shp; 2 shafts (reversible gear box)
Speed, knots: 28
Range, miles: 5 000 at 18 knots
Complement: 900 (31 officers, 265 senior ratings, 604 junior ratings) (excluding aircrew)

The history of this class is a long and complex one starting almost sixteen years ago. The first of class, the result of many compromises, was ordered from Vickers on 17 April 1973. At that time completion might have been expected in 1977-78 but changes in design and labour problems have delayed this by probably two years. The results of this have been the running-on of *Hermes* and the recommissioning of *Bulwark* as well as *Blake's* continuation in service to provide the necessary aircraft platforms at sea. The order for the second ship, *Illustrious,* was placed on 14 May 1976, whilst the third, *Ark Royal,* was placed in December 1978. *Invincible* sea trials started May 1979. *Illustrious* is planned to carry out trials in 1980.
The primary task of this class, apart from providing a command centre for maritime air forces, is the operation of both helicopters and VTOL/STOL aircraft. Provision has been made for sufficiently large lifts and hangars to accommodate the next generation of both these aircraft.
The design allows for an open foc's'le head and a slightly angled deck which will allow the Sea Dart launcher to be set almost amidships.

Aircraft: The second squadron of Sea Harriers will be embarked in *Invincible* and subsequently all such squadrons will be deployed in ships of this class. (See *Aircraft* note under *Hermes* for further details.)

Cost: Although originally estimated at approximately £60 million the estimated cost of *Invincible* at 1976 prices = £167 million and later ships at £200+ million.

Design: In 1976-77 an amendment was incorporated to allow for the transport and landing of a Commando.

Electrical: Eight diesel generators = 14 000 kW.

Flight deck: Various angles of lift have been tested for the forward end of the flight-deck, (Ski-jump) to allow V/STOL aircraft of greater all-up weight to operate more efficiently. *Invincible* has been fitted with a 7 degree Ski-jump and the other two are to have 15 degree Ski-jumps. This will involve resiting the Sea Dart launcher.

Future: It now appears to be the intention to retain three carriers in commission which will normally allow for at least two being available. With *Hermes* and *Bulwark* running and *Illustrious* commissioning in 1980 it seems probable that *Blake* will be paid off well before the latter event.

Missiles: Original drawing shows four Exocet launchers subsequently apparently deleted.

Radar: Surveillance: One Type 1022.
Search: One Type 992 R.
Fire control: Two Type 909 for Sea Dart.
Navigation: One Type 1006.

Sonar: Type 2016.

INVINCIBLE 3/1979, MOD(N) (Jack Dewis)

INVINCIBLE 3/1979, Michael D. J. Lennon

INVINCIBLE 3/1979, MOD(N) (Jack Dewis)

UK / Aircraft carriers 595

INVINCIBLE 3/1979, Michael D. J. Lennon

INVINCIBLE 3/1979, K. Royall

INVINCIBLE 3/1979, Michael D. J. Lennon

CRUISERS

2 "TIGER" CLASS (HELICOPTER CRUISERS)

Name	No.	Builders	Laid down	Launched	Commissioned
TIGER (ex-*Bellerophon*)	C 20	John Brown Ltd, Clydebank	1 Oct 1941	25 Oct 1945	18 Mar 1959
BLAKE (ex-*Tiger*, ex-*Blake*)	C 99	Fairfield S.B. & Eng, Govan	17 Aug 1942	20 Dec 1945	8 Mar 1961

Displacement, tons: 9 500 standard; 12 080 full load
Length, feet (metres): 538·0 *(164·0)* pp; 550·0 *(167·6)* wl; 566·5 *(172·8)* oa
Beam, feet (metres): 64·0 *(19·5)*
Draught, feet (metres): 23·0 *(7·0)*
Aircraft: 4 Sea King helicopters
Missiles: SAM; 40 Sea Cat (2 quad launchers)
Guns: 2—6 in *(152 mm)*/52 (twin Mk 26); 2—3 in *(76 mm)*/70 (twin Mk 6)
Armour: Belt 3·5 in—3·2 in *(89—83 mm)*; deck 2 in *(51 mm)*; turret 3 in—1 in *(76—25 mm)*
Main engines: 4 Parsons geared turbines; 4 shafts; 80 000 shp
Boilers: 4 Admiralty 3-drum type
Speed, knots: 30
Oil fuel, tons: 1 850
Range, miles: 2 000 at 30 knots; 4 000 at 20 knots; 6 500 at 13 knots
Complement: 85 officers, 800 ratings

This design was originally an improvement on that of *Superb*/*Swiftsure*. *Bellerophon* and *Hawke* of a similar design were cancelled in 1945-46 as were the projected ships *Centurion*, *Edgar*, *Mars* and *Neptune*. There was much juggling of names between ships; *Blake* was renamed *Tiger* in December 1944 and back to *Blake* in February 1945. *Defence* was renamed *Lion* in October 1957. *Bellerophon* was renamed *Tiger* in February 1945. Work on all three of the surviving ships was suspended in July 1946, the decision to complete them being announced on 15 October 1954. Subsequent redesign delayed work even further and it was not completed until 1959-61. By this time *Tiger* had cost £13·113 million and *Blake* £14·940 million. The next stage was conversion to command helicopter cruisers (official title). *Lion* was not converted and was eventually sent for scrap in April 1975. *Blake* was transformed by Portsmouth Dockyard at a cost of £5·5 million from early 1965 until recommissioning on 23 April 1969. *Tiger* was in hand from 1968 to 1972 at Devonport Dockyard, her cost reaching the staggering sum of £13·25 million. (As a considerable amount of equipment from *Lion* was used in *Tiger's* conversion the latter was unofficially known for a time as "Liger"). *Tiger* to reserve in June 1978 to provide part of the manpower needed for *Bulwark*. *Blake* will probably pay off in time for *Illustrious* to be manned up for commissioning in 1980.

Electrical: Four turbo-generators provide 4 000 kW AC, the first time this type of power had been used in British cruisers although it was already in use in the "Daring" class destroyers.

Engineering: Main machinery is largely automatic and can be remotely controlled. Steam conditions 400 psi pressure and 640°F. Propellers 11 ft diameter, 285 rpm. The engineering departments of this class have not been without their continuing difficulties.

Guns: Unique in mounting 6 in (Mk 26). The only other ships with 3 in (Mk 6) are Canadian.

Radar: Search: One Type 965 and one Type 993.
Height finder: One Type 278.
Fire control: Four MRS 3 fire control directors.
Navigation: One Type 978.

Turning circle: 800 yards.

BLAKE 6/1977, C. and S. Taylor

TIGER 6/1977, John G. Calli

TIGER 6/1977, C. and S. Taylor

LIGHT CRUISERS

1 TYPE 82

Name	No.	Builders	Laid down	Launched	Commissioned
BRISTOL	D 23	Swan Hunter Ltd	15 Nov 1967	30 June 1969	31 Mar 1973

Displacement, tons: 6 100 standard; 7 100 full load
Length, feet (metres): 507·0 *(154·5)*
Beam, feet (metres): 55·0 *(16·8)*
Draught, feet (metres): 16·8 *(5·2)* (keel); 23 *(7)* (sonar dome)
Aircraft: Landing platform for 1 Wasp helicopter
Missiles: SAM; Est 30 Sea Dart (twin launcher)
A/S weapons: 1 Ikara single launcher fwd;
 1 Limbo 3-barrelled depth charge mortar (Mark 10) aft
Guns: 1—4·5 in *(115 mm)*/55 (single Mk 8); 2—20 mm
Main engines: COSAG arrangement (combined steam and gas turbines) 2 sets Standard Range geared steam turbines, 30 000 shp; 2 Bristol-Siddeley marine Olympus TMIA gas turbines, 56 000 shp; 2 shafts
Boilers: 2
Speed, knots: 29
Fuel, tons: 900
Range, miles: 5 000 at 18 knots
Complement: 407 (29 officers, 378 ratings)

Designed around Sea Dart GWS 30 weapons system. Fully stabilised to present a steady weapon platform. The gas turbines provide emergency power and high speed boost. The machinery is remotely-controlled from a ship control centre. Automatic steering, obviating the need for a quartermaster. Many labour-saving items of equipment fitted to make the most efficient and economical use of manpower resulting in a smaller ship's company for tonnage than any previous warship. Fitted with Action Data Automation Weapon System. Started trials 10 April 1972. Remainder of class cancelled owing to high cost and cancellation of aircraft-carrier building programme for which they were intended as escorts. Officially listed as "destroyer" which is in some measure borne out by her limited fire-power, lack of embarked helicopter and limited ESM.

Appearance: Three funnels, one amidships and two aft abreast the mainmast.

A/S weapons: Ikara is GWS 40.

Communications: By GEC-Marconi to include SCOT satellite system compatible with both SKYNET and the US Defence satellites.

Cost: £22·5 million (£27 million overall). GEC-Marconi equipment for radar, weapons and communications cost over £3 million.

Missiles: The Sea Dart ship missile system has a reasonable anti-ship capability. GWS30.

Radar: Surveillance: One Type 965 with double AKE array and IFF.
Search: One Type 992.
Fire control: Two Type 909 (Sea Dart).
Navigation: One Type 1006.

Sonar: Types 162, 170, 182, 184, 185, 189.

BRISTOL 7/1978, Michael D. J. Lennon

BRISTOL 7/1978, Michael D. J. Lennon

BRISTOL (On Queen Mother's birthday) 8/1978, Michael D. J. Lennon

598 UK / Light cruisers

6 "COUNTY" CLASS

Name	No.	Builders	Laid down	Launched	Commissioned
KENT	D 12	Harland & Wolff Ltd, Belfast	1 Mar 1960	27 Sep 1961	15 Aug 1963
LONDON	D 16	Swan, Hunter & Wigham Richardson, Wallsend	26 Feb 1960	7 Dec 1961	4 Nov 1963
ANTRIM	D 18	Fairfield S.B. & Eng Co Ltd, Govan	20 Jan 1966	19 Oct 1967	14 July 1970
GLAMORGAN*	D 19	Vickers (Shipbuilding) Ltd, Newcastle-upon-Tyne	13 Sep 1962	9 July 1964	11 Oct 1966
FIFE	D 20	Fairfield S.B. & Eng Co Ltd, Govan	1 June 1962	9 July 1964	21 June 1966
NORFOLK	D 21	Swan, Hunter & Wigham Richardson, Wallsend	15 Mar 1966	16 Nov 1967	7 Mar 1970

* Refit

Displacement, tons: 5 440 standard; 6 200 full load
Length, feet (metres): 520·5 (158·7)
Beam, feet (metres): 54·0 (16·5)
Draught, feet (metres): 20·5 (6·3) screws; 16·8 (5·1) keel
Aircraft: 1 Wessex helicopter
Missiles: SAM; 4 Exocet (single cells) (except Kent and London) (see Missiles note);
SAM; 36 Seaslug (twin launcher aft);
Sea Cat (two quad launchers).
Guns: 4—4·5 in (115 mm)/45 (twin Mk 6) (2—4·5 only in ships with Exocet)
Main engines: Combined steam and gas turbines;
2 sets geared steam turbines, 30 000 shp;
4 gas turbines, 30 000 shp; 2 shafts
Boilers: 2 Babcock & Wilcox
Speed, knots: 30
Complement: 471 (33 officers and 438 men)

Fife, Glamorgan, Antrim and *Norfolk*, have the more powerful Seaslug II systems. All fitted with stabilisers and are fully air-conditioned. Original cost varied from £13·8 million (*Hampshire*) to £16·8 million (*Antrim*). Officially rated as "destroyers".

Appearance: *Kent* and *London* have mainmast stepped further aft than remainder. The last four of the class have distinctive tubular foremast and twin AKE radar aerial.

Costs: Running costs (at 1976 prices, excluding helicopter) £4·9 million per ship.

Disposal: As a result of the Defence Review *Hampshire* was paid off in April 1976—at least seven years before she might have been expected on the disposal list. *Devonshire* paid off for de-storing on 38 July 1978 and to disposal list 13 September 1978 and it is possible that about 1980 *Kent* and *London* may be deleted. *Devonshire* is still retained as "stand-by" in the Defence White Paper

Electrical: Two 1 000 kW turbo-alternators and three gas turbines alternators total 3 750 kW, at 440 V a/c SCOT fitted in *London*.

Engineering: These were the first ships of their size to have COSAG (combined steam and gas turbine machinery). Boilers work at a pressure of 700 psi and a temperature of 950°F. The steam and gas turbines are geared to the same shaft. Each shaft set consists of a high pressure and low pressure steam turbine of 15 000 shp combined output plus two G.6 gas turbines each of 7 500 shp. The gas turbines are able to develop their full power from cold within a few minutes, enabling ships lying in harbour without steam to get under way instantly in emergency.

Gunnery: The 4·5 in guns are radar controlled fully automatic dual-purpose. The 20 mm guns were added for picket duties in South East Asia, but have been retained for general close range duties.

Missiles: Four Exocet fitted in *Norfolk, Antrim, Glamorgan* and *Fife*. No reloads carried. *Norfolk* Exocet trials on French missile range (Mediterranean) in April 1974.
Seaslug Mk 2 except in *Kent* and *London* with Mk 1.

Radar: Air search: One type 965 (double AKE-2 array in *Norfolk, Glamorgan, Antrim* and *Fife*—remainder single AKE-1).
Surveillance: One Type 992 Q.
Height finder: One Type 278.
Seaslug fire control: One Type 901.
Gunnery fire control: MRS 3 (forward) with Type 903.
Sea Cat fire control: GWS 23 in *London*; GWS 22 with Type 904 in *Kent, Norfolk, Antrim, Fife* and *Glamorgan*; GWS 21 in *Devonshire*.
Navigation: One Type 978 or 1006.

Sonar: Type 184.

LONDON 5/1977, C. and S. Taylor

NORFOLK 7/1978, Michael D. J. Lennon

FIFE 5/1978, John G. Callis

KENT 1978, C. and S. Taylor

DESTROYERS

1 + 5 "BROADSWORD" CLASS (TYPE 22)

Name	No.	Builders	Laid down	Launched	Commissioned
BROADSWORD	F 88	Yarrow (Shipbuilders) Ltd, Glasgow	7 Feb 1975	12 May 1976	21 Feb 1979
BATTLEAXE	F 89	Yarrow (Shipbuilders) Ltd, Glasgow	4 Feb 1976	12 May 1977	1980
BRILLIANT	F 90	Yarrow (Shipbuilders) Ltd, Glasgow	24 Mar 1977	15 Dec 1978	1981
BRAZEN	F 91	Yarrow (Shipbuilders) Ltd, Glasgow	19 Aug 1978	—	1982
—	—	Yarrow (Shipbuilders) Ltd, Glasgow	—	—	—
—	—	Yarrow (Shipbuilders) Ltd, Glasgow	—	—	—

Displacement, tons: 3 500 standard; 4 000 full load
Dimensions, feet (metres): 430 × 48·5 × 14 (keel); 19·9 (screws); *(131·2 × 14·8 × 4·3; 6)*
Aircraft: 2 Lynx Mk 2 helicopters with ASM and A/S torpedoes
Missiles: SSM; 4 Exocet (single cells); SAM; Sea Wolf (two 6-barrelled launchers)
Guns: 2—40 mm/70
A/S weapons: 6 (2 triple) Mk 32 torpedo tubes for Mk 46; helicopter-carried A/S torpedoes
Main engines: COGOG arrangement of 2 Rolls-Royce Olympus gas turbines; 56 000 bhp and 2 Rolls-Royce Tyne gas turbines; 8 500 bhp; 2 shafts; cp propellers
Speed, knots: 30+ (18 on Tynes)
Range, miles: 4 500 at 18 knots (on Tynes)
Complement: 223 (18 officers, 205 ratings)

Designed as successors to the "Leander" class, the construction of which ceased with the completion of the scheduled programme of 26 ships. Order for the first of class, *Broadsword*, was placed on 26 February 1974, *Battleaxe* ordered 5 September 1975. Order for *Brilliant* 7 September 1976, *Brazen* on 21 October 1977 and the fifth and sixth ships on 25 April 1979. This class is primarily designed for A/S operations and is capable of acting as OTC and helicopter control ship. These are the first major ships for the Royal Navy which have no main gun armament (apart from the "Blackwood" class.)
It is reported that nine of this class are planned. The fifth and subsequent ships will probably be an enlarged version of this class, which is already 20 ft longer than the Type 42.
Any extension of 20 ft or more will mean that these so-called "frigates" are of greater length than the "light-cruisers" of sixty years ago and over 100 ft longer than the "Tribal" class of the last war.

Aircraft: Although capable of carrying two helicopters normal complement only one. Helicopters will probably carry Sea Skua air-to-surface missiles.

Cost: Approx £40 million.

Electrical: Four diesel generators = 4 000 kW.

Launch: Launch of *Brilliant* delayed from 31 October 1978 to 15 December 1978 by industrial action.

Fire control: Sea Wolf, GWS 25; Exocet, GWS 50.

Radar: Surveillance: Two Type 967/8.
Sea Wolf control: Two Type 910.
Navigation: One Type 1006.

Sonar: Type 2016 and VDS.

BROADSWORD 9/1978, MOD(N)

BROADSWORD 9/1978, MOD(N)

BROADSWORD 2/1979, Michael D. J. Lennon

BROADSWORD 2/1979, Michael D. J. Lennon

600 UK / Destroyers

6 + 8 "SHEFFIELD" CLASS (TYPE 42)

Name	No.	Builders	Laid down	Launched	Commissioned
SHEFFIELD	D 80	Vickers (Shipbuilding) Ltd, Barrow-in-Furness	15 Jan 1970	10 June 1971	16 Feb 1975
BIRMINGHAM	D 86	Cammell Laird & Co Ltd, Birkenhead	28 Mar 1972	30 July 1973	3 Dec 1976
NEWCASTLE	D 87	Swan Hunter Ltd, Wallsend-on-Tyne	21 Feb 1973	24 Apr 1975	23 Mar 1978
GLASGOW	D 88	Swan Hunter Ltd, Wallsend-on-Tyne	7 Mar 1974	14 Apr 1976	9 Mar 1979
EXETER	D 89	Swan Hunter Ltd, Wallsend-on-Tyne	22 July 1976	25 Apr 1978	—
SOUTHAMPTON	D 90	Vosper Thornycroft Ltd	21 Oct 1976	29 Jan 1979	—
CARDIFF	D 108	Vickers (Shipbuilding) Ltd Barrow-in-Furness (see note)	3 Nov 1972	22 Feb 1974	1979
COVENTRY	D 118	Cammell Laird & Co Ltd, Birkenhead	22 Mar 1973	21 June 1974	20 Oct 1978
NOTTINGHAM	D 91	Vosper Thornycroft Ltd	6 Feb 1978	—	—
LIVERPOOL	D 92	Cammell Laird & Co Ltd, Birkenhead	5 July 1978	—	—
MANCHESTER	D 95	Vickers (Shipbuilding) Ltd, Barrow-in-Furness	May 1979	—	—
—	—	Vosper Thornycroft Ltd	1979	—	—
—	—	Cammell Laird & Co Ltd, Birkenhead	—	—	—
—	—	Swan Hunter Ltd, Wallsend-on-Tyne	—	—	—

Displacement, tons: 3 150 standard; 4 100 full load
Length, feet (metres): 410·0 *(125·0)*
 463 *(141) (Manchester)*
Beam, feet (metres): 47 *(14·3)*; 49 *(14·9) (Manchester)*
Draught, feet (metres): 19 *(5·8)* (screws); 12·5 *(3·8)* (keel)
Aircraft: 1 Lynx Mk 2 helicopter
Missiles: SAM; Est 24 Sea Dart (1 twin launcher) (surface-to-surface capability)
Guns: 1—4·5 in *(115 mm)*/55 (Mk 8); 2—20 mm Oerlikon; 2 saluting
A/S weapons: Helicopter-launched Mk 44 torpedoes; 6 A/S torpedo tubes (triples) for Mk 46 (in some)
Main engines: COGOG arrangement of Rolls-Royce Olympus gas turbines for full power 50 000 shp; 2 Rolls-Royce Tyne gas turbines for cruising 8 000 shp; cp propellers; 2 shafts
Speed, knots: 30
Range: 4 000 miles at 18 knots
Complement: 268 (accommodation for 312)

This class is fitted with four sets of stabilisers and twin rudders. The helicopter will carry the Sea Skua (CK 834) air-to-surface weapon for use against lightly defended surface ship targets such as fast patrol boats. Advantages include ability to reach maximum speed with great rapidity, reduction in space and weight and 25 per cent reduction in technical manpower. Originally to cost approximately £23· million per ship.
Exeter ordered 22 January 1976. *Southampton* ordered 18 March 1976. *Nottingham* ordered 1 March 1977 *Liverpool* on 27 May 1977, *Manchester* 10 November 1978, and No. 12 on 27 March 1979. Nos. 13 and 14 ordered 25 April 1979.
Glasgow damaged by fire whilst fitting out 23 September 1976.
Southampton was due to be launched 17 October 1978 but this was delayed by industrial problems until 29 January 1979. Further problems beset this event which finally took place overnight 29/30th January 1979.

Class: In the same way as it was found necessary to enlarge the "Leanders" a similar but more radical change is being made to this class. From *Manchester* onwards the beam will be increased by 2 ft and the length by 53 ft with little change in displacement.
Completion: *Cardiff*, whose completion was delayed by lack of man-power at Vickers Ltd, Barrow, was towed to Swan Hunters, Ltd, Wallsend in February 1976 for completion.

Costs: Building costs—*Sheffield* £23·2 million; *Birmingham* £30·9 million. Running costs (1976 prices, excluding helicopter) £5·2 million per year per ship.

Electrical: Four diesel generators = 4 000 kW.

Electronics: Twin SCOT Skynet satellite communication aerials; ADAWS 4 for coordination of action information. ECM D/F.

Engineering: Considerable automation has allowed a number of machinery spaces to be operated unmanned. Cp propellers by Stone Manganese (Type XX).

Missiles: GWS 30 control.

Radar: Search: One Type 965 with double AKE-2 array and IFF.
Surveillance and target indication: One Type 992Q.
Sea Dart fire control and target: Two Type 909.
Navigation, HDWS and helicopter control: One Type 1006.

Sonar: Type 184 hull-mounted. Type 162 classification.

COVENTRY 10/1978, Michael D. J. Lennon

GLASGOW 3/1979, Michael D. J. Lennon

NEWCASTLE 3/1979, C. and S. Taylor

BIRMINGHAM 6/1977, C. and S. Taylor

UK / Frigates 601

FRIGATES

Note: A new Type 24 design is under discussion although details are not yet published.

8 "AMAZON" CLASS (TYPE 21)

Name	No.	Builders	Laid down	Launched	Commissioned
AMAZON	F 169	Vosper Thornycroft Ltd, Woolston	6 Nov 1969	26 Apr 1971	11 May 1974
ANTELOPE	F 170	Vosper Thornycroft Ltd, Woolston	23 Mar 1971	16 Mar 1972	19 July 1975
ACTIVE	F 171	Vosper Thornycroft Ltd, Woolston	23 July 1971	23 Nov 1972	17 June 1977
AMBUSCADE	F 172	Yarrow (Shipbuilders) Ltd, Glasgow	1 Sep 1971	18 Jan 1973	5 Sep 1975
ARROW	F 173	Yarrow (Shipbuilders) Ltd, Glasgow	28 Sep 1972	5 Feb 1974	29 July 1976
ALACRITY	F 174	Yarrow (Shipbuilders) Ltd, Glasgow	5 Mar 1973	18 Sep 1974	2 July 1977
ARDENT	F 184	Yarrow (Shipbuilders) Ltd, Glasgow	26 Feb 1974	9 May 1975	13 Oct 1977
AVENGER	F 185	Yarrow (Shipbuilders) Ltd, Glasgow	30 Oct 1974	20 Nov 1975	15 Apr 1978

Displacement, tons: 2 750 standard; 3 250 full load (see note)
Length, feet (metres): 384·0 (117·0)
Beam, feet (metres): 40·5 (12·3)
Draught, feet (metres): 19 (5·8)
Aircraft: 1 Lynx Mk 2 helicopter (see note)
Missiles: SSM; 4 Exocet (single cells) (see note); SAM; Est 20 Sea Cat (1 quad launcher)
Guns: 1—4·5 in (115 mm)/55 (single Mk 8); 2—20 mm Oerlikon (singles)
A/S weapons: Helicopter launched torpedoes; 6 (2 triple) torpedo tubes for Mk 46 (in some later ships)
Main engines: COGOG arrangement of 2 Rolls-Royce Olympus gas turbines 56 000 bhp; 2 Rolls-Royce Tyne gas turbines for cruising 8 500 shp; 2 shafts; cp, 5-bladed propellers
Speed, knots: 30; 18 on Tyne GTs
Range, miles: 4 000 at 17 knots; 1 200 at 30 knots
Complement: 175 (13 officers, and 162 ratings) (accommodation for 192)

A contract was awarded to Vosper Thornycroft, on 27 February 1968 for the design of a patrol frigate to be prepared in full collaboration with Yarrow Ltd. This is the first custom built gas turbine frigate (designed and constructed as such from the keel up, as opposed to conversion) and the first warship designed by commercial firms for many years.

A/S weapons: Torpedo tubes to be fitted in all ships.
Costs: Building costs between £14·4 million (Antelope) and £27·7 million (Avenger). Running costs (at 1976 prices, excluding helicopter) £3·3 million per ship per year.
Displacement: The inclusion of permanent ballast to improve stability has increased displacement above the designed figures shown.
Electronics: SCOT satellite communication fitted in several ships, CAAIS fitted.
Helicopter: Provided with Wasp until Lynx is available in Antelope, Active and Ambuscade.
Missiles: Although Sea Wolf was planned for the last four, it was not ready in time so all will mount Sea Cat. A retro-fitting will take place at second major refit. All fitted with Exocet from Active onwards. Remainder to be fitted at first major refit.
Radar: Surveillance and target Indicator: One Type 992Q.
Navigation: One Type 978.
Sea Cat control: Two GWS 24.
Gun fire control: Orion RTN-10X WSA 4 system.
IFF Interrogator: Cossor Type 1010.
IFF Transponder: Plessey PTR 461.
Sonar: Type 184M hull-mounted.
Type 162M classification.

ALACRITY
6/1977, C. and S. Taylor

AVENGER
9/1978, Michael D. J. Lennon

ACTIVE
9/1978, Michael D. J. Lennon

ARROW
1/1979, Michael D. J. Lennon

602 UK / Frigates

26 "LEANDER" CLASS

IKARA GROUP

Name	No.	Builders	Laid down	Launched	Commissioned
AURORA	F 10	John Brown & Co (Clydebank) Ltd	1 June 1961	28 Nov 1962	9 Apr 1964
EURYALUS	F 15	Scotts Shipbuilding & Eng Co, Greenock	2 Nov 1961	6 June 1963	16 Sep 1964
GALATEA	F 18	Swan Hunter & Wigham Richardson, Wallsend	29 Dec 1961	23 May 1963	25 Apr 1964
ARETHUSA	F 38	J. Samuel White & Co Ltd, Cowes	7 Sep 1962	5 Nov 1963	24 Nov 1965
NAIAD	F 39	Yarrow & Co Ltd, Scotstoun, Glasgow	30 Oct 1962	4 Nov 1963	15 Mar 1965
DIDO	F 104	Yarrow & Co Ltd, Scotstoun, Glasgow	2 Dec 1959	22 Dec 1961	18 Sep 1963
LEANDER	F 109	Harland & Wolff Ltd, Belfast	10 Apr 1959	28 June 1961	27 Mar 1963
AJAX	F 114	Cammell Laird & Co Ltd, Birkenhead	12 Oct 1959	16 Aug 1962	10 Dec 1963

EXOCET GROUP

Name	No.	Builders	Laid down	Launched	Commissioned
CLEOPATRA	F 28	HM Dockyard, Devonport	19 June 1963	25 Mar 1964	4 Jan 1966
SIRIUS	F 40	HM Dockyard, Portsmouth	9 Aug 1963	22 Sep 1964	15 June 1966
PHOEBE	F 42	Alex Stephen & Sons Ltd, Glasgow	3 June 1963	8 July 1964	15 Apr 1966
MINERVA*	F 45	Vickers-Armstrong Ltd, Newcastle	25 July 1963	19 Dec 1964	14 May 1966
DANAE*	F 47	HM Dockyard, Devonport	16 Dec 1964	31 Oct 1965	7 Sep 1967
JUNO	F 52	John I. Thornycroft Ltd, Woolston	16 July 1964	24 Nov 1965	18 July 1967
ARGONAUT*	F 56	Hawthorn Leslie Ltd, Hebburn-on-Tyne	27 Nov 1964	8 Feb 1966	17 Aug 1967
PENELOPE*	F 127	Vickers-Armstrong Ltd, Newcastle	14 Mar 1961	17 Aug 1962	31 Oct 1963

BROAD-BEAMED GROUP

Name	No.	Builders	Laid down	Launched	Commissioned
ACHILLES	F 12	Yarrow & Co Ltd, Scotstoun, Glasgow	1 Dec 1967	21 Nov 1968	9 July 1970
DIOMEDE	F 16	Yarrow & Co Ltd, Scotstoun, Glasgow	30 Jan 1968	15 Apr 1969	2 Apr 1971
ANDROMEDA*	F 57	HM Dockyard, Portsmouth	25 May 1966	24 May 1967	2 Dec 1968
HERMIONE	F 58	Alex Stephen & Sons Ltd, Glasgow	6 Dec 1965	26 Apr 1967	11 July 1969
JUPITER	F 60	Yarrow & Co Ltd, Scotstoun, Glasgow	3 Oct 1966	4 Sep 1967	9 Aug 1969
BACCHANTE	F 69	Vickers-Armstrong Ltd, Newcastle	27 Oct 1966	29 Feb 1968	17 Oct 1969
APOLLO	F 70	Yarrow & Co Ltd, Scotstoun, Glasgow	1 May 1969	15 Oct 1970	28 May 1972
SCYLLA	F 71	HM Dockyard, Devonport	17 May 1967	8 Aug 1968	12 Feb 1970
ARIADNE	F 72	Yarrow & Co Ltd, Scotstoun, Glasgow	1 Nov 1969	10 Sep 1971	10 Feb 1973
CHARYBDIS	F 75	Harland & Wolff Ltd, Belfast	27 Jan 1967	28 Feb 1968	2 June 1969

* Refit or conversion (F 57 and F 127)

Displacement, tons: 2 450 standard; 2 860 full load (Ikara); 3 200 full load (Exocet); 2 500 standard; 2 962 full load (Broad-beamed)
Length, feet (metres): 372 (113·4)
Beam, feet (metres): 41 (12·5) (Leanders) 43 (13·1) (Broad-beamed)
Draught, feet (metres): 14·8 (4·5) (keel) 18 (5·5) (screws); 18·5 (5·6) (screws) (Exocet)
Aircraft: 1 Lynx Mk 2 (Phoebe and Sirius) or Wasp helicopter
Missiles: Ikara Group: 2 quad Sea Cat Exocet Group: 4 MM 38 Exocet (fwd); 3 quad Sea Cat (2 aft, 1 fwd) Broad-Beamed Group: 1 quad Sea Cat
Guns: Ikara Group: 2—40 mm/70 Exocet Group: 2—40 mm/70 Broad-Beamed Group: 2—4·5 in (115 mm)/45 (twin Mk 6); 2—20 mm/70
A/S weapons: Ikara Group: Ikara (fwd); 1 Limbo (aft) Exocet Group: 2 triple Mk 32 torpedo tubes Broad-Beamed Group: 1 Limbo
Main engines: 2 double reduction geared turbines; 2 shafts; 30 000 shp (see notes)
Boilers: 2
Speed, knots: 27
Oil fuel, tons: 460
Range, miles: 4 000 at 15 knots
Complement: 223 (Exocet Group) (20 officers, 203 ratings); 257 (Ikara Group); 260 (Broad-beamed) (19 officers, 241 ratings)

This class, whose construction extended over ten years, was an improvement on the Type 12. As originally designed there were several significant improvements—a helicopter, VDS and long-range air warning radar being the most important. Recently a number of conversions have been put in hand (see notes below).

Conversions:
(a) Ikara Group
Leander (Devonport) completed December 1972;
Ajax (Devonport) completed September 1973;
Galatea (Devonport) completed September 1974;
Naiad (Devonport) completed July 1975;
Euryalus (Devonport) completed March 1976;
Aurora (Chatham) completed March 1976;
Arethusa (Portsmouth) completed April 1977;
Dido (Devonport) completed October 1978;
(b) Exocet Group
Cleopatra (Devonport) completed 28 November 1975;
Phoebe (Devonport) completed April 1977;
Sirius (Devonport) completed October 1977.
Argonaut (Devonport) completed October 1978;
Minerva (Chatham) completed October 1978;
Juno (Portsmouth) to complete 1979;
Danae (Devonport) to complete 1979;
Penelope to complete 1981.
(c) The conversion of the Broad-beamed Group started with *Andromeda* (late 1977) and will include the provision of four MM 38 Exocet launchers, the Sea Wolf SAM system, improved sonar and modern EW equipment, ASW torpedo tubes. At the same time the 4·5 in turret, Sea Cat and Limbo will be removed.

Conversion Costs: Ikara—£8-16 million; Exocet—£16-28 million; Broad-beamed—£40 million (1978). These wide brackets of costs are due in great part to inflation for conversions extending from 1972-85.

Costs: Building costs—earlier ships averaged £4·7 million, later ones £7·0 million. Running costs (at 1976 prices, excluding helicopter)—£2·9 million per ship per year.

Electrical: 440 volts, 60 cycle AC. 1 900 kW in earlier ships, 2 500 kW in later ones.

Electronics: SCOT satellite communications being fitted at later conversions.

ARETHUSA (Ikara Group)   9/1978, Michael D. J. Lennon

CLEOPATRA (Exocet Group)   6/1977, C. and S. Taylor

ARIADNE (Broad-beamed Group)   10/1978, J. L. M. van der Bur

Engineering: The first ten have Y-100 machinery, the remainder of the "Leanders" Y-136. "Broad-beamed Leanders" have Y-160 machinery.

Gunnery: 4·5 in turret removed in Exocet and Ikara conversions and in *Penelope*. 40 mm are not fitted in unconverted ships mounting Sea Cat. Conversions mount 2 single 40 mm abaft the bridge.

Radar: Air surveillance: One Type 965 with single AKE array (except in Ikara ships).
Combined air/surface warning: One Type 993.
Fire control: MRS 3/GWS 22.
Navigation: One Type 978. Type 1006 (conversions).

Sonar: Type 199 VDS was originally fitted in all but *Diomede*. some the VDS has been removed leaving the well—in other the well has been plated over to provide extra accommodation for RMs. Can be replaced. Currently all Ikara conversions have VDS. Type 2016 in Broad-beamed Group.

UK / Frigates 603

7 "TRIBAL" CLASS (TYPE 81)

Name	No.	Builders	Laid down	Launched	Commissioned
ASHANTI	F 117	Yarrow & Co Ltd, Scotstoun	15 Jan 1958	9 Mar 1959	23 Nov 1961
ESKIMO	F 119	J. Samuel White & Co Ltd, Cowes	22 Oct 1958	20 Mar 1960	21 Feb 1963
GURKHA	F 122	J. I. Thornycroft & Co Ltd, Woolston	3 Nov 1958	11 July 1960	13 Feb 1963
ZULU	F 124	Alex Stephen & Sons Ltd, Govan	13 Dec 1960	3 July 1962	17 Apr 1964
MOHAWK	F 125	Vickers-Armstrong Ltd, Barrow	23 Dec 1960	5 Apr 1962	29 Nov 1963
NUBIAN	F 131	HM Dockyard, Portsmouth	7 Sep 1959	6 Sep 1960	9 Oct 1962
TARTAR*	F 133	HM Dockyard, Devonport	22 Oct 1959	19 Sep 1960	26 Feb 1962

* Refit

Displacement, tons: 2 300 standard; 2 700 full load
Length, feet (metres): 360·0 (109·7)
Beam, feet (metres): 45·5 (13)
Draught, feet (metres): 18 (5·5) (screws); 12·5 (3·8) (keel)
Aircraft: 1 Wasp helicopter
Missiles: SAM; Est 16 Sea Cat (quad launcher)
Guns: 2—4·5 in (singles); 2—20 mm
A/S weapons: 1 Limbo 3-barrelled mortar
Main engines: Combined steam and gas turbine; Metrovick steam turbine; 12 500 shp; Metrovick gas turbine; 7 500 shp; 1 shaft
Boilers: 1 Babcock & Wilcox (plus 1 auxiliary boiler)
Speed, knots: 25 (17 max on gas turbines)
Oil fuel, tons: 400
Complement: 253 (13 officers and 240 ratings)

Ashanti, Eskimo and *Gurkha* were ordered under the 1955-56 estimates, *Nubian* and *Tartar* 1956-57, and *Mohawk* and *Zulu* 1957-58. Designed as self-contained units for service in such areas as the Persian Gulf. *Ashanti* cost £5·22 million, *Tartar*, £4·14 million. Some still have 4 in flare rocket launchers.

Construction: All-welded prefabrication. Denny Brown stabilisers fitted. Enclosed bridge and twin rudders.

Corvus: Two Knebworth Corvus Chaff launchers fitted.

Electrical: Generator capacity of 1 500 kW.

Engineering: The gas turbine is used to boost the steam turbines for sustained bursts of high speed and also enables the ship lying in harbour without steam up to get under way instantly in emergency. The machinery is remotely controlled. The main boiler works at a pressure of 550 psi and a temperature of 850°F. Five-bladed propeller, 11·75 ft diameter, 280 rpm. The forward funnel serves the boilers, the after one the gas turbine.

Radar: Search: One Type 965 with single AKE 1 array and IFF.
Air and surface warning: One Type 993.
Navigation: One Type 978.
Fire control: MRS 3 system.
Sea Cat: GWS 21.

Sonar: Types 177, 170 and 162. Type 199. VDS fitted in *Ashanti* and *Gurkha* in 1970.

ZULU 7/1978, Leo van Ginderen

ASHANTI 5/1978, J. L. M. van der Burg

MOHAWK (at Melbourne) 1/1978, Ron Wright

ESKIMO 7/1978, C. and S. Taylor

604 UK / Frigates

9 "ROTHESAY" CLASS (MODIFIED TYPE 12)

Name	No.	Builders	Laid down	Launched	Commissioned
YARMOUTH*	F 101	John Brown & Co Ltd, Clydebank	29 Nov 1957	23 Mar 1959	26 Mar 1960
LOWESTOFT	F 103	Alex Stephen & Sons Ltd, Govan	9 June 1958	23 June 1960	18 Oct 1961
BRIGHTON	F 106	Yarrow & Co Ltd, Scotstoun	23 July 1957	30 Oct 1959	28 Sep 1961
ROTHESAY*	F 107	Yarrow & Co Ltd, Scotstoun	6 Nov 1956	9 Dec 1957	23 Apr 1960
LONDONDERRY	F 108	J. Samuel White & Co Ltd, Cowes	15 Nov 1956	20 May 1958	22 July 1960
FALMOUTH	F 113	Swan Hunter, Wigham Richardson	23 Nov 1957	15 Dec 1959	25 July 1961
BERWICK	F 115	Harland & Wolff Ltd, Belfast	16 June 1958	15 Dec 1959	1 June 1961
PLYMOUTH*	F 126	HM Dockyard, Devonport	1 July 1958	20 July 1959	11 May 1961
RHYL	F 129	HM Dockyard, Portsmouth	29 Jan 1958	23 Apr 1959	31 Oct 1960

* Refit

Displacement, tons: 2 380 standard; 2 800 full load
Length, feet (metres): 370·0 *(112·8)*
Beam, feet (metres): 41·0 *(12·5)*
Draught, feet (metres): 17·3 *(5·3)*
Aircraft: 1 Wasp helicopter
Missiles: SAM; Est 16 Sea Cat (quad launcher)
Guns: 2—4·5 in *(115 mm)*/45 (twin Mk 6)
A/S weapons: 1 Limbo 3-barrelled DC mortar
Main engines: 2 double reduction geared turbines; 2 shafts; 30 000 shp
Boilers: 2 Babcock & Wilcox
Speed, knots: 30
Oil fuel, tons: 400
Complement: 235 (15 officers and 220 ratings)

Provided under the 1954-55 programme. Originally basically similar to the "Whitby" class but with modifications in layout.

Cost: £3·6 million average building cost.

Electrical: Two turbo generators and two diesel generators in all ships. Total 1 140 kW. Alternating current, 440 volts, three phase, 60 cycles per second.

Engineering: Two Admiralty Standard Range turbines each rated at 15 000 shp. Propeller revolutions 220 rpm. Boilers 550 psi *(38·7 kg/cm²)* pressure and 850°F *(450°C)* temperature.

Modernisation: The "Rothesay" class was reconstructed and modernised from 1966-72 during which time they were equipped to operate a Wessex Wasp helicopter armed with homing torpedoes. A flight deck and hangar were built on aft, necessitating the removal of one of their anti-submarine mortars. A Sea Cat replaced the 40 mm gun. A new operations room, new GFCS and full air-conditioning were provided.

Radar: Search: One Type 993.
Fire control: MRS 3.
Navigation: One Type 978.

Sea Cat: Optical Director—GWS 20.

Sonar: New sonar fitted aft in *Lowestoft*.

Special Refits: *Londonderry* refitted at Rosyth from November 1975 to mid-1979 to become trials ship for Admiralty Surface Weapons Establishment. *Rothesay* started similar refit in 1978. *Yarmouth* started two year refit February 1979.

YARMOUTH 8/1978, Michael D. J. Lennon

RHYL (at Melbourne) 1/1978, Ron Wright

BRIGHTON 1/1978, Wright and Logan

LOWESTOFT 6/1978, C. and S. Taylor

UK / Frigates 605

2 "SALISBURY" CLASS (TYPE 61)

Name	No.	Builders	Laid down	Launched	Commissioned
SALISBURY	F 32	HM Dockyard, Devonport	23 Jan 1952	25 June 1953	27 Feb 1957
LINCOLN	F 99	Fairfield S.B. & Eng Co Ltd, Govan	20 May 1955	6 Apr 1959	7 July 1960

Displacement, tons: 2 170 standard; 2 408 full load
Length, feet (metres): 320·0 (97·5) pp; 330·0 (100·6) wl; 339·8 (103·6) oa
Beam, feet (metres): 40·0 (12·2)
Draught, feet (metres): 15·5 (4·7) (screws); 11·7 (3·6) (keel)
Missiles: SAM; Est 16 Sea Cat (quad launcher)
Guns: 2—4·5 in (115 mm)/45 (twin Mk 6); 2—20 mm
A/S weapons: 1 Squid triple-barrelled DC mortar (only Lincoln)
Main engines: 8 ASR 1 diesels in three engine rooms; 2 shafts; 14 400 bhp; 4 engines geared to each shaft
Speed, knots: 24
Oil fuel, tons: 230
Range, miles: 2 300 at full power; 7 500 at 16 knots
Complement: 237 (14 officers and 223 ratings)

Originally class of three designed primarily for the direction of carrier-borne and shore-based aircraft. Lincoln ordered on 8 June 1951. Construction was all welded and largely prefabricated. The construction of three other ships Exeter, Gloucester and Coventry cancelled in 1957 being replaced by first three "Leander" class. Salisbury fitted with stabilisers. Original lattice masts replaced by tower masts during 1960s. Lincoln was fitted with wooden bow sheathing for Cod War 1976 but has subsequently been returned to reserve in the Stand-by Squadron at Chatham.

Cost: £3·3 million building cost.

Fire control: Sea Cat control. GWS 20 (optical).

Radar: Long range surveillance: One Type 965P with double AKE 2 array with IFF.
Combined warning: One Type 993.
Height-finder: One Type 278.
Target indication: One Type 982.
Fire control: Mk 6M director with Type 275.
Navigation: One Type 978.

SALISBURY
6/1977, Michael D. J. Lennon

Sonar: Types 174 and 170B.

Transfers: Llandaff to Bangladesh as Oomar Farooq (F 16) on 1 Dec 1976. Salisbury and Lincoln were to have been transferred to Egypt, a move that was not cancelled until Salisbury had reached Gibraltar. The latter now listed as "Stand-by etc".

1 "LEOPARD" CLASS (TYPE 41)

Name	No.	Builders	Laid down	Launched	Commissioned
LYNX	F 27	John Brown & Co Ltd, Clydebank	13 Aug 1953	12 Jan 1955	14 Mar 1957

Displacement, tons: 2 300 standard; 2 520 full load
Length, feet (metres): 320 (97·5) pp; 330 (100·6) wl; 339·8 (103·6) oa
Beam, feet (metres): 40 (12·2)
Draught, feet (metres): 16 (4·9) (screws); 11·9 (3·7) (keel)
Guns: 4—4·5 in (115 mm)/45 (twin Mk 6); 1—40 mm/70
A/S weapons: 1 Squid 3-barrelled DC mortar
Main engines: 8 ASR 1 diesels in 3 engine rooms; 14 400 bhp; 2 shafts; 4 engines geared to each shaft
Speed, knots: 24
Oil fuel, tons: 220
Range, miles: 2 300 at full power; 7 500 at 16 knots
Complement: 235 (15 officers, 220 ratings)

Originally a class of four, a fifth ship having been cancelled for a "Leander" class. Designed primarily for anti-aircraft protection. All welded. Fitted with stabilisers. Lynx to Stand-by Squadron June 1977 at Chatham.

Cost: Average £3·2 million building cost.

Radar: Air search: One Type 965 with single AKE 1 array and IFF.
Combined warning: Type 993 (AKD aerial).
Fire control: Mk 6 M I-band. Type 275.
Navigation: One Type 978.

LYNX
6/1977, Dr. Giorgio Arra

Reconstruction: Lynx was extensively refitted in 1963 with new mainmast.

Sonar: Types 174 and 170.

Transfers: Another ship of this class, Panther, was transferred to India while building and renamed Brahmaputra. Jaguar to Bangladesh July 1978.

1 "WHITBY" CLASS (TYPE 12)

Name	No.	Builders	Laid down	Launched	Commissioned
TORQUAY	F 43	Harland & Wolff Ltd, Belfast	11 Mar 1953	1 July 1954	10 May 1956

Displacement, tons: 2 150 standard; 2 560 full load
Length, feet (metres): 360·0 (109·7) wl; 369·8 (112·7) oa
Beam, feet (metres): 41·0 (12·5)
Draught, feet (metres): 17 (5·2) (screws); 12·9 (3·9) (keel)
Guns: 2—4·5 in (115 mm)/45 (twin Mk 6)
A/S weapons: 1 Limbo 3-barrelled DC mortar
Main engines: 2 sets dr geared turbines; 2 shafts; 30 430 shp
Boilers: 2 Babcock & Wilcox; pressure 550 psi (38·7 kg/cm²); temperature 850°F (454°C)
Speed, knots: 31
Oil fuel, tons: 370
Complement: 225 (12 officers, and 213 ratings)

Ordered in 1951. Twin-rudders.

Class: Originally class of six. Torquay used as Navigation/Direction training and trials ship at Portsmouth, having a large deck-house aft and carrying the first CAAIS (Computer Assisted Action Information System) to go to sea. Eastbourne, alongside at Rosyth for engine-room trainees from HMS Caledonia and approved for disposal, 1978. Scarborough and Tenby scrapped after transfer to Pakistan due to the high quoted cost of modernisation.

Radar: Search: One Type 993.
Navigation: Type 1006.
Fire control: Type 275 (Mk 6M DCT).

TORQUAY
8/1978, Michael D. J. Lennon

Sonar: Types 177, 170 and 162.

UK / Amphibious warfare forces

AMPHIBIOUS WARFARE FORCES

2 ASSAULT SHIPS (LPD)

Name	No.	Builders	Laid down	Launched	Commissioned
FEARLESS	L 10 (ex-L 3004)	Harland & Wolff Ltd, Belfast	25 July 1962	19 Dec 1963	25 Nov 1965
INTREPID	L 11 (ex-L 3005)	John Brown & Co (Clydebank) Ltd	19 Dec 1962	25 June 1964	11 Mar 1967

Displacement, tons: 11 060 standard; 12 120 full load; 16 950 ballasted
Length, feet (metres): 500 *(152·4)* wl; 520 *(158·5)* oa
Beam, feet (metres): 80 *(24·4)*
Draught, feet (metres): 20·5 *(6·2)*
Draught, ballasted: 32 *(9·8)* aft; 23 *(7·0)* fwd
Landing craft: 4 LCM(9) in dock; 4 LCVP at davits
Vehicles: Specimen load: 15 tanks, seven 3 ton and 20 quarter-ton trucks
Aircraft: Flight deck facilities for 5 Wessex helicopters
Missiles: SAM; Sea Cat (4 quad launchers)
Guns: 2—40 mm/70 Bofors
Main engines: 2 EE turbines; 22 000 shp; 2 shafts
Boilers: 2 Babcock & Wilcox
Speed, knots: 21
Range, miles: 5 000 at 20 knots
Complement: 580 (see *Troops* note)

FEARLESS *11/1978, Michael D. J. Lenno*

They carry landing craft which are floated through the open stern by flooding compartments of the ship and lowering her in the water; are able to deploy tanks, vehicles and men; have seakeeping qualities much superior to those of tank landing ships, and greater speed and range. Capable of operating independently. Another valuable feature is a helicopter platform which is also the deckhead of the dock from which the landing craft are floated out. Officially estimated building cost: *Fearless* £11·25 million; *Intrepid* £10·5 million.
Intrepid to reserve in 1976 for refit in 1977-1978—relieved *Fearless* (to refit and reserve) November 1978.

Countermeasures: Mount 2 Knebworth Corvus launchers.

Electrical: Power at 440V 60c/s 3-phase a/c is supplied by four 1 000 kW AE1 turbo-alternators.

Electronics: Fitted with CAAIS.

Engineering: The two funnels are staggered across the beam of the ship, indicating that the engines and boilers are arranged *en echelon,* two machinery spaces having one turbine and one boiler installed in each space. The turbines were manufactured by the English Electric Co, Rugby, the gearing by David Brown & Co, Huddersfield. Boilers work at a pressure of 550 psi and a temperature of 850°F. Two five-bladed propellers, 12·5 ft diameter, 200 rpm in *Fearless*.

Operational: Each ship is fitted out as a Naval Assault Group/Brigade Headquarters with an Assault Operations Room from which naval and military personnel can mount and control the progress of an assault operation.

Radar: Air and surface search: One Type 993.
Navigation: One Type 975.

Satellite system: The Royal Navy fitted its first operational satellite communications system in *Intrepid* in 1969, the contract having been awarded to Plessey Radar—now removed.

Training: *Intrepid* used for the sea training of officers from the Britannia Royal Naval College, Dartmouth, retaining full amphibious capabilities.

Troops: Each ship can carry 380 to 400 troops at ship's company standards, and an overload of 700 marines and military personnel can be accommodated for short periods.

INTREPID *3/1979, Michael D. J. Lenno*

INTREPID *3/1979, Michael D. J. Lenno*

UK / Amphibious warfare forces 607

1 AMPHIBIOUS TRANSPORT (LPA) (RFA MANNED)

Name	No.	Builders	Laid down	Launched	Commissioned
TARBATNESS	A 345	Swan Hunter and Wigham Richardson, Wallsend-on-Tyne	1966	22 Feb 1967	10 Aug 1967

Displacement, tons: 9 010 light; 16 792 full load (14 000 normal operating)
Measurement, tons: 7 782 deadweight; 12 359 gross; 4 744 net
Dimensions, feet (metres): 524 × 72 × 22 (159·7 × 22 × 6·7)
Aircraft: 3 Gazelle helicopters
Main engines: Wallsend-Sulzer 8-cyl RD.76 diesel; 11 520 bhp = 18 knots
Range, miles: 12 000 at 16 knots
Complement: 150

As *Tarbatness* will be surplus to requirements as a Stores Support Ship in the near future she is being taken in hand in August 1979 for conversion to an amphibious transport, a somewhat late recognition of the Royal Marines urgent requirement for sea-borne mobility. In her new role she will have an Amphibious Command centre, improved communications, a flight-deck and hangar for three Gazelle helicopters, access to the flight-deck for vehicles requiring vertical lift and six LCVPs at davits. Accommodation will be available for a full Commando Group including artillery and vehicles. Completion date is as yet uncertain.

TARBATNESS   5/1978, Wright and Logan

6 LOGISTIC LANDING SHIPS (RFA MANNED)

Name	No.	Builders	Laid down	Launched	Commissioned
SIR BEDIVERE	L 3004	Hawthorn Leslie, Hebburn-on-Tyne	Oct 1965	20 July 1966	18 May 1967
SIR GALAHAD	L 3005	Alex Stephen, Glasgow	Feb 1965	19 Apr 1966	17 Dec 1966
SIR GERAINT	L 3027	Alex Stephen, Glasgow	June 1965	26 Jan 1967	12 July 1967
SIR LANCELOT	L 3029	Fairfield, Glasgow	Mar 1962	25 June 1963	16 Jan 1964
SIR PERCIVALE*	L 3036	Hawthorn Leslie, Hebburn-on-Tyne	Apr 1966	4 Oct 1967	23 Mar 1968
SIR TRISTRAM	L 3505	Hawthorn Leslie, Hebburn-on-Tyne	Feb 1966	12 Dec 1966	14 Sep 1967

*Refit

Displacement, tons: 3 270 light; 5 674 full load (3 370 and 5 550 in *Sir Lancelot*)
Dimensions, feet (metres): 412·1 × 59·8 × 13·0 (135·1 × 19·6 × 4·3)
Guns: Fitted for 2—40 mm—not normally carried
Main engines: 2 Mirrlees 10-cyl diesels; 9 400 bhp; 2 shafts; (2 Denny/Sulzer diesels; 9 520 bhp in *Sir Lancelot*)
Speed, knots: 17
Oil fuel, tons: 850
Range, miles: 8 000 at 15 knots
Complement: 68 (18 officers, 50 ratings)
Military lift: 340 (534 with hard lying)

Sir Lancelot was the prototype of this class which was originally built for the Army but transferred to RFA in Jan and March 1970. Fitted for bow and stern loading with drive-through facilities and deck-to-deck ramps. Facilities provided for on-board maintenance of vehicles and for laying out pontoon equipment.

Aircraft: Helicopters can be operated from the well-deck and the after platform by day or night in the later ships. In *Sir Lancelot* well-deck operations are limited to fair weather-day conditions. If required to carry helicopters, 11 can be stowed on the Tank Deck and nine on the Vehicle Deck.

SIR PERCIVALE   4/1978, Michael D. J. Lennon

Cranes: One 20 ton, two 4½ ton cranes.

Load: Can carry 16 main battle tanks, 34 mixed vehicles, 120 tons POL and 30 tons ammunition.

2 LOGISTIC LANDING CRAFT (RCT)

Name	No.	Builders	Laid down	Launched	Commissioned
DENNES	L 4001	Brooke Marine, Lowestoft	27 Aug 1975	29 July 1976	1977
ARAKAN	L 4003	Brooke Marine, Lowestoft	16 Feb 1976	23 May 1977	1978

Displacement, tons: 870 light; 1 413 full load
Dimensions, feet (metres): 240 × 45·9 × 5·8 (73·2 × 14 × 1·8)
Main engines: 2 Mirrlees-Blackstone ESL8 MGR diesels; 2 000 bhp = 10·3 knots
Fuel, tons: 150 dieso
Range, miles: 4 000 at 10 knots
Complement: 35 (4 officers, 31 men) (plus 34 troops)

Both ordered in October 1974. Can carry 350 ton of stores, five Chieftain tanks or eleven 8 ton lorries.

ARAKAN   1978, Brooke Marine Ltd

1 LCT (8) TYPE (RCT)

AGHEILA L 4002

Displacement, tons: 657 light; 895 to 1 017 loaded
Dimensions, feet (metres): 231·2 × 39 × 3·2 fwd; 6·5 aft (70·5 × 11·9 × 1 fwd; 2·0 aft) Beaching draughts
Main engines: 4 Paxman diesels; 1 840 bhp; 2 shafts = 10 knots
Range, miles: 3 000 at 9·5 knots
Complement: 33 to 37

Originally nine of these ships were operated by the RCT having been transferred from the Royal Navy. *Agheila* has low bridge with radar central and platform forward of bridge. Can carry five Chieftain tanks or eight light tanks or fifteen 4 ton trucks or eleven DUKW or 250 tons stores.

AGHEILA   5/1978, C. and S. Taylor

608   UK / Amphibious warfare forces — Helicopter support ship

14 LCM (9) TYPE

Name	No.	Builders	Commissioned
—	L 700	Brooke Marine Ltd	1964
—	L 701	Brooke Marine Ltd	1964
—	L 702	Brooke Marine Ltd	1965
—	L 703	Brooke Marine Ltd	1965
—	L 704	R. Dunston (Thorne)	1964
—	L 705	R. Dunston (Thorne)	1965
—	L 706	R. Dunston (Thorne)	1965
—	L 707	R. Dunston (Thorne)	1965
—	L 708	R. Dunston (Thorne)	1966
—	L 709	R. Dunston (Thorne)	1966
—	L 710	J. Bolson (Poole)	1965
—	L 711	J. Bolson (Poole)	1965
—	L 3507	Vosper Ltd	1963
—	L 3508	Vosper Ltd	1963

Displacement, tons: 75 light; 176 loaded
Dimensions, feet (metres): 85 × 21·5 × 5·5 *(25·7 × 6·5 × 1·7)*
Capacity: 2 tanks or 100 tons of vehicles
Main engines: 2 Paxman 6-cyl YHXAM diesels; 2 shafts; 624 bhp = 10 knots. Screws enclosed in Kort nozzles to improve manoeuvrability

LCM (9) 3507 and LCM (9) 3508 were the first operational minor landing craft to be built since the Second World War. Ramped in the traditional manner forward, a completely enclosed radar-fitted wheelhouse is positioned aft. Upon completion they carried out familiarisation trials to perfect the new techniques required in launching and recovering LCMs from the flooded sterns of the parent assault ships. Now operated by the Royal Marines. Four each of the 700 Series allocated to assault ships.

LCM 704 (from HMS *Fearless*)   11/1978, Michael D. J. Lenno

LCM 3507 (RCT)   7/1978, Leo van Ginderen

2 LCM (7)

7037   7100

Displacement, tons: 28 light; 63 loaded
Dimensions, feet (metres): 60·2 × 16 × 3·7 *(18·4 × 4·9 × 1·2)*
Main engines: 290 bhp = 9·8 knots

Employed as naval servicing boats and store carriers. Re-engined with Gray Marine diesels.

12 "AVON" CLASS RPL (RCT)

AVON RPL 01	**GLEN** RPL 07
BUDE RPL 02	**HAMBLE** RPL 08
CLYDE RPL 03	**ITCHEN** RPL 09
DART RPL 04	**KENNET** RPL 10
EDEN RPL 05	**LODDON** RPL 11
FORTH RPL 06	**MEDWAY** RPL 12

Displacement, tons: 100 (full load) (approx)
Dimensions, feet (metres): 72·2 × 20·5 × 5·5 *(22 × 6·2 × 1·7)*

Diesel-driven Ramp Powered Lighters (RPL) manned by RCT and available for short coastal hauls. *Itchen*, *Clyde* and *Dart* stationed in Hong Kong, *Eden* and *Forth* in Cyprus, remainder in UK. *Avon* used for experimental work.

BUDE   10/1978, Michael D. J. Lennon

26 LCVP (1) (2) and (3)

LCVP (1) 102, 112, 118, 120, 123, 127, 128, 134, 136
LCVP (2) 142-149
LCVP (3) 150-158

Displacement, tons: 8·5 light; 13·5 full load
Dimensions, feet (metres): 41·5 (LCVP (2)); 43 (LCVP (3)) × 10 × 2·5 *(12·7; 13·1 × 3·1 × 0·8)*
Main engines: 130 bhp = 8 knots; 2 Foden diesels; 200 bhp = 10 knots (LCVP (2))

LCVP (2)s carried by *Intrepid* and *Fearless* can carry 35 troops or two Land Rovers. Crew three. LCA (2)s were redesignated LCVPs (Landing Craft Vehicle and Personnel) in 1966. There were also a number of variations and prototypes of about the same length (43 ft).

Note: Raiding Landing Craft, including LCR 5507 and 5508, and Navigational Landing Craft, including LCN 604 (ex-LCR 5505).

LCVP (alongside LCM (9))   9/1978, John G. Callis

3 LCP (L) (3)

LCP (L) (3) 501, 503, 556

Displacement, tons: 6·5 light; 10 loaded
Dimensions, feet (metres): 37 × 11 × 3·2 *(11·3 × 3·4 × 1)*
Main engines: 225 bhp = 12 knots

HELICOPTER SUPPORT SHIP

Name	No.	Builders	Commissioned
ENGADINE	K 08	Henry Robb Ltd, Leith	15 Dec 1967

Displacement, tons: 9 000 full load (approx)
Measurement, tons: 6 384 gross; 2 848 net; 4 520 deadweight
Dimensions, feet (metres): 424·0 × 58·4 × 22·1 *(129·3 × 17·8 × 6·7)*
Aircraft: 4 Wessex and 2 Wasp or 2 Sea King helicopters
Main engine: 1 Sulzer two stroke, 5-cyl turbocharged 5RD68 diesel; 5 500 bhp = 14·5 knots
Complement: RFA: 63 (15 officers, 48 men); RN: 14 (2 officers, 12 ratings)
   Accommodation for a further RN 113 (29 officers and 84 ratings)

Projected under the 1964-65 Navy Estimates. Ordered on 18 August 1964. Laid down on 9 August 1965. Officially named on 15 September 1966. Largest ship then built by the company. Intended for the training of helicopter crews in deep water operations. She does not carry her own flight but embarks aircraft as necessary. Fitted with Denny Brown stabilisers, the only RFA vessel so equipped. Also fitted with PTA hangar immediately abaft the funnel.

ENGADINE   5/1977, Michael D. J. Lennon

MINE WARFARE FORCES

Name	No.	Builders	Commissioned
ABDIEL	N 21	John I. Thornycroft Ltd, Woolston, Southampton	17 Oct 1967

Displacement, tons: 1 375 standard; 1 500 full load
Dimensions, feet (metres): 265 × 38·5 × 10 *(80·8 × 11·7 × 3)*
Mines: 44 carried
Main engines: 2 Paxman Ventura 16-cyl pressure charged diesels; 1 250 rpm; 2 690 bhp = 16 knots
Complement: 77

Exercise minelayer ordered in June 1965. Laid down on 23 May 1966. Launched on 27 January 1967. Main machinery manufactured by Davey Paxman, Colchester. Main gearing supplied by Messrs Wisemans. Her function is to support mine countermeasure forces, maintain these forces when they are operating away from their shore bases and minelaying. Cost £1·5 million.

ABDIEL   *1978, MOD(N)*

1 + 4 "HUNT" CLASS (MINESWEEPERS/MINEHUNTERS—COASTAL)

Name	No.	Builders	Commissioned
BRECON	M 29	Vosper Thornycroft Ltd	1979
LEDBURY	—	Vosper Thornycroft Ltd	1980
CATTISTOCK	—	Vosper Thornycroft Ltd	—
COTTESMORE	—	Yarrow, Glasgow	—
MIDDLETON	—	Yarrow, Glasgow	—

Displacement, tons: 615 standard; 725 full load
Dimensions, feet (metres): 197 × 32·3 × 7·3 *(60 × 9·9 × 2·2)*
Gun: 1—40 mm
Main engines: 2 Ruston-Paxman Deltic diesels; 2 000 bhp = 15 knots (a third Deltic for slow running)
Range, miles: 1 500 at 12 knots
Complement: 45 (6 officers, 39 ratings)

A new class of MCM Vessels combining both hunting and sweeping capabilities. Hulls of GRP. Equipped with two French PAP 104 mine destructor outfits. Have slow speed drive available up to 8 knots. *Brecon* laid down 15 September 1975, launched 21 June 1978. *Ledbury* ordered 31 March 1977, laid down 5 October 1977. *Brecon* trials May-June 1979. It is reported that 12 of this class are planned. Agreement of March 1976 provided for Yarrow Ltd equipping their yard to build ships of this class. *Cattistock*, *Cottesmore* and *Middleton* ordered February 1979.

Cost: Reported as £18 million for *Brecon* and £12/15 million for remainder.

BRECON   *7/1978, Leo van Ginderen*

1 MINESWEEPER/MINEHUNTER (COASTAL)

Name	No.	Builders	Commissioned
WILTON	M 1116	Vosper Thornycroft Ltd, Woolston	14 July 1973

Displacement, tons: 450 standard
Dimensions, feet (metres): 153·0 × 28·8 × 8·5 *(46·3 × 8·8 × 2·5)*
Gun: 1—40 mm Mark 7
Main engines: 2 English Electric Deltic 18-7A diesels; 2 shafts; 3 000 bhp = 16 knots
Range, miles: 2 300 at 13 knots
Complement: 37 (5 officers and 32 ratings)

The world's first GRP warship. Contract signed on 11 February 1970. Laid down 16 November 1970 and launched on 18 January 1972. Prototype built of glass reinforced plastic to the existing minehunter design by Vosper Thornycroft at Woolston. Similar to the "Ton" class and fitted with reconditioned machinery and equipment from the scrapped *Derriton*.

Cost: Building cost £2·3 million.

Radar: Types 975 and 955M (IFF).

Sonar: Type 193M.

WILTON   *7/1978, Leo van Ginderen*

0 + 12 "EDATS" CLASS

To counter the increasing threat of minelaying in deeper waters procurement is planned in 1979-80 of twelve ships based on a commercial trawler design. The title of this class, the Extra Deep Armed Team Sweep vessels (EDATS) does little to clarify their form or method of operation, except for the words "Extra Deep" and "Sweep". Whether the "Armed Team" indicates that the ships will be armed or that the sweeps will be armed is far from clear. What is clear is that *St Davids* and *Venturer* (later in this section) are involved in trials for this new class.

610 UK / Mine warfare forces

32 "TON" CLASS
15 MINEHUNTERS

Name	No.	Builders	Commissioned
BILDESTON	M 1110	J. S. Doig (Grimsby) Ltd	28 Apr 1953
BRERETON†	M 1113	Richards Ironworks	9 July 1954
BRINTON	M 1114	Cook Welton and Gemmell	4 Mar 1954
BRONINGTON	M 1115	Cook Welton and Gemmell	4 June 1954
BOSSINGTON	M 1133	J. I. Thornycroft & Co, Southampton	11 Dec 1956
GAVINTON	M 1140	J. S. Doig (Grimsby) Ltd	14 July 1954
HUBBERSTON	M 1147	Fleetlands Shipyards Ltd, London	14 Oct 1955
IVESTON	M 1151	Philip & Sons Ltd, Dartmouth	29 June 1955
*KEDLESTON	M 1153	William Pickersgill & Son	2 July 1955
*KELLINGTON	M 1154	William Pickersgill & Son	4 Nov 1955
KIRKLISTON	M 1157	Harland & Wolff Ltd, Belfast	21 Aug 1954
MAXTON	M 1165	Harland & Wolff Ltd, Belfast	19 Feb 1957
NURTON	M 1166	Harland & Wolff Ltd, Belfast	21 Aug 1957
SHERATON	M 1181	White's Shipyard Ltd, Southampton	24 Aug 1956
SHOULTON	M 1182	Montrose Shipyard Ltd	16 Nov 1955

† Refit
* = RNR Training Ship

SHOULTON — 10/1978, Michael D. J. Lennon

17 MINESWEEPERS—COASTAL

Name	No.	Builders	Commissioned
*ALFRISTON	M 1103	J. I. Thornycroft & Co., Southampton	16 Mar 1954
BICKINGTON	M 1109	White's Shipyard Ltd, Southampton	27 May 1954
CRICHTON	M 1124	J. S. Doig (Grimsby) Ltd	23 Apr 1954
CUXTON	M 1125	Camper and Nicholson Ltd, Gosport	1953
GLASSERTON	M 1141	J. S. Doig (Grimsby) Ltd	31 Dec 1954
*HODGESTON	M 1146	Fleetlands Shipyards Ltd, London	17 Dec 1954
*LALESTON	M 1158	Harland and Wolff	1954
REPTON	M 1167	Harland & Wolff Ltd, Belfast	12 Dec 1957
POLLINGTON	M 1173	Camper & Nicholson Ltd, Gosport	5 Sep 1958
SHAVINGTON	M 1180	White's Shipyard Ltd, Southampton	1 Mar 1956
*UPTON	M 1187	J. I. Thornycroft & Co, Southampton	24 July 1956
WALKERTON	M 1188	J. I. Thornycroft & Co, Southampton	10 Jan 1958
WOTTON	M 1195	Philip & Sons Ltd, Dartmouth	13 June 1957
SOBERTON†	M 1200	Fleetlands Shipyards Ltd, Gosport	17 Sep 1957
STUBBINGTON	M 1204	Camper & Nicholson Ltd, Gosport	30 July 1957
LEWISTON	M 1208	Herd & Mackenzie, Buckie, Banff	16 June 1960
*CROFTON	M 1216	J. I. Thornycroft & Co, Southampton	26 Aug 1958

† Refit
* = RNR Training Ship

Displacement, tons: 360 standard; 440 full load
Dimensions, feet (metres): 153·0 × 27·7 × 8·2 (46·3 × 8·5 × 2·5)
Guns: Vary in different ships, some sweepers having no 40 mm, some 1—40 mm and 2—20 mm whilst hunters have 1—40 mm
Main engines: 2 diesels; 2 shafts; 2 500 bhp (JVSS 12 Mirrlees); 3 000 bhp (18A-7A Deltic)
Speed, knots: 15
Oil fuel, tons: 45
Range, miles: 2 500 at 12 knots
Complement: 29 (38 in minehunters, 5 officers and 33 ratings)

The survivors of a class of 118 built between 1953 and 1960, largely as a result of lessons from the Korean War. John I. Thornycroft & Co Ltd, Southampton were the lead yard for these ships which have double mahogany hull and incorporate a considerable amount of non-magnetic material. Fitted with Vospers stabilisers. The majority has now been fitted with "Cascover" nylon in place of copper sheathing. *Cuxton* commissioned finally in October 1975 after 22 years in "moth-balls". *Glasserton* in the Stand-by Squadron.

Appearance: Frigate-type enclosed bridges in *Bildeston, Brereton, Brinton, Crofton, Cuxton, Iveston, Kellington, Kirkliston, Lewiston, Bossington, Bronington, Gavinton, Hubberston, Kedleston, Maxton, Repton, Pollington, Nurton, Sheraton, Shoulton, Soberton, Stubbington, Walkerton, Wiston.*
Enclosed bridges being fitted in remainder.

Conversions: *Beachampton, Monkton, Wasperton, Wolverton* and *Yarnton* were converted into coastal patrol vessels late in 1971, (see *Light Forces*). *Laleston* was converted into diving training ship in 1966-67. *Walkerton* used by Dartmouth RN College as Navigation Training Ship, to be relieved by *Alfriston* in 1978. *Shoulton* was the original minehunter conversion, fitted with pump-jet and bow thruster.

Cost: Average running cost at 1976 prices £0·3 million per ship.

Diving: *Laleston* is diving training ship, attached to Ulster RNR.

Engineering: Earlier vessels had Mirrlees diesels, but later units had Napier Deltic lightweight diesels. *Highburton*, the first with Deltic diesels, was accepted on 21 April 1955. All minehunters have Deltics and active rudders. Generators for electrical power are in a separate engine room in Mirrlees, Deltic-conversions and minehunters. Deltic built minesweepers have a generator in the main engine-room and two generators in the generator-room. Mirrlees still fitted in *Glasserton, Laleston, Cuxton* and *Repton*. Three-bladed propellers, 6 ft diameter, 400 rpm. *Shoulton,* refitted 1965-67, has pump-jet propulsion.

Fishery protection: Under the command of Captain FPS and based at Rosyth this duty is carried out by the Offshore Division ("Island" class under Light Forces) and the Coastal Division consisting of "Ton" class. In 1979 these duties are carried out by *Bickington, Brereton, Brinton, Cuxton, Crichton, Pollington, Repton, Shavington, Stubbington* and *Wotton*. All FPS ships carry a large Signal Projector (searchlight).

Osbourne sweep: *Glasserton* is fitted with derricks for Osbourne sweep. *Highburton* used in initial trials.

Radar: Type 975 (*Kirkliston,* Type 1006).

Royal Naval Reserve: The practice of temporarily renaming ships attached to RNR divisions has been abandoned. The seven ships now operate as follows: *Kedleston*—Forth; *Upton*—Tay; *Kellington*—Sussex; *Alfriston*—Solent; *Crofton*—Mersey; *Hodgeston*—Clyde; *Laleston*—Ulster. Other RNR training ships are provided from the "Kingfisher" class (see *Light Forces*) and "Venturer" class.

Sonar: Type 193 in minehunters (Type 193M in *Iveston*).

Transfers: Argentina (six in 1968), Australia (six in 1962), Ghana (one in 1964), India (four in 1956), Ireland (three in 1971), Malaysia (seven in 1960-68), South Africa (ten in 1958-59).

CRICHTON — 11/1978, Michael D. J. Lennon

GLASSERTON — 11/1977, Michael D. J. Lennon

IVESTON — 11/1978, Michael D. J. Lennon

POLLINGTON — 6/1978, Wright and Logan

LALESTON — 11/1978, Michael D. J. Lennon

UK / Mine warfare forces — Maintenance ships 611

2 "VENTURER" CLASS (MINESWEEPERS—STEEL—MEDIUM)

Name	No.	Builders	Commissioned
ST. DAVID	M 07	Cubow Ltd, Woolwich	1972
	(ex-Suffolk)		
VENTURER	M 08	Cubow Ltd, Woolwich	1973
	(ex-Suffolk)		

Measurement, tons: 392 gross; 134 net
Dimensions, feet (metres): 120·7 × 29·2 × 12·8 (36·6 × 8·9 × 3·9)
Main engines: 2 Mirrlees-Blackstone diesels; 2 000 hp = 14 knots

Both were designed as stern trawlers. *St. David* was converted into a Stand-by Safety Vessel for offshore installations in 1976. Purchased by Ministry of Defence in 1978. Unarmed with navigational radar. Act as RNR training ships—*Venturer* with Severn Division and *St David* with South Wales Division.

Future: It is reported that these were the forerunners of the "EDATS" class of comparatively inexpensive minesweepers to back up the very costly "Hunt" class and listed separately earlier in this section. These two ships are certainly involved in successful trials of deep-sweeping gear and techniques.

ST. DAVID   12/1978, Michael D. J. Lennon

3 "HAM" CLASS (MINESWEEPERS—INSHORE)

Name	No.	Builders	Commissioned
DITTISHAM	M 2621	Fairlie Yacht Slip	1954
FLINTHAM	M 2628	Bolson & Co	1955
THORNHAM (Aberdeen)	M 2793	Taylor, Shoreham	1957

Displacement, tons: 120 standard; 159 full load
Dimensions, feet (metres): 2601 Series: 106·5 × 21·2 × 5·5 (32·5 × 6·5 × 1·7); Thornham: 107·5 × 22 × 5·8 (32·8 × 6·7 × 1·8)
Gun: 1—20 mm Oerlikon fwd
Main engines: 2 Paxman diesels; 1 100 bhp = 14 knots
Oil fuel, tons: 15
Complement: 15 (2 officers, 13 ratings)

The first inshore minesweeper, *Inglesham*, was launched by J. Samuel White & Co Ltd, Cowes, on 23 April 1952. The 2601 series were of composite construction. In all 95 of this class were built.
Thornham attached to Aberdeen University RNU, other two at Plymouth, (*Raleigh*).

Conversions: As a result of a decision in 1962 several of this class were saved from deletion and converted for other tasks (listed separately later—six TRVs, three DGVs, six RNXS tenders (now reduced to two) and two survey craft).

Transfers: Australia (three in 1966-68), France (15 in 1954-55), Ghana (two in 1959), India (two in 1955), Libya (two in 1963), Malaysia (four in 1958-59), South Yemen (three in 1967). Ships subsequently returned are not listed.

DITTISHAM   6/1977, Dr. Giorgio Arra

2 "LEY" CLASS M 2001 SERIES (MINEHUNTERS—INSHORE)

Name	No.	Builders	Commissioned
AVELEY	M 2002	J. S. White & Co Ltd, Cowes	1953
ISIS (ex-Cradley)	M 2010	Saunders Roe Ltd	1955

Displacement, tons: 123 standard; 164 full load
Dimensions, feet (metres): 107 × 21·8 × 5·5 (32·3 × 6·5 × 1·7)
Gun: 1—40 mm (*Isis*); 1—20 mm (*Aveley*)
Main engines: 2 Paxman diesels; 700 bhp = 13 knots
Complement: 15 (2 officers, 13 ratings)

The "Ley" class, originally of ten ships, differed from the "Ham" class. They were of composite non-magnetic metal and wooden construction, instead of all wooden construction. Their superstructure and other features also differed. They had no winch or sweeping gear, as they were minehunters, not sweepers. *Aveley* is attached to Plymouth. *Isis*, renamed in 1963, has been affiliated with Southampton University RNU since 1 April 1974. Royal Navy crew.

ISIS   6/1977, Dr. Giorgio Arra

MAINTENANCE SHIPS

Name	No.	Builders	Laid down	Launched	Commissioned
TRIUMPH	A 108 (ex-R 16)	R & W Hawthorn Leslie, Hebburn	27 Jan 1943	2 Oct 1944	9 Apr 1946

Displacement, tons: 13 500 standard; 17 500 full load
Length, feet (metres): 699·0 (213·1)
Beam, feet (metres): 80·0 (24·4)
Draught, feet (metres): 23·7 (7·2)
Width, feet (metres): 112·5 (34·3) oa
Aircraft: 3 helicopters in flight deck hangar
Guns: 4—40 mm; 3 saluting (now removed)
Main engines: Parsons geared turbines; 2 shafts; 40 000 shp
Boilers: 4 Admiralty 3-drum type; pressure 400 psi (28·1 kg/cm²); temperature 700°F (371°C)
Speed, knots: 24·25
Oil fuel, tons: 3 000
Range, miles: 10 000 at 14 knots; 5 500 at full speed
Complement: 500 (27 officers, 473 men) plus 285 (15 officers, 270 men) on maintenance staff

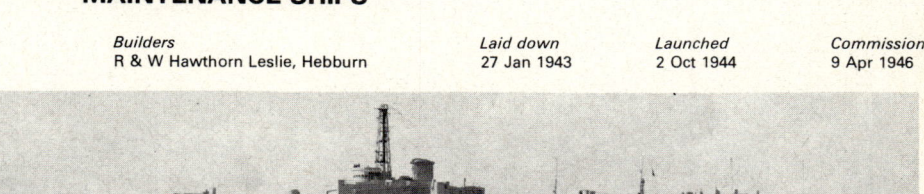
TRIUMPH   9/1974, Dr Giorgio Arra

Originally an aircraft carrier of the "Colossus" class. Converted for present role at a cost of £10·2 million. at Portsmouth between 1958 and 1965. Now in reserve at Chatham in preservation.

2 "HEAD" CLASS

Name	No.	Builders	Laid down	Launched	Commissioned
RAME HEAD	A 134	Burrard D.D. Co, Vancouver	12 July 1944	22 Nov 1944	18 Aug 1945
BERRY HEAD	A 191	North Vancouver Ship Repairers	15 June 1944	21 Oct 1944	30 May 1945

Displacement, tons: 9 000 standard; 11 270 full load
Length, feet (metres): 441·5 (134·6)
Beam, feet (metres): 57·5 (17·5)
Draught, feet (metres): 22·5 (6·9)
Guns: 11—40 mm
Main engines: Triple expansion; 2 500 ihp
Boilers: 2 Foster-Wheeler
Speed, knots: 10 approx
Oil fuel, tons: 1 600 capacity
Complement: 425

Escort Maintenance Ships. To reserve in 1972. *Rame Head* accommodation ship at Portsmouth since June 1976. *Berry Head*, at Devonport.

RAME HEAD   8/1978, J. L. M. van der Burg

612 UK / Royal yacht — Hovercraft and hydrofoil

ROYAL YACHT

Name	No.	Builders	Laid down	Launched	Commissioned
BRITANNIA	A 00	John Brown & Co Ltd, Clydebank	July 1952	16 Apr 1953	14 Jan 1954

Displacement, tons: 3 990 light; 4 961 full load
Measurement, tons: 5 769 gross
Dimensions, feet (metres): 412·2 × 55·0 × 17·0 (125·7 × 16·8 × 5·2)
Main engines: Single reduction geared turbines; 2 shafts; 12 000 shp = 21 knots (22·5 trials)
Boilers: 2
Oil fuel, tons: 330 (510 with auxiliary fuel tanks)
Range, miles: 2 800 at 20 knots; 3 200 at 18 knots; 3 675 at 14 knots
Complement: 277 (21 officers, 256 ratings)

Designed as a medium sized naval hospital ship for use by Her Majesty The Queen in peacetime as the Royal Yacht. Construction conformed to mercantile practice. Fitted with Denny-Brown single fin stabilisers to reduce roll in bad weather from 20 to 6 degrees. Cost £2·098 million. To pass under the bridges of the St. Lawrence Seaway when she visited Canada, the top 20 ft of her mainmast and the radio aerial on her foremast were hinged in November 1958 so that they could be lowered as required.

BRITANNIA   6/1977, John Mortimer

ICE PATROL SHIP

Name	No.	Builders	Laid down	Launched	Commissioned
ENDURANCE (ex-*Anita Dan*)	A 171	Krögerwerft, Rendsburg	1955	May 1956	Dec 1956

Displacement, tons: 3 600
Measurement, tons: 2 641 gross
Length, feet (metres): 300 *(91·5)*; 305 *(93)* including helicopter deck extension
Beam, feet (metres): 46 *(14)*
Draught, feet (metres): 18 *(5·5)*
Aircraft: 2 Wasp helicopters
Guns: 2—20 mm
Main engine: 1 Burmester & Wain 550 VTBF diesel; 3 220 ihp; 1 shaft
Speed, knots: 14·5
Range, miles: 12 000 at 14·5 knots
Complement: 119 (13 officers, 106 men, including a small Royal Marine detachment) plus 12 spare berths for scientists

Purchased from J. Lauritzen Lines, Copenhagen (announced on 20 February 1967). Strengthened for operation in ice. Converted by Harland & Wolff, Belfast 1967-68 into an ice patrol ship for southern waters, undertaking hydrographic and oceanographic surveys and acting as support ship for the British Antarctic Survey and guard vessel. Original cost £1·8 million.
An unusual feature for one of HM ships is her hull painted a vivid red for easy identification in the ice.

Communications: At 1978 refit in Chatham was fitted with Marisat communication system.

ENDURANCE   11/1978, Michael D. J. Lennon

HOVERCRAFT AND HYDROFOIL

Notes: (a) The Royal Navy Hovercraft Trials Unit was established at Lee-on-the-Solent in 1974.
(b) MCM trials with SR.N4 *Sir Christopher* carried out in 1976.

BOEING JETFOIL 929-100

SPEEDY

Displacement, tons: 110
Dimensions, feet (metres): 99 × 31 × 16·3 *(30·1 × 9·5 × 5)* (foils extended); 90 × 31 × 4·8 *(27·4 × 9·5 × 1·5)* (foils retracted)
Main engines: 2 Allison 501-K20A gas turbines (6 600 shp) connected to 2 Rocketdyne Powerjet 20 pumps for waterjet propulsion = 50 knots

Ordered in 1978 for evaluation in the offshore protection role. Launched 9 July 1979.
Armament: Not yet announced but designed to carry six SSMs and a 76 mm Compact gun.

JETFOIL   1979, Jane's Surface Skimmers

UK / Hovercraft and hydrofoil 613

1 VOSPER THORNYCROFT (VT2) TYPE

001

Operating weight, tons: 100 (all-up, starting)
Dimensions, feet (metres): 100·3 × 43·5 *(31·2 × 13·3)*
Main engines: 2 Rolls-Royce Proteus gas turbines (lift and propulsion);
4 500 shp = 60 knots
Endurance: 5 hours at max power with 10·5 tons fuel
Capacity: 130 troops or 23·5 tons installed armament

First chartered by MOD in 1976 and purchased in April 1979. Trials of the several possible tasks—patrol, MCM, logistic support, troop landings—will continue.

VT2   1978, Vosper Thornycroft Ltd

3 WINCHESTER (SR.N6) TYPE

Operating weight, tons: 10 normal gross weight
Dimensions, feet (metres): 60·7 × 25·3 *(18·5 × 7·7)*
Main engine: 1 Rolls-Royce Gnome 1301 gas turbine; 1 400 shp = 50 knots
Range, miles: 200

Modified with radar and military communications equipment for the primary role of fast amphibious communication craft to support Royal Marine units. (Mark 2/3.)

SR.N6 Mk 6   1975, BHC

1 WELLINGTON (BH.7) TYPE

Operating weight, tons: 55
Dimensions, feet (metres): 78·3 × 45·5 × 34·0 oa (height); 5·5 (skirt) *(23·9 × 13·9 × 10·4; 1·7)*
Main engine: 1 Rolls-Royce Proteus 15M541 gas turbine; 4 250 shp = 58 knots
Endurance: 8 hours at max power with 8 tons fuel
Capacity: 60 troops or 7 tons installed armament
Complement: 14

Costing about £700 000, delivered to the inter-Service Hovercraft Trials Unit at the Royal Naval Air Station, Lee-on-Solent, in April 1970. She could be used as a missile armed fast patrol craft, an amphibious assault craft or for MCM tasks. Winter trials in Swedish waters in February 1972. Records established: longest open sea voyage, furthest north, and sustained speeds of over 55 knots in the Baltic.

BH.7   6/1977, Dr. Giorgio Arra

1 SR.N5 TYPE

This small hovercraft is used for crew training.

SR.N5   4/1976, C. and S. Taylor

DIVING SUPPORT SHIPS

Name	No.	Builders	Commissioned
RECLAIM (ex-*Salverdant*)	A 231	Wm Simons & Co Ltd, Renfrew	Oct 1948

Displacement, tons: 1 200 standard; 1 800 full load
Dimensions, feet (metres): 217·8 × 38 × 15·5 *(66·4 × 11·6 × 4·7)*
Main engines: Triple expansion; 2 shafts; 1 500 ihp = 12 knots
Oil fuel, tons: 310
Range, miles: 3 000
Complement: 100

Engined by Aitchison Blair Ltd. Laid down on 9 April 1946. Launched on 12 March 1948. Construction based on the design of a "King Salvor" class naval ocean salvage vessel. First deep diving and submarine rescue vessel built as such for the Royal Navy. Fitted with sonar, radar, echo-sounding apparatus for detection of sunken wrecks, and equipped for submarine rescue work. Due for replacement, a design contract for a "sea-bed operations vessel" having been awarded to Scotts, Greenock in June 1977. Order to be placed in 1979. This design includes a central diving well in addition to all normal diving support equipment.

RECLAIM   6/1977, Dr. Giorgio Arra

Name	No.	Builder	Commissioned
SEAFORTH CLANSMAN	—	Cochranes, Selby, N. Yorks	1977

Measurement, tons: 1977 gross; 577 net; 1 180 deadweight
Dimensions, feet (metres): 257·8 × 46·2 × 16·4 *(78·6 × 14·1 × 5)*
Main engines: Four 12-cyl diesels; 1 830 bhp; 2 cp propellers = 13 knots

Built for Seaforth Maritime Ltd, Aberdeen. Taken over for the RFA on charter 1978, for one year with option for extensions. Based at Aberdeen with naval diving party. With main engines forward she is fitted as a diving support ship with a stern ramp, moonpool, anti-pollution gear, fire-fighting gear and bow-thruster.

SEAFORTH CLANSMAN   5/1978, A. Denholm

LIGHT FORCES

(See Deletion List for "Dark" and "Brave" classes).
(See Tenders section for "Alert" patrol craft).

Note: A design study is in hand for a new class of patrol vessels to succeed the "Ton" class MCMVs used for Fishery Protection. As these are described in the Defence White Paper as "Offshore Patrol Vessels—to succeed vessels used for coastal fishery protection" it is not possible to make any estimate of their particulars.

7 "ISLAND" CLASS (OFFSHORE PATROL CRAFT)

Name	No.	Builders	Commissioned
JERSEY	P 295	Hall Russell & Co Ltd	15 Oct 1976
GUERNSEY	P 297	Hall Russell & Co Ltd	28 Oct 1977
SHETLAND	P 298	Hall Russell & Co Ltd	14 July 1977
ORKNEY	P 299	Hall Russell & Co Ltd	25 Feb 1977
LINDISFARNE	P 300	Hall Russell & Co Ltd	3 Mar 1978
ANGLESEY	P 277	Hall Russell & Co Ltd	June 1979
ALDERNEY	P 278	Hall Russell & Co Ltd	Nov 1979

Displacement, tons: 925 standard; 1 260 full load
Dimensions, feet (metres): 195·3 × 34·2 × 14 *(59·6 × 10·4 × 4·3)*
Gun: 1—40 mm
Main engines: 2 diesels; 1 shaft; 4 380 hp = 16 knots
Range, miles: 7 000 at 12 knots
Complement: 34 (accommodation for 40)

Order for first five announced 11 February 1975. Order placed 2 July 1975. *Jersey* launched 18 March 1976, *Orkney* 29 June 1976, *Shetland* 22 October 1976 *Guernsey* 17 February 1977 and *Lindisfarne* 1 June 1977. Can carry small RM detachment.
Two more of class ordered 21 October 1977. *Anglesey* laid down 6 February 1978, launched 18 October 1978—*Alderney* 11 June 1978, 27 February 1979.
The earlier ships of this class were retrofitted and the remainder built with enlarged bilge keels to damp down their motion in heavy weather. Last pair to be fitted with stabilisers.

Cost: For *Jersey* and *Orkney* building cost £3·3 million. Running cost £0·5 million per ship per year at 1976 prices.

ORKNEY   10/1978, Michael D. J. Lennon

1 VOSPER THORNYCROFT (FAST ATTACK CRAFT—PATROL)

Name	No.	Builders	Commissioned
TENACITY	P 276	Vosper Thornycroft Ltd	17 Feb 1973

Displacement, tons: 165 standard; 220 full load
Dimensions, feet (metres): 144·5 × 26·6 × 7·8 *(44·1 × 8·1 × 2·4)*
Guns: 1—40 mm; 2 MGs
Main engines: 3 Rolls-Royce Proteus gas turbines; 3 shafts; 12 750 bhp = 40 knots; 2 Paxman Ventura 6-cyl diesels on wing shafts for cruising = 16 knots
Range, miles: 2 500 at 15 knots
Complement: 32 (4 officers, 28 ratings)

Built as a private venture and launched on 18 February 1969 at Camber Shipyard, Portsmouth. Steel hull and aluminium alloy superstructure. Purchased by the Ministry of Defence (Navy) on 25 January 1972 for approximately £750 000 "as lying" and refitted with minor alterations and additions to meet naval requirements. Fishery protection vessel. Decca navigation radar.

Armament: Fitted with 40 mm gun in 1978.

Cost: After conversion £1·26 million.

TENACITY (with 40 mm gun)   9/1978, John G. Callis

UK / Light forces 615

3 FAST TRAINING BOATS

Name	No.	Builders	Commissioned
SCIMITAR	P 271	Vosper Thornycroft Group, Porchester Shipyard	19 July 1970
CUTLASS	P 274	Vosper Thornycroft Group, Porchester Shipyard	12 Nov 1970
SABRE	P 275	Vosper Thornycroft Group, Porchester Shipyard	5 Mar 1971

Displacement, tons: 102 full load
Dimensions, feet (metres): 100·0 × 26·6 × 6·4 *(30·5 × 8·1 × 1·9)*
Main engines: 2 Rolls-Royce Proteus gas turbines; 9 000 hp = 40 knots (2 Foden diesels for cruising in CODOG arrangement)
Range, miles: 425 at 35 knots; 1 500 at 11·5 knots
Complement: 12 (2 officers, 10 ratings)

Hull of glued laminated wood construction. Design developed from that of "Brave" class fast patrol boats. Design permits fitting of third gas-turbine and a gun armament if required. Launch dates:— *Cutlass* 19 February 1970, *Sabre* 21 April 1970, *Scimitar* 4 December 1969. Training craft at Portland.

SCIMITAR   7/1978, Leo van Ginderen

4 "BIRD" CLASS (LARGE PATROL CRAFT)

Name	No.	Builders	Commissioned
KINGFISHER	P 260	R. Dunston Ltd, Hessle	8 Oct 1975
CYGNET	P 261	R. Dunston Ltd, Hessle	8 July 1976
*PETEREL	P 262	R. Dunston Ltd, Hessle	7 Feb 1977
*SANDPIPER	P 263	R. Dunston Ltd, Hessle	16 Sep 1977

*RNR

Displacement, tons: 194 full load
Dimensions, feet (metres): 120 × 21·7 × 6·5 *(36·6 × 6·6 × 2)*
Guns: 1—40 mm; 2 MG
Main engines: 2 Paxman 16YJCM diesels; 4 200 bhp = 18 knots
Oil fuel, tons: 35
Range, miles: 2 000 at 14 knots
Complement: 19 (3 officers, 16 ratings)

Based on the smaller "Seal" class RAF rescue launches with some improvement to sea-keeping qualities and fitted with stabilisers. *Kingfisher* launched 20 September 1974. *Cygnet* 6 October 1975. *Peterel* 14 May 1976. *Sandpiper* 20 January 1977.
Cost: Average cost for building £1·1 million each. *Sandpiper* cost £1·4 million.
Design: Comparison of later craft with *Kingfisher* shows an expected attempt to cut down topweight eg radar cross-trees, deletion of scuttles.
Duties: *Kingfisher* and *Cygnet* attached to MCM Rosyth having been found unsuitable for Fishery Protection; *Peterel* RNR North Western group (Clyde); *Sandpiper* RNR Channel group (London).

SANDPIPER   2/1978, Wright and Logan

5 MODIFIED "TON" CLASS (LARGE PATROL CRAFT)

Name	No.	Builders	Commissioned
BEACHAMPTON	P 1007 (ex-M 1107)	Goole S.B. Co	1953
MONKTON	P 1055 (ex-M 1155)	Herd & Mackenzie, Buckie	1956
WASPERTON	P 1089 (ex-M 1189)	J. Samuel White & Co Ltd	1956
WOLVERTON	P 1093 (ex-M 1193)	Montrose S.Y. Co	1957
YARNTON	P 1096 (ex-M 1196)	Pickersgill	1956

Displacement, tons: 360 standard; 425 full load
Dimensions, feet (metres): 153·0 × 28·8 × 8·2 *(46·3 × 8·8 × 2·5)*
Guns: 2—40 mm Bofors (single, 1 fwd, 1 aft)
Main engines: 2 diesels; 2 shafts; 3 000 bhp = 15 knots
Oil fuel, tons: 45
Range, miles: 2 300 at 13 knots
Complement: 30 (5 officers and 25 ratings, but varies)

Former coastal minesweepers of the "Ton" class, refitted at the end of 1971, re-designated as coastal patrol vessels with limited wire-sweeping capability. Fitted with limited armour in bridge area. Form 6th Patrol Squadron Hong Kong.

BEACHAMPTON (Hong Kong)   11/1978, Lawrence Phillips

2 "FORD" CLASS (LARGE PATROL CRAFT)

Name	No.	Builders	Commissioned
DEE (ex-*Beckford*)	P 3104	Wm. Simons, Renfrew	1953
DROXFORD	P 3113	Pimblott, Northwich	1954

Displacement, tons: 120 standard; 142 full load
Dimensions, feet (metres): 117·2 × 20·0 × 7·0 *(35·7 × 6·1 × 2·1)*
A/S weapons: DC rails; large and small DC
Main engines: Davey Paxman diesels. Foden engine on centre shaft. 1 100 bhp = 18 knots
Oil fuel, tons: 23
Complement: 19

Built in 1953-57. Last survivors of a class of 20. *Dee* attached to Liverpool University RNU (administered by RNR Mersey) and *Droxford* to Glasgow University RNU (administered by RNR Clyde). *Dee* renamed 1965, this name having been used for *Droxford* 1955-65.

DROXFORD   11/1978, Michael D. J. Lennon

SURVEY SHIPS

1 IMPROVED "HECLA" CLASS

Name	No.	Builders	Commissioned
HERALD	A 138	Robb Caledon, Leith	31 Oct 1974

Displacement, tons: 2 000 standard; 2 945 full load
Dimensions, feet (metres): 260·1 × 49·1 × 15·6 *(79·3 × 15 × 4·7)*
Aircraft: 1 Wasp helicopter
Main engines: Diesel-electric drive; 1 shaft
Speed, knots: 14
Range, miles: 12 000 at 11 knots
Complement: 128

A later version of the "Hecla" class design. Fitted with Hydroplot Satellite navigation system, computerised data logging, gravimeter, magnetometer, sonars, echo-sounders, coring and oceanographic winches, passive stabilisation tank, bow thruster and two 35 ft surveying motor-boats.
Laid down 9 November 1972. Launched by Mrs Mary Hall, wife of the Hydrographer, on 4 October 1973.

Cost: £5·2 million building cost.

HERALD — 4/1977, Wright and Logan

3 "HECLA" CLASS

Name	No.	Builders	Commissioned
HECLA	A 133	Yarrow & Co, Blythswood	9 Sep 1965
HECATE	A 137	Yarrow & Co Ltd, Scotstoun	20 Dec 1965
HYDRA	A 144	Yarrow & Co, Blythswood	5 May 1966

Displacement, tons: 1 915 light; 2 733 full load
Measurement, tons: 2 898 gross
Length, feet (metres): 260·1 *(79·3)*
Beam, feet (metres): 49·1 *(15·0)*
Draught, feet (metres): 15·6 *(4·7)*
Aircraft: 1 Wasp helicopter
Main engines: Diesel-electric drive; 1 shaft; 3 Paxman Ventura 12-cyl Vee turbocharged diesels; 3 840 bhp; 1 electric motor; 2 000 shp
Speed, knots: 14
Oil fuel, tons: 450
Range, miles: 12 000 at 11 knots
Complement: 127

The first Royal Navy ships to be designed with a combined oceanographical and hydrographic role. Of merchant ship design and similar in many respects to the Royal Research ship *Discovery*. The hull is strengthened for navigation in ice, and a bow thruster is fitted. The fore end of the superstructure incorporates a Landrover garage and the after end a helicopter hangar with adjacent flight deck. Equipped with chartroom, drawing office and photographic studio; two laboratories, dry and wet; electrical, engineering and shipwright workshops, large storerooms and two surveying motor-boats. Air-conditioned throughout.
Average cost £1·25 million. *Hecate* laid down 26 October 1964, launched 31 March 1965. *Hecla;* 6 May 1964, 21 December 1964; *Hydra* 14 May 1964, 14 July 1965.

HECATE — 6/1977, C. and S. Taylor

COASTAL SURVEY SHIPS

4 "BULLDOG" CLASS

Name	No.	Builders	Commissioned
BULLDOG	A 317	Brooke Marine Ltd, Lowestoft	21 Mar 1968
BEAGLE	A 319	Brooke Marine Ltd, Lowestoft	9 May 1968
FOX	A 320	Brooke Marine Ltd, Lowestoft	11 July 1968
FAWN	A 335	Brooke Marine Ltd, Lowestoft	10 Sep 1968

Displacement, tons: 800 standard; 1 088 full load
Dimensions, feet (metres): 189 × 36·8 × 12 *(57·6 × 11·2 × 3·7)*
Guns: Fitted for 2—20 mm
Main engines: 4 Lister-Blackstone ERS8M, 8-cyl, 4 stroke diesels, coupled to 2 shafts; cp propellers; 2 640 bhp = 15 knots
Range, miles: 4 500 at 12 knots
Complement: 39 (5 officers, 34 ratings)

Originally designed for duty overseas, working in pairs. Launch dates: *Bulldog* on 12 July 1967, *Beagle* on 7 September 1967, *Fox* on 6 November 1967 and *Fawn* on 29 February 1968. Built to commercial standards. Fitted with passive tank stabilizer, precision ranging radar, Decca "Hifix" system, automatic steering. Air-conditioned throughout. Carry 28·5 ft surveying motor-boat.

BULLDOG — 11/1978, Michael D. J. Lennon

INSHORE SURVEY CRAFT

Note: Orders expected for two inshore survey craft to replace *Waterwitch* and *Woodlark* with three to follow to replace the "E" class.

3 "E" CLASS

Name	No.	Builders	Commissioned
ECHO	A 70	J. Samuel White & Co Ltd, Cowes	12 Sep 1958
ENTERPRISE	A 71	M. W. Blackmore & Sons Ltd, Bideford	1959
EGERIA	A 72	Wm. Weatherhead & Sons Ltd, Cockenzie	1959

Displacement, tons: 120 standard; 160 full load
Dimensions, feet (metres): 106·8 × 22·0 × 6·8 *(32·6 × 6·7 × 2·1)*
Gun: Fitted for 1—40 mm
Main engines: 2 Paxman diesels; 2 shafts; cp propellers; 1 400 bhp = 14 knots
Oil fuel, tons: 15
Range, miles: 1 600 at 10 knots
Complement: 18 (2 officers, 16 ratings); accommodation for 22 (4 officers, 18 ratings)

Built to same design as "Ham" Class MSIs.
Echo, the first Inshore Survey Craft, was launched on 1 May 1957. Equipped with two echo sounding machines, sonar, radar, wire sweep gear and surveying motor boat.

EGERIA — 6/1977, Michael D. J. Lennon

UK / Inshore survey craft — Large fleet tankers 617

2 "HAM" CLASS

Name	No.	Builders	Commissioned
WATERWITCH (ex-*Powderham*)	M 2720	J. Samuel White & Co Ltd, Cowes	1959
WOODLARK (ex-*Yaxham*)	M 2780	J. Samuel White & Co Ltd, Cowes	1958

Displacement, tons: 120 standard; 160 full load
Dimensions, feet (metres): 106·5 × 21·2 × 5·5 *(32·5 × 6·5 × 1·7)*
Main engines: Diesels; 2 shafts; 1 100 bhp = 14 knots
Range, miles: 1 500 at 12 knots
Complement: 18 (2 officers, 16 ratings)

Former inshore minesweepers of the "Ham" class converted to replace the old survey motor launches *Meda* and *Medusa* for operation in inshore waters at home. *Waterwitch* operated by RMAS.

WATERWITCH   11/1978, Michael D. J. Lennon

ROYAL FLEET AUXILIARY SERVICE

Notes: (a) Many of large RFAs carry two boxed 40 mm guns
(b) Two support tankers are to be ordered in March 1979.
(c) In 1978 it was announced that after the departure of *Ark Royal* the seagoing air strength of the RN would be augmented by putting at least four Sea Kings in all large RFAs. An RN air detachment will be with each flight. If available space in the hangars is devoted solely to helicopters each ship should be able to carry six aircraft.

Commodore, RFA: Commodore S. C. Dunlop, MBE

LARGE FLEET TANKERS (AOF(L))

3 "OL" CLASS

Name	No.	Builders	Commissioned
OLWEN (ex-*Olynthus*)	A 122	Hawthorn Leslie, Hebburn	21 June 1965
OLNA*	A 123	Hawthorn Leslie, Hebburn	1 Apr 1966
OLMEDA (ex-*Oleander*)	A 124	Swan Hunter, Wallsend	18 Oct 1965

* Refit

Displacement, tons: 10 890 light; 36 000 full load
Measurement, tons: 25 100 deadweight; 18 600 gross
Dimensions, feet (metres): 648·0 × 84·0 × 36·4 *(197·5 × 25·6 × 11·1)*
Aircraft: 4 Sea King helicopters
Main engines: Pametrada double reduction geared turbines; 26 500 shp = 19 knots
Boilers: 2 Babcock & Wilcox; 750 psi; 950°F
Complement: 87 (25 officers and 62 ratings)

Largest and fastest ships when they joined the Royal Fleet Auxiliary Service. *Olmeda* was launched on 19 November 1964, while *Olna* and *Olwen* were launched on 28 July 1965 and 10 July 1964, respectively.
Designed for underway replenishment of the Fleet both alongside or by helicopter. Specially strengthened for operations in ice, fully air-conditioned. *Olna* has a transverse bow thrust unit for improved manoeuvrability in confined waters and a new design of replenishment-at-sea systems.

Capacity: Original figures as follows; 18 400 tons FFO; 1 720 tons diesel; 130 tons lub oil; 3 730 tons Avcat; 280 tons Mogas. The proportions of FFO and diesel may now be changed.

Hangar: On port side of funnel can house three helicopters. On starboard side acts as garage for vehicles or for three more helicopters.

OLWEN   9/1978, Wright and Logan

2 LATER "TIDE" CLASS

Name	No.	Builders	Commissioned
TIDESPRING	A 75	Hawthorn Leslie, Hebburn	18 Jan 1963
TIDEPOOL	A 76	Hawthorn Leslie, Hebburn	28 June 1963

Displacement, tons: 8 531 light; 27 400 full load
Measurement, tons: 18 900 deadweight; 14 130 gross
Dimensions, feet (metres): 583·0 × 71·0 × 32·0 *(177·6 × 21·6 × 9·8)*
Aircraft: 4 Sea King helicopters
Main engines: Double reduction geared turbines; 15 000 shp = 18·3 knots
Boilers: 2 Babcock & Wilcox
Complement: 110 (30 officers and 80 ratings)

Highly specialised ships for fuelling (13 000 tons cargo fuel) and storing naval vessels at sea. *Tidespring* was laid down on 24 July 1961, launched on 3 May 1962. *Tidepool* was laid down on 4 December 1961, launched on 11 December 1962.

Hangar: On port side of funnel can house three helicopters. On starboard side acts as garage for vehicles or for three more helicopters.

TIDESPRING   8/1978, Michael D. J. Lennon

UK / Small fleet tankers — Support tankers

SMALL FLEET TANKERS (AOF(S))

5 "ROVER" CLASS

Name	No.	Builders	Commissioned
GREEN ROVER*	A 268	Swan Hunter, Hebburn-on-Tyne	15 Aug 1969
GREY ROVER	A 269	Swan Hunter, Hebburn-on-Tyne	10 Apr 1970
BLUE ROVER	A 270	Swan Hunter, Hebburn-on-Tyne	15 July 1970
GOLD ROVER	A 271	Swan Hunter, Wallsend-on-Tyne	22 Mar 1974
BLACK ROVER	A 273	Swan Hunter, Wallsend-on-Tyne	23 Aug 1974

* Refit

Displacement, tons: 4,700 light; 11 522 full load
Measurement, tons: 6 692 (A 271 and 273), 6 822 (remainder) deadweight; 7 510 gross; 3 185 net
Dimensions, feet (metres): 461·0 × 63·0 × 24·0 *(140·6 × 19·2 × 7·3)*
Aircraft: 1 Sea King helicopter
Main engines: 2 Pielstick 16-cyl diesels; 1 shaft; cp propeller; 15 360 bhp = 19 knots
Oil fuel: 950 tons
Range, miles: 15 000 at 15 knots
Complement: 47 (16 officers and 31 men)

Small fleet tankers designed to replenish HM ships at sea with fuel, fresh water, limited dry cargo and refrigerated stores under all conditions while underway. A helicopter landing platform is provided served by a stores lift, to enable stores to be transferred at sea by "vertical lift". *Green Rover* was launched on 19 December 1968, *Grey Rover* on 17 April 1969, *Blue Rover* on 11 November 1969. *Gold Rover* on 7 March 1973 and *Black Rover* on 30 October 1973. Cargo capacity 6 600 tons fuel with varying proportions of FFO, Dieso, Avcat, Avtur, Gasoline and Lub oil.

Cost: *Gold Rover* cost £7·7 million, an increase of £4·7 million over *Green Rover*. Running costs at 1976 prices £1·0 million per ship per year.

Engineering: A 268-270 re-engined 1973-74.

Training: *Gold Rover* employed on training duties at Portland.

GREY ROVER (in Hong Kong)   1/1978, Dr. Giorgio Arr

BLUE ROVER   7/1978, Michael D. J. Lennon

SUPPORT TANKERS (AOS)

Note: Majority under long-term charter.

Name	No.	Builders	Commissioned
PEARLEAF	A 77	Blythswood Shipbuilding Co Ltd, Scotstoun	Jan 1960

Displacement, tons: 25 790 full load
Measurement, tons: 18 711 deadweight; 12 353 gross; 7 215 net
Dimensions, feet (metres): 568 × 71·7 × 30 *(173·2 × 21·9 × 9·2)*
Main engine: 1 Rowan Doxford 6-cyl diesel; 8 800 bhp = 16 knots
Complement: 55

Chartered from Jacobs and Partners Ltd, London on completion. Launched on 15 October 1959. Can carry three different grades of cargo. Astern and abeam fuelling.

PEARLEAF   8/1978, J. L. M. van der Burg

Name	No.	Builders	Commissioned
PLUMLEAF	A 78	Blyth D.D. & Eng Co Ltd	July 1960

Displacement, tons: 26 480 full load
Measurement, tons: 19 430 deadweight; 12 459 gross
Dimensions, feet (metres): 560 × 72 × 30 *(170·8 × 22 × 9·2)*
Main engine: 1 N.E. Doxford 6-cyl diesel; 9 500 bhp = 15·5 knots
Complement: 55

Launched 29 March 1960. Astern and abeam fuelling.

PLUMLEAF   9/1978, Wright and Logan

2 SUPPORT TANKERS

Name	No.	Builders	Commissioned
– (ex-*Hudson Deep*)	—	Cammell Laird & Co Ltd, Birkenhead	1976
– (ex-*Hudson Cavalier*)	—	Cammell Laird & Co Ltd, Birkenhead	1976

Measurement, tons: 19 976 gross; 13 642 net; 33 750 deadweight

Chartered in 1979 to replace *Orangeleaf* (ex-*Southern Satellite*) and *Cherryleaf* (ex-*Overseas Adventurer*) returned to their owners, former in May 1978 and subsequently scrapped, the latter in April 1979. Both to be converted, ex-*Hudson Deep* at Cammell Lairds and the second at Swan Hunters. They were of a four-ship order cancelled by Hudson Bay Co but these two were completed by the shipbuilders, being the only order then in hand.

COASTAL TANKER (AO(H))

1 "EDDY" CLASS

Name	No.	Builders	Commissioned
EDDYFIRTH	A 261	Lobnitz & Co Ltd, Renfrew	10 Feb 1954

Displacement, tons: 1 960 light; 4 160 full load
Measurement, tons: 2 200 deadweight; 2 222 gross
Dimensions, feet (metres): 286 × 44 × 17·2 *(87·2 × 13·4 × 5·2)*
Main engines: 1 set triple expansion; 1 shaft; 1 750 ihp = 12 knots
Boilers: 2 oil burning cylindrical

The last of a class of eight, all completed 1952-54. Cargo capacity: 1 650 tons oil.

EDDYFIRTH 10/1976, Wright and Logan

FLEET REPLENISHMENT SHIPS (AEFS)

Name	No.	Builders	Commissioned
FORT GRANGE	A 385	Scott-Lithgow, Greenock	6 Apr 1978
FORT AUSTIN	A 386	Scott-Lithgow, Greenock	1979

Displacement, tons: 21 000 standard; 23 600 full load
Measurement, tonnes: 8 160 deadweight
Dimensions, feet (metres): 603 × 79 × 29·5 *(183·9 × 24·1 × 9)*
Aircraft: 1 Sea King helicopter
Main engine: 1—8-cyl 8RND90 Sulzer diesel; 23 200 bhp; 1 shaft = 20 knots
Range, miles: 10 000 at 20 knots
Complement: 140 RFA, 45 RN supply and aircraft detachments

Ordered in November 1971. Fitted with a helicopter flight-deck and hangar, thus allowing not only for vertical replenishment but also a base for Force A/S helicopters. *Fort Grange* laid down November 1973, launched 9 December 1976. *Fort Austin* laid down 9 December 1975, launched 9 March 1978, started sea trials November 1978—due for delivery mid-1979. A/S stores for helicopters carried on board. To replace *Resurgent*, *Retainer* and *Tabatness*.

Engineering: Bow thruster fitted.

FORT GRANGE 10/1978, Michael D. J. Lennon

Name	No.	Builders	Commissioned
RESOURCE	A 480	Scotts Shipbuilding & Eng Co, Greenock	16 May 1967
REGENT	A 486	Harland & Wolff, Belfast	6 June 1967

Displacement, tons: 22 890 full load
Measurements, tons: 18 029 gross
Dimensions, feet (metres): 640·0 × 77·2 × 26·1 *(195·1 × 23·5 × 8)*
Aircraft: 2 Sea King helicopters
Guns: Fitted for 2—40 mm Bofors (single) which are not carried in peacetime
Main engines: AEI steam turbines; 20 000 shp = 21 knots
Complement: 119 RFA officers and ratings; 52 Naval Dept industrial and non-industrial civil servants; RN detachment for helicopter flying and maintenance

Ordered on 24 January 1963. They have lifts for armaments and stores, and helicopter platforms for transferring loads at sea. Designed from the outset as Fleet Replenishment Ships (previous ships had been converted merchant vessels). Air-conditioned. *Resource* was launched at Greenock on 11 February 1966, *Regent* at Belfast on 9 March 1966. Official title is Ammunition, Explosives, Food, Stores Ship (AEFS).

RESOURCE 8/1978, Michael D. J. Lennon

ARMAMENT SUPPORT SHIP (AE)

Name	No.	Builders	Commissioned
RESURGENT (ex-*Changchow*)	A 280	Scotts Shipbuilding & Eng Co Ltd, Greenock	1951

Displacement, tons: 14 400
Measurement, tons: 9 357 gross
Dimensions, feet (metres): 477·2 × 62 × 29 *(145·8 × 18·9 × 8·8)*
Main engine: Doxford diesel; 1 shaft; 6 500 bhp = 16 knots
Oil fuel, tons: 925
Complement: 107

Resurgent was taken over on completion. Being replaced by "Fort" class.

RESURGENT 9/1977, Michael D. J. Lennon

620 UK / Stores support ships — (RMAS) Mooring, salvage and boom vessels

STORES SUPPORT SHIPS (AVS/AFS)

Name	No.	Builders	Commissioned
LYNESS	A 339	Swan Hunter & Wigham Richardson Ltd, Wallsend-on-Tyne	22 Dec 1966
STROMNESS	A 344	Swan Hunter & Wigham Richardson Ltd, Wallsend-on-Tyne	21 Mar 1967

Displacement, tons: 9,010 light; 16 792 full load (14 000 normal operating)
Measurement, tons: 7 782 deadweight; 12 359 gross; 4 744 net
Dimensions, feet (metres): 524 × 72 × 22 *(159·7 × 22 × 6·7)*
Aircraft: 1 Sea King helicopter
Main engine: 1 Wallsend-Sulzer 8-cyl RD.76 diesel; 11 520 bhp = 18 knots
Range, miles: 12 000 at 16 knots
Complement: 151 (25 officers, 82 ratings, 44 stores personnel)

Lifts and mobile appliances provided for handling stores internally, and a new replenishment at sea system and a helicopter landing platform for transferring loads at sea. A novel feature of the ships is the use of closed-circuit television to monitor the movement of stores. All air-conditioned. *Lyness* was launched on 7 April 1966, *Stromness* on 16 September 1966. *Lyness* is an Air-Stores Support Ship and cost £3·5 million.

Cost: Running cost, at 1976 prices, £1·6 million per ship per year.

LYNESS 9/1978, Michael D. J. Lenno

STORE CARRIER (AK)

Name	No.	Builders	Commissioned
BACCHUS	A 404	Henry Robb Ltd, Leith	Sep 1962

Displacement, tons: 2 740 light; 8 173 full load
Measurement, tons: 5 312 deadweight; 4 823 gross; 2 441 net
Dimensions, feet (metres): 379 × 55 × 22 *(115·6 × 16·8 × 6·7)*
Main engine: Swan Hunter Sulzer diesel; 1 shaft; 5 500 bhp = 15 knots
Oil fuel, tons: 720
Complement: 57

Built for the British India Steam Navigation Co for charter to the Royal Navy on completion. Crew accommodation and engines aft as in tankers. Purchased in 1973 by P & O SN Co, remaining on charter to MOD (N). Boxed 40 mm guns carried on board. Sister ship *Hebe* deleted 1979.

HEBE (deleted 1979) 6/1977, Dr. Giorgio Arr

ROYAL MARITIME AUXILIARY SERVICE

Notes: (a) The Royal Maritime Auxiliary Service and Port Auxiliary Service were combined as RMAS on 1 October 1976.
(b) To avoid over complication the ships and vessels of the Royal Naval Auxiliary Service and some of the Royal Corps of Transport are included here.

MOORING, SALVAGE AND BOOM VESSELS

Note: *Scarab* ("Insect" class tender) with bow sheave acts as mooring vessel at Pembroke Dock. *Cricket* (no bow sheave) acts as mooring vessel in the Clyde.

2 "WILD DUCK" CLASS (A)
2 "IMPROVED WILD DUCK" CLASS (B)
2 "LATER WILD DUCK" CLASS (C)

Name		No.	Builders	Commissioned
MANDARIN		P 192	Cammell Laird & Co Ltd, Birkenhead	5 Mar 1964
PINTAIL	A	P 193	Cammell Laird & Co Ltd, Birkenhead	Mar 1964
GARGANEY		P 194	Brooke Marine Ltd, Lowestoft	20 Sep 1966
GOLDENEYE	B	P 195	Brooke Marine Ltd, Lowestoft	21 Dec 1966
GOOSANDER		A 164	Robb Caledon Ltd	10 Sep 1973
POCHARD	C	A 165	Robb Caledon Ltd	11 Dec 1973

Displacement, tons: (A) 750 light; 1 200 full load. (B) 850 light; 1 300 full load. (C) 941 light; 1 622 full load
Dimensions, feet (metres): (A) 181·8 × 36·6 × 13 *(55·4 × 11·2 × 4)*. (B) 189·8 × 36·6 × 13 *(57·9 × 11·2 × 4)*. (C) 197·6 × 40·1 × 13·8 *(60·2 × 12·2 × 4·2)*
Main engine: 1 Davey Paxman 16-cyl diesel; 1 shaft; cp propeller; 550 bhp (A and B); 750 bhp (C)
Speed, knots: 10 (A and B); 10·8 (C)
Range, miles: 3 260 at 9·5 knots (C); 3 000 at 10 knots (A and B)
Complement: 26

Mandarin was the first of a new class of marine service vessels. Launched on 17 September 1963. *Pintail* was launched on 3 December 1963. *Garganey* and *Goldeneye* were built in 1965-67. *Goosander* and *Pochard* of the later "Later Wild Duck" class were launched 12 April 1973 and 21 June 1973 respectively. Previously their three tasks were separately undertaken by specialist vessels. Capable of laying out and servicing the heaviest moorings used by the Fleet and also maintaining booms for harbour defence. Heavy lifting equipment enables a wide range of salvage operations to be performed, especially in harbour clearance work. The special heavy winches have an ability for tidal lifts over the apron of 200 tons. Boxed 40 mm guns carried on board.

GOLDENEYE 8/1978, J. L. M. van der Burg

4 "KIN" CLASS

Name	No.	Builders	Commissione
KINGARTH	A 232	A. Hall, Aberdeen	1944
KINBRACE	A 281	A. Hall, Aberdeen	1945
KINLOSS	A 482	A. Hall, Aberdeen	1945
UPLIFTER	A 507	Smith's Dock Co Ltd	1944

Displacement, tons: 950 standard; 1 050 full load
Measurement, tons: 262 deadweight; 775 gross
Dimensions, feet (metres): 179·2 × 35·2 × 12·0 *(54 × 10·6 × 3·6)*
Main engine: 1 British Polar Atlas M44M diesel; 630 bhp = 9 knots
Complement: 34

Originally a class of eight classified as Coastal Salvage Vessels, but re-rated Mooring, Salvage and Boom Vessels in 1971. Equipped with horns and heavy rollers. Can lift 200 tons deadweight over the bow. *Kinbrace*, *Kingarth* and *Uplifter* were refitted with diesel engines in 1966-67, and *Kinloss* in 1963-64.

KINLOSS 5/1977, Michael D. J. Lenno

UK (RMAS) / Mooring, salvage and boom vessels — Trials ships

"LAY" CLASS

Name	No.	Builders	Commissioned
LAYMOOR (RN)	P 190	Wm. Simons & Co Ltd (Simons-Lobnitz Ltd)	9 Dec 1959

Displacement, tons: 800 standard; 1 050 full load
Dimensions, feet (metres): 192·7 × 34·5 × 11·5 (59 × 10·3 × 3·4)
Main engines: Triple expansion; 1 shaft; 1 300 ihp = 10 knots
Boilers: 2 Foster-Wheeler "D" type; 200 psi
Complement: 26 (4 officers; 22 ratings)

Building cost £565 000. Designed for naval or civilian manning. Good accommodation enables her to be operated in any climate. Oil-fuelled.

LAYMOOR   11/1978, Michael D. J. Lennon

COASTAL TANKERS

6 "OILPRESS" CLASS

Name	No.	Builders	Commissioned
OILPRESS	Y 21	Appledore Shipbuilders Ltd	1969
OILSTONE	Y 22	Appledore Shipbuilders Ltd	1969
OILWELL	Y 23	Appledore Shipbuilders Ltd	1969
OILFIELD	Y 24	Appledore Shipbuilders Ltd	1969
OILBIRD	Y 25	Appledore Shipbuilders Ltd	1969
OILMAN	Y 26	Appledore Shipbuilders Ltd	1969

Displacement, tons: 280 standard; 530 full load
Dimensions, feet (metres): 139·5 × 30·0 × 8·3 (41·5 × 9 × 2·5)
Main engine: 1 Lister-Blackstone ES6 diesel; 1 shaft; 405 shp at 900 rpm
Complement: 11 (4 officers and 7 ratings)

Ordered on 10 May 1967. Three are diesel oil carriers and three FFO carriers. Launched:— Oilbird 21 November 1968, Oilfield 5 September 1968, Oilman 18 February 1969, Oilpress 10 June 1968, Oilstone 11 July 1968, Oilwell 20 January 1969. Near sisters to "Water" class.

OILSTONE   9/1978, Michael D. J. Lennon

TRIALS SHIPS

Note: *Endsleigh* operates from Rosyth for A.C.R.E.

Name	No.	Builders	Commissioned
NEWTON	A 367	Scott Lithgow Ltd	17 June 1976

Displacement, tons: 3 940
Dimensions, feet (metres): 323·5 × 53 × 18·5 (98·6 × 16 × 5·7)
Main engines: Diesel-electric; 3 Mirrlees-Blackstone diesels; 1 shaft; 4 350 bhp = 14 knots
Range, miles: 5 000 at 14 knots
Complement: 64 (including 12 scientists)

Ordered November 1971. Laid down 19 December 1973. Launched 25 June 1975. Fitted with bow thruster and Kort nozzle. Propulsion system is very quiet. Passive tank stabilisation. Prime duty sonar propagation trials. Can serve as cable-layer with large cable tanks. Special winch system. Based at Plymouth.

NEWTON   2/1979, A. Denholm

Name	No.	Builders	Commissioned
WHITEHEAD	A 364	Scotts Shipbuilding Co Ltd, Greenock	1971

Displacement, tons: 3 040 full load
Dimensions, feet (metres): 319·0 × 48·0 × 17·0 (97·3 × 14·6 × 5·2)
Torpedo tubes: 1—21 in (bow, submerged); 3 (1 triple) Mk 32 A/S mounting
Main engines: 2 Paxman 12 YLCM diesels; 1 shaft; 3 400 bhp = 15·5 knots
Range, miles: 4 000 at 12 knots
Complement: 10 officers, 32 ratings, 15 trials and scientific staff

Designed to provide mobile preparation, firing and control facilities for weapons and research vehicles. Launched on 5 May 1970. Named after Robert Whitehead, the torpedo development pioneer and engineer. Fitted with equipment for tracking weapons and target and for analysing the results of trials. Based at Plymouth.

WHITEHEAD   9/1977, Michael D. J. Lennon

Name	No.	Builders	Commissioned
AURICULA	A 285	Ferguson Bros, Glasgow	1980

Displacement, tons: 1 100
Dimensions, feet (metres): 170·5 × — × — (52 × — × —)
Main engines: 2 Mirrlees-Blackstone diesels; 2 shafts; 1 300 hp

Ordered 5 January 1978 as sonar trials and experimental ship for delivery early 1980.

Name	No.	Builders	Commissioned
CRYSTAL	RDV 01	HM Dockyard, Devonport	30 Nov 1971

Displacement, tons: 3 040
Dimensions, feet (metres): 413·5 × 56·0 × 5·5 (126·1 × 17·1 × 1·7)
Complement: 60, including scientists

Unpowered floating platform for Sonar Research and Development. Ordered in December 1969. Launched 22 March 1971. A harbour-based laboratory without propulsion machinery or steering which provides the Admiralty Underwater Weapons Establishment at Portland with a stable platform on which to carry out acoustic tests and other research projects. Under Dockyard Control.

CRYSTAL   7/1978, Wright and Logan

2 "MINER" CLASS

Name	No.	Builders	Commissioned
BRITANNIC (ex-*Miner V*)	—	Philip & Son Ltd, Dartmouth	26 June 1941
STEADY (ex-*Miner VII*)	—	Philip & Son Ltd, Dartmouth	31 Mar 1944

Displacement, tons: 300 standard; 355 full load
Dimensions, feet (metres): 110·2 × 26·5 × 8·0 (33·6 × 8·1 × 2·4)
Main engines: Ruston & Hornsby diesels; 2 shafts; 360 bhp = 10 knots

Last of a class of eight small controlled-minelayers. *Miner V* was converted into a harbour cable-layer and renamed *Britannic* in 1960. *Miner VII* was adapted as a stabilisation trials ship at Portsmouth and renamed *Steady* in 1960. *Britannic* laid-up at Portland as spare ship for *Steady* who normally operates off the Channel Islands.

BRITANNIC   8/1976, Wright and Logan

622   UK (RMAS) / Trials ships — Cable ship

1 Ex-LCT (3)

WHIMBREL (ex-NSC (E) 1012) A 179

Displacement, tons: 300
Dimensions, feet (metres): 187 × 29.5 × 5 (57 × 9 × 1.5)
Main engines: Diesels; 2 shafts

Employed for weapon research by Underwater Weapons Establishment, Portland.

WHIMBREL   1974, Michael D. J. Lennon

TORPEDO RECOVERY VESSELS

4 NEW CONSTRUCTION

Displacement, tons: 660
Dimensions, feet (metres): 155.8 × 28 × — (47.4 × 8.5 × —)
Main engines: 2 diesels; 2 200 hp = 14 knots
Complement: 17

Ordered from Hall Russell, Aberdeen on 1 July 1977.

Name	No.	Builders	Commissioned
TORRENT	A 127	Cleland S.B. Co, Wallsend	10 Sep 1971
TORRID	A 128	Cleland S.B. Co, Wallsend	Jan 1972

Measurement, tons: 550 gross
Dimensions, feet (metres): 151.0 × 31.5 × 11 (46.1 × 9.6 × 3.4)
Main engines: Paxman diesels; 700 bhp = 12 knots
Complement: 19

Torrent was launched on 29 March 1971 and *Torrid* on 7 September 1971. These ships have a stern ramp for torpedo recovery—can carry 22 torpedoes in hold and ten on deck.
Torrent—Clyde. *Torrid*—Portsmouth.

TORRID   6/1977, Michael D. J. Lennon

6 "HAM" CLASS

BUCKLESHAM M 2614	**EVERINGHAM** M 2626	**HAVERSHAM** M 2635
DOWNHAM M 2622	**FRITHAM** M 2630	**LASHAM** M 2636

Details similar to other "Ham" class in Mine Warfare section but converted for TRV in 1964 onwards. Now fitted with stern ramp.

LASHAM   7/1978, A. Denholm

Ex-RAF CRAFT

OSPREY (Ex-RAF RTTL 2770) (RMAS)   **L 72** (RMAS)

Two craft operating on the Clyde. For details see RAF section at end—*Osprey*, RTTL Mk 2 Type; L 72, 1300 Series Pinnace Type.

L 72   7/1978, A. Denholm

ENDEAVOUR

Displacement, tons: 88
Dimensions, feet (metres): 76 × 14.5 × 9.8 (23.2 × 4.4 × 3)
Main engine: 1 Lister-Blackstone diesel; 337 hp; 1 shaft = 10.5 knots

Built for Liverpool Customs by R. Dunston & Co in 1966. Subsequently bought by M.O.D. Operates as TRV and range safety craft at Bincleaves Torpedo Range, Portland.

ENDEAVOUR   8/1977, Michael D. J. Lennon

CABLE SHIP

Name	No.	Builders	Commissioned
ST. MARGARETS	A 259	Swan Hunter & Wigham Richardson Ltd	1944

Displacement, tons: 1 300 light; 2 500 full load
Measurement, tons: 1 524 gross; 1 200 deadweight
Dimensions, feet (metres): 252 × 36.5 × 16.3 (76 × 10.9 × 4.8)
Main engines: Triple expansion; 2 shafts; 1 250 ihp = 12 knots

Provision was made for mounting one 4 in gun and four 20 mm guns but no armament is fitted. Sister ship *Bullfinch* paid off at Plymouth.

ST. MARGARETS   8/1978, Michael D. J. Lennon

SUBMARINE TENDER

WAKEFUL (ex-*Dan*, ex-*Heracles*) A 236

Displacement, tons: 900 approx
Measurement, tons: 492 gross
Dimensions, feet (metres): 127·5 × 35 × 15·5 *(38·9 × 10·7 × 4·7)*
Main engines: 2—9-cyl Ruston diesels; 4 750 bhp
Complement: 18

Purchased from Sweden in 1974 at cost of £600 000. Built as a tug by Cochranes, Selby, N. Yorks and now operated as Submarine Target Ship in the Clyde after undergoing a £1·6 million refit.

WAKEFUL   2/1979, Michael D. J. Lennon

ARMAMENT STORE CARRIERS (AKF)

Note: All AKFs have a red band on their buff funnel.

Name	No.	Builders	Commissioned
THROSK	A 379	Cleland S.B. Co, Wallsend	20 Sep 1977

Displacement, tons: 1 968 full load
Measurement, tons: 1 150 deadweight
Dimensions, feet (metres): 231·2 × 39 × 15 *(70·5 × 11·9 × 4·6)*
Main engines: 2 Mirrlees-Blackstone diesels; 3 000 bhp; 1 shaft = 14 knots
Range, miles: 5 000 at 10 knots
Complement: 22 (plus 10 spare bunks)

Ordered 9 December 1975. Laid down 25 August 1976, launched 31 March 1977. To carry armament stores in two holds. Two 5 tonne derricks.

THROSK   8/1977, Michael D. J. Lennon

Name	No.	Builders	Commissioned
MAXIM	A 377	Lobnitz & Co Ltd, Renfrew	1945

Displacement, tons: 604
Measurement, tons: 340 deadweight
Dimensions, feet (metres): 144·5 × 25 × 8 *(44·1 × 7·6 × 2·4)*
Main engines: Reciprocating; 500 ihp = 9 knots
Complement: 13

Launched 6 August 1945. Laid up at Pembroke Dock.

WATER CARRIERS

"SPA" CLASS

Name	No.	Builders	Commissioned
SPAPOOL	A 222	Charles Hill & Sons Ltd, Bristol	1947

Displacement, tons: 1 219 full load
Measurement, tons: 630 deadweight; 672 to 719 gross
Dimensions, feet (metres): 172 × 30 × 12 *(52·5 × 9·2 × 3·6)*
Main engines: Triple expansion; 675 ihp = 9 knots
Coal, tons: 90

Reported as based in Mombasa. Originally class of six with one 3 in and two 20 in guns. *Spabeck* carried HTP for submarines *Explorer* and *Excalibur*. Deleted May 1977.

7 "WATER" CLASS

Name	No.	Builders	Commissioned
WATERCOURSE	Y 15	Drypool Engineering & Drydock Co, Hull	1974
WATERFOWL	—	Drypool Engineering & Drydock Co, Hull	25 May 1974
WATERFALL	Y 17	Drypool Engineering & Drydock Co, Hull	1967
WATERSHED	Y 18	Drypool Engineering & Drydock Co, Hull	1967
WATERSPOUT	Y 19	Drypool Engineering & Drydock Co, Hull	1967
WATERSIDE	Y 20	Drypool Engineering & Drydock Co, Hull	1968
WATERMAN	A 146	R. Dunston (Hessle) Ltd	June 1978

Measurement, tons: 285 gross
Dimensions, feet (metres): 131·5 × 24·8 × 8 *(40·1 × 7·5 × 2·3)*
Main engine: 1 diesel; 1 shaft; 600 bhp = 11 knots
Complement: 11

Y 19-20 have after deck-house extended forward. *Waterman* ordered 3 February 1977, laid down 19 June 1977 and launched 24 November 1977. She is a modified ship, having a store-carrying capability.

WATERMAN   10/1978, Wright and Logan

3 "FRESH" CLASS

FRESHBURN   FRESHLAKE   FRESHSPRING

Displacement, tons: 594
Dimensions, feet (metres): 126·2 × 25·5 × 10·8 *(38·5 × 7·8 × 3·3)*
Main engines: Triple expansion; 450 ihp = 9 knots

Freshspring was converted from coal to oil fuel, in 1961. *Freshburn* and *Freshlake* at Chatham, *Freshspring* at Faslane. Last of a wartime class of 14.

FRESHSPRING   11/1978, Michael D. J. Lennon

TUGS

Note: (a) Appearance of RMAS tugs—black hull with white line, buff upperworks, buff funnel with black top. The blue band on the funnel varies between ports.
(b) Four twin unit Tractor Tugs ordered from Richard Dunston (Hessle) on 22 February 1979 for service in 1980. To have single diesel with two Voith-Schneider units. Primarily for harbour work with coastal towing capacity. The first of a new generation of tugs.

3 OCEAN TUGS

Name	No.	Builders	Commissioned
ROYSTERER	A 361	C. D. Holmes, Beverley, Humberside	26 Apr 1972
ROLLICKER	A 502	C. D. Holmes, Beverley, Humberside	Feb 1973
ROBUST	A 366	C. D. Holmes, Beverley, Humberside	6 Apr 1974

Displacement, tons: 1 630 full load
Dimensions, feet (metres): 179·7 × 38·5 × 18·0 *(54 × 11·6 × 5·5)*
Main engines: 2 Mirrlees KMR 6 diesels (by Lister-Blackstone Mirrlees Marine Ltd); 2 shafts; 4 500 bhp at 525 rpm = 15 knots
Range, miles: 13 000 at 12 knots
Complement: 31 (10 officers and 21 ratings) (and able to carry salvage party of 10 RN officers and ratings)

Bollard pull—50 tons. Designed principally for salvage and long-range towage but can be used for general harbour duties, which *Robust* now undertakes at Devonport. *Roysterer* based at Devonport, *Rollicker* in the Clyde. Cost well over £2 million apiece. Ordered November 1968 *(Rollicker, Roysterer)* and May 1970 *(Robust)*. Launch dates: *Robust* 7 October 1971, *Rollicker* 29 January 1971, *Roysterer* 20 April 1970.

ROYSTERER   7/1977, Michael D. J. Lennon

624 UK (RMAS) / Tugs

Name	No.	Builders	Commissioned
TYPHOON	A 95	Henry Robb & Co Ltd, Leith	1960

Displacement, tons: 800 standard; 1 380 full load
Dimensions, feet (metres): 200·0 × 40·0 × 13·0 *(60·5 × 12 × 4)*
Main engines: 2 turbocharged Vee type 12-cyl diesels; 1 shaft; 2 750 bhp = over 16 knots

Launched on 14 October 1958. The machinery arrangement of two diesels geared to a single shaft was an innovation for naval ocean tugs in the Royal Navy. Cp propeller, 150 rpm. Fitted for fire-fighting, salvage and ocean rescue, with a heavy mainmast and derrick attached. Bollard pull 32 tons.

TYPHOON 1977, Michael D. J. Lennon

5 "CONFIANCE" CLASS

Name	No.	Builders	Commissioned
AGILE	A 88	Goole S.B. Co.	July 1959
ADVICE	A 89	A. & J. Inglis Ltd, Glasgow	Oct 1959
ACCORD	A 90	A. & J. Inglis Ltd, Glasgow	Sep 1958
CONFIANCE	A 289	A. & J. Inglis Ltd, Glasgow	27 Mar 1956
CONFIDENT	A 290	A. & J. Inglis Ltd, Glasgow	Jan 1956

Displacement, tons: 760 full load
Dimensions, feet (metres): 154·8 × 35·0 × 11·0 *(47·2 × 10·7 × 3·4)*
Main engines: 4 Paxman HAXM diesels; 2 shafts; 1 800 bhp = 13 knots
Complement: 29 plus 13 salvage party

Fitted with 2·5 m diameter Stone Kamewa cp propellers. *Accord, Advice* and *Agile,* formerly rated as dockyard tugs were officially added to the "Confiance" class in 1971 as part of the Royal Maritime Auxiliary Service ocean towing force although there are minor differences between these three and the "Confiance" pair. Fitted for one 40 mm gun.

Appearance: *Agile* is the only one with a tall mainmast. *Confiance* now fitted with a "Roysterer" type rubber bow fender.

ADVICE 10/1978, Michael D. J. Lennon

1 "SAMSON" CLASS

Name	No.	Builders	Commissioned
SEA GIANT	A 288	Alexander Hall & Co Ltd, Aberdeen	1955

Displacement, tons: 1 200 full load
Measurement, tons: 850 gross
Dimensions, feet (metres): 180 × 37 × 14 *(54 × 11·2 × 4·3)*
Main engines: Triple expansion; 2 shafts; 3 000 ihp = 15 knots
Complement: 30

Superman laid up in reserve at Devonport.

SEA GIANT 3/1978, Michael D. J. Lennon

1 "BUSTLER" CLASS

Name	No.	Builders	Commissioned
CYCLONE (ex-*Growler*)	A 111	Henry Robb Ltd, Leith	Sep 1943

Displacement, tons: 1 118 light; 1 630 full load
Dimensions, feet (metres): 205·0 × 40·2 × 16·8 *(62·5 × 12·3 × 5·1)*
Main engines: 2 Atlas Polar 8-cyl diesels; 1 shaft; 4 000 bhp = 16 knots
Oil fuel, tons: 405
Range, miles: 17 000 (economical)
Complement: 42

Last of class of eight. In Gibraltar. Launch date: 10 September 1942.

CYCLONE 1975, Michael D. J. Lennon

3 "DIRECTOR" CLASS (PAS)

Name	No.	Builders	Commissioned
FAITHFUL	A 85	Yarrow & Sons Ltd	1958
FORCEFUL	A 86	Yarrow & Sons Ltd	1958
DEXTEROUS	A 93	Yarrow & Sons Ltd	1957

Displacement, tons: 710 full load
Dimensions, feet (metres): 157·2 × 30 (60 over paddle boxes) × 10 *(47·9 × 9·2 (18·4) × 3·)*
Main engines: Paxman diesels and BTH motors; diesel-electric; 2 shafts; 2 paddle wheels, 2 000 bhp = 13 knots
Complement: 21

Dexterous at Gibraltar. The only class of paddlers run by any navy in the world, this bein considered the best arrangement for working with aircraft carriers.

Reserves: *Grinder* and *Griper* are laid up at Portsmouth, *Favourite* at Devonport and *Director* Rosyth.

FAITHFUL 10/1978, Michael D. J. Lennon

19 "DOG" CLASS

AIREDALE A 102	**HUSKY** A 178	**SPANIEL** A 201
ALSATIAN A 106	**MASTIFF** A 180	**SHEEPDOG** A 250
CAIRN A 126	**SALUKI** A 182	**BASSET** (ex-*Beagle*) A 327
DALMATIAN A 129	**POINTER** A 188	**COLLIE** A 328
DEERHOUND A 155	**SETTER** A 189	**CORGI** A 330
ELKHOUND A 162	**SEALYHAM** A 197	**FOXHOUND** (ex-*Boxer*) A —
LABRADOR A 168		

Displacement, tons: 170 full load
Dimensions, feet (metres): 94 × 24·5 × 12 *(28·7 × 7·5 × 3·7)*
Main engines: Lister-Blackstone diesels; 1 320 bhp = 12 knots
Complement: 8

Harbour berthing tugs. *Airedale* and *Sealyham* at Gibraltar. Bollard pull 16 tons. Complete 1962-72. *Foxhound* renamed 22 October 1977 to free the name *Boxer* for new Type 22 frigate.

Appearance: Varies considerably, some with mast, some with curved upper-bridge work, som with flat monkey-island.

LABRADOR 11/1978, Michael D. J. Lennon

UK (RMAS) / Tugs — Fleet tenders 625

8 "GIRL" CLASS

| ALICE A 113 | AUDREY A 117 | BETTY A 322 | BARBARA A 324 |
| AGATHA A 116 | AGNES A 121 | BRIDGET A 323 | BRENDA A 335 |

Of 40 tons. 495 bhp = 10 knots. "A" names built by P. K. Harris, "B" names by Dunstons. Completed 1962-72. *Barbara* in Chatham.

5 "FELICITY" CLASS

| FELICITY A 112 | GEORGINA A 152 | HELEN A 198 |
| FIONA A 148 | GWENDOLINE A 196 | |

"Water tractors". Of 80 tons. 600 bhp = 10 knots. *Felicity* built by Dunstons and remainder by Hancocks. Completed 1973.

BARBARA   6/1977, Michael D. J. Lennon

HELEN   6/1976, Michael D. J. Lennon

8 "MODIFIED GIRL" CLASS

| DAISY A 145 | DOROTHY A 173 | CHARLOTTE A 210 | CLARE A 228 |
| DAPHNE A 156 | EDITH A 177 | CHRISTINE A 217 | DORIS A 252 |

Of 38 tons. 495 bhp = 10 knots. *Clare* in Hong Kong. *Edith* at Gibraltar. "C" names built by Pimblott and "D" and "E" names by Dunstons. Completed 1971-72. *Celia* sold to Sembawang Dockyard, Singapore in 1971.

FLEET TENDERS

DOLWEN (ex-*Hector Gull*)

Displacement, tons: 602 full load
Measurement, tons: 354·6 gross; 115·9 net
Dimensions, feet (metres): 135 × 29·5 × 14·5 *(41·1 × 9·0 × 4·4)*
Main engine: 1 National FSSM6 diesel; 1 shaft (cp propeller)

Built at Appledore by P. K. Harris in 1962 as stern trawler. Converted to buoy tender and now operates as range safety ship for RAE, Aberporth.

DOROTHY   9/1978, Michael D. J. Lennon

DOLWEN   1/1978, Michael D. J. Lennon

12 "TRITON" CLASS

KATHLEEN A 166	LILAH A 174	ISABEL A 183	MYRTLE A 199
KITTY A 170	MARY A 175	JOAN A 190	NANCY A 202
LESLEY A 172	IRENE A 181	JOYCE A 193	NORAH A 205

All completed by August 1974 by Dunstons. "Water-tractors" with small wheelhouse and adjoining funnel. 58 ft *(17·7 m)* and of 107·5 tons. 330 bhp = 8 knots.

7 "INSECT" CLASS

Name	No.	Builders	Commissioned
BEE	A 216	C. D. Holmes Ltd, Beverley, Humberside	1970
CICALA	A 263	C. D. Holmes Ltd, Beverley, Humberside	1971
COCKCHAFER	A 230	C. D. Holmes Ltd, Beverley, Humberside	1971
CRICKET	A 229	C. D. Holmes Ltd, Beverley, Humberside	1972
GNAT	A 239	C. D. Holmes Ltd, Beverley, Humberside	1972
LADYBIRD	A 253	C. D. Holmes Ltd, Beverley, Humberside	1973
SCARAB	—	C. D. Holmes Ltd, Beverley, Humberside	1973

Displacement, tons: 450 full load
Dimensions, feet (metres): 111·8 × 28 × 11 *(34·1 × 8·5 × 3·4)*
Main engine: 1 Lister-Blackstone diesel; 1 shaft; 660 bhp = 10·5 knots
Complement: 10

First three built as stores carriers, three as armament carriers and *Scarab*, as mooring vessel capable of lifting 10 tons over the bows. *Cricket* acts as a mooring vessel in the Clyde while *Gnat* and *Ladybird* operate as armament carriers with a red funnel band.

ISABEL   6/1977, Wright and Logan

GNAT   7/1978, A. Denholm

626 UK (RMAS) / Fleet tenders

1 DIVING TENDER

Name	No.	Builders	Commissioned
DATCHET	—	Vospers Ltd (Singapore)	1972

Main engines: 2 Gray diesels, 2 shafts, 450 bhp = 12 knots

DATCHET 7/1978, Leo van Ginderen

4 DIVING TENDERS

Name	No.	Builders	Commissioned
ILCHESTER	A 308	Gregson Ltd, Blyth	1974
INSTOW	A 309	Gregson Ltd, Blyth	1974
IRONBRIDGE (ex-*Invergordon*)	A 310	Gregson Ltd, Blyth	1974
IXWORTH	A 318	Gregson Ltd, Blyth	1974

Of similar characteristics to "Clovelly" class. Royal Navy manned except *Ilchester* (RMAS).

IXWORTH 2/1979, A. Denholm

8 + 2 "LOYAL" CLASS (RNXS)

VIGILANT (ex-*Loyal Factor*) A 382
ALERT (ex-*Loyal Governor*) A 510
LOYAL HELPER A 157
LOYAL CHANCELLOR A 1770
LOYAL WATCHER A 159
LOYAL VOLUNTEER A 160
LOYAL MEDIATOR A 161
LOYAL MODERATOR A 220
SUPPORTER (ex-*Loyal Supporter*) A 158
LOYAL PROCTOR A 1771

Details as for "Clovelly" class. *Alert* and *Vigilant* classified as "Patrol Craft" as they carry out patrols off Ulster. (Royal Navy manned.) *Loyal Helper* completed 10 February 1978 and last four later in 1978.

Bases: Portsmouth: *Loyal Mediator*.
Plymouth: *Loyal Moderator, Loyal Watcher* (Birkenhead).
Medway: *Loyal Helper*.
Scotland: *Loyal Volunteer, Loyal Proctor, Supporter* (Belfast).

LOYAL HELPER 8/1978, Michael D. J. Lennon

27 "CLOVELLY" CLASS

Name	No.	Builders	Commissioned
ETTRICK	A 274	J. Cook, Wivenhoe	1972
ELSING	A 277	J. Cook, Wivenhoe	1971
FELSTED	A 348	R. Dunston, Thorne	1972
ELKSTONE	A 353	J. Cook, Wivenhoe	1971
FROXFIELD	A 354	R. Dunston, Thorne	1972
EPWORTH	A 355	J. Cook, Wivenhoe	1972
CLOVELLY	A 389	I. Pimblott & Sons, Northwich	1972
DUNSTER	A 393	R. Dunston, Thorne	1972
HOLMWOOD	A 1772	R. Dunston, Thorne	1973
HORNING	A 1773	R. Dunston, Thorne	1973
CRICCIETH	A 391	I. Pimblott & Sons, Northwich	1972
CRICKLADE	A 381	C. D. Holmes, Beverley, Humberside	1971
CROMARTY	A 488	J. Lewis, Aberdeen	1972
DENMEAD	A 363	C. D. Holmes, Beverley, Humberside	1972
DORNOCH	A 490	J. Lewis, Aberdeen	1972
FINTRY	A 394	J. Lewis, Aberdeen	1972
FOTHERBY	A 341	R. Dunston, Thorne	1972
FULBECK	A 365	C. D. Holmes, Beverley	1972
GLENCOE	A 392	I. Pimblott & Sons, Northwich	1972
GRASMERE	A 402	J. Lewis, Aberdeen	1972
HAMBLEDON	A 1769	R. Dunston, Thorne	1973
HARLECH	A 1768	R. Dunston, Thorne	1973
HEADCORN	A 1776	R. Dunston, Thorne	1973
HEVER	A 1767	R. Dunston, Thorne	1973
LAMLASH	A 208	R. Dunston, Thorne	1974
LECHLADE	A 211	R. Dunston, Thorne	1974
LLANDOVERY	A 207	R. Dunston, Thorne	1974

Displacement, tons: 143 full load
Dimensions, feet (metres): 80 × 21 × 6·6 *(24·1 × 6·4 × 3)*
Main engine: 1 Lister-Blackstone diesel; 1 shaft; 320 bhp = 10·5 knots
Complement: 6

All fleet tenders of an improved "Aberdovey" class. *Elsing* and *Ettrick* at Gibraltar (Royal Navy manned), used for patrol duties. Can be used for varying tasks—cargo, passenger, training, diving (*Dornoch* and *Fotherby*).

CRICKLADE 11/1978, Michael D. J. Lennon

14 "ABERDOVEY" CLASS

Name	No.	Builders	Commissioned
ABERDOVEY	Y 10	I. Pimblott & Sons, Northwich	1963
ABINGER	Y 11	I. Pimblott & Sons, Northwich	1964
ALNESS	Y 12	I. Pimblott & Sons, Northwich	1965
ALNMOUTH	Y 13	I. Pimblott & Sons, Northwich	1966
APPLEBY	Y 14	I. Pimblott & Sons, Northwich	1967
ASHCOTT	Y 16	I. Pimblott & Sons, Northwich	1968
BEAULIEU	A 99	J. S. Doig, Grimsby	1966
BEDDGELERT	A 100	J. S. Doig, Grimsby	1967
BEMBRIDGE	A 101	J. S. Doig, Grimsby	1968
BIBURY	A 103	J. S. Doig, Grimsby	1969
BLAKENEY	A 104	J. S. Doig, Grimsby	1970
BRODICK	A 105	J. S. Doig, Grimsby	1971
CARTMEL	A 350	I. Pimblott & Sons, Northwich	1971
CAWSAND	A 351	I. Pimblott & Sons, Northwich	1971

Displacement, tons: 117·5 full load
Dimensions, feet (metres): 79·8 × 18 × 5·5 *(24 × 5·4 × 2·4)*
Main engine: 1 Lister-Blackstone diesel; 1 shaft; 225 bhp = 10·5 knots
Complement: 6

Multi-purpose for stores (25 tons), passengers (200 standing) plus a couple of torpedoes. *Alness* and *Ashcott* at Gibraltar (Royal Navy manned). *Alnmouth* operates from Devonport for Sea Cadet Corps training. *Bembridge* at Portsmouth for Sea Cadet Corps. *Aberdovey* with RMs Poole.

BRODICK 7/1978, A. Denholm

UK (RMAS) / Fleet tenders — Scottish fishery protection vessels 627

"HAM" CLASS (RNXS)

SHIPHAM M 2726   PORTISHAM M 2781

Details in Mine Warfare section. Being replaced by new construction "Loyal" class. *Shipham* based in Medway and *Portisham* at Portsmouth.

SHIPHAM   8/1978, J. L. M. van der Burg

MFV TYPES

A number of MFV types are used in dockyard ports, not necessarily under naval control.

FV 1021   9/1978, A. Denholm

TRANSPORT

SANDRINGHAM M 2791

Of the "Ham" class of Inshore Minesweepers. For details see Mine Warfare section. Used as personnel transport in the Clyde. There is also FDC 7001 (commonly known as *James Bond*) which also acts as a transport in the Clyde/Faslane area.

SANDRINGHAM   5/1978, A. Denholm

TANK CLEANING VESSELS

"ISLES" CLASS

Name	No.	Builders	Commissioned
BALDY	A 332	John Lewis and Sons	1943
INDY	A 336	Cook Welton and Gemmell	1943
COMER	A 338	John Lewis and Sons	1943
SWITHA	A 346	A. and J. Inglis Ltd	1942

Displacement, tons: 770 full load
Dimensions, feet (metres): 164 × 27.5 × 14 *(49 × 8.4 × 4.2)*
Main engines: Triple expansion; 1 shaft; 850 ihp = 12 knots
Boiler: 1 cylindrical
Coal, tons: 183

Last survivors, in UK service, of a class of 145 built for minesweeping and escort duties during the war. Most of them were employed on wreck dispersal after the war until conversion to their present role in 1951-57.

INDY   11/1978, Michael D. J. Lennon

DEGAUSSING VESSELS

Note: Two degaussing vessels ordered from Cleland S.B. Co Ltd, Wallsend mid-1978.

3 "HAM" CLASS

FORDHAM M 2717   WARMINGHAM M 2737   THATCHAM M 2790

Of the "Ham" class of Inshore Minesweepers. For details see Mine Warfare section. *Fordham* at Devonport, *Warmingham* at Portsmouth, *Thatcham* in the Clyde.

THATCHAM   11/1978, Michael D. J. Lennon

SCOTTISH FISHERY PROTECTION VESSELS

2 "JURA" CLASS

Name	No.	Builders	Commissioned
JURA	—	Hall, Russell & Co, Aberdeen	1973
WESTRA	—	Hall, Russell & Co, Aberdeen	1975

Displacement, tons: 778 light; 1 285 full load
Measurement, tons: 942 gross
Dimensions, feet (metres): 195.3 × 35 × 14.4 *(59.6 × 10.7 × 4.4)*
Main engines: 2 British Polar SP112VS-F diesels; 4 200 bhp; 1 shaft = 17 knots
Complement: 28

Jura was leased by the Ministry of Defence for oil-rig patrol and armed with one 40 mm. Returned from Royal Navy service January 1977 and disarmed. *Westra* was launched on 6 August 1974. Four other ships are operated by Department of Agriculture and Fisheries for Scotland—*Brenda* of 181 ft, *Norma*, *Vigilant* and *Switha*. The last of these is due for replacement by a new *Switha*, shortly to be built and fitted with a helicopter platform for a BO 105.

JURA   5/1978, A. Denholm

BRENDA   9/1978, A. Denholm

628 UK / Royal Corps of Transport

ROYAL CORPS OF TRANSPORT

As well as "Ardennes", "Agheila" and "Avon" classes listed in the Amphibious Warfare section the following craft are operated by the RCT.

1 "HAM" CLASS

R. G. MASTERS V.C. (ex-RAF 5012, ex-HMS *Halsham*)

Details in Mine Warfare section. Communications vessel. Built by Buckie S.Y. 1953. Speed—13 knots.

R. G. MASTERS V.C. 1976, Michael D. J. Lennon

1 "90 ft" MFV

YARMOUTH NAVIGATOR

Navigation training vessel. Built in 1944 by Richards Ironworks. Speed—8 knots.

YARMOUTH NAVIGATOR 1976, Michael D. J. Lennon

1 RANGE SAFETY CRAFT

ALFRED HERRING V.C.

Dimensions, feet (metres): 77·7 × 18 × 4·9 *(23·7 × 5·5 × 1·5)*
Main engines: 2 Paxman 8YJ CM 4 diesels; 2 000 bhp = 26 knots

Built by James and Stone, Brightlingsea. Commissioned 1978. Serves at the Royal Artillery Missile Range in the Outer Hebrides. Similar design to RAF "Spitfire" class RTTL Mk 3.

ALFRED HERRING V.C. 10/1978, Michael D. J. Lennon

1 + (12) RANGE SAFETY CRAFT

SAMUEL MORLEY V.C. (+ 12)

Dimensions, feet (metres): 49·2 × 14·9 × 6·5 *(15 × 4·6 × 2)*
Main engines: 2 Rolls Royce C8M410 diesels; 820 bhp = 22 knots
Complement: 3

13 building by Fairey Marine as replacements for present craft.

SAMUEL MORLEY V.C. 1978, Michael D. J. Lennon

1 GENERAL SERVICE LAUNCH

TREVOSE

Of 72 ft. Navigation training vessel. Built by Vospers Ltd in 1964.

7 GENERAL SERVICE LAUNCHES

JACKSON	RADDLE
MARTIN	SMIKE
NEWMAN NOGGS	URIAH HEEP
OLIVER TWIST	

Of 50 ft. *Oliver Twist* due for deletion after damage.

SMIKE 12/1978, Michael D. J. Lennon

7 GENERAL DUTIES LAUNCHES

CARP WB 01	ROACH WB 05
CHUB WB 02	PERCH WB 06
BREAM WB 03	PIKE WB 07
BARBEL WB 04	

47 ft work-boats.

BARBEL 7/1978, Leo van Ginderen

6 COMMAND and CONTROL CRAFT

PETREL L 01	SKUA L 04
TERN L 02	SHEARWATER L 05
FULMAR L 03	SHELDUCK L 06

41 ft craft.

PETREL 2/1977, Michael D. J. Lennon

Ex-SAR CRAFT

HYPERION (ex-1385)
MINORU (ex-1667)
JOSEPH HUGHES G.C. (ex-1648)

Hyperion of 1300 Series RAF Pinnaces; other pair of 1600 Series Range Safety Launches. Details under RAF Marine Craft below. *Hyperion* in Cyprus.

JOSEPH HUGHES G.C. 2/1978, Michael D. J. Lennon

ROYAL AIR FORCE MARINE CRAFT

Officer-in-Charge: Group Captain J. F. Burgess

New Construction: All wooden craft to be replaced by "Seal" class, "Spitfire" class and 27 ft work-boats by end 1981.

"SEAL" CLASS (LRRSC)

Name	No.	Builders	Commissioned
SEAL	5000	Brooke Marine, Lowestoft	Aug 1967
SEAGULL	5001	Fairmile Construction, Berwick-on-Tweed	1970
SEA OTTER	5002	Fairmile Construction, Berwick-on-Tweed	1970

Displacement, tons: 159 full load
Dimensions, feet (metres): 120·3 × 23·5 × 6·5 *(36·6 × 7·2 × 2)*
Main engines: 2 Paxman diesels; 2 200 hp = 21 knots
Complement: 18

All welded steel hulls. Aluminium alloy superstructure.

SEA OTTER 4/1978, Michael D. J. Lennon

"SPITFIRE" CLASS (RTTL Mk 3)

Name	No.	Builders	Commissioned
SPITFIRE	4000	James and Stone, Brightlingsea	1972
SUNDERLAND	4001	James and Stone, Brightlingsea	1976
STIRLING	4002	James and Stone, Brightlingsea	1976
HALIFAX	4003	James and Stone, Brightlingsea	1977

Displacement, tons: 70
Dimensions, feet (metres): 77·7 × 18 × 4·9 *(23·7 × 5·5 × 1·5)*
Main engines: 2 Paxman diesels; 2 100 hp = 22 knots
Complement: 9

All welded steel hulls; aluminium alloy superstructure. *Spitfire* has twin funnels, remainder one.

STIRLING 1/1978, Michael D. J. Lennon

4 RESCUE TARGET TOWING LAUNCHES Mk 2 (RTTL Mk 2)

2752, 2757, 2768, 2771

Displacement, tons: 34·6
Dimensions, feet (metres): 68 × 19 × 6 *(20·7 × 5·8 × 1·8)*
Main engines: 2 Rolls-Royce Sea Griffon; 1 100 bhp = 30 knots
Complement: 9

Hard chine, wooden hulls. Built by Vospers, Saunders Roe and Groves and Gutteridge. To be replaced by RTTL Mk 3.

10 PINNACES 1300 SERIES

Displacement, tons: 28·3
Dimensions, feet (metres): 63 × 15·5 × 5 *(19·2 × 4·9 × 1·5)*
Main engines: 2 Rolls-Royce C6 diesels; 190 bhp = 13 knots
Complement: 5

Hard chine, wooden hulls. Built by Groves and Gutteridge, Robertsons (Dunoon) and Dorset Yacht Co (Poole). 5 ton cargo capacity.

1300 Series Pinnace 1975, RAF

7 RANGE SAFETY LAUNCHES 1600 SERIES

Displacement, tons: 12 full load
Dimensions, feet (metres): 43 × 13 × 4 *(13·1 × 4 × 1·2)*
Main engines: 2 Rolls-Royce C6 diesels; 190 bhp = 16 knots
Complement: 4

Hard chine, wooden double diagonal hulls.

RANGE SAFETY LAUNCH 1976, RAF

HARBOUR CRAFT

24 ft tenders and Gemini craft in current use. To be replaced by 27 ft Cheverton work-boats by 1980-81.

HM CUSTOMS

The Customs and Excise (Waterguard) of HM Treasury operate a considerable number of craft around the UK, including Fairey Marine Trackers.

POLICE SERVICE

Police craft of many sizes operate in all the major ports, although rarely met with beyond the port limits.

TRINITY HOUSE

A number of vessels of varying types—buoy-layers, pilot craft, lighthouse tenders—may be met throughout the waters of the UK.

UNITED STATES OF AMERICA

Administration

Secretary of the Navy:
  Hon. W. Graham Claytor Jr

There are one Under Secretary and four Assistant Secretaries.

Principal Appointments by Flag Officers' Seniority

Chief of Naval Operations:
  Admiral Thomas B. Hayward
Commander-in-Chief, Pacific:
  *Admiral Maurice F. Weisner
Commander-in-Chief, Allied Forces, Southern Europe:
  Admiral Harold E. Shear
Vice-Chief of Naval Operations:
  Admiral Robert L. J. Long
Commander-in-Chief, US Pacific Fleet:
  Admiral Donald C. Davis
Chief of Naval Material:
  Admiral Alfred J. Whittle, Jr
Commander-in-Chief, Atlantic, Commander-in-Chief, US Atlantic Fleet and Supreme Allied Commander, Atlantic (NATO):
  Admiral Harry D. Train II
Commander-in-Chief, US Naval Forces, Europe:
  *Vice-Admiral Joseph P. Moorer
Commander Sixth Fleet and Commander Strike Force South (NATO):
  Vice-Admiral James D. Watkins
Commander Naval Air Force, US Pacific Fleet:
  Vice-Admiral Robert P. Coogan
Commander Naval Air Systems Command:
  Vice-Admiral Forrest S. Petersen
Commander Naval Sea Systems Command:
  Vice-Admiral Clarence R. Bryan
Commander Submarine Force, US Atlantic Fleet:
  Vice-Admiral Kenneth M. Carr
Commander Naval Surface Force, US Atlantic Fleet:
  Vice-Admiral William L. Read
Commander, Second Fleet:
  Vice-Admiral Wesley L. McDonald
Commander Third Fleet:
  Vice-Admiral Kinnaird R. McKee
Commander Naval Air Force, US Atlantic Fleet:
  Vice-Admiral George E. R. Kinnear II
Commander Seventh Fleet:
  Vice-Admiral Sylvester R. Foley, Jr
Commander Naval Surface Force, US Pacific Fleet:
  Vice-Admiral Lee Baggett Jr
Commander, Naval Forces, Japan:
  Rear-Admiral Lando W. Zech, Jr
Commander Military Sealift Command:
  Rear-Admiral John D. Johnson, Jr
Commander Naval Electronics Systems Command:
  Rear-Admiral Earl B. Fowler, Jr
Commander Mine Warfare Command:
  Rear-Admiral Albert J. Monger
Commander US Naval Forces, Caribbean:
  Rear-Admiral Arthur K. Knoizen
Commander Middle East Force:
  Rear-Admiral Samuel H. Packer II
Commander South Atlantic Force:
  Rear-Admiral John J. Ekelund
Commander Submarine Force, US Pacific Fleet:
  Rear-Admiral Nils R. Thunman

Note: *Unified Command with the Commander-in-Chief directing all US Navy, Army, and Air Force activities in the area.

Marine Corps

Commandant:
  General Louis H. Wilson, Jr
Assistant Commandant:
  General Robert H. Barrow

Diplomatic Representation

Naval Attaché and Naval Attaché for Air in London:
  Captain T. M. Vojtek
Naval Attaché and Naval Attaché for Air in Moscow:
  Captain Leonard A. Braken
Naval Attaché and Naval Attaché for Air in Paris:
  Captain Neil L. Harvey

Personnel

	30 Sep 1977 (Actual)	30 Sep 1978 (Actual)	30 Sep 1979 (Planned)
Navy			
Officers	63 312	62 973	63 000
Enlisted	461 571	464 502	456 125
Marine Corps			
Officers	18 584		
Enlisted	173 057	191 500	191 250

Mercantile Marine

Lloyd's Register of Shipping:
  4 746 vessels of 16 187 636 tons gross

US Commerce Department (vessels over 1 000 tons) (1 Oct 1978):
  Active: 599 vessels of 11 827 160 tons gross
  Reserve: 156 vessels of 1 227 912 tons gross

Strength of the Fleet

Number of ships listed in the table are actual as of 1 February 1979, based on official tabulation and include ships and craft attached to the Naval Reserve Force (NRF).

Type		Active	Building	Reserve	Conversion
Strategic Missile Submarines					
SSBN	Ballistic Missile Submarines (nuclear-powered)	41	7	—	—
Attack Submarines					
SSN	Submarines (nuclear-powered)	72	24	2	—
SS	Submarines (conventionally-powered)	7	—	—	—
SSG	Guided Missile Submarine (conventionally-powered)	—	—	1	—
Auxiliary Submarines					
AGSS	Auxiliary Submarines	1	—	1	—
Aircraft Carriers					
CVN	Multi-purpose Aircraft Carriers (nuclear-powered)	3	1	—	—
CV	Multi-purpose Aircraft Carriers	10	—	1	—
CVA	Attack Aircraft Carrier	—	—	1	—
CVS	ASW Aircraft Carriers	—	—	4	—
Battleships					
BB	Battleships	—	—	4	—
Cruisers					
CGN	Guided Missile Cruisers (nuclear-powered)	8	1	—	—
CG	Guided Missile Cruisers	20	—	—	1
CA	Gun Cruisers	—	—	2	—
Destroyers					
DDG	Guided Missile Destroyers	37	1	—	—
DD	Destroyers	59	13	—	—
Frigates					
FFG	Guided Missile Frigates	7	25	—	—
FF	Frigates	58	—	—	—
Light Forces					
PHM	Guided Missile Patrol Combatants (hydrofoil)	1	5	—	—
PG	Patrol Combatants	2	—	2	—
PCH	Patrol Craft (hydrofoil)	1	—	—	—
PTF	Fast Patrol Craft	4	—	—	—
Amphibious Warfare Forces					
LCC	Amphibious Command Ships	2	—	—	—
LHA	Amphibious Assault Ships (GP)	3	—	2	—
LKA	Amphibious Cargo Ships	6	—	—	—
LPA	Amphibious Transports	2	—	—	—
LPD	Amphibious Transport Docks	14	—	—	—
LPH	Amphibious Assault Ships (helicopter)	7	—	—	—
LSD	Dock Landing Ships	13	—	—	—
LST	Tank Landing Ships	20	—	—	—
Mine Warfare Forces					
MSO	Minesweepers—Ocean	25	—	—	—
Auxiliary Ships					
AD	Destroyer Tenders	9	3	1	—
AE	Ammunition Ships	13	—	—	—
AFS	Combat Stores Ships	7	—	—	—
AG	Miscellaneous	1	—	1	—
AGDS	Auxiliary Deep Submergence Support Ship	1	—	—	—
AGF	Miscellaneous Command Ship	1	—	—	—
AH	Hospital Ship	—	—	1	—
AO	Oilers	6	—	—	—
AOE	Fast Combat Support Ships	4	—	—	—
AOR	Replenishment Oilers	7	—	—	—
AR	Repair Ships	4	—	—	—
ARL	Repair Ship, small	—	—	1	—
ARS	Salvage Ships	9	—	—	—
AS	Submarine Tenders	12	2	2	—
ASR	Submarine Rescue Ships	6	—	—	—
ATF	Fleet Ocean Tugs	6	—	—	—
ATS	Salvage and Rescue Ships	3	—	—	—
AVM	Guided Missile Ship	1	—	—	—
AVT	Auxiliary Aircraft Landing Training Ship	1	—	—	—
Service Craft					
All Types		1 102*	3	1 102*	
Military Sealift Command (nucleus)		69	12	—	2

Note: *Total Number of service craft in US Navy. Breakdown for each category not available

USA/ Introduction

Special Notes

To provide similar information to that included in other major Navies' Deployment Tables the fleet assignment (abbreviated "F/S") status of each ship in the US Navy has been included. The assignment appears in a column immediately to the right of the commissioning date. In the case of the Floating Drydock section this system is not used. The following abbreviations are used to indicate fleet assignments:

AA	Active, Atlantic Fleet
AR	In Reserve, Out of Commission, Atlantic Fleet
ASA	Active, In Service, Atlantic Fleet
ASR	In Reserve, Out of Service, Atlantic Fleet
Bldg	Building
CONV	Ship undergoing conversion
LOAN	Ship or craft loaned to another government, or non-government agency, but US Navy retains title and the ship or craft is on the NVR
MAR	In Reserve, Out of Commission, Atlantic Fleet and laid up in the temporary custody of the Maritime Administration
MPR	Same as "MAR", but applies to the Pacific Fleet
NRF	Assigned to the Naval Reserve Force (ships so assigned are listed in a special table, at the end of each major category, that indicates NRF homeport, date assigned to NRF and which ship, if any, it replaced)
Ord	The contract for the construction of the ship has been let, but actual construction has not yet begun
PA	Active, Pacific Fleet
PR	In Reserve, Out of Commission, Pacific Fleet
Proj	The ship is scheduled for construction at some time in the immediate future
PSA	Active, In Service, Pacific Fleet
PSR	In Reserve, Out of Service, Pacific Fleet
TAA	Active, Military Sealift Command, Atlantic Fleet
TAR	In Ready Reserve, Military Sealift Command, Atlantic Fleet
TPA	Active, Military Sealift Command, Pacific Fleet
TPR	In Ready Reserve, Military Sealift Command, Pacific Fleet
TWWR	Active, Military Sealift Command, World-wide Routes

Ship Status Definitions

In Commission: As a rule any ship, except a Service Craft, that is active, is in commission. The ship has a Commanding Officer and flies a commissioning pennant. "Commissioning date" as used in this section means the date of being "In Commission" rather than "completion" or "acceptance into service" as used in some other navies.

In Service: All Service Craft (Drydocks and with classifications that start with "Y"), with the exception of *Constitution*, that are active, are "in service". The ship has an Officer-in-Charge and does not fly a commissioning pennant.

Ships "in reserve, out of commission" or "in reserve, out of service" are put in a state of preservation for future service. Depending on the size of the ship or craft, a ship in "mothballs" usually takes from 30 days to nearly a year to restore to full operational service.

The above statuses do not apply to the Military Sealift Command.

Shipbuilding/Conversion Programmes

Planned Five Year Shipbuilding/Conversion Programme (Fiscal Year 1980/1984)

Shipbuilding*
- 6 "Ohio" Class SSBNs
- 5 "Los Angeles" Class SSNs
- 1 Aircraft Carrier (Medium) (CVV)
- 10 Guided Missile Destroyers ("DDG 47" Class)
- 1 Destroyer (DDX)
- 25 "Oliver Hazard Perry" Class Guided Missile Frigates (FFG)
- 5 Mine Countermeasures Vehicles (MCM)
- 4 "Cimarron" Class Oilers (AO)
- 10 Ocean Surveillance Ships (AGOS)

Conversions*
- 2 Aircraft Carrier Service Life Extension Programme (SLEP)
- 10 Anti-Air Warfare Modernisation "Charles F. Adams" Class (DDG)
- 1 Cargo Ship (AK)

Revised Five Year Shipbuilding/Conversion Programme (Fiscal Year 1979/1983)

Shipbuilding**
- 5 "Ohio" Class SSBNs
- 5 "Los Angeles" Class SSNs
- 1 Aircraft Carrier (Medium) (CVV)
- 1 Improved "Virginia" Class Guided Missile Cruiser (nuclear-powered) (CGN)
- 26 "Oliver Hazard Perry" Class Guided Missile Frigates (FFG)
- 2 Dock Landing Ships (LSD)
- 5 Mine Countermeasures Vehicles (MCM)
- 1 "Yellowstone" Class Destroyer Tender (AD)
- 1 "Cimarron" Class Oiler (AO)
- 2 Utility Ocean Tugs (ATU)
- 11 Ocean Surveillance Ships (AGOS)
- 1 Cable Repair Ship (ARC)

Conversion**
- 2 Aircraft Carrier Service Life Extension Programmes (SLEP)
- 0 Anti-Air Warfare Modernisation "Charles F. Adams" Class (DDG)
- 1 Cargo Ship (AK)

Approved Fiscal Year 1979 Programme

Shipbuilding

1	"Los Angeles" Class SSN (SSN 720)	325·6
8	"Oliver Hazard Perry" Class FFGs (FFG 36/43)	1,493·1
1	"Yellowstone" Class AD (AD 44)	318·0
2	Ocean Surveillance Ships (AGOS 1/2)	69·0

Shipbuilding Long Term Lead Items

1	"Ohio" Class SSBN (SSBN 733)	198·0
1	"Los Angeles" Class SSN (SSN 721)	26·3

Conversion Long Term Lead Items

1	Aircraft Carrier Service Life Extension Programme (SLEP)	32·2
1	Anti-Air Warfare Modernisation "Charles F. Adams" Class (DDG)	128·0

Proposed Fiscal Year 1979 Supplemental Programme

Shipbuilding*

		Appropriations***
2	Improved "Spruance" Class Guided Missile Destroyers (DDG) (ex-*Iranian*)	1,086

Proposed Fiscal Year 1980 Programme

Shipbuilding*

1	"Ohio" Class SSBN (SSBN 733)	1,414·6
1	"Los Angeles" Class SSN (SSN 721)	517·9
1	Aircraft Carrier, Medium (CVV)	1,617·1
1	Guided Missile Destroyer ("DDG 47" Class)	820·2
6	"Oliver Hazard Perry" Class Guided Missile Frigates (FFG) (FFG-44/49)	1,258·8
5	Ocean Surveillance Ships (AGOS 3/7)	154·0

Conversion*

1	Anti-Air Warfare Modernisation "Charles F. Adams" Class (DDG)	223·8

Notes:

* As of 25 January 1979. ** As of March 1978. *** Amount is in millions of US$.

Source: Data based on Department of Defense Annual Report FY 1980 and material from the Office of Chief of Naval Operations.

Naval Aviation

US Naval Aviation currently consists of approx 7 000 aircraft flown by the Navy and Marine Corps. The principal naval aviation organisations are 13 carrier air wings, 24 maritime reconnaissance/patrol squadrons, and three Marine Aircraft Wings. In addition, the Naval Reserve and Marine Corps Reserve operate 7 fighter squadrons, 11 attack squadrons, and 12 patrol squadrons, plus various reconnaissance, electrical warfare, tanker, helicopter and transport units.

Fighter: 26 Navy squadrons with F-4 Phantom and F-14 Tomcat aircraft; 12 Marine squadrons with F-4 Phantoms.
Attack: 39 Navy squadrons with A-6 Intruder and A-7 Corsair aircraft; 13 Marine squadrons with A-4 Skyhawk, A-6 Intruder, AV-8 Harrier aircraft.
Reconnaissance: 10 Navy RA-5C Vigilante and RF-8G Crusader aircraft; 3 Marine squadrons with RF-4B Phantoms.
Airborne Early Warning: 12 Navy squadrons with E-2 Hawkeye aircraft.
Electronic Warfare: 8 Navy squadrons with EA-6B Prowler aircraft (Marines operate EA-6A Intruder aircraft in composite reconnaissance squadrons).
Anti-Submarine: 9 Navy squadrons with S-3 Viking aircraft replacing S-2 Trackers.
Maritime Patrol: 24 Navy squadrons with P-3 Orion aircraft.
Helicopter Anti-Submarine: 16 Navy squadrons with SH-3 Sea King and SH-2 LAMPS helicopters.
Helicopter Mine Countermeasures: 1 Navy squadron with RH-53 Sea Stallion.
Helicopter Support: 4 Navy squadrons with UH-46 Sea Knight helicopters.
Electronic Reconnaissance: 2 Navy squadrons with EP-3E Orion and EC-121 Warning Star aircraft.
Communications Relay: 2 Navy squadrons with EC-130 Hercules aircraft.
Observation: 3 Marine squadrons with OV-10 Bronco aircraft.
Helicopter Gunship: 3 Marine squadrons with AH-1 Sea Cobra helicopters.
Helicopter Transport: 21 Marine squadrons with UH-1 Iroquois (Huey), CH-46 Sea Knight, and CH-53 Sea Stallion helicopters.

BASES

Naval Air Stations and Air Facilities (44)

NAS Alameda, Calif; NAF China Lake, Calif; NAF El Centro, Calif; NAS Los Alamitos, Calif; NAS Mirimar, Calif; NAS Moffett Field (San Jose), Calif; NAS Point Mugu, Calif; NAS North Island (San Diego), Calif; NAF Andrews, Washington DC; NAS Cecil Field (Pensacola), Fla; NAS Jacksonville, Fla; NAS Key West, Fla; NAS Whiting Field (Milton), Fla; NAS Saufley Field (Pensacola), Fla; NAS Pansacola, Fla; NAS Atlanta (Marietta), Ga; NAS Glenview, Ill; NAS Barbers Point (Oahu), Hawaii; NAS New Orleans, La; NAS Brunswick, Me; NAS Paxtuxent River, Md; NAS South Weymouth, Mass; NAF Detroit, Mich; NAS Meridan, Miss; NAS Fallon, Nev; NAS Lakehurst, NJ; NAF Warminster, Penna; NAS Willow Grove, Penna; NAS Memphis (Millington), Tenn; NAS Chase Field (Beeville), Texas; NAS Corpus Christi, Texas; NAS Dallas, Texas; NAS Kingsville, Texas; NAS Norfolk, Va; NAS Whidbey Island (Oak Harbor), Wash; NAF Lajes, Azores; NAS Bermuda; NAS Guantanamo Bay, Cuba; NAF Naples, Italy; NAF Atsugi, Japan; NAS Agana, Guam; NAF Okinawa; NAS Subic Bay, Philippines; NAF Mildenhall (Suffolk), England.

Naval Stations and Naval Bases (25)

Yokosuka, Japan; Subic Bay, Philippines; Apra Harbour, Guam; Midway Is; Adak, (Alaska); Pearl Harbor, (Hawaii); Treasure Is (San Francisco) Calif; San Diego, Calif; Coronado (San Diego) Calif (Amphibs); Long Beach (Calif); Mayport, Fla; Roosevelt Roads, Puerto Rico; Guantanamo Bay, Cuba; Charleston, SC; Norfolk, Va; Little Creek (Norfolk) Va (Amphibs); Philadelphia, Pa; Brooklyn, NY; New London (Conn) (Submarines); Newport, RI; Boston, Mass; Argentia, Newfoundland; Keflavik, Iceland; Rota, Spain; Naples, Italy.

Strategic Missile Submarine Bases (6)

Holy Loch, Scotland; Apra Harbour, Guam; Rota, Spain (being phased out by 1980); Charleston, SC; Bangor, Wash (under construction as Trident base); Kings Bay, Ga (projected).

Navy Yard (1)

Washington, DC (administration and historical activities only).

Naval Shipyards (Refitting and repair) (8)

Pearl Harbor, Hawaii; Puget Sound, Bremerton, Wash; Long Beach, Calif; Mare Is, Vallejo, Calif; Charleston, SC; Norfolk, Va; Philadelphia, Pa; Portsmouth, NH (located in Kittery, Me).

Naval Ship Repair Facilities (2)

Subic Bay, Philippines; Yokosuka, Japan.

Marine Air Stations and Air Facilities (7)

El Toro (Santa Ana), Calif; Kaneohe Bay (Oahu), Hawaii; Cherry Point, NC; New River (Jacksonville), Fla; Quantico, Va; Iwakuni, Japan; Futema, Okinawa.

Marine Corps Bases (5)

Camp Pendleton, Calif; Twentynine Palms, Calif; Camp H.M. Smith (Oahu), Hawaii; Camp Lejeune, NC; Camp Smedley D. Butler (Kawasaki), Okinawa.

CLASSIFICATION OF NAVAL SHIPS AND SERVICE CRAFT

The following is the official US Navy list of classifications of naval ships and service craft as promulgated by the Secretary of the Navy on 11 January 1978 and periodically amended. The following data should be noted: the use of an "E" before a classification indicates that the ship or craft is experimental in nature; the use of a "T" indicates that the ship or craft is assigned to the Military Sealift Command and is civilian manned. In either case the letters "E" and "T" are not an official part of the ship classification.

From time to time classifications, such as AGOS, appear which are not an official classification. These classifications indicate new ship types which were developed after the last official list was published. They are usually added to the list by change or revision. Some classifications listed below are no longer employed in the US Navy, but are retained because the classification is still in official use in correspondence, notices, etc and/or are still on the Naval Vessel Register (NVR) in some other capacity than as a US Naval Ship. In some cases, there are no more ships of the type in any capacity. Examples are MSC, MCS, ATA, LSIL. The letter "X" is often added to existing classifications, such as FFGX and ARX, to indicate a new class whose characteristics have not been defined.

COMBATANT SHIPS CATEGORY

Warship Classification

Aircraft Carrier Type
CTOL Conventional Take Off and Landing Aircraft Carriers
- Multi-purpose Aircraft Carrier — CV
- Multi-purpose Aircraft Carrier (nuclear propulsion) — CVN
- ASW Aircraft Carrier — CVS
- (Attack Aircraft Carrier) — (CVA)*

Surface Combatant Type
Battleships
- Battleship — BB

Cruisers
- Gun Cruiser — CA
- Guided Missile Cruiser — CG
- Guided Missile Cruiser (nuclear propulsion) — CGN

Destroyers
- Destroyer — DD
- Guided Missile Destroyer — DDG

Frigates
- Frigate — FF
- Guided Missile Frigate — FFG

Submarine Type
Attack Submarines
- Submarine (conventionally-powered) — SS
- Guided Missile Submarine (conventionally-powered) — SSG
- Submarine (nuclear-powered) — SSN

Ballistic Missile Submarines
- Ballistic Missile Submarine (nuclear-powered) — SSBN

Auxiliary Submarine
- Auxiliary Submarine — AGSS

Other Combatant Classification

Patrol Combatant Type
Patrol Ships
- Patrol Combatant — PG
- Guided Missile Patrol Combatant (hydrofoil) — PHM

Amphibious Warfare Type Ships
Amphibious Helicopter/Landing Craft Carriers
- Amphibious Assault Ship (general purpose) — LHA
- Amphibious Assault Ship (helicopter) — LPH
- Amphibious Transport Dock — LPD

Landing Craft Carriers
- Amphibious Cargo Ship — LKA
- Amphibious Transport — LPA
- Dock Landing Ship — LSD
- Tank Landing Ship — LST

Miscellaneous
- Amphibious Command Ship — LCC

Mine Warfare Type Ship
Minesweepers
- Minesweeper, Ocean (non-magnetic) — MSO

AUXILIARY SHIPS CATEGORY

Auxiliary Classification

Mobile Logistic Type Ships
Underway Replenishment
- Ammunition Ship — AE
- Store Ship — AF
- Combat Store Ship — AFS
- Oiler — AO
- Fast Combat Support Ship — AOE
- Replenishment Oiler — AOR

Material Support
- Destroyer Tender — AD
- Repair Ship — AR
- Submarine Tender — AS

Support Type Ships
Fleet Support
- Salvage Ship — ARS
- Submarine Rescue Ship — ASR
- Auxiliary Ocean Tug — ATA
- Fleet Ocean Tug — ATF
- Salvage and Rescue Ship — ATS
- (Utility Ocean Tug) — (ATU)*

Other Auxiliaries
- Miscellaneous — AG
- Deep Submergence Support Ship — AGDS
- Hydrofoil Research Ship — AGEH
- Miscellaneous Command Ship — AGF
- Frigate Research Ship — AGFF
- Missile Range Instrumentation Ship — AGM
- Oceanographic Research Ship — AGOR
- Surveying Ship — AGS
- Hospital Ship — AH
- Cargo Ship — AK
- Vehicle Cargo Ship — AKR
- Gasoline Tanker — AOG
- Transport Oiler (effective 30 September 1778) — AOT
- Transport — AP
- Self-propelled Barracks Ship — APB
- Cable Repairing Ship — ARC
- Repair Ship, Small — ARL
- Guided Missile Ship — AVM
- Auxiliary Aircraft Landing Training Ship (effective 1 July 1978) — AVT
- Training Aircraft Carrier (deleted 1 July 1978) — CVT

COMBATANT CRAFT CATEGORY

Combatant Craft Classification

Patrol Type Craft
Coastal Patrol Combatants
- Patrol Boat — PB
- Patrol Craft (fast) — PCF
- Patrol Craft (hydrofoil) — PCH
- Patrol Gunboat (hydrofoil) — PGH
- Fast Patrol Craft — PTF

River/Roadstead Craft
- Mini-Armoured Troop Carrier — ATC
- River Patrol Boat — PBR

Amphibious Warfare Type Craft
Landing Craft
- Amphibious Assault Landing Craft — AALC
- Landing Craft, Air Cushion — LCAC
- Landing Craft, Mechanised — LCM
- Landing Craft, Personnel, Large — LCPL
- Landing Craft, Personnel, Ramped — LCPR
- Landing Craft, Utility — LCU
- Landing Craft, Vehicle, Personnel — LCVP
- Amphibious Warping Tug — LWT

Special Warfare Craft
- Light Seal Support Craft — LSSC
- Medium Seal Support Craft — MSSC
- Swimmer Delivery Vehicle — SDV
- Special Warfare Craft, Light — SWCL
- Special Warfare Craft, Medium — SWCM

Mine Warfare Type Craft
Mine Countermeasures Craft
- Minesweeping Boat — MSB
- Minesweeping, Drone — MSD
- Minesweeper, Inshore — MSI
- Minesweeper, River (converted LCM-6) — MSM
- Minesweeper, Patrol — MSR

SUPPORT CRAFT CATEGORY

Support Craft Classification (Non self-propelled craft are indicated)

Service Craft Type
Drydocks
- Large Auxiliary Floating Dry Dock (non self-propelled) — AFDB
- Small Auxiliary Floating Dry Dock (non self-propelled) — AFDL
- Medium Auxiliary Floating Dry Dock (non self-propelled) — AFDM
- Auxiliary Repair Dry Dock (non self-propelled) — ARD
- Medium Auxiliary Repair Dry Dock (non self-propelled) — ARDM
- Bowdock — YBD
- Yard Floating Dry Dock (non self-propelled) — YFD

Tugs
- Large Harbour Tug — YTB
- Small Harbour Tug — YTL
- Medium Harbour Tug — YTM

Tankers
- Fuel Oil Barge — YO
- Gasoline Barge — YOG
- Water Barge — YW

Lighters
- Open Lighter (non self-propelled) — YC
- Car Float (non self-propelled) — YCF
- Aircraft Transportation Lighter (non self-propelled) — YCV
- Covered Lighter — YF
- Covered Lighter — YFN
- Floating Dry Dock Workshop (Hull) — YRDH
- Floating Dry Dock Workshop (Machine) — YRDM
- Radiological Repair Barge (non self-propelled) — YRR
- Salvage Craft Tender (non self-propelled) — YRST
- Seaplane Wrecking Derrick — YSD
- Large Covered Lighter (non self-propelled) — YFNB
- Lighter (special purpose) (non self-propelled) — YFNX
- Refrigerated Covered Lighter — YFR
- Refrigerated Covered Lighter (non self-propelled) — YFRN
- Harbour Utility Craft — YFU
- Garbage Lighter — YG
- Garbage Lighter (non-self-propelled) — YGN
- Gasoline Barge (non self-propelled) — YOGN
- Fuel Oil Barge (non self-propelled) — YON
- Oil Storage Barge (non self-propelled) — YOS
- Sludge Removal Barge (non self-propelled) — YSR
- Water Barge (non self-propelled) — YWN

Miscellaneous
- Barracks Craft (non self-propelled) — APL
- Deep Submergence Rescue Vehicle — DSRV
- Deep Submergence Vehicle — DSV
- Unclassified Miscellaneous (self and non self-propelled) — IX
- Submersible Research Vehicle — NR
- Miscellaneous Auxiliary — YAG
- Floating Crane (non self-propelled) — YD
- Diving Tender (non self-propelled) — YDT
- Ferry Boat or Launch — YFB
- Dry Dock Companion Craft (non self-propelled) — YFND
- Floating Power Barge (non self-propelled) — YFP
- Covered Lighter (Range Tender) — YFRT
- Salvage Lift Craft, Heavy (non self-propelled) — YHLC
- Dredge — YM
- Salvage Lift Craft, Medium (non self-propelled) — YMLC
- Gate Craft (non self-propelled) — YNG
- Patrol Craft — YP
- Floating Pile Driver (non self-propelled) — YPD
- Floating Workshop (non self-propelled) — YR
- Repair and Berthing Barge (non self-propelled) — YRB
- Repair, Berthing and Messing Barge (non self-propelled) — YRBM

*Classification not or no longer official but included in this list because of usage in the US section text.

ELECTRONIC EQUIPMENT CLASSIFICATION

The "AN" nomenclature was designed so that a common designation could be used for Army, Navy and Air Force equipment. The system indicator "AN" does not mean that the Army, Navy and Air Force use the equipment, but means that the type number was assigned in the "AN" system.

"AN" nomenclature is assigned to complete sets of equipment and major components of military design; groups of articles of either commercial or military design which are grouped for military purposes; major articles of military design which are not part of or used with a set; and commercial articles when nomenclature will not facilitate military identification and/or procedures.

"AN" nomenclature is not assigned to articles catalogued commercially except as stated above; minor components of military design which other adequate means of identification are available; small parts such as capacitors and resistors; and articles having other adequate identification in joint military specifications. Nomenclature assignments remain unchanged regardless of later installation and/or application.

Installation

- A Airborne (installed and operated in aircraft).
- B Underwater mobile, submarine.
- C Air transportable (inactivated, do not use).
- D Pilotless carrier.
- F Fixed.
- G Ground, general ground use (includes two or more ground-type installations).
- K Amphibious.
- M Ground, mobile (installed as operating unit in a vehicle which has no function other than transporting the equipment).
- P Pack or portable (animal or man).
- S Water surface craft.
- T Ground, transportable.
- U General utility (includes two or more general installation classes, airborne, shipboard, and ground).
- V Ground, vehicular (installed in vehicle designed for functions other than carrying electronic equipment, etc, such as tanks).
- W Water surface and underwater.

Type of Equipment

- A Invisible light, heat radiation.
- B Pigeon.
- C Carrier.
- D Radiac.
- E Nupac.
- F Photographic.[1]
- G Telegraph or teletype.
- I Interphone and public address.
- J Electromechanical or inertial wire covered.
- K Telemetering.
- L Countermeasures.
- M Meteorological.
- N Sound in air.
- P Radar.
- Q Sonar and underwater sound.
- R Radio.
- S Special types, magnetic, etc, or combinations of types.
- T Telephone (wire).
- V Visual and visible light.
- W Armament (peculiar to armament, not otherwise covered).
- X Facsimile or television.
- Y Data processing.

Purpose

- A Auxiliary assemblies (not complete operating sets used with or part of two or more sets or sets series).
- B Bombing.
- C Communications (receiving and transmitting).
- D Direction finder, reconnaissance and/or surveillance.
- E Ejection and/or release.
- G Fire-control or searchlight directing.
- H Recording and/or reproducing (graphic meteorological and sound).
- K Computing.
- L Searchlight control (inactivated, use G).
- M Maintenance and test assemblies (including tools).
- N Navigational aids (including altimeters, beacons, compasses, racons, depth sounding, approach, and landing).
- P Reproducing (inactivated, do not use).
- Q Special, or combination of purposes.
- R Receiving, passive detecting.
- S Detecting and/or range and bearing, search.
- T Transmitting.
- W Automatic flight or remote control.
- X Identification and recognition.

1. Not for US use except for assigning suffix letters to previously nomenclatured items.

Example: AN/URD-4A. AN: "AN" System; U: General Utility; R: Radio; D: Direction Finder, Reconnaissance, and/or Surveillance; 4: Model Number; A: Modification Letter.

CLASSIFICATION OF MARITIME ADMINISTRATION SHIP DESIGNS

The US Maritime Administration is a Division of the US Department of Commerce. All US flag merchant vessels are built under the jurisdiction of the US Maritime Administration and are assigned Maritime Administration design classifications. These classifications consist of three groups of letters and numbers.

A number of US Naval Auxiliaries were originally built to Maritime Administration specifications and were acquired during construction or after the ship was completed. It should be noted that the Maritime Administration acts as a "ship broker" for the US government and does not build ships for itself. The Maritime Administration generally oversees the operation and administration of the US Merchant Marine.

Merchant Ship Design Classifications

Type and Length of Vessel

		Length in Feet at Load Water Line			
Type		1	2	3	4
C	Cargo	Under 400	400-450	450-500	500-550
P	Passenger	Under 500	500-600	600-700	700-800
N	Coastal Cargo	Under 200	200-250	250-300	300-350
R	Refrigerated Cargo	Under 400	400-450	450-500	500-550
S	Special (Navy)	Under 200	200-300	300-400	400-500
T	Tanker	Under 450	450-500	500-550	550-600

Type of Propulsion; Number of Propellers and Passengers

	Single Screw		Twin Screw	
	1/12	13+	1/12	13+
Power	Passengers	Passengers	Passengers	Passengers
Steam	S	S1	ST	S2
Motor (Diesel)	M	M1	MT	M2
Turbo-Electric	SE	SE1	SET	SE2

Example: C4-S-B1. C4: Cargo Ship between 500 and 550 ft long; S: steam powered; B1: 1st variation ("1") of the original design ("B"). If the third group of letters and numbers read BV1 instead of B1, the translation of the code would be, the 1st variation ("1") of the 22nd modification ("V") of the original design ("B").

MAJOR COMMERCIAL SHIPYARDS

Avondale Shipyards, Inc, New Orleans, Louisiana
Bath Iron Works Corp, Bath, Maine
Bethlehem Steel Corp, Sparrows Point, Maryland
General Dynamics Corp, Electric Boat Division, Groton, Connecticut (formerly Electric Boat Company)
General Dynamics Corp, Quincy Shipbuilding Division, Quincy, Massachusetts (formerly Bethlehem Steel Corp Yard)
Ingalls Shipbuilding Division (Litton Industries), Pascagoula, Mississippi
Lockheed Shipbuilding & Construction Co, Seattle, Washington
National Steel & Shipbuilding Co, San Diego, California
Newport News Shipbuilding & Dry Dock Co, Newport News, Virginia
Todd Shipyards Corp, San Pedro, California
Todd Shipyards Corp, Seattle, Washington

Note: All of the above yards have engaged in naval shipbuilding, overhaul, or modernisation except for the General Dynamics/Electric Boat yard which is engaged only in submarine work.

SHIPBOARD SYSTEMS

AEGIS (formerly Advanced Surface Missile System). Advanced surface-to-air missile system intended for use in guided missile destroyer (DDG 47 class) and cruisers (CGN 42 class) scheduled for delivery during the 1980s. To have a capability against high-performance aircraft and air, surface and sub-surface launched, anti-ship missiles. Launcher is Mk 26. AEGIS will have an electronic scanning radar with fixed antenna which will be capable of controlling friendly aircraft as well as surveillance, detection and tracking. Elements will include the AN/UYK-7 computer and illuminators for missile guidance for use with Standard surface-to-air missile.
Status: Development.

ASROC (Anti-Submarine Rocket). Anti-Submarine weapon launched from surface ships with homing torpedo or nuclear depth charge as warhead. Launcher is Mk 10 or Mk 26 combination ASROC/surface-to-air missile launcher or Mk 16 eight-cell "pepper box". Installed in US Navy cruisers, destroyers, and frigates; Japanese, Italian, West German, and Canadian destroyer-type ships.
Weight of missile approximately 1 000 lb; length 15 ft; diameter 1 ft; span of fins 2·5 ft. Payload: Mk 44 or Mk 46 acoustic-homing torpedo or nuclear depth charge; range one to six miles.
Designation: RUR-5.
Status: Operational.

BPDMS (Basic Point Defence Missile System). Close-in-air-defence system employing the Sparrow AIM-7E or 7F series missile designated Sea Sparrow and a modified ASROC-type "pepper box" launcher. Installed in aircraft carriers, ocean escorts, and amphibious ships.
Status: Operational.

CAPTOR (Encapsulated Torpedo). Mk 46 torpedo inserted in mine casing. Can be launched by aircraft or submarine.
Status: Operational.

CIWS (Close-in Weapon System). "Family" of advanced gun and missile systems to provide close-in or "point" defence for ships against anti-ship missiles and aircraft. Specific weapons being developed or evaluated under this programme include the Chaparral, Hybrid launcher, Pintle, Vulcan Air Defence, Phalanx, and OTO Melara 35 mm twin gun mount.

LAMPS (Light Airborne Multi-Purpose System). Ship-launched helicopter intended for anti-submarine and missile-defence missions, with secondary roles of search-and-rescue and utility (eg, parts and personnel transfer). For use aboard destroyer-type ships with hangars. Sensors include Magnetic Airborne Detection (MAD), and sonobuoys with digital relays to permit control and attack direction by launching ship. Radar provided to extend detection range.
Weapons: 2 Mk 46 ASW torpedoes. Crew: pilot, co-pilot, one operator.
Status: 105 Kaman Seasprite helicopters being modified to SH-2 configuration as interim LAMPS. Deployed in cruisers, destroyers, and frigates.
LAMPS III Improved Light Airborne Multi-Purpose System based on Army Utility Tactical Transport Aircraft System (UTTAS) helicopter.
Status: Development.

MCLWG (Major Calibre Light-Weight Gun). Light-weight 8 in gun (Mk 71) planned for advanced surface combatants.
Status: Evaluation in destroyer *Hull* (DD 945).

NTDS (Naval Tactical Data System). Combination of digital computers, displays, and transmission links to increase an individual ship commander's capability to assess tactical data and take action by integrating input from various sensors (eg, radars) and providing display of tactical situation and the defence or offence options available. Data can be transmitted among NTDS equipped ships. An automatic mode initiates action to respond to greatest threats in a tactical situation. Also can be linked to airborne Tactical Data System (ATDS) in E-2 Hawkeye aircraft. Fitted in US Navy aircraft carriers, missile-armed cruisers, destroyers ("Coontz" class) amphibious command ships, and two frigates (*Voge* [FF 1047] and *Koelsch* [FF 1049]).
Status: Operational.

NATO SEA SPARROW Follow-on to BPDMS with a Target Acquisition System (TAS), powered director, smaller launcher, and control console combined with the Sea Sparrow missile. Planned for US amphibious and auxiliary ships.
Status: Under development; also a NATO co-operative programme with Belgium, Denmark, Italy, Netherlands and Norway. Being evaluated in *Downes* (FF 1070).

PHALANX Rapid-fire, close-in gun system being developed to provide close range defence against anti-ship missiles. Fires 20 mm ammunition from six-barrel "gatling" gun with "dynamic gun aiming" with fire control radar tracking projectiles and target(s). Theoretical rate of fire 3 000 rounds-per-minute. Initially planned for "Spruance" class destroyers, frigates, and some auxiliary ships; tentative programme calls for approx 359 units in 192 ships and three trainers.
Status: Development.
Average cost for installation: $100 000 (new construction), $150 000 (retrofitting).

QUICKSTRIKE Advanced mine system; details classified.
Status: Development.

SINS (Ships' Inertial Navigation System). Navigation system providing exact navigation information without active input from terrestrial sources. Prime components are gyroscopes and accelerometers that relate movement of the ship in all directions, ship speed through water and over the ground, and true north to give a continuous report of the ship's position.
Status: Operational.

SIRCS (Shipboard Intermediate Range Combat System). Programme to integrate shipboard self-defence systems (existing and planned).
Status: Development.

SUBROC (Submarine Rocket). Anti-submarine missile launched from submarines with nuclear warhead. Launched from 21 in torpedo tube. Carried in US Navy submarines of "Thresher" and later classes with amidships torpedo tubes, BQQ 2 or BQQ 5 sonar and Mk 113 or later torpedo fire control systems. The missile is fired from the submerged submarine, rises up through the surface, travels through air towards the hostile submarine, and then re-enters the water to detonate.
Weight of missile approximately 4 000 lb, length 21 ft; diameter 1·75 ft (maximum); estimated range 25 to 30 miles.
Designation: UUM-44.
Status: Operational.

TACTAS (Tactical Towed Array Sonar). Ship-towed long-range acoustic detection system.

TOMAHAWK A cruise missile whose details are listed below. Both submarines and surface ships will be able to launch the SLCM version. Mentioned here as one of the most significant advances in missile design of the last ten years.

NAVAL MISSILES

Type(a)	Designation	Name	Launch Platform (tubes/launchers)	Range miles (km)	Length feet (metres)	Weight lb (kg)	Notes(b)
SLBM	UGM-27C	Polaris A-3	"Ethan Allen", "George Washington" submarines (16)	2 500 (4 023)	32 (9·8)	30 000 (13 608)	Thermo-nuclear; MRV warhead
SLBM	UGM-73A	Poseidon C-3	"Lafayette" submarines (16)	approx 2 500 (4 023)	34 (10·4)	65 000 (29 484)	Thermo-nuclear; MIRV warhead
SLBM	UGM-96A	Trident (I) C-4	"Ohio" submarines (24)	approx 4 000 (6 432)	34·1 (10·4)	70 000 (31 752)	Thermo-nuclear; MIRV and MARV warhead
SLBM	UGM	Trident (II) D-5	Trident submarines (24)	approx 6 000 (9 656)	45·75 (13·9)	126 000 (57 153)	Proposed
SLCM	BGM-109	Tomahawk	Attack submarines (torpedo tubes) Surface ships (box launchers)	approx 1 500 (2 414)	20·5 (6·3)	2 400-2 700 (1 088-1 224)	Nuclear land attack and 300 mile (HE) anti-ship; under development
SSM	RGM-66D/E	Standard-ARM	Some surface ships (ASROC launcher)	15 (24·14)	15 (4·6)	1 400 (635)	HE
SSM	RGM-84	Harpoon	Surface ships	50 (80·5)	15 (4·6)	1 470 (666·1)	Operational; HE
USM	RGM-84	Encapsulated Harpoon	Attack submarines (torpedo tubes)	60 (96·6)	21 (6·4)	2 355 (1 068)	Development; HE; operational 1978-79
SAM	RIM-2	Terrier	Cruisers (1 or 2 twin); "Coontz" destroyers (1 twin); "Kitty Hawk", "America" carriers (2 twin)	20+ (32·2+)	26·1 (8)	3 000 (1 361)	Nuclear or HE
SAM	RIM-7	Sea Sparrow	Surface ships	8 (12·9)	12 (3·7)	500 (226·8)	HE; Mk 25 or Mk 29 (NATO) multiple launcher; Basic Point Defence Missile System
SAM	RIM-8	Talos	"Albany", "Long Beach" cruisers (2 twin)	65+ (104·6+)	31·2 (9·5)	7 000 (3 175)	Nuclear or HE
SAM	RIM-24	Tartar	"Albany" cruisers (2 twin); "Chas. Adams" destroyers (1 twin or single); "Brooke" frigates (1 single); later cruisers	10+ (16·1+)	15 (4·6)	1 425 (646·4)	HE
SAM	RIM-66	Standard-MR (SM-1)	Tartar replacement	20+ (32·2+)	14·4 (4·4)	1 200-1 400 (546·3-635)	HE
SAM	RIM-66C	Standard (SM-2)	Talos replacement	60+ (96·6+)			Long range with mid-course guidance; development
SAM	RIM-66C	Standard (SM-2MR)	Aegis	20+ (32·2+)			Medium range—development
SAM	RIM-67	Standard-ER (SM-1)	Terrier replacement	35+ (56·3+)	26·2 (8)	2 900 (1 315·4)	HE
SAM	RIM-67B	Standard (SM-2ER)	Talos replacement	60+ (96·6+)			Long range—development
AAM	AIM-7	Sparrow III	F-4/F-14/F-15 fighters	9-16 (14·5-25·8)	12 (3·7)	500 (226·8)	
AAM	AIM-9C/D	Sidewinder-1B	F-4/F-14/F-15/F-16 fighters	8 (12·9)	9·5 (2·9)	185 (83·9)	
AAM	AIM-54	Phoenix	F-14 fighter (6)	60+ (96·6+)	13 (4)	985 (446·8)	
ASM	AGM-12B	Bullpup-A	Attack/patrol aircraft	7 (11·3)	10 (3·1)	571 (259)	

NAVAL MISSILES

Type(a)	Designation	Name	Launch Platform (tubes/launchers)	Range miles (km)	Length feet (metres)	Weight lb (kg)	Notes(b)
ASM	AGM-12D	Bullpup-B	Attack/patrol aircraft	10 (16.1)	13.5 (4.1)	1 785 (809.7)	Nuclear or HE
ASM	AGM-45	Shrike	Attack/patrol aircraft	8–10 (12.9–16.1)	10 (3.1)	390 (176.9)	Anti-radiation
ASM	AGM-53	Condor	Attack/patrol aircraft	40–60 (64.4–96.6)	13.8 (4.2)	2 130 (966.2)	Nuclear or HE; production planned
ASM	AGM-62	Walleye I	Attack/patrol aircraft	16 (25.7)	11.2 (3.5)	1 100 (499)	Nuclear or HE
ASM	AGM-62	Walleye II	Attack/patrol aircraft	35 (56.3)	13.2 (4.0)	2 400 (1 089)	Nuclear or HE
ASM	AGM-78	Standard-ARM	Attack/patrol aircraft	35 (56.3)	15 (4.6)	1 356 (615.1)	Anti-radiation
ASM	AGM-83	Bulldog	Attack/patrol aircraft	35 (56.3)	9.8 (3.0)	600 (272.1)	Modified Bullpup
ASM	AGM-84	Harpoon	Attack/patrol aircraft	120 (193.1)	12.6 (3.8)	1 168 (529.8)	Operational; HE
ASM	AGM-88	Harm	Attack/patrol aircraft		13.7 (4.2)	780 (353.8)	Development; High-speed Anti-Radiation Missile; larger than Shrike
ASW	RUR-5	ASROC	Cruisers, destroyers, frigates	1–6 (1.6–9.7)	15 (4.6)	1 000 (453.6)	Nuclear depth charge, Mk 44, or Mk 46 torpedo; multiple launcher in most ships; Mk 26 launcher in later ships; 570 lb (256.5 kg) with Mk 46
ASW	UUM-44	SUBROC	"Thresher" and later attack submarines (torpedo tubes)	25–30 (40.2–48.3)	21 (6.4)	4 000 (1 814.4)	Nuclear

(a) FBM = Fleet Ballistic Missile; SLCM = Sea-Launched Cruise Missile; SSM = Surface-to-Surface Missile; SAM = Surface-to-Air Missile; AAM = Air-to-Air Missile; ASM = Air-to-Surface Missile; ASW = Anti-Submarine Warfare.
(b) MRV = Multiple Re-entry Vehicle; MIRV = Multiple Independently Targeted Re-entry Vehicle; MARV = Maneouvring Re-entry Vehicle; HE = High Explosive.

TORPEDOES

Designation	Launch Platform	Weight lb (kg)	Length feet (metres)	Diameter, in (mm)	Propulsion	Guidance	Notes
Mk 37 Mod 2	Submarines	1 690 (766.6)	13.4 (4.1)	19 (482.6)	Electric	Wire; active-passive acoustic homing	Anti-submarine
Mk 37 Mod 3	Submarines	1 430 (648.6)	11.25 (3.4)	19 (482.6)	Electric	Active-passive acoustic homing	Anti-submarine
Mk 37C	Submarines				Liquid mono-propellant	Active-passive acoustic homing	Anti-submarine; modified Mk 37-2/3 for allied navies; in production
Mk 44 Mod 1	Surface ships (Mk 32 tubes and ASROC); aircraft	433 (196.4)	8.4 (2.6)	12.75 (323.9)	Electric	Active acoustic homing	Anti-submarine
Mk 45 Mod 1 & Mod 2 (ASTOR)	Submarines	2 213 (1 003.8)	18.9 (5.8)	19 (482.6)	Electric	Wire	Anti-submarine; nuclear warhead; 10+ mile range; being replaced by Mk 48
Mk 46 Mod 0	Surface ships (Mk 32 tubes and ASROC); aircraft	568 (257.6)	8.5 (2.6)	12.75 (323.9)	Solid-propellant	Active-passive acoustic homing	Anti-submarine; successor to Mk 44
Mk 46 Mod 1 & Mod 2	Surface ships (Mk 32 tubes and ASROC); aircraft	508 (230.4)	8.5 (2.6)	12.75 (323.9)	Liquid mono-propellant	Active-passive acoustic homing	Anti-submarine; successor to Mk 44; Mod 4 used in CAPTOR (Encapsulated Torpedo) mine
Mk 48 Mod 1 & Mod 3	Submarines	3 480 (1 578.5)	19.1 (5.8)	21 (533.6)	Liquid mono-propellant	Wire/terminal acoustic homing	Anti-submarine and anti-shipping; in production; range approx 20 miles
ALWT	Aircraft; submarines						Advanced Light-Weight Torpedo; to replace Mk 46; in design stage

WILLIAM V. PRATT, DUPONT and BOWEN

9/1978, USN (PH1. A. C. Matthews)

636 USA/ Introduction

DELETIONS

Note: Disposals listed in parentheses after each entry. For those ships whose disposal is indicated as "transfer", see succeeding pages for further details on the transfer.

Submarines

1976   31 Jan *Scabbardfish* (SS 397) (transfer)
1977   1 Oct *Salmon* (SS 573) (transfer); 5 Dec *Capitaine* (SS 336), *Pickerel* (SS 524) and *Volador* (SS 490) (all transfer)
1978   15 July *Lizardfish* (SS 373) (transfer); 30 Sep *Sailfish* (SS 572) (pending)

Aircraft Carriers

1976   31 Jan *Hancock* (CV 19) (scrapped)
1977   30 Sep *Franklin D. Roosevelt* (CV 42) (scrapped)

Cruisers

1976   9 Aug *Columbus* (CG 12) (scrapped); 22 Nov *Little Rock* (CG 4) (memorial at Buffalo, NY as of 21 June 1977)
1978   31 July *Providence* (CG 6), *Springfield* (CG 7) and *St. Paul* (CA 73) (all scrap), *Canberra* (CA 70) and *Newport News* (CA 148) (possible memorials)

Guided Missile Destroyers

1978   29 Apr *John S. McCain* (DDG 36) (scrapped); 1 June *Mitscher* (DDG 35) (scrapped)

Destroyers

1976   23 Jan *Wiltsie* (DD 716) (transfer); 30 Jan *Gurke* (DD 783) (transfer); 1 July *Stribling* (DD 867) (target); *New* (DD 818), *Richard E. Kraus* (DD 849) (both transfer); 30 Sep *Brownson* (DD 868) (pending); 1 Oct *Glennon* (DD 840) (scrapped), *George K. MacKenzie* (DD 836) (sunk as target 17 Oct 1976); *Holder* (DD 819) (transfer), 2 Nov *Leonard F. Mason* (DD 852) (transfer); 1 Dec *Vesole* (DD 878), *William M. Wood* (DD 715) (both pending)
1977   1 Feb *Bordelon* (DD 881) (transfer); 1 Oct *Power* (DD 839), *Sarsfield* (DD 837) (both transfer); 1 Nov *Basilone* (DD 824) (scrapped); 15 Dec *Rich* (DD 820) (scrapped)
1978   30 May *Bausell* (DD 845) (target); 1 July *William R. Rush* (DD 714) (transfer); 1 Dec *Agerholm* (DD 826) (target)

Frigate

1978   15 July *Booth* (FF 170) (transfer)

Command Ships

1977   1 Dec *Northampton* (CC 1), *Wright* (CC 2) (scrapped)

Light Forces

1977   31 Jan *Ashville* (PG 84), *Marathon* (PG 89) (to Massachusetts Maritime Academy as training ships 11 and 18 Apr 1977 respectively); *Gallup* (PG 85), *Canon* (PG 90) (pending), *Crockett* (PG 88) (to Environmental Protection Agency 18 Apr 1977. Based Lake Michigan); 1 Oct *Antelope* (PG 86) (transferred to Environmental Protection Agency 17 Jan 1978); *Ready* (PG 87) (to Massachusetts Maritime Academy 1 Mar 1978 as training ship), *Grand Rapids* (PG 98) (reclassified as "boat" and assigned to Naval Ship Research and Development Center as M/V *Athena II* this date), *Douglas* (PG 100) (scheduled for transfer to Naval Ships Research and Development Center as M/V *Athena III* in early 1979)
1979   PTF 23, 24 and 26 (all sold)

Amphibious Command Ships

1976   30 July *Mount McKinley* (LCC 7), *Estes* (LCC 12) (scrapped); 1 Dec *Pocono* (LCC 16), *Taconic* (LCC 17) (scrapped)

Amphibious Cargo Ships

1976   1 Sep *Seminole* (LKA 104), *Union* (LKA 106), *Washburn* (LKA 108), *Merrick* (LKA 97), *Winston* (LKA 94) (all scrapped)
1977   1 Jan *Thuban* (LKA 19), *Algol* (LKA 54), *Capricornus* (LKA 57), *Muliphen* (LKA 61), *Yancey* (LKA 93), *Rankin* (LKA 103), *Vermillion* (LKA 107) (all scrapped)

Amphibious Transports

1976   1 Sep *Magoffin* (LPA 199), *Talladega* (LPA 208), *Navarro* (LPA 215), *Pickaway* (LPA 222), *Bexar* (LPA 237) (all scrapped); 1 Dec *Sandoval* (LPA 194), *Mountrail* (LPA 213) (all scrapped)

Amphibious Transports (small)

1977   31 Oct *Ruchamkin* (LPR 89) (transfer)
1978   31 Mar *Enright* (APD 66) (transfer)

Amphibious Transport Submarine

1977   15 Mar *Sealion* (LPSS 315) (target)

Dock Landing Ships

1976   15 Apr *Whitemarsh* (LSD 8) (transfer); 30 Apr *Whetstone* (LSD 27) (laid up Maritime Administration, Suisun Bay, Calif); 30 June *Comstock* (LSD 19) (laid up Maritime Administration); 15 Oct *Cabildo* (LSD 16), *Colonial* (LSD 18), *Tortuga* (LSD 26) (all laid up Maritime Administration, Suisun Bay, Calif); 1 Nov *Rushmore* (LSD 14), *Shadwell* (LSD 15) (laid up Maritime Administration, James River, Va); 11 Nov *Donner* (LSD 20) (same as *Rushmore* and *Shadwell*)

Tank Landing Ships

1976   15 Aug *Whitfield County* (LST 1169), *Terrell County* (LST 1157) (both transfers); 1 Nov *Terrebonne Parish* (LST 1156), *Tom Green County* (LST 1159), *Wexford County* (LST 1168), *Summitt County* (LST 1146) (all transfers), *Duval County* (LST 578) (pending)
1977   30 Dec *Grant County* (LST 1174) (transfer)
1978   15 Apr *Page County* (LST 1076), *Park County* (LST 1077) (both transfers)

Mine Warfare Forces

1976   1 May *Falcon* (MSC 190), *Frigate Bird* (MSC 191), *Hummingbird* (MSC 192), *Jacana* (MSC 193), *Limpkin* (MSC 195), *Meadowlark* (MSC 196) (returned from loan to Indonesia; scrapped); 15 May *Lucid* (MSO 458), *Acme* (MSO 508), *Advance* (MSO 510) (all scrapped); 15 Aug *Chickadee* (MSF 59) (transfer); 1 Nov *Nimble* (MSO 459) (scrapped)
1977   1 July *Energy* (MSO 436), *Firm* (MSO 444) (returned from loan to Philippines; scrapped); 1 Aug *Thrush* (MSC 204) (returned from lease to Virginia Institute of Marine Science where employed as AGOR; transferred to Institute permanently this date); 1 Sep *Agile* (MSO 421), *Observer* (MSO 461), *Pinnacle* (MSO 462), *Skill* (MSO 471), *Vital* (MSO 474), *Sturdy* (MSO 494), *Swerve* (MSO 495), *Venture* (MSO 496) (all scrapped)

Destroyer Tenders

1976   15 Sep *Isle Royal* (AD 29) (sold)
1978   15 June *Tidewater* (AD 31) (transfer)

Ammunition Ships

1976   15 July *Firedrake* (AE 14) (sold)
        1 Oct *Mauna Loa* (AE 8), *Wrangell* (AE 12) (both sold)

Store Ships

1976   30 Apr *Denebola* (AF 56) (scrapped); 1 June *Zelima* (AF 49), *Pictor* (AF 54), *Aludra* (AF 55), *Procyon* (AF 61) (all sold); 1 Oct *Arcturus* (AF 52), *Hyades* (AF 28) (both sold)
1977   29 Apr *Vega* (AF 59) (pending)

Miscellaneous

1976   15 Aug *Pvt Jose E. Valdes* (AG 169) (sold)
1977   30 Sep *Alacrity* (AG 520), *Assurance* (AG 521) (both ex-MSO; both scrap)

Hydrofoil Research Ship

1978   30 Sep *Plainview* (AGEH 1) (stripped; hulk sold)

Major Communications Relay Ship

1976   15 Oct *Annapolis* (AGMR 1) (ex-CVE: scrapped)

Oceanographic Research Ships

1977   15 Feb *Josiah Willard Gibbs* (AGOR 1) (transfer); 30 Dec *Chain* (AGOR 17) (scrapped)

Patrol Craft Tender

1977   1 Mar *Graham County* (AGP 1176) (scrapped)

Survey Ships

1976   15 Apr *Sgt George D. Keathley* (AGS 35) (transfer); 30 Apr *Coastal Crusader* (AGS 36) (ex-AGM; sold)

Light Cargo Ship

1976   15 Apr *Mark* (AKL 12) (transfer)

Oilers

1976   15 July *Kennebec* (AO 36) (sold); *Tappahannock* (AO 43) (pending)
1977   1 Dec *Sabine* (AO 25), *Chikaskia* (AO 54), *Aucilla* (AO 56) (all sold)

Gasoline Tankers

1977   15 Apr *Elkhorn* (AOG 7), *Namakagon* (AOG 53), *Pecatonica* (AOG 57) (all transfer)
1978   15 Apr *Tombigbee* (AOG 11) (transfer)

Repair Ships

1976   1 Sep *Markab* (AR 23) (sold); 1 Nov *Amphion* (AR 13) (transfer)
1977   1 Jan *Briareus* (AR 12) (sold); 1 Oct *Delta* (AR 9) (retained)
1978   1 Sep *Grand Canyon* (AR 28) (sold)

Battle Damage Repair Ships

1976   15 Apr *Midas* (ARB 5) (pending); *Sarpedon* (ARB 7) (scrap); 10 Dec *Helios* (ARB 12) (transfer)

Cable Repairing Ship

1977   20 Dec *Thor* (ARC 4) (sold)

Repair Ships, Small

1976   1 Nov *Minotaur* (ARL 15) (transfer)
1977   1 Oct *Egeria* (ARL 8), *Belerophon* (ARL 31) (scrapped); 31 Dec *Indra* (ARL 37) (retained)
1978   15 June *Askari* (ARL 30) (transfer)

Salvage Ships

1977   15 Apr *Cable* (ARS 19) (sunk as target 7 Aug 1978); 1 Dec *Grapple* (ARS 7) (transfer)
1978   31 Mar *Grasp* (ARS 24) (transfer); 1 Sep *Escape* (ARS 6) (pending)

USA/ Introduction

Submarine Rescue Ships

1977 15 Sep *Coucal* (ASR 8) (target); 30 Sep *Tringa* (ASR 16) (pending)

Auxiliary Ocean Tugs

1976 15 Apr *Cahokia* (ATA 186), *Mahopac* (ATA 196) (both transfer)
1977 1 Oct *Tatnuck* (ATA 195) (sold); 31 Oct *Kalmia* (ATA 184) (transfer)
1978 1 July *Samoset* (ATA 190) (transfer)

Fleet Ocean Tugs

1976 15 Apr *Chickasaw* (ATF 83) (transfer)
1977 1 Oct *Chowanoc* (ATF 100) (transfer); *Mataco* (ATF 86) (sold); 31 Oct *Choctaw* (ATF 70) (transfer); 1 Dec *Bannock* (ATF 81) (transfer)
1978 31 Mar *Cusabo* (ATF 155) (transfer); 21 Apr *Cree* (ATF 84) (accidentally bombed 18 Jan; seriously damaged; scrapped); 1 Aug *Molala* (ATF 106) (transfer); 1 Sep *Nipmuc* (ATF 157), *Salinan* (ATF 161) (both transfer); 30 Sep *Abnaki*, *Cocopa* (ATF 101), *Hitchiti* (ATF 103) (all transfer)

SERVICE CRAFT

Floating Docks

1976 15 Apr ARD 9, *Windsor* (ARD 22) (both transfer); 15 Sep *Arco* (ARD 29) (transfer)
1977 1 June AFBD 1 (Sections A, G/J) (sold); 1 Sep AFDL 26 (transfer); 15 Nov AFDL 30 (transfer); 1 Dec AFDL 28, AFDL 29, ARD 15, ARD 17, ARD 28 (all transfer)
1978 17 Feb AFDL 43 (pending); 15 Nov YFD 9 (sold)

Unclassified Miscellaneous

1977 1 Dec IX 505 (ex-YTM 759) (sold)

Covered Lighters

1976 1 Feb YC 1322, 1392, 1441 (all sold); 1 Aug YC 978 (sold)
1977 1 Feb YC 763 (sold); 15 Feb YC 706 (sold); 1 Aug YC 316 (sold)
1978 15 July YC 1516 (sold)

Car Floats

1976 1 Aug YCF 14, 15 (both sold)

Aircraft Transport Lighter

1977 15 Dec YCV 18 (sold)

Floating Cranes

1976 1 June YD 207 (sold); 15 July YD 174 (sold)
1977 15 Aug YD 75 (sold); 1 Dec YD 180, 183, 156, 157, 203 (all transfer)

Covered Lighters (self-propelled)

1977 15 Mar YF 328 (target)

Ferryboat or Launch

1976 1 Sep YFB 82, 86 (both transfer)

Covered Lighters (non self-propelled)

1976 1 May YFN 1172 (sold)
1977 15 Feb YFN 922 (sold); 10 Dec YFN 903 (transfer)

Large Covered Lighters (non self-propelled)

1976 1 Mar YFNB 2 (transferred to Pacific Trust Territories); 15 July YFNB 22 (scrapped)
1977 1 May YFNB 23 (transferred to Maritime Administration, Suisun Bay, Calif for service)

Dry Dock Companion Craft

1977 31 Oct YFND 6 (transfer); 1 Dec YFND 19 (transfer)

Lighter (special purpose)

1978 15 July YFNX 21 (sold)

Refrigerated Covered Lighter

1977 31 Oct YFR 443 (transfer)

Harbour Utility Craft

1976 1 Apr YFU 67 (target); 15 Nov YFU 99 (sold)
1977 1 Apr YFU 88 (sold); 1 July YFU 55 (sold); 15 Sep YFU 44 (sold)
1978 1 Oct YFU 93 (sold)

Salvage Craft Lift, Medium

1975 15 Feb YMLC 5, 6 (both sold)

Fuel Oil Barges

1976 1 June YO 227 (sunk as target 19 Mar 1977); 1 July YO 199 (sunk as target Aug 1976)
1977 1 Mar *Crownblock* (YO 48) (target); 15 June YO 205 (sunk as target 25 Oct 1977); 1 July YO 219 (target)

Gasoline Barge

1976 5 Apr YOG 80 (transfer)

Oil Storage Barge

1976 1 Aug YOS 22 (sold)

Patrol Craft

1976 1 July YP 589, 590 (both sold)
1977 1 Sep YP 587 (transferred 28 Nov 1977 to Navy Sea Cadet Corp, Southfield, Mich. for use as training ship)
1978 1 June YP 591 (sold)

Floating Workshops

1976 1 Sep YR 32 (transfer)
1977 1 Dec YR 34 (transfer)

Repair and Berthing Barge

1976 1 Mar YRB 28 (sold)

Seaplane Wrecking Derricks

1976 1 Feb YSD 42 (sold)
1977 1 Dec YSD 60 (sold)
1978 15 Apr YSD 34 (sold); 15 Aug YSD 72 (sold)

Small Harbour Tugs

1976 1 Sep YTL 211, 567 (both transfer)

Medium Harbour Tugboats

1976 1 Mar *Wabanaquet* (YTM 525) (sold); 1 Apr YTM 510 (target); *Hisada* (YTM 518) (sunk as target 23 May 1976); 15 May *Satago* (YTM 414) (sunk as target 21 Jan 1977); 1 July *Tensaw* (YTM 418) (target)
1977 15 Apr *Panameta* (YTM 402) (sunk as target 4 Sep 1977); 1 May *Chilkat* (YTM 773) (transferred Maritime Administration, Suisun Bay, Calif for service), *Oomulgee* (YTM 532) (sold); 1 Oct *Mahoa* (YTM 519) (sunk as target 21 Apr 1978); 1 Dec *Ankachak* (YTM 767) (transfer)
1978 1 May *Anamos* (YTM 409) (target); 15 Nov *Manktao* (YTM 734) (target)

Water Barges (self-propelled)

1977 1 Dec YW 131 (transfer)

638 USA/ Introduction

US NAVAL SHIPS AND CRAFT TRANSFERRED TO FOREIGN COUNTRIES

This section comprises a list of ships and craft, arranged by date transferred, to a foreign country, since 1 January 1976. All transfers, except where noted took place under the International Logistics Programme (formerly the Military Defense Assistance Pact). The six methods of transfer are as follows:

Sale: The recipient buys the vessel(s) and receives the title(s). Most ship sales usually fall in this category.
Loan: Vessel(s) is loaned to recipient. US Navy retains title; recipient pays operating and maintenance costs.
Grant Aid: The recipient receives the vessel(s) in lieu of a grant of money. The USA does not retain title, but pays for activation (if needed), modernisation, and all other costs to make the vessel(s) suitable for transfer. After the transfer, the recipient country assumes all costs.
Lease: Similar to a loan, only the navy of the recipient country, rather than its government, makes the request to lease a vessel(s) directly to the US Navy rather than to the US government.
Off-Shore Procurement (OSP): Vessel(s) built in a foreign yard (usually in a yard in country of the recipient) and the United States pays half the costs of construction and/or provides equipment and technical assistance. US Navy hull numbers are assigned for accounting purposes.
Special: Vessel(s) transferred under methods other than the five listed above will be listed in the "Mode" column as Special.

For the last several years the most common method of transfer has been by sale.

Notes:
(a) A single asterisk before a date in the "Date of Transfer" column indicates that the ship in question had previously been loaned or leased to the indicated country at an earlier date.
(b) In the "USN Name/Hull Number" column asterisks appearing after the former USN name/hull number indicate the following: * formerly with the Republic of South Viet-Nam Navy; ** formerly with the Khmer Republic (ex-Cambodia) Navy; *** formerly with the Japanese Maritime Self-Defense Force.
(c) Those ships indicated as transferred by "Special*" in the "Mode" column were transferred to the indicated country via the Agency for International Development (AID).
(d) A "—" in the "Recipient Name/Hull Number" column indicates that as of writing the foreign name and pennant number were unknown.

Date of Transfer	Recipient	USN Name/Hull Number	Recipient Name/Hull Number	Mode
1976				
6 Jan	Barbados	Kemper County (LST 854)	Commercial	Special*
*14 Feb	Argentina	Salish (ATA 187)	Comodoro Somellera (A 10)	Sale
*14 Feb	Argentina	Catawba (ATA 210)	Alfrez Sobral (A-9)	Sale
*14 Feb	Argentina	M/V Dry Tortugas (ATF)	Goyena (Q 17)	Sale
*14 Feb	Argentina	M/V Sombrero Key (ATF)	Thompson (A 14)	Sale
Mar	Philippines	LT 1976 (ex-US Army)	Tiboli (YQ 58)	Sale
* Mar	Ethiopia	Orca (AVP 49)	Ethiopia (A 01)	Sale
5 Apr	Philippines	Camp (FFR 251)*	Rajah Lakandula (PS 4)	Sale
5 Apr	Philippines	Chincoteague (WHEC 375)*	Andres Bonifacio (PS 7)	Sale
5 Apr	Philippines	Yakutat (WHEC 380)*	(for cannibalisation and scrapping)	Sale
5 Apr	Philippines	Bering Strait (WHEC 382)*	Diego Silang (PS 9)	Sale
5 Apr	Philippines	Castle Rock (WHEC 383)*	Francisco Dagahoy (PS 10)	Sale
5 Apr	Philippines	Cook Inlet (WHEC 384)*	(for cannibalisation and scrapping)	Sale
5 Apr	Philippines	McCulloch (WHEC 386)*	Gregorio de Pilar (PS 8)	Sale
5 Apr	Philippines	Amherst (PCER 853)*	Datu Marikudo (PS 23)	Sale
5 Apr	Philippines	Jerome County (LST 848)*	Ilicos Norte (LT 98)	Sale
5 Apr	Philippines	Garrett County (AGP 786)*	—	Sale
5 Apr	Philippines	Harnett County (AGP 821)*	Dumagat (AE 57)	Sale
5 Apr	Philippines	YOG 80*	(for cannibalisation and scrapping)	Sale
* Apr	Greece	Lapon (SS 260)	(for cannibalisation and scrapping)	Sale
* Apr	Greece	Scabbardfish (SS 397)	Triaina (S 86)	Sale
*19 May	Taiwan	White Marsh (LSD 8)	Chung Cheng (LSD 191)	Sale
*19 May	Taiwan	Chickasaw (ATF 83)	Ta Tung (ATF 548)	Sale
*19 May	Taiwan	Pecatonica (AOG 57)	Chang Pei (AOG 507)	Sale
*19 May	Taiwan	Namakagon (AOG 53) (ex-HMNZS)	Lung Chuan (AOG 515)	Sale
*19 May	Taiwan	Mahopac (ATA 196)	Ta Peng (ATA 549)	Sale
*19 May	Taiwan	Mark (AKL 12)	Yung Kang (AKL 514)	Sale
*19 May	Taiwan	Cahokia (ATA 186)	Ta Teng (ATA 550)	Sale
*19 May	Taiwan	Elkhorn (AOG 7)	Hsing Lung (AOG 517)	Sale
*19 May	Taiwan	Windsor (ARD 22)	Fo Wu No 6	Sale
*19 May	Taiwan	Sgt George D. Keathley (AGS 35)	Chu Hwa (AGS 564)	Sale
*19 May	Taiwan	Placerville (PC 1087)	—	Sale
*19 May	Taiwan	Hanford (PC 1142)	—	Sale
*19 May	Taiwan	Susanville (PC 1149)	—	Sale
4 June	Singapore	USNS LST 579 (T-LST 579)	Intrepid (L 203)	Sale
4 June	Singapore	USNS LST 613 (T-LST 613)	Persistance (L 205)	Sale
4 June	Singapore	USNS LST 623 (T-LST 623)	Perseverence (L 206)	Sale
4 June	Singapore	USNS LST 629 (T-LST 629)	Excellence (L 202)	Sale
4 June	Singapore	USNS LST 649 (T-LST 649)	Resolution (L 204)	Sale
17 June	Fiji	Woodpecker (MSC 209)	Kikau (204)	Sale
*23 June	Uruguay	Chickadee (MSF 59)	Cdmt Pedro Campbell (MSF 1)	Sale
8 July	Saudi Arabia	Unnamed (LCU type)	Al-Uqair (LCU 311)	Grant Aid
Aug	Spain	LCU 1471	—	Sale
Aug	Spain	LCU 1491	—	Sale
13 Sep	Philippines	Amick (DE 168)***	—	Sale
13 Sep	Philippines	Atherton (DE 169)***	—	Sale
13 Sep	Philippines	USNS LST 47 (T-LST 47)	Tarlac (LT 500)	Sale
13 Sep	Philippines	USNS LST 230 (T-LST 230)	Laguna (LT 501)	Sale
13 Sep	Philippines	USNS LST 287 (T-LST 287)	Samar Oriental (LT 502)	Sale
13 Sep	Philippines	USNS LST 491 (T-LST 491)	Lanao Del Sur (LT 503)	Sale
13 Sep	Philippines	USNS LST 566 (T-LST 566)	Lanao Del Norte (LT 504)	Sale
13 Sep	Philippines	USNS LST 607 (T-LST 607)	Leyte Del Sur (LT 505)	Sale
13 Sep	Philippines	USNS Davies County (T-LST 692)	Benegut (LT 507)	Sale
13 Sep	Philippines	USNS Harris County (T-LST 822)	Aurora (LT 508)	Sale
13 Sep	Philippines	USNS Orleans Parish (T-LST 1069)	Northern Cotabato (LT 511)	Sale
13 Sep	Philippines	USNS LST 1072 (T-LST 1072)	Tani-Tawi (LT 512)	Sale
16 Sep	Peru	Tench (SS 417)	(for cannibalisation and scrapping)	Sale
24 Sep	Philippines	Nansemond County (LST 1064)***	—	Sale
24 Sep	Philippines	LSSL 87***	—	Sale
24 Sep	Philippines	YTL 750***	—	Sale
24 Sep	Philippines	FS 408***	—	Sale
29 Sep	Dominican Republic	Etlah (AN 79)	Cambiaso (P 207)	Sale
29 Sep	Dominican Republic	Passaconaway (AN 86)	Separacion (P 208)	Sale
29 Sep	Dominican Republic	Passaic (AN 87)	Caleras (P 209)	Sale
7 Oct	Malaysia	Henry County (LST 824)	Sri Banggi (A 1501)	Sale
7 Oct	Malaysia	Sedgewick County (LST 1123)	Rajah Jarom (A 1502)	Sale
1977				
*12 Jan	Taiwan	ARD 9	Fo Wu No 5	Sale
*14 Jan	Argentina	Heermann (DD 532)	Brown (D 20)	Sale
*14 Jan	Argentina	Dortch (DD 670)	(for cannibalisation and scrapping)	Sale
*14 Jan	Argentina	Stembel (DD 644)	Rosales (D 22)	Sale
24 Jan	Philippines	Satyr (ARL 23)	Yakal	Sale
*31 Jan	South Korea	Minotaur (ARL 15)	Duk Su (ARL 1)	Sale
*31 Jan	South Korea	Erben (DD 631)	Chung Mu (DD 91)	Sale
*31 Jan	South Korea	Hickox (DD 673)	Pusan (DD 93)	Sale
*31 Jan	South Korea	Halsey Powell (DD 686)	Seoul (DD 92)	Sale
*31 Jan	South Korea	Chevalier (DD 805)	Chung Buk (DD 95)	Sale
*31 Jan	South Korea	Everett F. Larson (DD 830)	Jeong Buk (DD 96)	Sale
*11 Feb	Paraguay	YFB 82	—	Sale
*11 Feb	Paraguay	YFB 86	—	Sale
*11 Feb	Paraguay	YTL 211	YTL 559	Sale
*11 Feb	Paraguay	YTL 567	—	Sale
*11 Feb	Paraguay	YR 37	—	Sale
*11 Feb	Paraguay	AFDL 26	—	Sale
14 Feb	Ecuador	Summit County (LST 1148)	Hualcopo (T 55)	Sale

USA/ Introduction 639

Date of transfer	Recipient	USN Name/Hull Number	Recipient Name/Hull Number	Mode
23 Feb	South Korea	New (DD 818)	Taejon (DD 99)	Sale
23 Feb	South Korea	Richard E. Kraus (DD 849)	Kwang Ju (DD 90)	Sale
Feb	Colombia	Hale (DD 642)	(for cannibalisation and scrapping)	Sale
1 Mar	Iran	Amphion (AR 13)	Chahbahar (A 41)	Sale
1 Mar	Iran	Arco (ARD 29)	FD 4	Sale
7 Mar	West Germany	Ringgold (DD 500)	Z 2 (D 171)	Sale
7 Mar	West Germany	Wadsworth (DD 516)	Z 3 (D 172)	Sale
7 Mar	West Germany	Claxton (DD 571)	Z 4 (D 178)	Sale
7 Mar	West Germany	Dyson (DD 572)	Z 5 (D 179)	Sale
17 Mar	Greece	Gurke (DD 783)	Tombazis (D 215)	Sale
17 Mar	Greece	Terrell County (LST 1157)	Oinoussa (L 104)	Sale
17 Mar	Greece	Whitfield County (LST 1169)	Kos (L 116)	Sale
15 Apr	Taiwan	Fort Marion (LSD 22)	— (LSD 618)	Sale
25 Apr	Greece	Aulick (DD 569)	Sfendoni (D 85)	Sale
25 Apr	Greece	Charette (DD 581)	Velos (D 16)	Sale
25 Apr	Greece	Conner (DD 582)	Aspis (D 06)	Sale
25 Apr	Greece	Hall (DD 583)	Lonchi (D 56)	Sale
25 Apr	Greece	Brown (DD 546)	Navarinon (D 63)	Sale
25 Apr	Greece	Bradford (DD 545)	Thyella (D 28)	Sale
29 Apr	Pakistan	Wiltsie (DD 716)	Tariq (D 165)	Sale
29 Apr	Pakistan	Epperson (DD 719)	Taimur (D 166)	Sale
May	Greece	Josiah Willard Gibbs (AGOR 1)	(for cannibalisation and scrapping)	Sale
10 June	Taiwan	Rowan (DD 782)	Chao Yang	Sale
10 June	Taiwan	Richard B. Anderson (DD 786)	Kai Yang	Sale
16 June	Argentina	YTL 426	Chulupi (R 10)	Sale
16 June	Argentina	YTL 441	Mocovi (R 5)	Sale
16 June	Argentina	YTL 443	Capayan (R 16)	Sale
16 June	Argentina	YTL 444	Chiquiyon (R 18)	Sale
16 June	Argentina	YTL 445	Calchaqui (R 6)	Sale
16 June	Argentina	YTL 448	Morcoyan (R 19)	Sale
1 Oct	Taiwan	Sarsfield (DD 837)	Te Yang	Sale
1 Oct	Taiwan	Powers (DD 839)	Shen Yang	Sale
1 Oct	Ecuador	Chowanoc (ATF 100)	Chimborazo (106)	Sale
1 Dec	Taiwan	Grapple (ARS 7)	Ta Hu	Sale
5 Dec	Italy	Capitaine (SS 336)	Alfredo Cappellini (S 507)	Sale
5 Dec	Italy	Volador (SS 490)	Gianfranco Gazzana Priaroggia (S 501)	Sale
5 Dec	Italy	Pickerel (SS 524)	Primo Longobardo (S 502)	Sale
28 Dec	Brazil	Helios (ARB 12)	Belmonte (G 24)	Sale
28 Dec	Brazil	YFN 903	—	Sale
30 Dec	Venezuela	Vernon County (LST 1161)	Amazonas (T 21)	Sale
30 Dec	Venezuela	Quirinus (ARL 39)	Guyana (T 18)	Sale
30 Dec	Venezuela	ARD 13	DF 11	Sale
30 Dec	Venezuela	YR 48	—	Sale
30 Dec	Venezuela	Wannalancet (YTM 385)	Fabrio Gallipoli (R 14)	Sale
30 Dec	Venezuela	Sassacus (YTM 193)	Diana III (R 15)	Sale
30 Dec	Venezuela	Oswegatchie (YTM 778)	Jose Felix Ribas (R 13)	Sale
30 Dec	Venezuela	Utina (ATF 163)	Felipe Larrazabal (R 21)	Sale
30 Dec	Venezuela	Marietta (AN 82)	Puerto Santos (H 01)	Sale
30 Dec	Venezueal	Tunxis (AN 90)	(for cannibalisation and scrapping)	Sale
30 Dec	Venezuela	Waxsaw (AN 91)	(for cannibalisation and scrapping)	Sale

1978

Date of transfer	Recipient	USN Name/Hull Number	Recipient Name/Hull Number	Mode
10 Mar	Taiwan	Leonard F. Mason (DD 852)	—	Sale
31 Mar	South Korea	Grasp (ARS 24)	Chang Won (ARS 5)	Sale
31 Mar	Colombia	Ruchamkin (LPR 89)	Cordoba (DT 15)	Sale
31 Mar	Colombia	Choctaw (ATF 70)	Pedro De Heredia (RM 72)	Sale
31 Mar	Colombia	Kalmia (ATA 184)	Bahia Utria (RM 75)	Sale
31 Mar	Colombia	YTL 231	Teniente Ricardo Sorzano (RM 73)	Sale
31 Mar	Colombia	YFR 443	Quindio (RM 153)	Sale
31 Mar	Colombia	YFND 6	Victor Cubillos	Sale
3 Apr	Taiwan	YFND 19	—	Sale
3 Apr	Taiwan	LCU 1212	Ho Chi (LCU 401)	Sale
3 Apr	Taiwan	LCU 1218	Ho Huei (LCU 402)	Sale
3 Apr	Taiwan	LCU 1244	Ho Yao (LCU 403)	Sale
3 Apr	Taiwan	LCU 1367	Ho Deng (LCU 404)	Sale
3 Apr	Taiwan	LCU 1397	Ho Feng (LCU 405)	Sale
3 Apr	Taiwan	LCU 1429	Ho Chao (LCU 406)	Sale
3 Apr	Taiwan	LCU 1452	Ho Teng (LCU 407)	Sale
17 May	Spain	Noa (DD 841)	Blas De Lezo (D 65)	Sale
17 May	Spain	Eugene A. Greene (DD 711)	Churruca (D 61)	Sale
17 May	Spain	Furse (DD 882)	Gravina (D 62)	Sale
17 May	Spain	Leary (DD 879)	Langara (D 64)	Sale
17 May	Spain	O'Hare (DD 889)	Mendez Nunez (D 63)	Sale
17 May	Spain	Tom Green County (LST 1159)	Conde De Venadito (L 13)	Sale
17 May	Spain	Wexford County (LST 1168)	Martin Alvarez (L 12)	Sale
17 May	Spain	Terrebonne Parish (LST 1156)	Velasco (L 11)	Sale
1 June	Taiwan	Tawakoni (ATF 114)	Ta Han (ATF 324)	Sale
1 July	South Korea	William R. Rush (DD 714)	Kang Won (DD 922)	Sale
11 July	Greece	Rupertus (DD 851)	Kontouriotis (D 213)	Sale
11 July	Greece	Arnold J. Isbell (DD 869)	Sachtouris (D 214)	Sale
11 July	Greece	Tombigbee (AOG 11)	Ariadni (A 414)	Sale
11 July	Greece	Page County (LST 1076)	Kriti (L 171)	Sale
11 July	Greece	Ankachak (YTM 767)	Aias (A 412)	Sale
12 July	Mexico	AFDL 28	—	Sale
12 July	Mexico	Park County (LST 1077)	Rio Panuco (IA 01)	Sale
12 July	Mexico	YD 156	—	Sale
12 July	Mexico	YD 157	—	Sale
12 July	Mexico	YD 180	—	Sale
12 July	Mexico	YD 183	—	Sale
12 July	Mexico	YD 203	—	Sale
1 Aug	Mexico	Molala (ATF 106)	R-7 (chg. to OTOMI (A 17) within after transfer)	Sale
30 Aug	Ecuador	Enright (APD 66)	Moran Valverde (D 01)	Sale
30 Aug	Ecuador	Cusabo (ATF 155)	Cayambe (R 101)	Sale
30 Aug	Ecuador	Army FS 525	Calicuchima (T 53)	Sale
30 Aug	Ecuador	Mulberry (AN 27)	Orion (0 111)	Sale
30 Aug	Ecuador	Eunice (PCE 846)	Esmeraldes (P 22)	Sale
30 Aug	Ecuador	Pascagoula (PCE 874)	Manabi (P 23)	Sale
31 Aug	Philippines	Booth (FF 170)	Datu Kalantiaw (PS 76)	Sale
31 Aug	Philippines	USCG Nettle (WAK 169)	Limasawa (TK 79)	Sale
1 Sep	Ecuador	Holder (DD 819)	Presidente Eloy Alfaro	Sale
1 Sep	Venezuela	Nipmuc (ATF 157)	Antonio Picardi (R 22)	Sale
1 Sep	Venezuela	Salinan (ATF 161)	Miguel Rodriquez (R 23)	Sale
30 Sep	Mexico	Abnaki (ATF 96)	Yaqui (A 18)	Sale
30 Sep	Mexico	Cocopa (ATF 101)	Seri (A 19)	Sale
30 Sep	Mexico	Hitchiti (ATF 103)	Cora (A 20	Sale
16 Oct	Dom. Republic	Samoset (ATA 190)	—	Sale
19 Dec	Iran	Trout (SS 566)	Kousseh (S 101)	Sale

UNITED STATES SHIP HULL NUMBERS

(Type designations in order of arrangement within this volume; ships are in numerical sequence)

Strategic Missile Submarines

SSBN—Fleet Ballistic Missile Submarines

"George Washington" Class
598 George Washington
599 Patrick Henry
600 Theodore Roosevelt
601 Robert E. Lee
602 Abraham Lincoln

"Ethan Allen" Class
608 Ethan Allen
609 Sam Houston
610 Thomas A. Edison
611 John Marshall

"Lafayette" Class
616 Lafayette
617 Alexander Hamilton

"Ethan Allen" Class (Cont'd)
618 Thomas Jefferson

"Lafayette" Class (Cont'd)
619 Andrew Jackson
620 John Adams
622 James Monroe
623 Nathan Hale
624 Woodrow Wilson
625 Henry Clay
626 Daniel Webster
627 James Madison
628 Tecumseh
629 Daniel Boone
630 John C. Calhoun
631 Ulysses S. Grant
632 Von Steuben
633 Casimir Pulaski
634 Stonewall Jackson
635 Sam Rayburn
636 Nathanael Greene
640 Benjamin Franklin
641 Simon Bolivar
642 Kamehameha
643 George Bancroft
644 Lewis and Clark
645 James K. Polk
654 George C. Marshall
655 Henry L. Stimson
656 George Washington Carver
657 Francis Scott Key
658 Mariano G. Vallejo
659 Will Rogers

"Ohio" Class
726 Ohio
727 Michigan

Submarines

SS/SSN—Attack Submarines
AGSS—Auxiliary Submarines
SSG—Guided Missile Submarines

"Dolphin" Class (AGSS)
555 Dolphin

"Tang" Class (SS)
563 Tang
565 Wahoo
567 Gudgeon (AGSS)

"Albacore" Class (AGSS)
569 Albacore

"Nautilus" Class (SSN)
571 Nautilus

"Grayback" Class (LPSS)
574 Grayback SS

"Seawolf" Class (SSN)
575 Seawolf

"Darter" Class (SS)
576 Darter

"Grayback" Class (SSG)
577 Growler

"Skate" Class (SSN)
578 Skate
579 Swordfish

"Barbel" Class (SS)
580 Barbel
581 Blueback
582 Bonefish

"Skate" Class (SSN) (Cont'd)
583 Sargo
584 Seadragon

"Skipjack" Class (SSN)
585 Skipjack

"Triton" Class (SSN)
586 Triton

"Halibut" Class (SSN)
587 Halibut

"Skipjack" Class (SSN) (Cont'd)
588 Scamp
590 Sculpin
591 Shark
592 Snook

"Thresher" Class (SSN)
594 Permit
595 Plunger
596 Barb

"Tullibee" Class (SSN)
597 Tullibee

"Thresher" Class (SSN) (Cont'd)
603 Pollack
604 Haddo
605 Jack
606 Tinosa
607 Dace
612 Guardfish
613 Flasher
614 Greenling
615 Gato
621 Haddock

"Sturgeon" Class (SSN)
637 Sturgeon
638 Whale
639 Tautog
646 Grayling
647 Pogy
648 Aspro
649 Sunfish
650 Pargo
651 Queenfish
652 Puffer
653 Ray
660 Sand Lance
661 Lapon
662 Gurnard
663 Hammerhead
664 Sea Devil
665 Guitarro
666 Hawkbill
667 Bergall
668 Spadefish
669 Seahorse
670 Finback

"Narwhal" Class (SSN)
671 Narwhal

"Sturgeon" Class (SSN) (Cont'd)
672 Pintado
673 Flying Fish
674 Trepang
675 Bluefish
676 Billfish
677 Drum
678 Archerfish
679 Silversides
680 William H. Bates
681 Batfish
682 Tunny
683 Parche
684 Cavalla

"Glenard P. Lipscomb" Class (SSN)
685 Glenard P. Lipscomb

"Sturgeon" Class (SSN) (Cont'd)
686 L. Mendel Rivers
687 Richard B. Russell

"Los Angeles" Class (SSN)
688 Los Angeles
689 Baton Rouge
690 Philadelphia
691 Memphis
692 Omaha
693 Cincinnati
694 Groton
695 Birmingham
696 New York City
697 Indianapolis
698 Bremerton
699 Jacksonville
700 Dallas
701 La Jolla
702 Phoenix
703 Boston
704 Baltimore
711 San Francisco

Aircraft Carriers

CV, CVA, CVN—Attack Aircraft Carriers
CVS—ASW Aircraft Carriers
AVT—Auxiliary Aircraft Landing Training Ship

"Intrepid" Class
11 Intrepid (CVS)

"Essex" Class
12 Hornet (CVS)

"Intrepid" Class (Cont'd)
16 Lexington (AVT)

"Essex" Class (Cont'd)
20 Bennington (CVS)

"Hancock" Class
31 Bon Homme Richard (CVA)
34 Oriskany (CV)

"Intrepid" Class (Cont'd)
38 Shangri-La (CVS)

"Midway" Class (CV)
41 Midway
43 Coral Sea

"Forrestal" Class (CV)
59 Forrestal
60 Saratoga
61 Ranger
62 Independence

"Kitty Hawk" Class (CV)
63 Kitty Hawk
64 Constellation

"Enterprise" Class (CVN)
65 Enterprise

"Kitty Hawk" Class (CV) (Cont'd)
66 America

"John F. Kennedy" Class (CV)
67 John F. Kennedy

"Nimitz" Class (CVN)
68 Nimitz
69 Dwight D. Eisenhower
70 Carl Vinson

Battleships

BB—Battleships

"Iowa" Class
61 Iowa
62 New Jersey
63 Missouri
64 Wisconsin

Cruisers

CG/CGN—Guided Missile Cruisers

Converted "Cleveland" Class (CG)
5 Oklahoma City

"Long Beach" Class (CGN)
9 Long Beach

"Albany" Class (CG)
10 Albany
11 Chicago

"Leahy" Class
16 Leahy
17 Harry E. Yarnell
18 Worden
19 Dale
20 Richmond K. Turner
21 Gridley
22 England
23 Halsey
24 Reeves

"Bainbridge" Class (CGN)
25 Bainbridge

"Belknap" Class (CG)
26 Belknap
27 Josephus Daniels
28 Wainwright
29 Jouett
30 Horne
31 Sterett
32 William H. Standley
33 Fox
34 Biddle

"Truxtun" Class (CGN)
35 Truxtun

USA/ Introduction

"California" Class (CGN)
- 36 California
- 37 South Carolina

"Virginia" Class (CGN)
- 38 Virginia
- 39 Texas
- 40 Mississippi
- 41 Arkansas

—Gun Cruisers

"Des Moines" Class
- 134 Des Moines
- 139 Salem

Destroyers

DG—Guided Missile Destroyers

"Charles F. Adams" Class
- 2 Charles F. Adams
- 3 John King
- 4 Lawrence
- 5 Claude V. Ricketts
- 6 Barney
- 7 Henry B. Wilson
- 8 Lynde McCormick
- 9 Towers
- 10 Sampson
- 11 Sellers
- 12 Robison
- 13 Hoel
- 14 Buchanan
- 15 Berkeley
- 16 Joseph Strauss
- 17 Conyngham
- 18 Semmes
- 19 Tattnall
- 20 Goldsborough
- 21 Cochrane
- 22 Benjamin Stoddert
- 23 Richard E. Byrd
- 24 Waddell

Converted "Forrest Sherman" Class
- 31 Decatur
- 32 John Paul Jones
- 33 Parsons
- 34 Somers

"Coontz" Class
- 37 Farragut
- 38 Luce
- 39 MacDonough
- 40 Coontz
- 41 King
- 42 Mahan
- 43 Dahlgren
- 44 William V. Pratt
- 45 Dewey
- 46 Preble

D—Destroyers

"Gearing" Class
- 718 Hamner
- 743 Southerland
- 763 William C. Lawe
- 784 McKean
- 785 Henderson
- 788 Hollister
- 806 Higbee
- 817 Corry
- 821 Johnston
- 822 Robert H. McCard

"Carpenter" Class
- 825 Carpenter
- 827 Robert A. Owens

"Gearing" Class (Cont'd)
- 829 Myles C. Fox
- 835 Charles P. Cecil
- 842 Fiske
- 862 Vogelgesang
- 863 Steinaker
- 864 Harold J. Ellison
- 866 Cone
- 871 Damato
- 873 Hawkins
- 876 Rogers
- 880 Dyess
- 883 Newman K. Perry
- 885 John R. Craig
- 886 Orleck
- 890 Meredith

"Forrest Sherman" Class
- 931 Forrest Sherman
- 933 Barry
- 937 Davis
- 938 Jonas Ingram
- 940 Manley
- 941 Dupont
- 942 Bigelow
- 943 Blandy
- 944 Mullinnix

"Hull" Class
- 945 Hull
- 946 Edson
- 948 Morton
- 950 Richard S. Edwards
- 951 Turner Joy

"Spruance" Class
- 963 Spruance
- 964 Paul F. Foster
- 965 Kinkaid
- 966 Hewitt
- 967 Elliot
- 968 Arthur W. Radford
- 969 Peterson
- 970 Caron
- 971 David R. Ray
- 972 Oldendorf
- 973 John Young
- 974 Comte de Grasse
- 975 O'Brien
- 976 Merrill
- 977 Briscoe
- 978 Stump
- 979 Conolly
- 980 Moosburgger
- 981 John Hancock
- 982 Nicholson
- 983 John Rodgers
- 984 Leftwich
- 985 Cushing
- 986 Harry W. Hill
- 987 O'Bannon
- 988 Thorn
- 989 Deyo
- 990 Ingersoll
- 991 Fife
- 992 Fletcher

Frigates

FFG—Guided Missile Frigates

"Brooke" Class
- 1 Brooke
- 2 Ramsey
- 3 Schofield
- 4 Talbot
- 5 Richard L. Page
- 6 Julius A. Furer

"Oliver Hazard Perry" Class
- 7 Oliver Hazard Perry
- 8 McInerney
- 9 Wadsworth
- 10 Duncan
- 11 Clark
- 12 George Philip
- 13 Samuel E. Morison
- 14 Sides
- 20 Antrim

FF—Frigates

"Bronstein" Class
- 1037 Bronstein
- 1038 McCloy

"Garcia" Class
- 1040 Garcia
- 1041 Bradley
- 1043 Edward McDonnell
- 1044 Brumby
- 1045 Davidson
- 1047 Voge
- 1048 Sample
- 1049 Koelsch
- 1050 Albert David
- 1051 O'Callahan

"Knox" Class
- 1052 Knox
- 1053 Roark
- 1054 Gray
- 1055 Hepburn
- 1056 Connole
- 1057 Rathburne
- 1058 Mayerkord
- 1059 W. S. Sims
- 1060 Lang
- 1061 Patterson
- 1062 Whipple
- 1063 Reasoner
- 1064 Lockwood
- 1065 Stein
- 1066 Marvin Shields
- 1067 Francis Hammond
- 1068 Vreeland
- 1069 Bagley
- 1070 Downes
- 1071 Badger
- 1072 Blakely
- 1073 Robert E. Peary
- 1074 Harold E. Holt
- 1075 Trippe
- 1076 Fanning
- 1077 Ouellet
- 1078 Joseph Hewes
- 1079 Bowen
- 1080 Paul
- 1081 Aylwin
- 1082 Elmer Montgomery
- 1083 Cook
- 1084 McCandless
- 1085 Donald B. Beary
- 1086 Brewton
- 1087 Kirk
- 1088 Barbey
- 1089 Jesse L. Brown
- 1090 Ainsworth
- 1091 Miller
- 1092 Thomas C. Hart
- 1093 Capodanno
- 1094 Pharris
- 1095 Truett
- 1096 Valdez
- 1097 Moinester

"Glover" Class
- 1098 Glover

Patrol Ships and Craft

PHM—Guided Missile Patrol Combatants (Hydrofoil)

"Pegasus" Class
- 1 Pegasus
- 2 Hercules
- 3 Taurus
- 4 Aquila
- 5 Aries
- 6 Gemini

PCH—Patrol Craft (Hydrofoil)

"High Point" Class
- 1 High Point

PG—Patrol Combatants

"Asheville" Class
- 92 Tacoma
- 93 Welch
- 99 Beacon
- 101 Green Bay

Amphibious Warships

LCC—Amphibious Command Ships (ex-AGC)

"Blue Ridge" Class
- 19 Blue Ridge
- 20 Mount Whitney

LHA—Amphibious Assault Ships (General Purpose)

"Tarawa" Class
- 1 Tarawa
- 2 Saipan
- 3 Belleau Wood
- 4 Nassau
- 5 Peleliu

LKA—Amphibious Cargo Ships

"Tulare" Class
- 112 Tulare

"Charleston" Class
- 113 Charleston
- 114 Durham
- 115 Mobile
- 116 St. Louis
- 117 El Paso

LPH—Amphibious Assault Ships (Helicopter)

"Iwo Jima" Class
- 2 Iwo Jima
- 3 Okinawa
- 7 Guadalcanal
- 9 Guam
- 10 Tripoli
- 11 New Orleans
- 12 Inchon

LPA—Amphibious Transports

"Paul Revere" Class
- 248 Paul Revere
- 249 Francis Marion

LPD—Amphibious Transport Docks

"Raleigh" Class
- 1 Raleigh
- 2 Vancouver

"Austin" Class
- 4 Austin
- 5 Ogden
- 6 Duluth
- 7 Cleveland
- 8 Dubuque
- 9 Denver
- 10 Juneau
- 11 Coronado
- 12 Shreveport
- 13 Nashville
- 14 Trenton
- 15 Ponce

USA / Introduction

LSD—Dock Landing Ships

"Thomaston" Class
- 28 Thomaston
- 29 Plymouth Rock
- 30 Fort Snelling
- 31 Point Defiance
- 32 Spiegel Grove
- 33 Alamo
- 34 Hermitage
- 35 Monticello

"Anchorage" Class
- 36 Anchorage
- 37 Portland
- 38 Pensacola
- 39 Mt Vernon
- 40 Fort Fisher

LST—Tank Landing Ships

"De Soto County" Class
- 1173 Suffolk County
- 1177 Lorain County
- 1178 Wood County

"Newport" Class
- 1179 Newport
- 1180 Manitowoc
- 1181 Sumter
- 1182 Fresno
- 1183 Peoria
- 1184 Frederick
- 1185 Schenectady
- 1186 Cayuga
- 1187 Tuscaloosa
- 1188 Saginaw
- 1189 San Bernardino
- 1190 Boulder
- 1191 Racine
- 1192 Spartanburg County
- 1193 Fairfax County
- 1194 La Moure County
- 1195 Barbour County
- 1196 Harlan County
- 1197 Barnstable County
- 1198 Bristol County

Mine Warfare Ships

MSO—Ocean Minesweepers

"Aggressive" and "Dash" Classes
- 427 Constant
- 428 Dash
- 429 Detector
- 430 Direct
- 431 Dominant
- 433 Engage
- 437 Enhance
- 438 Esteem
- 439 Excel
- 440 Exploit
- 441 Exultant
- 442 Fearless
- 443 Fidelity
- 446 Fortify
- 448 Illusive
- 449 Impervious
- 455 Implicit
- 456 Inflict
- 464 Pluck
- 488 Conquest
- 489 Gallant
- 490 Leader
- 492 Pledge

"Acme" Class
- 509 Adroit
- 511 Affray

Auxiliary Ships

AD—Destroyer Tenders

"Dixie" Class
- 14 Dixie
- 15 Prairie
- 17 Piedmont
- 18 Sierra
- 19 Yosemite

"Klondike" and "Shenandoah" Classes
- 24 Everglades
- 26 Shenandoah
- 36 Bryce Canyon

"Samuel Gompers" Class
- 37 Samuel Gompers
- 38 Puget Sound

"Yellowstone" Class
- 41 Yellowstone
- 42 Acadia

AE—Ammunition Ships

"Suribachi" Class
- 21 Suribachi
- 22 Mauna Kea
- 23 Nitro
- 24 Pyro
- 25 Haleakala

"Kilauea" Class
- 26 Kilauea
- 27 Butte
- 28 Santa Barbara
- 29 Mount Hood
- 32 Flint
- 33 Shasta
- 34 Mount Baker
- 35 Kiska

AFS—Combat Store Ships

"Mars" Class
- 1 Mars
- 2 Sylvania
- 3 Niagara Falls
- 4 White Plains
- 5 Concord
- 6 San Diego
- 7 San Jose

AG—Miscellaneous

"Compass Island" Class
- 153 Compass Island

"Vanguard" Class
- 194 Vanguard

AGF—Miscellaneous Flagship

- 3 La Salle

AH—Hospital Ship

- 17 Sanctuary

AO—Oilers

"Jumboised Cimarron" Class
- 51 Ashtabula
- 98 Caloosahatchee
- 99 Canisteo

"Neosho" Class
- 143 Neosho (MSC)
- 144 Mississinewa (MSC)
- 145 Hassayampa (MSC)
- 146 Kawishiwi
- 147 Truckee
- 148 Ponchatoula

"Cimarron" Class
- 177 Cimarron
- 178 Monongahela
- 179 Merrimack

AOE—Fast Combat Support Ships

"Sacramento" Class
- 1 Sacramento
- 2 Camden
- 3 Seattle
- 4 Detroit

AOR—Replenishment Oilers

"Wichita" Class
- 1 Wichita
- 2 Milwaukee
- 3 Kansas City
- 4 Savannah
- 5 Wabash
- 6 Kalamazoo
- 7 Roanoke

APB/IX—Self-Propelled Barracks Ships

- 502 Mercer
- 503 Nueces
- 504 Echols

AR—Repair Ships

"Vulcan" Class
- 5 Vulcan
- 6 Ajax
- 7 Hector
- 8 Jason

ARL—Repair Ship, Small

"Achelous" Class
- 24 Sphinx

ARS—Salvage Ships

"Diver" and "Bolster" Classes
- 8 Preserver
- 23 Deliver
- 25 Safeguard
- 33 Clamp
- 34 Gear
- 38 Bolster
- 39 Conserver
- 40 Hoist
- 41 Opportune
- 42 Reclaimer
- 43 Recovery

AS—Submarine Tenders

"Fulton" Class
- 11 Fulton
- 12 Sperry
- 15 Bushnell
- 16 Howard W. Gilmore
- 17 Nereus
- 18 Orion

"Proteus" Class
- 19 Proteus

"Hunley" Class
- 31 Hunley
- 32 Holland

"Simon Lake" Class
- 33 Simon Lake
- 34 Canopus

"L.Y. Spear" Class
- 36 L.Y. Spear
- 37 Dixon

"Emory S. Land" Class
- 39 Emory S. Land
- 40 Frank Cable
- 41 McKee

ASR—Submarine Rescue Ships

"Chanticleer" Class
- 9 Florikan
- 13 Kittiwake
- 14 Petrel
- 15 Sunbird

"Pigeon" Class
- 21 Pigeon
- 22 Ortolan

ATA—Auxiliary Tugs

"Sotoyomo" Class
- 181 Accokeek
- 193 Stallion
- 213 Keywadin

ATF—Fleet Tugs

"Cherokee" and "Abnaki" Classes
- 76 Ute
- 84 Cree
- 85 Lipan
- 91 Seneca
- 110 Quapaw
- 113 Takelma
- 149 Atakapa
- 158 Mosospelea
- 159 Paiute
- 160 Papago
- 162 Shakori

"Powhatan" Class
- 166 Powhatan
- 167 Narragansett
- 168 Catawba
- 169 Navajo

ATS—Salvage and Rescue Ships

"Edenton" Class
- 1 Edenton
- 2 Beaufort
- 3 Brunswick

USA/ Introduction

Military Sealift Command

Note: All ships of MSC have T prefix.

AF—Store Ship

"Rigel" Class
58 Rigel

AG—Miscellaneous

164 Kingsport

AGM—Range Instrumentation Ships

8   Wheeling
9   General H. H. Arnold
10 General Hoyt S. Vandenberg
20 Redstone
22 Range Sentinel

AGOR—Oceanographic Research Ships

3   Robert D. Conrad
4   James M. Gilliss
7   Lynch
9   Thomas G. Thompson
11 Mizar
12 De Steiguer
13 Bartlett
14 Melville
15 Knorr
16 Hayes
21 Gyre
22 Moana Wave

AGS—Surveying Ships

21 Bowditch
22 Dutton
26 Silas Bent
27 Kane
29 Chauvenet
32 Harkness
33 Wilkes
34 Wyman
38 H. H. Hess

AK—Cargo Ships

"Greenville Victory" Class
237 Greenville Victory

240 Pvt. John R. Towle
242 Sgt. Andrew Miller
254 Sgt. Truman Kimbro

"Private Leonard C. Brostrom" Class
255 Pvt. Leonard C. Brostrom

"Eltanin" Class
271 Mirfak

"Greenville Victory" Class (Cont'd)
274 Lieut. James E. Robinson

"Schuyler Otis Bland" Class
277 Schuyler Otis Bland

"Norwalk" Class
279 Norwalk
280 Furman
281 Victoria
282 Marshfield

"Wyandot" Class
283 Wyandot

AKR—Vehicle Cargo Ships

"Comet" Class
7   Comet

"Meteor" Class
9   Meteor

AOT—Transport Oilers

"Suamico" Class
50 Tallulah

"Cimarron" Class
57 Marias
62 Taluga

"Suamico" Class (Cont'd)
67 Cache
73 Millicoma
75 Saugatuck
76 Schuylkill
78 Chepachet

"Jumboised Mispillion" Class
105 Mispillion
106 Navasota
107 Pasumpsic
108 Pawcatuck
109 Waccamaw

"Mission" Class
134 Mission Santa Ynez

"Maumee" Class
149 Maumee
151 Shoshone
152 Yukon

"American Explorer" Class
165 American Explorer

"Sealift" Class
168 Sealift Pacific
169 Sealift Arabian Sea
170 Sealift China Sea
171 Sealift Indian Ocean
172 Sealift Atlantic
173 Sealift Mediterranean
174 Sealift Caribbean
175 Sealift Arctic
176 Sealift Antarctic

"Potomac" Class
181 Potomac

"Columbia" Class
182 Columbia
183 Neches
184 Hudson
185 Susquehanna

AOG—Gasoline Tankers

"Peconic" Class
77 Rincon
78 Nodaway
79 Petaluma

"Alatna" Class
81 Alatna
82 Chattahoochee

ARC—Cable Ships

2 Neptune
3 Aeolus
6 Albert J. Meyer

KITTY HAWK AND SAMPLE REFUELLING   1978

644 USA/ Introduction

AIRCRAFT CARRIERS

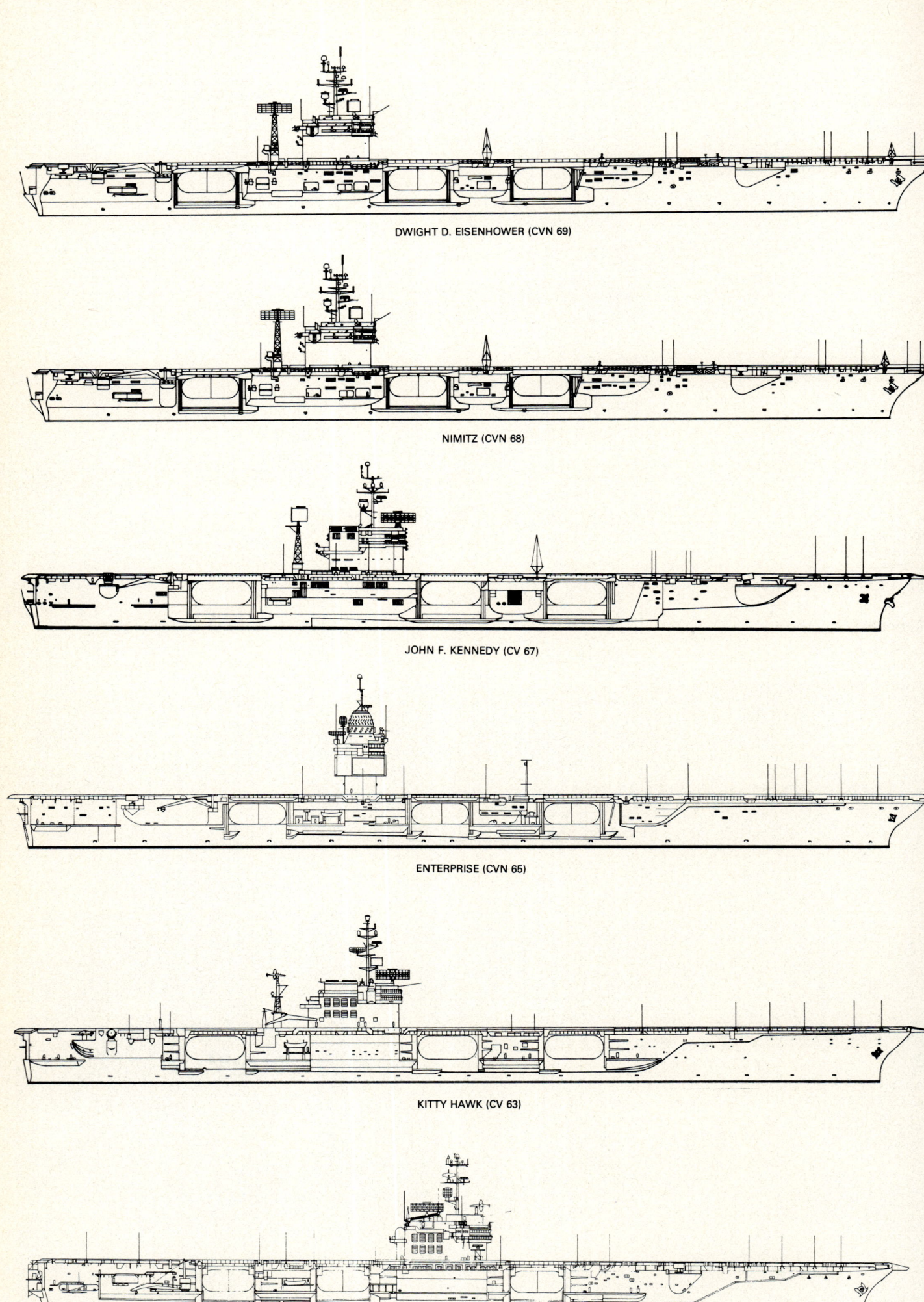

DWIGHT D. EISENHOWER (CVN 69)

NIMITZ (CVN 68)

JOHN F. KENNEDY (CV 67)

ENTERPRISE (CVN 65)

KITTY HAWK (CV 63)

INDEPENDENCE (CV 62)

Scale: 1 inch = 150 feet (1 : 1 800)

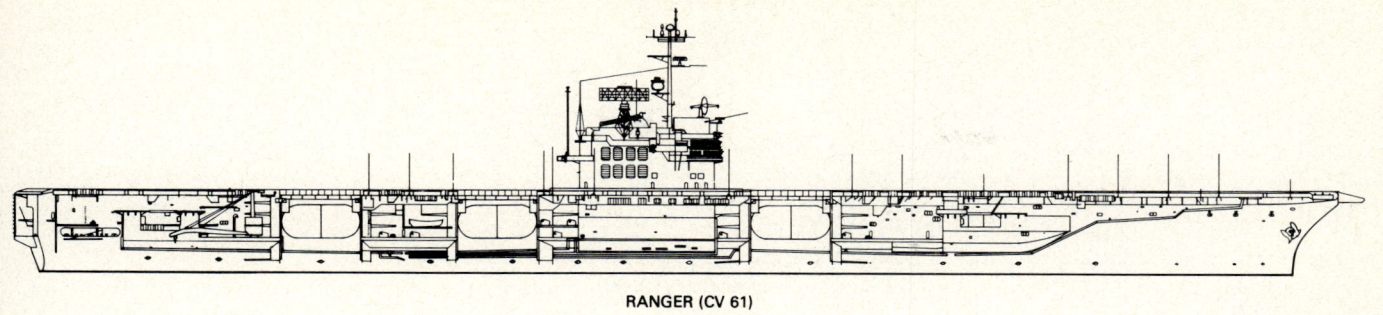
RANGER (CV 61)

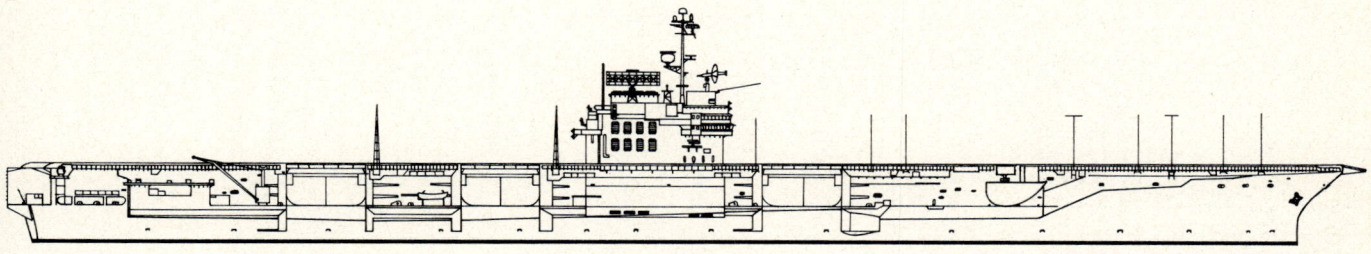
SARATOGA (CV 60)

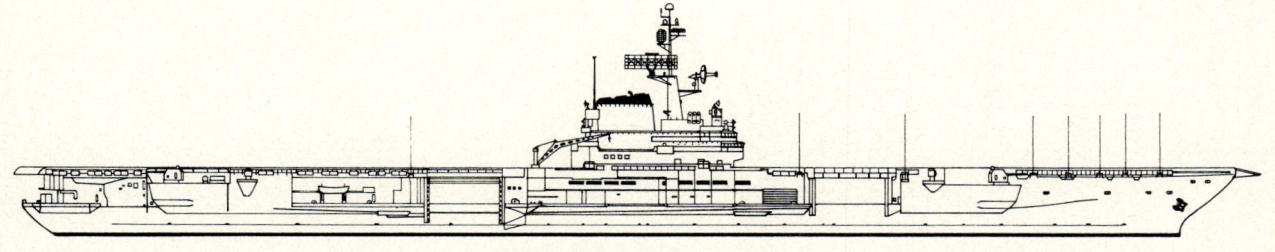
CORAL SEA (CV 43) "Midway" Class

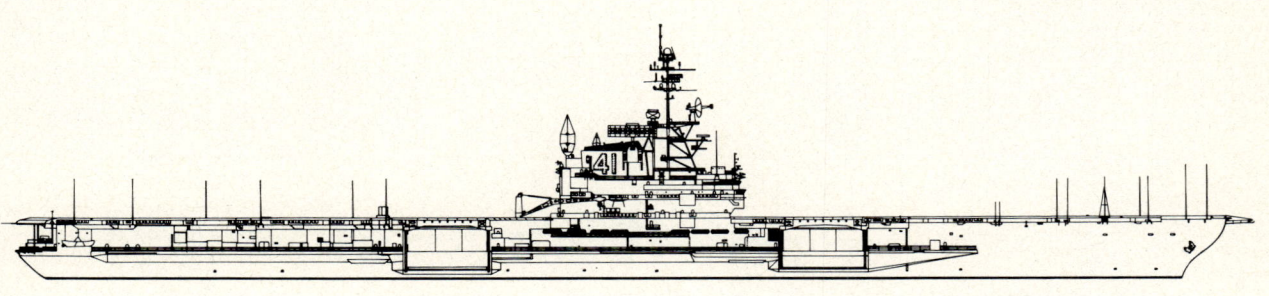
MIDWAY (CV 41)

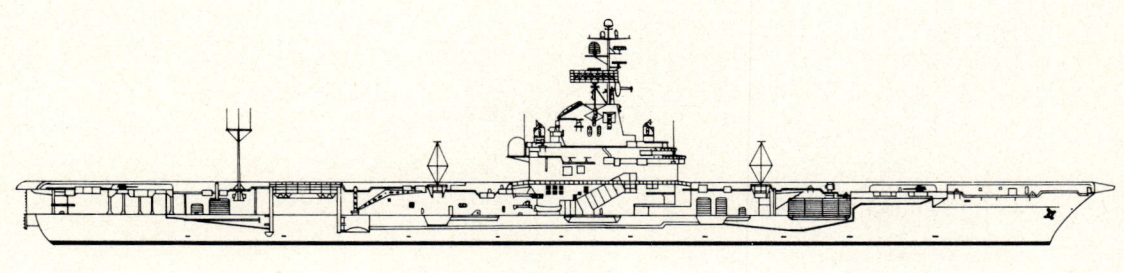
"HANCOCK" Class

Scale: 1 inch = 150 feet (1 : 1 800)

BATTLESHIPS

NEW JERSEY (BB 62)

CRUISERS

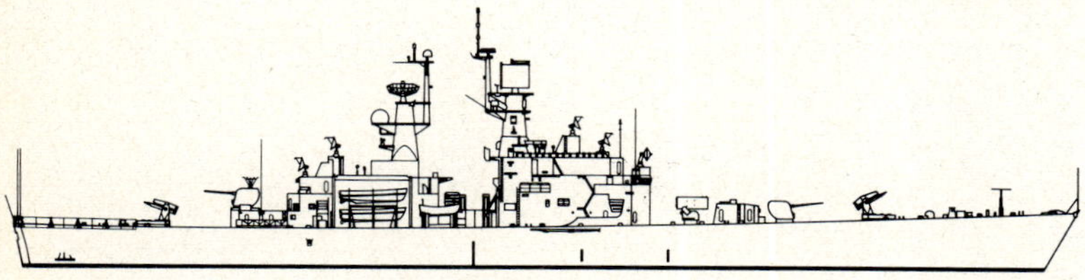

CALIFORNIA (CGN 36)

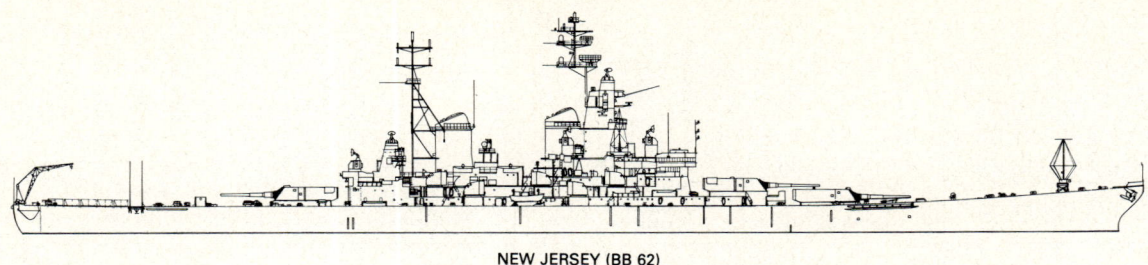

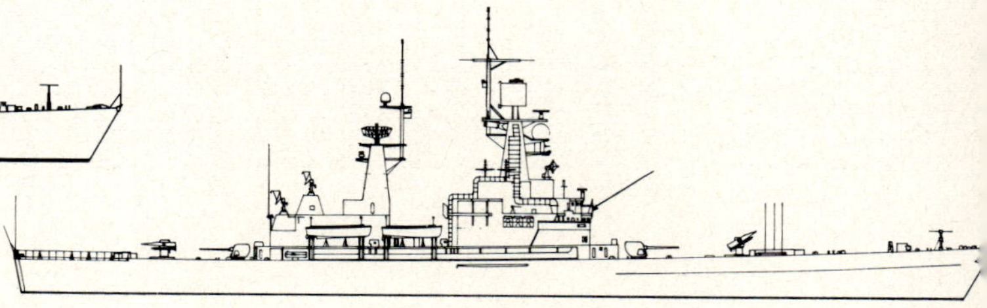

VIRGINIA (CGN 38)

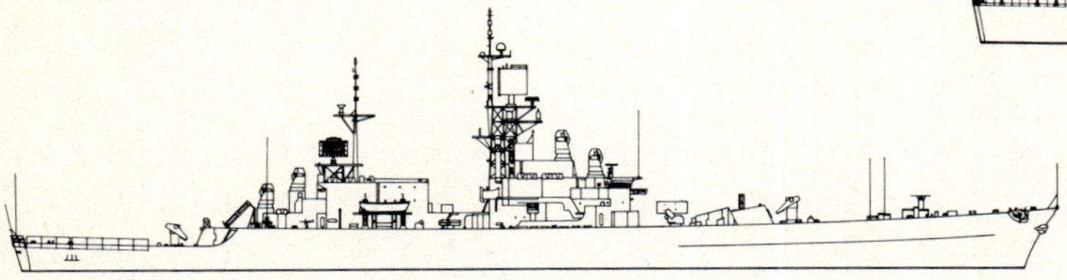

BAINBRIDGE (CGN 25)

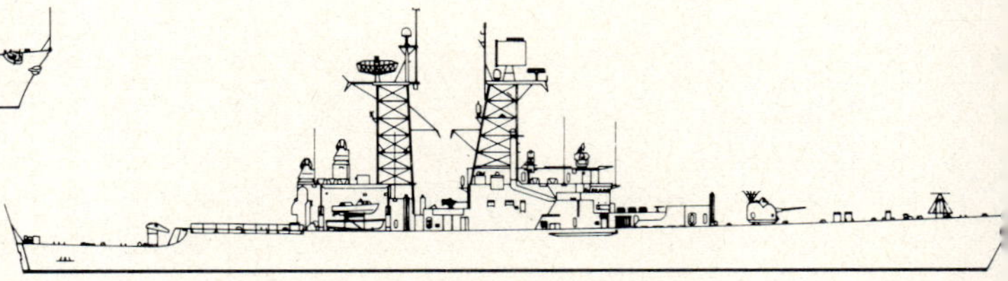

TRUXTUN (CGN 35)

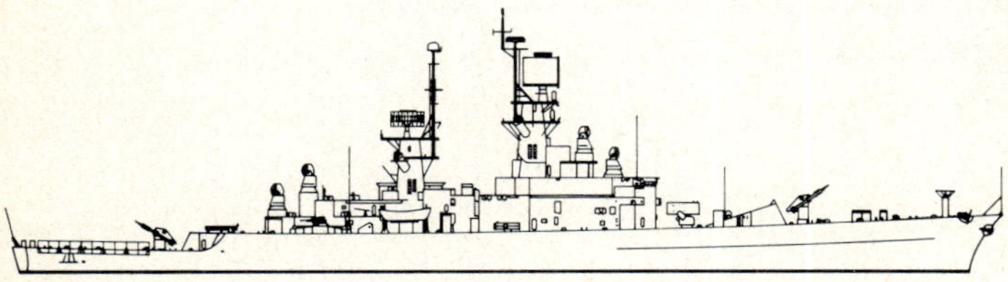

LEAHY (CG 16)

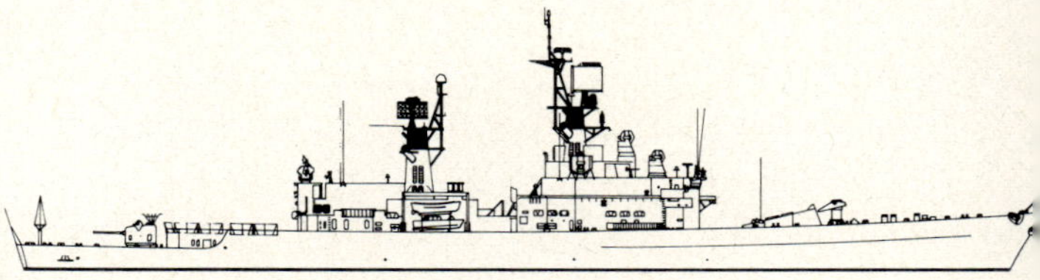

WAINWRIGHT (CG 28)

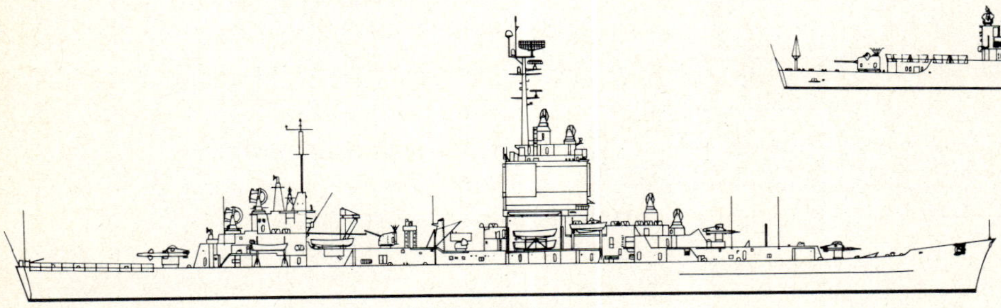

LONG BEACH (CGN 9)

DESTROYERS

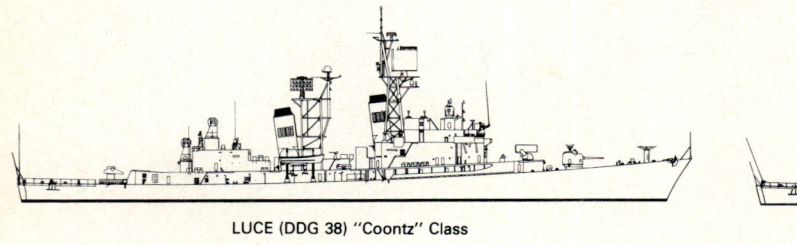

LUCE (DDG 38) "Coontz" Class

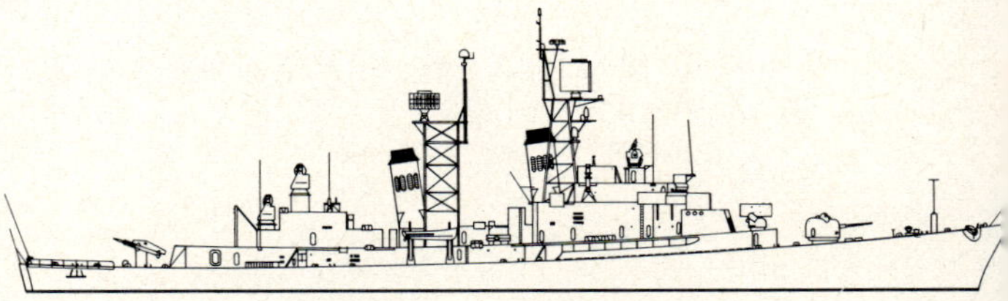

FARRAGUT (DDG 37) "Coontz" Class

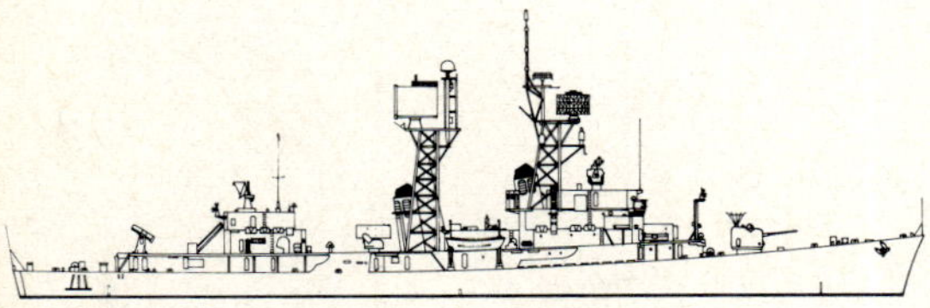

DECATUR (DDG 31)

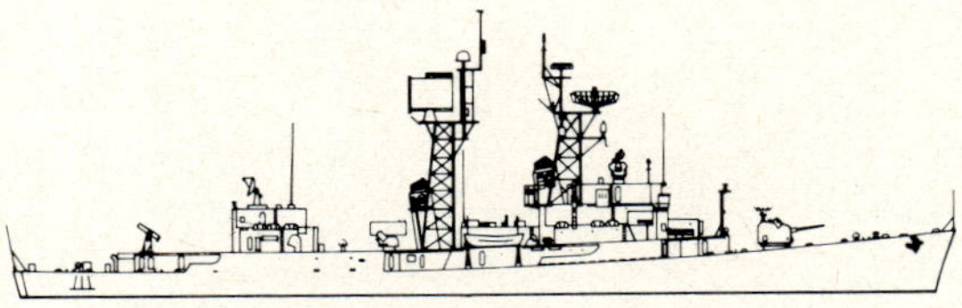

SOMERS (DDG 34) Converted "Forrest Sherman" Class

Scale: 1 inch = 150 feet (1 : 1 800)

USA/ Introduction 647

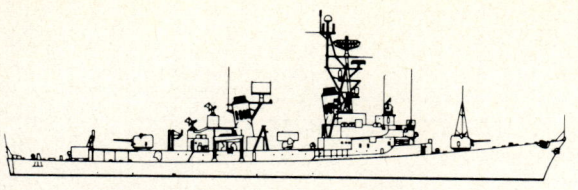
WADDELL (DDG 24) "Charles F. Adams" Class

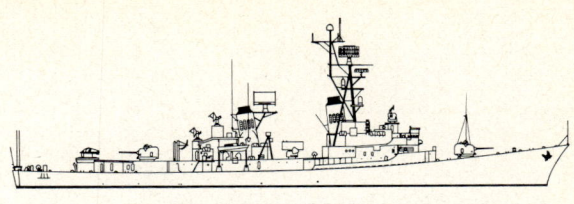
BARNEY (DDG 6) "Charles F. Adams" Class

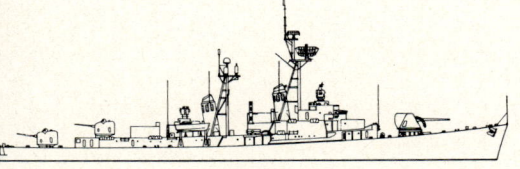
HULL (DD 945)

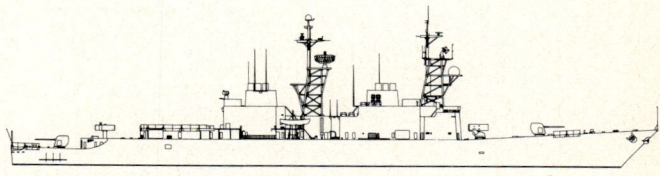
SPRUANCE (DD 963)

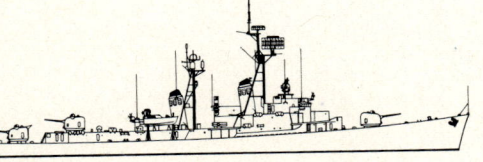
TURNER JOY (DD 951) "Forrest Sherman" Class

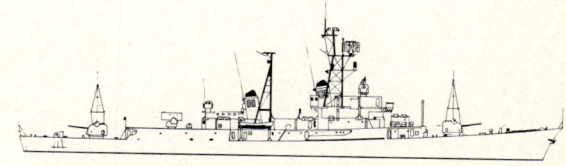
JONAS INGRAM (DD 938) "Forrest Sherman" Class (ASW)

BARRY (DD 933) "Forrest Sherman" Class (ASW)

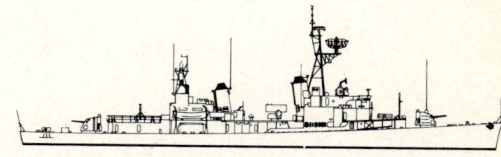
"GEARING" Class FRAM I (all guns forward and aft)

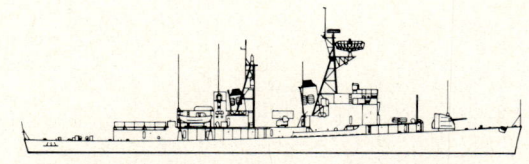
ROBERT A. OWENS (DD 827) "Carpenter" Class FRAM I

FRIGATES

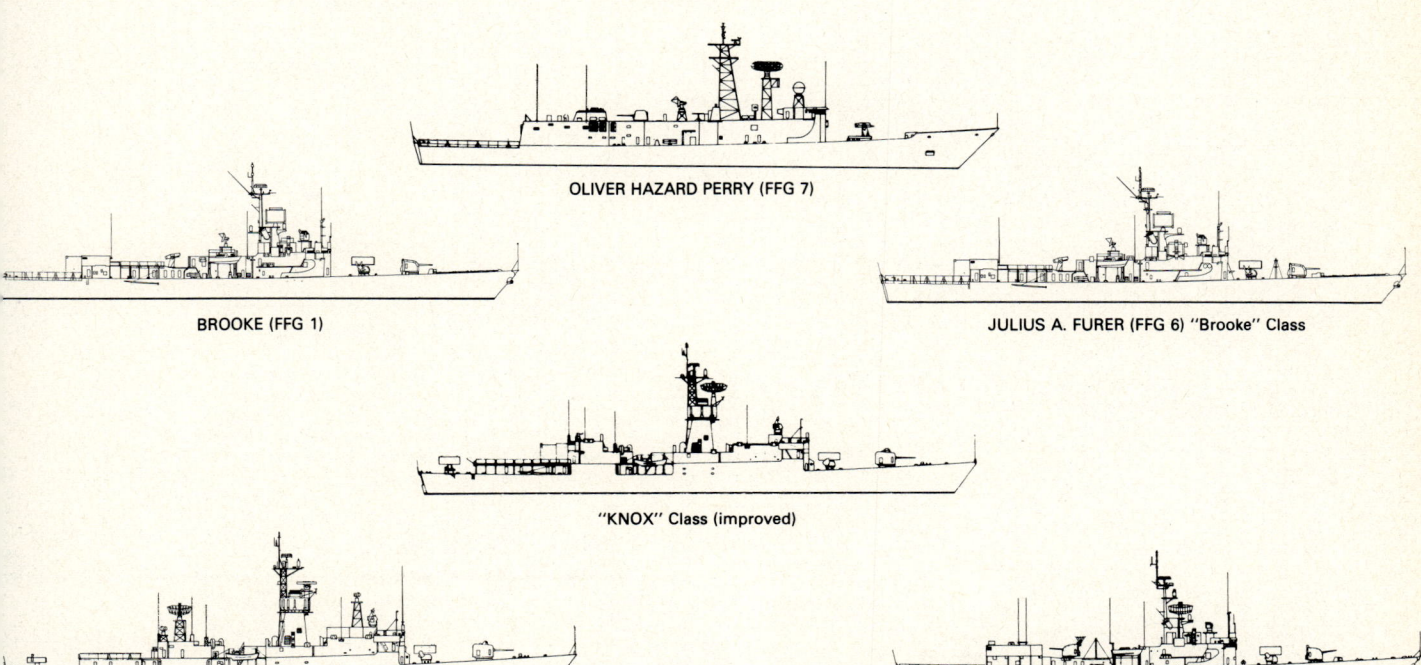

OLIVER HAZARD PERRY (FFG 7)

BROOKE (FFG 1)

JULIUS A. FURER (FFG 6) "Brooke" Class

"KNOX" Class (improved)

DOWNES (FF 1070) NATO Sea Sparrow

"GARCIA" Class (LAMPS Modification)

SAMPLE (FF 1048) "Garcia" Class

Scale: 1 inch = 150 feet (1 : 1 800)

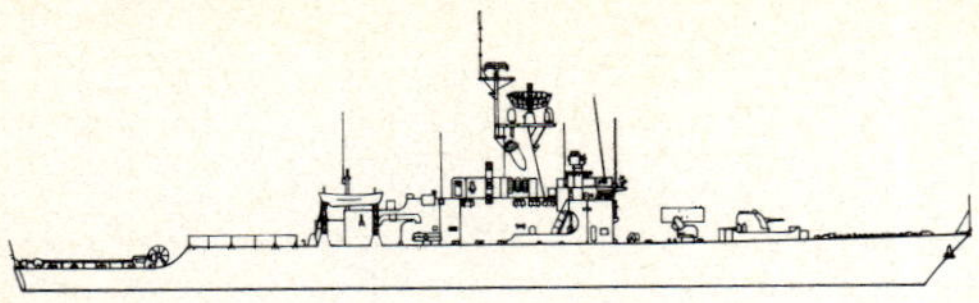

BRONSTEIN (FF 1037)

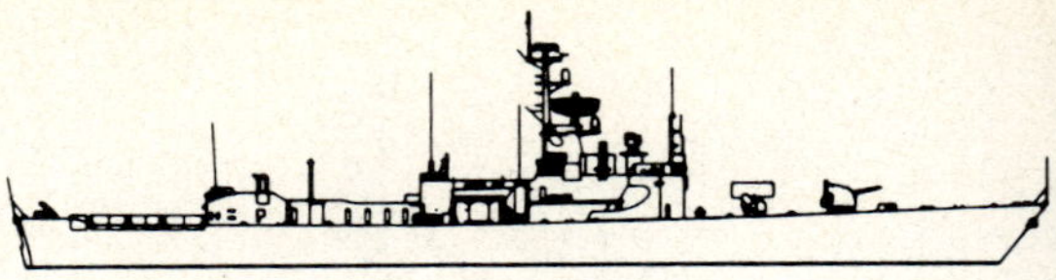

GLOVER (AGFF 1)

COMMAND SHIP

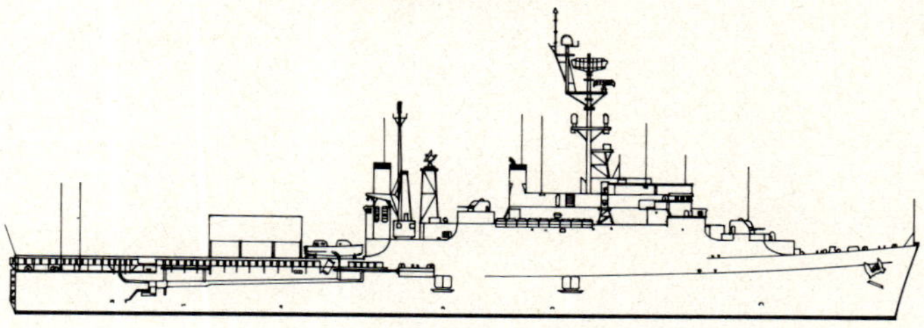

LASALLE (AGF 3)

AMPHIBIOUS WARFARE SHIPS

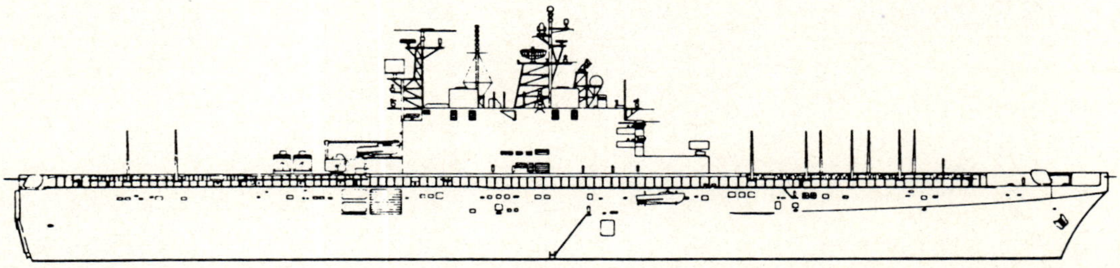

TARAWA (LHA 1)

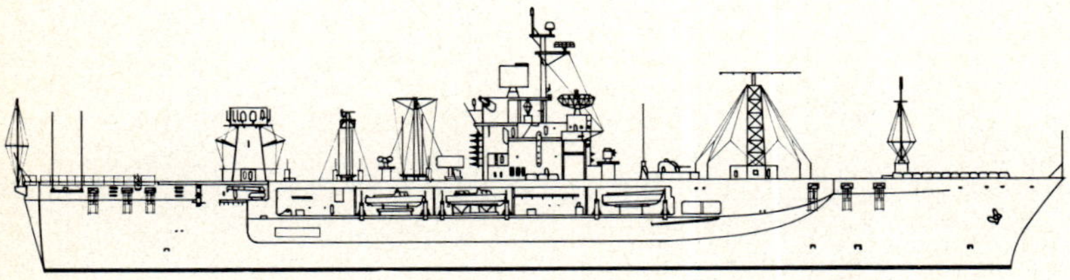

BLUE RIDGE (LCC 19)

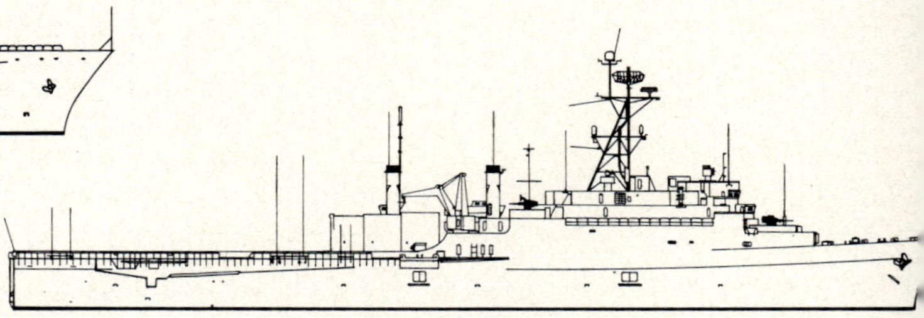

NASHVILLE (LPD 13)

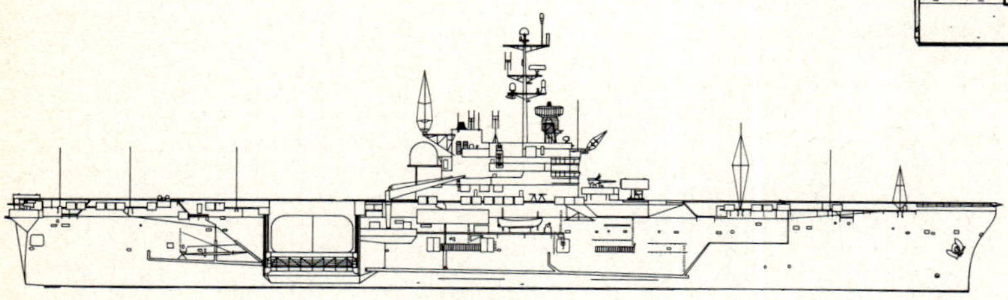

TRIPOLI (LPH 10)

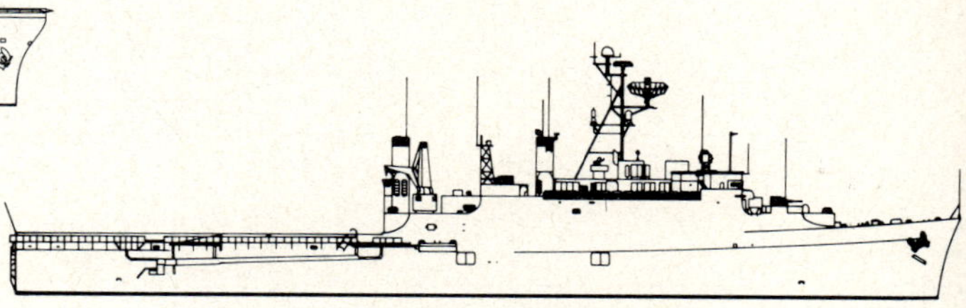

RALEIGH (LPD 1)

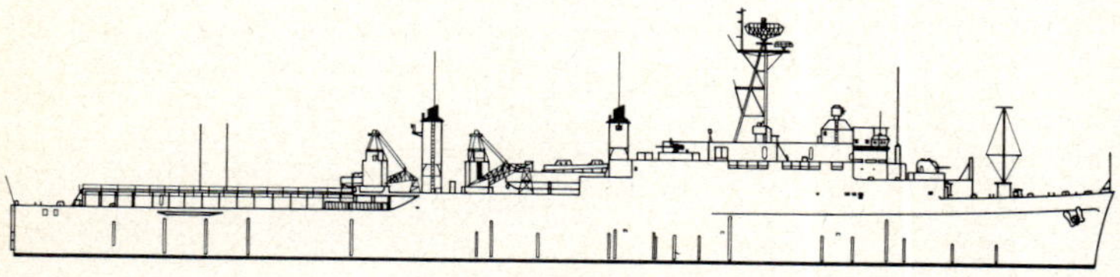

ANCHORAGE (LSD 36)

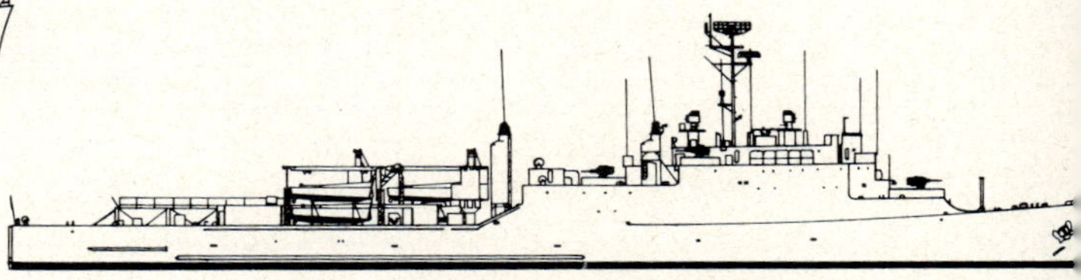

HERMITAGE (LSD 34) "Thomaston" Class

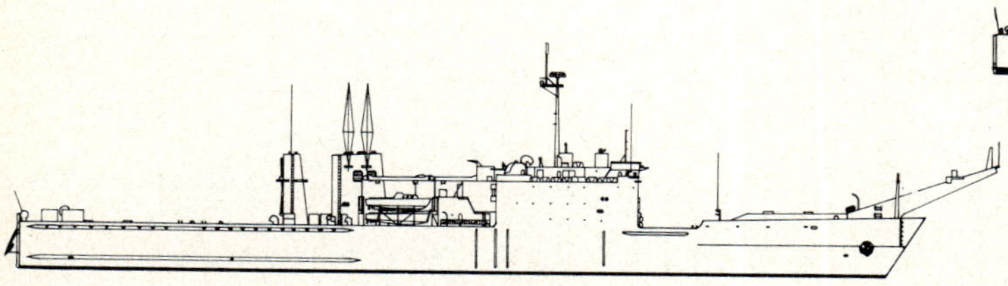

NEWPORT (LST 1179)

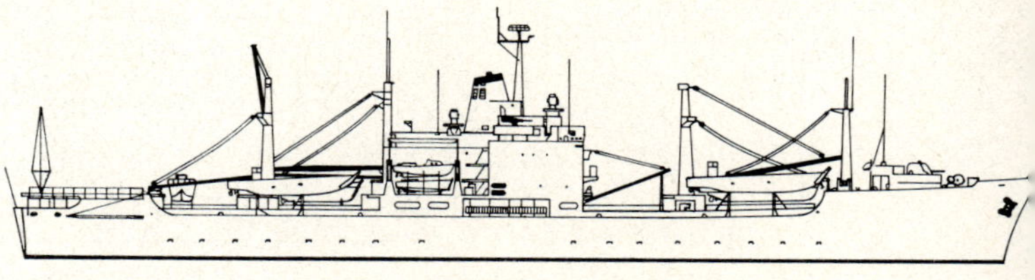

CHARLESTON (LKA 113)

Scale: 1 inch = 150 feet (1 : 1 800)

PATROL SHIPS AND CRAFT

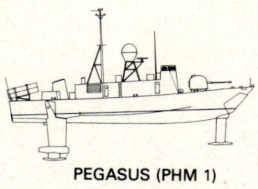
PEGASUS (PHM 1)

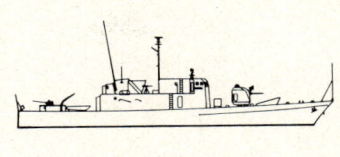
"ASHEVILLE" Class

"AGGRESSIVE" Class MSO

Scale: 1 inch = 100 feet (1 : 1 200)

AUXILIARY SHIPS

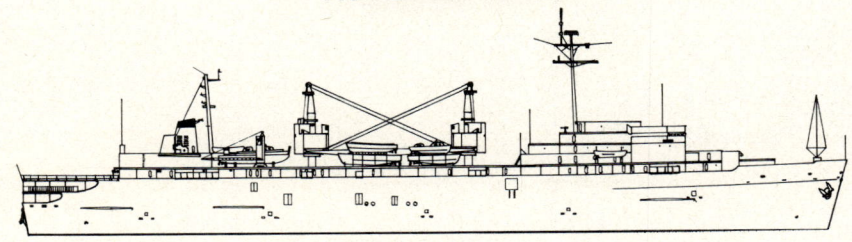
"SAMUEL GOMPERS" Class

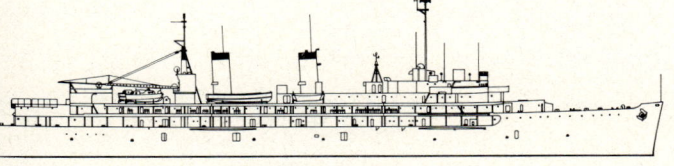
YOSEMITE (AD 19) "Dixie" Class

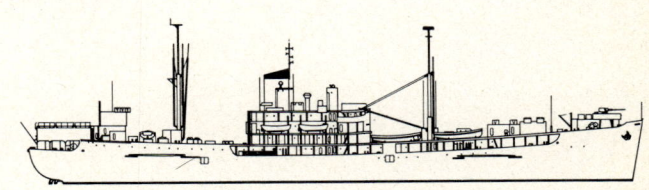
BRYCE CANYON (AD 36) "Shenandoah" Class

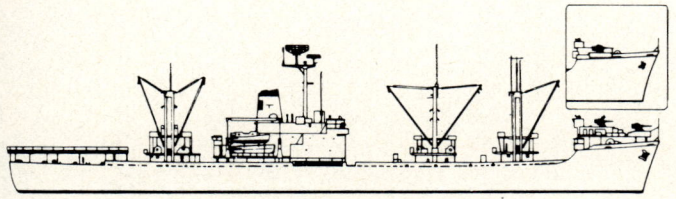
MAUNA KEA (AE 22) "Suribachi" Class
(inset shows gun variation)

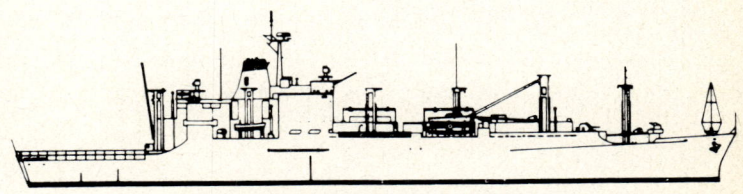
SANTA BARBARA (AE 28) "Kilauea" Class

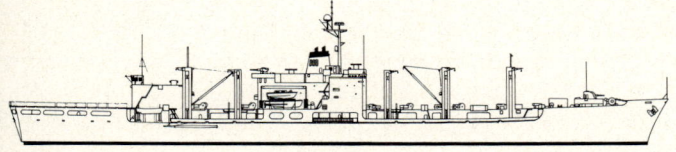
MARS (AFS 1)

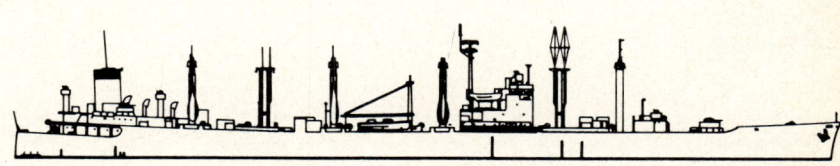
CANISTEO (AO 99) Jumboised T3-S2-A1

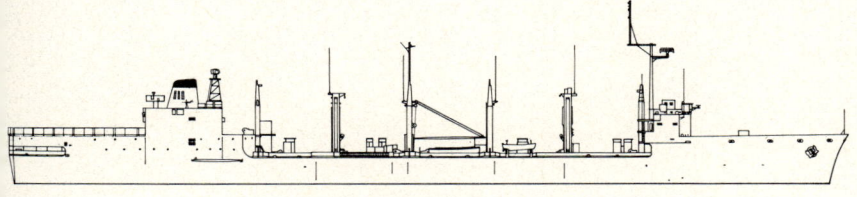
ROANOKE (AOR 7) "Wichita" Class

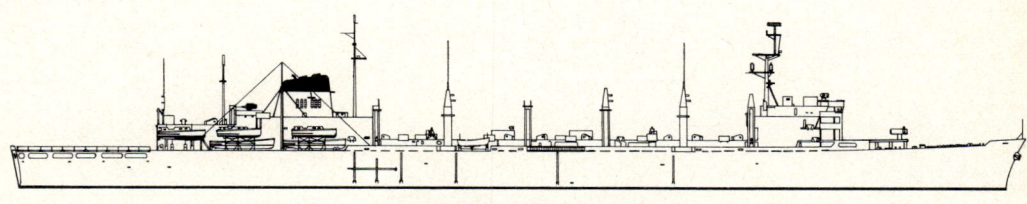
CAMDEN (AOE 2) "Sacramento" Class

Scale: 1 inch = 150 feet (1 : 1 800)

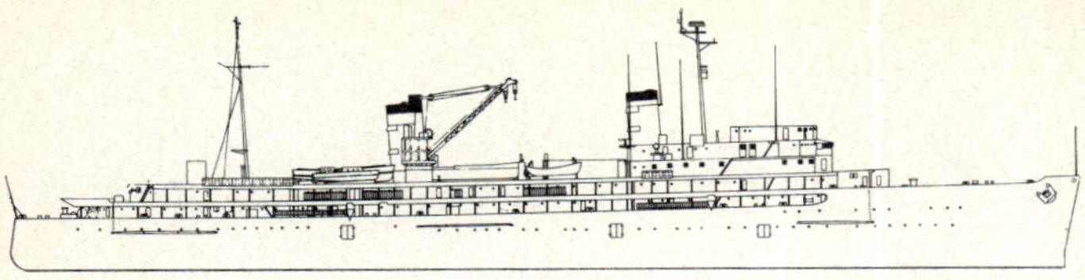

650 USA/ Introduction

VULCAN (AR 5)

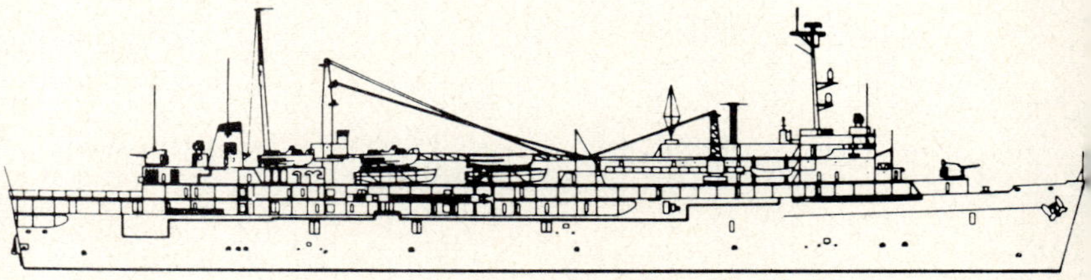

L. Y. SPEAR (AS 36)

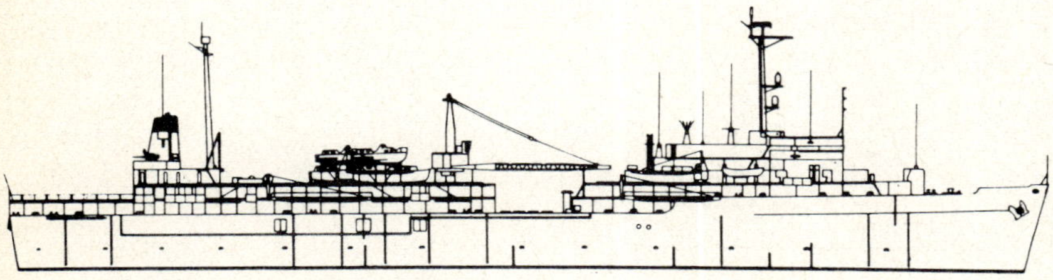

CANOPUS (AS 34) "Simon Lake" Class

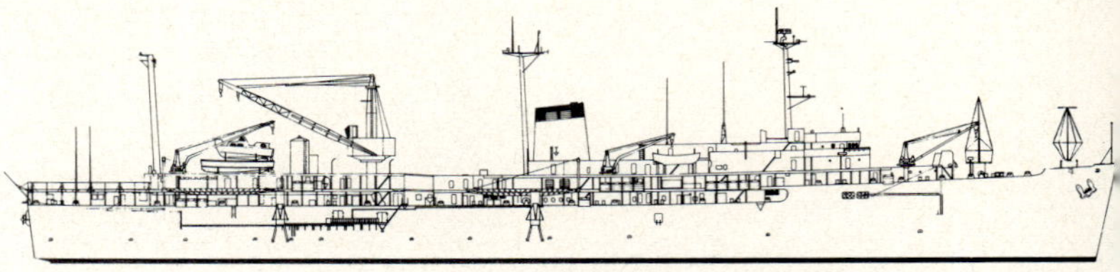

HUNLEY (AS 31)

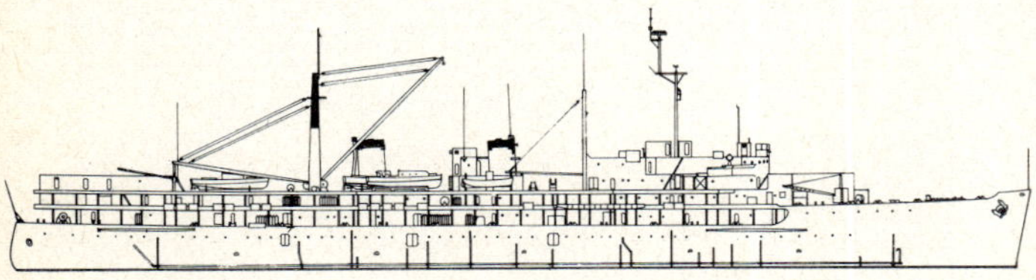

HOWARD W. GILMORE (AS 16) "Fulton" Class

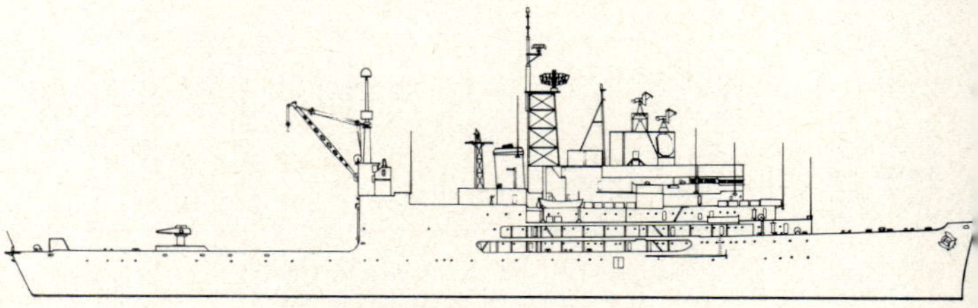

NORTON SOUND (AVM 1)

Scale: 1 inch = 150 feet (1 : 1 800)

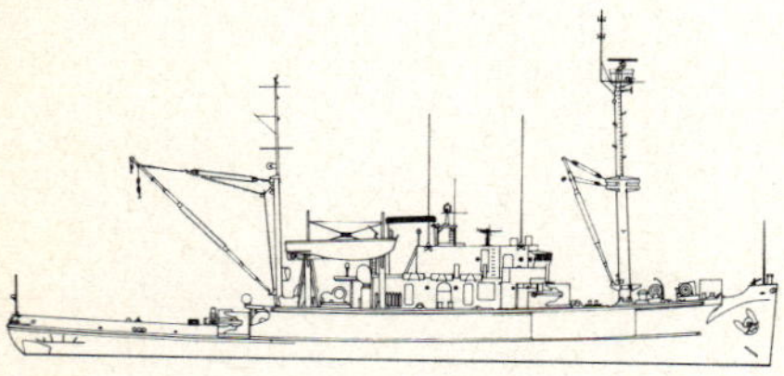

CONSERVER (ARS 39)

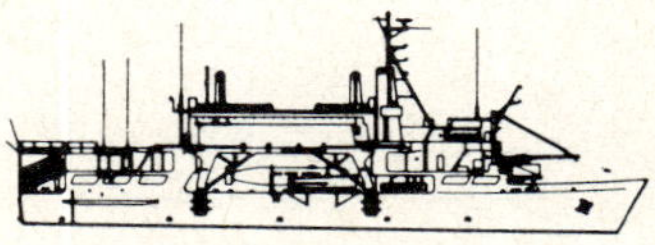

PIGEON (ASR 21)

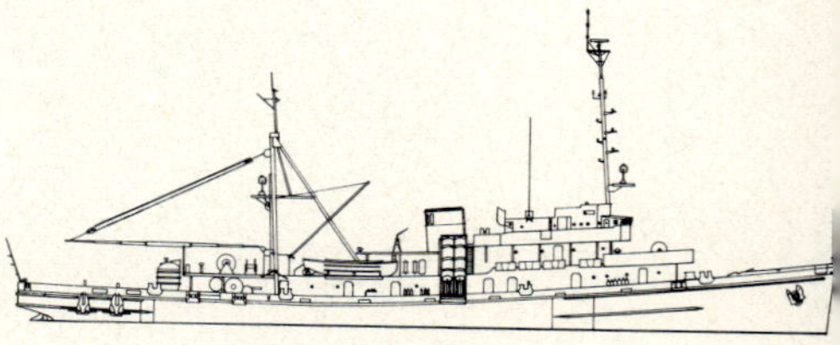

SUNBIRD (ASR 15)

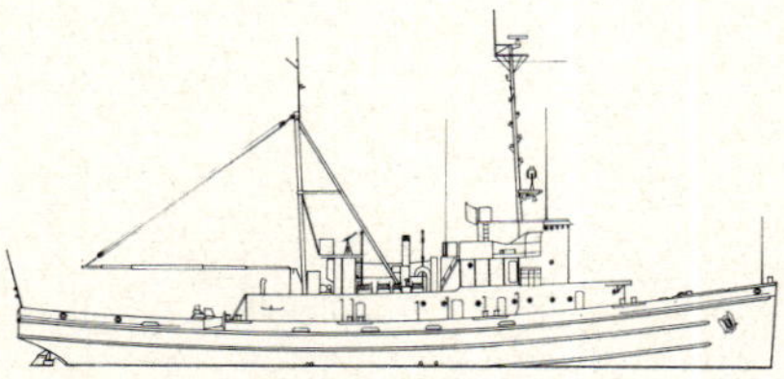

"ABNAKI" Class ATF

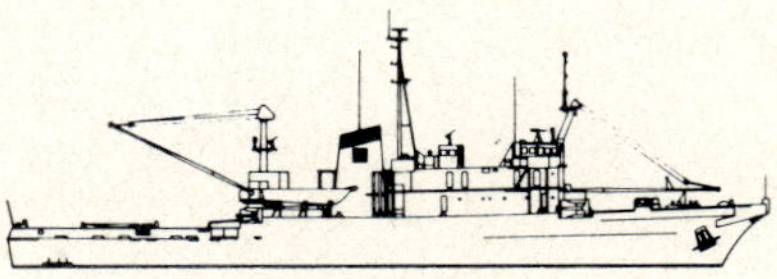

EDENTON (ATS 1)

Scale: 1 inch = 100 feet (1 : 1 200)

MILITARY SEALIFT COMMAND

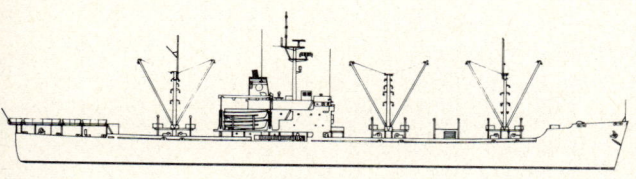
RIGEL (T-AF-58)

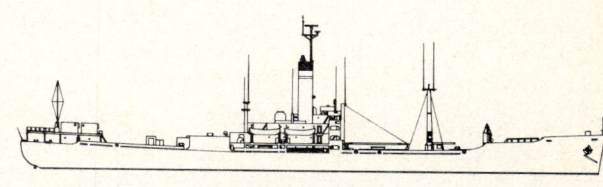
KINGSPORT (T-AG-164)

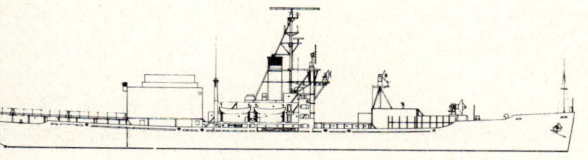
WHEELING (T-AGM-8)

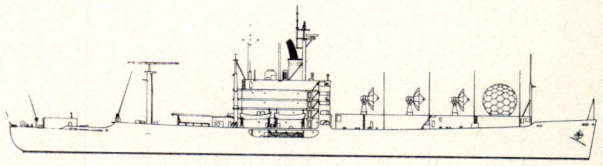
RANGE SENTINEL (T-AGM-22)

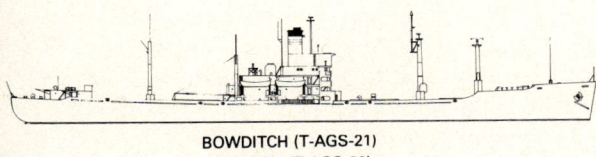
BOWDITCH (T-AGS-21)
DUTTON (T-AGS-22)

H. H. HESS (T-AGS-38)

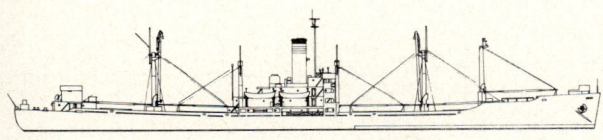
PVT. JOHN R. TOWLE (T-AK-240)

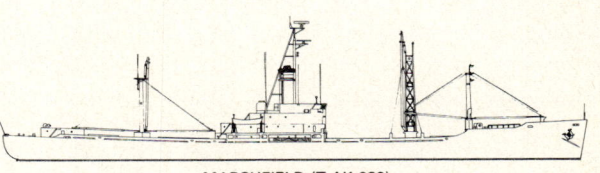
MARSHFIELD (T-AK-282)

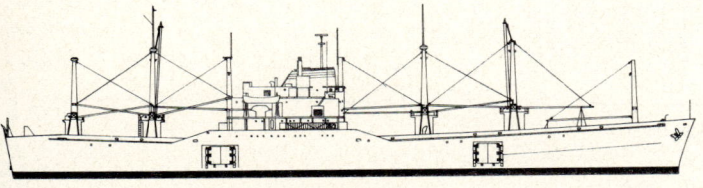
COMET (T-AKR-9)

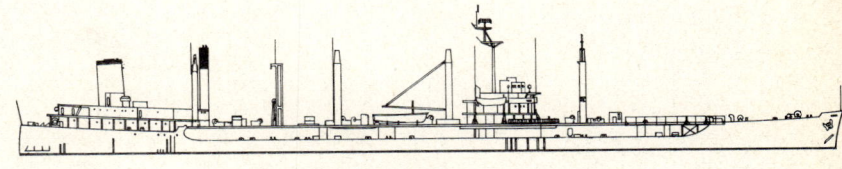
MISPILLION (T-AO 105) Jumboised T3-S2-A3

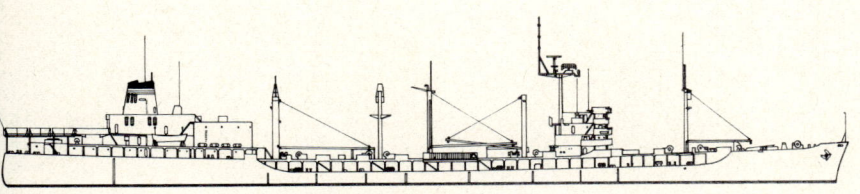
MISSISSINEWA (T-AO-144)

Scale: 1 inch = 150 feet (1 : 1 800)

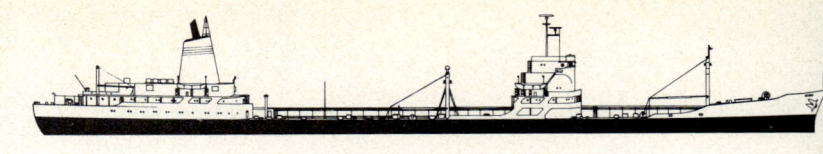
MAUMEE (T-AO-149)

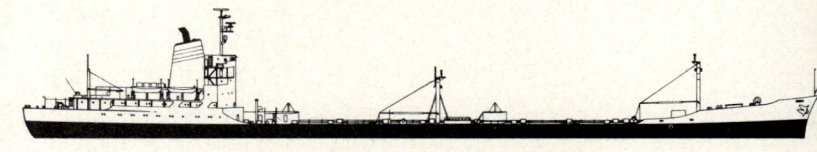
SEALIFT PACIFIC (T-AO-168)

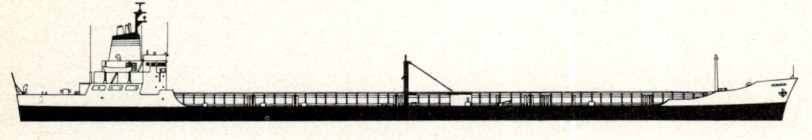
POTOMAC (T-AO-181)

COLUMBIA (T-AC-182)

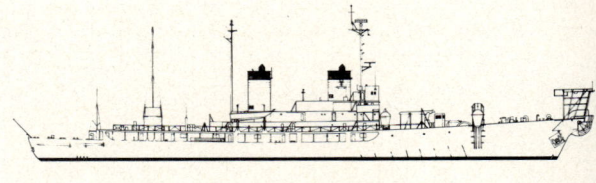
AEOLUS (T-ARC-3)

Scale: 1 inch = 150 feet (1 : 1 800)

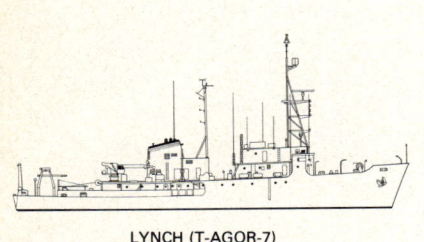
LYNCH (T-AGOR-7)

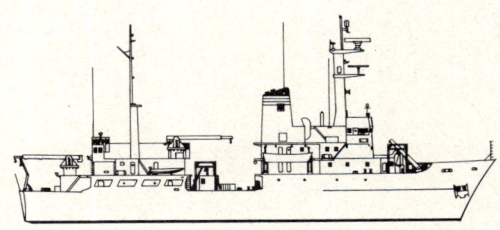
HAYES (T-AGOR-16)

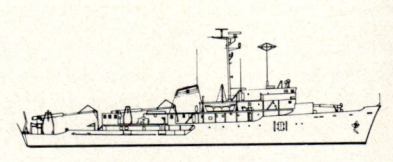
WILKES (T-AGS-33)

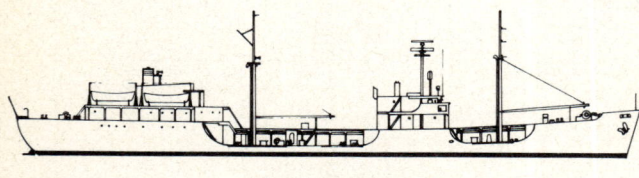
PETALUMA (T-AOG-79)

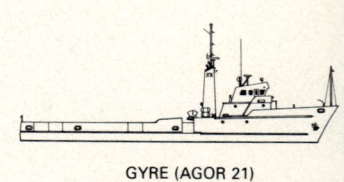
GYRE (AGOR 21)
MOANA WAVE (AGOR 22)

Scale: 1 inch = 100 feet (1 : 1 200)

All drawings by A. D. Baker III

SUBMARINES

STRATEGIC MISSILE SUBMARINES (SSBN)

The current SSBN force, with the completion of the last Poseidon conversion in 1977, provides over 5 000 separate warheads or "re-entry" vehicles, or about 55 per cent of US strategic warheads. (Each Poseidon missile is believed normally to carry ten separately targetable RVs, while the Polaris A-3 missile delivers three RVs on the same target, thus the latter weapon is considered to deliver only one warhead).

The Trident strategic missile submarine programme has been initiated to replace the older Polaris/Poseidon submarines from about 1980 onwards. All 41 existing submarines will reach their 20th year of active service between 1981 and 1987. The urgency of the original SSBN programme will thus result in block obsolescence at this time causing a substantial decrease in overall SLBM capability in the late 1980s and early 1990s.

Trident Programme: The Trident programme provides for an improved nuclear-propelled submarine and longer-range missiles. The Trident submarine is described below; the Trident I missile now under development will have a nominal range of approximately 4 000 n. miles. This missile will be installed in the new construction submarines and retrofitted in ten of the Poseidon-armed submarines. The longer range (approx 6 000 mile) Trident II missile is under study. This weapon, which could be available in the mid-1980s, would also have a greater throw weight and accuracy than the Trident I.

When the Trident programme was initiated, the Navy planned to construct the first submarine with the Fiscal Year 1974 funding and three submarines each year thereafter for the initial ten SSBN class. However, in 1974 the Department of Defense slowed the rate to 1-2-2-2-2-1; in 1975 this was again revised to 1-2-1-2-1-2-1.

In early 1976, Secretary of Defense Donald H. Rumsfeld announced that for planning purposes additional submarines beyond the ten-submarine force would be procured at the 1-2-1-2 rate continuously consistent with Strategic Arms Limitation Talks (SALT) agreements.

In March 1978 Secretary of Defense Harold Brown further reduced the building rate to 1-1-1-1-1-2-1-2 beginning with the FY 1980 budget. This was done to allow the sole prime contractor, General Dynamics, to catch up with the programme which is now running 18-24 months behind delivery date schedules.

Future SLBN Programme: Proposals to develop a type of smaller Trident-carrying submarines from the "Los Angeles" or "Narwhal" class designs had been dropped because of the increased costs which would result but in 1978 were reopened for re-examination.

WILL ROGERS in Holy Loch, Scotland   1972, USN

Strategic Cruise Missiles: The US Navy is in advanced development of a strategic Sea-Launched Cruise Missile (SLCM) (Tomahawk). This is an underwater-launched weapon with ram-jet propulsion which could deliver nuclear warheads to a range of approximately 1 500 n. miles. A shorter-range (300 mile) version of the weapon with a conventional warhead is planned for use as an over-the-horizon anti-ship weapon. The strategic cruise missile would have a low-level, terrain following flight path over land, much like that of a manned bomber in contrast to the ballistic trajectory of a Polaris/Poseidon/Trident missile.

Names: US ballistic missile submarines (SSBN) have been named for "distinguished Americans who were known for their devotion to freedom" since 1958 when the Polaris submarine programme was initiated. Included as "Americans" were Latin American and Hawaiian leaders, and several Europeans who supported the American fight for independence. In 1976 the SSBN name source was changed to States of the Union with the first Trident submarine (SSBN 726) being named *Ohio*.

OHIO   4/1979, Electric Boat Division

0 + 7 + ? "OHIO" CLASS (BALLISTIC MISSILE SUBMARINES (SSBN))

Name	No.	Builders	Laid down	Launch	Commission	F/S
OHIO	SSBN 726	General Dynamics (Electric Boat)	10 Apr 1976	mid-1979	late 1980	Building
MICHIGAN	SSBN 727	General Dynamics (Electric Boat)	4 Apr 1977	mid-1980	late 1981	Building
	SSBN 728	General Dynamics (Electric Boat)	9 June 1977	early 1981	mid-1982	Building
	SSBN 729	General Dynamics (Electric Boat)	—	late 1981	early 1983	Ord
	SSBN 730	General Dynamics (Electric Boat)	—	mid-1982	late 1983	Ord
	SSBN 731	General Dynamics (Electric Boat)	—	mid-1983	mid-1984	Ord
	SSBN 732	General Dynamics (Electric Boat)	—	late 1983	early 1985	Ord
	SSBN 733	Requested FY 1980 programme				Proj
	SSBN 734	Proposed FY 1981 programme				Proj
	SSBN 735	Proposed FY 1982 programme				Proj
	SSBN 736	Proposed FY 1983 programme				Proj
	SSBN 737	Proposed FY 1984 programme				Proj
	SSBN 738	Proposed FY 1984 programme				Proj

Displacement, tons: 16 600 surfaced; 18 700 dived
Length, feet (metres): 560 (170·7)
Beam, feet (metres): 42 (12·8)
Draught, feet (metres): 35·5 (10·8)
Missiles: 24 tubes for Trident I Submarine-Launched Ballistic Missile (SLBM)
Torpedo tubes: 4—21 in (533 mm) Mk 68 (bow)
Main machinery: 1 pressurised-water cooled S8G (General Electric) reactor; geared turbines; 1 shaft; 60 000 shp
Complement: 133 (16 officers, 117 enlisted men)

These submarines will be the largest undersea craft yet constructed, being significantly larger than the Soviet "Delta" class missile submarines which are now the largest afloat. The lead submarine was contracted to the Electric Boat Division of the General Dynamics Corp (Groton, Connecticut) on 25 July 1974. The only other US shipyard currently capable of building submarines of this class is the Newport News S.B. & D.D. Co in Virginia.
A series of problems both in Washington and in the shipbuilding yards has resulted in progressive delays to this class.
Ohio herself is scheduled to begin deployment from the Trident base at Bangor, Washington in 1981. As each "Ohio" class is commissioned a Polaris-armed SSBN ("SSBN 598" and "608" classes) will be withdrawn from service.

Class: The total number of ships of this class to be built has not yet been decided.

Design: The size of the Trident submarine is dictated primarily by the larger size missile required for 4 or 6 000 mile range and the larger reactor plant to drive the ship. The submarine will have 24 tubes in a vertical position.
The principal characteristics of the Trident concept as proposed were: (1) long-range missile (eventually of 6 000 miles (Trident II)) to permit targeting the Soviet Union while the submarine cruises in remote areas, making effective ASW virtually impossible for the foreseeable future, (2) extremely quiet submarines, (3) a high at-sea to in-port ratio.

Designation: Initially the hull number SSBN 711 was planned for the first Trident submarine. However, on 21 February 1974 the designation SSBN 1 was assigned, confusing the Navy's submarine designation system which goes back to USS *Holland* (SS 1), commissioned in 1900. Subsequently, the designation was again changed on 10 April 1974, with the "block" SSBN 726-735 being reserved for the Trident programme. Three more 736-738 now added.

Electronics: UYK-7 computer is provided to support electronic and weapon systems. Mk 118 digital torpedo fire control system is installed.

Engineering: These submarines will have a nuclear core life of about nine years between refuellings. A prototype of the S8G reactor plant has been constructed at West Milton, New York.

Fiscal: Costs of the first four SSBNs have increased over the initial appropriations. See 1975-76 edition for initial costs. SSBNs 731 and 732 in FY 1978 are funded at $1 703 million for the pair.

Originally requested under FY 1979 was $911·9 million for SSBN 733 construction and $274·8 million for advance procurement of SSBN 734. However, because of construction delays, design problems, settlement claims, etc, with previously authorised SSBNs, Congress refused to authorise the $911·9 million to build SSBN 733. Instead it approved $198·0 million for further advance procurement of SSBN 733 and the money for SSBN 734. The FY 1980 budget requests $1,414·0 million to construct SSBN 733 and $64·0 million for further advance procurement of SSBN 734.

Missiles: The Trident submarines will be armed initially with the Trident I missile, scheduled to become operational late in 1978. This missile is expected to have a range of 4 000 n. miles, a range already exceeded by the SS-N-8 missile in the Soviet "Delta" class submarines. However, the US missile will have a MIRV warhead, which at present is not fitted to SS-N-8, although SS-N-6 (Mod III) has an MRV head.
The Trident missile is expected to carry more than the 10 to 14 re-entry vehicles that the Poseidon can lift. In addition, the Mk 500 MARV (Manoeuvring Re-entry Vehicle) is under development for the purpose of demonstrating its compatability with the Trident I missile. This re-entry vehicle intended to evade ABM interceptor missiles and is not terminally guided to increase its accuracy.

Navigation: Each submarine will have two Mk 2 Ships Inertial Navigation Systems; to be fitted with satellite navigation receivers.

Sonar: BQQ 5 (passive only).

OHIO (roll-out)   4/1978, Electric Boat Division

USA / Submarines 655

31 "BENJAMIN FRANKLIN" and "LAFAYETTE" CLASSES (BALLISTIC MISSILE SUBMARINES (SSBN))

Name	No.	Builders	Laid down	Launched	Commissioned	F/S
LAFAYETTE	SSBN 616	General Dynamics (Electric Boat Div)	17 Jan 1961	8 May 1962	23 Apr 1963	AA
ALEXANDER HAMILTON	SSBN 617	General Dynamics (Electric Boat Div)	26 June 1961	18 Aug 1962	27 June 1963	AA
ANDREW JACKSON	SSBN 619	Mare Island Naval Shipyard	26 Apr 1961	15 Sep 1962	3 July 1963	AA
JOHN ADAMS	SSBN 620	Portsmouth Naval Shipyard	19 May 1961	12 Jan 1963	12 May 1964	AA
JAMES MONROE	SSBN 622	Newport News Shipbuilding & D.D. Co	31 July 1961	4 Aug 1962	7 Dec 1963	AA
NATHAN HALE	SSBN 623	General Dynamics (Electric Boat Div)	2 Oct 1961	12 Jan 1963	23 Nov 1963	AA
WOODROW WILSON	SSBN 624	Mare Island Naval Shipyard	13 Sep 1961	22 Feb 1963	27 Dec 1963	AA
HENRY CLAY	SSBN 625	Newport News Shipbuilding & D.D. Co	23 Oct 1961	30 Nov 1962	20 Feb 1964	AA
DANIEL WEBSTER	SSBN 626	General Dynamics (Electric Boat Div)	28 Dec 1961	27 Apr 1963	9 Apr 1964	AA
JAMES MADISON	SSBN 627	Newport News Shipbuilding & D.D. Co	5 Mar 1962	15 Mar 1963	28 July 1964	AA
TECUMSEH	SSBN 628	General Dynamics (Electric Boat Div)	1 June 1962	22 June 1963	29 May 1964	AA
DANIEL BOONE	SSBN 629	Mare Island Naval Shipyard	6 Feb 1962	22 June 1963	23 Apr 1964	AA
JOHN C. CALHOUN	SSBN 630	Newport News Shipbuilding & D.D. Co	4 June 1962	22 June 1963	15 Sep 1964	AA
ULYSSES S. GRANT	SSBN 631	General Dynamics (Electric Boat Div)	18 Aug 1962	2 Nov 1963	17 July 1964	AA
VON STEUBEN	SSBN 632	Newport News Shipbuilding & D.D. Co	4 Sep 1962	18 Oct 1963	30 Sep 1964	AA
CASIMIR PULASKI	SSBN 633	General Dynamics (Electric Boat Div)	12 Jan 1963	1 Feb 1964	14 Aug 1964	AA
STONEWALL JACKSON	SSBN 634	Mare Island Naval Shipyard	4 July 1962	30 Nov 1963	26 Aug 1964	AA
SAM RAYBURN	SSBN 635	Newport News Shipbuilding & D.D. Co	3 Dec 1962	20 Dec 1963	2 Dec 1964	AA
NATHANAEL GREENE	SSBN 636	Portsmouth Naval Shipyard	21 May 1962	12 May 1964	19 Dec 1964	AA
BENJAMIN FRANKLIN	SSBN 640	General Dynamics (Electric Boat Div)	25 May 1963	5 Dec 1964	22 Oct 1965	AA
SIMON BOLIVAR	SSBN 641	Newport News Shipbuilding & D.D. Co	17 Apr 1963	22 Aug 1964	29 Oct 1966	AA
KAMEHAMEHA	SSBN 642	Mare Island Naval Shipyard	2 May 1963	16 Jan 1965	10 Dec 1965	AA
GEORGE BANCROFT	SSBN 643	General Dynamics (Electric Boat Div)	24 Aug 1963	20 Mar 1965	22 Jan 1966	AA
LEWIS AND CLARK	SSBN 644	Newport News Shipbuilding & D.D. Co	29 July 1963	21 Nov 1964	22 Dec 1965	AA
JAMES K. POLK	SSBN 645	General Dynamics (Electric Boat Div)	23 Nov 1963	22 May 1965	16 Apr 1966	AA
GEORGE C. MARSHALL	SSBN 654	Newport News Shipbuilding & D.D. Co	2 Mar 1964	21 May 1965	29 Apr 1966	AA
HENRY L. STIMSON	SSBN 655	General Dynamics (Electric Boat Div)	4 Apr 1964	13 Nov 1965	20 Aug 1966	AA
GEORGE WASHINGTON CARVER	SSBN 656	Newport News Shipbuilding & D.D. Co	24 Aug 1964	14 Aug 1965	15 June 1966	AA
FRANCIS SCOTT KEY	SSBN 657	General Dynamics (Electric Boat Div)	5 Dec 1964	23 Apr 1966	3 Dec 1966	AA
MARIANO G. VALLEJO	SSBN 658	Mare Island Naval Shipyard	7 July 1964	23 Oct 1965	16 Dec 1966	AA
WILL ROGERS	SSBN 659	General Dynamics (Electric Boat Div)	20 Mar 1965	21 July 1966	1 Apr 1967	AA

Displacement, tons: 6 650 light surfaced; 7 250 standard surfaced; 8 250 dived
Length, feet (metres): 425 (129·5)
Beam, feet (metres): 33 (10·1)
Draught, feet (metres): 31·5 (9·6)
Missile launchers: 16 tubes for Poseidon C-3 SLBM (see *Missile* notes)
Torpedo tubes: 4—21 in (533 mm) Mk 65 (bow)
Main machinery: 1 pressurised-water cooled S5W (Westinghouse) reactor; 2 geared turbines; 15 000 shp; 1 shaft
Speed, knots: 20 surfaced; approx 30 dived
Complement: 168 (20 officers, 148 enlisted men) (SSBN 640 onward); 140 (14 officers, 126 enlisted men) (remainder)

These submarines were the largest undersea craft to be completed in the West. The first four submarines (SSBN 616, 617, 619, 620) were authorised in the Fiscal Year 1961 shipbuilding programme with five additional submarines (SSBN 622-626) authorised in a supplemental to the FY 1961 programme; SSBN 627-636 (ten) in the FY 1962, SSBN 640-645 (six) in the FY 1963, and SSBN 654-659 (six) in the FY 1964. Cost for the earlier ships of this class was approximately $109·5 million per submarine.

Design: *Benjamin Franklin* and later submarines are officially considered a separate class; however, differences are minimal (eg, quieter machinery).

Electronics: Fitted with Mk 113 Mod 9 torpedo fire control system.

Engineering: *Benjamin Franklin* and subsequent submarines of this class have been fitted with quieter machinery. All SSBNs have diesel-electric stand-by machinery, snorts, and "outboard" auxiliary propeller for emergency use.
The nuclear cores inserted in refuelling these submarines during the late 1960s and early 1970s cost approximately $3·5 million and provide energy for approximately 400 000 miles.

Missiles: Polaris; The first eight ships of this class were fitted with the Polaris A-2 missile (1 500 n. mile range) and the 23 later ships with the Polaris A-3 missile (2 500 n. mile range). SSBN 620 and SSBN 622-625 (five ships) were rearmed with the Polaris A-3 missile during overhaul-refuellings from 1968 to 1970. *Andrew Jackson* launched the first Polaris A-3 missile on 26 October 1963. *Daniel Webster* was the first submarine to deploy with the A-3 missile, beginning her first patrol on 28 September 1964. *Daniel Boone* was the first SSBN to deploy to the Pacific, beginning her first patrol with the A-3 missile on 25 December 1964.
Poseidon (C3); *James Madison* was the first submarine to undergo conversion to carry the Poseidon missile. She launched the first Poseidon missile on 3 August 1970 and began the first Poseidon patrol on 31 March 1971. Poseidon conversion, overhaul, and reactor refuelling are conducted simultaneously. In addition to changes in missile tubes to accommodate larger Poseidon, the conversion provides replacement of Mk 84 fire control system with Mk 88 system (see Conversion Table on the following page).
Trident I (C4); Current planning provides for 12 units of these two classes to be fitted with the Trident I missile. *Francis Scott Key* is the first SSBN to be converted to fire the Trident I missile. Six of the conversions, namely those of SSBN-627, 632, 633, 640/641 and 643 will take place during the regularly scheduled overhauls of the submarines (hence the longer conversion periods) and the remainder during tender availabilities alongside an AS (FBM) (hence the shorter conversion periods). The actual industrial time spent on the conversion package is about one month. The conversion includes minor modifications to the launcher and to the ballasting of the submarine to accommodate the greater weight of the Trident missile as well as extensive modifications to the installed fire control, instrumentation and missile checkout subsystems to support the increased sophistication of the longer range missile. A tentative conversion schedule is indicated on the following page. *Francis Scott Key* received her Trident conversion during her tender availability and will serve as a sea-going test bed for the sea testing phase of the Trident I missile. During this time she will not be employed on deterrent patrols. *Francis Scott Key*

SIMON BOLIVAR　　　　　　　　　　　　　　　　　9/1976, Dr. Giorgio Arra

SIMON BOLIVAR　　　　　　　　　　　　　　　　　9/1976, Dr. Giorgio Arra

will complete her role as a sea going test bed and return to her deterrent mission in December 1979 when she will be the first SSBN to deploy with the Trident I missile. All Trident equipped SSBN's of this class will be based at Kings Bay, Georgia beginning in spring 1979.
Navigation: These submarines are equipped with an elaborate Ship's Inertial Navigation System (SINS), a system of gyroscopes and accelerometers which relates movement of the ship in all directions, true speed through the water and over the ocean floor, and true north to give a continuous report of the submarine's position. Navigation data produced by SINS can be provided to each missile's guidance package until the instant the missile is fired.
As converted, all Poseidon submarines have three Mk 2 Mod 4 SINS; all fitted with navigational satellite receivers.

Personnel: Each submarine is assigned two alternating crews designated "Blue" and "Gold". Each crew mans the submarine during a 60 day patrol and partially assists during the intermediate 28 day refit alongside a Polaris tender.

MARIANO C. VALLEJO 1974, USN

POSEIDON CONVERSION SCHEDULE

No.	Programme	Conversion Yard	Start	Complete
SSBN 616	FY 1973	General Dynamics Corp (Electric Boat)	15 Oct 1972	7 Nov 1974
SSBN 617	FY 1973	Newport News S.B. & D.D. Co	15 Jan 1973	11 Apr 1975
SSBN 619	FY 1973	General Dynamics Corp (Electric Boat)	19 Mar 1973	15 Aug 1975
SSBN 620	FY 1974	Portsmouth Naval Shipyard	1 Feb 1974	15 Apr 1976
SSBN 622	FY 1975	Newport News S.B. & D.D. Co	15 Jan 1975	14 May 1977
SSBN 623	FY 1973	Puget Sound Naval Shipyard	15 June 1973	27 June 1975
SSBN 624	FY 1974	Newport News S.B. & D.D. Co	1 Oct 1973	23 Oct 1975
SSBN 625	FY 1975	Portsmouth Naval Shipyard	29 Apr 1975	29 July 1977
SSBN 626	FY 1975	General Dynamics Corp (Electric Boat)	1 Dec 1975	21 Feb 1978
SSBN 627	FY 1968	General Dynamics Corp (Electric Boat)	3 Feb 1969	28 June 1970
SSBN 628	FY 1970	Newport News S.B. & D.D. Co	10 Nov 1969	18 Feb 1971
SSBN 629	FY 1968	Newport News S.B. & D.D. Co	11 May 1969	11 Aug 1970
SSBN 630	FY 1969	Mare Island Naval Shipyard	4 Aug 1969	22 Feb 1971
SSBN 631	FY 1970	Puget Sound Naval Shipyard	3 Oct 1969	16 Dec 1970
SSBN 632	FY 1969	General Dynamics Corp (Electric Boat)	11 July 1969	19 Nov 1970
SSBN 633	FY 1970	General Dynamics Corp (Electric Boat)	10 Jan 1970	30 Apr 1971
SSBN 634	FY 1971	General Dynamics Corp (Electric Boat)	15 July 1970	29 Oct 1971
SSBN 635	FY 1970	Portsmouth Naval Shipyard	19 Jan 1970	2 Sep 1971
SSBN 636	FY 1971	Newport News S.B. & D.D. Co	22 July 1970	21 Sep 1971
SSBN 640	FY 1971	General Dynamics Corp (Electric Boat)	25 Feb 1971	15 May 1972
SSBN 641	FY 1971	Newport News S.B. & D.D. Co	15 Feb 1971	12 May 1972
SSBN 642	FY 1972	General Dynamics Corp (Electric Boat)	15 July 1971	27 Oct 1972
SSBN 643	FY 1971	Portsmouth Naval Shipyard	28 Apr 1971	31 July 1972
SSBN 644	FY 1971	Puget Sound Naval Shipyard	30 Apr 1971	21 July 1972
SSBN 645	FY 1972	Newport News S.B. & D.D. Co	15 July 1971	17 Nov 1972
SSBN 654	FY 1972	Puget Sound Naval Shipyard	14 Sep 1971	8 Feb 1973
SSBN 655	FY 1972	Newport News S.B. & D.D. Co	15 Nov 1971	22 Mar 1973
SSBN 656	FY 1972	General Dynamics Corp (Electric Boat)	12 Nov 1971	7 Apr 1973
SSBN 657	FY 1972	Puget Sound Naval Shipyard	20 Feb 1972	17 May 1973
SSBN 658	FY 1973	Newport News S.B. & D.D. Co	21 Aug 1972	19 Dec 1973
SSBN 659	FY 1973	Portsmouth Naval Shipyard	16 Oct 1972	8 Feb 1974

TENTATIVE TRIDENT CONVERSION SCHEDULE

No.	Programme	Occasion	Start	Complete
SSBN 627	FY 1979	During ship overhaul	3 Aug 1979	4 Dec 1980
SSBN 629	FY 1980	During tender availability	3 Apr 1980	22 June 1980
SSBN 630	FY 1980	During tender availability	28 June 1980	16 Sep 1980
SSBN 632	FY 1980	During ship overhaul	12 Jan 1980	15 May 1981
SSBN 633	FY 1980	During ship overhaul	1 July 1980	4 Nov 1981
SSBN 634	FY 1981	During tender availability	27 Oct 1981	20 Jan 1982
SSBN 640	FY 1980	During ship overhaul	2 Oct 1979	2 Jan 1981
SSBN 641	FY 1979	During ship overhaul	5 Jan 1979	3 July 1980
SSBN 643	FY 1980	During ship overhaul	1 Apr 1980	1 July 1981
SSBN 655	FY 1980	During tender availability	4 Dec 1979	23 Feb 1980
SSBN 657	FY 1979	During tender availability	2 Oct 1978	20 Dec 1979
SSBN 658	FY 1979	During tender availability	1 Sep 1979	19 Nov 1980

Note: Completion dates in Trident conversion include the conducting of sea and missile firing trials and in the case of SSBN 657 her service as a test platform for the missile.

5 "ETHAN ALLEN" CLASS (BALLISTIC MISSILE SUBMARINES (SSBN))

Name	No.	Builders	Laid down	Launched	Commissioned	F/S
ETHAN ALLEN	SSBN 608	General Dynamics (Electric Boat Div, Groton)	14 Sep 1959	22 Nov 1960	8 Aug 1961	PA
SAM HOUSTON	SSBN 609	Newport News Shipbuilding & D.D. Co	28 Dec 1959	2 Feb 1961	6 Mar 1962	PA
THOMAS A. EDISON	SSBN 610	General Dynamics (Electric Boat Div, Groton)	15 Mar 1960	15 June 1961	10 Mar 1962	PA
JOHN MARSHALL	SSBN 611	Newport News Shipbuilding & D.D. Co	4 Apr 1960	15 July 1961	21 May 1962	PA
THOMAS JEFFERSON	SSBN 618	Newport News Shipbuilding & D.D. Co	3 Feb 1961	24 Feb 1962	4 Jan 1963	PA

Displacement, tons: 6 955 surfaced; 7 880 dived
Length, feet (metres): 410 *(125)*
Beam, feet (metres): 33 *(10·1)*
Draught, feet (metres): 32 *(9·8)*
Missiles: 16 tubes for Polaris A-3 SLBM
Torpedo tubes: 4—21 in *(533 mm)* bow
Main machinery: 1 pressurised-water cooled S5W (Westinghouse) reactor;
2 geared turbines (General Electric); 15 000 shp; 1 shaft
Speed, knots: 20 surfaced; 30 dived
Complement: 142 (15 officers, 127 enlisted men) (operate with two separate crews) (see note under "Lafayette" class)

These submarines were designed specifically for the ballistic missile role and are larger and better arranged than the earlier "George Washington" class submarines. The first four ships of this class were authorised in the Fiscal Year 1959 programme; *Thomas Jefferson* was in the FY 1961 programme. These submarines and the previous "George Washington" class will not be converted to carry the Poseidon missile because of material limitations and the age they would be after conversion.

Design: These submarines and the subsequent "Lafayette" class have a depth capability similar to the "Thresher" class attack submarines; pressure hulls of HY-80 steel.

Missiles: These ships were initially armed with the Polaris A-2 missile (1 500 n. mile range). *Ethan Allen* launched the first A-2 missile fired from a submarine on 23 October 1961. She was the first submarine to deploy with the A-2 missile, beginning her first patrol on 26 June 1962. *Ethan Allen* fired a Polaris A-2 missile in the Christmas Island Pacific Test Area on 6 May 1962 in what was the first complete US test of a ballistic missile including detonation of the nuclear warhead. All five of these submarines have been modified to fire the A-3 missile (2 500 n. mile range).

Navigation: Fitted with two Mk 2 Ship's Inertial Navigation Systems (SINS) and navigational satellite receiver.

THOMAS JEFFERSON 9/1977, USN

ETHAN ALLEN 1971, USN

THOMAS JEFFERSON 6/1976, USN

658 USA / Submarines

5 "GEORGE WASHINGTON" CLASS (BALLISTIC MISSILE SUBMARINES (SSBN))

Name	No.	Builders	Laid down	Launched	Commissioned	F/S
GEORGE WASHINGTON	SSBN 598	General Dynamics (Electric Boat Div, Groton)	1 Nov 1957	9 June 1959	30 Dec 1959	PA
PATRICK HENRY	SSBN 599	General Dynamics (Electric Boat Div, Groton)	27 May 1958	22 Sep 1959	9 Apr 1960	PA
THEODORE ROOSEVELT	SSBN 600	Mare Island Naval Shipyard	20 May 1958	3 Oct 1959	13 Feb 1961	PA
ROBERT E. LEE	SSBN 601	Newport News Shipbuilding & D.D. Co	25 Aug 1958	18 Dec 1959	16 Sep 1960	PA
ABRAHAM LINCOLN	SSBN 602	Portsmouth Naval Shipyard	1 Nov 1958	14 May 1960	11 Mar 1961	PA

Displacement, tons: 6 019 standard surfaced; 6 888 dived
Length, feet (metres): 381·7 *(116·3)*
Beam, feet (metres): 33 *(10·1)*
Draught, feet (metres): 29 *(8·8)*
Missiles: 16 tubes for Polaris A-3 SLBM
Torpedo tubes: 6—21 in *(533 mm)* Mk 59 (bow)
Main machinery: 1 pressurised-water cooled S5W (Westinghouse) reactor;
   2 geared turbines (General Electric); 15 000 shp; 1 shaft
Speed, knots: 20 surfaced; 31 dived
Complement: 112 (12 officers, 100 enlisted men)

George Washington was the West's first ship to be armed with ballistic missiles. A supplement to the Fiscal Year 1958 new construction programme signed on 11 February 1958 provided for the construction of the first three SSBNs. The Navy ordered the just-begun attack submarine *Scorpion* (SSN 589) to be completed as a missile submarine on 31 December 1957. The hull was redesignated SSGN 598 and completed as *George Washington*. *Patrick Henry* similarly was re-ordered on the last day of 1957, her materials having originally been intended for the not-yet-started SSN 590. These submarines and three sister ships (two authorised in FY 1959) were built to a modified "Skipjack" class design with almost 130 ft being added to the original design to accommodate two rows of eight missile tubes, fire control and navigation equipment, and auxiliary machinery. All are depth limited compared with later designs.

Appearance: Note that the "hump" of hull extension for housing missile tubes is more pronounced in these submarines than later classes.

Designation: Originally classified SSGN 598-600. Reclassified SSBN 598-600 on 26 June 1958.

Engineering: *George Washington* was the first FBM submarine to be overhauled and "refuelled". During her 4½ years of operation on her initial reactor core she carried out 15 submerged missile patrols and steamed more than 100 000 miles.

Missiles: These ships were initially armed with the Polaris A-1 missile (1 200 n. mile range). *George Washington* successfully fired two Polaris A-1 missiles while submerged off Cape Canaveral on 20 July 1960 in the first underwater launching of a ballistic missile from a US submarine. She departed on her initial patrol on 15 November 1960 and remained submerged for 66 days, 10 hours. All five submarines of this class have been refitted to fire the improved Polaris A-3 missile (2 500 n. mile range). Missile refit and first reactor refuelling were accomplished simultaneously during overhaul. *George Washington* from 20 June 1964 to 2 February 1966, *Patrick Henry* from 4 January 1965 to 21 July 1966, *Theodore Roosevelt* from 28 July 1965 to 14 January 1967, *Robert E. Lee* from 23 February 1965 to 2 July 1966, and *Abraham Lincoln* from 25 October 1965 to 3 June 1967, four at Electric Boat yard in Groton, Connecticut, and *Robert E. Lee* at Mare Island Naval Shipyard (California). These submarines all have Mk 84 fire control systems and gas-steam missile ejectors (originally fitted with Mk 80 fire control systems and compressed air missile ejectors, changed during A-3 missile refit).
These submarines will not be modified to carry and launch the advanced Poseidon ballistic missile.

Navigation: Fitted with three Mk 2 Mod 4 Ship's Inertial Navigation System (SINS) and navigational satellite receiver.

ABRAHAM LINCOLN   USN

GEORGE WASHINGTON   USN

ROBERT E. LEE   USN

SUBMARINES (SSN and SS)

The US Navy's submarine forces consist of two principal categories: ballistic missile submarines (SSBN), listed in the previous section, and attack submarines (SS and SSN). The Navy's attack submarine force is almost entirely nuclear. The few remaining diesel-electric submarines are all of post-World War II construction. The stated goal of the US Navy is to attain a force level of 90 SSNs ("Skipjack" class and later) by the mid-1980s, but because of construction problems there is bound to be a delay in this programme.

A construction rate of one SSN per year from FY 1979 for the foreseeable future has been proposed by the Department of Defense.

Construction of the submarines recently has been slowed by the late delivery of component equipment and problems in the shipyards. Further complicating the situation has been the start of the Trident missile submarine programme and the loss to the SSN construction programme of the Litton/Ingalls yard at Pascagoula, Mississippi, which delivered its last nuclear submarine in 1974. This leaves only two shipyards in the USA building nuclear submarines. (No diesel-propelled submarines have been built in the USA since 1959).

In January 1977 Secretary of Defense D. H. Rumsfeld reported it has been decided to continue the production of the SSN 688 (Los Angeles) class until at least the mid-1980s rather than to introduce a new generation submarine. We plan to procure eight SSN 688s in the five year programme. A faster building rate will be necessary in the 1980s." In March 1978 Secretary of Defense Harold Brown reduced the procurement rate from eight to five.

The initial sea trials of *Los Angeles* gave an increase over the designed speed and showed improved sound quieting.

Ancillary Programmes: These include development of a wide-aperture array sonar for rapid localisation of targets and attack, the retrofitting of BQQ 5 sonar in all submarines and deployment of submarine-launched Harpoon.

Anti-ship Missiles: An encapsulated version of the Harpoon anti-ship missile has been developed for launching from submarines. The Harpoon, also capable of surface ship and aircraft launch, is a 15 ft weapon carrying a conventional high-explosive warhead. In the encapsulated version (length 21 ft), the Harpoon is launched from a torpedo tube and travels to the surface where the protective capsule is discarded, the missile's fins extend, and the rocket engine ignites. The Harpoon has a range of about 60 n. miles and will be operational in FY 1978/9.

Deep Submergence Vehicles: The US Navy's Deep Submergence Vehicles (DSV), including the nuclear-propelled *NR-1*, are rated as Service Craft and are listed at the end of this section.

Force Levels: As of 1 February 1979 there were 79 SS/SSNs in commission. In addition 24 SSN were under construction and 2 SSN and 1 SSG in reserve.

Names: US submarines generally have been named for fish and other marine life except that fleet ballistic missile submarines have been named for famous Americans. The tradition of naming "fleet" and "attack" submarines for fish was broken in 1971 when three submarines of the "Sturgeon" class and the one-of-a-kind SSN 685 were named after deceased members of Congress. Previously US destroyer-type ships have been named after members of Congress.

Later in 1971 the SSN 688, lead ship for a new class of attack submarines, was named *Los Angeles*, introducing "city" names to US submarines.

Transfers: Three of the four remaining "Tang" class submarines (*Tang, Wahoo* and *Trout*) were scheduled for transfer to the Imperial Iranian navy in 1978-79. *Trout* has been transferred and the other transfers cancelled.

10 + 21 + (7) "LOS ANGELES" CLASS: SUBMARINES (nuclear-powered) (SSN)

Name	No.	Builders	Laid down	Launched	Commissioned	F/S
LOS ANGELES	SSN 688	Newport News S.B. & D.D. Co	8 Jan 1972	6 Apr 1974	13 Nov 1976	PA
BATON ROUGE	SSN 689	Newport News S.B. & D.D. Co	18 Nov 1972	26 Apr 1975	25 June 1977	AA
PHILADELPHIA	SSN 690	General Dynamics (Electric Boat)	12 Aug 1972	19 Oct 1974	25 June 1977	AA
MEMPHIS	SSN 691	Newport News S.B. & D.D. Co	23 June 1973	3 Apr 1976	17 Dec 1977	AA
OMAHA	SSN 692	General Dynamics (Electric Boat)	27 Jan 1973	21 Feb 1976	11 Mar 1978	PA
CINCINNATI	SSN 693	Newport News S.B. & D.D. Co	6 Apr 1974	19 Feb 1977	10 June 1978	AA
GROTON	SSN 694	General Dynamics (Electric Boat)	3 Aug 1973	9 Oct 1976	8 July 1978	AA
BIRMINGHAM	SSN 695	Newport News S.B. & D.D. Co	26 Apr 1975	29 Oct 1977	1y Dec 1978	AA
NEW YORK CITY	SSN 696	General Dynamics (Electric Boat)	15 Dec 1973	18 June 1977	17 Feb 1979	AA
INDIANAPOLIS	SSN 697	General Dynamics (Electric Boat)	19 Oct 1974	30 July 1977	3 Mar 1979	AA
BREMERTON	SSN 698	General Dynamics (Electric Boat)	8 May 1976	22 July 1978	1979	Bldg
JACKSONVILLE	SSN 699	General Dynamics (Electric Boat)	21 Feb 1976	18 Nov 1978	1980	Bldg
DALLAS	SSN 700	General Dynamics (Electric Boat)	9 Oct 1976	1979	1980	Bldg
LA JOLLA	SSN 701	General Dynamics (Electric Boat)	16 Oct 1976	1979	1980	Bldg
PHOENIX	SSN 702	General Dynamics (Electric Boat)	30 July 1977	1979	1981	Bldg
BOSTON	SSN 703	General Dynamics (Electric Boat)	11 Aug 1978	1980	1981	Bldg
BALTIMORE	SSN 704	General Dynamics (Electric Boat)	1979	1980	1982	Bldg
—	SSN 705	General Dynamics (Electric Boat)	1979	1981	1982	Bldg
—	SSN 706	General Dynamics (Electric Boat)	1979	1981	1982	Ord
—	SSN 707	General Dynamics (Electric Boat)	1980	1981	1983	Ord
—	SSN 708	General Dynamics (Electric Boat)	1980	1982	1983	Ord
—	SSN 709	General Dynamics (Electric Boat)	1981	1982	1984	Ord
—	SSN 710	General Dynamics (Electric Boat)	1981	1983	1984	Ord
SAN FRANCISCO	SSN 711	Newport News S.B. and D.D. Co	26 May 1977	1979	1980	Bldg
—	SSN 712	Newport News S.B. and D.D. Co	17 Aug 1978	1980	1981	Bldg
—	SSN 713	Newport News S.B. and D.D. Co	1979	1980	1982	Ord
—	SSN 714	Newport News S.B. and D.D. Co	1979	1981	1982	Ord
—	SSN 715	Newport News S.B. and D.D. Co	1980	1981	1983	Ord
—	SSN 716	Newport News S.B. and D.D. Co	1980	1982	1983	Ord
—	SSN 717	Newport News S.B. and D.D. Co	1981	1982	1984	Ord
—	SSN 718	Newport News S.B. and D.D. Co	1981	1983	1984	Ord
—	SSN 719	Approved FY 1978 programme				
—	SSN 720	Approved FY 1979 programme				
—	SSN 721	Proposed FY 1980 programme				
—	SSN 722	Proposed FY 1981 programme				
—	SSN 723	Proposed FY 1982 programme				
—	SSN 724	Proposed FY 1983 programme				
—	SSN 725	Proposed FY 1984 programme				

Displacement, tons: 6 000 standard; 6 900 dived
Length, feet (metres): 360 *(109.7)*
Beam, feet (metres): 33 *(10.1)*
Draught, feet (metres): 32.3 *(9.85)*
Missiles: Tube launched Harpoon
Torpedo tubes: 4—21 in *(533 mm)* amidships
A/S weapons: SUBROC and Mk 48 A/S torpedoes
Main machinery: 1 pressurised-water cooled S6G (GE) reactor; 2 geared turbines; 1 shaft
Speed, knots: 30+ dived
Complement: 127 (12 officers, 115 enlisted men)

SSN 688-690 were authorised in the Fiscal Year 1970 new construction programme, SSN 691-694 in the FY 1971, SSN 695-699 in the FY 1972, SSN 700-705 in the FY 1973, SSN 706-710 in the FY 1974, SSN 711-713 in the FY 1975, SSN 714-715 in the FY 1976, SSN 716-718 in the FY 1977, SSN 719 in the FY 1978 and SSN 720 in the FY 1979 programme. Additional submarines are planned at the rate of one unit per year into the mid-1980s and then at a faster rate.

Detailed design of the "SSN 688" class as well as construction of the lead submarine was contracted to the Newport News Shipbuilding & Dry Dock Company, Newport News, Virginia. Due to controversy in Washington, strikes and other shipyard problems these submarines are considerably behind schedule with the lead ship being completed over two years behind the original date. Thus, *Los Angeles* was nearly five years from keel laying to commissioning while *Birmingham* took only three years.

Design: Every effort has been made to improve sound quieting and the trials of *Los Angeles* have shown success in this area.

Electronics: UYK-7 computer is installed to assist command and control functions: Mk 113 Mod 10 torpedo fire control system fitted in SSN 688-699 (to be replaced by Mk 117 in near future); Mk 117 in later submarines.

Engineering: The S6G reactor is reportedly a modified version of the D2G type fitted in *Bainbridge* and *Truxtun*. The D2G reactors each produce approximately 30 000 shp. Reactor core life between refuellings is estimated at ten years.

Fiscal: The costs of these submarines have increased in every fiscal year programme. In FY 1976 an average cost of $221.25 million per unit was estimated for a 38-submarine class. However, FY 1977 units are estimated to cost approximately $330 million each, the single FY 1979 unit is estimated at $325.6 million and the single FY 1980 unit $517.9 million.

Radar: BPS 15.

Sonar: BQQ 5 long range acquisition; BQS 15 close range; Towed array fitted.

PHILADELPHIA 5/1977, USN

JACKSONVILLE (alongside *Ohio*) 11/1978, General Dynamics

BIRMINGHAM 2/1979, USN

USA / Submarines 661

1 "GLENARD P. LIPSCOMB" CLASS: SUBMARINE (nuclear-powered) (SSN)

Name	No.	Builders	Laid down	Launched	Commissioned	F/S
LENARD P. LIPSCOMB	SSN 685	General Dynamics (Electric Boat)	5 June 1971	4 Aug 1973	21 Dec 1974	AA

Displacement, tons: 5 813 standard; 6 480 dived
Length, feet (metres): 365 (111·3)
Beam, feet (metres): 31·7 (9·7)
Missiles: To be fitted for Harpoon
Torpedo tubes: 4—21 in (533 mm) amidships
A/S weapons: SUBROC and A/S torpedoes
Main machinery: 1 pressurised-water cooled S5Wa (Westinghouse) reactor. Turbine-electric drive (General Electric); 1 shaft
Speed, knots: approx 25+ dived
Complement: 120 (12 officers, 108 enlisted men)

Studies of a specifically "quiet" submarine were begun in October 1964. After certain setbacks approval for the construction of this submarine was announced on 25 October 1968 and the contract awarded to General Dynamics on 14 October 1970. The Turbine-Electric Drive Submarine (TEDS) was constructed to test "a combination of advanced silencing techniques" involving "a new kind of propulsion system, and new and quieter machinery of various kinds", according to the Department of Defense. The TEDS project will permit an at-sea evaluation of improvements in ASW effectiveness due to noise reduction.
No further class of turbine-electric nuclear submarines has been proposed. Rather, quieting features developed in *Glenard P. Lipscomb* which do not detract from speed have been incorporated in the "Los Angeles" design.
Authorised in the Fiscal Year 1968 new construction programme, estimated construction cost was approximately $200 million.

Electronics: Mk 113 Mod 8 TFCS. To be replaced by Mk 117 Mod 3.

Engineering: Turbine-electric drive eliminates the noisy reduction gears of standard steam turbine power plants. The turbine-electric power plant is larger and heavier than comparable steam turbine submarine machinery.
Tullibee (SSN 597) was an earlier effort at noise reduction through a turbine-electric nuclear plant.

GLENARD P. LIPSCOMB 1974, General Dynamics, Electric Boat Division

1 "NARWHAL" CLASS: SUBMARINE (nuclear-powered) (SSN)

Name	No.	Builders	Laid down	Launched	Commissioned	F/S
NARWHAL	SSN 671	General Dynamics (Electric Boat)	17 Jan 1966	9 Sep 1967	12 July 1969	AA

Displacement, tons: 4 450 standard; 5 350 dived
Length, feet (metres): 314·6 (95·9)
Beam, feet (metres): 37·7 (11·5)
Draught, feet (metres): 27 (8·2)
Missiles: To be fitted for Harpoon
Torpedo tubes: 4—21 in (533 mm) amidships
A/S weapons: SUBROC and A/S torpedoes
Main machinery: 1 pressurised water-cooled S5G (General Electric) reactor. 2 steam turbines; 17 000 shp; 1 shaft
Speed, knots: 20+ surfaced; 30+ dived
Complement: 107 (12 officers, 95 enlisted men)

Authorised in the Fiscal Year 1964 new construction programme.

Design: *Narwhal* is similar to the "Sturgeon" class submarines in hull design.

Electronics: Mk 113 Mod 6 torpedo fire control system. To be replaced by Mk 117 system.

Engineering: *Narwhal* is fitted with the prototype sea-going S5G natural circulation reactor plant. According to Admiral H. G. Rickover the natural circulation reactor "offers promise of increased reactor plant reliability, simplicity, and noise reduction due to the elimination of the need for large reactor coolant pumps and associated electrical and control equipment by making maximum advantage of natural convection to circulate the reactor coolant".
The Atomic Energy Commission's Knolls Atomic Power Laboratory was given prime responsibility for development of the power plant. Construction of a land-based prototype plant began in May 1961 at the National Reactor Testing Station in Idaho. The reactor achieved initial criticality on 12 September 1965.

Sonar: BQS 8 upward-looking sonar for under-ice work (photo). BQQ 2 system (BQS 6 active and BQR 7 passive). BQS 6 is fitted in a 15 ft sphere and BQR 7 with conformal hydrophone array forward.

NARWHAL 2/1974, USN

37 "STURGEON" CLASS: SUBMARINES (nuclear-powered) (SSN)

Name	No.	Builders	Laid down	Launched	Commissioned	F/S
STURGEON	SSN 637	General Dynamics (Electric Boat)	10 Aug 1963	26 Feb 1966	3 Mar 1967	AA
WHALE	SSN 638	General Dynamics (Quincy)	27 May 1964	14 Oct 1966	12 Oct 1968	AA
TAUTOG	SSN 639	Ingalls Shipbuilding Corp	27 Jan 1964	15 Apr 1967	17 Aug 1968	PA
GRAYLING	SSN 646	Portsmouth Naval Shipyard	12 May 1964	22 June 1967	11 Oct 1969	AA
POGY	SSN 647	Ingalls Shipbuilding Corp	4 May 1964	3 June 1967	15 May 1971	PA
ASPRO	SSN 648	Ingalls Shipbuilding Corp	23 Nov 1964	29 Nov 1967	20 Feb 1969	PA
SUNFISH	SSN 649	General Dynamics (Quincy)	15 Jan 1965	14 Oct 1966	15 Mar 1969	AA
PARGO	SSN 650	General Dynamics (Electric Boat)	3 June 1964	17 Sep 1966	5 Jan 1968	AA
QUEENFISH	SSN 651	Newport News S.B. & D.D. Co	11 May 1965	25 Feb 1966	6 Dec 1966	PA
PUFFER	SSN 652	Ingalls Shipbuilding Corp	8 Feb 1965	30 Mar 1968	9 Aug 1969	PA
RAY	SSN 653	Newport News S.B. & D.D. Co	1 Apr 1965	21 June 1966	12 Apr 1967	AA
SAND LANCE	SSN 660	Portsmouth Naval Shipyard	15 Jan 1965	11 Nov 1969	25 Sep 1971	AA
LAPON	SSN 661	Newport News S.B. & D.D. Co	26 July 1965	16 Dec 1966	14 Dec 1967	AA
GURNARD	SSN 662	San Francisco NSY (Mare Island)	22 Dec 1964	20 May 1967	6 Dec 1968	PA
HAMMERHEAD	SSN 663	Newport News S.B. & D.D. Co	29 Nov 1965	14 Apr 1967	28 June 1968	AA
SEA DEVIL	SSN 664	Newport News S.B. & D.D. Co	12 Apr 1966	5 Oct 1967	30 Jan 1969	AA
GUITARRO	SSN 665	San Francisco NSY (Mare Island)	9 Dec 1965	27 July 1968	9 Sep 1972	PA
HAWKBILL	SSN 666	San Francisco NSY (Mare Island)	12 Sep 1966	12 Apr 1969	4 Feb 1971	PA
BERGALL	SSN 667	General Dynamics (Electric Boat)	16 Apr 1966	17 Feb 1968	13 June 1969	AA
SPADEFISH	SSN 668	Newport News S.B. & D.D. Co	21 Dec 1966	15 May 1968	14 Aug 1969	AA
SEAHORSE	SSN 669	General Dynamics (Electric Boat)	13 Aug 1966	15 June 1968	19 Sep 1969	AA
FINBACK	SSN 670	Newport News S.B. & D.D. Co	26 June 1967	7 Dec 1968	4 Feb 1970	AA
PINTADO	SSN 672	San Francisco NSY (Mare Island)	27 Oct 1967	16 Aug 1969	11 Sep 1971	PA
FLYING FISH	SSN 673	General Dynamics (Electric Boat)	30 June 1967	17 May 1969	29 Apr 1970	AA
TREPANG	SSN 674	General Dynamics (Electric Boat)	28 Oct 1967	27 Sep 1969	14 Aug 1970	AA
BLUEFISH	SSN 675	General Dynamics (Electric Boat)	13 Mar 1968	10 Jan 1970	8 Jan 1971	AA
BILLFISH	SSN 676	General Dynamics (Electric Boat)	20 Sep 1968	1 May 1970	12 Mar 1971	AA
DRUM	SSN 677	San Francisco NSY (Mare Island)	20 Aug 1968	23 May 1970	15 Apr 1972	PA
ARCHERFISH	SSN 678	General Dynamics (Electric Boat)	19 June 1969	16 Jan 1971	17 Dec 1971	AA
SILVERSIDES	SSN 679	General Dynamics (Electric Boat)	13 Oct 1969	4 June 1971	5 May 1972	AA
WILLIAM H. BATES (ex-*Redfish*)	SSN 680	Ingalls Shipbuilding (Litton)	4 Aug 1969	11 Dec 1971	5 May 1973	PA
BATFISH	SSN 681	General Dynamics (Electric Boat)	9 Feb 1970	9 Oct 1971	1 Sep 1972	AA
TUNNY	SSN 682	Ingalls Shipbuilding (Litton)	22 May 1970	10 June 1972	26 Jan 1974	PA
PARCHE	SSN 683	Ingalls Shipbuilding (Litton)	10 Dec 1970	13 Jan 1973	17 Aug 1974	PA
CAVALLA	SSN 684	General Dynamics (Electric Boat)	4 June 1970	19 Feb 1972	9 Feb 1973	PA
L. MENDEL RIVERS	SSN 686	Newport News S.B. & D.D. Co	26 June 1971	2 June 1973	1 Feb 1975	AA
RICHARD B. RUSSELL	SSN 687	Newport News S.B. & D.D. Co	19 Oct 1971	12 Jan 1974	16 Aug 1975	AA

Displacement, tons: 3 640 standard; 4 640 dived
Length, feet (metres): 292·2 *(89·0)* (see *Design* notes)
Beam, feet (metres): 31·7 *(9·5)*
Draught, feet (metres): 26 *(7·9)*
Missiles: Being fitted for Harpoon (already in SSN 638, 662, 663, 686, 687)
Torpedo tubes: 4—21 in *(533 mm)* Mk 63 amidships
A/S weapons: SUBROC and A/S torpedoes
Main machinery: 1 pressurised-water cooled S5W (Westinghouse) reactor; 2 steam turbines; 15 000 shp; 1 shaft
Speed, knots: 20+ surfaced; 30+ dived
Complement: 107 (12 officers, 95 enlisted men)

The 37 "Sturgeon" class attack submarines comprise the largest US Navy group of nuclear-powered ships built to the same design to date.
SSN 637-639 were authorised in the Fiscal Year 1962 new construction programme. SSN 646-653 in FY 1963, SSN 660-664 in FY 1964, SSN 665-670 in FY 1965, SSN 672-677 in FY 1966, SSN 678-682 in FY 1967, SSN 683-684 in FY 1968, and SSN 686-687 in FY 1969.

Construction: *Pogy* was begun by the New York Shipbuilding Corp (Camden, New Jersey), contract with whom was terminated on 5 June 1967; contract for completion awarded to Ingalls Shipbuilding Corp on 7 December 1967.
Guitarro sank in 35 ft of water on 15 May 1969 while being fitted out at the San Francisco Bay Naval Shipyard. According to a congressional report, the sinking, caused by Shipyard workers, was "wholly avoidable". Subsequently raised; damage estimated at $25 million. Completion delayed more than two years.

Design: These submarines are slightly larger than the previous "Thresher" class and can be identified by their taller sail structure and the lower position of their diving planes on the sail (to improve control at periscope depth). Sail height is 20 ft, 6 in above deck. Sail-mounted diving planes rotate to vertical for breaking through ice when surfacing in arctic regions.
These submarines probably are slightly slower than the previous "Thresher" and "Skipjack" classes because of their increased size with the same propulsion system as in the earlier classes.
SSN 678/684, 686 and 687 are ten feet longer than remainder of class to accommodate extra sonar and electronic gear.

Electronics: Mk 113 torpedo fire control system is being replaced by Mk 117 (already in SSN 638, 639, 646-9, 652, 662-3, 665, 668-9, 673).

Name: *William H. Bates* (SSN 680) previously *Redfish* renamed 25 June 1971.

Operational: *Whale, Pargo*, and older nuclear submarine *Sargo* conducted exercises in the Arctic ice pack during March-April 1969. *Whale* surfaced at the geographic North Pole on 6 April, the 60th anniversary of Rear-Admiral Robert E. Peary's reaching the North Pole. This was the first instance of single-screw US nuclear submarines surfacing in the Arctic ice.

Radar: BPS 14 Search.

Sonar: BQQ 2 sonar system. Principal components of the BQQ 2 include the BQS 6 active sonar, with transducers mounted in a 15 ft diameter sonar sphere, and BQR 7 passive sonar, with hydrophones in a conformal array on sides of forward hull. The active sonar sphere is fitted in the optimum bow position, requiring placement of torpedo tubes amidships. These submarines also have BQS 8 under-ice sonar and BQS 12 (first 16 units) or BQS 13 active/passive sonars. Transducers for the BQS 8, intended primarily for under-ice navigation, are in two small domes aft of the sail structure.
Sonar suites of the *Guitarro* and *Cavalla* have been modified. All "Sturgeon" class submarines are to be refitted with replacement of the BQQ 2 by BQQ 5 during regular overhauls.

GUITARRO
6/1978, Dr. Giorgio Arr

BILLFISH (at Zeebrugge)
11/1978, Leo van Ginderen

HAWKBILL
10/1978, Dr. Giorgio Arra

Submersibles: *Hawkbill* and *Pintado* have been modified to carry and support the Navy's Deep Submergence Rescue Vehicles (DSRV). See section on Deep Submergence Vehicles for additional DSRV details.

USA / Submarines 663

13 "THRESHER" CLASS: SUBMARINES (nuclear-powered) (SSN)

Name	No.	Builders	Laid down	Launched	Commissioned	F/S
PERMIT	SSN 594	Mare Island Naval Shipyard	16 July 1959	1 July 1961	29 May 1962	PA
PLUNGER	SSN 595	Mare Island Naval Shipyard	2 Mar 1960	9 Dec 1961	21 Nov 1962	PA
BARB	SSN 596	Ingalls Shipbuilding Corp	9 Nov 1959	12 Feb 1962	24 Aug 1963	PA
POLLACK	SSN 603	New York Shipbuilding Corp	14 Mar 1960	17 Mar 1962	26 May 1964	AA
HADDO	SSN 604	New York Shipbuilding Corp	9 Sep 1960	18 Aug 1962	16 Dec 1964	PA
JACK	SSN 605	Portsmouth Naval Shipyard	16 Sep 1960	24 Apr 1963	31 Mar 1967	AA
TINOSA	SSN 606	Portsmouth Naval Shipyard	24 Nov 1959	9 Dec 1961	17 Oct 1964	AA
DACE	SSN 607	Ingalls Shipbuilding Corp	6 June 1960	18 Aug 1962	4 Apr 1964	AA
GUARDFISH	SSN 612	New York Shipbuilding Corp	28 Feb 1961	15 May 1965	20 Dec 1966	AA
FLASHER	SSN 613	General Dynamics (Electric Boat)	14 Apr 1961	22 June 1963	22 July 1966	PA
GREENLING	SSN 614	General Dynamics (Electric Boat)	15 Aug 1961	4 Apr 1964	3 Nov 1967	PA
GATO	SSN 615	General Dynamics (Electric Boat)	15 Dec 1961	14 May 1964	25 Jan 1968	AA
HADDOCK	SSN 621	Ingalls Shipbuilding Corp	24 Apr 1961	21 May 1966	22 Dec 1967	AA

Displacement, tons: 3 750 standard; *Flasher, Greenling* and *Gato* 3 800; 4 300 dived except *Jack* 4 470 dived, *Flasher, Greenling* and *Gato* 4 242 dived
Length, feet (metres): 278·5 *(84·9)* oa except *Jack* 297·4 *(90·7)* oa, *Flasher, Greenling* and *Gato* 292·2 *(89·1)*
Beam, feet (metres): 31·7 *(9·6)*
Draught, feet (metres): 28·4 *(8·7)*
Missiles: To be fitted for Harpoon
Torpedo tubes: 4—21 in *(533 mm)* Mk 63 amidships
A/S weapons: SUBROC and A/S torpedoes
Main machinery: 1 pressurised-water cooled S5W (Westinghouse) reactor; 2 steam turbines, 15 000 shp; 1 shaft
Speed, knots: 20+ surfaced; 30+ dived
Complement: 103 (12 officers, 91 enlisted men)

They have a greater depth capability than previous SSNs and are the first to combine the SUBROC anti-submarine missile capability with the advanced BQQ 2 sonar system. The lead ship of the class, *Thresher* (SSN 593), was authorised in the Fiscal Year 1957 new construction programme, the SSN 594-596 in FY 1958, SSN 603-607 in FY 1959, SSN 612-615 in FY 1960, and SSN 621 in FY 1961.
Thresher (SSN 593) was lost off the coast of New England on 10 April 1963 while on post-overhaul trials. She went down with 129 men on board (108 crewmen plus four naval officers and 17 civilians on board for trials).

Construction: *Greenling* and *Gato* were launched by the Electric Boat Division of the General Dynamics Corp (Groton, Connecticut); towed to Quincy Division (Massachusetts) for lengthening and completion.

Design: *Jack* was built to a modified design to test a modified power plant (see *Engineering* notes).
Flasher, Gato and *Greenling* were modified during construction; fitted with SUBSAFE features, heavier machinery, and larger sail structures.
These submarines have a modified "tear-drop" hull design. Their bows are devoted to sonar and their four torpedo tubes are amidships, angled out, two to port and two to starboard. The sail structure height of these submarines is 13 ft 9 in to 15 ft above the deck, with later submarines of this class having a sail height of 20 ft.

Electronics: Mk 113 torpedo fire control system which is being replaced by Mk 117 (already in SSN 594 and 621).

Engineering: *Jack* is fitted with two propellers on one shaft (actually a single shaft within a sleeve-like shaft) and a counter-rotating turbine without a reduction gear. Both innovations are designed to reduce operating noises. To accommodate the larger turbine, the engine spaces were lengthened by 10 ft and the shaft structure was lengthened 7 ft to mount the two propellers. The propellers are of different size and are smaller than in the other submarines of this class. Also eliminated in *Jack* was a clutch and secondary-propulsion electric motor. *Jack's* propulsion arrangement provides a 10 per cent increase in power efficiency, but no increase in speed. The arrangement was not a success and was not repeated.

Names: Names changed during construction: *Plunger* ex-*Pollack*; *Barb* ex-*Pollack* ex-*Plunger*; *Pollack* ex-*Barb*.

Sonar: BQQ 2 (BQS 6 active and BQR 7 passive). The positioning of the conformal array for BQR 7 in the bow dictates the use of midships tubes.

BARB 9/1977, Dr. Giorgio Arra

FLASHER 7/1978, Dr. Giorgio Arra

1 "TULLIBEE" CLASS: SUBMARINE (nuclear-powered) (SSN)

Name	No.	Builders	Laid down	Launched	Commissioned	F/S
TULLIBEE	SSN 597	General Dynamics (Electric Boat)	26 May 1958	27 Apr 1960	9 Nov 1960	AA

Displacement, tons: 2 317 standard; 2 640 dived
Length, feet (metres): 273 *(83·2)*
Beam, feet (metres): 23·3 *(7·1)*
Draught, feet (metres): 21 *(6·4)*
Torpedo tubes: 4—21 in *(533 mm)* Mk 64 amidships
A/S weapons: A/S torpedoes
Main machinery: 1 pressurised-water cooled S2C (Combustion Engineering) reactor; turbo-electric drive with steam turbine (Westinghouse); 2 500 shp; 1 shaft
Speed, knots: 15+ surfaced; 20+ dived
Complement: 56 (6 officers, 50 enlisted men)

Tullibee was designed specifically for anti-submarine operations and was the first US submarine with the optimum bow position devoted entirely to sonar. No additional submarine of this type was constructed because of the success of the larger, more-versatile "Thresher" class. *Tullibee* was authorised in the Fiscal Year 1958 new construction programme. She is no longer considered a "first line" submarine.

Design: She has a modified, elongated "tear-drop" hull design. Originally she was planned as a 1 000 ton craft, but reactor requirements and other considerations increased her size during design and construction.
Her four amidships torpedo tubes are angled out from the centreline two to port and two to starboard. Not fitted to fire SUBROC.

Electronics: Mk 112 torpedo fire control system.

Engineering: She has a small nuclear power plant designed and developed by the Combustion Engineering Company. The propulsion system features turbo-electric drive rather than conventional steam turbines with reduction gears in an effort to reduce operating noises.

Navigation: Fitted with Ship's Inertial Navigation System (SINS).

Sonar: BQQ 2 system (BQS 6 active and BQR 7 passive) the first submarine so fitted.
BQG 4 passive (PUFFS—Passive Underwater Fire Control Feasibility System) with three (originally two) domes on top of hull.

TULLIBEE 1968, USN

664 USA / Submarines

5 "SKIPJACK" CLASS: SUBMARINES (nuclear-powered) (SSN)

Name	No.	Builders	Laid down	Launched	Commissioned	F/S
SKIPJACK	SSN 585	General Dynamics (Electric Boat)	29 May 1956	26 May 1958	15 Apr 1959	AA
SCAMP	SSN 588	Mare Island Naval Shipyard	23 Jan 1959	8 Oct 1960	5 June 1961	AA
SCULPIN	SSN 590	Ingalls Shipbuilding Corp	3 Feb 1958	31 Mar 1960	1 June 1961	AA
SHARK	SSN 591	Newport News S.B. & D.D. Co	24 Feb 1958	16 Mar 1960	9 Feb 1961	AA
SNOOK	SSN 592	Ingalls Shipbuilding Corp	7 Apr 1958	31 Oct 1960	24 Oct 1961	PA

Displacement, tons: 3 075 surfaced; 3 513 dived
Length, feet (metres): 251·7 *(76·7)*
Beam, feet (metres): 31·5 *(9·6)*
Draught, feet (metres): 29·4 *(8·9)*
Torpedo tubes: 6—21 in *(533 mm)* bow (Mk 59)
A/S weapons: A/S torpedoes
Main machinery: 1 pressurised-water cooled S5W (Westinghouse) reactor; 2 steam turbines (Westinghouse in *Skipjack*; General Electric in others); 15 000 shp; 1 shaft
Speed, knots: 16+ surfaced; 30+ dived
Complement: 93 (8 officers, 85 enlisted men)

Combine the high-speed endurance of nuclear propulsion with the high-speed "tear-drop" "Albacore" hull design. *Skipjack* was authorised in the Fiscal Year 1956 new construction programme and the five other submarines of this class were authorised in FY 1957.
These submarines are still considered suitable for "first line" service.
Each cost approximately $40 million.
Scorpion (SSN 589) of this class was lost some 400 miles southwest of the Azores while *en route* from the Mediterranean to Norfolk, Virginia, in May 1968. She went down with 99 men on board.

Construction: *Scorpion's* keel was laid down twice; the original keel, laid down on 1 November 1957, was renumbered SSBN 598 and became the Polaris submarine *George Washington;* the second SSN 589 keel became *Scorpion*. *Scamp's* keel laying was delayed when materiel for her was diverted to SSBN 599. This class introduced the Newport News Shipbuilding and Dry Dock Company and the Ingalls Shipbuilding Corporation to nuclear submarine construction. Newport News had not previously built submarines since before World War I.

Design: *Skipjack* was the first US nuclear submarine built to the "tear-drop" design. These submarines have a single propeller shaft (vice two in earlier nuclear submarines) and their diving planes are mounted on sail structures to improve underwater manoeuvrability. No after torpedo tubes are fitted because of their tapering sterns.

Electronics: Fitted with Mk 101 Mod 17 TFCS.

Engineering: The "Skipjack" class introduced the S5W fast attack submarine propulsion plant which has been employed in all subsequent US attack and ballistic missile submarines except the "Los Angeles" class (SSN 688) *Narwhal* (SSN 671) and *Glenard P. Lipscomb* (SSN 685). The plant was developed by the Bettis Atomic Power Laboratory.

Sonar: Modified BQS 4.

SCAMP   12/1976, Dr. Giorgio Arra

SCAMP   12/1976, Dr. Giorgio Arra

SCAMP   12/1976, Dr. Giorgio Arra

USA / Submarines 665

1 "HALIBUT" CLASS: SUBMARINE (nuclear-powered) (SSN)

Name	No.	Builders	Laid down	Launched	Commissioned	F/S
HALIBUT	SSN 587 (ex-SSGN 587)	Mare Island Naval Shipyard, Vallejo, Calif.	11 Apr 1957	9 Jan 1959	4 Jan 1960	PR

Displacement, tons: 3 850 standard; 5 000 dived
Length, feet (metres): 350 (106·6)
Beam, feet (metres): 29·5 (8·9)
Draught, feet (metres): 21·5 (6·5)
Torpedo tubes: 6—21 in (533 mm) 4 bow (Mk 61); 2 stern (Mk 62)
Main machinery: 1 pressurised-water cooled S3W (Westinghouse) reactor; 2 steam turbines (Westinghouse); 6 600 shp; 2 shafts
Speed, knots: 15+ surfaced; 20+ dived
Complement: 98 (10 officers, 88 enlisted men)

Halibut is believed to have been the first submarine designed and constructed specifically to fire guided missiles.
She was originally intended to have diesel-electric propulsion but on 27 February 1956 the Navy announced she would have nuclear propulsion. She was the US Navy's only nuclear-powered guided missile submarine (SSGN) to be completed. Authorised in the Fiscal Year 1956 new construction programme and built for an estimated cost of $45 million.
She was reclassified as an attack submarine on 25 July 1965 after the Navy discarded the Regulus submarine-launched missile force. Her missile equipment was removed. Reportedly she has been fitted with a ducted bow thruster to permit precise control and manoeuvring, when active employed on research duties.
She can carry the 50 ft Deep Submergence Rescue Vehicle (DSRV) and other submersibles on her after deck and operate these while dived.
Decommissioned on 30 June 1976 and laid up at Bremerton.

Design: Built with a large missile hangar faired into her bow (see *picture*). Her hull was intended primarily to provide a stable surface launching platform rather than for speed or manoeuvrabilty.

Electronics: Mk 101 Mod 11 torpedo fire control system (removed 1977).

Missiles: Designed to carry two Regulus II surface-to-surface missiles. The Regulus II was a transonic missile which could carry a nuclear warhead and had a range of 1 000 miles. The Regulus II was cancelled before becoming operational and *Halibut* operated from 1960 to 1964 carrying five Regulus I missiles, subsonic cruise missiles which could deliver a nuclear warhead on targets 575 n miles from launch.
During this period the US Navy operated a maximum of five Regulus guided (cruise) missile submarines, *Halibut*, the post-war constructed *Grayback* (SSG 574 now SS 574) and *Growler* (SSG 577), and the World War II-built *Tunny* (SSG 282 subsequently LPSS 282) and *Barbero* (SSG 317).
As SSGN *Halibut* carried a complement of 11 officers and 108 enlisted men.

Navigation: Fitted with Ship's Inertial Navigation System (SINS).

Sonar: BQS 4.

HALIBUT (with DSRV embarked) *1970, USN*

1 "TRITON" CLASS: SUBMARINE (nuclear-powered) (SSN)

Name	No.	Builders	Laid down	Launched	Commissioned	F/S
TRITON	SSN 586 (ex-SSRN 586)	General Dynamics (Electric Boat)	29 May 1956	19 Aug 1958	10 Nov 1959	AR

Displacement, tons: 5 940 surfaced; 6 670 dived
Length, feet (metres): 447 (136·2)
Beam, feet (metres): 37 (11·3)
Draught, feet (metres): 24 (7·3)
Torpedo tubes: 6—21 in (533 mm) 4 bow; 2 stern (Mk 60)
Main machinery: 2 pressurised-water cooled S4G (General Electric) reactors;
2 steam turbines (General Electric); 34 000 shp; 2 shafts
Speed, knots: 27+ surfaced; 20+ dived
Complement as SSRN: 170 (14 officers, 156 enlisted men)

Triton was designed and constructed to serve as a radar picket submarine to operate in conjunction with surface carrier task forces.

Authorised in the Fiscal Year 1956 new construction programme and built for an estimated cost of $109 million.
Triton circumnavigated the globe in 1960, remaining submerged except when her sail structure broke the surface to enable an ill sailor to be taken off near the Falkland Islands. The 41 500 mile cruise took 83 days and was made at an average speed of 18 knots.
Reclassified as an attack submarine (SSN) on 1 March 1961 as the Navy dropped the radar picket submarine programme. She is no longer considered a "first line" submarine and was decommissioned on 3 May 1969 to become the first US nuclear submarine placed in preservation. Laid up at Norfolk.
There had been proposals to operate the *Triton* as an underwater national command post afloat, but no funds were provided.

Design: *Triton* was fitted with an elaborate combat information centre and large radar antenna which retracted into the sail structure. Until the Trident SSBN programme *Triton* was the longest US submarine ever constructed.

Electronics: Mk 101 Mod 11 torpedo fire control system.

Engineering: *Triton* is the only US submarine with two nuclear reactors. The Atomic Energy Commission's Knolls Atomic Power Laboratory was given prime responsibility for development of the power plant. After 2½ years of operation, during which she steamed more than 110 000 miles, *Triton* was overhauled and refuelled from July 1962 to March 1964.

Sonar: BQS 4.

TRITON *1959, USN*

4 "SKATE" CLASS: SUBMARINES (nuclear-powered) (SSN)

Name	No.	Builders	Laid down	Launched	Commissioned	F/S
SKATE	SSN 578	General Dynamics (Electric Boat)	21 July 1955	16 May 1957	23 Dec 1957	PA
SWORDFISH	SSN 579	Portsmouth Naval Shipyard	25 Jan 1956	27 Aug 1957	15 Sep 1958	PA
SARGO	SSN 583	Mare Island Naval Shipyard	21 Feb 1956	10 Oct 1957	1 Oct 1958	PA
SEADRAGON	SSN 584	Portsmouth Naval Shipyard	20 June 1956	16 Aug 1958	5 Dec 1959	PA

Displacement, tons: 2 310 light; 2 360 full load (578-9); 2 384 light; 2 547 full load (583-4)
Length, feet (metres): 267·7 *(81·5)*
Beam, feet (metres): 25 *(7·6)*
Draught, feet (metres): 22 *(6·7)*
Torpedo tubes: 8—21 in *(533 mm)* 6 bow; 2 stern (short)
Main machinery: 1 pressurised-water cooled S3W (Westinghouse) reactor in *Skate* and *Sargo*, 1 pressurised-water cooled S4W (Westinghouse) in *Swordfish* and *Seadragon*; 2 steam turbines (Westinghouse); 6 600 shp; 2 shafts
Speed, knots: 20+ surfaced; 25+ dived
Complement: 87 (11 officers, 76 enlisted men)

The first production model nuclear-powered submarines, similar in design to *Nautilus* but smaller. *Skate* and *Swordfish* were authorised in the Fiscal Year 1955 new construction programme and *Sargo* and *Seadragon* in FY 1956.
Skate was the first submarine to make a completely submerged transatlantic crossing. In 1958 she established a (then) record of 31 days submerged with a sealed atmosphere, on 11 August 1958 she passed under the ice at the North Pole during a polar cruise, and on 17 March 1959 she became the first submarine to surface at the North Pole. *Sargo* undertook a polar cruise during January-February 1960 and surfaced at the North Pole on 9 February 1960.
Seadragon sailed from the Atlantic to the Pacific via the Northwest Passage (Lancaster Sound, Barrow and McClure Straits) in August 1960. *Skate,* operating from New London, Connecticut and *Seadragon,* based at Pearl Harbour, rendezvoused under the ice at the North Pole on 2 August 1962 and then conducted anti-submarine exercises under the polar ice pack and surfaced together at the North Pole.
Skate also operated in the Arctic Ocean during April-May 1969, conducting exercises under the Arctic ice pack with the later nuclear-powered attack submarines *Pargo* and *Whale;* and again during the spring of 1971 with the nuclear attack submarine *Trepang.*

Electronics: Fitted with Mk 101 Mod 19 torpedo fire control system.

Engineering: The reactors for this class were developed by the Atomic Energy Commission's Bettis Atomic Power Laboratory, the new propulsion system was similar to that of *Nautilus* but considerably simplified with improved operation and maintenance. The propulsion plant developed under this programme had two arrangements, the S3W configuration in *Skate, Sargo* and *Halibut* and the S4W configuration in *Swordfish* and *Seadragon.* Both arrangements proved satisfactory. *Skate* began her first overhaul and refuelling in January 1961 after steaming 120 862 miles on her initial reactor core during three years of operation. *Swordfish* began her first overhaul and refuelling in early 1962 after more than three years of operation in which time she steamed 112 000 miles.

Sonar: BQS 4.

SWORDFISH 8/1977, Dr. Giorgio Arra

1 "SEAWOLF" CLASS: SUBMARINE (nuclear-powered) (SSN)

Name	No.	Builders	Laid down	Launched	Commissioned	F/S
SEAWOLF	SSN 575	General Dynamics (Electric Boat)	15 Sep 1953	21 July 1955	30 Mar 1957	PA

Displacement, tons: 3 765 surfaced; 4 200 dived
Length, feet (metres): 337·5 *(102·9)*
Beam, feet (metres): 27·7 *(8·4)*
Draught, feet (metres): 23 *(7)*
Torpedo tubes: 6—21 in *(533 mm)* bow
Main machinery: 1 pressurised-water cooled S2Wa (Westinghouse) reactor; 2 steam turbines (General Electric), 15 000 shp; 2 shafts
Speed, knots: 20+ surfaced; 20+ dived
Complement: 101 (11 officers, 90 enlisted men)

Seawolf was the world's second nuclear-propelled vehicle; she was constructed almost simultaneously with *Nautilus* to test a competitive reactor design. Funds for *Seawolf* were authorised in the Fiscal Year 1952 new construction programme.
She is no longer considered a "first line" submarine and has been engaged primarily in research work since 1969.

Design: GUPPY-type hull with stepped sail.

Electronics: Mk 101 Mod 8 torpedo fire control system.

Engineering: Initial work in the development of naval nuclear propulsion plants investigated a number of concepts, two of which were of sufficient interest to warrant full development: the pressurised water and liquid metal (sodium). *Nautilus* was provided with a pressurised-water reactor plant and *Seawolf* was fitted initially with a liquid-metal reactor. Originally known as the Submarine Intermediate Reactor (SIR), the liquid-metal plant was developed by the Atomic Energy Commission's Knolls Atomic Power Laboratory.
The SIR Mark II/S2G reactor in *Seawolf* achieved initial criticality on 25 June 1956. Steam leaks developed during the dock-side testing. The plant was shut down and it was determined that the leaks were caused by sodium-potassium alloy which had entered the super-heater steam piping. After repairs and testing *Seawolf* began sea trials on 21 January 1957. The trials were run at reduced power and after two years of operation *Seawolf* entered the Electric Boat yard for removal of her sodium-cooled plant and installation of a pressurised-water plant similar to that installed in *Nautilus* (designated S2Wa). When the original *Seawolf* plant was shut down in December 1958 the submarine had steamed a total of 71 611 miles. She was recommissioned on 30 September 1960. The pressurised-water reactor was refuelled for the first time between May 1965 and August 1967, having propelled *Seawolf* for more than 161 000 miles on its initial fuel core.

Sonar: BQS 4.

SEAWOLF 1974, William Whalen, Jr.

USA / Submarines 667

1 "NAUTILUS" CLASS: SUBMARINE (nuclear-powered) (SSN)

Name	No.	Builders	Laid down	Launched	Commissioned	FiS
NAUTILUS	SSN 571	General Dynamics (Electric Boat)	14 June 1952	21 Jan 1954	30 Sep 1954	AA

Displacement, tons: 3 764 surfaced; 4 040 dived
Length, feet (metres): 319·4 *(97·4)*
Beam, feet (metres): 27·6 *(8·4)*
Draught, feet (metres): 22 *(6·7)*
Torpedo tubes: 6—21 in *(533 mm)* bow (Mk 50)
Main machinery: 1 pressurised-water cooled S2W (Westinghouse) reactor; 2 steam turbines (Westinghouse), approx 15 000 shp; 2 shafts
Speed, knots: 20+ surfaced; 20+ dived
Complement: 105 (13 officers, 92 enlisted men)

Nautilus was the world's first nuclear-propelled vehicle. She predated the first Soviet nuclear-powered submarine by an estimated five years.
The funds for her construction were authorised in the Fiscal Year 1952 budget. She put to sea for the first time on 17 January 1955 and signalled the historic message: "Underway on nuclear power".
On her shakedown cruise in May 1955 she steamed submerged from London, Connecticut, to San Juan, Puerto Rico, travelling more than 1 300 miles in 84 hours at an average speed of almost 16 knots; she later steamed submerged from Key West, Florida, to New London, a distance of 1 397 miles, at an average speed of more than 20 knots.
During 1958 she undertook extensive operations under the Arctic ice pack and in August she made history's first polar transit from the Pacific to the Atlantic, steaming from Pearl Harbour to Portland, England. Under the ice she passed the geographic North Pole on 3 August 1958.
During 1972-74 she underwent a 30 month overhaul and modification at the Electric Boat yard in Groton, Connecticut, where the submarine was built. Modified for submarine communications research. Scheduled for decommissioning at Mare Island on 30 September 1979, to become a memorial at the US Naval Academy, Annapolis.

Electronics: Mk 101 Mod 6 torpedo fire control system.

Engineering: In January 1948 the Department of Defense requested the Atomic Energy Commission to undertake the design, development, and construction of a nuclear reactor for submarine propulsion. Initial research and conceptual design of the Submarine Thermal Reactor (STR) was undertaken by the Argonne National Laboratory. Subsequently the Atomic Energy Commission's Bettis Atomic Power Laboratory, operated by the Westinghouse Electric Corporation, undertook development of the first nuclear propulsion plant.
Nautilus STR Mark II nuclear plant (redesignated S2W) was first operated on 20 December 1954 and first developed full power on 3 January 1955.
After more than two years of operation, during which she steamed 62 562 miles, she began an overhaul which included refuelling in April 1957. She was again refuelled in 1959 after steaming 91 324 miles on her second fuel core, and again in 1964 after steaming approximately 150 000 miles on her third fuel core.

Sonar: BQS 4.

NAUTILUS   *1975, General Dynamics, Electric Boat Division*

NAUTILUS   *1975, General Dynamics, Electric Boat Division*

3 "BARBEL" CLASS: SUBMARINES (SS)

Name	No.	Builders	Laid down	Launched	Commissioned	FiS
BARBEL	SS 580	Portsmouth Naval Shipyard	18 May 1956	19 July 1958	17 Jan 1959	PA
BLUEBACK	SS 581	Ingalls Shipbuilding Corp	15 Apr 1957	16 May 1959	15 Oct 1959	PA
BONEFISH	SS 582	New York Shipbuilding Corp	3 June 1957	22 Nov 1958	9 July 1959	PA

Displacement, tons: 2 145 surfaced; 2 894 dived
Length, feet (metres): 219·1 *(66·8)*
Beam, feet (metres): 29 *(8·8)*
Draught, feet (metres): 28 *(8·5)*
Torpedo tubes: 6—21 in *(533 mm)* bow (Mk 58)
Main machinery: 3 diesels; 4 800 bhp (Fairbanks-Morse); 2 electric motors (General Electric); 3 150 shp; 1 shaft
Speed, knots: 15 surfaced; 21 dived
Complement: 77 (8 officers, 69 men)

These submarines were the last non-nuclear combatant submarines built by the US Navy. All three were authorised in the Fiscal Year 1956 new construction programme.

Construction: *Blueback* was the first submarine built by the Ingalls Shipbuilding Corp at Pascagoula, Mississippi, and *Bonefish* was the first constructed at the New York Shipbuilding Corp yard in Camden, New Jersey. None of the three shipyards that built this class is now employed in submarine construction.

Design: These submarines have the "tear drop" hull design which was tested in the experimental submarine *Albacore*. As built, their fore planes were bow-mounted; subsequently moved to the sail.
They introduced a new concept in centralised arrangement of controls in an "attack centre" to increase efficiency; which has been adapted for all later US combat submarines.

Electronics: Mk 101 Mod 20 torpedo fire control system.

Sonar: BQS 4.

BLUEBACK   *12/1978, Lawrence Phillips*

1 "GRAYBACK" CLASS: GUIDED MISSILE SUBMARINE (SSG)

Name	No.	Builders	Laid down	Launched	Commissioned	F/S
GROWLER	SSG 577	Portsmouth Naval Shipyard	15 Feb 1955	5 Apr 1958	30 Aug 1958	PR

Displacement, tons: 2 540 standard; 3 515 dived
Length, feet (metres): 317·6 (96·8)
Beam, feet (metres): 27·2 (8·2)
Draught, feet (metres): 19 (5·8)
Torpedo tubes: 6—21 in (533 mm) 4 bow; 2 stern
Main machinery: 3 diesels (Fairbanks-Morse); 4 600 bhp; 2 electric motors (Elliott); 5 500 shp; 2 shafts
Speed, knots: 20 surfaced; 17 dived
Complement: 87 (9 officers, 78 enlisted men)

Growler was authorised in the Fiscal Year 1955 new construction programme; completed as a guided missile submarine to fire the Regulus surface-to-surface cruise missile (see Halibut, SSN 587 for Missile notes).

When the Regulus submarine missile programme ended in 1964, Growler and her near-sister Grayback were withdrawn from service, Growler being decommissioned on 25 May 1964. Grayback was subsequently converted to an amphibious transport submarine (LPSS). Growler was scheduled to undergo a similar conversion when Grayback was completed, but the second conversion was deferred late in 1968 because of rising ship conversion costs.

Growler is in reserve at Bremerton.

Design: Grayback and Growler were initially designed as attack submarines of the "Darter" class. Upon redesign as missile submarines they were cut in half on the building ways and were lengthened approximately 50 ft, two cylindrical hangars, each 11 ft high and 70 ft long, were superimposed on their bows, a missile launcher was installed between the hangars and sail structure, and elaborate navigation and fire control systems were fitted. The height of the sail structure on Growler is approximately 30 ft above the deck; Grayback's lower sail structure was increased during LPSS conversion.

Electronics: Mk 106 Mod 13 torpedo fire control system.

Sonar: BQS 4.

GROWLER 1958, USN

1 "GRAYBACK" CLASS: SUBMARINE (SS, ex-LPSS)

Name	No.	Builders	Laid down	Launched	Commissioned	F/S
GRAYBACK	SS 574 (ex-LPSS 574, ex-SSG 574)	Mare Island Naval Shipyard	1 July 1954	2 July 1957	7 Mar 1958	PA

Displacement, tons: 2 670 standard; 3 650 dived
Length, feet (metres): 334 (101·8)
Beam, feet (metres): 27 (8·2)
Draught, feet (metres): 19 (5·8)
Torpedo tubes: 8—21 in (533 mm) 6 bow (Mk 52); 2 stern (Mk 53)
Main machinery: 3 diesels (Fairbanks-Morse); 4 500 bhp; 2 electric motors (Elliott); 5 500 shp; 2 shafts
Speed, knots: 20 surfaced; 16·7 dived
Complement: 89 (12 officers, 77 enlisted men)
Troops: 67 (7 officers, 60 enlisted men)

Grayback was originally intended to be an attack submarine of the "Darter" class, being authorised in the Fiscal Year 1953 new construction programme, but redesigned in 1956 to provide a Regulus missile launching capability; completed as SSG 574 in 1958, similar in design to Growler (SSG 577). See Growler listing above for basic design notes. Homeported in Sasebo.

Classification: Grayback was reclassified as an attack submarine (SS) on 30 June 1975 although she retains a transport configuration and capabilities. The reclassification was an administrative change associated with funding support.

Conversion: She began conversion to a transport submarine at Mare Island in November 1967. The conversion was originally estimated at $15·2 million but was actually about $30 million. She was reclassified from SSG to LPSS on 30 August 1968 (never officially designated APSS).

During conversion she was fitted to berth and mess 67 troops and carry their equipment including landing craft or swimmer delivery vehicles (SDV). Her torpedo tubes and hence attack capability are retained. As completed (SSG) she had an overall length of 322 ft 4 in; lengthened 12 ft during LPSS conversion. Conversion was authorised in the FY 1965 programme and completed with her new commissioning on 9 May 1969; delayed because of higher priorities being allocated to other submarine projects.

Electronics: Mk 106 Mod 12 torpedo fire control system.

Sonar: BQS 2; BQS 4 (PUFFS).

GRAYBACK 5/1978, Dr. Giorgio Arra

USA / Submarines 669

1 "DARTER" CLASS: SUBMARINE (SS)

Name	No.	Builders	Laid down	Launched	Commissioned	F/S
DARTER	SS 576	General Dynamics (Electric Boat)	10 Nov 1954	28 May 1956	26 Oct 1956	PA

Displacement, tons: 1 720 surfaced; 2 388 dived
Length, feet (metres): 284·5 (86·7)
Beam, feet (metres): 27·2 (8·3)
Draught, feet (metres): 19 (5·8)
Torpedo tubes: 8—21 in (533 mm) 6 bow; 2 stern
Main machinery: 3 diesels (Fairbanks-Morse); 4 500 bhp; 2 electric motors (Elliott); 5 500 shp; 2 shafts
Speed, knots: 19·5 surfaced; 14 dived
Complement: 83 (8 officers, 75 men)

Designed for high submerged speed with quiet machinery. Planned sister submarines *Growler* and *Grayback* were completed to missile-launching configuration.
Basic design of *Darter* is similar to the "Tang" class described later.
Authorised in the Fiscal Year 1954 shipbuilding programme. No additional submarines of this type were built because of shift to high-speed hull design and nuclear propulsion.
Home port shifted to Sasebo, Japan in March 1979 making her and *Grayback* the only US submarines homeported overseas.

Electronics: Mk 106 Mod 11 torpedo fire control system.

Sonar: BQG 4 (PUFFS).

DARTER 1967, Dr. Giorgio Arra

3 "TANG" CLASS: SUBMARINES (SS and AGSS)

Name	No.	Builders	Laid down	Launched	Commissioned	F/S
TANG	SS 563	Portsmouth Naval Shipyard	18 Apr 1949	19 June 1951	25 Oct 1951	PA
WAHOO	SS 565	Portsmouth Naval Shipyard	24 Oct 1949	16 Oct 1951	30 May 1952	PA
GUDGEON	AGSS 567	Portsmouth Naval Shipyard	20 May 1950	11 June 1952	21 Nov 1952	PA

Displacement, tons: 2 050 standard; 2 700 dived
Length, feet (metres): 287 (87·4)
Beam, feet (metres): 27·3 (8·3)
Draught, feet (metres): 19 (6·2)
Torpedo tubes: 8—21 in (533 mm) 6 bow; 2 stern
Main machinery: 3 diesels (Fairbanks-Morse); 4 500 bhp; 2 electric motors; 5 600 shp; 2 shafts
Speed, knots: 15·5 surfaced; 16 dived
Complement: 83 (8 officers, 75 men)

Six submarines of this class were constructed, incorporating improvements based on German World War II submarine developments. *Tang* was authorised in the Fiscal Year 1947 new construction programme, *Wahoo* and *Trout* in FY 1948, and *Gudgeon* in FY 1949. *Gudgeon* was the first US submarine to circumnavigate the world during September 1957-February 1958. All modernised under FRAM II programme.

Classification: *Tang* was reclassified as a research submarine (AGSS) on 30 June 1975 for use in acoustic research. She reverted to SS classification on 15 August 1978. On 1 April 1979 *Gudgeon* reclassified as AGSS as replacement for *Tang*.

Electronics: Mk 106 Mod 18 torpedo fire control system.

Sonar: BQG 4 (PUFFS).

Transfers: *Trigger* (SS 564) transferred to Italy on 10 July 1973; *Harder* (SS 568) transferred to Italy on 15 March 1974. (These were the first US submarines of past-World War II construction to be transferred to foreign navies).
Trout to Iran on 19 December 1978, *Wahoo* was scheduled to follow in late 1979 but this has been cancelled. The transfer of *Tang* to Iran was cancelled on 3 February 1979.

GUDGEON

670 USA / Submarines

1 "ALBACORE" CLASS: AUXILIARY SUBMARINE (AGSS)

Name	No.	Builders	Laid down	Launched	Commissioned	F/S
ALBACORE	AGSS 569	Portsmouth Naval Shipyard	15 Mar 1952	1 Aug 1953	5 Dec 1953	AR

Displacement, tons: 1 500 standard; 1 850 dived
Length, feet (metres): 204 *(62·2)*
Beam, feet (metres): 22 *(6·7)*
Draught, feet (metres): 18·5 *(5·6)*
Torpedo tubes: None
Main machinery: 2 diesels; radial pancake type (General Motors); 1 electric motor (Westinghouse); 1 shaft
Speed, knots: 25 surfaced; 33 dived
Complement: 54 (5 officers, 49 men)

Built as a high-speed experimental submarine to test an advanced hull form. Officially described as a hydrodynamic test vehicle. Streamlined, whale shaped hull without casing.

Decommissioned and placed in reserve on 1 September 1972 at Philadelphia.

Experimental: She has been extensively modified to test advanced submarine design and engineering concepts.
Phase I modifications were made from July 1954 to February 1955 to eliminate the many bugs inherent with completely new construction and equipment.
Phase II modifications from December 1955 to March 1956 during which conventional propeller-rudder-stern diving plane arrangement was modified; the new design provided for the propeller to be installed aft of the control surfaces. (At this time a small auxiliary rudder on the sail was removed).
A concave bow sonar dome was fitted for tests in 1960. Phase III modifications from November 1960 to August 1961 during which an entirely new stern was installed featuring the stern planes in an "X" configuration, a system of ten hydraulic operated dive brakes around the hull amidships, a dorsal rudder, and a new bow sonar dome. Phase IV modifications from December 1962 to March 1965 during which a silver-zinc battery was installed and counter-rotating stern propellers rotating around the same axis were fitted.
Albacore conducted trials with towed sonar arrays from May to July 1966.
All modifications were made at the Portsmouth Naval Shipyard.

ALBACORE

1 "DOLPHIN" CLASS: AUXILIARY SUBMARINE (AGSS)

Name	No.	Builders	Laid down	Launched	Commissioned	F/S
DOLPHIN	AGSS 555	Portsmouth Naval Shipyard	9 Nov 1962	8 June 1968	17 Aug 1968	PA

Displacement, tons: 800 standard; 930 full load
Length, feet (metres): 152 *(46·3)*
Beam, feet (metres): 19·3 *(5·9)*
Draught, feet (metres): 18 *(5·5)*
Torpedo tubes: Removed
Main machinery: Diesel-electric (2 Detroit 12 V71 diesels), 1 650 hp; 1 shaft
Speed, knots: 15+ dived
Complement: 22 (7 officers, 15 enlisted men) plus 4 to 7 scientists

Specifically designed for deep-diving operations. Authorised in the Fiscal Year 1961 new construction programme but delayed because of changes in mission and equipment coupled with higher priorities being given to other submarine projects. Fitted for deep-ocean sonar and oceanographic research. She is highly automated and has three computer-operated systems, a safety system, hovering system, and one that is classified. The digital-computer submarine safety system monitors equipment and provides data on closed-circuit television screens; malfunctions in equipment set off an alarm and if they are not corrected within the prescribed time the system, unless overridden by an operator, automatically brings the submarine to the surface. There are several research stations for scientists and she is fitted to take water samples down to her operating depth.
Underwater endurance is limited (endurance and habitability were considered of secondary importance in design).
Assigned to Submarine Development Group 1 at San Diego.

Design: Has a constant diameter cylindrical pressure hull approximately 15 ft in outer diameter closed at both ends with hemispherical heads. Pressure hull fabricated of HY-80 steel with aluminium and fibre-glass used in secondary structures to reduce weight. No conventional hydroplanes are mounted, improved rudder design and other features provide manoeuvring control and hovering capability.

Engineering: Fitted with 330 cell silver-zinc battery. Submerged endurance is approximately 24 hours with an at-sea endurance of 14 days.

DOLPHIN   USN

GUPPY SUBMARINES

All 52 submarines modernised to the GUPPY (Greater Underwater Propulsion Project) configurations have been deleted or transferred to other navies. The last GUPPY submarines to serve with the US Navy were *Clamagore* (SS 343) deleted on 27 June 1975 and *Tiru* (SS 416) deleted on 1 July 1975. They were not transferred to Turkey, as planned, but are still (1979) berthed at Norfolk awaiting a decision on their future.
Corrections to the comprehensive list of GUPPY submarine disposals and transfers provided in the 1974-75 edition include: *Blenny* (SS 324) deleted on 15 August 1973 (sunk as target); *Sea Poacher* (SS 406) transferred to Peru on 1 July 1974; *Atule* (SS 403) transferred to Peru on 31 July 1974. *Tench* (SS 417) to Peru 16 September 1976 for spares.

DEEP SUBMERGENCE VEHICLES

The US Navy operates several deep submergence vehicles for scientific, military research, and operational military missions. The US Navy acquired its first deep submergence vehicle with the purchase of the bathyscaph *Trieste* in 1958. *Trieste* was designed and constructed by Professor Auguste Piccard. The US Navy sponsored research dives in the Mediterranean Sea with *Trieste* in 1957 after which the bathyscaph was purchased outright and brought to the USA.

Trieste reached a record depth of 35 800 ft *(10 910 m)* in the Challenger Deep off the Marianas on 23 January 1960, being piloted by Lieutenant Don Walsh, USN, and Jacques Piccard (son of Auguste). Rebuilt and designated *Trieste II,* the craft was subsequently used in the search for wreckage of the nuclear-powered submarine *Thresher* (SSN 593) which was lost in 1963 and *Scorpion* (SSN 589) lost in 1968.

After the loss of *Thresher* the US Navy initiated an extensive deep submergence programme that led to construction of two Deep Submergence Rescue Vehicles (DSRV); however, other vehicles proposed in the recommended programme were not built because of a lack of interest, changing operational concepts, and funding limitations.

Several of these deep submergence vehicles and other craft and support ships are operated by Submarine Development Group One at San Diego, California. The Group is a major operational command that includes advanced diving equipment; divers trained in "saturation" techniques; the DSVs *Trieste II, Turtle, Sea Cliff,* DSRV-1, DSRV-2; the submarine *Dolphin* (AGSS 555); several submarine rescue ships.

The hull of the original *Trieste* and Krupp sphere are in the Navy Yard in Washington, DC.

1 NUCLEAR-POWERED RESEARCH VEHICLE: HTV TYPE

A nuclear-powered hull research vehicle has been proposed by Admiral H. G. Rickover, Deputy Commander for Nuclear Propulsion, Naval Sea Systems Command. The craft would have a greater depth capability than the NR 1 (described below) and would employ a nuclear plant similar to that of the earlier craft.

Reportedly, Admiral Rickover began development of the design in 1971. The term HTV for Hull Test Vehicle has been used for this vehicle, reportedly to avoid critical association with the NR 1 programme.

Estimated construction time is 2½ years, construction having been approved in the FY 1978 programme. To be built of HY 130 steel reportedly at General Electric, Electric Boat Division. Unofficial estimates of construction costs were more than $300 million. At the beginning of 1979 the HTV was still in the design stage.

1 NUCLEAR-POWERED OCEAN ENGINEERING AND RESEARCH VEHICLE

Name	Builders	F/S
NR 1	General Dynamics (Electric Boat), Groton	ASA

Displacement, tons: 400 submerged
Length, feet (metres): 136·4 × 12·4 × 14·6 *(41·6 × 3·8 × 4·5)*
Diameter, feet (metre): 12 *(3·7)*
Reactor: 1 pressurised-water cooled
Machinery: Electric motors; 2 propellers; four ducted thrusters
Complement: 7 (2 officers, 3 enlisted men, 2 scientists)

NR 1 was built primarily to serve as a test platform for a small nuclear propulsion plant; however, the craft additionally provides an advanced deep submergence ocean engineering and research capability. Vice-Admiral Rickover conceived and initiated NR 1 in 1964-65 (the craft was not proposed in a Navy research or shipbuilding budget).

Laid down on 10 June 1967; launched on 25 January 1969; placed in service 27 October 1969. Commanded by an officer-in-charge vice commanding officer. First nuclear-propelled service craft.

Describing the craft Admiral Rickover has stated: "The (NR 1) will be able to perform detailed studies and mapping of the ocean bottom, temperature, currents, and other oceanographic parameters for military, commercial, and scientific use. The submarine (NR 1) will have viewing ports for visual observation of its surroundings and the ocean bottom. In addition, a remote grapple will be installed to permit collection of marine samples and other items. With its depth capability, the NR 1 is expected to be capable of exploring areas of the Continental Shelf.

Construction: Originally costed at $30 million in March 1965. During detailed design of NR 1 the Navy determined that improved equipment had to be developed and a larger hull than originally planned would be required. Consequently, in July 1967 the Navy obtained Congressional approval to proceed with construction of NR 1 at an estimated cost of $58·03 million. The final estimated ship construction cost at time of launching was $67 million plus $19·9 million for oceanographic equipment and sensors, and $11·8 million for research and development (mainly related to the nuclear propulsion plant), for a total estimated cost of $99·2 million.

Design: The NR 1 is fitted with wheels beneath the hull to permit "bottom crawling". This will obviate the necessity of hovering while exploring the ocean floor. Submarine wheels, a concept proposed as early as the first decade of this century by submarine inventor Simon Lake, were tested in the small submarine *Mackerel* (SST 1).

The NR 1 is fitted with external lights, external television cameras, a remote-controlled manipulator, and various recovery devices. No periscopes, but fixed television mast. Credited with a 30 day endurance, but limited habitability makes missions of only a few days feasible. Reportedly, a surface "mother" ship is required to support the NR 1.

Engineering: The NR 1 reactor plant was designed by the Atomic Energy Commission's Knolls Atomic Power Laboratory. She is propelled by two propellers driven by electric motors outside the pressure hull with power provided by a turbine generator within the pressure hull. Four ducted thrusters, two horizontal and two vertical, are provided for precise manoeuvring.

NR 1   *1969, General Dynamics, Electric Boat*

NR 1   *1969, General Dynamics, Electric Boat*

2 DEEP SUBMERGENCE RESCUE VEHICLES

No.	Builders	F/S
DSRV 1	Lockheed Missiles and Space Co	PSA
DSRV 2	(Sunnyvale, Calif)	ASA

Weight in air, tons: 32
Length, feet (metres): 49·2 *(15·0)*
Diameter, feet (metres): 8 *(2·4)*
Propulsion: Electric motors, propeller mounted in control shroud and four ducted thrusters
Speed, knots: 5 (maximum)
Endurance: 12 hours at 3 knots
Operating depth, feet (metres): 5 000 *(1 525)*
Complement: 3 (pilot, co-pilot, rescue sphere operator) +24 rescued men

The Deep Submergence Rescue Vehicle is intended to provided a quick-reaction world-wide, all-weather capability for the rescue of survivors in a disabled submarine. The DSRV is transportable by road, aircraft (in C 141 and C 5 jet cargo aircraft), surface ship (on "Pigeon" ASR 21 class submarine rescue ships), and specially modified submarines (SSN type).

The operational effectiveness of the craft is limited severely by the lack of large numbers of ships and submarines that can transport and support the craft. They will be used for the forseeable future for evaluation and research.

The carrying submarine will launch and recover the DSRV while submerged and, if necessary, while under ice. A total of six DSRVs were planned, but only two were funded. DSRV 1 was placed in service 7 August 1971 and DSRV 2 on 7 August 1972. DSRV 1 activated for rescue duty on 4 November 1977 and DSRV 2 on 1 January 1978. They will alternate their duties every two months.

Cost: The construction cost for the DSRV 1 was $41 million and for the DSRV 2 $23 million. The development, construction, test, and support of both vehicles through FY 1975 was $220 million. This expenditure includes the design and construction, research, spares and training.

Design: The DSRV outer hull is constructed of formed fibreglass. Within this outer hull are three interconnected spheres which form the main pressure capsule. Each sphere is 7·5 ft in diameter and is constructed of HY-140 steel. The forward sphere contains the vehicle's control equipment and is manned by the pilot and co-pilot, the centre and after spheres accommodate 24 passengers and a third crewman. Under the DSRVs centre sphere is a hemispherical protrusion or "skirt" which seals over the disabled submarine's hatch. During the mating operation the skirt is pumped dry to enable personnel to transfer.

Electronics: Elaborate search and navigational sonar, and closed-circuit television (supplemented by optical devices) are installed in the DSRV to determine the exact location of a disabled submarine within a given area and for pinpointing the submarine's escape hatches. Side-looking sonar can be fitted for search missions.

672 USA / Deep submergence vehicles

Engineering: Propulsion and control of the DSRV are achieved by a stern propeller in a movable control shroud and four ducted thrusters, two forward and two aft. These, plus a mercury trim system, permit the DSRV to manoeuvre and hover with great precision and to mate with submarines lying at angles up to 45 degrees from the horizontal. An elaborate Integrated Control and Display (ICAD) system employs computers to present sensor data to the pilots and transmit their commands to the vehicle's control and propulsion system.

Names: Unofficially named *Avalon* (DSRV 1) and *Mystic* (DSRV 2).

DSRV 1 on HAWKBILL (SSN 666)   1971, USN

2 DEEP SUBMERGENCE VEHICLES: MODIFIED "ALVIN" TYPE

Name	No.	Builders	F/S
TURTLE (ex-*Autec II*)	DSV 3	General Dynamics (Electric Boat), Groton, Conn	PA
SEA CLIFF (ex-*Autec I*)	DSV 4	General Dynamics (Electric Boat), Groton, Conn	PSA

Weight, tons: 21
Length, feet (metres): 25 *(7·6)*
Beam, feet (metres): 8 *(2·4)*
Propulsion: Electric motors, trainable stern propeller; 2 rotating propeller pods
Speed, knots: 2·5
Endurance: 8 hours at 2 knots
Operating depth, feet (metres): 6 500 *(1 980)*
Complement: 2 (pilot, observer)

Intended for deep submergence research and work tasks. Designated *Autec I* and *Autec II* during construction, but assigned above names in dual launching on 11 December 1968. Designated DSV 4 and DSV 3, respectively, on 1 June 1971 when they were placed in service. DSV 3 placed in commission (miscellaneous) in January 1973 and DSV 4 placed in service (miscellaneous) in the same month.

Construction: Three pressure spheres were fabricated for the *Alvin* submersible programme, one for installation in *Alvin*, a spare, and one for testing. The second and third spheres subsequently were allocated to these later submersibles.

Design: Twin-arm manipulator fitted to each submersible. Propulsion by stem propeller and two smaller, manoeuvring propeller "pods" on sides of vehicles; no thrusters.

SEA CLIFF   USN

1 DEEP SUBMERGENCE VEHICLE: "ALVIN" TYPE

Name	No.	Builders	F/S
ALVIN	DSV 2	General Mills Inc, Minneapolis, Minn	PSA

Weight, tons: 16
Length, feet (metres): 22·5 *(6·9)*
Beam, feet (metres): 8·5 *(2·6)*
Propulsion: Electric motors; trainable stern propeller; 2 rotating propeller pods
Speed, knots: 2
Endurance: 8 hours at 1 knot
Operating depth, feet (metres): 12 000 *(3 658)*
Complement: 3 (1 pilot, 2 observers)

Alvin was built for operation by the Woods Hole Oceanographic Institution for the Office of Naval Research. Original configuration had an operating depth of 6 000 ft. Named for Allyn C. Vine of Woods Hole Oceanographic Institution.
Alvin accidentally sank in 5 051 ft of water on 16 October 1968; subsequently raised in August 1969; refurbished 1970-71 in essentially original configuration. Placed in service on Navy List 1 June 1971. Subsequently refitted with titanium pressure sphere to provide increased depth capability and again operational in November 1973.

ALVIN   1974

1 DEEP SUBMERGENCE VEHICLE: "TRIESTE" TYPE

Name	No.	F/S
TRIESTE II	DSV 1 (ex-X-2)	PSA

Weight, tons: 84
Displacement, tons: 303 dived
Length, feet (metres): 78·6 *(24·0)*
Beam, feet (metres): 15·3 *(4·7)*
Propulsion: Electric motors, 3 propellers aft, ducted thruster fwd (see *Design* notes)
Speed, knots: 2
Endurance: 10-12 hours at 2 knots
Operating depth, feet (metres): 12 000 *(3 658)* (see *Design* notes)
Complement: 3 (2 operators, 1 observer)

Trieste II is the successor to *Trieste I* which the US Navy purchased in 1958 from Professor Auguste Piccard. The original *Trieste* was built at Castellammare, Italy; launched on 1 August 1953.
The vehicle is operated by Submarine Development Group One at San Diego, California, and is used primarily as a test bed for underwater equipment and to train deep submergence vehicle operators (hydronauts).
Designated as a "submersible craft" and assigned the designation X-2 on 1 September 1969; subsequently changed to DSV 1 on 1 June 1971. Placed in service, (miscellaneous) January 1973.
Used in location of wreckage of *Scorpion* and *Thresher*.

Design: *Trieste II* is essentially a large float with a small pressure sphere attached to the underside. The float, which is filled with aviation petrol, provides buoyancy. Designed operating depth is 20 000 ft but dives have been limited to approximately 12 000 ft. (The record-setting Challenger Deep dive was made with a Krupp sphere which has a virtually unlimited depth capability.)
Trieste II was built at the Mare Island Naval Shipyard in September 1965-August 1966 with a modified float, pressure sphere, propulsion system, and mission equipment being fitted. In the broadside view the sphere is now largely hidden by protective supports to keep the sphere clear of the welldeck when the craft rests in a floating dry dock.
Fitted with external television cameras and mechanical manipulator; computerised digital navigation system installed.

Transfers: The 600 ft capability *Nemo* DSV 5 is on loan to the Southwest Research Institute, San Antonio, Texas, since 1974.

TRIESTE II   1970, USN

AIRCRAFT CARRIERS

The US Navy currently operates 13 aircraft carriers: eleven ships of post-World War II construction (including three nuclear powered) and two "Midway" class ships completed shortly after the war. In addition, an obsolescent "Intrepid" class ship serves as a training carrier. *Coral Sea* has no assigned air wing and is kept available for contingency use. The additional nuclear carrier is under construction, *Carl Vinson* (CVN 70), to commission in 1981.

With the ever increasing size and costs of aircraft carriers, alternative designs to the "Nimitz" class have been sought to maintain a planned force level of 12 carriers beyond the mid-1980s when the first of the "Forrestal" class nears the end of its service life. Among the alternatives discussed was a concept known as "CVNX". A Navy study group, at the request of the then Secretary of Defense, James R. Schlesinger, was formed and directed to examine the feasibility of constructing "medium" size aircraft carriers of approx 50 000 tons standard displacement as an alternative to the "Nimitz" class. The group submitted its report in January 1976. Known collectively as the "CVNX" concept, it proposed three designs for further development (see 1976-77 edition of Jane's, page 560, bottom for further details). This concept was later discarded only to be resurrected in 1978. The current planned procurement of a fourth "Nimitz" class (CVN 71), for which long term lead items were requested under the FY 1977, had been held in abeyance while the "Medium-sized" aircraft carrier was re-evaluated. The procurement of a fourth "Nimitz" class, added to the FY 1979 budget by Congress was cancelled on 17 August 1978 when the entire FY 1979 defense budget was vetoed by President Carter. One CVV is to be requested under the FY 1980 programme (see under CVV, "Nimitz" class and "CV 67" class for additional comments). It is the US Navy's plan to rely on a force of 12 CVN/CVs through the 1990s.

Air Wings: Each large aircraft carrier (CV/CVN) normally operates an air wing of some 85 to 95 aircraft: two fighter squadrons of 24 F-4 Phantom or F-14 Tomcats; two light attack squadrons of 24 A-7 Corsairs; one medium attack squadron of 12 A-6 Intruders; one anti-submarine squadron of ten S-3 Viking aircraft; one A/S squadron of eight SH-3 Sea King helicopters; and smaller squadrons or detachments of three RA-5C Vigilante reconnaissance aircraft, four EA-6B Prowler electronic warfare aircraft, four KA-6 Intruder tankers, and four E-2 Hawkeye early-warning/control aircraft.
The "Midway" class carriers cannot accommodate the full wing described above, and normally would not operate the Vigilante and Viking aircraft.
The carriers generally also embark a Carrier On-board Delivery (COD) aircraft in addition to the air wing.

Classification: From 1972 onward attack aircraft carriers (CVA) were reclassified as aircraft carriers (CV) upon being fitted with anti-submarine control centres and facilities to support A/S aircraft and helicopters (in addition to fighter/attack aircraft). The multi-purpose configuration was dictated by the phasing out of dedicated anti-submarine aircraft carriers (CVS), the last being decommissioned in 1974.
All active ships still classified as attack aircraft carriers (CVA/CVAN) on 30 June 1975 were changed to CV/CVN regardless of their ability to support anti-submarine aircraft.

Service Life Extension Programme (SLEP): Beginning with the FY 1980 programme, the Carrier Service Life Extension Programme (SLEP) will be initiated. Each carrier, beginning with *Saratoga* (CV 60), will undergo a two year modernisation and overhaul which is designed to extend each ship's life by 10-15 years. The chart below shows the long term implications of the SLEP programme. Also shown are the projected retirement dates of the ships after they have been through the SLEP programme as well as the retirement dates of the two remaining "Midway" class ships (for further data on this programme see "Forrestal" class CVs).

Training Carrier: The "Intrepid" class carrier *Lexington* (AVT 16) operates as a training ship and is based at Pensacola, Florida. The ship has no aircraft maintenance or arming capabilities, and is not considered as a combat ship. In an emergency, aircraft could be embarked on a very restricted operational basis.
It is anticipated that *Coral Sea* (CV 43) will replace *Lexington* in the training role about 1983.

Names: US aircraft carriers traditionally have been named for American battles and earlier Navy ships. However, during the past few years they have increasingly been named for statesmen and naval leaders.

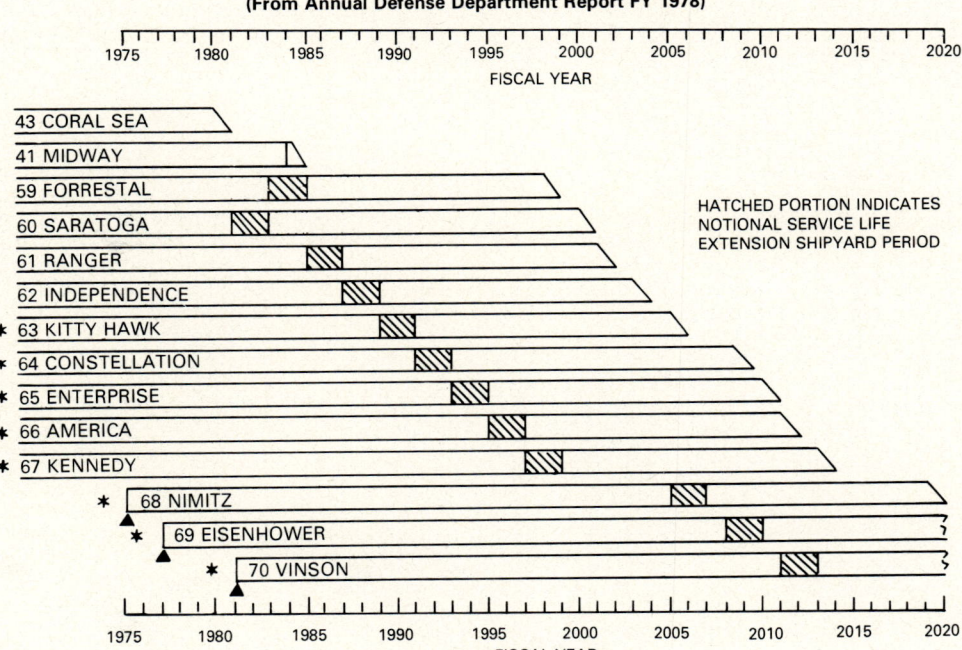

CARRIER SERVICE LIFE EXTENSION PROGRAMME
(From Annual Defense Department Report FY 1978)

(1) AIRCRAFT CARRIER (MEDIUM) (CVV): PROPOSED

Displacement, tons: 52 200 standard; 62 427 full load
Length, feet (metres): 912 *(278)*
Beam, feet (metres): 126 *(38·4)*
Flight deck, feet (metres): 256·5 *(78·2)*
Draught, feet (metres): 34 *(10·4)*
Aircraft: 55–65
Catapults: 2 steam (C-13)
Elevators: 2
Main engines: Steam turbines; 100 000 shp; 2 shafts
Speed, knots: 27–29
Range, miles: 8 000 at 20 knots
Complement: 3 400–3 900 (including air wing)

One Aircraft Carrier, Medium (CVV) has been requested in the FY 1980 Shipbuilding programme. This ship would be capable of operating Vertical and Short Take-off and Landing (V/STOL) aircraft and helicopters as well as modern fixed wing aircraft. The original concept for this type of ship was developed in 1975/76, but was later discarded. However, with the increasing costs of the "Nimitz" class CVN, the concept was re-evaluated. With the aircraft carrier still the backbone of the fleet and faced with a need to continue construction of aircraft carriers to replace its older units, the Navy, in the person of the Secretary of the Navy, pushed the CVV design when it was evident that after the President vetoed the fourth "Nimitz" class he would not fund another CVN. In this the Navy had the backing of Secretary of Defense Harold Brown. However, Navy and Defense Department's detailed examination of the proposed CVV design revealed many weaknesses which included the following: The CVV would have to be designed from keel up and would take longer to complete than a ship based on the ten year old "John F. Kennedy" class design, the youngest of the Navy's conventional carriers. Also, the 82,000 full load "John F. Kennedy" carries approximately 85 aircraft and has four catapults for launching them while the 62,500 full load CVV would carry between 55 and 65 aircraft and have only two catapults. Finally, the CVV would be less versatile, than the "John F. Kennedy" class. Critics of this design say it would make sense to build the CVV only if the ship was to be followed by additional carriers of the same design, but the Carter Administration's long range Navy shipbuilding programme makes no provision for any additional carriers of this design (the second unit, originally intended to be authorised under the FY 1982 budget, has been deleted). Another factor of interest discovered in the detailed examination of the CVV design was that a "John F. Kennedy" class CV would only cost $100 million more to construct than a new CVV. Upon conclusion of their study Navy leaders convinced the Secretary of the Navy and the Secretary of Defense of the cost effectiveness of constructing a second "John F. Kennedy" class unit in place of the CVV. This was recommended to the President in the proposed FY 1980 Shipbuilding programme. However, the President rejected the suggestion and is insisting on building the single unit of the CVV design at a cost of $1·5 billion.

Design: The projected mission of the CVV design would be for sea control, amphibious assault, close air support, mine countermeasures and low intensity Anti-Air Warfare (AAW) operations.
This multi-mission concept overcomes many of the objections which led to Congressional refusal to fund the smaller Sea Control Ship previously proposed by the Navy. In addition, the CVV would have sufficient speed to accompany carrier task forces or fast merchant ships.

Aircraft: The V/STOL strike aircraft is the AV-8 Harrier or successor; the large anti-submarine helicopter is the SH-3 Sea King or SH-53 Sea Stallion (in an A/S configuration); the LAMPS (Light Airborne Multi-Purpose System) is actually a medium-size helicopter primarily configured for A/S search and attack. The current LAMPS helicopter is the SH-2, while later aircraft based on the Army's Utility Tactical Transport Aircraft System (UTTAS) programme is being developed as the LAMPS III.
The Department of Defense requested that $200 million be included in the FY 1980 budget for further development of the AV-8B Harrier, but the request was denied leaving the Navy and Marine Corps with the British built AV-8A Harrier for some years to come. Other V/STOL designs such as the Hawker Siddeley/McDonnel-Douglas AV-16 Advanced Harrier, have also had their development slowed by the lack of R & D funds in recent Defense Department budgets.

Gunnery: The CVV design provides for the installation of at least two Close-In Weapon Systems (CIWS), the rapid-fire multi-barrel 20 mm Phalanx gun system.

Missiles: Harpoon anti-ship missiles in storage/launcher canisters could be fitted.

Propulsion: Despite the Title VIII legislation passed by Congress which encourages nuclear propulsion for surface combatants, all CVV designs provide for fossil-fuel propulsion. This is the prime reason why this design costs only $1·5 billion compared with $2·4 billion for the fourth "Nimitz" class CVN.

CVV (Artist's concept)

3 "NIMITZ" CLASS: MULTI-PURPOSE AIRCRAFT CARRIERS (nuclear propulsion) (CVN)

Name	No.	Builders	Laid down	Launched	Commissioned	F/S
NIMITZ	CVN 68	Newport News Shipbuilding & Dry Dock Co	22 June 1968	13 May 1972	3 May 1975	AA
DWIGHT D. EISENHOWER	CVN 69	Newport News Shipbuilding & Dry Dock Co	15 Aug 1970	11 Oct 1975	18 Oct 1977	AA
CARL VINSON	CVN 70	Newport News Shipbuilding & Dry Dock Co	11 Oct 1975	Oct 1979	1982	Bldg

Displacement, tons: 72 700 light (condition A); 81 600 standard; 91 487 full load
Length, feet (metres): 1 092 *(332·0)*
Beam, feet (metres): 134 *(40·8)*
Draught, feet (metres): 37 *(11·3)*
Flight deck width, feet (metres): 252 *(76·8)*
Catapults: 4 steam (C13-1)
Aircraft: 90+
Missiles: 3 Basic Point Defence Missile System (BPDMS) launchers with Sea Sparrow missiles (Mk 25 in *Nimitz*; Mk 29 in remainder) (see notes)
Guns: See notes
Main engines: Geared steam turbines; 280 000 shp; 4 shafts
Nuclear reactors: 2 pressurised-water cooled (A4W/A1G)
Speed, knots: 30+
Complement: 3 300 plus 3 000 assigned to air wing for a total of 6 300 per ship

The lead ship for this class and the world's second nuclear-powered aircraft carrier was ordered 9½ years after the first such ship, *Enterprise* (CVN 65). *Nimitz* was authorised in the Fiscal Year 1967 new construction programme; *Dwight D. Eisenhower* in the FY 1970 programme; and *Carl Vinson* in the FY 1974 programme. The builders are the only US shipyard now capable of constructing large, nuclear-propelled warships.
The completion of the first two ships has been delayed almost two years because of delays in the delivery and testing of nuclear plant components. *Eisenhower* was contracted for delivery to the Navy 21 months after *Nimitz*. However, the official Navy construction schedule notes that past undermanning by the shipbuilder has resulted in slippage beyond contract delivery date.
Originally it was planned to procure two more ships of this class (CVN 71 and 72). Long lead items for CVN 71 were requested under FY 1977 and $350 million were authorised. President Ford's request to cancel CVN 71 was backed by President Carter but Congress allowed $268·4 million of the original authorisation to stand, a sum already contractually agreed. The stipulation was made that this sum should be used for spare components for CVN 68/70 or for long lead items for CVN 71 should the Administration decide to go ahead with her. This all came about at a time when Congress and the Pentagon were debating the future Carrier programme in the light of increasing cost, size and building time of the CVNs. After examining all the alternatives, including the Aircraft Carrier, Medium (CVV), a majority of Congress decided that the nuclear-powered aircraft carrier was the most cost effective platform even with the long period of time necessary for construction. When President Carter failed to request money for the construction of an aircraft carrier under the FY 1979 programme, both houses of Congress attached $2·0 billion to the Defense Department budget for the construction of a fourth "Nimitz" class CVN. President Carter vetoed this bill on 17 August 1978.

Classification: *Nimitz* and *Eisenhower* were ordered as attack aircraft carriers (CVAN): reclassified CVN on 30 June 1975. First two ships will be refitted with A/S control centre and facilities for A/S aircraft and helicopters for their new multi-mission role (attack/ASW). *Vinson* will be completed with these facilities.

Electronics: These ships have the Naval Tactical Data System (NTDS).

Endurance: 13 years for reactors, 16 days for aviation fuel (steady flying).

Engineering: These carriers have only two nuclear reactors compared with the eight reactors required for *Enterprise*. The nuclear cores for the reactors in these ships are expected to provide sufficient energy for the ships each to steam for at least 13 years, an estimated 800 000 to 1 million miles between refuelling.

Fiscal: A number of cost growth factors have had an impact on these ships, including delays in schedule. The cost of *Nimitz* in FY 1976 dollars was equivalent to $1 881 million; the two later ships will cost in excess of $2 000 million each in equivalent dollars.

Gunnery: It is planned to add three 20 mm Mk 15 CIWS to each ship, which at present have only two 40 mm saluting guns.

Missiles: *Nimitz* will shortly receive Mk 29 Sea Sparrow in place of Mk 25.

Names: *Dwight D. Eisenhower* is believed to be the first major US surface warship to be named after an Army officer.
Carl Vinson is believed to be the first US naval ship to be named after a living person since the American Revolution. Carl Vinson was a member of the House of Representatives from Georgia from 1914-65; he served as Chairman of the House Naval Affairs Committee and later the House Armed Services Committee.

Protection: Sides with system of full and empty compartments. Full compartments can contain aviation fuel. 2·5 in approx plating over certain areas of side shell. Box protection over magazine and machinery spaces.

Radar: 3D air search: SPS 48.
Air search: SPS 43A.
Surface search: SPS 10.
Navigational: SPN 42, 43 and 44.

Sonar: None.

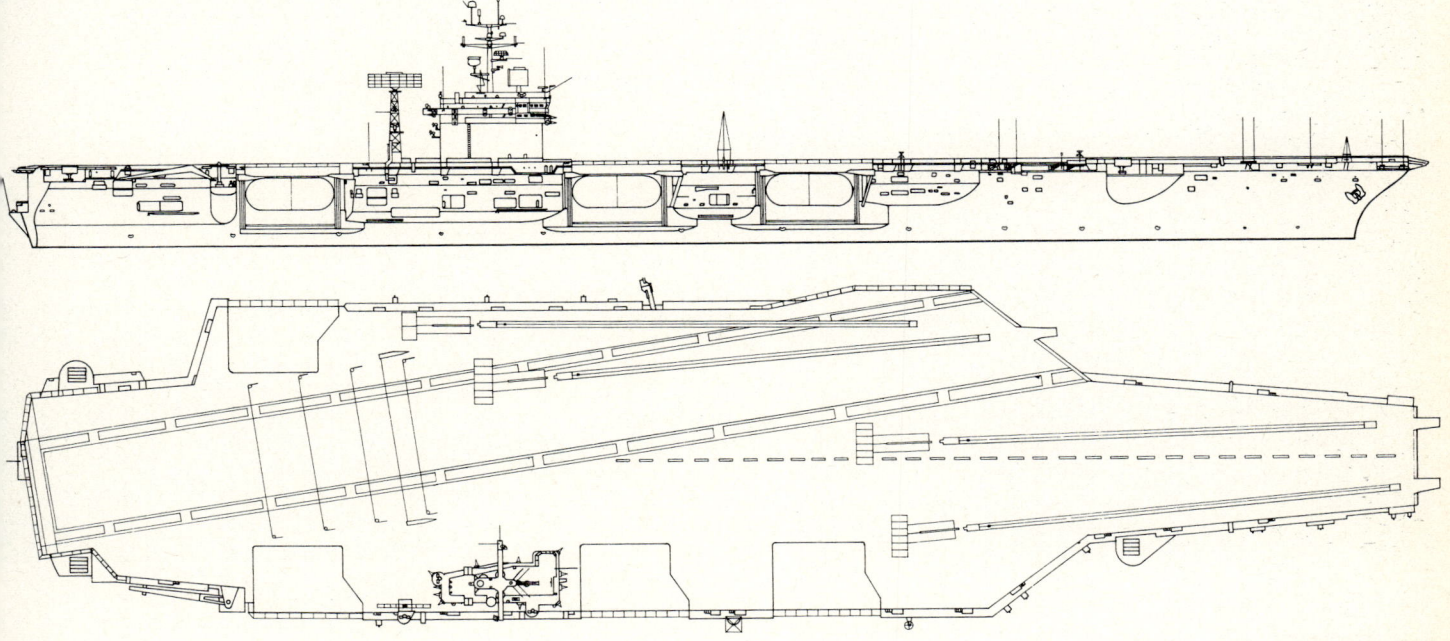

NIMITZ *Drawing, A. D. Baker III*

NIMITZ *6/1978, Wright and Logan*

USA / Aircraft carriers

NIMITZ
6/1978, Wright and Logan

NIMITZ
4/1975, USN

DWIGHT D. EISENHOWER
8/1977, USN

USA /Aircraft carriers 677

1 "ENTERPRISE" CLASS: MULTI-PURPOSE AIRCRAFT CARRIER (nuclear propulsion) (CVN)

Name	No.	Builders	Laid down	Launched	Commissioned	F/S
ENTERPRISE	CVN 65	Newport News Shipbuilding & Dry Dock Co	4 Feb 1958	24 Sep 1960	25 Nov 1961	PA

Displacement, tons: 75 700 standard; 89 600 full load
Length, feet (metres): 1 102 *(335·9)*
Beam, feet (metres): 133 *(40·5)*
Draught, feet (metres): 35·8 *(10·8)*
Flight deck width, feet (metres): 252 *(76·8)* maximum
Aircraft: approx 84
Catapults: 4 steam (C 13)
Missile launchers: 2 Basic Point Defence Missile Systems (BPDMS) launchers (Mk 25) with Sea Sparrow missiles
Main engines: 4 geared steam turbines (Westinghouse); approx 280 000 shp; 4 shafts
Nuclear reactors: 8 pressurised-water cooled A2W (Westinghouse)
Speed, knots: approx 35
Complement: 3 100 (162 officers, approx 2 940 enlisted men) plus 2 400 assigned to attack air wing for a total of 5 500

At the time of her construction, *Enterprise* was the largest warship ever built and is rivalled in size only by the nuclear-powered "Nimitz" class ships. *Enterprise* was authorised in the Fiscal Year 1958 new construction programme. She was launched only 31 months after her keel was laid down.
The cost of *Enterprise* was $451·3 million.
Currently undergoing a two year refit/overhaul at Puget Sound Naval S.Y., Bremerton, Washington. Completion January 1981.
The FY 1960 budget provided $35 million to prepare plans and place orders for components of a second nuclear-powered carrier, but the project was cancelled.

Armament: *Enterprise* was completed without any armament in an effort to hold down construction costs. Space for Terrier missile system was provided. Mk 25 Sea Sparrow BPDMS subsequently was installed in late 1967 and this is planned to be replaced by Mk 29 and to be supplemented with three 20 mm Mk 15 CIWS during her current refit.

Classification: Originally classified as CVAN; reclassified as CVN on 30 June 1975.

Design: Built to a modified "Forrestal" class design. The most distinctive feature is the island structure. Nuclear propulsion eliminated requirement for smoke stack and boiler air intakes. Rectangular fixed-array radar antennae ("billboards") are mounted on sides of island; electronic countermeasure (ECM) antennae ring dome-shaped upper levels of island structure. A re-shaping of the island will take place in her current refit. This includes the removal of the mast and dome (which carries obsolete ECM gear) which will be replaced with a mast similar to that of the "Nimitz" class. The "billboards" of the SPS 32 and 33 radars will also be removed to be replaced by the antennas of SPS 48 and 49 radars on the new mast.
Enterprise has four deck-edge lifts (as shown in the drawing)—two forward of the island and one on each side abaft the island.

Electronics: Fitted with the Naval Tactical Data System (NTDS); Tacan.

Engineering: *Enterprise* was the world's second nuclear-powered warship (the cruiser *Long Beach* was completed a few months earlier). Design of the first nuclear-powered aircraft carrier began in 1950 and work continued until 1953 when the programme was deferred pending further work on the submarine reactor programme. The large ship reactor project was reinstated in 1954 on the basis of technological advancements made in the previous 14 months. The Atomic Energy Commission's Bettis Atomic Power Laboratory was given prime responsibility for developing the nuclear power plant.
The first of the eight reactors installed in *Enterprise* achieved initial criticality on 2 December 1960, shortly after the carrier was launched. After three years of operation during which she steamed more than 207 000 miles, *Enterprise* was overhauled and refuelled from November 1964 to July 1965. Her second set of cores provided about 300 000 miles steaming. The eight cores initially installed in *Enterprise* cost $64 million; the second set cost about $20 million.
Enterprise underwent an extensive overhaul from October 1969-January 1971, which included installation of a new set of uranium cores in the ship's eight nuclear reactors. The overhaul and refuelling took place at the Newport News shipyard. Estimated cost of the overhaul was approximately $30 million, with $13 million being for non-nuclear repairs and alterations, and $17 million being associated with installation of the new nuclear cores (the latter amount being in addition to the $80 million cost of the eight cores). This third set of cores is expected to fuel the ship for 10 to 13 years.
There are two reactors for each of the ship's four shafts. The eight reactors feed 32 heat exchangers.

Radar: Search: SPS 32 and 33 ("billboards").
Low level search: SPS 58.
Search: SPS 10 and 12.
Navigational radars: SPN 10.

ENTERPRISE 8/1978, Dr. Giorgio Arra

ENTERPRISE 4/1978, USN (PH2. P. J. Salesi)

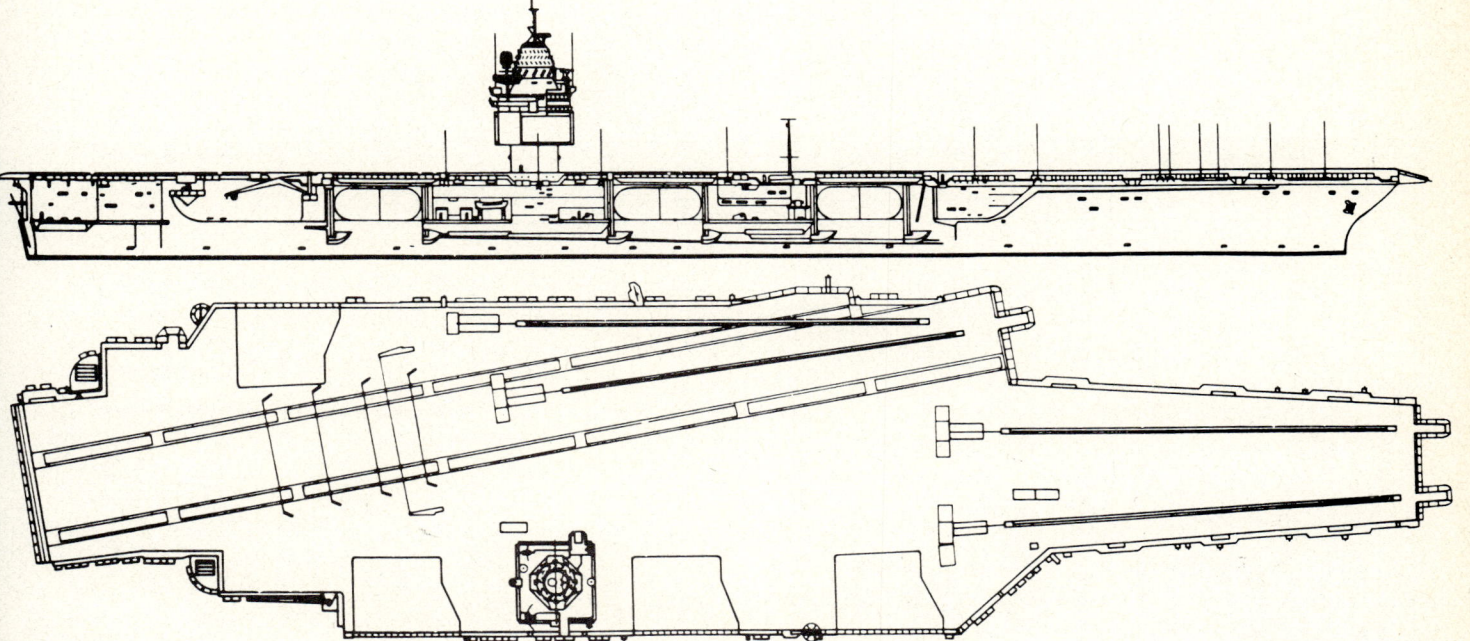

ENTERPRISE Drawing, A. D. Baker III

4 "KITTY HAWK" and "JOHN F. KENNEDY" CLASSES: MULTI-PURPOSE AIRCRAFT CARRIERS (CV)

Name	No.	Builders	Laid down	Launched	Commissioned	F/S
KITTY HAWK	CV 63	New York Shipbuilding Corp, Camden, NJ	27 Dec 1956	21 May 1960	29 Apr 1961	PA
CONSTELLATION	CV 64	New York Naval Shipyard	14 Sep 1957	8 Oct 1960	27 Oct 1961	PA
AMERICA	CV 66	Newport News Shipbuilding & Dry Dock Co	9 Jan 1961	1 Feb 1964	23 Jan 1965	AA
JOHN F. KENNEDY	CV 67	Newport News Shipbuilding & Dry Dock Co	22 Oct 1964	27 May 1967	7 Sep 1968	AA

Displacement, tons:
 Kitty Hawk: 60 100 standard; 80 800 full load
 Constellation: 60 100 standard; 80 800 full load
 America: 60 300 standard; 78 500 full load
 John F. Kennedy: 61 000 standard; 82 000 full load
Length, feet (metres):
 Kitty Hawk and *Constellation:* 1 046 *(318·8)*
 America: 1 047·5 *(319·3)*
 J. F. Kennedy: 1 052 *(320·7)*
Beam, feet (metres): 130 *(39·6)*
Draught, feet (metres):
 J. F. Kennedy: 35·9 *(10·9)*
 Remainder: 37 *(11·3)*
Flight deck width, feet (metres): 252 *(76·9)*
Catapults: 4 steam
Aircraft: approx 85
Missile launchers: 2 twin Terrier surface-to-air launchers (Mk 10) in *Constellation, America* (40 missiles per twin launcher)
 3 Basic Point Defence Missile System (BPDMS) launchers (Mk 25) with Sea Sparrow missiles in *John F. Kennedy*;
 3 Mk 29 BPDMS launchers in *Kitty Hawk*
Guns: See note
Main engines: 4 geared turbines (Westinghouse) 280 000 shp; 4 shafts
Boilers: 8 (Foster-Wheeler)
Speed, knots: 30+
Complement: 2 800 (150 officers, approx 2 645 enlisted men) plus approx 2 150 assigned to attack air wing for a total of 4 950 officers and enlisted men per ship

CONSTELLATION
8/1977, Dr. Giorgio Arra

CONSTELLATION
8/1977, Dr. Giorgio Arra

These ships were built to an improved "Forrestal" design and are easily recognised by their smaller island structure which is set farther aft than the superstructure in the four "Forrestal" class ships. Lift arrangements also differ (see *Design* notes). *Kitty Hawk* was authorised in the Fiscal Year 1956 new construction programme, *Constellation* in FY 1957, *America* in FY 1961, and *John F. Kennedy* in FY 1963. Completion of *Constellation* was delayed because of a fire which ravaged her in the New York Naval Shipyard in December 1960. Construction of *John F. Kennedy* was delayed because of debate over whether to provide her with conventional or nuclear propulsion.
The construction of a second "John F. Kennedy" class unit was proposed in place of the much criticized Medium Aircraft Carrier (CVV), to President Carter for submission in the FY 1980 defense budget. However, he rejected the submission and decided on the construction of the CVV.

Classification: As completed, all four ships were classified as attack aircraft carriers (CVA); first two changed to multi-mission aircraft carriers (attack and anti-submarine) when modified with A/S command centres and facilities for S-3 Viking fixed-wing aircraft and SH-3 Sea King helicopters. *Kitty Hawk* to CV vice CVA on 29 April 1973; *John F. Kennedy* to CV vice CVA on 1 Dec 1974; *Constellation* and *America* from CVA to CV on 30 June 1975, prior to A/S modifications.

Design: They have two deck-edge lifts forward of the superstructure, a third lift aft of the structure, and the port-side lift on the after quarter. This arrangement considerably improves flight deck operations. Four C13 catapults (with one C13-1 in each of later ships). *John F. Kennedy* and *America* have stern anchors as well as bower anchors because of their bow sonar domes (see *Sonar* notes). All have a small radar mast abaft the island.

Electronics: All four ships of this class have highly sophisticated electronic equipment including the Naval Tactical Data System (NTDS). Tacan in all ships.

Fire Control: *Kitty Hawk:* Two Mk 91 MFCS for Mk 29 BPDMS.
Constellation: Four Mk 76 MFCS for Terrier.
America: Three Mk 76 MFCS for Terrier.
John F. Kennedy: Three Mk 115 MFCS for Mk 25 BPDMS.
It is planned to replace Mk 76 and Mk 115 systems with Mk 91 in *Constellation* and *John F. Kennedy.*

Fiscal: Construction costs were $265·2 million for *Kitty Hawk*, $264·5 million for *Constellation*, $248·8 million for *America*, and $277 million for *John F. Kennedy*.

Gunnery: Planned to mount three 20 mm Mk 15 CIWS in each ship. All currently have only 40 mm saluting guns (two in 63 and 64, four in 66 and one in 67).

Missiles: The two Terrier-armed ships have a Mk 10 Mod 3 launcher on the starboard quarter and a Mod 4 launcher on the port quarter.
America has updated Terrier launchers and guidance system that can accommodate Standard missiles; *Constellation* retains older Terrier HT systems which will be replaced by three NATO Sea Sparrow launchers (Mk 29).
Three Sea Sparrow BPDMS launchers were fitted in *John F. Kennedy* early in 1969. It is planned to replace *Constellation's* Terrier system with Mk 29 BPDMS and *John F. Kennedy's* Mk 25 with Mk 29 BPDMS. *America* is to retain her Terrier until 1979-80.

Names: *Kitty Hawk* honours the site where the Wright brothers made their historic flights.

Radar: 3D search: SPS 52 (3 ships).
Search: SPS 43.
Search: SPS 30 (3 ships).
Search: SPS 48 and 58 *(John F. Kennedy).*

Rockets: Mk 28 Mod 5 rocket launching systems fitted in *America* and *John F. Kennedy.*

Sonar: SQS 23 *(America* only).
This is the only US attack carrier so fitted, although it was planned also for *John F. Kennedy.*

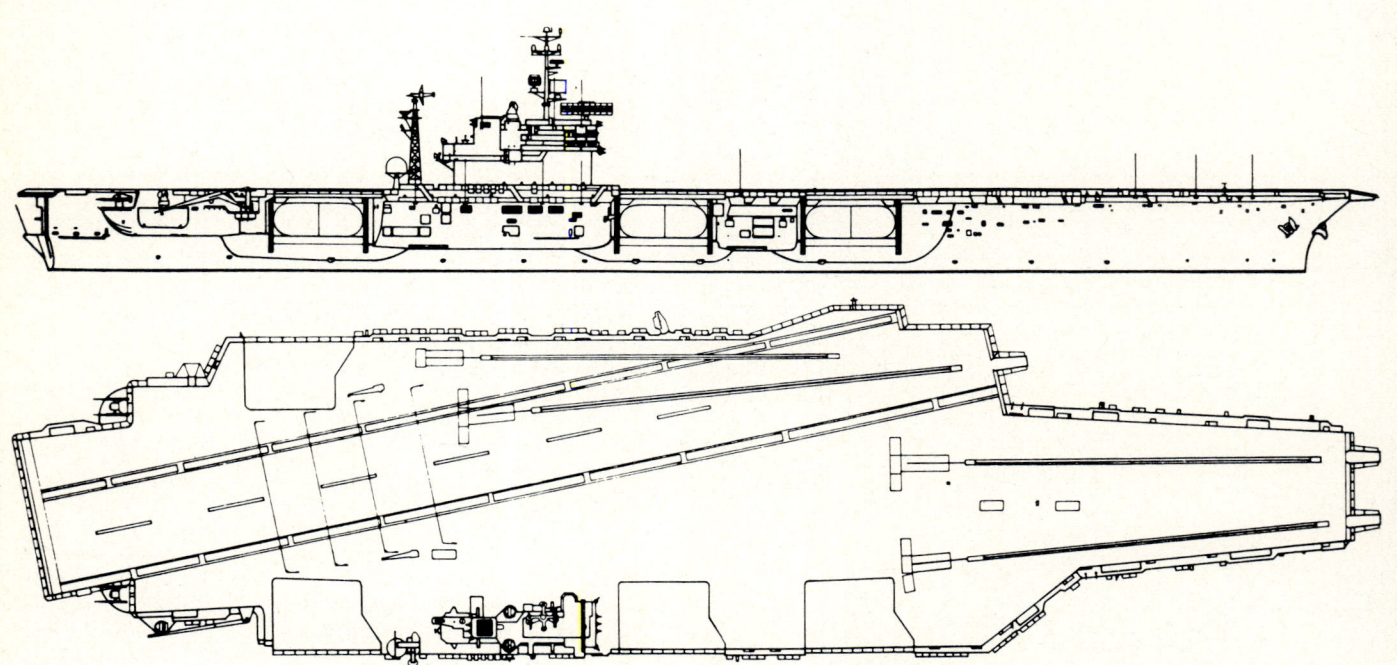

AMERICA

Drawing by A. D. Baker III

USA /Aircraft carriers 679

JOHN F. KENNEDY 3/1978, USN (PH1. Osborne)

AMERICA 10/1974, USN

KITTY HAWK 1/1978, Dr. Giorgio Arra

680 USA /Aircraft carriers

4 "FORRESTAL" CLASS: AIRCRAFT CARRIERS (CV)

Name	No.	Builders	Laid down	Launched	Commissioned	F/S
FORRESTAL	CV 59	Newport News S.B. & D.D. Co	14 July 1952	11 Dec 1954	1 Oct 1955	AA
SARATOGA	CV 60	New York Naval Shipyard	16 Dec 1952	8 Oct 1955	14 Apr 1956	AA
RANGER	CV 61	Newport News S.B. & D.D. Co	2 Aug 1954	29 Sep 1956	10 Aug 1957	PA
INDEPENDENCE	CV 62	New York Naval Shipyard	1 July 1955	6 June 1958	10 Jan 1959	AA

Displacement, tons:
 Forrestal and *Saratoga*: 59 060 standard; 75 900 full load
 Others: 60 000 standard; 79 300 full load
Length, feet (metres):
 Forrestal: 1 086 *(331)*
 Ranger: 1 071 *(326·4)*
 Saratoga: 1 063 *(324)*
 Independence: 1 070 *(326·1)*
Beam, feet (metres): 129·5 *(39·5)*
Draught, feet (metres): 37 *(11·3)*
Flight deck width, feet (metres): 252 *(76·8)* maximum
Catapults: 4 steam (2—C7 and 2—C11 in 59 and 60; 4—C7 others)
Aircraft: approx 70
Guns: 2—5 in *(127 mm)*/54 (Mk 42) (single) in *Ranger*
Missile launchers: 2 Basic Point Defence Missile Systems (BPDMS) launchers (Mk 25) with Sea Sparrow missiles in all except *Ranger* (Mk 29)
Main engines: 4 geared turbines (Westinghouse) 4 shafts; 260 000 shp *(Forrestal)*; 280 000 shp (remainder)
Boilers: (Babcock & Wilcox)
Speed, knots:
 Forrestal; 33
 Others; 34
Complement: 2 790 (145 officers, approx 2 645 enlisted men) plus approx 2 150 assigned to attack air wing for a total of 4 940+ per ship

FORRESTAL 7/1976, A. D. Baker III

Forrestal was the world's first aircraft carrier built after World War II. The *Forrestal* design drew heavily from the aircraft carrier *United States* (CVA 58) which was cancelled immediately after being laid down in April 1949. *Forrestal* was authorised in the Fiscal Year 1952 new construction programme; *Saratoga* followed in the FY 1953 programme, *Ranger* in the FY 1954 programme, and *Independence* in the FY 1955 programme.

Classification: *Forrestal* and *Saratoga* were initially classified as Large Aircraft Carriers (CVB); reclassified as Attack Aircraft Carriers (CVA) on 1 October 1952 to reflect their purpose rather than size.
Saratoga redesignated CV on 30 June 1972; *Independence* on 28 Feb 1973; *Forrestal* and *Ranger* on 30 June 1975.

Design: The "Forrestal" class ships were the first aircraft carriers designed and built specifically to operate jet-propelled aircraft. *Forrestal* was redesigned early in construction to incorporate British-developed angled flight deck and steam catapults. These were the first US aircraft carriers built with an enclosed bow area to improve seaworthiness. Other features include armoured flight deck and advanced underwater protection and internal compartmentation to reduce effects of conventional and nuclear attack. Mast configurations differ; *Forrestal* originally had two masts, one of which was removed in 1967.

Electronics: Naval Tactical Data System (NTDS); Tacan.

Engineering: *Saratoga* and later ships have an improved steam plant; increased machinery weight of the improved plant is more than compensated for by increased performance and decreased fuel consumption. *Forrestal* boilers are 615 psi *(42·7 kg/cm²)*; 1 200 psi *(83·4 kg/cm²)* in other ships. Four 5-bladed propellers of 21 ft diameter.

Fiscal: Construction costs were $188·9 million for *Forrestal*, $213·9 million for *Saratoga*, $173·3 million for *Ranger*, and $225·3 million for *Independence*.

Gunnery: All four ships initially mounted eight 5 in guns (Mk 42) in single mounts, two on each quarter and two on each bow. The forward sponsons carrying the guns interfered with ship operations in rough weather, tending to slow the ships down. The forward sponsons and guns were subsequently removed (except in *Ranger*), reducing armament to four guns per ship. The after guns were removed with installation of BPDMS launchers (see below). *Ranger's* remaining 5 in guns removed in 1976. Each ship carries four 40 mm saluting guns. It is planned to fit all these ships with three 20 mm Mk 15 CIWS in the immediate future.

Missiles: The four after 5 in guns were removed from *Forrestal* late in 1967 and a single BPDMS launcher for Sea Sparrow missiles was installed forward on the starboard side. An additional launcher was provided aft on the port side in 1972. Two BPDMS launchers fitted in *Independence* in 1973; *Saratoga* in 1974; *Forrestal* in 1976. These are soon to be replaced by three Mk 29 BPDMS launchers—the same fitting in *Ranger*.

Names: *Forrestal* is named after James V. Forrestal, Secretary of the Navy from 1944 until he was appointed the first U Secretary of Defense in 1947.

Radar: Low angle air search: SPS 58.
Search: SPS 30 and 43 (*Saratoga* —to be replaced by SPS 4 and 49 during SLEP); SPS 48 and 49 in remainder.
Navigation: SPN 10.

Rockets: One Mk 28 rocket launching system fitted in all bu *Ranger*.

Service Life Extension Programme (SLEP): Owing to curren building costs this programme is intended to extend carriers lives from 30 to 45 years. The "Forrestal" class will be the firs to undergo this modernisation—*Saratoga* first under FY 198 *Forrestal* in FY 1983, *Independence* in FY 1984 and *Ranger* in F 1986.
Each modernisation will last 18-24 months and include exten sive re-cabling and renovation. Cost approx $496 million eac (FY 1980 dollars). $32·2 million advance funding approved i FY 1979 for first SLEP which was to be *Saratoga* at Philadelphi NY. Protests at this choice from Newport News resulted i Congress deciding to make their own decision—if this is no forthcoming by April 1979 SLEP will be postponed to FY 1982 will start with *Forrestal* while *Saratoga* has a major overhaul

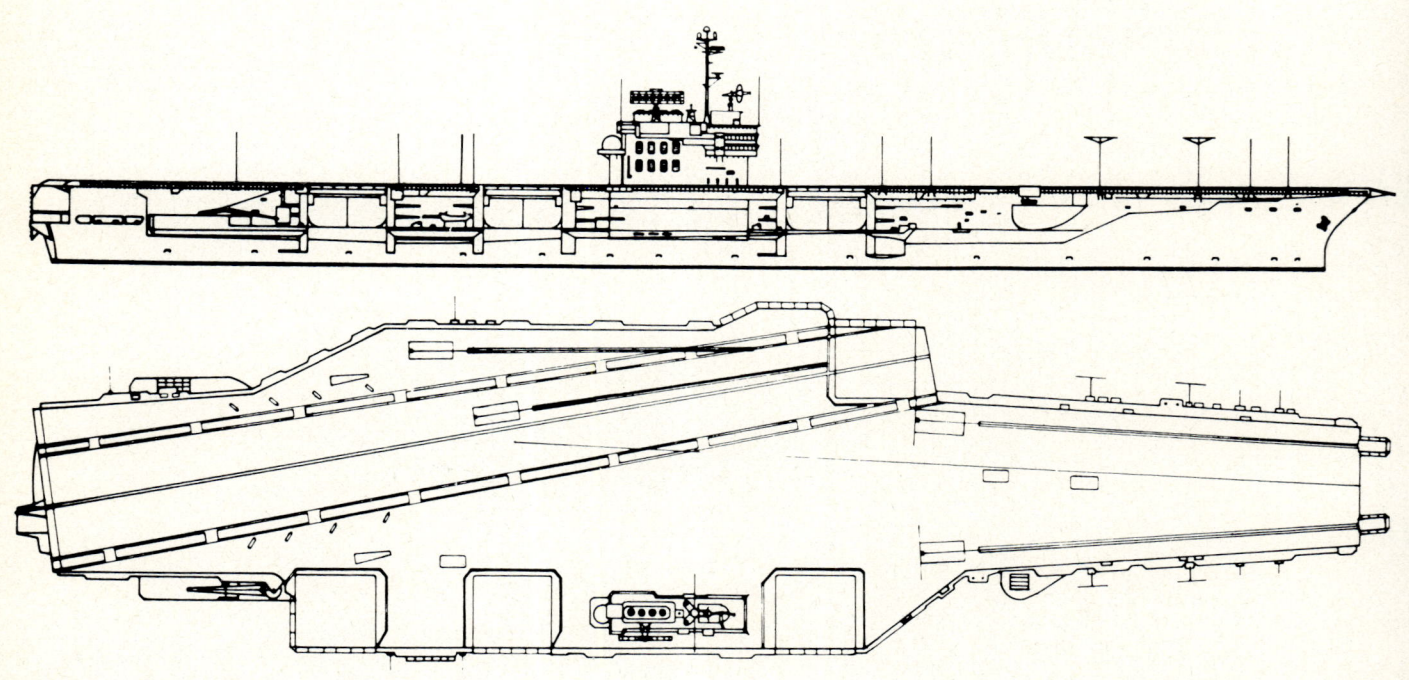

FORRESTAL Drawing, A. D. Baker III

USA /Aircraft carriers 681

SARATOGA 1975, USN

INDEPENDENCE 2/1976, USN

RANGER 9/1976, Dr. Giorgio Arra

USA / Aircraft carriers

2 "MIDWAY" CLASS: MULTI-PURPOSE AIRCRAFT CARRIERS (CV)

Name	No.	Builders	Laid down	Launched	Commissioned	F/S
MIDWAY	CV 41	Newport News S.B. & D.D. Co	27 Oct 1943	20 Mar 1945	10 Sep 1945	PA
CORAL SEA	CV 43	Newport News S.B. & D.D. Co	10 July 1944	2 Apr 1946	1 Oct 1947	AA

Displacement, tons: *Midway:* 51 000 standard; *Coral Sea:* 52 500 standard; 62 200 full load
Length, feet (metres): 979 *(298·4)*
Beam, feet (metres): 121 *(36·9)*
Draught, feet (metres): 35·3 *(10·8)*
Flight deck width, feet (metres): 238 *(72·5)* maximum
Catapults: 2 steam in *Midway* (C 13); 3 in *Coral Sea* (C 11)
Aircraft: approx 75
Guns: See notes
Main engines: 4 geared turbines (Westinghouse); 212 000 shp; 4 shafts
Boilers: 12 (Babcock & Wilcox)
Speed, knots: 30+
Complement: *Midway* 2 615 (140 officers, approx 2 475 enlisted men); *Coral Sea* 2 710 (165 officers, approx 2 545 enlisted men) plus approx 1 800 assigned to air wing

The original three carriers of this class were the largest US warships constructed during World War II. Completed too late for service in that conflict, they were the backbone of US naval strength for the first decade of the Cold War. The entire class has been in active service (except for overhaul and modernisation) since the ships were completed. *F. D. Roosevelt* deleted in 1977.

Midway was homeported at Yokosuka, Japan, in October 1973; she is the only US aircraft carrier to be based overseas.
Midway will probably be retained in service until 1985 to provide a 13 carrier force level. *Coral Sea* is currently active but has no air wing and is used for contingencies. She will be replaced in the active fleet by *Carl Vinson*.

The unnamed CVB 44, 56 and 57 of this class were cancelled prior to the start of construction.

Classification: These ships were initially classified as large Aircraft Carriers (CVB); reclassified as Attack Aircraft Carriers (CVA) on 1 October 1952. Both ships reclassified as Aircraft Carriers (CV) on 30 June 1975.

Design: These ships were built to the same design with a standard displacement of 45 000 tons, full load displacement of 60 100 tons, and an overall length of 968 feet. They have been extensively modified since completion (see notes below). These ships were the first US aircraft carriers with an armoured flight deck and the first US warships with a designed width too large to enable them to pass through the Panama Canal.

Electronics: Naval Tactical Data System (NTDS); Tacan.

Fire control: One Mk 37 and one Mk 56 GFCS.

Fiscal: Construction cost of *Midway* was $85·6 million and *Coral Sea* $87·6 million.

Gunnery: As built, these ships mounted 18—5 in guns (14 in *Coral Sea*), 84—40 mm guns, and 28—20 mm guns. In 1978 the last 5 in guns were removed.
Both are to be fitted with three 20 mm Mk 15 CIWS in near future.
Both ships carry two 40 mm saluting guns.

Missiles: Both are to be fitted with two Mk 25 Sea Sparrow launchers (BPDMS) in near future.

Modernisation: All were extensively modernised. Their main conversion gave them angled flight decks, steam catapults, enclosed bows, new electronics, and new lift arrangement (*Franklin D. Roosevelt* from 1954 to 1956, *Midway* from 1955 to 1957, and *Coral Sea* from 1958 to 1960; all at Puget Sound Naval Shipyard). Lift arrangement was changed in *Franklin D. Roosevelt* and *Midway* to one centreline lift forward, one deck-edge lift aft of island on starboard side, and one deck-edge lift at forward end of angled deck on port side. *Coral Sea* has one lift forward and one aft of island on starboard side and third lift outboard on port side aft. *Midway* began another extensive modernisation at the San Francisco Bay Naval Shipyard in February 1966; she was recommissioned on 31 January 1970 and went to sea in March 1970.
Her modernisation included widening the flight deck, provisions for handling newer aircraft, new catapults, new lifts (arranged as in *Coral Sea*), and new electronics.
Midway is now the more capable of the two ships.

Radar: Low angle air search: SPS 58.
Search: SPS 10, 30 and 43.
Navigation: SPN 6 and 10.

MIDWAY
1/1979, Dr. Giorgio Arra

MIDWAY
1/1979, Dr. Giorgio Arra

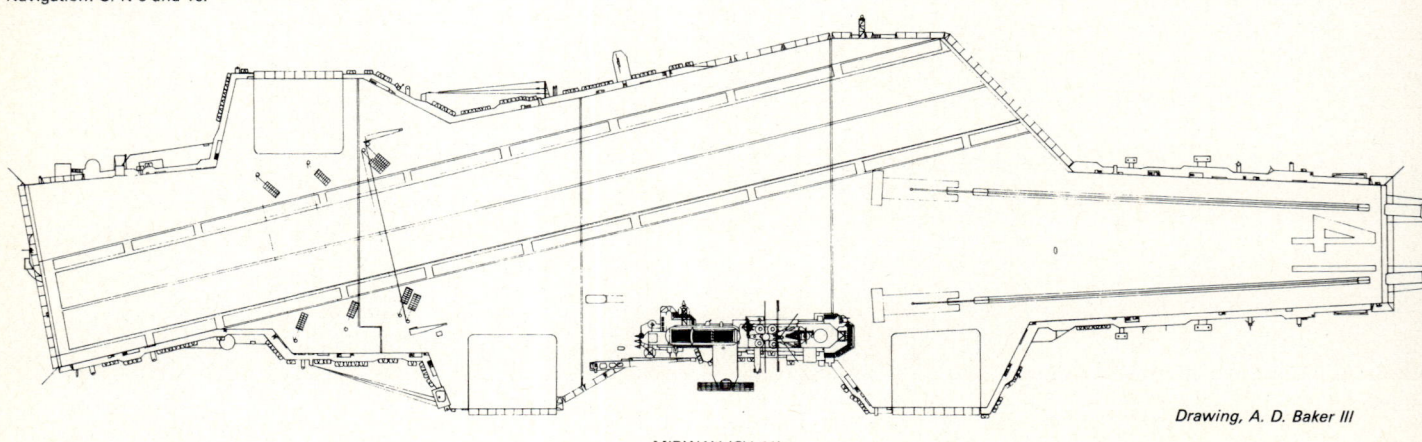
Drawing, A. D. Baker III
MIDWAY (CV 41)

USA /Aircraft carriers 683

5 "HANCOCK" and "INTREPID" CLASSES: AIRCRAFT CARRIERS (2 CVA/CV, 2 CVS, 1 AVT)

Name	No.	Builders	Laid down	Launched	Commissioned	F/S
INTREPID	CVS 11	Newport News Shipbuilding & Dry Dock Co	1 Dec 1941	26 Apr 1943	16 Aug 1943	AR
LEXINGTON	AVT 16	Bethlehem Steel Co, Quincy, Mass	15 July 1941	26 Sep 1942	17 Feb 1943	AA
BON HOMME RICHARD	CVA 31	New York Navy Yard	1 Feb 1943	29 Apr 1944	26 Nov 1944	PR
ORISKANY	CV 34	New York Navy Yard	1 May 1944	13 Oct 1945	25 Sep 1950	PR
SHANGRI-LA	CVS 38	Norfolk Navy Yard	15 Jan 1943	24 Feb 1944	15 Sep 1944	AR

Displacement, tons: 29 600 light; 41 900 full load. (Oriskany 28 200 light; 40 600 full load)
Length, feet (metres): 820 (249·9) wl; 899 (274) oa (889 (270·9) Shangri-La, Lexington)
Beam, feet (metres): 103 (30·8) except Oriskany 106·5 (32·5)
Draught, feet (metres): 31 (9·4)
Flight deck width, feet (metres): 172 (52·4) except Lexington 192 (58·5) and Oriskany 195 (59·5)
Catapults: 2 steam
Aircraft: 70 to 80 for CVA/CV type; approx 45 for CVS type; none assigned to Lexington
Guns: 2—5 in (127 mm)/38 (single Mk 24) in Oriskany; 4 guns in other ships except all removed from Lexington
Main engines: 4 geared turbines (Westinghouse) 150 000 shp; 4 shafts
Boilers: 8 (Babcock & Wilcox)
Speed, knots: 30+
Complement: CVA/CV type: 2 090 (110 officers, 1 980 enlisted men); plus approx 1 185 (135 officers, 1 050 enlisted men) in air wing for a total of approx 3 200 per ship
CVS type: 1 615 (115 officers, approx 1 500 enlisted men) plus approx 800 assigned to ASW air group for a total of 2 400 per ship
Lexington: 1 440 (75 officers, 1 365 enlisted men); no air unit assigned

LEXINGTON 5/1975, USN

These ships (formerly six including Hancock) originally were "Essex" class aircraft carriers; extensively modernised during 1950s, being provided with enclosed bow, angled flight deck, improved elevators, increased aviation fuel storage, and steam catapults. Construction of Oriskany suspended after World War II and she was completed in 1950 to a modified "Essex" design.
Bon Homme Richard decommissioned on 2 July 1971, Shangri-La on 30 July 1971, Intrepid on 15 March 1974, Oriskany on 30 September 1976; Lexington will remain in commission as a training carrier (with no aircraft support capability) until FY 1984. She was originally scheduled for deletion in FY 1979 but is now to be overhauled in FY 1980.

Classification: All "Essex" class ships originally were designated as Aircraft Carriers (CV); reclassified as Attack Aircraft Carriers (CVA) on 1 Oct 1952. Intrepid reclassified as ASW Support Aircraft Carrier (CVS) on 31 March 1962, Lexington on 1 October 1962, Shangri-La on 30 June 1969. Lexington became the Navy's training aircraft carrier in the Gulf of Mexico on 29 December 1962; reclassified CVT on 1 January 1969 and AVT on 1 July 1978.
Oriskany redesignated as CV on 30 June 1975 (as was now-stricken Hancock).

Electronics: Oriskany conducted the initial sea trials of the Naval Tactical Data System (NTDS) in 1961-62; Tacan.

Fire control: Fitted with one Mk 37 gunfire control system and two Mk 56 GFCS except Oriskany with two Mk 37 GFCS.

ORISKANY 8/1970, USN

Modernisation: These ships have been modernised under several programmes to increase their ability to operate more-advanced aircraft. Oriskany was completed with some post-war features incorporated. The most prominent difference from their original configuration is angled flight deck and removal of twin 5 in gun mounts from flight deck forward and aft of island structure. Three elevators fitted; "Pointed" centreline lift forward between catapults, deckedge lift on port side at leading edge of angled deck, and deckedge lift on starboard side aft of island structure. Minimal gun battery retained (see description of original armament under "Essex" class listings). Remaining guns removed from Lexington in 1969; by 1975 Oriskany had only two 5 in guns fitted.

Radar: Search: SPS 10, 30 and 43.
Navigation: SPN 10.
Lexington:
Search: SPS 10, 12 and 43.
Navigation: SPN 10.

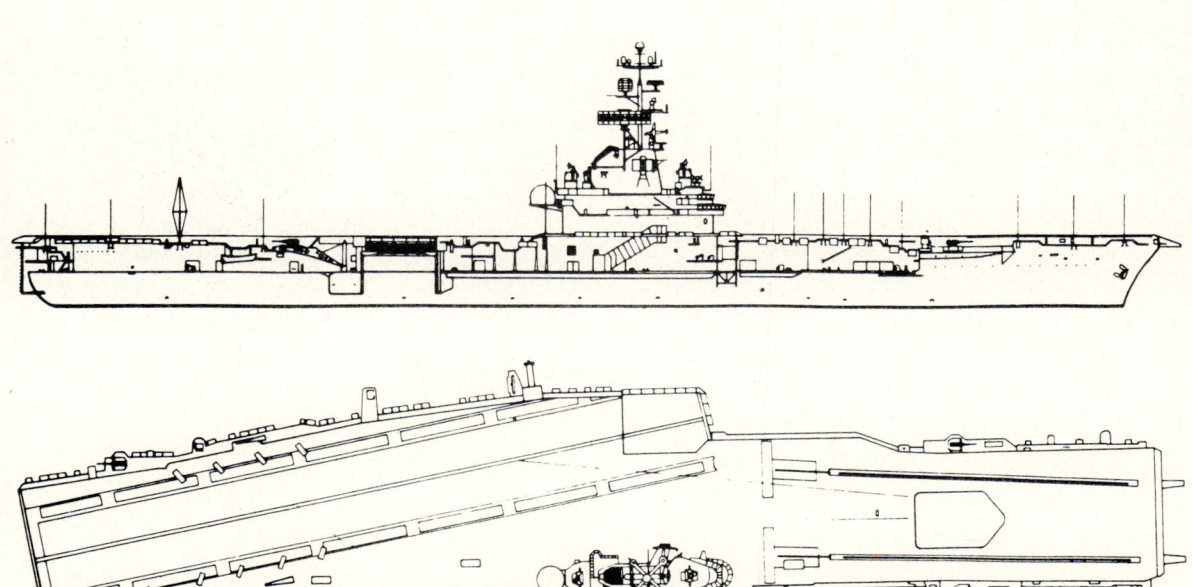

ORISKANY Drawing, A. D. Baker III

684 USA /Aircraft carriers

2 MODERNISED "ESSEX" CLASS: ASW AIRCRAFT CARRIERS (CVS)

Name	No.	Builders	Laid down	Launched	Commissioned	F/S
HORNET	CVS 12	Newport News Shipbuilding & Dry Dock Co	3 Aug 1942	29 Aug 1943	29 Nov 1943	PR
BENNINGTON	CVS 20	New York Navy Yard	15 Dec 1942	26 Feb 1944	6 Aug 1944	PR

Displacement, tons: approx 33 000 standard; approx 40 600 full load
Length, feet (metres): 899 *(274)*
Beam, feet (metres): 101 *(30·7)*
Draught, feet (metres): 31 *(9·4)*
Flight deck width, feet (metres): 172 *(52·4)*
Catapults: 2 hydraulic (H-8)
Aircraft: 45 (including 16 to 18 helicopters)
Guns: 4—5 in *(127 mm)*/38 (single Mk 24)
Main engines: 4 geared turbines (Westinghouse); 150 000 shp; 4 shafts
Boilers: 8 (Babcock & Wilcox)
Speed, knots: 30+
Complement: 1 615 (115 officers, approx 1 500 enlisted men) plus approx 800 assigned to ASW air group for a total of 2 400 per ship

The two above ships and the previously listed "Hancock" and "Intrepid" classes are the survivors of the 24 "Essex" class fleet carriers built during World War II (with one ship, *Oriskany*, not completed until 1950). Both of the above ships were extensively modernised during the 1950s; however, they lack the steam catapults and other features of the "Hancock" and "Intrepid" classes.
Bennington was decommissioned on 15 January 1970 and *Hornet* on 26 June 1970. Both laid up at Bremerton, Wash.

Classification: These ships originally were designated as Aircraft Carriers (CV); reclassified as Attack Carriers (CVA) on 1 October 1952. Subsequently they became ASW Support Aircraft Carriers (CVS): *Hornet* on 27 June 1958, and *Bennington* on 30 June 1959.

Design: All 24 "Essex" class ships were built to the same basic design except for the delayed *Oriskany*. Standard displacement as built was 27 100 tons, full load displacement was 36 380 tons, and overall length 888 or 872 ft.

Fire control: One Mk 37 and three Mk 56 GFCS.

Modernisation: These ships have been modernised under several programmes to increase their ability to operate advanced aircraft and to improve sea keeping. Also modernised to improve anti-submarine capabilities under the Fleet Rehabilitation and Modernisation (FRAM II) programme.

Radar: Search: SPS 10, 30 and 43; Tacan.

Sonar: SQS 23 (bow-mounted).

BENNINGTON (starboard lift raised during replenishment)   1968, USN

HORNET   1968, USN

BATTLESHIPS

4 "IOWA" CLASS

Name	No.	Builders	Laid down	Launched	Commissioned	F/S
IOWA	BB 61	New York Navy Yard	27 June 1940	27 Aug 1942	22 Feb 1943	AR
NEW JERSEY	BB 62	Philadelphia Navy Yard	16 Sep 1940	7 Dec 1942	23 May 1943	PR
MISSOURI	BB 63	New York Navy Yard	6 Jan 1941	29 Jan 1944	11 June 1944	PR
WISCONSIN	BB 64	Philadelphia Navy Yard	25 Jan 1941	7 Dec 1943	16 Apr 1944	AR

Displacement, tons: 45 000 standard; 58 000 full load
Length, feet (metres): 887·2 (270·4) except New Jersey 887·6 (270·5)
Beam, feet (metres): 108·2 (33·0)
Draught, feet (metres): 38 (11·6)
Guns: 9—16 in (406 mm)/50 (triple); 20—5 in (127 mm)/38 (twin Mk 38); 20—40 mm/60 in Missouri only
Main engines: 4 geared turbines (General Electric in BB 61 and BB 63; Westinghouse in BB 62 and BB 64); 212 000 shp; 4 shafts
Boilers: 8 (Babcock & Wilcox)
Speed, knots: 33 (all may have reached 35 knots in service)
Oil fuel, tons: 9 000
Range, miles: 5 000 at 30 knots; 15 000 at 17 knots
Complement: Designed complement varied, averaging 95 officers and 2 270 enlisted men in wartime; New Jersey was manned by 70 officers and 1 556 enlisted men (requirements reduced with removal of all light anti-aircraft weapons, floatplanes, and reduced operational requirements) in 1968-69.

These ships were the largest battleships ever built except for the Japanese Yamato and Musashi (64 170 tons standard, 863 ft overall, nine 18·1 in guns). All four "Iowa" class ships were in action in the Pacific during World War II, primarily screening fast carriers and bombarding amphibious invasion objectives. Three were mothballed after the war with Missouri being retained in service as a training ship. All four ships again were in service during the Korean War (1950-53) as shore-bombardment ships; all mothballed 1954-58.

New Jersey began reactivation in mid-1967 at a cost of approximately $21 million; recommissioned on 6 April 1968. Iowa and Wisconsin remained in reserve at the Philadelphia Naval Shipyard where New Jersey had been berthed and reactivated; and the mothballed Missouri at the Puget Sound Naval Shipyard, Bremerton, Washington.

New Jersey was again decommissioned on 17 December 1969 and mothballed at Bremerton with Missouri. Two additional ships of this class were laid down, but never completed: Illinois (BB 65), laid down 15 January 1945, and Kentucky (BB 66), laid down 6 December 1944. Illinois was 22 per cent complete when cancelled on 11 Aug 1945. Kentucky was 69·2 per cent complete when construction was suspended late in the war; floated from its building dock on 20 January 1950. Conversion to a missile ship (BBG) was proposed but no work was undertaken and she was stricken on 9 June 1958 and broken up for scrap. The engines for Kentucky and Illinois were used in the "Sacramento" class fast combat support ships.

Approximate construction cost was $114·485 million for Missouri; other ships cost slightly less.

Aircraft: As built, each ship carried three floatplanes for scouting and gunfire spotting and had two quarterdeck catapults. Catapults removed and helicopters carried during the Korean War.

Armour: These battleships are the most heavily armoured US warships ever constructed, being designed to survive ship-to-ship combat with enemy ships armed with 16 in guns. The main armour belt consists of Class A steel armour 12·1 in thick tapering vertically to 1·62 in; a lower armour belt aft of Turret No. 3 to protect propeller shafts is 13·5 in; turret faces are 17 in; turret tops are 7·25 in; turret backs are 12 in; barbettes have a maximum of 11·6 in of armour; second deck armour is 6 in; and the three-level conning tower sides are 17·3 in with an armoured roof 7·25 in (the conning tower levels are pilot house, navigation bridge and flag-signal bridge).

Design: These ships carried heavier armament than previous US battleships and had increased protection and larger engines accounting for additional displacement and increased speed. All fitted as fleet flagships with additional accommodations and bridge level for admiral and staff. When New Jersey was reactivated in 1967-68 this accommodation remained mothballed.

Gunnery: The Mk 7 16 in guns in these ships fire projectiles weighing up to 2 700 lb (1 225 kg) (armour piercing) a maximum range of 23 miles (39 km). As built, these ships had 40—40 mm and 49 to 60—20 mm anti-aircraft guns (except Iowa, only 19 quad 40 mm mounts); all 20 mm guns now removed.

When recommissioned in 1968 New Jersey was fitted with two Mk 38 fire control directors in addition to the Mk 40 and four Mk 51 previously installed. Mk 48 shore bombardment computer installed when reactivated. Also fitted with four Mk 37 and six Mk 56 GFCS.

Operational: New Jersey made one deployment to the Western Pacific during her third commission (1968-69). During the deployment she was on the "gun line" off South Viet-Nam for a total of 120 days with 47 days being the longest sustained period at sea.

While in action New Jersey fired 5 688 rounds of ammunition from her 16 in main battery guns and a total of 6 200 rounds during the commission, the additional firings being for tests and training. While off Viet-Nam she also fired some 15 000 rounds from her 5 in secondary battery guns.

In comparison, during World War II New Jersey fired 771 main battery rounds and during two deployments in the Korean War and midshipmen training cruises she fired 6 671 main battery rounds.

Radar: SPS 6 and 10 (fitted in New Jersey 1968-69).

NEW JERSEY (off Viet-Nam)   4/1969, USN

WISCONSIN   USN

USA / Cruisers

CRUISERS

The US Navy's active cruiser force consists of 28 guided missile ships. Only five of these ships (all nuclear-powered) have been completed during the past five years with the three older ships being modernised World War II-built cruisers. All of these ships are oriented primarily toward Anti-Air Warfare (AAW) with the three older ships additionally configured to serve as flagships for the US Navy's numbered fleets. In addition, the collision-damaged *Belknap* (CG 26) is undergoing a two-year repair/modernisation programme (1978-80).

One additional nuclear propelled missile cruiser is under construction. With nine nuclear cruisers available by 1980 the Navy could operate two all-nuclear carrier task forces.

On 22 February 1977 Secretary of Defense Harold Brown announced the cancellation of the nuclear strike cruiser (CSGN) programme preferring the option of two DDG-47 Aegis-equipped destroyers for the price of one CSGN. In January 1979 the construction of the four "Modified Virginia" class CGNs was cancelled. They were originally designed to replace the CSGN programme but, according to official sources the construction of the class was "overtaken by events." (Details of the proposed CSGN are in *Jane's Fighting Ships* 1976-77 and of the "Modified Virginia" class in 1978-79.)

3 + 1 "VIRGINIA" CLASS: GUIDED MISSILE CRUISERS (nuclear propulsion) (CGN)

Name	No.	Builders	Laid down	Launched	Commissioned	F/S
VIRGINIA	CGN 38 (ex-*DLGN 38*)	Newport News S.B. and D.D. Co	19 Aug 1972	14 Dec 1974	11 Sep 1976	AA
TEXAS	CGN 39 (ex-*DLGN 39*)	Newport News S.B. and D.D. Co	18 Aug 1973	9 Aug 1975	10 Sep 1977	AA
MISSISSIPPI	CGN 40 (ex-*DLGN 40*)	Newport News S.B. and D.D. Co	22 Feb 1975	31 July 1976	5 Aug 1978	AA
ARKANSAS	CGN 41	Newport News S.B. and D.D. Co	17 Jan 1977	21 Oct 1978	June 1980	Bldg

Displacement, tons: 10 000 full load
Length, feet (metres): 585 *(177·3)*
Beam, feet (metres): 63 *(18·9)*
Draught, feet (metres): 29·5 *(9·0)*
Aircraft: 2 (see *Helicopter* notes)
Missiles: SAM/ASW; Standard-MR/ASROC (2 twin Mk 26 launchers)
Guns: 2—5 in *(127 mm)*/54 (single Mk 45)
A/S weapons: ASROC (see above);
2 triple torpedo tubes (Mk 32)
Main engines: 2 geared turbines; 60 000 shp; 2 shafts
Reactors: 2 pressurised-water cooled D2G (General Electric)
Speed, knots: 30+
Complement: 442 (27 officers, 415 enlisted men)

Virginia was authorised in the Fiscal Year 1970 new construction programme, *Texas* in the FY 1971, *Mississippi* in the FY 1972, and *Arkansas* in the FY 1975.
CGN 42 was proposed in the FY 1976 new construction programme but was not funded by the Congress.
Construction of this class has been delayed because of a shortage of skilled labour in the shipyard. Newport News S.B. & D.D. Co (Virginia) is the only shipyard in the USA now engaged in the construction of nuclear surface ships. The first three ships of the class were more than one year behind their original construction schedules.

Classification: These ships were originally classified as guided missile frigates (DLGN); subsequently reclassified as guided missile cruisers (CGN) on 30 June 1975.

Design: The principal differences between the "Virginia" and "California" classes are the improved anti-air warfare capability, electronic warfare equipment, and anti-submarine fire control system. The deletion of the separate ASROC Mk 16 launcher permitted the "Virginia" class to be 10 ft shorter.

Electronics: Naval Tactical Data System (NTDS).

Fiscal: These ships have incurred major cost growth/escalation during their construction. Fiscal data on the earlier ships were in the 1974-75 and earlier editions.

Fire control: Mk 74 missile control directors.
Digital Mk 116 ASW FCS.

Gunnery: Mk 86 gunfire control directors. Two 20 mm Mk 15 CIWS will be fitted in each ship.
Each ship has two 40 mm saluting guns.

Helicopters: A hangar for helicopters is installed beneath the fantail flight-deck with a telescoping hatch cover and an electro-mechanical elevator provided to transport helicopters between the main deck and hangar. These are the first US post-World War II destroyer/cruiser ships with a hull hangar.

Missiles: The initial design for this class provided for a single surface-to-air missile launcher; revised in 1969 to provide two Mk 26 launchers that will fire the Standard-Medium Range (MR) surface-to-air missile and the ASROC anti-submarine missile. "Mixed" Standard/ASROC magazines are planned for each launcher.
Harpoon SSM will be fitted in the immediate future and it is planned to fit the Tomahawk cruise missile.

Radar: 3D search: SPS 48A.
Search: SPS 40B and 55.

Rockets: Mk 36 "Chaffroc" RBOC (Rapid Bloom Overhead Chaff) to be fitted.

Sonar: SQS 53A (bow-mounted).

VIRGINIA 9/1978, J. L. M. van der Burgh

MISSISSIPPI 6/1978, Newport News S.B. and D.D. Co

MISSISSIPPI 6/1978, Newport News S.B. and D.D. Co

2 "CALIFORNIA" CLASS: GUIDED MISSILE CRUISERS (nuclear propulsion) (CGN)

Name	No.	Builders	Laid down	Launched	Commissioned	F/S
CALIFORNIA	CGN 36	Newport News Shipbuilding Co	23 Jan 1970	22 Sep 1971	16 Feb 1974	AA
SOUTH CAROLINA	CGN 37	Newport News Shipbuilding Co	1 Dec 1970	1 July 1972	25 Jan 1975	AA

Displacement, tons: 9 561 standard; 11 100 full load
Length, feet (metres): 596 *(181·7)*
Beam, feet (metres): 61 *(18·6)*
Draught, feet (metres): 31·5 *(9·6)*
Missiles: SSM; Harpoon to be fitted in near future; SAM; 80 Standard-MR (two single Mk 13 launchers) (see note)
Guns: 2—5 in *(127 mm)*/54 (single Mk 45)
A/S weapons: 4 torpedo tubes (Mk 32); 1 ASROC 8-tube launcher (Mk 16)
Main engines: 2 geared turbines; 60 000 shp; 2 shafts
Nuclear reactors: 2 pressurised-water cooled D2G (General Electric)
Speed, knots: 30+
Complement: 540 (28 officers, 512 enlisted men)

California was authorised in the Fiscal Year 1967 new construction programme and *South Carolina* in the FY 1968 programme. The construction of a third ship of this class (DLGN 38) was also authorised in FY 1968, but the rising costs of these ships and development of the DXGN/DLGN 38 design (now "Virginia" class) caused the third ship to be cancelled.

Classification: These ships were originally classified as guided missile frigates (DLGN); subsequently reclassified as guided missile cruisers (CGN) on 30 June 1975.

Design: These ships have tall, enclosed towers supporting radar antennae in contrast to the open lattice masts of the previous nuclear frigates *Truxtun* and *Bainbridge*. No helicopter support facilities provided.

Electronics: Fitted with the Naval Tactical Data System (NTDS).

Engineering: Estimated nuclear core life for these ships provides 700 000 miles range; estimated cost is $11·5 million for the two initial nuclear cores in each ship.

Fire control: Two Mk 74 MFCS; one Mk 86 GFCS; one Mk 11 weapons direction system (to be replaced by Mk 13).

Fiscal: Estimated cost is $200 million for *California* and $180 million for *South Carolina*.

Gunnery: Two Phalanx 20 mm CIWS (Mk 15) to be fitted. Each ship carries two 40 mm saluting guns.

Missiles: Reportedly, these ships carry some 80 surface-to-air missiles divided equally between a magazine beneath each launcher.

Radar: 3D air search: SPS 48.
Search: SPS 10 and 40.
Fire control: SPG 51D, SPG 60 and SPQ 9A.

Rockets: Mk 36 Chaffroc RBOC to be fitted in place of Mk 28 system.

Sonar: SQS 26CX (bow-mounted).

CALIFORNIA 6/1977, C. and S. Taylor

SOUTH CAROLINA 9/1976, USN

CALIFORNIA 6/1977, C. and S. Taylor

688   USA / Cruisers

1 "TRUXTUN" CLASS: GUIDED MISSILE CRUISER (nuclear propulsion) (CGN)

Name	No.	Builders	Laid down	Launched	Commissioned	F/S
TRUXTUN	CGN 35	New York SB Corp (Camden, New Jersey)	17 June 1963	19 Dec 1964	27 May 1967	PA

Displacement, tons: 8 200 standard; 9 127 full load
Length, feet (metres): 564 *(171·9)*
Beam, feet (metres): 58 *(17·7)*
Draught, feet (metres): 31 *(9·4)*
Aircraft: 1 helicopter
Missiles: SSM; Harpoon to be fitted;
  SAM/ASW; 60 Standard-ER/ASROC (1 twin Mk 10 launcher)
Guns: 1—5 in *(127 mm)*/54 (single Mk 42)
  2—3 in *(76 mm)*/50 (single Mk 34)
A/S weapons: ASROC (see above);
  4 fixed torpedo tubes (Mk 32)
Main engines: 2 geared turbines; 60 000 shp; 2 shafts
Nuclear reactors: 2 pressurised-water cooled D2G (General Electric)
Speed, knots: 29
Complement: 528 (36 officers, 492 enlisted men)
Flag accommodations: 18 (6 officers, 12 enlisted men)

TRUXTUN   1/1977, Dr. Giorgio Arra

Truxtun was the US Navy's fourth nuclear-powered surface warship. The Navy had requested seven oil-burning frigates in the Fiscal Year 1962 shipbuilding programme; Congress authorised seven ships, but stipulated that one ship must be nuclear-powered.
Although the *Truxtun* design is adapted from the "Belknap" class design, the nuclear ship's gun-missile launcher arrangement is reversed from the non-nuclear ships.
Construction cost was $138·667 million.

Ammunition: Of the 60 rounds for the missile launcher no more than 20 can be ASROC.

Classification: *Truxtun* was originally classified as a guided missile frigate (DLGN); subsequently reclassified as a guided missile cruiser (CGN) on 30 June 1975.

Electronics: Naval Tactical Data System (NTDS); Tacan.

Engineering: Power plant is identical to that of the cruiser *Bainbridge*.

Fire control: Two Mk 76 missile control systems, one Mk 68 gunfire control system, one Mk 11 weapon direction system, one SPG 53A and two SPG 55B weapon control radars (Mk 11 WDS to be replaced by Mk 14).

Gunnery: 2 Phalanx 20 mm systems (Mk 15) to be fitted. Two 40 mm saluting guns fitted.

Name: *Truxtun* is the fifth ship to be named after Commodore Thomas Truxton (sic) who commanded the frigate *Constellation* (38 guns) in her successful encounter with the French frigate *L'Insurgente* (44) in 1799.

Radar: 3D search: SPS 48.
Search: SPS 10 and 40.

Rockets: Mk 36 Chaffroc RBOC will be fitted soon replacing the Mk 28 system.

Sonar: SQS 26 (bow-mounted).

Torpedoes: Fixed Mk 32 tubes are below 3 in gun mounts, built into superstructure.

TRUXTUN   8/1978, Dr. Giorgio Arra

TRUXTUN   8/1978, Dr. Giorgio Arra

USA / Cruisers 689

9 "BELKNAP" CLASS: GUIDED MISSILE CRUISERS (CG)

Name	No.	Builders	Laid down	Launched	Commissioned	F/S
BELKNAP	CG 26	Bath Iron Works Corporation	5 Feb 1962	20 July 1963	7 Nov 1964	AR
JOSEPHUS DANIELS	CG 27	Bath Iron Works Corporation	23 Apr 1962	2 Dec 1963	8 May 1965	AA
WAINWRIGHT	CG 28	Bath Iron Works Corporation	2 July 1962	25 Apr 1964	8 Jan 1966	AA
JOUETT	CG 29	Puget Sound Naval Shipyard	25 Sep 1962	30 June 1964	3 Dec 1966	PA
HORNE	CG 30	San Francisco Naval Shipyard	12 Dec 1962	30 Oct 1964	15 Apr 1967	PA
STERETT	CG 31	Puget Sound Naval Shipyard	25 Sep 1962	30 June 1964	8 Apr 1967	PA
WILLIAM H. STANDLEY	CG 32	Bath Iron Works Corporation	29 July 1963	19 Dec 1964	9 July 1966	PA
FOX	CG 33	Todd Shipyard Corporation	15 Jan 1963	21 Nov 1964	8 May 1966	PA
BIDDLE	CG 34	Bath Iron Works Corporation	9 Dec 1963	2 July 1965	21 Jan 1967	AA

Displacement, tons: 6 570 standard; 7 900 full load
Length, feet (metres): 547 (166·7)
Beam, feet (metres): 54·8 (16·7)
Draught, feet (metres): 28·8 (8·7)
Aircraft: 1 SH-2D LAMPS helicopter
Missiles: SSM; Harpoon to be fitted;
 SAM; 60 Standard-ER/ASROC (1 twin Mk 10 launcher)
Guns: 1—5 in (127 mm)/54 (Mk 42)
 2—3 in (76 mm)/50 (single Mk 34)
A/S weapons: ASROC (see above); 2 triple torpedo tubes (Mk 32)
Main engines: 2 geared turbines (General Electric except De Laval in CG 33); 85 000 shp; 2 shafts
Boilers: 4 (Babcock & Wilcox in CG 26-28, 32-34; Combustion Engineering in CG 29-31)
Speed, knots: 32·5
Complement: 418 (31 officers, 387 enlisted men) including squadron staff
Flag accommodations: 18 (6 officers; 12 enlisted men)

These ships were authorised as guided missile frigates; DLG 26-28 in the Fiscal Year 1961 shipbuilding programme; DLG 29-34 in the FY 1962 programme.
All ships of this class are active except *Belknap*, which was severely damaged in a collision with the carrier *John F. Kennedy* (CV 67) on 22 November 1975 near Sicily; the cruiser was towed back to the USA for rebuilding at Philadelphia Naval Shipyard. Placed "Out of Commission—Special" 20 December 1975. Repair and modernisation began 9 January 1978. Estimated completion 8 January 1980. Estimated cost is $213 million and includes new improved 5 in gun (probably light-weight in).

Ammunition: 60 missiles for Mk 10 launcher of which only 20 can be ASROC.

Classification: These ships were originally classified as guided missile frigates (DLG); reclassified as guided missile cruisers (CG) on 30 June 1975.

Design: These ships are distinctive by having their single missile launcher forward and 5 in gun mount aft. This arrangement allowed missile stowage in the larger bow section and provided space aft of the superstructure for a helicopter hangar and platform. The reverse gun-missile arrangement, preferred by some commanding officers, is found in *Truxtun*.

Electronics: Naval Tactical Data System (NTDS); Tacan.

Fire control: Two Mk 76 missile control systems, one Mk 68 gunfire control system, two Mk 51 gun directors (removed from *Sterett* in 1976 and *Josephus Daniels*, *Belknap* and *Fox* in 1977), one Mk 11 weapon direction system (Mk 7 in *Josephus Daniels* and *Belknap*), one SPG 53A and two SPG 55B weapon control radars. (Mk 14 WDS to be fitted in place of present system in all ships soon).

Gunnery: All of this class will be fitted with two Phalanx 20 mm Mk 15 CIWS as will *Belknap* during rebuilding. Two 76 mm 50 calibre removed from *Sterett* in 1976 and replaced by Harpoon.

Helicopters: These ships are the only conventionally powered US cruisers with a full helicopter support capability. All fitted with the Light Airborne Multi-Purpose System, now the SH-2D helicopter. *Belknap* embarked the first operational SH-2D/LAMPS in December 1971.

Missiles: A "triple-ring" rotating magazine stocks both Standard anti-craft missiles and ASROC anti-submarine rockets, feeding either weapon to the launcher's two firing arms. The rate of fire and reliability of the launcher provide a potent AAW/ASW capability to these ships.
Fox was fitted with an experimental Tomahawk cruise-missile system in 1977.

Radar: 3D search: SPS 48.
Search: SPS 10 and 37 (26-28) or 40 (remainder).

Rockets: Mk 36 Chaffroc RBOC to be fitted in place of Mk 28.

Sonar: SQS 26 (bow-mounted).

Torpedoes: As built, these ships each had two 21 in tubes for anti-submarine torpedoes installed in the structure immediately forward of the 5 in mount, one tube angled out to port and one to starboard; subsequently removed.

JOUETT 11/1978, Dr. Giorgio Arra

BIDDLE 11/1978, Leo van Ginderen

HORNE 10/1978, Dr. Giorgio Arra

9 "LEAHY" CLASS: GUIDED MISSILE CRUISERS (CG)

Name	No.	Builders	Laid down	Launched	Commissioned	F/S
LEAHY	CG 16	Bath Iron Works Corporation	3 Dec 1959	1 July 1961	4 Aug 1962	PA
HARRY E. YARNELL	CG 17	Bath Iron Works Corporation	31 May 1960	9 Dec 1961	2 Feb 1963	AA
WORDEN	CG 18	Bath Iron Works Corporation	19 Sep 1960	2 June 1962	3 Aug 1963	PA
DALE	CG 19	New York S.B. Corporation	6 Sep 1960	28 July 1962	23 Nov 1963	AA
RICHMOND K. TURNER	CG 20	New York S.B. Corporation	9 Jan 1961	6 Apr 1963	13 June 1964	AA
GRIDLEY	CG 21	Puget Sound Bridge & Dry Dock Co	15 July 1960	31 July 1961	25 May 1963	PA
ENGLAND	CG 22	Todd Shipyards Corporation	4 Oct 1960	6 Mar 1962	7 Dec 1963	PA
HALSEY	CG 23	San Francisco Naval Shipyard	26 Aug 1960	15 Jan 1962	20 July 1963	PA
REEVES	CG 24	Puget Sound Naval Shipyard	1 July 1960	12 May 1962	15 May 1964	PA

Displacement, tons: 5 670 standard; 7 800 full load
Length, feet (metres): 510 pp *(155·5)*; 533 *(162·5)* oa
Beam, feet (metres): 54·9 *(16·6)*
Draught, feet (metres): 24·8 *(7·6)*
Missiles: SSM; Harpoon to be fitted;
 SAM; 80 Standard-ER (Mk 10 launcher)
Guns: 4—3 in *(76 mm)*/50 (twin Mk 33)
A/S weapons: 1 ASROC 8-tube launcher;
 2 triple torpedo tubes (Mk 32)
Main engines: 2 geared turbines (see *Engineering* notes);
 85 000 shp; 2 shafts
Boilers: 4 (Babcock & Wilcox in CG 16-20, Foster-Wheeler in 21-24)
Speed, knots: 32·7
Fuel, tons: 1 800
Range, miles: 8 000 at 20 knots
Complement: 377 (18 officers, 359 enlisted men) (16, 17, 21, 23); 413 (32 officers, 381 men) (18-20, 22, 24)
Flag accommodations: 18 (6 officers, 12 enlisted men)

These ships are "double-end" missile cruisers especially designed to screen fast carrier task forces. They are limited in only having 3 in guns. Authorised as DLG 16-18 in the Fiscal Year 1958 new construction programme and DLG 19-24 in the FY 1959 programme.

Classification: These ships were originally classified as guided missile frigates (DLG); reclassified as guided missile cruisers (CG) on 30 June 1975.

Design: These ships are distinctive in having twin missile launchers forward and aft with ASROC launcher between the forward missile launcher and bridge on main deck level.
There is a helicopter landing area aft but only limited support facilities are provided; no hangar.

Electronics: Naval Tactical Data System (NTDS) fitted during AAW modernisation.

Engineering: General Electric turbines in CG 16-18, De Laval turbines in CG 19-22, and Allis-Chalmers turbines in CG 23 and CG 24.

Fire control: Four Mk 76 missile control systems, two Mk 63 gunfire control systems (*Reeves* only), one Mk 11 weapon direction system, (to be replaced by Mk 14 WDS) and four SPG 55 radars. Mk 114 ASW fire control system.

Gunnery: Two Phalanx 20 mm CIWS Mk 15 to be fitted.
Two 40 mm saluting guns fitted.

Modernisation: These ships were modernised between 1967 and 1972 to improve their Anti-Air Warfare (AAW) capabilities. Superstructure enlarged to provide space for additional electronic equipment, including NTDS; improved Tacan fitted and improved guidance system for Terrier/Standard missiles installed, and larger ship's service turbo generators provided.
All ships modernised at Bath Iron Works except *Leahy* at Philadelphia Naval Shipyard.
Cost of *Leahy* modernisation was $36·1 million.

Radar: 3D search: SPS 48 (replacing SPS 39 or 52 in some ships).
Search: SPS 10, 37.

Rockets: Mk 36 Chaffroc RBOC to be fitted.

Sonar: SQS 23 bow-mounted.

WORDEN   11/1978, Lawrence Phillip

ENGLAND   1/1978, Dr. Giorgio Arr

LEAHY   10/1977, Dr. Giorgio Arra

USA / Cruisers 691

1 "BAINBRIDGE" CLASS: GUIDED MISSILE CRUISER (nuclear propulsion) (CGN)

Name	No.	Builders	Laid down	Launched	Commissioned	F/S
BAINBRIDGE	CGN 25	Bethlehem Steel Co, Quincy, Mass	15 May 1959	15 Apr 1961	6 Oct 1962	PA

Displacement, tons: 7 600 standard; 8 580 full load
Length, feet (metres): 565 *(172·5)*
Beam, feet (metres): 57·9 *(17·6)*
Draught, feet (metres): 25·4 *(7·7)*
Missiles: SSM; Harpoon;
SAM; 80 Standard-ER (2 twin Mk 10 launchers)
Guns: 2—20 mm (twin)
A/S weapons: 1 ASROC 8-tube launcher;
2 triple torpedo tubes (Mk 32)
Main engines: 2 geared turbines, approx 60 000 shp; 2 shafts
Nuclear reactors: 2 pressurised-water cooled D2G (General Electric)
Speed, knots: 34
Complement: 470 (34 officers, 436 enlisted men)
Flag accommodations: 18 (6 officers, 12 enlisted men)

Bainbridge was the US Navy's third nuclear-powered surface warship (after the cruiser *Long Beach* and the aircraft carrier *Enterprise*). Authorised in the Fiscal Year 1956 shipbuilding programme. Construction cost was $163·61 million.

Classification: *Bainbridge* was originally classified as a guided missile frigate (DLGN); reclassified as a guided missile cruiser (CGN) on 30 June 1975.

Engineering: Development of a nuclear power plant suitable for use in a large "destroyer type" warship began in 1957. The Atomic Energy Commission's Knolls Atomic Power Laboratory undertook development of the destroyer power plant (designated D1G/D2G).

Fire control: Four Mk 76 missile control systems, one Mk 14 weapons direction system, four SPG 55A weapon control radars.

Gunnery: Four 3 in *(76 mm)* in twin mountings removed during modernisation. Two 40 mm saluting guns carried.

Missiles: Terrier system replaced by Standard SM-1.

Modernisation: *Bainbridge* underwent an Anti-Air Warfare (AAW) modernisation at the Puget Sound Naval Shipyard from 30 June 1974 to 24 September 1976. The ship was fitted with the Naval Tactical Data System (NTDS) and improved guidance capability for missiles. Estimated cost of modernisation $103 million.

Radar: 3D search: SPS 52.
Search: SPS 10 and 37.

Rockets: Mk 36 Chaffroc RBOC to be fitted.

Sonar: SQS 23 (bow-mounted).

BAINBRIDGE 4/1978, Dr. Giorgio Arra

1 "LONG BEACH" CLASS: GUIDED MISSILE CRUISER (nuclear propulsion) (CGN)

Name	No.	Builders	Laid down	Launched	Commissioned	F/S
LONG BEACH	CGN 9 (ex-CGN 160, CLGN 160)	Bethlehem Steel Co, Quincy, Mass	2 Dec 1957	14 July 1959	9 Sep 1961	PA

Displacement, tons: 14 200 standard; 15 540 light; 17 100 full load
Length, feet (metres): 721·2 *(219·8)*
Beam, feet (metres): 73·2 *(22·3)*
Draught, feet (metres): 29·7 *(9·1)*
Aircraft: Deck for utility helicopter
Missiles: SAM; 120 Terrier/Standard-ER
(2 twin Mk 10 launchers) (see note)
Guns: 2—5 in *(127 mm)*/38 (single Mk 30)
A/S weapons: 1 ASROC 8-tube launcher;
2 triple torpedo tubes (Mk 32)
Main engines: 2 geared turbines (General Electric); 80 000 shp; 2 shafts
Nuclear reactors: 2 pressurised-water cooled C1W (Westinghouse)
Speed, knots: 30
Complement: 1 160 (79 officers, 1 081 enlisted men)
Flag accommodations: 68 (10 officers, 58 enlisted men)

Long Beach was the first ship to be designed as a cruiser for the USA since the end of World War II. She is the world's first nuclear-powered surface warship and the first warship to have guided missile main battery. She was authorised in the Fiscal Year 1957 new construction programme. Estimated construction cost was $332·85 million.

Aegis: Long-lead funding for the installation of an Aegis system was provided in the FY 1977 programme. The conversion was due to start in October 1978 for completion in October 1981. It was cancelled in December 1976 and the authorised funds rescinded (see *Conversion* note below).

Conversion: As a result of the Aegis cancellation (above) *Long Beach* is to undergo a mid-life modernisation in FY 1980. This is planned to include updating of missile systems, restoration of the missile radars, the present SPS 32 and 33 air search to be replaced by SPS 48 and 49 systems, replacement of the ship's computer and modernisation of the communications system. Estimated cost of modernisation—$267 million. Estimated length of modernisation—two years (September 1980–September 1982).

Classification: Ordered as a guided missile light cruiser (CLGN 160) on 15 October 1956; reclassified as a guided missile cruiser (CGN 160) early in 1957 and renumbered (CGN 9) on 1 July 1957.

Design: Initially planned at about 7 800 tons (standard) to test the feasibility of a nuclear-powered surface warship. Early in 1956 her displacement was increased to 11 000 tons and a second Terrier missile launcher was added. A Talos missile launcher was also added which, with other features, increased displacement to 14 200 tons.

Electronics: Naval Tactical Data System (NTDS).

Fire control: Four Mk 76 missile fire control systems, one Mk 77 Mod 4 missile fire control system, two Mk 56 gunfire control systems, one Mk 6 weapon direction system, two SPG 49B and four SPG 55A weapon control radars.

Engineering: The reactors are similar to those of *Enterprise* (CVN 65). *Long Beach* first got underway on nuclear power on 5 July 1961. After four years of operation and having steamed more than 167 700 miles she underwent her first overhaul and refuelling at the Newport News Shipbuilding and Dry Dock Company from August 1965 to February 1966.

Gunnery: Completed with an all-missile armament. Two single 5 in mounts were fitted during 1962-63. Two Phalanx 20 mm CIWS Mk 15 to be fitted. Two 40 mm saluting guns carried.

Missiles: *Long Beach* has two Terrier twin missile launchers stepped forward and one Talos twin missile launcher aft. Reportedly, her magazines hold 120 Terrier missiles and approx 46 Talos missiles. Harpoon to be fitted.
Talos system was inactivated in FY 1978—to be removed in 1980-82 modernisation.

Radar: Long range fixed air search: SPS 32.
Long range target tracking: SPS 33.
(Fixed arrays "billboards" on bridge, SPS 32 horizontal and 33 vertical—both modified in 1970).
Search: SPS 10 and 12.

Rockets: Mk 36 Chaffroc RBOC to be fitted in place of Mk 28.

Sonar: SQS 23.

LONG BEACH 8/1978, Dr. Giorgio Arra

692 USA / Cruisers

2 "ALBANY" CLASS: GUIDED MISSILE CRUISERS (CG)

Name	No.	Builders	Laid down	Launched	Commissioned	F/S
ALBANY	CG 10 (ex-CA 123)	Bethlehem Steel Co, Fore River	6 Mar 1944	30 June 1945	15 June 1946	AA
CHICAGO	CG 11 (ex-CA 136)	Philadelphia Navy Yard	28 July 1943	20 Aug 1944	10 Jan 1945	PA

Displacement, tons: 13 700 standard;
17 700 full load *(Chicago)* 18 240 *(Albany)*
Length, feet (metres): 674 *(205·4)*
Beam, feet (metres): 71 *(21·6)*
Draught, feet (metres): 33·5 *(10·2)*
Missiles: SAM; 84 Tartar (2 twin Mk 11 launchers)
Guns: 2—5 in *(127 mm)*/38 (single Mk 24)
A/S weapons: 1 ASROC 8-tube launcher;
2 triple torpedo tubes (Mk 32)
Helicopters: Deck for utility helicopters
Main engines: 4 geared turbines General Electric;
120 000 shp; 4 shafts
Boilers: 4 Babcock & Wilcox
Speed, knots: 32
Complement: 1 222 (72 officers, 1 150 enlisted men)
Flag accommodations: 68 (10 officers, 58 enlisted men)

These ships were fully converted from heavy cruisers, *Albany* having been a unit of the "Oregon City" class and *Chicago* of the "Baltimore" class. Although the two heavy cruiser classes differed in appearance they had the same hull dimensions and machinery. These ships form a new, homogeneous class. Both used solely as flagships—to be deleted in FY 1980.
Albany is 6th Fleet flagship in the Mediterranean and *Chicago* is 3rd Fleet flagship in the Pacific

Conversion: During conversion these ships were stripped down to their main hulls with all cruiser armament and superstructure being removed. New superstructures make extensive use of aluminium to reduce weight and improve stability. *Albany* was converted at the Boston Naval Shipyard between January 1959 and new commissioning on 3 November 1962; *Chicago* at San Francisco Naval Shipyard from July 1959 to new commissioning on 2 May 1964.

Electronics: Naval Tactical Data System (NTDS) is fitted in *Albany*.

Fire control: Two Mk 77 missile fire control systems, four Mk 74 missile fire control systems, two Mk 56 gunfire control systems, one Mk 6 weapon direction system, four SPG 49B and four SPG 51C weapon control radars.

Gunnery: No guns were fitted when these ships were converted to missile cruisers. Two single open-mount 5 in guns were fitted subsequently to provide low-level defence.
Two 40 mm saluting guns fitted.

Missiles: One twin Talos launcher is forward and one aft, a twin Tartar launcher is on each side of the main bridge structure. During conversion, space was allocated amidships for installation of eight Polaris missile tubes, but the plan to install ballistic missiles in cruisers was cancelled in mid-1959. Reportedly 104 Talos were embarked and 84 Tartar missiles are carried.
Talos system in both ships inactivated in FY 1978. Launchers and associated equipment to be left on board until both are disposed of. Meanwhile systems will be used for spares for the Talos in *Oklahoma City*.

Modernisation: *Albany* underwent an extensive anti-air warfare modernisation at the Boston Naval Shipyard, including installation of NTDS, a digital Talos fire control system and improved radars. This began in February 1967 and was completed in August 1969. She was formally recommissioned on 9 November 1968.
Both were due for major overhauls—*Albany* July 1978-June 1979, *Chicago* beginning March 1979. Due to the age and material condition of these ships both major overhauls have been cancelled.

Radar: *Albany:*
3D search: SPS 48.
Search: SPS 10, 30 and 43.
Chicago:
Search: SPS 10, 30, 43 and 52.

Rockets: Mk 28 Chaffroc RBOC.
Sonar: SQS 23 (bow-mounted).

CHICAGO 2/1978, Dr. Giorgio Arr

ALBANY 1976, Michael D. J. Lenno

CHICAGO 2/1978, Dr. Giorgio Arr

USA / Cruisers 693

1 CONVERTED "CLEVELAND" CLASS: GUIDED MISSILE CRUISER (CG)

Name	No.	Builders	Laid down	Launched	Commissioned	F/S
OKLAHOMA CITY	CG 5 (ex-CLG 5, ex-CL 91)	Cramp Shipbuilding, Philadelphia	8 Mar 1942	20 Feb 1944	22 Dec 1944	PA

Displacement, tons: 10 670 standard; 15 200 full load
Length, feet (metres): 610 *(185.9)*
Beam, feet (metres): 66.3 *(20.1)*
Draught, feet (metres): 25 *(7.6)*
Aircraft: Utility helicopter carried
Missiles: SAM; 46 Talos (1 twin Mk 7 launcher)
Guns: 3—6 in *(152 mm)*/47 (triple);
2—5 in *(127 mm)*/38 (twin Mk 32)
Main engines: 4 geared turbines (General Electric); 100 000 shp; 4 shafts
Boilers: 4 (Babcock & Wilcox)
Speed, knots: 30.6 knots (CG 5); 32 (others)
Complement: Approx 1 350
Flag accommodations: 216 (50 officers; 166 enlisted men)

Originally a series of six ships were converted from light cruisers of the "Cleveland" class; three ships converted to Terrier missile configuration aft and three ships to Talos missile aft, with two ships of each missile type configured to serve as fleet flagships.
Oklahoma City the sole survivor is flagship of the US Seventh Fleet in the Western Pacific (homeported in Yokosuka, Japan). She is to be deleted in FY 1980 and replaced as flagship by *Blue Ridge* (LCC 19).

Classification: Upon conversion to missile configuration was reclassified as guided missile light cruiser (CLG). On 30 June 1975 the surviving three ships were reclassified as guided missile cruisers (CG).

Conversion: All six ships of this class had their two after 6 in gun turrets replaced by a twin surface-to-air missile launcher, superstructure enlarged to support missile fire control equipment, lattice masts fitted to carry antennae, 5 in battery reduced from original 12 guns and all 40 mm and 20 mm light anti-aircraft guns removed. The four ships fitted as fleet flagships additionally had their No 2 turret of 6 in guns removed and their forward superstructure enlarged to provide command and communications spaces. *Oklahoma City* began conversion at the Bethlehem Steel shipyard in San Francisco in May 1957 and was commissioned on 7 September 1960. There is a helicopter landing area on the fantail, but only limited support facilities are provided; no hangar.

Fire control: CG 5 has one Mk 77 missile fire control system and the Terrier ships one Mk 73; CG 5 has one Mk 2 weapon direction system and two SPG 49A weapon control radars; Terrier ships one Mk 3 weapon direction system and two SPQ 5A radars.

Gunnery: Two 40 mm saluting guns fitted in each ship.

OKLAHOMA CITY *12/1978, Lawrence Phillips*

Missiles: As of FY 1979 *Oklahoma City* is the only US Navy ship fitted with an active Talos system, spares for which are to be taken from *Albany* and *Chicago*.

Radar: Search: SPS 10, 30 and 43.
Sonar: None.

2 "DES MOINES" CLASS: HEAVY CRUISERS (CA)

Name	No.	Builders	Laid down	Launched	Commissioned	F/S
DES MOINES	CA 134	Bethlehem Steel Co, Fore River	28 May 1945	27 Sep 1946	16 Nov 1948	AR
SALEM	CA 139	Bethlehem Steel Co, Fore River	4 July 1945	25 Mar 1947	14 May 1949	AR

Displacement, tons: 17 000 standard; 20 950 full load
Length, feet (metres): 716.5 *(218.4)*
Beam, feet (metres): 76.3 *(23.3)*
Draught, feet (metres): 25.4 *(7.7)*
Guns: 9—8 in *(203 mm)*/55 (triple); 12—5 in *(127 mm)*/38 (twin Mk 32); 20—3 in *(76 mm)*/50 (twin Mk 33) *(Des Moines)*; 22—3 in *(Salem)*
Main engines: 4 geared turbines (General Electric); 120 000 shp; 4 shafts
Boilers: 4 (Babcock & Wilcox)
Speed, knots: 31.5
Complement: 1 803 (116 officers, 1 687 enlisted men) *(Des Moines)*
1 738 (115 officers, 1 623 enlisted men) *(Salem)*

These ships were the largest and most powerful 8 in gun cruisers ever built. Completed too late for World War II, they were employed primarily as flagships for the Sixth Fleet in the Mediterranean and the Second Fleet in the Atlantic. *Salem* was decommissioned on 30 January 1959 and *Des Moines* on 14 July 1961. Both laid up at Philadelphia. A third ship of this class, *Newport News,* was deleted in 1978.

Aircraft: As completed *Des Moines* had two stern catapults and carried four floatplanes; catapults later removed.

Design: These ships are an improved version of the previous "Oregon City" class. The newer cruisers have automatic main batteries, larger main turrets, taller fire control towers, and larger bridges. *Des Moines* is fully air-conditioned.
Additional ships of this class were cancelled: *Dallas* (CA 140) and the unnamed CA 141-142, CA 149-153.

Electronics: Tacan.

Fire control: Four Mk 56 gunfire control systems, two Mk 54 gunfire control directors and four Mk 37 GFCS.

Gunnery: These cruisers were the first ships to be armed with fully automatic 8 in guns firing cased ammunition. The guns can be loaded at any elevation from −5 to +41 degrees; rate of fire is four times faster than earlier 8 in guns. Mk 16 8-in guns in these ships; other heavy cruisers remaining on Navy List have Mk 15 guns.
As built, these ships mounted 12—5 in guns, 24—3 in guns (in twin mounts), and 12—20 mm guns (single mounts). The 20 mm guns were removed almost immediately and the 3 in battery was reduced gradually as ships were overhauled. With full armament the designed wartime complement was 1 860.

DES MOINES *USN*

DESTROYERS

The rapid drop in destroyer numbers began to slow in September 1975 when the first of 31 "Spruance" class destroyers was commissioned. These ships will be completed at regular intervals through 1979. At this time the Navy plans to follow the "Spruance" class with a guided missile destroyer based on the same hull and machinery, but employing the Aegis missile system.

Increasingly the Navy is using frigates for operations that previously required destroyers. Although the frigates have modern anti-submarine weapons and sensors similar to destroyers, and in some classes superior, the frigates lack the guns, electronics, 30 knot speeds, and in most cases the surface-to-air missiles considered necessary for modern anti-air warfare and surface warfare operations.

Soon after the last of the "Spruance" class ships are complete in 1979, the destroyer force is expected to consist of 70 ships the 39 missile-armed DDG type and the 31 "Spruance" class non-missile DD type. Most or all of the "Forrest Sherman" class destroyers and the few surviving "Gearing" class ships will probably be assigned to the Naval Reserve Force by that time.

CLASSIFICATION

All guided missile frigates (DLG/DLGN) on the Navy List as of 30 June 1975 were reclassified as guided missile cruisers (CG/CGN) except for the ten ships of the "Coontz" class which were reclassified as guided missile destroyers (DDG).

DESTROYER (DDX): PROPOSED

Under the FY 1984 programme, the construction of the lead ship of a new class of destroyer is to be requested. The class planned to augment the new "DDG 47" class. Further details are not available.

1 + 15 GUIDED MISSILE DESTROYERS (AEGIS) (DDG)

Name	No.	Builder	Laid down	Launched	Commission	F/S
—	DDG 47	Ingalls Shipbuilding Corporation	1979	1981?	Jan 1983	Ord
—	One ship	Requested FY 1980	—	—	—	Proj
—	Two ships	Proposed FY 1981	—	—	—	Proj
—	Two ships	Proposed FY 1982	—	—	—	Proj
—	Three ships	Proposed FY 1983	—	—	—	Proj
—	Two ships	Proposed FY 1984	—	—	—	Proj
—	Five ships	Future programmes	—	—	—	Proj

Displacement, tons: 9 055 full load
Length, feet (metres): 563·3 (171·7)
Beam, feet (metres): 55 (16·8)
Draught, feet (metres): 31 (9·5)
Aircraft: 2 LAMPS helicopters
Missiles: SSM; 16 Harpoon (8-tube launchers);
SAM/ASW: 88 Standard-MR/ASROC
(2 twin Mk 26 launchers) (see notes)
Guns: 2—5 in (127 mm)/54 (single Mk 45); 2—20 mm/76 Phalanx Close-In Weapon Systems (6-barrelled Mk 15 CIWS)
A/S weapons: ASROC; torpedo tubes (Mk 32)
Main engines: 4 LM 2500 gas turbines; 80 000 shp; 2 shafts
Speed, knots: 30+
Complement: 316 (27 officers, 289 enlisted men)

The "DDG 47" class fulfils the proposal for a non-nuclear Aegis-armed ship as proposed in the early 1970s with the designation DG, but subsequently dropped to avoid conflict with the Navy's nuclear propelled cruiser programme.
The "DDG 47" budget request is for $938 million for the lead ship; follow-on ships will cost between $800-850 million each, still many times that of the late DG proposal. The high cost of these ships and the view that all high-capability Aegis ships should have nuclear propulsion have made the class the target of intensive Congressional criticism. The Navy-Department of Defense plan provides for sixteen of these ships.

Design: The "DDG 47" design is a modification of the "Spruance" class (DD 963). The same basic hull will be used, with the same gas turbine propulsion system. The design calls for 1 in steel armour plate to protect the magazines.

Electronics: Aegis is described under "Shipboard Systems". DDG 47 will have the full Aegis electronics suite.

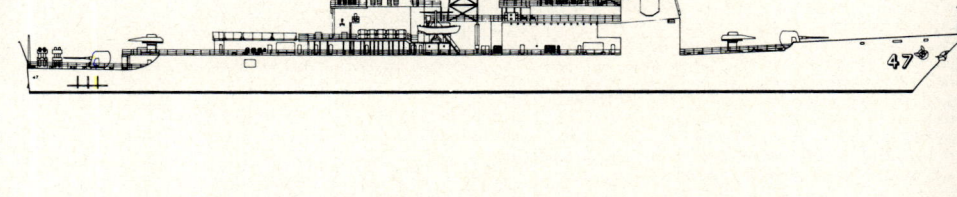

"DDG 47" Class — A. D. Baker III

Fire control: Aegis Weapons Control System Mk 7 with UYK-7 computers to control radar phasing, Mk 86 gunfire control system, four Mk 99 missile guidance illuminators. Mk 116 Underwater FCS.

Radar: SPY 1A paired arrays (one forward, one aft).
Search: SPS 49.
Weapons: SPQ 9.

Sonar: SQS 53 (bow-mounted) and TACTAS towed array.

2 IMPROVED "SPRUANCE" CLASS GUIDED MISSILE DESTROYERS (DDG): PROPOSED

Name	No.	Builders	Laid down	Launched	Commissioned	F/S
— (ex-Iranian *Nader*)	— 995, (ex-US DD 996)	Ingalls Shipbuilding Corporation	Apr 1979	mid-1980	mid-1981	Bldg
—(ex-Iranian *Anoushirvan*)	— 996, (ex-US DD 998)	Ingalls Shipbuilding Corporation	July 1979	mid-1980	late 1981	Bldg

Displacement, tons: 8,230 full load, 6,210 light
Length, feet (metres): 563 (171·6)
Beam, feet (metres): 55 (16·8)
Draught, feet (metres): 29 (8·8)
Missiles: SAM/ASW; 52 Standard-ER/16 ASROC;
(twin Mk 26 launchers) (see *Missile* notes)
Guns: 2—5 in (127 mm)/54 (single Mk 45)
A/S weapons: 2 triple Mk 32 torpedo tubes; ASROC
Main engines: 4 GE LM-2500 gas turbines; 80,000 shp; 2 shafts
Speed, knots: 30+
Range, miles: 3,300 at 30 knots
Complement: Approx 245

Under a revised FY 1979 supplemental budget request the US Navy will take over the contracts of the two improved "Spruance" class DD's that were under construction for Iran. The contract for the construction of these ships had been awarded to Ingalls on 23 April 1978, but cancelled by the new Iranian government on 3 February 1979. These ships are optimised for general warfare instead of anti-submarine warfare as the "Spruance" class. These ships will be the most powerful destroyer type ships in the fleet.

Classification: This class is sometimes referred to as the "DD 993" class. Both ships originally assigned the hull numbers DD 996 and 998 respectively for accounting purposes. When DD 995 and 997 of this class were cancelled by the Iranian government in June 1976, DD 996 and 998 were reclassified DD 995 and DD 996 on 23 April 1978. Both will be allocated DDG hull numbers in the US Navy.

Design: The modular concept will be used extensively to facilitate construction and future modernisation.

Electronics: Both will be equipped with Automatic Data Action Systems.

Engineering: The plant duplicates that of the "DD 963" and "DDG 47" classes.

Fire control: Will be fitted with two Mk 74 missile fire control systems, two Mk 86 gun fire control systems and one Mk 116 underwater fire control system.

Missiles: The Standard missile load would be split between two magazines. Harpoon SSM system and Tomahawk cruise missiles will probably be fitted.

Gunnery: Space and weight are reserved for the installation of two 20 mm CIWS (Mk 15).

Radar (est): Navigation and surface search: SPS 55.
Air search/height: SPS 52.
Fire control: SPG 51.

Rockets: Mk 36 Chaffroc system to be fitted.

Sonar: Probably SQS 53 (bow-mounted).

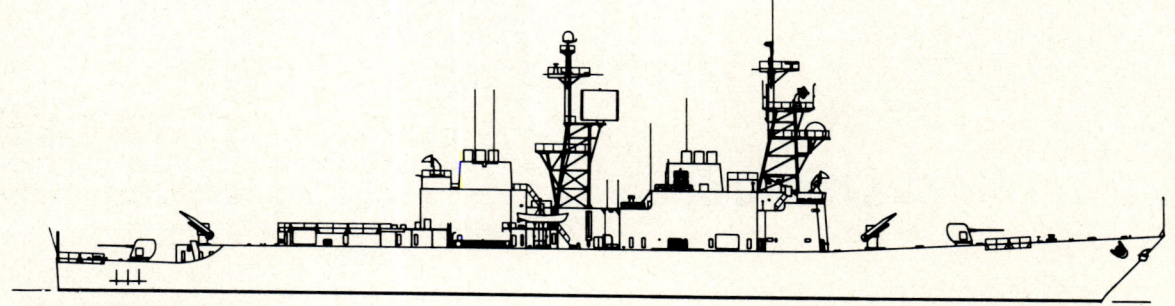

"Improved Spruance" Class

1976, A. D. Baker III

USA / Destroyers

23 "CHARLES F. ADAMS" CLASS: GUIDED MISSILE DESTROYERS (DDG)

Name	No.	Builders	Laid down	Launched	Commissioned	F/S
CHARLES F. ADAMS	DDG 2	Bath Iron Works, Bath, Maine	16 June 1958	8 Sep 1959	10 Sep 1960	AA
JOHN KING	DDG 3	Bath Iron Works, Bath, Maine	25 Aug 1958	30 Jan 1960	4 Feb 1961	AA
LAWRENCE	DDG 4	New York Shipbuilding Corporation	27 Oct 1958	27 Feb 1960	6 Jan 1962	AA
CLAUDE V. RICKETTS	DDG 5	New York Shipbuilding Corporation	18 May 1959	4 June 1960	5 May 1962	AA
BARNEY	DDG 6	New York Shipbuilding Corporation	18 May 1959	10 Dec 1960	11 Aug 1962	AA
HENRY B. WILSON	DDG 7	Defoe Shipbuilding Co	28 Feb 1958	23 Apr 1959	17 Dec 1960	PA
LYNDE McCORMICK	DDG 8	Defoe Shipbuilding Co	4 Apr 1958	9 Sep 1960	3 June 1961	PA
TOWERS	DDG 9	Todd Shipyards Inc, Seattle	1 Apr 1958	23 Apr 1959	6 June 1961	PA
SAMPSON	DDG 10	Bath Iron Works, Bath, Maine	2 Mar 1959	9 Sep 1960	24 June 1961	AA
SELLERS	DDG 11	Bath Iron Works, Bath, Maine	3 Aug 1959	9 Sep 1960	28 Oct 1961	AA
ROBISON	DDG 12	Defoe Shipbuilding Co	23 Apr 1959	27 Apr 1960	9 Dec 1961	PA
HOEL	DDG 13	Defoe Shipbuilding Co	1 June 1959	4 Aug 1960	16 June 1962	PA
BUCHANAN	DDG 14	Todd Shipyards Inc, Seattle	23 Apr 1959	11 May 1960	7 Feb 1962	PA
BERKELEY	DDG 15	New York Shipbuilding Corporation	1 June 1960	29 July 1961	15 Dec 1962	PA
JOSEPH STRAUSS	DDG 16	New York Shipbuilding Corporation	27 Dec 1960	9 Dec 1961	20 Apr 1963	PA
CONYNGHAM	DDG 17	New York Shipbuilding Corporation	1 May 1961	19 May 1962	13 July 1963	AA
SEMMES	DDG 18	Avondale Marine Ways Inc	18 Aug 1960	20 May 1961	10 Dec 1962	AA
TATTNALL	DDG 19	Avondale Marine Ways Inc.	14 Nov 1960	26 Aug 1961	13 Apr 1963	AA
GOLDSBOROUGH	DDG 20	Puget Sound Bridge & Dry Dock Co	3 Jan 1961	15 Dec 1961	9 Nov 1963	PA
COCHRANE	DDG 21	Puget Sound Bridge & Dry Dock Co	31 July 1961	18 July 1962	21 Mar 1964	PA
BENJAMIN STODDERT	DDG 22	Puget Sound Bridge & Dry Dock Co	11 June 1962	8 Jan 1963	12 Sep 1964	PA
RICHARD E. BYRD	DDG 23	Todd Shipyards Inc, Seattle	12 Apr 1961	6 Feb 1962	7 Mar 1964	AA
WADDELL	DDG 24	Todd Shipyards Inc, Seattle	6 Feb 1962	26 Feb 1963	28 Aug 1964	PA

Displacement, tons: 3 370 standard; 4 500 full load
Length, feet (metres): 437 *(133·2)*
Beam, feet (metres): 47 *(14·3)*
Draught, feet (metres): 27·2 *(8·3)*
Missiles: SSM; Harpoon to be fitted;
 DDG 2-14; SAM; 42 Tartar (1 twin Mk 11 launcher)
 DDG 15-24: SAM; 40 Tartar (1 single Mk 13 launcher) (see *Missile* note)
Guns: 2—5 in *(127 mm)*/54 (single Mk 42)
A/S weapons: 1 ASROC 8-tube launcher;
 2 triple torpedo tubes (Mk 32)
Main engines: 2 geared steam turbines (General Electric in DDG 2, 3, 7, 8, 10-13, 15-22; Westinghouse in DDG 4-6, 9, 14, 23, 24); 70 000 shp; 2 shafts
Boilers: 4 (Babcock & Wilcox in DDG 2, 3, 7, 8, 10-13, 20-22; Foster-Wheeler in DDG 4-6, 9, 14, 23, 24; Combustion Engineering in DDG 15-19)
Speed, knots: 30
Complement: 354 (24 officers, 330 enlisted men)

DDG 2-9 were authorised in Fiscal Year 1957 new construction programme, DDG 10-14 in FY 1958, DDG 15-19 in FY 1959, DDG 20-22 in FY 1960, DDG 23-24 in FY 1961. Excellent general-purpose ships.

Classification: The first eight ships were to be a continuation of "Hull" class DDs and carried hull numbers DD 952-959. Redesigned as Guided Missile Destroyers and assigned DDG numbers. DDG 1 was *Gyatt* (ex-DD 712), which operated as a missile destroyer from 1956 to 1962 armed with a twin Terrier launcher.

Design: These ships were built to an improved "Forrest Sherman" class design with aluminium superstructures and a high level of habitability including air conditioning in all living spaces. DDG 20-24 have stem anchors because of sonar arrangement.
Several ships have been modified with an extension of the bridge structure on the starboard side on the 02 level.

Fire control: Two Mk 74 MFCS, one Mk 68 GFCS (to be replaced by Mk 86), one Mk 4 weapon system (to be replaced by Mk 13 which is already fitted in DDG 9, 12, 15 and 21), one SPG 51C, one SPG 53A weapon control radars and one Mk 114 ASW FCS.

Missiles: Ships equipped with either launcher can load, direct, and fire about six missiles per minute. *Lawrence* and *Hoel* fitted in 1972-1973 with multiple launcher for Chaparral (MIM-72A) for operational testing, in addition to their Tartar launcher.

Modernisation: Beginning in FY 1980 it is planned to give certain ships of this class a mid-life modernisation, officially known as "DDG upgrade", to improve their capabilities, ease the maintenance and extend their service lives by 15 years over the current estimate of 20. This modernisation will include installation of the Harpoon SSM/Standard ARM missile system (both to be launched from the Mk 11 or Mk 13 launcher), replacing the existing EW arrangements with the Anti-Ship Missile Defense (ASMD) EW system (including SLQ 31/32 (V) systems), replacing the radar with SPS 40C/D and SPS 52B, installing SPS 58 radar (high data rate search radar with short range detection of air targets in all types of clutter), installation of an Integrated Automatic Detection and Tracking System (SYS 1), replacing the radar receivers in the CIC with UYA 4 consoles for real-time tactical data processing, replacing the Mk 4 WDS by Mk 13, installing Mk 86 FCS for the Standard ARM missiles and gun armament and fitting two SQQ 23 sonar domes with control units.
Originally all twenty three ships of the class were to be modernised but, as a result of the current Administration's defence cuts, only ten will be so treated. The programme for these is:-
FY 1980—*John King*, October 1979 at Philadelphia, Naval Shipyard; FY 1981—*Sampson, Tattnall* and *Cochrane*; FY 1982—*Joseph Strauss, Semmes* and *Goldsborough*; FY 1983—*Conyngham, Benjamin Stoddert* and *Waddell*. The remaining thirteen ships are due to be deleted beginning in the late 1980s.
Each modernisation will take 20-24 months and cost $125·7-178·5 million (1979$). $167 million for advance procurement was authorised under the FY 1979 programme.

Names: DDG 5 was originally named *Biddle*; renamed *Claude V. Ricketts* on 28 July 1964.

Radar: 3D search: SPS 39 (52 being fitted).
 Search: SPS 10 and 37 (2-14).
 SPS 10 and 40 (15-24); SPS 39.

Rockets: Mk 36 Chaffroc (RBOC) will be fitted.

Sonar: SQS 23 (bow-mounted) (20-24).
 SQS 23 (hull-mounted) (remainder).

GOLDSBOROUGH *1/1978, Dr. Giorgio Arra*

LYNDE McCORMICK *9/1978, Dr. Giorgio Arra*

TATTNALL *10/1978, J. L. M. van der Burgh*

10 "COONTZ" CLASS: GUIDED MISSILE DESTROYERS (DDG)

Name	No.	Builders	Laid down	Launched	Commissioned	F/S
FARRAGUT	DDG 37 (ex-DLG 6)	Bethlehem Co, Quincy, Mass	3 June 1957	18 July 1958	10 Dec 1960	AA
LUCE	DDG 38 (ex-DLG 7)	Bethlehem Co, Quincy, Mass	1 Oct 1957	11 Dec 1958	20 May 1961	AA
MACDONOUGH	DDG 39 (ex-DLG 8)	Bethlehem Co, Quincy, Mass	15 Apr 1958	9 July 1959	4 Nov 1961	AA
COONTZ	DDG 40 (ex-DLG 9)	Puget Sound Naval Shipyard	1 Mar 1957	6 Dec 1958	15 July 1960	AA
KING	DDG 41 (ex-DLG 10)	Puget Sound Naval Shipyard	1 Mar 1957	6 Dec 1958	17 Nov 1960	AA
MAHAN	DDG 42 (ex-DLG 11)	San Francisco Naval Shipyard	31 July 1957	7 Oct 1959	25 Aug 1960	AA
DAHLGREN	DDG 43 (ex-DLG 12)	Philadelphia Naval Shipyard	1 Mar 1958	16 Mar 1960	8 Apr 1961	AA
WILLIAM V. PRATT	DDG 44 (ex-DLG 13)	Philadelphia Naval Shipyard	1 Mar 1958	16 Mar 1960	4 Nov 1961	AA
DEWEY	DDG 45 (ex-DLG 14)	Bath Iron Works, Maine	10 Aug 1957	30 Nov 1958	7 Dec 1959	AA
PREBLE	DDG 46 (ex-DLG 15)	Bath Iron Works, Maine	16 Dec 1957	23 May 1959	9 May 1960	PA

Displacement, tons: 4 150/4 580 standard; 5 709/5 907 full load
Length, feet (metres): 512·5 *(156·2)*
Beam, feet (metres): 52·5 *(15·9)*
Draught, feet (metres): 23·4 *(7·1)*
Missiles: SSM; Harpoon to be fitted;
 SAM; 40 Terrier/Standard-ER (1 twin Mk 10 Launcher)
 (see *Missile* note)
Gun: 1—5 in *(127 mm)*/54 (Mk 42) (see *Gunnery* note)
A/S weapons: 1 ASROC 8-tube launcher;
 2 triple torpedo tubes (Mk 32)
Main engines: 2 geared turbines; 85 000 shp; 2 shafts
Boilers: 4 (Foster-Wheeler in DDG 37-39; Babcock & Wilcox in DDG 40-46)
Speed, knots: 33
Fuel, tons: 900
Range, miles: 5 000 at 20 knots
Flag accommodations: 19 (7 officers, 12 enlisted men)
Complement: 377 (21 officers, 356 enlisted men)

These ships are an improvement of the "Mitscher" class (DL/DDG). DDG 37-42 were authorised in the Fiscal Year 1956 programme; DDG 43-46 in the FY 1957 programme. Average cost per ship was $52 million.
Although now classified as "destroyers", these ships have many of the capabilities of the larger US cruiser classes, including the Terrier/Standard-ER missile system and Naval Tactical Data System (NTDS).

Classification: *Farragut, Luce* and *MacDonough* were initially classified as frigates (DL 6-8, respectively); changed to guided missile frigate (DLG) 6-8 on 14 November 1956. The first ship ordered as a missile frigate was *Coontz* which became the name ship for the class. All ten ships were classified as guided missile frigates (DLG 6-15) from completion until 30 June 1975 when reclassified as guided missile destroyers (DDG 37-46).

Design: These ships were the only US guided missile "frigates" with separate masts and funnels. They have aluminium superstructures to reduce weight and improve stability. Early designs for this class had a second 5 in gun mount in the "B" position; design revised when ASROC launcher was developed.
Helicopter landing area on stern, but no hangar and limited support capability.

Electronics: *King* and *Mahan* along with the aircraft carrier *Oriskany* (CV 34) were the first ships fitted with the Naval Tactical Data System (NTDS), conducting operational evaluation of the equipment in 1961-62. NTDS now in all ships.

Engineering: De Laval turbines in DDG 37-39 and DDG 46; Allis-Chalmers turbines in DDG 40-45.

Fire control: Two Mk 76 missile fire control systems, one Mk 68 gunfire control system, one SPG 53A and two SPG-55B weapon control radars (plus two SPG 50—*Macdonough* only). One Mk 11 WDS and one Mk 111 ASW FCS.

Gunnery: The original four 3 in/50 guns were removed during modernisation.
King was fitted with the 20 mm Phalanx Mk 15 CIWS for at-sea evaluation from August 1973 to March 1974.
Two 40 mm saluting guns fitted.

Missiles: The first five ships of this class originally fitted with Terrier BW-1 beam-riding missile systems; five later ships built with Terrier BT-3 homing missile systems. Reportedly, each ship carries 40 missiles (BT-3).

Modernisation: These ships have been modernised to improve their Anti-Air Warfare (AAW) capabilities. Superstructure enlarged to provide space for additional electronic equipment, including NTDS (previously fitted in *King* and *Mahan*); improved Tacan installed, improved guidance system for Terrier/Standard missiles (SPG 55 fire control radar), and larger ship's service turbo generators fitted. *Farragut* also had improved ASROC reload capability provided (with additional structure forward of bridge) and second mast increased in height. (Other ships do not carry ASROC reloads).
All ships modernised at Philadelphia Naval Shipyard, except *Mahan* at Bath Iron Works, Bath; Maine, and *King* at Boland Machine & Manufacturing Co, New Orleans, Louisiana between 1969 and 1977.
Cost of modernisation was $39 million per ship in the FY 1970 conversion programme.

Names: DDG 38 was to have been named *Dewey*; renamed *Luce* in 1957.

Radar: (After modernisation).
3D search: SPS 48 (SPS 52 in *King* and *Pratt*).
Search: SPS 10 and 37.

Rockets: Mk 36 Chaffroc (RBOC) system to be fitted.

Sonar: SQS 23.

WILLIAM V. PRATT 7/1976, A. D. Baker III

MACDONOUGH 10/1977, C. and S. Taylor

PREBLE 10/1977, Dr. Giorgio Arra

DEWEY 8/1977, USN (PH1. F. S. Osborne)

4 CONVERTED "FORREST SHERMAN" AND "HULL" CLASSES: GUIDED MISSILE DESTROYERS (DDG)

Name	No.	Builders	Laid down	Launched	Commissioned	F/S
DECATUR	DDG 31 (ex-DD 936)	Bethlehem Steel Co, Quincy, Mass	13 Sep 1954	15 Dec 1955	7 Dec 1956	PA
JOHN PAUL JONES	DDG 32 (ex-DD 932)	Bath Iron Works, Maine	18 Jan 1954	7 May 1955	5 Apr 1956	PA
PARSONS	DDG 33 (ex-DD 949)	Ingalls Shipbuilding Corporation	17 June 1957	19 Aug 1958	29 Oct 1959	PA
SOMERS	DDG 34 (ex-DD 947)	Bath Iron Works, Maine	4 Mar 1957	30 May 1958	3 Apr 1959	PA

Displacement, tons: 4 150 full load
Length, feet (metres): 418·4 (127·5)
Beam, feet (metres): 44 (13·4)
Draught, feet (metres): 20 (6·1)
Missiles: SAM; 40 Tartar (1 single Mk 13 launcher)
Gun: 1—5 in (127 mm)/54 (Mk 42)
A/S weapons: 1 ASROC 8-tube launcher;
   2 triple torpedo tubes (Mk 32)
Main engines: 2 geared turbines (Westinghouse in *John Paul Jones* and *Decatur*; General Electric in others); 70 000 shp; 2 shafts
Boilers: 4 (Foster-Wheeler in *Decatur*; Babcock & Wilcox in *John Paul Jones, Somers* and *Parsons*)
Speed, knots: 31 knots
Fuel, tons: 500
Range, miles: 4 500 at 20 knots
Complement: 337 (22 officers, 315 enlisted men) (*Decatur* and *John Paul Jones*)
   364 (25 officers and 339 enlisted men) (*Parsons* and *Somers*)

"Forrest Sherman" and "Hull" class destroyers that have been converted to a guided missile and improved ASW configuration. Plans for additional DDG conversions of this type were dropped. *Decatur* was reclassified as DDG 31 on 15 September 1966; *John Paul Jones, Somers* and *Parsons* became DDG on 15 March 1967. See "Forrest Sherman" class DDs for additional notes.

Conversion: *Decatur* began conversion to a DDG at the Boston Naval Shipyard on 15 June 1965, *John Paul Jones* at the Philadelphia Naval Shipyard on 2 December 1965, *Parsons* at the Long Beach (California) Naval Shipyard on 30 June 1965, and *Somers* at the San Francisco Bay Naval Shipyard on 30 March 1966.
Recommissioned as DDGs on 29 April 1967, 23 April 1967, 2 November 1967 and 10 February 1968 respectively.
During conversion all existing armament was removed except the forward 5 in gun; two triple ASW torpedo tubes were installed forward of the bridge; two heavy lattice masts fitted; ASROC launcher mounted aft of second stack; single Tartar Mk 3 launcher installed aft (on 01 level; system weighs approximately 135 000 lb).
Original DDG conversion plans provided for Drone Anti-Submarine Helicopter (DASH) facilities; however, ASROC was substituted in all four ships as DASH lost favour in the Navy.

Fire control: One Mk 74 missile fire control system, one Mk 68 gunfire control system, one SPG 51C and one SPG 53B weapon control radars.
One Mk 4 WDS and one Mk 114 ASW FCS.

Gunnery: These ships and the "Coontz" class are the only US destroyers with one 5 in gun.

Radar: 3D search: SPS 48.
Search: SPS 10 and 37 (40 in *Somers*).

Rockets: Mk 36 Chaffroc (RBOC) to be fitted.

Sonar: SQS 23 (hull-mounted).

SOMERS
8/1978, Dr. Giorgio Arra

DECATUR
1/1977, Dr. Giorgio Arra

JOHN PAUL JONES
6/1978, Dr. Giorgio Arra

19 + 12 "SPRUANCE" CLASS: DESTROYERS (DD)

Name	No.	Builders	Laid down	Launched	Commissioned	F/S
SPRUANCE	DD 963	Ingalls Shipbuilding Corporation	17 Nov 1972	10 Nov 1973	20 Sep 1975	AA
PAUL F. FOSTER	DD 964	Ingalls Shipbuilding Corporation	6 Feb 1973	23 Feb 1974	21 Feb 1976	PA
KINKAID	DD 965	Ingalls Shipbuilding Corporation	19 Apr 1973	25 May 1974	10 July 1976	PA
HEWITT	DD 966	Ingalls Shipbuilding Corporation	23 July 1973	24 Aug 1974	25 Sep 1976	PA
ELLIOTT	DD 967	Ingalls Shipbuilding Corporation	15 Oct 1973	19 Dec 1974	22 Jan 1976	PA
ARTHUR W. RADFORD	DD 968	Ingalls Shipbuilding Corporation	14 Jan 1974	1 Mar 1975	16 Apr 1977	AA
PETERSON	DD 969	Ingalls Shipbuilding Corporation	29 Apr 1974	21 June 1975	9 July 1977	AA
CARON	DD 970	Ingalls Shipbuilding Corporation	1 July 1974	24 June 1975	1 Oct 1977	AA
DAVID R. RAY	DD 971	Ingalls Shipbuilding Corporation	23 Sep 1974	23 Aug 1975	19 Nov 1977	PA
OLDENDORF	DD 972	Ingalls Shipbuilding Corporation	27 Dec 1974	21 Oct 1975	4 Mar 1978	PA
JOHN YOUNG	DD 973	Ingalls Shipbuilding Corporation	17 Feb 1975	7 Feb 1976	20 May 1978	PA
COMTE DE GRASSE	DD 974	Ingalls Shipbuilding Corporation	4 Apr 1975	26 Mar 1976	5 Aug 1978	AA
O'BRIEN	DD 975	Ingalls Shipbuilding Corporation	9 May 1975	8 July 1976	3 Dec 1977	PA
MERRILL	DD 976	Ingalls Shipbuilding Corporation	16 June 1975	1 Sep 1976	11 Mar 1978	PA
BRISCOE	DD 977	Ingalls Shipbuilding Corporation	21 July 1975	15 Dec 1976	3 June 1978	AA
STUMP	DD 978	Ingalls Shipbuilding Corporation	25 Aug 1975	29 Jan 1977	19 Aug 1978	AA
CONOLLY	DD 979	Ingalls Shipbuilding Corporation	29 Sep 1975	19 Feb 1977	14 Oct 1978	AA
MOOSBURGGER	DD 980	Ingalls Shipbuilding Corporation	3 Nov 1975	23 July 1977	16 Dec 1978	AA
JOHN HANCOCK	DD 981	Ingalls Shipbuilding Corporation	16 Jan 1976	29 Oct 1977	1 Mar 1979	AA
NICHOLSON	DD 982	Ingalls Shipbuilding Corporation	20 Feb 1976	11 Nov 1977	1979	Bldg
JOHN RODGERS	DD 983	Ingalls Shipbuilding Corporation	12 Aug 1976	25 Feb 1978	1979	Bldg
LEFTWICH	DD 984	Ingalls Shipbuilding Corporation	12 Nov 1976	8 Apr 1978	1979	Bldg
CUSHING	DD 985	Ingalls Shipbuilding Corporation	27 Dec 1976	17 June 1978	1979	Bldg
HARRY W. HILL	DD 986	Ingalls Shipbuilding Corporation	3 Jan 1977	10 Aug 1978	1979	Bldg
O'BANNON	DD 987	Ingalls Shipbuilding Corporation	21 Feb 1977	25 Sep 1978	1979	Bldg
THORN	DD 988	Ingalls Shipbuilding Corporation	29 Aug 1977	14 Nov 1978	1980	Bldg
DEYO	DD 989	Ingalls Shipbuilding Corporation	14 Oct 1977	27 Jan 1979	1980	Bldg
INGERSOLL	DD 990	Ingalls Shipbuilding Corporation	5 Dec 1977	1979	1980	Bldg
FIFE	DD 991	Ingalls Shipbuilding Corporation	6 Mar 1978	1979	1980	Bldg
FLETCHER	DD 992	Ingalls Shipbuilding Corporation	24 Apr 1978	1979	1980	Bldg
—	DD 997	Ingalls Shipbuilding Corporation	1979	—	1982	Ord

Displacement, tons: 5 830 light; 7 810 full load
Length, feet (metres): 529 *(161·3)* wl; 563·2 *(171·7)* oa
Beam, feet (metres): 55·1 *(16·8)*
Draught, feet (metres): 29 *(8·8)*
Aircraft: 1 SH-3 Sea King or 2 SH-2D LAMPS helicopters
Guns: 2—5 in *(127 mm)*/54 (single Mk 45)
A/S weapons: 1 ASROC 8-tube launcher
2 triple torpedo tubes (Mk 32)
Main engines: 4 General Electric LM2500 gas turbines; 80 000 shp; 2 shafts
Speed, knots: 33
Range, miles: 6 000 at 20 knots
Complement: 296 (24 officers, 272 enlisted men)

According to official statements, "the primary mission of these ships is anti-submarine warfare including operations as an integral part of attack carrier task forces."
The Fiscal Year 1969 new construction programme requested funding for the first five ships of this class, although, funds were denied by Congress. In the FY 1970 programme Congress approved funds for five ships, but increasing costs forced the Department of Defense to construct only three ships under the FY 1970 programme (DD 963-965); six ships were authorised in the FY 1971 programme (DD 966-971); seven ships (DD 972-978) in the FY 1972 programme; seven ships (DD 979-985) in the FY 1974 programme, and seven ships (DD 986-992) in the FY 1975 programme.
DD 997 was added to the Navy's FY 1978 programme by Congress and is not Navy initiated. Known as an "air capable" *Spruance*, she was to have an enlarged hangar and flight deck and be able to accommodate up to four LAMPS III ASW helicopters.

Originally two of this class were added by the US Senate. The House of Representatives failed to approve funds for any of this class. During the House-Senate Conference about the FY 1978 Military Budget, agreement was reached to provide $310 million for one ship. This sum was authorised with the proviso that no more than this should be spent on this ship. When bids were solicited from shipbuilders should they be over the $310 million, weapons, electronics and other equipment would have to be deleted to bring the cost under the limit.
Since the 1978-79 edition of Jane's the cost of constructing this ship has escalated beyond the $310 million limit imposed by Congress. As a result, to cut costs, the "air capable" portions of the design have been reduced and the ship will be constructed as a 31st "Spruance" class DD (see 1978-79 edition for illustration of "air capable" design).

A/S weapons: The ASROC reload magazine is located under the launcher with the twin-cell launcher nacelles depressing to a vertical position. Capacity 24 rounds. 14 torpedoes carried for Mk 32 tubes.

Design: Extensive use of the modular concept is used to facilitate initial construction and block modernisation of the ships. The ships are highly automated, resulting in about 20 per cent reduction in personnel over a similar ship with conventional systems.

Engineering: These ships are the first large US warships to employ gas turbine propulsion. Each ship has four General Electric LM2500 marine gas turbine engines, a shaft-power version of the TF39 turbofan aircraft engine, and cp propellers, because gas turbine engines cannot use a reversible shaft. Fitted with advanced self-noise reduction features.

Fire control: Mk 116 digital underwater fire control system and one Mk 86 gunfire control system, one Mk 91 missile FCS, one SPQ 60 and one SPQ 9 radars.

Gunnery: An improved 5 in/54 (Mk 65) gun is being considered for use in later ships of the class. The "Spruance" design can accommodate the 8 in Major Calibre Light-Weight Gun (MCLWG) (Mk 71). There are now plans to install that weapon in DD 963, 965, 973, 974, 977, 985-7, 991 during each overhaul after 1980. The 5 in mount will be retained aft. 600 rounds per gun carried (5 in).
Two 20 mm Phalanx Mk 15 CIWS are planned for installation.

Helicopters: Full helicopter facilities are provided to accommodate the Light Airborne Multi-Purpose System (LAMPS) now the SH-2D helicopter. However, the ship can handle the larger SH-3 Sea King series.

Missiles: The NATO Sea Sparrow multiple missile launcher (Mk 29) is planned for installation in these ships (between helicopter deck and after 5 in gun mount).

Radar: Search: SPS 40 and SPS 55.

Rockets: Mk 36 Chaffroc system is to be retrofitted in 1978-79 in DD 963-972 (in place of Mk 33) and in remainder during construction.

Sonar: SQS 53 (bow mounted) (SQS 35 VDS not fitted due to success with SQS 53).

Torpedoes: The triple Mk 32 torpedo tubes are inside the superstructure to facilitate maintenance and reloading; they are fired through side ports.

HEWITT

1/1979, Dr. Giorgio Arra

USA / Destroyers 699

COMTE DE GRASSE 1/1979, Ingalls S.B. Divn. Litton Industries

DAVID R. RAY 1/1979, Ingalls S.B. Divn. Litton Industries

700 USA / Destroyers

14 "FORREST SHERMAN" and "HULL" CLASSES: DESTROYERS (DD)

Name	No.	Builders	Laid down	Launched	Commissioned	F/S
FORREST SHERMAN	DD 931	Bath Iron Works, Bath, Maine	27 Oct 1953	5 Feb 1955	9 Nov 1955	AA
BIGELOW	DD 942	Bath Iron Works, Bath, Maine	6 July 1955	2 Feb 1957	8 Nov 1957	AA
MULLINNIX	DD 944	Bethlehem Steel Co, Quincy, Mass	5 Apr 1956	18 Mar 1957	7 Mar 1958	AA
HULL	DD 945	Bath Iron Works, Bath, Maine	12 Sep 1956	10 Aug 1957	3 July 1958	PA
EDSON	DD 946	Bath Iron Works, Bath, Maine	3 Dec 1956	1 Jan 1958	7 Nov 1958	NRF
TURNER JOY	DD 951	Puget Sound Bridge & Dry Dock Co	30 Sep 1957	5 May 1958	3 Aug 1959	PA

ANTI-SUBMARINE MODERNISATION

Name	No.	Builders	Laid down	Launched	Commissioned	F/S
BARRY	DD 933	Bath Iron Works, Bath, Maine	15 Mar 1954	1 Oct 1955	31 Aug 1956	AA
DAVIS	DD 937	Bethlehem Steel Co, Quincy, Mass	1 Feb 1955	28 Mar 1956	28 Feb 1957	AA
JONAS INGRAM	DD 938	Bethlehem Steel Co, Quincy, Mass	15 June 1955	8 July 1956	19 July 1957	AA
MANLEY	DD 940	Bath Iron Works, Bath, Maine	10 Feb 1955	12 Apr 1956	1 Feb 1957	AA
DUPONT	DD 941	Bath Iron Works, Bath, Maine	11 May 1955	8 Sep 1956	1 July 1957	AA
BLANDY	DD 943	Bethlehem Steel Co, Quincy, Mass	29 Dec 1955	19 Dec 1956	26 Nov 1957	AA
MORTON	DD 948	Ingalls Shipbuilding Corporation	4 Mar 1957	23 May 1958	26 May 1959	PA
RICHARD S. EDWARDS	DD 950	Puget Sound Bridge & Dry Dock Co	20 Dec 1956	24 Sep 1957	5 Feb 1959	PA

Displacement, tons: 2 800/3 000 standard; 3 960/4 200 full load
Length, feet (metres): 418 (127·4)
Beam, feet (metres): 45 (13·7)
Draught, feet (metres): 20 (6·1)
Guns: A/S Mod; 2—5 in (127 mm)/54 (single Mk 42)
DD 945; 1—8 in (203 mm)/55 (single Mk 71);
2—5 in (127 mm)/54 (single Mk 42);
Others; 3—5 in (127 mm)/54 (single Mk 42);
1—3 in (76 mm)/50 (single Mk 33) (in DD 931, 946 and 951 only)
A/S weapons: 2 triple torpedo tubes (Mk 32);
1 ASROC 8-tube launcher in A/S modified ships
Main engines: 2 geared turbines (Westinghouse in DD 931, 933, 937 and 938; General Electric in others); 70 000 shp; 2 shafts
Boilers: 4 Babcock & Wilcox (Foster-Wheeler in DD 937, 938, 940-942)
Speed, knots: 33 knots
Oil fuel, tons: 750
Range, miles: 4 500 at 20 knots
Complement: 292 (17 officers, 275 enlisted men) in unmodified ships; 304 in A/S Mod ships (17 officers, 287 enlisted men)

These ships were the first US destroyers of post-World War II design and construction to be completed with the DD designation. Four have been converted to a guided missile configuration (DDGs) and are listed separately. They were authorised in the Fiscal Year 1952-56 new construction programmes. These ships each cost approximately $26 million.
Edson was assigned to the NRF on 1 April 1977 for employment as school ship for engine-room training and for reservist training at Newport, Rhode Island.

Armament: As built all 18 ships of this class had three single 5 in guns, two twin 3 in mounts, four fixed 21 in ASW torpedo tubes (amidships); two ASW Hedgehogs (forward of bridge), and depth charge racks.

Design: The entire superstructure of these ships is of aluminium to obtain maximum stability with minimum displacement. All living spaces are air conditioned. *Davis* and later ships have higher bows; *Hull* and later ships have slightly different bow designs. *Barry* had her sonar dome moved forward in 1959 and a stem anchor fitted.

Electronics: Several of the unmodified ships have elaborate electronic warfare antennas on the main mast.

Fire control: One Mk 56 and one Mk 68 GFCS, one Mk 114 ASW FCS (except in DD 942, 944 and 951 which have Mk 105 and DD 931, 945 and 946 which have no ASW FCS), one Mk 5 target designation system, one SPG 53A radar (SPG 50 in *Hull*).

Gunnery: With original armament of one 5 in mount forward and two 5 in mounts aft, these were the first US warships with more firepower aft than forward. Note that *Barry* and later ships have their Mk 68 gunfire control director forward and Mk 56 director aft; positions reversed in earlier ships.
During 1974-75 *Hull* was fitted with an 8 in gun forward to determine feasibility of installing a Major Calibre Light Weight Gun (MCLWG) in destroyer-type ships for shore bombardment. Forward 5 in gun removed. There are no plans to remove the 8 in gun.
Single Phalanx 20 mm Mk 15 CIWS to be installed in *Bigelow*.

Modernisation: Eight ships of this class were extensively modified in 1967-71 to improve their anti-submarine capabilities: *Barry, Davis, Du Pont* at the Boston Naval Shipyard; *Jonas Ingram, Manley, Blandy* at the Philadelphia Naval Shipyard; and *Morton, Richard S. Edwards* at the Long Beach (California) Naval Shipyard. During modernisation the anti-submarine torpedo tubes installed forward of bridge (on 01 level), deckhouse aft of second funnel extended to full width of ship, ASROC launcher installed in place of after gun mounts on 01 level, and variable depth sonar fitted at stern. Six ships of this class were not modernised because of increased costs.

Radar: Search: SPS 10, 37 or 40.

Sonar: SQS 23 (bow-mounted in *Barry*, the first US ship so fitted).
VDS in ASW ships.

HULL with 8 in gun forward   6/1978, Dr. Giorgio Arra

MULLINNIX   1976, Michael D. J. Lennon

MORTON (ASW modernisation)   8/1978, Dr. Giorgio Arra

USA / Destroyers 701

28 "GEARING" CLASS (FRAM I): DESTROYERS (DD)

Name	No.	Builders	Laid down	Launched	Commissioned	F/S
*HAMNER	DD 718	Federal S.B & D.D. Co	23 Apr 1945	24 Nov 1945	11 July 1946	NRF
*SOUTHERLAND	DD 743	Bath Iron Works Corporation	27 May 1944	5 Oct 1944	22 Dec 1944	NRF
*WILLIAM C. LAWE	DD 763	Bethlehem, San Francisco	12 Mar 1944	21 May 1945	18 Dec 1946	NRF
*McKEAN	DD 784	Todd Pacific Shipyards	15 Sep 1944	31 Mar 1945	9 June 1945	NRF
HENDERSON	DD 785	Todd Pacific Shipyards	27 Oct 1944	28 May 1945	4 Aug 1945	NRF
*HOLLISTER	DD 788	Todd Pacific Shipyards	27 Dec 1944	9 Oct 1945	26 Mar 1946	NRF
*HIGBEE	DD 806	Bath Iron Works Corporation	26 June 1944	12 Nov 1944	27 Jan 1945	NRF
CORRY	DD 817	Consolidated Steel Corporation	5 Apr 1945	28 July 1945	26 Feb 1946	NRF
*JOHNSTON	DD 821	Consolidated Steel Corporation	6 May 1945	19 Oct 1945	10 Oct 1946	NRF
*ROBERT H. McCARD	DD 822	Consolidated Steel Corporation	20 June 1945	9 Nov 1945	26 Oct 1946	NRF
*MYLES C. FOX	DD 829	Bath Iron Works Corporation	14 Aug 1944	13 Jan 1945	20 Mar 1945	NRF
*CHARLES P. CECIL	DD 835	Bath Iron Works Corporation	2 Dec 1944	22 Apr 1945	29 June 1945	NRF
*FISKE	DD 842	Bath Iron Works Corporation	9 Apr 1945	8 Sep 1945	28 Nov 1945	NRF
VOGELGESANG	DD 862	Bethlehem, Staten Island	3 Aug 1944	15 Jan 1945	28 Apr 1945	NRF
STEINAKER	DD 863	Bethlehem, Staten Island	1 Sep 1944	13 Feb 1945	26 May 1945	NRF
*HAROLD J. ELLISON	DD 864	Bethlehem, Staten Island	3 Oct 1944	14 Mar 1945	23 June 1945	NRF
*CONE	DD 866	Bethlehem, Staten Island	30 Nov 1944	10 May 1945	18 Aug 1945	NRF
*DAMATO	DD 871	Bethlehem, Staten Island	10 May 1945	21 Nov 1945	27 Apr 1946	NRF
*HAWKINS	DD 873	Consolidated Steel Corporation	14 May 1944	7 Oct 1944	10 Feb 1945	NRF
*ROGERS	DD 876	Consolidated Steel Corporation	3 June 1944	20 Nov 1944	26 Mar 1945	NRF
*DYESS	DD 880	Consolidated Steel Corporation	17 Aug 1944	26 Jan 1945	21 May 1945	NRF
NEWMAN K. PERRY	DD 883	Consolidated Steel Corporation	10 Oct 1944	17 Mar 1945	26 July 1945	NRF
*JOHN R. CRAIG	DD 885	Consolidated Steel Corporation	17 Nov 1944	14 Apr 1945	20 Aug 1945	NRF
ORLECK	DD 886	Consolidated Steel Corporation	28 Nov 1944	12 May 1945	15 Sep 1945	NRF
MEREDITH	DD 890	Consolidated Steel Corporation	27 Jan 1945	28 June 1945	31 Dec 1945	NRF

* To be deleted in FY 1980

Displacement, tons: 2 425 standard; 3 480 to 3 520 full load
Length, feet (metres): 390·5 (119·0)
Beam, feet (metres): 41·2 (12·6)
Draught, feet (metres): 19 (5·8)
Guns: 4—5 in (127 mm)/38 (twin Mk 38)
A/S weapons: 1 ASROC 8-tube launcher; 2 triple torpedo tubes (Mk 32)
Main engines: 2 geared turbines (General Electric; Westinghouse in DD 743, 822, 871, 880 and Allis-Chalmers in DD 788); 60 000 shp; 2 shafts
Boilers: 4 (Babcock & Wilcox)
Speed, knots: 32·5
Range, miles: 5 800 at 15 knots
Complement: 274 (14 officers, 260 enlisted men); 307 in Naval Reserve training ships (12 officers, 176 enlisted active duty; 7 officers, 112 enlisted reserve)

The US Navy survivors of the several hundred destroyers constructed in the USA during World War II.
The "Gearing" class initially covered hull numbers DD 710-721, 742, 743, 763-769, 782-791, 805-926. Forty-nine of these ships were cancelled in 1945 (DD 768, 769, 809-816, 854-856, and 891-926); four ships were never completed and were scrapped in the 1950s; Castle (DD 720), Woodrow R. Thompson (DD 721), Lansdale (DD 766), and Seymour D. Owens (DD 767).
Two similar ships completed to a modified design after World War II are listed separately as the "Carpenter" class.
All ships are assigned to Naval Reserve training and are manned by composite active duty-reserve crews.

Armament-Design: As built, these ships had a pole mast and carried an armament of six 5 in guns (twin mounts), 12—40 mm guns (2 quad, 2 twin), 11—20 mm guns (single), and 10—21 in torpedo tubes (quin). After World War II, the after bank of tubes was replaced by an additional quad 40 mm mount. All 40 mm and 20 mm guns were replaced subsequently by six 3 in guns (2 twin, 2 single) and a tripod mast was installed to support heavier radar antennae. The 3 in guns and remaining anti-ship torpedo tubes were removed during FRAM modernisation.

Electronics: Electronic warfare equipment fitted to most ships.

Engineering: During November 1974 Johnston conducted experiments using liquefied coal as fuel in one boiler (Project Seacoal).

Fire control: Single Mk 37 gunfire control system, Mk 114 ASW FCS (Mk 111 in DD 763, 785, 788 and 890) and Mk 5 target designation system.

Helicopters: Fitted to operate the Drone Anti-Submarine Helicopter (DASH) during FRAM modernisation—never carried.

Modernisation: All of these ships underwent extensive modernisation under the Fleet Rehabilitation and Modernisation (FRAM I) programme between 1961 and 1965.
There are two basic FRAM I configurations: Some ships had twin 5 in mounts in "A" and "B" positions and Mk 32 torpedo launchers abaft second funnel; others have twin 5 in mounts in "A" and "Y" positions and Mk 32 launchers on 01 level in "B" position.

Radar: SPS 10, 37 or 40.

Sonar: SQS 23.

Transfers: Ships of this class serve with Brazil, Ecuador, Greece, South Korea, Pakistan, Taiwan and Turkey.

HAWKINS
9/1976, Dr. Giorgio Arra

HIGBEE
12/1978, USN

HAMNER
3/1976, USN

2 "CARPENTER" CLASS (FRAM I): DESTROYERS (DD)

Name	No.	Builders	Laid down	Launched	Commissioned	F/S
CARPENTER	DD 825	Consolidated Steel Corporation, Orange, Texas	30 July 1945	30 Dec 1945	15 Dec 1949	NRF
ROBERT A. OWENS	DD 827	Bath Iron Works Corporation	29 Oct 1945	15 July 1946	5 Nov 1949	NRF

Displacement, tons: 2 425 standard; 3 540 full load
Length, feet (metres): 390·5 *(119·0)*
Beam, feet (metres): 41 *(12·5)*
Draught, feet (metres): 20·9 *(6·4)*
Guns: 2—5 in *(127 mm)*/38 (twin Mk 38)
A/S weapons: 1 ASROC 8-tube launcher; 2 triple torpedo tubes (Mk 32)
Main engines: 2 geared turbines (General Electric) 60 000 shp; 2 shafts
Boilers: 4 (Babcock & Wilcox)
Speed, knots: 33
Complement: 282 (12 officers, 176 enlisted active duty; 8 officers, 86 enlisted reserve)

These ships were laid down as units of the "Gearing" class. Their construction was suspended after World War II until 1947 when they were towed to the Newport News Shipbuilding and Dry Dock Co for completion as DDK. As specialised ASW ships they mounted 3 in *(76 mm)* guns in place of 5 in mounts and were armed with improved ahead-firing anti-submarine weapons (Hedgehogs and Weapon Able/Alfa); special sonar equipment installed. The DDK and DDE classifications were merged in 1950 with both of these ships being designated DDE on 4 March 1950. Upon being modernised to the FRAM I configuration they were reclassified DD on 30 June 1962. Both of these ships are assigned to Naval Reserve training; they are manned by composite active duty and reserve crews.

Carpenter is to be deleted in FY 1980.

Electronics: These ships have electronic warfare antennas on smaller tripod mast forward of their second funnel.

Fire control: One Mk 56 gunfire control system, one Mk 11 ASW FCS, Mk 1 target designation system and one SPG 35 fire control radar.

Radar: Search: SPS 10 and 40.

Sonar: SQS 23.

CARPENTER

"ALLEN M. SUMNER" CLASS (FRAM II)

All surviving ships of the 70-destroyer "Allen M. Sumner" class have been stricken or transferred to other navies. Between 1943 and 1945, 58 destroyers and 12 minelayers were completed to this design. See 1974-75 and earlier editions for characteristics.

Ships of this class serve in the navies of Argentina, Brazil, Chile, West Germany, Greece, Italy, South Korea, Mexico, Peru, Spain, Taiwan and Turkey.

"FLETCHER" CLASS

The survivors of 175 "Fletcher" class destroyers have been stricken or transferred to other navies. See 1975-76 and previous editions for characteristics.

Ships of this class serve in the navies of Argentina, Brazil, Chile, Colombia, West Germany, Greece, Italy, South Korea, Mexico, Peru, Spain, Taiwan and Turkey.

NAVAL RESERVE FORCE TRAINING DESTROYERS

Name/Hull No.	NRF Homeport	Date of Assignment	Remarks
HAMNER (DD 718)	Portland, Oreg	1 June 1975	Replaced *Ozbourn* (DD 846)
SOUTHERLAND (DD 743)	San Diego, Calif	2 July 1973	Replaced *Bridget* (DE 1024)
WILLIAM C. LAWE (DD 763)	New Orleans, La	31 Aug 1973	Replaced *Putnam* (DD 757)
McKEAN (DD 784)	Seattle, Wash	1 Oct 1975	Replaced *Epperson* (DD 719)
HENDERSON (DD 785)	Long Beach, Calif	1 Oct 1973	Replaced *Arnold J. Isbell* (DD 869)
HOLLISTER (DD 788)	Long Beach, Calif	2 July 1973	Replaced *Hooper* (DE 1026)
HIGBEE (DD 806)	Seattle, Wash	1 July 1975	Replaced *Theodore E. Chandler* (DD 717)
CORRY (DD 817)	Philadelphia, Pa	31 Aug 1973	Replaced *Lowry* (DD 770)
JOHNSTON (DD 821)	Philadelphia, Pa	1 July 1972	Replaced *Hank* (DD 702)
ROBERT H. McCARD (DD 822)	Tampa, Fla	18 Dec 1972	Replaced *Beatty* (DD 756)
CARPENTER (DD 825)	San Francisco, Calif	15 Jan 1973	Replaced *Perkins* (DD 877)
ROBERT A. OWENS (DD 827)	Pensacola, Fla	15 June 1977	
MYLES C. FOX (DD 829)	New York City	2 July 1973	Replaced *John R. Pierce* (DD 753)
CHARLES P. CECIL (DD 835)	New London, Conn	2 July 1973	Replaced *Gearing* (DD 710)
FISKE (DD 842)	Bayonne, NJ	31 Aug 1973	Replaced *Robert K. Huntington* (DD 781)
VOGELGESANG (DD 862)	Newport, RI	1 Mar 1974	
STEINAKER (DD 863)	Baltimore, Md	2 July 1973	Replaced *Allan M. Sumner* (DD 692)
HAROLD J. ELLISON (DD 864)	Philadelphia, Pa	30 Nov 1974	Replaced *Robert L. Wilson* (DD 847)
CONE (DD 866)	Charleston, SC	31 Aug 1973	Replaced *Strong* (DD 758)
DAMATO (DD 871)	Newport, RI	1 Feb 1974	
HAWKINS (DD 873)	Philadelphia, Pa	15 Dec 1977	Replaced *Rich* (DD 820)
ROGERS (DD 876)	Portland, Oreg	1 Oct 1973	Replaced *Wallace L. Lind* (DD 703)
DYESS (DD 880)	Brooklyn, NY	16 Feb 1971	Replaced *Zellars* (DD 777)
NEWMAN K. PERRY (DD 883)	Newport, RI	1 July 1975	
JOHN R. CRAIG (DD 885)	San Diego, Calif	26 Aug 1973	Replaced *Bauer* (DE 1025)
ORLECK (DD 886)	Tacoma, Wash	1 Oct 1973	Replaced *Brinkley Bass* (DD 887)
MEREDITH (DD 890)	Mayport, Fla	31 Aug 1973	Replaced *Waldron* (DD 699)
EDSON (DD 946)	Newport, RI	1 Apr 1977	Replaced *Holder* (DD 819)

USA / Frigates 703

FRIGATES

There are 65 frigates (FF/FFG) in commission with another 73 ships planned for construction during the next few years. All ships now in commission have the large SQS 26 sonar, ASROC anti-submarine rockets, and a helicopter capability. However, only seven have a surface-to-air missile capability for limited area defence. The projected 74 ships of the "Oliver Hazard Perry" class (FFG 7) will have the smaller SQS 56 sonar. The ASROC will be deleted but the ships will be able to operate two LAMPS (Light Airborne Multi-Purpose System) helicopters and will have a surface-to-air/surface-to-surface missile capability. The "Perry" class ships will be more versatile than the previous "Knox" class frigates and several other navies have expressed interest in the newer design. The Royal Australian Navy has ordered three of the ships.

The US Navy's frigates could be supplemented in the ocean escort role by the 12 "Hamilton" class high-endurance cutters operated by the Coast Guard. The Coast Guard ships are fitted with sonar and are armed with Mk 32 torpedo tubes (as well as a single 5 in gun). They also have facilities for operating a large helicopter.

Future Programmes: Preliminary studies for a successor class to the "Oliver Hazard Perry" class, currently known as the "FFGX" programme are in hand.

2 + 24 + (33) "OLIVER HAZARD PERRY" CLASS: GUIDED MISSILE FRIGATES (FFG)

Name	No.	Builders	Laid down	Launched	Commission	F/S
OLIVER HAZARD PERRY	FFG 7 (ex-PF 109)	Bath Iron Works, Bath, Maine	12 June 1975	25 Sep 1976	17 Dec 1977	AA
McINERNEY	FFG 8	Bath Iron Works, Bath, Maine	7 Nov 1977	4 Nov 1978	1979	Bldg
WADSWORTH	FFG 9	Todd Shipyards Corporation, San Pedro	13 July 1977	29 July 1978	1980	Bldg
DUNCAN	FFG 10	Todd Shipyards Corporation, Seattle	29 Apr 1977	1 Mar 1978	1980	Bldg
CLARK	FFG 11	Bath Iron Works, Bath, Maine	1978	1979	1980	Bldg
GEORGE PHILIP	FFG 12	Todd Shipyards Corporation, San Pedro	1978	1978	1980	Bldg
SAMUEL E. MORISON	FFG 13	Bath Iron Works, Bath, Maine	4 Dec 1978	1979	1980	Bldg
SIDES	FFG 14	Todd Shipyards Corporation, San Pedro	7 Aug 1978	1979	1980	Bldg
—	FFG 15	Bath Iron Works, Bath, Maine	1979	1979	1981	Bldg
—	FFG 16	Bath Iron Works, Bath, Maine	1979	1980	1981	Bldg
ANTRIM	FFG 19	Todd Shipyards Corporation, San Pedro	19 Dec 1978	1978	1981	Bldg
—	FFG 20	Todd Shipyards Corporation, Seattle	21 June 1978	1979	1981	Bldg
—	FFG 21	Bath Iron Works, Bath, Maine	1979	1980	1981	Bldg
AHRION	FFG 22	Todd Shipyards Corporation, Seattle	1 Dec 1978	1979	1981	Bldg
—	FFG 23	Todd Shipyards Corporation, San Pedro	1979	1980	1981	Bldg
—	FFG 24	Bath Iron Works, Bath, Maine	1980	1980	1981	Bldg
—	FFG 25	Todd Shipyards Corporation, San Pedro	1979	1980	1982	Bldg
—	FFG 26	Bath Iron Works, Bath, Maine	1980	1980	1982	Bldg
—	FFG 27	Todd Shipyards Corporation, San Pedro	1980	1981	1982	Bldg
—	FFG 28	Todd Shipyards Corporation, Seattle	1979	1979	1982	Ord
—	FFG 29	Bath Iron Works, Bath, Maine	1980	1981	1982	Ord
—	FFG 30	Todd Shipyards Corporation, San Pedro	1980	1981	1982	Ord
—	FFG 31	Todd Shipyards Corporation, Seattle	1979	1980	1982	Ord
—	FFG 32	Bath Iron Works, Bath, Maine	1981	1981	1982	Ord
—	FFG 33	Todd Shipyards Corporation, San Pedro	1981	1981	1983	Ord
—	FFG 34	Bath Iron Works, Bath, Maine	1981	1981	1983	Ord
Eight ships	FFG 36/43	Approved FY 1979 programme				Proj
Six ships	FFG 44/49	Proposed FY 1980 programme				Proj
Six ships	FFG 50/55	Proposed FY 1981 programme				Proj
Six ships	FFG 56/61	Proposed FY 1982 programme				Proj
Four ships	FFG 62/65	Proposed FY 1983 programme				Proj
Three ships	FFG 66/68	Proposed FY 1984 programme				Proj

Displacement, tons: 3 605 full load
Length, feet (metres): 445 *(135·6)*
Beam, feet (metres): 45 *(13·7)*
Draught, feet (metres): 24·5 *(7·5)* (sonar); 14·8 *(4·5)* (keel)
Missiles: SSM/SAM; 40 Harpoon/Standard/Tartar (1 single Mk 13 launcher)
Gun: 1—76 mm/62 (Mk 75)
A/S weapons: 2 triple torpedo tubes (Mk 32)
Main engines: 2—LM 2500 gas turbines (General Electric); 41 000 shp; 1 shaft (cp propeller)
Speed, knots: 29
Range, miles: 4 500 at 20 knots
Complement: 164 (11 officers, 153 enlisted men)

They are follow-on ships to the large number of frigates (formerly DE) built in the 1960s and early 1970s, with the later ships emphasising anti-ship/aircraft/missile capabilities while the previous classes were oriented primarily against submarines (eg, larger SQS 26 sonar and ASROC).

The lead ship (FFG 7) was authorised in the Fiscal Year 1973 shipbuilding programme; three ships (FFG 8-10) in the FY 1975 programme; and six ships (FFG 11-16) in the FY 1976 programme. Congress authorised nine ships in the FY 1976, but cost escalation permitted the construction of only six ships; eight ships in the FY 1977 (FFG 19-26); eight ships in the FY 1978 (FFG 27-34) and nine ships in the FY 1979 (FFG 36-43).

The Navy proposes to build 48 additional ships of this class. The three additional ships of this class under construction at the Todd-Seattle shipyard for the Royal Australian Navy are assigned US Navy hull numbers FFG 17, 18 and 35 for accounting purposes. In addition to the three Australian units, three other units (with no US Navy hull numbers assigned) are being built for Spain in Spain.

Aircraft: LAMPS III is scheduled to enter service about 1985. Starting in FY 1985 FFG 7-34 (excluding FFG 17 and 18) will be retro-fitted to support LAMPS III which includes the installation of the Rapid Hauldown and Traversing System (RAST) which is equipment designed for safe helicopter operations in high seas. At the same time the SQR 19 (TACTAS) sonar will be fitted on FFG 7-34. The entire retro-fit will cost $13 million (1979$) per unit. LAMPS III support facilities, RAST and the TACTAS sonar will be fitted in all ships authorised from FY 1979 onwards, during construction.

Classification: These ships were originally classified as "patrol frigates" (PF) at a time when the term "frigate" was used in the US Navy for the DL/DLG/DLGN. *Oliver Hazard Perry* was designated PF 109 at time of keel laying and designated FFG 7 on 30 June 1975.

Design: These ships are slightly longer but lighter than the earlier "Knox" class. The original single hangar has been changed to two adjacent hangars, each to house an SH-2 or follow-on LAMPS helicopters.
Several weapon and sensor systems for this class were evaluated at sea in the guided missile frigate *Talbot* (FFG 4). Fin stabilisers may be fitted at a later date (space and weight reserved).

Engineering: Two auxiliary retractable propeller pods are provided aft of the sonar dome to provide "get home" power in the event of a casualty to the main engines or propeller shaft. Each pod has a 325 hp engine to provide a ship speed of 3 to 5 knots.

Fire control: The Mk 92 weapons control system is installed with a dome-shaped antenna atop the bridge. (The Mk 92 is the Americanised version of the WM-28 system developed by NV Hollandse Signaalapparaten). Mk 13 weapon direction system.

Fiscal: The design-to-cost estimate of $45·7 million in the Fiscal Year 1973 dollars based on a 49-ship programme has increased to $55·3 million in the same dollars due to design and cost estimating changes. However, adding the estimated inflation and contract escalation factors brings the estimated cost per ship in the FY 1979 programme to $186·6 million.

Gunnery: The principal gun on this ship is the single 76 mm OTO Melara with a 90-round-per-minute firing rate (designated Mk 75 in US service). Space and weight are reserved for one 20 mm Phalanx Mk 15 CIWS.

Missiles: The single-arm Tartar-type missile launcher will be capable of firing both Tartar/Standard-MR surface-to-air and Harpoon surface-to-surface missiles. "Mixed" missile magazines will be provided.

Radar: Long-range search: SPS 49.
Search and navigation: SPS 55.
Weapons control: STIR (modified SPG 60).

Rockets: Mk 36 Chaffroc RBOC launcher fitted.

Sonar: SQS 56 (hull-mounted). To be fitted with SQR 19 TACTAS (towed passive sonar) starting in mid-1980s.

OLIVER HAZARD PERRY   12/1977, USN

704 USA / Frigates

6 "BROOKE" CLASS: GUIDED MISSILE FRIGATES (FFG)

Name	No.	Builders	Laid down	Launched	Commissioned	F/S
BROOKE	FFG 1	Lockheed S.B. & Construction Co	10 Dec 1962	19 July 1963	12 Mar 1966	PA
RAMSEY	FFG 2	Lockheed S.B. & Construction Co	4 Feb 1963	15 Oct 1963	3 June 1967	PA
SCHOFIELD	FFG 3	Lockheed S.B. & Construction Co	15 Apr 1963	7 Dec 1963	11 May 1968	PA
TALBOT	FFG 4	Bath Iron Works, Bath, Maine	4 May 1964	6 Jan 1966	22 Apr 1967	AA
RICHARD L. PAGE	FFG 5	Bath Iron Works, Bath, Maine	4 Jan 1965	4 Apr 1966	5 Aug 1967	AA
JULIUS A. FURER	FFG 6	Bath Iron Works, Bath, Maine	12 July 1965	22 July 1966	11 Nov 1967	AA

Displacement, tons: 2 640 standard; 3 426 full load
Length, feet (metres): 414·5 *(126·3)*
Beam, feet (metres): 44·2 *(13·5)*
Draught, feet (metres): 24·2 *(7·4)*
Aircraft: 1 SH-2D LAMPS helicopter
Missiles: SAM; 16 Tartar/Standard-MR (1 single Mk 22 launcher)
Gun: 1—5 in *(127 mm)*/38 (Mk 30)
A/S weapons: 1 ASROC 8-tube launcher; 2 triple torpedo tubes (Mk 32)
Main engines: 1 geared turbine (Westinghouse in FFG 1-3, General Electric in others); 35 000 shp; 1 shaft
Boilers: 2 (Foster-Wheeler)
Speed, knots: 27·2
Complement: 248 (17 officers, 231 enlisted men)

These ships are identical to the "Garcia" class escorts except for the Tartar missile system in lieu of a second 5 in gun mount and different electronic equipment. Authorised as DEG 1-3 in the Fiscal Year 1962 new construction programme and DEG 4-6 in the FY 1963 programme. Plans for ten additional DEGs in the FY 1964 and possibly three more DEGs in a later programme were dropped because of the $11 million additional cost of a DEG over FF. In 1974-75 *Talbot* was reconfigured as test and evaluation ship for systems being developed for the "Oliver Hazard Perry" class (FFG 7) frigates and "Pegasus" class (PHM 1) hydrofoil combatants.

Classification: Reclassified as FFG 1-6 on 30 June 1975.

Fire control: One Mk 74 MFCS, one Mk 56 GFCS, one Mk 114 ASW FCS, one Mk 4 weapon direction system, one SPG 51 and one SPG 35 fire control radars.

Helicopters: These ships were designed to operate Drone Anti-Submarine Helicopters (DASH), but the programme was cut back before helicopters were provided. They were fitted to operate the Light Airborne Multi-Purpose System (LAMPS), currently the SH-2D helicopter during 1972-75 refits.

Missiles: These ships have a single Tartar Mk 22 launching system which weighs 92 395 lb. Reportedly, the system has a rate of fire similar to the larger Mk 11 and Mk 13 systems installed in guided missile destroyers, but the FFG system has a considerably smaller magazine capacity (16 missiles according to unofficial sources).
The FFG 4-6 have automatic ASROC loading system (noted angled base of bridge structure aft of ASROC in these ships).

Radar: 3D search: SPS 52.
Search: SPS 10.
Missile control: SPG 51C.

Rockets: Mk 33 Chaffroc RBOC. Mk 36 to replace Mk 33 in FFG 1 and 3.

Sonar: SQS 26 AX (bow-mounted). (SQS 56 evaluated in *Talbot*).

JULIUS A. FURER 10/1978, Leo van Ginderen

RICHARD L. PAGE 2/1976, USN

JULIUS A. FURER 10/1978, Leo van Ginderen

46 "KNOX" CLASS: FRIGATES (FF)

USA / Frigates 705

Name	No.	Builders	Laid down	Launched	Commissioned	F/S
KNOX	FF 1052	Todd Shipyards, Seattle	5 Oct 1965	19 Nov 1966	12 Apr 1969	PA
ROARK	FF 1053	Todd Shipyards, Seattle	2 Feb 1966	24 Apr 1967	22 Nov 1969	PA
GRAY	FF 1054	Todd Shipyards, Seattle	19 Nov 1966	3 Nov 1967	4 Nov 1970	PA
HEPBURN	FF 1055	Todd Shipyards, San Pedro	1 June 1966	25 Mar 1967	3 July 1969	PA
CONNOLE	FF 1056	Avondale Shipyards	23 Mar 1967	20 July 1968	30 Aug 1969	AA
RATHBURNE	FF 1057	Lockheed S.B. & Construction Co	8 Jan 1968	2 May 1969	16 May 1970	PA
MEYERKORD	FF 1058	Todd Shipyards, San Pedro	1 Sep 1966	15 July 1967	28 Nov 1969	PA
W. S. SIMS	FF 1059	Avondale Shipyards	10 Apr 1967	4 Jan 1969	3 Jan 1970	AA
LANG	FF 1060	Todd Shipyards, San Pedro	25 Mar 1967	17 Feb 1968	28 Mar 1970	PA
PATTERSON	FF 1061	Avondale Shipyards	12 Oct 1967	3 May 1969	14 Mar 1970	AA
WHIPPLE	FF 1062	Todd Shipyards, Seattle	24 Apr 1967	12 Apr 1968	22 Aug 1970	PA
REASONER	FF 1063	Lockheed S.B. & Construction Co	6 Jan 1969	1 Aug 1970	31 July 1971	PA
LOCKWOOD	FF 1064	Todd Shipyards, Seattle	3 Nov 1967	5 Sep 1964	5 Dec 1970	PA
STEIN	FF 1065	Lockheed S.B. & Construction Co	1 June 1970	19 Dec 1970	8 Jan 1972	PA
MARVIN SHIELDS	FF 1066	Todd Shipyards, Seattle	12 Apr 1968	23 Oct 1969	10 Apr 1971	PA
FRANCIS HAMMOND	FF 1067	Todd Shipyards, San Pedro	15 July 1967	11 May 1968	25 July 1970	PA
VREELAND	FF 1068	Avondale Shipyards	20 Mar 1968	14 June 1969	13 June 1970	AA
BAGLEY	FF 1069	Lockheed S.B. & Construction Co	22 Sep 1970	24 Apr 1971	6 May 1972	PA
DOWNES	FF 1070	Todd Shipyards, Seattle	5 Sep 1968	13 Dec 1969	28 Aug 1971	PA
BADGER	FF 1071	Todd Shipyards, Seattle	17 Feb 1968	7 Dec 1968	1 Dec 1970	PA
BLAKELY	FF 1072	Avondale Shipyards	3 June 1968	23 Aug 1969	18 July 1970	AA
ROBERT E. PEARY	FF 1073	Lockheed S.B. & Construction Co	20 Dec 1970	23 June 1971	23 Sep 1972	PA
HAROLD E. HOLT	FF 1074	Todd Shipyards, San Pedro	11 May 1968	3 May 1969	26 Mar 1971	PA
TRIPPE	FF 1075	Avondale Shipyards	29 July 1968	1 Nov 1969	19 Sep 1970	AA
FANNING	FF 1076	Todd Shipyards, San Pedro	7 Dec 1968	24 Jan 1970	23 July 1971	PA
OUELLET	FF 1077	Avondale Shipyards	15 Jan 1969	17 Jan 1970	12 Dec 1970	PA
JOSEPH HEWES	FF 1078	Avondale Shipyards	15 May 1969	7 Mar 1970	24 Apr 1971	AA
BOWEN	FF 1079	Avondale Shipyards	11 July 1969	2 May 1970	22 May 1971	AA
PAUL	FF 1080	Avondale Shipyards	12 Sep 1969	20 June 1970	14 Aug 1971	AA
AYLWIN	FF 1081	Avondale Shipyards	13 Nov 1969	29 Aug 1970	18 Sep 1971	AA
ELMER MONTGOMERY	FF 1082	Avondale Shipyards	23 Jan 1970	21 Nov 1970	30 Oct 1971	AA
COOK	FF 1083	Avondale Shipyards	20 Mar 1970	23 Jan 1971	18 Dec 1971	PA
McCANDLESS	FF 1084	Avondale Shipyards	4 June 1970	20 Mar 1971	18 Mar 1972	AA
DONALD B. BEARY	FF 1085	Avondale Shipyards	24 July 1970	22 May 1971	22 July 1972	AA
BREWTON	FF 1086	Avondale Shipyards	2 Oct 1970	24 July 1971	8 July 1972	PA
KIRK	FF 1087	Avondale Shipyards	4 Dec 1970	25 Sep 1971	9 Sep 1972	PA
BARBEY	FF 1088	Avondale Shipyards	5 Feb 1971	4 Dec 1971	11 Nov 1972	PA
JESSE L. BROWN	FF 1089	Avondale Shipyards	8 Apr 1971	18 Mar 1972	17 Feb 1973	AA
AINSWORTH	FF 1090	Avondale Shipyards	11 June 1971	15 Apr 1972	31 Mar 1973	AA
MILLER	FF 1091	Avondale Shipyards	6 Aug 1971	3 June 1972	30 June 1973	AA
THOMAS C. HART	FF 1092	Avondale Shipyards	8 Oct 1971	12 Aug 1972	28 July 1973	AA
CAPODANNO	FF 1093	Avondale Shipyards	12 Oct 1971	21 Oct 1972	17 Nov 1973	AA
PHARRIS	FF 1094	Avondale Shipyards	11 Feb 1972	16 Dec 1972	26 Jan 1974	AA
TRUETT	FF 1095	Avondale Shipyards	27 Apr 1972	3 Feb 1973	1 June 1974	AA
VALDEZ	FF 1096	Avondale Shipyards	30 June 1972	24 Mar 1973	27 July 1974	AA
MOINESTER	FF 1097	Avondale Shipyards	25 Aug 1972	12 May 1973	2 Nov 1974	AA

Displacement, tons: 3 011 standard; 3 877 (1052-1077) 4 200 (remainder) full load
Length, feet (metres): 438 *(133·5)*
Beam, feet (metres): 46·75 *(14·25)*
Draught, feet (metres): 24·75 *(7·55)*
Aircraft: 1 SH-2 LAMPS helicopter
Missiles: SAM; 1 Sea Sparrow BPDMS multiple launcher (Mk 25) in 1052-1069 and 1071-1083; 1 NATO Sea Sparrow multiple launcher (Mk 29) in *Downes*; SSM; Harpoon in FF 1055, 1057, 1060, 1070, 1082, 1085, 1090, 1092 and 1096 (see *Missile* note)
Gun: 1—5 in *(127 mm)*/54 (Mk 42)
A/S weapons: 1 ASROC 8-tube launcher; 4 fixed torpedo tubes (Mk 32)
Main engines: 1 geared turbine (Westinghouse) 35 000 shp; 1 shaft
Boilers: 2 Combustion Engineering (except FF 1056, 1057, 1061, 1063, 1065, 1072, 1073, 1075, 1077 which have Babcock & Wilcox)
Speed, knots: 27
Complement: 245 (17 officers, 228 enlisted men); increased to 283 (22 officers, 261 enlisted men) with BPDMS and LAMPS installation; (as built 12 ships had accommodation for 2 staff officers)

The 46 frigates of the "Knox" class comprise the largest group of destroyer or frigate type warships built to the same design in the West since World War II. These ships are similar to the previous "Garcia" and "Brooke" classes, but slightly larger because of the use of non-pressure-fired boilers.

Although now classified as frigates they were authorised as DE 1052-1061 (10 ships) in the Fiscal Year 1964 new construction programme, DE 1062-1077 (16 ships) in FY 1965, DE 1078-1087 (10 ships) in FY 1966, DE 1088-1097 (10 ships) in FY 1967, and DE 1098-1107 (10 ships) in FY 1968. However, construction of six ships (DE 1102-1107) was deferred in 1968 as US Navy emphasis shifted to the more versatile and faster ships; three additional ships (DE 1098-1100) were cancelled on 24 February 1969 to finance cost overruns of the FY 1968 nuclear-powered attack submarines and to comply with a Congressional mandate to reduce expenditures; the last ship of the FY 1968 programme (DE 1101) was cancelled on 9 April 1969.

The DEG 7-11 guided missile "frigates" constructed in Spain are similar to this design.

Classification: Originally classified as ocean escorts (DE); reclassified as frigates (FF) on 30 June 1975.

Construction: The ships built at Avondale Shipyards in Westwego, Louisiana, were assembled with mass production techniques. The hulls were built keel-up to permit downhead welding. Prefabricated, inverted hull modules were first assembled on a permanent platen, then lifted by hydraulic units and moved laterally into giant turning rings which rotated the hull into an upright position. Avondale, which also built the "Hamilton" class cutters for the Coast Guard, side launched these ships.

Design: A 4 000 lb lightweight anchor is fitted on the port side and an 8 000 lb anchor fits into the after section of the sonar dome.

BADGER (with Sea Sparrow)   3/1978, USN (PH1 A. E. Legare)

OUELLET (with Sea Sparrow)   10/1977, Dr. Giorgio Arra

Engineering: DE 1101 was to have had gas turbine propulsion; construction of the ship was cancelled when decision was made to provide gas turbine propulsion in the "Spruance" class (DD 963) destroyers.

These ships can steam at 22 knots on one boiler. They have a single 5-blade, 15 ft diameter propeller.

Fire control: One Mk 68 gunfire control with SPG 53A radar, one Mk 115 MFCS, one Mk 114 ASW FCS and one Mk 1 target designation system.

Fiscal: These ships have cost considerably more than originally estimated. Official programme cost for the 46 ships as of January 1974 was $1 424 million an average of $30·959 million per ship not including the LAMPS, Standard missile, VDS, or BPDMS installation.

Helicopters: These ships were designed to operate the now-discarded DASH unmanned helicopter. From FY 1972 to FY 1976 they were modified to accommodate the Light Airborne Multi-Purpose System, the SH-2D anti-submarine helicopter; hangar and flight deck are enlarged. Cost approximately $1 million per ship for LAMPS modification. Modification of FF 1061 and 1070 cancelled.

Missiles: Sea Sparrow Basic Point Defence Missile System (BPDMS) launcher installed in 31 ships from 1971-75 (FF 1052-1069, 1071-1083).
Modified NATO Sea Sparrow installed in *Downes* for evaluation.
In addition, some ships are being fitted with the Standard interim surface-to-surface missile which is fired from the ASROC launcher forward of the bridge. Two of the eight "cells" in the launcher are modified to fire a single Standard.
Cost was approximately $400 000 per ship for BPDMS and $750 000 for Standard missile modification.
Downes and *Lockwood* have been used in at-sea firing tests and shipboard compatability for the Harpoon ship-to-ship missiles.
Harpoon fitted in *Ainsworth* in August 1976 (first production model in US Navy) followed by *Thomas C. Hart*. To be fitted in all other ships in immediate future.

Names: DE 1073 originally was named *Conolly;* changed on 12 May 1971.

Radar: Search: SPS 10 and 40.
(**Note:** *Downes* has SPS 58 threat detection radar, and Improved Point Defence/Target Acquisition System (IPD/TAS) radar).

Rockets: Mk 36 Chaffroc RBOC to be fitted in near future replacing Mk 33 system in FF 1052, 1055, 1061, 1065, 1068, 1072, 1074-76, 1078-1085 and 1087.

Sonar: SQS 26 CX (bow-mounted).
SQS 35 (Independent VDS) (except FF 1053-55, 1057-62, 1072 and 1077).

In FY 1980 funds are requested to retro-fit twelve sets of SQR 18-A TACTAS towed array sonar in twelve "Knox" class ships. All ships of this class are planned eventually to be supplied with SQR 18-A.

Torpedoes: Improved ASROC-torpedo reloading capability as in some ships of previous "Garcia" class (note slanting face of bridge structure immediately behind ASROC). Four Mk 32 torpedo tubes are fixed in the amidships structure, two to a side angled out at 45 degrees. The arrangement provides improved loading capability over exposed triple Mk 32 torpedo tubes

WHIPPLE (with Sea Sparrow) — 4/1978, USN (PH2 L. B. Foster)

BREWTON (no Sea Sparrow) — 3/1978, Dr. Giorgio Arr

PHARRIS (no Sea Sparrow) — 6/1978, Michael D. J. Lennon

USA / Frigates 707

10 "GARCIA" CLASS: FRIGATES (FF)

Name	No.	Builders	Laid down	Launched	Commissioned	F/S
GARCIA	FF 1040	Bethlehem Steel, San Francisco	16 Oct 1962	31 Oct 1963	21 Dec 1964	AA
BRADLEY	FF 1041	Bethlehem Steel, San Francisco	17 Jan 1963	26 Mar 1964	15 May 1965	PA
EDWARD McDONNELL	FF 1043	Avondale Shipyards	1 Apr 1963	15 Feb 1964	15 Feb 1965	AA
BRUMBY	FF 1044	Avondale Shipyards	1 Aug 1963	6 June 1964	5 Aug 1965	AA
DAVIDSON	FF 1045	Avondale Shipyards	20 Sep 1963	2 Oct 1964	7 Dec 1965	PA
VOGE	FF 1047	Defoe Shipbuilding Co	21 Nov 1963	4 Feb 1965	25 Nov 1966	AA
SAMPLE	FF 1048	Lockheed S.B. & Construction Co	19 July 1963	28 Apr 1964	23 Mar 1968	PA
KOELSCH	FF 1049	Defoe Shipbuilding Co	19 Feb 1964	8 June 1965	10 June 1967	AA
ALBERT DAVID	FF 1050	Lockheed S.B. & Construction Co	29 Apr 1964	19 Dec 1964	19 Oct 1968	PA
O'CALLAHAN	FF 1051	Defoe Shipbuilding Co	19 Feb 1964	20 Oct 1965	13 July 1968	PA

Displacement, tons: 2 620 standard; 3 403 full load
Length, feet (metres): 414·5 *(126·3)*
Beam, feet (metres): 44·2 *(13·5)*
Draught, feet (metres): 24 *(7·3)*
Aircraft: 1 SH-2D LAMPS helicopter (except *Sample* and *Albert David*)
Guns: 2—5 in *(127 mm)*/38 (single Mk 30)
A/S weapons: 1 ASROC 8-tube launcher;
2 triple torpedo tubes (Mk 32)
Main engines: 1 geared turbine (Westinghouse in 1040, 1041, 1043-1045; GE in others); 35 000 shp; 1 shaft
Boilers: 2 (Foster-Wheeler)
Speed, knots: 27·5
Complement: 239 (13 officers, 226 enlisted men (1040, 1041, 1043, 1044)
247 (16 officers, 231 enlisted men) (remainder)

These ships exceed some of the world's destroyers in size and ASW capability, but are designated as frigates by virtue of their single propeller shaft and limited speed. The FF 1040 and FF 1041 were authorised in the Fiscal Year 1961 new construction programme, FF 1043-1045 in FY 1962, and FF 1047-1051 in FY 1963.

Classification: Originally classified as ocean escorts (DE); reclassified as frigates (FF) on 30 June 1975. The hull numbers DE 1039, 1042, and 1046 were assigned to frigates built overseas for Portugal to US "Dealey" design.

Design: Anchors are mounted at stem and on portside, just forward of 5 in gun. Hangar structure of this class modified during the early 1970s to handle LAMPS except in *Sample* and *Albert David*.

Electronics: *Voge* and *Koelsch* are fitted with a specialised ASW Naval Tactical Data System (NTDS).

Fire control: One Mk 56 gunfire control system, one Mk 114 ASW FCS and one Mk 1 target designation system, one SPG 35 fire control radar.

Helicopters: The Drone Anti-Submarine Helicopter (DASH) programme was cut back before these ships were provided with helicopters. Reportedly only *Bradley* actually operated with DASH.
All but two of these ships were fitted to operate the Light Airborne Multi-Purpose System (LAMPS), now the SH-2D helicopter between FY 1972-75.

Missiles: *Bradley* was fitted with a Sea Sparrow Basic Point Defense Missile System (BPDMS) in 1967-68; removed for installation in the carrier *Forrestal* (CV 59).

Radar: Search: SPS 10 and 40.

Sonar: SQS 26 AXR (bow-mounted) in FF 1040-1041, 1043-1045.
SQS 26 BR (bow-mounted) in FF 1047-1051.

Torpedoes: Most of these ships were built with two Mk 25 torpedo tubes built into their transom for launching wire-guided ASW torpedoes. However, they have been removed from the earlier ships and deleted in the later ships. *Voge* and later ships have automatic ASROC reload system (note angled base of bridge structure behind ASROC in these ships).

DAVIDSON
3/1978, USN (PH2 L. B. Foster)

SAMPLE
3/1978, USN (PH2 A. E. Legare)

EDWARD McDONNELL
1976, Leo van Ginderen

708 USA / Frigates

1 "GLOVER" CLASS: FRIGATE (FF)

Name	No.	Builders	Laid down	Launched	Commissioned	F/S
GLOVER	FF 1098 (ex-AGFF 1, ex-AGDE 1, ex-AG 163)	Bath Iron Works, Bath, Maine	29 July 1963	17 Apr 1965	13 Nov 1965	AA

Displacement, tons: 2 643 standard; 3 426 full load
Length, feet (metres): 414·5 *(126·3)*
Beam, feet (metres): 44·2 *(13·5)*
Draught, feet (metres): 24 *(7·3)*
Gun: 1—5 in *(127 mm)*/38 (Mk 30)
A/S weapons: 1 ASROC 8-tube launcher;
  2 triple torpedo tubes (Mk 32);
  facilities for small helicopter
Main engines: 1 geared turbine (Westinghouse); 35 000 shp;
  1 shaft
Boilers: 2 (Foster-Wheeler)
Speed, knots: 27
Complement: 248

Glover was built to test an advanced hull design and propulsion system, and has a full combat capability.

The ship was originally authorised in the Fiscal Year 1960 new construction programme, but was postponed and re-introduced in the FY 1961 programme. Estimated construction cost was $29·33 million.
On 1 October 1979 *Glover* ceased her experimental role and assumed the status of a Frigate (FF). It is not known whether she will have capabilities updated by having facilities for LAMPS II installed or her electronic equipment modernised.

Classification: *Glover* was originally classified as a miscellaneous auxiliary (AG 163); completed as an escort research ship (AGDE 1). Subsequently changed to frigate research ship on 30 June 1975 and reclassified as a regular frigate on 1 October 1979.

Design: *Glover* has a massive bow sonar dome integral with her hull and extending well forward underwater.

Electronics: The ship has a prototype tactical assignment console that integrates signals from the three sonars and radars present combined and coordinated tactical situation presentations in the Combat Information Centre (CIC). Reportedly, th increases the combat effectiveness of the ship to a consi erable extent.

Fire control: Mk 56 GFCS with SPG 35; one Mk 114 ASW F(and one Mk 1 target designation system.

Radar: Search: SPS 10 and 40.

Sonar: Bow-mounted SQS 26 AXR active sonar, hull-mount SQR 13 Passive/Active Detection and Location (PADLO sonar, and SQS 35 Independent Variable Depth Sonar (IVD lowered from the stern.

GLOVER (Old hull number as AGFF 1)   1974, USN

2 "BRONSTEIN" CLASS: FRIGATES (FF)

Name	No.	Builders	Laid down	Launched	Commissioned	F/S
BRONSTEIN	FF 1037	Avondale Shipyards	16 May 1961	31 Mar 1962	16 June 1963	PA
McCLOY	FF 1038	Avondale Shipyards	15 Sep 1961	9 June 1962	21 Oct 1963	AA

Displacement, tons: 2 360 standard; 2 650 full load
Length, feet (metres): 371·5 *(113·2)*
Beam, feet (metres): 40·5 *(12·3)*
Draught, feet (metres): 23 *(7·0)*
Guns: 2—3 in *(76 mm)*/50 (twin Mk 33)
A/S weapons: 1 ASROC 8-tube launcher;
  2 triple torpedo tubes (Mk 32);
  facilities for small helicopter
Main engines: 1 geared turbine (De Laval); 20 000 shp; 1 shaft
Boilers: 2 (Foster-Wheeler)
Speed, knots: 26
Complement: 196 (16 officers, 180 enlisted men)

These two ships may be considered the first of the "second generation" of post-World War II frigates which are comparable in size and ASW capabilities to conventional destroyers. *Bronstein* and *McCloy* have several features such as hull design, large sonar and ASW weapons that subsequently were incorporated into the mass-produced "Garcia", "Brooke", and "Knox" classes.
Both ships were built under the Fiscal Year 1960 new construction programme.

Classification: These ships were originally classified as ocean escorts (DE); reclassified as frigates (FF) on 30 June 1975.

Design: Position of stem anchor and portside anchor (ju forward of gun mount) necessitated by large bow sonar dom€ As built, a single 3 in (Mk 34) open mount was aft of tF helicopter deck; removed for installation of towed sonar.

Fire control: One Mk 56 gunfire control system, one Mk 1" ASW FCS, Mk 1 target designation system and SPG 35 fi control radar.

Radar: Search: SPS 10 and 40.

Sonar: SQS 26 (bow-mounted).
TASS (Towed Array Surveillance System) installed mid-1970 Cable reel on quarterdeck.

BRONSTEIN   7/1975, US

LIGHT FORCES

The US Navy's programme to construct a series of 30 hydrofoil missile ships has been sharply curtailed, with only six units now planned probably as a result of a 130 per cent increase in estimated unit costs. Designated "patrol combatant missile (hydrofoil)".

Initial problems in the pump, gearbox, and electrical system of the prototype PHM have been overcome.

PHM 1-5 will be operated as a tactical squadron to develop tactics and gain technical experience with this type of craft. *Gemini* will be operated as a High Speed Test Vehicle in place of *Pegasus*.

In earlier hydrofoil craft, *High Point* (PCH 1) is operated in a test and evaluation status. During 1974-75 *High Point* was evaluated by the US Coast Guard (subsequently returned to Navy control). Finally, several patrol and riverine warfare craft are operated by the Naval Reserve Force, and one new design (PB) is being developed for US and foreign use. US use of these craft will be minimal; rather they are intended to compete with contemporary small craft built overseas in the foreign sales market.

1 + 5 PATROL COMBATANTS MISSILE (HYDROFOILS)

Name	No.	Builders	Commissioned	F/S
PEGASUS	PHM 1	Boeing Co, Seattle	9 July 1977	AA
HERCULES	PHM 2	Boeing Co, Seattle	1982	Bldg
TAURUS	PHM 3	Boeing Co, Seattle	1981	Bldg
AQUILA	PHM 4	Boeing Co, Seattle	1981	Bldg
ARIES	PHM 5	Boeing Co, Seattle	1981	Ord
GEMINI	PHM 6	Boeing Co, Seattle	1982	Ord

Displacement, tons: 239 full load
Dimensions, feet (metres):
  foils extended: 131·2 *(40·0)* oa × 28·2 *(8·6)* hull × 23·2 *(7·1)*
  foils retracted: 147·5 *(45·0)* oa × 28·2 *(8·6)* hull × 6·2 *(1·9)*
Missiles: SSM; 8 canisters (quad) for Harpoon
Gun: 1—76 mm/62 (Mk 75)
Main engines: Foil borne; 1 gas turbine (General Electric LM 2500); 18 000 shp; 2 waterjet propulsion units = 48 knots
  Hull borne; 2 diesels (Mercedes-Benz); 1 600 bhp; 2 waterjet propulsion units = 12 knots
Range, miles: 1 700 at 9 knots; 700 at 40 knots
Complement: 21 (4 officers, 17 enlisted men)

The PHM design was developed in conjunction with the Italian and West German navies in an effort to produce a small combatant that would be universally acceptable to NATO navies with minor modifications.

The US Navy plans to construct six ships of this class. *Pegasus* and *Hercules* were authorised in the Fiscal Year 1973 R and D programme, and four additional ships in the FY 1975 shipbuilding programme. Planning for 24 additional units was cancelled in 1975. *Pegasus* was laid down on 10 May 1973 and launched on 9 November 1974 and made her first foil-borne trip on 25 February 1975. *Hercules* was laid down on 30 May 1974. Due to cost increases and inflation her construction was suspended in August 1975 when 40·9 per cent complete. Later *Hercules* was to be completed with funds from the FY 1976 shipbuilding programme, but a further re-examination of this programme led to the cancellation of all but *Pegasus* on 6 April 1977. *Pegasus* was to serve as a High Speed Test Vehicle. In August 1977, the Secretary of Defense released the $272·7 million appropriated to complete the six ship programme. Subsequently, a contract to complete *Hercules* and construct PHM 3/6 was awarded to Boeing Co on 20 October 1977. *Gemini* will be completed for use as test ship and will be unarmed while the remainder will be operational. *Pegasus* was transferred from the Pacific to the Atlantic in July 1979. The others will be assigned to the Atlantic on commissioning.

Classification: The designation PHM originally was for Patrol Hydrofoil-Missile; reclassified Patrol Combatant Missile (Hydrofoil) on 30 June 1975.

Fire control: Fitted with the Mk 92 fire control system (Americanised version of the WM-28 radar and weapons control system developed by NV Hollandse Signaalapparaten).

Missiles: PHM 1-5 will have two lightweight four-tube canister launchers. This is double the Harpoon armament originally planned.

Name: PHM 1 was originally named *Delphinus*—renamed 26 April 1974.

Rockets: Mk 34 Chaffroc to be fitted.

PEGASUS 4/1978, USN (PH2 L. B. Foster)

PEGASUS 10/1975, USN

710 USA / Light forces

4 "ASHEVILLE" CLASS: PATROL COMBATANTS (PG)

Name	No.	Builders	Commissioned	F/S
TACOMA	PG 92	Tacoma Boatbuilding	14 July 1969	AA
WELCH	PG 93	Peterson Builders	8 Sep 1969	AA
BEACON	PG 99	Peterson Builders	21 Nov 1969	AR
GREEN BAY	PG 101	Peterson Builders	5 Dec 1969	AR

Displacement, tons: 225 standard; 235 full load
Dimensions, feet (metres): 164·5 × 23·8 × 9·5 *(50·1 × 7·3 × 2·9)*
Guns: 1—3 in *(76 mm)*/50 (single Mk 34); 1—40 mm (single Mk 10); 4—·50 cal MG (twin)
Main engines: CODAG: 2 diesels (Cummins); 1 450 shp; 2 shafts = 16 knots
   1 gas turbine (General Electric LM 2500); 13 300 shp; 2 shafts = 40+ knots
Range, miles: 1 700 at 16 knots; 325 at 37 knots
Complement: 24 (3 officers, 21 enlisted men)

Originally a class of 17 patrol gunboats (PG ex-PGM) designed to perform patrol, blockade, surveillance, and support missions. No anti-submarine capability. Requirement for these craft was based on the volatile Cuban situation in the early 1960s.
PG 92 and 93, authorised in the Fiscal Year 1966 programme. Ships took approximately 18 months from keel laying to completion. Cost per ship approximately $5 million.
Tacoma and *Welch* are at Little Creek, Virginia, involved in training Saudi Arabian naval personnel.
Chehalis (PG 94) was stripped of armament and assigned as a research craft to the Naval Scientific Research & Development Center in Annapolis, Maryland, on 21 August 1975; renamed *Athena* (no hull number assigned) and civilian manned. *Grand Rapids* followed her on 1 October 1977 (as *Athena II*) and *Douglas* (PG 100) (as *Athena III*) in early 1979. *Antelope* (PG 86) transferred to US Environmental Protection Agency 17 January 1978. All 17 of this class still exist, some with other Government agencies or foreign navies (see *Deletion* list).

Classification: These ships were originally classified as motor gunboats (PGM); reclassified as patrol boats (PG) with same hull numbers on 1 April 1967 and as Patrol Combatants (PG) on 30 June 1975.

Design: All aluminium hull and aluminium-fibreglass superstructure. Because of the heat-transmitting qualities of the aluminium hull and the amount of waste heat produced by a gas turbine engine the ships are completely air conditioned.

Engineering: The transfer from diesel to gas turbine propulsion (or vice versa) can be accomplished while under way with no loss of speed. From full stop these ships can attain 40 knots in one minute; manoeuvrability is excellent due in part to cp propellers.

Fire control: Mk 63 Gunfire Control System with SPG 50 fire control radar.

Gunnery: 3 in (Mk 34) gun forward in closed mount with 40 mm (Mk 3) gun in open mount aft.

"ASHEVILLE" Class   7/1976, Dr. Giorgio Arr

"ASHEVILLE" Class (with missiles)   6/1973, USN

Missiles: *Benicia* (PG 96) was experimentally fitted with a single launcher aft for the Standard interim anti-ship missile in 1971; removed prior to transfer to South Korea later that year.

1 "HIGH POINT" CLASS: PATROL CRAFT (HYDROFOIL) (PCH)

Name	No.	Builders	In Service	F/S
HIGH POINT	PCH 1	Boeing Co, Seattle	15 Aug 1963	PSA

Displacement, tons: 110 full load
Dimensions, feet (metres): 115 *(35)* × 31 *(9·4)* × 6 *(1·8)* (foils retracted) or 17 *(5·2)* (foils extended)
Guns: removed
A/S weapons: removed
Main engines: Foil borne; 2 gas turbines (Bristol Siddeley Marine Proteus); 6 200 shp;
   2 paired counter-rotating propellers = 48 knots
   Hull borne; diesel (Packard); 600 bhp; retractable outdrive with 1 propeller = 12 knots
Complement: 13 (1 officer, 12 enlisted men)

Experimental craft authorised under the Fiscal Year 1960 programme. Built at Martinac Boatyard, Tacoma. Laid down 27 February 1961, launched 17 August 1962. During March 1975 *High Point* was evaluated by the Coast Guard. *High Point* was due to be deleted on 30 September 1978. However Congress provided additional funds in the FY 1979 budget despite there being no request from the Defense Department.

Design: *High Point's* forward foil is supported by a single strut and the after foil by twin struts. Twin underwater nacelles at the junction of the vertical struts and main foil housed contra-rotating, super-cavitating propellers for foil-borne propulsion. After foils modified in 1973 and nacelles repositioned to improve performance in heavy sea states. Also, forward foil strut made steerable to improve manoeuvrability.

Gunnery: A single 40 mm gun was mounted forward in 1968; subsequently removed.

Missiles: During 1973-74 *High Point* was employed as a test ship for the lightweight canister launchers for the Harpoon surface-to-surface missile intended for the PHM.

HIGH POINT   1975, USCG

1 "OSPREY" CLASS: FAST PATROL CRAFT (PTF)

PTF 25

Displacement, tons: 105 full load
Dimensions, feet (metres): 94·7 × 23·2 × 7 *(28·8 × 7·1 × 2·1)*
Guns: removed
Main engines: Gas turbines; 2 shafts
Complement: approx 20

Built by Sewart Seacraft Division of Teledyne Inc of Berwick, Louisiana. Completed in 1968. Aluminium hull. Commercial name is "Osprey".
PTF 25 fitted with gas turbines on an experimental basis in early 1978. Used solely for experimental purposes.

"OSPREY" Class   1976, Dr. Giorgio Arra

COASTAL PATROL AND INTERDICTION CRAFT (CPIC)

The US Navy's prototype CPIC was transferred to South Korea on 1 August 1975. No additional craft of this type is planned for the US Navy.

15 PATROL BOATS Mk I (2) and III (13) Series (PB)

Displacement, tons:
 Mk I: 26·9 light; 36·3 full load
 Mk III: 31·5 light; 41·25 full load
Dimensions, feet (metres):
 Mk I: 65 × 16 × 4·9 (19·8 × 4·9 × 1·5)
 Mk III: 65 × 18 × 5·9 (19·8 × 5·5 × 1·8)
Guns: 6—20 mm or ·50 cal MG (1 twin, 4 single)
Main engines: Diesel (Detroit); 1 635 bhp; 3 shafts = 26 knots

The PB series is being developed as replacements for the "Swift" type inshore patrol craft (PCF). Mk I built by Sewart Seacraft, Berwick, Louisiana; Mk III by Peterson Builders Sturgeon Bay, Wisconsin. Two Mark I prototypes completed in 1972 and delivered to the Navy in 1973 for evaluation; assigned to Naval Reserve Force. Procurement of the PB Mk III for the US Navy is under consideration. (The PB Mark II design was not built).
The Mk III design has the pilot house offset to starboard to provide space on port side for installation of additional weapons.

PB Mk III 9/1976, Dr. Giorgio Arra

5 INSHORE PATROL CRAFT Mk I and II Series (PCF)

Displacement, tons: 22·5 full load
Dimensions, feet (metres): 50·1 × 13 × 3·5 (15·3 × 4·0 × 1·1)
Guns: 1—81 mm mortar, 3—·50 cal MG (twin MG mount atop pilot house and single MG mounted over mortar)
Main engines: 2 geared diesels (General Motors); 960 shp; 2 shafts = 28 knots
Complement: 6 (1 officer, 5 enlisted men)

The PCF design is adapted from the all-metal crew boat which is used to support off-shore drilling rigs in the Gulf of Mexico. Approximately 125 built since 1965.
Designation changed from Fast Patrol Craft (PCF) to Inshore Patrol Craft (PCF) on 14 August 1968.
Transfers: PCF 33, 34, and 83-86 transferred to the Philippines in 1966. Additional PCFs of this type constructed specifically for transfer to Thailand, the Philippines, and South Korea; not assigned US hull numbers in the PCF series; 104 PCFs formerly manned by US Navy personnel transferred to South Viet-Nam in 1968-1970.

PCF Mk I Type 1969, USN

38 RIVER PATROL BOATS Mk I and II Series (PBR)

Displacement, tons: 8
Dimensions, feet (metres): 32 × 11 × 2·6 (9·8 × 3·4 × 0·8)
Guns: 3—·50 cal MG (twin mount fwd; single aft); 1—40 mm grenade launcher; 1—60 mm mortar in some boats
Main engines: 2 geared diesels (General Motors); water jets = 25+ knots
Complement: 4 or 5 (enlisted men)

Fibreglass hull river patrol boats. Approximately 500 built 1967-73; most transferred to South Viet-Nam.

PBR Mk II Type USN

2 COMMAND AND CONTROL BOATS (CCB)

Displacement, tons: 80 full load
Dimensions, feet (metres): 61 × 17·5 × 3·4 (18·6 × 5·3 × 1·0)
Guns: 3—20 mm; 2—·30 cal MG; 2—40 mm high velocity-grenade launchers
Main engines: 2 diesels (Detroit); 2 shafts = 8·5 knots max (6 knots sustained)
Complement: 11

This craft serves as afloat command post providing command and communications facilities for ground force and boat group commanders. Heavily armoured. Armament changed to above configuration in 1968. Converted from LCM-6 landing craft. Both are in poor condition and due for deletion in FY 1979.

Note: All other small craft, ie Assault Support Patrol Boats (ASPB), "Mini" Armoured Troop Carriers (ATC) and Swimmer Support Craft were disposed of 1976-77.

COMMAND AND CONTROL BOAT USN

AMPHIBIOUS WARFARE FORCES

The relatively large and modern US amphibious warfare force is being improved with deliveries now under way of the five large, "Tarawa" class amphibious assault ships (LHA). These ships are the size (and configuration) of aircraft carriers, and each can embark a reinforced Marine battalion complete with equipment, trucks, landing craft, and helicopters.

The current force of 65 large amphibious ships can simultaneously lift the assault elements of slightly more than one Marine Amphibious Force (MAF) even when one includes a ship non-availability factor of 15 per cent for overhauls. An MAF is a division/aircraft wing team and their supporting elements with a total of approximately 45 000 troops.

Upon completion of all five "Tarawa" class assault ships, the amphibious lift will be sufficient for one and one-third division/wing teams(excluding ships in overhaul). When the last LHA is delivered, the amphibious force will have 66 active ships and three Naval Reserve Force (NRF) ships. All are capable of 20 knot or higher sustained speeds and have helicopter facilities.

Although the MAF lift capability is used as measurement criteria for US Navy amphibious ships by defence officials, a more realistic consideration is the number of reinforced battalions which can be maintained afloat in forward areas, primarily the Mediterranean and the Western Pacific. The US Navy is now able to keep two reinforced battalions continuously afloat in "WesPac" and one in the "Med", albeit one of the former without helicopters because of a shortage of LPH/LHA-type ships. In addition, a reinforced battalion is intermittently deployed in the Atlantic, generally without helicopters. The availability of the five "Tarawa" class LHAs will alleviate the lack of helicopter ships in the deployed forces. NRF assignments are listed at end of section.

"LSD 41" Class: The Navy planned to begin replacement of the "Thomaston" class dock landing ships (LSD) in the mid-1980s as they reach the end of their 30 year service life. First ship was scheduled for construction under the Fiscal Year 1980 programme; at least six ships were being planned but this was cut to two by the Secretary of Defense who considered the technology being used was outmoded and all were finally deleted as the project was shelved indefinitely.

V/STOL operations: *Guam* (LPH 9) operated as an interim sea control ship from 1972 to 1974, during which period she operated AV-8A Harrier V/STOL (Vertical/Short Take-Off and Landing) aircraft in the light attack and intercept role, and SH-3 Sea King helicopters in the anti-submarine role. See 1974-75 edition for additional data.

Guam has continued to carry 12 Marine-flown Harriers upon return to the LPH role. Increasing V/STOL aircraft operations from the LPH/LHA ships have been undertaken.

Minesweeping Operations: Several LPHs were used to operate RH-53D Sea Stallion helicopters in the mine countermeasures role during the 1973 sweeping of North Vietnamese ports and the 1974 sweeping of the Suez Canal.

Transport submarines: The transport submarine *Grayback* (SS 574, ex-*LPSS 574*) is in active commission and is listed in the Submarine section of this edition.

2 "BLUE RIDGE" CLASS: AMPHIBIOUS COMMAND SHIPS (LCC)

Name	No.	Builders	Laid down	Launched	Commissioned	F/S
BLUE RIDGE	LCC 19	Philadelphia Naval Shipyard	27 Feb 1967	4 Jan 1969	14 Nov 1970	PA
MOUNT WHITNEY	LCC 20	Newport News Shipbuilding & Dry Dock Co.	8 Jan 1969	8 Jan 1970	16 Jan 1971	AA

Displacement, tons: 17 100 full load
Length, feet (metres): 620 *(188·5)*
Beam, feet (metres): 82 *(25·3)*
Main deck width, feet (metres): 108 *(32·9)*
Draught, feet (metres): 25·5 *(7·8)*
Aircraft: Utility helicopter can be carried
Missiles: 2 Basic Point Defence Missile System (BPDMS) launchers for Sea Sparrow missile (Mk 25)
Guns: 4—3 in *(76 mm)*/50 (twin Mk 33)
Main engine: 1 geared turbine (General Electric); 22 000 shp; 1 shaft
Boilers: 2 (Foster-Wheeler)
Speed, knots: 23
Range, miles: 13 000 at 16 knots
Complement: 720 (40 officers, 680 enlisted men)
Flag accommodations: 700 (200 officers, 500 enlisted men)

These are large amphibious force command ships of post-World War II design. They can provide integrated command and control facilities for sea, air and land commanders in amphibious operations. *Blue Ridge* was authorised in the Fiscal Year 1965 new construction programme, *Mount Whitney* in FY 1966. One more was planned but cancelled late in 1969. It was proposed that the last ship combine fleet as well as amphibious force command-control facilities. The phasing out of the converted "Cleveland" class (CG) fleet flagships has fostered discussion of the potential use of these ships in that role. Their capabilities are greater than would be required by a fleet commander while they are considered too slow for striking fleet operations.

Blue Ridge will replace *Oklahoma City* as Seventh Fleet flagship in FY 1980.

Classification: Originally designated Amphibious Force Flagships (AGC); redesignated Amphibious Command Ships (LCC) on 1 January 1969.

Design: General hull design and machinery arrangement are similar to the "Iwo Jima" class assault ships.

Electronics: Tactical Aircraft Navigation (Tacan).
These ships have three computer systems to support their Naval Tactical Data System (NTDS), Amphibious Command Information System (ACIS), and Naval Intelligence Processing System (NIPS).

Fire control: Each ship has two Mk 56 gunfire control systems, two Mk 115 missile fire control systems and one Mk 1 target designation system. SPG 35 radar also carried.

Gunnery: At one stage of design two additional twin 3 in mounts were provided on forecastle; subsequently deleted from final designs. Antennae and their supports severely restrict firing arcs of guns. Two 20 mm Mk 15 CIWS to be fitted. Two 40 mm saluting guns carried.

Missiles: Two BPDMS launchers installed on each ship during 1974 (on antenna deck, aft of superstructure).

Personnel: The ships' complements includes one Marine officer and 12 enlisted men to maintain communications equipment for use by Marine Corps command and staff.

Radar: 3D search: SPS 48.
Search: SPS 10 and 40.

Rockets: One Mk 36 Chaffroc (RBOC) launcher to be fitted.

MOUNT WHITNEY 10/1978, Michael D. J. Lennon

BLUE RIDGE 1/1977, Dr. Giorgio Arra

MOUNT WHITNEY 10/1978, Michael D. J. Lennon

USA / Amphibious warfare forces 713

3 + 2 "TARAWA" CLASS: AMPHIBIOUS ASSAULT SHIPS G.P. (LHA)

Name	No.	Builders	Erection of First Module	Launched	Commissioned	F/S
TARAWA	LHA 1	Ingalls Shipbuilding Corporation	15 Nov 1971	1 Dec 1973	29 May 1976	PA
SAIPAN	LHA 2	Ingalls Shipbuilding Corporation	21 July 1972	18 July 1974	15 Oct 1977	AA
BELLEAU WOOD	LHA 3	Ingalls Shipbuilding Corporation	5 Mar 1973	11 Apr 1977	23 Sep 1978	PA
NASSAU	LHA 4	Ingalls Shipbuilding Corporation	13 Aug 1973	21 Jan 1978	late 1979	Bldg
PELILEU (ex-Da Nang)	LHA 5	Ingalls Shipbuilding Corporation	12 Nov 1976	25 Nov 1978	mid-1980	Bldg

Displacement, tons: 39 300 full load
Length, feet (metres): 820 *(250)*
Beam, feet (metres): 106 *(32·3)*; 118·1 *(36)* (flight deck)
Draught, feet (metres): 26 *(7·9)*
Aircraft: See *Aircraft* note for helicopters. Harrier AV-8A V/STOL aircraft in place of some helicopters as required
Missiles: 2 Basic Point Defence Missile Systems (BPDMS) launchers firing Sea Sparrow missiles (Mk 25)
Guns: 3—5 in *(127 mm)*/54 (single Mk 45)
 6—20 mm (Mk 67) (single)
Main engines: 2 geared turbines (Westinghouse); 140 000 shp; 2 shafts
Boilers: 2 (Combustion Engineering)
Speed, knots: 24
Range, miles: 10 000 at 20 knots
Complement: 902 (90 officers, 812 enlisted men)
Troops: 1 903 (172 officers, 1 731 enlisted men)

LHA 1 was authorised in the Fiscal Year 1969 new construction programme, the LHA 2 and LHA 3 in FY 1970 and LHA 4 and LHA 5 in FY 1971. The Navy announced on 20 January 1971 that four additional ships of this type previously planned would not be constructed. All ships of this class are under construction at a new ship production facility known as "Ingalls West". The new yard was developed specifically for multi-ship construction of the same design.
A sixth LHA was initially included in the FY 1979 programme at the behest of Senator Gary Hart. She was to have been the replacement for an LPH (next page) but was deleted from the finally approved FY 1980 budget. LHA 5 renamed 15 February 1978.

Aircraft: The flight deck can operate a maximum of 9 CH-53 Sea Stallion or 12 CH-46 Sea Knight helicopters; the hangar deck can accommodate 19 CH-53 Sea Stallion or 30 CH-46 Sea Knight helicopters. A mix of these and other helicopters and at times AV-8A Harriers could be embarked.

Contract: These ships were procured by the US Navy with the acquisition processes known as Concept Formulation, Contract Definition, and Total Package Procurement. The proposals of Litton Systems Inc, and two other shipbuilding firms were submitted in response to specific performance criteria. The firms submitted detailed designs and cost estimates for series production of not less than five ships of this type. This procurement process has subsequently been abandoned.

Design: Beneath the full-length flight deck are two half-length hangar decks, the two being connected by an elevator amidships on the port side and a stern lift; beneath the after elevator is a floodable docking well measuring 268 ft in length and 78 ft in width which is capable of accommodating four LCU 1610 type landing craft. Also included is a large garage for trucks and AFVs and troop berthing for a reinforced battalion.

TARAWA 7/1976, USN

Storage for 10 000 gallons (US) of vehicle petrol and 400 000 gallons (US) of JP-5 helicopter petrol.

Electronics: Helicopter navigation equipment provided. Each ship also will have an Integrated Tactical Amphibious Warfare Data System (ITAWDS) to provide computerised support in control of helicopters and aircraft, shipboard weapons and sensors, navigation, landing craft control, and electronic warfare.

Engineering: A 900 hp fixed bow thruster is provided for holding position while unloading landing craft.

Fire control: One Mk 86 gunfire control system and two Mk 15 Missile fire control systems; also one SPG 60 and one SPG 9A weapon control radars.

Fiscal: In early 1974 the estimated total cost to the government of the five LHAs was $1 145 million or an average of $229 million per ship. A cancellation fee of $109·7 million was due to the shipyard for cancellation of LHA 6-9.

Gunnery: To be fitted with two 20 mm Mk 15 CIWS. Two 40 mm saluting guns fitted.

Medical: These ships are fitted with extensive medical facilities including operating rooms, X-ray room, hospital ward, isolation ward, laboratories, pharmacy, dental operating room and medical store rooms.

Radar: 3D search: SPS 52.
Search: SPS 10 and 40.
Air/navigation: SPN 35.

Rockets: One Mk 36 Chaffroc (RBOC) to be fitted.

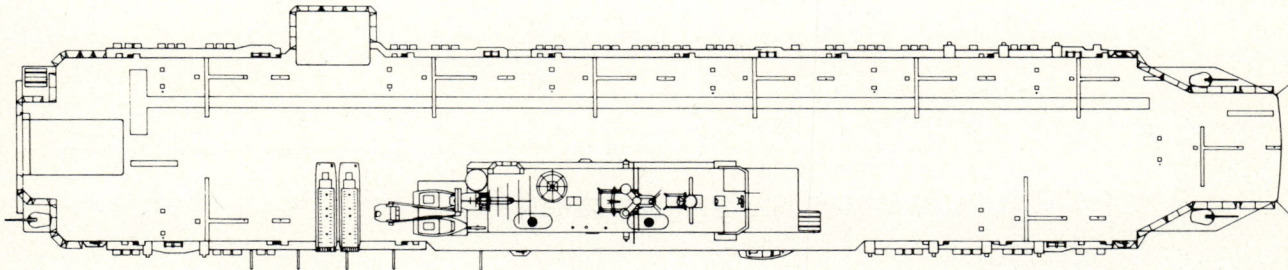

"TARAWA" Class Drawing, A. D. Baker III

BELLEAU WOOD 6/1978, Litton Industries

7 "IWO JIMA" CLASS: AMPHIBIOUS ASSAULT SHIPS (LPH)

Name	No.	Builders	Laid down	Launched	Commissioned	F/S
IWO JIMA	LPH 2	Puget Sound Naval Shipyard	2 Apr 1959	17 Sep 1960	26 Aug 1961	AA
OKINAWA	LPH 3	Philadelphia Naval Shipyard	1 Apr 1960	14 Aug 1961	14 Apr 1962	PA
GUADALCANAL	LPH 7	Philadelphia Naval Shipyard	1 Sep 1961	16 Mar 1963	20 July 1963	AA
GUAM	LPH 9	Philadelphia Naval Shipyard	15 Nov 1962	22 Aug 1964	16 Jan 1965	AA
TRIPOLI	LPH 10	Ingalls Shipbuilding Corp	15 June 1964	31 July 1965	6 Aug 1966	PA
NEW ORLEANS	LPH 11	Philadelphia Naval Shipyard	1 Mar 1966	3 Feb 1968	16 Nov 1968	PA
INCHON	LPH 12	Ingalls Shipbuilding Corp	8 Apr 1968	24 May 1969	20 June 1970	AA

Displacement, tons: 17 000 light; 18 000 (2, 3 and 7), 18 300 (9 and 10), 17 706 (11), 17 515 (12) full load
Length, feet (metres): 602·3 *(183·0)*
Beam, feet (metres): 84 *(25·6)*
Draught, feet (metres): 26 *(7·9)*
Flight deck width, feet (metres): 104 *(31·7)* maximum
Aircraft: For helicopters see *Aircraft* note
4 AV-8A Harriers in place of some troop helicopters
Missiles: 2 Basic Point Defence Missile System (BPDMS) launchers firing Sea Sparrow missiles (Mk 25)
Guns: 4—3 in *(76 mm)*/50 (twin Mk 33)
Main engines: 1 geared turbine (De Laval in *Tripoli*, GE in *Inchon*, Westinghouse in others); 22 000 shp; 1 shaft
Boilers: 2 (Combustion Engineering; Babcock & Wilcox in *Guam*)
Speed, knots: 23
Complement: 609 (47 officers, 562 enlisted men)
Troops: 1 731 (143 officers, 1 588 enlisted men)

Iwo Jima was the world's first ship designed and constructed specifically to operate helicopters. Each LPH can carry a Marine battalion landing team, its guns, vehicles, and equipment, plus a reinforced squadron of transport helicopters and various support personnel.
Iwo Jima was authorised in the Fiscal Year 1958 new construction programme, *Okinawa* in the FY 1959, *Guadalcanal* in the FY 1960, *Guam* in the FY 1962, *Tripoli* in the FY 1963, *New Orleans* in the FY 1965, and *Inchon* in the FY 1966.
Estimated cost of *Iwo Jima* was $40 million.
Guam was modified late in 1971 and began operations in January 1972 as an interim sea control ship. She operated Harrier AV-8 V/STOL aircraft and SH-3 Sea King A/S helicopters in convoy escort exercises; she reverted to the amphibious role in 1974 but kept 12 AV-8As on board. Several of these ships operated RH-53 minesweeping helicopters to clear North Vietnamese ports in 1973 and the Suez Canal in 1974.
The conversion of one of this class into a V/STOL carrier was put into the FY 1979 building programme at the behest of Senator Gary Hart. The cost would have been $45 million and a sixth "Tarawa" class was requested as a replacement. The whole of this plan was dropped from the final programme.

Aircraft: The flight decks of these ships provide for simultaneous take off or landing of seven CH-46 Sea Knight or four CH-53 Sea Stallion helicopters during normal operations. The hangar decks can accommodate 19 CH-46 Sea Knight or 11 CH-53 Sea Stallion helicopters, or various combinations of helicopters.

Design: Each ship has two deck-edge lifts, one to port opposite the bridge and one to starboard aft of island. Full hangars are provided; no arresting wires or catapults. Two small elevators carry cargo from holds to flight deck. Storage provided for 6 500 gallons (US) of vehicle petrol and 405 000 gallons (US) of JP-5 helicopter petrol.

Electronics: Tacan; advanced electronic warfare equipment fitted.

Fire control: As rearmed with BPDMS these ships have two Mk 115 missile fire control systems.

Gunnery: As built, each ship had eight 3 in guns in twin mounts, two forward of the island structure and two at stern. Gun battery reduced by half with substitution of BPDMS launchers (see *Missiles* note). Two 20 mm Mk 15 CIWS to be fitted. Two 40 mm saluting guns fitted.

Medical: These ships are fitted with extensive medical facilities including operating room, X-ray room, hospital ward, isolation ward, laboratory, pharmacy, dental operating room, and medical store rooms.

Missiles. One Sea Sparrow launcher forward of island structure and one on the port quarter. *Okinawa* had one BPDMS launcher fitted in 1970 and the second in 1973; *Tripoli* and *Inchon* rearmed in 1972, *Iwo Jima* and *New Orleans* in 1973, *Guam* and *Guadalcanal* in 1974.

Radar: Search: SPS 10 and 40.
Navigation: SPN 10.

Rockets: One Mk 36 Chaffroc (RBOC) to be fitted.

OKINAWA   *12/1978, Lawrence Phillips*

GUADALCANAL   *10/1978, Michael D. J. Lennon*

TRIPOLI   *1/1978, Dr. Giorgio Arra*

12 "AUSTIN" CLASS: AMPHIBIOUS TRANSPORT DOCKS (LPD)

Name	No.	Builders	Commissioned	F/S
AUSTIN	LPD 4	New York Naval Shipyard	6 Feb 1965	AA
OGDEN	LPD 5	New York Naval Shipyard	19 June 1965	PA
DULUTH	LPD 6	New York Naval Shipyard	18 Dec 1965	PA
CLEVELAND	LPD 7	Ingalls Shipbuilding Corp	21 Apr 1967	PA
DUBUQUE	LPD 8	Ingalls Shipbuilding Corp	1 Sep 1967	PA
DENVER	LPD 9	Lockheed S.B. & Construction Co	26 Oct 1968	PA
JUNEAU	LPD 10	Lockheed S.B. & Construction Co	12 July 1969	PA
CORONADO	LPD 11	Lockheed S.B. & Construction Co	23 May 1970	AA
SHREVEPORT	LPD 12	Lockheed S.B. & Construction Co	12 Dec 1970	AA
NASHVILLE	LPD 13	Lockheed S.B. & Construction Co	14 Feb 1970	AA
TRENTON	LPD 14	Lockheed S.B. & Construction Co	6 Mar 1971	AA
PONCE	LPD 15	Lockheed S.B. & Construction Co	10 July 1971	AA

Displacement, tons: 10 000 light;
   13 900 (4-6), 16 550 (7-10), 16 900 (11-13), 17 000 (14 and 15) full load
Length, feet (metres): 570 *(173·3)*
Beam, feet (metres): 100 *(30·5)*
Draught, feet (metres): 23 *(7·0)*
Aircraft: up to 6 UH-34 or CH-46 helicopters
Guns: 2—3 in *(76 mm)*/50 (twin Mk 33) (8—3 in (4 twin) in LPD 10 and 15)
Main engines: 2 steam turbines (De Laval); 24 000 shp; 2 shafts
Boilers: 2 Foster-Wheeler (Babcock & Wilcox in LPD 5 and 12)
Speed, knots: 21
Complement: 473 (27 officers, 446 enlisted men)
Troops: 930 in LPD 4-6 and LPD 14-15; 840 in LPD 7-13
Flag accommodations: Approx 90 in LPD 7-13

These ships are enlarged versions of the earlier "Raleigh" class; most notes for the "Raleigh" class apply to these ships.
The dates of laying down and launching are: *Austin* and *Ogden* 4 February 1963 and 27 June 1964; *Duluth* 18 December 1963 and 14 August 1965; *Cleveland* 30 November 1964 and 7 May 1966; *Dubuque* 25 January 1965 and 6 August 1966; *Denver* 7 February 1964 and 23 January 1965; *Juneau* 23 January 1965 and 12 February 1966; *Coronado* 3 May 1965 and 30 July 1966; *Shreveport* 27 December 1965 and 25 October 1966; *Nashville* 14 March 1966 and 7 October 1967; *Trenton* 8 August 1966 and 3 August 1968; *Ponce* 31 October 1966 and 20 May 1970. *Duluth* completed at Philadelphia Naval Shipyard.
LPD 4-6 were authorised in the Fiscal Year 1962 new construction programme, LPD 7-10 in FY 1963, LPD 11-13 in FY 1964, LPD 14 and LPD 15 in FY 1965, and LPD 16 in FY 1966. LPD 16 was deferred in favour of LHA programme; officially cancelled in February 1969.

Fire control: One Mk 56 GFCS, two Mk 63 GFCS with two SPG 50 and one SPG 35 radars. One Mk 1 target designation system. (None of the foregoing in LPD 6, 7 and 9).

Gunnery: Two 20 mm Mk 15 CIWS to be fitted.

Rockets: Each ship will be fitted with Mk 36 Chaffroc. Mk 28 already fitted in *Coronado* and *Nashville*.

SHREVEPORT 10/1978, Michael D. J. Lennon

DULUTH 1/1978, Dr. Giorgio Arra

CLEVELAND 2/1978, Dr. Giorgio Arra

2 "RALEIGH" CLASS: AMPHIBIOUS TRANSPORT DOCKS (LPD)

Name	No.	Builders	Commissioned	F/S
RALEIGH	LPD 1	New York Naval Shipyard	8 Sep 1962	AA
VANCOUVER	LPD 2	New York Naval Shipyard	11 May 1963	PA

Displacement, tons: 8 040 light; 13 600 full load
Length, feet (metres): 521·8 *(158·4)*
Beam, feet (metres): 100 *(30·5)*
Draught, feet (metres): 22 *(6·7)*
Aircraft: up to 6 UH-34 or CH-46 helicopters
Guns: 8—3 in *(76 mm)*/50 (twin Mk 33)
Main engines: 2 steam turbines; (De Laval); 24 000 shp; 2 shafts
Boilers: 2 (Babcock & Wilcox)
Speed, knots: 21
Complement: 490 (30 officers, 460 enlisted men)
Troops: 1 139 (143 officers, 996 enlisted men)

The amphibious transport dock was developed from the dock landing ship (LSD) concept but provides more versatility. The LPD replaces the amphibious transport (LPA) and, in part, the amphibious cargo ship (LKA) and dock landing ship. The LPD can carry a "balanced load" of assault troops and their equipment, has a docking well for landing craft, a helicopter deck, cargo holds and vehicle garages. *Raleigh* was authorised in the Fiscal Year 1959 new construction programme, *Vancouver* in the FY 1960. *Raleigh* was laid down on 23 June 1960 and launched on 17 March 1962; *Vancouver* on 19 November 1960 and 15 September 1962. Approximate construction cost was $29 million per ship.
A third ship of this class, *La Salle* (LPD 3), was reclassified as a miscellaneous command ship (AGF 3) on 1 July 1972.

Design: These ships resemble dock landing ships (LSD) but have fully enclosed docking well with the roof forming a permanent helicopter platform. The docking well is 168 ft long and 50 ft wide *(51·2 × 15·2)*, less than half the length of wells in newer LSDs; the LPD design provides more space for vehicles, cargo and troops. Ramps allow vehicles to be driven between helicopter deck, parking area and docking well, side ports provide roll-on/roll-off capability when docks are available. An overhead monorail in the docking well with six cranes facilitates loading landing craft. The docking well in these ships can hold one LCU and three LCM-6s or four LCM-8s or 20 LVTs (amphibious tractors). In addition, two LCM-6s or four LCPLs are carried on the boat deck which are lowered by crane.

Gunnery: Two 20 mm Mk 15 CIWS to be fitted.

Helicopters: These ships are not normally assigned helicopters because they lack integral hangars and maintenance facilities. It is intended that a nearby amphibious assault ship (LHA or LPH) would provide helicopters during an amphibious operation. Telescoping hangars have been fitted.

Rockets: Mk 36 Chaffroc system to be fitted.

RALEIGH 1/1976, USN

VANCOUVER 12/1978, Lawrence Phillips

716   USA / Amphibious warfare forces

"LSD 41" CLASS DOCK LANDING SHIPS (LSD): PROPOSED

Displacement, tons: 10 976 light; 15 774 full load
Dimensions, feet (metres): 608 × 84 × 19·7 (185·3 × 25·6 × 6·0)
Guns: 2—20 mm Mk 15 CIWS
Main engines: Not available; about 36 000 shp; 2 shafts = 23 knots
Complement: 423 (22 officers, 401 enlisted men)
Troops: 338 (25 officers, 313 enlisted men)

Originally six of this class were to be constructed as replacements for the "Thomaston" class. However, upon examination of the design by Secretary of Defense Harold Brown, construction was cut back to two units as it was considered the technology used in the design was outmoded. The lead ship was originally to be requested in the Fiscal Year 1981 programme and the second unit under the FY 1983 programme. However, the LSD 41 class was not included "in this year's program and will not until we assess the changes in future amphibious lift requirements . . . . ." Cost per ship about $300 million.

Design: Based on the previous "Anchorage" class which was designed over ten years ago. Well deck measures 440 ft × 50 ft. The ship will be able to handle the CH-53E helicopter and/or the AV-8A Harrier V/STOL aircraft as well as air cushion landing craft vehicles.

Electronics: Will be fitted with the SPS 55 and SPS 65V radars as well as the SLQ 32V electronic countermeasures systems.

Engineering: The type of propulsion plant to be used in the design is still open to question. Originally it was intended to fit diesel propulsion.

Rockets: To be fitted with Mk 36 Chaffroc (RBOC) system.

"LSD 41" Class   USN drawing

5 "ANCHORAGE" CLASS: DOCK LANDING SHIPS (LSD)

Name	No.	Builders	Commissioned		F/S
ANCHORAGE	LSD 36	Ingalls Shipbuilding Corp	15 Mar	1969	PA
PORTLAND	LSD 37	General Dynamics, Quincy, Mass	3 Oct	1970	AA
PENSACOLA	LSD 38	General Dynamics, Quincy, Mass	27 Mar	1971	AA
MOUNT VERNON	LSD 39	General Dynamics, Quincy, Mass	13 May	1972	PA
FORT FISHER	LSD 40	General Dynamics, Quincy, Mass	9 Dec	1972	PA

Displacement, tons: 8 600 light; 13 600 full load
Dimensions, feet (metres): 553·3 × 84 × 20 (168·6 × 25·6 × 6)
Guns: 6—3 in (76 mm)/50 (twin Mk 33) (8 (twins) in LSD 38)
Main engines: Steam turbines (De Laval); 24 000 shp; 2 shafts = 20 knots sustained, 22 max
Boilers: 2 (Foster-Wheeler except Combustion Engineering in *Anchorage*)
Complement: 397 (21 officers, 376 enlisted men)
Troops: 376 (28 officers, 348 enlisted men)

These ships are similar in appearance to earlier classes but with a tripod mast. Helicopter platform aft with docking well partially open; helicopter platform can be removed. Docking well approximately 430 × 50 ft (131·1 × 15·2 m) can accommodate three LCU-type landing craft. Space on deck for one LCM, and davits for one LCPL and one LCVP. Two 50 ton capacity cranes. LSD 36 was authorised in the Fiscal Year 1965 shipbuilding programme; LSD 37-39 in the FY 1966 programme; LSD 40 in the FY 1967 programme.
Anchorage was laid down on 13 March 1967 and launched in 5 May 1968; *Portland* on 21 September 1967 and 20 December 1969; *Pensacola* on 12 March 1969 and 11 July 1970; *Mount Vernon* on 29 January 1970 and 17 April 1971; and *Fort Fisher* on 15 July 1970 and 22 April 1972. Estimated minimum construction cost is $11·5 million per ship.

Gunnery: Two 20 mm Mk 15 CIWS to be fitted.

Rockets: One Mk 36 Chaffroc (RBOC) to be fitted.

MOUNT VERNON   1/1978, Dr. Giorgio Arra

PORTLAND   10/1978, J. L. M. van der Burg

8 "THOMASTON" CLASS: DOCK LANDING SHIPS (LSD)

Name	No.	Builders	Commissioned		F/S
THOMASTON	LSD 28	Ingalls Shipbuilding Corp	17 Sep	1954	PA
PLYMOUTH ROCK	LSD 29	Ingalls Shipbuilding Corp	29 Nov	1954	AA
FORT SNELLING	LSD 30	Ingalls Shipbuilding Corp	24 Jan	1955	AA
POINT DEFIANCE	LSD 31	Ingalls Shipbuilding Corp	31 Mar	1955	PA
SPIEGEL GROVE	LSD 32	Ingalls Shipbuilding Corp	8 June	1956	AA
ALAMO	LSD 33	Ingalls Shipbuilding Corp	24 Aug	1956	PA
HERMITAGE	LSD 34	Ingalls Shipbuilding Corp	14 Dec	1956	AA
MONTICELLO	LSD 35	Ingalls Shipbuilding Corp	29 Mar	1957	PA

Displacement, tons: 6 880 light; 12 000 full load
Dimensions, feet (metres): 510 × 84 × 19 (155·5 × 25·6 × 5·8)
Guns: 6—3 in (76 mm)/50 (twin Mk 33) (8 (twins) in LSD 32)
Main engines: Steam turbines (General Electric); 24 000 shp; 2 shafts = 22·5 knots
Boilers: 2 (Babcock & Wilcox)
Range, miles: 10 000+ (cruising)
Complement: 400
Troops: 340

LSD 28-31 launched in 1954 on 9 February, 7 May, 16 July and 28 September respectively; LSD 32 launched on 10 November 1955; LSD 33-35 launched in 1956 on 20 January, 12 June and 10 August. Fitted with helicopter platform over docking well; two 5 ton capacity cranes; can carry 21 LCM-6 or 3 LCU and 6 LCM landing craft or approximately 50 LVTs (amphibious tractors) in docking well plus 30 LVTs on mezzanine and super decks (with helicopter landing area clear). Welldeck measures 391 × 48 ft.
Note pole mast compared to tripod mast of "Anchorage" class which have enclosed 3 in gun mounts forward of bridge.

Gunnery: As built, each ship had 16—3 in guns subsequently reduced to present fitting.

Rockets: One Mk 36 Chaffroc (RBOC) to be fitted.

PLYMOUTH ROCK   9/1978, Michael D. J. Lennon

MONTICELLO   12/1978, Lawrence Phillips

USA / Amphibious warfare forces 717

20 "NEWPORT" CLASS: TANK LANDING SHIPS (LST)

Name	No.	Laid down	Launched	Commissioned	F/S
NEWPORT	LST 1179	1 Nov 1966	3 Feb 1968	7 June 1969	AA
MANITOWOC	LST 1180	1 Feb 1967	4 June 1969	24 Jan 1970	AA
SUMTER	LST 1181	14 Nov 1967	13 Dec 1969	20 June 1970	AA
FRESNO	LST 1182	16 Dec 1967	28 Sep 1968	22 Nov 1969	PA
PEORIA	LST 1183	22 Feb 1968	23 Nov 1968	21 Feb 1970	PA
FREDERICK	LST 1184	13 Apr 1968	8 Mar 1969	11 Apr 1970	PA
SCHENECTADY	LST 1185	2 Aug 1968	24 May 1969	13 June 1970	PA
CAYUGA	LST 1186	28 Sep 1968	12 July 1969	8 Aug 1970	PA
TUSCALOOSA	LST 1187	23 Nov 1968	6 Sep 1969	24 Oct 1970	PA
SAGINAW	LST 1188	24 May 1969	7 Feb 1970	23 Jan 1971	AA
SAN BERNARDINO	LST 1189	12 July 1969	28 Mar 1970	27 Mar 1971	PA
BOULDER	LST 1190	6 Sep 1969	22 May 1970	4 June 1971	AA
RACINE	LST 1191	13 Dec 1969	15 Aug 1970	9 July 1971	PA
SPARTANBURG COUNTY	LST 1192	7 Feb 1970	11 Nov 1970	1 Sep 1971	AA
FAIRFAX COUNTY	LST 1193	28 Mar 1970	19 Dec 1970	16 Oct 1971	AA
LA MOURE COUNTY	LST 1194	22 May 1970	13 Feb 1971	18 Dec 1971	AA
BARBOUR COUNTY	LST 1195	15 Aug 1970	15 May 1971	12 Feb 1972	PA
HARLAN COUNTY	LST 1196	7 Nov 1970	24 July 1971	8 Apr 1972	AA
BARNSTABLE COUNTY	LST 1197	19 Dec 1970	2 Oct 1971	27 May 1972	AA
BRISTOL COUNTY	LST 1198	13 Feb 1971	4 Dec 1971	5 Aug 1972	PA

HARLAN COUNTY   10/1978, J. L. M. van der Burg

Displacement, tons: 8 450 full load
Dimensions, feet (metres): 522·3 hull oa × 69·5 × 17·5 (aft) (159·2 × 21·2 × 5·9)
Guns: 4—3 in (76 mm)/50 (twin Mk 33)
Main engines: 6 diesels (General Motors in 1179-1181, Alco in others); 16 000 bhp, 2 shafts; (cp propellers) = 20 knots
Range, miles: 2 500+ (cruising)
Complement: 196 (12 officers, 174 enlisted men)
Troops: 431 (20 officers, 411 enlisted men)

These ships are of an entirely new design, larger and faster than previous tank landing ships. They operate with 20 knot amphibious squadrons to transport tanks, other heavy vehicles, engineer equipment, and supplies which cannot be readily landed by helicopters or landing craft. These are the only recent construction amphibious ships with a pole mast instead of tripod-lattice mast.
Newport was authorised in the Fiscal Year 1965 new construction programme. LST 1180-1187 (eight ships) in FY 1966, and LST 1188-1198 (11 ships) in FY 1967. LST 1179-1181 built by Philadelphia Naval Shipyard, LST 1182-1198 built by National Steel & S.B. Co, San Diego, California. Seven additional ships of this type that were planned for the FY 1971 new construction programme were cancelled.

Design: These ships are the first LSTs to depart from the bow-door design developed by the British early in World War II. The hull form required to achieve 20 knots would not permit bow doors, thus these ships unload by a 112 ft ramp over their bow. The ramp is supported by twin derrick arms. A ramp just forward of the superstructure connects the lower tank deck with the main deck and a vehicle passage through the superstructure provides access to the parking area amidships. A stern gate to the tank deck permits unloading of amphibious tractors into the water, or unloading of other vehicles into an LCU or onto a pier. Vehicle stowage is rated at 500 tons and 19 000 square ft (5 000 square ft more than previous LSTs). Length over derrick arms is 562 ft; full load draught is 11·5 ft forward and 17·5 feet aft. Bow thruster fitted to hold position offshore while unloading amphibious tractors.

Fire control: One Mk 1 Target Designation System in LST 1179 and 1190.

Gunnery: Two 20 mm Mk 15 CIWS to be fitted.

Rockets: One Mk 36 Chaffroc RBOC to be fitted.

SUMTER   10/1978, Michael D. J. Lennon

PEORIA   10/1978, Dr. Giorgio Arra

3 "DE SOTO COUNTY" CLASS: TANK LANDING SHIPS (LST)

Name	No.	Builders	Commissioned	F/S
SUFFOLK COUNTY	LST 1173	Boston Navy Yard	15 Aug 1957	AR
LORAIN COUNTY	LST 1177	American S.B. Co, Lorain, Ohio	3 Oct 1959	MAR
WOOD COUNTY	LST 1178	American S.B. Co, Lorain, Ohio	5 Aug 1969	MAR

Displacement, tons: 4 164 light; 7 100 full load
Dimensions, feet (metres): 445 × 62 × 17·5 (138·7 × 18·9 × 5·3)
Guns: 6—3 in (76 mm)/50 (twin Mk 33)
Main engines: 6 diesels (Fairbanks-Morse in 1173, Cooper Bessemer in others); 13 700 bhp; 2 shafts; (cp propellers) = 16·5 knots
Complement: 188 (15 officers, 173 men)
Troops: 634 (30 officers, 604 enlisted men)

Originally a class of seven tank landing ships (LST 1171, 1173-1178 with LST 1172 not built). They were faster and had a greater troop capacity than earlier LSTs; considered the "ultimate" design attainable with the traditional LST bow-door configuration.
Suffolk County launched on 5 September 1956, *Lorain County* on 22 June 1957, and *Wood County* on 14 December 1957.
Suffolk County decommissioned 25 August 1972, *Lorain County* on 1 September 1972 and *Wood County* on 1 May 1972. All in reserve.

Conversion: *Wood County* was to have been converted to Patrol Combatant Support Ship (AGHS) under the original FY 1978 programme but this was deleted by the new administration.

Design: High degree of habitability with all crew and troop living spaces air conditioned. Can carry 23 medium tanks or vehicles up to 75 tons on 288 ft long (lower) tank deck. Davits for four LCVP-type landing craft. Liquid cargo capacity of 170 000 gallons (US) diesel or jet fuel plus 7 000 gallons (US) of petrol for embarked vehicles; some ships had reduced troop spaces to carry additional 250 000 gallons (US) of aviation petrol for pumping ashore or to other ships.

SUFFOLK COUNTY   1971, USN

718 USA / Amphibious warfare forces

5 "CHARLESTON" CLASS: AMPHIBIOUS CARGO SHIPS (LKA)

Name	No.	Builders	Commissioned	F/S
CHARLESTON	LKA 113	Newport News S.B. & D.D. Co	14 Dec 1968	AA
DURHAM	LKA 114	Newport News S.B. & D.D. Co	24 May 1969	PA
MOBILE	LKA 115	Newport News S.B. & D.D. Co	29 Sep 1969	PA
ST. LOUIS	LKA 116	Newport News S.B. & D.D. Co	22 Nov 1969	PA
EL PASO	LKA 117	Newport News S.B. & D.D. Co	17 Jan 1970	AA

Displacement, tons: 10 000 light; 18 600 full load
Dimensions, feet (metres): 575·5 × 62 × 25·5 (175·4 × 18·9 × 7·7)
Guns: 6—3 in (76 mm)/50 (twin Mk 33) (8 (4 twins) in LKA 115 and 116)
Main engines: 1 steam turbine (Westinghouse); 19 250 shp; 1 shaft = 20 knots
Boilers: 2 (Combustion Engineering)
Complement: 334 (24 officers, 310 enlisted men)
Troops: 226 (15 officers, 211 enlisted men)

Charleston laid down 5 December 1966, launched 2 December 1967; *Durham* laid down 10 July 1967, launched 29 March 1968; *Mobile* laid down 15 January 1968, launched 19 October 1968; *St. Louis* 3 April 1968 and 4 January 1969 and *El Paso* 22 October 1968 and 17 May 1969. These ships are designed specifically for the attack cargo ship role; can carry nine landing craft (LCM) and supplies for amphibious operations. Design includes two heavy-lift cranes with a 78·4 ton capacity, two 40 ton capacity booms, and eight 15 ton capacity booms; helicopter deck aft.
The LKA 113-116 were authorised in the Fiscal Year 1965 shipbuilding programme; LKA 117 in the FY 1966 programme.
Cost of building was approximately $21 million per ship.

Classification: Originally designated Attack Cargo Ship (AKA), *Charleston* redesignated Amphibious Cargo Ship (LKA) on 14 December 1968; others to LKA on 1 January 1969.

Engineering: These are among the first US Navy ships with a fully automated main propulsion plant; control of plant is from bridge or central machinery space console. This automation permitted a 45 man reduction in complement.

Fire control: One Mk 1 Target Designation System (LKA 116 only).

Gunnery: Two 20 mm Mk 16 CIWS to be fitted.

Rockets: One Mk 36 Chaffroc RBOC to be installed.

MOBILE   2/1978, Dr. Giorgio Arre

ST. LOUIS   1978, Michael D. J. Lennon

1 "TULARE" CLASS: AMPHIBIOUS CARGO SHIP (LKA)

Name	No.	Builders	Commissioned	F/S
TULARE (ex-*Evergreen Mariner*)	LKA 112	Bethlehem, San Francisco	13 Jan 1956	NRF

Displacement, tons: 9 050 light; 17 500 full load
Dimensions, feet (metres): 564 × 80 × 28 (171·9 × 24·4 × 8·5)
Guns: 6—3 in (76 mm)/50 (twin Mk 33)
Main engines: Steam turbine (De Laval); 22 000 shp; 1 shaft = 23 knots
Boilers: 2 (Combustion Engineering)
Complement: 393 (10 officers, 154 enlisted active duty; 21 officers, 208 enlisted reserve)
Troops: 319 (18 officers, 301 enlisted men)

Laid down on 16 February 1953; launched on 22 December 1953; acquired by Navy during construction; C4-S-1A type. Has helicopter landing platform and booms capable of lifting 60 ton landing craft. Carries 9 LCM-6 and 11 LCVP landing craft as deck cargo. Designation changed from AKA 112 to LKA 112 on 1 January 1969.
Tulare was assigned to the Naval Reserve Force on 1 July 1975 and is partially manned by reserve personnel. To be deleted in FY 1980.

Class: Thirty-five "Mariner" design C4-S-1A merchant ships built during the early 1950s; five acquired by Navy, three for conversion to amphibious ships (AKA-APA) and two for support of Polaris-Poseidon programme (designated AG). Acquisition of sixth ship cancelled.

TULARE   1969, USN

2 "PAUL REVERE" CLASS: AMPHIBIOUS TRANSPORTS (LPA)

Name	No.	Builders	Commissioned	F/S
PAUL REVERE (ex-*Diamond Mariner*)	LPA 248	New York S.B. Corp	3 Sep 1958	NRF
FRANCIS MARION (ex-*Prairie Mariner*)	LPA 249	New York S.B. Corp	6 July 1961	NRF

Displacement, tons: 10 709 light; 16 838 full load
Dimensions, feet (metres): 563·5 × 76 × 27 (171·8 × 23·2 × 8·2)
Guns: 8—3 in (76 mm)/50 (twin Mk 33)
Main engine: Steam turbine (General Electric); 22 000 shp; 1 shaft = 22 knots
Boilers: 2 (Foster-Wheeler)
Complement: 452 (13 officers, 187 enlisted active duty; 15 officers, 237 enlisted reserve)
Troops: 1 657 (96 officers, 1 561 enlisted men)

Paul Revere launched 13 February 1954, *Francis Marion* launched 11 April 1953. "Mariner" C4-S-1A merchant ships acquired for conversion to attack transports; *Paul Revere* converted by Todd Shipyard Corporation, San Pedro, California, under the Fiscal Year 1957 conversion programme; *Francis Marion* converted by Bethlehem Steel Corp, Key Highway Yard, Baltimore, Maryland, under the FY 1959 programme. Helicopter platform fitted aft; seven LCM-6 and 16 LCVP landing craft carried as deck cargo; each ship has four Mk 63 gunfire control systems. Fitted to serve as force flagships.
Designation of both ships changed from APA to LPA on 1 January 1969.
Assigned to the Naval Reserve Force are partially manned by reserve personnel.
Both to be deleted in FY 1980—one may be transferred to Spain as a replacement for *Aragon* (ex-USS *Noble*, APA 218).

Fire control: Four Mk 63 GFCS, one Mk 5 Target Designation System and four SPG 50 radars (LPA 249 only).

FRANCIS MARION   10/1978, Leo van Ginderen

USA / Landing craft   719

LANDING CRAFT

1 AMPHIBIOUS ASSAULT LANDING CRAFT (AALC)
AEROJET-GENERAL DESIGN (JEFF-A)

Weight, tons: 90 empty; 167 gross
Dimensions, feet (metres): 96·2 oa × 48 × (height) 23·2 *(29·3 × 14·6 × 7·1)*
Main engines: 4 gas turbines (Avco-Lycoming T40); 15 000 hp; 4 aircraft-type propellers in rotating shrouds for propulsive thrust = approx 50 knots cruising
Lift engines: 2 gas turbines (Avco-Lycoming T40); 7 500 hp; 8 horizontal fans (2 sets) for cushion lift
Range, miles: 200
Complement: 6

This is an Air Cushion Vehicle (ACV) landing craft being developed by the Aerojet-General Corporation and being built by Todd Shipyards, Seattle, Washington, under Navy contract. Construction completed in February 1975 with one year of contractor testing before delivery to Navy in February 1976. (Construction shifted from Tacoma Boatbuilding Co).
Above dimensions are for craft on air cushion; when at rest dimensions will be 97 × 44 × 19 ft. Designed to carry 120 000 lb payload at a design speed of 50 knots (same as Jeff-B). Design features include aluminium construction, bow and stern ramps, cargo deck area of 2 100 square ft; two sound-insulated compartments each hold four persons; three engines housed in each side structure; two propellers in rotating shrouds provide horizontal propulsion and steering. Performance parameters include four-hour endurance (200 n. mile range), 4 ft obstacle clearance, and capability to maintain cruise speed in Sea State 2 with 25 knot headwind.
Delivered 1976.

Project: Aerojet-General and Bell Aerosystems were awarded contracts in 1971 to design competitive assault landing craft employing ACV technology and to build and test one craft per company.

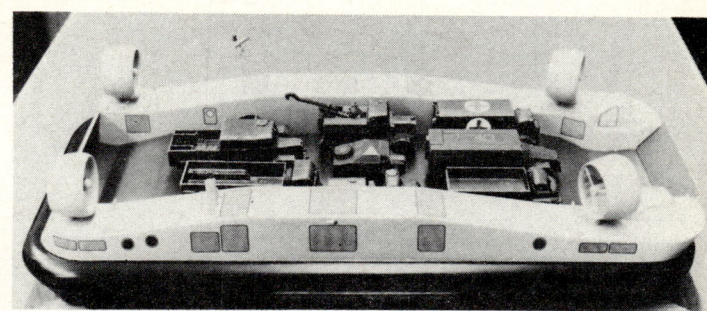
AEROJET-GENERAL DESIGN (Model)

These are air cushion or bubble craft, supported above the land or water surface by a continuously generated cushion or bubble of air held by flexible "skirts" that surround the base of the vehicle. According to US Navy usage, they differ from surface effect ships (SES) which have rigid sidewalls that penetrate the water surface to help hold the cushion or bubble. Official designation of these craft is Amphibious Assault Landing Craft (AALC), with the Aerojet-General design being referred to as AALC—Jeff(A) and the Bell Aerosystems craft as AALC—Jeff(B). Tests are to be run with both craft until FY 1982 when the best of each will be incorporated in a design which will then be mass-produced. $18·3 million appropriated under FY 1979 for these tests.

1 AMPHIBIOUS ASSAULT LANDING CRAFT (AALC)
BELL DESIGN (JEFF-B)

Weight, tons: 165 gross
Dimensions, feet (metres): 86·75 oa × 47 × (height) 23·5 *(26·4 × 14·3 × 7·2)*
Main/lift engines: 6 gas turbines (Avco-Lycoming T40); 16 800 hp; interconnected with 2 aircraft-type propellers in rotating shrouds for propulsive thrust and 4 horizontal fans for cushion lift = approx 50 knots cruising
Range, miles: 200
Complement: 6

ACV landing craft built by Bell Aerosystems. Completed 1976. Above dimensions are for craft on air cushion; when at rest dimensions are 80 × 43 × 19 ft *(24·4 × 13·1 × 5·8 m)* Aluminium construction; bow and stern ramps; cargo area of 1 738 square ft; three engines housed in each side structure with raised pilot house on starboard side. Performance parameters similar to Jeff (A).
Distinguished from Aerojet-General craft by having only two shrouded propellers for thrust and steering. Delivered 1976. Currently running extensive trials.

BELL AEROSYSTEMS DESIGN

60 "LCU 1610" CLASS: UTILITY LANDING CRAFT (LCU)

LCU 1613	LCU 1627	LCU 1641	LCU 1651	LCU 1661	LCU 1671
LCU 1614	LCU 1628	LCU 1642	LCU 1652	LCU 1662	LCU 1672
LCU 1616	LCU 1629	LCU 1643	LCU 1653	LCU 1663	LCU 1673
LCU 1617	LCU 1630	LCU 1644	LCU 1654	LCU 1664	LCU 1674
LCU 1618	LCU 1631	LCU 1645	LCU 1655	LCU 1665	LCU 1675
LCU 1619	LCU 1632	LCU 1646	LCU 1656	LCU 1666	LCU 1676
LCU 1621	LCU 1633	LCU 1647	LCU 1657	LCU 1667	LCU 1677
LCU 1623	LCU 1634	LCU 1648	LCU 1658	LCU 1668	LCU 1678
LCU 1624	LCU 1635	LCU 1649	LCU 1659	LCU 1669	LCU 1679
LCU 1626	LCU 1637	LCU 1650	LCU 1660	LCU 1670	LCU 1680

Displacement, tons: 200 light; 375 full load
Dimensions, feet (metres): 134·9 × 29 × 6·1 *(41·1 × 8·8 × 1·9)*
Guns: 2—50 cal machine guns
Main engines: 4 diesels (Detroit); 1 000 bhp; 2 shafts (Kort nozzles) = 11 knots
Range, miles: 1 200 at 8 knots
Complement: 12 to 14 (enlisted men)

Improved landing craft, larger than previous series; can carry three M-103 or M-48 tanks (approx 64 tons and 48 tons respectively). Cargo capacity 170 tons.
LCU 1610-1612 built by Christy Corp, Sturgeon Bay, Wisconsin; LCU 1613-1619, 1623, 1624 built by Gunderson Bros Engineering Corp, Portland, Oregon; LCU 1620, 1621, 1625, 1626, 1629, 1630 built by Southern Shipbuilding Corp, Slidell, Louisiana; LCU 1622 built by Weaver Shipyards, Texas; LCU 1627, 1628, 1631-1636 built by General Ship and Engine Works (last six units

LCU 1661   *1976, Dr. Giorgio Arra*

completed in 1968); LCU 1638-1645 built by Marinette Marine Corp, Marinette, Wisconsin (completed 1969-70); LCU 1646-1666 built by Defoe Shipbuilding Co, Bay City, Michigan (completed 1970-71). The one-of-a-kind aluminium hull, 133·8 ft LCU 1637 built by Pacific Coast Engineering Co, Alameda, California; LCU 1667-1670 built by General Ship & Engine Works, East Boston, in 1973-74; LCU 1671-1680 built by Marinette Marine Corp, 1974-76.
LCU 1636, 1638, 1639, 1640 reclassified as YFB 88-91 in October 1969 LCU 1620 and 1625 to YFU 92 and 93 respectively, in April 1971; LCU 1611, 1615, 1622 to YFU 97-99 in February 1972; LCU 1610, 1612 to YFU 100 and 101 respectively, in August 1972.

Engineering: Only two diesels fitted with vertical cycloidal propellers shipped in LCU 1621 and ex-LCUs 1620 and 1625.

31 "LCU 1466" CLASS: UTILITY LANDING CRAFT (LCU)

LCU 1466	LCU 1473	LCU 1487	LCU 1505	LCU 1539	LCU 1558
LCU 1467	LCU 1477	LCU 1488	LCU 1532	LCU 1547	LCU 1559
LCU 1468	LCU 1482	LCU 1489	LCU 1535	LCU 1548	LCU 1563
LCU 1469	LCU 1484	LCU 1490	LCU 1536	LCU 1552	LCU 1564
LCU 1470	LCU 1485	LCU 1492	LCU 1537	LCU 1554	LCU 1578
LCU 1472					

Displacement, tons: 180 light; 360 full load
Dimensions, feet (metres): 119 × 34 × 6 *(36·3 × 10·4 × 1·8)*
Guns: 2—20 mm
Main engines: 3 diesels (Gray Marine); 675 bhp; 3 shafts = 10 knots
Complement: 14

These are enlarged versions of the World War II-built LCTs; constructed during the early 1950s. LCU 1608 and 1609 have modified propulsion systems; LCU 1582 and later craft have Kort nozzle propellers. LCU 1496 reclassified as YFU 70 on 1 March 1966; LCU 1471 to YFU 88 in May 1968; LCU 1576, 1582 and 1608 to YFU 89-91, respectively, in June 1970; LCU 1488, 1491, and 1609 to YFU 94-96 on 1 June 1971; YFU 94 reverted to LCU 1488 on 1 February 1972.
LCUs 1473, 1505, 1532, 1537, 1548, 1552, 1554, 1558, 1563, 1564 and 1578 acquired from the US Army in September 1978. All are classified as LCUs although not all are actually employed as such.

Classification: The earlier craft of this series were initially designated as Utility Landing Ships (LSU); redesignated Utility Landing Craft (LCU) on 15 April 1952 and classified as service craft.

LCU 1488   *1965, USN*

720 USA / Landing craft

23 UTILITY LANDING CRAFT: LCU 501 SERIES

LCU 539	LCU 660	LCU 768	LCU 1124	LCU 1430
LCU 588	LCU 666	LCU 803	LCU 1241	LCU 1451
LCU 599	LCU 667	LCU 871	LCU 1348	LCU 1462
LCU 608	LCU 674	LCU 893	LCU 1348	
LCU 654	LCU 742	LCU 1045	LCU 1387	

Displacement, tons: 143-160 light; 309 to 320 full load
Dimensions, feet (metres): 119 × 32·7 × 5 *(36·3 × 10·7 × 1·5)*
Guns: 2—20 mm
Main engines: 3 diesels (Gray Marine); 675 bhp; 3 shafts = 10 knots
Complement: 13 (enlisted men)

Formerly LCT(6) 501-1465 series; built in 1943-44. Can carry four tanks or 200 tons of cargo.

LCU 524, 529, 550, 562, 592, 600, 629, 664, 666, 668, 677, 686, 742, 764, 776, 788, 840, 869, 87█ 960, 973, 974, 979, 980, 1056, 1082, 1086, 1124, 1136, 1156, 1159, 1162, 1195, 1224, 1236, 125█ 1283, 1286, 1363, 1376, 1378, 1384, 1386, 1398, 1411, and 1430 reclassified as YFU 1 through 4█ respectively, on 18 May 1958; LCU 1040 reclassified YFB 82 on 18 May 1958; LCU 144█ reclassified YFU 53 in 1964; LCU 509, 637, 646, 709, 716, 776, 851, 916, 973, 989, 1126, 1165, 120█ 1232, 1385, and 1388 reclassified as YFU 54 through 69, respectively, on 1 March 1966; LCU 78█ reclassified as YFU 87. YFU 9 reverted to LCU 666 on 1 January 1962; LCU 1459 converted t█ YLLC 4; LCU 1462 to YFU 102 on 1 August 1973. Changes reflect employment as general carg█ craft assigned to shore commands (see section on Service Craft).

Classification: All LCUs were originally rated as Landing Craft, Tank (LCT(6)); redesignate█ Utility Landing Ships (LSU) in 1949 to reflect varied employment; designation changed to Utili█ Landing Craft (LCU) on 15 April 1952 and classified as Service Craft.

MECHANISED LANDING CRAFT: LCM 8 TYPE

Displacement, tons: 115 full load (steel) or 105 full load (aluminium)
Dimensions, feet (metres): 73·7 × 21 × 5·2 *(22·5 × 6·4 × 1·6)*
Main engines: 2 diesels (Detroit or General Motors); 650 bhp; 2 shafts = 9 knots
Complement: 5 (enlisted men)

Constructed of welded-steel or (later units) aluminium. Can carry one M-48 or M-60 tank (both approx 48 tons) or 60 tons cargo; range is 150 nautical miles at full load. Also operated in large numbers by the US Army.

LCM 8 1976, Dr. Giorgio Arr█

MECHANISED LANDING CRAFT: LCM 6 TYPE

Displacement, tons: 60 to 62 full load
Dimensions, feet (metres): 56·2 × 14 × 3·9 *(17·1 × 4·3 × 1·2)*
Main engines: Diesels; 2 shafts; 450 bhp = 9 knots

Welded-steel construction. Cargo capacity is 34 tons or 80 trops.

LCM 6 9/1976, Dr. Giorgio Arra█

LANDING CRAFT VEHICLE AND PERSONNEL (LCVP)

Displacement, tons: 13·5 full load
Dimensions, feet (metres): 35·8 × 10·5 × 3·5 *(10·9 × 3·2 × 1·1)*
Main engine: Diesel; 325 bhp; 1 shaft = 9 knots

Constructed of wood or GRP. Fitted with 30-calibre machine guns when in combat areas. Cargo capacity, 8 000 lb; range, 110 n. miles at full load.

2 WARPING TUGS (LWT)

LWT 1	LWT 2

Displacement, tons: 61 (hoisting weight)
Dimensions, feet (metres): 85 × 22 × 6·8 *(25·9 × 6·7 × 2·1)*
Main engines: 2 diesels (Harbormaster); 420 bhp; 2 steerable shafts = 9 knots
Complement: 6 (enlisted men)

These craft are employed in amphibious landings to handle pontoon causeways. The LWT 1 and 2 are prototypes of an all-aluminium design completed in 1970. A collapsible A-frame is fitted forward to facilitate handling causeway anchors and ship-to-shore fuel lines. They can be "side loaded" on the main deck of an LST 1179 class ship or carried in an LPD/LSD type ship. The propulsion motors are similar to outboard motors, providing both steering and thrust, obviating the need for rudders.
Built by Campbell Machine, San Diego, California.

LWT 2 USN

WARPING TUGS (LWT)

Displacement, tons: approx 120
Dimensions, feet (metres): 92·9 × 23 × 6·5 *(28·3 × 7 × 2)*
Main engines: 2 outboard propulsion units = 6·5 knots

These craft are fabricated from pontoon sections and are assembled by the major amphibious commands as required.

LWT 85 USN

NAVAL RESERVE FORCE TRAINING AMPHIBIOUS WARFARE SHIPS

Name/Hull No.	NRF Homeport	Date of Assignment	
TULARE (LKA 112)	San Francisco, Calif	1 July 1975	Replaced *Hamner* (DD 718)
PAUL REVERE (LPA 248)	Long Beach, Calif	1 July 1975	Replaced *Higbee* (DD 806) and *McKean* (DD 784)
FRANCIS MARION (LPA 249)	Norfolk, Va	14 Nov 1975	

USA/ Mine warfare forces 721

MINE WARFARE FORCES

The US Navy has initiated a programme to construct a new class of mine countermeasures ships especially for deep water operations.
Currently the Navy operates three active and 22 Naval Reserve Force (NRF) minesweepers. The active ships provide support for mine research and development activities at the Naval Coastal Systems Laboratory in Panama City, Florida; the NRF ships are manned by composite active-reserve crews. In addition, the Navy flies 21 specially equipped RH-53D Sea Stallion helicopters. These helicopters, which tow mine countermeasure devices, are readily deployable to aircraft carriers or amphibious ships in overseas areas. They can counter mines laid in shallow waters but have no capability against deep-water mines.

The US Navy maintains no surface ships with a minelaying capability. Rather, the Navy can plant mines by carrier-based aircraft, land-based maritime patrol aircraft, and attack submarines. The large B-52 Stratofortress bombers of the Strategic Air Command can also plant sea mines.

MINE COUNTERMEASURE SHIPS (MCM): PROPOSED

Displacements, tons: 1 640 standard; 2 200 full load
Length, feet (metres): 239·5 (73·0)
Beam, feet (metres): 44·3 (13·5)
Draught, feet (metres): 11·2 (3·4)
Gun: Probably one 20 mm
Main engines: 2 diesels; 6 800 bhp; 2 shafts (cp propellers) = 18 knots
Complement: About 100

At least fifteen ships of a new class of US Mine Warfare vessel is to be constructed over the next 10-15 years. The class is planned as replacements for the "Aggressive", "Dash" and "Acme" classes now some 20-25 years old. One ship is requested under the Fiscal Year 1981 Shipbuilding programme while two ships are planned for the FY 1983 programme and two more for the FY 1984 programme. Cost to be about $100-110 million per ship (FY 1979$). Construction of the first ship originally to be authorised under the FY 1980 programme but delayed to FY 1981 while the design was altered and new minesweeping gear developed.

Sonar: Probably SQQ 14.

2 "ACME" CLASS: OCEAN MINESWEEPERS (MSO)

Name	No.	Launched	Commissioned	F/S
DROIT	MSO 509	20 Aug 1955	4 Mar 1957	NRF
AFFRAY	MSO 511	18 Dec 1956	8 Dec 1958	NRF

Displacement, tons: 633 light; 750 full load
Dimensions, feet (metres): 173 × 35 × 14 (52·7 × 10·7 × 4·3)
Guns: 2—20 mm (twin)
Main engines: 2 diesels (Packard), 2 280 bhp; 2 shafts; (cp propellers) = 15 knots
Complement: 81 (7 officers, 37 enlisted active duty; 4 officers, 33 enlisted reserve)

Built by Frank L. Sample, Jr, Inc, Boothbay Harbor, Maine. Plans to modernise these ships were cancelled (see notes under "Aggressive" class).
Droit and Affray are assigned to Naval Reserve training, manned partially by active and partially by reserve personnel (see notes under "Aggressive" class).

AFFRAY   1969, USN

23 "AGGRESSIVE" and "DASH" CLASSES: OCEAN MINESWEEPERS (MSO)

Name	No.	Launched	Commissioned	F/S
CONSTANT	MSO 427	14 Feb 1952	8 Sep 1954	NRF
DASH	MSO 428	20 Sep 1952	14 Aug 1953	NRF
DETECTOR	MSO 429	5 Dec 1952	26 Jan 1954	NRF
DIRECT	MSO 430	27 May 1953	9 July 1954	NRF
DOMINANT	MSO 431	5 Nov 1953	8 Nov 1954	NRF
ENGAGE	MSO 433	18 June 1953	29 June 1954	NRF
ENHANCE	MSO 437	11 Oct 1952	16 Apr 1955	NRF
ESTEEM	MSO 438	20 Dec 1952	10 Sep 1955	NRF
EXCEL	MSO 439	25 Sep 1953	24 Feb 1955	NRF
EXPLOIT	MSO 440	10 Apr 1953	31 Mar 1954	NRF
EXULTANT	MSO 441	6 June 1953	22 June 1954	NRF
FEARLESS	MSO 442	17 July 1953	22 Sep 1954	NRF
FIDELITY	MSO 443	21 Aug 1953	19 Jan 1955	AA
FORTIFY	MSO 446	14 Feb 1953	16 July 1954	NRF
ILLUSIVE	MSO 448	12 July 1952	14 Nov 1953	AA
IMPERVIOUS	MSO 449	29 Aug 1952	15 July 1954	NRF
IMPLICIT	MSO 455	1 Aug 1953	10 Mar 1954	NRF
INFLICT	MSO 456	6 Oct 1953	11 May 1954	NRF
PLUCK	MSO 464	6 Feb 1954	11 Aug 1954	NRF
CONQUEST	MSO 488	20 May 1954	20 July 1955	NRF
GALLANT	MSO 489	4 June 1954	14 Sep 1955	NRF
LEADER	MSO 490	15 Sep 1954	16 Nov 1955	AA
PLEDGE	MSO 492	20 July 1955	20 Apr 1956	NRF

Displacement, tons: 620 light; 735 full load (428-431); 720 (remainder)
Dimensions, feet (metres): 172 × 36 × 13·6 (52·4 × 11·0 × 4·2)
Gun: 1—20 mm Mk 68 (single); (all modernised ships are unarmed)
Main engines: 4 diesels (Packard) (Waukesha in modernised ships); 2 280 bhp; 2 shafts; cp propellers = 14 knots; Dash, Detector, Direct and Dominant, have 2 diesels (General Motors); 1 520 bhp (see Modernisation notes)
Range, miles: 2 400 at 10 knots
Complement: 76 (6 officers, 70 enlisted men); 86 in NRF ships (3 officers, 36 enlisted active duty; 3 officers, 44 enlisted reserve) (see Modernisation note)

These ships were built on the basis of mine warfare experience in the Korean War (1950-53); 58 built for US service and 35 transferred upon completion to NATO navies.(One ship cancelled, MSO 497). They have wooden hulls and non-magnetic engines and other equipment. All surviving ships were built in private shipyards.
Initially designated as minesweepers (AM); reclassified as ocean minesweepers (MSO) in February 1955. Originally fitted with UQS 1 mine detecting sonar. Active MSOs serve as tenders to various research facilities.
On 14 August 1978, Leader (MSO 490) and Illusive (MSO 448) deployed to Europe for operations with the NATO STANAVFORCHAN (MCM) and for exercises with various European navies. This is the first deployment made by US Mine Warfare vessels since 1973. One of the prime reasons this year long deployment was undertaken was because the experiences gained will be used in development of the new class of Mine Countermeasures Ships (MCM) (above).

Engineering: Diesel engines are fabricated of non-magnetic stainless steel alloy.

Modernisation: All the ocean minesweepers in commission during the mid-1960s were to have been modernised; estimated cost and schedule per ship were $5 million and ten months in shipyard. However, some of the early modernisations took as long as 26 months which, coupled with changes in mine countermeasures techniques, led to cancellation of programme after 13 ships were modernised: MSO 433, 437, 438, 441-443, 445, 446, 448, 449, 456, 488, and 490. The modernisation provided improvements in mine detection, engines, communications, and habitability: four Waukesha Motor Co diesel engines installed (plus two or three diesel generators for sweep gear), SQQ 14 sonar with mine classification as well as detection capability provided, twin 20 mm in some ships (replacing single 40 mm because of space requirements for sonar hoist mechanism), habitability improved, and advanced communications equipment fitted; bridge structure in modernised ships extended around mast and aft to funnel. Complement in active modernised ships is six officers and 70 enlisted men.
Some MSOs have received SQQ 14 sonar but not full modernisation.

LEADER   11/1978, Leo van Ginderen

ILLUSIVE   9/1978, Michael D. J. Lennon

Transfers: Ships of this class serve in the navies of Belgium, France, Italy, Netherlands, Norway, Portugal, Spain, and Uruguay.

2 Ex-MINESWEEPERS: RESEARCH SHIPS (MSI)

Name	No.	Builders	In service
COVE	MSI 1	Bethlehem Shipyards Co, Bellingham	20 Nov 1958
CAPE	MSI 2	Bethlehem Shipyards Co, Bellingham	27 Feb 1959

Displacement, tons: 120 light; 240 full load
Dimensions, feet (metres): 105 × 22 × 10 *(32·0 × 6·7 × 3·0)*
Guns: Removed
Main engine: Diesel (General Motors); 650 bhp; 1 shaft = 12 knots
Complement: 21 (3 officers, 18 men)

These ships were prototype inshore minesweepers (MSI) authorised under the Fiscal Year 1956 new construction programme. *Cape* laid down on 1 May 1957 and launched on 5 April 1968; *Cove* laid down 1 February 1957 and launched 8 February 1958.
Cape is operated by the Naval Undersea Research Development Center, San Diego, California; neither in service nor in commission. *Cove* transferred to Johns Hopkins Applied Physics Laboratory on 31 July 1970 with the same status. Both conduct Navy research.
Neither ship is now in the Navy List but are rated as "floating equipment". Both active.

CAPE   1968, US

8 MINESWEEPING BOATS (MSB)

MSB 15	MSB 25	MSB 29	MSB 51
MSB 16	MSB 28	MSB 41	MSB 52

Displacement, tons: 30 light; 39 full load except MSB 29, 80 full load
Dimensions, feet (metres): 57·2 × 15·5 × 4 *(17·4 × 4·7 × 1·2)*
  (MSB 29; 82 × 19 × 5·5 *(25 × 5·8 × 1·7)*
Guns: Several MG
Main engines: 2 geared diesels (Packard); 600 bhp; 2 shafts = 12 knots
Complement: 6 (enlisted)

Wooden hull minesweepers intended to be carried to theatre of operations by large assault ships; however, they are too large to be easily handled by cranes and are assigned to sweeping harbours. From 1966 to 1972 they were used extensively in Viet-Nam for river minesweeping operations.
Of 49 minesweeping boats of this type built only eight remain in active service, all based at Charleston, South Carolina.
MSB 29 built to enlarged design by John Trumpy & Sons, Annapolis, Maryland, in an effort to improve seakeeping ability.
Normally commanded by chief petty officer or petty officer first class.

NAVAL RESERVE FORCE TRAINING MINE WARFARE SHIPS

Name/Hull No.	NRF Homeport	Date of Assignment	Remarks
CONSTANT (MSO 427)	Long Beach, Calif	1 July 1972	Replaced *Embattle* (MSO 434)
DASH (MSO 428)	Newport, RI	1 Mar 1976	Replaced *Jacana* (MSC 193)
DETECTOR (MSO 429)	Newport, RI	15 Aug 1977	Exchanged with *Adroit* (MSO 509)
DIRECT (MSO 430)	Perth Amboy, NJ	1 Sep 1971	
DOMINANT (MSO 431)	Perth Amboy, NJ	1 Sep 1971	
ENGAGE (MSO 433)	St. Petersburg, Fla	1 Aug 1974	
ENHANCE (MSO 437)	San Diego, Calif	1 July 1974	
ESTEEM (MSO 438)	Seattle, Wash	1 Sep 1975	Replaced *Vireo* (MSC 205), *Warbler* (MSC 206) and *Woodpecker* (MSC 209)
EXCEL (MSO 439)	San Francisco, Calif	1 July 1972	
EXPLOIT (MSO 440)	Portland, Me	30 Sep 1973	
EXULTANT (MSO 441)	St. Petersburg, Fla	1 July 1972	
FEARLESS (MSO 442)	Charleston, SC	1 July 1974	
FORTIFY (MSO 446)	Little Creek, Va	1 Aug 1974	
IMPERVIOUS (MSO 449)	Mayport, Fla	1 Aug 1974	
IMPLICIT (MSO 455)	Tacoma, Wash	1 July 1972	
INFLICT (MSO 456)	Little Creek, Va	1 Aug 1974	
PLUCK (MSO 464)	San Diego, Calif	1 July 1972	
CONQUEST (MSO 488)	Seattle, Wash	1 Sep 1975	
GALLANT (MSO 489)	San Francisco, Calif	1 July 1972	Replaced *Reaper* (MSO 467)
PLEDGE (MSO 492)	Long Beach, Calif	1 July 1972	
ADROIT (MSO 509)	Portsmouth, NH	15 Aug 1977	Exchanged with *Detector* (MSO 429)
AFFRAY (MSO 511)	Portland, Me	30 June 1973	

AUXILIARY SHIPS

The Auxiliary Ships of the US Navy are usually divided into two broad categories, Underway Replenishment Ships and Fleet Support Ships. Underway Replenishment Ships are distinguished by their primary role, the direct support of deployed forces in the forward area of operations.

Most US Navy replenishment ships are fitted with helicopter platforms to allow the transfer of supplies by vertical replenishment (VERTREP). Helicopters are carried specifically for this purpose by the newer ammunition ships (AE), the combat store ships (AFS), the fast combat support ships (AOE), and some replenishment oilers (AOR). Carrier-based helicopters are sometimes employed in this role.

Planned Underway Replenishment (UNREP) ship force levels provide a wartime capability to support deployed carrier and amphibious task groups in up to four or five locations simultaneously. This plan is based on the availability of some storage depots on foreign territory, and the use of Military Sealift Ships to carry fuels, munitions, and the stores from the USA or overseas sources for transfer to UNREP ships in overseas areas.

During peacetime some 16 to 18 UNREP ships normally are forward deployed in the Mediterranean and western Pacific areas in support of the 6th and 7th Fleets, respectively.

The Navy's plan for modernisation of the UNREP forces provides for 14 fleet oilers (AO) in the new construction programme.

Fleet support ships provide primarily maintenance and related towing and salvage services at advanced bases and at ports in the USA. These ships normally do not provide fuel, munitions, or other supplies except when ships are alongside for maintenance.

Most fleet support ships operate from bases in the USA. The five Polaris/Poseidon submarine tenders (AS) are based at Holy Loch, Scotland; Rota, Spain; Charleston, South Carolina; and Apra harbour, Guam, with one ship generally in transit or overhaul. The Rota facility will be disestablished in about 1980. In addition, two support ships (AD/AR/AS type) generally are forward deployed in the Mediterranean and two in the western Pacific.

Underway replenishment ships and fleet support ships are mainly Navy manned and armed; however, an increasing number are being operated by the Military Sealift Command (MSC) with civilian crews. The latter ships are not armed and have T- prefix before their designations.

2 + 3 + (1) "YELLOWSTONE" and "SAMUEL GOMPERS" CLASSES: DESTROYER TENDERS (AD)

Name	No.	Builders	Laid down	Commissioned	F/S
SAMUEL GOMPERS	AD 37	Puget Sound Naval S.Y., Bremerton	9 July 1964	1 July 1967	PA
PUGET SOUND	AD 38	Puget Sound Naval S.Y., Bremerton	15 Feb 1965	27 Apr 1968	AA
YELLOWSTONE	AD 41	National Steel B.B. Co, San Diego	2 June 1977	early 1980	Bldg
ACADIA	AD 42	National Steel B.B. Co, San Diego	14 Feb 1978	mid-1980	Bldg
CAPE COD	AD 43	National Steel B.B. Co, San Diego	—	late 1980	Bldg
	AD 44	Approved FY 1979 programme	—	1981	Proj

Displacement, tons: 20 500 full load
Dimensions, feet (metres): 644 × 85 × 22·5 (196·3 × 25·9 × 6·9)
Guns: 1—5 in (127 mm)/38 (Mk 30) (Puget Sound only); 4—20 mm (Mk 67)
Missile launchers: 1 NATO Sea Sparrow system planned for AD 41 and later ships
Main engines: Steam turbines (De Laval); 20 000 shp; 1 shaft = 18 knots
Boilers: 2 (Combustion Engineering)
Complement: 1 803 (135 officers, 1 668 enlisted men)

These are the first US destroyer tenders of post-World War II design; capable of providing repair and supply services to new destroyer classes. The tenders also have facilities for servicing nuclear power plants. Services can be provided simultaneously to six guided-missile destroyers moored alongside. Basic hull design similar to "L. Y. Spear" and "Simon Lake" submarine tenders. Provided with helicopter platform and hangar; two 7 000 lb capacity cranes.

Samuel Gompers authorised in the FY 1964 new construction programme and Puget Sound in the FY 1965 programme.

Two sisters of Samuel Gompers were cancelled—AD 39 of the FY 1960 programme on 11 December 1965 prior to start of construction to provide funds for overruns in other new ship programmes and AD 40, authorised in the FY 1973 programme, in April 1974. AD 41 was included in the FY 1975 programme and AD 42 in the FY 1976 programme with two additional ships planned. (AD 41 and later ships of a slightly modified design.)

Estimated cost of AD 43 (ordered 30 September 1977) is $260·4 million and estimated cost of AD 44 is $318 million.

Gunnery: Proposed armament of AD 41-43 is two 20 mm Phalanx CIWS, two 40 mm Mk 64 (singles), two 20 mm Mk 67 (singles). Two 40 mm saluting guns (AD 37 and 38).

Particulars: Apply only to "Samuel Gompers" class.

SAMUEL GOMPERS   8/1978, Dr. Giorgio Arra

SAMUEL GOMPERS   1/1977, Dr. Giorgio Arra

3 "KLONDIKE" and "SHENANDOAH" CLASSES: DESTROYER TENDERS (AD)

Name	No.	Builders	Commissioned	F/S
EVERGLADES	AD 24	Los Angeles S.B. & D.D. Co	25 May 1951	AR
SHENANDOAH	AD 26	Todd Shipyards, Los Angeles	13 Aug 1945	AA
BRYCE CANYON	AD 36	Charleston NY	15 Sep 1950	PA

Displacement, tons: 8 165 standard; 14 700 full load (15,460 AD 24)
Dimensions, feet (metres): 492 × 69·5 × 27·2 (150·0 × 21·2 × 8·3)
Guns: 1—5 in (127 mm)/38 (Mk 37) (AD 36)
2—3 in (76 mm)/50 (Mk 26) (AD 24)
4—20 mm (Mk 68) (AD 26)
Main engines: Steam turbines (Westinghouse); (General Electric in AD 24); 8 500 shp; 1 shaft = 18·4 knots
Boilers: 2 Foster-Wheeler; (Babcock & Wilcox in AD 24)
Complement: 778 to 918

These ships are of modified C-3 design completed as destroyer tenders. Originally class of four. Everglades launched 28 January 1945, Shenandoah 29 March 1945; Bryce Canyon 7 March 1946.

Originally 13 ships of two similar designs, the "Klondike" class of AD 22-25 and "Shenandoah" class of AD 26, 31, 33, 35, 36. Great Lakes (AD 30), Canopus (AD 33, ex-AR 27), Arrow Head (AD 35) cancelled before completion; Klondike (AD 22) reclassified AR 22 (since deleted); Grand Canyon (AD 28) reclassified AR 28 (since deleted).

Two ships remain in active service with Everglades in reserve as accommodation and depot ship at Philadelphia Navy Yard. Yellowstone (AD 27) paid off 12 September 1974. Shenandoah to be deleted in FY 1980.

Gunnery: Original armament for "Klondike" class was one 5 in gun, four 3 in guns, and four 40 mm guns; for "Shenandoah" class was two 5 in guns and eight 40 mm guns. One Mk 52 FCS and one Mk 26 FC radar fitted in AD 36.

Two 40 mm saluting guns in AD 24 and 26.

Modernisation: These ships have been modernised under the FRAM II programme to service modernised destroyers fitted with ASROC, improved electronics, helicopters etc.

BRYCE CANYON   6/1978, USN (PhAn J. Mason)

724 USA / Auxiliary ships

5 "DIXIE" CLASS: DESTROYER TENDERS (AD)

Name	No.	Builders	Commissioned	F/S
DIXIE	AD 14	NY Shipbuilding Corp, NJ	25 Apr 1940	PA
PRAIRIE	AD 15	NY Shipbuilding Corp, NJ	5 Aug 1940	PA
PIEDMONT	AD 17	Tampa Shipbuilding Co, Florida	5 Jan 1944	AA
SIERRA	AD 18	Tampa Shipbuilding Co, Florida	20 Mar 1944	AA
YOSEMITE	AD 19	Tampa Shipbuilding Co, Florida	25 Mar 1944	AA

Displacement, tons: 9 450 standard; 17 190 to 18 000 full load
Dimensions, feet (metres): 530·5 × 73·3 × 25·5 *(161·7 × 22·3 × 7·8)*
Guns: 4—20 mm (single Mk 67)
Main engines: Steam turbines (New York S.B. Corp in AD 14 and 15; Allis Chalmers in remainder); 12 000 shp; 2 shafts = 18·2 knots
Boilers: 4 (Babcock & Wilcox)
Complement: 1 131 to 1 271

Launched on 27 May 1939, 9 December 1939, 7 December 1942, 23 February 1943 and 16 May 1943 respectively. Near sisters of "Vulcan" and "Fulton" classes.
All five ships are active with *Dixie* the oldest ship currently in service with the US Navy except for the sail frigate *Constitution*. Two 40 mm saluting guns carried.

Modernisation: All of these ships have been modernised under the FRAM II programme to service destroyers fitted with ASROC, improved electronics, helicopters, etc. Two or three 5 in guns and eight 40 mm guns removed during modernisation.

DIXIE   4/1976, USN

8 "KILAUEA" CLASS: AMMUNITION SHIPS (AE)

Name	No.	Builders	Commissioned	F/S
KILAUEA	AE 26	General Dynamics Corp, Quincy, Mass	10 Aug 1968	PA
BUTTE	AE 27	General Dynamics Corp, Quincy, Mass	14 Dec 1968	AA
SANTA BARBARA	AE 28	Bethlehem Steel Corp, Sparrows Pt, Md	11 July 1970	AA
MOUNT HOOD	AE 29	Bethlehem Steel Corp, Sparrows Pt, Md	1 May 1971	PA
FLINT	AE 32	Ingalls S.B. Corp, Pascagoula, Miss	20 Nov 1971	PA
SHASTA	AE 33	Ingalls S.B. Corp, Pascagoula, Miss	26 Feb 1972	PA
MOUNT BAKER	AE 34	Ingalls S.B. Corp, Pascagoula, Miss	22 July 1972	AA
KISKA	AE 35	Ingalls S.B. Corp, Pascagoula, Miss	16 Dec 1972	PA

Displacement, tons: 18 088 full load (17 931, AE 26 and 27)
Dimensions, feet (metres): 564 × 81 × 28 *(171·9 × 24·7 × 8·5)*
Helicopters: 2 UH-46 Sea Knight cargo helicopters normally embarked
Guns: 8—3 in *(76 mm)*/50 (twin Mk 33) (AE 28-33); 4—3 in (twin) (remainder)
Main engines: Geared turbines (General Electric); 22 000 shp; 1 shaft = 20 knots
Boilers: 3 (Foster-Wheeler)
Complement: 411 (38 officers, 373 enlisted men)

Fitted for rapid transfer of missiles and other munitions to ships alongside or with helicopters in vertical replenishment operations (VERTREP). Helicopter platform and hangar aft. AE 26 and 27 authorised in the Fiscal Year 1965 new construction programme, AE 28 and 29 in the FY 1966, AE 32 and 33 in the FY 1967, and AE 34 and 35 in the FY 1968. AE 26 laid down 10 March 1966; AE 27, 21 July 1966; AE 28, 20 December 1966; AE 29, 8 May 1967; AE 32, 4 August 1969; AE 33, 10 November 1969; AE 34, 10 May 1970; AE 35, 4 August 1971.

SHASTA   10/1978, Dr. Giorgio Ar

Fire control: One Mk 56 GFCS, one Mk 1 Target Designation System and one SPG 35 radar (A 27, 29, 34 and 35 only).
Gunnery: The 3 in guns are arranged in twin closed mounts forward and twin open mounts a between funnel and after booms. Two 20 mm Mk 15 CIWS to be fitted.
Missiles: Plans to instal NATO Sea Sparrow cancelled.
Rockets: Mk 36 Chaffroc (RBOC) to be fitted.

5 "SURIBACHI" and "NITRO" CLASSES: AMMUNITION SHIPS (AE)

Name	No.	Builders	Commissioned	F/S
SURIBACHI	AE 21	Bethlehem Steel Corp, Sparrows Pt, Md	17 Nov 1956	AA
MAUNA KEA	AE 22	Bethlehem Steel Corp, Sparrows Pt, Md	30 Mar 1957	PA
NITRO	AE 23	Bethlehem Steel Corp, Sparrows Pt, Md	1 May 1959	AA
PYRO	AE 24	Bethlehem Steel Corp, Sparrows Pt, Md	24 July 1959	PA
HALEAKALA	AE 25	Bethlehem Steel Corp, Sparrows Pt, Md	3 Nov 1959	PA

Displacement, tons: 7 470 light; 10 000 standard; 15 500 full load (21 and 22), 15 900-16 083 (rest)
Dimensions, feet (metres): 512 × 72 × 29 *(156·1 × 21·9 × 8·8)* (21 and 22); 502 *(153)* (rest)
Guns: 4—3 in *(76 mm)*/50 (twin Mk 33)
Main engines: Geared turbines (Bethlehem); 16 000 shp; 1 shaft = 18 knots (AE 21 and 22); 20·6 (rest)
Boilers: 2 (Combustion Engineering)
Complement: 386 (16 officers, 370 enlisted men) (AE 21 and 22); 350 (20 officers, 330 enlisted men) (rest)

Designed specifically for underway replenishment. A sixth ship of this class to have been built under the Fiscal Year 1959 programme was cancelled.
All five ships were modernised in the 1960s, being fitted with high-speed transfer equipment, three holds configured for stowage of missiles up to and including the 33 ft Talos, and helicopter platform fitted aft (two after twin 3 in gun mounts removed).
Arrangements of twin 3 in gun mounts differ, some ships have them in tandem and others side-by-side.

PYRO   7/1978, Dr. Giorgio Arr

Fire control: One Mk 1 Target Designation System (AE 22 only).
Rockets: Mk 36 Chaffroc (RBOC) to be fitted.

7 "MARS" CLASS: COMBAT STORE SHIPS (AFS)

Name	No.	Builders	Commissioned	F/S
MARS	AFS 1	National Steel and S.B. Co, San Diego	21 Dec 1963	PA
SYLVANIA	AFS 2	National Steel and S.B. Co, San Diego	11 July 1964	AA
NIAGARA FALLS	AFS 3	National Steel and S.B. Co, San Diego	29 Apr 1967	PA
WHITE PLAINS	AFS 4	National Steel and S.B. Co, San Diego	23 Nov 1968	PA
CONCORD	AFS 5	National Steel and S.B. Co, San Diego	27 Nov 1968	AA
SAN DIEGO	AFS 6	National Steel and S.B. Co, San Diego	24 May 1969	AA
SAN JOSE	AFS 7	National Steel and S.B. Co, San Diego	23 Oct 1970	AA

Displacement, tons: 16 500 full load (1-3) 15 900 (remainder)
Dimensions, feet (metres): 581 × 79 × 24 *(177·1 × 24·1 × 7·3)*
Guns: 8—3 in *(76 mm)*/50 (twin Mk 33)
Helicopters: 2 UH-46 Sea Knight helicopters normally assigned
Main engines: Steam turbines (De Laval except AFS 6—Westinghouse); 22 000 shp; 1 shaft = 20 knots
Boilers: 3 (Babcock & Wilcox)
Complement: 486 (45 officers, 441 enlisted men)

On building represented a new design with a completely new replenishment at sea system. "M" frames replace conventional king posts and booms, which are equipped with automatic tensioning devices to maintain transfer lines taut. Computers provide data on stock status with data displayed by closed-circuit television. Five holds (one refrigerated). Cargo capacity 2 625 tons dry stores and 1 300 tons refrigerated stores (varies with specific loadings).
Automatic propulsion system with full controls on bridge. The large SPS 40 radars fitted in *Mars* and *Sylvania* have been removed; some ships have Tacan (tactical aircraft navigation) radar.
Mars authorised in the Fiscal Year 1961 shipbuilding programme, *Sylvania* in FY 1962, *Niagara Falls* in FY 1964, *White Plains* and *Concord* in FY 1965, *San Diego* in FY 1966, *San Jose* in FY 1967.

MARS   9/1978, Dr. Giorgio Ar

Rockets: Mk 36 Chaffroc (RBOC) to be fitted.

USA / Auxiliary ships 725

1 MISCELLANEOUS (AG)
Ex-MERCHANT DEEP SALVAGE SHIP

Name	No.	Builders	Completed	F/S
Ex-M/V *Hughes Glomar Explorer*	AG 193	Sun S.B. and Drydock Co, Chester, Pa	July 1973	MPR

Displacement, tons: 63 300 full load
Measurement, tons: 27 445 gross; 18 511 net; 39 705 deadweight
Dimensions, feet (metres): 618·8 × 115·7 × 50·8 *(188·6 × 35·3 × 15·5)*
Aircraft: Landing area for 1 medium helicopter; no support facilities
Main engines: 5 Nordberg diesels, 6 electric motors (diesel-electric drive); 13 200 shp; 2 shafts = approx 15 + knots
Boilers: 4
Complement: Not available

Built for the Summa Corporation 1972-73, this vessel was officially classified by the American Bureau of Shipping as a "Survey Ship". After her actual mission and career as a salvage ship for a Soviet "Golf" class submarine had been widely disclosed 1975-76, the US Navy took her over on 30 September 1976 and classified her as AG 193. She was then inactivated and transferred to the Maritime Administration on 17 January 1977 for lay-up at the reserve fleet in Suisun Bay, Cal. On 1 June 1978 she was leased to Global Marine Development Inc, Newport Beach, Cal. The company will pay all reactivation and overhaul costs as well as the cost of cocooning when she is returned to the navy. While on lease she is to be used for "scientific and mineral exploration and mining in the deep ocean".

1 "COMPASS ISLAND" CLASS: MISCELLANEOUS (AG)

Name	No.	Builders	Commissioned	F/S
COMPASS ISLAND (ex-*Garden Mariner*)	AG 153 (ex-YAG 56)	New York S.B. Corporation, NJ	3 Dec 1956	AA

Displacement, tons: 17 600 full load
Dimensions, feet (metres): 564 × 78 × 31 *(171·6 × 23·8 × 9·5)*
Main engines: Geared turbines (General Electric); 19 250 shp; 1 shaft = 20 knots
Boilers: 2 (Foster-Wheeler)
Complement: 250 (18 officers, 232 enlisted men)

Originally a "Mariner" class merchant ship (C4-S-1a type). Acquired by the Navy on 29 March 1956.
Converted by New York Naval Shipyard for the development of the Fleet Ballistic Missile guidance and ship navigation systems. Her mission is to assist in the development and valuation of a navigation system independent of shore-based aids. Navy manned.
Observation Island (AG 154), a sister ship, serves with the Military Sealift Command.
To be replaced by *Vanguard* (AG 194) (see MSC section) and deleted in FY 1980.

COMPASS ISLAND   6/1978, Wright and Logan

1 "POINT BARROW" CLASS: AUXILIARY DEEP SUBMERGENCE SUPPORT SHIP (AGDS)

Name	No.	Builders	Commissioned	F/S
POINT LOMA (ex-*Point Barrow*)	AGDS 2 (ex-AKD 1)	Maryland S.B. & D.D. Co	28 Feb 1958	PA

Displacement, tons: 9 415 standard; 14 000 full load
Dimensions, feet (metres): 492 × 78 × 22 *(150·0 × 23·8 × 6·7)*
Guns: None
Main engines: Steam turbines (Westinghouse); 6 000 shp; 2 shafts = 15 knots
Boilers: 2 (Foster-Wheeler)
Complement: 160 (Including scientific personnel and submersible operators)

A docking ship designed to carry cargo, vehicles, and landing craft (originally designated AKD). Built for the Military Sea Transportation Service (now Military Sealift Command); launched on 25 May 1957 decommissioned and delivered to MSTS on 29 May 1958. Maritime Administration T2-ST-23A design; winterised for arctic service. Fitted with internal ramp and garage system. Subsequently refitted with hangar over docking well and employed in transport of large booster rockets to Cape Kennedy Space Center. Primarily used to carry the second stage of the Saturn V moon rocket and Lunar Modules. Placed out of service in reserve on 28 September 1972.
Transferred from Military Sealift Command to Navy on 28 February 1974 for modification to support deep submergence vehicles, especially the bathyscaph *Trieste II*. Placed in commission "special" on 28 February 1974 as the AGDS 2; renamed *Point Loma* for the location of the San Diego submarine base where Submarine Development Group 1 operates most of the Navy's submersibles. *Point Loma* was placed in commission on 30 April 1975. Aviation gas capacity increased to approximately 100 000 gallons (US) to support *Trieste II* which uses lighter-than-water avgas for flotation.

POINT LOMA   6/1976, J. L. M. van der Burg

Classification: The designation AGDS was established on 3 January 1974; originally it was a service craft designation rather than a ship designation. AGDS 1 was assigned briefly to the floating dry dock *White Sands* (ARD 20), the previous *Trieste II* support ship. *Point Loma* renamed and reclassified AGDS 2 on 28 February 1974.

1 CONVERTED "RALEIGH" CLASS: COMMAND SHIP (AGF)

Name	No.	Builders	Laid down	Launched	Commissioned	F/S
LA SALLE	AGF 3 (ex-LPD 3)	New York Naval Shipyards	2 Apr 1962	3 Aug 1963	22 Feb 1964	AA

Displacement, tons: 8 040 light; 13 900 full load
Length, feet (metres): 521·8 *(158·4)*
Beam, feet (metres): 104 *(31·7)*
Draught, feet (metres): 21 *(6·4)*
Guns: 8—3 in *(76 mm)*/50 (Mk 33 twin)
Main engines: Steam turbines (De Laval); 24 000 shp; 2 shafts
Boilers: 2 (Babcock & Wilcox)
Speed, knots: 20
Complement: 387 (18 officers, 369 enlisted men)
Flag accommodation: 59 (12 officers, 47 enlisted men)

La Salle is a former amphibious transport dock (LPD) of the "Raleigh" class. Authorised in the Fiscal Year 1961 new construction programme. *La Salle* served as an amphibious ship from completion until 1972; the ship retains an amphibious assault capability.
La Salle serves as flagship for the US commander Middle East Force, operating in the Persian Gulf, Arabian Sea, and Indian Ocean and is designated as flagship of the new 5th Fleet.

Conversion: Converted in 1972 at Philadelphia Navy Yard. Elaborate command and communications facilities installed; accommodations provided for admiral and staff; additional air-conditioning fitted; painted white to help retard heat of Persian Gulf area. Reclassified as a flagship and designated AGF 3 on 1 July 1972 keeping previous "3" hull number.

Fire control: One Mk 56 and one Mk 70 gunfire control system.

Gunnery: Has two 40 mm saluting guns. To be fitted with 20 mm Mk 15 CIWS.

Radar: Search: SPS 10 and 40.

Rockets: One Mk 36 Chaffroc (RBOC) to be fitted.

LA SALLE   8/1975, USN

USA / Auxiliary ships

1 "HAVEN" CLASS: HOSPITAL SHIP (AH)

Name	No.	Builders	Commissioned	F/S
SANCTUARY (ex-*Marine Owl*)	AH 17	Sun S.B. & D.D. Co, Chester	20 June 1945	RR

Displacement, tons: 11 141 standard; 15 100 full load
Dimensions, feet (metres): 520 × 71·5 × 24 *(158·5 × 21·8 × 7·3)*
Main engines: Steam turbines (General Electric); 9 000 shp; 1 shaft = 18·33 knots
Boilers: 2 (Babcock & Wilcox)
Complement: 675 (87 officers, 588 enlisted)

SANCTUARY 1974, U.

Sanctuary is the survivor of six hospital ships (AH) of the "Haven" class. Built on C4-S-B2 merchant hull and launched on 15 August 1944. *Sanctuary* recommissioned from reserve in 1966 for service off Viet-Nam; decommissioned on 15 December 1971 for modification to "dependent support ship" at Hunter's Point Naval Shipyard, San Francisco, California. Subsequently recommissioned on 18 November 1972.
As a dependent support ship *Sanctuary* had special facilities for obstetrics, gynaecology, maternity, and nursery services; fitted as a 74 bed hospital which can be expanded to 300 beds in 72 hours. She was the first US Navy ship with mixed male-female crew (although previously female nurses have been assigned to hospital ships and transports). The medical personnel consisted of 50 officers and approximately 120 enlisted including several female nurse officers; the ship's company consisted of 20 officers (including two women) and approximately 330 enlisted (including 60 women). The ship was modified to support US dependents of ships homeported in Piraeus, Greece. However, she was not deployed to Greece, but was decommissioned on 28 March 1974 and laid up at Philadelphia.

0 + 5 + 9 "CIMARRON" CLASS: OILERS (AO)

Name	No.	Builder	Commissioned	F/S
CIMARRON	AO 177	Avondale Shipyards	late 1979	Bldg
MONONGAHELA	AO 178	Avondale Shipyards	mid-1980	Bldg
MERRIMACK	AO 179	Avondale Shipyards	late 1980	Ord
	AO 180	Avondale Shipyards	late 1981	Ord
	AO 186	Avondale Shipyards	mid-1982	Ord
	AO 187	Planned FY 1981 programme		
	AO 188	Planned FY 1982 programme		
	AO 189	Planned FY 1983 programme		
	AO 190	Planned FY 1984 programme		
	AO 191-195	Future programmes		

Displacement, tons: 27 500 full load
Dimensions, feet (metres): 588·5 × 88 × 35 *(179·4 × 26·8 × 10·7)*
Guns: 2—20 mm Phalanx CIWS
Rockets: 1—Mk 36 Chaffroc
Main engine: 1 geared turbine; 24 000 shp; 1 shaft = 20 knots
Boilers: 2
Complement: 135

This class of fleet oilers is significantly smaller than the previous built-for-the-purpose AOs the "Neosho" class; the newer ships are "sized" to provide two complete refuellings of fossil-fuelled aircraft carrier and six to eight accompanying destroyers. The lead ship w requested in the Fiscal Year 1975 new construction programme but was not approved Congress. Subsequently, two ships (AO 177 and AO 178) approved in FY 1976, one ship in 1977 (AO 179) and two ships in FY 1978 (AO 180 and 186).
A contract for the construction of AO 177 and 178 was awarded to Avondale Shipyards I Westwego, Louisiana on 9 August 1976 for AO 179 on 25 January 1977 and for AO 180 and on 11 April 1978. AO 177 laid down 18 May 1978 and AO 178 on 15 August 1978. Fifteen more this class planned or proposed.
Each ship has a capacity of 120 000 barrels and will have a helicopter platform aft.

Classification: The hull numbers AO 168-176 are assigned to the "Sealift" class tankers; AO 1 is USNS *Potomac*; AO 182-185 assigned to "Columbia" class. All listed under Military Sea Command section.

"CIMARRON" Class Drawing, A. D. Baker III

6 "NEOSHO" CLASS: OILERS (AO)

Name	No.	Launched	Commissioned	F/S
NEOSHO	T-AO 143	10 Nov 1953	24 Sep 1954	TAA
MISSISSINEWA	T-AO 144	12 June 1954	18 Jan 1955	TAA
HASSAYAMPA	T-AO 145	12 Sep 1954	19 Apr 1955	TPA
KAWISHIWI	AO 146	11 Dec 1954	6 July 1955	PA
TRUCKEE	AO 147	10 Mar 1955	23 Nov 1955	AA
PONCHATOULA	AO 148	9 July 1955	12 Jan 1956	PA

Displacement, tons: 11 600 light; 38 000 full load
Dimensions, feet (metres): 655 × 86 × 35 *(199·6 × 26·2 × 10·7)*
Guns: 8—3 in *(76 mm)*/50 (twin Mk 33) (4—3 in in AO 145; none in T-AO 144)
Main engines: Geared turbines (General Electric); 28 000 shp; 2 shafts = 20 knots
Boilers: 2 (Babcock & Wilcox)
Complement: 324 (21 officers and 303 enlisted men including staff) when navy manned

HASSAYAMPA 1/1978, Dr. Giorgio Arr

Neosho built by Bethlehem Steel Co, Quincy, Massachusetts; others by New York Shipbuilding Corporation, Camden, New Jersey. These are the largest "straight" fleet oilers (AO) constructed specifically for the Navy. Cargo capacity is approximately 180 000 barrels of liquid fuels. Original armament was two 5 in guns and twelve 3 in guns; former removed in 1969. Two twin 3 in gun mounts removed from *Neosho*, *Mississinewa*, and *Truckee* and helicopter platform installed. Those ships also have additional superstructure installed forward of after superstructure. All fitted to carry a service force commander and staff (12 officers).
Mississinewa assigned to Military Sealift Command on 15 November 1976 (guns remove civilian manned); *Neosho* on 25 May 1978 and *Hassayampa* on 17 November 1978. Remaind will follow.

Fire control: Armed ships except T-AO 145 have two Mk 56 GFCS.

3 "JUMBOISED CIMARRON" CLASS: OILERS (AO)

Name	No.	Launched	Commissioned	F/S
ASHTABULA	AO 51	22 May 1943	7 Aug 1943	PA
CALOOSAHATCHEE	AO 98	2 June 1945	10 Oct 1945	AA
CANISTEO	AO 99	6 July 1945	3 Dec 1945	AA

Displacement, tons: 34 040 full load
Dimensions, feet (metres): 644 × 75 × 35 *(196·3 × 22·9 × 10·7)*
Guns: 4—3 in *(76 mm)*/50 (single Mk 26)
Main engines: Geared turbines (Bethlehem); 13 500 shp; 2 shafts = 18 knots
Boilers: 4 (Foster-Wheeler)
Complement: 317 (19 officers and 298 enlisted men)

All built by Bethlehem Steel Co, Sparrows Point, Maryland. Originally T3-S2-A1 oilers; converted during mid-1960s under "jumbo" programme. Enlarged midsections added to increase cargo capacity to approximately 143 000 barrels plus 175 tons of munitions and 100 tons refrigerated stores. No helicopter platform fitted.
All three ships naval manned.

ASHTABULA 5/1978, USN (PH1 L. B. Foster)

4 "SACRAMENTO" CLASS: FAST COMBAT SUPPORT SHIPS (AOE)

Name	No.	Laid down	Launched	Commissioned	F/S
SACRAMENTO	AOE 1	30 June 1961	14 Sep 1963	14 Mar 1964	PA
CAMDEN	AOE 2	17 Feb 1964	29 May 1965	1 Apr 1967	PA
SEATTLE	AOE 3	1 Oct 1965	2 Mar 1968	5 Apr 1969	AA
DETROIT	AOE 4	29 Nov 1966	21 June 1969	28 Mar 1970	AA

Displacement, tons: 19 200 light; 51 400-53 600 full load
Dimensions, feet (metres): 793 × 107 × 39·3 *(241·7 × 32·6 × 12·0)*
Aircraft: 2 UH-46 Sea Knight normally assigned
Missiles: One Mk 29 Nato Sea Sparrow System (AOE 1, 2 and 4)
Guns: 4—3 in *(76 mm)/*50 (twin Mk 33) (4 twins in AOE 3)
Main engines: Geared turbines (General Electric); 100 000 shp; 2 shafts = 26 knots
Boilers: 4 (Combustion Engineering)
Complement: 600 (33 officers, 567 enlisted men) (AOE 1 and 2);
680 (33 officers, 647 enlisted men) (AOE 3 and 4)

These ships provide rapid replenishment at sea of petroleum, munitions, provisions, and fleet freight. Fitted with helicopter platform, internal arrangements, and large hangar for vertical replenishment operations (VERTREP). Cargo capacity 177 000 barrels plus 2 150 tons munitions, 500 tons dry stores, 250 tons refrigerated stores (varies with specific loadings).
Built by Puget Sound Naval Shipyard except *Camden* by New York Shipbuilding Corporation, Camden, New Jersey. *Sacramento* authorised in the Fiscal Year 1961 new construction programme; *Camden* in FY 1963, *Seattle* in FY 1965, and *Detroit* in FY 1966. Construction of AOE 5 in FY 1968 was deferred and then cancelled in November 1969. No additional ships of this type were planned because of high cost, the availability of new-construction ammunition ships, and the great success of the smaller "Wichita" class replenishment oilers. Approximate cost of *Camden* was $70 million.

Appearance: These ships can be distinguished from the smaller "Wichita" class replenishment oilers by their larger superstructures and funnel, helicopter deck at higher level, and hangar structure aft of funnel.

SACRAMENTO   3/1978, USN (PH1 A. E. Legare)

Engineering: *Sacramento* and *Camden* have machinery taken from the cancelled battleship *Kentucky* (BB 66)—*Seattle* and *Detroit* from *Illinois* (BB 65).

Fire control: One Mk 91 MFCS (except AOE 3).

Gunnery: Two Phalanx 20 mm CIWS to be fitted.

Missiles: NATO Sea Sparrow system with Mark 91 director to be fitted in AOE 2 and 3.

Rockets: One Mk 36 Chaffroc (RBOC) to be fitted.

7 "WICHITA" CLASS: REPLENISHMENT OILERS (AOR)

Name	No.	Laid down	Launched	Commissioned	F/S
WICHITA	AOR 1	18 June 1966	18 Mar 1968	7 June 1969	PA
MILWAUKEE	AOR 2	29 Nov 1966	17 Jan 1969	1 Nov 1969	AA
KANSAS CITY	AOR 3	20 Apr 1968	28 June 1969	6 June 1970	PA
SAVANNAH	AOR 4	22 Jan 1969	25 Apr 1970	5 Dec 1970	AA
WABASH	AOR 5	21 Jan 1970	6 Feb 1971	20 Nov 1971	PA
KALAMAZOO	AOR 6	28 Oct 1970	11 Nov 1972	11 Aug 1973	AA
ROANOKE	AOR 7	19 Jan 1974	7 Dec 1974	30 Oct 1976	PA

Displacement, tons: 37 360 full load
Dimensions, feet (metres): 659 × 96 × 33·3 *(200·9 × 29·3 × 10·2)*
Aircraft: 2 UH-46 Sea Knight can be embarked
Missiles: 1 NATO Sea Sparrow system (Mk 29) in *Roanoke* and *Kansas City*
Guns: 4—3 in *(76 mm)/*50 (twin) (Mk 33) (in AOR 1, 5-6); 4—20 mm Mk 67 single (AOR 2 and 7)
Main engines: Geared turbines (General Electric); 32 000 shp;
2 shafts = 20 knots (18 knots on 2 boilers)
Boilers: 3 (Foster-Wheeler)
Complement: 390 (27 officers, 363 enlisted men); 457 (30 and 427 in AOR 7)

These ships provide rapid replenishment at sea of petroleum and munitions with a limited capacity for provision and fleet freight. Fitted with helicopter platform and internal arrangement for vertical replenishment operations (VERTREP), but no hangar originally provided: all will subsequently be fitted with hangar. Cargo capacity 175 000 barrels of liquid fuels plus 600 tons munitions, 425 tons dry stores, 150 tons refrigerated stores.
All built by General Dynamics Corporation, Quincy Massachusetts except AOR 7 by National Steel and Shipbuilding Co, San Diego, California. *Wichita* and *Milwaukee* authorised in the Fiscal Year 1965 new construction programme, *Kansas City* and *Savannah* in FY 1966, *Wabash* and *Kalamazoo* in FY 1967, and *Roanoke* in FY 1972. Approximate cost of *Milwaukee* was $27·7 million.

Fire control: One Mk 91 MFCS (AOR 3 and 7).

Gunnery: Two 20 mm Mk 15 CIWS to be fitted; four 20 mm Mk 67 (single) to be fitted in AOR 1 and 3-6.

Rockets: One Mk 36 Chaffroc (RBOC) to be fitted.

ROANOKE   7/1976, National Steel and S.B. Co San Diego

KALAMAZOO   2/1978, USN (PH1 Osborne)

REPAIR SHIPS (AR) NEW CONSTRUCTION

Navy plans to build a new class of repair ships have been deferred indefinitely. The first unit of the class was to have been requested in the Fiscal Year 1979 programme.

4 "AJAX" CLASS: REPAIR SHIPS (AR)

Name	No.	Builders	Commissioned	F/S
VULCAN	AR 5	New York S.B. Corp	16 June 1941	AA
AJAX	AR 6	Los Angeles S.B. & D.D. Corp	30 Oct 1942	PA
HECTOR	AR 7	Los Angeles S.B. & D.D. Corp	7 Feb 1944	PA
JASON	AR 8 (ex-ARH 1)	Los Angeles S.B. & D.D. Corp	19 June 1944	PA

Displacement, tons: 9 140 standard; 16 160-16 380 full load
Dimensions, feet (metres): 529·3 × 73·3 × 23·3 (161·3 × 22·3 × 7·1)
Guns: 4—20 mm (singles) (Mk 67)
Main engines: Steam turbines (Allis-Chalmers except AR 5—New York S.B. Corp); 11 000 shp; 2 shafts = 19·2 knots
Boilers: 4 (Babcock & Wilcox)
Complement: 1 336 (63 officers, 1 273 enlisted men)

Vulcan was built under the 1939 programme and the other three under the 1940 programme. Launched on 14 December 1940, 22 August 1942, 11 November 1942 and 3 April 1943 respectively. All carry a most elaborate equipment of machine tools to undertake repairs of every description. *Jason,* originally designated ARH 1 and rated as heavy hull repair ship, was reclassified AR 8 on 9 September 1957. Eight 40 mm guns (twin) have been removed; the four 5 in guns previously fitted were the standard main battery of large fleet support ships and oilers during World War II.

HECTOR   3/1977, USN (PhAn T. Pfrang)

2 "ACHELOUS" CLASS: REPAIR SHIPS: SMALL (ARL)

Name	No.	Builders	Commissioned	F/S
SPHINX	ARL 24 (ex-*LST 963*)	Bethlehem Steel Co, Higham, Mass	12 Dec 1944	PR
INDRA	ARL 37 (ex-*LST 1147*)	Chicago Bridge & Iron Co, Seneca, Illinois	28 May 1945	None

Displacement, tons: 1 625 light; 4 325 full load
Dimensions, feet (metres): 328 × 50 × 11 (100·0 × 15·2 × 3·4)
Guns: 8—40 mm (quad)
Main engines: Diesels (General Motors); 1 800 bhp; 2 shafts = 12 knots
Complement: 266 (18 officers, 248 enlisted men)

Tank landing ships converted during construction to landing craft repair ships (ARL). Rerated as Repair Ships, Small (ARL) on 11 January 1978. Launched 21 May 1945 and 18 November 1944 respectively. Fitted with machine shops, parts storage, lifting gear, etc and 60 ton capacity booms. The ARLs cater for small amphibious, minesweeping, and riverine craft. Tripod mast in 37. Both reactivated during Viet-Nam War.
Indra was stricken on 31 December 1977 but retained indefinitely as Station Ship at Norfolk. Va.

Fire control: Two Mark 51 directors.

Transfers: Former US Navy LSTs modified to fleet support ships (AGP-ARB-ARL-ARVE) are operated by the navies of Greece, Indonesia, South Korea, Malaysia, Philippines, Taiwan, Turkey and Venezuela.

SPHINX   1968, USN

11 "DIVER" and "BOLSTER" CLASSES: SALVAGE SHIPS (ARS)

Note: Plans for new Salvage Ships indefinitely postponed.

Name	No.	Builders	Commissioned	F/S
PRESERVER	ARS 8	Basalt Rock Co, Napa, Calif	11 Jan 1944	AA
DELIVER	ARS 23	Basalt Rock Co, Napa, Calif	18 July 1944	PA
SAFEGUARD	ARS 25	Basalt Rock Co, Napa, Calif	31 Oct 1944	PA
CLAMP	ARS 33	Basalt Rock Co, Napa, Calif	23 Aug 1943	MPR
GEAR	ARS 34	Basalt Rock Co, Napa, Calif	24 Sep 1943	Loan
BOLSTER	ARS 38	Basalt Rock Co, Napa, Calif	1 May 1945	PA
CONSERVER	ARS 39	Basalt Rock Co, Napa, Calif	9 June 1945	PA
HOIST	ARS 40	Basalt Rock Co, Napa, Calif	21 July 1945	AA
OPPORTUNE	ARS 41	Basalt Rock Co, Napa, Calif	5 Oct 1945	AA
RECLAIMER	ARS 42	Basalt Rock Co, Napa, Calif	20 Dec 1945	PA
RECOVERY	ARS 43	Basalt Rock Co, Napa, Calif	15 May 1946	AA

Displacement, tons: 1 530 standard; 1 970 full load (ARS 38-43 2 040)
Dimensions, feet (metres): 213·5 × 41 (except later ships, 44) × 13 (65·1 × 12·5 (or 13·4) × 4·0)
Guns: 2—20 mm
Main engines: Diesel-electric (Cooper Bessemer); (Caterpillar in ARS 23, 25, 38, 39, 42); 2 440 shp; 2 shafts = 14·8 knots
Complement: 96-157

These ships are fitted for salvage and towing; equipped with compressed air diving equipment. Launched on 1 April 1943, 25 September 1943, 20 November 1943, 24 October 1942, 24 October 1942, 23 December 1944, 27 January 1945, 31 March 1945, 31 March 1945, 25 June 1945 and 4 August 1945 respectively. Early ships have 8 ton and 10 ton capacity booms; later ships have 10 ton and 20 ton booms.
ARS 38 and later ships are of a slightly different design, known as the "Bolster" class.
Preserver (ARS 8) to be deleted in FY 1980.
Gear is operated by a commercial firm in support of Navy activities; *Curb* ARS 21 on loan to private salvage firm, supports naval requirements as needed. *Clamp* was stricken from the Navy List in 1963 but reacquired in 1973 and is still laid up in Maritime Administration Reserve Fleet.

RECLAIMER   8/1978, Dr. Giorgio Arra

USA / Auxiliary ships 729

2 + 3 "L. Y. SPEAR" and "EMORY S. LAND" CLASSES: SUBMARINE TENDERS (AS)

Name	No.	Builders	Commissioned	F/S
L. Y. SPEAR	AS 36	General Dynamics Corp, Quincy	28 Feb 1970	AA
DIXON	AS 37	General Dynamics Corp, Quincy	7 Aug 1971	PA
EMORY S. LAND	AS 39	Lockheed S.B. & Cons Co, Seattle	26 Mar 1979	AA
FRANK CABLE	AS 40	Lockheed S.B. & Cons Co, Seattle	1979	Bldg
McKEE	AS 41	Lockheed S.B. & Cons Co, Seattle	1981	Bldg

Displacement, tons: 13 000 standard (13 840, later ships); 22 640 full load (AS 36 and AS 37); 24 000 (AS 39-41)
Dimensions, feet (metres): 643·8 × 85 × 28·5 *(196·2 × 25·9 × 8·7)*
Guns: 4—20 mm (Mk 67 single) (AS 37); 2—40 mm (Mk 64 single) (AS 39-41)
Main engines: Steam turbines (General Electric); 20 000 shp; 1 shaft = 20 knots
Boilers: 2 (Foster-Wheeler)
Complement: 1 348 (96 officers, 1 252 enlisted men) (AS 36 and 37); 1 158 (50 officers, 1 108 enlisted men) (AS 39-41)
Flag accommodation: 69 (25 officers, 44 enlisted men)

L. Y. SPEAR 9/1976, Dr. Giorgio Arra

These ships are the first US submarine tenders designed specifically for servicing nuclear-propelled attack submarines. Basic hull design similar to "Samuel Gompers" class destroyer tenders. Provided with helicopter deck but no hangar. Each ship can simultaneously provide services to four submarines moored alongside. AS 39 and later ships ("Emory S. Land" class) are especially configured to support "SSN 688" class submarines.
L. Y. Spear authorised in the Fiscal Year 1965 shipbuilding programme, laid down 5 May 1966 and launched 7 September 1967; *Dixon* authorised in the FY 1966, laid down 7 September 1967 and launched 20 June 1970; AS 38 of FY 1969 not built to provide funds for cost increases in other ship programmes. Cancelled 27 March 1969. *Emory S. Land* authorised in FY 1972, and *Frank Cable* in FY 1973 both laid down on 2 March 1976 and launched on 4 May 1977 and 14 January 1978 respectively. *McKee* authorised FY 1977, ordered 29 April 1977 and laid down 14 January 1978. No additional submarine tenders planned through FY 1983.
Estimated cost of AS 41 is $260·9 million.

2 "SIMON LAKE" CLASS: SUBMARINE TENDERS (AS)

Name	No.	Builders	Commissioned	F/S
SIMON LAKE	AS 33	Puget Sound Naval Shipyard	7 Nov 1964	AA
CANOPUS	AS 34	Ingalls S.B. Co, Pascagoula	4 Nov 1965	AA

Displacement, tons: 19 934 full load (AS 33); 21 089 (AS 34)
Dimensions, feet (metres): 643·7 × 85 × 30 *(196·2 × 25·9 × 9·1)*
Guns: 4—3 in *(76 mm)*/50 (twin Mk 33)
Main engines: Steam turbines (De Laval); 20 000 shp; 1 shaft = 20 knots
Boilers: 2 (Combustion Engineering)
Complement: 1 428 (90 officers, 1 338 men) (AS 33); 1 421 (95 officers, 1 326 enlisted men) (AS 34)

These ships are designed specifically to service fleet ballistic missile submarines (SSBN), with three submarines alongside being supported simultaneously.
Simon Lake was authorised in the Fiscal Year 1963 new construction programme, laid down on 7 January 1963 and launched 8 February 1964. *Canopus* was authorised in FY 1964, laid down on 2 March 1964 and launched on 12 February 1965. AS 35 was authorised in the FY 1965 programme, but her construction was cancelled 3 December 1964.

Conversions: Conversions to permit of Poseidon C-3 missile handling and repairing and support of related systems carried out at Puget Sound Navy yard as follows: *Canopus*, completed 3 February 1970; *Simon Lake*, completed 9 March 1971.

CANOPUS 1966, USN

2 "HUNLEY" CLASS: SUBMARINE TENDERS (AS)

Name	No.	Builders	Commissioned	F/S
HUNLEY	AS 31	Newport News S.B. & D.D. Co	16 June 1962	PA
HOLLAND	AS 32	Ingalls S.B. Co, Pascagoula	7 Sep 1963	AA

Displacement, tons: 10 500 standard; 19 000 full load
Dimensions, feet (metres): 599 × 83 × 27 *(182·6 × 25·3 × 8·2)*
Guns: 4—20 mm (singles)
Main engines: Diesel-electric (6 Fairbanks-Morse diesels); 15 000 bhp; 1 shaft = 19 knots
Complement: 2 568 (144 officers, 2 424 enlisted men)

These are the first US submarine tenders of post-World War II construction; they are designed specifically to provide repair and supply services to fleet ballistic missile submarines (SSBN). Have 52 separate workshops to provide complete support. Helicopter platform fitted aft but no hangar. Both ships originally fitted with a 32 ton capacity hammerhead crane; subsequently refitted with two amidships cranes as in "Simon Lake" class.
Hunley authorised in the Fiscal Year 1960 shipbuilding programme, laid down on 28 November 1960 and launched on 28 September 1961; *Holland* authorised in the FY 1962 programme, laid down on 5 March 1962 and launched on 19 January 1963. Former ship cost $24 359 800.

Conversions: Conversions to provide for Poseidon C-3 missile handling and repairing and support of related systems carried out at Puget Sound Navy Yard as follows: *Hunley*, completed 22 January 1974; *Holland*, completed 20 June 1975.

HOLLAND USN

730   USA / Auxiliary ships

7 "FULTON" and "PROTEUS" CLASSES: SUBMARINE TENDERS (AS)

Name	No.	Builders	Commissioned	F/S
FULTON	AS 11	Mare Island Navy Yard	12 Sep 1941	AA
SPERRY	AS 12	Moore S.B. & D.D. Co, Oakland	1 May 1942	PA
BUSHNELL	AS 15	Mare Island Navy Yard	10 Apr 1943	AR
HOWARD W. GILMORE (ex-*Neptune*)	AS 16	Mare Island Navy Yard	24 May 1944	AA
NEREUS	AS 17	Mare Island Navy Yard	27 Oct 1945	PR
ORION	AS 18	Moore S.B. & D.D. Co, Oakland	30 Sep 1943	AA
PROTEUS	AS 19	Moore S.B. & D.D. Co, Oakland	31 Jan 1944	PA

Displacement, tons: 9 734 standard; 16 230-17 020 full load (19 200, AS 19)
Dimensions, feet (metres): 530·5 (except *Proteus* 574·5) × 73·3 × 25·5 (161·7 (*Proteus* 175·1) × 22·3 × 7·8)
Guns: 2—5 in (*127 mm*)/38 in AS 15 and 17; 4—20 mm (Mk 67) (single) in active ships; 2—20 mm (Mk 24) (twin) in AS 17 only
Main engines: Diesel-electric (General Motors) (Allis Chalmers in AS 19); 11 200 bhp; 2 shafts = 15·4 knots
Complement: 1 286-1 937 (except *Proteus* 1 300 (86 officers, 1 214 enlisted men))

These venerable ships are contemporaries of the similar-design "Dixie" class destroyer tenders and the "Vulcan" class repair ships. Launched on 27 December 1940, 17 December 1941, 14 September 1942, 16 September 1943, 12 February 1945, 14 October 1942 and 12 November 1942 respectively. As built, they carried the then-standard large auxiliary armament of four 5 in guns plus eight 40 mm guns (twin). The original 20 ton capacity cylinder cranes have been replaced in *Howard W. Gilmore,* who is to be inactivated in FY 1980 and replaced by *Emory S. Land* (AS 39).

Conversion: *Proteus* AS 19 was converted at the Charleston Naval Shipyard, under the Fiscal Year 1959 conversion programme, at a cost of $23 million to service nuclear-powered fleet ballistic missile submarines (SSBN). Conversion was begun on 19 January 1959 and she was recommissioned on 8 July 1960. She was lengthened by adding a 44 ft section amidships, and the bare hull weight of this six-deck high insertion was approximately 500 tons. Three 5 in guns were removed and her upper decks extended aft to provide additional workshops. Storage tubes for Polaris missiles installed; bridge crane amidships loads and unloads missiles for alongside submarines.

Modernisation: All except *Proteus* have undergone FRAM II modernisation to service nuclear-powered attack submarines. Additional maintenance shops provided to service nuclear plant components and advanced electronic equipment and weapons. After two 5 in guns and eight 40 mm guns (twin) removed.

HOWARD W. GILMORE   6/1976, Dr. Giorgio Arra

SPERRY   3/1973, USN

2 "PIGEON" CLASS: SUBMARINE RESCUE SHIPS (ASR)

Name	No.	Builders	Commissioned	F/S
PIGEON	ASR 21	Alabama D.D. & S.B. Co, Mobile	28 Apr 1973	PA
ORTOLAN	ASR 22	Alabama D.D. & S.B. Co, Mobile	14 July 1973	AA

Displacement, tons: 3 411 full load
Dimensions, feet (metres): 251 × 86 (see *Design* notes) × 21·25 (*76·5 × 26·2 × 6·5*)
Guns: 2—20 mm (single)
Main engines: 4 diesels (Alco); 6 000 bhp; 2 shafts = 15 knots
Range, miles: 8 500 at 13 knots
Complement: 115 (6 officers, 109 enlisted men)
Staff accommodation: 14 (4 officers, 10 enlisted men)
Submersible operators: 24 (4 officers, 20 enlisted men)

These are the world's first ships designed specifically for this role, all other ASR designs being adaptations of tug types. The "Pigeon" class ships serve as (1) surface support ships for the Deep Submergence Rescue Vehicles (DSRV), (2) rescue ships employing the existing McCann rescue chamber, (3) major deep-sea diving support ships and (4) operational control ships for salvage operations. Each ASR is capable of transporting, servicing, lowering, and raising two Deep Submergence Rescue Vehicles (DSRV) (see section on Deep Submergence Vehicles). The Navy had planned in the 1960s to replace the 10 ship ASR force with new construction ASRs. However, only two ships were funded, with procurement of others cancelled.
Pigeon authorised in the Fiscal Year 1967 new construction programme and *Ortolan* in the FY 1968 programme. *Pigeon* was laid down on 17 July 1968 and launched on 13 August 1969; *Ortolan* was laid down on 22 August 1968 and launched on 10 September 1969; they were delayed more than two years by a shipyard strike and technical difficulties; additional delays encountered in special equipment installation.

Design: These ships have twin, catamaran hulls, the first ocean-going catamaran ships to be built for the US Navy with the exception of AGOR *Hayes* of the MSC, since Robert Fulton's steam gunboat *Demologos* of 1812. The design provides a large deck working area, facilities for raising and lowering submersibles and underwater equipment, and improved stability when operating equipment at great depths. Each of the twin hulls is 251 ft long and 26 ft wide. The well between the hulls is 34 feet across, giving the ASR a maximum beam of 86 ft. Fitted with helicopter platform and with precision three-dimensional sonar system for tracking submersibles.

Diving: These ships have been fitted with the Mk II Deep Diving System to support conventional or saturation divers operating at depths to 850 ft. The system consists of two decompression chambers, two personnel transfer capsules to transport divers between the ship and ocean floor, and the associated controls, winches, cables, gas supplies etc. Submarine rescue ships are the US Navy's primary diving ships and the only ones fitted for helium-oxygen diving.

Engineering: Space and weight are reserved for future installation of a ducted thruster in each bow to enable the ship to maintain precise position while stopped or at slow speeds.

ORTOLAN   9/1976, Dr. Giorgio Arra

PIGEON   12/1977, USN (PH2 R. Weissleder)

USA / Auxiliary ships 731

4 "CHANTICLEER" CLASS: SUBMARINE RESCUE SHIPS (ASR)

Name	No.	Builders	Commissioned	F/S
FLORIKAN	ASR 9	Moore S.B. & D.D. Co, Oakland	5 Apr 1943	PA
KITTIWAKE	ASR 13	Savannah Machine & Foundry Co	18 July 1946	AA
PETREL	ASR 14	Savannah Machine & Foundry Co	24 Sep 1946	AA
SUNBIRD	ASR 15	Savannah Machine & Foundry Co	28 Jan 1947	AA

Displacement, tons: 1 653 standard; 2 320 full load
Dimensions, feet (metres): 251·5 × 44 × 16 (76·7 × 13·4 × 4·9)
Guns: 2—20 mm (single) (Mk 68)
Main engines: Diesel-electric (Alco ARS 9 and 15; General Motors remainder); 3 000 bhp; 1 shaft = 15 knots
Complement: 116-221

Large tug-type ships equipped with powerful pumps, heavy air compressors, and rescue chambers for submarine salvage and rescue operations. Launched on 14 June 1942, 10 July 1945, 29 September 1945 and 3 April 1945 respectively.
Fitted for Helium-oxygen diving.
As built, each ship was armed with two 3 in guns; removed 1957-58. Some ships subsequently fitted with two 20 mm guns.

SUNBIRD 9/1975, Dr. Giorgio Arra

Transfers: Former US Navy submarine rescue ships serve in the navies of Brazil and Turkey—*Tringa* to Iran late 1978.

3 "SOTOYOMO" CLASS: AUXILIARY TUGS (ATA)

Name	No.	Builders	Commissioned	F/S
ACCOKEEK	ATA 181	Levingston S.B. Co, Orange, Texas	7 Oct 1944	MAR
STALLION	ATA 193	Levingston S.B. Co, Orange, Texas	26 Feb 1945	MAR
KEYWADIN	ATA 213	Gulfport Boiler & Welding Works, Port Arthur, Texas	1 June 1945	MAR

Displacement, tons: 534 standard; 860 full load
Dimensions, feet (metres): 143 × 33·9 × 13 (43·6 × 10·3 × 4·0)
Main engines: Diesel-electric (General Motors diesels); 1 500 bhp; 1 shaft = 13 knots
Complement: 49 (7 officers, 42 enlisted men)

Steel-hulled tugs formerly designated as rescue tugs (ATR); designation changed to ATA in 1944. Launched on 27 July 1944, 14 December 1944, and 9 April 1945 respectively. During 1948 they were assigned names that had been carried by discarded fleet and yard tugs.
All of the surviving ships were decommissioned in 1969-71 and placed in reserve. Two ships of this class serve in the Coast Guard.

Transfers: Ships of this class serve with Argentina, Colombia, Dominican Republic and Taiwan.

ACCOKEEK 1970, USN

0 + 7 "POWHATAN" CLASS: FLEET OCEAN TUGS (ATF)

Name	No.	Builders	Laid down	Completed	F/S
POWHATAN	ATF 166	Marinette Marine Corp, Wisc	30 Sep 1976	mid-1979	Bldg
NARRAGANSETT	ATF 167	Marinette Marine Corp, Wisc	5 May 1977	mid-1979	Bldg
CATAWBA	ATF 168	Marinette Marine Corp, Wisc	14 Dec 1977	mid-1979	Bldg
NAVAJO	ATF 169	Marinette Marine Corp, Wisc	14 Dec 1977	late 1979	Bldg
—	ATF 170	Marinette Marine Corp, Wisc	20 Feb 1979	mid-1980	Bldg
—	ATF 171	Marinette Marine Corp, Wisc	mid-1979	late 1980	Bldg
—	ATF 172	Marinette Marine Corp, Wisc	late 1979	mid-1981	Bldg

Displacement, tons: 2 400 full load
Dimensions, feet (metres): 240 × 48 × 17 (73·2 × 14·6 × 5·2)
Guns: (see notes)
Main engines: 2 diesels (General Motors); 4 500 bhp; 2 shafts; (cp propellers) = 15 knots
Complement: 47 (43 civilians, 4 Navy communications ratings)

A new class of fleet tugs built to commercial standards originally intended as successors to the "Cherokee" and "Abnaki" class ATFs. However, procurement was halted at seven ships with no more planned. All will be transferred to MSC upon completion for operational service. A 300 bhp bow thruster is fitted along with a 10 ton capacity crane.

Gunnery: Space provided to fit two 20 mm (single) amd two ·50 calibre machine guns in war. Unarmed during peacetime.

Fiscal: Estimated cost of the lead ship is $11·5 million. The ATF 170-172 will cost about $17·2 million each.

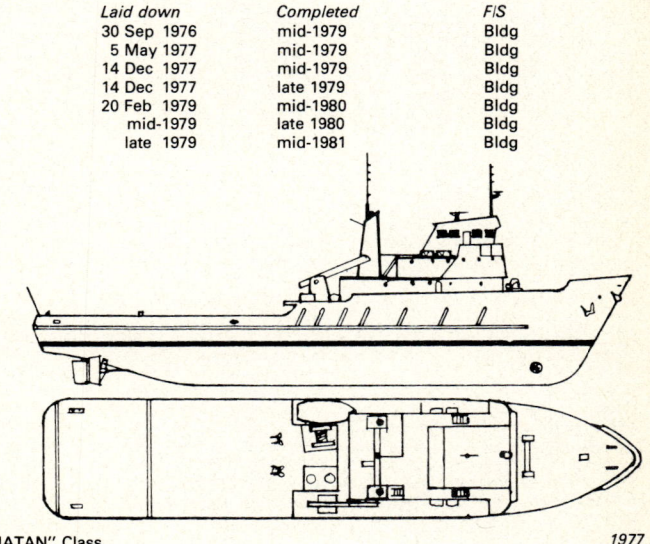
"POWHATAN" Class 1977

11 "CHEROKEE" and "ABNAKI" CLASSES: FLEET TUGS (ATF)

Name	No.	Builders	Commissioned	F/S
UTE	T-ATF 76	United Engineering Co, Alameda, Calif	31 Dec 1942	TPA
LIPAN	T-ATF 85	United Engineering Co, Alameda, Calif	29 Apr 1943	TPA
SENECA	ATF 91	Cramp S.B. Co, Philadelphia	30 Apr 1943	MAR
MOCTABI	ATF 105	Charleston S.B. & D.D. Co, SC	25 July 1944	NRF
QUAPAW	ATF 110	United Engineering Co, Alameda, Calif	6 May 1944	NRF
TAKELMA	ATF 113	United Engineering Co, Alameda, Calif	3 Aug 1944	PA
ATAKAPA	T-ATF 149	Charleston S.B. & D.D. Co, SC	8 Dec 1944	TAA
MOSOPELEA	T-ATF 158	Charleston S.B. & D.D. Co, SC	28 July 1945	TAA
PAIUTE	ATF 159	Charleston S.B. & D.D. Co, SC	27 Aug 1945	NRF
PAPAGO	ATF 160	Charleston S.B. & D.D. Co, SC	3 Oct 1945	NRF
SHAKORI	ATF 162	Charleston S.B. & D.D. Co, SC	20 Dec 1945	AA

Displacement, tons: 1 235 standard; 1 640 full load
Dimensions, feet (metres): 205 × 38·5 × 17 (62·5 × 11·7 × 5·2)
Gun: 1—3 in (76 mm)/50 (Mk 22) (gun removed from MSC ships and ATF 105 and 159)
Main engines: Diesel-electric drive (General Motors or Alco); 3 000 bhp; 1 shaft = 15 knots
Complement: 75 (5 officers, 70 enlisted men) navy; 24 civilians plus 6 navy communications personnel in MSC ships.

Large ocean tugs fitted with powerful pumps and other salvage equipment. ATF 96 and later ships ("Abnaki" class) have smaller funnel. As built these ships mounted two 40 mm guns in addition to 3 in gun. Launched on 24 June 1942, 17 September 1942, 22 January 1943, 25 March 1944, 15 May 1943, 18 September 1943, 11 July 1944, 7 March 1945, 4 June 1945, 21 June 1945 and 9 August 1945 respectively.
Beginning in 1973 several fleet tugs have been assigned to the Military Sealift Command and provided with civilian crews; these ships are designated T-ATF and are unarmed. ATF 85 and ATF 158 assigned to MSC in July 1973; ATF 76, and ATF 149 to MSC in July-August 1974. Three ships of this class serve with the US Coast Guard.

Deletions: On 18 January 1978 after slipping an old YO hulk at the bombing range near San Diego *Cree* (ATF 84) was accidentally bombed by a US A-6 Intruder aircraft. After the investiga-

SHAKORI 6/1978, Michael D. J. Lennon

tion *Cree* was deleted and sold for scrap.
Ute and *Lipan* to be deleted in FY 1980.

Naval Reserve: Following transferred to Naval Reserve Force: *Moctabi*, 1 January 1977; *Paiute*, 1 February 1977; *Papago*, 1 August 1977; *Quapaw*, 30 September 1977.

Transfers: Ships of this class serve with Argentina, Chile, Dominican Republic, Peru, Turkey, Taiwan and Venezuela.

732 USA / Auxiliary ships

3 "EDENTON" CLASS: SALVAGE AND RESCUE SHIPS (ATS)

Name	No.	Builders	Commissioned	F/S
EDENTON	ATS 1	Brooke Marine, Lowestoft, England	23 Jan 1971	AA
BEAUFORT	ATS 2	Brooke Marine, Lowestoft, England	22 Jan 1972	PA
BRUNSWICK	ATS 3	Brooke Marine, Lowestoft, England	19 Dec 1972	PA

Displacement, tons: 2 929 full load
Dimensions, feet (metres): 282·6 × 50 × 15·1 (86·1 × 15·2 × 4·6)
Guns: 2—20 mm (Mk 68 single) (ATS 2 and 3); 2—20 mm (twin Mk 24) (ATS 1)
Main engines: 4 diesels (Paxman); 6 000 bhp; 2 shafts; (cp propellers) = 16 knots
Complement: 100 (9 officers and 91 enlisted men)

These ships are designed specifically for salvage operations and are capable of (1) ocean towing, (2) supporting diver operations to depths of 850 ft, (3) lifting submerged objects weighing as much as 600 000 lb from a depth of 120 ft by static tidal lift or 30 000 lb by dynamic lift, (4) fighting ship fires, and (5) performing general salvage operations. Fitted with 10 ton capacity crane forward and 20 ton capacity crane aft.
ATS 1 was authorised in the Fiscal Year 1966 shipbuilding programme; ATS 2 and ATS 3 in the FY 1967 programme. Laid down on 1 April 1967, 19 February 1968 and 5 June 1968 respectively; launched on 15 May 1968, 20 December 1968 and 14 October 1969. In service the British-made components have created certain supply problems.
ATS 4 was authorised in the FY 1972 new construction programme and ATS 5 in the FY 1973 programme, with several additional ships being planned. However, construction of these ships was deferred in 1973 with the smaller modification of a commercial design ATF being substituted in their place.
Classification changed from salvage tug (ATS) to salvage and rescue ship (ATS) on 16 February 1971.

Diving: These ships can carry the air-transportable Mk 1 Deep Diving System which can support four divers working in two-man shifts at depths to 850 ft. The system consists of a double-chamber recompression chamber and a personnel transfer capsule to transport divers between the ship and ocean floor. The ships' organic diving capability is compressed air only.

Engineering: Fitted with tunnel bow thruster for precise manoeuvring.

EDENTON 9/1978, John G. Callis

1 CONVERTED "CURRITUCK" CLASS: GUIDED MISSILE SHIP (AVM)

Name	No.	Builders	Commissioned	F/S
NORTON SOUND	AVM 1 (ex-AV 11)	Los Angeles S.B. & D.D. Co, San Pedro	8 Jan 1945	PA

Displacement, tons: 9 106 standard; 15 170 full load
Dimensions, feet (metres): 540·6 × 71·6 × 23·5 (164·8 × 21·8 × 7·2)
Missiles: 1 twin Standard surface-to-air launcher (Mk 26)
Machinery: Geared turbines (Allis-Chalmers); 12 000 shp; 2 shafts = 19 knots
Boilers: 4 (Babcock & Wilcox)
Complement: 750 (86 officers, 664 enlisted men)

Norton Sound is a seagoing laboratory and test centre for advanced weapon systems. Constructed as a seaplane tender (AV 7); laid down 7 September 1942, launched 28 November 1943. After operating briefly in the Pacific War and afterward as a seaplane tender; in 1948 she was converted to a guided missile test ship.
Subsequently served as test ship for a number of research and weapon programmes, and is currently employed as a test platform for the Aegis advanced fleet defence system.

Classification: Changed from AV 11 to AVM 1 on 8 August 1951.

Conversion: Norton Sound was initially fitted as a guided missile (test) ship in 1948 during a seven month conversion at the Philadelphia Naval Shipyard; 30 ton capacity boom removed from fantail (similar boom retained on hangar structure); helicopter deck provided forward; provision for fuelling, checking out, monitoring, and firing rockets and missiles.
Converted from November 1962 to June 1964 at Maryland S.B. & D.D. Co, Baltimore, Maryland, to test ship for the Typhon advanced weapons control system (intended for a new class of nuclear-powered guided missile cruisers); Typhon system removed in July 1966.
Modified in 1974 to serve as test ship for the Aegis advanced fleet defence system. SPY-1 paired radar arrays to provide 180 degree coverage (12 × 12 ft, six-sided "faces") installed atop forward superstructure; Mk 110 radar control system installed (including five UYK-7 computers to control phase steering of radars). Twin Standard surface-to-air missile launcher fitted on stern. SPS 52 radar also fitted.

Gunnery: Fitted in 1968 with light-weight 5 in 54 calibre gun and associated Mk 86 gunfire control system for operational test and evaluation.

Missiles: Missiles and rockets test fired from Norton Sound include the Aerobee, Loon (US version of the German V-1), Lark, Regulus, Terrier, Tartar, and Sea Sparrow. During Project Argus in 1958 from a position south of the Falkland Islands she launched three multi-stage missiles carrying low-yield nuclear warheads which were detonated approximately 300 miles above the earth. (The ship was also used to launch high-altitude balloons in Project Skyhook during 1949).

NORTON SOUND 11/1974, USN

NAVAL RESERVE FORCE TRAINING AUXILIARY SHIPS

Name/No.	NRF Homeport	Date of Assignment
MOCTABI (ATF 105)	Everett, Wash	1 Jan 1977
QUAPAW (ATF 110)	Port Hueneme, Calif	30 Sep 1977
PAIUTE (ATF 159)	Mayport, Fla	1 Feb 1977
PAPAGO (ATF 160)	Little Creek, Va	1 Aug 1977

USA / Special vessels 733

SPECIAL VESSELS

ADVANCED NAVAL VEHICLES

(Not included in US Naval Vessels Register)

The US Navy has applied the term Advanced Naval Vehicles (ANV) to a number of platforms being considered for future construction programmes. These include airships, Small Waterplane Area Twin Hull (SWATH) ships, hydrofoils, Surface Effect Ships (SES), Air Cushion Vehicles (ACV), and Wing-In-Ground (WIG) effect machines, among others.

Some of these concepts are relatively old, such as the airship (which the US Navy discarded in 1962) and hydrofoils; the latter now being in production for the US Navy after several years of experimentation. After successful tests of two 100 ton SES designs the US Navy had planned to construct prototypes of a 2 000 ton ocean-going SES combatant. Preliminary characteristics of such an Advanced Naval Vehicle are provided below and the artist concept is shown on this page.

Navy plans for the 3 000 ton SES have been consistently slowed down since 1975 by a Department of Defense decision that the Navy should undertake a comprehensive analysis of all advanced platform concepts, determine their potential roles, and relate estimated costs. Accordingly, in 1975 the Navy established the Advanced Naval Vehicles Concept Evaluation effort.

The Navy's overall SES programme continues to be the largest ANV effort in terms of current funding, with $48 million requested for the Fiscal Year 1977. Still, this is a paltry sum when compared to research and development efforts in a number of other areas.

3 000 ton SURFACE EFFECT SHIP (SES)

Weight, tons: 3 000
Length, feet (metres): 270 *(82·3)*
Beam, feet (metres): 105 *(32)*
Skirt height, feet (metres): 18 *(5·5)*
Helicopters: 2 SH-3 Sea King
Missiles: Harpoon surface-to-surface launchers; Sea Sparrow surface-to-air launchers
Main/lift engines: gas turbines
Speed, knots: 85 (calm)

The above characteristics are those of a national combat-capable surface effect ship. Contracts were awarded to the Bell Aerospace Division of Textron and to Rohr Industries to undertake the development and design of such a ship. Although the nominal weight of 2 000 tons is in general use, it has become obvious that the SES will in reality be close to 3 000 tons.
After evaluation of the designs submitted by Rohr and Bell a contract for design with option to construct was awarded to Rohr Marine Inc, San Diego.
Money to build a prototype was to be requested under the FY 1979 budget, cost was to be about $90 million. However, the Carter Administration deleted all building funds from the FY 1979 request in December 1977. Instead $80 million was appropriated for continued research work. Under the FY 1980 research and development programme this craft was deleted from the Department of Defense request. (See *USSR* section.)
In A/S operations the large SES would employ the sprint-and-drift technique, whereby it would travel at high speeds to an area, slow to use its sensors to search the area, and then move on to another area.

Classification: During the early 1970s the Navy used the classification DSX for planning purposes to indicate a large SES employed in destroyer/frigate roles.

Design: The SES concept differs from the Air Cushion Vehicle (ACV) by having rigid "sidewalls" that pentrate into the water to provide stability for high-speed operation. Flexible "skirts" forward and aft trap the air bubble under the hull.

3 000 ton SES   *1977, Rohr Marine Inc*

1 EXPERIMENTAL SURFACE EFFECT SHIP (SES) AEROJET-GENERAL DESIGN

SES-100A

Weight, tons: 100 gross
Dimensions, feet (metres): 81·9 × 41·9 *(25·0 × 12·8)*
Main/lift engines: 4 gas turbines (Avco-Lycoming) 12 000 hp; three fans for lift and two water-jet propulsion systems = 80+ knots (designed)

Surface effect ship developed by Aerojet-General Corporation, and built by Tacoma Boatbuilding Co, Tacoma, Washington, to test feasibility of large SES for naval missions. Christened in July 1971; underway in mid-1972 in competition with the Bell design described below. Aluminium construction with rigid sidewalls to hold cushion or bubble of air. Cargo capacity ten tons (instrumentation during evaluation); provision for crew of four and six observers. Fitted with four TF-35 gas turbine engines, marine version of the T55-L-11A developed for the CH-47C helicopter. The SES-100A is reported to have reached 76 knots on trials. Overhauled at NAS Patuxent River in 1979. Under operational control of Naval Sea Systems Command.

SES-100A   *11/1978, USN*

1 EXPERIMENTAL SURFACE EFFECT SHIP (SES) BELL AEROSYSTEMS DESIGN

SES-100B

Weight, tons: 100 gross
Dimensions, feet (metres): 78 × 35 *(23·8 × 10·7)*
Main engines: 3 gas turbines (Pratt & Whitney); 13 500 hp; 2 semi submerged, super cavitating propellers = 80+ knots
Lift engines: 3 gas turbines (United Aircraft of Canada); 1 500 hp; eight lift fans

Surface effect ship developed by Bell Aerospace Division of the Textron Corp; built at Bell facility in Michoud, Louisiana. Christened on 6 March 1971; underway in February 1972 as competitive development platform for Navy.
Aluminium hull with rigid sidewalls to hold cushion or bubble of air. Cargo capacity ten tons (instrumentation during evaluation); provision for crew of four and six observers.
Fitted with three Pratt & Whitney FT-12 gas turbine engines and three United Aircraft of Canada ST-6J-70 gas turbine engines.
The SES-100B set an SES speed record of 89·48 knots during trials on 30 June 1976. During the same year she successfully made a vertical launch of a Standard missile while moving at 60 knots. Overhauled at NAS Patuxent River in 1979. Under operational control of Naval Sea Systems Command.

SES-100B   *1974, Bell Aerosystems*

SERVICE CRAFT

As of 1 January 1979, the US Navy has 1 102 service craft, primarily small craft, on the US Naval Vessel Register. A majority of them provide services to the fleet in various harbours and ports. Others are ocean going ships such as *Elk River* that provide services to the fleet in the research area. Only the self-propelled craft and relics are listed here. The non-self-propelled craft, such as floating cranes, dredges are not included. Most of the service craft are rated as "Active, in Service", but a few are rated as "in commission".

FLOATING DRY DOCKS

The US Navy operates a number of floating dry docks to supplement dry dock facilities at major naval activities, to support fleet ballistic missile submarines (SSBN) at advanced bases, and to provide repair capabilities in forward combat areas.

The larger floating dry docks are made sectional to facilitate movement overseas and to render them self docking. The ARD-type docks have the forward end of their docking well closed by a structure resembling the bow of a ship to facilitate towing. Berthing facilities, repair shops, and machinery are housed in sides of larger docks. None is self-propelled.

Nineteen floating dry docks are in Navy service (including one partial dock), eight are out of service in reserve (including two partial docks), and 27 are on lease to commercial firms for private use. Several are on loan to other US services and foreign navies (including one partial dock).

ARDM 4 was built at the Bethlehem Steel Co, Sparrows Point, Maryland. Designed specifically to service "Los Angeles" class (SSN 688) submarines. Completed January 1979.

Figures in parenthesis indicate the number of sections for sectional docks. Each section of the AFDB docks has a lifting capacity of about 10 000 tons. Four sections of the AFDB 7 form the floating dry dock *Los Alamos* at Holy Loch, Scotland and two sections are in reserve. (The AFDB sections each are 256 ft long, 80 ft in width, with wing walls 83 ft high; the wing walls, which contain compartments, fold down when the sections are towed).

White Sands (ARD 20) was reclassified as auxiliary deep submergence support vehicle (AGDS 1) on 1 August 1973; subsequently stricken. ARD 5 named *Waterford* 16 November 1976, ARD 7 *West Milton* on 18 May 1976 and ARD 30 *San Onofre* on 7 March 1975.

Transfers: The following floating dry docks are in foreign service: ARD 23 to Argentina; AFDL 39, ARD 14 to Brazil; ARD 32 to Chile; ARD 28 to Columbia; ARD 13 to Ecuador; AFDL 11 to Kampuchea (Cambodia); ARD 15, AFDL 28 to Mexico; ARD 6 to Pakistan; AFDL 26 to Paraguay; AFDL 33, ARD 8 to Peru; AFDL 20, AFDL 44 to Philippines; ARD 9, *Windsor* (ARD 22) to Taiwan; ARD 13 to Venezuela; AFDL 22 to South Viet-Nam; ARD 12 to Turkey; *Arco* (ARD 29) to Iran; ARD 25 to Chile; AFDL 24 to Philippines; ARD 11 to Mexico. Some of these have recently been bought outright from US Navy and have been deleted from US Naval Ship Register.

LARGE AUXILIARY FLOATING DRY DOCKS (AFDB)

Name-No.	Completed	Capacity	Construction	Notes
AFDB 1	1943	90 000 tons	Steel (5)	Navy Reserve (B/F only)
AFDB 2	1944	90 000 tons	Steel (10)	Navy Reserve
AFDB 3 (partial)	1944	81 000 tons	Steel (6)	Navy Reserve (Sections B, C, E/H)
AFDB 3 (partial)	1944	81 000 tons	Steel (3)	Maritime Reserve (Sections A, D and I)
AFDB 4	1944	55 000 tons	Steel (9)	Reserve
AFDB 5	1944	55 000 tons	Steel (7)	Navy Reserve
AFDB 7 (partial)	1944	20 000 tons	Steel (2)	Navy Reserve (C and D)
LOS ALAMOS AFDB 7 (partial)	1944	40 000 tons	Steel (4)	Navy Holy Loch, Scotland (A, B, E and G only)

MEDIUM AUXILIARY FLOATING DRY DOCKS (AFDM)

Name-No.	Completed	Capacity	Construction	Notes
AFDM 1 (ex-YFD 3)	1942	15 000 tons	Steel (3)	Commercial lease
AFDM 2 (ex-YFD 4)	1942	15 000 tons	Steel (3)	Commercial lease
AFDM 3 (ex-YFD 6)	1943	18 000 tons	Steel (3)	Commercial lease
AFDM 5 (ex-YFD 21)	1943	18 000 tons	Steel (3)	Subic Bay, Philippines
AFDM 6 (ex-YFD 62)	1944	18 000 tons	Steel (3)	Subic Bay, Philippines
AFDM 7 (ex-YFD 63)	1945	18 000 tons	Steel (3)	Norfolk, Va
RICHLAND AFDM 8 (ex-YFD 64)	1944	18 000 tons	Steel (3)	Guam, Marianas
AFDM 9 (ex-YFD 65)	1945	18 000 tons	Steel (3)	Commercial lease
AFDM 10	1945	18 000 tons	Steel (3)	Commercial lease

AFDM 6   8/1978, Dr. Giorgio Arra

SMALL AUXILIARY FLOATING DRY DOCKS (AFDL)

Name-No.	Completed	Capacity	Construction	Notes
AFDL 1	1943	1 000 tons	Steel	Guantanamo Bay, Cuba
AFDL 2	1943	1 000 tons	Steel	Commercial lease
AFDL 6	1944	1 000 tons	Steel	Little Creek, Virginia
AFDL 7	1944	1 900 tons	Steel	Subic Bay, Philippines
AFDL 8	1943	1 000 tons	Steel	Commercial lease
AFDL 9	1943	1 000 tons	Steel	Commercial lease
AFDL 10	1943	1 000 tons	Steel	Reserve
AFDL 12	1943	1 000 tons	Steel	Commercial lease
AFDL 15	1943	1 000 tons	Steel	Commercial lease
AFDL 16	1943	1 000 tons	Steel	Commercial lease
AFDL 19	1944	1 000 tons	Steel	Commercial lease
AFDL 21	1944	1 000 tons	Steel	Commercial lease
AFDL 23	1944	1 900 tons	Steel	Subic Bay, Philippines
AFDL 25	1944	1 000 tons	Steel	Loaned to Army
AFDL 29	1943	1 000 tons	Steel	Commercial lease
AFDL 35	1944	2 800 tons	Concrete	Commercial lease
AFDL 37	1944	2 800 tons	Concrete	Commercial lease
AFDL 38	1944	2 800 tons	Concrete	Commercial lease
AFDL 40	1944	2 800 tons	Concrete	Commercial lease
AFDL 41	1944	2 800 tons	Concrete	Commercial lease
AFDL 45	1944	2 800 tons	Concrete	Commercial lease
AFDL 47	1946	6 500 tons	Steel	Reserve
AFDL 48	1956	4 000 tons	Concrete	Long Beach Naval Shipyard

AFDL 6   9/1976, Dr. Giorgio Arra

AUXILIARY REPAIR DRY DOCKS and MEDIUM AUXILIARY REPAIR DRY DOCKS (ARD and ARDM)

Name-No.	Completed	Capacity	Construction	Notes
WATERFORD (ARD 5)	1942	3 000 tons	Steel	New London, Connecticut
WEST MILTON (ARD 7)	1943	3 000 tons	Steel	New London, Connecticut
ARDM 3 (ex-ARD 18)	1944	3 000 tons	Steel	Charleston, South Carolina
ARDM 4	1979		Steel	New London, Connecticut
OAK RIDGE ARDM 1 (ex-ARD 19)	1944	3 000 tons	Steel	King's Bay, Georgia
ARD 24	1944	3 000 tons	Steel	San Francisco, Calif
ALAMAGORDO ARDM 2 (ex-ARD 26)	1944	3 000 tons	Steel	Charleston, South Carolina
SAN ONOFRE (ARD 30)	1944	3 000 tons	Steel	Pearl Harbor Naval Shipyard

SAN ONOFRE (ARD 30)   6/1970, USN

USA / Floating dry docks — Unclassified miscellaneous 735

YARD FLOATING DRY DOCKS (YFD)

Name-No.	Completed	Capacity	Construction	Notes
YFD 7	1943	18 000 tons	Steel (3)	Commercial lease
YFD 8	1942	20 000 tons	Wood	Commercial lease
YFD 23	1943	10 500 tons	Wood	Commercial lease
YFD 54	1943	5 000 tons	Wood	Commercial lease
YFD 68	1945	14 000 tons	Steel (3)	Commercial lease
YFD 69	1945	14 000 tons	Steel (3)	Commercial lease
YFD 70	1945	14 000 tons	Steel (3)	Commercial lease
YFD 71	1945	14 000 tons	Steel (3)	San Diego Naval Base
YFD 83 (ex-AFDL 31)	1943	1 000 tons	Steel	US Coast Guard

1 "ADMIRAL W. S. BENSON" CLASS: UNCLASSIFIED MISCELLANEOUS (IX)

Name	No.	Builders	Commissioned	F/S
GENERAL HUGH J. GAFFEY (ex-*Admiral W. L. Capps*)	IX 507 (ex-AP 121)	Bethlehem Steel Co, Alameda	18 Sep 1944	PSA

Displacement, tons: 22 574 full load; 12 657 light
Dimensions, feet (metres): 609 × 76 × 29 *(185·6 × 23·2 × 8·8)*
Main engines: Turbo-electric (General Electric); 18 000 shp; 4 shafts = 21 knots
Boilers: 4 Combustion Engineering
Complement: 2 076 (499 officers, 1 577 enlisted) (includes troop berthing)

Former Transport (AP). Served with the US Navy from 1944-46; operated by the Army Transportation Corp. 1946-50. Reacquired by the Navy on 1 March 1950 for operation by the Military Sea Transportation Service (now the Military Sealift Command). Served continuously until laid up in early 1969 and stricken 9 October 1969. Laid up in the Maritime Administration Reserve Fleet, Suisun Bay. Reacquired by the navy on 1 November 1978 and reinstated on the Naval Vessel Register on the same date. Reclassified from AP 121 to IX 507 on 1 November 1978. Reacquired for service as a Barracks Ship at Bremerton Naval Shipyard, Bremerton, Washington for the crew of USS *Enterprise* (CVN 65) which started a two year overhaul at Bremerton in January 1979. Portions of the ship is still inactivated. Only the berthing areas, crew quarters and necessary supporting areas have been activated. All topside gear and most of the superstructure, as well as portions of the hull remain inactivated. Placed "in service" in mid-1979. She will remain in service at least through FY 1983.

3 "BENEWAH" CLASS: UNCLASSIFIED MISCELLANEOUS (IX)

Name	No.	Builders	Commissioned	F/S
MERCER	IX 502 (ex-APB 39, ex-APL 39)	Boston Navy Yard	19 Sep 1945	PSA
NUECES	IX 503 (ex-APB 40, ex-APL 40)	Boston Navy Yard	30 Nov 1945	PSA
ECHOLS	IX 504 (ex-APB 37, ex-APL 37)	Boston Navy Yard	1 Jan 1947	ASA

Displacement, tons: 4 080 full load
Dimensions, feet (metres): 328 × 50 × 11 *(100·0 × 15·2 × 3·4)*
Guns: Vary
Main engines: Diesels (General Motors); 1 600 to 1 800 bhp; 2 shafts = 10 knots
Complement: 193 (13 officers, 180 enlisted men) as APB
Troops: 1 226 (26 officers, 1 200 enlisted men) as APB

Originally built as self-propelled barracks ships (APB) built to provide support and accommodation for small craft and riverine forces. Launched on 30 July 1945, 17 November 1944, 6 May 1945, respectively. *Echols* placed in reserve January 1947. All ex-LST type ships of the same basic characteristics. *Mercer* and *Nueces* recommissioned in 1968 for service in Viet-Nam; decommissioned in 1969-71 as US riverine forces in South Viet-Nam were reduced.
Each APB has troop berthing and messing facilities, evaporators which produce up to 40 000 gallons of fresh water per day, a 16 bed hospital, X-ray room, dental room, bacteriological laboratory, pharmacy, laundry, library, and tailor shop; living and most working spaces are air-conditioned.

MERCER (as APB 39)   1968, USN

Mercer and *Nueces* again reactivated in 1974 to serve as barrack ships for ships in overhaul at Puget Sound Naval Shipyard, Bremerton, Washington. *Echols* reactivated in 1976 to provide berthing for crews of Trident missile submarines being built by General Dynamics Electric Boat Division in Groton, Connecticut.

Classification: *Mercer* and *Nueces* reclassified as "unclassified miscellaneous" (IX) on 1 November 1975; *Echols* changed to IX on 1 February 1976.

1 CONVERTED "ELK RIVER" CLASS: UNCLASSIFIED MISCELLANEOUS (IX)

Name	No.	Builders	Commissioned	F/S
ELK RIVER	IX 501 (ex-LSMR 501)	Brown S.B. Co, Houston	27 May 1945	PSA

Displacement, tons: 1 785 full load
Dimensions, feet (metres): 229·7 × 50 × 9·2 *(70 × 15·2 × 2·8)*
Main engines: Diesels; 1 400 bhp; 2 shafts = 11 knots
Complement: 25 + 20 technical personnel

Elk River is a former rocket landing ship specifically converted to support Navy deep submergence activities on the San Clemente Island Range off the coast of southern California. Launched 21 April 1945.
The ship is capable of supporting (1) deep diving for man-in-the-sea programmes, (2) deep diving for salvage programmes, (3) submersible test and evaluation, (4) underwater equipment testing, and (5) deep mooring operations. Operated by combined Navy-civilian crew.

Conversion: She was withdrawn from the Reserve Fleet and converted to a range support ship in 1967-68 at Avondale Shipyards Inc, Westwego, Louisiana, and the San Francisco Bay Naval Shipyard.
The basic LSMR hull was lengthened and eight-foot sponsons were added to either side to increase deck working space and stability; superstructure added forward. An open centre well was provided to facilitate lowering and raising equipment; also fitted with 65 ton capacity gantry crane (on tracks) to handle submersibles and active positioning mooring system to hold ship in precise location without elaborate mooring and permit shifting within the moor. Five anchors including bow anchor. Fitted with prototype Mk 2 Deep Diving System.

ELK RIVER   1978, Dr. Giorgio Arra

1 CONVERTED "MARK" CLASS: UNCLASSIFIED MISCELLANEOUS (IX)

Name	No.	F/S
NEW BEDFORD	IX 308 (ex-AKL 17, ex-FS 289)	PSA

Displacement, tons: Approx 700
Dimensions, feet (metres): 176·5 × 32·8 × 10 *(53·8 × 10·0 × 3·1)*
Main engines: Diesel; 1 000 bhp; 1 shaft = 10 knots

Former Army cargo ship (freight and supply) acquired by the Navy on 1 March 1950 for cargo work and subsequently converted to support torpedo testing. Operated since 1963 by Naval Torpedo Station, Keyport, Washington. Employed as Torpedo Test ship.

NEW BEDFORD   1973, USN

736 USA / Miscellaneous

1 CONVERTED ARMY SUPPLY SHIP TYPE: UNCLASSIFIED MISCELLANEOUS (IX)

IX 306 (ex-FS 221)

Displacement, tons: 906 full load
Dimensions, feet (metres): 179 × 33 × 10 (54·6 × 10·1 × 3·1)
Main engine: Diesel; 1 shaft = 12 knots

Former Army cargo ship (freight and supply) acquired by the Navy in January 1969 and subsequently converted to a weapon test ship, being placed in service late in 1969. Conducts research for the Naval Underwater Weapons Research and Engineering Station, Newport, Rhode Island; operates in Atlantic Underwater Test and Evaluation Centre (AUTEC) range in Caribbean. Manned by Navy and civilian RCA personnel. Note white hull with blue bow and torpedo tube opening on starboard side just aft of hull number.

IX 306   1969, USN

1 UNCLASSIFIED MISCELLANEOUS: BARGE GROUP (IX)

IX 310

A group of barges used by Naval Underwater Sound Laboratory, Newport, Rhode Island. Placed "in service" 1 April 1971. Consists of two barges joined by a deckhouse. Based on Lake Seneca, NY.

1 UNCLASSIFIED MISCELLANEOUS: SAIL FRIGATE (IX)

(See frontispiece)

Name	No.	Under Way	F/S
CONSTITUTION	None	23 July 1798	AA

The oldest ship remaining on the Navy List. *Constitution* is one of the six frigates authorised by act of Congress on 27 March 1794. Has been in full commission since October 1971, having been "in commission, special" prior to that date. Served as Flagship of the First Naval District until 1 October 1977 when she was transferred to the control of the Director of Naval History, Department of the Navy. Every year she is taken out into Boston Harbor and "turned around" so she will wear evenly on both sides of her masts. Overhauled at the former Boston Naval Shipyard from April 1973 to early 1975 at the cost of $4·2 million to "spruce her up" for the American Bicentennial. The "Unclassified Miscellaneous" classification of IX-21, assigned to her on 8 January 1941 was dropped on 1 September 1975 for some unfathomable reason. With her classification dropped, she is the only US Navy ship carried on the Naval Vessel Register without a classification. Since a ship in commission can not be on the Naval Register without a classification, her legal status as a naval ship is hazy.

The sailing ship *Constellation*, which survives under private ownership at Baltimore, Maryland, is apparently the last sailing man-of-war built for the US Navy; she was constructed at the Norfolk (Virginia) Navy Yard in 1853-54, built in part with material from the earlier frigate *Constellation* (launched 1797).

1 CONVERTED "YW 83" CLASS: MISCELLANEOUS AUXILIARY (YAG)

Name	No.	F/S
MONOB I	YAG 61 (ex-IX 309, ex-YW 87)	ASA

Displacement, tons: 440 light; 1 390 full load
Dimensions, feet (metres): 174 × 33 (53 × 10·8)
Main engine: 1 diesel = 7 knots

Monob I is a mobile listening barge converted from a self-propelled water barge. Built in 1943 and completed conversion for acoustic research in May 1969, being placed in service in May 1969. Conducts research for the Naval Mine Defence Laboratory, Panama City, Fla. Designation changed from IX 309 to YAG 61 on 1 July 1970.

MONOB I   1969, USN

2 DIVING TENDERS (YDT)

Tenders used to support shallow-water diving operations. Two self-propelled diving tenders are on the Navy List: *Phoebus* YDT 14 (ex-YF 294), and *Suitland* YDT 15 (ex-YF 336). (Two non-self-propelled YDTs are in service.)

3 COVERED LIGHTERS (YF)

Lighters used to transport material in harbours; self-propelled; three are on the Navy List: YF 862, YF 866 and *Keyport* (YF 885). Only *Keyport* is in service.

6 FERRYBOATS (YFB)

Ferryboats used to transport personnel and vehicles in large harbours; self-propelled; YFB 83 and 87-91; all are active. In service. YFB 88-91 are the former LCU 1636, 1638-1640, all reclassified on 1 September 1969. *Aquidneck* (YFB 14) transferred to State of Washington on 23 December 1975.

YFB 88 (ex-LCU 1636)   USN

USA / Miscellaneous 737

1 REFRIGERATED COVERED LIGHTER (YFR)

...ed to store and transport food and other materials which require refrigeration. *YFR 888* ...mains on the Navy List in reserve.

5 COVERED LIGHTERS (RANGE TENDER (YFRT))

...ghters used for miscellaneous purposes; YFRT 287, 451, 520, and 523 active; YFRT 418 is in ...serve. Note Mk 32 torpedo tubes on YFRT 520.

YFRT 520   1969, USN

10 HARBOUR UTILITY CRAFT (YFU): 1 UNCLASSIFIED MISCELLANEOUS (IX)

...U 71	YFU 74	YFU 76	YFU 79	YFU 81
...U 72	YFU 75	YFU 77	YFU 80	IX 506 (ex-*YFU 82*)
				YFU 83

Dimensions, feet (metres): 125 × 36 × 7·5 *(38·1 × 10·9 × 2·3)*
Main engines: Diesels = 8 knots
Guns: 2—·50 cal MG

...ilitarised versions of a commercial lighter design and a single craft *(YFU 83)* built to LCU 1646 ...esign and of similar characteristics. Used for off-loading large ships in harbours and ferrying ...argo from one coastal port to another. Built by Pacific Coast Engineering Co, Alameda, ...alifornia; completed 1967-1968. Can carry more than 300 tons cargo; considerable cruising ...nge.
...FU 71-77 and *YFU 80-82* loaned to US Army in 1970 for use in South Viet-Nam; returned to ...avy control in 1973. Only *YFU 81* and *83* are active—rest in reserve. YFU 82 reclassified IX 506 ...1 April 1978. Assigned in active status to Naval Oceanographic Systems Center.

YFU 75   1968, USN

8 HARBOUR UTILITY CRAFT LCU TYPE (YFU)

YFU 50 (ex-LCU 1486)	YFU 97 (ex-LCU 1611)	YFU 101 (ex-LCU 1612)
YFU 91 (ex-LCU 1608)	YFU 98 (ex-LCU 1615)	YFU 102 (ex-LCU 1462)
YFU 93 (ex-LCU 1625)	YFU 100 (ex-LCU 1610)	

Former utility landing craft employed primarily as harbour and coastal cargo craft (see section on Landing Craft for basic characteristics).
Several YFUs were loaned to the US Army in 1970 for use in Viet-Nam after withdrawal of US Navy riverine and coastal forces. *YFU 91, 98, 100-102* active; rest in reserve.

18 FUEL OIL BARGES (YO)

Small liquid fuel carriers intended to fuel ships where no pierside fuelling facilities are available; self-propelled. 11 units active, remainder in reserve.

8 GASOLINE BARGES (YOG)

Similar to the fuel barges (YO), but carry gasoline and aviation fuels; self-propelled; four are active with four in reserve.

22 PATROL CRAFT (YP)

...P 654	YP 657	YP 661	YP 665	YP 669	YP 673
...P 655	YP 658	YP 662	YP 666	YP 670	YP 674
...P 656	YP 659	YP 663	YP 667	YP 671	YP 675
	YP 660	YP 664	YP 668	YP 672	

...P 654 series:

Displacement, tons: 69·5 full load
Dimensions, feet (metres): 80·4 × 18·8 × 5·3 *(24·5 × 5·7 × 1·6)*
Main engines: 4 diesels (General Motors); 660 bhp; 2 shafts = 13·5 knots

...P 673 series:

Displacement, tons: 68 full load
Dimensions, feet (metres): 80·6 × 17·8 × 5·3 *(24·6 × 5·4 × 1·6)*
Main engines: 2 Detroit diesels; 680 bhp; 2 shafts = 12 knots

YP 669   1971, Peterson Builders

These craft are used for instruction in seamanship and navigation at the Naval Academy, Annapolis, Maryland; Naval Officer Candidate School, Newport, Rhode Island; and Surface Warfare Officers School at Newport. Fitted with surface search radar, Fathometer, gyro compass, and UHF and MF radio; *YP 655* additionally fitted for instruction in oceanographic research at the Naval Academy.
YP 654-663 built by Stephens Bros, Inc, Stockton, California; completed in 1958; *YP 664* and *665* built by Elizabeth City Shipbuilders, Inc, Elizabeth City, North Carolina; *YP 666* and *667* built by Stephens Bros; *YP 668* built by Peterson Boatbuilding Co, Tacoma, Washington, completed in 1968; *YP 669-672* built by Peterson completed in 1971-1972. *YP 673-675* authorised in FY 1977. Builders, Peterson Builders Inc, Sturgeon Bay, Wisconsin——laid down April-December 1978 and completed June-September 1979.
These craft are of wooden construction with aluminium deck houses.

738 USA/ Tugs — Miscellaneous

81 LARGE HARBOUR TUGS (YTB)

EDENSHAW	YTB 752	TAMAQUA	YTB 797
MARIN	YTB 753	OPELIKA	YTB 789
PONTIAC	YTB 756	NATCHITOCHES	YTB 799
OSHKOSH	YTB 757	EUFAULA	YTB 800
PADUCAH	YTB 758	PALATKA	YTB 801
BOGALUSA	YTB 759	CHERAW	YTB 802
NATICK	YTB 760	NANTICOKE	YTB 803
OTTUMWA	YTB 761	AHOSKIE	YTB 804
TUSCUMBIA	YTB 762	OCALA	YTB 805
MUSKEGON	YTB 763	TUSKEGEE	YTB 806
MISHAWAKA	YTB 764	MASSAPEQUA	YTB 807
OKMULGEE	YTB 765	WENATCHEE	YTB 808
WAPAKONETA	YTB 766	AGAWAN	YTB 809
APALACHICOLA	YTB 767	ANOKA	YTB 810
ARCATA	YTB 768	HOUMA	YTB 811
CHESANING	YTB 769	ACCONAC	YTB 812
DAHLONEGA	YTB 770	POUGHKEEPSIE	YTB 813
KEOKUK	YTB 771	WAXAHATCHIE	YTB 814
NASHUA	YTB 774	NEODESHA	YTB 815
WAUWATOSA	YTB 775	CAMPTI	YTB 816
WEEHAWKEN	YTB 776	HAYANNIS	YTB 817
NOGALES	YTB 777	MECOSTA	YTB 818
APOPKA	YTB 778	IUKA	YTB 819
MANHATTAN	YTB 779	WANAMASSA	YTB 820
SAUGUS	YTB 780	TONTOGANY	YTB 821
NIANTIC	YTB 781	PAWHUSKA	YTB 822
MANISTEE	YTB 782	CANONCHET	YTB 823
REDWING	YTB 783	SANTAQUIN	YTB 824
KALISPELL	YTB 784	WATHENA	YTB 825
WINNEMUCCA	YTB 785	WASHTUCNA	YTB 826
TONKAWA	YTB 786	CHETEK	YTB 827
KITTANNING	YTB 787	CATAHECASSA	YTB 828
WAPATO	YTB 788	METACOM	YTB 829
TOMAHAWK	YTB 789	PUSHMATHA	YTB 830
MENOMINEE	YTB 790	DEKANAWIDA	YTB 831
MARINETTE	YTB 791	PETALESHARO	YTB 832
ANTIGO	YTB 792	SHABONEE	YTB 833
PIQUA	YTB 793	NEWGAGON	YTB 834
MANDAN	YTB 794	SKENANDOA	YTB 835
KETCHIKAN	YTB 795	POKAGON	YTB 836
SACO	YTB 796		

KALISPELL 8/1978, Dr. Giorgio Arr

Displacement, tons: 350 full load
Dimensions, feet (metres): 109 × 30 × 13·8 (33·2 × 9·1 × 4·2)
Main engines: 2 diesels; 2 000 bhp; 2 shafts
Complement: 10 to 12 (enlisted)

Large harbour tugs; 81 are in active service. YTB 752 completed in 1959, YTB 753 in 1960, YT 756-762 in 1961, YTB 763-766 in 1963, YTB 770 and YTB 771 in 1964, YTB 767-769, 776 in 196 YTB 774, 775, 777-789 in 1966, YTB 790-793 in 1967, YTB 794 and 795 in 1968, YTB 796-803 1969, and YTB 804-815 completed in 1970-72, YTB 816-827 completed 1972-73, YTB 828-83 completed 1974-75. YTB 837 and YTB 838 transferred upon completion in late 1975 to Sau Arabia.

63 MEDIUM HARBOUR TUGS (YTM)

HOGA (YTM 146)	WINGINA (YTM 395)	NAHOKE (YTM 536)
TOKA (YTM 149)	YANEGUA (YTM 397)	CHEGODEGA (YTM 542)
KONOKA (YTM 151)	NATAHKI (YTM 398)	ETAWINA (YTM 543)
JUNALUSKA (YTM 176)	NUMA (YTM 399)	YATANOCAS (YTM 544)
DEKAURY (YTM 178)	OTOKOMI (YTM 400)	ACCOHANOC (YTM 545)
MADOKAWANDO (YTM 180)	PITAMAKAN (YTM 403)	TAKOS (YTM 546)
NEPANET (YTM 189)	COSHECTON (YTM 404)	YANABA (YTM 547)
SASSACUS (YTM 193)	CUSSETA (YTM 405)	MATUNAK (YTM 548)
DEKANISORA (YTM 252)	KITTATON (YTM 406)	MIGADAN (YTM 549)
HIAWATHA (YTM 265)	POROBAGO (YTM 413)	ACOMA (YTM 701)
RED CLOUD (YTM 268)	SECOTA (YTM 415)	ARAWAK (YTM 702)
PAWTUCKET (YTM 359)	TACONNET (YTM 417)	MORATOC (YTM 704)
SASSABA (YTM 364)	— (YTM 496)	YUMA (YTM 748)
WAUBANSEE (YTM 366)	NABIGWON (YTM 521)	HACKENSACK (YTM 750)
CHEPANOC (YTM 381)	SAGAWAMICK (YTM 522)	MASCOUTAH (YTM 760)
COATOPA (YTM 382)	SENASQUA (YTM 523)	MENASHA (YTM 761)
COCHALI (YTM 383)	TUTAHACO (YTM 524)	APOHOLA (YTM 768)
WANNALANCET (YTM 385)	WAHAKA (YTM 526)	MIMAC (YTM 770)
GANADOGA (YTM 390)	WAHPETON (YTM 527)	HIAMONEE (YTM 776)
ITARA (YTM 391)	NADLI (YTM 534)	LELAKA (YTM 777)
MECOSTA (YTM 392)		POCASSET (YTM 779)
WINAMAC (YTM 394)		

ETAWINA (YTM 543) 1975, Dr. Giorgio Arra

Former YTBs renumbered YTMs in the mid-1960s. Some are former Army Tugboats. About half are in reserve (US Navy and Maritime) and half active.

10 SMALL HARBOUR TUGS (YTL)

Unnamed. Five are active and five in reserve.

11 WATER BARGES (YW)

Barges modified to carry water to ships in harbour; self-propelled. Three active, eight in reserve.

TORPEDO WEAPONS RETRIEVERS (TWR)

Displacement, tons: 97·4 light; 152 full load
Dimensions, feet (metres): 102 × 21 × 7·8 (31·1 × 6·4 × 2·4)
Main engines: 4 diesels; 2 shafts = 18 knots
Range, miles: 1 900 at 10 knots
Complement: 15 (enlisted)

These are the largest of several types of torpedo recovery craft operated by the Navy. They are fitted to recover torpedoes and perform limited torpedo maintenance during exercises. An internal stern ramp facilitates recovery and up to 17 tons of torpedoes can be carried. These large TWRs also perform harbour utility duties. Range is 1 900 miles at 10 knots. Some are numbered—one is given the distinguished Royal Naval name of "Diamond". None carried on Naval Vessel Register.

TWR 9/1975, Dr. Giorgio Arra

MILITARY SEALIFT COMMAND
(See also under Auxiliaries Section)

Sealift ships provide ocean transportation for all components of the Department of Defense. These ships are operated by the Navy's Military Sealift Command (MSC), renamed on 1 August 1970 from Military Sea Transportation Service (MSTS). Sealift cargo ships and tankers are not configured to provide underway replenishment (UNREP) of other ships, or land stores over the beach in amphibious landings. Four MSC-operated cargo ships are fitted to carry Submarine-Launched Ballistic Missiles (SLBM) and other supplies for US Polaris/Poseidon submarines. On 1 February 1979 there was a total of 69 ships active in the MSC nucleus fleet of which 66 were fully active and three in reduced operating status. Four MSC ships are scheduled for deletion and one inactivated in FY 1980.

Most US defence cargo is carried in commercial merchant ships under charter to the government (through the Military Sealift Command).
The Commander, Deputy Commander, and Area Commanders of the MSC (Atlantic, Pacific, and Far East) are flag officers of the Navy on active duty. All ships are civilian manned with most of their crews being Civil Service employees of the Navy. However, the tankers are operated under contract to commercial tanker lines and are manned by merchant seamen.
The Military Sealift Command also operates a number of underway replenishment (UNREP) ships, fleet support ships, and special projects ships that support other defence-related activities, mostly research, surveying and missile-range support ships.
This section also includes research ships on loan to various civilian research institutions.

Armament: No ship of the Military Sealift Command is armed.

Classification: Military Sealift Command ships are assigned standard US Navy hull designations with the added designation prefix "T". Ships in this category are referred to as "USNS" (United States Naval Ship) instead of "USS" (United States Ship) which is used for Navy-manned ships.

1 "RIGEL" CLASS: STORE SHIP (AF)

Name	No.	Launched	Commissioned	F/S
RIGEL	T-AF 58	15 Mar 1955	2 Sep 1955	TAA

Displacement, tons: 7 950 light; 15 540 full load
Dimensions, feet (metres): 502 × 72 × 29 *(153·0 × 22·0 × 8·8)*
Guns: none
Main engine: Geared turbine (General Electric); 16 000 shp; 1 shaft = 20 knots
Boilers: 2 (Combustion Engineering)
Complement: approx 350

Built by Ingalls Shipbuilding Co, Pascagoula. R3-S-A4 type. Helicopter platform fitted aft. *Rigel* was assigned to Military Sealift Command on 23 June 1975 (guns removed).

"RIGEL" Class 1974, USN

1 CONVERTED "MISSION" CLASS: MISCELLANEOUS (AG)

In 1979 *Vanguard* (AGM 19) was reclassified AG 194. She will replace *Compass Island* (AG 153) as test ship for Fleet Ballistic Missile guidance and ship navigation systems. For further data see under "Vanguard" class AGM/AG.

1 CONVERTED "VICTORY" TYPE: MISCELLANEOUS (AG)

Name	No.	Builders	F/S
KINGSPORT (ex-*Kingsport Victory*)	T-AG 164	California S.B. Corp	TAA

Displacement, tons: 7 190 light; 10 680 full load
Dimensions, feet (metres): 455 × 62 × 22 *(138·7 × 18·9 × 6·7)*
Main engines: Geared turbines; 8 500 shp; 1 shaft = 15·2 knots
Boilers: 2
Complement: 73 (13 officers, 42 men, 15 technicians)

Maritime Administration type VC2-S-AP3. Employed as cargo ship by Military Sea Transportation Service prior to conversion. Name shortened, ship reclassified and converted in 1961-62 by Willamette Iron & Steel Co, Portland, Oregon, into the world's first satellite communications ship, for Project Advent, involving the promotion of a terminal to meet the required military capability for high capacity, world-wide radio communications using high altitude hovering satellites, and the installation of ship-to-shore communications facilities, additional electric power generating equipment, a helicopter landing platform, aerological facilities, and a 30 ft parabolic communication antenna housed in a 53 ft diameter plastic radome abaft the superstructure. Protect Advent Syncom satellite relay operations were completed in 1966, and *Kingsport* was reassigned to hydrographic research. Antenna sphere now removed.
Note antenna mast on helicopter platform in photograph; exhaust ducts fitted to funnel.
Operated by Military Sealift Command for Naval Electronic Systems Command.

KINGSPORT 1/1976, Michael D. J. Lennon

1 "OBSERVATION ISLAND" CLASS: MISCELLANEOUS (AG)

Name	No.	Builders	Commissioned	F/S
OBSERVATION ISLAND (ex-*Empire State Mariner*)	AG 154 (ex-YAG 57)	New York S.B. Corp, NJ	5 Dec 1958	Conv

Displacement, tons: 16 076 full load
Dimensions, feet (metres): 563 × 76 × 29 *(171·6 × 23·2 × 8·8)*
Main engines: Geared turbines (General Electric); 19 250 shp; 1 shaft = 20 knots
Boilers: 2 (Foster-Wheeler)
Complement: 428 (35 officers, 393 enlisted men)

Built as a "Mariner" class merchant ship (C4-S-1A type); launched on 15 August 1953; acquired by the Navy on 10 September 1956 for use as a Fleet Ballistic Missile (FBM) test ship. Converted at Norfolk Naval Shipyard.
Was fitted to test fire Polaris and later Poseidon missiles. Navy manned. Decommissioned on 29 September 1972 and placed in Maritime Administration reserve; remains in Navy List.
On 18 August 1977, *Observation Island* was reacquired by the US Navy from the Maritime Administration and was transferred to the Military Sealift Command for administrative control. She will undergo a two to three year conversion for operation as a Missile Range Instrumentation Ship (AGM) beginning in July 1979. She will probably be reclassified AGM 23 towards the end of her conversion. Upon completion she will be under the operational control of the US Air Force. US Navy will retain title.

Missile Testing: The ship was fitted with complete missile testing, servicing and firing systems. She fired the first ship-launched Polaris missile at sea on 27 August 1959. Refitted to fire the improved Poseidon missile in 1969 and launched the first Poseidon test missile fired afloat on 16 December 1969.

OBSERVATION ISLAND 1971, USN

740 USA / Military Sealift Command

1 CONVERTED "HASKELL" CLASS: MISSILE RANGE INSTRUMENTATION SHIP (AGM)

Name	No.	Builders	Commissioned	F/S
RANGE SENTINEL (ex-*Sherburne*)	T-AGM 22 (ex-APA 205)	Permanente Metals Corp, Richmond, Calif	20 Sep 1944	TAA

Displacement, tons: 11 800 full load
Dimensions, feet (metres): 455 × 62 × 23 *(138·7 × 18·9 × 7·0)*
Main engine: Turbine (Westinghouse); 8 500 hp; 1 shaft = 17·7 knots
Boilers: 2 (Combustion Engineering)
Complement: 95 (14 officers, 54 men, 27 technical personnel)

Former attack transport (APA) converted specifically to serve as a range instrumentation ship in support of the Poseidon Fleet Ballistic Missile (FBM) programme. Maritime Administration VC2-S-AP5 type. Renamed *Range Sentinel* on 26 April 1971.
Stricken from the Navy List on 1 October 1958 and transferred to Maritime Administration reserve fleet; reacquired by the Navy on 22 October 1969 for AGM conversion.
Converted from October 1969 to October 1971; placed in service as T-AGM 22 on 14 October 1971. Operated by Military Sealift Command.

RANGE SENTINEL　　　　　　　　　　　　　　　　　　　1973, USN

2 CONVERTED "MISSION" CLASS: 1 MISSILE RANGE INSTRUMENTATION SHIP (AGM), 1 MISCELLANEOUS (AG)

Name	No.	Builders	Delivered	F/S
VANGUARD (ex-*Muscel Shoals*, ex-*Mission San Fernando*)	AG 194 (ex-T-AGM 19, ex-T-AO 122)	Marine Ship Corp, Sausalito, Calif	29 Feb 1944	TAA
REDSTONE (ex-*Johnstown*, ex-*Mission de Pala*)	T-AGM 20 (ex-T-AO 114)	Marine Ship Corp, Sausalito, Calif	22 Apr 1944	TAA

Displacement, tons: 22 310 full load
Dimensions, feet (metres): 595 oa × 75 × 25 *(181·4 × 22·9 × 7·6)*
Main engines: Turbo-electric (Westinghouse); 10 000 shp; 1 shaft = 14 knots
Boilers: 2 (Babcock & Wilcox)
Complement: *Vanguard* 19 officers, 71 enlisted men, 108 technical personnel; *Redstone* 20 officers, 71 enlisted men, 120 technical personnel

Former "Mission" class tankers converted in 1964-66 to serve as mid-ocean communications and tracking ships in support of the Apollo manned lunar flights. Maritime Administration T2-SE-A2 type.
Converted to range instrumentation ships by General Dynamics Corp, Quincy Division, Massachusetts; each ship was cut in half and a 72 ft mid-section was inserted, increasing length, beam, and displacement; approximately 450 tons of electronic equipment installed for support of lunar flight operations, including communications and tracking systems; balloon hangar and platform fitted aft. Cost of converting these two ships and *Mercury* (their sister deleted in 1969) was $90 million. *Redstone* is operated by Military Sealift Command for NASA Goddard Space Flight Center.
Vanguard was transferred to the Navy's Strategic Systems Project office on 1 October 1978. The contract for her overhaul and modification for this new mission as replacement for *Compass Island* (AG 153) was awarded to Todd Shipyard Corp, Brooklyn on 12 January 1979. The main change in *Vanguard's* appearance will be the removal of her two radar antennae and pedestals amidships.
Note different bow structure configurations and deck houses.

REDSTONE　　　　　　　　　　　　　　　9/1976, Michael D. J. Lennon

VANGUARD　　　　　　　　　　　　　　　　　　　　1976, USN

2 CONVERTED C4-S-A1 TYPE: MISSILE RANGE INSTRUMENTATION SHIPS (AGM)

Name	No.	Builders	Commissioned	F/S
GENERAL H. H. ARNOLD (ex-USNS *General R. E. Callan*)	T-AGM 9 (ex-T-AP 139)	Kaiser Co, Richmond Calif	17 Aug 1944	TAA
GENERAL HOYT S. VANDENBERG (ex-USNS *General Harry Taylor*)	T-AGM 10 (ex-T-AP 145)	Kaiser Co, Richmond Calif	1 Apr 1944	TAA

Displacement, tons: 16 600 full load
Dimensions, feet (metres): 552·9 × 71·5 × 26·3 *(168·5 × 21·8 × 8·0)*
Main engines: Geared turbines (Westinghouse); 9 000 shp; 1 shaft = 14 knots
Boilers: 2 (Babcock & Wilcox)
Complement: 205 (21 officers, 71 men, 113 technical personnel)

Former troop transports converted in 1962-63 for monitoring Air Force missiles firing and satellite launches. Maritime Administration C4-S-A1 type. Upon conversion to range instrumentation ships they were placed in service in 1963 under Air Force operation, however assigned to MSTS for operation on 1 July 1964 (*Arnold*) and 13 July 1964 (*Vandenberg*).
Both ships are operated by Military Sealift Command for Air Force Eastern Test Range in Atlantic.

GEN. HOYT S. VANDENBERG　　　　　　　　　　　　　USN

1 "VICTORY" CLASS: MISSILE RANGE INSTRUMENTATION SHIP (AGM)

Name	No.	Builders	Completed	F/S
WHEELING (ex-*Seton Hall Victory*)	T-AGM 8	Oregon SB Corp, Portland	June 1945	TPA

Displacement, tons: 11 500 full load
Dimensions, feet (metres): 455·3 × 62·2 × 22 *(138·8 × 19·0 × 6·7)*
Main engines: Geared turbines (Westinghouse); 8 500 shp; 1 shaft = 17 knots
Boilers: 2 (Combustion Engineering)
Complement: 107 (13 officers, 46 men, 48 technical personnel)

Wheeling is the only survivor of six "Victory" type military cargo and merchant ships converted to missile range instrumentation ships during the massive US space and military missile programmes of the 1960s. Maritime Administration VC2-S-AP3 type. Assigned to Military Sea Transportation Service on 28 May 1964; operated in support of Pacific Missile Range. Fitted with helicopter hangar and platform aft. Employed to test AWG-9 fire control system for use in the F-14 Tomcat fighter aircraft.

WHEELING　　　　　　　　　　　　　　　　　　　　USN

USA / Military Sealift Command 741

2 "GYRE" CLASS: OCEANOGRAPHIC RESEARCH SHIPS (AGOR)

Name	No.	Builders	Completed	F/S
GYRE	AGOR 21	Halter Marine Service, New Orleans	14 Nov 1973	Loan
MOANA WAVE	AGOR 22	Halter Marine Service, New Orleans	16 Jan 1974	Loan

Displacement, tons: 950 full load
Dimensions, feet (metres): 165 × 36 × 14·5 *(50·3 × 11·0 × 4·4)*
Main engines: Turbo-charged diesels (Caterpillar); 1 700 bhp; 2 shafts;
(cp propellers) = 12 knots
Complement: 21 (10 crew, 11 scientists)

Laid down on 9 October 1972 and 10 October 1972 respectively; launched on 25 May 1973 and 18 June 1973. They are based on a commercial ship design. Fitted with a 150 hp retractable propeller pod for low-speed or station keeping with main machinery shut down. Open deck aft provides space for equipment vans to permit rapid change of mission capabilities. Each ship cost approximately $1·9 million.
They are assigned for operation to Texas A & M University and the University of Hawaii, respectively.

GYRE 1973, Halter Marine Services

1 "HAYES" CLASS: OCEANOGRAPHIC RESEARCH SHIP (AGOR)

Name	No.	Builders	Completed	F/S
HAYES	T-AGOR 16	Todd Shipyards, Seattle	21 July 1971	TAA

Displacement, tons: 2 876 full load
Dimensions, feet (metres): 246·5 × 75 (see *Design* notes) × 22 *(75·1 × 22·9 × 6·7)*
Main engines: Geared diesels (General Motors); 5 400 bhp; 2 shafts;
(cp propeller) = 15 knots
Range, miles: 6 000 at 13·5 knots
Complement: 74 (11 officers, 33 men, 30 scientists)

Hayes is one of two classes of modern US naval ships to have a catamaran hull, the other being the ASR 21 class submarine rescue ships. Laid down 12 November 1969; launched 2 July 1970. Estimated cost was $15·9 million.
Operated by the Military Sealift Command for the Office of Naval Research under the Technical control of the Oceanographer of the Navy.

Design: Catamaran hull design provides large deck working area, centre well for operating equipment at great depths, and removes laboratory areas from main propulsion machinery. Each hull is 246·5 ft long and 24 ft wide (maximum). There are three 36 in diameter instrument wells in addition to the main centre well.

Engineering: An auxiliary 165 bhp diesel is fitted in each hull to provide "creeping" speed of 2 to 4 knots. Separation of cp propellers by catamaran hull separation provides high degree of manoeuvrability eliminating the need for bow thrusters.

HAYES 1971, Todd Shipyards Corp

7 "ROBERT D. CONRAD" CLASS: OCEANOGRAPHIC RESEARCH SHIPS (AGOR)

Name	No.	Builders	Completed	F/S
ROBERT D. CONRAD	AGOR 3	Gibbs Corp, Jacksonville	29 Nov 1962	Loan
JAMES M. GILLISS	AGOR 4	Christy Corp, Sturgeon Bay	5 Nov 1962	Loan
LYNCH	T-AGOR 7	Marinette Mfg Co, Point Pleasant	27 Mar 1965	TAA
THOMAS G. THOMPSON	AGOR 9	Marinette Marine Corp, Wisc	24 Aug 1965	Loan
THOMAS WASHINGTON	AGOR 10	Marinette Marine Corp, Wisc	27 Sep 1965	Loan
DE STEIGUER	T-AGOR 12	Northwest Marine Iron Works, Portland, Oregon	28 Feb 1969	TPA
BARTLETT	T-AGOR 13	Northwest Marine Iron Works, Portland, Oregon	31 Mar 1969	TAA

Displacement, tons: 950-1 200 light; 1 362-1 370 full load
Dimensions, feet (metres): 208·9 × 40 × 15·3 *(63·7 × 12·2 × 4·7)*
Main engines: Diesel-electric (Caterpillar Tractor Co diesels (3 and 4); Cummins in rest);
1 000 bhp; 1 shaft = 13·5 knots
Range, miles: 12 000 at 12 knots
Complement: 41 (9 officers, 17 men, 15 scientists except *De Steigeur* and *Bartlett*, 8 officers, 18 men)

This is the first class of ships designed and built by the US Navy for oceanographic research. Fitted with instrumentation and laboratories to measure gravity and magnetism, water temperature, sound transmission in water, and the profile of the ocean floor. Special features include 10 ton capacity boom and winches for handling over-the-side equipment; bow thruster; 620 hp gas turbine (housed in funnel structure) for providing "quiet" power when conducting experiments; can propel the ship at 6·5 knots.
Robert D. Conrad laid down on 19 January 1961 and launched on 26 May 1962. Operated by Lamont Geological Observatory of Columbia University under technical control of the Oceanographer of the Navy.
James H. Gilliss laid down on 31 May 1961 and launched on 19 May 1962. Operated by the University of Miami (Florida) since 1970 in support of Navy programmes.
Lynch laid down on 7 September 1962 and launched on 17 March 1964. Operated by Military Sealift Command under the technical control of the Oceanographer of the Navy.
Thomas G. Thompson laid down on 12 September 1963 and launched on 18 July 1964. Operated by University of Washington (State) under technical control of the Oceanographer of the Navy.
Thomas Washington laid down on 12 September 1963 and launched on 1 August 1964. Operated by Scripps Institution of Oceanography (University of California) under technical control of the Oceanographer on the Navy.
De Steiguer and *Bartlett* laid down on 12 November 1965 and 18 November 1965 and launched on 21 March 1966 and 24 May 1966. Operated by Military Sealift Command under the technical control of the Oceanographer of the Navy.

Transfers: Ships of this class are in service with Brazil *(Sands)* and New Zealand *(Charles H. Davies)*.

DE STEIGUER 1978, Dr. Giorgio Arra

LYNCH 1974, Dr. Giorgio Arra

742 USA / Military Sealift Command

2 "MELVILLE" CLASS: OCEANOGRAPHIC RESEARCH SHIPS (AGOR)

Name	No.	Builders	Completed	F/S
MELVILLE	AGOR 14	Defoe S.B. Co, Bay City, Mich	27 Aug 1969	Loan
KNORR	AGOR 15	Defoe S.B. Co, Bay City, Mich	14 Jan 1970	Loan

Displacement, tons: 1 915 full load
Dimensions, feet (metres): 244·9 × 46·3 × 15 (74·7 × 14·1 × 4·6)
Main engines: 2 diesels (De Laval); 2 500 bhp; 2 cycloidal propellers = 12·5 knots
Range, miles: 10 000 at 12 knots
Complement: 50 (9 officers, 16 men, 25 scientists)

Oceanographic research ships of an advanced design fitted with internal wells for lowering equipment, underwater lights and observation ports. Facilities for handling small research submersibles.
Melville and *Knorr* laid down on 12 July 1967 and 9 August 1967 respectively; launched 10 July 1968 and 21 August 1968. *Melville* operated by Scripps Institution of Oceanography and *Knorr* by Woods Hole Oceanography Institution for the Office of Naval Research, under technical control of the Oceanographer of the Navy.

Engineering: First US Navy ocean-going ships with cycloidal propellers permitting the ships to turn 360 degrees in their own length. One propeller is fitted at each end of the ship, providing movement in any direction and optimum station keeping without use of thrusters. They have experienced engineering difficulties.

MELVILLE 1969, Defoe Shipbuildin

1 CONVERTED "ELTANIN" CLASS: OCEANOGRAPHIC RESEARCH SHIP (AGOR)

Name	No.	Builders	In Service	F/S
MIZAR	T-AGOR 11 (ex-T-AK 272)	Avondale Marine Ways, New Orleans	7 Mar 1958	TPA

Displacement, tons: 2 036 light; 3 481 full load
Dimensions, feet (metres): 262·2 × 51·5 × 18·7 (79·9 × 15·7 × 5·7)
Main engines: Diesel-electric (ALCO diesels, Westinghouse electric motors) 2 700 bhp; 2 shafts = 12 knots
Complement: 56 (11 officers, 30 enlisted men, 15 scientists)

Built for Military Sea Transportation Service. Designed for Arctic operation with hull strengthened against ice. C1-ME2-13a type. Delivered as cargo ship to MSTS and subsequently converted to oceanographic research ship.
Mizar was operated by the Military Sealift Command for Naval Research Laboratory, under technical control of the Oceanographer of the Navy. Transferred to technical control of Naval Electronics Command on 1 July 1975.

Conversion: *Mizar* converted in 1962 into deep sea research ship. Equipped with centre well for lowering oceanographic equipment including towed sensor platforms, fitted with laboratories and elaborate photographic facilities, hydrophone system and computer for seafloor navigation and tracking towed vehicles. *Mizar* had key roles in the searches for the US nuclear submarines *Thresher* and *Scorpion*, the French submarine *Eurydice*, and recovery of the H-bomb lost at sea off Palomares, Spain.

MIZAR 1973, Wright and Logan

0 + 2 + 10 OCEAN SURVEILLANCE SHIPS (AGOS)

Name	No.	Builders
—	AGOS 1 and 2	Approved FY 1979 programme
—	AGOS 3-7	Proposed FY 1980 programme
—	AGOS 8-12	Proposed FY 1981 programme

Displacement, tons: 2 500 approx
Length, feet (metres): 217 (66·1) approx
Beam, feet (metres): 42 (12·8)
Main engines: Diesel-electric; 2 shafts = 11 knots

The Navy plans to construct 12 ocean surveillance ships to operate the new SURTASS (Surface Towed Array Surveillance System). These ships will have a hull design similar to but slightly smaller than the "Powhatan" class (ATF) now under construction, but will be specially configured for the ocean surveillance mission. They will be operated by the Military Sealift Command, apparently with civilian crews and Navy personnel to operate the classified SURTASS equipment.

1 CONVERTED MERCHANT TYPE: SURVEYING SHIP (AGS)

Name	No.	Builders	In Service	F/S
H. H. HESS (ex-*Canada Mail*)	T-AGS 38	National Steel & S.B. Co.	16 Jan 1978	TPA

Displacement, tons: 22 625 full load
Measurement, tons: 14 747 deadweight
Dimensions, feet (metres): 535·7 × 76 × 41 (163·3 × 23·2 × 12·5)
Main engines: Geared turbines (GE); 19 250 shp; 1 shaft = 20 knots
Boilers: 2 (Foster-Wheeler)
Complement: 57

Merchant ship completed in 1965 and acquired by the Navy 9 July 1976 for conversion to replace the "Victory" class surveying ship *Michelson* (T-AGS 23). Above data as merchant ship. As a hydrographic survey ship she is operated by the Military Sealift Command (Pacific Fleet) for the Oceanographer of the Navy. Converted at National Steel and S.B. Co San Diego between March 1977 and January 1978.

H. H. HESS 1978, USN

USA / Military Sealift Command 743

2 "CHAUVENET" CLASS: SURVEYING SHIPS (AGS)

Name	No.	Builders	Completed	F/S
CHAUVENET	T-AGS 29	Upper Clyde Shipbuilders, Glasgow	13 Nov 1970	TPA
HARKNESS	T-AGS 32	Upper Clyde Shipbuilders, Glasgow	29 Jan 1971	TAA

Displacement, tons: 3 670 full load
Dimensions, feet (metres): 393·2 × 54 × 16 *(119·8 × 16·5 × 4·9)*
Main engine: 1 Alco diesel; 3 600 bhp; 1 shaft = 15 knots
Complement: 175 (13 officers, approx 150 men and technical personnel, 12 scientists)

Capable of extensive military hydrographic and oceanographic surveys, supporting coastal surveying craft, amphibious survey teams and helicopters. Fitted with two helicopter hangars and platform.
Chauvenet authorised in the Fiscal Year 1965 new construction programme; Harkness in the FY 1966 programme. Laid down on 24 May 1967 and 30 June 1967 respectively; launched on 13 May 1968 and 12 June 1968.
These ships are operated by the Military Sealift Command for the Oceanographer of the Navy with Navy detachments on board. Harkness scheduled to be inactivated in FY 1980.

CHAUVENET 1971, USN

4 "SILAS BENT" and "WILKES" CLASSES: SURVEYING SHIPS (AGS)

Name	No.	Builders	Completed	F/S
SILAS BENT	T-AGS 26	American S.B. Co, Lorain	23 July 1965	TPA
KANE	T-AGS 27	Christy Corp, Sturgeon Bay	19 May 1967	TAA
WILKES	T-AGS 33	Defoe S.B. Co, Bay City, Mich	28 June 1971	TAA
WYMAN	T-AGS 34	Defoe S.B. Co, Bay City, Mich	3 Nov 1971	TAA

Displacement, tons: 1 935 standard; 2 420-2 580 full load
Dimensions, feet (metres): 285·3 × 48 × 15·1 *(87·0 × 14·6 × 4·6)*
Main engines: Diesel-electric (diesels; Westinghouse in 26; Alco in 27; GE in others); 3 000 bhp; 1 shaft = 15 knots
Complement: 77/78 (12 officers, 35 or 36 men, 30 scientists)

These ships were designed specifically for surveying operations. Bow propulsion unit for precise manoeuvrability and station keeping. All four ships operated by Military Sealift Command for the Oceanographer of the Navy.
Laid down on 2 March 1964, 19 December 1964, 18 July 1968 and 18 July 1968 respectively; launched on 16 May 1965, 20 November 1965, 31 July 1969 and 30 October 1969.
Wilkes laid up in ready reserve.

WILKES 6/1971, USN

2 "BOWDITCH" CLASS: SURVEYING SHIPS (AGS)

Name	No.	Builders	Completed	F/S
BOWDITCH (ex-SS *South Bend Victory*)	T-AGS 21	Oregon S.B. Co	July 1945	TAA
DUTTON (ex-SS *Tuskegee Victory*)	T-AGS 22	South Coast Co, Newport Beach	June 1945	TPA

Displacement, tons: 13 050 full load
Dimensions, feet (metres): 455·2 × 62·2 × 25 *(138·7 × 19·0 × 7·6)*
Main engine: Geared turbine (GE in 21; Westinghouse in 22); 8 500 shp; 1 shaft = 15 knots
Boilers: 2
Complement: 100 (13 officers, 47 men, approx 40 technical personnel)

VC2-S-AP3 type ships. Converted to support the Fleet Ballistic Missile Programme, Dutton at Philadelphia Naval Shipyard 8 November 1957 to 16 November 1958 and Bowditch at Charleston Naval Shipyard 10 October 1957 to 30 September 1958.
Designed for general surveying and to record magnetic fields and gravity.
Operated by Military Sealift Command for the Oceanographer of the Navy.

BOWDITCH 1976, Michael D. J. Lennon

1 CARGO SHIP (AK) PROPOSED CONVERSION

Under the Fiscal Year 1981 programme it is proposed to convert a merchant freighter to a Cargo Ship (AK 284). Estimated cost of conversion $50 million. Details and planned task not available, but it is probable that she will be converted to a supply tender for Fleet Ballistic Missile submarines carrying Trident missiles.

1 CONVERTED "ANDROMEDA" CLASS: CARGO SHIP (AK)

Name	No.	Builders	Commissioned	F/S
WYANDOT	T-AK 283 (ex-T-AKA 92)	Moore D.D. Co, Oakland	30 Sep 1944	MPR

Displacement, tons: 7 430 light; 11 000 full load
Dimensions, feet (metres): 459·2 × 63 × 28 *(140·0 × 19·2 × 8·5)*
Main engines: Geared turbines (General Electric); 6 000 shp; 1 shaft = 16·5 knots
Boilers: 2 (Combustion Engineering)
Complement: 423 (38 officers, 385 enlisted men) (as AKA)

Former attack cargo ship (AKA) of the "Andromeda" class; C2-S-B1 type. Launched on 28 June 1944; commissioned as AKA 92. Designation changed to T-AK 283 on 1 January 1969. Winterised for arctic service.
On 5 March 1976 was transferred to Maritime Administration for lay-up in the fleet at Suisun Bay. Remains on Navy List.

744 USA / Military Sealift Command

4 "NORWALK" CLASS: CARGO SHIPS (AK)

Name	No.	F/S
NORWALK (ex-*Norwalk Victory*)	T-AK 279	TAA
FURMAN (ex-*Furman Victory*)	T-AK 280	TPA
VICTORIA (ex-*Ethiopia Victory*)	T-AK 281	TAA
MARSHFIELD (ex-*Marshfield Victory*)	T-AK 282	TAA

Displacement, tons: 6 700 light; 11 000/11 300 full load
Dimensions, feet (metres): 455·25 × 62 × 22 *(138·8 × 18·9 × 6·7)*
Main engine: Geared turbine; 8 500 shp; 1 shaft = 17 knots
Boilers: 2 (Babcock & Wilcox, 279-280; Combustion Engineering, 281-282)
Complement: 80 to 90 plus Navy detachment

Former merchant ships of the VC2-S-AP3 "Victory" type built during World War II. Extensively converted to supply tenders for Fleet Ballistic Missile (FBM) submarines. Fitted to carry torpedoes, spare parts, packaged petroleum products, bottled gas, black oil and diesel fuel, frozen and dry provisions, and general cargo as well as missiles. No 3 hold converted to carry 16 Polaris missiles in vertical position; tankage provided for 355 000 gallons (US) of diesel oil and 430 000 gallons (US) of fuel oil (for submarine tenders). All subsequently modified to carry Poseidon missiles. All four ships are operated by the Military Sealift Command with civilian operating crews; a small Navy detachment in each ship provides security and technical services. *Norwalk* scheduled for deletion in FY 1980.

Conversion: *Norwalk* converted to FBM cargo ship by Boland Machine & Manufacturing Co, and accepted for service on 30 December 1963; *Furman* converted by American Shipbuilding Co, and accepted on 7 October 1964; *Victoria* converted by Philadelphia Naval Shipyard, and accepted on 15 October 1965; and *Marshfield* converted by Boland Machine & Manufacturing Co, and accepted on 28 May 1970.

NORWALK 9/1976, Michael D. J. Lenno

1 "SCHUYLER OTIS BLAND" CLASS: CARGO SHIP (AK)

Name	No.	F/S
SCHUYLER OTIS BLAND	T-AK 277	TPA

Displacement, tons: 15 910 full load
Dimensions, feet (metres): 454 × 66 × 27 *(138·4 × 20·1 × 8·2)*
Main engine: Geared turbine (GE); 13 750 shp; 1 shaft = 18·5 knots
Boilers: 2 (Foster-Wheeler)
Complement: 51 (14 officers, 37 enlisted men)

Acquired from the Maritime Administration by the Military Sea Transportation Service on 20 July 1961. The only ship of the type (C3-S-DX1) built; prototype of the "Mariner" cargo ship design.

SCHUYLER OTIS BLAND 1/1978, V. H. Young

1 "ELTANIN" CLASS: CARGO SHIP (AK)

Name	No.	Builders	In Service	F/S
MIRFAK	T-AK 271	Avondale Marine Ways, New Orleans	30 Dec 1957	TAA

Displacement, tons: 2 022 light; 3 886 full load
Dimensions, feet (metres): 262·2 × 51·5 × 18·7 *(79·9 × 15·7 × 5·7)*
Main engines: Diesel-electric (ALCO diesels with Westinghouse electric motors); 2 700 bhp; 2 shafts = 13 knots
Complement: 48

Built for Military Sea Transportation Service, Louisiana. Designed for Arctic operation with hull strengthened against ice. C1-M E2-13a type. Launched on 5 August 1957. Note icebreaking prow in photo.

Conversion: Two other ships of this class converted for oceanographic research: *Eltanin*, reclassified from T-AK 270 to T-AGOR 8 on 15 November 1962 loaned to Argentina as *Islas Orcadas*; *Mizar* T-AK 272 was reclassified T-AGOR 11 on 15 April 1964 (see AGORs "Eltanin" class).

MIRFAK USN

1 "PRIVATE LEONARD C. BROSTROM" CLASS: CARGO SHIP (AK)

Name	No.	Acquired	F/S
PVT. LEONARD C. BROSTROM (ex-*Marine Eagle*)	T-AK 255	9 Aug 1950	TPA

Displacement, tons: 8 590 light; 12 056 full load
Dimensions, feet (metres): 520 × 71·5 × 33 *(158·5 × 21·8 × 10·1)*
Main engine: Geared turbine (GE); 9 000 shp; 1 shaft = 15·8 knots
Boilers: 2 (Babcock & Wilcox)
Complement: 57 (14 officers, 43 men)

She is fitted with 150 ton capacity booms, providing the most powerful lift capability of any US ship. C4-S-B1 type built in 1943.

PVT. LEONARD C. BROSTROM USN

USA / Military Sealift Command 745

5 "GREENVILLE VICTORY" CLASS: CARGO SHIPS (AK)

Name	No.	F/S
GREENVILLE VICTORY	T-AK 237	MAR
PVT. JOHN R. TOWLE (ex-*Appleton Victory*)	T-AK 240	TAA
SGT. ANDREW MILLER (ex-*Radcliffe Victory*)	T-AK 242	MAR
SGT. TRUMAN KIMBRO	T-AK 254	MPR
LT. JAMES E. ROBINSON (ex-T-AG 170, ex-T-AK 274, ex-AKV 3, ex-*Czechoslovakia Victory*)	T-AK 274	MAR

Displacement, tons: 6 700 light; 15 199 full load
Dimensions, feet (metres): 455·5 × 62 × 28·5 *(138·9 × 18·9 × 8·9)*
Main engine: Geared turbine (GE in 240 and 242, Westinghouse in others); 8 500 shp (242 and 254; 6 000 shp); 1 shaft = 17 knots except T-AK 254 15 knots
Boilers: 2

Former merchant ships of the "Victory" type built during World War II. All near sisters. VC2-S-AP3 type capable of 17 knots except T-AK 254 is VC2-S-AP2 type capable of 15 knots. All acquired 1 March 1950 (T-AK 254, in August). "Victory" type cargo ships configured as Fleet Ballistic Missile (FBM) cargo ships are listed separately.

Classification: The former Military Sea Transportation Service aircraft cargo and ferry ships *Lt. James E. Robinson* AKV 3 reclassified as cargo ship on 7 May 1959. *Kingsport Victory* T-AK 239, was renamed and reclassified *Kingsport* T-AG 164 in 1962.
Lt. James E. Robinson T-AK 274, was to have been transferred to the Maritime Administration, but was modified for special project work and reclassified as T-AG 170 in 1963, and reverted to the original classification T-AK 274 on 1 July 1964. Transferred to Maritime Administration for lay-up at James River. Ship remains on Navy List.
Sgt. Truman Kimbro, Sgt. Andrew Miller and *Greenville Victory* transferred to Maritime Administration on 6, 22 and 23 March 1976 for lay-up at Suisun Bay and James River (last two). Remain on Navy List.

PVT. JOHN R. TOWLE *1978, Michael D. J. Lennon*

1 "METEOR" CLASS: VEHICLE CARGO SHIP (AKR)

Name	No.	Builders	Delivered	F/S
METEOR (ex-*Sea Lift*)	T-AKR 9 (ex-LSV 9)	Puget Sound Bridge & D.D. Co	25 Apr 1967	TPA

Displacement, tons: 11 130 light; 16 940 standard; 21 700 full load
Dimensions, feet (metres): 540 × 83 × 27 *(164·7 × 25·5 × 8·2)*
Main engines: Geared turbines; 19 400 shp; 2 shafts = 20 knots
Boilers: 2
Complement: 54
Passengers: 12

Maritime Administration C4-ST-67a type. Roll-on/roll-off vehicle cargo ship. Cost of $15 895 500. Authorised under the Fiscal Year 1963 programme. Laid down on 19 May 1964 and launched on 18 April 1965. Delivered to Military Sea Transportation Service on 25 April 1967. Designed for point-to-point sea transportation of Department of Defense self-propelled, fully loaded, wheeled, tracked and amphibious vehicles and general cargo. Internal ramps, stern ramp and side openings provide for quick loading and unloading. Originally authorised as AK-278, changed to LSV on 1 January 1963 and to AKR 9 on 1 January 1969.

METEOR *1966, Lockheed Shipbuilding*

Name: Originally named *Sea Lift*. Renamed *Meteor* on 12 September 1975 to avoid confusion with "Sealift" class tankers.

1 "COMET" CLASS: VEHICLE CARGO SHIP (AKR)

Name	No.	Builders	Commissioned	F/S
COMET	T-AKR 7 (ex-T-LSV 7, ex-T-AK 260)	Sun S.B. & D.D. Co, Chester, Penn	27 Jan 1958	TAA

Displacement, tons: 7 605 light; 18 286 full load
Dimensions, feet (metres): 499 × 78 × 28·8 *(152·1 × 23·8 × 8·8)*
Main engines: Geared turbines (General Electric); 13 200 shp; 2 shafts = 18 knots
Boilers: 2 (Babcock & Wilcox)
Complement: 73

Roll-on/roll-off vehicle carrier built for Military Sea Transportation Service C3-ST-14A type. Laid down on 15 May 1956. Launched on 31 July 1957. Maritime Administration Design includes ramp system for loading and discharging. The hull is strengthened against ice. Can accommodate 700 vehicles in two after holds; the forward holds are for general cargo. Equipped with Denny-Brown stabilisers. Reclassified from T-AK to T-LSV on 1 June 1963, and changed to T-AKR on 1 January 1969.

COMET USN

1 "CALLAGHAN" CLASS: VEHICLE CARGO SHIP (AKR)

Name	No.	Builders	F/S
ADMIRAL WM. M. CALLAGHAN	—	Sun S.B. & D.D. Co, Chester, Penn	TAA

Displacement, tons: 24 500 full load
Dimensions, feet (metres): 694 × 92 × 29 *(211·5 × 28·0 × 8·8)*
Main engines: 2 LM2500 gas turbines (General Electric); 50 000 shp; 2 shafts = 26 knots
Complement: 33

Roll-on/roll-off vehicle cargo ship built specifically for long-term charter to the Military Sealift Command. Launched on 17 October 1967. Internal parking decks and ramps for carrying some 750 vehicles on 167 537 square ft of parking area; unloading via four side ramps and stern ramp, she can off load and reload full vehicle capacity in 27 hours.
This ship is not on the Naval Vessels Register but is included here for information.

Engineering: She was the first Navy-sponsored all gas-turbine ship; has similar turbines to those of the "Spruance" class destroyers (DD 963) and "Oliver Hazard Perry" class frigates (FFG 7).

ADM. WM. M. CALLAGHAN USN

746 USA / Military Sealift Command

5 "JUMBOISED MISPILLION" CLASS: OILERS (AO)

Name	No.	Launched	Commissioned	F/S
MISPILLION	T-AO 105	10 Aug 1945	29 Dec 1945	TPA
NAVASOTA	T-AO 106	30 Aug 1945	27 Feb 1946	TPA
PASSUMPSIC	T-AO 107	31 Oct 1945	1 Apr 1946	TPA
PAWCATUCK	T-AO 108	19 Feb 1945	10 May 1946	TAA
WACCAMAW	T-AO 109	30 Mar 1946	25 June 1946	TAA

Displacement, tons: 11 600 light; 34 179 full load (33 750 in T-AO 106 and 109)
Dimensions, feet (metres): 644 × 75 × 35·5 (196·3 × 22·9 × 10·8)
Guns: Removed
Main engines: Geared turbines (Westinghouse); 13 500 shp; 2 shafts = 16 knots
Boilers: 4 (Babcock & Wilcox)
Complement: 290 (16 officers, 274 men) when Navy manned

NAVASOTA 2/1977, Dr. Giorgio Arr.

All built by Sun Shipbuilding & Dry Dock Co, Chester, Pennsylvania. Originally T3-S2-A3 oilers; converted during mid-1960s under "jumbo" programme. Enlarged mid-sections added to increase cargo capacity to approximately 150 000 barrels. Helicopter platform fitted forward. As "jumboised" these ships had four 3 in single gun mounts; removed in MSC service.
Passumpsic was assigned to the Military Sealift Command on 24 July 1973. *Mispillion* on 26 July 1974, *Waccamaw* on 24 February 1975, *Pawcatuck* on 15 July 1975 and *Navasota* on 13 August 1975. All operate in fleet support with civilian crews and naval detachments.

PASSUMPSIC 1978, J. A. Verhoog

2 "JUMBOISED CIMARRON" CLASS: OILERS (AO)

Name	No.	Launched	Commissioned	F/S
MARIAS	T-AO 57	21 Dec 1943	12 Feb 1944	TAA
TALUGA	T-AO 62	10 July 1944	25 Aug 1944	TPA

Displacement, tons: 25 450 full load
Dimensions, feet (metres): 553 × 75 × 33 (168·6 × 22·9 × 10·1)
Guns: Unarmed
Main engines: Geared turbines (Bethlehem); 13 500 shp; 2 shafts = 18 knots
Boilers: 4 (Foster-Wheeler)
Complement: 274 (14 officers, 260 enlisted men)

These ships are survivors of a class of 26 of twin-screw (S2) fleet oilers built during World War II; some converted to escort carriers. Both ships were built by Bethlehem Steel Co, Sparrows Point, Maryland. Original armament consisted of one 5 in gun, four 3 in guns and up to eight 40 mm guns. Cargo capacity 145 000 barrels of liquid fuels.
Marias and *Taluga* were assigned to the Military Sealift Command (MSC) on 2 October 1973 and 4 May 1972 respectively; guns removed. Operate in fleet support.
To be deleted in FY 1980.

MARIAS 10/1976, Michael D. J. Lennor

4 "COLUMBIA" CLASS: TRANSPORT OILERS (AOT, ex-AO)

Name	No.	Builders	Delivered	F/S
COLUMBIA (ex-*Falcon Lady*)	T-AOT 182	Ingalls S.B. Co, Pascagoula	11 Mar 1971	TWWR
NECHES (ex-*Falcon Duchess*)	T-AOT 183	Ingalls S.B. Co, Pascagoula	4 Aug 1971	TWWR
HUDSON (ex-*Falcon Princess*)	T-AOT 184	Ingalls S.B. Co, Pascagoula	4 May 1972	TWWR
SUSQUEHANNA (ex-*Falcon Countess*)	T-AOT 185	Ingalls S.B. Co, Pascagoula	13 Jan 1972	TWWR

Displacement, tonnes: 8 730 light; 46 600 full load
Dimensions, feet (metres): 672 × 89 × 36 (204·8 × 27·1 × 11·0)
Main engines: Two 16-cyl Pielstick diesels; 15 000 bhp = 16·5 knots
Oil fuel, tons: 2 600
Complement: 23 (11 officers, 12 sailors)

Former merchant tankers originally chartered to the Military Sealift Command. All four acquired on bareboat charter on 3 May 1974 (182 and 183), 10 April 1974 (184) and 17 April 1974 (185). Acquired by US Navy for MSC service on 15 January 1976 (182), 11 February 1976 (183), 23 April 1976 (184) and 11 May 1976 (185). Operated under contract by Cove Shipping Inc. Cargo capacity 310 000 barrels. All reclassified AOT on 30 September 1978.

HUDSON (as *Falcon Princess*)

1 "POTOMAC" CLASS: TRANSPORT OILER (AOT, ex-AO)

Name	No.	Acquired	F/S
POTOMAC (ex-*Shenandoah*)	T-AOT 181	12 Jan 1976	TWWR

Displacement, tons: 27 467 deadweight
Dimensions, feet (metres): 620 × 83·5 × 34 (189·0 × 25·5 × 10·4)
Main engine: Geared turbine; 20 460 shp; 1 shaft = 18 knots
Boilers: 2

The merchant tanker *Shenandoah* was built from the stern of the naval tanker *Potomac* (T-AO 150) destroyed by fire on 26 September 1961, and new bow and mid-body sections. After being chartered by the Military Sealift Command since 14 December 1964 the ship was formally acquired on 12 January 1976, assigned the name *Potomac* and placed in MSC service. Cargo capacity 200 000 barrels. Operated under charter by Hudson Waterways Corp. Reclassified AOT on 30 September 1978.

POTOMAC 1977, USN

USA / Military Sealift Command 747

9 "SEALIFT" CLASS: TRANSPORT OILERS (AOT, ex-AO)

Name	No.	Builders	Delivered	F/S
SEALIFT PACIFIC	T-AOT 168	Todd Shipyards	14 Aug 1974	TWWR
SEALIFT ARABIAN SEA	T-AOT 169	Todd Shipyards	6 May 1975	TWWR
SEALIFT CHINA SEA	T-AOT 170	Todd Shipyards	9 May 1975	TWWR
SEALIFT INDIAN OCEAN	T-AOT 171	Todd Shipyards	29 Aug 1975	TWWR
SEALIFT ATLANTIC	T-AOT 172	Bath Iron Works, Bath, Maine	26 Aug 1974	TWWR
SEALIFT MEDITERRANEAN	T-AOT 173	Bath Iron Works, Bath, Maine	6 Nov 1974	TWWR
SEALIFT CARIBBEAN	T-AOT 174	Bath Iron Works, Bath, Maine	10 Feb 1975	TWWR
SEALIFT ARCTIC	T-AOT 175	Bath Iron Works, Bath, Maine	22 May 1975	TWWR
SEALIFT ANTARCTIC	T-AOT 176	Bath Iron Works, Bath, Maine	1 Aug 1975	TWWR

Displacement, tons: 34 100 full load
Measurement, tons: 27 500 deadweight
Dimensions, feet (metres): 587 × 84 × 34·6 (178·9 × 25·6 × 10·6)
Main engines: Two 14-cyl Pielstick turbo-charged diesels; 19 200 bhp; 1 shaft; (cp propeller) = 16 knots
Range, miles: 12 000 at 16 knots
Complement: 30 + 2 Maritime Academy cadets

SEALIFT ANTARCTIC 1975, USN

Built specially for long term-charter by the Military Sealift Command. T-AO 168 launched on 13 October 1973; others launched in 1974 on 26 January, 20 April, 27 July, 26 January, 9 March, 8 June, 31 August and 26 October respectively. Operated for MSC under charter by Marine Transport Lines Inc.
Fitted with bow thruster to assist docking; automated engine room. Cargo capacity 225 154 barrels. Estimated cost $146·5 million for the nine ship class. All reclassified AOT on 30 September 1978.

1 "AMERICAN EXPLORER" CLASS: TRANSPORT OILER (AOT, ex-AO)

Name	No.	Builders	Completed	F/S
AMERICAN EXPLORER	T-AOT 165	Ingalls S.B. Co, Pascagoula	27 Oct 1959	TWWR

Displacement, tons: 8 400 light; 31 300 full load
Measurement, tons: 22 525 deadweight
Dimensions, feet (metres): 615 × 80 × 32 (187·5 × 24·4 × 9·8)
Main engines: Steam turbines (De Laval); 22 000 shp; 1 shaft = 20 knots
Boilers: 2 (Babcock & Wilcox)
Complement: 53

AMERICAN EXPLORER USN

T5-S-RM2A type. Laid down on 9 July 1957; launched on 11 April 1958. Built for the Maritime Administration, but acquired by Military Sea Transportation Service. Cargo capacity 190 300 barrels.
Operated for Military Sealift Command under charter by Hudson Waterways Corp.
Reclassified AOT on 30 September 1978.

3 "MAUMEE" CLASS: TRANSPORT OILERS (AOT, ex-AO)

Name	No.	Builders	Delivered	F/S
MAUMEE	T-AOT 149	Ingalls S.B. Co, Pascagoula	12 Dec 1956	TWWR
SHOSHONE	T-AOT 151	Sun S.B. & D.D. Co, Chester	15 Apr 1957	TWWR
YUKON	T-AOT 152	Ingalls S.B. Co, Pascagoula	17 May 1957	TWWR

Displacement, tons: 7 761 light; 32 953 full load
Measurement, tons: 25 000 deadweight
Dimensions, feet (metres): 620 × 83·5 × 32 (189·0 × 25·5 × 9·8)
Main engine: Geared turbine (Westinghouse); 18 600 shp; 1 shaft = 18 knots
Boilers: 2 (Combustion Engineering)
Complement: 53

MAUMEE 1978, Michael D. J. Lennon

Yukon laid down 16 May 1955, launched 16 March 1956; Maumee laid down 8 March 1955, launched 16 February 1956; Shoshone laid down 15 August 1955, launched 17 January 1957. T5-S-12A type. Potomac T-AO 150 sank after explosion in 1961, but was rebuilt in 1963-64; see previous listing for Potomac (T-AO 181). Cargo capacity 203 216 barrels.
Maumee provided with ice-strengthened bow during 1969-70 modification at Norfolk S.B. & D.D. Co; employed in transporting petroleum products to Antarctica in support of US scientific endeavours.
These ships are operated for the Military Sealift Command under charter by Hudson Waterways Corp. Reclassified AOT on 30 September 1978.

1 "MISSION" CLASS: TRANSPORT OILER (AOT, ex-AO)

Name	No.	Builders	Completed	F/S
MISSION SANTA YNEZ	T-AOT 134	Marineship Corp, Sausalito, Calif	13 Mar 1944	MPR

Displacement, tons: 5 730 light; 22 380 full load
Dimensions, feet (metres): 524 × 68 × 31 (159·7 × 20·7 × 9·5)
Main engines: Turbo-electric (General Electric); 10 000 shp; 1 shaft = 16 knots
Boilers: 2 (Babcock & Wilcox)
Complement: 52

Built to a T2-SE-A2 design. She is the sole survivor of a class of 27 ships (AO 111-137). Acquired from the Naval Overseas Transportation Service on 1 October 1949. Transferred to the Maritime Administration, Suisun Bay on 6 March 1975 for lay-up. Reclassified from AO to AOT on 30 September 1978.

Note: Civilian oiler *Williamsburg* chartered by MSC early 1978 for transport and storage of oil on East Coast/Gulf of Mexico.

5 "SUAMICO" CLASS: TRANSPORT OILERS (AOT, ex-AO)

Name	No.	Builders	Commissioned	F/S
TALLULAH (ex-Valley Forge)	T-AOT 50	Sun S.B. & D.D. Co, Chester	5 Sep 1942	MAR
MILLICOMA (ex-Conestoga, ex-King's Mountain)	T-AOT 73	Sun S.B. & D.D. Co, Chester	5 Mar 1943	MAR
SAUGATUCK (ex-Newton)	T-AOT 75	Sun S.B. & D.D. Co, Chester	19 Feb 1943	MAR
SCHUYLKILL (ex-Louisburg)	T-AOT 76	Sun S.B. & D.D. Co, Chester	9 Apr 1943	MAR
CHEPACHET	T-AOT 78	Sun S.B. & D.D. Co, Chester	27 Apr 1943	Loan

Displacement, tons: 5 252 light; 21 880 full load
Dimensions, feet (metres): 523·5 × 68 × 33 (159·6 × 20·7 × 10·1)
Main engines: Turbo-electric drive (GE except Westinghouse in 75); 6 000 shp; 1 shaft = 15 knots
Boilers: 2 (Babcock & Wilcox)
Complement: 52

SCHUYLKILL USN

T2-SE-A1 tankers begun as merchant ships but acquired by Navy and completed as fleet oilers. During the post World War II period, all of these ships were employed in the tanker role, carrying petroleum point-to-point. Launched on 25 June 1942, 21 January 1943, 7 December 1942, 16 February 1943, 10 March 1943 respectively.
Cargo capacity approximately 134 000 barrels.
Transferred to Maritime Administration for lay-up at James River—T-AOT 50, 29 May 1975; T-AOT 73, 16 July 1975; T-AOT 75, 5 November 1974; T-AOT 76, 8 September 1975 and T-AOT on 13 March 1972. Chepachet (T-AOT 78) was transferred to the Department of Energy on 9 November 1978 as a loan. The ship will be used in Geothermal research. Specifically, she will be used as a test platform in ocean thermal energy conversion (OTEC). After five years, the ship will be returned to the US Navy. Her conversion into the world's first electrical generating platform will cost about $25 million. All remain on Navy List—replaced by "Sealift" class AOs.

748　USA / Military Sealift Command

2 "ALATNA" CLASS: GASOLINE TANKERS (AOG)

Name	No.	Completed	F/S
ALATNA	T-AOG 81	July 1957	MPR
CHATTAHOOCHEE	T-AOG 82	Oct 1957	MPR

Displacement, tons: 7 300 (81); 5 720 (82) full load
Measurement, tons: 3 659 gross
Dimensions, feet (metres): 302 × 61 × 19 (92·1 × 18·6 × 5·8)
Main engines: Turbo-electric (Alco built diesels); 4 000 bhp; 2 shafts = 13 knots
Complement: 51

Built as T1-MET-24a type gasoline tankers by Bethlehem Steel Co, Staten Island. Bows strengthened for navigation in ice. Equipped with small helicopter deck. *Chattahoochee* transferred to the temporary custody of the Maritime Administration on 8 August 1972 for lay-up at Suisun Bay. *Alatna* followed on 8 August 1972. Both reacquired by the US Navy in early 1979 for reactivation and operation by MSC. Scheduled to be in service by mid-1979. Both ships may have their main engines replaced during reactivation overhaul. Cargo capacity 30 000 barrels.

ALATNA　　　1978, US

3 "TONTI" CLASS: GASOLINE TANKERS (AOG)

Name	No.	Builders	Completed	F/S
RINCON (ex-*Tarland*)	T-AOG 77	Todd Shipyards, Houston	Oct 1945	TPA
NODAWAY (ex-*Belridge*)	T-AOG 78	Todd Shipyards, Houston	Sep 1945	TPA
PETALUMA (ex-*Raccoon Bend*)	T-AOG 79	Todd Shipyards, Houston	Nov 1945	TPA

Displacement, tons: 2 100 light; 6 047 full load
Dimensions, feet (metres): 325·2 × 48·2 × 19·1 (99·1 × 14·7 × 5·8)
Main engine: 1 diesel (Nordberg); 1 400 bhp; 1 shaft = 10 knots
Complement: 41

T1-M-BT2 gasoline tankers. Launched as merchant tankers on 5 January 1945, 15 May 1945 and 9 August 1945 respectively. All acquired by Navy 1 July 1950 (77) and 7 September 1950 (78 and 79) and assigned to Military Sea Transportation Service and employed in point-to-point carrying of petroleum. Cargo capacity approximately 30 000 barrels.
These are the only survivors in US service of a once large number of small gasoline tankers. *Rincon* and *Petaluma* are to be replaced by the two "Alatna" class AOGs in late 1979-early 1980 when both will be scrapped. Several survive in foreign navies.

RINCON　　　US

0 + 1 CABLE REPAIR SHIP (ARC)

Displacement, tons: 8 370 light; 14 157 full load
Dimensions, feet (metres): 502·5 × 73 × 24 (153·2 × 22·3 × 7·3)
Main engines: Diesel-electric; 10 200 shp; 2 shafts = 15 knots
Range: 10 000 at 15 knots
Complement: 126 (88 MSC crew, 6 USN contingent and 32 technicians)

Originally two units of this class were to be built as replacement for *Thor* (ARC 4) (since deleted) and *Aeolus* (ARC 3). However, under recent Administration economies only one will be built. She was authorised in the Fiscal Year 1979 programme. Estimated construction cost is $17 million. Pennant number will be ARC 7. Upon completion she will be operated by the Military Sealift Command (MSC). Ship will be fitted with bow thrusters and stern thrusters (two at either end) as well as a remotely manned engineering room controllable from the bridge.

1 "AEOLUS" CLASS: CABLE REPAIR SHIP (ARC)

Name	No.	Builders	Commissioned
AEOLUS (ex-*Turandot*)	T-ARC 3 (ex-AKA 47)	Walsh-Kaiser Co, Providence, RI	18 June 1945

Displacement, tons: 7 810 full load
Dimensions, feet (metres): 438 × 58·2 × 19·25 (133·5 × 17·7 × 5·9)
Main engines: Turbo-electric (Westinghouse); 6 000 shp; 2 shafts = 14 knots
Boilers: 2 (Wickes)
Complement: 221 (23 officers, 198 enlisted men)

Built as S4-SE2-BE1 attack cargo ship. Transferred to Maritime Administration and laid up in reserve from 1946 until reacquired by Navy for conversion to cable repair ship in 1955-56 at the Key Highway Plant of Bethlehem Steel Corp, Baltimore, Maryland, being recommissioned on 14 May 1955. Fitted with cable-laying bow sheaves, cable stowage tanks, cable repair facilities, and helicopter platform aft.
Employed in hydrographic and cable operations. Naval manned until 1973 when transferred to Military Sealift Command and provided with civilian crew.

AEOLUS　　　USN

2 "NEPTUNE" CLASS: CABLE REPAIR SHIPS (ARC)

Name	No.	Builders	Commissioned
NEPTUNE (ex-*William H. G. Bullard*)	T-ARC 2	Pusey & Jones Corp, Wilmington, Del	1 June 1953
ALBERT J. MEYER	T-ARC 6	Pusey & Jones Corp, Wilmington, Del	13 May 1963

Displacement, tons: 7 810 full load
Dimensions, feet (metres): 370 × 47 × 25 (112·8 × 14·3 × 7·6)
Main engines: Reciprocating (Skinner); 4 800 ihp; 2 shafts = 14 knots
Boilers: 2 (Combustion Engineering)
Complement: 173

Built as S3-S2-BP1 type cable ships for the Maritime Administration.
Neptune acquired by the Navy from the Maritime Administration in 1953 and sister ship *Albert J. Meyer* from US Army in 1966. They have been fitted with electric cable handling machinery (in place of steam equipment) and precision navigation equipment; helicopter platform in *Neptune*.
Both ships are operated by the Military Sealift Command. *Neptune* was naval-manned until 8 November 1973 when transferred to MSC.
The USNS *Neptune* (T-ARC 2) should not be confused with the commercial cable ship *Neptun* of the United States Undersea Cable Corp.

NEPTUNE　　　1975, Dr. Giorgio Arra

USA (USCG) / Introduction

COAST GUARD

Senior Officers

Commandant:
 Admiral John B. Hayes
Vice Commandant:
 Vice-Admiral Robert H. Scarborough
Chief of Staff:
 Rear-Admiral James P. Stewart
Commander, Atlantic Area:
 Vice-Admiral Robert I. Price
Commander, Pacific Area:
 Vice-Admiral James S. Gracey

Establishment

The United States Coast Guard was established by an Act of Congress approved 28 January 1915, which consolidated the Revenue Cutter Service (founded in 1790) and the Life Saving Service (founded in 1848). The act of establishment stated the Coast Guard "shall be a military service and a branch of the armed forces of the USA at all times. The Coast Guard shall be a service in the Treasury Department except when operating as a service in the Navy". Congress further legislated that in time of national emergency or when the President so directs, the Coast Guard operates as a part of the Navy. The Coast Guard did operate as a part of the Navy during the First and Second World Wars.
The Lighthouse Service (founded in 1789) was transferred to the Coast Guard on 7 July 1939.
The Coast Guard was transferred to the newly established Department of Transportation on 1 April 1967.

Missions

The current missions of the Coast Guard are to (1) enforce or assist in the enforcement of applicable Federal laws upon the high seas and waters subject to the jurisdiction of the USA including environmental protection; (2) administer all Federal laws regarding safety of life and property on the high seas and on waters subject to the jurisdiction of the USA, except those laws specifically entrusted to other Federal agencies; (3) develop, establish, maintain, operate, and conduct aids to maritime navigation, ocean stations, icebreaking activities, oceanographic research, and rescue facilities; and (4) maintain a state of readiness to function as a specialised service in the Navy when so directed by the President.

Personnel

31 Dec 1978: 4 759 officers, 1 356 warrant officers, 30 778 enlisted men.

Aviation

Only the larger "Hamilton" class cutters and certain classes of icebreakers can support helicopters at sea.
As of 1 January 1979 the Coast Guard's aviation strength consisted of 55 fixed-wing aircraft and 18 helicopters:

25 HC-130 Hercules
17 HC-131 Convair
 1 HU-16   Albatross
 1 VC-4A   Gulfstream I
 1 VC-11A Gulfstream II
38 HH-3F   Pelican
30 HH-52A Sea Guard

The Coast Guard plans to acquire approximately 40 land-based patrol and rescue aircraft in the period 1979-83 to replace the long-serving HU-16 Albatross amphibians.

Cutter Strength

All Coast Guard vessels are referred to as "cutters". Cutter names are preceded by USCGC. Cutter serial numbers are prefixed with letter designations similar to the US Navy classification system with the prefix letter "W". The first two digits of serial numbers for cutters less than 100 ft in length indicate their approximate length overall. All Coast Guard cutters are active unless otherwise indicated.
Approximately 600 small rescue and utility craft also are in service.

The following table provides a tabulation of the ship strength of the United States Coast Guard. Ship arrangement is based on function and employment. Numbers of ships listed are actual as of 1 January 1979. Some projections of changes are also included.

Category/Classification		Active*	Reserve	New Construction
Cutters				
WHEC	High Endurance Cutters	17	1	—
WMEC	Medium Endurance Cutters	23	—	6
Icebreakers				
WAGB	Icebreakers	6	—	—
WTGB	Icebreaking Tugs	1	—	5
Patrol Craft				
WPB	Patrol Craft, Large	76	—	—
Training Cutters				
WIX	Training Cutter	1	—	—
WTR	Reserve Training Cutter	1	—	—
Oceanographic Cutters				
WAGO	Oceanographic Cutters	2	—	—
Buoy Tenders				
WLB	Buoy Tender, Seagoing	29	4	—
WLM	Buoy Tender, Coastal	15	—	—
WLI	Buoy Tender, Inland	13	—	—
WLR	Buoy Tender, River	22	—	—
Construction Tenders				
WLIC	Construction Tender, Inland	14	—	—
Lightships				
WLV	Lightships	2	1	—
Harbour Tugs				
WYTM	Harbour Tugs, Medium	14	—	—
WYTL	Harbour Tugs, Small	15	—	—

Shipbuilding Programmes

Approved FY 1979 Programme

2 WMEC ("270 ft" Class)
2 WTGB ("140 ft" Class)

Proposed FY 1980 Programme

3 WMEC ("270 ft" Class)

DELETIONS

Icebreakers

1976 Edisto (WAGB 284) and Staten Island (WAGB 278) (both sold)
1978 9 May Burton Island (WAGB 283) (sold)

High Endurance Cutters

1976 Chautauqua (WHEC 41) (scrapped), Mendota (WHEC 69), Minnetonka (WHEC 67), Ponchartrain (WHEC 70) and Winona (WHEC 65), (all pending)

Patrol Craft

1976 Cape Higgon (WPB 95302), Cape Gull (WPB 95304), Cape Upright (WPB 95303) and Cape Hatteras (WPB 95305) (hulks stripped; sold)
1978 18 Sep Flagstaff (WPGH 1) (pending)

Buoy Tenders

1976 30 Sep Loganberry (WLI 65305) (sold); 12 Nov Clematis (WLI 74286) (sold), Shadbush (WLI 74287) and Blueberry (WLI 65302) (both sold)
1977 1 June Oleander (WLR 73264) (sold); 30 June Sycamore (WLR 268) (sold); 1 July Tern (WLI 80801) (sold); 8 July Foxglove (WLR 285) (sold); 12 Aug Forsythia (WLR 63) (sold); 1 Sep Verbena (WLI 317) (sold)
1978 31 Oct Azalea (WLI 641) (sold), Juniper (WLM 224)

Training Cutters

1978 3 Nov Cuyahoga (WIX 157) (sunk in collision 20 Oct 1978; raised; hulk target)

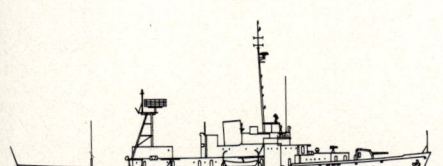
"Campbell" Class

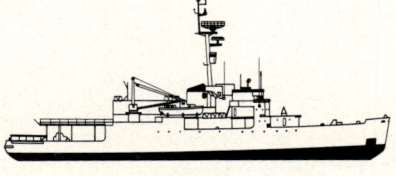
"Wind" Class

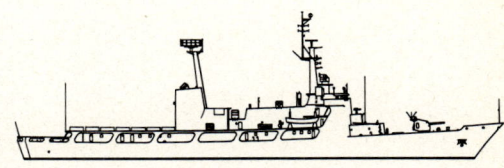
"Hamilton" Class

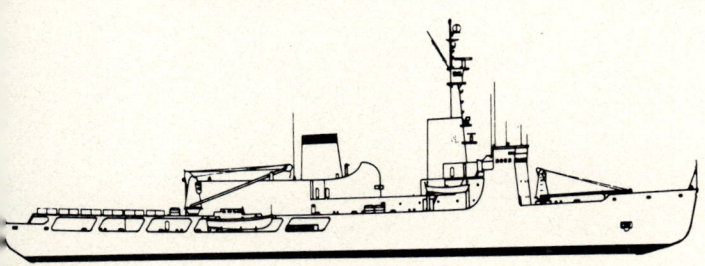
POLAR STAR

"Reliance" Class

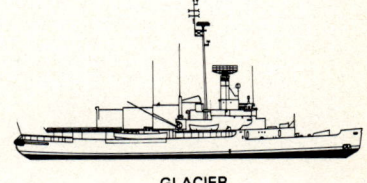
GLACIER

Scale: 1 inch = 150 feet (1 : 1 800)

Drawings, A. D. Baker III

HIGH ENDURANCE CUTTERS

12 "HAMILTON" and "HERO" CLASSES: HIGH ENDURANCE CUTTERS (WHEC)

Name	No.	Builders	Laid down	Launched	Commissioned	F/S
HAMILTON	WHEC 715	Avondale Shipyards Inc, New Orleans, Louisiana	Jan 1965	18 Dec 1965	20 Feb 1967	AA
DALLAS	WHEC 716	Avondale Shipyards Inc, New Orleans, Louisiana	7 Feb 1966	1 Oct 1966	1 Oct 1967	AA
MELLON	WHEC 717	Avondale Shipyards Inc, New Orleans, Louisiana	25 July 1966	11 Feb 1967	22 Dec 1967	PA
CHASE	WHEC 718	Avondale Shipyards Inc, New Orleans, Louisiana	15 Oct 1966	20 May 1967	1 Mar 1968	AA
BOUTWELL	WHEC 719	Avondale Shipyards Inc, New Orleans, Louisiana	12 Dec 1966	17 June 1967	14 June 1968	PA
SHERMAN	WHEC 720	Avondale Shipyards Inc, New Orleans, Louisiana	13 Feb 1967	23 Sep 1967	23 Aug 1968	AA
GALLATIN	WHEC 721	Avondale Shipyards Inc, New Orleans, Louisiana	17 Apr 1967	18 Nov 1967	20 Dec 1968	AA
MORGENTHAU	WHEC 722	Avondale Shipyards Inc, New Orleans, Louisiana	17 July 1967	10 Feb 1968	14 Feb 1969	PA
RUSH	WHEC 723	Avondale Shipyards Inc, New Orleans, Louisiana	23 Oct 1967	16 Nov 1968	3 July 1969	AA
MUNRO	WHEC 724	Avondale Shipyards Inc, New Orleans, Louisiana	18 Feb 1970	5 Dec 1970	10 Sep 1971	PA
JARVIS	WHEC 725	Avondale Shipyards Inc, New Orleans, Louisiana	9 Sep 1970	24 Apr 1971	30 Dec 1971	PA
MIDGETT	WHEC 726	Avondale Shipyards Inc, New Orleans, Louisiana	5 Apr 1971	4 Sep 1971	17 Mar 1972	PA

Displacement, tons: 3 050 full load
Length, feet (metres): 378 *(115·2)*
Beam, feet (metres): 42·8 *(13·1)*
Draught, feet (metres): 20 *(6·1)*
Guns: 1—5 in *(127 mm)*/38 (Mk 30); 2—20 mm in 715, 716, 718, 720-722; 2—·50 MGs
A/S weapons: 2 triple torpedo tubes (Mk 32)
Helicopters: 1 HH-52A or HH-3 helicopter
Main engines: Combined diesel and gas turbine (CODAG): 2 diesels (Fairbanks-Morse) 7 000 bhp; 2 gas turbines (Pratt & Whitney FT-4A), 36 000 shp; 2 shafts; (cp propellers)
Speed, knots: 29, 20 cruising
Oil fuel: 800 tons
Range, miles: 14 000 at 11 knots (diesels); 2 400 at 29 knots (gas)
Complement: 164 (15 officers, 149 enlisted)

All active. In the fall of 1977 *Gallatin* and *Morgenthau* were the first of the Coast Guard ships to have women assigned as permanent members of the crew.

Anti-submarine armament: Hedgehog anti-submarine weapons have been removed from earlier ships during overhaul and Mk 309 fire control system for Mk 32 torpedo tubes are installed. Hedgehogs deleted in later ships. *Hamilton* was first to drop hedgehogs and receive Mk 309 during 1970 overhaul.

Design: These ships have clipper bows, twin funnels enclosing a helicopter hangar, helicopter platform aft. All are fitted with oceanographic laboratories, elaborate communications equipment, and meteorological data gathering facilities. Superstructure is largely of aluminium construction. Bridge control of manoeuvring is by aircraft-type joy-stick rather than wheel.

Engineering: The "Hamiltons" were the largest US "military" ships with gas turbine propulsion prior to the Navy's "Spruance" class destroyers. The Fairbanks-Morse diesels are 12-cylinder.
Engine and propeller pitch consoles are located in wheelhouse and at bridge wing stations as well as engine room control booth.
A retractable bow propulsion unit is provided for station keeping and precise manoeuvring (unit is located directly forward of bridge, immediately aft of sonar dome).

Gunnery: Planned to ship two 40 mm guns in all vessels and to replace two 81 mm mortars with two 20 mm in ships that had them. Mk 56 GFCS and SPG 35 fire control radar.

Radar: Search: SPS 29 and 51.

Sonar: SQS 38.

GALLATIN   1978, USCG

CHASE   1976, Michael D. J. Lennon

USA (USCG) / High endurance cutters 751

6 "CAMPBELL" (327 ft) CLASS: HIGH ENDURANCE CUTTERS (WHEC)

Name	No.	Builders	Laid down	Launched	Commissioned	F/S
BIBB (ex-*George M. Bibb*)	WHEC 31	Charleston Navy Yard	10 May 1935	14 Jan 1937	10 Mar 1937	AA
CAMPBELL (ex-*George W. Campbell*)	WHEC 32	Philadelphia Navy Yard	1 May 1935	3 June 1936	16 June 1936	PA
DUANE (ex-*William J. Duane*)	WHEC 33	Philadelphia Navy Yard	1 May 1935	3 June 1936	16 Aug 1936	AA
INGHAM (ex-*Samuel D. Ingham*)	WHEC 35	Philadelphia Navy Yard	1 May 1935	3 June 1936	12 Sep 1936	AA
SPENCER (ex-*John C. Spencer*)	WHEC 36	New York Navy Yard	11 Sep 1935	3 Jan 1936	1 Mar 1937	AR
TANEY (ex-*Roger B. Taney*)	WHEC 37	Philadelphia Navy Yard	1 May 1935	3 June 1936	20 Nov 1936	AA

Displacement, tons: 2 216 standard; 2 656 full load
Length, feet (metres): 327 *(99·7)*
Beam, feet (metres): 41 *(12·5)*
Draught, feet (metres): 15 *(4·6)*
Guns: 1—5 in *(127 mm)*/38 (Mk 30); 2—81 mm mortars (except 35) (see notes)
A/S weapons: Removed
Main engines: Geared turbines (Westinghouse); 6 200 shp; 2 shafts
Boilers: 2 (Babcock & Wilcox)
Speed, knots: 19·8
Range, miles: 4 000 at 19 knots; 8 000 at 10·5 knots
Complement: 144 (13 officers, 131 enlisted men)

These were the Coast Guard's largest cutters until *Hamilton* was completed in 1967.
Duane served as an amphibious force flagship during the invasion of Southern France in August 1944 and was designated AGC 6; the other ships of this class, except the lost *Alexander Hamilton* (PG 34), were similarly employed but retained Coast Guard number with WAGC prefix (amidships structure built up and one or two additional masts installed); all reverted to gunboat configuration after war (WPG). Redesignated WHEC on 1 May 1966.
All of these cutters remain in active service except *Spencer*, decommissioned on 1 February 1974 and placed in reserve at the Coast Guard Yard, Curtis Bay, Maryland. *Spencer* is employed as a stationary engineering school ship.

Anti-submarine armament: During the 1960s these ships each had an ASW armament of one ahead-firing fixed hedgehog and two Mk 32 triple torpedo tube mounts; subsequently removed from all ships.

Gunnery: As built these ships had two 5 in/51 guns (single mounts forward) and two 6 pdr guns; rearmed during World War II with an additional single 5 in/51 gun installed aft plus two or three 3 in/50 anti-aircraft guns, and several 20 mm anti-aircraft guns (depth charge racks installed); *Taney* was experimentally armed with four 5 in/38 guns in single mounts. Present armament fitted after World War II.
Planned to fit all of class with two 40 mm Mk 64 (single).

TANEY   1975, USCG

INGHAM   6/1976, C. and S. Taylor

1 "CASCO" (311 ft) CLASS: HIGH ENDURANCE CUTTER (WHEC)

Name	No.	Builders	Laid down	Launched	Commissioned	F/S
UNIMAK	WHEC 379 (ex-WTR 379, ex-WHEC 379, ex-AVP 31)	Associated Shipbuilders, Seattle, Wash	15 Feb 1942	27 May 1942	31 Dec 1943	AA

Displacement, tons: 1 766 standard; 2 800 full load
Length, feet (metres): 310·75 *(94·7)*
Beam, feet (metres): 41 *(12·5)*
Draught, feet (metres): 13·5 *(4·1)*
Guns: 1—5 in *(127 mm)*/38 (Mk 30); 2—81 mm mortars
A/S weapons: Removed
Main engines: Diesels (Fairbanks-Morse); 6 080 bhp; 2 shafts
Speed, knots: 18
Range, miles: 8 000 at 18 knots
Complement: 150 (13 officers; 137 enlisted men)

Unimak is the sole survivor of 18 former Navy seaplane tenders (AVP) transferred to the Coast Guard in 1946-48 (WAVP/WHEC 370-387). *Unimak* operated as a training cutter (WTR) from 1969 until decommissioned on 30 May 1975 at Baltimore. Replaced by *Reliance* WTR 615. Towed to Boston in January 1977 for reactivation which was delayed by a serious engineroom fire. Recommissioned 15 August 1977 to assist in patrolling the 200 mile EEZ. Due to her age and engineering problems in wake of the fire her active career may be short.

Classification: The former Navy AVPs were designated WAVP by the Coast Guard until changed to high endurance cutters (WHEC) on 1 May 1966. *Unimak* subsequently became a training cutter (WTR) on 28 November 1969. Reclassified WHEC on 15 August 1977.

Transfers: Ships of this class (originally "Barnegat" class) serve in the navies of Ethiopia, Italy, Philippines and Viet-Nam and commercially.

UNIMAK   1977, USCG

MEDIUM ENDURANCE CUTTERS

0 + 4 + 9 "BEAR" (270 ft) CLASS: MEDIUM ENDURANCE CUTTERS (WMEC)

Name	No.	Builders	Laid down	Launched	Commissioned	F/S
BEAR	WMEC 901	Tacoma Boatbuilding Co, Tacoma	21 Mar 1979	20 Feb 1980	28 Nov 1980	Bldg
TAMPA	WMEC 902	Tacoma Boatbuilding Co, Tacoma	17 Dec 1979	30 June 1980	23 Feb 1981	Bldg
HARRIET LANE	WMEC 903	Tacoma Boatbuilding Co, Tacoma	21 Mar 1980	30 Nov 1980	29 June 1981	Bldg
NORTHLAND	WMEC 904	Tacoma Boatbuilding Co, Tacoma	25 Aug 1980	9 Mar 1981	2 Nov 1981	Bldg
SENECA	WMEC 905	Approved FY 1979 programme	—	—	—	Ord
PICKERING	WMEC 906	Approved FY 1979 programme	—	—	—	Ord
ESCANABA	WMEC 907	Requested FY 1980 programme	—	—	—	Proj
LEGARE	WMEC 908	Requested FY 1980 programme	—	—	—	Proj
ARGUS	WMEC 909	Requested FY 1980 programme	—	—	—	Proj
Seven ships (minimum)	WMEC 910-916	Planned FY 1981-1984 programmes	—	—	—	Proj

Displacement, tons: 1 780 full load
Dimensions, feet (metres): 270 × 38 × 13·5 *(82·3 × 11·6 × 4·1)*
Aircraft: 1 HH-52A or 1 LAMPS III helicopter
Missiles: (see note)
Gun: 1—3 in *(76 mm)*/62 (Mk 75) (see note)
A/S weapons: (see note)
Main engines: Diesels; 7 000 bhp; 2 shafts = 19·5 knots
Complement: 95 (13 officers, 82 enlisted men)

The Coast Guard plans to construct up to 25 medium endurance cutters of this class over a seven year period. They will replace the "Campbell" class and other older medium and high endurance cutters when they become operational from about 1981 onwards.

A/S weapons: These ships will have no shipboard A/S weapons, but will rely on helicopters to deliver torpedoes against submarines detected by the ships' towed sonar array operations.

Design: They will be the only medium endurance cutters with helicopter hangars, and the first cutters with automated command and control centre. Fin stabilisers to be fitted.

Electronics: Fitted with Mk 92 weapons control system, easily identified by radome above the bridge. These ships will not have hull-mounted sonar, but instead the tactical Towed Array Sonar System (TASS), capable of providing long-range targeting data for A/S helicopter attack.

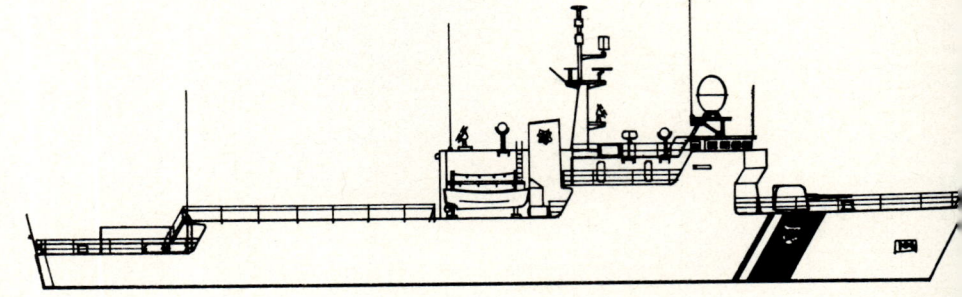

"BEAR" Class *1978, A. D. Baker III*

Engineering: Diesels were selected over gas turbine propulsion because of the Coast Guard requirement for long on-station time at slow speeds as opposed to high-speed naval operations.

Fiscal: The Coast Guard Fiscal Year 1977 programme provided $49 million for the first two ships of this class.

Gunnery: Weight and space for CIWS.

Helicopters: The plans are designed to accommodate the HH-52 Sea Guard helicopter or its Coast Guard successor, or the Navy's planned LAMPS III (Light Airborne Multi-Purpose System) helicopter. The helicopter hangar is extendable. Weight and space reserved for helicopter landing and traversing system.

Missiles: Weight and space reserved for Harpoon.

16 "RELIANCE" (210 ft) CLASS: } 15 MEDIUM ENDURANCE CUTTERS (WMEC) / 1 TRAINING CUTTER (WTR)

Name	No.	Builders	Commissioned	F/S	Name	No.	Builders	Commissioned	F/S
RELIANCE	WTR 615	Todd Shipyards	20 June 1964	AA	STEADFAST	WMEC 623	American Shipbuilding Co	25 Sep 1968	AA
DILIGENCE	WMEC 616	Todd Shipyards	26 Aug 1964	AA	DAUNTLESS	WMEC 624	American Shipbuilding Co	10 June 1968	AA
VIGILANT	WMEC 617	Todd Shipyards	3 Oct 1964	AA	VENTUROUS	WMEC 625	Coast Guard Yard, Curtis Bay, Baltimore	16 Aug 1968	PA
ACTIVE	WMEC 618	Christy Corp	17 Sep 1966	AA					
CONFIDENCE	WMEC 619	Coast Guard Yard, Curtis Bay, Baltimore	19 Feb 1966	PA	DEPENDABLE	WMEC 626	American Shipbuilding Co	22 Nov 1968	AA
					VIGOROUS	WMEC 627	American Shipbuilding Co	2 May 1969	AA
RESOLUTE	WMEC 620	American Shipbuilding Co	8 Dec 1966	PA	DURABLE	WMEC 628	Coast Guard Yard, Curtis Bay, Baltimore	8 Dec 1967	AA
VALIANT	WMEC 621	American Shipbuilding Co	28 Oct 1967	AA					
COURAGEOUS	WMEC 622	American Shipbuilding Co	10 Apr 1968	AA	DECISIVE	WMEC 629	Coast Guard Yard, Curtis Bay, Baltimore	23 Aug 1968	AA
					ALERT	WMEC 630	American Shipbuilding Co	4 Aug 1969	AA

Displacement, tons: 950 standard; 1 007 full load (except WTR and WMEC 616-619, 970 full load)
Dimensions, feet (metres): 210·5 × 34 × 10·5 *(64·2 × 10·4 × 3·2)*
Aircraft: 1 HH-52A helicopter embarked as required
Guns: 1—3 in *(76 mm)*/50; 2—40 mm (single Mk 64) (see *Gunnery* note)
Main engines: 2 turbo-charged diesels (ALCO 251B); 2 shafts; 5 000 bhp = 18 knots (WTR 615 and WMEC 616-619 have 2 Solar gas turbines in addition (4 000 shp))
Range, miles: 6 100 at 13 knots (615-619); 6 100 at 14 knots; 2 700 at 18 knots (remainder)
Complement: 61 (7 officers, 54 enlisted men)

Designed for search and rescue duties. Design features include 360 degree visibility from bridge; helicopter flight deck (no hangar); and engine exhaust vent at stern in place of conventional funnel. Capable of towing ships up to 10 000 tons. Air-conditioned throughout except engine room; high degree of habitability.
Launched, respectively, on the following dates: 25 May 1963, 20 July 1963, 24 December 1963, 21 July 1965, 8 May 1965, 30 April 1966, 14 January 1967, 18 March 1967, 24 June 1967, 21 October 1967, 11 November 1967, 16 March 1968, 4 May 1968, 29 April 1967, 14 December 1967, 19 October 1968.
All these cutters are active. *Reliance* is the Coast Guard's reserve training cutter based at Yorktown, Virginia, and retains full search, rescue, and patrol capabilities.

Designation: These ships were originally designated as patrol craft (WPC); changed to WMEC on 1 May 1966.

Gunnery: Two 20 mm single (Mk 67) to be fitted in all ships.

Helicopters: *Alert* was the first US ship fitted with the Canadian-developed "Beartrap" helicopter hauldown system. No further procurement of this system has been funded.

VIGILANT *9/1976, Dr. Giorgio Arra*

ICEBREAKERS

2 "POLAR STAR" CLASS: ICEBREAKERS (WAGB)

Name	No.	Builders	Commissioned	F/S
POLAR STAR	WAGB 10	Lockheed Shipbuilding Co, Seattle, Wash	19 Jan 1976	PA
POLAR SEA	WAGB 11	Lockheed Shipbuilding Co, Seattle, Wash	23 Feb 1978	PA

Displacement, tons: 12 087 full load
Dimensions, feet (metres): 399 × 86 × 31 (121·6 × 26·2 × 9·5)
Aircraft: 2 HH-52A helicopters
Guns: None
Main engines: Diesel-electric; 6 ALCO diesels; 18 000 shp; 3 gas turbines (Pratt & Whitney FT4A-12); 60 000 shp; 3 shafts; (cp propellers) = 18 knots
Range, miles: 28 000 at 13 knots
Complement: 163 (13 officers, 125 enlisted men plus 10 scientists and 15 flight crew)

These ships are the first icebreakers built for US service since *Glacier* was constructed two decades earlier. The programme is intended to replace the World War II-built "Wind" class icebreakers. *Polar Star* authorised in the Fiscal Year 1971 budget of the Department of Transportation; *Polar Sea* in the FY 1973 budget. *Polar Star* was laid down on 15 May 1972 and launched on 17 November 1973; *Polar Sea* was laid down on 27 November 1973 and launched on 24 June 1975. No additional ships are planned for the near future. *Polar Star* based at Seattle.

Design: The "Polar Star" class icebreakers are the largest ships operated by the US Coast Guard. At a continuous speed of 3 knots these ships can break ice 6 ft thick and by riding on the ice they can break 21 ft pack.
These ships have a conventional icebreaker hull form with cutaway bow configuration and well rounded body sections to prevent being trapped in ice. Two 15 ton capacity cranes fitted aft; hangar and flight deck aft; extensive research laboratories provided for arctic and oceanographic research.

Engineering: This CODOG design provides for conventional diesel engines for normal cruising in field ice and gas turbines for heavy icebreaking. The diesel engines drive generators producing AC power; the main propulsion DC motors draw power through rectifiers permitting absolute flexibility in the delivery of power from alternate sources. The use of controllable-pitch propellers on three shafts will permit manoeuvring in heavy ice without the risk to the propeller blades caused by stopping the shaft while going from ahead to astern. The Coast Guard had given consideration to the use of nuclear power for an icebreaker; however, at this time the gas turbine-diesel combination can achieve the desirable power requirements without the added cost and operating restrictions of a nuclear powerplant. From January 1976 until November 1977 (her first deployment) *Polar Star* had serious engineering problems which resulted in her being alongside for most of that period. *Polar Star* was still experiencing problems with her propellers in 1979.

Gunnery: Two single 40 mm and four 20 mm guns to be fitted.

POLAR STAR 1978, V. H. Young

POLAR STAR 6/1976, USCG

1 "GLACIER" CLASS: ICEBREAKER (WAGB)

Name	No.	Builders	USN Commissioned	F/S
GLACIER	WAGB 4 (ex-AGB 4)	Ingalls Shipbuilding Corp, Pascagoula, Mississippi	27 May 1955	PA

Displacement, tons: 8 449 full load
Dimensions, feet (metres): 309·6 × 74 × 29 (94·4 × 22·6 × 8·8)
Aircraft: 2 helicopters normally embarked
Main engines: Diesel-electric (10 Fairbanks-Morse diesels and 2 Westinghouse electric motors); 21 000 hp; 2 shafts = 17·6 knots
Range, miles: 29 200 at 12 knots; 12 000 at 17·6 knots
Complement: 241 (15 officers, 226 enlisted men)

The largest icebreaker in US service prior to the "Polar Star" class; laid down on 3 August 1953 and launched on 27 August 1954. Transferred from Navy (AGB 4) to Coast Guard on 30 June 1966. During 1972 *Glacier* and assigned helicopters were painted red to improve visibility in Arctic regions. All other icebreakers except *Mackinaw* painted red during 1973.

Engineering: When built *Glacier* had the largest capacity single-armature DC motors ever built and installed in a ship.

Gunnery: As built *Glacier* was armed with two 5 in guns (twin), six 3 in guns (twin), and four 20 mm guns; lighter weapons removed prior to transfer to Coast Guard; 5 in guns removed in 1969. Two single 40 mm guns to be fitted.

GLACIER 1976, John A. Jedrlinic

754 USA (USCG) / Icebreakers

2 "WIND" CLASS: ICEBREAKERS (WAGB)

Name	No.	Builders	Launched	F/S
WESTWIND	WAGB 281 (ex-AGB 6)	Western Pipe & Steel Co, San Pedro, California	31 Mar 1943	GLA
NORTHWIND	WAGB 282	Western Pipe & Steel Co, San Pedro, California	25 Feb 1945	AA

Displacement, tons: 3 500 standard; 6 515 full load
Dimensions, feet (metres): 269 × 63·5 × 29 (82·0 × 19·4 × 8·8)
Aircraft: 2 helicopters normally embarked (HH 52 A)
Main engines: Diesel-electric; 4 diesels (Enterprise); 10 000 bhp; 2 shafts = 16 knots
Range, miles: 38 000 at 10·5 knots; 16 000 at 16 knots
Complement: 135

Originally seven ships in this class built. Five ships were delivered to the US Coast Guard during World War II and two to the US Navy in 1946. *Westwind* served in the Soviet Navy from 1945 to 1951 (named *Severni Polus* in Soviet service) and with *Northwind* are last of the class. *Westwind* operates on the Great Lakes. Crews of *Northwind* and *Westwind* reduced from 181 to approximately 135 during 1975.

Engineering: These ships were built with a bow propeller shaft in addition to the two stern shafts; bow shaft removed from all units because it would continually break in heavy ice. *Westwind* re-engined in 1973-74, and *Northwind* in 1974-75.

Gunnery: As built the one Coast Guard ship mounted four 5 in guns (one twin mount forward and one twin mount aft on 01 level) and twelve 40 mm guns (quad); the Navy Ships were completed with only forward twin 5 in mount (as built a catapult and cranes were fitted immediately abaft the funnel and one floatplane was carried). Armament reduced after war and helicopter platform eventually installed in all ships.
During the 1960s *Northwind* carried two 5 in guns (twin), and the other ships each mounted one 5 in gun; all primary gun batteries removed in 1969-70. Two single 40 mm guns to be shipped in *Westwind* and *Northwind*.

NORTHWIND   12/1976, V. H. Young

1 "MACKINAW" CLASS: ICEBREAKER (WAGB)

Name	No.	Builders	Commissioned	F/S
MACKINAW (ex-*Manitowac*)	WAGB 83	Toledo Shipbuilding Co, Ohio	20 Dec 1944	GLA

Displacement, tons: 5 252
Dimensions, feet (metres): 290 × 74 × 19 (88·4 × 22·6 × 5·8)
Aircraft: 1 helicopter
Main engines: 2 diesels (Fairbanks-Morse); with electric drive (Elliot); 3 shafts (1 fwd, 2 aft); 10 000 bhp = 18·7 knots
Range, miles: 60 000 at 12 knots; 10 000 at 18·7 knots
Complement: 127 (10 officers, 117 enlisted men)

Laid down on 20 March 1943; launched 6 March 1944. Specially designed and constructed for service as icebreaker on the Great Lakes. Equipped with two 12 ton capacity cranes. Clear area for helicopter is provided on the quarterdeck.

MACKINAW   USCG

1 "STORIS" CLASS: MEDIUM ENDURANCE CUTTER (WMEC)

Name	No.	Builders	Commissioned	F/S
STORIS (ex-*Eskimo*)	WMEC 38 (ex-WAGB 38, ex-WAGL 38)	Toledo Shipbuilding Co, Ohio	30 Sep 1942	PA

Displacement, tons: 1 715 standard; 1 925 full load
Dimensions, feet (metres): 230 × 43 × 15 (70·1 × 13·1 × 4·6)
Guns: 2—40 mm (single Mk 64)
Main engines: Diesel-electric; 1 shaft; 1 800 bhp = 14 knots
Range, miles: 22 000 at 8 knots; 12 000 at 14 knots
Complement: 106 (10 officers, 96 enlisted men)

Laid down on 14 July 1941; launched on 4 April 1942. Ice patrol tender. Strengthened for ice navigation and sometimes employed as icebreaker. Employed in Alaskan service for search, rescue and law enforcement.
Designation changed from WAG to WAGB on 1 May 1966; redesignated as medium endurance cutter (WMEC) on 1 July 1972.

STORIS   1975, USCG

4 + 4 + 1 "140 ft" CLASS: ICEBREAKING TUGS (WTGB)

Name	No.	Builders	Laid down	Commissioned	F/S
KATMAI BAY	WTGB 101	Tacoma Boatbuilding Co, Tacoma	7 Nov 1977	8 Jan 1979	GLA
BRISTOL BAY	WTGB 102	Tacoma Boatbuilding Co, Tacoma	13 Feb 1978	5 Apr 1979	Bldg
MOBILE BAY	WTGB 103	Tacoma Boatbuilding Co, Tacoma	13 Feb 1978	6 May 1979	Bldg
BISCAYNE BAY	WTGB 104	Tacoma Boatbuilding Co, Tacoma	29 Aug 1978	6 Aug 1979	Bldg
NEAH BAY	WTGB 105	Tacoma Boatbuilding Co, Tacoma	—	mid-1980	Ord
MORRO BAY	WTGB 106	Tacoma Boatbuilding Co, Tacoma	—	late 1980	Ord
PENOBSCOT BAY	WTGB 107	Tacoma Boatbuilding Co, Tacoma	—	—	Ord
THUNDER BAY	WTGB 108	Approved FY 1979 programme	—	—	Ord
STURGEON BAY	WTGB 109	Planned FY 1981-84 programmes	—	—	Proj

Displacement, tons: 662 full load
Dimensions, feet (metres): 140 × 37·6 × 12·5 (42·7 × 11·4 × 3·8)
Main engines: Diesel-electric; 2 500 bhp; 1 shaft =14·7 knots
Endurance: 14 days
Complement: 17 (3 officers, 14 enlisted men)

This class is designed to replace the "110 ft" class WYTMs. Originally classified as WYTMs. Reclassified WTGBs on 5 February 1979. The size, manoeuvrability and other operational characteristics of these new vessels are tailored for operations in harbours and other restricted waters and for fulfilling present and anticipated multi-mission requirements. All units are ice strengthened for operation on the Great Lakes, coastal waters and in rivers. Painted white. WTGB 101 authorised in the FY 1976 programme, WTGB 102-104 in the FY 1977 programme, WTGB 105-106 in the FY 1978 programme, WTGB 107 in the FY 1979 programme.

KATMAI BAY   1/1979, USCG

PATROL CRAFT

23 "CAPE" CLASS: PATROL CRAFT—LARGE (WPB)

Name	No.	Builders	F/S
"A" Series			
CAPE SMALL	95300	Coast Guard Yard, Curtis Bay, Maryland	PA
CAPE CORAL	95301	Coast Guard Yard, Curtis Bay, Maryland	PA
CAPE GULL	95304	Coast Guard Yard, Curtis Bay, Maryland	AA
CAPE GEORGE	95306	Coast Guard Yard, Curtis Bay, Maryland	AA
CAPE CURRENT	95307	Coast Guard Yard, Curtis Bay, Maryland	AA
CAPE STRAIT	95308	Coast Guard Yard, Curtis Bay, Maryland	AA
CAPE CARTER	95309	Coast Guard Yard, Curtis Bay, Maryland	PA
CAPE WASH	95310	Coast Guard Yard, Curtis Bay, Maryland	PA
CAPE HEDGE	95311	Coast Guard Yard, Curtis Bay, Maryland	PA
"B" Series			
CAPE KNOX	95312	Coast Guard Yard, Curtis Bay, Maryland	AA
CAPE MORGAN	95313	Coast Guard Yard, Curtis Bay, Maryland	AA
CAPE FAIRWEATHER	95314	Coast Guard Yard, Curtis Bay, Maryland	AA
CAPE FOX	95316	Coast Guard Yard, Curtis Bay, Maryland	AA
CAPE JELLISON	95317	Coast Guard Yard, Curtis Bay, Maryland	AA
CAPE NEWAGEN	95318	Coast Guard Yard, Curtis Bay, Maryland	PA
CAPE ROMAIN	95319	Coast Guard Yard, Curtis Bay, Maryland	PA
CAPE STARR	95320	Coast Guard Yard, Curtis Bay, Maryland	AA
"C" Series			
CAPE CROSS	95321	Coast Guard Yard, Curtis Bay, Maryland	AA
CAPE HORN	95322	Coast Guard Yard, Curtis Bay, Maryland	AA
CAPE SHOALWATER	95324	Coast Guard Yard, Curtis Bay, Maryland	AA
CAPE CORWIN	95326	Coast Guard Yard, Curtis Bay, Maryland	PA
CAPE HENLOPEN	95328	Coast Guard Yard, Curtis Bay, Maryland	AA
CAPE YORK	95332	Coast Guard Yard, Curtis Bay, Maryland	AA

Displacement, tons: 105
Dimensions, feet (metres): 95 × 20 × 6 *(29·0 × 6·1 × 1·8)*
Guns: 2—50 cal MG
Main engines: 4 diesels (Cummings); 2 324 bhp; 2 shafts = 20 knots (21 knots, C series)
Range, miles: 2 600 (A series); 3 000 (B series); 2 800 (C series); all at 9 knots (economical); 460 at 20 knots (C Series 500 at 21 knots)
Complement: 14 (1 officer, 13 enlisted)

Designed for port security, search, and rescue. Steel hulled. A series built in 1953; B series in 1955-56, and C series in 1958-59.
Plans to dispose of this class from 1974-75 onward in favour of new WPB construction have been cancelled; instead all twenty three remaining craft will be modernised (see below). Some

CAPE FAIRWEATHER   7/1976, A. D. Baker III

CAPE GEORGE   1976, USCG

ships carry women officers and/or enlisted ladies as part of the crew. Eight "Cape" class cutters serve in the South Korean Navy.

Modernisation: All 23 craft will be modernised to extend their service life for an estimated ten years. Cost in 1976 was estimated at $500 000 per cutter. They will receive new engines, electronics, and deck equipment; superstructure will be modified or replaced; and habitability will be improved. The programme began in July 1977 and will be complete by 1981. Each craft will take five months to modernise.

53 "POINT" CLASS: PATROL CRAFT—LARGE (WPB)

Name	No.	Builders	F/S
"A" Series			
POINT HOPE	82302	Coast Guard Yard, Curtis Bay, Maryland	AA
POINT VERDE	82311	Coast Guard Yard, Curtis Bay, Maryland	AA
POINT SWIFT	82312	Coast Guard Yard, Curtis Bay, Maryland	AA
POINT THATCHER	82314	Coast Guard Yard, Curtis Bay, Maryland	AA
"C" Series			
POINT HERRON	82318	Coast Guard Yard, Curtis Bay, Maryland	AA
POINT ROBERTS	82332	Coast Guard Yard, Curtis Bay, Maryland	AA
POINT HIGHLAND	82333	Coast Guard Yard, Curtis Bay, Maryland	AA
POINT LEDGE	82334	Coast Guard Yard, Curtis Bay, Maryland	PA
POINT COUNTESS	82335	Coast Guard Yard, Curtis Bay, Maryland	PA
POINT GLASS	82336	Coast Guard Yard, Curtis Bay, Maryland	PA
POINT DIVIDE	82337	Coast Guard Yard, Curtis Bay, Maryland	PA
POINT BRIDGE	82338	Coast Guard Yard, Curtis Bay, Maryland	PA
POINT CHICO	82339	Coast Guard Yard, Curtis Bay, Maryland	PA
POINT BATAN	82340	Coast Guard Yard, Curtis Bay, Maryland	AA
POINT LOOKOUT	82341	Coast Guard Yard, Curtis Bay, Maryland	AA
POINT BAKER	82342	Coast Guard Yard, Curtis Bay, Maryland	AA
POINT WELLS	82343	Coast Guard Yard, Curtis Bay, Maryland	AA
POINT ESTERO	82344	Coast Guard Yard, Curtis Bay, Maryland	PA
POINT JUDITH	82345	Martinac S.B., Tacoma, Washington	PA
POINT ARENA	82346	Martinac S.B., Tacoma, Washington	AA
POINT BONITA	82347	Martinac S.B., Tacoma, Washington	PA
POINT BARROW	82348	Martinac S.B., Tacoma, Washington	PA
POINT SPENCER	82349	Martinac S.B., Tacoma, Washington	AA
POINT FRANKLIN	82350	Coast Guard Yard, Curtis Bay, Maryland	AA
POINT BENNETT	82351	Coast Guard Yard, Curtis Bay, Maryland	PA
POINT SAL	82352	Coast Guard Yard, Curtis Bay, Maryland	PA
POINT MONROE	82353	Coast Guard Yard, Curtis Bay, Maryland	AA
POINT EVANS	82354	Coast Guard Yard, Curtis Bay, Maryland	PA
POINT HANNON	82355	Coast Guard Yard, Curtis Bay, Maryland	AA
POINT FRANCIS	82356	Coast Guard Yard, Curtis Bay, Maryland	AA
POINT HURON	82357	Coast Guard Yard, Curtis Bay, Maryland	AA
POINT STUART	82358	Coast Guard Yard, Curtis Bay, Maryland	PA
POINT STEELE	82359	Coast Guard Yard, Curtis Bay, Maryland	AA
POINT WINSLOW	82360	Coast Guard Yard, Curtis Bay, Maryland	PA
POINT CHARLES	82361	Coast Guard Yard, Curtis Bay, Maryland	AA
POINT BROWN	82362	Coast Guard Yard, Curtis Bay, Maryland	AA
POINT NOWELL	82363	Coast Guard Yard, Curtis Bay, Maryland	AA
POINT WHITEHORN	82364	Coast Guard Yard, Curtis Bay, Maryland	AA
POINT TURNER	82365	Coast Guard Yard, Curtis Bay, Maryland	AA
POINT LOBOS	82366	Coast Guard Yard, Curtis Bay, Maryland	AA
POINT KNOLL	82367	Coast Guard Yard, Curtis Bay, Maryland	AA
POINT WARDE	82368	Coast Guard Yard, Curtis Bay, Maryland	AA
POINT HEYER	82369	Coast Guard Yard, Curtis Bay, Maryland	PA
POINT RICHMOND	82370	Coast Guard Yard, Curtis Bay, Maryland	AA
"D" Series			
POINT BARNES	82371	Coast Guard Yard, Curtis Bay, Maryland	AA
POINT BROWER	82372	Coast Guard Yard, Curtis Bay, Maryland	PA
POINT CAMDEN	82373	Coast Guard Yard, Curtis Bay, Maryland	PA
POINT CARREW	82374	Coast Guard Yard, Curtis Bay, Maryland	PA
POINT DORAN	82375	Coast Guard Yard, Curtis Bay, Maryland	PA
POINT HARRIS	82376	Coast Guard Yard, Curtis Bay, Maryland	PA
POINT HOBART	82377	Coast Guard Yard, Curtis Bay, Maryland	AA
POINT JACKSON	82378	Coast Guard Yard, Curtis Bay, Maryland	AA
POINT MARTIN	82379	Coast Guard Yard, Curtis Bay, Maryland	AA

POINT FRANKLIN   9/1977, USCG (CWO. J. Greco Jr)

POINT BRIDGE   1/1977, USCG

Displacement, tons: A series 67; C series 66; D series 69
Dimensions, feet (metres): 83 × 17·2 × 5·8 *(25·3 × 5·2 × 1·8)*
Guns: 1—50 cal MG or 2—50 cal MG; some boats unarmed
Main engines: 2 diesels; 1 600 bhp; 2 shafts = 23·5 knots except D series 22·6 knots
Range, miles: 1 500 at 8 knots (1 200 D series)
Complement: 8 (1 officer, 7 enlisted) (see notes)

Designed for search, rescue, and patrol. Of survivors, A series built 1960-61; C series in 1961-67; and D series in 1970.
26 cutters of the "A" and "B" series were transferred to South Viet-Nam in 1969-70.

Names: WPB 82301-82344 were assigned "Point" names in January 1964.

Personnel: Most of these units now have an officer assigned; a few still operate with an all-enlisted crew. Some carry women as officers or enlisted personnel.

756 USA (USCG) / Training cutter — Seagoing tenders

TRAINING CUTTER

1 "EAGLE" CLASS: SAIL TRAINING CUTTER (WIX)

Name	No.	Builders	F/S
EAGLE (ex-*Horst Wessel*)	WIX 327	Blohm & Voss, Hamburg	AA

Displacement, tons: 1 784 full load
Dimensions, feet (metres): 231 wl; 295·2 oa × 39·1 × 17 *(90·0 × 11·9 × 5·2)*
Sail area, square feet: 25 351
Height of masts, feet (metres): fore and main 150·3 *(45·8)*; mizzen 132 *(40·2)*
Main engine: Auxiliary diesel (MAN); 700 bhp; 1 shaft = 10·5 knots (as high as 18 knots under full sail alone)
Range, miles: 5 450 at 7·5 knots (diesel only)
Complement: 245 (19 officers, 46 enlisted men, 180 cadets)

Former German training ship. Launched on 13 June 1936. Taken by the USA as part of reparations after the Second World War for employment in US Coast Guard Practice Squadron. Taken over at Bremerhaven in January 1946; arrived at home port of New London, Connecticut, in July 1946.
(Sister ship *Albert Leo Schlageter* was also taken by the USA in 1945 but was sold to Brazil in 1948 and re-sold to Portugal in 1962. Another ship of similar design, *Gorch Foch*, transferred to the USSR in 1946 and survives as *Tovarisch*).

Appearance: When the Coast Guard added the orange-and-blue marking stripes to cutters in the 1960s *Eagle* was exempted because of their affect on her graceful lines; however, in early 1976 the stripes and words "Coast Guard" were added in time for the July 1976 Operation Sail in New York harbour.

EAGLE   5/1978, (PH1 L. H. Sallion)

SEAGOING TENDERS

Note: *Acushnet* WAGO 167 serves as Oceanographic cutter with *Evergreen* WAGO 295 from class below. *Acushnet* operates from Gulfport, Miss and *Evergreen* from New London, Conn.

33 "BALSAM" CLASS: BUOY TENDERS (SEAGOING) (WLB)/OCEANOGRAPHIC CUTTER (WAGO)

Name	No.	Launched	F/S	Name	No.	Launched	F/S
BALSAM*	WLB 62	1942	PR	BITTERSWEET	WLB 389	1944	AA
LAUREL	WLB 291	1942	PA	BLACTHAW*	WLB 390	1944	AA
CLOVER	WLB 292	1942	PA	BLACKTHORN	WLB 391	1944	AA
EVERGREEN	WAGO 295	1943	AA	BRAMBLE*	WLB 392	1944	GLA
SORREL*	WLB 296	1943	AA	FIREBUSH	WLB 393	1944	AA
IRONWOOD	WLB 297	1944	PA	HORNBEAM	WLB 394	1944	AA
CITRUS*	WLB 300	1943	PA	IRIS	WLB 395	1944	PA
CONIFER	WLB 301	1943	AA	MALLOW	WLB 396	1944	PA
MADRONA	WLB 302	1943	AA	MARIPOSA	WLB 397	1944	GLA
TUPELO	WLB 303	1943	PR	SAGEBRUSH	WLB 399	1944	AA
MESQUITE	WLB 305	1943	GLA	SALVIA	WLB 400	1944	AA
BUTTONWOOD	WLB 306	1943	PA	SASSAFRAS	WLB 401	1944	AA
PLANETREE	WLB 307	1943	PA	SEDGE*	WLB 402	1944	PA
PAPAW	WLB 308	1943	AA	SPAR*	WLB 403	1944	AA
SWEETGUM	WLB 309	1943	AA	SUNDEW*	WLB 404	1944	AA
BASSWOOD	WLB 388	1944	PA	SWEETBRIER	WLB 405	1944	AA
				WOODRUSH	WLB 407	1944	GLA

Displacement, tons: 935 standard; 1 025 full load
Dimensions, feet (metres): 180 × 37 × 13 *(54·9 × 11·3 × 4)*
Guns: 1—3 in *(76 mm)*/50 in *Citrus,* (original armament); 2—20 mm guns in *Ironwood, Bittersweet, Firebush, Sedge* and *Sweetbrier* rest unarmed
Main engines: Diesel-electric; 1 000 bhp in tenders numbered WLB 62-303 series, except *Ironwood;* 1 shaft = 12·8 knots; others 1 200 bhp; 1 shaft = 15 knots
Complement: 53 (6 officers, 47 enlisted men)

Seagoing buoy tenders. *Ironwood* built by Coast Guard Yard at Curtis Bay, Maryland; others by Marine Iron & Shipbuilding Co, Duluth, Minnesota, or Zeneth Dredge Co, Duluth, Minnesota. Completed 1943-45. Eight ships indicated by asterisks are strengthened for icebreaking. Three ships, *Cowslip, Bittersweet,* and *Hornbeam,* have controllable-pitch, bow-thrust propellers to assist in manoeuvring. All WLBs have 20 ton capacity booms. *Evergreen* has been refitted as an oceanographic cutter (WAGO) and is painted white.

Modernisation: All of this class will undergo, are undergoing or have completed modernisation. This has involved a rebuilding of the main engines and overhaul of the propulsion motors, improvement of habitability, installation of hydraulic cargo-handling equipment and the addition of a bow thruster. *Sorrel* completed in mid-1977 under the FY 1977 programme, *Sundew* is to be completed under the FY 1978 and *Firebush* and *Woodrush* under the FY 1979 programme.

MARIPOSA   1975, USCG

COASTAL TENDERS

5 "RED" CLASS: BUOY-TENDERS COASTAL (WLM)

Name	No.	Launched	F/S	Name	No.	Launched	F/S
RED WOOD	WLM 685	1965	AA	RED CEDAR	WLM 688	1971	AA
RED BEECH	WLM 686	1965	AA	RED OAK	WLM 689	1972	AA
RED BIRCH	WLM 687	1966	AA				

Displacement, tons: 471 standard; 512 full load
Dimensions, feet (metres): 157 × 33 × 6 *(47·9 × 10·1 × 1·8)*
Main engines: 2 diesels; 2 shafts; 1 800 hp = 12·8 knots
Range, miles: 3 000 at 11·6 knots
Complement: 31 (4 officers, 27 enlisted men)

All built by Coast Guard Yard, Curtis Bay, Maryland. WLM 685-7 completed 1965-66 and others 1971-72. Fitted with cp propellers and bow thrusters; steel hulls strengthened for light icebreaking. Steering and engine controls on each bridge wing as well as in pilot house. Living spaces are air conditioned. Fitted with 10 ton capacity boom.

RED CEDAR 1976, Dr. Giorgio Arra

3 "HOLLYHOCK" CLASS: BUOY-TENDERS COASTAL (WLM)

Name	No.	F/S
FIR	WLM 212	PA
HOLLYHOCK	WLM 220	AA
WALNUT	WLM 252	PA

Displacement, tons: 989
Dimensions, feet (metres): 175 × 34 × 12 *(53·4 × 10·4 × 3·7)*
Main engines: 2 diesels; 2 shafts; 1 350 bhp = 12 knots
Complement: 40 (5 officers, 35 enlisted men)

Launched in 1937 *(Hollyhock)* and 1939 *(Fir and Walnut)*. *Walnut* was re-engined by Williamette Iron & Steel Co, Portland, Oregon, in 1958. Redesignated coastal tenders, (WLM), instead of buoy tenders, (WAGL) on 1 January 1965. Fitted with 20 ton capacity boom.

WALNUT 1976, John A. Jedrlinic

7 "WHITE SUMAC" CLASS: BUOY-TENDERS COASTAL (WLM)

Name	No.	F/S	Name	No.	F/S
WHITE SUMAC	WLM 540	AA	WHITE HEATH	WLM 545	AA
WHITE BUSH	WLM 542	PA	WHITE LUPINE	WLM 546	AA
WHITE HOLLY	WLM 543	AA	WHITE PINE	WLM 547	AA
WHITE SAGE	WLM 544	AA			

Displacement, tons: 435 standard; 600 full load
Dimensions, feet (metres): 133 × 31 × 9 *(40·5 × 9·5 × 2·7)*
Main engines: Diesels; 2 shafts; 600 bhp = 9·8 knots
Complement: 21 (1 officer, 20 enlisted men)

All launched in 1943. All seven ships are former US Navy YFs, adapted for the Coast Guard. The *White Alder* (WLM 541) was sunk in a collision on 7 December 1968. Fitted with 10 ton capacity boom.

WHITE SAGE 1976, USCG

BUOY-TENDERS (INLAND) (WLI)

Name	No.	F/S
AZALEA	WLI 641	AA

Displacement, tons: 200 full load
Dimensions, feet (metres): 100 × 24 × 5 *(30·5 × 7·3 × 1·5)*
Main engines: Diesels; 2 shafts; 440 bhp = 9 knots
Complement: 14 (1 officer, 13 enlisted men)

Built in 1958. Fitted with pile driver.

Name	No.	F/S
COSMOS	WLI 293	AA
RAMBLER	WLI 298	AA
BLUEBELL	WLI 313	AA
SMILAX	WLI 315	AA
PRIMROSE	WLI 316	AA

Displacement, tons: 178 full load
Dimensions, feet (metres): 100 × 24 × 5 *(30·5 × 7·3 × 1·5)*
Main engines: Diesels; 2 shafts; 600 bhp = 10·5 knots
Complement: 15 (1 officer, 14 enlisted men)

Cosmos completed in 1942, *Bluebell* in 1945, others in 1944. *Primrose* fitted with pile drivers.

PRIMROSE (with pile driver) 1976, John A. Jedrlinic

Name	No.	F/S
BUCKTHORN	WLI 642	GLA

Displacement, tons: 200 full load
Dimensions, feet (metres): 100 × 24 × 4 *(30·5 × 7·3 × 1·2)*
Main engines: Diesels; 2 shafts; 600 bhp = 7·3 knots
Complement: 14 (1 officer, 13 enlisted men)

Completed in 1963.

BUCKTHORN 1975, USCG

Name	No.	F/S
BLACKBERRY	WLI 65303	AA
CHOKEBERRY	WLI 65304	AA

Displacement, tons: 68 full load
Dimensions, feet (metres): 65 × 17 × 4 *(19·8 × 5·2 × 1·2)*
Main engines: Diesels; 1 shaft; 220 hp = 9 knots
Complement: 5 (enlisted men)

Completed in 1946.

Name	No.	F/S
BAYBERRY	WLI 65400	PA
ELDERBERRY	WLI 65401	AA

Displacement, tons: 68 full load
Dimensions, feet (metres): 65 × 17 × 4 *(19·8 × 5·2 × 1·2)*
Main engines: Diesels; 2 shafts; 400 hp = 11·3 knots
Complement: 5 (enlisted men)

Completed in 1954.

758 USA (USCG) / Buoy tenders (river) — Oceangoing tugs

BUOY TENDERS (RIVER) (WLR)

Note: All are based on rivers of USA especially the Mississippi and the Missouri and its tributaries.

SUMAC WLR 311

Displacement, tons: 404 full load
Dimensions, feet (metres): 115 × 30 × 6 (35·1 × 9·1 × 1·8)
Main engines: Diesels; 3 shafts; 960 hp = 10·6 knots
Complement: 23 (1 officer, 22 enlisted men)

Built in 1943.

GASCONADE	WLR 75401	CHEYENNE	WLR 75405
MUSKINGUM	WLR 75402	KICKAPOO	WLR 75406
WYACONDA	WLR 75403	KANAWHA	WLR 75407
CHIPPEWA	WLR 75404	PATOKA	WLR 75408
		CHENA	WLR 75409

Displacement, tons: 145 full load
Dimensions, feet (metres): 75 × 22 × 4 (22·9 × 6·7 × 1·2)
Main engines: Diesels; 2 shafts; 600 hp = 10·8 knots
Complement: 12 (enlisted men)

Built 1964-71.

OUACHITA	WLR 65501	SCIOTO	WLR 65504
CIMARRON	WLR 65502	OSAGE	WLR 65505
OBION	WLR 65503	SANGAMON	WLR 65506

Displacement, tons: 139 full load
Dimensions, feet (metres): 65·6 × 21 × 5 (20 × 6·4 × 1·5)
Main engines: Diesels; 2 shafts; 600 hp = 12·5 knots
Complement: 10 (enlisted men)

Built in 1960-62.

OBION 1/1978, USCG

DOGWOOD WLR 259

Displacement, tons: 230 full load
Dimensions, feet (metres): 114 × 26 × 4 (34·8 × 7·9 × 1·2)
Main engines: Diesels; 2 shafts; 2 800 hp = 11 knots
Complement: 21 (1 officer, 20 enlisted men)

Built in 1940.

LANTANA WLR 80310

Displacement, tons: 235 full load
Dimensions, feet (metres): 80 × 30 × 6 (24·3 × 9·1 × 1·8)
Main engines: Diesels; 3 shafts; 10 000 hp = 10 knots
Complement: 20 (1 officer, 19 enlisted men)

Built in 1943.

CONSTRUCTION TENDERS (INLAND) (WLIC)

Name	No.	F/S	Name	No.	F/S
PAMLICO	WLIC 800	AA	KENNEBEC	WLIC 803	AA
HUDSON	WLIC 801	AA	SAGINAW	WLIC 804	AA

Displacement, tons: 413 light
Dimensions, feet (metres): 160·9 × 30 × 4 (49 × 9·1 × 1·2)
Main engines: 2 diesels = 11·5 knots
Complement: 15

Built in 1975-78 at the Coast Guard Yard, Curtis Bay, Maryland. *Saginaw* completed as last of class 6 February 1978.

Name	No.	F/S	Name	No.	F/S	Name	No.	F/S
ANVIL	WLIC 75301	AA	MALLET	WLIC 75304	AA	WEDGE	WLIC 75307	AA
HAMMER	WLIC 75302	AA	VISE	WLIC 75305	AA	SPIKE	WLIC 75308	AA
SLEDGE	WLIC 75303	AA	CLAMP	WLIC 75306	AA	HATCHET	WLIC 75309	AA
						AXE	WLIC 75310	AA

Displacement, tons: 145 full load
Dimensions, feet (metres): 75 (WLIC 75306-75310 are 76) × 22 × 4 (22·9 × 6·7 × 1·2)
Main engines: Diesels; 2 shafts; 600 hp = 10 knots
Complement: 9 or 10 (1 officer in *Mallet, Sledge* and *Vise;* 9 enlisted men in all)

Completed 1962-65.

SPIKE pushing barge 1971, USCG

OCEANGOING TUGS

2 "DIVER" CLASS: MEDIUM ENDURANCE CUTTER (WMEC)/OCEANOGRAPHIC CUTTER (WAGO)

Name	No.	Builders	USN Comm.	F/S
ACUSHNET (ex-USS *Shackle*)	WAGO 167 (ex-WAT 167, ARS 9)	Basalt Rock Co, Napa, California	5 Feb 1944	AA
YOCONA (ex-USS *Seize*)	WMEC 168 (ex-WAT 168, ARS 26)	Basalt Rock Co, Napa, California	3 Nov 1944	PA

Displacement, tons: 1 557 standard; 1 745 full load
Dimensions, feet (metres): 213·5 × 39 × 15 (65·1 × 11·9 × 4·6)
Guns: Removed
Main engines: Diesels (Cooper Bessemer); 3 000 bhp; 2 shafts = 15·5 knots
Complement: *Acushnet* 64 (7 officers, 57 enlisted men); *Yocona* 72 (7 officers, 65 enlisted men)

Large, steel-hulled salvage ships transferred from the Navy to the Coast Guard after World War II and employed in tug and oceanographic duties. Launched 1 April 1943 and 8 April 1944 respectively. *Acushnet* modified for handling environmental data buoys and reclassified WAGO in 1968; *Yocona* reclassified as WMEC in 1968.

ACUSHNET 12/1978, V. H. Young

3 "CHEROKEE" CLASS: MEDIUM ENDURANCE CUTTERS (WMEC)

Name	No.	Builders	USN Comm.	F/S
CHILULA	WMEC 153 (ex-WAT 153, ATF 153)	Charleston Shipbuilding & Drydock Co, Charleston, South Carolina	5 Apr 1945	AA
CHEROKEE	WMEC 165 (ex-WAT 165, ATF 66)	Bethlehem Steel Co, Staten Island, New York	26 Apr 1940	AA
TAMAROA (ex-*Zuni*)	WMEC 166 (ex-WAT 166, ATF 95)	Commercial Iron Works, Portland, Oregon	9 Oct 1943	AA

Displacement, tons: 1 731 full load
Dimensions, feet (metres): 205 × 38·5 × 17 (62·5 × 11·7 × 5·2)
Guns: 1—3 in/50; 2—·50 cal MG
Main engines: Diesel-electric (General Motors diesel); 3 000 bhp; 1 shaft = 16·2 knots
Complement: 72 (7 officers, 65 enlisted men)

Steel-hulled tugs transferred from the Navy to the Coast Guard on loan in 1946; transferred permanently 1 June 1969. Classification of all three ships changed to WMEC in 1968. Launched on 1 December 1944, 10 November 1939, and 13 July 1943, respectively.

TAMAROA 1977, USCG

USA (USCG) / Oceangoing tugs — National Oceanic and Atmospheric Administration 759

2 "SOTOYOMO" CLASS: MEDIUM ENDURANCE CUTTERS (WMEC)

Name	No.	Builders	USN Comm.	F/S
MODOC (ex-USS Bagaduce)	WMEC 194 (ex-WATA 194, ATA 194)	Levingston Shipbuilding Co, Orange, Texas	14 Feb 1945	PA
COMANCHE (ex-USS Wampanoag)	WMEC 202 (ex-WATA 202, ATA 202)	Gulfport Boiler & Welding Works, Port Arthur, Texas	8 Dec 1944	AA

Displacement, tons: 534 standard; 860 full load
Dimensions, feet (metres): 143 × 33·8 × 14 (43·6 × 10·3 × 4·3)
Armament: 2—·50 cal MG
Main engines: Diesel-electric (General Motors diesel); 1 shaft; 1 500 hp = 13·5 knots
Complement: 47 (5 officers, 42 enlisted men)

Steel-hulled tugs. Launched on 4 December 1944 and 10 October 1944, respectively. *Modoc* was stricken from the Navy List after World War II and transferred to Maritime Administration; transferred to Coast Guard on 15 April 1959. *Comanche* transferred on loan from Navy to Coast Guard from 25 February 1959 until stricken from Navy List on 1 June 1969 and transferred permanently. Both ships reclassified as WMEC in 1968.

1 "85 ft" CLASS: HARBOUR TUG MEDIUM (WYTM)

MESSENGER   WYTM 85009

Displacement, tons: 230 full load
Dimensions, feet (metres): 85 × 23 × 9 (25·9 × 7 × 2·7)
Main engine: Diesel; 1 shaft; 700 hp = 9·5 knots
Complement: 10 (enlisted)

Built in 1944. Active in the Atlantic Fleet.

15 "65 ft" CLASS: HARBOUR TUGS SMALL (WYTL)

CAPSTAN	WYTL 65601	CATENARY	WYTL 65606	LINE	WYTL 65611
CHOCK	WYTL 65602	BRIDLE	WYTL 65607	WIRE	WYTL 65612
SWIVEL	WYTL 65603	PENDANT	WYTL 65608	BITT	WYTL 65613
TACKLE	WYTL 65604	SHACKLE	WYTL 65609	BOLLARD	WYTL 65614
TOWLINE	WYTL 65605	HAWSER	WYTL 65610	CLEAT	WYTL 65615

Displacement, tons: 72 full load
Dimensions, feet (metres): 65 × 19 × 7 (19·8 × 5·8 × 2·1)
Main engine: Diesel; 1 shaft; 400 hp = 9·8 knots except WYTL 65601-65606 10·5 knots
Complement: 10 (enlisted men)

Built from 1961 to 1967. All active in the Atlantic Fleet.

MODOC   1977, USCG

HARBOUR TUGS

13 "110 ft" CLASS: HARBOUR TUGS MEDIUM (WYTM)

MANITOU	WYTM 60	MOHICAN	WYTM 73	CHINOOK	WTYM 96
KAW	WYTM 61	ARUNDEL	WYTM 90	OBJIBWA	WYTM 97
APALACHEE	WYTM 71	MAHONING	WYTM 91	SNOHOMISH	WYTM 98
YANKTON	WYTM 72	NAUGATUCK	WYTM 92	SAUK	WYTM 99
		RARITAN	WYTM 93		

Displacement, tons: 370 full load
Dimensions, feet (metres): 110 × 27 × 11 (33·5 × 8·2 × 3·4)
Main engines: Diesel-electric; 1 shaft; 1 000 hp = 11·2 knots
Complement: 20 (1 officer, 19 enlisted men)

Built in 1943 except WYTM 90-93 built in 1939. WYTM 60, 71-73, 91, 96, 98, 99 active in the Atlantic Fleet. Remainder active on inland waterways. Class to be phased out in early 1980s.

LINE   7/1976, A. D. Baker III

CHINOOK   1/1977, USCG

LIGHTSHIPS (WLV)

WLV 604 (Columbia)
WLV 612 (Nantucket)
WLV 613 (Relief)

Displacement, tons: 607 full load (except WLV 604; 617 full load)
Dimensions, feet (metres): 128 × 30 × 11 (39 × 9·1 × 3·4)
Main engine: Diesel; 550 bhp; 1 shaft = 11 knots

All launched 1950. WLV 604 assigned to Astoria, Oregon; others to Boston, Massachusetts. Coast Guard lightships exchange names according to assignment; hull numbers remain constant.

NATIONAL OCEANIC AND ATMOSPHERIC ADMINISTRATION

Command

Director, National Ocean Survey:
   Rear-Admiral Allen L. Powell
Associate Director, Office of Fleet Operations:
   Rear-Admiral Herbert R. Lippold, Jnr.
Director, Atlantic Marine Center:
   Rear-Admiral Robert C. Munson
Director, Pacific Marine Center:
   Rear-Admiral Eugene A. Taylor

Establishment

The "Survey of the Coast" was established by an act of Congress on 10 February 1807. Renamed US Coast Survey in 1834 and again renamed Coast and Geodetic Survey in 1878. The commissioned officer corps was established in 1917. The Coast and Geodetic Survey was made a component of the Environmental Science Services Administration on 13 July 1965, when that agency was established within the Department of Commerce. The Environmental Science Services Administration subsequently became the National Oceanic and Atmospheric Administration in October 1970 with the Coast and Geodetic Survey being renamed National Ocean Survey and its jurisdiction expanded to include the US Lake Survey, formerly a part of the US Army Corps of Engineers; the Coast Guard's national data buoy development project; and the Navy's National Oceanographic Instrumentation Centre.

Missions

The National Ocean Survey operates the ships of the National Oceanic and Atmospheric Administration (NOAA), a federal agency created in 1970. During 1972-73 the National Marine Fisheries Service (formerly the Bureau of Commercial Fisheries of the Department of Interior) was consolidated into the NOAA fleet which is operated by the National Ocean Survey. Approximately 15 small ships and craft 65 ft or longer are counted in the National Marine Fisheries Service. The former National Marine Fisheries vessels are not described because of the specialised, non-military nature of their work.
The National Ocean Survey prepares nautical and aeronautical charts; conducts geodetic, geophysical, oceanographic, and marine surveys; predicts tides and currents; tests, evaluates, and calibrates sensing systems for ocean use; and conducts the development of and eventually will operate a national system of automated ocean buoys for obtaining environmental information.

The National Ocean Survey is a civilian agency that supports national civilian and military requirements. During time of war the ships and officers of NOAA can be expected to operate with the Navy, either as a separate service or integrated into the Navy.

Ships

The following ships may be met with at sea.
Oceanographic Survey Ships: *Researcher, Oceanographer, Discoverer, Surveyor.*
Hydrographic Survey Ships: *Fairweather, Rainier, Mt. Mitchell.*
Coastal Survey Ships: *McArthur, Davidson, Peirce, Whiting.*
Coastal Vessels: *Rude, Heck, Ferrel.*

Personnel

The National Ocean Survey has approximately 225 commissioned officers and 250 officers and 2 250 civil service personnel. In addition, another 125 commissioned officers serve elsewhere in NOAA and several US Navy officers are assigned to NOAA.

URUGUAY

Headquarters Appointment

Commander-in-Chief of the Navy:
Vice-Admiral Victor González Ibargoyen

Diplomatic Representation

Naval Attaché in Washington:
Captain Jorge Laborde

Personnel

(a) 1979: Total: 3 500 officers and men (including Naval Infantry)
(b) Voluntary service

Base

Montevideo: Main naval base with a drydock and a slipway

Coast Guard

The Prefectura Maritima operates six coastal patrol craft.

Naval Air Arm

2 SH-34C helicopters
2 Bell 47G
3 Grumman S-2A Tracker (ASW)
4 Beech SNB-5 (Training-Transport)
3 North American SNJ (Training)
1 Beech T-34 B Mentor (Training)
1 EMB-110B Bandeirante ordered (further orders expected)

Prefix to Ships' Names

R.O.U.

Strength of the Fleet

	Active	Building
Frigates	3	—
Corvettes	2	—
Large Patrol Craft	1	—
Coastal Patrol Craft	6	—
Survey Ships	2	—
Salvage Vessel	1	—
Tankers	3	—
Tenders	3	—
Landing Craft	2	—

Mercantile Marine

Lloyd's Register of Shipping:
48 vessels of 174 357 tons gross

DELETIONS

Frigate

1975 *Montevideo*

Tanker

1978 *President Oribe* (scrapped)

FRIGATES

1 Ex-US "DEALEY" CLASS

Name	No.	Builders	Laid down	Launched	Commissioned
18 DE JULIO (ex-USS *Dealey*, DE 1006)	DE 3	Bath Iron Works Corporation	15 Oct 1952	8 Nov 1953	3 June 1954

Displacement, tons: 1 450 standard; 1 900 full load
Length, feet (metres): 314·5 *(95·9)*
Beam, feet (metres): 36·8 *(11·2)*
Draught, feet (metres): 13·6 *(4·2)*
Guns: 4—3 in *(76 mm)*/50 (twin Mk 33)
A/S weapons: 2 triple torpedo tubes (Mk 32)
Main engine: 1 De Laval geared turbine; 20 000 shp; 1 shaft
Boilers: 2 Foster-Wheeler
Speed, knots: 25
Complement: 165

Purchased 28 July 1972. *Dealey* was the first US escort ship built after the war.

Fire control: Mk 63 forward and aft with SPG 34 radar.

Radar: SPS 6, SPS 10.

18 DE JULIO   1975, Uruguayan Navy

2 Ex-US "CANNON" CLASS

Name	No.	Builders	Laid down	Launched	Commissioned
URUGUAY (ex-USS *Baron*, DE 166)	DE 1	Federal S.B. & D.D. Co, Pt Newark	Dec 1942	9 May 1943	5 July 1943
ARTIGAS (ex-USS *Bronstein*, DE 189)	DE 2	Federal S.B. & D.D. Co, Pt Newark	Aug 1943	14 Nov 1943	13 Dec 1943

Displacement, tons: 1 240 standard; 1 900 full load
Length, feet (metres): 306·0 *(93·3)*
Beam, feet (metres): 37·0 *(11·3)*
Draught, feet (metres): 17·1 *(5·2)*
Guns: 3—3 in *(76 mm)*/50 (single Mk 22);
2—40 mm/60 (twin Mk 1) (see *Gunnery* notes)
A/S weapons: Hedgehog; 8 DCT; (see *Torpedo tubes* note)
Main engines: Diesel-electric; 2 shafts; 6 000 bhp
Speed, knots: 19
Oil fuel, tons: 315 (95 per cent)
Range, miles: 8 300 at 14 knots
Complement: 160

Appearance: Practically identical, but *Uruguay* can be distinguished by the absence of a mainmast, whereas *Artigas* has a small pole mast aft.

Gunnery: Formerly also mounted ten 20 mm guns, but these have been removed.

Radar: Search: SPS 6.
Tactical: SPS 10.

Torpedo tubes: The three 21 in torpedo tubes in a triple mounting, originally carried, were removed.

Transfers: *Uruguay*, May 1952; *Artigas*, March 1952.

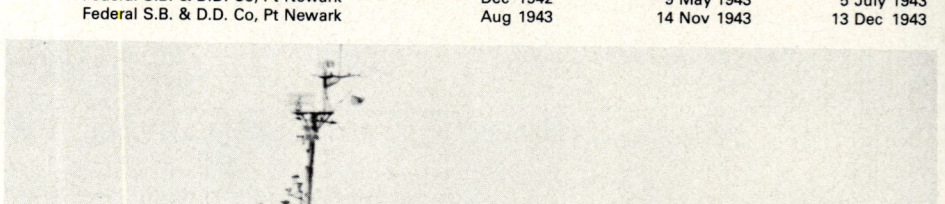

URUGUAY   1975, Uruguayan Navy

CORVETTES

1 Ex-US "AUK" CLASS

Name	No.	Builders	Commissioned
COMANDANTE PEDRO CAMPBELL (ex-USS *Chickadee* MSF 59)	MS 31 (ex-MSF 1)	Defoe B & M Works	9 Nov 1942

Displacement, tons: 890 standard; 1 250 full load
Dimensions, feet (metres): 221·2 × 32·2 × 10·8 *(67·5 × 9·8 × 3·3)*
Guns: 1—3 in/50; 4—40 mm (twin); 4—20 mm (twin)
Main engines: Diesel-electric; 2 shafts; 3 118 bhp = 18 knots
Complement: 105

Former US fleet minesweeper. Launched on 20 July 1942. Transferred on loan and commissioned at San Diego on 18 August 1966. Purchased 15 August 1976.

COMANDANTE PEDRO CAMPBELL   1971

1 Ex-US "AGGRESSIVE" CLASS

Name	No.	Builders	Commissioned
MALDONADO (ex-*Bir Hakeim* M 614, ex-USS *MSO 451*)	MS 33	USA	24 Feb 1954

Displacement, tons: 700 standard; 795 full load
Dimensions, feet (metres): 171·0 × 35·0 × 10·3 *(52·1 × 10·7 × 3·1)*
Gun: 1—40 mm
Main engines: 2 General Motors diesels; 2 shafts; 1 600 bhp = 13·5 knots
Range, miles: 3 000 at 10 knots
Complement: 54

Former US ocean minesweeper launched 1 October 1953 and transferred to France in February 1954. Returned to the US Navy and transferred to Uruguay in September 1970. All sweeping gear removed.

MALDONADO   1975, Uruguayan Navy

LIGHT FORCES

0 + 3 LARGE PATROL CRAFT

Length, feet (metres): about 150 *(45)*
Speed, knots: 25
Endurance, days: 10

Ordered in 1979.

1 US "ADJUTANT" CLASS (LARGE PATROL CRAFT)

Name	No.	Builders	Commissioned
RIO NEGRO (ex-*Marguerite*, ex-USS *MSC 94*)	MS 32	USA	1954

Displacement, tons: 370 standard; 405 full load
Dimensions, feet (metres): 141·0 × 26·0 × 8·3 *(43 × 8 × 2·6)*
Guns: 2—20 mm
Main engines: 2 General Motors diesels; 2 shafts; 1 200 bhp = 13 knots
Oil fuel, tons: 40
Range, miles: 2 500 at 10 knots
Complement: 38

Built for France under MDAP. Returned to USA in 1969. She was transferred to Uruguay at Toulon on 10 November 1969. All sweeping gear removed.

RIO NEGRO   1975, Uruguayan Navy

1 Ex-US 63 ft AVR (COASTAL PATROL CRAFT)

COLONIA PR 10 (ex-*AR 1*)

Displacement, tons: 25 standard; 34 full load
Dimensions, feet (metres): 63 × 15 × 3·8 *(19·2 × 4·6 × 1·2)*
Guns: 4 MGs
Main engines: 2 Hall Scott Defender; 1 260 bhp = 33·5 knots
Range, miles: 600 at 15 knots
Complement: 8

Launched 4 July 1944.

COLONIA   1975, Uruguayan Navy

762 URUGUAY / Light forces — Survey ships

1 COASTAL PATROL CRAFT

Name	No.	Builders	Commissioned
CARMELO	PR 11	Lürssen, Vegesack	1957

Displacement, tons: 70
Dimensions, feet (metres): $93.0 \times 19.0 \times 7.0$ $(28.4 \times 5.8 \times 2.1)$
Gun: 1—20 mm
Speed, knots: 25

CARMELO 1975, Uruguayan Navy

1 COASTAL PATROL CRAFT

Name	No.	Builders	Commissioned
PAYSANDU	PR 12	Sewart, USA	1968

Displacement, tons: 60
Dimensions, feet (metres): $83.0 \times 18.0 \times 6.0$ $(25.3 \times 5.5 \times 1.8)$
Guns: 3—50 cal MG
Main engines: 2 General Motors diesels; 2 shafts = 22 knots

PAYSANDU 1975, Uruguayan Navy

3 COASTAL PATROL CRAFT

701   702   703

43 ft craft transferred by US Navy in February 1970.

SURVEY SHIPS

Name	No.	Builders	Commissioned
CAPITAN MIRANDA	GS 20 (ex-GS 10)	Sociedad Espanola de Construccion Naval, Matagorda, Cadiz	1930

Displacement, tons: 516 standard; 527 full load
Dimensions, feet (metres): $179 \times 26 \times 10.5$ $(54.6 \times 7.9 \times 3.2)$
Main engine: 1 MAN diesel; 500 bhp = 11 knots
Oil fuel, tons: 37
Complement: 49

Originally a three-masted schooner with pronounced clipper bow used as a cadet training ship.

CAPITAN MIRANDA (old pennant number) 1971

Name	No.	Builders	Commissioned
SALTO	GS 24 (ex-PR 2)	Cantieri Navali Riuniti, Ancona	1936

Displacement, tons: 150 standard; 180 full load
Dimensions, feet (metres): $137 \times 18 \times 10$ $(41.8 \times 5.5 \times 3.1)$
Gun: 1—40 mm
Main engines: 2 Germania-Krupp diesels; 2 shafts; 1 000 bhp = 17 knots
Range, miles: 4 000 at 10 knots
Complement: 26

Now used also as a buoy-tender.

SALTO (old pennant number) 1971

URUGUAY / Salvage vessel — Tenders   763

SALVAGE VESSEL

1 Ex-US "COHOES" CLASS

Name	No.	Builders	Commissioned
HURACAN (ex-USS *Nahant* AN 83)	AM 25 (ex-*BT 30*)	Commercial Ironworks, Portland, Oregon	1945

Displacement, tons: 650 standard; 855 full load
Dimensions, feet (metres): 168·5 × 33·8 × 11·7 *(51·4 × 10·3 × 3·6)*
Guns: 3—20 mm (single)
Main engines: Diesel-electric; 1 shaft; 1 200 bhp = 11·5 knots
Complement: 48

Former US netlayer, transferred December 1968 for salvage services carrying divers and underwater swimmers. In 1954 diving equipment and a recompression chamber were installed.

HURACAN   1975, Uruguayan Navy

AMPHIBIOUS CRAFT

2 Ex-US "LCM 6" CLASS

LD 40   **LD 41**

Transferred on lease October 1972.

TANKERS

Note: Both operate under commercial charter to ANCAP (State Oil Company) when not required for naval purposes.

Name	No.	Builders	Commissioned
JUAN A. LAVALLEJA (ex-MV *Solfonn*)	AO 27	Kawasaki, Kobe	1975

Measurement, tons: 68 931 gross; 131 663 deadweight
Dimensions, feet (metres): 895·8 × 144·6 × 51·6 *(273 × 44·1 × 15·7)*
Main engines: 2 steam turbines; 24 500 shp = 15·5 knots

Former Norwegian tanker laid-up on 13 October 1975. Bought by Uruguayan Navy 13 January 1977.

JUAN A. LAVALLEJA   1977, J. van der Woude

Name	No.	Builders	Commissioned
PRESIDENTE RIVERA	AO 28	EN Bazán, Spain	1971

Measurement, tons: 19 686 gross; 31 885 deadweight
Dimensions, feet (metres): 636·3 × 84 × 32 *(194 × 25·6 × 9·8)*
Main engines: 15 300 bhp = 15 knots
Complement: 58

PRESIDENTE RIVERA   1975, Uruguayan Navy

TENDERS

VANGUARDIA AM 26 (ex-US YTL 589)

Transferred September 1965.

Following also reported: UA 12 (ex-US) repair ship, *Anapal* No 1, ex-US 20 LH, ex-US 26 MW, *Banco Ingles,* LV 21 (ex-US WLV *Portland*) (no longer a light-ship).

VENEZUELA

Administration

Commander General of the Navy (Chief of Naval Operations):
 Vice-Admiral Magin La Grave Fry
Deputy Chief of Naval Operations:
 Rear-Admiral Ernesto Reyes Leal
Chief of Naval Staff:
 Rear-Admiral Alfredo Bello Borges

Diplomatic Representation

Naval Attaché in London:
 Captain Ramon Sanoja Medina
Naval Attaché in Washington:
 Rear-Admiral Rafael Silveira
Assistant Naval Attaché in Washington:
 Commander Carlos A. Colmenares

Personnel

(a) 1979: 7 500 officers and men including 4 000 of the Marine Corps (3 battalions)
(b) 2 years national service

National Guard

The Fuerzas Armadas de Cooperacion, generally known as the National Guard, is a paramilitary organisation, 10 000 strong. It is concerned, amongst other things, with customs and internal security—the Maritime Wing operates the Coastal Patrol Craft listed under Light Forces, though these nominally belong to the Navy.

Bases

Caracas: Main HQ.
Puerto Cabello: Main Naval Base (Dockyard, 1 Drydock, 1 synchrolift, 1 floating crane).
La Guaira: Small Naval Base (Naval Academy).
Puerto de Hierro: Naval Supply Base.

Naval Air Arm

2 Bell 47J helicopters
6 Grumman S-2E Trackers (ASW)
4 Grumman Hu-16A Albatros (SAR)
2 Douglas C-47 (Transports)
1 HS-748 (Transport)
2 Cessna 337 (Liaison)

Strength of the Fleet

Type	Active	Building
Submarines, Patrol	4	2
Destroyers	4	—
Frigates	5	5
Fast Attack Craft—Missile/Gun	6	—
Coastal Patrol Craft	21	—
LST	1	—
LSMs	4	—
Transport Landing Ship	1	—
Transports	4	—
Survey Ships and Craft	3	—
Ocean Tug	1	—
Harbour Tugs	13	—
Floating Dock	1	—
National Guard CPC	16	—

Mercantile Marine

Lloyd's Register of Shipping:
 201 vessels of 823 543 tons gross

DELETIONS

Submarine

1977 Carite (ex-USS *Tilefish*) (28 Jan)

Destroyer

1975 Aragua (D 31)

Light Forces

1976-77 Albatros, Alcatraz, Calamar, Camaron, Caracol, Gaviota, Mejillon, Petrel, Pulpo, Togogo (US "PC-461" class)

Frigates

1976 General José de Austria
1977 General José Garcia

Survey Ships

1975 Puerto Miranda (H 03), Puerto de Nutrius (H 02)

PENNANT LIST

Submarines

S 21	Tiburon
S 22	Picuda
S 31	Sabalo
S 32	Caribe

Destroyers

D 11	Nueva Esparta
D 12	Zulia
D 21	Carabobo
D 22	Falcon

Frigates

—	Sucre
—	Urdaneto
—	New "Lupo" class
F 11	Almirante Clemente
F 12	General José Trinidad Moran
F 13	General Juan José Flores
F 14	Almirante Brion

Light Forces

C 87	Rio Orinoco
C 88	Rio Ventuari
C 89	Rio Caparo
C 90	Rio Venamo
C 91	Rio Torres
C 92	Rio Escalante
C 93	Rio Limon
C 94	Rio San Juan
C 95	Rio Tucuyo
C 96	Rio Turbio
C 128-138	"Rio Orinoco" class
P 11	
P 12	
P 13	
P 14	
P 15	
P 16	
P 119	Gabriela (Survey)
P 121	Lely (Survey)

Amphibious Forces

T 21	Los Monjes
T 22	Los Roques
T 23	Los Frailes
T 24	Los Testigos
T 31	Guyana
T 51	Amazonas

Transports

T 12	Las Aves
T ?	Punta Cabana
T 41	Maracaibo
T ?	New ship

Survey Ships

H 01	Puerto Santo
P 119	Gabriela
P 212	Lely

Tugs

C 139-142	Harbour Tugs
R 11	Fernando Gomes
R 13	General José Felix Ribas
R 14	Fabrio Gallipoli
R 21	Felipe Larrazabal
R ?	Diana III

Floating Dock

DF 11	Golfo de Carriaco

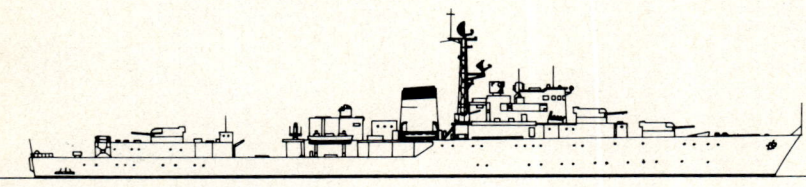

NUEVA ESPARTA

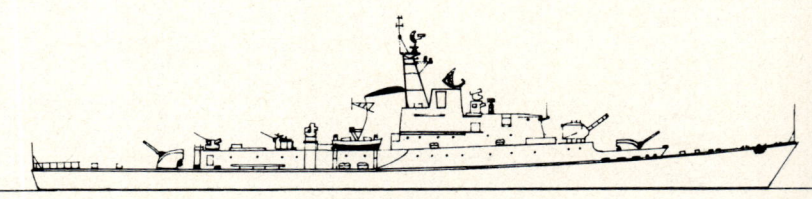

ALMIRANTE BRION

Scale: 1 inch = 100 feet (1 : 1 200)

Drawings by James Goldrick

VENEZUELA / Submarines — Destroyers 765

SUBMARINES

2 + 2 HOWALDTSWERKE TYPE 209

Name	No.	Builders	Laid down	Launched	Commissioned
SABALO	S 31 (ex-S 21)	Howaldtswerke, Kiel	1973	21 Aug 1975	6 Aug 1976
CARIBE	S 32 (ex-S 22)	Howaldtswerke, Kiel	1973	16 Dec 1975	11 Mar 1977

Displacement, tons: 990 surfaced; 1 350 dived
Dimensions, feet (metres): 177·1 × 20·3 × 18 *(54·0 × 6·2 × 5·5)*
Torpedo tubes: 8—21 in (with reloads) bow
Main machinery: Diesel-electric; 4 MTU-Siemens diesel generators; 1 Siemens electric motor 5 000 hp; 1 shaft
Speed, knots: 10 surfaced; 22 dived
Range, miles: 50 days
Complement: 31

Type 209, IK81 designed by Ingenieurkontor Lübeck for construction by Howaldtswerke, Kiel and sale by Ferrostaal, Essen, all acting as a consortium.
A single-hull design with two main ballast tanks and forward and after trim tanks. Fitted with snort and remote machinery control. Slow revving single screw. Very high capacity batteries with GRP lead-acid cells and battery-cooling—by W. Hagen and VARTA. Active and passive sonar, sonar detection set, sound-ranging equipment and underwater telephone. Have two periscopes, radar and Omega receiver. Fore-planes retract. Ordered in 1971.
Second pair ordered 10 March 1977.

CARIBE and SABALO   1978, Venezuelan Navy

2 Ex-US "GUPPY II" CLASS

Name	No.	Builders	Laid down	Launched	Commissioned
TIBURON (ex-USS *Cubera*, SS 347)	S 21 (ex-S 12)	Electric Boat Co, Groton	11 May 1944	17 June 1945	19 Dec 1945
PICUDA (ex-USS *Grenadier*, SS 525)	S 22 (ex-S 13)	Boston Navy Yard	8 Feb 1944	15 Dec 1944	10 Feb 1951

Displacement, tons: 1 870 surfaced; 2 420 dived
Length, feet (metres): 307·5 *(93·8)*
Beam, feet (metres): 27·0 *(8·2)*
Draught, feet (metres): 18·0 *(5·5)*
Torpedo tubes: 10—21 in *(533 mm)* (6 bow, 4 stern)
Main machinery: 3 diesels; 4 800 shp;
  2 electric motors; 5 400 shp; 2 shafts
Speed, knots: 18 surfaced; 15 dived
Range, miles: 12 000 at 10 knots
Oil fuel, tons: 300
Complement: 80

Transferred as follows—*Tiburon* 5 January 1972, *Picuda* 15 May 1973.

PICUDA (as GRENADIER)   USN

DESTROYERS

2 "ARAGUA" CLASS

Name	No.	Builders	Laid down	Launched	Commissioned
NUEVA ESPARTA	D 11	Vickers Armstrong Ltd, Barrow	24 July 1951	19 Nov 1952	8 Dec 1953
ZULIA	D 12 (ex-D 21)	Vickers Armstrong Ltd, Barrow	24 July 1951	29 June 1953	15 Sep 1954

Displacement, tons: 2 600 standard; 3 670 full load
Length, feet (metres): 402·0 *(122·5)*
Beam, feet (metres): 43·0 *(13·1)*
Draught, feet (metres): 19·0 *(5·8)*
Missiles: SAM; Est. 8 Sea Cat (2 quad launchers) (D 11 only)
Guns: 6—4·5 in *(114 mm)*/45 (twin Mk 4); 16—40 mm/60 (twin Mk 5) in D 12; 4—40 mm/60 (twin Mk 5) in D 11
A/S weapons: 2 Hedgehogs; 2 DCT; 2 DC racks
Main engines: Parsons geared turbines; 2 shafts; 50 000 shp
Boilers: 2 Yarrow
Speed, knots: 34
Range, miles: 5 000 at 10 knots
Complement: 256 (20 officers, 236 men)

ZULIA (old pennant number)   7/1976, A. D. Baker III

Ordered in 1950 as class of three. *Aragua* deleted 1975. Air conditioned. Two engine rooms and two boiler rooms served by a single uptake. The 4·5 in guns are fully automatic.

Fire control: Two UK type 276 on DCT for 4·5 in.
Two optical GWS 20 directors for Sea Cat in D 11.

Radar: Search: AWS 2 *(Nueva Esparta)* SPS 6 *(Zulia)*. SPS 12 (both).
Fire control: I Band.

Refits: Both refitted at Palmers Hebburn Works, and Vickers in 1959, and at New York Navy Yard in 1960 to improve antisubmarine and anti-aircraft capabilities. *Nueva Esparta* at Cammell Laird in 1968-69 when Sea Cat launchers were fitted and some 40 mm and the torpedo tubes removed. *Zulia* refitted at Puerto Cabello in 1972-73. Torpedo tubes removed.
In the near future *Nueva Esparta* is to undergo another refit at which she will be re-engined with diesels to fit her for her new training role.

VENEZUELA / Destroyers — Frigates

1 Ex- US "ALLEN M. SUMNER (FRAM II)" CLASS

Name	No.	Builders	Laid down	Launched	Commissioned
FALCON (ex-USS *Robert K. Huntington* DD 781)	D 22 (ex-D 51)	Todd Pacific Shipyards	1944	5 Dec 1944	3 Mar 1945

Displacement, tons: 2 200 standard; 3 320 full load
Dimensions, feet (metres): 376·5 × 40·9 × 19 (114·8 × 12·4 × 5·8)
Guns: 6—5 in (127 mm)/38 (twin Mk 38)
A/S weapons: 2 Hedgehogs; 2 triple torpedo tubes (Mk 32); facilities for small helicopter
Main engines: 2 geared turbines; 60 000 shp; 2 shafts
Boilers: 4
Speed, knots: 34
Range, miles: 4 600 at 15 knots
Complement: 274

Purchased from US Navy 31 October 1973. Modernised under the FRAM II programme. Refitted in USA in 1977.

Radar: SPS 40 and SPS 10.

Sonar: Hull-mounted; SQS 29 series. VDS.

FALCON 1978, Venezuelan Navy

1 Ex-US "ALLEN M. SUMNER" CLASS

Name	No.	Builders	Laid down	Launched	Commissioned
CARABOBO (ex-USS *Beatty*, DD 756)	D 21 (ex-D 41)	Bethlehem, Staten Island	1944	30 Nov 1944	31 Mar 1945

Displacement, tons: 2 200 standard; 3 320 full load
Dimensions, feet (metres): 376·5 × 40·9 × 19·0 (114·8 × 12·4 × 5·8)
Guns: 6—5 in (127 mm)/38 (twin Mk 38)
A/S weapons: 2 fixed Hedgehogs; DCs; 2 triple torpedo tubes (Mk 32)
Main engines: 2 geared turbines; 60 000 shp; 2 shafts
Boilers: 4
Speed, knots: 34
Range, miles: 4 600 at 15 knots
Complement: 274

Transferred from US Navy 14 July 1972. Refitted in USA in 1977.

Fire control: Mk 37 GFCS forward with Mk 25 radar; Mk 51 GFCS aft (no radar).

Radar: SPS 6, SPS 10.

Sonar: SQS 29 series.

CARABOBO (as *Beatty*) 1965, Dr. Giorgio Arra

FRIGATES

1 + 5 "LUPO" CLASS

Name	No.	Builders	Laid down	Launched	Commissioned
MARISCAL SUCRE	F 21	CNR, Riva Trigoso	19 Nov 1976	28 Sep 1978	1979
ALMIRANTE BRION	F 22	CNR, Riva Trigoso	June 1977	—	—
GENERAL URDANETA	F 23	CNR, Riva Trigoso			
GENERAL SOUBLETTE	F 24	CNR, Riva Trigoso			
GENERAL SALOM	F 25	CNR, Riva Trigoso			
GENERAL JOSÉ FELIX RIBAS	F 26	CNR, Riva Trigoso			

Displacement, tons: 2 208 standard; 2 500 full load
Dimensions, feet (metres): 366 × 39·4 × 11·8 (111·6 × 12 × 3·6)
Aircraft: 1 AB212 helicopter (fixed hangar)
Missiles: SSM; 4 Otomat (single launchers); SAM; 8 Aspide (8-cell launcher for Albatros system)
Guns: 1—5 in (127 mm)/54 (Compact); 4—40 mm/70 (singles)
Rocket launchers: 2 SCLAR 4·1 in multi-tube mountings
A/S weapons: 6 tubes for A/S torpedoes (triples)
Main engines: CODAG. 2 Fiat/GEI LM 2 500 gas turbines; 34 400 bhp; 2 GMT A230/20M diesels; 7 800 hp; 2 shafts
Speed, knots: 35; 21 on diesels
Range, miles: 5 000 at 15 knots
Complement: 185

Letter of intent signed 24 October 1975.

Missiles: With fixed hangar only 4 Otomat carried with no reloads for Albatros system.

Radar: Search: Selenia MM/SPS 74.
Navigation: SMA SPQ/2F.
Fire control (guns): Elsag Mark 10 Mod O Argo.
Fire control (missiles): EX 77 Mod O.

Sonar: SQS 29.

MARISCAL SUCRE 11/1978, Commander Aldo Fraccaroli

VENEZUELA / Frigates — Light forces   767

4 "ALMIRANTE CLEMENTE" CLASS

Name	No.	Builders	Laid down	Launched	Commissioned
ALMIRANTE CLEMENTE	F 11 (ex-D 12)	Ansaldo, Leghorn	5 May 1954	12 Dec 1954	1956
GENERAL JOSÉ TRINIDAD MORAN	F 12 (ex-D 22)	Ansaldo, Leghorn	5 May 1954	12 Dec 1954	1956
GENERAL JUAN JOSÉ FLORES	F 13 (ex-D 13)	Ansaldo, Leghorn	5 May 1954	7 Feb 1955	1956
ALMIRANTE BRION	F 14 (ex-D 23)	Ansaldo, Leghorn	12 Dec 1954	4 Sep 1955	1957

Displacement, tons: 1 300 standard; 1 500 full load
Length, feet (metres): 325·11 *(99·1)*
Length, feet (metres): 35·5 *(10·8)*
Draught, feet (metres): 12·2 *(3·7)*
Guns: 4—4 in *(102 mm)*/46 (twin) or 2—76 mm/62 (single Compact); 4—40 mm/70 (twin); 8—20 mm/70 (twin HSS) (modified group 40 mm only) (see note)
A/S weapons: 2 Hedgehogs, 4 DCT and 2 DC racks in original group; 1 A/S Mortar, 4 DCT and 2 DC racks in modified group
Torpedo tubes: 3—21 in *(533 mm)* triple (only F 13)
Main engines: 2 sets geared turbines; 2 shafts; 24 000 shp
Boilers: 2 Foster-Wheeler
Speed, knots: 32
Oil fuel, tons: 350
Range, miles: 3 500 at 15 knots
Complement: 162 (12 officers, 150 men)

The first three of this class of six were ordered in 1953. Three more were ordered in 1954. Aluminium alloys were widely employed in the building of all superstructure. All ships fitted with Denny-Brown fin stabilisers and air conditioned throughout the living and command spaces.

Gunnery: The 4 in guns are fully automatic and radar controlled—replaced by two OTO Melara 76 mm in F 11 and 12.

Modernisation: *Almirante José Garcia, Almirante Brion* and *General José de Austria* were refitted by Ansaldo, Leghorn, in 1962 to improve their anti-submarine and anti-aircraft capabilities: the survivor of this group is known as "Modified Almirante Clemente" type. *Almirante Clemente* and *General José Trinidad Moran* were taken in hand for refit by Cammell Laird/Plessey group in April 1968. 4 in guns replaced by 76 mm OTO Melara Compact. *Almirante Clemente* started her post-refit trials in February 1975 and *General Jose Moran* after trials sailed mid-January 1976 for Venezuela.

Radar: Search: MLA 1—some, Plessey AWS-1.
Fire control: I Band.

ALMIRANTE CLEMENTE   1978, Venezuelan Navy

LIGHT FORCES

Note: Also reported three ex-US 43 ft PBs transferred February 1970

6 VOSPER-THORNYCROFT "121 ft" CLASS (FAST ATTACK CRAFT—MISSILE AND GUN)

Name	No.	Builders	Laid down	Launched	Commissioned
CONSITUCION	P 11	Vosper-Thornycroft Ltd	Jan 1973	1 June 1973	16 Aug 1974
*FEDERACION	P 12	Vosper-Thornycroft Ltd	Aug 1973	26 Feb 1974	25 Mar 1975
INDEPENDENCIA	P 13	Vosper-Thornycroft Ltd	Feb 1973	24 July 1973	20 Sep 1974
*LIBERTAD	P 14	Vosper-Thornycroft Ltd	Sep 1973	5 Mar 1974	12 June 1975
PATRIA	P 15	Vosper-Thornycroft Ltd	Mar 1973	27 Sep 1973	9 Jan 1975
*VICTORIA	P 16	Vosper-Thornycroft Ltd	Mar 1974	3 Sep 1974	22 Sep 1975

* Missile craft

Displacement, tons: 170
Dimensions, feet (metres): 121 × 23·3 × 6 *(36·9 × 7·1 × 1·8)*
Missiles: SSM; 2 Otomat (P 12, 14 and 16) (single cells)
Gun: 1—76 mm/62 (Compact) (P 11, 13 and 15); 1—40 mm gun (P 12, 14 and 16)
Main engines: 2 MTU diesels; 7 200 hp; 2 shafts
Speed, knots: 27; 31 max
Range, miles: 1 350 at 16 knots
Complement: 17 (3 officers, 14 men)

A £6 million order the first laid down in January 1973. A new design, fitted with Elsag fire control system NA 10 mod 1 and Selenia radar in 76 mm gun craft. Ten more fast attack craft (missile) projected.

Radar: SPQ 2D.

LIBERTAD   1978, Venezuelan Navy

21 "RIO ORINOCO" CLASS (COASTAL PATROL CRAFT)

Name	No.	Builders	Commissioned
RIO ORINOCO	C 87	Inma, La Spezia	1974
RIO VENTUARI	C 88	Inma, La Spezia	1974
RIO CAPARO	C 89	Inma, La Spezia	1974
RIO VENAMO	C 90	Inma, La Spezia	1974
RIO TORRES	C 91	Inma, La Spezia	1974
RIO ESCALANTE	C 92	Inma, La Spezia	1975
RIO LIMON	C 93	Inma, La Spezia	1975
RIO SAN JUAN	C 94	Inma, La Spezia	1975
RIO TUCUYO	C 95	Inma, La Spezia	1975
RIO TURBIO	C 96	Inma, La Spezia	1975
	C 128-138	Dianca, Puerto Cabello	—

Displacement, tons: 65
Dimensions, feet (metres): 92·8 × 15·7 × 4·9 *(28·3 × 4·8 × 1·5)*
Main engines: 2 MTU diesels; 2 200 bhp = 25 knots

Ordered in May 1973. Assistance given in overseeing at Puerto Cabello by Inma. First Cabello built craft launched March 1974 and six were completed by end 1975.

768 VENEZUELA / Amphibious forces — Survey ships

AMPHIBIOUS FORCES

1 Ex-US "TERREBONNE PARISH" CLASS (LST)

Name	No.	Builders	Commissioned
AMAZONAS	T 51	Ingalls Shipbuilding	1953
(ex-USS *Vernon County* LST 1161)	(ex-T 21)	Corporation	

Displacement, tons: 2 590 light; 5 800 full load
Dimensions, feet (metres): 384 × 55 × 17 *(117.4 × 16.8 × 5.2)*
Guns: 6—3 in/50 (twins)
Main engines: 4 General Motors diesels; 2 shafts; cp propeller; 6 000 bhp = 15 knots
Complement: 116
Troops: 395

Built 1952-53. Carries four LCVP landing craft. Transferred on loan 29 June 1973. Purchased 30 December 1977.

1 Ex-US "ACHELOUS" CLASS

Name	No.	Builders	Commissioned
GUYANA	T 31	Chicago Bridge & Iron Co,	1945
(ex-USS *Quirinus*, ARL 39, ex-*LST 1151*)	(ex-T 18)	Seneca, Illinois	

Displacement, tons: 1 625 light; 4 100 full load
Dimensions, feet (metres): 328 × 50 × 11.2 *(100 × 15.2 × 3.4)*
Guns: 8—40 mm (two quad mountings)
Main engines: General Motors diesels; 2 shafts; 1 800 bhp = 11.6 knots
Complement: 81 (11 officers, 70 men)

Former US Navy landing craft repair ship. Laid down on 3 March 1945. Loaned to Venezuela in June 1962 and now used as a transport. Purchased 30 December 1977.

4 Ex-US "LSM I" CLASS

Name	No.	Builders	Commissioned
LOS MONJES	T 21	Brown Shipbuilding Co,	1945
(ex-USS *LSM 548*)	(ex-T 13)	Houston, Texas	
LOS ROQUES	T 22	Brown Shipbuilding Co,	1945
(ex-USS *LSM 543*)	(ex-T 14)	Houston, Texas	
LOS FRAILES	T 23	Brown Shipbuilding Co,	1945
(ex-USS *LSM 544*)	(ex-T 15)	Houston, Texas	
LOS TESTIGOS	T 24	Brown Shipbuilding Co,	1945
(ex-USS *LSM 545*)	(ex-T 16)	Houston, Texas	

Displacement, tons: 743 beaching; 1 095 full load
Dimensions, feet (metres): 203.5 × 34.5 × 8.3 *(62.1 × 10.5 × 2.5)*
Guns: 1—40 mm; 4—20 mm
Main engines: Direct drive diesels; 2 shafts; 2 800 bhp = 12 knots
Range, miles: 9 000 at 11 knots
Complement: 59

Transferred to Venezuela under MAP—February 1959 (T 21), September 1959 (T 22), December 1959 (T 23), January 1960 (T 24).

LOS FRAILES   1978, Venezuelan Navy

12 LCVPS

Built by Dianca, Puerto Cabello 1976-77.

TRANSPORTS

2 CANADIAN TYPE

Name	No.	Builders	Commissioned
MARACAIBO	T 41 (ex-T 19)	Vickers, Canada	1949
(ex-M/V *Ciudad de Maracaibo*)			
VALENCIA	T 42	Vickers, Canada	1953
(ex-M/V *Ciudad de Valencia*)			

Measurement, tons: 4 297 gross; 5 885 deadweight
Dimensions, feet (metres): 420.5 × 55 × 22.3 *(128.15 × 16.76 × 6.78)*
Main engine: 1 Nordberg diesel; 4 275 hp = 15 knots

Acquired from state shipping company in 1973 and 1977 respectively.

VALENCIA   1978, Venezuelan Navy

1 JAPANESE TYPE

Name	No.	Builders	Commissioned
PUNTA CABANA	T ? (ex-T 17)	Uraga Dockyard, Japan	—

Displacement, tons: 3 200
Dimensions, feet (metres): 373.9 × 52.5 × 22.9 *(114 × 16 × 7)*
Main engine: Diesel; 5 500 hp = 17 knots
Range, miles: 6 000 at 15 knots

Name	No.	Builders	Commissioned
LAS AVES (ex-*Dos de Diciembre*)	T ? (ex-T 12)	Chantiers Dubigeon, Nantes-Chantenay	1955

Displacement, tons: 944
Dimensions, feet (metres): 234.2 × 33.5 × 10 *(71 × 10.2 × 3.1)*
Guns: 4—20 mm (2 twin)
Main engines: 2 diesels; 2 shafts; 1 600 bhp = 15 knots
Range, miles: 2 600 at 11 knots

Launched in September 1954. Light transport for naval personnel. Renamed *Las Aves* in 1961. Can be used as Presidential Yacht.

LAS AVES   1970, Venezuelan Navy

SURVEY SHIPS

1 OCEANOGRAPHIC SHIP

Dimensions, feet (metres): 224.4 × 38.7 × 13.8 *(68.4 × 11.8 × 4.2)*
Main engines: 2 diesels; 2 180 hp; 1 shaft; cp propeller = 14 knots
Complement: 60

This design is apparently the result of enquiries in Argentina, France, W. Germany, UK and USA. The order is now reported as placed, either in Argentina or France—it is also reported that the operation and maintenance of this ship will be co-ordinated with the USA.

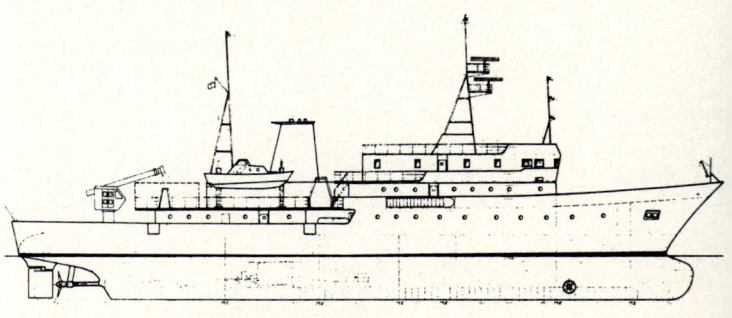
New Oceanographic Ship (preliminary drawing)   1978

Ex-US "COHOES" CLASS

Name	No.	Builders	Commissioned
PUERTO SANTO (ex-USS *Marietta*, AN 82)	H 11 (ex-H 01)	Commercial Iron Works, Portland, Oregon	1945

Displacement, tons: 650 standard; 855 full load
Dimensions, feet (metres): 168·5 × 33·8 × 11·7 *(51·4 × 10·2 × 3·6)*
Guns: 3—20 mm
Main engines: Bush-Sulzer diesel-electric; 1 shaft; 1 500 bhp = 12 knots
Complement: 46

Puerto Santo loaned from USA in Jan 1961 under MAP and converted into Hydrographic survey vessel and buoy tender by US Coast Guard Yard, Curtis Bay, Maryland, in February 1962. Originally carried one 3 in/50 gun. Since 1977 used full-time as a buoy tender. Acquired by sale 30 December 1977. The bow horns now removed.

PUERTO SANTO   1978, Venezuelan Navy

2 SURVEY LAUNCHES

Name	No.	Builders	Commissioned
GABRIELA	P 119	Abeking and Rasmussen, Lemwerder	5 Feb 1974
NELY	P 121	Abeking and Rasmussen, Lemwerder	7 Feb 1974

Displacement, tons: 90
Dimensions, feet (metres): 88·6 × 18·4 × 4·9 *(27 × 5·6 × 1·5)*
Main engines: 2 diesels; 2 300 hp = 20 knots
Complement: 16

Nely laid down 28 May 1973, launched 12 December 1973 and *Gabriela* laid down 10 March 1973, launched 29 November 1973. Non-naval—civilian manned by Instituto de Canalizaciones.

TUGS

Ex-US "CHEROKEE" CLASS

Name	No.	Builders	Commissioned
FELIPE LARRAZABAL (ex-USS *Utina*, ATF 163)	R 21	Charleston S.B. and D.D. Co	1945
ANTONIO PICARDI (ex-USS *Nipmuc*, ATF 157)	R 22	Charleston S.B. and D.D. Co	8 July 1945
MIGUEL RODRIGUEZ (ex-USS *Salinan*, ATF 161)	R 23	Charleston S.B. and D.D. Co	9 Nov 1945

Displacement, tons: 1 235 standard; 1 675 full load
Dimensions, feet (metres): 205 × 38·5 × 15·5 *(61·7 × 11·6 × 4·7)*
Gun: 1—3 in *(76 mm)*/50 (in R 21)
Main engines: Diesel-electric; 3 000 bhp; 1 shaft
Speed, knots: 15
Complement: 85

R 21 transferred 3 September 1971. This is the third tug of this name. The first (ex-USS *Discoverer*) was deleted in 1962. The second (ex-USS *Tolowa*, ATF 116) was deleted in 1972 after damage when grounded. R 21 purchased 30 December 1977; other two 1 September 1978.

ANTONIO PICARDI   1978, Venezuelan Navy

1 HARBOUR TUG

C 142

Built by Dianca, Puerto Cabello. Two Werkspoor diesels; two shafts; 1 600 bhp. Ordered in 1973. Commissioned as dockyard tug with Dianca in 1978. Three similar tugs, C 139, 140 and 141 are run by Ministry of Communications.

1 Ex-US HARBOUR TUG

FERNANDO GOMEZ (ex-YTM 744) R 11 (ex-R 12)

Displacement, tons: 161
Dimensions, feet (metres): 80 × 19 × 8 *(24·5 × 5·8 × 2·4)*
Main engines: Clark diesel; 6-cyl, 315 rpm; 380 bhp = 15 knots
Complement: 10

2 Ex-US MEDIUM HARBOUR TUGS

FABRIO GALLIPOLI (ex-USS *Wannalancet* YTM 385) R 14
DIANA III (ex-USS *Sassacus* YTM 193)

Leased to Venezuela in August 1965. Purchased 30 December 1977.

5 Ex-US "YTL 421" CLASS (SMALL HARBOUR TUGS)

Ex-US YTL 446, 451, 455, 590, 592

80 ft long, leased in January 1963.

REPAIR CRAFT

DF 11 (ex-USS *ARD 13*, ex-DF 1)
Floating dock of 3 000 tons and built of steel. Transferred on loan to Venezuela in February 1962. Purchased 30 December 1977.

Ex-US YR 48 (Floating Workshop) transferred 1965. Purchased 30 December 1977.

One Floating Crane with 40 ton lift.

SAIL TRAINING SHIP

Displacement, tons: 934
Dimensions, feet (metres): 249·9 × 34·8 × 13·4 *(76·2 × 10·6 × 4·2)*
Auxiliary engine: 1 General Motors diesel; 700 hp = 10 knots

Ordered from Astilleros Celaya, Spain in 1978.

NATIONAL GUARD

12 COASTAL PATROL CRAFT

RIO META   RIO URIBANTE
RIO PORTUGUESA   + 9

Displacement, tons: 45
Dimensions, feet (metres): 88·6 × 16 × 4·9 *(27 × 4·9 × 1·5)*
Guns: 1—20 mm; 1 MG
Main engines: 2 diesels; 3 300 hp = 30 knots
Range, miles: 1 500 at 15 knots
Complement: 12

Built at Chantiers Navals de l'Esterel first six 1970-71, second six 1976-77.

8 "RIO" CLASS (COASTAL PATROL CRAFT)

Name	No.	Builders	Commissioned
RIO APURE	—	Chantiers Navals de l'Esterel, Cannes	1955
RIO ARAUCA	—	Chantiers Navals de l'Esterel, Cannes	1955
RIO CABRIALES	—	Chantiers Navals de l'Esterel, Cannes	1955
RIO CARONI	—	Chantiers Navals de l'Esterel, Cannes	1955
RIO GUARICO	—	Chantiers Navals de l'Esterel, Cannes	1955
RIO NEGRO	—	Chantiers Navals de l'Esterel, Cannes	1955
RIO NEVERI	—	Chantiers Navals de l'Esterel, Cannes	1955
RIO TUX	—	Chantiers Navals de l'Esterel, Cannes	1955

Displacement, tons: 38
Dimensions, feet (metres): 80·3 × 15·3 × 4·2 *(24·5 × 4·7 × 1·3)*
Main engines: 2 Mercedes diesels; 1 500 bhp; 2 shafts = 27 knots
Complement: 15

"RIO" Class   1978, Ch. Navals de L'Esterel

1 COASTAL PATROL CRAFT

GOLFO DE CARIACO

Displacement, tons: 37
Dimensions, feet (metres): 65 × 18 × 9 *(20 × 5·5 × 2·8)*
Main engines: Diesels; speed = 19 knots
Complement: 10

1 COASTAL PATROL CRAFT

RIO SANTO DOMINGO

Displacement, tons: 40
Dimensions, feet (metres): 70 × 15 × 6 *(22 × 4·6 × 1·9)*
Main engines: 2 General Motors diesels; 1 250 bhp = 24 knots
Complement: 10

VIET-NAM

Administration

Commander in Chief of the Navy:
Rear-Admiral Ta Xuan Thu

Strength of the Fleet

It is impossible to give an accurate estimate of this fleet—except for the recent Soviet transfers the details following refer to the known classes in 1975 including their names and pennant numbers at that time. There is no evidence as to which ships have been made operational. All that can be said is that those listed consist of the original North Viet-Nam fleet plus those that failed to escape from South Viet-Nam.
So far as operational availability is concerned only a very small proportion of this considerable force can be considered fit for sea. Of those that are seaworthy very few can steam any distance due to a chronic lack of fuel oil.

Personnel

1979: ?

Mercantile Marine

Lloyd's Register of Shipping:
80 vessels of 162 585 tons gross

FRIGATES

2 Ex-SOVIET "PETYA II" CLASS

Displacement, tons: 950 standard; 1 100 full load
Dimensions, feet (metres): 268·9 × 29·9 × 10·5 *(82·3 × 9·1 × 3·2)*
Guns: 4—76 mm (twins)
A/S weapons: 10—406 mm torpedo tubes (quin); 2—MBU 2500
Main engines: 2 gas turbines; 1 diesel; 3 shafts; 36 000 shp = 35 knots
Complement: 98

Transferred in 1978.

"PETYA II" Class

1 Ex-US "BARNEGAT" CLASS

Name	No.	Builders	Launched	Commissioned
THAM NGU LAO (ex-USCGC *Absecon*, WHEC 374, ex-AVP 23)	HQ 15	Lake Washington S.Y.	8 Mar 1942	28 Jan 1943

Displacement, tons: 1 766 standard; 2 800 full load
Length, feet (metres): 310·75 *(94·7)*
Beam, feet (metres): 41·1 *(12·5)*
Draught, feet (metres): 13·5 *(4·1)*
Guns: 1—5 in *(127 mm)*/38; 2—81 mm mortars; several MG
Main engines: Diesels (Fairbanks-Morse); 6 080 bhp; 2 shafts
Speed, knots: Approx 18
Complement: Approx 200

Last of a group built as seaplane tenders for the US Navy. Transferred to US Coast Guard in 1948, initially on loan designated WAVP and then on permanent transfer subsequently redesignated as high endurance cutter (WHEC). Transferred from US Coast Guard to South Vietnamese Navy in 1971.

Ex-US "BARNEGAT" Class   1971, Vietnamese Navy

1 Ex-US "SAVAGE" CLASS

Name	No.	Builders	Launched	Commissioned
TRAN KHANH DU (ex-USS *Forster*, DER 334)	HQ 04	Consolidated Steel Corporation, Orange, Texas	13 Nov 1943	25 Jan 1944

Displacement, tons: 1 590 standard; 1 850 full load
Length, feet (metres): 306 *(93·3)*
Beam, feet (metres): 36·6 *(11·2)*
Draught, feet (metres): 14 *(4·3)*
Guns: 2—3 in *(76 mm)*/50 (single)
A/S weapons: 6 (Mk 32 triple) torpedo tubes; 1 trainable Hedgehog (Mk 15); depth charge rack
Main engines: Diesel (Fairbank-Morse); 6 000 bhp; 2 shafts
Speed, knots: 21
Complement: Approx 170

Former US Navy destroyer escort of the FMR design group. Employed during 1960s in Indochina for coastal patrol and interdiction by US Navy (Operation MARKET TIME). Transferred to South Vietnamese Navy on 25 September 1971. Was in overhaul at time of occupation of South Viet-Nam.

Radar: Search: SPS 10 and 28.

TRAN KHANH DU   1971, Vietnamese Navy

VIET-NAM / Corvettes — Light forces 771

CORVETTES

2 Ex-US "ADMIRABLE" CLASS

Name	No.	Launched
HA HOA (ex-USS *Sentry*, MSF 299)	HQ 09	15 Aug 1943
HA HOI (ex-USS *Prowess*, IX 305, ex-MSF 280)	HQ 13	17 Feb 1944

Displacement, tons: 650 standard; 945 full load
Dimensions, feet (metres): 184.5 × 33 × 9.75 *(56.3 × 10 × 3)*
Guns: 1—3 in *(76 mm)*/50; 2—40 mm (single); up to 8—20 mm (twin)
A/S weapons: 1 fixed Hedgehog; depth charges
Main engines: Diesel (Cooper Bessemer); 1 710 bhp; 2 shafts = 14 knots
Complement: Approx 80

Former US Navy minesweepers of the "Admirable" class (originally designated AM). *Ky Hoa* built by Winslow Marine Railway & S.B. Co, Winslow, Washington, and *Ha Hoi* by Gulf S.B. Corp, Chicasaw, Alabama.
Ky Hoa transferred in August 1962, *Ha Hoi* transferred on 4 June 1970. Minesweeping equipment has been removed and two depth charge racks fitted on fantail; employed in patrol and escort roles.

LIGHT FORCES

Ex-SOVIET "SO 1" CLASS

Displacement, tons: 170 standard; 215 full load
Dimensions, feet (metres): 137.8 × 19.7 × 5.9 *(42 × 6 × 1.8)*
Guns: 4—25 mm (2 twin mountings)
A/S weapons: 4—5-barrelled MBU; 2 DCT
Mines: Can carry 20
Main engines: 3 diesels; 7 500 hp = 28 knots
Range, miles: 1 100 at 13 knots
Complement: 30

Four of Soviet "SO 1" class were originally transferred to North Viet-Nam, two in 1960-61 and two in 1964-65, but one was sunk by US Navy aircraft on 1 February 1966.

Ex-US "PGM 59" and "71" CLASSES (LARGE PATROL CRAFT)

Name	No.	Transferred
VU DU	HQ 600 (PGM 64)	Feb 1963
TIEN MOI	HQ 601 (PGM 65)	Feb 1963
MINH HOA	HQ 602 (PGM 66)	Feb 1963
KIEN VANG	HQ 603 (PGM 67)	Feb 1963
KEM QUI	HQ 605 (PGM 59)	May 1963
MAY RUT	HQ 606 (PGM 60)	May 1963
NAM DU	HQ 607 (PGM 61)	May 1963
HOA LU	HQ 608 (PGM 62)	July 1963
TO YEN	HQ 609 (PGM 63)	July 1963
DINH HAI	HQ 610 (PGM 69)	Feb 1964
TRUONG SA	HQ 611 (PGM 70)	Apr 1964
THAI BINH	HQ 612 (PGM 72)	Jan 1966
THI TU	HQ 613 (PGM 73)	Jan 1966
SONG TU	HQ 614 (PGM 74)	Jan 1966
TAT SA	HQ 615 (PGM 80)	Oct 1966
HOANG SA	HQ 616 (PGM 82)	Apr 1967
PHU QUI	HQ 617 (PGM 81)	Apr 1967
PHO CHAU	HQ 619 (PGM 91)	Apr 1967

Displacement, tons: 117 full load
Dimensions, feet (metres): 100.3 × 21.1 × 6.9 *(30.6 × 6.4 × 2.1)*
Guns: 1—40 mm; 2 or 4—20 mm (twin); 2—MG
Main engines: Diesel; 1 900 bhp; 2 shafts = 17 knots
Complement: Approx 15

Welded-steel patrol gunboats built in the USA specifically for foreign transfer; assigned PGM numbers for contract purposes. Enlarged version of US Coast Guard 95 ft patrol boats with commercial-type machinery and electronic equipment. HQ 600-605 built by J. M. Martinac S.B. Corp, Tacoma, Washington; HQ 606-610 built by Marinette Marine Corp, Wisconsin. HQ 604 scuttled at sea—1975.

Ex-SOVIET "KOMAR" CLASS (FAST ATTACK CRAFT—MISSILE)

Displacement, tons: 70 standard; 80 full load
Dimensions, feet (metres): 87.9 × 20.3 × 4.9 *(26.8 × 6.2 × 1.5)*
Missiles: SSM; 2 SS-N-2 (single launchers)
Guns: 2—25 mm (twin fwd)
Main engines: 4 diesels; 4 shafts; 4 800 hp = 40 knots
Range, miles: 400 at 30 knots
Complement: 19

A sister ship was reported sunk on 19 December 1972.

Ex-SOVIET "P 4" CLASS (FAST ATTACK CRAFT—TORPEDO)

Displacement, tons: 25 full load
Dimensions, feet (metres): 62.3 × 10.8 × 3.3 *(19 × 3.3 × 1)*
Guns: 2—14.5 mm (1 twin)
Torpedo tubes: 2—18 in *(457 mm)*
Main engines: 2 diesels; 2 200 bhp = 50 knots

Approximately a dozen aluminium hulled motor torpedo boats were transferred from the Soviet Union in 1961 and 1964 and some from China. A number have been lost in action.

6 Ex-CHINESE "P 6" CLASS (FAST ATTACK CRAFT—TORPEDO)

Displacement, tons: 66 standard; 75 full load
Dimensions, feet (metres): 85.3 × 20 × 4.9 *(26 × 6.1 × 1.5)*
Guns: 4—25 mm (2 twin)
Torpedo tubes: 2—21 in *(533 mm)* (single)
Mines: 4
Main engines: 4 diesels; 4 800 bhp; 4 shafts = 41 knots
Range, miles: 450 at 30 knots
Complement: 20

Built in China and transferred in 1967. Some may have been lost in action.

8 Ex-CHINESE "SHANGHAI" CLASS (FAST ATTACK CRAFT—GUN)

Displacement, tons: 155 full load
Dimensions, feet (metres): 127.3 × 17.7 × 5.2 *(38.8 × 5.4 × 1.6)*
Guns: 4—37 mm (twins); 4—25 mm (twins)
Main engines: 4 diesels; 4 800 bhp = 30 knots
Complement: 25

Four were received from the People's Republic of China in May 1966 and four more in 1968.

14 Ex-CHINESE "SWATOW" CLASS (FAST ATTACK CRAFT—GUN)

Displacement, tons: 80 full load
Dimensions, feet (metres): 83.6 × 19 × 6.6 *(25.5 × 5.8 × 2)*
Guns: 4—37 mm; 2—20 mm
A/S weapons: 8 depth charges
Main engines: 4 diesels; 4 800 bhp = 40 knots
Range, miles: 750 at 15 knots
Complement: 17

Approximately 30 "Swatow" class built in China were transferred in 1958, and 20 were delivered in 1964 to replace those lost in action. Pennant numbers run in a 600 series.

3 Ex-SOVIET "ZHUK" CLASS (FAST ATTACK CRAFT—PATROL)

Displacement, tons: 60
Dimensions, feet (metres): 75 × 16 × 6 *(24.6 × 5.2 × 1.9)*
Guns: 4—14.5 mm (twins)
Main engines: 2 M50 diesels; 2 400 hp; 2 shafts = 34 knots
Complement: 18

Transferred 1978.

26 Ex-USCG 82 ft "POINT" CLASS (COASTAL PATROL CRAFT)

Name	No.
LE PHUOC DUI	HQ 700 (ex-*Point Garnet* 82310)
LE VAN NGA	HQ 701 (ex-*Point League* 82304)
HUYNH VAN CU	HQ 702 (ex-*Point Clear* 82315)
NGUYEN DAO	HQ 703 (ex-*Point Gammon* 82328)
DAO THUC	HQ 704 (ex-*Point Comfort* 82317)
LE NGOC THANH	HQ 705 (ex-*Point Ellis* 82330)
NGUYEN NGOC THACH	HQ 706 (ex-*Point Slocum* 82313)
DANG VAN HOANH	HQ 707 (ex-*Point Hudson* 82322)
LE DINH HUNG	HQ 708 (ex-*Point White* 82308)
THUONG TIEN	HQ 709 (ex-*Point Dume* 82325)
PHAM NGOC CHAU	HQ 710 (ex-*Point Arden* 82309)
DAO VAN DANG	HQ 711 (ex-*Point Glover* 82307)
LE DGOC AN	HQ 712 (ex-*Point Jefferson* 82306)
HUYNH VAN NGAN	HQ 713 (ex-*Point Kennedy* 82320)
TRAN LO	HQ 714 (ex-*Point Young* 82303)
BUI VIET THANH	HQ 715 (ex-*Point Patrige* 82305)
NGUYEN AN	HQ 716 (ex-*Point Caution* 82301)
NGUYEN HAN	HQ 717 (ex-*Point Welcome* 82329)
NGO VAN QUYEN	HQ 718 (ex-*Point Banks* 82327)
VAN DIEN	HQ 719 (ex-*Point Lomas* 82321)
HO DANG LA	HQ 720 (ex-*Point Grace* 82323)
DAM THOAI	HQ 721 (ex-*Point Mast* 82316)
HUYNH BO	HQ 722 (ex-*Point Grey* 82324)
NGUYEN KIM HUNG	HQ 723 (ex-*Point Orient* 82319)
HO DUY	HQ 724 (ex-*Point Cypress* 82326)
TROUNG BA	HQ 725 (ex-*Point Maromc* 82331)

Displacement, tons: 64 standard; 67 full load
Dimensions, feet (metres): 83 × 17.2 × 5.8 *(25.3 × 5.2 × 1.8)*
Guns: 1—81 mm mortar/50 cal MG (combination) plus 2 to 4—50 cal MG (single) or 1—20 mm
Main engines: 2 diesels; 1 200 bhp; 2 shafts = 16.8 knots
Complement: 8 to 10

Former US Coast Guard 82 ft patrol boats (designated WPB). All served in Vietnamese waters, manned by US personnel, comprising Coast Guard Squadron One. HQ 700-707 transferred to South Vietnamese Navy in 1969, HQ 708-HQ 725 in 1970.

30 MOTOR LAUNCH TYPES (COASTAL PATROL CRAFT)

Some 30 motor launches were reported to have been incorporated into the North Viet-Nam Navy before May 1966, but not all are still in service.

AMPHIBIOUS FORCES

3 Ex-US "501-1152" CLASS (LSTs)

Name	No.	Launched
DA NANG (ex-USS *Maricopa County*, LST 938)	HQ 501	15 Aug 1944
VUNG TAU (ex-USS *Cochino County*, LST 603)	HQ 503	14 Mar 1944
QUI NHON (ex-USS *Bullock County*, LST 509)	HQ 504	23 Nov 1943

Displacement, tons: 2 366 beaching; 4 080 full load
Dimensions, feet (metres): 328 × 50 × 14 *(100 × 15·2 × 4·3)*
Guns: 7 or 8—40 mm (1 or 2 twin; 4 or 5 single); several 20 mm
Main engines: General Motors diesel; 1 700 bhp; 2 shafts = 11 knots
Complement: 110

Former US Navy tank landing ships HQ 501 built by Bethlehem Steel Co, Hingham, Massachusetts; HQ 504 by Jeffersonville B & M Co, Jeffersonville, Indiana; HQ 503 by Chicago Bridge & Iron Co. Illinois. Lattice tripod masts.

11 Ex-US "LSM 1" CLASS

Name	No.	Launched
HAN GIANG (ex-LSM 9012, ex-USS LSM 110)	HQ 401	28 Oct 1944
NINH GIANG (ex-USS LSM 85)	HQ 403	15 Sep 1944
TIEN GIANG (ex-USS LSM 313)	HQ 405	24 May 1944
HAU GIANG (ex-USS LSM 276)	HQ 406	20 Sep 1944
+ 7		

Displacement, tons: 743 beaching; 1 095 full load
Dimensions, feet (metres): 203·5 × 34·5 × 8·3 *(62 × 10·5 × 2·5)*
Guns: 2—40 mm; 4—20 mm
Main engines: Diesel; 2 shafts; 2 800 bhp = 12 knots
Complement: 73

First two transferred to French Navy for use in Indo-China, January 1954. *Han Giang* transferred to Viet-Nam Navy, December 1955. *Tien Giang* transferred in 1962, *Hau Giang* on 10 June 1965. *Lam Giang* of this class scuttled at sea after the North Vietnamese victory. Additional seven ships believed held by North Viet-Nam in 1974-75.

6 Ex-US "LSSL 1" CLASS

Name	No.	Launched
NGUYEN NGOC LONG (ex-USS LSSL 96)	HQ 230	6 Jan 1945
+ 5		

Displacement, tons: 227 standard; 383 full load
Dimensions, feet (metres): 158 × 23·7 × 5·7 *(48·3 × 7·2 × 1·7)*
Guns: 1—3 in; 4—40 mm; 4—20 mm; 4 MG
Main engines: Diesel; 2 shafts; 1 600 bhp = 14 knots
Complement: 60

Served in Japanese Navy in 1953 to 1964; retransferred to South Viet-Nam in 1965. Additional five ships believed held by North Viet-Nam in 1974-75.

18 Ex-US LCU TYPE

HQ 533 (ex-US LCU 1479)	HQ 543 (ex-US LCU 1493)
HQ 534 (ex-US LCU 1480)	HQ 544 (ex-US LCU 1485)
HQ 535 (ex-US LCU 1221)	HQ 545 (ex-US LCU 1484)
HQ 536 (ex-US LCU 1595)	HQ 546 (ex-US YFU 90, ex-LCU 1582)
HQ 537 (ex-US LCU 1501)	HQ 547 (ex-US LCU 1481)
HQ 538 (ex-US LCU 1594)	HQ 548 (ex-US LCU 1498)
HQ 539 (ex-US LCU 1502)	HQ 560 (ex-US YLLC 1, LCU 1348)
HQ 540 (ex-US LCU 1475)	HQ 561 (ex-US YLLC 5, YFU 2, LCU 529)
HQ 542 (ex-US LCU 1494)	HQ 562 (ex-US YLLC 3, YFU 33, LCU 1195)

LCU 501 series

Displacement, tons: 309 to 320 full load
Dimensions, feet (metres): 119 × 32·7 × 5 *(36·3 × 10 × 1·5)*
Main engines: Gray Marine diesels; 675 bhp; 3 shafts = 10 knots

LCU 1466 series

Displacement, tons: 360 full load
Dimensions, feet (metres): 119 × 34 × 5·25 *(36·3 × 10·6 × 1·7)*
Main engines: Gray Marine diesels; 675 bhp; 3 shafts = 8 knots

501 series built during World War II with LCT (6) designation; 1466 series built during the early 1950s. Transferred to South Viet-Nam from 1954 to 1971, with some of the earlier craft serving briefly in French Navy in Indo-China waters.

Most units armed with two 20 mm guns.

Note: It is probable that in 1975 North Viet-Nam held an additional group of five LCI/LSIL Type, one LCT(6) and six LCT(7). Whether these still exist is not known.

RIVERINE CRAFT

The US Navy transferred approximately 700 armed small craft to South Viet-Nam since 1965. A few former French riverine craft also survive. The exact number of these craft now in service is not known.

In addition to the armed craft grouped here under the category of Riverine (Warfare) Craft, there are numerous small landing craft which are armed.

107 Ex-US "SWIFT" CLASS

Displacement, tons: 22·5 full load
Dimensions, feet (metres): 50 × 13 × 3·5 *(15·2 × 3·9 × 1·1)*
Guns: 1—81 mm mortar/1—50 cal MG combination mount; 2—·50 cal MG (twin)
Main engines: 2 General Motors geared diesels; 960 bhp; 2 shafts = 28 knots
Complement: 6

All-metal inshore patrol craft (PCF). Transferred to South Viet-Nam from 1968 to 1970. Numbered in HQ 3800-3887 and later series.

293 Ex-US PBR TYPE

Displacement, tons: PBR I series: 7·5; PBR II series: 8
Dimensions, feet (metres): PBR I series: 31 × 10·5 × 2·5 *(9·5 × 3·2 × 0·8)*
 PBR II series: 32 × 11 × 2·6 *(9·8 × 3·4 × 0·8)*
Guns: 3—·50 cal MG (twin mount fwd; single gun aft)
Main engines: 2 geared diesels; 440 bhp; water-jet propulsion = 25+ knots
Complement: 4 or 5

River patrol boats (PBR) with fibreglass (plastic) hulls. Transferred to South Viet-Nam from 196■ to 1970. Numbered in HQ 7500-7749 and 7800 series.

27 Ex-US RCP TYPE

Displacement, tons: 15·6
Dimensions, feet (metres): 35·8 × 10·3 × 3·6 *(10·9 × 3·1 × 1·1)*
Guns: Varies: 2—·50 cal MG (twin mount aft and single gun at conning station); some units have additional twin ·30 cal mount in place of ·50 cal MH
Main engines: 2 geared diesels; 2 shafts = 14 knots

River patrol craft (RPC); predecessor to PBR type. Welded-steel hulls. Few used by US Navy a minesweepers, but most of the 34 units built were transferred to South Viet-Nam upon completion in 1965; others in 1968-69. Numbered HQ 7000-7028.

84 Ex-US ASPB TYPE

Displacement, tons: 36·25 full load
Dimensions, feet (metres): 50 × 15·6 × 3·75 *(15·2 × 4·8 × 1·1)*
Guns: Varies: 1 or 2—20 mm (with 2—·50 cal MG in boats with one 20 mm); 2—·30 cal MG; 2—40 mm grenade launchers
Main engines: 2 geared diesels; 2 shafts = 14 knots sustained
Complement: 6

Assault support patrol boats (ASPB) with welded-steel hulls. Transferred to South Viet-Nam from 1969 to 1970. Numbered in HQ 5100 series.

42 Ex-US MONITORS

Displacement, tons: 80 to 90 full load
Dimensions, feet (metres): 60·5 × 17·5 × 3·5 *(18·3 × 5·3 × 1·1)*
Guns: 1—105 mm howitzer; 2—20 mm; 3—·30 cal MG; 2—40 mm grenade launchers
Main engines: 2 geared diesels; 2 shafts = 9 knots
Complement: 11

River monitors (MON). Transferred to South Viet-Nam in 1969-70. Numbered in HQ 6500 series.

22 Ex-US LCM MONITORS

Displacement, tons: 75 full load
Dimensions, feet (metres): 60 × 17 × 3·5 *(18·3 × 5·2 × 1·1)*
Guns: Varies: 1—81 mm mortar or 2 M10-8 flame throwers; 1—40 mm; 1—20 mm; 2—·50 c. MG; possibly 2 to 4—·30 cal MG
Main engines: 2 geared diesels; 2 shafts = 8 knots
Complement: Approx 10

24 LCM 6 landing craft converted to this configuration from 1964 to 1967. Predecessor to th Monitor listed above. Transferred to South Viet-Nam from 1965 to 1970. Numbered in HQ 180 series.

100 Ex-US ATC TYPE

Displacement, tons: 66 full load
Dimensions, feet (metres): 65·5 × 17·5 × 3·25 *(20 × 5·4 × 1)*
Guns: Varies: 1 or 2—20 mm; 2—·50 cal MG; several ·30 cal MG; 2—40 mm grenade launcher
Main engines: 2 geared diesels; 2 shafts = 8·5 knots (6 knots sustained)

Armoured troop carriers (ATC). Some fitted with steel helicopter platforms for evacuation o wounded. Transferred to South Viet-Nam in 1969. Numbered in HQ 1200 series.

9 Ex-US CCB TYPE

Displacement, tons: 80 full load
Dimensions, feet (metres): 61 × 17·5 × 3·4 *(18·6 × 5·4 × 1·1)*
Guns: 3—20 mm; 2—·30 cal MG; 2—40 mm grenade launchers
Main engines: 2 geared diesels; 2 shafts = 8·5 knots maximum (6 knots sustained)
Complement: 11

Transferred to South Viet-Nam in 1969-70. Numbered HQ 6100-6108.

4 Ex-US CSB TYPE

Dimensions, feet (metres): 56 × 18·75 × 6 *(17·1 × 5·7 × 1·8)*
Guns: 4—·50 cal MG (twin)
Main engines: 2 geared diesels; 2 shafts = 6 knots
Complement: 6

Combat salvage boats (CSB) converted from LCM-6 landing craft; configured for river salvage and to support diving operations. Ten ton capacity "A" frame forward.

Ex-FRENCH CRAFT

The Vietnamese Navy listed 43 ex-French STCAN/FOM and 14 LCM Commandement as being in service. The latter are converted LCM-3 landing craft.

MINESWEEPING LAUNCHES

Before cessation of hostilities 24 minesweeping launches were listed in the South Vietnamese Navy; ten MLMS 50 ft type transferred in 1963 from US Navy (numbered HQ 150-155, 157-160); HQ 156 and 161 stricken in 1971); eight MSM 56 ft type transferred in 1970 (numbered HC 1700-1707); six MSR 50 ft type transferred in 1970 (numbered HQ 1900-1905). Other riverine craft had a minesweeping capability.

VIET-NAM / Tankers — YEMEN (NORTH) / Light forces 773

TANKERS

Ex-US YOG TYPE

HQ 472 (ex-US YOG 67)　　　　　　HQ 475 (ex-YOG 56)
HQ 473 (ex-US YOG 71)

Displacement, tons: 450 light; 1 253 full load
Dimensions, feet (metres): 174·0 × 32·0 × 10·9 (53 × 9·8 × 3·3)
Main engines: Diesels; 1 shaft = 10 knots
Cargo Capacity: 6 570 barrels

Former US Navy small gasoline tankers.
Transfers: HQ 472 in July 1967, HQ 473 in March 1970; HQ 474 in April 1971, and HQ 475 in June 1972. HQ 474 scuttled at sea in 1975.

WATER CARRIERS

2 Ex-US YW TYPE

HQ 9118 (ex-US YW 152)　　　　　　HQ 9113 (ex-US YW 153)

Former US Navy self-propelled water carriers. Transferred to South Viet-Nam in 1956.

HARBOUR TUGS

9 Ex-US YTL TYPE

HQ 9500 (ex-US YTL 152)　　HQ 9508 (ex-US YTL 452)
HQ 9501 (ex-US YTL 245)　　HQ 9509 (ex-US YTL 456)
HQ 9502 (ex-US YTL)　　　　HQ 9510 (ex-US YTL 586)
HQ 9503 (ex-US YTL 200)　　HQ 9511 (ex-US YTL 457)
HQ 9504 (ex-US YTL 206)

Former US Navy harbour tugs. HQ 9500 transferred to South Viet-Nam in 1955; HQ 9501, 9503, 9504 in 1956; others from 1968 to 1970.

VIRGIN ISLANDS

An area of some 40 islands, large and small.

Chief of Police:
Rex K. Jones, MVO, QPM

Base
Road Town

1 BROOKE MARINE PATROL CRAFT

VIRGIN CLIPPER

Displacement, tons: 15
Dimensions, feet (metres): 40 × 12 × 2 (12·2 × 3·7 × 0·6)
Gun: 1 MG
Main engines: 2 diesels; 370 hp = 22 knots
Complement: 4

Standard Brooke Marine patrol craft attached to the Royal Virgin Islands Police Force.

VIRGIN CLIPPER　　　　　　　　　1975, Virgin Islands Police Force

YEMEN—NORTH
(Arab Republic)

Personnel
(a) 1979: 200 officers and men
(b) 3 years national service

Base
Hodeida

Mercantile Marine
Lloyd's Register of Shipping:
4 vessels of 1 436 tons gross

LIGHT FORCES

4 Ex-SOVIET "P 4" CLASS (FAST ATTACK CRAFT—TORPEDO)

Displacement, tons: 25 full load
Dimensions, feet (metres): 62·3 × 10·8 × 3·3 (19 × 3·3 × 1)
Guns: 2 MG
Torpedo tubes: 2—18 in
Main engines: 2 M50 diesels; 2 shafts; 2 200 hp = 50 knots
Range, miles: 400 at 13 knots
Complement: 12

Transferred by USSR in late 1960s.

2 Ex-SOVIET "ZHUK" CLASS (FAST ATTACK CRAFT—PATROL)

Displacement, tons: 60 full load
Dimensions, feet (metres): 75 × 16 × 6 (24·6 × 5·2 × 1·9)
Guns: 4—14·5 mm (twins)
Main engines: 2 M50 diesels; 2 400 hp; 2 shafts = 34 knots
Complement: 18

Transferred in 1978.

4 Ex-SOVIET "POLUCHAT" CLASS (LARGE PATROL CRAFT)

Displacement, tons: 70 standard; 90 full load
Dimensions, feet (metres): 98·4 × 19 × 5·9 (30 × 5·8 × 1·8)
Guns: 2—14·5 mm (twin)
Main engines: 2 diesels; 2 shafts; 2 400 shp = 20 knots
Complement: 20

Transferred 1970.

Note: In addition a dozen smaller Patrol Craft and two small landing craft have been reported.

YEMEN—SOUTH
(People's Democratic Republic)

Personnel
(a) 1979: 450 officers and men
(b) 2 years national service

Bases
Aden, Mukalla

Mercantile Marine
Lloyd's Register of Shipping:
24 vessels of 10 061 tons gross

LIGHT FORCES

2 Ex-SOVIET "SO I" CLASS (LARGE PATROL CRAFT)

Displacement, tons: 170 standard; 215 full load
Dimensions, feet (metres): 137·8 × 19·7 × 5·9 *(42 × 6 × 1·8)*
Guns: 4—25 mm (twins)
A/S weapons: 2—5-barrelled RBUs; 2 DC racks
Main engines: 3 diesels; 7 500 shp = 28 knots
Range, miles: 1 100 at 13 knots
Complement: 31

Transferred in April 1972.

2 Ex-SOVIET "P 6" CLASS (FAST ATTACK CRAFT—TORPEDO)

111   112

Displacement, tons: 64 standard; 73 full load
Dimensions, feet (metres): 85·3 × 20 × 4·9 *(26 × 6·1 × 1·5)*
Guns: 4—25 mm (twins)
Torpedo tubes: 2—21 in *(533 mm)*
Main engines: 4 diesels; 4 shafts; 4 800 bhp = 41 knots
Range, miles: 450 at 30 knots
Complement: 20

Transferred 1971.

2 Ex-SOVIET "ZHUK" CLASS (FAST ATTACK CRAFT—PATROL)

Displacement, tons: 60 full load
Dimensions, feet (metres): 75 × 16 × 6 *(24·6 × 5·2 × 1·9)*
Guns: 4—14·5 mm (twin)
Main engines: 2 M50 diesels; 2 400 hp; 2 shafts = 34 knots
Complement: 18

Transferred February 1975.

1 Ex-SOVIET "POLUCHAT" CLASS (LARGE PATROL CRAFT)

Displacement, tons: 70 standard; 90 full load
Dimensions, feet (metres): 97·1 × 19 × 4·8 *(29·6 × 5·8 × 1·5)*
Guns: 2—14·5 mm (twin)
Main engines: 2 diesels; 2 shafts; 2 400 shp = 20 knots
Complement: 15

1 FAIREY MARINE "TRACKER 2" CLASS (COASTAL PATROL CRAFT)

Displacement, tons: 31
Dimensions, feet (metres): 63·1 × 16·3 × 4·8 *(19·3 × 5 × 1·5)*
Gun: 1—20 mm
Main engines: 2 General Motors 12V 71TI diesels; 1 800 hp; 2 shafts = 25 knots
Range, miles: 650 cruising
Complement: 11

Delivered 1978.

4 FAIREY MARINE "SPEAR" CLASS (COASTAL PATROL CRAFT)

Dimensions, feet (metres): 29·8 × 9·2 × 2·6 *(9·1 × 2·8 × 0·8)*
Guns: 3—7·62 mm MG
Main engines: 2 diesels; 290 hp = 25 knots

Three delivered 30 September 1975—one in 1978.

1 FAIREY MARINE "INTERCEPTOR" CLASS

Of 25 ft *(7·6 m)* with a catamaran hull. Can carry eight 25 man life-rafts or a platoon of troops. Twin 135 outboard motors = 30 knots. Delivered 27 July 1975.

AMPHIBIOUS FORCES

2 Ex-SOVIET "POLNOCHNIY" CLASS (LCT)

Displacement, tons: 780 standard; 1 000 full load
Dimensions, feet (metres): 246 × 29·5 × 4·7 *(73 × 9 × 1·8)*
Guns: 4—25 mm (twin); 2—18-barrelled 140 mm rocket launchers
Main engines: 2 diesels; 5 000 bhp = 18 knots
Complement: 40

Can carry six tanks. Transferred in August 1973.

3 Ex-SOVIET "T 4" CLASS (LCVPs)

Displacement, tons: 35 standard; 93 full load
Dimensions, feet (metres): 65·3 × 19·3 × 4·5 *(19·9 × 5·6 × 1·4)*
Main engines: 2 diesels; 2 shafts; 600 bhp = 10 knots
Range, miles: 1 500 at 10 knots

Transferred November 1970.

1 "Z" LIGHTER

MINE WARFARE FORCES

1 Ex-SOVIET "T 58" CLASS (OCEAN MINESWEEPER)

Displacement, tons: 900 full load
Dimensions, feet (metres): 229·6 × 29·5 × 7·9 *(70 × 9 × 2·4)*
Guns: 4—57 mm (twins); 4—25 mm (twins)
Main engines: 2 diesels; 4 000 shp; 2 shafts = 17 knots
Complement: 82

Transferred 1978

3 Ex-BRITISH "HAM" CLASS (MSI)

JIBLA (ex-HMS *Bodenham*, ex-*Al Saqr*)
SOCOTRA (ex-HMS *Blunham*, ex-*Al Dairak*)
ZINGAHAR (ex-HMS *Elsenham*, ex-*Al Ghazala*)

Displacement, tons: 120 standard; 160 full load
Dimensions, feet (metres): 106·5 × 21·2 × 5·5 *(32·4 × 6·5 × 1·7)*
Gun: 1—20 mm
Main engines: 2 Paxman diesels; 1 100 bhp = 14 knots
Oil fuel, tons: 15
Complement: 15 officers and men

Transferred to the South Arabian Navy established by the Federal Government in 1967. All three were renamed after local islands in 1975. They must now be candidates for deletion.

YUGOSLAVIA

Ministerial

Federal Secretary for People's Defence:
General Nikola Ljubicic
Assistant Secretary for Naval Affairs:
Admiral Branko Mamula (see *Flag Officers*)

Headquarters Appointments

Chief of General Staff:
Colonel General Stane Potocar

Flag Officers

Commander-in-Chief and Commander of Split Naval Region:
Admiral Branko Mamula
Fleet Commander:
Vice-Admiral Sveto Letica

Diplomatic Representation

Defence Attaché in London:
Colonel M. Surlan
Naval, Military and Air Attaché in Moscow:
Colonel S. Krivokapic
Naval, Military and Air Attaché in Washington:
Colonel Milan Mavric

Personnel

(a) 1979: 14 000 (1 500 officers and 12 500 men)
(b) 18 months national service

Bases and Organisation

Split Naval Region: Major commands are the Fleet, Pula Naval District (HQ at Pula), Sibenik Naval District (HQ at Sibenik), Boka Naval Sector (HQ at Kumbor).
River Flotilla (Novi Sad) under operational command of Belgrade Army Region.
Main bases: Lora/Split: Minor bases: Pula, Sibenik, Ploce, Gulf of Cattaro.

Naval Air Arm

ASW helicopter squadron (Divulje) was formed in 1974-75 and has a number of Ka-25 Hormones.
There is also an air-liaison detachment (Divulje) composed of a few Mi-8 and S-55 helicopters and DHC-2 Beavers.

New Construction

As well as the new submarines, fast attack craft and LSTs it is reported that the first of a new class of surface ship, possibly of some 1 800 tons with two diesels and one Olympus gas turbine, is planned although funds are temporarily lacking. One of this class building for Indonesia.

Strength of the Fleet

Type	Active	Building (Planned)
Submarines—Patrol	6	1 + ?
Destroyer	1	—
Corvettes	3	—
Fast Attack Craft—Missile	14	6
Fast Attack Craft—Gun	6	—
Fast Attack Craft—Torpedo	14	—
Large Patrol Craft	24	—
Minesweepers—Coastal	4	—
Minesweepers—Inshore	10	—
River Minesweepers	17	?
LSTs	—	1
LCTs/Minelayers	24	—
LCAs	8	?
Training Ships	2	(1)
Survey Ship	1	—
HQ Ships	2	—
Salvage Vessel	1	—
Tankers	6	—
Transports	10	—
Ammunition Transports	4	—
Tugs	12	—
Water Carriers	3	—
Presidential Yacht	1	—

Mercantile Marine

Lloyd's Register of Shipping:
468 vessels of 2 365 630 tons gross

DELETIONS

Large Patrol Craft

1975 Two "Kraljevica" class to Bangladesh, one to Ethiopia

SUBMARINES

1 + 1 + ? "SAVA" CLASS

Name	No.	Builders	Laid down	Launched	Commissioned
SAVA	831	S. and D.E. Factory, Split	1975	1977	1978
—	832	S. and D.E. Factory, Split	—	—	—

Displacement, tons: 964 dived
Dimensions, feet (metres): 215·8 × 22·9 × — (65·8 × 7 × —)
Torpedo tubes: 6—21 in *(533 mm)* (10 reloads or 20 mines)
Main machinery: Diesel-electric; 1 shaft
Speed, knots: 16·1 dived
Complement: 35

A new class of diesel propelled submarine with a diving depth of 1 000 ft. Have Soviet electronic equipment and armament. Further construction planned.

3 "HEROJ" CLASS (PATROL SUBMARINES)

Name	No.	Builders	Laid down	Launched	Commissioned
HEROJ	821	Uljanik Shipyard, Pula	1964	1967	1968
JUNAK	822	Split S.Y.	1965	1968	1969
USKOK	823	Uljanik Shipyard, Pula	1966	1969	1970

Displacement, tons: 1 068 dived
Length, feet (metres): 210·0 *(64)*
Beam, feet (metres): 23·6 *(7·2)*
Draught, feet (metres): 16·4 *(5·0)*
Torpedo tubes: 6—21 in *(533 mm)* (bow)
Main machinery: Diesels; electric motors; 2 400 hp; 1 shaft
Speed, knots: 16 surfaced; 10 dived
Complement: 55

Have Soviet electronic equipment and armament.

JUNAK   *1972, S. and DE. Factory, Split*

2 "SUTJESKA" CLASS (PATROL SUBMARINES)

Name	No.	Builders	Laid down	Launched	Commissioned
SUTJESKA	811	Uljanik Shipyard, Pula	1957	28 Sep 1958	16 Sep 1960
NERETVA	812	Uljanik Shipyard, Pula	1957	1959	1962

Displacement, tons: 820 surfaced; 945 dived
Length, feet (metres): 196·8 *(60·0)*
Beam, feet (metres): 22·3 *(6·8)*
Draught, feet (metres): 16·1 *(4·9)*
Torpedo tubes: 6—21 in *(533 mm)* (bow)
Main machinery: Diesels; electric motors; 1 800 hp
Speed, knots: 14 surfaced; 9 dived
Range, miles: 4 800 at 8 knots
Complement: 38

The first class of submarines to be built in a Yugoslav yard. Were later modernised and received Soviet electronic equipment and armament.

NERETVA   *1969, Dr. Giorgio Arra*

776 YUGOSLAVIA / Submarines — Corvettes

"MALA" CLASS (2 MAN SUBMARINES)

Dimensions, feet (metres): 25 × 6 approx (7·6 × 1·8 approx)
Main motor: 1 electric motor; single screw
Complement: 2

This is a free-flood craft with the main motor, battery, navigation-pod and electronic equipment housed in separate watertight cylinders. Constructed of light aluminium it is fitted with fore- and after-hydroplanes, the tail being a conventional cruciform with a single rudder abaft the screw. Large perspex windows give a good all-round view.

"MALA" Class *1973, S. and DE. Factory, Split*

DESTROYER

1 "SPLIT" CLASS

Name	No.
SPLIT (ex-*Spalato*)	R 11

Builders	Laid down	Launched	Commissioned
Brodogradiliste, Rijeka (see note)	July 1939	1940	1959 (see note)

Displacement, tons: 2 400 standard; 3 000 full load
Length, feet (metres): 376·3 (114·7) pp; 393·7 (120·0) oa
Beam, feet (metres): 36·5 (11·1)
Draught, feet (metres): 12·3 (3·8)
Guns: 4—5 in (127 mm); 10—40 mm (twins)
A/S weapons: 2 Hedgehogs; 6 DCT; 2 DC racks
Torpedo tubes: 5—21 in (533 mm)
Mines: Capacity 40
Main engines: Geared turbines; 2 shafts; 50 000 shp
Boilers: 2 water-tube type (1 operational)
Speed, knots: 24
Oil fuel, tons: 590
Complement: 240

Built by Brodogradiliste "3 Maj", Rijeka. The original ship was laid down in July 1939 by Chantieres de Loire, Nantes, in 1939 at Split Shipyard. Completed on 4 July 1958. Ready for operational service in 1959. The original design provided for an armament of five 5·5 in guns, ten 40 mm guns and six 21·7 in torpedo tubes (tripled), but the plans were subsequently modified.
Only one boiler now operational. Serves as flagship of the Torpedo Boat Brigade.

Fire control: Mk 37 GFCS forward with Mk 12 and 22 radars; Mk 51 GFCS for 40 mm.

Radar: SC and SG1.

SPLIT *Commander Aldo Fraccaroli*

CORVETTES

2 "MORNAR" CLASS

Name	No.
MORNAR	PBR 551
BORAC	PBR 552

Builders	Laid down	Launched	Commissioned
Tito S.Y., Kraljevica	1957	1958	10 Sep 1959
Tito S.Y., Kraljevica	1964	1965	1965

Displacement, tons: 330 standard; 430 full load
Dimensions, feet (metres): 174·8 × 23 × 6·6 (53·3 × 7 × 2)
Guns: 1—76 mm; 2—40 mm (single); 3—20 mm (triple, aft)
A/S weapons: 4 MBU-1200; 2 DCT; 2 DC racks
Main engines: 4 SEMT-Pielstick diesels; 2 shafts; 3 240 bhp
Speed, knots: 20
Range, miles: 3 000 at 12 knots; 2 000 at 15 knots
Complement: 60

The design is an improved version of that of *Udarnik*.
Modernised in 1970-73 at Naval repair yard, "Sava Kovacevic", Tivat, Gulf of Cattaro. Probably now fitted with Soviet sonar equipment.

Type name: Patrolni Brod.

BORAC (before modernisation) *Commander Aldo Fraccaroli*

YUGOSLAVIA / Corvettes — Light forces 777

1 "LE FOUGUEUX" CLASS

Name	No.	Builders	Laid down	Launched	Commissioned
UDARNIK (ex-P 6)	PBR 581	F.C. Mediterranee (Le Havre)	1954	1 June 1954	1955

Displacement, tons: 325 standard; 400 full load
Dimensions, feet (metres): 174·8 × 23 × 6·6 (53·3 × 7 × 2)
Guns: 2—40 mm; 2—20 mm
A/S weapons: 1 Hedgehog; 4 DCT; 2 DC racks
Main engines: 4 SEMT-Pielstick diesels; 3 240 bhp = 18·7 knots
Range, miles: 3 000 at 12 knots; 2 000 at 15 knots
Complement: 62

USA offshore procurement.

UDARNIK   1972, Yugoslav Navy

LIGHT FORCES

Note: The recent order from Yugoslavia for a considerable number of Pielstick diesels may indicate a change of policy over the type of Light Forces to be built.

4 +6 "RADE KONCAR" CLASS (Type 211) (FAST ATTACK CRAFT—MISSILE)

Name	No.	Builders	Commissioned
RADE KONCAR	401	Tito S.Y., Kraljevica	Apr 1977
VLADO CETKOVIC	402	Tito S.Y., Kraljevica	1978
—	403	Tito S.Y., Kraljevica	1979
—	404	Tito S.Y., Kraljevica	1979

Displacement, tons: 240 full load
Dimensions, feet (metres): 147·6 × 27·6 × 7·5 (45 × 8·4 × 2·5)
Missiles: 2 launchers for SS-N-2
Guns: 2 Bofors 57 mm/L 70
Main engines: 2 Rolls-Royce Proteus gas turbines; 11 600 shp; 2 MTU diesels; 7 200 shp
Speed, knots: 40
Range, miles: 500 at 35 knots
Complement: 30

Designed by the Naval Shipping Institute in Zagreb based on Swedish "Spica" class with bridge amidships like Malaysian boats. *Rade Koncar* launched 16 October 1976. *Vlado Cetkovic* launched 28 August 1977.

Radar: Philips TAB in radome.

Type name: Raketna Topovnjaca.

RADE KONCAR   1978, Front

10 Ex-SOVIET "OSA" CLASS (FAST ATTACK CRAFT—MISSILE)

M. ACEV RC 301	V. SKORPIK RC 305	K. ROJC RC 308
V. BAGAT RC 302	N. MARTINOVIC RC 306	F. ROZMAN-STANE RC 309
P. DRAPSIN RC 303	J. MAZAR RC 307	Z. JOVANOVIC-SPANAC RC 310
S. FILIPOVIC RC 304		

Displacement, tons: 160 standard; 210 full load
Dimensions, feet (metres): 127·9 × 26·6 × 5·9 (39 × 8·1 × 1·8)
Missiles: SSM; 4—SS-N-2 (single launchers)
Guns: 4—30 mm (2 twin, 1 fwd, 1 aft)
Main engines: 3 diesels; 13 200 bhp = 40 knots
Fuel, tons: 40
Range, miles: 800 at 25 knots
Complement: 29 (4 officers, 25 men)

Acquired between 1965 and 1969.

Names: Named after war heroes.

Radar: Search: Square Tie.
Fire control: Drum Tilt.
IFF: High Pole.

Type name: Raketni Camac.

N. MARTINOVIC   1972, Yugoslav Navy

K. ROJC   1972

14 Ex-SOVIET "SHERSHEN" CLASS (201 TYPE) (FAST ATTACK CRAFT—TORPEDO)

CRVENA ZVIJEZDA TC 220	KORNAT
PARTIZAN II TC 222	PROLETER
BIKOVAC	STRELJKO
IVAN	+ 7

Displacement, tons: 145 standard; 160 full load
Dimensions, feet (metres): 118·1 × 25·3 × 4·9 (36 × 7·7 × 1·5)
Guns: 4—30 mm (2 twin)
Torpedo tubes: 4—21 in (single)
Mines: 4-6
Main engines: 3 diesels; 3 shafts; 13 200 bhp = 41 knots
Fuel, tons: 30
Range, miles: 800 at 30 knots
Complement: 16

Four craft (TC 211, 212, 215, 216) acquired from USSR, 1965. Remainder built under licence by Tito Shipyard, Kraljevica between 1966 and 1971.

Names: Named after partisan craft of World War II.

Pennant numbers: TC 211-224.

CRVENA ZVIJEZDA   1972

Radar: Search: Pot Head.
Fire control: Drum Tilt.
IFF: High Pole.

Type name: Torpedni Camac.

778 YUGOSLAVIA / Light forces — Mine warfare forces

6 "158" CLASS (Ex-108) (FAST ATTACK CRAFT—GUN)

TOP 146, 154, 162, 168, 169, 174

Displacement, tons: 50 standard; 60 full load
Dimensions, feet (metres): 78 × 21·3 × 4·5 *(23·8 × 6·5 × 1·3)*
Guns: 2—40 mm Bofors L 60; 4—12·7 mm Browning MGs (twins)
Mines: 2-4
Main engines: 3 Packard motors; 3 shafts; 4 500 bhp = 26 knots
Range, miles: 320 at 21 knots
Complement: 14

Of the same class as US "Higgins". Built in Yugoslavia 1951-60 as "108" class. About 25 were reconstructed from 1963 on as gunboats classified as "158" class. Now considered obsolete and mainly used for auxiliary duties.

Transfers: Six to Sudan in April 1970. Two to Ethiopia in 1960 (deleted 1969).

Type name: Topovnjaca.

"158" Class *Yugoslav Navy*

14 "KRALJEVICA" CLASS ("501" and "509" TYPES) (LARGE PATROL CRAFT)

501, 503-4, 506-8 ("501" Type)

510-12, 519-21, 523, 524 ("509" Type)

Displacement, tons: 180 standard; 202 (full load) ("501" Type); 195; 245 "509" Type)
Dimensions, feet (metres): 134·5 × 20·7 × 5·5 *(41 × 6·3 × 1·7)* ("501" Type)
 141·4 × 20·7 × 5·7 *(43·1 × 6·3 × 1·8)* ("509" Type)
Guns: 1—40 mm; 4—20 mm ("501" Type);
 1—3 in *(76 mm)* US Mk 22; 1—40 mm; 4—20 mm ("509" Type)
A/S weapons: 2 Mousetraps (or 1 Hedgehog); 2 DCT; 2 DC Racks
Main engines: 2 diesels; 2 shafts; 3 000 bhp = 17 knots ("501" Type);
 3 300 bhp = 19 knots ("509" Type)
Range, miles: 500 at 12 knots
Complement: 45 ("501" Type); 49 ("509" Type)

Built at Tito SY, Kraljevica—"501" Type 1953-56 and "509" Type 1957-59.

Modernisation: Two MBU 1200 being fitted as elderly 3 in guns are replaced by extra 40 mm. All export models have this 40 mm shipped.

Radar: Search: Decca 45.

Sonar: QCU 2.

Transfers: Six to Indonesia in 1959 (built as separate order); two to Sudan in 1969; one to Ethiopia in 1975; two to Bangladesh in 1975.

"KRALJEVICA" Class *Yugoslav Navy*

10 TYPE 131 (LARGE PATROL CRAFT)

KALNIK PC 132	COPAONIK
LOVCEN PC 136	KOZUF
DURMITOR PC 139	ROMANIJA
CER	+ 3

Displacement, tons: 85 standard; 120 full load
Dimensions, feet (metres): 91·9 × 14·8 × 8·3 *(28 × 4·5 × 2·5)*
Guns: 6—20 mm (triple Hispano-Suiza HS 831 mounts)
Main engines: 2 diesels; 900 bhp = 15 knots

Built at Trogir S.Y. between 1965 and 1968. Serve in Maritime Border Brigade.

Type name: Patrolni Camac.

Pennant numbers: 131-140.

Type 131 *1968, Yugoslav Navy*

MINE WARFARE FORCES

4 "VUKOV KLANAC" CLASS (MINESWEEPERS—COASTAL)

Name	No.	Builders	Commissioned
VUKOV KLANAC (ex-*Hrabri*)	M 151 (ex-*D 25*)	A. Normand, France	Sep 1957
PODGORA (ex-*Smeli*)	M 152 (ex-*D 26*)	A. Normand, France	Sep 1957
BLITVENICA (ex-*Slobodni*)	M 153 (ex-*D 27*)	A. Normand, France	Sep 1957
GRADAC (ex-*Snazni*)	M 161	Mali Losinj SY, Yugoslavia	1960

Displacement, tons: 365 standard; 424 full load
Dimensions, feet (metres): 152 × 28 × 8·2 *(46·4 × 8·6 × 2·5)*
Guns: 2—20 mm
Main engines: SIGMA free piston generators; (gas turbines in *Gradac*);
 2 shafts; 2 000 bhp = 15 knots
Oil fuel, tons: 48
Range, miles: 3 000 at 10 knots
Complement: 40

The first three were built as US "off-shore" orders. *Gradac* (ex-*Snazni*) was built in Yugoslavia in 1960 with French assistance.

BLITVENICA (ex-*Slobodni*) *1966, Yugoslav Navy*

6 "M 117" CLASS (MINESWEEPERS—INSHORE)

M 117   M 118   M 119   M 121   M 122   M 123

Displacement, tons: 120 standard; 131 full load
Dimensions, feet (metres): 98·4 × 18 × 4·9 *(30 × 5·5 × 1·5)*
Guns: 1—40 mm; 2—12·7 mm MG
Main engines: 2 General Motors diesels; 1 000 bhp = 12 knots
Complement: 25

Built in Yugoslav shipyards between 1966 and 1968.

M 121 *1968, Yugoslav Navy*

YUGOSLAVIA / Mine warfare forces — Amphibious forces   779

4 BRITISH "HAM" CLASS (MINESWEEPERS—INSHORE)

M 141   M 142   M 143   M 144

Displacement, tons: 123 standard; 164 full load
Dimensions, feet (metres): 106·5 × 21·2 × 5·5 *(32·4 × 6·5 × 1·7)*
Guns: 2—20 mm
Main engines: 2 Paxman diesels; 1 100 bhp = 14 knots
Range, miles: 2 000 at 9 knots
Complement: 22

Built in Yugoslavia 1964-66 under the US Military Aid Programme. Of same design as British 'Ham' class.

M 142   1968, Yugoslav Navy

3 + ? "NESTIN" CLASS (RIVER MINESWEEPERS)

Name	No.	Builders	Commissioned
NESTIN	M 331	Brodotehnika, Belgrade	20 Dec 1975
MOTAJICA	M 332	Brodotehnika, Belgrade	18 Dec 1976
BELEGIS	M 333	Brodotehnika, Belgrade	Jan 1977

Displacement, tons: 65
Dimensions, feet (metres): 88·6 × 20·7 × 5·2 *(27 × 6·3 × 1·6)*
Guns: 3—20 mm Hispano (triple, aft)
Main engines: 2 diesels; 520 bhp = 15 knots

Continuing programme.

24 "M 301" CLASS (RIVER MINESWEEPERS)

M 301-324

Displacement, tons: 38
Guns: 2—20 mm
Main engines: Speed = 12 knots

All launched in 1951-53. Serve on the Danube.

"M 301" Class   1978, Front

AMPHIBIOUS FORCES

NEW CONSTRUCTION LST

Displacement, tons: 2 980
Dimensions, feet (metres): 334·6 × 46·6 × 10·2 *(102 × 14·2 × 3·1)*
Guns: 2—40 mm
Main engines: 2 diesels; 6 800 shp

A new class capable of carrying six tanks, a number of LCAs and fitted with a helicopter deck now being built in Yugoslavia. Of merchant ship appearance—apparently LCAs are hoisted out by derricks.

24 DTM 211 TYPE (LCT/MINELAYERS)

DTM 215, 217-223, 229-31 +13

Displacement, tons: 410
Dimensions, feet (metres): 155·1 × 21 × 7·5 *(47·3 × 6·4 × 2·3)*
Guns: 2—40 mm (single); 2—12·7 mm
Mines: Can carry 100
Speed, knots: 9
Complement: 15

Capable of carrying at least two, possibly three of the heaviest tanks. Unlike other tank landing craft in that the centre part of the bow drops to form a ramp down which the tanks go ashore, the vertical section of the bow being articulated to form outer end of ramp. Built in Yugoslavia. Can also act as minelayers.

DTM 230   B. Hinchcliffe

Transfers: Two to Sudan in 1969.

15 + ? "601" TYPE (LCAs)

DJC 601-615

Displacement, tons: 32
Dimensions, feet (metres): 70·2 × 15·1 × 2 *(21·4 × 4·6 × 0·6)*
Gun: 1—20 mm
Main engines: Diesels; 1 125 shp = 22 knots

A programme is under way for the construction of a considerable number of LCAs built of polyester and glass fibre. Probably to be carried in the new class of LSTs. First in service September 1976, second 1977. 612 in service June 1978.

YUGOSLAVIA / Miscellaneous — Transports

MISCELLANEOUS

Note: The 1 850 tonnes Training Ship design is under construction for Indonesia and Iraq. It is not known if the Yugoslav navy intends to build one of this class.

TRAINING SHIPS

1 "GALEB" CLASS

Name	No.	Builders	Commissioned
GALEB (ex-*Kuchuk*, ex-*Ramb III*)	M 11	Ansaldo, Genoa	1939

Displacement, tons: 5 182 standard
Measurement, tons: 3 667 gross
Length, feet (metres): 384·8 *(117·3)*
Beam, feet (metres): 51·2 *(15·6)*
Draught, feet (metres): 18·4 *(5·6)*
Main engines: 2 diesels; 2 shafts; 7 200 bhp
Speed, knots: 17

Ex-Italian. Launched in 1938. Sunk as an auxiliary cruiser in 1944, refloated and reconstructed in 1952. Serves as fleet flagship, Presidential Yacht and training ship. Former armament was four 3·5 in, four 40 mm and 24—20 mm (six quadruple) guns. The guns were landed. Can act as minelayer.

GALEB   1976, Dhr J. van der Woude

JADRAN (ex-*Marco Polo*)

Displacement, tons: 720
Dimensions, feet (metres): 190 × 29·2 × 13·8 *(58 × 8·8 × 4·2)*
Sail area: 8 600 sq ft *(800 sq m)*
Main engine: 1 Linke-Hofman Diesel; 375 hp = 8 knots

Topsail schooner. Built by Blohm and Voss, Hamburg. Served in Italian navy during World War II (*Marco Polo*). Launched in 1932. Accommodation for 150 Cadets.

PRESIDENTIAL YACHT

Name	No.	Builders	Commissioned
JADRANKA (ex-*Bjeli Orao*)	—	C. R. dell Adriatico, San Marco, Trieste	Oct 1939

Displacement, tons: 567 standard; 660 full load
Dimensions, feet (metres): 213·2 × 26·5 × 9·3 *(60·5 × 7·9 × 2·8)*
Main engines: 2 Sulzer diesels; 1 900 bhp = 18 knots

Launched on 3 June 1939. While in Italian hands was named *Alba*, for some days only, then *Zagaria*. Fitted for two 40 mm and two MGs—not mounted in peace-time.

JADRANKA   1978, Reinhard Nerlich

HQ SHIPS

KOZARA

Former Presidential Yacht on Danube. Now acts as flagship of the river flotilla.

VIS

Built in 1956. Serves as flagship of missile boat brigade.

SURVEY SHIP

Name	No.	Builders	Commissioned
ANDRIJA MOHOROVICIC	PH 33	Gdansk Shipyard, Poland	1972

Displacement, tons: 1 240 standard; 1 700 full load
Dimensions, feet (metres): 240 × 32·8 × 13·2 *(67 × 10·5 × 4)*
Main engines: 2 diesels; 3 000 hp = 15 knots
Complement: 37

Built in 1971 at the shipyard in Gdansk, Poland, and added to the Yugoslav Navy List in 1972. Of Soviet "Moma" class.

A. MOHOROVICIC   1972, Yugoslav Navy

SALVAGE VESSEL

SPASILAC PS 12

New construction to replace ship of same name which was built in Kiel in 1929-30 and is now deleted. Built at Tito SY, Belgrade. In service 10 September 1976. Diesel propulsion.

TANKERS

2 PN 24 TYPE (HARBOUR TANKERS)

PN 24   PN 25

Built at Split in mid-1950s.

4 PN 13 TYPE (HARBOUR TANKERS)

PN 13 (ex-*Lovcen*)   PN 14   PN 15   PN 16

Displacement, tons: 695 standard
Speed, knots: 8·5

PN 13 (ex-*Lovcen*) was launched in 1932. PN 17 was transferred to the Sudanese Navy in 1969.

TRANSPORTS

4 PT 71 TYPE

PT 71—PT 74

Displacement, tons: 310 standard; 428 full load
Dimensions, feet (metres): 141·5 × 22·2 × 16 *(46·4 × 7·2 × 5·2)*
Main engines: 300 bhp = 7 knots

Built in 1953.

6 PT 61 TYPE

PT 61—66

Built at Pula and Sibenik 1951-54.

4 PO TYPE (AMMUNITION TRANSPORTS)

PO 52—55

Of 600 tons.

TUGS

4 COASTAL TUGS

PR 37—40

Speed, knots: 11
Type name: PR = Pomorski Remorker.

8 HARBOUR TUGS

LR 67—74

Displacement, tons: 130
Type name: LR = Lucki Remorker.

WATER CARRIERS

PV 11   PV 12   PV 13

Of various types and of modern construction.

ZAIRE

Ministerial

State Commissioner for Defence:
Lieutenant-General Mobuto Sese Seko (President)

Personnel

(a) 1979: 200 officers and men
(b) Voluntary service

Bases

Matadi; Lake Tanganyika

Mercantile Marine

Lloyd's Register of Shipping:
34 vessels of 109 785 tons gross

LIGHT FORCES

Note: Also reported, but not confirmed, that three ex-Chinese "Hu Chwan" class hydrofoils have been transferred.

1 COASTAL PATROL CRAFT

ZAIRE (ex-*President Mobuto*, ex-*General Olsen*, ex-*Congo*)

A 70 ton craft, the first in this naval force.

6 SEWART TYPE (COASTAL PATROL CRAFT)

Displacement, tons: 33
Length, feet (metres): 65 *(19·8)*
Guns: 6 MG
Main engines: 2 General Motors diesels = 26 knots
Range, miles: 1 000 at 18 knots

Purchased in USA in 1971.

3 Ex-KOREAN (N) "P 4" CLASS

Displacement, tons: 25 full load
Dimensions, feet (metres): 62·3 × 10·8 × 3·3 *(19 × 3·3 × 1)*
Guns: 2—14·7 mm MG
Torpedo tubes: 2—18 in *(457 mm)*
Main engines: 2 M50 diesels; 2 shafts; 2 200 hp = 50 knots
Range, miles: 400 at 13 knots
Complement: 12

Transferred 1974.

12 COASTAL PATROL CRAFT

Ordered in 1974 in France. No further information.

1 COASTAL PATROL CRAFT

Of 18 tons, 25 knots and mounting three MG. Purchased in USA in 1968.

3 Ex-US COASTAL PATROL CRAFT

Purchased in 1974. Of same type as Swiftboats.

4 COASTAL PATROL CRAFT

Reported as transferred by China in late 1960s.

ZANZIBAR

(see also Tanzania)

Although part of the United Republic of Tanzania, Zanzibar retains a separate Executive and Legislature, the President of Zanzibar being First Vice-President of Tanzania.

4 VOSPER THORNYCROFT 75 ft TYPE

Displacement, tons: 70
Dimensions, feet (metres): 75 × 19·5 × 8 *(22·9 × 6·0 × 2·4)*
Guns: 2—20 mm
Main engines: 2 diesels; 1 840 hp
Speed, knots: 24·5
Range, miles: 800 at 20 knots
Complement: 11

This was one of the first orders for the new Keith Nelson 75 ft craft. First pair delivered 6 July 1973, second pair 1974.

75 ft Type   *1974, Vosper Thornycroft*

NAVAL STRENGTHS

NAVAL STRENGTHS

Figures in brackets indicate ships under construction or planned.

	Ballistic Missile Submarines (N = Nuclear D = Diesel)	Cruise Missile Submarines (N = Nuclear D = Diesel)	Fleet Submarines	Patrol Submarines	Aircraft Carriers (L=light)	Cruisers and Light Cruisers	Destroyers	Frigates	Corvettes	FAC Missile	FAC Torpedo	FAC Gun	Patrol Craft	Mine-layers
ALBANIA				3						4	39	6	4	
ARGENTINA			4 (1)	1 (L)		2	8 (1)	(2)	10		2	2	36	
AUSTRALIA			6	1 (L)			5	6 (3)					13 (14)	
BELGIUM								4					8	
BRAZIL			8	1 (L)			12		6	10			22	
BULGARIA			2					2	3	4	10		6	
CANADA			3				4	16					13	
CHILE			3			3	6	5	3		4		15	
CHINA, PEOPLE'S REPUBLIC	1 (D)	1 (?)		79 (6)			11	14 (4?)		172 (20)	200 (10)	404 (10)	140+	
COLOMBIA				2+4 (small)		3	2	3					23	
CUBA								1 Res		30	24	8	30	
DENMARK				6				7 (3)	2	10	6		63	7
ECUADOR				2			1	1	2	3	3		7	
EGYPT				12 (2)			5	3 (2)		21 (6)	26	4	21	
FINLAND								2	2	4+1		14	5	2
FRANCE	4 (1) (N)	1 (D)	(2)	23	2	2	20 (3)	23 (4)		5			27	
GERMANY (Democratic)								2		15	61		32	
GERMANY (Federal)				24			11	6 (12)	5	30	10			
GREECE				9 (2)			12	4	5	10 (6)	14		12	2
INDIA				8	1 (L)	1	1	29 (2)	4	16			11 (2)	
INDONESIA				3 (2)				9 (3)		9 (4)	4		30	
IRAN				1			3 (2)	4	4	10			7	
IRAQ										14	10	4	31	
ISRAEL				3				(2)		20 (4)			39 (2)	
ITALY				10 (2)		3 (1)	7	14 (1)	8		7			
JAPAN				13 (2)			32 (3)	15 (1)	12		5		10	
KOREA (North)				16 (2)				4		18	165 (2)	134 (4)	56	
KOREA (South)							10	7 (1)	6	8			34 (1)	
LIBYA				3				1	3 (2)	11 (14)			11	
MALAYSIA								2		8		6	22	
MEXICO							2	5	34				36 (9)	
NETHERLANDS				6 (2)			10	8 (10)	6				5	
NEW ZEALAND								4					4	
NIGERIA								1 (1)	4	0 (6)			12 (15)	
NORWAY				15				5	3	28 (12)	17			3
PAKISTAN				4 (2) + 6 small		1	6	1			4	14	3	
PERU				8 (4)		4	5	2		(6)			10 (6)	
PHILIPPINES								8	11	(3)		9	73 (5)	
POLAND				4			1			12	21		31	
PORTUGAL				3				17					27	
ROMANIA									3	5	23	18	31	
SAUDI ARABIA								(4)		(9)	3		116	
SOUTH AFRICA				3				3		6 (6)			4	
SPAIN				8 (4)	1 (L) (1)		11	17 (6)					78 (10)	
SWEDEN				11 (3)			1 (5 res)	1 (2 res)		10 (7)	25		38	48
SYRIA								2		12	8		3	
TAIWAN				2			22	11	3	1 (1)	9		14	
THAILAND								6		6			47	2
TURKEY				12 (2)			12	2		8	13		49 (11)	7
UNION OF SOVIET SOCIALIST REPUBLICS	69 (3) (N) 20 (D)	45 (2) (N) 24 (D)	42 (2)	147 (2) (+100 res)	2 (2)	39 (4)	114 (4)	108 (1) (? res)	116 (2)	120	61	50	170	2
UNITED KINGDOM	4		11 (3)	16	3 (2) (L)	8	8 (3)	51 (4)					21	1
UNITED STATES OF AMERICA	41 (N) (7N)	1 res (D)	72 (24+2 res)	8 (1 res)	13 (3N) +(1N) +6 res	28 (1) (+3 res)	96 (14)	65 (25)					6 (2 res)	
VENEZUELA				4 (2)			4	4 (6)		3		3	21	
YUGOSLAVIA				6 (1)			1		3	13 (3)	14	20	23	

Note: The Type headings used necessarily include ships with wide variations in capability. This table therefore gives only a general indication of the make-up of these navies. For an accurate comparison reference must be made to the individual national sections.

NAVAL STRENGTHS

Ocean Mine-sweepers	Coastal Mine-sweepers/ Mine-hunters	Inshore Mine-sweepers	Mine-sweeping Boats	Assault Ships	Landing Ships	Landing Craft	Depot Repair Main-tenance Ships	Survey Research Ships (Large and Small)	Supply Ships	Large Tankers	Small Tankers	Hydrofoils and ACVs	Misc-ellaneous	
2		6	11								4		20	ALBANIA
	4/2				5	29		9		3			27 (1)	ARGENTINA
	3				(1)	6	1	4 (1)		1			43 (3)	AUSTRALIA
7	4 (10)	14						2	2				14	BELGIUM
	6				2	48	2	14	1	1	2		64	BRAZIL
2	4		12			20		3			3		30	BULGARIA
							1	4	3		2	1	39	CANADA
					4	7	2	1		2	2		14	CHILE
17					29	467	1	20	24 (?12)		18	70	400+	CHINA, PEOPLE'S REPUBLIC
							1	3			1		22	COLOMBIA
	2					7		12					22	CUBA
	8										2		11 (1)	DENMARK
					3			2	1				12	ECUADOR
10		4				7						3	9	EGYPT
		6				13							84	FINLAND
4	22/12 (15)			2	7	48	7	9	2	4 (1)	5		153 (10)	FRANCE
	51				12 (1)	2		23	4		4		55	GERMANY (Democratic)
	40	19				50	13	1	8	5	5		90	GERMANY (Federal)
	14			1	16	67	1	6			8		30 (1)	GREECE
2 (3)	4	4			1	9	2	4 (2)		2	2		13	INDIA
5	2				9	41	4	4		1	5		11 (1)	INDONESIA
	3	2			2 (1)	1	1	3	2 (1)	1	1	14	7	IRAN
2	3					3							3	IRAQ
					3	9						2 (2)	9	ISRAEL
4	27/3 (4)	10			2	56	7	4	1	2		3 (4)	100	ITALY
	31 (3)		6		6		4	7	(1)	(1)	1		36 (2)	JAPAN
						70							105	KOREA (North)
	8		1		20	1	1	6	6		4		2	KOREA (South)
					3	2 (1)	1						4	LIBYA
	5				3		1	1					28 (3)*	MALAYSIA
					3			2			2		18	MEXICO
	11/4 (15)	16				10	3	3	2				51	NETHERLANDS
								4 (2)					7	NEW ZEALAND
					1 (1)	0 (2)		1					11	NIGERIA
	10					7	1	1					14	NORWAY
	7							1			2		7	PAKISTAN
					4			2			8		17 (2)	PERU
	2				35	71	3	4			4	4	18	PHILIPPINES
24			20			38		1			8		74+1 AGI	POLAND
	4					15 (1)		4		1	1		4	PORTUGAL
	4	10	8										4+	ROMANIA
	2 (2)					4						8	3	SAUDI ARABIA
	10							2	1				9	SOUTH AFRICA
4	12			1	5	33	1 (2)	6		1	13 (2)		80 (4)	SPAIN
	12	18				144		6	1		1		48	SWEDEN
1	2												1	SYRIA
	14		8		29	22	1	4			7		42	TAIWAN
	4		10		10	41		4			4		13	THAILAND
	21	4	9 (Hunters)		5	68	4	4	2		6		35	TURKEY
177 (3)	113 (3)	123			1 (1)	25 (1)	150	63 (1)	172 (2)	9	23	24	52 +41	400+ 54 AGIs	UNION OF SOVIET SOCIALIST REPUBLICS
	19/17 (4)	5		2	7	61	3	14	8 (1)	15	6	6	183	UNITED KINGDOM
25				14	53 (2 res)	100	21 (5) (23 res)	40	20	17	2 (5)		1 093 plus MSC	UNITED STATES OF AMERICA
					6			3					18	VENEZUELA
	4	10	17 (river)		(1)	25		1			10		30	YUGOSLAVIA

* Police

NAVAL EQUIPMENT

AIRCRAFT

Notes: (a) For technical details see under country of origin; (b) Class: A Carrier based   B Helicopters   C Land based

Country/Manufacturer	Strength	Role	Class (See note)	Country of Origin	Max Speed	Service Ceiling	Range	Max Endurance	T/O Weight
ARGENTINA									
McDonnell Douglas Skyhawk (A-4Q)	15	F/W Attack Bomber	A	USA	(a)				
Grumman Tracker (S-2A/E)	6	F/W A/S	A	USA					
Grumman Albatross (HU-16B)	3	F/W Search and Rescue Amphibian	C	USA					
Aerospatiale Alouette III	6	Helicopter	B	France					
Sikorsky Sea King (S-61D-4)	4	Helicopter	B	USA					
Westland Lynx Mk 23	2	A/S Helicopter	B	UK					
Aermacchi MB 326GB	12	F/W Trainer and Light Attack	C	Italy					
Lockheed Neptune (P-2H)	8	F/W Maritime Patrol	C	USA					
AUSTRALIA									
McDonnell Douglas Skyhawk (A-4G)	13	F/W Attack Bomber	A	USA	Plus 3 TA-4G trainers				
Lockheed Orion (P-3B/C)	19	F/W Maritime Patrol	C	USA	Operated by Air Force				
Grumman Tracker (S-2E/G)	19	F/W Maritime Patrol	A, C	USA					
Government Aircraft Factories (GAF) Search Master B		F/W Maritime Patrol	C	Australia	168 knots (cruising)	22 500 ft (6 860 m)	730 n. miles at 10 000 ft (3 050 m)		8 500 lb (3 855 kg)
Bell Iroquois (UH-1)	5	Helicopter	B	USA					
Westland Wessex (HAS 31B)	6	Helicopter	B	UK					
Westland Sea King (HAS 50)	7	Helicopter	B	UK					
BELGIUM									
Aerospatiale Alouette III	3	Coast Guard Helicopter	B	France					
Westland Sea King Mk 48	5	Search and Rescue Helicopter	B	UK	Operated by Air Force				
BRAZIL									
Embraer EMB-111 (P-95)	12	F/W Maritime Reconnaissance	C	Brazil	Operated by Air Force 218 knots (cruising)	27 000 ft (8 230 m)	1 470 n. miles at 10 000 ft (3 050 m)		15 432 lb (7 000 kg)
Grumman Tracker (S-2A/E)	16	F/W Maritime Patrol	A	USA	Operated by Air Force				
Bell 47G-2 & 47J	2	Helicopter	B	USA					
Bell JetRanger II	18	Helicopter	B	USA					
Hughes 269/300	6	Helicopter	B	USA					
Sikorsky Sea King (SH-3D)	5	Helicopter	B	USA					
Westland Wasp	5	A/S Helicopter	B	UK					
Westland Whirlwind	3	Helicopter	B	UK					
Westland Lynx	9	A/S Helicopter	A	UK/France	Carried on new destroyers				
CANADA									
Sikorsky CHSS-2 Sea King (CH-124)	32	Helicopter	B	USA					
Canadair Argus (CP-107)	26	F/W Maritime Patrol	C	Canada	20 000 ft 274 knots	20 000 ft plus (6 100 m plus)	5 124 n. miles at 194 knots		148 000 lb (67 130 kg)
Canadair CL-215		F/W Amphibian	C	Canada	157 knots (cruising)		1 220 n. miles		Land 43 500 lb (19 731 kg) Sea 37 700 lb (17 100 kg)
Grumman CS2F-3 Tracker (CP-121)	28	F/W A/S	C	USA	Some in storage				
Lockheed Aurora (CP-140)	18	F/W Maritime Patrol	C	USA	Deliveries to begin in 1980 to replace Argus				
CHILE									
Embraer EMB-111N	6	F/W Maritime Reconnaissance	C	Brazil					
Bell JetRanger	4	Helicopter	B	USA					
Grumman Albatross (HU-16B)	8	F/W Maritime Amphibian	C	USA	Operated by Air Force				
Lockheed Neptune (SP-2E)	4	F/W Maritime Patrol	C	USA					

NAVAL EQUIPMENT / Aircraft 789

Wing span rotor diameter	Length	Height	Power Plant	Armament Capacity	Remarks
54 ft 0 in (16·46 m)	41 ft 2·4 in (12·56 m)	18 ft 1·5 in (5·52 m)	2 × 400 shp Allison 250-B17B turboprop engines	Provision for underwing stores	Used by Indonesian Navy (Not by Australia)
52 ft 4·5 in (15·96 m)	48 ft 7·75 in (14·83 m)	15 ft 6·5 in (4·74 m)	2 × 750 shp Pratt & Whitney (Canada) PT6A-34 turboprop engines		
142 ft 3·5 in (43·38 m)	128 ft 9·5 in (39·25 m)	36 ft 8·5 in (11·19 m)	4 × Wright R-3350 EA-1 turbo-compound radial piston engines 3 700 hp each	15 600 lb of weapons (7 075 kg)	In service with 4 Sqdns. (Nos. 404, 405, 407 and 415)
93 ft 10 in (28·6 m)	65 ft (19·82 m)	29 ft 3 in (8·92 m)	2 × 2 100 hp Pratt & Whitney R-2800 radial piston engines		Used by Greek and Spanish Air Forces and Royal Thai Navy for search and rescue (Not by Canada)

NAVAL EQUIPMENT / Aircraft

Country/Manufacturer	Strength	Role	Class (See note)	Country of Origin	Max Speed	Service Ceiling	Range	Max Endurance	T/O Weight
CHINA (PEOPLE'S REPUBLIC)									
Ilyushin Il-28T	130	F/W Torpedo Bomber	C	USSR (built in China)	14 765 ft (4 000 m) 485 knots	40 350 ft (12 300 m)	at 415 knots (770 km/h) 1 175 n. miles		46 300 lb (21 000 kg)
Shenyang F-6 (MiG-19SF) ("Farmer")	300	F/W Fighter	C	USSR (built in China)	32 800 ft (10 000 m) 783 knots	58 725 ft (17 900 m)	with ext tanks 1 187 n. miles	2 hrs 38 min	19 180 lb (8 700 kg)
Shenyang F-9 ("Fantan")	50	F/W Fighter	C	China	nearly Mach 2		combat radius 430 n. miles		22 050 lb (10 000 kg)
DENMARK									
Aerospatiale Alouette III	8	Helicopter	B	France	Flown from frigates				
Westland Lynx	7	Helicopter	B	UK	Delivery in 1979, for fishery patrol				
EGYPT									
Westland Sea King Mk 47	6	A/S Helicopter	B	UK					
FRANCE									
Breguet Br 1050 Alizé	24	F/W A/S	A	France	10 000 ft (3 050 m) 254 knots	26 250 ft (8 000 m)	normal 1 350 n. miles	7 hrs 40 min	18 100 lb (8 200 kg)
Vought Crusader F-8E(FN)	20	F/W Interceptor	A	USA					
Dassault Etendard IV-M, IV-P	42	F/W Attack Recce	A	France	36 000 ft (11 000 m) Mach 1·02	49 000 ft (15 000 m)	at 442 knots (820 km/h) with ext tanks 1 520 n. miles		22 650 lb (10 275 kg)
Dassault Super Etendard	71 ordered	F/W Fighter	A	France	36 000 ft (11 000 m) approx Mach 1	45 000 ft (13 700 m)	with anti-ship missile 350 n. miles		26 455 lb (12 000 kg)
Aerospatiale Super Frelon SA321G	21	A/S and Minesweeping Helicopter	B	France	at S/L 148 knots	10 325 ft (3 150 m)	at S/L 442 n. miles		28 660 lb (13 000 kg)
Aerospatiale Alouette III	20	General-Purpose Helicopter	B	France	at S/L 113 knots	10 500 ft (3 200 m)	290 n. miles		4 840 lb (2 200 kg)
Westland/Aerospatiale Lynx	26 ordered	A/S Helicopter	B	UK/France					
Breguet Br 1150 Atlantic	35	F/W Long-Range Maritime Patrol	C	France	High Altitude 355 knots	32 800 ft (10 000 m)	4 854 n. miles	at 169 knots 18 hours	95 900 lb (43 500 kg)
Aerospatiale N262/Frégate	20	F/W Transport	C	France	208 knots	23 500 ft (7 160 m)	with max payload 525 n. miles		23 370 lb (10 600 kg)
Lockheed Neptune (P-2H)	20	F/W Maritime Patrol	C	USA					
GERMANY (FEDERAL REPUBLIC)									
Westland Sea King (HAS Mk 41)	21	Search and Rescue Helicopter	B	UK					
Breguet Br 1150 Atlantic	19	F/W Maritime Patrol and Elint	C	France					
Dornier Do 28D-2 Skyservant	20	F/W General Duty	C	Germany	10 000 ft (3 050 m) 175 knots	25 200 ft (7 680 m)	1 090 n. miles		8 470 lb (3 842 kg)
Lockheed Starfighter (F-104G)	115	F/W Fighter	C	USA (built in Germany)	To be replaced by Panavia Tornado Includes RF-104G				
Panavia Tornado	112	Swing-wing Strike and Reconnaissance	C	Germany/Italy/UK	36 000 ft (11 000 m) 1 108 knots		750 n. miles radius of action		45 000–58 400 lb (20 411–26 490 kg)
GREECE									
Grumman Albatross (HU-16B)	8	F/W Maritime Patrol Amphibian	C	USA	Equipped for A/S role				
Aerospatiale Alouette III	4	A/S and Search and Rescue Helicopter	B	France	Operated from ships				
INDIA									
Ilyushin Il-38 ("May")	4	F/W Maritime Patrol	C	USSR					
Breguet Br 1050 Alizé	17	F/W A/S	A	France					
Armstrong Whitworth Sea Hawk	22	F/W Fighter-Bomber	A	UK	Max cruise speed at S/L 512 knots				16 200 lb (7 355 kg)
Aerospatiale Alouette III/Chetak	20	Helicopter	B	France	Chetak is Indian-built Alouette III				
Westland Sea King Mk 42/42A	15	A/S Helicopter	B	UK					

NAVAL EQUIPMENT / Aircraft

Wing span rotor diameter	Length	Height	Power Plant	Armament Capacity	Remarks
0 ft 4·75 in (21·45 m)	57 ft 10·75 in (17·65 m)		2 × Klimov VK-1 turbojets	2 torpedoes	
9 ft 6·5 in (9·00 m)	48 ft 10·5 in (14·90 m)	13 ft 2·25 in (4·02 m)	2 × Klimov R-9B turbojets (Chinese-built)	3 × 30 mm cannon, rockets, bombs	Limited all-weather version also operational
3 ft 5 in (10·20 m)	50 ft 0 in (15·25 m)		2 × unidentified turbojets		Evolved from F-6
51 ft 2 in (15·6 m)	45 ft 6 in (13·86 m)	16 ft 5 in (5·00 m)	1 × 2 100 eshp Rolls-Royce Dart R.Da 21 turboprop	Depth charges, torpedo, rockets, AS.12 missiles	Those embarked on *Clemenceau* and *Foch* are fitted to carry 2 Matra R530 missiles each
31 ft 6 in (9·60 m)	47 ft 3 in (14·40 m)	14 ft 1 in (4·30 m)	1 × SNECMA Atar 8B turbojet	2 × 30 mm cannon, 3 000 lb (1,360 kg) rockets, bombs, Sidewinder missiles	
31 ft 6 in (9·60 m)	46 ft 11·5 in (14·31 m)	12 ft 8 in (3·85 m)	1 × SNECMA Atar 8K-50 turbojet	2 × 30 mm cannon, rockets, bombs, missiles	Deliveries started in 1978
62 ft 0 in (18·90 m)	Inc tail rotor 65 ft 10·75 in (20·08 m)	21 ft 10·25 in (6·66 m)	3 × 1 550 shp Turbomeca Turmo III C6 turboshaft engines	Four homing torpedoes, search radar, sonar Provision for 27 passengers	
36 ft 1·75 in (11·02 m)	42 ft 1·5 in (12·84 m)	9 ft 10 in (3·00 m)	1 × 570 shp Turbomeca Artouste IIIB turboshaft engine	Provision for gun, missiles, torpedoes, MAD equipment	
119 ft 1 in (36·3 m)	104 ft 2 in (31·75 m)	37 ft 2 in (11·33 m)	2 × 6 106 ehp Rolls-Royce Tyne R.Ty.20 Mk 21 turboprop engines	Bombs, depth charges, homing torpedoes, rockets or ASMs	
71 ft 10 in (21·90 m)	63 ft 3 in (19·28 m)	20 ft 4 in (6·21 m)	2 × 1 080 hp Turbomeca Bastan VIC turboprop engines	Seating for 29	Used by French Navy as light transports and aircrew trainers
51 ft 0·25 in (15·55 m)	37 ft 5·25 in (11·41 m)	12 ft 9·5 in (3·90 m)	2 × 380 hp Lycoming IGSO-540-A1E piston engines	Seating for 12 or 13	
Swept: 28 ft 2·5 in (8·60 m)	54 ft 9·5 in (16·70 m)	18 ft 8·5 in (5·70 m)	2 × Turbo-Union RB.199-34R-4 turbojets	2 × 27 mm cannon, bombs, missiles	To equip MFG1 and 2 Performance achieved with development engines
39 ft (11·89 m)	39 ft 8 in (12·09 m)	8 ft 8 in (2·64 m)	1 × Rolls-Royce Nene 103 turbojet	Cannon, bombs or rockets	Operational in carrier *Vikrant*

792 NAVAL EQUIPMENT / Aircraft

Country/Manufacturer	Strength	Role	Class (See note)	Country of Origin	Max Speed	Service Ceiling	Range	Max Endurance	T/O Weight
INDONESIA									
Aerospatiale Alouette III	3	Helicopter	B	France					
Grumman Albatross (HU-16A)	5	F/W Maritime Patrol Amphibian	C	USA					
GAF Search Master B	12	F/W Maritime Patrol	C	Australia					
IRAN									
Lockheed Orion (P-3F)	6	F/W Maritime Patrol	C	USA	Operated by Air Force				
Sikorsky Sea King (SH-3D)	20	A/S Helicopter	B	USA (built in Italy)					
Sikorsky RH-53D	6	Mine Countermeasures Helicopter	B	USA					
Agusta-Bell 212ASW	6	Anti-ship Helicopter	B	Italy					
ISRAEL									
IAI 1124 Sea Scan	3	F/W Coastal Patrol	C	Israel	at S/L 471 knots			7 hrs 30 min	22 850 lb (10 364 kg)
ITALY									
Agusta-Sikorsky SH-3D	33	A/S Helicopter	B	USA (built in Italy)					
Agusta-Bell 204AS	32	A/S Helicopter	B	Italy	at S/L 104 knots	4 500 ft (1 370 m)	340 n. miles		9 500 lb (4 310 kg)
Agusta-Bell 212ASW	84 ordered	A/S Helicopter	B	Italy	at S/L 106 knots		360 n. miles	5 hrs	11 176 lb (5 070 kg)
Breguet Br 1150 Atlantic	18	F/W Long-Range Maritime Patrol	C	France	Operated by Air Force				
Piaggio P.166S Albatross		F/W Coastal Patrol	C	Italy	9 500 ft (2 900 m) 193 knots	25 500 ft (7 770 m)			8 115 lb (3 680 kg)
JAPAN									
Sikorsky Sea King (SH-3A)	61	A/S Helicopter	B	USA (built in Japan)					
Kawasaki-Boeing KV 107/II-3	7	Mine Countermeasures Helicopter	B	Japan USA					
Grumman Tracker (S-2A)	24	F/W A/S	C	USA					
Kawasaki-Lockheed P-2J	82	F/W A/S and Maritime Patrol Bomber	C	Japan	Max cruising 217 knots	30 000 ft (9 150 m)	with max fuel 2 400 n. miles		75 000 lb (34 019 kg)
Lockheed Neptune (P-2H)	19	F/W A/S and Maritime Patrol Bomber	C	USA					
Shin Meiwa PS-1	22	F/W A/S Flying-Boat	C	Japan	Max level at 5 000 ft (1 525 m) 295 knots	29 500 ft (9 000 m)	1 169 n. miles	15 hrs	94 800 lb (43 000 kg)
MEXICO									
Grumman Albatross (HU-16A)	12	F/W Search and Rescue Amphibian	C	USA					
Aerospatiale Alouette III	2	Helicopter	B	France					
NETHERLANDS									
Westland Wasp (HAS Mk 1)	11	Helicopter	B	UK					
Westland Lynx (SH-14B/C)	24	A/S Helicopter	B	UK/France	First six (UH-14A) used for Search and Rescue				
Breguet Br 1150 Atlantic	8	F/W A/S	C	France					
Lockheed Neptune (SP-2H)	13	F/W Maritime Patrol	C	USA					
Fokker-VFW F.27MPA		F/W Maritime Patrol	C	Netherlands	230 knots (cruising)	23 200 ft (7 070 m)	2 400 n. miles		45 000 lb (20 410 kg)
NEW ZEALAND									
Westland Wasp (HAS Mk 1)	2	A/S Helicopter	B	UK					
Lockheed Orion (P-3B)	5	F/W Maritime Patrol	C	USA	Operated by RNZAF				
NORWAY									
Westland Sea King (Mk 43)	10	Search and Rescue Helicopter	B	UK	Operated by Norwegian Air Force				
Westland Lynx	4	A/S Helicopter	B	UK/France					
Lockheed Orion (P-3B)	5	F/W Maritime Patrol	C	USA	Operated by Norwegian Air Force				

NAVAL EQUIPMENT / Aircraft

Wing span Rotor diameter	Length	Height	Power Plant	Armament Capacity	Remarks
44 ft 9·5 in (13·65 m)		15 ft 9·5 in (4·81 m)	Two Garrett-AiResearch TFE 731 turbofans	Equipment includes search radar, flare dispensers	
48 ft (14·63 m)	57 ft (17·37 m)		1 × 1 290 shp General Electric T58-GE-3 turboshaft	2 × Mk 44 torpedoes, dipping sonar	
48 ft (14·63 m)	57 ft 1 in (17·40 m)	14 ft 5 in (4·40 m)	1 × 1 875 shp Pratt & Whitney (Canada) PT6T-6 Turbo Twin Pac twin turboshaft	2 × Mk 44 or Mk 46 torpedoes, depth charges, missiles, dipping sonar	
46 ft 9 in (14·25 m)	38 ft 1 in (11·60 m)	16 ft 5 in (5·00 m)	Two 340 hp Lycoming GSO-480-B1C6 piston engines		Used by South African Air Force (not by Italy)
97 ft 8·5 in (29·78 m)	95 ft 10·75 in (29·23 m)	29 ft 3·5 in (8·93 m)	Two General Electric T64-IHI-10E turboprop engines and two pod-mounted J3-IHI-7D turbojets	Classified; equipment includes radar, smoke detector and MAD	
108 ft 9 in (33·15 m)	109 ft 9·25 in (33·46 m)	32 ft 2·75 in (9·82 m)	Four Ishikawajima-built General Electric T64-IHI-10 turboprop engines each 3 060 ehp	Torpedoes, air-to-surface rockets, bombs, radar, MAD, sonobuoys	Also 4 US-1 search and rescue amphibians
95 ft 2 in (29·00 m)	77 ft 3·5 in (23·56 m)	27 ft 11 in (8·50 m)	Two 2 140 shp Rolls-Royce Dart 532-7R turboprop engines	Normally unarmed. Equipment includes underfuselage radome	Used by Peruvian Navy, Spanish Navy (not by Netherlands)

NAVAL EQUIPMENT / Aircraft

Country/ Manufacturer	Strength	Role	Class (See note)	Country of Origin	Max Speed	Service Ceiling	Range	Max Endurance	T/O Weight
PAKISTAN									
Breguet Br 1150 Atlantic	3	F/W A/S	C	France	Operated by Pakistan Air Force				
Westland Sea King (Mk 45)	6	A/S Helicopter	B	UK					
Grumman Albatross (HU-16A)	2	F/W Maritime Patrol Amphibian	C	USA	Operated by Pakistan Air Force				
PERU									
Grumman Tracker (S-2E)	9	F/W A/S	C	USA					
Agusta-Bell 212ASW	6	A/S Helicopter	B	Italy					
Bell UH-1D/H	6	Helicopter	B	USA					
Bell JetRanger	10	Helicopter	B	USA					
Aerospatiale Alouette III	2	Helicopter	B	France					
Grumman Albatross (HU-16B)	4	F/W Maritime Patrol Amphibian	C	USA	Operated by Peruvian Air Force				
Fokker-VFW F.27MPA	2	F/W Maritime Patrol	C	Netherlands					
POLAND									
Ilyushin Il-28 ("Beagle")	8	F/W Recce and ECM	C	USSR					
PORTUGAL									
Lockheed Neptune (SP-2E)	4	F/W Long-range Maritime Patrol	C	USA	Operated by Portuguese Air Force				
SOUTH AFRICA									
Westland Wasp (HAS Mk 1)	11	A/S Helicopter	B	UK	Embarked in Destroyers: *Jan Van Riebeeck; Simon van der Stel* Embarked in Frigates: *President Kruger; President Pretorius; President Steyn*				
Avro Shackleton MR.3	7	F/W Long-range Maritime Patrol	C	UK	Operated by SAAF				
Piaggio P.166S Albatross	18	F/W Coastal Patrol	C	Italy					
SPAIN									
Hawker Siddeley Matador (Harrier)	10	F/W V/STOL Strike/Recce	A	UK	Supplied via USA for operation from carrier *Dedalo* (+2 Harrier TAV-8A)				
Agusta-Bell 212ASW	12	A/S Helicopter	B	Italy					
Agusta-Bell 204AS	4	Search and Rescue Helicopter	B	Italy					
Bell AH-1G HueyCobra	6	Armed Helicopter	B	USA					
Sikorsky Sea King (SH-3D)	22	A/S Helicopter	B	USA					
Lockheed Orion (P-3A)	2	F/W Maritime Patrol	C	USA	Operated by Spanish Air Force				
Canadair CL-215	10	Search and Rescue, F/W Amphibian	C	Canada					
Fokker-VFW F.27MPA	3	F/W Search and Rescue	C	Netherlands	Operated by Spanish Air Force				
Grumman Albatross (HU-16B)	8	F/W Maritime Patrol Amphibian	C	USA	Operated by Spanish Air Force				
Hughes 500 M	12	A/S Helicopter	B	USA					
SWEDEN									
Agusta-Bell 206A JetRanger	10	Search and Rescue Helicopter	B	USA					
Boeing Vertol-Kawasaki 107-II	10	A/S and General Duty Helicopter	B	USA Japan					
Saab-Scania SH-37 Viggen	18	F/W Maritime Recce	C	Sweden	Mach 2				
SYRIA									
Kamov Ka-25 ("Hormone")	9	A/S Helicopter	B	USSR					
THAILAND									
Grumman Tracker (S-2F)	10	F/W A/S, Maritime Patrol	C	USA					
Canadair CL-215	2	Search and Rescue, F/W Amphibian	C	Canada					
Grumman Albatross (HU-16B)	2	F/W Search and Rescue Amphibian	C	USA					
TURKEY									
Agusta-Bell 205AS	3	A/S Helicopter	B	Italy					
Agusta-Bell 212ASW	6	A/S Helicopter	B	Italy					
Grumman Tracker (S-2A/E)	20	F/W A/S	C	USA					

Wing span / Rotor diameter	Length	Height	Power Plant	Armament Capacity	Remarks
34 ft 9·25 in (10·60 m)	53 ft 5·75 in (16·30 m)	19 ft 0·25 in (5·80 m)	One Volvo Flygmotor RM8A turbofan	Two air-to-air missiles Provision for attack weapons	Operated by Swedish Air Force

NAVAL EQUIPMENT / Aircraft

Country/Manufacturer	Strength	Role	Class (See note)	Country of Origin	Max Speed	Service Ceiling	Range	Max Endurance	T/O Weight
UNION OF SOVIET SOCIALIST REPUBLICS									
Yakovlev Yak-36 ("Forger-A")	50	F/W VTOL Attack and Reconnaissance	A	USSR	Mach 1·3				22 050 lb (10 000 kg)
Mil Mi-14 ("Haze")	75	A/S Helicopter	C	USSR					26 455 lb (12 000 kg)
Kamov Ka-25 ("Hormone")	300 approx	A/S and missile guidance Helicopter	B	USSR	119 knots	11 500 ft (3 500 m)	350 n. miles		16 100 lb (7 300 kg)
Tupolev Tu-26 ("Backfire")	50	V/G Recce Bomber	C	USSR	approx Mach 2		approx 4 350 n. miles		270 000 lb (122 500 kg)
Tupolev Tu-16 ("Badger")	450	F/W Long-Range Bomber Maritime Recce	C	USSR	at 35 000 ft 510 knots	42 650 ft (13 000 m)	with max bomb load 2 605 n. miles		150 000 lb (68 000 kg)
Tupolev Tu-95 ("Bear")	75	F/W Long-Range Bomber Maritime Recce	C	USSR	Cruising at 32 000 ft 410 knots		with max load 6 775 n. miles		340 000 lb (154 220 kg)
Tupolev Tu-22 ("Blinder")	60	F/W Recce Bomber	C	USSR	at 40 000 ft Mach 1·4	60 000 ft (18 300 m)	1 215 n. miles		185 000 lb (83 900 kg)
Sukhoi Su-17 ("Fitter-C/D")	30	V/G A/S and close support Fighter	C	USSR	Mach 2·17	59 050 ft (18 000 m)	Combat radius 195-340 n. miles		41 887 lb (19 000 kg)
Beriev M-12 ("Mail")	90	F/W A/S Recce Amphibian	C	USSR	329 knots	39 977 ft (12 185 m)	2 160 n. miles		65 035 lb (29 500 kg)
Ilyushin Il-18 ("Coot-A")	10	F/W Maritime Recce, Elint	C	USSR	360 knots				141 100 lb (64 000 kg)
Ilyushin Il-38 ("May")	60	F/W A/S Recce	C	USSR	365 knots	32 800 ft (10,000 m)	3 900 n. miles		
UNITED KINGDOM									
Hawker Siddeley Harrier (AV-8A)		F/W V/STOL Strike and Recce	A	UK	over 640 knots	over 50 000 ft (15 240 m)	over 3 000 n. miles with one flight refuelling		over 25 000 lb (11 339 kg)
Hawker Siddeley Sea Harrier (FRS.1)	34 ordered	F/W V/STOL Strike and Recce	A	UK					
Westland/Aerospatiale Gazelle HT.2	29	Training Helicopter	B	UK France	at S/L 167 knots	16 400 ft (5 000 m)	at S/L with full fuel 361 n. miles		3 970 lb (1 800 kg)
Westland Lynx (HAS.2)	60 ordered	Search and Strike Helicopter	B	UK	145 knots (cruising)		Mission radius 154 n. miles	2 hrs 24 min	9 500 lb (4 309 kg)
Westland Sea King (HAS.1 and HAS.2)	69	A/S Helicopter	B	UK	Normal operating 112 knots	10 000 ft (3 050 m)	664 n. miles with normal fuel		21 000 lb (9 525 kg)
Westland Sea King (HAR.3)	16	Search and Rescue Helicopter	B	UK	cruising speed at S/L 112 knots	10 000 ft (3 050 m)	664 n. miles with normal fuel		21 000 lb (9 525 kg)
Westland Wasp (HAS.1)	80	General Purpose and A/S Helicopter	B	UK	at S/L 104 knots		approx 234 n. miles		5 600 lb (2 495 kg)
Westland Wessex (HAS.1/3 & HU.5)	150	A/S, Assault and General Purpose Helicopter	B	UK	at S/L 115 knots	(HAS.1) 14 000 ft (4 300 m)	Max fuel 10% reserve 415 n. miles		13 500 lb (6 120 kg)
Hawker Siddeley Nimrod (MR.1)	28	F/W Long Range Maritime Recce	C	UK	500 knots	42 000 ft (12 800 m)	Ferry 4 500-5 000 n. miles	12 hrs (typical)	177 500-192 000 lb (80 510-87 090 kg)
Avro Shackleton (MR.3)	(SAAF)	F/W Long Range Maritime Patrol	C	UK	at S/L 152 knots		2 515 n. miles		
Hawker Siddeley (Avro) Shackleton (AEW.2)	11	F/W Airborne Early Warning	C	UK	226 knots			10 hrs	98 000 lb (44 452 kg)

NAVAL EQUIPMENT / Aircraft

Wing span Rotor diameter	Length	Height	Power Plant	Armament Capacity	Remarks
23 ft 0 in (7.00 m)	49 ft 3 in (15.00 m)		One conventional turbojet and two lift-jets	Gun pods and rocket pods	Also a two-seat training version ("Forger-B")
69 ft 10.25 in (21.29 m)			Two 1 500 shp Isotov turboshaft		Similar to Mi-8 transport, but with retractable landing gear, undernose radome, towed MAD, boat hull, etc.
51 ft 8 in (15.75 m)	32 ft 0 in (9.75 m)	17 ft 7.5 in (5.37 m)	Two 900 shp Glushenkov GTD-3 turboshaft	A/S torpedoes, flares, small stores	
*113 ft (34.45 m)	132 ft (40.23 m)	33 ft (10.06 m)	Possibly two Kuznetsov turbofans	Air-to-surface missiles. Two guns in tail mounting	
110 ft (33.5 m)	120 ft (36.5 m)	35 ft 6 in (10.8 m)	Two Mikulin AM-3M turbojets	Up to 7 × 23 mm cannon in dorsal, ventral and tail turrets and nose. 19 800 lb (9 000 kg) of bombs or missiles	Total includes 90 flight refuelling tankers
159 ft (48.5 m)	155 ft 10 in (47.5 m)	39 ft 9 in (12.12 m)	Four 14 795 ehp Kuznetsov NK-12MV turboprops	Bombs, missiles, 2 to 6 × 23 mm cannon	
90 ft 10.5 in (27.70 m)	132 ft 11.5 in (40.53 m)		Two turbojets with afterburners	Cameras. Provision for bombs and missiles	Data for "Blinder-C"
*45 ft 11.25 in (14.00 m)	61 ft 6.25 in (18.75 m)	15 ft 7 in (4.75 m)	One Lyulka AL-21F-3 afterburning turbojet	Two 30 mm cannon. 11 023 lb (5 000 kg) of bombs, rockets, missiles	Data for "Fitter-C". "Fitter-D" has undernose radar
122 ft 8.5 in (37.4 m)	117 ft 9 in (35.9 m)	33 ft 4 in (10.17 m)	Four 4 250 ehp Ivchenko AI-20 turboprops	Equipment includes side-looking radar	
97 ft 6 in (29.70 m)	107 ft 11.25 in (32.90 m)	22 ft 11.5 in (7.00 m)	Two 4 000 shp Ivchenko AI-20D turboprops	Torpedoes, depth charges, sonobuoys, MAD gear, nose radome	
122 ft 8.5 in (37.4 m)	129 ft 10 in (39.6 m)	33 ft 4 in (10.15 m)	Four 4 250 ehp Ivchenko AI-20 turboprops	A/S weapons, MAD gear, undernose radar	

*wings spread

Wing span Rotor diameter	Length	Height	Power Plant	Armament Capacity	Remarks
25 ft 3 in (7.70 m)	45 ft 6 in (13.87 m)	11 ft 4 in (3.45 m)	One Rolls-Royce Pegasus 103 vectored-thrust turbofan engine	Aden gun pods, bombs, rockets, Sidewinder missiles, flares, camera	In service with USMC and Spain (Matador). Total includes 8 TAV-8As
25 ft 3.25 in (7.70 m)	47 ft 7 in (14.50 m)	12 ft 2 in (3.71 m)	One Rolls-Royce Pegasus 104 vectored-thrust turbofan engine	Aden gun pods, bombs, rockets, Sidewinder missiles, air-to-surface missiles, etc	For service from 1979
34 ft 5.75 in (10.50 m)	39 ft 3.25 in (11.97 m)	10 ft 2.25 in (3.15 m)	One 590 shp Turbomeca Astazou IIIA turboshaft engine		
42 ft (12.80 m)	49 ft 9 in (15.16 m)	11 ft 9.75 in (3.60 m)	Two 900 shp Rolls-Royce BS 360.07.26 Gem turboshaft engines	Two Mk 44 or Mk 46 homing torpedoes, depth charges or missiles	
62 ft 0 in (18.90 m)	72 ft 8 in (22.15 m)	16 ft 10 in (5.13 m)	Two 1 660 shp Rolls-Royce Gnome H 1400-1 turboshaft engines	Dipping sonar type 195 system, radar, smoke floats, AD580 doppler navigation, torpedoes, depth charges, machine gun	Data for current Mk 2 version.
62 ft 0 in (18.90 m)	72 ft 8 in (22.15 m)	16 ft 10 in (5.13 m)	Two 1 660 shp Rolls-Royce Gnome H 1400-1 turboshaft engines		
32 ft 3 in (9.83 m)	40 ft 4 in (12.29 m)	11 ft 8 in (3.56 m)	One Rolls-Royce Bristol Nimbus 503 turboshaft engine, derated to 710 shp	Two Mk 44 homing torpedoes or other stores	
56 ft 0 in (17.07 m)	65 ft 9 in (20.03 m)	16 ft 2 in (4.93 m)	One Rolls-Royce Bristol Gnome 112 and one Gnome 113 turboshaft engines, each 1 350 shp	Up to 13 troops or 7 stretchers A/S version (HAS.1) can carry weapons	
114 ft 10 in (35.3 m)	126 ft 9 in (38.63 m)	29 ft 8.5 in (9.08 m)	Four Rolls-Royce RB168 Spey Mk 250 turbofan engines	Bombs, mines, depth charges, MAD, full range ASW detection equipment	Operated by RAF. Being uprated to MR.2
119 ft 10 in (36.52 m)	87 ft 4 in (26.52 m)	23 ft 4 in (7.11 m)	Four Rolls-Royce Griffon 57A piston engines, 2 455 hp each		Operated by SAAF
119 ft 10 in (36.52 m)	92 ft 6 in (28.19 m)	23 ft 4 in (7.11 m)	Four Rolls-Royce Griffon 67 piston engines, 2 450 hp each	Early warning electronics	Operated by RAF

NAVAL EQUIPMENT / Aircraft

Country/Manufacturer	Strength	Role	Class (See note)	Country of Origin	Max Speed	Service Ceiling	Range	Max Endurance	T/O Weight
UNITED STATES OF AMERICA									
Rockwell International Bronco OV-10A	114 built	F/W Multi-purpose Counter Insurgency	C	USA	at S/L W/O Weapons 244 knots		Ferry with aux. fuel 1 240 n. miles	Combat radius with max weapon load 198 n. miles	14 466 lb (6 563 kg)
Vought A-7E Corsair II	950 built	F/W Attack Aircraft	A	USA	at S/L 600 knots		Ferry 2 800 n. miles		42 000 lb (19 050 kg)
RF-8G Crusader	40	F/W Recce	A	USA	870 knots				34 000 lb (15 420 kg)
Grumman C-2A Greyhound	25	F/W COD Transport	A	USA	at 11 000 ft (3 450 m) 306 knots		at cruising speed and height 1 432 n. miles		54 830 lb (24 870 kg)
Grumman Hawkeye E-2B/C	94	F/W Airborne Early Warning	A	USA	325 knots	30 800 ft (9 390 m)	Ferry 1 394 n. miles		51 569 lb (23 391 kg)
Grumman A-6E Intruder	Total 546 built	F/W Strike and Recce	A	USA	at S/L 563 knots	47 500 ft (14 480 m)	2 365 n. miles		60 400 lb (27 400 kg)
McDonnell Douglas F-4B Phantom II	Total built 1 264	F/W All Weather Fighter	A	USA	Mach 2·5	54 400 ft (16 580 m)	Ferry 1 718 n. miles		54 600 lb (24 765 kg)
McDonnell Douglas A-4M Skyhawk	500	F/W Attack Bomber	A	USA	with 4 000 lb of bombs 561 knots		Ferry 1 740 n. miles		24 500 lb (11 113 kg)
McDonnell Douglas EA-3B Skywarrior	60	F/W Electronic Countermeasures	A	USA	at 10 000 ft (3 050 m) 530 knots	45 000 ft (13 780 m)	Normal 2 520 n. miles		73 000 lb (33 112 kg)
Grumman F-14A Tomcat	390 ordered	F/W All Weather Fighter	A	USA	Mach 2·40	over 56 000 ft (17 070 m)			74 348 lb (33 724 kg)
Grumman S-2E Tracker	180	F/W A/S	A	USA	at S/L 230 knots	21 000 ft (6 400 m)	Ferry 1 128 n. miles	Max endurance 9 hrs	29 150 lb (13 222 kg)
Lockheed S-3A Viking	187 built	F/W A/S	A	USA	450 knots	over 35 000 ft (10 670 m)	Ferry 3 000 n. miles+		42 500 lb (19 277 kg)
Rockwell International RA-5C Vigilante	25	F/W Tactical Recce	A	USA	Mach 2·1	64 000 ft (19 500 m)	2 600 n. miles		66 800 lb (30 300 kg)
Sikorsky SH-34 Seabat/Seahorse (S-58)		A/S and General Purpose Helicopter	B	USA	at S/L 107 knots	9 000 ft (2 740 m)	214 n. miles +10% reserve		14 000 lb (6 350 kg)
Bell AH-1J Sea Cobra	Total 101	Close Support Helicopter	B	USA	180 knots	10 550 ft (3 215 m)	310 n. miles		10 000 lb (4 535 kg)
Sikorsky SH-3A/D/G Sea King	325	A/S and Transport Helicopter	B	USA	144 knots	14 700 ft (4 480 m)	542 n. miles 10% reserve		18 626 lb (8 450 kg)
Boeing Vertol UH-46D Sea Knight	450 built	Transport and Utility Helicopter	B	USA	144 knots	14 000 ft (4 265 m)	approx 198 n. miles		Max 23 000 lb (10 433 kg)
Kaman SH-2F Seasprite	100	A/S Helicopter	B	USA	at S/L 143 knots	22 500 ft (6 860 m)	367 n. miles		12 800 lb (5 805 kg)
Sikorsky CH-53A/D Sea Stallion	275	Assault Transport Helicopter	B	USA	170 knots	21 000 ft (6 400 m)	223 n. miles		42 000 lb (19 050 kg)
Sikorsky RH-53D	30	Mine Countermeasures Helicopter	B	USA				over 4 hr	50 000 lb (22 680 kg)
Bell UH-1E	190	Assault Support Helicopter	B	USA	140 knots	21 000 ft (6 400 m)	248 n. miles		9 500 lb (4 309 kg)
Hawker Siddeley AV-8A Harrier	80	F/W V/STOL Strike/Recce	A	UK					
Grumman EA-6A/B Prowler	104	F/W ECM/Elint	A	USA	566 knots at S/L	44 500 ft (13 565 m)	955 n. miles with max load		65 000 lb (26 535 kg)
Lockheed C-130 Hercules	117	F/W Transport and Recce and Tanker	C	USA	335 knots	33 000 ft (10 060 m)	4 460 n. miles		155 000 lb (70 310 kg)
Lockheed SP-2H Neptune		F/W Long Range Maritime Patrol	C	USA	at 10 000 ft (3 050 m) 350 knots	22 000 ft (6 700 m)	3 200 n. miles		79 895 lb (36 240 kg)
Lockheed P-3A/B/C and EP-3E Orion	400	F/W A/S Recce	C	USA	at 15 000 ft (4 570 m) 411 knots	28 300 ft (8 625 m)	Mission radius 2 070 n. miles		142 000 lb (64 410 kg)
URUGUAY									
Bell 47G-2	2	Helicopter	B	USA					
Sikorsky SH-34J	2	A/S and Search and Rescue Helicopter	B	USA					
Grumman Tracker (S-2A)	3	F/W A/S Patrol	C	USA					
VENEZUELA									
Agusta-Bell 212ASW	10	A/S Helicopter	B	Italy					
Bell 47G	4	Helicopter	B	USA					
Grumman Tracker (S-2E)	6	F/W A/S Patrol	C	USA					

NAVAL EQUIPMENT / Aircraft

Wing span / Rotor diameter	Length	Height	Power Plant	Armament Capacity	Remarks
40 ft 0 in (12·19 m)	41 ft 7 in (12·67 m)	15 ft 2 in (4·62 m)	Two 715 ehp Garrett AiResearch T76-G-416/417 turboprops	4 × 0·30 in machine guns, air-to-air missiles, bombs, rockets, etc. Max weapon load 3,600 lb (1,633 kg)	
38 ft 9 in (11·80 m)	46 ft 1·5 in (14·06 m)	16 ft 0·75 in (4·90 m)	One Allison TF41-A-2 turbofan	Air-to-air, air-to-surface missiles, guns, rockets, bombs, drop tanks	Total includes A-7A/B/C
35 ft 8 in (10·87 m)	54 ft 6 in (16·61 m)	15 ft 9 in (4·80 m)	One Pratt & Whitney J57-P-20 turbojet		
80 ft 7 in (24·56 m)	56 ft 8 in (17·27 m)	15 ft 11 in (4·85 m)	Two 4 050 ehp Allison T56-A-8A turboprops	10 000 lb freight	
80 ft 7 in (24·56 m)	57 ft 7 in (17·55 m)	18 ft 4 in (5·59 m)	Two 4 910 ehp Allison T56-A-425 turboprops	Early warning and command electronics	Data for E-2C
53 ft 0 in (16·15 m)	54 ft 9 in (16·69 m)	16 ft 2 in (4·93 m)	Two Pratt & Whitney J52-P-8A turbojets	Bombs, missiles and other stores	Total includes A-6A/B/C
38 ft 5 in (11·70 m)	58 ft 0 in (17·76 m)	16 ft 0 in (4·96 m)	Two General Electric J79-GE-8 turbojets with afterburners	Missiles, bombs, rockets	Also F-4J/N and 50 RF-4Bs
27 ft 6 in (8·38 m)	40 ft 4 in (12·27 m)	15 ft 0 in (4·57 m)	One Pratt & Whitney J52-P-408A turbojet	Cannon, bombs, rockets, missiles	Total includes A-4C/E/F/L
72 ft 6 in (22·07 m)	76 ft 4 in (23·27 m)	22 ft 8 in (6·91 m)	Two Pratt & Whitney J57-P-10 turbojets	Provision for bombs, torpedoes, cannon	Total includes tankers
64 ft 1·5 in (19·54 m) Unswept	61 ft 11·9 in (18·89 m)	16 ft 0 in (4·88 m)	Two Pratt & Whitney TF30-P-412A turbofans with afterburners	Guns, missiles, bombs	
72 ft 7 in (22·13 m)	43 ft 6 in (13·26 m)	16 ft 7 in (5·06 m)	Two 1 525 hp Wright R-1820-82WA piston engines	Depth charges, torpedoes, rockets, sonobuoys	Total includes S-2D/G
68 ft 8 in (20·93 m)	53 ft 4 in (16·26 m)	22 ft 9 in (6·93 m)	Two General Electric TF34-GE-2 turbofan engines	Bombs, depth bombs, rockets, missiles, mines, torpedoes, flares	
53 ft 0 in (16·15 m)	76 ft 7·25 in (23·35 m)	19 ft 5 in (5·92 m)	Two General Electric J79-GE-10 turbojets	Variety of weapons inc. thermonuclear bombs	
56 ft 0 in (17·07 m)	56 ft 8·25 in (17·27 m)	15 ft 11 in (4·85 m)	One 1 525 hp Wright R-1820-84B/D piston engine	12 passengers	
44 ft 0 in (13·41 m)	53 ft 4 in (16·26 m)	13 ft 8 in (4·15 m)	One 1 800 shp Pratt & Whitney T400-CP-400 turboshaft	Cannon and rockets	Total includes improved AH-1T
62 ft 0 in (18·90 m)	72 ft 8 in (22·15 m)	16 ft 10 in (5·13 m)	Two 1 400 shp General Electric T58-GE-10 turboshaft	Torpedoes, missiles, total 840 lb (381 kg) of weapons	Data for SH-3D
60 ft 0 in (18·29 m)	Fuselage 51 ft 0 in (15·54 m)	16 ft 8·5 in (5·09 m)	Two 1 400 shp General Electric T58-GE-10 turboshaft	Up to 10 000 lb load	Total includes CH-46s
44 ft 0 in (13·41 m)	52 ft 7 in (16·03 m)	15 ft 6 in (4·72 m)	Two 1 350 shp General Electric T58-GE-8F turboshaft	LAMPS equipment. Details in JAWA	
72 ft 3 in (22·02 m)	88 ft 3 in (26·90 m)	24 ft 11 in (7·60 m)	Two 2 850 shp GE T64-GE-6 turboshaft	37 passengers or 24 stretchers with 4 attendants	Data for CH-53D
72 ft 3 in (22·02 m)			Two 4 380 shp GE T64-GE-415 turboshaft	Two machine-guns	
44 ft 0 in (13·41 m)	53 ft 0 in (16·15 m)	12 ft 7·25 in (3·84 m)	One Lycoming T53-L-11 turboshaft	Machine guns, rockets, 8 passengers or 4 000 lb cargo	Total includes UH-1D/H/L
53 ft 0 in (16·15 m)	59 ft 5 in (18·11 m)		Two Pratt & Whitney J52-P-408 turbojets	Normally unarmed ECM equipment	Data for EA-6B
132 ft 7 in (40·41 m)	97 ft 9 in (29·78 m)	38 ft 3 in (11·66 m)	Four 4 508 ehp Allison T56-A-15 turboprop	Cargo up to 26 640 lb (12 080 kg) 92 troops, 64 paras or 74 stretchers	Data for late-model transport
103 ft 10 in (31·65 m) inc. tip tanks	91 ft 8 in (27·94 m)	29 ft 4 in (8·94 m)	Two 3 500 hp Wright R-3350-32W radial piston + 2 Westinghouse J34 turbojets	8 000 lb (3 630 kg) bombs, torpedoes, depth charges and rockets	
99 ft 8 in (30·37 m)	116 ft 10 in (35·61 m)	33 ft 8·5 in (10·29 m)	Four 4 910 ehp Allison T56-A-14 turboprops	Mines, depth bombs, torpedoes	Data for P-3C. Improved CP-140 Aurora under development for Canada

NAVAL EQUIPMENT / Aircraft — Guns

Country/Manufacturer	Strength	Role	Class (See note)	Country of Origin	Max Speed	Service Ceiling	Range	Max Endurance	T/O Weight
YUGOSLAVIA									
Kamov									
Ka-25 ("Hormone")		A/S Helicopter	B	USSR					
Mil									
Mi-8 ("Hip")		Coastal Patrol Helicopter	B	USSR					

GUNS

Calibre mm (inch)	Length in Calibres	Country and Year Introduced	No. of Barrels Mk. of Mtg.	Elevation Degrees	Rate of Fire per Barrel (Rounds per Minute)	Weight of Shell kg (Explosive Charge)	Range km (Surface/Height)	Range km AA Slant	Associated Radar/Director
HEAVY									
406 (16)	50	US Navy, 1936	Triple	45	2	1 225 AP 862 HC	39		Mk 34 Fire Control Director
203 (8)	55	US Navy, 1971	Single Mk 71	—5, +65, 20/sec	10-12 rpm	118 max	Estimated over 55		Mk 68 fire control system on destroyer *Hull*
203 (8)	55	US Navy, 1927, 1944	3 Mk 15 Mk 16	30 41	5 10 cased	125	23 28		Mk 34 fire control director with Mk 13 radar
152 (6)	53	Bofors, Sweden 1942	Triple and twin	70 60	10-15	46	18/10 26 max		
152 (6)	50	Vickers, UK 1951	Twin Mk 26	80	20	59	23		MRS-3 F.C.S.
152 (6)	50	Vickers, UK, 1934	Triple Mk 23	45	8	50	23 max		
152 (6)	50	Vickers, UK	Twin Mk 21	60	8	45	23 max		
152 (6)	47	US Navy, 1933	Triple Mk 16		10	47	23 max		Mk 33 F.C.S. Mk 34 Director
150 (5·9)	50	USSR, 1938	Triple Semi-auto	50	4/10	50	27 max		26 foot range finder (built-in)
MEDIUM									
133 (5·25)	50	UK, (1939)	Twin Mk 1	70	12	36	21	13 ceiling	
130 (5·1)	60	USSR, 1953	Twin Auto	70	15	27	17/8 28/13 max		
130 (5·1)	50	USSR, 1936	Twin semi-auto single	40	10	27	24 max 15 opt		
130 (5·1)	58	USSR	Twin semi-auto Dual purpose	50	15	27	28 max 18 opt	13 max	Sun Visor, Egg Cup and Wasp Head
127 (5)	54	US Navy, 1969	Single Mk 45	+65— −15	20	32			Mk 86 F.C.3 with AN/SPG-60 radar
127 (5)	54	OTO Melara, 1968	Single	85	45	32	15/7		
127 (5)	54	US Navy, 1953	Single Mk 42	+85— −15	40	46	24/14 max		Mk 68 Director with AN/SPG-53 radar
127 (5)	54	France, 1948	Twin semi-auto	80	18	32	18/9 22/13 max		
127 (5)	54	US Navy, 1944	Single Mk 39	80	15	32	12/8 22/13 max		
127 (5)	38	US Navy, 1935	Single Mk 30 Twin Mk 38	80	15	37	13/8 17/11		
127 (5)	50	US Navy, 1923	Single		8	27			
120 (4·7)	50	Bofors, Sweden, 1950	Twin	85	42	24	13/7 20/12 max		Dutch fire control Director L.A.-01. See note
120 (4·7)	50	San Carlos, Spain, 1950	Twin NG-53	80	15	25	18/11		
120 (4·7)	50	Bofors, Sweden, 1934	Single	70	12	24	20 max		
120 (4·7)	45	Vickers, UK, 1931	Single	40	12	23	18		
120 (4·7)	50	Ansaldo, Italy, 1926	Twin			23			
120 (4·7)	46	Bofors, Sweden, 1967	Single	80	80	21 (3·2)	12/8 19/12		
120 (4·7)	45	Bofors, Sweden, 1945	Twin	80	20	24	19/13		
114 (4·5)	55	Vickers, UK, 1971	Single Mk 8	+55- −10	25	21	22		

Wing span / Rotor diameter	Length	Height	Power Plant	Armament Capacity	Remarks

Remarks

US Navy Reserve Battleships of "Iowa" class.

MCLWG (Major Calibre Lightweight Gun) at present only in destroyer *Hull* for trials. Destined for "Spruance" class if accepted. Intended for surface fire. Digital Mk 86 GFCS in new constructions.

Mk 15 manually operated fitted to *Saint Paul* and *Canberra*. Mk 16 automatically operated on US cruisers of "Salem" class.

Fitted in cruisers *A. Grau* (Peru) and *A. Latorre* (Chile). *A. Latorre* has the only existing triple mount. Single Bofors 152 mm open shielded mountings in Swedish minelayer *Alvsnabben* are believed to belong to the same general type.

Only on board cruisers HMS *Blake* and *Tiger*. One mounting per ship.

Now only found in British-built cruisers—Indian *Mysore* and Peruvian "Bolognesi" class. Mk 23 gun on Mk 23 mounting.

Only aboard Indian Navy cruiser *Delhi*.

Only aboard US cruiser "Brooklyn" class owned by Argentina (2) and Chile (1).

Independent-elevating barrels often referred as L.57 long. On "Chapaiev" and "Sverdlov" classes of Soviet cruisers.

Dual purpose mounting exists only aboard British built cruiser *Babur* (Pakistan).

"Kotlin" class and variants (USSR and Polish "Warszawa"). Sometimes referred to as 58 calibres long × 50.

"Skory" class destroyers (USSR). "Luta" class Chinese Navy. Single only on Ex-Soviet "Gordy" class of Chinese Navy.

"Skory" (Mod) and "Kotlin" classes.

Ordered by US Navy ("Virginia", "California", "Spruance" and "Tarawa" classes) also Iran "Spruances", Mk 65 improvement, proposed for late "Spruance" class.

In use by Canada (four "Iroquois" class destroyers) and Italy (two "Audace" class) ordered for "Lupo" class frigates of Italy, Peru and Venezuela. Probably for Italian "Maestrale" class.

Aboard US carriers, cruisers, destroyers and frigates of post war design. Also in Australia, West Germany, Japan and Spain.

Twin gun using American ammunition only remaining aboard four T53 destroyers ("La Bourdonnais" class).

Aboard US carriers of the original "Midway" class and in Japanese "Akizuki" and "Murasame" classes (five destroyers). Semi-automatic.

Twin Mk-38 aboard US-built destroyers "Gearing" and "Sumner" classes in many navies; Danish, Italian and Spanish built escorts. Single Mk 30 on other wartime escorts; US built in many foreign navies. Cruisers, "Long Beach", "Brooke" and "Garcia" classes of frigates, auxilaries, and a few Spanish and Yugoslav built frigates. Both models employ Mk 12 barrel and usually Mk 37 fire control director, sometimes complemented for Mk 56. In austere installations Mk 52 fire control system, including Mk 51 manual director. Other variants of this widely used wartime gun are Mk 32 in several old US cruisers. Single Mk 24 in "Albany" class cruisers also "Hancock"/"Essex" classes of carriers. Open mountings without shield are used in auxiliaries and known as either Mk-37 or Mk-30 Mod 24, both singles.

Single open mountings used (eight per ship) in US built "Brooklyn" class cruisers remaining in Argentine Navy (2) and Chilean Navy (1).

Dutch fire control director LA-01 aboard destroyers of the "Halland" class. (Sweden 2, Columbia 2) and of the Dutch "Tromp", "Holland" and "Friesland" classes.

Data is estimated. Derived from NG-50. NG-53 is semi-automatic. Only in service in Spanish destroyer *Oquendo*.

Only aboard *Halsingborg* and *Kalmar* frigates of the Royal Swedish Navy.

Manually operated. Surface fire only in "R" class destroyers of the Indian Navy (3). Mk 9 gun on Mk CP-18 mounting.

Believed to be used in the two "Paraguay" class gunboats of Paraguayan Navy.

Turret has a 4 mm shield 51 rounds per minute. Private venture only mounted in the two Finnish "Turunmaa" class escorts. One mounting per ship.

Swedish destroyers of "Öland" and "Östergotland" classes. Semi-automatic light shield. Originally employing Mk-45 fire control.

Developed from the "Abbot" field gun. Aboard British "Amazon", "Bristol" and "Sheffield" classes.

NAVAL EQUIPMENT / Guns

Calibre mm (inch)	Length in Calibres	Country and Year Introduced	No. of Barrels Mk. of Mtg.	Elevation Degrees	Rate of Fire per Barrel (Rounds per Minute)	Weight of Shell kg (Explosive Charge)	Range km (Surface/Height)	Range km AA Slant	Associated Radar/Director
MEDIUM									
114 (4·5)	50	Vickers, UK, 1946	Twin Mk 6	80	11-25	25	13/6 19		
114 (4·5)	45	Vickers, UK, 1942	Twin Mk 4	80	15	25	18		"Battle" class
114 (4·5)	45	Vickers, UK, 1943	Single Mk 5	55		25	17		"Tribal" class
105 (4·1)	50	Bofors, Sweden, 1932	Single						
102 (4)	60	Vickers, UK, 1955	Single	75	40	16	12/8 18/12		
102 (4)	45	Vickers, UK, 1935	Twin Mk 19	80	up to 16	16	19/13		
102 (4)	40	Vickers, UK, 1940	Single Mk 23	60	15	16	9		
100 (3·9)	60	USSR, 1942	Twin	80 or 90	15-20	16	11/8 18/12 max		Sun Visor
100 (3·9)	56	China							
100 (3·9)	55	France 1959	Single, various versions	80	60	13·5	13/7 17/11 max		DRBC 32
100 (3·9)	50	USSR	Twin	80	15	16	20 12	15 000 max 9,000 Slant	Sun Visor
100 (3·9)	50	USSR, 1947	Single	40 or 80	15	13·5	18/11 16/6	6,000	Sun Visor
85 (3·4)	55	USSR, 1943	Single, Twin	70 or 75	10-20	9·5	9/6 14/9	6,000	
76 (3)	70	Vickers, UK, 1951	Twin Mk 6	80 or 90	90	7	17		
76 (3)	62	OTO Melara, Italy, 1964	Single	85	85	6	8/5 16/12 max		
76 (3)	62	OTO Melara, Italy, 1961	Single	85	60	6	8/5 16/12 max		
76 (3)	60	USSR, 1961	Twin	85	60	6	15/10		
76 (3)	50	Bofors, Sweden, 1965	Single	30	30	5·9 (0·6)	7·5/— 13/— max	6 000	
76 (3)	50	US Navy, 1944	See Note	85	45 or 50	6	7/5·5 13/8		
76 (3)	50	US Navy, 1936	Single Mks 21-22 & 26	85	20 or 33	6	12/9		Mk 52
LIGHT									
57 (2·2)	80	USSR, about 1965	Twin	85	120	2·7	5/1 12/5 max		Muff Cobb
57 (2·2)	70	USSR, 1959	Single, Twin, Quad	85	120	2·8	—/4 9/6 max	6 000	Hawk Screech
57 (2·2)	70	Bofors, Sweden, 1971	Single	75	200	2·4 (0·4)	14/—		Dutch M-20 series
57 (2·2)	60	Bofors, Sweden, 1950	Twin	90	120-130	2·6	—/5 14/9		
45 (1·8)	85	USSR, 1953	Quad	90	160-220	1·5	—/4 9/6 max	7 000	Hawk Screech
40 (1·6)	70	Bofors, Sweden, 1946	Single 2·4-3·3 Also Twin	80-90	240-300	2·4	4/— 13/9		
40 (1·6)	60	Bofors, Sweden, 1942	Various	80	120-160	0·89	—12·7 10/4·5 max		
37 (1·5)	80	Krupp, Germany, 1932	Single	85	80	0·745	4/3		
37 (1·5)	63	USSR, 1944	Twin	80	130	0·7	8/5 max	3 000	Eye Shooting
37 (1·5)	63	USSR, 1944	Single	80	130	0·7	8/5 max	3 000	Eye Shooting
35 (1·5)	90	Oerlikon, Switzerland, 1972	Twin	85	550	1·55	6/5 max		
30 (1·2)	75	Oerlikon, Switzerland, 1974	Twin	80-85	650	1 0·36	3 10·2 max		

NAVAL EQUIPMENT / Guns 803

Remarks

...emi-automatic aboard escorts of Australia (where it was locally built under licence) Brazil, Chile, India, Iran, Netherlands, New Zealand, Peru, South Africa and UK navies.

...is assumed that closed twin turrets in "Battle" class destroyers of Iran and Pakistan navies and Venezuelan "Aragua" class use the same gun but are semi-automatic.

...tted to British "Tribal" class, Pakistan "C" class and Malaysian frigate *Rahmat*; open turret hand loaded.

...wo Argentine "King" class frigates. Three guns per ship. Hand loaded. Open shield.

...sed exclusively aboard two "Almirante Williams" class destroyers of Chilean Navy. Closed turrets. Four mountings per ship.

...hese performance figures belong to the pre-war 2·1 ton 4 in barrel made by Vickers. The twin Mk 19 can be found in the navies of Ecuador, Egypt, India, Malaysia, Nigeria, Pakistan, Peru and South ...frica. Fitted in ex-British frigates of Burma, Dominican Republic, Egypt, India and Thailand.

...short barrelled ex-submarine type mounting, serves in "Vosper Mk 1" class corvettes owned by Libya and Ghana. Sometimes referred to as the 102 or 100 mm are the twin guns of the ...talian-made frigates owned by Venezuela ("A. Clemente" class) and Indonesia ("Surapati" type).

...nly in Russian cruisers ("Sverdlov" and "Chapaev" class) and "Kotlin" class destroyers. The gunnery of the Chinese "Kiangtung" class could be considered as a local development. Each turret ...ses its own Egg Cup radar. Fire control is managed with Sun Visor radars.

...nown to exist in Chinese "Kiang-Nan" class. Probably the same as those aboard North Korean frigates of "Najin" class and corvettes of the "Sariwan" and "Tral" classes. The last being Russian ...uilt. The guns are thought to be a Chinese refit of a Soviet weapon, possibly the 100/50 1947 model.

...wo versions: *Modèle 1953* with analogue fire control and *Modèle 68* associated with digital fire control. Integrating DRBC 32 radar. Aboard two ("Clémenceau") carriers, one "Colbert" cruiser, two "Suffren" frigates, *Jeanne d'Arc* and escorts of the "C 65", "C 70", "A 69", "F 67", "T 47", "ASW", "T 53 ASW", "T 56" and "Commandant Rivière" classes. Total of 36 ships including those under ...onstruction in French Navy. Also fitted in Belgian "E 71" class (4); Federal Germany ("Hamburg", "Köln" and "Rhein" classes and *Deutschland,* Portugal ("C. João Belo" and "João Coutinho" ...lasses); Tunisia; South Africa (A69 class new Avisos); and Turkish ("Rhein") class. The newest 1976 turret, which is lighter than its predecessors is claimed to reach 90 rounds per minute.

"Sverdlov" and "Chapaev" classes.

"Riga", "Kola", "Don" and "Purga" class ships of Soviet Navy. Semi-automatic.

Twin mounts in "Skory" class. Single mounts in "Kronshtadt" class. New enclosed mounting, single, on "Krivak" class ships built since 1976.

Fully automatic aboard Canadian frigates and HMS *Blake* and *Tiger* cruisers.

Ordered by Argentina, Denmark, Federal Germany, Iran, Israel, Italy, Libya, Morocco, Netherlands, Nigeria, Oman, Spain, Turkey, Venezuela and USA. The USA has standardised the weapon as the Mk 75 to start its employment in "Pegasus" and "WMEC-630" classes; a variety of fire control systems is used, notably the Dutch M.20 series.

Aboard Italian Navy ships "V Veneto," "A. Doria," "Impavido," "Alpino," "Bergamini," "Centauro" and "De Cristofaro" classes. Sometimes referred to as Brescia model. Also in use on ships of Greek and Ecuadorian Navies.

"Kiev", "Kara", "Kynda", "Krivak", "Kashin", converted "Kildin", "Mirka", and "Petya" classes.

Surface fire only. Used aboard fast attack craft of Norwegian "Storm" class (20) and Singapore "Type B" Vosper class (3).

Most usual versions are single Mk 34 single mount (weight 7·7 tons). Mk 27 and Mk 33 twin mounts (weight 14·5 tons). In both open and semi-protected versions, the last using a fibre-glass shield. Aboard US-built cruisers, destroyers, frigates and auxiliaries. Extensively used in foreign navies and foreign-built ships; notably Japan. Built under licence (Mk 34) in Spain. Mk 56 and Mk 63 gunfire control systems usually employed.

Semi-automatic; intended for surface fire only; widely used in many obsolete ships of US Navy (auxiliary, amphibious) and abroad including wartime-built escort destroyers. Also Greek "Algerine" class. Many other 76 mm of obsolete types remain in service in small quantities. A single 76/40, probably OTO Melara-built, is used aboard Italian built corvettes ("Albatross" class) owned by Denmark (4) and Indonesia (2). Also a 76/40, probably Vickers' 1914 model is used by the Paraguayan Navy on its "Humaita" and "C. Cabral" classes. These have single mounts. Another 76 mm tank turret 76/41·2 is used by Soviet river patrol launches of "Shmel" and "PB" classes. "Trad" and "Bangrachan" classes of Thai Navy probably use Japanese wartime guns of 76 or 75 mm by 40 or 50 calibres long.

Soviet Navy "Moskva", "Kresta I" and "Kresta II", "Grisha I" and "Grisha II", "Nanuchka", "Poti", "Turya" and "T 58" classes. Amphibious and auxiliary ships sometimes referred to as 73 calibres long. Water-cooled.

Only twin mod. has muzzle brake. This and quadruple are aboard Soviet "Kildin", "Kanin" and "Kotlin" classes. Singles are aboard Soviet "Skory" (modified) destroyers and various classes of minesweepers. Also East Germany's amphibious ships. A single Chinese 57 mm gun is used in "Shanghai II" class fast attack craft (including some transferred to Albania) and the new "Luta" class.

Plastic-enclosed turret used by navies of Denmark *(Willemoes)* Malaysia *(Perdana)*; Singapore ("Sea" class); Sweden ("Visby", class frigates and 38 fast attack craft); Thailand's "Prabarapak" class. Single 57 mm guns in Sweden's "Alvsnabben" class are of unidentified model—they have very long barrels.

Current Swedish original turret for this gun weighs 20-24 tons and is aboard Peruvian "A Grau" class and Chilean *A Latorre* Sweden's "Halland" class destroyers use French turret weighing 15 tons with only 80 degree elevation. Also fitted to French cruiser *Colbert* and escorts of the T47, T53, E50 and E52 classes. Open, unprotected, small and obsolete single 57 mm mountings are operated in five patrol vessels of Icelandic Navy. A similar weapon of 47 mm calibre is aboard its sixth fishery protection vessel. Peruvian "Loreto" class (2 ships) also use a similar 47 mm gun but might be of the American 30 calibre long model.

"Kildin" and "Kotlin" classes. Semi-automatic.

The original 1946 model has appeared in a very wide range of variations built in many western countries. Usually 1958 versions: SP-48 type built in Spain, British Mk 7 and Italian Breda improvements. (106 twin and 107 single) with 32 ready use rounds per barrel; Twin type 64 (200 ready use rounds/barrel) and type 350P/564 single (144 ready use rounds). Latest improvement is Breda Compatto twin 40/70 using either 736 ready use rounds or 444 ru rounds. Ordered for Italy, Peru and Venezuela ("Lupo" class) and Libya. This weapon uses "Dardo" system. Non-Italian models use 20 ready use rounds.

Many local versions have been manufactured from the original system. Most common are the American (twin Mk 1 and quad Mk 2 water-cooled mountings, single Mk 3 air-cooled.) Other variants are the British twin Mk 5 weighing 3 tons and a French single.

Single mounting built in Spain around 1950. Derived from standard German twin mounting. Remaining examples aboard seven Spanish patrol and auxiliary ships. Semi-automatic.

"Sverdlov", "Chapaev", "Skory (modified)" and "Riga" classes. Twin Chinese mountings in "Whampoa", "Shantung" and "Shanghai", "Swatow" classes.

"Kronshtadt", "T301" class. Minesweepers use new enclosed version turret called 70-K.

The original weapon (GDM-A) is only found in Greek "Navsithoi" class fast attack craft, Iranian "Saam" class Libyan *Dat Assawari*, Turkish "Dogan" class and Ecuadorean Lurssen craft. Also possibly in two Japanese "Improved Haruna" class. An Italian mounting variant (Oerlikon OTO) was proposed for Peruvian "Lupo" and Libyan 550 ton corvettes. Probably abandoned in favour of twin Breda 40/70 KDC barrel weighing 120 kg. Has 112 ready use rounds per barrel.

GMC-A muzzle braked barrel KCB, HEX, HS 8, 31SLH. Manufactured in UK and in service. In Abu Dhabi patrol craft and Indonesian "Surapati" class frigates. American Emerlec Mk 74 twin mounting (950 ready use rounds) was first embarked in South Korean "Gireogi" coastal patrol craft. Now also used on Greek FPBs.

NAVAL EQUIPMENT / Guns — Missiles

Calibre mm (inch)	Length in Calibres	Country and Year Introduced	No. of Barrels Mk. of Mtg.	Elevation Degrees	Rate of Fire per Barrel (Rounds per Minute)	Weight of Shell kg (Explosive Charge)	Range km (Surface/Height)	Range km AA Slant	Associated Radar/Director
LIGHT									
30 (1·2)	70	Hispano Suiza, France, 1962	Single	·83	600	0·42	2·8 8·5 max		
30 (1·2)	65	USSR, 1960	Twin	80 or 85	500		2·5 4 max		Drum Tilt
20 (0·8)	70	Oerlikon, Switzerland, 1938	Twin	85	465	0·12	5	1 000	

MISSILES

Further details can be found in the current edition of JANE'S WEAPON SYSTEMS
Note: Maximum range given can be up to twice the optimum range.

Country/ Manufacturer	Classification	Name	No.	Length ft	Launch weight lb	Power plant	Guidance	Max Range n. miles	Mach speed	Warhead	Remarks
AUSTRALIA											
Dept of Productivity	A/S	Ikara	—	11·3		Solid fuel rocket	Command link	13	—	Torpedo-HE	Acoustic homing torpedo. Digital control system in RAN. In RN version computer service from ADAS. Branik system in Brazilian "Niteroi" class linked to ships WCS with two Ferranti FM1600B computers.
FRANCE											
Aerospatiale	SLBM	MSBS	M1	34·1	39 683	Solid fuel rocket 2 stage	Inertial	1 350	—	Nuclear 500 KT	In "Le Redoubtable" class SSBN.
	SLBM	MSBS	M2	34·1	44 000	as above	Inertial	1 860	—	Nuclear 500 KT	In production to replace M1.
	SLBM	MSBS	M20	34·1	44 000	as above	Inertial	1 860	—	Thermonuclear 1 MT	First embarked mid-1976.
	SLBM	MSBS	M4	34·1	73 300	as above with 3 stages	Inertial	2 500+	—	Thermonuclear with seven MRV each of 150 KT	Production by late 1970s.
CNIM	SSM	—	RP14	6·5	118	Solid fuel rocket	Nil	9	—	HE	22 rocket multiple launcher.
Matra (with Oto Melara)	SSM	Otomat	—	14·6	1 694	Turbojet	Inertial cruise Active homer	112	0·9	132 lb HE	Sea-skimmer for last 2 miles; can be ASM.
Aerospatiale	SSM	Exocet	MM38	17·1	1 617	2 stage solid fuel rocket	Inertial cruise Active radar homer	26	0·9	363 lb HE	Sea-skimmer throughout flight. Variants — AM 39, air-launched; MM 39, ship-launched version of AM 39; MM 40, improved MM 38 with 40 n. mile range; SM 39, projected submarine launched MM 39.
	SSM	—	SS11	3·9	66	2 stage solid fuel rocket	Wire-guided	2·0	330 knots	HE or torpedo	Same characteristics as AS-11. Harpon is very similar with improved guidance.
	SSM	—	SS12	6·2	165	2 stage solid fuel rocket	Wire-guided	4·4	—	66 lb HE	Same characteristics as AS-12.
Ecan Ruelle	SAM	Masurca	Mk 2	28·2 (with booster)	4 070	2 stage solid fuel rocket	Mod 2 Beam rider. Mod 3. semi active homer	25 (slant)	2·5	105 lb HE	Mounted in *Colbert*, *Suffren* and *Duquesne*.
	SAM	Hirondelle Super 530	—	—	—	—	—	—	—	—	Project for PDMS for small ships and craft.
	SAM	Catulle	—	—	—	—	—	—	—	—	Development. Multi-barrelled rocket system firing salvoes of 40 mm shells.
Matra	SAM	Crotale Navale	R440	9·5	176	Solid fuel rocket	Infra-red/ command	10	0·9 to 1·2	33 lb HE	Being installed in French Navy.
Matra-Hawker Siddeley	ASM	Martel	AS37/ AJ168	13·8 12·8	1 165	Solid fuel rocket	TV on AJ168; passive radar homing on AS37	?30	2 to 0·8	HE	Air-to-surface weapon also in service with RAF.
Aerospatiale	ASM	—	AS20	8·5	315	2 solid fuel rocket	Radio command	4	—	66 lb HE	In service.
	ASM	—	AS30	12·4	1 100	2 stage solid fuel rocket	Radio command	6	1·5	506 lb HE	In service.
Matra	AAM	Magic	R550	9·2	200	Solid fuel rocket	Infra-red	4	—	HE	In service 1975.
	AAM	—	R530	10·8 11·6 (Super)	430	Solid fuel rocket	Infra-red or semi-active radar. EMD electro-magnetic, semi-active in Super 530	9·5	2·7	HE	Proximity fused head. Being replaced by Super 530.
Latecoere	A/S	Malafon Mk 2	—	20·1	3 300	2 stage solid fuel rocket and booster	Radio/acoustic homing	8·1	450 knots	Torpedo	Torpedo dropped by parachute 300 yards from target.
GERMANY (FEDERAL REPUBLIC)											
Messerschmitt-Bölkow-Blöhm	ASW	Kormoran	—	14·4	1 323	3 stage solid fuel rocket	Active or passive radar	20	0·95	350 lb HE	Suitable for all fixed and rotary-wing aircraft.
ISRAEL											
Israel Aircraft Industries	SSM	Gabriel I and II	—	11·0	882 (I) 1 100 (II)	Two stage solid fuel rocket	Active radar or optical	14 (I) 26 (II)	0·7	400 lb HE	Mounted in "Saar" and "Saar IV" classes. Now being exported, eg Singapore, South Africa.

NAVAL EQUIPMENT / Guns — Missiles

Remarks

Mounting (215 ready use rounds) in French "Commandant Rivière" class. "Ouragan" class and single "La Combattante" fast attack craft. Hispano Suiza system is now owned by Oerlikon.

Water cooled. Small enclosed turret used in Soviet ships of "Kanin" some "Kotlin" and "Sverdlov" (CC version) classes. Also some "Rigas", fast attack craft, minesweepers and amphibious craft. In the German "Hai" class and patrol ships is a 30 mm single mounting which was introduced in the new Polish (series 500) landing craft. This might belong to the same system.

Country/Manufacturer	Classification	Name	No.	Length ft	Launch Weight, lb	Powerplant	Guidance	Max Range n. mile	Mach Speed	Warhead	Remarks
ITALY											
Sistel	SSM	Sea Killer I (Nettuno)	—	12·3	375	1 stage solid fuel rocket	Beam rider/radio-command or optical	6+	1·9	77 lb HE	Operational for use in ships or helicopters (Marte). Five round launcher in ships.
	SSM	Sea Killer II (Vulcano)	—	15·4	660	2 stage solid rocket motor	as above	13	1·9	155 lb HE	
	SSM	Sea Killer III	—	17·4	1 200	1 booster 2 sustainers	Active homer	24	1·9	330 lb HE	Under development.
Otomat (with Matra)	SSM	Otomat (see "France")									
Sistel	SAM	Sea Indigo	—	11	266	1 stage solid fuel rocket	Radio command/beam rider	5·5 (slant)	2·5	46 lb HE	Automatic reloading in ships over 500 tons.
	ASM	Airtos	—	12·8	421	1 stage solid fuel rocket	Active radar homing	6	1·5	77 lb HE	All-weather system under development.
NORWAY											
Kongsberg Vaapenfabrikk	SSM	Penguin I and II	—	9·8	726	2 stage solid fuel rocket	Inertial/infra-red homing	14·5 20 (II)	0·7	264 lb HE	Fitted in frigates and fast attack craft.
	A/S	Terne III	—	6·6	298	2 stage solid fuel rocket	Nil	1·5	—	110 lb HE depth charge	Full salvo of six can be fired in 5 seconds. Reload time 40 seconds.
SWEDEN											
Saab-Scania	SSM	—	RB 08A	18·8	1 984	Marboré turbo-jet	Radar homing	?100	0·85	HE	For ship and coast artillery use. Entered service 1967.
Bofors	A/S	—	Type 375	—	550	Rocket	Nil	0·5/1·0/2·2	—	HE	Have three different rocket motors M50 (0·5 m), Erika (1·0 m), Nelli (2·2 m).
UNION OF SOVIET SOCIALIST REPUBLICS											
(NATO designations used—further details at head of USSR section)	SLBM	Sark	SS-N-4	42·5	41 000 app.	2 stage solid fuel rocket	Inertial	370	—	Nuclear megaton	Tested 1955. Operational 1958 Obsolete. Surface launched.
	SLBM	Serb	SS-N-5	42·5	41 000 app.	2 stage solid fuel rocket	Inertial	700	—	Nuclear megaton	Operational 1963. Dived launched.
	SLBM	Sawfly	SS-N-6	31·6	44 000	2 stage liquid fuel rocket	Inertial	1 300 (1 600 Mks II and III)	—	Nuclear Megaton (3 MRV in Mk III)	Operational 1967. "Yankee" class. (Mks II and III in 1974-75).
	SLBM	—	SS-N-8	42·5	45 000	2 stage liquid fuel rocket	Stellar-Inertial	4 200	—	Nuclear Megaton	Operational 1972, "Delta" and "Delta II" class.
	SLBM	—	SS-N-X-13	?32	?	2 stage	Inertial	370	—	Nuclear	Appears to have been unsuccessful. Never operational. Possibly anti-task force.
	SLBM	—	SS-N-17	36·3	?	2 stage solid fuel rocket with Post Boost Vehicle (PBV)	Inertial	2 400	—	Nuclear MRV or MIRV	Now being deployed in "Yankee" class from 1977.
	SLBM	—	SS-N-18	46·3	44 000	2 stage liquid fuel rocket with Post Boost Vehicle (PBV)	Inertial	5 200	—	Nuclear MRV	Sea trials Nov 1976—deployed in "Delta III" class and for "Typhoon" class.
	SSM	Scrubber	SS-N-1	22·5	—		Radar Infra-red homing	130	0·9	—	Operational 1958. Soon obsolete
	SSM	Styx	SS-N-2	15	5 100	2 stage solid fuel rocket	Active radar homing	23	0·9	HE	Operational 1960 SS-N-2 B and C (once designated SS-N-11) now in service.

NAVAL EQUIPMENT / Missiles

Country/ Manufacturer	Classifi- cation	Name	No.	Length ft	Launch Weight, lb	Powerplant	Guidance	Max Range n. mile	Mach Speed	Warhead	Remarks
USSR											
	SSM	Shaddock/Sepal	SS-N-3	36	9 900	2 boosters Turbojet sustainer	Radar head, mid- course guidance Radar or IR homing	150-250	1·5	HE or Nuclear	Operational 1961-62. Surface launch in submarines.
	SLCM	—	SS-N-7	22	—	—	Autopilot radar homing	30	1·5	—	Operational 1969-70. submarine launched from dived.
	SSM	Siren	SS-N-9	30	—	Ramjet	Radar head with mid-course guidance or inertial	150 (with relay)	1·0+	HE or Nuclear	Operational 1968-69. In "Nanuchka" class.
	SSM	—	SS-N-12	—	—	—	? Radar—mid course guidance	250	—	HE or Nuclear	Replacement for Shaddock in both s/ms and surface ships including "Kiev" class.
	SAM	Goa	SA-N-1	22 (booster)	—	2 stage solid fuel rocket	Beam-rider semi-active radar	17 (slant)	2	HE	Operational 1961.
	SAM	Guideline	SA-N-2	34·7	5 000	Solid booster liquid sustainer	Radar	25	3·5	HE (290 lb)	Only in *Dzerzhinsky*.
	SAM	Goblet	SA-N-3	20	1 200	2 stage solid fuel rocket	Rocket/ramjet	20-30	1·5/2·8	HE (90 lb)	Probably similar to SA-6 (Gainful). Operational 1967.
	SAM	—	SA-N-4	10·5?	—	—	Radar-command	8?	2?	HE	Probably PDMS. Operational 1969.
	SAM	—	SA-N-5	4·9	32	Rocket	Optical with IR homing	5·6	?1·5	HE	Seaborne form of SA-7 (Grail) in Light and Amphibious forces.
	SAM	—	SA-N-10	23	—	1 stage rocket	Active radar homing	31	6	?	Operational 1979. Anti-cruise-Missile- missile. Probably used in conjunction with Head Nev C radar. In new "Kara" class and *Provorny*.
	ASM	Kennel	AS-1	29	6 000?	1 Turbojet	Beam-rider with radar homing	55	0·9	HE	Obsolete. Used by Badger aircraft.
	ASM	Kipper	AS-2	33	7 700	1 Turbojet	Autopilot. Radar homing	115	1·0+	HE or Nuclear	Operational 1960. Used by Badger C aircraft.
	ASM	Kangaroo	AS-3	49·2	17 600	1 Turbojet	—	? 350	1·5+	Nuclear	Operational 1961. Used by Bear aircraft.
	ASM	Kitchen	AS-4	37	13 000 ?	1 stage liquid fuel rocket	Inertial guidance, radar homing	145	2+	Nuclear	Operational 1965. Used by Bear, Blinder and Backfire aircraft.
	ASM	Kelt	AS-5	28	—	1 stage liquid fuel rocket	Active radar homing	85	0·9	HE or Nuclear	Operational 1968. Used by Badger C and G aircraft.
	ASM	Kingfish	AS-6	—	11 000	1 stage	Inertial Mid- course active radar homing	120	3	HE or Nuclear	Operational 1970-71. Used by Badger C and Backfire aircraft.
	ASM	Kerry	AS-7	—	260	1 stage solid fuel rocket	Active radar homing	6	1	HE	Used by Forger aircraft.
	ASM	—	AS-9	—	330	1 Turbojet	Passive homing on radar	60		HE	Used by Badger and Backfire aircraft.
	A/S	—	FRAS I	—	—	—	?Pre-programme	15	—	?Nuclear	Operational 1968 in "Moskva" and "Kiev" classes on SUWN-1 mounting. Similar to USN ASROC.
	A/S	—	SSN-14	—	—	—	—	30	—	Torpedo	Operational 1968. Now in "Kresta II", "Kara" and "Krivak" classes and also in place of FRASI (above). Almost certainly has an anti-surface ship capabili- ty.
	A/S	—	SSN-15	—	—	—	—	20	—	?Nuclear	Operational 1974. for use from "Victor II", "Charlie II" and "Tango" class submarines in A/S operations. When fitted with a torpedo in place of war head known as SS-N-16.
UNITED KINGDOM											
	SLBM	Polaris A3 (see USA)	—	—	—	—	—	—	—	UK made 3×200 KT Thermo- nuclear MRV	Carried in "Resolution" class.
Hawker Siddeley	SAM/ SSM	Sea Dart	CF 299	14·3	1 212	Solid fuel booster Liquid ramjet sustainer	Radar guidance (Type 909) semi-active radar homing	25	—	HE	Fitted in *Bristol* and Type 42 destroyers with GWS 30 system.

NAVAL EQUIPMENT / Missiles

Country/ Manufacturer	Classification	Name	No.	Length ft	Launch Weight, lb	Powerplant	Guidance	Max Range n. mile	Mach speed	Warhead	Remarks
UK											
	SAM	Sea Slug Mk 1 and 2	—	19.7	About 4 400	4 solid fuel boosters, solid fuel sustainer	Beam-riding (Type 901)	24(Mk 1) approx	2+	HE Proximity fuse	Surface-to-surface capability. Mk 2 has a longer range and better low-level capability.
British Aircraft Corp	SAM	Sea Wolf	PX 430	6.5	176	Solid fuel rocket	Radio command with TV or radar tracking (Type 910)	—	2+	HE	Entire system GWS 25. (Normally to be used from 6-barrelled launcher). Lightweight version for ships smaller than frigates Sea Wolf VM 40 — under study.
Short Bros and Harland	SAM	Sea Cat	—	4.9	140	2 stage solid fuel rocket	Optical, Radar or TV	2.9		HE	Fitted in many systems GWS 20 (visual) GWS 22 and 24 (Radar). Signaal M40 (Radar). Normally 4-barrelled launcher. 3-barrelled launcher (less than half the weight) in service.
	ASM	Sea Skua	CL 834	9.2	462	Solid fuel rocket	Radar/radio control radar homing	?5	—	45 lb HE	Developed for use from helicopters with Sea Spray radar.
Hawker-Siddeley	AAM	Firestreak	—	10.5	320	Solid fuel rocket	Infra-red homing	4.3	2+	50 lb HE	Being replaced by Red Top (below).
	AAM	Red Top	—	10.8	330	Solid fuel rocket	Infra-red homing	6	3	68 lb HE	A much improved version of Firestreak.
Short Bros and Harland	SAM	Slam (Blow Pipe)	—	4.6	40	2 stage solid fuel rocket	Optical with radio guidance	—	—	4.8 lb HE	Privately developed system. Suitable for submarines or surface ships.
UNITED STATES OF AMERICA											
Lockheed	SLBM	Polaris A3	UGM 27C	32	30 000(3)	2 stage solid fuel rocket	Inertial	2 500	10 at burn-out	Thermonuclear MRV head	See USA and UK sections for fitting policy.
	SLBM	Poseidon (C-3)	UGM 73A	34	65 000	2 stage solid fuel rocket	Inertial	2 500	—	Thermonuclear MIRV head	As above. Double A3 payload.
	SLBM	Trident I (C-4)	UGM 96A	34.1	70 000	3 stage solid fuel rocket	Inertial	4 000 approx		Thermonuclear MIRV and MARV head	To replace Poseidon using same tubes and for "Ohio" class.
	SLBM	Trident II (D-5)	UGM	45.8	126 000	3 stage solid fuel rocket	Inertial	6 000 approx		Thermonuclear	For fitting in "Ohio" class SSBNs.
McDonnell Douglas	SSM/ USM	Harpoon	RGM 84	15 21 (s/m)	1 470 2 355 (s/m)	Solid fuel booster Turbojet sustainer	Pre-programmed Active radar homing	50 60 (s/m)	0.9	HE 500 lb	For general surface-ship fitting. Submarine version under trial.
GDC-Convair	SLCM	Tomahawk	BGM 109	20.5	2 400-2 700	Solid boost-turbofan cruise	TAINS (Strat) Inertial with radar homing (Tact)	1 750 (Strat) 275 (Tact)	475 knots	HE (Tact) Nuclear (Strat)	Under development in both strategic and tactical forms in parallel with ALCM.
	ASM	Harpoon	AGM 84	12.6	1 168	As RGM 84	As RGM 84	120	0.9	HE	
	ASM	Condor	AGM 53	5.5	2 130	1 solid fuel rocket	Radio control TV homing	40-60	1.1	HE or nuclear	For carrier-borne A/C particularly A6. Production planned.
Maxson	ASM	Bullpup A and B	AGM 12B and C	10(A) 13.5(B)	571(A) 1 785(B)	1 liquid fuel rocket	Command	7(A) 10(B)	2	HE 250 lb(A) 1 000 lb(B) or nuclear	Operational 1959.
Texas Instruments Inc	ASM	Harm	AGM 88	13.7	780	1 liquid fuel rocket	—	—	—	—	High-speed anti-radiation missile Development
	ASM	Bulldog	AGM 83	9.8	600	1 liquid fuel rocket	Command	35	—	—	Modified Bullpup.
NASC/NWC	ASM	Shrike	AGM 45	10	390	1 solid fuel rocket	Passive radar homing	8-10	2	HE	Production 1963. Anti-radiation.
Martin, Marietta	ASM	Walleye I and II	AGM 62	11.2 (I) 13.2 (II)	1 100 (I) 2 400 (II)	Nil	TV guided	16 (I) 35 (II)	—	HE or nuclear	Glide bombs.
GDC-Pomona	ASM	Standard ARM	AGM 78	15	1 356	Dual thrust solid fuel rocket	Passive Radar homing	35	2	HE	Production 1968.
GDC-Pomona	SAM	Standard-MR (SM-1)	RIM 66	14.4	1 300	Dual thrust solid fuel rocket	Semi-active radar homing	20+	—	HE	Tartar replacement.
GDC-Pomona	SAM	Standard (SM-2)	RIM 66C					60+			Mid-course guidance for long-range. Talos replacement. Standard-MR (SM-2) with 20+ range for Aegis. Standard-ER (SM-2) (RIM 67B) under development SSM capability. Terrier replacement (ER).
GDC-Pomona	SAM	Standard-ER (SM-1)	RIM 67	26.2	2 900	2 stage solid fuel rocket	Semi-active radar homing	35+	—	HE	
Raytheon	SAM	Seasparrow	RIM 7H	12	500	1 solid fuel rocket	Semi-active radar homing	12(E) 24+(F)	—	HE	Can also be used as UK version. XJ 521. Mk 25 or 29 (NATO) launcher. BPDMS
Bendix	SAM	Talos	RIM 8F, G and H	31.3 (booster)	7 000	Solid fuel booster ram-jet sustainer	Beam rider semi-active radar homing	65+	2.5	HE or nuclear	SSM capability. RIM H has anti-radiation housing. Replacement by RIM 66C.
GDC-Pomona	SAM	Tartar	RIM 24B	15	1 425	Dual thrust solid fuel rocket	Semi-active radar homing	14	2	HE	Ceiling 40 000 ft Replacement by RIM 66.
GDC-Pomona	SAM	Terrier	RIM 2F	26.1 (booster)	3 000	2 stage solid fuel rocket	Semi-active radar homing	20+	2.5	HE	Ceiling 65 000 ft. Operational 1963. Replacement by RIM 67.
NWC-Hughes	AAM	Agile	AIM 95	8	250	Solid fuel	Infra-red	2	—	HE	Planned replacement for Sidewinder.
Hughes	AAM	Phoenix	AIM 54	13	985	1 solid fuel rocket	Radar homing	60+	2+	HE	In use in F14 Operational 1973.
Raytheon/NWC/ Philco Ford	AAM	Sidewinder-1B	AIM 9G, J H and L	9.5	185	1 solid fuel rocket	Infra-red	8	2	HE	Ceiling 50 000 ft+. First AIM9B entered service 1962.
Raytheon	AAM	Sparrow III	AIM 7E and F	12	450(E) 500(F)	1 solid fuel rocket	Semi-active radar homing	9(E) 16(F)	3.5	HE	For carrier-borne aircraft.
Honeywell	A/S	ASROC	RUR 5	15.4	1 000(Mk 44) 570(Mk 46)	1 solid fuel rocket	Pre-programme	1—6	—	Mk 44 or 46 torpedo or Nuclear D/C	Fired from multi-barrelled launcher. Mk 26 in later ships. 10 mile version under development.
Goodyear	A/S or anti-surface-ship	SUBROC	UUM 44	21	4 000	2 stage solid fuel rocket	Pre-programme inertial	25-30	1+	Nuclear	Fired from 21 in torpedo tubes.

RADAR

Country/Number	Type	Transmitter frequency	Transmitter peak power	Range
DENMARK				
20T48 Super/Pilot	Navigation Radar	9 375±30 MHz I Band	20 KW± 1dB Measured at output flange	48 n. miles
FRANCE				
ELI 4	Naval IFF Interrogator	1 030± 0·5 Mcs	Selectable 0·5 or 2 kW	—
ELR 3	IFF Transponder	—	—	—
Triton	C band surface search radar	C Band	250 kW	—
Castor I and II	TRS 3200 fire control radar	I Band	36 kW	—
Pollux	I Band fire control radar	I Band	200 kW	20 m
Pollux II	Improved version of above fire control	Probably I Band	—	—
Calypso II	TRS 1030 Surface search	I/J Band	70 kW	30 km for 10 m² air target
Calypso III	TRS 3100 Surface search	I/J Band	—	35 km for 10 m² air target
Calypso IV	Surface search	I/J Band	—	—
Jupiter I	TH D 1077 long range surveillance Radar C Band 2 MW	C/D Band 23 cm	2 MW	180 km for 2 m² air target
Jupiter II	TRS 3010 air search radar	D Band	—	—
Ramses	TH D 1022 short range nav & surveillance radar	I Band	36 kW	60 n. miles
Lynx	TH D 1051	—.	—	—
Saturne I-II	TH D 1041. TRS 3043	E/F Band	1 MW	—
Sea Tiger	Surveillance radar. TRS 3001	E/F Band	Average 1 kW	60 n. miles on 2 m² fluctuation target—with P.D 50%
DRBC 31	Gun fire control radar	I Band	—	—
DRBC 32	Gun fire control radar	I Band	—	—
DRBI 10	Height finder	E/F Band	Between 1 and 2 MW	Between 100 and 140 n. miles
DRBI 23	Surveillance and target designator—3D	C/D Band (23 cm)	—	—
DRBN 30	Navigation	—	7 kW	—
DRBN 31	Navigation	—	—	—
DRBN 32	Navigation	—	—	—
DRBV 13	Air search radar	E/F Band	—	—
DRBV 20	Long range search radar	Metric	—	—
DRBV 22	Air search radar	C Band	—	—
DRBV 23	Air search and surveillance	C Band	—	—
DRBV 26	Air search	—	—	—
DRBV 31	Air search	—	—	—
DRBV 50-51	Surface search	—	—	—
DRBR 50-51	Missile guidance	I Band	—	—
GERMANY (Federal)				
Atlas 1555	Navigation radar	—	—	—
INTERNATIONAL				
EX 77 Mod O	Director for NATO Sea Sparrow	Probably I Band	—	—
ITALY				
Argus 5000	Early warning radar	—	5 MW	—
Orion 250	Fire control radar	I Band	200 kW	—
Orion RTN 10X	Fire control radar	I Band	—	40 n. miles
Orion RTN 16X	Monopulse fire control radar	I Band	—	—
Orion RTN 20 X	Fire control radar	I Band	—	—
Orion RTN 30X	Fire control radar	I Band	—	—
RAN 2C	Surveillance radar	G Band	—	—
RAN 3L	Early warning radar	C/D Band	—	Approx 200 n. miles
RAN 7S	10 cm air and surface search radar	10 cm	—	—
RAN 10S	Air and sea search on small ships	E/F Band	—	40 n. miles
RAN 11L/X	Air warning and weapons control	C and D Bands	28 kW C Band, 80 kW I Band	35 n. miles
RAN 13X	Search radar	I Band	—	—
RAN 14X	Low altitude and surface search	I Band	—	—
RAN 57	Surface search radar	—	—	—
Sea Hunter	Search radar	I/J Band	180 kW	—
Sea Hunter	Tracker radar	I/J Band	—	—
SPQ 2D	Search radar	I Band	—	—
3 RM	Navigation radar	—	7 or 20 kW	—
MM/BPS704	Navigation radar	—	—	—
JAPAN				
OPS 1	Air search	—	—	—
OPS 2	Air search	—	—	—
OPS 11	Air search	—	—	—
OPS 12	Air search	—	—	—
OPS 14	Air search	—	—	—
OPS 15	Surface search	—	—	—
OPS 16	Surface search	—	—	—
OPS 17	Surface search	—	—	—
OPS 28	Not available	—	—	—
OPS 35	Surface search	—	—	—
OPS 37	Surface search	—	—	—
ZPS 2	Surface search	—	—	—
ZPS 3	Surface search	—	—	—
—	Fire control	—	—	—
—	Fire control	—	—	—
—	Fire control	—	—	—
—	Fire control	—	—	—
NETHERLANDS				
DA 01	Surface search	—	—	—
DA 02	Surface search	—	—	—
DA 04	Surface search	—	—	—
DA 05	Surface search	E/F Band	—	—
DA 08	Air search	E/F Band	—	—
LW 01	Air search	Probably D Band	—	—
LW 02	Air search	D Band	500 kW	100 n. miles
LW 03-04	Air search	D Band	—	—
LW 06	Air search	D Band	—	—
LW 08	Air search	D Band	—	145 n. miles
SD-X	Surface search	I Band	—	—
SGR 101 (M1)	Fire control	I Band	—	—
SGR 107 (M2)	Fire control	I Band	—	—
SGR 108 (M4)	Fire control	I Band	—	—
SGR 120	Fire control	I Band	—	—
VI 01 (SGR 104)	Height finder	E/F Band	400 kW	150 n. miles
WM 4/42	Fire control	I Band	—	—
ZW 01	Surface search	Probably I Band	—	—
ZW 06	Surface search	I Band	—	—
ZW 07	Surface search	I Band	—	—
ZW 08	Surface search	I Band	—	—
3D MTTR	Multi target tracking radar	—	—	—

NAVAL EQUIPMENT / Radar

P.R.F.	Manufacturer	Remarks
Short NOM 400 Hz±200 Hz Long NOM 2000 Hz±200 Hz	TERMA	
—	LMT	Receiver frequency: 1 090 Mc/s
—	LMT	Includes selective identification feature and side lobe suppression
—	Thompson CSF	Associated with Thompson fire control systems
Variable	Thompson CSF	Used in some versions of Vega series fire control system; 20 kW
—	Thompson CSF	Used in some versions of Vega series fire control system; 200 kW
Variable	Thompson CSF	Used for surface search. Used on board submarines
Variable	Thompson CSF	Improvement of above
—	—	Improved Calypso II
Variable	Thompson CSF	Used in submarines
450 per sec	Thompson CSF	Naval air surveillance radar (long range)
—	Thompson CSF	
—	Thompson CSF	
—	Thompson CSF	Dual radar. Coastal mine watching system
—	Thompson CSF	Medium range air and surface surveillance radar
—	Thompson CSF	Can be used in Thompson CSF series ship fire control systems
—	Thompson CSF	A, B and D versions for 57 and 100 mm guns
—	Thompson CSF	A, C and D, versions fitted in various classes of French ships
—	Thompson CSF	Robinson scanner mounted on French carriers and *Jeanne d'Arc*
—	Thompson CSF	3D surveillance-target designator radar. Stacked beam system mounted on board "Sufren" class
—	Thompson CSF	Obsolescent
—	Thompson CSF	Fitted in smaller ships
—	Thompson CSF	Introduced 1969
—	Thompson CSF	Pulse doppler air search radar. Multi mode operation
—	Thompson CSF	Operates in metric wave band A, B and C versions C model on aircraft carriers
—	Thompson CSF	Search radar A, C and D versions in service on French and other vessels
—	Thompson CSF	Long range naval air search and surveillance radar
—	Thompson CSF	B and C; C transistorised
—	Thompson CSF	Type 67 frigates
—	Thompson CSF	50 in T47 class
—	Thompson CSF	Part of Masurca surface-to-air missile system
—	Krupp Atlas Elektronic	
—	NATO Consortium	Provides search, target designation tracking and illumination for Sea Sparrow point defence missile system
—	Selenia	High power. Ship's early warning radar
—	Selenia	Used in NA 9. System conical scan; 200 kW
—	Selenia	Fire control radar used by RN as Type 912
—	Selenia	
—	Selenia	Used in Dardo system
—	Selenia	Used in Albatros system
—	Selenia	Dual purpose air and surface surveillance radar
—	Selenia	Digital. Signal processing
—	Selenia	Air and surface target warning
—	Selenia	Air and surface surveillance
—	Selenia	D Band air detection, I/J Band surface detection
—	Selenia	Surface and low flying search
—	Selenia	Low altitude and surface search radar
—	Selenia	
Variable	Contraves	
—	Contraves	
—	SMA	Surface search and short range air search
750-6 000 Hz range	SMA	Series of I Band navigation and surface warning radars
—	Selenia	For submarines
—	—	Similar in appearance to US AN/SPS 6; parameters are probably also similar
—	—	
—	—	Not yet operational
—	—	Similar in appearance to US AN/SPS 5; parameters are probably also similar
—	—	
—	—	Not yet operational
—	—	Found on board old patrol craft
—	—	Employed by submarines
—	—	Associated with fire control director
—	—	Associated with fire control director Type 0
—	—	Associated with fire control director Type 1
—	—	Associated with fire control director Type 2
—	Hollandse Signaalapparaten	On board Colombian "Halland" class plus numerous Dutch and West German units
—	Hollandse Signaalapparaten	
—	Hollandse Signaalapparaten	
—	—	Land version designated DA 05/M
—	Hollandse Signaalapparaten	
—	Hollandse Signaalapparaten	Only on board Argentine *25 de Mayo* and Peruvian *Almirante Grau* and *Aguirre*
—	Hollandse Signaalapparaten	Designed for destroyer size ships. Employed by numerous navies
—	Hollandse Signaalapparaten	
—	Hollandse Signaalapparaten	
—	Hollandse Signaalapparaten	
—	Hollandse Signaalapparaten	
—	Hollandse Signaalapparaten	Associated with fire control directors M1, M2, M3
—	Hollandse Signaalapparaten	Associated with fire control director M3
—	Hollandse Signaalapparaten	Associated with fire control director M4
—	Hollandse Signaalapparaten	Associated with fire control director M2
1 000	Hollandse Signaalapparaten	Only on board Argentine *25 de Mayo* and Peruvian *Almirante Grau*
—	Hollendse Signaalapparaten	Radar for most M20 series and WM series fire control
—	Hollandse Signaalapparaten	Alternative designation SGR 103
—	Hollandse Signaalapparaten	
—	Hollandse Signaalapparaten	Submarine radar
—	Hollandse Signaalapparaten	Anti submarine radar
—	Hollandse Signaalapparaten	3D air search

NAVAL EQUIPMENT / Radar

Country/Number	Type	Transmitter frequency	Transmitter peak power	Range
SWEDEN				
9 GR 600	Transmitter/receiver	I Band	200 kW	—
9 LV 200	Mk 2 Tracking radar/Fire control	J Band	65 kW	—
SUBFAR	Air search	D Band	—	—
UNION OF SOVIET SOCIALIST REPUBLICS				
Square Tie	Lightweight search radar	I Band	—	—
Square Head	IFF	—	—	—
Pop Group	Fire control radar	Probably I Band	—	—
Head Net	Air surveillance radar	Probably D or E/F Band	—	—
Drum Tilt	Fire control radar	Probably I Band	—	—
Sun Visor	Fire control radar	Probably I or G Band	—	—
Cylinder Head	Fire control radar	—	—	—
Big Net	Air search radar	C Band	—	—
Fan Song E	Fire control radar	G Band	—	—
Hair Net	Naval radar	E Band	—	—
Plinth Net	Target acquisition radar	—	—	—
Pot Drum	Naval radar	Probably I Band	—	—
Pot Head	Naval radar	Probably I Band	—	—
Scoop Pair	Missile control radar	—	—	—
Hawk Screech	Gun fire control	Probably I Band. Possibly G Band	—	—
Owl Screech	Gun fire control	Probably I Band. Possibly G Band	—	—
High Lune	Naval height finder	Probably E/F Band	—	—
Muff Cob	Fire control radar	G/H or I Band	—	—
Slim Net	Air warning radar	Probably E/F Band	—	—
Flat Spin	Surveillance radar	D or E/F Band	—	—
Top Sail	3D radar	Probably C Band	—	—
Head Light	Fire control	Probably I and G/H Band	—	—
Strut Curve	Air search radar	Probably E/F Band	—	—
Peel Group	Fire control radar	Probably E Band and I Band	—	40
Boat Sail	Submarine radar air search	D or E Band	—	—
Skin Head	Target acquisition radar	Probably I/J Band	—	—
Top Trough	Surface surveillance radar	—	—	—
Knife Rest B	Early warning radar	—	—	—
High Sieve	Surface search radar	—	—	—
Top Bow	Gun fire control radar	—	—	—
Seagull	Air search	—	—	—
Top Steer	3D air search radar	—	—	—
Trap Door	Missile control radar	—	—	—
Eye Bowl	Missile control radar	—	—	—
Band Stand	Missile control radar	—	—	—
Bass Tilt	Gun control radar	—	—	—
UNITED KINGDOM				
AWS/2	Surface search and target indication	E/F Bands	—	60 n. miles
Decca 45	Navigation	—	—	—
Decca 202	Navigation	—	—	—
Decca 212	Navigation	—	—	—
Decca 303	Navigation	—	—	—
Decca 416	Navigation	—	—	—
Decca 909	Navigation	—	—	—
Decca 1226	Navigation	—	—	—
Decca 2400	Navigation	—	—	—
RN Type 268	Surface search	—	—	—
RN Type 278	Height finder	—	—	—
RN Type 285	Fire control	—	—	—
RN Type 291	Air search	—	—	—
RN Type 901	Fire control	Possibly G Band	—	—
RN Type 903	Fire control	—	—	—
RN Type 904	Fire control	—	—	—
RN Type 909	Fire control	Possibly G Band	—	—
RN Type 910	Fire control	I Band	—	—
RN Type 912	Fire control	I Band	—	—
RN Type 965	Air search, long range, early warning	Metric	—	—
RN Type 967	Air search	E/F Bands	—	—
RN Type 968	Surface search	C/D Bands	—	—
RN Type 974	Navigation (Decca 12)	—	—	—
RN Type 975	Surface search/navigation	I Band	50 kW	48 n. miles
RN Type 978	Navigation	I Band	—	—
RN Type 982	Low angle, air warning	—	—	—
RN Type 983	Height finder	—	—	—
RN Type 992Q	Air/Surface search and target indication	E/F Bands	—	—
RN Type 993	Air/Surface search	—	—	—
RN Type 994	Air/Surface search	—	—	—
RN Type 1003	Submarine search/navigation	—	—	—
RN Type 1006	Navigation	I Band	—	—
RN Type 1022	Surveillance	—	—	—
S 604 HN	Surface search	I Band	2/3 MW	—
S 810	Surface search	I Band	200 kW	—
SNW 12	Air search	—	—	—
14/9	Navigation	—	—	—
UNITED STATES OF AMERICA				
RTN 10	Fire control for Sea Sparrow III	I Band	—	—
SPG 49	Guidance for Talos and Terrier. Surface-to-air	Used with SPW 2	—	120 km
SPG 51	Tartar missile guidance	I Band	—	—
SPG 53	Fire control radar	—	—	—
SPG 55	Terrier guidance radar	G/H Band	Approx 50 kW	50 km
SPG 60	Doppler search and tracking	I Band	—	93 km
SPQ 9	Lockheed MK 86 fire control system	I/J Band	—	37 km
SPQ 5	Missile guidance	G/H Band	—	—
SPS 6	Air surveillance	D Band	Approx 500 kW	100-200 km
SPS 10	Surface search	G/H Band	—	—
SPS 12	Long range air search	D Band	0.1 and 1.0 MW	—
SPS 30	Long range 3D radar	—	—	—
SPS 32	Air and surface surveillance	—	—	—
SPS 33	Fire control radar	—	—	—
SPS 37	Long range air surveillance	—	—	—
SPS 39	3D radar air surveillance	—	—	200-300 km
SPS 40	Search and surveillance for air targets	? E/F Band	? 1 MW	—
SPS 43	High power very long range search radar	? Metric	1-2 MW	—
SPS 48	Air surveillance radar	? E/F Band	—	—
SPS 49	Air search radar	—	—	—
SPS 52	3D air surveillance	? E/F Band	—	—
SPS 55	Surface search and navigation	—	130 kW	—
SPS 58	Pulse Doppler air search and target acquisition radar	D Band	—	—
SPY 1	Multi function array radar	E/F Band	Several MW	—

NAVAL EQUIPMENT / Radar

P.R.F.	Manufacturer	Remarks
2-3 000 Hz	Philips	
Approx 2 000 Hz	Philips	Frequency agility naval fire control
Variable 250-3 000/sec	Philips	Air and surface search
—	—	Probably include target detection and tracking for anti-ship missile direction
—	—	IFF interrogator
—	—	Associated with Soviet Navy's SAN-4 surface-to-air missile system
—	—	Air search and surveillance
—	—	For twin 30 mm guns. Head Net B has two A antennae back-to-back and in horizontal plane
—	—	For 100 mm and 130 mm guns. C has second antenna inclined
—	—	Believed now obsolete
—	—	Very large long range air surveillance radar
—	—	Shipboard version of Guideline surface-to-air missile radar—now obsolete
—	—	Medium range general purpose search and surveillance radar—now obsolete
—	—	Medium range general purpose search radar—probably obsolete
—	—	Small surface search radar for light forces
—	—	Surface target detection; short range for light forces
—	—	Twin radar group for Shaddock SSM
—	—	For 45 and 76 mm guns
—	—	For 76 mm guns
—	—	Gun fire control for 57 mm
—	—	High definition surface target radar in earlier classes
—	—	Long range air search radar
—	—	Long range 3D air surveillance radar
—	—	Missile fire control group for SA-N-3 and SS-N-14
—	—	Lightweight search radar
—	—	Missile control group for SA-N-1
—	—	Air search for submarine pickets
—	—	Surface target detection radar for light forces
—	—	High definition surface target radar
—	—	Long wavelength early warning radar
—	—	Target acquisition radar for 152 mm guns
—	—	Long range air search radar—now obsolete
—	—	Possibly air control radar. In "Kiev" class
—	—	Control for SS-N-12 in "Kiev" class
—	—	Control for SS-N-14 in "Krivak" class
—	—	Control for SS-N-9 in "Nanuchka" and "Sarancha" classes
—	—	For 30 mm Gatling guns
400-1 000 pps		Plessey AWS5, later version
—	Decca	
—	Decca	
—	Decca	
—	Decca	
—	Decca	On board some modern French ships
—	Decca	
—	Decca	On board some modern French ships
—	Decca	
—	Marconi	Introduced during WW II now obsolete
—	—	"Tiger" and "County" classes
—	—	Mainly obsolete still found on Egyptian and South American units
—	—	Introduced during WW II now obsolete
—	Marconi	Guidance for Sea Slug missile
—	Sperry	With MRS 3 system
—		Guidance for Sea Slug missiles, GWS22
—	Marconi	Guidance for Sea Dart
—	Marconi	Guidance for Sea Wolf
—	—	RN version of Orion RTN 10X (Italy)
—	Marconi	Long range air search also target designation for guided weapons and IFF Mk 10 facilities. Can be combined with Type 968 for medium to short range defence radar
—	Marconi	Fitted back-to-back. 965Q is single array (Hermes, "Leanders", "Tribals")
—	Marconi	Fitted back-to-back. 965R is double array (Bristol, "Sheffields")
—	Decca	Obsolete
—	Kelvin Hughes	
—	Decca	
—	—	"Salisbury" class
—	—	
—	Marconi	"County" class
—	—	"Leander" class
—	Plessey	AWS 4 below decks plus 993 aerial
—	Kelvin Hughes	
—	Marconi	To replace Type 965
—	Marconi	Long range surveillance
1 500 or 4 400 Hz	Marconi	Lightweight surveillance
—	Marconi	
—	Kelvin Hughes	
—	Raytheon	
—	Sperry	
—	Raytheon	Part of Mk 73 FCS
—	—	Associated with Mk 68 fire control system
—	Sperry	
—	Lockheed	
—	Lockheed	
—	Sperry	Now obsolescent
—	Westinghouse	Now obsolescent. Found in a number of Latin American navies
—	Sylvania	First produced in late 1940s extensively modified through Model F
—	RCA Moorestown	Used on older units of Japanese MSDF
—	GEC	
—	Hughes	Companion in use with SPS 33
—	Hughes	
—	Westinghouse	
—	Hughes	Now obsolete
—	Lockheed	
—	Westinghouse	Generally carries IFF antenna
—	ITT-Gilfillan	3D long range air surveillance
—	Raytheon	Narrow beam very long range for air search
—	Hughes	In use in NATO navies
750-2 250 pps	Cordion Electronics	Replacement for SPS 10
—	Westinghouse	Designed to operate with US Navy point defence Surface Missile System
—	—	Under development for US Navy Aegis fleet air defence missile system

SONAR

Country/Designation	Description	Manufacturer	Mounting
AUSTRALIA			
Mulloka	Sonar project for RAN	—	—
Barra	Project Barra is RAAF/RAN project to develop advanced sonobuoy and airborne detection system	Amalgamated Wireless	—
CANADA			
HS 1000	Lightweight search and attack sonar either hull mounted or towed	Canadian Westinghouse	—
SQS 505	Medium search/attack sonar	Canadian Westinghouse	—
SQS 507 (Helen)	Lightweight variable depth towed sonar	Canadian Westinghouse	—
FRANCE			
DUBV/23D	Active surface vessel search/attack sonar	CIT/ALCATEL	Bow mounted
DUBV/43B	Variable depth sonar	CIT/ALCATEL	Towed
DUUX 2A/B/C	Passive sonar. Submarine detection system	CIT/ALCATEL	—
DUBV 24/C	Low frequency panoramic search/attack sonar	CIT/ALCATEL	—
PASCAL Sonar	Surveillance and tracking sonar for small and medium ships	CIT/ALCATEL	—
DUUA 2A	Simultaneous search and attack sonar for modernised "Daphne" class S/M	CIT/ALCATEL	—
DUUA 2B	Passive detection 1·5-15 kHz	CIT/ALCATEL	Hull
HS-71/DUAV-4	Helicopter Sonar	CIT/ALCATEL	—
TSM 2 400/DUBA 25	Surface vessel sonar (TARPON). Attack sonar	Thomson CSF	Hull or towed
Diodon (TSM 2314)	Submarine detection, target tracking and attack operations	Thomson CSF	Hull or towed
Piranha (TSM 2140)	Attack sonar	Thomson CSF	Hull
DUBM 41A	Side looking sonar	Thomson CSF	Towed
DUBM 21A IBIS	Mine counter measure sonar	Thomson CSF	Hull mounted
DUBM 40B	Active mine hunting sonar	Thomson CSF	Towed
ITALY			
IP 64 MD 64	Submarine sonars	USEA	—
NETHERLANDS			
LWS 30	Passive sonar/intercept system. Omni-directional surveillance against surface or sub-surface targets	Hollandse Signaalapparaten BV	—
PSH 32	High performance search and attack sonar	Hollandse Signaalapparaten BV	Hull
UNITED KINGDOM			
PMS 26/27	Lightweight search/attack sonar	Plessey	Hull
Type 195	Helicopter sonar	Plessey	Dunking type
PMS 32	Active/passive panoramic sonar	Plessey	Hull
Type 162M	Sideways looking sonar (classification)	Kelvin Hughes	Hull
Type 170B	Short range search and attack	—	Hull
Type 177	Medium range search, panoramic	—	Hull
Type 184M	Medium range panoramic search and attack	Graseby	Hull
Type 186	Submarine sonar	EMI	Hull
Type 187	Submarine attack sonar	EMI	Hull
Type 193	RN mine hunting system (Acoustic)	Plessey	Hull
Type 193M	Solid state improved version of type 193 mine hunting sonar	Plessey	Hull
Type 199	Variable depth towed sonar	EMI	Towed
Type 719	Submarine sonar	EMI	Hull
Type 2001	Active/passive, submarine	—	Hull
Type 2007	Long range passive, submarine	GAC	Hull
Type 2016	Long range panoramic search	Plessey/Graseby	Hull
SADE	Sensitive Acoustic Detection Equipment. Intruder detection system	Plessey	—
Project 35	Advanced fleet escort sonar in development	Plessey	—
GI 738	Towed decoy	Graseby	Towed
GI 750	Solid state panoramic search and attack	Graseby	Hull/VDS
GI 768	Solid state panoramic search and attack	Graseby	Hull/VDS
GI 777 K and C	Solid state panoramic search and attack	Graseby	Hull/VDS
GI 780	Solid state passive	Graseby	Bow
UNITED STATES OF AMERICA			
AQS 13	Helicopter sonar	Bendix	Dunking type
BQG 1/4	Submarine passive fire control sonars	Sperry/Raytheon	Hull
BQQ 1	Search and fire control sonars	Raytheon	Hull
BQQ 2	Sonar for Subroc system	Raytheon	Hull
BQQ 5	Nuclear attack submarine sonar	Hughes/GE/IBM	Hull
BQR 2B	Submarine passive sonar	EDO	Hull
BQR 3	Submarine passive sonar	Raytheon	Hull
BQR 7	Passive sonar. Part of BQQ 2 system	EDO	Hull
BQR 15	Towed submarine sonar	Western Electric	Towed
BQR 19	Submarine sonar	Raytheon	Hull
BQR 21	Submarine passive detection and tracking set (DIMUS)	Honeywell	Hull
BQS 6	Active submarine sonar. Part of BQQ 2 system	Raytheon	Hull
BQS 8	Under ice navigation sonar	EDO/Hazeltine	Hull
BQS 13	Submarine search sonar. Passive/active	IBM	Hull
SQA 10	Variable depth sonar	Litton	Towed
SQA 13	Variable depth sonar Hoist	EDO/Litton	Hull
SQA 14	"Searchlight" sonar	Raytheon	Towed
SQA 16	"Searchlight" sonar	Raytheon	Hull
SQA 19	Variable depth sonar	Litton	Towed
SQG 1	A/S attack sonar	Raytheon	Hull
SQQ 14	Mine hunting and classification sonar	GE	Hull
SQQ 23	Sonar for A/S patrol ships	—	Hull
SQR 14	Surface sonar	—	Hull
SQR 18	Passive towed array	EDO	VDS
SQS 4	Short range active sonar	Sangamo/GE	Hull
SQS 23	Long range active sonar	Sangamo	Hull
SQS 26	Bow mounted "Bottom Bounce" mode sonar to replace SQS 23	EDO/GE	Hull
SQS 29/32	Surface vessel active sonars. Numbers relate to differing frequencies	—	—
SQS 35	Variable depth towed sonar	—	Towed
SQS 36	Medium range hull sonar	EDO	Hull
SQS 38	Medium range hull sonar	EDO	Hull
SQS 56	Lightweight sonar under development for USN PF ships	Raytheon	Hull
UQS 2	Mine hunting sonar	GE	Hull
610	Long range hull sonar	EDO	Hull
700 series	Medium range hull and variable depth versions	EDO	Hull and towed
780 Series	Computer-aided medium range light weight	EDO	Hull and towed
Model 900	Submarine mine avoidance	EDO	Hull
Model 910	Surface ship mine avoidance	EDO	Hull
1102/1105	Submarine active/passive medium range	EDO	Hull

Frequency	Power	Ship Type	Remarks
—	—	—	
—	—	—	
—	—	—	
—	—	—	
4 operating frequencies around 5 kHz, 2 of which are operational	96 kW (2 × 48 kW)	A/S escorts Types T47/T56 "Suffren" class frigates and type C67 and corvettes type C70 of French Navy	
	—	A/S escorts T47 and T56 also C67 series and C70 series	
4 operating frequencies around 5 kHz, 2 of which are operational	48 kW (2 × 24 kW)	—	
10 and 11·5 kHz	5 kW	—	
8·4 kHz	30 kW	"Daphne" class S/M	
—	—	"Agosta" class S/M	
—	—	Helicopter	
—	—	"Aviso" type	
Selectable: 11·12 or 13 kHz	—	ASW small or medium tonnage	
11, 12 or 13 kHz	10 kVA	Small ship	
8, 9 or 10 kHz	5 kVA	Small ship	
100 kHz mod ±10 kHz	2 kW	Mine hunters	
730 kHz	1 kW	Mine hunters	
—	—	Small or medium size S/M	
—	—	—	
—	—	Corvette to frigate size ships	
10 kHz	13 kW	Ships and patrol craft over 150 tons—PMS 27 = PMS 26 with different hull outfit	
—	—	Westland Sea King ASW	
—	50 kW	A/S escort ships	
50 kHz	—	—	
—	—	Frigates with Mk 10 mortar	
—	—	Older frigates	
—	—	Destroyers and frigates	
—	—	Frigates and above	
—	—	Patrol Submarines	
—	—	Vosper mine hunter	
—	—	Mine hunters	
—	—	Frigates ("Leanders" and "Tribals")	
—	—	Bow array	
—	—	Beam array	
—	—	"Invincible" class and Type 22	
—	—	Shore based	
—	—	—	
—	—	Corvettes and above	
—	—	Frigates and above	
—	—	Corvettes	
—	—	Large patrol craft	
—	—	Small submarines	
—	—	Helicopter	
—	—	S/M	
—	—	—	
—	—	S/M	
—	—	S/M	
—	—	S/M	
—	—	S/M	
—	—	—	
—	—	SSBNs	
—	—	S/M	
—	—	SSBNs and SSNs	
—	—	S/M	
—	—	S/M	
—	—	S/M	
—	—	—	
—	—	—	
—	—	—	
—	—	—	
—	—	MCM	
—	—	—	
—	—	—	
—	—	—	
—	—	—	Re-designated AN/SQS 53. Specified for 30 "Spruance" class DD 963 destroyers
—	—	—	
—	—	—	
—	—	—	
—	—	—	
—	—	—	
—	—	—	
—	—	Surface ships	
—	—	—	
—	—	Submarine	

TORPEDOES

No.	Name/Note	Length cm	Diameter mm	Weight kg	Speed knots	Range km	Explosive charge kg	Guidance	Target/Role	Carrier
FRANCE										
Z 16	Now probably obsolete	720	550	1 700	30	10	300	Preset plus Pattern	A/S	S/M
E 14	Acoustic Torpedo	429·1	550	900	25	5·5	200	Acoustic	A/Surface (up to 20 knots) +S/M at shallow depth	S/M
E 15	Acoustic Torpedo	600	550	1 350	25	12	300	Acoustic	A/Surface 0-20 knots +S/M at shallow depth	S/M
L 3	Acoustic Torpedo	430	550	910	25	5·5	200	Acoustic	A/S 0-20 knots up to 300 m depth	S/M only
L 4	Acoustic Torpedo	313 inc parachute stabiliser	533	540	30			Acoustic	A/S up to 20 knots	Airborne
L 5 Mod 1	Multi purpose		533	1 000	35			Direct Attack or Programmed Search		Ship
L 5 Mod 3			533	1 300	35					S/M
GERMANY (FEDERAL REPUBLIC)										
SST 4	Wire Guided Torpedo	639 inc 46 wire casket	533				260	Wire Guided Active/Passive Sonar Homing	A/Surface	Ship or S/M
	Sea Eel	639	533	1 370	35/23	13/28		Wire guided Active/Passive Sonar Homing	A/S	S/M or FPBs
	Sut	613 and 670 inc wire casket	533							S/M or ship
	Seal	639 inc wire casket	533	1 370			260	Wire		Ships
	Seeschlange	400 inc wire casket	533				100	Wire	A/S	
ITALY										
G 6E	Kangaroo	620	533					Wire Guided	Obsolescent	
A 184		600	533					Wire Guided Active/Passive Sonar	A/S or A/Surface	Ship or S/M
A 244		270	324					Homing Course and Depth		Ship or aircraft
SWEDEN										
Type 41		244	400	250				Passive Homing Sonar	Limited A/Surface or A/S	S/M
Type 42		244 + 18 wire section	400	270				Passive Homing Sonar or Wire Guidance	A/S	Ship S/M and helicopter
Type 61		70·25	533	1 765			250	Wire Guided	A/Ship	Ship or S/M

NAVAL EQUIPMENT / Torpedoes

No.	Name/Note	Length cm	Diameter mm	Weight kg	Speed knots	Range km	Explosive charge kg	Guidance	Target/Role	Carrier
UNION OF SOVIET SOCIALIST REPUBLICS										
—	—	—	533	—	—	—	—	—	—	Surface ships, submarines and aircraft
—	—	?500	406	—	—	—	—	—	—	
UNITED KINGDOM										
Mark 8		670	533	1 535	45	4·5		Preset Course Angle & Depth	A/Surface	S/M
Mark 20	—	411	533	821	20	11	91 kg HE	Pre-set/Homing	A/Surface, A/S	S/M
Mark 23	—	—	533	—	20	—	91 kg HE	Wire Guided Homing	A/S	S/M
Mark 24 Mod O	Tigerfish	646·4	533	1 550	Dual high or low	32		Wire Guided Acoustic Homing	Primarily A/S	S/M
MW 30 Mark 44	Drill and Practice	256	324	233				Active/Acoustic Homing	A/Surface	Aircraft, ship, helicopter
UNITED STATES OF AMERICA										
Mark 14	Mod 5	525	533	1 780	32-46	46·9	230	Preset depth & Course Angles	A/Surface	S/M
Mark 37	Mod 3	340	484·5	649	24	—	150 HE	Free running then Sonar Auto Homing	A/S	S/M
Mark 37	Mod 2	409	484·5	766	24	—	150 HE	Wire Guidance Active/Passive Sonar Homing	A/S	S/M
NT 37 2C Dimensions and warheads as for Mk 37 Mod 2/3 but speed increased by 40%, range by over 100% and wire guided capability in excess of 13 000 yds. Improvements to sonar and homing logic plus additional A/Ship attack modes									A/Surface, A/S	Ship or S/M
Mark 44	Mod 1	260	324	196·4	—	—		Active Acoustic	A/S	Ships (Mk 32 or Asroc), aircraft
Mark 45	Mod 1 Astor (Mod 2)	580	484·5	1 003·8		approx 11	Nuclear Warhead	Wire Guided	A/S	S/M being replaced by Mk 48
Mark 46	Mod 0, 1 and 2	260	324	257 230 (1 and 2)	—	—		Active/Passive Acoustic Homing	A/S	Ships, (Mk 32 or Asroc), aircraft, helicopter Mod 1 and 2 have liquid propellant
Mark 46	Captor Mod 4	Mk 46 inserted in mine casing and sown in narrow seas. See Jane's Weapon System 2541.441.								
Mark 48	Mod 1 and 2	580	533	1 579	50	46	—	Wire Guided and Active/Passive Acoustic Homing	A/Surface, A/S	S/M
—	Freedom Torpedo	572	484·5	1 237	40	18·5	minimum of 295 kg	Wire Guided to hit or free run to intercept followed by pattern run if target missed	A/Surface, A/S	Ship or S/M

DEXTOR (Deep EXperimental TORpedo) Mk 48 replacement
ALWT (Advanced LightWeight Torpedo) Mk 46 replacement

ADDENDA

ALBANIA

Pennant numbers:—"Whiskey" class submarines; 512, 514, 516. "Hu Chwan" class hydrofoils; 100 and 300 series. "Shanghai" class fast attack craft; 101-106 "T301" class minesweepers; 153, 154 and 345.
Naval bases:—Add Sazan Island, Sarande, Shinjin and Pasha Liman.

ARGENTINA

German frigates to be CODOG powered with two Olympus gas turbines (27 700 hp each) and two MTU diesels (10 680 hp). Contract signed 15 February 1979. Names of "A69" frigates—*Drummond* and *Guerrico*. Five offshore patrol ships of 65 metres 900 tons and 20 knots + ordered from Bazán, Ferrol, Spain.
New 1 700 ton submarines (Thyssen—Nordseewerke) to have range of 15 000 miles surfaced at 5 knots with a diving depth of 300 metres.
Two 1 400 ton submarines (of same design but 6 metres shorter with reduced range and 21 knots dived) to be built in Argentina.
Second Wärtsila icebreaker ordered.

AUSTRALIA

Fremantle launched 15 February 1979. *Tobruk* laid down 7 February 1979.

BARBADOS

New 103 ft patrol craft to be ordered mid-1979.

BELGIUM

Correction to text:—*Spa* is degaussing vessel and *Heist* is guided missile transport (page 56).

BRUNEI

Add third "Waspada" class name *Pejuang* P03. Two new coastal patrol craft for Police Force launched 2 February 1979. Names—*Tenang* and *Abadi*. Dimensions 18 × 4·9 × ? ft. Two diesels, water jets = 28 knots. Complement 5.

BULGARIA

Naval bases:—Add Atiya.
Submarine pennant number, 13 and 14.
"Osa" class delete No 24 (1978).

CHINA

Second "Han" class submarine completed 1977. Reported to have been built at Wahan.
Up to 68 "Romeo" class submarines reported.
"An Shan" class destroyer pennant numbers 101-104.
Class totals for "Osa" class to 84, "Hai Nan" class to 24, "P4" class to 80 (approx 50 in reserve), "Shanghai" class to 295 (taking account of transfer and deletion of early ships of class).

COLOMBIA

Carib, Hidasta, Jicarilla—ATFs—transferred by sale from USA 15 March 1979. Transfer of ARB *Midas* cancelled.

CUBA

Naval bases:—Delete Cabanas and Varadero. Add Punta Ballenatos, and Canasi.
Reported deletions:—Four "Komar" class, two "Kronshtadt" and two "SO 1" class.
Add:—one ex-Polish "K8" class minesweeper, two ex-Soviet "Yelva" class diving ships, two "Turya" class hydrofoils.

DENMARK

"Niels Juel" class frigates to receive General Dynamics RAM-ASMD SAM when available.

DOMINICAN REPUBLIC

Deletions 1978—*Capitan-General Pedro Santana, Gregorio Luperon* (both "Tacoma" class), *Cristobal Colon, Juan Alejandro Acosta* (both Canadian "Flower" class), *Rigel* (coastal patrol craft) and *Maguana* (harbour Tug). "Carite" class coastal patrol craft used for SEAL support as is new *Nube del Mar* BA7 of 42 × 12 × 1 ft, and two ex-fishing craft *Alto Velo* BA11 and *Saona* BA12. New harbour Tug *Puerto Hermoso* RP 22.

ECUADOR

Manabi decommissioned 1978—used as alongside training ship at Guayaquil.

FINLAND

Recent programme announced for design of prototype 30 ton 20 metre fast attack craft and the modernisation of frigate *Hämeenmaa*, six "Nuoli" class and two "Ruissalo" class.

FRANCE

1979 New Construction programme includes 1 SSBN (*Inflexible*), 1 DDG ("George Leygues" AA version), 1 MHC (second "Eridan" class), 2 "Champlain" class LSTs. Second "Eridan" laid down 5 February 1979.
SNA-3 to be ordered in 1979.

GERMANY (FDR)

Procurement of General Dynamics RAM-ASMD SAM when available.
Marburg completed hunter-conversion as last ship of the series 28 March 1979.
Gauss (research ship) to be replaced by new construction of same name ordered December 1978 for delivery March 1980. Building by Schlichting. Of 1 600 tons, 68·7 metres long with diesel-electric propulsion for 13½ knots.

GUINEA

Two "Shershen" class transferred by USSR 1978.

GUINEA BISSAU

Two "T 4" class landing craft transferred by USSR 1978.

INDIA

Reported that six additional "Polnochniy" class LCTs ordered in USSR in July 1977 for construction in Poland. *Trishul* converted with two SS-N-2 launchers as in *Talwar*.
Reported that *Dharini* (repair ship) has been deleted.

INDONESIA

Further orders for Wilton, Fijenoord frigates—definitely three and possibly five.

IRAN

Cancellations of orders—*Andoushirvan, Nader* (3 February 1979), *Kouroosh, Daryush* (31 March 1979). Transfer of submarines cancelled as follows: *Tang* (3 February 1979), *Wahoo* (31 March 1979).

IRAQ

"SO 1" class pennant numbers now 310, 311, 312.
"Osa" class:—"Osa I", *Haziran* 1, *Kanun ath-Thani* 6, *Nisan* 7, *Tamuz* 17, "Osa II", *Sa'd, Khalid ibn al-Walid*.
"P6" class:—Pennant numbers include 217-222.

ISRAEL

Seventh "Reshef" named *Nitzhon*.

ITALY

"Maestrale" class to be fitted with Raytheon 1164 VDS and Raytheon 1160 series hull-mounted sonar.

JAPAN

Dimensions of *Tsugaru* (MSA) differ from *Sooya* due to some of class being ice-strengthened. *Tsugaru* (launched 6 December 1978), 3 700 tons full load, 105·4 × 14·6 × 4·9 metres, 16 000 hp = 22 knots.

KAMPUCHEA

Bases:—Ream, Chrui Chang War, Phnom Pehn.
"Swift" class coastal craft, delete 9 from total; remainder, P 122, 124, 126-132.
"PBR Mark I and II" class river patrol craft. Delete 40 from total. Remainder VP 29-31, 33, 34 (Mark I), VP 5, 8-10, 25, 26, 36, 37, + 12 (Mark II).
All amphibious forces probably deleted.

KOREA (NORTH)

Reported size of small submarines building 40-45 metres.
Add two "Hai Nan" class—total six in 1978.
Add six "Chaho" class—total 66.
"Taechong" class—total four, two in 1975 and two in 1978.
"Sin Hung" class—total 72.
"Nampo" class—total 80.

KUWAIT

Order for new fast attack craft probably to be placed with Hong Leong-Lürssen, Malaysia.

MEXICO

Add three ex-US "Abnaki" class tugs:—*Yaqui* (ex-*Hichiti*) A18, *Seri* (ex-*Abnaki*) A19, *Cora* (ex-*Cocopa*) A20.

MOROCCO

"Descubierta" class frigate ordered from Bazán on 7 June 1977.

NIGERIA

Meko 306 frigate to be laid down May 1979.
Armament: 1—76 mm Oto Melara, 2 twin 40 mm, 16 Harpoon, Sea Sparrow, 2 triple ASW torpedo tubes, 1—105 mm Breda rocket launcher.
Second LST launched 7 December 1978 named *Ofiom*.

NORWAY

Two Lynx helicopters ordered spring 1979.
Third "Hauk" class—*Terne* (988)—commissioned 13 March 1979.
Ørn commissioned 19 January 1979.

PAKISTAN

Asroc retained in "Gearing" class destroyers with stock of projectiles.
Breguet Atlantics and some Sea King helicopters now refitted to carry Exocet MM 39 ASM.

PHILLIPPINES

Two ex-Korean (South) "Cannon" class frigates overhauled and transferred early 1979—*Kang Won* and *Kyong Ki*.

POLAND

Pennant number "Kotlin" class *Warszawa* now 278. "Polnochniy" class LCTs—*Balas* 823, *Brda* 814, *Grunwald* 862 or 882, *Janow* 817, *Lenin* 811, *Narwik* 818, *Studzianki* 812, *Warta* 831. "Modified Obluze" class—*Wytrwaly* 302, *Zawiety* 303, *Zreczni* 306.
"K8" class. Built 1955-60. Pennants in 800-900 series.
Add "Marabut" class LCMs. Pennant numbers 516-519. "Eichstaden" class confirmed as class name for LCPs. *Hydrograf*—add as third "Moma" class.
"Pilica" class coastal patrol craft. Add new pennant number 724. Reported as carrying two 21 in (533 mm) torpedo tubes.

ROMANIA

"Hu Chwan" class hydrofoils—total 15, pennant numbers VT 51-65.
River patrol craft—total 16, pennant numbers VB 76-91.
Add five "SD 200" class patrol craft. Pennant numbers SD 270, 274, 275, 277, 278.
Add 8 + "VD" class inshore minesweepers. Pennant numbers VD 141-148. A new class in production.
Voinicul ("Roslavl" class tug) pennant number NS 116.

SEYCHELLES

Reported transfer of one ex-French minesweeper and one ex-UK coastal patrol craft as well as purchase of one Britten-Norman "Defender" aircraft.

SOUTH AFRICA

Tug *De Mist* completed by Dorman Long (SA) Ltd December 1978.

SPAIN

"Descubierta" class—*Vencedora* launched 29 March 1979, to commission September 1981; F 37 to commission January 1982; F 38 launch date November 1979, to commission May 1982.

SRI LANKA

Delete coastal patrol craft PB 102 sunk in collision. Five new coastal patrol craft ordered early 1979 from Colombo Dockyard.

SWEDEN

"Jagaren" class. After first four remainder of class to complete at 3-monthly intervals programme to finish in 1982. These craft are being engined with diesels from deleted "Plejad" class after refit and up-rating by MTU.
"Spica T131" class to be rearmed with Harpoon and not Penguin missiles.

TURKEY

Unconfirmed report of four missile-armed "Kartal" class ordered from Lürssen, Vegesack.

UNITED KINGDOM

Sixth "Hunt" class *Brocklesby* ordered from Vosper Thornycroft Ltd 24 April 1979.

818 ADDENDA

UNITED STATES OF AMERICA

John Hancock (DD 981) was commissioned on 10 March not 1 March 1979.

Second "DDG 47" class number DDG 48.

AG 193 (ex-M/V *Hughes Glomar Explorer*) is operated under contract by Lockheed Missiles and Space Co Inc for Global Marine Development Inc.

SSBN 729 has been named *Georgia*. Her keel was laid on 7 April 1979.

Ohio (SSBN 726) was launched on 7 April 1979.

Emory S. Land (AS 39) was commissioned on 15 March not 26 March 1979. Active Atlantic Fleet.

Francis Marion (LPA 249) and the Greek merchant freighter *Starlighter* collided on 4 March 1979. Spain had actively expressed an interest in acquiring *Francis Marion* as a replacement for *Aragon* (ex-USS *Noble*, APA 218) because of the *Marion's* flagship accommodations. However, if the damage is too expensive to repair, Spain may decide to take the *Paul Revere* (LPA 248) which has no flag accommodations.

A contract for the construction of six YRBM's hull numbers YRBM 31-36) was awarded to Marinette Marine Corp., Marinette, Wisconsin on 12 March 1979.

The ex-USCGC *Cuyahoga* (WIX 157) was scuttled on 19 March 1979, 30 miles off Cape Charles on the Virginia Coast to form part of a man-made fishing reef.

Haven (AH 17) transferred to Maritime Administration, James River 23 August 1978.

Clark (FFG 11) was launched on 24 March 1979 at Bath, Maine.

Antrim (FFG 20) was launched on 27 March 1979.

Also included in the Proposed Fiscal Year 1980 programme are long term lead items for the Carrier Service Life Extension Program (SLEP) and a Supply Ship Conversion (AK 284)—$50·5 million; cost growth and escalation for prior year programmes—$300·0 million and construction of landing craft, service craft and miscellaneous items—$223·9 million.

YTL 435 was striken from the Naval Vessel Register on 1 February 1979.

Admiral Robert L. J. Long, USN, currently Vice Chief of Naval Operations, will relieve Admiral Maurice F. Weisner, USN, as Commander-in-Chief, Pacific.

The transfer of *Wahoo* (SS 565) to Iran was cancelled on 31 March 1979. The transfer of *Tang* (SS 563) to Iran was cancelled on 3 February 1979. *Wahoo* will be decommissioned prior to 1 October 1979 and *Tang* prior to 1 October 1980. Both ships will be sold under FMS to a foreign country. The ex-*Trout* (SS 566) which was transferred to Iran on 19 December 1978, may never sail to Iran. The Iranian government has requested that she be bought back.

The third and fourth units of the Iranian ordered "Improved Spruance" class (DD 993), USN hull numbers DD 995 and 996 respectively, were cancelled by the new Iranian regime on 3 February 1979. The acquisition of the first and second units of this class, hull numbers DD 993 and 994 respectively, by the Iranian government was cancelled on 31 March 1979. The US Navy now has a requirement for all four ships. The third and fourth units, as indicated in the text, were included in the amended FY 1979 supplemental budget request at a cost of $1·1 billion. On 12 April 1979, the House and Senate Armed Forces Committees approved their acquisition, but the Budget Committee rejected their acquisition. The House and Senate Appropriations Committee have not yet acted on the supplemental budget request. A final decision on the request to be made later. The Administration intends to submit an amendment to the FY 1980 Department of Defense Budget Request providing for the acquisition of DD 993 and DD 994 at a total cost of $725 million. If the acquisition of any or all of these units is rejected, the Navy will try to sell the contracts to another country. If this fails, the contracts will be terminated, the completed portions of the ship scrapped and the parts and usable material absorbed by the US Navy.

As of 1 February 1979, the construction status of DD 993-996, was as follows:

Hull No.	Per Cent Completed	Keel Laid	Launched	Completion
DD 993	48·4	26 June 1978	25 Aug 1979	21 Nov 1980
DD 994	43·5	23 Oct 1978	26 Jan 1980	27 Mar 1981
DD 995	42·5	9 Apr 1979	26 Apr 1980	26 June 1981
DD 996	42·3	9 July 1979	26 July 1980	25 Sep 1981

First of this class renumbered DDG 998.

Since preparation of the manuscript for the US section (January/February 1979) it has been decided not to reclassify *Vanguard* (AGM 19) as AG 194 for her new mission as replacement for *Compass Island* (AG 153). She will remain as AGM 19. Despite her new mission, *Vanguard* will still be manned by MSC. Otherwise all other data in the text still applies.

AFDB 3 (Section E) transferred to the Maritime Administration, James River for layup on 14 February 1979.

AFDB 3 (Section H) was transferred to the Maritime Administration, James River, on 22 March 1979 for layup.

Only *Tarawa* (LHA 1) of the "Tarawa" class is fully configured to carry the Harrier (AV 8A) VSTOL aircraft. She was converted in 1979 at Subic Bay, Philippines for deployment to the Commander, Middle East Force in the Indian Ocean. None of the other units of the class has yet been fitted to carry the Harrier. Prior to 1979, all the units of the "Iwo Jima" Class LPH's had been given "Jury Rig" conversions to handle four Harrier (AV 8A), in place of helicopters, for special occasions. In 1979, *Tripoli* (LPH 10) was given a full conversion to handle the AV-8A. She is the first of the class to have a full conversion. Other units of the class will follow. *Tripoli* is scheduled to deploy to the Indian Ocean, with *Tarawa*, in late 1979. During the FY 1979/80 period, it has been reported that the Middle East Force will be disestablished and replaced by a new fleet to be called the Fifth Fleet. *Lasalle* (AGF 3) will remain as Flagship Commander, Fifth Fleet. At the same time the base at Diego Garcia will be enlarged so it can fully support large "Forrestal" class carriers.

The following are the projected ship status changes in the US Navy from 12 May 1979 to 30 September 1980. All dates are subject to change.

Date	Name/Hull Number	From	To
12 May 1979	NICHOLSON (DD 982)	Building	Active
30 May 1979	POWHATAN (ATF 166)	Building	MSC
1 June 1979	TAKELMA (ATF 113)	Active	NRF
29 June 1979	MEREDITH (DD 890)	NRF	Strike
15 July 1979	HIGBEE (DD 806)	NRF	Strike
21 July 1979	JOHN RODGERS (DD 0983)	Building	Active
27 July 1979	JOHN R. CRAIG (DD 885)	NRF	Strike
1 Aug 1979	NORWALK (T AK 279)	MSC	MA
4 Aug 1979	INDIANAPOLIS (SSN 697)	Building	Active
15 Aug 1979	DELIVER (ARS 23)	Active	Strike
18 Aug 1979	NASSAU (LHA 4)	Building	Active
1 Sep 1979	SHAKORI (ATF 162)	Active	NRF
1 Sep 1979	LEFTWICH (DD 984)	Building	Active
20 Sep 1979	TRUCKEE (AO 147)	Active	MSC
30 Sep 1979	SAFEGUARD (ARS 25)	Active	Strike
30 Sep 1979	NARRAGANSETT (ATF 167)	Building	MSC
30 Sep 1979	NAUTILUS (SSN 571)	Active	Reserve Fleet
1 Oct 1979	MAUNA KEA (AE 22)	Active	NRF
1 Oct 1979	KAWISHIWI (AO 146)	Active	MSC
1 Oct 1979	HAMNER (DD 718)	NRF	Strike
1 Oct 1979	WILLIAM C. LAWE (DD 763)	NRF	Strike
1 Oct 1979	HOLLISTER (DD 788)	NRF	Strike
1 Oct 1979	JOHNSTON (DD 821)	NRF	Strike
1 Oct 1979	ROBERT H. McCARD (DD 822)	NRF	Strike
1 Oct 1979	MYLES C. FOX (DD 829)	NRF	Strike
1 Oct 1979	CHARLES P. CECIL (DD 835)	NRF	Strike
1 Oct 1979	FISKE (DD 842)	NRF	Strike
1 Oct 1979	HAROLD J. ELLISON (DD 864)	NRF	Strike
1 Oct 1979	CONE (DD 866)	NRF	Strike
1 Oct 1979	DAMATO (DD 871)	NRF	Strike
1 Oct 1979	HAWKINS (DD 873)	NRF	Strike
1 Oct 1979	ROGERS (DD 876)	NRF	Strike
1 Oct 1979	DYESS (DD 880)	NRF	Strike
1 Oct 1979	DURHAM (LKA 114)	Active	NRF
1 Oct 1979	PAUL REVERE (LPA 248)	NRF	MA
13 Oct 1979	FRANK CABLE (AS 40)	Building	Active
13 Oct 1979	CUSHING (DD 985)	Building	Active
27 Oct 1979	BREMERTON (SSN 698)	Building	Active
15 Nov 1979	SOUTHERLAND (DD 743)	NRF	Strike
15 Nov 1979	McKEAN (DD 784)	NRF	Strike
21 Nov 1979	CHARLESTON (LKA 113)	Active	NRF
30 Nov 1979	CATAWBA (ATF 168)	Building	MSC
1 Dec 1979	PRESERVER (ARS 8)	Active	MA
1 Dec 1979	HARRY W. HILL (DD 986)	Building	Active
9 Dec 1979	McINERNEY (FFG 8)	Building	Active
15 Dec 1979	OKLAHOMA CITY (CG 5)	Active	Strike
29 Dec 1979	O'BANNON (DD 987)	Building	Active
15 Jan 1980	YELLOWSTONE (AD 41)	Building	Active
1 Feb 1980	ALBANY (CG 10)	Active	Strike
15 Feb 1980	CARPENTER (DD 825)	NRF	Strike
15 Feb 1980	TULARE (LKA 112)	NRF	MA
16 Feb 1980	THORN (DD 988)	Building	Active
23 Feb 1980	JACKSONVILLE (SSN 699)	Building	Active
1 Mar 1980	CHICAGO (CG 11)	Active	Strike
8 Mar 1980	WADSWORTH (FFG 9)	Building	Active
14 Mar 1980	FRANCIS MARION (LPA 249)	NRF	MA
15 Mar 1980	DEYO (DD 989)	Building	Active
1 Apr 1980	SHENANDOAH (AD 26)	Active	Strike
12 Apr 1980	DUNCAN (FFG 10)	Building	Active
1 May 1980	COMPASS ISLAND (AG 153)	Active	MA
1 May 1980	CIMARRON (AO 177)	Building	Active
3 May 1980	INGERSOLL (DD 990)	Building	Active
30 May 1980	NAVAJO (ATF 169)	Building	MSC
7 June 1980	FIFE (DD 991)	Building	Active
21 June 1980	PELELIU (LHA 5)	Building	Active
21 June 1980	DALLAS (SSN 700)	Building	Active
30 June 1980	ARKANSAS (CGN 41)	Building	Active
30 June 1980	WAHOO (SS 565)	Active	Strike
12 July 1980	CLARK (FFG 11)	Building	Active
2 Aug 1980	FLETCHER (DD 992)	Building	Active
9 Aug 1980	MONONGAHELA AO 178)	Building	Active
9 Aug 1980	GEORGE PHILIP (FFG 12)	Building	Active
14 Aug 1980	TATTNALL (DDG 19)	Active	Conversion
15 Aug 1980	BELKNAP (CG 26)	Conversion	Active
31 Aug 1980	ATF 170	Building	MSC
1 Sep 1980	PYRO (AE 24)	Active	NRF
1 Sep 1980	PONCHATULA (AO 148)	Active	MSC
1 Sep 1980	MOBILE (LKA 115)	Active	NRF
30 Sep 1980	MARIAS (T AO 57)	MSC	MA
30 Sep 1980	TALUGA (T AO 62)	MSC	MA
30 Sep 1980	HOWARD W. GILMORE (AS 16)	Active	Reserve Fleet
30 Sep 1980	UTE (T ATF 76)	MSC	MA
30 Sep 1980	LIPAN (T ATF 85)	MSC	MA

Active Fleet Total
30 Sep 1979: 535 ships
30 Sep 1980: 528 ships

INDEXES

COUNTRY ABBREVIATIONS

Alb	Albania	Gra	Grenada	PNG	Papua New Guinea
Alg	Algeria	Gre	Greece	Pol	Poland
Ana	Anguilla	Gua	Guatemala	Por	Portugal
Ang	Angola	Guy	Guyana	Qat	Qatar
Arg	Argentina	Hai	Haiti	RoC	Taiwan
Aus	Austria	HK	Hong Kong	RoK	Korea, Republic (South)
Aust	Australia	Hon	Honduras	Rom	Romania
Ban	Bangladesh	Hun	Hungary	SA	South Africa
Bar	Barbados	IC	Ivory Coast	Sab	Sabah
Bel	Belgium	Ice	Iceland	SAr	Saudi Arabia
Ben	Benin	Ind	India	Sen	Senegal
Bhm	Bahamas	Indo	Indonesia	Sey	Seychelles
Bhr	Bahrain	Iran	Iran	Sin	Singapore
Blz	Belize	Iraq	Iraq	SL	Sierra Leone
Bol	Bolivia	Ire	Ireland	Sol	Solomon Islands
Bru	Brunei	Isr	Israel	Som	Somalia
Brz	Brazil	Ita	Italy	Spn	Spain
Bul	Bulgaria	Jam	Jamaica	Sri	Sri Lanka
Bur	Burma	Jap	Japan	StK	St Kitts
Cam	Cameroon	Jor	Jordan	StL	St Lucia
Can	Canada	Kam	Kampuchea	StV	St Vincent
Chi	Chile	Ken	Kenya	Sud	Sudan
Col	Colombia	Kwt	Kuwait	Sur	Surinam
Com	Comoro Islands	Lao	Laos	Swe	Sweden
Con	Congo	Lbr	Liberia	Syr	Syria
CPR	China, People's Republic	Lby	Libya	Tan	Tanzania
CR	Costa Rica	Leb	Lebanon	Tld	Thailand
Cub	Cuba	Mad	Madagascar	Tog	Togo
Cyp	Cyprus	Mex	Mexico	Ton	Tonga
Cz	Czechoslovakia	Mlt	Malta	TT	Trinidad and Tobago
Den	Denmark	Mlw	Malawi	Tun	Tunisia
DPRK	Korea, Democratic People's Republic (North)	Mly	Malaysia	Tur	Turkey
		Mnt	Montserrat	UAE	United Arab Emirates
DR	Dominican Republic	Mor	Morocco	Uga	Uganda
Ecu	Ecuador	Moz	Mozambique	UK	United Kingdom
Egy	Egypt	Mrt	Mauritius	Uru	Uruguay
ElS	El Salvador	Mtn	Mauritania	USA	United States of America
EqG	Equatorial Guinea	Nic	Nicaragua	USSR	Union of Soviet Socialist Republics
Eth	Ethiopia	Nig	Nigeria	Ven	Venezuela
Fij	Fiji	Nld	Netherlands	VI	Virgin Islands
Fin	Finland	Nor	Norway	Vtn	Viet-Nam
Fra	France	NZ	New Zealand	YAR	Yemen Arab Republic (North)
Gab	Gabon	Omn	Oman	YPDR	Yemen, People's Democratic Republic (South)
Gam	Gambia	Pak	Pakistan		
GB	Guinea Bissau	Pan	Panama	Yug	Yugoslavia
GDR	Germany, Democratic Republic	Par	Paraguay	Zai	Zaire
GFR	Germany, Federal Republic	Per	Peru	Zam	Zambia
Gha	Ghana	Plp	Philippines	Zan	Zanzibar
Gn	Guinea				

NAMED SHIPS

3 De Noviembre (Ecu) 139
6 October (Egy) 142
9 De Octubre (Ecu) 139
10 De Agosto (Ecu) 139
18 De Julio (Uru) 760

A

A. Barbosa (Brz) 68
A. Chirikov (USSR) 558
A. F. Dufour (Bel) 54
A. Smirnov (USSR) 560
A. Vilkitsky (USSR) 558
Aarøsund (Den) 131
AB 21-24 (Tur) 491
AB 25-34 (Tur) 490
Ababeh Ibn Nefeh (Syr) 464
Abaco (Bhm) 50
Abcoude (Nld) 359
Abd Al Rahman (Iraq) 261
Abdiel (UK) 609
Abdul Aziz (SAr) 420
Abdullah Ibn Arissi (Syr) 464
Abeille Normandie (Fra) 190
Aber Wrach (Fra) 183
Aberdovey (UK) 626
Abhay (Ind) 240
Abinger (UK) 626
Abkhaziya (USSR) 562
Abnegar (Iran) 259
Abou Abdallah El Ayachi (Mor) 351
Abra (Plp) 401
Abraham Crijnssen (Nld) 356
Abraham Lincoln (USA) 658
Abrolhos (Brz) 65
Abtao (Per) 388
Abu El Ghoson (Egy) 146
Abu Obaidah (SAr) 420
Abukuma (Jap) 306
Acacia (Fra) 180
Acadia (USA) 723
Acadian (Can) 84
Acajou (Fra) 190
Acanthe (Fra) 180
Acara (Brz) 65
Acchileus (Gre) 224
Acco (Isr) 265
Accohanoc (USA) 738
Accokeek (USA) 731
Acconac (USA) 738
Accord (UK) 624
Acevedo (Spn) 440
Acharné (Fra) 190
Achat (GFR) 210
Acheron (GFR) 206
Achilles (Swe) 462
Achilles (UK) 602
Achziv (Isr) 267
Acklins (Bhm) 50
Acoma (USA) 738
Aconit (Fra) 173
Acor (Por) 413
Actif (Fra) 190
Active (UK) 601
Active (USA) 752
Acushnet (USA) 758
Acute (Aust) 44
Adam Kuckhoff (GDR) 194
Adamidis (Gre) 224
Adatepe (Tur) 488
Addriyah (SAr) 420
Adelaide (Aust) 43
Adige (Ita) 285
Admiral Fokin (USSR) 526
Admiral Golovko (USSR) 526
Admiral Isachenkov (USSR) 524
Admiral Isakov (USSR) 524
Admiral Lazarev (USSR) 527
Admiral Makarov (USSR) .. 524, 576
Admiral Nakhimov (USSR) 524
Admiral Oktyabrsky (USSR) 524
Admiral Pershin (USSR) 545
Admiral Senyavin (USSR) 527
Admiral Ushakov (USSR) 527
Admiral Vladimirsky (USSR) ... 562
Admiral Wm. M. Callaghan (USA) 745
Admiral Yumaschev (USSR) ... 524
Admiral Zozulya (USSR) 525
Adolf Bestelmeyer (GFR) 212
Adroit (Aust) 44
Adroit (USA) 721, 722
Advance (Aust) 44
Advent (Can) 93
Adversus (Can) 84
Advice (UK) 624
Adzhariya (USSR) 562
Aedon (Gre) 222
Aegeon (Gre) 223
Aeger (Nor) 370
Aegir (Ice) 232
Aeolus (USA) 748
Aetos (Gre) 219
Afanasy Nikitin (USSR) 578
Affray (USA) 721, 722
Afif (SAr) 422
Afonso Cerqueira (Por) 412
Afonso de Albuquerque (Por) .. 414
Afonso Pena (Brz) 68
AG 1, 4 (Tur) 498
AG 5, 6 (Tur) 497
Agatan (USSR) 579
Agatha (UK) 625
Agave (Ita) 281
Agawan (USA) 738
Agdleq (Den) 128
Agheila (UK) 607
Agile (UK) 624
Agnes (UK) 625
Agosta (Fra) 162
Agosto, De 10 (Ecu) 139
Agpa (Den) 128
Aguascalientes (Mex) 347
Aguia (Por) 413
Aguila (Chi) 100
Aguilucho (Spn) 447
Aguirre (Per) 389
Agulha (Brz) 65
Agulhas (SA) 430
Agusan (Plp) 400
Ah San (RoK) 323
Ahmed Es Sakali (Mor) 351
Ahoskie (USA) 738
Ahrenshoop (GDR) 195
Aias (Gre) 224
Aigli (Gre) 222
Aigrette (Fra) 190
Aiguiere (Fra) 190
Ainsworth (USA) 705
Aiolos (Gre) 220
Air Sprite (Aust) 48
Airedale (UK) 624
Airone (Ita) 279
Aisberg (USSR) 578
Aitape (PNG) 384
Aiyar Lulin (Bur) 75
Ajax (Swe) 462
Ajax (UK) 602
Ajax (USA) 728
Ajonc (Fra) 188
Akademik Arkhangelsky (USSR) 561
Akademik Korolev (USSR) 564
Akademik Kovalevsky (USSR) .. 560
Akademik Krilov (USSR) 562
Akademik Kurchatov (USSR) ... 564
Akademik L. Orbeli (USSR) 560
Akademik Sergei Korolev (USSR) 566
Akademik Shirshov (USSR) 564
Akademik Vavilov (USSR) 560
Akademik Vernadsky (USSR) ... 564
Akademik Voeykov (USSR) 565
Akagi (Jap) 309
Akashi (Jap) 303
Akbas (Tur) 498
Akhisar (Tur) 491
Akhtuba (USSR) 569
Akigumo (Jap) 294, 309
Akin (Tur) 496
Akiyoshi (Jap) 308
Akizuki (Jap) 295, 309
Akpinar (Tur) 495
Akrama (Lby) 334
Aktion (Gre) 222
Al Adrisi (Iraq) 261
Al Ahad (Lby) 332
Al Aqab (UAE) 582
Al Bachir (Mor) 350
Al Badr (Lby) 332
Al Emlaka (Lby) 335
Al Farouq (SAr) 420
Al Fateh (Lby) 332
Al Fulk (Omn) 376
Al Ghazi (Iraq) 261
Al Ghullan (UAE) 581
Al Jabbar (Omn) 376
Al Jala (Tun) 485
Al Kadisia (Iraq) 262
Al Keriat (Lby) 335
Al Makas (Egy) 146
Al Mansur (Omn) 376
Al Mubaraki (Kwt) 329
Al Mujahid (Omn) 376
Al Munassir (Omn) 377
Al Nasiri (Omn) 376
Al Nasser (Egy) 142
Al Nejah (Omn) 376
Al Qiaq (SAr) 422
Al Quysumah (SAr) 420
Al Riyadh (SAr) 422
Al Said (Omn) 376
Al Salemi (Kwt) 329
Al Salihi (Omn) 376
Al Sansoor (Omn) 377
Al Shaab (Iraq) 261
Al Shurti (Kwt) 329
Al Shaheen (UAE) 582
Al Shweirif (Lby) 335
Al Sultana (Omn) 377
Al Tami (Iraq) 261
Al Thawra (Iraq) 262
Al Ula (SAr) 422
Al Wadeeah (SAr) 420
Al Wafi (Omn) 376
Al Wusaail (Qat) 415
Al Yarmouk (Iraq) 262
Al Yarmouk (SAr) 420
Al Zaffer (Egy) 142
Alabarda (Por) 414
Alacrity (UK) 601
Alagoas (Brz) 62
Alain Kobis (GDR) 194
Alakush (Arg) 31
Alamagordo (USA) 734
Alambai (USSR) 571
Alamgir (Pak) 381
Alamo (USA) 716
Alarich (GFR) 210
Alatna (USA) 748
Alatyr (USSR) 570
Albacora (Por) 411
Albacore (USA) 670
Albany (USA) 692
Albardão (Brz) 65
Albatros (Ita) 279
Albatros (Pol) 407
Albatros (Spn) 447
Albatros II (Spn) 447
Albatros III (Spn) 447
Albatros (Tur) 490
Albatroz (Por) 413
Albay Hakki Burak (Tur) 495
Albenga (Ita) 286
Albert David (USA) 707
Albert Gast (GDR) 194
Albert J. Meyer (USA) 748
Alblas (Nld) 359
Alcatraz (Spn) 441
Alcalá Galiano (Spn) 436
Alcione (Ita) 279
Aldan (USSR) 579
Aldebarán (DR) 135
Aldebaran (Fra) 178
Aldebaran (Swe) 455
Alderney (UK) 614
Ale (Swe) 460
Alef (Iraq) 261
Aleksandr Nevski (USSR) 527
Aleksandr Suvorov (USSR) 527
Aleksandr Tortsev (USSR) 550
Alençon (Fra) 179
Alert (Can) 92
Alert (Lbr) 331
Alert (UK) 626
Alert (USA) 752
Alexander Hamilton (USA) 655
Alexander Henry (Can) 90
Alexander Mackenzie (Can) 92
Alferez Sobral (Arg) 29
Alfonso Vargas (Col) 117
Alfred Herring VC (UK) 628
Alfred Merz (GDR) 196
Alfriston (UK) 610
Algarna III (Tur) 498
Alghero (Ita) 281
Algonquin (Can) 80
Ali Haider (Ban) 51
Alice (UK) 625
Alicudi (Ita) 284
Alidada (USSR) 557
Aliseo (Ita) 276
Alkmaar (Nld) 358
Alkyon (Gre) 222
Alloro (Ita) 281
Alma (USSR) 557
Almirante Brasil (Brz) 68
Almirante Brion (Ven) 766
Almeida Carvalho (Por) 414
Almirante Brion (Ven) 767
Almirante Camara (Brz) 66
Almirante Clemente (Ven) 767
Almirante Domecq Garcia (Arg) 28
Almirante Gago Coutinho (Por) 412
Almirante Garcia de los Reyes (Spn) 434
Almirante Grau (Bol) 57
Almirante Grau (Per) 389
Almirante Irizar (Arg) 33
Almirante Jeronimo Goncalves (Brz) 68
Almirante Lynch (Chi) 98
Almirante Magalhaes Correa (Por) 412
Almirante Pereira Da Silva (Por) 412
Almirante Riveros (Chi) 97
Almirante Saldanha (Brz) 66
Almirante Storni (Arg) 28
Almirante Valdes (Spn) 436
Almirante Williams (Chi) 97
Alness (UK) 626
Alnmouth (UK) 626
Alor Star (Mly) 340
Alouette (Fra) 190
Alphée (Fra) 188
Alpino (Ita) 277
Alsatian (UK) 624
Alsedo (Spn) 439
Alsfeld (GFR) 213
Alssund (Den) 131
Alste (GFR) 212
Alta (Nor) 372
Altai (USSR) 572
Altair (Fra) 178
Altair (USSR) 558
Altay (USSR) 570
Altenburg (GDR) 195
Altentreptow (GDR) 195
Alunya (Plp) 404
Alvaro Alberto (Arg) 32
Alvaro Alberto (Brz) 65
Alvin (USA) 672
Alvsborg (Swe) 456
Alvsnabben (Swe) 457
AMI-8 (Mex) 346
Amakusa (Jap) 308
Amami (Jap) 300, 307
Aman (Kwt) 329
Amapa (Brz) 65
Amar (Mrt) 343
Amatsukaze (Jap) 295
Amazon (UK) 601
Amazonas (Brz) 60
Amazonas (Ecu) 140
Amazonas (Per) 392
Amazonas (Ven) 768
Amazone (Fra) 163
Amazone (GFR) 206
Amba (Ind) 242
Ambe (Nig) 367
Ambuscade (UK) 601
America (Per) 392
America (USA) 678
American Explorer (USA) 747
Amerigo Vespucci (Ita) 284
Ametyst (USSR) 539
Amga (USSR) 554
AMI-8 (Mex) 346
Amilcare (Tur) 484
Amindivi (Ind) 237
Amini (Ind) 237
Amiral Charner (Fra) 173
Ammersee (GFR) 208
Ammiraglio Magnaghi (Ita) 282
Ampermetr (USSR) 557
Amphitriti (Gre) 216
Amrum (GFR) 211
Amsel (GFR) 210
Amsterdam (Nld) 356
Amur (USSR) 579
Amurang (Indo) 249
Amvrakia (Gre) 222
Amyot D'Inville (Fra) 175
Amyr (SAr) 420
An Yang (RoC) 467
Anadir (USSR) 558
Anapal (Uru) 763
Anchorage (USA) 716
Anchova (Brz) 65
Andagoya (Col) 119
Andalucia (Spn) 438
Andaman (Ind) 237
Andenes (Nor) 374
Andenne (Bel) 55
Anders Bure (Swe) 461
Andorinha (Por) 413
Andrea Bafile (Ita) 280
Andrea Doria (Ita) 273
Andres Bonifacio (Plp) 398
Andres Quintana Roos (Mex) ... 346
Andrew Jackson (USA) 655
Andrija Mohorovicic (Yug) 780
Andromeda (Gre) 220
Andromeda (USSR) 558
Andromeda (UK) 602
Andros (Bhm) 50
Androth (Ind) 237
Ane (Swe) 459
Aneriod (USSR) 557
Ang Pangulo (Plp) 403
Angamos (Chi) 101
Angamos (Per) 388
Anglesey (UK) 614
Angostura (Brz) 64
Angthong (Tld) 479
Anhatomirim (Brz) 65
Anita Garibaldi (Brz) 68
Anjadip (Ind) 237
Annapolis (Can) 81
Anoa (Indo) 247
Anoka (USA) 738
Anshan (CPR) 105
Antaios (Gre) 224
Antar (Egy) 146
Antares (Spn) 444
Antares (USSR) 558
Antarktyda (USSR) 558
Antelope (UK) 601
Anteo (Ita) 284
Anthiploiarhos Anninos (Gre) .. 219
Antigo (USA) 738
Antiopi (Gre) 222
Antiploiarhos Laskos (Gre) 219
Antiploiarhos Pezopoulos (Gre) 221
Antizana (Ecu) 140
Anton Dohrn (GFR) 213
Anton Saefkow (GDR) 194
Antonio Enes (Por) 412
Antonio de la Fuente (Mex) 346
Antonio Picardi (Ven) 769
Antrim (UK) 598
Antrim (USA) 703
Anvil (USA) 758
Aoif (Ire) 263
Aokumo (Jap) 294
Apalachee (USA) 759
Apalachicola (USA) 738
Ape (Ita) 279
Apohola (USA) 738
Apollo (UK) 602
Apopka (USA) 738
Appleby (UK) 626
Aprendiz Ledio Conceiçao (Brz) 68
Apsheron (USSR) 562
Apu (Fin) 153
Aquila (Ita) 279
Aquila (USA) 709
Aquiles (Chi) 101
Ar Rakib (Lby) 334
Ara (Fra) 190
Aracatuba (Brz) 65
Aragon (Spn) 441
Aragosta (Ita) 282
Aragui (USSR) 571
Araka (Tan) 474
Arakan (UK) 607
Arashio (Jap) 292
Arataki (NZ) 364
Aratu (Brz) 65
Arau (Mly) 340
Arauca (Col) 117
Araucano (Chi) 101
Arawak (USA) 738
Arcata (USA) 738
Archerfish (USA) 662
Archimède (Fra) 186
Arcona (GFR) 212
Arcturus (Fra) 178
Arcturus (Swe) 455
Ardang (Tld) 480
Ardennes (UK) 607
Ardent (Aust) 44
Ardent (UK) 601
Ardhana (UAE) 581
Ardito (Ita) 274
Arenque (Brz) 65
Arethousa (Gre) 223
Arethusa (UK) 602
Aréthuse (Fra) 163
Arg (Nor) 371
Argens (Fra) 176
Argentina (Brz) 68
Argo (Gre) 222, 224
Argonaut (GFR) 210
Argonaut (UK) 602
Argonaute (Fra) 163
Argungu (Nig) 367
Argus (Brz) 66
Argus (Nld) 361
Argus (USA) 752
Arhikelefstis Maliopoulos (Gre) 221
Arhikelefstis Stassis (Gre) 221
Ariadne (GFR) 206
Ariadne (UK) 602
Ariadni (Gre) 223
Ariane (Fra) 163
Arica (Per) 388
Ariel (Fra) 188
Aries (Indo) 250
Aries (USA) 709
Arild (Swe) 456
Arinya (Plp) 404
Aris (Gre) 223
Ark Royal (UK) 594
Arkansas (USA) 686
Arkhipelag (USSR) 556
Arkö (Swe) 458
Arkona (GDR) 197
Arktika (USSR) 576
Armoise (Fra) 189
Arnala (Ind) 237
Arrow (UK) 601
Artemiz (Iran) 255
Artevelde (Bel) 54
Arthur Becker (GDR) 194
Arthur W. Radford (USA) 698
Artigas (Uru) 760
Artika (USSR) 558
Aruana (Brz) 65
Arundel (USA) 759
Arvakur (Ice) 232
Arvid Harnack (GDR) 194
Ary Parreiras (Brz) 67
Arzachena (Ita) 286
As Saddiq (SAr) 420
As Sulayel (SAr) 422

INDEXES / Named Ships 821

Asagiri (Jap) 310
Asagumo (Jap) 294, 309
Asakaze (Jap) 293
Asama (Jap) 309
Asashio (Jap) 292
Ashanti (UK) 603
Ashcott (UK) 626
Ashdod (Isr) 267
Ashitaka (Jap) 308
Ashkelon (Isr) 267
Ashtabula (USA) 726
Asinara (Ita) 286
Askar (Bhr) 50
Askø (Den) 130
Askold (USSR) 558
Asoyuki (Jap) 310
Aspis (Gre) 218
Aspö (Swe) 458
Aspro (USA) 662
Assail (Aust) 44
Assiniboine (Can) 82
Assiut (Egy) 145
Astice (Ita) 282
Astore (Ita) 279
Astrapi (Gre) 220
Astrea (Swe) 455
Asturias (Spn) 438
ASU 81-85 (Jap) 303
Asuantsi (Gha) 214
Aswan (Egy) 145
Atada (Jap) 304
Atahualpa (Ecu) 140
Atair (GFR) 206, 213
Atakapa (USA) 731
Atalaia (Brz) 65
Atalanti (Gre) 223
ATB 1, 2, 3 (Swe) 462
Athabaskan (Can) 80
Atico (Per) 393
Atika (Iraq) 260
Atilay (Tur) 487
Atlante (Ita) 285
Atlantis (GFR) 206
Atlas (Gre) 224
Atlas (Swe) 462
Atlas (USSR) 557
Atle (Swe) 460
Atmaca (Tur) 490
Atrevida (Spn) 439
Atromitos (Gre) 224
Atsumi (Jap) 299
Attack (Aust) 44
Attilio Bagnolini (Ita) 271
Attock (Pak) 383
Atum (Brz) 65
Atún (DR) 136
Atyimba (Plp) 404
Audace (Ita) 274
Audaz (Brz) 68
Audrey (UK) 625
Augsburg (GFR) 203
August Lüttgens (GDR) 194
Augusto de Castilho (Por) 412
Aunis (Fra) 185
Auricula (UK) 621
Aurora (Plp) 401
Aurora (UK) 602
Ausonia (Ita) 286
Austin (USA) 715
Aveley (UK) 611
Avenger (UK) 601
Averof (Gre) 225
Avon (UK) 608
Avra (Gre) 222
Awaji (Jap) 300, 307
Aware (Aust) 44
Axe (USA) 758
Ayabane (Jap) 314
Ayanami (Jap) 296
Ayanasi (Pan) 384
Ayase (Jap) 297
Aylwin (USA) 705
Aysberg (USSR) 559
Aytodor (USSR) 558
Azalea (USA) 757
Azalée (Fra) 180
Azimut (USSR) 559
Azor (Spn) 445
Azov (USSR) 522
Azueta (Mex) 346
Azuma (Jap) 301
Azumanche (Gua) 226

B

Baagø (Den) 130
Babr (Iran) 255
Babur (Pak) 379
Baccarat (Fra) 179
Bacchante (UK) 602
Bacchus (UK) 620
Bad Bramstedt (GFR) 213
Bad Doberan (GDR) 193
Badek (Mly) 338
Badger (USA) 705
Badr (Pak) 380
Badr (SAr) 420
Baffin (Can) 93
Bagley (USA) 705
Bahaira (Egy) 145
Bahawalpur (Pak) 382
Bahia (Brz) 60
Bahia Aguirre (Arg) 32
Bahia Buen Suceso (Arg) 32
Bahia Camarones (Arg) 32
Bahia San Blas (Arg) 32
Bahia Utria (Col) 119
Bahmanshir (Iran) 259
Bahaira (Egy) 145
Bahram (Iran) 256
Bahrain I (Bhr) 50
Baiana (Brz) 64
Baikal (USSR) 563
Bainbridge (USA) 691
Bakan (USSR) 556
Bakasi (Cam) 76
Balas (Pol) 408
Balawatha (Sri) 448
Balder (Nld) 358
Balder (Swe) 459
Baleares (Spn) 438
Baleno (Ita) 280
Baler (Plp) 400
Balikpapan (Aust) 47
Balikpapan (Indo) 251
Balizador (Par) 386
Balkhash (USSR) 563
Balny (Fra) 173
Balsa (Fra) 190
Balsam (USA) 756
Baltimore (USA) 659
Baltrum (GFR) 211
Baltyk (Pol) 408
Baluchistan (Pak) 381
Bambu (Ita) 281
Banba (Ire) 263
Banckert (Nld) 356
Banco Ingles (Uru) 763
Bandar Abbas (Iran) 258
Bangeko (Tld) 479
Banggai (Indo) 251
Bangrachan (Tld) 478
Bangpakong (Tld) 480
Bani Yas (UAE) 581
Banks (Aust) 47
Bannu (Pak) 382
Bansin (GDR) 195
Banten (Indo) 249
Baptiste de Andrade (Por) 412
Baraka (Sud) 450
Barakuda (Indo) 247
Barb (USA) 663
Barbara (GFR) 212
Barbara (Ita) 283
Barbara (UK) 625
Barbe (GFR) 205
Barbel (UK) 628
Barbel (USA) 667
Barbette (Aust) 44
Barbey (USA) 705
Barbour County (USA) 717
Barcelo (Spn) 440
Barguzin (USSR) 571
Barney (USA) 695
Barnstable County (USA) 717
Barograf (USSR) 557
Barometr (USSR) 557
Barq (Ind) 243
Barracuda (Gua) 226
Barracuda (Por) 411
Barricade (Aust) 44
Barroso Pereira (Brz) 67
Barry (USA) 700
Barsø (Den) 129
Barsuk (USSR) 538
Bartlett (Can) 91
Bartlett (USA) 741
Barzan (Qat) 415
Basanta (Spn) 447
Basaran (Tur) 496
Basento (Ita) 285
Bashkiriya (USSR) 562
Basilan (Plp) 400
Baskunchak (USSR) 562
Bass (Aust) 47
Bassein (Ind) 241
Basset (UK) 624
Basswood (USA) 756
Bat Sheva (Isr) 267
Bat Yam (Isr) 267
Batanes (Plp) 402
Batangas (Plp) 399
Batiray (Tur) 487
Batfish (USA) 662
Baton Rouge (USA) 659
Battleaxe (UK) 599
Baung (Mly) 338
Bauru (Brz) 67
Bauten (Indo) 236
Bayandor (Iran) 256
Bayberry (USA) 757
Bayern (GFR) 202
Bayfield (Can) 93
Baykalsk (USSR) 579
Bayonet (Aust) 44
Bayovar (Peru) 394
Bayraktar (Tur) 493
Bayreuth (GFR) 213
BDI-4 (Arg) 30
Bditelny (USSR) 535
BDK 2, 3, 4, 5, 6, 7 & 8 (Spn) 442
Beachampton (UK) 615
Beacon (USA) 710
Beagle (Chi) 101
Beagle (UK) 616
Beamsville (Can) 86
Bear (USA) 752
Beas (Ind) 238
Beaufort (USA) 732
Beaulieu (UK) 626
Beauport (Can) 93
Beddgelert (UK) 626
Bedovy (USSR) 530
Bee (UK) 625
Belbek (USSR) 559
Beledau (Mly) 338
Belegis (Yug) 779
Belikawa (Sri) 448
Belize (Blz) 57
Belknap (USA) 689
Bellatrix (DR) 135
Belleau Wood (USA) 713
Bellona (Den) 127
Belmonte (Brz) 67
Belmopan (Blz) 57
Belos (Swe) 461
Bembridge (UK) 626
Bendahara (Bru) 69
Bendigo (Aust) 43
Bengali (Fra) 190
Benin (Nig) 367
Benina (Lby) 334
Benjamin Franklin (USA) 655
Benjamin Stoddert (USA) 695
Bennington (USA) 684
Bentang Kalungkang (Indo) 248
Bentang Silungkang (Indo) 248
Bentang Waitatire (Indo) 248
Bentara (Mly) 340
Berezan (USSR) 558
Berezina (USSR) 568, 574
Berezinsk (USSR) 579
Bergall (USA) 662
Bergen (GDR) 195
Bergen (Nor) 369
Berk (Tur) 489
Berkel (Nld) 348
Berkeley (USA) 695
Berlaimont (Fra) 179
Berlayer (Sin) 425
Berlin (GDR) 197
Bernau (GDR) 195
Berneval (Fra) 179
Bernhard Bästlein (GDR) 194
Berry (Fra) 185
Berry Head (UK) 611
Bertha (Cub) 123
Beruang (Indo) 247
Berwick (UK) 604
Beskytteren (Den) 126
Bessmenny (USSR) 535
Betano (Aust) 47
Betelgeuse (DR) 135
Bételgeuse (Fra) 180
Betty (UK) 625
Betwa (Ind) 238
Bévéziers (Fra) 162
Beyrouth (Leb) 331
Bezhitsa (USSR) 567
Bezukoriznenny (USSR) 534
Bezuprechniy (USSR) 534
Bhaktal (Ind) 241
Bholu (Pak) 383
Bi Bong (RoK) 326
Bibb (USA) 751
Bibury (UK) 626
Bickington (UK) 610
Bidassoa (Fra) 176
Biddle (USA) 689
Biduk (Indo) 251
Bielik (Pol) 405
Bigelow (USA) 700
Bihoro (Jap) 306
Bij (Bel) 56
Bikovac (Yug) 777
Bilbino (USSR) 579
Bildeston (UK) 610
Bille (Den) 127
Billfish (USA) 662
Bimbia (Cam) 76
Bimlipitan (Ind) 241
Binbasi Saadettin Gurcan (Tur) 495
Birinci Inönü (Tur) 487
Birmingham (UK) 600
Birmingham (USA) 659
Biscayne Bay (USA) 754
Bitol (Gua) 226
Bitt (USA) 759
Bitterfeld (GDR) 195
Bittersweet (USA) 756
Bizan (Jap) 309
Bizerte (Tun) 485
Bizon (Pol) 407
Black Rover (UK) 618
Blackan (Swe) 458
Blackberry (USA) 757
Blackthorn (USA) 756
Blacthaw (USA) 756
Blagorodny (USSR) 533
Blake (UK) 596
Blakely (USA) 705
Blakeney (UK) 626
Blanco Encalada (Chi) 96
Blandy (USA) 700
Blas de Lezo (Spn) 436
Blavet (Fra) 176
Blestyashchy (USSR) 533
Blidö (Swe) 458
Blink (Nor) 371
Blitvenica (Yug) 778
Blois van Treslong (Nld) 356
Blommendal (Nld) 360
Blue Ridge (USA) 712
Blue Rover (UK) 618
Blueback (USA) 667
Bluebell (USA) 757
Bluefish (USA) 662
Bluethroat (Can) 84
Bobr (Pol) 407
Bodry (USSR) 535
Boeo (Ita) 286
Bogalusa (USA) 738
Bogra (Ban) 52
Bohechio (DR) 136
Bojeador (Plp) 403
Bollard (USA) 759
Bolshevetsk (USSR) 579
Bolster (USA) 728
Boltenhagen (GDR) 195
Bombard (Aust) 44
Bombarda (Por) 414
Bon Homme Richard (USA) 683
Bonefish (USA) 667
Bonifaz (Spn) 439
Bonite (Fra) 190
Bonny (Nig) 367
Bontoc (Plp) 400
Booshehr (Iran) 258
Bora (Tur) 490
Borac (Yug) 776
Borasco (GFR) 210
Bore (Swe) 459
Borgen (Nor) 372
Borgsund (Nor) 372
Boris Butoma (USSR) 569
Boris Chilikin (USSR) 569
Boris Davidov (USSR) 558
Bormida (Ita) 285
Borodino (USSR) 553
Borovichi (USSR) 567
Bossington (UK) 610
Boston (USA) 659
Bouchard (Arg) 28
Boulanouar (Mtn) 342
Boulder (USA) 717
Bouleau (Fra) 190
Boussole (Fra) 181
Boutwell (USA) 750
Bouvet (Fra) 172
Bowditch (USA) 743
Bowen (USA) 705
Boyaca (Col) 117
Boyky (USSR) 531
Bradano (Ita) 285
Bradley (USA) 707
Brahmaputra (Ind) 238
Bramastra (Indo) 245
Bramble (USA) 756
Brani (Sin) 425
Brann (Nor) 371
Brännaren (Swe) 461
Bras (Nig) 367
Bras D'Or (Can) 84
Brask (Nor) 371
Brasse (GFR) 205
Braunschweig (GFR) 203
Bravy (USSR) 532
Brazen (UK) 599
Bream (UK) 628
Brecon (UK) 609
Bredal (Den) 127
Breitling (GDR) 197
Bremerton (USA) 659
Brenda (UK) 625, 627
Brenta (Ita) 285
Brereton (UK) 610
Breshtau (USSR) 572
Brewton (USA) 705
Breydel (Bel) 54
Bridget (UK) 625
Bridle (USA) 759
Brigadier M'Bonga Tounda (Cam) 76
Brigant (GFR) 210
Brighton (UK) 604
Brillant (USSR) 539
Brilliant (UK) 599
Brinchang (Mly) 339
Brinton (UK) 610
Brisbane (Aust) 40
Briscoe (USA) 698
Bristol (UK) 597
Bristol Bay (USA) 754
Bristol County (USA) 717
Britannia (UK) 612
Brittanic (UK) 621
Broadsword (UK) 599
Brodick (UK) 626
Bromo (Indo) 252
Bronington (UK) 610
Bronstein (USA) 708
Brooke (USA) 704
Brott (Nor) 371
Brumby (USA) 707
Brunei (Aust) 47
Bruno Kühn (GDR) 194
Bruno Racua (Bol) 57
Brunswick (USA) 732
Bryce Canyon (USA) 723
Buccaneer (Aust) 44
Buccoo Reef (TT) 482
Buchanan (USA) 695
Bucklesham (UK) 622
Buckthorn (USA) 757
Bude (UK) 608
Bui Viet Thanh (Vtn) 771
Buk (GDR) 196
Buk Han (RoK) 326
Bukindon (Plp) 401
Bula (Indo) 251
Bulgia (Nld) 358
Bulldog (UK) 616
Bulsar (Ind) 241
Bulwark (UK) 593
Buna (PNG) 385
Bunbury (Aust) 43
Burak Reis (Tur) 487
Buran (USSR) 578
Burdjamhal (Indo) 250
Burlivy (USSR) 533
Burrard (Can) 86
Burudjulasad (Indo) 249
Bushnell (USA) 730
Bussemaker (Nld) 359
Butt (GFR) 205
Butte (USA) 724
Buttonwood (USA) 756
Bützow (GDR) 193
Buyskes (Nld) 360
Buyvol (USSR) 538
Byblos (Leb) 331
Byk (USSR) 538
Byvaly (USSR) 533

C

Cabo Fradera (Spn) 441
Cabo Odger (Chi) 99
Cabo Roxo (GB) 227
Cabo San Antonio (Arg) 30
Cabo San Gonzalo (Arg) 30
Cabo San Pio (Arg) 30
Cabo San Vincente (Arg) 30
Cabocla (Brz) 64
Cabrakan (Gua) 225
Cacine (Por) 413
Cadarso (Spn) 439
Cagayan (Plp) 401
Caio Duilio (Ita) 273
Cairn (UK) 624
Çakabey (Tur) 494
Cakra (Indo) 245
Calchaqui (Arg) 34
Calderas (DR) 134, 136
Caldy (UK) 627
Calibio (Col) 117
Calicuchima (Ecu) 140
California (USA) 687
Callenburgh (Nld) 356
Calliope (Fra) 179
Calmar (Fra) 187
Caloosahatchee (USA) 726
Camalote (Gua) 226
Camarines Norte (Plp) 402
Camarines Sur (Plp) 402
Cambiaso (DR) 134
Camboria (Brz) 64
Camden (USA) 727
Camélia (Fra) 180
Camiguin (Plp) 400
Camilo Cienfuegos (Cub) 123
Camocim (Brz) 66
Camoudie (Guy) 228
Campbell (USA) 751
Campti (USA) 738
Camsell (Can) 89
Canakkale (Tur) 487
Canal Beagle (Arg) 32
Canberra (Aust) 43
Candarli (Tur) 495
Candido De Lasala (Arg) 30
Candido Leguizamo (Col) 119
Candido Pérez (Spn) 440
Candrasa (Indo) 245
Canisteo (USA) 726
Cannamore (Ind) 241
Canonchet (USA) 738
Canopo (Ita) 278
Canopus (Brz) 66
Canopus (Fra) 178
Canopus (USA) 729
Canterbury (NZ) 362

822 INDEXES / Named Ships

Cantho (Fra) 179
Caonabo (DR) 137
Caorle (Ita) 280
Capayan (Arg) 34
Cape (Can) 92
Cape (USA) 722
Cape Breton (Can) 83
Cape Carter (USA) 755
Cape Cod (USA) 723
Cape Coral (USA) 755
Cape Corwin (USA) 755
Cape Cross (USA) 755
Cape Current (USA) 755
Cape Fairweather (USA) 755
Cape Fox (USA) 755
Cape George (USA) 755
Cape Gull (USA) 755
Cape Harrison (Can) 92
Cape Hedge (USA) 755
Cape Henlopen (USA) 755
Cape Horn (USA) 755
Cape Jellison (USA) 755
Cape Knox (USA) 755
Cape Louisburg (Can) 92
Cape Morgan (USA) 755
Cape Newagen (USA) 755
Cape Rogers (Can) 92
Cape Romain (USA) 755
Cape Shoalwater (USA) 755
Cape Small (USA) 755
Cape Starr (USA) 755
Cape Strait (USA) 755
Cape Wash (USA) 755
Cape York (USA) 755
Capella (DR) 135
Capella (Fra) 180
Capella (Swe) 454
Capitan Alsina (DR) 135
Capitan Alvaro Ruiz (Col) 119
Capitan Beotegui (DR) 136
Capitan Cabral (Par) 386
Capitan Castro (Col) 119
Capitan General Pedro
Santana (DR) 134
Capitan Meza (Par) 385
Capitan Miranda (Uru) 762
Capitan Parra (Spn) 447
Capitan Quiñones (Per) 389
Capitan R. D. Binney (Col) 117
Capitan Rigoberto Giraldo
(Col) 119
Capitan Vladimir Valek
(Col) 119
Capitan W. Arvelo (DR) 136
Capiz (Plp) 399
Capodanno (USA) 705
Capotillo (DR) 136
Caprera (Ita) 286
Capricorne (Fra) 180
Capstan (USA) 759
Captor (Can) 84
Capucine (Fra) 189
Carabiniere (Ita) 277
Carabobo (Ven) 766
Caravelas (Brz) 66
Carbonara (Ita) 286
Cardenas (Per) 393
Cardiff (UK) 600
Caribe (Cub) 123
Caribe (Ven) 765
Carite (DR) 136
Carl Vinson (USA) 675
Carlo Bergamini (Ita) 278
Carlo Margottini (Ita) 278
Carlos Alban (Col) 118
Carlos E. Restrepo (Col) 118
Carlos Galindo (Col) 117
Carmelo (Uru) 762
Caron (USA) 698
Carp (UK) 628
Carpenter (USA) 702
Carsamba (Tur) 495
Cartagena (Col) 117
Cartmel (UK) 626
Casabianca (Fra) 172
Casamance (Sen) 422
Cascade (Fra) 190
Casimir Pulaski (USA) 655
Castagno (Ita) 281
Castelhanos (Brz) 66
Castilla (Spn) 441
Castor (Chi) 102
Castor (GFR) 206
Castor (Spn) 444
Castor (Swe) 454
Castore (Ita) 278
Catahecassa (USA) 738
Cataluña (Spn) 438
Catanduanes (Plp) 400
Catawba (USA) 731
Catenary (USA) 759
Cattistock (UK) 609
Cavalla (USA) 662
Cavilla (Lbr) 331
Cawsand (UK) 626
Cayambe (Ecu) 140
Cayuga (USA) 717
Cazadora (Spn) 437
Ceara (Brz) 60
Cebu (Plp) 399
Cedro (Ita) 281
Centaure (Fra) 189
Centauro (Brz) 68
Centauro (Ita) 278
Céphée (Fra) 180
Cer (Yug) 778
Cerbe (Tur) 487
Ceres (Fra) 179
Cessnock (Aust) 43
Cezayirli Gazi Hasan Paşa (Tur) . 495
Chaco (Arg) 31
Chaguaramus (TT) 482
Chahbahar (Iran) 258
Chaleur (Can) 85
Chamak (Ind) 240
Chamois (Fra) 184
Champion (UK) 629
Champlain (Fra) 176
Chandhara (Tld) 480
Chang (Tld) 479
Chang Chiang (CPR) 107
Chang Chun (CPR) 105
Chang Pai Shan (CPR) 112
Chang Pei (RoC) 473
Chang Pi (CPR) 107
Chapare (Bol) 57
Chapal (Ind) 240
Charag (Ind) 240
Charkieh (Egy) 145
Charles F. Adams (USA) 695
Charles P. Cecil (USA) 701, 702
Charleston (USA) 718
Charlotte (UK) 625
Charme (Fra) 190
Charn (Tld) 481
Charybdis (UK) 602
Chase (USA) 750
Chataigner (Fra) 190
Chatak (Ind) 240
Chatoyer (St V) 419
Chattahoochee (USA) 748
Chaudiere (Can) 81
Chauvenet (USA) 743
Chazhma (USSR) 565
Chegodega (USA) 738
Cheleken (USSR) 558
Chen Hai (RoC) 470
Chena (USA) 758
Chène (Fra) 190
Ch'eng Tu (CPR) 106
Chepachet (USA) 747
Chepanoc (USA) 738
Cheraw (USA) 738
Cheremshan (USSR) 571
Cherokee (USA) 758
Chesaning (USA) 738
Chetek (USA) 738
Chevreuil (Fra) 184
Cheyenne (USA) 758
Chi Lin (CPR) 105
Chi Nam Po (Rok) 327
Chi Nan (CPR) 107
Chiang Sha (CPR) 107
Chiburi (Jap) 300
Chicago (USA) 692
Chien Yang (RoC) 466
Chifuri (Jap) 308
Chignecto (Can) 85
Chihaya (Jap) 302
Chihuahua (Mex) 345
Chikugo (Jap) 297, 306
Chilula (USA) 758
Chimborazo (Ecu) 140
Chimbote (Per) 392
Chimère (Fra) 189
Chinaltenango (Gua) 226
Ch'ing Kang Shan (CPR) 112
Ching Yang (RoC) 467
Chinguetti (Mtn) 343
Chinook (USA) 759
Chioggia (Ita) 286
Chios (Gre) 221
Chippewa (USA) 758
Chiquillan (Arg) 34
Chiriguano (Arg) 34
Chitose (Jap) 297, 307
Chiu Hua (RoC) 472
Chiu Lien (RoC) 472
Chock (USA) 759
Chokeberry (USA) 757
Chömpff (Nld) 359
Chowl (Ire) 263
Chr Ju (RoK) 323
Christina (Gre) 224
Christine (UK) 625
Chu Yung (RoC) 468
Chuang (Tld) 481
Chub (UK) 628
Chubut (Arg) 31
Chui (Ken) 316
Chula (Tld) 480
Chulupi (Arg) 34
Chulym (USSR) 573
Chumikan (USSR) 565
Chun Ji (RoK) 327
Chung Buk (RoK) 322
Chung Cheng (RoC) 470, 471
Chung Chi (RoC) 471
Chung Chiang (RoC) 471
Chung Chien (RoC) 471
Chung Chih (RoC) 471
Chung Chuan (RoC) 471
Chung Fu (RoC) 471
Chung Hai (RoC) 471
Chung Hsing (RoC) 471
Chung Kuang (RoC) 471
Chung Lien (RoC) 471
Chung Ming (RoC) 471
Chung Mu (RoK) 322
Chung Nam (RoK) 323
Chung Pang (RoC) 471
Chung Shan (RoC) 468
Chung Sheng (RoC) 471
Chung Shu (RoC) 471
Chung Shun (RoC) 471
Chung Suo (RoC) 471
Chung Ting (RoC) 471
Chung Tung (CPR) 106
Chung Wan (RoC) 471
Chung Yeh (RoC) 471
Chung Yung (RoC) 471
Churchill (UK) 590
Churruca (Spn) 436
Cicala (UK) 625
Ciclope (Ita) 285
Cidade de Natal (Brz) 68
Cigale (Fra) 187
Cigno (Ita) 278
Cigogne (Fra) 190
Cimarron (USA) 726, 758
Cincinnati (USA) 659
Cinq Juin (Sey) 423
Circé (Fra) 179
Circeo (Ita) 286
Cirujano Videla (Chi) 101
Cisne (Por) 413
Citadelle Henry (Hai) 228
Citrus (USA) 756
Ciudad de Quibdo (Col) 119
Clamp (USA) 728, 758
Clare (UK) 625
Clark (USA) 703
Claude V. Ricketts (USA) 695
Cleat (USA) 759
Clemenceau (Fra) 164
Cleopatra (UK) 602
Cleveland (USA) 715
Clio (Fra) 179
Clovelly (UK) 626
Clover (USA) 756
Clyde (UK) 608
Coahuila (Mex) 345
Coatopa (USA) 738
Coburg (GFR) 209
Cochali (USA) 738
Cochrane (Chi) 96
Cochrane (USA) 695
Cockhafer (UK) 625
Colac (Aust) 48
Colbert (Fra) 167
Colibri (Fra) 190
Colleen (Ire) 263
Collie (UK) 624
Colocolo (Chi) 102
Colonia (Uru) 761
Colosso (Ita) 286
Columbia (Can) 81
Columbia (USA) 746
Comanche (USA) 759
Comandante Arandia (Bol) 57
Comandante Araya (Chi) 100
Comandante Hemmerdinger
(Chi) 100
Comandante Hermenegildo
Capelo (Por) 411
Comandante João Belo (Por) 411
Comandante Pedro Campbell
(Uru) 761
Comandante Roberto Ivens
(Por) 411
Comandante Sacadura Cabral
(Por) 411
Comet (USA) 745
Commandant Blaison (Fra) 175
Commandant Bory (Fra) 173
Commandant Bourdais (Fra) 173
Commandant de Pimodan (Fra) 175
Commandant Rivière (Fra) 173
Commandante General
Irigoyen (Arg) 29
Commander Marshall (Bar) 53
Como Manuel Azueta (Mex) 344
Comodoro Py (Arg) 28
Comodoro Rivadavia (Arg) 32
Comodoro Somellera (Arg) 29
Compass Island (USA) 725
Comte de Grasse (USA) 698
Concord (USA) 724
Conde de Venadito (Spn) 442
Condell (Chi) 98
Condor (Ita) 279
Condor (Por) 413
Cone (USA) 701, 702
Confiance (UK) 624
Confidence (USA) 752
Confident (UK) 624
Conifer (USA) 756
Connole (USA) 705
Conolly (USA) 698
Conqueror (UK) 590
Conquest (USA) 721, 722
Conserver (USA) 728
Constant (USA) 721, 722
Constellation (USA) 678
Constitucion (Ven) 767
Constituição (Brz) 63
Constitution (USA) 736
Contromestre Navarro (Per) 394
Conyngham (USA) 695
Cook (Aust) 44
Cook (USA) 705
Coontz (USA) 696
Copaonik (Yug) 778
Cora (Mex) 345
Corail (Fra) 182
Coral Sea (USA) 682
Cordoba (Col) 116
Corgi (UK) 624
Cormier (Fra) 190
Cormoran (Arg) 32
Cormorant (Can) 85
Cornelis Drebbel (Nld) 361
Coronado (USA) 715
Coronel Bolognesi (Per) 389
Coronel Edvardo Avaroa (Bol) 57
Corrillo (Per) 395
Corry (USA) 701, 702
Corsaro II (Ita) 284
Cortez (Chi) 102
Coshecton (USA) 738
Cosme Garcia (Spn) 434
Cosmos (USA) 757
Cotopaxi (Ecu) 140
Cottesmore (UK) 609
Courageous (UK) 590
Courageous (USA) 752
Courageux (Fra) 190
Courland Bay (TT) 483
Cove (USA) 722
Coventry (UK) 600
Cowichan (Can) 85
Crame Jean (Sen) 423
Cree (Can) 86
Criccieth (UK) 626
Crichton (UK) 610
Cricket (UK) 620, 625
Cricklade (UK) 626
Criquet (Fra) 187
Cristobal Colon (DR) 135
Crofton (UK) 610
Croix du Sud (Fra) 178
Cromarty (UK) 626
Crotone (Ita) 281
Crvena Zvijezda (Yug) 777
Crystal (UK) 621
Cuanza (Por) 413
Cuartel Moncada (Cub) 123
Cuauthemoc (Mex) 344
Cuddalore (Ind) 241
Cuenca (Ecu) 139
Cuitlahuac (Mex) 344
Cunene (Por) 413
Curlew (Aust) 43
Cushing (USA) 698
Cusseta (USA) 738
Custódio de Mello (Brz) 67
Cutlass (UK) 615
Cuxhaven (GFR) 205
Cuxton (UK) 610
Cybèle (Fra) 179
Cyclamen (Fra) 180
Cyclone (UK) 624
Cygne (Fra) 190
Cygnet (UK) 615
Czajka (Pol) 407
Czalpa (Pol) 407

D

10 De Agosto (Ecu) 139
D'Entrecasteaux (Fra) 180
D'Estienne D'Orves (Fra) 175
D'Estrées (Fra) 172
D'Iberville (Can) 89
Da Nang (Vtn) 772
Dacca (Pak) 383
Dace (USA) 663
Dachs (GFR) 205
Dae Gu (RoK) 323
Dafni (Gre) 222
Dahlgren (USA) 696
Dahlia (Fra) 189
Dahlonega (USA) 738
Daio (Jap) 305
Daisy (UK) 625
Daito (Jap) 308
Dakhla (Egy) 145
Daksaya (Sri) 448
Dale (USA) 690
Dallas (USA) 659, 750
Dalmatian (UK) 624
Dalnevostochny Komsomolets
(USSR) 533
Dam Thoai (Vtn) 771
Damato (USA) 701, 702
Dammam (SAr) 420
Damman (Swe) 458
Damuan (Bru) 70
Danae (UK) 602
Danbjørn (Den) 132
Dang Van Hoanh (Vtn) 771
Dang Yang (RoC) 466
Daniel Boone (USA) 655
Daniel Webster (USA) 655
Dankwart (GFR) 210
Dannebrog (Den) 132
Dao Thuc (Vtn) 771
Dao Van Dang (Vtn) 771
Daoud Ben Aicha (Mor) 351
Daphne (Den) 128
Daphné (Fra) 163
Daphne (UK) 625
Dar El Barka (Mtn) 342
Dareen (SAr) 422
Daring (Can) 92
Daring (Sin) 424
Darshak (Ind) 241
Dart (UK) 608
Darter (USA) 669
Daryush (Iran) 254
Dash (USA) 721, 722
Dasser Ort (GDR) 197
Dastoor (Kwt) 329
Dat Al Diyari (Iraq) 261
Dat Assawari (Lby) 332
Datchet (UK) 626
Datu Kalantiaw (Plp) 398
Datu Marikudo (Plp) 399
Dauntless (Sin) 424
Dauntless (USA) 752
Dauphin (Fra) 163
Dauriya (USSR) 562
David R. Ray (USA) 698
Davidson (USA) 707, 759
Davis (USA) 700
Dawson (Can) 93
De Brouwer (Bel) 54
De Grasse (Fra) 170
De Julio, 18 (Uru) 760
De Neys (SA) 430
De Noorde (SA) 430
De Ruyter (Nld) 355
De Steiguer (USA) 741
Decatur (USA) 697
Decisive (USA) 752
Dédalo (Spn) 435
Dee (UK) 615
Deepak (Ind) 242
Deerhound (UK) 624
Defensora (Brz) 63
Deflektor (USSR) 557
Deirdre (Ire) 263
Dekanawida (USA) 738
Dekanisora (USA) 738
Dekaury (USA) 738
Dela (Gha) 214
Delfin (Arg) 31
Delfin (Nor) 371
Delfin (Pol) 407
Delfin (Por) 411
Delfin (Spn) 433
Delfinen (Den) 125
Delfinen (Swe) 453
Delfzijl (Nld) 358
Delhi (Ind) 225
Deliver (USA) 728
Delphin (GFR) 205
Demirhisar (Tur) 491
Demmin (GDR) 195
Democratia (Rom) 418
Dempo (Indo) 252
Deneb (GFR) 206
Denizkusu (Tur) 490
Denmead (UK) 626
Denver (USA) 715
Dependable (USA) 752
Derwent (Aust) 42
Derzky (USSR) 531
Des Moines (USA) 693
Descatusaria (Rom) 418
Descubierta (Spn) 437
Desh Deep (Ind) 243
Desna (USSR) 570
Desrobirea (Rom) 418
Dessau (GDR) 195
Detector (Can) 84
Detector (USA) 721, 722
Detroit (USA) 727
Détroyat (Fra) 175
Deutschland (GFR) 210
Deviator (USSR) 559
Dewarutji (Indo) 251
Dewey (USA) 696
Dexterous (UK) 624
Deyatelny (USSR) 535
Deyo (USA) 698
Dhafeer (UAE) 582
Dharini (Ind) 242
Dhofar (Omn) 377
Diaguita (Arg) 29
Diamantina (Aust) 45
Diamiette (Egy) 142
Diamont (GFR) 210

INDEXES / Named Ships 823

Diana (GFR) 206
Diana (Spn) 437
Diana III (Ven) 769
Diane (Fra) 163
Dido (UK) 602
Diego Silang (Plp) 398
Dietrich (GFR) 210
Diez Canseco (Per) 395
Diez De Agosto (Ecu) 139
Dikson (USSR) 562
Diligence (USA) 752
Diligente (Col) 117
Dilos (Gre) 224
Dinant (Bel) 55
Dinder (Sud) 450
Dinh Hai (Vtn) 771
Dintel (Nld) 361
Diombos (Sen) 423
Diomede (UK) 602
Diomo Antoniou (Gre) 220
Diou Loulou (Sen) 423
Direct (USA) 721, 722
Dirna (GDR) 193
Discoverer (USA) 759
Discovery Bay (Jam) 288
Dittisham (UK) 611
Dives (Fra) 176
Dixie (USA) 724
Dixon (USA) 729
Diyakawa (Sri) 448
Djerv (Nor) 371
DM01-06 (Mex) 346
DM10-19 (Mex) 346
Dmitri Galkin (USSR) 553
Dmitri Laptev (USSR) 560
Dmitri Mendeleyev (USSR) 564
Dmitri Ovstyn (USSR) 560
Dmitri Pozharski (USSR) 527
Dmitri Sterlegov (USSR) 560
Dnestr (USSR) 569
Dnog (Brz) 68
Do Bong (RoK) 328
Doblestny (USSR) 535
Dobrinya Nikitch (USSR) 578
Dogan (Tur) 489
Dogwood (USA) 758
Doirani (Gre) 224
Dokkum (Nld) 359
Dolfijn (Nld) 354
Dolfin (Iran) 254
Dolgota (USSR) 557
Dolphin (USA) 670
Dolwen (UK) 625
Dom Aleixo (Por) 413
Dom Jeremias (Por) 413, 414
Dominant (USA) 721, 722
Dommel (Nld) 361
Dompaire (Fra) 179
Dompfaff (GFR) 210
Don (USSR) 571
Donald B. Beary (USA) 705
Donatan (Tur) 496
Donau (GFR) 207
Donbass (USSR) 562
Donchedi (Tld) 479
Donetsky Shakhter (USSR) 550
Donetz (USSR) 568
Dorade (Alg) 21
Dorang (Indo) 248
Dordrecht (Nld) 358
Dore (Indo) 249
Dorina (Nig) 366
Doris (Fra) 163
Doris (Gre) 223
Doris (UK) 625
Dornbusch (GDR) 196
Dornoch (UK) 626
Dorothy (UK) 625
Dorsch (GFR) 205
Dos de Mayo (Per) 388
Dostoyny (USSR) 535
Doudart de LaGrée (Fra) 173
Downes (USA) 705
Downham (UK) 622
Dr. Gondim (Brz) 68
Dr. Jamot (Cam) 76
Drachten (Nld) 359
Draga (Par) 386
Draken (Swe) 453
Draug (Nor) 373
Dreadnought (UK) 590
Dreg IV (Nld) 361
Drejø (Den) 129
Drenthe (Nld) 356
Dreptatea (Rom) 418
Drogou (Fra) 175
Drossel (GFR) 210
Droxford (UK) 615
Drum (USA) 662
Drunen (Nld) 359
Druzhny (USSR) 535
Druzki (Bul) 70
Dryade (Fra) 188
Dryaden (Den) 128
Du Chayla (Fra) 172
Duane (USA) 751
Duarte (DR) 137
Dubbo (Aust) 43
Dubna (USSR) 569
Dubuque (USA) 715
Duderstadt (GFR) 213
Duenas (Per) 395
Duero (Spn) 443
Duguay-Trouin (Fra) 170
Duk Bong (RoK) 326
Duk Su (RoK) 327
Duluth (USA) 715
Dumagat (Plp) 401
Dumai (Indo) 251
Dumit (Can) 93
Dunagiri (Ind) 237
Dunay (USSR) 570, 578
Duncan (USA) 703
Dundalk (Can) 83
Dundurn (Can) 83
Dunster (UK) 626
Duperré (Fra) 171
Dupetit Thouars (Fra) 172
Dupleix (Fra) 168
Dupont (USA) 700
Duque de Caxais (Brz) 64
Duquesne (Fra) 169
Durable (USA) 752
Durance (Fra) 182
Durban (SA) 429
Düren (GFR) 205
Durgham (UAE) 582
Durham (USA) 718
Durmitor (Yug) 778
Dutton (USA) 743
Duyong (Mly) 339
Dwight D. Eisenhower (USA) 675
Dyess (USA) 701, 702
Dzato (Gha) 214
Dzerzhinski (USSR) 527
Dzik (Pol) 407

E

E 6 (Arg) 34
E. Panagopoulos (Gre) 221
E. Toll (USSR) 560
Eagle (USA) 756
East London (SA) 429
Eastwood (Can) 86
Ebano (Ita) 281
Ebène (Fra) 190
Eberswalde (GDR) 195
Ebro (Spn) 443
Eceabad (Tur) 497
Echo (UK) 616
Echols (USA) 735
Eckaloo (Can) 93
Eckero (Fin) 155
Edda (Swe) 462
Eddyfirth (UK) 619
Eden (UK) 608
Edenshaw (USA) 738
Edenton (USA) 732
Edera (Ita) 281
Edgar André (GDR) 194
Edith (UK) 625
EDM 1, 2, 3, 4 (Arg) 30
Edson (USA) 700, 702
EDVP 1, 3, 7, 8, 9, 10, 12, 13, 17, 19, 21, 24, 28, 29, 30 (Arg) 30
Edward Cornwallis (Can) 91
Edward McDonnell (USA) 707
Efficace (Fra) 190
Egeria (UK) 616
Egernsund (Den) 131
Eglantine (Fra) 180
Eider (Fra) 190
Eifel (GFR) 208
Eilat (Isr) 265
Eilenburg (GDR) 195
Eisbar (GDR) 197
Eisbar (GFR) 211
Eisleben (GDR) 195
Eisvogel (GDR) 197
Eisvogel (GFR) 211
Ejura (Gha) 214
Ekholot (USSR) 557
Ekster (Bel) 56
Ekvator (USSR) 558
El Austral (Arg) 32
El Fasher (Sud) 449
El Fateh (Egy) 142
El Fayoud (Egy) 146
El Harris (Mor) 350
El Horriya (Egy) 146
El Jail (Mor) 350
El Khafir (Mor) 350
El Khartoum (Sud) 449
El Manufieh (Egy) 146
El Mikdam (Mor) 350
El Paso (USA) 718
El Sabiq (Mor) 350
El Tami (Iraq) 260
El Wacil (Mor) 350
Elan (Fra) 184
Elbe (GFR) 207
Elbjørn (Den) 132
Elderberry (USA) 757
Eléphant (Fra) 190
Eléphant (IC) 287
Elevthera (Bhm) 50
Elew (Pol) 409
Elfe (Fra) 188
Elicura (Chi) 100
Elk River (USA) 735
Elkhound (UK) 624
Elkstone (UK) 626
Ellerbek (GFR) 211
Elliott (USA) 698
Elmer Montgomery (USA) 705
Elmina (Gha) 214
Elsing (UK) 626
Elton (USSR) 558
Embrun (Fra) 190
Emden (GFR) 203
Emer (Ire) 263
Emerald Star (Mnt) 348
Emily Hobhouse (SA) 428
Emory S. Land (USA) 729
Endeavour (Can) 84
Endeavour (Sin) 425
Endeavour (UK) 622
Endurance (Sin) 425
Endurance (UK) 612
Engadine (UK) 608
Engage (USA) 721, 722
Engageante (Fra) 189
England (USA) 690
Engoulevent (Fra) 190
Enhance (USA) 721, 722
Enø (Den) 130
Enrico Dandolo (Ita) 271
Enrico Toti (Ita) 271
Enrique Collazo (Cub) 123
Enseigne de Vaisseau Henry (Fra) 173
Enseigne de Vaisseau Jacoubet (Fra) 175
Enterprise (UK) 616
Enterprise (USA) 677
Enugu (Nig) 367
Enyimiri (Nig) 366
Epe (Nig) 367
Epée (Fra) 177
Epworth (UK) 626
Equator (USSR) 567
Equeurdiville (Fra) 190
Erable (Fra) 190
Ercole (Ita) 286
Erdek (Tur) 497
Erezcano (Arg) 31
Eridan (Fra) 179
Erimo (Jap) 301, 305
Erin'mi (Nig) 366
Erkin (Tur) 496
Erle (Nor) 371
Ernest Grube (GDR) 194
Erns Haeckel (GDR) 197
Ernst Krenkel (USSR) 564
Ernst Schneller (GDR) 194, 197
Ernest Thälmann (GDR) 193, 197
Ersen Bayrak (Tur) 498
Ertugrul (Tur) 493
Eruslan (USSR) 574
Esan (Jap) 305
Escambray (Cub) 123
Escanaba (USA) 752
Eschwege (GFR) 213
Escuintla (Gua) 226
Eskimo (UK) 603
Esmeralda (Chi) 100
Esmeraldas (Ecu) 138
Espadon (Alg) 21
Espadon (Fra) 163
Espartana (Col) 117
Espérance (Fra) 181
Esper Ort (GDR) 197
Espirito Santo (Brz) 62
Esplora (DR) 136
Essahir (Mor) 350
Essaouira (Mor) 351
Estafette (Fra) 181
Esteban Baca Calderon (Mex) 346
Esteban Jaramillo (Col) 118
Esteem (USA) 721, 722
Etawina (USA) 738
Etchbarne (Brz) 68
Ethan Allen (USA) 657
Ethiopia (Eth) 148
Étoile Polaire (Fra) 178
Ettrick (UK) 626
Etzion Gueber (Isr) 267
Eufaula (USA) 738
Euro (Ita) 276
Euryalus (UK) 602
Everglades (USA) 723
Evergreen (USA) 756
Everingham (UK) 622
Evertsen (Nld) 357
Evros (Gre) 223
Excel (USA) 721, 722
Excellence (Sin) 425
Exeter (UK) 600
Exploit (USA) 721, 722
Extremadura (Spn) 438
Exultant (USA) 721, 722
Exuma (Bhm) 50

F

F. Bovesse (Bel) 54
F. Litke (USSR) 558
F. Rozman-Stane (Yug) 777
F. L. Jahn (GDR) 197
Fabrio Gallipoli (Ven) 769
Faedra (Gre) 222
Fafnir (GFR) 210
Faggio (Ita) 281
Fahrion (USA) 703
Fairfax County (USA) 717
Fairweather (USA) 759
Faisal (SAr) 420
Faithful (UK) 624
Falakhon (Iran) 256
Falcon (Ven) 766
Falcone (Ita) 279
Falk (Nor) 371
Falken (Swe) 462
Fällaren (Swe) 459
Falmouth (UK) 604
Falster (Den) 130
Fan Kong (RoC) 469
Fanantenana (Mad) 336
Fanning (USA) 705
Faramarz (Iran) 255
Fareed (Kwt) 330
Farfadet (Fra) 189
Farm (Nor) 374
Farø (Den) 129
Faroleiro Areas (Brz) 66
Faroleiro Nascimento (Brz) 66
Farragut (USA) 696
Farwa (Lby) 334
Fashoda (Sud) 450
Fata Hilla (Indo) 245
Fateh-Al-Khair (Qat) 415
Fatsa (Tur) 493
Faune (Fra) 188
Fauvette (Fra) 190
Favignana (Ita) 286
Fawn (UK) 616
FB 1, 2, 3, 5-10 (RoK) 325
Fearless (UK) 606
Fearless (USA) 721, 722
Fecia di Cossato (Ita) 271
Federacion (Ven) 767
Fedor Litke (USSR) 578
Fedor Matisen (USSR) 560
Fedor Vidyaev (USSR) 553
Fehmarn (GFR) 211
Felchen (GFR) 205
Felicity (UK) 625
Felipé Larrazabal (Ven) 769
Felix Romero (Mex) 346
Felsted (UK) 626
Feolent (USSR) 571
Fernando Gomez (Ven) 769
Fernando Lizardi (Mex) 346
Ferré (Per) 390
Ferrel (USA) 759
Fethiye (Tur) 493
Fidelity (USA) 721
Fiete Schulze (GDR) 194
Fife (UK) 598
Fife (USA) 698
Finback (USA) 662
Finike (Tur) 493
Fink (GFR) 210
Finlay (Cub) 123
Fintry (UK) 626
Fiona (UK) 625
Fir (USA) 757
Firebush (USA) 756
Firtina (Tur) 490
Fische (GFR) 206
Fiske (USA) 701, 702
Fjøløy (Nor) 373
Flaggtief (GDR) 196
Flamingo (Bhm) 49
Flasher (USA) 663
Flensburg (GFR) 205
Fletcher (USA) 698
Fleur (SA) 429
Flibustier (GFR) 210
Flinders (Aust) 45
Flint (USA) 724
Flintham (UK) 611
Flore (Fra) 163
Florikan (USA) 731
Flunder (GFR) 205
Flying Fish (USA) 662
Fo Wu 5-6 (RoC) 473
Foça (Tur) 493
Foch (Fra) 164
Föhr (GFR) 211
Foka (Pol) 407
Fóla (Ire) 263
Forbin (Fra) 171
Forceful (UK) 624
Förde (GFR) 212
Fordham (UK) 627
Forelle (GFR) 205
Formosa (Arg) 31
Forrest Sherman (USA) 700
Forrestal (USA) 680
Fort Austin (UK) 619
Fort Charles (Jam) 288
Fort Fisher (USA) 716
Fort Grange (UK) 619
Fort Snelling (USA) 716
Fort Steele (Can) 85
Forte (Ita) 286
Forte de Coimbra (Brz) 64
Forth (UK) 608
Fortify (USA) 721, 722
Fortuna I (Arg) 34
Fortuna II (Arg) 34
Fotherby (UK) 626
Fourmi (Fra) 187
Fox (UK) 616
Fox (USA) 689
Foxhound (UK) 624
Francis Garnier (Fra) 176
Francis Hammond (USA) 705
Francis Marion (USA) 718, 720
Francis Scott Key (USA) 655
Francisco Dagahoy (Plp) 398
Francisco de Gurruchaga (Arg) 29
Francisco J. Mujica (Mex) 346
Francisco Zarco (Mex) 345
Franco (Per) 395
Frank Cable (USA) 729
Franklin (Can) 88
Fraser (Can) 82
Frassino (Ita) 281
Frauenlob (GFR) 206
Freccia (Ita) 279
Frederick (USA) 717
Freedom (Sin) 424
Freesendorf (GDR) 197
Freibeuter (GFR) 210
Freiburg (GFR) 209
Frej (Swe) 460
Freja (Swe) 461
Fremantle (Aus) 43
Fréne (Fra) 190
Freshburn (UK) 623
Freshlake (UK) 623
Freshspring (UK) 623
Fresia (Chi) 99
Fresno (USA) 717
Fret (Nld) 357
Frettchen (GFR) 205
Freundschaft (GDR) 196, 197
Freya (GFR) 206
Freyr (Nld) 358
Friedrich Schulze (GDR) 194
Friedrich Voge (GFR) 212
Friesland (Nld) 356
Fritham (UK) 622
Frithjof (GFR) 213
Fritz Behn (GDR) 194
Fritz Gast (GDR) 194
Fritz Hagale (Col) 117
Fritz Heckert (GDR) 194
Froxfield (UK) 626
Fryken (Swe) 463
Fu Chou (CPR) 114
Fu Chun (CPR) 105
Fu Kuo (RoC) 469
Fu Shan (RoC) 468
Fu Yang (RoC) 466
Fuh Chow (RoC) 469
Fuji (Jap) 304, 306
Fukue (Jap) 300
Fulbeck (UK) 626
Fulda (GFR) 205
Fulmar (UK) 628
Fulton (USA) 730
Fundy (Can) 85
Furman (USA) 744
Fusimi (Jap) 301
Futami (Jap) 303
Fuyushio (Jap) 292
FW 1 (GFR) 209
FW 4 (GFR) 209
FW 5 (GFR) 209
FW 6 (GFR) 209
Fyen (Den) 130
Fylla (Den) 127

G

G. Truffaut (Bel) 54
Gaash (Isr) 265
Gabriela (Ven) 769
Gadebusch (GDR) 193
Gaeta (Ita) 281
Gafsah (Tun) 484
Gaggia (Ita) 281
Gagliardo (Ita) 286
Gaj (Ind) 243
Gal (Isr) 264
Galatea (UK) 602
Galatée (Fra) 163
Galeb (Yug) 780
Galicia (Spn) 442
Gallant (USA) 721, 722
Gallatin (USA) 750
Galten (Swe) 458
Galvez (Chi) 102
Galvez (Per) 395
Gama (Pak) 383
Gambero (Ita) 282

824 INDEXES / Named Ships

Ganadoga (USA) 738
Ganas (Mly) 338
Ganda (Iraq) 260
Gangut (USSR) 553
Ganyang (Mly) 338
Garcia (USA) 707
Garcia D'Avila (Brz) 64
Garcia y Garcia (Per) 390
Gardénia (Fra) 188
Gardouneh (Iran) 256
Garganey (UK) 620
Garian (Lby) 334
Garigliano (Fra) 179
Garonne (Fra) 183
Gasconade (USA) 758
Gässten (Swe) 458
Gastao Moutinho (Brz) 67
Gästrikland (Swe) 453
Gatineau (Can) 82
Gato (USA) 663
Gauss (GFR) 213
Gave (Fra) 190
Gavilan I, II (Spn) 447
Gavinton (UK) 610
Gaviota (Spn) 441
Gavril Sarychev (USSR) 556
Gawler (Aust) 43
Gayret (Tur) 488
Gayundah (Aust) 48
Gazal (Tur) 498
Gazelle (Fra) 184
Gazelle (GFR) 206
GB 21, GB 22, GB 23, GB 24 (Eth) 149
GC 2, 3, 4, 5, 6, 7, 8 (ELS) 147
Gear (USA) 728
Geba (Por) 413
Geelong (Aus) 43
Gefion (GFR) 206
Geir (Nor) 371
Geiserich (GFR) 210
Gelderland (Nld) 361
Gelderland (SA) 428
Gelinotte (Fra) 190
Gelso (Ita) 281
Gelsomino (Ita) 281
Gema (Sin) 425
Gemini (USA) 709
Gemert (Nld) 359
Gemma (GFR) 206
Gen J. T. Cabanas (Hon) 229
General Belgrano (Arg) 27
General H. H. Arnold (USA) 740
General Hoyt S. Vandenberg (USA) 740
General Hugh J. Gaffey (USA) 735
General José Felix Ribas (Ven) 766
General José Trinidad Moran (Ven) 767
General Juan José Flores (Ven) 767
General Pereira D'Eca (Por) 412
General Salom (Ven) 766
General San Martin (Arg) 34
General Soublette (Ven) 766
General Urdaneta (Ven) 766
General Vasques Cobo (Col) 118
General Vincente Guerrero (Mex) 347
Genil (Spn) 443
Genrik Gasanov (USSR) 569
Genthin (GDR) 195
Genun (Jap) 314
George Bancroft (USA) 655
George C. Marshall (USA) 655
George Ferguson (Bar) 53
George Philip (USA) 703
George Washington (USA) 658
George Washington Carver (USA) 655
Georges Leygues (Fra) 168
Georgi Ushakov (USSR) 564
Georgina (UK) 625
Georgy Sedov (USSR) 563
Gepard (GFR) 205
Gepard (USSR) 538
Geraldtown (Aust) 43
Géranium (Fra) 178
Gerda (Swe) 462
Gerhard Prenzier (GDR) 195
Gernot (GFR) 210
Geuse (GFR) 210
Geyser (Fra) 190
Ghadunfar (UAE) 582
Ghanadhah (UAE) 581
Gharbia (Egy) 145
Gharial (Ind) 240
Ghazi (Pak) 379
Gheppio (Ita) 279
Ghorpad (Ind) 240
Giaggiolo (Ita) 281
Gianfranco Gazzana Priaroggia (Ita) 272
Gidrofon (USSR) 557
Gidrograf (USSR) 556
Gidrosat (USSR) 559
Giena (USSR) 538
Giethoorn (Nld) 359
Gigas (Gre) 224
Gigrometr (USSR) 559
Gihad (Sud) 450
Gilgit (Pak) 382
Gillöga (Swe) 458
Ginga (Jap) 313
Girelle (Fra) 189
Gireogi (RoK) 325
Girne (Tur) 490
Girorulevoy (USSR) 557
Giselher (GFR) 210
Giuseppe Garibaldi (Ita) 272
Giza (Egy) 145
Glacier (USA) 753
Gladan (Swe) 462
Gladstone (Aust) 43
Glaive (Fra) 177
Glamorgan (UK) 598
Glasgow (UK) 600
Glasserton (UK) 610
Glavkos (Gre) 216
Glen (UK) 608
Glenard P. Lipscomb (USA) 661
Glenbrook (Can) 86
Glencoe (UK) 626
Glendada (Can) 93
Glendale (Can) 86
Glendyne (Can) 86
Glenevis (Can) 86
Glenside (Can) 86
Glicine (Ita) 281
Glimt (Nor) 371
Glomma (Nor) 372
Gloria (Col) 119
Glover (USA) 708
Glubomer (USSR) 559
Glücksburg (GFR) 209
Glycine (Fra) 180
Gnat (UK) 625
Gnevny (USSR) 531
Gnist (Nor) 371
Godavari (Ind) 239
Godetia (Bel) 55
Gödicke (GFR) 210
Goeland (Fra) 190
Go-Go (Jap) 303
Goiaz (Brz) 60
Gölçük (Tur) 496
Gold Rover (UK) 618
Goldeneye (UK) 620
Goldsborough (USA) 695
Golfo de Cariaco (Ven) 769
Goliath (Fra) 190
Golwitz (GDR) 197
Goosander (UK) 620
Gorch Fock (GFR) 210
Gordy (USSR) 531
Gorgona (Col) 118
Gorizont (USSR) 559, 567
Gorz (Iran) 256
Göttingen (GFR) 205
Goyena (Arg) 32
Graal-Müritz (GDR) 195
Graça Aranha (Brz) 66
Grad (USSR) 540
Gradac (Yug) 778
Grado (Ita) 280
Gradus (USSR) 559
Gráinne (Ire) 263
Gral (Hon) 229
Granaten (Swe) 462
Granchio (Ita) 282
Grand Duc (Fra) 190
Granma (Cub) 123
Gransee (GDR) 195
Grasmere (UK) 626
Grass Ort (GDR) 197
Gravesmühlen (GDR) 193
Gravina (Spn) 436
Gray (USA) 705
Grayback (USA) 668
Grayling (USA) 662
Grecale (Ita) 276
Green Bay (USA) 710
Green Rover (UK) 618
Greenling (USA) 663
Greenville Victory (USA) 745
Gregorio de Pilar (Plp) 398
Gregorio Luperon (DR) 134
Greifswald (GDR) 195
Gremyashchy (USSR) 531
Grenfell (Can) 92
Grey Rover (UK) 618
Gribb (Nor) 371
Gridley (USA) 690
Griep (GFR) 212
Griffon (Can) 89
Griffon (Fra) 185
Grifone (Ita) 279
Grillon (Fra) 187
Grim (Swe) 459
Grimma (GDR) 195
Grimmen (GDR) 195
Gripen (Swe) 453
Gromky (USSR) 535
Groningen (Nld) 356
Grønsund (Den) 131
Grot (USSR) 559
Groton (USA) 659
Growler (USA) 668
Grozny (USSR) 526
Grozyashchy (USSR) 535
Grua Flotante (Par) 386
Grumete (Brz) 68
Grumete Perez (Chi) 101
Grunwald (Pol) 408
Gryf (Pol) 408
Grypskerk (Nld) 361
Guacanagarix (DR) 137
Guacolda (Chi) 99
Guadalcanal (USA) 714
Guadalete (Spn) 443
Guadalmedina (Spn) 443
Guadalquivir (Spn) 443
Guadiana (Spn) 443
Guairia (Brz) 68
Guam (USA) 714
Guanabacoa (Cub) 123
Guanabara (Brz) 60
Guarani (Brz) 68
Guarapari (Brz) 64
Guardfish (USA) 663
Guardian Rios (Per) 394
Guawidjaja (Indo) 247
Guayaquil (Ecu) 139
Guayas (Ecu) 140
Guaycuru (Arg) 34
Guben (GDR) 195
Gudgeon (USA) 669
Guépratte (Fra) 172
Guernsey (UK) 614
Guglielmo Marconi (Ita) 271
Guillermo Prieto (Mex) 345
Guise (Per) 391
Guitarro (USA) 662
Guldar (Ind) 240
Guldborgsund (Den) 131
Gunnar (GFR) 210
Gunter (GFR) 210
Gurkha (UK) 603
Gurnard (USA) 662
Gustaf af Klint (Swe) 461
Gustav Zedé (Fra) 186
Gutierriez Zamora (Mex) 345
Guyana (Ven) 767
Gwendoline (UK) 625
Gymnote (Fra) 162
Gyre (USA) 741

H

H. C. Oersted (GFR) 212
H. H. Hess (USA) 742
H. U. Sverdrup (Nor) 373
Ha Hoi (Vtn) 771
Haarlem (Nld) 358
Hachi-Go (Jap) 300
Hachijo (Jap) 308
Hackensack (USA) 738
Hadda (Nld) 358
Haddo (USA) 663
Haddock (USA) 663
Hadejia (Nig) 366
Hadubrand (GFR) 210
Haerlem (SA) 428
Hagen (GFR) 210
Hägern (Swe) 462
Hai (Nor) 371
Hai Chiu (CPR) 113
Hai Pao (RoC) 465
Hai Sheng (CPR) 113
Hai Shih (RoC) 465
Hai Yu (CPR) 114
Hai Yun (CPR) 113
Haifa (Isr) 265
Hait'se (CPR) 113
Haiti Cherie (Hai) 228
Haku (NZ) 364
Hakuun (Jap) 314
Haleakala (USA) 724
Halibut (USA) 665
Halifax (UK) 629
Halland (Swe) 453
Halmstad (Swe) 454
Halsey (USA) 690
Hälsingland (Swe) 453
Hamagiri (Jap) 310
Hamana (Jap) 302
Hamanami (Jap) 310
Hamayuki (Jap) 310
Hamazuki (Jap) 309
Hamble (UK) 608
Hambledon (UK) 626
Hamburg (GFR) 202
Hameenmaa (Fin) 150
Hamilton (USA) 750
Hammer (Den) 127
Hammer (USA) 758
Hammerhead (USA) 662
Hamner (USA) 701, 702
Han Giang (Vtn) 772
Han Jih (RoC) 473
Han Yang (RoC) 466
Hang Tuah (Mly) 337
Hangor (Pak) 379
Hanhak Sattru (Tld) 476
Hanit (Isr) 265
Hannibal (Tun) 484
Hanö (Swe) 455
Hans Bürkner (GFR) 204
Hans Coppi (GDR) 194
Hansa (GFR) 207
Hansaya (Sri) 448
Hanse (GFR) 211
Harambee (Ken) 316
Haras 1-5 (Omn) 377
Harimau (Indo) 247
Harischi (Iran) 258
Harkness (USA) 743
Harlan County (USA) 717
Harlech (UK) 626
Harlingen (Nld) 358
Harold E. Holt (USA) 705
Harold J. Ellison (USA) 701, 702
Harriet Lane (USA) 752
Harry E. Yarnell (USA) 690
Harry W. Hill (USA) 698
Hartnaut (GFR) 210
Harukaze (Jap) 296
Haruna (Jap) 293
Harusame (Jap) 295
Harushio (Jap) 292
Haruzuki (Jap) 310
Harz (GFR) 208
Hashira (Jap) 300
Hassayampa (USA) 726
Hasselt (Bel) 55
Hasslö (Swe) 458
Hatagumo (Jap) 309
Hatchet (USA) 758
Hathi (Ind) 243
Hatsukari (Jap) 297
Hatsushima (Jap) 299
Hau Giang (Vtn) 772
Hauk (Nor) 370
Haversham (UK) 622
Havfruen (Den) 128
Hawea (NZ) 363
Hawkbill (USA) 662
Hawkins (USA) 701, 702
Hawser (USA) 759
Hay Tan (RoC) 473
Hayabusa (Jap) 303
Hayagiri (Jap) 310
Hayagumo (Jap) 309
Hayannis (USA) 738
Hayase (Jap) 299
Hayes (USA) 741
Hazran Nauni (Iraq) 260
Hazza (UAE) 582
Headcorn (UK) 626
Hebe (Swe) 462
Hecate (UK) 616
Heck (USA) 759
Hecla (UK) 616
Hector (Swe) 462
Hector (USA) 728
Hefring (Nld) 358
Heimdal (Nor) 374
Heimdal (Swe) 459
Heinrich Dorrenbach (GDR) 194
Heinz Kapelle (GDR) 194
Heinz Roggenkamp (GFR) 212
Heist (Bel) 56
Heiyo (Jap) 312
Hekura (Jap) 308
Helen (StL) 419
Helen (UK) 625
Helgoland (GFR) 211
Hellevotsluis (Nld) 358
Helmut Just (GDR) 196
Henderson (USA) 701, 702
Hengam (Iran) 258
Heng Yang (RoC) 467
Henri Poincaré (Fra) 184
Henrik (Swe) 462
Henry B. Wilson (USA) 695
Henry Clay (USA) 655
Henry L. Stimson (USA) 655
Hepburn (USA) 705
Hephestos (Gre) 223
Heppens (GFR) 211
Hera (Swe) 462
Heraklis (Gre) 224
Herald (UK) 616
Hercule (Fra) 190
Hercules (Arg) 27
Hercules (DR) 137
Hercules (Pol) 409
Hercules (Swe) 462
Hercules (USA) 709
Herev (Isr) 265
Heriberto Jara Corona (Mex) 346
Herkules (GFR) 206
Herluf Trolle (Den) 126
Hermelijn (Nld) 357
Hermelin (GFR) 205
Hermenegildo Galena (Mex) 345
Hermes (GFR) 203
Hermes (Swe) 462
Hermes (UK) 592
Hermione (UK) 602
Hermitage (USA) 716
Hernando Gutierrez (Col) 119
Heroj (Yug) 775
Héron (Fra) 190
Heros (Swe) 462
Herstal (Bel) 55
Hertha (GFR) 206
Hesperos (Gre) 220
Hessen (GFR) 202
Hêtre (Fra) 190
Hetz (Isr) 265
Hévéa (Fra) 190
Hever (UK) 626
Hewitt (USA) 698
Hiamonee (USA) 738
Hiawatha (USA) 738
Hibiscus (Fra) 189
Hidaka (Jap) 308
Hiei (Jap) 293
Hiev (GFR) 212
Higbee (USA) 701, 702
High Point (USA) 710
Hilderbrand (GFR) 210
Himgiri (Ind) 237
Hippopotame (Fra) 190
Hirado (Jap) 308
Hiryu (Jap) 311
Hisingen (Swe) 458
Hitteen (SAr) 420
Hiu (Indo) 247
Hiyama (Jap) 308
Hiyodori (Jap) 297
Hjortø (Den) 130
Ho Chang (RoC) 471
Ho Chao (RoC) 471
Ho Cheng (RoC) 471
Ho Chi (RoC) 471
Ho Chie (RoC) 471
Ho Chien (RoC) 471
Ho Chuan (RoC) 471
Ho Chun (RoC) 471
Ho Chung (RoC) 471
Ho Dang La (Vtn) 771
Ho Deng (RoC) 471
Ho Duy (Vtn) 771
Ho Feng (RoC) 471
Ho Hoei (RoC) 471
Ho Meng (RoC) 471
Ho Mou (RoC) 471
Ho Seng (RoC) 471
Ho Shan (RoC) 471
Ho Shou (RoC) 471
Ho Shun (RoC) 471
Ho Teng (RoC) 471
Ho Tsung (RoC) 471
Ho Yao (RoC) 471
Ho Yung (RoC) 471
Hoa Lu (Vtn) 771
Hoang Sa (Vtn) 771
Hobart (Aust) 40
Hodgeston (UK) 610
Hoel (USA) 695
Hoga (USA) 738
Hoist (USA) 728
Hokuto (Jap) 313
Holland (USA) 729
Holland Bay (Jam) 288
Hollister (USA) 701, 702
Hollyhock (USA) 757
Holmwood (UK) 626
Holnis (GFR) 207
Hommel (Bel) 56
Homs (Lby) 334
Honorio Barreto (Por) 412
Hoogeveen (Nld) 359
Hoogezand (Nld) 359
Horand (GFR) 210
Hormuz (Iran) 259
Hornbeam (USA) 756
Horne (USA) 689
Hornet (USA) 684
Horning (UK) 626
Horobutsu (Jap) 306
Horonai (Jap) 307
Horria (Tun) 485
Horriya (Sud) 450
Horten (Nor) 372
Hortensia (Fra) 189
Hos Durg (Ind) 239
Hotaka (Jap) 301
Houma (USA) 738
Houn (Jap) 314
Houtepen (Nld) 359
Howard W. Gilmore (USA) 730
Howar (Bhr) 50
Hsi An (CPR) 107
Hsiang Yang (RoC) 467
Hsiang Yang Hung San (CPR) 113
Hsiang Yang Hung Wu (CPR) 113
Hsin Lung (RoC) 473
Hsueh Chih (RoC) 469
Hua Shan (RoC) 468
Hua Yang (RoC) 467
Hualcopo (Ecu) 139
Huancavilca (Ecu) 138
Huarpe (Arg) 34
Huascar (Chi) 102
Hubberston (UK) 610
Hudson (Can) 93
Hudson (USA) 746, 758
Huei Yang (RoC) 467
Hugin (Swe) 454
Hugo Eckener (GDR) 196
Hui An (CPR) 107
Huitfeld (Den) 127

INDEXES / Named Ships 825

Hull (USA) 700
Hulubalang (Mly) 340
Humaita (Brz) 60
Humaita (Par) 385
Humberto Cortes (Col) 117
Humming Bird II (TT) 483
Hunahpu (Gua) 225
Hunding (GFR) 210
Hung Hsing (RoC) 473
Hunley (USA) 729
Huracan (Uru) 763
Huron (Can) 80
Husky (UK) 624
Hussein Abdallah (Jor) 314
Huy (Bel) 55
Huynh Bo (Vtn) 771
Huynh Van Cu (Vtn) 771
Huynh Van Ngan (Vtn) 771
Hval (Nor) 371
Hvalorg (Ice) 232
Hvass (Nor) 371
Hvidbjørnen (Den) 127
Hwa Chon (RoK) 328
Hwa San (RoK) 326
Hwar (Qat) 415
Hyäne (GFR) 205
Hyatt (Chi) 95
Hydra (Nld) 361
Hydra (UK) 616
Hydrograf (Pol) 409
Hydrograf (Nor) 375
Hydrograph (GDR) 196
Hydrograph Pahlavi (Iran) 259
Hydrograph Shahpour (Iran) 259
Hyperion (Gre) 224
Hyperion (UK) 629

I

I. Karavoyiannos
Theophilopoulos (Gre) 224
I. Meng Shan (CPR) 112
Iason (Gre) 224
Ibare (Bol) 57
Ibis (Aust) 43
Ibn Al Hadrami (Lby) 335
Ibn Haritha (Lby) 335
Ibn Ouf (Lby) 335
Ibn Said (Iraq) 261
Ibuki (Jap) 300, 308
Icel (Tur) 489
Ichi-Go (Jap) 303
Ichilo (Bol) 57
Idini (Mtn) 342
Ierax (Gre) 219
Ifugao (Plp) 404
Iggö (Swe) 458
Ignacio Altamirano (Mex) 345
Ignacio de la Llave (Mex) 345
Ignacio L. Vallarta (Mex) 345
Ignacio Lopez Rayon (Mex) 346
Ignacio Mariscal (Mex) 346
Ignacio Ramirez (Mex) 346
Ignacio Zaragoza (Mex) 346
Igorot (Plp) 404
Iguassu (Brz) 68
Iguatemi (Brz) 64
Ijssel (Nld) 361
Ikaria (Gre) 221
Iki (Jap) 308
Ikinci Inönü (Tur) 487
Ilchester (UK) 626
Ile d'Oléron (Fra) 185
Ilha de Poilão (GB) 227
Ilia Muromets (USSR) 578
Iliki (Gre) 224
Illusive (USA) 721
Illustrious (UK) 594
Ilmen (USSR) 556
Ilo (Per) 393
Ilocos Norte (Plp) 401
Iloilo (Plp) 399
Ilongot (Plp) 404
Im Raq Ni (Mtn) 343
Iman (USSR) 570
Imeni XXV Svezda KPSS
(USSR) 578
Impavido (Ita) 275
Imperial Marinheiro (Brz) 64
Impervious (USA) 721, 722
Impetuoso (Ita) 276
Implicit (USA) 721, 722
In Cheon (RoK) 323
In Chon (RoK) 327
Inagua (Bhm) 50
Inchon (USA) 714
Indépendance (Cam) 76
Independence (Sin) 424
Independence (USA) 680
Independencia (Bol) 57
Independencia (Brz) 63
Independencia (DR) 135
Independencia (Per) 393
Independencia (Ven) 767
Indianapolis (USA) 659
Indiga (USSR) 571
Indomable (Col) 115
Indomita (Arg) 31
Indomito (Ita) 276
Indra (USA) 728
Inebolu (Tur) 496
Infanta Cristina (Spn) 437
Infanta Elena (Spn) 437
Inflict (USA) 721, 722
Ingeniero Mery (Chi) 102
Inger (GFR) 205
Ingersoll (USA) 698
Ingham (USA) 751
Ingolf (Den) 127
Ingul (USSR) 568
Inguri (USSR) 568
Inlay (Bur) 74
Inma (Bur) 74
Inouse (Gre) 221
Insar (USSR) 573
Instow (UK) 626
Intisar (Kwt) 329
Intishat (Egy) 146
Intrepid (Sin) 425
Intrepid (UK) 606
Intrepid (USA) 683
Intrepida (Arg) 31
Intrepido (Col) 115
Intrepido (Ita) 275
Intrépido (Spn) 437
Invincible (UK) 594
Inya (Bur) 74
Iou (Jap) 300
Iowa (USA) 685
Ipiranga (Brz) 64
Ipoploiarhos Arliotis (Gre) 219
Ipoploiarhos Batsis (Gre) 219
Ipoploiarhos Daniolos (Gre) 222
Ipoploiarhos Grigoropoulos
(Gre) 222
Ipoploiarhos Konidis (Gre) 219
Ipoploiarhos Kristalidis (Gre) 222
Ipoploiarhos Mikonios (Gre) 219
Ipoploiarhos Roussen (Gre) 222
Ipoploiarhos Tournas (Gre) 222
Ipoploiarhos Troupakis (Gre) 219
Ipswich (Aust) 43
Iquique (Per) 388
Irene (UK) 625
Iris (USA) 756
Irkut (USSR) 569
Ironbridge (UK) 626
Ironwood (USA) 756
Iroquis (Can) 80
Isaac Peral (Spn) 434
Isaac Sweers (Nld) 357
Isabel (UK) 625
Isabela (DR) 136
Isabela (Plp) 402
Isar (GFR) 207
Isard (Fra) 184
Isbjørn (Den) 132
Isenami (Jap) 310
Isère (Fra) 182
Iseyuki (Jap) 309
Ishikari (Jap) 306
Ishim (USSR) 573
Isis (UK) 611
Iskenderun (Tur) 489
Iskra (Pol) 408
Isku (Fin) 151
Isla de la Plata (Ecu) 140
Isla Puna (Ecu) 140
Islas de Noronha (Brz) 68
Islas Orcadas (Arg) 32
Islay (Per) 388
Isonami (Jap) 296
Isoshio (Jap) 292
Isoyuki (Jap) 310
Isozuki (Jap) 309
Issole (Fra) 177
Istanbul (Tur) 489
Istiklal (Tur) 485
Istiqlal (Sud) 450
Isuzu (Jap) 297, 306
Itacurussa (Brz) 66
Itapura (Brz) 68
Itara (USA) 738
Itati (Arg) 34
Itchen (UK) 608
Itenez (Bol) 57
Iuka (USA) 738
Ivan (Yug) 777
Ivan Bubnov (USSR) 569
Ivan Kireyev (USSR) 560
Ivan Kolyshkin (USSR) 553
Ivan Kruzenstern (USSR) 562, 578
Ivan Kucherenko (USSR) 553
Ivan Moskvitin (USSR) 578
Ivan Susanin (USSR) 578
Ivan Vadremeev (USSR) 553
Iveston (UK) 610
Iwai (Jap) 300
Iwase (Jap) 297
Iwo Jima (USA) 714
Ixinche (Gua) 226
Ixworth (UK) 626
Izhora (USSR) 570
Izmeritel (USSR) 557
Izmir (Tur) 489
Izmit (Tur) 489
Izu (Jap) 305
Izumrud (USSR) 539, 564

J

J. E. Bernier (Can) 89
J. E. Van Haverbeke (Bel) 54
J. Mazar (Yug) 777
J. T. C. Ramsey (Bar) 53
Jacinthe (Fra) 189
Jacinto Candido (Por) 412
Jack (USA) 663
Jackdaw (Ire) 263
Jackson (UK) 628
Jacksonville (USA) 659
Jade (GFR) 212
Jadran (Yug) 780
Jadranka (Yug) 780
Jägaren (Swe) 454
Jaguar (Guy) 228
Jaguar (Nld) 357
Jahangir (Pak) 381
Jalanidhi (Indo) 250
Jambeli (Ecu) 140
James K. Polk (USA) 655
James M. Gilliss (USA) 741
James Madison (USA) 655
James Monroe (USA) 655
Jamhuri (Ken) 316
Jamuna (Ind) 242
Jan Van Brakel (Nld) 356
Jannada (Iraq) 261
Janow (Pol) 408
Jaquel El Bahr (Tun) 485
Jarvis (USA) 750
Jaskolka (Pol) 407
Jasmin (Fra) 178
Jason (USA) 728
Jaspis (GFR) 210
Jastrab (Pol) 407
Jato (Gam) 192
Javier Quiroga (Spn) 440
Jaya Wijaya (Indo) 250
Jean Bourdon (Can) 93
Jean Moulin (Fra) 175
Jeanne d'Arc (Fra) 166
Jebba (Nig) 366
Jebel Antar (Alg) 21
Jebel Honda (Alg) 21
Jeddah (SAr) 422
Jeong Buk (RoK) 322
Jerijih (Mly) 339
Jerong (Mly) 338
Jersey (UK) 614
Jervis Bay (Aust) 46
Jesse L. Brown (USA) 705
Jesus G. Ortega (Mex) 345
Jibla (YPDR) 774
Jida (Bhr) 50
Jihad (Leb) 330
Jo (Nor) 371
Joan (UK) 625
Joao Coutinho (Por) 412
Joao Roby (Por) 412
Joe Mann (Aust) 48
Johan Krüger (GDR) 196
Johan Mansson (Swe) 461
Johanna Van Der Merwe (SA) 428
Johannesburg (SA) 429
John A. MacDonald (Can) 88
John Adams (Ire) 263
John Adams (USA) 655
John Cabot (Can) 88
John C. Calhoun (USA) 655
John F. Kennedy (USA) 678
John Hancock (USA) 698
John King (USA) 695
John Marshall (USA) 657
John Paul Jones (USA) 697
John R. Craig (USA) 701, 702
John Rodgers (USA) 698
John Young (USA) 698
Johnston (USA) 701, 702
Johore Bahru (Mly) 340
Jonas Ingram (USA) 700
Jonnam (RoK) 323
Jonny Scheer (GDR) 197
Jonquille (Fra) 178
Jordan (GDR) 196
Jorge Juan (Spn) 436
Jorge Soto del Corval (Col) 118
Jos Sudarso (Indo) 246
Jose Maria del Castillo
Velasco (Mex) 346
Jose Maria Izazagu (Mex) 346
Jose Maria Maja (Mex) 346
Jose Natividad Macias (Mex) 346
Josef Schares (GDR) 194
Joseph Hewes (USA) 705
Joseph Hughes GC (UK) 629
Joseph Strauss (USA) 695
Josephus Daniels (USA) 689
Joshan (Iran) 256
Jouett (USA) 689
Joumhouria (Tun) 485
Joves Fiallo (Col) 119
Joyce (UK) 625
Juan A. Lavalleja (Uru) 763
Juan Aldama (Mex) 345
Juan Alejandro Acosta (DR) 135
Juan Bautista Morales (Mex) 346
Juan Lucio (Col) 117
Juan N. Alvares (Mex) 345
Juan Sebastian de Elcano (Spn) 445
Jucar (Spn) 443
Juist (GFR) 211
Jules Verne (Fra) 184
Julio, De 18 (Uru) 760
Julius A. Furer (USA) 704
Junak (Yug) 775
Junaluska (USA) 738
Juneau (USA) 715
Juno (UK) 602
Junon (Fra) 163
Jupiter (Bul) 73
Jupiter (GFR) 206
Jupiter (Pan) 384
Jupiter (Sin) 424
Jupiter (UK) 602
Jura (UK) 627
Jurel (DR) 136
Justice (Sin) 424
Jüterbog (GDR) 195
Jyuu-Go (Jap) 300
Jyuu-Ichi-Go (Jap) 300
Jyuu-Ni-Go (Jap) 300

K

K. Rojc (Yug) 777
Ka Tok (RoK) 327
Kaakkuri (Fin) 155
Kaapstad (SA) 429
Kabashima (Jap) 306
Kadet (Pol) 409
Kadmath (Ind) 237
Kae Bong (RoK) 326
Kahlid (SAr) 420
Kahnamuie (Iran) 256
Kai Feng (CPR) 113
Kai Yang (RoC) 466
Kaibilbalam (Gua) 226
Kain Ji-Dam (Nig) 367
Kaio (Jap) 313
Kairyu (Jap) 311
Kaivan (Iran) 256
Kaiyo (Jap) 312
Kakalang (Indo) 247
Kakap (Indo) 247
Kakinada (Ind) 241
Kala 1-6 (Fin) 154
Kala Hitam (Indo) 248
Kalamazoo (USA) 727
Kalamisani (Indo) 247
Kalanada (Indo) 247
Kalar (USSR) 568
Kalat (Pak) 382
Kalinga (Plp) 404
Kalispell (USA) 738
Kalkan (Tur) 490
Kalliroe (Gre) 224
Kallisto (USSR) 565
Kalnik (Yug) 778
Kalvari (Ind) 235
Kama (USSR) 571
Kamagong (Plp) 402
Kaman (Iran) 256
Kamchatka (USSR) 573, 579
Kamchatsky Komsomolets
(USSR) 553
Kamehameha (USA) 655
Kamenz (GDR) 195
Kamishima (Jap) 307
Kamorta (Ind) 237
Kampela 1 (Fin) 154
Kampela 2 (Fin) 154
Kamui (Jap) 308
Kanaris (Gre) 218
Kanarya (Tur) 497
Kanawa (Jap) 304
Kanawha (USA) 758
Kanderi (Ind) 235
Kane (USA) 743
Kang Won (RoK) 322
Kangan (Iran) 259
Kania (Pol) 407
Kanjar (Ind) 237
Kansas City (USA) 727
Kao Hsiung (RoC) 471
Kaparen (Swe) 454
Kaper (GFR) 210
Kapi I, II, III (Tur) 498
Kapitan A. Radzabov (USSR) 578
Kapitan Belousov (USSR) 577
Kapitan Bukaev (USSR) 578
Kapitan Chadaev (USSR) 578
Kapitan Chechkin (USSR) 578
Kapitan Kosolapov (USSR) 578
Kapitan Krutov (USSR) 578
Kapitan M. Izmaylov (USSR) 578
Kapitan Melekhov (USSR) 577
Kapitan Nikolaev (USSR) 577
Kapitan Plahin (USSR) 578
Kapitan Sorokin (USSR) 577
Kapitan Voronin (USSR) 577
Kapitan Zarubin (USSR) 578
Kara (Tog) 481
Karamürsel (Tur) 493
Karanj (Ind) 235
Karato (Jap) 301
Karatsu (Jap) 307
Karayel (Tur) 490
Karhu (Fin) 153
Karimata (Indo) 251
Karimudjawa (Indo) 251
Karjala (Fin) 151
Karkas (Iran) 257
Karl F. Gauss (GDR) 196
Karl Meseberg (GDR) 194
Karlskrona (Swe) 456
Karlsö (Swe) 458
Karlsøy (Nor) 373
Karlsruhe (GFR) 203
Karnaphuli (Ban) 52
Karpathos (Gre) 222
Karpaty (USSR) 573
Karpfen (GFR) 205
Kartal (Tur) 490
Karwar (Ind) 241
Kasar (Kwt) 329
Kasasagi (Jap) 297
Kasha (USSR) 557
Kasirga (Tur) 490
Kassos (Gre) 222
Kastor (Gre) 220
Kastoria (Gre) 224
Kataigis (Gre) 220
Katchal (Ind) 237
Kathleen (UK) 625
Katmai Bay (USA) 754
Katori (Jap) 301
Katsonis (Gre) 217
Katsura (Jap) 300, 306
Katun (USSR) 568
Katuren (Jap) 314
Kaura (Nor) 369
Kavaratti (Ind) 237
Kave 1-4 and 6 (Fin) 154
Kaveri (Ind) 239
Kavkaz (USSR) 556
Kaw (USA) 759
Kawishiwi (USA) 726
Kawkab (UAE) 581
Kedleston (UK) 610
Kedma (Isr) 267
Kegon (Jap) 311
Kegostrov (USSR) 567
Keihässalmi (Fin) 152
Kelabang (Indo) 248
Kelang (Mly) 340
Kelaplintah (Indo) 247
Kelefstis Stamou (Gre) 220
Kelewang (Mly) 338
Kellington (UK) 610
Kemaindera (Bru) 69
Kemper County (Bar) 53
Kennebec (USA) 758
Kennet (UK) 608
Kenoki (Can) 92
Kent (UK) 598
Kentauros (Gre) 220
Keokuk (USA) 738
Kepez (Tur) 498
Kerambit (Mly) 338
Keravnos (Gre) 224
Kerch (USSR) 522
Kerempe (Tur) 493
Kerkini (Gre) 224
Kersaint (Fra) 172
Kesari (Ind) 240
Keshet (Isr) 265
Kessaraya (Isr) 267
Keta (Gha) 213
Ketchikan (USA) 738
Keywadin (USA) 731
Khabar (SAr) 420
Khabarov (USSR) 575
Khadang (Iran) 256
Khanjar (Iran) 256
Kharg (Iran) 258
Khariton Laptev (USSR) 556, 578
Kharkov (USSR) 518
Khasab (Omn) 377
Khataf (Bhr) 50
Khawlan (Lby) 334
Khazbek (USSR) 573
Khersones (USSR) 557
Khibiny (USSR) 573
Khirirat (Tld) 475
Khobi (USSR) 571
Ki Rin (RoK) 327
Kichli (Gre) 222
Kickapoo (USA) 758
Kidon (Isr) 265
Kien Vang (Vtn) 771
Kiev (USSR) 518, 577
Kiisla (Fin) 155
Kikau (Fij) 149
Kikuchi (Jap) 306
Kikuzuki (Jap) 294
Kilauea (USA) 724
Kildin (USSR) 558
Kiliç (Tur) 490
Kilimli (Tur) 493
Kilklops (Gre) 224

826 INDEXES / Named Ships

Kiltan (Ind) 237
Kilya (Tur) 497
Kim Men (RoC) 473
Kim Qui (Vtn) 771
Kimberley (SA) 429
Kimbla (Aust) 45
Kimolos (Gre) 222
Kinabalu (Mly) 339
Kinbrace (UK) 620
King (Arg) 29
King (USA) 696
Kingarth (UK) 620
Kingfisher (UK) 615
Kingsport (USA) 739
Kinkaid (USA) 698
Kinloss (UK) 620
Kinn (Nor) 369
Kinugasa (Jap) 314
Kinzeer Al Bahr (Omn) 377
Kirk (USA) 705
Kirkliston (UK) 610
Kiro (Fij) 149
Kirov (USSR) 521
Kirpan (Ind) 238
Kish (Iran) 259
Kiska (USA) 724
Kissa (Gre) 222
Kistna (Ind) 239
Kitagumo (Jap) 309
Kitakami (Jap) 297
Kithnos (Gre) 222
Kittanning (USA) 738
Kittaton (USA) 738
Kittiwake (USA) 731
Kitty (UK) 625
Kitty Hawk (USA) 678
Kiyonami (Jap) 310
Kiyozuki (Jap) 310
Kjapp (Nor) 371
Kjekk (Nor) 371
Kled Keo (Tld) 481
Klipper (GFR) 210
Klueng Baden (Tld) 481
Klütz (GDR) 195
Klyasma (USSR) 571
Kmasan (USSR) 567
Knechtsand (GFR) 211
Knechtsand II (GDR) 197
Knorr (USA) 742
Knossos (Gre) 224
Knox (USA) 705
Knurr (Nor) 371
Knurrhahn (GFR) 212
Ko Hung (RoK) 326
Ko Mun (RoK) 327
Kobben (Nor) 369
Kobchik (USSR) 538
Koblenz (GFR) 205
Kocatepe (Tur) 488
Kochisar (Tur) 491
Koelsch (USA) 707
Koida (USSR) 570
Koje (RoK) 324
Kojima (Jap) 306
Koksijde (Bel) 54
Kola (USSR) 570
Kolesnikov (USSR) 559
Kolguev (USSR) 558
Köln (GFR) 203
Kolum (Tld) 480
Komayuki (Jap) 310
Komenda (Gha) 214
Komet (GDR) 196
Komet (GFR) 213
Kompas (Indo) 248
Kompas (Pol) 409
Kompas (USSR) 559
Komsomolets (USSR) 528
Komsomolets Ukrainy (USSR) 529
Konda (USSR) 571
Kondor (Pol) 405
Konoka (USA) 738
Konstanz (GFR) 205
Kontre Admiral
Choroshkin (USSR) 545
Kontroller (Pol) 409
Kootenay (Can) 82
Kopernik (Pol) 408
Korawakka (Sri) 448
Kormoran (Pol) 407
Kornat (Yug) 777
Korrigan (Fra) 188
Korsar (GFR) 210
Korsholm (Fin) 154
Kortenaer (Nld) 356
Kortryk (Bel) 55
Kos (Gre) 221
Koshiki (Jap) 304, 308
Koskelo (Fin) 155
Kosmonavt Georgy
Dobrovolsky (USSR) 567
Kosmonavt Pavel
Belyayev (USSR) 567
Kosmonavt Sayev (USSR) 567
Kosmonavt Vladimir Komarov
(USSR) 566
Kosmonavt Vladklav
Volkov (USSR) 567
Kosmonavt Yuri Gagarin (USSR) 566
Kosoku 6 (Jap) 298
Kota Bahru (Mly) 340
Kotobiki (Jap) 311
Kountouriotis (Gre) 218
Koura (NZ) 364
Kouroosh (Iran) 254
Kouzu (Jap) 300
Kozara (Yug) 780
Kozlu (Tur) 493
Kozu (Jap) 308
Kozuf (Yug) 778
Kr. Tønder (Nor) 374
Krab (Pol) 409
Kram (Tld) 479
Krapu (Indo) 248
Krasin (USSR) 576
Krasnaya Presnya (USSR) 550
Krasny-Kavkaz (USSR) 529
Krasny-Krim (USSR) 529
Krekel (Bel) 56
Krenometr (USSR) 557
Krieger (Den) 127
Krilon (USSR) 558
Kris (Mly) 338
Kriti (Gre) 221
Krogulec (Pol) 407
Kromantse (Gha) 213
Kronos (Gre) 224
Kronshtadt (USSR) 524
Krøttøy (Nor) 373
Krym (USSR) 556
Krymsky Komsomolets (USSR) 550
Ku San (RoK) 327
Ku Yong (RoK) 328
Kuala Kangsar (Mly) 340
Kuala Trengganu (Mly) 340
Kuang Chou (CPR) 107
Kuban (USSR) 574
Kuching (Mly) 340
Kuchkuch (GFR) 210
Kudako (Jap) 300
Kudret (Tur) 498
Kuei Lin (CPR) 106
Kuei Yang (CPR) 106
Kuha 21-26 (Fin) 153
Kuhlungsborn (GDR) 195
Kuikka (Fin) 155
Kukolkan (Gua) 225
Kula (Fij) 149
Kum Kok (RoK) 326
Kum San (RoK) 326
Kuma (Jap) 306
Kumano (Jap) 297,306
Kumataka (Jap) 298
K'un Ming (CPR) 106
Kun Yang (RoC) 467
Kunashiri (Jap) 307
Kunimi (Jap) 308
Kunna (Nor) 369
Kuovi (Fin) 155
Kuparu (NZ) 364
Kurama (Jap) 308
Kurki (Fin) 155
Kurobe (Jap) 306
Kurokami (Jap) 308
Kuroshio (Jap) 292
Kurs (USSR) 557
Kursograf (USSR) 557
Kursura (Ind) 235
Kurtaran (Tur) 496
Kusadasi (Tur) 493
Kusakaki (Jap) 308
Kusseh (Iran) 254
Kut (Tld) 479
Kuthar (Ind) 238
Kuznetsky (USSR) 573
Kuzuryu (Jap) 306
Kuvvet (Tur) 498
Kvalsund (Nor) 372
Kvarven (Nor) 373
Kvikk (Nor) 371
Kvina (Nor) 372
KW3 (GFR) 210
KW15-KW20 (GFR) 210
Kwang Ju (RoK) 322
Kwei Yang (RoC) 467
Ky Hoa (Vtn) 771
Kya (Nor) 369
Kyklon (Gre) 220
Kyknos (Gre) 220
Kyong Nam (RoK) 323
Kyong Puk (RoK) 323
Kyritz (GDR) 195
Kyuu-Go (Jap) 300

L

L. Mendel Rivers (USA) 662
L. Y. Spear (USA) 729
L'Adroit (Fra) 178
L'Agenais (Fra) 174
L'Alsacien (Fra) 174
L'Archéonaute (Fra) 186
L'Ardent (Fra) 178
L'Ardent (IC) 287
L'Astrolabe (Fra) 181
L'Audacieux (Cam) 76
L'Etoile (Fra) 189
L'Indomptable (Fra) 161
L'Inflexible (Fra) 161
L'Intrepide (IC) 287
La Belle Poule (Fra) 189
La Charente (Fra) 182
La Combattante (Fra) 177
La Crete a Pierrot (Hai) 228
La Dieppoise (Fra) 178
La Dunkerquoise (Fra) 178
La Falence (Sen) 423
La Fidèle (Fra) 186
La Galissonière (Fra) 170
La Grande Hermine (Fra) 189
La Jolla (USA) 659
La Lorientaise (Fra) 178
La Moure County (USA) 717
La Paimpolaise (Fra) 178
La Pedrera (Per) 388
La Persévérante (Fra) 186
La Praya (Fra) 162
La Prudente (Fra) 186
La Recherche (Fra) 181
La Salle (USA) 725
La Saône (Fra) 182
Labana (Guy) 228
Laborieux (Fra) 190
Labrador (Can) 89
Labrador (UK) 624
Labuan (Aust) 47
Lac Tonlé Sap (Fra) 183
Lachs (GFR) 205
Lacomble (Nld) 359
Ladava (PNG) 384
Ladislao Cabrea (Bol) 57
Ladoga (USSR) 557
Ladya (Tld) 479
Ladybird (UK) 625
Lae (PNG) 384
Laesø (Den) 129
Lafayette (USA) 655
Lagoa (Por) 413
Laguna (Plp) 401
Lahmeyer (Brz) 68
Lahn (GFR) 207
Lahore (Pak) 382
Lai Yang (RoC) 466
Lake Buhi (Plp) 403
Lake Buluan (Plp) 403
Lake Lanao (Plp) 403
Lake Mainit (Plp) 403
Lake Naujan (Plp) 403
Lake Paoay (Plp) 403
Laks (Nor) 371
Laksamana (Mly) 340
Laleston (UK) 610
Lamego (Brz) 68
Lamaki (Iraq) 261
Lambung Mangkurat (Indo) 246
Lamlash (UK) 626
Lampedusa (Ita) 286
Lampo (Ita) 280
Lampo Batang (Indo) 252
Lana (Nig) 367
Lanao del Norte (Plp) 401
Lancha Ecografa (Par) 386
Landtieff (GDR) 197
Lang (USA) 705
Langara (Spn) 436
Langeland (Den) 131
Langeness (GFR) 211
Langeoog (GFR) 211
Lanta (Tld) 479
Lantana (USA) 758
Lao Yang (RoC) 466
Lapon (USA) 662
Lapseki (Tur) 497
Lapwing (Ana) 23
Larak (Iran) 258
Larice (Ita) 281
Larkana (Pak) 382
Las Aves (Ven) 768
Lasham (UK) 622
Latanier (Fra) 190
Latorre (Chi) 96
Lauis Ledge (Plp) 403
Launceston (Aust) 43
Laurel (USA) 756
Laurier (Fra) 180
Laurindo Pitta (Brz) 68
Lautaro (Chi) 98
Lavan (Iran) 258
Lawrence (USA) 695
Lawrenceville (Can) 86
Laya (Spn) 440
Layang (Indo) 248
Laymoor (UK) 621
Lazaga (Spn) 439
Lazzaro Mocenigo (Ita) 271
Le Basque (Fra) 174
Le Béarnais (Fra) 174
Le Dgoc An (Vtn) 771
Le Dinh Hung (Vtn) 771
Le Fort (Fra) 190
Le Foudroyant (Fra) 161
Le Fringant (Fra) 178
Le Ngoc Thanh (Vtn) 771
Le Normand (Fra) 174
Le Picard (Fra) 174
Le Phuoc Dui (Vtn) 771
Le Provençal (Fra) 174
Le Redoubtable (Fra) 161
Le Savoyard (Fra) 174
Le Terrible (Fra) 161
Le Tonnant (Fra) 161
Le Valeureux (Cam) 76
Le Valeureux (IC) 287
Le Van Nga (Vtn) 771
Le Vendéen (Fra) 174
Le Vigilant (IC) 287
Leader (USA) 721
Leahy (USA) 690
Leander (UK) 602
Leandro Valle (Mex) 345
Lech (GFR) 207
Lech (Pol) 409
Lechlade (UK) 626
Ledang (Mly) 339
Ledbury (UK) 609
Leftwich (USA) 698
Legare (USA) 752
Legazpi (Spn) 424
Leie (Bel) 55
Lelaka (USA) 738
Lelaps (Gre) 220
Lely (Ven) 769
Lemadang (Indo) 248
Lembing (Mly) 338
Lena (USSR) 570
Lengeh (Iran) 259
Lenin (Pol) 408
Lenin (USSR) 576
Leningrad (USSR) 520, 577
Leningradski Komsomolets
(USSR) 535
Leon (Gre) 219
Leon (Spn) 437
Leon Guzman (Mex) 346
Leonardo Da Vinci (Ita) 271
Leonid Dymeen (USSR) 562
Leonid Sobolev (USSR) 562
Lepanto (Spn) 436
Lerche (GFR) 210
Lerice (Ita) 281
Lerida (Aust) 48
Les Almadies (Sen) 423
Lesbos (Gre) 221
Lesley (UK) 625
Leticia (Col) 117
Letuchky (USSR) 535
Levanzo (Ita) 286
Lewis and Clark (USA) 655
Lewiston (UK) 610
Lexington (USA) 683
Leyte (Plp) 399
Liao Yang (RoC) 466
Libeccio (Ita) 276
Libellule (Fra) 187
Liberal (Brz) 63
Liberation (Bel) 55
Libertad (Arg) 33
Libertad (DR) 135
Libertad (Ven) 767
Licio Visintini (Ita) 278
Lien Chang (RoC) 472
Lientur (Chi) 98
Lieutenant James E.
Robinson (USA) 745
Lieutenant de Vaisseau
Lavallée (Fra) 175
Lieutenant Malghagh (Mor) 351
Lieutenant Riffi (Mor) 350
Lightship Columbia (USA) 759
Lightship Nantucket (USA) 759
Lightship Relief (USA) 759
Ligia Elena (Pan) 383
Lihiniya (Sri) 448
Likendeeler (GFR) 210
Lilah (UK) 625
Lilas (Fra) 180
Liman (USSR) 558
Limasawa (Plp) 403
Limburg (Nld) 356
Limnos (Can) 93
Limnos (Gre) 221
Limpopo (Por) 413
Lin I (CPR) 107
Linaro (Ita) 286
Lincoln (UK) 605
Lindau (GFR) 205
Lindisfarne (UK) 614
Lindormen (Den) 131
Lindos (Gre) 224
Line (USA) 759
Ling Yuen (RoC) 472
Liniers (Spn) 438
Linza (USSR) 557
Lipan (USA) 731
Lisa (USSR) 538
Liseron (Fra) 188
Listerville (Can) 86
Litoral (Bol) 57
Liulom (Tld) 477
Liverpool (UK) 600
Livio Piomarta (Ita) 271
Llandovery (UK) 626
Llobregat (Spn) 443
Lo Yang (RoC) 467
Lobélia (Fra) 180
Lobitos (Per) 394
Lockwood (USA) 705
Loddon (UK) 608
Loganville (Can) 86
Loire (Fra) 183
Lok Adhar (Ind) 243
Loke (Swe) 459
Lokeren (Bel) 55
Lokodjo (IC) 287
Lomas (Per) 393
Lommen (Swe) 462
Lonchi (Gre) 218
London (UK) 598
Londonderry (UK) 604
Long Beach (USA) 691
Longlom (Tld) 477
Lorain County (USA) 717
Loreley (GFR) 206
Loreto (Per) 392
Loriot (Fra) 190
Los (Pol) 407
Los Alamos (USA) 734
Los Angeles (USA) 659
Los Frailes (Ven) 768
Los Monjes (Ven) 768
Los Roques (Ven) 768
Los Testigos (Ven) 768
Lossen (Den) 131
Lotlin (USSR) 557
Loto (Ita) 281
Lotsman (USSR) 556
Louhi (Fin) 154
Louis St. Laurent (Can) 88
Lovat (USSR) 571
Lovcen (Yug) 778
Lowestoft (UK) 604
Loyal Chancellor (UK) 626
Loyal Helper (UK) 626
Loyal Mediator (UK) 626
Loyal Moderator (UK) 626
Loyal Proctor (UK) 626
Loyal Volunteer (UK) 626
Loyal Watcher (UK) 626
Loyang (CPR) 107
LP 1, 2 & 3 (GFR) 212
LS 9-12 (Tur) 491
Lu Shan (RoC) 468
Lübben (GDR) 195
Lübeck (GFR) 203
Lübz (GDR) 193
Luce (USA) 696
Luciole (Fra) 187
Ludwigslust (GDR) 193
Luigi Rizzo (Ita) 278
Luis Manuel Rojas (Mex) 346
Lulea (Swe) 454
Lumme (GDR) 197
Lundy (UK) 627
Lüneburg (GFR) 209
Lung Chiang (RoC) 469
Lung Chuan (RoC) 473
Lupo (Ita) 277
Lutin (Fra) 188
Lütjens (GFR) 201
Lütjie Horn (GFR) 211
Lutteur (Fra) 190
Lynch (Arg) 31
Lynch (USA) 741
Lynde McCormick (USA) 695
Lyness (UK) 620
Lynx (UK) 605
Lyø (Den) 130
Lyr (Nor) 371
Lyre (Fra) 178

M

M. Acev (Yug) 777
M. Fevzi Cakmak (Tur) 488
Ma San (RoK) 327
Ma'oz (Isr) 267
Maagen (Den) 128
Maassluis (Nld) 358
Maccah (SAr) 420
Macdonough (USA) 696
Maceo (Cub) 123
Mackenzie (Can) 81
Mackinaw (USA) 754
Machtigal (Cam) 76
Macorix (DR) 137
Macreuse (Fra) 190
Mactan (Plp) 403
Madadgar (Pak) 383
Madang (PNG) 384
Madaraka (Ken) 316
Madera (Bol) 57
Madokawando (USA) 738
Madrona (USA) 756
Maeklong (Tld) 480
Maestrale (Ita) 276
Magar (Ind) 240
Magat Salamat (Plp) 399
Magellan (GFR) 210
Magne (Swe) 454
Magnetologe (GDR) 196
Magnolia (Fra) 188
Magomed Gadzhiev (USSR) 553

INDEXES / Named Ships 827

Maguana (DR) 136
Mahamiru (Mly) 339
Mahan (Iran) 256
Mahan (USA) 696
Maharajalela (Bru) 69
Maharajalela (Mly) 340
Maharajasetia (Mly) 340
Mahkota (Mly) 340
Mahmood (Pak) 382
Mahnavi-Hamraz (Iran) 259
Mahnavi-Taheri (Iran) 259
Mahnavi-Vahedi (Iran) 259
Mahoning (USA) 759
Mahroos (Kwt) 329
Mahu (Nld) 359
Maille Brézé (Fra) 172
Main (GFR) 207
Makigumo (Jap) 294, 309
Makinami (Jap) 296
Makishio (Jap) 292
Makkum (Nld) 358
Makrele (GFR) 205
Makurdi (Nig) 366
Makut Rajakumarn (Tld) 475
Mala Hayati (Indo) 245
Malabar (Fra) 189
Malaika (Mad) 336
Malaspina (Spn) 444
Maldonado (Uru) 761
Maliopoulos (Gre) 223
Mallard (Can) 92
Mallemukken (Den) 128
Mallet (USA) 758
Mallow (USA) 756
Mamba (Ken) 316
Manabi (Ecu) 138
Manatee Bay (Jam) 288
Manawanui (NZ) 364
Manchester (UK) 600
Mandan (USA) 738
Mandarin (UK) 620
Mandorlo (Ita) 281
Mandovi (Por) 413
Manga (NZ) 364
Mango (Ita) 281
Mangro (Pak) 379
Manhattan (USA) 738
Manistee (USA) 738
Manitou (USA) 759
Manitowoc (USA) 717
Manley (USA) 700
Manø (Den) 130
Mano (Lbr) 331
Manoka (Cam) 76
Manquier (Fra) 190
Mansa Kila IV (Gam) 192
Manta (Ecu) 139
Manterola (Chi) 102
Mantilla (Col) 119
Mantilla (Per) 395
Manual Doblado (Mex) 345
Manuel Crecencio Rejon (Mex) 346
Manuel Lara (Col) 119
Manuel Villavicencio (Per) 391
Manych (USSR) 569
Manzanillo (Mex) 347
Mapiri (Bol) 57
Maquindanao (Plp) 401
Marabout (Fra) 190
Maracaibo (Ven) 768
Marajo (Brz) 67
Maranhao (Brz) 62
Marañón (Per) 391
Marburg (GFR) 205
Marcilio Dias (Brz) 62
Mardan (Pak) 382
Mardjan (Iran) 259
Margaree (Can) 82
Margay (Guy) 228
Maria Quiteria (Brz) 68
Maria Van Riebeeck (SA) 428
Mariano Escobedo (Mex) 345
Mariano G. Vallejo (USA) 655
Mariano Metamoros (Mex) 347
Marias (USA) 746
Marin (USA) 738
Marinduque (Plp) 402
Marinero Fuentealba (Chi) 99
Marinette (USA) 738
Mario Serpa (Col) 119
Mariposa (USA) 756
Mariscal Santa Cruz (Bol) 57
Mariscal Sucre (Ven) 766
Marisco (Brz) 68
Mariz E. Barros (Brz) 62
Marlin (Bhm) 49
Marmaris (Tur) 492
Marn Vichai (Tld) 481
Maronnier (Fra) 190
Marqués De La Ensenada (Spn) 435
Mars (GFR) 206
Mars (USA) 724
Mars (USSR) 558
Mårsgarn (Swe) 462
Marshal Timoshenko (USSR) 524
Marshal Voroshilov (USSR) 524
Marshfield (USA) 744
Marsopa (Spn) 433
Marsouin (Fra) 163
Marsquin (Alg) 21
Marsteinen (Nor) 373
Martadinata (Indo) 246
Marti (Cub) 123
Marti (Pan) 384
Marti (Tur) 489
Martin (UK) 628
Martin Alvarez (Spn) 442
Martin Pécheur (Fra) 190
Martinet (Fra) 190
Martins de Oliveira (Brz) 67
Marvin Shields (USA) 705
Mary (UK) 625
Marysville (Can) 86
Marzook (Kwt) 329
Mascoutah (USA) 738
Mashhoor (Kwt) 329
Mashtan (Bhr) 50
Mashuk (USSR) 579
Masna (Bru) 69
Massapequa (USA) 738
Mastiff (UK) 624
Mata Ikan (Sin) 425
Matanga (Ind) 243
Mataphon (Tld) 480
Matias de Cordova (Mex) 346
Matjan Kumbang (Indo) 247
Mato Grosso (Brz) 62
Matra (Tld) 480
Matsunami (Jap) 310
Matsuura (Jap) 307
Matsuyuki (Jap) 310
Matunak (USA) 738
Maumee (USA) 747
Mauna Kea (USA) 724
Maursund (Nor) 372
Max Reichpietsch (GDR) 194
Max Reichpietsch II (GDR) 197
Maxim (UK) 623
Maxton (UK) 610
Maxwell (Can) 93
May Rut (Vtn) 771
Mayak (USSR) 561
Maymoon (Kwt) 329
Mayor Arias (Col) 119
Mayta Kapac (Bol) 57
Mayu (Bur) 73
Mazatenango (Gua) 226
McArthur (USA) 759
McCandless (USA) 705
McCloy (USA) 708
McInerney (USA) 703
McKean (USA) 701, 702
McKee (USA) 729
Mearim (Brz) 64
Mechelen (Bel) 56
Mecosta (USA) 738
Medusa (GFR) 206
Medusa (Pol) 409
Medved (USSR) 538
Medway (UK) 608
Meerkatze (GFR) 213
Meersburg (GFR) 209
Mehmetcik (Tur) 492
Mehr (Iran) 259
Mehran (Iran) 256
Mei Lo (RoC) 471
Mei Ping (RoC) 471
Mei Sung (RoC) 471
Mei Tseng (RoC) 471
Meise (GFR) 210
Meiyo (Jap) 311
Melaban (Mly) 339
Melbourne (Aust) 39
Melchor Ocampo (Mex) 345
Mélèze (Fra) 190
Meliton Carvajal (Per) 391
Mella (DR) 134
Mellon (USA) 750
Mellum (GFR) 211
Meltem (Tur) 490
Mélusine (Fra) 188
Melville (USA) 742
Memmert (GFR) 207
Memphis (USA) 659
Menasha (USA) 738
Mendez Nuñez (Spn) 436
Mendieta (Gua) 226
Menominee (USA) 738
Mentawai (Indo) 251
Menzel Bourguiba (Tun) 485
Merawa (Lby) 334
Mercer (USA) 735
Mercure (Fra) 180
Mercury (Sin) 424
Mercuur (Nld) 361
Meredith (USA) 701, 702
Meric (Tur) 492
Meridian (USSR) 567
Merisier (Fra) 190
Merksem (Bel) 55
Merle (Fra) 190
Merlin (Fra) 188
Merrickville (Can) 86
Merrill (USA) 698
Merrimack (USA) 726
Mersin (Tur) 492
Mesaha 1-2 (Tur) 495
Mésange (Fra) 190
Mesco (Ita) 286
Mesquite (USA) 756
Messenger (USA) 759
Mestre Joao Dos Santos (Brz) 66
Metacom (USA) 738
Metan (USSR) 571
Meteor (GDR) 196
Meteor (GFR) 213
Meteor (USA) 745
Meteoro (Chi) 101
Meuse (Bel) 55
Meuse (Fra) 182
Meyerkord (USA) 705
Mezen (USSR) 574
Mgla (USSR) 561
Miaoulis (Gre) 217
Michel (GFR) 210
Michelangelo (Iran) 259
Michigan (USA) 654
Michishio (Jap) 292
Middelburg (Nld) 358
Middleton (UK) 609
Midgett (USA) 750
Midway (USA) 682
Mier (Bel) 56
Migadan (USA) 738
Miguel dos Santos (Brz) 68
Miguel Malvar (Plp) 399
Miguel Ramos Arizpe (Mex) 346
Miguel Rodriguez (Ven) 769
Mikhail Kutusov (USSR) 527
Mikhail Lomonosov (USSR) 560
Mikhail Somov (USSR) 564
Mikula (Can) 93
Mikuma (Jap) 297
Mikura (Jap) 304, 308
Milanian (Iran) 256
Milano (Spn) 447
Milazzo (Ita) 281
Miller (USA) 705
Millicoma (USA) 747
Milsø 101, 102 (Den) 133
Milwaukee (USA) 727
Mimac (USA) 738
Mime (GFR) 210
Mimosa (Fra) 180
Minabe (Jap) 307
Minas Gerais (Brz) 61
Minase (Jap) 300
Mincio (Ita) 285
Minden (GFR) 205, 213
Mindoro Occidental (Plp) 401
Minegumo (Jap) 294, 310
Miner (USSR) 545
Minerva (GFR) 206
Minerva (UK) 602
Minh Hoa (Vtn) 771
Ministro Portales (Chi) 97
Ministro Zenteno (Chi) 97
Miño (Spn) 443
Minoo (Jap) 311
Minören (Swe) 459
Minoru (UK) 629
Minotauros (Gre) 224
Minsk (USSR) 518
Mira (Por) 414
Miramichi (Can) 85
Mircea (Rom) 418
Mirfak (USA) 744
Mirto (Ita) 282
Misamis Occidental (Plp) 402
Miseno (Ita) 286
Misgav (Isr) 265
Mishawaka (USA) 738
Miskanaw (Can) 93
Mispillion (USA) 746
Mission Santa Ynez (USA) 747
Mississinewa (USA) 726
Mississippi (USA) 686
Missouri (USA) 685
Mistral (GFR) 210
Misurata (Lby) 334
Mitilo (Ita) 282
Mitzahon (Isr) 265
Miura (Jap) 298, 305
Mivtach (Isr) 265
Miyake (Jap) 300, 307
Miyato (Jap) 300
Mizar (USA) 742
Miznach (Isr) 265
Mizrak (Tur) 490
Mizutori (Jap) 297
Mjölner (Swe) 454
Moana Wave (USA) 741
Mobile (USA) 718
Mobile Bay (USA) 754
Mochizuki (Jap) 294, 310
Mocovi (Arg) 34
Moctabi (USA) 731, 732
Mode (Swe) 454
Modoc (USA) 759
Møen (Den) 130
Mogami (Jap) 297
Mogano (Ita) 281
Møgsterfjord (Nor) 374
Mohawk (UK) 603
Mohican (USA) 759
Moineau (Fra) 190
Moinester (USA) 705
Mok Po (RoK) 327
Moksha (USSR) 571
Moldavya (USSR) 562
Mölders (GFR) 201
Mollendo (Per) 394
Momin (Pak) 382
Monastir (Tun) 485
Mongisidi (Indo) 246
Mongol (USSR) 573
Monkton (UK) 615
Mono (Tog) 481
Monob I (USA) 736
Monongahela (USA) 726
Monowai (NZ) 363
Monsun (GFR) 210
Montcalm (Can) 90
Montcalm (Fra) 168
Monte Cristo (Ita) 286
Monticello (USA) 716
Montmagny (Can) 92
Montmorency (Can) 91
Moorhen (Can) 92
Moosburgger (USA) 698
Moran Valverde (Ecu) 138
Moratoc (USA) 738
Morcoyan (Arg) 34
Mordogan (Tur) 492
Moresby (Aust) 44
Morgane (Fra) 188
Morgenthau (USA) 750
Mornar (Yug) 776
Morona (Per) 395
Morro Bay (USA) 754
Mors (Pol) 407
Morse (Fra) 163
Morsoviets (USSR) 558
Morton (USA) 700
Morvarid (Iran) 259
Morzhovets (USSR) 567
Mosel (GFR) 207
Moshal (Pak) 382
Moskovsky Komsomolets (USSR) 533
Moskva (USSR) 520, 577
Mosopelea (USA) 731
Mosselbaai (SA) 429
Motajica (Yug) 779
Motobu (Jap) 299, 305
Mouette (Fra) 190
Mount Baker (USA) 724
Mount Hood (USA) 724
Mount Mitchell (USA) 759
Mount Samat (Plp) 403
Mount Vernon (USA) 716
Mount Whitney (USA) 712
MS 41 (Eth) 148
Muavenet (Tur) 488
Mubarak (Pak) 382
Muchula (Bol) 57
Muguet (Fra) 180
Mujahid (Pak) 382
Mukhtar (Pak) 382
Mul 11 (Swe) 457
Mul 12-19 (Swe) 457
Mullinnix (USA) 700
Multan (Pak) 382
Multatuli (Indo) 250
Mungo (Cam) 76
Munin (Swe) 454
Munro (USA) 750
Munsif (Pak) 382
Murakumo (Jap) 294, 309
Muräne (GFR) 205
Murasame (Jap) 295
Murat Reis (Tur) 487
Murature (Arg) 29
Murayjib (UAE) 582
Murban (UAE) 581
Murcia (Spn) 437
Mürefte (Tur) 492
Murene (Alg) 21
Murene (Fra) 190
Murene (Mor) 351
Murmansk (USSR) 527, 577
Muroto (Jap) 305
Murotsu (Jap) 300
Murshed (Kwt) 329
Murtaja (Fin) 153
Murtala Muhamed (Nig) 367
Muskegon (USA) 738
Muskingum (USA) 758
Musson (USSR) 564
Mutiara (Mly) 339
Mutilla (Chi) 102
Mutin (Fra) 189
Mutis (Indo) 252
Mutsuki (Jap) 310
Mutsure (Jap) 300
Muzuki (Jap) 300
Myles C. Fox (USA) 701, 702
Myojo (Jap) 313
Myosotis (Fra) 189
Myrtle (UK) 625
Mysing (Swe) 454
Mysore (Ind) 235
Mytho (Fra) 179

N

9 De Octubre (Ecu) 139
N.B. McLean (Can) 90
N. I. Goulandris I (Gre) 221
N. I. Goulandris II (Gre) 221
N. Kolomeytsev (USSR) 560
N. Martinovic (Yug) 777
N. Yevgenov (USSR) 560
N'Gombe (Gab) 192
N'Guene (Gab) 191
Na Dong (RoK) 326
Naaldwijk (Nld) 359
Naarden (Nld) 359
Nabigwon (USA) 738
Nachi (Jap) 311
Nachtigall (GFR) 210
Näcken (Swe) 452
Nadli (USA) 738
Nafkratoussa (Gre) 221
Naftilos (Gre) 223
Naga Banda (Indo) 245
Naga Pasa (Indo) 247
Nagakyay (Bur) 74
Nagatsuki (Jap) 294
Naghdi (Iran) 256
Nahang (Iran) 254
Nahid (Iran) 256
Nahidik (Can) 93
Nahoke (USA. 738
Naiad (UK) 602
Najad (Swe) 452
Najade (GFR) 203
Najaden (Den) 128
Nakha (Tld) 480
Nakhodchivy (USSR) 532
Nakhodka (USSR) 556
Nala (Indo) 245
Nalón (Spn) 443
Nam Du (Vtn) 771
Nam Yang (RoK) 326
Namao (Can) 92
Namdö (Swe) 458
Nan Chang (CPR) 107
Nan Yang (RoC) 467
Nana-Go (Jap) 300
Nanawa (Par) 385
Nancy (UK) 625
Nanryu (Jap) 311
Nanticoke (USA) 738
Naparima (TT) 483
Naporisty (USSR) 533
Nara (USSR) 571
Narhvalen (Den) 125
Narra (Plp) 402
Narragansett (USA) 731
Narushio (Jap) 292
Narval (Fra) 163
Narval (Spn) 433
Narvik (Fra) 179
Narvik (Nor) 369
Narwhal (Can) 90
Narwhal (USA) 661
Narwik (Pol) 408
Nashat (Ind) 240
Nashua (USA) 738
Nashville (USA) 715
Nassau (USA) 713
Nastoychivy (USSR) 532
Natahki (USA) 738
Natchitoches (USA) 738
Natek (Pol) 409
Nathan Hale (USA) 655
Nathanael Greene (USA) 655
Natick (USA) 738
Natori (Jap) 307
Natsugumo (Jap) 294, 309
Natuna (Indo) 251
Naugatuck (USA) 759
Nautilus (GFR) 206
Nautilus (Nld) 361
Nautilus (SA) 428
Nautilus (Spn) 439
Nautilus (USA) 667
Navajo (USA) 731
Navarinon (Gre) 218
Navarra (Spn) 437
Navasota (USA) 746
Navodvhik (USSR) 545
Navigator (Pol) 408
Navigator (SA) 430
Nawarat (Bur) 74
Nazario Sauro (Ita) 271
Ndjole (Gab) 192
Ndovu (Ken) 316
Neah Bay (USA) 754
Nebli (Spn) 447
Neches (USA) 746
Neckar (GFR) 207
Negba (Isr) 267
Negros Occidental (Plp) 399
Negros Oriental (Plp) 399
Nemuro (Jap) 299
Neodesha (USA) 738
Neosho (USA) 726
Nepanet (USA) 738
Neptun (Den) 128
Neptun (GFR) 206
Neptun (Rom) 418

828 INDEXES / Named Ships

Neptun (Swe) 452
Neptune (USA) 748
Neptunia (Pol) 409
Neptuno (DR) 136
Neptuno (Per) 395
Nercha (USSR) 571
Nereida (Spn) 447
Nereide (Fra) 188
Neretva (Yug) 775
Nereus (Gre) 216
Nereus (USA) 730
Nerey (USSR) 561
Nereida (Spn) 447
Nerz (GFR) 205
Nesokrushimy (USSR) 532
Nestin (Yug) 779
Neuende (GFR) 211
Neuderzhimy (USSR) 530
Neukrotimy (USSR) 535
Neulovimy (USSR) 530
Neuquen (Arg) 31
Neuruppin (GDR) 195
Neustadt (GFR) 213
Neustrelitz (GDR) 195
Neuwerk (GFR) 211
Nevel (USSR) 567
Nevelskoy (USSR) 563
New Bedford (USA) 735
New Jersey (USA) 685
New Orleans (USA) 714
New York City (USA) 659
Newcastle (UK) 600
Newgagon (USA) 738
Newman K. Perry (USA) 701, 702
Newman Noggs (UK) 628
Newport (USA) 717
Newton (UK) 621
Neyzeh (Iran) 256
Ngahau Koula (Ton) 482
Ngahan Siliva (Ton) 482
Ngo Van Quyen (Vtn) 771
Ngolo (Gab) 191
Ngurah Rai (Indo) 246
Nguyen An (Vtn) 771
Nguyen Dao (Vtn) 771
Nguyen Han (Vtn) 771
Nguyen Kim Hung (Vtn) 771
Nguyen Ngoc Long (Vtn) 772
Nguyen Ngoc Thach (Vtn) 771
Nhong Sarhai (Tld) 478
Ni-Go (Jap) 303
Niagara Falls (USA) 724
Niantic (USA) 738
Nibbio (Ita) 279
Nicholson (Can) 84
Nicholson (USA) 698
Nicolas Suarez (Bol) 57
Nicolet (Can) 93
Niederösterreich (Aus) 49
Niels Juel (Den) 126
Nienburg (GFR) 209
Nieuwpoort (Bel) 54
Nigeria (Nig) 365
Nikolai Filchenkov (USSR) 550
Nikolai Obyekov (USSR) 550
Nikolai Vilkov (USSR) 550
Nikolai Zubov (USSR) 558
Nikolay Stolbov (USSR) 553
Nikolayev (USSR) 522
Nilgiri (Ind) 237
Nils Strömcrona (Swe) 461
Nimitz (USA) 675
Nimpkish (Can) 86
Nimr (Egy) 145
Ninh Giang (Vtn) 772
Niobe (GFR) 207
Niovi (Gre) 222
Nipat (Ind) 240
Nipigon (Can) 81
Nirbhik (Ind) 240
Nirghat (Ind) 240
Nisan (Iraq) 260
Nisida (Ita) 286
Nisr (Egy) 145
Nistar (Ind) 242
Niteroi (Brz) 63
Nito Restrepo (Col) 118
Nitro (USA) 724
Nivelir (USSR) 561
Nixe (GFR) 206
Niyodo (Jap) 297
Njord (Swe) 460
Noakhali (Ban) 52
Nobaru (Jap) 308
Noce (Ita) 281
Nodaway (USA) 748
Nogah (Isr) 267
Nogales (USA) 738
Nogueira Da Gama (Brz) 66
Noguera (Per) 395
Nojima (Jap) 306
Nokomis (Can) 92
Noon (Bhr) 50
Norah (UK) 625
Norain (Bru) 69
Norby (Den) 127
Norderney (GFR) 211
Nordkaperen (Den) 125
Nordkaperen (Swe) 453
Nordkapp (Nor) 374
Nordstrand (GFR) 211
Nordwind (GFR) 210
Norfolk (UK) 598
Norge (Nor) 373
Norma (UK) 627
Norman McLeod Rogers (Can) 88
Nornen (Nor) 374
Norrköping (Swe) 454
Norrtälje (Swe) 454
Norsten (Swe) 458
Northland (USA) 752
Northwind (USA) 754
Norton Sound (USA) 732
Norviking (Nor) 374
Norwalk (USA) 744
Noshiro (Jap) 297
Noto (Jap) 308
Nottingham (UK) 600
Novator (USSR) 561
Noviembre, De 3 (Ecu) 139
Novorossiisk (USSR) 518
Noyer (Fra) 190
NR 1 (USA) 671
Nubian (UK) 603
Nueces (USA) 735
Nueva Esparta (Ven) 765
Nueve de Julio (Arg) 27
Nueva Viscaya (Plp) 399
Nuevo Rocafuerte (Ecu) 139
Nuku (Indo) 246
Numa (USA) 738
Numana (Ita) 281
Nung Ra (RoK) 327
Nunobiki (Jap) 311
Nuoli 1-13 (Fin) 151
Nurton (UK) 610
Nusa Telu (Indo) 251
Nusret (Tur) 492
Nymfen (Den) 128
Nymphe (GFR) 206
Nynäshamn (Swe) 454

O

18 De Julio (Uru) 760
O/Lt Valcke (Bel) 56
Oak Ridge (USA) 734
Ob (USSR) 573
O'Bannon (USA) 698
Oberon (UK) 591
Oberst Brecht (Aus) 49
Obion (USA) 758
Objibwa (USA) 759
Obraztsovy (USSR) 529
O'Brien (Chi) 95
O'Brien (USA) 698
Observation Island (USA) 739
Ocala (USA) 738
O'Callahan (USA) 707
Oceanografico (Mex) 347
Oceanographer (USA) 759
Ocelot (Guy) 228
Ocelot (UK) 591
Ochakov (USSR) 522
Ocoa (DR) 136
Octant (Fra) 181
October, 6 (Egy) 142
Octubre, De 9 (Ecu) 139
Odarenny (USSR) 529
Odd (Nor) 371
Oden (Swe) 460
Odenwald (GFR) 209
Odev (Tur) 498
Odiel (Spn) 443
Odin (GFR) 207
Odin (UK) 591
Odinn (Ice) 232
Odisseus (Gre) 224
Oeillet (Fra) 189
Ofanto (Ita) 285
Offenburg (GFR) 209
Ogden (USA) 715
Ogna (Nor) 372
Ognenny (USSR) 534
Ognevoy (USSR) 529
Oguta (Nig) 366
O'Higgins (Chi) 96
Ohio (USA) 653, 654
Oilbird (UK) 621
Oilfield (UK) 621
Oilman (UK) 621
Oilpress (UK) 621
Oilstone (UK) 621
Oilwell (UK) 621
Ojibwa (Can) 79
Ojika (Jap) 298, 306
Ok Cheon (RoK) 326
Oka (USSR) 571
Okanagan (Can) 79
Okba (Mor) 349
Okean (USSR) 558, 564
Okeanos (Gre) 216
Oker (GFR) 212
Oki (Jap) 308
Okinami (Jap) 310
Okinawa (Jap) 307
Okinawa (USA) 714
Okitsu (Jap) 300
Oklahoma City (USA) 693
Okmulgee (USA) 738
Okoume (Fra) 190
Oktyabrskaya Revolutsiya (USSR) 527
Okushiri (Jap) 308
Olaya (Per) 395
Olaya Herrera (Col) 118
Oldendorf (USA) 698
Olekma (USSR) 570
Olfert Fischer (Den) 126
Oliveira E. Carmo (Por) 412
Oliver Hazard Perry (USA) 703
Oliver Twist (UK) 628
Olivier (Fra) 190
Oljevern 02 (Nor) 375
Oljevern 03 (Nor) 375
Oljevern 04 (Nor) 375
Olmeda (UK) 617
Olmo (Ita) 281
Olna (UK) 617
Olwen (UK) 617
Olympus (UK) 591
Omaha (USA) 659
Ombouf (Gab) 192
Ombrine (Alg) 21
Ommen (Nld) 359
Omøsund (Den) 131
Onaran (Tur) 496
Onbevreesd (Nld) 358
Öncu (Tur) 498
Ondine (Fra) 188
Onega (USSR) 574
Onondaga (Can) 79
Onslaught (UK) 591
Onslow (Aust) 38
Ontano (Ita) 281
Onverdroten (Nld) 358
Onvervaard (Nld) 358
Onyx (UK) 591
Ooi (Jap) 297
Oonami (Jap) 296
Ooshio (Jap) 292
Oosterland (SA) 428
Ootsu (Jap) 300
Opelika (USA) 738
Operario Luis Leal (Brz) 68
Opossum (UK) 591
Opportune (UK) 591
Opportune (USA) 728
Oqbah (SAr) 420
Oracle (UK) 591
Orage (Fra) 176
Oranienburg (GDR) 195
Ordóñez (Spn) 440
Orella (Chi) 98
Oriental Mindoro (Plp) 402
Origny (Fra) 181
Oriole (Can) 86
Orion (Aust) 38
Orion (Brz) 66
Orion (Ecu) 140
Orion (USA) 730
Oriskany (USA) 683
Orkney (UK) 614
Orleck (USA) 701, 702
Orlik (Pol) 407
Ørn (Nor) 370
Ornö (Swe) 455
Orompello (Chi) 100
Orpheus (UK) 591
Orsa (Ita) 277
Orsha (USSR) 571
Orsk (USSR) 571
Ortolan (USA) 730
Ortwin (GFR) 210
Oruc Reis (Tur) 487
Orzel (Pol) 405
Osage (USA) 758
Oshkosh (USA) 738
Osiris (UK) 591
Oslo (Nor) 369
Osprey (UK) 622
Oste (GFR) 212
Östergötland (Swe) 453
Ostorozny (USSR) 534
Ostseeland (GDR) 197
Ostwind (GFR) 210
Otago (NZ) 363
Otaka (Jap) 298
Otama (Aust) 38
Otobo (Nig) 366
Otokomi (USA) 738
Otori (Jap) 297
Otowa (Jap) 311
Ottawa (Can) 82
Otter (UK) 591
Otto Meycke (GFR) 212
Otto Schmidt (USSR) 577
Otto Tost (GDR) 194
Otto von Guericke (GDR) 197
Ottumwa (USA) 738
Otus (UK) 591
Otvetstvenny (USSR) 534
Otway (Aust) 38
Ouachita (USA) 758
Oudenaarde (Bel) 55
Oued (Fra) 190
Ouellet (USA) 705
Ouessant (Fra) 162
Ougree (Bel) 55
Ouistreham (Fra) 179
Oumi (Jap) 300
Ouragan (Cam) 76
Ouragan (Fra) 176
Ouranos (Gre) 224
Ourthe (Bel) 55
Ovens (Aust) 38
Overijssel (Nld) 356
Oxley (Aust) 38
Ozelot (GFR) 205
Ozhestochenny (USSR) 534
Ozhivlenniy (USSR) 534

P

P. Drapsin (Yug) 777
Pabna (Ban) 52
Pacocha (Per) 388
Paderborn (GFR) 205
Padma (Ban) 52
Paducah (USA) 738
Paea (NZ) 364
Paek Ku II, 12, 13, 15, 16, 17, 18, 19 (RoK) 324
Pahlawan (Mly) 340
Paita (Per) 393
Paiute (USA) 731, 732
Pakan Baru (Indo) 251
Palacios (Per) 390
Palang (Iran) 255
Palangrin (Fra) 186
Palatka (USA) 738
Palawan (Plp) 400
Palétuvier (Fra) 190
Palinuro (Ita) 284
Palma (Ita) 281
Palmer Ort (GDR) 197
Pamban (Ind) 240
Pamir (USSR) 579
Pamlico (USA) 758
Pampeiro (Brz) 65
Pampero (GFR) 210
Pamyat Merkuryia (USSR) 559
Panah (Mly) 338
Panaji (Ind) 240
Panaria (Ita) 286
Pandora (Gre) 224
Pandorong (Indo) 247
Pandrosos (Gre) 224
Pangan (Tld) 479
Pangasinan (Plp) 399
Panglima (Sin) 425
Panquiaco (Pan) 383
Pansio (Fin) 154
Pantelleria (Ita) 286
Panter (Nld) 357
Pantera (USSR) 538
Panthir (Gre) 219
Panvel (Ind) 240
Papago (USA) 731, 732
Papanikolis (Gre) 217
Papaw (USA) 756
Papayer (Fra) 190
Papenoo (Fra) 183
Papudo (Chi) 99
Paquerette (Fra) 178
Paraguassu (Brz) 68
Paraguay (Par) 385
Paraibano (Brz) 66
Parana (Brz) 62
Parati (Brz) 65
Parche (USA) 662
Parchim (GDR) 193
Pargo (USA) 662
Pari (Mly) 338
Parinas (Per) 394
Parizeau (Can) 93
Parksville (Can) 86
Parnaiba (Brz) 64
Parramatta (Aust) 42
Parsons (USA) 697
Partisan (GDR) 197
Partizan II (Yug) 777
Parvin (Iran) 256
Pasewalk (GDR) 195
Pasopati (Indo) 245
Passat (USSR) 564
Passereau (Fra) 190
Passero (Ita) 286
Passo da Patria (Brz) 68
Passop (Swe) 462
Passumpsic (USA) 746
Pastor Rouaix (Mex) 346
Pat 01, 02, 03, 04, 05, 05, 06 (Indo) 252
Pathfinder (Plp) 404
Patoka (USA) 758
Patos (Alb) 19
Patria (Nld) 361
Patria (Ven) 767
Patrick Henry (USA) 658
Patron (Mex) 348
Patterson (USA) 705
Pattimura (Indo) 246
Patuakhali (Ban) 52
Paul (USA) 705
Paul Eisenschneider (GDR) 194
Paul F. Foster (USA) 698
Paul Revere (USA) 718, 720
Paul Wieczorek (GDR) 194
Paulo Afonso (Brz) 68
Paus (Mly) 338
Pavel Bashmakov (USSR) 560
Pawcatuck (USA) 746
Pawhuska (USA) 738
Pawtucket (USA) 738
Paysandu (Uru) 762
PB 3, 5, 6, 8-12 (RoK) 325
PB 19-27 (Jap) 298
PC 11 (Eth) 149
PC 13 (Eth) 149
PC 14 (Eth) 149
PC 15 (Eth) 149
Pearl Bank (Plp) 403
Pearleaf (UK) 618
Peccari (Guy) 228
Pechenga (USSR) 569
Peder Skram (Den) 126
Pedro de Heredia (Col) 119
Pedro Gual (Col) 118
Pedro Teixeira (Brz) 64
Pegas (USSR) 565
Pegase (Fra) 188
Pegasus (USA) 709
Pehuenche (Arg) 34
Peirce (USA) 759
Pekan (Mly) 340
Peleng (USSR) 556
Pélican (Fra) 187
Pelikan (Pol) 407
Pelikan (Tur) 490
Pelikanen (Swe) 462
Pelileu (USA) 713
Pellinki (Fin) 154
Pelorus (USSR) 556
Pemburu (Bru) 69
Pendant (USA) 759
Penedo (Brz) 65
Penelope (UK) 602
Penobscot Bay (USA) 754
Pensacola (USA) 716
Penyarang (Bru) 69
Peoria (USA) 717
Perch (UK) 628
Perdana (Mly) 338
Perekop (USSR) 567
Peresvet (USSR) 578
Perkun (Pol) 409
Perleberg (GDR) 193
Permit (USA) 663
Pernambuco (Brz) 62
Perseo (Ita) 277
Perseus (GFR) 206
Perseverance (IC) 287
Perseverence (Sin) 425
Persistence (Sin) 425
Pertanda (Mly) 340
Perth (Aust) 40
Pertuisane (Fra) 177
Pervenche (Fra) 180
Pervenets (USSR) 560
Perwira (Bru) 69
Perwira (Mly) 340
Peshawar (Pak) 383
Petalesharo (USA) 738
Petaluma (USA) 748
Peter Tordenskjold (Den) 126
Peterel (UK) 615
Peterson (USA) 698
Petr Ilichev (USSR) 550
Petr Lebedev (USSR) 564
Petr Pakhtusov (USSR) 563
Petrel (Arg) 32
Pétrel (Fra) 188
Petrel (UK) 628
Petrel (USA) 731
Petrodvorets (USSR) 562
Petropavlovsk (USSR) 522
Pétunia (Fra) 178
Peyk (Tur) 489
Peykan (Iran) 256
Phai (Tld) 479
Phali (Tld) 477
Pham Ngoc Chau (Vtn) 771
Pharris (USA) 705
Phénix (Fra) 180
Phetra (Tld) 480
Philadelphia (USA) 659
Philips van Almonde (Nld) 356
Phoebe (UK) 602
Phoenix (USA) 659
Phosamton (Tld) 480
Phu Du (Vtn) 771
Phu Qui (Vtn) 771
Pi Bong (RoK) 326
Pian (RoK) 327
Pianosa (Ita) 286
Piast (Pol) 409
Piaui (Brz) 62
Piave (Ita) 285
Pickering (USA) 752
Picúa (DR) 136
Picuda (Gua) 226

INDEXES / Named Ships 829

Picuda (Ven) 765
Piedmont (USA) 724
Piedra Buena (Arg) 28
Pierre Radisson (Can) 88
Piet Heyn (Nld) 356
Pieter Floresz (Nld) 356
Pietro Cavezzale (Ita) 283
Pietro de Christofaro (Ita) 278
Pigassos (Gre) 220
Pigeon (USA) 730
Pijao (Col) 115
Pike (UK) 628
Pikkala (Fin) 154
Pil (Nor) 371
Piloto Pardo (Chi) 101
Pimentel (Per) 394
Pin (Fra) 190
Pin Klao (Tld) 476
Ping Jin (RoC) 468
Pingouie (Kam) 315
Pingouin (Fra) 190
Pingvinen (Swe) 462
Pinna (Ita) 282
Pino (Ita) 281
Pinson (Fra) 190
Pintado (USA) 662
Pintail (UK) 620
Piombino (Ita) 286
Pionier (GDR) 197
Pioppo (Ita) 282
Piqua (USA) 738
Piraja (Brz) 65
Piratini (Brz) 65
Pirol (GFR) 210
Pirttisaari (Fin) 154
Pishin (Pak) 382
Pitamakan (USA) 738
Piteå (Swe) 454
Pivert (Fra) 190
Pivoine (Fra) 180
PK 10, 11 (RoK) 325
Plainsville (Can) 86
Plamenny (USSR) 533
Planet (GFR) 212
Planetree (USA) 756
Platana (Fra) 190
Platano (Ita) 281
Pledge (USA) 721, 722
Pleias (Gre) 222
Ploiarhos Arslanoglou (Gre) 221
Ploiarhos
Chadzikonstandis (Gre) 221
Plon (GFR) 211
Plotarhis Blessas (Gre) 219
Plotze (GFR) 205
Pluck (USA) 721, 722
Plug (USSR) 578
Plumleaf (UK) 618
Plunger (USA) 663
Pluto (GFR) 206
Plymouth (UK) 604
Plymouth Rock (USA) 716
Po Yang (RoC) 467
Pobeda (Bul) 70
Pocasset (USA) 738
Pochard (UK) 620
Podchorazy (Pol) 409
Podgora (Yug) 778
Podor (Sen) 422
Pogy (USA) 662
Point Arena (USA) 755
Point Baker (USA) 755
Point Barnes (USA) 755
Point Barrow (USA) 755
Point Batan (USA) 755
Point Bennet (USA) 755
Point Bonita (USA) 755
Point Bridge (USA) 755
Point Brower (USA) 755
Point Brown (USA) 755
Point Camden (USA) 755
Point Carrew (USA) 755
Point Charles (USA) 755
Point Chico (USA) 755
Point Countess (USA) 755
Point Defiance (USA) 716
Point Divide (USA) 755
Point Doran (USA) 755
Point Estero (USA) 755
Point Evans (USA) 755
Point Francis (USA) 755
Point Franklin (USA) 755
Point Glass (USA) 755
Point Hannon (USA) 755
Point Harris (USA) 755
Point Herron (USA) 755
Point Heyer (USA) 755
Point Highland (USA) 755
Point Hobart (USA) 755
Point Hope (USA) 755
Point Huron (USA) 755
Point Jackson (USA) 755
Point Judith (USA) 755
Point Knoll (USA) 755
Point Ledge (USA) 755
Point Lobos (USA) 755
Point Loma (USA) 725
Point Lookout (USA) 755
Point Martin (USA) 755
Point Monroe (USA) 755
Point Nowell (USA) 755
Point Richmond (USA) 755
Point Roberts (USA) 755
Point Sal (USA) 755
Point Spencer (USA) 755
Point Steele (USA) 755
Point Stuart (USA) 755
Point Swift (USA) 755
Point Thatcher (USA) 755
Point Turner (USA) 755
Point Verde (USA) 755
Point Warde (USA) 755
Point Wells (USA) 755
Point Whitehorn (USA) 755
Point Winslow (USA) 755
Pointer (UK) 624
Pokagon (USA) 738
Polar Sea (USA) 753
Polar Star (USA) 753
Polemistis (Gre) 224
Polimar 1-4 (Mex) 346
Polipo (Ita) 282
Pollack (USA) 663
Pollington (UK) 610
Pollux (GFR) 206
Pollux (Spn) 444
Polyarnik (USSR) 559, 570
Polyus (USSR) 563
Ponce (USA) 715
Ponchatoula (USA) 726
Ponciano Arriaga (Mex) 345
Pondicherry (Ind) 241
Ponoi (USSR) 574
Pontiac (USA) 738
Pontos (Gre) 216
Poolster (Nld) 360
Popenguine (Sen) 422
Porbandar (Ind) 241
Porkkala (Fin) 154
Porobago (USA) 738
Porpoise (Aust) 48
Porpoise (UK) 591
Porpora (Ita) 282
Port Elizabeth (SA) 429
Port Said (Egy) 143
Porte Dauphine (Can) 85
Porte de la Reine (Can) 85
Porte Quebec (Can) 85
Porte St. Jean (Can) 85
Porte St. Louis (Can) 85
Portisham (UK) 627
Portland (USA) 716
Porto D'Ischia (Ita) 286
Porto Pisano (Ita) 286
Porto Recanati (Ita) 286
Poseidon (Fra) 189
Poseidon (GFR) 213
Poseidon (Pol) 409
Poseidón (Spn) 446
Possidon (Gre) 216
Potengi (Brz) 67
Poti (Brz) 65
Potok (USSR) 574
Potomac (USA) 746
Potsdam (GDR) 197
Potvis (Nld) 354
Poughkeepsie (USA) 738
Powhatan (USA) 731
Pozzi (Ita) 286
Prab (Tld) 479
Prabal (Ind) 240
Prabparapak (Tld) 476
Prachand (Ind) 240
Pradeepa (Sri) 448
Pradhayak (Ind) 243
Pragmar (Mex) 348
Prairie (USA) 724
Pralaya (Ind) 240
Prasae (Tld) 476
Prat (Chi) 96
Pratap (Ind) 240
Prathong (Tld) 479
Preble (USA) 696
Premier Maitre l'Her (Fra) 175
Prerow (GDR) 195
Preserver (Can) 83
Preserver (USA) 728
President Albert Bernard
Bongo (Gab) 191
President Bourguiba (Tun) 484
President El Hadj
Omar Bongo (Gab) 191
President Kruger (SA) 428
President Leon M'ba (Gab) 191
President Pretorius (SA) 428
President Steyn (SA) 428
Presidente Busch (Bol) 57
Presidente Eloy Alfaro (Ecu) 138
Presidente Kennedy (Bol) 57
Presidente Rivera (Uru) 763
Presidente Sarmiento (Arg) 34
Presidente Stroessner (Par) 386
Prespa (Gre) 224
Prestol Botello (DR) 134
Pretoria (SA) 429
Preveze (Tur) 487
Priboi (USSR) 564
Priliv (USSR) 564
Primo Longobardo (Ita) 272
Primorsky Komsomolets
(USSR) 545
Primorye (USSR) 556
Primrose (USA) 757
Princesa (Spn) 439
Pritzwalk (GDR) 195
Private John R. Towle (USA) 745
Private Leonard C. Brostrom
(USA) 744
Prizma (USSR) 561
Procion (DR) 135
Proet (Tld) 480
Professor Anichkov (USSR) 567
Professor Bogorov (USSR) 560
Professor Khlyustin (USSR) 567
Professor Krümmel (GDR) 196
Professor Kudrevich (USSR) 567
Professor Kurentsov (USSR) 560
Professor Minyayev (USSR) 567
Professor Pavlenko (USSR) 567
Professor Rybaltovsky (USSR) 567
Professor Schyogolev (USSR) 567
Professor Ukhov (USSR) 567
Professor Vodnanitsky (USSR) 560
Professor Vize (USSR) 564
Professor Yushenko (USSR) 567
Professor Zubov (USSR) 564
Proleter (Yug) 777
Prometeo (Ita) 285
Protea (SA) 429
Protecteur (Can) 83
Proteo (Ita) 285
Protet (Fra) 173
Proteus (Gre) 216
Proteus (USA) 730
Protraktor (USSR) 557
Provider (Can) 83
Provo Wallis (Can) 91
Provorny (USSR) 529
Prozorlivy (USSR) 530
Prut (USSR) 570
Psyché (Fra) 163
PT 11-15 (Jap) 298
Puerto Deseado (Arg) 32
Puerto Santo (Ven) 769
Puffer (USA) 662
Puget Sound (USA) 723
Pukaki (NZ) 363
Pukkio (Fin) 154
Pulang Geni (Indo) 247
Pulau Raja (Indo) 249
Pulau Rani (Indo) 249
Pulau Rapat (Indo) 249
Pulau Ratewo (Indo) 249
Pulau Rengat (Indo) 249
Pulau Roon (Indo) 249
Pulau Rorbas (Indo) 249
Pulicat (Ind) 240
Puma (GFR) 205
Punaruu (Fra) 183
Pung To (RoK) 327
Puni (Bru) 70
Punta Alta (Arg) 33
Punta Cabana (Ven) 768
Punta Delgada (Arg) 33
Punta Medanos (Arg) 33
Puran (Ind) 243
Purha (Fin) 154
Puri (Ind) 240
Purus (Brz) 64
Pusan (RoK) 322
Pushmatha (USA) 738
Putri Sabah (Sab) 419
Putsaari (Fin) 154
Putumayo (Ecu) 140
Pyhtää (Fin) 154
Pylky (USSR) 535
Pyok Pa (RoK) 324
Pyro (USA) 724
Pyrpolitis (Gre) 224

Q

Qena (Egy) 145
Qeshm (Iran) 257
Quadra (Can) 87
Quapaw (USA) 731, 732
Qu'Appelle (Can) 81
Quartier Maitre Alfred Motto
(Cam) 76
Quartier Maitre Anquetil (Fra) 175
Quarto (Ita) 283
Queenfish (USA) 662
Queensville (Can) 86
Querandi (Arg) 34
Quercia (Ita) 281
Quest (Can) 84
Quetta (Pak) 382
Quezon (Plp) 398
Qui Nhon (Vtn) 772
Quidora (Chi) 99
Quilmes (Arg) 34
Quindio (Col) 118
Quita Sueno (Col) 115
Quito (Ecu) 139

R

R-1, 3, 5, 6 (Mex) 348
R. G. Masters (UK) 628
Racer (Can) 92
Racine (USA) 717
Rad (Tld) 481
Raddle (UK) 628
Rade Koncar (Yug) 777
Radoom (UAE) 581
Raduga (USSR) 540
Rafiki (Tan) 474
Raftsund (Nor) 372
Raffello (Iran) 259
Rahav (Isr) 264
Rahmat (Mly) 337
Raimundo Nonato (Brz) 68
Rainier (USA) 759
Raisio (Fin) 152
Rajah Jarom (Mly) 339
Rajah Lakandula (Plp) 397
Rajshahi (Pak) 382
Rakata (Indo) 252
Raleigh (USA) 715
Rally (Can) 92
Ramadan (Iraq) 261
Ramakami (Sri) 448
Rambler (USA) 757
Rame Head (UK) 611
Ramsey (USA) 704
Ramzow (GDR) 197
Ran (Den) 128
Ran (Swe) 460, 462
Rance (Fra) 183
Rang Kwien (Tld) 479
Rangamati (Ban) 52
Range Sentinel (USA) 740
Ranger (USA) 680
Ranjit (Ind) 236
Rapid (Can) 92
Raposo Tavares (Brz) 64
Rapp (Nor) 371
Raritan (USA) 759
Ras Adar (Tun) 485
Ras El-Helal (Lby) 335
Rashid (Egy) 143
Rask (Nor) 371
Ratcharit (Tld) 476
Rathburne (USA) 705
Rathenow (GDR) 195
Rattler (Guy) 228
Ratulangi (Indo) 250
Raven (Ire) 263
Ravn (Nor) 371
Rawi (Tld) 480
Ray (USA) 662
Razumny (USSR) 535
Razyashchy (USSR) 535
Razytelny (USSR) 535
Ready (Can) 92
Reasoner (USA) 705
Rebun (Jap) 300, 308
Recalde (Spn) 439
Reclaim (UK) 614
Reclaimer (USA) 728
Recovery (USA) 728
Red Beech (USA) 757
Red Birch (USA) 757
Red Cedar (USA) 757
Red Cloud (USA) 738
Red Oak (USA) 757
Red Wood (USA) 757
Redstone (USA) 740
Reduktor (USSR) 557
Redwing (USA) 738
Reeves (USA) 690
Regent (UK) 619
Regga (Kwt) 330
Regulus (GFR) 206
Reimei (Jap) 314
Reinøysund (Nor) 372
Reiun (Jap) 314
Relay (Can) 92
Reliance (USA) 752
Remada (Tun) 485
Renchong (Mly) 338
Renke (GFR) 205
Renown (UK) 588
Rentaka (Mly) 338
Repiter (USSR) 557
Repton (UK) 610
Repulse (UK) 588
Repulsor (Par) 386
Requin (Alg) 21
Requin (Fra) 163
Researcher (USA) 759
Réséda (Fra) 180
Reshef (Isr) 265
Reshitelny (USSR) 529
Resolute (USA) 752
Resolution (Sin) 425
Resolution (UK) 588
Resource (UK) 619
Restauracion (DR) 135
Restigouche (Can) 82
Resurgent (UK) 619
Retalhuleu (Gua) 226
Retivy (USSR) 535
Rettin (GFR) 213
Reunification (Cam) 76
Revenge (UK) 588
Reyes (Chi) 102
Rezky (USSR) 535
Rezvy (USSR) 535
Rhein (GFR) 207
Rhenen (Nld) 359
Rhin (Fra) 183
Rhinocéros (Fra) 190
Rhon (GFR) 208
Rhône (Fra) 183
Rhyl (UK) 604
Riachuelo (Brz) 60
Riazi (Iran) 258
Ribadu (Nig) 367
Ribeira Grande (Por) 413
Ribnitz-Damgarten (GDR) 193
Riccio (Ita) 282
Richard B. Russell (USA) 662
Richard E. Byrd (USA) 695
Richard L. Page (USA) 704
Richard S. Edwards (USA) 700
Richard Sorge (GDR) 194
Richardson (Can) 93
Richland (USA) 734
Richmond K. Turner (USA) 690
Rider (Can) 92
Riesa (GDR) 195
Rig Tugger (Nor) 374
Rigel (DR) 136
Rigel (Ecu) 140
Rigel (GFR) 206
Rigel (Spn) 444
Rigel (USA) 739
Rihtniemi (Fin) 152
Rijger (SA) 428
Rimfaxe (Den) 131
Rincon (USA) 748
Ring (Swe) 459
Rio Apure (Ven) 769
Rio Arauca (Ven) 769
Rio Branco (Brz) 66
Rio Cabriales (Ven) 769
Rio Canete (Per) 395
Rio Caparo (Ven) 767
Rio Caroni (Ven) 769
Rio Chicama (Per) 396
Rio Chira (Per) 396
Rio Chui (Brz) 68
Rio Cruta (Nic) 364
Rio Das Contas (Brz) 68
Rio Doce (Brz) 68
Rio Escalante (Ven) 767
Rio Formoso (Brz) 68
Rio Grande Do Norte (Brz) 62
Rio Guarico (Ven) 769
Rio Huaura (Per) 396
Rio Ica (Per) 396
Rio Illave (Per) 392
Rio Kuringwas (Nic) 364
Rio Limon (Ven) 767
Rio Locumba (Per) 396
Rio Meta (Ven) 769
Rio Minho (Por) 413
Rio Negro (Arg) 31
Rio Negro (Brz) 68
Rio Negro (Uru) 761
Rio Negro (Ven) 769
Rio Neveri (Ven) 769
Rio Oiapoque (Brz) 68
Rio Orinoco (Ven) 767
Rio Panuco (Mex) 347
Rio Pardo (Brz) 68
Rio Pativilca (Per) 396
Rio Piura (Per) 392
Rio Portuguesa (Ven) 769
Rio Ramis (Per) 392
Rio Real (Brz) 68
Rio Sama (Per) 396
Rio San Juan (Ven) 767
Rio Santo Domingo (Ven) 769
Rio Torres (Ven) 767
Rio Tucuyo (Ven) 767
Rio Tumbes (Per) 392
Rio Turbio (Ven) 767
Rio Turvo (Brz) 68
Rio Tux (Ven) 769
Rio Uribante (Ven) 769
Rio Venamo (Ven) 767
Rio Ventuari (Ven) 767
Rio Verde (Brz) 68
Rio Vitor (Per) 396
Rio Zarumilla (Per) 392
Riohache (Col) 117
Rishiri (Jap) 300, 308
Ristna (USSR) 567
Ritsa (USSR) 574
Riva Trigoso (Ita) 286
Riverton (Can) 86
Rizal (Plp) 398
Rizzuto (Ita) 286
Roach (UK) 628
Roanoke (USA) 727
Roark (USA) 705
Robel (GDR) 195
Robert A. Owens (USA) 702
Robert D. Conrad (USA) 741
Robert E. Lee (USA) 658

830 INDEXES / Named Ships

Robert E. Peary (USA) 705
Robert Foulis (Can) 92
Robert H. McCard (USA) 701, 702
Robert Koch (GDR) 197
Robison (USA) 695
Robust (UK) 623
Robuste (Fra) 190
Robusto (Ita) 286
Rochefort (Bel) 54
Rochen (GFR) 205
Rödlöga (Swe) 458
Rodos (Gre) 221
Rodriguez (Col) 118
Rodriguez Zamora (Col) 119
Rodriquez (Per) 394
Rodsteen (Den) 127
Roermond (Nld) 359
Roger De Lauria (Spn) 435
Rogers (USA) 701, 702
Rokk (Nor) 371
Rokko (Jap) 308
Roku-Go (Jap) 303
Rolf Peters (GDR) 195
Rollicker (UK) 623
Romah (Isr) 265
Romaleus (Gre) 224
Romanija (Yug) 778
Romblon (Plp) 400
Romeo Romei (Ita) 271
Rommel (GFR) 201
Romø (Den) 129
Romsø (Den) 129
Roncador (Col) 115
Rondonia (Brz) 65
Roraima (Brz) 65
Rosales (Arg) 28
Rosario (Por) 413
Rosenheim (GFR) 213
Rosen Ort (GDR) 197
Rosslau (GDR) 195
Rossosh (USSR) 571
Rostam (Iran) 255
Rostock (GDR) 193, 197
Rota (Den) 128
Rotersand (GFR) 213
Rothesay (UK) 604
Rotoiti (NZ) 363
Rotsund (Nor) 372
Rotterdam (Nld) 356
Rotvaer (Nor) 373
Rouget (Fra) 190
Rovuma (Por) 413
Roysterer (UK) 623
Röyttä (Fin) 152
Rozmak (Pol) 407
Rubin (USSR) 539
Rude (USA) 759
Ruden (GDR) 196
Rudolf Breitscheid (GDR) 194
Rudolf Diesel (GFR) 212
Rudolf Egelhofer (GDR) 194
Ruediger (GFR) 210
Ruissalo (Fin) 152
Rulevoy (USSR) 545
Rumb (USSR) 559
Ruotsinsalmi (Fin) 152
Rupel (Bel) 55
Rush (USA) 750
Ruslan (USSR) 578
Rustom (Pak) 383
Ruve (Fiji) 149
Ruwan Yaro (Nig) 367
Ruza (USSR) 557
Ryadh (SAr) 421
Rybachi (USSR) 558
Rymättylä (Fin) 152
Rys (Pol) 407
Ryul Po (RoK) 324

S

6 October (Egy) 142
S. Chelyuskin (USSR) 558
S. Filipovic (Yug) 777
S. Krakov (USSR) 560
S41-S60 (GFR) 204
S61-S70 (GFR) 204
Sa Chon (RoK) 324
Saam (Iran) 255
Saar (GFR) 207
Saar (Isr) 265
Saarburg (GFR) 209
Sabalo (Ven) 765
Saban (Bur) 75
Sabback El Bahr (Tun) 485
Sabogal (Col) 119
Sabola (Indo) 248
Sabratha (Lby) 334
Sabre (UK) 615
Sachsenwald (GFR) 209
Sachtouris (Gre) 218
Sackville (Can) 84
Saco (USA) 738
Sacramento (USA) 727
Sacre (Spn) 447
Sadaf (Iran) 259
Sadarin (Indo) 248
Sadko (USSR) 578
Sado (Jap) 306
Saetta (Ita) 279
Safaga (Egy) 146
Safeguard (USA) 728
Safra (Bhr) 50
Safwa (SAr) 420
Sagami (Jap) 302, 306
Sagawamick (USA) 738
Sagebrush (USA) 756
Saginaw (USA) 717, 758
Sagiri (Jap) 310
Sagittaire (Fra) 178
Sagittario (Ita) 277
Sagres (Por) 415
Sagu (Bur) 75
Saguenay (Can) 82
Saham (Bhr) 50
Sahel (Fra) 183
Sahene (Gha) 214
Sahin (Tur) 490
Sahiwal (Pak) 382
Saikai (Jap) 314
St. Anthony (Can) 86
St. Charles (Can) 86
St. Croix (Can) 81
St. David (UK) 611
St. Likoudis (Gre) 224
St. Louis (Sen) 422
St. Louis (USA) 718
St. Margarets (UK) 622
St. Paul (Lbr) 331
St. Sylvestre (Cam) 76
Saintonge (Fra) 184
Saipan (USA) 713
Sakate (Jap) 300
Sakhalin (USSR) 565, 579
Sakhalinsky Komsomolets (USSR) 545
Sakiet Sidi Youssef (Tun) 484
Sakito (Jap) 301
Salaam (Tan) 474
Salamaua (PNG) 385
Salami (Leb) 330
Saldiray (Tur) 487
Saleha (Bru) 69
Salem (USA) 693
Salisbury (UK) 605
Salm (GFR) 205
Salmaneti (Indo) 248
Salmone (Ita) 281
Salta (Arg) 26
Salto (Uru) 762
Saluki (UK) 624
Salvatore Todaro (Ita) 278
Salvia (USA) 756
Salvora (Spn) 440
Salvore (Ita) 286
Sam Chok (RoK) 326
Sam Houston (USA) 657
Sam Rayburn (USA) 655
Samadar (Indo) 248
Samadikun (Indo) 246
Samae San (Tld) 481
Samana (DR) 136
Samandira (Tur) 498
Samarai (PNG) 384
Sambre (Bel) 55
Samed (Tld) 480
Samos (Gre) 221
Sample (USA) 707
Sampo (Fin) 153
Sampson (USA) 695
Samsø (Den) 129
Samson (Gre) 224
Samsun (Tur) 492
Samudra Devi (Sri) 448
Samuel E. Morison (USA) 703
Samuel Gompers (USA) 723
Samuel Morley VC (UK) 628
Samum (GFR) 210
San Andres (Col) 118
San Benedetto (Ita) 286
San Bernardino (USA) 717
San Diego (USA) 724
San Francisco (USA) 659
San Francisco dos Santos (Brz) 68
San Giusto (Ita) 286
San-Go (Jap) 303
San Jose (USA) 724
San Luis (Arg) 26
San Onofre (USA) 734
San Salvador (Bhm) 50
Sanaga (Cam) 76
Sanaviron (Arg) 34
Sancaktar (Tur) 493
Sanctuary (USA) 726
Sandalo (Ita) 281
Sand Lance (USA) 662
Sandhayak (Ind) 241
Sandpiper (UK) 615
Sandringham (UK) 627
Sangamon (USA) 758
Sangay (Ecu) 140
Sangsetia (Mly) 340
Sangual (Spn) 447
Sans Souci (Hai) 228
Sanson Gri (Spn) 447
Santa Barbara (USA) 724
Santa Catarina (Brz) 62
Santal (Fra) 190
Santander (Col) 116
Santaquin (USA) 738
Santa Fe (Arg) 26
Santiago del Estero (Arg) 26
Santisima Trinidad (Arg) 27
Santos Degollado (Mex) 345
Sao Gabriel (Por) 414
Sao Roque (Por) 413
Sao Tang (RoC) 469
Sapanca (Tur) 492
Sapele (Nig) 367
Saphir (GFR) 210
Sapri (Ita) 281
Sarasin (Tld) 477
Saratoga (USA) 680
Sarcelle (Fra) 190
Sardius (Aust) 47
Sargo (USA) 666
Sariyer (Tur) 492
Sarköy (Tur) 497
Sarobetsu (Jap) 307
Saros (Tur) 492
Sarpamina (Indo) 247
Sarpawasesa (Indo) 247
Sarpen (Nor) 373
Sasiga (USSR) 571
Sasila (Indo) 248
Saskatchewan (Can) 81
Sassaba (USA) 738
Sassacus (USA) 738
Sassafras (USA) 756
Satakut (Tld) 479
Satsuma (Jap) 298, 305
Sattahip (Tld) 477
Satzhaff (GDR) 197
Sauda (Nor) 372
Saugatuck (USA) 747
Saugus (USA) 738
Sauk (USA) 759
Saule (Fra) 190
Sava (Yug) 775
Savannah (USA) 727
Save (Por) 413
Sawangi (Indo) 248
SB 1, 2, 3, 5 (RoK) 325
Scamp (USA) 664
Scampo (Ita) 282
Scarab (UK) 620, 625
Scarabée (Fra) 187
Sceptre (UK) 589
Scharhörn (GFR) 211
Schelde (Bel) 55
Schenectady (USA) 717
Scheveningen (Nld) 358
Schiedam (Nld) 358
Schirocco (GFR) 210
Schlei (GFR) 205
Schleswig (GFR) 205
Schleswig-Holstein (GFR) 202
Schofield (USA) 704
Schönebeck (GDR) 195
Schuiling (Nld) 359
Schultz Xavier (Por) 415
Schütze (GFR) 206
Schuyler Otis Bland (USA) 744
Schuylkill (USA) 747
Scimitar (UK) 615
Scioto (USA) 758
Scirocco (Ita) 276
Scorpios (Gre) 220
Sculpin (USA) 664
Scylla (UK) 602
Sderzhanny (USSR) 529
Sea Cliff (USA) 672
Sea Devil (USA) 662
Sea Dog (Gam) 192
Sea Dragon (Sin) 424
Sea Giant (UK) 624
Sea Hawk (Sin) 424
Sea Lion (Sin) 424
Sea Otter (UK) 629
Sea Scorpion (Sin) 424
Sea Spray (TT) 483
Sea Tiger (Sin) 424
Sea Wolf (Sin) 424
Seadragon (USA) 666
Seaforth Clansman (UK) 614
Seagull (UK) 629
Seahorse (USA) 662
Seal (Aust) 48
Seal (UK) 629
Sealift Antarctic (USA) 747
Sealift Arabian Sea (USA) 747
Sealift Arctic (USA) 747
Sealift Atlantic (USA) 747
Sealift Caribbean (USA) 747
Sealift China Sea (USA) 747
Sealift Indian Ocean (USA) 747
Sealift Mediterranean (USA) 747
Sealift Pacific (USA) 747
Sealion (UK) 591
Sealyham (UK) 624
Seattle (USA) 727
Seawolf (USA) 666
Sebastian L. de Tejada (Mex) 345
Sebha (Lby) 334
Sebo (Gha) 214
Second Maitre le Bihan (Fra) 175
Secota (USA) 738
Seddulbahir (Tur) 492
Sedge (USA) 756
Seeteufel (GFR) 210
Segui (Arg) 28
Sehested (Den) 127
Sehwan (Pak) 382
Seid Bereil (GDR) 197
Seima (USSR) 571
Seinda (Bur) 75
Seiun (Jap) 314
Sekiun (Jap) 314
Sel (Nor) 371
Selcuk (Tur) 492
Selendon (Per) 395
Selenga (USSR) 571
Seliger (USSR) 556
Sellers (USA) 695
Semani (Alb) 19
Sembilang (Indo) 247
Semmes (USA) 695
Semois (Bel) 55
Semyen Chelyuskin (USSR) 578
Semyen Dezhnev (USSR) 558, 578
Senasqua (USA) 738
Senckenburg (GFR) 213
Sendai (Jap) 307
Seneca (USA) 731, 752
Senja (Nor) 374
Seoul (RoK) 322
Separacion (DR) 134
Seraing (Bel) 55
Serampang (Mly) 338
Serang (Mly) 338
Serdar (Tur) 493
Sergei Vavilov (USSR) 564
Sergej Lazo (USSR) 550
Serdity (USSR) 534
Sergento Aldea (Chi) 99
Sergipe (Brz) 62
Seri (Mex) 345
Serrano (Chi) 98
Seruwa (Sri) 448, 449
SES-100A (USA) 733
SES-100B (USA) 733
Setanta (Ire) 263
Seteria (Bru) 69
Setkaya (Bur) 75
Setogiri (Jap) 310
Setter (UK) 624
Setyahat (Bur) 75
Sevan (USSR) 562
Sevastopol (USSR) 525
Sever (USSR) 558
Seyhan (Tur) 492
Seymen (Tur) 492
Sfendoni (Gre) 218
Sgombro (Ita) 281
Sgt. Andrew Miller (USA) 745
Sgt. Truman Kimbro (USA) 745
Shaab (Sud) 450
Shabonee (USA) 738
Shacha (USSR) 571
Shackle (USA) 759
Shah Jahan (Pak) 381
Shahbandar (Mly) 340
Shaheed Ruhul Amin (Ban) 52
Shahrokh (Iran) 257
Shahsavar (Iran) 259
Shakal (USSR) 538
Shakori (USA) 731
Shakti (Ind) 242
Shamshir (Iran) 256
Shangri-La (USA) 683
Sharab (Ind) 240
Sharada (Ind) 240
Shardul (Ind) 240
Shark (USA) 664
Shasta (USA) 624
Shavington (UK) 610
Shearwater (UK) 628
Sheepdog (UK) 624
Sheffield (UK) 600
Sheksna (USSR) 570
Shelduck (UK) 628
Shelon (USSR) 571
Shen Yang (RoC) 466
Shenandoah (USA) 723
Sheraton (UK) 610
Sherman (USA) 750
Shetland (UK) 614
Shih Jian (CPR) 112
Shikinami (Jap) 296, 310
Shikine (Jap) 301, 308
Shilka (USSR) 573
Shimanami (Jap) 309
Shimayuki (Jap) 310
Shin Song (RoK) 324
Shinano (Jap) 306
Shinonome (Jap) 309
Shipham (UK) 627
Shiqmona (Isr) 267
Shiraito (Jap) 311
Shirakami (Jap) 306
Shiramine (Jap) 309
Shirane (Jap) 293
Shirasagi (Jap) 314
Shiratori (Jap) 297
Shiretoko (Jap) 305
Shisaka (Jap) 301, 304
Shobo (Jap) 302
Shoryu (Jap) 311
Shoshone (USA) 747
Shou Shan (RoC) 468
Shoulton (UK) 610
Shoun (Jap) 314
Shoyo (Jap) 311
Shreveport (USA) 715
Shu Kuang (CPR) 113
Shulab (Iraq) 261
Shushuk (Pak) 379
Shwepazun (Bur) 75
Shwethida (Bur) 75
Shyri (Ecu) 138
Si Hung (RoK) 326
Sibarau (Indo) 248
Sibir (USSR) 565, 576
Sichang (Tld) 481
Sides (USA) 703
Sidney (Can) 84
Sidon (Leb) 331
Siegfried (GFR) 210
Siegmund (GFR) 210
Siegura (GFR) 210
Sierra (USA) 724
Siete de Agosto (Col) 116
Sifnos (Gre) 222
Sigacik (Tur) 492
Signalchik (USSR) 545
Sigrun (Swe) 462
Sil (Spn) 443
Silas Bent (USA) 743
Silifke (Tur) 492
Silinan (Indo) 248
Silmä (Fin) 155
Silny (USSR) 535
Silva (Spn) 447
Silversides (USA) 662
Sima (USSR) 559
Simba (Ken) 316
Simcoe (Can) 91
Simeto (Ita) 285
Simon Bolivar (Bol) 57
Simon Bolivar (USA) 655
Simon Fraser (Can) 91
Simon Lake (USA) 729
Simorgh (Iran) 257
Simpson (Chi) 95
Simsek (Tur) 490
Sin Mi (RoK) 327
Sinai (Egy) 145
Sind (Pak) 381
Sine-Saloum (Sen) 422
Sinhu Durg (Ind) 239
Sinmin (Bur) 75
Sinop (Tur) 492
Siquijor (Plp) 400
Sir Bedivere (UK) 607
Sir Cecil Romer (Ire) 263
Sir Galahad (UK) 607
Sir Geraint (UK) 607
Sir Humphrey Gilbert (Can) 90
Sir James Douglas (Can) 92
Sir Lancelot (UK) 607
Sir Percivale (UK) 607
Sir Tristram (UK) 607
Sir William Alexander (Can) 90
Sira (Nor) 372
Sirena (USSR) 558
Sirène (Fra) 163
Sirio (DR) 136
Sirios (Gre) 224
Sirius (Brz) 66
Sirius (GFR) 206
Sirius (Swe) 454
Sirius (UK) 602
Sirte (Lby) 334
Sisu (Fin) 153
Sittard (Nld) 359
Sivrihisar (Tur) 491
Sjaelland (Den) 130
Sjöbjörnen (Swe) 452
Sjødrag (Nor) 375
Sjødrev (Nor) 375
Sjøfalk (Nor) 375
Sjöhästen (Swe) 452
Sjöhunden (Swe) 452
Sjölejonet (Swe) 452
Sjømaleren (Nor) 375
Sjöormen (Swe) 452
Sjørokk (Nor) 375
Sjøskuett (Nor) 375
Sjøtroll (Nor) 375
Sjøvern (Nor) 375
Ska 3, 4, 5, 6, 7, 8 (Den) 133
Skaftö (Swe) 458
Skagul (Swe) 459
Skanör (Swe) 456
Skate (USA) 666
Skeena (Can) 82
Skenandoa (USA) 738
Skenderbeu (Alb) 20
Skiathos (Gre) 222
Skidegate (Can) 92
Skilak (Kam) 315
Skinfaxe (Den) 131
Skipjack (USA) 664

INDEXES / Named Ships 831

Skjold (Nor) 371
Sklinna (Nor) 369
Skolpen (Nor) 369
Skomer (UK) 627
Skorpion (GFR) 206
Skory (USSR) 529
Skrei (Nor) 371
Skromny (USSR) 532
Skrytny (USSR) 532
Skua (Can) 93
Skua (UK) 628
Skudd (Nor) 371
Skuld (Swe) 462
Slava (Bul) 70
Slavny (USSR) 529
Sledge (USA) 758
Sleipner (Den) 131
Sleipner (Nor) 370
Sleipner (Swe) 459
Slimak (Pol) 409
Sloughi (Mtn) 343
Småland (Swe) 453
Smaragd (GFR) 210
Smeli (Bul) 70
Smely (USSR) 529
Smetlivy (USSR) 529
Smike (UK) 628
Smilax (USA) 757
Smok (Pol) 409
Smolny (USSR) 567
Smotryashchy (USSR) 534
Smyge (Swe) 456
Smyshleny (USSR) 529
Snapphanen (Swe) 454
Snar (Nor) 371
Snipe (Aust) 43
Snögg (Nor) 371
Snohomish (USA) 759
Snook (USA) 664
Soares Dutra (Brz) 67
Sobat (Sud) 450
Sobenes (Chi) 102
Soberton (UK) 610
Søbjornen (Den) 128
Socorro (Col) 119
Socotra (YPDR) 774
Södermanland (Swe) 453
Soemba (Nld) 361
Sogut (Tur) 497
Sohag (Egy) 145
Søhesten (Den) 128
Søhunden (Den) 128
Sokol (Pol) 405
Sokrushitelny (USSR) 534
Solea (GFR) 213
Solidny (USSR) 534
Solimoes (Brz) 64
Søløven (Den) 128
Somers (USA) 697
Somerset (SA) 430
Sömmera (GDR) 195
Song Tu (Vtn) 771
Sonduren (Tur) 498
Songhee (Can) 86
Soobrazitelny (USSR) 529
Sooraya (Sri) 448
Sorachi (Jap) 307
Sørfold (Nor) 374
Søridderen (Den) 128
Sorong (Indo) 251
Sørøysund (Nor) 372
Sorrell (USA) 756
Sorsogon (Plp) 402
Sosva (USSR) 571
Souellaba (Cam) 76
Soufa (Isr) 265
Søulven (Den) 128
Sour (Leb) 331
Sousse (Tun) 484
South Carolina (USA) 687
Southampton (UK) 600
Southerland (USA) 701, 702
Souya (Jap) 299
Sovereign (UK) 589
Sovereignty (Sin) 424
Sovershenny (USSR) 534
Sovietsky Dagestan (USSR) 538
Sovietsy Azerbaijan (USSR) 538
Sovietsy Turkmenestan (USSR) 538
Soya (Jap) 305
Soyanna (USSR) 571
Soznatelny (USSR) 532
Spa (Bel) 56
Spadefish (USA) 662
Spaekhuggeren (Den) 125
Spaniel (UK) 624
Spapool (UK) 623
Spar (USA) 756
Sparö (Swe) 458
Spartan (UK) 589
Spartanburg County (USA) 717
Sparviero (Ita) 279
Spasilac (Yug) 780
Spassk (USSR) 565
Speedy (UK) 612
Spejaren (Swe) 454
Spencer (USA) 751
Sperone (Ita) 286
Sperry (USA) 730
Speshny (USSR) 533
Spessart (GFR) 208
Sphinx (USA) 728
Spica (GFR) 206
Spica (Swe) 454
Spiegel Grove (USA) 716
Spiekeroog (GFR) 211
Spike (USA) 758
Spin (Bel) 56
Spindrift (Can) 92
Spiro (Arg) 30
Spitfire (UK) 629
Splendid (UK) 589
Split (Yug) 776
Spokojny (USSR) 533
Sposobny (USSR) 529
Spoven (Swe) 462
Spray (Can) 92
Springaren (Swe) 453
Springeren (Den) 125
Spruance (USA) 698
Spume (Can) 92
Squalo (Ita) 281
Sri — (Mly) 340
Sri Banggi (Mly) 339
Sri Bangji (Sab) 419
Sri Gumantong (Mly) 340
Sri Gumantong (Sab) 419
Sri Johor (Mly) 338
Sri Kelantan (Mly) 338
Sri Kudat (Mly) 340
Sri Labuan (Mly) 340
Sri Labuan (Sab) 419
Sri Langkawi (Mly) 339
Sri Melaka (Mly) 338
Sri Menanti (Mly) 340
Sri Negri Sembilan (Mly) 338
Sri Perak (Mly) 338
Sri Perilis (Mly) 338
Sri Sabah (Mly) 338
Sri Sarawak (Mly) 338
Sri Selangor (Mly) 338
Sri Semporna (Sab) 419
Sri Tawau (Mly) 340
Sri Trengganu (Mly) 338
Stadt (Nor) 369
Stalbas (Nor) 374
Stallion (USA) 731
Stalwart (Aust) 46
Staphorst (Nld) 359
Star (GFR) 210
Starkodder (Swe) 454
Statny (USSR) 534
Stavanger (Nor) 369
Stavelot (Bel) 54
Staverman (Nld) 359
Steadfast (USA) 752
Steady (UK) 621
Stefan Malygin (USSR) 560
Stegg (Nor) 371
Steigerwald (GFR) 209
Steil (Nor) 371
Stein (USA) 705
Steinaker (USA) 701, 702
Stella Polare (Ita) 284
Stepenny (USSR) 534
Stephan Jantzen (GDR) 197
Steregushchy (USSR) 529
Sterett (USA) 689
Sternberg (GDR) 193
Stieglitz (GFR) 210
Stier (GFR) 206
Stirling (UK) 629
Stonewall Jackson (USA) 655
Stör (GFR) 205
Stord (Nor) 369
Storetbecker (GFR) 210
Storione (Ita) 281
Storis (USA) 754
Storm (Nor) 371
Storozhevoy (USSR) 535
Stoyky (USSR) 534
Stralsund (GDR) 195
Strasburg (GDR) 195
Streljko (Yug) 777
Stremitelny (USSR) 534, 579
Strogiy (USSR) 529
Stromboli (Ita) 282
Stromness (UK) 620
Strömstad (Swe) 454
Stroyny (USSR) 529
Stuart (Aust) 42
StubbenKammer (GDR) 197
Stubbington (UK) 610
Stump (USA) 698
Stura (Ita) 285
Sturgeon (USA) 662
Sturgeon Bay (USA) 754
Sturkö (Swe) 455
Stvor (USSR) 558
Styrbjörn (Swe) 454
Styrsö (Swe) 458
Su Yong (RoK) 326
Subteniente Usorio Saravia (Gua) 225
Suchan (USSR) 565
Süderoog (GFR) 213
Suenson (Den) 127
Suffolk County (USA) 717
Suffren (Fra) 169
Suiryu (Jap) 311
Sukanya (Ind) 240
Sukkur (Pak) 382
Sukrip (Tld) 477
Sulhafa Al Bahr (Omn) 377
Sultan Hasanudin (Indo) 246
Sultan Kudarat (Plp) 399
Sultanhisar (Tur) 491
Sulu (Plp) 402
Sumac (USA) 758
Sumida (Jap) 307
Sumter (USA) 717
Sunbird (USA) 731
Sunchon (RoK) 324
Sund (Den) 133
Sundang (Mly) 338
Sunderland (UK) 629
Sundew (USA) 756
Sundsvall (Swe) 454
Sunfish (USA) 662
Sungai Gerong (Indo) 251
Superb (UK) 589
Suphairin (Tld) 476
Supply (Aust) 46
Supporter (UK) 626
Sura (Indo) 247
Suribachi (USA) 724
Surigao Del Norte (Plp) 401
Surigao Del Sur (Plp) 401
Surma (Ban) 52
Surmene (Tur) 492
Suro 2, 3, 5-8 (RoK) 328
Surotama (Indo) 247
Surovy (USSR) 534
Surubi (Arg) 31
Surveyor (USA) 759
Susa (Lby) 334
Susquehanna (USA) 746
Sutjeska (Yug) 775
Sutlej (Ind) 242
Suwad (Bhr) 50
Svartlöga (Swe) 458
Svedujschy (USSR) 533
Svenner (Nor) 369
Sverdlov (USSR) 527
Svetly (USSR) 533
Svirepy (USSR) 535
Sviyaga (USSR) 558
Svobodny (USSR) 534
Swan (Aust) 42
Swarozyc (Pol) 409
Sweetbrier (USA) 756
Sweetgum (USA) 756
Swiatowid (Pol) 409
Swiftsure (UK) 589
Switha (UK) 627
Swivel (USA) 759
Swordfish (USA) 666
Sycomore (Fra) 190
Sylphe (Fra) 188
Sylt (GFR) 211
Sylvania (USA) 724
Syros (Gre) 221
Sysola (USSR) 571
Szu Ch'ing Shan (CPR) 112
Szu Ming (RoC) 473

T

3 De Noviembre (Ecu) 139
T. Bellingsgausen (USSR) 558
T.T. Lewis (Bar) 53
Ta Chih (CPR) 112
Ta Hu (RoC) 473
Ta Peng (RoC) 473
Ta Pieh Shan (CPR) 112
Ta Sueh (RoC) 473
Ta Teng (RoC) 473
Ta Tung (RoC) 473
Ta Wan (RoC) 473
Ta Yu (RoC) 473
Tabarzin (Iran) 256
Tabkah (Lby) 335
Tabuk (SAr) 420
Tachikaze (Jap) 293
Tackle (USA) 759
Tacoma (USA) 710
Taconnet (USA) 738
Tadindeng (Tld) 479
Tae Cho (RoK) 327
Taejon (RoK) 322
Tafelberg (SA) 429
Tagbanua (Plp) 404
Tagil (USSR) 569
Tahan (Mly) 339
Tahchin (Tld) 476
Taheri (Iran) 259
Tahuamanu (Bol) 57
Tai Hsing Shan (CPR) 112
Tai Shan (RoC) 468
Tai Yuan (RoC) 468
Taifun (GFR) 210
Taifun (USSR) 559
Taimur (Pak) 380
Tajo (Spn) 443
Takami (Jap) 300
Takanami (Jap) 296, 310
Takanawa (Jap) 308
Takane (Jap) 300
Takapu (NZ) 363
Takashio (Jap) 292
Takatori (Jap) 306
Takatsuki (Jap) 294, 308
Takelma (USA) 731
Takos (USA) 738
Taku Shan (CPR) 112, 114
Takuyo (Jap) 311
Talara (Per) 394
Talaud (Indo) 251
Talbot (USA) 704
Talibong (Tld) 480
Tallin (USSR) 522
Tallulah (USA) 747
Taluga (USA) 746
Talwar (Ind) 238
Taman (USSR) 562
Tamanami (Jap) 310
Tamaqua (USA) 738
Tamaroa (USA) 758
Tamayuki (Jap) 310
Tambora (Indo) 252
Tampa (USA) 752
Tamrau (Indo) 252
Tamur (Iraq) 261
Tamuz (Iraq) 260
Tana (Nor) 372
Tanaro (Ita) 285
Taney (USA) 751
Tang (USA) 669
Tangerhütte (GDR) 195
Tanin (Isr) 264
Tapi (Tld) 475
Tarablous (Leb) 331
Taragiri (Ind) 237
Tarak (Tur) 498
Tarakan (Aust) 47
Tarakan (Indo) 251
Taranaki (NZ) 363
Tarapunga (NZ) 363
Tarawa (Sri) 448, 449
Tarawa (USA) 713
Tarbatness (UK) 607
Tarek Ibn Zayed (Syr) 464
Tareq Ben Zaid (Iraq) 261
Tariq (Egy) 142
Tariq (Pak) 380
Tariq (Qat) 415
Tariq (SAr) 420
Tarkhankut (USSR) 570
Tarmo (Fin) 153
Tärnö (Swe) 455
Tarqui (Ecu) 140
Tarshish (Isr) 265
Tartar (UK) 603
Tartu (Fra) 171
Tartu (USSR) 571
Tasaday (Plp) 404
Tashiro (Jap) 300
Tashkent (USSR) 522
Tat Sa (Vtn) 771
Tatsuta (Jap) 307
Tattnall (USA) 695
Taupo (NZ) 363
Taurus (Brz) 66
Taurus (USA) 709
Tautog (USA) 662
Tautra (Nor) 373
Tavda (USSR) 568
Tavi (Fin) 155
Tawfic (Mor) 349
Tawi-Tawi (Plp) 401
Tayfun (Tur) 489
Taymyr (USSR) 558
Tayrona (Col) 115
Tazarka (Tun) 485
TB 1 (GFR) 212
Te Yang (RoC) 466
Tebuk (SAr) 422
Tecumseh (USA) 655
Tecunuman (Gua) 226
Tegernsee (GFR) 208
Tegualda (Chi) 99
Tehuantepec (Mex) 345
Tehuelche (Arg) 34
Teide (Spn) 444
Teja (GFR) 210
Tekirdag (Tur) 492
Tekkä (Fin) 155
Teluk Amboina (Indo) 249
Teluk Bajur (Indo) 249
Teluk Bone (Indo) 249
Teluk Kau (Indo) 249
Teluk Langsa (Indo) 249
Teluk Manado (Indo) 249
Teluk Ratai (Indo) 249
Teluk Saleh (Indo) 249
Teluk Tomini (Indo) 249
Tembah (Can) 93
Temenggong (Mly) 340
Templin (GDR) 195
Tenace (Fra) 189
Tenacity (UK) 614
Tenente Claudio (Brz) 68
Tenente Fabio (Brz) 68
Tenente Raul (Brz) 68
Teniente Farina (Par) 385
Teniente Luis Bernal (Col) 119
Teniente Miguel Silva (Col) 119
Teniente Pratts Gil (Par) 386
Tenente O. Carreras Saguier (Par) 386
Teniente Sorzano (Col) 119
Tenyo (Jap) 312
Teodolit (USSR) 557
Terek (USSR) 570
Teriberka (USSR) 574
Terme (Tur) 492
Termoli (Ita) 281
Tern (UK) 628
Terra Nova (Can) 82
Teruzuki (Jap) 295
Teshio (Jap) 297, 307
Teterow (GDR) 193
Teuri (Jap) 300
Texas (USA) 686
TF 1-6 (GFR) 210
TF 101-102 (GFR) 210
TF 104-108 (GFR) 210
Thai Binh (Vtn) 771
Thalia (Gre) 222
Tham Ngu Lao (Vtn) 770
Thar (Egy) 145
That Assuari (Qat) 415
Thatcham (UK) 627
Thayanchon (Tld) 477
The Luke (Aust) 48
Themistocles (Gre) 218
Theodore Roosevelt (USA) 658
Theseus (GFR) 203
Theseus (Gre) 224
Thetis (GFR) 203
Thetis (Gre) 224
Thi Tu (Vtn) 771
Thoaban (UAE) 581
Tho Chau (Vtn) 771
Thomas A. Edison (USA) 657
Thomas C. Hart (USA) 705
Thomas Carleton (Can) 91
Thomas G. Thompson (USA) 741
Thomas Jefferson (USA) 657
Thomas Washington (USA) 741
Thomaston (USA) 716
Thompson (Arg) 32
Thor (Ice) 232
Thorn (USA) 698
Thornham (UK) 611
Throsk (UK) 623
Thu Tay Thi (Bur) 75
Thule (Swe) 460
Thuong Tien (Vtn) 771
Thunder (Can) 85
Thunder Bay (USA) 754
Thurø (Den) 129
Thyella (Gre) 218
Tian Kuo (RoC) 469
Tianée (Fra) 187
Tiboli (Plp) 404
Tiburon (Pan) 384
Tiburon (Ven) 765
Tichitt (Mtn) 342
Ticino (Ita) 285
Tidepool (UK) 617
Tidespring (UK) 617
Tien Giang (Vtn) 772
Tien Moi (Vtn) 771
Tien Shan (RoC) 468
Tienga (Sud) 450
Tierra Del Fuego (Arg) 31
Tiger (UK) 596
Tijgerhaai (Nld) 354
Tikal (Gua) 226
Timavo (Ita) 285
Timban (Brz) 64
Timo (Ita) 281
Timsah (UAE) 582
Tinaztepe (Tur) 488
Tino (Ita) 286
Tinosa (USA) 663
Tippu Sultan (Pak) 381
Tir (Ind) 239
Tiran (Iran) 256
Tirebolu (Tur) 492
Tirfing (Swe) 454
Tista (Ban) 52
Tista (Nor) 372
Titan (Gre) 224
Titan (USSR) 571
Tjeld (Nor) 371
Tjerk Hiddes (Nld) 357
Tjurkö (Swe) 455
Tlaxcala (Mex) 347
To Yen (Vtn) 771
Toba (Arg) 34
Tobol (USSR) 553
Tobruk (Aust) 47
Tobruk (Lby) 333
Todak (Indo) 248
Todak (Mly) 338
Tofino (Spn) 444
Tohok (Indo) 247
Toka (USA) 738
Tokachi (Jap) 297, 307
Toky (Mad) 336
Toll (Arg) 31

832 INDEXES / Named Ships

Tomahawk (USA) 738
Tombak (Mly) 338
Tomonami (Jap) 310
Tompazis (Gre) 218
Tomsky Komsomolets (USSR) 550
Tonb (Iran) 258
Tone (Jap) 306
Tonelero (Brz) 60
Tongeren (Bel) 55
Tongpliu (Tld) 477
Tonijn (Nld) 354
Tonina (Arg) 31
Tonina (Spn) 433
Tonkawa (USA) 738
Tonocote (Arg) 34
Tontogany (USA) 738
Topas (GFR) 210
Topater (Bol) 57
Tor (Swe) 460
Torani (Indo) 247
Tordön (Swe) 454
Toribio (Bol) 57
Tornade (Cam) 76
Tornadon (GFR) 210
Torpen (Nor) 373
Torquay (UK) 605
Torrens (Aust) 42
Torrent (UK) 622
Torrid (UK) 622
Tortuguero (DR) 134
Totila (GFR) 210
Toucan (Fra) 190
Toufan (Iran) 259
Toumi (Jap) 308
Toun (Jap) 314
Tourmaline (Fra) 178
Tourterelle (Fra) 190
Tourville (Fra) 170
Tousan (Iran) 259
Toushi (Jap) 300
Towara (Arg) 31
Towers (USA) 695
Towline (USA) 759
Townsville (Aust) 43
Toxotis (Gre) 220
Trabzon (Tur) 492
Tracy (Can) 90
Trafalgar (UK) 589
Tramandai (Brz) 64
Tran Khanh Du (Vtn) 770
Tran Lo (Vtn) 771
Traust (Nor) 371
Travailleur (Fra) 190
Traverz (USSR) 557
Trenton (USA) 715
Trepang (USA) 662
Trevose (UK) 628
Triaina (Gre) 217
Trident (Fra) 177
Tridente (Brz) 68
Trieste II (USA) 672
Trieux (Fra) 176
Trifoglio (Ita) 281
Triki (Mor) 349
Trinity (TT) 483
Tripoli (USA) 714
Trippe (USA) 705
Trischen (GFR) 211
Trishul (Ind) 238
Tritao (Brz) 68
Triton (Den) 127
Triton (Fra) 185
Triton (GFR) 203
Triton (Gre) 216
Triton (Nld) 361
Triton (USA) 665
Triumph (UK) 611
Triunfo (Brz) 68
Tromp (Nld) 355
Trondheim (Nor) 369
Tropik (USSR) 559
Tross (Nor) 371
Troung Ba (Vtn) 771
Truckee (USA) 726
Truett (USA) 705
Truong Sa (Vtn) 771
Truxtun (USA) 688
Trygg (Nor) 371
Tsna (USSR) 568
Tsugaru (Jap) 302
Tsukuba (Jap) 308
Tsukumi (Jap) 301
Tsurugi (Jap) 308
Tsushima (Jap) 312
Tübingen (GFR) 205
Tufan (Tur) 490
Tui (NZ) 364
Tuima (Fin) 151
Tuisku (Fin) 151
Tukan (Pol) 407
Tulagaq (Den) 128
Tulare (USA) 718, 720
Tulcan (Ecu) 139
Tulipe (Fra) 189
Tullibee (USA) 663
Tuloma (USSR) 574
Tumaco (Col) 118
Tumleren (Den) 125
Tümmler (GFR) 205
Tunda Satu (Mly) 339
Tung An (CPR) 107
Tung Fan Hung (CPR) 112
Tunguska (USSR) 571
Tunny (USA) 662
Tupa (Fra) 187
Tupelo (USA) 756
Tupper (Can) 91
Tur (Pol) 407
Turia (Spn) 443
Turman (USSR) 538
Turner Joy (USA) 700
Turnhout (Bel) 55
Turtle (USA) 672
Turunmaa (Fin) 151
Turva (Fin) 155
Tuscaloosa (USA) 717
Tuscumbia (USA) 738
Tuskegee (USA) 738
Tutahaco (USA) 738
Tuuli (Fin) 151
Tuwaig (SAr) 422
Tuzla (Tur) 497
Tydeman (Nld) 360
Tyfon (Gre) 220
Tyo To (RoK) 327
Typhoon (UK) 624
Tyr (Ice) 232
Tyrsky (Fin) 151
Tzacol (Gua) 226

U

U1-U2 (GFR) 200
U9-U12 (GFR) 200
U13-U30 (GFR) 200
Ubirajara dos Santos (Brz) 68
Ucayali (Per) 391
Uckermünde (GDR) 195
Udarnik (Yug) 777
Udaygiri (Ind) 237
Udomdet (Tld) 476
Ueltzen (GFR) 213
Ufa (USSR) 557
Ugra (USSR) 557
Uhuru (Tan) 474
Uisko (Fin) 155
Ul Rung (RoK) 327
Ul San (RoK) 327
Ula (Nor) 369
Ulabat (Tur) 497
Ülkü (Tur) 497
Ulla (Spn) 443
Ulm (GFR) 205
Uluç Ali Reis (Tur) 487
Ulvsund (Den) 131
Ulyana Gromova (USSR) 558
Ulysses S. Grant (USA) 655
Umar Farooq (Ban) 51
Umberto Grosso (Ita) 278
Umeå (Swe) 454
Umidori (Jap) 297
Umigiri (Jap) 310
Umitaka (Jap) 298
Umurbey (Tur) 497
Un Pong (RoK) 326
Unanue (Per) 393
Unden (Swe) 463
Undine (GFR) 206
Ung Po (RoK) 323
Uniao (Brz) 63
Unimak (USA) 751
Unja (USSR) 574
Uplifter (UK) 620
Uporny (USSR) 531
Upton (UK) 610
Ural (USSR) 571
Uranami (Jap) 296, 310
Urania (Nld) 361
Urayuki (Jap) 309
Urazuki (Jap) 310
Urd (Swe) 462
Urho (Fin) 153
Uriah Heep (UK) 628
Uribe (Chi) 98
Urk (Nld) 358
Uruguay (Arg) 34
Uruguay (Uru) 760
Urume (Jap) 300
Usedom (GDR) 196
Uskok (Yug) 775
Ustica (Ita) 286
Usumacinta (Mex) 345
Utara (Sin) 425
Utatlan (Gua) 225
Ute (USA) 731
Uthaug (Nor) 369
Uthörn (GFR) 213
Utile (Fra) 190
Utla (Nor) 372
Utö (Swe) 455
Utone (Jap) 300
Utrecht (Nld) 356
Utsira (Nor) 369
Utstein (Nor) 369
Utvaer (Nor) 369
Uusimaa (Fin) 150
Uzushio (Jap) 292

V

24 De Mayo (Ecu) 139
25 De Julio (Ecu) 139
V. Bagat (Yug) 777
V. Golovnin (USSR) 558
V. Skorpik (Yug) 777
V. Sukhotsky (USSR) 560
Vadso (Nor) 370
Vaedderen (Den) 127
Vagach (USSR) 559
Vagir (Ind) 235
Vagli (Ind) 235
Vagsheer (Ind) 235
Väktaren (Swe) 454
Val (USSR) 556
Valday (USSR) 573
Valdez (USA) 705
Valdivia (Chi) 100
Vale (Nor) 371
Vale (Swe) 454
Valencia (Ven) 768
Valentin G. Farias (Mex) 345
Valerian Albanov (USSR) 560
Valerian Uryvaev (USSR) 560
Valeureux (Fra) 190
Valiant (UK) 590
Valiant (USA) 752
Vällö (Swe) 458
Valpas (Fin) 155
Vampire (Aust) 41
Van (Tur) 497
Van Bochove (Nld) 361
Van der Wel (Nld) 359
Van Dien (Vtn) 771
Van Galen (Nld) 357
Van Hamel (Nld) 359
Van Kinsbergen (Nld) 356
Van Moppes (Nld) 359
Van Nes (Nld) 357
Van Speijk (Nld) 357
Van Straelen (Nld) 359
Van 'T Hoff (Nld) 359
Van Versendaal (Nld) 359
Van Well Groenveld (Nld) 359
Vancouver (Can) 87
Vancouver (USA) 715
Vanguard (USA) 740
Vanguardia (Uru) 763
Vanneau (Fra) 190
Vapcarov (Bul) 73
Varberg (Swe) 454
Vargen (Swe) 453
Varma (Fin) 153
Varyag (USSR) 526
Vasama 2 (Fin) 152
Vasiliy Chapaev (USSR) 524
Vasily Poiarkov (USSR) 578
Vasily Pronchishtchev (USSR) 578
Vasouya (Alg) 21
Västerås (Swe) 454
Västervik (Swe) 454
Vauquelin (Fra) 172
Vdokhnovenny (USSR) 533
Vdumchivy (USSR) 534
Vector (Can) 93
Vedushchy (USSR) 534
Veer (Ind) 240
Veere (Nld) 358, 359
Vega (Fra) 178
Vega (Swe) 454
Vega (USSR) 558
Veinte de Julio (Col) 116
Veintencinco De Julio (Ecu) 139
Veinticinco de Mayo (Arg) 26
Vejrø (Den) 129
Vela (Ind) 235
Velasco (Spn) 442
Velos (Gre) 218
Vencedora (Spn) 437
Vendetta (Aust) 41
Vengadora (Col) 117
Venlo (Nld) 359
Ventimiglia (Ita) 286
Venturer (UK) 611
Venturous (USA) 752
Venus (Fra) 163
Venuta (USSR) 555
Verendrye (Can) 92
Vernøy (Nor) 373
Verny (USSR) 534
Verseau (Fra) 180
Vertieres (Hai) 228
Vertikal (USSR) 556
Verviers (Bel) 54
Vesky (USSR) 533
Vessletz (Bul) 73
Vesuvio (Ita) 282
Vetluga (USSR) 554
Veurne (Bel) 54
Viareggio (Ita) 281
Vice-Admiral Drozd (USSR) 525
Vicente Yañez Pinzon (Spn) 439
Victor Cubillos (Col) 119
Victor Hensen (GFR) 213
Victor Schoelcher (Fra) 173
Victoria (USA) 744
Victoria (Ven) 767
Vidar (Nor) 371
Vidar (Swe) 454
Vidyut (Ind) 240
Vieste (Ita) 281
Vigilant (UK) 626, 627
Vigilant (USA) 752
Vigilante (Fra) 189
Vigoroso (Ita) 286
Vigorous (USA) 752
Viima (Fin) 155
Vijay Durg (Ind) 239
Vijeta (Ind) 240
Viken (Swe) 456
Vikrant (Ind) 235
Viksten (Swe) 458
Viktor Bugaev (USSR) 564
Viktor Kotelnikov (USSR) 553
Villa de Bilbao (Spn) 439
Villaamil (Spn) 439
Villapando (Mex) 346
Villar (Per) 391
Ville Marie (Can) 93
Vilm (GDR) 196
Vilsund (Den) 131
Vilyui (USSR) 555
Vinash (Ind) 240
Vindhyagiri (Ind) 237
Vineta (GFR) 206
Vinh Long (Fra) 179
Vinö (Swe) 458
Violette (Fra) 189
Virgin Clipper (VI) 773
Virginia (USA) 686
Virginio Fasan (Ita) 278
Virgo (Swe) 454
Vis (Yug) 780
Visborg (Swe) 456
Visby (Swe) 454
Vischio (Ita) 281
Vise (Bel) 55
Vise (USA) 758
Vishera (USSR) 570
Vitalienbrüder (GFR) 210
Viteazul (Rom) 418
Vitsgarn (Swe) 462
Vitte (GDR) 195
Vittorio Veneto (Ita) 272
Vityaz (USSR) 564
Vivies (Gre) 224
Vlaardingen (Nld) 358
Vladimir Kavraysky (USSR) 563
Vladimir Kolechitsky (USSR) 569
Vladimir Obruchev (USSR) 565
Vladimir Rusanov (USSR) 578
Vladimir Trefolev (USSR) 572
Vladimir Zaimov (Bul) 73
Vladivostock (USSR) 577
Vladivostok (USSR) 525
Vlado Cetkovic (Yug) 777
Vlijatelny (USSR) 533
Vnimatelny (USSR) 534
Voge (USA) 707
Vogelgesang (USA) 701, 702
Vogelsand (GFR) 211
Voima (Fin) 153
Voinicul (Rom) 418
Volga (USSR) 553
Volk (USSR) 538
Volkan (Tur) 489
Volker (GFR) 210
Volkhov (USSR) 570
Völklingen (GFR) 205
Volna (USSR) 564
Volstad Jr (Nor) 374
Voluntario (Brz) 68
Volvi (Gre) 224
Von Steuben (USA) 655
Voronezhsky Komsomolets (USSR) 550
Vos (Nld) 357
Vosso (Nor) 372
Vostok (USSR) 559
Vozbuzhdenny (USSR) 532
Vozmushchenny (USSR) 533
Vrazumitelny (USSR) 534
Vreeland (USA) 705
Vsevolod Beryozkin (USSR) 560
Vukov Klanac (Yug) 778
Vulcan (USA) 728
Vung Tau (Vtn) 772
Vyderzhanny (USSR) 533
Vyuga (USSR) 578
Vyzyvayuschy (USSR) 533

W

W. S. Sims (USA) 705
Waage (GFR) 206
Wabash (USA) 727
Waccamaw (USA) 746
Waddell (USA) 695
Wadi M'ragh (Lby) 333
Wadi Majer (Lby) 333
Wadsworth (USA) 703
Wahaka (USA) 738
Waheed (Kwt) 330
Wahoo (USA) 669
Wahpeton (USA) 738
Waikato (NZ) 362
Wainwright (USA) 689
Wakagumo (Jap) 310
Wakanami (Jap) 310
Wakasa (Jap) 305
Wakataka (Jap) 298
Wakeful (UK) 623
Walchensee (GFR) 208
Walkerton (UK) 610
Walnut (USA) 757
Walrus? (Nld) 354
Walrus (UK) 591
Walter (GFR) 210
Walter E. Foster (Can) 91
Walther Hertwig (GFR) 213
Walther Von Ledebur (GFR) 212
Walvisbaai (SA) 429
Wamandai (Nld) 361
Wambrau (Nld) 361
Wan Shou (RoC) 472
Wanamassa (USA) 738
Wandenkolk (Brz) 68
Wandelaar (Bel) 53
Wangerooge (GFR) 211
Wannalancet (USA) 738
Wapakoneta (USA) 738
Wapato (USA) 738
Warmingham (UK) 627
Warnemünde (GDR) 195
Warrnambool (Aust) 43
Warspite (UK) 590
Warszawa (Pol) 405
Warta (Pol) 408
Washtucna (USA) 738
Waspada (Bru) 69
Wasperton (UK) 615
Wate (GFR) 210
Watercourse (UK) 623
Waterfall (UK) 623
Waterford (USA) 734
Waterfowl (UK) 623
Waterman (UK) 623
Watershed (UK) 623
Waterside (UK) 623
Waterspout (UK) 623
Waterwitch (UK) 617
Wathah (Kwt) 329
Wathena (USA) 738
Waubansee (USA) 738
Wauwatosa (USA) 738
Waxahatchie (USA) 738
Wedge (USA) 758
Wee Bong (RoK) 326
Weehawken (USA) 738
Weeraya (Sri) 448
Wega (GFR) 206, 213
Weilheim (GFR) 205
Weisswasser (GDR) 195
Welch (USA) 710
Wels (GFR) 205
Wen Shan (RoC) 468
Wenatchee (USA) 738
Werra (GFR) 207
Wesp (Bel) 56
West Milton (USA) 734
Westdiep (Bel) 53
Westensee (GFR) 208
Western Samar (Plp) 402
Westerwald (GFR) 209
Westgat (Nld) 361
Westhinder (Bel) 53
Westra (UK) 627
Westwind (GFR) 210
Westwind (USA) 754
Wetzlar (GFR) 205
Wewak (Aust) 47
Whale (USA) 662
Wheeling (USA) 740
Whimbrel (UK) 622
Whipple (USA) 705
White Bush (USA) 757
White Heath (USA) 757
White Holly (USA) 757
White Lupine (USA) 757
White Pine (USA) 757
White Plains (USA) 724
White Sage (USA) 757
White Sumac (USA) 757
Whitehead (UK) 621
Whiting (USA) 759
Whyalla (Aust) 43
Wichita (USA) 727
Widder (GFR) 206
Wielingen (Bel) 53
Wielingen (Nld) 361
Wiernier (USSR) 559
Wiesel (GFR) 205
Wiking (GFR) 210
Wildwood (Can) 86
Wilhelm Bauer (GFR) 200
Wilhelm Pieck (GDR) 197
Wilhelm Pieckstadt (GDR) 195
Wilhelm Pullwer (GFR) 212
Wilkes (USA) 743
Will Rogers (USA) 653, 655
Willem van der Zaan (Nld) 356
Willemoes (Den) 127

INDEXES / Named Ships — Classes 833

Willemstad (Nld) 358
Willi Bansch (GDR) 194
William C. Lawe (USA) 701, 702
William H. Bates (USA) 662
William H. Standley (USA) 689
William J. Stewart (Can) 93
William V. Pratt (USA) 696
Williamsburg (USA) 747
Wilton (UK) 609
Winamac (USA) 738
Windhoek (SA) 429
Wingina (USA) 738
Winnemucca (USA) 738
Wire (USA) 759
Wisconsin (USA) 685
Wismar (GDR) 193, 197
Wisting (Nor) 373
Witte de With (Nld) 356
Wittensee (GFR) 208
Witthayakhom (Tld) 476
Wittigo (GFR) 210
Wittstock (GDR) 195
Wodnik (Pol) 408
Woerden (Nld) 359
Wol Mi (RoK) 327
Wolf (Nld) 357
Wolfe (Can) 90
Wolfsburg (GFR) 205
Wolgast (GDR) 195
Wollongong (Aust) 43
Wolverton (UK) 615
Wood County (USA) 717
Woodlark (UK) 617
Woodrow Wilson (USA) 655
Woodrush (USA) 756
Worden (USA) 690
Wotan (GFR) 207
Wotton (UK) 610
Wu Chang (CPR) 107
Wu Kang (RoC) 472
Wu Sheng (RoC) 468
Wu Tai (RoC) 472
Wyaconda (USA) 758
Wyandot (USA) 743
Wyman (USA) 743

X

Xucuxuy (Gua) 226

Y

Yacuma (Bol) 57
Yaegumo (Jap) 309
Yaeshio (Jap) 292
Yaeyama (Jap) 307
Yaffo (Isr) 265
Yagui (Mex) 345
Yahagi (Jap) 307
Yahiko (Jap) 305
Yakal (Plp) 402
Yakhroma (USSR) 571
Yakov Gakkel (USSR) 560
Yakov Smirnitsky (USSR) 560
Yama (Isr) 267
Yamadori (Jap) 297
Yamagumo (Jap) 294
Yamakuni (Jap) 306
Yamal (USSR) 562
Yamana (Arg) 29
Yamayuki (Jap) 310
Yamayuri (Jap) 310
Yan Gyi Aung (Bur) 74
Yan Lon Aung (Bur) 75
Yan Myo Aung (Bur) 74
Yan Taing Aung (Bur) 74
Yana (USSR) 568
Yanaba (USA) 738
Yanegua (USA) 738
Yankton (USA) 759
Yarden (Isr) 267
Yarhisar (Tur) 491
Yarmouk (Syr) 464
Yarmouth (UK) 604
Yarmouth Navigator (UK) 628
Yarnton (UK) 615
Yarra (Aust) 42
Yashiro (Jap) 304
Yatanocas (USA) 738
Yavdezan (Alg) 21
Yavza (USSR) 573
Yay Bo (Bur) 75
YDT 11 & 12 (Can) 86
Yedekci (Tur) 498
Yegorlik (USSR) 570
Yelcho (Chi) 100
Yellowstone (USA) 723
Yelnya (USSR) 570
Yemelyan Pugatchev (USSR) 578
Yen Lun (CPR) 113
Yenisey (USSR) 571
Yermak (USSR) 576
Yerofei Khabarov (USSR) 578
Yildiray (Tur) 487
Yildirim (Tur) 490
Yildiz (Tur) 490
Ymer (Swe) 460
Yocona (USA) 758
Yodo (Jap) 311
Yokose (Jap) 300
Yola (Nig) 367
Yon-Go (Jap) 303
Yong Dong (RoK) 326
Yong Mun (RoK) 328
Yosemite (USA) 724
Yoshino (Jap) 297, 306
Youth of Oman (Omn) 377
Youville (Can) 86
Ystad (Swe) 454
Yu (Mly) 338
Yu Shan (RoC) 468
Yu Tai (RoC) 472
Yubari (Jap) 307
Yudachi (Jap) 295
Yuen Yang (RoC) 467
Yug (USSR) 559, 562
Yukigumo (Jap) 309
Yukikaze (Jap) 296
Yukon (Can) 81
Yukon (USA) 747
Yuma (USA) 738
Yung An (RoC) 470
Yung Cheng (RoC) 470
Yung Chi (RoC) 470
Yung Ching (RoC) 470
Yung Chou (RoC) 470
Yung Fu (RoC) 470
Yung Hsin (RoC) 470
Yung Jen (RoC) 470
Yung Ju (RoC) 470
Yung Kang (RoC) 473
Yung Lo (RoC) 470
Yung Nien (RoC) 470
Yung Ping (RoC) 470
Yung Shan (RoC) 470
Yung Sui (RoC) 470
Yupiter (USSR) 556
Yuri M. Shokalsky (USSR) 565
Yurij Godin (USSR) 561
Yurik Lisyanskiy (USSR) 578
Yuugumo (Jap) 294
Yuushio (Jap) 292
Yuzbasi Tolunay (Tur) 495
Yuzuki (Jap) 309

Z

Z2-Z5 (GFR) 202
Z. Jovanovic-Spanac (Yug) 777
Zaal (Iran) 255
Zabaikalye (USSR) 556
Zacatecas (Mex) 347
Zafer (Tur) 488
Zafona (Isr) 267
Zaire (Por) 413
Zaire (Zai) 781
Zakarpatye (USSR) 556
Zambales (Plp) 401
Zambeze (Por) 413
Zamboanga del Norte (Plp) 401
Zander (GFR) 205
Zangezur (USSR) 573
Zaporozhiye (USSR) 556
Zapoylara (USSR) 558
Zarnitsa (USSR) 562
Zarti (Pan) 384
Zarya (USSR) 561
Zbik (Pol) 407
Zeefakkel (Nld) 361
Zeehond? (Nld) 354
Zeisig (GFR) 210
Zeitz (GDR) 195
Zelonodolsk (USSR) 536
Zeltin (Lby) 333
Zemchug (USSR) 539
Zenit (USSR) 559, 567
Zenobe Gramme (Bel) 56
Zerbst (GDR) 195
Zeus (Gre) 224
Zeya (USSR) 568
Zharki (USSR) 535
Zhdanov (USSR) 527
Zhguchy (USSR) 531
Zhiguili (USSR) 572
Zingahar (YPDR) 774
Zingst (GDR) 195
Zinnia (Bel) 55
Zleiten (Lby) 335
Zobel (GFR) 205
Zolotoy Rog (USSR) 570
Zomer (Nld) 359
Zond (USSR) 557
Zorky (USSR) 531
Zorritos (Per) 394
Zoubin (Iran) 256
Zubr (Pol) 407
Zuiderkruis (Nld) 360
Zuiun (Jap) 314
Zulfiquar (Pak) 382
Zulia (Ven) 765
Zulu (UK) 603
Zum Zum (Pak) 383
Zurara (UAE) 581
Zuraw (Pol) 407
Zvezda (USSR) 562
Zwaardvis (Nld) 354

CLASSES

A

A 17 (Swe) 452
A 20 (Spn) 444
A 30 (Spn) 444
A 69 (Arg, Fra) 29, 175
Aberdovey (UK) 626
Abhay (Ind, Mrt) 240, 343
Abkhaziya (USSR) 562
Abnaki (Mex, USA) 345, 348, 731
Abtao (Per) 388
Achelous (Indo, RoK, Plp, RoC, USA, Ven) 250, 327, 402, 472, 728, 768
Acme (USA) 721
Adjutant (Bel, Den, Fra, Gre, Ita, Nor, Pak, Spn, RoC, Tun, Tur, Uru) 54, 131, 180, 188, 222, 281, 372, 382, 443, 470, 484, 492, 761
Admirable (Bur, DR, Mex, Plp, RoC, Vtn) 74, 134, 346, 347, 399, 403, 473, 771
Admiral W. S. Benson (USA) 735
Aeolus (USA) 748
Agave (Ita) 281
Agdleq (Den) 128
Aggressive (Bel, Fra, Ita, Nld, Spn, USA, Uru) 54, 179, 281, 358, 443, 721, 761
Agosta (Fra, Pak, Spn) 162, 379, 433
Aguilucho (Spn) 447
Aist (USSR) 552
Ajax (USA) 728
Akademik Krilov (USSR) 562
Akademik Kurchatov (USSR) 564
Akademik L. Orbeli (USSR) 560
Akagi (Jap) 309
Akashi (Jap) 303, 312
Akizuki (Jap) 295, 309
Akshay (Ban) 52
Alatna (USA) 748
Alava (Spn) 438
Albacore (USA) 670
Albany (USA) 692
Albatros (Ita) 279
Albatroz (Por) 413
Alesha (USSR) 545
Alfa (USSR) 511
Alfange (Ang) 23
Algerine (Bur, Gre, Tld) 74, 224, 480
Alicudi (Ita) 284
Alkmaar (Nld) 358
Allen M. Sumner (Arg, Brz, Gre, RoC, Ven) 28, 61, 217, 467, 766
Allen M. Sumner Fram II (Brz, Chi, Col, Iran, RoK, Tur, USA, Ven) 61, 97, 116, 255, 323, 488, 702, 766
Alligator (USSR) 550
Almirante (Chi) 97
Almirante Clemente (Ven) 767
Almirante Pereira da Silva (Por) 412
Aloe (Ecu) 140
Alpino (Ita) 277
Altay (USSR) 570
Alvin Type (USA) 672
Alvin Type (Modified) (USA) 672
Alvsborg (Swe) 456
Amatsukaze (Jap) 295
Amazon (UK) 601
American Explorer (USA) 747
Amga (USSR) 554
Amphion (Iran, RoC) 258, 472
Amur (USSR) 554
Anchorage (USA) 716
Anchova (Brz) 65
Andizhan (Mod) (USSR) 555
Andrea Doria (Ita) 273
Andromeda (Spn) 441
Andromeda (Converted) (USA) 743
Andryusha (USSR) 546
Ane (Swe) 459
Angeln (Tur) 497
An Ju (DPRK) 321
Annapolis (Can) 81
Anshan (CPR) 105
An Tung (CPR) 113
Ape (Ita) 279
Aragosta (Ita) 282
Aragua (Ven) 765
Arauca (Col) 117
ARD 12 (Ecu) 140
Aréthuse (Fra) 163
Argo (DR) 135
Argos (Ang) 22
Argus (Brz) 66
Ariadne (GFR) 206
Aristaeus (Col, GFR) 119, 207
Arktika (USSR) 576
Arkö (Swe) 458
Artillerist (DPRK) 319
Asashimo (Jap) 310
Ash (Isr) 267
Asheville (RoK, Tur, USA) 324, 490, 710
Ashland (RoC) 470
Atlantik (USSR) 564
Atrevida (Spn) 439
Atsumi (Jap) 299
Attack (Aust, Indo, PNG) 44, 248, 384
Audace (Ita) 274
Audaz (Spn) 437
Auk (RoK, Mex, Per, Plp, RoC, Tur, Uru) 324, 345, 347, 395, 398, 468, 495, 761
Austin (USA) 715
Avon (UK) 608
Ayanami (Jap) 296
Azteca (Mex) 346
Azueta (Mex) 346

B

Babochka (USSR) 543
Baglietto Type (Alg) 21
Baikal (USSR) 573
Bainbridge (USA) 691
Balao (Chi, Gre, Spn) 95, 217, 434
Balder (Nld) 358
Baleares (Spn) 438
Ballatrix (Moz) 351
Balsam (Plp, USA) 404, 756
Bangor (Moz) 351
Bangrachan (Tld) 478
Baptista De Andrade (Por) 412
Bar (CPR, Tur) 113, 498
Barbel (USA) 667
Barcelo (Mtn) 342
"Barcelo (P 10)" (Spn) 440
Barnegat (Eth, Gre, Ita, Vtn) 148, 223, 283, 770
Barranquilla (Col) 117
Barrosa Pereira (Brz) 67
Barsø (Den) 129
Baskunchak (GDR) 196
Bathurst (CPR) 107
Batral (Fra, Mor) 176, 351
Batram (Mad) 336
Bat Sheva (Isr) 267
Battle (Iran, Pak) 255, 380
Bat Yam (Isr) 267
Bay (Can, Por) 85, 414
Bear (USA) 752
Belknap (USA) 689
Bellatrix (Ang, DR, Per) 23, 135, 393
Benewah (USA) 735
Benjamin Franklin (USA) 655
Berezina (USSR) 568
Bergamini (Ita) 278
Berk (Tur) 489
Berneval (Fra) 181
Bertram Type (Egy, Jor) 145, 314
Bezhitsa (USSR) 567
Bihoro (Jap) 306
Bird (UK) 615
Biya (USSR) 559
Bizan (Jap) 309
Black Swan (Egy, Ind) 142, 239
Blackwood (Ind, UK) 238
Blue Ridge (USA) 712
Bluebird (Tld) 479
Bodensee (GFR) 208
Bolster (USA) 728
Bombarda (Por) 414
Boris Chilikin (USSR) 569
Bouchard (Arg, Par) 30, 385
Bowditch (USA) 743
Brave (Gre) 220
Bravo (USSR) 514
Broadsword (Gua, UK) 225, 599
Bronstein (USA) 708
Brooke (USA) 704
Brooklyn (Arg, Chi) 27, 96
Bryza (Pol) 409
Bulldog (UK) 616
Bustler (UK) 624
Buyskes (Nld) 360
Byblos (Leb) 331

C

C/Kaibokan I (CPR) 107
C 65 (Fra) 173
C 70 (Fra) 168
C 80 (SAr) 421
Cabildo (Gre, Spn, RoC) 221, 442, 470
Cacine (Por) 413
Cakabey (Tur) 494
California (USA) 687
Callaghan (USA) 745
Campbell (USA) 751
Cannon (Gre, Per, Plp, Tld, Uru) 219, 394, 398, 476, 760
Cape (Can, Eth, Hai, Iran, RoK, Tld, Tur, USA) 83, 149, 228, 256, 258, 325, 477, 493, 755
Carpentaria (Bur, Sol) 74, 425
Carpenter (Fram I) (USA) 702
Casco (Plp, USA) 398, 751
Castle (CPR) 107
Castor (Spn) 444
Centauro (Ita) 278
Ceylon (Per) 389
CGC (Bur) 74
CH (Pak) 381
Chaho (DPRK) 320
Chan Tou (CPR) 113
Chanticleer (Tur, USA) 496, 731
Chapaev (USSR) 528
Charles F. Adams (USA) 695
Charles F. Adams (Modified) (GFR) 201
Charles Lawrence (Chi, Ecu, Mex, RoK, RoC) 98, 138, 323, 345, 468
Charleston (USA) 718
Charlie I (USSR) 507
Charlie II (USSR) 507
Chauvenet (USA) 743
Chayka (Indo) 252
Ch'eng Tu (CPR) 106
Cherokee (Arg, Chi, Col, DR, Ecu, Indo, Pak, Per, RoC, USA) 29, 99, 100, 117, 137, 140, 252, 383, 394, 473, 731, 758
Chifuri (Jap) 308
Chikugo (Jap) 297
Chiyokaze (Jap) 310
Chodo (DPRK) 319
Chong-Jin (DPRK) 320
Chulym (USSR) 573
Cimarron (USA) 726
Cimarron (Jumboised) (USA) 726, 746
Circe (Fra) 179
Claud Jones (Indo) 246
Clemenceau (Fra) 164
Cleveland (Converted) (USA) 693
Clovelly (UK) 626
Cohoes (DR, Uru, Ven) 134, 763, 769
Colossus (Arg, Brz) 26, 61
Columbia (USA) 746
Comandante Joao Belo (Por) 411
Combattante IIG (Lby) 333
Combattante IIIB (Nig) 366
Comet (USA) 745
Commandant Rivière (Fra) 173
Compass Island (USA) 725
Confiance (UK) 624
Coontz (USA) 696
Costa Sur (Arg) 32
County (UK) 598
Courtney (Col) 117
CR (Pak) 381
Crosley (Col, RoC, RoK) 116, 323, 468
Currituck (Converted) (USA) 732
Cutlass (Gua) 226

D

D/Kaibokan II (CPR) 107
D 20 (Spn) 436
D 60 (Spn) 436
Dabur (Arg, Isr) 31, 266
Daio (Jap) 305
Daldyn (USSR) 557
Daphne (Den) 128
Daphné (Fra, Pak, Por, SA, Spn) 163, 379, 411, 428, 433

834 INDEXES / Classes

Daring (Aust, Per) 41, 390
Darter (USA) 669
Dash (USA) 721
DD 280 (Can) 80
DE 226 (Jap) 296
De Cristofaro (Ita) 278
De Ruyter (Per) 389
De Soto County (Brz, Ita, USA) 64, 280, 717
Dealey (Uru) 760
Deirdre (Ire) 263
Delfinen (Den) 125
Delta I (USSR) 503
Delta II (USSR) 503
Delta III (USSR) 503
Des Moines (USA) 693
Descubierta (Modified) (Mor) 349
Desna (USSR) 565
Deutschland (GFR) 210
Dhafeer (UAE) 582
Dido (Modified) (Pak) 379
Director (UK) 624
Diver (RoC, USA) 473, 728, 758
Dixie (USA) 724
DKN Type (Indo) 252
Dmitri Ovstyn (USSR) 560
Dnepr (USSR) 554, 557
Dobrynya Nikitch (GDR) 197
Dog (UK) 624
Dokkum (Nld) 359
Dolfijn (Nld) 354
Dolphin (USA) 670
Dom Aleixo (Por) 413
Don (Indo, USSR) 250, 553
Draken (Swe) 453
Dreadnought (UK) 590
DTK 221 (Sud) 450
DTM 231 (Sud) 450
Dubna (USSR) 569
Dun (Can) 83
Durance (Fra) 182
Dvora (Isr) 266

E

E (UK) 616
E 52 (Fra) 174
E 52B (Fra) 174
Eagle (USA) 756
Echo (USSR) 512
Echo II (USSR) 508
Edats (UK) 609
Eddy (UK) 619
Edenton (USA) 732
Edsall (Mex) 344
Elk River (RoK) 326
Elk River (Converted) (USA) 735
Elk River (Modified) (Pan) 384
Eltanin (USA) 744
Eltanin (Converted) (USA) 742
Emory S. Land (USA) 729
Enforcer (Hai) 228
Enterprise (USA) 677
Eridan (Fra) 179
Erimo (Jap) 305
Essex (Modernised) (USA) 684
Ethan Allen (USA) 657
Etorofu (CPR) 107

F

F 30 (Spn) 437
F 60 (Spn) 439
F 67 (Fra) 170
Fabius (Mex) 347
Falster (Den) 130
Felicity (UK) 625
Feolent (USSR) 571
Ferocity (Gre) 220
FFG 7 (Aust, Spn) 43, 437
Fiji (Ind) 235
Flagstaff 2 (Isr) 266
Fletcher (Arg, Brz, Chi, GFR, Gre, RoK, Mex, Per, RoC, Spn, Tur, USA) 28, 62, 96, 202, 218, 322, 344, 391, 436, 467, 489, 702
Flower (CPR, DR, Tld) 107, 113, 135, 480
Ford (Gha, Nig, Sin, SA, UK) 214, 367, 425, 428, 615
Forrestal (USA) 680
Forrest Sherman (USA) 700
Forrest Sherman (Converted) (USA) 697
Fort (Can) 85
Foxtrot (Ind, Lby, USSR) 235, 332, 514
Frauenlob (GFR) 206
Freccia (Ita) 279
Fremantle (Aust) 43
Fresh (UK) 623
Friesland (Nld) 356
Frösch (GDR) 195
Fu Chou (CPR) 114
Fukae (Jap) 312
Fukien (CPR) 111
Fulton (USA) 730
Fushun (CPR) 111
Futami (Jap) 303
Fuyushio (Jap) 292
FW (GFR) 209

G

Gagarin (USSR) 566
Galeb (Yug) 780
Galati (CPR) 113, 114
Garcia (USA) 707
Garian (Lby) 334
Gdansk (Pol) 407
Gearing Fram I (Brz, Ecu, Gre, RoK, Pak, Spn, RoC, Tur, USA) 62, 138, 218, 322, 380, 436, 466, 488, 701
Gearing Fram II (Arg, Gre, RoK, RoC, Tur) .. 28, 218, 322, 466, 488
George Washington (USA) 658
Girl (UK) 625
Girl (modified) (UK) 625
Glacier (USA) 753
Glavkos (Gre) 216
Glen (Can) 86
Glenard P. Lipscomb (USA) 661
Glover (USA) 708
Golf (CPR) 104
Golf I and II (USSR) 506
Goryn (USSR) 579
Gota Lejon (Chi) 96
Grayback (USA) 668
Greenville Victory (USA) 745
Grisha I, II & III (USSR) 539
Gromovoy (CPR) 114
Guardian (Bar) 53
Guppy IA (Arg, Per) 26, 388
Guppy II (Arg, Brz, RoC, Ven) 26, 60, 465, 765
Guppy IIA (Gre, Spn, Tur) 217, 434, 487
Guppy III (Brz, Gre, Ita, Tur) 60, 217, 272, 487
Gus (USSR) 552
Gyre (USA) 741

H

H (Fin) 154
Ha T'se (CPR) 113
Habicht I (GDR) 197
Hai (GDR) 193
Hai Dau (CPR) 108
Hai Kou (CPR) 109
Hai Nan (DPRK, Pak) 318, 381
Hai Ping (CPR) 114
Hainan (CPR) 108
Halibut (USA) 665
Halland (Swe) 453
Halland (Modified) (Col) 116
Ham (Fra, Ind, UK, YPDR, Yug) 178, 189, 241, 611, 617, 622, 627, 628, 774, 779
Hamakaze (Jap) 310
Hamashio (Jap) 312
Hamburg (GFR) 202
Hamilton (USA) 750
Han (CPR) 104
Hanchon (DPRK) 321
Hancock (USA) 683
Hanö (Swe) 455
Harukaze (Jap) 296
Haruna (Jap) 293
Hashidate (CPR) 107
Hashima (Jap) 312
Haskell (Spn) 441
Haskell (Converted) (USA) 740
Hatsushima (Jap) 299
Hauk (Nor) 370
Hauki (Fin) 154
Haven (USA) 726
Hayabusa (Jap) 303
Hayase (Jap) 299
Hayes (USA) 741
Head (UK) 611
Hecla (UK) 616
Hecla (Improved) (UK) 616
Hercules (DR) 137
Hero (USA) 750
Heroj (Yug) 775
Herstal (Bel) 55
Hidaka (Jap) 308
Higgins (Arg, Ita) 31, 280
High Point (USA) 710
Hiryu (Jap) 311
Hoku (Alb, CPR) 18, 108
Hola (CPR) 108
Holland (Per) 390
Hollyhock (USA) 757
Homa (CPR) 108
Hotel II and III (USSR) 505
Hu Chwan (Alb, CPR, Pak, Rom, Tan) 19, 110, 382, 417, 474
Hugin (Swe) 454
Hull (USA) 700
Hull (Converted) (USA) 697
Humaita (Par) 385
Hunley (USA) 729
Hunt (Egy, Ind, UK)) .. 143, 239, 609
Huntress (SAr, Sen) 421, 423
Huntsman (Ana) 23
Hvidbjørnen (Den) 127
Hvidbjørnen (Modified) (Den) .. 126

I

Ilo (Per) 393
Iltis (GDR) 194
Ilyusha (USSR) 548
Impavido (Ita) 275
Imperial Marinheiro (Brz) 64
Impetuoso (Ita) 276
Independence (Spn) 435
India (USSR) 517
Ingul (USSR) 579
Insect (UK) 620, 625
Interceptor (Cmn, Qat, UAE, YPDR) 76, 416, 582, 774
Intrepid (USA) 683
Iowa (USA) 685
Ishim (USSR) 573
Island (UK) 614
Isles (UK) 627
Isuzu (Jap) 297
Ivan Rogov (USSR) 548
Iwo Jima (USA) 714
Iwon (DPRK) 321
Izu (Jap) 305

J

Jaguar (Gre, SAr, Tur) 220, 420, 490
Jerong (Mly) 338
Joao Coutinho (Por) 412
John F. Kennedy (USA) 678
Juliett (USSR) 509
Jupiter (Ang, Moz) 23, 351
Jura (UK) 627

K

K 8 (Egy, Pol, USSR) . 146, 407, 548
K 48 (DPRK) 319
KB 123 (GDR) 194
Kaibokan (CPR) 113
Kala (Fin) 154
Kaman (Iran) 256
Kamchatka (USSR) 573
Kamenka (GDR, USSR) 196, 559
Kamishima (CPR) 107
Kampela (Fin) 154
Kan-Chu (CPR) 113
Kanin (USSR) 531
Kapitan Belousov (USSR) 577
Kapitan Chechkin (USSR) 578
Kapitan Izmaylov (USSR) 578
Kapitan Sorokin (USSR) 577
Kara (USSR) 522
Karhu (Fin) 153
Kartal (Tur) 490
Kasado (Jap) 300, 303, 304
Kashin (Ind, USSR) 236, 529
Kashin (Modified) (USSR) 529
Katun (USSR) 580
Kave (Fin) 154
Kazbek (USSR) 570
Kedah (Mly) 338
Kedma (Isr) 267
Kelabang (Indo) 248
Kellar (Por) 414
Kenneth Whiting (Ita) 280
Keyla (USSR) 574
Khabarov (USSR) 575
Khobi (Alb, Indo, USSR) 19, 251, 571
Kiang Hu (CPR) 106
Kiang Nan (CPR) 106
Kiang Tung (CPR) 106
Kiev (USSR) 518
Kilauea (USA) 724
Kildin (USSR) 530
Kildin (Modified) (USSR) 530
Kin (UK) 620
King (Arg) 29
Kirov (USSR) 521
Kitty Hawk (USA) 678
Klasma (USSR) 568
Klasma (Modified) (USSR) 568
Klickitat (Arg) 33
Klondike (USA) 723
Klongyai (Tld) 477
KM-4 (DPRK) 321
Knox (USA) 705
Kojima (Jap) 306
Kola (USSR) 538
Köln (GFR) 203
Kolomna (USSR) 560
Komar (Alg, CPR, Cub, Egy, Indo, DPRK, Syr, Vtn) 20, 108, 121, 143, 247, 318, 464, 771
Komarov (USSR) 566
Konda (USSR) 571
Kondor I (GDR) 195, 196, 197
Kondor II (GDR) 195
Koni (GDR, USSR) 193, 536
Korolev (USSR) 566
Kortenaer (Nld) 356
Koskelo (Fin) 155
Kosmonavt Pavel Belyayev (USSR) 567
Kotlin (USSR) 533
Kouzu (Jap) 300
Krake (GDR) 197
Kraljevica (Ban, Eth, Indo, Sud, Yug) 52, 149, 248, 449, 778
Kresta I (USSR) 525
Kresta II (USSR) 524
Kris (Mly) 338
Krivak I (USSR) 535
Krivak II (USSR) 535
Krogulec (Pol) 407
Kromantse (Gha) 213
Kronshtadt (Alb, CPR, Cub, Indo, Rom, USSR) 18, 108, 121, 247, 416, 574
Ku Song (DPRK) 321
Kuha (Fin) 153
Kümo (GDR) 196
Kunashiri (Jap) 307
Kvalsund (Nor) 372
KW (Gre) 221
Kynda (USSR) 526

L

L. Y. Spear (USA) 729
La Combattante I (Fra) 177
La Combattante II (Gre) 219
La Combattante III (Gre) 219
La Dunkerquoise (Fra) 178
Labo (GDR) 195
Lafayette (USA) 655
Lake (NZ) 363
Lama (USSR) 554
Lampo (Ita) 280
Lance (Gam, Sen) 192, 423
Langeland (Den) 131
Lay (UK) 621
Lazaga (Modified) (Mor) 349
Lazaga (P-00) (Spn) 439
LCM 3 (Bur) 74
LCM-6 (Plp, Sen, Tld, Uru) 402, 423, 480, 763
LCM-8 (Pan, Plp, Spn) 384, 402, 443
LCT (8) (Com) 119
LCU (Bur, Plp, SAr, Tld) 74, 402, 422, 480
LCU 501 (Gre, Kam, RoK, Par, RoC, Tur) 222, 315, 327, 386, 471, 494
LCU 1466 (Kam, Leb, RoC, USA) 315, 331, 471, 719
LCU 1610 (Brz, USA) 64, 719
LCVP (Plp) 402
LDM 100 & 400 (Por) 414
LDP 200 (Por) 414
Le Fougueux (Fra, Tun, Yug) 178, 484, 777
Leahy (USA) 690
Leander (Chi, Ind, NZ, UK) 98, 237, 362, 602
Leander, Broad-Beamed (NZ) .. 362
Leander (Modified) (Ind) 236
Lebed (USSR) 552
Lebedev (USSR) 564
Lei Chou (CPR) 114
Lentra (USSR) 557, 559, 574
Leopard (Ban, Ind, UK) 51, 238, 605
Leskov (USSR) 564
Ley (UK) 611
Libau (USSR) 568
Libelle (GDR) 194
Lindau (GFR) 205
Lindormen (Den) 131
Liulom (Tld) 477
Loadmaster (Bhr, Bru, Omn) 50, 70, 377
Long Beach (USA) 691
Loreto (Per) 392
Los Angeles (USA) 659
Loyal (UK) 626
LPI-1 (Spn) 440
LSD 41 (USA) 716
LSIL 351 (Plp, RoC, Tld) 402, 472, 479
LSM 1 (DR, Ecu, Gre, Isr, RoK, Par, Per, Plp, RoC, Tld, Ven, Vtn) 136, 140, 222, 267, 327, 386, 393, 402, 471, 479, 767, 772
LSM 1 (Modified) (Tur) 492
LSSL-1 (Plp, Vtn) 402, 772
LST 1 (Per) 392
LST (3) (Ind) 240
LST 1-511 (Indo, Plp) 249, 401
LST 1-510 (Gre, RoK, RoC, Tld) 221, 326, 471, 479
LST 511 (Per) 393
LST 501-1152 (Vtn) 772
LST 511-1152 (Brz, Chi, CPR, Col, Ecu, Gre, Indo, RoK, Mly, Mex, Plp, Sin, RoC, Tld, Tur) 64, 100, 112, 118, 139, 221, 249, 326, 339, 347, 401, 425, 471, 493
Luchecorsk (USSR) 564
Lüneburg (GFR) 209
Lupo (Ita, Ven) 277, 766
Lupo (Modified) (Per) 391
Lürssen TNC 45 (Indo, Tld) 247, 476
Lürssen (Ecu) 139
Lürssen S-143 (Nig) 366
Luta (CPR) 105
Luza (USSR) 571
LVC (Spn) 440
LVE (Spn) 440
LVI (Spn) 441
Lynch (Arg) 31

M

M 3 (Aus) 49
M 15 (Swe) 459
M 20 (Spn) 443
M 31 (Swe) 458
M 40 (Rom) 418
M 43 (Swe) 458
M 47 (Swe) 458
M 117 (Yug) 778
M 301 (Yug) 779
Maagen (Den) 128
Machete (Gua) 226
Mackenzie (Can) 81
Mackinaw (USA) 754
Maestrale (Ita) 276
Majestic (Ind) 235
Majestic (Modified) (Aust) 39
Mala (Yug) 776
Malaspina (Spn) 444
Manta (Ecu) 139
Manych (USSR) 569
Maranon (Per) 391
Mark (RoC) 473
Mark (Converted) (USA) 735
Mars (USA) 724
Matka (USSR) 543
Matsuura (Jap) 307
Matsuyuki (Jap) 310
Mattawee (CPR) 114
Maumee (USA) 747
Mayak (USSR) 557, 574
Mayakovsky (USSR) 564
Mayakovsky (Modified) (USSR). 565
Meko 360 Type (Arg) 27
Melitopol (USSR) 561
Melville (USA) 742
Meteor (USA) 745
MHV 20 (Den) 130
MHV 70 (Den) 130
MHV 80 (Den) 130
MHV 90 (Den) 129
Midway (USA) 682
Mikhail Kalinin (USSR) 574
Minegumo (Jap) 294
Miner (UK) 621
Ming (CPR) 104
Mirka I & II (USSR) 536
Mirny (Mtn, USSR) 342, 556
Mispillion (Jumboised) (USA) .. 746
Mission (Pak, USA) 383, 747
Mission (Converted) (USA) 739, 740
Miura (Jap) 298
Mizutori (Jap) 297
Mol (Eth, Som, Sri) 148, 426, 448
Moma (Bul, Pol, USSR) 73, 408, 556, 558
Mornar (Yug) 776
Moskit (Pol) 409
Moskva (USSR) 520, 577
MO IV (DPRK) 320
MO VI (Gn) 227
MP 4 (USSR) 551
MP 6 (USSR) 574
Mrowka (Pol) 409
MS 501 (Alb) 19
MSC 218 (Plp) 401
MSC 268 (Pak, Spn, RoC) 382, 443, 470
MSC 268 & 292 (Iran) 257
MSC 268 & 294 (RoK, Tur). 326, 492
MSC 294 (Gre) 222
MSC 322 (SAr) 420
Muna (USSR) 574
Murakumo (Jap) 309
Murasame (Jap) 295

N

Näcken (Swe) 452
Najin (DPRK) 317
Nalon (Spn) 443
Nampo (DPRK) 321
Nana-Go (Jap) 300
Nanuchka (Ind) 239
Nanuchka I (USSR) 540
Nanuchka II (USSR) 540
Narhvalen (Den) 125

INDEXES / Classes 835

Narval (Fra) 163
Narwhal (USA) 661
Nasty (Gre, Tur) 220, 490
Natya (Ind, USSR) 241, 545
Nautilus (USA) 667
Nawarat (Bur) 74
Neosho (USA) 726
Nepa (USSR) 573
Neptun (USSR) 572
Neptune (USA) 748
Nercha (USSR) 571
Nestin (Yug) 779
Nevelskoy (USSR) 563
Newport (USA) 717
Nikolai Zubov (USSR) 556, 558
Nils Juel (Den) 126
Nimitz (USA) 675
Niobe (GFR) 207
Niteroi (Brz) 63
Nitro (USA) 724
Nogekaze (Jap) 310
Nojima (Jap) 306
Nordseewerke Type (Arg) 26
Norton (Can) 86
Norwalk (USA) 744
November (USSR) 512
Nunobiki (Jap) 311
Nuoli (Fin) 151
Nyryat (Alb, Alg, Egy) 20, 21, 146
Nyryat I (Cub, USSR) 123, 575
Nyryat II (Iraq) 261

O

Oberon (Brz, Can, Chi, UK) 60, 79, 95, 591
Obluze (Pol) 406
Obluze (Modified) (Pol) 406
Observation Island (USA) 739
October (Egy) 144
Ohio (USA) 654
Oilpress (UK) 621
Okean (USSR) 557
Okhtensky (Cub, Egy, Indo, USSR) 123, 146, 252, 579
Oksywie (Pol) 407
OL (UK) 617
Olekma (Improved) (USSR) 570
Olekma/Pevek (USSR) 570
Oliver Hazard Perry (USA) 703
Olya (USSR) 548
Onega (USSR) 560
Ooshio (Jap) 292
Orel (USSR) 579
Osa (CPR, Pol, Rom, Yug) 108, 406, 417, 777
Osa I (Alg, Bul, Cub, Egy, GDR, Ind, Iraq, DPRK, Syr, USSR) 20, 71, 121, 143, 194, 240, 260, 318, 464, 541
Osa II (Alg, Cub, Eth, GDR, Ind, Lby, Som, Syr, USSR) 20, 121, 148, 194, 240, 334, 426, 464,541
Oskol (USSR) 555
Oslo (Nor) 369
Osprey (Den, USA) 132, 710
Oxley (Aust) 38

P

P 4 (Alb, Bul, CPR, Cub, Egy, DPRK, Rom, Syr, Tan, Vtn, YAR, Zai) 19, 71, 110, 122, 144, 321, 417, 464, 474, 771, 773, 781
P 6 (Alg, CPR, Cub, Egy, EqG, Gn, GB, Iraq, DPRK, Pol, Som, Tan, USSR, Vtn, YPDR) 20, 21, 110, 122, 144, 147, 227, 227, 261, 320, 406, 426, 474, 544, 771, 774
P 21 (Ire) 263
P 48 (Sen, Tun, UAE) 422, 485, 581
PA 75 (Fra) 165
Pabna (Ban) 52
Pajak (Pol) 409
Pamir (USSR) 556, 579
Papa (USSR) 507
Parinas (Per) 394
Passat (USSR) 564
Pat (Indo) 252
Patapsco (Chi, Col, Gre, RoC) 101, 118, 223, 473
Patra (IC) 287
Pattimura (Indo) 246
Paul Revere (USA) 718
PC-461 (Indo, Plp, RoC) 247, 399, 473
PC 1638 (Chi, Tur) 99, 491
PCE 827 (Bur, Ecu, RoK, Plp) 74, 138, 324, 399
Pchela (USSR) 543
Peder Skram (Den) 126
Pedro Teixeira (Brz) 64
Pei Hai (CPR) 111
Perdana (Mly) 338
Perth (Aust) 40
Perwira (Bru) 69
Petya I (Syr, USSR) 463, 537
Petya I (Mod) (USSR) 537
Petya II (Ind, USSR, Vtn) 237, 537, 770
Petya II (Mod) (USSR) 537
PF 103 (Iran, Tld) 256, 475
PGM (Bur) 75
PGM-9 (Gre) 221
PGM 39 (Indo, Plp) 248, 400
PGM-53 (Eth) 149
PGM 59 (Vtn) 771
PGM-71 (DR, Ecu, Lbr, Per, Plp, Tld, Tur, Vtn) 135, 139, 331, 396, 400, 477, 491,771
PGM-71 (Improved) (Iran) 256
Pigeon (USA) 730
Pilica (Pol) 407
Piratini (Brz) 65
Pirttisaari (Fin) 154
Pizarro (Modernised) (Spn) 439
Plejad (Swe) 455
PO 2 (Alb, Bul, Iraq) 19, 72, 261
Podzharny (Indo) 251
Point (USA, Vtn) 755, 771
Point Barrow (USA) 725
Polar Star (USA) 753
Polimar (Mex) 346
Polnochniy (Alg, Ang, Egy, Ind, Iraq, Lby, Pol, Som, USSR, YPDR) 21, 23, 145, 240, 260, 335, 408, 426, 551, 774
Poluchat (Alg, EqG, Ind, Moz, Syr, Tan, YAR, YPDR) 21, 147, 240, 351, 464, 474, 773, 774
Poluchat I (Alb, Gn, Iraq, Som, USSR) 20, 227, 261, 426, 574
Poluchat II (Egy) 146
Polyus (USSR) 563
Poolster (Nld) 360
Porpoise (UK) 591
Porte (Can) 85
Poti (Bul, Rom, USSR) 71, 416, 540
Potok (USSR) 574
Potomac (USA) 746
Potvis (Nld) 354
Povenets (USSR) 567
Powhatan (USA) 731
Pozharny I (USSR) 575
PR 72 (Mor) 349
PR-72P (Per) 391
President (SA) 428
Primorye (USSR) 556
Private Leonard C. Brostrom (USA) 744
Proteus (USA) 730
Prut (USSR) 572
PS 700 (Lby) 335
Puerto Deseado (Arg) 32
Pukkio (Fin) 154
Purga (USSR) 577
PX (Mly) 340
PX (Improved) (Mly) 340

Q

Quebec (USSR) 517
Quilmes (Arg) 34

R

R (Ind, Indo) 236, 249
Rade Koncar (Yug) 777
Raleigh (USA) 715
Raleigh (Converted) (USA) 725
Rapier (SAr) 421
Rebun (Jap) 308
Red (USA) 757
Redwing (Fij, Sin, Spn) 149, 424, 443
Reinøysund (Nor) 372
Reliance (USA) 752
Reshef (Isr, SA) 265, 428
Resolution (UK) 588
Restigouche (Can) 81
Restigouche (Improved) (Can) 82
Rhein (GFR) 207
Rhin (Fra) 183
Riga (Bul, CPR, Fin, GDR, Indo, USSR) 70, 106, 150, 193, 246, 538
Rigel (USA) 739
Rihtniemi (Fin) 152
Rio (Ven) 769
Rio Doce (Brz) 68
Rio Orinoco (Ven) 767
River (Aust, Bur, DR, Egy, Ind) 42, 73, 134, 143, 239
Robbe (GDR) 195
Robert D. Conrad (Brz, USA) 66, 741
Robert H. Smith (Tur) 488
Roger de Lauria (Spn) 435
Romeo (Bul, CPR, Egy, DPRK, USSR) 70, 104, 141, 317, 515
Ropucha (USSR) 549
Roraima (Brz) 65
Roslavl (CPR, Rom) 114, 418
Rothesay (UK) 604
Rover (UK) 618
Rudderow (RoK, RoC) 323, 468
Ruissalo (Fin) 152
RV 4 (Fin) 155
RV 8 (Fin) 155
RV 9 (Fin) 155
RV 10 (Fin) 155
RV 30 (Fin) 155
RV 37 (Fin) 155
RV 41 (Fin) 155

S

S 1 (CPR) 104
S 30 (Spn) 434
S 60 (Spn) 433
S 70 (Spn) 433
Saam (Iran) 255
Saar 1, 2, 3 (Isr) 265
Sabah (Mly) 338
Sachsenwald (GFR) 209
Sacramento (USA) 727
Saint (Can) 86
St. Laurent (Can) 82
Salisbury (Ban, UK) 51, 605
Salta (Arg) 26
Samara (USSR) 559
Sam Kotlin (Pol, USSR) 405, 532
Samson (UK) 624
Samuel Gompers (USA) 723
Sandhayak (Ind) 241
Sao Roque (Por) 413
Sarancha (USSR) 541
Sariwan (DPRK) 318
Sasha (USSR) 547
Sauda (Nor) 372
Sauro (Ita) 271
Sava (Yug) 775
Savage (Plp, Tun, Vtn) 397, 484, 770
Schoolboy (RoK) 325
Schütze (Brz, GFR) 64, 206
Schuyler Otis Bland (USA) 744
Schwalbe (Tan) 474
SDB Mark 2 (Ind) 240
Sealift (USA) 747
Seal (UK) 629
Seawolf (USA) 666
Sechura (Per) 394
Sekstan (Alb, Alg, Egy) 19, 21, 146
Sewart (Eth, Iran, Nic, RoK) 149, 259, 325, 364
Shanghai (Cam, CPR, Con, DPRK, Rom, Vtn) 76, 109, 120, 319, 417, 771
Shanghai II (Alb, CPR, Gn, Pak, SL, Sri, Tan, Tun) 19, 109, 227, 382, 423, 448, 474, 484
Shantung (CPR) 110
Sharada (Ind) 240
Sheffield (UK) 600
Shenandoah (Indo, USA) 251, 723
Shershen (Ang, Bul, DPRK, Egy, GDR, USSR, Yug) 22, 71, 144, 194, 320, 543, 777
Shih Jian (CPR) 112
Shikinami (Jap) 310
Shirane (Jap) 293
Shiretoko (Jap) 305
Shmel (USSR) 544
Shu Kuang (CPR) 113
Sibir (USSR) 565
Silas Bent (USA) 743
Simon Lake (USA) 729
Sinpo (DPRK) 320
Sirius (Brz, Fra, Mor) 66, 178, 180, 349
Sithole (Indo) 252
Sjöormen (Swe) 452
Skate (USA) 666
Skipjack (USA) 664
Skory (Egy, USSR) 142, 534
Sleipner (Nor) 370
Slepen (USSR) 542
SM 165 (Rom) 418
SMB I (Egy, USSR) 145, 551
Smolny (USSR) 567
Smuggler 21SS (Ice) 232
SNA 72 (Fra) 162
Snogg (Nor) 371
Södermanland (Swe) 453
Sofia (USSR) 569
SO-I (Alg, Bul, Cub, Egy, Iraq, DPRK, USSR, Vtn, YPDR) 20, 71, 121, 144, 260, 319, 542, 771, 774
Søløven (Den) 128
Sonya (USSR) 547
Sooraya (Sri) 448
Sorum (USSR) 579
Sotoyomo (Arg, Brz, Chi, DR, Per, RoC, RoK, USA) 29, 34, 68, 98, 137, 328, 393, 472, 473, 731, 759
Souya (Jap) 299
Soya (Jap) 305
Spa (UK) 623
Sparviero (Ita) 279
Spear (Bhr, Indo, Mlw, Qat, StK, Sen, UAE, YPDR) 50, 248, 336, 416, 419, 423, 582, 774
Spear 2 (Gha) 214
Spica-M (Mly) 338
Spica T 121 (Swe) 454
Spica T 131 (Swe) 454
Spitfire (UK) 629
Split (Yug) 776
Spruance (USA) 698
Spruance (Improved) (USA) 694
Spruance (Modified) (Iran) 254
Stenka (USSR) 542
Storis (USA) 754
Storm (Nor) 371
Sturgeon (USA) 662
Suamico (USA) 747
Suffren (Fra) 169
Sura (USSR) 572
Suribachi (USA) 724
Susa (Lby) 334
Susanin (USSR) 578
Susanin (Modified) (USSR) 563
Sutjeska (Yug) 775
Sutlej (Ind) 242
Sverdlov (USSR) 527
Swatow (CPR, DPRK, Vtn) 109, 319, 771
Swift (Hon, Kam, Mlt, Tld, Vtn) 229, 315, 341, 478, 772
Swiftsure (UK) 589
Sword (TT) 483
SX 404 (Pak) 379
SX 506 (Col) 115

T

T 4 (Cub, Som, YPDR) 122, 426, 774
T 42 (Swe) 455
T 43 (Alb, Alg, Bul, CPR, Egy, Indo, Iraq, Pol, Syr, USSR) 19, 21, 72, 111, 145, 249, 262, 407, 464, 546, 573
T 43/AGR (USSR) 546
T 47 (Fra) 172
T 53 (Fra) 171
T 56 (Fra) 170
T 58 (USSR, YPDR) 545, 774
T 58 (Mod) (Ind) 242
T 301 (Alb, Egy, Rom) 19, 146, 418
Tachikaze (Jap) 293
Tacoma (DR, RoK, Tld) 134, 324, 476
Tai Shan (CPR) 111
Takami (Jap) 300
Takatori (Jap) 306
Takatsuki (Jap) 294
Talara (Per) 394
Tan Lin (CPR) 114
Tang (Iran, Ita, USA) 254, 271, 669
Tango (USSR) 513
Tarantul (USSR) 539
Tarawa (USA) 713
Tarmo (Fin) 153
Taucher (GDR) 197
Telkka (Fin) 155
Telnovsk (USSR) 558, 574
Terrebonne Parish (Gre, Spn, Tur, Ven) 221, 442, 493, 768
Teshio (Jap) 307
Thetis (GFR) 203
Thomaston (USA) 716
Thresher (USA) 663
Tide (Aust) 46
Tide (Later) (UK) 617
Tiger (UK) 596
Ting Hai (CPR) 114
Tisza (Indo) 251
Tjeld (Nor) 371
TM (CPR) 114
TNC 45 (Sin) 424
Tokachi (Jap) 307
Tomba (USSR) 555
Ton (Arg, Aust, Gha, Ind, Ire, Mly, SA, UK) 31, 43, 214, 241, 263, 339, 429, 610
Ton (Modified) (Aust, UK) 43, 615
Tonti (USA) 748
Toplivo I (Alb) 19
Toplivo 3 (Alb) 19
Toti (Ita) 271
Town (Pak) 382
Tracker (Bhr, SA) 50, 430
Tracker 2 (Gam, YPDR) 192, 774
TR 40 (Rom, USSR) 418, 548
Trafalgar (UK) 589
Tral (DPRK) 318
Tree (CPR) 113
Tribal (UK) 603
Trident (Fra) 177
Trieste Type (USA) 672
Tripartite (Bel, Fra, Nld) 54, 179, 358
Triton (Den, UK, USA) 127, 625, 665
Tromp (Nld) 355
Tropik (USSR) 564, 565
Truxtun (USA) 688
Tsukuba (Jap) 308
Tugur (Indo) 252
Tuima (Fin) 151
Tulare (USA) 718
Tullibee (USA) 663
Turunmaa (Fin) 151
Turya (USSR) 543
Tydeman (Nld) 360
Type A (Sin) 424
Type B (Sin) 424
Type XXI (Converted) (GFR) 200
Type 42 (Arg) 27
Type 82 (UK) 597
Type 122 (GFR) 203
Type 143 (GFR) 204
Type 143A (GFR) 204
Type 148 (GFR) 204
Type 205 (GFR) 200
Type 206 (GFR) 200
Type 210 (GFR) 200
Type 520 (GFR) 205
Type 521 (GFR) 205
Type 207 (Nor) 369
Type 209 (Col, Ecu, Indo, Per, Tur, Ven) 115, 138, 245, 388, 487, 765
Type 210 (GFR) 200
Type TNC 45 (Arg) 31
Typhoon (USSR) 503

U

Uda (Indo, USSR) 251, 570
Ugra (Ind, USSR) 242, 553
Ukuru (CPR) 107
Umitaka (Jap) 298
Ural (USSR) 571
Urho (Fin, Swe) 153, 460
Uzushio (Jap) 292

V

V 01 (Swe) 456
V 4 (Mex) 348
Vadsø (Nor) 370
Valday (USSR) 573
Valerian Uryvaev (USSR) 560
Valiant (UK) 590
Van Speijk (Nld) 357
Van Straelen (Nld) 359
Vanya (Bul, Syr, USSR) 72, 464, 547
Vasama (Fin) 152
Vasily Pronchishtchev (USSR) 578
VC (Spn) 447
Vegesack (Tur) 493
Ventura (UK) 611
VG (Rom) 418
Victor I (USSR) 511
Victor II (USSR) 511
Victory (USA) 740
Victory (Converted) (USA) 739
Ville (Can) 86
Virginia (USA) 686
Visby (Swe) 454
Voda (USSR) 575
Voima (Fin) 153
Vukov Klanac (Yug) 778
Vydra (Bul, Egy, USSR) 72, 145, 551
Vytegrales (USSR) 562, 567

W

Walchensee (GFR) 208
Waspada (Bru) 69
Water (UK) 623
Wellington (Iran) 257
Westerwald (GFR) 209
Whampoa (CPR) 110
Whiskey (Alb, CPR, DPRK, Egy, Indo, Pol, USSR) 18, 104, 141, 245, 317, 405, 516
Whiskey Canvas Bag (USSR) 517
Whiskey Long-Bin (USSR) 510
Whiskey Twin Cylinder (USSR) 510
Whitby (Ind, NZ, UK) 238, 363, 605
White Sumac (USA) 757
Wichita (USA) 727
Wielingen (Bel) 53
Wild Duck (UK) 620
Wild Duck (Improved) (UK) 620
Wild Duck (Later) (UK) 620
Wildervank (Eth, Omn) 148, 376
Wilkes (USA) 743
Willemoes (Den) 127
Winchester (Iran) 257
Wind (USA) 754
Wisla (Pol) 406
Wisting (Nor) 373
Wodnik (Pol) 408
Wolf (Nld) 357
Wood (Can) 86